The Victoria History of the
Counties of England
EDITED BY WILLIAM PAGE, F.S.A.

A HISTORY OF

WORCESTERSHIRE

VOLUME III

THE
VICTORIA HISTORY
OF THE COUNTIES
OF ENGLAND

WORCESTERSHIRE

PUBLISHED FOR
THE UNIVERSITY OF LONDON
INSTITUTE OF HISTORICAL RESEARCH
REPRINTED FROM THE ORIGINAL EDITION OF 1913
BY
DAWSONS OF PALL MALL
FOLKESTONE & LONDON
1971

Issued by
Archibald Constable and Company Limited
in 1913
Reprinted for the University of London
Institute of Historical Research
by
Dawsons of Pall Mall
Cannon House
Folkestone, Kent, England
1971

ISBN: 0 7129 0481 6

Printed in Great Britain
by photolithography
Unwin Brothers Limited
Woking and London

INSCRIBED
TO THE MEMORY OF
HER LATE MAJESTY
QUEEN VICTORIA
WHO GRACIOUSLY GAVE
THE TITLE TO AND
ACCEPTED THE
DEDICATION OF
THIS HISTORY

Dudley Castle Worcester
From an engraving by F. Eastes 1753

THE
VICTORIA HISTORY
OF THE COUNTY OF
WORCESTER

GENERAL EDITOR : WILLIAM PAGE, F.S.A.

LOCAL EDITOR : J. W. WILLIS-BUND, M.A., LL.B., F.S.A.

VOLUME THREE

PUBLISHED FOR
THE UNIVERSITY OF LONDON
INSTITUTE OF HISTORICAL RESEARCH

REPRINTED BY
DAWSONS OF PALL MALL
FOLKESTONE & LONDON

CONTENTS OF VOLUME THREE

CONTENTS OF VOLUME THREE

CONTENTS OF VOLUME THREE

LIST OF ILLUSTRATIONS

LIST OF ILLUSTRATIONS

LIST OF ILLUSTRATIONS

LIST OF ILLUSTRATIONS

LIST OF ILLUSTRATIONS

LIST OF ILLUSTRATIONS

LIST OF ILLUSTRATIONS

LIST OF MAPS

EDITORIAL NOTE

THE Editors are indebted to the following, who by reading the proofs of this volume have added much to the accuracy of the work. They especially wish to express their thanks to Sir Richard C. Temple, Bart., Sir Richard B. Martin, Bart., Mr. John Amphlett, M.A., J.P., the Rev. E. R. Dowdeswell, M.A., and Mr. R. Vaughan Gower, and also to Sir Harry F. Vernon, Bart., Mr. T. A. C. Attwood, M.A., F.S.A., the Rev. Hugh F. Bennett, B.A., Mr. R. V. Berkeley, F.S.A., D.L., J.P., the Rev. J. J. Burton, M.A., Mr. Thomas Cave, the Rev. W. K. W. Chafy, D.D., F.S.A., the Rev. F. S. Colman, M.A., Mr. John H. Crane, J.P., Mrs. Dalgleish, Lt.-Gen. H. F. Davies, D.L., J.P., Mr. G. H. Simpson-Hayward, the Rev. H. J. Kelsall, M.A., the Rev. H. M. Niblett, M.A., the Rev. Gordon H. Poole, B.A., Mr. Michael Tomkinson, D.L., J.P., Mr. H. E. Taylor and Mr. R. Bruce Ward.

They also desire to acknowledge the assistance and information given by the Rev. G. le Strange Amphlett, M.A., the late Rear-Admiral R. F. Britten, Mr. John Brinton, D.L., J.P., Mr. B. C. Cobb, Mr. Bickerton H. Deakin, the Rev. K. A. Deakin, M.A., the Rev. W. A. Edwards, M.A., the Rev. R. C. Garnett, M.A., the Rev. A. G. Grisewood, M.A., Mr. Gainsborough Harward, Mr. John Hill, Messrs. Holloway, Blount and Duke, the late Mr. John H. Hooper (Chapter Clerk of Worcester), the late Rev. H. Housman, the Rev. W. Hawker Hughes, M.A. (Bursar of Jesus College, Oxford), Mr. T. W. Whitmore Jones, Mr. James Morton (formerly Town Clerk of Kidderminster), Mr. L. F. Lambert, J.P., Mr. Arthur E. Lord, Mr. F. A. Manley and Miss Caroline Staunton.

For illustrations and plans the Editors are indebted to the Society of Antiquaries, Mr. R. V. Berkeley, F.S.A., D.L., J.P., the Editor and Proprietors of *Country Life* (for photographs of Cleeve Prior Manor and Old Granary, Earl's Croome Court, Hadzor House and Hewell Grange, Tardebigge), the Countess of Coventry, Miss Lucy C. Davies, Mr. W. W. Harris, Mr. G. H. Simpson-Hayward and the Royal Archæological Institute.

A HISTORY OF

WORCESTERSHIRE

TOPOGRAPHY

THE HUNDRED OF HALFSHIRE

CONTAINS THE FOLLOWING PARISHES [1]

UPPER ARLEY [2] (transferred from Staffordshire)
BELBROUGHTON
BROMSGROVE
BROOM
CHADDESLEY CORBETT
CHURCHILL
CHURCH LENCH
CLENT
COSTON OR COFTON HACKETT
CRUTCH
DODDERHILL WITH ELMBRIDGE
DOVERDALE
DROITWICH BOROUGH

DUDLEY BOROUGH
ELMLEY LOVETT
FECKENHAM
FRANKLEY
GRAFTON MANOR
HADZOR
HAGLEY
HALESOWEN WITH CRADLEY, LUTLEY AND WARLEY WIGORN
HAMPTON LOVETT
KIDDERMINSTER BOROUGH AND FOREIGN WITH LOWER MITTON

KING'S NORTON
KINGTON
NORTHFIELD
PEDMORE
RUSHOCK
SALWARPE
STONE
OLD SWINFORD WITH STOURBRIDGE
TARDEBIGGE
UPTON WARREN
WESTWOOD PARK
YARDLEY

The origin of Halfshire Hundred cannot be traced as a collection of lands belonging to one owner or group of owners, as is the case with other Worcestershire hundreds. At the time of the Domesday Survey Pershore comprised the lands of the abbeys of Westminster and Pershore, Blackenhurst those of Evesham Abbey, Oswaldslow the possessions of the Bishop and priory of Worcester, but Halfshire was made up of the lands of various holders, of whom the Crown and William Fitz Ansculf were the chief.

Halfshire includes part of the parish of Dudley which is a detached part of Worcestershire lying within the boundary of the county of Stafford. It is irregularly shaped, parishes in the hundreds of Pershore and Oswaldslow being situated in the midst of Halfshire parishes.

In 1086 most of the parishes now included in the hundred of Halfshire were contained in the hundreds of Came (Kamel, Camele), Clent, Cresselau (Kerselau) and Esch (Aesc, Naisse, Leisse, del Eisse).[3] The union of these hundreds had not been effected before the time of Stephen,[4] but it had taken place before 1175-6.[5]

Alvechurch and Stoke Prior in Came Hundred, Cleeve Prior with Lench, Hanbury, Phepson in Himbleton, and parts of Crowle and Inkberrow in Esch Hundred, and Hartlebury and Wolverley in Cresselau Hundred belonged to

---

[1] This list, with the exception of Upper Arley, Broom, Clent and Crutch, represents the extent of the hundred in 1831.

[2] Upper Arley was transferred for civil purposes from Staffordshire to Worcestershire in 1895 and is locally in Halfshire Hundred.

[3] Clent Hundred apparently took its name from the manor of Clent which was included in it, and Esch perhaps from the manor of Heisse mentioned in a survey of the hundred of the Norman period (Cott. MS. Vesp. B. xxiv, fol. 6).

[4] V.C.H. Worcs. i, 326, 328 ; Cott. MS. Vesp. B. xxiv, fol. 6 et seq.

[5] Pipe R. 22 Hen. II (Pipe R. Soc.), 36.

the church of Worcester,[6] and with the two manors of Eardiston and Knighton in Doddingtree Hundred, forming the whole of the Worcestershire possessions of the church of Worcester outside its hundred of Oswaldslow,

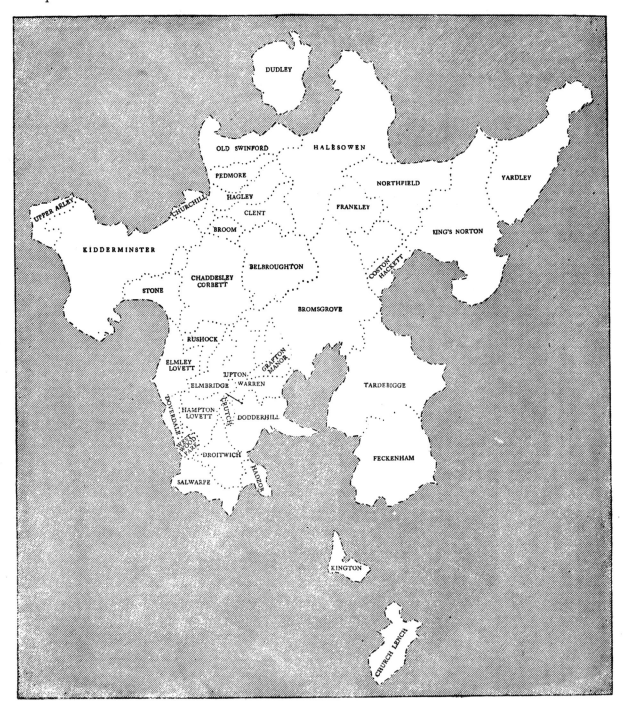

INDEX MAP TO THE HUNDRED OF HALFSHIRE

were included in the reign of Henry I under the name Kinefolka.[7] Subsequently all these manors were transferred to the Bishop of Worcester's hundred of Oswaldslow. It is not known when these changes were made. Most of the parishes seem to have been wholly or in part in Halfshire

[6] *V.C.H. Worcs.* i, 287-98.   [7] Ibid. 325-6.

Hundred in 1220 and 1274.[8] Alvechurch, Hanbury, and Inkberrow were wholly in Oswaldslow in 1346,[9] and are included in it at the present day, but Crowle, Hartlebury and Woverley remained partly in Halfshire Hundred. Cleeve Prior and Stoke Prior,[10] which by a charter of King John in 1207 had been freed from suits at the hundred court,[11] were transferred to Oswaldslow before 1603.[12] The process by which these changes took place was probably gradual; something of the kind was evidently going on at the end of the reign of Henry III, for in 1275 it was presented at the hundred court of Halfshire that Godfrey, Bishop of Worcester in 1272, had attached to his hundred of Oswaldslow Walter de Hurstheye, John de Hurstheye and Roger de Pressian of Coston, who had formerly been accustomed to answer with the men of Halfshire.[13] William de Valence had also included in his liberty of Newbury the men of Morton, Shell and Witton, who had formerly been accustomed to answer with the men of Halfshire.[14]

The manors in Esch Hundred belonging to Evesham Abbey, Abbots Morton and Sheriff's and Atch Lench[15] were transferred to the abbot's hundred of Blackenhurst before 1280.[16] The greater part of Church Lench remained and still remains in Halfshire Hundred.

That part of the parish of Halesowen which belonged to the Earl of Shrewsbury in 1086 was annexed by him to Shropshire,[17] although it is some miles from the nearest place in that county.

Clent was in the hundred of Clent in Worcestershire in 1086,[18] but with Tardebigge it was farmed by the Sheriff of Stafford with Kingswinford in Staffordshire.[19] This probably accounts for Clent having been subsequently transferred to Staffordshire, in which county it remained until 1832.

In 1266 the king had granted that the Abbot of Bordesley and his men of Tardebigge might answer to the Sheriff of Warwickshire for their farm instead of to the Sheriff of Staffordshire, and part of the parish seems to have remained in Warwickshire until the 19th century.[20]

In 1760 it was provided that Yardley, which, as a member of Beoley and a possession of the Abbot of Pershore, had been in Pershore since the formation of that hundred,[21] should be 'rated and assessed' in Halfshire Hundred,[22] and the parish seems to have been finally considered part of Halfshire for all purposes.

In 1603 and 1782[23] the extent of Halfshire Hundred was practically the same as in 1831.[24] Halesowen with its hamlet of Warley Salop was in Shropshire, but its hamlets of Lutley, Cradley, Oldbury and Warley Wigorn were in Halfshire; Kingsford in Wolverley was in Halfshire, the

[8] Assize R. 1021, m. 8, 8 d. ; 1026, m. 42 d., 43, 44. [9] *Feud. Aids,* v, 306, 307.
[10] Stoke Prior seems still to have been for purposes of assessment in Halfshire Hundred in 1798 (*Bibl. of Worc.* [Worcs. Hist. Soc.], 80). [11] *Cal. Rot. Chart.* 1199–1216 (Rec. Com.), 168.
[12] *Lay Subs. R. Worcs.* 1603 (Worcs. Hist. Soc.). [13] *Hund. R.* (Rec. Com.), ii, 284.
[14] Ibid. [15] *V.C.H. Worcs.* i, 307. [16] *Lay Subs. R. Worcs. c.* 1280 (Worcs. Hist. Soc.), 86.
[17] *V.C.H. Worcs.* i, 238. [18] Ibid. 287.
[19] For the monks of Worcester's account of the reason of this see *V.C.H. Worcs.* i, 238.
[20] See under the manor of Tardebigge. [21] *V.C.H. Worcs.* i, 305.
[22] Stat. 1 Geo. III, cap. 2. The Act was confirmed by 5 Geo. III, cap. 5 ; 8 Geo. III, cap. 8 ; 38 Geo. III, cap. 5. [23] Grafton being extra-parochial is not included in Nash's list of the hundred.
[24] *Lay Subs. R. Worcs.* 1603 (Worcs. Hist. Soc.) ; Nash, *Hist. of Worc.* Introd. 59.

rest of the parish being in Oswaldslow. Hartlebury was in Oswaldslow, but its hamlet of Over Mitton was in Halfshire.

The Shropshire part of Halesowen with Tardebigge, Clent and Broom was transferred to Worcestershire under the Acts of 1832 and 1844.[25]

Crutch was formerly extra-parochial, but is now a parish in the hundred of Halfshire.

The manors of Feckenham and Holloway in Hanbury were surveyed in 1086 under Herefordshire.[26] The cause of this was that they had belonged to the Earl of Hereford, and though they still remained in the hundred of Esch in Worcestershire, he had so far annexed them to his lordship of Hereford that they were surveyed under that county.[27]

The boroughs of Droitwich, Dudley and Kidderminster, which are all in Halfshire Hundred, were represented at the assize courts from early times by their own twelve jurors.[28] The hundred of Halfshire was known in the 13th century as the hundred of Wych,[29] and in 1280 the hundred is called 'Dimidii Comitatus de Wych.'[30] In 1275 the hundred of Dudley is mentioned.[31]

The hundred of Halfshire seems always to have belonged to the Crown,[32] and was under the sheriff of the county and his officers.[33] The hundred has been divided since the end of the 17th century into the two divisions of Upper and Lower Halfshire,[34] and there appears to have been a separate court for each division, that of the Lower Division being sometimes held at Churchill 'under a great tree.'[35]

---

[25] Stat. 2 & 3 Will. IV, cap. 64 ; 7 & 8 Vict. cap. 61. [26] *V.C.H. Worcs.* i, 320, 321.
[27] Ibid. 240. [28] Assize R. 1021, m. 8 d., 9. [29] *Abbrev. Plac.* (Rec. Com.), 63*b*.
[30] *Lay Subs. R. Worcs. c.* 1280 (Worcs. Hist. Soc.), 6. [31] *Hund. R.* (Rec. Com.), ii, 285.
[32] Chan. Inq. p.m. (Ser. 2), clxv, 192.
[33] Cox and Hall, *Magna Brit.* vi, 229. In 1315 the hundred of Halfshire or Demi Counte was enumerated among the possessions of Guy de Beauchamp Earl of Warwick, sheriff of the county. It was held of the king in chief (*Cal. Inq. p.m.* 1–9 *Edw. II*, 397). It is curious that Halfshire was not surveyed with the king's other property in 1650 ; the reason possibly was that the greater part of it lay in the forest of Feckenham, over which Charles I had sold all his forest rights.
[34] The Bromsgrove Division of Halfshire is mentioned in 1760 and 1798. *Bibl. of Worc.* (Worcs. Hist. Soc.), i, 55, 80. [35] Lyttelton MS. (Soc. of Antiq.) ; Exch. Dep. 5 Will. and Mary, East. no. 24.

UPPER ARLEY

Earnleia (x cent.) ; Ernlege (xi cent.) ; Erleia, Ernelea (xii cent.) ; Arleg, Erdele, Arnlee de Port (xiii cent.) ; Aerley (xv cent.) ; Over Areley (xvi cent.).

Upper Arley is a parish containing 3,969 acres, of which 50 acres are covered with water, on the Shropshire border of the county. It was included in the county of Staffordshire until 1895, when it was transferred to Worcestershire.[1] It is watered on the west by the Severn and three of its tributaries, and on the east by a tributary of the Stour. The parish abounds in woods, especially that part on the right bank of the Severn which was formerly and is still partly in Wyre Forest. Shatterford and Arley Woods in the east of the parish were formerly in Kinver Forest.[2] In 1905 the parish included 875 acres of arable land, 1,945 acres of permanent grass and 838 acres of woodland.[3]

The village is well wooded and charmingly situated in the Severn valley, on the left bank of the river, about 5 miles north of Bewdley and 6 miles north-west of Kidderminster. It is built along the road running south-west from Shatterford, which after entering the village runs for nearly 100 yards along the side of the river, and taking a bend to the north-west rises up-hill to the church and Arley Castle, both of which are built on high ground at the western extremity of the settlement. It thus takes the form of a horseshoe. None of the cottages are of any great antiquity, and are chiefly built of red brick with tile roofs.

The Grange, the residence of the Misses Corser, is a small 18th-century red brick house on the west side of the road leading to the church. The roof is tiled and the house contains a good oak staircase having a moulded handrail and turned balusters. The station is on the opposite side of the river to the village, and is reached by a ferry which was a source of revenue to the lords of the manor in the 14th century.

Arley Castle stands on high ground to the east of the church, and commands a good view of the Severn valley and forest of Wyre. The greater part of the present house, now the residence of Mr. R. Woodward, D.L., J.P., was built of sandstone in the Gothic style by Lord Mountnorris in 1844. The only ancient feature remaining is a part of the Old Hall, formerly the dower house of the Lytteltons of Hagley, now forming the south wing. It is a two-storied building, erected apparently in the latter part of the 16th century, and enlarged in the reign of James I. The roof is tiled, and externally the hall has been refaced with stucco. The windows have been renewed in most cases with sashes, and the moulded label of the early Gothic revivalists has been inserted over them. With the exception of two staircases the interior was entirely remodelled in 1844. Both

these staircases are on the eastern side of the house. That on the north is Elizabethan, in two flights, with a moulded handrail, shaped flat balusters and square newels, capped with turned finials. The other, or principal staircase, is of a more pretentious design, and was added early in the 17th century. It ascends to the first floor in three flights, with square landings at each turn. The strings and handrail are moulded, and the newel posts, which have shaped finials incised with an arabesque enrichment, are ornamented in a similar manner. The balusters are shaped and have small Ionic capitals. The panelled risers are a peculiar feature of the staircase. A considerable amount of 17th-century woodwork has been re-used in the old part of the house, especially in the library, a room in the north-west corner of the original block, where a cleverly constructed fireplace might be taken for original Jacobean work. Several tombstones taken from the churchyard have been utilized in the building of a cellar in the additions made by Lord Mountnorris.

The soil varies, the subsoil being sandstone rock. The chief crops are wheat, barley, oats and beans. Cider apples were formerly grown at Arley, and Sir Henry Lyttelton cultivated vines from which were produced light wines equal to those of France.[4] There is a freestone quarry on the estate of Mr. Woodward, from which grindstones, millstones and building stone are obtained. A thin stratum of coal was worked in the middle of the 19th century.[5]

There are ancient earthworks in Arley Wood and Hawkbatch.

Place-names occurring in deeds relating to Upper Arley are Elarenesland, le Wheolares,[6] Rylondbrugge, Wudres (xv cent.),[7] Quateway, Frenchman Street, Whitnells, Popehouse Lane (xvi cent.).[8]

MANORS The manor of *UPPER ARLEY* was given to the college of Wolverhampton by Wulfrun, the founder, about 996.[9] The clerks of Wolverhampton held 2 hides at Arley in 1086, and to this manor belonged half a hide in 'the other Arley,' which Osbert Fitz Richard took by force from the canons.[10]

The college of Wolverhampton with all its possessions was granted by William Rufus to Samson Bishop of Worcester.[11] Samson gave the college to the Prior and convent of Worcester,[12] and from them it was unlawfully taken by Roger Bishop of Salisbury in the reign of Stephen.[13] The college was restored to the priory of Worcester by King Stephen, but Upper Arley was apparently given by Bishop Roger to Henry de Port, for his son Adam was in possession in 1166-7,[14] and it appears that Henry de Port had formerly held it.[15] Adam de Port forfeited all his possessions in 1172,[16] when Upper or Over Arley

---

[1] Local and Personal Act, 58 & 59 Vict. cap. 86.

[2] Nash, *Hist. of Worc.* ii, App. ii ; *Cal. Chart. R.* 1226–57, p. 154.

[3] Statistics from Bd. of Agric. (1905).

[4] Nash, op. cit. ii, App. i.

[5] Lewis, *Topog. Dict.*

[6] Jeayes, *Lyttelton Chart.* no. 349.

[7] Ibid. no. 373.

[8] Misc. Bks. Ld. Rev. clxxxv, fol. 149 et seq.

[9] Dugdale, *Mon. Angl.* vi, 1443. At this time pannage for thirty pigs at 'Scipricga' belonged to the manor of Arley. The bounds of the manor are given in Wulfrun's charter (ibid. 1445).

[10] *Dom. Bk.* (Rec. Com.), i, 247 d.

[11] Heming, *Chartul.* (ed. Hearne), 537 ; Oliver, *Hist. of Church of Wolverhampton*, 24, 25. [12] Ibid.

[13] Heming, loc. cit. ; Oliver, op. cit. 28.

[14] *Pipe R.* 13 *Hen. II* (Pipe R. Soc.), 56.

[15] Nash, op. cit. ii, App. vii. Adam grants the church 'cum bosco quod prefata ecclesia habuit tempore patris mei, scilicet Henrici de Port.'

[16] *Pipe R.* 18 *Hen. II* (Pipe R. Soc.), 106 ; Eyton, *Domesday Studies, Staff.* 67.

passed to the Crown. During the early years of the reign of Richard I it appears to have been farmed by the men of the manor,[17] but in 1194 it was granted to William de Braose at a rent of £15 10s. 7d. yearly.[18]　He held it until 1198–9, when it was resumed by the Crown, probably on account of the debts owed by William to the king.[19]　In the following year it was granted by King John to Thomas de Burgh. He held it of the king in chief for the service of one knight's fee,[20] and from that time it was always held of the king in chief either for knight service or at a fee-farm rent.[21] Thomas

DE BURGH. *Gules seven lozenges vair.*

de Burgh was still holding the manor in 1225,[22] but in March 1227 it was granted by the king to Hubert de Burgh, Earl of Kent, brother of Thomas,[23] and the grant was confirmed in 1228.[24] In 1232 the king freed from regard of the forest the wood of Arley belonging to Hubert de Burgh in the forest of Kinver.[25] On the fall of Hubert in 1232 he surrendered all his possessions to the king,[26] and, though they were restored to him in the same year,[27] this manor was granted in June 1233 to Anketil Mallore and his heirs, to be held at a fee farm of 10 marks yearly.[28] In 1235–6, however, as the result of an action between Hubert and Anketil, the manor was restored to the earl,[29] who was succeeded in 1243 by his son John.[30]　John de Burgh granted this manor to Robert Burnell, Bishop of Bath and Wells, who surrendered it to King Edward I.[31] In 1274 the king granted it to Letard Hanyn and his issue,[32] and in 1276 Letard obtained licence to grant it to Roger de Mortimer.[33]　It passed from Roger to his son Edmund in 1282,[34] and was granted by the latter to his daughter Iseult and her first husband Walter de Balun for their lives.[35] After Walter's death Iseult married Hugh de Audley, and on his forfeiture in 1322 the manor was granted by the king to Iseult,[36] who held it until her death about 1339–40.[37]　The reversion after her death, during the minority of

Roger de Mortimer, had been granted in 1336 to William de Bohun[38] Earl of Northampton, who had married Elizabeth widow of Edmund de Mortimer, grandson of the Edmund who had granted the manor to Iseult.[39]　Roger came of age about 1348, but Elizabeth held the manor until her death in 1356, when it passed to her son Roger,[40] who had become Earl of March by the reversal of his grandfather's attainder in 1354.[41]　It passed with the title of Earl of March[42] until it was sold by Richard Duke of York and Earl of March in 1448 to William Boerley or Burley.[43]　William died in 1458–9,[44] but he had apparently before his death conveyed the manor to trustees for Thomas Lyttelton, who had married Joan, William's eldest daughter and co-heir.[45]　Sir Thomas died seised of the manor in 1481, when he was succeeded by his son William.[46]　From him it passed in 1507 to his son John,[47] and from that time the descent of the manor is identical with that of Frankley (q.v.) until the death of Thomas Lord Lyttelton in 1779.[48]

The manor then passed to his sister Lucy Fortescue, wife of Sir Arthur Annesley, Viscount Valentia.[49]　She and her husband were dealing with half the manor in 1782–3,[50] but she died in 1783,[51] and the manor passed to her son George,[52] who succeeded his father as Earl of Mountnorris in 1816.[53]　He built the present Arley Castle in 1844, but died in that year at Arley without surviving issue.[54] The manor then passed to his nephew Arthur Lyttelton

ANNESLEY, Viscount Valentia. *Paly argent and azure a bend gules.*

Annesley,[55] who sold it in 1852 to Robert Woodward. He died in 1882, when Arley passed to his son Robert,[56] the present owner of the manor.

The lords of the manor of Arley claimed there pleas of the Crown, free warren, market and fair and waifs and strays, view of frankpledge, infangenthef and gallows.[57] There is no indication, however, that a market or fair was ever held at Arley. There was a wood belonging to the manor in the bounds of

[17] Hunter, *Gt. R. of the Pipe,* 1 *Ric. I* (Rec. Com.), 248 ; *Will. Salt Arch. Soc. Coll.* ii, 3.
[18] *Will. Salt Arch. Soc. Coll.* ii, 55, 61.
[19] Ibid. 65, 72, 79, 86.
[20] Ibid. 91, 97 ; *Testa de Nevill* (Rec. Com.), 55.
[21] *Cal. Chart. R.* 1226–57, p. 182 ; *Cal. Pat.* 1272–81, p. 145 ; *Feud. Aids,* v, 9, 18 ; Chan. Inq. p.m. 22 Ric. II, no. 34 ; 37 Hen. VI, no. 11 ; (Ser. 2), xxii, 36 ; liii, 42.
[22] Maitland, *Bracton's Note Bk.* iii, 530.
[23] Jeayes, op. cit. no. 12 ; *Cal. Chart. R.* 1226–57, p. 25.
[24] *Cal. Chart. R.* 1226 57, p. 81.
[25] Ibid. 154.
[26] Matt. Paris, *Chron. Maj.* (Rolls Ser.), iii, 232.
[27] Ibid. 233.
[28] *Cal. Chart. R.* 1226–57, p. 182.
[29] Maitland, op. cit. iii, 200–1.
[30] *Excerpta e Rot. Fin.* (Rec. Com.), i, 406. Margaret widow of Hubert released all her claim to dower in this manor in 1247 (*Will. Salt Arch. Soc. Coll.* iv, 239).

[31] *Cal. Pat.* 1272–81, p. 145 ; *Plac. de Quo Warr.* (Rec. Com.), 718.
[32] *Cal. Chart. R.* 1257–1300, p. 187.
[33] *Cal. Pat.* 1272–81, p. 145.
[34] G.E.C. *Complete Peerage,* v, 379.
[35] Add. MS. 5485, fol. 160 ; *Cal. Close,* 1323–7, p. 467.
[36] *Cal. Close,* 1323–7, p. 467.
[37] *Abbrev. Rot. Orig.* (Rec. Com.), ii, 130.
[38] Duchy of Lanc. Royal Chart. no. 277.
[39] *Cal. Close,* 1354–60, p. 271 ; G.E.C. *Complete Peerage,* v, 379.
[40] *Cal. Close,* 1354–60, p. 271.
[41] G.E.C. *Complete Peerage,* v, 243.
[42] Chan. Inq. p.m. 34 Edw. III (1st nos.), no. 86 ; 22 Ric. II, no. 34 ; 3 Hen. VI, no. 32 ; *Cal. Pat.* 1429–36, p. 186.
[43] Jeayes, op. cit. no. 351, 353, 354 ; Close, 49 Hen. VI, m. 14 d.
[44] Chan. Inq. p.m. 37 Hen. VI, no. 11.
[45] Chan. Inq. p.m. 37 Hen. VI, no. 11 ; *Cal. Pat.* 1461–7, pp. 94, 459. In 1464–5 Margaret widow of William

Burley was summoned to answer for damages done in Arley, which she held for life. The plaintiffs, Thomas Lyttelton and William Trussell, complained that she had wasted the estate by allowing the buildings to remain unroofed, and by cutting down eighty oaks and 100 elms (*Will. Salt Arch. Soc. Coll.* [new ser.], iv, 131).
[46] Chan. Inq. p.m. 21 Edw. IV, no. 55.
[47] Ibid. (Ser. 2), xxii, 36.
[48] Ibid. liii, 42 ; ccxxix, 140 ; cclvii, 71 ; Pat. 1 Jas. I, pt. i ; 34 Chas. II, pt. ix, no. 7 ; Feet of F. Staffs. Trin. 6 Anne ; Recov. R. East. 5 Geo. II, rot. 31 ; 5 Geo. III, rot. 174.
[49] G.E.C. *Complete Peerage,* v, 406.
[50] Feet of F. Staffs. Mich. 23 Geo. III.
[51] G.E.C. *Complete Peerage,* v, 406.
[52] Feet of F. Staffs. Hil. 55 Geo. III.
[53] G.E.C. loc. cit.　[54] Ibid.
[55] Burke, *Extinct Peerage* ; Lewis, *Topog. Dict.*
[56] Burke, *Landed Gentry,* 1906.
[57] *Plac. de Quo Warr.* (Rec. Com.), 718. Mr. Woodward has the original grant of these.

Upper Arley Church : The Nave looking East

Arley Castle : Principal Staircase

Wyre Forest,[58] and the weirs and fishing in the Severn and a ferry over the river formed valuable appurtenances of the manor.[59] In 1602 'a passage called the Ferry boate' over the Severn was held by the parish at the will of the lord of the manor.[60]

A water corn-mill at Arley is first mentioned in 1425,[61] and in 1602 the site of the old mill is mentioned, together with mills near Bulfield and Arley Wood.[62] Mills are also mentioned in the 17th and 18th centuries.[63] There is now a disused corn-mill called Worralls on a tributary of the Severn on the Kidderminster boundary, and Arley Mill, a corn-mill, on another tributary, is on the east of the park at Arley Castle.

The manor of *EXTONS* (Heyston, xiii cent.; Hexston, xiv cent.) was held of the manor of Upper Arley.[64] It originated in land held by a family named Hexton or Hekstane, probably as early as the 12th century. Hubert de Burgh, who became lord of Arley in 1227, granted to Robert son of Robert de Gloucester all the land in Arley which Robert had held of Thomas de Burgh, and which had formerly been held by Osbert de Hexton.[65] Robert gave this land to Dametta de Hexton[66] for life, with remainder to Avelina de Hexton. Dametta seems to have died about 1292, when Avelina successfully sued Henry de Hexton for a messuage and lands.[67] Roger son of Henry de Hexton received a grant of land in Arley from William de Gerrus in 1295.[68] It was probably this Roger who in 1312–13 obtained from Henry son of Henry de Hexton, his brother, a recognition of his right to land in Arley.[69] His widow Idonea was holding the estate in 1327,[70] but it had passed by 1332–3 to Henry de Hexton, probably son of Roger.[71] Before 1383 the Hextons had added to their estate at Arley a tenement called Silvestres, formerly belonging to John Gunny,[72] and at that date John de Hexton granted to his son William the reversion of a tenement which John atte Brok and his wife Maud then held.[73] William was succeeded by a son John,[74] who settled his land in 1406.[75] Isabel his wife appears to have survived him and granted the estate to trustees, who gave it in 1439 to John Hexton and his wife Agnes daughter of John Horewode.[76] John Hexton was dealing with land at Arley in 1449,[77] and in 1482 his son Thomas, a merchant and burgess of Bristol, leased 'Hextons Place' to Thomas Holowey of Alveley, co. Salop, and Joan his wife, at a yearly rent of £5.[78] Three years later he granted it to John Alcock, Bishop of Worcester, and others[79] in trust for the Dean and

college of Westbury.[80] In 1496 the dean leased 'the manor in the lordship of Arley called Hexteyns Place'[81] at a rent of £80 to Thomas Wildecote of Highley, co. Salop, with the condition that if Thomas should cause to be appropriated to the college any church in the diocese of Worcester of the annual value of 10 marks the rent should be returned to him.[82] This or some similar condition may have been fulfilled by Thomas, for in 1501 the dean re-leased to him all his estate in Arley,[83] and Thomas sold the manor in 1520–1 to John Pakington.[84] John gave the estate to his daughter Bridget on her marriage with John Lyttelton, lord of Arley,[85] and it apparently afterwards followed the descent of the manor of Upper Arley, though it is not mentioned in deeds relating to the manor until 1707.[86]

The value of the estate at Hextons increased greatly about 1680, when freestone was discovered there[87] suitable for making grindstones, which were much in demand in the neighbourhood owing to the local hardware trade.

PICKARDS TENEMENT and *THE MORE* originated in land granted by Letard de Hanyn to Hugh de Picard, also known as Hugh de Waban.[88] In 1276 an assize was taken to find whether Letard and Hugh had disseised Roger de Cruce of land in 'Shutenearelegh,' or South Arley,[89] and Roger de Mortimer, to whom Letard sold the manor in that year, granted to Hugh for his homage and service all the land which Alexander de Colrugge held in Arley Manor, with land called 'terra de la More' held by Richard Hyrlaund and his wife Maud.[90] John Picard, son and heir of Hugh, leased the estate called the More and a carucate of land in Arley in 1323 to Thomas son of William Bromley of Arley and Margaret his wife for their lives, and his grant was ratified by his daughters Isabel and Joan in 1338.[91] In the following year Thomas and Margaret granted their interest in the estate to Thomas Lestrange.[92] Nothing further is known of it until 1357, when Roger son of Hugh de Wyre gave to his son Richard all his land in Arley called 'More or Woddus or Pykaslonde' with contingent remainders to Richard and John, brothers of the grantor, and to his sisters Juliana and Margaret.[93] In 1460 John Kocke granted 'Le More and Le Wodehouse *alias* Picarslond' to Gilbert Talbot and others,[94] evidently in trust, for in 1476 John Goode recovered this property from John Cokkes of Chetton, probably to be identified with the above John Kocke.[95] In 1485 John Goode's son Thomas sold a messuage called Lee Pykardes with land called

[58] Inq. a.q.d. 19 Edw. II, no. 144; *Cal. Close*, 1323–7, p. 467; Chan. Inq. p.m. 6 Edw. III (1st nos.), no. 86; Feet of F. Staffs. Hil. 55 Geo. III.
[59] *Cal. Close*, 1323–7, p. 467; Chan. Inq. p.m. 6 Edw. III (1st nos.), no. 86.
[60] Misc. Bks. Ld. Rev. clxxxv, fol. 149–55.
[61] Chan. Inq. p.m. 3 Hen. VI, no. 32.
[62] Misc. Bks. Ld. Rev. clxxxv, fol. 149–55.
[63] Recov. R. Mich. 15 Jas. I, rot. 25; East. 5 Geo. II, rot. 31.
[64] Jeayes, op. cit. no. 12.   [65] Ibid.
[66] She is called the aunt of Alan son of Guy de Glaseleye.
[67] *Will. Salt Arch. Soc. Coll.* vi (1), 217.
[68] Jeayes, op. cit. no. 42; see also no. 60.

[69] Ibid. no. 69; *Will. Salt Arch. Soc. Coll.* ix (1), 43.
[70] *Will. Salt Arch. Soc. Coll.* vii (1), 247.
[71] Ibid. x (1), 128; Jeayes, op. cit. no. 90. Henry son of Roger de Hexton witnessed a charter of 1323.
[72] John gave it in 1315 to his servant John son of Joan le Kynges (Jeayes, op. cit. no. 71), who granted it in 1316 to William de la Lowe (ibid. no. 74). John Gunny sold it in 1319 to Thomas Conan and Lawrentia his wife (ibid. no. 84).
[73] Jeayes, op. cit. no. 224.
[74] Ibid. no. 233.   [75] Ibid. no. 261.
[76] Ibid. no. 335, 336.
[77] Ibid. no. 373.
[78] Ibid. no. 417, 424.
[79] Ibid. no. 424; *Will. Salt Arch. Soc. Coll.* xi, 252.

[80] Jeayes, op. cit. no. 429.
[81] This is the first time the estate is called a manor.
[82] Jeayes, op. cit. no. 429.
[83] Ibid. no. 430.
[84] Feet of F. Staffs. Mich. 12 Hen. VIII.
[85] Nash, op. cit. ii, App. vi.
[86] Nash, loc. cit.; Feet of F. Staffs. Trin. 6 Anne; Mich. 23 Geo. III; Hil. 55 Geo. III; Recov. R. East. 5 Geo. II, rot. 31; 5 Geo. III, rot. 174.
[87] Nash, op. cit. ii, App. i.
[88] Jeayes, op. cit. no. 90.
[89] *Will. Salt Arch. Soc. Coll.* vi (1), 77.
[90] Jeayes, op. cit. no. 59.
[91] Ibid. no. 90, 32, 109.
[92] Ibid. no. 110.
[93] Ibid. no. 156.
[94] Ibid. no. 367.
[95] Ibid. no. 408.

Lee Doddes and Lee Annottes Ruddyng to Thomas Wildecote and his wife Elizabeth.[96] Pickards Tenement from that time followed the descent of Extons.[97] The name still survives at Pickard's Farm, to the north of the village of Upper Arley.

A weir at Arley and a messuage and a carucate of land at *LE BOURE*, sometimes called a manor, belonged in the 13th century to Adam de la Bure or Boure. He granted the weir in 1236 to Laurence de Alveley at a rent of 2*s.* yearly,[98] and at the same date Laurence released to Adam a curtilage at Arley.[99] In 1304–5 and 1326 weirs and land belonging to Adam de la Boure were excepted from the estate of the Audleys in Arley,[100] and in 1331–2 their custody was granted to Iseult de Audley.[1] On her death it passed under her will to William de Bohun Earl of Northampton.[2] In 1333 it was found by

beginning of the 14th century, some small pieces of Norman ornament built into the south nave wall at its eastern end (when it was heightened early in the 16th century) point to a church of 12th-century erection. This building no doubt consisted of a nave and chancel only, and the thickness of the south wall of the present nave suggests that it belongs to the original structure.

The first enlargement appears to have taken place *circa* 1325, when a north aisle was added and at the same time the chancel arch was rebuilt. Early in the 16th century the aisle was extended eastward and the walls of the nave were heightened by the addition of a clearstory, probably necessitated by the building of a 15th-century tower which kept out the light previously obtained through a large west window. The present tower was not built until late in the 16th

UPPER ARLEY CHURCH FROM THE NORTH-WEST

inquisition that the land at la Boure was member of the manor of Cleobury and that Edmund de Mortimer had died seised of it in fee.[3]

The church of *ST. PETER* consists of a modern chancel, south vestry and organ chamber, a nave 32 ft. 5 in. by 19 ft. 5 in., a north aisle 51 ft. 10 in. by 14 ft. 2 in. (the full length of the nave and extending eastwards nearly to the end of the chancel), a south porch and a tower 18 ft. by 17 ft. 3 in. at the west end of the nave. These measurements are all internal.

Though the earliest detail *in situ* dates from the

century, but the foundations of the earlier one can still be seen. At the same time as the raising of the nave walls the church was reroofed and the aisle wall heightened by the addition of an embattled parapet. No further structural alterations appear to have been made until 1885, when the present chancel was built together with the vestry, organ chamber and south porch, while at the same time the building was generally restored.

These modern enlargements have been made in red and grey sandstone from the Hexton quarries, a stone used throughout in the original building.

[96] Jeayes, op. cit. no. 423 ; Add. MS. 31314, fol. 73.
[97] Nash, op. cit. ii, App. vi.
[98] *Will. Salt Arch. Soc. Coll.* iv, 233.

[99] Ibid. 229. Laurence in 1238 claimed land in Arley which had belonged to his great-grandfather Orme in the time of Henry II (ibid. 89).

[100] Ibid. vii (1), 138; *Cal. Close,* 1323–7, p. 467.
[1] *Abbrev. Rot. Orig.* (Rec. Com.), ii, 56.
[2] Ibid. 130. [3] *Cal. Close,* 1333–7, p. 143.

Between the chancel and the north chapel is a modern arcade of two pointed arches. The chancel arch is pointed and of two orders, the mouldings of the outer being continuous and those of the inner stopped on the capitals of the respond shafts. The latter are half-round on plan with moulded bases on square plinths.

The arcade between the nave and aisle is in three bays with pointed arches of two chamfered orders carried on piers, quatrefoil on plan with a small roll between each shaft and having moulded capitals and bases of simple section. The responds are similar and almost the whole arcade is original 14th-century work. In the east end of the south nave wall is a small blocked doorway with a drop rear arch, which probably opened into the rood-stair, as it is invisible outside. Immediately over this doorway is a blocked window, its opening visible externally. The doorway within the modern porch is new, but in the wall above can be seen the segmental relieving arch of an older opening.

The clearstory on each side is pierced with two pairs of square-headed four-light windows with vertical tracery in the heads. The jambs of these windows differ slightly on the two sides of the church.

The added clearstory on the north is slightly thicker than the wall below, the junction being masked by a small chamfer. The embattled parapet to the north and south walls, which is also returned across the east wall of the nave, is original, with a continuous coping. The merlons are enriched by a sunk trefoiled panel under a pointed head. A massive buttress terminates the south wall of the nave towards the west.

Of the aisle windows, the eastern retains its original opening with a segmental head, but the mullions, &c., are modern. Of the three in the north wall, the first from the east has three lights and a square head with panelled spandrels. The other two date from the 14th century, having two lights each with a quatrefoil in the head. Further west is a blocked pointed doorway with a segmental rear arch, which has been restored externally.

The west window of the aisle is similar to the two last described in the north wall. Externally the nave aisle is finished with a chamfered plinth and supported by five simple buttresses terminated with gabled copings. The parapet is similar to that of the main nave walls; at the west end it is sloped up to meet the tower, but the east wall of the quire aisle has a low gable.

The tower stands on a moulded plinth, and is externally divided by moulded strings into four stages and crowned with a low parapet. At the south-east angle is an octagonal stair turret, and from the western corners project diagonal buttresses, stopping at the level of the bell-chamber windows, the string-courses being carried round them. The pointed tower arch, of two square orders, springs from square responds with moulded bases and abaci. The west window is modern, though set within the pointed head and jambs of the original work. In the north and south walls of the first stage is a small pointed window of a single uncusped light, with an external moulded architrave stopping on a slightly projecting sill. Under the tower was formerly a gallery (removed in recent years), and the set-offs which supported it are still visible. The ringing chamber is lighted by two small windows similar to those in the ground stage, while in each wall of the bell-chamber are coupled semicircular openings with plain imposts and key-stones, which seem to have been inserted in the 18th century. The floor of the bell-chamber appears to have been raised at some period, as shown by the holes in the east and west walls of the ringing chamber for the reception of the joists of the older floor.

The roof of the chancel is modern, but the roofs (both of elm) over the nave and aisle are of the early 16th century, though the latter has been considerably restored. The nave roof is of very low pitch, and is divided into four bays by heavy moulded rafters. Those against the end walls and in the centre are supported by carved spandrel braces and wall-posts carried on stone corbels. The corbels to the centre one are carved with saltire crosses, but the others are plain. The ridge, wall-plates and purlins are all moulded. The aisle roof is flat, and is divided into five main bays, each of which is further subdivided into four panels by moulded beams. All the roofs are covered with lead.

The font and the pulpit are both modern.

Built high up in the north wall of the nave is a small stone on which is carved a circle inclosing a dove. In the floor of the aisle under the easternmost arch opening into the chancel are a few mediaeval tiles.

Over the chancel arch is a very dilapidated wall painting of the Judgement. In the centre of the picture, seated on a rainbow and clad in a red robe, is the figure of the Almighty with both hands upraised. The figures of the doomed are on the south side of the arch, with the righteous to the north. The painting was uncovered in 1884, but has since that date much faded, and is now very indistinct.

Under the west arch opening into the chancel is a fine effigy of an early 14th-century knight. The figure, set on a modern base, is in the attitude of prayer, the legs crossed and resting on the back of a small lion. Over the mail is a long surcoat, and upon the head, which rests on a cushion, is a bascinet. The sword hangs at the left side, and on the left arm is strapped a shield charged with his arms,[4] barry dancetty, which are also repeated on the ailettes.

On the south wall of the nave is a mural monument to Sir Henry Lyttelton, bart., who died 24 June 1693. The monument also records the burials of Captain William Lyttelton, brother of the above, and his nephew Henry son of Sir Charles Lyttelton.

There is a ring of six bells by Abel Rudhall, 1753. The treble is inscribed 'When you us ring we'll sweetly sing A.R. 1753'; the second 'Peace and good neighbourhood A.R. 1753'; the third 'Prosperity to this Parish A.R. 1753'; the fourth 'Abel Rudhall cast us all 1753'; the fifth 'Wm. Hill and Thomas Brooks Churchwardens A.R. 1753,' and the tenor 'I to the Church the living call and to the grave do summon all. A.R. 1753.'

---

[4] From his arms the knight is probably Sir Walter de Balun of Much Marcle, co. Hereford, first husband of Iseult daughter of Edmund Mortimer of Wigmore. He was living and married to her in 1286–7 (Add. MS. 5485, fol. 160). The story that he died on his wedding day at Southampton seems to have no foundation.

The plate consists of two silver cups, two silver patens—one large – and a silver flagon, each inscribed 'The Gift of George Mountnorris to the Parish of Over Arley 1817,' and stamped with the date letter of the previous year, a small glass water-cruet having a plated stopper, and a modern brass almsdish.

The registers previous to 1812 are as follows : (i) all entries 1564 to 1719 ; (ii) baptisms and burials 1720 to 1812, marriages 1720 to 1754 ; (iii) marriages 1754 to 1799 ; (iv) marriages 1799 to 1812.

ADVOWSON The advowson of the church of Upper Arley was originally annexed to the manor and was given in the middle of the 12th century to the Dean and Chapter of Lichfield by Adam de Port and his wife Sybil.[5] The church was confirmed to the dean and chapter by Pope Honorius III in 1221[6] and by Boniface Archbishop of Canterbury (1245–70)[7] and Alexander Bishop of Coventry and Lichfield (1224–38).[8] In 1225 Thomas de Burgh, lord of the manor, un-

In 1676 the Dean of Lichfield claimed the advowson and rectory of Arley on the grounds that they were held by the Lytteltons under a lease only. On search being made in the cathedral registers a memorandum was found by which it appeared that Gilbert Lyttelton had purchased the advowson in fee, a condition of the purchase being that he should pay to the dean and vicar annual rents of £10 each and should entertain the former as often as he came to visit the church.[17] In 1675 Sir Henry Lyttelton gave the vicar the great tithes of the part of the parish which lies on the west side of the Severn, together with the small tithes of the whole parish, in lieu of the yearly pension of £10.[18]

CHARITIES The Poor's Land.—The parish is in possession of two cottages with gardens at the Herne, three cottages with gardens at Arley, and a house and 10 a. at Nash End, derived in part from the benefaction of a Mr. Longmore and of other donors, bringing in an income of £50 a year or thereabouts. The trustees have also

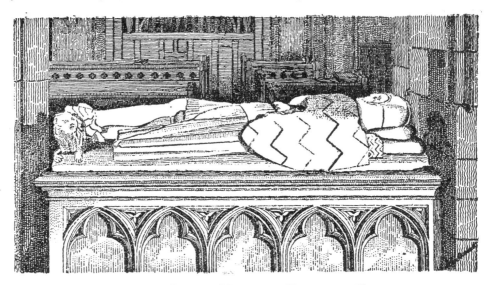

UPPER ARLEY CHURCH : TOMB WITH EFFIGY OF A KNIGHT

successfully claimed the church of Arley.[9] The advowson was included in the grant of the manor to Anketil Mallore in 1233,[10] and it would appear that the de Burghs also claimed it, for in 1259–60 the king, at the instance of John de Burgh, acknowledged the dean's right,[11] and in 1260 John confirmed this.[12] The dean had again to make good his right against the king in 1292–3.[13]

The dean and chapter remained in possession of the advowson and rectory until 1548,[14] when they were sold to Gilbert son of John Lyttelton.[15] They then followed the descent of the manor[16] until the sale of the latter to Robert Woodward. The rectory passed with the manor, but the advowson was retained by Arthur Lyttelton Annesley and now belongs to his son Lieut.-Gen. Sir Arthur Lyttelton Lyttelton-Annesley.

a sum of £110 2s. on deposit at a bank arising from accumulations of income. In 1909 a sum of £33 was distributed among fifty-five poor people.

In 1811 Thomas Corbyn by his will bequeathed £60, the interest to be distributed among the poor on St. Thomas's Day yearly. The legacy with an addition by the executors is now represented by £100 consols. In 1909 the annual dividends of £2 10s. were divided among five poor women in sums varying from 5s. to 15s.

In 1886 the Rev. Edward Whieldon by a codicil to his will proved at London 28 September bequeathed £100, now represented by £99 2s. 8d. consols, the annual dividends amounting to £2 9s. 4d. to be distributed among aged and deserving poor. In 1910 the distribution was made among seven widows in sums varying from 4s. to 12s. 6d.

[5] Maitland, op. cit. iii, 530.
[6] Hist. MSS. Com. Rep. xiv, App. viii, 216.
[7] Dugdale, Mon. Angl. vi, 1245.
[8] Ibid. 1251.
[9] Maitland, loc. cit.
[10] Cal. Chart. R. 1226–57, p. 182.
[11] Plac. de Quo Warr. (Rec. Com.), 711; Will. Salt Arch. Soc. Coll. iv, 249.
[12] Dugdale, Mon. Angl. vi, 1250.
[13] Plac. de Quo Warr. (Rec. Com.), 711.
[14] Valor Eccl. (Rec. Com.), iii, 132.
[15] Jeayes, op. cit. no. 438 ; Nash, op. cit. ii, App. viii.
[16] For references see manor.
[17] Nash, op. cit. ii, App. viii.
[18] Ibid.

BELBROUGHTON

Broctune (ix cent.); Brotune (xi cent.); Bellenbrokton (xiv cent.).

The parish of Belbroughton has an area of 4,748 acres, comprising, in 1905, 2,012¾ acres of arable land, 2,195½ acres of permanent grass and 321½ acres of woodland.[1] It occupies the lower slopes of the Clent range, its height varying from 332 ft. on the western border to 700 ft. in the extreme northeast. The village is situated close to the western border of the parish. The church stands on high ground on the west side of the by-road running south out of the settlement. Immediately opposite is the rectory, a plain three-story red brick building of the late 18th century, to the north of which stands the old tithe-barn, now in a very dilapidated condition and shortly to be pulled down to make room for a parish hall. The cottages are of no great antiquity and are mostly of red brick, although half-timber construction is also to be seen; they are generally roofed with tiles. At the northern extremity of the village, at the junction of the roads from Holy Cross and Bell End, is the 'Talbot,' a small late 17th or early 18th-century inn built of red brick and having a tiled roof. It is of no architectural interest, but the stables which are attached to the building on the east, and are of the same date (though built of stone), merit attention on account of the attempt at symmetry displayed in the design of their elevations.

The greater part of the Bell Inn at Bell End was rebuilt late in the 17th or early 18th century, though parts are of much earlier date. It is of L-shaped plan, two stories high, and is built of red brick with a tile roof; the older walls are, however, of half-timber construction. The interior has been completely modernized. The windows are divided into lights by wooden transoms and mullions. This is one of the many inns in which King Charles is incorrectly said to have rested in his flight from Worcester.

Moor Hall, now a farm-house, is situated a little way off the east side of the Bromsgrove and Stourbridge road. It was surrounded by a moat, now filled in on the north and east sides. The house, which was erected late in the 17th century, is of two stories and built of red brick with a tiled roof. It is of little architectural interest, having been added to on the north-east and completely modernized in the 19th century. Over the entrance doorway is a small stone panel inscribed with the following : 'Non Domus Dominum sed Dominus Domum Honestat, $_{I}^{T}_{E}$ 1680.'

Fairfield Court stands back on the west side of the Bromsgrove and Stourbridge road, about 5 miles north of the latter town. It is now a farm-house, and until recent years was entirely surrounded by a moat, access to the house being obtained by a drawbridge, but all traces of this have now disappeared and the moat along the north side of the building has been filled in. The principal front of the house, with the porch, faces north and two wings project southward from the rear of the building. To the

original house, probably erected early in the 16th century, belong the whole of the east end of the building and the central chimney stack in the middle of the western portion, but most of the remainder of the structure was entirely rebuilt in the early part of the following century and remains in a good state of preservation. In the 18th century the ends of the east wall of the eastern wing were refaced with red brickwork and about the same time the dairy (adjoining the south-west corner of the house) was erected, while the modern work consists of the outhouse at the end of the dairy and various minor alterations.

BELBROUGHTON : DOORWAY OF BELL END CHAPEL AT BELL HALL

The plan of the original house is now a matter of conjecture, but from the disposition of the chimneys it does not seem to have been very dissimilar from the existing arrangement. The projecting porch in the middle of the Jacobean part of the north front opens into a large hall extending in length entirely across the building with windows at both ends. In the centre of the west wall is the old chimney stack, against the south side of which, rising to the first floor and the attics in the roof, is a fine Jacobean staircase of oak. The strings and handrail of the stair are moulded and the balusters turned, while the square newel posts are surmounted by shaped finials of a pleasing design. In an irregular-shaped room on the west of the hall is an original square-headed doorway, still retaining its 17th-century nail-studded door and a blocked-up three-light window. The east wall of the hall marks

[1] Statistics from Bd. of Agric. (1905).

the division between the 16th and 17th-century work, and to the former belong the two original stacks, built against the external east wall. Round the walls of a room to the east of the hall, known as the 'oak room,' is some late 16th or early 17th-century panelling, but this is not *in situ*, though it was no doubt taken from some other part of the house. A partition on the west of the room is likewise made up of 16th-century panelling. It screens off a passage from which the hall is entered. The bedrooms are of little interest ; they generally communicate with a passage running along the south side of the building.

The exterior of the house is picturesque. The oldest part is of half-timber and brick construction, though this on the south is covered by an 18th-century brick facing. The whole of the old framing is built with horizontal and vertical timbers, the panels being tall and

addition are low and divided into lights by sandstone mullions. The windows lighting the hall are, however, higher than the others and transomed. The porch is carried up two stories high and finishes with a pointed gable. The entrance archway is round-headed, with a slightly projecting keystone and impost blocks. The west end of the house has a pointed gable of half-timber construction, and the south front of the west wing is also gabled. All the roofs are tiled.

The Ram Alley Brook flows through the parish westward. At intervals it has been widened into ponds, which furnish the motive power for several mills, as in the 17th and 18th centuries all the small streams in this part of the county were utilized for forges. As early as the 16th century we have a reference to a Blade Mill in Brian's Bell in this parish.[2]

The main road from Stourbridge to Bromsgrove

MOOR HALL, BELBROUGHTON

narrow. The first floor on the south side of the east wing overhangs, and is carried on long curved braces projecting from the main uprights at the end of the side walls. The east block is gabled towards the north and south. The northern stack on the east wall is built of stone up to the eaves, but above this point are two square brick chimneys, carried up independently of one another, but joined by an oversailing brick coping at the top. Both chimneys have an angular rib of brickwork carried up each face. The central stack, above the roof, is of the same design, but the coping is modern. The walls of the 17th-century addition are built of red sandstone up to the level of the first floor, while the upper part is of red brick with red sandstone quoins and dressings to the windows. Round the base of the walls is a slightly projecting plinth. All the original windows in this

runs south-eastward through the parish, the village, situated close to the western border of the parish, being connected with it by several branch roads.

Nash states that the parish was in the forests of Feckenham and Piperode[3] and some of the large woodlands, the survival of the forest in Chaddesley Corbett and Bromsgrove, run into this parish. In the 17th century Morehall Bell and Brian's Bell were looked upon as being ' in the King's Holt.'[4]

The surface soil is loamy and the subsoil varies from the bunter pebble beds of the eastern part of the parish to Keuper Marl in the south-west and Keuper Sandstone in the north-west.

One industry of the neighbourhood is the manufacture of scythes, hay and chaff knives and edge tools of all kinds for agricultural purposes. This industry was carried on at Belbroughton at least as early as

[2] Chan. Proc. (Ser. 2), bdle. 34, no. 6.   [3] Nash, *Hist. of Worc.* i, 56–7.   [4] Exch. Dep. 5 Will. and Mary, East. no. 24.

1564, when 'John Smythe, sythesmythe,' was the defendant in a suit respecting a messuage called 'Hollies.'[5] There used to be a good deal of nail-making, but this has died out.

There are brickworks near Bradford and glass is made on a small scale at Fairfield.

Agriculture, especially on allotments and small holdings, furnishes employment for a number of the inhabitants. Wheat, barley and oats are the chief crops raised on the farms, while vegetables and fruit are grown on the small holdings. Part of the land is under pasture.

Fairs, at which horned cattle, horses and cheese were sold, were held at Belbroughton in the 19th century on the first Monday in April and the Monday before St. Luke's Day.[6]

Wildmoor, Bromeheath and Madley Heath were

where there was a mill.[10] At this time the Earl of Shrewsbury owned 240 acres of woodland in Belbroughton which he was entitled to inclose for seven years after each 'fall' of timber.[11]

A Roman urn with over 100 coins of various emperors was found near Fairfield in 1833.[12]

MANORS King Coenwulf in 817 exempted the Bishop of Worcester's estate at 'Beolne, Broctun and Forfeld' from all secular services except military service and the maintenance of bridges and strongholds.[13] His charter implies that the bishop was already in possession of these lands; the means by which he acquired them are unknown. Subsequently the monastery lost these manors and they passed to Earl Leofwin, but his son Leofric promised to restore them to the monks after

BELBROUGHTON : FAIRFIELD COURT FROM THE NORTH

commons belonging to the manor of Belbroughton,[7] Bell Heath to Brian's Bell, and Hollis Hill, Gosty Green and the Sling to Morehall Bell. The commons all adjoined and had no hedges or fences between.[8] In 1799, when an Act was passed for their inclosure,[9] the commons at Belbroughton contained about 500 acres. Under the award the lords of Brian's Bell were always to have the use of the pools on the common belonging to that manor and of the brook running from Shuts Mill and Farely Coppice over the common to Lower Fen Pool and to the Bell Inn,

his death.[14] He died in 1057[15] 'in a good old age, a man of no less virtue than power in his time—religious, prudent and faithful to his country, happily wedded to Godiva, a woman of great praise.'[16] She, on the death of her husband, requested to be allowed to retain the manors for her life, with reversion to the priory, on payment of a money rent. To this the monks agreed,[17] but it is doubtful whether they ever obtained possession of the manors, for shortly afterwards the land was ravaged by Edwin and Morcar, who occupied these manors.[18] Godiva seems, however,

[5] Chan. Proc. (Ser. 2), bdle. 188, no. 59. See also *Quart. Sess. Rec.* (Worcs. Hist. Soc.), p. xxxvi et seq.

[6] Lewis, *Topog. Dict.*; Brayley and Britton, *Beauties of Engl. and Wales*, xv (2), 204.

[7] Close, 17 Chas. I, pt. viii, no. 26.

[8] Exch. Dep. 5 Will. and Mary, East. no. 24.

[9] The award is dated 19 Mar. 1803 (*Blue Bk. Incl. Awards*, 188).

[10] Priv. Act, 39 Geo. III, cap. 54.

[11] Ibid.   [12] *V.C.H. Worcs.* i, 218.

[13] Heming, *Chartul.* (ed. Hearne), 449–

50; Kemble, *Codex Dipl.* no. 212; Birch, *Cart. Sax.* i, 500–1.

[14] Heming, op. cit. 261.

[15] *Angl.-Sax. Chron.* (Rolls Ser.), ii, 159.

[16] Thomas, *Surv. of Worc.* A. 69–70.

[17] Heming, op. cit. 261.

[18] Ibid.

to have retained possession of *BROUGHTON*, for in 1086 2 hides there which she had held belonged to Urse the sheriff.[19] A hide which was held under Urse by Robert in Clent Hundred,[20] following as it does in the Domesday Survey immediately after the entry for Broughton, may refer to land in this neighbourhood. *FAIRFIELD* (Forteld, ix cent.; Fornelde, xiv cent.) is not separately mentioned in Domesday, but was evidently then included in Broughton, which subsequently became known as the manor of Fairfield or Belbroughton or Belbroughton and Fairfield.[21] To it were appurtenant five salt-pans at Droitwich, which rendered 100 mits of salt and 5 ounces of silver.

This manor passed with Urse's other possessions to the Beauchamps and the overlordship followed the descent of the barony of Elmley.[22] In 1572–3 the

BELBROUGHTON : FAIRFIELD COURT FROM THE NORTH-WEST

manor was said to be held of the queen as of her hundred of Halfshire.[23]

The Beauchamps probably held the manor in demesne until the reign of Henry II, when on the marriage of Emma daughter of William de Beauchamp with Ralph de Sudeley [24] the manor was apparently given to Ralph, for his great-grandson Bartholomew de Sudeley, who died in 1280, was said to be holding the manor of William de Beauchamp without service because it was given in free marriage to his ancestors.[25]

The manor passed at Bartholomew's death to his son John,[26] who died in 1336 [27] and was succeeded by his grandson John son of Bartholomew de Sudeley.[28]

SUDELEY. *Or two bends gules.*

John died in 1340–1,[29] leaving a son John, but his widow Eleanor held the manor until her death in 1361,[30] when it passed to John. On his death in February 1366–7 he left as his heirs his nephew Thomas Boteler, aged ten years, son of his eldest sister Joan, and his younger sister Margery, aged thirty years.[31] In the following year a partition was made of John de Sudeley's lands,[32] and Fairfield seems to have been assigned to Thomas Boteler. John and William, the two elder sons of Sir Thomas Boteler, died without issue,[33] and Alice wife of Edmund Chesney, who was holding the manor in 1431 [34] and presented to the church in 1422,[35] may have been William's widow, the manor having been settled on William and his wife Alice in 1417–18.[35a] The manor afterwards passed to Sir Ralph Boteler of Sudeley, third son of Sir Thomas, who dealt with it in 1464 and 1467–8.[36] Sir Ralph Boteler had an only son Thomas, who died during his father's lifetime, probably between 1449 and 1460, without issue.[37] Sir Ralph died on 2 May 1473 seised of the manor, and, as he left no surviving issue, John Norbury, grandson of his sister Elizabeth, and William Belknap, son of his sister Joan, became joint heirs to his possessions.[38]

[19] *V.C.H. Worcs.* i, 319a. This holding has been wrongly identified in a former volume as Broughton Hackett.

[20] *V.C.H. Worcs.* i, 319a.

[21] The two manors were evidently distinct in 817 and in the middle of the 11th century, and, though united from 1086 to about 1538, have since remained separate, though always in the same ownership.

[22] *Cal. Inq. p.m.* 1–19 *Edw.* I, 197; 1–9 *Edw. II*, 403; Chan. Inq. p.m. 2 Hen. IV, no. 58; 8 Hen. IV, no. 68; 13 Edw. IV, no. 58. In 1361 and 1367 the manor was said to be held

of the Prior of Coventry (ibid. 35 Edw. III, pt. ii [1st nos.], no. 59; 41 Edw. III [1st nos.], no. 54). [23] Ibid. (Ser. 2), clxv, 192.

[24] Dugdale, *Hist. of Warw.* 1073; *Visit. of Essex* (Harl. Soc. xiv), 563.

[25] *Cal. Inq. p.m.* 1–19 *Edw.* I, 197.

[26] *Worc. Inq. p.m.* (Worcs. Hist. Soc.), pt. i, 24.

[27] *Abbrev. Rot. Orig.* (Rec. Com.), ii, 104.

[28] Chan. Inq. p.m. 10 Edw. III (1st nos.), no. 32.

[29] Ibid. 14 Edw. III (1st nos.), no. 10.

[30] Ibid. 35 Edw. III, pt. ii (1st nos.), no. 59.

[31] Ibid. 41 Edw. III (1st nos.), no. 54.

[32] *Abbrev. Rot. Orig.* (Rec. Com.), ii, 296. It is not very clear from this to whom Fairfield was assigned, but Margery was not holding it in 1379, when she died without issue, her heir being Thomas Boteler (Chan. Inq. p.m. 3 Ric. II, no. 63).

[33] Dugdale, *Hist. of Warw.* 1073.

[34] *Feud. Aids*, v, 331.

[35] Nash, op. cit. i, 59.

[35a] Close, 5 Hen. V, m. 16.

[36] Chan. Inq. p.m. 13 Edw. IV, no. 58.

[37] Pat. 8 Edw. IV, pt. iii, m. 12.

[38] Chan. Inq. p.m. 13 Edw. IV, no. 58.

His wife Alice survived him, dying 10 February 1473-4.[39] On 11 February 1477 Sir John Norbury and William Belknap had licence to enter into possession of the lands of Ralph Boteler of Sudeley,[40] but it does not appear to which of the two Fairfield passed. Probably Sir John Norbury held it, as it is not mentioned in the inquisition taken on the death of William Belknap in 1484.[41] In 1496 a partition took place between Edward Belknap, William's nephew, and Sir John Norbury, and it is interesting to note that the manor which for over two centuries had been known as 'Forfeld' was then called Belbroughton.[42] By this partition it was agreed that Sir John Norbury should hold Belbroughton.[43] In 1500 the manor was secured to Sir John Norbury's daughter and heir Anne wife of Richard Halliwell.[44] From Anne it passed to her daughter Jane, who married Sir Edmund Bray,[45] created Lord Bray in 1529.[46] Lord Bray died in 1539, and Fairfield was held by Jane Lady Bray until her death on 24 October 1558.[47] Her only son John Lord Bray having died without issue in the previous year, her six daughters became her heirs. In 1560-1 they agreed that Edmund Lord Chandos and Dorothy his wife, the fifth daughter, should have the manors of Fairfield, Belbroughton and Broomhill.[48] In 1574 Dorothy, then a widow, jointly with her son Giles Lord Chandos conveyed the manors of Fairfield and Belbroughton to Ann Petre,[49] widow of Sir William Petre, kt., Secretary of State to Henry VIII and Edward VI, Mary and Elizabeth. Anne left the manors to her daughter Catherine, who married John Talbot of Grafton.[50] John conveyed them in 1595 to Richard Leveson and John Brooke.[51] In 1609 Jane Watson, widow, and Sarah Watson conveyed these manors to Sir Richard Greaves,[52] who held them until his death on 10 July 1632, when his son Thomas Greaves succeeded.[53] In 1641-2 the latter, with Martha his wife, conveyed them to Thomas Rant and Thomas Hammond,[54] who were evidently

BRAY, Lord Bray. *Argent a cheveron between three eagles' legs sable razed at the thigh.*

CHANDOS, Lord Chandos. *Or a pile gules.*

trustees for William Ward, a wealthy goldsmith of London.[55] Fairfield and Belbroughton were probably included in certain manors unnamed which were conveyed by Thomas Rant and others to William's son Humble, Lord Ward of Birmingham, in 1649.[56] Lord Ward married Frances Lady Dudley, and seems to have settled Fairfield and Belbroughton on his third son William Ward, who was in possession in 1700.[57] John Ward, grandson of William, succeeded to the barony of Ward in 1740 on the death of his cousin,[58] and the manors from that time followed the descent of Dudley Castle [59] (q.v.), William Humble Ward, Earl of Dudley, being the present owner.

In the 16th century a 'manor or capital messuage' called Fairfield Court belonged to Henry James, who left four daughters—Elizabeth wife of Humphrey Perrott, Dorothy wife of Henry Greswolde, Martha wife of John Perrott, and Anne. It was agreed in 1596 that the capital messuage should belong to Humphrey Perrott and Elizabeth, and the former was still holding it in 1610.[60]

Tradition says there was once a chapel at Fairfield Court.[61]

The manor of BELNE (Beolne, ix cent. ; Bellem, Belna, xi cent.), afterwards BRIAN'S BELL (Broyns-belne, Brunesbell, xvi cent.) and BELL HALL, between 817 and 1057 appears to have followed the same descent as Fairfield (q.v.). The Danes probably deprived either Godiva or the monks of Worcester of this manor, for it was held before the Conquest by Leofnoth, a thegn of King Edward the Confessor. It afterwards passed to Ralf Fitz Hubert, who held it for more than five years. The Domesday Survey states that he was wrongfully dispossessed of it by William Fitz Osbern.[62] William Fitz Ansculf was in possession of it at the time of the Survey.[63] The overlordship passed with Dudley to Fulk Paynel,[64] and afterwards descended with the manor of Northfield [65] (q.v.). This overlordship is last mentioned in 1428.[66] In 1491-2 the manor was said to be held of the Duke of Buckingham.[67]

The 3 hides which the manor comprised in 1086 were held of these overlords by Robert,[68] who, from the fact of Belbroughton being afterwards held by the Beauchamps, may have been Robert le Despenser, brother of Urse D'Abitot.[69] A survey of a later date than Domesday states that William de Beauchamp held 8 hides at Belne of the fief of Fulk Paynel.[70] The large increase of 5 hides in its extent is not explained, but possibly the 2 or 3 hides contained in Belbroughton and Fairfield, also held by William de Beauchamp, were included in this return, though they were not of Fulk Paynel's fee.

[39] Pat. 16 Edw. IV, pt. ii, m. 10.
[40] Ibid.
[41] Chan. Inq. p.m. 2 Ric. III, no. 16.
[42] B.M. Add. Chart. 5684.
[43] Ibid.
[44] Ibid. ; *Visit. of Surr.* (Harl. Soc. xliii), 220.
[45] *Visit. of Surr.* (Harl. Soc. xliii), 220.
[46] G.E.C. *Complete Peerage,* ii, 11.
[47] Chan. Inq. p.m. (Ser. 2), clxv, 192.
[48] Ibid. clxix, 40 ; see also Feet of F. Worcs. Hil. 11 Eliz.
[49] Feet of F. Worcs. Hil. 16 Eliz.
[50] Burke, *Peerage* ; Chan. Inq. p.m. (Ser. 2), cccv, 108.
[51] Recov. R. East. 37 Eliz. rot. 55.
[52] Feet of F. Worcs. Hil. 6 Jas. I.

Habington states that the manor was sold by John Earl of Shrewsbury to Sir Richard Greaves (*Surv. of Worc.* i, 46).
[53] Chan. Inq. p.m. (Ser. 2), cccclxx, 58.
[54] Feet of F. Worcs. East. 17 Chas. I.
[55] Close, 17 Chas. I, pt. viii, no. 26.
[56] Recov. R. D. Enr. East. 1649, m. 4 d.
[57] Exch. Dep. East. 5 Will. and Mary, no. 24 ; Feet of F. Worcs. East. 12 Will. III.
[58] G.E.C. *Complete Peerage,* viii, 49.
[59] John Viscount Dudley left Belbroughton and Fairfield to a younger son William, Dudley passing first to his eldest son John, but eventually to

William ; Nash, op. cit. i, 57 ; Recov. R. Trin. 44 Geo. III, rot. 339.
[60] Recov. R. D. Enr. Hil. 8 Jas. I, m. 10 d.
[61] Noake, *Guide to Worc.* 25.
[62] See V.C.H. *Worcs.* i, 316b n.
[63] Ibid. 316b.
[64] See Dudley.
[65] V.C.H. *Worcs.* i, 316b, 328b ; *Testa de Nevill* (Rec. Com.), 40b ; *Worc. Inq. p.m.* (Worcs. Hist. Soc.), pt. i, 37 ; pt. ii, 115 ; *Feud. Aids,* v, 302, 323.
[66] *Feud. Aids,* v, 323.
[67] Cal. Inq. p.m. Hen. VII, i, 345.
[68] V.C.H. *Worcs.* i, 316b.
[69] Ibid. 328 n.
[70] Ibid. 328b.

Brian's Bell was held by the Beauchamps under the Paynels for the service of one knight, and descended with the barony of Elmley,[71] this mesne lordship being mentioned for the last time in 1546.[72]

Under the lords of Elmley, Brian's Bell was held by the family of Belne. The earliest mention of these under-tenants in connexion with land in Belbroughton occurs early in the 13th century, when Hugh de Belne was holding a knight's fee in Belne.[73] Hugh was succeeded by a son Simon before 1254–5,[74] and at that date made an agreement with William le Bruyn as to estovers in William's wood of Belne.[75] The Bruyns seem afterwards to have acquired this manor,[76] as in 1280 Simon le Bruyn and Margery widow of William Bruyn contributed to the subsidy for the tithing of Belne Bruyn,[77] and Simon le Bruyn was holding the manor in 1299–1300.[78] From this date Brian's Bell followed the same descent as the manor of Ab Lench[79] in Fladbury (q.v.) until the death of Edward Conway in 1546.[80] Sir John Conway, son and successor of Edward, and his son Edward conveyed it in 1592 to Humphrey Perrott.[81] It descended in this family from father to son[82] until 1776, when John Perrott died, leaving a daughter Katherine.[83] By her marriage with Walter Noel of Hilcote the manor of Brian's Bell passed to the Noel family, in whose possession it remained until the death of Charles Perrott Noel in 1908.[84] He left

PERROTT. *Gules three pears or and a chief argent with a demi-lion sable therein.*

NOEL. *Or fretty gules with a quarter ermine.*

this manor by will to his widow for life, with reversion to Sir Neville Lyttelton and remainder in default of heirs male to Lord Cobham.[85] Mrs. Noel is the present owner of the estate.

At Bell Hall, attached to the modern mansion of the Noels, are the remains of an ancient chapel.[86] This chapel existed in Habington's time, but was then 'desolate.'[87]

The manor of *MOREHALBENE* or *MOORHALL BELL* was held of the manor of Brian's Bell for scutage and suit of court and rent of 20*s*.[88] The earliest tenant of the manor whose name is known is Richard Rugge, who held it at the end of the 15th century.[89] It passed from him to his daughter Joan wife of Sir William Molyneux,[90] who in 1539 gave the manor to his son Richard.[91] Richard and his mother Joan sold it in 1539 to Humphrey Pakington and Rowland Hill,[92] who transferred it in 1540 to John Pakington.[92a] It then descended with the manor of Chaddesley Corbett (q.v.) until 1723.[93] In that year Sir Robert Throckmorton sold it to Joseph Cox,[94] who some years later purchased the manor of Stone, and seems to have settled both manors on his daughter Mary and her husband Stephen Beckingham.[95] The latter in 1738 conveyed Moorhall to Robert Aglionby Slaney[96] and others, apparently for settlement on his son Stephen, who was holding it with him in 1751.[97] The manor shortly afterwards passed to the Tristrams,[98] who seem to have resided there at the beginning of the 18th century.[99] John Tristram was in possession in 1771–2,[100] and the manor still belonged to this family in 1780,[1] but after

TRISTRAM. *Argent three roundels gules and a label azure.*

this date there is a difficulty in tracing its descent. It had passed before 1814 to William Hooper,[2] and belonged in 1868 to Miss Durant of Clent.[3]

The inhabitants of Moorhall and Brian's Bell owed suit at the hundred court held at Churchill for part of Halfshire Hundred.[4] The two villages of Moorhall and Brian's Bell formed one constablewick, and the constable was chosen one year in Moorhall Bell and the next in Brian's Bell, and was elected at the king's leet at Churchill.[5]

An estate at *BRADFORD* is first mentioned in the 13th century. In 1274–5 William de Hurst brought

---

[71] *V.C.H. Worcs.* i, 328*b*; *Worc. Inq. p.m.* (Worcs. Hist. Soc.), pt. i, 37; pt. ii, 115; Exch. Inq. p.m. (Ser. 2), file 1198, no. 12.

[72] Exch. Inq. p.m. (Ser. 2), file 1198, no. 12.

[73] *Testa de Nevill* (Rec. Com.), 40*b*.

[74] Assize R. 1022, m. 22 d.

[75] Ibid.; Feet of F. Worcs. 39 Hen. III, no. 33.

[76] The Belnes were still holding land in the parish in 1280 and 1361, but it does not appear to have been the manor (*Worc. Subs. R. c.* 1280 [Worcs. Hist. Soc.], 11; Chan. Inq. p.m. 35 Edw. III, pt. i, no. 26).

[77] *Worc. Subs. R. c.* 1280 (Worcs. Hist. Soc.), 11.

[78] Habington, *Surv. of Worc.* (Worcs. Hist. Soc.), i, 46–7.

[79] *Feud. Aids*, v, 331; Chan. Inq. p.m. 17 Edw. IV, no. 66; De Banco R. East. 1 Ric. III, m. 2 (Chart. Enr.); *Cal. Inq. p.m. Hen. VII*, i, 345.

[80] Exch. Inq. p.m. (Ser. 2), file 1198, no. 12.

[81] Feet of F. Worcs. East. 34 Eliz.

[82] For pedigree see Burke, *Landed Gentry*; Recov. R. Mich. 13 Chas. II, rot. 191; Mich. 7 Geo. II, rot. 34. William Sebright died in 1620 holding land called 'Bryans Bill' in Belbroughton (Chan. Inq. p.m. [Ser. 2], ccclxxxvi, 85).

[83] Burke, *Landed Gentry.*

[84] Recov. R. Hil. 35 Geo. III, rot. 174; East. 56 Geo. III, rot. 243; Burke, *Landed Gentry.*

[85] Inform. by Mr. J. W. Willis-Bund.

[86] Noake, op. cit. 24.

[87] Habington, op. cit. i, 47, and see p. 18 below.

[88] De Banco R. Mich. 20 Hen. VIII, m. 409.

[89] Ibid.   [90] Ibid.

[91] Recov. R. D. Enr. Hil. 33 Hen. VIII, m. 8.

[92] Recov. R. Trin. 31 Hen. VIII, rot. 351; Add. MS. 31314, fol. 27.

[92a] Add. MS. 31314, fol. 29 d.

[93] Add. MS. 31314, fol. 29 d., 197*b*, 102; Feet of F. Worcs. East. 5 Edw. VI; Trin. 1 Jas. I; East. 2 Jas. I; Mich. 6 Chas. I; Hil. 35 & 36 Chas. II.

[94] Feet of F. Worcs. Hil. 10 Geo. I; Close, 10 Geo. I, pt. xxv, no. 8.

[95] Nash, op. cit. ii, 386.

[96] Feet of F. Worcs. Trin. 11 & 12 Geo. II.

[97] Recov. R. Trin. 24 & 25 Geo. II, rot. 159.

[98] The Tristrams were holding land in this manor as early as 1693–4 (Exch. Dep. East. 5 Will. and Mary, no. 24).

[99] Prattinton Coll. (Soc. of Antiq.). J. Tristram, writing in 1736, says: 'The little spot which I occupy called Moorhall we purchased of the Barnabys of Herefordshire and of Edward Boughton.'

[100] Nash, op. cit. i, App. 23.

[1] Ibid. i, 57.

[2] Recov. R. Hil. 54 Geo. III, rot. 36.

[3] Noake, op. cit. 25.

[4] Exch. Dep. East. 5 Will. and Mary, no. 24.   [5] Ibid.

BELBROUGHTON CHURCH : THE OLD NAVE AND CHANCEL LOOKING EAST

BELBROUGHTON CHURCH : THE PULPIT

an action against John son of Simon de Bradford and Christine his wife for obstructing a road at Belbroughton.[6] Roger Lord of la More paid a subsidy of 4s. 8d. at Belne Simonis in 1280,[7] while William de la Hurst paid 10s. at Belne Bruyn,[8] and John and Christine de Bradford paid subsidy at Belbroughton.[9] Robert and Ellen de la Hurst recovered seisin of a carucate of land at Belne Bruyn against William de la Hurst in 1292–3.[10]

Margaret the wife of Henry de Bradford, sen., died in 1379 seised of tenements in Belbroughton, which she held of Thomas le Boteler by knight's service. Her son and heir William de Bradford died three years later, and was succeeded by a sister Margaret.[11] Possibly the land at Belbroughton held in 1431 by Edmund Shyne of Droitwich for a sixth of a knight's fee may refer to this property.[12] Nothing further is known of the estate until 1650, when William Penn of Bradford begged to compound, his estate being discharged five years later.[13]

In 1795 Elizabeth Mariana Harris, eldest daughter of Aston and Mary Harris, both deceased, conveyed to William Morland and others the capital messuage or mansion-house called Bradford and lands, &c., in Belbroughton parish,[14] as trustees for its sale. The property had been settled by John Harris on the said Aston and Mary, and Aston by his will dated 1 March 1794 had left it to Elizabeth in trust that she should sell it and give £1,000 to each of her sisters Anne, Harriet and Penelope.[15] The house was put up for sale in February 1818.[16]

The origin of the manor of *BROMHILL* [17] is not known. In 1473 Sir Ralph Boteler of Sudeley died seised of land at Bromhill,[18] which subsequently followed the descent of Fairfield.[19] The estate, called a manor since 1574,[20] now belongs to the Earl of Dudley.

The church of the *HOLY TRINITY* **CHURCHES** is built of stone and consists of a modern chancel and nave 88 ft. long and 21 ft. wide, to the south of which are the old chancel and nave, 90 ft. long and about 19 ft. wide, with a west tower 10 ft. deep and 9 ft. wide, and a south aisle 8½ ft. wide. These measurements are all internal.

The existence of a 12th-century church is clear from the portions of the south door, the window west of it, and from various carved fragments at the rectory of the same or earlier date. The earliest part of the existing building is the south aisle, which dates from the 13th century. The old chancel, which is of the 14th century, would therefore occupy the position of the 12th-century chancel, to which the south aisle was added. The modern chancel and nave are mainly in the 14th-century style, but parts of the north door of the modern nave, including its ogee head, are old. Preparations have been made to add a north aisle and western porch to this part of the church. The old 14th-century chancel has a three-light window with modern geometric tracery and old jambs. In the north wall is a large ogee-headed,

moulded recess and on the south are 15th-century sedilia, a piscina and three 14th-century windows of two trefoiled lights with a quatrefoil over. Here also is a door, probably of the same date. In the south-west angle is the entrance to the rood stair, to which there is a small trefoil-headed window. The chancel arch is probably of the 16th century, but has been much restored. It is of two chamfered orders, two-centred, with moulded capitals and semi-octagonal responds. The north arcade of the old nave is of three bays. It is of a curious design, of two unbroken chamfered orders, and has been reconstructed from the remains of a similar arcade, dating probably from the 15th century, which were found in the wall when pierced for the modern part of the church. The south arcade, the greater part of which is modern, is similar to the chancel arch and has concave octagonal piers with moulded capitals, but the label appears to be of an earlier date, though much restored, and the stops in some cases renewed. The tower arch is of the 15th century. The windows in the south aisle are modern, but in the south wall is a 13th-century piscina. The south door has been restored from some 12th-century fragments, and has a round head, double-shafted jambs and two roll mouldings to the head. The porch and external doorway are modern. West of the porch is a round-headed single-light window, partly old and dating from the 12th century. This window and the fragments of the south door appear to have been recently discovered and inserted in this wall.

The 15th-century tower is of three stages, with a stair turret in the south-east angle, and has angle buttresses. It has an embattled parapet and the octagonal spire has ogee-headed lights, with the remains of crocketed gables.

The belfry windows are of two lights with trefoiled ogee heads and quatrefoils over. The stage below has square-headed loophole lights.

The 14th-century chancel has a 17th-century roof inscribed on the western beam 'Laus Deo This roofe was new built at the charge of Richard Tristram Rector 1660.' A part of the nave roof is also old, the eastern beam being inscribed 'w.t. 1654 g.w.' On the eastern respond of the south aisle are remains of a painting showing a female figure with a floral pattern. The font is of the 15th century with octagonal bowl and quatrefoiled panels, a stem and moulded base.

There is a good 17th-century pulpit with dragons and grotesque corbels, round arches in panels and a moulded dentil course.

On the eastern exterior of the south aisle is a monument to Richard Tristram, 1691. Preserved at the rectory are various fragments of 12th and 13th-century work, including a grotesque animal, dog-tooth moulding, etc. There is also a piece of a pre-Conquest cross, with interlacing ornament.

There is a peal of six bells. The first five are by Thomas Rudhall of Gloucester, 1781, and the tenor

---

[6] Assize R. 1026, m. 10.
[7] Lay Subs. R. Worcs. c. 1280 (Worcs. Hist. Soc.), 11.
[8] Ibid.
[9] Ibid. 6.
[10] Assize R. 1030, m. 1.
[11] Chan. Inq. p.m. 7 Ric. II, no. 19.

[12] Feud. Aids, v, 331.
[13] Cal. Com. for Comp. 2675.
[14] Recov. R. D. Enr. East. 35 Geo. III, m. 30.
[15] Ibid.
[16] Prattinton Coll. (Soc. of Antiq.).
[17] Walter de Bromhull paid a subsidy

of 3s. at Belbroughton in 1280 (Worc. Subs. R. c. 1280 [Worcs. Hist. Soc.], 6).
[18] Chan. Inq. p.m. 13 Edw. IV, no. 58.
[19] For references see Fairfield.
[20] Feet of F. Worcs. Hil. 16 Eliz.

recast by Thomas Mears, 1840. The treble is inscribed 'The Rev.d Mr. John Wylde gave 5 : 5 : 0 1781'; the second, 'The Rev.d M.r Tho.s Tristram gave 5 : 5 : 0 1781'; the third, 'Aston Harris Esq.r gave 7 : 7 : 0 1781'; the fourth, 'John Tristram junr. Esq.r gave 10 : 10 : 0 1781'; and the fifth, 'John Tristram senr. Esq.r gave 50 : 0 : 0 1781.' The tenor is inscribed 'I to the Church the living call and to the grave do summon all ⸫ T.M. 1840 : W.m Clinton Gent. gave 5 : 5 : 0.'

The plate consists of a silver cup of the Restoration period, the date letter being illegible; an 1809 silver cup on which is engraved a monogram of the initials 'E.B.'; a 1701 silver salver standing on a foot, and a modern silver paten and chalice presented to the parish by the present rector.

The registers previous to 1812 are as follows : (i) all entries 1540 to 1649; (ii) 1650 to 1738; (iii) baptisms and burials 1739 to 1800, marriages 1739 to 1753; (iv) baptisms and burials 1801 to 1812; (v) marriages 1754 to 1812.

BELL END CHAPEL stands in the grounds of Bell Hall. It is a small early chapel, now disused, overgrown by ivy and in a very dilapidated condition. It was erected *circa* 1200, and apart from the insertion of mullioned windows in the east and west walls, the addition of buttresses to the west wall and the re-roofing at a later period, it has been left much in its original state. It is rectangular on plan, and is built of red sandstone, the roof being tiled.

The east window is of 16th-century date and was divided by mullions into three square-headed lights, but these are now blocked up with brickwork. In the north wall are two small round-headed windows with splayed inner jambs, and to the west of these is a blocked-up semicircular doorway with an external double-chamfered hood mould. The openings in the south wall correspond in size and position to those in the wall opposite, though the windows have external rebates for shutters and the doorway is far more ornate. This doorway is of two orders; the inner one, the edge of which has been rounded off, is continuous, while the outer, which is stopped at the springing by moulded abaci now much decayed, is elaborately moulded, and the jambs below are worked in a sunk quarter round. The west window is similar to the east, being of three square-headed lights.

The building has an external plinth, but through the raising of the ground this is now only visible at the north end of the east wall. The north and south walls have been continued westward (probably at the same time as the insertion of the east and west windows) to form buttresses. These are now greatly damaged, and only portions of them remain *in situ*.

ADVOWSON There were a church and priest at Belbroughton in 1086,[21] and the advowson was annexed to the manor of Belbroughton and Fairfield until about 1595,[22] when the manor was sold by John Talbot. He retained the advowson and died in 1607, when it passed to his son John,[23] by whom it was sold in 1624 to Thomas Tristram, clerk.[24] Between this date and 1731 the presentations were made by various people,[25] who were probably feoffees of the Tristrams, for in 1731 Bridget Tristram presented to the church,[26] and in 1733 she sold the advowson to the President and scholars of St. John's College, Oxford,[27] with whom it has since remained.[28] Dr. Gibbons, of St. John's College, gave £1,000 and his widow £300 of the purchase money. The advowson is subject to the condition that 'the person to be presented from time to time shall be one of the fellows of the college who has been or is at such time Dean of Divinity in the said college.'[29]

St. Mark's chapel of ease was erected at Fairfield in 1854.

There is a Primitive Methodist chapel at Belbroughton.

CHARITIES The parish is in possession of 2 a. 0 r. 16 p. called Breach Farm, and 2 a. 1 r. 3 p. called Brookfield Farm, producing a gross rent of £12.

In 1691 Dame Mary Yate by deed gave an annuity of £2 10s., charged on Cakebold Farm in Chaddesley Corbett, to be applied in the distribution of bread.

In 1750 George Garbett by will bequeathed £100, now represented by £138 8s. 2d. consols, the annual dividends, amounting to £3 9s., to be applied in bread and clothes.

Joseph Smith—as appeared from the Church Table—by will (date not stated) demised an annuity of £5, issuing out of the Clock House Estate at Fockbury, to be expended in woollen material for garments for poor widows, fatherless children and other poor.

The Rev. Thomas Welsh by will (date not stated) bequeathed £20 stock, now £23 18s. 8d. consols, the dividends of 12s. a year to be given to the poor at Easter.

In 1832 Benjamin Brecknell, by will proved in the P.C.C. 26 January, bequeathed £1,000, now £1,134 11s. 2d. consols in the names of administering trustees, producing £28 7s. yearly, to be distributed in money, bread and other articles in kind.

In 1883 Miss Elizabeth Hunt by deed declared the trusts of a sum of £497 10s. 3d. consols, producing £12 8s. 8d. yearly, to be distributed in sums of not less than 5s. each to poor widows, irrespective of age, and to men of not less than seventy years of age on 24 December yearly. The income of the several charities is applied for the benefit of the poor in accordance with their respective trusts.

The several sums of stock, unless otherwise stated, are held by the official trustees, who also hold a sum of £132 18s. consols arising from a legacy of £100 to the Free School by will of George Garbett above

21 *V.C.H. Worcs.* i, 319a.

22 *Worc. Epis. Reg. Ginsborough* (Worcs. Hist. Soc.), 148; Chan. Inq. p.m. 41 Edw. III (1st nos.), no. 54; Nash, op. cit. i, 58–9; Add. Chart. 5684; Chan. Inq. p.m. (Ser. 2), clxv, 192; clxix, 40.

23 Chan. Inq. p.m. (Ser. 2), cccv, 108.

24 Feet of F. Worcs. Trin. 22 Jas. I. J. Tristram, writing in 1736, states that the purchase took place in 1610 (Prattinton Coll. [Soc. of Antiq.]).

25 Inst. Bks. (P.R.O.). John Hill, who presented in 1701, held the advowson under a mortgage from Henry Tristram

5 Feb. 1697 (*Diary of Francis Evans* [Worcs. Hist. Soc.], 47).

26 Inst. Bks. (P.R.O.).

27 Feet of F. Worcs. Trin. 6 & 7 Geo. II.

28 Inst. Bks. (P.R.O.).

29 *Diary of Francis Evans* (Worcs. Hist. Soc.), 47, quoting Dr. Gibbons's will.

mentioned, and a legacy of £20 to the same school by will of Thomas Griffen in 1758. The dividends, amounting to £3 6s. 4d., are applied for educational purposes.

In 1903 Miss Phoebe Lucy Baker by deed conveyed to trustees three cottages in Wood Lane to be used as almshouses for aged and infirm women, and by a deed of trust 18 January 1904 a sum of £1,045 7s. 7d. consols was transferred to trustees, the dividends, amounting to £26 2s. 6d. yearly, to be applied in insurance and keeping the almshouses in repair.

BROMSGROVE

Bremesgrave (xi cent.) ; Brumesgrave (xiii cent.) ; Brymmesgrove (xv cent.).

From the ancient parish of Bromsgrove the civil parish of North Bromsgrove was formed in 1894,[1] Catshill, a separate ecclesiastical parish since 1844,[2] being included in it in 1895. In 1880 Crowfield was transferred from Dodderhill to Bromsgrove and at the same date part of Chaddesley Wood, formerly in Upton Warren, became part of Bromsgrove. Two years later parts of Bromsgrove were transferred to Upton Warren.[3]

The Spadesbourne brook, rising in the Lickey Hills, flows south-west through the parish, and passing through the centre of the town of Bromsgrove, is joined there by the Battlefield brook, which comes from Chadwick, the united streams forming the River Salwarpe. Dyers Bridge, at the bottom of the town, which in 1778 was the largest bridge in the parish, was built of sandstone in one span of 20 ft. It formed the boundary between the manors of Bromsgrove and Dyers.

The land falls from 940 ft. at Windmill Hill in the north to the south, the lowest point, 261 ft., being in the town of Bromsgrove. The parish lies on the Keuper Marls and Sandstone, and much of the land in the rural districts is agricultural. Catshill is on the Bunter Pebble Beds, and the soil is loam and clay, producing crops of wheat and turnips.

The parishes of Bromsgrove and North Bromsgrove cover an area of 11,656 acres,[4] of which Bromsgrove includes 196½ acres of arable land and 396¾ acres of permanent grass, while North Bromsgrove has 3,241¾ acres of arable, 4,998¾ of permanent grass and 434½ of woods and plantations.[5] Bromsgrove was formerly divided into yields named Burnford, Fockbury,[6] Catshill, Chadwick, Shepley, Burcot,[7] Padestones or Spadesbourne, Timberhonger, Woodcote and Town Yield, which were recognized at least as late as the end of the 18th century,[8] and some of which are hamlets of Bromsgrove at the present day.[9] Bromsgrove was inclosed under an Act of 1799, the award being dated 25 December 1802.[10] The award for Bonehill is dated 19 November 1813, that for Woodcote Green Common, Great Wood, Little Wood and Hopping Hill Coppice 5 July 1855, and for Chadwick, including parts of Lickey,[11] Etchy and Wildmoor, 10 December 1795.[12]

In the 18th century the 'customary or Whitsun ale' was no longer held in the parish, but the custom survived among the farmers of distributing all the milk of their cows on Whitsunday morning to any of their poor neighbours who chose to go for it.[13]

The town of Bromsgrove is situated about 6 miles north of Droitwich, upon the Worcester and Birmingham road, along which the chief and older part of the town lies. The church stands in a commanding position on the summit of rising ground to the south of the main road, which in its course through the town is known as Worcester Street,[14] and is approached from St. John Street, a turning leading southwards out of the Market Place by a picturesque flight of steps. On the north side of St. John Street is a house with a brick nogged half-timber gable end, on the tie-beam of which is carved R. D. 1674. The lower part of the house has been faced with red sandstone and all the openings appear to be modern. At the junction of St. John Street with the Market Place a stream which runs at the back of the houses in Worcester Street is crossed by a rebuilt bridge. A stone tablet preserved from the former bridge and reset in the parapet records its erection in the year 1755 with the names of the churchwardens of that date. The town hall is a dreary building coated with unpainted stucco, standing in Worcester Street at the corner of the Market Place. At the opposite corner of the Market Place is a picturesque group of gabled half-timber houses probably dating from the early years of the 17th century. They are of three stories with tiled roofs, but appear to have been much tampered with and restored. In the same street is some excellent Georgian work, notably the Red Lion and Green Dragon Inns. Much half-timber work still survives, of which the best example is, perhaps, the Castle Inn and the two adjoining houses. These are of three stories, the upper stories gabled and oversailing, supported by console brackets. In Hanover Street is a row of red brick cottages. An oval tablet in the wall is inscribed 'Neare St Johns Cross Hanover Street Anno Domini 1715.' The Grammar School stands on the east side of the Worcester Street, near the southern extremity of the town. The oldest part of the buildings dates from 1693 and contains the original schoolroom ; this block was originally of

---

[1] *Census of Engl. and Wales, Worc.* 1901, p. 28.
[2] Ibid. 5.
[3] *Census of Engl. and Wales,* 1891, ii, 658.
[4] Figures taken from census of 1901.
[5] Statistics from Bd. of Agric. (1905).
[6] Focheberie was a berewick of Bromsgrove in 1086 (*V.C.H. Worcs.* i, 285).
[7] Bericote in 1086 (ibid.).
[8] Prattinton Coll. (Soc. Antiq.) ; Recov. R. East. 3 Geo. II, rot. 24.

[9] The present Linthurst is probably to be identified with Lindeorde, a berewick of Bromsgrove in 1086 (*V.C.H. Worcs.* i, 285).
[10] Priv. Act, 39 Geo. III, cap. 32 ; *Blue Bk. Incl. Awards,* 189.
[11] In 1340 Roger son of John de Bishopsdon obtained seisin of the bailiwick of the forestry of 'la Leek hay,' which was in the king's hay (*Cal. Close,* 1339–41, p. 552).
[12] *Blue Bk. Incl. Awards,* 192, 189.

The Act for Chadwick was passed in 1791 (Priv. Act, 31 Geo. III, cap. 31), that for Bunhill in 1810 (Priv. Act, 50 Geo. III, cap. 45 [not printed]).
[13] Prattinton Coll. (Soc. Antiq.).
[14] In 1635 the parish was in default for not repairing the Spittle causeway, being the church way to the market, for want of which the passengers were forced to break through the adjoining lands (*Quart. Sess. Rec.* [Worcs. Hist. Soc.], 600).

two stories, with an attic, but an extra story has been added. A portion of the head master's house appears to be of the same date.

At the north of the town, on the east side of the Birmingham road, is the modern church of All Saints. The building occupied by Lloyds Bank at the corner of Worcester Street and the road leading to the railway station is constructed out of the materials of the Hop Pole Inn, a 16th-century structure of half-timber taken down about 1870 and re-erected. The design appears to have been much altered in the process of re-erection. The almshouses in the Alcester road are modern—one pair was erected in 1820, another pair in 1825 and a third pair in 1842. The remaining blocks were built in 1883. The railway station is about a mile to the east of the town and is really in Finstall, formerly a hamlet in the parish of Stoke Prior, but now a separate ecclesiastical parish. The district which has sprung up in the neighbourhood is known as Aston Fields. At Great Dodford are remains of the priory of Augustine canons established here at the end of the 12th century and incorporated in 1464 with Halesowen Abbey.[15] The part remaining is of stone and may perhaps have been the refectory. At the south-east angle are buttresses of two offsets and at the south-west is a doorway with a chamfered two-centred segmental head and jambs. In the 16th century the buildings appear to have been razed to the ground with the exception of this portion, which was then converted into a dwelling-house. There is a large stone chimney stack on the south with three diagonal shafts of brick and a smaller stack with similar shafts to the west of this; both belong to the 16th-century reconstruction. At the east end of this main block is a wing of half-timber work projecting northwards, which does not appear to be part of the original establishment. The course of the surrounding moat can still be traced at the south-east, and it seems not improbable that the present road to the west of the house follows the line of the moat on this side. Chadwick Manor House, about 3½ miles north of Bromsgrove, on the west side of the Halesowen road, is a late 17th-century building of brick with stone dressings. Chadwick Grange is a modern farm-house of no particular interest.

Sarah Bache, the hymn-writer, was born at Bromsgrove about 1771,[16] as were also John Flavel, the Presbyterian divine, about 1630, and William Dugard, the 17th-century schoolmaster and printer.[17] Benjamin Maund, botanist and fellow of the Linnean Society, carried on the combined businesses of chemist, bookseller, printer and publisher in the town in the middle of the 19th century,[18] and Elijah Walton the artist resided at Bromsgrove Lickey during the last years of his life, and died there in 1880.[19]

Among former place-names in the parish were Asseberga and Tuneslega (xi cent.)[20]; Wrante and Brandelay (xiii cent.); Kingstotenhull, Chirnemore Bagfeld, Barneslade, Olde Lynde, Le Beokes, Tylamesland, Baynardesgrove and Lamesey (xv cent.)[21]; Le Stapull and Kylbarnes (xvi cent.).[22]

BOROUGH There is evidence that a borough existed at Bromsgrove during the 12th and 13th centuries, but it was short lived, and little is known of its history. The mention of a reeve and beadle in the manor in 1086 indicate that it was even then of somewhat greater importance than an ordinary royal manor.[23] In 1156 the 'men of Bromsgrove' paid 10s. to the Sheriff of Worcestershire,[24] in 1169 the 'vill of Bromsgrove' rendered account of £4,[25] and during the latter part of the century 'the men of Bromsgrove' or 'the town of Bromsgrove' paid tallage which amounted to 20 marks with Norton in 1177,[26] to 8 marks in 1187,[27] 100s. in 1195[28] and £7 12s. 2d. two years later.[29] After this time, possibly owing to the fact that the manor was granted out by the Crown, the prosperity of the town diminished, and by 1227 its inhabitants had become so poor that tallage was reduced from 37 to 20 marks, and afterwards from 27½ to 18 marks.[30] Later an attempt was made to restore the fortunes of the town, and Henry III in 1260–1 granted the manor to the men of Bromsgrove at fee farm for five years,[31] and two members, Thomas Rastel and Thomas de Burneford, represented the borough in the Parliament of 1295.[32] This was, however, the only occasion on which Bromsgrove returned members.

In the 15th and 16th centuries three courts were held for the borough—the great court, the smaller court and the view of frankpledge. The great courts were held at Lickey, and at them were elected the bailiff, reeve, two constables and two aletasters, the common name for the last being 'crab nabbers.'[33]

John Lacey, writing in 1778, said that the Town Yield, then containing about 400 houses, was governed by a bailiff, recorder, alderman and other officers, and that as they then had no powers a proverb had arisen, 'The bailiff of Bromsgrove has no fellow.'[34] The bailiffs continued, however, to hold a court in the town hall for the recovery of small debts every three weeks.[35] Prattinton, writing a little later, states that a court leet and court baron were then held at Whitsuntide and Michaelmas.[36] Courts leet are held at the present day, and the bailiff and other officers are duly elected, the jury making their presentments at the half-yearly courts.[37]

James I granted the tolls to John How of Longer Castle, whose heirs sold them to Thomas Earl of Plymouth, who continued to take them until they were abolished.[38] The tolls were regulated by an Act of 1816,[39] and three years later the royal family was exempted from paying tolls.[40]

In 1533 Bromsgrove is mentioned as one of the towns in Worcestershire in which cloth was permitted

[15] See below under Dodford.
[16] *Dict. Nat. Biog.*
[17] Ibid. [18] Ibid.
[19] Ibid.
[20] *V.C.H. Worcs.* i, 285.
[21] Ct. R. (Gen. Ser.), portf. 210, no. 36; Add. Chart. (Brit. Mus.), 23855.
[22] *L. and P. Hen. VIII*, xiv (2), g. 619 (65); Memo. R. (L.T.R.), Mich. Recorda 6 Eliz. rot. 162.
[23] *V.C.H. Worcs.* i, 285.

[24] Hunter, *Gt. R. of the Pipe*, 2, 3, 4 Hen. II, 62.
[25] *Pipe R.* 15 Hen. II (Pipe R. Soc.), 138. [26] Pipe R. 23 Hen. II, m. 4 d.
[27] Ibid. 33 Hen. II, m. 15 d.
[28] Ibid. 7 Ric. I, m. 1 d.
[29] Ibid. 9 Ric. I, m. 13 d.
[30] *Rot. Lit. Claus.* (Rec. Com.), ii, 184, 185b.
[31] *Abbrev. Rot. Orig.* (Rec. Com.), i, 17; *Cal. Pat.* 1258–66, p. 167.

[32] *Ret. of Memb. of Parl.* 6.
[33] Ct. R. (Gen. Ser.), portf. 210, no. 36; Prattinton Coll. (Soc. Antiq.).
[34] Prattinton Coll. (Soc. Antiq.).
[35] Ibid.
[36] Ibid.
[37] Information supplied by Mr. R. Forrest.
[38] Prattinton Coll. (Soc. Antiq.).
[39] Stat. 56 Geo. III, cap. 67.
[40] Ibid. 59 Geo. III, cap. 49.

BELBROUGHTON : FRAGMENTS OF EARLY CARVED STONES

BROMSGROVE CHURCH : THE NAVE LOOKING EAST

to be manufactured,[41] and a flourishing trade in narrow cloth and friezes then existed, and continued till towards the end of the 18th century. In 1778 the manufacture of linsey occupied only about 140 hands, while that of linen employed about 180 hands, and the making of nails about 900 hands.[42] This last had already been introduced in the 17th century,[43] and was, until the end of the 19th century, the staple trade of the town. There are now also a silk button manufactory and a brewery.

The right to hold a weekly market at Bromsgrove on Wednesdays was granted in 1200 to Hugh Bardulf,[44] and in 1317 John de Mortimer obtained from the king a Tuesday market and a fair for three days at the feast of the Decollation of St. John the Baptist (29 August).[45] In 1468 the market seems to have been held on Thursday.[46] The market day was Tuesday in 1792,[47] and has so remained to the present day. Fairs were held on 24 June and 1 October in 1792,[48] and in 1814,[49] and on 24 June in 1888.[50] The June fair is still continued as a horse and pleasure fair.

A Statute fair for the hiring of servants was first held on 24 September 1777 and continued to be held on the Wednesday before Michaelmas Day. Lacey states that in 1778 'a rabbling kind of wake' was held on the third Sunday in July at a place called Sythemore near the church, and also at Catshill, 2 miles out of the town, where bull baiting, bowling, wrestling and cock fighting took place. He adds that on Shrove Tuesday 'that most cruel and inhuman, cowardly and shameful pastime of throwing at cocks is used throughout the parish to the great grief and discontent of all good Christian people.'[51]

Cattle fairs are now held on alternate Tuesdays, except in December, when they are held on the first three Tuesdays of the month.

In 1846 an Act was passed for improving the town of Bromsgrove,[52] and under the Local Government Act of 1858 it became a separate district. Provisional orders were made in 1861 and 1863 for extending the boundaries of the district.[53] The urban district was governed by a local board of fifteen members and the rural district by one of twelve members, but under the provisions of the Local Government Act of 1894 these have been superseded by the urban district councils of Bromsgrove and North Bromsgrove.

The town is lighted with gas by the Bromsgrove Gas Light and Coke Company, incorporated in 1882.[54] An Act was first passed in 1866 to enable the town to obtain a better water supply,[55] and water is now obtained from the East Worcestershire

Water Works, the reservoirs of which are situated at the top of the Lickey and at Burcot and Headless Cross.

A cemetery under the control of the Bromsgrove Burial Joint Committee was formed in 1857, and in 1878 the volunteer fire brigade was established with two manual engines and a fire escape. The petty sessions formerly held in the old town hall are now held in the public office adjoining the police station erected in 1890. The Institute, founded in 1859, was removed to New Road in 1894, and the school of art adjoining it was built in 1895. In the same road is the cottage hospital, founded in 1878 at Mount Pleasant and removed in 1891 to its present site.

A great cross standing before the market-house was taken down in 1832, at which time the present town hall was built. A prison called the Tolhouse is mentioned in 1468.[56]

BROMSGROVE was among the possessions of Ethelric, son of Ethelmund, who in 804 announced his intention of giving eleven 'manses' at Bromsgrove and Feckenham (Feccanhom) to Wœrferth for his life with reversion to the church of Worcester.[57] According to the annals of Worcester Priory, this disposition of Bromsgrove had been ordained by Ethelmund in his will,[58] but there is no evidence that it ever took effect. According to an endorsement of a charter relating to Inkberrow, Bromsgrove afterwards belonged to Wulfheard, son of Cussa, and was given by him at the request of King Ceolwulf I of Mercia (821–3) to Heaberht or Eadberht Bishop of Worcester in exchange for Inkberrow.[59]

In the time of King Edward the Confessor Bromsgrove was held by Earl Edwin, but it passed at the Conquest into the hands of the king, and in 1086 heads the list of the king's lands in Worcestershire. Attached to it were eighteen berewicks, which, with the manor lands, were assessed at 30 hides.[60] To the manor belonged 13 salt-pans in Droitwich and three salt workers who rendered 300 mits of salt.[61] The manor also contained four eyries of hawks. It evidently remained in the hands of the Crown until the beginning of the 13th century.[62] In 1176 lands to the value of £50 in this manor and Martley were granted to Roger de Mortimer by Henry II,[63] and he was still in possession of lands of half that value in 1194.[64] In 1200 King John granted the manor at fee farm to Hugh Bard or Bardulf and his heirs to be held of the king, rendering for it the ancient farm and the increment of 20 marks made in the time of King Richard.[65] Hugh Bard held the manor until 1204,[66] when he presumably died without heirs,[67] for

[41] Stat. 25 Hen. VIII, cap. 18. The Act also provides that the rents of houses in the town should not be raised.

[42] Prattinton Coll. (Soc. Antiq.).

[43] *Quart. Sess. Rec.* (Worcs. Hist. Soc.), Introd. p. xxxviii.

[44] Chart. R. 1 John, m. 4.

[45] *Cal. Chart. R.* 1300–26, p. 367.

[46] Mins. Accts. bdle. 1067, no. 15.

[47] *Rep. of Roy. Com. on Market Rts. and Tolls,* i, 215.

[48] Ibid.

[49] Brayley and Britton, *Beauties of Engl. and Wales,* xv (2), 200.

[50] *Rep. on Market Rts.* i, 215.

[51] Prattinton Coll. (Soc. Antiq.).

[52] Loc. and Personal Act, 9 & 10 Vict. cap. 124.

[53] Priv. Act, 24 & 25 Vict. cap. 39; 26 & 27 Vict. cap. 32.

[54] Loc. and Personal Act, 45 & 46 Vict. cap. 40.

[55] Ibid. 34 & 35 Vict. cap. 51.

[56] Mins. Accts. bdle. 1067, no. 15.

[57] Heming, *Chartul.* (ed. Hearne), ii, 447; Kemble, *Codex Dipl.* no. 186; Birch, *Cart. Sax.* i, 438.

[58] Dugdale, *Mon. Angl.* i, 608.

[59] Birch, *Cart. Sax.* i, 428. Both this charter and that of 804 are certainly genuine.

[60] *V.C.H. Worcs.* i, 285.

[61] In 1236 the bailiffs of Droitwich were commanded not to permit any salt to be sold in Droitwich until the king's salt which he had in that vill, belonging to his manor of Bromsgrove, should be sold (*Cal. Close,* 1234–7, p. 370).

[62] Pipe R. 23 Hen. II, m. 4 d.; 33 Hen. II, m. 15 d.; 7 Ric. I, m. 1 d.; 9 Ric. I, m. 13 d.; 1 John, m. 6 d.

[63] Ibid. 22 Hen. II, m. 3.

[64] Ibid. 6 Ric. I, m. 9.

[65] Ibid. 2 John, m. 2 d.; *Rot. de Oblat. et Fin.* (Rec. Com.), 68; Chart. R. 1 John, m. 4.

[66] Pipe R. 4, 5, 6 John.

[67] *Rot. de Oblat. et Fin.* (Rec. Com.), 244. In 1203 the rent which Hugh Bard paid for the manor was granted to Everard de Bevere and Waleran de Cotes during pleasure. The manor was then said to have lately belonged to Gilbert de Ayre (*Rot. de Liberate* [Rec. Com.], 69).

it was granted in that year to William de Furnell, clerk, at farm for his life.[68] The manor was granted in 1215 by King John to his brother William Earl of Salisbury, saving to William de Furnell his right of holding the vill for his life.[69] William de Furnell, who was rector of Bromsgrove,[70] continued to hold Bromsgrove at farm until his death in 1236, when it was given by the king to Nicholas Poynz and his coparceners, who seem to have been William's heirs.[71]

William Earl of Salisbury joined Louis of France against King John, and forfeited the manor of Bromsgrove, which was granted in 1216 to Gilbert de Ayre.[72] The earl was restored to favour on the accession of Henry III, and this manor was given back to him in 1217.[73] He died in 1226,[74] when the manor again came to the Crown. Friar Geoffrey, the king's almoner, was appointed as custodian of the manor in 1236,[75] and two years later it was given as security to Henry de Hastings and his wife Ada until the latter should have obtained her share of the lands of John, late Earl of Chester, her brother.[76] The manor returned into the king's possession in 1244–5,[77] and from that time until 1260–1 remained in the hands of farmers appointed from time to time by the Crown.[78] At the latter date Henry III granted it to the men of Bromsgrove, to be held at farm for five years.[79]

Henry III assigned the manor to Queen Eleanor, but it was found in 1274 that for some unexplained reason she had not received it.[80] In 1263 Henry III granted to Roger de Mortimer an annual rent of £100 from the manors of Bromsgrove and Norton,[81] and in 1278 Edward I handed over both these manors to his mother Eleanor, on condition that she paid the rent due to Roger de Mortimer.[82] In 1299 Edward I assigned it to Queen Margaret as dower,[83] but when it was found that it was burdened with a rent to the Mortimers other land was granted to her in exchange.[84]

MORTIMER. *Barry or and azure a chief or with two pales between as many gyrons azure therein and a scutcheon argent over all.*

In 1302 Edmund de Mortimer granted the rent from Bromsgrove to Isabel de Clare for life.[85] His son Roger de Mortimer, who succeeded him in 1304,[86] granted this rent in 1315 to his brother John in tail-male with remainder to his mother Margaret, Edmund de Mortimer's widow, for life.[87] In 1317 John obtained from the Crown a grant of the manors of Bromsgrove and Norton to be held in fee at a fee-farm rent of £10 yearly.[88] John was accidentally slain at a tournament at Worcester in 1318–19 and was succeeded by his son John,[89] from whom the manor apparently passed to his uncle Roger de Mortimer, Earl of March, for in 1329 the king remitted to the earl the fee-farm rent of £10, which Queen Isabella, to whom it then belonged, had already remitted during her lifetime.[90] Roger Earl of March was attainted and executed in 1330,[91] and all his lands were forfeited to the Crown. In 1332–3 the custody of the manors of Bromsgrove and Norton, from which Margaret de Mortimer was still receiving £100, was granted to John son of Guy de Beauchamp Earl of Warwick for eight years.[92] Four years later the custody of Roger, grandson and heir of the Earl of March, was entrusted to William de Montagu and these manors were assigned to the support of the child.[93] Roger gave his grandmother, Joan Countess of March, for life 100 marks of land and rent in Bromsgrove and Norton in 1347,[94] and in 1350 he granted to her the whole manor in exchange for lands in Ireland.[95]

On her death in 1356 it reverted to Roger, then Earl of March.[96] He died in 1360 and was succeeded by his son Edmund, third Earl of March,[97] who died in 1381.[98] The executors of his will granted the manor to Margaret Countess of Norfolk and others for eight years in 1387–8.[99]

Roger son and successor of Edmund was slain by the Irish at Kenlis in 1398,[100] but it seems probable that he never held this manor, for in 1403 it was granted by the king during the minority of the heir to Richard Lord Grey of Wilton, being then described as lately the property of Sir Edmund Mortimer, kt.,[1] who had leased it to William Latimer of Danby and others. This heir was Edmund, fifth Earl of March, son of Roger, who received seisin about 1409.[2] Edmund, owing to his claim to the throne, was long kept in prison at Trim Castle by Henry IV,[3] but was released by Henry V in 1413. He conveyed the manor of Bromsgrove in 1415 to trustees,[4] and after his death in 1424[5] his nephew and heir Richard Duke of York sued them for this manor.[6] Nine years later an agreement was made by which these trustees received from the manor a

[68] Chart. R. 5 John, m. 10; Pipe R. 6 John, m. 7 d.; *Testa de Nevill* (Rec. Com.), 44.
[69] *Rot. Lit. Claus.* (Rec. Com.), i, 223.
[70] Nash, *Hist. of Worc.* i, 160.
[71] Pipe R. 7–17 John; *Rot. Lit. Claus.* (Rec. Com.), ii, 106; *Excerpta e Rot. Fin.* (Rec. Com.), i, 297.
[72] *Rot. Lit. Claus.* (Rec. Com.), i, 262.
[73] Ibid. i, 299, 333.
[74] G.E.C. *Complete Peerage*, vii, 32.
[75] *Cal. Pat.* 1232–47, p. 147.
[76] Anct. D. (P.R.O.), A 6313; *Cal. Pat.* 1232–47, p. 224. Henry's grandson John de Hastings petitioned for the manor in 1318–19 (Inq. a.q.d. 12 Edw. II, no. 123; Council Proc. 12 Edw. II).
[77] *Abbrev. Rot. Orig.* (Rec. Com.), i, 7.
[78] Ibid. 8; *Cal. Pat.* 1247–58, pp. 111, 493.
[79] *Abbrev. Rot. Orig.* (Rec. Com.), i, 17; *Cal. Pat.* 1258–66, p. 167.

[80] *Cal. Pat.* 1272–81, p. 71.
[81] Ibid. 1258–66, p. 303. In 1275–6 it was stated at the Hundred Court that Roger de Mortimer held the manor of Bromsgrove (*Hund. R.* [Rec. Com.], ii, 282).
[82] *Cal. Pat.* 1272–81, p. 271.
[83] Ibid. 1292–1301, p. 453.
[84] Ibid. 1301–7, p. 118.
[85] Ibid. 70.
[86] Chan. Inq. p.m. 32 Edw. I, no. 63a.
[87] *Cal. Pat.* 1313–17, p. 276.
[88] *Cal. Chart. R.* 1300–26, p. 366. This fee-farm rent was granted by Parliament in 1327 to Queen Isabella in recognition of her services in suppressing the Despensers' rebellion (*Cal. Pat.* 1327–30, p. 68).
[89] Chan. Inq. p.m. 12 Edw. II, no. 11; *Abbrev. Rot. Orig.* (Rec. Com.), i, 246; Burke, *Extinct Peerage*, 373.
[90] *Cal. Pat.* 1327–30, pp. 366, 440.

[91] G.E.C. *Complete Peerage*, v, 379.
[92] *Abbrev. Rot. Orig.* (Rec. Com.), ii, 63.
[93] Ibid. 105; *Cal. Close*, 1343–6, p. 531. Complaints of waste and destruction were made during the minority of Roger, and an inquiry ordered (*Cal. Pat.* 1340–3, p. 203).
[94] *Cal. Pat.* 1345–8, p. 349.
[95] Ibid. 1348–50, p. 545.
[96] Chan. Inq. p.m. 30 Edw. III (1st nos.), no. 30.
[97] G.E.C. *Complete Peerage*, v, 243; *Cal. Close*, 1360–4, p. 114.
[98] Chan. Inq. p.m. 5 Ric. II, no. 43.
[99] Close, 11 Ric. II, pt. i, m. 10 d.
[100] G.E.C. *Complete Peerage*, v, 244.
[1] *Cal. Pat.* 1401–5, p. 267.
[2] Ibid. 1408–13, p. 146.
[3] G.E.C. *Complete Peerage*, v, 244.
[4] Feet of F. Div. Co. Trin. 3 Hen. V.
[5] Chan. Inq. p.m. 3 Hen. VI, no. 32.
[6] Wrottesley, *Ped. from Plea R.* 342.

certain yearly rent for twenty years.[7] Richard's son Edward succeeded to the estate in 1460,[8] and on his accession as King Edward IV Bromsgrove became part of the crown estates.

It was granted by Edward IV in 1461 to his mother Cicely Duchess of York for her life,[9] and Richard III confirmed this grant in 1483–4.[10]

Edward IV appears to have settled it on his daughters Katherine Countess of Devon and Anne the wife of Sir Thomas Howard, from whom in 1511 Henry VIII recovered it, giving them other lands in exchange.[11]

RICHARD, Duke of York. *The royal arms with the difference of a label argent with three roundels gules on each pendant.*

Before obtaining this release from the heirs of Edward IV, Henry VIII had granted land and rent in Bromsgrove in 1509 to Katherine of Aragon.[12] Jane Seymour held the manor until her death in 1537[13] and Anne of Cleves received it on her marriage in 1540,[14] Katherine Howard in the following year[15] and Katherine Parr in 1544.[16]

In 1553 Edward VI sold the manor to John Dudley Duke of Northumberland,[17] but on the attainder of the duke in the same year his property reverted to the Crown. The estate was restored to his son Ambrose Earl of Warwick by Elizabeth in 1564,[18] but he died without surviving issue in 1589.[19] His widow Anne Countess of Warwick held it until her death in 1603–4,[20] when the manor reverted once more to the Crown.[21] James I gave it in 1611 to Sir Richard Grobham[22] and he held it until his death in 1629,[23] leaving it by will to his nephew Sir John Howe, who was created a baronet in 1660.[24] His grandson Sir Scrope Howe sold the estate in 1682 to Thomas Lord Windsor,[25] who was created Earl of Plymouth in that year.[26] On his death in 1687 the property passed to his grandson Other.[27] The four succeeding Earls of Plymouth inherited the property,[28] but the sixth earl died without issue in 1833, when this estate passed to his younger sister Harriet wife of Hon. Robert Henry Clive. The abeyance of the barony of Windsor was terminated in her favour 25 October 1855. She was succeeded in 1869 by her grandson Robert George,[29] fourteenth Lord Windsor, who was created Earl of Plymouth in 1905 and is the present lord of the manor of Bromsgrove.

A few court rolls of this manor between 1389 and 1546 have been preserved at the Public Record

WINDSOR. *Gules a saltire argent between twelve crosslets or.*

CLIVE. *Argent a fesse sable with three molets or thereon.*

Office,[30] and there are others (1473–1502) at the British Museum.[31]

The court rolls and records of the manor of Bromsgrove were formerly kept in the steeple of Bromsgrove Church in a chest of which the steward, bailiff, and reeve had the keys. It was only opened in their presence and in that of four tenants of the manor.[32]

In the Domesday Survey it is stated that 3 hides at *CHADWICK* (Celdwic, xi cent.; Chadelwic, Chadleswich, Chadeleiwyz, Chadewyz, xiii cent.; Chadeleswych, xiv cent.; Chaddyswyche, xv cent.) had been formerly held by thegns of Earl Eadwine, but in 1086 it was part of the royal manor of Bromsgrove, and Urse held it of the king, Alvred being the tenant under Urse.[33] The interest of Urse passed to the Beauchamps and followed the descent of Elmley Castle.[34]

In the 12th century Ralph de Lens was holding the vill of Chadwick in demesne, and in 1195,[35] after his death, his widow Beatrice of London held Chadwick and Willingwick as dower, with reversion to her son Roger.[36] In 1232 Roger son of Ralph de Lens gave to the hospital of St. Wulfstan, Worcester, his capital messuage and lands in Chadwick.[37] Roger's son Ralph, who probably succeeded him shortly after,[38] was also a benefactor of the hospital, and in 1248 he gave to it the dower lands of his mother Felicia. In return for this the hospital gave to him and his wife Mary a corner house in Worcester, opposite that of Hugh de Pakenton, and a corrody, half of which was to cease on the death of either Ralph or Mary, and the other half on the death of the survivor.[39] Thomas de Lens appears at one time to have held the manor,[40] but

[7] Harl. Chart. 53 H. 17; *Cal. Pat.* 1429–36, p. 514; Feet of F. Div. Co. East. 14 Hen. VI.

[8] G.E.C. *Complete Peerage*, v, 244.

[9] *Cal. Pat.* 1461–7, p. 131.

[10] Pat. 1 Ric. III, pt. v, m. 10, 9.

[11] Feet of F. Div. Co. Mich. 3 Hen. VIII. He further obtained an Act of Parliament in 1536 to assure to himself and his heirs certain lands including Bromsgrove formerly belonging to the earldom of March (Stat. 28 Hen. VIII, cap. 39). [12] *L. and P. Hen. VIII*, i, 155.

[13] Ibid. xiv (1), g. 1192 (20).

[14] Ibid. xv, g. 144 (2).

[15] Ibid. xvi, g. 503 (25); Pat. 32 Hen. VIII, pt. vi.

[16] Pat. 35 Hen. VIII, pt. xvii, m. 9; *L. and P. Hen. VIII*, xix (1), g. 141 (65).

[17] Pat. 7 Edw. VI, pt. viii.

[18] Ibid. 6 Eliz. pt. iv, m. 32.

[19] G.E.C. *Complete Peerage*, viii, 65.

[20] Ibid.

[21] Exch. Dep. Mich. 19 Jas. I, no. 37.

[22] Pat. 9 Jas. I, pt. v.

[23] Feet of F. Div. Co. Hil. 2 Chas. I; Chan. Inq. p.m. (Ser. 2), ccccllx, 53. In 1627 the manor was settled on his wife, provision being made for his brother John, for the maintenance of his almshouses at Burtpage, Somerset, with remainder to George, the son of John Grobham, and his younger brothers successively. [24] Burke, *Peerage.*

[25] Recov. R. Trin. 34 Chas. II, rot. 183; Feet of F. Worcs. East. 34 Chas. II.

[26] G.E.C. *Complete Peerage*, vi, 257.

[27] Ibid.

[28] Recov. R. East. 3 Geo. II, rot. 24; Trin. 25 & 26 Geo. II, rot. 329.

[29] Burke, *Peerage.*

[30] Ct. R. (Gen. Ser.), portf. 210, no. 34, 35, 36, 37, 38, 39, 40.

[31] Add. Chart. 23855.

[32] Exch. Dec. and Orders (Ser. iv), no. 1, fol. 125 d. In 1609 the king's auditor had some difficulty in seeing them.

[33] *V.C.H. Worcs.* i, 286a.

[34] *Red Bk. of Exch.* (Rolls Ser.), 567; *Testa de Nevill* (Rec. Com.), 40; Exch. K. R. Misc. Bks. xxii, fol. 1; Chan. Inq. p.m. 7 Hen. V, no. 46.

[35] At this date half a salt-pan at Droitwich belonged to this manor (Feet of F. Worcs. 7 Ric. I, no. 1).

[36] Feet of F. Worcs. 7 Ric. I, no. 1.

[37] *Cal. Chart. R.* 1226–57, p. 172.

[38] *Testa de Nevill* (Rec. Com.), 40.

[39] Feet of F. Worcs. 33 Hen. III, no. 56.

[40] *Feud. Aids*, v, 303.

before 1274 it seems probable that the Master of St. Wulfstan's had acquired it, for at about that time he appropriated to himself the assize of bread and ale at Chadwick, and unsuccessfully tried to withdraw his suit at Bromsgrove.[41] Successive Masters of St. Wulfstan's held the manor until the hospital was dissolved in the 16th century.[42] Henry VIII sold the manor to Richard Morrison in 1540, adding in 1544 a rent reserved in 1540.[43] In the following year Richard Morrison released it again to the king, receiving other lands in exchange,[44] and in 1546 Chadwick was given to the Dean and Canons of Christ Church, Oxford.[45] The whole of the Chadwick estate was sold by the Dean and Canons in 1904 to the Chadwick Estate Ltd., with the exception of the site of the reservoir, which is on lease to the East Worcestershire Waterworks Co. for 99 years from 1902.[46]

John Lacey, writing in 1778, states that the ancient mansion-house had belonged in the 17th century to the Lowe family,[47] from whom it came by marriage to Henry Vaughan Jeffries. His son Humphrey sold the lease of it in 1777 to John Hutton of Birmingham.[48] In 1813 the manor-house was put up for sale.[49] It afterwards came into the hands of John Carpenter,[50] a gentleman farmer, the author of a treatise on agriculture,[51] who mortgaged it to Mr. Penn. On the bankruptcy of the latter it was bought by Mr. Wilcox,[52] who left it to his nephew John Osborne, the owner in 1826. In 1849 Manor Hall was the property of Francis T. Rufford.[53] Chadwick Manor is now a farm-house.

In 1086 there were two holdings at *WILLING-WICK* (Willingewic, xi cent.; Welingewic, xii cent.; Wylincwyke, xiii cent.; Winlyngwyche, xiv cent.; Welynchewyk, xv cent.), each being parcel of the royal manor of Bromsgrove. One part, held by thegns of Earl Eadwine in the time of Edward the Confessor, was in 1086 held by Urse, whose knight Walter then held 2 hides and 3 virgates there.[54] The other holding of 3 virgates had been held by Wulfwine, a thegn of Earl Eadwine, and was in 1086 among the lands of William Fitz Ansculf, Baldwin holding it of him.[55] That part of the vill held under Urse evidently followed the same descent as the manor of Chadwick (q.v.) in the Lens family,[56] by some

member of which it was evidently granted to the hospital of St. Wulfstan, for the master of the hospital was in possession of it in 1346.[57] It probably became incorporated after 1428 with the manor of Chadwick, for no further mention of it has been found.[58] In the early 16th century a tenement called 'Wylengeswyke' belonged to William Curtes 'of old enheritaunce.'[59]

Of the land at Willingwick held in 1086 under William Fitz Ansculf no further mention is found,[60] unless, as appears probable, it is to be identified with land at Willingwick held in 1431 for a sixth of a knight's fee by Joan Lady Beauchamp,[61] to whom it may have passed from William Fitz Ansculf in the same way as Northfield. Joan died in 1435,[62] and this manor apparently passed to her grandson James Earl of Ormond, for it belonged to his brother Thomas, who eventually succeeded as Earl of Ormond and died in 1515.[63] This manor passed to his youngest daughter Margaret wife of Sir William Boleyn of Blickling, co. Norfolk, and was sold in 1518 by her sons Sir James and Sir Thomas Boleyn to Richard Fermour.[64] From this time all references to it cease.

TIMBERHONGER (Tymberhongle, Tymberhonghre, xiv cent.), a berewick of the royal manor of Bromsgrove in 1086,[65] was held of that manor until near the end of the 15th century, the last mention of the overlordship occurring in 1473.[66] The earliest tenants who held this manor of whom there is record are the Portes. Elizabeth de Portes held Timberhonger in 1297–8 and 1300.[67] In 1332 Richard de Portes had land there,[68] and five years later William de Portes and his wife Maud sold the manor to Hugh de Cooksey.[69] From that time the manor followed the same descent as the manor of Cooksey in Upton Warren [70] (q.v.), and it now belongs to the Earl of Shrewsbury and Talbot.

The manor of *WOODCOTE* is partly in Upton Warren and partly in Bromsgrove, the manor-house being in the latter parish. Before 1066 the manor belonged to Wulfsige, a thegn of Edward the Confessor, but by 1086 it had passed to Herlebald, who held it of Urse D'Abitot.[71] The overlordship passed from Urse to the Beauchamps as in Elmley Castle [72] (q.v.). The next mention of Herlebald's successor

[41] *Hund. R.* (Rec. Com.), ii, 283.

[42] *Feud. Aids*, v, 303, 324; *Valor Eccl.* (Rec. Com.), iii, 228.

[43] *Pat.* 32 Hen. VIII, pt. v, m. 1; 36 Hen. VIII, pt. xxiv, m. 2.

[44] *Pat.* 37 Hen. VIII, pt. vii, m. 10; *L. and P. Hen. VIII*, xx (2), g. 266 (32).

[45] *Pat.* 38 Hen. VIII, pt. viii; *L. and P. Hen. VIII*, xxi (2), g. 648 (25); Private Act, 31 Geo. III, cap. 31; Lewis, *Topog. Dict.* The manorial rights seem now to have lapsed.

[46] Information from the Treasurer, Christ Church, Oxford.

[47] Prattinton Coll. (Soc. Antiq.); notes by John Lacey. In 1646 the estate of Roger Lowe of Bromsgrove was sequestered, but eighteen months after his death it was restored to his widow. The question of Roger's sequestration arose again five years later when his cousin Roger Lowe claimed this property (*Cal. Com. for Comp.* 425, 2725). See also Feet of F. Worcs. East. 1655; Trin. 25 Chas. II; Mich. 32 Chas. II; Chan. Proc. (Ser. 2), bdle. 448, no. 39.

[48] Prattinton Coll. (Soc. Antiq.).

[49] Ibid.

[50] Private Act, 31 Geo. III, cap. 31.

[51] Brayley and Britton, op. cit. xv (2), 200.

[52] Ibid. Note by Mr. Penn.

[53] Lewis, *Topog. Dict.*

[54] *V.C.H. Worcs.* i, 286a.

[55] Ibid. 286, 316.

[56] Feet of F. Worcs. 7 Ric. I, no. 1; *Testa de Nevill* (Rec. Com.), 40.

[57] *Feud. Aids*, v, 303.

[58] Ibid. 324.

[59] Early Chan. Proc. bdle. 297, no. 56.

[60] William Clopton died about 1420 holding a sixth of the manors of Chadwick and Willingwick in right of his wife Joan, who survived, of Richard Earl of Warwick for knight service (Chan. Inq. p.m. 7 Hen. V, no. 46).

[61] *Feud. Aids*, v, 330.

[62] G.E.C. *Complete Peerage*, i, 14. Dugdale gives her will dated 1434 at length (*Baronage*, i, 140).

[63] G.E.C. *Complete Peerage*, vi, 141–3; Close, 12 Hen. VIII, no. 15. Land, sometimes called a manor, at Chadwick passed with this estate at Willingwick.

[64] G.E.C. loc. cit.; Close, 12 Hen. VIII, no. 15; Feet of F. Worcs. Trin. 10 Hen. VIII.

[65] *V.C.H. Worcs.* i, 285.

[66] Chan. Inq. p.m. 50 Edw. VI (1st nos.), no. 20; 24 Hen. VI, no. 36; 38 & 39 Hen. VI, no. 49; 13 Edw. IV, no. 32.

[67] Add. MS. 28024, fol. 148; Habington, *Surv. of Worc.* (Worcs. Hist. Soc.), i, 85.

[68] Feet of F. Worcs. East. 6 Edw. III.

[69] Ibid. 11 Edw. III, no. 27.

[70] For references see Cooksey. In 1537 inquiry was made as to whether Timberhonger was parcel of the manor of Cooksey or whether it was a manor of itself (*L. and P. Hen. VIII*, xii [2], g. 411 [5]).

[71] *V.C.H. Worcs.* i, 318b. 'Wdecote' was one of the berewicks of Bromsgrove (ibid. 285).

[72] *Testa de Nevill* (Rec. Com.), 40; *Cal. Inq. p.m.* 1–9 Edw. II, 403; *Cal. Close*, 1313–18, p. 277.

as underlord occurs about the middle of the 13th century when Richard de Montviron was tenant of the manor.[73] He or a successor of the same name was impleaded for common of pasture at Woodcote by William son of Warin de Upton in 1254-5,[74] and was holding in 1299-1300.[75] He had been succeeded before 1315-16 by John de Bishopston,[76] who was said to be his heir.[77] John settled the manor in 1316-17 on Joan daughter of Edmund de Grafton,[78] afterwards married to his son Roger. John de Bishopston was living in 1319, when he obtained a grant of free warren in the manor.[79] Roger de Bishopston and Joan, having no son, settled the manor in 1345 on their only daughter Alice and her husband Walter, son of Richard de Clodeshale.[80] Richard de Clodeshale, great-grandson of Alice, left Woodcote to his only child Elizabeth [81] wife of Sir Thomas Aston, kt., and she in 1410 settled it on her daughter Margaret wife of Richard Brace and their heirs.[82] Richard Brace and Margaret had two daughters, Elizabeth, who married John Ewnet, and Margaret, who married firstly Robert Bromwich and secondly Reginald Monington, and they claimed the manor after her death under the above settlement, their right to it being confirmed in 1472 by Walter Arderne,[83] son of Elizabeth Clodeshale by another husband, Robert Arderne of Park Hall, co. Warw.[84] In 1504 John Arderne son of Walter [85] tried to obtain the manor from Rowland Ewnet son of Elizabeth and William Bromwich, grandson of Margaret, but a case before the King's Bench was decided in favour of the defendants.[86] In 1494 William Bromwich sold his share of Woodcote to Thomas Bromwich,[87] who in 1521-2 acquired the other half from Rowland Ewnet son of the above Rowland.[88] Nothing further is known of the manor until 1550, when Ralph Fane and Elizabeth his wife released their interest in it to Anne wife of Edmund Horne, to whom the reversion, after Elizabeth's death, belonged. Edmund and Anne [89] in 1551 sold Woodcote to Sir John Pakington, kt.,[90] who appears to have settled it on his daughter Bridget when she married Sir John Lyttelton of Frankley, kt.[91] The latter died seised in 1591, and by his will left the manor to his second son George and Margaret his wife, with reversion to their son Stephen and his heirs male, and contingent remainders to John, another son of George and Margaret, and to Gilbert eldest son of the testator.[92]

Stephen Lyttelton was one of the conspirators in the Gunpowder Plot, and was arrested with Robert Winter at Hagley [93] through the treachery of one of his mother's servants at Holbeach.[94] Woodcote is not mentioned in the list of his lands forfeited to the Crown, probably because his mother, Margaret Lyttelton, was still living and held it for her life. After her death it passed to Gilbert Lyttelton and Etheldreda his wife.[95] Gilbert in 1617 became bound in the sum of £2,000 in trust for the use of Anne Lyttelton, widow, who afterwards became the wife of Francis Fowke, and of her two daughters Frances and Elizabeth. Woodcote appears to have been mortgaged on this account, but Gilbert afterwards sold it to Sir Brian Cave of Ingarsby (co. Leic.).[96] Sir Brian does not seem to have obtained possession, for the manor was afterwards held in moieties by Elizabeth wife of Walter Fowke and Frances wife of Henry Cupper,[97] evidently the two daughters of Anne Lyttelton mentioned above. Henry and Frances gave up their share to Walter Fowke and Elizabeth,[98] who conveyed the whole to John Cupper and Leonard Chamberlain in 1641.[99] This conveyance was apparently made for the purpose of paying Walter's debts, and in 1652 Cupper and Chamberlain were sued for not fulfilling the trusts of this conveyance.[100] Chamberlain, however, stated that Walter Fowke sold the manor to him in 1639, and that he maintained the said Walter and his wife 'weekly in theyre expences in London for a long tyme.' When the Civil War began Walter Fowke became an officer in the royal army, and Henry Cupper also took up arms for the king, and begged Chamberlain's estate in the manor from the king, taking the profits until Worcester was besieged in 1646, when the manor was sequestered. It was subsequently restored to Henry Cupper, who went to the Isle of Man with the Earl of Derby, thus preventing Chamberlain from suing him.[1] It would seem that Chamberlain never recovered seisin, for in 1668 John Baker and his wife Sarah sold the manor to Thomas Foley, and a clause is inserted in the conveyance assuring it from all claims by Walter Fowke and his wife Elizabeth and Henry Cupper and his wife Frances.[2] From that time it evidently passed in the Foley family, following the descent of Oddingley (q.v.), being in the possession of Thomas Lord Foley in 1802. About 1820 it was purchased by James Deakin, who sold it in 1828 to John Earl of Shrewsbury. It has since descended with the title.[3]

The early history of the manor of *GANNOW* is uncertain. In 1330 Hugh de Mortimer obtained a grant of free warren at 'Gamion,'[4] and in 1407 the manor of Gannow was said to have been held of the Earl of Warwick by Richard Ruyhale and his wife Elizabeth.[5] James Butler, Earl of Wiltshire, forfeited this manor on his attainder in 1461,[6] and it was given by Edward IV to Fulk Stafford.[7] He died without heirs in 1463, and the king then gave two-

[73] *Testa de Nevill* (Rec. Com.), 40.
[74] Assize R. 1022, m. 4 d.
[75] Habington, *Surv. of Worc.* (Worcs. Hist. Soc.), i, 85.
[76] *Cal. Inq. p.m.* 1–9 *Edw. II*, 403.
[77] Add. MS. 28024, fol. 190 d.
[78] Feet of F. Worcs. case 259, file 16, no. 4.
[79] *Cal. Chart. R.* 1300–26, p. 415.
[80] Feet of F. Worcs. Trin. 19 Edw. III; *Visit. of Warw.* (Harl. Soc. xii), 74.
[81] *Visit. of Warw.* (Harl. Soc. xii), 74.
[82] Feet of F. Worcs. case 260, file 26, no. 23. In 1431 Miles Water of Stone was holding certain land in Woodcote for the service of an eighth of a knight's fee.
[83] Close, 12 Edw. IV, m. 31.

[84] *Visit. of Warw.* (Harl. Soc. xii), 73.
[85] Ibid.
[86] De Banco R. 20 Hen. VII, m. 397; Early Chan. Proc. bdle. 120, no. 54.
[87] Close, 23 Hen. VII, pt. i, no. 37.
[88] Ibid. 13 Hen. VIII, no. 6.
[89] Feet of F. Worcs. Mich. 4 Edw. VI.
[90] Ibid. East. 5 Edw. VI.
[91] Jeayes, *Lyttelton Chart.* no. 15.
[92] P.C.C. 26 Drury.
[93] *Cal. S. P. Dom.* 1603–10, p. 281.
[94] Ibid. 1580–1625, p. 474.
[95] Notes of F. Worcs. Mich. 20 Jas. I.
[96] Chan. Proc. Jas. I, C 22, no. 26.
[97] Feet of F. Worcs. Mich. 9 Chas. I; Trin. 11 Chas. I; Mich. 13 Chas. I.
[98] Ibid. East. 12 Chas. I

[99] Ibid. Trin. 17 Chas. I.
[100] Chan. Proc. (Ser. 2), bdle. 439, no. 66.
[1] Ibid.
[2] Feet of F. Worcs. East. 20 Chas. II.
[3] Inform. from Mr. Bickerton H. Deakin.
[4] Chart. R. 4 Edw. III, m. 38, no. 96.
[5] Chan. Inq. p.m. 9 Hen. IV, no. 26. Richard Oldcastle, to whom the Ruyhales' lands passed (see Birtsmorton), was dealing with land at Gannow in 1421 (Sir T. Phillipps, *Index to Worc. Fines*, 2).
[6] Chan. Inq. p.m. 3 Edw. IV, no. 12. The manor was then said to be held of the manor of Frankley.
[7] *Cal. Pat.* 1461–7, p. 112.

thirds of it to Sir John Scott, with the reversion of the remaining third on the death of Margaret the widow of Fulk.[8]   Sir John Scott surrendered the manor to the king in 1481 in exchange for other lands,[9] and the king then gave it to the Dean and Canons of St. George's Chapel, Windsor,[10] with the reversion of the third part, still in the hands of Margaret Stafford.   The manor does not appear to have remained long in the hands of the dean and chapter, for, according to Nash, it was granted, like the manor of Old Swinford, to Thomas Earl of Ormond,[11] and it subsequently passed with the manor of Willingwick to Richard Fermour,[12] a wea¹thy merchant who was amassing vast property in land at that time.   He was later convicted under the Statute of Provisors and deprived of his property, Gannow being given by Henry VIII in 1545 to John Dudley, Viscount Lisle, Great Admiral of England,[13] but in 1550 Richard Fermour's property was restored.[14]   He died in 1552[15] and was succeeded by his son John, who was knighted in the following year.[16]   Thomas Fermour, who was holding it in 1571 and died in 1580, was apparently brother of John.[17]   He left it to his son Richard,[18] who probably sold it to the Lloyd family.   In 1624 Thomas and Robert Lloyd and William Porter conveyed it to Anne Porter, a widow.[19]   In 1650 Henry Porter owned land in Gannow.[20]   Nash, writing about 1782, states that the manor was owned by Thomas Jolliffe,[21] and it is probably to be identified with the manor of Ganway which he was holding in 1720-1.[22]   The manor passed with that of Coston Hackett (q.v.) to Robert Biddulph, who was in possession in 1795.[23]   It is believed to have passed with Coston Hackett to the Earl of Plymouth in the 19th century.   A court was still held for it once a year in the early 19th century.[24]

The Prior of Dodford had land and rents at *DODFORD* to the yearly value of £4 17s. in 1291.[25] The priory with all its possessions was granted to the abbey of Halesowen in 1464,[26] and Dodford Priory then became a cell of that abbey.[27]   In 1538 the Abbot of Halesowen surrendered the manor and priory of Dodford to the king,[28] who granted them in the same year to Sir John Dudley.[29]   In the following year he gave the manor to his brother Andrew,[30] who in 1551 sold it, with the exception of the mansion-

house, by which the site of the priory was perhaps meant, to Thomas and Hugh Wylde.   The latter sold the estate in 1559 to Thomas and Robert Wylde   Thomas died before 1561 and Robert was distrained for homage for it in 1564.[31]   It remained in this family until, in the middle of the 17th century, it passed to Richard Bourne of Acton Hall on his marriage with Anne daughter of Robert Wylde.[32]   Page Bourne, a descendant of this lady, owned it at the beginning of the 19th century, when the manor courts were still held.[33]   The Rt. Hon. William Sturges Bourne, who died in 1845, left it to his wife and daughter, but it was soon afterwards sold, a farm forming part of it being bought in 1856 by Mr. Robert Deakin.[34]

The *SITE OF THE PRIORY OF DODFORD* was granted with the manor in 1538 to Sir John Dudley, and alienated by him to Andrew Dudley, who sold his 'chief mansion house or messuage' at Dodford to John Fownes in 1539.[35]   His son or grandson Thomas Fownes, sen., at the time of his death in 1631, held the reversion of this estate after the death of Jane wife of Henry Dyson, widow of Thomas's son Thomas, on whom it had been settled at the time of her marriage with Thomas.[36]   Thomas, the son, had died without issue in 1620,[37] and in 1633 livery of the manor was made to his brother John Fownes,[38] who continued to hold it as late as 1664.[39]   He was succeeded by Thomas Fownes, who was living in 1675,[40] after which all trace of this property is lost.

The priory is now a farm.   The walls to a height of about 6 ft. are those of the old priory.   The chapel has entirely disappeared, but stood on the left of the court.[41]

The earliest mention of the so-called manor of *DYERS* is in 1537, when Edward Dewpy or Bewpye and his wife Elizabeth sold it to John Pakington.[42]   John Pakington was knighted in 1545, and died fifteen years later, leaving two daughters, of whom Bridget, who married Sir John Lyttelton, inherited this manor.[43]   Her grandson, John Lyttelton, was attainted in 1601, owing to his share in Essex's rebellion.[43a]   James I granted the manor to his widow Muriel in 1603,[44] her son, Sir Thomas Lyttelton, afterwards holding the manor.   He sold it in 1639 to Ralph and John Taylor.[45]   Ralph Taylor conveyed

[8] *Cal. Pat.* 1461-7, pp. 221, 297; 1467-77, p. 18.
[9] Ibid. 1476-85, p. 281.
[10] Ibid. 285.   [11] Nash, op. cit. i, 155.
[12] Feet of F. Worcs. Trin. 10 Hen. VIII. The manor was claimed in 1579 by Henry Lord Hunsdon as one of the heirs of the Earl of Ormond (Chan. Proc. [Ser. 2], bdle. 211, no. 102).
[13] *L. and P. Hen. VIII*, xx (2), 412 (ii); g. 1068 (41).
[14] Pat. 4 Edw. VI, pt. ix.
[15] Edmondson, *Baronagium Gen.* iii, 225.
[16] Pat. 1 Mary, pt. xi, m. 19.
[17] Recov. R. Mich. 12 & 13 Eliz. rot. 1308; Chan. Proc. (Ser. 2), bdle. 211, no. 102; Edmondson, loc. cit.
[18] Chan. Inq. p.m. (Ser. 2), cxc, 66.
[19] Feet of F. Worcs. Mich. 22 Jas. I.
[20] Ibid. 1650.
[21] Nash, op. cit. i, 155.
[22] Recov. R. D. Enr. Trin. 7 Geo. I, m. 15.
[23] Recov. R. Mich. 36 Geo. III, rot. 141.
[24] Prattinton Coll. (Soc. Antiq.).
[25] *Pope Nich. Tax.* (Rec. Com.), 231.

[26] Worc. Epis. Reg. Carpenter, fol. 186 d.; *Cal. Pat.* 1461-7, p. 321.
[27] Dugdale, *Mon. Angl.* vi, 944.
[28] Feet of F. Div. Co. Trin. 30 Hen. VIII.
[29] *L. and P. Hen. VIII*, xiii (2), g. 491 (1).
[30] Ibid. xiv (1), g. 651 (8).
[31] Memo. R. (L.T.R.), Mich. Recorda, 6 Eliz. rot. 162.
[32] *Visit. of Worcs.* (Harl. Soc. xxvii), 152; Feet of F. Worcs. Hil. 2 & 3 Jas. II.
[33] Prattinton Coll. (Soc. Antiq.). In 1785 'the manor of Dodford' was conveyed by Wilson Aylesbury Roberts and Betty Carolina his wife to John Thomas Batt (Feet of F. Worcs. Mich. 26 Geo. III), and in 1804 a property called the manor of Dodford passed from Thomas and Mary Gem to Robert Mynors (ibid. East. 44 Geo. III).
[34] Inform. from Mr. Bickerton H. Deakin.
[35] *L. and P. Hen. VIII*, xiii (2), g. 491 (1); xiv (1), g. 651 (8); xiv (2), g. 619 (65).
[36] Chan. Inq. p.m. (Ser. 2), ccclxii, 77.

[37] Ibid.
[38] Fine R. 9 Chas. I, pt. ii, no. 27.
[39] Habington, *Surv. of Worc.* (Worcs. Hist. Soc.), i, 87; Feet of F. Worcs. Mich. 16 Chas. II.
[40] Feet of F. Worcs. Hil. 26 & 27 Chas. II.
[41] MSS. at Soc. of Antiq. no. 153, Bp. Lyttelton's church notes.
[42] Feet of F. Worcs. Trin. 29 Hen. VIII; Add. MS. 31314, fol. 50-1, 72.
[43] *Dict. Nat. Biog.*; *Visit. of Worc.* 1569 (Harl. Soc. xxvii), 94.
[43a] Exch. Spec. Com. 44 Eliz. no. 2519.
[44] Pat. 1 Jas. I, pt. i; Feet of F. Div. Co. Trin. 3 Jas. I.   In 1599 Thomas Cornwall claimed the manor in right of his wife Anne (a daughter of Gilbert Lyttelton, father of John who was attainted in 1601), upon whom he said Gilbert had settled the manor (Chan. Proc. Eliz. L.l. 8, no. 60).   Thomas and Anne gave up their claim in 1605 in favour of Muriel (Feet of F. Div. Co. Trin. 3 Jas. I).
[45] Feet of F. Worcs. Trin. 15 Chas. I; Recov. R. Mich. 16 Chas. I, rot. 43.

it in 1664 to Nicholas and Edmund Lechmere,[46] and in 1692 Edward Taylor conveyed it to Sandys Lechmere and Edward Milles.[47] The manor of Dyers still existed at the end of the 18th century when Nash wrote his *History of Worcester*,[48] but he does not give the name of the owner. The old manor-house was pulled down in 1777, and the Golden Lion Inn was built on its site.[49] Prattinton calls this manor 'Diocese or Dyers manor,' and in his time two courts were held yearly.[50]

The manor of *BUNHILL* (Bollenhill, xv cent. ; Bovenhill, Bonehill, xvi cent. ; Bornehill, Beaconhill, Bavenhill, xviii cent.) seems to have originated in land at 'Bollenhull' held at the time of his death in 1473 by Sir Ralph Boteler of Sudeley.[51] It was appurtenant to the manor of Fairfield in Belbroughton (q.v.) until the latter was sold by John Talbot about 1595,[52] but it is mentioned as a separate manor in 1560–1.[53] It must have been sold by the Talbots to Robert Caldwell, for in 1619 and 1630 he made conveyances of it to John Westwood.[54] It was in the possession of Thomas Jolliffe of Coston Hackett in 1720–1,[55] and passed with Coston Hackett to Robert Biddulph, who was holding it in 1795.[56] No further mention of this manor has been found.

The Abbot of Bordesley had lands in Bromsgrove at least as early as 1155.[57] In the 13th century Alured Jordan sold land which he held of the king there to the abbot.[58] In 1267 the convent quit-claimed to Henry III 24*s*. which 'they were wont to receive from the king's manor of Bromsgrove of the king's appointed alms,' and received other lands and rent in return.[59] The abbot attended the court of Bromsgrove in 1389,[60] but nothing further is known of his estate here.

During the 15th century land in this parish, occasionally described as the manor of Bromsgrove, was in the hands of the Staffords. Sir Humphrey Stafford of Grafton bequeathed it by his will dated 1442 to his son Richard, but Richard died without issue, and the manor passed to his brother Sir Humphrey.[61] It then followed the same descent as Kenswick in the parish of Knightwick (q.v.) until 1546, when Humphrey Stafford succeeded his father Sir Humphrey in this manor.[62] This Humphrey forfeited all his possessions by an attainder, and Bromsgrove was granted in 1592 to William Tipper and Robert Dawe.[63] From this time the estate disappears.

BARNSLEY HALL was held during the 17th century by the Barnsley family, who are known to have been holding land in Bromsgrove in the 15th and 16th centuries.[64] Their pedigree is entered in the Worcestershire Visitation of 1569.[65] John Lacey, writing in 1778, states that the Barnsleys sold the hall to the Lowes, from whom it was bought by Edward Knight of Wolverley. The old hall was taken down in 1771 and a large farm erected near its site.[66] It was purchased about 1900 by the Worcestershire County Council, who erected a large lunatic asylum upon the site.

BARNSLEY. *Sable a cross between four roses argent with a molet gules for difference.*

There were three mills in the manor of Bromsgrove in 1086, worth 13*s*. 4*d*.[67] Bromsgrove Mill, 'on the churche and markett waye,'[68] was given with the manor to Ambrose Earl of Warwick by Elizabeth. James I separated the mill from the manor in 1609 and gave the former to Edward Ferrers and Francis Philipps.[69] In the following year Edward and Francis sold the mill to Giles Richards, but ten years later the mill-house and buildings were in ruins and the footbridge and horsebridge and floodgates had entirely disappeared.[70] A water corn-mill at Bromsgrove was advertised for sale in 1817.[71] Mr. W. A. Cotton, writing in 1888, stated that this mill had been recently removed to effect a public improvement.[72]

The Lower Mills at Bromsgrove were held of Edward Knight at a fee-farm rent of £1 16*s*. 6*d*. in 1769.[73] Fockbury Mill was leased by Sir John Lyttelton in the 14th century to Joan widow of Gilbert Penn, who left it in her will to Gilbert Barnsley.[74] Fockbury Mill, a corn-mill on the Battlefield Brook, still exists. A mill existed at Whitford[75] or Wyteford in 1266.[76] There is now a corn-mill called Whitford Mill on the Battlefield Brook.

The tithe of the mill of Chadwick was granted with the manor in 1232 to the hospital of St. Wulfstan by Roger de Lens,[77] and in 1271–2 Walter de Montviron and Annora his wife gave a mill at Chadwick to the hospital.[78] The present Chadwick Mill is on Battlefield Brook near Chadwick Farm. A corn-mill at Wildmoor[79] in Chadwick belonged in 1791 to William Viscount Dudley and Ward.[80]

There is a corn-mill at Lickey End on the Spadesbourne Brook, and there are many mills in the

[46] Feet of F. Worcs. Mich. 16 Chas. II.

[47] Recov. R. Mich. 4 Will. and Mary, rot. 273 ; Recov. R. D. Enr. Mich. 4 Will. and Mary, m. 4.

[48] op. cit. i, 159.

[49] Prattinton Coll. (Soc. Antiq.).

[50] Ibid.

[51] Chan. Inq. p.m. 13 Edw. IV, no. 58.

[52] Feet of F. Div. Co. Hil. 3 Eliz. ; Chan. Inq. p.m. (Ser. 2), clxix, 40 ; Feet of F. Worcs. Hil. 16 Eliz. ; Recov. R. East. 37 Eliz. rot. 55.

[53] Feet of F. Div. Co. Hil. 3 Eliz.

[54] Ibid. Worcs. Mich. 17 Jas. I ; Recov. R. Hil. 6 Chas. I, rot. 3.

[55] Recov. R. D. Enr. Trin. 7 Geo. I, m. 15.

[56] Recov. R. Mich. 36 Geo. III, rot. 141.

[57] Hunter, *Great Roll of Pipe*, 2, 3, 4 *Hen. II*, 62, 91, 92, &c. ; Pipe R. 22 Hen. II, m. 3 ; 23 Hen. III, &c. ; *Red Bk. of Exch.* (Rolls Ser.), 661.

[58] *Testa de Nevill* (Rec. Com.), 43 ; *Cal. Pat.* 1232–47, pp. 171, 172.

[59] *Cal. Chart. R.* 1257–1300, p. 73.

[60] Ct. R. (Gen. Ser.), portf. 210, no. 34.

[61] Chan. Inq. p.m. (Ser. 2), lxxv, 96.

[62] Pat. 2 Hen. VII, pt. i, m. 8 ; *Cal. Inq. p.m. Hen. VII*, i, 545 ; Chan. Inq. p.m. (Ser. 2), xxxiii, 4 ; Exch. Inq. p.m. (Ser. 2), file 1198, no. 8.

[63] Pat. 34 Eliz. pt. iv.

[64] Add. Chart. 23855 ; Ct. R. (Gen. Ser.), portf. 210, no. 35, 36, 40, &c. ; Chan. Proc. (Ser. 2), bdle. 63, no. 5 ; Star Chamber Proc. Hen. VIII, bdle. 29, no. 109 ; Habington, op. cit. i, 88 ; *Cal. Com. for Comp.* 2913.

[65] op. cit. (Harl. Soc. xxvii), 15.

[66] Prattinton Coll. (Soc. Antiq.).

[67] *V.C.H. Worcs.* i, 286.

[68] Hardy and Page MSS. file 347*a*.

[69] Pat. 7 Jas. I, pt. xvi.

[70] Exch. Dep. East. 18 Jas. I, no. 19 ; Mich. 19 Jas. I, no. 37.

[71] Prattinton Coll. (Soc. Antiq.).

[72] Hardy and Page MSS. file 347*a*.

[73] Prattinton Coll. (Soc. Antiq.).

[74] Chan. Proc. (Ser. 2), bdle. 63, no. 5.

[75] Witeurde was one of the berewicks of the manor of Bromsgrove in 1086 (*V.C.H. Worcs.* i, 285).

[76] *Worc. Inq. p.m.* (Worcs. Hist. Soc.), pt. i, 10.

[77] *Cal. Chart. R.* 1226–57, p. 172.

[78] Feet of F. Worcs. 56 Hen. III, no. 36.

[79] In 1269–70 John Carbonel obtained licence to inclose land called Wildmore in the forest of Lickey. Inq. a.q.d. 54 Hen. III, file 3, no. 15.

[80] Priv. Act, 31 Geo. III, cap. 31.

town, including Townsend Mill and Blackmore Mill, corn-mills on the Spadesbourne Brook, and in the south of the town Moat Mill, Lint Mill and Bant Mill. Sugarbrook Mill lies on the boundary between this parish and Stoke Prior, and there is a disused cotton-mill at the junction of the Spadesbourne and Battlefield Brooks.

After Henry III granted the church of Bromsgrove to the priory of Worcester in 1232 [81] the monastery appropriated the tithes and lands belonging to it, a portion being set aside for the payment of a vicar.[82] From this appropriation the *RECTORY MANOR* appears to have arisen. It was leased in 1253 to Samson de Bromsgrove for two years,[83] and in 1306 it was found that the prior and convent had had the amercements under the assize of bread and ale among the men and tenants of their appropriate church of Bromsgrove until Queen Eleanor had the custody of the manor of Bromsgrove.[84] The priory retained the rectory until its dissolution, when Henry VIII granted it in 1542 to the Dean and Chapter of Worcester,[85] in whose possession it remained until the manorial rights lapsed.[86] The Ecclesiastical Commissioners still hold the rectorial tithes and about 40 acres of glebe land. Both have been for many years leased to the lord of the manor for the time being. Prattinton, writing in the beginning of the 19th century, states that the rectory manor was formerly part of Feckenham Forest, and that a court leet was held twice a year.[87] Lord Plymouth still holds courts annually.[88]

The church of *ST. JOHN BAPTIST* consists of chancel 40 ft. 6 in. by 32 ft. 3 in., north vestry, clear-storied nave 67 ft. 6 in. by 36 ft. 6 in., a north aisle 20 ft. 3 in. wide and a south aisle 20 ft. 9 in. wide, a south porch, and west tower 19 ft. 6 in. by 18 ft. These measurements are all internal.

The earliest church, of which there are remains in the south door and the eastern respond of the north arcade of the nave, was a late 12th-century cruciform aisleless building, having a chancel smaller than the present one.

In the middle of the 13th century the chancel was rebuilt, lengthened and widened on the south side, a 13th-century arch replacing the Norman one to the nave. The south aisle is also of this date, and it may be presumed that a narrow north aisle was added at this time.

The position of the piscina here may indicate that the old transept was retained and used as a chapel. There is no evidence of an early tower. In the 14th century the vestry was added to the chancel, and late in the same century the present west tower and spire were built. In the 15th century the north wall of the north aisle was probably rebuilt in line with the north wall of the transept, the west wall of which was then removed and windows were spaced along the wall, using up two 14th-century windows from the former aisle and perhaps the jambs of the north transept window. Later in the century the aisle was carried on by the side of the chancel as far as the

vestry, though it is possible that a chapel already existed east of the transept at this point, before the east wall of the transept was removed.

During the 15th century a steep-pitched ceiling existed over the nave, but at the end of that century or the beginning of the next this was removed, the south arcade being rebuilt at the same time and a clearstory added.

In the south aisle the square projecting tomb recess was added to the south wall and a porch built to replace the earlier one. The church was thoroughly restored by Sir Gilbert Scott in 1858, and the upper part of the spire was rebuilt in 1892.

The east window of the chancel consists of five modern lancets grouped under a pointed head, part of the exterior of the window being old.

In the north wall is a two-light trefoiled window of about 1300 with a quatrefoil over. The vestry is lighted by a three-light trefoiled east window and a similar two-light window in the north wall, with a modern door below. The doorway communicating with the chancel is also modern. West of the vestry is a wide four-centred arch with panelled soffit, moulded ribs and carved bosses opening into the eastern end of the north aisle. In the wall round it are traces of a previous arch of higher pitch, suggesting the existence of a chapel to the east of the north transept, previous to the 15th century. A rib on the east wall of the north aisle and corbels with angels, set in the north-east and south-east angles, are perhaps remains of the chapel vault. The segmental arch from the east wall, now blocked, originally connected with the vestry.

The south wall of the chancel has two windows similar to that on the north. The sedilia are composed of old work re-used and carved with quatrefoils inclosing shields. There is also a trefoiled piscina, the drain of which is old. At the south-west end of the wall is an arch, apparently of the 14th century, opening into the aisle. The chancel arch is two-centred and of three moulded orders with labels; the responds have three half-shafts with moulding and nail-heads on the capitals. Above the arch on the west side is the line of the steep pitch 13th-century ceiling. On the north side is the opening of the rood-loft, with the stair passing up through the wall.

The north arcade is of five bays, the eastern arch having square moulded abaci of late 12th-century type. All except the arch, however, is now modern. West of this is a small trefoiled arch forming a second bay inserted by Scott at the restoration of the church. The three western bays are of late 13th-century date, and have two-centred arches of two chamfered orders, supported by piers of quatrefoil plan which have been much restored. The south arcade consists of four bays of about the year 1500, with small moulded capitals and shafts similar to the arch mouldings. The clearstory has five two-light windows on each side of the nave, contemporary with the south arcade.

The east window of the north aisle is of the 15th century, with two lights and tracery in the head, and the first two windows in the north wall are of similar date. This part of the aisle is occupied by the organ. The third window has also 15th-century

[81] *Cal. Chart. R.* 1226–57, p. 154.
[82] *Reg. Priory Worc.* (Camden Soc.), 30; *Ann. Mon.* (Rolls Ser.), iv, 427.
[83] *Ann. Mon.* (Rolls Ser.), iv, 442.
[84] Chan. Inq. p.m. 35 Edw. I, no. 70;

Inq. a.q.d. 35 Edw. I, file 63, no. 10. The Prior of Worcester was fined by the bailiffs of Bromsgrove for taking these amercements in 1290. *Abbrev. Plac.* (Rec. Com.), 220.

[85] *L. and P. Hen. VIII*, xvii, g. 71 (29).
[86] The manor still existed in 1779 (Nash, op. cit. i, 161).
[87] Prattinton Coll. (Soc. Antiq.).
[88] Information by Mr. J. Willis-Bund.

tracery, but its jambs are perhaps those of the original transept window, and are similar to the jambs of the corresponding windows of the south aisle. The fourth and fifth windows are of about 1320, and consist of three lights, a central cinquefoiled light flanked by trefoiled lights. Between these windows is a blocked 14th-century door, the stones of the outside arch numbered for re-setting. The west window of the aisle is 15th-century work of four lights with cinquefoiled heads and tracery over. The tower arch of three moulded orders dates from the end of the 14th century. In the south aisle the east window with three uncusped lights and intersecting mullions is of 13th-century date; the first window in the south wall of three lights with tracery over is of the 15th century, and is similar in detail to the four-light

that the door has been reset in its present position. In the north and south walls of the ground stage of the tower are three-light windows of 14th-century date with cinquefoiled lights and intersecting mullions. A door leads to the belfry stair in the south-west angle. In the north and south faces of the second stage are small pointed windows, and on the west three crocketed niches with figures of St. Peter, St. Paul, and an unidentified saint, and a small arched recess on either side. In the third stage the belfry windows are of two lights with quatrefoils over. On either side of these is blank arcading with tracery, crockets and finials. The porch itself is of 15th-century date; but traces of that which it replaces are to be seen on the wall above. It is lit by two-light windows in the side walls, and to the east

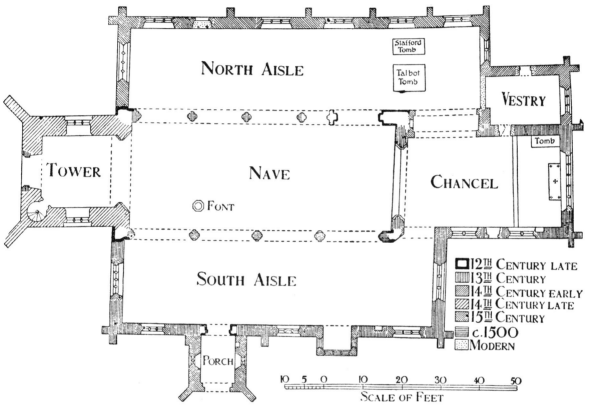

PLAN OF BROMSGROVE CHURCH

window in the west wall. West of this is a piscina, partly old, of about 1300, and a square projecting bay, probably for a tomb, with a three-light, square-headed window in its south wall and similar single-light windows in its east and west walls, all of 15th-century date. Above the south porch and on either side of it are three 15th-century windows of three lights each with square heads. The south door appears to be late 12th-century work re-used when the original nave door was moved out to the aisle wall. The late 14th-century west tower is of three stages, with diagonal buttresses of four offsets and panelled battlements having pinnacles at the angles, above which rises a lofty octagonal spire of stone with roll-moulded angles, and two sets of finialled lights. The moulded west doorway of the tower, with an obtuse pointed head externally, may be 13th-century work. The Roman numerals on the stones of the arch suggest

of the door is a stoup with a niche for an image on the other side. The roof of cambered beams is old, and above the outer doorway is a canopied niche. Generally the exterior of the church is faced with large sandstone, and the walls, with the exception of the chancel, have embattled parapets, surmounted by pinnacles marking the bays. The south aisle retains its 13th-century buttresses to the south and west walls, and on the latter is the line of an earlier roof. On each side of the tower are straight joints in the masonry. The chancel roof is apparently old, those of the aisles and nave modern. In the chancel is a 17th-century desk with a chained copy of Jewell's *Apology*, and in the vestry is an old poor-box. The font and fittings of the church are modern.

In the north aisle is a large alabaster altar tomb with effigies of Sir John Talbot and his two wives (Margaret Troutbeck and Elizabeth Wrottesley).

The north and part of the east sides of the tomb are modern and blank. On the west are three cusped and traceried panels inclosing shields; the first has three piles and a quarter ermine, for Wrottesley; the second, a large shield, quarterly of nine, for Talbot, 1, a lion, 2, a lion, 3, bendy, 4, barry ten martlets, 5, a saltire with a martlet, 6, a bend between six martlets, 7, a fret, 8, two lions passant, 9, a lion; the third is a small shield, quarterly, 1, a fleur de lis between three men's heads, 2, three piles, 3, two cheverons with a crosslet fitchy in the quarter, 4, a lion passant. On the south side of the tomb are four traceried panels, the first and third with a talbot, the second blank, and the fourth, in a cabled circle, three trout interlaced, which are the arms of

BROMSGROVE CHURCH FROM THE NORTH-WEST

tomb to Sir Humphrey Stafford and Elizabeth his wife, ob. 1450, in stone, the east and west ends only, which have quatrefoiled panels, being old. On it are two fine alabaster effigies of a man and woman. The man wears a pointed bascinet with orle and raised visor; his plate armour shows traces of gilding, the hands are gloved with finger tips exposed and the feet have pointed sollerets. The head rests on a helmet crested with a boar's head. The lady has a mitred head-dress, and at her feet are a griffin and a talbot. In the north-east corner of the chancel is a white alabaster altar tomb with the effigy of a lady. The tomb has probably been shortened, and has a double row of cinquefoiled panels, three angels with blank shields and a small image bracket. The figure wears a jewelled head-dress and long mantle; a metal necklace and cloak clasp as well as the brass inscription have been removed. The figure represents Elizabeth daughter of Ralph Lord Greystock and first wife of Sir Gilbert Talbot of Grafton, ob. 1517. On the wall above is a good monument in grey marble to John Hall, Bishop of Bristol, with the arms of his see, three crowns, impaling crusilly three talbots' heads razed. He died in 1710.

In the north aisle is a brass tablet to Dame Bridget Talbot, wife of Sir John Talbot of Castle Ring, Ireland, daughter of Sir John Talbot the elder of Grafton, ob. 1619. Another tablet is to Dame Margrete Lygon, wife of Sir Arnould Lygon, of Beauchamp Court, ob. 1632.

In the south aisle is the marble and alabaster monument of George Lyttelton (1600) with his effigy. Behind is a panelled arch (wherein is a slab with an inscription) between Corinthian columns with a cornice over, supporting a shield of the cheveron and scallops of Lyttelton, quartered with the old coat, Argent a bend cotised sable in a border engrailed gules bezanty.

Outside the north wall of the north aisle is a much-worn red sandstone effigy of a woman. On the south aisle wall is a sundial.

In the tower are ten bells, the first, second and seventh cast by T. Mears of London, 1816; the third, fourth (with inscription 'When you us ring, We'll sweetly sing'), sixth, and tenth by Thomas Rudhall of Gloucester, 1773; the ninth ('I to the church the living call, And to the grave do summon all') by John Rudhall, 1790; the eighth was recast by Barwell of Birmingham in 1897, and the fifth, the only remnant of the original ring, by Abraham Rudhall, 1701, inscribed 'God prosper this parish.' There is also a priest's bell bearing merely the date 1816.

The bells of Bromsgrove Church were recast about 1622 by John Tydman for £61 2s. 4d. The old bells weighed: the great bell 19 cwt. 1 qr. 4 lb. 10 oz., the second 15 cwt. 13 lb., the third 14 cwt. 1 qr. 14 lb., and the fourth 9 cwt. 3 qr. 8 lb. When they had been recast, however, they were found to be worthless, and

Troutbeck. On the east face of the tomb one panel only is left and bears the letter M. The marginal inscription, cut in raised letters on the slab, runs: 'Hic jacent corpora Johannis Talbot militis et domine Margarete prime uxoris atque domine Elizabethe uxoris secunde filie Walteri Wrocheley armigeri qui quidem Johannes obiit X° die Septembris Anno Domini M°CCCCL°. Quorum animabus propicietur deus amen.' The effigy of Sir John is placed between those of his wives and is in plate armour with hauberk, the head and hands being bare. He wears a collar of SS, and his feet with rounded sabbatons rest on a lion. The figure on his right has a kennel head-dress with veil. The lady on his left wears a jewelled coif. To the north is a second

the five contained far less weight than the four old ones.[89]

The plate is all of 1876 and consists of two silver chalices, two patens and a flagon. The old plate is said to have been melted down.

The registers previous to 1812 are as follows: (i) all entries 1590 to 1652; (ii) 1653 to 1719; (iii) 1719 to 1733; (iv) 1734 to 1754, also baptisms and burials 1783 to 1793; (v) baptisms and burials 1753 to 1803; (vi) baptisms and burials 1774 to 1783; (vii) marriages 1754 to 1773; (viii) marriages 1773 to 1812; (ix) baptisms and burials 1793 to 1806; (x) baptisms and burials 1806 to 1815.

The church of *ALL SAINTS*, erected 1872–4, consists of an apsidal chancel, with a north organ chamber and a south vestry, north and south transepts, nave, north and south aisles and a north-west tower. The nave is of six bays. The design is in the style of the late 13th century and the materials are quarry faced and coursed rubble, with wrought stone dressings and tiled roofs.

ADVOWSON There was probably a church at Bromsgrove in 1086,[90] as there was then a priest in the manor. The advowson apparently remained in the Crown until 1232, when Henry III granted the church of Bromsgrove to the Prior and monks of Worcester,[91] who appropriated it in 1235.[91a] This gift was confirmed by Gregory IX in 1237[92] and by Bishop William de Blois, who assigned the chapel of Grafton to the sacristan of the church of Worcester instead of 10 marks which the sacristan used to receive from the church of Bromsgrove for finding tapers at the tomb of King John.[93]

The advowson of the church remained in the possession of the prior and convent[94] until the dissolution of their house, and was granted in 1542 by Henry VIII to the Dean and Chapter of Worcester.[95] This was confirmed by James I in 1608,[96] and they continue to hold it at the present day.

In 1669 the advowson fell to the king, no presentation having been made for eighteen months.[97] The vicarage of Bromsgrove was held together with the bishopric of Rochester by special licence from 1544 to 1550,[98] and again from 1828 to about 1846, when George Murray, Bishop of Rochester, was vicar of Bromsgrove. The Trustees for Ministers recommended an augmentation of £50 to the living of Bromsgrove in 1656, as it was a great market town and the means small.[99]

There were five chapels dependent on the church of Bromsgrove, i.e. Chadwick, Moseley, Wythall, Grafton, and King's Norton. The last four have become parochial.[100]

The chapel of St. James in Chadwick was given by Roger son of Ranulf de Lens to the hospital of St. Wulfstan, and his gift was confirmed by the king in 1232.[1] In 1401 the Preceptor of St. Wulfstan's was sued by the inhabitants of Chadwick and Willingwick for not providing a chaplain to serve the chapel of Chadwick.[2] The Prior of Worcester seems to have claimed the advowson of the chapel in the 15th century, but renounced it in 1432.[3] Nash states that the chapel was in ruins at the end of the 18th century. He adds that it was said to be the duty of the Dean of Christ Church, Oxford, to keep the chapel in repair and to find a chaplain, but that service had not been performed nor the chapel been fit for service within living memory.[4]

In 1405 the Bishop of Worcester licensed those of the parishioners of Bromsgrove who lived near King's Norton to attend service at the chapel of Moseley, as being nearer and more convenient for them than the church of Bromsgrove.[5]

Richard de la Lynde endowed a chantry in the church of St. John the Baptist of Bromsgrove in 1304–5,[6] and in 1335 Richard, called the clerk of Bromsgrove, obtained licence to have divine service celebrated in an oratory in his manor of Bromsgrove.[7]

In 1447 Sir Humphrey Stafford of Grafton obtained licence of the king to found a perpetual chantry of two chaplains in the church of Bromsgrove, at the altar of St. Mary, to celebrate divine service for the good estate of the king and queen and of Humphrey and Eleanor his wife, to be called 'the chantry of Humphrey Stafford of Grafton kt.'[8] The chantry was not actually founded until 1476-8, when Eleanor, Sir Humphrey's widow, endowed a chaplain with a rent of £6 13s. 4d. from the manor of Dodford, co. Northants.[9] The advowson of this chantry belonged to the Staffords, lords of Dodford.[10] In the reign of Edward VI, when the chantry was dissolved, £7 was being paid to a priest who was bound to keep a school and assist the curate at Bromsgrove, while there was also a chantry priest receiving a stipend of £6 13s. 4d. A sum of 6s. 8d. was given to the poor and 6s. was reserved for lamps, the remainder being employed for the 'repairs of the church, sending soldiers to the wars, repairing highways, and bridges, and suchlike charitable deeds within the parish.'[11] Lands forming part of the endowment of this chantry were sold in 1550 to William Winlove and Richard Feild,[12] but in 1556-7 the school was re-endowed by Queen Mary, as the 'free grammar school of King Philip and Queen Mary,' with £7 per annum, and the government of it was entrusted to six men of the town.[13]

[89] Chan. Proc. (Ser. 2), bdle. 363, no. 8.
[90] *V.C.H. Worcs.* i, 285.
[91] *Cal. Chart. R.* 1226-57, p. 154.
[91a] *Ann. Mon.* (Rolls Ser.), iv, 427.
[92] Nash, op. cit. i, 168.
[93] Heming, *Chartul.* (ed. Hearne), ii, 644; *Reg. Priory Worc.* (Camden Soc.), 30a.
[94] The advowson of Bromsgrove was claimed by Edward I in 1279 and at about the same time by the Master of the Temple, who stated that his order had held it in the time of Richard I. *Reg. G. Giffard* (Worcs. Hist. Soc.), 106; *Cal. Close,* 1272-9, p. 556; De Banco R. 30, m. 11.
[95] Pat. 33 Hen. VIII, pt. v; *L. and P. Hen. VIII,* xvii, g. 71 (29).

[96] Pat. 6 Jas. I, pt. xii, no. 2.
[97] *Cal. S. P. Dom.* 1668-9, p. 573.
[98] *L. and P. Hen. VIII,* xix (1), g. 1035 (51).   [99] *Cal. S. P. Dom.* 1656-7, p. 15.
[100] See under Grafton Manor and King's Norton.
[1] *Cal. Chart. R.* 1226-57, p. 172.
[2] Worc. Epis. Reg. Clifford, fol. 2; Bodl. Lib. Chart. 42*.
[3] Worc. Epis. Reg. Pulton, fol. 134 d. A full account of this dispute may be found in the *Annals of S. Wulstan,* by F. T. Marsh.
[4] Nash, op. cit. Supp. 17.
[5] *Cal. Papal Letters,* vi, 29.
[6] Chan. Inq. p.m. 33 Edw. I, no. 204; Inq. a.q.d. file 54, no. 10.

[7] Worc. Epis. Reg. Montagu (1333-7), fol. 10 d.
[8] *Cal. Pat.* 1446-52, p. 108.
[9] Worc. Epis. Reg. Alcock, fol. 102; *Cal. Pat.* 1476-85, pp. 11, 57. The lord of Dodford, co. Northants, was sued for this rent in 1577 (Memo. R. Mich. Recorda 20 Eliz. rot. 34).
[10] Worc. Epis. Reg. Silvester de Gigliis, fol. 35, 86 d.
[11] Chant. Cert. 25, no. 19; 60, no. 11; 61, no. 10.
[12] Aug. Off. Misc. Bks. ccclxxiv, fol. 52. An account of this chantry may be found in *N. and Q.* (Ser. vii), ii, 149, 218.
[13] Pat. 3 & 4 Phil. and Mary, pt. ii, m. 22.

The ecclesiastical parish of All Saints was formed in 1875.[14] The vicarage is in the gift of the vicar of Bromsgrove. Christ Church, Catshill, Holy Trinity, Lickey, and St. Mary, Dodford, are parishes formed from Bromsgrove in 1844, 1858, and 1908 respectively.[15] The livings are vicarages, the first two in the gift of the vicar of Bromsgrove and the third in the gift of the Rev. W. G. Whinfield. There are chapels of ease at Linthurst and at Rubery in Lickey, and a mission chapel at Sidemoor. The Roman Catholic church at Bromsgrove was erected in 1860.

There are Baptist,[15a] Congregational,[16] Wesleyan Methodist and Primitive Methodist chapels in Bromsgrove, a Baptist chapel at Dodford, founded 1865,[16a] and a Methodist chapel at Sidemoor. At Catshill and Bourneheath are Baptist,[16b] Wesleyan, and Primitive Methodist chapels, and at Lickey Wesleyan, Congregational and Primitive Methodist chapels.

The Free Grammar School.[17]

CHARITIES   The consolidated charities are regulated by a scheme of the Charity Commissioners 1 March 1907. They include certain donations for the poor, recorded on a table of benefactions in the church, dated 1636 ; also the charities of Anthony Cole, will, 1660, Mrs. Roberts, will (date unknown), Humphrey Cooke, will, 1720, and other charities referred to below.

The properties originally belonging to the charities have undergone considerable changes by allotments on the inclosure, exchanges and sales and accumulations of income, and now consist of the almshouses, erected for the most part from accumulations of income ; land situated at Sidemoor, Bourneheath and Bromsgrove containing in the aggregate 17 acres or thereabouts, two houses in St. John's Street and a house in Birmingham Road producing a gross rental of £92 ; an annuity of £3 issuing out of land at Wildmoor in respect of Anthony Cole's Charity ; an annuity of £5 out of an estate at Fockerby in respect of Joseph Smith's Charity ; and an annuity of £1 out of land at Shepley mentioned in the ancient table of benefactions as 'worthy Stafford's dole.' Also £171 8s. 4d. India 3 per cent. stock derived under the will of Mary Kettle, 1791 ; £1,019 5s. 1d. like stock under the will of Thomas Haukes, 1809 ; £112 10s. 3d. like stock by will of Elizabeth Moore, 1819 ; £354 6s. 5d. like stock by will of James Ridgeway, 1837 ; and £1,956 1s. 11d. like stock under the will of James Holyoake, proved at Birmingham 2 April 1859. The several sums of stock are held by the official trustees, who also hold a further sum of £968 16s. 5d. India 3 per cent. stock and a sum of £3,352 19s. 7d. Bank of England stock, producing together in annual dividends £457 18s. 6d.

In 1910, in pursuance of the scheme, a sum of £50 was paid in grants to institutions, about £350 in stipends, in coals, and for nursing the almspeople, who by a scheme of 17 August 1909 may be forty in number, reckoning a married couple as two ; a sum of £76 19s. in pensions to poor people of sixty years and upwards.

An annual sum of £2 is paid to the churchwardens of St. John's for distribution among poor widows in respect of Mrs. Roberts's Charity and £3 a year is distributed among poor widows resident in Chadwick Yield in respect of Anthony Cole's Charity.

The two charities next mentioned are likewise administered by the trustees of the consolidated charities under the scheme of 1907, namely—

Joseph Martin's Charity, founded by will, proved at Worcester 19 February 1881. The legacy of £1,500, owing to insufficiency of assets, is represented by £858 3s. 2d. India 3 per cent. stock, the annual dividends of which, amounting to £25 14s. 8d., are applicable under the scheme in pensions to poor widows resident in the town of Bromsgrove, as defined in 1881.

Hannah Richardson's Poor Widows' Trust, founded by declaration of trust 1862, consisting of £101 8s. 3d. like stock, the annual dividends of £3 0s. 8d. being applicable in payments of 2s. each to poor widows at Christmas.

Bishop Hall's Charity, founded by deed poll 19 March 1708 by John Hall, Bishop of Bristol, consists of 66 a. 3 r. at or near Elmbridge, comprised in deed of 21 March 1711, producing about £50 a year, and a sum of £100 consols. Out of the income £20 a year is expended in clothing poor men and women of Bromsgrove and the residue in the distribution of Bibles in Bromsgrove, Kidderminster, Worcester, Stourbridge, Bewdley and Droitwich.

In 1787 Simon Crane by deed charged his houses in Bromsgrove with 20s. yearly for the benefit of the quire of the parish church. The annuity is paid out of a house in the High Street.

In 1800 the Rev. John Welch by his will left £20 for the poor at Christmas, represented by £23 18s. 8d. consols, producing 12s. a year, which is distributed in sums of 2s. to each recipient.

In 1821 James Wilkinson, by his will proved in the P.C.C. 10 April, bequeathed an annuity of £2 to be applied, subject to keeping in repair his parents' tomb in the churchyard, for the benefit of the poor inmates of the almshouses in Alcester Road. In 1909 a sum of 17s. 6d. was expended in repairs of the tomb and £3 2s. 6d. in coal to the almspeople, of which £2 was received from land in Kidderminster Road and £2 from houses in St. John Street, presumably in respect of this and some other charity.

In 1832 Mary Makeg, by her will proved in the P.C.C. 14 December, bequeathed £200, the interest —subject to the repair of her brother's tomb in the churchyard—to be distributed to the poor in sums not exceeding 3s. to any one family. The sum of £180, being the legacy less duty, is secured by a mortgage of premises at Lickey End at 4½ per cent., and is distributed in certain proportions by the vicars of the several ecclesiastical districts.

In 1874 the Rev. Thomas Warren, by his will proved at Worcester 15 September, left £200, now represented by £212 4s. 4d. consols, the annual dividends, amounting to £5 6s., to be applied— subject to the repairs of tombstone to his wife in the cemetery—in supplying warm clothing for the poor of the congregation of St. John's. In 1910 flannel was distributed to about forty recipients.

---

[14] *Census of Engl. and Wales, Worc.* 1901, p. 5.   [15] Ibid. 5, 6.
[15a] Founded 1666 (*Baptist Hd. Bk.* 1912, p. 134).
[16] In 1672 three houses at Bromsgrove were licensed for Congregational worshippers (*Cal. S. P. Dom.* 1672, pp. 578, 676, 678). The present church was founded in 1833 (*Congregational Yr.Bk.* 1912, p. 307).
[16a] *Baptist Hd. Bk.* 1912, p. 134.

[16b] The Baptist chapel at Catshill was founded in 1830 (*Baptist Hd. Bk.* 1912, p. 134).
[17] See article on 'Schools,' *V.C.H. Worcs.* iv.

Broom Church : The Font

Bromsgrove Church : Monument to Lady Talbot

In 1903 Robert Anthony Hall, by his will proved at Worcester 8 December, left £500 to be placed to the endowment fund of the Cottage Hospital. The legacy with other gifts, amounting together to £1,200, has been invested on mortgage in the names of the trustees of the hospital. The trustees of the Cottage Hospital, under the terms of the will of the late Mr. James Lea, proved at Worcester 12 January 1905, acquired for the sum of £50 the testator's dwelling-house, known as 'Fernleigh,' and other land adjoining on the New Road, and subsequently sold the same for £871 2s., of which £471 2s. was transferred to the extension and improvement fund and the sum of £400 invested on mortgage as an endowment fund.

Nonconformist charities :—

The Baptist Ministers' Endowment Fund consists of a sum of £591 14s. 10d. consols, including the charities of Richard Johns, founded in 1772, originally a cottage sold for £50 ; of Jonathan Bell, originally nine cottages comprised in deed 1808, sold in 1883 for £370, and of Humphry Potter, originally a dwelling-house, sold in 1883 for £176.

By a scheme of the Charity Commissioners 1 May 1906 the annual dividends, amounting to £14 15s. 8d., are applicable towards the support of the minister of the Baptist Chapel in New Road.

In 1872 the Rev. Thomas Warren by deed gave £150 for the benefit of the congregation of the old Baptist Chapel. The principal sum has been lent on mortgage at 4 per cent. By a scheme of the Charity Commissioners 3 May 1910 the income of £6 a year is made applicable for the benefit of poor members of the Baptist Chapel in New Road.

The several sums of stock, unless otherwise stated, are held by the official trustees.

BROOM

Brom (xii cent.).

Broom is a small parish beautifully situated to the west of the Clent Hills. A small stream rises on the eastern boundary, and running through three pools forms a slight valley through the centre of the parish, which it leaves on its western boundary. The parish has an area of only 730½ acres, of which 576 acres are arable and the rest pasture.[1] The soil is a sandy loam and the subsoil chiefly New Red Sandstone, which in places is very near the surface. A little inferior gravel is worked in the direction of Clent. Although lying geographically in Worcestershire, Broom was included in Staffordshire from the 12th century until the middle of the 19th century, when it was transferred to Worcestershire under the Acts of 1832 and 1844.[1a] Like most of the other parishes in the north of Halfshire it is hilly, the land rising from 276 ft. above the ordnance datum in the west to 400 ft. in the east. The village is in the centre of the parish among some rather good timber, and formerly contained no large house of any importance except the rectory [2] and Broom House. Noake, writing in 1868, describes the parish as having 'no manufactures or public works, no local squire, no mansion, no Dissenter's chapel, no church-rate disturbances, no Fenianism or agitation of any sort.' [3]

Broom House, the residence of Mr. John Alexander Holder, stands in beautifully-kept grounds on the opposite side of the road to the church. It is a three-story building of late 18th-century erection. The south or principal front is faced with stone and has a semicircular porch of Adam style. The east front is of red sandstone and the back is of red brick. The roofs are tiled.

A very old and almost disused pack-horse track called Honal Lane forms part of the eastern boundary of the parish, and was formerly an important road known as the Horse Wall or Walk.[4]

The following are noteworthy field-names : Nailer's Close, Kiln Pit, The Feathers, Tinker's Bush, Great Kite Furlong, Mins Yard Field or 'Little Gain,' Hazel Wicket Sling and Little Coney Gree. The cross-roads at one boundary of the parish are called Hackman's Gate, formerly the Hangman's Gate, situated on the edge of the Bleak Down, now Blake Down.[5] Close by is Yielding Tree (Ildyngtre, xv cent.).

BROOM has always been held of the MANOR king in chief, the overlordship being last mentioned in 1617.[6] At the time of the Domesday Survey it formed part of the manor of Clent, and was not separated from it until 1154, when Henry II granted it to Maurice de Ombersley at a fee-farm rent of £1 13s. 4d. to be paid to the Sheriff of Staffordshire.[7] This rent occurs on the Pipe Rolls of Staffordshire until 1200.[8] In 1193 Richard I granted the rent with that of other manors to his aunt Emma, wife of David, King of North Wales.[9] Maurice de Ombersley was followed by his son Richard, who, however, must have died without issue or forfeited this property before 1200, when it was in the king's hands. In that year King John granted land there worth 2½ marks to the nuns of Brewood in Staffordshire,[10] to whom it belonged until the Dissolution.[11] Broom was granted to Charles Duke of Suffolk in 1538.[12] He sold it a few days later to William Whorwood, the solicitor-general,[13] who left all his property, after the death of Maud his wife, to his two daughters Anne and Margaret. Neither of them seems to have left children, and on the death of Anne, then the widow of Ambrose Dudley, about 1554–5, Broom passed to her cousin Thomas Whorwood,[14] in whose family it remained until 1672,[15] when Wortley Whorwood, his great-

---

[1] Statistics from Bd. of Agric. (1905).
[1a] Stat. 2 & 3 Will. IV, cap. 64 ; 7 & 8 Vict. cap. 61.
[2] Noake, *Guide to Worc.* 78.
[3] Ibid.
[4] Inform. from the Rev. J. H. Bourne.
[5] Ibid.
[6] Chan. Inq. p.m. (Ser. 2), cccliv, 104.
[7] *Will. Salt Arch. Soc. Coll.* ii, 16.
[8] Ibid. 117 ; *Pipe R.* 13 Hen. II (Pipe R. Soc.), 57 ; 23 *Hen. II*, 140 ; Hunter, *Gt. R. of the Pipe*, 1 Ric. I, 245.
[9] *Will. Salt Arch. Soc. Coll.* ii, 27. £2 6s. 8d. was charged on Broom and Rowley Regis. This grant was during the king's pleasure only.
[10] Chart. R. 2 John, m. 20 ; *Cal. Chart. R.* 1257–1300, p. 79.
[11] *Valor Eccl.* (Rec. Com.), iii, 103.
[12] *L. and P. Hen. VIII*, xiii (2), g. 1182 (18 K). It is in this grant that Broom is first described as manor.
[13] Close, 30 Hen. VIII, pt. ii, no. 30 ; *L. and P. Hen. VIII*, xiii (2), 1118.
[14] Chan. Inq. p.m. (Ser. 2), civ, 76. Thomas was the eldest son of John, a younger brother of William Whorwood.
[15] Pat. 22 Eliz. pt. ix, m. 26 ; Chan. Inq. p.m. (Ser. 2), cccliv, 104 ; ccccxxxii, 109 ; Feet of F. Staffs. Trin. 23 Chas. I ; Recov. R. Staff. Trin. 23 Chas. I, rot. 83.

A HISTORY OF WORCESTERSHIRE

great-grandson, conveyed it to Philip Foley.[16] After that date the manor seems to have changed hands very frequently. In 1727 a moiety belonged to a Nicholas Pigge and Mary[17] his wife, whether by purchase or inheritance does not appear. The whole manor was held in 1762 by Samuel Hellier,[18] from whom it passed to Thomas Shaw Hellier and Mary his wife, who conveyed it in 1786 to Thomas Burne, jun.[19] In 1822 Thomas Hill the younger and Thomas Hill his son were holding it,[20] and about 1852[21] it passed to the Earl of Dudley, to whom it now belongs.

In the 13th and 14th centuries the Dunclents and Staffords held lands in Broom of the prioress and convent,[22] the Dunclent property including certain fish-ponds there.[23]

A water-mill belonged to the lords of the manor in the 18th century,[24] but is no longer used.

CHURCH The church of *ST. PETER* consists of a chancel[25] with a north vestry, a nave and a west tower.

The church was built at the end of the 18th century and was restored in 1861, when the vestry was added and the stair to the tower built. At this restoration the chancel appears to have been considerably modernized, the present chancel arch then being inserted and the east window 'Gothicized' internally; the oak panelling now round the vestry walls was then no doubt taken from the chancel and placed in its present position. The chancel is lighted by round-headed windows, one in the east and two in the south wall, and the nave by three—one on the north and two on the south. Between the windows in the south wall of the chancel is a priest's doorway. The first stage of the tower is used as the main entrance to the building and has immediately over it a small organ gallery, seen from the body of the church through the tower arch, which is tall with a semicircular head.

All the walls are of red brick with stone dressings and are plastered internally. With the exception of those on the south side of the chancel, which have flat external architraves on the outside, all the windows have moulded archivolts with flat keystones. At the eaves level is a stone cornice of a simple cavetto section. Over the chancel is a segmental barrel vault of oak divided into panels by moulded ribs. The nave is roofed in a similar manner, but the vault is more modern. All the roofs are tiled.

The tower is thickly overgrown with ivy. The ringing stage is lighted by three small circular windows and the bell-chamber by four round-headed ones.

The bowl and upper part of the stem of the font date from the middle of the 12th century, but the lower part is modern. On plan it is circular and is rudely carved in low relief with a continuous arcade of fifteen interlacing arches, and a band of

flowing leaf enrichment above. A modern stone rim has been fixed round the top of the bowl, and the cover is also new. Below the bowl is a narrow necking, and at the head of each of the six panels of the modern stem is a grotesque face, the upper part of the series being original.

There appear to be two bells, the smaller, probably of the 17th century, with an unintelligible inscription, and the larger by John Martin of Worcester, 1671.

The plate consists of an 1839 silver chalice, a modern silver paten, an electro-plated flagon, an electro-plated paten with a cover, a large brass almsdish and two smaller ones.

The registers previous to 1812 are as follows : (i) baptisms and burials 1664 to 1785; marriages 1664 to 1753; (ii) baptisms and burials 1785 to 1812; (iii) marriages 1755 to 1809.

ADVOWSON Maurice de Ombersley, to whom the manor was granted in 1154, is said to have 'founded' the church of Broom.[26] His son Richard forfeited the advowson with the manor, and it appears to have been granted with it by King John to the nuns of Brewood, though it is not mentioned in the charter.[27] In 1203-4, after the death of Alexander de Bransford, whom Richard de Ombersley had presented to the church of Broom, a dispute arose between the Prioress of Brewood and Herbert parson of Clent as to the advowson of Broom. The latter claimed it on the grounds that Broom was a chapelry of Clent, but the prioress stated that Alexander was parson of Broom, and that on his death the bishop had sequestered the church as vacant.[28] It would seem that the prioress won the suit, for there is no indication that the church of Broom[29] was ever subsequently looked upon as a chapelry of Clent. The nuns probably held the advowson until the Dissolution,[30] but it was not granted with the manor to Charles Duke of Suffolk. The rectory was granted in 1543 to William Whorwood,[31] who perhaps obtained the advowson at about the same time, but the latter is not mentioned until 1617, when it belonged to Thomas Whorwood.[32] From that time it followed the same descent as the manor until 1627,[33] when Gerard Whorwood granted the next two presentations to Margaret Jevons.[34] William Hamerton presented in 1662 and John Dolman in 1681.[35] Members of the Dolman family occur as patrons until 1709.[36] Samuel Fletcher, who presented in 1745, and Richard Clive and John Tibbatts, who were patrons in 1770,[37] probably held the advowson by grant of the Dolmans, for the trustees of Mr. Dolman were said to be patrons about 1786,[38] and Joseph Scott of Great Barr, who with others (probably the trustees of Mr. Dolman) presented to the church in 1783,[39] is said by Shaw to have been related to Rev. Thomas Dolman, rector of Broom.[40] Mr. Dolman was said to be patron in 1808.[41]

---

[16] Feet of F. Staffs. Trin. 24 Chas. II; Recov. R. Staff. Mich. 24 Chas. II, rot. 47.
[17] Feet of F. Div. Co. East. 13 Geo. I; Recov. R. East. 13 Geo. I, rot. 331.
[18] Recov. R. Hil. 2 Geo. III, rot. 267.
[19] Feet of F. Staffs. Mich. 27 Geo. III.
[20] Recov. R. Worc. Trin. 3 Geo. IV, rot. 130.
[21] Noake, op. cit. 78. Information by Mr. J. Willis-Bund.
[22] Jeayes, *Lyttelton Chart.* no. 148, 201, 237, 238, 240; Chan. Inq. p.m. 8 Hen. V, no. 36.

[23] Jeayes, op. cit. no. 121, 201.
[24] Feet of F. Staffs. Trin. 24 Chas. II; Recov. R. Staff. Mich. 24 Chas. II, rot. 47; Hil. 2 Geo. III, rot. 267; Trin. 3 Geo. IV, rot. 130.
[25] Chancel measures 20 ft. 6 in. by 12 ft., the nave 25 ft. 6 in. by 15 ft., all internal measurements.
[26] *Will. Salt Arch. Soc. Coll.* iii, 127.
[27] Ibid.
[28] *Abbrev. Plac.* (Rec. Com.), 44a.
[29] It is called 'Capella de Brome' in the 14th century. *Inq. Non.* (Rec. Com.), 131.

[30] *Sede Vacante Reg.* (Worcs. Hist. Soc.), 235; *L. and P. Hen. VIII,* xviii (1), g. 981 (30).
[31] *L. and P. Hen. VIII,* loc. cit.
[32] Chan. Inq. p.m. (Ser. 2), ccdliv, 104.
[33] Ibid. ccccxxxii, 109; Feet of F. Staffs. East. 3 Chas. I; Inst. Bks. P.R.O.
[34] Feet of F. Staffs. East. 3 Chas. I.
[35] Inst. Bks. P.R.O. [36] Ibid. [37] Ibid.
[38] Bacon, *Liber Regis,* 969.
[39] Inst. Bks. P.R.O.
[40] *Hist. of Staff.* ii (1), 251.
[41] Carlisle, *Topog. Dict.*

Lord Dudley presented in 1810,[42] probably for that turn only, since in 1849 Sir Edward Dolman Scott, son of Joseph Scott (afterwards Sir Joseph), was patron of Broom.[43] The advowson was purchased from his trustees in 1859[44] by Mr. J. G. Bourne, who presented his son, the Rev. Joseph Green Bourne. The Rev. Joseph Handforth Bourne, son of the latter,[45] is the present patron.

CHARITIES An annuity of £1 10s., known as Harris's Charity, is received from the Earl of Dudley, and distributed in loaves to about fifty poor and in sixpences to about twelve householders on 21 December annually.

The Parish Charity Fund consists of £5 and £19 19s. given for the poor by John Sparry and Mrs. Betty Sutherland respectively. It is now accumulating in the Post Office Savings Bank.

The Day and Sunday Schools' Fund consists of £19 19s. bequeathed for the schools by the said Mrs. Sutherland. This sum is also in the savings bank, the income being applied in supplying Bibles and Prayer-books to scholars.

CHADDESLEY CORBETT

Ceadresleage (ix cent.); Cedeslaeh, Cedeslai (xi cent.); Cheddesleg (xii and xiii cent.); Chedeslea, Claydesle (xiii cent.); Chaddeslegh Corbett (xiv cent.).

Chaddesley Corbett is a large parish covering 6,079 acres, of which 3,065¼ are arable land, 2,247¼ pasture and 242¾ woodland.[1] The Elmley or Doverdale Brook, which rises in Belbroughton, flows through the south of the parish, forming part of the southern boundary. Barnett Brook, which also rises in Belbroughton and joins the Stour near Kidderminster, waters the northern part of Chaddesley Corbett. The principal road is the main road from Kidderminster to Bromsgrove which enters the parish near the hamlet of Mustow Green. Another road crosses it at Mustow Green and passes through Harvington to Broom. The village lies to the south of the Doverdale Brook, and consists of one street lying on a road running off the Kidderminster and Bromsgrove road to Stourbridge. On either side of the street are red brick and timber and brick houses and cottages of various dates. The church stands on the west side at the south end of the village. In the churchyard are the steps and base of a mediaeval cross, the shaft and head of which were erected in 1903. Opposite the church is the Talbot Inn, a well-preserved timber and brick house on a base of sandstone built about 1600. It has two porches approached by steps. A short distance further south is Brockencote Hall, situated in extensive grounds to which the Doverdale Brook forms the eastern boundary. Standing on the north side of the Bromsgrove road to the south-west of the church is the Lodge, the residence of Mr. James Meredith. Most of the house was rebuilt early in the last century, though the north-west corner dates from early in the 17th century. The walls of this part of the house are of half-timber and brick construction, considerably modernized when the 19th-century alterations were made. To the north-west of the house is a large half-timber barn. It is L-shaped in plan, and was no doubt erected when the original house was built. West of the church to the north of the Bromsgrove road are the almshouses, built in 1637.

The hamlet of Harvington is rather more than a mile north-west of the village. Harvington Hall, formerly the seat of the Yates, Pakingtons, and Throckmortons, is approached by a small by-road running north off the main road from Kidderminster to Bromsgrove, and is built at the south-east corner of the area inclosed by the surrounding moat. This moat has been in places partly filled in, and, though comparatively narrow on the south and east, it is much wider on the west, while on the north it stretches away in a large sheet of water, now divided into two by the road. The Hall itself is in a very dilapidated condition, and much of the older part—though still roofed and retaining all its floors—is in a ruinous state and overgrown with ivy. The general plan of the buildings takes the form of the letter L, the east block being built along the side of the moat, the south some few yards back from the water's edge.

The latter is the original building, and is late Elizabethan. About the middle of the 17th century from the east end of this block a low wing was thrown out on the north, while early in the following century a tall three-story building was erected at the end of this addition. The later buildings, with a part of the original block, have been divided up into tenements, but the rest of the house is quite uninhabitable. The interior has been stripped of its panelling, and the fine oak staircase is now at Coughton Court, Warwickshire.

The Elizabethan building is three stories high with attics in the roof. It is built of red brick with red sandstone quoins, dressings and plinth. The walls are generally carried up in pointed gables, and the tiled roofs are of a fairly high pitch. The original windows throughout were mullioned with the larger ones subdivided by transoms. On plan it is an irregular H, and the principal rooms appear to have been on the first floor. Two interesting features of the building are the hiding-places and the number of entrances or exits. One of these is in the middle of the south front, one on the west, and one in each of the side walls of the projecting wings on the north; these last two entrances face each other. The main staircase was in the north-west corner of the house, and a second, built round a central newel, is in the south-east corner of the central block. There is a third staircase in the east wing. The whole of the ground floor was probably given up to the domestic offices, the kitchen occupying the east wing.

The principal room on the first floor was the hall, a large T-shaped apartment extending over the whole of the central block and lighted by large transomed and mullioned windows from both the north and south. It was entered on the west, directly off the principal staircase, while another doorway in the south wall gave access to the central newelled stair. Opposite

[42] Inst. Bks. P.R.O.

[43] Lewis, *Topog. Dict. of Engl.*; Burke, *Peerage.*   [44] *Clergy Lists.*

[45] Burke, *Landed Gentry.*
[1] Statistics from Bd. of Agric. (1905).

this doorway high up in the north wall is one of the hiding holes, now exposed to view through the dismantling of the building. The fireplace is in the centre of the south wall. A small room on the south side of the principal staircase gives access to a large hiding-place, situated above an adjoining passage.

In the 17th-century extension the same materials have been used as in the original building, though the mullioned windows here are of oak. At the north end of this wing is a large square-headed entrance to the courtyard in the angle of the two blocks. The wing contains two principal apartments, one above the other, the upper being ceiled with a segmental barrel vault of plaster. On the north side is a hiding hole, now blocked up, and at the same end is a tall

HARVINGTON HALL FROM THE SOUTH-EAST

brick chimney stack of an ornamental design. The 18th-century addition is built of the same materials as the older portions and is rectangular on plan.

The malt-house stands at the south-west corner of the site and is contemporary with the Elizabethan building. It is two stories high, the lower one being built of red sandstone and the upper of half-timber, much of the brick filling in being laid diagonally. The roof is tiled and the floor of the upper story is plastered.

Another outbuilding, now used as a school, stands to the north of the malt-house, but this is an 18th-century erection. Quite close to the house is a Roman Catholic chapel dedicated to St. Mary, built by Sir George Throckmorton in 1825.[2] Near the chapel is a memorial crucifix to Father Wall, who officiated at Harvington in the 17th century, and was executed at Worcester in 1679. Many of the inhabitants of Chaddesley Corbett during the 16th and 17th centuries were presented for recusancy, among them being Humphrey Pakington.[3] A Roman Catholic congregation flourished at Harvington in the early 18th century. Father Charles Dodd, author of *English Church History*, succeeded in 1726 to this cure, and during his residence at Harvington finished his great work. He was buried in 1742–3 at Chaddesley Corbett.[4]

Winterfold, which has for some years been the seat of the Harwards,[5] is a red brick mansion standing in a well-wooded deer park.

Chaddesley Corbett once formed part of the forest of Piperode, which was later absorbed in Feckenham Forest.

The land is undulating, varying in height from about 180 ft. above the ordnance datum in the south near Doverdale Brook to 400 ft. in the north. The soil is loamy and the subsoil red sandstone, raising good crops of wheat, barley, beans, oats and potatoes. Agriculture is the chief industry, but the steam saw and cornmills of William Seager, Ltd., at Cakebole and the scythe works of Isaac Nash at Drayton give employment to some of the inhabitants.

Noake writing in 1868 states that the parish wake at Whitsuntide was then still held.[6] Among the place-names are:—Clatcote, Berehull, Taggeburne,[7] Derewalle, Monkeswall, Wallersrudyng, Truggesrudyng, Grimbaldesmede[8] and Fresefield.[9] The name of the hamlet of Drayton occurs as early as the 13th century,[10] while Woodrow (Woderowe) and Cakebole (Cakeball, Cakbawle) are mentioned in the 15th and 16th centuries[11] and Brockencote in the 16th century.[12]

MANORS — In 816 King Coenwulf of Mercia exempted twenty-five 'manentes' at 'Ceadres leage' from various royal services.[13] The land at that date evidently belonged to the Bishop or church of Worcester. Heming, in his chartulary of the possessions of Worcester Priory, states that *CHADDESLEY* was taken away from that church by Earl Leofric, but that his wife Godiva restored it to the priory after his death. Shortly afterwards it was again seized by Edwin and Morcar,

[2] *Catholic Directory*, 1908, p. 151.
[3] Recusant Roll (Pipe Office Ser.), no. 2; *Var. Coll.* (Hist. MSS. Com.), i, 314, 319, 325.
[4] *Dict. Nat. Biog.*
[5] John Harward appears to have been holding land at Chaddesley Corbett in

1565 (Chan. Proc. [Ser. 2], bdle. 49, no. 41). [6] Noake, *Guide to Worc.* 83.
[7] Mins. Accts. bdle. 645, no. 10464.
[8] Ibid. bdle. 1067, no. 17.
[9] Pat. 36 Hen. VIII, pt. viii.
[10] Feet of F. Worcs. case 258, file 8, no. 14.

[11] Mins. Accts. bdles. 645, no. 10464; 1067, no. 17; Chan. Proc. (Ser. 2), bdles. 49, no. 41; 138, no. 6; 194, no. 43.
[12] Ibid. bdle. 49, no. 41.
[13] Birch, *Cart. Sax.* i, 497; Heming, *Chartul.* (ed. Hearne), 381.

but 'to their swift confusion,' the former being murdered and the latter dying in captivity,[14] when their lands, including Chaddesley, passed to the Crown.[15] The overlordship of Chaddesley Corbett was apparently granted by William I or William II to Robert Fitz Hamon,[16] whose eldest daughter Mabel married Robert Earl of Gloucester, natural son of Henry I.[17] William Earl of Gloucester, son of Robert, died in 1183, leaving three daughters and co-heirs, Mabel wife of the Count of Evreux in Normandy, Amice wife of Richard de Clare Earl of Hertford, and Isabel divorced wife of King John, and afterwards wife of Geoffrey de Mandeville Earl of Essex.[18] The overlordship eventually passed to Gilbert de Clare Earl of Hertford, son of Amice, who became Earl of Gloucester, and it descended with the earldom of Gloucester till the death of Gilbert de Clare in 1314,[19] when the fee at Chaddesley Corbett was assigned to his widow Maud, daughter of the Earl of Ulster.[20] After her death it probably passed to

above, for he was holding it at the time of his death in 1348–9,[24] and it was assigned as dower to his widow Elizabeth.[25] It passed on her death in 1359 [26]

CLARE. *Or three cheverons gules.*

DESPENSER. *Quarterly argent and gules fretty or with a bend sable over all.*

to Edward le Despenser, nephew of Hugh, who died seised of it in 1375, leaving a son Thomas, his heir.[27]

HARVINGTON HALL FROM THE NORTH-EAST

Eleanor wife of Hugh le Despenser, jun., eldest sister of Gilbert de Clare, as the manor was said in 1323–4 to be held of Hugh le Despenser, jun., as of the honour of Gloucester.[21] Hugh was executed in 1326, and the fee seems then to have passed to Margaret, second sister and co-heir of Gilbert de Clare, and her second husband Hugh Audley, who was created Earl of Gloucester in 1336–7,[22] as at the time of Hugh's death in 1347 he was said to be holding this fee at Chaddesley.[23] He left no male issue, and the fee was evidently restored to Hugh le Despenser, son of Hugh and Eleanor mentioned

Elizabeth Lady le Despenser, widow of Edward, appears to have had some interest in this fee, for in 1394 she allowed William de Beauchamp to grant the church of Chaddesley to the college of Warwick.[28] The agreement of her son Thomas was also obtained.[29] It is difficult to account for the fact that before this date the fee had passed to Thomas Earl of Stafford, great-grandson of Hugh Audley and Margaret de Clare,[30] for at the time of his death in 1392 he was said to be holding a fee at Chaddesley.[31] His widow Anne by special dispensation of the pope married her late husband's brother Edmund,[32] and was holding this

[14] Heming, *Chartul.* (ed. Hearne), 261 ; Dugdale, *Mon.* i, 595.
[15] *V.C.H. Worcs.* i, 320a.
[16] *Rot. Cur. Reg.* (Rec. Com.), ii, 175.
[17] G.E.C. *Complete Peerage*, iv, 38.
[18] Ibid. 38, 39, 40 ; Burke, *Extinct Peerage* ; *Dict. Nat. Biog.*
[19] *Cal. Inq. p.m. Hen. III*, 158 ; 1–19 *Edw. I*, 466, 488 ; 1–9 *Edw. II*, 341.

[20] *Cal. Close*, 1313–18, p. 136.
[21] Inq. a.q.d. file 162, no. 15, 17 Edw. II.
[22] G.E.C. *Complete Peerage*, iv, 42.
[23] Chan. Inq. p.m. 21 Edw. III (1st nos.), no. 59.
[24] Ibid. 23 Edw. III, pt. ii (1st nos.), no. 169.
[25] *Cal. Close*, 1349–54, p. 36.
[26] G.E.C. *Complete Peerage*, iii, 92.

[27] Chan. Inq. p.m. 49 Edw. III (1st nos.), pt. ii, no. 46.
[28] Exch. K.R. Misc. Bks. xxii, fol. 104.
[29] Ibid. fol. 104 d.
[30] G.E.C. op. cit. vii, 211.
[31] Chan. Inq. p.m. 16 Ric. II (1st nos.), no. 27.
[32] G.E.C. loc. cit.

fee as dower at the time of Edmund's death in 1403.[33] She died in 1438,[34] but before that time her right in the fee at Chaddesley seems to have lapsed. After 1403 no connected descent of the overlordship can be traced. In 1410–11 the manor was said to be held of Richard Earl of Warwick for a rent of a rose,[35] and in 1435–6 of the Prior of Little Malvern.[36] It was stated in 1439 and in 1446 that it was not held of the king in chief, but neither the lord nor the service due for it was known.[37] In

AUDLEY. *Gules fretty or.*

1487–8 it was held of the king as of the earldom of March,[38] in 1492–3 of the king in chief for service unknown,[39] and in 1505 of the king as of the manor of Elmley.[40]

Before the Conquest 'a certain woman' Eadgifu held Chaddesley, and was still holding it in 1086.[41] At that time it seems to have been a place of considerable importance, having eight berewicks attached to it, and consisting of 25 hides, of which 10 were free from geld, the value of the whole being £12.[42] The manor passed in the 12th century to Robert son of Payn, who was succeeded by his son and grandson, both named Richard Folliott.[43] By the latter's daughter Hawise, who married firstly Robert son of Richard, and secondly, before 1199, Roger Corbett,[44] the manor came to the Corbett family. William Corbett appears to have been in possession of the manor in 1235, as at that date an agreement was made between him and the Abbot of Tewkesbury as to a rent and tenement which the abbot's men held in the manor of Chaddesley.[45] He still held it in 1261–2,[46] but had been succeeded before 1266 by Robert Corbett.[47] This Robert died without issue about 1270, and the manor passed to his nephew William, son of William Corbett.[48] On his death about 1282–3 [49] a third of the manor was assigned to his widow Ada.[50] She outlived her son Roger, who died in 1289–90,[51] and on her death about 1290–1

CORBETT of Chaddesley Corbett. *Or a raven sable in a border engrailed gules.*

the whole manor passed to her grandson William Corbett.[52]

The inquisition taken in 1290 after the death of Roger Corbett gives a good idea of the value and extent of the manor. It contained a capital messuage worth 10s., four vineyards worth 26s. 8d., and two water-mills worth 26s. 8d. 'if they are kept in repair'; the tenant of each virgate of land ought among other services 'to do average to the bridge of Tewkesbury' twice a year, 'to get the lord's cloth within the county,' and to give the lord two hens at Christmas worth 2d. in return for which he gave them 'reasonable furze and dead wood'; twelve cotarii each paid yearly 11s. 6d. and 'ought to do lesser service to mend the lady's linen.'[53]

William Corbett, son and heir of Roger, appears to have lived to a great age. In 1304 he obtained a grant of free warren at Chaddesley Corbett.[54] He had been knighted before 1314-15,[55] and appears to have been implicated in the rebellion against the Despensers, for in 1322 his estates were seized.[56] In 1328-9 he made three separate grants of rents of £200 annually from his manor of Chaddesley Corbett.[57] In 1330 he complained of Roger de Mortimer Earl of March and John Wyard,[58] who enticed him to Berkeley, where they detained him for four days, took away his seal, and forced him to make a recognizance to John Wyard for 1,350 marks.[59] In 1340 William Corbett's conduct to his wife drew down episcopal censure and he was ordered to amend under penalty of £40.[60] He was appointed in 1340 one of the commissioners in Worcester to value the king's ninths.[61] In 1351, when he was said to be an octogenarian, he was exempted for life from public services.[62] Four years later, however, William Corbett of Chaddesley is mentioned as a justice of the peace,[63] and in 1358-9 he settled the manor on himself for life with reversion to Thomas de Beauchamp Earl of Warwick.[64]

The latter settled this property, described as a fee in Chaddesley Corbett, and the advowson of the church in tail-male upon his younger son William Lord Bergavenny and his wife Joan, with contingent remainder to himself.[65] William died in 1411,[66] and the manor was held by his wife Joan until her death in 1435.[67] As her only son Richard had died without male issue in 1422, the manor reverted to Richard Earl of Warwick, grandson and heir male of Thomas Earl of Warwick mentioned above.[68] The manor then descended in the same way as Elmley Castle (q.v.) to George Duke of Clarence and his wife Isabel Nevill.[69]

[33] Chan. Inq. p.m. 4 Hen. IV, no. 41.
[34] Ibid. 17 Hen. VI, no. 54.
[35] Ibid. 12 Hen. IV, no. 34. Richard was probably not the true overlord, the manor being then held by his uncle William in tail-male with reversion to Richard under a settlement made by his grandfather Thomas.
[36] Ibid. 14 Hen. VI, no. 35.
[37] Ibid. 17 Hen. VI, no. 54; 24 Hen. VI, no. 43.
[38] Cal. Inq. p.m. Hen. VII, i, 155.
[39] Ibid. 339.
[40] Chan. Inq. p.m. (Ser. 2), xviii, 87.
[41] V.C.H. Worcs. i, 320a.   [42] Ibid.
[43] Rot. Cur. Reg. (Rec. Com.), ii, 175-6.
[44] Ibid. 175.
[45] Ann. Mon. (Rolls Ser.), i, 97.
[46] Cal. Inq. p.m. Hen. III, 158.
[47] Cal. Pat. 1258-66, p. 631.

[48] Cal. Chart. R. 1257-1300, p. 140; Roberts, Cal. Gen. 145; Excerpta e Rot. Fin. (Rec. Com.), ii, 506.
[49] Roberts, op. cit. 337; Abbrev. Rot. Orig. (Rec. Com.), i, 46.
[50] Reg. G. Giffard (Worcs. Hist. Soc.), 257; Cal. Inq. p.m. 1-19 Edw. I, 466.
[51] Cal. Inq. p.m. 1-19 Edw. I, 466.
[52] Ibid. 488.
[53] Worc. Inq. p.m. (Worcs. Hist. Soc.), pt. i, no. 20.
[54] Cal. Chart. R. 1300-26, p. 48.
[55] Cal. Inq. p.m. 1-9 Edw. II, 341, 342.
[56] Abbrev. Rot. Orig. (Rec. Com.), i, 262.
[57] Cal. Close, 1327-30, pp. 357, 518, 519.
[58] One of the grants of £200 had been made to John Wyard (ibid. 519).
[59] Parl. R. ii, 38a.

[60] Worc. Epis. Reg. Braunsford, flyleaf.
[61] Cal. Pat. 1340-3, p. 153.
[62] Ibid. 1350-4, p. 32. He must have been just over seventy at this time.
[63] Ibid. 1354-8, p. 298.
[64] Feet of F. Worcs. Mich. 32 Edw. III.
[65] Exch. K.R. Misc. Bks. xxii, fol. 1; Chan. Inq. p.m. 12 Hen. IV, no. 34.
[66] Chan. Inq. p.m. 12 Hen. IV, no. 34.
[67] Ibid. 14 Hen. VI, no. 35.
[68] G.E.C. Complete Peerage, viii, 57-8; i, 14-16. Under a fine of 1425 the reversion of the manor after Joan's death had been settled on the Bishop of Winchester and other trustees for Richard Earl of Warwick. Feet of F. Div. Co. Mich. 4 Hen. VI; Chan. Inq. p.m. 14 Hen. VI, no. 35.
[69] Chan. Inq. p.m. 17 Hen. VI, no. 54; 24 Hen. VI, no. 43.

CHADDESLEY CORBETT : THE TALBOT INN

CHADDESLEY CORBETT CHURCH : 12TH CENTURY FONT

Isabel died in 1476 and the duke in 1477–8,[70] when the manor passed into the hands of the king on account of the minority of their son Edward.[71] It apparently remained in the king's hands until about 1481,[72] and it was probably at about this time that the heirs of Henry Duke of Warwick—namely, the descendants of his sister Anne and of his half-sisters Margaret and Elizabeth—claimed the manor under a settlement made by Richard father of Henry.[73] These co-heirs were Anne wife of Richard Duke of Gloucester (afterwards Richard III), Edward son of George Duke of Clarence, Elizabeth wife of Edward Grey Lord Lisle, and Elizabeth Lady Latimer. The manor of Chaddesley seems to have been assigned to Elizabeth Lady Lisle, for she died seised of it in September 1487.[74] It is difficult to explain the fact that in December of the same year Anne Countess of Warwick, having obtained an Act of Parliament for her restoration to the Beauchamp estates,[75] conveyed the manor, together with nearly all her other recovered property, to Henry VII,[76] for the ownership certainly remained with the Greys. Edward Viscount Lisle held the manor by courtesy until his death in 1492, when it passed to his son John,[77] who died in 1504. A daughter Elizabeth was born shortly after his death,[78] but she died without issue in 1519,[79] and the manor passed to her aunt Elizabeth, then wife of Arthur

GREY, Lord Lisle. *Barry argent and azure with three roundels gules in the chief and a label argent.*

Plantagenet,[80] who was created Viscount Lisle in 1523.[81] In 1522 and 1528–9 the manor was settled upon Arthur Viscount Lisle for life, with reversion to John Dudley son of Elizabeth by her first husband Edmund Dudley.[82] Sir Arthur and John leased the manor for forty years in 1527 to John Pakington,[83] but in 1529 John Pakington and Lord Lisle released their claims in the manor to Sir John Dudley,[84] who in the same year sold it to John Pakington, at first retaining a yearly rent of £40, but later compounding for it.[85]

As he had no children Sir John settled the manor in 1538 on John son of his brother Humphrey in tail-male.[86] Humphrey, who succeeded his father

John in 1578,[87] died without male issue in 1631,[88] leaving the manor to his eldest daughter Mary wife of Sir John Yate. She, being a staunch Roman Catholic, was prohibited in 1680 from leaving England, which she desired to do on account of her health. At length she was permitted by special leave of the Secretary of State—on condition that she left within fourteen days—'to imbarque with her trunks of Apparel and other necessaries not prohibited at any port of this kingdom.'[89]

She was succeeded in 1696 by her granddaughter and heir, Mary wife of Sir Robert Throckmorton,[90] whose descendant Sir Nicholas William George Throckmorton, bart., is now lord of the manor,[91] and until recently held most of the land in the parish.

THROCKMORTON, baronet. *Gules a cheveron aregnt with three gimel bars sable thereon.*

The Court Rolls from the time of Henry IV and other deeds relating to the manor are in the possession of Sir N. W. G. Throckmorton, bart., at Coughton Court, Warwick.[92]

A deer park at Chaddesley Corbett, held with the manor in the 15th century,[93] was sold with it to John Pakington.[94] In 1417 repairs were done to the 'Dere house' in the park.[95]

Three mills rendering twelve horseloads of grain belonged to Eadgifu, lady of the manor, at the time of the Domesday Survey.[96] In 1290 Roger Corbett held only two mills,[97] but another mill possibly belonged to his mother Ada Corbett, who had one third of the manor in dower.[98] Humphrey Pakington had three mills near Barnettbrook in Chaddesley and Moorhall Bell in 1604,[99] and 'certain mills' in Chaddesley belonged to Lady Mary Yate in 1675 [100] and to Sir Robert Thockmorton in 1747.[1] These probably survive in Lower Bellington, Bellington and Barnett mills, the first of which is now disused. A mill called 'Sythemill' belonged to the manor in 1481,[2] and a mill at Drayton is still used for scythe grinding.

In 1544 a water-mill called Walke Mill or Heth Mill in Chaddesley, with land called Mawtes Furlong in Chaddesley in the lordship of Dunclent, and Spelley Hull in Chaddesley in the lordship of Stone, was granted to John Maynard and William Breton,[3] who

[70] G.E.C. *Complete Peerage*, ii, 272.
[71] *Cal. Pat.* 1476–85, pp. 136, 211.
[72] Mins. Accts. bdle. 645, no. 10464.
[73] Early Chan. Proc. bdle. 66, no. 376.
[74] *Cal. Inq. p.m. Hen. VII*, i, 155.
[75] G.E.C. *Complete Peerage*, viii, 63.
[76] Anct. D. (P.R.O.), A 11056; Close, 3 Hen. VII, m. 11.
[77] *Cal. Inq. p.m. Hen. VII*, i, 339.
[78] Chan. Inq. p.m. (Ser. 2), xviii, 87.
[79] G.E.C. *Complete Peerage*, v, 117.
[80] Anct. D. (P.R.O.), A 12551.
[81] G.E.C. op. cit. v, 118.
[82] Add. MS. 31314, fol. 15b, 16, 18.
[83] Ibid. fol. 16.
[84] Ibid. fol. 19b.
[85] Ibid. fol. 20, 21.
[86] Ibid. fol. 102b. Nash gives this John Pakington as purchaser of the manor. *Hist. of Worc.* i, 185.
[87] Chan. Inq. p.m. (Ser. 2), clxxxiii, 76.
[88] Ibid. ccclxxxvi, 113.
[89] Noake, op. cit. 84. Her passport is

still among the Sessions Records at the shire hall, Worcester, and her monument is in the church of Chaddesley Corbett.
[90] *Index to Worc. Feet of F.* (Worcs. Hist. Soc.), 340; Feet of F. Worcs. Hil. 6 Geo. I; Close, 10 Geo. I, pt. xxv, no. 8.
[91] Recov. R. Trin. 21 Geo. II, rot. 163; Recov. R. D. Enr. Trin. 21 Geo. II, m. 9; Recov. R. Trin. 22 Geo. III, rot. 30; Mich. 7 Geo. IV, rot. 264. For pedigree of the Throckmortons see Burke's *Peerage*; G.E.C. *Complete Baronetage*, ii, 198–9; see also under Throckmorton in the parish of Fladbury.
[92] *Hist. MSS. Com. Rep.* iii, App. 257. A manor called Chaddesley Coll, Chaddesley Colles or Chaddesley Collectour appears in the 15th and 16th centuries, but is probably a variant of Chaddesley Corbett, whose descent it follows. Early Chan. Proc. bdle. 66, no. 376; *Cal. Inq. p.m. Hen. VII*, i, 155; Anct. D. (P.R.O.), A 12551.

[93] *Cal. Pat.* 1441–6, p. 433; Mins. Accts. bdle. 1067, no. 17; *Cal. Pat.* 1476–85, p. 136.
[94] Add. MS. 31314, fol. 16.
[95] Mins. Accts. bdle. 1067, no. 17; Add. MS. 31314, fol. 16.
[96] *V.C.H. Worcs.* i, 320a.
[97] *Worc. Inq. p.m.* (Worcs. Hist. Soc.), pt. i, no. 20.
[98] Ibid.
[99] Recov. R. Worc. East. 2 Jas. I, rot. 77. See also ibid. Trin. 1656, rot. 157.
[100] Exch. Dep. Spec. Com. Trin. 27 Chas. II, no. 8.
[1] Recov. R. Worc. Trin. 20 & 21 Geo. II, rot. 163.
[2] Mins. Accts bdle. 645, no. 10464. A number of the local mills were used for the manufacture of scythes and iron implements.
[3] *L. and P. Hen. VIII*, xix (1), g. 1035 (48); Pat. 36 Hen. VIII, pt. iii, m. 21.

sold it in the same year to Thomas Vaughan of St. Albans.[4]

It is not known of whom the reputed manor of *HARVINGTON* (Herewynton, Herwinton, xiii cent.; Hervyngton, xv cent.) was held in early times, but from 1410–11, when the overlordship is first mentioned, until the manorial rights of Harvington lapsed it was identical with that of Chaddesley Corbett.[5]

John de Harvington held land at Harvington in 1280.[6] Adam son of William de Harvington,[7] probably a descendant, held the manor in the middle of the 14th century. He was a clerk in holy orders, and became chancellor of the Exchequer in 1327.[8] He had been appointed chancellor of the Exchequer at Dublin in 1326. In 1342 he conveyed the reversion of the manor after his death to Thomas Beauchamp Earl of Warwick.[9] The earl apparently afterwards sold or leased the manor to Richard de Stonleye, for in 1346 Richard released to the earl all

'to th'end he may have conference with som learned devines to work him (if possibly yt may be) to som conformity.'[15]

The church of *ST. CASSIAN* consists of a chancel 44 ft. 2 in. by 18 ft. 11 in., modern north vestry, north chapel 31 ft. 10 in. by 15 ft. 11 in., nave about 54 ft. 6 in. by 20 ft. 3 in., north aisle of nearly the same length, 14 ft. 1 in. wide, south aisle 56 ft. 5 in. by 10 ft. 1 in., and a west tower 15 ft. by 14 ft. 10 in. These measurements are all internal.

CHURCH

The north arcade of the nave, which is the earliest portion of the existing building, dates from the first half of the 12th century. At this period the nave had a north aisle only, but before the close of the century an important enlargement took place. The west wall was taken down and the nave lengthened by one broad bay, and at the same time the southern arcade and aisle were added. During the following century a chapel of two bays was built on the north

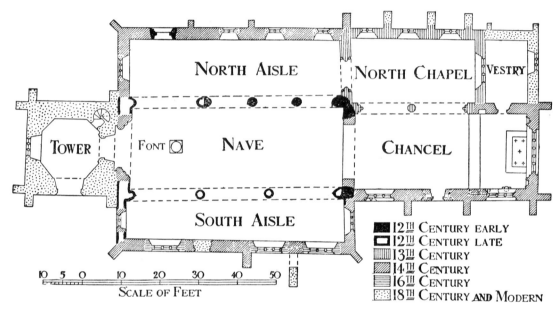

NORTH AISLE   NORTH CHAPEL | VESTRY

TOWER   FONT   NAVE   CHANCEL

SOUTH AISLE

■ 12TH CENTURY EARLY
□ 12TH CENTURY LATE
▦ 13TH CENTURY
▧ 14TH CENTURY
▤ 16TH CENTURY
▨ 18TH CENTURY AND MODERN

10 5 0   10   20   30   40   50

SCALE OF FEET

PLAN OF CHADDESLEY CORBETT CHURCH

his lands in England, except his estate in the manor of Harvington.[10] The manor reverted before 1357–8 to the Earl of Warwick, for in that year he leased it at a rent of £10 a year to Edmund de Brugg and Joan his wife.[11]

From that time it followed the descent of Chaddesley Corbett Manor[12] (q.v.), but all manorial rights apparently lapsed before 1578.[13] The manor-house seems to have been the seat of the Pakingtons and of Lady Mary Yate.[14]

Humphrey Pakington of Chaddesley Corbett was confined at his mansion-house at Harvington for recusancy in 1595, and on 9 November in that year the council ordered him to be brought to London

side of the Norman quire, and this was suffered to remain when the early chancel was replaced by the present handsome structure in the 14th century. The same century saw the rebuilding of the outer walls of both the nave aisles, only the west end of the southern being left of the 12th-century work, and the tower arch was reconstructed at the same time. Early in the 16th century the southern windows of the south aisle were inserted and in the 18th the existing tower was built.

The chancel throughout, with the exception of the arcade shafts, is of early 14th-century date, very rich in detail, the tracery of the four windows being remarkable for its elegance and variety.

[4] *L. and P. Hen. VIII,* xix (2), g. 340 (60), p. 196.

[5] Chan. Inq. p.m. 12 Hen. IV, no. 34; 14 Hen. VI, no. 35; 17 Hen. VI, no. 54; 24 Hen. VI, no. 43; (Ser. 2), xviii, 87; clxxxiii, 76.

[6] *Lay Subs. R. Worc.* c. 1280 (Worcs. Hist. Soc.), 15.

[7] Jeayes, *Lyttelton Chart.* no. 131.

[8] *Cal. Pat.* 1324–7, pp. 197, 295; 1327–30, p. 58.

[9] Add. MS. 28024, fol. 162; Feet of F. Worcs. case 260, file 21, no. 17.

[10] Add. MS. 28024, fol. 9b.

[11] Ibid. fol. 10b.

[12] Feet of F. Div. Co. Mich. 4 Hen. VI,

no. 45; Early Chan. Proc. bdles. 58, no. 156; 66, no. 376; Chan. Inq. p.m. (Ser. 2), clxxxiii, 76.

[13] Chan. Inq. p.m. (Ser. 2), clxxxiii, 76.

[14] Close, 10 Geo. I, pt. xxv, no. 8; Chan. Inq. p.m. (Ser. 2), clxxxiii, 76; ccclxxxvi, 113.

[15] *Acts of P. C.* 1595–6, pp. 50, 51.

The five-light east window has flowing tracery of the 14th century, and on each side is a niche with a crocketed canopy over and a foliated bracket.

In the north wall is a round-headed late 14th-century door, opening into a modern vestry, which occupies the site of an earlier one.

In the same wall is a recess, with trefoiled ogee head and a crocketed canopy above. An arcade of two bays divides the north chapel from the chancel. The responds are formed with three engaged shafts, but the column is octagonal. Up to the capitals the work is of the 13th century, but the arches above are 14th-century work and the capitals were probably re-cut at the same period. The three plain lancet lights under a segmental rear arch, in the east wall of the chapel, date from c. 1250, and the three windows in the north wall are of similar date and description, but of two lights only. Below the east window is a moulded ledge, which probably carried a decorated beam above the chapel altar.

The arch between the chapel and the north aisle is of the same type as the chancel arcade.

In the south chancel wall are three windows, of three lights each, the heads filled with flowing and geometric tracery. The label of the centre window is stopped on carved masks, but the others have stops of foliage. Below the third can be traced the position of a 'low-side' window, which has been restored, externally, as a two-light square-headed window. Beneath the centre window is a doorway similar to that at the north-east.

The chancel arch is pointed, of two plain chamfered orders, the inner dying on to the walls, the outer continuing down as chamfered responds. The exterior is very rich in appearance. The buttresses have each two gabled offsets filled with tracery, the upper finished with crockets and finials.

The northern arcade of the nave consists of three bays, with round arches of two plain orders and a fourth and larger bay at the west end, with a similar but pointed arch. The cylindrical columns and responds of the three earlier bays have scalloped capitals slightly differing in design. The western half of the third pier, where the work of the two periods joins, has also a scalloped capital, and the west respond is similar.

The southern arcade consists of three bays, with tall pointed arches of two plain orders, similar to the western bay of the north arcade in spacing and detail of capitals.

The four windows of the north aisle are modern restorations in the style of the 14th century, and the three-light west window in the tower is likewise modern. The north doorway appears to be of the original 12th-century date. The head is semi-circular, and the external jambs are shafted, the shafts having scalloped capitals.

In the south aisle the three-light windows in the south wall date from the early 16th century. The east window is modern, but at the west end is a two-light 14th-century window inserted in the earlier wall. The aisle walls were raised in the 16th century, and the earlier roof line is still visible at the west end. There are traces of a south door, now blocked. Externally there is a tomb recess with a crocketed canopy, with a buttress springing over the opening to the wall above. In the west window are some fragments of old glass.

The tower, with embattled parapet and spire, was built in the 18th century.

The chancel has a plaster barrel-ceiling with wood ribs. The nave roof is modern, but the pent over the south aisle is ancient. At the intersections of the moulded beams are roses, with carved bosses at the wall plate on the ends of the intermediate timbers. These bosses, with one exception, bear angels, some with shields and one holding a censer.

The font is of red sandstone, circular in shape, and a fine piece of 12th-century work. On the rim of the bowl is a double band of interlaced work, and below this five dragons with knotted tails. The stem has a deep band of interlaced work, and the base a double row of 'Stafford knots.'

In the chapel are two life-size effigies: a priest in mass vestments, and a late 13th-century knight in chain mail. The latter wears a mail coif, knee cops, a long surcoat, and a shield on the left arm. The feet with prick spurs rest on a dog, and a line of rosettes extends along the edge of the slab on which the effigy rests.

In the south aisle is a tomb slab of a man and his wife with a broken inscription round the edge, running: 'Thome Fforest Parcarii de Dunclent et Margaritae uxoris ejus et omnium puerorum suorum quorum . . . .' Between the words are arrows, hunting horns, leaves, &c., and at the four corners the symbols of the Evangelists.

In the north chapel is a monument in alabaster and black marble to Elizabeth daughter of Thomas Holt of Aston, bart., died 1647, with arms: Azure two bars or in chief a cross paty. Another monument commemorates Humphrey Pakington (died 1631) and his wife (died 1657), with arms: Party cheveronwise sable and or with three mullets or in the chief, and three sheaves gules in the foot. A fourth monument is to Ann wife of Sir Henry Audley of Burechurch, Essex, and daughter of Humphrey Pakington, died 1642.

An ancient altar slab about 5 ft. long and 13 in. thick is preserved here.

In the tower is a fragment of a 12th-century 'Majesty' in a vesica.

There is a peal of eight bells and a small ringing-in bell. The treble and second are dated 1783, and encircled with bands of ornament; the third is by Abraham Rudhall, and inscribed 'I sweetly sing when you mee ring A.R. 1701'; the fourth and fifth are also by Abraham Rudhall, and are respectively inscribed 'Wee all to ring God save the King 1701' and 'God prosper this Church and Parish 1701'; both the sixth and seventh are by C. G. Mears, 1856; and the tenor, which was originally by Abraham Rudhall, 1701, and inscribed with the names of the vicar and churchwardens and 'God save the King,' was recast by Messrs. Stainbank in 1905. The small bell is by Mears & Stainbank, 1891.

The plate consists of a chalice dated 1571 and made in the preceding year, a paten of 1724, a modern chalice, paten and cruet.

The registers previous to 1812 are as follows: (i) mixed entries 1538 to 1727 (this book is preceded by a note that the injunction for keeping registers was first read at Chaddesley Corbett 24 November 1538); (ii) baptisms and burials 1728 to 1812, marriages 1728 to 1753; (iii) marriages 1754 to 1812.

ADVOWSON From the mention of two priests at Chaddesley Corbett in the Domesday Survey[16] it may perhaps be inferred that there was a church there in 1086. The advowson appears at first to have belonged to the lords of the manor. In 1200 the Abbot of Tewkesbury sued Roger Corbett and Hawise his wife for the right of presentation, which he claimed to have been given to one of his predecessors by Robert Fitz Hamon, and to have been confirmed to the monastery by Henry I, William Duke of Gloucester, the heir of Robert and Simon Bishop of Worcester.[17] Roger Corbett and Hawise opposed this on the ground that Robert Fitz Payn, great-grandfather of Hawise, Richard Folliott the elder, her grandfather, and Richard Folliott the younger, her father, had each in turn presented to the church, and that when a dispute about the advowson arose between Robert son of Richard, her former husband, and Fromund, predecessor of the abbot, the former presented Ralph Folliott, who was admitted by the bishop.[18] The claim of the Corbett family was probably well founded, and the dispute was amicably settled by the abbot surrendering his rights in return for 4 virgates of land in 'Wadehamet' and 4 in 'Dreiton.'[19]

The advowson remained with the lords of the manor[20] until 1385, when the king granted licence to William de Beauchamp, Lord Bergavenny, to alienate it to the collegiate church of St. Mary, Warwick, which had been founded by one of his ancestors.[21] This gift was confirmed in 1397 by the king,[22] and by Sir William and his wife Joan in 1410.[23]

The dean and chapter probably appropriated the rectory of Chaddesley Corbett in 1394, and the vicarage was ordained in the same year.[24] At the Dissolution they were receiving a rent of £24 16s. 8d. from the rectory of Chaddesley.[25]

The college of Warwick was dissolved in 1544,[26] and the advowson of Chaddesley Corbett was granted in 1545 to the burgesses of Warwick.[27] They appear to have presented for the last time in 1639,[28] and the advowson has since that time been vested in the Crown.[29]

The rectory was granted with the advowson to the burgesses of Warwick,[30] who retained the rectorial tithes after parting with the advowson.[31] The great tithes are now in the hands of the Warwick Municipal Charity Trustees.

About twenty years before the dissolution of chantries a certain William Newman gave tenements in Chaddesley Corbett worth £5 3s. 8d. yearly to trustees for the maintenance of a school there.[32] Land at Chaddesley Corbett called 'Our Ladyes Lands,' given for the maintenance of a priest, obits and lights, was granted in 1562 to Cicely Pickerell.[33]

The churches of Rushock and Stone were at one time chapelries of Chaddesley Corbett.[34]

At Bluntington there is a Primitive Methodist chapel, erected in 1873, and at Drayton there is a Church mission-room.

CHARITIES The School and Poor's Lands are regulated by a scheme dated 29 June 1878.[35] By the scheme trustees were appointed and the following charities were merged in the foundation, namely :

Humphrey Westwood's, will, proved in the P.C.C. 1622, consisting of a rent-charge of 50s. payable out of a messuage known as the Horseshoes ;

Simon Westwood's, being originally a rent-charge of 50s. issuing out of lands at Harborne, of which 18s., part thereof, was in 1895 redeemed by the transfer to the official trustees of £36 2½ per cent. annuities ;

Gilbert Penn's, will, 1653, now consisting of £43 12s. 8d. consols, with the official trustees, producing £1 1s. 9d. yearly, arising from redemption in 1867 of original rent-charge of 26s. ;

James Pratt's, will, proved 1828, consisting of £678 0s. 10d. consols, with the official trustees, of which one moiety (£339 0s. 5d.) belongs to the Delabere Almshouses (see below).

Out of the income of the foundation a sum of £50 a year is distributed in doles to about 120 poor people, and the balance in scholarships, technical education and prizes for the children of parishioners.

The almshouses founded by Margaret Delabere in 1637 for five poor widows are endowed with a house with 2 a. 1 r. 19 p., and 14 a. 0 r. 35 p. of the annual rental value of £40 18s. ; also with £357 5s. 9d. consols and £36 2½ per cent. annuities, producing together £9 16s. 8d. a year. The stock is held by the official trustees, and includes a sum of £339 0s. 5d. consols, being a moiety of £678 0s. 10d. consols representing a legacy by will of James Pratt, proved in the P.C.C. 29 October 1828. The other moiety is included in the property of the Endowed Schools (see above).

The inmates receive £2 each a quarter.

The almshouses founded in 1691 by Dame Mary Yate for four poor widows are endowed with six pieces of land with buildings thereon, containing 19 a. 2 r. 15 p., and a house and garden, the whole producing £35 yearly. Each inmate receives £6 per annum and £4 is spent on coal for their use.

The Dame Mary Yate Charity for apprenticing, founded by indentures of lease and release 18 and 19 August 1674, is endowed with 16 a. 2 r., seven cottages and salt works at Droitwich, producing £48 a year, and 22 a. 3 r. 13 p. at Chaddesley Corbett, let at £52 a year ; also £1,647 5s. 7d. consols, with

[16] *V.C.H. Worcs.* i, 320a.

[17] Dugdale, *Mon.* ii, 70 ; *Rot. Cur. Reg.* (Rec. Com.), ii, 175–6.

[18] *Rot. Cur. Reg.* (Rec. Com.), ii, 175 ; *Testa de Nevill* (Rec. Com.), 23.

[19] Dugdale, *Mon.* ii, 76. It should be noticed, however, that the church of Chaddesley is mentioned in a charter confirming the Abbot and convent of Tewkesbury in their possession dated in 1300. It is difficult to explain this, as the Corbett family undoubtedly held the advowson before this date ; *Cal. Chart. R.* 1257–1300, p. 490.

[20] Feet of F. Worcs. case 260, file 22, no. 32 ; *Cal. Inq. p.m.* 1–19 *Edw. I,* 466 ; Exch. K.R. Misc. Bks. xxii, fol. 1.

[21] *Cal. Pat.* 1381–5, p. 580.

[22] Ibid. 1396–9, p. 270.

[23] Feet of F. Div. Co. East. 11 Hen. IV, no. 62.

[24] Exch. K.R. Misc. Bks. xxii, fol. 106, 108 d., 109.

[25] *Valor Eccl.* (Rec. Com.), iii, 83.

[26] *V.C.H. Warw.* ii, 129.

[27] Pat. 37 Hen. VIII, pt. v, m. 23 ; *L. and P. Hen. VIII,* xx (1), g. 846 (41).

[28] Inst. bks. P.R.O.

[29] Ibid.

[30] *L. and P. Hen. VIII,* xx (1), g. 846 (41).

[31] Nash, *Hist. of Worc.* i, 187.

[32] Chant. Cert. 60, no. 21 ; Chan. Proc. (Ser. 2), bdle. 194, no. 43.

[33] Pat. 4 Eliz. pt. iii, m. 40.

[34] *Reg. G. Giffard* (Worcs. Hist. Soc.), 30 ; Habington, *Surv. of Worc.* (Worcs. Hist. Soc.), ii, 276 ; Worc. Epis. Reg. Reynolds (1308–13), fol. 88 ; ibid. Wakefield (1375–95), fol. 63 d., 64 d.

[35] See article on 'Schools.'

CHADDESLEY CORBETT CHURCH : SOUTH WALL OF CHANCEL

CHADDESLEY CORBETT CHURCH : THE NAVE LOOKING EAST

the official trustees, producing £41 3s. 8d. a year, arising in part from sale of land and in part from accumulations of income.

In 1909 the sum of £104 was expended in apprenticeship premiums.

Eleemosynary Charities :

In 1620 William Seabright by will devised an annuity of £3 0s. 8d. payable out of property in Bethnal Green to be applied in the distribution of fourteen penny loaves every Sunday to fourteen poor. The parish clerk also receives 6s. 8d. for selecting the recipients.

In 1687 John Taylor by his will gave 40s. yearly out of two fields called the Off Meadows in Stone to the poor.

In 1732 Jonathan Harrison, by his will proved at Worcester 25 March, bequeathed £5, the interest to be laid out in bread on 21 December yearly. To secure punctual payment a sum of 5s. a year was charged by the testator's son, John Harrison, upon certain property in Lower Chaddesley, and this is distributed in twenty loaves to twenty poor.

In 1817 William Wheeler, by a codicil to his will, left a legacy for the poor, now represented by £191 2s. 2d. consols with the official trustees. The annual dividends, amounting to £4 15s. 4d., are distributed among the poor in sums varying from 2s. 6d. to 10s. In 1909 there were fourteen recipients.

In 1836 Mrs. Elizabeth Pratt by her will bequeathed £700, the income on £300 to be applied for the organist, on another £300 for poor parishioners, and on £100 for singers. The legacy was invested in £754 15s. consols with the official trustees, producing £18 17s. 4d. yearly. The proportion due to the poor is applied in the distribution of coal, meat, groceries and cash.

In 1899 John Giles, by his will proved at London 28 June, gave a sum of £2 yearly to bell-ringers for ringing a muffled peal of bells annually on the date of testator's decease. A sum of £80 consols is held by the official trustees in respect of this charity.

The parish is in possession of 2 a. 0 r. 15 p. of land of the annual letting value of £2 10s. which is applicable towards the repairs of the highways.

CHURCHILL

Cercehalle (xi cent.) ; Chirhulle (xii cent.).

The parish of Churchill, containing 954 acres, of which 721 acres are arable land, 160¾ permanent grass, and 8 acres woodland,[1] is on the Staffordshire border, about 3½ miles north-east of Kidderminster. It is generally known as Churchill near Kidderminster or Churchill in Halfshire to distinguish it from Churchill near Worcester in the hundred of Oswaldslow. In 1306 it was referred to as 'Churchill in the forest of Kinver,'[2] and some years later was amerced with neighbouring townships for non-attendance at the court of the regarder of that forest.[3] It was still described as in Kinver Forest in 1604.[4]

An Act for inclosing Churchill Common was passed in 1773.[5]

Churchill is watered by 'a quick and clear stream,'[6] which rises in the Clent Hills and forms the eastern boundary of the parish, occasionally artificially widened into pools ; about 2 miles from Churchill it flows into the River Stour. The land slopes upwards from the valley of this stream, and at its lowest level towards the west and north is 211 ft. above the ordnance datum, while near the northern boundary of the parish it attains a height of 400 ft.

The village of Churchill stands on the right bank of this stream, and consists of one rather straggling street continued southward as a branch road joining the main road from Kidderminster to Halesowen near Blakedown. At the north of the village three roads diverge, going respectively to Cookley, Kinver, and Stakenbridge.

The nearest station to Churchill is at Blakedown.

The hamlets of Blakedown, Stakenbridge, and Harborough in the civil parish of Hagley were in 1888 transferred to Churchill for ecclesiastical purposes by Order in Council. In Blakedown is a chapel of ease to the parish church.

The subsoil consists of Bunter Pebble Beds ; the surface is very dry and is mostly sand. The parish is mainly agricultural, wheat, barley and green crops being raised, but there are spade and shovel works on a small scale in the village. It is said that during the 18th century Churchill so abounded in damsons and plums that all the neighbouring markets were supplied from it.[7]

MANOR At the time of the Domesday Survey the manor of *CHURCHILL* was held by Walter of William Fitz Ansculf, the lord of Dudley ; it had formerly belonged to Wigar,[8] who had also held the adjacent manor of Cradley.[9]

The overlordship followed the descent of the barony of Dudley until the partition of John de Somery's lands in 1323,[10] when it was assigned to his younger sister Joan de Botetourt, but from that time it appears to have lapsed. The manor was held of these overlords for the service of a fourth of a knight's fee.[11]

About the middle of the 12th century Agnes de Somery bequeathed half a hide of land at Churchill 'and the rest of that vill' towards the foundation of the monastery of St. James at Dudley, desiring to be buried there.[12] She was probably related to John de Somery, who had married Hawise, the sister of Gervase Paynel. Her gift was confirmed before 1161 by Gervase as lord of the fee,[13] and afterwards by Pope Lucius III in 1182.[14]

At the Dissolution the possessions of Dudley Priory in Churchill included assize rents amounting to 17s.,[15]

[1] Statistics from Bd. of Agric. (1905).
[2] Worc. Epis. Reg. Gainsborough, fol. 43b.
[3] Forest R. Staffs. 19 Edw. I, quoted in Lyttelton MSS. (Soc. Antiq.).
[4] Exch. Dep. Spec. Com. East. 2 Jas. I, no. 4.
[5] Private Act, 13 Geo. III, cap. 21.
[6] Lyttelton MSS. (Soc. Antiq.).
[7] Ibid.
[8] V.C.H. Worcs. i, 316b.
[9] Ibid. 317a.
[10] Cal. Inq. p.m. 1–19 Edw. I, 495; Cal. Close, 1318–23, p. 631.
[11] Cal. Close, 1318–23, p. 631.
[12] Dugdale, Mon. v, 83.
[13] Ibid.
[14] Ibid. ; V.C.H. Worcs. ii, 159.
[15] Valor Eccl. (Rec. Com.), iii, 104.

which were granted in 1541 to Sir John Dudley, afterwards Duke of Northumberland,[16] and after his attainder to Thomas Reve and George Cotton.[17] The latter are said to have sold the rent to Humphrey Dickens,[18] but this seems improbable, as the estate of Dudley Priory in the manor passed to the Lytteltons, being forfeited by John Lyttelton in 1601 [19] and restored to his widow Muriel two years later.[20] Thomas son of John purchased the manor in 1605–6, when the fee-farm rent would have lapsed. A rent of 6s. 8d. appears to have been reserved by the Crown on one of these grants, for in 1635–6 6s. 8d. yearly from the vill of Churchill was granted to William Scriven and Philip Eden and their heirs.[21]

Shortly after the grant of Gervase Paynel, the Prior of Wenlock, to which Dudley was a cell, gave the manor to Robert de Hurcott (Hurchote), probably of the adjoining parish of Kidderminster, for a rent of half a mark yearly to the monks of Dudley.[22] Robert seems to have been succeeded by Adam de Hurcott, who conveyed Churchill to his son Robert.[23] It was probably this Robert de Hurcott who in 1234–5 dealt with the adjoining vill of Hurcott.[24] A few years later he granted 'the land of Churchill' with the advowson of the church to Hugh Drugel in free marriage with his sister Margery.[25]

John Drugel or Drobul, who was possibly the son of Hugh and Margery, presented to the church in 1298 and again in the following year, when he was described as being of the manor of Suckley.[26] Probably therefore he did not reside at Churchill, and he seems to have leased the land to one John de Melford.[27] John Drugel afterwards conveyed the rent of 60s. 8d., payable by John de Melford, with the advowson, to the family of Bastenhall of Suckley.[28] Giles de Bastenhall presented to the church in 1340 [29] and had been succeeded in 1350 by Joan widow of John de Bastenhall. In that year Joan conveyed the advowson and the rent of 60s. 8d. to Edmund de Dunclent and his wife Joan, apparently for three lives.[30] It was probably this Edmund de Dunclent who presented to the church in 1361 [31] and who was succeeded by his son John, lord of Churchill in 1368.[32] Churchill was settled in 1397 on John de Dunclent and his wife Joan, with reversion to John Wythall and his wife Alice and their heirs, and remainder to Elizabeth the daughter of John de Dunclent.[33] John Bilington was lord of Churchill and presented to the church in 1422,[34] but before 1429 the manor had passed to Thomas Dickens of Bobbington, co. Stafford,[35] but whether by sale or otherwise does not appear. Thomas Dickens seems to have been succeeded in Churchill by his second

son Thomas, who occurs as lord of the manor in 1471.[36] Thomas had died leaving a son Richard before 1483, when his widow Elizabeth held the manor.[37] In the following year she granted an annual rent of 20s. from lands in Churchill held by Thomas Willot to her son Richard.[38]

DICKENS of Bobbington. *Ermine a cross paty sable.*

From this time until 1561 the history of the manor is a blank, but it probably reverted to the elder branch of the Dickens family, as Hugh [39] Dickens held it in 1561, and granted it that year to a younger son Thomas Dickens and his wife Philippa in tail-male.[40] Richard Dickens, who succeeded, and held the manor in 1601, may have been son of Thomas and Philippa.[41] He had been succeeded before 1605–6 by John Dickens, who conveyed the manor in that year to Thomas Lyttelton.[42]

From that date it has descended with the manor of Hagley [43] (q.v.), and now belongs to Viscount Cobham.

At the end of the 18th century a court was still occasionally held for the Crown at the Bell Inn. There was no court leet, and the court baron of the Lytteltons was then falling into disuse, 'there being no copyholders within the manor.' [44]

A mill held by the lord of the manor by payment of 20s. yearly to the lord of Hagley is mentioned in the 13th century.[45] A blade-mill and mill pool at Churchill are mentioned at the end of the 16th century.[46]

There is now a mill at Churchill about a quarter of a mile to the south of the village.

CHURCH The church of *ST. JAMES* is a modern building, and consists of a chancel with a north vestry, above which is the tower, and a nave with a wooden south porch. The material of the building is red sandstone, and the design is in the style of the early 14th century. In the nave is a modern octagonal font.

In the church was formerly an ancient parish chest rudely hollowed out of a single block of oak.[47]

There are two bells. The treble bears the name of John Cox, churchwarden, and the date 1722 ; the second is by John Martin of Worcester, and bears his stamp.

The church plate consists of a three-legged salver hall marked for 1808, a cup with a cover of the

[16] *L. and P. Hen. VIII*, xvi, g. 678 (47).

[17] Pat. 1 Mary, pt. iv, m. 27.

[18] Prattinton Coll. (Soc. Antiq.).

[19] Misc. Bks. Ld. Rev. ccxxviii, fol. 235 ; Exch. Spec. Com. 44 Eliz. no. 2519.

[20] Pat. 1 Jas. I, pt. i, m. 30.

[21] Ibid. 11 Chas. I, pt. i, no. 1.

[22] Jeayes, *Lyttelton Chart.* no. 1.

[23] Ibid. no. 15.

[24] Feet of F. Worcs. 19 Hen. III, no. 28.

[25] Jeayes, op. cit. no. 10.

[26] *Reg. G. Giffard* (Worcs. Hist. Soc.), 496, 511.

[27] In the Lay Subsidy Roll of c. 1280 (Worcs. Hist. Soc.) Richard de Melford paid a mark ; John was probably his descendant. He is described as 'lord of

Churchill' in the 14th century (Jeayes, op. cit. no. 179).

[28] Jeayes, op. cit. no. 146.

[29] Nash, *Hist. of Worc.* i, 193.

[30] Jeayes, op. cit. no. 146. The grant was said to be 'for lives.'

[31] Nash, loc. cit.

[32] Jeayes, op. cit. no. 178, 179.

[33] Ibid. 239. According to Nash (*Hist. of Worc.* i, 190–1) the Dunclents held this manor till the reign of Henry VI.

[34] Nash, op. cit. i, 191, quoting from Worc. Ep's. Reg. Morgan, fol. 10b.

[35] Jeayes, op. cit. no. 315, 316, 322, 323, 338.

[36] Ibid. 397 ; 'Visit. of Staffs. 1583,' *Will. Salt Arch. Soc. Coll.* iii (2), 67.

[37] Jeayes, op. cit. no. 420.

[38] Ibid. 422.

[39] He was son of John, eldest son of Thomas Dickens, the first holder of the manor (*Will. Salt Arch. Soc. Coll.* iii [2], 67).

[40] Misc. Bks. Ld. Rev. ccxxviii, fol. 237.

[41] Ibid. ; Exch. Spec. Com. 44 Eliz. no. 2519.

[42] Feet of F. Worcs. East. 3 Jas. I.

[43] Recov. R. Mich. 9 Chas. I, rot. 86 ; Pat. 34 Chas. II, pt. ix ; Feet of F. Worcs. Trin. 6 Anne.

[44] Prattinton Coll. (Soc. Antiq.), quoting Lyttelton MSS.

[45] Jeayes, op. cit. no. 10.

[46] Misc. Bks. Ld. Rev. ccxxviii, fol. 237 d.

[47] Lyttelton MSS. (Soc. Antiq.).

usual Elizabethan type on which the hall marks are obliterated, a modern glass flagon with a silver top and handle and a modern chalice, gilt inside, with the Birmingham hall marks for 1861.

The registers before 1812 are as follows : (i) all entries 1540 to 1712 ; (ii) all entries 1715 to 1813.

ADVOWSON The advowson of Churchill apparently followed the descent of the manor[48] until 1561. It seems to have been retained by Hugh Dickens when he granted the manor to his younger son Thomas, as Hugh presented to the church in 1571.[49] It passed from him to his grandson William, son of his eldest son Humphrey.[50]

William Dickens presented in 1584,[51] and the advowson probably passed at about the same time as the manor to Thomas Lyttelton, as he presented in 1618.[52] From that time the advowson has descended with the manor,[53] Viscount Cobham being the present patron.

Richard Penne,[54] by his will dated 1470, desired to be buried in the churchyard of St. James the Apostle of Churchill and left 12d. to the high altar, two torches and 4 acres of land and a tenement in Kidderminster.[55]

CHARITIES The charities of Richard Penne and Roger Bennett (1602) are comprised in a scheme of the County Court of Worcestershire holden 24 September 1856, supplemented by a scheme of the Charity Commissioners 29 May 1894. The trust property consists of school with site, 1 a. 2 r. 2 p. near St. George's Church, Kidderminster, let at £6 10s. a year, £2,712 10s. 9d. consols, and £267 14s. 9d. Local Loans 3 per cent. stock, producing together £75 16s. 8d. in annual dividends.

The sums of stock are held by the official trustees, and arise from sales in 1872, 1874 and 1876 of lands, houses and cottages, and of the Britannia Inn in 1881, and from accumulations of income.

By an order of the Charity Commissioners 5 December 1905 the portion applicable for educational purposes is to be designated 'The Penne and Bennett Educational Foundation,' the remainder being applicable for church purposes.

CHURCH LENCH

Circelenz (xi cent.) ; Ciricleinc, Lench Roculf (xiii cent.).

The parish of Church Lench lies on the eastern border of the county. The parish includes the hamlets of Ab Lench or Hob Lench,[1] Atch Lench and Sheriff's Lench, the first being a chapelry of Fladbury until 28 December 1865, when, for ecclesiastical purposes, it became part of Church Lench.[2] The Whitsun Brook flows northward and then westward through the parish, and the land gradually rises from the valley of this stream, which near the western boundary of the parish is 154 ft. above the ordnance datum. Sheriff's Lench is 378 ft. above the same level. Church Lench has an area of 2,572 acres, of which, in 1905, 1,321 acres were arable land, 1,130¼ permanent grass and 90¾ acres woodland.[3] Ab Lench includes 884 acres. The subsoil is lower lias clay, the surface clay and sand. Farming is the chief occupation ; wheat, barley and beans are grown.

The Inclosure Act for Church Lench was passed in 1783,[4] and the award is dated 19 December in that year.[5]

17th-century place-names are : Hommeangswicke, Golden Butts, Hippitts, Woodcocke Thorne Coppice, Balloe Hill.[6]

MANORS It is stated in the Evesham Chronicle that CHURCH LENCH formed part of the gift made by Kenred of Mercia in 708 to Evesham Abbey,[7] but Church Lench is not mentioned in the grant as given in the Harleian Manuscript.[8] A grant of five 'manentes' at Lench was made to the abbey by King 'Eadward' of Mercia between 860 and 865.[9] No such king is known, and the charter is an obvious forgery. Church Lench seems to have been afterwards alienated, as Abbot Mannig (1044–54) is stated to have recovered this township for his church.[10] His successor, Æthelwig II, is also said to have acquired at great cost certain lands, among them Church Lench, from 'King Edward and other good men.'[11] In 1086 it was held by the abbot and convent in demesne,[12] but it was shortly afterwards granted by Ab᾿ot Walter (1077–86) to Urse d'Abitot the Sheriff of Worcestershire 'for service' for the term of his life only.[13] His heirs, the Beauchamps, apparently retained it, however, as a survey of the lands of the abbey of Evesham, the probable date of which is about 1150, states that William de Beauchamp, grandson of Urse, held 4 hides at Church Lench of the abbey.[14]

The rights of the Abbot of Evesham in the overlordship were recognized until the 13th century at least, when William de Beauchamp was said to be holding Church Lench by gift of Robert the Abbot.[15] After that time the rights of the abbot in the manor appear to have lapsed.

The Beauchamps continued as overlords, and occasional owners in demesne,[16] of the manor until the 14th century.[17]

Under them the manor was held by the Roculfs, from whom Church Lench took the alternative name of Lench Roculf.[18] During the early part of the

---

[48] *Reg. G. Giffard* (Worcs. Hist. Soc.), 496, 511; *Sede Vacante Reg.* (Worcs. Hist. Soc.), 209, 426 ; Jeayes, op. cit. no. 10.
[49] Nash, op. cit. i, 193.
[50] *Will. Salt Arch. Soc. Coll.* iii (2), 67.
[51] Nash, loc. cit.
[52] Inst. Bks. P.R.O.
[53] Ib᾿d. ; *Clergy Lists.*
[54] The Pennes held land at Churchill in the 15th, 16th and 17th centuries (Early Chan. Proc. bdle. 219, no. 72 ; Exch. Spec. Com. 44 Eliz. no. 2519).

[55] Prattinton Coll. (Soc. of Antiq.).
[1] Now known as Abbots Lench.
[2] *Parl. Papers* (1872), xlvi, 27.
[3] Statistics from Bd. of Agric. (1905).
[4] Priv. Act. 23 Geo. III, cap. 25.
[5] *Blue Bk. Incl. Awards,* 189.
[6] Close, 1651, pt. lvi, no. 19.
[7] *Chron. de Evesham* (Rolls Ser.), 72.
[8] Op. cit. 3763, fol. 59.
[9] Birch, *Cart. Sax.* ii, 122.
[10] *Chron. de Evesham* (Rolls Ser.), 86.

[11] Ibid. 94 ; Harl. MS. 3763, fol. 59.
[12] *V.C.H. Worcs.* i, 307b.
[13] Cott. MS. Vesp. B. xxiv, fol. 49 d.
[14] *V.C.H. Worcs.* i, 328b and n.
[15] Harl. MS. 3763, fol. 61 d., 68.
[16] Add. MS. 28024, fol. 158, 160.
[17] *Cal. Inq. p.m.* 1–9 Edw. II, 403 ; Exch. K.R. Misc. Bks. xxii, fol. 1.
[18] *Reg. G. Giffard* (Worcs. Hist. Soc.), 116 ; *Pope Nich. Tax.* (Rec. Com.), 217, 239.

reign of Henry III it appears to have been held by Roger Roculf or Rotulf, who in 1229–30 conveyed certain land to Ellis son of Giffard.[19] About the same time the recently founded abbey of Halesowen received from him several grants in which he is designated 'lord of Church Lench.'[20] The property which the abbot and convent thus received appears to have afterwards become a distinct manor (q.v.), now the capital manor of Church Lench.

The Roculfs continued to hold the manor, and William Roculf paid a subsidy at Lench Roculf in 1280,[21] and in 1299–1300 he was in possession of the manor,[22] and was succeeded before 1315 by his son Thomas. It seems to have next passed to John Roculf, who in 1346 held the fourth part of a knight's fee there.[23]

The next mention of this property is in 1428, when Thomas Serchesdene held John Roculf's estate.[24] Thomas was still in possession in 1431.[25] After this time nothing is known of this manor, which may have become incorporated with Rous Lench, a manor also held by Thomas Serchesdene, or perhaps lapsed to the overlords, the Earls of Warwick, and became annexed to Sheriff's Lench.

The present manor of *CHURCH LENCH* seems to have originated in land at Church Lench granted in the reign of Henry III by Roger Roculf, lord of Church Lench, to the abbey of Halesowen.[26]

In 1272–3 William Abbot of Halesowen conveyed a messuage and 3 carucates of land in Church Lench and a carucate of land in Ab Lench to Ralph de Hengham, afterwards chief justice of the Common Pleas, who was to hold the estate for life, with reversion to the abbot.[27]

No mention is made in Pope Nicholas's *Taxatio* of any property held in Church Lench by the Abbot and convent of Halesowen. The land and tenements granted by Roger Roculf appear to have been retained by them,[28] however, until in 1538 it was surrendered to the king by William Taylor, the last abbot.[29] It was granted in the same year to Sir John Dudley.[30] It was probably sold by him to William Scudamore, who died seised of it in 1560, when it passed to his son John.[31] He in 1596 settled the manor in tailmale on his son Sir James, with remainder to his brothers George and Roland.[32] Sir James died in 1619 in the lifetime of his father, leaving a son John,[33] who was created a baronet in 1620.[34] In 1627 he sold the manor to William Keyt,[35] who died seised of it 12 October 1632.[36] He left a son and heir John, who had livery of the manor of Church Lench in 1635.[37] He died in 1660, and was succeeded by his son John, who was created a baronet in 1662.[38]

Sir John Keyt was succeeded in 1662 by his son William,[39] who survived his four sons and died in 1702, when his estates passed to his grandson Sir William.[40] Sir William Keyt was burned to death at Norton, co. Gloucester, in September 1741, being supposed to have been a lunatic and to have set fire to the house,[41] and Nash states that the manor was then sold to Sir Dudley Ryder,[42] whose son Nathaniel, created Lord Harrowby in 1776, was the owner of it in 1779.[43] In 1793 John Callow and Ellen his wife conveyed 'the manor of Church Lench' to John Clarke.[44]

KEYT, baronet. *Azure a cheveron between three kites' heads razed or with three trefoils gules on the cheveron.*

The Rev. William Chafy, D.D., of Sherborne, co. Dorset, master of Sidney-Sussex College, Cambridge, purchased part of the manor about 1826, and more has since been acquired by his grandson the Rev. William Kyle Westwood Chafy, D.D., of Sherborne and of Rous Lench.[45] About a third of the manor was purchased by the Duc d'Aumale and on his death passed by will to the Duc d'Orleans. This part was sold in 1912 to Sir Charles Swinfen Eady.

SHERIFF'S LENCH (Lenche, xi cent.; Shyreveslench, xiv cent.; Shrewlenche, xvi cent.) is said to have been the Lench, Lench Bernardi or 'Lench Alnoth juxta Chadelbure' (Chadbury in Norton parish) asserted to have been given by Ethelbald of Mercia to the abbey of Evesham in 716,[46] but it must afterwards have been lost by the abbey, as it was among the lands recovered by Abbot Æthelwig (1070–7) from King Edward and other good men.[47] The manor comprised 4 hides and was acquired in moieties by Æthelwig; 2 hides he held in the time of King Edward and the other two he bought with the money of the church from Gilbert Fitz Turold with the permission of King William.[48] The Domesday Survey gives the additional information that the proceeds of the latter moiety of the manor supported one monk in Evesham Abbey.[49] It does not, however, agree with the chronicles of Evesham as to the acquisition of the other 2 hides, which are here stated to have been bought of King William for 1 mark of gold.[50] The whole manor was held by Abbot Æthelwig until his death in 1077,[51] when it was stolen from the church by Odo Bishop of Bayeux, who gave it to Urse the Sheriff.[52] It is difficult to decide to what period to assign the statement made in the Domesday Survey that Lench had been held as three manors, 2 hides being held by two

[19] Feet of F. Worcs. 14 Hen. III, no. 8.
[20] Jeayes, *Lyttelton Chart.* no. 23, 24, 25.
[21] *Lay Subs. R. c.* 1280 (Worcs. Hist. Soc.), 19.
[22] Nash, *Hist. of Worc.* ii, 80.
[23] *Feud. Aids*, v, 303.
[24] Ibid. 324. [25] Ibid. 331.
[26] Jeayes, op. cit. pp. 8, 9; Nash, op. cit. ii, 80; App. 20.
[27] Feet of F. Worcs. 1 Edw. I, no. 1.
[28] *Valor Eccl.* (Rec. Com.), iii, 207. In 1535 it was valued at 10l. 5½d.
[29] Feet of F. Div. Co. Trin. 30 Hen. VIII.
[30] Pat. 30 Hen. VIII, pt. iii, m. 16; *L. and P. Hen. VIII*, xiii (2), g. 491 (1).
[31] Chan. Inq. p.m. (Ser. 2), cxxvi, 82; Chan. Proc. (Ser. 2), bdle. 131, no. 7.

[32] Feet of F. Div. Co. Trin. 39 Eliz.
[33] Chan. Inq. p.m. (Ser. 2), ccclxxiv, 85.
[34] G.E.C. *Complete Baronetage*, i, 146.
[35] Feet of F. Worcs. Trin. 3 Chas. I.
[36] Chan. Inq. p.m. (Ser. 2), dx, 40.
[37] Fine R. 11 Chas. I, pt. iii, no. 47.
[38] G.E.C. *Complete Baronetage*, iii, 140; Feet of F. Div. Co. Trin. 14 Chas. II.
[39] G.E.C. *Complete Baronetage*, iii, 140; Feet of F. Worcs. Mich. 20 Chas. II.
[40] G.E.C. *Complete Baronetage*, iii, 140.
[41] Ibid.
[42] Nash, op. cit. ii, 81. Bishampton, which followed the same descent as Church Lench during the 17th century, was sold in 1753 by Sir Thomas Charles Keyt, son of Sir William, to Sir Dudley Ryder (Feet of F. Worcs. Trin. 26 & 27

Geo. II), and Church Lench was probably sold at about the same time.
[43] Nash, loc. cit.; Supp. 51; G.E.C. *Complete Peerage*, iv, 175.
[44] Feet of F. Worcs. Trin. 33 Geo. III.
[45] Information supplied by Dr. W. K. W. Chafy.
[46] *Chron. de Evesham* (Rolls Ser.), 72; *V.C.H. Worcs.* i, 308a, 290, n. 3; Harl. MS. 3763, fol. 59, 62 d.; Kemble, *Codex Dipl.* no. 65.
[47] *Chron. de Evesham* (Rolls Ser.), 94, 97.
[48] Cott. MS. Vesp. B. xxiv, fol. 10 d.; Harl. MS. 3763, fol. 60 d.
[49] *V.C.H. Worcs.* i, 308. [50] Ibid.
[51] Harl. MS. 3763, fol. 60 d.
[52] Ibid.; Cott. MS. Vesp. B. xxiv, fol. 10 d.; *V.C.H. Worcs.* i, 308.

thegns and two by a certain woman named Aelfgifu,[53] as in the Cotton MS. it is clearly stated that the church of Evesham held the manor in demesne after its acquisition by Æthelwig.[54]

In 1086 the manor of Sheriff's Lench was returned among the possessions of Odo, Bishop of Bayeux, then in the king's hands. Urse was still sub-tenant,[55] and the Evesham Chronicle states that he held it 'contra Rotulum Winton' in the time of Abbot Walter towards the end of the 11th century.[56] In spite of the title to the manor, which the monks of Evesham had made out at the time of the Survey, they seem never to have recovered it from Urse, though they must evidently have extorted some acknowledgement of seignorial rights, for Urse's successors the Beauchamps recognized the Abbots of Evesham as their overlords.[57] Though the manor was said to be held for the service of half a knight's fee, 'because it was in the hands of the mighty it does nothing for the abbot except homage, and the men of Lench do suit at Blakenhurst.'[58] The abbot's overlordship is mentioned for the last time in 1316, and afterwards, though it was known that the manor was not held of the king in chief, it could never be discovered who was the true overlord.[59]

EVESHAM ABBEY. *Azure a chain with its padlock set saltirewise between three mitres argent.*

From Urse the manor passed to the Beauchamps, the hereditary Sheriffs of Worcester, and thus doubtless acquired its name Sheriff's Lench. It passed with Elmley Castle in the Beauchamp family until about the middle of the 13th century, when William de Beauchamp gave to his brother James the manors of Sheriff's Lench and Church Lench and the advowson of the church, with the exception of the land which he had given to Bartholomew de Sudeley.[60] By an undated charter James de Beauchamp granted Sheriff's Lench to his nephew William Earl of Warwick and Maud his wife,[61] and the manor descended with Elmley Castle [62] until it was granted in tail-male by Thomas de Beauchamp Earl of Warwick to his younger son William, afterwards Lord Bergavenny.[63] It then passed with Chaddesley Corbett[63] (q.v.) and was

BEAUCHAMP. *Gules a fesse between six crosslets or.*

claimed with that manor by the co-heirs of Henry Duke of Warwick, and evidently assigned to Edward Earl of Warwick, who was attainted in 1499.[64] It was, however, like Chaddesley Corbett, granted by Anne Countess of Warwick to Henry VII in 1487–8.[65]

In July 1511 the manor was leased for forty years to George Throckmorton.[66] In November of the same year it was granted in fee to William Dineley of Charlton,[67] and this grant was confirmed in 1514, a rent of £5 a year being reserved to the Crown.[68]

From that time the manor followed the same descent as Charlton in Cropthorne (q.v.) to John Dineley.[69]

From deeds among the Prattinton Collection it appears that Sheriff's Lench was sold by a Mrs. Johnson towards the end of the 18th century to — Masefield, and that it afterwards passed to a Mr. Pulteney, who sold it to different owners, the greater part passing to a Mr. Stokes, who sold it to a Mr. Edwin, the owner in 1812. Half the manor was purchased about 1824 by the Rev. Dr. William Chafy, and the other half, including the old manor-house, now called the Manor Farm, and about 500 acres of land, was bought of Mr. Winnall in 1873 by the Rev. William K. W. Chafy, D.D., who now owns the whole.[70] The manor-house is now undergoing restoration, but contains nothing of interest except a well-preserved dog-gate at the foot of the stairs.

By an undated charter, probably about 1253, William de Beauchamp granted to Bartholomew de Sudeley in free marriage with his daughter Joan 10 virgates of land and a messuage in SHERIFF'S LENCH, with reversion to the donor in case Joan had no children.[71] The manor, which was held of the lords of Elmley Castle by the service of a pair of spurs,[72] then followed the same descent as Fairfield in Belbroughton [73] until 1496, when the lands of Ralph Lord Sudeley were divided between Edward Belknap and Sir John Norbury. Sheriff's Lench was assigned to the former.[74] It was perhaps this manor which as 'the manor of Shrewlinche parcel of Warwick and Spenser's land' was granted in 1560 to Sir Nicholas Throckmorton and his heirs.[75] Sir Nicholas left the manor in 1571 to his second son, Arthur Throckmorton,[76] and in 1596 he and his wife Anne were in possession of it,[77] but nothing further is known of the estate.

The sacrist of Evesham Abbey held an estate at Lench during the 13th century, and before 1206 had purchased of the commoners of Lench the right to assart certain common land there.[78] In 1206 he held 3½ hides of land at Lench.[79] In the Subsidy Roll of 1280 this estate is called 'Lenche Sacriste de

[53] *V.C.H. Worcs.* i, 308.
[54] Cott. MS. Vesp. B. xxiv, fol. 10 d.
[55] *V.C.H. Worcs.* i, 308.
[56] *Chron. de Evesham* (Rolls Ser.), 97.
[57] Harl. MS. 3763, fol. 168 d.; *Cal. Inq. p.m.* 1–9 Edw. II, 398.
[58] Harl. MS. 3763, fol. 168 d.
[59] Chan. Inq. p.m. 12 Hen. IV, no. 34; 17 Hen. VI, no. 54; 24 Hen. VI, no. 43.
[60] Add. MS. 28024, fol. 158 d. For Sudeley's manor see below.
[61] Add. MS. 28024, fol. 160.
[62] Harl. MS. 3763, fol. 168 d.; *Cal. Inq. p.m.* 1–9 Edw. II, 410.
[63] Chan. Inq. p.m. 12 Hen. IV, no. 34; 14 Hen. VI, no. 35.
[63a] Ibid. 17 Hen. VI, no. 54; 24 Hen. VI,

no. 43; Early Chan. Proc. bdle. 58, no. 156; bdle. 66, no. 376.
[64] Early Chan. Proc. bdle. 66, no. 376; Chan. Inq. p.m. (Ser. 2), lxxix, 170.
[65] Close, 3 Hen. VII, m. 11.
[66] *L. and P. Hen. VIII,* i, 1895.
[67] Ibid. 1959.
[68] Ibid. 5361.
[69] For references see Charlton. Arthur Throckmorton conveyed a rent of £5 from the manor of Sheriff's Lench (evidently the rent reserved by the Crown on the grant of the manor to William Dineley in 1514) to Francis Dineley (Feet of F. Worcs. Hil. 28 Eliz.). In 1588–9 the manor of Sheriff's Lench 'late in the tenure of William Dineley'

was granted by the queen to William Tipper and Robert Dawe (Pat. 31 Eliz. pt. v).
[70] Information by the Rev. W. K. W. Chafy, D.D.
[71] Add. MS. 28024, fol. 158.
[72] Chan. Inq. p.m. 10 Edw. III (1st nos.), no. 32; 2 Ric. III, no. 16; 13 Edw. IV, no. 58.
[73] Ibid.; Close, 13 Hen. VII, m. 10.
[74] Close, 13 Hen. VII, m. 10.
[75] Pat. 2 Eliz. pt. xii, m. 24.
[76] Chan. Inq. p.m. (Ser. 2), clvii, 104.
[77] Feet of F. Div. Co. East. 38 Eliz.
[78] *Chron. de Evesham* (Rolls Ser.), 212.
[79] Ibid. 211.

Evesham' and the Abbot of Evesham paid a subsidy of 22*s*. there.[80]

ATCH LENCH (Eccheslenc, viii cent.; Eacesleinc, Achelenz, xi cent.) was given to the abbey of Evesham by Kenred son of Wulfhere, King of Mercia, in 708,[81] and like Church Lench was afterwards alienated but recovered by Abbot Æthelwig II (1070–7).[82] It was held by the abbot and convent in demesne at the time of the Survey, its assessment being 4½ hides.[83]

Atch Lench was probably the Lench which was appropriated to the use of the pittancer of the abbey, to whom, it is stated in a survey of the abbey made in 1206, Prior Thomas had granted the wood in Atch Lench which he bought of Peter de Lens.[84] In the reign of Henry III William Meldrope held half a hide there by gift of Robert the Abbot.[85] Atch Lench remained in the possession of the abbey of Evesham until the dissolution of that house.[86]

On 15 August 1542 Henry VIII granted it to the Dean and Chapter of Westminster.[87] Queen Mary, who refounded the abbey, regranted it to the abbot and convent,[88] but on the accession of Elizabeth the abbey was again dissolved, and Atch Lench was once more in May 1560 granted to the dean and chapter.[89] It remained in their possession until the Commonwealth, when, their lands being sequestered, the manor of Atch Lench was in 1650 sold to Sir Cheyney Colepeper of Hollingbourne, Kent.[90] At the Restoration the manor was restored to the dean and chapter. Their estates were vested in the Ecclesiastical Commissioners about 1858,[91] and the manor of Atch Lench has since belonged to the Ecclesiastical Commissioners.[92] It has for many years been held under the Commissioners by members of the family of Bomford.[92a] Among the dean and chapter's documents at Westminster are court rolls of Atch Lench from 1666 to 1802.[93]

DEAN AND CHAPTER OF WESTMINSTER. *Azure a cross paty between five martlets or and a chief or with a pale of the arms of France and England between two roses gules.*

In the time of Bishop Werefrith (873–915) Ethelred the Earl gave to the church of Worcester Cleeve Prior with *LENCH*.[94] This was evidently the half-hide which was held by Godric under Fritheric, custodian of the church of St. Helen, Worcester, and was restored to the monks in the 12th century by Fritheric because it justly belonged to them.[95] This half-hide at Lench was still held with Cleeve in 1086 by the monks of Worcester,[96] and continued to be so held until 1253,[97] when it is mentioned for the last time.

The church of *ALL SAINTS* consists *CHURCH* of a chancel 27 ft. by 15 ft. 6 in., with a modern north organ chamber and vestry, a nave 45 ft. by 16 ft. 6 in., a south aisle 9 ft. wide, a western tower about 8 ft. square, and a south porch, all measurements being internal.

In the 12th century the church consisted of a nave and a short chancel, but rebuilding has destroyed almost all traces of its early history. A south transept was added at some date previous to the 15th century, in the early part of which the south aisle was built to line with the transept end, the 12th-century south door being reset in the later wall. Subsequent 15th-century alterations included the rebuilding of the chancel arch, the addition of the nave clearstory with the insertion of a large window in the north wall, and probably the erection of the lower part of the tower, the latter being completed in the 16th century. In modern times the chancel and the parapet of the tower have been rebuilt and the organ chamber and vestry added.

All the windows of the chancel are modern, in 14th and 15th-century style, though a few old stones have been used up in their jambs. The chancel arch has a slightly blunted two-centred head of two chamfered orders. A projecting block of masonry in the north wall of the nave contains the rood-stair, and west of this is a single-light window with a modern head. Half-way along the north wall is a large 15th-century window of three lights with rectilinear tracery under a four-centred head, and further west is the original 12th-century north door. The lower part is now blocked up, and the round head forms a lunette window in which are inserted some fragments of 15th-century glass. The wall of the clearstory above, being somewhat thinner, is set back externally, and contains two 15th-century windows of two lights each, with quatrefoils under the four-centred heads. The south wall of the nave is pierced with an arcade of three bays, the first arch, of wider span, being the original entrance to the transept. It is four-centred, with two chamfered orders, and dates from the middle of the 15th century. In its eastern respond is the canopy of an elaborate 15th-century image niche with a foliated finial, embattled cornice and cusped panels to the soffit. The two western bays of the arcade are of early 15th-century date, with pointed arches of two continuous chamfered orders stopped with a single broach stop. The low, late 15th-century opening to the tower has plain square jambs and a four-centred head, and to the south of it is a door leading to an open wooden belfry stair.

The three-light east window of the south aisle is of late 14th-century date, with flowing tracery and a four-centred head. To the south of it is a moulded image bracket of slightly later date. The three 15th-century windows in the south wall are all square-headed, the westernmost having two lights and the others one only. The west window, of the same date, has been considerably restored. The 12th-century south door was reset at the building of the south aisle, and the round head is now the only unrestored portion.

The south porch and the font are both modern.

[80] *Lay Subs. R. Worcs.* 1280 (Worcs. Hist. Soc.), 86.
[81] *Chron. de Evesham* (Rolls Ser.), 72; Harl. MS. 3763, fol. 59.
[82] *Chron. de Evesham* (Rolls Ser.), 94.
[83] *V.C.H. Worcs.* i, 307*b*.
[84] *Chron. de Evesham* (Rolls Ser.), 214.
[85] Harl. MS. 3763, fol. 61 d.

[86] *Valor Eccl.* (Rec. Com.), iii, 250.
[87] *L. and P. Hen. VIII*, xvii, g. 714 (5).
[88] Pat. 3 & 4 Phil. and Mary, pt. v.
[89] Ibid. 2 Eliz. pt. xi.
[90] Close, 1651, pt. lvi, no. 19; 1654, pt. xi, no. 13.
[91] *Lond. Gaz.* 2 Aug. 1858, p. 3610.
[92] Information from Ecclesiastical Commissioners.

[92a] Information from Dr. Chafy.
[93] Doc. at Westminster, Press 10, shelf 4.
[94] Heming, *Chartul.* (ed. Hearne), 516.
[95] Ibid. 428.
[96] *V.C.H. Worcs.* i, 297*a*.
[97] Ibid. 326*a*; Hale, *Reg. of Worc. Priory* (Camden Soc.), 80*a*, 155*a*.

The tower, three stages high, with angle buttresses, has a single-light transomed west window of 16th-century date, and similar lights to the two upper stages, all with square heads. The embattled parapet and pinnacles are modern.

Preserved in a glass case in the nave are the remains of an early 16th-century cope made into a desk cloth. The material is blue velvet embroidered with a floral pattern. The orphrey of the cope has been cut in half and sewed on as a border to both edges. It has six figures of saints under canopies on a gold ground.[98] After a precarious existence of many years the cope came under the custody of Dr. W. K. W. Chafy, who exhibited it to the Society of Antiquaries at Burlington House, when they reported on it. Dr. Chafy handed it to the then rector, and had the case made for it and the particulars attached.

The tower contains six bells, the treble, second,

points to the existence of a church there at that date.

The advowson belonged to the Abbots of Evesham, and was claimed by them in 1208.[99] It must shortly afterwards have passed into the hands of the Beauchamps, for William Beauchamp was patron in 1261 when the Bishop of Worcester assigned to the nunnery of Cookhill the great tithes of Church Lench. A vicarage was then ordained,[100] the ordination being confirmed by Bishop Giffard in 1279, when the vicar's portion was assigned and a piece of land upon which to erect tithe barns granted to the nuns.[1] Though the rectorial tithes were thus granted to Cookhill Nunnery, the advowson remained with the Beauchamps, descending with the manor of Sheriff's Lench.[2] On the attainder of Edward Earl of Warwick in 1499 it passed to the Crown, in which it remained until 7 November 1865, when

ALL SAINTS, CHURCH LENCH : NAVE AND TOWER FROM THE NORTH-EAST

third, fourth and sixth of which were cast by Taylor of Loughborough in 1869 and 1870. The fifth is dated 1600 and bears the inscription 'give thanke to God' and the churchwardens' names.

The church plate is modern and consists of a silver cup and paten with a silver-mounted glass flagon.

The registers before 1812 are as follows : (i) baptisms 1692 to 1754, burials and marriages 1702 to 1754 ; (ii) baptisms and burials 1755 to 1812 ; (iii) marriages 1755 to 1812.

ADVOWSON   A priest at Church Lench is mentioned in 1086, and the fact that it then bore its distinguishing prefix

the patronage was transferred to the Bishop of Worcester.[3]

The tithes of Church Lench which had been granted to the nuns of Cookhill remained in their possession until the Dissolution.[4]

The messuage and lands in Church Lench held by the nunnery were granted on 1 July 1542 to Nicholas Fortescue[5] and confirmed to John Fortescue in 1663–4[6] ; their tithes of grain and hay in Church Lench and Atch Lench, in the tenure of William Milner, were granted in November 1561 to the Bishop of Worcester and his successors in part compensation for manors retained by Queen Elizabeth.[7]

[98] It is fully described in *Proc. Soc. of Antiq.* (Ser. 2), xix (2), 189.
[99] *Chron. de Evesham* (Rolls Ser.), 229.
[100] Nash, op. cit. ii, 15.   [1] Ibid.
[2] *Reg. G. Giffard* (Worcs. Hist. Soc.), 368 ; *Sede Vacante Reg.* (Worcs. Hist.

Soc.), 205 ; Add. MS. 28024, fol. 158 d., 160 ; *Cal. Inq. p.m.* 1–9 *Edw. II*, 410 ; Exch. K.R. Misc. Bks. xxii, fol. 1 ; Chan. Inq. p.m. (Ser. 2), lxxix, 170.
[3] Inst. Bks. (P.R.O.) ; *Lond. Gaz.* 7 Nov. 1865, p. 5189.

[4] *Pope Nich. Tax.* (Rec. Com.), 217, 239 ; *Valor Eccl.* (Rec. Com.), iii, 262, 263.
[5] Pat. 34 Hen. VIII, pt. i.
[6] Ibid. 15 Chas. II, pt. ix.
[7] Ibid. 4 Eliz. pt. vi.

William Roculf by his will provided for the establishment of a chantry, to which a chaplain was admitted in 1269.[8] The church in which the foundation took place is not stated, but the name Roculf suggests that it may have been at Church Lench.

On 26 May 1574 a chapel in Sheriff's Lench, formerly belonging to Evesham Monastery, was granted to John and William Mersh.[9]

At Atch Lench is a Baptist chapel, dating from 1825.

CHARITIES

In 1886 the Rev. Martin Amphlett, by his will proved at Worcester 9 October, bequeathed £198 10s. 2d. consols, the annual dividends, amounting to £4 19s., to be applied towards maintaining and keeping the churchyard in good order. The stock is held by the official trustees.

CLENT [1]

Clent is a hilly parish containing besides the village of Clent the hamlets of Upper Clent, where is situated the church, Lower Clent, Adam's Hill, Holy Cross and Rumbold, divided from the rest of the parish by Walton Hills, of which Holy Cross is the most populous. Although surveyed in Worcestershire in Domesday Book the parish was soon afterwards annexed to Staffordshire, evidently owing to the fact that it paid the farm it rendered to the king, through the manor of Kingswinford in that county. It remained part of Staffordshire until 1832, when it was again annexed to Worcestershire for Parliamentary purposes.[2] In 1844 it became part of Worcestershire for all purposes.[3] The soil is gravel, marl and clay and the subsoil clay and stone. Agriculture is the only industry, the chief crops being wheat, oats and potatoes, which latter have largely supplanted the barley which used to be grown. In the 16th and 17th centuries the chief trade was scythe-making, which was followed by nail-making,[4] and this in its turn died out late in the 19th century. The parish covers an area of 2,424 acres, which includes 755½ acres of arable land, 911½ of grass land, 81 acres of woods and plantations[5] and 7 acres covered by water, the last being made up by several ponds, two of which work mills.

The whole of the eastern part of the parish is on the Clent Hills, which at some points attain to a height of over 1,000 ft. above the ordnance datum and afford wide and beautiful views. The hills are rounded in outline and covered with grass and gorse. On these hills the Britons are said to have encamped before a battle thought to have been fought on Clent Heath. The tradition is supported by the fact that five tumuli formerly existed on the heath and were opened by Bishop Lyttelton, who attributed them to the Romans. In all of them he found the remains of human bones and burnt wood, and one contained an urn filled with bones.[6] There is a description of the Clent Hills and the country to be seen from them in Drayton's *Polyolbion*.[7] The origin of four upright stones on the summit of the Hills was the subject of some discussion in 1865 and again in 1883. The statement that they were placed there

by George first Lord Lyttelton is the correct one, but his successor Lord Lyttelton claimed for them a much earlier origin and they are sometimes said to be Druidical remains.[8]

According to tradition the Kings of Mercia had at one time a residence in Clent and the parish was the scene of the murder of St. Kenelm. The legend states that on the death of Kenulf, King of Mercia, in 819 his son Kenelm, then a child of eight, became king. His sister Quendreda wishing to be queen persuaded her lover Ascobert to take the child into the woods and kill him and bury him under a thorn tree. The body was miraculously discovered by the appearance of a dove at Rome bearing a scroll on which were the words

'In Clentho vaccae valli Kenelmus regius natus,
    Jacet sub spino, capite truncatus.'

Thereupon messengers were sent to England to remove the body to Winchcombe Abbey and in the place where it was found 'a sacred fountain[9] burst out from the dry cave and flowed away in a stream, which brought health to many who drank it.'[10]

The chief road in the parish is from Stourbridge through Lower Clent and Holy Cross to Bromsgrove, but the main road from Birmingham to Kidderminster bounds and passes through a small portion of the western extremity of the parish. At Holy Cross the Stourbridge road is intersected by a road from Birmingham which passes through the village of Clent. Clent House stands back on the east side of the Bromsgrove and Stourbridge road to the west of the church. The older portion of the building dates from the early 18th century, but the main structure was not erected till later in the same century. The materials of both portions are red brick and stone. The present owner is Mr. John Amphlett.

In 1788[11] the common of Lower Clent was inclosed and certain roads appointed.[12]

A common called Calcot Hill is mentioned in a survey taken in 1553 as containing 100 acres and being able to keep 400 sheep.[13] The owners of certain land in Clent still have rights of common on the Clent and Walton Hills.

---

[8] *Reg. G. Giffard* (Worcs. Hist. Soc.), 34.
[9] Pat. 16 Eliz. pt. xii.
[1] The spelling of the name has remained the same from the time of the Conquest.
[2] Stat. 2 & 3 Will. IV, cap. 64.
[3] Ibid. 7 & 8 Vict. cap. 61.
[4] Harris, *Clentine Rambles*.
[5] Statistics from Bd. of Agric. (1905).
[6] Lyttelton MSS. (Soc. Antiq.), fol. 2.
[7] Song xiv.

[8] *N. and Q.* (Ser. 3), vii, 323, 365, 389, 507 ; viii, 18 ; (Ser. 6), viii, 247, 349.
[9] The well is on the boundary between this parish and Romsley.
[10] The legend, taken from Bodl. MS. Douce 368, fol. 79–82b, is printed in full in Amphlett, *Short Hist. of Clent*, App. A. See also Matt. Paris, *Chron. Maj.* (Rolls Ser.), i, 372–3. The date of Kenulf's death is given as it appears in the *Anglo-*

Sax. Chron. (Rolls Ser.) ii, 52. The outline of this story can be traced back to Florence of Worcester (fl. 1118). Its origin has not yet been satisfactorily explained, and the introduction of Clent into the tale is remarkable.
[11] *Blue Bk. Incl. Awards*, 189.
[12] Prattinton, quoting the Worc. Journ. 7 Sept. 1788, gives full details as to these roads.
[13] Lyttelton MSS. (Soc. Antiq.), fol. 79.

MANORS

Heming, the Worcester chronicler, states, on the testimony of Bishop Wulfstan, that the manor of *CLENT* with Tardebigge and Kingswinford was purchased from King Ethelred by Æthelsige (Ægelsinus), Dean of Worcester, for the use of his monastery, but that when he died during the war between Edmund Ironside and Cnut, Ævic Sheriff of Staffordshire, 'because there was no one who would do justice to the Holy Church,' seized them from the monastery,[14] probably for the use of the king. Clent was still a royal possession at the time of the Domesday Survey, when the farm of £4 yearly was paid at the manor of Kingswinford, in Staffordshire.[15] Its name occurs regularly on the early Pipe Rolls of Staffordshire[16] as part of the king's demesnes, 1 mark being rendered from it, and in 1193 it was among the places from which the annuity of £22 6s. 8d. granted to Emma wife of David King of North Wales was to be paid.[17] In 1204 King John granted it to Ralph de Somery to be held by a rent of £4 13s. 4d., paid by the hands of the Sheriff of Staffordshire.[18] Roger de Somery, who was probably the son of this Ralph, obtained a grant of a fair at Clent in 1253.[19] In the 13th century the Somerys held the manors of Clent and Mere, co. Staffs., by rendering yearly 40 marks, and had in Clent free warren and tallage when the king tallaged his manors, and owed suit at two general hundreds.[20]

Since that date the manor followed the same descent as that of Northfield[21] (q.v.) until about 1431, when the possessions of Joyce wife of Sir Hugh Burnell were divided between Joan Lady Beauchamp and Maurice Berkeley.[22] Clent was assigned to Lady Beauchamp,[23] and passed to her grandson James Butler, created Earl of Wiltshire in 1449.[24] On his attainder in 1461[25] Clent passed into the hands of the king, and was granted in 1462 to Fulk Stafford,[26] but on his death without issue male in the following year two thirds of the manor and the reversion of one third after the death of Margaret widow of Fulk Stafford were granted to Sir Walter Wrottesley.[27] The whole manor was confirmed in tail-male to Sir Walter in 1466.[28] He died in 1473,[29] and though he left a son Richard the manor was granted in 1474 to Humphrey Stafford of Grafton and his heirs male.[30] Humphrey Stafford was executed for treason soon after the accession of Henry VII,[31] and in 1485 the Earl of Wiltshire's attainder was reversed in favour of his brother Thomas Earl of Ormond,[32] Clent with the earl's other property being granted to him.[33] Clent

has since followed the same descent as Hagley,[34] the present owner of the manor being Charles George Viscount Cobham.

The rent reserved to the Crown, when the manor was given to Ralph de Somery, was granted in 1351 to Hugh de Wrottesley for life only, the grant being confirmed in 1378-9,[35] and in 1442 to William Burley for life.[36] It remained with the Crown for more than 200 years, being sold by the Parliamentary Commissioners to Christopher Howling in 1649,[37] but returning to the Crown at the Restoration. Under the Act of 1670 for the sale of fee-farm rents,[38] that of Clent appears to have been sold to the Pagets of Beaudesert, afterwards Earls of Uxbridge,[39] and in that family it remained until 1769, when Henry Paget second Earl of Uxbridge died childless.[40] He apparently left it to his kinsman Sir William Irby, created Lord Boston in 1761,[41] to whom it was paid in the time of Bishop Lyttelton.[42] Towards the end of the 19th century it was purchased from Lord Boston by Lord Lyttelton.[43]

IRBY, Lord Boston. *Argent fretty sable a quarter gules with a chaplet or therein.*

In the reign of Henry VIII the inhabitants of Clent petitioned for a confirmation of their rights as dwelling on ancient demesne of the Crown and obtained a charter in 1566, which was confirmed in 1625.[44]

The charter was granted to the inhabitants of Clent *alias* 'Chenett' through a curious mistake which arose from the transfer of the manor from Worcestershire to Staffordshire. When search was made for Clent in Domesday Book, the fact that it had originally been in Worcestershire was overlooked, and it was identified with Chenet in Staffordshire, the only place in that county to which its name bore any resemblance.[45] By the charter the inhabitants were exempted from the payment of toll, stallage, passage, pontage, &c., from contributing to the expenses of sending knights to Parliament, and from serving on any juries except those in their own parish.

The four days' fair at the feast of St. Kenelm (17 July), granted in 1253 to Roger Somery as lord of Clent,[46] was always held in St. Kenelm's Chapel Yard just within Romsley,[47] and was continued until the middle of the 19th century.[48] In the middle of

14 Heming, *Chartul.* (ed. Hearne), i, 276; *V.C.H. Worcs.* i, 238-9.
15 *V.C.H. Worcs.* i, 287.
16 *Pipe R.* 15 *Hen. II* (Pipe R. Soc.), 71; 19 *Hen. II*, 61; 23 *Hen. II*, 26; *Pipe R.* 23 Hen. II, m. 8 d., 11 d.; 5 Ric. I, m. 6 d.
17 *Pipe R.* 5 Ric. I, m. 6 d.
18 *Chart. R.* 6 John, m. 11, no. 1; Cart. Antiq. (P.R.O.), G. 12.
19 *Chart. R.* 37 & 38 Hen. III, pt. i, m. 15. This charter is not given in the printed calendar of Charter Rolls.
20 *Cal. Inq. p.m.* 1-19 *Edw. I*, 14; *Will. Salt Arch. Soc. Coll.* v (1), 116-17.
21 *Cal. Chart. R.* 1226-57, p. 97; *Feud. Aids*, v, 9, and see Northfield.
22 See Northfield.
23 Early Chan. Proc. bdle. 19, no. 6.
24 G.E.C. *Complete Peerage*, viii, 165.
25 Chan. Inq. p.m. 3 Edw. IV, no. 12.

26 *Cal. Pat.* 1461-7, p. 112.
27 Ibid. p. 217. See also p. 297.
28 Ibid. 485.
29 Chan. Inq. p.m. 13 Edw. IV, no. 23.
30 *Cal. Pat.* 1467-77, p. 470.
31 *Dict. Nat. Biog.*
32 G.E.C. *Complete Peerage*, vi, 142; *Parl. R.*, vi, 296a.
33 *Parl. R.* vi, 554a.
34 Chan. Inq. p.m. (Ser.2),lv, 2; Recov. R. Hil. 10 Eliz. rot. 157; Trin. 28 Eliz. rot. 64; Chan. Inq. p.m. (Ser. 2), cclvii, 71; Feet of F. Staffs. Trin. 6 Anne; Recov. R. Mich. 25 Geo. III, rot. 416.
35 *Cal. Pat.* 1377-81, p. 105. In 1313 the king exempted John de Somery from the payment of this farm for life on account of his good service in Scotland; ibid. 1307-13, p. 564.
36 Ibid. 1441-6, p. 73.
37 Lyttelton MSS. (Soc. Antiq.), fol. 68.

38 Stat. 22 Chas. II, cap. 6; Palmer's Indices, lxxiii, fol. 82a.
39 Lyttelton MSS. (Soc. Antiq.), fol. 68.
40 G.E.C. *Complete Peerage*, viii, 12.
41 Ibid. i, 380.
42 Lyttelton MSS. (Soc. Antiq.), fol. 68.
43 Amphlett, op. cit. 152.
44 Ibid. 126-9, quoting the charter, a copy of which is in the possession of one of the inhabitants of Clent.
45 Ibid.; Lyttelton MSS. (Soc. Antiq.), fol. 68.
46 *Cal. Pat.* 1247-58, p. 253.
47 Lyttelton MSS. (Soc. Antiq.), fol. 68.
48 Amphlett, op. cit. 26-7. Shaw, writing in 1801, says that at the wake called Kenelm's Wake or Crab Wake the custom prevailed among the inhabitants of pelting each other and the parson with crabs (Shaw, *Hist. of Staffs.* ii, 243; *Gent. Mag.* lxvii, 738).

the 18th century fairs were also held by prescriptive right at Holy Cross on the second Wednesday in April and the first Wednesday in September.[49] In 1868 Clent had a cattle and cheese fair 'at which the inhabitants are allowed by an old charter to sell beer without licence,'[50] but this fair with those at Holy Cross has been discontinued.

Besides the Domesday manor of Clent there is in the parish a manor known as *CHURCH CLENT* or *KINGS HOLT*. There was a court baron, but as regards view of frankpledge it was always under the jurisdiction of the lords of the ancient manor.[51] At the time of the dissolution of the monasteries this manor belonged to the abbey of Halesowen.[52]

CLENT CHURCH : THE CHANCEL

Charles I in 1633 gave this estate, with a tenement called Calcot Hill, to William Scrivener and Philip Eden.[53] They appear to have sold it to a Mr. Norrice, from whom it was purchased in 1660[54] by John Underhill, whose father John Underhill and grandfather William Underhill had lived at Calcot Hill House.[55] It passed successively from the Underhills to Dr. Samuel Barton, Sarah French, John Wowen[56] and Jane his wife and three maiden ladies, Jane, Ann and

Matilda Manning.[57] Before 1799 Ann Manning's share had been sold to John Hollington, whose descendant William Hollington purchased the other two thirds about 1878.[58] The Calcot Hill estate, 198 acres in extent, together with the manor of Church Clent, in which are contained other lands in the parish, mostly glebe,[59] was sold by Mr. Hollington in 1893 to Thomas Jarvis Hodgetts for £4,200.[60]

Bishop Lyttelton gives a list of some of the customs of the manor of Church Clent in the 16th century from a manuscript formerly in the possession of a Mr. Tyrer, steward of the court.[61]

At the time when Nash wrote his *History of Worcester* (c. 1782) the manor comprised only three cottages and four farm-houses, of which Calcot Hill Farm was the largest.[62]

The church of *ST. LEONARD* consists of a chancel 23 ft. by 15 ft., with an organ chamber on the north, a nave 46 ft. by 15 ft., north and south aisles, the latter 12 ft. wide, a west tower 11 ft. by 10½ ft., the ground floor of which is used as a vestry, and a south porch. These measurements are all internal.

The 12th-century church probably consisted of a chancel and nave only, to which a south aisle was added about 1170. There is no evidence of further structural alterations until early in the 15th century, when the tower was built and the south aisle widened, the chancel being reconstructed about 1440. The north aisle was added in 1837, but this, together with the nave, was rebuilt during the years 1864–5. The organ chamber and porch were erected at the same time.

The chancel axis inclines to the south. In the east wall is an original traceried window of five lights, with a segmental-pointed head ribbed on the inside and ornamented at the apex with a small carved angel holding what appears to be a paten. The external hood is finished with a finial. In the west end of the north wall a modern arch opens into the organ chamber. The chancel is lit from the south by two square-headed two-light windows, the inner jambs of which are splayed below, but shouldered at the head. Under the sill of the easternmost is an ogee-headed piscina. The basin appears to have been quatrefoiled, but has been broken off flush with the wall face. Between the windows is a very flat ogee-headed doorway of the same date as the chancel, the external label of which returns on itself. Cut on the eastern inner jamb is a black-letter inscription

[49] Nash, *Hist. of Worc.* ii, App. 14.
[50] Harris, op. cit.
[51] Information by Mr. John Amphlett.
[52] Pat. 9 Chas. I, pt. viii, no. 4.
[53] Ibid.
[54] This date is given as 1676 in *A Short History of Clent.*
[55] Exch. Dep. by Com. Mich. 30 Chas. II, no. 7 ; Hil. 30 & 31 Chas. II, no. 1. The lord of the manor held a court there at this date.
[56] John Wowen was holding the manor in 1765 (Feet of F. Staffs. Hil. 5 Geo. III).
[57] Amphlett, op. cit. 163. See also

Shaw, *Hist. of Staffs.* ii, 241 ; Lyttelton MSS. (Soc. Antiq.).
[58] Feet of F. Staffs. Mich. 45 Geo. III.
[59] Inform. by Mr. John Amphlett.
[60] Ibid.
[61] Lyttelton MSS. (Soc. Antiq.), fol. 78.
[62] Nash, op. cit. App. xv.

reading, 'Juxta hunc lapidem jacet corpus johannis cleye.' In the opposite jamb is a large groove cut to receive a wooden bar. The chancel arch, of three chamfered orders, is 15th-century work. The chancel walls are built of sandstone with a moulded plinth, stepped to the fall of the ground from east to west, and diagonal buttresses at the east end. The coping of the eastern gable is finished, at the apex, with a crocketed pinnacle and with carved grotesques at the eaves.

The nave arcades are in three bays. That on the north is entirely modern, but portions of 12th-century masonry have been retained in the southern. The pointed arches of two square orders rest on circular piers with scalloped capitals and moulded bases raised on square plinths. Parts of the capitals of both piers are old, and a few stones in the piers and arches appear to have been re-used. The west respond, with the exception of the abacus, is original 12th-century work. The two-light east window in the south aisle is contemporary with the widening, but the tracery and mullions have been restored. At the east end of the south wall is a small piscina, with a pointed head and broken bowl, and in the same wall are two 15th-century windows of two lights each. The pointed south door between them has been much restored, and the south porch is modern. Externally the walls of this aisle have a double chamfered plinth, with a diagonal buttress at the south-west angle and a second in a line with the east wall.

The tower, divided into three stages by moulded strings, has an embattled parapet and a moulded plinth, with diagonal buttresses at the angles. In the south-west corner is a small vice. The tower arch is pointed and of two orders, the outer continuous but the inner interrupted by a moulded cap. The south wall is pierced by a modern doorway, but the three-light traceried west window is original. The ringing stage is lit from the north and south by a single square-headed light, and in each wall of the bell-chamber is a two-light pointed opening of the early 15th century. Projecting from each face of the tower below the parapet is a much-weathered gargoyle, carved in the form of a grotesque beast. The nave roofs are modern, but that over the chancel is of early 15th-century date and of the trussed rafter type. Each pair of rafters is trussed by a collar and two curved braces, which spring from the moulded wall-plates and form a series of semicircular arches.

There is a peal of eight bells, two of which were added in 1902 by Taylor of Loughborough. The old bells are inscribed as follows : (1) 'Mr John Waldron de Field, Mr Wm Cole, Zeph Creswell 1718'; (2) 'Cantate Domino Canticum Novum. 1681'; (3) 'Henricus Bagley mee fecit 1681'; (4) 'Henry Bagley made me 1681'; (5) 'Henry Bagley made me 1681'; (6) 'John Perry vicar, John Cresswell John Waldron Churchwardens, John Amphlett Esquire' and on the lip of the bell 'John Gopp,

Abraham Hill, Richard Wight, Joseph Waldron, Thomas Waldron, Richard Hill. Richard Bagley made mee 1743.'

The plate consists of a mid-16th-century silver cup unstamped, a silver salver of 1693 inscribed 'Donum Mariae Amphlett Ecclesiae Clent 1750,' a modern silver flagon of 1907, an electro-plated paten and an electro-plated flagon.

The registers previous to 1813 are as follows : (i) all entries 1562 to 1619, also for year 1626 ; (ii) baptisms 1637 to 1642, marriages and burials 1637 to 1641, also all 1654 to 1729 ; (iii) baptisms 1729 to 1775 (no entries for 1738), also for year 1782, marriages 1729 to 1754, burials 1729 to 1757, for the year 1768, 1774 to 1776 and 1780 to 1782 ; (iv) baptisms and burials 1783 to 1812 ; (v) marriages 1754 to 1787 ; (vi) marriages 1787 to 1798 ; (vii) marriages 1798 to 1812. The earlier books have been handsomely bound.

ADVOWSON The advowson of Clent followed the descent of the manor,[63] until John Botetourt granted it in 1340 to the abbey of Halesowen,[64] his gift being confirmed in 1340 and 1393.[65] The rectory was appropriated to Halesowen Abbey in 1343–4 and a vicarage was ordained in 1344.[66] In 1291 the church with the chapel of Rowley, which was annexed to Clent until 1841,[67] was said to be worth £18 13s. 4d.[68] The advowson was granted with the rectory in 1538 to Sir John Dudley,[69] and on his attainder in 1553 it fell to the Crown, to which it has since belonged.[70] In 1558 the advowson and rectory were temporarily granted to the Bishop of Worcester.[71] The rectory was granted in 1609 to Francis Phillips and Richard Moore,[72] and thus became separated from the advowson. Before 1726 it had been bought by Joseph Amphlett of Clent,[73] and the great tithes have since remained in his family, being now in the possession of Mr. John Amphlett of Clent House.[74]

CHARITIES The Church Lands, which were originally derived from a surrender in 1616 by Humphrey Penn at a court baron, now consist of four cottages with gardens producing £13 a year and a sum of £2,815 4s. 6d. consols with the official trustees, arising from sales of land from time to time. The dividends, amounting to £70 7s. 4d. yearly, together with the rents, are carried to the churchwardens' account to maintain the services and fabric of the church.

In 1654 Hester Cordiwen at a court baron surrendered 4 a. 2 r. for some charitable purposes. The trust property was sold in 1902 and proceeds invested in £228 1s. 8d. consols, producing £5 14s. yearly, which is applied under a scheme of the Charity Commissioners 26 March 1897 for the benefit of the poor.

In 1712 John Maris by his will devised several parcels of land in Clent for the poor not in receipt of parochial relief, and in 1713 William Cole by his will devised other lands for the same purpose. In

[63] *Reg. G. Giffard* (Worcs. Hist. Soc.), 193 ; *Will. Salt Arch. Soc. Coll.* iii (1), 39 ; *Cal. Pat.* 1272–81, pp. 53, 184 ; 1330–4, p. 321.
[64] *Cal. Pat.* 1338–40, p. 443.
[65] Ibid. ; 1391–6, p. 249.
[66] Worc. Epis. Reg. Braunsford (1339–

49), fol. 59 d., 83 ; Nash, op. cit. App. xi.
[67] *Feud. Aids,* v, 312 ; *Pope Nich. Tax.* (Rec. Com.), 217 ; Priv. Act, 4 & 5 Vict. cap. 24. The actual separation did not take place until 1848. *Parl. Papers* (1872), xlvi, 18 d.

[68] *Pope Nich. Tax.* (Rec. Com.), 217.
[69] *L. and P. Hen. VIII,* xiii (2), g. 491 (1). [70] Inst. Bks. P.R.O.
[71] Pat. 5 & 6 Phil. and Mary, pt. ii, m. 30. [72] Ibid. 7 Jas. I, pt. ix, no. 12.
[73] Priv. Act, 13 Geo. I, cap. 21.
[74] Information by Mr. John Amphlett.

1903 a piece of land known as Sandfield containing 2 a. 2 r. 31 p. was sold and the proceeds invested in £1,192 8s. 3d. consols, leaving 11 a. 2 r. belonging to the charity, producing about £32 a year. This rent and the annual dividends, amounting to £29 16s., are applied in the distribution of doles.

In 1843 John Harris, by his will proved in the P.C.C. 26 August, bequeathed a legacy now represented by £501 18s. 7d. consols, the annual dividends, amounting to £12 10s. 8d., to be applied in winter in good warm clothing. In 1908–9 300 yards of flannel were distributed.

In 1865 Miss Susanna Goodman, by her will proved at Worcester 28 March, bequeathed £100, now represented by £110 17s. 7d. consols, the annual dividends, amounting to £2 15s. 4d., to be distributed on 4 April among poor widows and old men over sixty years of age, in sums of not less than 2s. 6d. each.

At the inclosure of Lower Clent Common in 1788 a sum of £15 was charged by the award on one of the fields formed out of it, to go in ease of the poor rates of persons who did not benefit by the inclosure, those persons to whom lands were allotted being excepted, and also tenants of the manor of Church Clent. The field in question having come into the possession of Lord Cobham, the charge was redeemed by him in 1909 by the transfer to the official trustees of £600 consols.

Educational Charities :

In 1704 John Amphlett by deed gave the site and school building thereon for the use of the parish, and endowed the same with a rent-charge of £8.

In 1797 Thomas Waldron bequeathed £500, the income to be applied in maintaining a Sunday school and for other purposes. The legacy is now represented by £732 12s. consols, producing £18 6s. 8d. yearly.

COSTON or COFTON HACKETT

Coftun (x cent.) ; Costone (xi cent.).

Coston Hackett, a small and hilly parish, covers an area of 1,299 acres, which includes 224 acres of arable land, 766 acres of pasture and 90 acres of woods and plantations.[1] In 1911 a small part of King's Norton was added to this parish. Bilberry Hill (800 ft.) and Coston Hill (800 ft.), part of the Lickey Hills, bound Coston Hackett on the west. The former evidently derived its name from the bilberry, which gave its name also to 'Bilberry wake,' held on the three Sundays following Midsummer.

The chief road is a branch from the main road between Birmingham and Bromsgrove, which enters the parish near Rednal and passes south through Kendal End to Alvechurch. From this road there are two branches, Groveley Lane, which cuts through the parish in a north-easterly direction and joins the main road from Birmingham to Evesham, and another which passes through the village of Coston Hackett to Coston Richard Farm.

The village of Coston Hackett is situated about 9 miles south-west of Birmingham on the eastern slopes of the Lickey Hills. The village is small and scattered. It presents no features of interest, with the exception of Coston Hall, formerly the manor-house of the Leicesters and Jolliffes, in which Charles I is said to have spent the night after Hawkesley House was taken 14 May 1645.[1a] Though otherwise completely modernized it still retains its original late 14th-century hall. On the north-west of the hall, parallel and of equal length with it, is an L-shaped block of buildings, which appears to be part of the original house. This is now occupied by the kitchen and offices, and has been so completely altered internally, and re-faced externally with stone in the quasi-Gothic taste of the early 19th century, that all trace of the original arrangement has been obliterated. The material of this portion of the house is probably half-timber, though concealed by modern casings of stone and brick. On the north-east side of the hall an early 19th-century house, three stories high, has replaced the original buildings, some of the cellars of which remain, though no work here appears to be

earlier than the end of the 16th century. The hall, recently restored, measures about 38 ft. by 21 ft. The roof is a splendid specimen of mediaeval carpentry. There are nine hammer-beam trusses, two of which are good copies of the 18th century, the hall, as originally constructed, being of six bays only. The hammer-beams are strutted from each main upright by solid moulded braces resting upon octagonal corbels of wood, beneath each of which is a shield-shaped block of the same material. Immediately below this level a deep and elaborately moulded wooden cornice runs round the walls of the hall ; a cornice of equal elaboration marks the wall-plates. At about one-third the height of the roof are moulded and cambered collars, strutted from the hammer-beams by curved braces, forming depressed four-centred arches, having at their centres carved pentagonal bosses. The spandrels between the collars and the ridge are occupied by slender wooden uprights. Each slope of the roof is divided into three compartments by two heavily-moulded purlins. The framing of the original louvre opening still survives between the fourth and fifth trusses from the east. Upon the corbels are shields with the following charges : an eagle displayed ; party-palewise indented ; a bend cotised ; a cheveron ; the bend cotised quartering and impaling the cheveron ; and a cheveron between three lilies. The lower part of the walls has been recently panelled, and at the south-east is a modern fireplace. All the windows are modern. Externally no original detail remains.

The Upper Bittell reservoir, a feeder of the Worcester and Birmingham Canal, is partly in Coston parish, and there is also a smaller reservoir which lies to the east of Bilberry Hill and from which the water is conveyed by the little River Arrow to the Lower Bittell reservoir in Alvechurch parish.

The soil is marl and the subsoil gravel, sand and clay. There is a small quarry where Wenlock limestone was worked at the time of the making of the Worcester and Birmingham Canal, and there are some gravel-pits. The population is entirely agricultural, the chief crops raised being wheat, barley and beans.

[1] Statistics from Bd. of Agric. (1905).

[1a] *Symonds' Diary* (Camden Soc.), 167.

There are also large orchards of apples and pears. The inclosure award for the parish is dated 1 June 1831.[2]

A pasture called Erneys *alias* Ernest occurs among the place-names.[3] There also may be mentioned The Lady Field, Moat Close and The Spiights.[4]

MANORS Five *cassata* of land in the vill of *COFTON* were given in 780 by King Offa to the church of St. Peter, which his grandfather Eanulf had founded at Bredon.[5] When this monastery became annexed to that of St. Mary of Worcester the property at Cofton passed to the latter church and as five *cassata* 'on Coftune aet tham hamstealle' was leased for five lives by Bishop Aelhun in 849 to Berhtwulf, King of Mercia, in exchange for his protection for the church of Worcester.[6] Berhtwulf appears immediately to have transferred his interest to his servant Egbert.[7] The land afterwards passed to King Athelstan, who in 930 granted it to the church of St. Mary, Worcester.[8] It still belonged to the church of Worcester as a berewick of the manor of Alvechurch in 1086.[9] At the same time Urse D'Abitot was holding 3 hides of land there, of which Turold held two and Walter one, and which Leofgeat, Ælfric and Æthelric had held as three manors before the Conquest.[10]

A hide of land at Coston, which appears to have formed the manor subsequently known as *COSTON HACKETT*, remained a member of the Bishop of Worcester's manor of Alvechurch at least as late as the end of the 13th century,[11] and was held of that manor. Under the bishop this manor was held by the Beauchamps, Urse's successors, as of their barony of Elmley, and the mesne overlordship followed the descent of the honour of Elmley Castle until 1637, when it is mentioned for the last time.[12]

Under these lords the manor of Coston Hackett was held by the Hacket family for knight service. The knight's fee in Worcestershire, held of William de Beauchamp in 1166 by William Hacket,[13] included this manor. Early in the 13th century Ralph Hacket held it as 1 hide of land,[14] and it was probably he who in 1226–7 agreed with Alda widow of Thomas Hacket that she should hold half a knight's fee in Coston in part satisfaction of her dower.[15] The manor probably belonged to Walter Hacket in 1270, when he was summoned by the Bishop of Worcester to be at London with horse and arms 'for the honour of the Holy Church and peace of the land.'[16] Some interest

in Coston Hackett seems to have passed like Oddingley to the Mortimers, and was confirmed in 1284 by Edmund Mortimer to his brother Roger.[17] About 1280 it was in the hands of Maud Hacket.[18] As at Oddingley some right in this manor passed to John de Costentyn and his wife Margery, for in 1293–4 Robert Leicester and Catherine his wife claimed 2 carucates of land in Coston and Alvechurch against John de Costentyn and Margery.[19] Their claim was quashed owing to an error in the spelling of Alvechurch, and John Costentyn seems to have remained in possession of the manor until 1299.[20] Robert Leicester held half a knight's fee at Coston Hackett in 1316,[21] and in 1346 the manor belonged to his widow Maud, who is styled 'Maud Hacket, who was the wife of Robert de Leicester.'[22] It would seem possible that the name Maud is given in error for Katherine, for in a return of knights' fees of the same date Katherine Hacket was said to be holding land in Coston which had formerly been held by Ralph Hacket[23] and Katherine Hacket paid a subsidy of 2s. at Coston in 1327.[24]

The manor evidently descended in the Leicester family. In 1431 it was held by Henry Leicester,[25] and William Leicester, lord of Coston Hackett, died in 1508.[26] On the death of William Leicester in 1525 it passed, after provision being made for his wife Anne, to his nephew John More,[27] who was succeeded in 1535 by three daughters, Jane wife of Michael Ashfield, formerly wife of James Dineley, Margaret wife of William Stanford, and Eleanor wife of John Folliott.[28] The Folliotts seem to have retained their share at any rate until 1620, when Thomas Folliott son of John and Eleanor[29] died seised of a capital messuage or farm in Coston Hackett, which was settled on his eldest son John.[30]

The rest of the manor was conveyed in 1573 by Jane Parker, widow, the eldest daughter of John More, who had married as a third husband Thomas Parker, and Thomas Dineley, evidently her son by her first husband, to Ralph Sheldon and John Middlemore,[31] evidently for settlement on Thomas Dineley and his wife Jane. Their daughter Mary married John Childe and she and her husband conveyed the manor to Edward Skinner, a clothier of Ledbury, in 1594.[32] The latter appears to have settled most of the property on his eldest son Richard,[33] and at the time of his death in 1631 held only Coston Hall and the advowson of the

---

[2] *Blue Bk. Incl. Awards,* 189.

[3] Chan. Proc. (Ser. 2), bdle. 152, no. 33.

[4] Inform. from Rev. K. A. Deakin.

[5] Kemble, *Codex Dipl.* no. 138; Heming, *Chartul.* (ed. Hearne), ii, 454; Birch, *Cart. Sax.* i, 327.

[6] Kemble, *Codex Dipl.* no. 262; Birch, *Cart. Sax.* ii, 40, 41; Heming, op. cit. i, 6. Birch and Heming give the boundaries of the land.

[7] Heming, op. cit. 8.

[8] Kemble, *Codex Dipl.* no. 351; Heming, op. cit. i, 10; Birch, *Cart. Sax.* ii, 400.

[9] *V.C.H. Worcs.* i, 298b.

[10] Ibid. 318a.

[11] Red Bk. of Bishopric of Worcester (Eccl. Com. Rec. Var. bdle. 121, no. 43698), fol. 126; *Testa de Nevill* (Rec. Com.), 42.

[12] Nash, *Hist. of Worc.* i, 21, 22; *Red Bk. of Exch.* (Rolls Ser.), 299; *Testa de*

Nevill (Rec. Com.), 40b, 41b; *Cal. Inq. p.m.* 1–9 *Edw. II,* 403; Exch. Inq. p.m. (Ser. 2), file 1190, no. 3; Chan. Inq. p.m. (Ser. 2), dlvii, 4; Add. MSS. (B.M.), 28024, fol. 290.

[13] *Red Bk. of Exch.* (Rolls Ser.), 299; Red Bk. of Bishopric of Worc. &c., fol. 253.

[14] *Testa de Nevill* (Rec. Com.), 41b.

[15] Feet of F. Worcs. 11 Hen. III, no. 15.

[16] *Reg. G. Giffard* (Worcs. Hist. Soc.), i, 45. Walter had been married in 1269 to Joan daughter of Simon de Otindon, and there seems to have been some dispute as to the legality of the marriage (ibid. 25).

[17] De Banco R. 55, m. 107 d.

[18] *Lay Subs. R. Worcs. c.* 1280 (Worcs. Hist. Soc.), 19.

[19] Assize R. 1030, m. 6 d.

[20] Red Bk. of Bishopric of Worc. fol. 126.

[21] *Cal. Inq. p.m.* 1–9 *Edw. II,* 403.

[22] *Feud. Aids,* v, 303.

[23] Ibid. 308.

[24] *Lay Subs. R. Worcs. c.* 1280 (Worcs. Hist. Soc.), 18.

[25] *Feud. Aids,* v, 330.

[26] Nash, op. cit. i, 252.

[27] P.C.C. 39 Bodfelde; Exch. Inq. p.m. (Ser. 2), file 1183, no. 6.

[28] Exch. Inq. p.m. (Ser. 2), file 1190, no. 3.

[29] *Visit. of Worc.* 1569 (Harl. Soc. xxvii), 55, 56.

[30] Chan. Inq. p.m. (Ser. 2), ccclxxviii, 137.

[31] Feet of F. Worcs. East. 15 Eliz.; *Visit. of Worc.* 1569 (Harl. Soc. xxvii), 55.

[32] Recov. R. D. Enr. East. 36 Eliz. m. 12 d.; Recov. R. Worc. East. 36 Eliz. rot. 77; Feet of F. Worcs. East. 36 Eliz.

[33] Feet of F. Worcs. Trin. 9 Jas. I; East. 18 Jas. I; Mich. 8 Chas. I.

chapel.[34] Richard Skinner died in 1633, leaving four daughters, Elizabeth, Mary, Margaret and Theodocia.[35] Coston Hackett passed to Margaret and her husband Thomas Jolliffe, a favourite of Charles I, whom he attended on the scaffold. He is said by Nash to have been represented in a picture formerly in the dining room of Coston Hall 'with a melancholy despairing countenance with his pistols and sword hanging on a pillar before him' and holding 'a key in his hand which the tradition of the family says was given to him by Charles I when in prison that he might have access to him when he pleased.'[36] Benjamin Jolliffe son of Thomas and Margaret died in 1719, leaving three sons and two daughters.[37] The eldest son Thomas succeeded,[38] but died childless in 1758, leaving the manor to Rebecca Lowe, the daughter of one of his sisters, for life, with reversion to Michael Biddulph, the son of his other sister.[39] Rebecca Lowe died in 1791,[40] and Michael Biddulph, after the death of his son Thomas in 1793,[41] seems to have settled it on his grandson Robert Biddulph,[42] and with him sold it about 1812 to Other Archer, sixth Earl of Plymouth.[43] From the latter it has descended to the fourteenth Lord Windsor, the present Earl of Plymouth.

The manor of COSTON RICHARD, which was held for knight service under the lords of Elmley Castle,[44] was probably included in a knight's fee held in 1166 by Richard de Coston of William de Beauchamp.[45] John de Coston, witness to a grant to Dudley Priory [1160-1206],[46] may have been owner of the manor which was in the possession of Richard de Coston early in the 13th century.[47] Walter de Coston, who in 1256 was exempted from being put on assizes, &c., against his will, was possibly lord of Coston.[48] In 1262-3 John de Coston granted this manor for life to Richard de Coston, who was to render for it the service of half a knight's fee.[49] Richard son of Alexander de Coston still held land at Coston in 1283-4.[50] Sybil eldest daughter of John de Coston was holding the manor in 1316.[51] She appears to have been succeeded before 1327[52] by Lucy wife of Alexander de Hodington, possibly her daughter or sister, who was

JOLLIFFE. *Argent a pile vert with three right hands argent thereon.*

still holding the manor in 1346, when she is called the heir of John de Coston.[53] In 1428 it was held by the heirs of Lucy de Hodington,[54] and in 1431 Thomas Webb held certain lands at Coston, and John Walsingham held a quarter of a knight's fee in Coston Richard.[55] John Walsingham was apparently lord of the manor in 1525,[56] and it was held in 1567 by Edward Walsingham, who had inherited it from his brother John and his father John.[57] Before 1594 it had been acquired by William Child, the lord of Coston Hackett,[58] and has since followed the same descent as that manor.[59] Coston Richard is not mentioned as a separate manor after the end of the 18th century, but the name still survives in a farm-house which lies near the boundaries of Alvechurch.

A water-mill belonged to one of the manors at the time of the Domesday Survey[60] and seems to have passed with Coston Hackett to the Leicesters.[61] It is last mentioned in 1573, when it was settled with the manor on Thomas Dineley and Jane his wife.[62] There are now no mills in existence in the parish, but there was probably at one time a windmill, as a field still bears the name Windmill Field.

The manor of GROVELEY belonged to the college of Westbury in co. Gloucester in 1536,[63] and was granted with it in 1544 to Sir Ralph Sadleir,[64] who sold it in 1548-9 to John Combes.[65] The latter died in 1550, leaving a son John,[66] who evidently sold the manor to Sir John Lyttelton. Sir John in 1590 left it by his will to his nephew George, the eldest son of Roger Lyttelton,[67] whose brother Humphrey seems to have sold it to Francis Heton.[68] Early in the 19th century the estate then known as Groveley Hall was in the possession of Robert Middleton Biddulph, who sold it to John Pickering. His trustees conveyed it in 1820 to John Merry,[69] who added to it by the purchase of adjoining land. John Merry died in 1856 and left the estate to his son William Lucas Merry, who sold it in 1872 to Ambrose Biggs of Birmingham. It was purchased of him in 1883 by Joseph Billing Baldwin of King's Norton, who left it to his son and daughter Major James Baldwin and Mrs. Fanny Jolly, who are the present joint owners.[70]

CHURCH
The church of ST. MICHAEL consists of a chancel 20 ft. by 16 ft. 6 in. with a modern organ chamber on the north side, and a nave 38 ft. 6 in. by 20 ft. 6 in. having a bell-turret at the west end. These measurements are all internal.

[34] Chan. Inq. p.m. (Ser. 2), dlii, 116.
[35] Ibid. dxlix, 64.
[36] op. cit. i, 252.
[37] Ibid. 250, 252.
[38] Recov. R. D. Enr. Trin. 7 Geo. I, m. 15 ; Recov. R. East. 6 Geo. I, rot. 84 ; East. 7 Geo. I, rot. 221.
[39] Nash, op. cit. i, 251. The validity of the will was contested unsuccessfully on the plea that Thomas Jolliffe was insane.
[40] Prattinton Coll. (Soc. Antiq.), quoting parish reg.
[41] Ibid.
[42] Recov. R. Mich. 36 Geo. III, rot. 141.
[43] Prattinton Coll. (Soc. Antiq.).
[44] Red Bk. of Exch. (Rolls Ser.), 299 ; Testa de Nevill (Rec. Com.), 40b.
[45] Red Bk. of Exch. (Rolls Ser.), 299.
[46] Will. Salt Arch. Soc. Coll. iii (1), 214-15.

[47] Testa de Nevill (Rec. Com.), 40b.
[48] Cal. Pat. 1247-58, p. 497.
[49] Feet of F. Worcs. case 258, file 8, no. 20.
[50] Ibid. case 259, file 11, no. 3.
[51] Cal. Inq. p.m. 1-9 Edw. II, 403.
[52] De Banco R. Trin. 1 Edw. III, m. 109 d.
[53] Feud. Aids, v, 303
[54] Ibid. 324.
[55] Ibid. 332, 330.
[56] Chan. Inq. p.m. (Ser. 2), xlvii, 19.
[57] Chan. Proc. (Ser. 2), bdle. 186, no. 11.
[58] Feet of F. Worcs. East. 36 Eliz.
[59] For references see Coston Hackett.
[60] V.C.H. Worcs. i, 318a.
[61] P.C.C. 39 Bodfelde ; Chan. Inq. p.m. (Ser. 2), xlvii, 19 ; Exch. Inq. p.m. (Ser. 2), file 1190, no. 3.
[62] Feet of F. Worcs. East. 15 Eliz.
[63] Valor Eccl. (Rec. Com.), ii, 433.

The nett value of Groveley and Monyhull in King's Norton was at that time £17 16s. 10d.
[64] L. and P. Hen. VIII, xix (1), g. 278 (68).
[65] Pat. 2 Edw. VI, pt. iv, m. 10.
[66] Chan. Inq. p.m. (Ser. 2), xciv, 98 ; Fine R. 7 Edw. VI, no. 18.
[67] Chan. Inq. p.m. (Ser. 2), ccxxix, 140.
[68] Habington, Surv. of Worc. (Worcs. Hist. Soc.), i, 168. Francis Heton died in 1625, leaving two sons Robert and William, the former of whom also left two sons, Francis and William. Prattinton Coll. (Soc. Antiq.), quoting parish reg.
[69] This purchase is probably referred to by Prattinton when he says an estate called Groveley Hall was sold by Mr. Biddulph to Mr. Merry of Birmingham (Prattinton Coll. [Soc. Antiq.]).
[70] Information by Mrs. Jolly.

Coston Hackett : Late 14th-century Roof at Coston Hall

The building was restored in 1861 and the earliest remaining portions date from the latter half of the 14th century. The east window is of three lights, with modern tracery under a pointed head. The walling and moulded jambs are old and appear to date from the 14th century. In the modern north wall is an arch opening into the organ chamber, and to the east of it a pointed window. The south wall is old, but the two windows are modern. Between them is a pointed doorway with a moulded label and head stops, and further east is a piscina. The chancel arch is modern.

In the north wall of the nave are two square-headed windows of three and two lights respectively, the tracery in each case being modern, and a low square-headed door. Externally the wall has been straightened by a facing 9 in. thick for most of its height. In the south wall are two windows similar to those opposite. A 15th-century doorway, with a moulded label and head stops, opens into an ancient porch built of wood. The west wall of the nave has been rebuilt; it has square angle buttresses and a large reconstructed 15th-century central buttress under a 16th-century bell-turret containing two bells.

The font is modern, and the pulpit and the communion rail are made up of old oak.

In the chancel is an incised alabaster slab to William Leicester and his wives Eleanor and Anne, with three effigies under canopies. William Leicester wears plate armour with scalloped tuiles and rounded sabbatons. His head rests on a tilting helm crested with a roebuck and his feet on a dog. His wives wear kennel head-dresses and from their girdles hang pomanders. Below the first wife Eleanor is a scroll, partly illegible, inscribed 'Non intres in judicium cū aīabus tuorum . . . ,' and below William Leicester and his second wife are a boy and girl. The marginal inscription reads :—'Hic jacent corpora Wiłłmi Leysestur dñi de Coston hacket Elinore et Anne uxorum suarum qui quidem Wiłłmus obiit [blank] die [blank] anno dñi miłłmo ccccc [blank] et dicta Elionora fuit filia Edmundi (?) Worley Armig⁹i et obiit 7 die mensis Januarii (?) a° dñi miłłmo ccccxiiii quorum aīabȝ ppicietur deus Amen.' Above the canopies are shields, the husband bearing : quarterly (1) a fesse between three fleurs de lis, (2) a lion passant, (3) ermine a bend, (4) a bend engrailed ermine. Above the first wife is the coat : a chief with a raven impaling a cheveron between three bulls' heads cabossed ; and over the second : a cheveron between three hunting horns.

In the nave is an alabaster tablet to William Babington, 1625, and his wife Eleanor daughter of Sir Edward Lyttelton, who died 1671 ; this was formerly in the chancel. There are also monuments to various members of the Jolliffe family.

The two bells are dated 1717.

The plate consists of a small paten, date probably about 1520, a cup with the hall mark of 1661, presented in 1827, a paten of 1827, and a modern flagon.

The registers before 1812 are as follows : (i) (much injured by damp) contains all entries 1550 to 1629 ; (ii) 1630 to 1651 ; (iii) 1654 to 1683, when there is a blank until 1702 ; (iv) 1702 to 1712 ; (v) 1712 to 1754 ; (vi) baptisms and burials 1785 to 1812 ; (vii) marriages 1755 to 1812.

In the churchyard is the base of an old cross.

ADVOWSON The church of Coston Hackett was a chapel annexed to the church of Northfield[71] until 1866, when it was separated from Northfield.[72] It is now a vicarage in the gift of Mrs. Deakin.

There are no endowed charities.

CRUTCH

Cruch (xiii cent.) ; la Crouche (xiv cent.) ; Croyche, Crouch next le Wich (xvi cent.) ; Crutch *alias* St. James (xvii cent.).

Crutch probably became extra-parochial in 1178, when the tithes were assigned to the nuns of Westwood in exchange for their claim on the church of Dodderhill,[1] and remained so until 1857, when it was formed into a civil parish.[2] It is a small parish, having an area of only 327 acres, with a population of 4 in 1901. The soil and subsoil are strong clay marl, and agriculture is the only industry. A road from Droitwich passes through Crutch on its way to Grafton Manor, Upton Warren and Elmbridge. Crutch Hill is over 200 ft. above the ordnance datum, and is said to have been a camp, but the traces, if any, of intrenchment are now very faint. The parish is watered by the Capel or Chapel Ditch and another small tributary of the Salwarpe.

There is no church and only one farm-house, known as Crutch Farm, which stands near the site of the ancient manor-house. All trace of this manor-house has now disappeared ; it is said to have stood on the top of some rising ground immediately to the south-west of the present building and adjoining the road known as Crutch Lane. A considerable indentation of the ground by the roadside may indicate a moat, though no return line can now be distinguished, and it may be the remains of a marl-pit. The farm-house is apparently a building of the late 17th century, though much modernized. The materials are red brick, with a tiled roof.

MANOR CRUTCH was no doubt included in the manor of Dodderhill in 1086, and so remained until the time of Henry II, when Osbern Fitz Hugh and Eustacia de Say, his mother, granted it to the nunnery at Westwood,[3] their gift being confirmed by Edward I and other later kings.[4] In 1535 the manor and chapel were valued at £7 6s. 8d.[5] The manor having passed at the Dissolution to the king, he sold it in 1538[6] to Robert Acton and his son Charles. It passed with Elmley Lovett to the four daughters and co-heirs of Sir John Acton, Elizabeth wife of Henry Townsend, Anne wife of Walter Colles, Helen wife of

[71] Worc. Epis. Reg. Silvester de Gigliis, (1498–1521), fol. 25 ; Pat. 13 Jas. I, pt. xv, no. 9.
[72] Parl. Papers (1872), xlvi, no. 227, p. 12. Another order for this separation was issued in 1871 (ibid.).

[1] V.C.H. Worcs. ii, 149 ; Thomas, Surv. of Cath. Church of Worc. A 111, 115.
[2] Stat. 20 Vict. cap. 19.
[3] Cal. Chart. R. 1257–1300, p. 320.

[4] Ibid. ; Cal. Pat. 1391–6, p. 582.
[5] Valor Eccl. (Rec. Com.), iii, 276.
[6] L. and P. Hen. VIII, xiii (1), g. 1309 (26) ; Pat. 30 Hen. VIII, pt. ii, m. 7.

Thomas Thornburgh, and Penelope wife of John Lench.[7] As in the case of Elmley Lovett the descent after this date becomes obscure. There is no further record of its ownership until 1765, when it belonged to Robert Cliffe.[8] About three years later he sold it to Mr. Vaughan Jefferies, a surgeon of Worcester.[9] By the beginning of the 19th century it seems to have been divided into five parts, one of which was conveyed by Thomas Philpott and Mary his wife to Humphrey Philpott in 1803.[10]

In 1850 the Rev. H. Douglas settled part of the manor[11] on the Rev. W. W. Douglas on his marriage. The latter purchased another portion[12] from the Rev. H. T. Philpott in 1879.[13] The rest of the manor was held in 1872 by R. A. Douglas Gresley, who still held it at his death in 1885.[14] The whole was purchased of these owners in February and April 1885 by John Corbett,[15] on whose death in 1901 it passed to his brother Thomas Corbett. He died in 1906,[16] and the manor was sold by his trustees in March 1909 to Mr. Edward Partington of Westwood,[17] who now owns it.

CHAPEL The date at which the chapel of Crutch was built is not known, but it was certainly before 1335, when Richard de Aston bequeathed 2d. to each of the altars of the Blessed Virgin and St. Katherine in 'la Crouche.'[18] The chapel was dedicated in honour of St. James, and was numbered among the possessions of Westwood Priory at the Dissolution.[19] It was granted with the manor to Robert and Charles Acton in 1538.[20] It descended with the manor until 1621,[21] but is not mentioned, and was probably disused, after that date.

There are no endowed charities.

DODDERHILL

Dudrenhull, Doderhull, Dudrenhulla (xii cent.).

Dodderhill, which now includes the formerly extra-parochial district of Malborough in the Vines, in 1831 comprised the now separate ecclesiastical parishes of Elmbridge and Wychbold. With the last-named place and Rashwood, which are still included in the civil parish, it has an area of 3,512 acres, of which 1,086¼ acres are arable land, 1,955¼ permanent grass and 21 woodland.[1] The River Salwarpe enters the parish near the Stoke Prior Mills. It forms part of the northern boundary, and then flows across the parish in a south-westerly direction towards Droitwich. Just above Impney it is joined by the Salty Brook, a continuation of the Capel Ditch, which forms the boundary between Crutch and Dodderhill. Body Brook, another tributary, rises in the parish, and, flowing along the south-eastern boundary, joins the Salwarpe in the parish of Droitwich.

The Worcester and Birmingham Canal and branches of the Midland and Great Western railways pass through the parish, and the Stoke Prior Works station on the Midland is just within the boundaries of Dodderhill. The main road from Droitwich to Bromsgrove cuts across the parish in a north-easterly direction. At Rashwood a branch from it connects it with the road from Bromsgrove to Alcester, and another branch from it leads to Elmbridge. The ground is undulating, and is generally higher in the east than in the west, the highest point being about 200 ft. above the ordnance datum between Wychbold and Astwood and the lowest 144 ft. on the road from Droitwich to Crutch.

There is no village of Dodderhill; the church of St. Augustine stands on a hill immediately north of Droitwich and just without the boundaries of the borough. Wychbold, which gave its name to the most important manor in the parish, is on the Bromsgrove road. Wychbold Hall, the residence of His Honour Judge Amphlett, K.C., J.P., is a modern house which lies to the south of the village. The house at Impney, on the same road about half a mile from Droitwich, is also modern, and stands in a deer park of nearly 200 acres. It is a fine red brick house built about 1875 by the late John Corbett, a great salt manufacturer, after the model of a French château from plans by Richard Phené Spiers.[1a]

Obden House is an early 17th-century house with stone gables.

The hamlets of Rashwood, between Droitwich and Wychbold, Astwood and Shaw Lane in the north-west are now in the ecclesiastical parish of Wychbold. At Astwood is Astwood Farm, an H-shaped half-timbered house of the early 17th century, re-fronted with brick about 1700. The house is of two stories with an attic, and the plan is of the normal central hall type of the period. In the southern ground-floor room of the west wing is some good Jacobean panelling. The chimney stacks are of stone, surmounted by tall brick shafts formed on the plan of two intersecting squares. Astwood and Shaw Lane increased very much in size during the last century owing to their proximity to the Stoke Prior Salt Works, which are just over the borders of Stoke Prior parish and were opened in 1828.[2] The works formerly belonged to John Corbett, who built numerous cottages in Dodderhill for the workmen in his employ, but about 1890 he sold all his salt works to the Salt Union, who now carry them on. The salt works give employment to a number of people, but agriculture is still one of the most important industries, the chief crops being wheat, beans, barley and turnips. The soil varies from strong clay marl to sandy loam, while the subsoil is marl, clay and gravel.

Huntingdrop, formerly Huntingthorpe, 2 miles east of Droitwich and at one time a detached part of Dodderhill, was annexed to Hanbury in 1880[3] and

[7] Chan. Proc. (Ser. 2), bdle. 139, no. 11. For other references see Elmley Lovett.

[8] Recov. R. Hil. 5 Geo. III, rot. 384.

[9] Nash, Hist. of Worc. i, 350.

[10] Feet of F. Worcs. Mich. 44 Geo. III.

[11] Probably five-tenths.

[12] Apparently three-tenths.

[13] Information supplied by Mr. R. Bruce Ward.

[14] Ibid.   [15] Ibid.

[16] Burke, Landed Gentry (1906).

[17] Information supplied by Mr. R. Bruce Ward.

[18] Worc. Epis. Reg. Montagu (1333–7), fol. 22.

[19] Dugdale, Mon. Angl. vi, 1010.

[20] Pat. 30 Hen. VIII, pt. ii, m. 7; L. and P. Hen. VIII, xiii (1), g. 1309 (26).

[21] For references see Elmley Lovett.

[1] Statistics from Bd. of Agric. (1905).

[1a] The plans were exhibited at the Royal Academy.

[2] V.C.H. Worcs. ii, 263.

[3] Census of Engl. and Wales, 1891, ii, 658.

four years later Paper Mills was transferred from Hampton Lovett to Dodderhill.[4] In 1880 Crowfield was transferred from Dodderhill to Bromsgrove,[5] and part of Dodderhill was transferred to Grafton Manor at the same date.[6] The southern part of the parish, which was in the borough of Droitwich and known as the In-liberties, was added to the adjoining parishes of St. Nicholas, St. Peter, and St. Andrew Droitwich in 1884.[7]

Elmbridge, formerly a chapelry annexed to Dodderhill, became a separate parish in 1877.[8] It has an area of about 1,778¼ acres, including 608 acres of arable land, 1,116 acres of permanent grass and 8¼ acres of woods and plantations.[9] The parish is watered by tributaries of the Salwarpe. The main road from Droitwich to Kidderminster passes through Cutnall Green, a hamlet in the south-west of Elmbridge. Broad Common in Elmbridge was inclosed

MANORS Dodderhill is not mentioned in the Domesday Survey,[16] the chief manor at the time of the Conquest being *WYCHBOLD* (Wicbold, vii cent. ; Wicelbold, xi cent. ; Wichebald, xii cent. ; Wychebaud, xiii cent.). Land at Wychbold near the River Salwarpe was granted by King Ethelred in 692 to the priory of Worcester, at the request of his former servant Oslaf, then a monk at Worcester.[17] It is said to have belonged to the priory until the 11th century, when Edwin, brother of Earl Leofric, wrested it from them.[18] The truth of this story is somewhat discredited by the fact that in 815 and 831 Wychbold appears as a royal residence, from which Kings Coenwulf and Wiglaf of Mercia executed charters.[18a] Edwin, according to the Worcester historian, did not live long to enjoy his ill-gotten lands, being put to death by Griffin, king of the Britons.[19] Instead of being restored to the

DODDERHILL : ASTWOOD FARM

under an Act of 1865,[10] and the award is dated 27 January 1874.[11] There is a common of about 24 acres at Purshull Green and another small common called Brians Green.[12] The inclosure award and tithe map are in the custody of the vicar of Elmbridge.

Among the place-names are Colleyhull and Churchbruggemede[13] (xiv cent.), Le More[14] (xvi cent.), Harpe Furlonge *alias* Hadfurlonge, Olloxhey or Ulloxhey, and Bibbs tenement[15] (xvii cent.).

priory, Wychbold seems to have been claimed by Earl Godwin and after the Conquest was granted to Osbern Fitz Richard.[20] On the death of the latter the manor, which was held of the king in chief,[21] passed to his son Hugh Fitz Osbern, who married Eustacia de Say. Their two sons Osbert and Hugh assumed their mother's surname. Osbert, dying without issue, was succeeded by his brother Hugh, who had two sons, Richard and Hugh.[22] The former died issueless, and

[4] *Census of Engl. and Wales,* 1891, ii, 658.

[5] Ibid.

[6] Ibid.

[7] Ibid.

[8] *Parl. Papers* (1890–1), lxi, 50.

[9] Statistics from Bd. of Agric. (1905).

[10] Priv. Act, 28 & 29 Vict. cap. 20.

[11] *Blue Bk. Incl. Awards,* 189. A small part of Broad Common still remains uninclosed.

[12] Information supplied by the Rev. J. H. L. Booker, late vicar of Elmbridge.

[13] Mins. Accts. bdle. 1067, no. 22.

[14] Pat. 7 Edw. VI, pt. iv, m. 13.

[15] Chan. Inq. p.m. (Ser. 2), cccclv, 66.

[16] In 1274–5 it was stated that Dodderhill was no vill but a certain place near the church of St. Augustine thus named (Assize R. 1026, m. 5).

[17] Birch, *Cart. Sax.* i, 112 ; Heming, *Chartul.* (ed. Hearne), 384.

[18] Heming, op. cit. 278.

[18a] Birch, *Cart. Sax.* i, 492, 557. As both these documents are preserved in contemporary texts, their authenticity is beyond question.

[19] Heming, loc. cit.

[20] *V.C.H. Worcs.* i, 314a.

[21] *Cal. Inq. p.m. Hen. III,* 120 ; 1–19 Edw. I, 87 ; Chan. Inq. p.m. 29 Edw III (1st nos.), no. 42.

[22] Nash, *Hist. of Worc.* i, 241.

the latter died at the end of the 12th century,[23] leaving three daughters.[24] This manor passed to Margery, who married firstly Hugh de Ferrers, secondly Robert Mortimer, and thirdly William Stutevill.[25] In 1199 Mabel daughter of Robert Marmion and widow of Hugh de Say had £11 3s. 11d. in the manor of Wychbold except the capital messuage which belonged to Hugh de Ferrers,[26] and in 1222–3 a moiety of the manor was conveyed to her for her lifetime by her daughter Margery and her husband William Stutevill.[27]

The latter held Margery's estates after her death by courtesy; in a fine of 1243–4,[28] in which he made certain grants to Hugh Mortimer, her son and heir by her second marriage, Wychbold was confirmed to him by Hugh, and he died seised of it in 1259, when it was valued at £15 5s.[29] The manor then passed to Hugh Mortimer, who received a grant of free warren there in 1266.[30] On his death in 1275 Wychbold passed to his son Robert,[31] who died in 1287,[32] when the estates were held by the king during the minority of the heir Hugh.[33] The latter died in 1304, it is said from poison administered by Maud his wife, who was only pardoned at the instance of Margaret, the queen consort.[34] In the inquisition taken after Hugh's death the manor is said to have been a member of Burford, held of the king by barony. His heirs were his daughters Joan and Margaret,[35] during whose minority the custody of their possessions was granted in 1304 to Queen Margaret.[36] In the same year, at the king's request, she transferred a moiety of the lands, during the minority of the elder daughter, with her marriage, to Thomas Bykenore,[37] and sold the custody of the remaining moiety, with the marriage of the younger daughter, to Walter, Bishop of Coventry and Lichfield.[38] Soon after, the escheator was ordered to deliver the manor of Wychbold to Maud widow of Hugh Mortimer,[39] and she remained in possession of it, including a capital messuage and toll paid by persons crossing the Salwarpe, until her death in 1308.[40] The manor was then assigned to the elder daughter of Hugh Mortimer, Joan, then wife of Thomas Bykenore.[41]

After Thomas Bykenore's death, Joan, his widow, married Sir Richard Talbot,[42] and in 1320 Wychbold was settled on them and their issue.[43] In 1325–6 the manor of Wychbold was conveyed by Sir Richard Talbot and Joan to Isabel Mortimer for her life.[44]

Isabel was still living in 1329, when Joan Talbot, after the death of her husband, settled the reversion on her eldest son John and Juliana his wife.[45] Joan was followed in 1341 by her son John Talbot,[46] after whose death in 1355[47] his widow Juliana held it in dower until her death in 1362, when their son John succeeded.[48] He died 18 February 1375, the custody of his son Richard[49] being granted by Edward III to his daughter Isabella.[50]

Wychbold was retained by Katharine, Sir John Talbot's widow, in dower.[51] Her son Richard Talbot died 13 September 1382,[52] when Alice, widow of Peter Preston, was granted the custody of John brother and heir of Richard.[53] On her complaint that certain persons schemed to dispossess her of his marriage and took him from place to place, Robert Beverley, serjeant-at-arms, was ordered to arrest the young heir and bring him before the king and council.[54]

John Talbot died a minor, 3 July 1388, and his three sisters became his co-heirs: Elizabeth wife of Warin Archdekne, Philippa wife of Matthew Gurney, and Eleanor.[55] Eleanor died unmarried in 1390,[56] and the lands were divided between Elizabeth and Philippa, the former receiving Wychbold, which passed to the Lucys through the marriage of her eldest daughter Eleanor with Sir Walter Lucy.[57] Sir Walter and Eleanor left three children, Sir William Lucy, who died childless in 1461, Eleanor the wife of Thomas Hopton, and Maud the wife of William Vaux of Harrowden.[58] On Sir William Lucy's death his estates passed to Elizabeth wife of Sir Roger Corbett of Moreton Corbet, co. Salop, and daughter of Eleanor Hopton and to Sir William Vaux, son of Maud.[59] According to Habington, Wychbold was then 'by sale transferred to others.'[60] The sale took place soon after Sir William Lucy's death, since in 1463–4 the manor was in the possession of Joan widow of Sir Robert Vere, who conveyed it to Nicholas Carew, Alexander and William Carew, two of his younger sons, and others,[61] evidently for the use of William Carew. It remained in his family for almost a century. In 1523 John Carew, his son, settled it on Margery Kelly, whom he afterwards married.[62] She was still holding it in 1547,[63] but before 1562 had been succeeded by her grandson Thomas Carew, who with Elizabeth his wife conveyed it in that year to Edward Villiers and Thomas Savage.[64]

²³ *Abbrev. Plac.* (Rec. Com.), 24; Assize R. 1026, m. 5.
²⁴ *Rot. Lit. Claus.* (Rec. Com.), i, 12, 5b.
²⁵ Ibid. i, 394–5, 407; *Excerpta e Rot. Fin.* (Rec. Com.), i, 34; *Red Bk. of Exch.* (Rolls Ser.), 287.
²⁶ *Abbrev. Plac.* (Rec. Com.), 24.
²⁷ Feet of F. Div. Co. 7 Hen. III, no. 29.
²⁸ Ibid. 28 Hen. III, no. 192.
²⁹ *Cal. Inq. p.m. Hen. III*, 120.
³⁰ *Cal. Chart. R.* 1257–1300, p. 62.
³¹ *Cal. Inq. p.m.* 1–19 *Edw. I*, 87.
³² G.E.C. *Complete Peerage*, v, 380.
³³ Pat. 22 Edw. I, m. 19.
³⁴ *Cal. Pat.* 1301–7, p. 378.
³⁵ Chan. Inq. p.m. 32 Edw. I, no. 48.
³⁶ *Cal. Pat.* 1301–7, p. 257.
³⁷ Ibid. 261.   ³⁸ Ibid. 265.
³⁹ *Cal. Close*, 1302–7, p. 181.
⁴⁰ Chan. Inq. p.m. 1 Edw. II, no. 59b.
⁴¹ *Cal. Close*, 1307–13, p. 36; see also *Cal. Pat.* 1307–13, pp. 45, 47.
⁴² G.E.C. *Complete Peerage*, v, 380, n. (g).

⁴³ *Cal. Pat.* 1317–21, p. 502. The manor, with that of Cotheridge, seems to have been claimed and held in 1315 by Roger Mortimer of Wigmore (ibid. 1313–17, pp. 424, 429, 600).
⁴⁴ Feet of F. Worcs. case 259, file 18, no. 28; *Cal. Pat.* 1324–7, p. 212.
⁴⁵ Pat. 3 Edw. III, pt. ii, m. 9.
⁴⁶ Chan. Inq. p.m. 14 Edw. III (1st nos.), no. 30.
⁴⁷ Ibid. 29 Edw. III (1st nos.), no. 42.
⁴⁸ Ibid. 35 Edw. III, pt. ii (1st nos.), no. 70.
⁴⁹ Ibid. 49 Edw. III, pt. ii (1st nos.), no. 50.
⁵⁰ Pat. 6 Ric. II, pt. i, m. 3. Ingelran de Couci, Isabella's husband, granted the custody of two-thirds to Peter Preston in 1375.
⁵¹ Chan. Inq. p.m. 4 Ric. II, no. 56.
⁵² Ibid. 6 Ric. II, no. 73.
⁵³ Pat. 6 Ric. II, pt. i, m. 3.
⁵⁴ Ibid. pt. ii, m. 16d.; see also 7 Ric. II, pt. i, m. 10.

⁵⁵ Chan. Inq. p.m. 12 Ric. II, no. 53.
⁵⁶ Ibid. 14 Ric. II, no. 49.
⁵⁷ Ibid. 9 Hen. IV, no. 39.
⁵⁸ Baker, *Hist. of Northants*, i, 130; Clutterbuck, *Hist. of Herts.* i, 395.
⁵⁹ Ibid. Since Wychbold is not mentioned in the inquisition taken after Sir William's death (1 Edw. IV, no. 16), it is possible that it was sold during his lifetime.
⁶⁰ *Surv. of Worc.* (Worcs. Hist. Soc.), ii, 310.
⁶¹ Feet of F. Worcs. East. 3 Edw. IV, no. 12. Wychbold is said to have come to the Carews through Sir Nicholas Carew's marriage with Joan daughter of Sir Hugh Courtney of Haccombe (Burke, *Commoners*, i, 267). The above fine is probably a settlement of the manor on William, her fifth son.
⁶² Chan. Inq. p.m. (Ser. 2), lxxxv, 78.
⁶³ Ibid. She is called Margery Tirrill in 1546 (ibid. lxxv, 101).
⁶⁴ Feet of F. Worcs. Trin. 4 Eliz.

DODDERHILL : PANELLING AT ASTWOOD FARM

The manor was afterwards purchased by the Pakingtons.[65] Sir John Pakington held it in 1610–11[66] and obtained licence in 1618–19 to impark 1,000 acres of arable land in Hampton Lovett, Westwood, Dodderhill and Droitwich.[67] He died seised of the manor in 1625, leaving it to his grandson John.[68] In this family it probably remains, but it has long been extinct.

Wychbold Hall is now the property and seat of His Honour Judge R. H. Amphlett, K.C., who inherited it in 1883 from his uncle the Rt. Hon. Sir Richard Paul Amphlett.[69] Wychbold Court is a fine old timber black and white house near ; it also belongs to the Amphletts.

The manor of *ELMBRIDGE* (Ambruge, xiii cent. ; Elmerugge, Elmbrugge, xiv cent. ; Elyngbrigge, xvi cent.) belonged before the Conquest to a certain Ældiet and in 1086 to Osbern Fitz Richard,[70] who held the adjoining manor of Wychbold. Elmbridge was held of the lords of Wychbold[71] (q.v.) by a family who took their name from the manor. Inard de Elmbridge was holding a quarter of a third of a fee of William de Stutevill about 1212.[72] He seems to have been succeeded by Stephen son of Inard, who went by the name of Stephen de Ellebrug,[73] or Stephen Fitz Inard.[74] Adam Elmbridge paid a subsidy of 1 mark at Elmbridge in 1280,[75] and died seised of the manor in 1308, leaving a son Roger.[76] The inquisition taken after his death shows that he had in the manor a capital messuage and free tenants, but no perquisites of court, because the tenants did suit at Wychbold.[77] Roger Elmbridge died

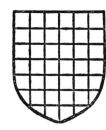

ELMBRIDGE. *Checky argent and sable.*

in 1327–8, leaving a son also called Roger,[78] who received a grant of free warren in his manor of Elmbridge in 1337[79] and held it until 1375, when he was succeeded by his brother John Elmbridge.[80] The latter died before 1379,[81] but had previously granted the manor to Sir Thomas Astley and Katherine his wife for the life of John Cassy, at a yearly rent of £10, with reversion to Roger[82] son and heir of John de Elmbridge, who was proved to be of age in 1398.[83] No mention of the manor occurs between this date and the 16th century, but it evidently continued in

the Elmbridge family,[84] who acquired the manor of Croham and other property in Surrey, and seem to have lived there.[85] A Roger 'Elingbridge' of Croydon, who may possibly be the same as the last-named Roger, was appointed to tender the oath of allegiance in 1443.[86] He seems to have had three sons, Roger, who died childless about 1437, John and William.[87] John succeeded to the Surrey estates,[88] and probably also to Elmbridge and left them successively to his son and grandson, both called Thomas.[89] The latter died seised of Elmbridge in 1507, and since a son, John, born after his death, died in infancy in the same year, the manor passed to his daughter Anne, at that time only three years old.[90] Before 1525 she married Sir John Dannet of Dannet Hall, co. Leicester,[91] and seems to have settled Elmbridge on one of her younger sons, Gerard Dannet,[92] who died in 1610,[93] leaving it to his younger son Gerard for life with reversion to his son and heir John.[94] The latter died in 1628, while his brother was still living, leaving a son and heir Thomas,[95] who was living in 1649,[96] but apparently died childless, leaving his property to a younger brother Gerard Dannet.[97] John Dannet, son of Gerard, seems to have left Elmbridge to his daughter Frances, who with her husband Edward Bookey sold it in 1769 to John Penrice,[98] in whose family it long remained, being until recently in the hands of the representatives of the late Edward Penrice. It now belongs to the Corbett trustees.

DANNET. *Sable sprinkled with drops argent a quarter ermine.*

PENRICE. *Party indented argent and gules with a wolf's head sable in the quarter.*

During the 13th century a tenth of a fee at Elmbridge, held of the honour of Richards Castle, was held by members of the Hanewode family. Early in the century it was held by Reginald de Hanewode[99] and in 1211–12 by Richard de Hanewode.[100] Joan de Hanewode held it in 1274–5,[1] John de Hanewode in

[65] Habington, op. cit. i, 310.
[66] Chan. Inq. p.m. (Ser. 2), cccxiv, 147.
[67] Pat. 16 Jas. I, pt. iv.
[68] Chan. Inq. p.m. (Ser. 2), ccccxviii, 69.
[69] Burke, *Landed Gentry* (1906).
[70] V.C.H. Worcs. i, 314.
[71] *Testa de Nevill* (Rec. Com.), 39*b* ; Chan. Inq. p.m. 1 Edw. II, no. 59*a* ; 2 Edw. II, no. 18 ; *Feud. Aids*, v, 302, 323 ; Chan. Inq. p.m. 49 Edw. III, pt. i, no. 43 ; 3 Ric. II, no. 2 ; 21 Ric. II, no. 21 ; 9 Hen. IV, no. 39 ; Chan. Inq. p.m. (Ser. 2), xxiv, 60 ; cccxiv, 147.
[72] *Testa de Nevill* (Rec. Com.), 39*b*, 42*b*.
[73] Ibid. 40*b*.　[74] Ibid. 131.
[75] *Lay Subs. R. c.* 1280 (Worcs. Hist. Soc.), 24. Philip de Elmbridge paid 3*s.* 6*d.* at the same date at Wychbold (ibid.).
[76] Chan. Inq. p.m. 2 Edw. II, no. 18.
[77] Ibid.
[78] *Cal. Inq. p.m.* 1–10 Edw. III, 13.

[79] Chart. R. 11 Edw. III, m. 32, no. 65.
[80] Chan. Inq. p.m. 49 Edw. III, pt. i, no. 43.
[81] Ibid. 3 Ric. II, no. 2. Elizabeth widow of Roger had held the manor until her death in 1379 (ibid. 21 Ric. II, no. 21).
[82] Ibid. 3 Ric. II, no. 2.
[83] Ibid. 21 Ric. II, no. 21.
[84] Roger Arderne was holding land in Elmbridge in 1431 (*Feud. Aids*, v, 331), and Richard Burdett died seised of the manor of Elmbridge held of the ' baron of Carue' in 1491–2 (*Cal. Inq. p.m. Hen. VII*, i, 345).
[85] *Coll. Topog. et Gen.* v, 170.
[86] Ibid.　[87] Ibid.
[88] Ibid.
[89] Ibid.
[90] Chan. Inq. p.m. (Ser. 2), xxiv, 60.
[91] Feet of F. Worcs. Mich. 20 Hen. VIII. Sir John and Anne had livery of her lands

in 1525 (*L. and P. Hen. VIII*, iv [1], g. 1533 [12]).
[92] *Coll. Topog. et Gen.* v, 170.
[93] Chan. Inq. p.m. (Ser. 2), cccxiv, 147 ; Nash, in his *Hist. of Worc.* i, 347, gives a pedigree of the family of Dannet, but the first part of it is obviously incorrect. It is possible that the Gerard Dannet who died in 1610 was grandson, not son, of Anne Elmbridge, since his eldest son John was only twelve years old at his death.
[94] Chan. Inq. p.m. (Ser. 2), cccxiv, 147.
[95] Ibid. ccccxliii, 63.
[96] *Index to Worc. Fines*, 1649–1714 (Worcs. Hist. Soc.), 5, 7.
[97] Feet of F. Worcs. East. 22 Chas. II ; Exch. Dep. by Com. Mich. 1659, no. 20.
[98] Feet of F. Worcs. East. 9 Geo. III ; Nash, op. cit. i, 347.
[99] *Testa de Nevill* (Rec. Com.), 39*b*.
[100] *Red Bk. of Exch.* (Rolls Ser.), 605.
[1] *Cal. Inq. p.m.* 1–19 Edw. I, 87.

1280,[2] and Robert de Hanewode in 1286–7.[3] Before 1308 it had passed to William de Hanewode,[4] and in 1327 and 1328 Robert son of William de Hanewode was dealing with land and rent at Elmbridge.[5]

The manor of IMPNEY (Ymeney, xiii cent.; Emeneye, xiv cent.; Imney, Yemmey, xvi cent.) was held by the Corbett family of the lords of Wychbold.[6] Robert Corbett, who was holding it c. 1210–12,[7] was succeeded shortly after by William Corbett, who in 1211–12 was holding it under Thomas Corbett.[8] Thomas was succeeded by Peter Corbett,[9] under whom William Corbett held the manor until about 1280.[10] His widow Alda died seised of it in 1290, her heir being William son of Roger Corbett.[11] In 1329 William received a grant of free warren in Impney.[12] He seems to have been succeeded by Roger, the custody of whose land and son and heir Walter was granted to Richard Ruyhale in 1383.[13] From Walter, who was still living in 1416[14] and 1431,[15] the manor passed to Thomas Corbett, possibly his son, and to William Corbett, son of Thomas. The latter died childless, leaving his property to his two sisters: Elizabeth, or Isabel, who married Ralph Hacklute, and Eleanor, who married Roger Harewell.[16] Walter Hacklute, son of Ralph and Isabel,[17] apparently left two daughters: Margaret, who married Richard Colley, and Eleanor, who married Thomas Rotsey, to whom Richard Colley and Margaret gave up their share of the manor in 1542.[18] In the same year Thomas Harewell, grandson of Eleanor, Edmund his son and heir,[19] and the above Thomas Rotsey and Eleanor his wife conveyed three fourths of the manor to George Wall,[20] to whom Thomas and Edmund sold their half in 1544[21] and Thomas Rotsey and Eleanor theirs in 1546.[22] George Wall was succeeded by a son George, who died without issue before 1564, when the manor passed to his four sisters.[23] One of them, Eleanor wife of Edward Corbett,[24] afterwards married Thomas Wylde, who seems to have acquired the whole manor.[25] It passed from him to his son George Wylde, serjeant-at-law,[26]

and to his son John Wylde,[27] who was appointed chief baron of the Exchequer in 1646.[28] The latter died in 1669[29] and was succeeded by an only daughter, Anne wife of Charles West Lord De La Warr,[30] who conveyed it in the same year to Elizabeth Knightley.[31] From her it passed to the Foleys, possibly through the marriage of Anne daughter and heir of Essex Knightley of Fawsley with Thomas Foley, eldest son of Paul Foley of Stoke Edith.[32] One of the Foleys exchanged it for certain lands in Martley and Shrawley, with Richard Nash, father of Treadway Nash, the celebrated historian of Worcestershire.[33] In 1785 Dr. Nash settled the manor on his only daughter Margaret[34] on her marriage with John Lord Somers, and she in 1811 settled it on her son Edward Charles Somers.[35] The latter was killed at the siege of Burgos in the following year,[36] and subsequently Lord Somers sold the manor to John Corbett, of the same name as, but not descended from, the feudal owners.[37] From the latter it passed by his will to Thomas Corbett, his brother,[38] whose trustees now hold it.

A several fishery which was claimed by William Corbett in 1274–5[39] belonged to the manor in the 14th,[40] 18th[41] and 19th[42] centuries. A fee-farm rent of £10 yearly, paid by the lord of Impney to the Crown, was sold in 1673 to John Kent, Roger Reeve and Richard Hawkins.[43]

PURSHULL (Purteshull, xiii cent.), now a farmhouse, is another estate in Elmbridge, which was held under the manor of Wychbold.[44] It is first mentioned about 1210, when John de Montviron held half a knight's fee there.[45] The estate passed at about that time to Sibyl de Peremort,[46] who was perhaps the wife of John de Peremort (Porinore), who was said to be holding a fifth of a knight's fee of the honour of Richards Castle in 1211–12.[47] John was still in possession in 1220–1,[48] and had been succeeded by Henry Peremort before 1274–5.[49] It was possibly this Henry who granted to his son Walter certain land in Purshull.[50] Alice widow of Walter de Peremort paid a subsidy of 12d. at Wychbold in 1280.[51]

---

[2] Lay Subs. R. Worcs. c. 1280 (Worcs. Hist. Soc.), 24.

[3] Cal. Inq. p.m. 1–19 Edw. I, 386.

[4] Ibid. 1–9 Edw. II, 24.

[5] De Banco R. East. 1 Edw. III, m. 25; Mich. 2 Edw. III, m. 159.

[6] Red Bk. of Exch. (Rolls Ser.), ii, 567, 605; Testa de Nevill (Rec. Com.), 39b, 40b; Feud. Aids, v, 302, 323; Cal. Inq. p.m. 1–9 Edw. II, 24.

[7] Red Bk. of Exch. (Rolls Ser.), 567; Testa de Nevill (Rec. Com.), 44 a.

[8] Testa de Nevill (Rec. Com.), 39b, 40b, 42b; Red Bk. of Exch. (Rolls Ser.), 605.

[9] Cal. Inq. p.m. 1–19 Edw. I, 87, 396.

[10] Assize R. 1026, m. 19 d.; Lay Subs. R. Worcs. c. 1280 (Worcs. Hist. Soc.), 24. He was dead by 1281 (Reg. G. Giffard [Worcs. Hist. Soc.], 128).

[11] Cal. Inq. p.m. 1–19 Edw. I, 488.

[12] Chart. R. 3 Edw. III, m. 6, no. 15.

[13] Cal. Pat. 1381–5, p. 320.

[14] Anct. D. (P.R.O.), C 3260.

[15] Feud. Aids, v, 330.

[16] Nash, op. cit. i, 348; Habington, op. cit. i, 463.

[17] Weaver, Visit. of Heref. 1569, p. 36.

[18] Feet of F. Div. Co. Mich. 34 Hen. VIII. Habington (i, 464) makes Eleanor Rotsey, Margaret Colley and

another sister Elizabeth Pychard the daughters of Roger Harewell, but Margaret is said to be daughter of Walter Hacklute in the above fine.

[19] Nash, op. cit. i, 77; Visit. of Worc. (Harl. Soc. xxvii), 71–2.

[20] Feet of F. Worcs. East. 34 Hen. VIII.

[21] Ibid. Trin. 36 Hen. VIII.

[22] Ibid. Mich. 38 Hen. VIII. Thomas Rotsey and Eleanor reserved to themselves an annuity of £10 out of their share of the manor and afterwards sold the annuity to Sir Thomas Palmer (Com. Pleas D. Enr. Mich. 1 Edw. VI, m. 20 d.; Feet of F. Worcs. Hil. 1 Edw. VI).

[23] Close, 6 Eliz. pt. xvi, no. 47.

[24] Visit. of Worcs. 1569 (Harl. Soc. xxvii), 151.

[25] Eleanor and her first husband bought a quarter of the manor in 1564 from George Davis, son of Jane, one of the sisters of George Wall (Close, 6 Eliz. pt. xvi, no. 47).

[26] Recov. R. Worc. Mich. 19 Jas. I, rot. 48.

[27] Visit. of Worc. 1569 (Harl. Soc. xxvii), 151.

[28] Dict. Nat. Biog.

[29] Ibid.

[30] G.E.C. Complete Peerage, iii, 50.

[31] Feet of F. Worcs. Mich. 21 Chas. II.

[32] Burke, Peerage.

[33] Nash, op. cit. i, 348.

[34] Recov. R. Worc. Hil. 25 Geo. III, rot. 381.

[35] Ibid. East. 51 Geo. III, rot. 24.

[36] Burke, Peerage.

[37] Burke, Landed Gentry (1906).

[38] Ibid.

[39] Assize R. 1026, m. 19 d.

[40] De Banco R. 491, m. 230.

[41] Recov. R. Worc. Hil. 25 Geo. III, rot. 381; East. 26 Geo. III, rot. 433; East. 51 Geo. III, rot. 24.

[42] Ibid. East. 52 Geo. III, rot. 127.

[43] Close, 25 Chas. II, pt. xi, no. 3.

[44] Testa de Nevill (Rec. Com.), 40, 42b; Feud. Aids, v, 302, 323; Chan. Inq. p.m. 1 Edw. II, no. 59a.

[45] Testa de Nevill (Rec. Com.), 40, 42b.

[46] Ibid. 40b.

[47] Red Bk. of Exch. (Rolls Ser.), 605.

[48] Assize R. 1021, m. 5.

[49] Cal. Inq. p.m. 1–19 Edw. I, 87.

[50] Habington, op. cit. i, 461. Habington gives other deeds relating to the Peremorts and Purshull, but none are dated (ibid. 460–1).

[51] Lay Subs. R. Worcs. c. 1280 (Worcs. Hist. Soc.), 24.

Henry Peremort held the estate in 1308.[52] Richard de Portes was dealing with land at Purshull and Timberhonger in 1332–3,[53] and Purshull was perhaps sold in 1337 with Timberhonger by William de Portes to Hugh de Cooksey, for Hugh de Cooksey obtained a grant of free warren at Purshull in 1335,[54] and in 1349 Hugh and William de Cooksey were dealing with land at Purshull.[55] Nash, however, quotes a deed of 1324–5 by which Walter de Cooksey released to Walter son of John de Peremort the capital messuage of Purshull, which lately formed the dower of Joan wife of John de Peremort.[56] From the Peremorts Purshull passed to the Purshulls through the marriage of Margaret daughter and heir of John de Peremort with a member of that family.[57] Habington quotes an undated deed by which this Margaret granted to her son John de Purshull all her lands within the manor of Wychbold,[58] and in 1398[59] Sir Walter de Cooksey granted to John de Purshull a tenement called the Hull of Purshull and other lands at Purshull.[60] John de Purshull held land at Purshull in 1431,[61] and it continued with the family of Purshull until the 18th century.[62] In 1781 it was the seat of Mrs. Purcell of Worcester.[63] John Baynham of Purshull Hall certified in 1791 that he had set apart for Roman Catholic worship a room in his house, which still exists in its ancient state.[64]

Purshull Hall stands about 2½ miles north-east of the church and a mile south of the main road from Bromsgrove to Kidderminster. It is a rectangular two-story house of red brick with tiled roofs and faces north-east. It was built in the early part of the 17th century, and somewhat enlarged and restored early in the 18th century. It has a projecting central porch with a window over, surmounted by a gable having a cross in the centre, a ball at each foot and a face finial. The dressings of the round-arched doorway and the window lintels are covered with plaster, and there is a brick string-course over the windows at both stages. Two chimneys project at the back, one of which, near the centre, is of ashlar sandstone to the first floor and is continued above in brickwork as an engaged group of three diagonal shafts the tops of which are modern ; the other at the south is rectangular and entirely of brickwork ; while a third at the north end is rectangular to the first floor and continued above as two separate shafts of the intersecting diagonal plan. On the west side of the house are many long, narrow windows of the Queen Anne period. The hall has a large stone fireplace with a deep moulded flat arch and jambs with moulded stops, and a deep cornice ; the whole is now painted black. The oak stairway, which is of late 17th-century date, has a long circular newel. The stairway at the top has some re-used mitred oak panelling of about 1630, and leads to a compartment in the roof over the kitchen wing which

contains an early 17th-century oak altar and rails ; the latter are in almost perfect condition and measure 10 ft. 8 in. along the front and 8 ft. 4 in. at the returned sides. They have plain top rails with projecting upper moulding, flat shaped and pierced balusters and a kneeling pace which returns all round. The altar has two turned and moulded legs and an incised frieze ; it has evidently been added to at some period and altered from its original form, some of the frieze being used up in the legs. The top has a piece cut out in the centre about 12 in. by 8¼ in., and still retains some fragments of old cloth covering. The iron knocker and some of the oak doors are probably of 17th-century date.

In the middle of the 14th century Thomas Cassy granted to Thomas Beauchamp Earl of Warwick land which he held for life at Purshull.[65] The earl appears to have settled it as the 'manor' of Purshull on William Lord Bergavenny and Joan his wife.[66] It is mentioned among the possessions of Joan Lady Bergavenny on her death in 1435,[67] and from an inquisition of 1476 appears to have passed to her granddaughter Elizabeth wife of Edward Nevill, afterwards Lord Bergavenny, for the latter was holding it by the courtesy at his death in 1476.[68] It is, however, enumerated among the possessions in 1439 of Richard Beauchamp Earl of Warwick,[69] who was the heir male of William Beauchamp Lord Bergavenny, and it was granted in 1447 as a late possession of Henry Duke of Warwick to Cecily Duchess of Warwick.[70]

The so-called manors of *SAGEBURY* and *OBDEN* have always followed the same descent, but the name of Obden does not occur until the 16th century. Sagebury, as its former name of Savagebury proves, must have at one time belonged to the family of Savage, and evidently to that branch of it which was settled at Newton, co. Warwick. Of this family Geoffrey Savage died about 1230, when the custody of his land and heir was granted to his father-in-law, Hugh le Despenser.[71] His son, also called Geoffrey, died without issue in 1248, and was succeeded by his uncle, William Savage, rector of Newton.[72] On the death of the latter in 1259[73] his property was divided between Thomas de Ednisoure, son of his sister Lucy, and Hugh Meynill, who had married Philippa, another sister,[74] Sagebury evidently being assigned to the latter, and passing from him to his son William and grandson Hugh.[75] Hugh Meynill, probably son of the last-named Hugh, received a grant of free warren there in 1350,[76] and this is the first mention of Sagebury which has been found.[77] He left two sons, William, who died without issue before 1363, and Richard,[78] who was succeeded before 1403 by four granddaughters, Joan, Elizabeth, Margaret, and Thomasine.[79] At first Sagebury seems to have been

[52] *Cal. Inq. p.m. 1–19 Edw. I,* 396.
[53] Feet of F. Worcs. East. 6 Edw. III.
[54] Chart. R. 9 Edw. III, m. 1, no. 3.
[55] Feet of F. Worcs. East. 23 Edw. III.
[56] Nash, op. cit. i, 348–9.
[57] Habington, op. cit, i, 461.
[58] Habington, loc. cit.
[59] The Cookseys retained some interest in Purshull until 1404–5 or later (Chan. Inq. p.m. 6 Hen. IV, no. 32).
[60] Nash, op. cit. i, 349, quoting deeds in possession of the late Dr. Purcell of Worcester.
[61] *Feud. Aids,* v, 331.

[62] Habington, op. cit. i, 462 ; Nash, op. cit. i, 346.
[63] Nash, loc. cit.
[64] *Worc. N. and Q.* 126.
[65] Add. MS. 28024, fol. 7.
[66] Chan. Inq. p.m. 12 Hen. IV, no. 34.
[67] Ibid. 14 Hen. VI, no. 35.
[68] Ibid. 16 Edw. IV, no. 66.
[69] Ibid. 17 Hen. VI, no. 54.
[70] *Cal. Pat.* 1446–52, p. 38.
[71] *Excerpta e Rot. Fin.* (Rec. Com.) i, 205. Newton was in the possession of a Geoffrey Savage in the time of Henry II and King John (*Pipe R. 5 Hen. II* [Pipe

R. Soc.], 25 ; 27 Hen. II, 73 ; Hunter, *Great R. of the Pipe,* 1 Ric. I [Rec. Com.], 117 ; *Rot. de Oblatis et Fin.* [Rec. Com.], 172).
[72] *Excerpta e Rot. Fin.* (Rec. Com.), ii, 31.
[73] Ibid. 313.   [74] Ibid. 323.
[75] Dugdale, *Hist. of Warw.* 229.
[76] Chart. R. 44 Edw. III, m. 4, no. 8 ; De Banco R. 420, m. 147.
[77] Philippa de Sagebury paid a subsidy of 20s. at Elmbridge in 1280 (*Lay Subs. R. Worcs. c.* 1280 [Worcs. Hist. Soc.], 24).
[78] *Plac. in Canc.* iii, 9.
[79] Wrottesley, *Ped. from the Plea R.* 229.

divided among them,[80] but it finally passed to Margaret, who married John Dethick,[81] son of Ralph Dethick of Dethick Hall, co. Derby. Richard Dethick, grandson of John and Margaret, settled it on his son Richard on his marriage with Elizabeth daughter of John Newport in 1526,[82] and the last-named Richard died seised of the manors of Sagebury and Obden in 1544, leaving a son William.[83] The latter dealt with the manor in 1583, when he held with it free fishing in Henbrook.[84] His son George had succeeded him before 1597,[85] and mortgaged his

DETHICK. *Argent a fesse vairy or and gules between three water bougets sable.*

estates at Sagebury and Obden,[86] and finally sold them in 1605 [87] to Edward Smyth and Dorothy his wife. They in 1613 conveyed half the property to George Smythes, citizen and alderman of London,[88] who purchased the other half from Henry Miles and Elizabeth his wife in the following year.[89] George Smythes died in 1615, leaving a son Arthur,[90] who got into debt partly by 'the cunning practise of others,' and partly by his own 'over liberall expenses,'[91] and was put into prison 'by the meanes of his father-in-law.'[92] Before he was of age he had married Elizabeth Chaffin, widow, daughter of a certain Giles Tooker, and according to her relations treated her very badly, refusing to pay for her maintenance and 'threatening her in verye evill termes and words unbeseeminge a husband.'[93] Soon after his marriage he had been persuaded by his father-in-law to settle his estates in Sagebury and Obden on his wife Elizabeth and their son Arthur,[94] and in 1622 he tried to re-settle them to make provision for a younger son George.[95] Arthur Smythes was knighted in 1624 and was Sheriff of Worcestershire in 1630.[96] In 1637 he, with Arthur his son and heir, sold Sagebury and Obden to Thomas Nott,[97] who was still holding them in 1683.[98] In 1746 both estates were in the possession of Pynson Wilmot, clerk.[99] On his death in 1784 they passed to his only son Robert Wilmot, who died intestate, when they passed to his sister Anne Wilmot,[100] who in 1802 married Thomas Henry

Bund. By her will she left them to her second daughter Ursula, who married the Rev. T. H. Hill, and they about 1875 sold them to John Corbett. The estates passed by his will to his brother Thomas Corbett, and are now the property of the Corbett trustees, Viscount Cobham and Mr. J. Willis-Bund.[100a]

The manor of *ASTWOOD* from early times consisted of two parts, one known as Astwood Robert and the other as Astwood Savage or Astwood Meynill. Both were held of the lords of Wychbold.[1] Little is known of Astwood Robert. Early in the 13th century it was held by Robert de Astwood,[2] and about the same time Richard de Astwood (Estwood) paid a mark for half a fee in Astwood.[3] The other estate must in early times have been closely connected with the manor of Sagebury (q.v.). Under the lords of Wychbold it was held during the 13th century by the Ardernes, Thomas Arderne being named as mesne lord in 1211–12, 1258–9, 1274–5, 1286–7 and 1308.[4] Under the Ardernes the estate was held by the Savages. Early in the 13th century Geoffrey Despenser held a fourth of a knight's fee at Astwood which shortly afterwards passed to Parnel Savage.[5] William Savage died in 1258–9 seised of 2 carucates of land in Astwood, and this estate like Sagebury was evidently assigned to his sister Philippa wife of Sir Hugh Meynill.[6]

It then followed the descent of Sagebury [7] until 1365–6, when Richard Meynill recovered it against John de Stoke and John de Blacklegh, who claimed it under a grant by Richard's brother William.[8] A quarter of a fee in Astwood held in 1431 by Thomas Gevettes[9] may perhaps be identified with this estate. Habington states that Astwood was held in the middle of the 17th century by the Wheelers,[10] but according to the visitation of Worcestershire in 1682 the Wyldes were seated there at that time, John Wylde of Astwood, Dodderhill, being succeeded by a son Thomas, who died about 1652. It passed from him to his son John, who was residing there in 1682.[11]

WYLDE of Astwood. *Argent a chief sable with three martlets argent therein.*

---

[80] There are settlements of one fourth of Sagebury on Roger Bradshaw and Elizabeth his wife in 1411 (Feet of F. Div. Co. East. 12 Hen. IV), and on Roger Aston, kt., and Elizabeth his wife in 1425 (ibid. Hil. 3 Hen. VI). Elizabeth was probably one of the co-heirs mentioned above, but if so must have been married three times, since in the pedigree given in a De Banco R. her husband is said to have been William Croweshawe (Wrottesley, op. cit. 229).

[81] *Feud. Aids*, v, 331. There is a pedigree of the Dethick family in *Visit. of Worc.* 1569 (Harl. Soc. xxvii), 47.

[82] Exch. Inq. p.m. (Ser. 2), file 1198, no. 1. Richard Dethick and his son are mentioned in a muster of 1539 (*L. and P. Hen. VIII*, i, 305).

[83] Exch. Inq. p.m. (Ser. 2), file 1198, no. 1. William's right to a part of Obden was disputed by his cousin William Dethick in 1560 (Chan. Proc. [Ser. 2], bdle. 56, no. 3), and by John Dethick son of William in 1571 (ibid. bdle. 53, no. 32; see also bdle. 54, no. 48, 49).

[84] Feet of F. Worc. Mich. 25 & 26 Eliz.

[85] Ibid. 39 & 40 Eliz.; Hil. 40 Eliz.

[86] Ibid.; *Acts of Parl. Relating to Worc.* (Worcs. Hist. Soc.), 11; Chan. Proc. Jas. I, H ix, 57; S xiii, 27.

[87] Feet of F. Worcs. Mich. 2 Jas. I.

[88] Ibid. 10 Jas. I; Trin. 11 Jas. I; Mich. 11 Jas. I.

[89] Ibid. Mich. 12 Jas. I. Elizabeth was probably the daughter of Edward Smith.

[90] Chan. Inq. p.m. (Ser. 2), cccxlvii, 93. His widow Sarah afterwards married Sir Arthur Savage, kt. (Chan. Proc. Jas. I, S xviii, 34).

[91] Chan. Proc. Jas. I, S xviii, 34.

[92] Ibid. xxvii, 15.   [93] Ibid.

[94] Ibid.; Feet of F. Worcs. Trin. 16 Jas. I. In 1621 Arthur Savage and Sarah his wife gave up their right to the property to Arthur Smythes and his trustees (ibid. Mich. 19 Jas. I).

[95] Chan. Proc. Jas. I, S xviii, 34.

[96] Shaw, *Knights of Engl.* ii, 184; *List of Sheriffs*, 159.

[97] Feet of F. Worcs. Mich. 13 Chas. I; Recov. R. Mich. 13 Chas. I, rot. 57.

[98] Recov. R. Hil. 35 & 36 Chas. II, rot. 96.

[99] Feet of F. Worcs. Mich. 20 Geo. II.

[100] Recov. R. Worc. Hil. 42 Geo. III, rot. 235.

[100a] Information by Mr. J. Willis-Bund.

[1] *Testa de Nevill* (Rec. Com.), 39b, 40b, 42b; *Red Bk. of Exch.* (Rolls Ser.), 605; *Feud. Aids*, v, 302, 323.

[2] *Testa de Nevill* (Rec. Com.), 39b, 42b.

[3] Ibid. 40b.

[4] *Red Bk. of Exch.* (Rolls Ser.), 605; *Cal. Inq. p.m.* Hen. III, 125; 1–19 Edw. I, 87; 1–9 Edw. II, 24.

[5] *Testa de Nevill* (Rec. Com.), 40b, 42b.

[6] *Cal. Inq. p.m.* Hen. III, 125.

[7] Feet of F. Worcs. 11 Edw. II, no. 25.

[8] De Banco R. 420, m. 147.

[9] *Feud. Aids*, v, 331.

[10] Habington, op. cit. i, 464–5.

[11] Metcalfe, *Visit. of Worc.* 1682, p. 103.

The manor of *PIPERS HILL* is mentioned in 1819, when it belonged to Thomas Shrawley Vernon.[12] It passed from him with the Hanbury estate to Sir Henry Foley Vernon.

CASHIES or *CASSIES FARM* probably took its name from the family of Cassy, of whom Thomas Cassy occurs as lord of Hadzor in the 14th century.[13] He seems to have had no children and gave up the reversion of most of his property, which may have included Cashies Farm, to Thomas Beauchamp Earl of Warwick.[14] The Earls of Warwick probably held the estate until the attainder of 1499.[15] It was leased by the Crown for twenty-one years to Richard Camme in 1515 and to John Borneford in 1526.[15a] In 1543 Henry VIII granted it to Richard Andrews and Nicholas Temple,[16] who in the following year sold it to Walter Talbot and Elizabeth his wife.[17] It is last mentioned in 1624, when John Talbot, son of Walter, died seised, leaving a son Francis.[18]

Mills seem to have been attached to each of the manors of Wychbold, Elmbridge and Impney. There were five mills at Wychbold in 1086,[19] and a rent of 50*s.* from the mill was settled on Mabel de Say in 1222–3.[20] The mill is mentioned again in the 13th century.[21] The mill of Elmbridge is first mentioned in 1376,[22] and still belonged to the manor in 1707.[23] In the 19th century four mills belonged to the manors of Impney and Barnes or Barnes Hall.[24]

A mill in the parish which had been granted to Haughmond Abbey, co. Salop, by Osbert Fitz Hugh, and confirmed to it by Hugh de Say his brother, remained in the possession of the abbey until its dissolution,[24a] and was granted to John Wright and Thomas Holmes in 1553–4.[25] There are now two corn-mills on the River Salwarpe near Wychbold Court, and Walkmill Farm, further south, probably indicates the site of a former mill. In Elmbridge there is a corn-mill near Elmbridge Green.

CHURCHES The church of *ST. AUGUSTINE* consists of a chancel 38 ft. 9 in. by 19 ft. 6 in., a nave, or more properly a central crossing, about 18 ft. square, north transept 23 ft. by 25 ft. 6 in., and a massive tower, the lower part of which serves as a south transept, 24 ft. by 16 ft., all internal measurements.

The church is of late 12th-century foundation, having probably been begun about 1180, though not dedicated till 1220.[26] At that time it must have been a large and important edifice of a complete cruciform plan with a central tower, but at the present time no part of the former nave is above ground.

This first building has undergone considerable alteration, and at the present time the arches of the crossing (below the former central tower) and some of the internal stonework of the north transept are the only portions of it which survive. In 1313 the church was appropriated to the Prior and convent of Worcester,[27] and in consequence the chancel was enlarged and new altars were consecrated there in 1322.[28]

The central tower is said to have been demolished during the Civil War, and there is no doubt that the nave and other parts suffered at the same time. The

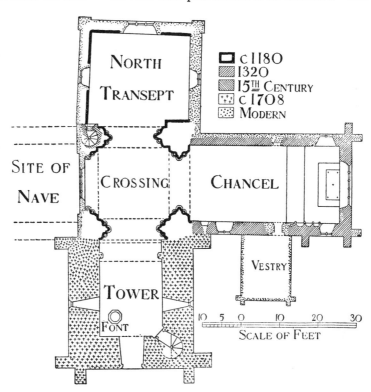

PLAN OF DODDERHILL CHURCH

present tower was erected about 1708, in the place of the south transept, which presumably was in ruins at that time.

The north transept appears to have been entirely rebuilt early in the 19th century, when it was refaced externally with plain red brick. The outer face of the north wall of the chancel has also been bricked.

Owing to the contiguity of the salt mines of Droitwich parts of the building have sunk to an alarming extent. The tower in spite of its massive walls (8 ft.

[12] Recov. R. East. 59 Geo. III, rot. 289.   [13] Add. MS. 28024, fol. 7*b*.
[14] Ibid. See also under Hadzor.
[15] *L. and P. Hen. VIII*, xviii (1), g. 981 (57).
[15a] Ibid. ii, 667 ; iv, g. 2002 (23).
[16] Ibid. xviii (1), g. 981 (57).
[17] Ibid. xix (1), g. 141 (77). Walter died in 1586–7 (Chan. Inq. p.m. [Ser. 2], ccxix, 99).

[18] Chan. Inq. p.m. (Ser. 2), ccccxvi, 68. The property then consisted of a capital messuage and 80 acres of land.
[19] *V.C.H. Worcs.* i, 314.
[20] Feet of F. Div. Co. 7 Hen. III, no. 29.
[21] Chan. Inq. p.m. 1 Edw. II, no. 59*b*.
[22] Mins. Accts. bdle. 1067, no. 22.
[23] Recov. R. Worc. Mich. 6 Anne, rot. 34.

[24] Ibid. East. 51 Geo. III, rot. 24 ; East. 52 Geo. III, rot. 127.
[24a] *Cal. Pat.* 1317–21, p. 434 ; Dugdale, *Mon. Angl.* vi, 110, 113.
[25] Pat. 7 Edw. VI, pt. iv, m. 13.
[26] *Ann. Mon.* (Rolls Ser.), iv, 413.
[27] Worc. Epis. Reg. Reynolds, fol. 97 d.
[28] Ibid. Cobham, fol. 28 d.

thick) has had to be strengthened by bolts and ties. The east end of the chancel is some 20 in. lower than the west, but the floor has been levelled again, and a curious illusion is caused by the falling of the string-courses eastward, which makes the floor appear to rise towards the east end.

A vestry was built to the south of the chancel fifteen years ago, on the site of one erected in 1820, which then replaced an old vestry and porch.

The five-light east window is of 14th-century date with leaf tracery which has been renewed outside but may be old internally. The pointed arch has a moulded label on stops carved as bishops' heads. The inner jambs have moulded angles with bases and capitals, supporting a moulded rear-arch. Internally on either side of this window were formerly canopied niches, but these have been entirely removed and the spaces filled with modern stonework. The three side windows in the chancel, one in the north and two in the south wall, have internal mouldings of similar detail to those of the east window but partly repaired. All are of 14th-century date, and of two lights with pointed heads and tracery of varying design. In the middle of the north wall is a small blocked doorway, with a depressed head. In the south wall are a piscina and two sedilia, forming three bays. The westernmost seat has been replaced by the vestry door, probably before the present doorway was inserted. Owing to the sinking of the wall the seats and sill are now lost in the floor. The heads are trefoiled and ogee shaped. Carried round the inside of the walls, below the windows, is a moulded string-course, which leaps the sedilia and the vestry doorway; the string is repeated externally on the south and east sides. Above the modern vestry doorway the blocked remains of a former window arch are visible outside. It was lower and smaller than the other two south windows. In the western end of the same wall is a small low-side window, now blocked, and obscured outside by the tower buttress. The internal jambs have roll mouldings with bases and capitals.

The chancel is ashlar faced internally, and externally on the south and east walls, which are strengthened by buttresses, the two eastern being modern. Evidence that the 12th-century chancel was vaulted is afforded by the additional order or wall rib on the east face of the chancel arch. The four arches forming the crossing are of late 12th-century or early 13th-century date, but parts of them have been renewed. The responds have detached keeled side-shafts with moulded bases, some of which are sunk below the floor level, and a half-round shaft against the inner face. Most of the capitals are scalloped, with carvings of varying design above; but one on the west jamb of the northern arch is carved with stiff upright foliage, typical of very early 13th-century work. Almost all the capitals of the inner half-round shafts are restorations, the shafts themselves, in the north and west arches, being later renewals. The arches were, no doubt, formerly semicircular, but owing to either subsidence or rebuilding they are now four-centred. The inner order of each arch evidently dates from late in the 17th century, when the central tower was removed. A thin wall, in which is a four-light traceried window, now closes the archway to the former nave. The gabled roof above the crossing and the flat panelled ceiling below are modern.

The north transept is lighted by three modern windows, and in the south-west corner is a blocked doorway, with four-centred head and rebated jambs, which gave access to the vice of the former central tower. Above it is a small trefoiled light. The transept is ashlar faced inside, the east wall being wholly modern, and the outside is faced with brick, with stone clasping buttresses at the angles. The tower is of three stages, of which the lowest forms the south transept. It has a separate archway towards the crossing standing free of the 12th-century work. It is lit to the east and west by plain narrow lancets and to the south by a traceried two-light window above the south doorway, which comes within the plinth and has moulded jambs and a pointed head. The upper part of the lowest stage, which is strengthened by the addition of two buttresses to each of its outer faces, is lit by single-light windows in the three free sides. The second stage has small square-headed lights to the south and east, and the windows to the bell-chamber are of two lights with pointed heads. The parapet is embattled and formerly had pinnacles at the corners, but these have perished, with most of the coping stones. The stonework of the tower is of ashlar, and each face is dotted with iron plates, to which the tie rods are bolted.

All the roofs and furniture of the church are modern, the pulpit being of iron.

There are a few fragments of old glass mixed with modern in the east window of the north transept.

The most interesting monument is an undated one of about 1620 on the north wall of the chancel to a Dannet; it is carved with four kneeling figures in relief, all defaced, with a Latin doggerel inscription. Over it is a shield of nine quarters : 1, Dannet; 2, two bars ; 3, three flying birds ; 4, three eagles between two bends ; 5, two bends ; 6, bendy of ten ; 7, a fesse checky between six crosslets ; 8, checky ; 9, six rings. Also on this wall is a mural monument to Philip Brace, died 1671, with his arms above, and another to Gilbert Penrice, died 1726, and his wife Mary Watkins, died 1722.

In the north transept is a Latin inscription to Edward and Arthur, sons of the Rev. Edward Philipps, died 1656 and 1664, and in the south transept (tower) are a small Latin inscription to a Dannet (undated) and a small brass to Samuel Sandes, 1636. There are also gravestones to the Rev. Henry Jones of Droitwich, died 1665, and various members of the Wylde family.

Of the six bells the treble and third are by Richard Sanders of Bromsgrove, dated 1708 ; the second by Mears, 1814 ; the fourth a 1708 bell recast in 1830 by J. Rudhall ; the fifth by Abel Rudhall, 1754 ; and the tenor a Rudhall bell of 1756 recast in 1893.

The communion plate includes a cup and cover paten of 1571, also two flagons and a plate of 1797, given by Thomas Holbeche, whose arms are engraved on the plate.

The registers previous to 1812 are as follows : (i) all entries 1651 to 1722 ; (ii) all entries 1723 to 1743 ; (iii) marriages 1744 to 1754, baptisms and burials 1744 to 1804 ; (iv) marriages 1754 to 1776 ; (v) marriages 1776 to 1812 ; (vi) baptisms and burials 1805 to 1812.

There are also two overseers' books : (i) 1652 to 1724, with list of briefs and copies of the award in the

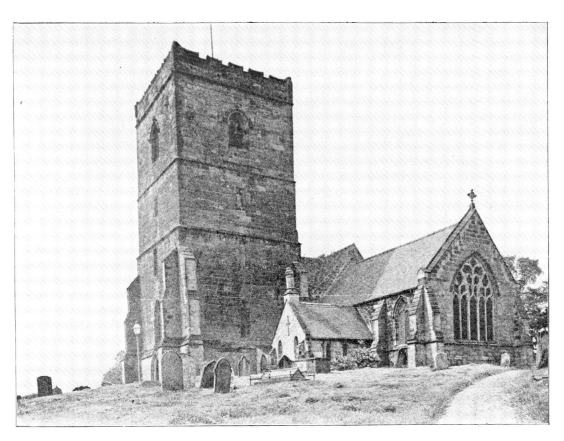

DODDERHILL CHURCH FROM THE SOUTH-EAST

DODDERHILL CHURCH : THE CHANCEL ARCH

matter of Elmbridge and its contribution ; (ii) 1738 to 1834.

The church of *ST. MARY*, Elmbridge, consists of a continuous chancel and nave 42 ft. 7 in. by 16 ft. 6 in., a north aisle of nearly the same length 16 ft. wide, and a stone bellcote surmounting the western gable. These measurements are all internal. The church was entirely rebuilt in 1872 in the 13th-century style with the exception of the north arcade of the nave, the columns and responds of which, dating from about 1200, have been preserved in their original positions. The fine south doorway of the latter half of the 12th century has also been re-set in the new south wall of the nave. It is of three round-arched orders, the outer moulded with the lozenge and the second with the cheveron ; the innermost order is quite plain, and the stones of the head are for the most part modern. The two outer orders have jamb shafts with bell-capitals and moulded bases with leaf-spurs at the angles. Outside all is a label curiously moulded with a succession of fluted cones.

The font and altar are modern. In the vestry, which is partitioned off at the west end of the aisle, is a chest of c. 1600, much cut down.

On the north wall of the aisle is an elaborate mural tablet to the memory of Edmund Purshull of Purshull Hall, 'who was buried,' as the inscription states, 'May y 21st 1650, Aged 96 years, being y first that was interred in this Church (at least for many ages).' Upon the same tablet are commemorated Gerard Purshull, his eldest son, who died in 1685, and Mary, the wife of James Purshull, eldest son of Gerard Purshull, who died in 1675. The inscription states that she was the daughter of John Wood, rector of Clent, by his first wife Bridget, widow of William Parrott of Bell Hall, and daughter of Francis Conyers, whose son Sir John Conyers, kt. and bart., was 'sometyme Lieutenant of the Tower of London and Captain of the king's life-guard of horse and Governor of Berwick-upon-Tweed.' Above the tablet is a shield of Purshull, Barry wavy argent and gules a bend sable with three boars' heads or thereon. To the east of this is a small brass plate commemorating John Dannet of Elmbridge Hall, who died in 1752, his wife, who died in 1760, two daughters of the name of Elizabeth, Edward Bookey, 'wine merchant of London,' buried 'in a cave near this place,' who died in 1774, and his wife Frances, daughter of the above-mentioned John Dannet, who died in 1782. In the church-yard east of the church is a large table-tomb, much decayed, and without inscription, probably of the mid-17th century.

There are two bells ; the first has no date or inscription upon it, and the second is inscribed 'W. B. 1750.'

The plate consists of a silver cup and cover paten of 1571 of the usual type, a modern silver flagon and paten and a mounted cruet.

The registers are as follows : (i) all entries 1570 to 1645 (with a gap from 1626 to 1631), fragmentary 1645 to 1663 and all entries 1663 to 1719 ; (ii) all entries 1720 to 1754, baptisms and burials to 1771 ; (iii) marriages 1755 to 1812 ; (iv) baptisms and burials 1773 to 1812.

The church of *ST. MARY DE WYCHE*, Wychbold, is a building of stone in late 14th-century style, consisting of a chancel, nave, aisles, transepts, vestry and organ chamber, south porch and west tower. The advowson is the property of the Corbett trustees.

ADVOWSON The advowson of the church of Dodderhill was given by Osbern Fitz Richard, lord of Wychbold, to the priory of Worcester,[29-30] and the gift was confirmed by Bishop Samson (1096–1112)[31] and by his successors Theulf (1115–23)[32] and Simon (1125–50).[33] About 1158 Osbert son of Hugh, with the advice of Alfred Bishop of Worcester, and with the consent of Henry I, granted the church of Dodderhill to the nuns of Westwood, and at the time the monks of Worcester made no protest.[34] Later, however, the church was restored to them by a judgement of Bishop Roger in 1178, the nuns being compensated with land and tithes in Clethall, Westwood and Crutch.[35] The monks obtained a confirmation of their right by Bishop Roger and Pope Lucius.[36] Osbert son of Hugh confirmed the church to the priory, reserving to himself the next two presentations,[37] and a further confirmation was obtained from Hugh Fitz Osbert.[38]

Baldwin Bishop of Worcester (1180-5) appropriated 100s. yearly from the church of Dodderhill to the Prior and convent of Worcester, and this was confirmed by Osbert de Say and his brother Hugh.[39]

The advowson was claimed in 1220–1 by William de Stutevill and his wife Margery, but they lost the suit,[40] and, though the claim was renewed by Robert de Mortimer in 1274–5, the monks seem to have had no difficulty in establishing their right.[41]

The church of Dodderhill was appropriated in 1301 to the Prior and convent of Worcester.[42] The appropriation was made without royal licence, and in 1302 the Archbishop of Canterbury, probably at the king's request, deprived the priory of the church.[43] It was decided in 1303–4 that the priory by this unauthorized appropriation had forfeited the church to the Crown.[44] The monks were pardoned for this trespass in 1305, and the church was restored,[45] and again appropriated to them in 1313.[46] In the following year a vicarage was ordained.[47]

Even then the monks seem to have had some difficulty in establishing their right to the church, for in 1333 the king presented John de Cokham by Letters Patent,[48] which were, however, revoked some days later on evidence that the advowson did not belong to the king.[49] This was followed by a confirmation from the king of the licence granted by

---

[29-30] Thomas, *Surv. of Worc. Cath.* A 104.
[31] Ibid.
[32] Ibid. A 106.
[33] Ibid. A 110.
[34] Ibid. A 111.
[35] Ibid. A 115.
[36] Ibid. A 114 ; Heming, *Chartul.* (ed. Hearne), 532, 536.
[37] Nash, op. cit. i, 332 ; Assize R. 1021, m. 4.

[38] Prattinton MSS. (Soc. of Antiq.), Deeds of D. and C. of Worc. no. 311; *Hist. MSS. Com. Rep.* xiv, App. viii, 192.
[39] Nash, op. cit. i, 333 ; Assize R. 1021, m. 4.
[40] Assize R. 1021, m. 4.
[41] Ibid. 1026, m. 5 ; Feet of F. Worcs. Trin. 3 Edw. I.
[42] *Reg. G. Giffard* (Worcs. Hist. Soc.), i, Introd. p. lvi. This appropriation is the last recorded act of Bishop Giffard.

[43] *Sede Vacante Reg.* (Worcs. Hist. Soc.), 30, 35, 41, 43, 44 ; *Ann. Mon.* (Rolls Ser.), iv, 556.
[44] *Abbrev. Plac.* (Rec. Com.), 250.
[45] *Cal. Pat.* 1301-7, p. 361.
[46] Worc. Epis. Reg. Reynolds (1308–13), fol. 97 d.
[47] Ibid. Maydston (1313–17), fol. 15 d.
[48] *Cal. Pat.* 1330-4, p. 413.
[49] Ibid. p. 416.

Edward I to appropriate the church,[50] and by another appropriation made on the mandate of the pope that the eight manors and five churches which belonged to the priory were not enough 'to support fifty monks and to give hospitality to the many strangers who visited the city.'[51] After this date the prior and monks seem to have held the advowson peaceably until the Dissolution.[52] It was granted in 1542, with the other property which had belonged to the priory, to the Dean and Chapter of Worcester,[53] who some years later surrendered it to the king 'in consideration of his acquittance of their obligation to maintain students at Oxford.'[54] In 1550 it was purchased with the rectory by Robert Catlin and Peter Wainwright,[55] who a few months later sold it to William and Gilbert Dethick,[56] the owners of an estate at Sagebury and Obden in the parish. They appear to have sold it to Henry Field, from whom it was purchased in 1574 by Philip Brace.[57] It remained in his family until the end of the 17th or beginning of the 18th century,[58] when it was again sold to Gilbert Penrice, who presented to the living in 1717.[59] Henry Penrice was the patron in 1771 and Harriet Holbeche in 1774.[60] According to Nash it 'came by a female to Thomas Holbecke,' the father of Harriet.[61] The advowson belonged to Thomas Holbeche in 1789[62] and 1831,[63] but had been sold before 1849, when the Rev. John Jackson was the patron and vicar of the church.[64] It was afterwards purchased by John Corbett of Impney.[65] He devised it to his brother Thomas, whose trustees are the patrons at the present day.

When William de Dover was rector of the church of Dodderhill, c. 1275, he founded and endowed a hospital there for a master and a certain number of brethren 'to minister divine service for ever,' the master being appointed by the Prior and Convent of Worcester.[66] The hospital was the subject of several disputes immediately after the Dissolution.[67] The late prior and convent were accused of suppressing the hospital without the king's licence, of turning out the poor people who lived there 'to their utter destruction,' of pulling down the buildings and selling the materials for their own use, of withholding the hospital lands from Richard Cornwall, the master, and of causing Richard Dethick and others to mow a meadow called 'Preastmeadow.'[68] About the same time Humphrey Stafford seems to have laid claim to the advowson of the hospital, and to a messuage called the chantry house with land belonging. It was shown that the advowson of the chantry or hospital, which was dedicated in honour of the Virgin Mary, belonged to the prior and convent, who presented a certain John

Sewell, and at the same time Humphrey Stafford presented John Marshall. A jury was appointed to settle the disputes which arose, but they were still undecided six months later, when the king having the bishopric in his hands presented Richard Cornwall to the hospital.[69] The house seems to have been finally dissolved with the chantries, and in 1548 its site and possessions were granted to Peter Wainwright and Robert Catlin.[70] According to Nash the property afterwards passed to the Braces, and in his time belonged to Mr. Gilbert Penrice,[71] from which it would appear that the site of the hospital followed the same descent as the advowson (q.v.). Nash also says that the 'edifice is still subsisting as a pigeon-house near the bridge.'[72]

In 1322 William de Thorntoft, rector of the church of Dodderhill, obtained licence to consecrate an altar in the church of Dodderhill.[73]

The chapel of Elmbridge annexed to the church of Dodderhill existed in 1274-5.[74] It remained a chapelry of Dodderhill[75] until 1877, when it was severed from the mother church and constituted a separate benefice.[76] It is now a vicarage in the gift of the trustees of the late Thomas Corbett. A curate to serve the chapel at Elmbridge was provided by the vicar of Dodderhill.[77]

In 1637, in settlement of a long-standing controversy, the inhabitants of Elmbridge were ordered to pay a third part towards the repairs of the church of Dodderhill and the ornaments thereof.[78]

The new ecclesiastical parish of Wychbold was formed from Dodderhill in 1888, and the church was consecrated in that year.[79] In Wychbold is a Congregational chapel dating from 1836.

CHARITIES

In 1624 Thomas Wylde by deed conveyed to trustees certain lands and hereditaments in this parish and Astwood, the rents to be applied towards reparation of the parish church, or maintenance and relief of poor people, or some other charitable or godly use, according to the discretion of the trustees. The trust property has been sold and the proceeds invested in £575 2s. consols with the official trustees, producing £14 7s. 4d., which in 1910 was applied in moieties for the church reparation and for the poor.

In 1655 Jane Murrall by her will left £5 for the poor, which with £9 collected by the parish was applied towards the purchase money of some cottages, which were conveyed by deed dated 1 November 1659 to trustees for the parish, the rents to be applied for such charitable uses as the minister and churchwardens and others should agree upon, reserving 5s. a year for distribution among the poor.

[50] *Cal. Pat.* 1330-4, p. 521.
[51] Worc. Epis. Reg. Horlton, 1327-33, i, fol. 27 ; ii, fol. 53 ; *Cal. Papal Letters,* ii, 381. At that time the church was valued at £30.
[52] *Valor Eccl.* (Rec. Com.), iii, 225. At that time the church was worth £18 10s.
[53] *L. and P. Hen. VIII,* xvii, g. 71 (29).
[54] *Hist. MSS. Com. Rep.* xiv, App. viii, 185.
[55] Pat. 4 Edw. VI, pt. viii.
[56] Nash, op. cit. i, 333.
[57] Feet of F. Worcs. Mich. 16 & 17 Eliz.
[58] Inst. Bks. (P.R.O.).
[59] Ibid.   [60] Ibid.
[61] op. cit. i, 333. See also under Charities.

[62] Inst. Bks. (P.R.O.).
[63] Gorton, *Topog. Dict. of Great Britain.*
[64] Lewis, *Topog. Dict.*
[65] Burke, *Landed Gentry* (1906).
[66] Chant. Cert. 25, no. 22; Nash, op. cit. i, 343, quoting the register of the Dean and Chapter of Worcester ; Worc. Epis. Reg. Silvester de Gigliis (1498-1521), fol. 25 d.
[67] In the *Valor Eccl.* (Rec. Com.), iii, 270, the yearly value is said to have been £8, but in the Chant. Cert. 25, no. 22, it is said to have amounted to £16 2s. 4d. after certain rents had been paid to the Prior and convent of Worcester.
[68] *L. and P. Hen. VIII,* xi, 1429 ; Star Chamb. Proc. Hen. VIII, ix, fol. 190-201 ; xii, fol. 210-11 ; bdle. 31, no. 84.

[69] Star Chamb. Proc. Hen. VIII, bdle. 28, no. 72.
[70] Pat. 4 Edw. VI, pt. viii. In 1590 there is a grant of all the lands belonging to the late chapel of Dodderhill to William Tipper and others (ibid. 32 Eliz. pt. iv).
[71] op. cit. i, 343.
[72] Ibid.
[73] Worc. Epis. Reg. Cobham (1317-27), fol. 28 d.
[74] Assize R. 1026, m. 9 d.
[75] Inst. Bks. (P.R.O.) ; Feet of F. Worcs. Mich. 16 & 17 Eliz. ; Exch. Dep. Mich. 1659, no. 20.
[76] *Parl. Papers* (1890-1), lxi, 50.
[77] Exch. Dep. Mich. 1659, no. 20.
[78] Nash, op. cit. i, 346.
[79] *Parl. Papers* (1890-1), lxi, 44.

In 1698 Catherine Talbot, as appeared from the Church Table, by will gave 20s. to be distributed on 1 May yearly to the poor of the In-liberties. The annuity is paid out of the Oakley Estate and duly applied.

The gift of Thomas Sanders of 10s. 6d. for bread to ten poor widows, and of Joseph Bache of 20s. for bread, also mentioned on the Church Table, have ceased to be paid.

In 1784 Thomas Holbeche in confirmation of a gift of £5 a year by will of his sister, Sarah Penrice, by deed charged his estate called Gateley Farm with an annuity of £5 for the poor of Dodderhill and Elmbridge.

In 1910 £3 was distributed among the poor of this parish and £2 among the poor of the chapelry of Elmbridge.

Chapelry of Elmbridge:

The church lands, referred to on the Church Table, consist of 9 a. 1 r. 20 p. let at £18 a year, which is applied towards the repairs of the church.

The Church Table also mentioned a gift by Edmund Brod to the poor of 3s. 4d. yearly charged upon his estate at Dunclent in the parish of Stone. The annuity has ceased to be paid.

Mr. Touch Bourne, as mentioned on the Church Table, gave a meadow containing 2 a. for the poor. It is let at £5 a year and the rent is duly applied.

The Church Table also mentioned that William Norris of this chapelry erected and endowed a school at Cutnall Green, to which Elmbridge was entitled to send fifteen children. For further details see below under parish of Rushock.

DOVERDALE

Doferdæl (ix cent.); Lunvredele (xi cent.); Douredela (xii cent.); Doveresdale.

Doverdale is a small parish a few miles north-west of Droitwich, and has an area of only 749 acres, of which 304 are arable land, about 400 permanent grass and 6 woods and plantations.[1] In 1901 the population was only 58, a slight increase on that of the middle of the 19th century. Noake states that in his time the parish consisted of only six houses and one labourer's cottage, 'the only one ever known there.'[2] The parish is watered by the Elmley or Doverdale Brook, which forms the boundary between Ombersley and Doverdale for some distance. The chief road is that from Hampton Lovett, on a branch of which to the south is the church of Doverdale. The old Moat Farm, possibly the manor-house, was burned down about 1850. The moat is now dry and the house has never been rebuilt.

The land is undulating, and varies from a height of 87 ft. above the ordnance datum on the banks of the Doverdale Brook to about 150 ft. in the north of the parish. The soil is clay and sandy loam, the subsoil clay and sandstone rock, raising crops of wheat, beans and barley. Agriculture is the only industry. Flax and hemp were cultivated in Worcestershire towards the end of the 18th century. Thomas Brooks of Doverdale claimed a bounty under the Act of 1780 in 1782 and some of the following years, and his claim was allowed at quarter sessions.[3]

In the time of King Edward the *MANOR* Confessor *DOVERDALE* was held by Thurbern, a thegn of the king. It had passed before 1086 to Urse D'Abitot,[4] from whom the overlordship passed to the owners of Elmley Castle.[5] The Savages of Elmley Castle claimed the overlordship at the time when Nash wrote his *History of Worcestershire* (c. 1780).[6]

The under-tenant mentioned in 1086 was a certain William,[7] whose successors, lords of the manor in the 12th and 13th centuries, were called 'de Doverdale.' In the reigns of John and Henry III, however, Richard de Ombersley held the manor as mesne lord under William de Beauchamp.[8]

In 1166 Walter de Doverdale held the manor by the service of one knight's fee,[9] and early in the 13th century William and Hugh Blund were in possession.[10] In a dispute as to the advowson of the church of Doverdale which arose in 1274 it was stated that the vill of Doverdale[10a] had been divided (apparently in the time of Henry III) between two sisters, Aline and Idonea.[11] Ralph de Doverdale, great-grandson of Aline, who is probably to be identified with Ralph de Doverdale, who was deputed to inspect certain salt-pits at Droitwich in 1264,[12] died about 1274, leaving a son William, a minor, whose custody was in the hands of Richard de Ombersley.[13] William de Doverdale, coroner for Worcestershire, died about 1303,[14] and is probably to be identified with William de Sodington, who died at this time seised of the manors of Sodington and Doverdale, leaving as his heirs his nephew Richard, son of Reynold le Porter and Marisca eldest sister of William, and his sisters Eustacia wife of William de Doverdale and Joan wife of Walter Blount.[15] Doverdale was held jointly by these co-heirs about 1316,[16] but the Blounts[17] subsequently acquired the whole manor of Sodington, Eastham passed to the Porters, and Doverdale was apparently assigned to Eustacia and William de Doverdale. Although William had two sons[18] the manor became divided into moieties, passing to the

[1] Statistics from Bd. of Agric. (1905).
[2] Guide to Worcs.
[3] Worc. N. and Q. 102; Stat. 21 Geo. III, cap. 58.
[4] V.C.H. Worcs. i, 318b.
[5] Red Bk. of Exch. (Rolls Ser.), 299, 567; Testa de Nevill (Rec. Com.), 40b, 43b; Cal. Inq. p.m. 1–9 Edw. II, 403; Chan. Inq. p.m. 3 Edw. IV, no. 15; (Ser. 2), cccl, 51.
[6] op. cit. i, 293.
[7] V.C.H. Worcs. i, 318b.

[8] Testa de Nevill (Rec. Com.), 40b; Assize R. 1026, m. 1.
[9] Red Bk. of Exch. (Rolls Ser.), i, 299; Pipe R. 13 Hen. II (Pipe R. Soc.), 68.
[10] Testa de Nevill (Rec. Com.), 40b.
[10a] By the references in Birch, Cart. Sax. i, 172, 502, it appears that Doverdale was originally a river name, tributary to the Salwarpe.
[11] Assize R. 1026, m. 1.
[12] Habington, Surv. of Worc. (Worcs. Hist. Soc.), ii, 299.

[13] Assize R. 1025, m. 1.
[14] Cal. Close, 1302–7, p. 32.
[15] Reg. W. Ginsborough (Worcs. Hist. Soc.), 75; Add. MS. 28024, fol. 190a.
[16] Add. MS. 28024, fol. 190a.
[17] A knight's fee at Doverdale was included among the possessions of Sir John Blount at the time of his death in 1425 (Chan. Inq. p.m. 3 Hen. VI, no. 17).
[18] Feet of F. Worcs. case 260, file 20, no. 26. They may have been sons by a former marriage.

families of Braz or Brace and Lench. Possibly Margery wife of Richard Brace of Droitwich, on whom half the manor was settled in 1335,[19] was a daughter of William de Doverdale, and Eustacia wife of Thomas Lench of Droitwich, on whom the other moiety was settled in 1371–2, may have been her sister.[20]

In 1428 the half a fee which Richard Brace had held belonged to his heir,[21] who was probably his son John, escheator of Worcestershire in 1403–4 and 1408–9 and justice of the peace in 1428–9.[22] John still held the manor in 1431,[23] but had probably been succeeded before 1434 by a son John.[24] This John was twice married. By his first wife he had a son Richard, whose daughters Margaret and Elizabeth married Robert Bromwich and John Ewnet respectively, and their representatives, William Bromwich, grandson of Margaret, and Rowland Ewnet, son of Elizabeth, claimed the manor at the beginning of the 16th century.[25] It seems, however, to have been settled upon John Brace, son of John Brace by his second wife, the settlement having probably been made about 1434, when Sir Humphrey Stafford of Grafton, father in-law of the younger John, presented with other trustees to the church of Doverdale.[26]

William Brace, who contributed six archers to the muster of 1539, was probably grandson of the younger John.[27] He died in 1543,[28] and his grandson Francis Brace[29] settled the manor in 1588 on his son Thomas on his marriage with Frances daughter of William Freer of Oxford, with contingent remainders in default of heirs male to Philip Brace, brother of Francis.[30] Thomas Brace died in his father's lifetime, leaving no son, so that on the death of Francis Brace in 1599 this moiety of the manor passed to Philip.[31] John Brace son of Philip held the manor in 1607,[32] and died in 1632.[33] His son Philip Brace compounded for his estates in 1646[34] and died in 1671.[35] His two eldest sons having died without issue it passed to his third son Philip, who also died without issue in 1674.[36] His heirs were his four sisters, Penelope Brace, Mercy wife of Sir Simon Clarke of Salford Priors, co. Warwick, Elizabeth wife of William Mills

BRACE. *Sable a bend argent between two armed arms in their proper colours.*

of Mickleton and Welford, co. Gloucester, and Eleanor wife of Francis Woolmer of Grafton,[37] who all conveyed their shares of the manor in 1677 to Thomas Tyrer, Gerard Dannet and Ralph Taylor,[38] apparently for the use of Ralph Taylor, who was in possession in 1684.[39] It was possibly this moiety of the manor which was conveyed in 1772 by John Hill, John Taylor and his wife Anne and others to Wilson Aylesbury Roberts and Rowland Hill.[40] Nash states that South Hall, the manor-house of the Braces, was once held by a Mr. Clifton,[41] and that in 1780 it was held by James Newnham.[42] Later it was purchased by William Prattinton of Bewdley from Mr. Amphlett, and belonged in 1816 to P. Prattinton.[43] It was perhaps this part of the manor which was subsequently purchased by Sir John Somerset Pakington.[44] It then followed the same descent as the other part of the manor.[45]

The other half of the manor had probably passed from Thomas Lench and Eustacia to Henry Lench before 1422–3.[46] He was still holding it in 1431,[47] but it had passed before 1434 to John Lench.[48] On the accession of Edward IV John Lench was attainted and 'suffered deathe and losse of all in the quarrell of sayntly Kinge Henry the syxt,' being found strangled in prison soon after he was condemned.[49] Doverdale with other property was granted to Sir Walter Scull and Frances his wife,[50] but on the accession of Henry VII was restored to John Lench, son of the above John.[51] He was succeeded by a son William, who held the manor in 1541,[52] and a grandson Ralph, who held it in 1603.[53] John Lench, who may have been son of Ralph, was lord of the manor in 1655 and 1673,[54] and by 1676 had been succeeded by George Lench.[55] He died in 1704, apparently leaving a son George,[56] who dealt with a mill in the manor in 1709.[57] This moiety of the manor passed to Captain Burrish and was sold towards the end of the 18th century by his son George.[58] It was probably this part of the manor which was sold in 1804 by John Mackmillan to Sir John Pakington, bart.[59] Sir John died without issue in 1830, and the manor passed to his nephew John Somerset Russell, who assumed the name Pakington and was created Lord Hampton.[60] He subsequently acquired the rest of the manor of Doverdale,[61] and from that time it followed the same descent as Hampton Lovett (q.v.), and was sold in 1902 to Mr. Edward Partington with the rest of the Westwood estate.

There was a mill worth 4s. at Doverdale in 1086.[62] It is not mentioned again until 1670, when it was

[19] Feet of F. Worcs. case 260, file 20, no. 15.
[20] Feet of F. Worcs. 45 Edw. III, no. 11.
[21] Feud. Aids, v, 324.
[22] Habington, op. cit. i, 191.
[23] Feud. Aids, v, 330.
[24] Sede Vacante Reg. (Worcs. Hist. Soc.), 414.
[25] Early Chan. Proc. bdle. 120, no. 54; bdle. 287, no. 18.
[26] Sede Vacante Reg. (Worcs. Hist. Soc.), 414.
[27] L. and P. Hen. VIII, xiv (1), p. 306; Visit. of Worc. 1569 (Harl. Soc. xxvii), 24.
[28] Nash, op. cit. i, 335.
[29] Close, 12 Eliz. pt. i, Brace and Russell.
[30] Feet of F. Worcs. Mich. 30 & 31 Eliz.
[31] Chan. Inq. p.m. (Ser. 2), cccxxv, 186.

[32] Feet of F. Worcs. East. 5 Jas. I.
[33] Nash, op. cit. i, 335.
[34] Cal. of Com. for Comp. pt. ii, 1414.
[35] Nash, op. cit. i, 335. Metcalfe gives the date as 1673 (Visit. of Worc. 1682–3, p. 23).
[36] Metcalfe, loc. cit.; Nash, loc. cit.
[37] Metcalfe, loc. cit.
[38] Feet of F. Trin. 29 Chas. II.
[39] Exch. Dep. East. 36 Chas. II, no. 31.
[40] Feet of F. Worcs. Hil. 12 Geo. III.
[41] op. cit. i, 293.   [42] Ibid.
[43] Prattinton Coll. (Soc. Antiq.).
[44] Information supplied by Mr. R. Bruce Ward.
[45] See below.
[46] Nash, op. cit. i, 292.
[47] Feud. Aids, v, 330.
[48] Sede Vacante Reg. (Worcs. Hist. Soc.), 414.

[49] Habington, op. cit. ii, 58; Chan. Inq. p.m. 3 Edw. IV, no. 15.
[50] Cal. Pat. 1467–77, p. 110; Rolls of Parl. v, 583.
[51] Rolls of Parl. vi, 334b.
[52] L. and P. Hen. VIII, xvi, 617.
[53] Lay Subs. R. 1603 (Worcs. Hist. Soc.), 5.
[54] Feet of F. Worcs. Trin. 1655; Mich. 21 Chas. II.
[55] Feet of F. Worcs. East. 25 Chas. II; Recov. R. D. Enr. Hil. 27 & 28 Chas. II, m. 1.
[56] Prattinton Coll. (Soc. Antiq.); Feet of F. Worcs. Trin. 4 Will. and Mary.
[57] Feet of F. Worcs. Mich. 8 Anne.
[58] Prattinton Coll. (Soc. Antiq.).
[59] Recov. R. East. 44 Geo. III, rot. 234.
[60] Burke, Peerage.   [61] See above.
[62] V.C.H. Worcs. i, 318b.

DOVERDALE CHURCH C. 1810
(*From a Water-colour by Thos. Rickards in Prattinton Collection*)

DROITWICH: ST. ANDREW'S CHURCH FROM THE SOUTH-WEST

conveyed by John Lench and his wife Sarah to Philip Brace and Thomas Symonds.[63] It apparently remained annexed to the Lench moiety of the manor, for George Lench was dealing with it in 1709,[64] and it is mentioned in conveyances of the manor in 1772 and 1804.[65] There is at the present day a water-mill on the Elmley Brook at Doverdale.

The little church of *ST. MARY THE VIRGIN* consists of a chancel, nave and modern south vestry, with a western wood steeple.

Some of the walling of the nave appears to date from the end of the 12th century, and the small round arch to the blocked north doorway is evidently of that date. Beyond this there are no distinctive features left of any age. The nave windows have old stonework, perhaps of the 14th or 15th century, but have been much altered. The chancel was rebuilt about the middle of the last century, and the church has undergone several restorations.

The chancel arch and chancel are modern, with a traceried east window of three lights. The first windows in the north and south walls of the nave have each three plain rectangular lights with a pointed segmental rear arch, and near the west end on either side is a plain rectangular single light; between the two north windows is a blocked doorway, the head of which is semicircular, with a filleted angle roll. The entrance is by a doorway in the west wall, with a round window over, both modern. The bell-turret is of modern woodwork and is supported on heavy wood posts in the nave and capped by a four-sided spire covered with lead.

The font is modern. The nave walls are panelled all round with 17th-century woodwork; the panelling along the north wall and about half the south has a fluted top rail, and the rest is carved with semicircular interlacing arches filled with foliage.

In the north-west window of the nave is an ancient stained glass figure of our Lady surrounded by scrolls inscribed 'Emanuel.'

There are three bells; the treble inscribed 'God be our speed 1660 I M' (John Martin of Worcester); the second, dated 1615 and bearing the initials of the churchwardens and the founder, Godwin Baker, with his mark the cross keys; the tenor inscribed 'Sancte Thome, ora pro nobis,' preceded b a flowered saltire.

The plate consists of an Elizabethan cup with hall mark of 1571, the stem of which has at some time been broken, and a large paten, 1868.

The only copy of the old registers preserved is the one containing marriages from 1756 to 1812. Some 17th-century entries will be found among the bishop's transcripts.

ADVOWSON There were a church and priest at Doverdale at the time of the Domesday Survey.[66] The advowson was apparently held with the manor until in the reign of Henry III William de Doverdale, on succeeding to the estates of his grandmother Aline, gave the advowson to his cousin John, son of Idonea,[67] because John offered such opposition to his succession.[68] In 1274 the advowson belonged to William de Doverdale, evidently a descendant of John, but it was claimed by Simon de Ombersley, to whom certain lands in the manor had been demised during the minority of the heir of Ralph de Doverdale by the overlord, Richard de Ombersley. William was able to make good his right to the advowson.[69] He presented to the church in 1275,[70] and may possibly be identified with William called le Wyte of Doverdale, who presented in 1294.[71] William son of Ralph de Doverdale, who married Eustacia, one of the daughters and co-heirs of William de Sodington, was probably a descendant of William le Wyte, and by his marriage the advowson and the manor once more became united. The advowson seems to have become annexed to the moiety of the manor held by the Braces,[72] and descended with it until nearly the end of the 17th century. It was included with the manor in a conveyance of 1677,[73] but seems to have been sold shortly after. John Price presented for one turn in 1688, and Thomas Egginton presented in 1704 and 1716.[74] He conveyed the advowson in 1722 to Thomas Brett.[75] Peter Cassey and Mercy his wife and others presented in 1744 and William Griffin in 1750 and 1762.[76] It had passed from him before 1765 to Robert Harrison,[77] who conveyed the advowson and rectory in 1770 to Richard Harrison.[78] This conveyance may have been made with a view to the purchase of the advowson by Hugh Laurents, for he presented to the church in 1771 and 1788,[79] and conveyed the advowson in 1789 to Richard Fuller.[80] The Rev. P. Laurents was said to be patron in 1808,[81] though George Thomas presented to the church in 1807,[82] and was patron in 1829.[83] The advowson had passed before 1849 to the Oldham family,[84] one of whom, Mrs. Curtler, was patron in 1868.[85] About ten years later the advowson was purchased of the representatives of the Oldhams by Mrs. C. P. Mottram, the present patron.

In the 15th century the rector of Doverdale paid 2s. yearly to the church of Hartlebury.[86]

CHARITIES In 1892 the Rev. James Oldham, by his will proved at Worcester 17 March, left £300, the interest to be applied towards the repair of the fabric of the church and of the fences and gates of the churchyard. The legacy was invested in £278 14s. 11d. consols with the official trustees, producing £6 19s. 4d. yearly.

---

[63] Feet of F. Worcs. Mich. 21 Chas. II.
[64] Ibid. 8 Anne.
[65] Ibid. Hil. 12 Geo. III; Recov. R. East. 44 Geo. III, rot. 234.
[66] V.C.H. Worcs. i, 318b.
[67] Aline and Idonea had held the manor jointly. See under manor.
[68] Assize R. 1026, m. 1.
[69] Ibid.
[70] Reg. G. Giffard (Worcs. Hist. Soc.), 78.

[71] Ibid. 438.
[72] Feet of F. Worcs. Hil. 9 Edw. III; Sede Vacante Reg. (Worcs. Hist. Soc.), 414; Early Chan. Proc. bdle. 120, no. 54; Chan. Inq. p.m. (Ser. 2), cccxxv, 186.
[73] Feet of F. Worcs. Trin. 29 Chas. II.
[74] Inst. Bks. (P.R.O.).
[75] Feet of F. Worcs. Hil. 8 Geo. I.
[76] Inst. Bks. (P.R.O.).
[77] Ibid.

[78] Feet of F. Worcs. Hil. 10 Geo. III.
[79] Inst. Bks. (P.R.O.).
[80] Feet of F. Worcs. Trin. 29 Geo. III.
[81] Carlisle, Topog. Dict. of Engl.
[82] Inst. Bks. (P.R.O.).
[83] Gorton, Topog. Dict. of Great Britain.
[84] Information by Mr. J. Willis-Bund.
[85] Noake, Guide to Worc.
[86] Worc. Epis. Reg. Carpenter, i, fol. 84.

THE BOROUGH OF DROITWICH

Wic, Saltwic (ix cent.) ; Wich, Wiche, Wyȝ, Wichium (xi to xiii cent.) ; Drightwich, Drutwich (middle of xiv cent.) ; Dertwich, Drightwich, Droitwich (xv cent.).

Droitwich lies on the banks of the River Salwarpe on undulating ground in the central Worcestershire plain. The streets of the old town are narrow and hilly ; the town conforms to no regular plan, and has no open market-place. The original main street, High Street and Friar Street, lies to the west of the ancient road to Bromsgrove and south of the Salwarpe, the principal side streets branching south from the High Street. The town lies on the main road from Worcester to Birmingham, and was in Roman times well placed for trade purposes[1] ; the Upper and Lower Saltways of later times indicate the principal road routes by which Droitwich salt was carried to the neighbouring counties. The small river was the only means of water communication until the Salwarpe and Droitwich Canal was begun by Brindley in 1767 and opened in 1771. From the 17th century there had been schemes for better water communication, connected with the names of Endymion Porter, Yarranton and Wall, Lord Windsor and Baker,[2] but all these were unsuccessful.

In 1852 the position of Droitwich was further improved by the creation of the Droitwich Junction Canal[3] to join the existing canal with the Worcester and Birmingham Canal at Hanbury Wharf. The railroad connexion is also good ; the station on the West Midland section of the Great Western is connected with the Midland by a loop line.

The brine baths and salt manufacture lend to the town all its characteristic features and give it two very different aspects. The pleasant surroundings necessary for a health resort are offered near the baths, while in the lower part of the town the decay caused by abandoned salt works and ruined buildings gives it a desolate appearance. When the salt trade was carried on by John Corbett there were several salt manufactories at work, and Droitwich was a prosperous place. Now (1912) there is only one salt manufactory, the Covercroft Works, in use. The main pumping of brine is for the use of the baths, and it seems likely that in a few years salt will cease to be made at Droitwich, and it will become solely a health resort. The spread of the town is to the higher lands, to the south towards Witton, and west to the railway station, where the risks of subsidence, much felt in the old part of the town, are not incurred, as they lie outside the salt area, which is very clearly defined.

BOROUGH Droitwich was the site of a Roman villa or spa,[4] but how far its salt was worked on a commercial scale there is nothing to show. The Anglo-Saxon charters give the first direct evidence proving that the salt springs had given the place commercial importance, but most of those which enter into detail are open to suspicion.[5] A forged Evesham charter[6] of date 716 refers to a grant of Hampton *juxta Wiccium emptorium*, and in another[7] of date 716-17 a part of a 'mansio in Wico emptorio salis quem nos Saltwic vocamus'; in the same charter 'illa portio quam nostratim *Sele* nuncupamus' is freed from tribute. The *salinae* or 'seals' of a later time will often come under notice below, and this early definition is important.[8] In a list of Worcester charters[9]

BOROUGH OF DROITWICH. *Gules a sword point downwards argent with its hilt and pommel or surmounted by two lions passant or.*

a grant is calendared by which Ethelbald of Mercia gave two *camina* or furnaces in Wich to Worcester Priory and *gustarium salis*, perhaps a measure of the salt water to be boiled in the furnaces. In a genuine charter[10] of date 888 the signatures are stated to be given 'in publico conventu ad Saltwic congregato,' and the place of the Witan's assembly is identified by Kemble as Droitwich.

But the best evidence of the value set in early English times upon the salt springs of Droitwich is to be found in the Domesday Book. In 1086 Droitwich was assessed at 10 hides, and of these 10 a quarter, 2½ hides, lay in Witton,[11] so that this hamlet had already become associated, for fiscal purposes at all events, with the more important though possibly later settlement of Droitwich. Droitwich is not styled 'burgus' in Domesday Book, neither is it treated as a royal manor. The king had rights in it but did not 'lord' it. Of the 10 hides which rendered geld, a half-hide was attached to the king's hall at Gloucester ; the remaining hides were distributed among certain churches and tenants in chief of the king. What William I held in demesne was the whole of the salt springs, the 'pits.' To other men had been given *salinae*, seals, portions of the salt water ; but in the wells or pits at that time sunk the Norman king had undivided lordship.[12] King Edward the Confessor had held a share only in the springs ; he had shared with the earl, whose right may have been that of the original under-king. Both king and earl had farmed their rights in the Confessor's time for a total farm of £76. That the king's total had once been £80 is indicated by the claim of the Abbey of Westminster to a tenth, £8,[13] a sum which was still being paid in the time of Edward III.[14] There had been further decline since the Confessor's day, for William's farm from the sheriff was 65 pounds

[1] *V.C.H. Worcs.* i, 210.
[2] Nash, *Hist. of Worc.* i, 306.
[3] Local and Personal Act, 15 & 16 Vict. cap. 22.   [4] *V.C.H. Worcs.* i, 210.
[5] Kemble, *Codex Dipl.* no. 67 (716–17) and 1358 (no date given) are passed by Kemble as genuine ; and the 'Wich' mentioned can be identified with Droitwich.

[6] Ibid. no. 65.   [7] Ibid. no. 68.
[8] See also *Evesham Chron.* (Rolls Ser.), 73.
[9] Hickes, *Thes.* iii, 299.
[10] Kemble, *Codex Dipl.* no. 1068.
[11] *V.C.H. Worcs.* i, 236, 268.
[12] The only conflicting evidence is that the monks of Bordesley sank a new pit

on an island (see below, p. 77) and at a later time the 'sheriffs' sele' seems to have been regarded as a pit (see below, p. 77).
[13] *V.C.H. Worcs.* i, 302.
[14] *Rot. Lit. Claus.* (Rec. Com.), ii, 6 ; i, 294, 346*b* ; *Cal. Close*, 1302–7, p. 26 ; 1323–7, p. 238 ; 1327–30, p. 57.

by weight. The king had eight pits or wells, five unnamed, three named, Upwic, Midelwic and Helperic. This last must be a personal name. Later we shall find pits in three districts known as Upwich, Middlewich and Nethermostwich, or Netherwich, and we shall find that it is shares in these pits that carry the burgess-ship. Upwich lay on the north side of the Salwarpe, Middlewich probably on the south. Netherwich is still a district, and lies west of the old site of St. Nicholas's Church. From each spring the king in the Confessor's time had a certain number of *salinae* or 'seals,' shares of salt water to be boiled in houses which later got the name of 'seals.' The yield of 'seals' from the five unnamed pits appears in Domesday as small compared with that from the named pits. Besides his 'seals' the king had also *hocci*, a word which occurs only in connexion with royal rights and is given once as *hoch*.[15]

The enjoyment of *salinae* had been originally due, in all probability, to royal grant ; and in 1086 many persons had rights to *salinae* and also to renders of salt in *mitts*, horse-loads, sextaries, or to renders of money's worth from *salinae*, renders due in some cases to estates in distant counties. The word 'wich' having by this time come to mean a salt spring,[16] it cannot always be definitely determined whether the salt springs of Droitwich or those of Cheshire are indicated, unless it can be shown that the manor which had 'seals' appurtenant belonged to a lord who had land in Droitwich.

The tenants in chief who held lands in Droitwich had 'burgesses' in Droitwich in varying numbers. A hundred burgesses can be thus assigned, and thirteen can be added as appurtenant to the neighbouring manor of Wychbold and answerable for certain agricultural services there at fixed seasons. The king's eleven houses probably also contained burgesses, but it is not certain that all 'houses' in Droitwich can be reckoned as 'burgesses'' houses, for in 1240 the Worcester Register states that the ten houses in Droitwich attached to the manor of Hallow were of 'servile condition' and paid merchet, toll and 'thac' and 'sok.'[17]

Salinarii were held by some of the owners of properties to which salt rights attached, and it may be that to the burgesses we may add the *salinarii* as members of the same class. The question of the precise meaning of the word 'burgess' in Domesday Book is wrapped in doubt, and can in all likelihood only be explained, more or less speculatively, case by case. In the case of Droitwich the evidence points to the fact that burgherhood has always been closely associated with certain franchises connected with the salt trade ; possibly the Domesday burgess of Droitwich was enfranchised with but one franchise, and that a franchise which made him more free than other men in respect of the salt trade. We have seen that the king had in 1086 a farm of 65 pounds weight from Droitwich ; the men answerable for this payment were presumably the payers of salt-gafol, persons who in return for their gafol shared in the monopoly of

the Droitwich salt springs and salt trade. One evidence for this theory is offered by a comparison of the terms in which Domesday describes Droitwich and Nantwich. In the description of the Cheshire Wiches there is a very elaborate statement on the subject of toll ; here there were no burgesses, at least none is named. Now in the description of Droitwich, on the other hand, there is not a word of toll, but here there are burgesses. Having regard to the usual burghal arrangement, it is natural to suppose that, though some persons might incur toll when carrying Droitwich salt through the gates of Droitwich, these persons would not be burgesses. The case of the Gloucester monks goes further to suggest that this was so. It is noticeable that the half-hide attached to the king's hall at Gloucester and the half-hide attached to the monastery at Gloucester, unlike most of the Droitwich hides, had no burgesses appurtenant. The two burgessless half-hides are described as being in one *consuetudo*.[18] The Gloucester monks, having no Droitwich burgesses, and having, perhaps for that reason, no means of escaping toll on the salt they obtained from Droitwich, were at the pains to get a charter exempting them from Droitwich toll. In Stephen's reign Waleran Count of Mellent, addressing his reeve and servants of Droitwich, ordered all the Gloucester monks' demesne —whatever their men could 'affy' to be theirs—to be quit of toll and custom at Droitwich, as it had been in the time of King Henry ; and King Stephen, visiting Droitwich, probably before 1139, gave the men of the Abbot of Gloucester their lands in Droitwich to hold freely as under Henry I.[19] The mention of Henry I seems to point to the fact that then first had the Gloucester monks found a means to escape toll, probably by royal grant. Later on, when the burgesses of Droitwich purchased the *firma burgi*, the monks of Gloucester will be found contributing to the farm,[20] and this, the price that others had to pay, may have been the price they paid for an effective release from toll. In 1215 we shall find John granting in fee farm to the burgesses the whole of his rights in the salt of Droitwich, and he does it by giving the vill *cum salsis et salinis*. By the *salsae* he seems to indicate his salt dues, the gafol paid for a share in the control of the springs, perhaps also the toll paid by the carriers of salt. He gives also his seals (*salinae*), these being the shares of brine drawn into his own vats and boiled in his own houses. This interpretation seems to be supported by the *salsa* rolls which are preserved among the Droitwich records.[21] These give the names of persons who appear to be contributing their shares of salt-gabelle to the farm of the borough. There are other lists of payers of *consuetudines* who appear to be non-burgesses. For further evidence it may be pointed out that the Worcester monks' payment of *salsa*, recorded in their own and in the borough MSS., may well have been in return for their right to use the 'common bucket,' to hire Droitwich men to draw their salt water (*salsa*) and to boil their salt (*sal*) and

[15] *Dom. Bk.* (Rec. Com.), fol. 180b. See below, p. 77, on 'hocksilver.'

[16] Ibid. 268a.

[17] Hale, *Worc. Reg.* (Camden Soc.), 52a.

[18] *Dom. Bk.* (Rec. Com.), fol. 174a.

[19] *Hist. et Cartul. Mon. S. Petri, Glouc.* (Rolls Ser.), i, 119 ; ii, 71, 143, 144.

[20] See below, p. 74.

[21] The collection of records in the town clerk's office at Droitwich is a remarkable one. The learned Dr. Pratinton made extracts from the same in the earlier part of the 19th century, and his volume (not paged) is in the possession of the Society of Antiquaries. Mr. W. de

Gray Birch has put the collection at Droitwich roughly into order, and copied the more important MSS. into a volume prepared for the use of the corporation. Many of the rolls are fragmentary, but from what remains a detailed history of the borough could be written.

repair their boilers, rights which Henry III interfered to defend by writ when the bailiffs of Droitwich sought to hinder them.[22]

Droitwich is explicitly called a 'burgus' for the first time, and as far as we know the only time before the charter of 1215, in the Pipe Roll of 1155–6, when an aid of 20s. was paid ; in later Pipe Rolls Droitwich, without the description 'burgus,' appears, somewhat irregularly, as contributing to aids and tallages.[23] The seemingly exceptional case in which the term 'burgus' is applied to Droitwich, and the terms of John's charter of 1215, may raise a doubt whether the burgesses of Droitwich enjoyed before 1215 the jurisdictional privileges of a borough court. The relation of the men of Droitwich to the king may have been a peculiar one, and if they were burgesses merely in respect of their salt franchise this would be accounted for. Their enjoyment of certain privileges in the working of the king's salt springs laid them under contribution to his aids. More cannot be said with safety until John in 1215[24] freed the burgesses from suits of shires and hundreds. Thenceforward Droitwich appears as a hundred co-ordinate with the hundred of Halfshire.[25]

The charter of John saved the pleas of the Crown, but the burgesses were given sac and soc and toll and team and infangthef, the last giving jurisdiction over thieves caught with stolen goods upon them within the area of the borough, but not over other criminal cases in which life and limb were at stake ; 'team' gave the borough court power to call vouchers to warrant and in so far to deal with real actions ; 'sac and soc' enforced the attendance of the burgesses as suitors to the borough court at fixed terms—terms at which the view of frankpledge would be held. A borough court was thus established which was of the humbler order of borough courts. 'Toll' made the burgesses quit of toll throughout the king's realm, and gave them liberty to sell all kinds of merchandise in England, in cities and boroughs and elsewhere, in markets and out of markets.

The trade which the burgesses desired to carry on was mainly no doubt a trade in salt. The salt could now not be taxed at the gates of other boroughs, so far as it was in the king's power by his grant to prevent this.[25a] The vill, that is to say what was the king's to give away in it, was made over to the burgesses in fee farm, *cum salsis et salinis* and all appurtenances and other liberties and free customs belonging to the king's part of the town, for a payment of £100 a year, to be paid at Michaelmas and Easter. When at the close of the 17th century the claim of one Steynor to sink a salt-pit on his land was contested by

the corporation, the words of this charter were closely canvassed by the parties to the action. As has been explained above, the burghal monopoly could probably find its best warrant in the phrase *cum salsis*, but we cannot cross-examine the lawyers of John's time on the precise meaning they attached to the phrase. In return for the *salsae* and *salinae* and their appurtenances which the sheriff till now had farmed, the burgesses promised to pay a higher farm than the sheriff had paid, that they might manage their own affairs. The creation of new pits was not contemplated, but there can be little doubt that a royal right to all salt springs which had not been given away already could have been maintained.[26]

This charter remained the governing charter of the borough till the time of Mary. It was confirmed by Edward III,[27] Richard II,[28] Henry IV,[29] Henry VI,[30] Edward IV,[31] Henry VII[32] and Henry VIII.[33] For the original charter the burgesses paid 50 marks.[34] On the morrow of the grant John gave William Longsword Earl of Salisbury the £100 of yearly fee farm.[35]

About this date the reeve and burgesses of Droitwich agreed with the monks of Gloucester that they would pay the monks' 20s. due to the earl's farm, if the abbot and monks would help to get the receipt at the king's Exchequer. The abbot and monks were to be quit of toll and all exactions and be of the Droitwich *communa* on the same footing as the burgesses ('habebunt communam inter nos sicut unus nostrum ').[36] The monks of Gloucester had by that time added to their half-hide the half-hide attached to the king's hall at Gloucester,[37] so that their Droitwich interests were considerable.

After the purchase of the fee farm, the town's prosperity seems to have diminished. In 1227 the king pardoned 28 marks of the 32 due as tallage.[38] In 1238 the town was in arrears over £23 for the farm, and the Sheriff of Worcestershire was ordered to distrain the burgesses. The bailiff of the town, Thomas Fitz Hugh, had 'affied' at the Exchequer for the debt, and was sent back to Droitwich as a prisoner, in order that he might attempt to recover the money.[39] In 1257 Droitwich was let to the burgesses to farm at the king's will, the sheriff being ordered not to interfere as to the farm or amercements from the farm till he was ordered to do so.[40] In 1262 two burgesses named, probably the bailiffs, rendered account for £80 blanche or £84 by tale,[41] which was probably the farm required under Henry's grant of 1257. Again in 1265 the farm failed, and the king complained to the sheriff that the seals were diminishing in value, and ordered him to view the pits with some

[22] *Hist. MSS. Com. Rep.* xiv, App. viii, 173.

[23] 8 Hen. II, 100s. for aid ; 23 Hen. II, 40 marks for aid ; 7 Ric. I, 20 marks of tallage ; and among the tallaged royal manors on the Pipe Rolls of 1, 5, 12, 16 John.

[24] The charter is printed *Cal. Rot. Chart.* 1199–1216 (Rec. Com.), 216b.

[25] Dugdale, *Mon. Angl.* vi, 1009 gives a conveyance of land in the hundred of Wich, and Anct. D. (P.R.O.), B 3717, one which was sealed in the hundred of Wich, before Adam Clerk, bailiff of Wich. As this last deed names the fee of Reynold Pauncefoot, it probably dates from soon after the grant of the charter of John.

[25a] When Worcester was the place at which a good deal of the salt was put on board boats for carriage to the various markets, in order to avoid the payment of toll on the salt if brought into Worcester, a lane just outside Worcester led down to the Severn, and by it the salt was taken to the boats. It was known as 'Salt Lane' and when the new county prison was built the Worcester Corporation changed the name to 'Castle Street.'

[26] Brunner, *Deutsche Rechtsgeschichte*, ii, 75–6, and the authorities there cited.

[27] Chart. R. 4 Edw. III, no. 22.

[28] *Cal. Pat.* 1377–81, p. 117.

[29] Ibid. 1399–1401, p. 60.

[30] Ibid. 1422–9, p. 489.

[31] Ibid. 1476–85, p. 336.

[32] Confirm. R. 5 Hen. VII, pt. i, no. 10.

[33] Ibid. 7 Hen. VIII, pt. i, no. 3.

[34] *Rot. de Oblatis et Fin.* (Rec. Com.), 561.

[35] *Rot. Lit. Pat.* (Rec. Com.), 151.

[36] *Glouc. Cartul.* (Rolls Ser.), ii, 145–6.

[37] Ibid. ii, 143.

[38] *Rot. Lit. Claus.* (Rec. Com.), ii, 185.

[39] Madox, *Firma Burgi*, 182, citing Memo. R. 22 Hen. III, rot. 11b foot.

[40] Ibid. 20, citing Pas. Communia 41 Hen. III, rot. 14b.

[41] The correct proportion, 1s. in the pound. See *Red Bk. of the Exch.* (Rolls Ser.), 781, on the assessment of Droitwich at this figure, and Madox, op. cit. 182.

knights and report. The sheriff reported that the pits needed thorough renewal, as the wood was old and they had never been repaired. The cost would be £40, for it would be necessary to destroy and afterwards rebuild some houses in the neighbourhood which were not of the king's demesne, in order to dig round and get to the bottom. The sheriff reported that the repairs once done would last a lifetime, and that they must be done before the boiling season began at Midsummer,[42] or the king's rent from the town would fall to 20s.[43] In 1271 the borough was let to Simon Aleyn and Richard Fitz Joce, probably the two bailiffs of the borough, and the town was committed to them to farm for five years.[44] At the end of this time the borough appears to have recovered the fee farm.

In 1274 complaint was made[45] that the community of the town subtracted money due from a 'seal,' and that men who ought to answer with the hundred of Halfshire had been appropriated by William de Valence at Goseford, for the men dwelling there did not answer with the men of Droitwich as they always used to do. The complaint presumably means that the tallage and the 'murdrum' fines of the rest of the hundred were affected by this 'subtraction.' Goseford, represented by Gosford Street, now Queen's Street, at the east end of Droitwich, going down to Chapel Bridge, in the parish of St. Peter of Witton, had paid with Droitwich as one unit; a loss on this unit had to be distributed over the rest of the hundred of Halfshire. The hundred of Halfshire also noted that the burgesses of Droitwich and other boroughs were distraining one neighbour for another, although the man distrained was neither himself the debtor nor the pledge of the debtor. The 'neighbour' was no doubt a suitor to the same court as the debtor, and by this rough-and-ready means of self-help remedies were obtained for wrongs. The practice was maintained in the boroughs after it had ceased in the county, though burgesses were among the first to secure their own chartered privilege from similar treatment.

The burgesses of Droitwich in their turn made complaint that Sir William de Valence, after the battle of Evesham, had appropriated part of the vill of Goseford to the damage of the king's farm. The men of Goseford were constrained to go to his court outside the town, and he appointed his own bailiffs and regulated his own measures. Goseford used always to answer with Droitwich. The town ultimately recovered control of Goseford, for St. Peter's, Goseford, was one of the parishes on which pavage was levied in 1380. Besides this complaint, which seems to hint that the jurisdictional and fiscal boundary of the borough was somewhat indeterminate, two further complaints show the burgesses' anxiety to prevent any reduction of the number of houses on which the borough could levy tallage. One man had alienated his house outside the community of the town into another liberty, to the damage of the king 4s. a year for tallage. The Hospitallers of Grafton had appropriated a tenement in Droitwich and damaged the king's tallage in the same way. Probably this last was a grant in mortmain[46] un-

licensed by the borough court; other boroughs were seeking to make grants in mortmain illegal unless they had been licensed by the borough court. In 1290 a fire began at St. Andrew's Church and destroyed the greater part of the town.[47]

In 1316 the town received the first grant of pavage,[48] a royal licence to take certain tolls on vendible goods, the money collected to be spent on paving. These grants were made for terms of years and frequently renewed. In 1327 the bailiffs, John Cassy the elder and the younger, were suspected of diverting pavage from its purpose, and a royal order for an inquiry was issued[49]; so also in 1341[50] and 1346.[51] A grant of pontage was made in 1331, and an inquiry of a similar kind was made as to the expenditure of the money in 1366.

The constitution of the borough in mediaeval and Tudor times is well exhibited in a fine series of borough records preserved at Droitwich; the earliest borough court rolls and accounts date from the beginning of the reign of Edward III. The importance of their monopoly and the comparative smallness of the number of burgesses made the borough one of the so-called 'democratic' type. No powerful council was developed, and the burgesses always retained a share in the government of the borough. There were two bailiffs and twelve jurats, but the bailiffs, at all events, were annually elected by the burgesses, and the jurats appear to have been persons of importance in the borough court, where they made the presentments rather than in the borough council.

For the government of the salt trade and for the issue of by-laws affecting the borough the burgesses met at the 'Chequer' or Exchequer building, built, as the Droitwich accounts show, in 1327. The Chequer was at Droitwich the equivalent of the Guildhall of other places, the Guildhall generally including a chequer chamber. The reckonings were made, no doubt, upon a chequered cloth as at the Westminster Exchequer. The assembly of the community meeting at the Chequers was called a 'burgess chamber,' a 'great house' or a 'common hall.' At the 'halls' it was determined when the salt boiling or 'walling' (A.-S. 'weallan') should begin and end, the term being usually about 25 June to 25 December; the price of salt was fixed and rules for its sale were drawn up, as also for the cleaning and mending of the pits. These last were duties performed at the expense of the borough, and annually accounted for with the other borough expenses by the bailiffs. In the 'halls' gifts of salt were agreed to, and on one occasion it was ruled that there should be gifts only to the four orders of mendicants (Franciscan, Dominican, Carmelite and Augustinian). One by-law ordered that none might monger salt for pears and apples, perhaps to prevent small retailing, and because it was thought injurious to the borough to exchange the precious salt for perishable goods. It was ordered that the friar who preached on St. Richard's Day should be paid, a reference, no doubt, to the feast of St. Richard of Wich, Bishop of Chichester. Leland

---

[42] The boiling lasted from Midsummer to Christmas.
[43] Nash, op. cit. i, 308.
[44] Madox, op. cit. 20, from the Pipe R.
[45] *Hund. R.* (Rec. Com.), ii, 284-5.
[46] The Hospitallers had land in Droit-

wich at the Dissolution. It was granted Pat. 4 Eliz. pt. vi.
[47] *Ann. Mon.* (Rolls Ser.), iv, 503.
[48] *Cal. Pat.* 1313-17, p. 469. A pavage patent of 14 Hen. VI is found at Droitwich and given a place of dignity on

the supposition that it is the earliest extant borough record and of date 14 Hen. III.
[49] Close, 14 Edw. II, m. 7.
[50] *Cal. Pat.* 1340-3, p. 217.
[51] Ibid. 1345-8, p. 116.

has set on record [52] that games were annually played at St. Richard's salt springs and certain vats called by his name.[53] The belief that when the chief spring failed St. Richard started it again does not appear to have any basis recorded in the biography of the saint.[54]

The early records do not appear to contain any entries to show by what means the body of burgesses was renewed and enlarged, other than an order from the Earl of Warwick (as sheriff) in 1370, that a certain man be made a commoner and admitted to the burgesses' privilege. In the early 16th century owners of boilers (*plumbi*) appear to have been burgesses, and there were many country burgesses. All were assessed to the king's 'lewne' or levy.

The burgesses' prerogative which gave them control of the salt trade necessitated the creation of an executive specially designed for the protection and control of the springs. From the 14th century there come lists of the presentments of the 'tractatores' or 'teyzemen,' 'tymen' or 'tiesmen,' the 'drawers' of brine (A.-S. 'teon' = to draw). It was the business of the 'tractatores' to control the drawing of the brine and see to its distribution in due proportions, as also to prevent fraud in the process of salt-making. The rules to secure equality in the draughts of good, middle and inferior qualities of brine to be supplied to each of the seals were elaborate [55]; and the 'dalls' and 'priors' mentioned in the Worcester Register and elsewhere in connexion with Droitwich salt may have reference to this.[56]

The drawers of the three wiches, Up-, Middle- and Netherwich, made the lists of presentments,[57] and appear to have acted as constables of the wards did in other towns, and the three 'wiches' seem to have been treated as wards. The drawers' presentments are not confined to offences in salt manufacture or salt trading. The presentments make known the existence of a school in the 14th century, for the carrying off of doors and windows from the 'schools' is made a ground of accusation. The borough's corporate ownership of property is similarly noticed; the parson of St. Andrew's was charged with building on the community's ground.[58]

The court of the borough was known as the law hundred, *hundredum legale*, in the 14th century. Like other borough courts, it had a certain amount of control over burgesses' wills, and some early wills are enrolled among the Droitwich records. The rolls of the time of Henry VIII show that the *hundredum legale* had by that time divided into two distinct

sessions, one a *curia parva* for the recovery of small debts, the other a great court, or king's court, in which the view of frankpledge was held and conveyances recorded and seisin delivered. Before the charter of James I the bailiffs doubtless exercised some of the powers of justices of the peace, but there was no chartered grant.

The special nature of the burgesses' monopoly and trade accounts for the absence of any mention of a merchant gild or of craft gilds.

From the time of John's grant of the farm to the Earl of Salisbury its descent can be traced with little breach of continuity.[59] The grant to the earl was confirmed by Henry III in 1217.[60] On the earl's death in 1226 it probably reverted to the Crown. In 1236 it was granted to Eleanor, queen of Henry III.[61] The farm, which had fallen to £80 blanche, rose to £85 blanche in 1280,[62] and to £89 5s. in 1290, and at this figure Eleanor held the 'manor' till her death in 1291.[63]

In 1299 Margaret, queen of Edward I, received the farm.[64] She died in 1317 and Isabella, queen of Edward II, seems to have held it for two years.[65] In 1319–27 the farm was held by the king's half-brother Edmund of Woodstock, Earl of Kent, by knight service.[66] On Edmund's execution in 1330 his enemy Roger Earl of March obtained the farm and held till his execution in the same year. Margaret Countess of Kent, Edmund's widow, then held till her death in 1350.[67] The grant passed to her son John till his death in 1352, when the farm had risen to £100. John's sister Joan held till her death in 1385, her husbands, Sir Thomas Holand and Edward Prince of Wales, in turn acknowledging her receipts. Her heir, Thomas Holand, half-brother of Richard II, held till his death in 1397. His widow Alice held in dower, and their daughters and their descendants afterwards held in shares. By their several marriages the following persons became recipients: Roger Mortimer and Edmund Earl of March, Sir John Grey and his descendants the Greys of Powys, Edmund of Langley Duke of York, Sir Henry Bromflete, George Duke of Clarence, the Dukes of Somerset and their descendants. John Tiptoft, Earl of Worcester, receiving a charge on the dower of Edmund of Langley's widow, had £5 charged on the fee farm. The mother of Edward IV had £70 17s. 10d. charged on the farm, and Elizabeth, queen of Henry VII, and Katherine of Aragon, Jane Seymour, Anne of Cleves and the Duke of Richmond succeeded to this share.[68]

[52] Leland, *Itin.* (ed. 2), iv (2), fol. 185.
[53] The chaplain who served the chantry in honour of St. Richard (see below) received the profits from the four bullaries called 'St. Richardes Vawtes' and 4 marks a year (*L. and P. Hen. VIII*, xvii, g. 283 [33]).
[54] *Acta Sanctorum*, App. i, 276–318. The chapel of the Sacred Heart in Worcester Road is the modern Roman Catholic Church.
[55] Nash, op. cit. i, 298.
[56] Hale, *Worc. Reg.* 95b, and the citations from the Westwood cartulary in *Mon. Angl.* vi, 1008. The latter source mentions 'helflingis' of salt. The 'wrthin' mentioned in the *Worc. Reg.* and in Anct. D. (P.R.O.), B 3717, is puzzling. In the case of the place-name Hlappawurthin (Kemble, op. cit. 209), 'wurthin' seems to have the double sense

of wich, village and salt spring. Possibly the mysterious 'v' of Dom. Bk. 163b, under Sopberie, which rendered twenty-five sextaries of salt, was a 'wrthin.'
[57] There are long lists of *wernatores* and *ernatores* whose offences are presumably to be connected with the salt trade.
[58] The perambulation of the time of Henry VI (see below, p. 79) and Dethick's suit in the 16th century show that there were some commons; Prattinton MSS.; Droitwich MSS. no. 416, 429. The burgesses claimed common on Dethick's lands 'after sickle and scythe.'
[59] A mass of receipts for the fee farm is included in the collection of municipal records at Droitwich. As the farm was frequently let to queens, Droitwich has a particularly fine collection of queens' seals.
[60] *Rot. Lit. Claus.* (Rec. Com.), i, 299, 333.

[61] *Cal. Chart. R.* 1226–57, p. 218.
[62] Madox, op. cit. 182.
[63] *Cal. Pat.* 1281–92, p. 368.
[64] Cole, *Illus. Doc.* 349; *Cal. Pat.* 1292–1301, p. 453.
[65] *Cal. Pat.* 1317–21, p. 116.
[66] *Cal. Chart. R.* 1300–26, p. 416; *Cal. Inq. p.m.* 1–10 Edw. III, 222.
[67] *Cal. Close*, 1330–3, p. 85.
[68] The above account is compiled from the Droitwich receipts, the Patent Rolls, Nash's *Hist. of Worc.* and other records. See *Cal. Close*, 1360–4, p. 176; Chan. Inq. p.m. 4 Hen. V, no. 51; (Ser. 2), ccxxxv, 94; 18 Edw. IV, no. 47; *Cal. Inq. p.m. Hen. VII*, i, 420, 487; *Cal. Pat.* 1422–9, p. 341; 1461–7, p. 131; Pat. 7 Hen. VII, pt. i, m. 8; Stat. 25 Hen. VIII, cap. 28; *L. and P. Hen. VIII*, iv, 737; xiv, g. 1192 (20); xv, g. 144 (2, p. 52); xviii (2), g. 107 (12).

Droitwich : St. Andrew's Church : Tower Arches and North Chapel

The payment seems then to have been allowed to fall into arrears, and in the 17th century £9,000 was charged against the bailiffs.[69] The Stuarts revived among the ancient claims one to a 'lewne' for provisioning the royal household, and Charles I granted Queen Henrietta for life £82 1s. 10d. from the vill.[70] The trustees of the Commonwealth in 1650 sold this yearly sum to the chief baron of the Exchequer, John Wilde, for £738 16s. 6d. A patent of 1670–1 appointed trustees for the sale of the same.[71] The fee farm continued to be a charge upon the borough during the 18th century. In 1704 Sir John Pakington sued the burgesses for his share of the fee farm, then divided among a number of persons.[72] It was stated then that 5s. 10d. a year per vat was the usual contribution to the farm[73]; complaint was made by the plaintiff that many newly-sunk pits were not contributing. In 1708 a bill was brought to the House of Commons to make the new pits contributory, but it was thrown out. How the payment of farm gradually lapsed does not appear, but the fact that it had lapsed is made known in the evidence on Sir John Pakington's petition, 1747,[74] and in the report of the commissioners in 1835.

The long descent of the farm of the 'sheriff's seal,' later called 'shrethales,' 'shrefvessel,' 'shervesputt,' and perhaps identical with the 'sheriff's walling,' which is often mentioned, can also be traced through many centuries. The right of Urse D'Abitot, Sheriff of Worcester, passed with Elmley Castle and the hereditary shrievalty to his descendants the Beauchamps, afterwards Earls of Warwick. During the reign of Stephen William de Beauchamp seems to have lost the sheriffdom and the appurtenant seals, but they were restored to him in 1141 by the Empress Maud,[75] to hold as his father Walter had held. The payment of £20 to Warwick Castle for a seal and bullary of eight vats called 'shirrevesele' appears on the early borough accounts.[76] It was in the neighbourhood of the sheriff's seal, within the borough, that Steynor at the close of the 17th century sank a pit on his own land, which was the means of breaking the burgesses' monopoly.

The king's farm was made up in part by levies of land gafol (longavel), paid at the close of the 13th century by thirty or forty persons, and of 'salsa,' which we take to be a 'gabelle' on salt, each person paying about 1s. The 'salsa' rolls appear to represent in early times the later 'salt rolls of farm assessed,' rolls giving the shares which burgesses contributed to the farm. There was also a render of 'hocksilver,' 'hokeselver,' 'hooselver,' paid by the Prior and convent of Worcester,[77] the Prioress of Westwood and the Abbot of Bordesley. Possibly this 'hocksilver' may be connected with the mysterious 'hocci,' 'hoch' of Domesday Book. The Abbot of

Bordesley's rights in Droitwich salt were derived from Waleran of Mellent, who allowed the monks to keep the new pit, made by their own work, on an island at Droitwich 'near Cholevilla,' the salt to be for their own use 'sine venditione quam inde faciant ibi.'[78] Possibly by the payment of hocksilver the monks were admitted to the right to sell salt by retail.

The rolls which record the payment of 'longavel,' 'salsa' and 'hocksilver' name also a 'ledsmyth' payment of 20s.—a payment perhaps for the monopoly of making or mending the boilers. They name also the 140 or more persons who paid *consuetudo*, which we take to be a fee in the nature of toll from country burgesses or non-burgesses who were admitted to the salt trade. Toll *eo nomine* forms a distinct account and probably refers to other wares; the toll was farmed for £36 in the reign of Edward III. An account of 1345–6 shows that with 'perquisites' from foreigners, fines for evasion (*asportatio*) of toll, stallage, pickage and amercements, the borough receipts amounted to £132 10s. 7½d.

By the Letters Patent of 1553–4,[79] confirming the charter of John, the burgesses were formally incorporated under the name of the bailiffs and burgesses of the borough of Wich. The two bailiffs were to be annually elected at the Exchequer, or some other convenient place, on the Tuesday after Michaelmas, and sworn in before the recorder and burgesses. The burgesses were to choose a recorder learned in the law from time to time, also a clerk of the borough court. In the borough court meeting on Tuesdays the bailiffs and burgesses were to have jurisdiction in all actions under the value of £5, and were authorized to make by-laws. Two serjeants-at-mace were to act as executive officers, and the borough was to be represented by two members elected by the bailiffs and burgesses. The market was to be held on Monday and to enjoy the same privileges as the markets of Wenlock and Ludlow.

The charter of 1625 is of a fuller and more formal character.[80] It recites the charter of John and explicitly forbids the sinking of new pits. The bailiffs and burgesses assembled in the Exchequer House were given power to make trade regulations and to sell and let lands. View of frankpledge was granted and a court leet twice a year, and the town clerk was ordered to act as steward in this court. Both this court and the pie-powder court had fallen into disuse in 1835. The two bailiffs were to be elected annually and were to act as coroners. They were given power to enroll bonds obligatory under a statute merchant seal, and had the authority of clerks of the market. The recorder, bailiffs and last two bailiffs, or any two of them, had full power to act as justices of the peace. The borough court was to be held weekly on Thursday, and its competence was to extend over all

---

[69] Droitwich MSS. 655–7.
[70] Pat. 2 Chas. I, pt. iv.
[71] Ibid. 22 Chas. II, pt. ii (1st roll).
[72] Exch. Dep. Mich. 2 Anne, no. 20.
[73] 5s. 8d. a 'plumb' or vat appears to have been the rate in the time of Edward IV; Prattinton MSS.
[74] Prattinton MSS.
[75] Round, *Geoffrey de Mandeville*, 313, 440. In the grant the empress warranted the shrievalty to William de Beauchamp against all men, naming specially Waleran Count of Mellent. Waleran may have received a grant of the office from Stephen,

but more probably he is mentioned as the owner of royal rights in Droitwich, which seem to have been granted to him by Stephen, for in a charter addressed to his bailiffs and servants of Droitwich he released the monks of Gloucester from tolls in Droitwich. See above, *Glouc. Cartul.* (Rolls Ser.), ii, 71.
[76] For later grants of the sheriff's seal, which appears to have become appurtenant to the manor of Salwarpe, see *L. and P. Hen. VIII*, ii, 4496; iii, g. 2927 (18), g. 5510 (28); xiii (1), g. 1115 (16); xviii (2), g. 449 (29); xx (1), g. 1081 (11).

[77] Besides the entry on the Droitwich rolls there is reference to the Worcester Priory's payment of hocksilver in Hale, *Worc. Reg.* 153b. Worcester Priory paid 'salsa' as well.
[78] Dugdale, *Mon. Angl.* v, 410; see also *Cal. Chart. R.* 1257–1300, p. 63; cf. *V.C.H. Worcs.* ii, 151.
[79] Pat. 1 Mary, pt. xv. This charter has escaped notice by the historians of the county and of Droitwich.
[80] Pat. 22 Jas. I, pt. iii, no. 6. It is translated in Nash, op. cit. i, 309.

actions not exceeding £10 in the amount at issue. The borough was to have a common prison for the custody of persons fined before its courts.

The oaths of the borough officers, preserved in a Droitwich minute book, of the time of Charles II, add some further details of the municipal executive. The bailiffs served all warrants and held the assizes of bread, beer and victuals, punished brawlers and swore to make just account and to see 'that the pit goes straight,' and that none occupy 'walling' other than his own inheritance. The burgess swore to be ready to come at the common bell [81] to attend at the Chequer and confer on any controversy, and to be privy to no wrong or oppression upon the pit. The oaths of the drawers at Upwich and Netherwich (Middlewich then lying waste) required them to watch the masters of 'le bechin,' 'beachin' or 'beargin,' [82] and the middlemen who bore the brine, and to see to the fair filling of the vessels. There were also sealers of leather, showing that a tanning industry had begun. [83]

By a Private Act of 1689-90, of which only the title appears to be known, new regulations were made for the salt works [84]; the bailiffs seem to have been discharged from their responsibility for the government of the pits, and governors were appointed in their stead. But in 1704 the governors ceased to exist. Robert Steynor's suits in Chancery and the King's Bench 1690-5, finally determined by the Lord Keeper's decision 24 January 1695, completely altered the character of the salt trade, which now ceased to be a monopoly of the burgesses.

At the time of the Municipal Reform Act the charter of James I was still the governing charter. The bailiffs and recorder received no salary and the serjeants-at-mace acted as constables without other salary than the fees which they claimed from persons who needed their services. The charter of James I gave no power to levy a rate for police or general purposes, and in 1835 the only source of municipal income was the rent of some cottages, about £10 a year. In 1835 it was reported that the bailiffs applied these rents to their own use, but spent far more at their own charges in keeping the court-house and prison in repair. When Droitwich was brought under the scheme of municipal reform the town clerk of the old régime made strenuous resistance, conveyed the site of the town hall to himself and refused to give up the documents. [85]

The charter of James I laid down no rule for the creation of burgesses or for the inheritance of the burgess-ship, and numerous disputes arose as to the law of the Droitwich burgess-ship and parliamentary franchise. Habington, writing in the 17th century, asserts that the first burgesses, who claimed other than by inheritance or marriage, were created by election in 1570, but an earlier case (1370) has been mentioned above. As soon as the burgess-ship ceased to have a commercial value and became valuable as a means to the parliamentary franchise the by-laws on the subject of admission to burgess-ship began to vary with the strength of political feeling or rival family interests. In the 16th century or later it seems to have been an accepted custom that every burgess must own a quarter of a vat in the 'original springs,' and when the borough monopoly had ended and the original springs ceased to be worked, those who were anxious to secure the parliamentary franchise used various legal but highly artificial means to comply with the condition. Any number of imaginary quarter-vats could be charged on non-existent springs, and passed from hand to hand for peppercorn rents and the like. As early as 1632 by-laws were made to prevent irregular creations of new burgesses, but none remained permanently effective. [86] In 1692 and 1747 the House of Commons agreed that the right to elect members of Parliament was in 'the burgesses of the corporation of the saltsprings of Droitwich,' but one of the issues in the Earl of Shrewsbury's case, 1686, [87] against the burgesses, as to whether 'proprietors,' persons inheriting shares in the springs, needed no formal admission and were by inheritance alone made burgesses, appears to have been still doubtful when Sir John Pakington presented a petition on this question in 1747. [88] In 1835 there were five resident and about thirty non-resident burgesses. In the 18th-century 'book of minutes of common halls' will be found the signatures of the electors on each occasion of a parliamentary election, and little further record of municipal government. The borough had been represented by two members in the Parliaments of Edward I and II, but not again till Mary's reign, when two members began to be sent regularly until 1832. Only one member was returned from 1832 to 1885, when the parliamentary representation of the borough was merged in that of a county division.

The best mediaeval evidence as to the population of Droitwich is provided by the Lay Subsidy Rolls published by the Worcestershire Historical Society, but the information they furnish is imperfect. The earliest roll is of about 1276-82 and names eighty-seven persons who paid a total of £26 13s. 2d. In 1327 a roll of ninety persons paid £5, Witton then paying apart from the borough. In 1340 the burgesses declared the ninth of their goods to be worth 20 marks. [89] Nash quotes records which give Droitwich 151 families in the four parishes in 1563 and 249 families in 1781. The parliamentary returns of 1801 [90] give 439 houses and 1,845 inhabitants. The population at the census of 1901 was 4,201, and in 1911 was 4,146.

John's charter of 1215 had granted to the burgesses a fair beginning at the feast of the Translation of St. Andrew and St. Nicholas (9 May), to last for eight days. Edward III in 1330 [91] gave instead a fair on the vigil and day of St. Thomas the Martyr (29 December) and on the vigil and day of St. Simon and St. Jude (28 October) and three days after. Mary's charter granted three fairs, on the vigil of St. Philip and St. James (1 May) and two days after, the vigil

---

[81] The common bell is mentioned in 1404, when it was rung by certain malefactors to summon their accomplices to break the houses of the Earl of Warwick at Droitwich (*Cal. Pat.* 1401-5, p. 423).

[82] The meaning of this word is uncertain. Possibly they were 'basin' masters, controllers of that 'common bucket' in which the monks of Worcester claimed their share (*Hist. MSS. Com. Rep.* xiv, App. viii, 173). In a borough account of 12 Ric. II the purchase of a 'bechen,' apparently for the salt pit, is recorded.

[88] In 1535-6 an attempt was made to start a cloth industry. Noake, *Worc. N. and Q.* 305.

[84] 1 Will. and Mary, cap. 19; *Hist. MSS. Com. Rep.* xii, App. vi, 110.

[85] Droitwich Minute Book.

[86] There is a full account in the Prattinton MSS.

[87] Droitwich Records.

[88] Prattinton MSS.

[89] *Inq. Non.* (Rec. Com.), 301.

[90] Prattinton MSS.

[91] Chart. R. 4 Edw. III, m. 11.

of St. Peter and St. Paul (29 June) and two days after, and the vigil of St. Simon and St. Jude (28 October) and two days after. The fairs were to be as open as those of Wenlock and Ludlow and under the same regulations. The charter of James I changed the market day from Monday to Friday and formally granted a pie-powder court for the same. In 1792 the fairs were held on Friday in Easter week, 22 September, 21 December and 23 September for hiring.[92] The present-day fairs are the Monday before 20 June, and for cattle only 12 December,[93] superseded by the fortnightly stock sales.

The agricultural system of the early community has left no such clear and definite traces as to encourage the hope that the arable area of the mediaeval borough can be divided into its original fields. It is even possible that Witton was the original agricultural centre. There are some few traces of the open-field system in the chartularies which describe the lands of the neighbourhood, but nothing of so definite and satisfactory a kind as to make it certain that Droitwich was not a district of isolated farmsteads, but a settlement equipped with arable hides on the Germanic model.

The territorial area of the borough at present covers 1,856 acres, or less than three square miles. An enlargement followed the Reform Act, which, however, affected the population rather than acreage, and the mediaeval acreage appears to have been approximately what it is now. It does not appear that the urban inhabited area of the Middle Ages was inclosed by any wall; a ditch and toll gates were probably its sole defences.[94] No murage grant was made to the borough.

In 1456 the boundaries of the borough were thus described[95]: from the stone wall of the churchyard of St. Augustine's, Dodderhill, on the south of the church at the stile by the priest's house, down by the common way to the church towards the east, by a tenement lying behind that of the Prior and convent of Worcester, up to the 'marestake' at the top of the hill. And so by the old boundaries down to the hall, lately rebuilt, of John Meredith's house, through the middle of the hall to the road called the common cart-way from Wich to Bromsgrove, to John Walker's old house, now Alice Pershore's. And so across the highway to a short lane leading to the wood there called Purdesore,[96] to the east. And so by the lane under the wood of the pasture called the Fordmill meadow next the Floodgates pit, on the south. And so down by the ditch of Purdesore wood to the ditch between the meadow called the Millmeadow on the west and the lord of Impney's meadow on the east. And so down by the ditch of Purdesore Wood to the River Salwarpe otherwise called the Mill Pond. And so up by the footbridge at the end of the Millmeadow by Wich highway on the south of the river and by the river up between Impney's meadow on the north and 'le Ruddecroft' on the south. And so up by the river to the 'Clerkenbath' where sheep are washed; and up the river to a little 'sechet' of water called Bottybroke under Impney on the west, which sechet descends by the Gerveysecroft into the Salwarpe, down by a small parcel of land lately inclosed by

Thomas Corbett lord of Impney. And so up at the end of the sechet of Bottybroke, where it enters the Salwarpe by Thomas Corbett's parcel on the west, and the custumary land of the lord of Impney on the east, by Gerveysecroft and Peter Cassey's pasture on the south of the sechet and up by the sechet to the upper end of a pasture by the side of the sechet called Blackmoor by Hanbury Field called the Westfield, by the Corbett place of Impney. And so up by the Bottybrook to the upper end of the Blackmoor pasture next the court place of Impney, to the king's highway on the south of Blackmoor pasture, and on the west of a certain common pasture called Nomansland to the east of Blackmoor pasture. And so up straight from Nomansland turning back by the said highway stretching between the demesne land of Hadsor to the south and the Blackmoor to the north, to the sechet called Grytenbrook, at the east end of Gerveyscroft. And so up straight on the west side of the sechet to the Cokescroft, leaving the croft to the east. And so up by the said croft and sechet stretching between the demesne land of Hadsor on the east and a field of Wich called Le Byttomfeld on the west. And so up between the Hadsor demesne land on the east and a certain common pasture there and a piece of land called Canonys land on the west to the field called Willot's Field towards the south. And so down from the upper end of the piece of Canonys land stretching by Willot's Field up to a short lane between the said field on the south and the field called Betemefield on the north. And so beyond the highway there called Prymmes Lane[97] to a field called Le Redefeld to a parcel of land in the lower part of the said field called Froxemere's Slough. And so up by Wynturesland on the north and the land called Lenchesland on the south, and straight to the short lane lying between the field called Littlefield on the south and La Redefield to the north. And so down the said lane by the upper end of a croft called Locarescroft and down under the foot of Tagwall Hill to the spring called Tagwall; and then down to the highway under Brazecroft, and leaving that croft on the north side of a lane called Le Thorny Lane stretching towards a meadow called Banardesmore and the field there called Loweshull Field on the south, to the sechet in Banardesmore under Spitalcroft with the culver-house to the north of the sechet. And so down by the sechet between Banardesmore and Falshamfield to the west, to the marl-pit called Falfordespit, within the franchise of Wich. And so down by the said sechet to the pool called Newpool by the Salwarpe demesne, and through the middle of the pool as far as Le Boltes-hede, and from this head, at the pool's head straight down from Boltesede by the gutter of the same to a sechet there towards the north called Northbrook, stretching straight to the Salwarpe under the park pale of Salwarpe by the bridge there called Cowbridge. And so up from the end of the sechet entering the river of Salwarpe, to the end of the Haymeadow, and straight by the river between the Brademeadow on the south of the park pale on the north, to the upper end of Overham meadow inclosed within the park pale by Breryhill land on the north of the meadow. And so down by the river to the sechet called Bile-

[92] *Rep. of Roy. Com. on Fairs and Markets* (1888), i, 215.
[93] In 1849 the Wednesday before St. Thomas's Day (Lewis, *Topog. Dict.*).
[94] In an account of 1633 there is an allusion to the 'filling of the pit at Worcester gate.'
[95] De Banco R. 35 Hen. VI, no. 784, m. 304.   [96] Now Pridzorwood.
[97] A farm called Primsland End marks this site.

borne to the end of Micham meadow. And so up by the sechet called Bilborne under the hill called Appellerhill to Boycotebridge, by the old messuage called Le Alfordsland in the Over Boycote.[98] And so across the common way leading to Ombersley towards the west and from Boycotebridge towards the tenement lying in Le Overboycote, and under it and a piece of land called Bruggesland on the south. And so by the old lane at the head of the marl-pit there by the head, and by the lane to the 'meseplace,' late John Selling's. And so by the old water-lane stretching towards the arable field called Le Hydefurlong. And so up by a sechet descending from Honeybornebridge [99] and from that bridge to a selion called the headland lying between two big pieces of arable called Fekenaputreeland. And so up by the headland to Cokeseysland to a footway called 'a mereway' [100] between the land called Blackfurlong to the north and Burfordsacre to the south by the Buryefield. And so up by the Buryfield on the north up to a new ditch between Cassy's land on the west and the demesne land of the rectory of Dodderhill on the east. And so under the rectory close to the west end of Dodderhill Church. And so round by the stone wall of the churchyard on the south of the church up to the priest's house.

From the perambulation above quoted, and from the chartularies which refer to Droitwich lands, it would be gathered that there was much pasture and much inclosure at an early date. 'Le Wychfeld' is named in a deed of 1346–7,[1] and through it passed a road called 'Ermyngwey.' From the 15th century come Wychefeld, Falshamfeld,[2] Astewodfeld. Loulleleye, Lulleleye, Lelyfield appears in records from the 14th to the 16th century, and may perhaps claim the Lollaycross. Souggenhyde or Suggenhyde comes from the 14th century. Masgundry or Masguntreefield, Sucknelfield,[3] and Falshamfield appear in the 18th-century parochial terriers of which Prattinton preserved copies.

Rafunestreet is named in 1236 as running from St. Mary's Witton to 'Luthbridge' and so to 'Letherenebruge.' [4] 'Le Ruinestreet' occurs continually in the conveyances and chartularies, with Froglane (running from Gosford Street to the Salwarpe); Froxmere; Le Barrestreet, perhaps marking a toll-bar; 'Wawenham' lane; and Vallance End, probably the Queen Street end where the Valence property lay. The corn-mills Frogmill *alias* the King's Mill [5] and Briarmill are named in mediaeval records and still exist. Besides the Chapelbridge and the Newbridge at the end of Froglane there was a Bagbridge, and Bagbridge Lane running from it where now is Asylum Lane, and a Lychebridge and others over the numerous brooks and winding streams of the borough area.

The town of Droitwich, though not wholly lacking in architectural interest, contains, apart from the churches of St. Andrew and St. Peter, little that is worthy of special remark. At the corner of High Street and Queen Street are some half-timbered houses of a comparatively early type. In the High Street, immediately to the east of St. Andrew's Church, is a good block of red brick Georgian houses.

The church and town hall face each other at the foot of St. Andrew's Street where it joins the High Street, and here the weekly market is held. The town hall is an uninteresting structure of the early 19th century. Friar Street, as the western continuation of the High Street is named, contains some work of the 16th and 17th centuries. Of the latter date perhaps the best example is a three-storied gabled house of brick, with a two-storied central porch and arched outer doorway. The string-courses and quoins are of stone. The original stone-mullioned windows have been replaced on the front elevation by large sash windows of the 18th century. The house is now divided into two. The Priory House, in the same street, is a half-timbered house of similar date. The Hope Inn, a Georgian building of three stories with a projecting hood to the doorway, is a good example of the period. The Raven Hotel, at the top of St. Andrew's Street, is a much modernized half-timber building, the original part probably dating from the early 16th century. St. Peter's Church is situated about three-quarters of a mile south-east of the main portion of the town, on the west side of the lane known as the 'Holloway.' To the east of the church stands the Manor House, the former seat of the Nash family. It is of half-timber, of three stories. The house, which appears to have been erected in 1618,[6] was restored in 1867, when the interior appears to have been wholly remodelled. Some panelling still survives, and over the fireplace of the room on the left-hand side of the entrance hall is an original plaster panel with strap-work ornamentation. On the panel is painted the following inscription : 'When you sit by this fire | Yourself to warm | Take care that yͬ tongue | Do your neighbour no harm.'

The lettering appears to be modern, but there seems to be little doubt that it is a more or less faithful copy of a preceding inscription. In a room on the first floor is a fireplace with a very similar panel above it. Adjoining the house is a fine brick barn, lighted by small windows with plastered mullions. At the north end of the Holloway, near its junction with the Alcester and Stratford road, are the 17th-century almshouses known as the Coventry Hospital. They form a range of eighteen two-storied houses, built of brick with plain casement windows and tiled roofs. A modern marble tablet on the front wall states that they were founded by the 'Right Honourable Henry Coventry, son of the Right Honourable Thomas Lord Coventry, Lord Keeper of the Great Seal of England, in the reign of King Charles I.' Below, and apparently of original date, is the Coventry shield : Sable a fesse ermine between three crescents or.

The newer portion of the town, which is almost entirely of a residential character, shows a tendency to spread in a southerly direction along the Worcester road and between it and the Holloway. A new district has also grown up within the last thirty years along the Ombersley Road and in the neighbourhood of the Great Western railway station.

The old Chequer House built in 1581, no doubt on the site of the Chequer of 1327, was swept away

---

[98] A Boycote farm still exists.
[99] Now Honeymansbridge.
[100] Mere = boundary.
[1] Anct. D. (P.R.O.), C 165.

[2] The name is preserved in the Falsam Pits on the southern borough boundary.
[3] Possibly this is the Suggenhyde of early documents.
[4] *Cal. Chart. R.* 1226–57, p. 102.

[5] Pat. 7 Jas. I, pt. xvi.
[6] This date, which tallies with the general style, is carved upon the modern entrance doorway.

about 1825, together with the market-house, part of the same building put up in 1628.[7] A cross is named in 1629.

The earliest allusion to the common seal of Droitwich comes from about 1220,[8] and it is probably the seal bearing the legend *Sigillum communitatis de Wycho* which has been figured.[9] It was a round seal bearing a shield of the ancient arms of the town with the sword and two passant lions between two wyverns. The matrix of a second seal,[10] of the early 15th century, is in the British Museum. It is 2⅛ in. in diameter; within a cusped circle a shield of the town arms as on the first seal, impaling quarterly (1) and (4) Checky argent and sable, (2) and (3) Gules two salt-barrows[11] or. The legend is *Sigillum commune ville Wychie*. It has been suggested that the checkers refer to the Droitwich Chequer where the accounts were made up. Soon after the grant of the charter of James I a third seal was made with arms as above, with the legend *Sigillum commune ville Wytchie*,[12] and a statute merchant seal exists of the same date, with the checkers impaling two salt-barrows.

There are two silver maces bearing the date 1646, when they were made, and 1660, when the royal arms superseded the 'state's arms.' There are three trade tokens of the 17th century bearing the town arms[13] and an ancient measure for salt.

Of the early history of the formation of the numerous parishes included in the borough of Droitwich little is known beyond what the history of the descent of the advowsons suggests. Inasmuch as the sole element of unity was the unity of the royal demesne in the salt-pits, and the lands over which burghal jurisdiction extended formed part of the demesne of many lords, no unity of parochial development is to be expected. There seem, however, to have been distinct manors or so-called manors at Witton St. Mary and Witton St. Peter.

MANORS   The manor of *WITTON*, or Witton St. Mary, probably originated in the land at Witton asserted to have been given to the abbey of Evesham in 716 by Ethelbald son of Alewi, King of the Mercians.[14] The manor afterwards seems to have been lost by the church of Evesham, and to have been restored to it in 1046 by Wulfgeat, when his son Aelfgeat became a monk at Evesham.[15] Abbot Alwin leased the land to his uncle for life, but on the death of the latter in Harold's battle against the Northmen the manor returned to the abbey.[16] It

was among the lands taken from the abbey by Odo of Bayeux and given to Urse the Sheriff,[17] who was in possession in 1086, his sub-tenant there being Gunfrei.[18] Theobald and Peter held this half-hide in Witton of Urse's successor, William de Beauchamp, at the end of the reign of Henry I.[19] Possibly this estate afterwards became annexed to the sheriff's seals at Droitwich, held by the Beauchamp family (see above).

It appears to have been distinct from the half-fee at Witton, to which the advowson of the church of St. Mary was in early times annexed, held under the lords of Richards Castle.[20] This estate was held early in the 13th century by the Pauncefoots,[21] apparently a branch of the family who held Bentley Pauncefoot. Grimbald Pauncefoot of Bentley was in possession in 1307-8,[22] and from that time the manor seems to have descended with the advowson of St. Mary's Witton[23] (q.v.). The tenant of the manor (Thomas Earl of Warwick) is mentioned for the last time in 1378-9, but the half-fee was still held of the lords of Richards Castle in 1407-8,[24] the tenant's name not being given.

The manor of *ST. PETER WITTON* originated in 2 hides at Witton held in the time of Edward the Confessor by his thegn Tuini. At the Conquest the estate passed to William son of Corbucion,[25] and was given, as half the vill of Witton, by his successor Peter Corbezun,[26] or Peter de Studley, to the priory which he founded at Witton St. Peter.[27] Peter also gave the prior ten 'junctis' of salt in Droitwich, two seals and places for firewood.[28] The priory was subsequently moved to Studley in Warwickshire, and its estate at Witton was augmented by a gift of land and a capital messuage at Witton by John le Roter, son of Hubert Balistarius.[29] Successive priors of Studley remained in possession of this estate until the Dissolution.[30] There was then a house on the manor called Canons Place, which was granted in 1545 to John Bellow and John Broxholme.[31] They sold it in the same year to Sir Humphrey Stafford.[32] John Wythe or Withy was dealing with half the estate in 1576-7,[33] and died seised of it in 1591,[34] leaving a son Thomas. The other moiety of the estate was held in 1581-2 by Anne Woodward, daughter and heir of William Woodward.[35] From this time until the beginning of the 19th century no deeds have been found relating to this estate, but it seems to have been annexed to the advowson of the church of St. Peter Witton, a quarter of which was held in 1621-2 by John Wylde.[36] He died in

[7] The bailiffs responsible for the buildings inscribed them with their names and dates. Prattinton gives an account of the arms in the stained glass of the destroyed Chequer.

[8] *Glouc. Cartul.* (Rolls Ser.), ii, 146.

[9] *Gent. Mag.* 1795, lxv (1), 13, as quoted in Jewitt and Hope, *Corporation Plate*.

[10] Figured in Nash, op. cit. i, 295.

[11] Barrow is the local name for the conical basket in which the salt is set to drain.

[12] Figured in Nash, op. cit. i, 295.

[13] *Assoc. Archit. Soc. Trans.* xi, 172.

[14] Dugdale, *Mon. Angl.* ii, 14; *Chron. of Evesham* (Rolls Ser.), 72.

[15] *V.C.H. Worcs.* i, 319*b*; *Chron. of Evesham* (Rolls Ser.), 94.

[16] *V.C.H. Worcs.* i, 319*b*.

[17] Harl. MS. 3763, fol. 60 d.; *Chron. of Evesham* (Rolls Ser.), 97.

[18] *V.C.H. Worcs.* i, 319*b*.

[19] Ibid. 330.

[20] *Cal. Inq. p.m.* 1-9 Edw. II, 24; Chan. Inq. p.m. 49 Edw. III, pt. ii, no. 50; 9 Hen. IV, no. 39.

[21] Assize R. 1021, m. 12; Anct. D. (P.R.O.), B 3717; Habington, op. cit. i, 486.

[22] *Cal. Inq. p.m.* 1-9 Edw. II, 24; *Cal. Close,* 1307-18, p. 98.

[23] Feet of F. Worcs. Trin. 22 Edw. III; Add. MS. 28024, fol. 5*b*; Chan. Inq. p.m. 2 Ric. II, no. 42.

[24] Chan. Inq. p.m. 9 Hen. IV, no. 39.

[25] *V.C.H. Worcs.* i, 317.

[26] Ibid. 330.

[27] Dugdale, *Mon. Angl.* vi, 185, 186; Chart. R. 1 Edw. III, m. 2, no. 3.

[28] This seems to have been the mean-ing of the *finstallum* found in many grants of land in Droitwich. Prattinton gives several mentions of *vinstalstedes* in the neighbourhood of the seals, and the Beauchamp Chartulary also refers to a *finstalstede*. See also *Reg. G. Giffard* (Worcs. Hist. Soc.), 467.

[29] Dugdale, *Mon. Angl.* vi, 185, 186.

[30] *Valor Eccl.* (Rec. Com.), iii, 87.

[31] *L. and P. Hen. VIII,* xx (1), g. 1335 (11).

[32] Ibid. (55).

[33] Habington, op. cit. i, 485.

[34] Chan. Inq. p.m. (Ser. 2), ccxxxiii, 111.

[35] Nash, op. cit. i, 326.

[36] Feet of F. Worcs. Mich. 19 Jas. I. John Wylde and his father George lived at the Harriots in Droitwich (Chan. Inq. p.m. [Ser. 2], ccclvi, 104).

1669,[37] and his share of the estate was purchased by Richard Nash,[38] who acquired the rest by descent from his father, James Nash.[39] His great-grandson, Treadway Nash, D.D., was owner of the whole manor in 1779.[40] It then passed with the manor of Impney until 1811, when it is mentioned for the last time.[41] The parish covers the eastern side of the borough, originally called Goseford.

NASH. *Sable a cheveron between three greyhounds standing argent with three sprigs of ash vert upon the cheveron.*

In the In-Liberties in the neighbourhood of what is now called the Vines lay the house of the *AUSTIN FRIARS* to the south of the river.[42] Its earlier history has been told elsewhere.[43] In 1543 the friary was given by the king to John Pye of Chippenham and Robert Were of Marlborough.[44] Their

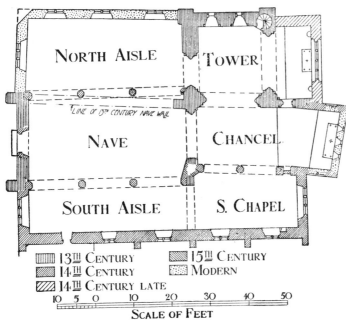

NORTH AISLE

TOWER

LINE OF 13TH CENTURY NAVE WALL

NAVE

CHANCEL

SOUTH AISLE

S. CHAPEL

13TH CENTURY   15TH CENTURY
14TH CENTURY   MODERN
14TH CENTURY LATE

10 5 0   10   20   30   40   50
SCALE OF FEET

PLAN OF ST. ANDREW'S CHURCH, DROITWICH

grant included the friars' orchard, Vine Close, and Barley Close. In the following year Were released his claim to Pye, who sold the site to Sir John Pakington in 1549.[45] Sir John gave it to his daughter Bridget on her marriage with John Lyttelton of Frankley.[46] They evidently sold it before 1579 to Thomas Gyerse, who settled it in that year upon himself and Margaret his wife for their lives with reversion to Francis Unett and his wife Jane and their issue.[47] Its further descent has not been traced.

CHURCHES

The church of ST. ANDREW consists of a chancel about 35 ft. 4 in. by 14 ft. 9 in., a north-east tower 16 ft. 3 in. by 16 ft. 5 in., a small chapel opening out of the east side of the tower 18 ft. 4 in. by 9 ft., a south chapel 25 ft. by 13 ft. 3 in., nave about 40 ft. by 20 ft. 9 in., north aisle 40 ft. by about 17 ft. 9 in., and a south aisle 41 ft. 4 in. by 11 ft. 4 in. These measurements are all internal.

The chancel, tower and west wall of the nave appear to date from the early 13th century. These, with the exception of a small portion of the east end of the north wall of the nave and the deeply weathered plinth of the north chapel, are the only parts that have survived a fire which occurred at the end of the same century; the width of the former north aisle is shown by the western tower arch, which is only about half the width of the present aisle. No evidence remains to show whether there was a south aisle previous to the fire. At the beginning of the 14th century a general rebuilding appears to have been entered upon, and to this date must be referred both arcades of the nave, including the whole of the north wall, the south chapel and south arcade of the chancel, and the south aisle. The nave was at the same time widened at the east end, the north wall now abutting clumsily upon the south limb and respond of the western tower arch. The buttress-like projection on the east wall of the nave to the north of the chancel arch is shown by the plan to line with the buttress at the north end of the west wall of the nave. As the present north wall is obviously outside the line of the former nave wall at the east, the presumption is that this otherwise unaccountable projection is a fragment of the 13th-century nave wall left by the 14th-century builders to give abutment to the southern tower arch. At the same time windows now blocked appear to have been inserted in the north and south walls of the chancel. In the last quarter of the 14th century the north chapel was rebuilt. About fifty years later the pitch of the roof seems to have been lowered, the north wall raised and a new window inserted in it at a considerable height from the floor. At the same period the upper stages of the tower were rebuilt. Early in the 16th century the chancel was treated in the same manner and some plain windows inserted in the clearstory. The roof then constructed still remains, though concealed by a flat plaster ceiling. It is evident that the chancel has been considerably altered and perhaps shortened at the east end, but at what period it is difficult to say. The present east

[37] *Dict. Nat. Biog.*
[38] Nash, op. cit. i, 326.
[39] Ibid. 326, 327.   [40] Ibid.
[41] Recov. R. D. Enr. East. 52 Geo. III, m. 7.
[42] A plan of the site is given in the Prattinton MSS.
[43] *V.C.H. Worcs.* ii, 173.
[44] *L. and P. Hen. VIII,* xviii (1), g.

226 (8). The name 'Marlborough' or Malborough, which afterwards attached to the ground, and the claim to be in the parish of Marlborough, seem to date from this grant. The commissioners of 1835 reported that the inhabitants of the Marlborough district contributed nothing to the rates of the borough and were not even assessed to the king's taxes. Cholera

broke out here, and the borough authorities having no authority were powerless to stop its spread. In 1880 the Marlborough was merged in the adjoining parish of St. Nicholas (*Pop. Ret.* [1891], ii, 658).
[45] Add. MS. 31314, fol. 187.
[46] Pat. 5 Edw. VI, pt. i, m. 13.
[47] Ibid. 21 Eliz. pt. vi, m. 37.

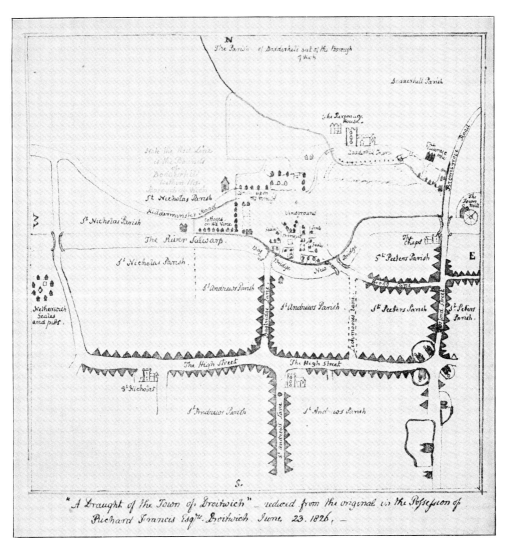

PLAN OF THE TOWN OF DROITWICH IN 1826

(*From the Prattinton Collection*)

wall, which follows the slant of the site, is of brick and dates from the 18th century. The three lancets in this wall and the west doorway and window of the nave are of the early 19th century. The jambs of these latter openings are probably of original 14th-century date. Within the last two years the tower has been restored and the north and west walls of the north aisle taken down and rebuilt.

At the north-east of the chancel is a blocked two-light window of the 14th century, the head of which can just be distinguished internally. To the westward of this is an opening into the north chapel, with boldly moulded jambs and acute two-centred head of early 13th-century date. The remainder of the wall is occupied by the southern arch of the tower. In the south wall is a blocked 14th-century window, visible only externally, similar in design and position to that in the opposite wall. A little to the west of this is a doorway of the 13th century, with chamfered jambs and two-centred head, blocked at the addition of the south chapel in the early part of the 14th century. Immediately adjoining is the east respond of the arcade of two bays pierced in the wall at the same period, to the width of which the west jamb of the doorway has been narrowed down. The arches of the arcade are two-centred and of two chamfered orders, with octagonal columns and responds. The capitals have plain bells and moulded abaci. Over the arcade are five square-headed clearstory windows, each of two plain lights, which belong to the 15th-century raising of the walls and lowering of the pitch of the chancel roof. The chancel arch is of two orders; the inner order is chamfered on both faces, but the outer order is chamfered only on the east face; the west face, where it overhangs the respond which fits the arch very ill, is moulded with a filleted bowtel, which is returned horizontally for a short distance upon the east wall of the nave. The north respond is contemporary in date with the tower, and continues the design of its north-west pier, the inner order being carried by a filleted attached column of semicircular section, and the outer order by a filleted nook shaft on the east side. On the west side the springing of the overhanging outer order is masked by two sculptured human heads. The south respond is similar on plan, but seems to be of slightly earlier date. The capital of the attached column is scalloped, and there are nook shafts on both east and west sides, carrying the outer orders. The lower half of the column has been cut away, and it now rests on a moulded corbel of the 15th century. Externally the north and south walls of the chancel are of large blocks of local sandstone, while the east wall is of red brick.

The ground stage of the tower is entirely of early 13th-century date. Two wide arches open into the north chapel on the east and the chancel on the south, while on the west is a narrower and acutely pointed two-centred arch of equal height opening into the north aisle. All are of two moulded orders, the inner carried by a filleted attached column of semicircular section, and the outer by filleted nook shafts projecting from a containing hollow. Their foliated capitals are of a fully developed Gothic type with square moulded abaci truncated at the angles. The bases are of the water-holding Attic form with square plinths. The mouldings of the east and south arches appear to have been cut away to form large casements at the end of the 14th century, to harmonize with the style of the north chapel, rebuilt at that period. The capitals of the eastern responds and of the north respond of the western arch have human heads mingled with the foliage. In the north wall are two wide lancet windows with shafted internal and external jambs, stepped sills, and external labels. The jamb shafts have foliated capitals, annulets, and moulded bases, and have been renewed externally. In the west wall to the north of the aisle arch is an aumbry recess. In the north-east angle a doorway with a two-centred head and label opens into the vice. Over the eastern face of the chapel arch are the marks of an earlier high-pitched roof. Externally the tower is divided into three receding stages by moulded strings. At the north-west angle is a large clasping buttress, extending about three-quarters the height of the ground stage, while a buttress-like projection at the north-east, stopping a little below the first string-course, contains the vice. The base of the tower is marked by a weathered plinth of considerable projection. The two upper stages appear to have undergone extensive alterations in the 15th century. The ringing stage is lighted by windows of two cinquefoiled lights with two-centred heads and vertical tracery, and the bell-chamber by windows of two similar lights with four-centred heads. Their tracery, together with the embattled parapet which crowns the tower, has been recently renewed.

The north chapel, which opens out of the tower, was rebuilt in the last quarter of the 14th century. The plinth of the north wall is a survival of the 13th-century chapel which it replaces. The east window is a fine example of transitional work. It has a two-centred head and is of four transomed lights, the upper cinquefoiled and the lower trefoiled. The tracery is of semi-vertical character, and there is an external label. The jambs are casement-moulded. On either side are image brackets. In the south-west angle is an early 13th-century shaft with a foliated capital forming part of the same suite with the south respond of the eastern tower arch. A fragment of shaft is supported on the capital, which most probably carried one of the corbels of the original roof.

High up in the north wall is a square-headed traceried window of two uncusped lights with an external label, later in date than the large east window. The sill string of this latter window is returned round the north wall. The walls are of the same local sandstone as the tower and the rest of the church, and are crowned by a cornice and parapet, gabled on the east and embattled on the north.

The south chapel is continuous with the south aisle, from which it is divided by a two-centred arch of two orders, the outer moulded with a plain and the inner with a swelled chamfer. The latter springs from plain square abaci supported by the head, shoulders, and upturned arms of two human figures; that on the south is crowned, while the northern figure wears a plain jerkin. The east window has a two-centred head and external label, and is of three trefoiled ogee lights with flowing tracery of a rather clumsy type. At the east of the north wall is the blocked chancel doorway, while the remainder of the wall is occupied by the arcade of two bays above described. At the south-east is a piscina with a trefoiled two-centred head; the basin is much decayed. The two south windows have two-centred heads, and are each of two trefoiled lights surmounted by a quatrefoil. Externally there are three buttresses of two offsets on the south, the westernmost taking the thrust of the dividing arch.

Immediately to the north of the nave face of the chancel arch is the truncated portion of the original 13th-century nave wall. The early 14th-century north arcade is of three bays with two-centred arches of two chamfered orders, and octagonal columns and responds. The east respond abuts clumsily upon the western tower arch, concealing the nook shaft which carries its outer order upon this side. The southern half is cut away immediately below the capital, and exposes a small circular shaft terminating in two human heads, placed by way of corbel to the respond capital. The shaft is evidently contemporary with the tower, but its original use and the reason for leaving its lower portion untouched are obscure. The central arch is very much distorted, its western half being appreciably the longer. The south arcade is of a similar number of bays, and has two-centred arches of like character supported by octagonal columns and responds, with plain bell capitals and moulded abaci and bases. The north side of the east respond is built into the slanting wall which fills the south-east internal angle of the nave. It seems probable that this is of the 15th century, and that rood stairs exist within this angle, though all trace of the entrance is concealed by the later plastering and the mural monument placed upon it. The west window has lost its tracery. The jambs and head of the doorway beneath have been stuccoed over, rendering it impossible to tell if it be original or not. Two 13th-century buttresses of two offsets, with chamfered angles, take the thrust of the arcades upon the west. A parapeted gable terminates the nave externally at this end.

The walls of the north aisle have been entirely rebuilt within the last two years upon the original foundations. Part of the north-west clasping buttress of the tower is visible at the north-east internal angle. In the north wall are three two-light windows, while on the west is a large window of three lights.

The south aisle is contemporary in date with the south chapel, and is lighted on the south by two two-light windows of the same design, to the west of which is a plain chamfered doorway. The three-light west window repeats the east window of the chapel. There are buttresses of two offsets between the windows and at the west end, the latter partially built into the brick wall of the adjoining vestry.

The early 16th-century timber roof of the chancel is now concealed by a plaster ceiling, a moulded tie-beam and carved boss being alone exposed. This boss, now whitewashed over, is carved with a figure, which may be intended for St. Andrew. The roofs of the nave, south chapel and south aisle are concealed by plaster ceilings. Those of the north chapel and north aisle are modern.

The painted stone font is of Jacobean date. The original Elizabethan altar table is now placed in the north chapel. In the upper lights of the east window of the north chapel are some pieces of heraldic glass, one of which, a shield, Gyronny gules and argent, is probably genuine, and may date from the early 16th

century; the remainder seem to be merely put together from fragments. There are also fragments of late 16th and early 17th-century heraldic glass in the east window of the south chapel.

There are no monuments earlier than the 17th century now remaining. On the south wall of the south chapel is an elaborate mural tablet to Mary wife of Henry Clifford and relict of Edward Wheeler, who died in 1680, and various other members of the Wheeler family. On the east wall of the nave to the south of the chancel arch is a large and elaborate mural monument to the memory of Coningesby Norbury, 'Captain of one of his Majesties Ships of War | and Envoy from King George the first to the Court of Morocco | to redeem the British Slaves.'

There is a peal of eight bells, inscribed as follows : Treble, 'God prosper this Corporation 1735 . R.S.,' for Richard Sanders. (2) 'Richard Bullock Richard Hale . Ch. Wd. 1735 . R.S.' (3) 'Richard Sanders cast us 3 . 1735. Bromsgrove.' (4) 'Jesus be our good speed (name erased) . . . churchwarden 1631.' Founder's mark, a shield with an anchor between the initials T.H. for Thomas Hancock. (5) 'Richd Norris Jno Phillips Ch . Wardens . A.R. 1759,' a Rudhall bell. (6) 'Robert Whieler John Gower Baylifes Peeter Wallwin Churchwarden 1631. Gloria Deo in Excelses' (*sic*). Same founder's mark[48] as (4). (7) 'God Save oure King. John Wheeler Edwin Barret, Bayles (Bailiffs) 1645 . I.M.,' for John Martin.[48a] Below the inscription is the shield of the corporation of Droitwich. Tenor, 'Thomas Street Esquier Recorder Edward Barrett and Thomas Rastell Baylifs Henry Clifford and Wintour Harris Justices 1676.'

The plate is entirely modern, the original plate having been disposed of within the last fifteen years.

The registers previous to 1812 are as follows : (i) baptisms and marriages 1571 to 1644, burials 1572 to 1644. Between 1644 and 1657 the entries are fragmentary. From the latter year all entries continue to 1692. (ii) all entries 1693 to 1769 ; (iii) all entries 1770 to 1787, baptisms and burials to 1804 (the marriages are entered in duplicate in this and the preceding volume from the year 1755) ; (iv) marriages 1755 to 1812 ; (v) baptisms and burials 1805 to 1812.

The church of *ST. PETER* consists of a chancel 26 ft. 6 in. by 16 ft. 1 in., a modern south vestry and organ chamber, north transept 19 ft. 4 in. by 18 ft., south transept 17 ft. by 19 ft. 4 in., nave 43 ft. 10 in. by 19 ft. 5 in., a west tower 10 ft. 9 in. square and a modern south porch. These measurements are all internal.

The nave and chancel date from the first half of the 12th century, though the western portion of the north wall of the nave seems to have been entirely rebuilt early in the 16th century. About 1220 a south aisle was added, the arcade of which still survives, though the aisle has been pulled down. The south transept may also be of this date; the earliest detail is the south-east window, which is of late 13th-century date, but this appears to be an insertion. Two blocked arches in the west wall of the transept point to the fo mer existence of a double south aisle, of a width nearly equal to the depth of the transept.

---

[48] On the waist of this and the fourth bell are various devices ; on the fourth is an impression of the shield of Bishop Scambler of Peterborough (1561–85), on the sixth an impression of the seal of the mediaeval gild of Corpus Christi at Coventry, representing St. Nicholas saying mass.

[48a] 1645 was the year Charles I was at Droitwich.

The presence of re-set 14th-century windows in the blocking of the bays of the nave arcade shows that the aisle was probably rebuilt at this period, a date with which the blocked arches in the transept wall would well accord. The north transept is of the same date, and the windows in the rebuilt portion of the north wall of the nave are also re-set work of the 14th century. At the close of the same century the west tower was added, and is an excellent specimen of early vertical work. Early in the 16th century very drastic alterations were made to the nave, entailing the rebuilding in brick of the whole of the north wall to the west of the north transept, and the addition of an elaborate timber roof of low pitch, raised on a clearstory of half-timber. It is probable that the south aisle was removed in the early 17th century, as the bricks which are used occasionally in the filling of the south arcade are of this date. The east window of the chancel and the south window of the south transept are modern, while a vestry and organ chamber have been added on the south side of the chancel.

In the north wall of the chancel are three round-headed windows of the early 12th century. At the south-east is a piscina of c. 1400 with a trefoiled head and a semicircular projecting basin. The head is surmounted by a finial which does not appear to belong to it. A doorway with a four-centred head of original 15th-century date opens into the modern vestry, which is on this side of the chancel, and adjoining it to the west is a modern opening into the organ chamber. The chancel arch is semicircular, and is contemporary with the three north windows. It is of two plain square orders, the inner order carried by coupled semicircular attached shafts with scalloped capitals, grooved and chamfered abaci and moulded bases of Attic type. The abacus-mould is carried round the responds of the otherwise continuous outer orders, and produced as a string-course upon the nave and chancel faces of the dividing wall. Above the arch is a modern triple opening, made with the intention of improving the acoustic properties of the chancel. Externally the north and east walls are plastered. The jambs and heads of the north windows, which are exposed, are grooved and chamfered, and at the west end of this wall is a small doorway, now blocked, and visible only externally, with a two-centred segmental head and chamfered jambs. The south wall, against which are built the modern vestry and organ chamber, is plastered on what was originally its outside face.

The north transept dates from c. 1340. In the east wall is a window with a two-centred head of two trefoiled ogee lights with flowing tracery over. The north window is of similar type, but of three lights. The west window is blocked by the large Wylde monument, and only the jambs and head are now visible. The transept opens into the nave by a two-centred arch of two chamfered orders, the inner order dying upon the flat face of the responds and the outer segmental and continuous. A small arch of similar character has recently been formed in the short length of wall to the eastward of it, where were formerly the rood-stairs. Externally the walls are faced with sandstone, and there is a straight joint between the east wall and the north wall of the chancel.

The south transept probably dates from the early 13th century and appears to have opened out of the now destroyed south aisle. It now opens into the nave by the eastern arch of the south arcade, its west wall abutting upon the eastern column of the arcade. In the east wall are two windows, the northernmost of three cinquefoiled lights with a square external head and segmental rear-arch, dating from the early 15th century. The south-east window appears to be an insertion of the late 13th century. It has a two-centred head and is of three uncusped lights, the side lights acutely pointed and the head of the centre light extending to the apex of the opening. Externally there is a label with a head-stop on the north ; the southern stop has disappeared. In the south wall is a two-centred window, probably an insertion of the 14th century, filled with modern tracery, and below it is a late 13th-century piscina with a trefoiled ogee head, the projecting basin of which has been cut away. Externally the walls are faced with sandstone, and there are buttresses of two offsets at either end of the south wall. In the west wall can be plainly traced the heads of an arcade of two bays which must have formerly opened into a double south aisle. The outer orders, which alone are visible, are two-centred and segmental.

At the east end of the north wall of the nave is the arch opening into the north transept. The rebuilt portion of the wall to the west is occupied by a re-set 14th-century window of two trefoiled ogee lights with flowing tracery within a two-centred head. The transept bay of the south arcade is the only one now open, the remaining two having been blocked on the demolition of the aisle. It is of three bays with two-centred arches of two chamfered orders, having labels on the nave side, and is supported by circular columns, of which only half of the eastern column and the upper part of the western column (where the wall has been recently cut away to show it) are now exposed. This arcade is of c. 1220. The east respond has a foliated cap of good early stiff-leaved character and a moulded semi-octagonal abacus. The east column has a plain bell capital and abacus of similar form, while the capital of the western column has human heads alternating with foliage in a manner very similar to the capitals of the responds of the tower arches at the neighbouring church of St. Andrew. The 14th-century window above described is in the blocking of the centre bay, and in the blocking of the west bay is a modern doorway. The north wall appears to have been entirely rebuilt at the period of the construction of the roof and clearstory. Externally piers of brickwork carry the wall-plate and are spaced with the roof principals. The lower courses of the wall are of red sandstone. The filling of the south arcade is of stone with occasional brick. The early 16th-century clearstory is of brick nogged half-timber.

The tower is divided externally into two stages by a moulded string-course, and has angle buttresses of four offsets on the west, the thrust of the tower arch being taken by large buttresses of a single offset at the east end of the north and south walls. The tower arch is of two moulded orders. The west window of the ground stage has a two-centred head and is of three trefoiled ogee lights with good early vertical tracery above. Below it is a doorway with a straight-sided four-centred head and casement-moulded jambs. The bell-chamber is lighted on the east, north and south by traceried windows with two-centred heads, each of two trefoiled ogee lights, and on the west by a square-headed window of two similar lights. The walls are of ashlar work, and are crowned by a 17th-century parapet of brick. The high-pitched roof of the chancel is modern. The north transept has a segmental plastered ceiling. The south transept has a roof of late 15th-century date. The nave roof dates from the early 16th century; there are five principals (two being against each end wall) trussed by curved braces from wall posts resting on stone corbels. Each bay is divided into eight compartments by the moulded ridge-piece, common rafters and purlins, which have carved bosses at their intersections. Each compartment is further subdivided into four by subsidiary moulded ribs, also with carved bosses at their intersections. This roof is covered externally with lead; the remaining roofs are tiled.

The font is a poor piece of Jacobean work. In the south-east window of the south transept are some fragments of original glass, comprising a piece of a Crucifixion with some canopy work of the 15th century, and some 14th-century black and white glass, including a pelican in her piety. There is also a shield erminois with a chief argent. Several interesting tiles of 15th-century date have been relaid in the floor of the vestry and on the step of the font. Most are of patterns found elsewhere in the neighbourhood, the most widely met with being a four-tile pattern containing four small shields, each charged with the monogram R E and surrounded by a circular border, inscribed in black letter 'In te dñe confidi.' At each corner is the initial M of our Lady. Another pattern contains four talbots drawn with great spirit and surrounded by a circular border inscribed in black letter 'Sir John Talbot.' Many have various heraldic charges, among which are the crest of an elephant's head cut off at the neck, and the upper part of a lion pattern within a circular border. There are two complete shields, the blazon of one of which is as follows : quarterly (1) and (4) a bend, (2) and (3) fretty impaling a fesse between six quatrefoils ; the other is also quarterly (1) and (4) a cheveron, (2) and (3) barry of six in chief three roundels. There is also a fragment of France quartering England, not to be confused with a mid-Victorian version of the same laid in the floor of the vestry.

The earliest monument in the church is a stone slab on the north wall of the tower to John Wythe and his wife Isabel ; the slab is much decayed and broken, and only the date of the latter's death is now legible. She died in the year 1545. The inscription, so much as now remains, is as follows : '. . . He was buried here yᵉ . . . | Novēbr in the yere . . . | & Isabell wyfe to yᵉ sayd Iõ wythe & dowgʳ & heyr to the | soone & heyre of Iohn moore | & Rose hiˢ wyfe wᶜʰ Rose was Daughtʳ & heyr to willã Brace | The sayd Isabel Was Buried yᵉ 30 day of Mach (sic) Anno Domini 1545.'

Below the inscription is a shield, quarterly : (1) and (4) Wythe, (2) Moore, (3) Brace. On either side of the shield is inscribed 'Iohn wythe | elldest sonne | to the sayde | Iohn Wythe | and Isabell | his wyfe.'

On the south wall is a slab of similar character, also much decayed, to Robert Wythe, son of the above, who died in 1586. The inscription is as follows : '. . . lyethe | . . . bodye of Robert | wythe esqui . . . the | seconde sonne of Iohn | wythe and Isobel | His wyfe wᶜʰ Robert dyed yᵉ

24 daye of | December Anno dñi | 1586 Anno Aetatis sue 63.'

Below is a shield, quarterly : (1) Wythe, (2) Wyche, (3) Moore, (4) Brace.

Against the west wall of the south transept is a large and elaborate monument to George Wylde, serjeant-at-law, who died in the year 1616. He is represented reclining at full length, his head supported on his left hand, wearing the robes of a serjeant-at-law. The figure is contained beneath an arched recess, flanked by Corinthian columns supporting an entablature. The spandrels and tympanum of the arch are ornamented with elaborate strap-work and arabesques, and the whole is picked out with colour. The inscription states that he married Frances the second daughter of Sir Edmund Huddlestone of Sawston in the county of Cambridge, by whom he had issue John (who married Ann, eldest daughter of Thomas Harries of Tong Castle, serjeant-at-law), George, Elizabeth (who married Walter Blount of Sodington), and Dorothy, who died young.

Above the monument is a shield of Wylde quartering Beaconsaw, on the dexter side Huddlestone, and on the sinister Beaconsaw.

In the chancel are slabs to many members of the Nash family. John Nash, who died in 1618; Elizabeth wife of James Nash, 1633 ; Anne wife of Richard Nash, daughter and heir of John Byrch of Cannock, 1651 ; Elizabeth second wife of Richard Nash, 1676 ; John, James and Thomas sons of John Nash, who died in 1660, 1661 and 1662 respectively ; Elizabeth daughter of Richard Nash, by his second wife, 1673 ; Richard Nash and Elizabeth his daughter, 1740; and Elizabeth his wife, 1741.

On the north wall of the chancel is an elaborate mural tablet to Richard Nash, who died in 1690, and to his son Richard, who died in 1696, and his wife Mary, who died in 1707.

There are three bells, inscribed as follows : Treble, 'God Save our Queene A | Lesabet,' probably by John Greene of Worcester about 1600; (2) ' + Celi Pande Fores Nobis Petre nobiliores' in Gothic capitals, with heads of Henry VI, Queen Margaret and Prince Edward as stops, probably cast at Worcester about 1480 ; (3) is a modern recasting of a bell of 1685, originally made by John Martin. There is also a small treble priest's bell, also a recast from a bell of 1692.

The plate consists of a silver cup of 1571, a modern copy of it with the mark of 1858, a silver paten of 1696, a silver flagon of 1781, presented to the church in 1883, and a modern silver paten of 1897.

The registers previous to 1812 are as follows : (i) baptisms, burials and marriages 1544 to 1760, baptisms and burials 1760 to 1792 ; (ii) marriages 1792 to 1812 ; (iii) baptisms and burials 1792 to 1812.

The modern church of *ST. NICHOLAS* consists of a chancel, north vestry and organ chamber, nave, north and south aisles and a south-west tower. The material is stone and the roofs are slated. The style is 'early Decorated.'

The original church of St. Nicholas lay to the west of the town adjoining Friary Street.

ADVOWSONS The church of St. Andrew in the centre of the original town, by which stood the 'Chequer' and market, was the church with which the corporation

DROITWICH : ST. PETER'S CHURCH FROM THE SOUTH

DROITWICH : ST. PETER'S CHURCH : THE NAVE LOOKING EAST

was closely connected in the 17th century and later. The advowson, before 1086 in all likelihood, and by royal grant, passed to the alien priory of Deerhurst.[49] Edward III and Richard II claimed the gift while the temporalities of the alien priory were theirs.[50] In 1467 Edward IV granted the priory of Deerhurst with the advowson of St. Andrew to the abbey of Tewkesbury,[51] with which it remained until the Dissolution. It then again passed to the Crown, in which it has remained until the present time.[52]

An agreement of 1359,[53] drawn up between the rector and the parishioners, throws light on the origin of the churchwarden's office and the history of the rights and duties of clergy and laity. The rector was to have the free custody of all books, vestments and other things, of which the finding and repairing belonged to him by law or by custom. For the custody of books and vestments provided by the parishioners a fit person was to be selected by the rector if he chose, or, if not, the custody of the same was to be arranged as the parishioners might wish, at their own risk in case of any loss. The necessaries of divine service, as prescribed by Archbishop Winchelsey's council of 1305,[54] were to be found by the parishioners. Oblations were not to be limited to 1d.—this, perhaps, because the borough had made a by-law attempting to limit the amount of the oblation.[55] No profane assemblies might gather in the church, and no stipendiary priests might celebrate without the rector's leave. There was to be no salt-boiling on Sunday, but there might be distribution of salt water to the seals.

In this church there was a chantry founded before 1491, when it was described as newly dedicated,[56] by Thomas Walker and his wife,[57] for their souls and the soul of Reginald Bray, famous councillor of Henry VII. It was dedicated in honour of Jesus Christ and the Blessed Virgin Mary, and a chantry-house and other endowments fell to the Crown at the dissolution of the chantries.[58] The presentation to this chantry passed from the founder to George Newport, who held it in 1506 and 1511 in right of his wife Joan.[59] Besides this chantry there was a foundation in honour of St. Richard, probably of earlier origin, in connexion with the parish church.[60] The number of communicants in the parish was in the reign of Edward VI 200.[61]

In 1548,[62] on the request of the parishioners, the parish of St. Mary de Witton (with the vicarage of St. Peter de Witton) was united to St. Andrew's by Letters Patent, but it was not till 1662 that the final union took place.[63] In the 17th century the borough accounts show that the corporation contributed

towards the repairs of St. Andrew's, and the claim to certain corporation pews was established.

The advowson of St. Peter de Witton, or de Wich, was granted by Peter de Studley to the priory of Studley,[64] and remained appropriate to the priory till the Dissolution.[65] The rectory and advowson of the vicarage followed the same descent as the manor of St. Peter's[66] until the disappearance of the latter in 1811.[67] The advowson then belonged to Lord Somers and descended with the title until its extinction on the death of Charles, the third earl, in 1883. It then passed to his eldest daughter Isabella Caroline Lady Henry Somerset, who held until 1906–7, when the patronage was transferred to the Bishop of Worcester.

An obit of small value is mentioned in St. Peter's Church in the 16th century.[68]

Dependent on Witton St. Peter was the bridge-chapel, on the bridge on the Bromsgrove road, still called Chapel Bridge. Nash says 'the public road with horses and carts passed through the chapel, the congregation sitting on one side of the road, the priest on the other, until in 1763 the chapel was pulled down.' The corporation contributed to its maintenance in the 17th century.[69]

The church of St. Nicholas is first heard of in connexion with a grant from Matthew Count of Boulogne, made about 1170, which gave the church to the nuns of Fontevrault settled at Westwood near Droitwich.[70] The gift was confirmed by the count's brother Philip and by Matthew's daughter Ida, and recorded in the Westwood chartulary together with the resignation (1186–91) of the rights of the parson, Master Pharicius, who appears to have held this 'chapel' (as it is then called) hereditarily by the gift of the count. Mr. Round has suggested[71] that the count's rights in St. Nicholas Church were perhaps appurtenant to his rights in Bampton, Oxon., which Domesday Book gives as a royal manor with salt rights in Droitwich.[72] This is borne out by a charter whereby Nicholas son of William granted to the nuns of Westwood all his land of 'Wichio,' within and without the town, which he had by grant of the nuns, *de feudo de Bampton*.[73]

The church remained appropriate to Westwood till the Dissolution. It must have been granted with the site of Westwood Priory to Sir John Pakington, though it is not mentioned in the grant, for he was in possession of it in 1542.[74] The advowson descended with Hampton Lovett Manor until 1643, when Sir John Pakington of Westwood sold it with the rectory to Thomas Pakington of Droitwich.[75] Thomas died in 1653, leaving two daughters, Mary, afterwards wife of Arthur Lowe, and Anne, who seems

[49] *Reg. G. Giffard* (Worcs. Hist. Soc.), 12, 337, 350. Deerhurst belonged to the monks of St. Denis, who had rights in Droitwich in 1086 (Dom. Bk. fol. 174a [2]; *V.C.H. Worcs.* i, 299).
[50] *Cal. Pat.* 1345–8, p. 165; 1348–50, p. 124; 1388–92, p. 124; 1396–9, p. 37.
[51] Ibid. 1467–77, pp. 66, 67; Nash, op. cit. i, 320.
[52] Inst. Bks. (P.R.O.); Nash, loc. cit.
[53] Worc. Epis. Reg. Brian (1352–61), fol. 93 d.
[54] Wilkins, *Concilia*, ii, 280.
[55] Many boroughs made ordinances as to the amount of the oblation.
[56] Worc. Epis. Reg. Moreton, fol. 44.
[57] Ibid.

[58] Pat. 3 Edw. VI, pt. vii. The endowment and chantry-house were granted to Silvester Taverner.
[59] Worc. Epis. Reg. Silvester de Gigliis (1498–1521), fol. 48, 72.
[60] Star Chamb. Proc. Edw. VI, bdle. 1, no. 91; see also *L. and P. Hen. VIII*, xvii, 1015.
[61] Chant. Cert. (Edw. VI), 61, no. 3.
[62] Pat. 2 Edw. VI, pt. v, m. 14.
[63] Priv. Act, 13 Chas. II, stat. i, cap. 10.
[64] Chart. R. 1 Edw. III, m. 2, no. 3. See above under manor of St. Peter's.
[65] *Reg. G. Giffard* (Worcs. Hist. Soc.), 383; *Sede Vacante Reg.* (Worcs. Hist. Soc.), 67; *Valor Eccl.* (Rec. Com.), iii, 86.

[66] *L. and P. Hen. VIII*, xx (i), p. 673. The advowson and rectory were included in the grant made by Queen Mary to Richard Bishop of Worcester in 1558 (Pat. 5 & 6 Phil. and Mary, pt. ii, m. 30).
[67] Inst. Bks. (P.R.O.).
[68] Chant. Cert. 60, no. 63.
[69] The arms in the window are described in the Prattinton MS.
[70] Dugdale, *Mon. Angl.* vi, 1006–7.
[71] *Peerage Studies*, 175.
[72] Dom. Bk. fol. 154b.
[73] Dugdale, op. cit. vi, 1007.
[74] *L. and P. Hen. VIII*, xvii, g. 1012 (28).
[75] Nash, op. cit. i, 331.

to have been unmarried.[76] Arthur Lowe and Mary and John Alderne and John Bath and his wife Elizabeth were dealing with the advowson in 1688.[77] From Mary Lowe the advowson passed with the Lowe in Lindridge to the Rev. William Cleiveland, who held it in 1779.[78] The church was in ruins long before this time, and no rector served the cure, the incumbent of St. Andrew's having the spiritual care of the parish.

In 1843 the parish was united to St. Andrew's,[79] but in 1870 it was again separated,[80] and a new church was built on the Ombersley road. The advowson of this living, which is a rectory, was in the Crown until 1907–8, when it was transferred to the Bishop of Worcester.

Parts of the parishes of Salwarpe and St. Andrew were transferred to the parish of St. Nicholas in 1880, and at the same date Park and Berry Hill Farms with part of Egg Hill, formerly in St. Peter's, became part of the parish of St. Nicholas.[81]

The church of St. Mary de Witton, called also St. Mary de Wich, is no longer in existence. It stood on the Worcester road to the south of the borough. The advowson passed to the Pauncefoot family, and Reynold Pauncefoot's right to the church was acknowledged by the Prior of Worcester at the Gloucester assize of 1203–4 in return for a composition.[82] The advowson belonged to Richard son of Reynold Pauncefoot in 1220-1,[83] but had passed before the end of the century to the Frenes, who presented to the church during the last decade of the 13th and at the beginning of the 14th century.[84] In 1348 John son of Ingram de Frene sold the advowson to Thomas Cassy of Droitwich,[85] who in 1355 sold it to Thomas Earl of Warwick.[86] The advowson was forfeited by his son in 1396,[87] and was granted in 1398 to the king's nephew, Thomas Duke of Surrey.[88] It was afterwards restored to the Earls of Warwick,[89] and passed with the rest of their possessions to Henry VII. The advowson seems to have remained in the Crown[90] until the union of the parish with that of St. Andrew in 1662. Already in 1349 the church was described as in bad repair,[91] and in 1427–8 it was said that there were not ten inhabitants.[92]

Droitwich Borough :

CHARITIES Coventry's Hospital, founded by will of the Right Hon. Henry Coventry, 1686, was the subject of a protracted suit in Chancery between the trustees and the Pakington family, involving the title to the entire property. A compromise was effected and the charity placed on a permanent basis in 1823 by the creation of an annuity of £473 charged upon certain farms.

In addition to the hospital the donor provided for the instruction and clothing of forty boys and forty girls of the borough. The trustees in exercise of their powers have closed the schools and appropriated the income formerly applicable for this purpose for increasing the number of the almspeople, for whose accommodation five new almshouses were erected in or about 1902, at a cost of £2,900, of which £2,000 is in course of being recouped.

The trust property now consists of twenty-three almshouses, each occupied by two inmates, and of the following securities arising in part from the redemption of the annuity of £473 above referred to and in part from investment by the Court of accumulations of income, namely—£10,920 India 3½ per cent. stock, £3,000 New Zealand 3 per cent. stock, £5,589 Middlesex County 3 per cent. stock, £4,000 Surrey County 3 per cent. stock, £133 6s. 6d. India 3 per cent. stock, and £110 East India Railway (Class B) annuities, and £885 12s. Metropolitan 3½ per cent. stock, producing together about £900 a year. Each of the inmates receives 3s. 6d. a week if under seventy years of age, and clothing and 5s. a week if above that age.

The several securities are held by the official trustees, who also hold a sum of £2,280 India 3½ per cent. stock on an Investment Account for recoupment of the £2,000 above mentioned. In 1910 a sum of £400 was also on deposit at a bank.

In 1789 Nathaniel George Petre, by his will, bequeathed £850 consols, to which £100 stock was added for the Sunday schools for boys, and in 1801 Mrs. Sarah Roberts by a codicil to her will bequeathed a further sum of £100 consols, making together £1,050 consols, which is held by the official trustees.

By a scheme of the Charity Commissioners 25 April 1899 the annual dividend, amounting to £26 5s., is made applicable in prizes or rewards of the value of 10s. each to children who attend a public elementary school and also attend a Sunday school, reserving £5 a year to St. Peter's Church Girls' Sunday School so long as it continues to be maintained.

In 1866 Alderman George Grove, by deed, declared the trusts of a sum of £1,000 given by him to the corporation, namely, that the income should be laid out in alternate years in the distribution of blankets, flannel and sheets on 5 November among deserving poor within the municipal borough or 500 yards thereof irrespective of religious creed.

St. Andrew :

In 1698 Catherine Talbot—as appeared from the Church Table—by her will bequeathed an annuity of £4 for the poor of this parish not receiving parish relief, and of £1 for the poor of St. Nicholas. See Lea's Provident Fund below.

The annuity of £5 is paid by the proprietor of the Oakley Estate, situate in this parish and Salwarpe.

In 1719 Talbot Barker, by his will, charged his estates in the parishes of Salwarpe and St. Andrew, Droitwich, with an annuity of £95, of which £40 is payable to the clergyman preaching a sermon on Sunday afternoon in St. Andrew's parish church, £20 for educational purposes in Droitwich, £20 for educational purposes in the parishes of Salwarpe and Martin Hussingtree, £10 for the poor of Droitwich and £5 for the poor of Salwarpe.

[76] Nash, op. cit. i, 331.
[77] Recov. R. Trin. 4 Jas. II, rot. 97.
[78] Nash, loc. cit.
[79] *Parl. Papers* (1872), xlvi, 13.
[80] Ibid. 17.
[81] *Pop. Ret.* (1891), ii, 657, 658.
[82] Habington, op. cit. i, 487 ; Reg. D. and C. Worc. i, fol. 24b, referred to in Nash, op. cit. i, 325.
[83] Assize R. 1021, m. 12.
[84] *Reg. G. Giffard* (Worcs. Hist. Soc.), 481, 496 ; Habington, op. cit. i, 487.
[85] Feet of F. Worcs. Trin. 22 Edw. III.
[86] Beauchamp Chartul. Add. MS. 28024, fol. 5b.
[87] Chan. Inq. p.m. 21 Ric. II, no. 137, m. 6 (e) and (f).
[88] *Cal. Pat.* 1396-9, p. 336.
[89] Nash, op. cit. i, 325 ; Chan. Inq. p.m. file 169, no. 58.
[90] Nash, op. cit. i, 326 ; Inst. Bks. (P.R.O.).
[91] *Sede Vacante Reg.* (Worcs. Hist. Soc.), 225.
[92] *Feud. Aids*, v, 315.

The several annuities which are vested in the official trustee of Charity Lands are paid out of the Oakley estate.

In 1859 Miss Harriet Ricketts, by her will, left a legacy in augmentation of this charity, which is represented by £55 7s. 11d. consols, of which two-fifths, £22 3s. 2d. stock, is applicable for educational purposes, under an order of the Charity Commissioners of 23 March 1906.

The stock is held by the official trustees, who also hold a sum of £110 16s. consols bequeathed by the same testatrix, producing £2 15s. 4d. yearly, administered by the vicar and churchwardens in clothing.

Giles Trimnall—as appeared from the Church Table—left to the poor of this parish several parcels of land, and a rent-charge of 6s. 8d. charged on a house, to be distributed on St. Thomas's Day. The land produces about £10 a year, and the official trustees hold a sum of £92 19s. 9d. consols, producing £2 6s. 4d. yearly. The income is duly applied. On 3 April 1912 a sum of £500 was paid by the Corbett Trustees, under the authority of the Charity Commissioners and of the High Court, to the account of the official trustees for investment in trust for Trimnall's Charity, as a compromise and an extinguishment of all claims on behalf of the charity trustees to the fee simple in two pieces of land in St. Andrew's parish, containing together rather more than an acre, which had apparently become merged in the Corbett estate.

In 1786 Mary Hickman, by her will, bequeathed £200, the interest to be applied for the benefit of the poor. The legacy, reduced by legal costs, is represented by a sum of £171 15s. 8d. consols standing in the name of the Paymaster-General of the High Court, producing £4 5s. 9d. yearly.

In 1756 Joseph Bache—as mentioned on the Church Table—by his will left the residue of his estate for the poor of this parish and Dodderhill. The sum of 50s. formerly received in respect of this charity has ceased to be paid.

In 1822 Mrs. Mary Wakeman, by deed, conveyed land near to a place called Cuckold's Corner, containing 1 a. 2 r., the annual rents to be applied in the purchase of bread among the virtuous poor. The land is let at £6 a year.

In 1797 Mrs. Sarah Roberts, by her will, left a yearly sum of £4 to be distributed on New Year's Day among the poor of St. Andrew and St. Nicholas by the minister of St. Andrew's. The legacy is represented by £133 6s. 8d. consols with the official trustees, producing £3 6s. 8d. yearly. See Lea's Provident Fund below.

In 1833 Miss Elizabeth Smithsend, by her will, bequeathed £45, the interest to be applied for the benefit of the poor of St. Andrew and St. Nicholas. The legacy is represented by two sums of £29 19s. 4d. consols, with the official trustees, producing 13s. each yearly for each parish.

Lea's Provident Fund :

In 1889 the Ven. Archdeacon William Lea, by his will proved at Worcester 11 December, bequeathed £100, represented by £107 16s. 4d. consols, with the official trustees, in augmentation of the charities of Mrs. Catherine Talbot and Mrs. Sarah Roberts, otherwise the 'May-day Money,' in accordance with the provisions of a scheme of the Charity Commissioners 26 June 1874.

Lea's Savings Bank Fund :

The official trustees also hold under this title a sum of £102 11s. 8d. consols, derived under the will of the same testator ;

Also a sum of £102 16s. 6d. consols, arising from the will of Mrs. Hannah Sophia Lea, proved at Worcester 11 May 1883.

A scheme dealing with all the charities in St. Andrew's parish is contemplated.

St. Nicholas :

Charity of Catherine Talbot.—The poor of this parish receive £1 a year, and also participate in the charity of Mrs. Sarah Roberts. (See under parish of St. Andrew.)

The charity of William Squire, founded by will dated 10 December 1716, was the subject of proceedings in the Court of Chancery. A sum of £1 6s. 8d. was applicable for the poor of St. Nicholas, £1 for the poor of Northfield, and the residue of the rents of 6 acres for the benefit of poor relations.

St. Peter :

In 1685 Mr. Tolley, as appeared from the Church Table, by his will devised 2 r. 12 p., the rents to be applied towards the repairs of the church. The land was sold with the sanction of the Charity Commissioners and the proceeds—less £30 remitted to the administering trustees—is represented by £198 6s. 7d. consols with the official trustees, who also hold a sum of £101 18s. 2d. consols in augmentation of this charity derived under the will of the Ven. Archdeacon Lea. The dividends, amounting to £7 9s. 10d., are applied in repairs to the church.

In 1698, as appeared from the Church Table, Catherine Talbot by her will gave 20s. a year to the poor of this parish.

In 1780 William Haseldine by his will directed that £100 should be placed out at interest, to be distributed in bread every Sunday to poor attending divine service. The legacy is represented by £110 19s. consols, producing £2 15s. 4d. yearly.

In 1789 Nathaniel George Petre, as mentioned on the Church Table—left £100, the interest to be given to the poor in bread on Christmas Eve. The legacy is represented by a sum of £150 consols, producing £3 15s. yearly.

In 1860 John Cole Wedgberrow by his will left a legacy, represented by £218 11s. 7d. consols, the annual dividends, amounting to £5 9s., to be applied (subject to repair of tomb) in the distribution of blankets.

In 1797 Mrs. Sarah Roberts by her will gave the yearly sum of £5 to be distributed to the poor on New Year's Day. The annuity was provided by the purchase of a sum of £166 13s. 4d. consols, which now produces £4 3s. 4d. yearly.

In 1889 the Ven. Archdeacon William Lea by his will proved at Worcester left a legacy represented by £203 16s. 5d. consols for the organist and quire of St. Peter's Church.

The five sums of stock above mentioned are held by the official trustees, who also hold a sum of £210 10s. 2d. consols, producing £5 5s. yearly, representing the gift of Mr. William Henry Ricketts and the educational foundations of Harriet Ricketts.

DUDLEY

Dudelei (xi cent.) ; Duddelœge (xii cent.).

Dudley forms a detached part of Worcestershire lying in the county of Stafford on the great South Staffordshire coalfield. The county boundary line makes a peculiar sweep on the north to exclude the portion known as Dudley Castle Hill, crowned by the ruins of the famous castle and containing the celebrated limestone caverns, now forming by itself a Staffordshire parish.[1] The parish of Dudley contains 3,546 acres, of which in 1905 47 acres were arable land, 1,387 acres permanent grass and 153 acres woodland.[2]

The land rises gradually from a height of a little over 300 ft. above the ordnance datum in the south to 700 ft. or 800 ft. in the north of the parish, which lies along the ridge of the Pennine Chain.

In the early 17th century Habington approached Dudley 'over hylls resembling with theyre black couller the Moores who are scorched with the Sun.'[3] From the various sidelights which the records throw on the position of Dudley and from the jealously guarded hunting rights of its lords it is clear that the surrounding country was once undulating forest land.

The town of Dudley has developed entirely to the south of the castle. It probably at first consisted of one long street, the present High Street, stretching between the two churches of St. Thomas and St. Edmund, from which other streets radiated to the south, east and west as the population increased and the coal workings developed.

The Market Place is at the north end of the High Street. The town hall was erected by the late Earl of Dudley and afterwards purchased and reconstructed by the corporation. Near it are the free library and school of art and the art gallery. The municipal technical school in Stafford Street was founded in 1896. The offices of the guardians and officers of the Dudley Union at the junction of St. James' Road and Parsons Street were erected in 1888.

The town is surrounded on all sides by factories and mines.

At Salt Well Wood in Netherton there are salt springs which resemble those at Cheltenham. There are baths in connexion with the springs.

Among the ancient place-names are La Leyne,[4] found in the 14th century, Yorke Park,[5] in the 15th century, Pewceter, Eryhytt,[6] Le Conigree Park,[7] The Talbott,[8] in the 16th and 17th centuries. The town cross is mentioned in a deed of 1338–9.[9]

BARONY CASTLE AND MANOR — DUDLEY was held before the Conquest by Earl Eadwine. At the time of the Domesday Survey the castle, which is specially mentioned, and the manor were in the hands of William Fitz Ansculf, son of Ansculf de Picquigny,[10] who may possibly have preceded his son in the possession of Dudley. William Fitz Ansculf in 1086 held in chief in the eleven counties of Stafford, Warwick, Worcester, Surrey, Berkshire, Northampton, Buckinghamshire, Rutland, Oxford, Middlesex and Huntingdon,[11] and his Worcester manors formed only a small portion of the vast estate which later became known as the barony or honour of Dudley. A large part of the barony was in the county of Buckinghamshire, but Dudley Castle in Worcestershire was the head of the honour, and there William held a manor assessed at 1 hide.[12]

When the barony was divided in 1323 the knights' fees and manors held by John de Somery lay in nine different counties.[13] In 1166 Gervase Paynel was the overlord of fifty fees which had been subinfeudated before the death of Henry I, as well as of five fees and two-thirds which had been granted to sub-tenants after the death of Henry I.[14]

The castle, with its members, of which the manor of Dudley was one, was held of the king in chief by the service of a whole barony.[15] In 1290–1 the castle was said to be held by barony of the king in chief by the service of three knights in time of war in Wales for forty days.[16]

The castle, barony and manor afterwards passed to Fulk Paynel, who is supposed to have acquired them by his marriage with Beatrice the daughter and heir of William Fitz Ansculf.[17] Fulk was succeeded by his son Ralf, who held his castle of Dudley in 1138 for the Empress Maud, and on this account the castle was attacked by King Stephen.[18] His son Gervase Paynel succeeded him, probably before 1160, when he founded the priory of Dudley in pursuance of the intent of his father.[19] He aided Prince Henry in his rising of 1173–4, and his castle of Dudley was demolished by Henry II in consequence,[20] but in 1176 he

---

[1] *Gazetteer of British Isles.*

[2] Statistics from Bd. of Agric. (1905).

[3] Habington, *Surv. of Worc.* (Worcs. Hist. Soc.), i, 195.

[4] *Cal. Pat.* 1327–30, p. 175.

[5] Chan. Inq. p.m. 8 Hen. IV, no. 46.

[6] Pat. 1 Edw. VI, pt. vi.

[7] Ibid. 8 Jas. I, pt. xlii.

[8] Ibid. 12 Jas. I, pt. xiv.

[9] Dugdale, *Baronage*, ii, 214.

[10] *V.C.H. Worcs.* i, 317a, 262. It has been asserted that Dudley was held at the beginning of the 8th century by 'great Dodo that famous Saxon' (Habington, op. cit. i, 196 ; also Nash, *Hist. of Worc.* i, 358), but the statement seems only a fanciful derivation of 'Dudley' from the name of Dodo or Dodda, a Mercian duke who with his brother Odda was said to have founded Tewkesbury Abbey about 700, and no authority has been found for the statement. Mr. H. S. Graze-

brook in his *Barons of Dudley* (Will. Salt Arch. Soc. Coll. ix [2], 3) states that Ferdinando Dudley Lea Smith, esq., of Halesowen Grange (representative of the eldest of the co-heirs of Ferdinando last Lord Dudley) has in his possession an illuminated manuscript pedigree, drawn up between the years 1643 and 1647, which is entitled 'The Genealogy, Antiquity, Arms, Succession and Creation of the ancient Lords and Barons of Dudley Castle, their princely alliances and honorable posterities : Shewing how the Barony of Dudley descends to the heirs general by letters Patent granted long before the Conquest.'

[11] *Dom. Bk.* (Rec. Com.), *passim.*

[12] *V.C.H. Worcs.* i, 317.

[13] *Cal. Close*, 1318–23, pp. 630–2.

[14] *Red Bk. of Exch.* (Rolls Ser.), 269–70. The court held for the barony was called the Court of Knights (*Curia militum*) or Knyghton Court (Cott. Chat. xxiii, 35 ; Anct. Pet. 4207).

[15] *Will. Salt Arch. Soc. Coll.* vi (1), 260 ; *Abbrev. Rot. Orig.* (Rec. Com.), i, 103b ; *Cal. Pat.* 1327–30, p. 270 ; 1334–8, pp. 101, 343 ; 1340–3, p. 11 ; *Feud. Aids*, v, 9 ; Chan. Inq. p.m. 33 Edw. III (1st nos.), no. 36 ; 2 Hen. IV, no. 49 ; 8 Hen. IV, no. 46 ; (Ser. 2), liv, 83 ; Exch. L.T.R. Memo. R. Trin. 33 Hen. VIII, rot. 58.

[16] *Cal. Inq. p.m.* 1–19 Edw. I, 494.

[17] Dugdale, *Mon. Angl.* v, 203 ; 'Coll. for a Hist. of Staffordshire,' *Will. Salt Arch. Soc. Coll.* ix (2), 6.

[18] John of Worcester, *Continuation of Chron. ex Chronicis* (ed. Weaver), 50.

[19] Dugdale, *Mon. Angl.* v, 203 ; *Red Bk. of Exch.* (Rolls Ser.), 269 ; *Will. Salt Arch. Soc. Coll.* ix (2), 8.

[20] Ralph de Diceto, *Opera Hist.* (Rolls Ser.), i, 404.

was restored to the king's favour.[21] Robert, his only child, predeceased him, and his sister Hawise, wife of John de Somery, became his heir.[21a] Although Hawise de Somery survived her brother, the barony passed on his death in 1194 to her son Ralph de Somery,[22] who in 1195–6 still owed 300 marks for relief of the barony of Gervase. Hawise married as her second husband Roger de Berkeley of Dursley,[23] and a portion of her brother's lands in Buckinghamshire were granted to her.[24]

On his mother's death in 1208–9 Ralph de Somery paid a fine of £100 and two palfreys for seisin of the lands which she had held.[25] He died about 1210, leaving a widow Margaret,[26] who afterwards married Maurice de Gaunt.[27]

Ralph de Somery appears to have left two sons, William and Roger, the former being known variously as Perceval de Somery and William Perceval de Somery.[28] Both were probably minors at the time of their father's death, for the barony of Dudley at about this time was in the hands of the Earl of Salisbury.[29] William died about 1222,[30] and the wardship of his son and heir Nicholas was granted to Ranulf Earl of Chester. Nicholas died without issue about 1229,[31] his uncle Roger de Somery doing homage for the barony on 10 July 1229.[32]

In 1230 Roger de Somery was abroad on the king's service,[33] and three years later the Sheriff of Worcestershire was commanded to seize his lands, 'because he came not to the king at the Feast of Pentecost to be girt with the belt of knighthood.'[34] Roger[35] had letters of protection for accompanying the expedition to Gascony in 1253.[36] Roger de Somery is said to have begun to make a castle of his manor-house in 1261–2, but was not allowed to continue it.[37] In 1264, in recognition of his services to the king in the Barons' War, he was allowed to inclose the dwelling-place of his manor of Dudley with a ditch and wall of stone and lime, and to fortify and crenellate it.[38] The new castle was apparently not built on the same site as the former one, as it was situated in the manor of Sedgley in Staffordshire.[39] It was still unfinished at the time of Roger's death in 1272,[40] but was completed by his son and successor Roger.[41] This Roger took an active part in the campaigns against the Welsh.[42] He died in 1291, leaving a son John, then only twelve years of age.[43]

SOMERY. *Or two lions passant azure.*

His widow Agnes survived him.[44] Besides John, Roger de Somery appears to have also left another son Roger and two daughters, who ultimately became their brother's co-heirs.[45] John de Somery took part in the Scotch War of 1303,[46] and in 1306 he received the honour of knighthood with Prince Edward.[47] In 1310 he was again employed in the Scotch wars,[48] and in 1314, immediately after the battle of Bannockburn, was summoned to attend at Newcastle to aid in defending the north of England. From that date he was in constant military employment.[49]

John de Somery seems to have been very overbearing with his tenants and neighbours. In 1310–11 William de Bereford and others alleged that ' he had taken upon him so great authority in Staffordshire that no man could have law or reason by means thereof, and that he domineered there more than a king ; as also that it was no abiding for any man in those parts except he well bribed the said John de Somery for protection, or yielded him much assistance towards the building of his castle, and that the said

[21] *Pipe R.* 21 *Hen. II* (Pipe R. Soc.), 69 ; 24 *Hen. II*, 98.
[21a] Grazebrook, 'The Barons of Dudley,' *Will. Salt Arch. Soc. Coll.* ix (2), 9.
[22] 'Pipe R. Staffs.' *Will. Salt Arch. Soc. Coll.* ii (1), 33, 58, 66, 67.
[23] Dugdale, *Baronage*, i, 612 ; *Mon. Angl.* v, 204.
[24] 'Pipe. R. Bucks.' *Will. Salt Arch. Soc. Coll.* ii (1), 150.
[25] 'Pipe R. Bucks. 10 John,' *Will. Salt Arch. Soc. Coll.* ii (1), 150.
[26] 'Pipe R. Berks. 12 John,' *Will. Salt Arch. Soc. Coll.* ii (1), 156.
[27] *Excerpta e Rot. Fin.* (Rec. Com.), i, 207 ; Smythe's *Lives of the Berkeleys* quoted in ' The Barony of Dudley,' *Will. Salt Arch. Soc. Coll.* ix (2), 13.
[28] *Rot. Lit. Claus.* (Rec. Com.), ii, 171, 500, 531 ; *Cal. Close*, 1227–31, p. 190 ; Nash (*Hist. of Worc.* ii, 207) mentions a deed among Lord Lyttelton's evidences at Hagley by which William de Somery leased a tenement in the manor of Swinford which Ranulf Langde had held in the reign of King John, from the death of the father of the said William de Somery. This deed does not appear in the *Lyttelton Charters* (ed. Jeayes). ' Dominus William de Sumeri' is a witness to an indenture between Roger the Abbot and the convent of Halesowen in the reign of Henry III. In 1349 Roger son of John Persevall de Somery granted to Simon son of Robert de Folewode de Toneworth all the lands and tenements which he held in Northfield and 6*s.* 6*d.* from tene-

ments which Anketin de Coventry formerly held in Birmingham.
[29] *Testa de Nevill* (Rec. Com.), 43.
[30] *Rot. Lit. Claus.* (Rec. Com.), i, 500, 531.
[31] *Excerpta e Rot. Fin.* (Rec. Com.), i, 185. The same Ranulf had held the manor of Dudley in 1216, probably during the minority of William de Somery (*Rot. Lit. Claus.* [Rec. Com.], i, 282).
[32] *Cal. Close*, 1227–31, p. 190. Just before, on 25 June, Roger de Somery had conveyed to Maurice de Gaunt, his stepfather, the manors of Dudley and Sedgley for seven years and had agreed that he would not marry during that time without the consent of Maurice (*Cal. Chart. R.* 1226–57, p. 97).
[33] *Will. Salt Arch. Soc. Coll.* viii (1), 2.
[34] Fine R. 17 Hen. III, m. 5.
[35] A Roger de Somery, who is identified by Glover with this Roger, died in 1235, but he belonged to another family, his father being Miles de Somery (Matt. Paris, *Hist. Angl.* [Rolls Ser.], ii, 385 ; *Excerpta e Rot. Fin.* [Rec. Com.], i, 182, 295 ; Grazebrook, 'Barons of Dudley,' *Will. Salt Arch. Soc. Coll.* ix [2], 16). It is to be observed, however, that in the inquisition taken on the death of Roger de Somery in 1272–3 Ralph de Somery is said to be his grandfather (*Cal. Inq. p.m.* 1–19 *Edw. I*, 14).
[36] *Will. Salt Arch. Soc. Coll.* viii (1), 3.
[37] Grazebrook, op. cit. 19.
[38] *Cal. Pat.* 1258–66, p. 307.
[39] *Cal. Inq. p.m.* 1–19 *Edw. I*, 14, 494.

This probably accounts for the fact that Dudley Castle Hill was extra-parochial.
[40] Ibid. 14.
[41] Ibid. 494. Building, however, seems to have been going on in 1310 when complaints were made about the conduct of John de Somery, who forced people to give him assistance in building his castle (Dugdale, *Hist. of Warw.* 501).
[42] *Coram Rege R.* 10 Edw. I ; *Will. Salt Arch. Soc. Coll.* vi (1), 123 ; viii (1), 10 ; ix (2), 30.
[43] *Cal. Inq. p.m.* 1–19 *Edw. I*, 493 ; *Worc. Inq. p.m.* (Worcs. Hist. Soc.), i, 34. The custody of the borough of Dudley and chase of Pensnett and of the manors of Cradley and Sedgley was granted to John de St. John (*Cal. Pat.* 1281–92, p. 465 ; 'Staff. Assize R. 21 Edw. I,' *Will. Salt Arch. Soc. Coll.* vi [1], 260). Before 1299 John de St. John, at that time a prisoner in France, had sold the custody to Agnes widow of Roger de Somery (*Abbrev. Rot. Orig.* [Rec. Com.], i, 103*b*).
[44] She died c. 1308 (' Fine R. 2 Edw. II,' *Will. Salt Arch. Soc. Coll.* ix [1], 121).
[45] G.E.C. *Complete Peerage*, vii, 190 ; Grazebrook, op. cit. 38 ; *Cal. Inq. p.m.* 10–20 *Edw. II*, 255.
[46] *Will. Salt Arch. Soc. Coll.* viii (1), 26.
[47] Ibid. ; Dugdale, *Baronage*, ii, 215.
[48] Dugdale, *Baronage*, ii, 215.
[49] *Parl. Writs* (Rec. Com.) ; Dugdale, *Baronage*, ii, 215 ; *Will. Salt Arch. Soc. Coll.* ix (2), 42.

John did use to beset men's houses in that county for to murther them, as also extorted large sums of money from them.'[50]

His unpopularity may account for a raid made upon the castle during his ownership of it. In 1321 Nicholas son of Robert de Somery and others were accused of breaking into John de Somery's castle of Dudley and carrying away £1,000 in money, and goods to the value of £200.[51]

Though until this time the Somerys had doubtless been barons by the tenure of the castle of Dudley, this John de Somery seems to have been the first member of the family summoned to Parliament as a baron. The writs were directed to John de Somery from 10 March 1307-8 until 14 March 1321-2, the last being three months after his death. He was never summoned as baron of Dudley.[52] John died without issue on 29 December 1321, leaving a widow Lucy, and, since his brother Roger had predeceased him, his heirs were his two sisters, Margaret wife of John de Sutton and Joan widow of Thomas de Botetourt.[53] On his death the barony created by the writ of 1307-8 became extinct, and the manors comprising the barony became divided.[54] Many of those in Worcestershire passed to Joan de Botetourt, but apparently Dudley Castle and Manor went to Margaret, the elder of the two sisters. It is noticeable, however, that Dudley is not mentioned in the Close Roll of 1323 among the lands so divided.[55]

John de Sutton and Margaret must, however, have held the castle and manor, for under the tyranny of the Despensers John was imprisoned until, through fear of death, he sealed a charter in 1325 by which the greater part of his wide possessions passed to them, the castle, manor and town of Dudley falling to the share of the younger Despenser.[56] After the downfall and execution of the Despensers,[57] John de Sutton and Margaret petitioned for the restoration of their lands, and the castle and town of Dudley were delivered to them in 1327.[58]

In 1328 John and Margaret settled the castle and manor on their son John and his wife Isabella, daughter of John de Cherleton, in tail,[59] and later John de Sutton seems to have mortgaged the castle to John de Cherleton, lord of Powis, to whom he owed the large sum of £3,000.[60] In 1330-1 William le Fisshere and others were summoned before the King's

Bench on a charge of besieging Dudley Castle. They assaulted the lord, John de Cherleton, besieged the castle for two days, shot arrows into it and cast stones against it.[61] John in 1331 again had occasion to complain that his castle at Dudley had been besieged and his goods carried away. Joan de Botetourt, daughter of Roger de Somery and sister of Margaret de Sutton, was chief among the besiegers.[62]

The castle had been recovered by John de Sutton before 1337, when he had licence to grant to his son John the castle and town of Dudley, which he held of the inheritance of Margaret his late wife, to hold during the lifetime of John de Sutton the elder.[63] John son of John obtained Letters Patent confirming his right to the castle and town of Dudley in May 1340,[64] a few days before settling both on his wife Isabel for her life.[65] John de Sutton, who was summoned to Parliament as Lord Dudley or Sutton de Dudley in 1341-2,[66] died in 1359,[67] and his widow Isabel under the settlement

SUTTON, Lord Dudley. *Or a lion vert with a forked tail.*

of 1340 continued to hold the castle and vill of Dudley until her death in 1397,[68] when it passed to her great-grandson, another John de Sutton.[69] He died in 1406, and was succeeded by a son of the same name,[70] who is said to have served for some time under Humphrey Duke of Gloucester in Guisnes Castle in France[71]; he was appointed Lieutenant of Ireland for two years in 1428.[72] During the Wars of the Roses John Dudley, one of the most zealous Lancastrians, was taken prisoner at Gloucester in 1451 and at the battle of St. Albans in 1455, and was afterwards wounded at Blore Heath.[73] However, in spite of his loyalty to Henry VI, he seems to have been immediately received into favour on the accession of Edward IV, who pardoned all the debts due from him to the Crown as Treasurer of the Household of Henry VI,[74] gave him £100 for his expenses in the king's service,[75] and in 1465 granted him £100 yearly for life from the customs and subsidies in the port of Southampton.[76] In 1487

---

[50] Dugdale, *Hist. of Warw.* under Billesley (1765), 501.

[51] De Banco R. and Coram Rege R. printed in *Will. Salt Arch. Soc. Coll.* ix (1), 88 ; x (1), 39.

[52] G.E.C. *Complete Peerage*, vii, 190 ; iii, 18.

[53] Ibid. vii, 190 ; *Cal. Inq. p.m.* 10-20 *Edw. II*, 255.

[54] In 1400 and 1406 the castle of Dudley was said to be held for the service of half a barony (Chan. Inq. p.m. 2 Hen. IV, no. 49 ; 8 Hen. IV, no. 46).

[55] *Cal. Close*, 1318-23, pp. 630-2.

[56] *Cal. Pat.* 1338-40, p. 521 ; *Cal. Close*, 1327-30, p. 63 ; 1323-7, p. 510. In 1322 the Sheriff of Staffordshire was ordered to arrest John de Sutton, and two years later Hugh le Despenser, jun., claimed that John de Sutton and Margaret had already made some agreement with him touching the castle and manor of Dudley and sued them for the fulfilment of the same (*Will. Salt Arch. Soc. Coll.* ix [1], 106).

[57] The custody of Dudley Castle after the death of Hugh le Despenser was granted to William de Birmingham ; *Abbrev. Rot. Orig.* (Rec. Com.), i, 301, 303.

[58] *Rolls of Parl.* ii, 435a ; Chan. Inq. p.m. 1 Edw. III (2nd nos.), no. 55 ; *Cal. Close*, 1327-30, p. 63.

[59] *Cal. Pat.* 1327-30, p. 270.

[60] *Cal. Close*, 1323-7, p. 660 ; cf. also Grazebrook, op. cit. 52.

[61] Coram Rege R. Mich. 4 Edw. III, m. 25, printed in *Will. Salt Arch. Soc. Coll.* xiv (1), 21.

[62] *Cal. Pat.* 1330-4, pp. 126-7. Joan appears to have laid claim to half the castle of Dudley (Assize R. 5 Edw. III, *Will. Salt Arch. Soc. Coll.* xi, 23).

[63] *Cal. Pat.* 1334-8, p. 343.

[64] Ibid. 1338-40, p. 521. In 1338 John son of John de Sutton had licence to clear and cultivate the wastes in several of his manors including Dudley (ibid. 101).

[65] Ibid. 530 ; 1340-3, p. 11 ; Feet of F. Div. Co. Mich. 14 Edw. III, no. 90.

[66] G.E.C. *Complete Peerage*, iii, 181.

[67] Chan. Inq p.m. 33 Edw. III (1st nos.), no. 36.

[68] Ibid. 2 Hen. IV, no. 49.

[69] Ibid.

[70] Ibid. 8 Hen. IV, no. 46.

[71] Dugdale, *Baronage*, ii, 215. Letters of protection granted to John Sutton for one year to go to the castle of Guisnes were revoked in 1424 because he 'tarried in his own castle of Dudley' (*Cal. Pat.* 1422-9, p. 204).

[72] *Cal. Pat.* 1422-9, pp. 475, 493.

[73] Grazebrook, op. cit. 66, 67 ; *Rolls of Parl.* v, 348a.

[74] *Cal. Pat.* 1461-7, p. 120.

[75] Ibid. 332.

[76] Ibid. 458. In 1474 Lord Dudley was one of the envoys appointed to treat with the Scotch about the marriage of the Princess Cecilia with James eldest son of James King of Scotland (*Cal. of Doc. rel. to Scotland*, iv, 288). In 1475 he received £43 6s. 8d. 'for the diet of Margaret lately called Queen' (ibid. 291).

he was succeeded by his grandson Edward Sutton *alias* Dudley,[77] who died in 1531–2, leaving a son John.[78]

Immediately after his succession John Lord Dudley, who was already very much in debt,[79] and is described by Dugdale as 'a weak man of understanding,'[80] seems to have mortgaged most of his estates to Sir John Dudley, afterwards Duke of Northumberland, for £2,000, for which he agreed to pay £400 yearly.[81] In 1532 Lord Dudley wrote to Cromwell begging him to use his influence with the king to persuade him to pay the £2,000 and to take in exchange the manor of Sedgley, worth £180 per annum, for twenty years.[82]

DUDLEY, Lord Dudley. *Or a lion azure with a forked tail vert.*

Evidently his request was not granted, since in 1533 Cromwell received another letter asking him to pay the £400 interest.[83] From a Close Roll of 1538–9 it appears that Cromwell lent him £1,000,[84] but in spite of this Lord Dudley's affairs soon became so much involved that he was obliged to make over most of his possessions to Sir John Dudley, being for the rest of his life dependent upon his friends and known by the name of Lord Quondam.[85] The castle and manor of Dudley were sold in 1535 to Sir John Dudley.[86] Cicely the wife of Lord Dudley with one of her daughters found refuge at Nuneaton, where the prioress gave them 'meat and drink free of cost,'[87] while his eldest son Edward obtained a commission as captain under his uncle Lord Leonard Grey in Ireland,[88] where he remained for several years. In 1547 he joined the expedition into Scotland and was appointed governor of Hume Castle. He succeeded his father as Lord Dudley in 1553,[89] and in 1554, after the attainder of John Dudley, then Duke of Northumberland, Queen Mary restored to him the manor and castle of Dudley.[90]

Dudley Castle was proposed as a prison for Mary Queen of Scots in 1585. Her keeper, Sir Amias Paulet,[91] visited the castle and reported that 'the lodginges . . . . . . are not so manye in number as I could wisshe and are also verie little and straight saving the lodginges wch must serve for this Q. wch

are so faire and commodious as she cannot desire to have them amended.' He then goes on to describe the defects of the castle ; there is plenty of coal and wood, but they can only be had for ready money ;

'also the howse ys utterlie destitute of Table boordes, cup boordes fourmes stooles and Bedstedes saving that the hall and greate chambre are provided with Table boordes . . . . A barne must be converted to a stable for the gouvernors horses . . . . . This Queenes gentlemen servantes will not like wth their straight lodginges because they have no ynner chambers. The brewing vesseles are somewhat decayed, and some are wanting wch may be supplied from Burton. The water for the kitchins and howshold must be sett owt of the dikes wthout the gate and yet some will say that the pump wch standeth in the middest of the court yf yt were clensed would furnishe sufficient and good water, but I find others that doubt thereof. The chamber windowes of this Q. lodginges are open upon the park as likewise the windowes of her kitchin, which I trust may be supplied by a good watche and a deepe ditche but especiallie by this Q. infirmities wch will not permitt her to run away on her owne feete. These defectes are recompenced yn parte with the strength of the howse in other respectes and with manie other good commodities.'[92]

It was finally decided to send the queen to Chartley.

Edward eighth Lord Dudley died in 1586,[93] and was succeeded by his eldest son, also called Edward.[94] Ferdinando, the only legitimate son of the last-named Edward, died of smallpox during his father's lifetime,[95] leaving an only daughter Frances, who married Humble Ward, son of William Ward, jeweller to Queen Henrietta Maria,[96] and to him the Dudley estates were evidently made over for the payment of Lord Dudley's debts.[97] To ensure Frances's succession a grant was obtained from the king in 1635, which provided that, although Ferdinando Dudley had died in his father's lifetime, Frances should have the same place as if her father had been Lord Dudley.[98] Humble Ward was created Lord Ward of Birmingham in 1644.[99]

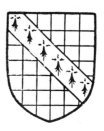

WARD, Lord Ward and Earl of Dudley. *Checky or and azure a bend ermine.*

During the Civil War the castle was garrisoned for Charles I, and was besieged in 1644, and again in 1646, from the Staffordshire side by the garrison at Wrottesley House,[100] and on the Worcestershire side by the Edgbaston garrison. The first time it was relieved by troops sent from Worcester by the

[77] *Cal. Inq. p.m. Hen. VII*, i, 125.
[78] Chan. Inq. p.m. (Ser. 2), liv, 83.
[79] *L. and P. Hen. VIII*, v, 1727.
[80] Dugdale, *Baronage*, ii, 216.
[81] *L. and P. Hen. VIII*, v, 1727.
[82] Ibid. The letter shows that Lord Dudley was afraid to go to London because 'Sir John Dudley lays wait for me . . . to keep me afore the days of payment.' [83] Ibid. vi, 467.
[84] Pt. vii, m. 3 d. ; *L. and P. Hen. VIII*, xiv (1), 357. In a list of Cromwell's 'Remembrances' there are the entries 'The yearly value of the lordships sold by the lord Dudley,' 'Supplications' of Lord Dudley and 'Paper of the value of Lord Dudley's debts' (*L. and P. Hen. VIII*, vii, 923 [ii, iii and xviii]).
[85] G.E.C. *Complete Peerage*, iii, 184.
[86] Close, 27 Hen. VIII, pt. i, no. 23 ; see also *L. and P. Hen. VIII*, xii (1), 1263, where the date is given as 1537. In 1532 Lord Dudley had conveyed the castle and manor to trustees apparently

for settlement on himself and his heirs (Feet of F. Div. Co. Trin. 24 Hen. VIII ; Recov. R. Worc. Trin. 24 Hen. VIII, rot. 424). Andrew Dudley was one of the trustees, and in 1534 and 1541 he and Lord Dudley were summoned to show why the castle and manor should not be taken into the king's hands because the fine had been levied without his licence (Memo. R. Mich. 26 Hen. VIII, rot. 12 ; Trin. 33 Hen. VIII, rot. 58).
[87] *L. and P. Hen. VIII*, xiii (2), App. 6.
[88] Ibid. xi, 934 ; xii (2), 382 ; xiv (2), App. 40. In 1545 he and his brother were commended in a letter from Sir William Paget to Lord Petre for 'forwardness in service' (ibid. xx [2], 919).
[89] G.E.C. op. cit. iii, 184.
[90] Orig. R. 2 & 3 Phil. and Mary, pt. i, rot. 94. In 1579–80 the castle and manor of Dudley were settled on Edward Lord Dudley and his heirs male with contingent remainders to the queen (Pat. 21 Eliz. pt. vi ; Feet of F.

Div. Co. Hil. 22 Eliz. ; Recov. R. Mich. 22 Eliz. rot. 1104). This remainder was granted by the queen in 1581 to William Lord Burghley and others (Pat. 23 Eliz. pt. iv, m. 3).
[91] State Papers (Scottish Ser.), xvi, 63.
[92] Ibid.
[93] Chan. Inq. p.m. (Ser. 2), ccxxxiv, 74. [94] Ibid. In 1612 the reversion and remainders depending upon the estates in fee tail belonging to Lord Dudley were granted to a certain George Baggeley, yeoman (Pat. 8 Jas. I, pt. xlii).
[95] *Cal. S. P. Dom.* 1619–23, p. 349.
[96] G.E.C. *Complete Peerage*, iii, 185.
[97] Feet of F. Div. Co. Trin. 5 Chas. I ; Mich. 11 Chas. I ; *Cal. S. P. Dom.* 1638–9, p. 511.
[98] *Cal. S. P. Dom.* 1635, p. 141.
[99] G.E.C. *Complete Peerage*, iii, 185.
[100] *Hist. MSS. Com. Rep.* xiii, App. ii, 306. The castle had been fortified by Colonel Leveson in 1643 (Add. MS. 5752, fol. 400–2).

king,[1] but in 1646 the governor, Sir Thomas Leveson, surrendered it by the king's orders after his surrender to the Scots 'to avoid bloodshed,' although it was 'provisioned for three years.'[2] The terms of surrender were accordingly very lenient, and included the stipulation that those who went to their own homes were to have 'unmolested peace' there, that passes were to be given to those who wished to go abroad, that 10 miles' march a day was to be the limit for those who went to join other garrisons, and that carriages should be provided for the officers.[3] After the second siege the castle was dismantled by order of Parliament.[4]

Lord Ward seems to have taken no active part in the Civil War, although he and his wife and children were living in Dudley Castle when it was garrisoned for Charles I and during the siege of 1646.[5] In 1651, in spite of his claim that his freedom from sequestration was one of the terms of the surrender of the castle to Sir William Brereton, and in spite of an order from Parliament for his discharge, Lord Ward's tenants were commanded not to pay him their rents, the county committee reporting that Sir William Brereton had only procured the order on the marriage of his daughter Frances with Lord Ward's eldest son Edward.[6] Lord Ward's estates do not seem to have been finally discharged until 1656.[7]

In 1660 Edward Gibson, grandson of John Sutton, second son of Edward eighth Lord Dudley, laid claim to the castle and barony of Dudley, saying that they had been entailed on the said Edward Sutton and his heirs male in the reign of Queen Mary.[8] His petition was referred to the Committee for Privileges,[9] but probably no further proceedings were taken, although in 1667 Frances Lady Dudley petitioned the king for the 'title, style and precedence of the barons of Dudley.'[10]

Edward Ward succeeded his father in the manor, castle and borough of Dudley and barony of Ward in 1670 and his mother in the barony of Dudley in 1697,[11] leaving them successively to his grandson[12] and great-grandson, both called Edward.[13] The latter died unmarried in 1731,[14] his heir being his uncle William Ward, fourteenth Lord Dudley and fifth Lord Ward, who also died unmarried in 1740.[15] The barony of Ward with the Dudley estates then passed to a cousin, John Ward,[16] who was created Viscount Dudley and Ward in 1763,[17] but the barony of Dudley, created by the writ of 1342, passed to the heir general, Ferdinando Dudley Lea, nephew of the last baron, on whose death without issue in 1757 it fell into abeyance between his five sisters, and still remains so, though the title Baroness Dudley was illegally assumed by Anne eldest sister and co-heir of the last lord.[18] From John first Viscount Dudley the manor passed to his sons John and William in succession. John William son and heir of William the third viscount succeeded in 1823, and was created

Earl of Dudley in 1827,[19] but died unmarried in 1833, when the barony of Ward, with his estates passed to his second cousin William Humble Ward. The viscounty of Dudley and Ward and earldom of Dudley of the 1827 creation became extinct, but the earldom was re-created in 1860 in favour of William son and heir of the last-named William Humble[20] and father of William Humble Ward, now Earl of Dudley and owner of the manor of Dudley and of the ruins of the castle.

DUDLEY CASTLE consists of an irregularly shaped walled inclosure, with its greatest length from north to south, having the keep on a mound at the south-west angle, the main gateway and barbican projecting from the external wall at the south-east, and a range of domestic buildings occupying the whole of the eastern side of the bailey, terminated by the chapel on the south and the postern gateway on the north. Near the north-west angle of the external wall is a small doorway, and there are traces of a building having formerly existed on the west side of the bailey about midway between this doorway and the keep. Immediately to the west of the main gateway the external wall is interrupted by a late block of domestic buildings. A deep moat surrounds this area on the east, north and west, commencing on the east side of the barbican and terminating at the north-west of the keep mound, which is unmoated. A considerable portion of the mound itself appears to have been faced with stone. On the northern side of the moat, opposite the north gateway, was a walled triangular outwork, covering the approaches from that direction; a road seems to have approached the castle from the north, passing round its eastern side, and so in by the north gate, where the moat was crossed by a drawbridge. On the edge of a steep slope, about 300 yards south of the keep, is a short piece of walling with a small angle tower and a two-storied gate-house; the work is poor, and seems to be all of late date. The modern approach to the castle leads by a short steep ascent to this gateway, and, turning there in a north-easterly direction, passes below the keep to the gate in the barbican.

Below and outside the chief moat is a second line of ditches, less regular and more difficult to trace clearly in their original outline. This is probably the limit to which the line of outer walls or palisading would have extended, though beyond them are still further ditches and escarpments, some natural and some probably quarries, which would all assist in making the site one of most remarkable strength.

The woods, which now cover the whole hill or ridge occupied by the defences, conceal to some extent, both on the ground and from a distance, the great natural advantages which the position must always have offered for any kind of fortification.

No part of the masonry defences appears to be of an earlier date than the latter half of the 13th century,

[1] *Cal. S. P. Dom.* 1644, p. 262. On pp. 235-6 there is a long account of a fight near Dudley in which the Parliamentary army under Lord Denbigh were victorious, only losing ten men, while the Royalists lost sixty or a hundred.
[2] *Hist. MSS. Com. Rep.* xiii, App. i, 570.
[3] *N. and Q.* (Ser. 5), xi, 156.
[4] *Hist. MSS. Com. Rep.* vi, App. i, 129b.
[5] *Cal. Com. for Comp.* iv, 2779.
[6] Ibid. In 1652 Humble Ward conveyed the castle, borough and manor of Dudley to Sir William Brereton and Thomas Brereton, probably for settlement on the said Edward and Frances (Feet of F. Div. Co. Trin. 1652).
[7] *Cal. Com. for Comp.* iv, 2780.
[8] *Hist. MSS. Com. Rep.* vii, 109a.
[9] Ibid.
[10] *Cal. S. P. Dom.* 1666-7, p. 477.
[11] G.E.C. *Complete Peerage,* iii, 185.
[12] Ibid.; Feet of F. Div. Co. Mich. 23 Chas. II; Mich. 26 Chas. II.
[13] G.E.C. op. cit. iii, 186.
[14] Ibid.
[15] Ibid. viii, 49.
[16] Ibid.; Recov. R. East. 14 Geo. II, rot. 199.
[17] G.E.C. op. cit. viii, 49; *Cal. of Home Office Papers,* 1760-5, p. 1154.
[18] G.E.C. op. cit. iii, 186-7.
[19] Ibid. viii, 49. [20] Ibid.

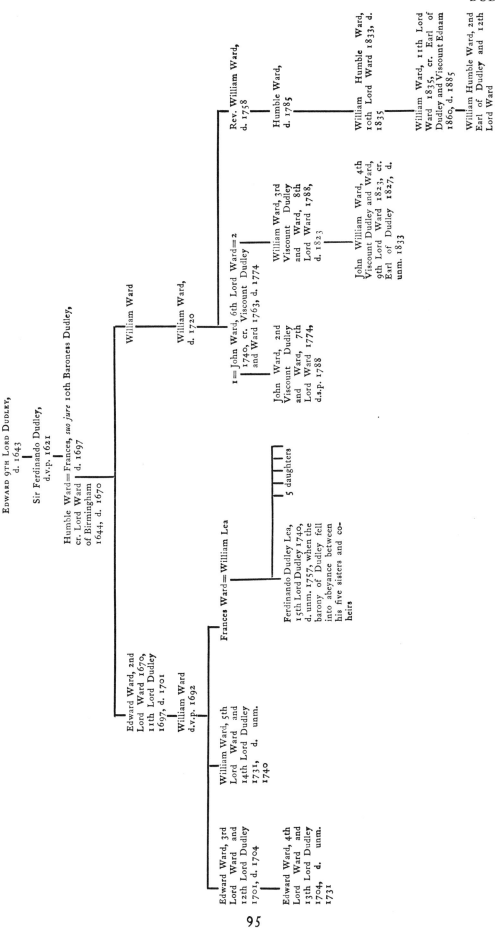

TABLE SHOWING DESCENT OF THE BARONIES OF DUDLEY AND WARD AND OF THE MANOR OF DUDLEY

Edward 9th Lord Dudley, d. 1643

Sir Ferdinando Dudley, d.v.p. 1621

Humble Ward = Frances, *suo jure* 10th Baroness Dudley, cr. Lord Ward d. 1697 of Birmingham 1644, d. 1670

Edward Ward, 2nd Lord Ward 1670, 11th Lord Dudley 1697, d. 1701

William Ward d.v.p. 1692

William Ward

William Ward, d. 1720

Frances Ward = William Lea

Ferdinando Dudley Lea, 15th Lord Dudley 1740, d. unm. 1757, when the barony of Dudley fell into abeyance between his five sisters and co-heirs

5 daughters

Edward Ward, 3rd Lord Ward and 12th Lord Dudley 1701, d. 1704

Edward Ward, 4th Lord Ward and 13th Lord Dudley 1704, d. unm. 1731

William Ward, 5th Lord Ward and 14th Lord Dudley 1731, d. unm. 1740

Rev. William Ward, d. 1758

Humble Ward, d. 1785

1 = John Ward, 6th Lord Ward = 2 1740, cr. Viscount Dudley and Ward 1763, d. 1774

John Ward, 2nd Viscount Dudley and Ward, 7th Lord Ward 1774, d.s.p. 1788

William Ward, 3rd Viscount Dudley and Ward, 8th Lord Ward 1788, d. 1823

John William Ward, 4th Viscount Dudley and Ward, 9th Lord Ward 1823, cr. Earl of Dudley 1827, d. unm. 1833

William Humble Ward, 10th Lord Ward 1833, d. 1835

William Ward, 11th Lord Ward 1835, cr. Earl of Dudley and Viscount Ednam 1860, d. 1885

William Humble Ward, 2nd Earl of Dudley and 12th Lord Ward

to which period the keep and gate-house with its barbican belong. The chapel block is of the early 14th century, while the buildings to the north between the chapel block and the postern are mainly reconstructions of the 16th century,[21] though the external wall against which they are built and some partition walls incorporated into their structure are of the original date. The dismantling of the castle in 1646 accounts largely for the ruinous state of the keep, main gateway, and wall of enceinte. The barons of Dudley and Ward continued to use the domestic portion as a residence until 1750, when it was devastated by fire. Tradition ascribes the fire, which lasted three days, to a set of coiners, who are said to have carried on their trade in the castle.

The keep stands on a mound partly artificial, overlooking the castle area, and forming the southern point of the main defences. The building is of limestone rubble with sandstone dressings, shaped angle pieces being occasionally introduced in the re-entering angles. The walls rise with a batter for about 4 ft. and are vertical above. The plan is rectangular, the longer sides running approximately east and west, and there are large circular towers at the four angles. Of these the northern two with the curtain wall between remain fairly complete as far as the battlements, which on the western tower have been rebuilt, but the rest of the walls and the southern towers have only 4 ft. or 5 ft. of masonry remaining above ground. A sloping approach leads east from the main gateway of the castle towards the keep, curving below a platform in front of the north-eastern tower, and leading to the gateway in the north curtain wall. Here the external doorway consists of a segmental arch of three orders, moulded with wide angle rolls, a 6-inch slot for the portcullis being placed between the second and third, and a rebate for a door inside all, with holes for the bar. The wall at this point is 11 ft. 4 in. thick, and the passage through it from the doorway is vaulted.

The interior of the keep had apparently two floors, without divisions, the towers forming a recess in each corner, and the battlements having a walled passage round the roof of the upper story. A newel stair on the eastern side of the entrance leads to the two floor levels and to the battlements, while a second newel stair adjoining it to the east leads from the first floor level to the battlements of the north-eastern tower. A stairway in each of the remaining towers, now blocked, leads from the ground to the first floor. The curtain and towers are variously pierced with loops and larger openings, and on the first floor above the gateway are two larger lights with moulded rear-arches, having their internal splays thrown to the westward by the position of the newel stairs above described. A blocked arch on the face of the north-west tower close above the moat seems to have been a drain shoot. The battlements are high, and the merlons are pierced with trefoil-headed loopholes, large on the western tower and small on the curtain, all being provided with rebates for shutters.

The remains of the thick wall of the enceinte, which is most probably contemporary with the keep, continue eastwards till they meet the block of 17th-century

buildings which adjoin the gate-house. On the inside, and parallel with it, is a short piece of wall, probably of the 15th century, which stops at the platform below the north-eastern tower. It is provided with two large cross loops, which appear to flank the slope leading to the gate of the keep. Perhaps a passage or covered way led down from the level of the keep towards the main gate, but subsequent alterations to the walls, which have been choked up in many places, render it impossible to state this with certainty At the point where this inner wall joins the 17th-century work is part of a buttress. The 17th-century work at this point consists of a thin-walled oblong block of buildings, two stories in height, extending up to the gate-house. On the side towards the bailey the principal floor is lighted by large mullioned and transomed windows of two lights, and the ground floor, where there are also two square-headed doorways, by smaller untransomed windows of the same number of lights.

The main gateway was originally three stories in height, but of the upper floor only a portion of the loopholed walls now survives. The entrance itself is a vaulted passage having doors and a portcullis at both ends, with a two-centred segmental external archway of three elaborately moulded orders, inclosed by a label with leaf stops, and on the bailey side an archway of two similar orders, the outer, which is raised considerably above the inner, being carried by small shafts with moulded capitals and bases, resting on carved corbels. It is protected on the external side by a barbican, having a large gateway flanked by small circular turrets, of which the foundations alone remain. This appears to have been an afterthought, though there is little difference in date. The walling is of rubble, with sandstone quoins, and of the same character as the keep. A doorway with a two-centred head and continuously moulded jambs, which must have been reached by an external staircase from the bailey, communicates with an apartment over the entrance lighted by twin trefoiled lights. The barbican is built with an inclination to the west to meet the curved approach leading to the gate.

East of the gateway and barbican there are now no buildings, and the main wall, which has been much restored, after continuing in a straight line for about 54 ft., trends to the northward and joins the chapel block. At the angle made by the change of inclination is a rounded mass of masonry, perhaps the base of a turret. The building containing the chapel and the domestic apartments adjoining is of the early 14th century. The first floor at the southern end, which is two stories in height, is occupied by the chapel, extending the full width of the building from west to east. It is lighted from the west by a large window with a two-centred head and external label, from which the tracery has disappeared. Sufficient remains to show that it was of three lights, and that the tracery was composed of sexfoiled spherical triangles. At the south-west is an ogee-headed doorway, entering the chapel either from buildings now gone or from an external stair. In the wall close to it is a recess for a water-stoup. A string-course runs round the west wall and what remains of the south wall, being slightly dropped to the north of the chapel. Beneath the chapel is a barrel-vaulted room, entered by a doorway with a two-centred head at the south-east, and lighted by plain square-headed

---

[21] An extant letter of Sir W. Sharington, dated 1553, mentions that Chapman (one of the masons working for him at Lacock) had gone to Dudley to set up a chimney-piece there.

Dudley Castle : The Keep from the North-east

Dudley Castle : The Great Hall : Interior looking North

lights, two in the west wall and one in the south wall to the east of the entrance.

The walls of the portion north of the chapel inclose a floorless area with a central dividing wall. The eastern part contained cellars on the ground floor, with two floors above, the east wall showing remains of two fireplaces on the first floor and one of wrought sandstone of more elaborate character on the second floor, all 16th-century work.

The western part has a ground floor room with two cross walls, and above this is what was probably the grand chamber, which is lighted by two large six-light mullioned and transomed windows in the west wall, inserted in the 16th century, with a small fireplace of the same date between. The masonry of this block is clumsy and coarse compared with that of the keep and gate-house. The north-west angle appears to have been cut back and refaced to square with the projecting rooms at the south-west of the hall. A passage in a three-sided turret projecting outside the wall of the enceinte leads from the north-west of the chapel block to the later buildings on the

often at the head of the hall stair, with traces of fan vaulting and carved work between the ribs. The eastern wall of the hall was formed by the main outer wall, and of this only the foundations remain; but the western preserves a row of six large four-light windows with mullions, transoms, and sloped sills. This wall has also small two-light mullioned windows on the ground floor. At the north end of the hall, on the level of the original floor, are three doorways with classical lintels opening into a kind of passage—the development of the earlier type of screens—and above these doors is a two-light pedimented window, which evidently overlooked the hall from a room above the passage.

On the west side of the west wall is a terrace extending about three-quarters the length of the hall. This has been restored, but there appears to have been originally a Corinthian arcade along the front, entered by a doorway at the south end, which communicated through the vestibule with the dais end of the hall. A doorway on the north communicated with a corresponding vestibule at the opposite end of

DUDLEY CASTLE FROM THE SOUTH-WEST

north. Its masonry, of neatly coursed limestone rubble, with regular sandstone quoins, shows it to be an addition of the same period.

At the south, in what was the basement beneath the hall, is a room running east and west with a rubble vaulted roof. Contained in a projection at the south-east were three small rooms, one above another, square in shape and lighted by small mullioned windows; the first floor room may have formed a vestibule to the hall. The floor above the vaulted room represents the southern or dais end of the hall, which extended northwards above a range of cellars, which, together with the floor of the hall, are now entirely gone. The south-eastern corner of the hall has required much repair, and the exact means of connexion between the dais and the chambers south of and above it are difficult to trace. There may have been a circular stair in the thick mass of wall at that corner, and there was apparently a passage in the projecting piece of wall, as on the ground floor level. At the top of this projection are the remains of a small room, such as was

the hall contained in a projecting building answering to that on the south. From the middle of the terrace a flight of steps led down to the level of the court, the terrace itself being supported by a line of arched recesses, which gave light to the small windows of the cellars below the hall.

At the north-east corner of the hall is a projection on the outer wall, part of which seems to have contained a newel stair, and from this point the wall trends to the north-west. This change of direction is followed by the building, with the result that a small triangular-shaped room is formed at this end of the hall, which probably served as a lobby, from which the hall was entered by the doors at that end.

The ground floor of the adjoining block of buildings contains the kitchen on the north, with a large room on the south, divided from the kitchen by a wide passage. This southern room, which, like the kitchen, occupies the whole width from west to east, is lighted by a large semicircular bay window of eight mullioned lights on the bailey side, while at the opposite end there are two arched recesses carrying the masonry floor of a serving lobby to the hall. A wide flight of steps appears to have originally led from this lobby down to the passage adjoining the kitchen. The northern wall is partly of the 12th century, and shows the remains of a large semicircular-headed doorway of this date. The jambs are gone, but a plain rear-arch is visible in its entirety on the south side and part of the roll-moulded external order on the north. The doorway has been built up, and the floor of the room above, now destroyed, was below the crown of its head. The north face of this wall has been much disturbed, and is corbelled back on the ground story, the thicker upper portion being carried by a pair of depressed arches of the 16th century, springing from a large central corbel of wrought sandstone.

The eastern wall of this block above the ground floor level appears to be entirely of the 16th century, and to be erected upon the original wall of enceinte. On the west the bay window is carried the whole height of the building, and the wall is crowned by large gables. At the north-east, against the external wall, is an ashlar-faced buttress of contemporary date. The kitchen has a large three-flue fireplace and oven in the north-east wall and a smaller one on the north-west. A small door from the kitchen opens into the court; the adjoining buildings on the north follow the trend of the external wall still further westward. The large room on the ground floor appears to have been a bakehouse, and contains two brick ovens on its south-east wall. Attached to the north-western angle is an octagonal turret with an external entrance door, extending the whole height of the building; the stairs which it contained have disappeared. The walling of the northern gate-house or postern block, though the details of the windows and of the gate-way itself show them to have been inserted in the 16th century, is of a much coarser character, and would appear to be of the 15th century. The original wall of enceinte has here been razed to the ground and replaced by a thinner wall. On the north side are two buttresses.

The northern gateway itself consists of two depressed arches about 6½ ft. wide, with a passage between them and a room above. The jambs and arches are very much worn and show evident marks of insertion. The eastern part of the block contains a series of rooms lighted by two-light mullioned windows; these were of small size, and probably servants' quarters. West of this gateway the buildings end. A passage in the wall of enceinte appears to have opened out of the gateway, which may, perhaps, have contained a flight of steps leading to a platform behind the battlements. The foundations of the wall can be traced in their original thickness along the whole of the west side of the bailey, but above ground, for the greater part of its length only a thin piece of wall on the inner side remains. Following this wall south-west and then south a small external doorway is reached; the head is rounded, and there are some traces of a projecting wall and arch to defend it close above the moat. Beyond this are a line of corbels and a large fireplace in the external wall;

the foundations of a small building probably of the 16th century, to which it belonged, measuring about 37 ft. 3 in. by 15 ft. 8 in., have been recently uncovered. The original thickness of the wall remains at this angle for a short distance. Approaching the keep the wall rises steeply up the keep mound, meeting its northern curtain west of the gateway.

The bailey may perhaps have been divided into two wards, but the surface has been much altered. There is a deep well in the centre of the present area.

The chapel of Dudley Castle is mentioned in 1323, when its advowson belonged to the lord of Dudley.[22]

When the manor and castle of Dudley were granted in 1554 to Edward Lord Dudley a rent of £12 5s. 8d. was reserved to the Crown.[23] This rent was probably included in annuities from the castle and manor granted by Queen Elizabeth in 1579 to Edward Lord Dudley for life with remainder to his daughter Anne, wife of Francis Throckmorton, and her heirs.[24] John Throckmorton was dealing with it in 1606,[25] but it apparently reverted to the Crown, for in 1650 it was sold by the trustees appointed by Parliament to Henry Sanders.[26] At the Restoration it again became a royal possession, and was vested in 1672 in trustees,[27] who sold it in that year to William Roberts, George Dashwood and Gabriel Roberts.[28] In 1700 this rent of £12 5s. 8d. was sold by Sir Samuel Dashwood to William Tempest, Richard Taylor and Richard Hoare.[29]

BOROUGH The borough grew up round the castle, the head of the great barony of Dudley, and the early working of coal and iron in the neighbourhood may have aided its development. There is no evidence to show that it was a borough at the time of the Domesday Survey or indeed until 1261–2, when Roger de Somery agreed that the Dean of Wolverhampton might establish a market in Wolverhampton on condition that he and his 'burgesses' of Dudley might be free from toll there.[30]

Though Dudley appeared by twelve separate jurors at the assizes in 1254–5,[31] it is not called a borough, but it is given that title in the eyre of 1274–5.[32]

It is not until the death of Roger de Somery in 1272 that any idea can be obtained of the actual value or importance of Dudley. The inquisition was taken in 1273, and, as the manor and borough were valued together, it is exceedingly difficult to get anything like a clear conception of the exact relationship of the two. It is probable, however, that the manorial tenants had obtained certain franchises from their lord, and in return for a fixed rent been freed from some or all of the services required of them as manorial tenants, becoming in fact tenants in burgage. The rents of the burgesses at that time produced yearly £5 15s. 5d.,[33] and the tolls of the markets 40s., while the pleas and perquisites of the hundred court were estimated at 30s. An inquisition taken in 1291 gives another account of the town, the borough being then extended at £30 17s. 3¾d. yearly. The rent of

[22] *Cal. Close*, 1318–23, p. 631.

[23] Pat. 2 & 3 Phil. and Mary, pt. ii, m. 11; Close, 1651, pt. viii, m. 7.

[24] Chan. Inq. p.m. (Ser. 2), ccxxxiv, 74.

[25] Feet of F. Div. Co. Trin. 4 Jas. I.

[26] Close, 1651, pt. viii, m. 7.

[27] Palmer's Indices (P.R.O.), lxxiii, fol. 18 d.

[28] Recov. R. D. Enr. Trin. 12 Will. III, m. 4.   [29] Ibid.

[30] Fine (1261), printed in *Will. Salt Arch. Soc. Coll.* iv (1), 250.

[31] Assize R. 1022, m. 25.

[32] Ibid. 1026, m. 35. In the 13th century Dudley seems to have ranked as a hundred (*Hund. R.* [Rec. Com.], ii, 285; *Worc. Inq. p.m.* [Worcs. Hist. Soc.], pt. i, 16, 34).

[33] *Worc. Inq. p.m.* (Worcs. Hist. Soc.), pt. i, 16.

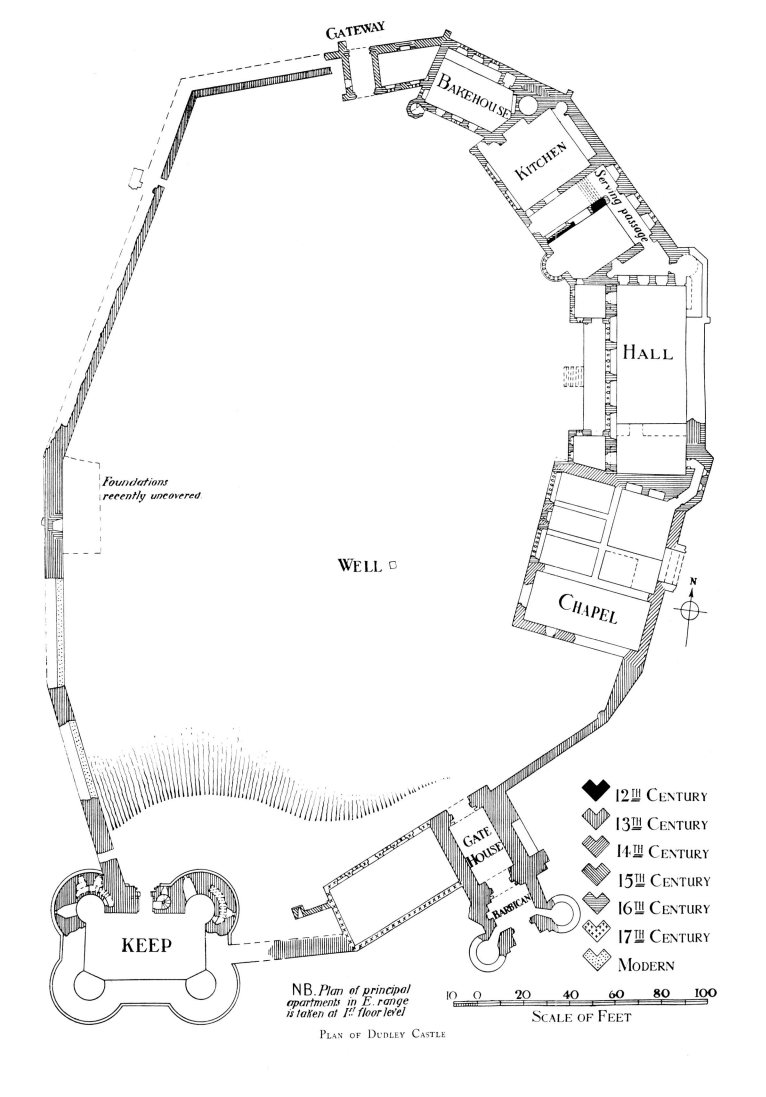

GATEWAY

BAKEHOUSE

KITCHEN

Serving passage

HALL

Foundations recently uncovered.

WELL □

CHAPEL

N

KEEP

GATE HOUSE

BARBICAN

◆ 12TH CENTURY
13TH CENTURY
14TH CENTURY
15TH CENTURY
16TH CENTURY
17TH CENTURY
MODERN

N.B. *Plan of principal apartments in E. range is taken at 1st floor level*

10 0   20   40   60   80   100

SCALE OF FEET

PLAN OF DUDLEY CASTLE

the burgesses was worth yearly £6 0s. 10d., an increase of 5s. 5d. on that paid in 1273. The tolls had decreased to 20s.,[34] but the pleas and perquisites of the hundred court had increased to 60s. A very significant entry tells us that there was one mine of sea-coal worth a mark a year, another valued at 40s., as well as two great smithies (*fabrice*) of the annual value of £4. The local coal and iron industry was already born.

It is very difficult to obtain any idea of the early constitution of the borough. Although there is no trace of an early incorporation charter, the town was governed in the 16th century by a mayor, bailiff and other officers, who were elected at the court leet of the lord of the manor, but had no magisterial authority.[35] A mayor is first mentioned in a list of Lord Dudley's possessions in 1591, which shows that this officer was elected every year and received £7 yearly from the burgesses as his fee.[36] This form of government seems to have continued until 1853, when a Local Board of Health, consisting of fifteen persons, was established under the Public Health Act.[37]

The incorporation charter, under which the town is now governed, was granted on 3 April 1865 by the title of the mayor, aldermen and burgesses of Dudley. It divided the town into the seven wards of St. Thomas, the Castle, Netherton, St. Edmund, St. James, St. John and Woodside, each of the first three being represented in the council by two aldermen and six councillors, the others by one alderman and three councillors.[38]

Dudley was represented in the Parliament of 1295,[39] but not again until the passing of the Reform Act in 1832, which allowed the burgesses to return one member, a privilege which is still continued. Dudley became a county borough under the Local Government Act of 1888, and has its own bench of magistrates. In 1907 it was granted a Court of Quarter Sessions.

The corporation plate consists of a gold chain and badge given to the town in 1882 by Lord Dudley, a mace and the common seal. The mace is 26 in. long, the upper part being encased with silver, surmounted by a royal crown, and bearing the inscription 'Presented by the Right Hon. William Viscount Dudley and Ward to the Town of Dudley on the 9th August 1798.'[40] The common seal is a round embossing stamp $2\frac{5}{16}$ in. wide, with the borough arms and crest, circumscribed 'The Mayor, Aldermen and Burgesses of the Borough of Dudley 1865.'

The town arms are Gules a fesse engrailed argent between Dudley Castle in the chief and a salamander in flames proper in the foot with a trilobite [41] between an anchor and a miner's lamp on the fesse. Crest, a lion's head razed.[42]

A market on Saturday had been established in Dudley before 1261.[43] Habington mentions a fair on St. James's Day,[44] and in 1684 Edward Lord Ward received a grant of two new fairs to be held on 21 April and 21 September.[45] Besides these three fairs, now held on the first Monday in May and October and the second Monday in August, a fourth fair has been established since 1792 and is held on the first Monday in March. They are all now chiefly pleasure fairs, very few cattle and horses being sold.[46]

The market was held in the High Street and in Netherton Square and Stone Street until 1848-9, when a market-place was formed by pulling down houses between High Street and Queen Street.[47]

The market rights and tolls were purchased by the corporation from Lord Dudley in 1870 at a cost of £10,000.[48]

Wakes used to be held annually at Netherton on the last Sunday in October, and at Kate's Hill on the Sunday before 21 October.

As at Kidderminster, the parish and manor, which in Dudley were at first co-extensive, were later divided into the borough and the foreign,[49] but by the beginning of the 19th century the borough had spread over the whole parish,[50] and in 1868 it was made to include, for Parliamentary purposes, the extra-parochial Dudley Castle Hill, the ecclesiastical districts of Pensnett, Brockmoor, Quarry Bank and Brierley Hill in the parish of Kingswinford and of Reddall Hill in Rowley Regis.[51]

Some idea of the population of Dudley in the 17th century can be obtained from the assessments of the hearth tax in the reign of Charles II. In 1662 there were two hundred and twenty-eight people who contributed to the tax,[52] while in 1674 there were only ninety-six,[53] a decrease which may have been due in part to the Great Plague of 1666.[54]

From the beginning of the 19th century the population seems to have steadily increased. Thus in 1831 there were 23,043 people in the town, in 1891 45,724, in 1901 48,733, and in 1911 51,092.[55]

During the 16th and 17th centuries Dudley seems to have sunk into great poverty. Sir Amias Paulet writing in 1585 describes it as 'one of the poorest townes that I have sene in my life,'[56] and in 1617 the inhabitants were obliged to petition for a collection in the county for their poor owing to an epidemic, the town depending 'principally upon poore handicrafts men who are nigh impoverished and now themselves waite ayde who heretofore did contribute to the refuge of the poore sorte.'[57] The state of affairs evidently considerably improved after the Civil War, when Dudley suffered severely, for Erdeswick writing in 1723 describes Dudley as a 'good handsome town,'[58] and its increased prosperity during the end of the 18th and the beginning of the 19th century is shown by its growing population and

---

[34] *Worc. Inq. p.m.* (Worcs. Hist. Soc.), pt. i, 34.

[35] Lewis, *Topog. Dict. of Engl.*; *Rep. on Publ. Rec.* (Rec. Com. 1837), 444.

[36] Exch. Spec. Com. 34 Eliz. no. 3106.

[37] Priv. Act, 16 & 17 Vict. cap. 24.

[38] Pat. 28 Vict. pt. iii, no. 9.

[39] *Ret. of Memb. of Parl.* i, 6. The two members returned were Benedict Andrew and Ralph 'Clericus.'

[40] Jewitt and Hope, *The Corp. Plate, &c., of the Cities and Corp. Towns of Engl. and Wales*, ii, 441.

[41] This fossil is found very extensively in the Dudley district and is locally called a Dudley Locust.

[42] Jewitt and Hope, loc. cit.

[43] Feet of F. Staffs. *Will. Salt Arch. Soc. Coll.* iv (1), 250-1. There is a curious entry on the Patent Roll of 1401 relating to attacks upon persons going to the markets of Dudley and other towns (*Cal. Pat.* 1399-1401, p. 552).

[44] *Surv. of Worc.* (Worcs. Hist. Soc.), i, 195.

[45] Pat. 36 Chas. II, pt. v, no. 10.

[46] *Rep. on Markets and Tolls*, viii, 210.

[47] Ibid.   [48] Ibid.

[49] Chan. Inq. p.m. 8 Hen. IV, no. 46; 9 Hen. V, no. 28; Exch. Spec. Com. 34 Eliz. no. 3106.

[50] *Index to Lond. Gaz.*

[51] Stat. 31 & 32 Vict. cap. 46.

[52] Lay Subs. R. Worcs. bdle. 260, no. 4.

[53] Ibid. no. 10.

[54] This decrease may have been also partly due to changed assessment.

[55] *Pop. Ret.*

[56] State Papers (Scottish Ser.), xvi, 63.

[57] *Quart. Sess. Rec.* (Worcs. Hist. Soc.), 229.

[58] *A Surv. of Staffs.* (1723), 117.

by the various Acts of Parliament which the inhabitants obtained for improving the roads leading to the town, for paving, cleansing and lighting it and for supplying it with water.[59]

The coal and iron mines for which Dudley is now so famous are known to have been worked in 1291, when, as already noted, Roger de Somery had a mine of 'sea coal' worth 13s. 4d. yearly, a mine of iron and sea coal worth 40s. yearly, and two great smithies of the annual value of £4.[60] From that time until the 17th century there are occasional references which show that the trade was increasing. Sir Amias Paulet in a letter to Walsingham says there is plenty of 'sea coal and charke coal' in Dudley,[61] while Habington in his survey of Worcester states that the inhabitants 'follow in profession Tabalcain the inventor of the Smythes hammer, the rest are myners delving into the bowells of the earthe for our fuell theyre profytt and have all of them the reputation of bould spirited men.'[62] But it was in the beginning of the 17th century that Dud Dudley, an illegitimate son of Edward Lord Dudley, made his great discovery that iron could be smelted with coal instead of charcoal, and in 1622 his father obtained a monopoly of the trade for fourteen years.[63] The work was begun in Lord Dudley's forges in Pensnett Chase, just within the borders of Staffordshire, a few miles from Dudley, and in Cradley, but partly owing to the enmity of the other ironmasters and to a great flood the trade did not prosper, and during the Civil War was stopped for a time,[64] though Dud declares he used his invention for founding cannon for the king in Worcester.[65] The discovery, however, made Dudley an important trade centre, although coal was not generally used for smelting iron until the middle of the 18th century.[66] Towards the end of the same century the trade was still further increased by the improvement of the roads leading to the town, and by the opening of two canals, one joining the Stourbridge Navigation in Kingswinford,[67] the other joining the Dudley Canal to the Worcester Canal at Selley Oak.[68] It is to the coal and iron trades that all the manufactures of Dudley owe their origin and development.] The manufacture of all kinds of hardware is extensively carried on.[69] Nails were made in Dudley at least as early as the 15th century, and in 1538 Reynold Ward of Dudley is said to have sold them at 11s. 4d. the thousand.[70] Nail and scythe making, when carried on by hand, gave employment to many of the families in the villages surrounding Dudley.[71] Of late years the hand-made nail trade has nearly ceased, except for some few specified sorts.

Dudley was visited by Edward III in 1328[72] and 1332,[73] and by Queen Elizabeth in 1575,[74] but the visits were probably made to the lords of Dudley rather than to the town.

The lords of Dudley had formerly two *PARKS* in this parish, one called the Old Park, which belonged to the castle and survives in the castle grounds, the other called the New Park, which was made by Roger de Somery between the wood of Pensnett and the town,[75] probably about 1247–8, when Roger acquired the deer with which to stock it from William Burdet in exchange for hunting rights in Dudley.[76] In 1253 he obtained a grant of free warren in all his demesne lands in England.[77] In 1275, after Roger's death and during the minority of his heir, the king granted twenty-four live deer out of the park and wood of Dudley to Roger de Mortimer.[78] The wood mentioned is probably the wood or chase of Pensnett which also descended with Dudley Manor, and which is described in the inquisition after Roger's death as being a league in length and half a league in breadth, stretching from the bounds of the manors of Kingswinford and Sedgley.[79] It was called a foreign wood in the inquisition taken on the death of Roger's son Roger in 1291.[80] In 1291 a grant of thirty live bucks from the parks of Sedgley and Dudley was made by the king to Bogo de Knovill.[81] The part of Pensnett Chase in Dudley called Pensnett Wood was inclosed with the other commons in 1783.[82]

A third park in Dudley called 'le Conyngre' is mentioned for the first time in 1553, when the custody of it was granted to John Lyttelton.[83] It was granted in 1554 to Edward Lord Dudley, and it then contained a house or lodge called the Wrennesnest.[84] It was probably the same as the park called the Quingedde, mentioned in an inquisition of 1592.[85]

The family of Burnell held property in Dudley in the 13th and 14th centuries. In 1293 Robert Burnell, Bishop of Bath, died seised of land there, which he held of John de Somery.[86] His heir was his nephew Philip Burnell, who died in the following year. The inquisition taken after the death of Philip states that he had a capital messuage in Dudley which he was 'unable to sustain,' and that the rents of the free tenants had decreased to 37s. 8½d.[87] The last mention of the Burnells holding land in Dudley occurs in 1315, when Edward Burnell son of Philip died seised of a messuage called 'Russelleshalle,' 128 acres of land and 52s. rent, leaving his sister Maud, who was the wife of John Lovel, as his heir.[88]

Sir John Sutton of Dudley died in 1487 seised of a messuage called *NETHERTON* (Nederton) within and parcel of the lordship of Dudley.[89] By a fine of 1579–80 the manor of Netherton and the 'boroughs of Dudley and Netherton' were settled in tail-male upon Edward Sutton Lord Dudley,[90] and in 1586 a

[59] Burton, *Bibliog. of Worc.* (Worcs. Hist. Soc.), pt. i, 76, 107.
[60] *Worc. Inq. p.m.* (Worcs. Hist. Soc.), i, 16.
[61] *Cal. S. P. Scottish Ser.* ii, 978.
[62] op. cit. i, 195.
[63] *Cal. S. P. Dom.* 1619–23, p. 349.
[64] Dudley, *Metallum Martis,* 12.
[65] Ibid. [66] *V.C.H. Worcs.* ii, 270.
[67] Burton, op. cit. pt. i, 67.
[68] Ibid. 77.
[69] *V.C.H. Worcs.* ii, 271.
[70] *L. and P. Hen. VIII,* xiii (2), pp. 132, 133.
[71] *V.C.H. Worcs.* ii, 272.

[72] *Cal. Pat.* 1327–30, pp. 277, 278, 299, 304, 307; *Cal. Close,* 1327–30, pp. 302, 303, 401.
[73] *Cal. Close,* 1330–3, pp. 486, 488, 489.
[74] *Cal. S. P. Dom.* 1547–80, p. 502.
[75] *Hund. R.* (Rec. Com.), ii, 284.
[76] Feet of F. Div. Co. 32 Hen. III, no. 21.
[77] Chart. R. 37 & 38 Hen. III, pt. i, m. 15. This charter does not appear in the printed Calendar of Charter Rolls.
[78] *Cal. Close,* 1272–9, p. 214.
[79] *Worc. Inq. p.m.* (Worcs. Hist. Soc.), i, 16.

[80] *Cal. Inq. p.m.* 1–19 *Edw. I,* 493.
[81] *Cal. Close,* 1288–96, p. 182.
[82] Priv. Act, 24 Geo. III, cap. 17.
[83] Pat. 2 & 3 Phil. and Mary, pt. ii, m. 11.
[84] Ibid. There is at the present day Wren's Nest Hill in Sedgley parish to the west of Dudley Castle.
[85] Chan. Inq. p.m. (Ser. 2), ccxxxiv, 74.
[86] Ibid. 21 Edw. I, no. 50.
[87] Ibid. 22 Edw. I, no. 45.
[88] *Cal. Inq. p.m.* 1–9 *Edw. II,* 393.
[89] Ibid. *Hen. VII,* i, 125.
[90] Feet of F. Div. Co. Hil. 22 Eliz.

house called Netherton, in the chase of Pensnett, was among the possessions of Edward Lord Dudley at the time of his death.[91] This house is again mentioned in 1610–11,[92] but after that all trace of it disappears. There is now, however, a manor at Netherton belonging to the Earl of Dudley.

PRIORY The advowson of the priory of Dudley seems to have belonged to Gervase Paynel, the founder, and his descendants, for in 1323 it was assigned to Margaret wife of John de Sutton as part of her share of the lands of her brother John de Somery.[93] In the 15th century the prior seems to have been appointed by the Prior of Wenlock, but the temporalities of the priory during a vacancy passed to the lords of Dudley.[94] At the Dissolution the possessions of the priory at Dudley were valued at 117s. 8d.,[95] and in 1541 they were granted with the site to Sir John Dudley.[96] On his forfeiture in 1553 the estate passed to the Crown, and was granted in 1554 to Edward Lord Dudley,[97] and it has since descended with the manor.[98] It is mentioned as recently as 1804.[99]

The priory church and buildings were allowed to fall into decay, and the lords of Dudley permitted various manufactures to be carried on in the church.

The priory was situated about half a mile west of the castle, but little is now left of the conventual church and offices. They now form a group of picturesque ivy-covered ruins standing in the grounds attached to the Priory House, the residence of Sir Gilbert Claughton, bart.

The remains show the church to have been cruciform with an aisleless nave and two chapels on the south side of the quire, the eastern chapel separated by a blank wall from the western chapel, which opened directly out of the south transept. Of the east and north walls of the quire nothing now remains above ground, while the north transept has entirely disappeared. The secular buildings were on the north side, but of these only a few foundations, overgrown by a thick bed of ivy, are left. Some of the corbels which supported the cloister roof remain on the outside of the north nave wall, and there are fragments of a central newel staircase at the northeast of the former north transept. It would appear, from what little detail remains, that the east end of the church was erected about 1190, while the building of the nave followed early in the 13th century, but the remains are not large enough to allow of this being stated with certainty, while the dating of the secular buildings is quite a matter of conjecture. The south and west windows of the nave, with the west doorway, are insertions of the early 14th century. The easternmost of the south chapels was not added until late in the 15th century. Most of the east and west and parts of the north and south walls of this chapel are left. It appears to have been in three bays and was vaulted possibly with a fan vault. In the east wall is a large four-centred window, the tracery of which was set in the

middle of the wall between shallow casements, while the outer order to both jambs was moulded with a double ogee. Over the window on the outside is a moulded label returning on itself in the form of a lozenge. Though the head and most of the jambs are left, all the tracery has been destroyed. On either side of the window were niches surmounted by tall canopies, the soffits of which were panelled in imitation of vaulting, but only the southern one now remains, and this much mutilated, while what is perhaps the soffit of the other, though of a slightly different design, can be seen used in the patching up of the south wall of the west chapel. The westernmost bay of the north wall remains fairly complete, and here the line of the vault can be traced as also on the east and west walls of the chapel. In this bay is a flat four-centred doorway opening into the quire. At the south-west are the remains of an octagonal stair turret, with the west jamb of a doorway, about 10 ft. above the ground level, which must have opened on to a small west gallery; the pockets for the joists which supported it can be clearly seen in the north and south walls. At the north end of the west wall are indications of a blocked opening leading from the chapel on the west. The shaped angle stones from which the capitals of the vaulting shafts at this end have almost entirely mouldered away show that the blank ashlar walling here is of original 15th-century date, and probably replaces the east wall of the earlier transept chapel. In the east wall of the south transept is a pointed arch of a single square order with quirked chamfered imposts, opening into the western chapel, the present south wall of which appears to be entirely modern. Against the east end of the south wall of the transept are the remains of a flat buttress, and at the south-west angle a flat clasping one. Most of the walls to the four westernmost bays of the nave are still standing. The sills of the windows in the north wall are at a higher level than those on the south, this being necessary to give sufficient height to the south wall of the cloisters. Only the lower parts of two of the windows remain. These appear to be of original early 13th-century date. In the west end of this wall is a pointed doorway set with deeply splayed external jambs and an external rebate, while the inner jambs have a continuous swelled chamfer. In the south wall are the lower parts of four early 14th-century windows which must have originally been of two lights each with external jambs of two chamfered orders and plain internal splays. Running below the sill on the outside is a string of semi-octagonal section. The sills to all these windows are broken and none of the heads are left, but an engraving of 1731 shows them to have been two-centred and filled with tracery.[100] At the west end of the wall and between the two centre windows are the remains of buttresses. Their stoppage a few feet above the level of the window sills tends to prove that the nave was never vaulted. In the west

[91] Chan. Inq. p.m. (Ser. 2), ccxxxiv, 74.
[92] Pat. 8 Jas. I, pt. xlii.
[93] *Cal. Close,* 1318–23, p. 630.
[94] *Cal. Pat.* 1408–13, p. 395; 1413–16, p. 304.
[95] *Valor Eccl.* (Rec. Com.), iii, 104.
[96] *L. and P. Hen. VIII,* xvi, g. 678 (47).
[97] Pat. 2 & 3 Phil. and Mary, pt. ii, m. 11.

[98] Ibid. 21 Eliz. pt. vi; Chan. Inq. p.m. (Ser. 2), ccxxxiv, 74; Feet of F. Div. Co. Mich. 11 Chas. I; Mich. 23 Chas. II.
[99] Recov. R. Trin. 44 Geo. III, rot. 339.
[100] 'The south-west view of Dudley Priory in the county of Stafford' (*sic*) by

Samuel and Nathaniel Buck, 1731. This engraving also shows the stair turret at the south-west of the eastern quire chapel, which has since been demolished to the foundation, with the exception of a portion of the west wall. It is represented with a crowning embattled cornice and ogee cupola.

wall is a large pointed doorway of three orders with an external hood, but the mouldings are too decayed to allow of identification. Above the doorway was a pointed gable, only traces of which are now visible, the apex of which must have risen above the sill of the large west window over it, and may perhaps have had open-work tracery. Both doorway and window appear to be insertions of the same date as the south windows. In the remaining portion of the nave are two 13th-century stone coffins. The larger one is broken into two, but the smaller one is in a fairly good state of preservation. There are also the remains of the upper part of a stone effigy of a priest dressed in ordinary ecclesiastical vestments. The head, which rests on a cushion, is broken off at the shoulders and is much mutilated.

There seems to have been no mill held by the lords of Dudley, but the Priors of Dudley seem to have possessed one in their manor in the parish, though it is not mentioned until after the Dissolution. In 1610–11 a windmill in Dudley which lately belonged to the priory was in the possession of Lord Dudley,[1] and in 1741 a water corn-mill was annexed to the site of the priory.[2] William Frebody died in 1437 seised of a water-mill there, which he held jointly with Margaret his wife of Sir John Sutton, kt.[3]

The church of *ST. EDMUND*
CHURCHES consists of a chancel with a south vestry and organ chamber, a nave, north and south aisles and a west tower. Over the aisles and at the west end of the nave are galleries. The old church was destroyed by Col. Leveson in 1646,[4] and from that date appears to have remained in ruins until rebuilt in 1724.[5] The galleries were erected early in the 19th century, but were considerably altered in 1864, when the building was restored and the wooden tracery inserted in the aisle windows.

The church is built of red bricks with stone dressings and has a tiled roof. The chancel is lighted by round-headed windows, and the chancel arch is of similar form with moulded archivolt and keystone.

The nave arcades are in four bays with semicircular arches, resting on square piers with moulded capitals and chamfered bases. The aisles are lit by large round-headed windows, one to each bay, and now filled with modern wood tracery of semi-Gothic character. At the west ends of both aisles are early 19th-century porches.

The main entrance to the church is under the tower, but there are also doorways in the west walls of the aisles. The square tower is divided externally by moulded stone cornices into three stages. Above the entrance doorway is a curved pediment with a second cleft pediment resting on three small Doric pilasters over it. The two upper stages of the tower are set back. Round-headed windows light the bell-chamber on each side and the shaped parapet above is finished with crocketed pinnacles at the angles. On one of the pilasters supporting the south aisle is set a sundial.

The plaster ceilings of the chancel and nave are coved at the sides but flat in the centre.

Under the tower arch is a screen with a round-headed doorway and Ionic pilasters on either side.

The front of the organ case is made up of pieces of the 18th-century oak reredos, and portions of an old ʻthree deckerʼ have been utilized in the present pulpit. In the chancel are two Jacobean chairs, both dated 1611.

A modern brass tablet in the chancel records the burial of Honor wife of Sir Ferdinando Dudley, died 1620.

In the vicarage is kept the old parish chest.

There is one bell, inscribed ʻR. Wells of Albourne fecit MDCCLXXVIII.ʼ

The plate consists of a 1748 silver cup and a paten of the same date (both are inscribed ʻThe Gift of John Hodgetts Gent. 1749ʼ) ; a silver chalice inscribed ʻThe Gift of Mrs. Phoebe Dixon to the Church of St. Edmund in Dudley 1801ʼ ; an 1872 silver flagon inscribed ʻThe Gift of Mrs. Elizabeth Benett To St. Edmund's Church Dudley 1872ʼ ; and an 1879 silver paten.

The early registers are in two books and are kept at St. Thomas's vicarage : (i) baptisms and burials 1540 to 1544 and 1547 to 1611, marriages 1542 to 1544 and 1547 to 1610, all entries for 1548 missing ; (ii) baptisms and burials 1611 to 1646, marriages 1611 to 1643. From 1650 until after 1812 the registers of St. Edmund's and St. Thomas's were kept conjointly at St. Thomas's.

In 1815 the parish church of *ST. THOMAS* was found to be in so dangerous a condition that an Act of Parliament was obtained for rebuilding it.[6] The present church was completed in 1817 at a cost of £12,650. It is now (1912) about to be enlarged.

The building comprises a shallow chancel, nave and aisles, with arcades of clustered shafts and wooden galleries, a west tower with spire and porches at the east end. The style is ʻlate Perpendicular.ʼ An ancient altar slab with its consecration crosses is preserved here.

The bells are ten in number, cast by Thomas Mears of London in 1818 ; the fifth bears the inscription ʻTo Doomsday may the name descend Dudley and the Poor Man's Friend, William, Viscount Dudley and Ward.ʼ

The plate includes an Elizabethan communion cup of 1571, another cup of the Puritan type with no hall mark, but inscribed 1626, and a flagon of unusual pear shape of 1724 (?), the gift of Gilbert Shaw in 1743, the later cup and the flagon having been gilt in 1864. There are three patens, the first of 1594, the second undated, but given by Samuel Shaw towards the middle of the 18th century, and the third of 1721.

The registers previous to 1813 are as follows : (i) all entries 1541 to 1610 ; (ii) all 1610 to 1629 ; (iii) all 1629 to 1650 ; (iv) all 1650 to 1653 ; (v) all 1653 to 1692 ; (vi) baptisms and marriages 1692 to 1714 ; (vii) baptisms and marriages 1715 to 1749 ; (viii) baptisms 1749 to 1771, marriages 1749 to 1754 ; (ix) baptisms

---

[1] Pat. 8 Jas. I, pt. xlii.
[2] Recov. R. East. 14 Geo. II, rot. 199.
[3] Chan. Inq. p.m. 15 Hen. VI, no. 46.
[4] The following is a note at the end of the second volume of the registers : ʻNote that ye Church of St. Edmund being demolished by Col. Levesson about

this time Both parishes did meet in ye St. Thomas & becam as one in all administraïons : & so in their offices within a few yeares after so that ye Registr books becam one also from thenceforth. Mr. John Tailor was settled in ye vicarage of Dudley & had possession

given him of ye Church of St. Thomas ye 17 day of ye same month . . .ʼ
[5] Built into the walls on the outside are several inscribed bricks laid by various people in 1724.
[6] Local and Personal Act, 55 Geo. III, cap. 44.

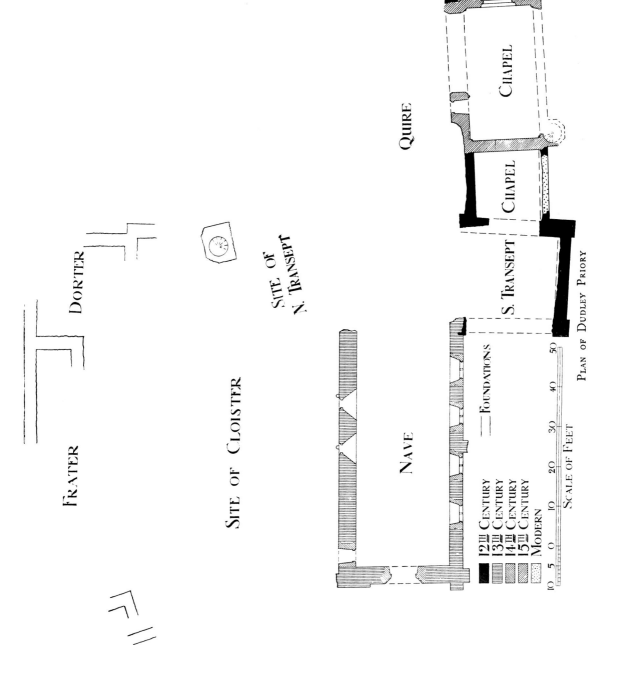

FRATER

DORTER

SITE OF CLOISTER

SITE OF
N. TRANSEPT

NAVE

QUIRE

S. TRANSEPT

CHAPEL

CHAPEL

12TH CENTURY
13TH CENTURY
14TH CENTURY
15TH CENTURY
MODERN
FOUNDATIONS

SCALE OF FEET
10 5 0 10 20 30 40 50

PLAN OF DUDLEY PRIORY

1772 to 1793; (x) baptisms 1794 to 1812; (xi) burials 1678 to 1712; (xii) burials 1713 to 1747; (xiii) burials 1747 to 1770; (xiv) burials 1771 to 1794; (xv) burials 1795 to 1812; (xvi) marriages 1754 to 1762; (xvii) marriages 1762 to 1770; (xviii) marriages 1770 to 1791; (xix) marriages 1791 to 1808; (xx) marriages 1808 to 1812. From the middle of the 17th century until after 1812 the entries for St. Thomas's and St. Edmund's are found together at St. Thomas's.

The church of *ST. LUKE* consists of a chancel with a south vestry and north organ chamber, a nave and north and south aisles. It was erected in 1878 and is built of red brick and roofed with slates.

The plate includes two cups, a salver-paten and flagon, all of 1863.

The church of *ST. JOHN*, Kate's Hill, consists of a chancel with a north organ chamber and south vestry, a nave with north and south aisles and a west tower; over the aisles and the west end of the nave are galleries. It was erected in 13th-century style in 1840, and is built of coursed ironstone rubble with ashlar dressings. The roofs are open and slated.

The plate includes a modern chalice and paten of the mediaeval type given in 1840.

The church of *ST. JAMES*, Eve Hill, consists of a chancel with a north vestry and south organ chamber, a nave with north and south aisles and a west tower. At the west end of the nave and over both the aisles are galleries. It was erected in 1840, apparently by the architect of St. John's, Kate's Hill, the designs being almost identical. The organ chamber and vestry were not added until 1869.

The plate includes a cup, paten and flagon given by the Cartwright family in 1840.

The church of *ST. AUGUSTINE*, Holly Hill, was built in 1884, and consists of a chancel with an organ chamber and vestry on the north and a small chapel on the south, a nave, north and south aisles, and porches and a baptistery at the west end of the nave. It is built of red brick with stone dressings in a free Gothic style and has wooden barrel ceilings and tiled roofs.

The church of *ST. ANDREW*, Netherton, was erected in 1830 on a site given by the late Earl of Dudley. It is a building of stone in 13th-century style, and consists of chancel, nave, aisles and an embattled tower with pinnacles. Connected with this church are chapels of ease, St. Peter's at Darby End and St. Barnabas at Dudley Wood.

From very early times there were *ADVOWSONS* two churches at Dudley. They were granted by Gervase Paynel in the middle of the 12th century to his newly-founded priory of Dudley,[7] and appear afterwards to have become annexed to the priory church of St. James, for when Pope Lucius confirmed the possessions of the priory in 1182 he included the church of St. James of Dudley with the chapels of St. Edmund and St. Thomas.[8] Both the churches were united in one vicarage,[9] and Bishop Sandys's survey states that St. Edmund's was the parish church and St. Thomas's a chapel dependent upon it.[10]

In 1238 an agreement was made between the Bishops of Worcester and of Coventry and Lichfield whereby it was agreed that the whole vill of Dudley with its churches should pertain to the bishopric of Worcester, while the site of the castle and the cell of monks belonging to it in the county of Stafford should belong to the bishopric of Coventry and Lichfield.[11]

The priory of Dudley had probably appropriated the rectory of Dudley as early as 1292, for Brother Robert de Malleye, Prior of Dudley, was then rector of the parish church of Dudley.[12] In 1342 the prior and monks appeared before the Bishop of Worcester to account for the appropriation of the church,[13] while in 1349 the sum of 200 marks was extorted from them for acquiring the advowson without the king's licence, and for licence to appropriate the church.[14] The advowson was retained by the priory until the Dissolution, when it passed to the Crown and was granted with the rectory in 1541 to Sir John Dudley.[15] On his forfeiture it again passed to the Crown, and was given by Queen Mary to Edward Lord Dudley in 1554.[16] It then followed the same descent as the manor,[17] William Earl of Dudley being now patron of the living.

In 1628 Edward Lord Dudley conveyed the rectory and tithes to Sir Miles Hobart,[18] probably for a certain term of years only, since, although they were in the possession of the Hobart family in 1668,[19] they were afterwards again held by Lord Dudley and commuted in 1783 when the parish was inclosed in return for the allotment of a certain portion of the common land.[20]

An Act of Parliament was obtained in 1836 authorizing the sale of glebe land in Dudley belonging to the vicarage there. It was purchased by the trustees of John William Earl of Dudley.[21]

In 1844 the four new parishes of St. Edmund, St. James, St. John and St. Andrew, Netherton, were formed out of the old parish of Dudley.[22] Since that date two other parishes have been formed, that of St. Luke in 1876[23] and that of St. Augustine in 1884.[24] The livings of all these churches are vicarages, and all are in the gift of the vicar of Dudley.

Land at Dudley called 'Our Ladyes lands' in the tenure of the churchwardens for the maintenance of a priest and obits was granted in 1562 to Cicely Pickerell.[25] She sold it about two years later to Thomas Watwood and Matthew Bysmere.[26]

The Society of Friends was established in Dudley before 1656, in which year the society's registers begin. The Meeting House was built in 1794.[27]

[7] *V.C.H. Worcs.* ii, 159.
[8] Ibid.
[9] Habington, op. cit. i, 197; Nash, op. cit. i, 360.
[10] Nash, loc. cit. In 1289 an institution was made to the vicarage of St. Edmund (*Reg. G. Giffard* [Worcs. Hist. Soc.], 333).
[11] *Ann. Mon.* (Rolls Ser.), iv, 429.
[12] *Reg. G. Giffard* (Worcs. Hist. Soc.), 426.

[13] Worc. Epis. Reg. Wulstan de Braunsford, fol. 56.
[14] *Cal. Pat.* 1348–50, p. 413; *Abbrev. Rot. Orig.* (Rec. Com.), ii, 205.
[15] *L. and P. Hen. VIII*, xvi, g. 678 (47).
[16] Pat. 2 & 3 Phil. and Mary, pt. ii, m. 11.
[17] Inst. Bks. (P.R.O.); Recov. R. East. 14 Geo. II, rot. 199; Trin. 44 Geo. III, rot. 339.
[18] Feet of F. Div. Co. East. 4 Chas. I.

[19] Ibid. 20 Chas. II.
[20] Priv. Act, 6 & 7 Will. IV, cap. 30.
[21] Ibid.
[22] *Lond. Gaz.* 15 Oct. 1844, p. 3519.
[23] Ibid. 5 Dec. 1876, p. 6744.
[24] *Census of Engl. and Wales* (1901), *Worc.* 6; *Parl. Papers* (1890–1), lxi, 19.
[25] Pat. 4 Eliz. pt. iii, m. 40.
[26] Chan. Proc. (Ser. 2), bdle. 13, no. 17.
[27] Rollason, *The Old Non-Parochial Reg. of Dudley.*

The Unitarian chapel, called the Old Meeting House, which was situated in Wolverhampton Street, was built in 1702 for the Presbyterians, and rebuilt in 1717 after being destroyed by rioters. The registers date from 1743.[28]

The Congregational chapel in King Street was built in 1839. An older chapel built in 1788 by the Countess of Huntingdon's students and ministers was acquired in the same year by the Independents, who in consequence of religious disagreements had seceded from the congregation of the Old Meeting House. The registers of this sect begin in 1803.[29]

There are also Congregational chapels in Himley Street and Woodside.

There is a Wesleyan Methodist chapel in King Street, built in 1788–90, and having registers commencing in 1804; a Baptist chapel in New Street built in 1778, having registers from 1814; and a Wesleyan chapel in Wolverhampton Street, which was built in 1828 and 1829, and belongs to the Methodist New Connexion.[30]

At Netherton there are Baptist, Congregational and Methodist chapels.

The Roman Catholic Church of Our Lady and St. Thomas of Canterbury in Porter's field was built in 1842,[31] and registered for marriages in 1847.[32]

CHARITIES In 1709 John Tandy, by will, devised a piece of land called the Furnace Piece, the rents to be applied in clothing for poor widows. Upon the inclosure about 2 acres of land were awarded in respect of this charity.

The endowment now consists of Queen's Cross Brewery and Lamp Tavern, let at £23 a year, cottages in Furnace Place, producing £17 a year, and 1 acre at Dudley Wood, producing £1 a year; also £1,615 11s. 5d. Queensland 3½ per cent. stock with the official trustees, producing £56 10s. 10d. in annual dividends, arising from sale of land in 1875, and sale of minerals from time to time.

In 1744 Elizabeth Hinckes, by will, bequeathed £40 for poor widows and housekeepers, and in 1762 Mrs. Parnell Taylor, by will, bequeathed £91 for providing hempen shifts for poor widows. A sum of £114 11s. 4d. Queensland 3½ per cent. stock is held by the official trustees in respect of these legacies, producing £4 0s. 2d. yearly.

The above-mentioned charities are administered together under a scheme of the Charity Commissioners 13 May 1887. In 1908 clothing of the value of £91 13s. was distributed among poor widows on St. Thomas's Day.

The Bread Charity comprises the charities of:

(1) Jasper Cartwright, founded by will, 1659;

(2) William Timmins, mentioned on the benefaction table in St. Edmund's Church; and

(3) The charity of Joshua Newborough the elder and Joshua Newborough the younger, founded by indentures of lease and release dated 3 and 4 July 1679 respectively.

The trust property now consists of 2 r. 10 p. near Mountsweet Brook, producing £1 1s. 6d. yearly, two cottages in Maughan Street, let at £9 2s. yearly, £1,394 18s. 7d. consols, belonging to Cartwright and Timmins charities, and £794 18s. 1d. consols, producing together £54 14s. 8d.

The sums of stock are held by the official trustees, representing sales of land and accumulations of income.

In 1908 the sum of £48 14s. 3d. was distributed in bread among the poor of the several ecclesiastical districts of the town.

The charities known as the Cartwright Clothing Charities are regulated by a scheme of the Charity Commissioners 10 April 1888.

They comprise the charities of:

(1) Mary Cartwright, by deed, 3 June 1818, trust fund, £600 consols with the official trustees, representing the redemption in 1905 of a rent-charge of £15 issuing out of the Yew Tree Farm at Rowley Regis;

(2) Henry Antrobus Cartwright, will proved at Worcester 6 August 1859, legacy of £100;

(3) Mary Anne Roberts, will proved at Worcester 11 July 1870, legacy of £100.

These legacies are represented by £213 11s. India 3 per cent. stock, producing £6 8s. yearly.

In 1908 the income was applied in the distribution of clothing and shoes to seven poor old men.

In 1745 Robert Baylies, by his will, directed (inter alia) that £30 should be paid to the trustees of Baylies' Charity School and the interest applied in relief of the poor.

A sum of £33 5s. 6d. consols was in 1905 set aside out of Baylies' Foundation in respect of this legacy, and is held by the official trustees, producing 16s. 8d. a year.

In 1875 Miss Rebecca Griffiths, by her will proved at Worcester 12 April, directed that stock sufficient to produce £50 a year should be purchased to be distributed in clothing on St. Thomas's Day among poor working people, under the title 'Mr. Thomas Griffiths' and Miss Rebecca Griffiths' Charity.'

The legacy is now represented by £1,525 4s. 4d. Queensland 3½ per cent. stock with the official trustees. The annual dividends, amounting to £53 7s. 8d., are duly applied.

In 1901 Dr. William Lewis Dudley, by his will, bequeathed £100, the interest thereof to be applied in repairing the tablet and casket containing the ashes of his wife in the parish church, and any surplus to be distributed to the poor. The legacy (less duty) was invested in £88 15s. 7d. India 3 per cent. stock with the official trustees, producing £2 13s. a year.

The following educational charities are dealt with under schools[33]: The Free Grammar School, the Blue Coat School, the School of Industry for Females, and the Baylies' Charity School.

The charities known as the Cartwright Educational Charity are regulated by scheme of the Charity Commissioners 29 August 1899.

They comprise the charities of:

(1) Mary Cartwright's School Charity, founded by deed 3 June 1819, whereby a rent-charge of £20 issuing out of land at Upper Oakham and a sum of £600 was given as an endowment of the school.

(2) Henry Antrobus Cartwright, by his will, bequeathed £200.

(3) Cornelius Cartwright, by his will proved at Worcester 13 November 1867, left £300.

(4) Mrs. Mary Anne Roberts, by her will, bequeathed £200.

[28] Rollason, The Old Non-Parochial Reg. of Dudley.   [29] Ibid.   [30] Ibid.   [31] Catholic Dir. (1908), p. 150.   [32] Lond. Gaz. 7 Sept. 1847, p. 3232.   [33] See article on 'Schools,' V.C.H. Worcs. iv.

ELMLEY LOVETT CHURCH FROM THE SOUTH-WEST

DUDLEY CASTLE : INTERIOR OF THE KEEP

The school buildings and house were sold, and the proceeds together with the gift and legacies above mentioned have been invested in £2,005 15s. 1d. India 3 per cent. stock with the official trustees, producing £60 3s. 4d. yearly, which with the rent-charge of £20 is made applicable under the scheme in providing clothing for girls attending some public elementary school of the Church of England, in granting prizes or rewards, and in the advancement in life of girls.

The hospital known as 'The Guest Hospital' was originally founded by the Earl of Dudley for the benefit of workmen who had become infirm from working in the limestone works. The land and buildings were subsequently conveyed to the trustees of a legacy of £20,000 bequeathed by will of the late Joseph Guest, for the endowment of a hospital. This hospital was further endowed with a sum of £5,095 10s. 9d. consols by will of Mrs. Elizabeth Bennett, proved 7 February 1879, and £10,204 1s. 8d. consols by will of Mrs. Mary Charlton, proved 15 November 1879 ; also with £1,150 Birmingham Canal Navigation stock by will of Miss Rebecca Griffiths, proved 12 April 1875. In 1876 an annuity of £94 of the Birmingham Corporation Water Board was acquired as an Alexander Brodie Cochrane Memorial Fund, for the assistance of poor patients and of deserving nurses, &c. In 1875 Thomas Roberts, by his will proved 3 December, likewise bequeathed £1,000 to this hospital.

The Dudley Dispensary is endowed with a sum of £3,092 15s. 6d. consols arising under the will of the above-mentioned Mrs. Elizabeth Bennett and that of Mrs. Mary Charlton, and with £1,173 6s. 3d. Birmingham Canal Navigation stock arising under the will of Miss Rebecca Griffiths, proved 12 April 1875, and other gifts.

In 1872 Miss Phoebe Fellowes, by her will proved 19 March, bequeathed £1,000, and the above-mentioned Thomas Roberts likewise bequeathed £500 to this dispensary.

In 1876 Edward Gittos Griffith, by his will proved at Lichfield, bequeathed a sum of money, the income to be applied towards the salary of a Scripture-reader. The legacy with accumulations is now represented by £519 0s. 9d. consols with the official trustees, producing £12 19s. 4d. yearly, which is duly applied.

Dudley, St. Edmund : In 1872 Miss Phoebe Fellowes, by her will proved 19 March, bequeathed £200 upon trust to be invested, and the income applied for the benefit of the poor of St. Edmund at Christmas. The trust fund consists of £214 15s. 3d. consols with the official trustees, producing £5 7s. 4d. yearly.

In 1879 Mrs. Elizabeth Bennett, by her will proved 7 February, left a legacy, now represented by £509 11s. consols with the official trustees, the annual dividends, amounting to £12 14s. 8d., to be distributed to the poor in money or kind at Christmas, at the discretion of the vicar.

St. Thomas : In 1879 Mrs. Mary Charlton, by her will proved 15 November, bequeathed £500 consols, the annual dividends, amounting to £12 10s., to be applied for the benefit of the poor of St. Thomas in money or kind, at the discretion of the vicar. The stock is held by the official trustees.

St. Luke : In 1906 Sarah Ann Waring, by will proved 30 October, bequeathed £200, the income to be applied at Christmas-time in clothing to poor attending St. Luke's Church, under the title of ' The William Waring Charity.' The legacy was invested in £201 9s. 2d. India 3½ per cent. stock with the official trustees, producing £7 1s. yearly.

St. John, Kate's Hill : In 1872 Miss Phoebe Fellowes, by her will proved 19 March, bequeathed £200 upon trust to be invested and the income applied for the benefit of the poor of St. John at Christmas. The legacy was invested in £215 12s. 8d. consols with the official trustees, producing £5 7s. 8d. yearly.

Netherton, St. Andrew : In 1872 Miss Phoebe Fellowes, by her will proved 19 March, bequeathed £200 upon trust to be invested and the income applied for the benefit of the poor of this parish at Christmas. The legacy was invested in £215 12s. 8d. consols with the official trustees, producing £5 7s. 8d. yearly.

The charities, founded by will of Mrs. Blanche Skidmore, proved 20 August 1873, consist of £107 13s. 5d. consols, the dividends, amounting to £2 13s. 10d., to be paid to the bell-ringers ; £107 13s. 5d. consols, the dividends to be applied in clothing for the poor in Christmas week, and £430 13s. 9d. consols, the dividends, amounting to £10 15s. 4d., to be applied towards the salary of the Bible-woman. The several sums of stock are held by the official trustees.

Nonconformist Charities : The Wesleyan chapel in King Street, founded by deed 1788, was vested in trustees appointed by order of the Charity Commissioners 20 January 1885, on trusts of ' The Wesleyan Chapel Model Deed.'

In 1844 Miss Ann Knight, by her will, bequeathed £100 5s. consols, now in the names of — Evans and two other trustees, the annual dividends of £2 10s. to be given on Christmas Day to poor of the congregation in bread.

In 1855 Benjamin Pitt, by will, bequeathed £500, the income to be applied in clothing for poor of the congregation on Christmas Day. The legacy is invested on mortgage at 3½ per cent. In 1909 £14 9s. was expended in flannel and calico and the balance in boots.

The Wesleyan chapel in Wolverhampton Street : In 1851 Thomas Fountain, by will proved at Worcester 26 June, bequeathed a legacy now represented by £98 7s. 2d. consols with the official trustees and £90 on deposit at Lloyds Bank. The income, amounting to £4 15s. 5d., is applicable in clothing on St. Thomas's Day for poor attending the chapel.

The Methodist chapel : The trustees are possessed of two cottages in Oakeywell Street derived under the will of Thomas Shaw 16 July 1797, producing £13 7s. yearly, one-half of the net income being applicable in clothing on Christmas Day for poor attending the chapel and the other half for the benefit of the Sunday school of the chapel.

ELMLEY LOVETT

Ælmeleia (xi cent.) ; Almelega Ricardi de Portes (xii cent.) ; Amelegh, Aumleye Lovet, Auneleg (xiii cent.).

The parish of Elmley Lovett, situated 5 miles north-west of Droitwich, has an area of 2,365 acres, which includes 664 acres of arable land, 1,443 acres of pasture and 49 acres of wood.[1]

The land is undulating at a height of 150 ft. to 200 ft. above the ordnance datum. The soil is clay and the subsoil marl, except in the north of the parish, where it is sandstone, and the chief crops raised are wheat, beans, oats and barley. The population is almost entirely engaged in agriculture, but sandstone quarries near the church are worked. The Elmley Brook runs through the parish and forms part of the eastern

Below the cornice on the south, east and west sides are square stone sundials. To the north-east of the church is an early 17th-century stone cottage, while opposite the rectory is a good house of similar date and material with mullioned windows and diagonal brick chimney stacks. The elementary school and post office are both at Cutnall Green, a mile to the south-east of the village. A second early 17th-century dovecote remains at a farm at the junction of the Hartlebury Road with that from Elmley Lovett to Kidderminster. It is a half-timber building on a brick base. The nearest railway station is at Hartlebury, 2 miles north-west of the village.

The inclosure award for the commons of Cutnall Green, part of which is in Elmbridge and Hampton

THE LODGE, ELMLEY LOVETT (NOW DESTROYED)

boundary. The main road from Kidderminster to Droitwich, dividing Elmley from Stone on the north, passes through the east of the parish. The village lies a little west of the Kidderminster road on the Elmley Brook. It consists only of the rectory, a fine red brick house of the Queen Anne period, and a few cottages. Elmley Lovett Lodge, said to have been built in 1635 by one of the Townshends and afterwards the seat of the Forresters, formerly stood to the south-east of the church, but was pulled down about 1890. It was a half-timber gabled house approached by an avenue of elms. Part of the inclosing walls only remain. Between it and the church is an early 17th-century dovecote of red brick with stone dressings. It is rectangular in plan with a pedimented doorway on the south and has a pyramidal tiled roof crowned by a timber lantern.

Lovett, Sneads Green and Broad Common, is dated 1874.[2] A detached part of the parish, consisting of about 5 acres of meadow land more than 2 miles from the nearest boundary of Elmley Lovett, was transferred to Hampton Lovett in 1884.[3]

Among the place-names are Appeloure, Boycote[4] (xiv cent.) ; Snede Blamorfield[5] (xv cent.) ; Polefield, Middil Rilande, Hynkesfield, le Stockyng, le Furriland,[6] Bawckryge, Jones Wodde,[7] Sapercotes[8] (xvi cent.).

MANORS In the reign of Edward the Confessor Alwold held ELMLEY LOVETT of Queen Edith, but by the time of the Domesday Survey the overlordship had passed to Ralph de Toeni,[9] standard-bearer of the Dukes of Normandy. He came over to England with the Conqueror, and, according to the Roman de Rou, when called upon to bear the standard at the battle of

[1] Statistics from Bd. of Agric. (1905).
[2] Blue Bk. Incl. Awards, 189.
[3] Census of Engl. and Wales (1891), ii, 657 ; Worc. N, and Q. 291.
[4] Anct. D. (P.R.O.), C 2954.
[5] Mins. Accts. bdle. 1068, no. 9.
[6] L. and P. Hen. VIII, iii, g. 3214 (3).
[7] Ibid. vi, 231.
[8] Ibid. xviii (2), g. 241 (9).
[9] V.C.H. Worcs. i, 310.

Hastings, excused himself from doing so in order that he might take a full share in the actual fighting.[10] He died in 1101–2, and was succeeded by his son Ralph, his eldest son Roger having died unmarried in 1093.[11] Ralph died about 1125,[12] and his son and successor Roger was holding this manor in the time of King Stephen.[13] Ralph de Toeni, who was holding Elmley in 1210,[14] was probably grandson of this Roger.[15] Matthew Paris relates that when this Ralph heard that his brother Roger lay at the point of death at Reading he hastened there to see him for the last time, but arriving too late he called upon the dead man with such vehemence that he returned to life to warn his brother of judgement to come. Thereupon Ralph vowed to found a religious house for the safety of the souls of his ancestors and his brother.[16]

TOENI.   *Argent a sleeve gules.*

In 1239, on the eve of a journey to the Holy Land,[17] he granted the marriage of his eldest son Roger to Humphrey Earl of Hereford and Essex, who married the boy to his daughter Alice.[18] Ralph died before reaching his destination.[19] On the death of his son Roger in 1277 the latter's son Ralph succeeded,[20] and, dying in 1294–5,[21] left two children, Robert and Alice. Robert succeeded to the manor and came of age in 1297, when seisin was given to him of his father's lands,[22] but he died without issue in 1309, when the overlordship of Elmley Lovett with his other estates passed to his sister and heir Alice, widow of Thomas de Leybourne,[23] who afterwards married Guy de Beauchamp Earl of Warwick.

After the earl's death in 1315[24] Alice married William la Zouche of Ashby,[25] and in 1318 during the absence of the latter at the Scotch wars the overlordship of Elmley Lovett seems to have been held by Hugh le Despenser Earl of Winchester.[26]

In 1321 Roger de Mortimer of Chirk seized the manor from William la Zouche and held it until the following year, when it was taken into the king's hands with his other property and restored to William.[27] In 1326 William la Zouche acquired from Eustace de Chapman and Alice his wife, the under-tenants, all their right in the manor, and his successors then held it of the king in chief, who is last mentioned as overlord in 1478.[28]

Walter, the tenant under Ralph de Toeni at the time of the Domesday Survey,[29] was represented in the time of King Stephen by Richard de Portes, after whom the manor was called 'Almelega Ricardi de Portes,'[30] and who is probably to be identified with the Richard who held Elmley in 1166–7.[31] Although the Portes continued to hold property in Elmley at least as late as 1327,[32] the branch of the family who held Elmley Lovett failed in the male line early in the 13th century, possibly on the death of Walter de Portes[33] in 1201, when Simon de Ribbesford received seisin of Walter's Worcestershire estates, having married Walter's heir.[34]

It would seem that this heir was Agnes de Portes, and that she married secondly a member of the Lovett family, for Henry Lovett, who is described as son and heir of Agnes de Portes, apparently held the manor.[35] Henry died before 1254–5,[36] and his widow Joan afterwards married Robert Stocumbe.[37] Henry and Joan had two sons, John, who died young, apparently without issue, and Henry, who succeeded his father,[38] but died a minor before 1260–1, leaving a widow Isabel and a son John, a minor.[39]

In 1260–1 Robert Stocumbe and Joan his wife sued Roger de Toeni and others for two-thirds of the manor of Elmley, of which they claimed part as Joan's dower and the rest in compensation for a third part of the stewardship of Roger de Toeni's land, which had been settled on Joan at her marriage.[40] Roger de Toeni, however, pleaded that Joan merely held the manor as custodian of Henry son of Henry Lovett. The result of the suit is not known. John son and heir of the younger Henry Lovett was still a minor in 1266, when his wardship passed from Walter de Mucegros to Roger de Clifford.[41] John Lovett recovered seisin of two-thirds of the manor against Roger de Clifford and the Prioress of Aconbury in 1274–5.[42] The other third was no doubt held by his mother Isabel, who, then the widow of William le Blount, presented to the church in 1316.[43]

LOVETT. *Argent three wolves passant sable.*

John Lovett in 1285 obtained possession of a messuage and a virgate of land at Elmley Lovett, which had belonged to John le Ken, a felon.[44] He apparently died soon after. According to Habington,

[10] F. Madan, *Gresleys of Drakelowe,* 10.
[11] Ibid. 11, 12.   [12] Ibid. 13.
[13] *V.C.H. Worcs.* i, 329b.
[14] *Testa de Nevill* (Rec. Com.), 44 ; *Red Bk. of Exch.* (Rolls Ser.), 567.
[15] Madan, op. cit. 223.
[16] Matt. Paris, *Chron. Maj.* (Rolls Ser.), iii, 144.
[17] Ibid. 540.
[18] *Excerpta e Rot. Fin.* (Rec. Com.), i, 327.
[19] Ibid. 334 ; Matt. Paris, op. cit. iii, 540.
[20] Madan, op. cit. 13.
[21] *Abbrev. Rot. Orig.* (Rec. Com.), i, 89.
[22] *Abbrev. Plac.* (Rec. Com.), 293a.
[23] *Cal. Inq. p.m.* 1–9 Edw. II, 101.
[24] Ibid. 397.
[25] *Cal. Pat.* 1318–23, p. 68.

[26] Ibid. 14, 544 ; 1321–4, pp. 168, 387.
[27] *Cal. Close,* 1318–23, p. 582.
[28] Chan. Inq. p.m. 18 Edw. IV, no. 47.
[29] *V.C.H. Worcs.* i, 310b.
[30] Ibid. 329b.
[31] *Pipe R.* 13 *Hen. II* (Pipe R. Soc.), 67.
[32] Walter son of Richard de Portes was holding property in co. Worcs. in 1241 (*Cal. Inq. p.m. Hen. III,* 3), and William de Portes had land in Elmley Lovett in 1270 (Feet of F. Worcs. case 258, file 8, no. 31). Master William de Portes paid a subsidy of 7s. at Elmley Lovett in 1280 (*Lay Subs. R. Worcs.* c. 1280 [Worcs. Hist. Soc.], 18, 19), and Roger de Portes paid 18d. in 1327 (*Lay Subs. R. Worcs.* 1327 [Worcs. Hist. Soc.], 42).
[33] Walter de Portes was murdered by Robert de Rushock (see Rushock).

[34] *Rot. de Oblatis et Fin.* (Rec. Com.), 144.
[35] *Abbrev. Plac.* (Rec. Com.), 355, 356.
[36] Assize R. 1022, m. 8 d.
[37] But see Hampton Lovett, where this name is given as Scotevill.
[38] Henry was alive and a minor in 1254–5 (Assize R. 1022, m. 8 d., 18).
[39] Ibid. 1192, m. 7.
[40] Ibid.
[41] *Cal. Pat.* 1258–66, p. 602.
[42] Assize R. 1026, m. 17 d.
[43] Nash, *Hist. of Worc.* i, 379 ; Betham, *Baronetage,* iv, 88, quoting deed by which John Lovett, lord of 'Aumell,' grants land at Timberlack to his mother Lady Isabel wife of William le Blount.
[44] *Cal. Close,* 1279–88, p. 319.

Nash and Betham he left two co-heirs, Cicely and Alice,[45] but no confirmation of this has been found, and it appears more probable that he died without issue.[46] After this date the descent of the manor becomes obscure. It seems to have passed to co-heirs,[47] and in 1326 Alice wife of Eustace le Chapman made good her claim as great-great-grand-daughter of Agnes de Portes[48] against John de Wolrinton and Stephen de la Lee and Alice his wife to two-thirds of the manor,[49] and in the same year granted the manor to William la Zouche of Ashby and Robert his son,[50] Lucy wife of Richard de Hodinton releasing her claim to the manor at the same time.[51]

It is probable that this purchase was made by Lord Zouche on behalf of his stepson Thomas de Beauchamp Earl of Warwick, who was then a minor, for the earl was holding land in Elmley Lovett in 1344–5,[52] and presented to the church in 1349.[53] In 1361 he settled the manor upon himself in tail-male.[54] His eldest son Guy predeceased him, and on his death in 1369 the manor passed to his second son Thomas.[55] From that time the descent of Elmley Lovett is identical with that of Elmley Castle[56] (q.v.) until 1487, when both were conveyed by Anne Countess of Warwick to Henry VII.[57]

Elmley Lovett remained in the Crown[58] until 1543, when it was sold to Sir Robert Acton, kt.,[59] who settled it in 1557–8 on his younger son Charles.[60] Sir Robert Acton died seised of the manor in 1558, when Charles succeeded.[61] After the death of Sir John Acton, son and heir of Charles,[62] in 1621 the manor was divided between his four daughters,[63] Elizabeth wife of Henry Townshend, Anne wife of Walter Colles, Helen wife of Thomas Thornburgh, afterwards kt., and Penelope wife of John Lench.[64]

From this date the descent of the manor becomes somewhat involved. According to Nash the whole manor came into the possession of Henry Townshend, who purchased the shares of the other co-heirs, but, although from certain fines levied in 1637–8 and 1639[65] this would seem to be correct, in later documents relating to the manor he and his successors are said to have held only half, and the Lenches are known to have held an estate in the parish at least as late as 1672.[66]

TOWNSHEND. *Azure a cheveron ermine between three scallops argent.*

Henry Townshend was one of the garrison of Worcester at the time of its surrender in 1646, and was in the city throughout the siege. He kept a regular diary, which Nash has partly printed in his *History of Worcestershire*.[67] Townshend was a commissioner for raising money for the king's forces and for the safeguarding of Worcestershire, but in 1646 he proved before the Parliamentary Commissioners that he had never borne arms in the war and had paid contributions to both sides. He was fined £285.[68] He survived his wife and died in 1663,[69] when his son Henry succeeded. He settled half the manor of Elmley Lovett in 1677 on his son and heir Henry on his marriage with Mary daughter of Thomas Vernon.[70] The younger Henry succeeded his father in 1685,[71] but his only child Ann died in infancy,[72] and on his death his property passed to his younger brother Robert Townshend, rector of Hanbury. The latter was succeeded by his eldest son Henry, and afterwards

---

[45] Habington, op. cit. i, 265, 368; Nash, op. cit. i, 377; Betham, op. cit. iv, 88.
[46] See manor of Hampton Lovett.
[47] See Advowson, p. 110.

mentioned in an Act of 1536 by which certain lands, sometime belonging to the earldom of Warwick, were assured to Henry VIII (28 Hen. VIII, cap. 22; Burton, *Bibliog. of Worc.* i, 9).

Memo. R. Mich. Recorda 8 Eliz. rot. 113.
[62] Chan. Inq. p.m. (Ser. 2), cclvii, 49.
[63] Ibid. cccxciv, 87.
[64] Feet of F. Div. Co. Mich. 4 Chas. I.

[48] The following pedigree compiled from the documents quoted above and Assize R. 1026, m. 9 d., will make the Lovett descent clearer.

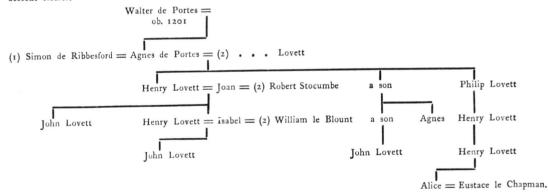

[49] *Abbrev. Plac.* (Rec. Com.), 356.
[50] Feet of F. Worcs. 19 Edw. II, no. 30.
[51] Ibid. no. 25.
[52] Anct. D. (P.R.O.), C 2954.
[53] *Sede Vacante Reg.* (Worcs. Hist. Soc.), 227.
[54] Feet of F. Div. Co. Mich. 35 Edw. III.
[55] Chan. Inq. p.m. 43 Edw. III (pt. i), no. 19.
[56] For references see Elmley Castle.
[57] Anct. D. (P.R.O.), A 11056. It is

[58] Star Chamb. Proc. Hen. VIII, bdle. 20, no. 148; *L. and P. Hen. VIII*, i, 130, 703. In 1523 the site of the manor was leased to Richard Hanbury for twenty-one years (*L. and P. Hen. VIII*, iii, g. 3214 [3]).
[59] Pat. 35 Hen. VIII, pt. xiii; Orig. R. 35 Hen. VIII, pt. iv, rot. 5.
[60] Pat. 4 & 5 Phil. and Mary, pt. xi, m. 28; Feet of F. Worcs. Hil. 1 Eliz.; Chan. Enr. Decree, bdle. 14, no. 11.
[61] Chan. Inq. p.m. (Ser. 2), cxix, 197;

[65] Ibid. Worc. Mich. 13 Chas. I; East' 14 Chas. I.
[66] See below.
[67] op. cit. App. 97 et seq.
[68] *Cal. Com. for Comp.* 1450.
[69] Metcalfe, *Visit. of Worc.* 1682–3, p. 92.
[70] Feet of F. Worcs. Hil. 28 & 29 Chas. II; Metcalfe, op. cit. 93.
[71] Prattinton Coll. (Soc. Antiq.).
[72] Nash, op. cit. i, 378, quoting M.I. in Elmley Lovett Church.

by a daughter Dorothy, who married Dr. Samuel Wanley, rector of Elmley Lovett,[73] and settled the moiety of the manor on him in 1744.[74] After Dorothy's death Dr. Wanley settled it on his second wife, Mary daughter of Sir Whitmore Acton of Aldenham, Shropshire, bart., but she also predeceased him by a few months.[75] He died in 1776, leaving this moiety to his friend the Rev. John Waldron, rector of Hampton Lovett, for life with reversion to his fourth and youngest son George Waldron.[76] The latter was holding it at the beginning of the 19th century,[77] but had sold it before 1809 to George Forrester.[78] Brooke Forrester was in possession in 1821 and 1828.[79] The Rev. Robert Thompson Forrester was lord of the manor in 1850,[80] and it was purchased of him in 1859 by William Orme Foster[81] of Apley Park, the great Stourbridge ironmaster, who left it to his second son, Captain James Foster, the present owner.[82]

The estate at Elmley Lovett which passed to the Lenches by the marriage of John Lench with Penelope Acton seems afterwards to have become known as SNEAD [83] or SNEAD'S GREEN. Habington states that it was added by the Lenches to their estate at Doverdale.[84] John Lench and Sarah his wife and William Lench were dealing with property described as a quarter of the manor of Elmley Lovett in 1655,[85] and in 1672 Elizabeth Lench conveyed 'the manor of Elme Lovett alias Snead' to Thomas Tyrer and Richard Avenant.[86] It was probably this estate which, under the name of the manor of Elmley Lovett or Snead's Green, belonged in 1802 to Thomas Lord Foley.[87] Three years later 'the manor of Snead's Green' was sold by Lord Foley to Francis Moule,[88] who in 1809 sold the manorial rights to George Forrester, then lord of the manor of Elmley Lovett.[89] Captain James Foster now receives the chief rents from the manor of Snead's Green.[90]

Snead's Green House, the seat of Francis Moule in 1809, had been in the possession of the family of Moule or Moyle since 1621, and was retained by Francis Moule when he sold the manorial rights of Snead's Green in 1809. On the death of his son, the last male heir of the family, the estate passed to his three sisters, and on their death to his niece Mrs. Stocks, the present owner.[91]

MERRINGTON lay in the parishes of Elmley Lovett, Hampton Lovett and Elmbridge.[92] The first mention of it occurs in 1375, when lands and tenements there and in several other places were settled by John Beauchamp of Holt in trust for the provision of a yearly payment of 12 marks to a chaplain to pray for the souls of the said John and his ancestors in Holt.[93]

John Beauchamp was attainted and forfeited all his possessions in 1387–8,[94] and in November 1389 the estate was granted by the king to Richard Wych, parson of Tredington, and others.[95] It subsequently, at some uncertain date, passed to the Cassy [96] family. It is first mentioned as a manor in 1530, when Robert Cassy appears to have conveyed it to William Brace.[97] In 1569 Henry Cassy and Francis Brace, who was probably the grandson of William mentioned above, were dealing with the manor of Merrington,[98] and in 1588 Francis Brace settled the manor on his son Thomas.[99] The manor then passed with the part of Doverdale held by the Braces to Ralph Taylor,[100] who was in possession in 1684.[1] In 1722 the messuage or farm called Merrington Farm in the tenure of Katherine Taylor was conveyed by Ralph Taylor to John Dovey, apparently for the purpose of settling an annuity from the estate upon Ralph and Katherine Taylor, his daughter by his first wife. By his second wife he had a son Hugh and a daughter Mary.[2] Merrington seems, however, to have passed to the lords of Elmley Lovett before this date, for in 1713 it was included in a conveyance of that manor made by Henry Townshend,[3] and it subsequently seems to have followed the same descent as Elmley Lovett.[4] The chief rents from the manor are now received by Captain James Foster, but the site of the manor is not known. As the rents are paid by the tenant of New House Farm, it may be concluded that Merrington was in that vicinity.[5]

It was stated in a deposition of 1684 that the waste grounds or commons called Cutnall Green and the Broad, which lay chiefly in Elmley Lovett parish, had always been owned by the lords of Merrington. Cutnall Green extended from a stone called Knaven Castle to a place called Black Lake. The two commons were divided by a ditch or bank, which formed the boundary between the parishes of Hampton Lovett and Elmley Lovett. Another deponent stated that he had never heard Merrington called a manor, but that it was formerly called Cutnall Green Farm.[6]

A park belonging to the manor is mentioned in 1395, when a certain William Porter paid 20s.

[73] Nash, op. cit. i, 378.
[74] Feet of F. Worcs. Trin. 17 & 18 Geo. II.
[75] Prattinton Coll. (Soc. Antiq.).
[76] P.C.C. 250 Bellas.
[77] Prattinton Coll. (Soc. Antiq.). He presented to the church in 1800.
[78] Information from Mrs. Stocks of Snead's Green House.
[79] Recov. R. Worc. Mich. 2 Geo. IV, rot. 122 ; Trin. 9 Geo. IV, rot. 24.
[80] P.O. Dir. Birmingham, 1850.
[81] Information supplied by Capt. James Foster.
[82] Burke, Landed Gentry (1906).
[83] A common called Snedys Wodde is mentioned in 1533, when it was part of Elmley Lovett Manor (L. and P. Hen. VIII, vi, 231).
[84] Habington, op. cit. i, 190.
[85] Feet of F. Worcs. Trin. 1655.
[86] Ibid. East. 24 Chas. II.

[87] Recov. R. Hil. 42 Geo. III, rot. 21.
[88] Information supplied by Mrs. Stocks.
[89] Ibid.
[90] Information supplied by Capt. James Foster.
[91] Information supplied by Mrs. Stocks.
[92] Exch. Dep. East. 36 Chas. II, no. 31.
[93] Anct. D. (P.R.O.), A 9774.
[94] G.E.C. Complete Peerage, i, 278.
[95] Cal. Pat. 1388–92, p. 146.
[96] John Cassy had been one of the feoffees of the settlement of 1375. Thomas son of John Cassy and Robert Cassy his brother were dealing with land at Elmley Lovett in 1344–5 (Anct. D. [P.R.O.], C 2954).
[97] Recov. R. Mich. 22 Hen. VIII, rot. 146.
[98] Ibid. Trin. 11 Eliz. rot. 129 ; Close, 12 Eliz. pt. i, Brace and Russell.
[99] Feet of F. Worcs. Mich. 30 & 31

Eliz. ; Chan. Inq. p.m. (Ser. 2), cccxxv, 186.
[100] Feet of F. Worcs. East. 5 Jas. I ; Hil. 12 Chas. II ; Recov. R. Mich. 15 Chas. II, rot. 209 ; Feet of F. Worcs. Trin. 29 Chas. II.
[1] Exch. Dep. East. 36 Chas. II, no. 31.
[2] Close, 10 Geo. I, pt. xxv, no. 24, 25.
[3] Recov. R. Mich. 12 Anne, rot. 30.
[4] Feet of F. Worcs. Trin. 14 Geo. III ; Recov. R. Mich. 2 Geo. IV, rot. 122 ; Trin. 9 Geo. IV, rot. 24.
[5] Information supplied by Capt. James Foster. It is to be noted, however, that this hardly agrees with what follows as to Merrington formerly being known as Cutnall Green Farm, for Cutnall Green lies to the south-east of the village of Elmley Lovett, while New House Farm is in the north-west.
[6] Exch. Dep. East. 36 Chas. II, no. 31.

yearly for its farm.[7] The office of parker was granted in 1446 to the king's servant Richard Frebody, page of the queen's chamber,[8] and in 1484 John Huddleston was made master of the game in the park.[9] The park, then containing 62½ acres, with its deer [10] was granted with the manor to Sir Robert Acton in 1543,[11] and belonged to his descendants until 1622,[12] after which all trace of it seems to have disappeared.

Three mills at Elmley Lovett rendering 109s. 4d. are mentioned in the Domesday Survey.[13] In 1260 a mill [14] passed with the manor,[15] and in 1543 was sold to Sir Robert Acton.[16] It still belonged to the lord of the manor in 1713,[17] but is no longer used. A mill-house and remains of a corn-mill with a stone dated 16— still exist at Elmley Lovett.

CHURCH The church of *ST. MICHAEL* consists of a chancel, nave, west tower with spire, and south porch. It was rebuilt in 1840, and is of little architectural interest. The tower is square, with single round-headed belfry windows, an embattled parapet with corner pinnacles and an octagonal spire. A 17th-century oak chest yet remains, and on the interior of the tower walls are five types of masons' marks. On the south wall of the chancel is a monument to Dorothy wife of Sir Henry Townshend, kt., with an inscription to her husband, who died 9 May 1685, aged sixty-one.

In the churchyard to the south of the church are the remains of a 15th-century cross with a tapering octagonal stem, and a base of the same form standing on two square steps. The cross itself is a modern restoration.

There is a peal of six bells, inscribed as follows : treble, 'Heaven fix when you hear us six, John Hemus, 1697'; (2) 'William Ince Hugh Arden Churchwardens, Peace to the church, 1696'; (3) 'Sing ye pleasantly unto God. William Baggley made mee 1696'; (4) 'Edward Best Rector, Thomas Baskervile, Humphrey England C.W. 16(9)6. William Baggley made mee'; (5) 'Omnibus gratia sed Henricus Townshend Armiger dominus mareni (maneri ?) ifact (facti ?) causa 1696'; tenor, 'Attend with diligence and prepare for the service of God according to the usage of the Church of England 1696. William Baggley made mee.'

The plate consists of a cup, salver, paten and flagon, all of plated ware.

The registers previous to 1812 are as follows : (i) mixed entries 1539 to 1730 ; (ii) baptisms and burials 1732 to 1804, marriages 1732 to 1753 ; (iii) baptisms and burials 1805 to 1812 ; (iv) marriages 1754 to 1812.

ADVOWSON A priest is mentioned at Elmley in the Domesday Survey, and from this the existence of a church at that date may perhaps be inferred. The advowson of Elmley Lovett Church followed the same descent as the manor [18] until the middle of the 18th century, passing to the Townshends after the death of John Acton in 1621.[19] Ann Townshend presented Samuel Wanley to the living in 1742,[20] but in 1776 the presentation for that turn was made by Robert Burgis, who then became the incumbent,[21] and was said to be patron in 1808,[22] though George Waldron presented in 1800.[23] By 1829 the patronage had passed to John Lynes,[24] who sold it probably about 1837 to Christ's College, Cambridge,[25] to which it still belongs.

In 1316 a dispute as to the rights of patronage between Isabel widow of Henry Lovett, Richard de Hodington and Lucy his wife, and William le Mol and Lucy his wife,[26] seems to have been decided in favour of Isabel, who presented to the church in that year.[27]

There was a chapel of St. Nicholas at Elmley in which a chantry was founded by Sir John Lovett, kt., at the end of the 13th or early in the 14th century.[28] The advowson of the chapel was said in 1327 to belong to the priory of Dodford.[29] No further mention has been found of this chantry, which was apparently not in existence in the reign of Edward VI when the chantries were suppressed. In 1562–3 Cicely Pickerell, widow, received a grant of 'all those chapels and les chappell yardes and one called the Rood Chappell yard' in Elmley Lovett.[30] This was probably all that remained of the chapel of St. Nicholas.

CHARITIES The Charity Estate, the particulars of the foundation of which are unknown, was formerly regulated by a decree of Commissioners for Charitable Uses, 1631–2, and is now regulated by scheme of the Charity Commissioners, 1871. The trust estate consists of 92 a., or thereabouts, let at £163 15s., also of a rent-charge of 6s. 8d. and a sum of £84 2s. 9d. consols held by the official trustees. Under the scheme a sum of £70 is applied for educational purposes, £40 for church purposes, and the balance distributed in clothes, &c., for the poor.

The official trustees also hold a sum of £445 3s. 10d. consols towards the replacement of a loan of £400.

The amount applied for education is paid to the Cutnall Green School, which was founded in 1863.

[7] Mins. Accts. bdle. 1123, no. 5.
[8] Cal. Pat. 1441–6, p. 433.
[9] Ibid. 1476–85, p. 379.
[10] Mins. Accts. Hen. VII, no. 990 ; Rentals and Surv. portf. 16, no. 81.
[11] L. and P. Hen. VIII, xviii (2), g. 241 (9) ; Pat. 35 Hen. VIII, pt. xiii, m. 5.
[12] Pat. 4 & 5 Phil. and Mary, pt. xi, m. 28 ; Chan. Inq. p.m. (Ser. 2), cclvii, 49 ; cccxciv, 87 ; Feet of F. Worcs. Trin. 5 Jas. I. [13] V.C.H. Worcs. i, 310.
[14] Assize R. 1192, m. 7.
[15] L. and P. Hen. VIII, iv, g. 5748 (8) ; Mins. Accts. Hen. VII, 990.

[16] L. and P. Hen. VIII, xviii (2), g. 241 (9).
[17] Feet of F. Worcs. Mich. 13 Chas. I ; Recov. R. Mich. 12 Anne, rot. 30.
[18] In 1291 the value of the church was £9 13s. 4d. (Pope Nich. Tax. [Rec. Com.], 217), a sum which had increased to £18 before 1535 (Valor Eccl. [Rec. Com.], iii, 274).
[19] See refs. under Manor ; Feet of F. Worcs. Mich. 22 Jas. I ; Recov. R. Hil. 15 Chas. I, rot. 45, &c. Presentations were made by members of the Best family from 1600 to 1663 and in 1708 Henry Toye presented (Nash, op. cit. i, 380).

[20] Inst. Bks. (P.R.O.).
[21] Ibid. ; Bacon, Liber Regis, 969.
[22] Carlisle, Topog. Dict.
[23] Inst. Bks. (P.R.O.).
[24] Clerical Guide, 1829.
[25] Clergy List, 1841.
[26] Worc. Epis. Reg. Maidstone (1313–17), fol. 44 d.
[27] Nash, op. cit. i, 379.
[28] Prattinton Coll. (Soc. Antiq.) ; Worc. Epis. Reg. Cobham (1317–27), fol. 121 ; Montagu (1333–7), fol. 15 d.
[29] Worc. Epis. Reg. Cobham, fol. 121.
[30] Pat. 5 Eliz. pt. v.

FECKENHAM

Feccanhom (ix cent.) ; Feccheham (xi cent.) ; Fekkeham, Fekeham (xii cent.) ; Feckeham, Feckaham, Fecham (xiii cent.) ; Flechenham (xvi cent.) ; Feckyngham (xvi and xvii cent.).

Feckenham is a large parish in the extreme east of the county on the borders of Warwickshire and has an area of 6,978 acres,[1] of which in 1905 1,035¾ were arable land, 4,680½ pasture and 87 woods and plantations.[1a] The civil parish of Feckenham Urban was formed in 1894 out of the part of Feckenham parish in Redditch Urban District,[1b] and is governed by the Redditch Urban District Council. The soil varies considerably in different parts of the parish, consisting chiefly of strong clay, gravel, marl and sand. The ground rises gradually from the west to the east, where the parish is bounded by a continuation of the Lickey Hills, which in some places rise to a height of 530 ft. Brandon Brook, a tributary of the Bow Brook, rises in the parish, which is also watered by the Bow Brook and other of its tributaries. The chief roads are one from Alcester through the village of Feckenham to Droitwich, which is sometimes called the Lower Salt Way and is said to be of Roman origin, and the Ridgeway, which passes along the eastern boundary of the parish to Redditch and divides Worcestershire from Warwickshire. There is no railway in the parish, the nearest station being at Redditch, 5 miles away.

The chief industries are the manufacture of needles and fish-hooks, for which the parish was well known in 1790.[2] A later development has been the manufacture of cycles and motors. Agriculture also gives employment to a number of people.

Besides the village there are the hamlets of Callow Hill and Hunt End in the north, and Astwood Bank and part of Crabbs Cross in the east, on the borders of Warwickshire.

The village of Feckenham is situated about 8 miles east of Droitwich upon the main road to Alcester. Of the houses which compose the village itself the majority are of red brick and include some good examples of late Georgian work. The principal street leads northwards from the main road to the church, on the south side of which is an open space surrounded by cottages, known as 'The Square.' At the bottom of a lane leading westwards from 'The Square' is the old grammar school, which seems originally to have consisted of one large room, the master's house being in the village. It has been turned into a cottage within the last forty years, and hardly any original details remain, with the exception of a fine oak door, with its moulded posts and head. Before being put to its present use, and while still the school-house, it had been drastically repaired, as recorded on a tablet fixed upon the south wall, inscribed as follows : 'Erected A.D. 1611. Repaired A.D. 1848.'

The church lies to the north, and near it is the site of the old prison, formerly known as ' Bennett's Bower,'[3] which consists of about 4 acres of land surrounded by a ditch, and was formerly used for the punishment of offenders in the forest.[4] In the 16th century the manorial courts were held in the upper part of the prison.[5] It was evidently allowed to fall into decay after the forest was disafforested in 1629, and in the time of Charles II the ground it had occupied is said to have been ' planted with tobacco which grew very well, till the planting of it was prohibited by Act of Parliament, 12 and 15 Ch. II.'[6] The parish is rich in fine examples of half-timber work, of which one of the most notable is Shurnock Court Farm, situated upon the main road about a mile to the west of the village. The house is of the normal central hall type of the 16th century, with the private apartments on the left hand of the entrance and the kitchen and offices on the right. Some good early 17th-century panelling remains in the room to the left of the entrance hall on the ground floor. A new entrance and staircase have been formed on the kitchen side, and the attic floor has been abolished to heighten the first floor. The stacks are of stone ashlar with good brick shafts. A moat, now partially filled up, surrounds the house. The farm buildings are modern. Some fragments of 15th-century tiles found in the house include the *In te dñe confidi* pattern, met with at St. Peter's Church, Droitwich, Salwarpe Church, Cookhill House and elsewhere in the neighbourhood. Astwood Court Farm, which stands about half a mile to the north of Shurnock Court, is a two-storied brick house of mid-17th-century date, surrounded by a moat still filled with water. In the central room on the ground floor are some fragments of original wainscoting re-set in modern work, on which is inscribed, without date, ' IOHN CVLPEPER.' Middle Bean Hall Farm, a two-storied house with attics and a tiled roof, is a fine example of early 16th-century half-timber work of the normal plan of the period. A row of attic gables were added in the first half of the 17th century, which give the front elevation a particularly elaborate and symmetrical appearance. These have carved barge-boards and ornamental curved strutting. The windows, with one exception, have been blocked, as this floor is no longer utilized for living rooms. On a rain-water head is the date 1635. The porch, of two stories, seems also to be an addition of this date, and contains original benches with baluster legs. There is some good Jacobean panelling in two of the upper rooms, though the interior has been for the most part completely modernized.

The most important house in the neighbourhood is Norgrove Court, a fine red brick mansion of mid-17th-century date, two stories in height with a mezzanine floor at the rear. The plan is oblong, with the entrance hall and principal stairs near the centre of the north side, occupying half the depth of the house from back to front. The principal rooms

---

[1] This includes Feckenham Urban, which comprises 127 acres.
[1a] Statistics from Bd. of Agric. (1905).
[1b] *Census of Engl. and Wales* (1901), *Warwick*, 28.

[2] *V.C.H. Worcs.* ii, 274. A weaver of Feckenham is mentioned in 1525 (*L. and P. Hen. VIII*, iv [1], g. 1466 [2]).
[3] *L. and P. Hen. VIII*, xviii (2), g. 107 (12) ; Prattinton Coll. (Soc. Antiq.),

quoting a survey of the manor taken 33 Eliz.
[4] Prattinton Coll. (Soc. Antiq.) ; *Cal. Close*, 1279–88, pp. 275, 380.
[5] Prattinton Coll. (Soc. Antiq.).
[6] Nash, *Hist. of Worc.* i, 439.

occupy the ground floor of the south or garden front. The kitchen was originally at the north-west angle, the accompanying offices being all on this side of the house. The principal staircase has oak newels with carved finials. The balusters and handrails have been much repaired and restored. The interior generally has suffered from alterations to suit it to the needs of a farm-house. Some fine plaster overmantels remain in two of the bedrooms on the first floor and in the panelled room on the mezzanine at the west side of the entrance hall. On the south or garden front the level of the first floor is marked by a moulded string-course of stone, and the windows have architraves, central mullions and transoms of the same material. On the first floor are two blocked doorways with moulded stone jambs and two-light openings above the lintels, which must have been

Tiled hipped roofs of uniform height crown all four elevations, and their projecting eaves are supported by carved console brackets of wood. From the central valley formed by the four roofs rises a large octagonal chimney stack. The remaining stacks are square on plan, with panelled sides, ornamented with geometrical patterns in lighter bricks. The house is a good example of the 'modernizing' plan of the first half of the 17th century, where, though the bedrooms are still 'en suite,' the later notions of domestic privacy are beginning to obtain, and the hall is reduced to a mere staircase.

Originally the whole of Feckenham was included in the extensive forest of the same name. About 1578 Sir John Throckmorton seems to have begun inclosing the common in the forest, but met with great opposition from the tenants, three of whom

MIDDLE BEAN HALL, FECKENHAM

originally intended to open on to flights of steps leading down to the garden. It is possible that a balcony may have connected the two flights, as the windows of the ground floor beneath this portion have evidently been disturbed, and have wooden frames in place of the original stone mullions. On either side of each doorway filled-up pockets in the brickwork mark the position of the handrails or balustrades. The bricks employed for the blocking of the doorways are of the same depth as those employed for the rest of the walling. It is, therefore, quite probable that the arrangement, though designed, was never carried out.

At the angles of the walls are plain stone quoins.

were committed to the Marshalsea for 'plucking downe of a frame of timber erected by Sir John Throgmorton in a copie holde of his.' [7] In 1579 Sir John was ordered to cease inclosing the commons until the suit between him and the tenants was determined.[8] The commons were finally inclosed under an Act of 1816, the award being dated 1832.[9] The forest was disafforested in 1629.[10]

Here, as elsewhere, the inclosures were followed by riots; 300 people with spades and armed with 'warlike munitions of all sorts' began throwing down inclosures. They were dispersed by thirty or forty men sent by the sheriff and justices of the county,

[7] *Acts of P.C.* 1577–8, pp. 375–6, 399.
[8] Ibid. 1579–80, p. 191.

[9] Priv. Act, 56 Geo. III, cap. 27; *Blue Bk. Incl. Awards*, 190. The common called Beanhall Fields had been inclosed in 1770 (Priv. Act, 11 Geo. III, cap. 60).
[10] *V.C.H. Worcs.* ii, 319.

but not before they had 'in most daring manner presented themselves armed with pikes, forest bills, and the like,' and not only slighted the power of the sheriff and justices, but 'assailed their persons and protested they would fight it out.'[11]

John de Feckenham, the last Abbot of Westminster and a celebrated divine, was born in the parish or forest of Feckenham.

Among the place-names are Wyshamclos,[12] Calnwehull[13] (xiv cent.) ; Ruyfel,[14] Harsfeldefurlonge,[15] in deeds without date ; Annetts Place,[16] Ruddyalls *alias* Broderiche[17] (xvi cent.) ; Lovelyne, Prestfield, Popeslade and the Burches,[18] Warkewoodes,[19] and Tookes Farm,[20] Cruse Hill[21] (xvii cent.). Lovelyne survives in the modern Love Lane Farm.

FECKENHAM, which like Bromsgrove was given by Ethelric son of MANORS Ethelmund to Wœrferth for life in 804

Roger forfeited it in 1074 for rebellion against the Conqueror.[25] It then appears to have been granted to Walter de Lacy, who died just before 1086, and is mentioned in the Domesday Survey as having granted 1 hide of land in Feckenham to a certain Hubert.[26] The manor did not, however, pass to his son Roger de Lacy, but belonged to the king in 1086,[27] and remained a royal possession, subject to various grants, for several centuries, probably on account of its position in the forest to which it gave its name. From 1191 to 1195 Elias de Etingehal paid £21 for the farm of Feckenham.[28]

During the early part of the 13th century Hugh de Nevill answered at the Exchequer for certain land in Feckenham, which had been granted to him, probably by King John,[29] and in 1217 the manor of Feckenham was granted during pleasure to John Marshall.[30] It was confirmed to him in 1221,[31] but

NORGROVE COURT, FECKENHAM : SOUTH FRONT

with reversion to the church of Worcester,[22] must have been a place of considerable size and importance in the reign of Edward the Confessor, when it was held of Eadwine, Earl of Mercia, by five thegns who 'could betake themselves with their land where they would,' and had under them four knights 'as free as themselves.'[23] Shortly after the Conquest it was granted to William Fitz Osbern,[24] Earl of Hereford, who died in 1071. His son

seems to have been taken from him in the following year in order that the manor might be granted at farm to the men of Feckenham.[32] They appear to have held it at farm for some years, being still in possession in 1229–30,[33] but their yearly fee-farm rent of £20 and a rent of 30s. a year which they had undertaken to pay to the abbey of Lire seem to have fallen into arrears.[34] Probably on this account the manor was taken from them and must have been

[11] *Cal. S. P. Dom.* 1631–3, p. 289.
[12] Chan. Inq. p.m. 46 Edw. III (2nd nos.), no. 63 ; 13 Ric. II, no. 64.
[13] Prattinton Coll. (Soc. Antiq.), Deeds of the D. and C. of Worc. no. 36. Now Callow Hill.
[14] Anct. D. (P.R.O.), B 3646.
[15] Ibid. B 3650.
[16] Chan. Proc. (Ser. 2), bdle. 4, no. 44.
[17] Com. Pleas D. Enr. East. 1 Mary, m. 10.

[18] Pat. 5 Jas. I, pt. xvi.
[19] Exch. Dep. Mich. 1656, no. 11.
[20] Ibid. 16 Jas. I, no. 26.
[21] Chan. Inq. p.m. (Ser. 2), cccxxii, 165.
[22] Dugdale, *Mon. Angl.* i, 608 ; Birch, *Cart. Sax.* i, 438 ; Kemble, *Codex Dipl.* no. 186.
[23] *V.C.H. Worcs.* i, 320b.
[24] Ibid.
[25] *Dict. Nat. Biog.*

[26] *V.C.H. Worcs.* i, 321.
[27] Ibid. 320b, 321.
[28] Pipe R. 3 Ric. I, m. 8, &c.
[29] Ibid. 4 John, m. 2, &c.
[30] *Cal. Pat.* 1216–25, p. 42.
[31] *Rot. Lit. Claus.* (Rec. Com.), i, 449, 454.
[32] Ibid. 506.
[33] Madox, *Firma Burgi*, 55.
[34] Ibid.

granted to Henry Earl of Arundel, for he surrendered it to the Crown about 1243, when Henry III granted it for life to his mother-in-law Beatrice Countess of Provence.[35] She was still holding it in 1257,[36] and it is difficult to account for a memorandum of 1250–1 to the effect that in 1248–9 Simon de Wautton, farmer of the manor, restored it to the king, who then granted it at farm to the men of Feckenham, who were in 1261–2 still owing £38 10s. for the years 1244–5 and 1246–7.[37]

It was granted in 1272 as dower to Queen Eleanor,[38] and in 1299 to Margaret of France.[39]

ELEANOR of Provence. *Or four pales gules.*

MARGARET of France. *Azure powdered with fleurs de lis or.*

In consideration of her services in suppressing the rebellion of the Despensers it was given by Parliament in 1327 to Queen Isabella.[40] On her fall in 1330 the manor again returned to the Crown, and was granted in 1331 to Queen Philippa, consort of Edward III.[41] Repairs were undertaken at the manor-house of Feckenham in 1355,[42] but in the following year the queen sold the hall to the Abbot of Evesham, who demolished it and carried away the materials.[43] In 1364 the queen granted the manor for her life to John Attwood, and in 1365 the king confirmed it to him for his life.[44] John surrendered his Letters Patent in 1377 in favour of William de Beauchamp,[45] to whom the manor was confirmed in 1399 quit of a rent of £37 14s. 4½d. which he had formerly paid.[46] The reversion after Sir William's death was granted in 1410 to Humphrey fourth son of Henry IV.[47] He was created Duke of Gloucester in 1414,[48] and the manor was settled on his second wife Eleanor Cobham in 1435.[49] On his death without issue in 1446–7 it would have again fallen to the Crown had not Henry VI granted the

PHILIPPA of Hainault. *Or a lion gules, for FLANDERS quartered with Or a sable lion for HOLLAND.*

reversion in case of failure of issue of the duke to Henry Duke of Warwick. His interest passed on his death in 1446 to his only daughter Ann,[50] and reverted to the king on her death without issue in 1449.[51] The manor was granted in dower to Elizabeth, consort of Edward IV, in 1465,[52] to Anne of Cleves in 1540,[53] to Katherine Howard in 1541,[54] and in 1544 to Katherine Parr.[55] In 1553 it was granted to John Duke of Northumberland,[56] but was forfeited by him in the same year and given by Queen Mary in 1558 to Sir John Throckmorton

WYDVILE. *Argent a fesse and a quarter gules.*

and Margery his wife and their heirs male,[57] although it is evident from a letter from Sir John to his brother Sir Nicholas Throckmorton that he did not obtain possession of the manor until about 1564.[58] He died in 1580, and in 1583 his eldest son Francis was arrested for a conspiracy against the queen and executed in the following year.[59] The reversion of the manor of Feckenham after the death of Dame Margery Throckmorton was then granted to Sir Thomas Leighton and Elizabeth his wife,[60] who seem to have had some difficulty in preserving their rights there. Lady Throckmorton was found to be cutting down and selling timber in the park 'to the utter spoileing and defacing thereof,'[61] and in 1594 Sir Thomas Leighton writing from Guernsey to Lord Burghley complained that he was 'continually wronged in his living at Feckenham by Sir Fulke Greville,' and prayed that 'the queen will command Sir Fulke to cease or allow him to come over and defend himself.'[62] Edward Leighton,

COVENTRY, Earl of Coventry. *Sable a fesse ermine between three crescents or.*

grandson and eventually heir of Sir Thomas, sold the manor in 1632 to Thomas Lord Coventry, Lord Keeper of the Great Seal,[63] in whose family it still remains, the present Earl of Coventry being now lord of the manor.

In 1086 there were at Feckenham a reeve, a beadle, a miller, a smith, and a radman.[64] In 1591 there were still a reeve and a beadle, who with the constable and other officers were elected by the tenants, and a bailiff[65] chosen by the lord from among the tenants and freeholders. The reeve and beadle were still elected in 1679.[66] All freeholders owed suit to

[35] *Cal. Pat.* 1232–47, p. 364.
[36] Ibid. 1247–58, p. 552.
[37] Madox, *Firma Burgi,* 55.
[38] *Cal. Pat.* 1272–81, pp. 27, 71.
[39] Ibid. 1292–1301, p. 453 ; 1307–13, p. 217.
[40] Ibid. 1327–30, p. 68.
[41] Ibid. 1330–4, p. 55.
[42] Ibid. 1354–8, p. 208.
[43] Ibid. 474, 545.
[44] Pat. 39 Edw. III, pt. i, m. 5.
[45] *Cal. Pat.* 1377–81, p. 73.
[46] Ibid. 1399–1401, p. 118 ; 1401–5, p. 47.

[47] Ibid. 1408–13, p. 164.
[48] G.E.C. *Complete Peerage,* iv, 44.
[49] Feet of F. Div. Co. Hil. 14 Hen. VI, no. 84 ; *Cal. Pat.* 1429–36, p. 504.
[50] Chan. Inq. p.m. 25 Hen. VI, no. 26.
[51] Ibid. 31 Hen. VI, no. 31.
[52] *Cal. Pat.* 1461–7, p. 445.
[53] *L. and P. Hen. VIII,* xv, g. 144 (2), p. 52.   [54] Ibid. xvi, g. 503 (25).
[55] Ibid. xix (1), g. 141 (65).
[56] Pat. 7 Edw. VI, pt. viii.
[57] Ibid. 5 & 6 Phil. and Mary, pt. i, m. 16.
[58] *Cal. S. P. Dom.* 1547–65, p. 574.

[59] *Dict. Nat. Biog.* ; *Cal. S. P. Dom.* 1581–90, pp. 130, 179, 184, 188.
[60] Pat. 27 Eliz. pt. xi, m. 30, no. 2 ; Exch. Spec. Com. no. 4774, 4777.
[61] *Acts of P.C.* 1587–8, p. 417 ; 1588, p. 90.
[62] *Cal. S. P. Dom.* 1580–1625, p. 363.
[63] Feet of F. Worcs. Mich. 8 Chas. I ; East. 9 Chas. I.
[64] *V.C.H. Worcs.* i, 320b, 321a.
[65] The bailiffs of Feckenham are mentioned in 1231 (*Cal. Close,* 1227–31, p. 480).
[66] Exch. Dep. Mich. 28 Chas. II, no. 22.

FECKENHAM : SHURNOCK COURT FARM

FECKENHAM : OVERMANTEL AT NORGROVE COURT

the court baron and all tenants of the manor were obliged to appear at the courts leet held on Whit Tuesday every year.[67] Six tenants who attended the court held every three weeks discharged the others from appearance. The heriot claimed by the lord on the death of every freeholder and every copyholder paying rent 'by the free roll,' and on the alienation of their land, was the best horse or gelding and best bull or ox at the will of the lord and the best saddle and bridle, the saddle going to the reeve and the bridle to the beadle.[68]

In 1237 the king caused a market and fair to be proclaimed in his manor of Feckenham. The market was to be on Thursday and the fair on the eve and day of the Nativity of St. John the Baptist and two days following.[69] In 1253 the market day was changed to Saturday.[70] The market seems to have died out before the end of the 18th century, but cattle fairs were held yearly on 26 March and 30 September until the middle of the 19th century,[71] and a wake is still held on the first Sunday after the feast of St. John the Baptist.

Owing to its situation in the forest, Feckenham was visited by all the early kings of England[72] who had a lodge in the park. There are several entries in Pipe Rolls and Patent Rolls relating to the repair of the king's houses in the manor,[73] and between the years 1166 and 1169 the sum of £29 14s. 5d. was expended on the king's chamber,[74] probably on the occasion of a visit from Henry II. That king granted a charter there in (probably) 1188.[74a] The manor-house was apparently not rebuilt after its demolition in 1356, for when the manor was granted in 1558 to John Throckmorton he complained of being 'forced to wander up and down like an Egyptian in other men's houses for want of one of my own.' He intended to build a house in Feckenham Park, and, since there was no water or spring there, wished to obtain the adjoining manor of Hanbury, from which water could be brought to Feckenham, agreeing in return to spend 1,000 marks on the house, which if he died without issue would revert to the Crown.[75]

A yearly rent of £58 17s. 8¾d. was reserved to the Crown when the manor was granted to Sir Thomas Leighton, and in 1672 was sold to a certain Richard Wiseman.[76] He appears to have left it to six daughters, who sold it to Thomas Harrison in 1681.[77]

An estate at *ASTWOOD*, now known as *AST-WOOD COURT*, was held partly of the manor of Inkberrow by suit at the court of Newbury and partly of the manor of Feckenham.[78] The first known tenants of the manor were members of the Musard family. In 1333-4 Nicholas de Wyshaw and his wife Agnes obtained licence to retain 40 acres of land in Feckenham which they had purchased without licence of John son of Masculinus Musard.[79] John retained land in Astwood,[80] and the estate bought by Wyshaw, afterwards known as Wyshamclos, later reverted to John or his heirs.[81] From John the manor passed to his son Masculinus,[82] who died before 1389, leaving a daughter Elizabeth wife of Roger Chaturley as his heir.[83] Elizabeth and Roger granted the manor in 1389 to Sir Nicholas de Stafford and Elizabeth his wife for their lives with reversion to Roger and Elizabeth.[84] Elizabeth daughter and heir of Roger Chaturley married John Huband, and she and her husband were holding the manor in 1446-7.[85] They granted it in 1470-1 to Humphrey and Edward Huband,[86] but Edward and his wife Mary lost it in 1495-6, when it was awarded to Thomas Kebell and others who claimed to have held it at the beginning of the reign of Henry VII and to have been disseised of it by Humphrey Huband.[87]

The manor is next found in the possession of Geoffrey Markham, who settled it in 1558 upon himself and Jane his wife and the heirs male of their son John.[88] Another conveyance of the manor was made in 1566, to which John Huband, John Bowes and John Markham and his wife Elizabeth were parties.[89] John and Jerome Markham sold the manor in 1587 to Ralph Bowes,[90] who leased it for 1,000 years in 1595 to Walter and Martin Culpeper.[91] In 1598 Martin Culpeper settled the manor on himself and his wife Lettice with remainder to their son Martin on the occasion of his marriage with Joyce daughter of Sir Edward Aston.[92] Lettice survived her husband and married secondly Sir Robert Purslowe, and they conveyed their life interest in the manor in 1616 to John Culpeper.[93] In 1634-5 Sir Alexander Culpeper

[67] The court leet is still held yearly in October at the 'Old Rose and Crown.'
[68] Prattinton Coll., quoting a MS. then in the possession of C. Hunt. No one but a tenant of the manor was supposed to hold the office of reeve (Exch. Dep. Hil. 16 Jas. I, no. 6 ; see also ibid. Mich. 1656, no. 11 ; Mich. 28 Chas. II, no. 22).
[69] Cal. Close, 1234-7, p. 429.
[70] Close, 37 Hen. III, m. 16.
[71] Rep. of Com. on Market Rts. i, 216 ; Carlisle, Topog. Dict. ; Lewis, Topog. Dict.
[72] Cal. Pat. 1292-1301, p. 78 ; Hist. MSS. Com. Rep. xi, App. vii, 144 ; Cal. Chart. R. 1257-1300, pp. 431, 488 ; Rot. Lit. Pat. (Rec. Com.), 150, 151 ; Cal. Pat. 1232-47, pp. 16, 154 ; Cal. Close, 1296-1300, p. 440 ; Cal. Pat. 1321-4, p. 365 ; Cal. Close, 1330-3, pp. 490, 594, 610 ; Cal. Pat. 1343-5, p. 195 ; 1377-81, p. 132. A valuable series of documents relating to the forest and courts of Feckenham are in the Record Room at Worcester.
[73] Pipe R. 8 Hen. II (Pipe R. Soc.), 56 ; 10 Hen. II, 4 ; 13 Hen. II, 64 ;

22 Hen. II, 34 ; 24 Hen. II, 44 ; Cal. Pat. 1377-81, p. 337 ; 1381-5, p. 230 ; 1391-6, p. 334 ; 1436-41, p. 90.
[74] Pipe R. 13 Hen. II (Pipe R. Soc.), 64 ; 14 Hen. II, 110 ; 15 Hen. II, 137.
[74a] Cal. Doc. of France, i, 11.
[75] Cal. S. P. Dom. 1547-65, pp. 574-5.
[76] Close, 24 Chas. II, pt. xv, m. 13. About 1546 the fee farm is said to have amounted to '£38 odd' (Exch. Dep. Mich. 1656, no. 11).
[77] Feet of F. Worcs. East. 34 Chas. II ; Mich. 33 Chas. II.
[78] Inq. a.q.d. file 224, no. 17 ; Hund. R. (Rec. Com.), ii, 284 ; Chan. Inq. p.m. 49 Edw. III, pt. i, no. 70 ; 14 Hen. VI, no. 35 ; 16 Edw. IV, no. 66.
[79] Nicholas Musard, grandfather of John, had also probably held an estate at Astwood (Wrottesley, Ped. from Plea R. 380).
[80] Inq. a.q.d. file 224, no. 17.
[81] Chan. Misc. bdle. 85, file 5, no. 125.
[82] Wrottesley, loc. cit.
[83] Chan. Inq. p.m. 15 Ric. II, pt. i, no. 70 ; Feet of F. Div. Co. East. 12 Ric. II.
[84] Feet of F. Div. Co. East. 12 Ric. II.

At the same date Maud wife of William Buyton released all her claim in the manor to Elizabeth Chaturley (ibid.).
[85] Wrottesley, op. cit. 380. In 1404-5 Sir Walter Cooksey died seised of the manor of 'Bastewode' held of Katherine Musard by service unknown (Chan. Inq. p.m. 6 Hen. IV, no. 32).
[86] Wrottesley, op. cit. 467 ; Feet of F. Div. Co. Mich. 49 Hen. VI.
[87] De Banco R. Trin. 11 Hen. VII, m. 220.
[88] Feet of F. Worcs. East. and Trin. 4 & 5 Phil. and Mary.
[89] Ibid. Mich. 8 & 9 Eliz.
[90] Ibid. Hil. 29 Eliz.
[91] Harl. Chart. 79 F 6.   [92] Ibid.
[93] Feet of F. Worcs. Mich. 14 Jas. I. In 1608 the manor was claimed by Elizabeth widow of Sir Stephen Culpeper, son of the elder Martin Culpeper (Chan. Proc. Jas. I, C 9, no. 26). Martin Culpeper the younger had died in 1604 and his son Martin in the following year, his sisters Lettice and Anne Culpeper being his heirs (Chan. Inq. p.m. [Ser. 2], ccxci, 118).

and Mary his wife and John and Thomas Culpeper sold the manor to Thomas Rich,[94] who was succeeded by his eldest son, also called Thomas.[95] The latter was created a baronet in 1660–1 for the help that he had rendered to the king when in exile.[96] On his death in 1667 the manor passed to his son William Rich, who sold it in 1707 to Thomas Vernon.[97] It then followed the same descent as Hanbury,[98] with which its manorial rights may have become merged, as it does not appear as a manor after 1819. Astwood Court, which was formerly the residence of George Webb, is now the property of George Hollington.

Another estate at *ASTWOOD*, afterwards called Astwodesstreche or Strecches Astwood, belonged from very early times to the Streche family. Osbert Streche was holding land in Worcestershire in 1201–2.[99] In 1220 Richard Streche was involved in a suit with John de Inkberrow as to land at Astwood, which John said had been held by a certain Sibilla in the time of Henry II, and on her death without issue had passed to her two aunts Edith and Edwina. Edith's right descended to her great-grandson John de Inkberrow, the claimant, and Edwina's right came to Walter de Portu. Richard refused to answer because Walter de Portu was not mentioned in the writ,[100] but he evidently gained the suit.[1] In 1243, however, the land which belonged to the wife of Richard Streche of Astwood was taken into the king's hands.[2] At the same date Robert Streche was paying relief for land in Worcestershire.[3] Robert died in 1261–2 holding in Feckenham certain land by service of being the king's woodward in the wood called 'Le Wercwode,' and the profits of the king's bailiwick of the forest of Feckenham with the lawing of dogs. He also held other land in Feckenham of Robert de Morton, and of the Abbot of Bordesley.[4] His son and successor Ralph Streche died about 1301 holding land in Feckenham, to which his son Robert succeeded.[5] Robert sold property in Astwood to Richard de Hawkeslow about 1319.[6]

Henry Winterfield was in possession of land at Astwood in 1375–6,[7] but it is possible that the Streches' estate at Astwood afterwards passed, like Hawkesley in King's Norton, from the Hawkeslows to the Staffords of Grafton, for in 1486–7 John Darell and John Pimpe obtained a grant of all the land in Feckenham forfeited in the previous year by Humphrey Stafford,[8] and this land then followed the descent of Hawkesley in King's Norton parish,[9] being apparently restored with it to Sir Humphrey Stafford, for in 1553 his son Sir Humphrey sold a messuage and land in Astwood to Thomas Clarke[10] and a farm called Ruddyalls or Broderiche in Feckenham to John

Morgan of Blatherwycke.[11] From that time the history of the former estate has not been traced. The latter was in 1618 in the possession of William Cookes of Norgrove,[12] and it probably became merged in that estate.

The Empress Maud seems to have given to her foundation at Bordesley certain rights in Feckenham Forest and a 'porcaria' and half a virgate of land at Feckenham. Nicholas son of Bernard gave the monks 12 acres at Feckenham.[13] These gifts were confirmed by Henry II and Richard I,[14] and seem to have included land at Astwood, for at the Dissolution the monks were receiving various rents from Feckenham and Astwood.[15] In 1538 the abbot conveyed this estate as the manor of Astwood and Feckenham to the king.[16] As the 'manor of Feckenham Astwood' it was held by John Phillips in 1809 and 1816 in right of his wife Emma,[17] the heiress of the Vernon family.

NORGROVE was held of the manor of Feckenham.[18] In the 14th century it seems to have belonged to a family called Northgrove, although Elizabeth de Northgrove and William her son are the only members of the family who are known to have held it. Elizabeth died about 1378[19] and William in 1381, leaving as his heirs his two sisters Catherine and Maud,[20] one of whom probably married one of the Jennetts, to whom Norgrove afterwards belonged. Richard Jennett of Norgrove received a general pardon from Edward IV in 1471,[21] and probably held the manor which afterwards belonged to Humphrey Jennett.[22] William son of Humphrey died seised of it in 1548, leaving his son Humphrey, then ten years old,[23] in the custody of his wife Elizabeth. She afterwards married Richard Hopton, and with him seems to

JENNETT of Norgrove. *Argent two cheverons between six martlets gules.*

have taken possession of Norgrove, refusing to give it up when her son Humphrey came of age.[24] Humphrey, having no son, settled it on his daughter Anne on her marriage with William son of Henry Cookes,[25] from whom it passed to their son Edward Cookes, who died in 1637.[26] His son William Cookes inherited the manor of Bentley Pauncefoot in Tardebigge parish from his uncle, and since that date Norgrove has descended with Bentley[27] (q.v.), now belonging to Mrs. Cheape of Bentley Manor.

SHURNOCK (SciranAc, x cent.; Shirnak, xiii cent.; Shurnak, xvi cent.) was granted before the

[94] Feet of F. Worcs. East. 10 Chas. I.
[95] G.E.C. *Complete Baronetage*, iii, 180.
[96] Ibid.
[97] Ibid.; Feet of F. Worcs. East. 6 Anne.
[98] Recov. R. Trin. 18 & 19 Geo. II, rot. 48 ; East. 59 Geo. III, rot. 289.
[99] *Rot. Canc.* (Rec. Com.), 129.
[100] Assize R. 1021, m. 13.
[1] Pipe R. 4 Hen. III, m. 14 d.
[2] *Excerpta e Rot. Fin.* (Rec. Com.), i, 398.   [3] Ibid. 397.
[4] *Cal. Inq. p.m. Hen. III*, 149.
[5] Chan. Inq. p.m. 28 Edw. I, no. 18 ; *Cal. Close*, 1296–1302, p. 456.
[6] *Cal. Pat.* 1317–21, p. 328.
[7] Inq. a.q.d. file 386, no. 16.
[8] Pat. 2 Hen. VII, pt. i.
[9] *Cal. Inq. p.m. Hen. VII*, i, 546 ;

L. and P. Hen. VIII, ii, 1182 ; Chan. Inq. p.m. (Ser. 2), xxiv, 83.
[10] Recov. R. D. Enr. East. 1 Mary, m. 9.   [11] Ibid. m. 10.
[12] Exch. Dep. Mich. 16 Jas. I, no. 26.
[13] *Cal. Chart. R.* 1257–1300, p. 63.
[14] Ibid. 63–6.
[15] Dugdale, *Mon. Angl.* v, 411, 412, 413 ; *Valor Eccl.* (Rec. Com.), iii, 272.
[16] Feet of F. Div. Co. Trin. 30 Hen. VIII.
[17] Prattinton Coll. (Soc. of Antiq.) ; Priv. Act, 56 Geo. III, cap. 27.
[18] Chan. Inq. p.m. 6 Ric. II, no. 59.
[19] Ibid. 2 Ric. II, no. 36.
[20] Ibid. 6 Ric. II, no. 59.
[21] *Cal. Pat.* 1467–77, p. 304.
[22] Exch. Dep. Mich. 34 & 35 Eliz. no. 21.

[23] Chan. Inq. p.m. (Ser. 2), lxxxvii, 96.
[24] Chan. Proc. (Ser. 2), bdle. 99, no. 57 ; Chan. Inq. p.m. (Ser. 2), cxxvi, 155.
[25] Chan. Proc. Jas. I, C 9, no. 24 ; Chan. Inq. p.m. (Ser. 2), ccclxxxi, 161.
[26] Ibid. ccclxxxiii, 91.
[27] Recov. R. Worc. Trin. 7 Geo. IV, rot. 134. Norgrove did not pass from the Cookes to the Hemmings at the same time as Bentley Pauncefoot. The latter was purchased about 1844 by Richard Hemming, needle-maker, Redditch. He afterwards bought Norgrove, and Mrs. Cheape, one of his daughters, succeeded under his will. See also Exch. Dep. Mich. 34 & 35 Eliz. no. 21 ; Mich. 16 Jas. I, no. 26.

Conquest to the Prior and convent of Worcester by a widow Wihburga.[28] It is not mentioned in the Domesday Book, being probably then included in the manor of Inkberrow, of which it was a constable-wick at the end of the 18th century.[29] In 1240 the prior was receiving a rent of 5s. from Shurnock,[30] and he was holding the manor in the time of Edward I,[31] and continued to do so until the Dissolution.[32]

Habington states that Shurnock was given to the priory of Worcester by William Molyns.[33] This William is probably to be identified with William de Molendinis, called lord of Shurnock in an undated deed of the 13th century,[34] who in 1292 obtained licence to give to the Prior and convent of Worcester land to the yearly value of 100s. in Shurnock.[35] At about the same time the prior and convent obtained grants of land at Shurnock from various donors.[36]

The manor was granted in 1542 to the Dean and Chapter of Worcester,[37] and confirmed to them in 1609.[38] In 1650 the capital messuage or farm-house of Shurnock was sold by the Parliamentary Commissioners to John Egiock of Inkberrow,[39] but it was restored to the dean and chapter on the accession of Charles II. At the end of the 18th century the estate passed to the Bearcrofts[40] of Mere Hall, who still hold it.[41]

A tenement called Beanhall, just within the borders of Feckenham, was formerly the residence of the Hanburys of Hanbury Hall.[42] It afterwards belonged to a certain Jane Shelley, who died in 1610, leaving it to her cousin Edward Lingen, son and heir of William brother of John Lingen, the father of Jane.[43]

A capital messuage in Feckenham called *TEMPLE ARDLEY* was inherited in 1616–17 by John Hanbury from his mother Margaret.[44] It evidently passed from the Hanburys to the Neales by the marriage of Anna Maria, daughter of John Hanbury, with Henry Neale about the end of the 17th century,[45] and is mentioned in the will of Mary Neale, who left it in 1805 to Edward Vansittart.[46] It is probably to be identified with the land in Feckenham returned in the *Testa de Nevill* as having been alienated by William son of Robert de Feckenham to the Templars of the Preceptory of Balsall,[47] but it is not known how it passed to the Hanburys.

The tenement called *WALLHOUSE*, formerly in Hanbury, now probably represented by Wallhouse Farm in Feckenham, appears to have belonged to the Rudings of Martin Hussingtree, for Edward second son of John Ruding is called 'of the Wallhouse' in

the visitation of 1569.[48] He left two daughters, Alice and Anne, the former of whom married Thomas Grant.[49] According to Nash the estate afterwards passed to the Cheatles of Worcester.[50] It seems to have belonged to a Thomas Cheatle, who agreed to settle it on his son Richard on his marriage with Margery daughter of Andrew Henley of Taunton, Somerset. Afterwards, however, Thomas settled the manor on another son Thomas, and early in the 17th century Margery and her son Richard sued Thomas for the estate.[51] Thomas Cheatle of Wallhouse died in 1690,[52] and it was probably his son Thomas who died in 1714, and appears to have been succeeded by John Cheatle.[53] From the Cheatles it passed to the Vernons of Hanbury.

The *PARK* at Feckenham is first mentioned in 1177–8,[54] and descended with the manor until the 17th century.

A mill is mentioned with the manor in 1086,[55] and seems to have followed the same descent until the 17th century.[56] About 1656 the lord of the manor expended £20 in repairing the mill, but it is not mentioned after this time.[57] There is now a corn-mill at Beanhall and a needle-mill in the town and another called Old Yarr Mill to the north-east of the town.

The fish-pond at Feckenham seems to have been of considerable importance. It was undergoing repairs in 1163–4 [58] and in many of the succeeding years, and appears to have been partially reconstructed in 1205.[59] It is constantly mentioned as an important appurtenance of the manor, and was known from the 14th century as Feckenham Pool.[60] It is mentioned as a mill-pool in 1585,[61] but had evidently been drained before 1656, when it is spoken of as grounds called 'Feckenham Pooles,' and was still appurtenant to the manor.[62] The site of the pool seems to have afterwards become a separate estate, and, according to Nash, was sold by one of the Leightons to the Vernons, and was held by Henry Cecil, in right of his wife Emma daughter of Thomas Vernon, at the end of the 18th century.[63] It must, however, at one time have belonged to Sir Thomas Cookes, who died in 1701, as he endowed the grammar school at Feckenham with £50 a year from the estate called Feckenham Pools.[64]

The church of *ST. JOHN THE BAPTIST* consists of a chancel 39 ft. by 19 ft., nave 49 ft. 6 in. by 26 ft., north aisle 12 ft. 9 in. wide, west tower 15 ft. by 14 ft. 6 in. and a south porch. These measurements are all internal.

CHURCH

[28] Heming, *Chartul.* (ed. Hearne), 336; Birch, *Cart. Sax.* iii, 206.

[29] Nash, op. cit. ii, 9.

[30] Hale, *Reg. of Worc. Priory* (Camden Soc.), 64b.

[31] Nash, op. cit. i, Introd. 36, quoting MSS. in Lord Shelburne's library.

[32] *Valor Eccl.* (Rec. Com.), iii, 223.

[33] op. cit. i, 131.

[34] Prattinton Coll. (Soc. Antiq.), Deeds of D. and C. of Worc. no. 280.

[35] *Cal. Pat.* 1281–92, p. 474.

[36] Prattinton Coll. (Soc. Antiq.), Deeds of D. and C. of Worc. no. 148, 214, 24, 147, 195, 119.

[37] Pat. 33 Hen. VIII, pt. v, m. 19.

[38] Ibid. 6 Jas. I, pt. xii, no. 2.

[39] Close, 1650, pt. xxiv, no. 18.

[40] Nash, op. cit. ii, 9.

[41] Information by Mr. J. Willis-Bund.

[42] Anct. D. (P.R.O.), C 2785 ; Nash, op. cit. i, 440.

[43] Chan. Inq. p.m. (Ser. 2), cccxxxii, 163.

[44] Fine R. 14 Jas. I, pt. ii, no. 14.

[45] Burke, *Landed Gentry* (1846) ; see under Advowson.

[46] P.C.C. 854 Nelson.

[47] op. cit. 43.

[48] *Visit. of Worcs.* 1569 (Harl. Soc. xxvii), 115.

[49] Ibid.

[50] Metcalfe, *Visit. of Worc.* 1682, p. 31.

[51] Chan. Proc. (Ser. 2), bdle. 398, no. 117, 119.

[52] Metcalfe, loc. cit. In 1693 the Wallhouse in the parish of Hanbury belonging to Dame Anne Rouse was certified as a place of worship for Nonconformists (Noake, *Guide to Worc.* 193).

[53] Nash, op. cit. i, 553, from monumental inscriptions in Hanbury Church.

[54] *Pipe R.* 24 *Hen. II* (Pipe R. Soc.), 44.

[55] *V.C.H. Worcs.* i, 321a.

[56] *Cal. Close,* 1296–1302, p. 341; Pat. 27 Eliz. pt. xi, no. 2 ; 7 Chas. I, pt. xix ; Exch. Spec. Com. no. 4774, 4777.

[57] Exch. Dep. Mich. 1656, no. 11.

[58] *Pipe R.* 10 *Hen. II* (Pipe R. Soc.), 4.

[59] *Rot. Lit. Claus.* (Rec. Com.), i, 19, 100b, 520 ; ii, 115.

[60] *Cal. Pat.* 1334–8, p. 372 ; Chan. Inq. p.m. 20 Ric. II, no. 97 ; *Cal. Pat.* 1405–8, p. 64 ; 1461–7, p. 45 ; Pat. 5 & 6 Phil. and Mary, pt. i, m. 16 ; 27 Eliz. pt. xi, m. 30, no. 2.

[61] Pat. 27 Eliz. pt. xi, m. 30, no. 2.

[62] Exch. Dep. Mich. 1656, no. 11.

[63] Nash, op. cit. i, 440.

[64] Ibid. 443.

The 12th-century church consisted of a chancel and nave, and the first tower was either contemporary with the nave or was added shortly afterwards. In the 13th century a north aisle was built, which was completely reconstructed in the 15th century, together with the tower, though here much of the earlier walling was retained.

The chancel was entirely rebuilt in 1853 and the south wall of the nave in 1866–7, when the porch was added and other repairs done to the stonework. All the chancel windows are modern, that in the east wall being of three lights with a traceried head.

The chancel arch is of two chamfered orders, apparently old, the inner order springing from modern moulded corbels.

The nave arcade consists of four bays of pointed arches with circular columns, the bases of which are, with one exception, modern. The first and second columns have moulded bell capitals sadly mutilated, while that to the eastern respond has been recut. The bell to the third column is carved with typical 13th-century trefoiled leaves, and towards the south-west a crowned head; the capital to the west respond is similar, but its very overhanging bell has a filleted round for the top member instead of the leaves. The three south windows and the porch are modern. The south doorway has a pointed head and is of two chamfered orders. The three-light east window of the north aisle appears to be all of 15th-century date and is built in red sandstone, with vertical tracery in the head and a two-centred drop arch. The quoin stones of the old nave angle (south of this window) are of several differently tinted stones, grey, red, and white in the lower parts and brown and green above. Most of the stonework of the first two north windows is modern, and both are of three lights with two-centred heads. The north doorway, like the south, has a pointed head, and appears to have been rebuilt with the old stones. The west and north-west windows of the aisle are each of two lights under a four-centred head, and have been much restored. The aisle is supported externally by modern buttresses. There are no quoin stones to the angle of the original nave at the west end of the aisle, but a straight joint is visible in the lias rubble walling.

The tower is of two stages. A pointed archway of two continuous chamfered orders opens into it from the nave. The 15th-century west window has three lights under a traceried head, and small rectangular lights pierce the side walls above the intermediate string-course. The bell-chamber is lighted towards the east by a pointed window, which has lost its tracery, and is partially blocked with stone to receive the head of the nave gable. The other three windows are of two ogee lights under a square head. Diagonal buttresses of four stages support the western angles of the tower, and above the roof are two early clasping buttresses to the eastern angles. The embattled parapet has panelled and crocketed pinnacles at the corners with angel corbels below. The walling of the tower to a line just below the belfry windows is of small coursed rubble with bands of larger stones,

but above this line the larger stones predominate. The roofs are modern, as are the font and cover. The sedilia and the east wall are panelled with 18th-century woodwork, and the benches are evidently cut down from the 18th-century box pews. There is an old chest with two lids formed out of a solid tree trunk, and preserved in the church is a pair of wafer irons [64a] having two moulds, the larger with a crucifix, the letters IHS and a heart, all within a radial circle, the smaller with the crucifix alone; its total length is 2 ft. 5 in.

In the easternmost arch of the arcade are traces of ancient red decoration, a wavy line and a band with scalloped edge. In the chancel was formerly a raised tomb with effigies of a knight in armour, and a lady with an infant and three daughters; this was swept away in 1853, and is said to be buried beneath the floor; the panel with the inscription belonging to the tomb still remains on the north wall. It commemorates Sir Martin Culpeper, kt., of Dean, in Oxfordshire, son and heir of Martin Culpeper of Astwood; he married Joyce eldest daughter of Sir Edward Aston of Tixall, Staffs., and died in 1604.

There are several other mural monuments and gravestones of the 18th and 19th centuries.

In the churchyard to the south-east of the chancel is the stump of an old cross.

There are eight bells, the treble and second cast by Taylor, 1866, the third inscribed 'Joseph Hemming and Edward Getley did contrive to have 6 where was but 5,' 1776, the fourth with inscription 'Cantate Domino Canticum Novum 1676,' the fifth by Henry Bagley, 1640, the sixth of the same date inscribed 'God save the King,' the seventh by T. Mears, 1841, and the tenor dated 1640 and inscribed 'By my voyce people may know to come to heare the word of God.'

The communion plate consists of a cup, paten, and flagon of modern date.

The registers previous to 1812 are as follows: (i) baptisms and burials 1538 to 1653, marriages 1538 to 1652; (ii) baptisms and marriages 1653 to 1664, burials 1653 to 1663; (iii) baptisms and marriages 1664 to 1704, burials 1663 to 1704; (iv) baptisms and burials 1705 to 1756, marriages 1705 to 1753; (v) baptisms and burials 1757 to 1791; (vi) marriages 1754 to 1790; (vii) marriages 1790 to 1812; (viii) baptisms and burials 1792 to 1812.

ADVOWSON The church and tithes of Feckenham were granted soon after the Conquest by William Fitz Osbern Earl of Hereford to the Abbot and convent of Lire in Normandy,[65] who continued to hold them until the 14th century.[66] During the 14th century all the abbey's possessions were taken into the king's hands on account of the war with France and remained in the Crown until 1414,[67] when Henry V granted them to the priory of Sheen in Surrey.[68] The advowson of Feckenham belonged to the priory until the Dissolution.[69] It was granted with the rectory in 1545 to Richard and Robert Taverner,[70] who in the same year sold them to Geoffrey Markham and

---

[64a] This was found some ten years ago in the thatch of a cottage and given to the church.

[65] *V.C.H. Worcs.* i, 321a.

[66] *Reg. G. Giffard* (Worcs. Hist. Soc.), 212, 541; but see *Cal. Pat.* 1232–47, p. 34; Close, 19 Hen. III, pt. i, m. 12.

[67] *Cal. Pat.* 1324–7, p. 248; 1338–40, p. 75; 1340–3, p. 288; 1348–50, p. 307; 1392–6, p. 19; 1399–1401, p. 248.

[68] *V.C.H. Surr.* ii, 89.

[69] Com. Pleas D. Enr. Hil. 3 Eliz. m. 10 d.; Dugdale, *Mon. Angl.* vi, 29, 34.

[70] Pat. 37 Hen. VIII, pt. iii; *L. and P. Hen. VIII,* xx (2), g. 496 (7).

Elizabeth his wife.[71] Geoffrey died in 1568.[72] John Markham, his eldest son, died two months after his father, leaving a son John,[73] who seems to have died before 1589, when his only surviving uncle Abraham Markham, with Anne his wife, sold the rectory and advowson to Humphrey Clerke.[74] The latter in 1590 conveyed them for 1,000 years to Martin Culpeper, son and heir of Martin Culpeper, and to Thomas Culpeper of Wilmington, co. Sussex, and in 1597–8 they were settled on Martin Culpeper, the father, and Lettice his wife with reversion to Martin the son in tail-male.[75] The latter died in 1604 and his only son Martin in the following year,[76] leaving this property to his uncle Stephen Culpeper, to whom Elizabeth Clerke had sold her right in the advowson and rectory in 1595–6. Stephen also died without issue in 1606,[77] and was succeeded by his cousin John Culpeper of Sussex, who held the advowson in 1625.[78] Mr. Robbins claimed the patronage in 1653,[79] and Henry Neale was patron in 1697.[80] According to Nash,[81] the Neales inherited the advowson and rectory from the Hanburys, therefore it is possible that both passed at the same time as Astwood to Thomas Rich,[82] and that he may have settled them on his daughter Anne and her second husband, John Hanbury of Feckenham, whose daughter Anne Maria married the above Henry Neale.[83] The advowson remained in his family for more than 100 years, passing from him in turn to his two sons, John, who died without issue male, and Thomas.[84] The latter was also succeeded by two sons, Joseph Macpherson Neale, who died unmarried in 1780, and John, who died childless in 1793, leaving most of his property, including the advowson of Feckenham, to his widow Mary.[85] By her will proved 1805 she left it to trustees for the use of the Rev. Edward Vansittart, a great-grandson of the first John Neale, in tail-male on condition that he would take the name of Neale.[86] He died in 1850,[87] and the advowson remained in the hands of trustees until 1909, when it was transferred to the Bishop of Worcester.

There was probably a private chapel in the Royal Lodge of Feckenham, for in 1176 a sum of £19 10s. was spent in works in the chapel of Feckenham.[88]

The church of St. Matthias and St. George at Astwood Bank was consecrated in 1884 by Dr. Philpott, Bishop of Worcester. It consists of a chancel and transept in the style of the 13th century. There is also a chapel of ease at Callow Hill.

In 1617 licence was given to the overseers of the poor of Feckenham to erect a cottage for a poor-house on waste land in the manor of Astwood.[89]

Parts of the parish of Feckenham were assigned to the new ecclesiastical parish of Headless Cross in 1850.[90]

There is a United Methodist chapel at Feckenham,

Wesleyan Methodist chapels at Ham Green and Astwood Bank, and a Baptist chapel, built in 1813, at Astwood Bank.

The Free School was founded by *CHARITIES* will of Richard Hanbury.[91]

The endowments consist of the old school building used as a cottage, let at £8 a year ; rent-charge of £6 13s. 4d. payable out of Warkwood Estate ; rent-charge of £50, payable out of Dunstall Court Estate, known as Thomas Cookes' endowment ; and a rent-charge of 6s. 8d., payable out of Irish's Close, known as the Arthur Bagshaw endowment.

The following charities are regulated by a scheme of the Charity Commissioners 14 June 1907, under the title of the United Charities, namely, the charities of :

1. Henry Hewes, will (date not mentioned), consisting of an annuity of £2 12s., issuing out of lands at Lentall, in the parish of Aymestrey, co. Hereford, for bread for six poor people every Sabbath Day ;

2. Sir John Hanbury, will, 1639, being an annual sum of £13 for distribution in bread, paid by the Merchant Taylors' Company ;

3. Job Burman, will, 1704, being an annual sum of 10s. on a house and land at Tamworth ;

4. John Wiggett, will, previous to 1765, being 20s. a year issuing out of land known as Cook's, for distribution on Sunday next after Candlemas Day to poor widows and widowers ;

5. Charities of William Butler, will, 1773, and Samuel Watts, consisting of a rent-charge of £4 10s. issuing out of a cottage and garden at Grafton Flyford ;

6. Robert Hunt, will, proved 21 October 1807, £100, interest to be applied every Christmas Eve in bread ;

7. Christopher Hunt, will, proved 22 August 1814, £100, interest to be applied every Christmas Eve in meat.

These legacies are represented by £199 10s. consols, producing yearly £4 19s. 8d.

By the scheme the vicar is appointed an *ex officio* trustee to act with four representative trustees, one to be appointed by the urban district council of Redditch and three to be appointed by the parish council of Feckenham, to be resident in each of the three wards of the parish. The income of the charities is applied mainly in the distribution of bread and meat.

In 1824 Robert Bolton Waldron, by codicils to his will proved in the P.C.C. 24 March, bequeathed £100, the interest to be applied for the benefit of the poor of the Callow Hill Division. The legacy, less duty, is represented by £85 7s. 10d. consols, producing £2 2s. 6d. yearly.

In 1890 the Rev. Alfred Marshall by his will left £50, invested in £51 4s. 1d. consols, the annual

[71] *L. and P. Hen. VIII*, xx (2), g. 910 (82).

[72] Chan. Inq. p.m. (Ser. 2), clxvii, 113. He is said to have made in 1554 a fraudulent conveyance of the rectory and advowson in order to settle it on his three younger sons Abraham, Anthony and Fulk (Pat. 1 Mary, pt. xiv, m. 21 ; 1 & 2 Phil. and Mary, pt. xi, m. 2). Anthony died without issue on 1 Dec. 1567.

[73] Chan. Inq. p.m. (Ser. 2), clxvii, 113. John had livery of a third of the rectory

and advowson in 1583, possibly on the death of his uncle Fulk (see foot-note above) ; Fine R. 25 Eliz. pt. i, no. 54.

[74] Pat. 31 Eliz. pt. xv, m. 21 ; Feet of F. Worcs. Trin. 31 Eliz.

[75] Harl. Chart. 79 F 6.

[76] Chan. Inq. p.m. (Ser. 2), ccxci, 118.

[77] Ibid.

[78] Inst. Bks. (P.R.O.).

[79] *Cal. S. P. Dom.* 1653–4, p. 164.

[80] Inst. Bks. (P.R.O.).

[81] op. cit. i, 442.

[82] Richard Robbins was a party to the

conveyance of Astwood (Feet of F. Worcs. East. 10 Chas. I).

[83] Burke, *Landed Gentry* (1846).

[84] Ibid. ; Inst. Bks. (P.R.O.).

[85] Burke, op. cit.

[86] Ibid. ; P.C.C. 854 Nelson.

[87] Burke, *Landed Gentry*, 1906.

[88] Pipe R. 22 Hen. II, m. 3.

[89] *Var. Coll.* (Hist. MSS. Com.), i, 294.

[90] *Lond. Gaz.* 11 Jan. 1850, p. 82, see Tardebigge.

[91] See article on Schools, *V.C.H Worcs.* iv.

dividends, amounting to £1 6s. 8d., to be distributed among poor members of the congregation of the parish church. The several sums of stock are held by the official trustees.

The Church Estate consists of two houses and about 30 a. let at £50 a year, which is applied in salaries of the organist and verger and towards repairs of the church.

FRANKLEY

Franchelie (xi cent.); Frangelee (xii cent.); Frankeleg, Francele, Fraunkel (xiii cent.).

The parish of Frankley is situated on high ground 3 miles south-east of Halesowen, the lowest part being in the north-west about 500 ft. above the ordnance datum, near the brook which divides the parish from Hunnington. The parish is situated on the east side of a continuation of the Clent and Lickey Hills. Frankley Beeches, a high point in the parish, is one of the great landmarks. The ridge from thence to Frankley Hill commands fine views, extending from the Cotswolds, Edge Hill, and the Leicestershire Hills by Barr Beacon and Dudley to the Wrekin and North Clee, and on a clear day as far as the Berwyn range, 70 miles away. The principal roads are a branch from Scotland Lane in Northfield, which cuts through the parish from east to west and then turns south towards Bromsgrove, and a road from Rubery station, which runs northward through the parish. This station, which is just within Frankley parish, is on a branch line of the Midland railway and was opened in 1881. There are reservoirs here for the storage of the water conveyed from Wales for the supply of Birmingham.

The village of Frankley, in the north-east of the parish, is very small and consists of the church, a farm called Westminster Farm, and a few cottages. The site of the old manor-house lies to the west of the church. It was formerly the chief seat of the Lyttelton family, but during the Civil War was occupied by Prince Rupert, who, on leaving it, burnt it to the ground to prevent its falling into the hands of the enemy. In 1601 the house was described as 'a very fair brick house and in good repair, and hath large and sufficient barns, stables, and outhouses.'[1] The tower of the present church was built out of the ruins of Frankley Hall.[2] The rectory is about a quarter of a mile further west, where the two principal roads intersect. The National school was built in 1865 and has since been enlarged.

Frankley Green[3] was formerly common land running on each side of the roadway now bearing the name. The irregular line of its boundaries can still be traced.

The parish, which is entirely agricultural, has an area of 1,934 acres, of which the greater part is pasture land, 682 acres being arable land and 112 wood.[4] The soil is chiefly clay and the subsoil sandstone and marl. A bed of running sand is found on Frankley Lower Hill Farm, near the railway, where it has caused landslips. A red stone from a quarry at

Holly Hill has been used for many years for road-making in the parish. The best of it has been taken by the Birmingham Corporation to make concrete for their reservoir.

The chief crops are oats, wheat, clover, roots, and recently potatoes. Certain old field-names such as the 'Hopyard,' now part of the station yard, and a 'Hop Leasowe' at Egg Hill suggest a former cultivation of this plant. There is a tradition of flax having been grown, as at the 'Whitening Ground,' and old women forty years ago used to talk of 'hurdening,' i.e. making hurden in their younger days. Some nail-making used to be carried on some thirty years ago.[5]

Among the place-names are Grandynneslone Road,[6] Whickeweye,[7] Bynghameslond, Berghenlond, Slowlond, Hullefeldes,[8] Brande Ground,[9] Hoblets,[10] Jounax, Hobacre, Sling, Welsh Meadow, Sollycroft, Kettles, Grumbling Leasowe, Price's Wood, or Priests' Wood, Ravenhays Wood, Scotland Lane, and California.

MANOR The manor of *FRANKLEY* belonged before the Conquest to a certain Wulfwine, but in 1086 was held by Baldwin of William Fitz Ansculf.[11] The overlordship followed the same descent as the barony of Dudley (q.v.) until 1323,[12] when on the division of John de Somery's lands it was assigned to his younger sister Joan de Botetourt.[13] The representatives of Joan de Botetourt held the overlordship until early in the 15th century.[14] The Bishop of Worcester was said to be overlord in 1481,[15] 1508,[16] and in 1599,[17] after which date the overlordship seems to have lapsed. Of these lords the manor was held by knight service. The amount of service said to be due for it varies in different deeds.

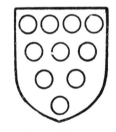

SEE OF WORCESTER.
Argent ten roundels gules.

The names of Baldwin's successors as underlords are not known before 1166, when Bernard de Frankley is mentioned as holding four knights' fees of Gervase Paynel.[18] This Bernard is known to have held the manor of Trysull, co. Stafford, at the same time and occurs about 1160 under the name of Bernard son of Giles de Trysull.[19] In 1196 Miles Pichard conveyed half a hide of land in Frankley to Stephen de Evercy and his wife Constance.[19a] Nash mentions a grant in the reign of Richard I by Philip de Frankley,

---

[1] Exch. Spec. Com. 44 Eliz. no. 2519.
[2] Noake, *Guide to Worc.* 168.
[3] Inform. from Rev. J. H. Bourlay.
[4] Statistics from Bd. of Agric. (1905).
[5] Inform. from Rev. J. H. Bourlay, late rector of Frankley.
[6] Jeayes, *Lyttelton Chart.* no. 67.
[7] Ibid. no. 131.

[8] Ibid. no. 265, 314.
[9] Exch. Spec. Com. 44 Eliz. no. 2519.
[10] Inform. from Rev. J. H. Bourlay.
[11] *V.C.H. Worcs.* i, 316a.
[12] *Red Bk. of Exch.* (Rolls Ser.), 269, 567; *Worc. Inq. p.m.* (Worcs. Hist. Soc.), pt. i, 58; Chan. Inq. p.m. 16 Edw. II, no. 72. [13] *Cal. Close*, 1318–23, p. 631.

[14] Chan. Inq. p.m. 35 Edw. III, pt. i, no. 34; *Feud. Aids*, v, 323.
[15] Chan. Inq. p.m. 21 Edw. IV, no. 55.
[16] Ibid. (Ser. 2), xxii, 48.
[17] Ibid. cclvii, 71.
[18] *Red Bk. of Exch.* (Rolls Ser.), 269.
[19] *Will. Salt Arch. Soc. Coll.* i, 200.
[19a] *Family of Picard*, 14.

son of Philip de Worcester, of land in Frankley to Simon de Heyles.[20] Philip was succeeded by Simon de Frankley,[21] who early in the 13th century gave a rent of 4s. to the Abbot and monks of Halesowen to pray for the souls of Rose his wife and of 'Elicia' his mother.[22] He is mentioned early in the 13th century as holding a quarter of a knight's fee in Frankley,[23] and was living in 1232,[24] but he must have died before 1233, when his son and heir is mentioned as having been given by Roger de Somery as a hostage to Walter de Beauchamp.[25] Simon's heir is generally supposed to have been a daughter Emma,[26] but the above entry shows that he had a son. Further, the Lyttelton charters show that the son's name was Philip and that Simon also had a daughter Margery.[27] Philip is called lord of Frankley in several charters,[28] and Emma lady of Frankley, who married Thomas de Lyttelton,[29] was evidently his heir, whether as his sister or daughter is not known. She too left an only daughter Emma, who married firstly Anger de Talton, who died before 1276,[30] and secondly Nicholas de Wheathampstead. In 1276 Emma, then a widow, gave to the Abbot and convent of Halesowen a rent of 2s. yearly from the land of Hugh de la Ruding in Frankley, for the soul of Anger de Talton, her late husband.[31] In 1280-1 she and her second husband settled the manor on themselves and the heirs of their bodies with remainders to Nicholas son of Emma[32] and to Emma's brother Edmund son of Thomas.[32a] In 1286, under an agreement between Nicholas de Wheathampstead and Nicholas de Talton (called de Frankley) son of Emma by her first husband,[33] it was provided that Nicholas de Wheathampstead was to hold the manor for his life, and that Nicholas de Frankley was to receive yearly from the manor of Frankley 5 marks until he should come of age, and afterwards all the rents of the manor.[34] Emma died in 1298, her son Nicholas being then twenty-eight years of age.[35]

He as Nicholas de Frankley sold the manor in 1299 to Sir Nicholas de Wymale,[36] to whom he also granted the wardship and marriage of his eldest son Thomas,[37] together with certain rents in Frankley which Christine, lady of Frankley (possibly the wife of Philip de Frankley), had held in dower.[38] These conveyances extended over the years 1299 to 1302, but before 1305 Sir Nicholas de Wymale must have exchanged the actual possession of the manor for a life estate in a rent of £25 from it, for in that year Nicholas de Frankley released to Sir John de Benstede, clerk, his right in the manor and the reversion of a yearly rent of £25 which Sir Nicholas de Wymale held for life of his grant.[39] At the same time Richard

de Capenore granted to Sir John a yearly rent of £5 15s. which Nicholas de Frankley had given him.[40]

John de Benstede, who was chief justice of the Common Pleas, received a grant of free warren at Frankley in 1305,[41] and sold the manor in 1308 to Adam de Harvington,[42] whose right in it was confirmed in 1319 by Thomas son of Nicholas de Frankley. In 1323-4 Adam granted the reversion of the manor after his death to Edmund de Grafton and his heirs,[43] and in 1344 Thomas son of Nicholas de Frankley confirmed the manor to Adam de Harvington and John de Grafton, who was presumably the successor of Edmund de Grafton.[44] John son of John de Grafton gave the manor to John Seers, Richard de Doverdale and other clerks, who were probably trustees, and they conveyed it in 1350 to Gilbert Chasteleyn,[45] who in the same year obtained a grant of free warren there.[46] Gilbert and his wife Margaret sold the manor in 1354 to Sir John Beauchamp,[47] who died seised of it in 1360.[48] His brother and heir, Thomas Earl of Warwick, must have sold it to Sir Richard Fitton, for in 1383 the executors of the will of Sir Richard were released by the overlord John de Botetourt from all claims in respect of the manor of Frankley.[49] Joan widow of Sir Richard Fitton in 1384 sold her right to William de Spernall,[50] who in 1399-1400 settled the manor on himself and his wife Alice and their issue male, with contingent remainder to his right heirs.[51] William died without issue male, leaving two daughters, Margaret, who married firstly Henry Hervyle, and secondly William Wybbe, and Joyce, who married William Swynfen.[52] Alice widow of William married Sir Thomas Stafford, and afterwards John Mulsho.[53] She apparently held the manor for life, and made various settlements of it, conveying it to William Sulney and John Alrewich as trustees, and in 1401-2 it was confirmed to them by Edward son of Thomas de Frankley.[54] Later Alice conveyed her claim in the manor to Cornelius de Wirleye, who reconveyed it to Sir Thomas Burdet, Edmund Stafford, Bishop of Exeter, and others, who were probably trustees for Alice's daughters.[55]

In 1405 the manor was claimed from these trustees by Thomas Lyttelton, grandson of the first Thomas Lyttelton of Frankley by his second wife Acelina, daughter of Warin Fitz William de Upton.[56] He based his claim on the fine levied in 1281 by which Nicholas de Wheathampstead and Emma his wife had settled Frankley on her son Nicholas de Frankley and his heirs, with contingent remainders to her half-brother Edmund Lyttelton. Lyttelton stated that

[20] Nash, *Hist. of Worc.* i, 458.

[21] Ibid.

[22] Jeayes, op. cit. no. 6. Rose was the daughter of Ralph de Chenduit and Elicia, who is probably the Elicia here mentioned (Wrottesley, *Ped. from the Plea R.* 480; Cur. Reg. R. Trin. 8 Hen. III, m. 11 d.).

[23] *Testa de Nevill* (Rec. Com.), 40b.

[24] *Cal. Pat.* 1225-32, p. 523.

[25] *Cal. Close,* 1231-4, p. 247.

[26] Burke, *Extinct Peerage,* under Lyttelton of Mownslow.

[27] Jeayes, op. cit. no. 21.

[28] Ibid. no. 19, 20, 21, 22.

[29] Burke, *Extinct Peerage,* loc. cit.

[30] Jeayes, op. cit. no. 37; Burke,

Peerage, under Cobham ; Nash, *Hist. of Worc.* i, 493.

[31] Jeayes, op. cit. no. 37.

[32] By her first husband.

[32a] Feet of F. Worcs. case 259, file 10, no. 21. Edmund was half-brother of Emma.   [33] *Cal. Close,* 1302-7, p. 319.

[34] Ibid. 1279-88, p. 410.

[35] *Worc. Inq. p.m.* (Worcs. Hist. Soc.), pt. i, 58.

[36] Jeayes, op. cit. no. 47, 46.

[37] Ibid. no. 48.

[38] Ibid. no. 50.

[39] *Cal. Close,* 1302-7, p. 319.

[40] Ibid.

[41] *Cal. Chart. R.* 1300-26, p. 59.

[42] Feet of F. Worcs. 2 Edw. II, no. 4.

[43] Ibid. Mich. 17 Edw. II, no. 8.

[44] Jeayes, op. cit. no. 126.

[45] Ibid. no. 144.

[46] Chart. R. 24 Edw. III, m. 4, no. 13.

[47] Jeayes, op. cit. no. 154.

[48] Chan. Inq. p.m. 35 Edw. III (pt. i), no. 34.

[49] Jeayes, op. cit. no. 223.

[50] Ibid. 225.

[51] De Banco R. East. 6 Hen. IV, m. 192 ; Trin. 9 Hen. IV, m. 319.

[52] Ibid.

[53] Ibid.

[54] Close, 4 Hen. IV, m. 39 d.

[55] De Banco R. East. 6 Hen. IV, m. 192.

[56] Aug. Off. Misc. Bks. lxi, fol. 29 ; Burke, *Extinct Peerage,* under Lyttelton of Mownslow.

Thomas son of Nicholas de Frankley and the said Edmund had both died without issue, though it has been seen above that Thomas had a son Edward, who was alive in 1401-2, and the defendants stated was still alive at the time of the suit. Thomas Lyttelton, the claimant, was nephew and heir of Edmund Lyttelton,[57] and, in spite of the numerous sales that had taken place, he recovered seisin of the manor, and in 1410 settled it on his wife Maud.[58] He is said to have died in 1422,[59] leaving an only daughter Elizabeth, who married Thomas Westcote *alias* Heuster.[60] His widow Maud granted the manor in 1429 to John Massy,[61] whom she is said to have married as her second husband.[62] John was holding the manor in 1431,[63] and granted it in that year to Thomas and Nicholas Burdet and others.[64] Possibly they were trustees for Elizabeth daughter of Thomas Lyttelton, for in 1461-2 the manor was settled upon her and her heirs,[65] and in 1476 Thomas Burdet gave up the manor to Elizabeth and her son Sir Thomas Lyttelton,[66] who was 'known by his mother's name on account of the importance of the property he inherited from her.[67]

He was made justice of the Common Pleas in 1466, and is famous for his book on Tenures, which he wrote for his son Richard, who was a barrister.[68] In 1476 he obtained an inspeximus from Edward IV confirming his right to the manor of Frankley.[69] He died seised of it in 1481 and was succeeded by his eldest son William,[70] who was knighted by Henry VII after the battle of Stoke in 1487.[71] Sir William died in 1507, having left the manor of Frankley to his wife Mary for her life.[72] His son John married Elizabeth daughter of Sir Gilbert Talbot, and settled the manor on her in 1531.[73] He died in the following year, and was succeeded by a son John,[74] who obtained livery of the manor in 1541.[75] The manor of Hagley was purchased by this John in 1565,[76] and the further descent of Frankley is identical with that of Hagley,[77] Viscount Cobham being at present lord of both manors.

A tenement called *OLDENHULL* in Frankley belonged to a family of that name in the 13th and 14th centuries.[78] John son of John de Oldenhull was outlawed in 1353 or 1363,[79] and his property was taken into the king's hands. In 1382 Oldenhull was claimed and recovered by Sir Richard Fitton as lord of Frankley,[80] and continued to be held with the manor.[81]

A deer park existed at Frankley in 1360, and it was then worth nothing beyond the keep of the deer.[82] At the beginning of the 17th century it is said to have contained twenty red deer and 200 fallow deer.[83] It seems to have been disparked after the house was burnt down during the Civil War.

A wood called Bromwich Wood containing 'seaven acres wherein are some few timber trees, some fire wood [and] oak trees, the underwood [being] for the most part alder trees,'[84] is mentioned in the 17th century.

CHURCH The church of *ST. LEONARD* consists of a chancel 24 ft. 7 in. by 13 ft. 2 in., a nave 41 ft. 6 in. by 21 ft. 6 in., a south porch and west tower about 8 ft. 6 in. square. These measurements are all internal.

The earliest details in the building date from the 15th century. The modern east window of the chancel is of three lights with old jambs, the stops to the external label being carved with butterflies. The five windows in the side walls are all modern, as is the chancel arch.

The nave is lit by three two-light windows with square heads in the north wall, with two similar windows and one single light in the south wall, but except for the jambs of the south-eastern window all are modern. The south door and porch are also modern. The modern tower opens with a round arch on to the nave with smaller arches on the north and south, the nave being prolonged on each side to the western face. The west window is of 15th-century date, of two lights, with a four-centred head. Both roofs are old, with arched braces to the principal rafters and moulded wall-plates. The chancel roof has two cambered tie-beams with braces.

The external facing of the church is of red and grey sandstone, and the tower is finished with a plain parapet with pinnacles at the angles.

There were formerly two bells; one being cracked was exchanged for a school bell about 1865. The remaining bell bears the inscription 'Sir IOHN LITTILTON 1588.'

The plate includes a large cup with cover paten of the Puritan type, hall mark 1707. On the foot of the cup is the inscription 'This belongs to Frankley in the County of Worcester and Chappel of St. Kenellum 1708.' The flagon is plated.

The registers before 1812 are as follows : (i) and (iA) bound together, containing baptisms 1598 to 1697, burials 1642 to 1695, marriages 1604 to 1695; baptisms and burials 1701 to 1748, marriages 1701 to 1745; (ii) baptisms and burials 1748 to 1812, marriages 1748 to 1794. The marriages overlap with volume iii, which includes marriages 1754 to 1812.

---

[57] Wrottesley, *Ped. from the Plea R.* 237-8.

[58] Jeayes, op. cit. no. 265.

[59] Burke, loc. cit.

[60] Elizabeth is generally supposed to have married Thomas Heuster as a second husband. The truth, however, appears to be that Thomas Westcote was known also as Thomas Heuster. Elizabeth is spoken of as Thomas Heuster's wife in 1417 (Jeayes, op. cit. no. 274) and as his widow in 1461 (Feet of F. Worcs. Mich. 1 Edw. IV, no. 1), while her son Thomas by Thomas Westcote was born in 1422 (*Dict. Nat. Biog.*). Moreover in 1436 Thomas Westcote *alias* Heuster is mentioned in a Lyttelton charter (no. 326), and in 1440 'Thomas Littulton son of

Thomas Heuster' occurs (Jeayes, op. cit. no. 337).

[61] Jeayes, op. cit. no. 314.

[62] Ibid. Introd. p. viii.

[63] *Feud. Aids*, v, 330.

[64] Jeayes, op. cit. no. 319.

[65] Feet of F. Worcs. Mich. 1 Edw. IV, no. 1.

[66] Jeayes, op. cit. no. 407.

[67] Her other children retained the name Westcote. [68] *Dict. Nat. Biog.*

[69] Jeayes, op. cit. no. 428.

[70] Chan. Inq. p.m. 21 Edw. IV, no. 55. William was married about 1469 to Ellen daughter and heir of Sir Thomas Walsh (Jeayes, op. cit. no. 391*b*).

[71] *Dict. Nat. Biog.* under Thomas Littleton.

[72] Chan. Inq. p.m. (Ser. 2), xxii, 48.

[73] Jeayes, op. cit. no. 434.

[74] Chan. Inq. p.m. (Ser. 2), liv, 137.

[75] Jeayes, op. cit. no. 436.

[76] Feet of F. Div. Co. Trin. 7 Eliz.

[77] For references see Hagley.

[78] Add. Chart. 17390; Jeayes, op. cit. no. 29, 72, 165; Chan. Inq. p.m. 1 Ric. II, no. 45; 2 Ric. II, no. 37.

[79] The inquisitions vary as to the date of his outlawry (Chan. Inq. p.m. 2 Ric. II, no. 37; 1 Ric. II, no. 45).

[80] Jeayes, op. cit. no. 217.

[81] Ibid. no. 223, 265, 314.

[82] Chan. Inq. p.m. 35 Edw. III, pt. i, no. 34.

[83] Exch. Spec. Com. 44 Eliz. no. 2519.

[84] Ibid.

ADVOWSON Frankley was formerly a chapelry annexed to the church of Halesowen. The chapel is first mentioned at the end of the 12th century, when Simon, lord of Frankley, granted to it certain lands in 'Cleilond in Frankley.'[85] Evidently the right of burial belonged to the mother church of Halesowen, since in 1236 Ralph, chaplain of Frankley, was accused of burying a dead body there to the detriment of the mother church, and was obliged to restore the mortuaries then made.[86] Nash mentions a confirmation of the chapel of Frankley to the monastery of Halesowen by Emma de Frankley in 1275–6.[87] This was probably in consequence of a claim by the prior and monks of Dudley to the advowson of Frankley as part of the church of Northfield, but they gave up their claim in 1297 to the Abbot and convent of Halesowen.[88] The advowson of the chapel has always followed the same descent as that of the church of Halesowen[89] (q.v.), and now belongs to Viscount Cobham. The chapelry was declared a rectory in 1866.[90]

By licence of Bishop Polton dated 1427 Maud Lyttelton had an oratory where mass was celebrated at Frankley.[91] A similar licence was granted to Thomas Lyttelton in 1443.[92] This chapel is mentioned in the will of Thomas Lyttelton in 1481 as Trinity chapel, Frankley. He bequeathed to it his 'gode litel massbook and gode vestment with the apparyl to an auter of the same sort of vestments which were my moder's,' while to the chapel of St. Leonard he left his 'great antiphoner.'[93] The Trinity chapel was probably destroyed with the manor-house.

In 1471–2 the Abbot of Halesowen was summoned to answer Sir Thomas Lyttelton why he did not find a priest during all the time Sir Thomas was at Frankley,[94] the reference probably being to the chapel of St. Leonard, as it appears from an earlier suit between the Abbot of Halesowen and the Archdeacon of Worcester that the abbot was bound to find a priest three days a week to perform divine service in St. Leonard's chapel.[95]

After the Dissolution Frankley was served by a perpetual curate, who was provided with a stipend of £10 by the Lytteltons. Sir Henry Lyttelton in the time of Charles II endowed the chapel with tithes amounting to about £40 a year, in lieu of this stipend.[96]

In 1738 Sir Thomas Lyttelton, bart., inclosed a plot of ground round the chapel for a cemetery, and with the bishop's permission it was used as a common burial-ground for the parishioners of Frankley.[97]

The vill of Frankley, being in the county of Worcester, but owning Halesowen, which was in Shropshire, as its parish church, was occasionally assessed for ninths in both counties. The inhabitants complained that this had happened in 1341, and prayed the king for a remedy.[98]

During the 15th century the inhabitants of Frankley subscribed 7d. yearly for the 'hye light.'[99] The church ale at Frankley is mentioned in churchwardens' accounts of Halesowen in 1497.[100]

There are no endowed charities.

GRAFTON MANOR

Grastone (xi cent.).

The parish of Grafton Manor situated to the southwest of Bromsgrove covers an area of 1,510 acres, of which 456 acres are arable land, 1,064 permanent grass and 41 woods and plantations.[1]

The ground is undulating, Breakback Hill, one of the highest points, being about 400 ft. above the ordnance datum. The soil is clay on a subsoil of clay and marl. Agriculture is the only industry.

Grafton originally formed part of the parish of Bromsgrove. The tithes of the chapel were separated from the church of Bromsgrove in the time of Bishop William de Blois (1218–36),[2] and it was probably at this time that Grafton Manor became extra-parochial. It became a civil parish in 1857.[3] Part of it was transferred to Bromsgrove in 1894.[4] There is no village or church and the only important building is the manor-house, standing in the south of the parish about a mile from Bromsgrove.

The present building is of L-shaped plan, with a main block running from east to west, and a wing at the west end projecting southwards. At the end of this wing, but quite independent of it, is the chapel. The greater part of what now survives of the original building appears to be of early 16th-century date. The house as then constructed would probably have consisted of a hall, with the great parlour at the east end, and the existing west wing containing the private apartments, with a small building connecting it with the chapel, which is of the early 15th century. In 1567 an important reconstruction was entered upon by John Talbot, who added the present entrance porch, inserted a new fireplace and south window in the great parlour, and refaced and put in new windows to the east wall of the west wing. All that portion lying between the entrance porch and the west wing, which probably contained the hall, was totally consumed by fire in 1710, the basement story alone surviving. No records remain to show what appearance the house presented previous to the fire, but it seems tolerably certain that this too was refaced in 1567. After the fire the west wing alone was inhabited, and in this ruinous state the building continued till the sixth decade of the last century, when the destroyed portion was rebuilt and the interior wholly remodelled, hardly an original feature surviving above the basement with the exception of the large shield in plaster over the fireplace in the great parlour, which is now known as

---

[85] Jeayes, op. cit. no. 2. The bounds of the land are given in the charter. Being included in the church of Halesowen, Frankley is not mentioned in the Taxation of Pope Nicholas or the *Valor Ecclesiasticus*.
[86] Jeayes, op. cit. no. 13.
[87] op. cit. i, 462.
[85] Jeayes, op. cit. no. 43.

[89] See Halesowen.
[90] *Lond. Gaz.* 14 Dec. 1866, p. 6942.
[91] Worc. Epis. Reg. Polton (1425–33), fol. 26.
[92] Nash, op. cit. i, 463.
[93] *Dict. Nat. Biog.*; Nicolas, *Test. Vetusta*, 365.
[94] Nash, op. cit. i, 463.
[95] Ibid.
[96] Ibid. 464.

[97] Ibid. 463.
[98] *Cal. Close*, 1341–3, p. 105.
[99] Nash, op. cit. ii, App. xxix.
[100] Ibid.
[1] Statistics from Bd. of Agric. (1905).
[2] Heming, *Chartul.* (ed. Hearne), 644.
[3] Stat. 20 Vict. cap. 19.
[4] *Census of England and Wales*, 1901, *Worc.* 28.

the 'music room.' In the rebuilding some of the old mullions appear to have been re-used. A good deal of the old panelling, &c., was taken away by the owner, Lord Shrewsbury.

The house is of two stories with a basement on the north and an attic floor in the roof. The west elevation of the west wing has remained untouched by the Elizabethan reconstruction. It is of red brick with occasional diapering of blue bricks, raised on a sandstone base with a chamfered plinth. The four windows of the attic floor are of two lights with chamfered stone mullions inclosed in stepped gables of brickwork with weathered copings. The chimney shafts consist on plan of two intersecting squares, a type common in the neighbourhood. The windows of the ground and first floors are modern, and many of the original openings have been blocked up. The interior of this wing has been so totally modernized as to completely obscure the original plan.

The entrance front of the house presents no features earlier than the Elizabethan period, with the excep-

and pediment over being supported by three fluted Ionic pilasters. The five-light transomed window of the great parlour to the east of the porch is contemporary with it in date and is finished with an entablature and pediment, the latter carved with the hound of the Talbots, and FIAT VOLVNTAS TVA inscribed below. On the frieze is the following quaint inscription : 'PLENTI : AND : GRASE : BI : IN : THIS : PLASE : WHYLE:EVERI:MAN:IS:PLESED:IN:HIS:DEGRE: | THERE:IS: BOTH PEASE : AND : VNETI : SALAMAN : SAITH :THERE:IS:NON: ACORDE : WHEN : EVERI : | MAN : (WOULDE : BE : A : LORDE).' The portion in brackets is continued on the frieze to the east of the window, which is partially obscured by ivy, so that the exact spelling cannot be vouched for.

In the gable over is a blocked two-light window of the earlier 16th-century date. Near the ground is a fanciful wall-fountain of carved stone with a semi-domed hood and a projecting fluted basin. An early 16th-century brick chimney stack (rebuilt at the top) on the east wall of the same building shows that the original house was conterminous, in this direction, with the present structure. The north or back elevation of the main block is devoid of interest, with the exception of the stone basement story, which is that of the original house, and has two four-centred doorways which have remained untouched. In the basement beneath the great parlour is a large room with a central octagonal post supporting a beam carrying the floor above. The great parlour itself has been entirely modernized,

GRAFTON MANOR HOUSE : WEST FRONT WITH CHAPEL

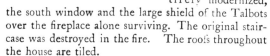

tion of the stepped brick gable of the great parlour and a small window in the east wall of the ground floor with a trefoiled ogee head. The buildings between the entrance porch and the west wing are entirely modern and are designed in harmony with the Elizabethan façade of this side of the wing, which is of brick with stone dressings, and has large two-light windows with ovolo-moulded mullions, and a doorway with flanking pilasters fancifully carved with strapwork. The whole has been crowned by a modern pierced parapet and is somewhat monotonous in appearance. The red sandstone entrance porch has a doorway with a semicircular head, with moulded imposts and archivolt, flanked by coupled and fluted Doric columns, elevated on pedestals and supporting an entablature proper to the order. Over the doorway are the arms of Queen Elizabeth carved with great spirit and beneath them the date 1567. The inner doorway appears to belong to the earlier work. It has moulded jambs and a depressed four-centred head. Above the porch is a small room lit by two transomed windows of two lights each, the entablature

the south window and the large shield of the Talbots over the fireplace alone surviving. The original staircase was destroyed in the fire. The roofs throughout the house are tiled.

The chapel is connected with the west wing by a small brick two-storied building of early 16th-century date, containing the sacristy and a priest's room over it. The chapel itself, measuring about 53 ft. by 17 ft. internally, is entirely of stone and dates from the first half of the 15th century. Though gutted by the fire, the tracery of the windows has survived. Those to the east and west are of four lights, each with vertical tracery under a two-centred head. In the north wall is one window and in the south two, all of similar character. In the north wall is a modern doorway opening into the later sacristy, and to the west of it the original north doorway with moulded jambs and four-centred head. At the west end of the same wall is a blocked doorway with an external two-centred head and a richly moulded rear arch. Immediately opposite in the south wall is a similar entrance with an original stoup to the west of it. The porch into which this opens is an early 19th-century addition. The eastern angles and the centres of the side walls are supported by buttresses of two offsets each. Over the west gable is an original stone bellcote containing one bell. In the north-west window are many pieces of 17th and 18th-century glass, including some Flemish medallions and a fine 16th-century shield of the royal arms encircled with the garter and ensigned with a crown. A shield with the arms of Worcester is probably of early date. To the south-west of the chapel is a large brick barn of the early 16th century similar in style to the earlier parts of the house. The walls are of red brick with occasional diapering and stand on a sandstone base. In the west wall are some original stone-mullioned windows, but the large doorway in the south wall is a modern insertion. On the south side of the chapel is a small burial-ground which has been disused since Grafton Manor ceased to be the head quarters of a Roman Catholic mission.

The disposition of the terraced gardens on the west side of the house does not appear to have been changed since the early 16th century. The walls are all of early bricks with diapering of blue brick, and the grounds are arranged in two broad terraces communicating with each other by stone steps, and leading down to a large lake at the bottom. In the lower terrace is the stew-pond, with rectangular sides of masonry, and stone steps in the centre of the west side, while on the border of the lake is a large circular dovecote of stone with a pyramidal tiled roof, still retaining its original stone cells.

Before the Conquest *MANOR GRAFTON*, a member of the manor of Bromsgrove, was held of Earl Edwin by five thegns, 'who could not withdraw from the lord of the manor.'[5] In 1086 Grafton was held of Urse D'Abitot by one of his knights called Roger.[6] The overlordship followed the same descent as Elmley Castle (q.v.) and is last mentioned in 1419.[7] In 1367–8 the manor was said to be held of the Bishop of Worcester, and in 1369–70 and 1517 of the king in chief.[8] During the 12th and 13th centuries Grafton belonged to a family who derived their name from the manor and may have been descendants of the Domesday tenant Roger. Henry de Grafton, who held a knight's fee of William de Beauchamp in 1166,[9] may have been succeeded

by Richard de Grafton, whose name occurs on a Pipe Roll of 1166–7.[10] In the reign of King John Grafton belonged to Ralph de Grafton[11] and afterwards to his son and grandson John.[12] Edmund de Grafton was holding it in 1315,[13] and in 1349–50 his son and successor John made a settlement of the manor.[14] He must have been succeeded shortly after by his son Roger, who granted the manor in 1350–1 to Thomas Beauchamp, Earl of Warwick,[15] who obtained a grant of free warren there in 1352–3.[16] John de Hastings died seised of it in 1367–8, leaving two daughters Maud and Joan.[17] Grafton was assigned to Maud, who married Ralph Stafford,[18]

Grafton Manor House : Entrance Porch and Great Parlour

and passed after the death of the latter in 1409–10 to their son Humphrey.[19] He was succeeded in 1419 by his son John Stafford,[20] who also inherited

[5] *V.C.H. Worcs.* i, 286a.
[6] Ibid.
[7] *Red Bk. of Exch.* (Rolls Ser.), 567 ; *Testa de Nevill* (Rec. Com.), 40, 43b ; Chan. Inq. p.m. 9 Edw. II, no. 71, m. 53 ; *Cal. Close*, 1313–18, p. 277 ; Chan. Inq. p.m. 11 Hen. IV, no. 38 ; 7 Hen. V, no. 18.
[8] Chan. Inq. p.m. 41 Edw. III (1st nos.), no. 33 ; 44 Edw. III (1st nos.), no. 31 ; (Ser. 2), xxxii, 96.

[9] *Red Bk. of Exch.* (Rolls Ser.), 299.
[10] *Pipe R.* 13 *Hen. II* (Pipe R. Soc.), 67.
[11] Assize R. 1026, m. 23 d.
[12] Ibid. ; Wrottesley, *Ped. from Plea R.* 145 ; *Testa de Nevill* (Rec. Com.), 40 ; *Cal. Pat.* 1232–47, p. 108.
[13] Chan. Inq. p.m. 9 Edw. II, no. 71, m. 53.
[14] Add. MS. 28024, fol. 135.
[15] Feet of F. Worcs. Trin. 24 Edw. III, no. 25.
[16] Chart. R. 26 Edw. III, m. 10, no. 23.

[17] Add. MS. 15663, fol. 181 d. ; Plac. in Canc. 6, no. 20. Two inquisitions were taken on the death of John Hastings, one giving the date of his death as 1367–8, the other 1369–70 (Chan. Inq. p.m. 41 Edw. III [1st nos.], no. 33 ; 44 Edw. III [1st nos.], no. 31).
[18] Chan. Inq. p.m. 48 Edw. III (1st nos.), no. 40.
[19] Ibid. 11 Hen. IV, no. 38.
[20] Ibid. 7 Hen. V, no. 18.

Upton Warren and died seised of both manors in 1422.[21] From his brother and successor Humphrey [22] the manor passed in 1449–50 [23] to his son Sir Humphrey,[24] who was attainted and executed for treason early in the reign of Henry VII.

Grafton and Upton Warren were granted in the same year to Sir Gilbert Talbot, second son of John Earl of Shrewsbury,[25] who died in 1517,[26] and was succeeded by his sons Gilbert [27] and John in turn.[28] John Talbot, grandson of the latter, who inherited the manors from his father John Talbot in 1555,[29] was imprisoned for many years as a recusant. In 1580

STAFFORD. *Or a cheveron gules.*

removed to Aldersgate Street, but owing to the Plague he was allowed to choose another house within 12 miles of London, where he was to remain a prisoner during the queen's pleasure.[31] In 1587 he was at Mitcham, co. Surrey, and he was allowed the liberty of going 'aboute the citie or suburbes of London.' [32] He was still a prisoner in 1588, but was allowed bail to go to Grafton on account of the 'longe sickenes and indisposicion' of his wife,[33] while in 1589 he was allowed to 'enjoy the libertie of six miles compasse' about his house in Clerkenwell on account of his own illness and on condition that he did not go to 'publicke places of assemblie of people as Paules Church and Westminster Hall.' [34] In 1592 he was sent to the prison at Ely,[35] and about 1596 to Banbury Castle.[36] During this time there are several licences allowing him to go into the country on private business, one occasion being a 'dangerous

GRAFTON MANOR HOUSE : TERRACED GARDEN AND LAKE

he was placed in the custody of the Dean of Westminster in order 'that he might not be forced on the soddaine to alter the Relligion he hathe ben broughte up in and ever professed, untill by conference with some learned men he might be resolved in conscience touching the Relligion now professed within the Realme.' [30] By the following year John Talbot had been

deseaze' for which he had 'great need to use the benefit of the Bathes,' [37] and another the death of his wife.[38] He appears to have been finally set at liberty in 1597–8, but in 1603–4 was still paying £20 a month for licence to be absent from church,[39] and later in the same year the benefit of his recusancy was granted to Sir William Anstruther.[40] The latter

[21] Chan. Inq. p.m. 10 Hen. V, no. 18.
[22] Ibid. In 1440–1 Humphrey Stafford had been exempted from serving on juries and other public offices (*Cal. Pat.* 1436–41, p. 540).
[23] Nash, *Hist. of Worc.* i, 157.
[24] Dugdale, *Hist. of Warw.* i, 316 ; Wrottesley, *Ped. from Plea R.* 420. There is a commission to the vicar of Bromsgrove for the marriage of Humphrey Stafford and Margaret daughter of William Stafford in 1482 (Worc. Epis. Reg. Alcock [1476–86], fol. 112).
[25] Pat. 1 Hen. VII, pt. iv.

[26] Exch. Inq. p.m. (Ser. 2), file 1178, no. 8 ; *L. and P. Hen. VIII,* ii, 3784. An inventory of his goods was taken soon after his death (*Var. Coll.* [Hist. MSS. Com.], ii, 308).
[27] Gilbert settled the manors on his brother John in 1529 (*Var. Coll.* [Hist. MSS. Com.], ii, 309), and in 1542 received a confirmation of the grant of both manors to his father (*L. and P. Hen. VIII,* xvii, p. 14).
[28] Chan. Inq. p.m. (Ser. 2), lxxxix, 160.
[29] W. and L. Inq. p.m. vii, 49.

[30] *Acts of P.C.* 1580–1, p. 169.
[31] Ibid. 1581–2, p. 219.
[32] Ibid. 1587–8, p. 102.
[33] Ibid. 1588, p. 389.
[34] Ibid. 1588–9, p. 198.
[35] Ibid. 1592–3, p. 76. See also ibid. 1592, p. 198.
[36] Ibid. 1596–7, p. 523.
[37] Ibid. 1592–3, p. 476.
[38] Ibid. 1596–7, p. 523. See also ibid. 1589–90, p. 9 ; 1590, p. 159 ; 1590–1, p. 142 ; 1597, p. 80.
[39] *Cal. S. P. Dom.* 1603–10, p. 87.
[40] Ibid. 146.

obtained for him a pardon for his recusancy and a discharge from all the forfeits and penalties which he owed,[41] but in 1606 he was again paying £260 a year.[42] He died in 1611, leaving a son George,[43] who succeeded to the title of Earl of Shrewsbury in 1618.[44] Both Grafton and Upton Warren have since remained in the possession of the Earls of Shrewsbury [45] and forming part of the estates settled by the Shrewsbury Estate Act, on the death of Bertram Arthur, the seventeenth earl, in 1856, passed with the title to the Earl Talbot, and did not pass under his will to Lord Edmund Howard. They now belong to Charles Henry John Chetwynd-Talbot twentieth Earl of Shrewsbury.

TALBOT, Earl of Shrewsbury. *Gules a lion and a border engrailed or.*

In 1542 there were two parks, called the Old and New Parks, in the manor of Grafton,[46] but they are not mentioned in any later documents.

CHAPEL The profits of the chapelry of Grafton annexed to the church of Bromsgrove were granted by William of Blois, Bishop of Worcester (1218–36), to the sacrist of St. Mary's, Worcester, who had to provide a taper to burn before the tomb of King John.[47] In 1275 there was a dispute about the advowson between John de Grafton, who claimed by descent from Ralph de Grafton, his grandfather, and the priory of St. Mary's,[48] but finally the former gave up his claim on payment of 35 marks.[49] Though the appropriation of the profits of the chapel of Grafton to the sacrist had been made with the consent of the convent,[50] in 1289 they complained that Bishop Godfrey Giffard had extorted from them the chapel of Grafton, and appropriated it to the use of the sacrist, without making any allowance for the expenses, amounting to £200, to which they had been put in recovering that chapel in the king's court.[51] The advowson next appears in the hands of the Staffords, and was among the possessions of Humphrey Stafford at the time of his attainder, and included in the grant to Sir Gilbert Talbot, kt., in 1486.[52] It then followed the same descent as the manor [53] (q.v.). The chapel, which was dedicated to St. Michael,[54] was still used in the time of Habington, who describes the arms and monuments of the Talbot family in it,[55] but it was in ruins before the end of the 18th century.[56]

In 1292 a sum of £10 was expended in rebuilding the chancel.[57]

There are no endowed charities.

HADZOR

Hadesour (xi cent.) ; Headdes Ofre (xii cent.) ; Haddesour, Hadeshore, Hadesovere (xiii cent.) ; Haddeshore, Haddesore (xiv cent.).

Hadzor is a small parish, well wooded in its western part, occupying an area of 996 acres, which in 1905 included 166¾ acres of arable land, 542 acres of permanent grass, and 32½ acres of woods and plantations.[1] The old road called the Salt Way, now the high road from Droitwich to Alcester, forms the northern boundary of Hadzor, and another road from Droitwich to Oddingley forms part of the western boundary, a branch from it crossing the parish and joining a road from the village.

The village of Hadzor is situated about a mile to the east of Droitwich, southward of the Alcester road. It is somewhat scattered and contains a few half-timbered cottages. The church stands within the park close upon the east side of Hadzor House, which is an 18th-century building with an addition designed by Matthew Habbershaw in 1827. The gardens were laid out at the same time. It is the residence of Major Hubert George Howard Galton, R.A., J.P., and contains a valuable collection of pictures and statuary. The Court Farm is an early 17th-century brick house much modernized.

The Roman Catholic chapel of St. Richard and St. Hubert, beautifully situated in Hadzor Wood, was built by the late Mr. T. H. Galton in 1878.[2] Attached to it is a small school, the only one in the parish. The Protestant children of the parish attend the school at Oddingley, which was annexed to Hadzor for ecclesiastical purposes in 1864.[3]

Dean Brook rises in Hadzor and flows south-east to Himbleton, and the Gitton Brook divides the parish from that of St. Peter, Droitwich. The Worcester and Birmingham Canal passes through Hadzor to the east of the village, and joins the Droitwich Junction Canal on the northern boundary. The parish is undulating, and lies at a height of about 200 ft. above the ordnance datum, the highest parts being in the south-west.

The parish was inclosed under an Act of 1773,[4] and the award, which is now in the custody of the clerk of the peace at Worcester, is dated 2 July 1773.[5] Agriculture is now the only industry, but salt [6] and clay were formerly worked. The soil is principally a stiff marl and the subsoil clay. The Bristol and Birmingham branch of the Midland railway passes through the parish, but the nearest passenger station is at Droitwich.

Among the early place-names are Shirreveshale,[7] found in the 13th century, Ovewood [8] in the 15th

[41] *Cal. S. P. Dom.*1603–10, pp. 157,173.
[42] Ibid. 1580–1625, p. 488.
[43] Chan. Inq. p.m. (Ser. 2), cccxlv, 146.
[44] G.E.C. *Complete Peerage,* vii, 142.
[45] Chan. Inq. p.m. (Ser. 2), dvi, 159.
[46] *L. and P. Hen. VIII,* xvii, p. 14.
[47] Heming, *Chartul.* (ed. Hearne), 644. In 1235 the king claimed the advowson as belonging to the church of Bromsgrove (*Cal. Pat.* 1232–47, p. 108).
[48] Assize R. 1026, m. 23 d.; Wrottesley, *Ped. from Plea R.* 145.

[49] Feet of F. Worcs. case 259, file 10, no. 22 ; *Abbrev. Plac.* (Rec. Com.), 191.
[50] Heming, *Chartul.* (ed. Hearne), 644.
[51] *Ann. Mon.* (Rolls Ser.), iv, 498 ; Thomas, *Surv. of Worc. Cath.* A 146.
[52] Pat. 1 Hen. VII, pt. iv.
[53] Chan. Inq. p.m. (Ser. 2), xxxii, 96 ; lxxxix, 160 ; dvi, 159 ; W. and L. Inq. p.m. vii, 49. [54] Nash, op. cit. i, 164.
[55] op. cit. i, 100–1.
[56] Nash, op. cit. i, 164; Carlisle, *Topog. Dict.*

[57] *Reg. G. Giffard* (Worcs. Hist. Soc.), 420.
[1] Statistics from Bd. of Agric. (1905).
[2] *Cath. Dir.* 1908, p. 151.
[3] *Parl. Papers* (1872), xlvi, 14 d.
[4] Priv. Act, 13 Geo. III, cap. 8.
[5] *Blue Bk. Incl. Awards,* 190.
[6] *V.C.H. Worcs.* i, 315 ; *Cal. Pat.* 1446–52, p. 38 ; *Cal. Inq. p.m. Hen. VII,* i, 1.
[7] Feet of F. Worcs. case 258, file 2, no. 2.
[8] Chan. Inq. p.m. (Ser. 2), clxviii, 58.

century, and Blackmore, Butts Field and Cookescroft[9] in the 16th century.

Before the Conquest Brihtwine held MANOR HADZOR 'as his paternal inheritance for which he owed service to no one but the King.'[10] He granted it to the priory of Worcester when his grandson Edwin became a monk there, and Bricsmaer, his son, the father of Edwin, confirmed the gift.[11] After the Conquest, however, William Earl of Hereford took it from the priory and gave it to his servant, Gilbert Fitz Turold,[12] who was holding it in 1086.[13] The descent of Gilbert Fitz Turold's land is obscure, and it is believed that he forfeited his fief.[14] Much of the land which he held in 1086 subsequently belonged to the honour of Gloucester,[15] but Hadzor passed into the possession of the family of Toeni, and the manor was held of their barony in the 13th century.[16] The overlordship passed from the Toenis to the Beauchamps[17] in the same way as that of Elmley Lovett, but lapsed in the middle of the 14th century, when the tenancy of the manor was acquired by Thomas Earl of Warwick, the manor after that time being held directly of the Crown.[18]

Walter, son-in-law of Gilbert Fitz Turold, was holding the manor as tenant under Gilbert in 1086,[19] but there is no record of his successors until the beginning of the 13th century, when William Fitz Warin was holding half a knight's fee in Hadzor.[20] In 1217–18 Hubert Balistarius granted to William Fitz Warin of Hadzor a wood in Hadzor called Shirreveshale,[21] and in 1256–7 an agreement was made between William Fitz Warin de Wick and William son of William Fitz Warin, by which the former was to hold land at Hadzor and elsewhere for life with reversion to the latter, who was probably his son.[22] William son of William Fitz Warin was in possession of the manor in 1300,[23] and in 1310 John de Burwell is called lord of Hadzor,[24] and was still holding the manor in 1318, when it was settled on himself and Maud his wife.[25] The manor must shortly afterwards have passed to the Cassys, for John Cassy of Droitwich and his son Thomas presented to the church, the advowson of which was annexed to the manor, in 1325 and 1329,[26] and Thomas Cassy was patron in 1349.[27] In 1357–8 Thomas Cassy and others granted certain land in Hadzor to John Alewy for life with reversion to Thomas Beauchamp Earl of Warwick.[28] Thomas Cassy had previously in 1348–9

settled the manor and advowson of the church on himself with reversion to his son John and Elizabeth his wife.[29] John probably died without issue, for Thomas had evidently before 1352 granted the reversion after his death to Thomas Beauchamp Earl of Warwick, who in that year obtained a grant of free warren over the manor.[30] Thomas Cassy was still holding the manor in 1361, when the earl settled it on himself for life, and on his son Thomas in tail-male.[31] From Thomas Beauchamp it followed the same descent as Elmley Castle[32] (q.v.) until it passed into the possession of Henry VII in 1487.[33] Hadzor was among the lands settled in 1533 on Katherine of Aragon, under the name of Katherine, Princess Dowager.[34] It was granted in 1546 to Richard Cupper,[35] who in the following year sold it to John Pakington of Westwood Park and Thomas Pakington his nephew.[36] The latter died in 1571,[37] and his son John sold the manor in 1579 to Nicholas Lewknor of Haseley, co. Oxford.[38] By his will dated 1 June 1580 Nicholas Lewknor left one-third of Hadzor, consisting of the site of the farm and manor, to his wife Mary, and the remaining two-thirds to his brother-in-law Thomas Copley, on condition that with part of the income of the estate he should build and endow an almshouse at Alvechurch.[39] Thomas Copley died in 1593 and his eldest son John, who succeeded him,[40] died without issue in 1606, leaving the two-thirds of Hadzor to his brother Thomas Copley,[41] who sold it to William Amphlett in 1633. The other third of Hadzor passed after Mary Lewknor's death to her husband's sister and heir Jane, wife of Anthony Sheldon, on whom it was settled in 1581.[42] Anthony survived his wife and held her share of the manor until his death in 1584,

CASSY. *Argent on a bend gules three buckles or.*

GALTON. *Ermine a fesse engrailed between six fleurs de lis gules with an eagle's head razed argent between two bezants on the fesse.*

[9] Pat. 21 Eliz. pt. vi, Pakington and Lewknor.

[10] *V.C.H. Worcs.* i, 267.

[11] Heming, *Chartul.* (ed. Hearne), 263–4; *V.C.H. Worcs.* i, 315 n.

[12] Heming, loc. cit.; *V.C.H. Worcs.* i, 266.

[13] *V.C.H. Worcs.* i, 315a.

[14] *V.C.H. Herefs.* i, 279.

[15] Ibid.; see *Testa de Nevill* (Rec. Com.), 40, 43, &c.

[16] *Testa de Nevill* (Rec. Com.), 40, 41; *Red Bk. of Exch.* (Rolls Ser.), 567.

[17] Add. MS. 28024, fol. 191b.

[18] Chan. Inq. p.m. 24 Hen. VI, no. 43; (Ser. 2), clvi, 1. In 1404 the manor was said to be held of the Abbot of Westminster (ibid. 5 Hen. IV, no. 68).

[19] *V.C.H. Worcs.* i, 315a.

[20] *Testa de Nevill* (Rec. Com.), 40, 41.

[21] Feet of F. Worcs. East. 2 Hen. III, no. 2.

[22] Ibid. Mich. 41 Hen. III, no. 1.

[23] *Reg. G. Giffard* (Worcs. Hist. Soc.), 527.

[24] *Cal. Close*, 1307–13, p. 251.

[25] Feet of F. Worcs. case 259, file 16, no. 17.

[26] Nash, *Hist. of Worc.* i, 484.

[27] Ibid.

[28] Add. MS. 28024, fol. 6b; see also fol. 6.

[29] Feet of F. Worcs. 22 Edw. III, no. 12.

[30] Chart. R. 26 Edw. III, m. 10, no. 23.

[31] Feet of F. Div. Co. Mich. 35 Edw. III, no. 83.

[32] Chan. Inq. p.m. 5 Hen. IV, no. 68; 24 Hen. VI, no. 43; Feet of F. Div. Co. Mich. 6 Edw. IV, no. 4; Chan. Inq. p.m. 18 Edw. IV, no. 47. It was granted in 1397 after the forfeiture of Thomas Earl of Warwick to John Earl

of Salisbury (*Cal. Pat.* 1396–9, p. 213).

[33] De Banco R. Hil. 3 Hen. VII, m. 208.

[34] Stat. 25 Hen. VIII, cap. 28. 'Hadser farme' was leased to William Newport and Philippa his wife in the same year (*L. and P. Hen. VIII*, vi, g. 196 [26]).

[35] Pat. 38 Hen. VIII, pt. iii, m. 49.

[36] Add. MS. 31314, fol. 184b, 185.

[37] Chan. Inq. p.m. (Ser. 2), clvi, 1. See also Ct. of Req. bdle. 62, no. 90.

[38] Pat. 21 Eliz. pt. vi, m. 32; Feet of F. Worcs. Mich. 21 & 22 Eliz.; Close, 22 Eliz. pt. ii.

[39] P.C.C. 20 Arundell.

[40] Chan. Inq. p.m. (Ser. 2), cccvi, 155.

[41] Ibid.; Fine R. 8 Jas. I, pt. i, no. 44.

[42] Feet of F. Div. Co. Mich. 23 & 24 Eliz.

Hadzor House : West Front

Hadzor Church : The Nave and Chancel looking North-east

when it passed to their son William,[43] who settled it on his wife Cicely in 1592,[44] and sold it in 1633 to William Amphlett, mentioned above.

The manor remained in his family until the beginning of the 19th century,[45] when it was sold to John Howard Galton, fifth son of Samuel Galton of Dudson, Birmingham, whose grandson Hubert George Howard Galton is now lord of the manor.[46]

The church of *ST. JOHN BAPTIST CHURCH* consists of a chancel 20 ft. by 14 ft. with a modern vestry to the north of it, nave 33 ft. by 20 ft., and a small modern west tower over a porch 7 ft. by 4 ft. These measurements are all internal.

The building is a fine example of the middle of the 14th century, and except for the modern additions is almost completely of that date. It has undergone several restorations, the first being in 1835.

The east wall appears to have been refaced outside, and the exterior of the three-light east window is apparently all new. It has a two-centred traceried head and moulded labels stopping on grotesque heads. On either side of the window inside are canopied niches with flattened ogee heads under crocketed gables terminating in carved finials. The foliated brackets of the niches appear to be modern restorations. In the south-east corner is a piscina recess. The side windows of the chancel, two on the south and one on the north side, are each of two lights with a quatrefoil over. The moulded labels, both inside and out, have ogee points and carved finials. The internal labels on the south stop on carved human heads and on the north side on beasts' heads. A moulded string runs all round the chancel externally under the window sills, and below it, in the south wall, is a small rectangular low-side window now blocked up and invisible internally. The two-centred chancel arch has continuously moulded jambs, and a moulded label on the west face, which terminates in an ogee point and a foliated finial.

There are three windows on each side of the nave, the tracery of which is more varied than that of the chancel windows. They are all original, except the one to the north-west, which is a modern copy, possibly replacing the north doorway mentioned by Dr. Prattinton in 1825 as being then blocked up. The internal labels are similar to those in the chancel

and stop on human heads. To the south-east is another piscina recess with a trefoiled head and ogee apex.

Between the first and second windows on the north side of the nave is an elaborate 14th-century tomb recess now occupied by a modern tomb. The wide two-centred arch has a moulded label finished with a carved finial. Above this is a niche for a figure, with a crocketed, finialled and gabled head, flanked by two other canopied niches of similar character. An outer crocketed label, in the form of a gable (springing from a grotesque head), with flanking pinnacles completes the composition, the space between it and the arch being filled in with blind tracery.

The vaulted porch under the tower and the west doorway are both modern. The small modern tower rises a single stage above the nave roof. The belfry is lighted by lancet windows.

The walling of the exterior generally is a mixture

HADZOR CHURCH FROM THE SOUTH-EAST

of white and red sandstone, ashlar faced. The western parts of the side walls of the nave seem to have been rebuilt when the tower was erected. There are two old buttresses at each corner of the chancel with moulded offsets, finished with trefoiled gablets. The similar buttresses at the angles of the nave have been more or less restored. The plinth, which surrounds the building, batters inward.

The external cornice is moulded with a hollow containing square flowers. Most of it is original, but the raking portion to the east gable is modern.

The roofs with the font, pulpit and altar table are all modern.

All the monuments to members of the Galton and Amphlett families and others are of the 18th and 19th centuries.

[43] Chan. Inq. p.m. (Ser. 2), ccviii, 199.
[44] Feet of F. Worcs. Trin. 34 Eliz.

[45] For pedigree see Burke, *Landed Gentry* (1906); Notes of F. Worc. Trin. 24 Chas. I.; Recov. R. Hil. 1

Geo. I, rot. 115; Hil. 24 Geo. II, rot. 170.
[46] Burke, *Landed Gentry* (1906).

The three windows on the north side of the nave contain a few fragments of fine 14th-century stained glass worked up with modern glass. Of the Annunciation in the westernmost window the old portions are the head of our Lady and a part of her dress. The head of St. Elizabeth and a few other fragments in the second window depicting the Visitation are old. The easternmost, representing the Purification, is all modern except a few pieces of the border.

In the head of the east window are remains of heraldic glass with the arms of Mortimer, Despenser, Beauchamp and Daubeney.

There is one bell,[47] recast in 1894. The inscription of the original bell has been reproduced upon it, and is as follows : 'John Grine Frances Hount 1668 . Soli Deo Gloria, Pax Hominibus.' Below on a shield are the founder's initials, 'J.M.,' for John Martin.

The plate includes a cup of peculiar pattern, with hall mark 1812, the gift of Rev. R. H. Amphlett, 1816, and a salver paten with the inscription on the foot 'The humble gift of Ester Paul to Hadzor Church August 4 1816.'

The registers previous to 1812 are as follows : (i) all entries 1554 to 1746 ; (ii) baptisms and burials 1750 to 1812, marriages 1750 to 1754 ; (iii) marriages 1754 to 1812.

ADVOWSON The advowson followed the descent of the manor,[48] and now belongs to Major H. G. H. Galton. Although the church is known to have existed in 1268,[49] it is not mentioned in the Taxation of Pope Nicholas in 1291. At the time of the Dissolution its value was £6 11s. 6d.[50]

In 1315 the bishop consecrated an altar at Hadzor.[51] An acre of meadow which had been given for the maintenance of lights in the church of Hadzor was valued in the middle of the 16th century at 20d.[52]

CHARITIES William Amphlett, by his will (without date), gave to the poor the sum of £3 6s. 8d. to remain as a certain stock for ever. No payment is now made in respect of this charity.

In 1745 Mrs. Mary Wood, by deed, conveyed to trustees 2 a. called Hempland upon trust out of the rents and profits to pay 20s. yearly to the poorest housekeepers, and the residue of the rents to the rector of the parish.

The land so charged is understood to be occupied by the rector for the time being, but the annuity is not now paid.

HAGLEY

Hageleia (xi cent.) ; Haggelegh (xiv cent.).

The parish of Hagley was at one time part of the forest of Kinver, but was disafforested in 1300-1, as it had only been included in the forest 'since the Coronation of King Henry.'[1]

It comprises an area of 2,431 acres, including 24 acres of inland water, 856 acres of arable land, 1,104 acres of pasture and 271 of wood.[2] The land rises gradually from the western border, where it varies from 270 ft. to 395 ft. above the ordnance datum, to the Clent Hills, just beyond the south-eastern border, where it rises to about 700 ft. Wychbury Hill, a detached hill partly in the parish of Pedmore, attains a height of 700 ft.

The Gallows Brook runs parallel with the southern boundary of the parish.

The main roads from Stourbridge to Bromsgrove and from Kidderminster to Halesowen pass through the parish, the village of Hagley being situated at the intersection of these roads. Hagley Hall and the church and rectory standing in Hagley Park are to the east of the village.

The old hall at Hagley, which is described in 1601 as ' a convenient house built for the most part of wood,'[3] was the scene of the capture of Stephen Lyttelton and Robert Winter, two of the conspirators in the Gunpowder Plot. They had escaped from Holbeach House, and, after wandering about the country for some time, came to Hagley, where a man called Peck concealed them in his house. During the absence of Mrs. Lyttelton they were taken to Hagley Hall, where they were betrayed by one of the servants.[4] Sir Charles Lyttelton made additions to the house

in the reign of William III, but it was taken down in 1760, when the present hall was built by George first Lord Lyttelton.

It stands in the fine park, facing the south-west, with a magnificent view over the undulating and well-wooded country which stretches away from the Clent Hills. The house, which is three stories high, with one in the roof, is built of sandstone, and is symmetrically designed both in plan and elevation. The kitchen and domestic offices occupy the ground floor, the principal apartments being placed on the floor above. The entrance or 'White' hall is reached from the park by two stone staircases, which meet on a wide landing or terrace in front. In the north-west wall of this apartment is a carved stone mantelpiece with a male figure on either side supporting a projecting shelf, above which is a carved panel of satyrs offering sacrifice to Diana. The cornice and ceiling are of elaborate design. Leading out of the hall on the south-east is the Van Dyck drawing room and on the north-west the library, both richly decorated. Occupying the whole of the south-east side of the house on this floor is the gallery, a finely-proportioned room, divided by fluted wooden columns of the Corinthian order into three bays. Behind the hall, in the middle of the north-east front, is the large dining room, and between this and the gallery the drawing room. The walls of the former are decorated with plaster swags and trophies, and the latter is hung with tapestry. The two main staircases are situated in the middle of the building and are top lighted. The northernmost is of stone with a simple iron balustrade, but the southern or

---

[47] There were formerly two, but it is said that one was removed within living memory and placed in the stable turret of the manor-house.

[48] Feet of F. Worcs. 22 Edw. III, no. 12 ; Chan. Inq. p.m. 2 Hen. IV, no. 58 ; Pat. 38 Hen. VIII, pt. iii ;

Close, 22 Eliz. pt. ii ; *Reg. G. Giffard* (Worcs. Hist. Soc.), 4, 527 ; Inst. Bks. (P.R.O.).

[49] *Reg. G.Giffard* (Worcs. Hist. Soc.), 4.
[50] *Valor Eccl.* (Rec. Com.), iii, 269.
[51] Worc. Epis. Reg. Maydston (1313–17), fol. 29.

[52] Aug. Off. Chant. Cert. 60, no. 64.
[1] Prattinton Coll. (Soc. Antiq.).
[2] Statistics from Bd. of Agric. (1905).
[3] Exch. Spec. Com. 44 Eliz. no. 2519.
[4] Lyttelton MSS. quoted by Prattinton in his collection at Soc. Antiq.

front staircase is of painted wood, with double-bellied balusters supporting a heavily moulded handrail. In the housekeeper's sitting room, which is on the ground floor, is a Jacobean fireplace—a relic of the former hall—the upper part only being original. The three panels, divided by Corinthian columns, bear coats of arms, that in the middle being Lyttelton impaling Bromley ; the dexter shield is Lyttelton surmounted by the crest of a blackamoor's head, while the sinister is a lozenge with the arms of Bromley, surmounted by the crest of a pheasant charged with a crescent. These are the achievements of John Lyttelton, esquire, and Muriel Bromley his wife, whom he married in 1590. The elevations are restrained and dignified. The ground stage is rusticated, and at the corners are carried up four square towers, each

are said to have been taken from the remains of the abbey at Halesowen.

Samuel Johnson visited William Henry Lyttelton, afterwards Lord Westcote, at Little Hagley in September 1774,[4a] and describes Lord Lyttelton's new house and the park as equalling his expectations, but states that the church is 'externally very mean, and is therefore diligently hidden by a plantation.'[5] The house he describes as 'one square mass,' with the offices below, and the rooms of elegance on the first floor, with two stories of bedchambers very well disposed above it. 'The bedchambers have low windows, which abates the dignity of the house. The Park has an artificial ruin, and wants water ; there is, however, one temporary cascade.'[6]

Charles Townshend gives the following account of

HAGLEY HALL FROM THE SOUTH

roofed with a low pyramidal roof of slate. The principal front has a slightly projecting façade in the centre, finished with a pediment, and the main cornice, running round the building, is surmounted by an open balustrade. All the windows are square-headed, and those to the first floor have entablatures. In the centre of the ground floor on the north-west front are three semicircular rusticated arches which give access to the servants' quarters and offices. The other elevations are of similar character to the front, and the whole building makes an imposing block.

Among the architectural features erected about the park is 'the castle,' a sham Gothic ruin into which have been built pieces of mediaeval masonry, which

an entertainment given by Lord Lyttelton soon after the house was finished :

'The invitation was universal to all ranks and all parties, and the plan was really magnificent. . . . . Some untoward accidents happened in the execution : for in the first place my lord forgot to have the beds aired ; in the second, he classed the company according to their birth and reputed estates into three divisions, and in the last Mr. Lyttelton, destined to have opened the ball with the first person of the first class, mutinied, and would only dance with a smart girl he had brought in the morning from a neighbouring village. . . . . Before the dinner was ended, everybody was talking of their private affairs and pedigree ; Bacchus's Hall was turned into the Herald's Office ; and the whole company became jealous and sulky. At the end of the three days my Lord's new palace was filled with disgust and complaints, and he is said to have confessed at last that distinctions are not prudent.'[7]

[4a] This was before he succeeded his nephew at Hagley.
[5] A Diary of a Journey into North Wales, 134-8.
[6] Ibid.

[7] MSS. of Marquess of Lothian (Hist. MSS. Com.), 241-2. There is an inventory of goods and furniture at Hagley dated 1750 in N. and Q. (Ser. 3), xi, 190. A full description of the new house is

given in Bishop Lyttelton's Hist. of Hagley, &c., Prattinton Coll. (Soc. Antiq.), and the grounds are described by Thomson in 'The Seasons' (Spring), lines 900-58.

Stakenbridge, Harborough and Blakedown form an almost detached portion of the parish in the south-west, near the Great Western railway station. This district was assigned in 1888 for ecclesiastical purposes to the parish of Churchill, but it is still for civil purposes in Hagley. Harborough Hall stands to the east of the high road from Kidderminster to Halesowen. The gabled front is of half-timber, and the porch, which projects from the centre, extends the whole height of the house. Over the doorway are the date 1635 and the initials W.A.P., probably referring to William and Anne Penn, the house having been long connected with that family. The inner door is plain and nail studded. To the right and left of this door are the two chief rooms of the ground floor, the chimneys forming a block opposite the entrance with the fireplaces back to back. In the centre room of the first floor is a remarkable set of 17th-century furniture, including a bedstead

barley being the chief crops raised. The surface soil varies from a stiff clay to a sandy loam, and the subsoil is breccia and sandstone.

An Act was passed in 1830 for the inclosure of the Brake and Warren lands in Hagley,[8] and the award for these commons is dated 10 November 1831.[9] In 1832 another Act legalized the inclosure of Harborough and Blakedown Commons,[10] the award for which is dated 16 October 1834.[11] In both cases arrangements were made for certain plots to be reserved for gravel-pits and quarries for the repair of the roads in the parish.

Wychbury Hill is the site of an early camp.[12] Several coins have been found here,[13] and in 1738 an iron chain in which was a 'large round Stone about the Size of a Man's head.'[14] A ball of baked clay, supposed to have been a weight for a fishing net, was found in Hagley Park about 1774.[15]

The following place-names occur: Le Vallyng[16]

HAGLEY : HARBOROUGH HALL, ENTRANCE FRONT

with a carved wood canopy and two chairs, one inscribed 'IH RH 1666.' The ceiling of this room is elaborately decorated in plaster-work, the two beams being enriched with a pattern of fir cones and roses.

In the garret is a hiding-place, and another, which contained some books, is stated to have been discovered early in the 19th century. East of the house is a large piece of artificial water.

There are many villa residences in the parish, but the population is mainly agricultural, wheat and

(xiv cent.); Stakynbroke, Hoore Stone[17] (xv cent.); Le Aspes or Lamp Land[18] (xvi cent.).

Before the Conquest *HAGLEY* was held by Godric, a thegn of King Edward the Confessor.[19] It appears in the Domesday Survey as the property of William Fitz Ansculf,[20] and was afterwards held as a knight's fee of the barony of Dudley.[21]

In 1086 it was held under William Fitz Ansculf by Roger.[22] The William de Hagley who was pardoned 3s. for danegeld in 1130–1, in the county

8 Priv. Act, 11 Geo. IV and 1 Will. IV, cap. 12.
9 *Blue Bk. Incl. Awards,* 190.
10 Priv. Act, 2 Will. IV, cap. 5.
11 *Blue Bk. Incl. Awards,* 190.
12 Prattinton Coll. (Soc. Antiq.), Bishop Lyttelton's Hist. of Hagley, &c., fol. 1. There is a tradition of an engagement

here between the Romans and Britons (ibid.).
13 Prattinton Coll. (Soc. Antiq.).
14 Ibid.
15 Soc. Antiq. MS. Min. xiii, 283.
16 Jeayes, *Lyttelton Chart.* no. 142.
17 Anct. D. (P.R.O.), C 732.

18 Prattinton Coll. (Soc. Antiq.).
19 *V.C.H. Worcs.* i, 317a.
20 Ibid.
21 *Red Bk. of Exch.* (Rolls Ser.), 269; *Testa de Nevill* (Rec. Com.), 40b; *Cal. Close,* 1288–96, p. 220; 1318–23, p. 631; Chan. Inq. p.m. (Ser. 2), lv, 8.
22 *V.C.H. Worcs.* i, 317.

of Stafford,[23] probably held this manor, for either he or a successor of the same name held a knight's fee here of Gervase Paynel in 1166.[24] Philip de Hagley occurs in 1187 as a witness to a charter of Gervase Paynel to the priory of Tickford, co. Bucks.[25] Robert de Hagley appears to have been lord of the manor early in the reign of Henry III,[26] and was possibly succeeded by Henry de Hagley,[27] who was in 1255 exempted for life from being put on assizes or from serving in any office against his will.[28] Henry son of Henry de Hagley in 1259 had seisin of the lands of his wife Lecia, daughter and heir of Henry de Linguire, in the county of Oxford.[29]

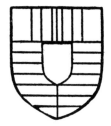

HAGLEY. *Party or and azure barry of eight pieces and a chief with two pales between two quarters all counter-coloured and a scutcheon argent over all.*

About 1280 Henry de Hagley paid a mark towards the subsidy and 4s. was paid by the lady of Hagley, probably the widow of the last owner.[30] In 1286 Henry de Hagley presented to the church,[31] and he was holding the manor in 1292.[32] He appears towards the end of the 13th century as the grantor of land in Harborough in Hagley Manor.[33] He was probably succeeded by Edmund de Hagley, who occurs in 1304 [34] and held Hagley in 1322.[35] Edmund appears to have died at about this time,[36] and to have been followed by another Edmund de Hagley, who held the manor in 1349[37] and surrendered it and the advowson two years later to Sir John de Botetourt, his overlord.[38]

BOTETOURT. *Or a saltire engrailed sable.*

Sir John de Botetourt [39] held the manor until 1370 or later, and Nash states that in 1373–4 Henry Hagley, heir of Edmund Hagley above mentioned, recovered the manor and advowson by a writ of right [40] ; but, though this statement appears to be correct, no confirmation of it has been found. Henry Hagley certainly presented to the church in 1380, 1382 and 1389.[41] A grant of protection for one year, which had been given him in December 1391 as staying on the king's service with Thomas Earl of Nottingham, Captain of Calais, was revoked in 1392 because he tarried in England on his own affairs.[42] Not long after he seems to have forfeited all his possessions on account of being concerned in the death of a certain Simon Cokkes.

He was pardoned in 1397 and his goods to the value of £20 were restored to him.[43] He seems to have been a man of some standing in Worcestershire, for he was sheriff in 1397,[44] and in the early 15th century was on the commission of the peace.[45]

In 1412 he with Alice his wife sold the manor to Thomas Walwyn of Much Marcle, William Biryton and Richard Peper,[46] who afterwards conveyed it to Joan Lady Bergavenny and to Thomas Arundel, Archbishop of Canterbury, Thomas Earl of Arundel, Walter Keble and others,[47] who were trustees for Joan and executors of her will. She was holding the manor in 1431,[48] and died in 1435,[49] having bequeathed Hagley to her grandson James Butler or Ormond, son of the Earl of Ormond.

On 20 November 1445 Walter Keble, apparently the only survivor of this settlement, conveyed Hagley to Sir James Butler with remainder to his brothers John and Thomas in succession, in default of issue.[50] Sir James Butler was created Earl of Wiltshire on 8 July 1449,[51] and succeeded his father as Earl of Ormond in 1452. Having been taken prisoner after the battle of Towton, he was attainted and beheaded in 1461, and his lands were forfeited.[52]

BUTLER, Earl of Ormond. *Or a chief indented azure.*

On 20 January 1462 Edward IV granted Hagley to Fulk Stafford and his heirs male.[53] He died shortly afterwards, leaving no male issue ; his widow Margaret was allowed to retain one-third of the manor in dower,[54] and on 27 January 1463 the remaining two-thirds were granted to Thomas Prout, the king's servant, and his heirs male, with the reversion of the share held by Margaret Stafford on her death.[55] Apparently Thomas Prout died without issue male shortly after receiving this grant, as early in 1474 his share of Hagley had reverted to the king. On 10 February Edward IV granted it to his consort, Queen Elizabeth, with the reversion of the third held by Margaret Stafford.[56] On 13 January 1479, at the request of the queen, the king granted the two-thirds held by her, with the reversion of the remaining third, to Westminster Abbey, on condition that the abbot should find two monks to celebrate daily in the chapel of St. Erasmus at Westminster, for the health of the king and queen.[57] The monastery does not appear to have long retained possession of Hagley ; on 4 July 1486, the attainder of James Earl of Ormond having been reversed the year before in favour of his brother Thomas, seventh earl,[58] the

23 *Gt. R. of the Pipe*, 31 *Hen. I* (Rec. Com.), 76.

24 *Red Bk. of Exch.* (Rolls Ser.), 269.

25 Dugdale, *Mon. Angl.* v, 204.

26 Jeayes, op. cit. no. 10.

27 *Testa de Nevill* (Rec. Com.), 40b.

28 *Cal. Pat.* 1247–58, p. 417.

29 *Excerpta e Rot. Fin.* (Rec. Com.), ii, 310.

30 *Lay Subs. R. c.* 1280 (Worcs. Hist. Soc.), 10–11.

31 *Reg. G. Giffard* (Worcs. Hist. Soc.), 282.

32 *Cal. Close*, 1288–96, p. 220.

33 Jeayes, op. cit. no. 45.

34 Ibid. no. 51.

35 Chan. Inq. p.m. 16 Edw. II, no. 72.

36 *Cal. Close*, 1318–23, p. 631.

37 Jeayes, op. cit. no. 142.

38 Ibid. no. 147, and Feet of F. Worcs. 24 Edw. III, no. 26.

39 Feet of F. Worcs. 33 Edw. III, no. 11, and Jeayes, op. cit. no. 159, 174, 186.

40 Nash, *Hist. of Worc.* i, 489.

41 Ibid. i, 507.

42 *Cal. Pat.* 1391–6, p. 63.

43 Ibid. 1396–9, p. 268.

44 P.R.O. *List of Sheriffs*, 157.

45 *Cal. Pat.* 1405–8, p. 499.

46 Feet of F. Div. Co. East. 13 Hen. IV.

47 Jeayes, op. cit. no. 343.

48 *Feud. Aids*, v, 330.

49 G.E.C. *Complete Peerage*, i, 14.

50 Jeayes, op. cit. no. 343.

51 G.E.C. *Complete Peerage*, viii, 165.

52 *Rolls of Parl.* v, 478a, 480b ; Chan. Inq. p.m. 3 Edw. IV, no. 12.

53 *Cal. Pat.* 1461–7, p. 112.

54 Ibid. 297.

55 Ibid. 223.

56 Ibid. 1467–77, p. 419.

57 Ibid. 1476–85, p. 133.

58 *Rolls of Parl.* vi, 296a.

latter received a grant of various liberties within his manor of Hagley.[59]

Thomas Earl of Ormond died in 1515, leaving as co-heirs his two daughters—Anne, widow of Sir James St. Leger, and Margaret, widow of Sir William Boleyn.[60] Hagley passed to the former, who died in 1532, her heir being her son Sir George St. Leger.[61] The latter was followed by a son John,[62] who in 1565 sold Hagley to John Lyttelton.[63] From John, then Sir John Lyttelton, Hagley passed in 1590 to his son Gilbert,[64] who was succeeded in 1599 by his son John.[65] The latter was afterwards concerned in Essex's plot,[66] and condemned to death for treason, but died in prison in 1601. His lands were forfeited to the Crown, but on the appeal of his widow Muriel were restored to her

LYTTELTON. *Argent a cheveron between three scallops sable.*

17 June 1603,[67] and his children were restored in blood in the same year.[68]

After John Lyttelton's death a survey was taken of Hagley and his other property. There was at Hagley a fishpool called 'Brodford Poole, lately broken by flood,' and a rabbit warren on 'Hagley Brak.'[69] Hagley was afterwards held by Thomas son of John and Muriel, who was created a baronet in 1618.[70] He was a noted Royalist, and colonel of the king's forces in Worcestershire. He was taken prisoner at Bewdley, and died in 1649–50.[71] His eldest son Henry was imprisoned in the Tower from 1651 to 1653 on a charge of supplying arms without licence to the Scottish army, but was finally released, since there was only 'one witness against him.'[72] In 1659 he was implicated, with two of his brothers, in General Booth's insurrection, and again sent to the Tower, where he seems to have remained until the Restoration. As before no one could be found to witness against him, his two servants who were in the rising and one Wright, a schoolmaster of Halesowen, who could have done so, having disappeared.[73] He died in 1693, and was succeeded by his brother Charles Lyttelton,[74] who was at one time Governor of Jamaica, and died in 1716. His son, Sir Thomas Lyttelton, was the father of Sir George Lyttelton, known as the 'good Lord Lyttelton,' who was an author of some repute, and the patron of James Thomson, who describes him in 'The Castle of Indolence.'[75] He was created Lord Lyttelton of Frankley in 1756,[76] but the barony

became extinct in 1779 on the death of his only son Thomas without issue,[77] being revived, however, in 1794 in favour of his brother, William Henry Lyttelton Lord Westcote, who had succeeded to many of his estates.[78] Charles George Lyttelton Viscount Cobham and Lord Lyttelton, great-grandson of the above,[79] is now lord of Hagley.

There has apparently never been a mill belonging to the manor of Hagley. Churchill Mill was in Hagley parish in the 16th century, and still lies on the border between Hagley and Churchill.[80]

Customs, called Beolawe and Bodelsilver, namely, the payment to the lord of 2s. or one sheep,[81] existed in the manor in the 14th century. There is a list of the customs of the manor in 1817 in the Prattinton MSS.[82]

A list of Lord Lyttelton's MSS. at Hagley is printed by the Historical MSS. Commission,[83] and a catalogue has been published.

HARBOROUGH belonged to the family of Penn from the reign of Edward III until the middle of the 18th century,[84] when William Penn left it to his two daughters. Anne, the elder, married Thomas Shenstone, and was the mother of William Shenstone the poet, and Mary, the younger, married Thomas Dolman, rector of Broom.[85] Sir Edward Dolman Scott, bart., owned an estate in the parish in 1832, when Harborough Common was inclosed.[86]

PENN. *Argent a fesse sable with three roundels argent thereon.*

CHURCHES The church of *ST. JOHN BAPTIST* consists of a chancel with a north vestry and organ chamber, a nave with north and south aisles, west tower and spire, and south porch. The church was almost completely rebuilt and considerably enlarged in 1860, the county doing the work in recognition of the great services Lord Lyttelton, who was Lord Lieutenant of the county for many years, had rendered to it. Sufficient fragments remain to indicate the existence of a late 13th-century building apparently consisting of chancel, nave and south aisle. The north aisle and arcade were added in 1826 by Rickman.[87] His original plan shows the church without a tower (though the thickness of the western wall of the nave rather suggests that one originally existed), and also one bay shorter than at present. The chancel is stated by Nash to have been rebuilt in 1754 by George Lord Lyttelton.

[59] Pat. 1 Hen. VII, pt. iv, m. 6 ; see also De Banco R. Chart. Enr. Trin. 10 Hen. VII, m. 1 ; Mich. 11 Hen. VII, m. 2, 3 d. ; Rolls of Parl. vi, 554a.
[60] G.E.C. Complete Peerage, vi, 143.
[61] Chan. Inq. p.m. (Ser. 2), lv, 8.
[62] Ibid.
[63] Feet of F. Div. Co. Trin. 7 Eliz.
[64] Chan. Inq. p.m. (Ser. 2), ccxxix, 140.
[65] Ibid. cclvii, 71.
[66] Acts of P.C. 1600–1, p. 489.
[67] Pat. 1 Jas. I, pt. i.
[68] Burton, Biblog. of Worc. i, 11.
[69] Exch. Spec. Com. 44 Eliz. no. 2519.
[70] G.E.C. Complete Baronetage, i, 117.
[71] Dict. Nat. Biog.
[72] Cal. Com. for Comp. 2898–9.

[73] Ibid. The title deeds of most of the Lytteltons' property were destroyed with Frankley House, therefore in 1682–3 Henry Lyttelton obtained a fresh grant from the Crown (Pat. 34 Chas. II, pt. ix, no. 7).
[74] G.E.C. Complete Baronetage, i, 117.
[75] Canto 1, stanzas lxv, lxvi. Stanza lxviii is a description of Thomson written by Lord Lyttelton.
[76] G.E.C. Complete Peerage, v, 185.
[77] Ibid.
[78] Ibid.
[79] Ibid. 186–7.
[80] Misc. Bks. Ld. Rev. ccxxviii, fol. 273.
[81] Jeayes, Lyttelton Chart. no. 186. The opinion of Dr. Thomas on these customs

was that Beolaw was a tax on every hive of bees and Bodelsilver a small piece of money paid annually to the lord by every tenant in consideration of his expenses in finding a bailey or steward to gather their rents, &c. (Prattinton Coll. [Soc. Antiq.]).
[82] (Soc. Antiq.), quoting a MS. belonging to 'the late George Clarke.'
[83] Rep. ii, App. 36.
[84] Lyttelton MSS. (Soc. Antiq.), fol. 5 ; Prattinton Coll. (Soc. Antiq.), quoting 'Hardwick's Deeds.'
[85] Dict. Nat. Biog.
[86] Priv. Act, 2 Will. IV, cap. 5.
[87] His original plan is preserved in the library of the Soc. of Antiq. London.

Hagley : Harborough Hall : 17th Century Bedstead

There is a ring of eight bells cast by Mears & Stainbank of London, 1885.

The plate includes a large silver-gilt cup, salver, paten and almsplate, all supposed to have been given to the church in 1746 by Sir Thomas Lyttelton.

The cup was sold some time ago, bought again at the sale of Prince Demidoff's effects at Florence by a London silversmith, and sold back to the parish. There are also two cups, a paten and a flagon in plated ware, and a brass almsdish.

The registers previous to 1812 are as follows : (i) baptisms 1538 to 1631, burials 1538 to 1630, marriages 1538 to 1631 ; (ii) fragments of four leaves only ; (iii) baptisms and burials 1731 to 1781, marriages 1731 to 1754 ; (iv) marriages 1754 to 1812 ; (v) baptisms and burials 1782 to 1812.

ST. JAMES THE GREAT, Blakedown, a chapel of ease to St. James, Churchill, is a building of stone, consisting of a chancel aisle, organ chamber, vestry and a western turret, the aisle, organ chamber and vestry having been added in 1905.

ADVOWSON From the fact that a priest is mentioned in the Domesday Survey at Hagley[88] it is probable that there was a church here in 1086. The first record of a presentation to the church occurs in 1286 when Henry de Hagley was patron.[89] From that time the advowson followed the descent of the manor[90] and is now held by Viscount Cobham.

In 1339 an altar in the church of Hagley was dedicated by the bishop.[91]

On 6 February 1562–3 a messuage and land and pasture called Lamp Close, formerly 'given to superstitious uses,' were granted to Cicely Pickerell, widow, and her heirs.[92]

An Act was passed in 1868 to render valid marriages formerly solemnized in the chapel of St. James the Great, Blakedown, then in the parish of Hagley.[93]

A church has recently been erected at Lower Hagley in place of a mission room which was opened there in 1882.

The house of Richard Serjeant at Hagley was licensed for Presbyterian worship in 1672,[94] but there are no Nonconformist chapels in the parish at the present day.

CHARITIES Margaret Goodyer, as stated in the table of benefactions placed in the church in 1792, by her will gave a rent-charge of 6s. yearly, issuing out of land in Hay Meadow and Summergate Meadow, to be distributed to the poor.

It is also stated in the same table that Samuel Hill by will bequeathed £20, the interest to be distributed to the poor on St. James's Day, and that Elizabeth Hollier by will left £100 for the poor at Christmas. These legacies are now represented by £129 11s. 1d. consols.

In 1800 Elizabeth Paget by her will bequeathed £100, the income to be distributed at Christmas to the poor. The legacy was invested in £107 13s. 5d. consols.

Thomas Webb Hodgett by his will (date not stated) bequeathed £333 6s. 8d. consols, the dividends to be applied in clothing and food at Christmas. The legacy, less duty, is represented by £301 4s. 2d. consols.

The several sums of stock are held by the official trustees, producing in annual dividends £13 8s. 8d.

HAGLEY CHURCH FROM THE NORTH-WEST

The parish is also possessed of land known as the Harbro' Allotments, producing £10 a year or thereabouts.

The income from the foregoing charities was in 1908–9 thus applied : £7 18s. 3d. in the relief of eighteen poor persons in Blakedown, £10 16s. in pensions to four widows, and the balance in gifts of meat at Christmas, and in medical relief to three persons.

In 1896 James Foster Bradley, by his will proved on 6 February, bequeathed £100, now represented

[88] *V.C.H. Worcs.* i, 317a.
[89] *Reg. G. Giffard* (Worcs. Hist. Soc.), 282.
[90] *Sede Vacante Reg.* (Worcs. Hist. Soc.), 182 ; Feet of F. Worcs. 24 Edw. III,

no. 26 ; Jeayes, op. cit. no. 343 ; Chan. Inq. p.m. (Ser. 2), ccxxix, 140 ; Inst. Bks. (P.R.O.).
[91] Worc. Epis. Reg. Wulstan de Braunsford (1339–49), fol. 12.

[92] Pat. 5 Eliz. pt. v.
[93] Priv. Act, 31 & 32 Vict. cap. 113 ; Burton, *Bibliog. of Worc.* i, 138.
[94] *Cal. S. P. Dom.* 1672, p. 399.

by £100 Birmingham Corporation 3 per cent. stock, the income of £3 a year, subject to repair of the family vault in the churchyard, to be applied for such charitable purposes as the rector and churchwardens should think fit. The testator further directed that, if the vault be neglected, the legacy should go over to the parish of Cheveley.

In 1884 the Hon. and Rev. William Henry Lyttelton, by his will proved 29 October, established a fund, to be called 'The Emily Lyttelton Fund,' for providing a nurse in midwifery cases and cases of non-infectious diseases. The endowment consists of £1,500 Worcester County Council 4 per cent. debentures, producing £60 a year.

HALESOWEN [1]

Hala (xi cent.) ; Hales Regis (xii cent.) ; Hales (xiii cent.) ; Halesoweyn, Halysoweyn (xiii and xiv cent.).

Part of Halesowen, which was wholly included in Worcestershire in 1086, formed part of Shropshire from the end of the 11th century to the beginning of the 18th, but was finally transferred to Worcestershire under the Acts of 1832 and 1844.[2] The first change was evidently due to the fact that the manor belonged to the powerful Earl of Shrewsbury, who annexed it to his county of Shropshire,[3] while Cradley, Warley Wigorn and Lutley, the parts of the parish which belonged to other lords, remained in Worcestershire. Halesowen is still a large parish, although considerable changes have been made in its boundaries during the last century. In 1831 it included the townships of Cakemore, Cradley, Hasbury, Hawn,[3a] Hill, Hunnington, Illey,[4] Lapal, Lutley, Oldbury, Ridgacre,[5] Romsley, Warley Wigorn and Warley Salop, its total area being 11,290 acres with a population of 11,839.[6] Since that date the seven new ecclesiastical parishes of Oldbury, Cradley, Quinton, Langley, Romsley, Blackheath and Round's Green have been formed.[7] The modern rural district of Halesowen has an area of 5,276 acres. The inclosure award for Offmoor Wood, Great Farley Wood and Winwood Heath in Romsley is dated 22 September 1859.[8] Oldbury was inclosed under an Act of 1829.[9]

The town is situated on the right bank of the River Stour in the midst of scenery which is still beautiful in spite of its proximity to the Black Country. There is now no trace of the boundaries of the ancient borough, but an Exchequer suit of the 17th century mentions crosses on the various roads leading into the town as the boundaries.[10] It is probable that the houses centred round the High Street, which is mentioned in the time of Edward III as the site of the market,[11] and possibly extended along Great and

Little Cornbow towards Cornbow Bridge over the Stour.[12] At the north end of High Street is the church of St. John the Baptist. In the middle of the 19th century the town is described as consisting 'chiefly of one street in which are some respectable houses, and of some smaller streets containing humbler dwellings irregularly built.'[13] Since that date it has been extended considerably towards the west.

There are several places of interest near the town, including the ruins of the once famous abbey. The Leasowes, 1½ miles to the north-east of the town, was at one time the home of William Shenstone, who spent many years of his life in beautifying the grounds, which are said to have been 'the envy of the great and the admiration of the skilful.'[14]

Halesowen Grange has long been the seat of the family of Lea Smith, representatives of the senior co-heir to the barony of Dudley.

The manufacture of nails, screws and screw-shafts for steamers, gun-barrels, files, chains and all kinds of hardware is carried on in Halesowen to some extent. Nail-making was an industry in Halesowen and the surrounding hamlets in the 17th century.[15] As early as 1625 Humphrey Hill of Cradley is described as 'a driver into the country with nails.'[16] During the Civil War Halesowen supplied shot to the garrison of Dudley Castle at £14 a ton.[17] Coal was found in the Hill township in the time of Edward I,[18] and in 1307 a mining lease at 'La Combes' was granted by the lord to Henry le Knyth and Henry del Hulle.[18a] In 1607 Muriel Lyttelton, then lady of the manor, brought an action against Thomas and John Low for sinking coal-pits in a field called 'Cole Pytt Leasow,' near Combes Wood, from which they made 40s. a week for two or three weeks.[19] Another attempt to work the mines was made in the 18th century, but it was found unprofitable.[20]

Oldbury, which is situated 5 miles north-east of Halesowen, has become an important manufacturing

---

[1] The account of Halesowen in Nash, *Hist. of Worc.* i, 508 et seq., was written by Charles Lyttelton, Bishop of Carlisle, whose MS. is preserved by the Soc. Antiq.

[2] Stat. 2 & 3 Will. IV, cap. 64 ; 7 & 8 Vict. cap. 61.

[3] *V.C.H. Worcs.* i, 238. Hales was accounted for under Worcestershire in 1154–5 (*Red Bk. of Exch.* [Rolls Ser.], 656). The change seems to have been the occasion of some difficulty in the collection of subsidies. In 1427–8 the collectors reported that they had not answered for any subsidy from the church of Halesowen because they did not know whether it was in the county of Worcester or Shropshire (*Lay Subs.* R. 1427–8 [Worcs. Hist. Soc.], 21. See also *Cal. Close*, 1341–3, p. 105).

[3a] Formerly spelt Halen. The greater part of this township belonged to the Attwoods (information by Mr. Thomas A. C. Attwood).

[4] In 1505 the Abbot of Halesowen leased the tithe barn of Illey with all tithes belonging to the township and elde of Illey to Richard Hawkys for twenty years (Jeayes, *Lyttelton Chart.* no. 431). A vill called Half Hide (dimidia hyda) in Halesowen is frequently mentioned in the 13th-century Court Rolls.

[5] Ridgacre is now Quinton, and is incorporated with Birmingham. The original name is retained only in a farm-house.

[6] *Pop. Ret.* (1831), 515. In 1563 there were 280 families in Halesowen (Harl. MS. 595, fol. 209).

[7] See under Advowson.

[8] *Blue Bk. Incl. Awards*, 191.

[9] Priv. Act, 10 Geo. IV, cap. 25.

[10] Exch. Dep. by Com. East. 31 Chas. II, no. 15.

[11] Jeayes, op. cit. no. 97. The High Street (*Alta via*) is mentioned in the Court Rolls of 1270 (*Ct. R. of Halesowen* [Worcs. Hist. Soc.], 11).

[12] Jeayes, op. cit. no. 190.

[13] Lewis, *Topog. Dict.*

[14] Boswell, *Life of Johnson* (ed. Hill), v, 457.

[15] *Quart. Sess.* R. (Worcs. Hist. Soc.), 89, 262. [16] Ibid. 397.

[17] Add. MS. 5752, fol. 402.

[18] Nash, op. cit. i, 508, quoting Court Rolls ; *Ct. R. of Manor of Hales* (Worcs. Hist. Soc.), 167, 168.

[18] *Ct. R. of Manor of Hales*, 566.

[19] Exch. Dep. Hil. 5 Jas. I, no. 17.

[20] Nash, op. cit. i, 508.

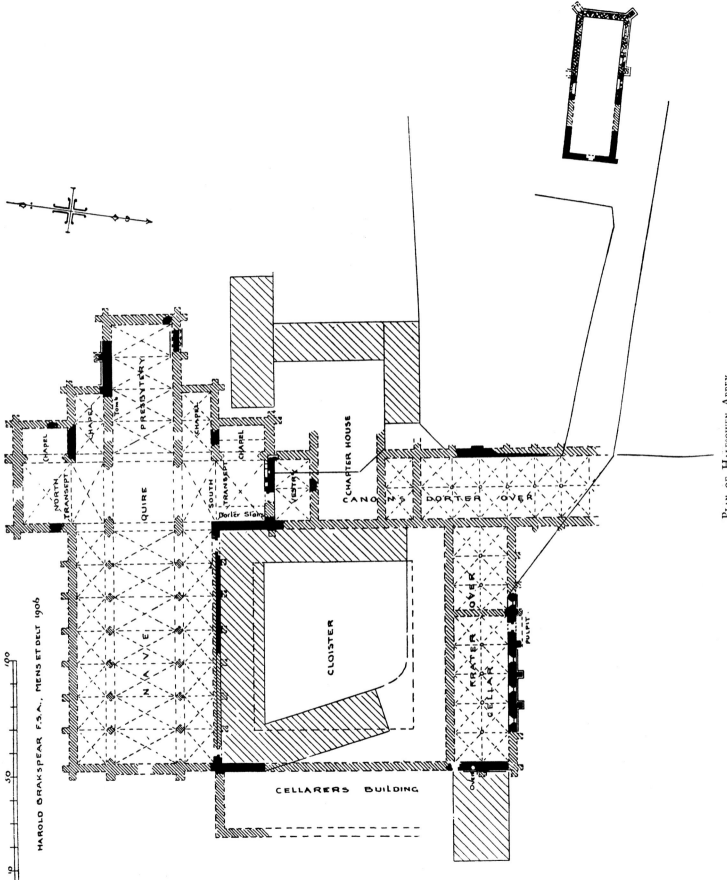

PLAN OF HALESOWEN ABBEY

The walls of the portions existing above ground are shown in solid black.

HAROLD BRAKSPEAR F.S.A., MENS ET DELT 1906

NORTH TRANSEPT

CHAPEL

CHAPEL

TOMB

PRESBYTERY

QUIRE

CHAPEL

SOUTH TRANSEPT

CHAPEL

VESTRY

Dorter Stairs

CHAPTER HOUSE

NAVE

CLOISTER

CANON'S DORTER OVER

FRATER OVER

CELLAR

PULPIT

OVEN

CELLARERS BUILDING

town owing to its situation in the great South Stafford-shire coalfield, and is now more populous than Halesowen. It is governed by an urban district council, formed under the Local Government Act of 1894, Langley constituting a ward of the Oldbury district. There are important brick-works, iron-foundries and chemical works in Oldbury and in the neighbouring parishes of Cradley, Langley, Black Heath and Quinton. It was at Cradley that Dud Dudley about 1619 set up one of his first forges for smelting iron with coal.[21]

Besides these busy manufacturing centres there are also in the parish purely agricultural districts raising crops of grain, roots, vegetables and other farm and dairy produce which find a ready market in the neighbouring towns.

Halesowen is connected with Birmingham and Dudley by the Birmingham Canal, opened at the end of the 18th century. The Halesowen branch of the Great Western railway, opened in 1878, and the Halesowen and Northfield railway, worked by the Great Western and Midland, have stations in Halesowen, and Rowley Regis station, on the Great Western railway, is just within the boundaries of the parish. There are also stations at Oldbury and Langley Green on the Great Western railway.

The chief roads are those from Dudley to Bromsgrove and from Birmingham to Kidderminster, which intersect near Halesowen station.

The scanty remains of the Premonstratensian *ABBEY OF HALES-OWEN* founded in 1215 are situated upon a slight eminence in a secluded valley about half a mile south-east of the village. The buildings appear to have been entirely surrounded by a moat fed from a stream running along the west side and joined by another bounding the abbey grounds on the south, but most of the moat is now either dried up or filled in. The conventual buildings were demolished shortly after the Dissolution, and from the churchwardens' accounts for 1539 it appears that the parish authorities took part in the spoliation. A modern farm-house stands a little to the south of the monastic remains. The arrangement of the original buildings is now somewhat conjectural, only fragments of the walls of the church, part of the south wall of the frater and a small building to the south-east of the claustral block being left standing above ground. The church apparently consisted of an aisled nave of seven bays, transepts, with two eastern chapels to each arm, the inner pair projecting two bays east, and an aisleless presbytery of four bays. The surviving remains include one bay of the north wall of the presbytery, the south-west corner of the south transept, the east end of the south wall of the south aisle and a small piece of walling at the south-west corner of the same

[21] *V.C.H. Worcs.* ii, 267–8 ; *Quart. Sess. R.* (Worcs. Hist. Soc.), Introd. p. lxvi.

aisle ; these are all *circa* 1220. The presbytery wall retains both the jambs of a tall lancet in the centre of the bay and the west jamb of another to the east, while on the west is the north-east angle of the inner transeptal chapel. The wall is broken off just below the heads of these windows. At the sill level was an internal moulded string. The presbytery was vaulted, the ribs springing from moulded corbels. Part of one of the buttresses supporting this wall remains, and the building was finished with an external chamfered plinth. The angle corbel and the springing of a low vault remain in the south-east corner of the transept chapel.

In the west wall of the south transept are two tall

HALESOWEN CHURCH FROM THE WEST

lancets, similar to those lighting the presbytery, and below them can be seen the outline of two pointed vaults under the rake of the night stairs to the dorter. The corbels and the springing of the ribs of the main vault, which appear to have been in one bay, also remain. The fragments of the south wall of the transept have been patched with modern work. In it is the doorway to an apartment on the south, either the cemetery passage or the vestry, which was formerly vaulted. To the east of the doorway is a small arched recess with a piscina basin. In the small piece of the return wall of the south nave aisle are the pointed arch and one jamb of the east processional doorway, now incorporated in the wall of a large barn which occupies the north side of the cloisters. A small fragment of the original walling at the south-west angle of the aisle determines the limits of the building in that direction. To the south of the remains of the church, and now forming a wall to the garden of the farm-house, is part of the south wall of the frater and its undercroft. The latter was eight bays long and vaulted, with a row of central columns and two-stage external buttresses. One of the moulded corbels supporting the vault remains in the south wall. Five bays of this wall are still standing with a much smaller portion of the frater above. The undercroft was divided by a wall across, five bays from the west end, and immediately west of this is a pointed doorway opening into a vaulted passage on the south. In the other remaining bays are small pointed windows. In the south-east angle of the cross wall is a moulded bracket, and behind it is a shallow

level, are similar windows, now blocked, and remains of a third, on the north side. In the west end of the same wall are the remains of a blocked-up two-light 13th-century window. In the south wall, and corbelled out at the floor level, is the lower part of a fireplace, and built into the jamb is a fine red sandstone grave-slab of 13th-century date. Carved in the lower part of the slab, under a trefoiled arch, is the kneeling figure of an angel, with the indent for a metal plate held originally in the hands. Below the figure is an open book, while carved in the upper part of the slab is a rood with the figures of our Lady and St. John. To the west of the fireplace is a range of three two-light transomed windows now somewhat damaged. Below the transoms the lights are rebated for shutters. In the west end of the wall is a single pointed opening divided by a transom, but the inner stones only are original. The ground floor is lit by

HALESOWEN ABBEY : SOUTH WALL OF FRATER

pointed recess. The frater was lighted by tall coupled lancets, of which five are left. The inner jambs have attached shafts with moulded capitals and bases. These lancets have both internal and external continuous strings and hood moulds.

To the south-east of the church is a two-story rectangular stone building of the latter part of the 13th century, though since that date it has been considerably altered. Its original use is uncertain, but it was probably the abbot's lodging. It is now used as a barn and is very dilapidated. Only a small part of the east end is now floored, the remainder being open to the roof.

From chases in the side walls the first floor appears to have been divided into two rooms. In the east wall is a two-light square-headed window lighting the first floor, an insertion of the 16th century. At the east end of the north and south walls, at the same

a 13th-century two-light window in the north wall and by three 16th-century windows in the south ; one of these a single light, the others of two each. Most of these openings are now blocked. Built into the south wall about half-way along is a curious little stone panel (17 in. by 6 in.) carved with the full-length figure of a late 13th-century knight. The figure is in mail, with legs crossed and a long shield on the left side. In the extreme west end of the south wall is a small 13th-century pointed window restored externally. An original pointed doorway with a segmental rear arch occupies the centre of the west wall.

Externally a chamfered base originally ran round the building, while at the east end were two-stage angle buttresses, the northern one being now broken away.

The roof is in a very dilapidated condition, and is now covered with corrugated iron, though many of the timbers are original. It is steep pitched and of the trussed-rafter type, the principal trusses having king posts supporting a longitudinal tie.

The abbey received several visits from Edward III on his expedition into Wales in 1332.[22] There is a tradition that King John intended to go there, but turned back on seeing it from Romsley Hill, 3 miles away, because he had wished it to be built in so retired a place that it could not be seen at a distance of 2 miles.[23] In the Halesowen churchwardens' book there is a record of the payment of 3d. 'to the ringers when the Prince came to Hales' in 1490.[24]

Among the famous men who lived or were born at Halesowen are Adam Littleton the lexicographer, Benjamin Green the mezzotint engraver, and Amos Green the painter, who was probably his brother. William Caslon the typefounder was born at Cradley

put,[29] Haraldeswelle,[30] Le Beroplas, Le Wytepole Bridge,[31] Steynesplace[32] (xiv cent.) ; Berehall[33] (xv cent.) ; and Le Bretche or the Breach[34] (xvii cent.). Le Heyfield, also called Heythefeld, Le Hyefelde, Le Hyghefeld, is mentioned in several of the Lyttelton charters[35] in the 13th, 14th and 15th centuries.

BOROUGH By the middle of the 13th century, although agriculture was still the chief employment of the men of Halesowen, other industries had already sprung up, as for example the making of cloth. Weavers are found in possession of plots of land, as Osbert and Hernald in the reign of Henry III, while dyers are frequently mentioned in the time of his successor.[36] Furthermore, a fulling-mill existed quite early, since Thomas the Skinner[37] (*Pelliparius*) wilfully drowned himself (*gratis se sub-*

HALESOWEN ABBEY : SOUTH WALL OF THE ABBOT'S LODGING

in 1692. Thomas Attwood the political reformer, called the 'Founder of Political Unions,' was born at Hawn House in 1783. He was the first representative in Parliament of the borough of Birmingham, and died in 1856. William Shenstone the poet was born at Halesowen in 1714, and was buried in Halesowen churchyard in 1763.

The numerous place-names which occur include la Hooly Welle,[25] Birimore, Cumbes,[26] Nonnemonnes Lydegate[27] (xiii cent.) ; Pendelston,[28] Trowesmarle-

mersit) in the 'Walkenmullenpol' in the later years of Edward I. Coal, again, was dug in Halesowen as early as at any place in Worcestershire, and certainly before the close of the 13th century.[38] It would have been naturally used by smiths for working up the iron smelted with charcoal at the local bloomeries. Great quantities of mediaeval *scoriae* have been found in the neighbourhood and either worked again or used for road metal. In 1304 Nicholas de [*sic*, le] Yrenmongere[39] witnessed a Halesowen deed.

[22] *Cal. Pat.* 1330–4, pp. 324, 326, 328.
[23] Prattinton Coll. (Soc. Antiq.).
[24] Printed in Nash, op. cit. ii, App. 29.
[25] *Ct. R. of Manor of Hales* (Worcs. Hist. Soc.), 334.
[26] Jeayes, op. cit. no. 17.
[27] Ibid. 62.
[28] Ibid. 133, 258.

[29] Ibid. 136.
[30] Ibid. 93.
[31] Ibid. 176.
[32] Ibid. 212.
[33] Ibid. 293.
[34] Chan. Inq. p.m. (Ser. 2), ccxliii, 47 ; Exch. Dep. by Com. Mich. 32 Chas. II, no. 1.

[35] (ed. Jeayes), no. 62, 63, 114, &c.
[36] Jeayes, op. cit. 6 et seq. and 16 ; *Ct. R. of Manor of Hales* (Worcs. Hist. Soc.), *passim*.
[37] Assize R. 739, m. 84.
[38] Nash, op. cit. i, 508 ; *Ct. R. of Manor of Hales*, 168, n. 2, 293.
[39] Jeayes, op. cit. 16 et seq.

The rise of such an industrial element must have made for change and increased independence, and at some time in the 13th century Henry III allowed[40] the Abbot and convent of Hales to create a borough, centrally situated within their manor. The rent of each burgage was fixed at 12d., and the holders were to enjoy such of the liberties and free customs of Hereford as they should choose,[41] and in addition the local privilege of common of pasture throughout Hales Manor as well as in the wood which stretched from the new mill of the abbey to Chatley Ford.[42] Although the burgages thus created are often referred to in local deeds[43] from the 13th century onwards, and grants of burgess right on conditions of a money payment frequently found on the Court Rolls[44] of the borough, the burgesses of Halesowen seem to have enjoyed little real independence. At the eyre[45] of 1255–6 Halesowen appeared as a 'villata' separate from the hundred by a bailiff and twelve jurors. At later eyres the 'manor' of Halesowen appeared in similar fashion. No important development, however, can be traced in the borough organization, and, as far as we know from existing records, Halesowen never sent representatives to Parliament even in the reign of Edward I. But the constant quarrels[46] between the men of Halesowen and the abbot suggest that during the 13th century at least there was a certain amount of vitality in the borough and the foreign manor adjacent.

Among the Court Rolls of the manor which are still in existence there are found courts and great courts[47] of the hundred and courts of the borough of Hales. Very little difference can be detected between these courts and the ordinary manor courts, the same offences being dealt with and the same men acting as jurors.[48] The extant rolls of the hundred of Hales begin in 1272[49] and those for the borough *eo nomine* in 1422. When the latter begin the former cease, so the jurisdiction of the two courts was probably identical.

The Court Rolls of the early 14th century show that the borough then possessed a high and low bailiff,[50] but little is known of its internal economy. The entries on the Court Rolls chiefly relate to pleas concerning land and the recovery of small debts. No one was allowed to exercise any trade in the town without obtaining licence from the abbot as lord of the borough.[51] Halesowen paid its subsidy in 1327–8 with the rest of the manors in the hundred of Brimstree,[52] and the fire which devastated the town about 1343[53] may have put an end to efforts at self-government.

Nothing is known of the number of burgages which existed in the borough at its first foundation. In the valors of the abbey lands in 1291 and 1535 no mention is made of any rents from such tenements. In the latter survey 'Halesburg,' though it is valued separately from Halesowen, would appear to be merely a second manor producing rents of assize £16 15s. 9d., rents from demesne lands 45s. 10d., and amercements of court estimated at 10s.[54]

As 'the manor of Halesburgh,' what remained of the borough was granted in 1538 with the rest of the abbey lands to Sir John Dudley,[55] and it appears as the manor of Halesborough in all deeds concerning the manor of Halesowen, the descent of which it follows until 1666. In a survey of the manor of Halesowen, taken in 1601 after the attainder of John Lyttelton, the tenants holding burgages, only four in number, were returned with the free tenants of the manor of Halesowen. In two cases the yearly rents paid were 12d. and in the other cases 12½d. and 16d.[56]

Before this time, however, the men of Halesowen appear to have made some attempts to recover their burghal rights. Richard Burleton paid 10s. to Sir John Lyttelton in the time of Queen Elizabeth for the right to become a burgess of Halesowen,[57] and in 1608 a proclamation of the borough of Halesowen, after setting forth that 'wee the Bayliffe, burgesses and inhabitants of Halesowen have had a long tyme a small meeting on the Sabothe Day for the buying and selling of butter cheese and fruite which was not allonely merely repugnante and contrary to the woord of God but also to our Kinges Majesties Laws,' and that Mrs. Lyttelton, then lady of the manor, was displeased at this breaking of the Sabbath, requested the townspeople in future to bring their goods to the Monday market and the fair on St. Barnabas Day,[58] which had evidently fallen into disuse.[59] An order of 1572 in the borough court that 'no Inhabitant or Craftsman within the borough shall kepe open their Shop Windows from ye tyme they ring into Servyse until Servyse be done, and likewyse after they ring into Evening Prayer they shall not kepe open the Shop windows until Servyse be done on pain of every Default 3s. 4d.,'[60] was evidently directed against this abuse, but had been ineffectual in stopping it.

At a court held at the same date it was ordered that 'no Person or Persons that brewe any weddyn Ale to sell shall brewe above twelve Strike of malt at the most and that the sayd Persons so married shall not kepe or have above eight Messe Persons at his

---

[40] Jeayes, op. cit. 9, from an Inspeximus by Abbot Nicholas of a notification by 'E. humilis Minister de Hales' of the royal charter. The date is unknown, but the market and fair were granted in 1220, though the dates of both fair and market were subsequently altered. *Vide infra.*

[41] 'Quas pro arbitrio suo predicti burgenses de Hales sibi eligerant.'

[42] It was returned in 1284–5 that Sir Stephen de Chatle had held Chatle in the manor of Hales of the king in chief, owing, in time of war, service for forty days with horse and arms, but that the fee had passed to the Abbot of Hales, who did no service for it (*Feud. Aids,* iv, 217). This Sir Stephen is perhaps to be iden-

tified with Stephen de Waresley, who in 1227 released to the Abbot of Halesowen all his right in 3 carucates of land and two mills in 'Chattel' and Lappol which the abbot claimed as appurtenant to the manor of Halesowen (*Rot. Lit. Claus.* [Rec. Com.], ii, 209).

[43] Jeayes, op. cit. 16 et seq.

[44] *Ct. R. of Manor of Hales* (Worcs. Hist. Soc.), 153.

[45] Assize R. 734, m. 5 (21).

[46] See below. As early as the eyre of 1255–6 the jury presented that 'Abbas de Hales non permittit homines de Hales placitare vetitum namium in com[itatu]. Immo capet namium eorum et non vult eos deliberare per ballivos domini Regis' (Assize R. 734, m. 5 [21]).

[47] The great courts were held twice a year, in April and October (*Ct. R. of Manor of Hales* [Worcs. Hist. Soc.], 10).

[48] Ibid. 9.   [49] Ibid. 243.

[50] Nash, op. cit. i, 514.

[51] Ibid.

[52] Lay Subs. R. 116, no. 1.

[53] *V.C.H. Worcs.* ii, 163.

[54] *Valor Eccl.* (Rec. Com.), iii, 206.

[55] *L. and P. Hen. VIII,* xiii (2), g. 491 (1).

[56] Misc. Bks. Ld. Rev. clxxxv, fol. 124–43.

[57] Nash, op. cit. i, 514.

[58] See below.

[59] Jeayes, op. cit. no. 445.

[60] Ct. R. quoted by Nash, op. cit. i, 515.

HALESOWEN ABBEY : 13TH CENTURY BUILDING

HALESOWEN ABBEY : SOUTH WALL OF FRATER

Dinner within the Burrowe and before his Bridall Day he shall kepe no unlawfull Games in his House nor sell any ale or Beer in his House out of his House on Pain of 20s.'[61] Eight years later it was found necessary to make the further regulations that no one should keep bride ales unless they were approved by the high bailiff and five other 'most substantial persons,' and afterwards by the lord of the borough, that no one should brew or sell ale except on the day of the wedding and one day before and after, and that the ale should only be sold at the price charged by the victuallers of the borough, the fine for each offence being this time 40s.[62]

The renewed prosperity of the borough at this time did not result in a new charter of incorporation, and at the end of the 17th century the borough boundaries were a matter of tradition, being supposed to be certain crosses [63] at the limits of the town, and though the constable for the borough and those for the manor were still separate officers, apparently appointed at the courts of the borough and the manor respectively, their functions had to a certain extent become amalgamated and there was considerable difference of opinion as to whether the borough constable had power to act in the parish and vice versa. The confusion seems to have arisen from the fact that only one constable attended at the county sessions, usually the constable of the parish,[64] and was accepted both for the borough and the parish. Further confusion was probably caused by the union of the borough and the parish for the maintenance of the poor. The burgesses never seem to have admitted any obligation to repair roads outside the borough, though they sometimes did so voluntarily, and a former overseer of roads for the parish admitted that, though he had often required the inhabitants of the borough to join in mending the roads in the parish, he had never prevailed on them to do so.[65]

The chief officer of the town at that time was the high bailiff, and, though no mention has been found of any other officer but the constable until the end of the following century when Nash wrote his 'History of Worcestershire,' it is probable that, in addition to the high bailiff and constable, a low bailiff and victual taster,[66] two overseers of swine and two searchers and sealers of leather [67] existed at the earlier date. All these officers were elected yearly at the lord's court,[68] and those who had served the office of high bailiff were afterwards reputed aldermen.[69] The aldermen and high bailiff proclaimed the yearly fair on St. Barnabas Day and appeared at

church on that occasion in their robes of office.[70] In 1822 the borough officers elected yearly at the court leet were the high and low bailiffs, a constable and head borough.[71] The high and low bailiffs were appointed at least as late as 1868,[72] but they had long ceased to exercise any magisterial function, if indeed they ever had done so. The borough court seems to have survived as a court of requests for the recovery of debts not exceeding 40s. until the middle of the 19th century.[73] The town is now governed by a rural district council of ten members.

The Abbot of Halesowen obtained from Henry III in 1220 licence to hold a market every week on Wednesdays and a fair lasting two days at the feast of St. Denis at Halesowen.[74] Three years later the date of the fair was altered to the feast of St. Kenelm (13 December).[75] It is probable that these fairs were granted before the constitution of the borough of Halesowen, but were afterwards looked upon as belonging to the borough. A grant in 1344 to the abbot and convent of a market weekly on Mondays and a fair for four days at the feast of St. Barnabas (11 June) [76] may have superseded the above. In this case the grant is specifically to the manor of Halesowen.

Owing to the declining prosperity of the borough the market and fair seem to have entirely fallen into disuse until they were revived by Mrs. Lyttelton in 1608 as mentioned above. In 1609 she obtained a confirmation of Edward III's grant of 1344,[77] and the Monday market day continued until the middle of the 19th century.[78] In 1868 the market day was Saturday,[79] and so continues. The fair of St. Barnabas probably survives in the Whitsun fair for horses, cattle, sheep and cheese. A pleasure fair has been held on Easter Monday since the early years of the 19th century.[80] Noake, writing in 1868, mentions a statute fair for the hiring of servants, held in October.[81]

A fair was still held at the feast of St. Kenelm in 1736, and took place in the chapel yard. Bishop Lyttelton, writing of it at that time, states that it was held by prescription and that there was no charter for it.[82] It was, however, probably a survival of the fair granted to the Abbot of Halesowen in 1223, or of that granted to Roger de Somery at Clent in 1253.[83]

MANORS The manor of *HALES*, which belonged in the reign of Edward the Confessor to a certain Olwine, was among the lands granted after the Conquest to Roger Earl of Shrewsbury,[84] who, as before mentioned,

---

[61] Ct. R. quoted by Nash, op. cit. i, 516; Prattinton Coll. (Soc. Antiq.).

[62] Ct. R. quoted by Nash, op. cit. ii, App. 26.

[63] The only one named is Hunter's Cross. A cross which used to stand at Cornbow may have been a boundary cross, and was removed to the churchyard in 1909. A cross called 'Crux coci' is mentioned in 1297 (Ct. R. of the Manor of Hales [Worcs. Hist. Soc.], 357), and 'Crux manicata' in 1298 (ibid. 384).

[64] One deponent stated that the constable of Halesowen parish and the constable of Oldbury attended alternately. From another witness it would seem that the constables of the borough and the parish attended in turn.

[65] Exch. Dep. East. 31 Chas. II, no. 5.

[66] For the purposes of the assize of beer the manor of Halesowen was divided into two parts, 'this side Stour' and 'beyond Stour' (see Ct. R. of Manor of Hales [Worcs. Hist. Soc.]).

[67] Some tanning was probably carried on at Halesowen from early times. Thomas Pelliparius occurs in 1291 (Assize R. 739, m. 84 d.; see also Ct. R. of Manor of Hales [Worcs. Hist. Soc.], 191), and in 1601-2 a free tenant of the manor held a house called a 'tanne house' (Misc. Bks. Ld. Rev. clxxxv, 124-43).

[68] Nash does not make it clear whether the court was that of the manor or the borough; probably, from what follows, the former.

[69] Nash, op. cit. i, 515.

[70] Ibid.

[71] Pigot, Commercial Dir. 1822-3.

[72] Noake, Guide to Worc. 180.

[73] Lewis, Topog. Dict.

[74] Fine R. 4 Hen. III, m. 3.

[75] Rot. Lit. Claus. (Rec. Com.), i, 553.

[76] Chart. R. 18 Edw. III, m. 5, no. 27. It may have been found that St. Kenelm's fair interfered with that held at Clent on the same day.

[77] Jeayes, op. cit. no. 446.

[78] Gorton, Topog. Dict.; Lewis, Topog. Dict.

[79] Noake, loc. cit.

[80] Pigot, Commercial Dir. 1822-3, p. 365.

[81] op. cit. 180.

[82] Prattinton Coll. (Soc. Antiq.).

[83] Cal. Pat. 1247-58, p. 253.

[84] V.C.H. Worcs. i, 303b, 309a.

annexed it to his county of Shropshire shortly after the date of the Domesday Survey.[85] It passed from Earl Roger to his two sons successively, Hugh, who died in 1098, and Robert de Belesme. On the forfeiture of the latter in 1102 it fell to the Crown.[86] Henry II gave it to his sister Emma, who had married David son of Owen Prince of Wales in 1174.[87] She restored it about 1193 to Richard I, who granted her in exchange rents amounting to its yearly value from this and other manors.[88] Emma was still holding the rents in 1202.[89] She left a son Owen, who is sometimes thought to have held the manor, owing to an entry in the Hundred Rolls, which states that King John had held it as an escheat from a certain Owen,[90] and to the addition of Owen to the name Hales.[91] In 1214 the king granted Halesowen to Peter des Roches, Bishop of Winchester, for the purpose of building and endowing a religious house,[92] and in the following year confirmed it to the Premonstratensian canons there.[93] In 1251 the abbot and convent received from Henry III a grant of free warren in the manor.[94]

Throughout the 13th and 14th centuries there were numerous disputes between the abbot and his tenants as to the services which the latter owed for their lands in the manor. About 1243 the tenants agreed that they owed the abbot merchet, suit at his mill,[95] unless it were manifestly out of repair, and six days' ploughing and six days' sowing in Lent, for each virgate of land. In return for this the abbot remitted 12½ marks tallage which they owed, and promised that they should only be tallaged when the men of the king's manors were, and that he would not enter into or in any way obstruct their common of pasture.[96] In spite of this agreement the quarrels still went on,[97] and about 1275 an inquisition was taken to ascertain what services and customs had been rendered when the manor belonged to King John. It was found that they had held their land of the

HALESOWEN ABBEY.
Azure a cheveron argent between three fleurs de lis or.

king by payment of 40d. yearly for every 'yard land,' by suit of court, heriot (the best horse and half the goats, hogs and bees and all the cocks) and relief. The tenants did six days' ploughing and five days' sowing for each whole yard land and one extra day's sowing by grace for which they had a feast at the manor-house. They had the right of grinding their corn where they would, because the king had no mill. They owed 12s. merchet if their daughters were married within the manor and 2s. if without.[98]

The abbot petitioned the king in 1278, stating that the men of Halesowen claiming to be of the ancient demesne[99] refused their customs and services, and prayed a remedy.[100] The result was a writ of quo warranto, in answer to which the abbot produced King John's charter and established his claim.[1] The disputes continued, however, until 1327, when the abbot commuted the services for a fixed rent.[2] In 1535 the abbot and convent received a revenue of £133 18s. 7¼d. from the manor of Halesowen with its hamlets.[3]

After the Dissolution Henry VIII granted the site of the abbey to Sir John Dudley, afterwards Duke of Northumberland.[4] While he held the manor he granted the 'mansion of the manor,' which was evidently what remained of the abbey, to his servant George Tuckey.[5]

After the Duke of Northumberland's attainder and execution in 1553 his widow Joan recovered Halesowen,[6] which had been settled on her in 1539.[7] She died in 1554–5, leaving the manor to trustees for the use of her three sons, who had been attainted for treason, Ambrose, the eldest, having the house and land to the value of £100.[8] Later in the same year Sir Ambrose Dudley[9] and his brother Sir Henry gave up their share to their younger brother Sir Robert Dudley, afterwards Earl of Leicester.[10] He appears to have settled it on his wife, the famous Amy Robsart, who with him conveyed the manor to Thomas Blount and George

DUDLEY. *Or a lion with a forked tail vert.*

[85] V.C.H. Worcs. i, 238.
[86] G.E.C. Complete Peerage, vii, 135; Dict. Nat. Biog.
[87] Cal. Rot. Chart. 1199–1216 (Rec. Com.), 44; Ralph de Diceto, Opera Historica (Rolls Ser.), i, 397.
[88] Pipe R. Staff. 5 Ric. I, m. 6 d. The manor is said to have been worth £17 6s. 8d.
[89] Rot. Canc. (Rec. Com.), 121.
[90] op. cit. (Rec. Com.), ii, 98. See Mr. J. R. Holliday's article in the Birmingham and Midl. Inst. Arch. Sect. Trans. 1871, p. 51.
[91] The suffix Owen was added to Hales as early as the middle of the 13th century, if not before; cf. Assize R. 734, m. 5 (21).
[92] Rot. Lit. Claus. (Rec. Com.), i, 174b; Cart. Antiq. NN 19; II, 30; Pipe R. 2 Hen. III, m. 1.
[93] Cal. Rot. Chart. 1199–1216 (Rec. Com.), 217; V.C.H. Worcs. ii, 163.
[94] Cal. Chart. R. 1226–57, p. 362. This grant was confirmed by Richard II in 1388 (Cal. Pat. 1385–9, p. 434).

[95] There are very frequent presentations on the Court Rolls of the 13th century on account of the failure of tenants to grind their corn at the abbot's mill.
[96] Cur. Reg. R. 28, m. 14 d.
[97] See De Banco R. 17, m. 99 d.; 57, m. 90 d.
[98] Chan. Inq. p.m. 4 Edw. I, no. 93; Hund. R. (Rec. Com.), ii, 98.
[99] It is to be noted that the abbot used this plea in 1228 to quash a claim made by Roger de Hales to land at Hales (Maitland, Bracton's Note Bk. ii, 244).
[100] Rolls of Parl. i, 10b.
[1] Abbrev. Plac. (Rec. Com.), 197; see also Anct. Pet. no. 2483.
[2] The agreement is entered on the Court Roll for that year. Two reeves were to be elected by the customary tenants at the great court after Michaelmas, one paying 20s. and the other 6s. 8d. for the office (Bp. Lyttelton's Hist. of Hagley, Halesowen, &c. [Soc. Antiq.], fol. 122; Nash, op. cit. i, 513).

[3] Valor Eccl. (Rec. Com.), iii, 206. In 1291 the rents of assize had been worth £4 and the pleas and perquisites of court 20s. (Pope Nich. Tax. [Rec. Com.], 230).
[4] L. and P. Hen. VIII, xiii (2), g. 491 (1).
[5] Charter quoted in Nash, op. cit. ii, App. 27. The site of the monastery was in the township of Lapal (Nash, op. cit. i, 517). For a description of the existing remains of the abbey see above p. 137.
[6] Chan. Inq. p.m. (Ser. 2), cx, 135.
[7] L. and P. Hen. VIII, xiv (1), g. 403 (21); Close, 30 Hen. VIII, pt. vii, no. 15.
[8] P.C.C. 26 More.
[9] One-third of the manor, being apparently the part which had been left to Sir Ambrose Dudley, was granted to his mother's trustees by the king and queen (Jeayes, op. cit. no. 439; Pat. 1 & 2 Phil. and Mary, pt. vi, m. 19).
[10] Bp. Lyttelton, Hist. of Hagley, Halesowen, &c. (Soc. Antiq.), fol. 130, quoting 'Lord Lyttelton's Evidences.'

HALESOWEN ABBEY : FRAGMENT OF NORTH WALL OF PRESBYTERY

HALESOWEN : ST. KENELM'S CHAPEL FROM THE NORTH-WEST

Tuckey in 1558.[11] In the same year Blount and Tuckey sold the manor to John Lyttelton,[12] and since that date it has followed the same descent as Hagley[13] (q.v.), Viscount Cobham being lord of the manor at the present day.

There is a list of the customs of the manor in 1817 among Prattinton's MSS.[14]

Court Rolls for the manor and borough of Halesowen are in the possession of Viscount Cobham at Hagley.[15]

When the possessions of the monastery of Halesowen were granted to Sir John Dudley a rent of £28 1s. 3d. yearly was reserved to the Crown. This was reduced to £20 in 1611, in consideration that part of the possessions of the monastery were no longer held by the Lytteltons. The £20 was paid to the Crown until 1650, when it was sold by order of Parliament.[16] On the Restoration it was restored to the king and settled on Queen Katherine in 1663-4.[17] Some years later an Act of Parliament was passed to enable the king to alienate fee-farm rents.[18] The purchaser of the rent from Halesowen is said to have been an ancestor of Sir Matthew Deeker,[19] to whose widow, Henrietta Deeker, the rent was paid in the time of Bishop Lyttelton.[20] It was finally purchased by Lord Lyttelton in the 19th century.

A park at Halesowen was made by the abbot and convent about 1290.[21] It was still in existence in 1601-2, and then contained some timber trees and firewood trees to the value of £40.[22]

There was no mill at Halesowen when the manor was granted to the abbot and convent,[23] but one seems to have been built very shortly afterwards.

In the reign of Henry III a Roger son of Roger the clerk of Hales gave the abbot certain lands in the parish with permission to erect a mill and mill pool, reserving to himself the rights of fishing in the overflow water and of having his corn ground in the mill without paying toll.[24]

The abbot had two mills worth 20s. a year in 1291,[25] and the new mill of Hales is mentioned in a Court Roll of 1293.[26] It was, however, burnt down in the same year.[27] In 1350 John de Peoleshal received licence to alienate to the abbot and convent three messuages and a mill in Halesowen, Oldbury and Warley.[28] These mills seem to have passed with the manor to the Lytteltons.

In 1672 there were, besides those belonging to the lord of the manor, three mills belonging to a certain Henry Haden, who had inherited two of them from his father.[29] These two are probably the 'Dalwyk Mulne'[29a] and 'le new Mulne' mentioned in an account roll dated 1369-70.[30] Mills called Birds' Mill (Bruddesmulne), Abbeley Mill, Greet Mill and Blakeley Mill are frequently mentioned in the 14th century Court Rolls.[30a]

Towards the end of the 18th century constables[31] were elected annually at the different courts for the manor of Halesowen, including all the Shropshire part of Halesowen except Oldbury, and for the manors of Cradley, Lutley and Warley Wigorn. Oldbury had its own constable, and third boroughs or deputy constables were elected yearly for each of the hamlets of Hawn and Hasbury, Hill, Ridgacre, Cakemore, Warley Salop, Lapal, Illey, Romsley and Hunnington.[32]

It seems to have been considered the duty of the Lytteltons to repair the Malt Mill and Cornbow bridges, which had only been needed since their mills had been built, the river having been formerly crossed by fords. In 1668-9 the bridges were in such bad repair that the constable prosecuted Sir Henry Lyttelton for refusing to restore them.[33]

In 1086 CRADLEY (Cradelie, xi cent.; Credelega, xiii cent.) formed part of the barony of Dudley, which belonged to William Fitz Ansculf. It was held of him by a certain Payn, who had succeeded the Saxon holder Wigar,[34] and, since no later underlord is mentioned, must have reverted to the barons of Dudley at an early date. It followed the same descent as the manor of Northfield[35] (q.v.) until the division of Joyce Burnell's estates between Maurice de Berkeley and Lady Joan Beauchamp took place in the middle of the 15th century. Cradley was then assigned with Northfield and Weoley (q.v.) to Maurice Berkeley,[36] but since Lady Beauchamp, who claimed some estate in Cradley, had previously settled it on her grandson James Butler Earl of Ormond and later Earl of Wiltshire, he afterwards successfully claimed it, and since then it has followed the same descent as Hagley[37] (q.v.), now belonging to Viscount Cobham.

In 1291 there was a capital messuage at Cradley worth 6d., one mill valued at 22s. and another at 12d., and mast in the park at 12d.[38]

The mill at Cradley is frequently mentioned in the Staffordshire Pipe Rolls. It yielded a rent of 3s. a year, which was granted about 1193 to Emma

[11] Pat. 4 & 5 Phil. and Mary, pt. xv, m. 19. The deed of sale bears her signature 'Amye Duddley,' and there is another deed of the same date, by which Anthony Forster, in whose house at Cumnor she lived for some time, gave up all his right in the manor (Jeayes, op. cit. no. 440, 441, 441b).
[12] Pat. 5 & 6 Phil. and Mary, pt. iv, m. 18.
[13] Chan. Inq. p.m. (Ser. 2), ccxxix, 140; cclvii, 71; Feet of F. Salop, East. 1652; Div. Co. Hil. 17 & 18 Chas. II; Recov. R. Mich. 5 Will. and Mary, rot. 88; 25 Geo. III, rot. 410.
[14] Soc. Antiq.; see also Exch. Dep. Hil. 5 Jas. I, no. 17.
[15] The earlier manorial rolls have been edited for the Worcester Historical Society by Mr. John Amphlett of Clent.
[16] Nash, op. cit. ii, App. 27.
[17] Pat. 15 Chas. II, pt. xiv.

[18] Stat. 22 Chas. II, cap. 6; Palmer's Indices (P.R.O.), lxxiii, fol. 82a.
[19] Bp. Lyttelton's Hist. of Hagley, &c. (Soc. Antiq.), fol. 147-8.
[20] Ibid.
[21] Assize R. 739, m. 85.
[22] Misc. Bks. Ld. Rev. clxxxv, fol. 143.
[23] Chan. Inq. p.m. 4 Edw. I, no. 93.
[24] Jeayes, op. cit. no. 17.
[25] Pope Nich. Tax. (Rec. Com.), 230a.
[26] Ct. R. of Manor of Hales (Worcs. Hist. Soc.), 240.
[27] Ibid. 246.
[28] Cal. Pat. 1348-50, p. 498; Chan. Inq. p.m. 24 Edw. III (2nd nos.), no. 24.
[29] Exch. Dep. East. 24 Chas. II, no. 4.
[29a] Possibly the Balwick or Walwyke Mill of 1302 (Ct. R. of Manor of Hales [Worcs. Hist. Soc.], 443, 465).
[30] Bp. Lyttelton's Hist. of Hagley, &c. (Soc. Antiq.), fol. 195.
[30a] Ct. R. of Manor of Hales (Worcs.

Hist. Soc.), 280, 350, 428, 443, 445, 471, 508, 543, 548.
[31] The first mention of the office of constable in the manor of Halesowen occurs in the Court Rolls of 1293 (Ct. R. of Manor of Hales [Worcs. Hist. Soc.], 250). Those of Romsley and Oldbury are mentioned at this date (ibid. 251). The office does not seem to have been in great request, as there are frequent records of payment for relief from its duties.
[32] Nash, op. cit. i, 527.
[33] Exch. Dep. by Com. East. 31 Chas. II, no. 15.
[34] V.C.H. Worcs. i, 317a.
[35] For references see Northfield.
[36] Early Chan. Proc. bdle. 19, no. 6.
[37] Cal. Pat. 1461-7, pp. 112, 223, 297; 1467-77, p. 419. For other references see Hagley.
[38] Worc. Inq. p.m. (Worcs. Hist. Soc.), i, 35. The park is mentioned in 1273 (ibid. 17).

wife of David King of North Wales in part exchange for the manor of Halesowen.[39] Its first assessment was in 1179.[40] A mill still belonged to the manor in 1338.[41] It was perhaps this mill from which John Wall was ejected by Thomas Nevill, Joan his wife and others in 1599.[42] No mill at Cradley is actually mentioned in the survey of John Lyttelton's lands taken in the reign of Elizabeth, but a memorandum was made that Thomas Birch claimed the liberty of making a fish-pond or stank or 'damme head' for the pond called Birches Mill Pond by rendering yearly 2d.[43] Just before the Dissolution the Abbot and convent of Halesowen had altered the course of the stream which formed the boundary between Cradley and Rowley and between the counties of Staffordshire and Worcestershire, and on account of this alteration paid to the lord of Cradley 12d. and 1 lb. of wax yearly.[44] In 1535 the abbot was paying to the king 16s. 4d. yearly for the farm of the mill of Cradley.[45]

According to Bishop Lyttelton the park was still in existence in the reign of Henry VIII,[46] but it is not mentioned in the survey taken in the reign of Elizabeth. Nash mentions that ruins of a manor-house with a moat existed on the estate called Cradley Park in his time, but were then much overgrown with wood.[47] Near these ruins was a field called Chapel Leasow, where tradition says there was once a chapel. The rectory and advowson of Cradley were included in the grant of Halesowen Abbey to Sir John Dudley in 1538,[48] so the mansion and chapel may perhaps have been on the abbot's estate at Cradley.[49] The chapel seems to have disappeared shortly after the Dissolution.

In 1535 the Abbot and convent of Halesowen were in receipt of rents amounting to 40s. from an estate in Cradley. It was probably held of the capital manor of Cradley, for a rent of 15d. was paid by the convent to 'Master Seleng'[50] (Saint Leger). This estate, which probably formed part of the manor of Halesowen, was granted as 'the manor of Cradley' to Sir John Dudley in 1538.[51] It is mentioned as a separate manor in 1556–7,[52] but evidently became incorporated with Halesowen shortly afterwards.

The manor of *LUTLEY* (Ludeleia, xi cent.; Lodeleye, xiv cent.; Ludley, xvii cent.) was perhaps granted by the Saxon lady Wulfrun in 996 to the college which she endowed at Wolverhampton, though it is not mentioned in the foundation charter.[53] At the time of the Domesday Survey the monastery was in the hands of secular canons of Wolverhampton, who were holding Lutley.[54] From 1086 until 1610

there is nothing to prove that the college continued to hold Lutley. At the later date the Dean of Wolverhampton granted a lease of the deanery to Sir Walter Levison, and tenements at Lutley were then included in the possessions of the deanery.[55] It is therefore probable that Lutley was granted with the college by Edward VI to John Duke of Northumberland.[56] The college was re-founded in 1553 by Queen Mary, who restored to the Dean and Prebendaries of Wolverhampton all their property,[57] which must have included Lutley, as it was in the possession of the dean in Nash's time.[58]

Under the Wolverhampton Rectory Act[59] of 1848 the college of Wolverhampton was dissolved and its estates vested in the Ecclesiastical Commissioners,[60] who were authorized in 1849 to sell the property belonging to the dean.[61] It is not known that Lutley was ever sold, and the manor is now extinct.

Lutley was held during the 18th century by the Earl of Bradford's family on lease from the Dean and Prebendaries of Wolverhampton.[62] It does not appear that there was ever a manor-house there.[63]

The monastery of Halesowen was receiving rents amounting to 26s. 8d. from an estate at Lutley at the time of the dissolution of their house.[64] It probably formed part of the manor of Halesowen, and was granted with it in 1538 to Sir John Dudley.[65]

The manor of *OLDBURY* (Aldeberia, xii cent.) was a member of the manor of Halesowen.[66] It evidently passed with Halesowen to the Crown in 1102, and from 1166[67] to 1173[68] the sum of 26s. 8d. was paid into the Exchequer from the farm of Oldbury. It was probably granted with Halesowen to the abbey of Halesowen, for the vill appeared at the courts of that manor from the time of Henry III.[69] Indeed, it is not described as a manor until 1557,[70] when Sir Robert Dudley settled it on himself and Amy his wife, with reversion to her right heirs, Arthur Robsart[71] being one of the trustees. The latter seems to have succeeded to Oldbury on Amy Dudley's death,[72] and had manorial rights, including frankpledge, there in 1573, when he settled it on his son Robert.[73] Robert died during his father's lifetime, leaving a son George, who in 1610 sold the reversion of Oldbury after Arthur Robsart's death to William Turton.[74] After Arthur's death George repented of the sale, and it was finally decided that certain messuages in the manor should belong to Turton, while the manor itself was settled on George and his wife Anne and their son Arthur.[75] In 1633 Arthur Robsart and William Turton, son and suc-

---

[39] *Will. Salt Arch. Soc. Coll.* ii (1), 2, 11, 18, 25, 28, 30–1, &c.
[40] Ibid. 175.
[41] Chan. Inq. p.m. 12 Edw. III (1st nos.), no. 40.
[42] *Quart. Sess. R.* (Worcs. Hist. Soc.), 18.
[43] Misc. Bks. Ld. Rev. ccxxviii, fol. 243b.
[44] Bp. Lyttelton, Hist. of Hagley, &c. (Soc. Antiq.), fol. 145, quoting Court Rolls.
[45] *Valor Eccl.* (Rec. Com.), iii, 207.
[46] Hist. of Hagley, &c. (Soc. Antiq.), fol. 146.
[47] Nash, op. cit. i, 526.
[48] *L. and P. Hen. VIII*, xiii (2), g. 491 (1).
[49] See below.
[50] *Valor Eccl.* (Rec. Com.), iii, 207.

[51] *L. and P. Hen. VIII*, xiii (2), g. 491 (1).
[52] Chan. Inq. p.m. (Ser. 2), cx, 135.
[53] Dugdale, *Mon.* vi, 1443.
[54] *V.C.H. Worcs.* i, 308b.
[55] Oliver, *Account of the Church of Wolverhampton*, 72.
[56] Pat. 7 Edw. VI, pt. viii, m. 25.
[57] Oliver, op. cit. 70.
[58] Nash, op. cit. i, 527.
[59] Stat. 11 & 12 Vict. cap. 95.
[60] *Index to Lond. Gaz.* 1830–83, p. 1927, under Wolverhampton.
[61] *Lond. Gaz.* 25 May 1849, p. 1711.
[62] Nash, op. cit. i, 527.
[63] Ibid.
[64] *Valor Eccl.* (Rec. Com.), iii, 207.
[65] *L. and P. Hen. VIII*, xiii (2), g. 491 (1).

[66] *Pipe R.* 19 Hen. II (Pipe R. Soc.), 108.
[67] Ibid. 13 Hen. II, 63.
[68] Ibid. 20 Hen. II, 108.
[69] *Ct. R. of Manor of Hales* (Worcs. Hist. Soc.).
[70] It was reserved from the sale of Halesowen to Thomas Blount and George Tuckey in 1558 (Feet of F. Salop, East. 4 & 5 Phil. and Mary).
[71] Com. Pleas D. Enr. East. and Trin. 3 & 4 Phil. and Mary; Feet of F. Salop, Trin. 3 & 4 Phil. and Mary; Mich. 3 Eliz.
[72] Memo. R. Mich. Recorda 10 Eliz. rot. 98; East. Recorda 20 Eliz. rot. 35.
[73] Feet of F. Salop, Mich. 15 Eliz.
[74] Chan. Inq. p.m. (Ser. 2), cccxc, no. 153; Feet of F. Salop, Mich. 8 Jas. I.
[75] Chan. Inq. p.m. (Ser. 2), cccxc, 153.

cessor of the above-mentioned William, sold it to Charles Cornwallis,[76] who held courts there in 1648.[77] He left two daughters, Anne wife of Anthony Mingay and Frances wife of William Fetherston,[78] the latter of whom finally succeeded to the whole of Oldbury.[79] From her it passed to her daughter Anne wife of William Addington,[80] who also left two daughters, Frances wife of Christopher Wright and Anne wife of Richard Grimshaw. Anne's son sold his share of Oldbury to Christopher Wright.[81] The latter was holding it in Nash's time.[82] He married as a second wife the widow of Richard Parrot of Hawkesbury, near Coventry.[83] The manor of Oldbury afterwards seems to have passed to the relatives of his second wife, for Francis Parrot of Hawkesbury Hall was lord of the manor in 1829.[84] His daughter Elizabeth married Major John Fraser of Hospital Field, Arbroath, and Oldbury passed from them to their daughter Elizabeth wife of Patrick Allan.[85] The latter assumed the additional surname of Fraser in 1851,[86] and Oldbury is now in the hands of the trustees of his will. Courts leet and baron are still held every year.

LANGLEY, which went by the name of *WALLEXHALL* (Wallokeshale, xiv cent.) *alias* Langley Wallexhall *alias* Langley and Wallexhall, and is described as a manor in the 16th and 17th centuries, has descended with Oldbury since the Dissolution. Before that date it apparently formed part of Oldbury.[87]

ROMSLEY (Rommesley, xiv cent.) may perhaps be identified with the hide and a half in the manor of Halesowen which was held in 1086 of Earl Roger by Roger the Huntsman.[87a] Since the 12th century it seems to have followed the same descent as Halesowen[88] and now belongs to Viscount Cobham. At the eyre of 1291–2 it was returned that Stephen de Asherug had held Romsley, Hampstead and Hazelbury (now Hasbury) by serjeanty of finding three foot soldiers for the king's army, one with a lance and two with bows and arrows, for forty days. These manors the Abbot of Halesowen then held, and for them he refused to render any service. The abbot, however, stated that he held the whole of the manor of Halesowen, of which these manors formed part,[89] free of all secular services, according to his foundation charter.[90] Romsley was, however, a separate manor, and its Court Rolls from 1277 for about 400 years are in the possession of Viscount Cobham. The Romsley rolls are sometimes written on the backs of the Halesowen rolls.[91]

From the time of Edward I to the 16th century occasional mention occurs of a hamlet in Romsley called *KENELMSTOWE* or Kelmystowe[92] which must have grown up round the chapel of St. Kenelm. In 1279 Kenelmstowe was evidently in the manor of Halesowen.[93] In a deed of 1462–3 'Kelmystowe' is said to be in the parish of Clent,[94] and in the reign of Queen Elizabeth it also appears to have been, partly at least, in Clent.[95] The truth appears to be that the hamlet lay partly in Clent and partly in Romsley. An inn called the 'Red Cow' at Kenelmstowe owed its name to the legend of the finding of St. Kenelm's body by a cow grazing in a meadow under Clent Hill, and its prosperity to the pilgrims visiting the shrine of St. Kenelm. It was probably this inn which as *hospitium Sancti Kenelmi* was rated at £5 in the rental of Romsley Manor in 1499.[96] It was leased by Lord Robert Dudley in 1556–7 to Richard Harris under the name of 'a mansion in Romsley near unto St. Kenelm's commonly called the sign of the red Cow.'[97] At the Reformation the pilgrimages to St. Kenelm's chapel ceased and the value of the inn declined.[98] The hamlet has now almost entirely disappeared.

The manor of *WARLEY WIGORN* (Werwelie, xi cent.; Wervelegh, Wervesley, xiii cent.; Wervelegh, xiv cent.), which had been held by Æthelward before the Conquest, belonged to William Fitz Ansculf at the time of the Domesday Survey,[99] and the fee formed part of the barony of Dudley (q.v.) until the death of John de Somery, without issue, in 1321.[100] This fee is not mentioned in the division of John de Somery's lands in 1323, and was evidently held jointly by his co-heirs, for when Richard de Fokerham granted the manor to Lady Joan Botetourt a moiety was said to be held of her and the other moiety of John de Sutton.[1] The overlordship seems to have lapsed when the manor was given to the abbey of Halesowen.[2]

Under these overlords the manor was held by knight's service.[3] In 1086 a certain Alelm held the manor,[4] and about the middle of the 13th century Margaret de Somery was holding it.[5] It afterwards passed to the Fokerhams, land at Warley being granted in 1276–7 by William de Fokerham and his wife Basil to Richard de Fokerham.[6] Richard died about 1289, and was succeeded by his son William,[7] who granted the manor of Warley with the chantry of Brendhall in 1309 to his son Richard.[8] Richard in 1320–1 conveyed the manor called Brendhall, which seems to have been identical with that of Warley, to his

[76] Feet of F. Salop, Mich. 9 Chas. I.
[77] Nash, op. cit. i, 521.
[78] Feet of F. Salop, East. 21 Chas. II.
[79] Ibid. Trin. 4 Will. and Mary.
[80] Ibid. East. and Trin. 2 Anne. A second daughter, Anne wife of — Paston, inherited half the manor, but died without issue (Nash, op. cit. i, 521).
[81] Nash, loc. cit.
[82] Ibid.
[83] Ibid.
[84] Priv. Act, 10 Geo. IV, cap. 25.
[85] Burke, *Landed Gentry* (ed. 5).
[86] Phillimore and Fry, *Changes of Name*, 4.
[87] Feet of F. Salop, Mich. 15 Eliz. and other references to Oldbury.
[87a] *V.C.H. Worcs.* i, 309.
[88] *Feud. Aids*, iv, 217; Feet of F. Div. Co. Trin. 28 Eliz.; Chan. Inq. p.m.

(Ser. 2), ccxxix, 140; Recov. R. East. 1652, rot. 197; East. 5 Geo. II, rot. 172.
[89] *Feud. Aids*, iv, 217.
[90] Assize R. 739, m. 85.
[91] *Ct. R. of the Manor of Hales* (Worcs. Hist. Soc.), 17, 163.
[92] Nash, op. cit. i, 519; Bp. Lyttelton's Hist. of Hagley, &c. (Soc. Antiq.), fol. 132. The termination 'stowe' very frequently means church.
[93] *Ct. R. of Manor of Hales* (Worcs. Hist. Soc.), 113.
[94] *Will. Salt Arch. Soc. Coll.* (New Series), iv, 124.
[95] Nash, op. cit. ii, App. 11, 12.
[96] Ibid. i, 519. The above form of the legend is a variant of that given under Clent *supra*, p. 50.
[97] Ibid.
[98] Ibid. Bishop Lyttelton accounts for

the final disappearance of the inn by the fact that the high road from Bromsgrove to Dudley, which had formerly passed through Kenelmstowe, had been diverted to pass through Halesowen.
[99] *V.C.H. Worcs.* i, 316b.
[100] *Cal. Inq. p.m.* 1–19 *Edw. I*, 495; *Testa de Nevill* (Rec. Com.), 40b, 43b.
[1] Nash, op. cit. i, 523.
[2] See below.
[3] *Testa de Nevill* (Rec. Com.), 40b; *Cal. Close*, 1288–96, p. 220.
[4] *V.C.H. Worcs.* i, 316b.
[5] *Testa de Nevill* (Rec. Com.), 40b.
[6] Feet of F. Div. Co. Mich. 4 & 5 Edw. I.
[7] *Cal. Close*, 1288–9, p. 2; *Cal. Inq. p.m.* 1–19 *Edw. I*, 495; Jeayes, op. cit. no. 65.
[8] Jeayes, op. cit. no. 65.

overlord John de Somery.[9] In 1337 Richard de Fokerham granted the manor of Warley to Lady Joan Botetourt,[10] younger sister and co-heir of John de Somery, and in the same year she granted it to the Abbot and convent of Halesowen on condition that they should find three canons to celebrate divine service in the abbey church and distribute 20s. to the poor on her anniversary.[11] In the same year John de Sutton,[12] who had married Margaret, the elder sister of John de Somery, quitclaimed his right in the manor, in return for

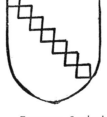

FOKERHAM. *Or a bend indented azure.*

which the abbot and convent promised him 'full participation in their prayers and spiritual benefits,' and when he died the same 'benefits' as an abbot.[13] Richard de Fokerham also confirmed the gift,[14] and in the same year received a grant of the manor for life from the abbot.[15]

At the Dissolution the abbot's estate at Warley was valued at £4 14s. 8d.[16] It was granted with Halesowen to Sir John Dudley in 1538,[17] and has since followed the same descent as Halesowen [18] (q.v.).

Brendhall, the capital messuage of this manor, the moat farm and other lands, and chief rents were sold by George Lord Lyttelton in 1772 to Mr. Robert Glover.[19] In 1485–6 the lord of the manor granted to William Hadley 'the manor called le Fotherhal de Wearley,' the waters of the moat and the fishery in it being reserved by the lord.[20] From the mention of the moat it may be inferred that Fotherhal was the moat farm mentioned above.

In the beginning of the reign of Charles I a Gilbert de Warley and Jane seem to have held the manor for a time, probably as lessees of the Lytteltons.[21]

Besides their manor of Halesowen the abbot and convent also had in the parish the granges of Blakeley in Oldbury, Owley in Lapal, Radewall in Ridgacre, Offmoor, Farley, Hamstead, Home Grange, New Grange and Warley Salop.[22] One carucate of land at Blakeley valued at 10s. belonged to the abbey in 1291.[23] Leases of the grange occur in 1329 [24] and 1343,[25] one including a water-mill. In 1340 the lessee was John Huwet of Rowley, who in that year obtained licence to have mass celebrated in his chapel of Blakeley Grange.[26] Owley Grange, the first mention of which occurs in 1415,[27] was leased in 1533 by the name of the manor of Owley Grange to William Geste and Elizabeth his wife for 8 marks yearly.[28] It is wrongly said to have been one of the

hiding-places of Charles II after the battle of Worcester. It belonged in 1680–1 to William Quest.[29]

Farley, Offmoor, Hamstead and Radewall Granges, Home Grange and New Grange belonged to the abbot and convent in 1291,[30] when Farley consisted of 2 carucates of land each worth 10s., Offmoor of 1 carucate, worth 1 mark, and Radewall of 1 carucate, worth 10s.[31] In the reign of Henry VII Radewall was let for 4 marks.[32]

Helle Grange was included in the grant of Halesowen Abbey to Sir John Dudley,[33] and descended in the same way as the manor of Halesowen, being last mentioned in 1598–9.[34]

CHURCHES The church of *ST. JOHN BAPTIST* consists of a chancel 29 ft. by 16 ft. 6 in., with vestry and organ chamber on the north, north chapel 16 ft. by 14 ft., south chapel 28 ft. 6 in. by 22 ft., nave, including the central tower, 85 ft. in length by 18 ft. at the east and 17 ft. 6 in. at the west, central tower dividing the nave into two portions 14 ft. 6 in. by 13 ft. 6 in., north aisle 14 ft. 9 in. wide, south aisle 21 ft. wide, with a modern addition at the south-east and a south porch. These measurements are all internal.

The earliest part of the present church is the short section of wall on the north side of the chancel containing a lancet window, parts of the east wall, and a portion of the walling joining the eastern respond on the south side. These represent the chancel of a church of about 1120, some 16½ ft. wide. Further remains of this church are to be found west of the central tower, where two bays of an arcade and a west wall are of a slightly later date.

The chancel arch, though almost entirely rebuilt, represents the eastern arch of the 12th-century central tower, and, from the spacing of the remaining original bays at the west end, the early nave must have been five bays long. The existence of a transept with eastern chapels is indicated by the remains of 12th-century arches to the north and south of the present chancel arch, and the pilaster buttresses at the west end of the present north aisle prove that the 12th-century aisle was about 11½ ft. wide. The early church was thus a large cruciform building, about 117 ft. long, with north and south aisles, transepts with eastern chapels, and central tower. The work was begun at the east end, but took long to complete, and the west door would hardly have been finished before 1200.

In the 14th century the south aisle was widened, its present width of about 21 ft. being probably the depth of the old transept then removed. It is not unlikely that the aisle was then carried on to the east end of the chancel by the insertion of two bays of

[9] Feet of F. Worcs. 14 Edw. II, no. 27 ; Nash, op. cit. i, 524 ; Bp. Lyttelton, Hist. of Hagley, &c. (Soc. Antiq.), fol. 141. The name still survives in a farm-house called Brand Hall.

[10] Jeayes, op. cit. no. 103.

[11] *Cal. Pat.* 1334–8, pp. 425, 461, 495 ; Jeayes, op. cit. no. 40.

[12] This John may have been the son of John de Sutton and Margaret de Somery, the date of the death of the elder John being uncertain.

[13] Jeayes, op. cit. no. 106.

[14] Ibid. 104.

[15] Ibid. 105.

[16] *Valor Eccl.* (Rec. Com.), iii, 206.

[17] *L. and P. Hen. VIII,* xiii (2), g. 491 (1).

[18] For references see Halesowen.

[19] Nash, op. cit. i, 524.

[20] Ibid.

[21] Feet of F. Div. Co. Trin. 5 Chas. I ; Mich. 8 Chas. I. Members of a family of this name were tenants in the manor in the 14th and 15th centuries (Nash, op. cit. i, 524 ; Jeayes, op. cit. no. 89, 92).

[22] Jeayes, op. cit. no. 273. Rental of the abbey quoted by Bp. Lyttelton in his Hist. of Hagley, &c. (Soc. Antiq.), App. 22.

[23] *Pope Nich. Tax.* (Rec. Com.), 230.

[24] *Cal. Pat.* 1327–30, p. 446.

[25] Jeayes, op. cit. no. 122.

[26] Worc. Epis. Reg. Wulstan de Brauns-ford (1339–49), fol. 37 d.

[27] Jeayes, op. cit. no. 273.

[28] Add. Chart. 7391.

[29] Exch. Dep. Mich. 32 Chas. II, no. 1

[30] *Pope Nich. Tax.* (Rec. Com.), 230. Farley Grange is mentioned in 1271 and Offmoor in 1302 (*Ct. R. of Manor of Hales* [Worcs. Hist. Soc.], 32, 456).

[31] *Pope Nich. Tax.* (Rec. Com.), 230.

[32] Bp. Lyttelton's Hist. of Hagley, &c. (Soc. Antiq.), fol. 200, quoting a rental of the abbey.

[33] *L. and P. Hen. VIII,* xiii (2), g. 491 (1).

[34] Chan. Inq. p.m. (Ser. 2), cclvii, 71.

arcading. At the end of the 14th or early in the 15th century the central tower was removed. It may possibly have fallen at that time and caused the partial ruin of the nave. Only the eastern arch of the old tower was suffered to remain, and, starting from this point, two bays of nave arcading were erected with the evident intention of subsequently building a west tower.

At the same time the north aisle was widened to its present size, 14¾ ft., and the north transept removed. Towards the end of the century the original idea of a western tower was abandoned and the present structure built half-way down the nave, leaving two bays only standing of the original 12th-century arcade, to the west of it.

A chapel dedicated to St. Katherine was next formed by extending the north aisle eastward to the chancel. In the gable is a small circular light in a square reveal, considerably repaired.

In the north wall are three shallow niches 5 ft. high, probably lockers, and above is an early 12th-century window with deeply splayed reveal. The head and rear arch are round, the latter showing traces of painting on the plaster. Beyond this window is a break in the masonry, and the small rubble work on the upper wall, which was above the vaulting, here changes to later ashlar. West of the modern vestry is the organ chamber opening from the chancel by a modern arch.

On the south side of the chancel is an arcade of two bays with pointed arches, probably of 14th-century date, of two chamfered orders resting on octagonal piers with capitals but no bases. The chancel arch has been greatly altered, and only

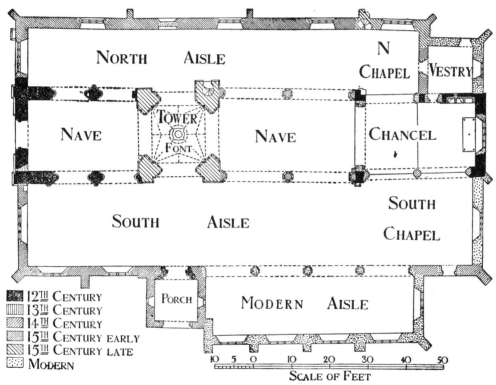

PLAN OF HALESOWEN CHURCH

wall of a vestry which was in existence on the site of the present one. A large window was inserted and an elaborate stair was built, in the north wall, to the rood-loft, which extended across the nave and both aisles.

The last important piece of work was the addition, after 1500, of a clearstory and a new roof to the nave, the line of the earlier roof being still visible on the tower wall. In modern times the church has been considerably restored and repaired, the north vestry rebuilt and a second aisle added on the south side.

The east window of the chancel is modern, of four lights, in 14th-century style. Above the window is the line of a round arch from wall to wall, which, together with the difference between the upper and lower masonry in the side walls of the chancel, proves the existence of a 12th-century barrel vault over the

portions of it appear to be the actual 12th-century work.

The first two bays on each side of the nave are of 15th-century date with two-centred arches of two orders. Above is a clearstory with three similar windows on each side, of two lights, under square heads.

The tower arches are of the same type as the nave arcade, but later, and have small capitals resembling a string-course which runs round the responds.

On the north side of the north-east pier of the tower is a door leading to the vice, and above it is a piece of old bell framing with the churchwardens' names for 1774. There is also an achievement of the royal arms. West of the tower are two bays of arcading of about 1150. Above the western respond on the north side is a round-headed opening, with traces of a corresponding one on the south side, these leading originally to a 12th-century gallery across the west end, which was approached by a stair in the south-west angle, now hidden. The west wall has three offsets, and is pierced by a large single lancet, below which is the west door with a round head of two zig-zag orders. Its jambs are shafted and have moulded abaci and scalloped capitals.

The east wall of the north aisle has been much repaired, but shows the join where it met the early vestry. The first north window is later and more elaborate than the rest, and is of four lights with a transom and late 15th-century tracery (most of which has been renewed) and a crocketed label. The three remaining windows in the north wall date from the 15th century, with a blocked north door between the second and third. The west window of the aisle has four lights. The tracery of these windows is for the most part modern, but the jambs are old.

side are small trefoiled lights. The external doorway is of 13th-century date. West of the door are two two-light windows with unusually wide splays and modern tracery. The west wall has a four-light window, and north of it a round-headed rebated recess in the wall.

The lofty tower shows externally three stages above the roofs. The lowest has on the north and south a three-light window of the 15th century. The second stage has square-headed two-light windows and a clock.

The belfry windows have two lights with 15th-century tracery and transoms with sub-cusping. The embattled parapet is modern.

The spire has three tiers of windows, all with foliated finials above.

On the exterior the east chancel wall has been much patched, but parts of the east window seem to

HALESOWEN CHURCH : WEST END OF THE NAVE SHOWING 12TH-CENTURY ARCADE

On the north side of the chancel arch is some broken masonry connected with the original transept and a later image bracket.

In the south aisle the east wall and window have been rebuilt in modern times. On the south side of the chancel arch is the offset of the original south transept, and at the point where the respond of the new 15th-century arcade was built against the chancel arch there is a straight joint. Breaks are also visible where the tower was built up to this arcade and where it meets the 12th-century work to the west. The second south aisle, with its arcade of four bays, was built in 1875. At the west end of this aisle is a porch with south door opening into the inner aisle. The doorway, which is reset 12th-century work, has a semicircular head, and is of three orders—one plain, one zigzag and one moulded—carried on double shafted jambs. Inserted in the porch walls are corbels with grotesque heads and beasts. On each

be old. Above it is a much restored 12th-century wall arcade of eight bays, consisting of round inter-lacing arches with cushion capitals, shafts and bases.

The north aisle has a gargoyle at the north-east angle ; the rood-loft stair is carried on corbels show-ing externally, and has a small trefoiled light with a foliated canopy.

At the western end of the nave on each side of the doorway are 12th-century pilaster buttresses and a plinth. On the western end of the north aisle is a 12th-century buttress, which is one of those at the north-west angle of the original church.

The interesting 12th-century font standing under the tower has a rounded bowl with a circular central shaft and four angle shafts with scalloped capitals. Round the bowl are four figures, much worn, which seem to represent our Lady, a king, a queen, and a priest holding a book, with interlaced strapwork between the figures. The roofs and furniture of the church are all modern. Among the monuments are a brass with the remains of an effigy to Rebekah wife of Thomas Littleton, rector, who died in 1669, an urn inscribed to the poet William Shenstone, who died in 1763, and a monument to Major Halliday (1794), by G. Banks, R.A.

There is a ring of eight bells : the first and sixth by John Warner of London, 1864, the second by Thomas Lester of London, 1753 ; the rest were cast by Joseph Smith of Edgbaston in 1707. On the fifth is ' Be it known to all, that doth me see that Ios. Smith in Edgbaston made all wee ' ; on the tenor : ' When sound of bell doth pearce your eare come to the church, God's Word to heare, my mournful sound doth warning give that here men cannot allwayes live.'

The plate consists of two chalices inscribed with the names of Francis Pierci, rector, and the church-wardens, 1684, and made two years previously, one large ancient flat paten (unmarked, but seems to be silver), a small flat paten of 1799, a modern silver flagon and a silver almsdish of 1730.

The registers before 1812 are as follows : (i) all entries 1559 to 1620, but leaves are missing from 1601 to 1609 and elsewhere ; (ii) 1620 to 1643, these two volumes having been re-bound (from 1643 to 1653 there is apparently a Civil War gap) ; (iii) baptisms 1661 to 1664, births 1653 to 1660, and burials and marriages 1653 to 1664 ; (iv) all entries 1665 to 1686 ; (v) 1687 to 1699 ; (vi) 1700 to 1716 ; (vii) 1717 to 1736 ; (viii) baptisms and burials 1736 to 1761 and marriages 1736 to 1754 ; (ix) marriages 1754 to 1762 ; (x) baptisms and burials 1761 to 1812 ; (xi) marriages 1762 to 1770 ; (xii) marriages 1770 to 1772 ; (xiii) marriages 1772 to 1783 ; (xiv) marriages 1783 to 1803 ; (xv) marriages 1804 to 1812.

The chapel of *ST. KENELM* lies in a picturesque hollow on the north-east slope of the Clent Hills. The stream which runs in the hollow below the church is fed by a spring which, according to tradition, rose on the spot where the body of Kenelm, murdered in 819, was found. A chamber, now filled with rubbish, below the east end of the chapel represents the shrine over the spring, which was much frequented by pilgrims.[35] The chapel consists of a continuous chancel and nave 46 ft. by 19 ft. wide, a space under the west tower, which projects over the nave, 18 ft. by 14 ft. wide, and a wooden south porch. These measurements are all internal.

The present north and south walls and the base of the tower, all built of red sandstone, are of 12th-century date. The east wall of the chancel was rebuilt in the 14th century, and the beautiful tower was added in the 15th century, a greenish sandstone being employed.

The interior of the chapel is uninteresting, being mostly modern. The walls are plastered and there are a modern roof and a large west gallery. On the south wall are the remains of rood screen corbels.

Externally the angles and gable of the east wall have 15th-century pinnacles. The three-light east window is modern and below it is an arched recess or doorway, which has had a wooden pentice over it. The entrance, which is now blocked, seems to have led to the well shrine.

In the north wall the first window is a 14th-

century lancet, and west of it is the jamb of a 12th-century light. Further west is a 12th-century pilaster buttress, the lower part being cut away for a 14th-century segmental archway, a feature repeated in the south wall. These were probably provided with steps leading down to the well under the chancel.

Of the two remaining windows on this side, the first, of two lights with a square head, is late 13th-century work, the second is modern. Two early buttresses remain, in one of which is a blocked 12th-century window, the other being a clasping buttress at the north-west angle. The plain 14th-century door is built within an earlier door of the 12th century. The tower wall sets back 1¼ ft. from the nave. The lower part of the tower, which is set astride of the west wall of the nave, is 12th-century work and has a plinth with wide flat angle buttress on the north-west. Over this is a 15th-century buttress with a modern pinnacle and one of the remarkable winged gargoyles which are repeated on the kneelers, angle buttresses, and window label at the west end.

Inside the west face of the tower is a large arched recess inclosing the modern west window, and a blocked round-headed door, which, though restored, represents the early west doorway. Above this the tower rises in two stages with diagonal buttresses. The lower stage has a large gargoyle on each buttress and the upper has a small belfry window in each face with rich crocketed canopy. Niches of similar type flank the belfry lights and are repeated on the buttresses. The embattled parapet has modern angle pinnacles and a line of trefoiled panelling below. The angle buttresses are terminated by smaller gargoyles of the type already noticed. Several of these gargoyles appear to represent butterflies.

The light but rich tower and the quaintly designed west end are very effective.

With the exception of a two-light 14th-century opening at the east end, all the windows in the south wall are modern restorations. Built into the wall is a small 12th-century figure of a priest in chasuble, stole and alb, a book in the left hand, and the right raised in benediction.

The 12th-century south door has a carved tympanum representing our Lord in glory with angels on each side. The arch has two orders, the outer with rays and fillets, the inner with beak heads. The side shafts appear to have been re-dressed. The porch is a 15th-century structure, with a four-centred outer arch of wood and a projecting cornice above, with plaster work and an embattled beam.

There is one bell, by Joseph Smith of Edgbaston, dated 1724.

The plate includes a curious cup of hammered silver with the hall mark of 1592, a silver paten with the hall mark of 1750, and an alms basin of repoussé work, possibly made in the early years of the 18th century. The flagon is plated.

The registers before 1812 are as follows : (i) baptisms and burials 1736 to 1783 ; (ii) baptisms 1783 to 1819. The second book contains also baptisms and burials of Frankley, 1813 to 1819.

ADVOWSONS A church and two priests at Halesowen are mentioned in the Domesday Survey.[36] Possibly the second priest served the chapel of St. Kenelm, which

---

[35] For an account of the legend of the murder of St. Kenelm see *supra*, p. 50, under Clent.

[36] *V.C.H. Worcs.* i, 309a.

is assumed to have been in existence at that time. The advowson belonged to the lord of the manor, and, while it was in the hands of David son of Owen, he, with the consent of Emma his wife, gave it to the Abbot of Pershore, who, however, restored it to King John in 1199.[37] It was included in the foundation charter of Halesowen Abbey in 1214.[38] The church seems to have been appropriated to the abbey about 1270, a vicarage being ordained in that year,[39] but the appropriation did not receive papal sanction until 1281.[40] The advowson belonged to the abbey until the Dissolution,[41] and was granted in 1538, with the rectory, to Sir John Dudley.[42] It has since followed the same descent as the manor,[43] Viscount Cobham being the present patron.

In 1291 and 1427 the church was taxed at £26 13s. 4d.,[44] and in 1535 the rectory was valued at £8 2s. 8d.[45]

In January 1864 a rearrangement of the tithes was made between Lord Lyttelton, the lay impropriator, and the incumbents of the three parishes of Halesowen, Quinton and St. Kenelm's.[46] Great tithes to the value of about £100 a year were conveyed to the clergy, Lord Lyttelton's estates being rendered tithe free.[47] Halesowen was constituted a rectory in 1866.[48]

The chapel of St. Kenelm in Romsley is not mentioned in the Domesday Survey, but may possibly have been served by one of the two priests at Halesowen.[49] In 1448 an indulgence was granted for the repair of the chapel,[50] and in 1473 the abbot and convent obtained licence to acquire lands worth £10 yearly for the maintenance of a chaplain.[51] The oblations offered at the chapel were valued at £10 in 1535.[52] The chapel was granted with Halesowen to Sir John Dudley,[53] the advowson belonging to the lords of Halesowen until 1866.[54] John Lyttelton and his successors held it as a free chapel in no way dependent on the church of Halesowen,[55] and his chaplains received no institution from the bishop. The stipend of the curate was formerly only £5, but in 1675 Sir Henry Lyttelton settled upon the curate and his successors, in lieu of this stipend, all the great tithes of Romsley.[56]

In 1841 St. Kenelm's was formed into a separate ecclesiastical parish,[57] and in 1863 the greater part of the township of Hunnington was added to it.[58] In the following year, as mentioned above, part of the tithes of Halesowen were assigned to St. Kenelm's,[59]

and in 1866 the parish was constituted a rectory.[60] It subsequently became known as the parish of Romsley. The rectory is now in the gift of the rector of Halesowen.

As mentioned above,[61] the chapel of Cradley seems to have disappeared shortly after the Dissolution. The ecclesiastical parish of Cradley was formed in 1841.[62] The present church of St. Peter was built by Thomas Best, clerk, and others in 1789, and was acquired from them in 1798, when the chapel was consecrated by the Bishop of Worcester. The patronage was secured to Thomas Best for three turns, and was then to pass to the Lytteltons.[63] The living is now a vicarage in the gift of the rector of Halesowen. The register begins in 1785.

A chapel at Oldbury was built in 1529 because during the winter and in the time of floods it was impossible for the inhabitants of Oldbury to attend the parish church.[64] It seems to have stood on copyhold land, since in 1574 William Feldon alias Carpenter made an agreement with Arthur Robsart and others that he would make no claim under any copy of court roll or other writing to the chapel croft except 'to hear God's service.'[65] The advowson was claimed by the patron of Halesowen, Oldbury being a chapelry of Halesowen,[66] but the presentations were probably irregularly made, and, according to Nash, the chapel came into the hands of Dissenters after the Revolution. The vicar of Halesowen reported in 1705 that the chapel of Oldbury was unendowed, and then served by nonconforming ministers,[67] but it was later taken over by Bishop Lloyd (1699–1717), who consecrated the chapel and cemetery.[68] The patronage was vested in the vicar of Halesowen in 1781,[69] but was said to have been in the Crown in 1808 and 1833.[70]

When the common of Oldbury was inclosed in 1829 it was arranged that half the proceeds of the sale of the inclosed lands should be assigned to building a new church at Oldbury, as the existing chapel was quite inadequate owing to the increasing population.[71] A new church, Christ Church, was built in 1841, and the patronage was vested in the vicars, afterwards the rectors, of Halesowen.[72] When the new diocese of Birmingham was formed in 1905 Oldbury was transferred to it, and the patronage vested in the bishop.

Oldbury was formed into a separate ecclesiastical parish in 1841,[73] and Langley was separated from it

[37] *Abbrev. Plac.* (Rec. Com.), 24 ; *Rot. Cur. Reg.* (Rec. Com.), ii, 157.
[38] *Rot. Lit. Claus.* (Rec. Com.), i, 174b ; *Cartae Antiquae*, NN 19.
[39] *Reg. G. Giffard* (Worcs. Hist. Soc.), 43 ; Nash, op. cit. ii, App. 29.
[40] *Reg. G. Giffard* (Worcs. Hist. Soc.), 71, 139, 177 ; Jeayes, op. cit. no. 39.
[41] *Reg. G. Giffard* (Worcs. Hist. Soc.), 177, 287 ; Worc. Epis. Reg. Hemenhall, fol. 14 d. ; *Valor Eccl.* (Rec. Com.), iii, 206 ; Feet of F. Div. Co. Trin. 30 Hen. VIII.
[42] Pat. 30 Hen. VIII, pt. iii ; *L. and P. Hen. VIII*, xiii (2), g. 491 (1).
[43] Inst. Bks. (P.R.O.).
[44] *Pope Nich. Tax.* (Rec. Com.), 217 ; *Lay Subs. R.*1427–9 (Worcs. Hist. Soc.), 21.
[45] *Valor Eccl.* (Rec. Com.), iii, 207.
[46] See below.
[47] Noake, op. cit. 182.
[48] *Lond. Gaz.* 1 May 1866, p. 2705.
[49] *V.C.H. Worcs.* i, 309a.

[50] Worc. Epis. Reg. Carpenter (1443–76), i, fol. 65.
[51] *Cal. Pat.* 1467–77, p. 396. Nash, in his *Hist. of Worc.* i, 520, quotes some Court Rolls of Romsley which show that various lands were acquired for the endowment of the chapel. The sacrist of Halesowen appears to have been curate of the chapel by virtue of his office (Nash, op. cit. i, 520).
[52] *Valor Eccl.* (Rec. Com.), iii, 207.
[53] *L. and P. Hen. VIII*, xiii (2), g. 491 (1).
[54] Chan. Inq. p.m. (Ser. 2), ccxxix, 140 ; Feet of F. Div. Co. Hil. 17 & 18 Chas. II ; Recov. R. Mich. 5 Will. and Mary, rot. 88.
[55] In 1705, however, the chapel of St. Kenelm was returned as a chapel of ease to the church of Halesowen (Nash, op. cit. i, 532).
[56] Ibid. i, 520.
[57] *Parl. Papers* (1872), xlvi, 17.

[58] Ibid. 27.
[59] Noake, op. cit. 181.
[60] *Lond. Gaz.* 25 May 1866, p. 3133.
[61] Under Cradley Manor.
[62] *Parl. Papers* (1872), xlvi, 17.
[63] Local and Personal Act, 39 Geo. III, cap. 72.
[64] Worc. Epis. Reg. printed in Nash, op. cit. ii, App. 27.
[65] Ibid. quoting MSS. formerly in the possession of J. Westwood, vicar of Halesowen.
[66] Feet of F. Div. Co. Hil. 17 & 18 Chas. II ; Recov. R. Mich. 5 Will. and Mary, rot. 88.
[67] op. cit. i, 532.
[68] Ibid. 522.
[69] Ibid. 532.
[70] Carlisle, *Topog. Dict.* ; Gorton, *Topog. Dict.*
[71] Priv. Act, 10 Geo. IV, cap. 25.
[72] Lewis, *Topog. Dict.*
[73] *Parl. Papers* (1872), xlvi, 17.

HALESOWEN CHURCH : THE SOUTH ARCADE

HAMPTON LOVETT CHURCH FROM THE NORTH-WEST

in 1846 and formed, with part of Halesowen, into an ecclesiastical parish.[74] The church of Holy Trinity, Langley, which was built in 1852, was formerly the parish church, but is now a chapel of ease to the church of St. Michael and All Angels erected in 1890–1. The living is a vicarage in the gift of the Crown and the bishop alternately. At Churchbridge is the chapel of ease of the Good Shepherd, built 1899.

A second ecclesiastical parish, that of Round's Green, was formed from Oldbury in 1905 with its church of St. James, built in 1892. The living is an incumbency in the gift of the vicar of Langley.[75]

The ecclesiastical parish of Quinton was formed in 1841,[76] and Christ Church was built in that year. It, like St. Kenelm's, became a rectory in 1866,[77] having had a portion of the tithes of Halesowen assigned to it in 1864.[78] Parts of Hill and Lapal were transferred to it from Halesowen in 1863.[79] The rectory is now in the gift of the Bishop of Birmingham. The parish includes Warley Salop and Warley Wigorn, which in 1884 were united under the name of Warley. A new ecclesiastical district of St. Hilda, Warley Woods, was formed in 1906[80] and is served by a curate in charge. Blackheath was formed out of Quinton, Halesowen and Rowley Regis in 1869,[81] and is a vicarage in the gift of the Bishop of Worcester. The church of St. Paul was built in the same year.

The advowson and rectory of the church of Lutley were included in the grant of Halesowen Abbey to Sir John Dudley in 1538.[82] The advowson and rectory are mentioned again in 1590–1,[83] but from that time they disappear.

In 1339 the bishop gave licence to a certain John de Honesworth to have divine service celebrated in his house of 'Walbrok' in the parish of Halesowen.[84]

In 1309 William Fokerham, lord of Warley Wigorn, gave his son Richard the chantry of Brendhall, belonging to the chapel of St. Katherine the Virgin.[85] In a rental of Halesowen Abbey of 1499–1500 a sum of 43s. 4d. was received from Margery Westwood for Warley Grange next the chapel of St. Michael.[86] This seems to indicate a second chapel at Warley. It is perhaps to be identified with the church of Warley, of which the advowson and rectory were included in the grant of Halesowen Abbey to Sir John Dudley in 1538.[87] No further mention of it has been found.

Nash[88] gives some interesting extracts from the churchwardens' books of Halesowen.[89] These show that there was a chancel dedicated in honour of St. Katherine and an image of that saint and lights dedicated in honour of St. Katherine and St. Stephen.

In 1469 William Pepwale granted land at Frankley and at Willingwick to trustees to hold for his wife Agnes while she lived and after her death for a chantry in the church of Halesowen.[90]

There is a Congregational chapel, built in 1807, and Baptist, Primitive Methodist and Wesleyan chapels in Halesowen, Langley, Cradley, Romsley and Oldbury, Unitarian chapels at Cradley and Oldbury, and United Methodist chapels at Blackheath, Cradley and Oldbury. A Roman Catholic church dedicated to St. Francis Xavier was built at Oldbury in 1865.

CHARITIES

The following charities are regulated by a scheme of the Charity Commissioners 27 November 1874, namely :

1. William Wight's, founded by deed 10 October 1614, consisting of a rent-charge of £1 for the poor, issuing out of a house in Cornbow Street.

2. The same donor, as recorded on a benefaction table, gave an annuity of £2 12s. for the poor and an annuity of £1 6s. 8d. for the minister for preaching sermons on the four quarter days. These payments are made out of the rent of 7 acres of land, known as the World's End, which is in the possession of the parish and is let at £20 a year, of which £3 13s. 4d. is applied towards the church expenses, £1 6s. 8d. to the minister, and the balance to the sick and needy.

3. Richard Dickins, will 1640, consisting of an annuity of 6s. 8d. for church expenses and of 10s. for the relief of the poor, issuing out of a house near Churchgates.

4. John Carpenter's, will 1726, consisting of a rent-charge of 20s. for twenty of the poorest housekeepers, on 2 February yearly, issuing out of a house in the High Street.

In 1789 Richard Green, by his will, gave an annuity of 52s. issuing out of land at Belle Vue, Halesowen, to be distributed in bread to the poor of the Hill and Lapal townships.

The Lea Charities : In 1701 William Lea, by will, devised land for charitable purposes. The endowment consists of about 26 acres of land at Frankley, let at £20 8s. a year, and £542 9s. 8d. consols, with the official trustees, producing £13 11s. yearly.

In 1704 Thomas Lea, by will, devised a rent-charge of £4 issuing out of houses in Cornbow Street.

These charities are regulated by a scheme of the Charity Commissioners 22 April 1910, whereby a moiety of the income is made applicable for the benefit of the poor of the town and borough, and the other moiety for the poor of Romsley Quarter, an annual sum of £2 out of each moiety to be applied in the distribution of clothes, &c., or medical aid in sickness, and the residue for the benefit of poor old men and women in clothing.

In 1906 Felix Smith, by his will, proved 12 May, bequeathed £10, the income to be applied in the upkeep of the parish churchyard. The legacy was invested in £11 17s. 4d. consols, with the official trustees, producing 5s. 8d. yearly.

In 1879 George Grainger, by will, proved 6 January, bequeathed £400, the income to be paid to the minister of the Congregational Chapel. The

[74] *Lond. Gaz.* 16 Jan. 1846, p. 156.
[75] *Clergy Lists.*
[76] *Parl. Papers* (1872), xlvi, 17.
[77] *Lond. Gaz.* 3 Apr. 1866, p. 2216.
[78] Noake, op. cit. 182.
[79] *Parl. Papers* (1872), xlvi, 27.
[80] *Pop. Ret.* (1891), ii, 656.
[81] *Lond. Gaz.* 13 July 1869, p. 3939.

[82] *L. and P. Hen. VIII*, xiii (2), g. 491 (1).
[83] Chan. Inq. p.m. (Ser. 2), ccxxix, 140.
[84] Worc. Epis. Reg. Wulstan de Braunsford (1339–49), fol. 3 d.
[85] Jeayes, op. cit. no. 65. This chapel was probably the chancel dedicated to St. Katherine in the parish church of Halesowen, mentioned below.

[86] Nash, op. cit. i, 524.
[87] *L. and P. Hen. VIII*, xiii (2), g. 491 (1).
[88] op. cit. ii, App. 29.
[89] Unfortunately these books, last mentioned about 1854, have disappeared, it is believed at one of the restorations to which the church has been subjected.
[90] Jeayes, op. cit. no. 392.

legacy was secured by a mortgage at 4½ per cent., producing £17 a year.

The same testator bequeathed £100 for the poor in warm garments on New Year's Day. It was represented by £114 13s. on mortgage at 4½ per cent., producing £5 13s. 2d. yearly.

Cradley : The following gifts were mentioned on the table of benefactions in the chapel at Cradley, namely :

John Sparry, will, 1659, the interest of £4 for the poor ;

Nicholas Holmer, will, 1673, the interest of 20s. to be given to the poor ;

Thomas Cox, will, 1695, the yearly profits of £10 to be given to the poor.

The legacies were paid to the parish officers and the income given on St. Thomas's Day to poor widows.

In 1705 John Mansell, by his will, devised an annuity of 40s. out of his lands and houses within the manor of Cradley to be distributed to forty poor householders in sums of 1s. each. The distribution takes place at Christmas time.

In 1806 John Townshend, by his will, proved at London, 11 September, bequeathed £70 consols, the annual dividends, amounting to £1 15s., to be applied towards the support of the National school, which was conveyed by deed, 9 October 1855.

In 1898 Charles Cockrane, by will, proved 5 July, bequeathed £2,000 (free of duty), the income to be applied for the benefit of the Unitarian Chapel at Netherend.

The Wesleyan Chapel and trust property, comprised in deeds, 1826, 1839 and 1860, was by order of the Charity Commissioners, 4 August 1869, vested in trustees thereby appointed on trusts of ' The Wesleyan Chapel Model Deed.'

Langley : In 1875 Samuel Clifton, by his will, proved at Lichfield, 11 November, bequeathed £100, represented by £106 7s. 8d. consols, with the official trustees, the annual dividends, amounting to £2 13s., to be applied towards the maintenance of such schools at Langley as the trustees should think proper. The income is applied to the Church schools.

The official trustees also hold £446 6s. 1d. consols, producing £11 3s. yearly, purchased with the proceeds of sale of part of the school site and building, and known as the Chance Scholarship Fund, founded by deed poll, 26 December 1851.

By schemes of the Board of Education, 1904 and 1910, the net income is to be applied in awarding secondary school and technical scholarships to children of persons in the employ of Messrs. Chance & Hunt, Limited, but failing suitable candidates therefrom, to children in the ecclesiastical parish of St. Michael and All Angels.

In 1902 Walter Showell, by will, proved at London, 3 January, bequeathed £2,000, the income to be paid to a Church of England clergyman for services in St. James's Church, Round's Green.

The legacy—less duty—is represented by £1,800 on mortgage of houses and land in Coventry Road, Aston-juxta-Birmingham, at 4 per cent., producing £72 a year.

Township of Oldbury : The Oldbury charity (including the benefaction of John Price, bequeathed by will, dated 11 February 1726) is regulated by a scheme of the Charity Commissioners, 28 February 1908.

By the scheme the endowments were divided into three portions :

(a) Site of schoolhouse and buildings thereon, house adjoining the Unitarian meeting-house, and the house and garden adjoining the schoolhouse, the whole producing £35 a year.

(b) A building estate, containing 5 acres in the centre of the town, nearly all built upon, gross yearly income £241 2s. 2d. A strip of land fronting Halesowen Street and Low Town, let on two building leases, yearly income £8 5s. 9d., and 1 r. 20 p., part of Furnace Field, let at 10s. a year, and the following sums of stock, held by the official trustees, namely, £966 13s. 4d. Birmingham 3 per cent. stock, £750 Birmingham Canal stock, £50 debenture stock of the Sharpness Docks and Gloucester and Birmingham Canal Company, and £257 1s. 5d. consols, producing in dividends £67 8s. yearly. At the date of the scheme there was also a sum of £102 11s. 3d. consols, accumulating with the official trustees and £1,000 on deposit at Lloyds Bank.

(c) Several pieces of land, containing 5 a. 2 r., fronting the road leading from Oldbury to Titford, gross yearly income £32 2s. 5d., and £250 Birmingham Corporation 3½ per cent. stock and £1,650 Birmingham Canal stock, held by the official trustees, producing in annual dividends £74 15s.

The scheme further provides that the endowments particularized under division (a) be held upon the trusts contained in an indenture of bargain and sale, dated 25 February 1784, that is to say for educational purposes ;

That those under (b) be held upon the trusts contained in an instrument of surrender, 6 April 1659, that is to say in the discretion of the trustees for educational purposes, the said educational endowments to be called ' The Oldbury Educational Foundation.'

That those under (c) be held upon trust for the support of the ministry of the meeting-house at Oldbury held upon the trusts of indentures of lease and release, dated respectively 25 and 26 March 1725.

Endowment for minister of congregation of Protestant Dissenters comprised in deed, 27 September 1817, consisted of land with buildings thereon, subsequently occupied as the Oldbury Institute, exchanged in 1888 for another piece of land adjoining, and a sum of £100 paid by way of equality of exchange, and invested in £103 7s. 2d. consols, with the official trustees, producing £2 11s. 8d. yearly.

The Primitive Methodist Chapel, comprised in indentures of 18 and 19 July 1836, was by a scheme of the Charity Commissioners, 20 October 1905, settled upon the trusts of ' The Primitive Methodist Chapel Model Deed.'

In 1801 Thomas Newby, by deed, gave 2 a. 2 r. or thereabouts in Oldbury, let at £42 a year, one moiety thereof to be distributed among the poor of Rowley Regis, Staffordshire, and the other moiety among the poor of Oldbury. It is applied in gifts of money averaging 5s. each.

In 1869 Mary Palmer, by her will, proved at Exeter, 9 December, left a legacy, now represented by £106 19s. 8d. consols, with the official trustees, the annual dividends, amounting to £2 13s. 4d., to be applied in the distribution of Bibles and New

Testaments about Christmas to such persons as the vicar should think proper.

In 1875 Samuel Clifton, by his will proved 11 November, bequeathed £100, the interest to be paid to the Christ Church National schools, Oldbury.

The township is possessed of 4 a. 1 r. 17 p. for public walks or pleasure grounds, acquired by deed 25 November 1892, and another piece of land containing 7,924 square yards, by deed, 10 November 1892.

Romsley : The charity founded in 1684 by William Smith is regulated by a scheme of the Charity Commissioners 10 November 1868. The trust property consists of 2 a. 3 r. at Romsley, let at £7 10s. a year, a rent-charge of £5 issuing out of Dove House Farm, and £10 rent from the master's house. The net income—subject to the payment of 20s. to the poor—is applied for educational purposes.[91]

In 1883 Thomas Jenks, by his will proved at Worcester 20 February, bequeathed £100, which has been invested in £99 10s. consols, with the official trustees ; the annual dividend, amounting to £2 9s. 8d., is applied in the distribution of bread and clothing to the poor on St. Thomas's Day.

Warley Wigorn : The charities known as Moore's Free School, founded by will, 1724, and Richard Powell's, founded by codicil to will proved at Worcester 20 June 1877, are regulated by a scheme of the Charity Commissioners 22 January 1901.

The trust fund consists of £1,563 1s. 1d. consols, with the official trustees, of which £994 1s. 7d. stock represents the proceeds of sale of site and school buildings thereon situated at Hill Top, Warley, and £348 5s. 8d. stock represents Richard Powell's legacy, and the balance accumulated income.

The scheme directs that the annual dividends, amounting to £39 1s. 6d., should be applied in prizes to children at a public elementary school, and in exhibitions not exceeding £10, tenable at any institution of education higher than elementary.

In 1801 Thomas Newby, by deed, gave an annuity of £4, one moiety thereof to be distributed to the poor on 26 December and 24 June annually, and the remaining moiety towards the support of a Sunday school.

HAMPTON LOVETT

Hamtona juxta Wiccium emptorium (viii cent.) ; Hamtun, Hamtune (xi cent.) ; Hampton Lovet (xiv cent.).

Hampton Lovett is a small parish containing 2,041 acres,[1] watered by the Hampton Brook. The land is undulating, rising from about 100 ft. above the ordnance datum on the banks of Hampton Brook to 200 ft. at certain points. The soil is mixed clay and the subsoil marl. Clay was worked on Stockend Farm, near the main road leading to Kidderminster, about fifty years ago, and there are other disused clay-pits in the parish, but now agriculture is the only industry.

Hampton Lovett village is situated to the east of the main road to Droitwich from Kidderminster ; it is small and very picturesque, consisting of only one group of houses, each of which stands in its own garden. The church is at the east end of the village and the rectory about a quarter of a mile north. There is now no school in the parish, that at Cutnall Green being supposed to serve it. A parish room was erected in 1897 on a site given by Lord Hampton with funds chiefly raised by Lady Godson, wife of Sir Frederick Godson, M.P. for Kidderminster, who was then residing at Westwood Park.

Boycott Farm, in the south of the parish, was transferred from Salwarpe to Hampton Lovett in 1880, and four years later part of Elmley Lovett was transferred to this parish.[2] There is apparently no inclosure award for Hampton Lovett.

William Thomas, who was Bishop of Worcester from 1683 to 1689, was presented to the rectory of Hampton Lovett in 1670.[3] Henry Hammond, the royalist divine, who was sheltered during the Commonwealth at Westwood, was buried in the church of Hampton Lovett in 1660 on the eve of the Restoration.[4]

MANORS In a spurious Evesham charter dated 716 Ethelbald of Mercia granted 'Hamtona juxta Wiccium emptorium' with other lands to Abbot Ecgwin.[5] The first authentic reference to HAMPTON LOVETT occurs in a charter of 817, when Coenwulf, King of Mercia, granted land at Salwarpe and 'Hamtun' to Bishop Deneberht of Worcester.[5a] According to the Chronicle of Evesham, however, the manor remained in the possession of the abbey until Abbot Æthelwig, who died in 1077,[6] gave it to Urse the Sheriff,[7] who was holding it in 1086.[8] According to the Domesday Survey Urse had succeeded Alwold in 4 hides at 'Hamtune' and the Abbot of Evesham in 4 hides at 'Hantune,' which is probably also to be identified with Hampton Lovett. With 'certain of his knights' he had held the manor of Hampton and those of Upton and Witton of Abbot Æthelwig II, but when the abbot died Urse 'invaded those lands and no service could be had.'[9] Hampton Lovett was subsequently held of the barony of Elmley Castle, and the overlordship is mentioned for the last time in 1626.[10]

Robert, tenant of both manors under Urse in 1086,[11] was evidently the Robert Parler who held other property of Urse in Worcestershire at that time,[12] as by Stephen's reign he had been succeeded by Isnard Parler.[13] It is uncertain whether William son of

91 See 'Schools,' V.C.H. Worcs. iv.

1 In this parish and Westwood there are 564¼ acres of arable land, 1,814¾ acres of permanent grass and 233 acres of woods (Statistics from Bd. of Agric. [1905]).

2 Census of Engl. and Wales (1891), ii, 657.

3 Dict. Nat. Biog.

4 Ibid. 5 Birch, Cart. Sax. i, 198.

5a Ibid. 501. For the identification of this Hamtun we are indebted to Mr. F. M. Stenton.

6 Chron. de Evesham (Rolls Ser.), 95.

7 Harl. MS. 3763, fol. 60 d.

8 V.C.H. Worcs. i, 318b, 319b.

9 Cott. MS. Vesp. B. xxiv, fol. 10 d. ; V.C.H. Worcs. i, 318b, 319b.

10 Testa de Nevill (Rec. Com.), 43, 40; Cal. Inq. p.m. 1–9 Edw. II, 403 ; Chan. Inq. p.m. 31 Hen. VI, no. 38 ; Cal. Inq. p.m. Hen. VII, i, 1 ; Chan. Inq. p.m. (Ser. 2), lv, 30 ; clvi, 1 ; ccccxviii, 69.

11 V.C.H. Worcs. i, 318b.

12 Ibid. 330.

13 Ibid. ; Cott. MS. Vesp. B. xxiv, fol. 10 d.

Guy de Offern, grandson of Isnard,[14] ever held this manor. An estate at Himbleton which Isnard had held was bequeathed by him to Brian de Brompton and his wife Margery,[15] and it would seem that Hampton Lovett followed the same descent, for it was settled by Brian de Brompton upon Henry Lovett and his wife Joan in tail, with reversion to the donor and his heirs.[16] John Lovett was dealing with land in Hampton Lovett in 1226–7,[17] and had been succeeded before the middle of the century [18] by his brother Henry.[19] John Lovett, who held the manor in 1256 and 1316, was son of Henry

LOVETT. *Argent three wolves passant sable.*

Lovett.[20] Part of the manor had passed before 1280 to the Blount family. This estate subsequently became known as the manor of Hampton Lovett, and its descent will be found below.

The manor retained by the Lovetts, which was afterwards called *OVER HALL* or *OVER COURT*,[21] passed on the death of John Lovett without issue [22] to the heirs of Brian de Brompton.[23] These heirs were his great-granddaughters Margaret and Elizabeth.[24]

Margaret, the eldest, married Sir Robert Harley, kt.,[25] and her half of Over Hall had passed to her son Robert Harley before 1361.[26] His only daughter and heir, Alice, married Sir Hamo Peshall,[27] and was succeeded before 1415–16 by her only child Elizabeth wife of Sir Richard Laken, kt.,[28] on whom half the manor was settled in 1431.[29] This moiety remained in the possession of the Lakens [30] until 1528, when Thomas Laken, great-grandson of the above Richard and Elizabeth, sold it to John Pakington.[31]

Elizabeth, the other heir of Brian de Brompton, married Sir Edmund Cornwall, kt., and they settled their half of Over Hall on their youngest son Peter,[32] who was granted free warren there in 1369.[33] Peter died in 1386, Edmund his grandson and heir being then two and a-half years old and in the custody of

Sir Brian Cornwall, lord of Burford.[34] This property remained with the Cornwalls, passing from Edmund Cornwall in 1452 to his son Thomas, and from Richard Cornwall in 1533 to his son George [35] until 1544, when George Cornwall sold it to John Pakington, who thus became possessed of the whole manor.[36]

The Blounts' manor of *HAMPTON* afterwards became more important than Over Hall. William Blount, husband of Isabel widow of Henry Lovett, who was seised of it about 1280,[37] was succeeded before 1316 by his son Peter [38]; he died without issue and was succeeded by his brother

CORNWALL. *Ermine a lion gules crowned or and a border engrailed sable bezanty.*

Sir Walter Blount, whose son William by his second wife Joan de Sodington was granted free warren there in 1327.[39] The manor apparently passed from William to his brother John Blount, who was in possession in 1346.[40] He was succeeded by a daughter Alice,[41] who presented to the church of Hampton Lovett in 1396 [42] and in 1414 founded a chantry at Hampton Lovett for the souls of Sir John Blount

BLOUNT. *Barry wavy or and sable.*

and Elizabeth his wife, her father and mother, and for Richard Stafford and Richard Stury, the two husbands of Alice.[43] Alice and her first husband, Richard Stafford, jun., were seised of the manor in 1370,[44] and in 1393 she settled it on her second husband, Sir Richard Stury, kt., with remainders to Elizabeth Blount, Walter Blount and to John son of Walter Blount.[45]

Alice died without issue in 1415, her heir being Sir John Blount of Sodington,[46] whose relationship to

[14] Habington, *Surv. of Worc.* (Worcs. Hist. Soc.), i, 285.
[15] Ibid.
[16] De Banco R. 423, m. 400 ; Wrottesley, *Ped. from Plea R.* 89.
[17] Cur. Reg. R. 97, m. 4 d.
[18] *Testa de Nevill* (Rec. Com.), 40.
[19] De Banco R. 423, m. 400. For pedigree of the Lovetts see Elmley Lovett, p. 108.
[20] De Banco R. 423, m. 400 ; Feet of F. Worcs. 41 Hen. III, no. 3 ; *Cal. Inq. p.m.* 1–9 Edw. II, 403.
[21] The name survived as Over or Upper Hall Manor until 1626, but the manor appears after that time to have become merged in Hampton Lovett Manor. The name Upper Hall still survives in a farm-house.
[22] De Banco R. 423, m. 400, but compare Elmley Lovett, where he is said to have left co-heirs. Possibly the statement in the De Banco R. that he died without issue may be assumed to mean that he died without issue male, the settlement by Brian de Brompton having perhaps been upon Henry Lovett and his issue male by Joan his wife.
[23] Ibid.
[24] Wrottesley, op. cit. 89 ; De Banco

R. 423, m. 400 ; see also Wrottesley, op. cit. 46 ; *Visit. of Shropshire,* 1623 (Harl. Soc.), ii, 304–6. Elsewhere Margaret and Elizabeth are said to be granddaughters of Brian ; Wrottesley, op. cit. 38.
[25] *Visit. of Shropshire,* 1623 (Harl. Soc.), i, 214 ; ii, 304.
[26] Ibid. ii, 305 ; Cott. Chart. xxvi, 3.
[27] *Visit. of Shropshire,* 1623 (Harl. Soc.), ii, 305. Joan widow of Robert de Harley the younger married as a second husband John Darras and seems to have been in possession of a moiety of the manor of Hampton Lovett in 1398 (Feet of F. Div. Co. East. 21 Ric. II ; *Visit. of Shropshire,* 1623 [Harl. Soc.], i, 214). In a fine of the same date, printed by Sir Thomas Phillipps, but not found among the feet of fines at the Public Record Office, Richard Maurdyn and Elizabeth his wife were dealing with a moiety of the manor (Sir T. Phillipps, *Index to Worc. Fines,* p. ix).
[28] *Visit. of Shropshire,* 1623 (Harl. Soc.), ii, 306 ; Wrottesley, op. cit. 289.
[29] Feet of F. Div. Co. East. 9 Hen. VI, no. 2.
[30] A pedigree of this family is given in *Visit. of Shropshire,* 1623 (Harl. Soc.), ii, 306–8.

[31] Ibid. ; Add. MS. 31314, fol. 11.
[32] De Banco R. 423, m. 400.
[33] Chart. R. 43 Edw. III, m. 6, no. 14.
[34] Marshall, *The Genealogist,* iii, 229.
[35] Chan. Inq. p.m. 31 Hen. VI, no. 38; (Ser. 2), lv, 30.
[36] Add. MS. 31314, fol. 56–60 ; Feet of F. Worcs. Trin. 36 Hen. VIII.
[37] *Lay Subs. R. Worcs.* c. 1280 (Worcs. Hist. Soc.), 22.
[38] Close, 9 Edw. II, pt. i, m. 13 ; *Cal. Inq. p.m.* 1–9 Edw. II, 403 ; Nash, *Hist. of Worc.* ii, 162a.
[39] Chart. R. 1 Edw. III, m. 31, no. 63; Nash, loc. cit.
[40] *Visit. of Worc.* 1569 (Harl. Soc. xxvii), 17 ; *Feud. Aids,* v, 303 ; Nash, op. cit. i, 536.
[41] The manor of Thickenappletree passed to Alice after the death of her brother William Blount (Habington, op. cit. i, 262), but there is nothing to show that William ever held Hampton Lovett.
[42] Nash, op. cit. i, 540.
[43] Chant. Cert. 25, no. 20.
[44] Feet of F. Div. Co. Mich. 44 Edw. III.
[45] Ibid. Trin. 17 Ric. II, no. 88.
[46] Chan. Inq. p.m. 2 Hen. V, no. 27.

her is not certain, but who was probably her nephew. It is difficult to account for the fact that the manor of Hampton Lovett passed a few years later (before 1419) to Thomas Blount, afterwards Sir Thomas, who was the grandson of Sir Walter Blount mentioned above by his first wife Eleanor, daughter and heir of John Beauchamp of Hatch, co. Somers.[47] He was succeeded in 1456 [48] by his son Sir Walter, who was created Lord Mountjoy in 1465 [49] and was followed in 1474 by his grandson Edward. The latter died in the following year, when the manor passed to his uncle John Blount,[50] who left it in 1485 to his son William fourth Lord Mountjoy.[51] In 1524 William sold the manor to Sir John Pakington above mentioned.[52]

PAKINGTON. *Party cheveronwise sable and argent with three molets or in the chief and three sheaves gules in the foot.*

Sir John Pakington built at Hampton Lovett a house called Hampton Court, which is described by Leland as 'a veri goodly new house of brike,'[53] and, having no sons, settled the reversion of the manor in 1542 upon his nephews Thomas and John Pakington, sons of his brother Robert, in tail-male with remainder to Humphrey, another brother of the elder John.[54] John died in 1560,[55] and the whole manor passed to Sir Thomas Pakington, who was Sheriff of Worcestershire in 1561.[56] On his death in 1571 the manor passed to his son John,[57] who was knighted in 1587.[58] He died in 1625, and was succeeded by his grandson Sir John Pakington, who had succeeded to the baronetcy on the death of his father in 1624.[59]

The estates of Sir John Pakington were sequestered three times for his loyalty to Charles I and Charles II,[60] and were not finally restored to him until the accession of Charles II. His wife Dorothy, daughter of Thomas Lord Coventry, has been said to have been the author of *The Whole Duty of Man*.[61] In 1669 Sir John settled the manor of Hampton Lovett on his son John,[62] who succeeded him in 1679–80 and died in 1688.[63] Sir John Pakington, his only son, supposed to be the original of Addison's Sir Roger de Coverley,[64] was succeeded in 1727 by his only surviving son Sir Herbert Perrott Pakington. The latter was succeeded in turn by his two sons—John, who died without issue in 1762, and Herbert Perrott, who died in 1795, leaving his property to his eldest son John.[65] In 1830 John also died without issue, and his

nephew John Somerset, son of William Russell of Powick and Elizabeth his wife, sister of the above John Pakington, succeeded as heir-at-law.[66] John Somerset Russell afterwards took the name of Pakington, and was created a baronet in 1846 and raised to the peerage as Lord Hampton in 1874.[67] As Sir John Pakington he was a minister of the Crown in several offices. He died in 1880, when Hampton Lovett passed to his son John Slaney Lord Hampton, who was succeeded in 1893 by his half-brother Herbert Perrott Murray Pakington,[68] from whom Mr. Edward Partington of Easton Glossop, co. Derby, the present owner of the manor, purchased it in July 1900.[69]

HORTON is now the name of two farms situated in the north of the parish. At the time of the Domesday Survey Robert held Horton of Urse D'Abitot. Aluric had held it before the Conquest,[70] but no other mention of the property has been found until the 16th century. In 1538 William Lygon of Madresfield mortgaged six messuages and land in Horton and Hampton Lovett to John Pakington,[71] and in the following year sold the estate to John.[72] In 1571 Sir Thomas Pakington, kt., nephew of John, died seised of the 'manor or farm' of Horton.[73] Since then it has belonged to the lords of the manor of Hampton Lovett,[74] but all manorial rights have long since lapsed.

THICKENAPPLETREE (Thiccan Apel Treo, Tichenapletreu, xi cent.; Thikenepeltre, xiii cent.; Fikelnapeltre, Thykenaptre, xiv cent.; Fykenapetre, Thirkenappeltre, xv cent.; Faukenapultre, Fekenapultre, xvi cent.), formerly a manor in the parish of Hampton Lovett, has now entirely disappeared. It was probably situated in the east of the parish, as, according to Habington in his *Survey of Worcestershire*, it was partly in the parishes of St. Peter and St. Augustine, Dodderhill.[75]

Before the Conquest Thickenappletree seems to have been held by the church of Worcester, having been acquired by Bishop Wulfstan from Erngeat son of Grim, who afterwards, with the help of Earl Leofric, regained the manor. Wulfstan retaliated by refusing to make Erngeat's son a monk, and the latter then promised that the manor should after his death belong to his son and through him to the monastery. This promise was not kept, and 'after a little while not one of all his children remained to succeed him and this land with his other property came to the hands of strangers.'[76] Thickenappletree probably passed to Alwold, who was mentioned in the Domesday Survey as a former lord of the manor.

[47] *Visit. of Worc.* 1569 (Harl. Soc. xxvii), 20; Nash, op. cit. i, 540; Worc. Epis. Reg. Morgan, fol. 3 d.
[48] Worc. Epis. Reg. Carpenter, i, fol. 113 d.; G.E.C. *Complete Peerage*, v, 398.
[49] G.E.C. loc. cit.; Feet of F. Div. Co. Hil. 11 Edw. IV, no. 80.
[50] G.E.C. *Complete Peerage*, v, 399.
[51] *Cal. Inq. p.m.* Hen. *VII*, i, 1.
[52] Recov. R. East. 17 Hen. VIII, rot. 457; Feet of F. Worcs. East. 17 Hen. VIII; Add. MS. 31314, fol. 8.
[53] Leland, *Itinerary* (ed. Hearne), vii, 13. This house was destroyed by Cromwell in the Civil War.
[54] Add. MS. 31314, fol. 89; Recov. R. D. Enr. Trin. 34 Hen. VIII, m. 1.
[55] From monument in the church. His will (16 Aug. 1551) enumerated

legacies, the non-payment of which was subsequently the cause of Chancery proceedings ([Ser. 2], bdle. 87, no. 58).
[56] P.R.O. *List of Sheriffs*, 158.
[57] Chan. Inq. p.m. (Ser. 2), clvi, 1. His widow Dorothy, who was his sole executrix, afterwards married Thomas Tasborow, and with him was sued in 1578 by Walter Longe and Mary his wife, one of the daughters of Sir Thomas Pakington, for the non-payment of legacies; Ct. of Req. bdle. 62, no. 90.
[58] Shaw, *Knights of Engl.* ii, 86.
[59] Chan. Inq. p.m. (Ser. 2), ccccxviii, 69; G.E.C. *Complete Baronetage*, i, 148.
[60] *Cal. Com. for Comp.* ii, 1194.
[61] *Dict. Nat. Biog.*
[62] Feet of F. Div. Co. Mich. 21 Chas. II.

[68] G.E.C. *Complete Baronetage*, i, 148.
[64] *Dict. Nat. Biog.*; G.E.C. *Complete Baronetage*, i, 149.
[65] G.E.C. *Complete Baronetage*, i, 149.
[66] G.E.C. *Complete Peerage*, iv, 156.
[67] Ibid.
[68] Burke, *Peerage*.
[69] Information supplied by Mr. R. Bruce Ward.
[70] *V.C.H. Worcs.* i, 318b.
[71] Add. MS. 31314, fol. 13. A family named Horton owned land in Hampton Lovett about this time (Chan. Proc. [Ser. 2], bdle. 23, no. 62).
[72] Add. MS. 31314, fol. 13 d., 51 d.
[73] Chan. Inq. p.m. (Ser. 2), clvi, 1.
[74] Ibid. ccccxviii, 69.
[75] Habington, op. cit. i, 242.
[76] Heming, *Chartul.* (ed. Hearne), 260.

In 1086 William was holding the manor of Hugh the Ass.[77] The Herefordshire manors of Hugh passed to the Chandos family,[78] but Thickenappletree does not seem to have done so, and one of the parts into which it subsequently became divided was held of the honour of Elmley Castle.[79]

This manor was known in later times as *GREAT THICKENAPPLETREE*. A John de Thickenappletree, who had some estate in the manor in 1248–9,[80] may possibly have held the manor itself; and Amicia de Thickenappletree was living in the parish of Hampton Lovett about 1280.[81]

In 1321 Richard le Boteler was holding Great Thickenappletree,[82] and he evidently sold it to Sir John Blount, kt., lord of Hampton Lovett, for in 1345–6 Joan le Boteler, Richard's widow, released her dower in Thickenappletree to Sir John,[83] who was in possession of the manor in 1346.[84] Thickenappletree then followed the same descent as the

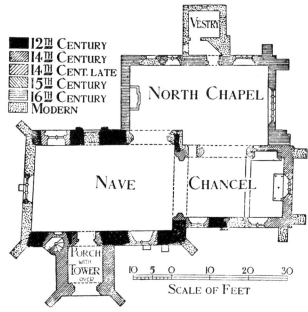

12TH CENTURY
14TH CENTURY
14TH CENT. LATE
15TH CENTURY
16TH CENTURY
MODERN

VESTRY

NORTH CHAPEL

NAVE   CHANCEL

PORCH
WITH
TOWER
OVER

10 5 0   10   20   30

SCALE OF FEET

PLAN OF HAMPTON LOVETT CHURCH

Blounts' manor of Hampton Lovett,[85] and is mentioned for the last time in 1626.

The second manor, known as *THICKENAPPLE-TREE NEXT WYCHE* or *KINGS THICKEN-APPLETREE*, was held of the manor of Inkberrow.[86] It probably originated in land in Thickenappletree in the demesne of Inkberrow. Such land was granted in 1371–2 by William de Brugge, parson of Martley, to his father Edward.[87] This estate was afterwards divided, part, as half the manor of Thickenappletree,

passing to Thomas Earl of Warwick, and the other as a knight's fee in Thickenappletree passing to the Sales, being held in 1375–6 by Sir Robert de Sale and in 1435–6 by John Sale.[88] The former moiety, which was held by Thomas Earl of Warwick at the time of his forfeiture in 1396,[89] followed the same descent as Elmley Castle until it was granted to Henry VII in 1487 by Anne Countess of Warwick.[90]

In 1525 the king granted a lease of the site of the manor of Thickenappletree 'parcel of Warwick's lands' to John Pakington for twenty-one years,[91] and a similar lease was made to John Wheeler in 1529–30[92] on the surrender of Pakington's lease. The manor was sold in 1545 to Richard and Walter Cupper,[93] and they in 1546 sold it to John Pakington and Thomas his nephew.[94] The manor then followed the same descent as Great Thickenappletree.[95]

CHURCH   The church of *ST. MARY* consists of a chancel 25 ft. 6 in. by 15 ft., a nave 37 ft. by 22 ft., a north chapel 36 ft. by 20 ft. with a modern vestry on the north side of it, and a tower 9 ft. by 10 ft. on the south side of the nave. These measurements are all internal.

Portions of the side walls of the nave and chancel remain of the early 12th-century church, which consisted of nave and chancel only. The plan remained unaltered till the 14th century, when a tower (forming a porch to the south doorway) was added on the south side of the nave; the east wall of the nave was rebuilt with a wider arch and the chancel perhaps lengthened eastwards. The east wall of the nave, which dates from the second quarter of the 14th century, is not set at right angles with the north and south walls, and corresponding irregularities in the east wall of the chancel and the west wall of the nave appear to be due to their being set out at equal distances from either end of this wall. About 1414[96] the chapel of St. Anne was built on the north side of the chancel; it was enlarged westward to its present size in 1561 by the Pakingtons.[97] In 1858–9 a careful restoration was undertaken. A vestry was added on the north side of the chapel, a window there being moved a little to the west and the old doorway walled up from the inside with the original oak door retained *in situ*. Owing to its bad condition the west end of the nave was entirely rebuilt and new tracery put into the old jambs of the west window. The wall between the nave and chapel was broken through and an arch inserted and the priest's doorway on the south of the chancel walled up at this time.

The east end of the chancel has been considerably restored, the large buttresses at the angles being

[77] *V.C.H. Worcs.* i, 320a.
[78] *V.C.H. Heref.* i, 276.
[79] *Cal. Inq. p.m. Hen. VII,* i, 1 ; Chan. Inq. p.m. (Ser. 2), clvi, 1 ; ccccxviii, 69.
[80] Feet of F. Worcs. case 258, file 6, no. 32.
[81] *Lay Subs. R. Worcs.* c. 1280 (Worcs. Hist. Soc.), 23.
[82] *Cal. Close,* 1318–23, pp. 359, 381.
[83] Habington, op. cit. i, 242.
[84] *Feud. Aids,* v, 303.
[85] Habington, loc. cit. ; Feet of F. Div. Co. Trin. 17 Ric. II ; Hil. 11 Edw. IV ;

Cal. Inq. p.m. Hen. VII, i, 1 ; Feet of F. Worcs. Mich. 34 Hen. VIII ; Chan. Inq. p.m. (Ser. 2), clvi, 1 ; ccccxviii, 69.
[86] Chan. Inq. p.m. 49 Edw. III, pt. i, 70; 14 Hen. VI, no. 35 ; 16 Edw. IV, no. 66.
[87] Add. MS. 28024, fol. 135.
[88] Chan. Inq. p.m. 49 Edw. III, pt. i, no. 70 ; 14 Hen. VI, no. 35.
[89] Chan. Inq. p.m. 21 Ric. II, no. 6.
[90] Ibid. 2 Hen. IV, no. 58 ; Feet of F. Div. Co. Mich. 2 Hen. VI ; Chan. Inq. p.m. 17 Hen. VI, no. 54 ; 18 Hen. VI, no. 3 ; *Cal. Pat.* 1446–52, p. 38 ; Feet of F. Div. Co. Mich. 6 Edw. IV, no. 41 ;

De Banco R. 903, m. 208 (Hil. 3 Hen. VII).
[91] Pat. 17 Hen. VIII, pt. i, m. 28 ; *L. and P. Hen. VIII,* iv (1), g. 1377 (12).
[92] Pat. 21 Hen. VIII, pt. i ; *L. and P. Hen. VIII,* iv (3), g. 6301 (16).
[93] Pat. 37 Hen. VIII, pt. xviii, m. 7 ; *L. and P. Hen. VIII,* xx (2), g. 910 (30).
[94] Add. MS. 31314, fol. 99 d.
[95] Chan. Inq. p.m. (Ser. 2), clvi, 1 ; ccccxviii, 69.
[96] Worc. Epis. Reg. Peverill, fol. 68, 81.
[97] Nash, op. cit. i, 544.

modern, but the east window is of late 14th-century date; it is of three lights with a traceried head under a two-centred arch. Above this is a small square-headed gable light, the gable itself terminating in a modern cross. On the north side of the chancel is a four-centred arch of two orders opening to the Pakington chapel; to the west of it is a smaller opening and to the east a recessed tomb. On the south side are two square-headed windows, each of two lights with tracery over. Between the windows the jambs of the blocked doorway are to be seen in the wall and further eastwards is a piscina. The chancel arch is of two continuous moulded orders and on the gable above it is a sanctus bellcote. The east window of the Pakington chapel is square-headed, of five lights, having a moulded label on the outside and a four-centred rear arch. The two north windows are similar to those on the south side of the chancel, except that the eastern one is of three lights. These windows, which are of 15th-century date, are not in their original positions, having been reset in the wall at the enlargement of the chapel in 1561, and the westernmost again moved when the vestry was added, as mentioned above. The blocked north doorway has a two-centred arch under a square head, with deep sunk moulded spandrels. At the southeast of the chapel is a piscina with an ogee head.

The nave is lighted by two ancient windows, one on each side, both probably of the late 14th century. The three-light west window has been rebuilt, the original jambs being re-used. On the north side of the nave is a fine early 12th-century doorway, having a semicircular head supported on shafts with cushion capitals and crude bases, the whole set in jambs slightly projecting from the wall face and continued upwards to the eaves as narrow pilaster buttresses. The door frame is flush with the outer face of the wall and has a tympanum under a segmental relieving arch.

The tower is of four stages, with an embattled parapet and a north-west cylindrical turret containing the stair. Its original entrance doorway within the church is blocked and an outer entrance has been made. The lower stage of the tower serves as a south porch, its outer doorway being pointed and double chamfered, while the inner doorway is of two moulded continuous orders. The belfry stage has windows of two lights with a quatrefoil over, and the two stories below have small chamfered square-headed windows. A peculiar feature is the saddle-backed roof running from north to south with small gables on the east and west.

There are two incised sundials on the south side of the chancel. Some of the pews are panelled in front with 15th-century tracery, probably remains of the chancel screen destroyed during the restoration of 1858. The oak altar table is of the 16th century, with carved baluster legs.

In the north-east window of the Pakington chapel is some heraldic glass dated 1561. The first piece is a much damaged and strangely arranged shield of Pakington quartered with Baldwin, Arden and Washbourne, and impaling a quartered coat whereof only the second and third quarters, which seem to be Donnington quartering Cretinge, survive. A second shield is quarterly: (1) lost. (2) Sable three fishes rising argent and a chief or with a lion sable between two roundels sable, the one charged with a martlet, the other with an anchor, impaling the second quarter

of the impaled coat on No. 1, for Kitson. (3) Partly lost, but apparently the third quarter of the Pakington coat on No. 1. (4) Quarterly, as the second quarter of the first shield but reversed. A third shield is Pakington impaling Washbourne, and a fourth shield is Arden quartering Washbourne impaling Azure ten billets or and a chief or with a demi-lion sable therein, for Dormer. A fifth shield is the quarterly coat of (1) and (4) Pakington, as on No. 1, with a mullet gules for difference. A sixth shield is the coat of Pakington quartering Washbourne, impaling Baldwin quartering Arden.

In the north wall of the chancel is a monument which was discovered behind the tomb of Sir John Pakington when that was removed to its present position in the west of the chapel. It is recessed into the wall and the lower part or pedestal is ornamented in front with four quatrefoils. The back of the recess is panelled in five compartments, and the insides of the jambs have similar panels continuing round the soffit of the four-centred arch. In the panelling at the back of the recess are three carved shields, repainted in modern times; the coats on them are: (1) Pakington; (2) Pakington impaling Dacres (the arms are wrongly painted); (3) Dacres. The tomb has been a good deal restored, and a brass inscription above it states that it was erected to Sir John Pakington, kt., of Hampton Lovett, who died in 1560. He was a judge, who received the grant of the Westwood property from Henry VIII, and according to the visitation pedigree of 1569 married Anne daughter of Henry Dacres, alderman of London.

The tomb at the west end of the chapel is to Sir John Pakington, who died in 1727; the monument is in the Renaissance style, with a reclining figure. On the south wall of the nave is a large wall monument to Henry Hammond, who died in 1660.

There are four bells: the first by John Martin of Worcester, 1664; the second by Richard Sanders of Bromsgrove, 1711; and the third inscribed 'SOM ROSA POLSATA MONDE MARIA VOCATA,' undated, but the ornamental borders at the end of the inscription show it to be the work of Thomas Hancox of Walsall, c. 1630. The fourth is a 'ting-tang' or sanctus bell, inscribed 'Indesinenter orate,' by John Martin, 1663.

The plate of the church was stolen in 1781, and then consisted of a large silver cup, a small silver paten, a large pewter flagon and two pewter plates; the present plate consists of a small cup with the 1755 hall mark, a small paten and flagon with the hall marks of 1895, and two pewter salvers each on three legs.

The registers before 1812 are as follows: (i) baptisms 1666 to 1766, burials 1666 to 1767, marriages 1666 to 1755; (ii) baptisms and burials 1766 to 1812; (iii) marriages 1755 to 1812.

ADVOWSON

The advowson of Hampton Lovett apparently belonged to the Lovetts, lords of the manor, for in 1269 a dispute about the right of patronage arose between Joan widow of Henry Lovett, then the wife of Robert de Scotevill,[98] and William Earl of Warwick, the guardian of the son and heir of Henry Lovett.

[98] This name is given as Stocumbe under Elmley Lovett.

It was determined in favour of the earl, and a writ was sent to the bishop commanding him to admit any person to the church of Hampton Lovett whom the earl might present.[99] The advowson afterwards became annexed to the Blounts' manor of Hampton Lovett, and has since followed its descent,[100] Edward Partington being now patron of the living.

Alice Stury, lady of the manor of Hampton Lovett, obtained licence in 1407 to found two chantries in the chapel of St. Anne in the church of Hampton Lovett dedicated in honour of St. John the Baptist and St. Anne.[1] The actual foundation does not appear to have taken place until 1414, when the bishop's licence was obtained[2] and the chantry of St. Anne was ordained.[3] The first admission to each chantry was made on 13 September 1414.[4] There are many subsequent references to these chantries, presentations to which were made by the lords of the Blounts' manor[5] of Hampton Lovett until the dissolution of the chantries about 1549, when the revenue of these two amounted to £16 14s. 7¾d. The chantry priests are said to be 'competently learnyd and of honest conversacon but not able to kepe a cure.'[6] In 1549 the chantry

house and lands belonging were granted to John Cupper and Richard Trevor.[7]

John Chapman, by his will dated February 1334, left £5 to the fabric of the church, 40s. to the high altar, 20s. to the light of the Cross and 6s. 8d. to the light of St. Nicholas and St. Margaret.[8]

CHARITIES
In 1830 Sir John Pakington, bart., by his will proved in the P.C.C. 16 July, bequeathed a sum of money, which was invested in £132 17s. 9d. consols, the dividends to be applied for the benefit of the poor in January and February.

In 1846 Miss Dorothy Pakington, by her will proved in the P.C.C. 25 September, left a legacy represented by £99 10s. consols for the use of the poor.

In 1891 the Rev. Joseph Amphlett, by his will proved at Worcester 19 February, bequeathed £200, which was invested in £206 19s. 9d. consols, the dividends to be applied in the same manner as the charity of Sir John Pakington above mentioned.

The several sums of stock are held by the official trustees, the annual dividends whereof, amounting to £10 19s. 4d., are applied in pursuance of the trusts of the respective charities.

KIDDERMINSTER

Chedeminstre (xi cent.) ; Kedeleministre, or Kideministre (xii–xiii cent.) ; Kidereministre (xiii–xv cent.) ; Kidderminster (xvi cent.).

The original ecclesiastical parish of Kidderminster covered all the land lying in the angle between the Severn and the Stour, with the exception of Over Mitton, a hamlet of Hartlebury situated in a bend of the latter river. An arm of the parish also extended eastwards, taking in the districts about Hurcott and Comberton. The northern boundary was formed by a chain of pools connected by a tributary of the Severn. The area of this triangular district is nearly 11,000 acres, of which 173 acres are covered with water, over 4,000 are arable land, 4,000 meadow and pasture and nearly 1,000 are covered with wood.[1]

MANORS
AND
BOROUGH
The present town of Kidderminster has developed from a settlement on the left bank of the Stour.[2] There is, however, evidence pointing to still earlier settlements elsewhere in the parish. In Mill Street, on the right bank of the river, there are caves in the sandstone cliff resembling the rock dwellings found in other parts of the country. The exact nature of the camps at Warshill near Trimpley[3] and of a tumulus near the Severn below the railway bridge is as yet undetermined.

Local tradition places at Broadwaters, on the

northern boundary of the parish, the site of a Saxon monastery. It is at least certain that the 10 cassates of land in the province of Usmere near the River Stour granted in 736 by Ethelbald, King of the Mercians, to his companion (comes) Cyniberht for the purpose of founding a monastery were near to Kidderminster. This land lay on both sides of the Stour and touched on the north 'Cynibre' wood (? Kinver), and on the west another wood called 'Moerheb,' part of which was also granted to Cyniberht.[4] Nothing is known of the monastery which Cyniberht was to have built. He had power to bequeath or alienate the land. It was certainly included in the 13 cassates at Stour-in-Usmere which his son, the Abbot Ceolfrith, gave to the Bishop and Cathedral Church of St. Peter, Worcester.[5]

In 781 Bishop Heathored, in consideration of the restoration of certain disputed lands, is stated to have obtained from King Offa a confirmation of the rights of the bishopric in 14 'mansae' at Stour-in-Usmere.[6] This document, however, is not certainly authentic, as are both the charters previously cited. There is no question as to the charter by which in 816 Denebert, then bishop, gave 14 cassates in two portions[7] at Stour to Coenwulf, King of the Mercians, in return for certain privileges to be enjoyed upon the lands of his see.[8]

[99] Reg. G. Giffard (Worcs. Hist. Soc.), i, 24, 32.
[100] Nash, op. cit. i, 540, 536 ; Cal. Inq. p.m. Hen. VII, i, 1 ; Feet of F. Worcs. East. 17 Hen. VIII ; Add. MS. 31314, fol. 8 ; Inst. Bks. (P.R.O.). The church, which was worth £27 1s. 4d. in 1291 (Pope Nich. Tax. [Rec. Com.], 217), had decreased in value to £10 6s. 8d. at the time of the Dissolution ; Valor Eccl. (Rec. Com.), iii, 268.
[1] Cal. Pat. 1405–8, p. 343.
[2] Nash, op. cit. i, 544 ; Worc. Epis. Reg. Peverill, fol. 68, 81.
[3] Worc. Epis. Reg. Peverill, fol. 81.

[4] Ibid. fol. 68.
[5] Ibid. fol. 75 ; Morgan, fol. 3 d. ; Polton, fol. 35, 144 d. ; Carpenter, i, fol. 11 d., 60 d., 62 d., 113 d. ; ii, 71 ; Moreton, fol. 45 ; Silvester de Gigliis, fol. 25, 39 d., 67 ; Feet of F. Worcs. East. 17 Hen. VIII ; Mich. 34 Hen. VIII.
[6] Chant. Cert. 25, no. 20 ; 60, no. 15 ; 61, no. 12.
[7] Pat. 3 Edw. VI, pt. vi.
[8] Worc. Epis. Reg. Wakefield, fol. 24 d.
[1] Statistics from Bd. of Agric. (1905).
[2] See below and cf. Leland, Itinerary (ed. 2), iv, 100.
[3] See V.C.H. Worcs. i, 191. Pigsty

Hill Coppice, adjoining Warshill or 'Wassell' Wood, was originally called Pict's Hill.
[4] It would therefore include Wolverley (Kemble, Cod. Dipl. no. 80 ; Birch, Cart. Sax. i, 222).
[5] Kemble, op. cit. 127 ; Birch, op. cit. i, 308.
[6] Kemble, op. cit. 143 ; Birch, op. cit. i, 335.
[7] cf. the two portions in Ethelbald's grant.
[8] Birch, op. cit. i, 497. The authenticity of these charters has been determined by Mr. F. M. Stenton.

The identification of Kidderminster with a part of the land at Stour-in-Usmere rests upon the fact that the name 'Ismere' is now applied to the series of pools at 'Broadwaters,'[9] and that Usmere was in 964 a part of the boundary between Kidderminster and Cookley in Wolverley.[10] The identification is supported by the fact that both Wolverley and Kidderminster were after 816 lands of the Crown.

No other record of Kidderminster is known before the Domesday Survey, in which it is described as a central 'manor' with sixteen outlying farms or 'berewicks.' These were Wannerton, Trimpley, Hurcott, 'Bristitune,' Habberley, 'Fastochesfeld,' Wribbenhall, Sutton, Oldington, Mitton, 'Teulesberge' and 'Sudwale,' and two berewicks each at Franche and Ribbesford.[11] In the time of Edward the Confessor the whole vill was possibly held by the king. In 1086 it was held by William I, but most of it lay waste and the king had added the woodland to his forest (of Feckenham). It had probably suffered from depredations by the Danes, who certainly ravaged Ribbesford, one of its berewicks.[12] Three small estates in the manor were separately held. The land of one 'radknight' was held by the reeve of the manor ; the land of another 'radknight' was held by a certain William, and Aiulf held a virgate of land. Moreover, two houses, one at Droitwich, the other at Worcester, belonged to the manor.[13]

The sheriff accounted to the king for the proceeds of the manor[14] until Henry II alienated it to his 'dapifer' or steward, Manasser Biset,[15] some time between 1156 and 1162.[16] Manasser had witnessed many of the king's charters,[17] and was present at Clarendon in 1164.[18] He died in or shortly before 1186.[19] The manor was to be held by knights' service, but the exact amount of the service is uncertain. In 1431, after its division into three portions, Lady Bergavenny, who held two portions, owed service for two-thirds of one half-fee.[20] The service from the whole manor was possibly that of half a fee. The statement made in 1428 that 'Hugh Cokesey, the Lady of Bergavenny and the Prior of Maiden Bradley hold one-third of a fee severally and none of them holds as much as a quarter'[21] should clearly read 'one-third of half a fee.'

In 1187 livery of Kidderminster was given to Manasser's heir,[22] who seems to have been his son Henry.[23] Henry Biset paid £8 as the farm of the town for one quarter in 1194.[24] In 1201, however, Geoffrey Fitz Piers was holding the manor at farm

from King John,[25] but Henry Biset the dapifer received a new grant from the king[26] of this and other manors, and agreed (May 1199) to pay 500 marks in instalments for the vills of Kidderminster and Sandhurst (co. Hants).[27]

Two suggestions may be made to account for this. One is that there were two Henry Bisets,[28] but this is weakened by the evidence of pedigrees produced in 13th-century pleas concerning the manor. More probably the manor was held in pledge for a debt due by Biset ; he still owed £100 14s. 8d. (? of the 500 marks) in 1201 when Geoffrey Fitz Piers accounted for a year's farm.[29] Shortly afterwards Henry Biset evidently recovered his lands, and upon his death the wardship of his heir was given to William of Huntingfield.[30]

Huntingfield was a prominent member of the baronial opposition to John.[31] Upon the outbreak of war the sheriff seized Kidderminster for the king. At Runnimede 21 June 1215, when Huntingfield had been appointed one of the 'conservators' of the Great Charter, the king restored the lands of which he had been dispossessed[32] ; but in the following November Kidderminster was delivered to Roger la Zouche 'during pleasure,'[33] and in 1216, when Huntingfield was subduing the eastern counties on behalf of Louis of France, John made a new grant of the town to his 'beloved and loyal' follower John L'Estrange.[34]

Kidderminster appears to have been restored to the Bisets after King John's death. It does not appear whether Henry Biset's heir, his son William,[35] ever actually held the manor. William's widow, Sarah, married Richard Keynes (de Cahannis),[36] and in 1223 failed to defend her claim to dower in Kidderminster against her daughter-in-law Isolde, widow of William Biset the younger, and her second husband, Aumary St. Amand.[37] Under an exchange with John Biset, brother and heir of the younger William, Aumary held the whole manor instead of the third which was his wife's dower.[38] In 1228 he had grant of free warren and a yearly fair.[39]

This grant was renewed to John Biset in 1238.[40] He also came to an agreement (1240) with the Prior and convent of Worcester as to the bounds of their respective lands on the heath between Wolverley and Kidderminster.[41] A year later (1241) he died,[42] leaving three daughters as co-heirs, of whom the eldest, Margery, was the wife of Robert Rivers, while Ela married firstly Ralph Nevill and afterwards John

[9] 'Ismere House' is situated near these pools.

[10] See Birch, op. cit. iii, 376.

[11] V.C.H. Worcs. i, 286b.

[12] Heming, Chartul. (ed. Hearne), i, 256.

[13] V.C.H. Worcs. i, 286b.

[14] Red Bk. of Exch. (Rolls Ser.), ii, 656.

[15] Copy of Chart. among Corp. Rec.

[16] The date is limited by the chancellorship of Becket, who appears as witness. Its authenticity is, however, doubtful, more especially as 'William' Earl of Leicester occurs among the witnesses, whereas Robert (de Beaumont) was then earl. The grant must have taken place before 1167 (cf. Pipe R. 13 Hen. II [Pipe R. Soc.], 57).

[17] Round, Cal. Doc. France, passim.

[18] Stubbs, Select Chart. (ed. 1888), 138.

[19] Pipe R. 32 Hen. II, m. 3 d.

[20] Feud. Aids, v, 329.

[21] Ibid. 323.

[22] Pipe R. 33 Hen. II.

[23] Add. MS. 37503, fol. 30 ; Dugdale, Mon. vi, 644.

[24] Pipe R. 6 Ric. I, m. 1.

[25] Rot. Canc. 3 John (Rec. Com.), 131.

[26] Cartae Antiq. SS. 12.

[27] Rot. de Oblatis et Fin. (Rec. Com.), 4.

[28] See below. Dugdale (Baronage, i, 632) makes the Henry Biset of 1199 nephew of Manasser's son Henry.

[29] Rot. Canc. 3 John (Rec. Com.), 133.

[30] Pipe R. 4 & 5 John ; Testa de Nevill (Rec. Com.), 44.

[31] Roger of Wendover, Flor. Hist. (Engl. Hist. Soc.), iii, 297, 356, 371.

[32] Rot. Lit. Claus. (Rec. Com.), i, 215b.

[33] Ibid. 237b.

[34] Ibid. 278b.

[35] Wrottesley, Ped. from Plea R. 481.

[36] Testa de Nevill (Rec. Com.), 40b.

[37] Maitland, Bracton's Note Bk. iii, 458 ; Assize R. 1021, m. 6 ; Rot. Lit. Claus. (Rec. Com.), i, 568. It is possible that this Isolde was identical with Isolde 'of Kidderminster,' who afterwards married Thomas Daniel and was 'with the Empress' in 1236 (Cal. Close, 1234-7, p. 241).

[38] But note that John Biset is called in another plea the grandson of Manasser (Cur. Reg. R. 135, m. 38 d.).

[39] Cal. Pat. 1225-32, p. 175. See below.

[40] Cal. Chart. R. 1226-57, p. 235.

[41] Ann. Mon. (Rolls Ser.), iv, 431 ; unfortunately the account of the boundary has not been found.

[42] Ibid. 433.

Wotton ; Isabel, the third daughter, became the wife of Hugh Pleseys,[43] probably the son of John Pleseys, who in 1241 had a grant of the custody and marriage of the two younger daughters.[44]

The division of the inheritance among the co-heirs caused some dissension.[45] The manor of Kidderminster was apportioned in three parts.

The share of the one daughter, Ela Wotton (second by birth), was known later as the manor of *KIDDERMINSTER BISET*.[46] John Wotton survived his wife, and settled her inheritance on their son John, who took the name of Biset, and on his wife Katharine.[47] John Biset died shortly before 1307, leaving a son John.[48] The latter alienated a messuage and certain of his lands in Kidderminster to Hugh Cooksey c. 1330.[49] Shortly afterwards Biset died, and the manor passed to his sister Margaret wife of Robert Martin of Yeovilton ('Yevelton'), co.

BISET. *Azure ten bezants.*

Somers.[50] She and her husband granted a lease of the manor to Hugh Cooksey and his wife Denise for their lives.[51] Denise Cooksey lived till 1376, when, owing to the fact that Robert Martin and his two sons Robert and William, to whom the manor should have reverted, were already dead,[52] Kidderminster Biset passed to the surviving heir of Margaret, Sir Walter Romsey, kt., her son by a second husband.[53] In 1380 Sir Walter settled the manor in tail-male on his son John and the latter's wife Alice,[54] but John Romsey died in his father's lifetime. His widow apparently married Malcolm de la Mare, for in 1385–6 Sir Walter sold the reversion of the manor contingent upon the death of Alice wife of Malcolm de la Mare to Sir John Beauchamp of Holt.[55]

Beauchamp also acquired a second share of the main manor, viz. the portion known as Burnells (q.v.). He had

BEAUCHAMP of Kidderminster. *Gules a fesse between six martlets or.*

been knighted during the Scottish expedition (1385)[56] of Richard II, and rose rapidly in the king's favour. In 1386 he had grant of free chase 'in vert and venison,' infangtheof, utfangtheof and the chattels of felons and fugitives in Kidderminster.[57]   In

October 1387 he was created Lord Beauchamp of Kidderminster 'in consideration of his good and gratuitous services, the trusty family from which he was descended and his great sense and circumspection.'[58] In the following May he fell a victim to the 'Merciless' Parliament, and in consequence of his attainder Kidderminster Burnell and the reversion of Kidderminster Biset were forfeited to the Crown.[59]

In 1389 his rights in Kidderminster were purchased by Thomas Earl of Warwick on behalf of John de Hermesthorpe and others,[60] who shortly afterwards conveyed to Nicholas Lilling and others as trustees for a reconveyance.[61] In June 1400, on the death of Alice widow of Malcolm de la Mare,[62] Lilling and his co-feoffees entered upon Kidderminster Biset, and settled it with Kidderminster Burnell on Warwick's younger brother, Sir William Beauchamp Lord Bergavenny.[63] His widow, Joan Lady Bergavenny, held both manors in dower[64] until her death, which took place 14 November 1435.[65] Kidderminster, apart from Bergavenny Castle and her other entailed estates, descended to her granddaughter Elizabeth wife of Sir Edward Nevill and daughter of Richard Earl of Worcester. Sir Edward was summoned by writ as Lord Bergavenny in 1450.[66] His son and heir George Lord Bergavenny (d. 1492) instructed his bailiff to allow the Priors of Maiden Bradley to take their part of the waifs and strays within their third of the manor and to avoid summoning the priors' tenants to Bergavenny's court.[67]

George Nevill Lord Bergavenny, a favourite with Henry VII and son of the first-named George, entailed all his estates upon himself and the heirs male of his body.[68] He died in 1535, and during the minority of his son Henry the king appointed John Avery to be bailiff of the lordship of Kidderminster Foreign.[69] Upon the death of Henry Lord Bergavenny in February 1586–7 the heir male to the estate was Edward Nevill of Newton St. Loe, Somerset, sometimes styled Lord Bergavenny.[70] His son Edward

NEVILL of Bergavenny. *Gules a saltire argent with a rose gules thereon.*

disputed the barony with the heir general and received a writ of summons as Lord Nevill of Bergavenny in 1604.[71] He died in London 1 December 1622, and was succeeded by his son Henry.[72] It was his son John Lord Bergavenny who in 1663 leased the

[43] *Hund. R.* (Rec. Com.), ii, 284 ; Cur. Reg. R. 137, m. 7 d.

[44] *Excerpta e Rot. Fin.* (Rec. Com.), i, 362.

[45] Cur. Reg. R. 137, m. 7 d.

[46] Chan. Inq. p.m. 16 Edw. IV, no. 66; the name has not been noted earlier than 1476.

[47] Chan. Inq. a.q.d. file 28, no. 12 ; Chan. Inq. p.m. 28 Edw. I, no. 30.

[48] Ibid. 35 Edw. I, no. 43.

[49] *Cal. Pat.* 1330–4, p. 3.

[50] *Cal. Inq. p.m.* 1–9 *Edw. III*, 412.

[51] *Cal. Pat.* 1338–40, p. 160 ; 1343–5, p. 110 ; *Cal. Close*, 1343–6, p. 239 ; Feet of F. Worcs. case 260, file 21, no. 21.

[52] Chan. Inq. p.m. 50 Edw. III (1st nos.), no. 20.

[53] Ibid. 47 Edw. III (1st nos.), no. 29 ; *Abbrev. Rot. Orig.* (Rec. Com.), ii, 347.

[54] *Cal. Pat.* 1377–81, p. 426.

[55] Ibid. 1381–5, p. 460 ; Feet of F. Worcs. case 260, file 25, no. 22.

[56] *Cal. Pat.* 1385–9, p. 16.

[57] Chart. R. 9 & 10 Ric. II, m. 6.

[58] *Cal. Pat.* 1385–9, p. 363.

[59] Chan. Inq. p.m. 12 Ric. II, no. 91.

[60] *Cal. Pat.* 1388–92, p. 80.

[61] Ibid. 307.

[62] Chan. Inq. p.m. 2 Hen. IV, no. 43.

[63] Ibid. 12 Hen. IV, no. 34. The attainder of the first Lord Kidderminster was reversed in 1398 in favour of his son

John ; but the proceedings of 1388 were reaffirmed in 1400 and John Beauchamp did not recover Kidderminster (ibid. 8 Hen. V, no. 70).

[64] *Feud. Aids*, v, 323, 329 ; Chan. Inq. p.m. 14 Hen. VI, no. 35.

[65] Chan. Inq. p.m. 14 Hen. VI, no. 35.

[66] G.E.C. *Complete Peerage*, i, 25.

[67] Add. MS. 37503, fol. 58, 59.

[68] See Priv. Act, 2 & 3 Phil. and Mary, cap. 22.

[69] *L. and P. Hen. VIII*, xiii (1), g. 646 (58).

[70] G.E.C. *Complete Peerage*, i, 19.

[71] Ibid.

[72] Chan. Inq. p.m. (Ser. 2), cccxcix, 157.

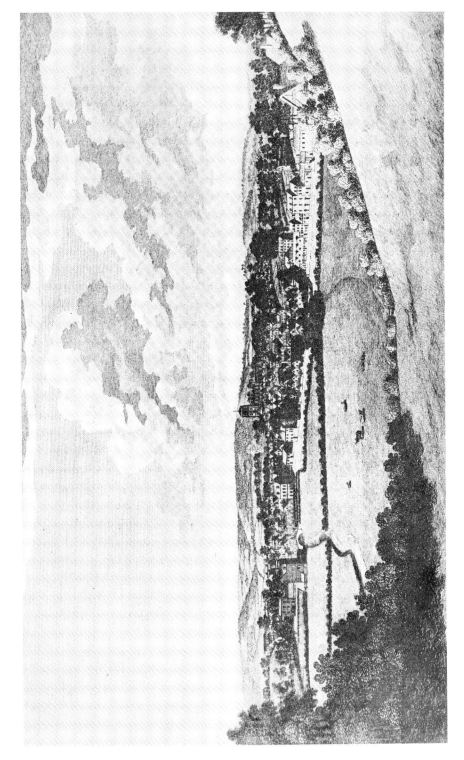

KIDDERMINSTER C. 1800
(*From the Prattinton Collection*)

manor and market tolls to William Dike for three lives.[73]

He was succeeded in the barony by his brother George, whose son and heir George Lord Bergavenny died without issue in 1695. Thereupon his estates passed to his kinsman, George Nevill, descendant and heir male of Sir Christopher Nevill, younger son of that Edward Lord Bergavenny who died in 1622. He died in 1721. His sons George and William died of smallpox in 1723 and 1724 respectively, whereupon their first cousin, William Nevill, inherited the entailed property and barony of Bergavenny.[74]

FOLEY of Kidderminster. *Argent a fesse engrailed between three cinqfoils and a border all sable.*

In 1733, under Act of Parliament, he sold his manorial rights in Kidderminster in order to purchase an estate in East Grinstead.[75] Conveyance was made to Edward Harley,[76] possibly in trust. Within the next forty years the manors were acquired by Thomas Foley, created Lord Foley of Kidderminster, 1776.[77]

Thenceforward these manors, with the remainder of Lord Foley's estate in Kidderminster, became entitled the manors of Kidderminster Borough and Foreign, and their history is coincident with that of the Great Witley estate (q.v.). The present owner of both is the Earl of Dudley.

The portion of the main manor assigned to Isabel Pleseys, the youngest daughter of John Biset, was known after 1476 by the name of *KIDDERMINSTER BUR-NELL*. It was evidently alienated before the death of Hugh Pleseys to Robert Burnell, Bishop of Bath and Wells, the great chancellor of Edward I, who purchased other lands in the county. He held one-third of Kidderminster at his death in 1292, 'doing for it to the king reasonable service with arms and horses in time of war, as the king may desire.'[78] He was succeeded by his nephew Philip Burnell of Holdgate, co. Salop, who rapidly wasted his estate.[79] His son Edward, left heir to his father in 1294,[80] was summoned to Parliament as

BURNELL of Holdgate. *Argent a lion sable with a crown or in a border azure.*

Lord Burnell in 1314,[81] but died without issue in the following year.[82] His sister and heir married firstly John Lovel, secondly John Handlo. In 1321 this portion of Kidderminster was entailed upon John and Maud Handlo and their heirs male[83]; in 1339 a new settlement was made upon their son Nicholas (afterwards called Burnell) and his wife Mary.[84] He entered upon the estate after his father's death in 1346,[85] served in the wars in France, and was summoned to Parliament as Lord Burnell in 1350.[86] In January 1382–3, upon the death of Nicholas Burnell, Kidderminster Burnell descended to his son Hugh.[87] Having no sons, he alienated it to his friend Sir John Beauchamp of Holt,[88] who also acquired the reversion of Kidderminster Biset. Thus two divisions of the original manor were re-united.

The third share, that of Margery Rivers, was inherited by her son John Rivers of Burgate.[89] He gave it to the Prior of Maiden Bradley, co. Wilts., and the leprous sisters in that house, which was of the foundation of Manasser·Biset, receiving in exchange land in Burgate.[90] In confirming to the priory the possession of the church of Kidderminster[91] he further granted the land and person of his villein, Hugh 'in la Grava.'[92] In 1270 Queen Eleanor confirmed to the priory the lands thus received,[93] and this portion of Kidderminster became merged in the priory's manor of Comberton.[94]

In the partition of the manor after John Biset's death the hall or manor-house seems to have been assigned to the lord of Kidderminster Biset.[95] It is said that a portion of the hall, including the kitchens, was converted into a Brussels carpet factory, which still existed in the last century.[96] The foundations of the old building were discovered when the savings bank was being built.[97] It lay in close proximity to the church on the sloping ground which rises from the left bank of the Stour. Hall Street, Dudley Street (formerly known as Barn Street),[98] and Orchard Street occupy the site of the demesne.

From early times the River Stour with its tributaries has been a source of industry. Two corn-mills were attached to the manor in 1086, while the reeve held another. The demesne mill, known as the Great Mill,[99] was burnt down late in the 14th century.[100] The Heathy mill south-east of the town was known as 'Walkmill,' and belonged to Bordesley Abbey.[1] In 1272 the Prior of Maiden Bradley had in view the building of a mill, probably Comberton Mill.[2] The mill at (Over) Mitton was known as 'le kylemilne.'[3]

The *TOWN* and *BOROUGH* of *KIDDER-MINSTER* owes its development to its position upon four main roads and on the River Stour, and

[73] Com. Pleas D. Enr. East. 15 Chas. II, m. 25.

[74] G.E.C. *Complete Peerage*, i, 23–4.

[75] Priv. Act, 6 Geo. II, cap. 10.

[76] Feet of F. Worcs. Trin. 6 & 7 Geo. II.

[77] Priv. Act, 14 Geo. III, cap. 52.

[78] Chan. Inq. p.m. Edw. I, file 63, no. 32.   [79] *Dict. Nat. Biog.*

[80] Chan. Inq. p.m. 22 Edw. I, no. 45.

[81] G.E.C. *Complete Peerage*, ii, 82.

[82] *Cal. Inq. p.m.* 1–9 Edw. II, no. 611.

[83] *Cal. Pat.* 1317–21, p. 601; Maud had a son John Lovel by her first husband (Chan. Inq. p.m. 20 Edw. III [1st nos.], no. 51).

[84] *Cal. Pat.* 1338–40, p. 302.

[85] *Cal. Close*, 1346–9, p. 110.

[86] G.E.C. *Complete Peerage*, vii, 82.

[87] Chan. Inq. p.m. 6 Ric. II, no. 20.

[88] Ibid. 12 Ric. II, no. 91. Lady Joan Bergavenny named Sir Hugh Burnell among 'her good-doers' for whom she founded a chantry at Hereford (*Test. Vetusta* [ed. Nicolas], 225).

[89] *Hund. R.* (Rec. Com.), ii, 284.

[90] Harl. Chart. 55 D 25.

[91] See below.

[92] Dugdale, *Mon.* vi, 644.

[93] Cott. Chart. Aug. ii, 14.

[94] See below.

[95] Chan. Inq. p.m. 28 Edw. I, no. 30; 35 Edw. I, no. 43; but the Bishop of Bath and Wells, when lord of Kidderminster Burnell, had a messuage worth

6d. (ibid. file 63, no. 32); his successor John Handlo had, however, no house or demesne land (ibid. 20 Edw. III [1st nos.], no. 51).

[96] Ric. Grove, *Hist. of the Old Minster Church at Kidderminster*, 20.

[97] Inform. kindly supplied by Miss Tomkinson.

[98] Grove, op. cit. 20.

[99] Add. MS. 37503, fol. 16 d.

[100] Chan. Inq. p.m. 6 Ric. II, no. 20.

[1] Pat. 31 Eliz. pt. vii, m. 31; *Cal. Com. for Comp.* iv, 3016. The name 'Walkmill' suggests that a fulling-mill was attached at one period.

[2] Anct. D. (P.R.O.), D 202.

[3] Ct. R. (Gen. Ser.), portf. 210, no. 70.

to the consequent early establishment of the cloth industry.

To the south of the site of the hall already referred to, and on the same bank of the Stour, was the old market-house, with the town hall and gaol, the last being a cellar which acquired, not without reason, the ill-omened name of the 'Blackhole.'[4]

The roads from Birmingham and Dudley meet in the old market-place and are crossed at their junction by a third road. This last is continued across the river by the curve of the 'Bull Ring'; on the right bank it branches into the main roads to Bewdley and Bridgnorth, on the left, but beyond the area of the old market, it leads to Worcester and to Bromsgrove. The old Worcester road formerly joined the Bromsgrove road at a point more distant from the market than at present. The new road was brought into the centre of the town about 1835.[5] In the immediate proximity of the old market-place the Dudley road is known as Blakewell Street, the Birmingham road as the High Street.

Standing at the bottom of the High Street is a small 16th-century inn, now known as the 'Three Tuns,' but formerly as the 'King's Head.'[5a] It is a two-storied gabled building, of half-timber and brick construction, though many of the uprights have been taken out and solid brickwork inserted, while the front to the ground floor is modern. On the east an archway through to the yard at the back divides the inn from another building of the same date, the front of which is entirely modern. The backs of both buildings overhang on the first floor.

On the south side of Church Street (no. 12) stands a small half-timber building, roofed with tiles, of early 17th-century date. It is rectangular on plan with a central stack, and is divided on the ground floor into four rooms, each having an angle fireplace, only one of which remains in its original state, the others having been blocked up. The front elevation is of symmetrical design, and it is in an excellent state of preservation. The upper floor projects over the street with small shaped brackets beneath the main beam. In the front are four windows of four lights each, with ovolo-moulded transoms. The timber framing to the walls is composed solely of vertical and horizontal members, there being no braces. The panels are all plastered.

The parish has from time immemorial been divided into the borough and the foreign.[6] The exact origin of the distinction is not clear. The earliest known record of the foreign as distinct from the borough is the 'Custom of the Lords of Kidderminster,'[7] which probably belongs to the fourth decade of the 14th century. Here it is stated that the profits of strays within the borough ought to be shared by the 'two lords' (possibly of Kidderminster Biset and Burnell), while strays on the commons or roads of the foreign belonged to the three lords

(including the Prior of Maiden Bradley) and each lord ought to have those on his own lordship within the foreign.

The borough evidently centred round the market-place. The lord had toll on all sales within certain bounds : 'Dakebroke in Blakestanstrete (? Blakewell Street), the Cross in Worcester Street, the Cross in Milstrete (? Proud Cross) or the barriers in Churchstrete.'[8] Leland, who visited the town about 1540, remarked that the 'fair and chief' part lay on the left side of the Stour; and in the centre of the market was a pretty cross with six pillars and arches of stone, with the seventh pillar in the middle to bear up the fornix.[9]

It remains uncertain whether the bounds given above were those of the original borough or only of the market. They were considerably smaller than those of the borough in 1837.[10] The borough and the foreign were distinct also for poor-law purposes and each had its own churchwardens. In 1616 the inhabitants of the borough petitioned that those of the foreign should contribute to the support of the poor of the whole parish.[11] The jealousy between the two districts was aggravated in the 18th century by the growth of considerable hamlets just outside the limits of the borough.[12] It was only partially allayed by a Boundary Act of 1841,[13] but is at last settled in 1912 by the incorporation into the borough of most of the outlying districts.

The division into two wards apparently dates only from the division of the borough for parliamentary purposes in 1832.[14]

Henry II in granting the manor to Manasser Biset gave him also full jurisdiction over his tenants, 'soke and sake, toll and theam, infangtheof and utfangtheof with all liberties and free customs whereof any of my Barons of England holds best.'[14a] John Beauchamp had a further grant of the goods and chattels of felons and fugitives within his manors (of Kidderminster Burnell and Biset).[14b]

The men of Kidderminster were slow to acquire any degree of independence. The possession of the manor by William I in 1086 gave them the position of tenants on ancient demesne of the Crown, rendering them free from toll, stallage, murage, &c., throughout the kingdom and exempting them from contributing to the expenses of knights of the shire or from sitting on juries outside the manor court. These privileges were confirmed to them in 1386, 1427, 1530 and in 1586.[15] The town was regularly tallaged by the king from 1177 onwards.[16]

The town was governed in the early period by a prepositus or reeve appointed by the lord. In 1086 he held the land of one radknight.[17] The reeve is again mentioned in 1221, when he with other freemen of the town 'testified that Robert Patrick's son had confessed himself a thief.'[18] Burgage tenure is frequently recorded. In the early 13th century

---

[4] *Parl. Papers* (1835), xxv, 1878; *Rep. of the Trial of Rev. H. Price* (1828), 23.

[5] Ebenezer Guest, 'Manners and Customs of Old Kidderminster'; see *Kidderminster Shuttle*, 22 Sept. 1906.

[5a] See the map surveyed by John Doharty, jun., and published in 1753.

[6] Boundary Rep. xi, pt. vi, Prattinton Coll. (Soc. of Antiq.).

[7] Corp. Rec.   [8] Ibid.

[9] *Itinerary* (ed. 2), iv, 100.

[10] *Parl. Papers* (1837), xxvii, 119.

[11] *Quart. Sess. R.* (Worcs. Hist. Soc.), i, 223.

[12] *Parl. Papers* (1835), xxv, 1877. The open commons of the foreign were inclosed in 1775, an Act for the inclosure having been passed in 1774 (*Blue Bk. Incl. Awards*, 190; Priv. Act, 14 Geo. III, cap. 47).

[13] Local and Personal Act, 4 & 5 Vict. cap. 72.

[14] See *Parl. Papers* (1837), xxvii, 119.

[14a] Corp. Rec.

[14b] Chart. R. 9 & 10 Ric. II, m. 6.

[15] Pat. 28 Eliz. pt. x, m. 43; Chart. R. 9 & 10 Ric. II, m. 6; *L. and P. Hen. VIII*, iv (3), 6248 (1).

[16] Pipe R. 33 Hen. II, m. 15 d., &c.

[17] *V.C.H. Worcs.* i, 286.

[18] Maitland, *Select Pleas of the Crown*, 140.

Wulfric gave to Maiden Bradley a 'burgage' held of the lord by 12*d.* rent yearly,[19] and in 1254 Richard of Trimpley enfeoffed Hugh Attwood (*de Bosco*) of another burgage.[20]

The extent of Kidderminster Biset drawn up in 1300 mentions only the rents of free tenants (40*s.*) and services of customary tenants [21]; but seven years later the rent of thirteen free tenants was 104*s.* 11*d.*, toll of market was worth 53*s.* 4*d.*, and there were sixty-three burgesses in addition to the free and customary tenants.[22]

Before the time of William de Cauntelow, who first took office as sheriff in 1200, the town was free from the sheriff's jurisdiction. In consideration of 16 marks of silver Walter Beauchamp (between 1237 and 1241) gave to John Biset and his heirs written acknowledgement of this exemption.[23] In 1275 it was recorded that the 'commonalty' of the borough had distraint save in cases of debt.[24] In 1305 the 'commonalty' joined the lord of Kidderminster Biset in presenting a chaplain to the chantry of St. Mary,[25] but what right they had to do so does not appear.

Two representatives, Walter Caldigan and Walter Lihtfot, were sent by Kidderminster to the 'Model' Parliament of 1295, but the burgesses were probably deterred by the contingent expense from returning a member to any other Parliament, until they sent a single member to the reformed Parliament of 1833.[26] The borough is still represented by one member.

The town probably owed its development during the 13th century to the valuable properties of the Stour water, which had already been recognized. In 1280 William the Dyer (*tinctore*) was assessed towards the payment of a subsidy,[27] and in 1292 a fulling-mill was standing.[28]

The town also received frequent visits from the king. Henry III was there in July 1221, when an expedition was proceeding against Llewelyn ap Iorwerth; the Welsh war brought him thither again in October 1223. He was there in September 1224 and 1226, August 1228, May 1231, August 1232, when there were renewed troubles with the Welsh and his visit seems to have been prolonged for at least ten days, and in June and September 1233.[29] He seems to have been entertained at the Hall [30] either by Aumary St. Amand, who took an active part in the Welsh negotiations in 1231,[31] or by John Biset, whose kinswoman Margaret saved him from an assassin when at her midnight devotions.[32]

The division of the manor between the three co-heirs of John Biset about the middle of the 12th century probably facilitated the growth of autonomy.

Each of the three lords had the amercements from his own free and customary tenants. They shared the waifs found on the highway or common lands of the foreign. They divided with the rector [33] the fines from burgesses who imperilled the town by stacking brushwood near the houses, and from buyers and sellers who did business without the prescribed limits.[34]

In 1333 the steward of the lord of Kidderminster Biset held an inquiry into the claims of the 'community of the burgesses.' From this it appears that they elected their own bailiff or reeve, and twice yearly sent six representatives chosen by the bailiff to the lord's view of frankpledge held on the hill. The bailiff also collected the lords' toll, placing it in a box without rendering any account, after deducting the payment for his own dinner. These customs were from time immemorial, and were held for law. The burgesses were also free from relief and heriot.[35]

To about the same date evidently belongs another account of the customs of the town known as the 'Composition of the manor and borough of Kidderminster,' which adds that the bailiff was to be chosen by twenty-four of the burgesses the Monday after Michaelmas. The bailiff was to choose an assistant (the 'low' bailiff) to make attachments and serve distraints, and two catchpolls 'to see the market in order.' Two honest burgesses were to walk the fairs and the markets, which were probably prescriptive in origin (see below) with the bailiff, and the three eldest burgesses were to aid him in keeping the peace.

The bailiff acted as clerk of the market, giving bread that fell short in weight and 'misselled' (measled) pork or brawn to the poor. He appointed a borough herdsman to keep the cattle on the lord's waste, and took half the fines from offenders against the regulations of the cloth trade, the lord taking the other half. Aided by six burgesses he appraised waifs and strays, and he 'took the advisament' of at least three of the elder burgesses in 'redressing of all matters for the prince [36] and the lord.' His gaoler handed over prisoners to the constable of the manor at Worcester Cross. He was allowed to hunt a couple of rabbits in the lord's warren three days in each week, whereas the ordinary burgess might only shoot one without going out of the highway, and the 'tenter' might not kill any.

Twice yearly at the great courts leet the town clerk, his wife and his man, the twelve men (of the jury) and their wives, the low bailiff and his wife dined at the expense of the bailiff. The officers were bound to present their accounts on these occasions.[37]

---

[19] Add. Chart. 20423.

[20] Feet of F. Worcs. case 258, file 7, no. 37.

[21] Chan. Inq. p.m. 28 Edw. I, no. 30.

[22] Ibid. 35 Edw. I, no. 43 ; see also *Cal. Close,* 1302–7, p. 518.

[23] Corp. Rec. 17th cent. transcript.

[24] *Hund. R.* (Rec. Com.), ii, 284.

[25] Worc. Epis. Reg. Gainsborough, ii, fol. 30.

[26] *Ret. of Memb. of Parl.* 6.

[27] *Lay Subs. R. Worcs.* c. 1280 (Worcs. Hist. Soc.), 9.

[28] Chan. Inq. p.m. Edw. I, file 63, no. 32. A witness to an early 13th-century Kidderminster charter was 'Hel-

fredus' the fuller (Add. Chart. 20423). Again Alfred (*Aluredus*) the fuller, possibly the same man, granted to Maiden Bradley a rent of 19*d.* in Kidderminster 'de placia ubi *domus hospitalis* quondam erat.' This site is described as 'ex directo magni molendini' (Add. MS. 37503, fol. 16).

[29] *Cal. Close,* 1227–31, *passim*; 1231–4, *passim*; *Cal. Pat.* 1216–25, pp. 295, 410, 471 ; 1225–32, *passim.*

[30] Upon one occasion he left a butt of wine in the 'lord's cellar'; *Cal. Close,* 1231–4, p. 271.

[31] *Cal. Pat.* 1225–32, p. 453.

[32] Matt. Paris, *Hist. Angl.* (Rolls Ser.), ii, 380, 412–13.

[33] But it is notable that the rector (the Prior of Maiden Bradley) himself held one-third of the manor (see above).

[34] Corp. Rec. ; Custom of the Lords of Kidderminster.

[35] Corp. Rec. : 17th-cent. transcript.

[36] Possibly the Prince of Wales ; see *V.C.H. Worcs.* ii, 211.

[37] Corp. Rec. The transcript of this custumal and of other documents relating to the borough was made on two vellum rolls, evidently for the purposes of the Exchequer Plea in 1653. These with the other records belonging to the corporation are kept in a glass case in the mayor's parlour, together with modern transcripts made by Mr. De Gray Birch.

The 'Twelve and the Twenty-four' presented to the lord's officers the man who desired to become a burgess, and if he could not pay the fine 'they ought to make him able.' [38]

In 1332, the year in which he took steps to introduce Flemish weavers into England, Edward III spent three days at Kidderminster.[39] The townsmen were then making broad and narrow cloths and kerseys and the trade of the 'tenters' (stretchers or dyers of cloth) was strictly regulated.[40]

There were at that time sixty-six men rated for the subsidy in the town itself, as opposed to fifty-eight in 1280.[41]

The commercial part of the town centred about the High Street, where the Prior of Maiden Bradley let land on a building lease in 1414.[42] The trades included those of draper, goldsmith, ironmonger and glover.[43]

A newly-built house in 'Blaxter Street' (? Blakewell Street) was owned by Sir Humphrey Stafford, a supporter of Richard III, attainted and executed at Tyburn, 17 November 1485. He also possessed a two-storied tavern, cottages in Worcester Street and Mill Street and the 'Courthouse' Tavern.[44] The rents of tenements in Shop Row were subsequently devoted to supporting obits,[45] while Sir Edward Blount bequeathed a tenement 'behind the shops' for the maintenance of his almshouses.[46]

Trade disputes arose between Kidderminster and Bewdley in the 15th century, and in January 1493–4 Prince Arthur of Wales is said to have made peace between the towns, commanding them 'to eschew all manner of debates and discords' and apply in future to himself and his council to settle all differences.[47] The quarrel apparently related to the toll on wool brought out of Wales across Bewdley Bridge.[48]

The cloth industry continued to flourish, and in 1533–4 an Act was passed limiting the industry to certain towns,[49] including Kidderminster. There were then in the town fifty-two men able to bear arms, and in the outlying hamlets forty-three.[50]

'By reason of the confluence of many thither daily' the town grew populous. In February 1632–3 the inhabitants petitioned for a royal charter.[51] They were probably influenced by disputes as to market-rights recently settled in favour of the lord of the borough. The charter was granted 4 August 1636. The town was incorporated under the name of 'the bailiff and burgesses of the borough of Kidderminster.' The bailiff[52] was to be chosen on the Monday after Michaelmas from the twelve capital burgesses, election being made by the whole of the burgesses. The capital burgesses were to hold office for life and join the bailiff in filling up vacancies in their number. The bailiff and burgesses chose a steward (Sir Ralph Clare of Caldwell being named in

the charter). He was assisted by an under steward learned in the law.

The bailiff and capital burgesses were to assemble in the gildhall or elsewhere to make by-laws for the government of the borough, and they might claim the advice of twenty-five assistant burgesses appointed by themselves from the more honest and upright inhabitants. The bailiff, his immediate predecessor and the under steward were to be justices of the peace within the borough, but the rights of the lords of the manor to court leet, &c., were reserved. To the bailiff and burgesses were granted fairs and markets 'as they had lawfully held the same.' [53] The twelve capital, and twenty-five assistant, burgesses may be compared with the 'Twelve and the Twenty-four' mentioned above.

The bailiff and capital burgesses aided by the 'assistants' proceeded to make by-laws at the 'courthouse,' the junior of the assistants speaking first. They provided themselves with 'comely and decent black gowns' in which to attend the bailiff to church on the Sabbath and festivals, and without which the bailiff might not walk the streets. They appointed a constable to keep order and bade every burgess keep at hand a club, bill or halbert. Innkeepers were forbidden to give entertainment on Sunday or holiday save 'due repose to strangers passengers and travellers'; and the churchwardens and constables left the church at the Second Lesson to make diligent search for such offenders. They ordered the cleansing of the streets on Saturday afternoons and the removal of standings from the street and market-place at night. Trading by any 'foreigner' not a burgess was prohibited unless he had been apprenticed seven years in the town or had gained permission from the burgesses and paid scot and lot.[54]

The position of Kidderminster at the meeting of three main roads rendered it of some importance during the Civil War.

In 1642 Essex, expecting that the king would advance on London by the Worcester road, sent a regiment to Kidderminster under Lord Brooke. He withdrew before a feigned advance on the part of Prince Rupert [55] with the loss of one soldier who fell down the steep cliff into Bewdley Street.[56] 'From haste or fear' some wagons and three or four pieces of ordnance were left behind,[57] and the townsmen hastened to deliver these to the Royalists.[58]

Many of the townsmen declared that they would have lived peaceably at home, but that they were driven by the 'rage of soldiers and drunkards' (who persisted in identifying the sober-minded with the rebellious) to take refuge with the Parliamentary garrison at Coventry.[59]

Early in June 1644 the men of Kidderminster were threatened with ruin by a troop of Royalist

[38] Corp. Rec. 'Custom of the Lords of Kidderminster.'
[39] Cal. Pat. 1330–4, p. 324 ; Cal. Close, 1330–3, pp. 594–8.
[40] Corp. Rec. 'Comp. of Manor and Borough' ; see V.C.H. Worcs. i, 284.
[41] Lay Subs. R. Worcs. 1280 (Worcs. Hist. Soc.), 12 ; ibid. 1327, 37.
[42] Anct. D. (P.R.O.), D. 394.
[43] Cal. Pat. 1429–36, pp. 228, 233, 239, 435 ; 1436–41, p. 118.
[44] Add. MS. 37503, fol. 59–60. John 'le Blaxtere' was living in Kidderminster

in 1281 (Mins. Accts. bdle. 1070, no. 5).
[45] Pat. 18 Eliz. pt. ii ; 19 Eliz. pt. v.
[46] Com. for Char. Uses, bdle. 35, no. 28 ; see account of charities below.
[47] Blakeway MS. quoted by Burton, Hist. of Bewdley, 83 ; for the prince's jurisdiction see V.C.H. Worcs. ii, 211.
[48] Ex inform. Mr. Willis-Bund.
[49] V.C.H. Worcs. i, 286.
[50] L. and P. Hen. VIII, xiv (i), 652 (M 25).
[51] Hist. MSS. Com. Rep. iii, App. 191.
[52] The charter makes no mention of a

low bailiff, but the office continued to exist (Exch. Dep. Trin. 1653, no. 2).
[53] Pat. 12 Chas. I, pt. ii, no. 1 ; the original charter is in the possession of the corporation.
[54] Corp. Rec. By-laws, 14 Dec. 1640.
[55] J. W. Willis-Bund, Civil War in Worc. 53.
[56] Parish reg. quoted by Burton, Hist. of Kidderminster, 77.
[57] Hist. MSS. Com. Rep. vii, App. 530b.
[58] Reliquiae Baxterianae (1696), 43.
[59] Ibid. 44.

PLAN OF KIDDERMINSTER IN 1753

(Surveyed by J. Doharty)

horse if they should send provisions to the Parliamentary army, while an order was issued to Parliamentary commanders to forbear from plundering the fulling-mills of Robert Wilmot, treasurer to the County Committee of Stafford, in Mitton.[60] A week later a Royalist force for the relief of Dudley marched through from Bewdley,[61] and when Waller arrived in the town next day he found it 'little better than an empty farm.' He took prisoner Lieut.-Col. Stamford and a captain of foot with 'some poor soldiers' and the French agent M. de Sabran,[62] and moved to Stourbridge next day.

In the following June Charles passed through the town on his way from Naseby to Bewdley, leaving behind a poor woman who had been wounded in the late battle.[63] Shortly afterwards there was skirmishing at Trimpley, and in November 1645 Sir Thomas Aston with a Royalist force encamped there, probably on the site of the ancient camp at Warshill. Attacked by the Parliamentarians under Captain Stone, Aston made a stout resistance, but was taken prisoner, his troops being routed.

A skirmish in the town itself, in which Captain Denham and two soldiers were killed,[64] may be that in which tradition relates that the beaten party were driven from Clensmore to take refuge in St. Mary's chantry.[65] In December the town was again molested by 'the most rude and ill-governed [Royalist] horse that . . . ever trod upon earth.'

Sir Ralph Clare of Caldwall and other residents at Kidderminster favoured the king's cause. Edward Broad of Dunclent was assisted in preparing guns to be used against the 'Roundhead rogues' by a Kidderminster man.[66] It was said, too, that Thomas Crane of Kidderminster sent horses and arms to Hartlebury Castle and to Bristol.[67]

In 1651 Charles II and his Scottish army, marching southwards, 'passed most by Kidderminster a field's breadth off.'[68] After their defeat at Worcester the fugitives fled back along the same road, although Charles himself turned off at Hartlebury.[69] Some of Cromwell's men, stationed at Bewdley Bridge, entered Kidderminster to cut off the retreat of the Royalists. Thirty troopers stationed in the market-place shot at many hundreds, who, ' not knowing in the dark what number it was that charged them, either hasted away or cried quarter.'[70] Subsequently the bailiffs were eager to show their zeal for the Commonwealth in searching for plots against Cromwell,[71] but they were backward in collecting the excise on ale.[72]

Though the name of 'gildhall' is applied by the charter of King Charles to the town hall or courthouse, no trace has been found of a gild-merchant in Kidderminster, but there is some later record of craft gilds. In 1650 the bailiff and capital burgesses drew up ordinances for the craft gilds which then existed in the town. There were companies of weavers, tailors, smiths and shoemakers. Each fraternity was governed by two wardens elected yearly. The annual assembly of each gild took place on the Monday after Midsummer, and the last man to arrive before 11 a.m. was made beadle or messenger to his company. There were strict rules against trading by non-members, half the fines being paid to the bailiff and burgesses, half to the fraternity. The wardens supervised the appointment of apprentices and journeymen, while the bailiff and capital burgesses could fine negligent wardens and control their expenses.[73]

Shortly after the Restoration the prosperity of the town was much increased through the completion of Andrew Yarranton's scheme for making the Stour navigable from Stourbridge to Kidderminster. Coal was first brought thither by water in 1665.[74] The construction of the Staffordshire and Worcestershire Canal brought not only a more satisfactory connexion with the Severn, but also a continuous stream of through traffic.[75]

The cloth trade, falling into decay early in the 18th century, was replaced by the manufacture of fancy materials, silk and woollen.[76] Carpet-weaving, introduced early in the 18th century by Pearsall and Broom, rapidly became the staple trade of the town.[77] New streets were built by Lord Foley within five years of the introduction of the first Brussels loom,[78] and the old streets were widened and improved.[79] Four-loomed shops were established in Dudley Street, Queen Street, Union Street and Broad Street.[80] With the rise of a new and important body of traders in the town, discontent at the exclusiveness of the governing body increased.[81] During the 18th century municipal elections were riotous. The mob threw cabbage-stalks at each other and respectable inhabitants were invited to pelt the bailiff-elect with apples.[82] In 1766 the high price of butter gave rise to serious disturbances, and the rioters visited neighbouring towns, forcing farmers to lower their prices.[83]

The capital burgesses were drawn chiefly from a single family; the assistant burgesses were not invited to vote in the common council, and, even after the repeal of the Test and Corporation Acts, it was long before a Dissenter was admitted as assistant.[84]

Ill-feeling was increased when, 6 August 1827, the corporation succeeded in gaining a new charter confirming their old constitution, save that the twelve capital burgesses gained the title of 'aldermen,' instituting the office of recorder and increasing the number of magistrates by creating the three senior aldermen ex officio justices of the peace.[85]

[60] Hist. MSS. Com. Rep. iv, App. 267. In the 17th century there were several fulling-mills on the Stour near Lower Mitton, in the occupation of different members of the Wilmot family, who appear to have been successful, as they registered their pedigree in the visitation of 1682.
[61] Willis-Bund, op. cit. 131, 133.
[62] Cal. S. P. Dom. 1644, p. 238.
[63] Parish reg. quoted by Burton, Hist. of Kidderminster, 217.
[64] Willis-Bund, op. cit. 170-3.
[65] Grove, op. cit.
[66] Willis-Bund, op. cit. 176, 204-5.

[67] Cal. Com. for Comp. iv, 2605.
[68] Reliquiae Baxterianae (1696), 68.
[69] Willis-Bund, op. cit. 256.
[70] Reliquiae Baxterianae, 69.
[71] Cal. S. P. Dom. 1655, pp. 31, 207.
[72] Ibid. 1658-9, p. 76.
[73] Corp. Rec. Ordinances 23 Aug. 1650; confirmed by Exch. Dec. 27 Aug. 1650.
[74] V.C.H. Worcs. ii, 252.
[75] Guest, 'Manners and Customs of Old Kidderminster,' Shuttle, 25 Aug. 1906.
[76] V.C.H. Worcs. ii, 295-6. A special

cloth manufactured at Kidderminster—a kind of linsey-woolsey—called 'Kidderminster stuff,' was very well known.
[77] Ibid. 297-9.
[78] See plan facing p. 164.
[79] Local and Personal Act, 17 Geo. III, cap. 75.
[80] Kidderminster Shuttle, 1 Sept. 1906.
[81] Exch. Dep. East. 6 Will. and Mary, no. 24.
[82] Gent. Mag. 1790, p. 1191.
[83] Prattinton Coll. (Soc. Antiq.).
[84] Parl. Papers (1835), xxv, 1877.
[85] Corp. Rec.; Pat. 8 Geo. IV, pt. ix, no. 1.

During the rioting which accompanied the great weavers' strike of 1828 the impartiality of the high bailiff was called into question.[86]

The local government was extended and reformed by the Municipal Reform Act of 1835,[87] which divided the borough into three wards represented by six aldermen and eighteen councillors.[88] The number of wards was doubled in 1880.

Previous to 1835 the sole jurisdiction possessed by the corporation was due to the charter of 1632–3, which constituted the bailiff, his predecessor and the under steward justices of the peace. Petty sessions had thenceforward been held weekly, but quarter sessions were regularly dismissed at once, owing to the lack of a sufficient gaol.[89] The Court of Requests

THE STAFFORDSHIRE AND WORCESTERSHIRE CANAL, KIDDERMINSTER

established in 1772 was held by a commission distinct from the borough magistrates.[90]

The corporation insignia include a silver-gilt mace, a Jubilee gift of Mr. George Houldsworth (mayor 1886–7), and the mayoral badge and chain purchased in 1875. The common seal given in 1775 bears an ornate cartouche with the town arms:

Azure two cheveronels or, between three bezants, and each charged with four roundels, and the legend ' Deo iuvante arte et industria floret.'

The corporation also possesses a beautiful Elizabethan loving-cup of silver-gilt with elaborately chased bowl and cover. Round the top is inscribed ' Given formerly p[er] Thomas Jennens of Kitterminster and inlarged p[er] his grandchild Thomas Jenens of the City of London Grocer A° Dm̄. 1623.' Hall-marks : London, 1611–12.[91]

During the 19th century Kidderminster increased rapidly in population and prosperity.

A period of depression from 1851 to 1861 was ended by the development of the railway, which had been constructed in 1852. Power loom machines were introduced 1860–5 and hand looms were entirely superseded. Not only was an impetus given to the carpet manufacture, which has since increased threefold, but also the town has expanded in all directions and especially upon the rising ground in the neighbourhood of the station. Much of the new town was built with bricks made near the Stour Vale Works, on the canal side and at Caldwall.[92.3]

The canal was almost superseded by the railway. The former donkey traffic[94] has quite disappeared and a system of electric tramways has been established. Moreover, the condition of the town has been immensely improved since the 17th century, when every burgess and innholder set a lantern before his door on dark nights.[95] Steps were taken for better lighting and paving in 1813,[96] and gas was introduced in 1818.[97] The old watch, consisting of about eight householders,[98] was replaced by professional watchmen before 1835.[99]

The town hall in High Street was replaced in 1877 by the present more spacious and commodious building in Vicar Street. It was erected on the site of the vicarage[100] and its frontage is adorned by a statue of Sir Rowland Hill, the great reorganizer of the postal system, who was born at Kidderminster 3 December 1795.[1] Near the town hall are the Corporation Buildings with the Corn Exchange, purchased in 1853.[2] At the corner of Market Street, near by, are the Science and Art Schools and the Borough Free Library, removed to its present position in 1894.

The town owes a part of this prosperity to the market, which was probably prescriptive in origin or due to the grant of toll made to Manasser Biset.[3]

The lord of the manor had a grant of a three days' fair at St. Bartholomewtide in 1228.[4] The (undated) ' Customs of the Lords of Kidderminster,'[5] which may probably be assigned to the 14th century, show that it was usual for each burgess to set up stalls before his tenement, but for the lord to receive 1d.

---

[86] *Rep. of the Trial of Rev. Humph. Price,* pr. 1829 for the Carpet Weavers' Committee.
[87] Stat. 5 & 6 Will. IV, cap. 76.
[88] Ibid.
[89] *Parl. Papers* (1835), xxv, 1877.
[90] Local and Personal Act, 12 Geo. III, cap. 66.
[91] Jewitt and Hope, *Corp. Plate,* ii, 443.

[92.3] *Kidderminster Shuttle,* 11 Aug. 1906.
[94] Ibid. 18 Aug. 1906.
[95] Corp. Rec. By-laws, 1640.
[96] Local and Personal Act, 53 Geo. III, cap. 83.
[97] Ibid. 58 Geo. III, cap. 83.
[98] By-laws, 1683.
[99] *Parl. Papers* (1835), xxv, 1878.
[100] Burton, *Hist. of Kidderminster,* 83.

[1] *Dict. Nat. Biog.*
[2] *Rep. of Roy. Com. on Markets and Tolls* (1891), viii, 160 ; *P.O. Dir.* 1854, p. 209.
[3] See above.
[4] *Cal. Pat.* 1225–32, p. 175 ; confirmed 1238 (*Cal. Chart. R.* 1226–57, p. 235).
[5] See above.

as toll from strangers and the low bailiff ½d. as stallage on fair and market days. The ambiguity of the charter of Charles I and the unsettled state of the town during the Civil War aggravated disputes between the burgesses and Lord Bergavenny's agent for the collection of tolls. About 1620 Lord Bergavenny offered the burgesses a lease of the tolls, but they refused, being under the impression that the high bailiff ought to receive the whole of the tolls towards his charges incurred in dining the lord's officers at the courts leet and baron and supping the low bailiff and the constable on market days.[6] The dispute was brought before the court of Exchequer and decrees given in favour of the lord,[7] who subsequently leased his rights to William Dike of Font, co. Sussex.[8] The latter sublet the tolls and court-house to the corporation,[9] who finally obtained from the lord a lease for 1,000 years.[10]

The general market is now held on Thursdays and Saturdays in a covered hall built by the corporation in 1822.[11] The cattle market, held fortnightly on Saturdays, was similarly moved from the streets to an inclosed space between Backmarket and Market Streets,[12] the new market being opened 26 October 1871.[13]

In 1694 there were three fairs yearly—one at Ascensiontide, one on Corpus Christi Day (Thursday after Trinity Sunday), and the third the chartered fair of St. Bartholomew.[14] The origin of the first two is unknown. The only existing fair is that which was formerly held in the town at Ascensiontide. It is now purely a pleasure fair, has been transferred to the third week in June, and is held in the suburbs.[15]

The cattle and cheese fair, held on 4 September until the middle of the last century, was probably a survival of the St. Bartholomew fair.[16] Early in the 19th century an additional fair was held on the Monday after Palm Sunday, and another, held on 29 June, may have been the original Corpus Christi fair, but these were all abolished before 1872, when a hiring fair was held the second Tuesday in each month and the pleasure fair was established in June. At Stourport the markets on Wednesdays and Saturdays, said to have been established in 1768, were at first well attended, especially in the hop season, but they are now almost extinct. There were also fairs on the first Tuesdays in April, July and October.[17]

The Grammar School was founded by charter, 1636; but it may have originated in the school held in St. Mary's Chantry.[18]

Pearsall's Endowed Grammar School, founded in 1795, is now merged in the 'New Meeting' Schools. There is a High School for Girls in the Chester Road. In addition to the Science and Art Schools there are seventeen elementary schools in Kidderminster and its hamlets, while Stourport has five and Wribbenhall three.

Some names of interest are Burlasshe, Conyngeshall and the Rose and Crown (temp. Charles II), Cross-of-the-Hands and Spout Inns.

Beyond the town itself lies the extensive parish of which it is the centre. Numerous outlying hamlets and farms represent the sixteen berewicks of the Domesday Survey. Two of these lay at Ribbesford across the Severn; the sites of three others—Bristitune, Fastochesfeld and Teulesberge—remain unknown.

The eastern arm of the parish contains Wannerton, still (as in 1086) no more than an isolated farm, and Hurcott, a hall with manorial rights of its own.[19] Near Hurcott, in a commanding position, stands Park Hall, the residence of Mr. G. E. Wilson, J.P.

South of Hurcott and Park Hall the parish is traversed by the Birmingham road and the Oxford, Worcester and Wolverhampton branch of the Great Western railway, and beyond these are the fertile fields and pasture-lands of the Little Dunclent, Offmoor and Comberton Farms.

Comberton itself is a residential district of Kidderminster which lies along the main road to Bromsgrove. Comberton Hall[20] is in the occupation of Mr. R. Howard Krause. It dates from about the year 1600. The house has been much altered by the removal of its curvilinear gables and the addition of bay windows, but retains generally its original plan of central hall with rooms on both sides, its old heavy beams, some of which are encased, and at the top of the stairway a moulded handrail and turned balusters of the early 18th century. At the back are the original brick stables with curvilinear gables.

Aggborough Farm lies on the hill-side between Comberton and the Stour, near the old Worcester road and the hamlet of Hoobrook, where there is a (now disused) paper-mill.

The low lands near the Worcester road, and indeed the whole valley of the Stour, are liable to floods, except in the town itself, where the stream is for the most part walled in. Such inundations frequently gave rise to 'malignant fevers' in the 18th century,[21] when many of the Kidderminster weavers lived in 'small nasty' houses along the river-side; but the townspeople declared that the high death-rate was due to smallpox.[22] The town, however, was thoroughly drained in 1872-3.

The road to Stourport following the river skirts Sutton Common, the 'Sudtone' of Domesday, near which is said to have been 'Sudwale,'[23] and, leaving on the left Brinton Park, given to the town in 1887 by Mr. John Brinton, D.L., J.P., formerly M.P., leads through Foley Park, a rapidly growing suburb of substantial houses, villas and small shops.

Beyond lies Oldington, another berewick; its woods extend from the road to the river-side. Oldington Farm, the probable site of the manor-house, stands

[6] See Exch. Dep. Mich. 1653, no. 2, 19.
[7] Corp. Rec. Dec. Mich. 8 Chas. I; Exch. Dec. Hil. 8 Chas. I (Ser. 3), xi, fol. 439.
[8] Com. Pleas D. Enr. East. 15 Chas. II, m. 25.
[9] Close, 20 Chas. II, pt. ix, no. 38.
[10] Parl. Papers (1835), xxv, 1877.
[11] Ibid.
[12] Rep. on Markets and Tolls (1891), viii, 160.

[13] 'Ephemerides,' Kidderminster Almanack, 1872, p. 14.
[14] Exch. Dep. East. 6 Will. and Mary, no. 24.
[15] Inform. kindly supplied by Mr. Ebenezer Guest.
[16] Brayley and Britton, Beauties of Engl. and Wales, xv (2), 239; allowing for the difference of thirteen days made by the alteration of the calendar, 1752.
[17] Pigot, Comm. Dir. 1822-3, p. 573;

National Dir. 1828-9, p. 879; P.O. Dir. 1872, p. 1452.
[18] V.C.H. Worcs. iv, under 'Schools.'
[19] See below.
[20] See below for manorial history.
[21] Jas. Johnstone, Hist. Dissertation concerning the Malignant Epidemical Fever of 1756.
[22] Prattinton Coll. (Soc. Antiq.), v, 3.
[23] Burton, Hist. of Kidderminster, 1.

back from the road. It has been converted into a sewage farm.

Stourport lies about the junction of the Stour and Severn, and is approached through Upper Mitton, formerly a part of Hartlebury parish. It is a town consisting mostly of modern houses, grouping generally on the road from the iron bridge over the Severn, which passes northward through Bridge Street, High Street and Lombard Street, and reaches the north end of the town in Foundry Street. In Lombard Street there is a fine square brick chimney, which rises to a great height, with perfectly plain sides, gradually diminishing in size. In 1863 Lower Mitton with Stourport adopted the Local Government Act of 1858,[24] uniting to form a local board of health, and in 1894 Lower and Upper Mitton were combined in the single urban district of Stourport.[25]

The town of Stourport grew up in consequence of Brindley's choice of the junction of the two rivers for the basin of the Staffordshire and Worcestershire Canal. The three great basins of the canal are the main feature of the town. There are large iron and carpet works built on the banks of the Stour. Green meadows sloping down to the left bank of the Severn form a pleasant contrast to the crowded shops and warehouses of the High Street and Bridge Street. The iron bridge was erected about 1870 to replace one which dated from about 1806.[26]

Lower Mitton is of older date than Stourport. It consists of a few scattered houses on the Wribbenhall road parallel with the Severn. Overlooking the river are Moor Hall, the residence of Mr. J. Brinton, and Lickhill Manor House, the seat of the ancient family of Folliott until the early part of the last century, when it became the property of the Craven family.[27]

On the way from Lower Mitton to Wribbenhall is Blackstone Rock, a massive sandstone cliff overlooking the river. A cave cut in its face is known as the Blackstone Hermitage.

Wribbenhall, another of the Domesday berewicks, a picturesque village on the Birmingham and Coventry road, is clustered about the bridge of Bewdley, where the main road to Birmingham crosses the Severn. The men of Kidderminster Foreign had to repair Wribbenhall bridge.[28] The older cottages with terraced gardens on the high banks of the Kidderminster road and the gabled houses facing the river are fast being replaced by modern villas, for Wribbenhall is practically a suburb of Bewdley, and since the construction of the Severn Valley Line about 1859[29] it has afforded the only approach to that town by rail. Wribbenhall was constituted a separate civil parish in 1901.[30]

On the outskirts of Wribbenhall is the small hamlet of Catchem's End, which is said to have been the limit of the sanctuary of Bewdley.[31] Beyond is the large park of Spring Grove, the residence of Mr. Thomas Wakefield Binyon, J.P.

When the high ground on the left bank of the Severn above Wribbenhall is reached the Bunter Pebble Beds, upon which lies the greater part of the parish, give way to a portion of the Forest of Wyre coalfield. The Coal Measures are covered by North Wood and Eymore Wood, east of which is a sill of basalt extending to Warshill Wood, where a ridge of breccia occurs.[32]

At North Wood a house with land was acquired by the Prior of Great Malvern about 1318.[33] Park Attwood, long the property of the Attwood family,[34] lies in the northern part of the parish. Local legend relates that a crusading member of the family, miraculously brought back from prison in a trance, delayed the fulfilment of a vow to devote his life to the protection of the Holy Sepulchre. He returned from a second imprisonment ragged and in chains, and was recognized by a faithful dog just in time to prevent the re-marriage of his despairing wife. The galloping of his horse and rattling of his chains are said to be still heard near Park Attwood.[35]

The chapelry of Trimpley marks the site of another of the Domesday berewicks. It consists of scattered farms and a few cottages lying near the road from Park Attwood to Kidderminster. The open common upon which the tenants of Trimpley Manor have common of pasture lies on either side of the road. During the last century it was planted with fine poplars by members of the Chillingworth family,[36] and in the midst are the grounds of Trimpley House, the residence of Mr Arnold Crane Rogers.

The road leads eastwards over Ridgstone Rock about 400 ft. above sea level. Thence is obtained a perfect panorama of the county, stretching eastwards to the Clent and the Lickey Hills and southwards to Worcester and Great Malvern. The steep incline below descends by the rough natural steps of 'Jacob's Ladder' into the wood and heathland of Habberley Valley, broken by a quaint peak called the Pekket Rock.

Low Habberley is a hamlet on the left of the road facing the present manor-house, while High Habberley lies on the cross-road leading to Catchem's End. The existence of one Habberley only is recorded in 1086, unless either hamlet is to be identified with one of the neighbouring berewicks of Franche.

Franche is a village 1 mile from the town of Kidderminster, and with its church, schools and club lies on either side of the Bewdley to Stourbridge road, extending from the cross-roads at Honeybrook Terrace to Franche Hall, built by Mr. Michael Tomkinson.

MANORS The lepers of Maiden Bradley acquired the manors of COMBERTON (Cumbrintun, xiii cent.; Comerton, Cumberton, xiii–xix cent.) and OLDINGTON (Aldintone, xi cent.; Oldinton, xiii–xiv cent.; Oldington, xv cent.) in the 13th century. Manasser Biset (d. about 1186) had enfeoffed Sir Ralph de Auxeville of these, together with Mitton Mill, and a rent-charge on the great mill of the manor,[37] and Sir Ralph

[24] Lond. Gaz. 27 Nov. 1863, p. 6055.
[25] Pop. Ret. (1901), 14.
[26] P.O. Dir. 1872, p. 1514; Pigot, Comm. Dir. 1822–3, p. 578. For markets and fairs at Stourport see above.
[27] Inform. kindly supplied by Mr. Campbell J. Craven of Clifton, co. Glos.
[28] Quart. Sess. R. (Worcs. Hist. Soc.), 512.

[29] B. Gibbons, Notes for a Hist. of Kidderminster (1859), 51.
[30] Loc. Govt. Bd. Order, 1 Apr. 1901.
[31] Inform. kindly supplied by Miss Tomkinson of Franche Hall; there is another 'Catchem's End' in Churchill parish.
[32] V.C.H. Worcs. i, 11, 14.
[33] Cal. Pat. 1317–21, p. 102.

[34] See below.
[35] Inform. kindly supplied by Miss Tomkinson; the story is given in a slightly different form in Gibbons, op. cit. 69. See also the account of Wolverley.
[36] Inform. kindly supplied by Miss Tomkinson.
[37] Add. MS. 37503, fol. 23 et seq.; Cal. Chart. R. 1226–57, p. 41.

KIDDERMINSTER : HOUSES AT WRIBBENHALL

had granted them piecemeal to the priory, partly in consideration of the payment of his ransom of 100 marks,[38] and partly for the welfare of his own soul and that of his lord, Henry Biset.[39] Already the prior had rights in Kidderminster Church (q.v.) of the gift of Manasser Biset.

From others the priory acquired various houses and pieces of land in the town,[40] and Margaret sister of Henry Biset, who built herself a house within the priory court in order to live a life of contemplation, gave rents in Kidderminster, assigned to her by her brother.[41] John Rivers of Burgate subsequently exchanged one-third of Kidderminster Manor with the same priory.

The prior's reeve had charge of the whole estate during the 13th and 14th centuries.[42] He collected rents and enforced services, kept the houses in repair, supervised the sale of wood (which in one year included as many as fifty-one oaks), provided for the wants of the prior when he visited the 'halls' of Oldington or Comberton, presided over the courts with the aid of a clerk, and disbursed liberal alms to the poor.

In 1390, however, the prior leased the third part of the manor of Kidderminster, with Oldington and Comberton and the tithes of Kidderminster, to Thomas Mal, chaplain, and John Mal for thirty-four years, subject to a rent, which was to be increased later unless 'great pestilence came to those parts.' Other tenements were also let out on lease.[43]

It became customary to let the estate for considerable terms of years.[44] John Blount was collector of rents, and held the rectory on lease in 1455–6,[45] and in 1522 Sir Thomas Blount and his son Edward had a lease of the whole estate for ninety-seven years.[46] Thus the property was little affected by the dissolution of Maiden Bradley Priory in 1535,[47] or by the subsequent grant of the rights of the priory to John Dudley, the Great Admiral of England, Viscount Lisle, and afterwards Duke of Northumberland,[48] then embarrassed by debts incurred in the king's service at Boulogne[49] (1544).

When in 1553 Northumberland was attainted and executed for his attempt to secure the throne for his daughter-in-law, the Lady Jane Grey, his lands were forfeited to the Crown, and in February 1559–60 Thomas Blount (said to be the grandson of the former lessee of 1522)[50] purchased all the property in Kidderminster which had formerly belonged to Maiden Bradley Priory.[51]

Thomas Blount died on 28 November 1568,[52] and was buried in the parish church. His son, Sir Edward Blount, kt., married (firstly) Mary Nevill, sister of Edward Lord Bergavenny,[53] and from him obtained a lease of the remainder of the original manor of Kidderminster.[54] In 1603 Sir Edward settled the reversion of his portion of the manor contingent upon his death on his kinsman Charles (Blount) Lord Mountjoy, who bequeathed his rights to his wife Penelope and her son Mountjoy Blount, afterwards created Earl of Newport.[55]

Sir Edward Blount died in 1630. In 1634 the Earl of Newport, then Master of the Ordnance, sold his estate at Kidderminster to Edmund Waller[56] the poet, who (either to raise money for the fine which purchased his safety after the discovery of his 'plot' against the Long Parliament, or to provide funds during his exile in France) split up the estate, selling it in three portions.

Daniel Dobbyns, a merchant of London, who was related to Waller by marriage,[57] purchased the 'fair house next the church'[58] and the manorial rights, apparently including Comberton. Dobbyns's house was pulled down shortly before 1782.[59] The site is now the property of the vicar.[60] Dobbyns reconveyed the 'moiety of the manor,' and possibly the manor of Comberton, to Waller, who sold it about 1652 with Comberton to Adam Hough and Thomas Hunt.[61] Adam Hough's descendant of the same name sold the 'manor of Comberton' to Samuel Steward c. 1772.[62] In this family it remained until about 1832.[63] It was bequeathed by two sisters and co-heirs, Mary Anne wife of Henry Evans and Charlotte Elizabeth Steward, to their kinsman Henry Steward Oldnall-Russell in tail. His son John Edwin took the name of Russell-Oldnall. Comberton is now the property of his brother Captain Roger William Oldnall of Stone[64] (q.v.).

It is not clear whether Oldington was sold to Daniel Dobbyns or not. It was certainly severed from Comberton by 1656, when William Bromhall and his wife Anne, Thomas Cowett and his wife Anne, John Somers (probably the father of the great chancellor)[65] and his wife Catherine, Francis Walker and Richard Whettall conveyed it to Thomas Foley, who was then sheriff of the county.[66]

It was thus among the first acquisitions of Thomas Foley in Kidderminster. It descended with the Foley estate till its purchase by the trustees of Lord Ward.[67] It is still the property of the Earl of Dudley.

[38] Add. MS. 37503, fol. 24. 'Ad redimendum corpus meum de carcere et de morte.'

[39] Madox, *Form. Angl.* 255 ; Add. MS. 37503, fol. 23 d., 24.

[40] Anct. D. (P.R.O.), B 2688 ; Feet of F. Unknown Co. 13 John, no. 59 ; Worcs. case 258, file 6, no. 22 ; Add. Chart. 20423.

[41] *Chart. of Salisbury* (Rolls Ser.), 74 ; this gift was probably the origin of the 'tradition of the leprous lady' of the Biset family (Nash, *Hist. of Worc.* ii, 36).

[42] Mins. Accts. bdle. 1070, no. 5 ; Ct. R. (Gen. Ser.), portf. 210, no. 70 ; Rentals and Surv. (P.R.O.), R. 719.

[43] Anct. D. (P.R.O.), D 339, 678, 930. An interesting account of the economic development of the estate is given by the Rev. J. R. Burton, *Hist. of Kidderminster*, 9–27.

[44] Mins. Accts. bdle. 1054, no. 11 ; 1055, no. 8 ; 1064, no. 7 n.

[45] Ibid. bdle. 1069, no. 8.

[46] Prattinton Coll. (Soc. Antiq.), Habington MS. v, 3.

[47] *L. and P. Hen. VIII*, ix, 168 ; x, 1238.

[48] Ibid. xx (2), 1068 (41).

[49] Ibid. 412 (ii).

[50] Burton, *Hist. of Kidderminster*, 49.

[51] Pat. 2 Eliz. pts. ix, x.

[52] Chan. Inq. p.m. (Ser. 2), clii, 173.

[53] There are effigies of himself and his two wives in the church, see below ; Exch. Dep. Mich. 1653, no. 19.

[54] Ibid. Trin. 1653, no. 2.

[55] Abstract of title quoted in Prattinton Coll. (Soc. Antiq.), Habington MS. v, 3.

[56] Prattinton Coll. (Soc. Antiq.), Habington MS. v, 3 ; Feet of F. Div. Co. Hil. 8 Chas. I ; East. 10 Chas. I, Hil. 8 Chas. I.

[57] *Visit. of London* (Harl. Soc. xv), 234.

[58] Possibly the house assigned to the vicar in 1336 ; see below.

[59] Nash, op. cit. ii, 37.

[60] Inform. kindly supplied by Mr. Tomkinson.

[61] Prattinton Coll. (Soc. Antiq.), Habington MS. v, 3 ; Habington, *Surv. of Worc.* (Worcs. Hist. Soc.), ii, 158 ; Feet of F. Worcs. East. 1652.

[62] Com. Pleas D. Enr. East. 12 Geo. III, m. 158 ; Recov. R. East. 12 Geo. III, rot. 492.

[63] Recov. R. Mich. 9 Geo. IV, rot. 382 ; Feet of F. Worcs. Mich. 3 Will. IV.

[64] Inform. kindly supplied by Mr. J. W. Stanier Jones of Dudley.

[65] G.E.C. *Complete Peerage*, vii, 166 ; see also parish reg. quoted by Burton, *Hist. of Kidderminster*, 152, 214.

[66] Feet of F. Worcs. Hil. 1656.

[67] See Great Witley.

The 'hall' at Oldington appears to have been the principal dwelling-house attached to the estate of Maiden Bradley Priory in Kidderminster. In 1281 a lock was bought for the door of a room in the hall, and thirty cuttings (*inserti*) for the lord's garden.[68] It was at Oldington that the vicar paid his yearly rent.[69]

In 1281 the prior had another hall at Kidderminster which may have been on the site either of Comberton Hall or of the house near the churchyard.[70]

The manor of *CALDWALL* (Caldewell, xiii cent.; Caldewall, xv cent.; or Cawdewall, xvi cent.) was held of the Prior of Maiden Bradley[71] in the 14th century. Possibly it was included in the lands given to the priory by John Rivers, for Henry 'of Caldwall' was one of the witnesses of his grants.[72]

Of its subinfeudation nothing is known. Henry of Caldwall settled a life interest in two messuages and land in Kidderminster, Caldwall and Franche upon William de Verdun and his wife Margery in 1248–9.[73] A Henry of Caldwall was a tenant of the prior in 1283–4.[74] The tenant in 1327 was evidently Hugh Cooksey of Cooksey in Upton Warren[75] (q.v.). In 1330 he acquired the services of a bondman of the lord of Kidderminster Biset,[76] and in 1335 he had a grant of free warren at Caldwall.[77] He also held the manor of Kidderminster Biset (q.v.) on lease. About 1376 Caldwall was the property of Denise widow of Hugh Cooksey.[78]

For two centuries the history of this manor was identical with that of Cooksey, being inherited by Roger Winter, kinsman of Joyce Beauchamp, sister and heir of the Sir Hugh Cooksey, kt., who had died in 1445.[79] Roger Winter's grandson George Winter sold Caldwall in 1589 to Francis Clare,[80] son of Simon Clare, lord of Over Mitton. Francis Clare died at Caldwall, 8 June 1608.[81] His son and heir, Sir Ralph Clare, kt., was a zealous supporter of the king and the most bitter opponent of Baxter. He took a prominent part in the defence of Worcester, 1642, but his presence there in 1651 is doubtful.[82] Baxter describes him as a courtier noted for his eminent civility and a churchman very zealous for conformity, the ruler of the vicar and of all business at Kidderminster.[83] His brother and heir Francis Clare was a captain of foot in the service of Charles I, and died in 1680.[84] His son Francis evidently succeeded to the manor.[85] It seems to have remained in the Clare family until 1777, when Antony Deane the younger, nephew of Francis Clare of Henwick in Hallow, sold it to Matthew Jeffries

CLARE of Caldwall. *Or three cheverons gules and a border engrailed azure.*

of Kidderminster and Thomas Jeffries of London, goldsmith.[86]

In 1897 the estate was purchased by the corporation from the trustees of George Turton.[87]

The park possibly dated from the grant of free warren to Hugh Cooksey in 1335.

Caldwall Castle stands on the low-lying land at the south end of the town. The site is bounded on the north-east and south-east by the Stour, which here takes a small bend. Of the mediaeval building only one octagonal tower remains, but this was added to in the latter part of the 17th century by the erection of a three-story brick building on the north-west. Beyond this a low castellated extension was built in the 19th century, containing a few offices. The original tower is built of red sandstone, is three stories high with an embattled parapet, and appears to have been erected early in the 15th century. The stonework on the outside is much decayed and greatly overgrown with ivy, while the interior of the two upper floors has been considerably modernized. In the north corner is a vice going the full height of the tower and crowned with an embattled parapet and a stone roof. The ground floor—now a basement—retains its original stone vault, the ribs springing from small moulded corbels and meeting in a boss carved with a lion's face. In the north-west wall is a pointed doorway, now leading up a few steps into the 17th-century addition. The vice opens, by an ogee-headed door, from the north side of the opening cut through the wall to this doorway. In the north-east wall are the jambs and pointed rear arch of an original opening, through which a modern doorway has been cut, while in the south wall is a three-centred opening in which are three steps leading up to the outside, but externally this is blocked up. In the west wall is a square-headed cupboard, divided in front by a central stone post, the jambs, head and sill being rebated for doors.

The upper floors are much modernized, but the second retains a late 16th-century window with four lights and a transom.

The road which runs along the north side of the castle is only a little below the level of the first floor and comes right up to the tower walls.[87a]

The staircase of the 17th-century addition was erected immediately against the tower and has moulded handrails and strings and heavy twisted balusters. The newels are square and have moulded cappings crowned with spherical finials and large acorn-shaped drops. Sash windows have been inserted throughout the addition, with the exception of the two upper floors fronting the road, where the original wooden transomed and mullioned window frames, fitted with iron casements, have been retained. Two chimney stacks have been carried up on the north-west wall through the centres of two stepped gables. The roof is tiled.

[68] Mins. Accts. bdle. 1070, no. 5.
[69] Add. MS. 37503, fol. 50 et seq.
[70] Mins. Accts. bdle. 1070, no. 5.
[71] Chan. Inq. p.m. 50 Edw. III (1st nos.), no. 20.
[72] Harl. Chart. 55 D 25; Dugdale, *Mon.* vi, 644; but Henry is not mentioned in the list of tenants, free or bond.
[73] Feet of F. Worcs. case 258, file 6, no. 25.
[74] Mins. Accts. bdle. 1070, no. 5, m. 2.

[75] Lay Subs. R. bdle. 200, no. 1.
[76] *Cal. Pat.* 1330–4, p. 3.
[77] Chart. R. 9 Edw. III, m. 1.
[78] Chan. Inq. p.m. 50 Edw. III (1st nos.), no. 20.
[79] See the account of the church below and *V.C.H. Worcs.* iii, 232.
[80] Feet of F. Worcs. Trin. 31 Eliz.; Pat. 31 Eliz. pt. xv.
[81] Chan. Inq. p.m. (Ser. 2), cccxli, 54.

[82] *Dict. Nat. Biog.*; Willis-Bund, *Civil War in Worc.* 227.
[83] *Reliquiae Baxterianae* (1696), 298, 301.
[84] Metcalfe, *Visit. of Worc.* 33.
[85] Recov. R. Trin. 3 Jas. II, rot. 36.
[86] Prattinton Coll. (Soc. Antiq.), v, 3.
[87] Inform. kindly supplied by Mr. Tomkinson.
[87a] The level of this road has been raised within the last few years.

A South-west Prospect of Stourport c. 1776

(From an engraving by Peter Mazell after James Sherrif)

The reputed manor of *EYMORE* (Eymer, xvii cent.) evidently originated in Edward Burnell's gift of 160 acres of wood, parcel of the manor of Kidderminster Burnell, to the Prior and convent of Worcester (*circa* 1312).[88] Shortly afterwards the prior had licence to impark his land at Kidderminster.[89] When the endowment of the priory was bestowed upon the dean and chapter [90] in January 1541–2 the lands in Eymore and Kidderminster were included.[91]

After the abolition of the chapter by the Long Parliament, Eymore was purchased (1649) by John Corbyn, the dean's lessee, for over £3,000.[92] The dean and chapter recovered their lands at the Restoration, and Eymore remained in their possession until 1861, when it was purchased by Mr. Edward Crane of Broom, who bequeathed it to his nephew, Mr. Arnold Crane Rogers of Trimpley House.[93]

HABBERLEY (Haburgelei, xi cent.; Haberlegh, xiii cent.; Haburley, xvi cent.),[94] a Domesday 'berewick' of Kidderminster, lay at least in part within the main manor of Kidderminster [95]; but Francis Clare is recorded to have possessed a separate 'manor' of Habberley in 1606,[96] part of which may have been the land in Habberley which formerly belonged to the chantry of St. Katherine in Kidderminster Church and was granted to Simon Clare after its suppression.[97] It subsequently descended with Caldwall Manor (q.v.) to Matthew and Thomas Jeffries. Reversionary rights were purchased by Thomas Crane of Habberley and Bewdley, who died 12 December 1824. Shortly before his death he made over the property to his nephew, John Crane, who died in 1866, leaving Habberley to his youngest brother, Henry Crane. Upon the latter's death in 1882 it descended to his son, Mr. John Henry Crane, of 'Oakhampton,' Stourport, the present owner.

The original manor-house was burnt down in 1718; it stood on the site of the present Low Habberley Farm and had been occupied by the Crane family since or before 1563. Of late years the tenant of Habberley House has called it the 'Manor House.' There seems no basis for a local tradition that an old house occupied by Mrs. Miller was at one time the manor-house.[98]

The reputed manor of *HEATHY* (Hetheye, xiii cent.; Dunclent Hethey, xiv cent.) lies near Dunclent on the borders of the parish of Stone. In 1275 Thomas Attwood granted a messuage, carucate of land and 2 marks rent in Heathy to Robert Attwood for life.[99] This was possibly identical with the quarter of a knight's fee in Dunclent which was held by Stephen Attwood (de Bosco) and subsequently passed to Avice Dunclent, 1346.[100]

The manor was held of Lord Bergavenny, 1544,[1] and therefore was doubtless a sub-manor of Kidderminster Biset or Burnell.

In 1524 John Hore and his wife Margaret conveyed the manor of Heathy to Gilbert Clare, Simon Rice and others with warrant against the heirs of Margaret.[2] Two-thirds of the manor subsequently came into the possession of Thomas Hey, and after his death in 1543 was divided between his three

CALDWALL CASTLE FROM THE NORTH

daughters, Elizabeth wife of Thomas Browne, Margaret wife of Peter Romney, and Joan Hey.[3]

The portion assigned to Elizabeth Browne descended to her son William,[4] who in 1574 conveyed it to Humphrey Doolittle of Stone.[5] His son John

[88] *Cal. Pat.* 1307–13, p. 505; 1313–17, p. 132; *Cal. Close*, 1313–18, p. 234.

[89] *Abbrev. Rot. Orig.* (Rec. Com.), i, 199.

[90] See *V.C.H. Worcs.* ii, 111.

[91] *L. and P. Hen. VIII*, xvii, g. 71 (29).

[92] Close, 1649, pt. xiv, no. 9.

[93] Inform. kindly supplied by Mr. Rogers.

[94] The form 'Abberley' sometimes occurs (ex inform. Mr. J. H. Crane).

[95] *Hist. MSS. Com. Rep.* xi, App. vii, 66.

[96] Feet of F. Worcs. Trin. 4 Jas. I.

[97] Aug. Off. Misc. Bks. ccclxxiv, fol. 30; Chan. Inq. p.m. (Ser. 2), cxci, 117; see below.

[98] Mr. Crane has kindly supplied the details of the 19th-century history of this manor.

[99] Feet of F. Worcs. case 258, file 9, no. 36.

[100] *Feud. Aids*, v, 303; another quarter-fee (? Dunclent Manor) was held at the same time by William de Hetheregh.

[1] *L. and P. Hen. VIII*, xix (1), g. 610 (43).

[2] Feet of F. Worcs. East. 16 Hen. VIII.

[3] *L. and P. Hen. VIII*, xix (1), g. 610 (43); Fine R. 30 Hen. VIII, no. 18; 38 Hen. VIII, no. 12; 3 Edw. VI, no. 4.

[4] Chan. Inq. p.m. (Ser. 2) cviii, 125; Fine R. 9 Eliz. no. 15.

[5] Feet of F. Worcs. Hil. 16 Eliz.

Doolittle had livery of it in 1583,[6] but died in January 1585–6, leaving an infant son John.[7] In 1607 this John had livery of his father's estate.[8] Its later history is unknown.

The portion of Heathy assigned to Margaret Romney was held after her death by her husband, and descended in 1577 to their son William.[9] In 1627 William and Paul Romney conveyed their interest in the manor of Heathy to Edward Broad of Dunclent,[10] who sold it with Dunclent[11] to Thomas Foley.[12]

The estate subsequently descended with that of Great Witley (q.v.), and is now the property of Lord Dudley.

The later history of the portion assigned to Joan Hey is unknown.

HURCOTT (Worcote, xi cent.; Hurecot, xiii cent.; Hurcott or Huthcott, xvii cent.) was a berewick of Kidderminster in 1086.[13]

The manor appears to have belonged for a considerable time to the successive incumbents, possibly since the time of Robert of Hurcott, who was rector when Manasser Biset (d. circa 1186) gave the church to Maiden Bradley Priory.[14]

In 1211, when Adam of Hurcott was vicar, Thomas Esturmi quitclaimed to the Prior of Maiden Bradley and to the church of Kidderminster all his rights in 2 virgates at Hurcott.[15] Robert son of Adam of Hurcott released his rights in the whole 'vill' to the vicar of Kidderminster and his successors in 1235.[16]

In the 14th century Hurcott Hall was the dwelling-place of the vicars. Their house with the demesne lands and fish-ponds was worth 40s., the rent from bond tenants 58s. 3d., the mill 20s. and pleas of court 18d.[17]

When in 1335 the vicarage was re-ordained Hurcott was not included in the vicar's portion, but was assigned to the Prior of Maiden Bradley. In 1340, however, Sir John de la Doune, the newly inducted vicar, obtained from the bishop an appropriation more favourable to himself, especially stipulating that the vicar should enjoy 'the manor of Hurcott where the rectors were formerly accustomed to reside.'[18] Subsequent ordinances[19] seem to have again deprived the vicar of the manor of Hurcott. About 1449 the Prior of Maiden Bradley let it to farm to the mother of Thomas Everdon.[20]

It remained in the possession of the prior and passed with his other estates in Kidderminster to Edmund Waller the poet. He sold Hurcott to William Walsh of Abberley.[21] It appears to have been purchased by George Evelyn, brother of the diarist, John Evelyn. The latter bought it from his brother 27 June 1648, and sold it six months later

at a profit of £100 to Colonel John Bridges,[22] who also purchased the jointure of Lady Mary widow of Sir Edward Blount in Kidderminster.[23]

Colonel Bridges was 'a prudent pious gentleman' who lived at Kidderminster and supported Baxter's work there.[24] In 1662 he sold the manor to Thomas Foley,[25] with whose estate at Great Witley it has since descended.

LOWER MITTON[26] was a berewick of Kidderminster in 1086.[27] Its early history is obscure; but it was clearly separate from Over Mitton by 1280, when the one township was styled Mitton and the other Mitton Walter.[28] Lower Mitton was the property of the Lygon family during the 16th century, and probably at an earlier date. Thomas Lygon died in 1507 holding two messuages in Lickhill and Lower Mitton.[29] He left a son Richard. A Richard Lygon died seised of the 'manor of Mitton' in 1556.[29a] His son William Lygon held the manor of 'Nether-mytton' in 1560.[30] He was evidently succeeded by Richard Lygon, whose son William ultimately inherited the manor.[30a] Sir William Lygon, kt., is said to have sold to every tenant the inheritance of his tenement.[31] This was probably the Sir William Lygon who in 1616 with his wife Elizabeth sold the manor to James Clent or Clint.[32]

Miles Clent and his wife Dorothy conveyed it to Thomas the second Lord Folliott, governor of Londonderry in 1662.[33] In March 1716–17 the barony of Folliott became extinct by the death of Henry the third Lord Folliott, only son and heir of the above Thomas.[34] Lower Mitton and Lickhill were inherited by his niece Rebecca wife of Arthur Lugg (who died at Lickhill in 1726) and daughter of Anne Soley, sister of Henry Lord Folliott.[35] In 1740 Rebecca Lugg, then a widow, made over the property to her 'kinsman John Folliott in consideration of her natural love and affection . . . and for his advancement in point of fortune,' reserving to herself for life the occupancy of Lickhill Manor House. He was lieutenant-colonel of the regiment of horse commanded by Lord Cathcart, and in 1750 devised his Worcestershire estates to Captain John Folliott of the Royal Hospital, near Dublin, with successive remainders to the latter's second son John, and eldest son Francis, in tail. Captain John Folliott entered upon the estate in 1762, and was succeeded by John his second son, who died at Lickhill unmarried in January 1814. The estate then descended to John Folliott of Sligo, grandson of Francis Folliott, and a minor. He resided mostly in Ireland, and represented the county of Sligo in Parliament. In 1822 he barred the entail on the Worcestershire property, and subsequently sold the Lickhill Estate with its manors of Lower Mitton and

[6] Fine R. 25 Eliz. pt. i, no. 49.
[7] Chan. Inq. p.m. (Ser. 2), cclxxvii, 31.
[8] Fine R. 5 Jas. I, pt. i, no. 10.
[9] Chan. Inq. p.m. (Ser. 2), clxxxiii, 103.
[10] Feet of F. Worcs. Trin. 3 Chas. I.
[11] See account of Stone; Cal. Com. for Comp. iv, 3014–16.
[12] Feet of F. Worcs. East. 18 Chas. I; Trin. 1655.
[13] V.C.H. Worcs. i, 286b.
[14] See below for the relations between the incumbents and the priory.
[15] Feet of F. Unknown Co. 13 John, no. 59.
[16] Ibid. Worcs. case 258, file 4, no. 26.
[17] Add. MS. 37503, fol. 43.

[18] Burton, op. cit. 111.
[19] See below.
[20] Mins. Accts. bdle. 1054, no. 11.
[21] Habington, Surv. of Worc. (Worcs. Hist. Soc.), ii, 158; Prattinton Coll. (Soc. Antiq.), v, 3.
[22] Evelyn, Diary (ed. Bray), i, 246–7; Feet of F. Worcs. Mich. 24 Chas. I.
[23] Cal. Com. for Comp. iv, 2736.
[24] Reliquiae Baxterianae (1696), 88.
[25] Feet of F. Worcs. East. 14 Chas. II.
[26] For Over Mitton see the account of Hartlebury.
[27] V.C.H. Worcs. i, 286b. It is there called 'Mitton' and may have included Over Mitton.

[28] Lay Subs. R. Worcs. 1280, p. 9.
[29] Chan. Inq. p.m. (Ser. 2), xxi, 19; see below under Lickhill.
[29a] Ibid. cx, 172.
[30] Feet of F. Worcs. Mich. 2 & 3 Eliz.
[30a] Recov. R. East. 21 Eliz. m. 537; Chan. Inq. p.m. (Ser. 2), ccvi, 8; cccvi, 161. [31] Burton, Hist. of Bewdley, 95.
[32] Feet of F. Worcs. Hil. 14 Jas. I.
[33] Ibid. East. 14 Chas. II.
[34] G.E.C. Complete Peerage, iii, 389.
[35] Inform. kindly supplied by Mr. Campbell J. Craven of Clifton, co. Glos.; cf. Feet of F. Worcs. Mich. 4 Geo. I; Mich. 7 Geo. I; Recov. R. Mich. 7 Geo. I, rot. 110.

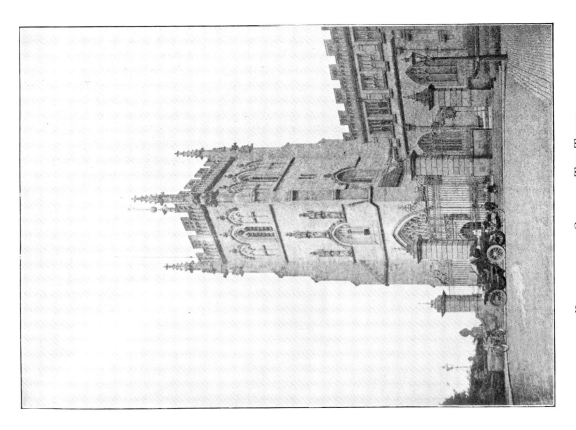

KIDDERMINSTER CHURCH : TOMB OF LADY JOYCE BEAUCHAMP

KIDDERMINSTER CHURCH : THE TOWER

Lickhill to Joseph Craven, J.P., of Steeton in Craven, co. Yorks.

Joseph Craven died 30 March 1867, having devised his Worcestershire property to his younger son John William Craven. The latter died in Scotland 12 October 1871, and the estate is now the property of his posthumous son, Mr. Campbell J. Craven.[36]

LICKHILL, also the property of Mr. Campbell J. Craven, has been accounted parcel of the Lower Mitton estate at least since 1429, when Robert Nelme of Worcester, who had in right of his wife Agnes the reversion of two messuages, a carucate of land, 6 acres of meadow and 11 marks rent in ' Leykhill,' Kidderminster, and Lower Mitton upon the death of Margaret wife of Walter Corbet, conveyed his title to Thomas Lygon, Thomas Heuster and others.[37] In 1507 Thomas Lygon's holding at Lower Mitton included a messuage at Lickhill.[38] Lickhill Manor House has long been the capital mansion of the Lower Mitton and Lickhill estate, and has been successively occupied by the Folliott and Craven families and their tenants. The house is of red brick, and is situated on the banks of the Severn between Stourport and Bewdley. It contains a fine oak staircase and some panelled rooms. During the time the Folliotts occupied it some choice tapestry covered the walls of the drawing-room. John Folliott, M.P., before referred to, removed the tapestry and Folliott family portraits to Hollybrook House, Sligo, his Irish seat, where they can still be seen.

At *WRIBBENHALL* the monks of Worcester had a small estate, which they asserted had been given to their monastery by King Offa.[39] It was assigned to the cellarer towards providing firewood for the use of the monks.[40] Its subsequent history is uncertain; possibly it was included in the land at Kidderminster and Eymore with which the dean and chapter was endowed in 1542.[41]

PARK ATTWOOD evidently originated in the licence granted in 1362 to John Attwood of Wolverley, the king's yeoman, to inclose 600 acres in his demesne lands at Kidderminster and Wolverley.[42] The reputed manor of Park Attwood remained in the Attwood family at least till 1595.[43] In 1661 John Attwood had rights in a considerable estate in Wolverley and Park Attwood,[44] and a John Attwood seems to have dealt with the manor in 1685.[45] The greater part of Park Attwood was purchased about 1797 by Henry Chillingworth of Holt Castle, and remained in the family until its recent sale by Lieut.-Col. William Henry Chillingworth. Thomas Hessin Charles, barrister-at-law, purchased the manor and lands of Park Attwood in 1912.[46]

TRIMPLEY (Trinpelei, xi cent.; Trimpelei, xiv cent.) was a berewick of Kidderminster in 1086,[47] and was probably the fee in Kidderminster granted by Manasser Biset to Stephen Attwood.[48] It descended to his grandson John Attwood in 1294,[49] and land at Trimpley remained in the Attwood family until the end of the 16th century.[50] The manorial rights were probably absorbed in those of Park Attwood.

Henry Chillingworth bought the bulk of the Trimpley estates about 1797. They remained with his descendants until recent times, when William Henry Chillingworth

ATTWOOD. *Gules a lion argent with a forked tail.*

sold Trimpley to Mr. Mills, whose daughter Mrs. Hudson is the present owner.

WANNERTON (Wenuerton, xi cent.; Wenfertone, xiii cent.; Wenforton or Wannerton, xvi cent.) is a reputed manor. It was one of the berewicks of Kidderminster in 1086,[52] and appeared as a separate hamlet on the Subsidy Roll of 1280.[53]

Three generations of the Wannerton family are said to have been lords of Wannerton during the 15th century.[54] John Wannerton, whose father and grandfather lived here, had a son John Wannerton of Worfield, co. Salop, whose daughter and heir Jane married Sir George Bromley, kt., justiciar of Chester.[55] The manor of Wannerton apparently formed her marriage portion.[56] She outlived her husband and settled Wannerton upon her grandson Thomas Bromley of Bridgnorth, who died without issue 20 February 1609–10.[57] He had settled the manor on his widow Eleanor, but it afterwards reverted to Sir Edward Bromley of Sheriff Hales, son of Sir George and Dame Jane, in accordance with the will of Thomas Bromley.[58] In 1677 William Bromley was in possession,[59] and in 1683 he conveyed Wannerton to Thomas Foley.[60] The manor has since descended with the Great Witley estate (q.v.).

The parish church of *ST. MARY* CHURCHES *AND ALL SAINTS* occupies a high position in the centre of the town, the tower being particularly prominent when approached by the wide street leading up to the fine wrought-iron gates of the churchyard.

The building consists of a chancel 43 ft. 6 in. long by 19 ft. 6 in. broad, with a south passage called ' the cloisters ' 8 ft. wide, a nave 81 ft. by 19 ft., north and south aisles and south-west tower. These measurements are all internal. There are further buildings at the eastern end of the chancel consisting

[36] The later history of the manor has been kindly supplied by Mr. Craven from his title-deeds and estate papers.

[37] Feet of F. Worcs. 8 Hen. V, no. 10.

[38] See above; cf. Feet of F. Worcs. Mich. 6 Chas. I.

[39] Dugdale, *Mon.* i, 608.

[40] Ibid. 607.

[41] See the account of Eymore above.

[42] Chart. R. 36 Edw. III, no. 13.

[43] Feet of F. Worcs. Trin. 38 Eliz. See the account of Wolverley.

[44] Feet of F. Worcs. East. 13 Chas. II.

[45] Recov. R. East. 1 Jas. II, m. 258; but cf. the account of Trimpley below.

[46] Inform. kindly supplied by Miss Tomkinson and Mr. John H. Crane.

[47] *V.C.H. Worcs.* i, 286b.

[48] Prattinton Coll. (Soc. Antiq.), *sub* Wolverley; but cf. the account of Heathy above.

[49] Ibid.

[50] See Wolverley; also Feet of F. Worcs. case 258, file 7, no. 37.

[51] Inform. kindly supplied by Miss Tomkinson and Mr. John H. Crane. Sir Ralph Clare's estate extended into Trimpley; a 'manor' of Trimpley descended with Caldwall Hall from 1654 onwards.

[52] *V.C.H. Worcs.* i, 286b.

[53] *Lay Subs. R. Worcs.* 1280 (Worcs. Hist. Soc.), 13.

[54] Hardwicke Coll. Add. MS. 31003, fol. 16.

[55] *Visit. of Shropshire* (Harl. Soc.), ii, 492.

[56] Feet of F. Worcs. Hil. 8 Eliz.; East. 38 Eliz.

[57] Chan. Inq. p.m. (Ser. 2), ccccxxiv, 88.

[58] Ibid.

[59] Recov. R. Mich. 29 Chas. II, rot. 168.

[60] Feet of F. Worcs. East. 35 Chas. II.

of a vestry and the 13th-century chantry of St. Mary, restored later. The church as a whole is very late in style and has been much rebuilt in modern times.

The six-light east window of the chancel is modern, and is designed in the style of the 14th century. The two piscinae, the sedilia and the side windows are all modern, but part of the walling is old. To the north side is an organ bay, built in 1874, and on the south side a modern arcade of three bays opening into an eastern extension of the south aisle, built in 1850, beyond which are 'the cloisters,' built in 1888. The chancel arch has been rebuilt. The nave has an arcade of six bays on the north and a similar arcade on the south, but the two western bays are replaced by the tower arch.

The arches are of two moulded orders with octagonal capitals and piers of about 1530. The north-east respond is cut back, probably to allow for a rood-loft, the entrance to which was by a stair behind the south-east respond. Above the arcade are clearstory windows of two lights with tracery and square heads of a late type.

The windows in the north wall of the north aisle are five in number, and are of three lights, with the exception of the westernmost, which is of four. The window in the west wall is of eight lights. All are modern, in the style of the 15th century.

The tower, as proved by the remains of an internal buttress, is slightly older than the arcades, and has an arch with multiple shafts. The west window is similar to that of the nave, but of five lights.

All the windows to the south nave aisle are modern restorations in 15th-century style, and to the south of the tower is a small modern porch, the roof of which abuts against a five-light window of the same date in the tower wall. The broken masonry on the south-west pier of the south aisle arcade seems to indicate an earlier arcade outside the present one. The roofs and fittings are modern, as is likewise the large font.

The church contains a number of fine monuments. In the chancel floor is a beautiful 15th-century brass consisting of a lady with a knight in plates on either side of her, and above them a triple canopy with a row of shields over. The brass is 8 ft. in length and has a Latin inscription in rhyming hexameters to John Phelip and his wife Matilda, formerly wife of Walter Cooksey. John Phelip died in 1415.

Above are the remains of six shields : the first, which had the arms of Phelip, is lost, the second is Phelip impaling Harmanville, the third Harmanville, the fourth Phelip, the fifth Cooksey and the last Cooksey impaling Harmanville.

On the north side of the chancel is a large monument to Sir Hugh Cooksey, lord of Caldwall Manor, and his wife, 1445. The figures lie in a recess under a four-centred arch. Above and on the sides the tomb is panelled and enriched with quatrefoils containing shields. In the centre above the tomb is a shield of the arms of Cooksey quartering Braose, supported by two others. On the east and west ends are angels holding shields ; the western is quarterly (1) and (3) Cooksey, (2) Boteler, (4) St. Piers. The eastern has quarterly (1) and (3) Cooksey, (2) Harmanville, (4) Argent a bend gules within a border checky or and azure.

West of this is a semicircular panelled arch in the wall containing a tomb with the effigies of Thomas Blount and his wife Margery with their five children. There is a defaced inscription on the wife's tomb, which states that she died November 1500. Above the figures is a shield : Quarterly (1) and (4) Blount ; (2) Cornwall of Kinlet ; (3) Argent three cheverons engrailed gules impaling Or a lion sable.

In the chancel is a carved chair which is said to have belonged to Richard Baxter, 1640.

On the south wall of the church are the marble effigies of Sir Edward Blount and his two wives (1630), with a shield, which, like all the rest of the heraldry of these monuments, has been repainted.

In the south aisle wall opposite the chancel arch are the mutilated remains of a 15th-century recessed tomb having four panels divided by groups of shafts, the lower panels with as many angels holding shields. Above these the panels are pierced and open on a recess with an effigy of Lady Joyce Beauchamp, who founded the chantry of St. Catherine. Above the opening are four figures, under rich crocketed canopies : the first two, perhaps, represent the Annunciation, the third is an angel, and the fourth figure, which holds the base of a chalice, may be St. John. The tomb extended above these, but is broken off, and has been inserted for preservation in its present position.

The exterior of the church has been to a great extent refaced at various dates in modern times. The tower, west front and clearstory were the last renovations. The former is a good copy of what the 15th-century tower was, and has three stages with crocketed angle pinnacles, canopied niches and panelled and embattled parapet, the latter feature being repeated to the nave clearstory. The wrought-iron gates of the churchyard are modern copies of an older pair.

There are eight bells, cast in 1754, and four more for chimes added in 1882.

The plate consists of a paten presented by Thomas Jennens, 1623, mark obliterated ; a second paten similar to this, but uninscribed and with obliterated mark ; a third, modern. There are three modern chalices, a modern flagon and three glass cruets with silver lids. There are also a silver straining spoon and six pewter plates marked S.H.B.

The registers are a remarkable set, being complete from 1539, and, besides being in excellent preservation, are enriched with colours in the titles and capitals and with various pen designs. Before 1812 they are as follows : (i) all entries 1539 to 1636 ; (ii) 1636 to 1672 ; (iii) 1672 to 1706 (these books, especially the first, being elaborately enriched) ; (iv) 1706 to 1722 ; (v) 1722 to 1761, the marriages stopping 1754 ; (vi) baptisms and burials 1761 to 1784 ; (vii) the same 1784 to 1800 ; (viii) the same 1801 to 1812. The marriage books from 1754 are five in number, 1754 to 1767, 1767 to 1777, 1777 to 1789, 1789 to 1802, 1802 to 1812.

The church of *ST. GEORGE* was erected in 1824 in early 15th-century Gothic, and consists of a short chancel, the sanctuary projecting into the body of the building, a nave, north and south aisles, a west tower—the bottom stage of which is used as the main vestibule—and vestries at the east end of the chancel. Over the aisles and the west end of the nave is a gallery.

The church of *ST. JOHN BAPTIST* consists of a chancel, with an organ chamber and vestries on the north, a nave, three aisles, one on the north of the nave and two on the south, a south transept, a south porch and a tower at the west end of the inner south aisle. The church was originally built in 1843, but was, with the exception of the tower, completely rebuilt and greatly enlarged from 1890 to 1894. It is a large and dignified structure in 14th-century style.

The church of *ST. JAMES* is a small red brick building erected in 1872 in the pointed style, and consists of chancel, nave, north vestries, with a small bell-turret and a west porch. The open pitch pine roof is tiled.

The church of *ST. BARNABAS*, Franche, which was consecrated in 1871, is a small red brick building, consisting of a chancel, a nave, a south porch—above which rises a small lead-covered bell-turret—and a north vestry. It is built in 13th-century style, and has an open pitch pine roof covered with tiles.

The old church of *ST. MICHAEL*, Lower Mitton, now disused, is a late 18th-century red brick building consisting of transepts, nave with galleries, north and south porches, and west tower, with an apsidal chancel added in the 19th century. The galleries are reached by two external stone stairways, one on each side of the nave. The tower is in three stages separated by stone strings. To the north is the new church, also dedicated to St. Michael, begun in 1887. It consists at present of a nave of six bays with clearstory, north and south aisles, and a vaulted south porch, built in the style of the 14th century, of ashlar sandstone dressed both internally and externally. The chancel and west tower included in the design have not yet been built.

The church of *HOLY TRINITY*, Trimpley, consisting of chancel, nave, and vestry, was built in 1844.

The church of *ALL SAINTS*, Wribbenhall, consisting of chancel, vestry, nave, south aisle, south porch, and north-east octagonal tower, is built of coursed sandstone rubble in the decorated style with tiled roofs. The lower part of the tower is square and serves as the organ chamber.

ADVOWSONS Manasser Biset had a church at Kidderminster of which he gave the reversion, contingent upon the death of Robert of Hurcott the Clerk, to his foundation for lepers at Maiden Bradley, co. Wilts., before 1175.[61] This grant was confirmed both by the king and by Bishop Roger.[62] Later Henry de Soilli, Bishop of Worcester, appropriated the church to the priory.[63]

The prior and monks pensioned Robert, appointing a vicar, Adam of Hurcott, who paid 100s. to him and 100s. to the priory yearly ; but when the vicar 'went away' John Biset claimed the right of presentation as lord of the manor, and the dispute resulted in the appointment by the bishop of a 'rector,' Master Thomas de Upton paying 20 marks yearly to the priory. Upon the death of this 'rector' John Biset presented another, the priory having certain tithes assigned to it (1241).[64]

The advowson formed part of the dower of Alice widow of John Biset, and litigation ensued, both in England and at Rome.[65] In spite of the prior's release of his rights in 1250 in return for 40s., land and rent in 'Wytford,'[66] a dispute arose about 1265 between the rector appointed by Alice Biset and the prior as to tithes,[67] and was finally settled by arbitrators appointed by the pope.[68]

After the death of Alice Biset two of the three co-heirs of John Biset surrendered all their rights in the advowson to John Rivers, the third co-heir, who re-granted the church, 'with all liberties rights and customs belonging thereto,' to the priory.[69] In 1270 the prior obtained royal confirmation of these grants.[70]

The prior subsequently petitioned the pope for a renewal of the former appropriation,[71] and in consequence a portion was assigned to the vicar, with a house, curtilage and dovecot adjoining the south side of the churchyard (1336).[72] In 1340 the recently presented vicar, John de la Doune, 'like an ungrateful man,' obtained for himself a larger portion, including the manor of Hurcott.[73] The Priors of Maiden Bradley continued to present until the dissolution of the house. An attempt to seize the advowson made by Richard II was reversed by Henry IV.[74]

A new ordination of the vicarage was made in 1401 and again in 1403.[75]

After the dissolution of Maiden Bradley Priory the rectorial rights and the advowson were granted, with the other property of the priory, to Viscount Lisle.[76] After his attainder Queen Mary granted the rectory and advowson to Richard Pates, Bishop of Worcester, 14 November 1558.[77] In June 1559, after Mary's death,[78] he was deprived and imprisoned, and Elizabeth granted the rectory and advowson to Thomas Blount, 1559–60.[79] The subsequent history of the advowson is identical with that of Hurcott (q.v.), but the rectorial tithes were sold by Edmund Waller to Daniel Dobbyns, who divided them into portions and bequeathed them to his several sons.[80]

The parishes of St. George, Kidderminster, and St. John the Baptist, Kidderminster, were chapelries of St. Mary and All Saints until 1867, when they were constituted separate parishes.[81] The livings are in the gift of the vicar of St. Mary and All Saints. St. James is a chapelry of St. Mary and All Saints.

St. Barnabas, Franche, is a chapelry of St. Mary and All Saints, dating from 1871.

Lower Mitton was a chapelry from very early times. A certain Philip was chaplain of Mitton

---

[61] The confirmatory charter of Henry II is witnessed by R[eginald] Earl of Cornwall, who died 1175. The terminal of the name proves the existence of a pre-Conquest church at Kidderminster.

[62] Add. MS. 37503, fol. 30 ; Dugdale, *Mon.* vi, 644.

[63] Dugdale, *Mon.* vi, 644 ; see *Cal. Pat.* 1334–8, p. 113 ; cf. Add. MS. 37503, fol. 31. The first appropriation seems to have been in the time of Henry de Soilli, who certainly admitted Adam of Hurcott.

[64] Add. MS. 37503, fol. 31 d., 32.

[65] Ibid. ; Cur. Reg. R. Mich. 33 Hen. III, m. 38 d.

[66] Cur. Reg. R. Hil. 34 Hen. III, m. 1.

[67] Anct. D. (P.R.O.), D 325.

[68] Add. MS. 37503, fol. 33 et seq.

[69] Dugdale, *Mon.* vi, 644.

[70] Cal. Chart. R. 1257–1300, p. 151.

[71] Add. MS. 37503, fol. 38.

[72] Worc. Epis. Reg. Monte Acuto, i, fol. 20 d., 21, 24.

[73] Ibid. Wulstan de Braunsford, i, fol. 21 f., ii, 21 d., and Add. MS. 37503, fol. 50.

[74] Cal. Pat. 1396–9, p. 444 ; 1399–1401, p. 116.

[75] Worc. Epis. Reg. Wynchecomb, fol. 61 d. ; Clifford, fol. 74.

[76] See above.

[77] Pat. 5 & 6 Phil. and Mary, pt. ii, m. 30.

[78] Dict. Nat. Biog. See V.C.H. Worcs. ii, 46.   [79] See Comberton.

[80] Prattinton Coll. (Soc. Antiq.), Habington MS. v, 3 ; Feet of F. Worcs. East. 1651.

[81] Lond. Gaz. 23 Aug. 1867, p. 4694 ; 10 Dec. 1867, p. 6766.

1200–14.[82] The chapelry was valued at 53s. 4d. circa 1334, and the altarage and the heriots in Mitton were set aside for the chaplain's use.[83] A burial-place was consecrated in 1625.[84]

In 1844 Lower Mitton was formed into a separate ecclesiastical district,[85] and in 1866 the living was declared a vicarage.[86] The vicar of St. Mary and All Saints, Kidderminster, was patron of the living until the building of the new church, the advowson now being vested in the bishop. Until 1860 the rectorial tithes formed a part of the Lower Mitton and Lickhill estate.[87]

Holy Trinity, Trimpley, is a chapel of ease to St. Mary and All Saints, Kidderminster. The chantry chapel of Trimpley was dedicated to the Virgin Mary.[88] Tradition locates this chapel near the present chapel of Holy Trinity, possibly on the site of the orchard now attached to the Trimpley post office. This supposition is borne out by the fact that the name 'Guyldones' is still applied to land in the neighbourhood, while land called 'Gyldons' lay near the chapel in 1501.[89]

John Attwood, usher of the king's chamber, of Wolverley and Trimpley, had licence to hear divine service in his oratory at Wood Acton, Wolverley, and Trimpley in 1357.[90] He built the chapel of Trimpley, endowing it with lands sufficient to maintain a priest to celebrate there daily for the souls of himself, his wife Alice, and his parents,[91] and obtaining indulgences and relaxation of penance for those who visited the chapel and gave alms for its repair.[92] The advowson of the chapel remained with the successive lords of Park Attwood (q.v.) until 1547, when it was seized by the Crown under the Chantries Act. In 1549 the messuage called the Chantry House, with the chapel yard and the land belonging to it, was purchased by John Cupper and Richard Trevor.[93] It subsequently came into the possession of Hugh Lee (d. 1576),[94] under whose will it ultimately passed to Sir Hugh Wrottesley, kt., who died seised of it in 1633.[95] By this time, however, the chapel had been pulled down.[96]

All Saints', Wribbenhall, is in the gift of the vicar of Kidderminster. The original chapel, built in 1719 upon ground leased by John Cheltenham from Lord Bergavenny, was for some time unconsecrated. The vicar of Kidderminster nominated two successive curates, but in 1742 and again in 1749 Lord Foley, as successor of Lord Bergavenny, nominated a curate and claimed the room as his private property.[97] In 1844 Wribbenhall was constituted a separate chapelry.[98]

There were two chantries attached to Kidderminster Church.[99] The one dedicated to the Virgin Mary existed in 1305, when the lord of the manor joined with the commonalty of the town in presenting a chaplain.[100] It was built within the churchyard,[1] and is now part of the main building. Apparently the patronage remained with the lords of Kidderminster Biset, although in 1499 a chaplain was presented by Sir John Mortimer, Thomas Jenyns, bailiff, William Colsell, and others of the more worthy parishioners,[2] doubtless reviving the former rights of the commonalty.

Simon Rice (who died in March 1529–30) of Over Mitton, rebuilt the chantry. It was suppressed in 1547, and the building was used as a school in the early part of the 17th century.[3]

The chantry of St. Catherine in the south aisle was founded by Lady Joyce Beauchamp in 1469, and was well endowed with lands at Trimpley, Puxton and Habberley,[4] which were granted after its suppression to Robert, Thomas and Andrew Salter, and afterwards became the property of Simon Clare.[5]

In 1401 a devotional gild of the Holy Trinity came into collision with the rector and vicar, and applied to the pope for licence to have mass celebrated very early in the morning by their own priest at the altar of the Holy Trinity in the parish church.[6]

The history of Nonconformity in Kidderminster dates from the time of Richard Baxter, the famous divine and author of 'The Saint's Everlasting Rest.' The corporation is justly proud in the possession of an autograph copy of the first edition of this book, and the townspeople have perpetuated his memory by erecting a statue in the Bull Ring.

He was appointed lecturer at Kidderminster in April 1641 by a committee of fourteen, in consequence of an agreement between the congregation of All Saints and their vicar, George Dance, whom they blamed for 'weakness in preaching, drunkeness and turning the table altar-wise.'

Baxter found in the town 'a small number of converts not much hated by the rest.' His eloquence in preaching, his diligence in catechizing and visiting, and his skill in medicine won the hearts of all classes; he persuaded the weavers to read or to enter into edifying converse at their looms, and his congregations were so large that 'they were fain to build galleries' in the church. Upon the outbreak of war he retired to Coventry, for the 'rabble,' who clung to their 'fooleries,' parading the streets yearly with painted forms of giants, were angry at the churchwardens' attempt to destroy the crucifix on the churchyard cross and vented their malice on Baxter, crying 'Down with the Roundhead!' In 1647 he returned, after 'the rabble had all gone into the King's army and been slain.'

---

[82] He witnessed the admission of the Prior of Maiden Bradley to the church and parsonage (Add. MS. 37003, fol. 30 d.). Mr. Campbell J. Craven states that the chapelry existed in 1195.

[83] Add. MS. 37503, fol. 44.

[84] Prattinton Coll. (Soc. Antiq.), Habington MS. v, 3.

[85] Lond. Gaz. 18 Sept. 1844, p. 3281.

[86] Ibid. 7 Aug. 1866, p. 4406.

[87] Inform. kindly supplied by Mr. C. J. Craven.

[88] Cal. Papal Pet. i, 350.

[89] Deed quoted by Burton, Hist. of Kidderminster, 97. It is noteworthy that Hugh son of Henry Mustell gave a messuage and land in Habberley to William

'le Gildon' temp. Edward I (Add. Chart. 24706).

[90] Epis. Reg. quoted by Burton, Hist. of Kidderminster, 96.

[91] Inq. a.q.d. file 363, no. 7; Prattinton Coll. (Soc. Antiq.).

[92] Cal. Papal Letters, iv, 36; Cal. Papal Pet. i, 350.

[93] Pat. 3 Edw. VI, pt. vi.

[94] Chan. Inq. p.m. (Ser. 2), clxxix, 67.

[95] Ibid. ccclxix, 194.

[96] Prattinton Coll. (Soc. Antiq.), Habington MS. v, 3.

[97] Prattinton Coll. (Soc. Antiq.); Lewis (Topog. Dict.) gives 1701 as the date of the erection of the chapel.

[98] Lond. Gaz. 18 Sept. 1844, p. 3281.

[99] Chant. Cert. 61, no. 15.

[100] Worc. Epis. Reg. Gainsborough, xi, 30.

[1] Ibid. Wulstan de Braunsford, i (3), fol. 116.

[2] Worc. Epis. Reg. Sede Vacante (Worcs. Hist. Soc.), 227, where 'Dokesey' is evidently an error for 'Cokesey'; list of patrons given by Nash, op. cit. i, 58.

[3] Habington, Surv. of Worc. (Worcs. Hist. Soc.), ii, 167.

[4] Burton, op. cit. 97; Valor Eccl. (Rec. Com.), iii, 274; Aug. Off. Misc. Bks. ccclxxiv, fol. 30.

[5] Pat. 4 Edw. VI, pt. iv; cf. the account of Habberley.

[6] Cal. Papal Letters, v, 411.

KIDDERMINSTER CHURCH : THE NAVE LOOKING EAST

KIDDERMINSTER CHURCH : NORTH WALL OF THE CHANCEL

About 1647 the vicarage was sequestered, and the townspeople, who had the sequestration, offered the living to Baxter, and ultimately procured it for him against his will.[7]

He allowed the vicar, Mr. Dance, to 'live a reformed life in peace,' at the old vicarage, himself occupying a few rooms in the top of another man's house.[8] This house is said to be the building at present occupied by a confectioner on the north side of the High Street.

At the restoration Mr. Dance became 'malapart' again, and supported by Sir Ralph Clare, whose zeal for conformity was greater than his (considerable) respect for Baxter, recovered the living, and prevented Baxter from resuming the lectureship.[9]

The 'Old Meeting' in Kidderminster is said to have been founded in Mill Street by the Rev. Thomas Baldwin, one of Baxter's assistants.[10] Certainly in 1672 Thomas Baldwin and Thomas Ware, Presbyterians, had licence to hold conventicles in their houses.[11] A site for a meeting-house was purchased in Bull Ring Street, 1694 ; the meeting-house was rebuilt in 1753 and 1824,[12] and the present 'Baxter Church' erected on the same site in 1884.

Another Congregational meeting in Park Street was founded in 1774, and a chapel was built at Stourport in Mitton Street, 1871.[13] A new Congregational Hall was opened at Kidderminster in 1907.

The Unitarian chapel in Church Street was built in 1782 and rebuilt in 1883. Its founders seceded from the 'Old Meeting' in 1780.[14] The chapel contains Baxter's pulpit, removed from the parish church at one of the restorations.

John Wesley frequently visited Kidderminster and Stourport. The Wesleyan chapel in Mill Street dates from 1803 ; it was built on the site of the Countess of Huntingdon's chapel,[15] and is regulated by a scheme of 4 November 1844. A second chapel has recently been built in the Birmingham Road. There are also a Wesleyan chapel at Stourport and Primitive Methodist chapels in George Street (1824) and at Lickhill Road, Stourport. New chapels have been built to supply the needs of Foley Park and other extensions of the town. The Baptists have a chapel in Church Street. Their first chapel was built in 1813 in Union Street. The present building was erected in part by proceeds of the sale of the former chapel under an order of the Charity Commissioners 2 April 1878, on land comprised in a deed of 1864. It has a subordinate meeting at Blakedown. Milton Hall was built in 1890.[16]

The Countess of Huntingdon's Free Church in Dudley Street was built in 1818 to replace the one sold to the Wesleyans.[17]

A Swedenborgian church was erected on Comberton Hill in 1908.

The Roman Catholic church of St. Ambrose, Leswell, built in 1858, through the efforts of Father Courtenay, replaced a chapel built in 1834.[18]

The Free Grammar School.[19]

CHARITIES Thomas Butcher, as appears from an inquisition of commissioners of charitable uses, 16 Charles I, by his will gave an annuity of £2 12s., issuing out of a public-house in Kidderminster, for poor every Sunday in bread.

In 1620 William Seabright, by his will, gave £3 0s. 8d. yearly for the poor in bread and 6s. 8d. yearly for the parish clerk for his trouble. The annuities are received from the governors of Seabright's Endowed School, Wolverley.

In 1690 John Oldnall, by his will proved at Worcester, gave 20s. yearly for the poor of the borough and 20s. yearly for the poor of the foreign of Kidderminster.

In 1693 Thomas Cook, by his will, gave £2 12s. yearly for the poor in bread issuing out of a house and garden in Church Street.

The rent-charges above mentioned are duly paid and distributed in bread together with the interest of a legacy of £100 in the Post Office Savings Bank by will of Edward Crane, dated in 1820.

In 1664 Abraham Plimley, by will, gave an annuity of £3 2s. issuing out of two houses in the Bull Ring for a poor person of the borough, the trustees to retain 2s. for their expenses.

In 1701 Elizabeth Bowyer, by deed, gave an annuity of £3 5s. for a poor man or woman, the trustees to retain 5s. for their expenses. The charge is now represented by £108 6s. 8d. consols with the official trustees, producing £2 14s. yearly.

In 1717 John Sparry, by his will, gave an annuity of £2 5s. issuing out of three houses at Stourbridge for a poor, honest man, the trustees to retain 5s. for their expenses.

In 1833 Joshua Cotton Cooper, by will, left a legacy, now represented by £105 10s. 8d. consols with the official trustees, the annual dividends amounting to £2 12s. 8d. to be given in equal parts to two poor persons not being man and wife.

The income of the four above-mentioned charities, together with the income of £110 16s. 6d. on deposit at the Metropolitan Bank, amounting to £3 6s. yearly, representing a legacy by will of Thomas Doolittle, is applied in the distribution of money.

In 1908 twenty-eight persons received about 10s. each.

In 1709 the Rev. Joseph Read, by deed, gave a yearly sum of £7, £5, part thereof, to be applied for the relief of a poor widow of the age of sixty years and upwards, or for apprenticing a poor boy, and the residue for the poor.

The legacy is now represented by £280 consols with the official trustees. In 1908 £5 was paid to a poor widow and £2 distributed among six poor persons.

In 1710 Edward Butler, by deed, gave an annuity of £2 2s. issuing out of two houses in the Bull Ring, to be distributed equally among six poor men or women on New Year's Day, the trustees to retain 2s. for their expenses. The charge is duly paid and applied.

[7] Reliquiae Baxterianae (1696), 79 ; see V.C.H. Worcs. ii, 69, 71.
[8] Reliquiae Baxterianae (1696), 20, 24, 40, 42, 79, 80, 83, 88–90, 97, 157, 299.
[9] Hist. MSS. Com. Rep. vii, App. i, 121a ; V.C.H. Worcs. ii, 79.
[10] Burton, Hist. of Kidderminster, 135.
[11] Cal. S. P. Dom. 1672, p. 473.
[12] Burton, Hist. of Kidderminster, 134.
[13] Congregational Yearbook, 1912, pp. 307–8.
[14] Dict. Nat. Biog. under 'Robert Gentleman' and 'Job Orton.'
[15] Burton, Hist. of Kidderminster, 138.
[16] Baptist Handbk. 1912, p. 135.
[17] Burton, Hist. of Kidderminster, 139
[18] Ibid.
[19] See 'Schools,' V.C.H. Worcs. iv.

In 1734 Mrs. Mary Glynn, by a codicil to her will, directed £200 to be invested in land, the rents thereof, subject to the repair of the vault of her husband and herself, to be divided yearly among ten poor old women. The land purchased was sold in 1880 and the proceeds invested in £551 14s. 4d. consols with the official trustees, producing £13 15s. 8d. yearly, which is duly applied.

Witnells.—The charities known as Witnells Alms, and the almshouses founded in 1670 by will of Sir Ralph Clare, are regulated by a scheme of the Charity Commissioners 15 May 1900. They comprise the charities of Edmund Broad, founded by deed, 1596-7 ; Edward Mills, will, 1614-15 ; Elizabeth Mills, will, 1626 ; Thomas Dawkes, will, 1611 ; Edward Dawkes, deed, 1632 ; Alice Dawkes, deed, 1614-15 ; and the charity of William Thomas Cowper, founded by will proved at London 21 January 1888.

The trust property consists of three almshouses in Church Street and a house in Hall Street used as an almshouse, fourteen cottages in St. Mary Street and Dudley Street, 2 a. 1 r. 34 p. in Broad Street, and small pieces of land in Dudley Street, Clensmore Lane, and Church Fields, producing a rental of £166 a year or thereabouts ; six rent-charges amounting together to £7 a year issuing out of certain properties ; also a sum of £1,745 12s. 7d. consols (including £281 0s. 8d. consols belonging to Cooper's charity), and £1,239 2s. 2d. Local Loans 3 per cent. stock, producing together £80 16s. in annual dividends.

The sums of stock which arise from sales of land from time to time and the investment of accumulations are held by the official trustees.

In 1909 a sum of £149 18s. was paid to the inmates of the almshouses, and a sum of £17 was applied in relief of the poor generally.

The almshouses founded in 1630 by will of Sir Edward Blount for six poor decayed housekeepers are endowed with a house now known as the Fox Inn, let at £55 a year, and a sum of £1,173 4s. 4d. consols, producing £29 6s. 8d. yearly arising from the sale of land.

The stock is held by the official trustees, who also hold a further sum of £146 19s. 7d. consols, arising from the sale in 1868 of four tenements used as almshouses devised in 1684 by will of Henry Higgins. The annual dividends amounting to £3 13s. 4d. are applied in coal to the inmates of Sir Edward Blount's almshouses.

The charities founded by Humphrey Burlton and Edward Burlton, by deeds, 1645 and 1707, now consist of a sum of £493 16s. 6d. consols held by the official trustees, arising from the sale in 1898 of 7 acres of land allotted on the inclosure of the foreign of Kidderminster. The annual dividends amounting to £12 6s. 8d. are distributed among the poor of the districts of Wribbenhall, Foley Park, Franche, Trimpley, &c.

In 1708 the Rev. John Hall, D.D., by his will, directed that the rents of his estate called Hollow Fields should be applied for charitable purposes, of which £5 was made applicable for the teaching of poor children.

The land was sold in 1865 and the proceeds invested in £1,553 8s. consols with the official trustees, of which £200 stock has been set aside as an endowment of Bishop Hall's Educational Foundation. The

dividends upon the residue of the stock, amounting to £33 16s. 8d. yearly, are applied in gifts of money and clothing tickets of the value of 6s. to 10s. each.

In 1776 John Brecknell, by his will, left £150, the interest to be applied in providing every child or unmarried person born in or an inhabitant of Church Street with a twopenny plum cake upon the eve of every Midsummer Day, and pipes and tobacco and ale for the male inhabitants then assembled, and the remainder to the poor in gifts of 2s. to 5s. The legacy is represented by £275 consols, producing £6 17s. 4d. yearly, of which about £2 is expended on a supper, £1 10s. in cakes and loaves, and the remainder in the distribution of money.

It further appears that a maiden lady gave 40s. a year for providing farthing cakes for every child born or living in Church Street.

In 1822 Joseph Lea, by will proved in the P.C.C. 17 January, bequeathed a legacy, now represented by £1,007 11s. 1d. consols with the official trustees. The charity is regulated by a scheme of the Charity Commissioners, whereby the annual dividends, amounting to £25 3s. 8d., are applicable in making grants of not less than £2 or more than £5 to poor persons resident in the borough, with a preference to persons who have been employed by any of the family or relatives of the founder.

Brinton Park consists of 23 a. 2 r. 31 p., comprised in the deed of gift by Mr. John Brinton, D.L., J.P., of Moor Hall, Stourport, then member of Parliament for the borough, dated 1 August 1887.

In 1837 Miss Sarah Colley, by will proved in the P.C.C., bequeathed £1,000, which was invested in £1,061 2s. consols in the names of trustees, the annual dividends, amounting to £26 10s., to be applied in warm clothing to old and infirm poor, each person to have a suit valued at £1 10s. on 24 December every year.

Charities of William Thomas Cooper.—William Thomas Cooper, by his will proved 21 January 1888, bequeathed a legacy of £400 to each of the following institutions, namely—the Children's Hospital, the Infirmary, the School of Art, the School of Science and to Witnells Alms Charity (see above). The several legacies were—owing to insufficiency of the personal estate, legacy duty and expenses—each reduced to £264 3s. 6d., which have been invested and the income applied for the benefit of the interested charities.

Nonconformist Charities : New Meeting Chapel.— In or about 1731 Jane Matthews gave £50 for the poor belonging to the New Meeting House. This gift, with accumulations, was invested in land, which has been sold, and the trust fund is now represented by £1,437 6s. 5d. consols with the official trustees, producing £35 18s. 8d. yearly, which is distributed to the poor in sums of about 5s. each.

In 1787 Serjeant Crane, by will, gave £100, now represented by £152 consols with the official trustees, the annual dividends, amounting to £3 16s., being applied in the same manner as the charity of Jane Matthews.

The same testator likewise bequeathed £200 towards the support of the 'New Meeting,' now represented by £357 2s. 10d. consols with the official trustees, the annual dividends of which, amounting to £8 18s. 4d., are paid to the treasurer of the chapel.

In 1798 Nicholas Pearsall, by his will, proved in the P.C.C. 20 October (among other things), bequeathed £300, the income to be applied in certain proportions in support of the New Meeting House, the Sunday schools and instruction of children in the borough or foreign of Kidderminster. The legacy is represented by £428 11s. 6d. consols, with the official trustees, producing £10 14s. a year, of which one-third is apportioned as the Pearsall Educational Foundation and two-thirds in support of the New Meeting House.

In 1868 George Talbot, by his will, proved 10 November, bequeathed a legacy, now represented by £531 1s. 3d. India 3 per cent. stock, standing in the names of A. G. Hopkins and three others, the annual dividends of which, amounting to £15 18s. 8d., are applicable as to three-fifths for the day schools and Sunday school in connexion with the chapel and two-fifths in support of the same chapel.

The same stockholders hold a sum of £460 stock for the benefit of the minister arising under the will of Richard Eve, proved at London, 28 August 1900.

The almshouses founded by Thomas Banks and endowed by his will, proved at London, 11 November 1891, are under the management of the deacons of the Baxter Congregational Church. They consist of six almshouses in Broad Street, and are endowed with £1,000, secured by a mortgage at £4 per cent. per annum. In 1909 the sum of £31 16s. was divided amongst the eleven inmates.

The minister of the Particular Baptist chapel in Church Street receives £20 a year from the charity of the Rev. George Brookes, founded by deed 2 October 1840 and will, proved 2 April 1844.

Lower Mitton.—The girls' Sunday school is endowed with a sum of £244 8s. 10d. consols, arising from the gifts of Mrs. Christie and Mary and Richard Barnett, producing £6 2s. yearly.

The National school was conveyed upon the trusts declared by deed 17 November 1842.

Stourport.—The Wesleyan chapel, school and trust property, comprised in deeds 1799, 1805, 1829 and 1831, were by an order of the Charity Commissioners 29 September 1882 vested in trustees, thereby appointed on the trusts of 'The Wesleyan Chapel Model Deed.'

Trimpley. — Henry Chillingworth, by deed, 11 July 1832, founded and endowed a school for this district. The endowments consist of the school buildings and schoolmistress's house, and a house given by John Crane of High Habberley, let at £8 a year, and by a further deed, dated 20 April 1838, the donor settled a sum of £500 consols, the annual dividends to be applied in payment of school-mistress and for books and clothing for eight poor scholars.

The official trustees also hold a sum of £839 17s. 11d. consols, producing £20 19s. 10d. a year, arising from the sale in 1891 of buildings and 13 a. 2 r. 15 p.

Wribbenhall.—In 1882 Mrs. Anne Hallen, by will, proved 2 November, bequeathed a legacy, now represented by £88 11s. 2d. consols, the annual dividends, amounting to £2 4s. 2d., to be applied for the benefit of the poor of this district.

The same testatrix bequeathed a further legacy, represented by £1,771 10s. consols, the annual dividends amounting to £44 5s. 8d. to be paid to the incumbent.

KING'S NORTON

Nortune (xi cent.); Norton (xi, xii and xiii cent.); Nortun, Norhton (xiii cent.); Kingesnorton (xiv cent.).

King's Norton, the greater part of which was included in the city of Birmingham under the Birmingham Extension Act, 1911, and so is now in Warwickshire, is a large parish situated immediately south of Birmingham, and included the now separate ecclesiastical parishes of Moseley, King's Heath and Wythall. The last was made into a separate civil parish in 1911 under the above-mentioned Act and is still in Worcestershire. In 1901 King's Norton covered an area of 11,726 acres,[1] of which 112 acres were covered with water, 1,251 were arable land, 7,810 pasture and 37½ woods.[2] Balsall Heath was formed into a separate civil parish in 1894 from King's Norton,[3] but is now a part of Birmingham.

The parish is watered by the River Rea, the Bournville River and the River Cole, which last divides it from Warwickshire on the east. The Worcester and Birmingham Canal and the Stratford-on-Avon Canal, which joins it to the north-east of King's Norton village, are fed by two reservoirs on the River Rea. The chief roads are the main road between Birmingham and Alcester and Icknield or Rycknield Street,[4] the Roman road which joins the same places. These run almost parallel, the first

passing through Moseley, King's Heath and Wythall Heath, the second through Stirchley Street and Walker's Heath.

The ground is hilly, being 400 ft. above the ordnance datum on the banks of the Rea, and varying from that to a height of about 600 ft. near Weatheroak Hill. The trade, and consequently the population, of the parish have increased enormously during the last century. Thus in 1831 the population was 3,977, while in 1891 it had increased to 17,750 and in 1901 to 35,790. The most populous parts are Moseley and King's Heath, which are the nearest to Birmingham. The chief manufactures are paper, metal and ammunition, gun-barrels and screws. Cadbury's cocoa and chocolate are made at the Bournville factory near Stirchley Street.

King's Norton is rapidly developing the monotonous appearance inseparable from the suburbs of a large town, though the older portion near the church still retains something of its original character. The houses are here grouped about a green stretching almost the length of the village, with the church standing in a large churchyard at the north-west corner.

The Saracen's Head Inn, adjoining the churchyard on the south, is a two-storied building of the late 15th century. The north wing, which fronts the churchyard and is now a separate tenement, retains

---

[1] The numbers are taken from the Census returns of 1901.

[2] Statistics from Bd. of Agric. (1905).

[3] *Census of Engl. and Wales,* 1901, *Worc.* 28.

[4] Called Ekelyngstret in 1535 (*Valor Eccl.* [Rec. Com.], ii, 433).

much of its original appearance, though the window openings have been altered and enlarged. The over-sailing upper story is supported by brackets springing from small attached columns cut out of the uprights. The southern portion of the house, which is occupied by the inn, has been encased with brick. A very similar house exists at Yardley in the same position relative to the church. On the north side of the churchyard is the building known as the 'old grammar school,' which seems to have been originally the priest's house. This is of two stories, each story containing one large room, with a projecting porch of the same height in the centre of the south front. The walls of the ground story are of brick, and have small plain stone-mullioned windows, while the upper story is entirely of half-timber. This upper story, curiously enough, appears to be of earlier date than the ground floor, which seems to have been under-built at the

anterior to this, so that it would rather appear that the window is of the later 15th century, or even of the 16th century. The form of the tracery would be naturally suggested by the material, and this would account for its 14th-century air. The walls of the ground story, which have evidently been under-built, are of red brick with stone quoins, and are crowned by a string-course of the same material. The entrance doorway of the porch has a straight-sided arched head with a projecting key-stone and jambs of stone. The windows throughout, with the exception of the east window of the first floor above described, appear to be contemporary with the rebuilding of the ground floor. The diagonal chimney shafts and fireplaces on the north side are modern. The upper floor is reached by an external staircase, not of original date. The building has recently been thoroughly and carefully restored.

KING'S NORTON : HOUSE ON SOUTH SIDE OF CHURCHYARD, ORIGINALLY FORMING PART OF SARACEN'S HEAD INN

time the porch was added, the detail of which shows it to be, at the earliest, of the late 16th century. The upper story, on the other hand, shows all the characteristics of the early 15th century. The roof principals have cambered collars strutted from the uprights by curved braces, forming in the central truss a two-centred arch of perfect curvature, and in the two intermediate trusses on either side segmental two-centred arches. The roof is further strengthened by curved wind-braces. The most remarkable feature is the window in the east wall, which is of three tre-foiled ogee lights, with foliated tracery under a pointed straight-sided head, both mullions and tracery being of timber. This appears to be an insertion, and upon its date depends the determination of that of the rest of the structure. The approach to reticulation which the tracery exhibits would at first sight suggest the middle of the 14th century. It does not seem likely that the roof above described is of a date

At Lifford, about three-quarters of a mile to the north of the main portion of the village, is Lifford Hall, a good brick Jacobean mansion of three stories, the attic story being gabled. The plan is of ⊔ type, the principal front facing north. The interior appears to have been wholly remodelled in the early years of the 19th century, when the original entrance doorway in the north front was built up and a new entrance hall and doorway formed in the west wing. The east wing at present consists of one large room with a modern bay window at the north end. The stone fireplace in this room is probably original. For some time previous to its restoration in the first half of the 19th century this wing appears to have been utilized as a barn. To the east of this wing is a range of stables and offices. The original windows have been altered to receive sash-frames, but the openings do not appear to have been enlarged, the original moulded stone sills remaining. In the garden is a small castellated octagonal turret, connected with the house by a fortress-like curtain wall, constructed of brick with a facing of stone. The size of the bricks shows this to be of original date with the house. The grounds are now partly occupied by a large reservoir and an adjoining mill-pond made on the formation of the neighbouring Worcester and Birmingham Canal. The head of water thus obtained has till recently been employed to work an india-rubber mill. The reservoir is used for pleasure-boating.

About 2 miles south of the main village, at Wythall is Blackgrave Farm, a moated brick house of the first half of the 17th century. The interior has been much altered. Weatheroak Hall, about half a mile south-west of Blackgrave Farm, and about the same distance east of the hamlet of Wythall, is an 18th-century house, almost entirely rebuilt in the year 1884. Hawkesley Hall is a modern house built upon the site of an older mansion. Highbury, the

on account of the resistance he met with, Rupert set fire to Birmingham.

King's Norton was visited by Queen Henrietta Maria in 1643.[5]

The commons, which are said in 1679 to have consisted of 2,000 acres of common and waste land, valued at £100 yearly,[6] were inclosed under an Act of 1772,[7] the award being dated 15 March 1774.[8]

Thomas Hall was vicar of King's Norton in 1660 when he wrote his treatise against May games. In this he says: 'There were two May-poles set up in my Parish, the one was stollen and the other was given by a profest Papist.'[9] He was ejected for nonconformity, and died in 1665, when he bequeathed his library for the use of the school and parishioners of King's Norton.[10]

William Lucas Sargent, the educational reformer and political economist, was born at King's Norton in 1809.[11]

KING'S NORTON : THE OLD GRAMMAR SCHOOL : INTERIOR LOOKING EAST

seat of the Rt. Hon. Joseph Chamberlain, is to the south of Moseley Hall.

A cavalry skirmish is said to have taken place at King's Norton in October 1642 between the Royalist cavalry under Rupert, who was advancing with the royal army towards Edgehill, and some Parliament Horse under Lord Willoughby of Parham, who surprised them, and, according to the Parliament accounts, utterly routed them. One of the Grevis family of King's Norton took a very conspicuous part for the Parliament in the fight at Camp Hill in this parish on Rupert's march to relieve Lichfield in 1643, when,

Among the place-names are Schoryebuttes,[21] Grendone,[13] Thorntenhulle, Rouacre[14] (xiii cent.) ; La Wychhalleacre,[15] Cokkismore,[16] Collebrugge, Litell Mayowes Grene,[17] Ivereslond or Inreslande[18] (xv cent.) ; Chyndehouse,[19] Seyes,[20] La Crosse House,[21] Broadford Bridge,[22] Yamfast Hurst, Heyden Hurst,[23] Harwicks,[24] Turvis *alias* Turvelond[25] (xvii cent.).

Before the Conquest and at the time *MANORS* of the Domesday Survey *KING'S NORTON* was a berewick of the manor of Bromsgrove.[26] It seems to have been held as a separate manor before the 13th century,[27] but followed

[5] Dugdale, *Diary*, 52.
[6] Exch. Spec. Com. 30 Chas. II, no. 6538.
[7] Priv. Act, 12 Geo. III, cap. 59.
[8] *Blue Bk. Incl. Awards*, 190.
[9] *Downfall of May Games.*
[10] *Dict. Nat. Biog.*
[11] Ibid.
[12] Anct. D. (P.R.O.), B 3275.

[13] Ibid. B 2454.
[14] Ibid. B 2594.
[15] *Cal. Close*, 1318–23, p. 574 ; Chan. Inq. p.m. 15 Edw. II, no. 86.
[16] Anct. D. (P.R.O.), A 6462.
[17] Ct. R. (Gen. Ser.), portf. 210, no. 35.
[18] Anct. D. (P.R.O.), B 1616, 3998.
[19] Chan. Proc. (Ser. 2), bdle. 5, no. 75.

[20] Pat. 10 Jas. I, pt. vi.
[21] Chan. Inq. p.m. (Ser. 2), ccccxxxii, 135 ; Com. Pleas D. Enr. East. 20 Jas. I, m. 9 d.
[22] Ct. R. (Gen. Ser.), portf. 210, no. 49.
[23] Ibid. [24] Ibid.
[25] Exch. Dep. Mich. 22 Jas. I, no. 41.
[26] *V.C.H. Worcs.* i, 285a.
[27] Pipe R. 2 John, m. 2 d.

the same descent as Bromsgrove (q.v.) until 1564,[28] when the latter was sold by Queen Elizabeth to Ambrose Earl of Warwick. King's Norton remained a royal manor until the beginning of the 19th century,[29] being settled on Queen Anne, consort of James I, in 1603,[30] on Queen Henrietta Maria in 1629[31] and on Queen Katherine.[32] On 8 October 1804 it was purchased of the Crown by John Taylor,[33] whose son James Taylor left it to William Francis, his eldest son by his second wife Anne Elizabeth daughter of Walter Michael Moseley. It now belongs to George William Taylor of Pickenham Hall, Swaffham, son of William Francis.[34] The manor is now practically extinct, the last court having been held in 1876,[35] and the manor pound having been appropriated by the district council as a depository for road materials.

The parish was formerly divided into five 'eldes' or 'yelds,' Lee, Rednal or Wrednall,[36] Headley, Moundsley and Moseley, for each of which there seem to have been an aletaster and a thirdborough.[37] The whole parish was governed by a bailiff, constable and reeve, elected every year by the tenants at the court leet.[38] There is one instance in the Court Rolls of the last-named office being held by a woman, or rather by her son as her deputy.[39] At a later date there were also a steward, who held the office during pleasure and received 53s. 4d. for keeping the court, a crier who received 6s. 8d., and a beadle who received 3s. 4d.[40]

The court leet was held every year on the Thursday in Whitsun week and the court baron every three weeks. The bailiff of the manor was allowed 66s. 8d. for providing a breakfast, dinner and supper for the judge on the leet day.[41] Before Bromsgrove was granted to Sir Richard Grobham the court for both Bromsgrove and King's Norton was held at 'the Lickie.'[42]

There is an interesting survey of the manor taken in 1650-1.[43] The soil of the heaths called Boswell Heath, Wake Green, Hayter's Heath, Kingswood, Norton Woods, &c., belonged to the lord of the manor and the trees to the tenants.

At the beginning of the reign of Edward III the tenants of the manors of King's Norton, Yardley and Solihull had been involved in a quarrel with Roger de Mortimer Earl of March, then lord of the manor, who had inclosed part of their common in King's Norton Wood.[44] He charged them with filling up a dyke he had made, and they were fined £300, afterwards reduced to 20 marks.

In 1616 James I granted to the men of King's Norton a market on Saturday and two fairs on the vigil and day of St. Mark and two days following, and on 5 August and two days following with a court of pie-powder.[45] The market was discontinued before the end of the 18th century, but fairs were still held on 25 April and 5 September.[46] These, though still held in 1849,[47] were obsolete before 1888,[48] but a statute fair is held on the first Monday in October at the present day.

The Abbot and convent of Bordesley had a grange at King's Norton in the 13th century.[49] This is no doubt to be identified with 'the whole demesne of Norton with the land of the forester and the beadle' granted to the abbey by the Empress Maud.[50] After the Dissolution this grange was included in the grant of the possessions of Bordesley Abbey in 1544 to Thomas Broke,[51] and passed from him to his sister and heir Jane Arrowsmith.[52] Her son John Arrowsmith sold it in 1550 to Alexander Avenon,[53] who died seised in 1580, and was succeeded by his son Alexander.[54] The latter settled it in 1604 on his wife Mary,[55] who survived him, and seems to have held the grange until 1628, when her son John Avenon had livery of it.[56] Two years later John Avenon and Elizabeth his wife conveyed it under fine to Anthony Slater and Anthony Alderson.[57] There is no further mention of it.

COLMERS (Colmore, Collemer, Colemares, Colemarsh, Chalmers), another estate in the parish, which is described as a manor from the 16th century, probably at first belonged to a family of the same name. Walter de Colmer was living c. 1280,[58] and John de Colmer, possibly his son, in 1327.[59] There is no trace of his successors until the 16th century, when John Rotsey mortgaged a capital messuage called Colmers to Robert Gower.[60] Robert Gower, son of William Gower of Boughton, St. John in Bedwardine, must have entered into possession of the manor before 1599, when he died seised of it.[61] His son

[28] *Rot. de Oblatis et Fin.* (Rec. Com.), 68; Chart. R. 5 John, m. 10; *Rot. Lit. Claus.* (Rec. Com.), i, 299; *Cal. Pat.* 1247-58, p. 111; 1272-81, pp. 71, 271; 1292-1301, p. 453; *Cal. Chart. R.* 1300-26, p. 366; *Cal. Pat.* 1327-30, p. 440; Chan. Inq. p.m. 30 Edw. III (1st nos.), no. 30; Feet of F. Div. Co. Hil. 48 Edw. III; Trin. 3 Hen. V; East. 14 Hen. VI; Mich. 3 Hen. VIII; Pat. 7 Edw. VI, pt. viii, and other references under Bromsgrove.

[29] *Cal. S. P. Dom.* 1547-80, p. 266; Pat. 33 Eliz. pt. v; 1 Chas. I, pt. iv, no. 14; Ct. R. (Gen. Ser.), portf. 210, no. 48, 49; Exch. Spec. Com. no. 6538; Misc. Bks. Ld. Rev. ccxxviii, fol. 303.

[30] Pat. 1 Jas. I, pt. xx; Add. MS. 6693, fol. 105.

[31] Pat. 5 Chas. I, pt. xv, no. 6; *Cal. S. P. Dom.* 1629-31, p. 37.

[32] Ct. R. (Gen. Ser.), portf. 210, no. 50. In 1650 the manor was sold by order of Parliament to Edward Moore and William Collins (Close, 1650, pt. xxxii, no. 25), but again came to the Crown at the Restoration.

[33] Information supplied by Mr. H. E. Taylor.

[34] Burke, *Landed Gentry.*

[35] Information supplied by Mr. H. E. Taylor.

[36] Land at 'Wreodanhale' was granted by King Offa in 780 to Bredon Monastery (Birch, *Cart. Sax.* i, 327). The Rednal area was excepted when the rest of King's Norton was taken into Birmingham, and is now for ecclesiastical purposes included in Lickey, and for civil purposes in Coston Hackett.

[37] Add. Chart. 23855; Ct. R. (Gen. Ser.), portf. 210, no. 35, 36, 37, 38, 49. The fine for refusing to execute the office of thirdborough was 20s.

[38] Ct. R. *ut supra*; Parl. Surv. Worc. 1650-1, no. 7.

[39] Ct. R. (Gen. Ser.), portf. 210, no. 35. The reeve had 1 mark yearly for his services (Parl. Surv. Worc. 1650-1, no. 7).

[40] Parl. Surv. Worc. 1650-1, no. 7.

[41] Ibid.

[42] Exch. Dep. Mich. 22 Jas. I, no. 41.

[43] Parl. Surv. Worc. 1650-1, no. 7.

[44] *Cal. Pat.* 1330-4, pp. 127, 268; Chan. Inq. p.m. 5 Edw. II (2nd nos.), no. 99.

[45] Pat. 14 Jas. I, pt. xiv, no. 13.

[46] *Rep. of Royal Com. on Market Rts. and Tolls*, i, 216. Carlisle, writing in 1808, however, states that there was a market held at King's Norton on Saturdays (*Topog. Dict.*).

[47] Lewis, *Topog. Dict.*

[48] *Rep. on Market Rts. and Tolls*, i, 216.

[49] Anct. D. (P.R.O.), B 2461.

[50] *Cal. Chart. R.* 1257-1300, p. 63.

[51] *L. and P. Hen. VIII*, xix (2), g. 166 (17).

[52] Chan. Inq. p.m. (Ser. 2), lxxv, 3.

[53] Pat. 4 Edw. VI, pt. ii, m. 26.

[54] Chan. Inq. p.m. (Ser. 2), cxc, 40.

[55] Feet of F. Worcs. East. 2 Jas. I. Alexander Avenon, the son, died in 1611 (Chan. Inq. p.m. [Ser. 2], dcclvii, 178).

[56] Fine R. 4 Chas. I, pt. iii, no. 2.

[57] Feet of F. Worcs. Mich. 6 Chas. I.

[58] *Lay Subs. R. Worcs. c.* 1280 (Worcs. Hist. Soc.), 66.

[59] Ibid. 1327, p. 18.

[60] Chan. Proc. (Ser. 2), bdle. 152, no. 48.

[61] *Visit. of Worc.* 1569 (Harl. Soc. xxvii), 61; Chan. Inq. p.m. (Ser. 2), cclvii, 74.

KING'S NORTON : THE OLD GRAMMAR SCHOOL FROM THE SOUTH

KING'S NORTON CHURCH : TOMB OF SIR RICHARD GREVIS OF MOSELEY, KT., AND HIS WIFE ANN

John had livery of it in 1602[62] and died in 1625.[63] The manor had been settled on Robert, his son and heir, and Frances Skinner, his intended wife.[64] Robert was succeeded by a son Richard who died in 1689, and was in turn succeeded by William Gower.[65] William Gower and his wife Ellen were among the Roman Catholic nonjurors who refused, after the insurrection of 1715, to take the oath of fealty to King George I. It is probable that Colmers was forfeited to the Crown, but afterwards compounded for.[65a] John Gower son of William, having predeceased his father, by his will dated in 1720 left his reversionary interest to his brother William Gower with contingent remainders if he should die unmarried to Edward Thomas Hawkins, second son of his cousin Thomas Hawkins of Nash, co. Kent, and to John elder brother of Edward.[66] William Gower, the father, gave his life interest in the estate in 1725 to his son William, who was killed in a duel in the same year. The elder William died in 1736, and the manor passed to Edward Thomas Hawkins, who assumed the name of Gower.[66a] He died unmarried, and Colmers belonged in 1788 to Thomas Hawkins, son of John, who in that year sold it to George Attwood.[67] Its further descent is not known.

HAZELWELL, which is not called a manor until the 17th century, probably derived its name from the family of Hazelwell who held it in the 14th century. In 1325 William de Hazelwell settled lands in King's Norton on himself and Margery his wife with reversion to his daughter Lucy and her husband William Benet.[68] Lucy was succeeded by a daughter, who married William Sye,[69] and left Hazelwell to her only child Alice, the wife of John Middlemore, who is said to have been the second son of John Middlemore of Edgbaston, in whose family it remained until the beginning of the 18th century.[70]

MIDDLEMORE of Edgbaston. *Party cheveronwise argent and sable with two moor-cocks in their proper colours in the chief.*

Alice Middlemore, who survived her husband, died about 1524, leaving her property to her eldest son John, who was succeeded about 1527 by his son George.[71] The latter died in 1566 and his widow Jane, the daughter of Hugh

Harman of Morehall, seems to have held Hazelwell until her death in 1591–2,[72] when it passed to her grandson George Middlemore, whose father Simon had died some years before.[73] George son of George Middlemore, who succeeded to Hazelwell about 1637, suffered much in the Civil War, his house at Hazelwell being plundered and his estate much reduced in value.[74] In 1646 his property was sequestered, but was finally discharged on payment of £10.[75] He was succeeded about 1652 by his son Robert,[76] and he in 1679–80 by his eldest son George,[77] who died unmarried in 1700, leaving his property to his nephew William, son of William Middlemore of London.[78] The latter died childless in 1709, having bequeathed his estate by a will without date to his brother George (who predeceased him) with remainder successively to his cousin George Middlemore, to Samuel Middlemore or his brother John, and to Richard Middlemore.[79] Since no executor was named in the will, administration of his goods was granted to his widow Margaret, the heirs being said to be Samuel and Thomas Middlemore. The former seems to have laid no claim to Hazelwell, and the latter, who was a soldier in Spain, did not hear of his cousin's death until some time after. However, on his return to England he brought a suit in Chancery in 1712 to recover the manor, which he claimed as being entailed on George Middlemore with remainder to him. It had been sold by Ellen Middlemore, sister of William, to George Birch, who already held a mortgage on it,[80] and Thomas in 1715 sold his interest to George Birch and confirmed the sale in 1722 to Thomas son of George, afterwards kt. and judge of the Common Pleas.[81] George Birch, son of Sir Thomas, succeeded him in 1757 and sold the manor to James Carden in 1785.[82]

The present Hazelwell Hall, which was probably built on the site of the old manor-house, is a modern structure belonging to the Cartland family.

The so-called manor of *HAWKESLEY*[83] (Hawekelowe, xiv cent.; Hawkeslowe, xvi cent.) was held of the manor of Bromsgrove.[84] Richard de Hawkeslow was assessed in the manor of Bromsgrove and King's Norton at 5s. 4d. in 1280.[85] He or a descendant of the same name held land at King's Norton in 1320–1,[86] and in 1323 William de Hazelwell obtained licence to grant a mill and land at King's Norton to Richard de Hawkeslow and his

[62] Fine R. 44 Eliz. pt. i, no. 9. In 1603 his lands in King's Norton were valued at £5 (*Lay Subs. R. Worcs.* 1603 [Worcs. Hist. Soc.], 13).

[63] Chan. Inq. p.m. (Ser. 2), cccliii, 71.

[64] Ibid.; and see Fine R. 6 Chas. I, pt. iii, no. 1a.

[65] Pedigree in possession of Mr. R. Vaughan Gower; Recov. R. D. Enr. Trin. 6 Geo. I, m. 15 d.

[65a] *Gent. Mag.* xcv (1), 604; see also Chan. Proc. 2727 Gower v. Gower.

[66] Recov. R. D. Enr. Trin. 6 Geo. I, m. 16 d.; Close, 7 Geo. I, pt. xxiii, no. 5.

[66a] Close, 12 Geo. I, pt. iv, no. 11; 10 Geo. II, pt. vi, no. 5; Burke, *Commoners,* ii, 44; *Gent. Mag.* 1736, p. 355.

[67] Inform. by Mr. R. Vaughan Gower; Com. Pleas D. Enr. East. 28 Geo. III, m. 15, 16.

[68] Inq. a.q.d. file 185, no. 3 (19 Edw. II);

[69] *Visit. of Worcs.* 1569 (Harl. Soc. xxvii), 96.

[69] *Visit. of Worcs.* 1569 (Harl. Soc. xxvii), 96.

[70] Pedigrees of this branch of the Middlemore family are published in *Harl. Soc.* xxvii, 96, and in Phillimore and Carter, *Account of the Family of Middlemore,* 91 et seq.

[71] Phillimore and Carter, loc. cit. The pedigree published by the Harl. Soc. does not mention John Middlemore, but gives George as the son and heir of Alice Hazelwell.

[72] Ibid.; George Middlemore and Joan his wife had a lease of King's Norton rectory in 1542 (*L. and P. Hen. VIII,* xvii, p. 702).

[73] Phillimore and Carter, op. cit. 98.

[74] Ibid. 103.

[75] Ibid. 103, 104; *Cal. of Com. for Comp.* ii, 1421.

[76] Phillimore and Carter, op. cit. 111; Feet of F. Worcs. Trin. 10 Chas. I.

[77] Hazelwell seems to have been settled on George in 1671 (Recov. R. Worc. Trin. 23 Chas. II, rot. 158).

[78] Phillimore and Carter, op. cit. 114.

[79] Ibid. 116.

[80] Ibid.; Chan. Dep. before 1714, Reynardson, 1033, no. 80.

[81] Recov. R. Trin. 1 Geo. I, rot. 90; Mich. 9 Geo. I, rot. 264; Burke, *Landed Gentry.*

[82] Feet of F. Div. Co. Mich. 26 Geo. III; see also Recov. R. Trin. 16 Geo. III, rot. 9.

[83] Chan. Inq. p.m. (Ser. 2), xxiv, 83; Feet of F. Worcs. Trin. 7 Edw. VI.

[84] Chan. Inq. p.m. (Ser. 2), xxiv, 83.

[85] *Lay Subs. R. Worcs.* 1280 (Worcs. Hist. Soc.), 67.

[86] Inq. a.q.d. file 145, no. 18.

sons John, Richard and William.[87] William de Hawkeslow paid a subsidy of 18*d.* at King's Norton in 1327,[88] and Richard de Hawkeslow in 1329 received from the Abbot of Bordesley a messuage and 2 carucates of land at King's Norton to hold during his life.[59] The former seems to have met with a violent death, for in 1344 his son Richard sued John Not for the death of his father.[90] According to a pedigree of the Hawkeslows given in *An Account of the Middlemore Family,* Richard Hawkeslow was succeeded by a son John,[91] and it was doubtless he who before 1424 granted seven messuages and certain land [92] in King's Norton, afterwards known as 'the manor of Hawkelowes,' to Humphrey Stafford.[93] Sir Humphrey, his son and successor, forfeited all his possessions on the accession of Henry VII, and the estate at Hawkesley was probably included in the land at King's Norton granted in 1485–6 as a forfeited possession of Humphrey Stafford to Sir Gilbert Talbot.[94] This grant does not seem, however, to have taken effect, for in the following year the land was granted to John Pympe and John Darell.[95] On the death of John Pympe in 1496 the estate is called the 'manor of King's Norton,'[96] but in the inquisition taken on the death of Sir John Darell in 1509 it is called the 'manor of Hawkelowes.'[97] Sir Humphrey Stafford, son of Humphrey mentioned above, was restored by Henry VIII in 1514–15,[98] and Hawkesley was evidently given back to him at that time, for in November 1515 John son of Sir John Darell obtained a pardon for all entries on the manor.[99] Sir Humphrey Stafford died in 1545 seised of the manor,[100] which must have been sold by his son Humphrey to a member of the Middlemore family. The purchaser was possibly William Middlemore, called in his will dated 1549 'of Hawkeslow.'[1] His son John Middlemore was dealing with the manor in 1553.[2]

Part of his house at Hawkesley was leased to his brother Henry, who seems to have held it until 1596.[3] John Middlemore died in 1597, and his son William settled the capital messuage and other property in

STAFFORD. *Or a cheveron gules and a border sable engrailed.*

Hawkesley on his son John when he married Bridget daughter of Thomas Betham of Rowington, co. Warwick.[4] John Middlemore succeeded to the whole of Hawkesley in 1633–4,[5] but his affairs seem to have become very much involved, and in 1637 he was imprisoned for debt in Worcester gaol, where he remained until his death about six years later.[6] His eldest son William was involved in still greater difficulties through his loyalty to the king in the Civil War. His house at Hawkesley was seized and garrisoned by the Parliamentary forces[7] early in 1645. In May in the same year the house was besieged by the Royalists, and surrendered to the king on the 15th, because 'the soldiers would not fight when they perceived it was the king's army,' although there 'was a month's provision and ammunition' in the house.[8] According to Clarendon 120 men, besides the governor, Captain Gouge, were taken prisoners.[9] The house was burnt after the surrender, and seems to have been rebuilt about 1654.[10] William Middlemore died in 1663, and was succeeded in turn by his three sons, John, who died in 1681, William, who died in 1711, and George.[11] The latter in 1723 settled Hawkesley on his eldest son John in tail-male.[12] Richard Middlemore, son of John, succeeded him about 1734.[13] In 1803, the year before his death, he conveyed Hawkesley to his second son Richard, who left it to his three daughters and co-heirs, Anne, Mary and Martha. Mary, afterwards the wife of Samuel Hoitt, died childless, leaving her share to her sisters, who in 1869 sold the whole to their kinsman William Middlemore of Birmingham, the father of Thomas Middlemore of Melsetter in Orkney, who now holds it.[14]

There is said to have formerly been a chapel at Hawkesley.[15]

At the time of the Domesday Survey *HOUNDES-FIELD* (Hundesfeld, xi and xiii cent. ; Hunckesfield, xviii cent.) was one of the eighteen berewicks annexed to Bromsgrove.[16] It belonged to the Crown until the Empress Maud granted it, as the land of Godric de Hundesfeld, to Bordesley Abbey,[17] probably at its foundation. It followed the same descent as the Grange belonging to the abbey at King's Norton[18] until John Arrowsmith sold it to a certain William Gilbert, whose son and heir Richard had livery of it in 1590.[19] William Gilbert, son of Richard, succeeded his father about 1629.[20] The estate belonged in 1717 to Elizabeth Byton,[21] and

[87] *Cal. Pat.* 1321–4, p. 321.
[88] *Lay Subs. R. Worcs.* 1327 (Worcs. Hist. Soc.), 18.
[89] *Cal. Pat.* 1327–30, p. 456.
[90] Phillimore and Carter, op. cit. 260.
[91] Ibid. 261–2.
[92] The estate comprised tenements called Usshes, Maynardes, Burdones, Clanfeld, Inkeford, Bradmedewe and Hullelond.
[93] Plac. in Canc. bdle. 26, no. 18.
[94] Pat. 1 Hen. VII, pt. iv.
[95] Ibid. 2 Hen. VII, pt. i, m. 8.
[96] *Cal. Inq. p.m. Hen. VII,* i, 545.
[97] Chan. Inq. p.m. (Ser. 2), xxiv, 83.
[98] Memo. R. Hil. Recorda, 6 Hen. VIII, rot. 53.
[99] *L. and P. Hen. VIII,* ii, 1182.
[100] Exch. Inq. p.m. (Ser. 2), file 1198, no. 8.
[1] Phillimore and Carter, op. cit. 174. It is to be noted, however, that a heriot was

paid at the end of the reign of Henry VIII for land at King's Norton held by Thomas Middlemore of Throckmorton (*L. and P. Hen. VIII,* xiv [1], 652 [M 25]), who was possibly father of William and may have been the purchaser of Hawkesley (Phillimore and Carter, op. cit. 167; Mins. Accts. Hen. VIII, no. 4029).
[2] Feet of F. Worcs. Trin. 7 Edw. VI; Phillimore and Carter, op. cit. 174.
[3] Recusant R. Exch. L.T.R. Pipe Ser. no. 1.
[4] Exch. Dep. by Com. Trin. 18 Chas. I, no. 2. William Middlemore is mentioned in the *Lay Subs. R. Worcs.* 1603 (Worcs. Hist. Soc.), and he was dealing with the manor in 1612–13 (Feet of F. Worcs. Mich. 10 Jas. I).
[5] P.C.C. 61 Seager.
[6] Phillimore and Carter, op. cit. 186.
[7] *Cal. S. P. Dom.* 1644–5, p. 393.

[8] Symonds, *Diary of the Marches of the Royal Army during the Civil War,* 167.
[9] *Hist. of the Rebellion,* iv, 38.
[10] Chan. Proc. Mitford, bdle. 134, no. 33.
[11] Phillimore and Carter, op. cit. 192–7.
[12] Ibid. 197. [13] Ibid. 201.
[14] Ibid. 205, 232.
[15] Ibid. 180 n.
[16] *V.C.H. Worcs.* i, 285*a.*
[17] *Cal. Chart. R.* 1257–1300, p. 63. The abbot afterwards claimed assize of bread and ale and view of frankpledge in the manor (*Hund. R.* [Rec. Com.], ii, 283).
[18] Anct. D. (P.R.O.), B 3967; *Valor Eccl.* (Rec. Com.), iii, 272; *L. and P. Hen. VIII,* xix (2), g. 166 (17); Chan. Inq. p.m. (Ser. 2), lxxv, 3; lxxxvii, 103.
[19] Fine R. 32 Eliz. pt. i, no. 26.
[20] Ibid. 5 Chas. I, pt. ii, no. 10.
[21] Recov. R. East. 3 Geo. I, rot. 86.

in 1737 it was conveyed by Richard Grevis and his wife Anne to William Salter.[22] In 1781 Thomas Heveningham and John Reeve conveyed it to Jacob Stokes.[23] The later descent of this estate has not been found.

KINGSUCH (Kingsitch, xvii cent.), another grange belonging to Bordesley Abbey, which was valued at £4 3s. at the time of the Dissolution,[24] was granted in 1544 to Thomas Broke,[25] who sold it in 1545 to Thomas Rotsey of King's Norton.[26] Ten years later it was purchased of the latter by Ralph Palmer,[27] whose son and heir William succeeded him in 1563,[28] but seems to have sold it soon afterwards to John Field, who in 1579 settled it on his daughter Anne on her marriage with William Whorwood.[29] The latter was afterwards knighted, and with his son and heir Thomas sold it in 1611 to Sir Clement Fisher,[30] who died seised in 1619.[31] In 1622 it was purchased from his son Sir Robert Fisher by John Turton of West Bromwich, co. Stafford, and William, his son and heir.[32] From William it passed to his son John, afterwards a baron of the Exchequer and justice of the King's Bench, who left his lands in King's Norton to his daughter Elizabeth Davies during the minority of his grandson John Turton.[33] The latter was holding the manor of Kingsuch in 1710.[34] It belonged to Robert Mynors, a surgeon of Birmingham, in 1865,[35] and is now in the possession of his descendants.

TURTON of West Bromwich. *Argent ten trefoils vert with a quarter gules.*

The manor of *MONYHULL* (Monehylls, xvi cent.) was held at the time of the Dissolution by the college of Westbury, co. Gloucester, but it is not known by whom it was given to the college. The farm of the manor, with Groveley, was £15 10s. 3d. a year, and from the capital messuage of Ekelyngstret a rent of £4 1s. 6d. was due, while the farm of the pasture of 'Brantyrene' was worth 13s. 4d.[36] Monyhull was granted with the site of the college to Sir Ralph Sadleir in 1544.[37] He sold it in 1547 to a certain William Sparry.[38] In the reign of Philip and Mary William Sparry sued Francis and Richard Rotsey and others for breaking down a seat in King's Norton Church which he had made for himself and his wife. The bill shows that he had been in the parish about thirty years and lived in a 'manor place' there called

'Puyhulls Hall.'[39] John Sparry and his wife Elizabeth conveyed the manor in 1590 to William Sparry,[40] and William Sparry died seised of Monyhull in 1610, leaving a son Daniel,[41] who appears to have sold it to William Child, who was dealing with it in 1650.[42] From him it passed to his son Peter.[43] By the middle of the 18th century the estate had come into the possession of James Arderne, whether by purchase or inheritance does not appear, and he conveyed it in 1762–3 to Girton Peake.[44] It is now the property of the city of Birmingham, and used as a colony for epileptics.

MOSELEY (Museleie, xi cent.) is also mentioned in the Domesday Survey as a berewick of Bromsgrove,[45] and probably remained part of that manor for some time, since no further mention of it occurs until the 15th century. In 1456–7 Baldwin Porter sold all his right in the 'manor' to Thomas Lyttelton, serjeant-at-law,[46] who died in 1481, leaving lands in Moseley to his son William.[47] Moseley Hall with an estate there afterwards came into the possession of a family called Grevis or Greaves, who are known to have held it in the 17th and 18th centuries.[48] The adjoining manor of Yardley (q.v.) also belonged to them. Moseley was purchased on 28 January 1767 of Ann Grevis and Henshaw Grevis by John Taylor.[49] From him it passed to his second son James, who died in 1852.[50] In 1854 the Hall

GREVIS of Moseley. *Argent a fesse azure between three roundels sable with a lion's head razed argent upon each and a griffon passant between two scallops or upon the fesse.*

was the seat of William Taylor. In the Priestley riots the Hall, which was then occupied by Lady Carhampton, was burnt by the rioters. It was rebuilt and was the seat of the Taylors until its recent purchase early in the 20th century by Mr. Richard Cadbury, who made it into a convalescent hospital for children, and gave it for that purpose to the Lord Mayor and Corporation of Birmingham.

In 1770 *MOUNDSLEY* was purchased from Honour, Edward and Frances Field by John Finch,[51] whose sister and heir Jane married John Simpson of Leicester.[52] Her son and heir John Finch Simpson was holding the property in 1803,[53] and in 1828 it was settled on his eldest daughter Mary[54] on her marriage with Edward Dawson of Whatton.[55] She

[22] Feet of F. Worcs. Trin. 10 & 11 Geo. II.
[23] Ibid. Trin. 21 Geo. III.
[24] Dugdale, *Mon. Angl.* v, 412.
[25] *L. and P. Hen. VIII,* xix (2), g. 166 (17).
[26] Ibid. xx (1), g. 125 (31).
[27] Pat. 1 & 2 Phil. and Mary, pt. xii, m. 7.
[28] Chan. Inq. p.m. (Ser. 2), cxxxvii, 53; Fine R. 6 Eliz. no. 37. In 1557 Ralph Palmer was the plaintiff in a suit in the court of Star Chamber against Thomas Baker and others who claimed the manor under a lease made by the late Abbot of Bordesley (Star Chamb. Proc. Phil. and Mary, bdle. 7, no. 30).
[29] Pat. 22 Eliz. pt. xii, m. 27.

[30] Feet of F. Worcs. Mich. 9 Jas. I.
[31] Chan. Inq. p.m. (Ser. 2), ccccxxxii, 135.
[32] Recov. R. D. Enr. East. 20 Jas. I, m. 9 d.; Feet of F. Worcs. East. 20 Jas. I.
[33] Shaw, *Hist. of Staffs.* i, 128.
[34] Recov. R. Trin. 9 Anne, rot. 78.
[85] Shaw, op. cit. i, 133.
[36] *Valor Eccl.* (Rec. Com.), ii, 433.
[37] *L. and P. Hen. VIII,* xix (1), g. 278 (68).
[38] Pat. 1 Edw. VI, pt. v, m. 15.
[39] Star Chamb. Proc. Phil. and Mary, bdle. 4, no. 22.
[40] Feet of F. Worcs. Mich. 32 & 33 Eliz.
[41] Chan. Inq. p.m. (Ser. 2), cccxxiv, 117; Fine R. 10 Jas. I, pt. i, no. 20.

[42] Feet of F. Worcs. Hil. 1650.
[43] Recov. R. Mich. 1 Jas. II, rot. 265.
[44] Feet of F. Div. Co. Hil. 3 Geo. III.
[45] *V.C.H. Worcs.* i, 285a.
[46] Close, 35 Hen. VI, m. 1.
[47] Chan. Inq. p.m. 21 Edw. IV, no. 56.
[48] *The Genealogist,* vi, 304; Chan. Proc. (Ser. 2), bdle. 77, no. 95.
[49] Information supplied by Mr. H. E. Taylor.
[50] Burke, *Landed Gentry,* 1906.
[51] Feet of F. Worcs. Trin. 10 Geo. III.
[52] Nichols, *Hist. of Leic.* iii (1), 326.
[53] Recov. R. Hil. 43 Geo. III, rot. 170.
[54] Ibid. East. 9 Geo. IV, rot. 48.
[55] Burke, *Landed Gentry* (1906) under Dawson.

died in 1843, and nine years later her husband sold Moundsley to Thomas Lane, to whose son Charles Pelham Lane it now belongs,[56] and he resides at the Hall.

TESSALL (Thesale, xi cent.; Teneshala, xii cent.), now only a farm-house, is mentioned in the Domesday Survey as a berewick of Bromsgrove.[57] With Houndesfield it was included in the foundation charter of the Empress Maud to Bordesley Abbey and in later confirmations by Henry II, Richard I and Henry III.[58] Walter son of Ralph de Tessall had in 1255–6 a messuage, rent and mill in Tessall[59] which he appears to have held of the king.[60] Before 1425 the manor seems to have been acquired by the lord of King's Norton and was granted by Edmund Earl of March to a certain Stephen Benet for life.[61] After that date it seems to have become merged in King's Norton Manor.

Besides the more important manors and granges there are in the parish several smaller estates which were the sites of reputed manors in the 17th and 18th centuries. Among these are Farmons, Weatheroak Hill, Wychall and Wythworth.

FARMONS in Moseley probably derived its name from John Farmon, who lived in King's Norton in 1327.[62] It afterwards belonged to James Earl of Wiltshire, and fell to the Crown on his attainder at the accession of Edward IV.[63] It belonged in 1777 to Richard Chambers and Anna Maria his wife,[64] and was purchased of them in 1780 by William Taylor.[65] It now belongs to George William Taylor, lord of King's Norton.

WEATHEROAK HILL belonged to the Fields. It is probable that it belonged to John Field c. 1280[66] and to Richard Field in 1327,[67] and descended from them to Henry Field, who died seised of it in 1584, leaving it to his brother John Field.[68] The latter left it before 1604 to his daughter Anne, the wife of Sir William Whorwood[69] of Bentley Pauncefoot, who settled it on Ursula wife of their son Thomas.[70] After that date there are no documents relating to it. Before 1806 it seems to have been purchased by Robert Mynors, from whom it has descended to the present owners, the Misses Emily Anne and Florence Annie Mynors, his great-granddaughters.[71]

WYCHALL (Wythalle, xiii cent.) may perhaps be identified with 'Warthvil,' one of the berewicks of Bromsgrove in 1086.[72] It was in the king's possession in 1237–8,[73] evidently as an appanage of Bromsgrove Manor. The king sued Richard son of Richard de Coston for a carucate of land at 'la Wythalle,' in the manor of Bromsgrove, in 1253, claiming it as an escheat, and promising that,

if he should recover it, it should belong to Paulinus de Bampton his serjeant.[74] It is possible that Richard de la Wychall, who gave an acre of land called 'la Wychhalleacre' to the Abbot of Bordesley early in the 14th century, was tenant of the manor.[75] The reversion of a moiety of Wychall Farm was bequeathed by Job Marston of Hall Green, Yardley, to his kinsman Joshua Avenant in 1701.[75a] The present Wychall Farm is an old moated half-timbered house not far from King's Norton railway station.

William Sheldon died in 1517 holding of the queen the so-called manor of WYTHWORTH, in King's Norton, which he bequeathed to his brother Ralph.[76] The manor with a water-mill called Kilcupps was sold in 1633 by William Cowper and his wife Martha to William Chambers,[77] and in 1711 Thomas and Edward Chambers conveyed it to John Holmden.[78] The name still survives at Wythwood Cottage in Wythall.

BLACKGRAVE was given by Richard I to Reginald de Bares. Reginald, after selling the land to Fulk de Wythworth, went on a crusade and never returned. Fulk apparently gave half the tenement, which consisted of a messuage and a carucate of land, to Emma de Alvechurch, against whom the king recovered it in 1237–8.[79] The king seemed to have based his claim on the fact that Reginald de Bares had broken prison at Feckenham, where he was detained for larceny, so that his land escheated to the king. In 1252 the king was said to have recovered the land from Hugh de Belne, who was vouched to warranty by his under-tenant Henry Lovett.[80] The king granted the land in that year to William son of Hugh de Belne for the service of rendering 22s. yearly at the Exchequer.[81] It was stated in 1275 by the 'elder people' of Alvechurch that the tenement of la Blackgrave which William de Belne then held was formerly demesne wood of the Bishop of Worcester, and that it had been alienated from the church by force by 'Folkwy de Wichford,'[82] and by the assent of Hugh formerly parson of Alvechurch, whose daughter Isabel married Hugh de Belne, and was succeeded by William de Belne her son and heir, who first obtained a charter of the king at the request of Sir John Mancel and others.[83] Hugh de Belne died about 1317–18 holding a messuage and land in King's Norton to which his son William succeeded.[84] William died seised of the estate in 1347–8,[85] when it passed to his brother Thomas, who died in 1361–2[86] His son William succeeded and did fealty for the land in 1362.[87]

Habington states that Blackgrave was lately the land of Mr. Gandy, from whom it passed to Sir Richard

[56] Burke, Landed Gentry (1906), under Lane.

[57] V.C.H. Worcs. i, 285a; Add. Chart. 20420.

[58] Cal. Chart. R. 1257–1300, pp. 63–4.

[59] Feet of F. Worcs. case 258, file 7, no. 41.

[60] Cal. Pat. 1422–9, p. 319.   [61] Ibid.

[62] Lay Subs. R. Worcs. 1327 (Worcs. Hist. Soc.), 17.

[63] Cal. Pat. 1461–7, pp. 261, 300; 1467–77, pp. 26, 441, 536; 1476–85, p. 416; Mins. Accts. bdle. 1067, no. 15.

[64] Recov. R. Mich. 18 Geo. III, rot. 514.

[65] Information supplied by Mr. H. E. Taylor.

[66] Lay Subs. R. Worcs. c. 1280 (Worcs. Hist. Soc.), 67.

[67] Ibid. 1327, 17.

[68] P.C.C. 41 Watson.

[69] Ibid. In 1603 Isabel Field, probably widow of John, was living at Weatheroak Hill (Lay Subs. R. 1603 [Worcs. Hist. Soc.], 14).

[70] Erdeswick, Surv. of Staffs. 394 n.

[71] Burke, Landed Gentry (1906).

[72] V.C.H. Worcs. i, 285a.

[73] Maitland, Bracton's Note Bk. no. 1234.

[74] Cal. Pat. 1247–58, pp. 193, 212.

[75] Cal. Close, 1318–23, p. 574; 1323–7, p. 83.

[75a] P.C.C. 100 Hern.

[76] Chan. Inq. p.m. (Ser. 2), xxxvii, 37.

[77] Feet of F. Div. Co. East. 8 Chas. I; Close, 7 Chas. I, pt. xix, no. 11.

[78] Recov. R. Mich. 10 Anne, rot. 93.

[79] Maitland, Bracton's Note Bk. no. 1234.

[80] Cal. Chart. R. 1226–57, p. 402.

[81] Ibid.; Excerpta e Rot. Fin. (Rec. Com.), i, 138.

[82] Possibly Fulk de Wythworth is meant.

[83] Sede Vacante Reg. (Worcs. Hist. Soc.), 75.

[84] Chan. Inq. p.m. 11 Edw. II, no. 16.

[85] Ibid. 21 Edw. III (1st nos.), no. 37.

[86] Ibid. 35 Edw. III, pt. i, no. 26.

[87] Cal. Close, 1360–4, p. 313.

Grevis, kt., and 'so descended to Mr. Grevis his son now livinge.'[88] It is perhaps to be identified with an estate called Walgrave, Whagrave, Bagrave, or Badgrave, which belonged in 1613 to Sir Thomas Palmer, and was then in the tenure of Thomas Grevis.[89]

There were formerly two mills belonging to the manor of King's Norton, one in Wrednall Elde, the other in Moundsley,[90] but there is no mention of them after the 17th century. Another mill belonged to Hawkesley and is first mentioned in 1323, when it was settled on Richard Hawkeslow and John, Richard and William his sons.[91]

In 1311 the king granted licence to William Jurdan to grant a mill and land in King's Norton to Richard de 'Brademedewe,'[92] but this was probably one of the mills belonging to the manor.

Henry Field left a mill called Hurste Mill to his

date, and the church would then have consisted of chancel, nave, and north aisle. In the beginning of the 14th century the south arcade was built and the south aisle added. The chancel was rebuilt in the 14th century, and the north aisle was either rebuilt or had windows inserted at the same time. The tower is a fine example of late 15th-century work, and the south porch is of similar date. Three gabled roofs were built to each aisle in the 17th century, those on the north being removed in modern times. The clearstory was probably built at the same time, for the windows are set out to space between the gables. A vestry existed on the north side of the chancel in the 16th or 17th century and was removed later. A modern vestry has been added at the north-west end of the north aisle and an organ bay built to the south of the chancel.

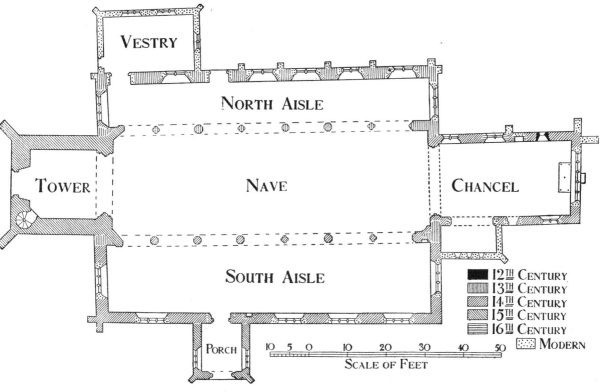

PLAN OF KING'S NORTON CHURCH

niece Anne and her husband William Whorwood in 1584,[93] and it was still in their family in 1625.[94] Hurste Mill is still in existence. Two 'grist mills' belonged to the rectory of King's Norton in 1651.[95]

CHURCH   The church of ST. NICHOLAS consists of a chancel 33 ft. by 18¾ ft., with a south organ bay, nave 82¼ ft. by 25 ft., north aisle 10½ ft. wide, south aisle 18½ ft. wide, west tower 17¼ ft. square, and a north vestry and south porch. These measurements are all internal.

The church is large, but with the exception of two 12th-century lancets in the chancel none of the work is earlier than the end of the 13th century. The north arcade of the nave is probably of that

The east window of the chancel is of five lancet lights grouped under a four-centred arch, all modern. In the north wall is a 12th-century round-headed single-light window reset, and below it is another smaller and now blocked. The blocked north door with a depressed arch led into the vestry now removed. East of this is a two-light 16th-century window, and a second with 14th-century jambs.

In the south wall is a restored two-light window, the sill being carried down to form sedilia. The south chancel door is modern. The chancel arch is of 14th-century date of two orders, the outer continuous, and the inner, with good ball flower ornament, springs from corbels.

[88] Habington, Surv. of Worcs. (Worcs. Hist. Soc.), ii, 219.
[89] Pat. 10 Jas. I, pt. vi.
[90] Ct. R. (Gen. Ser.), portf. 210, no. 35, 36. [91] Cal. Pat. 1321–4, p. 321.
[92] Ibid. 1307–13, p. 349.
[93] P.C.C. 41 Watson.
[94] Exch. Dep. by Com. Mich. 22 Jas. I, no. 41. [95] Close, 1651, pt. I, no. 16.

The nave is seven bays in length. The two-centred arcading on the north is of two chamfered orders, resting on capitals and piers of varying design. The first, fourth and sixth piers are of four engaged shafts harmonizing with the eastern respond, the second and fifth are octagonal, and the third round. The capitals and bases vary in moulding, but the whole of this arcade probably dates from the latter half of the 13th century. The south arcade, which is of a similar type, dates from the beginning of the 14th century ; the first and third piers are of four clustered shafts, the remainder, with the east respond, being octagonal. The west responds of both arcades are cut into by the diagonal buttresses of the tower. The clearstory on each side has three circular trefoiled and quatrefoiled lights, all probably of 17th-century date. The tower arch is of 15th-century date moulded on the splay.

relief. On each side is a three-light traceried window of the 15th century. In the northeast corner is a small recess, probably for a water stoup.

The west tower is in four stages with battlements, angle pinnacles and octagonal spire.

In the west wall of the ground stage is a doorway with a crocketed label much restored, and above it a large four-light window with a label formed by the second course rising above it.

To the north and south of the second stage is a two-light window in a deep reveal. The third stage has niches with crocketed canopies and finials, containing figures, apparently modern.

Two transomed windows of two lights pierce each face of the belfry stage. They are provided with crocketed labels and finials, flanked by similar blind windows.

KING'S NORTON : THE CHURCH FROM THE GREEN

The east window of the north aisle is of three lights with modern tracery. In the north wall, which has been much repaired, are five two-light windows with modern tracery. Between the fourth and fifth windows is a modern door, and at the northwest end a modern vestry. The west window of the aisle is similar to the eastern, but the tracery is apparently old.

The windows in the south aisle are of three lights each, and have all been restored in the style of the 14th century. The west window is similar, but of narrower proportions.

To the east of the south door is a 15th-century piscina, presumably not *in situ*, with an ogee head and remains of crockets.

The south door is of 15th-century date, and above it are fragments of a canopied and crocketed image bracket. The porch itself is of the 15th century, the roof showing traces of vaulting, and the angle corbels bearing the symbols of the Evangelists in high

The embattled parapet has trefoiled panels, the merlons being ornamented with quatrefoils. The spire has three bands of moulding, with ogee-headed lights and a line of crockets to each angle.

The modern roofs rest on carved corbels ; the north aisle has a pent roof, the south a roof of three transverse gables, all modern. The buttresses of the north aisle are modern.

The south aisle wall appears to have been refaced from the east end up to the porch, parts of the windows and labels being original. The porch has a crocketed label with finial, and the windows west of the porch have similar enrichment. The three gables over this aisle are of 17th-century date, with lines of trefoiled panels. On the western is a butterfly gargoyle of the type that occurs in several churches in the north of the county.

At the east end of the south aisle is a floor slab of a priest in mass vestments. The inscription is almost illegible, but the date seems to be 1508. On the south wall is a monument to John Middlemore of Edgbaston and Hazelwell Halls, ob. 1698.

High up on the arcade wall of the aisle is a wood painted heraldic tablet to Sarah wife of Henry Est of Slade Pool ; the date appears to be 1632.

On the north wall of the north aisle is a brass tablet inscribed—

Th' Ascension day on ninth of May
Third year of King James reign
To end my time & steal my coin
I William Greves was slain
· 1605 ·

On the north side of the tower is an altar tomb, with two life-size figures engraved on a flat alabaster slab, the lines being filled in with black composition. The man is in plate armour with his head upon his helmet. His wife is in the dress of the period with her head on a cushion.

An inscription in raised letters runs round the edge of the tomb, but is much defaced ; it reads ' Humphrey Littleton of (?) Groveley and Martha his wife, daughter of Robert Gower of Colemers Esq. . . . . ob. 1588.'[95a]

On the wall above this is a recess with effigies of a man and his wife in 17th-century costume, kneeling. The only clue to their identity is a shield quarterly or and (?) gules.

On the south side of the tower is a 17th-century altar tomb with two recumbent figures of Richard Grevis of Moseley, kt., and Ann his wife, daughter of Thomas Leighton of Wattlesborough. The figures are in the dress and armour of the period. The man's head rests on a mantled helmet, his feet on a gauntlet. The inscription is on a decorated slab above, with small kneeling effigies of four sons and four daughters. Above are the arms of Grevis impaling Leighton.

Above are two crested helms, the one with a two-headed eagle sable, for Grevis, the other with a wyvern sable, for Leighton.

There is a ring of eight bells cast by Chapman & Mears of London in 1783 ; the first and seventh were recast by Blews of Birmingham, 1867, and the fifth by Thomas Mears of London in 1826. The sixth has also been recently recast by Taylor.

The plate includes a good specimen of the Elizabethan cup with cover for paten, with the fringe or gadroon on the stem and the dotted line ornament. There is also a set of plated ware, including a cup, paten, flagon and almsdish.

The registers before 1812 are as follows : (i) all entries 1546 to 1791, marriage entries ceasing 1754 ; (ii) baptisms and burials 1792 to 1812 ; (iii) a marriage book 1754 to 1812.

The church of *ST. MARY, MOSELEY*, consists of a chancel, nave, north aisle, transept and tower.

The earliest part of the church is the Tudor tower, which is said to have been built in 1514. In the latter part of the 19th century the church was almost rebuilt. In 1876 the restoration was begun, the north aisle being added in 1886 and the organ chamber in the following year. In 1894 the vestry was built and in 1897 the present chancel and transept were erected. There are eight bells in the tower. The register begins in 1750.

The church of King's Norton *ADVOWSON* was formerly a chapel annexed to the church of Bromsgrove (q.v.), and has always followed the same descent.[96] It was severed from Bromsgrove in 1846,[97] and the living was declared a vicarage in 1866,[98] and is in the gift of the Dean and Chapter of Worcester. The chapel was not valued separately until 1536, when it was worth £15 10s.[99] In 1651 the parsonage-house and lands belonging were sold to Charles Cocks of the Middle Temple.[100]

In 1561-2 it was returned ' the Chappell and the Chappell More is hole 'the Quenes reserving one little plecke by the lane syde a nowte the well to T. (? J.) Middlemore.'[1]

The chapel of St. Mary Moseley was built by the parishioners of King's Norton because the parish was ' seven miles broad every way & 40 miles compass,' and many of the inhabitants lived 4 miles from the parish church.[2] In 1405 licence was given to the parishioners of Bromsgrove who lived near King's Norton to attend mass in the chapel of St. Mary, Moseley.[3] In 1494–5 the feoffees of the lands and tenements of St. Mary's chapel received from the queen certain pieces of waste land in Moseley.[4]

The salary of the chaplain was supplied by the parishioners from a fund amounting to £24 10s. 10½d., which had been granted to them by various ' deeds declaring no use,' with which they found one, two, or even three priests, the surplus when there were only one or two being used for the repair of the bridges and highways and 'relieving the poor and other charitable alms and good deeds.'[5] In 1562 land formerly belonging to the chapel of Moseley was granted to Cicely Pickerell and her heirs,[6] and in 1577-8 a 'house or room called the Lady Priest's Chamber ' in Moseley with land belonging was granted to John Mershe and others.[7] The chapel apparently continued to be used[8] and a brief for rebuilding was issued in 1780.[9]

Moseley was formed into a separate ecclesiastical parish in 1853.[10] The living is a vicarage in the gift of the Bishop of Birmingham. In 1875 the parish of St. Anne, Moseley, was constituted from this parish,[11] the living being a vicarage in the gift of the vicar of Moseley. The church consists of a chancel, nave, aisles and tower with spire, and is built of stone. The church of St. Agnes, erected in 1883-4, is a

[95a] The arms of Gower of Colmers as impaled by Humphrey Littleton in King's Norton Church are, barry argent and gules a cross paty sable, quartering Grindall, ermine a cross paty gules (Grazebrook, *Heraldry of Worcs.*; Burke, *Commoners*, ii, 44).
[96] Worc. Epis. Reg. Hemenhale, fol. 21; Carpenter (1444–72), i, 133 ; *L. and P. Hen. VIII*, xvii, g. 71 (29) ; xix (1), g. 1035 (51) ; *Cal. S. P. Dom.* 1611–18, p. 73 ; Inst. Bks. (P.R.O.).

[97] *Parl. Papers* (1872), xlvi, 18 d.
[98] *Lond. Gaz.* 3 Apr. 1866, p. 2214.
[99] *Valor Eccl.* (Rec. Com.), iii, 225. An inventory of the goods belonging to the church in 1552 is printed in *Trans. Birmingham and Midl. Inst.* 1872, p. 44.
[100] Close, 1651, pt. l, no. 16.
[1] Memo. R. Mich. Commissioners, 4 Eliz. rot. 3.
[2] Chant. Cert. 60, no. 10.
[3] *Cal. Papal Letters*, vi, 29

[4] Ct. R. (Gen. Ser.), portf. 210, no. 36.
[5] Chant. Cert. 60, no. 10.
[6] Pat. 4 Eliz. pt. iii.
[7] Ibid. 20 Eliz. pt. vii.
[8] *Cal. S. P. Dom.* 1656–7, p. 356 ; *Diary of Francis Evans* (Worcs. Hist. Soc.), 52.
[9] B. M. Chart. Pr. B xx, 6.
[10] *Lond. Gaz.* 18 Mar. 1853, p. 809.
[11] Ibid. 5 Feb. 1875, p. 272.

chapel of ease to St. Mary's, Moseley. The boundaries of Moseley were altered in 1879 to include part of Yardley.[12]

Samuel Shaw, the Nonconformist divine, was curate of Moseley in 1657.[13]

In 1344 a chaplain called William Paas received licence to alienate a messuage and land and rent in King's Norton to a chaplain for celebrating divine service daily at the altar of the Virgin Mary in King's Norton Church.[14] This is no doubt the chantry of St. Thomas the Martyr mentioned in a Chancery suit of 1485–1500,[15] whose invocation is said to have been afterwards changed to St. Michael,[16] the change doubtless taking place about 1538 in consequence of the proclamation of Henry VIII erasing the name of St. Thomas from the calendar of saints. At the time of its dissolution the chantry supported three stipendiary priests, one being the master of the grammar school and another the usher.[17] In 1549 rents amounting to 53s. 6d. from lands which had been given 'to maintain a priest in service of the Holy Trinity, Blessed Mary and St. Michael' were granted to Richard Field and others.[18]

St. Mary's, Wythall, became a separate ecclesiastical parish, formed from part of Alvechurch, King's Norton and Solihull, in 1853.[19] The living is a vicarage, the patron being the vicar of King's Norton. There was formerly a chapel there, which is first mentioned in the 17th century.[20] After the Restoration Richard Moore, the Nonconformist minister, obtained licence to preach in the chapel, which he described as 'his house and room at Withall,'[21] but the licence was withdrawn two years later.[22] In 1672 he was again presented to the chapel, where he remained for two years.[23] The present church, built in 1862, is of brick in 14th-century style, consisting of chancel, nave, transepts, south aisle, south porch and tower.

The parish of St. Paul, Balsall Heath, was also formed as a district chapelry from King's Norton in 1853.[24] It was declared a vicarage in 1867,[25] and the living is in the gift of the vicar of King's Norton. The church is of brick, consisting of chancel, nave, aisle, side chapel, baptistery and tower. The church of St. Thomas in the Moors, Balsall Heath, was built in 1883, and the living is a vicarage in the gift of trustees. The church is of brick and with slate roof, and consists of chancel, nave, aisles and north and south porches. The new parish of St. Barnabas was formed in 1905, and is a vicarage in the gift of the Bishop of Birmingham.

The ecclesiastical parish of King's Heath was formed in 1863[26] from Moseley and King's Norton. The living, which was declared a vicarage in 1866,[27] is now in the gift of the vicar of Moseley. All Saints' Church, built in 1859, is a building in 15th-century style, consisting of chancel, nave, aisles and tower with spire.

The church of the Ascension, Stirchley Street (1900), and St. Agnes, in the Cotteridge (1903), are chapels of ease to the parish church of Moseley.

In King's Norton there is a Roman Catholic church of St. Joseph and St. Helen, and also a Congregational and other Nonconformist chapels.

CHARITIES The school foundation, ascribed to Edward VI, but existing before the dissolution of the chantries, when it was provided for under the chantry endowments,[28] was formerly held in the ancient building in the churchyard already described, to which a library was bequeathed by Mr. Hall, a former clergyman of the parish. It was endowed with a rent-charge of £15, less land tax, paid by the receiver of the Crown rents. This has been redeemed by the transfer to the official trustees of £449 6s. 2d. consols, now producing £11 4s. 8d. yearly, which is applied for educational purposes under a scheme, 24 June 1884. The books which formed the library have been deposited in the Birmingham Public Library.

The almshouses, referred to in an ancient table of benefactions as founded by Mr. Avenant, are endowed with £926 2s. 11d. consols, with the official trustees, arising from sale of land and producing £23 3s. yearly, and with the remainder of the land let in allotments, of the annual rental value of £7 4s. The charity is regulated by a scheme of the Court of Chancery 25 May 1855. In 1910 £20 was paid to the alms-women.

In 1701 Job Marston by his will left £100 to be laid out in the purchase of land, the rents and profits whereof to be received by the minister of Moseley Chapel. The endowment now consists of 4 a. 3 r., let at £30 a year, which is paid to the minister, who also receives a rent-charge of £2 10s., supposed to have been created by one Samuel Wells.

The United Charities are regulated by a scheme, 26 August 1868, and comprise the following charities, namely :—

The Moseley Estate, containing 12 a. 2 r. ; the Red Hill Estate, containing 12 a. 1 r. ; the allotment, containing 4 a. 1 r., producing in the aggregate about £210 yearly ; Sir William Whorwood's charity, founded by will proved in the P.C.C. 16 February 1615, consisting of a rent-charge of £5 for the poor, paid by the Earl of Dartmouth ; the parish land, containing 19 p., in respect of which the annual sum of 15s. is received ; an annuity of £2 6s. 8d., mentioned in the table of benefactions as given by a Mr. Fox ; and an annuity of £2, stated to have been given by the will of John Field. The official trustees also hold a sum of £185 7s. 4d. consols, producing £4 12s. 8d., arising from the investment of accumulations of income.

By the scheme two-thirds of the income may be applied for educational purposes and the residue in general distribution among the poor.

The Kingswood Chapel Trust.—A meeting-house for Protestant Dissenters and a residence for the minister were built at King's Norton about 1712. In 1791 the meeting-house and the parsonage-house were attacked by the Priestley rioters and burnt down. Two separate actions under the Riot Act were

[12] *Lond. Gaz.* 30 May 1879, p. 3677.
[13] *Dict. Nat. Biog.*
[14] Inq. a.q.d. file 273, no. 16 (18 Edw. III) ; *Cal. Pat.* 1343–5, p. 309.
[15] Early Chan. Proc. bdle. 110, no. 58.
[16] Aug. Off. Proc. bdle. 36, no. 41.

[17] Chant. Cert. 60, no. 10.
[18] Pat. 3 Edw. VI, pt. v.
[19] *Lond. Gaz.* 26 Aug. 1853, p. 2858.
[20] *Cal. S. P. Dom.* 1656–7, p. 356.
[21] *Dict. Nat. Biog.* ; S. P. Dom. Chas. II, lxvi, 34.
[22] *Cal. S. P. Dom.* 1661–2, p. 613.

[23] *Dict. Nat. Biog.*
[24] *Census of Engl. and Wales,* 1901, *Worcs.* 5.
[25] *Lond. Gaz.* 27 Dec. 1867, p. 7073.
[26] Ibid. 13 Jan. 1863, p. 202.
[27] Ibid. 4 Dec. 1866, p. 6768.
[28] Chant. Cert. 60, no. 10.

commenced by the trustees against two inhabitants of the hundred, which resulted in £140 being recovered in respect of the meeting-house and £200 in respect of the parsonage-house. Both were rebuilt on land comprised in a deed of 23 January 1775. Other properties were subsequently acquired, and the trust estate now consists of three cottages and gardens, a field containing 2 acres and another field containing 3 acres, part of which is let on a building lease. The rents amount to £65 a year, which with collections and subscriptions are expended in ministerial supplies, salaries of the organist and chapel-keeper and the general maintenance of the chapel.

The Wythall Institute, which was erected in 1889 by public subscription and used for entertainments and concerts, was endowed by Mr. Mynors with £1,800 consols, producing £45 a year. The stock is standing in the names of the administering trustees.

The official trustees hold the sums of £176 16s. 11d. consols and £208 17s. 6d. consols, arising under the wills of Mrs. Sarah Jackson and William Humphrey Jackson (dates not stated), the annual dividends whereof, amounting together to £9 12s. 8d., are applicable towards the maintenance of the church and organ therein.

KINGTON

Chintune (xi cent.) ; Kinton, Kyneton (xiii cent.) ; Kynton (xiv cent.) ; Keynton (xvii cent.) ; Kington or Kineton (xix cent.).

Kington is a small parish covering an area of 1,071 acres, of which 264½ are arable land, 574½ permanent grass and 57 woods and plantations.[1] The subsoil is clay and sand, the chief crops raised being wheat, oats, beans and roots. The parish is watered by the Piddle Brook and two small tributaries which rise in Kington. The main road from Worcester to Alcester crosses the southern part of the parish, and on a branch road from it the village of Kington is situated. The land, like that of most of the Worcestershire parishes, is undulating, rising gradually from the banks of the Piddle Brook to a height of 200 ft. and more above the ordnance datum.

Before the Conquest *KINGTON* was *MANORS* held as three manors by Ælwig, Eilaf and Tori.[2] In 1086 there seem to have been only two manors, held by two knights of Roger de Lacy.[3]

The overlordship of one of these manors appears to have been given by one of the Lacys to Roger Pichard,[4] one of his tenants,[5] for at the beginning of the 13th century Kington was said to be held of the barony of Roger Pichard.[6] In 1290 John Pichard conveyed certain of his estates in Hereford to Philip ap Howell,[7] and the overlordship of Kington may have been included in this conveyance, for in 1315–16 it belonged to Philip ap Howell.[8] In 1578 a moiety of the manor was held of the queen as of the late dissolved monastery of Evesham.[9]

This manor had passed before 1212 to Robert Pipard,[10] who was still holding it in 1225,[11] and was succeeded by Guy Pipard, probably his son.[12] The latter left two daughters, Ivetta and Maud, between whom the manor seems to have been divided.[13]

Ivetta's half passed to her only daughter, also called Ivetta, wife of William Kardiff,[14] who was holding it c. 1280.[15] It passed with Queenhill in Ripple to Joan wife of John Wincote, who was holding her share of the manor in 1331,[16] but seems to have sold it before 1346 to John de Somerville,[17] in whose family it remained until the 16th century. A pedigree of the family is given by Dugdale in his *History of Warwickshire*.[18] William Somerville presented to the church in 1434,[19] and in 1491 Thomas Wolmer purchased the use of the mill stream in Kington of Thomas Somerville.[20] John Somerville, grandson of Thomas, died seised of the manor in 1578.[21]

SOMERVILLE. *Argent a fesse between three rings gules with three leopards' heads argent on the fesse.*

His son and heir John was arrested in 1583 for his share in a plot to kill the queen and committed to Newgate, where he was found strangled a few days after.[22] In 1609 James I granted his property in Kington to George Salter and John Williams,[23] who sold it in 1611 to William Turner and William Canning.[24] Turner gave up his right to Canning,[25] who in 1612 conveyed this half of the manor to Edward Canning of Enstone, co. Oxford,[26] and he with Richard and Robert Canning sold it in 1627 to Abel Gower.[27] By his will proved November 1632 the latter left it to his wife Mary, who seems to have settled it on Timothy Stampe, her son by a former husband.[28] In 1658 Timothy Stampe and Ann his wife conveyed it to Edward Heath and Thomas Yates,[29] apparently as a preliminary to its sale to William Bickerton in the following year.[30]

[1] Statistics from Bd. of Agric. (1905).
[2] V.C.H. Worcs. i, 312a.
[3] Ibid.
[4] In the 13th century Roger Pichard was holding in Almeley, co. Hereford, a fee which had formerly belonged to Walter de Lacy (Testa de Nevill [Rec. Com.], 68b).
[5] Ibid. 69.
[6] Ibid. 40b, 41a.
[7] Picards or Pichards of Stradewy, 29.
[8] Cal. Inq. p.m. 1–9 Edw. II, 372.
[9] Chan. Inq. p.m. (Ser. 2), clxxxiii, 89.
[10] Testa de Nevill (Rec. Com.), 40b.

[11] Feet of F. Worcs. 10 Hen. III, no. 11.
[12] Coll. Topog. et Gen. i, 260.
[13] Ibid.   [14] Ibid.
[15] Lay Subs. R. Worcs. c. 1280 (Worcs. Hist. Soc.), 19.
[16] Chan. Inq. p.m. 9 Edw. II, no. 42 ; Coll. Topog. et Gen. i, 260.
[17] Feud. Aids, v, 303, 330.
[18] op. cit. 829.
[19] Sede Vacante Reg. (Worcs. Hist. Soc.), 408.
[20] Prattinton Coll. (Soc. Antiq.), quoting the 'Hanbury Evidences'; Misc. Bks. Ld. Rev. ccxxviii, fol. 290.

[21] Chan. Inq. p.m. (Ser. 2), clxxxiii, 89 ; Dugdale, Hist. of Warw. 829.
[22] Dugdale, op. cit. 830.
[23] Pat. 7 Jas. I, pt. xxii, no. 2.
[24] Close, 9 Jas. I, pt. xviii, no. 19.
[25] Prattinton Coll. (Soc. Antiq.), quoting the 'Hanbury Evidences.'
[26] Ibid.
[27] Ibid. ; Feet of F. Worcs. Trin. 3 Chas. I.
[28] Prattinton Coll. as above ; see also Feet of F. Worcs. Mich. 16 Chas. I.
[29] Prattinton Coll. as above ; Feet of F. Worcs. Mich. 1658.
[30] Prattinton Coll. as above.

William Bickerton sold a moiety of 'the manor' of Kington in 1711 to Thomas Carpenter,[31] but in 1763 it seems to have belonged to Ann Millard, John Benton and John Haynes.[32] In 1814 it was advertised as being for sale.[33] Later in the same year John Jordan Haynes and Rebecca his wife sold it to Benjamin Littlewood of Amblecote.[34]

Maud, the other daughter of Robert Pipard, seems to have married Henry de Somery,[35] and her share of the manor followed the same descent as the Somerys' manor of Bishampton,[36] passing to the chantry priests of Hampton Lovett,[37] and after the Dissolution to the Scudamores and Keyts.[38] The last mention of it which has been found in original deeds occurs in 1662, when it belonged to Sir John Keyt.[39]

Nash does not mention the owner of this estate in his time, but a property in Kington which had formerly belonged to the Keyts was held in 1811 by a Mr. Freeman of Pedmore Hall.

The other manor of *KINGTON* was held of the manor of Inkberrow,[40] the overlordship of this manor having probably passed from Roger de Lacy to the Earls of Pembroke, lords of Inkberrow, in the same way as Himbleton and Spetchley (q.v.). It belonged in 1225 to William de Kington,[41] and seems to have passed successively to Nicholas Kington, who was in possession in 1327,[42] and the latter's son William and grandson Nicholas,[43] the last of whom was holding it in 1331.[44] In 1346 Hugh de Cooksey and Nicholas Somery were holding half a fee in Great Cooksey and Kington which had been the property of William de King-ton.[45] The manor then seems to have passed to the family of Toky, Thomas and Joan Toky being called 'of King-ton' in 1361.[46] Henry Toky, who settled land in Kington on his wife Isabel in 1392–3, perhaps succeeded Thomas.[47] It then went to his son John Toky,[48] who was holding the estate in 1431 [49] and died without issue male. His daughter and heir Maud brought the manor to the Wolmer family by her marriage with Thomas Wolmer,[50] whose son Thomas seems to have held it

TOKY. *Argent three cinqfoils sable.*

in 1491.[51] John Wolmer, grandson and heir of the last-named Thomas, died seised of the manor in 1518, leaving a son John,[52] whose grandson Anthony Wolmer was holding it in 1595 [53] and died before 1603.[54] In 1635 the manor belonged to Thomas Wolmer, grandson of Anthony, and Lucy his wife,[55] and their son John held it in 1659.[56] He died without issue, leaving the reversion after the death of his widow Philadelphia to his nephew Thomas Wolmer,[57] who by his will, dated 1707, left it to a cousin Thomas Wolmer.[58] The latter, with Philadelphia, widow of John Wolmer, sold it in 1714 to Thomas Vernon of Hanbury.[59] It then passed with Hanbury [60] (q.v.) until about 1857, when Thomas Bowater Vernon sold it to William Laslett of Abberton Hall,[61] M.P. for Worcester 1852–60 and 1868–74.[62] He married in 1842 Maria daughter of Dr. Carr, Bishop of Worcester, but died without issue in 1884.[63]

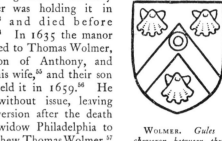

WOLMER. *Gules a cheveron between three scallops argent with a ring sable for difference.*

By his will this estate, which now seems to be the capital manor of Kington, passed to the Rev. Robert James Baker, who was succeeded in 1886–7 by Mrs. Baker Carr. The manor was purchased about 1905 by Mr. Lawrence C. Tipper, the present owner.

VERNON of Hanbury. *Or a fesse azure with three sheaves or thereon and a crosslet fitchy gules in the chief.*

CHURCH
The church of *ST. JAMES* is small, consisting of a chancel 16¾ ft. by 12½ ft., and nave 28¼ ft. by 17½ ft., with an additional western portion below the tower 7 ft. deep by 12 ft. wide. These measurements are all internal. The original church appears to have been erected in the 13th century and to have been a plain rectangular building, about 44 ft. by 12 ft.

---

[31] Feet of F. Worcs. Mich. 10 Anne.

[32] Ibid. 4 Geo. III. John Haynes was lord of the manor in 1781 (Priv. Act, 21 Geo. III, cap. 42).

[33] Prattinton Coll. (Soc. Antiq.), giving an extract from the *Worc. Journal*, 24 Feb. 1814.

[34] Feet of F. Worcs. Mich. 55 Geo. III.

[35] See Bishampton.

[36] *Feud. Aids*, v, 303, 324 ; *Lay Subs. R. Worcs.* 1327 (Worcs. Hist. Soc.), 22 ; *Cal. Close*, 1337–9, p. 145.

[37] Pat. 6 Edw. VI, pt. vi. It is to be noted that Kington Manor is not included in the conveyance of Bishampton by William de Bryan to Alice de Stury, nor in the grant by Alice to the chantry, but it certainly belonged to the chantry at the Dissolution, though it is not then called a manor.

[38] Add. MS. 31314, fol. 190, and see Bishampton for other references.

[39] Recov. R. Trin. 14 Chas. II, rot. 10.

[40] Chan. Inq. p.m. (Ser. 2), clxxix, 255.

[41] Feet of F. Worcs. case 258, file 2, no. 11.

[42] *Lay Subs. R. Worcs.* 1327 (Worcs. Hist. Soc.), 22 ; *Cal. Pat.* 1327–30, pp. 151, 222.

[43] *Coll. Topog. et Gen.* i, 260.

[44] Ibid.

[45] *Feud. Aids*, v, 303.

[46] *Sede Vacante Reg.* (Worcs. Hist. Soc.), 207.

[47] Assize R. 1035, m. 2 ; County Placita Chan. 12 Edw. IV, no. 10.

[48] Ibid.

[49] *Feud. Aids*, v, 330.

[50] *Visit. of Worcs.* 1569 (Harl. Soc. xxvii), 150, gives the following pedigree:—

Thomas Toky = Isabel
|
Thomas Toky
|
John Toky of Kenton = Mary
|
Thomas Wolmer = Maud

[51] Misc. Bks. Ld. Rev. ccxxviii, fol.

290 ; Prattinton Coll. (Soc. Antiq.), quoting the 'Hanbury Evidences.'

[52] Exch. Inq. p.m. (Ser. 2), file 1178, no. 5 ; *Visit. of Worcs.* 1569, loc. cit.

[53] Feet of F. Worcs. Trin. 37 Eliz. ; *Visit of Worcs.* 1569, pp. 150–1.

[54] *Lay Subs. R. Worcs.* 1603 (Worcs. Hist. Soc.), 15.

[55] Recov. R. Hil. 11 Chas. I, rot. 67 ; Feet of F. Worcs. Hil. 11 Chas. I ; Prattinton Coll. (Soc. Antiq.), quoting the 'Hanbury Evidences.'

[56] Prattinton Coll. (Soc. Antiq.), quoting the 'Hanbury Evidences.'

[57] Ibid.

[58] Ibid.

[59] Feet of F. Worcs. Mich. 1 Geo. I.

[60] Recov. R. Trin. 18 & 19 Geo. II, rot. 48.

[61] This estate evidently passed with the advowson, which was sold in 1857 (*Clergy Lists*).

[62] W. R. Williams, *Parl. Hist. of Worcs.* 112, 113.

[63] Burke, *Landed Gentry* (ed. 7).

KINGTON CHURCH C. 1810
(*From a Water-colour by Thos. Rickards in Prattinton Collection*)

The nave was probably lengthened about 7 ft. to the west and the small timber tower erected in the 15th century. During the 16th century the nave was widened southwards. A complete restoration took place in 1881, when the chancel was rebuilt with the old material mixed with new.

The east window is modern, of three lights under a traceried head, and on either side of it is an ancient image bracket. Of the two windows in the north wall the eastern is a pointed lancet, which appears to be of the 13th century; the other is a square-headed single light, also old. Between these windows, inside, is a recess with a two-centred drop arch. The south-east window is a late 13th-century trefoiled lancet with a restored head, and the south-west a round-headed light with a four-centred rear-arch. Between these windows is another recess (presumably an aumbry) with a triangular pointed head. The entrance to the chancel is spanned by a modern archway of wood. The north wall of the nave is thicker than that of the chancel, and on the south

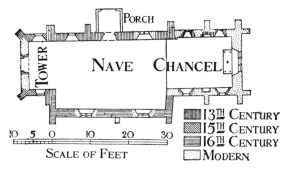

13ᵀᴴ CENTURY
15ᵀᴴ CENTURY
16ᵀᴴ CENTURY
MODERN

SCALE OF FEET

PLAN OF KINGTON CHURCH

side the building widens out some 5 ft. The first window in the north wall has two lights with a quatrefoil above and is largely modern. The north doorway is old, and the second window, a single-pointed light, is apparently 13th-century work. The two south windows are similar to the north-east and mostly modern. Part of the east face of the tower shows in the nave and has modern wood uprights on a timber girder. The nave narrows again on the south side to the space below the tower, which is lighted by a 15th-century window on either side with a square head. The west doorway is of a single chamfered order with a pointed head and the western angles are strengthened by diagonal buttresses, both apparently original, but the wall itself has been rebuilt or refaced. The tower over is of half-timber and plaster work. The sides of the bell-

chamber are pierced with plain square openings and the roof is gabled east and west. The walling of the nave is of large rough ashlar unevenly coursed. The five buttresses against the north wall are probably old ; a pair near the west end appear to mark the position of a former west wall. The three buttresses south of the nave have been considerably renewed. The roofs are gabled, with modern pointed wagon-headed ceilings.

The octagonal bowl of the font has been recut. On the north wall at the entrance to the chancel is a piece of 15th-century panelling, the cornice moulded and carved with a running vine pattern. Similar woodwork, which evidently formed part of an elaborate screen, is used up in the modern pulpit.

There are three bells, inscribed as follows : treble, 'W.H. R.D. November 22 1693 '; (2) the same ; (3) 'Will : Ocklei Thoˢ Farr, Church-wardens No : the 22 1693.'

The plate consists of a silver cup of 1784, inscribed 'Robert Baker, Robert Payten, church-wardens 1785,' a silver paten of 1875, a modern plated flagon, and two pewter almsdishes.

The registers before 1812 are as follows : (i) baptisms and marriages 1587 to 1735, with a gap, 1645 to 1653 ; (ii) baptisms 1735 to 1812, marriages 1735 to 1754 ; (iii) marriages 1754 to 1812.

The first mention of the church
ADVOWSON occurs in 1225, when William de Kington and Robert Pipard, who held the manors, agreed to present alternately, William having the first presentation.[64] From that time the advowson belonged in moieties to the lords of both manors, Robert Pipard's right descending to the Kardiffs and Somervilles.[65] After John Somerville's forfeiture in 1583 the advowson was not granted with his moiety of the manor to Salter and Williams, but seems to have been bought by Anthony Wolmer, who was dealing with the whole of the advowson in 1595.[66] It has since descended with his portion of the manor.[67]

The rectory of Kington was annexed to the vicarage of Dormston in 1874.[68] William Tyndal the antiquary was presented to the rectory of Kington by Henry Cecil in 1792.[69]

As early as 1291 the Prior of St. Guthlac near Hereford had tithes amounting to 13s. 4d. in Kington,[70] which after the Dissolution, when they had decreased in value to 10s.,[71] were granted in 1542 to John ap Rice with the site of the priory.[72] He sold them in 1600 to Anthony Wolmer for £30.[73]

There are no endowed charities.

[61] Feet of F. Worcs. case 258, file 3, no. 11. In 1285 the Bishop of Worcester presented to the living by lapse of time (*Reg. G. Giffard* [Worcs. Hist. Soc.], 272).
[65] *Coll. Topog. et Gen.* i, 260 ; *Sede Vacante Reg.* (Worcs. Hist. Soc.), 207, 408 ;

Chan. Inq. p.m. (Ser. 2), clxxxiii, 89 ; Feet of F. Worcs. Trin. 37 Eliz.
[66] Feet of F. Worcs. Trin. 37 Eliz.
[67] Ibid. Hil. 11 Chas. I ; Mich. 1 Geo. I ; Recov. R. Trin. 18 & 19 Geo. II, rot. 48 ; Inst. Bks. (P.R.O.) ; *Clergy Lists.*

[68] *Lond. Gaz.* 15 May 1874, p. 2556.
[69] *Dict. Nat. Biog.*
[70] *Pope Nich. Tax.* (Rec. Com.), 218.
[71] *Valor Eccl.* (Rec. Com.), iii, 263.
[72] Prattinton Coll. (Soc. Antiq.).
[73] *L. and P. Hen. VIII*, xvii, g. 1154 (42) ; see also xix (1), g. 444 (8).

NORTHFIELD

Nordfeld (xi cent.).

The parish of Northfield is situated on the northern border of the county, but with the exception of the Bartley Green area, which was annexed to Lapal, Northfield was incorporated in the city of Birmingham by the Birmingham Extension Act, 1911. It had in 1901 an area of 6,011 acres, of which 60 acres were covered with water, 968½ were arable land, 3,486 permanent grass, and 30½ woods and plantations.[1]

Until the 19th century Northfield was an agricultural parish, but by the rapid expansion of Birmingham it has become part of that city, and in the ten years between 1891 and 1901 its population increased from 9,907 to 20,767. This increase is partly due to the influx of a suburban population and partly to the erection of works in the neighbourhood. The change is manifested most strongly in the northern part of the parish, where Selly Oak, lying between Northfield and Birmingham, has sprung into such importance as quite to dwarf the ancient village of Northfield.

Bournbrook and Selly Park are continuations north-eastward of Selly Oak; California is a 'village of brickmakers' on the banks of the Birmingham and Worcester Canal in the north of the parish.

A supposed Roman road, called the Upper Saltway, passed from Selly Oak over the Lickey Hills on its way to Worcester, and can still be traced along the high road between Birmingham and Worcester.[2] This high road is joined in the village of Northfield by the Alcester and Birmingham road.

The pumping-station of the Birmingham Corporation water-works is at Selly Oak.

The Evans Cottage Homes at Selly Oak were founded in 1868 by the late Alfred Smith Evans for ladies of reduced fortunes. The homes consist of a group containing nine dwellings.

There are some old cottages called The Rookery in Bournbrook Lane, near Selly Oak, in which the bricks are disposed in herring-bone fashion.[3]

Among the place-names are 'Bromewychestude'[4] and Hatherleye,[5] which occur in the 14th century, and Brokhole tenement[6] in the 15th century.

MANORS   The manor of NORTHFIELD was held of the king in chief as part of the barony of Dudley.[7] In 1086 it was in the hands of William Fitz Ansculf, the Norman lord of Dudley, to whom it had passed from Aelfwold, the Saxon holder.[8] No under-tenant is mentioned.

Until the early 14th century this manor descended with the barony of Dudley (q.v.). During that period it is sometimes called the manor of Northfield, sometimes the manor of Weoley. It is clear, however, that only one chief manor existed, and that it was divided into the three tithings of Northfield, Selly and Middleton.[9] Of these Selly and Middleton were sub-manors, which owed suit at the court of the great manor held at Weoley. Selly was already in existence at the time of Domesday, while Middleton was carved out of the chief manor during the latter half of the 12th century.

When John de Somery died in 1322[10] the vill of Northfield was assigned to his younger sister Joan,[11] the widow of Thomas Botetourt, and she held it until her death in 1338.[12] Her son John being a minor,[13] Edward III granted the custody of her lands in 1339 to his kinswoman Eleanor Beaumont,[14] but in the following year John Botetourt, afterwards a knight, had livery of his lands.[15] He acted as justice of the peace for the county of Worcester, and as a commissioner of array in Warwickshire,[16] and died in 1386.[17] His only son John had predeceased him, leaving a daughter Joyce, the wife of Sir Hugh Burnell of Holdgate.[18] Joyce, therefore, became her grandfather's heir, and immediately after entering into possession settled Northfield on herself and her husband.[19] She died in 1407 without issue, leaving as heirs her aunts, Joyce wife of Sir Adam Peshall, Maud Botetourt a nun in Polesworth Abbey, and Agnes Botetourt a nun in Elstow Abbey, the sisters of her father John Botetourt, and her cousins Maurice Berkeley, the grandson of another sister Katharine, and Agnes and Joyce Wykes, the granddaughters of Alice, another sister.[20] Of these heirs Maud and Agnes Botetourt apparently could not or did not claim, and Agnes Wykes died unmarried shortly afterwards, so that the reversion of the manor after the death of Sir Hugh Burnell, who held it by the courtesy of England, belonged to Joyce Peshall, Joyce Wykes, who became the wife of Hugh Stranley or Stanley, and Maurice Berkeley. In 1417 Hugh Stranley and Joyce conveyed the reversion of their third part of the manor of Northfield to Nicholas Ruggeley and his wife Edith,[21] who immediately afterwards sold it to Joan Lady Beauchamp, widow of William Beauchamp of Bergavenny,[22] who in 1419 acquired another third from Sir Adam Peshall and Joyce.[23] Maurice Berkeley came into possession of his third on the death of Sir Hugh Burnell in 1419,[24] and shortly afterwards a dispute arose between him and Lady Beauchamp respecting this and other manors.[25] The exact cause of the dispute is not clear, but it may have arisen because of the difficulty of dividing Joyce Burnell's property. In 1431 Lady Beauchamp and Maurice held the manor jointly,[26] but by subsequent arbitration it was decided that the castle of Weoley and manors of Northfield and Cradley should pass

[1] Statistics from Bd. of Agric. (1905).
[2] V.C.H. Worcs. i, 212. Selly Cross on the highway leading to Birmingham is referred to in 1506 (Add. Chart. 15269).
[3] Mr. A. E. Everitt, in Trans. Arch. Sect. Birm. and Midl. Inst. 1871, p. 8.
[4] Jeayes, Lyttelton Chart. no. 145.
[5] Add. Chart. 15263, 15269.
[6] Prattinton Coll. (Soc. Antiq.).
[7] Cal. Inq. p.m. 1-19 Edw. I, 14, 493.
[8] V.C.H. Worcs. i, 316a.
[9] F. S. Pearson, LL.B., in Trans. Arch. Sect. Birm. and Midl. Inst. 1894, p. 31.

[10] Chan. Inq. p.m. 16 Edw. II, no. 72.
[11] Cal. Inq. p.m. 10-20 Edw. II, 256.
[12] Chan. Inq. p.m. 12 Edw. III (1st nos.), no. 40.
[13] Cal. Pat. 1338-40, p. 24.
[14] Ibid. 312.
[15] Burke, Extinct Peerage.
[16] Cal. Pat. 1377-81, p. 423; 1381-5, pp. 70, 71, 86, 590.
[17] Chan. Inq. p.m. 9 Ric. II, no. 4.
[18] Ibid.
[19] Feet of F. Div. Co. Trin. 10 Ric. II.

[20] Chan. Inq. p.m. 8 Hen. IV, no. 64.
[21] Feet of F. Div. Co. Mich. 5 Hen. V, no. 65.
[22] Ibid. 68.
[23] Feet of F. Div. Co. Mich. 7 Hen. V, no. 3; Jeayes, Lyttelton Chart. no. 287. Sir Hugh Burnell released all his right in these two thirds to Lady Beauchamp (ibid. no. 281, 288).
[24] Chan. Inq. p.m. 8 Hen. V, no. 116.
[25] Early Chan. Proc. bdle. 19, no. 6-8.
[26] Feud. Aids, v, 330.

to Maurice Berkeley as well as 40*s.* out of the manor of Old Swinford.[27]

Lady Beauchamp had previously conveyed the manor to trustees for her grandson James Butler,[28] and probably the settlement took place after her death in 1435, since the trustees appear to have acted alone.[29] Maurice Berkeley died seised of the manor in 1464 and was succeeded by his son and heir William Berkeley,[30] afterwards a knight, who on 7 November 1485 was attainted and forfeited his estates for his adherence to Richard III.[31] On 2 March 1486 Henry VII granted it to his uncle Jasper Tudor, Duke of Bedford, and his heirs male,[32] but ten days later sold it to John Lord Dudley.[33] This curious double dealing naturally led to complications, which were increased when in 1489 Sir William Berkeley was restored and the reversion of the manor after the death of the Duke of Bedford was granted to him.[34] It is not clear who received the issues of the manor, for in 1495 Edward Lord Dudley, who had succeeded his grandfather John Lord Dudley in 1487,[35] stated

BERKELEY. *Gules a cheveron between ten crosses formy argent.*

that he was unaware of the grant to Jasper Tudor,[36] and it could scarcely have remained unknown to him if he received no profits from Northfield. The approaching death of the Duke of Bedford induced both Lord Dudley and Sir William Berkeley in 1495 to present petitions to the king in the furtherance of their individual interests.[37] In reply to these petitions the king in 1495 confirmed the manor to Lord Dudley.[38] In spite of this, on the death of the Duke of Bedford, in December 1495, the king entered into possession of the manor, and on the death of Sir William Berkeley granted all his right in it to Richard Berkeley, son of William, in 1501.[39] Under an Act of 1523 Northfield was confirmed to Lord Dudley,[40] who dealt with it in 1531[41] and sold it at about this time to Richard Jervoise, citizen and mercer of London,[42] 'a man of grete power and having grete substance and a man of grete possessions.'[43] Richard Jervoise did not reside at Northfield,[44] but leased the site of the castle to John Churchman of Northfield[45] and the park to John Statham.[46]

For nearly three hundred years the manor of Northfield was held by the Jervoise family of Herriard and Britford.[47] On the death of Thomas Clarke Jervoise in 1809 it was purchased by Mr. Daniel Ledsam of Edgbaston, Birmingham,[48] with whose descendants it still remained in 1902.

JERVOISE of Herriard. *Sable a cheveron between three eagles close argent.*

The *CASTLE OF WEOLEY* has long since fallen into decay and little now remains of it except part of the south wall. Its site, somewhat difficult of access, is about a mile west of Selly Oak station and close to the northern boundary of the parish. It is surrounded by a large and deep moat fed by a small stream on the west. The Birmingham and Worcester Canal skirts its northern side and is separated from the moat by a narrow strip of land. To the south of the moat is Weoley Castle Farm, into the buildings of which a part of the stone belonging to the castle has been built.[49] The island on which the castle stood is now laid out as the kitchen garden of the farm. The area covered by the castle and moats is said to have been about 4 acres.[50]

Of the origin of Weoley Castle little is known. It is not mentioned in the Domesday Survey, and doubtless its history as a castle dates from the latter half of the 13th century, when in 1264 Roger de Somery had the royal licence to crenellate his manor-house of Weoley.[51]

In 1322 Weoley Castle was assigned with Northfield Manor to Joan Botetourt,[52] but it is not mentioned in the extent of the manor taken at her death in 1338.[53] Weoley Castle descended with the manor of Northfield and was involved with it in the dispute between Maurice Berkeley and Joan Lady Beauchamp. The Berkeleys resided there, Maurice Berkeley being described as of Weoley in 1464–5.[54] His son Sir William Berkeley also made Weoley Castle his home[55] until deprived of it by his attainder. Probably its decay dates from that period because of the uncertainty as to ownership which must have followed the king's various grants (see under Manor). Richard Jervoise apparently never resided there. Some Chancery proceedings of Elizabeth's reign refer to the site

---

[27] Early Chan. Proc. bdle. 19, no. 6–8.
[28] Ibid.
[29] Ibid. James Butler afterwards seized the manor contrary to the award, but Berkeley obtained redress about 1452 (ibid.).
[30] Chan. Inq. p.m. 4 Edw. IV, no. 29.
[31] *Rolls of Parl.* vi, 275–6.
[32] Pat. 1 Hen. VII, pt. ii.
[33] Ibid. pt. iii.
[34] Ibid. 4 Hen. VII, pt. i.
[35] *Cal. Inq. p.m. Hen. VII,* i, 125.
[36] *Rolls of Parl.* vi, 483–4.
[37] Ibid. 483–4, 487.
[38] Stat. 11 Hen. VII, cap. 47; see also cap. 50.
[39] *Rolls of Parl.* vi, 552–4. In 1501 Richard petitioned the king for licence to purchase the manor of Lord Dudley, but never seems to have taken advantage of the permission (ibid.; Stat. 19 Hen. VII, cap. 38).

[40] Stat. 14 & 15 Hen. VIII, cap. 21, proviso 35.
[41] Feet of F. Worcs. Trin. 23 Hen. VIII; Recov. R. East. 23 Hen. VIII, rot. 116.
[42] *L. and P. Hen. VIII,* v, 672; Pearson, in *Trans. Arch. Sect. Birm. and Midl. Inst.* 1896, p. 40.
[43] Star Chamb. Proc. Hen. VIII, bdle. 17, no. 79. In 1536–7 Richard Jervoise was confirmed in his possession of the manor by John son of Richard Berkeley (Close, 28 Hen. VIII, pt. ii, no. 18).
[44] See Star Chamb. Proc. Hen. VIII, bdle. 23, no. 78.
[45] In 1577 John Churchman and Margaret his wife conveyed or claimed to convey the manor of Northfield and Weoley to Richard Middlemore (Feet of F. Div. Co. Trin. 19 Eliz.).
[46] Star Chamb. Proc. Hen. VIII, bdle.

[17], no. 79; Chan. Proc. (Ser. 2), bdle. 104, no. 54; bdle. 158, no. 24.
[47] Chan. Inq. p.m. (Ser. 2), ccxviii, 50; Recov. R. Mich. 9 Jas. I, rot. 119; Feet of F. Div. Co. East. 13 Chas. I; Trin. 22 Chas. I; Worcs. Hil. 24 Chas. I; Div. Co. Mich. 1657; Recov. R. Hil. 1657, rot. 23; East. 29 Geo. III, rot. 196. A pedigree of this family is given in *Trans. Arch. Sect. Birm. and Midl. Inst.* 1896, p. 40.
[48] Pearson, in *Trans. Arch. Sect. Birm. and Midl. Inst.* 1902, p. 57.
[49] Ibid.
[50] Ibid. 58.
[51] *Cal. Pat.* 1258–66, p. 307.
[52] *Cal. Inq. p.m.* 10–20 *Edw. II,* 256.
[53] Chan. Inq. p.m. 12 Edw. III (1st nos.), no. 40.
[54] Ibid. 4 Edw. IV, no. 29.
[55] *Reg. of the Guild of Knowle,* 65.

of the castle[56] as if it had passed out of use as a residence.

It was probably in ruins by the middle of the 17th century, as Habington mentions no castle as being then in existence, and in draft particulars for a contemplated sale dated at about that time it is described as 'a ruyned castell.'[57]

In a survey of 1432-3 it is described as 'the Castell of Weoley with a water called the mote compassing the 1st Castell, in which is a great halle with a great chambre in the upper ende, . . . a Chapell set by hitselfe in the north part of the Castell covered wit lead, and a vestre adjoining the same Chapell, . . . vi turrets of stone whereof the gate at the entre of the sd Castell is one with 6 chambres and chymies in the same.'[58]

A deer park was in existence at Weoley as early as 1273.[59] In 1275-6 Sir Roger de Somery was said to have inclosed within it 40 acres of the common pasture.[60] The park appears to have been well stocked at that time, for in August 1273 the king sent John son of John to take venison in the park and to cause it to be salted and kept in barrels in a safe place until further orders,[61] and in the following year the keeper of the park was ordered to allow Robert Tiptot to have twenty does.[62] In 1291, however, it was stated that there were no deer in Weoley Park.[63] In 1386 it was returned that the pasture of the park was worth 20s. yearly beyond the sustenance of the animals there.[64] In 1425 William Lovecock was presented for shooting arrows at the lady's wild deer in the park and having his greyhound continually running there without licence, while John and Thomas Preston of Harborne chased hares, martens and 'fysshers' or polecats in the park.[65] When Richard Jervoise purchased the manor of Northfield there were about 100 deer in the park, but in a few years George Walsh, his bailiff, decreased their number to twenty.[66] The park is not mentioned after this time.

In the reign of Henry VI there are said to have been eight beer-tasters within the manor.[67] About the same time many of the manorial offices, such as constable, beadle and reeve, were held by women; thus in 1444 Margery Vytteshalle, widow, was elected reeve and Elizabeth Thicknesse constable, the latter appointing a male deputy.[68]

Two water-mills and a fishery were held with the manor in 1272-3 and 1338,[69] while in 1368 there were three mills worth 30s., a fishery worth 20s. at Weoley and two fishponds worth 6s. 8d.[70] One water corn-mill was sold with the manor to Richard Jervoise,[71] and still formed part of it in 1789.[72]

Two entries occur in Domesday Book respecting 'Escelie'; both may refer to SELLY OAK (Selleie, xii cent.; Selley,[73] xiii cent.), although it is also possible that one may be identifiable with the later Weoley, which is not otherwise mentioned in the Survey. Both 'Escelies' were held by William Fitz Ansculf. The larger and more valuable of the two contained 4 hides, and to it belonged the berewick of Bartley Green.[74] It was held under Fitz Anscuf by Wibert, who had succeeded one Wulfwine, by whom it had been bought for three lives from the Bishop of Chester. Although Wulfwine's last wish was that when his wife died the manor should return to the church from which he had it, and his son, the Bishop of Lichfield, knew of this wish, to which the chief men of the whole county could testify,[75] his desire remained unfulfilled, and once it had passed into the hands of the Norman lord of Dudley it remained in his possession and descended with his lands. The other 'Escelie' contained 1 hide, and had been held by Tumi and Eleva as two manors; from them it had passed to Robert, the Domesday under-tenant.[76]

Only one Selly, held of the manor of Northfield,[77] is afterwards mentioned. Although from 1086 until the middle of the 13th century there is no definite evidence to show who held Selly, its subsequent history shows that for a considerable part of that time it was held by a family who sometimes bore the name of Selly and sometimes that of Barnack, from the parish of that name in Northamptonshire, where they also held land. In 1166 Gervase de Barnack was one of the knights of Gervase Paynel.[78]

In 1231 Richard son of Gervase de Barnack made an agreement with the Abbot of Peterborough concerning a certain rent in Barnack,[79] and possibly he was the Richard de Selly who was one of the collectors in Worcestershire of the aid for the marriage of Isabella sister of Henry III.[80] Richard was succeeded by his son Peter, who in 1254 received a grant of free warren in his demesne lands of Selly and Barnack,[81] and was followed by Richard Selly, probably his son, who paid 20s. for his lands in 1280.[82] In 1274-5 it was presented that Richard Selly had made a warren at Selly, and that he was of full age, but not yet knighted.[83] A few years later Richard died, leaving a son John, a minor.[84] In 1291 John de Selly held half a knight's fee in Selly,[85] and in 1319-20 had been succeeded by his son Geoffrey,[86] who was accused in 1328 of having broken into the houses of Thomas de Blaunfront at Alvechurch,[87] and in 1331 aided in besieging the castle of Dudley.[88] He did not lose prestige by these

[56] Chan. Proc. (Ser. 2), bdle. 104, no. 54.

[57] Pearson, in Trans. Arch. Sect. Birm. and Midl. Inst. 1902, pp. 59, 60.

[58] Ibid. pp. 58-9.

[59] Worcs. Inq. p.m. (Worcs. Hist. Soc.), pt. i, 17.

[60] Hund. R. (Rec. Com.), ii, 284.

[61] Cal. Close, 1272-9, p. 30.

[62] Ibid. 137.

[63] Worcs. Inq. p.m. (Worcs. Hist. Soc.), pt. i, 36.

[64] Chan. Inq. p.m. 9 Ric. II, no. 4.

[65] Pearson, in Trans. Arch. Sect. Birm. and Midl. Inst. 1894, p. 41.

[66] Star Chamb. Proc. Hen. VIII, bdle. 23, no. 78.

[67] Pearson, in Trans. Arch. Sect. Birm. and Midl. Inst. 1894, p. 39.

[68] Ibid.

[69] Worcs. Inq. p.m. (Worcs. Hist. Soc.), pt. i, 16-17; Chan. Inq. p.m. 12 Edw. III (1st nos.), no. 40.

[70] Chan. Inq. p.m. 9 Ric. II, no. 4.

[71] Star Chamb. Proc. Hen. VIII, bdle. 17, no. 79.

[72] Recov. R. East. 29 Geo. III, rot. 196.

[73] Shelley occurs in 1546 (Chan. Inq. p.m. [Ser. 2], lxxv, 94).

[74] V.C.H. Worcs. i, 315b.

[75] Ibid. 316a. The reading of the words 'ep'o Li' as Bishop of Lichfield is only a rather remote possibility. See V.C.H. Worcs. i, 316, note 1.

[76] Ibid. 316b.

[77] Cal. Inq. p.m. 1-19 Edw. I, 495; 10-20 Edw. II, 257; Chan. Inq. p.m. (Ser. 2), lxxv, 94.

[78] Red Bk. of Exch. (Rolls Ser.), 269.

[79] Liber Swapham (Cartul. of Peterborough in custody of D. and C. of Peterborough), fol. 194b.

[80] Testa de Nevill (Rec. Com.), 41, 44. A Richard de Sulley occurs in 1221 (Select Pleas of the Crown [Selden Soc.], i, 87).

[81] Cal. Pat. 1247-58, p. 274. A Peter de Selle occurs in the Testa de Nevill (Rec. Com.), 46, as holding in Himley, Staffs.

[82] Lay Subs. R. 1280 (Worcs. Hist. Soc.), 17. [83] Assize R. 1026, m. 44 d

[84] Anct. D. (P.R.O.), A 4793.

[85] Cal. Inq. p.m. 1-19 Edw. I, 495.

[86] Feet of F. Worcs. 13 Edw. II, no. 4.

[87] Cal. Pat. 1327-30, p. 279.

[88] Ibid. 1330-4, p. 126.

Northfield Church :· The North Door

misdeeds, however, for in 1338–9 the king committed to him, under the name of Geoffrey de Barnack, jointly with Roger de Aylesbury, the custody of John Botetourt.[89]

After this the descent of Selly for some years is obscure. A Geoffrey de Selly and his son John were living in Northfield in 1362–3.[90] According to the Visitation of Surrey,[91] Geoffrey de Barnack was succeeded by his son John, who left a daughter and co-heir Joan, the wife of Thomas Vincent. The manor of Barnack certainly passed to the Vincent family,[92] but Selly followed a different descent. In 1402–3 a third part of it was in the hands of Henry Prest and his wife Joan, as the right of Joan, who then conveyed it to Henry Wybbe.[93] In 1482 the whole manor was in the hands of Thomas Jennett, who according to the Visitation of Worcester of 1569 married Alice the sister of Henry Wybbe,[94] and probably acquired the manor of Selly in this way. Thomas Jennett died in 1482, leaving a son William, who had been an idiot since his birth, but who nevertheless entered into possession of the manor,[95] and jointly with Agneta or Anne his wife dealt with land there in 1502.[96]

In 1508 William Jennett and Anne conveyed the manor to Sir Robert Throckmorton, Richard Throckmorton and Henry Durant.[97] In 1520 it had passed to William Gower and his wife Agnes.[98] William was succeeded in 1546 by a son Henry.[99] From Henry Gower the manor descended to his son William, whose son John appears to have been in possession in 1597.[100] John Gower was apparently succeeded before 1601 by his brother Robert,[1] and the manor evidently followed the same descent as Colmers in King's Norton (q.v.) from that time until 1719–20, when half the farm called Selly Hall was settled on William Gower of Colmers in King's Norton for life with reversion to John Gower.[2]

GOWER. *Azure a cheveron between three wolves' heads razed or.*

There are no later documents relating to this manor, which is not mentioned as such by Nash, and had probably before that time (1782) become merged in the manor of Northfield, as Mr. J. F. Ledsam was said to be lord of Selly Oak about the middle of the 19th century.

In 1835 Selly Park Farm was advertised for sale.[3]

The old manor-house at Selly had been converted into three cottages before 1896.[4]

It is probable that the manor of *MIDDLETON* (Middeltune, xii cent.) originally formed part of that of Northfield, of which it has always been held.[5] During the latter half of the 12th century Ralph Paynel gave 'the land of Middletune and lahaie,' the latter being probably the modern Hay Green, to Bernard Paynel.[6] Bernard was probably the Bernard son of William Paynel who occurs about 1187.[7] Between that date and 1194, when Gervase Paynel died, Bernard received from Gervase a confirmatory grant of Middleton and 'lahaie.'[8]

It is not clear how or when Middleton passed away from Bernard Paynel, but towards the end of the 13th century it was held by a family taking their name from the place. A John de Middleton occurs in 1273,[9] and in 1291 held the township of Middleton.[10] The Middleton family held the manor for a considerable time, but, as several members bore the name of John, it is not easy to distinguish one generation from another. John de Middleton occurs in 1298[11] and in 1310.[12] In 1315 John son of Philip de Tessall granted to John de Middleton and his heirs a rent of 20d. from land in Northfield.[13] In 1322 John de Middleton held a quarter of a knight's fee in Northfield.[14]

The manor of Middleton was settled in 1325–6 on John de Middleton for his life, with remainders to his sons Adam, Thomas and John.[15] Adam de Middleton probably, therefore, succeeded his father, and was followed in turn by his son Richard. The latter made a grant of land in Middleton in 1366,[16] and ten years later the 'manor of Middleton and Le Hay' was settled on him and his wife Margery.[17] Margery survived her husband, and afterwards married one William Ockam or Hoccam.[18] Richard Middleton had left no son, and Middleton was claimed by four co-heirs, apparently daughters of Richard,[19] Alice wife of Gerard Kyngeley, Joyce Pepwall, Alice wife of William Merston and Margaret wife of John Mollesley.[20] Margaret Ockam probably held the manor while she lived, under the settlement mentioned above, and when she died, about 1435, William Ockam prepared to sell it.[21] The co-heirs intervened, stating that the manor had descended to them as the heirs of Adam Middleton on Richard Middleton's death.[22] In exchange for a surrender by William Ockam of all his claim in the manor the co-heirs granted it to him for his life at a yearly rent of 6 marks.[23] Possibly Ockam died a few years later, as on 25 April 1443 one John Merston did homage

[89] *Abbrev. Rot. Orig.* (Rec. Com.), ii, 123.
[90] De Banco R. 411, m. 143 d.
[91] *Harl. Soc. Publ.* xliii, 55.
[92] See *V.C.H. Northants,* ii, 464.
[93] Feet of F. Worcs. 4 Hen. IV, no. 6.
[94] *Harl. Soc. Publ.* xxvii, 9.
[95] Chan. Inq. p.m. (Ser. 2), xix, 79. The visitation mentioned above does not agree with this inquisition.
[96] Add. Chart. 15268.
[97] De Banco R. 984, m. 116 d.
[98] Add. Chart. 15270. Gower had held land in Selly in 1506 (ibid. 15269).
[99] Chan. Inq. p.m. (Ser. 2), lxxv, 94.
[100] Feet of F. Worcs. Mich. 33 & 34 Eliz.; *Visit. of Worcs.* 1569 (Harl. Soc. xxvii), 61; Feet of F. Worcs. Mich. 39 & 40 Eliz.

[1] Feet of F. Worcs. Mich. 43 & 44 Eliz. ; *Visit. of Worcs.* 1569 (Harl. Soc. xxvii), 61; Recov. R. D. Enr. East. 44 Eliz. m. 20.
[2] Ibid. Mich. 6 Geo. I, m. 11.
[3] Extract from a local newspaper in the Prattinton Coll.
[4] Pearson, in *Trans. Arch. Sect. Birm. and Midl. Inst.* 1896, p. 43.
[5] *Cal. Inq. p.m.* 1–19 *Edw. I,* 495 ; Chan. Inq. p.m. 16 Edw. II, no. 72.
[6] Prattinton Coll. (Soc. Antiq.), from Rev. Denham Cookes' Evidences, 1813, no. 1.
[7] Dugdale, *Mon. Angl.* v, 203–4.
[8] Prattinton Coll. (Soc. Antiq.), from Rev. Denham Cookes' Evidences, 1813, no. 1.
[9] *Worcs. Inq. p.m.* (Worcs. Hist. Soc.), pt. i, 16.

[10] Ibid. 37.
[11] Ibid. 58.
[12] Prattinton Coll. (Soc. Antiq.), from Rev. Denham Cookes' Evidences, 1813, no. 2.
[13] Ibid. no. 3.
[14] Chan. Inq. p.m. 16 Edw. II, no. 72.
[15] Feet of F. Worcs. 19 Edw. II, no. 22.
[16] Prattinton Coll. (Soc. Antiq.), from Rev. Denham Cookes' Evidences, 1813, no. 5.
[17] Ibid. no. 6.
[18] Ibid. no. 11.
[19] Ibid. no. 12.
[20] Ibid. no. 10.
[21] Prattinton Coll. (Soc. Antiq.), from John Phillips' Evidences, 1814, no. 19.
[22] Ibid. from Rev. Denham Cookes' Evidences, no. 10.
[23] Ibid. 1813, no. 10, 11.

to the lord of Northfield and Weoley for a moiety of the manor of Middleton, and for the other moiety was summoned with Gerard Kyngeley and John Mollesley also to do homage.[24]

John Merston is described as a goldsmith of London.[25] It is not clear how he came to hold a share in the manor. He had some interest in it as early as 1437–8, when he joined with Richard Middleton's co-heirs in resisting William Ockam's claims.[25a] He could not have inherited Alice Merston's share, as she was still living in January 1456, when she 'in her pure widowhood' was holding land in Northfield,[26] and in April of the same year John Merston settled the manor on himself and his heirs.[27]

William Merston, son of Alice, dealt with lands there in 1473, and in 1477 with the whole manor of Middleton.[28] John Merston also held or claimed the whole manor several times during the same period,[29] and though in 1457 he executed a deed of sale of

the co-heirs, and that John and William Merston, though nominally dealing with the whole manor, in reality only held parts of it.

Middleton is next mentioned in 1522, when Elizabeth Edwards of Stratford-on-Avon leased her manor place there to Henry Morgan and his wife Agnes for sixty-one years.[32] Elizabeth was possibly the widow of John Edwards, and Agnes was probably his daughter.[33] A deed of 1526, by which Thomas Greville and his wife Elizabeth, who was perhaps the Elizabeth Edwards mentioned above, conveyed the manor of Middleton to Henry Morgan and Agnes,[34] may have been in confirmation of their lease. In 1538 the manor was settled on Thomas and Elizabeth Greville for their lives, with remainders to Henry and Agnes Morgan, and to their sons Edward and William.[35] Edward Morgan afterwards held Middleton, and about 1596 his son Edward is said to have granted a lease of all his lands in Worcestershire to Henry and William Cookes for 3,000 years.[36] In the same year the reversion of two-thirds of the manor was settled on Henry Cookes and his son William, and of the other third on Richard Vernon, the manor being then held for life by Edward Morgan, jun., and his wife Margaret.[37]

On 30 September 1598 the lease made in 1596 by Edward Morgan, jun., was cancelled and destroyed,[38] and apparently a new conveyance was made by which the manor of Middleton passed to the possession of Henry Cookes of Shiltwood in Tardebigge.[39] William Cookes, son of this Henry, died seised of the manor in 1619, leaving a son Edward,[40]

NORTHFIELD CHURCH : WINDOWS IN NORTH WALL OF THE CHANCEL

the manor to Thomas Morgan, in 1466 it was again in the hands of his trustees.[30] In 1471 Alice, formerly wife of Gerard Kyngeley, granted to John Russell for seventy-nine years certain land near the site of the manor of Middleton.[31] It would appear, therefore, that the manor had been divided among

on whose death in 1637 it passed to his son William.[40a] William succeeded his uncle Thomas in the manor of Bentley Pauncefoot, and the descent of Middleton is identical with that of Bentley Pauncefoot until about 1813.[41] The manorial rights of Middleton seem now to have lapsed, but the

[24] Pearson, in *Trans. Arch. Sect. Birm. and Midl. Inst.* 1894, pp. 32–3.

[25] Prattinton Coll. (Soc. Antiq.), from Rev. Denham Cookes' Evidences, 1813, no. 7.

[25a] Ibid. John Phillips' Evidences, 1814, no. 8.

[26] Ibid. Rev. Denham Cookes' Evidences, 1813, no. 12.

[27] Ibid. no. 7.

[28] Ibid. no. 14, 17.

[29] Ibid. no. 9 ; John Phillips' Evidences, 1814, no. 7, 21.

[30] Ibid. John Phillips' Evidences, 1814, no. 21, 7.

[31] Ibid. no. 13.

[33] *Visit. of Worcs.* 1569 (Harl. Soc. xxvii), 97.

[34] Feet of F. Worcs. Mich. 18 Hen. VIII.

[35] Prattinton Coll. (Soc. Antiq.), from John Phillips' Evidences, 1814, no. 5. In 1545 Rose Clayton was dealing with half the manor of Middleton (Recov. R. East. 37 Hen. VIII, rot. 123).

[36] Prattinton Coll. (Soc. Antiq.), John Phillips' Evidences, 1814, no. 43.

[37] Feet of F. Worcs. Trin. 38 Eliz. ; Chan. Inq. p.m. (Ser. 2), ccclxxxi, 161.

[38] Prattinton Coll. (Soc. Antiq.), John Phillips' Evidences, 1814, no. 43.

[32] Ibid. no. 6.

[39] Ibid. In the Prattinton Collection occurs a 'Scedull, Inventory or Roule of Deeds, &c., delivered by Edward Morgan the father and Edward Morgan the son concerning their lands in Worcester to the hands custody and possession of Henry Cookes.'

[40] Chan. Inq. p.m. (Ser. 2), ccclxxxi, 161 ; Metcalfe, *Visit. of Worcs.* 1682–3, p. 36.

[40a] G.E.C. *Complete Baronetage*, iii, 301.

[41] Recov. R. East. 17 Geo. II, rot. 324; Feet of F. Div. Co. Hil. 29 Geo. III ; Prattinton Coll. (Soc. Antiq.), from Rev. Denham Cookes' Evidences.

name survives at Middletonhall Farm, near the King's Norton boundary.

The church of *ST. LAWRENCE CHURCH* consists of a chancel 35½ ft. by 20½ ft., nave 51½ ft. by 23 ft., north and south aisles, south porch, and west tower 15½ ft. by 15 ft. These measurements are all internal. The earliest part of the existing building is the north doorway, of about 1170, which, with two carved heads, inserted in the south face of the tower, formed part of a 12th-century church.

Of the building which succeeded this there are ample remains in the complete 13th-century chancel, the south aisle added at the end of that century and the lower stage of the tower. In the 15th century the upper portion of the tower was rebuilt and at some later date the south arcade of the nave, perhaps owing to the failure of the walls. The north aisle with its arcade is a modern addition.

The east window of the chancel consists of three grouped lancets, with moulded heads and shafted jambs, inclosed by an outer arch having shafted jambs and a moulded label. In the north wall are three groups of three lancets, each lancet having shafts to the jambs, with moulded capitals and arches, and outside these a blank half-arch. Each group is inclosed under a segmental pointed arch springing from circular shafts. In the south wall are two similar sets of lancets, and a third containing a lancet light without shafts. The north aisle of the nave, with the arcade of four bays, is modern work in the style of the 14th century. The south arcade has also four bays, with octagonal columns, all of poor design.

The round-headed north door dates from about 1170 and has been reset in the modern aisle wall. The inner of the two orders has cheveron ornament and the outer a row of beak-heads. The jamb shafts are masked by cheveron work. The south aisle dates from late in the 13th century. The east window has three lights with intersecting mullions in the head, and in the south wall are three windows, and one at the west end, of similar type but of two lights each. At the south-east is a contemporary trefoiled piscina, grooved for a shelf. The south door is pointed with large crowned half-figure stops to the moulded label.

The porch is of good 15th-century woodwork on a stone base. The sides are panelled, the wall-plates embattled, and the roof has a braced tie-beam with moulded collars and wind-braces. On the wall above the doorway are traces of the position of a previous porch.

The tower arch is of three orders, springing from chamfered abaci, continued on as a moulded string-course. The first and part of the second stage of the tower are of 13th-century date, though the greater part of the west wall has been rebuilt. In the north and south walls are two-light windows, with a stair at the south-east angle and a west door. In the south wall is a wide-arched doorway now blocked. The internal fittings of the church are modern, with the exception of some 15th-century carved woodwork, from a screen, re-used in the pulpit, and a bench end. On the south chancel wall is a monument to John Hinckley, rector, 1660–95, and his two wives, and on the opposite wall another to Isabella wife of Stanford Wolferstan, minister of Wootton Wawen.

On the exterior there are traces of a building against the south chancel wall, opening from the south aisle by an arch, of which the northern springing remains. There are also traces of the bonding of the eastern wall; and, as this chamber must have been contemporary with the chancel, it proves the existence of an earlier south aisle, which, at the end of the 13th century, was replaced by the present one. The south chancel door has a flattened trefoiled head with the moulding continued on the jambs. The roofs are of steep pitch and covered externally with tiles.

The exterior of the tower is in three stages, the upper of grey, the lower two of red sandstone. On each side of the west door is a niche, about 6 ft. high, with a pointed head. In the second stage on the north

NORTHFIELD CHURCH : THE WEST TOWER

and south faces are plain lights with carved animal heads, apparently of the 12th century, inserted on either side. The upper stage has two-light belfry windows and an embattled parapet, on the west side of which a diminutive portcullis is cut in relief.

In the north chancel wall, below the third group of lancets, is a low-side window with a square external head, and in the south wall the corresponding lancet with a low sill would seem to have communicated with the chamber which stood on that side.

There is a ring of six bells, by Joseph Smith of Edgbaston, dated 1730. The inscriptions are famous as giving the history of the negotiations for the casting, as follows : (1) 'We now are six tho' once but five'; (2) 'and against our casting some did strive'; (3) 'but when a day for meeting there was fixt'; (4) 'apeared but nine against twenty six,' and so on.

The plate includes an old cup and cover for paten of later Elizabethan work, also a flagon and salver on feet, the gift of the Rev. H. Soley, a former rector, and a handsome modern silver-gilt cup with jewelled stem and a paten to match presented in memory of the Rev. H. Clarke.

The registers before 1812 are as follows : (i) all entries 1560 to 1654 ; (ii) baptisms 1654 to 1741, burials 1654 to 1678, marriages 1654 to 1741 ; (iii) burials 1678 to 1757; (iv) baptisms 1742 to 1758, marriages 1742 to 1754 ; (v) marriages 1754 to 1812 ; (vi) baptisms and burials 1758 to 1809 ; (vii) baptisms and burials 1810 to 1812.

ADVOWSON   The church of Northfield was granted to the priory of Dudley by Gervase Paynel when he founded the house about 1160,[42] and from that time until the Dissolution was held by the prior and convent,[43] who reserved to themselves a pension from it.[44] In 1294 a dispute arose between Bishop Giffard and the priory respecting the church[45] ; it is not clear what was the cause, but it seems probable that the bishop had infringed the right of the convent in the presentation. Again in 1342 the Prior and monks of Dudley were required by the Bishop of Worcester to show their right to receive a pension from Northfield Church.[46]

When the priory was dissolved, its rights in the church became vested in the Crown, and on 26 March 1541 Henry VIII granted to Sir John Dudley, afterwards Duke of Northumberland, a pension of 6s. 8d. issuing from it with all other possessions of the priory in Northfield,[47] this grant apparently including the advowson. When Northumberland was attainted and executed in 1553 his property came into the hands of the Crown. In 1554 the tithes of Northfield were granted to Edward Sutton Lord Dudley,[48] who seems to have also held the advowson, which was dealt with by his trustees in 1578–9 and in 1579–80.[49] In 1587 the queen presented to the living.[50] In 1595, however, Edward Sutton, the next Lord Dudley, conveyed the advowson with the yearly rent issuing from the rectory to Richard Hammett.[51] On 14 November 1608 Richard and Edward Hammett received from the Crown a grant of a yearly rent of £4 from the rectory and church.[52] In 1611 the reversion of the tithes of Northfield, after the expiry of the estate of Edward Lord Dudley, was granted to George Baggeley of Dudley, yeoman.[53]

On 11 July 1615 the advowson of Northfield was granted by the king to Sir Charles Montagu and Edward Sawyer of London, gentleman.[54] It had passed before 1621 to Edward Skinner, who died seised of it in 1631, leaving a son and heir Richard,[55] but in 1639 one Phineas White of the city of Coventry is said to have presented to the living by the grant of Thomas Jervoise of Herriard, then lord of the manor.[56] Jervoise himself presented in 1660, but in 1661 and 1663 the king is said to have presented, in the first case 'to corroborate title.'[57] In 1671 the advowson was dealt with by Edward Lord Ward of Birmingham,[58] the successor of Lord Dudley, but from 1695 until 1799 the presentations were made by the Jervoise family.[59] After that date Jervoise Clarke Jervoise seems to have sold the advowson to George Fenwick of Sunderland, who presented in 1805,[60] and in whose family it remained at any rate until 1877.[61] In the following year the advowson passed to Stephen Barker,[62] who sold or gave it in 1887–8 to Keble College, Oxford, the present patron.[63]

Selly Oak was constituted a separate ecclesiastical parish in 1862.[64] The living is a vicarage, in the gift of the Bishop of Birmingham and trustees. The church of St. Mary, consecrated in 1861, is a building in 14th-century style, consisting of chancel, nave, transepts and tower with spire.

Selly Hill, now a separate ecclesiastical parish, was formed in 1892 from Northfield.[65] The vicarage is in the gift of trustees. The church of St. Stephen, consecrated in 1871, consists of chancel, nave, vestry, organ chamber and tower with spire.

St. Michael's, Bartley Green, is a chapel of ease to Northfield Church, and there is a small mission chapel at West Heath. The mission church of St. Wulstan is a chapel of ease to St. Mary, Selly Oak.

There are Wesleyan chapels at Northfield and California and at Selly Oak, Primitive Methodist chapels at Woodgate and Selly Oak, a Friends' meeting-house and other Nonconformist places of worship at Selly Oak, and a Roman Catholic chapel under the invocation of St. Edward the Confessor at Selly Oak.

CHARITIES   The Educational Charities, founded by the wills of Dr. William Worth, archdeacon of Worcester and rector of this parish, dated in 1742, and of the Rev. Thomas Lockey Soley, proved in 1779, and of Thomas Lloyd, are represented by £433 6s. 8d. consols with the official trustees. The annual dividends, amounting to £11 18s. 4d., are carried to the credit of the North-field schools.

Eleemosynary Charities.— In 1662 John Norton — as stated in the table of benefactions — by deed charged his lands called Portlands with an annuity of 24s. for the poor. From the same table it appears that John Field charged an estate called Good-rest Farm with 40s. a year for the poor ; also that Henry Hinkley, by his will, gave eight half-crowns for eight poor people and 8s. to provide them with a dinner on 25 May yearly, if on a Sunday, or on the next Sunday after, to be paid out of an estate called Nether Holbach. The Parliamentary Returns of 1786 mention that Thomas Lloyd gave 2s. 6d. for the poor, and that William Squire, by his will, gave 20s. a year

---

[42] Dugdale, *Mon. Angl.* v, 83.

[43] *Reg. G. Giffard* (Worcs. Hist. Soc.), 65, 494 ; *Cal. Pat.* 1345–8, p. 144.

[44] Of 6 marks in 1291 (*Pope Nich. Tax.* [Rec. Com.], 217b), and in 1342 (Worc. Epis. Reg. Bransford, bk. i [3], fol. 56), but 46s. in 1535 (*Valor Eccl.* [Rec. Com.], iii, 104).

[45] *Reg. G. Giffard* (Worcs. Hist. Soc.), 441.

[46] Worc. Epis. Reg. Bransford, bk. i (3), fol. 56 ; see also *Sede Vacante Reg.* (Worcs. Hist. Soc.), 271.

[47] Pat. 32 Hen. VIII, pt. vi, m. 7 ; *L. and P. Hen. VIII*, xvi, g. 678 (47).

[48] Pat. 1 & 2 Phil. and Mary, pt. ii.

[49] Ibid. 21 Eliz. pt. vi ; Feet of F. Div. Co. Hil. 22 Eliz.

[50] Nash, *Hist. of Worcs.* ii, 192.

[51] Feet of F. Worcs. Mich. 37 & 38 Eliz.

[52] Pat. 6 Jas. I, pt. xxiii, no. 14.

[53] Ibid. 8 Jas. I, pt. xlii, no. 10.

[54] Ibid. 13 Jas. I, pt. xv, no. 9.

[55] Chan. Inq. p.m. (Ser. 2), ccclxxxii, 116.

[56] Nash, op. cit. ii, 192 ; Inst. Bks. (P.R.O.).

[57] Ibid.

[58] Feet of F. Div. Co. Mich. 23 Chas. II.

[59] See Nash, op. cit. ii, 192 ; Inst. Bks. (P.R.O.).   [60] Inst. Bks. (P.R.O.).

[61] *Trans. Arch. Sect. Birm. and Midl. Inst.* 1877, p. 4.

[62] Kelly, *Dir. of Birmingham*, 1878.

[63] *Clergy Lists.*

[64] *Lond. Gaz.* 10 June 1862, p. 2969.

[65] *Census of Engl. and Wales, Worc.* 1901, p. 7.

NORTHFIELD CHURCH : THE CHANCEL

PEDMORE CHURCH : TYMPANUM

for the poor of this parish (see under Droitwich St. Nicholas).

The official trustees also hold a sum of £12 7s. 6d. consols in respect of — Middlemore's charity, producing 6s. 8d. a year.

The income of these charities, amounting together to £6 1s. 2d., is applied as to £1 10s. 3d. among ten poor widows of Northfield, the same amount to ten poor widows of Bartley Green, and the remainder among the poor of Bournbrook, Selly Oak and Ten Acres.

PEDMORE

Pevemore (xi cent.); Pebmore, Pebbmer (xiii cent.).

The parish of Pedmore is situated in the northwest of the county adjoining Stourbridge. It comprises an area of 1,510 acres. The general slope of the land is from east to west, the greatest height being attained at Wychbury Hill, in the south-east of the parish. It forms the north-western end of the Clent Hills, and is 600 ft. above the ordnance datum. There is here a large earthwork on this hill where two bronze rings have been found. The western boundary varies in height from about 300 ft. in the north to 400 ft. in the south.

The subsoil is Keuper sandstone; the surface soil is light and suitable for the production of turnips, swedes, mangolds and barley. The stone with which Old Swinford Church was built was obtained from quarries at Pedmore. In 1905 the parish comprised 752 acres of arable land and 607 acres of permanent grass.[1] In 1300 part of the parish of Pedmore was included in the forest of Kinver,[2] but at the present day there are only 7½ acres of woodland.

Pedmore Hall stands on a small hill about a quarter of a mile east of the main road between Bromsgrove and Stourbridge and to the east of the church. It faces the west and is approached through an avenue of limes. Though the centre part of the present building was erected in 1670,[3] the house is now of little interest, having undergone considerable alteration in the 18th century. It is three stories high and stands on a basement. The front has been stuccoed and the windows modernized. Of the 17th-century fittings the staircase only remains. It is at the back of the house. The handrail and strings are moulded and the balustrade between is composed of one open panel to each flight following the rake of the stair.

Pedmore Common, in the north-west of the parish, and close to the road from Kidderminster to Stourbridge, is surrounded by a race-course.

Sixteenth-century place-names which occur in deeds relating to Pedmore are the Hides, Grymsmere Inneye, Olerne Coppice, Gostier,[4] Nednell or Knednell, and Foxcote.[5]

MANOR The manor of *PEDMORE* was held by Turgar in the time of Edward the Confessor. It appears in the Domesday Survey as one of the possessions of William Fitz Ansculf, of whom it was held by Acard.[6]

The overlordship descended with the manor of Northfield[7] (q.v.), being mentioned for the last time in 1547.[8] Early in the 13th century Geoffrey de Piringham[9] paid 20d. for three parts of a fee which he held of the barony of Dudley.[10] Geoffrey was probably descended from Giffard de Tiringham, who held three fees under Gervase Paynel in 1166.[11] This Giffard died about 1189, and occurs as Giffard 'de Pebmore' in a deed of 1179–89.[12]

Geoffrey de Piringham was probably succeeded by Philip de Pedmore, whose name occurs as a witness to an inspeximus charter of the borough of Halesowen in the latter part of the reign of Henry III,[13] and again in a grant of somewhat later date in which he is termed 'Philip lord of Pedmore.'[14] He paid a subsidy of 10s. for his land in Pedmore in 1280,[15] but he seems to have died before 1292, when 'the lady of Pebmore,' probably his widow, held the manor.[16]

In 1296–7 John son of John son of Philip jointly with Sarah his wife conveyed the reversion of the manor after Sarah's death to William de Simplingford.[17] William presented to the church in 1304,[18] and was said to be in possession of the manor in 1322,[19] but Sarah was still holding it in 1323.[20]

In 1339–40 John de Simplingford sold the manor to Walter Clodshall and his son Richard.[21] Richard Clodshall presented to the church of Pedmore in 1349, 1361 and 1401,[22] and appears to have been still alive in 1424–5.[23] By the marriage of his daughter Elizabeth with Robert Arderne of Park Hall[24] co. Warw. the manor of Pedmore passed to the Ardernes. After the death of Elizabeth, Robert Arderne held it by courtesy, but, having sided with the Yorkists, he

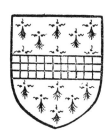

ARDERNE of Park Hall. *Ermine a fesse checky or and azure.*

[1] Statistics from Bd. of Agric. (1905).

[2] Nash, *Hist. of Worcs.* Introd. 68 n.

[3] See note in parochial register. It is here stated that the house was built by Mr. Samuel Wright, who at the same time planted 40 acres of orchard.

[4] Ct. of Req. bdle. 72, no. 48.

[5] Misc. Bks. Ld. Rev. ccxxviii, fol. 284 d.

[6] *V.C.H. Worcs.* i, 317. There were two messuages at Worcester appurtenant to the manor of Pedmore.

[7] *Worcs. Inq. p.m.* (Worcs. Hist. Soc.), i, 37; Chan. Inq. p.m. 16 Edw. II, no.

72; *Testa de Nevill* (Rec. Com.), 40b; Exch. Inq. p.m. (Ser. 2), file 1183, no. 7.

[8] Chan. Inq. p.m. (Ser. 2), lxxxv, 75.

[9] This name should probably be read as Tiringham.

[10] *Testa de Nevill* (Rec. Com.), 40b.

[11] *Red Bk. of Exch.* (Rolls Ser.), 269.

[12] *Will. Salt Arch. Soc. Coll.* iii, 218.

[13] Jeayes, *Lyttelton Chart.* no. 27.

[14] Ibid. no. 45.

[15] *Lay Subs. R. Worcs.* 1280 (Worcs. Hist. Soc.), 10.

[16] *Cal. Inq. p.m. 1–19 Edw. I,* 495.

[17] Feet of F. Worcs. 25 Edw. I, no. 7.

[18] Nash, op. cit. ii, 240.

[19] Chan. Inq. p.m. 16 Edw. II, no. 72.

[20] *Cal. Close,* 1318–23, p. 631.

[21] Feet of F. Worcs. 13 Edw. III, no. 34.

[22] *Sede Vacante Reg.* (Worcs. Hist. Soc.), 378; Nash, op. cit. ii, 240.

[23] Chan. Inq. p.m. 3 Hen. VI, no. 32

[24] Dugdale, *Antiq. of Warw.* 925–6; Burke, *Commoners,* i, 638; *Feud. Aids,* v, 330.

was attainted and executed in 1451–2.[25] The custody of his lands was granted for four years to Fulk Stafford and Thomas Young in 1454.[26] The manor seems to have been restored to Walter Arderne, son and heir of Robert and Elizabeth, and passed from him to his son John.[27] This John married Alice daughter of Richard Bracebridge, and their union was the cause of some dispute between their parents, Robert Arderne accusing Richard Bracebridge of stealing away his son.[28]

On John Arderne's death, 23 May 1525, his son Thomas succeeded to his estates,[29] and in 1539 settled Pedmore on his son William, who, however, predeceased him in 1544,[30] leaving a son Edward, who thus became heir-apparent to his grandfather, whom he succeeded in 1563.[31] In 1573 Edward Arderne settled Pedmore on his son Robert on the latter's marriage with Eleanor daughter of Reginald Corbett.[32] Edward was afterwards concerned in the plot of his son-in-law John Somerville to kill the queen, and was executed at Tyburn in October 1583.[33] Since the manor of Pedmore had been previously settled on Edward Arderne's son Robert and Elizabeth his wife in fee-tail, they were allowed to hold it with reversion to the Crown in case of their dying without issue.[34] On 27 January 1585–6 this reversion was granted in perpetuity to Edward D'Arcy,[35] to whom a fresh grant was made on 3 May 1609.[36] Robert Arderne, who died in 1635,[37] was succeeded by his grandson Robert, who received a grant of the reversion of the manor from Charles I in 1640,[38] and thus became seised of the manor in fee. He appears to have sided with the king in the Civil War, and died, probably in arms, in 1643,[39] leaving as co-heirs his four sisters, Anne wife of Sir Charles Adderley, whose share descended to their son Arderne Adderley, Elizabeth wife of Sir William Pooley, whose heir was their daughter Susannah, afterwards the wife of Anthony Maxey, Dorothy, who married Harvey Bagot, and Goditha or Judith, who married Herbert Price.[40] In the September following Robert Arderne's death his estate was sequestered by the county committee, and found to have been previously mortgaged for £2,000 to Sir William Boughton, who appears to have sold the mortgage to several persons. The various parties having compounded for their respective shares, three-fourths of the estate was discharged from sequestration on 30 November 1653,[41] and the remaining fourth pertaining to Herbert Price and Goditha, which appears to have been purchased from the Committee for Compounding by Humphrey Boughton, was also discharged in February following.[42]

In the early part of 1668 Thomas Foley purchased from the co-heirs the various shares of the manor,[43] and left it by his will dated January 1671 to trustees for the maintenance of boys at the Bluecoat School or Hospital, which he had founded at Old Swinford.[44] To the trustees of the school it still belongs.

CHURCH The church of *ST. PETER* consists of a chancel with north vestry and organ bay, a nave with north and south aisles, west tower and south porch.

The only remains of an early church are the arch and tympanum of the south door, which date from the 12th century, together with some fragments preserved in the tower. The building which preceded the existing one appears, from illustrations in the *Gentleman's Magazine*, &c., to have been of no architectural interest, and after being half rebuilt, owing to subsidence, was entirely pulled down in 1869. Much of the old material was re-used. The chancel arch of the older church, consisting of three square orders, now forms the organ bay, and has modern capitals and responds. During its demolition three layers of plaster, with texts and scrolls, were uncovered on the walls; a square two-light low-side window was also removed.

In the present south aisle wall is a trefoiled piscina, probably of the 14th century, moved from the earlier Lady chapel. The font, perhaps of the 15th century, is octagonal, with tracery in the panels on each face, and a thick octagonal stem with no base.

Some old glass from the previous east window is preserved in the vestry, and shows the arms of Arderne. A fragment of the Clare arms, or three cheverons gules, was also found. In the tower is an old clock, now disused, which may be the one for which new weights were purchased in 1694.

The south doorway, probably of late 12th-century date, has a round head of one order with a zigzag on the face and soffit. The tympanum represents our Lord in glory, the right hand raised in benediction, and the figure inclosed within a vesica formed of two serpents, with the feet of the figure resting on their heads. On either side are the symbols of the Evangelists.

The jambs have shafts with scalloped capitals, and are partly restored.

The bells are three in number: the first cast in 1736 by W. B. of Bromsgrove and recast 1897, the second cast 1735 and recast 1897, and the third cast 1735, and inscribed 'I to the Church the living call and to the grave do summon all.'

The plate consists of a cup made in 1571 and inscribed 'Gloria deo, ex dono Johannis Perrot

[25] Chan. Inq. p.m. 32 Hen. VI, no. 21; Fine R. 32 Hen. VI, m. 11.

[26] Fine R. 32 Hen. VI, m. 11.

[27] Ct. of Req. bdle. 72, no. 48.

[28] Dugdale, *Antiq. of Warw.* 928.

[29] Exch. Inq. p.m. (Ser. 2), file 1183, no. 7. The date of his death is given as 1526 in the inquisition taken on the death of his grandson William (Chan. Inq. p.m. [Ser. 2], lxxxv, 75).

[30] Chan. Inq. p.m. (Ser. 2), lxxxv, 75; Ct. of Req. bdle. 72, no. 48.

[31] Chan. Inq. p.m. (Ser. 2), cxxxv, 2 (2).

[32] Mins. Accts. 1 & 2 Jas. I, no. 35, m. 20 d.; Pat. 16 Chas. I, pt. ix, no. 4; Recov. R. Trin. 15 Eliz. rot. 628.

[33] *Cal. S. P. Dom.* 1581–90, pp. 140, 157; Camden (*Annals of Queen Eliz.* 495) states that his conviction was imputed to Robert Earl of Leicester, whose displeasure he had incurred.

[34] Pat. 28 Eliz. pt. x, no. 4.

[35] Ibid.

[36] Ibid. 7 Jas. I, pt. xliii.

[37] Dugdale, op. cit. 926.

[38] Pat. 16 Chas. I, pt. ix, no. 4.

[39] *Cal. Com. for Comp.* 1204.

[40] Ibid. See also Chan. Proc. (Ser. 2), bdle. 439, no. 3. Sir Charles Adderley and Anne and Dorothy Bagot, then Dorothy Arderne, had dealt with part of the manor in 1639 (Feet of F. Worcs. Mich. 15 Chas. I).

[41] *Cal. Com. for Comp.* 1205.

[42] Ibid. 2042. Previous to this there had been settlements of the parts of the manor belonging to the Bagots and Prices (Feet of F. Worcs. Trin. 1645; East. 1651). Herbert Price also dealt with one-fourth of the manor in 1660 (ibid. Trin. 12 Chas. II).

[43] Feet of F. Worcs. Hil. 19 & 20 Chas. II; Recov. R. Hil. 20 & 21 Chas. II, rot. 4. Thomas Foley is said to have bargained with the tenants of the manor to pay him £300 yearly (Prattinton Coll. [Soc. Antiq.], quoting information from Jacob White, Lord Foley's agent).

[44] See *V.C.H. Worcs.* iv, under Schools; Goodyear, *Stourbridge Old and New,* 97.

Armigeri,' a modern standing and flat paten, and a modern flagon.

The registers before 1812 are as follows: (i) all entries 1539 to 1705; (ii) 1705 to 1752; (iii) baptisms and burials 1752 to 1812. There is a marriage book 1754 to 1813.

ADVOWSON   There was a priest at Pedmore in 1086, but no mention is made of any church or chapel at that time.[45] In 1292 there was a chapel at Pedmore, the advowson of which belonged to the lady of the manor.[46] In 1339–40 it is called a church.[47] The advowson followed the same descent as the manor until 1668,[48] when it passed into the hands of Thomas Foley. His grandson Thomas was created Lord Foley of Kidderminster in 1711–12,[49] and the advowson descended with the title[50] until it was given by Lord Foley about 1857 to the feoffees of the hospital of Old Swinford,[51] in whose patronage it still remains.

Richard de Kingswood, rector of Pedmore, had licence to let his church to farm on 5 May 1335, the rectory being then in ruins and not to be repaired without great expense. Seven marks were to be devoted to its repair 'except 30s. which were to be paid to the said rector.'[52]

CHARITIES   In 1892 Mrs. Mary Cole, by her will proved at London 30 April, bequeathed £50 to be applied towards the support of the parish schools. The legacy was invested in £50 17s. 7d. consols.

The same testatrix bequeathed a further sum of £50 towards the general expenses of the parish church. This was likewise invested in £50 17s. 7d. consols.

The sums of stock are held by the official trustees; the annual dividends, amounting to £1 5s. 4d. in each case, are applied in accordance with the trusts of the respective charities.

RUSHOCK

Russococ (xi cent.); Rossoc (xii cent.); Roshock, Russok, Ruschok (xiii cent.); Ruschok (xiv cent.); Ryshok (xv cent.).

Rushock is a fertile and well-wooded parish, having an area of 1,257 acres, 538 acres being arable land and 597 pasture.[1] It is situated south of Chaddesley Corbett and was formerly a chapelry of that parish. When Ombersley Forest was partly disafforested in 1229 the new forest boundary passed through the middle of the town of Rushock to La Brodeford.[2] The other half of the town appears to have been in the forest of Feckenham.[3] The Elmley Brook and one of its tributaries are the only streams in the parish. The main road from Kidderminster to Droitwich is the chief road; it enters Rushock by the Bradford bridge. The village is situated almost in the centre of the parish, north-east of this road. The houses are scattered and surrounded by trees. In the south of the village there is a pound.

The parish lies about 200 ft. above the ordnance datum, the land falling slightly in the west to the bank of Elmley Brook. The inclosure award is dated 15 April 1812,[4] the Act having been passed in 1805.[5]

The soil is clay, the subsoil marl and clay. Agriculture is the only industry. In the 18th century flax and hemp were cultivated to a certain extent, and in 1782 and later Henry Ellins claimed the bounties offered for their cultivation in Rushock.[6]

Rushock Court was the scene of the arrest in 1679 of Father Wall, a Roman Catholic priest, who was afterwards tried at Worcester on the charge of remaining in England contrary to the statute of Queen Elizabeth, and executed at Red Hill near Worcester.[7]

The Rev. Timothy Goodwin, rector of Rushock, was consecrated Bishop of Kilmore and Ardagh in 1714. He became Archbishop of Cashel in 1727.[8]

MANOR   Before the Conquest RUSHOCK was held by Achil, but by the time of the Domesday Survey Hunulf was holding it of Urse D'Abitot.[9] The overlordship passed with the barony of Elmley Castle until 1512–13, when it is mentioned for the last time.[10]

Hunulf's successor in the manor was Robert de Rushock, who was holding it by the service of one knight's fee in 1166.[11] Early in the reign of King John Robert and his wife Alice were arrested for the murder of Walter de Portes. Robert's property was forfeited, but on payment of a fine he was allowed to take the habit of a monk, and retired to Worcester, where he died. His widow Alice, who had also apparently promised to assume the religious habit, tried unsuccessfully in 1220–1 to recover one third of the manor of Rushock in dower, stating that part of Robert's lands had been restored by King John to the daughter of Robert.[12] The whole manor had been granted after Robert de Rushock's forfeiture to William de Braose, but was seized with his other property by King John in 1208,[13] and granted by William de Beauchamp, the overlord, to Thomas Sturmy, to whom it was afterwards confirmed by Walter de Beauchamp.[14]

In the mean time William de Braose died, and in 1215 his property was restored to his second son and

---

[45] V.C.H. Worcs. i, 317.

[46] Worcs. Inq. p.m. (Worcs. Hist. Soc.), i, 37.

[47] Feet of F. Worcs. 13 Edw. III, no. 34.

[48] Sede Vacante Reg. (Worcs. Hist. Soc.), 378; Nash, op. cit. ii, 240; Chan. Inq. p.m. (Ser. 2), lxxxv, 75; Pat. 16 Chas. I, pt. ix, no. 4; Inst. Bks. (P.R.O.); Feet of F. Worcs. Hil. 19 & 20 Chas. II.

[49] Burke, Peerage.

[50] Inst. Bks. (P.R.O.); Recov. R. Hil. 45 Geo. III, rot. 21.

[51] Clergy Lists.

[52] Worc. Epis. Reg. Montacute, ii, fol. 10.

[1] Statistics from Bd. of Agric. (1905).

[2] Cal. Chart. R. 1226–57, p. 102.

[3] Nash, Hist. of Worcs. i, Introd. 65.

[4] Blue Bk. Incl. Awards, 191.

[5] Priv. Act, 45 Geo. III, cap. 30 (not printed).   [6] Worc. N. and Q. 102.

[7] Noake, Guide to Worcs. 313.

[8] Ibid.; Dict. Nat. Biog.

[9] V.C.H. Worcs. i, 318a.

[10] Red Bk. of Exch. (Rolls Ser.), 299;

Testa de Nevill (Rec. Com.), 40; Worcs. Inq. p.m. (Worcs. Hist. Soc.), pt. i, no. 39; Cal. Inq. p.m. 1–9 Edw. II, 403; Chan. Inq. p.m. 16 Edw. IV, no. 66; (Ser. 2), xxvii, 144.

[11] Red Bk. of Exch. (Rolls Ser.), i, 299; Pipe R. 13 Hen. II (Pipe R. Soc.), 67.

[12] Assize R. 1021, m. 13.

[13] Rot. Lit. Pat. 1201–16 (Rec. Com.), 87b.

[14] Maitland, Bracton's Note Bk. no. 250; Testa de Nevill (Rec. Com.), 43b; Red Bk. of Exch. (Rolls Ser.), 567.

heir, Giles Bishop of Hereford, on payment of a fine.[15] The bishop died in November of that year, and his brother Reynold de Braose was allowed to succeed to his estates in 1217,[16] and received seisin of Rushock in the following year.[17] He granted it to Alexander D'Abitot and the heirs of his body. Alexander died without issue, but his brother and heir Osbert claimed Rushock by another charter to Alexander and his heirs, and brought an unsuccessful action against Geoffrey, son of the above Thomas Sturmy,[18] and Reynold de Braose.[19] He was succeeded in 1246 by his son Henry,[20] who came of age in 1254,[21] and died seised of the manor about 1295.[22] It then passed to his son Henry Sturmy, who was succeeded about 1304–5 by a son Henry.[23] He settled the manor in 1325 on his eldest

STURMY. *Argent three demi-lions gules.*

son Henry and the latter's wife Margaret.[24] The elder Henry died about 1338–9,[25] and Henry Sturmy, his son, obtained in 1359 a grant of free warren in his demesne lands of Rushock.[26] This Henry, who died in 1381,[27] had granted the manor before his death to Sir John Attwood and his wife Lucy, and his grant was confirmed in 1379 by William Sturmy, his nephew and heir.[28]

By an undated charter Thomas Beauchamp Earl of Warwick (who died in 1369) granted a fee at Rushock to his younger son William Lord Bergavenny,[29] and it is probable that the manor lapsed to the overlord soon after this date, for in 1411 William Beauchamp Lord Bergavenny died seised of it. It then followed the descent of Kidderminster Biset[30] (q.v.) until it was sold, probably by George fifth Lord Bergavenny, to Sir Stephen Jenyns, kt., who in April 1513 obtained licence to grant it to the Merchant Taylors' Company, London, in trust for their grammar school at Wolverhampton.[31] This grant was confirmed by James I in 1619,[32] and the manor still belongs to the trustees of the school.

During the reign of Elizabeth Francis Brace was tenant of the manor of Rushock, and apparently resided there.[33] In 1619 the manor seems to have been occupied by Thomas Russell.[34] Later in the

17th century the manor was leased by the Finches. Francis Finch of Rushock was among the prisoners taken by the Parliamentary forces at Worcester in 1646,[35] and he seems to have been an ardent Royalist. He was fined 50s. in 1649 for the estate at Rushock,[36] and in 1658 was obliged to obtain a pass to come to London on business.[37] On the accession of Charles II he petitioned for the office of Grand Commissioner of Excise as a reward for seventeen years of faithful service.[38] Francis and his son Windsor Finch were dealing with the manor of Rushock in 1665,[39] and Windsor and his wife Margaret were in possession in 1681 and 1684.[40]

THE MERCHANT TAYLORS. *Argent a royal tent between two parliament robes all in their proper colours and a chief azure with a leopard or therein.*

CHURCH

The church of *ST. MICHAEL* stands on the edge of a ridge and is of no architectural interest, consisting of shallow chancel, north vestry, transepts, nave with west gallery and tower, all in poor modern Gothic.

There is a tall octagonal font of uncertain date, with trefoiled panels and a shallow bowl. In the chancel are two 17th-century chairs and a few other pieces of old woodwork. Built into the tower walls are also a few carved stone fragments of an earlier church, probably that known to have been consecrated in October 1285.[41]

There are two bells: treble, by C. & G. Mears, 1853; tenor (cracked), 'All prayse and glory be to God for ever D.L. C.W. 1681,' by John Martin.

The plated cup, paten, flagon and almsdish are modern but of mediaeval pattern.

The registers before 1812 are as follows: (i) all entries 1661 to 1681; (ii) 1685 to 1812.

ADVOWSON

The chapel of Rushock was consecrated by Bishop Giffard in 1285.[42] It was dependent on the church of Chaddesley Corbett,[43] and the rector of Chaddesley was patron until 1389 or later.[44] The advowson of Chaddesley had been granted in 1385 to the Dean and canons of Warwick, and they appear shortly after to have appropriated the rectory of Chaddesley,

[15] *Rot. Lit. Pat.* 1201–16 (Rec. Com.), 157.

[16] *Cal. Pat.* 1216–25, p. 72.

[17] *Rot. Lit. Claus.* (Rec. Com.), i, 378b.

[18] From an entry on the Close Rolls of the date it would seem that Geoffrey was the son of Henry Sturmy and that Thomas Sturmy was his uncle (*Rot. Lit. Claus.* [Rec. Com.], ii, 135).

[19] Maitland, *Bracton's Note Bk.* no. 250.

[20] *Excerpta e Rot. Fin.* (Rec. Com.), i, 451.

[21] Ibid. ii, 182.

[22] *Worcs. Inq. p.m.* (Worcs. Hist. Soc.), pt. i, no. 39. Laurentia Sturmy, who held Rushock in 1299 (Habington, *Surv. of Worcs.* [Worcs. Hist. Soc.], ii, 276) and contributed to the subsidy there in 1327 (*Lay Subs. R. Worcs.* 1327 [Worcs. Hist. Soc.], 41), may have been the widow of Henry de Sturmy, and is perhaps to be identified with Laurentia wife of Thomas

Conan, who held the manor in dower in 1325–6 (Feet of F. Worcs. 19 Edw. II, no. 31), and against whom Nicholas Webbe and Margaret his wife recovered a rent from land in Rushock in 1334–5 (*Abbrev. Rot. Orig.* [Rec. Com.], ii, 93).

[23] Chan. Inq. p.m. 33 Edw. I, no. 65.

[24] Feet of F. Worcs. case 259, file 18, no. 31.

[25] Chan. Inq. p.m. 12 Edw. III (1st nos.), no. 18.

[26] Chart. R. 33 Edw. III, m. 3, no. 2.

[27] Chan. Inq. p.m. 5 Ric. II, no. 21.

[28] Close, 2 Ric. II, m. 15 d.

[29] Exch. K. R. Misc. Bks. xxii, fol. 1.

[30] Chan. Inq. p.m. 12 Hen. IV, no. 34; 14 Hen. VI, no. 35; 16 Edw. IV, no. 66.

[31] *L. and P. Hen. VIII*, i, 3879; Chan. Inq. p.m. (Ser. 2), xxvii, 144; Prattinton Coll. (Soc. Antiq.), quoting a benefaction table in Wolverhampton Church. The

actual grant was apparently not made until 1515.

[32] Pat. 17 Jas. I, pt. viii.

[33] Chan. Proc. (Ser. 2), bdle. 109, no. 17; Close, 12 Eliz. pt. i, Brace and Russell.

[34] Pat. 17 Jas. I, pt. viii, grant to Merchant Taylors' Company.

[35] Nash, op. cit. App. 106.

[36] *Cal. Com. for Comp.* 2025.

[37] *Cal. S. P. Dom.* 1658–9, p. 576.

[38] Ibid. 1660–1, p. 150.

[39] Feet of F. Worcs. Hil. 16 & 17 Chas. II.

[40] Ibid. Mich. 33 Chas. II; East. 36 Chas. II.

[41] *Reg. G. Giffard* (Worcs. Hist. Soc.), 266.

[42] Ibid.

[43] Worc. Epis. Reg. Reynolds (1308–13), fol. 88; Wakefield (1375–95), fol. 63 d.

[44] Nash, op. cit. ii, 303.

and thus become patrons of Rushock, for they presented to Rushock from 1397 until 1512.[45] After that time they appear to have leased it, for their grantees are said by Nash to have presented in 1534, 1561 and 1587.[46] The connexion between Rushock and Chaddesley Corbett was apparently severed before 1535, probably at the time when Chaddesley Corbett was appropriated by the college of Warwick, for Rushock is called a rectory in 1535 and was then valued at £10.[47] The queen presented to the church in 1589,[48] and the advowson has since been in the Crown.[49]

CHARITIES The charity of William Norris, founded by deed 22 September 1702, and the subsidiary charities of Frances and John Aaron are regulated by schemes of the Charity Commissioners, 1878 and 1894.

The trust property consists of 4 a. 2 r. 30 p. at Cutnall Green in Elmley Lovett let at £20 a year, and a rent-charge of £5 10s. issuing out of Lowbridge Farm in Rushock; also £119 10s. consols with the official trustees, producing £2 19s. 8d. yearly, arising from a gift of 20 guineas by Frances Aaron in 1766 and a legacy of £100 by will of John Aaron, proved in 1771.

The income is applicable in support of the school at Cutnall Green for children from Rushock and Elmbridge, and any balance in grants for the benefit of the school at Rushock.

The bread money consists of a sum of 7s. 7d. paid quarterly out of Lowbridge Farm and applied in bread to seven widows or aged persons. This donation is attributed to a gift of William Norris in 1710.

SALWARPE

Salewearpe, Salowarpa (ix cent.); Salewarpe (xi, xiii and xiv cent.); Saltwarp (xiv cent.); Sulwarp (xvi cent.).

Salwarpe is a small well-wooded parish covering an area of 1,914 acres,[1] of which 20 acres are water, nearly one-third is arable land, about two thirds permanent grass and 45 acres woodland.[2] The soil is chiefly marl on a subsoil of marl and gravel, and produces crops of wheat and barley, agriculture being the chief industry. Salwarpe is well watered by the River Salwarpe and its tributary the Hadley Brook, the river itself forming part of the western boundary. The road from Droitwich to Oddingley forms part of the eastern and that from Ombersley to Droitwich part of the northern boundary. The main road from Worcester to Droitwich passes through the parish, and a branch from it runs north-west to the village. The land is undulating, rising gradually from the banks of the Salwarpe on the west, where the average height is about 100 ft. above the ordnance datum, to the east, where it attains to a height of 256 ft.

The small village of Salwarpe, distant about 1½ miles to the south-west of Droitwich, is picturesquely situated on the slope of a valley through which runs the River Salwarpe. To the north of the church, and separated from the churchyard by the now disused branch of the Worcester and Birmingham Canal, is Salwarpe Court, a fine half-timber house of the late 15th century, the ancient seat of the Talbots. The interior has been completely modernized and stripped of its original fittings. It is of two stories with a tiled roof. The original hall was doubtless in the centre, with the kitchen and offices on the east and the private apartments on the west. The exterior of this portion is in fine preservation. There is a deep bay window at the south-west, surmounted by a gable having a barge-board elaborately carved with a foliated

wave ornament. All the openings, which are now blocked, have moulded mullions and transoms. The interior of this portion is now occupied by store rooms. Over the entrance doorway is a projecting bay supported by brackets, forming an entrance porch. The doorway itself has moulded posts and a four-centred head, and still retains its original door, a fine specimen of the joinery of the period. Attached to a farm near Salwarpe Court is a large timber barn, used as a dwelling-house and of considerable age. The village itself, though prettily situated, contains no features of architectural interest. The canal runs through a cutting in the side of the valley, which enhances rather than detracts from the naturally picturesque situation of the village, bordered as it is by trees which have by now attained quite respectable proportions. The road along which the few cottages are grouped crosses the canal by a brick bridge, fast falling to decay, and descends to the level of the river by a winding slope, at the foot of which is a water-mill still in active use. Until the middle of the 19th century there were a whipping-post and stocks in the village near the bridge. There is still a pound at the cross roads. Richard Beauchamp thirteenth Earl of Warwick was born at Salwarpe on 28 January 1381. Under the will of Henry V he became guardian of the young king, Henry VI, until he reached the age of sixteen. Episodes in the life of Earl Richard are illustrated in the Rous Roll in the Cottonian Collection at the British Museum.[2a]

Salwarpe was inclosed under an Act of 1812–13,[3] and the award is dated 30 January 1817.[4] Boycott Farm was transferred from this parish to Hampton Lovett in 1880,[5] and part of the parish was transferred to St. Nicholas, Droitwich, and from St. Andrews, Droitwich, at the same date.[6]

Among the place-names are Coppecote,[7] Ladywood, formerly Levediwode,[8] Tilledon, Baggebruggestrete,[9]

45 Nash, op. cit. ii, 303.   46 Ibid.
47 Valor Eccl. (Rec. Com.), iii, 274.
48 Nash, loc. cit.
49 Inst. Bks. (P.R.O.).
1 This includes Chauson hamlet, which became a separate civil parish under the Local Government Act of 1894. Its area is 151 acres (Census of Engl. and Wales, 1901, Worc. 28).

2 Statistics from Bd. of Agric. (1905).
2a Cott. MS. Julius E. iv, 6.
3 Priv. Act, 53 Geo. III, cap. 16 (not printed).
4 Blue Bk. Incl. Awards, 191.
5 Census of Engl. and Wales, 1891, ii, 657.
6 Ibid. 658.
7 Cal. Inq. p.m. 1–9 Edw. II, 398;

Chan. Proc. (Ser. 2), bdles. 79, no. 12; 86, no. 24. A 'way toll' at Coppecote belonged to Guy Earl of Warwick in 1315.
8 Cal. Inq. p.m. 1–9 Edw. II, 410; L. and P. Hen. VIII, xx (1), g. 1081 (11); Mins. Accts. bdle. 645, no. 10461.
9 Mins. Accts. bdle. 645, no. 10461.

Swines,[10] Middleton,[11] Hyllend,[12] Le Courte Close,[13] Pulheye.[14]   Of these Copcut, Ladywood, Middleton, Hill End and Pulley still survive.

According to a Saxon charter, dated *MANORS* 817,[15] *SALWARPE* was granted by Coenwulf, King of the Mercians, to Deneberht, Bishop of Worcester, and his church.[16] The boundaries given in this charter show that at that time Salwarpe extended as far north as Doverdale, and that then, as now, it adjoined Ombersley, and that the River Salwarpe, from which the village

SALWARPE COURT : SOUTH-WEST FRONT

derived its name, formed one of the boundaries. Eight acres at Colford and a fourth part of the wood and pasture land at Witton (Wictune) belonged to the estate.[17]   The manor appears to have been taken from the church, probably by an ancestor of Earl Leofric and his brother Godwin, for Leofric held part of Salwarpe and Godwin held the principal manor there.   Godwin on his death-bed was persuaded by Saint Wulfstan, then Dean of Worcester, to restore it to the priory.[18]   Ethelwine, Godwin's son, evidently the Aelwinus cilt mentioned in the Domesday Survey as a former lord of Salwarpe, repudiated his father's will and retained the manor, but according to Heming, the Worcester chronicler, did not hold it for long, 'losing his lands with his life' soon after Godwin's death.[19]

Salwarpe was not, however, restored to the priory, but granted to Roger de Montgomery Earl of Shrewsbury, who was overlord in 1086.[20] On his death in 1094 his English titles and estates, according to the Norman custom, passed to his second son Hugh, who was killed four years later while fighting in Anglesey.[21]   His eldest brother Robert of Bellesme succeeded him, but in 1102 forfeited all his estates in England for rebellion against Henry I.[22]   The overlordship from this time remained with the Crown, and is last mentioned in 1571.[23]   In 1406 and 1440 the manor was said to be held of the Prior of Coventry.[24]

At the time of the Domesday Survey Urse D'Abitot, who probably lived at Droitwich,[25] was the under-tenant at Salwarpe,[26] and had a park there.   From him the manor passed to the Beauchamps and followed the same descent as Elmley Castle[27] (q.v.), passing into the hands of Henry VII in 1487.

Salwarpe was settled on Katherine of Aragon when

[10] Chan. Proc. (Ser. 2), bdle. 79, no. 12.

[11] Ibid. bdles. 79, no. 12 ; 86, no. 24.

[12] Ibid. bdle. 82, no. 47.

[13] *L. and P. Hen. VIII*, xix (1), g. 610 (86).

[14] Chan. Proc. (Ser. 2), bdle. 5, no. 1. This name as Pullelea occurs in the boundaries of Salwarpe given in a charter of 817 (Heming, *Chartul.* [ed. Hearne], 353).

[15] In a catalogue of charters given in Heming's Chartulary there is one by Ceolwulf King of Mercia dated 813 relating to Salwarpe (op. cit. 579).

[16] Heming, *Chartul.* (ed. Hearne), 449 ; Kemble, *Codex Dipl.* i, 268 ; Birch, *Cart. Sax.* i, 500, 501, 502.

[17] Heming, op. cit. 353 ; Nash, in his *Hist. of Worcs.* (ii, App. 50), gives the boundaries in English.

[18] Heming, op. cit. 259.

[19] *V.C.H. Worcs.* i, 309a n.; Heming, op. cit. 260.

[20] *V.C.H. Worcs.* i, 309a.

[21] G.E.C. *Complete Peerage*, vii, 135.

[22] Ibid.

[23] *Cal. Inq. p.m.* 1–9 *Edw. II*, 398 ; Chan. Inq. p.m. 18 Edw. IV, no. 47 ; (Ser. 2), clxii, 166.

[21] Chan. Inq. p.m. 8 Hen. IV, no. 68 ; 18 Hen. VI, no. 3 ; see below.

[25] *V.C.H. Worcs.* i, 265.

[26] Ibid. 309a.

[27] Ibid. 328 ; *Cal. Inq. p.m.* 1–9 *Edw. II*, 398, 410 ; Chan. Inq. p.m. 21 Ric. II, no. 137, m. 6 ; 2 Hen. IV, no. 58 ; 17 Hen. VI, no. 54 ; 24 Hen. VI, no. 43 ; 18 Edw. IV, no. 47 ; *Cal. Pat.* 1476–85, p. 136 ; Add. MS. 28024, fol. 15a ; Anct. D. (P.R.O.), A 11056.   Salwarpe was granted to Thomas Earl of Kent in 1397 on account of the forfeiture of Thomas Earl of Warwick (*Cal. Pat.* 1396–9, p. 200).

she married Prince Arthur, and she continued to hold it until her death.[28]

The manor was granted in 1545 to Hugh Davie and George Wall,[29] who sold it in 1546 to John Talbot,[30] a grandson of the second Earl of Shrewsbury.[31] John settled it in 1547 on his second wife Elizabeth, daughter of Walter Wrottesley, and their heirs.[32] She survived him, and on her death in 1559 Salwarpe passed to Gilbert Talbot, her son and heir.[33] He, however, died without issue in 1567 and was succeeded by his younger brother John,[34] who in 1574 married Olive third daughter of Sir Henry Sharington of Lacock, co. Wiltshire, and settled the manor on her.[35] After her husband's death in 1582 Olive married Sir Robert Stapleton, kt., and they appear to have conveyed her interest in Salwarpe to her eldest son Sharington.[36] His son and heir Sharington, a zealous Royalist, was taken prisoner in 1644 and confined in Warwick Castle. He afterwards compounded for the sum of £2,011.[37]

In 1653 Sharington settled the manor on his eldest son John with reversion to the latter's only son Sharington,[38] who died without issue in 1685.[39] John Talbot settled the manor in 1677 upon his second wife Barbara, daughter of Sir Henry Slingsby, kt.,[40] and mortgaged it in 1705 for £6,000. By his will, dated 31 August 1712, he directed that the manor should be sold for the payment of his debts.[41] It was purchased by his grandson John, son of Sir John Ivory, kt., and Anne his wife, who had taken the name of Talbot on succeeding to the manor of Lacock, co. Wiltshire.[42] In 1738 he settled Salwarpe on his son John Talbot,[43] who appears to have sold it to Philip Gresley, for he in 1822 settled it on Robert Archibald Douglas, son of General Archibald Douglas of Witham, co. Essex.[44] Philip Gresley died in 1825, leaving all his property to this Robert on condition that he would take the name of Gresley, and on the latter's death without issue in 1885 [45] Salwarpe passed to his nephew William Willoughby Douglas, rector

TALBOT. *Gules a lion and an engrailed border or.*

of Salwarpe, whose son Archibald Douglas now holds it.[46]

A hide of land at Salwarpe was given by Earl Leofric to the monastery of Coventry which he founded about 1043.[47] This hide was held in 1086 by Urse under the church of Coventry, but he had put it into his park.[48] The prior from that time probably lost possession, though some tradition of his overlordship survived until the 15th century, when the manor of Salwarpe is twice said to have been held of the Prior of Coventry.[49] In the reign of Stephen this hide in Salwarpe was held by William de Beauchamp 'of the fief of the bishop of Chester,' [50] and it probably became merged in the capital manor of Salwarpe, as it is not again mentioned separately.

A park in Salwarpe is mentioned in the Domesday Survey as belonging to Urse D'Abitot,[51] and followed the descent of the manor until the 16th century.[52] The last mention of it appears to be in 1559, when Elizabeth widow of John Talbot died seised of it.[53] Probably it was disparked when the family residence was removed from Salwarpe to Lacock, co. Wiltshire,[54] brought to the Talbots by the marriage of John son of the above John with Olive daughter and co-heir of Henry Sharington.

Urse D'Abitot had a mill in Salwarpe in 1086,[55] and it passed with the manor to the Beauchamps and Talbots.[56] Another mill in Salwarpe was granted by Wulfstan, Bishop of Worcester, to the Prior and monks of Worcester,[57] and confirmed to them by William the Conqueror, with special injunctions to Urse D'Abitot to permit them to hold it quietly and honourably.[58] This mill was not included among the possessions of the priory at the Dissolution. In 1322 two mills in Salwarpe were settled on Nicholas de Piry and Agnes his wife with reversion to Walter their son and his issue.[59] William Piry died seised of a mill at Salwarpe in 1402.[60]

Sir John Lyttelton of Frankley died in 1590 holding a windmill at Salwarpe.[61] His son Gilbert seems to have built two water-mills there, which he called Sowleys or New Mills.[62] They were forfeited by his son John on his attainder, but restored to Muriel widow of John in 1603.[63]

At the present day there are two water-mills at Salwarpe, one in the village and the other called New Mill on the borders of Ombersley.

[28] L. and P. Hen. VIII, vi, 529 (4); Stat. 25 Hen. VIII, cap. 28.

[29] Pat. 37 Hen. VIII, pt. ii, m. 6; L. and P. Hen. VIII, xx (1), g. 1081 (11).

[30] Pat. 37 Hen. VIII, pt. x, m. 6.

[31] Burke, Peerage, under Shrewsbury.

[32] Chan. Inq. p.m. (Ser. 2), lxxxix, 160; Exch. Inq. p.m. (Ser. 2), file 1205, no. 2.

[33] Exch. Inq. p.m. (Ser. 2), file 1205, no. 2.

[34] Chan. Inq. p.m. (Ser. 2), clxii, 166. There is an inventory taken in 1570 of the household goods of this John Talbot among the MSS. of Lord Edmund Talbot (Var. Coll. [Hist. MSS. Com.], ii, 310).

[35] Chan. Inq. p.m. (Ser. 2), cxcvii, 89.

[36] Feet of F. Worcs. Mich. 40 & 41 Eliz.   [37] Cal. Com. for Comp. 1035.

[38] Recov. R. Mich. 1653, rot. 217.

[39] Burke, Landed Gentry (1906), under Talbot of Lacock.

[40] Ibid.; Feet of F. Worcs. Trin. 29 Chas. II; Recov. R. Trin. 29 Chas. II, rot. 59.   [41] P.C.C. 104 Aston.

[42] Prattinton Coll. (Soc. Antiq.); Burke, Landed Gentry (1906).

[43] Recov. R. Hil. 12 Geo. II, rot. 264. The manor was advertised as being for sale on 5 May 1773. See Prattinton Coll. (Soc. Antiq.).

[44] Feet of F. Worcs. East. 3 Geo. IV.

[45] Will. Salt Arch. Soc. Coll. (New Ser.), i, 137.

[46] Burke, Landed Gentry (1906).

[47] Dugdale, Mon. Angl. iii, 177, 191.

[48] V.C.H. Worcs. i, 299.

[49] Chan. Inq. p.m. 8 Hen. IV, no. 68; 18 Hen. VI, no. 3.

[50] V.C.H. Worcs. i, 328.

[51] Ibid. 309a. The park contained 124 acres in 1545 (Pat. 37 Hen. VIII, pt. ii, m. 6).

[52] Cal. Inq. p.m. 1–9 Edw. II, 410; Cal. Pat. 1476–85, p. 136; Add. MS. 28024, fol. 67b; L. and P. Hen. VIII, i, 3490; iv, g. 1049 (28), 1676 (14), 3008 (12); xx (1), g. 1081 (11).

[53] Exch. Inq. p.m. (Ser. 2), file 1205, no. 2.

[54] Nash, op. cit. ii, 336.

[55] V.C.H. Worcs. i, 309a.

[56] Add. MS. 28024, fol. 67b; L. and P. Hen. VIII, i, 3490; xx (1), g. 1081 (11); Recov. R. Mich. 1653, rot. 217; Trin. 29 Chas. I, rot. 59; Mich. 4 Anne, rot. 88.

[57] Heming, op. cit. 523.

[58] Cal. Pat. 1281–92, p. 26; Cal. Chart. R. 1300–26, p. 206.

[59] Feet of F. Worcs. case 259, file 18, no. 6.

[60] Chan. Inq. p.m. 4 Hen. IV, no. 13. This may possibly be the mill which had belonged to the priory of Worcester.

[61] Chan. Inq. p.m. (Ser. 2), ccxxix, 140.

[62] Exch. Spec. Com. 44 Eliz. no. 2519. He may have purchased them from the descendants of Thomas Solley, who died seised of tenements and a free fishery at Salwarpe in 1557 (Chan. Inq. p.m. [Ser. 2], cxiv, 70).

[63] Pat. 1 Jas. I, pt. i, m. 31; Harl. Chart. 83 H 28.

A free fishery, mentioned first in 1315, was sold with the manor to Hugh Davie and George Wall in 1545 [64] and held by Philip Gresley and Ann his wife, lord and lady of the manor, in 1822.[65] Thomas Solley died in 1557 seised of a free fishery in Salwarpe which passed to his kinsman Edward Hanbury [66] and in 1559 Gregory Price conveyed a free fishery there to Gilbert Lyttelton.[67]

When the manor of Salwarpe was granted to the Bishop of Worcester in 817 the gift included ' below the greatest pit, four salt vat stalls and eight pits for brine, five on the east half, and three on the west half, and at the middle pit eight vat stalls and the brine thereto, that men may be well accommodated, and unseparated the brine.' [68] Five salt-pans at Droitwich belonged to the manor of Salwarpe at the time of the Domesday Survey,[69] and six were annexed to the hide which Urse held of the Prior of Coventry.[70] These vats afterwards became known as the Sheriffs' seals (Shref vessels or Shrefhales), and the further history of them is given under Droitwich (q.v.). They remained attached to the manor of Salwarpe probably as late as 1712, eleven salt-vats being mentioned in Sir John Talbot's will.[71]

OAKLEY, situated in the east of the parish and now only a farm-house, was the site of a reputed manor which probably at first belonged to a family of the same name. Richard son of William de Oakley recovered two parts of a carucate of land at Salwarpe in 1274–5,[72] and William de Quercu, who paid a subsidy of 4s. at Salwarpe in 1280,[73] may have been an owner of this estate. Avis de Oakley occurs in 1299–1300,[74] and John de Oakley paid a subsidy of 3s. at Salwarpe in 1327,[75] and was lord of Oakley in 1346.[76] From that time until the beginning of the 16th century there seems to be no record of their successors. In 1524–5 William Trimmell was holding lands worth £10 in Salwarpe,[77] and this probably refers to Oakley, which the Trimmells are known to have held. John Trympley, lord of Oakley in 1535,[78] is probably to be identified with John Trimmell, who was a resident at Salwarpe in 1539.[79] Richard Trimmell, son of the latter, was holding Oakley in 1555, when it appears as a manor for the first time.[80] Thomas son of Richard [81] left it to his only daughter Mary, who married John Talbot, a younger son of John Talbot of Salwarpe,[82] from whom it passed to John, their son, and to his son also called John. The latter was succeeded by an only daughter Olive,[83] but she died unmarried in 1681,[84] her heirs being her aunts Elizabeth and Katherine and her cousin Elizabeth daughter of

Mary, another aunt, by her second husband Sir John Tyas, kt.[85] Elizabeth and Katherine died unmarried, and the whole of the property passed to their niece Elizabeth, who married Simon Barker.[86] She seems to have been succeeded by a son Talbot Barker, who died in 1719, leaving his property in Worcestershire to his right heirs on his mother's side.[87] These must have been the descendants of Olive, Mary, Anne and Elizabeth, the daughters of John Talbot and Mary Trimmell,[88] and, since Pelham Maitland and Dorothea his wife were holding it in her right in 1760,[89] she was probably their only descendant. In 1770 the manor of Oakley with the manor-house and lands, let at a rent of £205 5s., then the property of Mary widow of George Burrish, were advertised as being for sale.[90] They have since passed through several hands and now are for the larger part the property of Mr. T. C. Quarrell.

In 1086 William Goizenboded held a hide of land at Celvestune, and William held it of 'him. As in the manor of Guiting in Gloucestershire, William had succeeded Richard the Youth (juvenis), the tenant before the Conquest.[91] In the time of Stephen this hide was held by William de Beauchamp 'of the fee of Robert Fitz Archembald.' [92] This Celvestune (Chalvestona) has been identified as *CHAUSON* in Salwarpe, but it does not occur later as a manor, and probably became absorbed in the manor of Salwarpe.[93] A place called Challesdon mentioned in a 15th-century survey of Salwarpe [94] is perhaps to be identified with it.

A house at Chauson of the late 16th or early 17th century is supposed to have been the residence of the Richardsons. Burke mentions a family of Richardson of 'Chawston' whose arms were recorded in the time of Charles I, giving a father, son and grandson named Stephen.[95] The Richardsons, who appear to have been citizens of Worcester,[96] were numbered among the gentry of the shire in 1660,[97] and perhaps built Chauson as a country residence. There is a monument in St. Helen's Church, Worcester, to Stephen Richardson of Chauson, Procurator-General of the Consistory Court of Worcester and chapter clerk, who died in 1665.

CHURCH The church of *ST. MICHAEL* consists of a chancel 28 ft. 6 in. by 16 ft. 9 in., north vestry, nave averaging 54 ft. by 15 ft. 11 in., north aisle 10 ft. 11 in. wide, south aisle 9 ft. 11 in. wide, west tower 11 ft. 11 in. square, and south porch. These measurements are all internal.

The earliest part of the present church is the nave arcade, dating from the 12th century. The north

[64] Chan. Inq. p.m. 9 Edw. II, no. 71 ; Pat. 37 Hen. VIII, pt. ii, m. 6.

[65] Feet of F. Worcs. East. 3 Geo. IV.

[66] Chan. Inq. p.m. (Ser. 2), cxiv, 70.

[67] Feet of F. Worcs. Mich. 1 & 2 Eliz.

[68] Heming, op. cit. 353 ; Translation in Nash, op. cit. ii, App. 50.

[69] V.C.H. Worcs. i, 309a.

[70] Ibid. 299.

[71] Cal. Inq. p.m. 1–9 Edw. II, 398, 410 ; L. and P. Hen. VIII, xiii (1), g. 1115 (16) ; xx (1), g. 1081 (11) ; P.C.C. 104, Aston.

[72] Assize R. 1026, m. 20.

[73] Lay Subs. R. Worcs. c. 1280 (Worcs. Hist. Soc.), 25.

[74] Habington, Surv. of Worcs. (Worcs. Hist. Soc.), i, 353.

[75] Lay Subs. R. Worcs. 1327 (Worcs. Hist. Soc.), 20.

[76] Habington, op. cit. i, 353.

[77] Lay Subs. R. Worcs. 200, no. 129.

[78] Valor Eccl. (Rec. Com.), iii, 270 ; Visit. of Worcs. 1569 (Harl. Soc. xxvii), 137.

[79] L. and P. Hen. VIII, xiv (1), p. 305.

[80] Visit. of Worcs. loc. cit. ; Feet of F. Worcs. East. 1 & 2 Phil. and Mary.

[81] Visit. of Worcs. loc. cit.

[82] Feet of F. Worcs. East. 15 Chas. I ; Exch. Dep. by Com. Mich. 19 Chas. II, no. 30.

[83] Exch. Dep. by Com. Mich. 19 Chas. II, no. 30.

[84] Prattinton Coll. (Soc. Antiq.), quoting a monument in the church.

[85] H. S. Grazebrook, 'The Talbots of Oakley,' Midland Antiq. ii, 156–61.

[86] Ibid. [87] P.C.C. 101 Shaller.

[88] Grazebrook, op. cit. 160.

[89] Feet of F. Div. Co. Mich. 34 Geo. II.

[90] Prattinton Coll. (Soc. Antiq.).

[91] V.C.H. Worcs. i, 317.

[92] Ibid. 328.

[93] Robert, Arnald and Walter de Chalveston paid subsidies at Salwarpe in 1280 (Lay Subs. R. Worcs. c. 1280 [Worcs. Hist. Soc.], 25) and Richard and Alice de Chalveston paid in 1327 (ibid. 1327, p. 20).

[94] Mins. Accts. bdle. 645, no. 10461.

[95] Burke, General Armoury, 853b.

[96] Chan. Proc. (Ser. 2), bdle. 458, no. 78.

[97] Harl. MS. 19816, fol. 125.

SALWARPE COURT : ENTRANCE FRONT

OLD TIMBER BARN NEAR SALWARPE COURT

aisle is mid-14th-century work, and the south of a few years later.

Traces of flying buttresses on the walls of both aisles, and carried across to the western piers, seem to point to the existence of a tower earlier than the present aisles, whose eastern arch, at some date after 1350, was in danger of spreading. The north and south walls of this tower being within the church would have formed bays similar to those of the arcade, but not in line with them.

In the middle of the 15th century a new tower was built immediately to the west of the older one, but not connected with it and not in line with the nave and previous tower. The older tower was then removed and the new one connected with the west ends of the aisle walls, and finally the north and south arches of the old tower were replaced by a continuation of the nave arcade built outside them. In order to keep these new bays of approximately equal width the responds were necessarily of unequal projection, and part of the last pier on the south side was cut away.

The present chancel was built in 1848. The east window is of three lights, with a two-light window in the south wall and one of one light on the north. Under a recess on the north side is a fine late 14th-century effigy of a priest in mass vestments holding a chalice.

The chancel arch is modern. The nave has an arcade of four bays on each side. The first three are similar, having obtuse pointed arches, of two square orders on the inner and one on the outer sides; the piers are circular with plain bell capitals. West of these there is a break, with a large square pier on the north and a smaller pier similar to it on the south.

The north aisle dates from the 14th century. The east and west windows, with the first two in the north wall, are of two lights with leaf tracery. The north door has a segmental head, and west of it is a wide single-light window. In the lower part of the north wall are four recesses with four-centred arches. Above the second is a cruciform cutting in the masonry, which probably contained an early stone rood.

There is a small trefoiled recess, perhaps for a piscina, at the eastern end of this wall.

The eastern bay of the aisle is fitted with a wood screen, mostly modern, but with pieces of 15th-century work re-used. The massive tower arch, of one pointed order, has panelled jambs, and the 15th-century west window is of four lights.

The south aisle dates from about 1370, and has an east window of two lights with a quatrefoiled head, three similar windows on the south and one in the west wall; the first window on the south is modern on the inside. At the east end, shut off by wrought-iron rails, is a black and white marble altar tomb with an inscription to Olive Talbot, 1681, and her mother Elizabeth, widow of John Talbot of Oakley, in the parish of Salwarpe, 1689. In the south-east corner

is a trefoiled piscina. The first bay of the aisle has a good 15th-century parclose screen, extensively repaired and patched. To the east of the south door, which is much restored, are three low recesses in the wall, similar to those in the north aisle. The west tower has an embattled parapet and angle buttresses. The tower arch is of a single two-centred order with panelled jambs. The west window of the ground stage is of four cinquefoiled lights with a traceried head. The vice is at the south-west. The bell-chamber has windows of two trefoiled lights, and the ringing chamber single square-headed lights.

At the west end of the aisle are some old tiles having cranes, hawks, a shield with three boars' heads, another of a fesse with three molets, and other devices. The south porch, roofs and font are modern.

On the south wall of the chancel is an alabaster monument to Thomas Talbot, 1613, with kneeling figures at a desk and children below. In the tower is a board, dated 1661, recording the benefactions of Thomas Trimmell, 1641.

There are two wooden chests, one dated 1697 and one earlier and longer with three locks.

The bells are six in number, the first four dating from 1684, the other two by Mears, 1846.

The plate consists of a cup and cover paten of the 1571 type, unmarked and apparently reworked; a flagon engraved with the Talbot arms impaling a cheveron between three wolves' heads razed, presented by Elizabeth Talbot; a restoration paten, a silver dish of 1820 and a silver-gilt chalice and paten presented in memory of the Rev. W. W. Douglas.

The registers before 1812 are as follows: (i) baptisms and burials 1666 to 1783, marriages 1666 to 1754; (ii) baptisms and burials 1783 to 1812; (iii) marriages 1754 to 1811.

ADVOWSON The advowson of Salwarpe belonged to the lords of the manor until about 1774,[98] when John Talbot sold it to Sir Herbert Perrott Pakington,[99] whose son Sir John Pakington sold it to Thomas Farley. The latter presented to the living in 1807, and in the same year sold the advowson to Admiral Rainier, who left it to his brother Dr. Rainier, from whom it was purchased by the Rev. Volvant Vashion, the rector as well as patron in 1826.[100] Mr. Vashion or his successor seems to have sold it to the Rev. Henry Douglas,[1] whose son the Rev. William Willoughby Douglas[2] inherited the manor of Salwarpe from his uncle in 1885, and left it with the advowson to his son Archibald Douglas, the present owner.[3]

In 1347 William de Salwarpe, clerk, and Thomas his brother obtained licence to grant certain land in Salwarpe to two chaplains to celebrate divine service daily in the parish church of St. Michael.[4] This grant was not made, and in 1356 William and Thomas on surrender of their Letters Patent obtained licence to grant the premises to the nuns of

[98] Chan. Inq. p.m. 9 Edw. II, no. 71, m. 153; *Cal. Pat.* 1327-30, p. 70; 1399-1401, p. 531; Feet of F. Div. Co. Mich. 2 Hen. VI; Chan. Inq. p.m. 18 Hen. VI, no. 3; *L. and P. Hen. VIII*, xx (1), g. 1081 (11); Inst. Bks. (P.R.O.). In 1291 the rectory was worth £7 (*Pope Nich. Tax.* [Rec. Com.], 217), and in 1535 had increased in value

to £15 7s. 10d. (*Valor Eccl.* [Rec. Com.], iii, 268).

[99] Nash, op. cit. ii, 337; Inst. Bks. (P.R.O.).

[100] Inst. Bks. (P.R.O.); Prattinton Coll. (Soc. Antiq.), quoting a letter from the Rev. H. Douglas. Henry Vaughan is said to have bought the advowson from Sir John Pakington, but apparently for

one presentation only. He presented the Rev. Robert Douglas, his son-in-law, the father of the above Henry.

[1] Lewis, *Topog. Dict. of Engl.*

[2] Noake, *Guide to Worcs.*

[3] See Burke, *Landed Gentry.*

[4] *Abbrev. Rot. Orig.* (Rec. Com.), ii, 190; Chan. Inq. p.m. 21 Edw. III (2nd nos.), no. 42; *Cal. Pat.* 1345-8, p. 336.

Westwood, who were to provide the two chaplains.[5] Subsequently the lands were seized by the king, on the plea that they had been alienated without licence, and granted in 1397 to John Bras and Geoffrey Mugge.[6] In 1368, however, certain salt-pits with which William brother and heir of Thomas Salwarpe had enfeoffed Thomas Earl of Warwick were given by the latter to the support of a chantry in Salwarpe dedicated to the Virgin Mary, to be served by one chaplain, who was to be nominated by the parishioners of Salwarpe but presented by the earl and his heirs.[7] Presentations were made to this chantry by the king after the attainder of the Earl of Warwick.[8] After the Dissolution the property belonging to this chantry was granted by Edward VI to Henry Tanner and Thomas Bocher.[9] 'The late chantry' is mentioned again in 1575, when Edward Corbett and Eleanor his wife and George Wylde her son conveyed it to Thomas Wylde.[10]

By his will, dated 1268, William de Beauchamp left a manse and garden adjoining the court of the rector to maintain a lamp in the church of Salwarpe, in honour of God Almighty, His Blessed Mother, and St. Katherine and St. Margaret the Virgins.[11]

CHARITIES

Charity of Talbot Barker. See under Droitwich St. Andrew.—The annual sum of £20 is applied for educational purposes in this parish, and an annual sum of £5 is applied for the benefit of the poor.

In 1698 Mrs. Catherine Talbot, by her will, gave to the poor of this parish the yearly sum of £4, which is paid by the proprietors of the Oakley estate. See under Droitwich St. Andrew.

It was stated on the church table, dated in 1757, that Margery Parker, by her will, gave 30s. a year to the poor to be raised out of land in the parish of Oddingley, and distributed at Christmas, Easter and Whitsuntide.

Other charitable gifts mentioned on the same table have been long lost, and appear to be irrecoverable.

Church Lands.—Upon the inclosure in 1813 of the commonable and waste lands in this parish about 8 a. were exchanged for some ancient property called Church Lands, the rents of which are carried to the churchwardens' accounts.

STONE

Stanes (xi and xiii cent.).

The parish of Stone has an area of 2,516 acres, of which 17 acres are covered by water, 1,405 acres are arable land, 415 permanent grass, and 90 wood.[1] It is situated immediately south-east of Kidderminster, from which it is divided by the River Stour and by one of its tributaries. There is a rifle range for volunteers on the left bank of the river. Besides the village there are three hamlets : Hoobrook in the west and partly in the foreign of Kidderminster, Dunclent half a mile north of the village, and Shenstone 1½ miles south. The village is in the north-east of the parish, and is 2 miles from each of the stations of Kidderminster and Hartlebury, and on the Kidderminster and Bromsgrove road. From this road Cursley Lane branches off near Mustow Green, and forming part of the eastern boundary of Stone runs south and joins the main road from Kidderminster to Droitwich. The last road, which passes through the west of Stone to Hartlebury, forms the southern boundary of this parish for some distance. Branches from it running in a north-easterly direction cross the parish, one called Stanklin Lane leading to the village of Stone, and the other passing through Shenstone to Chaddesley Corbett. The land rises gradually from the Stour to a height of 287 ft. above the ordnance datum in the east. Stour Hill, a little to the east of the river, is partly in this parish and partly in Hartlebury.

The parish was inclosed under an Act of 1762–3, and the award is dated 20 December 1763.[2] The soil is loamy, lying partly on the Keuper Sandstones and partly on the Bunter Pebble beds. The population is now chiefly engaged in agriculture, the most important crops being wheat, beans, barley and potatoes. Paper and yarn-mills were formerly worked at Hoobrook, but are now disused. There are two schools in the parish, one in the village of Stone, and the other, an infants' school, at Hoobrook. A third school was built at Shenstone in 1882, but never opened for want of funds, and is now used as a barn.

MANORS

Before the Conquest STONE was held as two manors by Tumi and Euchil, but in 1086 Herlebald was holding it as one manor of Urse D'Abitot,[3] from whom the overlordship passed with his other property to the Beauchamps and probably descended with their barony of Elmley Castle[4] (q.v.), although its connexion with the Beauchamp family is not mentioned after the 13th century. The manor was said in 1578, 1618 and 1636 to be held of the Crown as of the hundred of Halfshire in socage by fealty.[5]

Herlebald was succeeded by the family of Stone, who took their name from the manor, although there is no mention of their holding land in the parish until the beginning of the 13th century, when Walter Stone was holding half a knight's fee of William de Beauchamp.[6] This Walter was possibly a son of William de Stanes, who in 1200–1 confirmed a grant made by his father Walter (fl. 1178) and grandfather William of land at Osmerley to the monks of Bordesley.[7] In 1259 a Walter Stone and Aline his wife are mentioned as landowners in Worcestershire,[8] and were probably holding the manor of Stone. They were evidently succeeded by

[5] Cal. Pat. 1354–8, p. 470.
[6] Ibid. 1396–9, p. 190.
[7] Worc. Epis. Reg. Moreton, fol. 58 ; Nash, op. cit. ii, 339.
[8] Worc. Epis. Reg. Silv. de Gigliis, fol. 140. See also ibid. Alcock, fol. 106 d.; Cal. Pat. 1476–85, pp. 163, 211, 308.
[9] Pat. 3 Edw. VI, pt. vi, m. 37.

[10] Feet of F. Worcs. East. 17 Eliz.
[11] Reg. G. Giffard (Worcs. Hist. Soc.), 8.

[1] Statistics from Bd. of Agric. (1905).
[2] Blue Bk. Incl. Awards, 191; Burton, Bibl. of Worc. i, 56 ; Priv. Act, 3 Geo. III, cap. 33.
[3] V.C.H. Worcs. i, 318b.

[4] Testa de Nevill (Rec. Com.), 40 ; Red Bk. of Exch. (Rolls Ser.), 567.
[5] Chan. Inq. p.m. (Ser. 2), dxxxviii, 96 ; clxxxiii, 96 ; ccclxxviii, 137.
[6] Testa de Nevill (Rec. Com.), 40.
[7] Madox, Formulare, no. 5, 89, 462, 464.
[8] Excerpta e Rot. Fin. (Rec. Com.), ii, 307.

Salwarpe Church : 15th-century Screen in South Aisle

Thomas Stone, whose name occurs on a Lay Subsidy Roll, c. 1280.[9] According to Nash, William Stone held the manor in 1284–5 and Thomas Stone in 1299.[10] By 1327 the manor had passed to Thomas's son Richard Stone,[11] who in that year with his wife Cecilia settled tenements in Stone on their son Richard and his wife Joan.[12] Richard the son probably died in the lifetime of his father, for in 1341 the latter with Cecily his wife settled a messuage and 2 carucates of land in Stone upon Margaret wife of Roger Folliott for life with remainder to Thomas Folliott, Margaret's son, and his wife Elizabeth, who is stated by Habington to have been a daughter of Richard or William Stone.[13] William Fitz Warin, who is mentioned in 1346 as a former owner of the manor,[14] may have obtained it by marriage with a widow of one

FOLLIOTT. *Argent a lion with a forked tail purpure crowned or.*

of the Stones. Thomas Folliott was holding the manor in 1346,[15] and it continued in the Folliott family until the 17th century. Hugh Folliott, grandson or great-grandson of Thomas,[16] was lord of the manor in 1428,[17] and had been succeeded before 1431 by his eldest son Richard.[18] The latter settled it in 1468 on his son Nicholas,[19] from whom it passed to his grandson John Folliott, who died in 1578.[20] After the death of Thomas Folliott son of John in 1617 his son Sir John Folliott, kt., who had married Elizabeth daughter of John Aylmer, Bishop of London, succeeded to the manor,[21] and in 1624 sold it to Sir William Courteen, kt.,[22] a prominent merchant. He was succeeded in 1636 by his son William Courteen,[23] who, owing to the repeated losses incurred by his father, became bankrupt in 1643.[24] Stone was probably claimed with his other property by the Committee for Sequestration and was sold to Sir James Rushout, bart., son of John Rushout, a Flemish merchant, who had settled in London.[25] The exact date of the purchase by Sir James is not known, but he was dealing with land at Stone in 1662–3,[26] and was in possession of the manor in 1694.[27] He died in 1697–8, and was succeeded by his second but eldest surviving son James.[28] On the latter's marriage in 1699–1700 with Arabella daughter of Thomas Vernon the manor was settled upon her.[29] Both Sir James and Arabella died in 1705, and their only son James died in boyhood in 1711.[30] The manor passed to his sister Elizabeth, who married in 1731 Paulett St. John.[31] A settlement of the manor was made upon her at that date.[32]

Elizabeth died without issue in December 1733,[33] and in 1734 St. John sold the manor for £6,500 to Joseph Cox, an attorney of Kidderminster,[34] whose daughter and heir Mary married Stephen Beckingham, and was holding the manor with him in 1738.[35] In 1751 it belonged to Stephen Beckingham and his son Stephen.[36] It had passed before 1762–3 to John Baker,[37] who was lord of the manor in 1808.[38] Property at Stone was apparently held by the Misses Baker in 1868,[39] and they and Mrs. Bernard owned the manor in 1872. It had passed before 1876 to James Holcroft of Red Hill House, Stourbridge. He was succeeded in March 1894 by his brother Charles Holcroft of the Shrubbery, Kingswinford, who was created a baronet in 1905,[40] and is now lord of the manor of Stone.

HOLCROFT, baronet. *Argent a cross engrailed sable with an eagle rising sable in the first and fourth quarters.*

The manor of *DUNCLENT* (Duncklen, xvi cent.) belonged before the Conquest to the priory of St. Guthlac, Hereford, and Odo held it of the priory. In 1086 it was held under the priory by Nigel the physician, under whom it was held by Urse.[41] Since in 1212 the fee belonged to Walter de Beauchamp,[42] it is evident that the Urse who held the manor under Nigel was Urse D'Abitot. The overlordship is not again mentioned until 1476, when the manor was said to be held of the Prior of Lewes for the service of one knight.[43]

Dunclent evidently gave its name to the family of Dunclent, who were lords of the manor in the 13th and 14th centuries. About 1280 Robert de Dunclent paid a subsidy of a mark at Dunclent,[44] and in 1284 Mary Dunclent, probably his widow, owned property there.[45] Clement de Dunclent is the next owner of the manor whose name is known. He seems in 1294 and 1316 to have held it under the Burnells, who in turn held it of Stephen de Bosco.[46] Clement de Dunclent paid a subsidy of 3s. at Dunclent in 1327,[47]

[9] *Lay Subs. R. Worcs.* c. 1280 (Worcs. Hist. Soc.), 14.
[10] *Hist. of Worcs.* ii, 385.
[11] *Lay Subs. R. Worcs.* 1327 (Worcs. Hist. Soc.), 21; Feet of F. Worcs. Hil. 15 Edw. III, no. 3.
[12] Feet of F. Worcs. Trin. 1 Edw. III.
[13] Ibid. Hil. 15 Edw. III, no. 3; Habington, *Surv. of Worcs.* (Worcs. Hist. Soc.), i, 387; ii, 256. In the *Worcs. Visit.* Elizabeth is called daughter of William Stone (Harl. Soc. xxvii, 54).
[14] *Feud. Aids,* v, 303.
[15] Ibid.
[16] *Visit. of Worcs.* 1569 (Harl. Soc. xxvii), 54.
[17] *Feud. Aids,* v, 323.
[18] Ibid. 330; *Visit. of Worcs.* 1569, loc. cit.
[19] *Visit. of Worcs.* 1569, loc. cit.
[20] W. and L. Inq. p.m. xix, 172.

[21] Chan. Inq. p.m. (Ser. 2), ccclxxviii, 137; Chan. Proc. Jas. I, L 5–1.
[22] Feet of F. Worcs. Mich. 22 Jas. I; Recov. R. Trin. 22 Jas. I, rot. 65.
[23] Chan. Inq. p.m. (Ser. 2), dxxxviii, 96.
[24] *Dict. Nat. Biog.*
[25] G.E.C. *Complete Baronetage,* iii, 210.
[26] Feet of F. Worcs. Mich. 14 Chas. II.
[27] Ibid. Div. Co. Trin. 6 Will. and Mary.
[28] G.E.C. loc. cit.
[29] Ibid.; Recov. R. Hil. 11 Will. III, rot. 76; Close, 8 Geo. II, pt. xii, no. 13, 14.
[30] G.E.C. op. cit. iii, 211.
[31] Ibid.
[32] Recov. R. D. Enr. Mich. 5 Geo. II, m. 10, 11; see also Feet of F. Div. Co. Mich. 7 Geo. II.
[33] G.E.C. op. cit. iii, 211, note a.
[34] Close, 8 Geo. II, pt. iii, no. 5.

[35] Feet of F. Worcs Trin. 11 & 12 Geo. II; Nash, op. cit. ii, 386.
[36] Recov. R. Trin. 24 & 25 Geo. II, rot. 159.
[37] Priv. Act, 3 Geo. III, cap. 33.
[38] Recov. R. East. 48 Geo. III, rot. 372.
[39] Noake, *Guide to Worcs.* 329.
[40] P.C.C. 187 Worc.; Burke, *Peerage.*
[41] *V.C.H. Worcs.* i, 308.
[42] *Red Bk. of Exch.* (Rolls Ser.), ii, 567.
[43] Chan. Inq. p.m. 16 Edw. IV, no. 66.
[44] *Lay Subs. R. Worcs.* c. 1280 (Worcs. Hist. Soc.), 12.
[45] Feet of F. Worcs. case 259, file 11, no. 1.
[46] *Worcs. Inq. p.m.* (Worcs. Hist. Soc.), i, 50; Inq. a.q.d. file 114, no. 15; *Cal. Inq. p.m.* 1–9 *Edw. II,* 393.
[47] *Lay Subs. R. Worcs.* 1327 (Worcs. Hist. Soc.), 21.

and his widow Amice was still in possession of a quarter of a knight's fee there in 1346.[48] John de Dunclent son of Clement was probably lord of the manor in 1351, when he exchanged certain lands in Broom with his brother Edmund and Maud his wife for others in Dunclent,[49] and he was called lord of Dunclent in 1368.[50] The family appears to have died out in the 14th century, and the manor probably reverted to the Beauchamps as overlords, being settled, like Rushock, on William Beauchamp Lord Bergavenny.[51] It then followed the descent of Kidderminster Biset [52] (q.v.), Lord Bergavenny being the owner in the reign of Queen Elizabeth. It was probably sold after his death in 1586–7, and its descent becomes difficult to trace.

In the Visitation of Worcester, 1569, Elizabeth daughter and heir of John Moore of Dunclent is mentioned as having married John Folliott of Stone,[53] and Nash also states that Dunclent was at one time held by John Moore.[54] It afterwards passed to Edmund Brode, who left most of his property, including a park called Dunclent Park, by his will, dated 22 February 1599, to a younger son, Edward Brode.[55] He sold the manor in 1655 to Thomas Foley,[56] in whose family it remained [57] until about 1836, when it was purchased by the late Earl of Dudley.[58] It now belongs to his son William Humble Earl of Dudley.

SHENSTONE and HOO were regarded as manors during the 17th century.[59] Land at Shenstone was held in 1431 by Richard Folliott, lord of Stone, by knight service,[60] and both manors passed with Stone from the Folliott family to Sir William Courteen.[61] They are not mentioned after 1636.[62]

A mill at Stone worth three ounces of silver belonged to the manor in 1086.[63] Another mill in the parish called 'the water mill of Stone' appears to have belonged to the manor of Dunclent, for it was given by Edmund de Dunclent to his brother John in 1351.[64]

A disused paper-mill at Hoobrook is the only mill at present in the parish.

CHURCH The church of ST. MARY consists of a chancel, nave with a western gallery and a western tower and spire. The whole building is modern, and was built in 1831, when the old church was destroyed. A pencil drawing of the latter, still preserved, shows this to have been of some interest. The sketch does not give much detail, but the proportion of the tower and the general appearance of the belfry lights suggest a 12th-century date for this part of the church, while the east windows of the chancel appear to have been three grouped lancets. Prattinton, who visited the church, also mentions 'a Saxon door on the north wall,' a further suggestion of 12th-century work.[65]

The present church is ostensibly designed in 15th-century style, but is poor in both design and detail. The traceried east window of the chancel is of three lights, and in the south wall is a two-light window. There is no chancel arch, and the nave is lit by six two-light windows, three on either hand. At the west end of the nave is an organ gallery. The tower is of three stages, with lancet belfry lights and an embattled parapet, above which is a stone spire. The lowest stage serves as a porch. The belfry contains six bells, cast by Thomas Mears of London in 1832. The font is of 13th-century design, with a square bowl. Affixed to the north wall of the chancel are two small brass plates, the only relics of the old church, both removed from a monument. One is to Will Spicer, died 1656, and bears the inscription:

'Drawn from a martyrs bloud, from a generous line
Decended was this meek, this grave divine.'

Below are the arms, a battled fesse between three lions rampant. The second brass is to Ursula wife of the above, died 1663, and bears the Spicer arms impaling a cheveron between three roses with the difference of a crescent upon the cheveron. Over the west door is a small late 18th-century carving of the royal arms with the unusual arrangement of England quartering Scotland, Ireland, and France.

The church plate consists of a small three-legged salver of 1800 and a modern set of a chalice, paten, standing salver and flagon, presented in 1862 by the Rev. John Peel, vicar of Stone and Dean of Worcester.

The registers before 1812 are as follows: (i) all entries 1601 to 1709; (ii) baptisms and burials 1709 to 1785, marriages 1709 to 1752; (iii) baptisms and burials 1786 to 1812; and (iv) a printed marriage book 1754 to 1812.

ADVOWSON The chapel of Stone was dedicated in honour of the Virgin Mary by Godfrey Giffard, Bishop of Worcester, in 1269.[66] It was annexed to the church of Chaddesley Corbett,[67] and the presentations were made by the rectors of Chaddesley until 1392.[68] Like Rushock it probably became separated from Chaddesley when that rectory was appropriated to the college of St. Mary, Warwick, and in 1535 it was a vicarage valued at £17.[69] The presentations were made by the dean until the dissolution of the college,[70] and the advowson of Stone was then apparently granted like that of Chaddesley Corbett to the bailiff and burgesses of Warwick,[71] as they or their feoffees presented until 1622.[72] The king presented in 1662, and the advowson has since been in the Crown.[73]

CHARITIES The Parochial Charity, comprising the charities of Nicholas and Elizabeth Folliott, founded by deed 4 June 1501; John Wall, 1 February 1504; Richard

48 *Feud. Aids*, v, 303. Half a knight's fee in Dunclent held at that time by William de Heathy is probably to be identified with the manor of Heathy in Kidderminster.

49 Jeayes, *Lyttelton Chart.* no. 148.

50 Ibid. 179.

51 Chan. Inq. p.m. 12 Hen. IV, no. 34.

52 Ibid. 14 Hen. VI, no. 35; 16 Edw. IV, no. 66; *L. and P. Hen. VIII*, xiii (1), g. 646 (58); Chan. Proc. (Ser. 2), bdle. 167, no. 18.

53 *Harl. Soc. Publ.* xxvii, 55.

54 op. cit. ii, 387.

55 P.C.C. 25 Wallopp.

56 Feet of F. Worcs. Trin. 1655.

57 Ibid. East. 16 Chas. II; Recov. R. Trin. 13 Will. III, rot. 204; Hil. 10 & 11 Geo. IV, rot. 255.

58 Information supplied by Mr. W. F. Taylor.

59 Feet of F. Worcs. Mich. 22 Jas. I; Chan. Inq. p.m. (Ser. 2), dxxxviii, 96.

60 *Feud. Aids*, v, 330.

61 Feet of F. Worcs. Mich. 22 Jas. I.

62 Chan. Inq. p.m. (Ser. 2), dxxxviii, 96.

63 *V.C.H. Worcs.* i, 318b.

64 Jeayes, op. cit. no. 148.

65 Prattinton Coll. (Soc. Antiq.).

66 *Reg. G. Giffard* (Worcs. Hist. Soc.), 30.

67 Ibid.; Worc. Epis. Reg. Wakefield, 1375–95, fol. 64 d.

68 Nash, op. cit. ii, 387.

69 *Valor Eccl.* (Rec. Com.), iii, 274.

70 Nash, loc. cit.

71 A grant of the advowson of Stone was made to William Tipper and Robert Dawe in 1590–1 (Pat. 33 Eliz. pt. i, m. 34).

72 Nash, loc. cit.

73 Inst. Bks. (P.R.O.).

Thatcher (date unknown) ; John Oldnall, will, 1690 ; Richard Hill, will, proved 1730 ; and Thomas Pratt, will, proved 1802, is regulated by a scheme of the Charity Commissioners, 4 August 1882, whereby the charity is divided into the educational branch, the church branch and the eleemosynary branch.

The trust property consists of 47 a. 3 r. and buildings of the rental value of £120 ; a rent-charge of £2 issuing out of Dawkes Meadow in respect of Oldnall's charity ; £7,055 9s. 6d. India 3 per cent. stock, belonging to the other charities above mentioned, and including proceeds of sales of land and royalties, and £190 11s. 6d. consols, which sums of stock are held by the official trustees ; also £16 8s. 6d. consols and £48 17s. 8d. like stock in the name of the Paymaster-General (Chancery Division), the dividends amounting in the aggregate to £218 4s.

The Educational Foundation, under an order of the Charity Commissioners, 20 February 1906, was determined to consist of the school premises, the dividends on £190 11s. 6d. consols, amounting to £4 15s., and an annual sum of 15s. for every £1 awarded to the school by the Board of Education and two-fifths of the remainder of the net income ; the church branch to consist of one-fifth of the remainder of the net income, two-fifths of such remainder being assigned to the eleemosynary branch.

In 1910 a sum of £36 4s. 4d. represented one-fifth of the remainder of the net income.

In 1817 William Wheeler by his will left a legacy of £200 (less duty) for the use of the poor in such manner as his daughter should direct. A portion of the principal sum appears to have been expended, and the remainder is now represented by £76 8s. 11d. consols, the annual dividends of which, amounting to £1 18s., are applied for the benefit of necessitous poor under a scheme of the Charity Commissioners, 23 January 1883.

OLD SWINFORD

Swineforde (xi cent.).

The parish of Old Swinford is situated in the north-west of the county on the border of Staffordshire. The total area, including the hamlet of Amblecote, which is in Staffordshire, is 3,369 acres. In the Worcestershire part of the parish there were in 1905 615½ acres of arable, 966¾ of permanent grass and only 7 of woods and plantations, while Amblecote included 112½ acres of arable land and 304½ acres of grass.[1] The River Stour flows westward and then northward through the parish, separating it from Staffordshire. From its valley, which is about 200 ft. above the ordnance datum, the land gradually rises, especially towards the north-east of Amblecote, where heights of 400 ft. are reached. The south is undulating.

The subsoil of Old Swinford varies considerably ; the eastern portion is situated on the South Staffordshire coalfield, in the west the subsoil consists of Bunter Pebble beds, and in the south of Keuper Sandstone. Coal and iron are found and a peculiarly rich fireclay is mined in the district.

Old Swinford comprised the townships of Stourbridge, Upper Swinford, Wollaston, Lye and Wollescote, the hamlet of Amblecote in Staffordshire and that of Norton to the south of Stourbridge.

The first settlement in Old Swinford may have been on the higher ground, as the church of St. Mary the Virgin was placed in the south of the parish at more than 100 ft. above the level of the river, but even in the later mediaeval period houses and a chapel were built on the site of the present town of Stourbridge, and little by little the houses stretched along that portion of the Bromsgrove and Wolverhampton road known as the High Street. In modern times a lateral extension of Stourbridge joined it to the older settlements of Wollaston on the west and Lye on the east, and Stamber Mill became of some industrial importance.

In the 16th century there are said to have been 700 'houselyng people' in the parish.[2]

Among buildings of interest in Stourbridge the Talbot Inn in the High Street dates from the early 17th century, when it was the residence of the Foleys. The present front appears to have been added in the 18th century. The principal stairs are of the earlier date and have turned balusters and massive newel posts. Original panelling and plasterwork remain in some of the rooms. The buildings, which are partly of half-timber, are grouped round two courtyards. The Vine Inn, adjoining the grammar school on the east side of the High Street, is a good specimen of late 16th-century half-timber work. In Smithfield, at the back of the modern Market Hall, are some early 17th-century brick houses, including the Bell Inn, which has been very much altered and modernized.

The buildings of the grammar school were almost entirely rebuilt in 1862. The head master's house, though much altered internally and re-fronted at the same period, appears to be the sole remnant of the original structure. No detail of any interest remains here with the exception of the stairs, which are of the 18th century. The present front, facing on the High Street, is in the Perpendicular manner, with white brick facings and stone dressings. Various additions were made in 1883 and 1893, and in 1899 the Science buildings on the south side of the playground were erected. Quite recently additional property has been acquired on the north side of the school, on which four new class rooms, an Art room, and the necessary cloak rooms were erected in 1910. The initials S. J. on some panelling still preserved are said to have been carved by Samuel Johnson when at school here.

The buildings of Old Swinford Hospital consist at present of a northern and a southern block, connected by a covered corridor. The southern block is the building of the original foundation of 1670, the northern block and connecting corridor having been added in 1882, by which the school accommodation has been practically doubled. The original building, which is of brick with stone dressings, is three stories in height and faces east. The attic story was rebuilt

---

[1] Statistics from Bd. of Agric. (1905).

[2] Chant. Cert. 60, no. 20 ; 61, no. 16.

and heightened at the time of the additions above referred to. The plan is oblong and two rooms in depth. The eastern side of the ground floor is occupied by a large schoolroom, part of which is now used as a dining hall, and by the board room which opens out of it at the northern end. On the west, at the rear of the building, are the kitchen, staircase and the master's rooms. Some original wainscoting still remains in the large schoolroom, into which the main entrance opens directly. The board room, now used as the head master's study, has its original panelling in good preservation. Over the fireplace at the west end of the room hangs the portrait of the founder, Thomas Foley. The apartments at the north-west corner of the building seem to have originally formed the head master's house. The first and attic floors are occupied on the east side by large dormitories. The ground and first floors are lighted by small stone-mullioned windows, and the stories are marked externally by moulded string-courses of stone. The entrance doorway is in the centre of the east elevation, and has a moulded semicircular head springing from panelled pilasters, surmounted by an entablature, the centre of which is crowned by a curved pediment. The whole is flanked by large inverted consoles. In the head of the door itself, which is a fine piece of 17th-century joinery, is a small wooden figure of Charity. The walls of the attic floor have been entirely rebuilt. From the centre of the building rises a small brick turret, capped by a modern lantern. The roofs are tiled. At the rear of the main buildings is a small brick building of contemporary date, converted into class rooms about sixty years ago, and now utilized for play rooms. The modern northern block is designed in a style to correspond with the original southern block. In 1906 a new school hall, board room and head master's room were added.

At Wollaston, about a mile to the north-west of the centre of the town, is Wollaston Hall, a much modernized early 17th-century house of half-timber, L-shaped on plan, and two stories in height, facing north-west. The main limb of the L is two rooms in depth, and in the centre of the principal front is a recessed entrance porch, which probably opened in the first instance directly into the large room which occupies the southern end of this side of the building, out of which the present entrance corridor appears to have been taken. On the north side of the entrance are two large rooms *en suite*, making up the rest of the frontage, while to the rear of them are two narrower rooms of equal length. The stairs, which are of original date, are on the south side of the entrance corridor, at the back of the original entrance hall. The projecting wing on the east side of the house, containing the kitchen and offices, is of brick, and appears to be a later addition or rebuilding. With the exception of the stairs and some linen-pattern panelling in one of the rooms at the back, little original detail remains on the ground floor. In some of the first floor rooms the original roof-timbers are exposed, and the construction displays great ingenuity. The rooms to the south of the staircase are reached by a narrow and lofty central passage lighted by dormers. Generally the interior has been ruthlessly

restored and modernized. The front elevation is crowned by a range of five gables, filled with ornamental half-timbering disposed in quatrefoil panels with flat baluster-shaped uprights above them. On one of the beams is carved the date 1617, and in the apex of the southern gable are the initials R. M. The barge-boards and finials appear to be modern, but the carved brackets at the intersection of the gables are probably original. The back elevation is also gabled, but the wall has been covered with rough-cast, so that the timbering is concealed. The windows have in nearly every case been renewed and enlarged. The original brick chimney shafts have for the most part survived. The roofs are tiled. The garden slopes down in a succession of terraces to the valley of the Stour.

The Corbett Hospital in Amblecote was presented to the town by the late John Corbett. The house and grounds cover about 30 acres.

From the town of Stourbridge main roads pass to Dudley, Wolverhampton, Kidderminster and Bromsgrove. The Oxford, Worcester and Wolverhampton branch of the Great Western railway, opened to the town of Stourbridge in May 1852,[3] passes through the parish northward, with a station at Stourbridge Junction at the eastern end of the town. From this junction a branch known as the Stourbridge extension passes north-eastwards through the Black Country to Birmingham. There is a station at Lye on this line. Another branch known as the Town Extension passes through Stourbridge to the riverside, with a station at Foster Street.

Water communication is afforded by the River Stour and the Stourbridge Canal. An attempt was made, under the direction of Mr. Yarranton, towards the end of the 17th century, to make the River Stour navigable. It was made completely navigable from Stourbridge to Kidderminster, but the project then had to be given up for lack of funds.[4] In 1776 Acts were passed to make canals from Stourbridge to join the Staffordshire and Worcester Canal near Stourton, and from Dudley to join the first at Black Delph.[5] In 1785 this canal was extended to meet the Birmingham Canal.[6]

From the situation of a large part of the parish in the Black Country and the presence of minerals Old Swinford has become an important industrial centre. The clothing trade was once carried on in Stourbridge, but it died out at the beginning of the 19th century.[7] There are coal-mines and large iron-works; many of the inhabitants are employed in nail-making; chains, anvils, spades, shovels and scythes are also made. The district is especially noted for the manufacture of fire-bricks, made from the valuable fireclay which is mined here. The presence of this clay induced a number of refugees from Hungary and Lorraine, whose leader was Henzoil Henzey,[8] to take up their residence in 1556 on the piece of ground known as Lye Waste, and begin the manufacture of glass, which is still carried on, having increased greatly about 1845 owing to the abolition of the duties. The site of their first glass house is still known as Hungary Hill.

Lye Waste originally formed an uncultivated part of Lye, but became an irregular village on the

---

[3] Noake, *Guide to Worcs.* 332.
[4] Nash, *Hist. of Worcs.* ii, 45.
[5] Stat. 16 Geo. III, cap. 28, 66.

[6] Nash, loc. cit.   [7] Noake, op. cit. 331.
[8] The accounts of Mr. Thomas Milward show that Henzey's descendants still

owned glass houses at Stourbridge at the beginning of the 18th century (Prattinton Coll. (Soc. Antiq.).

Old Swinford Hospital : Entrance Front

Salwarpe Church : Altar Tomb to Olave Talbot and her
Mother Elizabeth

settlement of the glass-workers. Their right of separate freehold was established on the passing of an Inclosure Act.[9]

Stourbridge is the head of a county court district. Petty sessions are held weekly at the court-house in Hagley Road. Acts were passed in 1777 and 1846 to expedite the recovery of small debts in Old Swinford.[10]

Under an Act passed in 1825-6 [11] Stourbridge was governed by a board of commissioners, who established there a town hall with a corn exchange and market. Another Act was passed in 1866 dividing the town into three wards—East, West, and South—and arranging for the inclusion of Lye, Wollaston, or Amblecote if the ratepayers of those hamlets should at any future time desire it.[12] This Act was amended in 1891,[13] and in 1894 the government of the town was vested

house of a certain Edward Milward. He was defeated and almost taken prisoner in a battle fought on Stourbridge Common in 1645.[15] A Mr. Dovaston, clerk to Thomas Milward, grandson of the above Edward, gives the following account of the prince's escape: The prince 'riding very hard to get towards Wollescote was pursued very close by a Parliament Trooper with his sword drawn. When the Prince came to the Heath Gate leading off the Common to Old Swinford, the Gate being shut and the Trooper very near to him, and there being a Boy near the Gate, the Prince cried "Open the Gate," when the Boy opened it, and when he was through he said hastily "Shut the Gate," which the Boy immediately did. This stopped the Trooper and saved the Prince.' The defeat caused the prince to remove from Wollescote, and before his departure he gave a signet ring to

WOLLASTON HALL, STOURBRIDGE : ENTRANCE FRONT

in an urban district council. The town is now divided into five wards—East, South, West, Old Swinford, and Wollaston. An attempt is being made (1912) to have these wards incorporated into a borough. Lye is governed by a separate urban district council of nine members, formed in 1897.

During the Civil War Basil Earl of Denbigh retreated to Stourbridge after his victory at Dudley in 1644 to await the arrival of Sir William Waller.[14] Shortly afterwards Wollescote became the head quarters of Prince Rupert, who is said to have stayed at the

Edward Milward, with the promise 'that when the King's affairs turned out prosperously he should have his loss repaired on presenting the Ring to the King and stating the circumstances.' [16] Stourbridge was the first place at which Charles II halted on his flight from Worcester after the battle. The 'Talbot' was in his line of march from Worcester to Staffordshire, but whether it was the inn where the king stopped to refresh is uncertain.

Among the MSS. relating to Old Swinford in the Prattinton Collection [17] are some extracts from the

[9] The parish of Old Swinford was inclosed in 1782 (Blue Bk. Incl. Awards, 191) under an Act of 1780 (Priv. 20 Geo. III, cap. 37).
[10] Burton, Bibl. of Worcs. (Worcs. Hist. Soc.), i, 67, 113; Stat. 17 Geo. III, cap. 19; 9 & 10 Vict. cap. 95.
[11] Local and Personal Act, 6 Geo. IV, cap. 19.   [12] Ibid. 29 & 30 Vict. cap. 169.
[13] Ibid. 54 & 55 Vict. cap. 119.
[14] Cal. S. P. Dom. 1644, p. 236.
[15] Ibid. 1645-7, p. 243; Prattinton Coll. (Soc. Antiq.).
[16] Prattinton Coll. (Soc. Antiq.).
[17] Soc. Antiq.

account books of the above-named Thomas Milward, who was an attorney at Stourbridge. These include the following :—

> 1704, 20 Feb.—Paid at the Cocking at Naggs Head, 2s. 6d.
> 1717, 8 Mar.—To John Compton, junr., of Wollaston, which he paid me at last Worcester Assizes in order to have agreed with the Clerk of the Assizes for the indictment at the Riot and pulling down Meeting House etc. (He gave 3s. 9d. for my trouble), 14s. 9d.
> 1718, 23 Oct.—Paid for my ale and colt ale at Stourbridge Court Leet, being my first time, 3s.
> 1719, 17 Aug.—Lost at the Cocking at Thomas Blount's, 13s. 6d.
> 1719, 19 Sept.—From Thomas Blount of Holloway for baiting the bull on Monday and Tuesday, being Kinfare Wake, 9s. 6d.
> Thos. Yorke drawing my Tooth, being the furthermost on the upper and right side. He drew one for Duggall the servant at the same time to shew me how easie. 1s.
> 1717, 15 May.—Paid to Mr. Philip Yorke for bleeding me, tho' he first pricked my left arm and missed the vein, 1s.
> Mr. Hopkins the Barber 1 yrs shaving and powdring me, 2s. 6d.
> Gave in cash to my wife 2s. 6d. to be repaid as she said.

Samuel Rogers the poet (1763–1855) was a native of Stourbridge, his paternal grandfather being a glass manufacturer of that town.[17a]

Seventeenth-century place-names are Hillmans Close, Milwardes Meadow, Madewelles Meadow and Ardens Meadow.[18]

In the time of Edward the Confessor *MANORS* *OLD SWINFORD* was held by Wulfwine, but in 1086 William Fitz Ansculf was in possession. It was held of him by Acard,[19] probably the same who held the adjoining manor of Pedmore.[20] The overlordship of Old Swinford followed the descent of Dudley (q.v.) until it lapsed in 1320, when John de Somery acquired the manor in fee.[21]

In the 13th century Acard's successor as tenant was a certain Ralph de Merston,[22] from whom the manor passed before 1285 to Bernard de Bruys.[23] The latter was succeeded in 1300–1[24] by his son of the same name, who in 1320–1 surrendered the manor to John de Somery, his overlord.[25] From that date the manor followed the same descent as Northfield[26] (q.v.) until the beginning of the 15th century, when a third of both manors belonged to Maurice Berkeley and the remaining two thirds to James Earl of Wiltshire, on whom they had been settled by his grandmother Joan Lady Bergavenny.[27] It was decided in settlement of the disputes which followed that the Earl of Wiltshire should have Old Swinford and pay 40s. yearly to Maurice Berkeley.[28] The manor then passed with Hagley until the death of Fulk Stafford about 1462.[29] Margaret, widow of Fulk, was given one third of the manor as her dower.[30]

The remaining two thirds and the reversion of Margaret's share were granted on 22 January 1463 to Sir John Scott,[31] and confirmed to him in 1476.[32]

Sir John Scott appears to have held two thirds of Old Swinford until 1481; on 30 July of that year he had surrendered his grants and received another which did not include Old Swinford.[33] Margaret Stafford was then said to be dead, but on 21 November two thirds of the manor and the reversion of Margaret's third on her death were granted to the Dean and canons of St. George's Chapel,

BUTLER. *Or a chief indented azure.*

Windsor.[34] This grant was evidently cancelled, for in 1485 the Earl of Wiltshire's attainder was reversed in favour of his brother Thomas Earl of Ormond,[35] and this manor was restored to him.[36] It then followed the same descent as Hagley[37] (q.v.) until 1661, when Katherine Lady Lyttelton and her son Sir Henry Lyttelton, bart., sold Old Swinford to Thomas Foley.[38]

It passed in the same way as the advowson of the church of Pedmore (q.v.) to the Lords Foley, and remained in their possession[39] until 1844–5, when it was purchased by the trustees of William Lord Ward,[40] who was created Earl of Dudley in 1860.[41] The manor now belongs to his son William Humble Ward, the present earl, who succeeded to the peerage in 1885.[42]

On 14 November 1482 Edward IV granted to the Dean and canons of St. George's Chapel, Windsor, who then held the manor, a market weekly on Tuesdays at their town of Old Swinford and Stourbridge, and two fairs yearly, one on the feast of St. Edward the Confessor (18 March), and another on the feast of St. Augustine (28 August), with a court of pie-powder and all issues and tolls.[43] A similar grant was made in 1486 to Thomas Earl of Ormond.[44]

The right of a weekly market on Friday and two fairs yearly, as in 1482, was afterwards held by the Lytteltons.[45] The profits of the fairs belonged in the 17th century to the bailiff of the manor, who had no other fee.[46] In 1792 and 1888 the market day was Friday,[47] but markets are now held on Friday and Saturday. Fairs were held in 1792 on 29 March and 8 September, but since 1888 there has been only one fair on the last Monday in March.[48] The latter was formerly a noted horse fair. The market rights belong to the local authorities.[49]

[17a] *Dict. Nat. Biog.*
[18] Recov. R. D. Enr. Mich. 4 Chas. I, m. 12.
[19] *V.C.H. Worcs.* i, 317a.
[20] Ibid.
[21] *Red Bk. of Exch.* (Rolls Ser.), 567 ; *Testa de Nevill* (Rec. Com.), 40, 43.
[22] *Testa de Nevill* (Rec. Com.), 40b.
[23] *Reg. G. Giffard* (Worcs. Hist. Soc.), 262 ; Chan. Inq. p.m. 19 Edw. I, no. 14. In 1290 the manor with the advowson was worth £9.
[24] Chan. Inq. p.m. 12 Edw. II, no. 38.
[25] Feet of F. Worcs. 14 Edw. II, no. 25.
[26] Ibid. 33 Edw. III, no. 11 ; Div. Co. Mich. 3 Hen. V ; Chan. Inq. p.m. 9 Ric. II, no. 4 ; Pat. 9 Ric. II, pt. ii,

m. 10 ; Chan. Inq. p.m. 8 Hen. V, no. 116 ; 1 Hen. VI, no. 65. Lucy widow of John de Somery held the manor for life (Close, 16 Edw. II, m. 20).
[27] Early Chan. Proc. bdle. 19, no. 6.
[28] Ibid.
[29] Chan. Inq. p.m. 3 Edw. IV, no. 12 ; *Cal. Pat.* 1461–7, p. 112.
[30] Pat. 2 Edw. IV, pt. ii, m. 12 ; 3 Edw. IV, pt. ii, m. 5.
[31] Ibid. 2 Edw. IV, pt. ii, m. 12.
[32] Ibid. 16 Edw. IV, pt. ii, m. 21.
[33] Ibid. 21 Edw. IV, pt. ii, m. 7.
[34] Ibid. m. 3.
[35] *Rolls of Parl.* vi, 296a.
[36] Pat. 1 Hen. VII, pt. iv.
[37] For references see Hagley.

[38] Feet of F. Worcs. Hil. 12 Chas. II.
[39] Nash, op. cit. ii, 212 ; Recov. R. Hil. 42 Geo. III, rot. 21 ; Trin. 13 Will. III, rot. 204.
[40] *Clergy Lists.*
[41] Burke, *Peerage.*   [42] Ibid.
[43] Pat. 22 Edw. IV, pt. ii, m. 21.
[44] Ibid. 1 Hen. VII, pt. iv.
[45] Chan. Inq. p.m. (Ser. 2), cclvii, 7 ; Misc. Bks. Ld. Rev. ccxxviii, fol. 308–10.
[46] Exch. Spec. Com. Worc. no. 2519.
[47] *Rep. on Market Rts. and Tolls,* i, 216.
[48] Ibid. Pinnock mentions a fair held at Stourbridge on 8 January (*Hist. and Topog. of Engl. and Wales,* vi, 30).
[49] *Rep. on Market Rts. and Tolls,* xiii (1), 322–3.

The courts for the manor of Old Swinford were held in Sir John St. Leger's time at a house called the gate-house in Old Swinford, but Sir John Lyttelton instituted the practice of holding them in the town hall.[50] It was alleged in 1594 that the court for the manor of Old Swinford and Stourbridge used to be held at one end of the town hall of Stourbridge, and that for the manor of Bedcote at the other end.[51] No court for either manor has been held for many years.[52]

There was a mill in the manor of Old Swinford at the time of the Domesday Survey.[53] In 1338 Joan Botetourt, lady of the manor, granted a water-mill called Rotherford Mill with a stank, stew and watercourse, with suit of multure by her tenants in Old Swinford at the mill, to be held at a yearly rent of 14s.[54]

A mill at Bedcote is mentioned in deeds of 1317 and 1338,[55] and a water-mill belonged to the manor of Amblecote in 1636.[56] A mill at Amblecote is mentioned in deeds of 1663, 1680 and 1688.[57] There were two water-mills built under one roof in the manor of Wollaston in 1592 and 1628.[58] Bedcote and Wollaston Mills still exist on the River Stour, and near the former is a corn-mill.

Before the Conquest *AMBLECOTE* (Elmelcote, xi cent.; Emelecot, Amelecot, xiii cent.; Hamelcote, xiv cent.) was in the hands of two men of Earl Algar, who held it 'without soke.' It had passed before 1086 to William Fitz Ansculf, of whom it was then held by Payn.[59] It was held of the lords of Dudley, at first apparently of the honour of Dudley, but afterwards, probably from the beginning of the 14th century, of the manor of Old Swinford, and the overlordship followed the same descent as that manor,[60] being last mentioned in 1636.[61]

Under the lords of Dudley the manor was held by the Birminghams, lords of Birmingham,[62] co. Warwick, during the 12th, 13th and 14th centuries,[63] but their interest seems to have lapsed shortly after 1322, as it is not mentioned after that date.[64]

Under the Birminghams the manor was held early in the 13th century for knight's service by Robert de Wavere.[65] Robert was probably succeeded by Cecily, who was 'lady of Amblecote' in 1255.[66] She appears to have married

BIRMINGHAM. *Party indented argent and sable.*

William de Stafford, and is alluded to as Cecily de Stafford in 1271.[67] The manor was held by tenants named William de Stafford in 1284–5,[68] 1290,[69] and in 1316.[70] In 1317 Sir William de Stafford gave it to his grandson James son of William de Stafford,[71] and James apparently held it until 1322, when he forfeited it as a rebel, and it was granted by the king to John de Somery, the overlord of the fee.[72] James de Stafford was pardoned in October 1322, and Sir William de Stafford, probably the grandfather of James mentioned above, was pardoned and released from prison in March 1323.[73] It does not appear that the manor of Amblecote was ever restored to James, for in 1338 his father, William de Stafford, who, according to statements made later on by the Erdeswicks, descendants of James, had ousted the latter from the manor on the death of James's grandfather, Sir William de Stafford, was in possession of the manor.[74] He granted it in that year to another son, John de Stafford, and his wife Margaret in tail, with remainder in default of their issue to James de Stafford and his heirs.[75] John de Stafford seems to have remained in peaceful possession of the manor during his life, but after his death his widow Margaret, and later their son Humphrey de Stafford, had to make good their claim in a prolonged suit brought against them by James de Stafford's daughter Margaret, wife of Sir John de Hardeshull, and continued after her death by her son Thomas de Erdeswick.[76] The matter was finally settled in 1377 in favour of Humphrey de Stafford.[77] From him the manor passed in 1413 to his son Sir Humphrey Stafford of Hook,[78] known as Humphrey with the silver hand.

Before his death in 1442 [79] Sir Humphrey settled[80] the manor of Amblecote upon Amice, afterwards Countess of Wiltshire, daughter of his eldest son Richard, with remainder to the heirs of his other sons John and William, and failing such heirs to the Staffords of Grafton.[81] Amice died without issue, and Humphrey son of John de Stafford succeeded to the manor.[82] He also died without issue in 1461,[83] and was succeeded by his cousin Humphrey, son of William de Stafford, the youngest son of Sir Humphrey.[84]

On 7 July 1461 he received a grant from the Crown of all the manors and lands of which Humphrey Stafford had been seised,[85] and Amblecote appears to have been included. Sir Humphrey Stafford was created Lord Stafford of Southwick in 1464 and Earl of Devon in 1469. Shortly afterwards he fell under the king's displeasure through having refused to assist

---

[50] Nash, op. cit. ii, 208.
[51] Stowe MSS. (B.M.), 753, no.
[52] Noake, op. cit. 330.
[53] V.C.H. Worcs. i, 317.
[54] Cal. Pat. 1338–40, p. 4.
[55] Anct. D. (P.R.O.), A 9101, 9102.
[56] Chan. Inq. p.m. (Ser. 2), cccclxxxiii, 64.
[57] Feet of F. Staff. Trin. 15 Chas. II; Mich. 32 Chas. II; Trin. 4 Jas. II.
[58] Close, 34 Eliz. pt. xxii, Persehowse and Liddeatt; Recov. R. D. Enr. Mich. 4 Chas. I, m. 12.
[59] Dom. Bk. (Rec. Com.), 249b.
[60] Red Bk. of Exch. (Rolls Ser.), 269; Testa de Nevill (Rec. Com.), 46b; Feud. Aids, v, 9; Chan. Inq. p.m. 19 Edw. I, no. 14; 16 Edw. II, no. 72; 1 Edw. IV, no. 30; 12 Edw. IV, no. 27; (Ser. 2), cxxvii, 46.

[61] Chan. Inq. p.m. (Ser. 2), dliv, 64.
[62] Dugdale gives a pedigree of this family in his Hist. of Warw. 898.
[63] Red Bk. of Exch. (Rolls Ser.), 269; Feud. Aids, v, 9; Chan. Inq. p.m. 19 Edw. I, no. 14; 16 Edw. II, no. 72.
[64] Chan. Inq. p.m. 16 Edw. II, no. 72.
[65] Testa de Nevill (Rec. Com.), 46b.
[66] Will. Salt Arch. Soc. Coll. v (1), 111. Roger de Amblecote, 'brother of the lady of Amelecote,' is mentioned in 1262 (ibid. 138); so it would seem that Cecily inherited Amblecote under some settlement.
[67] Ibid. iv, 201.
[68] Feud. Aids, v, 9.
[69] Chan. Inq. p.m. 19 Edw. I, no. 14.
[70] Feud. Aids, v, 16.
[71] Anct. D. (P.R.O.), A 9101.
[72] Cal. Pat. 1321–4, p. 120.

[73] Cal. Close, 1318–23, p. 634.
[74] Will. Salt Arch. Soc. Coll. xiii, 109, 139.
[75] Anct. D. (P.R.O.), A 9102.
[76] Will. Salt Arch. Soc. Coll. xiii, 102, 105, 109, 110, 139.
[77] Ibid. 139.
[78] Chan. Inq. p.m. 1 Hen. V, no. 41; Wrottesley, Ped. from Plea R. 472.
[79] N. and Q. (Ser. 4), viii, 286.
[80] John Bishop of Bath and Wells and later Archbishop of Canterbury, brother of Humphrey Stafford with the silver hand, was one of the trustees in this settlement (Chan. Inq. p.m. 1 Edw. IV, no. 30; N. and Q. [Ser. 4], viii, 306).
[81] Chan. Inq. p.m. 1 Edw. IV, no. 30.
[82] Ibid.   [83] Ibid.
[84] Ibid.
[85] Pat. 1 Edw. IV, pt. iv, m. 7.

the Earl of Pembroke in suppressing Sir John Conyers' rebellion, and was beheaded and attainted on 24 August 1469. His lands were forfeited, but on 9 November the king granted licence to his heirs to take possession of them.[86] As he died without issue,[87] these heirs were the daughters of his aunt Alice Stafford, namely, Elizabeth, who married Sir John Coleshill and died without issue, Anne, who married Sir John Willoughby, and Eleanor, who became the wife of Thomas Strangways.[88] On the death of the Earl of Devon Humphrey Stafford of Grafton had entered into the manor, claiming it as the heir male under the settlement made by Sir Humphrey with the silver hand,[89] and in spite of the grant of 1469 he apparently enjoyed possession of the manor until 1473, when he was ejected by Robert Willoughby de Broke, son of Anne Willoughby.[90] In the reign of Richard III, however, Humphrey, being 'in favour and conceit' with the king, was able to eject Robert and his coparceners, and seems to have remained in possession of the manor until the beginning of the reign of Henry VII.[91] In 1485, on the petition of Robert Willoughby, Elizabeth Coleshill and Eleanor Strangways, the property was restored to them by Henry VII.[92] The Erdeswicks seem to

STRANGWAYS. *Sable two lions passant paly argent and gules.*

GREY of GROBY. *Barry argent and azure.*

have renewed their claim to the manor at about this time, but gave up all their right in exchange for 1,000 marks in 1481–2.[93]

The manor of Amblecote seems to have fallen to the share of Eleanor Strangways, for in 1504 her son[94] Henry Strangways died seised of it, leaving a son and heir Giles,[95] who as Sir Giles Strangways, kt., sold the manor in 1540 to Rowland Shakerley, who conveyed it in the same year to Thomas Grey.[96] It passed from him in 1559 to his son John.[97] In 1591 it was arranged that, as John Grey had no children, Mary the daughter of his younger brother George should marry either Henry son of Sir George Grey of

Pirgoe, co. Essex, or one of his brothers Ambrose and George. If this marriage did not take place the manor was to go to Henry, Ambrose and George in tail-male successively, and £1,000 was to be paid to Mary.[98] John conveyed the manor to Sir Henry Grey for the purposes of this trust in 1591–2,[99] and died in 1595.[100] Edward, his brother and heir, released all his right in the manor to Sir Henry Grey.[1] In March 1601 Mary, then aged about fourteen, expressed her determination not to marry any one of the three brothers.[2] Sir Henry Grey, who was created Lord Grey of Groby in 1603, probably held the manor until his death in 1614,[3] though Edward Grey was party to a fine dealing with it in 1606.[4] It passed on the death of Sir Henry to his son Ambrose Grey,[5] whose two brothers George and Henry had died without issue.[6] He died seised of it in 1636, when his son Henry succeeded.[7] In 1652 Henry Grey and his wife Mary conveyed the manor to Anne Gerrard, widow, for ninety-nine years, if she should live so long.[8]

Henry Grey died in 1686, and, his two children both having died unmarried,[9] the manor of Amblecote appears to have passed to his cousin John Grey of Enville, one of the grandsons of Sir John Grey, the eldest son of Sir Henry Grey, lord of Groby.[10] Harry Grey, son of this John, succeeded his cousin Thomas as Earl of Stamford in 1719–20.[11] The manor passed with the title[12] from that time until the death without issue of the seventh Earl of Stamford in 1883. It was held by his widow Catherine until her death in 1905,[13] and then passed under the will of the earl to his wife's grand-niece Catherine Sarah, wife of Sir Henry Foley Lambert, seventh baronet, daughter of the Rev. Alfred Payne, rector of Enville.[14] Sir Henry assumed the surname Grey in lieu of Lambert in 1905 in accordance with the terms of the earl's will, and his widow Lady Grey is now lady of the manor of Amblecote.

The manor of *BEDCOTE* (Bettecote, xiv cent.) was held of the manor of Old Swinford.[15] In 1289–90 William de Boys conveyed a messuage and land in Bedcote and Foxcote to Geoffrey de Kynsedele.[16] Early in the 14th century Sir William Stafford, who held the adjoining manor of Amblecote, appears to have held some property at Bedcote within the manor of Old Swinford. In 1317 he enfeoffed his grandson James Stafford of a mill, &c., there to hold in tail with reversion in default to himself.[17] This estate evidently descended with Amblecote[18] to Sir Humphrey Stafford of Hook, who granted it to his son Sir John Stafford and Anne

[86] Pat. 9 Edw. IV, pt. ii, m. 10.
[87] In the inquisition taken on his lands it is stated that Amblecote was entailed on the heirs male of Sir Humphrey Stafford with the silver hand (Chan. Inq. p.m. 12 Edw. IV, no. 27). In the inquisition taken on the death of his cousin Humphrey in 1461 no mention was made of male heirs in the entail.
[88] Pat. 9 Edw. IV, pt. ii, m. 10 ; Chan. Inq. p.m. 19 Edw. IV, no. 47.
[89] Chan. Inq. p.m. 12 Edw. IV, no. 27.
[90] *Will. Salt Arch. Soc. Coll.* (New Ser.), vi (1), 149 ; Coram Rege R. Rex, East. 1 Edw. V, m. 1 d.
[91] *Rolls of Parl.* vi, 325–6.
[92] Ibid.
[93] Feet of F. Staff. Mich. 7 Hen. VII.
[94] Hutchins, *Hist. of Dors.* ii, 662.

[95] Exch. Inq. p.m. (Ser. 2), file 1017, no. 19.
[96] Feet of F. Staff. Mich. 32 Hen. VIII ; Recov. R. D. Enr. Trin. 32 Hen. VIII, m. 6 d., 11, 14.
[97] Chan. Inq. p.m. (Ser. 2), cxxvii, 46.
[98] Ibid. dclxxx, 4.
[99] Recov. R. Trin. 34 Eliz. rot. 10 ; Close, 41 Eliz. pt. xxi, Graye and Graye.
[100] Chan. Inq. p.m. (Ser. 2), dclxxx, 4.
[1] Close, 41 Eliz. pt. xxi, Graye and Graye.
[2] Chan. Inq. p.m. (Ser. 2), dclxxx, 4. She married William Stanley of Bromwich (Shaw, *Hist. of Staff.* ii, 268).
[3] G.E.C. *Complete Peerage*, iv, 98.
[4] Feet of F. Div. Co. Trin. 4 Jas. I.
[5] Recov. R. D. Enr. Hil. 12 Jas. I, m. 7 d.

[6] Shaw, op. cit. ii, 269.
[7] Chan. Inq. p.m. (Ser. 2), dliv, 64.
[8] Feet of F. Staff. Mich. 1652.
[9] Shaw, op. cit. ii, 273. [10] Ibid. 269.
[11] G.E.C. *Complete Peerage*, vii, 230.
[12] Recov. R. Staff. Hil. 3 Geo. III, rot. 138 ; Trin. 37 Geo. III, rot. 143 ; Mich. 5 Geo. IV, rot. 321.
[13] Burke, *Peerage.*
[14] G.E.C. *Complete Peerage*, vii, 232, note f.
[15] Chan. Inq. p.m. 1 Edw. IV, no. 30 ; Nash, op. cit. ii, 208, 210.
[16] Feet of F. Worcs. 18 Edw. I, no. 17.
[17] Anct. D. (P.R.O.), A 9101.
[18] Ibid. 9102 ; Nash, op. cit. ii, 208. Humphrey Stafford mortgaged the manor in 1416 to Robert Daniel for 250 marks (Nash, loc. cit.).

Old Swinford : The Talbot Inn, Stourbridge

his wife in tail, with remainder to William Stafford, another son.[19] From Sir John Stafford and Anne his wife it passed to their son Humphrey, who died seised of it on 6 August 1461.[20] From this time it followed the same descent as the manor of Amblecote, to the co-heirs of Humphrey Earl of Devon,[21] and was apparently also assigned to Eleanor Strangways, as in 1541 William Strangways[22] of Stockstrete *alias* Lockets, in Dorset, sold the manor to Richard Jervois, merchant.[23] Bedcote was sold in 1626 by Sir Thomas Jervois,[24] grandson of Richard, to Nicholas Sparry.[25] The manor seems afterwards to have passed to the Lytteltons, for in 1660–1 it was conveyed with the manor of Old Swinford to Thomas Foley.[26] From that date the manor followed the same descent as that of Old Swinford.[27]

Bedcote Manor is mentioned in 1868, when it belonged to the Earl of Dudley, and its boundaries are said to have been identical with those of Stourbridge.[28] There appears to be no manor at the present day.

The manor of *STOURBRIDGE* (Steresbridge, xiv cent. ; Storebrige, Sturbrygge, xv cent.) is stated to have been dependent on the chief manor of Old Swinford, and to have been partly comprised within the manor of Bedcote.[29] It was probably this part which was granted with the manor of Bedcote by Sir Humphrey Stafford of Hook to Sir John Stafford and Anne his wife, from whom it descended to their son Humphrey, who died seised of it with Bedcote in 1461.[30] It passed with Bedcote to the co-heirs of Humphrey Stafford.[31] It seems to have become identical with the manor of Bedcote from this time, and no further mention of it occurs.

A second manor of Stourbridge followed the same descent as the manor of Old Swinford. The first mention of it occurs in 1482, when Edward IV granted to the Dean and Chapter of St. George's, Windsor, certain liberties in their manor of Old Swinford and Stourbridge.[32] It was restored with Old Swinford to Thomas Lord Ormond.[33] From that time it apparently followed the same descent as the manor of Old Swinford.[34] It still existed as a separate manor in 1866.[34a]

The earliest mention of *WOLLASTON* (Wullaston, xiii cent.) is in 1240–1, when William de la Platte and his wife Hawise conveyed land and rent there to Peter de Prestwood.[35] The manor afterwards belonged to the family of Perrott. William Perrott of Wollaston and his son John are mentioned

in a deed of 1442–3,[36] and it passed afterwards to Roger Perrott, who was succeeded by a son William and a grandson Humphrey.[37] Anne widow of William Perrott married John Persehowse, and in 1592 she and Humphrey, with Richard Persehowse, who then held the manor, but whose relationship to John does not appear, sold to George Liddeatt, a merchant tailor of London, the manor, with the capital messuage called Wollaston Hall.[38] It seems that George bought other property at Wollaston of John Taylor, sen., and John Taylor, jun.[39] George was succeeded by John Liddeatt of Cannock, co. Staff., who conveyed the manor in 1616 to Thomas Banneste,[40] probably for a settlement, as it was reconveyed to John in the same year.[41] He and his wife Jane mortgaged it in 1628 to Frances Manning, widow.[42]

PERROTT of Wollaston. *Gules three pears or and a chief argent with a demi-lion sable therein.*

John Liddeatt died in 1639,[43] and by his will, dated 19 June 1639, he bequeathed it to his son John for life, and then to 'such son of his said son as should be of best behaviour.' John was then eleven years of age. Edward Liddeatt was appointed executor of the will.[44] Edward Liddeatt and John Liddeatt and Elizabeth his wife dealt with the manor in 1672,[45] but after that date all trace of a manor here seems to have disappeared.

Wollaston Hall was the seat of the Wheeler family for some years at the end of the 17th and the beginning of the 18th century.[46] It passed from this family to the Addenbrooks.[47]

LIDDEATT. *Gules a fesse erminois between three wolves' heads or cut off at the neck.*

PIRCOTE GRANGE was held by the Abbot and convent of Halesowen in 1291 ; they had there a carucate of land, the value of which was 10s., and a fixed rent of 2s. 6d.,[48] but it does not appear how they gained possession of it. The abbey retained this property until the Dissolution[49] ; it was then let out at farm at a rent of 42s. Pircote Grange is not

[19] Chan. Inq. p.m. 1 Edw. IV, no. 30.
[20] Ibid.
[21] *Rolls of Parl.* vi, 325–6.
[22] He was probably son of Thomas Strangways son of Eleanor (Hutchins, *Hist. of Dors.* ii, 662).
[23] Close, 32 Hen. VIII, pt. ii ; Feet of F. Div. Co. Hil. 32 Hen. VIII. Richard is said to have been born at Kidderminster 'of mean parents.' He became 'apprenticed in London, by his industry got wealth and afterwards purchased the said manor of Bedcote' (Stowe MSS. [B.M.], 753, no. 9).
[24] At a court baron of Sir Thomas Jervois the boundaries of the manor of Bedcote are fully described, and printed by Nash, op. cit. ii, 208.
[25] Feet of F. Worcs. Hil. 1 Chas. I ; Prattinton Coll. (Soc. Antiq.), Deeds of D. and C. of Worc. no. 327.

[26] Feet of F. Worcs. Hil. 12 Chas. II.
[27] Ibid. East. 16 Chas. II ; Recov. R. Trin. 13 Will. III, rot. 204 ; Hil. 42 Geo. III, rot. 21.
[28] Noake, op. cit. 330.
[29] Nash, op. cit. ii, 207, quoting from an original MS. volume in the evidence chest of Stourbridge School.
[30] Chan. Inq. p.m. 1 Edw. IV, no. 30. In 1461 the manor was held of Fulk Stafford.
[31] *Rolls of Parl.* vi, 325–6 ; Pat. 1 Hen. VII, no. 54.
[32] *Cal. Pat.* 1476–85, p. 333. Stourbridge had not been included in the grant of the manor of Old Swinford to the dean and chapter in the previous year.
[33] Pat. 1 Hen. VII, pt. iv.
[34] For references see Old Swinford.
[34a] Loc. and Personal Act, 29 & 30 Vict. cap. 169.

[35] Feet of F. Worcs. 25 Hen. III, no. 27.
[36] Feet of F. Staff. 21 Hen. VI, no. 37 ; *Will. Salt Arch. Soc. Coll.* xi, 234.
[37] Close, 34 Eliz. pt. xxii, Persehowse and Liddeatt.   [38] Ibid.
[39] Close, 14 Jas. I, pt. vii, no. 35.
[40] Ibid.
[41] Feet of F. Div. Co. Trin. 14 Jas. I.
[42] Recov. R. D. Enr. Mich. 4 Chas. I. m. 12.
[43] Chan. Inq. p.m. (Ser. 2), ccccxcii, 79.
[44] Ibid.
[45] Feet of F. Div. Co. Hil. 23 & 24 Chas. II ; Trin. 24 Chas. II.
[46] Burton, *Bibl. of Worc.* (Worcs. Hist. Soc.), i, 28, 30, 33, 44 ; Nash, op. cit. ii, 212.
[47] Shaw, *Hist. of Staff.* ii, 237.
[48] *Pope Nich. Tax.* (Rec. Com.), 230a.
[49] *Valor Eccl.* (Rec. Com.), iii, 207.

mentioned in the conveyance of the abbey's property to the king, made in 1538 by William Taylor, the last abbot,[50] but it must have been included, as on 9 June the manor was granted with the other lands of the abbey to Sir John Dudley.[51] On his attainder in 1553 it reverted to the Crown, and so remained until 9 October 1557, when it was granted to Sir John Bourne, chief secretary to Queen Mary, and Dorothy his wife.[52] No further mention of this estate has been found.

The church of *ST. MARY THE VIRGIN* consists of a chancel with north vestry and south chapel, a wide nave with north, south and west galleries and a western tower, the whole building being modern

OLD SWINFORD CHURCH : WEST TOWER FROM THE SOUTH

except the tower. The present chancel was built in 1898 and has a large seven-light transomed east window with tracery of the 'perpendicular' type. In the north and south walls are two three-light windows with flowing tracery, that on the south opening into the south chapel. Two arches to the west open into the chapel and organ chamber. Against the walls are clusters of shafting, supporting a wood barrel ceiling. The nave, built in 1842, is extremely wide and lofty, the roof having elaborately cusped and traceried queen post trusses. It is lit by fourteen two-light windows on either side, divided horizontally by the north and south galleries. On the north is a pinnacled porch of 14th-century style.

In the westernmost window of the south chapel is preserved some heraldic glass taken from the older east window. Amongst the coats are those of Lyttelton, Foley and Dudley.

The western tower, the only ancient part of the church, is a fine example of late 14th-century work, and is of four stages with an embattled parapet, a stone spire and angle buttresses. The spire has small trefoil-headed lights at two levels and a little above the parapet four two-light openings. The belfry windows are of two lights with a quatrefoil over. There are also openings to the north and south of the second stage in which the tracery is modern. The west window is of three lights and below it is the modern west door.

The tower contains a ring of eight bells : the first and second cast in 1902, the third by Matthew Bagley, 1687, the fourth by Matthew or Henry Bagley in 1686, inscribed 'Cantate Dominum (*sic*) canticum novum,' the fifth by Henry Bagley, dated 1686, the sixth recast in 1902, the seventh by Matthew Bagley, 1686, and the eighth by Abel Rudhall, dated 1740, and inscribed 'I to the church the living call, and to the grave do summon all.'

The plate consists of a small chalice dated 1646 and inscribed $^{H}_{PA}$ with a shield, a bird in chief between three (?) acorns, a cup (Puritan pattern) with the letter R repeated four times, a standing paten made in 1780, a small modern paten, and a flagon given by John Wheeler in 1708.

The registers before 1812 are as follows : (i) all entries 1602 to 1692 (this is a large book enriched with elaborate capitals and pen work) ; (ii) 1693 to 1718 ; (iii) 1719 to 1735 ; (iv) 1736 to 1752 ; (v) baptisms and burials 1747 to 1783, marriages 1753 only ; (vi) baptisms and burials 1768 to 1800 ; (vii) baptisms and burials 1800 to 1808 ; (viii) baptisms and burials 1808 to 1813 ; (ix) marriages 1754 to 1762 ; (x) marriages 1762 to 1774 ; (xi) marriages 1774 to 1780 ; (xii) marriages 1780 to 1795 ; (xiii) marriages 1795 to 1813 and three duplicate books ; (xiv) baptisms, burials and marriages 1717 to 1746 ; (xv) baptisms and burials 1747 to 1783, marriages 1747 to 1753 ; (xvi) baptisms and burials 1783 to 1805.

The church of *ST. THOMAS*, Stourbridge, consists of a chancel with an apsidal end, a north vestry and south organ chamber, a nave, north and south aisles, and a west tower with gallery entrances on either side.

The church was erected in 1726 with a bequest of £300 from Mr. Biggs, a clothier of Stourbridge, augmented by subscriptions, and was enlarged in 1890, when the chancel was rebuilt, the original entrances at the east end of the aisles converted respectively into the organ chamber and vestry, and the present porches built.

[50] Feet of F. Div. Co. Trin. 30 Hen. VIII.   [51] Pat. 30 Hen. VIII, pt. iii, m. 16.   [52] Pat. 4 & 5 Phil. and Mary, pt. vi, m. 19.

The building is faced with red brick with stone dressings and the main cornice is carried round the building. The chancel is designed to harmonize with the older part of the building and is lighted by three large windows. The body of the church is divided into four bays by Doric columns raised on high plinths. The roof is a large plaster barrel vault, intersected on either side by similar vaults over each bay of the aisles, and continued eastward over the chancel, terminating in a semi-dome above the apse. The body of the building is lighted by large semicircular aisle windows, one to each bay, across which are carried the galleries. The oak fronts of the latter are original 18th-century work.

The tower is three stages high, finished with a balustraded parapet with stone vases at the angles. There is a peal of eight bells by Lester & Pack, 1759, of which the seventh was recast by Mears & Stainbank in 1901.

The plate consists of a silver salver probably of 1697, though the date letter is almost obliterated; a 1742 silver cup inscribed 'The Gift of Thomas Hill 1745'; a silver cup of 1749 inscribed 'Hanc Lagenam in Usum Capellae in Oppido de Stourbridge Dono dedit Johannes Cook de Stourton Generosus 1748'; a modern silver cup of the same pattern as the older one, and a modern electro-plated paten.

At the time of the Dissolution there was a chapel dedicated to the HOLY TRINITY at Stourbridge, which had been founded in 1430 by Philip Harely and Joan his wife and endowed by various other benefactors.[53] The priest who served in the chapel 'stood charged to teach the poor men's children of the same parish frely . . . to saye masse in the chapell there . . . to assist the curate of Old Swinford, ye parish beyng very large and brode.'[54] The chapel, which is said by Nash to have stood where the school now stands,[55] evidently disappeared soon after the Dissolution, the chantry priest's house being granted in 1550 to William Winlove and Richard Field.[56]

The ecclesiastical parish of HOLY TRINITY, Amblecote, was formed in 1842.[57] The church was erected on a site given by the Earl of Stamford and Warrington. It is built of brick in the 13th-century style, and consists of a chancel, nave, and west tower. The living is a vicarage in the gift of Lady Grey, the owner of the manor.

The ecclesiastical parish of CHRIST CHURCH, Lye, was formed in 1843[58] from the townships of Lye and Wollescote. The church was built and endowed by Thomas Hill of Dennis Park, co. Staffs. The living is a vicarage in the gift of the Bishop of Worcester.

The building consists of a chancel, nave, north and south transepts, a west tower and vestries, and three porches, one on either side of the chancel opening into the transepts and one on the south side of the nave. The body of the church was built in 1843, but the transepts and east end were not added until later. It is a red brick building in the 'pointed' style and has a slate roof, while above the tower rises a light coloured brick spire, apparently a later addition.

The ecclesiastical parish of ST. JAMES, Wollaston, was formed in 1860,[59] and the living is in the gift of William Henry Foster of Apley Park.

The church consists of a chancel, with a north vestry and south organ chamber, north and south transepts, a nave and aisles, a south porch and a north-west tower. At the west end of the nave is a gallery. It was erected in 1860 in the 'decorated' style, and is built in purple-coloured bricks with stone dressings, while the open pitch pine roofs are covered with tiles.

The parish of ST. JOHN THE EVANGELIST, Stourbridge, was formed in 1862,[60] the living being a vicarage in the gift of the Earl of Dudley.

The church consists of a chancel, a north vestry and south organ chamber, a nave, north and south aisles, and a south porch. Over the west end of the nave is a small flèche. It was built from the designs of George Street in 1860 in Early English Gothic, the material being mainly red sandstone.

The ecclesiastical parish of Stamber Mill was formed in 1873, the living being a vicarage in the gift of the Bishop of Worcester. The church of ST. MARK was built in 1870 on a site given by F. T. Rufford.

It is a small red brick and timber building consisting of a chancel with an apsidal end, an organ chamber at the north and a vestry on the south, a nave, north and south aisles, and a north porch. The piers of the nave arcades are of cast-iron and support pitch pine arches, above which are clearstories of the same material. The roofs are slated.

ADVOWSONS A priest is mentioned in Domesday[61] and a church was in existence at Old Swinford at least as early as 1284–5, when the Abbot of Missenden conveyed the advowson, which had been granted to him by the bishop in the same year,[62] to Bernard de Bruys and Agatha his wife.[63] From that time the descent of the advowson has been identical with that of the manor.[64]

The vicar of St. Thomas's, Stourbridge, was at first elected by the parishioners by vote, but, since this led to very unseemly consequences, the church was brought under the control of the Ecclesiastical Commissioners in the middle of the 19th century.[65] The building was claimed as a chapel of ease by the rector of Old Swinford, but it was arranged, on the petition of the inhabitants, that it should remain a free chapel vested in the townspeople.[66] The ecclesiastical parish of St. Thomas was formed in 1866,[67] the living being a vicarage in the gift of the Bishop of Worcester.

The mission chapel at Chawnhill was registered for marriages in 1877.[68] There are also mission chapels in Union Street and at Lye.

The Roman Catholic church in Stourbridge was established in 1823. The present church, dedicated

---

[53] Chant. Cert. 25, no. 30.
[54] Ibid. 60, no. 20; 61, no. 16.
[55] Nash, op. cit. ii, 210.
[56] Pat. 4 Edw. VI, pt. iv.
[57] Pop. Ret. Staff. 1901, p. 5.
[58] Pop. Ret. Worcs. 1901, p. 7.
[59] Ibid. 8.
[60] Lond. Gaz. 5 Sept. 1862, p. 4367.

[61] V.C.H. Worcs. i, 317a.
[62] Reg. G. Giffard (Worcs. Hist. Soc.), 227.
[63] Feet of F. Worcs. 13 Edw. I, no. 10.
[64] Ibid. 14 Edw. II, no. 25; Reg. G. Giffard (Worcs. Hist. Soc.), 262, 329; Worcs. Inq. p.m. (Worcs. Hist. Soc.), i, 37; Cal. Pat. 1385–9, p. 149; Feet of

F. Div. Co. Mich. 3 Hen. V; Cal. Pat. 1461–7, pp. 112, 297; Pat. 7 Eliz. pt. viii, m. 40; Inst. Bks. (P.R.O.); Clergy Lists. [65] Noake, op. cit. 333.
[66] Goodyear, Stourbridge Old and New, 78.
[67] Lond. Gaz. 27 July 1866, p. 4231.
[68] Ibid. 2 Nov. 1877, p. 6000.

under the invocation of Our Lady and All Saints, was consecrated in 1891.[69] Attached is a convent of sisters of St. Paul and a school rebuilt in 1911.

There are also chapels for Baptists, Friends, Congregationalists, Methodists, Presbyterians, Unitarians, Wesleyans, and Catholic Apostolic worshippers. At Amblecote there are Primitive Methodist and Wesleyan chapels.

The Quakers erected a meeting-house at Stourbridge in 1680,[70] and in 1689 it was certified that a newly-built house at Stourbridge was set apart as a Quaker meeting-place.[71] Presbyterians were established at Old Swinford in 1672, when the houses of Richard Beckes and Jarvis Bryan were licensed for their worship.[72] In 1698 a place of worship for Presbyterians was erected in Coventry Street, Stourbridge.[73]

The Presbyterian chapel at Lye Waste was built at the beginning of the 19th century with money left by a certain William Scott of Birmingham in 1792.[74] Before that date services had been held in a private house, but were discontinued owing to the outbreak of the Priestley riots near Birmingham. There was at that time no other place of worship, and the inhabitants are said to have ' become proverbial for their ignorance and profaneness and their incivility to the passing stranger.'[75]

Educational Foundations. — For
CHARITIES the Free Grammar School and Old Swinford Hospital, see ' Schools.'[76]

Wheeler's School.—The educational charity of John Wheeler, founded by deed 1708, and further endowed by will of Henry Glover, proved in the P.C.C. 1717, is regulated by schemes of the Charity Commissioners, 1884 and 1900. The trust estate, which formerly consisted of house property, is now represented by £2,459 Lancashire and Yorkshire Railway 3 per cent. stock, producing £73 15s. 4d. yearly.

The Waste Bank School, founded in 1782 by will of Thomas Hill, is endowed with a sum of £200 consols, the annual dividends of £5 being applicable for the instruction of poor children of the Waste, the Lye and Carless Green.

In 1835 Francis Hill, by his will, proved in the P.C.C. 29 October, bequeathed £333 6s. 8d. consols, the annual dividends, amounting to £8 6s. 8d., to be applied for charitable purposes at Lye School.

The Scott School, founded in 1792 by will of William Scott, is regulated by scheme of the Charity Commissioners, 1871. The trust property consists of £1,970 Birmingham Canal Navigation stock and £200 Great Western Railway 5 per cent. stock, producing together £88 16s. yearly, which under the scheme is applicable towards instruction of poor children of Stourbridge, or support of any public elementary school, or in scholarships for children attending such schools. The several sums of stock above mentioned are held by the official trustees, who also hold a sum of £316 Great Western Railway 5 per cent. stock, arising under the will of Sarah Scott, dated in 1872, the dividends, amounting to £15 16s. yearly, being applicable for the benefit of the Wollaston Road schools. The original school was closed by order of the Board of Education in 1912.

The hospital founded and endowed by John Corbett. By deed dated 13 September 1892 (enrolled) John Corbett conveyed to the Rt. Hon. Charles George, Viscount Cobham and nine others as trustees the mansion-house and estates of 30 a. 2 r. 26 p. situate at the Hill, Amblecote, upon trust for the establishment of a hospital for poor persons, inhabitants of Stourbridge, Brierley Hill, Kingswinford, Pedmore, Hagley, Lye Waste and Wollescote, irrespective of their religious tenets. The said John Corbett, by his will proved at London 30 October 1902, bequeathed to the trustees £10,000 as an Endowment Fund, which legacy was in fact superseded by a gift of £10,000 in his lifetime. The invested funds in 1909 exceeded £20,000.

Palmer and Seabright's Charity consists of four houses erected on land in the street of Stourbridge, comprised in a deed of feoffment, 1632. They are held upon a lease for ninety-nine years from 24 June 1839 at £15 5s. yearly. The income is applied in out-relief of widows and orphans of Old Swinford and Stourbridge, Lye and Wollescote.

The charity, founded by will, of John Iddins, 1795, consists of £257 17s. 9d. consols with the official trustees, the annual dividends of which, amounting to £6 8s. 8d., are in pursuance of a declaration of trust, 13 May 1817, distributed in bread to the poor monthly, some at St. Thomas's Church, Stourbridge, and some by the vicar of Lye.

In 1832 Anne Iddins, by her will, proved in the P.C.C. 22 August, left a legacy, now represented by £167 12s. 10d. consols with the official trustees, the annual dividends, amounting to £4 3s. 8d., to be applied in bread in equal proportions at the churches above mentioned monthly to poor widows and infirm persons.

In 1620 William Seabright, by his will (among other things), gave a yearly rent-charge of £3 7s. 4d. out of property in Bethnal Green, London, £3 0s. 8d. thereof to be distributed weekly in bread to poor of Old Swinford and 6s. 8d. to the parish clerk for his pains in the distribution. See also under Wolverley.

Edward Archbould—as appears from an old tablet in the church—gave 40s. a year for the poorest housekeepers in Old Swinford and Stourbridge in equal portions. This is paid out of a house adjoining the Talbot Inn.

In 1720 Thomas Milward, by his will, gave £1 yearly to poor housekeepers of Old Swinford and £1 yearly to poor housekeepers of Stourbridge, to be distributed on St. Thomas's Day. The annuities are paid out of three houses in the High Street, Stourbridge.

In 1781 John Wells, by his will, directed that £420 should be invested in the public funds, and that out of the dividends £6 should be distributed among 120 poor of Old Swinford and the remainder in bread every Sunday among the poor of Stourbridge. The legacy is represented by £735 consols with the official trustees, producing £18 7s. 4d. yearly.

In 1820 Joseph Lea, by his will, bequeathed £1,000, the income to be applied preferentially for the benefit of the poor resident at the Lye and Lye Waste. The legacy is now represented by £573 South Eastern Railway 5 per cent. stock, producing £28 13s.

[69] *Cath. Dir.* 1912, p. 186.
[70] Noake, op. cit. 334.
[71] *Var. Coll.* (Hist. MSS. Com.), i, 326.
[72] *Cal. S. P. Dom.* 1672, pp. 399, 402.
[73] Goodyear, op. cit.
[74] Prattinton Coll. (Soc. Antiq.).
[75] Ibid.
[76] *V.C.H. Worcs.* iv.

yearly. The charity is regulated by a scheme of the Charity Commissioners, 9 August 1910.

In 1825 James Batson, by his will, proved in the P.C.C. 15 January, left £100 for the poor of Old Swinford and Stourbridge. The legacy is represented by £82 10s. 8d. consols, producing £2 1s. yearly.

In 1843 John Harris, by his will, proved in the P.C.C., left a legacy, represented by £501 18s. 8d. consols, the annual dividends, amounting to £12 11s., to be applied during the winter in good warm clothing to destitute poor. The distribution is made in half-crown clothing tickets, two-thirds in the parish of St. Thomas and one-third in St. John's.

In 1857 John Hopkins, by his will, proved in the P.C.C. 13 November, left a share in the Birmingham Canal Navigation, now represented by £93 8s. 4d. consols, the annual dividends, amounting to £2 6s. 8d., to be distributed on 14 February in every year to poor regularly attending divine service.

In 1862 Henry Bate, by a codicil to his will, proved at Worcester 14 November, left a legacy, now represented by £891 14s. 1d. India 3 per cent. stock, the annual dividends, amounting to £26 15s., to be applied for the benefit of necessitous poor of the ecclesiastical districts within the parish of Old Swinford.

In 1866 Joseph Cole, by his will, proved 20 September, bequeathed £300, the interest to be applied in wearing apparel, bed-clothes, or food to poor men and women. The legacy was invested in £309 5s. consols, producing £7 14s. 4d. yearly.

In 1871 Elizabeth Hopkins, by her will, proved at London 24 February, left a share in the Birmingham Canal Navigation, now represented by £96 12s. 5d. consols, the dividends, amounting to £2 8s. 4d., to be distributed on 14 February yearly in sums of not less than 5s. each to the poor.

In 1873 Charles Grove, by his will, proved at Worcester 24 January, bequeathed £100, the interest to be applied in bread on Christmas Day to the poor of St. Thomas, Stourbridge. The legacy was invested in £101 13s. consols, producing £2 10s. 8d. yearly.

The several sums of stock are held by the official trustees, who also hold a sum of £1,037 12s. 3d.

consols, arising under the will of Elizabeth Hunt (date not stated), the dividends of which, amounting to £25 18s. 8d., are distributed in sums of not less than 5s. to widows and old men over seventy years of age.

The Presbyterian or Unitarian chapel at Stourbridge is endowed with £60 London and North Western Railway stock, purchased with a legacy by Miss Emma Evers ; also with freehold ground rent in Tiverton Road, Smethwick, amounting to £20 8s. yearly, purchased with a legacy of £500, bequeathed by will of John Richards, proved in the P.C.C. 29 June 1847, for the maintenance of the Sunday schools in connexion with the chapel or for the promotion of psalmody.

In 1874 the Rev. Thomas Warren, by his will, proved at Worcester 15 September, bequeathed £200, the income—subject to keeping in order a tomb in the burial yard of the Presbyterian chapel—to be applied in the distribution of warm clothing for the poor of the Presbyterian congregation. The legacy was invested in £209 3s. consols with the official trustees, producing £5 4s. 4d. yearly.

In 1898 Charles Cochrane, by his will, proved at Worcester 5 July, bequeathed £2,000, the income to be applied towards payment of minister's stipend, or expenses of management, or repairs of the Unitarian chapel at Stourbridge. The legacy was invested in £1,850 London and South Western Railway 3 per cent. stock, in the name of the treasurer of the chapel, producing £55 10s. yearly.

The same testator bequeathed £2,000 for the same purposes in connexion with the Unitarian chapel at the Lye. The legacy has been lent on mortgage of freehold property in Redcliff Street, Swindon, at 3½ per cent. interest.

In 1900 Miss Ellen Frances Lee, by her will, proved at Lichfield 15 October, left £400, the interest to be applied in augmentation of the stipend of the minister of the Presbyterian chapel at Stourbridge. The legacy was invested in £250 London County 3 per cent. stock and £120 Birmingham Canal stock, in the name of Thomas Grosvenor Lee, producing together £12 6s. yearly.

TARDEBIGGE

Taerdebicgan, Terdeberie (xi cent.) ; Terdebigge (xii cent.) ; Tardebick, Tarbick (xvi cent.) ; Tarbecke (xvii cent.).

Tardebigge, formerly a large parish situated on the borders of Warwickshire, included in 1831 the now separate civil parishes of Redditch, Bentley Paunce-foot, and Webheath and the township of Tutnall and Cobley, which now includes the ancient village of Tardebigge.[1]

Tardebigge some time after 1086 was annexed to Staffordshire, and paid its fee-farm rent through the sheriff of that county,[2] but in 1266 the king granted that the Abbot and convent of Bordesley and their men of Tardebigge should in future answer to the Sheriff of Warwickshire instead of to the Sheriff of

Staffordshire.[3] In 1292-3 the jurors of Seisdon Hundred in Staffordshire presented that the manor of Tardebigge, which was in Warwickshire and used to appear twice annually at the sheriff's tourn at Seisdon Hundred in the time of Henry III, had been withdrawn fifteen years before by the Abbot of Bordesley from Staffordshire and put into Warwickshire.[4]

Nash says : 'The line which divides the counties ran between the old church and the two chancels, the former being supposed to be in Worcestershire, the latter in Warwickshire ; from hence to Lord Plymouth's house the country runs in an irregular line ; the house itself is divided into nearly two equal parts ; the southern part in our county, the northern part in Warwickshire ; which county runs

[1] For ecclesiastical purposes Tardebigge parish still exists and includes Webheath, Bentley Pauncefoot and Tutnall and Cobley.

[2] V.C.H. Worcs. i, 238-9 ; Red Bk. of Exch. (Rolls Ser.), 652, 656.
[3] Cal. Chart. R. 1257-1300, p. 62.

[4] Will. Salt Arch. Soc. Coll. vi (1), 261.

like a peninsula, or rather an island, from Hipsley eastward, having on the north Beoly, and on the south Tardebigge, in Worcestershire.'[5]

Until 1831 the hamlet of Tutnall and Cobley was in Warwickshire, but by the Acts of 1832 and 1844[6] it was transferred to the county of Worcester.

Tutnall and Cobley cover an area of 3,511 acres, of which $839\frac{1}{2}$ acres are arable land, 2,255 grass, and $355\frac{3}{4}$ woods.[7] Redditch was divided in 1894 into the two civil parishes of Redditch, containing 657 acres, 307 acres being permanent grass, and North Redditch, containing 1,408 acres,[8] of which $235\frac{1}{4}$ acres are arable land, $787\frac{1}{2}$ acres permanent grass, and 273 acres woodland. The area of Bentley Pauncefoot is 1,688 acres, including $511\frac{1}{4}$ acres of arable land, $1,532\frac{1}{2}$ acres of permanent grass, and $63\frac{1}{4}$ acres of woods; and that of Webheath 2,185 acres, including 438 acres of arable land and 1,174 acres of permanent grass. The soil varies in different parts of the ancient parish. In Tutnall and Cobley it is mixed, on a subsoil of Keuper Sandstone ; in Bentley the soil is the same and the subsoil marl ; and in Webheath the soil is stiff loam and the subsoil Keuper Marl.

Agriculture is the chief industry except in Redditch, which from an insignificant hamlet has become a large manufacturing town, where the manufacture of needles, fish-hooks and fishing tackle is extensively carried on. This industry, for which Redditch is the most famous town in England, was introduced towards the end of the 18th century by needle-makers from Birmingham, who settled at Redditch on account of the water-power facilities given by the River Arrow. From that date the industry and consequent importance of the town have increased enormously. Some four hundred people were employed in the manufacture of needles and fish-hooks about 1782,[9] and this number by 1868 had increased to 10,000.[10] In 1901 the population of the town was 9,438, an increase of almost 1,000 on that of 1891.

The site of Bordesley Abbey is situated to the north-west of the town. It was excavated towards the middle of the 19th century, and a great part of the foundations were discovered.[11] Encaustic tiles found on the site are now preserved in the vestry of the church of Redditch. In the middle of the 17th century a ' greate owlde gate' still remained.[12]

A fair is said to have been held at Redditch on St. Stephen's Day in the 16th century,[13] and Habington mentions two on St. Stephen's Day, and on the Sunday after the feast of St. Peter ad Vincula,[14] but in the middle of the 19th century there were two fairs, held on the first Monday in August, and on the third Monday in September for cattle.[15] At present the fairs are held on the Saturday preceding the August Bank Holiday and on the third Monday in September. The town is not chartered to hold a market, but one is virtually held in the principal streets every Saturday. Petty sessions are held every Wednesday at Redditch, the county court district having been formed in 1847.[16] The town was formerly governed by a local board formed in 1859.[17] Under the Local Government Act of 1894 it is governed by an urban district council.

The village of Tardebigge is situated about $2\frac{1}{4}$ miles south-east of Bromsgrove and 7 miles north-east of Droitwich. The church stands in a picturesque position on the brow of a small hill overlooking the Worcester and Birmingham Canal, which here enters a tunnel. The village itself contains little of interest, with the exception of a fine red brick house with stone dressings of the early 18th century at its western extremity. Hewell Grange, the residence of the Earl of Plymouth, stands in a large park at the east end of the village, bounded on the west by the Bromsgrove and Alcester Road. It was erected during the years 1885 and 1892, and is a very elaborate building. The old house, designed by Thomas Cundy, was situated near the lake. The Duchess of Kent and Princess Victoria visited Hewell Grange on 5 November 1832. The park is about 850 acres in extent, and contains a large piece of ornamental water on the east side of the house. The grounds were laid out by Humphrey Repton in the early years of the 19th century.

At Bentley, about $1\frac{1}{4}$ miles south of Tardebigge, is some half-timber work. There is a moated inclosure to the north-west of Upper Bentley.

The River Arrow divides Tutnall and Cobley from Alvechurch and then flows south past Redditch to Alcester, where it is joined by the Alne. The Worcester and Birmingham Canal also passes through Tutnall and Cobley and near the village of Tardebigge. The commons were inclosed in 1772.[18]

Among the place-names are Himmingehale,[19] Rodeley, Bertefeld, a tenement called Wysamusplace,[20] Lukesfield, Colborn, Poersheye,[21] Lynewoode, Brokhyll, Foxenhale, Hentelows,[22] Lie Lane [23] and Rashill.[24]

MANORS The history of *TARDEBIGGE* begins in the later 10th century. The will of Wulfgeat of Donnington, co. Salop, accounts for 2 hides there. One hide was bestowed by Wulfgeat as 'soul scot' upon what religious body is not stated. The other hide was left by Wulfgeat to his daughter Wilflaed.[24a] Tardebigge is said to have been purchased from King Ethelred in the 10th century by Ethelsige, a Dean of Worcester, for his church, but after the death of the latter it was seized by Ævic, Sheriff of Staffordshire, during the war between Edmund Ironside and Cnut (c. 1016).[25] It belonged to the king before the Conquest, and in 1086 paid a farm of '11 pounds of pennies at

[5] Nash, *Hist. of Worcs.* ii, 402.
[6] Stat. 2 & 3 Will. IV, cap. 64 ; 7 & 8 Vict. cap. 61.
[7] Statistics from Bd. of Agric. (1905).
[8] *Census of Engl. and Wales*, 1901, *Worcs.* 28.
[9] Nash, op. cit. ii, 404.
[10] Noake, *Guide to Worcs.* 305.
[11] A full account is given in Woodward's *Hist. of Bordesley Abbey*, 90 et seq.
[12] Habington, *Surv. of Worcs.* i, 80.
[13] Woodward, op. cit. 84.

[14] Habington, op. cit. i, 80.
[15] Lewis, *Topog. Dict.* ; see also *Rep. of Royal Com. on Market Rts. and Tolls,* i, 216.
[16] *Lond. Gaz.* 10 Mar. 1847, p. 990.
[17] Ibid. 12 Feb. 1859, p. 678.
[18] Priv. Act, 12 Geo. III, cap. 65.
[19] Anct. D. (P.R.O.), B 4139.
[20] Ibid. C 2129.
[21] Ibid. D 933.
[22] Ct. R. (Gen. Ser.), portf. 210, no. 98. In 1464 the Abbot and convent of

Bordesley obtained licence to improve the waste called Lyndenwoode (*Cal. Pat.* 1461–7, p. 357).
[23] Pat. 31 Hen. VIII, pt. v.
[24] Ibid.
[24a] Birch, *Cart. Sax.* iii, 652 ; Harl. Chart. 83 A 2 ; Heming, *Chartul.* 582. The bounds of Tardebigge in Anglo-Saxon are given in Heming's *Chartul.* (362).
[25] Heming, *Chartul.* (ed. Hearne), 276–7, 362, 379 ; *V.C.H. Worcs.* i, 238, 239.

Tardebigge : Hewell Grange : South-east Façade

Tardebigge : Hewell Grange : North Side of the Great Hall

20 to the ounce' through the Sheriff of Staffordshire at Kingswinford Manor.[26] Tardebigge is said to have been included in the endowment of Bordesley Abbey, founded in 1138 by Waleran de Beaumont [27] Count of Mellent and Earl of Worcester.[28] The foundation of the abbey has also been attributed to Queen Maud, who granted another charter similar to that of 1138, and who with Henry II is recognized as the founder of the abbey.[29] These charters gave the Abbot of Bordesley and his men of Tardebigge freedom from toll in cities, boroughs and market towns throughout England, but in the reign of Edward I Robert de Mortimer exacted passage and toll from the abbot and his men passing by the town of Wychbold. The dispute was eventually settled in favour of the abbot.[30] The abbot and convent paid a farm of £10 through the Sheriff of Staffordshire for their possessions in Tardebigge throughout the 12th century.[31] In 1266 Henry III granted that the abbot and convent should not be distrained by their sheep as long as they had other animals and goods whereby they could be distrained,[32] the grant being of special importance to them, since wool-growing was the chief source of their revenue.[33]

The manor or grange of Tardebigge remained in the possession of the Abbot and convent of Bordesley[34] until the abbey was surrendered to the king in 1538,[35] and in 1542 Andrew Lord Windsor was obliged, much against his will, to exchange his manor of Stanwell, near Windsor, for the possessions of the abbey, including the manor of Tardebigge.[36]

Sir Andrew was succeeded in 1543 by his son William,[37] who was one of the twenty-six peers who signed the settlement of the Crown on Lady Jane Grey. He was, however, active in the proclamation of Queen Mary, at whose coronation he acted as Pantler.[38] On his death in 1558 Tardebigge passed to his son Edward, who was succeeded in 1574–5 by his son Frederick.[39] He died unmarried in 1585, when his brother Henry succeeded.[40] Thomas son of Henry, who followed his father in 1605, was Rear-Admiral of the Fleet sent in 1623 to bring Prince Charles from Spain, and is said to have spent £15,000 in entertainments on that occasion. He, having no children, settled the manor in 1641 upon Thomas Windsor Hickman, son of his sister Elizabeth, on condition that he assumed the name Windsor instead of Hickman.[41] Thomas, who succeeded to the estate in the same year, distinguished himself at the battle of Naseby in 1645 and relieved the king's garrison at High Ercall. Charles I is said to have ordered a patent to be prepared to grant him the

title of Lord Windsor, which had fallen into abeyance on the death of his uncle, but the dignity was not conferred upon him until the accession of Charles II.[42] He was created Earl of Plymouth in 1682,[43] and died in 1687, when his grandson Other succeeded.[44] From Other son and successor of Other, the second earl, the manor passed in 1732 to his son Other Lewis.[45] Other Hickman, son of the latter, was succeeded in 1799 by his son Other Archer, on whose death without issue in 1833 the barony of Windsor again fell into abeyance.[46] The abeyance was terminated in 1855 in favour of Lady Harriet Clive, younger sister of the last lord,[47] and her grandson Robert George Windsor-Clive, who succeeded to the title and estates on her death in 1869,[48] was created

WINDSOR. *Gules a saltire argent between twelve crosslets or.*   CLIVE. *Argent a fesse sable with three molets or thereon.*

Earl of Plymouth in 1905,[49] and is the present owner of the manor.

Lands at Bordesley formed part of the endowment of the abbey there,[50] and were granted in 1542 by the name of the manor of *BORDESLEY* to Andrew Lord Windsor, with the site of the abbey.[51] The site and manor of Bordesley followed the same descent as Tardebigge (q.v.).

Edward Lord Windsor obtained licence in 1561 to impark 1,000 acres of land in Bordesley and Tardebigge.[52] According to Nash, Bordesley Park was sold before his time to Lord Foley.[53] In the middle of the 18th century Bordesley Park was owned or occupied by the Taylors of Moseley. John Taylor, who died in 1814, and his son John both lived there.[54] The estate now known as Bordesley Hall, which stands in a park of about 200 acres, is in the parish of Alvechurch and belongs to Mr. Charles John Geast Dugdale.

REDDITCH (Le Rededych, le Redyche, xv cent.), which was held at the Dissolution by the Abbot of Bordesley, is not mentioned in the foundation charters

---

[26] *V.C.H. Worcs.* i, 287.

[27] He received a grant of the county and city of Worcester from King Stephen (Henry of Huntingdon, *Hist. Angl.* [Rolls Ser.], 282).

[28] Dugdale, *Mon. Angl.* v, 410 ; Harl. Chart. 45 I 30 ; Add. Chart. 20419.

[29] Cott. MS. Nero C. iii, fol. 176 ; *Cal. Chart. R.* 1257–1300, pp. 63–6 ; *Hund. R.* (Rec. Com.), ii, 284.

[30] Feet of F. Worcs. 3 Edw. I, no. 59.

[31] *Red Bk. of Exch.* (Rolls Ser.), 656 ; see Pipe Rolls.

[32] *Cal. Chart. R.* 1257–1300, p. 62.

[33] *V.C.H. Worcs.* ii, 152.

[34] *Cal. Pat.* 1354–8, p. 332 ; *Valor Eccl.* (Rec. Com.), iii, 271.

[35] *L. and P. Hen. VIII,* xiii (1), 1401 ; Feet of F. Div. Co. Trin. 30 Hen. VIII.

[36] Pat. 34 Hen. VIII, pt. x, m. 8 ; *L. and P. Hen. VIII,* xvii, g. 285 (18) ; see also 231.

[37] G.E.C. *Complete Peerage,* viii, 185.

[38] Ibid.

[39] Ibid. 186 ; Recov. R. Trin. 25 & 26 Eliz. rot. 158.

[40] G.E.C. op. cit. viii, 186 ; Feet of F. Div. Co. Hil. 31 Eliz.

[41] Chan. Inq. p.m. (Ser. 2), ccccxcix, 31.

[42] G.E.C. *Complete Peerage,* vi, 257.

[43] Ibid.

[44] Ibid. ; Feet of F. Warw. Trin. 1 Anne.

[45] G.E.C. op. cit. vi, 258.

[46] The earldom passed to Andrews Windsor, uncle and heir male of Other Archer, but became extinct on the death of his brother Henry in 1843 without male issue (ibid.).

[47] Ibid. viii, 188.

[48] Ibid.

[49] Burke, *Peerage.*

[50] *Cal. Chart. R.* 1257–1300, p. 63.

[51] *L. and P. Hen. VIII,* xvii, g. 285 (18).

[52] Pat. 4 Eliz. pt. vi. In 1230 Henry III granted that the Abbot of Bordesley and his successors should have the custody of their woods of 'Holeway, Tunneshal and Terdebig' in the forest of Feckenham, and that these woods should be quit of forest dues on condition that the monks should make no more clearings without the king's licence (Cart. Antiq. FF 17 ; QQ 1 ; *Cal. Chart. R.* 1226–57, p. 116 ; *Cal. Close,* 1227–31, p. 318).

[53] op. cit. ii, 404.

[54] Burke, *Landed Gentry* (1906).

of the abbey, and it is not known how or when it was acquired. It may have been originally included in the manor of Bordesley. The vill of Redditch is mentioned in the 14th and 15th centuries,[55] and it is first called a manor at the time of the Dissolution,[56] when it contributed £17 11s. 10d. yearly to the revenues of the abbot and convent.[57] It was granted with Tardebigge Manor to Lord Windsor, and has since followed the same descent as that manor (q.v.).

The manor of *BENTLEY PAUNCEFOOT* (Beneslei, xi cent. ; Benetlega Pancevot, Benetleye in Feckenham Forest, xiii cent.), which was held before the Conquest by Leofric of Earl Edwin of Mercia, had passed before 1086 to William, who held it of Urse D'Abitot.[58]

The overlordship followed the descent of Elmley Castle (q.v.) until it lapsed in the 16th century.[59] William, the Domesday tenant, was succeeded by the family of Pauncefoot, from whom the manor derives the second part of its name. Richard Pauncefoot held half a hide of land at Bentley in 1198,[60] and his son Richard had succeeded to Bentley before 1220.[61] It was perhaps this Richard who obtained a grant of free warren there in 1255.[62] His son and heir Grimbald Pauncefoot[63] was lord of the manor in 1275–6,[64] and is probably the Grimbald Pauncefoot who fought in the barons' war in the reign of Henry III, at first on the side of the barons and afterwards on that of the king, being knighted by Prince Edward.[65] His manor at Bentley was within the bounds of the forest of Feckenham, and in 1281 he obtained licence to have a rabbit warren there and to 'enclose places for the dwellings of the rabbits with a little dike and low hedge so that the king's deer may have entrance and exit.'[66] He had been succeeded before 1293–4 by a son of the same name, who in that year was going to Gascony on the king's service. He was apparently in want of money for the expedition, and tried to obtain licence to cut down and sell timber in his wood of Bentley to the value of 200 marks. It was found that pannage in the wood was due to the king and his tenants, and, as the wood was part of the royal forest of Feckenham, waste would prejudice the king's hunting. Further, as Sybil, mother of Grimbald, held one-third in dower and Richard Pauncefoot ought to have twelve good oaks there by charter of his father,

timber to the value of 200 marks could not be cut down without loss to them.[67] In 1294, however, Grimbald received licence to sell wood to the value of 100 marks.[68] He died about 1313–14, being succeeded by his brother Emery,[69] or Aymer, whose name was included in 1321 in a list of those receiving pardons for joining in the rising against the Despensers.[70] In the following year he was fined 200 marks as one of the followers of the Earl of Lancaster and released from prison upon payment of the same.[71] In 1325 he was summoned to

PAUNCEFOOT. *Gules three lions argent.*

perform military service in Guienne,[72] but in 1326 he is spoken of as an enemy of the king. At the same time William de Montagu, who was 'in the king's service pursuing the rebels,' was accused of taking stock and goods from the manor of Bentley, and he justified his action on the ground that no one pursuing the rebels should be molested for the possession of any of their goods.[73] In 1333, shortly before his death,[74] Emery Pauncefoot settled the manor on his son Grimbald, with contingent remainder to another son Hugh.[75] The former died childless in 1375,[76] and his brother Hugh, who succeeded him, died before 1379, when his widow Katherine was in possession.[77] Sir John Pauncefoot, son and heir of Hugh, settled the manor in 1417–18 on his son William and Margaret his wife and their issue,[78] but they evidently died childless, since Thomas, brother of William, was lord of the manor some years later.[79] John Pauncefoot, grandson of Thomas, died in 1516,[80] leaving a son Richard, then aged three. Richard was succeeded by his son John,[81] who sold the site of the manor to Thomas Jeffreys in 1556[82] and the rest to Ralph Sheldon and William Childe in 1560.[83]

It appears that the Jeffreys had before this time been tenants of the manor-house. As early as 1512 John Pauncefoot let it to William Jeffreys for forty years, and in 1544 Richard Pauncefoot let to Elizabeth Jeffreys 'the demesne lands of Bentley as held by her

---

[55] *Cal. Pat.* 1348–50, p. 112 ; 1391–6, p. 414 ; Anct. D. (P.R.O.), B 519, 3043 ; *Cal. Pat.* 1461–7, p. 357.

[56] Feet of F. Div. Co. Trin. 30 Hen. VIII.

[57] *Valor Eccl.* (Rec. Com.), iii, 271.

[58] *V.C.H. Worcs.* i, 318a.

[59] *Red Bk. of Exch.* (Rolls Ser.), ii, 567 ; *Testa de Nevill* (Rec. Com.), 40 ; Chan. Inq. p.m. 8 Edw. II, no. 8 ; *Cal. Close*, 1333–7, p. 36 ; Chan. Inq. p.m. (Ser. 2), xxxi, 115 ; Memo. R. Exch. (L.T.R.), East. 4 Eliz. rot. 34 d. ; 19 Eliz. rot. 76.

[60] Feet of F. Worcs. 9 Ric. I, no. 6.

[61] Ibid. 5 Hen. III, no. 28 ; 11 Hen. III, no. 26.

[62] *Cal. Chart. R.* 1226–57, p. 447.

[63] Berry, *Bucks. Gen.* 101.

[64] *Hund. R.* (Rec. Com.), ii, 284 ; Feet of F. Div. Co. 9 Edw. I, no. 32.

[65] *Worcs. Inq. p.m.* (Worcs. Hist. Soc.), i, 21.

[66] *Cal. Chart. R.* 1257–1300, p. 258.

[67] *Worcs. Inq. p.m.* (Worcs. Hist. Soc.), i, 52 ; Inq. a.q.d. file 21, no. 2.

[68] *Cal. Pat.* 1292–1301, p. 79.

[69] Chan. Inq. p.m. 8 Edw. II, no. 8.

[70] *Cal. Pat.* 1321–4, p. 19 ; *Parl. Writ* (Rec. Com.), ii (3), 1263.

[71] *Parl. Writ*, loc. cit. [72] Ibid.

[73] *Will. Salt Arch. Soc. Coll.* x (1), 65.

[74] *Cal. Inq. p.m.* 1–10 *Edw. III*, 317.

[75] Feet of F. Worcs. 6 Edw. III, no. 50. He had previously settled it on his wife Sybil (ibid. 16 Edw. II, no. 5), and she held it after his death (*Cal. Close*, 1333–7, p. 36 ; Chan. Inq. p.m. 7 Edw. III [2nd nos.], no. 46).

[76] Chan. Inq. p.m. 49 Edw. III, pt. ii (2nd nos.), no. 25.

[77] *Cal. Pat.* 1377–81, p. 345. She seems afterwards to have married Richard Ruyhall the younger (Chan. Inq. p.m. 13 Ric. II, no. 40), and in 1381 Parnel widow of Sir Grimbald granted to them all the lands which she held in dower in Bentley for the rent of 3 marks yearly (*Kyre Park Chart.* [Worcs. Hist. Soc.], 90).

[78] Feet of F. Worcs. 3 Hen. V, no. 3. In 1431 John obtained a confirmation of the charters granting free warren in Bentley to his ancestors Richard and Grimbald (*Cal. Pat.* 1429–36, p. 180).

[79] Early Chan. Proc. bdle. 44, no. 46.

[80] Chan. Inq. p.m. (Ser. 2), xxxi, 115. His widow Bridget married a certain John Browne and was still living in 1536 (Feet of F. Worcs. Mich. 27 Hen. VIII ; Close, 20 Hen. VIII, no. 54). John Pauncefoot had conveyed the manor before his death to Thomas Mervyn, evidently in trust for his infant son Richard, for Thomas Fermour, to whom Mervyn transferred the manor in 1518, restored it in 1528 to Richard Pauncefoot (Close, 20 Hen. VIII, no. 54 ; Memo. R. Exch. [L.T.R.], Trin. 33 Hen. VIII, rot. 18).

[81] Berry, *Bucks. Gen.* 102 ; Memo. R. Exch. (L.T.R.), Hil. 4 & 5 Phil. and Mary, rot. 34.

[82] Feet of F. Worcs. Trin. 3 & 4 Phil. and Mary.

[83] Ibid. Mich. 2 & 3 Eliz. ; East. 3 Eliz. ; Memo. R. Exch. (L.T.R.), East. 4 Eliz. rot. 34 d.

TARDEBIGGE CHURCH : THE CHANCEL ARCH

late husband William Jeffreys' at a yearly rent of £50 on condition that she would find 'house-room' for Richard, his steward, and servants when they came twice a year to hold courts.[84] The site remained in the Jeffreys family until 1606, when Edward Jeffreys and his eldest son Humphrey sold it to Henry Cookes.[85]

Before 1577 the manor of Bentley had been sold by Ralph Sheldon and William Childe to Henry Field,[86] through whose niece it passed to Sir William Whorwood.[87] He settled it in 1603 on his son Thomas and the latter's wife Ursula, daughter of George Brome.[88] Thomas Whorwood died in October 1634, leaving a son Brome,[89] who had been married the month before to Jane Ryder or Ryther, afterwards noted for her attempts to arrange the escape of Charles I.[90] They had one son and one daughter, but it is doubtful whether the former (who was drowned in 1657)[91] ever succeeded to Bentley, since it appears to have been sold before 1651 to Thomas Cookes,[92] grandson of the Henry Cookes who had purchased the site from Edward Jeffreys. He was made one of the commissioners for 'reducing co. Worcester to the obedience of Parliament' and afterwards sheriff of the county.[93] On his death without issue the manor seems to have passed to his nephew William Cookes, who was created a baronet in 1664 and died in 1672.[94] His son Sir Thomas Cookes,[95] the founder of Worcester College, Oxford, died without issue in 1701, leaving most of his property to his nephew Thomas Winford and his heirs male with contingent remainders to John and Harry Winford, his brothers, and to John Cookes, cousin of the testator, on condition that whoever inherited the manor should take the name of Cookes.[96] Thomas Winford, afterwards Sir Thomas Cookes Winford, and his two brothers died without issue and the manor passed to John Cookes, eldest son of the John Cookes mentioned in the will,[97] who was holding it in 1744.[98] He was succeeded in 1747[99] by his nephew the Rev. Thomas Cookes, rector of Notgrove, co. Gloucester,[100] whose

Cookes of Bentley, baronet. *Or two cheverons gules between six martlets sable.*

grandson Thomas Henry Cookes appears to have been lord of the manor in 1826,[1] though his father did not die until 1829.

Bentley was purchased before 1850 by Walter Chamberlain Hemming, and had passed before 1860 to Richard Hemming, to whose daughter Maud, widow of Major George C. Cheape of Wellfield, co. Fife, the manor now belongs.[2]

The Abbot and convent of Bordesley had several smaller manors or 'reputed manors' in the parish of Tardebigge.

The hamlets of *TUTNALL* and *COBLEY* (Tothehal and Comble) are mentioned in the Domesday Survey as berewicks of the manor of Bromsgrove and belonged before the Conquest to Earl Edwin of Mercia and in 1086 to the king.[3] Tutnall was later known as Totinhill.[4] 'Cobesleie' is included in the foundation charter of Bordesley Abbey as transcribed by Dugdale from deeds belonging to Sir Clement Throckmorton of Haseley, co. Warwick.[5] Both have since then followed the same descent as Tardebigge (q.v.).

STRECHE BENTLEY, so called after a family of the name of Streche or Estrech, probably belonged to Richard Streche, who is mentioned as rendering half a mark in Worcestershire on the Pipe Roll of 1167.[6] Another Richard Streche died seised of the bailiwick of the forest of Bentley in 1270–1.[7] His son, also called Richard, held Streche Bentley in 1274,[8] and in 1275–6 Robert Streche of Bentley held a virgate of land of the king without doing service for it.[9] Robert seems, however, to have held the land only under a ten years' lease granted by Richard Streche.[10] He was still called Robert Streche of Bentley in 1283–4,[11] but the manor seems afterwards to have passed to Walter de Aylesbury, who is called lord of Streche Bentley in an undated charter by which he granted to Robert Gest lands in Bentley Pauncefoot, holding by a rent of 4s. 6d. and by suit of court to the lord of Bentley Pauncefoot.[12] It was perhaps this property which John de Wysham and Hawise his wife held of Emery Pauncefoot at the time of John's death, c. 1332, and which passed to his son John.[13] By undated charters John the cook of Bentley and Reginald Long of Bentley granted rent and land at Bentley to Bordesley Abbey.[14] At the time of the Dissolution the so-called manor belonged

[84] Prattinton Coll. (Soc. Antiq.), quoting the Rev. D. Cookes' Evidences.
[85] Feet of F. Worcs. Mich. 4 Jas. I.
[86] Memo. R. Exch. (L.T.R.), East. 19 Eliz. rot. 76.
[87] P.C.C. 41 Watson.
[88] Feet of F. Worcs. Hil. 1 Jas. I; Chan. Inq. p.m. (Ser. 2), ccclxvii, 101.
[89] Chan. Inq. p.m. (Ser. 2), dv, 135.
[90] Dict. Nat. Biog.
[91] Ibid.
[92] Cal. Com. for Comp. 2714; Nash, op. cit. i, 440.
[93] Cal. Com. for Comp. 2714.
[94] G.E.C. Complete Baronetage, iii, 301.
[95] Feet of F. Div. Co. Hil. 29 & 30 Chas. II.
[96] P.C.C. 92 Dyer; Nash, op. cit. ii, 440. Sir Thomas Cookes also left money for one sermon to be preached every Easter Monday in Tardebigge, Feckenham, or Bromsgrove, which was to be attended by the masters and scholars of the schools he had endowed in Feckenham and Bromsgrove, each boy 'receiving

as encouragement for their so doing' a book 'treating either of the sacrament, charity, love, obedience, duty or a good life or such other good and godly books.' After the sermon the trustees of the school and the preacher were to dine together. He also provided for clothing a certain number of the Feckenham boys, a provision which is still (1912) in force.
[97] Prattinton Coll. (Soc. Antiq.), quoting Rev. Denham Cookes' Evidences.
[98] Recov. R. East. 17 Geo. II, rot. 324.
[99] Burke, Landed Gentry (1846).
[100] Ibid.; Recov. R. Mich. 29 Geo. III, rot. 288.
[1] Recov. R. Trin. 7 Geo. IV, rot. 134.
[2] Burke, Landed Gentry (1846).
[3] V.C.H. Worcs. i, 285a.
[4] Pat. 34 Hen. VIII, pt. x, m. 8.
[5] Dugdale, Mon. Angl. v, 409. Cobley is not mentioned in the original charters as preserved at the British Museum or in the confirmations by Henry III.

[6] Pipe R. 13 Hen. II (Pipe R. Soc.), 66.
[7] Cal. of Inq. p.m. Hen. III, 250. In the reign of Henry III Richard Streche of Bentley granted a house and land there to Emma and Eva, daughters of Thomas Streche (Anct. D. [P.R.O.], B 514).
[8] Feet of F. Worcs. case 258, file 9, no. 44.
[9] Hund. R. (Rec. Com.), ii, 284.
[10] Assize R. 1026, m. 18 d.
[11] Feet of F. Worcs. 12 Edw. I, no. 4.
[12] Prattinton Coll. (Soc. Antiq.), quoting the Rev. Denham Cookes' Evidences; see also Anct. D. (P.R.O.), B 3646.
[13] Chan. Inq. p.m. 6 Edw. III (1st nos.), no. 53; Cal. Close, 1330–3, p. 516; 1333–7, p. 454. John de Wysham is said in 1428 and 1431 to have held the manor of Bentley which Grimbald Pauncefoot had held, but at those dates Bentley Pauncefoot was still in possession of the Pauncefoots (Feud. Aids, v, 324, 330).
[14] Anct. D. (P.R.O.), B 515, 516.

to Bordesley Abbey,[15] and was granted in 1542 to Andrew Lord Windsor,[16] afterwards following the descent of Tardebigge (q.v.).

HEWELL GRANGE, now the Worcestershire seat of the Earl of Plymouth, was granted to his ancestor Andrew Lord Windsor with the other possessions of Bordesley Abbey.[17] Hewell Grange is not mentioned in the foundation charter of the abbey, but it was stated at the Hundred Court in 1275–6 that it had been granted to the abbey by the Empress Maud, and in 1291 the abbot held 7 carucates of land at Hewell cum Lega.[18] The present house was built on a new site in the park between 1885 and 1891.

SHELTWOOD (Saltwod, Syltwode, xiii cent.; Scheltewodde, xvi cent.), though not mentioned in the foundation charter, was granted to Bordesley Abbey by the Empress Maud.[19] In 1291 the abbot held 3 carucates of land and a dovecot there,[20] and about 1388–9 he granted 'Shiltewode Grange' to William de Buyton for life without obtaining the king's licence.[21] The estate remained in the possession of the abbey until the Dissolution.[22] It was not granted with the site of the abbey to Lord Windsor, but appears to have remained a Crown possession until 1551, when it was granted to Edward Lord Clinton.[23] It had passed before 1571 to Edward Lord Windsor,[24] but its further descent has not been traced. It probably became merged in the manor of Tardebigge.

A mill called Lea Mill, possibly in the parish of Tardebigge,[25] was given in 1180–1 by William the Baker to the abbey of Bordesley in consideration of an annuity of 12 quarters of wheat and 12 quarters of rye. William had received the mill some twenty years before from Walter Bishop of Chester.[26] The mill was confirmed to the abbey by Richard I, and is then said to have been given by Roger de Sandford.[27] A mill at Bordesley belonged to the abbey at the Dissolution,[28] and four water-mills were annexed to the manors of Tardebigge and Bordesley in 1589.[29] In 1752 Lord Windsor had a water grist-mill and a water paper-mill in Bordesley and Tardebigge.[30] Lea Mill may perhaps be identified with the old mill to the south of Hewell Grange. In 1678 there were two water corn-mills and three fulling-mills at Bentley Pauncefoot belonging to Sir Thomas Cookes, then lord of the manor,[31] and in 1826 Thomas Henry Cookes had three corn-mills there.[32] There is no mill at Bentley Pauncefoot at the present day, but Perrymill Farm may mark the site of a former one. There are numerous mills at Redditch on the Arrow and its tributaries. In the 14th century Robert, Abbot of Bordesley, had fishing rights in Tardebigge.[33]

The present church of *ST. BAR-CHURCH THOLOMEW*, erected about 1777, is a stone building, and consists of a chancel 18 ft. by 33 ft. with an apsidal east end, a nave 58½ ft. by 34½ ft., and a west tower 9 ft. square with side vestries, all in the Renaissance style. These measurements are all internal. The chancel has three semicircular-headed windows in the apse and a doorway on the south side. The nave is lit by four round-headed windows on each side, and at the west end is a gallery. The west door enters the tower, which is octagonal internally and forms a narthex with a vestry on each side. The arched doorway is flanked by columns carrying an entablature and pediment. The tower is of three stages, the two lower being square, with round-headed windows in the ringing chamber. The third has two columns standing free at each angle and carrying an entablature convex on plan, above which rises a tall octagonal spire having vases at each broach.

In the narthex is a mutilated kneeling effigy of a man in 16th-century armour. In the nave is a mural monument to Maria wife of Thomas Cookes of Bentley, daughter of Thomas Lord Windsor and his wife, the sister of George Marquess of Halifax, who died in 1694.

There are three bells: the first is inscribed 'Wm Callow, Saml Harris, Churchwardens 1774,' with Thomas Rudhall's mark; second, 'Jn° Rudhall fec^t, Saml Harris, Churchwarden, 1796'; and a third, 'Goodwin Nash, John Parke, Churchwardens, Henry Bagley made me, 1746.'

The plate consists of a plain cup, dish, paten and flagon, all inscribed 'Other, Earl of Plymouth 1790,' and bearing the hall-mark of that year, and also a modern paten.

The registers before 1812 are as follows: (i) baptisms 1566 to 1647, burials 1579 to 1647, marriages 1566 to 1647; (ii) baptisms and burials 1654 to 1671, marriages 1653 to 1671; (iii) all entries 1672 to 1692; (iv) 1693 to 1730; (v) baptisms and burials 1731 to 1770, marriages 1731 to 1751 (there is a gap in the marriages between 1751 and 1754); (vi) marriages 1754 to 1770; (vii) baptisms and burials 1770 to 1809; (viii) marriages 1770 to 1812; (ix) baptisms and burials 1809 to 1812.

From the description in Nash's *History of Worcestershire* [34] it would appear that the former church dated back to the Norman period. The tower of this church fell in 1774, and so damaged the remainder of the building that the whole had to be taken down. A brief was issued in 1777 for building a new church on a slightly different site wholly in Worcestershire.[35] In pulling down the old church the monuments of the Windsor family were so much damaged that they were not replaced in the new building. Some are described in Dugdale's *History of Warwickshire*.[36] Nash gives the following account of the old church: 'The church was dedicated to St. Bartholomew, and is supposed to have been built soon after the Conquest. The most ancient part was a circular arch over the south door with hatched

[15] Feet of F. Div. Co. Trin. 30 Hen. VIII.

[16] Pat. 34 Hen. VIII, pt. x, m. 8.

[17] Ibid.

[18] *Hund. R.* (Rec. Com.), ii, 284; *Pope Nich. Tax.* (Rec. Com.), 229.

[19] *Hund. R.* (Rec. Com.), ii, 284.

[20] *Pope Nich. Tax.* (Rec. Com.), 229.

[21] Chan. Inq. p.m. 12 Ric. II, no. 73.

[22] Feet of F. Div. Co. Trin. 30 Hen. VIII; *Valor Eccl.* (Rec. Com.), iii, 271.

[23] Pat. 5 Edw. VI, pt. vii.

[24] Recov. R. Trin. 13 Eliz. rot. 733. Henry Cookes called 'of Sheltwood' died there in 1616 (Chan. Inq. p.m. [Ser. 2], ccclxx, 51), and his son William also died there in 1619 (ibid. ccclxxxi, 161).

[25] Hewell Grange and 'Leya' were taxed together in 1291.

[26] *Anct. Chart.* (Pipe R. Soc.), 79, 80.

[27] Ibid.; *Cal. Chart. R.* 1257–1300, p. 66. [28] Dugdale, *Mon. Angl.* v, 412.

[29] Pat. 32 Eliz. pt. xvi.

[30] Recov. R. Trin. 25 & 26 Geo. II, rot. 329.

[31] Feet of F. Div. Co. Hil. 29 & 30 Chas. II.

[28] Recov. R. Trin. 7 Geo. IV, rot. 134.

[33] De Banco R. 356, m. 245 d.

[34] op. cit. ii, 408.

[85] B.M. Chart. Br. B. xvii, 9; see above under description of parish.

[36] op. cit. 734, 735.

TARDEBIGGE CHURCH FROM THE SOUTH-WEST

mouldings, and the supporting columns had the common rude Saxon capitals. The tower was partly octagonal, but from the style of the arch over the door at the west end of the tower, and the thin taper columns, one may conjecture it was built after the reign of Henry I. In the highest north window of the north side of the body of the church was a man with eight children, praying, and in the next pane a woman with three daughters in the same attitude, with the inscription, 'Seward and Agnet de Bedford,' the rest broken. In the lowest window of the same side a man and his wife praying, inscribed, 'Uxor ejus,' with eight sons and one daughter. [37]

ADVOWSONS The advowson of the church of Tardebigge was included in the foundation charter of Bordesley Abbey.[38] The church had been appropriated to the abbey and the vicarage ordained before 1245. To the vicar were assigned all obventions of the altar and of the chapel of St. Stephen, and all small tithes, but it was found that this endowment was insufficient, and in 1245 the bishop ordained that the vicar should receive in addition a mark yearly from the abbot and convent as rectors.[39]

In 1259 the advowson was claimed by Henry III on the ground that Richard I had presented, but he finally gave up his claim, 'having perceived that the said house was founded out of the said advowson.' [40] In 1291 the church of Tardebigge was worth £15 6s. 8d.,[41] but by the time of the Dissolution the rectory was only worth £4 1s. 5¼d.[42] The advowson with the rectory and tithes has followed the same descent as the manor [43] (q.v.).

There was formerly a chapel at Bentley Pauncefoot Manor, which at the beginning of the 14th century was served by the monks of Bordesley, who were obliged to find a priest to celebrate divine service every Sunday, Wednesday and Friday, and on all feast days. In 1332 Emery Pauncefoot granted the monks 2 marks yearly to find a chaplain for the remaining days of the week.[44]

There was also a chapel at Bordesley dedicated to St. Stephen,[45] the advowson of which was granted in 1542 to Andrew Lord Windsor.[46] There seems to have been a district assigned to this chapel which was in existence at least as early as 1245.[47] Nash gives the boundaries of this district as they existed in 1645.[48] The advowson belonged to the lords of the manor,[49] but the chapel was deserted after the Dissolution and used as a barn until 1687, when, upon the application of the inhabitants of Redditch to the Earl of Plymouth, it was endowed and used as a church.[50] The chapel was restored and further endowed in 1712 by Nathaniel Mugg. A tablet recording this gift was the only one which had escaped destruction at the time of the demolition of the chapel in 1805.[51] An Act for building a new chapel at Redditch was

obtained in 1805,[52] and the old one was taken down. Illustrations of the old chapel and the new one as it existed in 1807 are given in Woodward's *History of Bordesley Abbey.*[53] The present church of St. Stephen was built in 1854–5, and the ecclesiastical parish was formed from Tardebigge in 1855.[54] It is of stone in 14th-century style, and consists of chancel, nave, north and south aisles, chapel, south porch, and tower with spire at the west end of the north aisle.

On 13 August 1902 part of the ecclesiastical parish of St. Stephen, Redditch, was constituted the new parish of St. George, Redditch.[55] The church, built in 1876, is of stone in 14th-century style, consisting of chancel, nave, north and south aisles, and eastern bell-turret. The living is a vicarage in the gift of the vicar of St. Stephen, Redditch.

Parts of the ancient ecclesiastical parish of Tardebigge were assigned in 1850 to the new ecclesiastical parish of Headless Cross,[56] which was constituted from this parish and Feckenham in Worcestershire and Ipsley in Warwickshire. It is now comprised in the new civil parish of Upper Ipsley, which was formed from Ipsley in 1894.[57]

St. Philip's at Webheath is a chapel of ease to St. Bartholomew's, Tardebigge, and at Lower Bentley there is a small church where services are held on Sunday afternoons by the vicar of Tardebigge.

There is a Baptist chapel at Webheath. At Redditch there are numerous Nonconformist places of worship. The Baptist chapel in Ipsley Street was built in 1862 and rebuilt in 1897, the United Methodist in Mount Pleasant was built in 1833 and rebuilt in 1899, and the Wesleyan chapel in Bates Hill, built in 1842, has since been enlarged.

CHARITIES Endymion Canning—as appeared from an ancient table of benefactions in the church—by his will (dated in 1631) left £50 for the poor to be disposed of to such charitable uses as the Earl of Plymouth should think fit. In performance of the said will the Earl of Plymouth by deeds of lease and release granted a house and land in Redditch, the rents and profits to be applied in the distribution of bread. The trust property now consists of 3 r. 35 p., producing £2 13s. yearly, £1,208 16s. 5d. consols with the official trustees, arising from the sale in 1873 of a portion of the property, and also a sum of £102 18s. 9d. consols in the names of trustees. The annual dividends, amounting together to £32 17s. 11d., are, with the net rents, applied in moieties in the distribution of bread among the poor of Tardebigge and Redditch.

In 1859 James Holyoake by his will bequeathed £2,000 for the benefit of the poor. The legacy, less duty, is represented by £520 Birmingham Corporation 3 per cent. stock, £870 on mortgage, and £143 invested with the Land Securities Company.

[37] Nash, op. cit. ii, 408.
[38] Cott. MS. Nero C. iii, fol. 176; Add. Chart. 20419.
[39] Worc. Epis. Reg. Carpenter, i, fol. 131a. In Moreton's register the date of the appropriation is given as 1489 (ibid. Moreton, 40 d.).
[40] Cal. Chart. R. 1257–1300, p. 17.
[41] Pope Nich. Tax. (Rec. Com.), 217.
[42] Valor Eccl. (Rec. Com.), iii, 273.
[43] Pat. 34 Hen. VIII, pt. x, m. 8; Inst. Bks. (P.R.O.).
[44] Cal. Pat. 1330–4, p. 332.

[45] Valor Eccl. (Rec. Com.), iii, 273.
[46] Pat. 34 Hen. VIII, pt. x, m. 8.
[47] Worc. Epis. Reg. Carpenter, i, 131a.
[48] Nash, op. cit. ii, 404.
[49] Pat. 10 Jas. I, pt. iii, no. 8; Chan. Inq. p.m. (Ser. 2), ccccxcix, 31; Recov. R. Trin. 25 & 26 Geo. II, rot. 329.
[50] Woodward, Hist. of Bordesley Abbey, 87.
[51] A reproduction of it is given by Woodward, op. cit. 85.
[52] Local and Personal Act, 45 Geo. III, cap. 66.   [53] op. cit. 83, 88.

[54] Lond. Gaz. 21 Aug. 1855, p. 3175. The church possesses the following books of registers previous to 1812: (i) baptisms and burials 1770 to 1807; (ii) baptisms and burials 1808 to 1812; (iii) marriages 1808 to 1811. Marriages previous to 1808 were not solemnized at Redditch.
[55] Census of Engl. and Wales, 1901, Worcs. 7 n.
[56] Lond. Gaz. 11 Jan. 1850, p. 82.
[57] Census of Engl. and Wales, 1901, Warw. 28.

The income, amounting to about £65 a year, is distributed in blankets, sheets and other articles in kind to about seventy recipients.

Redditch.—In 1715 John Allen, by his will proved at Worcester, charged his customary lands at Foxlydiate with an annuity of £15 4s., of which £10 is receivable by the vicar and £5 4s. is applied to the National schools as John Allen's Educational Foundation.

Eleemosynary Charities.—This parish receives a moiety of the income of the charity of Endymion Canning. See above.

In 1826 Benjamin Sarson, by his will, left £30, now represented by £32 14s. 1d. consols, the annual dividends, amounting to 16s. 4d., to be distributed in bread on Easter Day, Trinity Sunday, Sunday after Michaelmas Day and Christmas Day among the oldest communicants.

In 1844 William Henry Boulton, by his will proved at Worcester 4 December, left £20, now £20 0s. 6d. consols, the annual dividends of 10s. to be distributed on New Year's Day to twelve poor widows, regular attendants at church and sacrament.

In 1856 William Field, by his will proved in the P.C.C. 22 January, left £100, invested in £108 5s. 1d. consols, the annual dividends, amounting to £2 14s., to be applied for the benefit of the aged and infirm poor.

In 1862 Miss Ellen Cicely Holyoake, by deed, gave £25, now £26 19s. 8d. consols, the annual dividends of 13s. 4d. to be distributed to twelve poor widows, regular attendants at church and sacrament.

In 1869 Mary Aston, by her will proved at Worcester 18 August, left £100, which, less duty, was invested in £95 14s. 11d. consols, the annual dividends, amounting to £2 7s. 8d., to be distributed after the Feast of the Epiphany to poor old men and women, constant attendants at service and Holy Communion, in bread, clothing, or money.

In 1870 Alfred Smallwood, by his will proved at Worcester in October, bequeathed £200, which was invested in £216 16s. 1d. consols, the annual dividends, amounting to £5 8s. 4d., to be applied in clothing, blankets, linen, bread, or coal about St. Thomas's Day.

In 1871 Henry Lewis, by his will, left £100 for the sick, aged, or infirm, represented by £107 10s. 7d. consols, producing £2 13s. 8d. yearly.

In 1882 William Wild, by his will proved at Worcester 25 September, bequeathed £50 to the vicar and churchwardens, the interest to be applied in equal proportions between the Society for the Propagation of the Gospel and the British and Foreign Bible Society. The legacy was invested in £49 6s. 2d. consols, producing £1 4s. 8d. yearly.

In 1887 Benjamin Sarson, by his will proved at Worcester 7 June, left £450, which was invested in £436 7s. 3d. consols, the dividends, amounting to £10 18s., to be applied in the purchase of tickets or in subscriptions to any hospital or charitable institution of a medical or surgical character in Birmingham or elsewhere, for securing benefits for the poor.

In 1909 Caroline Swann, by her will proved with a codicil at Worcester 4 May, bequeathed £160 4s. 9d. consols, the annual dividends of £4 to be applied in

pursuance of a scheme of the Charity Commissioners 15 March 1910, for the general benefit of the poor in one or more of the ways therein specified.

The several securities belonging to the eleemosynary charities are, unless otherwise stated, held by the official trustees.

The Milward Memorial Charity, comprised in deed 19 April 1880, was founded by the children of Henry Milward in memory of their father and mother. It consists of a freehold building used as a mission room, with a sum of £100 consols, the dividends to be applied in keeping the same in repair.

The Smallwood Hospital was founded and endowed by the will of Edwin Smallwood, proved at London 8 August 1892, and by gifts of William Smallwood, the residuary legatee, at a cost exceeding £10,000, leaving a sum of £11,260 available for investment in the names of the trustees, who also hold a sum of £551 10s. 1d. India 2½ per cent. stock as a special endowment fund by will of Edwin Smallwood, and £575 19s. 9d. like stock, arising from the sale of houses in Britten Street, conveyed in 1897 by Joseph Fessey for the benefit of the hospital. The official trustees also hold £104 11s. 6d. consols left by will of Richard Bennett, proved in 1891, and £107 4s. 9d. like stock given in 1902 by Walter Lewis towards the endowment of a bed in the women's ward in memory of his sister Elizabeth Clayton.

In 1902 the income from mortgages and all investments amounted to £503.

Nonconformist Charities.—In 1841 Joseph John Freeman, by deed, conveyed to trustees a dwelling-house with the shopping and other premises situate at Redditch upon trust that a moiety of the rents should be paid to the minister of the Congregational church, and the other moiety applied in upholding and keeping the said church in repair. The trust property produces £138 yearly.

In 1910 Miss Harriet Smith, by her will, left £50, the interest to be applied for the general purposes of the Dorcas Society in connexion with the Wesleyan chapel. The legacy was invested in £59 8s. 2d. India 3 per cent. stock with the official trustees, producing £1 15s. 8d. yearly.

St. Stephen's.—In 1880 Henry Smallwood, by his will proved at Worcester 26 June, left £50, the interest to be distributed at Christmas in coal to poor members of St. Stephen's Church. The legacy, less duty, was invested in £45 1s. 8d. consols, producing £1 2s. 4d. yearly.

In 1888 the Rev. George Frederick Fessey, by his will proved at Gloucester 27 December, left a legacy, now represented by £392 14s. 8d. consols with the official trustees, the annual dividends, amounting to £9 16s. 4d., to be distributed on 28 November among poor members of St. Stephen's Church, with a preference to communicants.

St. George.—In 1888 the Rev. George Frederick Fessey, by his will proved at Gloucester 27 December, left a legacy, now represented by £671 0s. 7d. consols with the official trustees, the annual dividends, amounting to £16 15s. 4d., to be distributed in bread among needy members of the congregation of St. George's Church. The distribution is made monthly to about twenty recipients.

UPTON WARREN

Houpton (viii cent.) ; Uptune (xi cent.) ; Shirrevesupton, Upton Fitz Waryn (xiv cent.) ; Upton Waryn (xv cent.).

Upton Warren is situated about 3¼ miles north of Droitwich, and has an area of 2,520 acres, of which only 4 are water. In 1905 there were about 886 acres of arable land, 1,398¼ acres of permanent grass and 31 acres of woodland.[1] The Salwarpe River forms part of its southern boundary and the Hampton Brook and one of its tributaries part of the western boundary. The main road from Kidderminster to Worcester forms the northern boundary, and a branch from it passes from north to south through the parish. The land is undulating at a height of about 200 ft. above the ordnance datum. The soil is clay, which at one time was worked, but now agriculture is the only industry, the most important crops being beans and wheat. The village is situated in the south-east of the parish on the River Salwarpe.

Badge Court, formerly Batchcott, is a half-timber and brick house, built about 1630, lying 3 miles west of Bromsgrove. According to Nash an Earl of Shrewsbury lived here, and in his time it was a large pile of buildings.[1a] It is H-shaped in plan and is of two stories with an attic, with tiled roofs and gables front and back. The original timbers are exposed at the back and on the east side, but elsewhere they are covered with ½-in. boards or thin lines have been painted on the brickwork. There is an original brick chimney projecting from the centre of the north side. The main doorway at the front admits to a small square porch, and then to a passage with the kitchen on the east, and the hall on the west occupying the centre of the house ; the stairway and parlour, reached through the hall, are in the west wing. The porch is entirely panelled, the lower part being of the 18th century, and the upper, with linenfold panelling, of the 17th century. In a diagonal panel in the ceiling is a painted shield of Winter of twelve quarters with a helm crested with an eagle coming out of a mural crown. The motto is 'Omnia Desuper.' The hall, parlour, and the room above the parlour are all entirely panelled in oak of the original date of the house. The fireplace is flanked by oak twin columns in two tiers rising to the full height of the room, each pair crowned by a single Ionic capital. In an 18th-century frame over the fireplace flanked by diamond-shaped projections is an achievement similar to that in the porch, but part of the motto is missing. The door to the passage is flanked by fluted oak pillars with Corinthian capitals. The heavy chamfered ceiling beams are now supported on 4-in. iron pillars. Over the entrance to the stairway and including some of the panelling is a segmental fanlight with carved angels in the spandrels. The panelling in the parlour is in small squares with a fluted frieze and moulded cornice, and over the fireplace are three semicircular-headed panels divided by fluted pilasters with Ionic capitals supporting consoles. The ceiling beams are moulded and there is a boss at their intersection in the centre of the room. The plain oak stairway leads to the wainscoted room over the parlour, which has three moulded panels over the fireplace divided by panelled pilasters. In the hearth are seventy-seven square tiles of the late 15th or early 16th century variously arranged ; some are of the four-tile Talbot pattern so often met with in this part of the county, while others have foliated and geometrical designs. Of the heraldic tiles five have a shield of Beauchamp and six a shield of Wyatt of Tewkesbury. The floors, ceiling beams, and roof timbers are of oak, and there are two original iron-studded doors, one with its original iron hinges in the dairy, and another constructed of two thicknesses of oak and heavily studded in an outhouse at the back. In the roof over the kitchen there is a closed chamber which has no entrance, and in which a bell can be rung from the outside.

The inclosure award for this parish is included with Bromsgrove and dated 5 July 1855.[2]

Among the 16th and 17th-century place-names are Nunchurch Meadow, Priors Field,[3] Barnsley,[4] Leverads, Wattlekens, Pyes Deane, Crowud Perry, Cattpurse Coppice.[5]

UPTON WARREN is included in a MANORS spurious grant which Ethelbald of Mercia is said to have made to Egwin, first Abbot of Evesham, in 716,[6] and is among the lands which Abbot Ethelwig redeemed from Edward the Confessor and others shortly before the Conquest.[7] After Ethelwig's death in 1077 Upton was seized by Odo, Bishop of Bayeux,[8] and he appears to have given it to Urse D'Abitot, who was holding it in 1086, although the Domesday Survey states that it ought then to have belonged to Evesham.[9] The overlordship passed from Urse to the Earls of Warwick and remained in their possession until the 15th century.[10] It then belonged to the Crown until it lapsed some time after 1630–1, when the last mention of it occurs.[11]

Herlebald was holding the manor under Urse in 1086. Warin Fitz William de Upton is the next under-tenant whose name is known, and he may have obtained it by gift of one of the Beauchamps on his marriage with Hawise de Beauchamp. He and his wife Hawise are mentioned in a charter of William Earl of Pembroke (1224–31), and were benefactors to the monastery of Pershore in the early 13th century.[12] Warin was succeeded in this manor by a son William called Fitz Warin,[13] who seems to have been a man of some note in Worcestershire,

---

[1] Statistics from Bd. of Agric. (1905).
[1a] *Hist. of Worcs.* i, 346 ; and see under manor.   [2] *Blue Bk. Incl. Awards*, 192.
[3] Pat. 32 Eliz. pt. v.
[4] Ibid. 8 Jas. I, pt. xlii.
[5] Parl. Surv. Worc. 1650–1, no. 4.
[6] Birch, *Cart. Sax.* i, 198 ; *Chron. de Evesham* (Rolls Ser.), 72.

[7] Ibid. 94.
[8] Ibid. 97.
[9] *V.C.H. Worcs.* i, 319a.
[10] *Testa de Nevill* (Rec. Com.), 40, 43b ; Chan. Inq. p.m. 7 Hen. V, no. 6 ; 10 Hen. V, no. 18 ; *Cal. Inq. p.m.* 1–9 Edw. II, 403 ; *Red Bk. of Exch.* (Rolls Ser.), 567.

[11] Chan. Inq. p.m. (Ser. 2), dvi, 159.
[12] Jeayes, *Lyttelton Chart.* no. 7 ; Aug. Off. Misc. Bks. lxi, fol. 28b, 29. See also an undated deed quoted by Prattinton by which Warin, lord of Upton, gave land there to Walter son of William de Colleshull (Prattinton Coll. [Soc. Antiq.]).
[13] *Testa de Nevill* (Rec. Com.), 40.

and was made sheriff of the county in 1229.[14] In 1254 William Fitz Warin de Upton was exempted for life from being put on juries, &c., against his will.[15] At about the same time he was engaged in a controversy with Richard de Montviron as to common at Woodcote.[16] Before 1315–16 the manor had passed to Edmund de Grafton,[17] and in 1319–20 John son of Edmund with his wife Alice granted the manor to William Fitz Warin for life, with reversion to John and Alice and their heirs.[18] William Fitz Warin died about 1338,[19] and the manor reverted to John de Grafton,[20] and subsequently followed the same descent as Grafton Manor[21] (q.v.).

Urse the sheriff was overlord of COOKSEY (Cochesei, Cochesie, xi cent.; Cokeseia, Kokeseye, xiii cent.), a member of the manor of Bromsgrove, at the time of the Domesday Survey,[22] and the overlordship afterwards formed part of the barony of Elmley, being mentioned for the last time in 1630.[23] Under the lords of Elmley the manor was held by knight service.

There were two manors at Cooksey, held before 1066 by Alfwine and Atilic, two thegns of Earl Edwin, and in 1086 by Herbrand and William.[24] About 1218 a controversy arose between Maud daughter of Henry and Richard de Montviron and others as to the title to a hide of land at Little Cooksey.[25] It seems probable that Richard de Montviron won the suit, for Little Cooksey appears to have subsequently followed the same descent as the manor of Woodcote, of which Richard was lord at that time, as it passed to the Bishopsdons in the 14th century.[26] Before 1346 it appears, however, to have passed to the Cookseys,[27] lords of Great Cooksey, and probably became merged in that manor after the middle of the 15th century.[28] Nash, writing in the latter part of the 18th century, says that 'the distinction of great and little Cokesey still prevails, though both are comprised in one manor.'[29]

The other manor, GREAT COOKSEY, gave its name to the important family of Cooksey. Walter de Cooksey held the manor about the middle of the 13th century,[30] and he or a descendant of the same name held it about 1280.[31] Elizabeth de Cooksey was lady of the manor in 1300,[32] and Walter son

of Walter was holding it in 1316,[33] and it was perhaps he who, as Walter de Cooksey, received the custody of the earldom of Warwick in 1325 during the minority of Thomas de Beauchamp[34] and paid a subsidy at Cooksey in 1327.[35] In 1335 Hugh, brother and successor of the last-mentioned Walter, who had succeeded him before 1333,[36] received a grant of free warren in Cooksey.[37] He died in 1356, and his wife Denise, one of the daughters and heirs of Edward le Boteler, who survived him, held the manor in dower until her death in 1376–7.[38] Walter, their son and heir, was only thirteen at the time of his father's death, but had been married three years before to Isabel daughter of Urrian de St. Peter.[39] He settled the manor on his son and heir Walter, who succeeded him in 1404.[40] Hugh son of Walter, who succeeded his father in 1406–7,[41] settled the manor on his wife Alice in 1441 and died four years later without issue.[42] Alice married Sir Andrew Ogard, and on her death in 1460 the manor passed to Joyce Beauchamp, widow, sister and co-heir of Hugh.[43] Joyce appears to have been married three times, first to — Beauchamp, secondly to Leonard Stapleton, and thirdly to John Grevill.[44] Her son and heir Sir John Grevill, kt., succeeded her in 1473, at the age of forty,[45] and died seised of the manor in 1480.[46] Owing to the importance of the estates which he had inherited from his mother his only son Thomas took the name of Cooksey,[47] but died without issue in 1498–9.[48] His property passed to Robert Russell and Roger Winter, the heirs of Cecily[49] wife of Thomas Cassy, another sister of Hugh Cooksey, the manor of Cooksey being assigned to Roger Winter.[50] The manor then followed the same descent as Huddington[50a] (q.v.).

There seems no longer to be a manor of Cooksey,[51] and probably when it passed into the hands of the Earls of Shrewsbury it became merged in the manor of Upton Warren.

COOKSEY. *Argent a bend azure with three cinqfoils or thereon.*

---

[14] *Cal. Pat.* 1225–32, p. 238.
[15] Ibid. 1247–58, p. 262.
[16] Assize R. 1022, m. 4 d.
[17] *Cal. Inq. p.m* 1–9 *Edw. II*, 403.
[18] Feet of F. Worcs. Trin. 13 Edw. II.
[19] *Cal. Close*, 1337–9, p. 417.
[20] *Feud. Aids*, v, 302; Add. MS. 28024, fol. 135.
[21] Feet of F. Worcs. Trin. 24 Edw. III; Chan. Inq. p.m. 41 Edw. III (1st nos.), no. 33; 44 Edw. III (1st nos.), no. 31; 10 Hen. V, no. 18; *Feud. Aids*, v, 323, 330; Pat. 1 Hen. VII, pt. iv; Exch. Inq. p.m. (Ser. 2), file 1178, no. 8; Star Chamb. Proc. Edw. VI, bdle. 4, no. 45; Chan. Inq. p.m. (Ser. 2), lxxxix, 160; W. and L. Inq. p.m. vii, 49; Exch. Spec. Com. no. 4770; Chan. Inq. p.m. (Ser. 2), cccxlv, 146; dvi, 159. Joan, the second daughter and co-heir of John de Hastings, who married firstly Sir John de Salesbury and secondly Sir Rustin Villeneuf, seems to have held the manor of Upton Warren during her lifetime (Chan. Inq. p.m. 12 Ric. II, no. 92; 7 Hen. V, no. 6), though it was assigned to her sister Maud in 1374–5 (ibid. 48 Edw. III [1st nos.], no. 40).

[22] *V.C.H. Worcs.* i, 286*a*, 319*a*.
[23] *Cal. Close*, 1313–18, p. 277; Chan. Inq. p.m. 50 Edw. III (1st nos.), no. 20; 6 Hen. IV, no. 32; 24 Hen. VI, no. 36; 13 Edw. IV, no. 32; 20 Edw. IV, no. 72; Chan. Inq. p.m. (Ser. 2), lvii, 11; lxxxix, 157; ccclxiv, 24*b*.
[24] *V.C.H. Worcs.* i, 286*a*, 319*a*.
[25] Pipe R. 2 Hen. III, m. 4; 4 Hen. III, m. 14 d.; *Excerpta e Rot. Fin.* (Rec. Com.), i, 9.
[26] *Cal. Chart. R.* 1300–26, p. 415.
[27] *Feud. Aids*, v, 303.   [28] Ibid. 323.
[29] op. cit. i, 346.
[30] *Testa de Nevill* (Rec. Com.), 40.
[31] Lay Subs. R. Worcs. c. 1280 (Worcs. Hist. Soc.), 18.
[32] Nash, op. cit. ii, 449.
[33] *Cal. Inq. p.m.* 1–9 *Edw. II*, 403; *Cal. Close*, 1313–18, p. 277.
[34] *Abbrev. Rot. Orig.* (Rec. Com.), i, 290*b*.
[35] *Lay Subs. R. Worcs.* 1327 (Worcs. Hist. Soc.), 41.
[36] *Her. and Gen.* vi, 659; Wrottesley, *Ped. from Plea R.* 17.
[37] Chart. R. 19 Edw. II, m. 1, no. 3.
[38] Chan. Inq. p.m. 30 Edw. III (1st

nos.), no. 54; *Cal. Close*, 1354–60, p. 286; Chan. Inq. p.m. 50 Edw. III (1st nos.), no. 20.
[39] Chan. Inq. p.m. 30 Edw. III (1st nos.), no. 54.
[40] Ibid. 6 Hen. IV, no. 32.
[41] *Her. and Gen.* vi, 659; see also Chan. Inq. p.m. 4 Hen. VI, no. 49.
[42] Chan. Inq. p.m. 24 Hen. VI, no. 36.
[43] Ibid. 38 & 39 Hen. VI, no. 49.
[44] Ibid. 24 Hen. VI, no. 36; *Her. and Gen.* vi, 169.
[45] Chan. Inq. p.m. 13 Edw. IV, no. 32.
[46] Ibid. 20 Edw. IV, no. 72.
[47] Ibid.   [48] *Her. and Gen.* vi, 169.
[49] The *Visit. of Worcester* 1569 gives this name as Elizabeth (Harl. Soc. xxvii), 118.
[50] *Her. and Gen.* vi, 659; Chan. Inq. p.m. (Ser. 2), lvii, 11. It is curious that this second sister should not have been mentioned in the inquisition taken on the death of Hugh Cooksey.
[50a] For references see Huddington.
[51] Cooksey Great Lodge, which was apparently the manor-house of Great Cooksey, was taken down before 1781 (Nash, op. cit. i, 346).

Cooksey with a house there called Batchcott (now Badge Court)[52] was left by Sir George Winter to his widow Mary for life with reversion to Gilbert Talbot, a younger brother of Francis Earl of Shrewsbury, who agreed to pay £1,500 for it.[53] On Sir George's death Gilbert at once laid claim to Badge Court, asserting that Sir George Winter had no power to leave it to his widow; but a suit which Mary Winter brought against him was 'after long debate' decided in her favour.[54]

The Winters had a park at Cooksey in the 16th century,[55] and closes called Little Park and Wood Park are mentioned in a survey of the manor taken in 1650.[56]

A mill was in existence at Upton Warren at the time of the Domesday Survey,[57] and another appears to have belonged to the manor of Cooksey during the 17th and 18th centuries.[58] There is now a corn-mill in the village on the Salwarpe.

CHURCH The church of *ST. MICHAEL* consists of a chancel 20 ft. by 15 ft., nave 50 ft. by 20 ft., small north vestry and a south tower 11½ ft. by 10 ft. These measurements are all internal.

A church probably existed here at the time of the Domesday Survey, but was rebuilt towards the end of the 13th century and consecrated in 1300.[59] The whole structure except the tower was rebuilt in the 18th century, the chancel in 1724 and the nave in 1798. The tower, which is of two stages, is evidently a late 14th-century rebuilding. The tower arch has a pointed head of two orders. The south window of the ground stage is of the same date, and has two ogee-headed lights with a quatrefoil above; a similar window on the east side has been filled in. In the west wall is a small circular light with a segmental rear arch, and below the offset on the south side is a small lancet window.

The windows to the bell-chamber, which have evidently been reset, are survivals from the earliest building on the site and date from c. 1220. Each has two trefoiled lancets inclosed by an outer order with a two-centred drop arch; the spandrel above the lancets is pierced by a trefoil. The embattled parapet is probably modern, and from it rises an octagonal stone spire of ashlar work.

The furniture is modern, the font being octagonal with panelled sides. The east window contains some remarkable modern glass.

In the chancel are several slabs, one to John Hill, son of John Hill, rector, and Sarah his wife, died 1667, aged six years, and another to the above-mentioned (rector for more than forty years), died 1699. In the nave is a mural monument to John Sanders, died 1670.

There are three bells: the first by John Martin of Worcester, 1653; the second by William Brooke of Bromsgrove, 1743; the third by John Greene the

younger of Worcester, 1618; this last bears his mark, three bells and I.G.

The plate includes a large Elizabethan cup and cover paten of the usual type, with the hall-mark and inscription of 1571.

The registers are as follows : (i) baptisms 1604 to 1645, burials and marriages 1605 to 1645 ; (ii) all entries 1657 to 1722 ; (iii) all 1722 to 1801 ; (iv) baptisms 1793 to 1812 ; (v) burials same period, and (vi) marriages 1754 to 1812.

ADVOWSON There was a priest at Upton in 1086.[60] The advowson apparently belonged originally to the lords of the manor,[61] and passed with the manor in 1350–1 to Thomas Earl of Warwick.[62] When the manor passed to the Hastings family the earl retained the advowson,[63]

UPTON WARREN CHURCH : THE TOWER

and it passed to his son Thomas Earl of Warwick, who forfeited it in 1396.[64] The glebe land and advowson were granted in 1398 to the king's nephew Thomas Duke of Surrey,[65] but the advowson was evidently restored to the earl in 1399, as he died seised of it in 1401,[66] and it afterwards passed to his descendants the Earls of Warwick.[67] Richard Nevill Earl of Warwick presented in 1463,[68] and the advowson probably passed on his death in 1471 to the

[52] A William de Bachecote paid a subsidy of 2s. at Cooksey in 1327 (*Lay Subs. R. Worcs.* 1327 [Worcs. Hist. Soc.], 41).
[53] Exch. Spec. Com. 28 Chas. II, no. 6531, 6532 ; 29 Chas. II, no. 6535 ; *Hist. MSS. Com. Rep.* x, App. iv, 198.
[54] Exch. Spec. Com. 28 Chas. II, no. 6531, 6532 ; 29 Chas. II, no. 6535.
[55] Chan. Inq. p.m. (Ser. 2), lxxxviii,

69 ; Chan. Proc. (Ser. 2), bdle. 163, no. 18 ; Feet of F. Worcs. Hil. 13 Eliz.
[56] Parl. Surv. Worc. 1650–1, no. 4.
[57] *V.C.H. Worcs.* i, 319a.
[58] Recov. R. Trin. 22 Chas. I, rot. 25 ; 12 Chas. II, rot. 108 ; Hil. 5 Geo. I, rot. 38 ; Parl. Surv. Worc. 1650–1, no. 4.
[59] *Reg. G. Giffard* (Worcs. Hist. Soc.), 518.
[60] *V.C.H. Worcs.* i, 319.

[61] Feet of F. Worcs. 13 Edw. II, no. 6 ; 24 Edw. III, no. 25.
[62] Ibid. 24 Edw. III, no. 25.
[63] Chan. Inq. p.m. 43 Edw. III, pt. i, no. 19.
[64] *Abbrev. Rot. Orig.* (Rec. Com.), ii, 308 ; Chan. Inq. p.m. 21 Ric. II, no. 137, m. 6 e and f.
[65] *Cal. Pat.* 1396–9, p. 336.
[66] Chan. Inq. p.m. 2 Hen. IV, no. 58.
[67] Nash, op. cit. ii, 451. [68] Ibid.

Crown, as it was included in 1485 in the grant of the manor to Gilbert Talbot.[69] Since that time the advowson has descended with the manor,[70] the Earl of Shrewsbury and Talbot being the present patron.

In the time of Edward VI a parcel of land at Cooksey given for the maintenance of a lamp in the church at Upton Warren was valued at 12*d*.[71]

CHARITIES John Saunders, some time alderman of the City of London—as appears on a monument in the church—settled an annuity of £10 to be for ever paid by the Grocers' Company, London, for placing out a boy of this parish as an apprentice in London, and for lack of such a boy, then a boy of Stoke Prior or Chaddesley. In 1910 a premium of £10 was paid, and there was a balance of £40 in hand.

Charities of Elizabeth Lacy, the Earl of Shrewsbury, Alice Nash and other benefactors mentioned in the Parliamentary Returns of 1786.—The endowment now consists of four cottages and gardens at Staple Hill and 2 a. 2 r. at Rock Hill, near Bromsgrove, of the annual rental value of £30 10s.

By an order of the Charity Commissioners 18 September 1906 five-sixths of the net income was determined to be the proportion applicable for educational purposes, under the title of the Lacy Educational Foundation, and the remainder for the poor.

The poor also receive a rent-charge of £1, paid out of land in Bromsgrove in respect of the charity of the Rev. John Hill.

In 1828 William Cole, by his will proved in the P.C.C. 18 February, left £30, now £30 consols, with the official trustees, the annual dividends of 15s. to be distributed on the first Sunday after Candlemas in bread to poor persons brought up to the Church of England.

WESTWOOD PARK

Westwude (xi-cent.).

The present parish of Westwood Park was originally included in Dodderhill, but became a separate extra-parochial district in 1178.[1] Habington says, 'Westwood in the territoryes of the Sayes, Barons of Bureford and Lordes of Wichbaud, was by their indulgence made a parish of it sealfe, including Westwood, Cruche, and Clerehall.'[2] For ecclesiastical purposes it was annexed to Hampton Lovett in 1541,[3] but it remained extra-parochial[4] until 1857,[5] when it became a parish.

It is situated immediately south of Hampton Lovett and covers an area of only 740 acres. The ground is undulating, but nowhere rises higher than about 185 ft. above the ordnance datum. The soil is marl, with patches of sandy gravel, the land being mostly pasture and park land. The house in the middle of the park, now the residence of Mrs. Bruce Ward, the daughter of the present owner, is on one of the highest points, and commands extensive and beautiful views of the surrounding country. The nucleus of the present mansion was erected early in the reign of Queen Elizabeth by Sir John Pakington (the Lusty Pakington), and seems to have been merely intended as a hunting-box. That this was, however, a building of considerable pretensions is apparent from the size and elaborate nature of the plan, which consists on the ground floor of a large entrance hall occupying the whole length of the principal front, with bay windows on either side of a central entrance doorway and in each end wall, and a similar block at the rear containing the kitchen and offices, separated from the front portion of the house by a narrow staircase hall in the centre of the building. The front block is of three stories with an attic floor, the kitchen block of four stories without an attic. There is a basement beneath the whole house. On the first floor is the saloon, an apartment of equal size with the entrance hall below it, measuring internally 46 ft. 6 in. by 22 ft. The bay windows throughout extend the whole height of the house. The materials are red brick with dressings of red sandstone. The house having suffered considerably during the Civil War, considerable alterations and repairs were undertaken about the time of the Restoration, with the double object of repairing the fabric and transforming it into the principal seat of the family, whose former house at Hampton Lovett had been destroyed by fire. Wings designed in a style to correspond with the existing house were added at each of the four corners of the building, projecting from the central mass at about the angle of 45°, and two diamond-shaped courts were formed at the front and back. At the north-east and south-west angles of the courts were square tower-like garden houses three stories high. The forecourt, with its garden towers and gate lodges, has survived in its entirety, but the court at the rear has disappeared. An engraving by Kip shows that the original arrangement of the courts was still preserved in the early years of the 18th century, about which period considerable internal repairs appear to have been entered upon. About 1840 a new kitchen was added at the rear of the house, contained in a one-story building occupying the portion of the court embraced by the wings on this side. The original panelling of the ground floor rooms was then replaced by painted deal 'Tudor' panelling of a singularly inappropriate type, and a plaster ceiling designed in the same style and grained in imitation of oak was substituted for the original ceiling of the staircase hall. A 'Tudor' bay window of stone was added to the room on the ground floor of the north wing, known as the 'chapel,' to bring it more into accordance with the notions of ecclesiastical propriety then prevalent. This room is now used as a servants' hall. These alterations were made under the direction of P. Hardwick, whose drawings are in the possession of the present owner.

From this it will be gathered that the ground floor rooms contain no features of particular interest, having been almost entirely modernized. The floors of the wings are at a higher level than those of the

[69] Pat. 1 Hen. VII, pt. iv.
[70] Recov. R. Hil. 21 Hen. VIII, rot. 129; Chan. Inq. p.m. (Ser. 2), lxxxix, 160; Inst. Bks. (P.R.O.). Members of the Cox and Ingram families who were patrons during the 18th and early 19th centuries were perhaps trustees of the Earls of Shrewsbury.
[71] Chant. Cert. 60, no. 65.
[1] See under Advowson.
[2] Habington, *Surv. of Worcs.* (Worcs. Hist. Soc.), i, 459.
[3] See under Advowson.
[4] Nash, *Hist. of Worcs.* i, 537.
[5] Stat. 20 Vict. cap. 19.

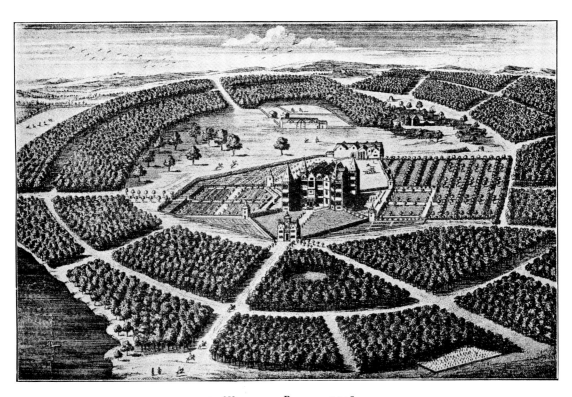

WESTWOOD PARK C. 1708

main building and are approached by short flights of steps. The kitchen, at the west of the central block, has been converted into a dining room, and the floor level of the 'chapel' has been re-arranged. The staircase-hall in the centre extends the whole length of the house at the first floor level, and the stairs rise to this height in successive flights of eight risers separated by landings of equal length. The handrails are supported by turned balusters, and the massive newel posts are surmounted by Corinthian columns with ball finials. The upper floors are

bay at the north-east of the ground story appears to be an addition of the latter half of the 17th century.

In the centre of the north-west wall of the saloon is an elaborate chimney-piece of carved oak, probably contemporary in date with the original building of this part of the house. It is of two superimposed orders, the lower Ionic and the upper Corinthian. The frieze of the entablature of the lower order, which spans the fireplace opening, is carved with a vine pattern in delicate relief, the shafts of the supporting

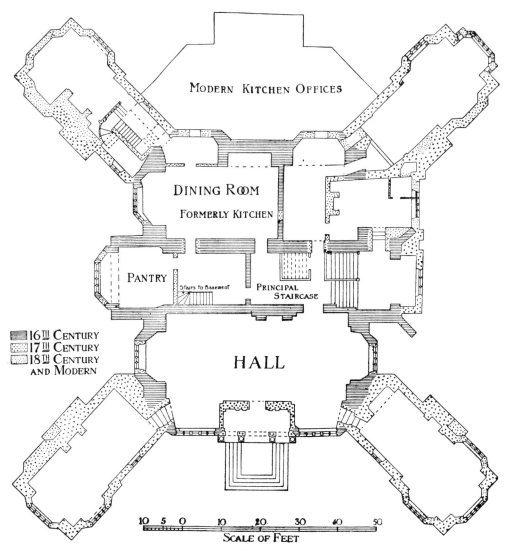

PLAN OF WESTWOOD PARK

reached by subsidiary stairs in the four-storied back portion of the house. Over the main stairs, at the level of the second floor of the front portion, is a long gallery, known as the 'Museum' gallery, with open wells at either end, railed with balustrading of a similar but slightly plainer design. The ceiling of the staircase formed by the floor of the latter, and the ceiling above, visible from below at either end, are of plaster, grained in imitation of oak, and date from the 19th-century restorations above referred to. Large four-light windows at the first and second floor levels light the staircase at either end. The square projecting

columns being ornamented with elaborate strap-work. The upper order has the frieze of its entablature decorated with grotesques and festoons and the shafts of its columns carved with the vine. The central panel, over the fireplace opening, has an enriched bolection moulding of bold section, and is filled by a modern portrait of Henry VIII; between the coupled columns on either side are semicircular-headed niches, fluted and elaborated with strapwork. The surfaces behind the columns and on the returns of the chimney breasts are ornamented with a design of oak leaves and acorns in

A HISTORY OF WORCESTERSHIRE

shallow relief. The fireplace opening itself has a grate and marble surround of the 18th century. A deep strapwork frieze of plaster runs round the walls of the room. This appears to be contemporary with the chimney-piece, the comparative coarseness of execution being due to the difference of material. Above this is the cove of the magnificent plaster ceiling, which seems to have been executed at the time the wings were added, or perhaps a few years earlier. In the centre is an oval wreath within a rectangular panel with curved ends. The soffit of the large and heavily moulded rib inclosing the panel is enriched with a garland of deeply undercut foliage, and the whole is inclosed by a modelled band of pointed leaves in high relief extending the length of the chimney breast. The remainder of the ceiling, and of those of the bay windows, is made out with wreaths and panels of slighter projection. The cove is ornamented with festoons of fruit and flowers. The walls still retain their original tapestry hangings, illustrating the life of Jacob. In the panelled jambs of the bays are fluted Corinthian pilasters. The tapestry hangings conceal the doorways at the south and east angles of the saloon leading to the rooms in the wings on this side of the house. Their addition has necessitated the blocking of the returns of the bays adjoining them.

The 'Japanese' room in the south wing has a ceiling of very similar type and of the same date as that of the saloon with a good modillion cornice. The room was re-decorated in the middle of the 18th century and remains to this day practically unaltered with its Oriental paper, marble bolection moulded chimney-piece, and elaborately enriched doorcase. The bay in the end wall is blocked. The room in the east wing, known as the 'White' room, has a ceiling of the same type, and white painted panelling of the 18th century, with a fine carved wood chimney-piece of contemporary date.

The less important rooms contain little of particular interest, though much good 18th-century work remains.

Externally the house presents a particularly imposing appearance with its four wings radiating from the central mass, and terminated at their extremities by tower-like projections having stone-mullioned bay windows in their side and end walls, and pyramidal slated roofs. In the first instance it is probable that these roofs were of a fanciful curved outline like those of the still remaining garden towers. Between the two stone-mullioned bay windows of the central block, which extend the whole height of the three principal stories, is the entrance porch, a charming piece of almost fully developed classical design, after the type of a triumphal arch in miniature, with a central and two side archways. An entablature, broken forward over four detached Corinthian columns and surmounted by a plain attic order, crowns the whole. The columns stand upon pedestals sculptured with lions' faces, and in each side opening are balustrades. Above the keystone of the central arch is a carved female figure riding upon an eagle with outstretched wings. The inner doorway is flanked by coupled Corinthian pilasters enriched with strapwork. The porch is elevated on a flight of steps. Over the porch, on the face of the blank wall of the first story between the bays, is the large shield of Pakington quartering Wash-

bourne, Baldwin and Arden, with the crest of an elephant. The floor levels are marked by moulded string-courses of stone, which on the walls of the wings are raised and dropped to correspond with the difference in level of the floors. The bay windows and the wing towers are finished with an elaborate carved parapet formed of the sheaves and molets of the Pakington shield. The attic windows of the central block are surmounted by curvilinear gables, crowned at the apex by circular panels, each inclosing a molet. Square bays forming the extremities of the staircase hall compose the central features of the side elevations. The angles of the bay on the north-east have buttresses extending to the first floor level. The ground story of this bay, as mentioned above, is further extended by a square projection containing a three-light transomed window with rusticated jambs and head, dating probably from the latter half of the 17th century. The bay windows of the wings have had their return lights blocked, probably in the 18th century, with the view of avoiding the window tax, and have been otherwise much altered in the 19th century, the sills having being lowered and extra mullions inserted; a drawing made about the year 1830 shows them to have been originally of two lights. The disposition of the plan renders all the elevations of equal size and importance, and was doubtless suggested by the site, which is on the summit of almost the highest ground in the whole extent of the park.

The twin-lodges on either side of the entrance gates are of brick with stone dressings, two stories in height, and have mullioned windows and curvilinear gables. They are joined by a semicircular archway containing the gates and surmounted by open stone screenwork filled with sheaves and molets. Above this an ornamental arched framing of timber supports a slated cupola. The garden towers at the north-east and south-west angles of the forecourt are of brick, three stories in height, with cornices of stone and curved slated roofs.

Mr. Edward Partington, J.P., is the present owner, having purchased it from the Pakingtons in 1900.

The exact site of the nunnery is unknown, but is supposed to be in the present kitchen garden.[6] A stone coffin has been found in Nunnery Wood, and there is a stone-lined well in a pool close by.

There are at present no roads in the parish, but a bridle-path from Hampton Lovett goes through the park. The main road from Ombersley to Droitwich passes along the southern boundary of the park. This road seems to have been made by Sir John Pakington before 1616, and was at that date the subject of some dispute between him and Sir Samuel Sandys, lord of Ombersley. It seems that there were formerly two roads through Westwood, one entering it at a bridge called Wadebridge, over Hadley Brook, and passing from there by Wadebridge Lane, Westwood Coppice and a field called Boycott to two bridges over a divided stream called 'Bryarmill' bridges, and from there to Droitwich, Bromsgrove, Kidderminster and Bewdley, the other from Ludlow, Bewdley and Ombersley, crossing Hadley Brook by a 'waynebridge made of stone' above Hadley Mill, passing the site of the nunnery and through woods called Westwood to Boycott Bridge, and so on to Droitwich and London. Sir John had inclosed these roads in his

[6] *Birm. and Midl. Inst. Arch. Sect. Trans.* 1880, p. 24.

WESTWOOD PARK : ENTRANCE FRONT

WESTWOOD PARK : THE SALOON

park, and 'drowned' a great part of one of them in 'a new great pool' there, but had made instead the present road, which is said to have been 'very narrow and very fowle in winter and a worse way and further about than the others.'[7] As a result Sir John is said to have had the embankments of his new lake cut through. The present park contains a lake of 60 acres.

During the Civil War and Commonwealth many eminent men visited Sir John Pakington at Westwood Park. Doctor Hammond, Bishop-designate of Worcester, spent the last years of his life there, and died there in 1660.[8] Bishops Morley, Fell and Gunning and Dean Hickes often visited at Westwood, and jointly with some of them Lady Dorothy Pakington is alleged to have written *The Whole Duty of Man*.[9]

Among the place-names are Ulnys Medowe, Byrchehyll, Boycote Felde, Ogans Medowe, Horsesiche, Banhamyshyll, Wynowynge Hylle, Dappyngs Medowe, Parsons Hill, Bryerhylle,[10] Le Pykes[11] (xvi cent.), Boycott[12] (xvii cent.), Cobbett's Corner, Nuns Harbour (xx cent.).

WESTWOOD is not mentioned in the *MANOR* Domesday Survey, being then probably included in the parish of Dodderhill,[13] but by the 12th century it was in the hands of Osbert Fitz Hugh, who with Eustacia de Say, his mother, granted it to the nunnery they founded there in the reign of Henry II.[14] This gift was confirmed by John, and subsequently by later kings.[15] After the Dissolution Sir John Pakington of Hampton Lovett petitioned that he might have the site of the nunnery in farm, 'since it was close to his house where he had no pasture for his horses although he was in the king's service in North Wales to his great charge.'[16] The manor with the site and demesne lands of the late nunnery was granted to him in 1539, and has since that date followed the same descent as Hampton Lovett[17] (q.v.).

The nuns of Westwood received a licence to make a *PARK* at Westwood, if they so chose, when the manor was granted to them,[18] but they do not seem ever to have done so. In 1618 Sir John Pakington obtained licence to impark 1,000 acres at Westwood, Hampton Lovett and other surrounding parishes,[19] and he impaled two great parks called Westwood Parks and stocked the one with red deer and the other with fallow deer. In doing this he met with some opposition from the burgesses of Droitwich, on account of rights of way which they had enjoyed over the manor of Westwood.[20]

The park was originally planted with oak woods radiating from the house. The oak is very rapidly growing but lacks durability, and this is so well known that it used to be specified in local building contracts that Westwood oak was not to be used. Since the present owner purchased the estate the park has gradually been reduced in area to 350 acres.[21]

A fee-farm rent of £5 16s., which must have been reserved when the manor was granted to Sir John Pakington, was vested in trustees for sale in 1670.[22] It was afterwards purchased by the Pakingtons.

A mill called Bierhalla in Westwood belonged to the nuns of Westwood in 1299,[23] and Henry Lovett by an undated charter remitted to them the foreign service which they owed him for it.[24] This mill, then called Bryer Mill, was valued at 48s. in 1535, when it still belonged to the nuns.[25] It was granted with the manor to Sir John Pakington in 1539.[26] The present Brier Mill is in the parish of Droitwich.

CHURCH The date of the building of a *AND* church at Westwood is not known. *ADVOWSON* In 1178 the tithes of Westwood, with sepulture and obventions of all the inhabitants, were assigned to the nuns of Westwood in exchange for their claim to the church of St. Augustine Dodderhill,[27] these tithes having formerly belonged to the church of Dodderhill. The conventual church or chapel of Westwood was valued at £2 in 1291.[28] The rectorial tithes were appropriated to the nunnery,[29] and the chaplain was provided at the expense of the nuns.[30] The chapel served as a parish church for the inhabitants of Crutch as well as those of Westwood, and had full parochial rights.[31] On the dissolution of Westwood nunnery the chapel was also suppressed, and the inhabitants of Westwood were left without any parish church. They petitioned the bishop that, as the tithes of Westwood were insufficient to support a priest, their hamlet might be annexed to the church of Hampton Lovett, which was conveniently near and accessible to them at any time of the year. Their petition was granted and the union was legalized in 1541.[32] The rectory and advowson had been granted in 1539 to John Pakington,[33] and his sanction was obtained to the union. The advowson and rectory of Westwood are mentioned in a deed of 1542,[34] but after that time all references to a church at Westwood cease, it having probably shared the fate of the conventual buildings. All remains of the church have disappeared.

There are no endowed charities.

[7] Exch. Dep. by Com. Worc. Mich. 14 Jas. I, no. 12.
[8] *Dict. Nat. Biog.*
[9] Nash, op. cit. i, 352–3.
[10] *Valor Eccl.* (Rec. Com.), iii, 276.
[11] Pat. 30 Hen. VIII, pt. vii.
[12] Exch. Dep. Mich. 14 Jas. I, no. 12.
[13] Habington speaks of Westwood as 'a lym of St. Augustin's paryshe named Duderhull of Wich' (*Surv. of Worcs.* [Worcs. Hist. Soc.], ii, 311).
[14] *V.C.H. Worcs.* ii, 148.
[15] Chart. R. 2 John, m. 28 ; *Cal. Chart. R.* 1257–1300, p. 320 ; *Cal. Pat.* 1391–6, p. 582 ; Pat. 14 Hen. VI, m. 15.

[16] *L. and P. Hen. VIII*, i, 386.
[17] Ibid. xiv (1), g. 651 (44) ; xvii, g. 1012 (28) ; Feet of F. Worcs. Mich. 34 Hen. VIII ; Com. Pleas D. Enr. Trin. 34 Hen. VIII, m. 1 ; Chan. Proc. (Ser. 2), bdle. 187, no. 72 ; *Cal. Com. for Comp.* 1194.
[18] *Cal. Chart. R.* 1257–1300, p. 320.
[19] Pat. 16 Jas. I, pt. iv.
[20] Chan. Proc. Jas. I, P 16, no. 53.
[21] Information supplied by Mr. R. Bruce Ward.
[22] Pat. 22 Chas. II, pt. ii, m. 2.
[23] Nash, op. cit. Introd. 65.
[24] Dugdale, *Mon. Angl.* vii, 1005.

[25] *Valor Eccl.* (Rec. Com.), iii, 276.
[26] *L. and P. Hen. VIII*, xiv, g. 651 (44).
[27] *V.C.H. Worcs.* ii, 149 ; Thomas, *Survey of Cath. Ch. of Worc.* A 111, 115.
[28] Worc. Epis. Reg. Thos. Hemenhale (1337–8), fol. 12 ; *Pope Nich. Tax.* (Rec. Com.), 239.
[29] *Valor Eccl.* (Rec. Com.), iii, 279.
[30] Nash, op. cit. i, 542, quoting Worc. Epis. Reg.
[31] Ibid. [32] Nash, loc. cit.
[33] *L. and P. Hen. VIII*, xiv (1), g. 651 (44).
[34] Feet of F. Worcs. Mich. 34 Hen. VIII.

YARDLEY

Gyrdeleahe (x cent.) ; Gerlei (xi cent.) ; Yerdel, Yerdelegh, Jerdel, Jerdelegh near Coleshull (xiii cent.); Erdeley (xv cent.) ; Yardell (xvii cent.).

The parish of Yardley, situated in the north-eastern corner of the county, became in 1911 part of the city of Birmingham under the Birmingham Extension Act.[1] The three chief roads are the main road from Birmingham to Coventry, which passes through Hay Mills in the north of the parish, and those from Birmingham to Warwick and from Birmingham to Stratford-on-Avon in the south of the parish. Yardley is watered by the River Cole, a tributary of the Avon.

The ground is lowest in the north on the banks of the river and rises gradually towards the south, being over 400 ft. above the ordnance datum in one part of the village and at Acock's Green, and reaching 500 ft. at Yardley Wood.

The area of the parish is 7,590 acres, which includes 60 acres of inland water, 1,595 acres of arable land, 4,163 of permanent grass and 12 of woods and plantations.[2] The commons, containing an area of 850 acres, were inclosed under an Act of 1833,[3] the award being dated 1847.[4]

The village of Yardley is now joined to Birmingham by a more or less continuous line of houses along the main road, though the original settlement near and around the church still retains a certain rural aspect. On the south side of the churchyard is the old schoolhouse, a fine half-timber building of the latter part of the 15th century. The plan is a narrow oblong, with an oversailing upper story, the moulded sill of which is supported by plain brackets springing from small octagonal shafts cut on the face of the main uprights of the ground story. The interior has been completely modernized. The upper story is open to the roof, which is supported by massive trusses with cambered tie-beams and collars. The principals are further strutted from both tie-beams and collars by curved struts. The chimney stacks have been rebuilt, and later brick buildings adjoin on the east side.

About a quarter of a mile south-west of the church, on the north side of the road named after it, is Blakesley Hall, a fine two-storied half-timber house of the 16th century, facing south. The plan is L-shaped, the centre being occupied by a hall with an entrance and porch at the south-east and a central newel-stair at the north-west angle. In the ground-floor room on the west side of the hall is a fireplace with moulded stone jambs and a four-centred head. The original kitchen was probably on the east side of the hall, but a new kitchen of brick appears to have been added on the north side of the house early in the 17th century. On the first floor the original partitions remain. This floor overhangs the ground floor, and the sills are supported by moulded brackets of unusually massive proportions. Over the outer doorway of the porch is the following inscription in

Roman characters, the work, doubtless, of some early 17th-century owner : ' OMNIPOTENS DEVS P'TECTOR SIT DOM' HVI' . R.S.' An ornamental character is imparted to the half-timbering by the short diagonal struts between the uprights, disposed herring-bone fashion. The upper part of the large brick chimney stack on the west side of the house has been rebuilt. Photographs taken previously to the repairs and restorations effected a few years since show this to have been surmounted by four diagonal chimney shafts of brick. The windows are all modern.

Near the church to the east is a moat surrounding the site of a house believed to have been once occupied by a family named Allstree.[5] Further to the east is another larger moat called Kent's Moat. There are also a moat at Glebe Farm in the north of the parish, a moated inclosure to the south of the village, and remains of moats at Broom Hall, Hyron Hall and near Highfield House in Hall Green.

At Hall Green, about 3 miles south of Yardley village, is Hall Green Hall, a two-storied half-timber house, some part of which appears to date from the 15th century. The house seems to have been added to and remodelled late in the 16th century and again in the early 18th century. At the end of the same century a fine staircase hall was added on the north side of the house. In the kitchen, which is in the centre of the house and was probably the original entrance hall, are a fine Elizabethan plaster ceiling and a large open fireplace. Many of the ceilings in the later parts of the house are good examples of the Adam style, and great ingenuity is shown in the planning of the staircase hall. The geometrical stairs have a central and two side flights, and in the rounded angles of the hall are doorways with doors following the curvature of the plan. All the joinery, though slight and attenuated to a degree, is fitted with marvellous precision. Many grates of the Adam period survive throughout the house. The farm-house adjoining on the south is of brick, and most probably dates from the 17th century. The stables at the rear of the house are of original mid-17th-century date. Over the main block is a good brick gable, stepped and curved.

Foxhollies Hall, which stands about a quarter of a mile to the north of Hall Green Hall, on the opposite side of the road, has been entirely remodelled and modernized. The original house, which forms the nucleus of the present building, is said to be of narrow bricks, but the walls have been stuccoed over, and no original detail is visible. With the exception of one or two early brick farm-houses, little else of interest remains in the parish, which is being rapidly covered with rows of dwelling-houses mostly of a rental of about £20. The erstwhile outlying hamlets, such as Stechford and Acock's Green, may still be traced by the examples of older work which occur here and there amid the surrounding waste of Victorian and Edwardian architecture.

---

[1] In 1857 Yardley was transferred to Warwickshire for the purposes of the several Acts relating to county and district constables, but on account of the inconvenience of this arrangement it was re-transferred to Worcestershire in 1899 (Local and Personal Act, 62 & 63 Vict. cap. 226).

[2] Statistics from Bd. of Agric. (1905).

[3] Priv. Act, 3 & 4 Will. IV, cap. 17.

[4] Blue Bk. Incl. Awards, 192.

[5] Birm. and Midl. Inst. Arch. Sect. Trans. 1880–1, p. 6.

Among the ancient place-names are Flaxbot,[6] le Bromilone,[7] le Hulbroc,[8] Hendeslond, Waxhullone,[9] Collelesewe,[10] Yarpesham-mede, Blakeley, Bondefeld,[11] Esson, Bromwall, Glascote, Colmedowe, Capcroft, Holkyron,[12] Brigfeld[13] and Kinkeswold.

YARDLEY evidently formed part of MANORS the original endowment of Pershore Abbey. By King Edgar's charter (972) 5 hides at Yardley were restored to the monks.[14] In 1086 Yardley was a member of the manor of Beoley, and still belonged to the monks of Pershore.[15] The connexion of Yardley with Beoley existed until the beginning of the 14th century,[16] and the tradition of the abbot's overlordship lasted still later, for in 1407 the manor was said to be held of the Abbot of Pershore by service unknown.[17] Subsequently, however, the manor was held of the king in chief by knight service.[18]

Early in the 13th century Beoley (and probably Yardley) was held by Robert son of Nicholas of William de Beauchamp, who was holding it of the Abbot of Pershore.[19] Robert son of Nicholas was perhaps the Robert son of Ralph son of Nicholas who with Felicia his wife obtained a grant of free warren in Beoley and Yardley in 1244.[20] Felicia, in whose right they held both manors, was daughter of Ralph de Limesi,[21] son of Geoffrey son of Geoffrey son of Hawise, who was living and probably held the manors in the time of Henry II.[22] Geoffrey de Limesi had certainly held the manor of Beoley, for by an undated charter Amabel de Limesi ratified the grants of her ancestors Geoffrey and John de Limesi by which they gave land in Beoley to Alexander son of Thany.[22a] Felicia died without issue, and was succeeded by her uncle Alan.[23] Ralph son of Alan, having no children,[24] sold Beoley and Yardley after 1267–8 to William Beauchamp Earl of Warwick,[25] to whom William son of Margery, wife of Walter

Comyn, sister of Ralph,[26] also released all the rights which he had in the manors.[27] The manor was granted for life by the above-mentioned William Earl of Warwick to Richard de Amundevill in 1296. On the death of Guy Earl of Warwick in 1315 it passed to his younger son John for life, with remainder to his eldest son Thomas. This John Beauchamp was at the naval victory off Sluys in 1340, and carried the Standard Royal at the battle of Cressy in 1346. He, with his brother Thomas Earl of Warwick, was one of the twenty-five original Knights of the Garter. In 1342 he obtained a grant of free warren in this manor. He died unmarried in 1360, when Yardley must have reverted to his brother Thomas Earl of Warwick.[27a] The Earls of Warwick continued to hold Yardley until 1487–8,[28] when, with their other possessions, it was given by Anne Countess of Warwick to Henry VII.[29]

In 1533 it was granted to Katherine of Aragon,[30] and was sold in 1553 to John Duke of Northumberland.[31] He was attainted and executed in the same year, but Yardley was evidently restored to his widow Joan, who exchanged it in 1553–4 with the queen for the manor of Claverdon, co. Warwick.[32] The queen then granted it to Edward Sutton Lord Dudley,[33] who died seised of it in 1586, leaving a son Edward.[34] In 1613 a writ was issued for inquiry as to who held the manor, which was supposed to be an escheat on account of defective title.[35] Lord Dudley's claim was established in 1616,[36] but he seems to have previously sold the manor to Sir Roland Lacy,[37] who in 1619 settled it on his eldest son Sir John on his marriage with Mary eldest sister of Sir William Withipoll.[38] In 1629, shortly after Sir Roland's death,[39] John Lacy sold the manor to Thomas[40] second son of Sir Richard Grevis of Moseley,[41] who in 1652 settled it on his brother Richard and Anne, afterwards his wife,[42] daughter of

---

[6] Anct. D. (P.R.O.), C 3028.

[7] Ibid. C 1346, 1355.

[8] Ibid. C 1522.   [9] Ibid. C 2761.

[10] Feet of F. Div. Co. Hil. 11 Edw. IV, no. 81.

[11] Mins. Accts. bdle. 645, no. 10461.

[12] Ct. R. (Gen. Ser.), portf. 210, no. 104.

[13] Star Chamb. Proc. Hen. VIII, bdle. 17, no. 50.

[14] Dugdale, *Mon.* ii, 416 ; Birch, *Cart. Sax.* iii, 585 ; Cott. MS. Aug. ii, 6. This document, written in a hand about a century later than its nominal date, no doubt gives with accuracy the possessions claimed by Pershore towards the middle of the 11th century. It is not evidence for the 10th. Evidently, however, the boundaries were based on local knowledge ; they include, for example, a reference to a River Colle (on Colle) which is no doubt the stream from which Coleshill in Warwickshire derives its name. (Note by Mr. F. M. Stenton.)

[15] *V.C.H. Worcs.* i, 305.

[16] Add. MS. 28024, fol. 114*a* ; Chan. Inq. p.m. 9 Edw. II, no. 71, m. 82.

[17] Chan. Inq. p.m. 8 Hen. IV, no. 68.

[18] Ibid. 17 Hen. VI, no. 54 ; 24 Hen. VI, no. 43.

[19] *Testa de Nevill* (Rec. Com.), 40. In a charter of about this date William de Beauchamp granted that the abbot and convent should levy and collect scutage and other services of him in Beoley and Yardley (Add. MS. 28024, fol. 150*b*).

[20] *Cal. Chart. R.* 1226–57, p. 277 ; Add. MS. 28024, fol. 112 *b*.

[21] The custody of the daughter of Ralph de Limesi had been granted to Ralph son of Nicholas in 1228 (*Excerpta e Rot. Fin.* [Rec. Com.], i, 177).

[22] Wrottesley, *Ped. from the Plea R.* 530. Geoffrey de Limesi was perhaps a younger son of the Domesday tenant Ralph de Limesi and his wife Hawise, who were benefactors of Hertford Monastery. The elder branch of the family appears to have held some rights of overlordship in Yardley, for John de Limesi presented to the church of Yardley as 'capital lord of the fee' during the minority of Ralph de Limesi (Maitland, *Bracton's Note Bk.* no. 1387). John de Limesi was great-grandson of the Ralph de Limesi of Domesday (Dugdale, *Mon.* iii, 300).

[22a] Add. MS. 28024, fol. 118 d.

[23] Wrottesley, op. cit. 530, 538.

[24] Ibid. 538.

[25] Add. MS. 28024, fol. 114*a*.

[26] *Cal. of Doc. Rel. to Scotland*, i, 910.

[27] Add. MS. 28024, fol. 111*b*, 112*a*.

[27a] Ibid. fol. 115*b*, 85*a* ; G.E.C. Complete Peerage, i, 276 ; *Cal. Inq. p.m.* 1–9 *Edw. II*, 410 ; Chart. R. 16 Edw. III, m. 3, no. 13.

[28] See Elmley Castle; *Abbrev. Plac.* (Rec. Com.), 197, 331*b* ; Chart. R. 26 Edw. III, m. 10, no. 23 ; Feet of F. Div. Co. Mich. 35 Edw. III ; Chan. Inq. p.m. 43 Edw. III, pt. i, no. 79 ; Close, 20 Ric. II, pt. ii,

m. 9 d. ; Chan. Inq. p.m. 2 Hen. IV, no. 58; 8 Hen. IV, no. 68 ; 17 Hen. VI, no. 54 ; 24 Hen. VI, no. 43 ; Close, 1 Hen. IV, pt. i, m. 18 ; Feet of F. Div. Co. Mich. 6 Edw. IV; Chan. Inq. p.m. 18 Edw. IV, no. 47 ; Mins. Accts. bdle. 645, no. 10461 ; *Cal. Pat.* 1446–52, p. 38 ; 1476–85, p. 96 ; Pat. 1 Ric. III, pt. iii, m. 22. In 1397, after the forfeiture of Thomas Earl of Warwick, Yardley Manor was granted to Thomas Earl Marshal and Earl of Nottingham (*Cal. Pat.* 1396–9, p. 220). He was created Duke of Norfolk in the same year, but was banished in 1398 (G.E.C. *Complete Peerage*, vi, 104), when Yardley was granted to Thomas Duke of Surrey (*Cal. Pat.* 1396–9, p. 429).

[29] Close, 3 Hen. VII, no. 11 ; Anct. D. (P.R.O.), A 11056.

[30] Palmer's Indices (P.R.O.), cxxxii, fol. 187.

[31] Pat. 7 Edw. VI, pt. viii, m. 25.

[32] Ibid. 1 Mary, pt. v, m. 1.

[33] Ibid. 1 & 2 Phil. and Mary, pt. ii ; 2 & 3 Phil. and Mary, pt. ii, m. 29.

[34] Chan. Inq. p.m. (Ser. 2), cxxxiv, 74.

[35] Exch. Spec. Com. Jas. I, no. 4774.

[36] Ibid. 4777.

[37] Feet of F. Worcs. East. 35 Eliz. ; Hil. 10 Jas. I.

[38] Chan. Inq. p.m. (Ser. 2), ccclix, 29.

[39] Ibid.

[40] Feet of F. Worcs. Mich. 5 Chas. I.

[41] *Gen.* vi, 304.

[42] Feet of F. Worcs. Mich. 1652.

Thomas Henshaw.[43] It then passed to Richard Grevis, son of Richard and Anne,[44] who died without issue in 1688,[45] being succeeded by his only surviving brother Benjamin Grevis.[46]

Charles Grevis, grandson of Benjamin, succeeded to the manor in 1759,[47] and sold it about 1768 to John Taylor, a manufacturer of Birmingham,[48] to whose great-grandson, Arthur James Taylor of Strensham Court,[49] it still belongs.

A fee-farm rent of £12 5s. 8d. was reserved when Yardley Manor was granted to Edward Lord Dudley, and was sold during the Commonwealth to Henry Sanders of Caldwell, co. Derby.[50]

GREET (Gritt, xvi cent.). About 1254 William de Edricheston granted land which he had newly acquired in Yardley and Greet to the Prior and convent of Studley.[51] He evidently held this land of Yardley Manor, for Robert son of Nicholas and Felicia his wife confirmed the grant in 1254.[52] Greet still belonged to Studley Priory at the time of the Dissolution,[53] and was sold in 1545 to Clement Throckmorton and Sir Alexander Avenon, ironmonger, afterwards Lord Mayor of London.[54] The latter in 1570 settled it on his son Alexander and Marjorie his wife.[55] Sir Alexander died in 1580,[56] and in 1586 his son pledged his so-called manor to cover a debt which he owed to a certain Thomas Starkey,[57] and in the same year sold the reversion to James Banks,[58] who sold it in 1601 to Henry Greswolde.[59] The latter died about a year later,[60] and by his will proved in May 1602 left Greet to his eldest son George, then thirteen years old.[61] Dorothy, widow of Henry, continued to live at Greet, having purchased from Joan, widow of Thomas Starkey, her interest in the manor.[62] George Greswolde died in 1612, and was succeeded by his brother Humphrey.[63] He died in 1660, and was succeeded in turn by his two sons Humphrey, who died without issue in 1671, and Henry, who died in 1700, leaving four sons, Humphrey who died unmarried in 1712, Henry who left a daughter Anne, Marshal and John.[64]

After this date the descent is not clear; in 1776 Henry Greswolde Lewis, grandson of the above Marshal, held a third.[65] The other two thirds were held in 1784[66] by William Richard Wilson and Jane Anne Eleanor his wife, who appear to have given up their share to Henry Greswolde Lewis. He was succeeded in 1829 by his kinsman Edmund Meysey Wigley,[67] who assumed the name Greswolde and died unmarried in 1833. On his death Henry Wigley, who also assumed the name Greswolde, became tenant for life under the will of Henry Greswolde Lewis, and he and his son Edmund

Greswolde, who was tenant in tail, barred the estate in tail and conveyed the estates to the use of Henry Greswolde for life, with remainder to Edmund Greswolde in fee simple. Edmund died in 1836, and on his decease his father succeeded to the estates in fee simple under the will of Edmund. In 1838 Henry settled a third of the estates on the marriage of his daughter Ann with Francis Edward Williams. Henry Greswolde died in 1849, and by his will he devised the remaining two thirds of the estates to his two daughters Mary and Elizabeth Greswolde in fee simple, and they succeeded thereto on his death. On the death of Elizabeth Greswolde in 1850 Francis Edward Williams succeeded to her third of the estate, and on his death in 1885 his son John Francis Greswolde Williams succeeded to two thirds. On the death of Mary Greswolde in 1859 Wigley Greswolde-Williams, eldest son of Francis Edward Williams, succeeded to her third, and on his death in 1875 his brother John Francis succeeded. He

GRESWOLDE of Yardley. *Argent a fesse gules between two running greyhounds sable.*

WILLIAMS. *Gyronny ermine and erminees a lion or sprinkled with drops of blood.*

died in 1892 without issue, and by his will devised the estate to his nephew Francis Wigley Greswolde Greswolde-Williams, now of Bredenbury Court (Herefs.).[68]

Besides the manors of Yardley and Greet there are in the parish the several smaller estates of Broom Hall, Greethurst, Lea Hall, Hay Place, now Hay Hall, and Stechford, the last four of which were called manors in the 15th and 16th centuries.

BROOM HALL (formerly Bromehale)[68a] was held in the 15th century by a family of the same name. About 1420 John Bromehale died seised of it, having held it of Richard Earl of Warwick, and leaving it to his three daughters—Juliana wife of William Northfolk, Elizabeth wife of John Shyngeler, and Isabel wife of Thomas Smith—and to his grandson John Coliton or Collecton *alias* Bromehale, son of Joan, another daughter.[69] John Coliton was out-

[43] *Gen.* vi, 304.
[44] Ibid.; Feet of F. Worcs. Trin. 30 Chas. II; 35 Chas. II. The latter is probably a settlement on his marriage with Eleanor daughter of Sir John Winford.
[45] *Gen.* vi, 306.
[46] Ibid.; Recov. R. Trin. 1 Will. and Mary, rot. 34.
[47] *Gen.* vi, 306.
[48] Nash, *Hist. of Worcs.* ii, 477.
[49] Burke, *Landed Gentry* (1906).
[50] Close, 1651, pt. viii, no. 7.
[51] Chart. R. 1 Edw. III, m. 2, no. 3; Feet of F. Worcs. case 258, file 7, no. 35.
[52] Feet of F. Worcs. case 258, file 7, no. 35.

[53] Dugdale, *Mon.* vi, 187; *Valor Eccl.* (Rec. Com.), iii, 87.
[54] *L. and P. Hen. VIII,* xx (1), g. 1335 (34).
[55] Pat. 13 Eliz. pt. ii, m. 26.
[56] Chan. Inq. p.m. (Ser. 2), cxc, 40.
[57] Ibid. cccli, 112.
[58] Ibid.; Feet of F. Div. Co. Mich. 28 & 29 Eliz.
[59] Feet of F. Worcs. Hil. 43 Eliz.
[60] P.C.C. 35 Montague; Chan. Inq. p.m. (Ser. 2), cccli, 112.
[61] Chan. Inq. p.m. (Ser. 2), cccli, 112.
[62] Ibid.
[63] Ibid.; Fine R. 14 Jas. I, pt. ii, no. 12; see also Feet of F. Worcs. Trin. 1650.

[64] Burke, *Landed Gentry,* 1906, under Greswolde-Williams; an inscription on a monument in Yardley Church quoted by Nash, op. cit. ii, 476, and by Prattinton (Soc. Antiq.).
[65] Recov. R. Trin. 16 Geo. III, rot. 151.
[66] Feet of F. Div. Co. East. 24 Geo. III.
[67] Burke, *Landed Gentry* (1906), under Greswolde-Williams.
[68] Information from Mr. A. Lord.
[68a] This is the 'bromhalas' mentioned in the boundaries of Yardley (Birch, *Cart. Sax.* iii, 589).
[69] Chan. Inq. p.m. 8 Hen. V, no. 100. The inquisition shows how the land was divided among the four co-heirs.

YARDLEY : BLAKESLEY HALL

YARDLEY : THE OLD SCHOOLHOUSE

lawed about 1422–3.[70]   The place is mentioned again in 1633–4, when Robert Yate died seised of it, leaving a son Robert.[71]   He held it of Ann Grevis as of the manor of Yardley.[72]

GREETHURST belonged from the 14th to the 16th century to the family of Holte, and was held of the manor of Yardley.[73]   Walter Holte died in 1379, leaving it to his wife Margaret for life with remainder in tail-male to his sons John and Simon.   John left a son Adelmare Holte, who died without issue and was succeeded by his uncle Simon Holte, from whom the estate passed to his son John and grandson and great-grandson, both called William.[74]   The latter about 1517 sued Richard Greswolde for taking possession of his 'dwelling house' called Greethurst and a mill called Holte's Mill.[75]   The plaintiff evidently recovered possession, for he died in 1517 seised of the capital messuage in Yardley called Holte's Place *alias* Greethurst.[76]   He left a son Thomas,[77] but there is no further mention of the place until 1664, when it was in the hands of Richard Grevis, lord of Yardley.[78]   It is mentioned again in 1678, when it belonged to Richard Grevis,[79] but after that date it seems to have become part of Yardley Manor, and the name has disappeared.

LEA HALL belonged to the Earls of Stafford in the 15th century,[80] while Hay Hall and Stechford (formerly Stitchford) were for a long time the property of the families of de la Hay and Este.[81]   In 1811 Hay Hall belonged to a Dr. Gilby.[82]

A messuage and mill in Stechford which belonged to Giles de Erdington are mentioned as early as 1249–50,[83] and in 1409–10 a messuage and land there belonged to John Smith, who settled them on his son, also called John.[84]

In 1385 Thomas de Beauchamp Earl of Warwick conveyed to Roger Bradewell at a rent of 6s. 8d. the site of a mill in Yardley called Wodemill, on which Roger was to build a mill, the timber being supplied by the earl.[85]   This is evidently the mill called 'Oldemylle' in 1479–80, when it still paid a rent of 6s. 8d. to the lord of Yardley.[86]   In 1593 two watermills were annexed to the manor, and in 1689 Benjamin Grevis, lord of the manor, had two watermills and one windmill in Yardley and Moseley.[87]   Another water-mill belonged to Edward Este in 1687.[88]   There are many mills at Yardley on the River Cole.   Titterford Mill, a corn-mill, is to the north of Yardley Wood, Sarehole Mill, another corn-mill, at Hall Green, Hay Mills (wire) and Washmill (corn) are in Hay Mills, and there is an old mill-pond to the north of Broom Hall.

Free fishing in Yardley was purchased from Robert Abney and Anne his wife by John Taylor in 1783.[89]

CHURCHES   The church of *ST. EDBURGH* consists of a chancel 38½ ft. by 17½ ft., with a north vestry and organ chamber, a nave 57½ ft. by 24½ ft., a north aisle 17 ft. wide, a

south transept 17 ft. by 16½ ft. and a west tower 14 ft. square.   These measurements are all internal.

The 13th-century remains include the south doorway, the south wall of the chancel, which contains a lancet window, and a similar window in the north wall of the vestry, formerly in the chancel.   They point to a simple church of that date, consisting probably of chancel and nave only.   In the 14th century north and south transepts seem to have been added and the chancel lengthened eastwards, and in the 15th century the west tower was built and the north aisle added.   In recent years the south transept and the east end of the chancel were rebuilt and the vestry added.

The east window of the chancel is of three lights, and at each angle of the east wall is a modern buttress.   In the north wall are a modern arch into the organ

YARDLEY CHURCH AND OLD SCHOOLHOUSE

chamber and a modern vestry door, while further east are the remains of a window with a semicircular head.   On the south side of the chancel the 13th-century rubble walling remains, while to the east is the coursed rubble of the 14th century.   In the earlier portion of the wall is a lancet opening, on each side of which is a 14th-century window of two lights with a quatrefoil in the head, and further east a modern window of two pointed lights.   The lofty chancel arch is of the late 14th century.

The western portion of the north arcade of the nave is of the 15th century; the east bay, which is

[70] Chan. Inq. p.m. 1 Hen. VI, no. 61.
[71] Ibid. (Ser. 2), ccccxcv, 53.   [72] Ibid.
[73] Exch. Inq. p.m. (Ser. 2), file 1178, no. 11.
[74] Court of Req. bdle. 3, no. 137.
[75] Ibid.
[76] Exch. Inq. p.m. (Ser. 2), file 1178, no. 11.   [77] Ibid.
[78] Recov. R. D. Enr. East. 16 Chas. II, m. 14 ; Recov. R. East. 16 Chas. II, rot. 197.

[79] Feet of F. Worcs. Trin. 30 Chas. II.
[80] Ibid. Div. Co. East. 12 Hen. VI.
[81] Ibid. Worcs. Trin. 15 Jas. I; Hil. 22 Jas. I; Prattinton Coll. (Soc. Antiq.), gives a pedigree of these two families.
[82] Prattinton Coll. (Soc. Antiq.).
[83] Feet of F. Div. Co. 34 Hen. III, no. 40.
[84] Anct. D. (P.R.O.), C 1510, 3020.
[85] Add. MS. 28024, fol. 111b.
[86] Mins. Accts. bdle. 645, no. 10461.

This mill appears to have been disused in 1485 (Mins. Accts. Hen. VII, no. 989).
[87] Feet of F. Worcs. East. 35 Eliz. ; Recov. R. Trin. 1 Will. and Mary, rot. 34.
[88] Recov. R. Mich. 3 Jas. II, rot. 75.
[89] Feet of F. Worcs. East. 23 Geo. III. The same right had been conveyed by Richard Eaves and John Baskerville and Sarah his wife to Joseph Tomkins in 1767 (ibid. Trin. 7 Geo. III).

the original transept arch, is of the 14th century. In the south wall of the nave are two 15th-century windows, each of two lights with quatrefoiled tracery over, and between them is a simple 13th-century pointed doorway, which has been rebuilt. It leads into a fine 15th-century oak porch with tracery at the sides and a carved barge-board. Further east is a chamfered arch opening into the south transept.

The north wall of the aisle is divided by buttresses into four bays; the walling in the eastern bay has wider joints than the others and contains a debased window of three lights. The other windows are similar to those in the south of the nave, and between them is a square-headed doorway with enriched spandrels. The west window of the aisle is of three lights, with rectilinear tracery, under a four-centred head.

The tower is of four stages, with a deep plinth and embattled parapet, surmounted by a tall crocketed hexagonal spire. The buttresses are diagonal, and the doorway has a four-centred head with a crocketed hood. Above it is a large pointed window of four lights with rectilinear tracery. The upper stages are lighted on all sides by transomed windows of two lights under four-centred heads with crocketed labels, and the staircase, which is at the south-west angle, has small trefoiled lights with canopied heads.

An inscription carved on the south wall-plate of the chancel roof states that it was 'ceiled at the cost and charge of Humphrey Griswould, gent., Will. Acock, sen., gent. and Will (Bissell ?), 1637.' On the opposite side it is stated that in 1797 'this chancel and vault was repaired by Henry Greswolde Lewis Esq. of Malvern Hall in the county of Warwick.' The font and pulpit are modern.

In the sanctuary are three floor slabs—one to Marshal Greswolde, 1728, another to Humphrey Greswolde, 1744, with his shield, and a third with the same arms but no inscription. A large monument in the south of the chancel commemorates Henry Greswolde, rector of Solihull, Warwick, and precentor of Lichfield, who died in 1700, with kneeling effigies of himself and his wife. Over this is another to Humphrey Greswolde, lay rector of Yardley, who died in 1671. To the north of the east window is a tablet erected by John Dodd in 1690 to various members of his family, with the arms of Cloverley quartering Dodd and Warren.

At the west end of the nave is the top slab of a 15th-century alabaster monument, now placed on end, bearing incised figures of a man and woman, apparently a member of the Este family and his wife. A brass inscription in the south transept commemorates Edward Este, utter barrister of the Inner Temple, 1625, and near it is a small 17th-century tablet to another Edward Este.

On the north wall of the chancel is a brass inscription commemorating Isabel Wheeler of Yardley, widow, 1598, and over it her effigy on brass between those of her two husbands, William Astell and Simon Wheeler.

In the tower are some masons' marks.

There is a peal of six bells : treble, 'The Bequest

of Aylmer Folliott Esquire, 1638'; (2) 'H.I.S. Nazarenus (sic), Rex Judaeorum, Fili Dei, Miserere Mei, 1638'; (3) 'Humphrey Hobday, and Richard Bissell, Churchwardens 1638'; (4) 'All praise and glori bee to God for ever, 1653, J.A.'; (5) 'William Bagly made mee, Richard Whitus, George Bissell Churchwardens 1691'; tenor, 'The gift of the parishioners in commemoration of the Coronation of King Edward the Seventh.'

The plate consists of two large silver flagons, each with the mark of 1650, and inscribed with a carefully composed Latin inscription to the effect that they were presented to the church of Yardley by Job Marston of Hall Green, a cup of 1728, inscribed 'Yardley Church,' a paten of 1727, similarly inscribed, a plated cup, and a modern glass flagon.

The registers previous to 1812 are as follows : (i) all entries 1539 to 1632 ; (ii) all 1633 to 1732 ; (iii) baptisms and burials 1733 to 1781, marriages 1733 to 1753 ; (iv) baptisms and burials 1782 to 1812 ; (v) marriages 1754 to 1785 ; (vi) marriages 1785 to 1812.

MARSTON CHAPEL, Hall Green, built in 1703 with money left for the purpose by Job Marston of Hall Green,[90] consists of a chancel, south organ chamber, and north and south transepts, added in the sixties of the last century, and an original nave and west tower. The materials are red brick with stone dressings. The chancel and transepts are designed in a style to harmonize with the original building, which is a pleasant example of the Queen-Anne style. The nave is lighted by three semicircular-headed windows in each side wall, with moulded stone architraves, imposts and archivolts. The wall is crowned by a stone entablature and balustrade, supported by plain Doric pilasters of the same material elevated upon pedestals. Over each pilaster the entablature is broken forward, and there are stone quoins at the angles of the walls. The interior is perfectly plain, and there is a gallery at the west end. The west tower rises square to the level of the main entablature, which is continued round it, above which it is surmounted by an octagonal turret of brick, containing one bell, crowned by a cupola. The roofs are slated.

No mention occurs of the church *ADVOWSON* of Yardley until the 13th century, when there were numerous disputes about the advowson. In 1220 Giles de Erdington[91] claimed it against the Abbot of Alcester, the Prior of Newport and Ralph de Limesi.[92] It probably at first belonged with the manor to the family of Limesi, and according to the Abbot of Alcester was a chapel annexed to the church of Beoley, which had been granted to his monastery by Geoffrey de Limesi, grandfather of Ralph, whose grant was confirmed by John Bishop of Worcester (1151–7) and by Hubert Walter, Archbishop of Canterbury (ob. 1205). However, as the Prior of Newport did not appear, and as Ralph and the abbot allowed that Thomas de Erdington, father of Giles, had made the last two presentations, the case was decided in favour of Giles, who at the same time gave the advowson to the Prior of Newport.[93] In 1263 Giles again claimed the advowson against the Priors of Newport

---

[90] Prattinton Coll. (Soc. Antiq.); P.C.C. 100 Hern.

[91] How the Erdingtons got possession of the church does not appear. It is possible that they claimed through Hawise, who was probably lady of the manor in the time of Henry II (see above under manor).

[92] Maitland, *Bracton's Note Bk.* iii, 347–9; Cur. Reg. R. 75, m. 5.

[93] Maitland, op. cit. iii, 349.

and Studley, and against Ralph de Limesi and William Comyn, and the case was again decided in his favour.[94]

In 1274 Ralph de Limesi sued Henry de Erdington son of Giles for the advowson of Yardley,[95] but in the same year a fine was levied by which Ralph gave up his claim.[96] Just before this, Henry had given the advowson to the Abbot and convent of Halesowen, but they had afterwards restored it to him with the charter,[97] and he gave it in 1279 to the nuns of Catesby.[98]

Before the nuns were allowed to enjoy the advowson their right was disputed in 1279 by the Abbot of Halesowen,[99] and in 1303 by the Prior of Newport [100] and by Henry de Erdington son of the last-named Henry.[1] Judgement was given in favour of the nuns in each case, but by 1346 the advowson had passed, probably by purchase, from them to Thomas Beauchamp Earl of Warwick, who in that year gave it to the newly-founded priory of Maxstoke,[2] Giles de Erdington giving up all his claim in the same year.[3] This led to another dispute, the claimant being the Prior of Tickford, who said that his priory had held the church of Yardley in the time of Henry III, but the jurors found for the Prior of Maxstoke,[4] to whom the advowson belonged until the Dissolution. The church was appropriated to the prior and convent in 1346,[5] and confirmed to them by the pope at the request of William de Clinton Earl of Hereford in 1349.[6]

In 1538 the site of Maxstoke Priory with all its possessions was granted to Charles Brandon Duke of Suffolk,[7] who two years later sold the site with the rectory of Yardley to Robert Trappes, a goldsmith of London.[8] The Duke of Suffolk died in 1545, and the dukedom became extinct on the death of his last surviving son in 1551,[9] when the advowson appears to have reverted to the Crown, for it was granted in 1554–5 with the manor to Sir Edmund Dudley.[10] It is included in conveyances of the manor until 1678,[11] but the presentations do not seem to have been made by the lords of the manor. Queen Mary granted the advowson in 1558 to Richard Bishop of Worcester,[12] and in 1596 William Swindles of Yardley, husbandman (agricola), presented.[13] William Parker Lord Monteagle was patron in 1612,[14] and his son Henry held the advowson in the middle of the 17th century.[15] Robert Dodd presented in 1675 and Thomas Habington in 1687.[16] Though presenta-

tions were made by the king in 1726, 1729 and 1766,[17] the advowson probably passed, through the marriage of Mary daughter of Thomas Habington with William Compton, to the Compton family,[18] for Sir Walter Habington Compton, bart., great-great-grandson of Mary Habington, was dealing with it in 1770,[19] and on his death without issue in 1773 it passed to his sister Jane, wife of John Berkeley.[20] She and her husband conveyed it to Rowland Berkeley in 1775,[21] evidently in trust for her daughter Catherine Berkeley, who was dealing with the advowson in 1798–9,[22] and apparently sold it to Edmund Wigley, who presented in 1805 and 1807.[23] He probably left it to his son Edmund Meysey-Wigley, but the latter died childless in 1833, leaving three sisters and co-heirs, Anne Maria, who married John Michael Severne, Caroline Meysey Wigley, and Mary Charlotte, who married Charles Wicksted.[24] Caroline died unmarried, and the youngest sister appears to have given up her right to Mrs. Severne, who was the only patron in 1868.[25] The advowson was purchased from the Severnes about 1871 by the Rev. J. Dodd, who left it to his sons Cyril Dodd, K.C., and the Rev. Frederick Sutton Dodd, the present vicar, to whom it now belongs.[26]

The rectory passed from Robert Trappes to his son Nicholas, after whose death, which took place before 1565, it was divided between his two daughters, Mary wife of Giles Paulet, son of the Marquess of Winchester, and Alice wife of Henry Browne of Maxstoke.[27] Alice seems to have married secondly William Byrde,[28] and with him settled half the rectory on themselves and their heirs, with contingent remainders to Thomas, Mary and Anne Umpton. Alice's share of the rectory passed eventually to Francis Browne,[29] probably her son, while the other half passed to William Paulet son of Giles.[30] In 1622 Francis sold his share to William Bissell and his son William,[31] who with Anne Walrond, widow, Humphrey Coles and John Griffith conveyed three-fourths of the rectory to Humphrey Greswolde in 1660.[32] William Rogerson, Nicholas Grimshaw and Henry Greswolde were dealing with the other quarter of the rectory in 1680,[33] and the whole belonged to Henry Greswolde in 1833, when the tithes were commuted for £525.[34]

During the last century new ecclesiastical parishes were formed from Yardley—St. Cyprian's Hay Mills

[94] Assize R. 1191, m. 15. William Comyn acknowledged that he had given up his right to the Prior of Studley.

[95] Wrottesley, Ped. from the Plea R. 529.

[96] Feet of F. Worcs. 3 Edw. I, no. 58.

[97] De Banco R. 31, m. 76.

[98] Ibid.; Dugdale, Mon. iv, 635.

[99] De Banco R. 29, m. 13; 31, m. 76; Feet of F. Worcs. 8 Edw. I, no. 18.

[100] De Banco R. 148, m. 39 d.

[1] Ibid. About 1279–1301 the prioress of Catesby petitioned for the restoration of the patronage of the church of Yardley 'unjustly' held by Ralph de Hengham the rector (Add. Chart. 20433). Ralph had been presented by Giles de Erdington (De Banco R. 29, m. 13).

[2] Cal. Pat. 1345–8, p. 135; Close, 20 Edw. III, pt. i, m. 4. The licence of the Abbot of Pershore as overlord of Yardley was obtained in 1346–7 (Habington, Surv. of Worcs. [Worcs. Hist. Soc.], i, 509).

[3] Cal. Close, 1346–9, p. 88.

[4] De Banco R. 349, m. 381; 354, m. 57; Cal. Close, 1346–9, p. 488.

[5] Worc. Epis. Reg. Wulstan de Bransford, i (3), fol. 105a.

[6] Cal. Papal Pet. i, 192; Cal. Papal Letters, iii, 333.

[7] L. and P. Hen. VIII, xiii (2), 1182 (18 m.n.w.).

[8] Ibid. xv, 895; Harl. Chart. 47 A. 53.

[9] G.E.C. Complete Peerage, vii, 310.

[10] Pat. 1 & 2 Phil. and Mary, pt. ii.

[11] Feet of F. Worcs. East. 35 Eliz.; Mich. 5 Chas. I; 20 Chas. II; Trin. 30 Chas. II.

[12] Pat. 5 & 6 Phil. and Mary, pt. ii, m. 30.

[13] Nash, op. cit. ii, 481.   [14] Ibid.

[15] Habington, op. cit. i, 511.

[16] Inst. Bks. (P.R.O.).

[17] Ibid. The University of Oxford presented in 1732.

[18] G.E.C. Complete Baronetage, iv, 141.

[19] Recov. R. Trin. 10 Geo. III, rot. 149.

[20] G.E.C. Complete Baronetage, iv, 141.

[21] Feet of F. Worcs. Trin. 15 Geo. III; Inst. Bks. (P.R.O.).

[22] Recov. R. Hil. 39 Geo. III, rot. 275.

[23] Inst. Bks. (P.R.O.).

[24] Burke, Commoners, ii, 676; Priv. Act, 3 & 4 Will. IV, cap. 17.

[25] Noake, op. cit. 358.

[26] Information supplied by the Rev. F. Sutton Dodd.

[27] Com. Pleas D. Enr. Mich. 7 & 8 Eliz. m. 15; Chan. Proc. (Ser. 2), bdle. 139, no. 26.

[28] Feet of F. Div. Co. Mich. 22 & 23 Eliz.; Pat. 22 Eliz. pt. i, m. 39.

[29] Notes of F. Div. Co. Mich. 12 Jas. I; Cal. S. P. Dom. 1619–23, p. 371.

[30] Exch. Dep. Trin. 12 Jas. I, no. 1.

[31] Feet of F. Worcs. East. 20 Jas. I.

[32] Ibid. Trin. 12 Chas. II.

[33] Ibid. Mich. 32 Chas. II.

[34] Priv. Act, 3 & 4 Will. IV, cap. 17. For pedigree of the Greswoldes see Burke, Landed Gentry, 1906, under Greswolde-Williams.

in 1878,[35] the advowson of which belongs to the Bishop of Birmingham. The church is built of red brick with stone dressings, and consists of chancel, nave, aisles, vestry, and tower with spire. Christ Church, Yardley Wood, was formed in 1849, and contains part of the ancient parish of King's Norton.[36] Christ Church was built and endowed by the late Mrs. Sarah Taylor, and is a building of stone consisting of chancel, nave, transepts and western bell-turret. The living is in the gift of Mr. A. J. Taylor, now lord of Yardley Manor. Part of Yardley became ecclesiastically annexed to Moseley in 1879,[37] and part to Acock's Green in 1867.[38] In 1894 the parish of St. John the Evangelist, Sparkhill, was constituted, the patronage being vested in five trustees.[39] The church is built of red brick with stone and terra cotta dressings, in 13th-century style, and consists of chancel, nave, transepts, vestry, organ chamber, and tower with spire.

There is in Yardley a Baptist Mission chapel served from Graham Street, Birmingham ; also a Congregational chapel.

CHARITIES The Yardley Charity Estates.— The inhabitants of this parish have from time immemorial received the benefit of certain lands and hereditaments granted to trustees for their use by various donors, the earliest deeds extant being temp. Henry VI. The trusts were definitely extended by deeds of lease and release 1 and 2 January 1766 to the support of the Yardley Free School and of the school at Hall Green. The latter school, however, was closed in or about 1899. The educational branch was regulated by certain schemes made under the Endowed Schools Acts and by a scheme confirmed by an Act of Parliament,[40] and is now governed by a scheme made by the Board of Education 12 August 1903.[41]

The non-educational branch is administered under an order of the Charity Commissioners 6 August 1901 as a separate charity under the title of the Yardley Charity Estates Almshouses.

The endowments consist of the new almshouses for six almswomen and a residence for a nurse, situate in Church Road, a yearly sum of £380 out of the general income of the charity estates, and a sum of £2,860 consols with the official trustees, producing £71 10s. yearly, representing the redemption of certain yearly sums of that amount specified in the scheme or schemes above referred to.

The scheme provides for the payment of £100 a year to the nurse, for a weekly payment of from 6s. to 10s. a week to each almswoman, also for medical attendance and appliances and funeral expenses of the almswomen ; also for the formation of a repair fund.

In 1671 Humphrey Greswolde, by his will, gave the yearly sum of £5 out of the rectory and great tithes of Yardley for providing four gowns for four poor aged men, one from each of the four quarters of the parish.

The charities of Job Marston were founded by will 24 May 1701, whereby a sum of £400 was directed to be laid out in lands, and the rents and profits to be applied as to one moiety for the vicar, subject to the distribution of £5 4s. yearly in bread to the poor attending church, and the other moiety in apprenticing or in the distribution of coats, &c., to poor attending church. The legacy was in 1728 laid out in the purchase of land, and the endowments now consist of a farm at Acock's Green, containing 40a. 2r. 34p. let at £95 a year, and 4,272 sq. yds. of building land, producing a yearly income of £23 7s. 8d., the legal estate in which was, by an order of the Charity Commissioners 24 July 1900, vested in the official trustee of charity lands. The net income is duly applied.

Marston's Chapel.—The same testator, by his will, devised land at Hall Green for the erection of a chapel thereon, and bequeathed £1,000 for that purpose, and further directed that £1,200 should be laid out in land, the rents and profits whereof should be applied for the repairs of the chapel and for the support of the minister. The intentions of the testator were carried into effect by an Act of 1702–3. The trust is regulated by a scheme of the Charity Commissioners 20 January 1903.

The trust estate now consists of the chapel, the parsonage-house at Hall Green, farm-house and land at Earlswood let at £80 a year and £4,265 14s. 7d. India 3½ per cent. stock with the official trustees, producing £149 6s. yearly, arising from the sale in 1903 of 6a. 2r. in Stoney Lane, Sparkbrook.

The trustees also receive £104 a year from the Governors of the grammar school, Handsworth, co. Staffs., being 4 per cent. interest on a sum of £2,600 advanced in 1906 on loan to that foundation, being part of the proceeds of sale in 1905 of 6a. in Showell Green Lane, Sparkbrook.

John Cottrell's Almshouses for two widows, founded by deed 1715, consist of two cottages used as alms-houses and a rent-charge of £5 issuing out of lands in Yardley, now the property of Colonel Jervoise.

In 1721 Joseph Fox by his will charged land at Showell Green with 20s. for the poor in bread and with 20s. for the master of Hall Green School, and, if there were no schoolmaster, then for coals for poor widows.

In 1727 John Bissell by his will gave an annuity of £2 for the master of Hall Green School and an annuity of £1 for a coat for a poor man in Swanhurst Quarter. By an order of the Charity Commissioners 27 June 1899 trustees of this charity were appointed and the rent-charges vested in the official trustee of charity lands.

A sum of £21 4s. 11d. consols, producing 10s. 4d. yearly, is also held by the official trustees in respect of Joseph Bissell's charity.

In 1829 Henry Greswolde Lewis, by his will proved in the P.C.C. 9 November, bequeathed £1,500, the income to be applied in the distribution of clothing and bread among six poor men and women of Yardley, and of the parishes of Radford Semele and Solihull in the county of Warwick. The share of this parish is represented by £571 3s. 9d. consols with the official trustees, producing £14 5s. 4d. yearly.

In 1837 Joseph Richards by his will left a legacy for the benefit of the poor of Bromwell End and

[35] Lond. Gaz. 1 Mar. 1878, p. 1578.
[36] Census of Engl. and Wales, 1901, Worc. 8.
[37] Lond. Gaz. 30 May 1879, p. 3677.
[38] Ibid. 1 Mar. 1867, p. 1442.
[39] Parl. Papers (1897), lxvii (6), no. 302, p. 14.
[40] Local and Personal Act, 2 Edw. VII, cap. 214.
[41] See 'Schools,' V.C.H. Worcs. iv.

Swanhurst End, which is represented by £83 6s. 8d. consols with the official trustees, producing £2 1s. 8d. yearly.

The Church of England Sunday School.—By an inclosure award made pursuant to an Act of Parliament,[42] a piece of land containing 37 p. or thereabouts was awarded to trustees, and on it a building was erected for the purposes of a Sunday school in connexion with the Church of England. By a scheme of the Charity Commissioners 16 August 1907 the trustees were authorized to use the same as a parish hall or to let the same to the local education authority, any rent received in respect thereof to be applied for the benefit of deserving poor.

The Church of England school is endowed with a

[42] Priv. Act, 3 & 4 Will. IV, cap. 17.

sum of £1,030 18s. 7d. consols by the will of John Francis Greswolde-Williams, dated 26 May 1891, proved at Worcester 12 August 1892. He also bequeathed a sum of £1,030 18s. 7d. consols for the benefit of the poor.

The sums of stock are held by the official trustees, producing £25 15s. 4d. yearly. The benefaction to the poor is distributed on 23 October in each year in the form of orders on shops for flannel, clothing, coats, dresses or food, or any other articles or things for domestic use or comfort, or money for paying rent.

Christchurch Yardley Wood. — In 1876 John Guest, by will proved at Birmingham 14 August, left for charitable purposes in this district a legacy which is represented by £355 4s. consols, producing £8 17s. 4d. yearly.

THE HUNDRED OF OSWALDSLOW

ALVECHURCH
BERROW
BISHAMPTON
BLOCKLEY
BREDICOT
BREDON with CUTSDEAN and NORTON-BY-BREDON
BROADWAS
CHURCHILL
CLAINES with WHISTONES
CLEEVE PRIOR
CROOME D'ABITÔT
EARL'S CROOME
HILL CROOME
CROPTHORNE with CHARLTON and NETHERTON
CROWLE
DAYLESFORD
ELMLEY CASTLE
EVENLODE
FLADBURY with HILL and MOOR, ABLENCH, STOCK and BRADLEY, THROCKMORTON, WYRE PIDDLE

GRIMLEY
HALLOW
HANBURY
HARTLEBURY
HARVINGTON
HIMBLETON with SHELL
HINDLIP
HOLT with LITTLE WITLEY
HUDDINGTON
ICCOMB [2]
INKBERROW
KEMPSEY
KNIGHTWICK with KENSWICK
LINDRIDGE with KNIGHTON ON TEME, NEWNHAM and PENSAX
LITTLE MALVERN
NORTON JUXTA KEMPSEY
ODDINGLEY
OMBERSLEY
OVERBURY with ALSTONE, CONDERTON, TEDDINGTON and LITTLE WASHBOURNE

PENDOCK
REDMARLEY D'ABITÔT
RIPPLE with HOLDFAST [3]
ROUS LENCH
ST. JOHN in BEDWARDINE
ST. MARTIN
ST. PETER with WHITTINGTON
SEDGEBERROW
SHIPSTON ON STOUR
SPETCHLEY
STOKE PRIOR
STOULTON
TIBBERTON
TIDMINGTON
TREDINGTON with ARMSCOTE, BLACKWELL, DARLINGSCOTT and NEWBOLD ON STOUR
WARNDON
WELLAND
WHITE LADIES ASTON
WICHENFORD
WOLVERLEY

Under a charter purporting to have been given by King Edgar in 964 [4] manors to the extent of 300 hides belonging to the church of Worcester were rearranged to form a triple hundred, to be known, according to the charter, as Oswaldslow, in memory of Bishop Oswald, in whose episcopate the arrangement took place. Three hundred courts were then assigned to the Bishop of Worcester and his monks, and from words in the charter it seems possible that this arrangement was made so that the church might have a full *scip socne* or district liable for supplying the king with one ship. [5] The names of the three hundreds thus united are said to have been Cuthbergehlawe, Wulfereslaw [6] and Winburntree (Winburgetrowe). The first of these would seem to have belonged to the monks as distinct from the bishop, their 50 hides at Cropthorne having formed half this hundred, which was completed by the addition of certain other of their manors [7] and confirmed to them by King Edgar. Winburntree evidently included the manors of Blockley and Tredington, the

---

[1] This list represents the extent of the hundred in 1831.

[2] Iccomb is now in Slaughter Hundred, co. Glouc.

[3] Queenhill with Holdfast, now a separate ecclesiastical parish, is and has been since the beginning of the 13th century in the hundred of Pershore (*Testa de Nevill* [Rec. Com.], 43).

[4] Heming, *Chartul.* (ed. Hearne), 517; Birch, *Cart. Sax.* iii, 379. For a discussion of the authenticity of this charter see *V.C.H. Worcs.* i, 246-7.   [5] See *V.C.H. Worcs.* i, 248.

[6] This hundred according to the charter the bishop had possessed freely from of old.

[7] The manors added amounted to 70 hides (*V.C.H. Worcs.* i, 247).

suitors at that hundred being the bishop's tenants of those manors, including
Evenlode, Daylesford, Dorn, Iccomb, Blackwell and Shipston on Stour,[8]
though these latter places, according to Edgar's charter, were among those
added to complete the half hundred belonging to the monks.[9]

Whatever may have been the origin of the hundred, in 1086, by the
testimony of the whole county, the church of Worcester held a hundred
called Oswaldslow, containing 300 hides, which the bishop held by ancient
custom.[10]   This hundred included all the estates of the bishop and prior in

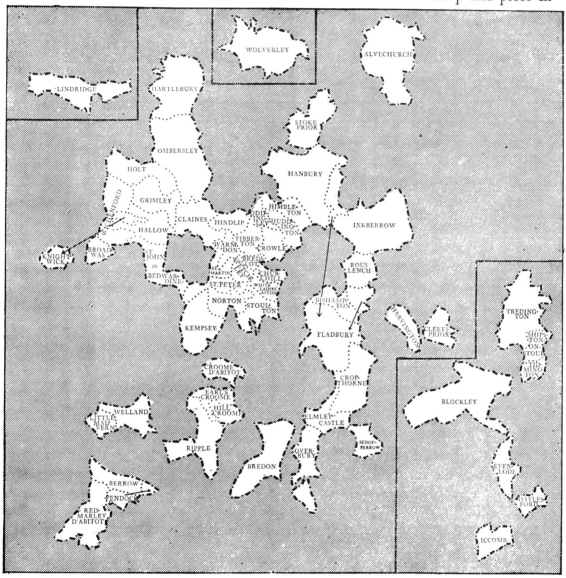

INDEX MAP TO THE HUNDRED OF OSWALDSLOW

Worcestershire except the following nine manors, viz. Crowle,[11] Cleeve Prior,
Phepson and Hanbury in Esch Hundred, Stoke Prior and Alvechurch in

---

[8] Eccl. Com. Ct. R. (P.R.O.), bdle. 189, no. 5 ; Chan. Inq. p m. 50 Edw. III (1st nos.), no. 21 ;
Hale, Reg. of Worc. Priory (Camd. Soc.), 64b, 68a, 104a.

[9] It is to be noted that these six estates contained together 20 hides, the amount by which the manors
said to have been added to complete the hundred of Cuthbergehlawe exceeded 50 hides.

[10] V.C.H. Worcs. i, 287 ; Heming, op. cit. 287, 288.

[11] Crowle is still partly in Halfshire Hundred, but the greater part of it had been transferred to
Oswaldslow before 1280 (Feud. Aids, v, 308 ; Lay Subs. R. Worcs. c. 1280 [Worcs. Hist. Soc.], 22, 39).

Came Hundred, part of Lindridge in Doddingtree, and Hartlebury and Wolverley in Cresselaw Hundred. These manors were still outside the hundred of Oswaldslow in the beginning of the 12th century, and were then included under the name 'Kinefolka.'[12] Alvechurch, Hanbury and Hartlebury were transferred to Oswaldslow before 1280,[13] except a part of Hartlebury which is still in Halfshire Hundred; Lindridge, Cleeve Prior, Stoke Prior and Wolverley were in 1207 constituted separate liberties with freedom from suit at shire and hundred courts,[14] and Phepson became part of the liberty of Stoke.[15]

Of the parishes added to Oswaldslow since 1086 Ombersley remained in Blackenhurst (Fishborough) Hundred until 1760, when for fiscal purposes it was transferred to Oswaldslow.[16] Part of Inkberrow in 1086 in Esch Hundred was transferred to Oswaldslow before 1280.[17] Cotheridge, now in Doddingtree Hundred, Bushley and Upton-on-Severn, now in Pershore, together with Hampton and Bengeworth, now in Blackenhurst, were in 1086 in Oswaldslow; Bushley was transferred before 1280,[18] Cotheridge before 1327,[19] and Upton-on-Severn for fiscal purposes in 1760.[20] Hampton and Bengeworth are said to have been in Oswaldslow Hundred before 1086,[21] and were in that hundred at the beginning of the 12th century.[22] William Beauchamp of Elmley was said to have withdrawn his part of Bengeworth from the bishop's hundred about the middle of the 13th century,[23] and in 1280 both Hampton and Bengeworth were in Blackenhurst.[24] Alderminster has been since the end of the 18th century partly in the hundred of Oswaldslow, but chiefly in Pershore Hundred.[24a]

By the witness of Domesday the king's sheriffs were excluded from all jurisdiction in the hundred of Oswaldslow.[25] The bishop had to collect the danegeld and supply military service. Under Edgar's charter the bishop claimed also fines for ecclesiastical offences, inflicted in the hundred court,[26] and fines called 'over-seunesse' and 'gylt wyt,' and everything else the king had in his hundreds. The Prior and monks of Worcester had the same rights and privileges. Domesday is, however, silent as to the rights of the monks in the jurisdiction of Oswaldslow, but in 1148 Bishop Simon confirmed to them the same liberties as he himself held in Oswaldslow and a third part of all forfeitures.[27] In the 13th and 14th centuries the Earl of Warwick's encroachments on the hundred were said to be to the prejudice of the convent as well as of the bishop,[28] and in 1301 one of the articles brought by the prior against the bishop was that the latter had granted to

[12] V.C.H. Worcs. i, 325, 326.   [13] Lay Subs. R. Worcs. c. 1280 (Worcs. Hist. Soc.), 29, 31, 33.
[14] Cal. Rot. Chart. 1199–1216 (Rec. Com.), 168.
[15] Phepson was said in 1240 to be in the liberty of the hundred of Stoke (Hale, op. cit. 57a).
[16] Stat. 1 Geo. III, cap. 2, confirmed by Stat. 5 Geo. III, cap. 5 ; 6 Geo. III, cap. 9 ; 38 Geo. III, cap. 5.
[17] Lay Subs. R. Worcs. c. 1280 (Worcs. Hist. Soc.), 34, 37.
[18] Ibid. 114.   [19] Ibid. c. 1327 (Worcs. Hist. Soc.), 52.
[20] Stat. 1 Geo. III, cap. 2.   [21] V.C.H. Worcs. i, 253–6 ; Heming, op. cit. 297.
[22] V.C.H. Worcs. i, 325b.   [23] Reg. G. Giffard (Worcs. Hist. Soc.), 75.
[24] Lay Subs. R. Worcs. c. 1280 (Worcs. Hist. Soc.), 81, 87.
[24a] Burton, Bibl. of Worcs. i, 80 ; Census of Engl. and Wales, 1831.
[25] V.C.H. Worcs. i, 287. The sheriff received no profits from Oswaldslow except amercements of the county, 'when they happen' (Cal. Inq. p.m. 1–9 Edw. II, 410).
[26] Hale, op. cit. 24a and note lv.   [27] Thomas, Surv. of Cath. Church of Worc. App. no. 18.
[28] Reg. G. Giffard (Worcs. Hist. Soc.), 75.

Simon de Croome the assize of bread and ale in one of his manors, without the assent of the prior.[29]

The bishop and the prior each had a beadle or serjeant (*serviens*) for the hundred, but there was a common bailiff[30] elected by the bishop with the consent of the prior and convent. These officers were presented to the sheriff after election.[31] The prior's beadle, the cellarer of the convent,[32] issued summonses to the hundred courts to the tenants of the prior, notice of the day being given him by the bishop's steward, who acted as bailiff. The prior's tenants brought their pledges to the steward, who delivered them to the cellarer.[33] The prior and convent claimed the amercements of their men and a third of those of strangers (*forinseci*).

About the middle of the 13th century the bishop seems to have asserted the privilege of holding pleas *de namio vetito*.[34] William de Beauchamp, the sheriff, successfully challenged the claim, and the bishop carried the case to the Roman Court, where he obtained a judgement in his favour,[35] and the right was confirmed by Henry III.[36]

In 1274–5 it appears that the bishop had usurped in his manorial courts jurisdiction as to the assize of bread and ale which properly belonged to the hundred.[37] There were occasional conflicts also as to the jurisdiction of the hundred and the borough of Worcester. In 1348 a dispute arose as to an inquest held by the coroner of the borough upon a man killed in the churchyard of the priory, which lay in Oswaldslow, where the county coroner had jurisdiction.[38]

The hundred of Oswaldslow, as a late possession of the bishopric, was sold by the Parliamentary Commissioners in 1649 to John Corbett.[39]

There does not seem to have been any permanently fixed place for holding the courts. In 1240 they appear to have been held at Oswaldslow, at St. John's and at Winburntree,[40] but in 1274–5 they were said to have been held outside Worcester, at Druhurst,[41] and at Winburntree.[42] Winburntree was evidently in the neighbourhood of Blockley and Tredington, and courts were held for this part of the hundred until the end of the 17th century.[43] Oswaldslow itself was in Wolverton,[44] in the manor of Kempsey,[45] and is mentioned in the boundaries of that manor in 977.[46] From the 15th to the 18th century the leets were held at Swinesherd in the parish of St. Peter, at Radford Bridge in Alvechurch, at Hill and Moor in

[29] *Reg. G. Giffard* (Worcs. Hist. Soc.), 548.

[30] In the 14th century the bailiff received all the fees and profits of the hundred court and of hues and cries and of bloodshed and waifs and strays, saving to the bishop chattels of felons and fugitives and amercements for breaches of the assize of bread and ale (*Cal. Pat.* 1350–4, p. 383).

[31] Assize R. 1022, m. 10 d.

[32] The beadle was found in meat and drink on the days of the county and hundred courts (Hale, op. cit. 124*a*).   [33] Hale, op. cit. 31*b*.

[34] *Ann. Mon.* (Rolls Ser.), iv, 439.   [35] Ibid. i, 140; iv, 440, 441; *Cal. Pat.* 1247–58, p. 68.

[36] *Cal. Chart. R.* 1226–57, p. 443; Hale, op. cit. 160*b*–162*a*; *Cal. Pat.* 1247–58, p. 610.

[37] *Hund. R.* (Rec. Com.), ii, 283.

[38] *Cal. Pat.* 1348–50, p. 245. The parish in which the priory was situated, St. Michael, Bedwardine, was wholly in the county, and so remained until the passing of the Municipal Reform Act.

[39] Close, 1649, pt. i, no. 7.   [40] Hale, op. cit. *passim.*

[41] The hundred of Druhurst is mentioned in 1319 (*Cal. Pat.* 1317–21, p. 389).

[42] *Hund. R.* (Rec. Com.), ii, 283.   [43] Eccl. Com. Ct. R. (P.R.O.) *passim.*   [44] In Stoulton.

[45] Red Bk. of Bishopric of Worcester, Eccl. Com. Rec. Var. bdle. 121, no. 43698, fol. 49.

[46] Kemble, *Cod. Dipl.* no. 612. It has been suggested that Oslafeshau mentioned in a record of 825 is identical with Oswaldslow (Haddan and Stubbs, *Councils*, iii, 596, 599, 601).

Fladbury, at Vernysyche near Pickt Oak, and at Bredon Hill at two large stones on the Hill called the King and Queen, at Rye Elm, and at Stoke Hill.[47]   The expense of holding the courts being found to exceed the profits, they were not held regularly at the end of the 18th century.[48]   High constables were regularly appointed until the middle of the 19th century.

Since the end of the 17th century the hundred has been divided into the three divisions of Upper, Middle, and Lower Oswaldslow.   Nash states that the court for the Upper Division, which is identical with the ancient Winburntree, was held at Shipston on Stour, that for the Middle Division at Wheelbarrow Castle, and that for the Lower Division outside Sidbury Gate, formerly at Swinesherd Green.[49]

[47] Eccl. Com. Ct. R. (P.R.O.), bdle. 195, no. 6 ; Nash, *Hist. of Worcs.*, Introd. p. lxi.
[48] Nash, op. cit. Introd. p. lxii.   [49] Ibid. p. lx.

ALVECHURCH

Aelfgithecirce (viii cent.) ; Aelfythecyrcan (x cent.) ; Aelfithe Cyrce (xi cent.) ; Alvithecherche (xii cent.) ; Alninechurch, Alvechirche (xiii cent.) ; Alvechchirche, Alvychurch, Alvenecherch, Alvethechirche, Alvynchurche, Alvythechurche (xiv cent.) ; Allchurch, Allewchurche, Alchurch (xvi cent.).

The parish of Alvechurch is situated in the north-east of the county of Worcester and has an area of 6,800 acres,[1] of which 896 acres are arable, 5,418 acres are permanent grass and 48 acres are wood.[2] The land is high, varying from 400 ft. above the ordnance datum in the south to 600 ft. in the north. The subsoil is clay and marl, and the chief crops are wheat, oats and beans.

Included in this parish are the village of Alvechurch and the hamlets of Forhill, Hopwood and Lea End in the north, Barnt Green in the west and Rowney Green and part of Weatheroak Hill in the south.

Between the years 1650 and 1660 a court of survey was held for the manor of Alvechurch, when the boundaries of the parish were accurately described. At the end of the 18th century attested copies of this survey were in the possession of several of the inhabitants.[3]

The River Arrow runs through the parish from north to south and forms part of the southern boundary, while one of its tributaries forms part of the eastern boundary.

The Worcester and Birmingham Canal, running through the western portion of the parish, is fed by two large reservoirs called Upper and Lower Bittell Reservoirs. South of Hopwood there are wharves on the canal, which enters the Westhill Tunnel to the north-east of Hopwood. On the banks of the canal, to the west of the village of Alvechurch, there are brickworks.

The chief road in the parish is the Birmingham and Evesham high road, which runs southwards from West Heath through the hamlet of Hopwood and the village of Alvechurch. Icknield Street, the old Roman road, runs through the hamlet of Forhill in the east of the parish.

The village of Alvechurch is situated about 4 miles north of Redditch in a hollow upon the main road to Birmingham. A cross-road leading eastwards in the direction of Bromsgrove constitutes the centre of the village, and here a small gore is formed, upon which is built an isolated block of red brick cottages. The church stands on high ground to the south of the Bromsgrove road, a little to the west of the cross-roads. On the north side of this road, between the church and the main part of the village, is a fine 16th-century half-timbered house, now divided into two. There is some good half-timber work in the main street, but the majority of the houses are of brick and of comparatively recent date. On an elevated plateau to the east of the village, immediately to the south of the cross-road mentioned above, is the site of the former palace of the Bishops of Worcester with the remains of fishponds. The buildings have disappeared, but the system of moats remains intact, inclosing a large rectangular area, subdivided by a cross moat. All but the trench on the north side are still filled with water. Just by the cross-road is a water-mill, still in use, worked by a stream which flows down the valley in which the village lies. Barnt Green House, close to the Barnt Green railway station, is a picturesque half-timbered house of the latter

BARNT GREEN HOUSE, ALVECHURCH

half of the 16th century. The plan is T-shaped and of the normal central hall type, with modern additions. There are two stories with an attic floor in the roof. The chimney stacks have bases of stone ashlar work surmounted by brick shafts of the intersecting diagonal type. Some original oak panelling remains, but most of the principal rooms appear to have been refitted in the 18th century with new panelling of the same material. The main staircase is a good example of the latter date.

On the northern boundary of the parish is Westhill Farm.[4] At Moorgreen Hall near Weatheroak Hill are the remains of a moat. In Rowney Green there are several gravel-pits.

The chief houses are Bordesley Hall with Bordesley Park belonging to Lieut.-Colonel H. C. Geast Dugdale, but now the residence of Mr. Alfred Harold Wiggin, J.P., and the Forhill House, the residence of Mr. Walter William Wiggin, J.P.

---

[1] Of these 162 acres are covered by water.
[2] Statistics from Bd. of Agric. (1905).
[3] Nash, *Hist. of Worcs.* i, 25. The survey is given in full.
[4] See below.

The Barnt Green, Evesham and Ashchurch branch of the Midland railway runs through the parish, and the Bristol and Birmingham branch of the same railway runs along a portion of the western boundary. There is a station on the former at Alvechurch opened in 1859, and on the latter at Barnt Green.

An Inclosure Act for Alvechurch was passed in 1819.[5]

The following place-names occur : Crukedebrugg, Levericheshull, Drayhulle, Pyrleye, Sandon, Ernaldescroft, and Pynyton (xiii cent.)[6] ; Le Graunge Wode, the Tirlewey,[7] Cockys Bache, the Ruddyng, Swanneshull,[8] Fraunces,[9] Webfeldes,[10] Coole Croft,[11] Awcott[12] (xvi cent.).

MANOR AND BOROUGH *ALVECHURCH* seems to have been originally included in 20 hides at Westhill (Wærsetfelda), Coston Hackett (Coftune),[13] and Rednal (Wreodanhale),[14] granted by Offa in 780 to the monastery of Bredon,[15] for later registers of Worcester Priory state that Offa gave to the church at Bredon, Alvechurch with the vills of Westhill, Coston, and Rednal,[16] but no separate charter has been found for Alvechurch. This estate passed like the rest of the possessions of the monastery of Bredon to the see of Worcester, and the 20 hides[17] were given by Aelhun (Ealhhun) Bishop of Worcester in 849, in exchange for a promise of protection, to King Berhtwulf for five lives, with reversion to the church of Worcester,[18] and Berhtwulf granted them to his thegn (*minister*) Egbert under the same conditions.[19] The land was restored to the church of Worcester in 930 by King Athelstan,[20] and a good argument for the identification of this estate with that afterwards known as Alvechurch is afforded by a later statement that Athelstan gave ' Ælfgythe Cyrcan,' as 20 hides, to the church of Worcester.[20a] In 1086 Alvechurch with its four berewicks, Coston Hackett, Westhill, Tonge and Overton, was numbered among the possessions of the see of Worcester.[21] It remained in the possession of successive bishops[21a] until 1648, when it was sold by the Parliamentary Trustees to William Combe,[22] the site of the manor and the park being sold at the same date to John Combe and Richard Quiney.[23]

SEE OF WORCESTER. *Argent ten rounde's gules.*

At the Restoration the manor was recovered by the bishop, and remained with the see of Worcester until 1860, when it was taken over by the Ecclesiastical Commissioners,[24] who are now lords of the manor.[25] Court leets for the manor were held yearly until about 1860.

Henry II seems to have afforested part of the manor of Alvechurch and annexed it to the neighbouring forest of Feckenham,[26] but Richard I freed 6½ acres within the bishop's manor of Alvechurch from fines due for their clearing[27] and confirmed the manor to the bishop.[28] John granted the bishop the same liberties in his manor of Alvechurch as he had in his other manors,[29] and freed 34½ acres there from payments for clearing and waste, pleas, and from all other forest exactions.[30]

In 1531 Alvechurch was exempted from contributing to the expenses of knights going to Parliament.[31]

The exact date of the formation of the mesne borough of Alvechurch is unknown, but the grant of burghal rights may have synchronized with or followed the establishment of a market and fair in the 13th century. In Bishop Giffard's Register[32] (1268–1302) the borough is recognized, and in the survey of Feckenham Forest given in the Beauchamp Chartulary it is admitted that the portion of Alvechurch which lay ' in foro' belonged to the see. By 1288 the rent[33] of the borough was valued at £4 2s. 9d. In 1299 there were about seventy-four burgage tenements, and their rents[34] ranged from 10d. to 15d. each. Three years after the pleas and perquisites[35] of the court of the manor and of the borough were worth £6 0s. 6d. The burgesses do not seem to have ever acquired any real independence, and the organization of the borough was mainly of the usual manorial type.

In 1529–30 the bishop received £3 18s. 10½d. from burgages in Alvechurch and 18s. 10d. in respect of two new ones.[36] A view of frankpledge was taken in 1537, in which William Staffordshire is stated to have paid 10d. for one burgage, and Thomas Aunge is mentioned as holding another of the bishop. In 1540–1 the rents of burgages in Alvechurch amounted to £3 18s. 10½d.[37] Bishop Silvester (1498–1521) granted a lease of a burgage in Alvechurch to Thomas Porter, who fifteen years later bequeathed it to his son William Porter. The latter granted it to Henry Porter, who in the reign of Elizabeth took proceedings against John Phillipps to recover possession of it.[38] The borough of Alvechurch never returned a member to Parliament. The town was governed by a bailiff chosen annually at the court leet of the manor and

[5] Private Act (N.P.), 59 Geo. III, cap. 60.

[6] Red Bk. of Bishopric of Worc. (Eccl. Com. Rec. Var. bdle. 121, no. 43698), fol. 125, 126, 142, 147 ; Cal. Pat. 1338–40, p. 464.

[7] L. and P. Hen. VIII, iii (1), g. 612 (4).

[8] Anct. D. (P.R.O.), A 4677.

[9] Ibid. A 6070.

[10] Pat. 3 Edw. VI, pt. iii.

[11] Ibid. 3 Eliz. pt. v.

[12] Anct. D. (P.R.O.), A 6070.

[13] Westhill and Coston Hackett were berewicks of Alvechurch in 1086.

[14] Now in King's Norton.

[15] Birch, Cart. Sax. i, 326, 327.

[16] Dugdale, Mon. Angl. i, 608.

[17] They then comprised 5 at Westhill, 5 at Coston Hackett, 5 at Rednal, 2 in Hopwood and 3 in Witlafesfeld, an un-

identified site, but there is no mention of Alvechurch.

[18] Birch, Cart. Sax. ii, 40. The charter is only preserved in a late copy, but is certainly authentic, and, from its subject matter, of unusual importance.

[19] Ibid.

[20] Birch, op. cit. ii, 400.; Heming, Chartul. (ed. Hearne), 10, 480.

[20a] Birch, op. cit. iii, 657.

[21] V.C.H. Worcs. i, 298; see also 326.

[21a] Mins. Accts. bdle. 1143, no. 18 ; Feud. Aids, v, 306, 318 ; Valor Eccl. (Rec. Com.), iii, 217.

[22] Close, 24 Chas. I, pt. xiii, no. 13.

[23] Ibid. pt. xiv, no. 29.

[24] Stat. 23 & 24 Vict. cap. 124.

[25] Information from Ecclesiastical Commissioners.

[26] Nash, Hist. of Worcs. i, 17b.

[27] Cart. Antiq. RR, 15.

[28] Ibid. D, 43.

[29] Cal. Rot. Chart. 1199–1216 (Rec. Com.), 10b ; Hist. MSS. Com. Rep. xiv, App. viii, 193.

[30] Cart. Antiq. I, 31.

[31] L. and P. Hen. VIII, v, g. 119 (5). The reason assigned for this exemption was that the manor was ancient demesne of the Crown.

[32] op. cit. (Worcs. Hist. Soc.), 536 ; Add. MS. 28024, fol. 148.

[33] Red Bk. of Bishopric of Worc. fol. 140.

[34] Ibid. 137.

[35] Mins. Accts. bdle. 1143, no. 18.

[36] Prattinton Coll. (Soc. Antiq.).

[37] Ibid.

[38] Chan. Proc. (Ser. 2), bdle. 139, no. 2.

appeared at the lord's court by a jury of its own inhabitants distinct from that of the manor.[39]   It was still styled a borough in 1808.[40]

In 1239 Walter, Bishop of Worcester obtained from Henry III a grant of a yearly fair at Alvechurch for three days at the feast of St. Lawrence (10 August) and a weekly market on Wednesdays.[41]   The grant was renewed to Bishop Godfrey in 1270, when the market day was changed to Saturday.[42]   The market had entirely disappeared before the end of the 18th century,[43] but two fairs were then held, one on St. Lawrence's Day and the other on 22 April, the latter being famous for the number of sheep and lambs sold.[44] The April and August fairs continued until about the middle of the 19th century[45]; but in 1850 a fair was held on 3 May, and statute fairs on Lady Day and Michaelmas Day.   In 1872 only one statute fair was held in October.   At the present day there are two fairs held at Alvechurch, one on the first Wednesday in May and the other on the first Wednesday in October.   They have, however, declined so much in importance that it is impossible to say there is any ownership in them at all.[46]

In 1299 the Bishop of Worcester owned two mills in one house in Alvechurch on the River Arrow.[47]   They are mentioned in a survey made in 1299 as worth £3 16s. yearly,[48] but in the reign of Henry VIII only brought in £1 6s. 8d.[49]   At the time of the sale of the bishops' lands in 1647 one mill was sold to Henry Haynes for £45 3s. 4d.[50]; the second, called the Town Mill, passed with the manor in 1648 to William Combe.[51] There are still two water corn-mills on the banks of the River Arrow, the one north and the other south of the village of Alvechurch.

The Bishops of Worcester had a *PARK* at Alvechurch in the reign of Henry II,[52] when one Reynold held half a hide of land for the service of being park-keeper.[53]   In 1213, the see of Worcester being then in his hands, the king granted to Robert de Rochelle (Ropella) three deer from the park of Alvechurch.[54]   Free warren was granted to the Bishop of Worcester in 1254 and in 1255.[55]   According to the above-mentioned survey of 1299 the park was then rated at 49s. 8d. and contained two ponds with islands in them.   The

fishing was worth 5s. and the pasture of the islands 2s.[56]   Bishop Giffard increased the park, giving to Nicholas de Norfolk land in Gomenhull in exchange for that added to the park.[57]   In 1529-30 and in 1535 the yearly rent of the park was £8.[58]   On 13 June 1538 Bishop Latimer wrote to Cromwell that he had intended to have asked for a good portion of the demesne lands of Bordesley, apparently to add to the park at Alvechurch.[59]   Edward VI confirmed the park to the bishop in 1552-3.[60]   In 1648 it was sold with the palace to John Combe and Richard Quiney.[61]   In 1652 there were proceedings in the Court of Exchequer between Richard Booth, then owner of Alvechurch Park, and the rector of Alvechurch with respect to tithes.[62]   The park had been converted into farms before the end of the 18th century.[63]

ALVECHURCH : 16TH-CENTURY HOUSE, NOW COTTAGES

The Bishops of Worcester had a palace at Alvechurch, at which they frequently resided.   William of Blois died there in 1236.[64]   Bishop Godfrey

[39] Nash, op. cit. i, 24 ; Carlisle, *Topog. Dict.*

[40] Carlisle, op. cit.

[41] *Cal. Chart. R.* 1226-57, p. 248.

[42] Ibid. 1257-1300, p. 139.

[43] It had probably disappeared before the middle of the 17th century, as Habington does not mention it.

[44] Nash, loc. cit.

[45] Lewis, *Topog. Dict.*; Carlisle, op. cit. ; Brayley and Britton, *Beauties of Engl. and Wales.*

[46] Information supplied by Rt. Rev. L. G. Mylne, D.D.

[47] Red Bk. of Bishopric of Worc. fol. 126 ; *Reg. G. Giffard* (Worcs. Hist. Soc.),

536.   They brought in a rent of £4 7s. in 1302 (Mins. Accts. bdle. 1143, no. 18).

[48] Prattinton Coll. (Soc. Antiq.).

[49] Ibid.   John Bedyll was the miller.

[50] *Coll. Topog. et Gen.* i, 4.

[51] Close, 24 Chas. I, pt. xiii, no. 13.

[52] Pipe R. 32 Hen. II, m. 3 d.

[53] Habington, *Surv. of Worcs.* (Worcs. Hist. Soc.), ii, 7 ; Red Bk. of Bishopric of Worc. fol. 141.

[54] *Rot. Lit. Claus.* (Rec. Com.), i, 147b.

[55] *Cal. Pat.* 1247-58, p. 345 ; *Cal. Chart. R.* 1226-57, p. 443.

[56] Prattinton Coll. (Soc. Antiq.).   In 1292 (*Cal. Pat.* 1281-92, p. 521), in 1334 (ibid. 1330-4, p. 584), and again in

1339 (ibid. 1338-40, p. 63) there is mention of a commission of oyer and terminer touching certain trespassers in the park of Alvechurch.

[57] Red Bk. of Bishopric of Worc. fol. 125.

[58] Prattinton Coll. (Soc. Antiq.) ; *Valor Eccl.* (Rec. Com.), iii, 217.

[59] *L. and P. Hen. VIII,* xiii (1), 1177.

[60] Pat. 6 Edw. VI, pt. vii.

[61] Close, 24 Chas. I, pt. xiv, no. 29.

[62] Exch. Dep. Trin. 28 Chas. II, no. 5.

[63] Nash, op. cit. i, 25.

[64] *Ann. Mon.* (Rolls Ser.), i, 101.

A HISTORY OF WORCESTERSHIRE

Giffard was often there,[65] many of his letters and deeds being dated at Alvechurch.[66] Reginald Brian, Bishop of Worcester, was at Alvechurch on 1 December 1356, when he received a letter from the Black Prince giving an account of the battle of Poictiers,[67] and he died there of the Plague in 1361.[68] Leland in his Itinerary mentions the palace and says, ' this place is made all of Tymbre and seemeth to be noe peice of ould Worke. It was lately in Decay and Bishop Latimer repaired it.'[69] In 1648 'the site of the manor or mansion-house of Alvechurch ' was sold by the trustees under the Act of 1646 to John Combe and Richard Quiney,[70] but at the Restoration it was recovered by the bishop. The palace soon afterwards fell into disrepair and by 1780 had been pulled down.[71] A chapel in the manor of Alvechurch is mentioned in 1447.[72]

BARNT GREEN (Brante, xiv cent.; Grene, xv cent.; Greane, xvi cent.; Barnte Green, xvii cent.) was probably included in Alvechurch in the early days of its history. It is first mentioned as a separate manor in 1450–1, when William Cecil and his wife Margaret conveyed it to William Cumberford.[73] The next owner mentioned is Christopher St. Germain, who demised it for forty years to William Willington in 1527–8.[74] William seems to have acquired half the manor in fee before 1542, when he made some settlement with regard to it to which his daughter Elizabeth and her husband Edward Boughton were parties.[75] Stephen Agard and his wife Elizabeth conveyed a moiety of the manor in 1547–8 to William Willington.[76] The latter apparently settled this manor on his youngest daughter Catherine, who married three times.[77] She and her third husband Anthony Throckmorton were dealing with land in Alvechurch in 1586,[78] and in 1589 Catherine, then a widow, with the consent of her sons John, Thomas and George, sold the manor to Anthony Tirringham and John Catesby,[79] and in the following year they sold it to Thomas Ridley, D.C.L., and Margaret his wife.[80] In 1660 the manor, then for the first time called Barnt Green, was conveyed by William Middlemore to Ralph Taylor the elder, Ralph Taylor the younger and William Moore.[81] Barnt Green seems, however, to have belonged to Henry Taylor, father of the younger Ralph, as he is called 'of Barn Green' in the Worcester visitation of 1682.[82] The younger Ralph died about 1670.[83] Shortly after the manor of Barnt Green seems to have passed to the Moore family. William Moore of Barnt Green died in 1714 and seems to have been succeeded by Edward Moore, who died in 1746.[84] An Edward Moore lived at Barnt Green in 1781,[85] but he and his ancestors were probably only tenants of the manor, for William Waldron was dealing with it in 1763.[86] William seems to have been succeeded by four co-heiresses—Ann wife of John Taylor, Mary wife of John Raybould, Elizabeth wife of Nathaniel Wright, and Sarah Waldron, since they were dealing with the manor in 1766.[87] John Taylor was in possession about 1814,[88] but in 1816 Joshua Yates and Ann Yates sold the manor to Other Archer Earl of Plymouth.[89] All manorial rights at Barnt Green have long since fallen into abeyance.

WINDSOR, Earl of Plymouth. *Gules a saltire argent between twelve crosslets or.*

HOPWOOD (Hopwuda, ix and x cent.), together with Westhill,[90] was granted by Bishop Aelhun to King Berhtwulf in 849,[91] and was restored to the church by King Athelstan in 930.[92]

It seems to have remained part of the demesne of the Bishops of Worcester until one of them gave it with his niece to William de Salesweres.[93] Thomas de Hopwood was impleaded for this manor by William of Blois, Bishop of Worcester (1218–36), but Thomas died while the suit was pending.[94] The bishop probably recovered it, for Bishop Giffard was in possession in 1299.[95] Hopwood seems again to have passed out of the hands of the bishop, for in 1344–5 Thomas de Grotene released to Bishop Wulstan all his claim in the manor of Hopwood.[96] After this date Hopwood probably merged into the manor of Alvechurch.

An estate at Hopwood was held in the 12th century by the lords of Talton, William de Armscote having acquired it before 1182 by exchange with Hamme and Roger for land in Fladbury.[97] It was held early in the 13th century by William son of Auger de Talton under the Bishop of Worcester's manor of Tredington.[98] It was evidently closely connected with the manor of Talton in Tredington, for it was held like that manor under Auger de Talton by Robert Waleraund in 1272–3,[99] and in 1299 Robert le Chaumbre held a hide of land at Hopwood.[100]

At the date of the Domesday Survey Urse D'Abitot owned a hide of land at *OSMERLEY* (Osmerlie, xi cent.; Osemeresleia, xii cent.) in Alvechurch, and Herlebald held it of him. Attached to this estate was a house in Worcester worth 16d. and a saltpan in Droitwich paying a rent of 12 'mits' of salt. There was also half a league (*lewa*) of wood.[1]

[65] *Reg. G. Giffard* (Worcs. Hist. Soc.), *passim.*
[66] Nash (op. cit. i, 24) says he died there.
[67] Worc. Epis. Reg. Brian, fol. 128. Nash gives the letter in full with a translation (op. cit. i, 35, 36).
[68] Noake, *Guide to Worcs.* 12.
[69] Leland, *Itin.* (ed. Hearne), iv, 108.
[70] Close, 24 Chas. I, pt. xiv, no. 29.
[71] Nash, op. cit. i, 25.
[72] Worc. Epis. Reg. Carpenter (1443–76), i, fol. 58.
[73] Feet of F. Div. Co. East. 29 Hen. VI.
[74] Anct. D. (P.R.O.), A 4688.
[75] Feet of F. Div. Co. Mich. 34 Hen. VIII; Burke, *Commoners,* iv, 527.
[76] Feet of F. Div. Co. Trin. 1 Edw. VI.

[77] Burke, loc. cit.
[78] Anct. D. (P.R.O.), A 6070.
[79] Ibid. A 12237; Feet of F. Worcs. Trin. 31 Eliz.
[80] Anct. D. (P.R.O.), A 12390; see also A 6602; Feet of F. Worcs. East. 35 Eliz.
[81] Feet of F. Worcs. Hil. 12 Chas. II.
[82] Metcalfe, *Visit. of Worcs.* 91.
[83] Ibid.
[84] Nash, op. cit. i, 30, 32, 33.
[85] Ibid. 26.
[86] Recov. R. Trin. 3 Geo. III, rot. 333.
[87] Feet of F. Worcs. Hil. 7 Geo. III.
[88] Prattinton Coll. (Soc. Antiq.).
[89] Feet of F. Worcs. Hil. 57 Geo. III.
[90] See below.

[91] Heming, *Chartul.* (ed. Hearne), i, 6.
[92] Ibid. 10.
[93] *Reg. G. Giffard* (Worcs. Hist. Soc.), 75; Red Bk. of Bishopric of Worc. fol. 145.
[94] *Reg. G. Giffard* (Worcs. Hist. Soc.), 75; Nash, op. cit. i, 22.
[95] Habington, op. cit. ii, 9.
[96] Red Bk. of Bishopric of Worc. fol. 146.
[97] Ibid. 83.
[98] *Testa de Nevill* (Rec. Com.), 42.
[99] *Cal. Inq. p.m.* 1–9 Edw. I, 6.
[100] Red Bk. of Bishopric of Worc. fol. 126.
[1] *V.C.H. Worcs.* i, 318a. Alwold had held this land.

254

The overlordship of this land remained with the Beauchamps, the descendants of Urse, until the end of the 12th century, when the estate was granted to the abbey of Bordesley.[2]

Urse's under-tenant Herlebald also held the manor of Stone in 1086, and Osmerley passed with that manor from him to the family of Stanes. William de Stanes gave the estate about the middle of the 12th century to the abbey of Bordesley at a rent of 4 marks, and his gift was confirmed in 1178 by his son Walter,[3] and in 1200–1 by his grandson William.[4] This grant was confirmed by various members of the Beauchamp family, as overlords of the fee.[5]

It remained with the abbey of Bordesley until the dissolution of the house in 1538,[6] and was granted in 1542 as land at Alvechurch, together with the other lands of the abbey, to Andrew Lord Windsor.[7] Land at Alvechurch still belongs to his descendant, the Earl of Plymouth, but the name Osmerley has disappeared.

WINDSOR-CLIVE, Earl of Plymouth. *Argent a fesse sable with three molets or thereon, quartered with* WINDSOR.

The early history of *WESTHILL* (Waersetfelda, viii cent.; Warstelle, xi cent.; Wasthull, xiii cent.) has been given under the manor of Alvechurch. At the date of the Domesday Survey Westhill was one of the berewicks attached to that manor,[8] and probably remained a part of the bishop's demesne until 1243–4, when the bishop granted land at Alvechurch to William de Norfolk and his wife Prudence.[9] Hugh de Norfolk sold an estate at Alvechurch to William son of William de Westhill in 1273–4.[10] He gave a messuage and land in Alvechurch to his eldest son William in 1275–6,[11] and the latter granted the same estate to his son, another William, in 1282–3.[12]

In 1283 William de Westhill and Matthew Cheker or del Excheker released to the Bishop of Worcester all their right to a messuage and 3 carucates of land in Westhill.[13] This grant was confirmed by the Crown in 1289,[14] but in the following year William de Westhill complained that Matthew Cheker had fraudulently obtained a fine conveying this estate to him, and that the conveyance to the bishop was made without his consent and to the disinheritance of his son William.[15] Judgement was given for William, but he seems never to have recovered the estate. In 1289 the bishop obtained from the commonalty of Westhill a release of all their right to common at Westhill.[16]

From that time Westhill seems to have been part of the manor of Alvechurch, and is possibly to be identified with the land of the Bishop of Worcester called 'hyghe Wastels,' mentioned in a deed of 1546.[17] In 1648 it was sold with the manor as part of the demesne called Wastills or Wastehills.[18] Its site is still marked by Westhill and Westhill Farm in the north of the parish.

Nicholas de Warwick was in possession of land at Alvechurch at the end of the 13th century. One hide he had acquired before 1299 of Nicholas de Norfolk, another half-hide he had bought of Hugh de Norfolk, whose predecessor in possession had been Hugh le Boteler.[19] Nicholas also held a messuage at 'Gouchmonesgreen' and half a virgate at Mornhill.[20] Nicholas de Warwick, by an undated charter, gave to Sir Thomas Blaunfront all the lands in Alvechurch which his father had held.[21] Thomas forfeited all his possessions about 1324,[22] but they were evidently restored to him or a descendant of the same name, for in 1329 Thomas Blaunfront obtained a grant of free warren at 'Gomondesgreen' at Alvechurch.[23] Thomas was still in possession of land at Alvechurch in 1332–3,[24] and purchased land at 'Gomondesgreen' in 1358.[25] By a deed, without date, he acquired land in Alvechurch and 'La Tange' from John Pichard.[26] Nothing further is known of this estate.

At the beginning of the 13th century Ralph Hacket was holding of William de Beauchamp a hide of land in Alvechurch,[27] which had probably been given to his ancestor William Hacket (see Coston Hackett) by Bishop Simon (1125–50).[28] Little is known of the descent of this estate, but it seems to have passed with the manor of Coston Hackett, of which it probably formed part, to the Leicester family.[29] It is mentioned for the last time in 1431, when it was held by Henry Leicester.[30]

CHURCH   The church of *ST. LAWRENCE* consists of a chancel 42 ft. by 20 ft., nave 51 ft. by 23 ft., north and south aisles, with chapels of two bays on either side of the chancel, about 75 ft. in total length by 16½ ft. wide on the north side and 10½ ft. on the south, and a west tower 15½ ft. square. These measurements are all internal.

The whole of the church, with the exception of the north aisle and the tower, was rebuilt in 1859 by the late Mr. W. Butterfield. The north aisle is of 14th-century date with later 15th-century insertions at the west end, and appears to have replaced a 12th-century building. The nave was probably of the same size as that of this building and had a 13th-century chancel to the east. The north arcade is modern, except the west respond, and is in

[2] Add. Chart. (B.M.), 20419 ; *Cal. Chart. R.* 1257–1300, pp. 64, 65.
[3] Madox, *Formulare Angl.* no. 5, 89.
[4] Ibid. 464.
[5] Ibid. 108 ; *Cal. Chart. R.* 1257–1300, p. 64.
[6] *V.C.H. Worcs.* ii, 153. At this time Osmerley and Nether Osmerley were worth £4 a year and Osmerley Grange £5 19s. (*Valor Eccl.* [Rec. Com.], iii, 271). In respect of the latter the monastery paid £2 6s. 8d. a year to the rector of Alvechurch (ibid.).
[7] *L. and P. Hen. VIII,* xvii, g. 285 (18).
[8] *V.C.H. Worcs.* i, 298b.

[9] *Feet of F. Worcs.* East. 28 Hen. III, no. 7.
[10] Ibid. 2 Edw. I, no. 5.
[11] *Reg. G. Giffard* (Worcs. Hist. Soc.), 418. [12] Ibid.
[13] *Chart. R.* 17 Edw. I, m. 1, no. 5 ; *Reg. G. Giffard* (Worcs. Hist. Soc.), 419, 420 ; *Abbrev. Plac.* (Rec. Com.), 227, 286 ; *Cal. Chart. R.* 1257–1300, p. 340.
[14] *Cal. Chart. R.* 1257–1300, p. 340.
[15] *Parl. R.* i, 22.
[16] *Reg. G. Giffard* (Worcs. Hist. Soc.), 329.
[17] *Anct. D.* (P.R.O.), A 4677.
[18] *Close,* 24 Chas. I, pt. xiii, no. 13.
[19] This was probably part of the land

which Norman Pincerna held in the 12th century (Red Bk. of Bishopric of Worc. fol. 141).
[20] Ibid. 128.
[21] Prattinton Coll. (Soc. Antiq.).
[22] *Mins. Accts.* bdle. 1148, no. 7.
[23] *Chart. R.* 3 Edw. III, m. 5, no. 4.
[24] *Feet of F. Worcs.* East. 6 Edw. III.
[25] Prattinton Coll. (Soc. Antiq.).
[26] Nash, op. cit. i, 31.
[27] *Testa de Nevill* (Rec. Com.), 41.
[28] Red Bk. of Bishopric of Worc. fol. 141.
[29] *Assize R.* 1030, m. 6 d. ; *Feud. Aids,* v, 307, 332.
[30] *Feud. Aids,* v, 307, 332.

the style of the 12th century, but in the rest of the church the later styles have been used. The tower is a rebuilding of the 15th-century work, bearing on the west face the date 1676.

The chancel is lit by lancet windows, and in the south wall is a sedile with a label enriched with re-used 'dog-tooth' ornament. Further west is a tomb recess of late date, partly original. Arcades of two bays with pointed arches open into the side chapels, and the chancel arch has responds of clustered shafts.

The modern north arcade of the nave is of three bays and has heavy round columns with scalloped capitals. The south arcade consists of three large bays and a small western one in the style of the 13th century. The clearstory is lighted by four windows on each side.

The east window of the north aisle is of five lights; the tracery appears to be later than the jambs, and may have been part of the east chancel window mentioned by Dr. Prattinton in 1826.[30a]

The first two north windows, which are largely original, are each of two lights, with cusped tracery under two-centred heads. Between is a recess containing a tomb. The north door has a plain ogee arch, and was blocked in 1869. The third north window is of three lights with 15th-century tracery under a four-centred head, and the west window is modern.

The south doorway, placed very close to the west end, is of 12th-century work re-used. It is recessed in two orders and has an original label with billet ornament and diapering and modern jamb shafts. A similar porch covers the doorway.

The tower is of three stages with diagonal buttresses to its western angles carried up to the parapet string, and a stair turret in the north-east angle. The doorway at the foot into the tower was blocked by Mr. Butterfield and an outer doorway substituted. The tower arch is of two continuous orders, and above it are marks of the former roof, and a window of two lights opening into the nave. The west window is of three lights with vertical tracery under a four-centred head. The jambs are evidently part of the original 15th-century work, perhaps re-worked, but the tracery appears to be later. The moulded string-course around the tower passes over the head as a crocketed label.

In the second stage are rectangular lights to the north, south and west, and over the last is a disused clock-dial in a square panel with an inscription above and the date 1676. A similar panel on the south face with an angel sculptured above it is partially hidden by a modern skeleton clock-face. The bell-chamber is lighted by windows of two lights each. The parapet is a 17th-century balustrade with crocketed angle and intermediate pinnacles. The roofs are all modern, those of the nave and chancel being gabled and open timbered below.

The rood screen is said to be old, but it is covered with modern paint.

The tomb in the north aisle is set in a wide recess flanked by diagonal pinnacles and having an ogee cinquefoiled arch crocketed and terminating in a carved finial. The whole appears to be work of about 1400. The recess contains an effigy of a knight in plate armour and jupon, with legs crossed, and two angels supporting the cushion. The head rests on a peaked bascinet with the visor raised. His shield, hung by a strap, on the left side is blank. A pleated short skirt reaches to the knee and is buttoned down the front. The legs and arms are cased in plate and the feet in pointed sollerets.

In the east part of the north aisle is a brass to Philip Chalwyn, gentleman usher to Henry VIII, died 1524, consisting of an armed figure with gauntlets at the feet, and four shields : the first of Chalwyn charged with a cheveron between three molets ; the second has the arms of Chalwyn quartering three defaced shields, impaling quarterly (1) and (4) three roses, (2) and (3) a fesse between three lions ; the third shield bears the impaled quarterly coat last mentioned ; the fourth is quartered, the first quarter Chalwyn, the second and fourth defaced, the third three fusils in a fesse.

In the chancel is the gravestone of a priest with a cross flory on a stepped calvary. On one side is a chalice and host and on the other a shield of the arms of John Carpenter, Bishop of Worcester (1446–76) : Paly azure and gules a cheveron argent with three crosslets gules thereon and a mitre or in the chief. Other late 17th and 18th-century stones and brass inscriptions also remain.

There are eight bells, six by Jos. Smith of Edgbaston, 1711, rehung and increased by two in 1890.

The communion plate is composed of two cups and patens of 1861 and a silver credence paten and cover and two silver-mounted cruets of later date ; the old plate is said to have been stolen about 1835.

The registers before 1812 are as follows : (i) mixed entries 1545 to 1652 ; (ii) baptisms and burials 1653 to 1797 and marriages to 1754 ; (iii) baptisms and burials 1798 to 1812 ; (iv) marriages 1754 to 1812.

There is a Mission church at Rowney Green. In Alvechurch is a Baptist chapel built in 1860, and at Rowney Green a Wesleyan chapel.

ADVOWSON At the date of the Domesday Survey there was a priest at Alvechurch.[31] The advowson belonged to the Bishop of Worcester, and it has remained with the see of Worcester until the present day.[32]

In 1288 the bishop instituted Robert de Wich to the church of Alvechurch,[33] and in the following year granted him a licence to be absent for three years and to let his benefice to farm.[31] In 1291 the church was taxed at the rate of £20,[35] and in 1328 the Bishop of Worcester appointed the Dean of Wich to inquire into the structural defects of the church, more particularly the chancel.[36]

There was a chantry of Saint Mary in the parish church of Alvechurch, which owned land in the

---

[30a] Prattinton Coll. (Soc. Antiq.).

[31] *V.C.H. Worcs.* i, 298b. From the name of the place it is evident that a church existed there at an early date, probably before 1000. The name may with absolute certainty be translated the 'church of Ælfgyth.' This is a feminine name, and we may infer that Ælfgyth founded the church. This event evidently brought the existing name into currency and explains the obscurity of the ancient Wastill and Hopwood (inform. from Mr. F. M. Stenton).

[32] *Ann. Mon.* (Rolls Ser.), iv, 430 ; Inst. Bks. (P.R.O.). In 1627 Sir Benjamin Thornburgh presented to the church, probably for that turn only.

[33] *Reg. G. Giffard* (Worcs. Hist. Soc.), 515.

[34] Ibid. 366.

[35] *Pope Nich. Tax.* (Rec. Com.), 217b. As also in 1340 (*Inq. Non.* [Rec. Com.], 295) and in the reign of Henry VIII (*Valor Eccl.* [Rec. Com.], iii, 217a).

[36] Worc. Epis. Reg. Orlton (1327–33), ii, fol. 20 d.

parish. There is no record of the donors, but it appears that at the date of the suppression of the chantries in the reign of Edward VI the lands of this chantry were worth £5 2*s.* 8*d.* a year.[37] These lands were granted to John Hereford and William Wilson in 1549,[38] and afterwards passed into the possession of Thomas Lewknor, who died in 1571, having settled them on his wife Jane, and after her death on his son Nicholas and his wife Margaret.[39] Nicholas Lewknor died without issue, and these lands passed to Jane, his sister and heir,[40] who married Anthony Sheldon of Broadway.[41] Anthony died seised of the chantry lands in 1584, when his son William succeeded.[42]

CHARITIES Educational Charities.—The grammar school is regulated by a scheme under the Endowed Schools Acts, 19 May 1899. The endowment consists of 11 a. 1 r. 26 p., known as Birchy Fields ; 1 a. 1 r. 23 p. at Hopwood, and five cottages, producing in rents £80 a year ; £779 Midland Railway 2½ per cent. stock, arising from the sales in 1901 and 1902 of the old schoolhouse erected in 1742 with a legacy by will of the Rev. William Wood, D.D., and land adjoining ; and £222 10*s.* 8*d.* consols, representing for the most part accumulations of income and proceeds of sale in 1883 of a garden at Withybed Green. The sums of stock are held by the official trustees, producing together £25 0*s.* 6*d.* yearly.

The scheme provides that a sum of £50 shall be applied towards the maintenance of an upper department in connexion with a public elementary school, and that the residue of the net income shall be applied in exhibitions.

A sum of about £16 a year from the income of the distributive charities is also applied for educational purposes, and the official trustees also hold a sum of £40 consols derived under the will of the Rev. John Welch, dated in 1800, the dividends of £1 a year being applicable towards the support of the Sunday school.

The distributive charities comprise the following charities, namely :—

Christian Smith, founded by will, 1634, consisting of an annuity of 20*s.* issuing out of lands and tenements near Rowney Green.

Thomas Jolliffe, will, 1693, annuity of 20*s.* paid by the Earl of Plymouth out of the Coston estates.

Job Marston, will, 1701, being 20*s.* received from the parish of Yardley.

John Smith, deed, 1713, being 20*s.* issuing out of a house in London Street, Alvechurch.

Parish House, cottage and garden, no. 31 on the tithe map, producing in weekly rents £7 16*s.* yearly.

Edward Moore, deed, 1746, consisting of an annuity of £2 10*s.* charged on land known as Pinton's Croft.

The Rev. John Welch, will, 1800, trust fund, £43 15*s.* 1*d.* consols, the annual dividends, amounting to £1 1*s.* 8*d.*, to be applied in the distribution of bread.

William Smith, will, proved in 1838, trust fund, £69 0*s.* 8*d.* consols, producing £1 14*s.* 4*d.* a year.

Out of the net income of these charities about £16 a year is applied for educational purposes, and the remainder is distributed among the poor in bread and other articles in kind.

The hospital of Nicholas Lewknor, founded by will, dated in 1580, was erected by Thomas Coploie under Letters Patent, 28 April 1588, upon 2 acres of land devised by the donor's will for a master, six brethren and two sisters. In the result of certain proceedings in Chancery an annuity of £33 6*s.* 8*d.* was settled as an endowment, which was redeemed in 1884 by the transfer of £1,111 8*s.* 3*d.* consols, now producing £27 15*s.* 8*d.* yearly, to the official trustees, who also hold a sum of £366 13*s.* 4*d.* consols, producing £9 3*s.* 4*d.* yearly, as a repair fund. The real estate consists of nine cottages and gardens, of which six are occupied by inmates of the hospital rent free, the remainder being let at £16 a year.

BERROW

Berga (xii cent.) ; Bereg, Bergh, Berewe Gefrey subtus Maluern, La Berewe (xiii cent.) ; Barwe, La Barewe, Berewe, Barowe, Baruwe, Borghe, La Bergh (xiv cent.) ; Berowe (xv cent.) ; Le Barowe, Netherberowe, Netherbury (xvi cent.).

This parish, in the south-west of the county on its western border, covers an area of 2,207 acres. The eastern part of Berrow is low lying, being only 50 ft. above the ordnance datum on the south-eastern boundary, but the land rises to the western boundary, which passes along the top of the Malvern Hills. No railway line passes through this parish, though in the middle of the 19th century a projected railway from Monmouth through the Forest of Dean to Worcester was to pass through Berrow and have a station near Rye Cross on the border of the parish.[1] The nearest station is at Upton-on-Severn, 7 miles distant, on the Tewkesbury and Malvern branch of

the Midland railway. The main road connecting Tewkesbury and Ledbury traverses the north side of the parish, and the little village of Berrow is on a branch road from it.

There are a large number of half-timber houses scattered throughout the parish. They are chiefly of the 17th century, but some are of a much earlier period. Berrow Court, near the church to the south-west, has been pulled down and a modern brick cottage now occupies part of the site. Part of the old garden wall remains on the east, and a long sheet of water at the north-east between the site of the court and the church may be part of a moat. Two barns, probably of the 16th century, stand to the east of the cottage, one of stone with a modern iron roof and the other of oak on a stone base, L-shaped on plan, and thatched. The vicarage, to the north of the church, is a 17th-century half-timber house with

[37] Chant. Cert. 60, no. 17. Of this the incumbent, Hugh Pryne, received £4 11*s.* 5*d.* (ibid. 61, no. 14). In 1553 he was in receipt of a pension of £4 yearly (Browne Willis, *Hist. of Abbies*, ii, 264).
[38] Pat. 3 Edw. VI, pt. vii.
[39] Chan. Inq. p.m. (Ser. 2), ccviii, 199.
[40] Ibid.
[41] Ibid.
[42] Ibid.
[1] Noake, *Guide to Worcs.* 29.

modern additions on both sides. A barn on the east side of the road between the church and the post office, constructed of heavy oak trusses with timbers about 15 in. by 8 in. forming pointed arches springing from the ground level, is probably of the 14th century. This barn, which is thatched and weather-boarded and stands on a stone base, is a fine example of its type. On the other side of the road a little farther north is another barn of somewhat similar character but not so perfect. Rye Court Farm, at the cross on the Ledbury road, is an early 17th-century half-timber and plaster house with 18th-century and modern brick additions. A projecting chimney on the south, which has a rectangular stone base and two diagonal brick shafts, is of the original date. Hollybush Manor, on the Ledbury road at the extreme west boundary of the parish, is a red brick house of two stories and an attic with twin tiled roofs. The southern portion was built early in the 18th century and the northern fronting the road was added about 1750. The centre of this elevation is slightly broken forward and contains a semicircular-headed doorway, surmounted by a pediment carried upon consoles and a 'Venetian' window above. In the hall, which is entered from the main doorway, is a good 18th-century square well stairway of oak with slender turned balusters and square newels. The windows retain their original wood frames with leaded lights in small squares. The Duke of York Inn, on the south side of the Ledbury road about a mile and a half west of the church, is a half-timber house of about 1600, with a modern brick front and modern additions at the back. On the opposite side of the road is a picturesque half-timber house of the central chimney type of about the same date, now divided into two cottages. On the north side of the Ledbury road about a mile to the east of the church is a T-shaped farm-house, now divided into two cottages, probably of stone and dating from the early 16th century, but repaired in half-timber and plaster about 100 years later. The north wing is still of stone and the stonework is carried along the lower part of the west wall, including the base of the north-west chimney. The heavy ceiling beams are of the original date, while three rectangular brick chimneys on the north are of the 17th century. A stone barn near the road with two tiers of long, narrow loopholes is probably of the original date of the house, though the roof timbers have been much repaired.

The greater part of the land is pasture, 1,545 acres being laid down in permanent grass. Of woods and plantations there are some 80 acres, the largest wood being Berrow Wood. The chief crops are wheat, barley and beans, the amount of arable land being about 490 acres.[2] The soil is mixed and the subsoil Keuper Marl. Quarries of limestone and road stone

were worked here in the middle of the 19th century,[3] and some are still worked.

In 1882 part of Pendock was transferred to Berrow.[4]

Among former place-names are Keysende and Keysendestrete[5] (xv cent.) ; Barne Close and Jackes[6] (xvii cent.); Mone Perry, Gibbert's Field, the Lynches, Billingsclose, Winning Leyes, Portnall, Organs, and the Conygree Hills[7] (xviii cent.). Berrow, which was formerly in Malvern Chase, was inclosed by an Act of 1855,[8] and the award is dated 1860.[9]

MANOR BERROW At the time of the Domesday Survey *BERROW* was evidently included in Overbury, of which parish it was a chapelry.[10] Overbury belonged to the Prior and convent of Worcester, and from an early date Berrow was held under the prior by suit and service at the prior's court of Overbury and the payment yearly of 40s. to the chamberlain and 3s. to the infirmarer of the monastery.[11] The overlordship of Berrow represented by this rent and service passed with the other possessions of the priory at the Dissolution to the Dean and Chapter of Worcester.[12] It was sold in 1651 with the rectory, which was also held by the dean and chapter, by the Parliamentary Trustees to

PRIORY OF WORCES-TER. *Argent ten roundels gules, which are the arms of the see, differenced with a quarter azure with our Lady and the Child or therein.*

Henry Perkins, as a quit-rent of 40s. due from Thomas Beale out of certain lands called Berrow Court.[13]

A Robert de Berrow was holding land in Worcestershire, probably this manor, in 1174-5,[14] and a Robert de Berrow, lord of the manor at the end of the 12th century,[15] was succeeded before 1224 by his son Roger.[16] Early in the reign of Edward I[17] the most wealthy resident in Berrow was Geoffrey de Berrow, who may have been son and heir of Roger. In an Assize Roll of this time Geoffrey's name is found attached distinctively to the name of the vill. In 1325 Edward II ordered that John de Berrow (atte Berghe), probably a descendant of Geoffrey, should have seisin of an acre of land in Berrow which had lately been held of him by William Rauwyn, hanged as a felon.[18] John died about three years later, leaving as his heir John, a boy twelve years old.[19] The custody and marriage of this minor, together with two parts of the manor, were granted to his mother Margaret.[20] In 1377, after the death of Simon de Berrow, perhaps the son of the last-mentioned John,[21] the prior and convent leased the manor, during

[2] Statistics from Bd. of Agric. (1905).

[3] Lewis, *Topog. Dict.*

[4] *Census of Engl. and Wales*, 1891, ii, 657.

[5] Add. Chart. 8452. Now Chase End and Chase End Street.

[6] Close, 1651, pt. xlix, no. 37.

[7] Recov. R. D. Enr. East. 11 Geo. II, m. 1.

[8] Private Act, 18 & 19 Vict. cap. 61.

[9] *Blue Bk. Incl. Awards*, 188.

[10] Berrow gelded with Overbury in the middle of the 13th century and was assessed at 1 hide (Hale, *Reg. of Worc. Priory* [Camd. Soc.], 74a).

[11] Ibid. 76a.

[12] *Pope Nich. Tax.* (Rec. Com.), 227 ; Chan. Inq. p.m. 2 Edw. III (1st nos.), no. 5 ; *Valor Eccl.* (Rec. Com.), iii, 223 ; Pat. 33 Hen. VIII, pt. v, m. 19 ; 6 Jas. I, pt. xii, no. 2 ; Chan. Inq. p.m. (Ser. 2), dxlviii, 11. The rent was only 40s. in the 16th century.

[13] Close, 1651, pt. xlix, no. 37. Beale was perhaps a tenant of the manor under the Nanfans.

[14] *Pipe R.* 21 *Hen. II* (Pipe R. Soc.), 129.

[15] Heming, *Chartul.* (ed. Hearne), 536, 537.

[16] Hale, *Reg. of Worc. Priory* (Camd. Soc.), 76b ; Cur. Reg. R. 86, m. 11 ; *Ann. Mon.* (Rolls Ser.), 416.

[17] *Lay Subs. R. Worcs.* c. 1280 (Worcs. Hist. Soc.), 44 ; Assize R. 1026, m. 22.

[18] *Cal. Close*, 1323-7, p. 421. This was probably the John de Berrow, lord of Berrow, who witnessed a grant to Worcester Priory in 1319 (Nash, op. cit. i, 74).

[19] Chan. Inq. p.m. 2 Edw. III (1st nos.), no. 5.

[20] Dugdale, *Mon. Angl.* i, 613.

[21] Habington, op. cit. i, 130.

the minority of Simon's son Thomas, to Robert Underhill and William Halliday at a yearly rent of 17 marks.[22] A dispute between Robert Whittington, lord of the manor of Staunton, and the Prior of St. Mary's, Worcester, concerning the overlordship of Berrow and the wardship and marriage of Simon's daughter Margaret (who had been forcibly taken away by the prior) was settled in favour of the latter, upon proof that Simon had done suit at his court at Overbury.[23] Thomas died without issue.[24] His sister Margaret then succeeded to the property and married William Golafre. In 1394 William and Margaret Golafre settled their property on the heirs of their bodies with remainder in default to Richard Ruyhale the younger.[25] William and Margaret appear to have died without issue, and the manor passed to the Ruyhales of Birtsmorton,[26] and has since followed

1671,[30] and it was perhaps his daughter who as Catherine Thackwell of Rye Court married the Rev. Lewis Terry of Longdon.[31] Her daughter Catherine married Paul Thackwell, and their son Stephen, who died in 1729,[32] was the father of John Thackwell,[33] who afterwards bought the manors of Berrow and Birtsmorton. Nash, writing towards the end of the 18th century, remarks that 'the Thackwells have now a good estate in this parish.'[34]

The families of Greenhill[35] and Clerk[36] held land in this parish from early times.

CHURCH The church of *ST. FAITH* consists of a chancel 23¾ ft. by 18½ ft., a nave 46 ft. by 18¾ ft., a south aisle 6¼ ft. wide, a west tower 10½ ft. square and a north porch. These measurements are all internal.

The mid-12th-century church consisted of an aisle-

BERROW CHURCH FROM THE NORTH-EAST

the same descent as that manor[27] (q.v.), Mr. F. B. Bradley-Birt being the present owner.

RYE COURT in this parish was formerly a seat of the Thackwell family,[28] but is now a farm-house. The Thackwells had owned land in Berrow as early as 1651, when John Thackwell dealt with an estate there.[29] William Thackwell held land at Berrow in

less nave and chancel, but of this only the north nave wall remains. The present chancel replaced the earlier one in the 14th century, the chancel arch being removed. The tower dates from the 15th century, and the earlier west window was probably then reset in its present position. The south aisle with its curious arcade is a 15th-century addition,

[22] Prattinton Coll. (Soc. Antiq.).
[23] Ibid. [24] Habington, op. cit. i, 130.
[25] Feet of F. Div. Co. 18 Ric. II, no. 91.
[26] Habington, op. cit. i, 125.
[27] Feet of F. Worcs. 3 Hen. VI, no. 14; 23 Hen. VI, no. 39, 40; Mich. 1659; Hil. 9 Geo. III; East. 19 Geo. III; De Banco R. Mich. 20 Hen. VII, m. 510; Hil. 20 Hen. VII, m. 488; Chan. Proc. (Ser. 2), bdle. 132, no. 42; Chan. Inq. p.m. (Ser. 2), ccccliii, 72.

[28] The manor of 'la Rye' held of John Nanfan is mentioned in 1513, when Christopher Throckmorton of Pendock died seised of it (Chan. Inq. p.m. [Ser. 2], xxix, 92). In 1605–6 it was settled on William Throckmorton and his heirs (Priv. Act, 3 Jas. I, cap. 16).
[29] Feet of F. Worcs. Trin. 1651.
[30] Ibid. Trin. 23 Chas. II.
[31] Burke, *Landed Gentry* (1906).
[32] Ibid. Called of Rye Court in M.I. in churchyard.

[33] Burke, op. cit.
[34] Nash, op. cit. i, 75.
[35] Assize R. 1026, m. 22; *Lay Subs. R. Worcs.* c. 1280 (Worcs. Hist. Soc.), 44.
[36] Add. Chart. 24750; Sloane Chart. (B.M.), xxxiii, 7; Chan. Inq. p.m. 8 Hen. V, no. 29; Pat. 37 Hen. VIII, pt. xii, m. 22; Exch. Dep. Trin. 13 Chas. II, no. 4; Feet of F. Worcs. Mich. 25 Chas. II; Trin. 3 Anne; Mich. 7 Geo. II.

which was subsequently extended westwards and the last bay of the arcade inserted.

The traceried east window of the chancel is of three lights of 15th-century date. In the north and south walls are two-light 14th-century windows, the southern much restored. The north door is partly modern, and in the south wall is a modern credence table. There is no chancel arch.

At the east end of the north wall of the nave is a square-headed low-side window of the squint type. West of this is a lancet window largely restored. The round-headed north door has side shafts with modern scalloped capitals.

The south arcade is of four bays, the first three arches having two chamfered orders. The red and yellow sandstone capitals are of rough and unusual cutting, being either very late in date or earlier capitals recut ; the piers are octagonal. The fourth bay is an extension, the narrow arch springing from the respond which now forms a third pier. The tower arch is of two chamfered orders, without capitals or bases.

The south aisle is lighted by windows of three lights with much restored tracery. The font is circular, with two rows of cable ornament encircling the bowl.

The embattled tower is two stages high, with large diagonal buttresses and a square turret for the newel stair at the north-east corner. The walls are of rubble and the roof is slated.

In 1818 there were four bells, two of which were mediaeval, but now there are only the treble, which is inscribed 'William Clark and William Morlee Churchwardens 1650,' and the tenor, by John Rudhall, 1825.

The plate consists of a standing paten, 1682, a flagon and almsdish given in 1750 and made in the preceding year, a knife engraved with the date 1750 and stamped with a lion passant, and a pewter plate dated 1750.

The registers before 1812 are as follows : (i) mixed entries 1698 to 1744 ; (ii) baptisms and burials 1745 to 1807, marriages 1745 to 1754 ; (iii) baptisms and burials 1808 to 1812 ; (iv) marriages 1754 to 1812.

ADVOWSON The chapel of Berrow was probably built by one of the lords of the manor, as it was said, in the 12th century, to have been built on the land of Robert de Berrow.[37] It was recognized as a chapel of Overbury in 1194, when Bishop Henry assigned a yearly pension of half a mark from the monks of Worcester for the improvement of their diet on certain anniversaries.[38] The lords of Berrow seem to have disputed the subjection of the chapel to Overbury, and claimed the advowson for themselves, for Robert de Berrow, by a charter confirmed by King John, acknowledged that Berrow was a chapelry of Overbury.[39] This acknowledgement is perhaps referred to in the registers of

Worcester Priory under date 1210, when it is stated that the prior received at farm the church of Berrow at a yearly rent of 18 marks.[40] This agreement was disputed by Robert's son Roger in 1224, but judgement was given in favour of the prior. At the same time the Prior of Little Malvern put in a claim to the advowson on the ground that it had been granted to his house by Robert de Berrow, but his claim was also quashed.[41] As a chapel of Overbury it was appropriated with that church in 1330 to the Prior and convent of Worcester.[42] After this time its connexion with Overbury seems to have been to a certain extent severed, and in 1535 the rectory of Berrow was returned as annexed to that of Stoke Prior.[43] At that time the whole of the tithes and glebe seem to have been held by the vicar or perpetual curate, who was appointed by the prior and convent, and made a payment of £7 yearly to them as impropriators.[44]

The rectory and advowson of the vicarage, having passed to the Crown at the Dissolution, were granted by Henry VIII in 1542 to the Dean and Chapter of Worcester.[45] This grant was confirmed by James I,[46] and the dean and chapter still hold the patronage, the Ecclesiastical Commissioners, to whom their estates were transferred in 1859, being now impropriators of the tithes.[46a]

The perpetual curacy of Berrow was a peculiar benefice, the Dean and Chapter of Worcester having concurrent jurisdiction with the chancellor in proving wills. It was visited by the bishop in his triennial visitation, and by the official of the dean and chapter in other years, but was exempt from archidiaconal jurisdiction.[47]

The Dean and Chapter of Worcester apparently claimed a rectorial manor at Berrow, for in the middle of the 17th century they held a court leet there.[48] The rectory and the mansion-house belonging to it were sold by the Parliamentary Trustees in 1651 to Henry Perkins.[49]

In 1656 a dispute came before the Court of Exchequer about the tithes and fee of the glebe lands in the parish which Henry Perkins had sold to John Woodley, yeoman, for three years.[50] Prattinton, writing about 1820, said that 'the late Mr. Boulter, of Welland, brother of the present, bought the great tithes.'[51] The tenant of the rectory, according to Nash, was bound to repair the chancel and the three bridges, Westbridge, Farley Bridge and Old Strike Bridge,[52] one of which was said to be out of repair in 1634.[53]

CHARITIES In 1743 Susannah Cocks Nanfan by will, devised a rent-charge of 40s. yearly issuing out of Upper Summers in Berrow. The income is applied in accordance with the scheme of the Charity Commissioners 6 November 1906, as to 10s. yearly to the vicar for a sermon on the first Sunday in February in each year, and the residue in coal to the poor.

[37] Habington, op. cit. i, 130.
[38] Prattinton Coll. (Soc. Antiq.), Deeds of D. and C. of Worc. no. 314 ; and see Overbury.
[39] Habington, loc. cit.; Cur. Reg R. 86, m. 11.
[40] Ann. Mon. (Rolls Ser.), iv, 399.
[41] Cur. Reg. R. 86, m. 11 ; Hale, Reg. of Worc. Priory (Camd. Soc.), 76b et seq. ; Ann. Mon. (Rolls Ser.), iv, 416.
[42] Cal. Pat. 132 -30, p. 536.
[43] Valor Eccl. (Rec. Com.), iii, 225.
[44] Ibid. 246.
[45] Pat. 33 Hen. VIII, pt. v, m. 19.
[46] Ibid. 6 Jas. I, pt. xii, no. 2.
[46a] Inform. by the Rev. H. E. Casey, vicar of Berrow.
[47] Valor Eccl. (Rec. Com.), iii, 512.
[48] Habington, op. cit. i, 126.
[49] Close, 1651, pt. xlix, no. 37.
[50] Exch. Dep. Hil. 1656-7, no. 3.
[51] Prattinton Coll. (Soc. Antiq.).
[52] op. cit. i, 75.
[53] Quarter Sess. R. (Worcs. Hist. Soc.), pt. ii, 568.

The parish has long been in possession of land known as the Poor's Land, consisting of 8 a., producing £10 8s. yearly, which is distributed in coal to the poor.

There are about 3½ acres belonging to the church, which produce £9 11s. 8d. yearly ; £5 is paid as the salary of the church clerk and the remainder is applied to church expenses.

BISHAMPTON

Bisantune[1] (xi cent.) ; Byshampton, Bihampton (xiii cent.) ; Bissehamton (xvi cent.).

The parish of Bishampton lies in the south-eastern part of the county of Worcester. It is bounded on the north by Whitsun Brook, which ultimately runs into the River Avon, and is divided on the east from Church Lench by some wooded hills 300 ft. above the ordnance datum. These hills form the highest part of the parish, the north and east being at about 100 ft. above the ordnance datum. The area of the parish is 1,910 acres ; 1,032 are arable, 733 acres are permanent grass, and 32 are woods.[1a] The soil is chiefly marl clay and the subsoil partly Lower Lias and partly Keuper Marl. The chief crops are wheat, beans, barley, turnips and garden produce.

The chief roads are Gunning Lane, running west, and Broad Lane, running east, from the village of Bishampton,[2] and a third road on which the village lies running due south through the parish to Fladbury.

The village is situated about 9 miles south-east of Worcester, some distance to the south of the Alcester and Stratford road. It is grouped along a by-road running from north to south with the church at the north end. The small half-timber farm-houses and cottages of which the settlement is composed combine to invest it with a picturesque and old-world air. The Manor Farm to the south-west of the church is a half-timber house, dating probably from the early 17th century, covered with rough-cast and modernized. Attached to a farm and fronting on the road is a fine timber barn, weather-boarded and standing on a sandstone base. On the east side of the village street is a good half-timber house of the early 17th century, two stories in height, with a tiled roof, showing the ornamental timbering characteristic of the period. The gabled end wings have richly carved barge-boards, and in the gable of the southern wing is the date 1629 ; the figures are obviously modern work, though probably copied from an older inscription. Hayes Farm, at the lower end of the village on the east side of the road, is a small rectangular building of half-timber of the late 16th century. The chimney stacks are surmounted by brick shafts of the intersecting diagonal type. Pebworth House, to the south of Hayes Farm and upon the same side of the road, is a modernized house now faced with brick, but still preserving a fine stone chimney stack of the late 16th century with shafts of brick. To the south of Pebworth House is a 17th-century H-shaped house faced with brick and having an elaborately panelled chimney stack of the same material on the north.

On the gable at this end is the date 1689 with the initials F. G.

An Inclosure Act for Bishampton was passed in 1795,[3] and the award is dated 1797.[4]

Seven *cassata* of land at BISHAMP-*MANORS TON* are said to have been given by King Edgar to the church of Worcester.[5] It is more probable, however, that Bishampton was in early times part of the manor of Fladbury, and came into the possession of the monastery when Fladbury was given to them.[6] In 1086 it was part of the manor of Fladbury, and one of the manors into which the parish afterwards became divided was held of the manor of Fladbury at least as late as 1419,[7] and probably later, as the overlordship of the Bishop of Worcester was recognized until 1525.[8]

At the date of the Domesday Survey the bishop's under-tenant at Bishampton was Roger de Lacy.[9] He was banished for his share in the rebellion against William Rufus, and his forfeited estates were bestowed on his brother Hugh de Lacy, who was the owner in 1108–18.[10] He died without male issue, and his estates passed to his two sisters.

Gilbert son of the second sister Emma assumed the name Lacy, and Roger de Lacy's interest in the manor passed in the Lacy family until the death of Walter de Lacy in 1241. The overlordship of Bishampton, which was attached to Weobly Castle, was assigned to Margery wife of John de Verdon, one of the granddaughters and co-heirs of Walter Lacy,[11] and passed from her to her son and grandson Theobald de Verdon. The last-named Theobald died without male issue in 1316,[12] and this fee was assigned in 1335–6 to one of his daughters, Elizabeth

LACY. *Quarterly or and gules a bend sable and a label argent.*

VERDON. *Or fretty gules.*

wife of Bartholomew de Burghersh.[13] Her son Bartholomew was succeeded by a daughter, Elizabeth

---

[1] This, the Domesday spelling of the name, is one of the very rare cases in which the scribes copied the old English form in the original return (inform. from Mr. F. M. Stenton).

[1a] Statistics from Bd. of Agric. (1905).

[2] In 1901 there were 83 houses and 340 inhabitants in the parish (*Census of Engl. and Wales*, 1901, *Worcs.* 23).

[3] Priv. Act, 35 Geo. III, cap. 4.

[4] *Blue Bk. Incl. Awards*, 188.

[5] Dugdale, *Mon. Angl.* i, 582 ; Heming, *Chartul.* (ed. Hearne), 583.

[6] See under Fladbury.

[7] *Testa de Nevill* (Rec. Com.), 41 ; Chan. Inq. p.m. 7 Hen. V, no. 57.

[8] Chan. Inq. p.m. (Ser. 2), xliii, 70.

[9] *V.C.H. Worcs.* i, 290b. These 10 hides were liable for service by land and water (see ibid. 249).

[10] Ibid. 324a ; Burke, *Extinct Peerage*.

[11] *Excerpta e Rot. Fin.* (Rec. Com.), i, 446.

[12] *Cal. Inq. p.m.* 10–20 Edw. II, 38.

[13] Ibid. 1–9 Edw. III, 496.

wife of Edward le Despenser, and Edward was holding the fee in her right at the time of his death, about 1375.[14] The Lacys' interest in the manor seems to have lapsed after this time.

Two Frenchmen were holding Bishampton of Roger de Lacy in 1086, and the parish remained divided into two manors until the 17th century. Half the parish, 5 hides, was held by the Pichard family,[15] tenants under the Lacys in the neighbouring manor of Kington and in various estates in Herefordshire. John Pichard held Bishampton about 1182 as mesne lord under Hugh de Lacy,[16] and as at Kington his interest passed to Philip ap Howel.[17]

As at Kington the Pipard family held Bishampton under the Pichards. Robert Pipard was the tenant towards the end of the 12th century under John Pichard.[18] A Robert Pipard held the manor for the service of a knight's fee at the beginning of the 13th century.[19] At this point the manor seems to have been divided, part passing with Kington to Guy Pipard and part to William Pipard, who may have been a younger brother of Guy.[20] The latter seems to have been involved in financial difficulties, for in 1237 his manor of Bishampton was valued as a preliminary to the settlement of debts which he owed to David of Oxford, a Jew.[21] Guy's manor passed with that of Kington to his daughters, thus becoming vested in the Kardiff and Somery families.[22]

Henry de Somery was dealing with land in Bishampton in 1275,[23] and the manor had passed before 1297–8 to Robert de Somery.[24] Roger de Somery of Bishampton is mentioned in 1313,[25] and Richard de Somery held land there in 1315–16.[26] Robert de Somery endowed a chantry with land at Bishampton in 1320–1.[27] It was probably the same Robert who in 1333 settled the manor on himself and his wife Sibyl with reversion to Thomas de Somery and Julia his wife and their heirs, with contingent remainder to the heirs of Robert.[28] Robert died before 1337, when Thomas son of Thomas de Somery granted to the Abbot of Pershore a rent of 10 marks for the life of Sibyl widow of Robert de Somery.[29] Thomas de Somery of Bishampton obtained in the following year a grant of the bailiwick of the hundred of Oswalds-

SOMERY. *Sable a bend between six martlets argent.*

low.[30] Thomas de Somery appears to have been lord of the manor in 1340,[31] but it had passed before 1356 to Thomas de Lyttelton,[32] who was holding it in 1363 in right of his wife Julia.[33] She is said to have been a daughter of Robert de Somery.[34] It was probably the Lytteltons' manor at Bishampton which was held in 1411–12 by William Bryan and Margery his wife in her right and conveyed by them in that year to Alice wife of Sir Richard Stury,[35] who in 1412 gave it to the chantry which she had founded at Hampton Lovett.[36] At the Dissolution of the chantries this manor passed to the Crown and was granted in 1549 to John Cupper and Richard Trevor.[37] They immediately sold the manor to Henry Jones and Adam Lutley, who were evidently trustees for Sir John Pakington.[38] In the following year Sir John settled this manor on his daughter Ursula and her husband William Scudamore.[39] The manor then followed the same descent as Church Lench (q.v.) until the death of Sir William Keyt in 1741.[40] His son and successor Sir Thomas Charles Keyt[41] sold the manor in 1753 to Sir Dudley Ryder.[42] He died in 1756 and was succeeded by his son Nathaniel Ryder, who was created Lord Harrowby in 1776.[43] On the death of the latter in 1803 his son Dudley[44] succeeded. He was created Viscount Sandon and Earl of Harrowby

RYDER, Earl of Harrowby. *Azure three crescents or with an ermine tail upon each.*

in 1809[45] and died in 1847, being succeeded by his son Dudley second Earl of Harrowby,[46] who sold the manor of Bishampton to the Duc d'Aumale about 1862. From him it passed to the Duc d'Orleans, who sold it in 1912 to Sir Charles Swinfen Eady.

The Kardiffs' moiety of the manor passed in the same way as Kington to William son of Paul de Kardiff, who succeeded to the estate in 1315.[47] It possibly passed from his descendants to the Somervilles in the same way as Kington, though little is known of their tenure of the manor. William Somerville of Aston Somerville was dealing with land at Bishampton in 1429–30,[48] and in 1561 John Somerville held 'the manor of Bishampton.'[49] At the time of his attainder in 1583 John Somerville was in possession of land in Bishampton which was parcel of the manor of Kington.[50] There is no further trace of this estate.

[14] Chan. Inq. p.m. 49 Edw. III, pt. ii, no. 46.
[15] Red Bk. of Bishopric of Worc. (Eccl. Com. Rec. Var. bdle. 121, no. 43698), fol. 253. [16] Nash, op. cit. i, 88.
[17] Cal. Inq. p.m. 1–9 Edw. II, 37; 10–20 Edw. II, 38; 1–9 Edw. III, 496, 284.
[18] Red Bk. of Bishopric of Worc. fol. 253; Habington, *Surv. of Worcs.* (Worcs. Hist. Soc.), i, 226, 227.
[19] *Testa de Nevill* (Rec. Com.), 41.
[20] For the descent of this part of the manor see below.
[21] *Cal. Close*, 1234–7, p. 467.
[22] See Kington in Halfshire Hundred. Red Bk. of Bishopric of Worc. fol. 68.
[23] *Abbrev. Plac.* (Rec. Com.), 188b.
[24] Add. MS. 28024, fol. 148.
[25] *Cal. Pat.* 1313–17, p. 74.

[26] Habington, op. cit. i, 58.
[27] *Abbrev. Rot. Orig.* (Rec. Com.), i, 258.
[28] Feet of F. Worcs. 7 Edw. III, no. 4.
[29] *Cal. Close*, 1337–9, p. 145.
[30] *Cal. Pat.* 1338–40, p. 90.
[31] Worc. Epis. Reg. Wulstan Bransford (1339–49), fol. 37 d.
[32] Ibid. Brian (1352–61), fol. 19 d.
[33] Feet of F. Worcs. East. 37 Edw. III.
[34] Burke, *Extinct Baronetage*, 314.
[35] Feet of F. Worcs. Trin. 13 Hen. IV.
[36] *Cal. Pat.* 1408–13, p. 450.
[37] Pat. 3 Edw. VI, pt. vi. This grant included the capital messuage called the Ferme Place and a water-mill, and many fields and closes whose names are given in the grant.
[85] Add. MS. 31314, fol. 190.
[39] Chan. Inq. p.m. (Ser. 2), cxxvi, 82.

[40] For references see Church Lench and Feet of F. Div. Co. Hil. 13 Will. III; Recov. R. Mich. 8 Anne, rot. 266; East. 15 Geo. II, rot. 252.
[41] G.E.C. *Complete Baronetage*, iii, 141.
[42] Feet of F. Worcs. Trin. 26 & 27 Geo. II.
[43] G.E.C. *Complete Peerage*, iv, 175.
[44] Ibid. Dudley Ryder seems to have held the manor before his father's death, for he was dealing with it in 1795 (Recov. R. Trin. 35 Geo. III, rot. 204).
[45] G.E.C. *Complete Peerage*, iv, 175.
[46] Ibid.
[47] *Cal. Inq. p.m.* 1–9 Edw. II, 372; Habington, op. cit. i, 227.
[48] Habington, op. cit. ii, 260.
[49] Recov. R. Mich. 3 & 4 Eliz. rot. 1160.
[50] Misc. Bks. Ld. Rev. Rec. ccxxviii, fol. 296.

The other part of the Pipards' manor was apparently held by William Pipard in 1234 and 1240–1.[51] It was, perhaps, this estate which was sold in 1313–14 as land at Bishampton by William son of Cecily Pipard, kinsman and one of the heirs of Robert Pipard, to Guy de Beauchamp Earl of Warwick.[52] At the same date Alexander de Ston-ington, another co-heir of Robert Pipard, released all his right in the manor to the earl, who assigned part of the capital messuage of Bishamp-ton as dower to the above-mentioned Cecily, who was the widow of Robert Pipard.[53] Guy Earl of Warwick died seised of this estate, then called the manor of Bishampton, in 1315.[54] It is uncertain whether this estate remained in the possession of the Earls of Warwick or whether it is to be identified with a knight's fee at Bishampton held in 1346 by William de Shobdon, and described as 'late of Robert Pipard.'[55] Thomas Earl of Warwick at the time of his attainder in 1396 was in possession of land in Bishampton which was granted in 1397 to Thomas Lyttelton.[56] William de Shobdon had ac-quired some land at Bishampton in 1331–2 of Nicholas de Wyshaw and his wife Agnes, who seem to have held it in her right.[57] He was dealing with land at Bishampton in 1352,[58] and his son Thomas was holding land there in 1374.[59] In 1411 Thomas son of Thomas de Shobdon paid 53s. 4d. to the barony of Elmley for land in Bishampton,[60] and in 1480 Thomas son of Thomas Sheldon (sic) paid rent to Elmley Castle for this land.[61]

BEAUCHAMP, Earl of Warwick. *Gules a fesse between six crosslets or.*

It was perhaps this estate which as the manor of Bis-hampton was held of the Bishop of Worcester in 1500–1 by Robert Throckmorton.[62] Thomas Throckmorton is said to have sold his land at Bis-hampton in 1594–5,[63] but Thomas Throckmorton died in 1615 holding rents from land in Bishampton,[64] and Habington, writing about the middle of the 17th century, states that Mr. Throck-

THROCKMORTON. *Gules a cheveron argent with three gimel bars sable thereon.*

morton held land there,[65] and Sir John Throckmorton in 1795 was holding certain quit-rents, heriots and services from land at Bishampton, due at his court of Throckmorton.[66]

The other manor at Bishampton was held under the Lacys by the family of Ferches or Furches, who were perhaps descendants of the second Frenchman who held of Roger de Lacy in 1086. The Lacys' overlordship seems to have lapsed before the beginning of the 13th century, the manor being held of the Bishop of Worcester as of the manor of Fladbury.[67] Herbert de Furches held it about 1182 as 5 hides under Hugh de Lacy,[68] and later it passed to Walter de Furches.[69] William de Furches held the manor at the beginning of the 13th century.[70] He had in 1200 succeeded his uncle Robert de Furches at Kings-ton in Herefordshire, and possibly also in this manor.[71] William or a descendant of that name was living in 1278,[72] but seems to have been suc-ceeded before 1290 by his grandson Fulk de Lucy.[73]

His grandson William Lucy owned a knight's fee in 1346,[74] and was succeeded by his son Thomas, who in his turn was followed by his son William.[75] This William was succeeded by his son Thomas Lucy,[76] who died in 1415–16, having settled the manor of Bishamp-ton on his brother William Lucy and his heirs.[77] William granted a third part of the manor to Alice, Thomas Lucy's widow, as her dower. William Lucy died in 1419, and Alice, who had married as her second husband Richard Archer, died in the following year. Both were succeeded by William Lucy, the son of Thomas and nephew of William.[78] This William Lucy was the owner in 1428,[79] and died in 1466, being succeeded by his son William.[80] He was created a knight of the Bath at the coronation of the queen of Henry VII,[81] and died in 1492, being succeeded by his son Edmund Lucy,[82] who in his turn was followed in 1495–6 by his son Thomas Lucy.[83] Thomas was knighted in 1512 by Henry VIII,[84] and died in 1525.[85] There was some objection taken to the way his will was administered and to his title to the manor of Bishampton,[86] which he had left to his son William Lucy.[87] Ultimately his grandson Thomas Lucy sold the manor of Bishampton to

LUCY. *Gules three luces rising argent.*

[51] *Cal. Pat.* 1232–47, p. 58; Feet of F. Worcs. East. 25 Hen. III.
[52] Add. MS. 28024, fol. 122 d.
[53] Ibid. fol. 123.
[54] *Cal. Inq. p.m.* 1–9 *Edw. II*, 411.
[55] *Lay Subs. R. Worcs.* 1346 (Worcs. Hist. Soc.), 24, 25. The name is errone-ously given as William Pipard in the *Feudal Aids* (v, 308).
[56] *Cal. Pat.* 1396–9, pp. 278, 280.
[57] Feet of F. Worcs. Mich. 5 Edw. III.
[58] Deeds relating to Bishampton in the possession of Mr. O. G. Knapp.
[59] Ibid.
[60] Add. R. 25962.
[61] Duchy of Lanc. Mins. Accts. bdle. 645, no. 10461.
[62] Chan. Inq. p.m. (Ser. 2), xiv, 6.
[63] Prattinton Coll. (Soc. Antiq.).
[64] Chan. Inq. p.m. (Ser. 2), ccclxvii, 100.

[65] Habington, op. cit. i, 57.
[66] Priv. Act, 35 Geo. III, cap. 4.
[67] See above.
[68] Red Bk. of Bishopric of Worc. fol. 253.
[69] Ibid.
[70] *Testa de Nevill* (Rec. Com.), 41.
[71] *Rot. de Oblatis et Fin.* (Rec. Com.), 77.
[72] *Abbrev. Plac.* (Rec. Com.), 195.
[73] Wrottesley, *Pedigrees from Plea R.* 51. In 1290 Philip Hacket died seised of land in Bishampton held of Fulk de Lucy (Chan. Inq. p.m. 18 Edw. I, no. 71). Fulk was holding part of the manor of Bishampton in 1297–8, and at the same time John Lovett had some estate there (Add. MS. 28024, fol. 148).
[74] *Feud. Aids*, v, 308. In the Lay Subsidy Roll of 1327 William Lucy is set down as the largest taxpayer in Bis-

hampton (p. 6). Dugdale, *Hist. of Warw.* 504; Wrottesley, loc. cit.
[75] *Visit. of Warw.* (Harl. Soc.), 287.
[76] Dugdale, *Hist. of Warw.* 504.
[77] Chan. Inq. p.m. 7 Hen. V, no. 57.
[78] Ibid. 8 Hen. V, no. 69.
[79] *Feud. Aids*, v, 319.
[80] Chan. Inq. p.m. 6 Edw. IV, no. 30.
[81] Shaw, *Knights of Engl.* i, 142.
[82] *Cal. Inq. p.m. Hen. VII*, i, 359. Edmund Lucy had held a court at Bishamp-ton in 1483 (Ct. R. [P.R.O.], portf. 210, no. 18). He was knighted in 1503 (Shaw, op. cit. ii, 33).
[83] Chan. Inq. p.m. (Ser. 2), xix, 29.
[84] Shaw, op. cit. ii, 35.
[85] Chan. Inq. p.m. (Ser. 2), xliii, 70.
[86] *L. and P. Hen. VIII*, iv (1), 1618.
[87] Chan. Inq. p.m. (Ser. 2), xliii, 70.

Francis Walshe in 1561.[88] Richard son of Francis was succeeded by two daughters, Anne wife of Sir Thomas Bromley, and Joyce wife of Sir Roland Cotton,[89] who with their mother Katherine, then wife of Roger Palmer, and their uncle Edmund Walshe sold the manor in 1615 to William Keyt,[90] who bought the other portion of the manor from Sir John Scudamore in 1627. The descent of the manor then follows that of the manor of Bishampton first described (q.v.), and Sir Charles Swinfen Eady is now owner.

There was a mill worth 12d. at Bishampton in 1086.[91] It appears to have passed with a moiety of the manor to the chantry of Hampton Lovett, and is mentioned in 1549 as a late possession of the chantry.[92] There is no mill in the parish at the present day.

The 12th-century north door, now blocked, has a round head, but has been rebuilt. To the west of it is a single-light window with some remains of original 12th-century work. The first and third windows on the south, which are almost entirely modern, have tracery of 14th-century character in 14th-century style, and between them is a restored round-headed light of the 12th-century type.

The south door of the nave has a round head and shafted external jambs, with scalloped capitals, mostly original 12th-century work. The porch is modern.

The large tower forms the only portion of the church not rebuilt in 1870. It is of three stages, with angle buttresses of four offsets and an embattled parapet finished with modern pinnacles at the angles. The tower arch is of two orders, and the west window of the ground stage is of three lights with vertical

BISHAMPTON CHURCH FROM THE SOUTH-WEST

CHURCH The church of *ST. JAMES* consists of a chancel with vestry, nave, south porch and a western tower. It appears to preserve the plan of a 12th-century building, to which a western tower was added c. 1400. The nave and chancel were, however, completely rebuilt in 1870, the stonework of the doors and windows being re-used where possible.

The modern east window of the chancel is of three lights, with tracery in the style of the 14th century. At the north-east is a single trefoiled light reset. The easternmost window of the south wall is a single trefoiled light with a deep reveal on both faces. Some of the stones appear to be old. The two westernmost windows in the wall are modern. The chancel arch is entirely modern. In the nave the first and second windows on the north are largely modern restorations.

tracery above. Each face of the belfry has a window of two lights, with a quatrefoil above. The southern has a sanctus bell, hung between the mullion and the western jamb, and below this window is another, with a plain single light. The belfry stair occupies the south-west angle of the tower. The circular bowl to the font is of the late 12th century, with roses, crosses and stars forming a band round the edge; the stem is modern.

The bells are six in number, inscribed as follows: the treble, 'Feare God, Honour the King 1690 Gulielmus Keyt Baronet Hujus Maneris 1690'; the second, the churchwardens' names 1690; the third, 'William Grimet 1690'; the fourth, 'William Bagley made me 1690'; the fifth, 'R. Sanders made me 1690'; the tenor, 'Fear God Honour yᵉ King 1690.' The sanctus bell has no inscription and is

[88] Chan. Inq. p.m. (Ser. 2), xciv, 89; Feet of F. Worcs. East. 3 Eliz.; Com. Pleas D. Enr. Hil. 3 Eliz. m. 9 d.

[89] Feet of F. Div. Co. Mich. 29 & 30 Eliz.; Recov. R. Mich. 40 Eliz. rot. 136.

[90] Close, 13 Jas. I, pt. xix, no. 12.
[91] *V.C.H. Worcs.* i, 291a.
[92] Pat. 3 Edw. VI, pt. vi.

of modern form. Till recently a muffled peal was rung commemorating the execution of Charles I.

The plate consists of a cup and cover paten made in 1778, inscribed 'John Windle A.M. Vicar,' with the churchwardens' names ; an interesting paten, shell shaped, with two flat handles and repoussé work which is inscribed ' I.W. 1684.' There are also a small modern silver flagon, almsdishes and a pewter plate.

The registers are as follows : (i) bound in a parchment volume, mixed entries from 1599 to 1667 ; (ii) 1668 to 1693 ; (iii) 1694 to 1738 ; (iv) 1738 to 1811, the marriage entries ceasing at 1754, when a printed marriage book begins extending to 1812.

ADVOWSON   There was a priest and possibly a church at Bishampton in 1086.[93]
The advowson evidently belonged to the Pipards' manor, for Robert de Somery presented in 1286 and 1290,[94] and in 1293–4 made an agreement with William de Kardiff and his wife Ivetta, co-heir of Guy Pipard, by which Somery and Kardiff were to present alternately, William and Ivetta making the first presentation.[95] It would seem, however, that a subsequent agreement must have vested the advowson in the Somerys, for it passed with their manor of Bishampton [96] until 1325–6, when Robert de Somery obtained licence to grant it to the nunnery of Cookhill.[97] The conveyance does not seem to have been completed until 1329.[98] The church was appropriated to the priory in 1331 [99] and the vicarage ordained in 1359.[100] For licence to appropriate the church the nuns undertook to pay the Bishop of Worcester 1 mark yearly.[1] The church of Bishampton remained appropriate to the priory of Cookhill until the Dissolution,[2] when it passed to the Crown. The advowson and rectory were granted in 1558 by Queen Mary to Richard Pates, Bishop of Worcester.[3] Pates was deprived on the accession of Elizabeth, but the rectory of Bishampton was granted to his successor Edwin Sandys in 1561.[4] Since this date the presentations to the church of Bishampton have always been made by the Bishop of Worcester with two exceptions, one in 1638, when Maurice Hiller presented, being patron in right of his wife, for one turn only, and the other in 1662, when the Crown presented,[5] the see of Worcester being vacant.

Bishampton appears at one time to have been a chapelry of Fladbury. In 1286 a composition was made between the rectors of Fladbury and Bishampton as to the profits of the chapel of Bishampton, and as a result the mortuaries of Bishampton were divided between the two rectors.[6]

A chantry of the Blessed Virgin in the parish church of Bishampton was founded by Robert de Somery in 1321, when he gave two messuages and lands and 20s. rent in Bishampton for that purpose.[7] The advowson descended with the Somerys' manor to Thomas Lyttelton,[8] and appears to have passed with it as the 'advowson of the church of the manor' to Alice Stury.[9] She must have conferred it upon the chantry of Hampton Lovett, for the chantry priests presented in 1424 and 1462.[10] The chantry was valued at the Dissolution at 40s. 2d.,[11] and was granted to John Cupper and Richard Trevor with the manor of Bishampton,[12] and afterwards passed with the manor to John Pakington.

There were 2 acres of arable land worth 8d. a year at Bishampton, given for the maintenance of certain lights.[13] This estate was granted in 1611 to Francis Morice and Francis Phillips.[14]

There is a Baptist mission chapel in the town of Bishampton in connexion with Pershore.[15]

CHARITIES   The charities subsisting in this parish are administered together, comprising the following, namely :—

Mrs. Mary Wallbank, mentioned on the church table, trust fund, £19 12s. 7d. consols ;

James Clarke, will, 1825, trust fund, £152 4s. 10d. consols.

Miss Phoebe Porter, will, proved at London 12 March 1861, trust fund, £333 6s. 8d. consols ; Miss Anne Porter, will, proved at London 27 March 1877, trust fund, £166 13s. 4d. consols.

The several sums of stock are held by the official trustees, producing in annual dividends £16 15s. 8d., which, together with the rents of the Poor's Land, containing 2 a. 1 r. 10 p., and of two cottages, called Babylon, producing about £10 a year, are applied in the distribution of articles in kind, chiefly in coal, clothing being given at Christmas to children attending the parish school in respect of Anne Porter's charity.

The Church Lands, consisting of about 4 a., are applicable for the repair of the church. This charity and the Poor's Land were recorded by an inscription on the gallery of the church.

BLOCKLEY

Bloccanleah (ix cent.); Blochlei (xi cent.); Blocclea (xii cent.) ; Blockelegh (xiii cent.).

The parish of Blockley, containing nearly 7,896 acres, of which 2,360 are arable, 4,128 permanent grass and 290½ woods and plantations,[1] lies among the Cotswolds to the north of Bourton-on-the-Hill,

---

93 *V.C.H. Worcs.* i, 291a.

94 *Reg. G. Giffard* (Worcs. Hist. Soc.), 287, 381.

95 Feet of F. Worcs. 22 Edw. I, no. 35.

96 *Reg. G. Giffard* (Worcs. Hist. Soc.), 537 ; *Ginsborough*, 135.

97 Inq. a.q.d. file 188, no. 4 ; Pat. 19 Edw. II, pt. ii, m. 13 ; Worc. Epis. Reg. Orlton (1327–33), ii, fol. 45 f.

98 Feet of F. Worcs. 3 Edw. III, no. 17 ; De Banco R. 278, m. 135.

99 Worc. Epis. Reg. Orlton (1327–33), i, fol. 23.

100 Ibid. Brian (1352–61), fol. 91 d.

1 Ibid.

2 *Valor Eccl.* (Rec. Com.), iii, 263.

3 Pat. 5 & 6 Phil. and Mary, pt. ii, m. 30.   4 Ibid. 4 Eliz. pt. vi.

5 Inst. Bks. (P.R.O.).

6 Nash, op. cit. i, 89 ; *Reg. G. Giffard* (Worcs. Hist. Soc.), 287.

7 *Cal. Pat.* 1317–21, p. 594 ; Worc. Epis. Reg. Cobham (1317–27), fol. 46 ; Inq. a.q.d. file 142, no. 20.

8 Worc. Epis. Reg. Cobham (1317–27), fol. 121 d. ; Orlton (1327–33), i, fol. 21 ; Bransford (1339–49), i (2), fol. 37 d. ; Brian (1352–61), fol. 19 d., 22 d.

9 Feet of F. Worcs. Trin. 13 Hen. IV.

10 Worc. Epis. Reg. Morgan (1419–25), fol. 26 d. ; Carpenter (1443–76), i, fol. 174.

11 Chant. Cert. 25, no. 18 ; 60, no. 27 ; 61, no. 23. In 1535 Henry Moore, rector of the church of Bredicot, held this chantry in augmentation of his rectory (*Valor Eccl.* [Rec. Com.], iii, 236).

12 Pat. 3 Edw. VI, pt. vi.

13 Chant. Cert. 60, no. 68.

14 Pat. 9 Jas. I, pt. ii.

15 *Baptist Handbook*, 1912.

1 Statistics from Bd. of Agric. (1905).

and is entirely surrounded by Gloucestershire and Warwickshire. The soil is light and fertile ; the subsoil is inferior oolite with beds of bunter pebble and Middle Lias ; the chief crops are cereals and beans, and there is much pasture for the famous Cotswold sheep. Stone quarries have been a feature of the parish since the 14th century : Norcombe Quarry and Blockley Quarries are mentioned as early as 1383[2] and White Quarry in 1506.[3]

The parish includes the hamlets of Aston Magna, Ditchford, Dorn, Draycott, Northwick and Paxford.

The village of Blockley lies in the south-west part of the parish on two hill-slopes and has a station nearly 2 miles away on the Great Western railway. The church stands at the top of the lower slope and adjoining the churchyard to the south is the old manor-house, built of native stone well weathered and stained with orange lichen. It is a good example of the local architecture of the early 17th century, though most of the window openings have been enlarged and sash windows inserted. A wide lawn stretches from the south-western front of the house to the edge of the slope where a flight of stone steps leads down to the lower garden overlooking the stream which runs through Dovedale Plantation. The majority of the houses in the village are of stone and date from the 16th and 17th centuries. The road to Chipping Camden skirts the edge of Northwick Park, whence a beautiful view of the country may be seen. The park stretches to the northern boundary of the parish and contains many fine trees, especially beeches and oaks ; there is a large herd of fallow deer, and the two pools—Northwick River and Upper Water—are well stocked with trout. The house was rebuilt about 1730 by Sir John Rushout, who, however, retained as much as possible of the appearance of the Elizabethan house which had belonged to the Childes. The west front is early Georgian. There is still a fine collection of pictures, though the great Northwick collection was moved to Thirlstane House, Cheltenham, and sold in 1859.

Upton Wold Farm lies about a mile due west of Blockley, near the Five Mile Drive, the main road to Broadway, which crosses the Buckle Street about a mile and a half north-west of the parish boundary. It is a 16th-century three-storied house of stone rubble masonry with ashlar quoins. The triple-gabled entrance front, with its central porch, extending the whole height of the building, is an excellent example of the symmetrical type of design which was beginning to prevail at the period of its erection. The outer doorway of the porch has a Tudor arch and the transomed windows of the ground floor are of five lights divided by stone mullions. The two upper floors are lighted by windows of three lights, those of the first floor being transomed. The chimney stacks are surmounted by diagonal shafts. The east side has been lately restored.

The hamlet of Aston is situated about 2 miles east of Blockley. The houses are mostly of stone, and many appear to be of the 16th and 17th centuries, and with their gabled roofs and stone-mullioned windows present a very picturesque appearance.

The railway now cuts the village in two, the greater portion of the houses being on the west side of the railway, while the church stands on the east side. The original chapel stands to the south-west of the present building and has been converted, probably at some time in the 17th century, into a pair of cottages, one occupying the chancel, which measures externally 22½ ft. by 17½ ft., and the other the nave, 24½ ft. by 22 ft. The building appears to date from the latter part of the 12th century. The only original detail remaining is the chancel arch, which is now blocked and partly concealed by a later chimney-breast. Enough is revealed, however, to show that the arch is two-centred and had shafted jambs with scalloped capitals and grooved and chamfered abaci. At the western end of the south wall of the nave is a blocked doorway, and all the window openings are later work. At the junction of the road leading from the main part of the village southwards past the church with the by-road leading eastwards over the railway are the base and part of the stem of a cross, probably of 14th-century date. On the west side of the railway line are some recently established brick and terra cotta works, to the influence of which is probably due a glaringly inharmonious row of red brick cottages which have just sprung into existence in the main street.

Draycott is north-east of Blockley village.

The hamlet of Paxford, which is in the extreme north of the parish on a hill overlooking the railway line, consists of a main street of plain stone houses. The school, built in 1866, is used for church services. Paxford House is of stone, partly old, with mullioned windows and a gable at either end. Upper Ditchford Farm, a 17th-century house of brick, stands to the north of Aston Magna, not far from Knee Brook.

Dorn is situated on the west side of the Fosse Way, which here forms the eastern boundary of the parish. It is traditionally the site of a Roman station, and coins and pottery have been found near Dorn Farm ; evidences of stone foundations have also been noticed, but these are not uncovered. Here, built into the outbuildings of an early 17th-century house, is a portion of the south wall of a 12th-century chapel. The masonry is of small rubble with wide joints and the original detail *in situ* comprises a small round-headed window, glazed, a square-headed window, a doorway with a wood lintel and a small ogee-headed light. These, with the exception of the first, are all blocked.

The following place-names occur in local records : Redlaund[4] (xiii cent.) ; Longehens House, Germyns[5] (xv cent.) ; Shipley Close, where the fairs were held,[6] Stapenhill, Cronynge, Crawe Meadow[7] (xvi cent.) ; Lady Homb, Chappell Ground, Dalby's Ditch,[8] Mapphale, Darton Hill and Callsham Cradles[9] (xvii cent.).

Leave to inclose a common leading from Blockley to Bourton-on-the-Hill was granted to Sir William Juxon, bart., in 1669, on condition that he made a road for travellers in his own grounds.[10] An Inclosure Act for Aston Magna was passed in 1733,[11] and for Blockley, Draycott and Paxford in 1772.[12]

---

[2] Mins. Accts. (Eccl. Com. Rec.), 92007.

[3] Ibid. 92009.

[4] Feet of F. Worcs. Hil. 38 Hen. III.

[5] Mins. Accts. (Eccl. Com. Rec.), 92008.

'Germyns' had been held in 1383 by William Germyn (ibid. 92007).

[6] Ibid. 92009.

[7] Pat. 30 Eliz. pt. iv, m. 20.

[8] Add. MS. 36645, fol. 152.

[9] Pat. 10 Chas. I, pt. xvi, no. 20.

[10] Cal. S. P. Dom. 1668–9, p. 390 ; 1672, p. 259.

[11] Priv. Act, 6 Geo. II, cap. 8.

[12] Ibid. 12 Geo. III, cap. 107.

BLOCKLEY MANOR HOUSE FROM THE SOUTH-WEST

MANORS Burhred, King of the Mercians, granted a monastery at Blockley in 855 to Aelhun, Bishop of Worcester, who paid 300 *solidi* of silver for it. Liberties of an archaic kind were granted with the estate to the bishop.[13] This gift was confirmed in the grant of the hundred of Oswaldslow to the church of Worcester made by the so-called charter of King Edgar.[14]

At the time of the Domesday Survey the Bishop of Worcester held 38 hides belonging to the manor of *BLOCKLEY*, including 1 hide at Iccomb which was appropriated to the support of the monks.[15] During the early part of the 12th century Ditchford, which had been held in 1086 by Richard,[16] was added to the bishop's demesne[17] together with 1½ hides of land[18] which had previously belonged to Ansgot.[19]

The manor continued in the possession of the Bishops of Worcester until 1648,[20] when it was sold by the Parliamentary Trustees to William Combe for £1,394 12*s*. 5*d*.[21] After the Restoration it was regranted to the church, and the bishops, as lords of the manor, held courts there at least as late as 1781.[22] The manorial rights are now in abeyance.

The hamlets of Aston Magna, Draycott, Upton Wold and Paxford belonged to the manor of Blockley, and the lands there were usually held of the Bishop of Worcester on leases of three lives. In some cases these leases were renewed time after time to members of the same family, so that it is possible to trace for many years the history of even a small holding. In 1282 Nicholas de Stanesby and Elizabeth his wife held, apparently in right of Elizabeth, 2 virgates of land in *ASTON MAGNA*[23] (Hangynde Aston, xiii cent. ; Aston by Blokeleye, xiv cent. ; Hanbury Aston, Hanging Aston, xvi cent.) which they granted to Adam and John, the two sons of Robert de Pirton,[24] whose family retained the estate until 1355, when it was given to the priest John Blockley by John de Upcote,[25] the son of another Robert de Pirton, and probably the grandson of one of the 13th-century grantees.[26] In 1356 the property was bestowed by John de Blockley on the chantry of St. Mary,[27] the descent of which (q.v. *infra*) it subsequently followed.

In the early part of the 12th century Jordan held 2 hides in Aston, of which he had been enfeoffed by Bishop Samson (d. 1112),[28] and he afterwards obtained another hide and a mill called Spina from Roger Golafre, whose sister he married.[29] Jordan was suc-

ceeded before 1182 by his son William,[30] who gave the property held of Hugh Golafre to his brother John.[31] The 2 hides which remained to him had passed before 1246 to another John de Aston,[32] who was perhaps William's son, and were held in 1299 by Adam de Aston.[33] Adam seems to have been succeeded by three daughters and co-heirs, for his land was held in 1346 by John Chester, John Bagge and John Wattes,[34] among whose heirs it was still divided in 1428,[35] though the whole of the property had come into the hands of Henry Chester by the middle of the 15th century.[36] It is, however, difficult to trace its history after this date.

The descent of the hide which was given with the mill to John the brother of William de Aston is even more obscure. Possibly it descended to Jordan de Hanging Aston *alias* Jordan de Blockley, whose son John, having shown title of sufficient patrimony, took priest's orders in 1305.[37] His property probably passed at his death to a brother or nephew,[38] as it seems to have been part of the land held in the middle of the 14th century by another John de Blockley, presumably a kinsman, who was also a clerk.[39] This John, who granted lands in Aston to the chantry of St. Mary in 1356[40] (*vide supra*), was still living in 1375 ; he then added to this gift the whole of his remaining estate,[41] which thus became merged in the chantry lands (q.v.).

In the time of Henry III Roger de Draycott held half a hide in Aston, which he had obtained in exchange for other lands from Iseult, the daughter of Samson, to whom it had been given as her marriage portion.[42] This holding, which belonged to William de Draycott in 1299,[43] probably followed the descent of his lands in Northwick (q.v.). Certain lands in Aston Magna were leased in 1587 to the Crown by Edmund Freke, Bishop of Worcester[44] ; these followed the descent of Blockley Park and the manor of Tredington[45] (q.v.).

A good deal of land in Aston was held in the 16th century by the Freeman family, who were said in 1526 to have been established in the parish 'from old time.'[46] Their name does not seem to occur on the earlier Court Rolls, but the statement as to their long connexion with Blockley was made on the authority of Thomas Freeman, at that time steward of the bishop's manor.[47] In 1565 another Thomas Freeman held lands in Aston[48] which eventually

[13] Birch, *Cart. Sax.* ii, 89. This charter has suffered from a bad copyist, but is certainly genuine. There is no further mention of this monastery.

[14] Hale, *Reg. of Worc. Priory* (Camd. Soc.), 23*b* ; Heming, *Chartul.* 520 ; Birch, op. cit. iii, 377.

[15] *V.C.H. Worcs.* i, 293.

[16] Ibid.   [17] Ibid. 325.

[18] Ibid.   [19] Ibid. 293.

[20] *Testa de Nevill* (Rec. Com.), 42 ; *Feud. Aids*, v, 306 ; Close, 21 Edw. III, pt. i, m. 2 ; Rentals and Surv. (Gen. Ser.), R. 724 ; Mins. Accts. (Eccl. Com. Rec.), 92007–9 ; Chan. Proc. (Ser. 2), bdle. 196, no. 73 ; Close, 24 Chas. I, pt. ix, no. 4. The mediaeval bishops paid fairly frequent visits to the manor (Worc. Epis. Reg. *passim*). Cantilupe died there in 1266 (*Dict. Nat. Biog.* ; *Ann. Mon.* [Rolls Ser.], iv, 452).

[21] Close, 24 Chas. I, pt. ix, no. 4.

[22] *Cal. S. P. Dom.* 1661–2, p. 366 ; Nash, *Hist. of Worcs.* i, 97.

[23] Feet of F. Worcs. East. 10 Edw. I ; East. 12 Edw. I.

[24] Ibid. This Robert was probably Robert de Gurnay of Purton (co. Glouc.), whose lands passed successively to his son Anselm (*Cal. Inq. p.m. Hen. III*, 226) and his grandson John the son of Adam (*Feud. Aids*, ii, 251).

[25] Close, 29 Edw. III, m. 24 d.

[26] *Abbrev. Rot. Orig.* (Rec. Com.), ii, 242 ; Inq. a.q.d. file 317, no. 13 ; Pat. 30 Edw. III, pt. i, m. 21.

[27] Ibid.

[28] Eccl. Com. Rec. bdle. 121, no. 43698, fol. 243.

[29] Ibid.

[30] Ibid. fol. 255, 256.

[31] Ibid.

[32] Ibid. fol. 261 ; *Testa de Nevill* (Rec. Com.), 42.

[33] Eccl. Com. Rec. bdle. 121, no. 43698, fol. 176.

[34] *Feud. Aids*, v, 307 ; *Lay Subs. R. 1346* (Worcs. Hist. Soc.), 27.

[35] *Feud. Aids*, v, 320.

[36] Habington, *Surv. of Worcs.* (Worcs. Hist. Soc.), i, 60. According to this historian the lands afterwards passed to John Bason *alias* Bucher (ibid. 59), but he gives no date.

[37] *Reg. Ginsborough* (Worcs. Hist. Soc.), 23.

[38] A William de Aston is mentioned in 1294 (*Reg. G. Giffard* [Worcs. Hist. Soc.], 448).

[39] *Abbrev. Rot. Orig.* (Rec. Com.), ii, 242, 340.

[40] Inq. a.q.d. file 317, no. 13.

[41] Ibid. files 387, no. 8 ; 390, no. 13.

[42] Anct. D. (P.R.O.), B 1935.

[43] Eccl. Com. Rec. bdle. 121, no. 43698, fol. 176.

[44] Pat. 30 Eliz. pt. iv, m. 20.

[45] Chan. Proc. (Ser. 2), bdle. 235, no. 1, &c.

[46] Mins. Accts. (Eccl. Com. Rec.), 92010.   [47] Ibid.

[48] Chan. Proc. (Ser. 2), bdle. 65, no. 84.

descended to Richard Freeman, whose lease for three lives was renewed by Bishop Hough in 1737.[49] His nephew Thomas Edwards Freeman of Batsford quarrelled with his own family and left his estates to his wife's nephew John Mitford, Lord Chancellor of Ireland, who was created Lord Redesdale in 1802. He assumed the additional name of Freeman, and was succeeded in 1830 by his son John Thomas created Earl of Redesdale in 1877. On his death in 1886 his estates passed to his cousin Algernon Bertram Mit-

FREEMAN. *Azure a fesse indented of three points or.*

MITFORD. *Argent a fesse between three moles sable.*

ford (now Freeman-Mitford), who was created Lord Redesdale in 1902,[50] and now holds an estate at Aston Magna.

UPTON WOLD (Upton, xiii cent. ; Upton Olde, xvi cent.) was held in the 13th century by a family which took its name from the place,[51] but it had passed by 1346 to John Gilbert,[52] and seems to have been afterwards held by Robert Prodehomme.[53] The mention of a reputed manor there occurs in 1608, when Ralph Sheldon was the owner.[54]

In the time of Henry II Haerte held half a hide in *DRAYCOTT* (Draycote, xii cent. ; Dracott, xvi cent.) of the gift of Bishop Simon (d. 1150),[55] and Roger de Draycott is mentioned in a fine of 1227.[56] Tedelm de Draycott (miswritten Braicota) held half a hide there in the later part of the reign of Henry III[57] ; this land had passed before 1295 to John de Draycott,[58] whose son and namesake afterwards held it.[59] The last member of this family of whom mention is made in local records was William Draycott, whose heirs were tenants of the property in 1431.[60]

In 1551 the so-called manor of Draycott was divided between William Freeman and Thomas Bushy, the latter of whom held in right of his wife Elizabeth.[61] The Bushys subsequently sold their moiety to Thomas Smith,[62] and in 1609 Anthony

Smith, probably the son of Thomas, died seised of the estate, leaving as his heir his son, another Thomas.[63] The descent of the property after this date is obscure, but it came ultimately to the owners of Northwick, and was held by Sir John Rushout at the end of the 18th century.[64]

Half a hide in *PAXFORD* was held in the middle of the 13th century by Robert son of William,[65] and afterwards descended to John Leger, who is said to have been Robert's son.[66] This land had been divided before 1346 between Gilbert Leger and Thomas atte Silver[67] ; and a virgate called 'Lyggers' subsequently came into the possession of the college of Westbury-on-Trym (co. Gloucester), to which it was granted probably during the latter half of the 15th century.[68] Another virgate, possibly that which had been held by Thomas atte Silver,[69] was held in 1358 by John Weleye, who granted it in that year to John Laurence.[70] This also formed part of the endowment of Westbury College, and at the Dissolution was granted together with Legers to Sir Ralph Sadleir.[71] He alienated both in 1556 to Richard and John Fletcher,[72] by whose family the joint estate was held for over a century.[73] It was afterwards sold by another John Fletcher to William Freeman,[74] and Mr. A. B. Freeman-Mitford (now Lord Redesdale) has property in the district and he and Major

FLETCHER. *Sable two battle axes argent crowned or crossed saltirewise.*

Knox, Mr. James Slatter, and the trustees of Mr. Joseph Crescens Reynolds now hold most of the land here.

Certain lands in Paxford were among those leased to the Crown in 1587,[75] and by Charles I to William Warmestry in 1634.[76] Thomas Warmestry, the younger son of William, in 1653 compounded as a delinquent for these lands[77] ; they afterwards followed the descent of Blockley Park (q.v.).

The manor of *DITCHFORD* (Dicford, xi cent.; Dicheford, xiii cent.) was held of the episcopal manor of Blockley in 1086 by Richard and previously by Alward ; it was assessed at 2 hides.[78] In the time of Edward I Geoffrey de Ditchford held 4 hides here,[79] which afterwards passed to William de Ditchford *alias* William Kynich.[80]

In 1319 this William settled the manor of *MIDDLE DITCHFORD* (Dichford Kenych, Mid-

---

[49] Add. MS. 36646, fol. 18.
[50] Burke, *Peerage* (1907) ; Collins, *Peerage* (ed. Brydges), ix, 184.
[51] *Testa de Nevill* (Rec. Com.), 42 ; *Feud. Aids*, v, 310.
[52] *Feud. Aids*, v, 310.
[53] Robert Prodehomme's holding is said to have belonged formerly to Gilbert de Draycott (Habington, op. cit. i, 60).
[54] Close, 6 Jas. I, pt. xvii, no. 23.
[55] Habington, op. cit. i, 438.
[56] Feet of F. Worcs. East. 12 Hen. III.
[57] *Testa de Nevill* (Rec. Com.), 42.
[58] *Reg. G. Giffard* (Worcs. Hist. Soc.), 453.
[59] Habington, op. cit. i, 59.
[60] *Feud. Aids*, v, 333.
[61] Habington, loc. cit.
[62] Feet of F. Div. Co. Mich. 5 Edw. VI.
[63] Chan. Inq. p.m. (Ser. 2), cccxxii, 152.

[64] Nash, op. cit. i, 100.
[65] *Testa de Nevill* (Rec. Com.), 42.
[66] Habington, op. cit. i, 63. It is called the 'manor of Paxford' in 1303 (*Reg. Ginsborough* [Worcs. Hist. Soc.], 34), but this seems to be the only occasion on which it is so described. It is, however, surveyed separately from Blockley in the Red Bk. of the Bishopric.
[67] *Feud. Aids*, v, 310.
[68] Pat. 35 Hen. VIII, pt. xii, m. 2.
[69] Habington (loc. cit.) says it had once been held by 'John son of William.'
[70] Feet of F. Worcs. East. 32 Edw. III.
[71] Pat. 35 Hen. VIII, pt. xii, m. 2 ; *L. and P. Hen. VIII*, xix (1), g. 278 (68).
[72] Pat. 3 & 4 Phil. and Mary, pt. iv, m. 14.

[73] Robert the son of John Fletcher (*Visit. of Shropshire* [Harl. Soc.], i, 185) held it in 1605 (*Cal. S. P. Dom.* 1603–10, p. 234), and in 1620 his widow Margery died seised of her jointure. Her son Thomas (Chan. Inq. p.m. [Ser. 2], cccxcvii, 3) was then in possession of the estate. In 1685 Arthur Fletcher and Dorothea his wife settled the property—which seems to have been the right of Dorothea—on Nicholas Fletcher and his heirs (Feet of F. Worcs. East. 1 Jas. II).
[74] Add. MS. 36646, fol. 140.
[75] Pat. 30 Eliz. pt. iv, m. 20.
[76] Ibid. 10 Chas. I, pt. xvi, no. 20.
[77] *Dict. Nat. Biog.*
[78] *V.C.H. Worcs.* i, 293, 325.
[79] *Testa de Nevill* (Rec. Com.), 42.
[80] Pat. 8 Edw. II, pt. i, m. 31 ; Inq. a.q.d. file 97, no. 10.

deldycheford, xiv cent. ; Freeman's Ditchford, xvi cent. ; Peshall Freeman's Ditchford, xix cent.) on himself and Joan his wife and the heirs of his body with remainder to John de Peyto and his heirs.[81] William de Ditchford, who was probably the son of this William, held half a knight's fee and one-tenth of a knight's fee in Ditchford in 1346.[82] He was succeeded by John de Ditchford, who died in 1376, leaving as his heir his son William.[83] William, still in his minority, died in 1381,[84] and his only child Katherine in 1383 ; the manor was then divided between his sisters Aline and Margaret.[85]

Robert de Clynton, who seems to have been the son of Margaret,[86] apparently succeeded to both portions of the estate. He held half a knight's fee in Ditchford in 1428, and in 1459 a Robert Clynton, perhaps his son, was described as farmer of the manor.[87] It passed shortly afterwards to William Ranes,[88] and was held in 1509 by Anne the daughter and heir of Thomas Ranes and the wife of Roger Cheverell.[89] She and her husband leased a moiety of the manor in that year to John Palmer and Mary his wife for their lives,[90] and in 1518 Anne, then a widow, granted half of the other moiety to John Grevell and his heirs.[91] This property seems afterwards to have been acquired by William Palmer and Anne his wife, who dealt with three-quarters of the manor by fine in 1555.[92] It subsequently passed to William Sheldon, who also obtained possession of the remaining quarter[93] and died seised of the whole estate in 1570.[94] The property then followed the same descent as the manor of Beoley (q.v. in Pershore Hundred) until 1649, when it was forfeited by William Sheldon to the Parliamentary Trustees, who sold it to Major John Wild-man.[95] After the Restoration it was, however, re-covered by Ralph the son and heir of William Sheldon,[96] in whose lifetime it was settled upon trustees to the use of Joseph Sheldon and Margaret his wife and their heirs.[97] In 1681 Sir Joseph Sheldon made a fresh settlement by which the

SHELDON. *Sable a fesse between three sheldrakes argent.*

trustees were to hold the manor after the death of Margaret to the use of his brother Daniel and Gilbert, Daniel's son, charged with a legacy of £3,000 to his own daughters Elizabeth and Anne to be paid within two years after his wife's death.[98] Gilbert Sheldon, who succeeded in 1696,[99] by his will in 1721 bequeathed the manor to his wife Elizabeth with the provision that it was to be sold after her death and the proceeds divided equally between his daughters Judith the wife of Paul Jodrell and Mary, who had married William Cradock.[100] Gilbert's debts, however, so far exceeded his personal estate that his widow and daughters agreed to forgo their interest in the manor in order that the money might be paid.[1] A Private Act of Parliament was accordingly passed to set aside the will of Gilbert Sheldon and allow the immediate sale of the property,[2] which was bought in 1726 by Thomas Lord Foley.[3] He sold it in 1742 to the trustees for the marriage settlement of Cosmas Henry Nevill and Lady Mary Lee, daughter of the Earl of Lichfield,[4] whose son Charles Nevill ' not being minded to marry ' made provision out of the estate for his sisters and younger brothers in 1772.[5] Charles Nevill was vouchee in a recovery of 1821,[6] but the subsequent history of the property is obscure and the manorial rights are now in abeyance.

The reputed manor of *OVER DITCHFORD* (Overdicheford, xiv cent.; Dycheforde Leasnes, Guyes Dycheford, xvi cent. ; Upper Dichford, xvii cent.) is not mentioned before the end of the 14th century.[7] It seems to have been held on lease from the Bishops of Worcester,[8] and may perhaps have been the quarter of a knight's fee held by — Skales in 1431.[9] In 1459 Thomas Hyckes was farmer of the manor,[10] and in 1526 Thomas Freeman, the steward of the bishop's lands, obtained a renewal of his lease for forty years.[11] A moiety of the estate was afterwards rented by William Grevell,[12] the other moiety being divided between John Freeman and John Herytage.[13] In 1550 Nicholas Heath, Bishop of Worcester, obtained licence from Edward VI to alienate the property to William Sheldon,[14] who died seised of it in 1570.[15] The so-called manor subsequently followed the descent of Middle Ditchford.

The manor of *DORN* (Dorene, xiv cent.; Doron, xv cent.) was among the lands mentioned in ' King

[81] Feet of F. Worcs. Hil. 12 Edw. II.
[82] *Feud. Aids*, v, 309.
[83] Chan. Inq. p.m. 50 Edw. III (1st nos.), no. 21.
[84] Ibid. 6 Ric. II, no. 32. [85] Ibid.
[86] ' Margaret widow of Henry Clinton' was living in 1405 (Pat. 11 Hen. VI, pt. i, m. 13 d.).
[87] Mins. Accts. (Eccl. Com. Rec.), 92008. Robert is said in 1428 to have succeeded to the land formerly held by William de Ditchford (*Feud. Aids*, v, 320), so that the descent seems clear, though William had died seised of one-quarter fee only, and one-quarter fee was held in Ditchford in 1431 by — Skales (ibid. 333). But there seems to have been some uncertainty as to the service : it was described in 1346 as one-half and one-tenth fee (*vide supra*), in 1376 as one-quarter fee with suit at court, scutage and rent of 8 dodokes of grain (Chan. Inq. p.m. 50 Edw. III, no. 21), and in 1381–3 as one quarter fee simply (ibid. 6 Ric. II, no. 32).

[88] Habington, op. cit. i, 60.
[89] Hutchins, *Hist. of Dorset*, i, 414.
[90] Feet of F. Worcs. Mich. 1 Hen. VIII.
[91] Ibid. Trin. 10 Hen. VIII.
[92] Feet of F. Div. Co. Trin. 1 & 2 Phil. and Mary.
[93] His son Ralph received a quitclaim from Hugh Cheverell, the grandson of Roger and Anne, in 1580 (Feet of F. Div. Co. East. 22 Eliz.).
[94] Chan. Inq. p.m. (Ser. 2), clix, 87.
[95] Feet of F. Div. Co. Mich. 10 Jas. I ; Chan. Inq. p.m. (Ser. 2), cccxxxiv, 58 ; *Cal. Com. for Comp.* 1955.
[96] Feet of F. Worcs. Hil. 13 & 14 Chas. II.
[97] Ibid. Trin. 30 Chas. II ; Add. MS. 34684.
[98] Add. MS. 34684.
[99] Ibid.
[100] Ibid.
[1] Ibid.
[2] Ibid.
[3] Close, 5 Geo. II, pt. xxi, m. 24.

[4] Recov. R. D. Enr. Trin. 12 Geo. III, m. 304.
[5] Ibid. ; Recov. R. East. 12 Geo. III, rot. 502.
[6] Recov. R. East. 2 Geo. IV, rot. 45.
[7] Mins. Accts. (Eccl. Com. Rec.), 92007.
[8] Ibid. 92010.
[9] *Feud. Aids*, v, 333.
[10] Mins. Accts. (Eccl. Com. Rec.), 92008.
[11] Ibid. 92010.
[12] Pat. 4 Edw. VI, pt. ii, m. 21.
[13] Ibid. ; Star Chamb. Proc. bdle. 20, no. 398.
[14] Pat. 4 Edw. VI, pt. ii, m. 21.
[15] Chan. Inq. p.m. (Ser. 2), clix, 87. The manors are here distinguished as ' Freeman's Ditchford ' and ' Guyes Ditchford,' and the former is distinctly stated to be Middle Ditchford ; possibly the Freemans had occupied it under the Palmers and Cheverells, but there seems to be no proof of this.

Edgar's Charter' to the church of Worcester,[16] and seems to have been included in the manor of Blockley in 1086.[17] It was subsequently taken out of the manor by Urse D'Abitot,[18] and was held in the time of Henry I by Walter de Beauchamp, when it was assessed at 5 hides.[19] It then became annexed to the honour of Elmley, but was said in 1428 to be held of the bishop in chief. Robert de Weteley held the estate in the time of Bishop Roger (1164–79),[20] and Richard de Walegh held it in the time of Henry III,[21] but by 1265 part of the property seems to have passed to Agatha the wife of Thomas le Blake,[22] who exchanged it for lands in Severnstoke with John D'Abitot[23]; possibly John had previously been a co-parcener of the estate. Another John D'Abitot held Dorn in 1316[24] and 1346,[25] and the name of 'Thomas Dapitot of Dorne' occurs in 1356,[26] but the manor seems to have passed before 1375 to John de Blockley, a priest.[27] Another John de Blockley held it in 1428[28]; he was succeeded by Thomas de Blockley, perhaps his brother, who died about 1478, leaving a widow Alice and two children, William and Sibyl.[29] Alice died seised of the manor in 1481, leaving as her heir her grandson John the son of William Blockley,[30] who was succeeded by his aunt Sibyl Malyns before 1509.[31] The estate was subsequently divided, and in 1544 Thomas Guise and Eleanor his wife held in right of Eleanor a moiety

PYE. *Ermine a bend indented gules.*

which they sold to William Gower[32]; this was bought from Robert Gower by John Woodward in 1568.[33] The other moiety was in the possession of Thomas Wye in 1576.[34] Both portions were bought in 1583 by John Throckmorton,[35] from whom they passed to John Croker,[36] who settled them in 1616 on his daughter Mary on her marriage to Robert Pye of Faringdon (co. Berks.).[37] This family remained in possession of the estate until 1767,[38] when Henry James Pye, the Poet Laureate, sold the manor to Thomas Edwards Freeman.[39] It then followed the descent of the Freemans' estate at Aston,[40] Lord Redesdale being the owner at the present day.

NORTHWICK was held in the time of Henry III of the manor of Blockley by Avice de Kingsford and Robert de Northwick,[41] whose ancestor Roger had held his share in 1182.[42] In 1227 Robert granted his land in marriage with his daughter Maud to Roger de Draycott, reserving a moiety to himself for life and dower for his wife Marjory.[43] This holding, which belonged to William de Draycott in 1299,[44] afterwards passed to Thomas de Clipstone, who held it as the fifth part of a knight's fee in 1346.[45] The land which had belonged to Avice de Kingsford perhaps passed to Richard Redlaund, who died seised of a carucate of land before 1254.[46] His widow Emma received dower therein, and the remainder was granted by Walter Cantilupe, Bishop of Worcester, to Richard de Crisetot.[47] By 1346 Avice de Kingsford's land had come into the possession of John de Clipstone,[48] and in 1383 John Childe, whose family had already been established for some years in the district, seems to have become tenant of the whole estate.[49]

Thomas Childe, 'gentilman,' succeeded before 1426 to the property,[50] which afterwards passed to Edmund Childe, who died about 1459, leaving as his heir his son William.[51] This William Childe in 1520 granted the reputed manor to Robert Haldyworth and other feoffees, on condition that they should pay 10 marks yearly to William Childe the younger and Anne (Hunckes) his wife,[52] who ten years later conveyed the estate to the feoffees, apparently for the purpose of a settlement[53] on his brother-in-law Thomas Hunckes. In 1558 Thomas Hunckes died seised of the manor, leaving as his heir his son Robert,[54] who having no children settled it in 1564 on his brother John.[55] In 1583 Robert and Thomas Hunckes, the sons of John, sold it to William Childe, the son of William and Anne,[56] from whose grandson and namesake it was bought in 1683 by Sir James Rushout, bart.[57] From that date until 1912 the property remained in the possession of the Rushout family.[58] On the death of

HUNCKES. *Argent three molets sable and a border gules bezanty.*

[16] Heming, *Chartul.* 520; Pat. 11 Edw. III, pt. iii, m. 30.

[17] *V.C.H. Worcs.* i, 293.

[18] Ibid. The overlordship was subsequently ascribed both to the Bishop of Worcester in 1346 (*Feud. Aids*, v, 306) and 1428 (ibid. 318) and the Earl of Warwick in 1316 (Chan. Inq. p.m. 9 Edw. II, no. 71) and 1481 (ibid. 22 Edw. IV, no. 40).

[19] *V.C.H. Worcs.* i, 325.

[20] Red Bk. of Bishopric of Worc. (Eccl. Com. Rec. Var. bdle. 121, no. 43698), fol. 252.

[21] *Testa de Nevill* (Rec. Com.), 41.

[22] Feet of F. Div. Co. Mich. 50 Hen. III. [23] Ibid.

[24] Chan. Inq. p.m. 9 Edw. II, no. 71, m. 53. [25] *Feud. Aids*, v, 306.

[26] *Cal. Pat.* 1354–8, p. 499.

[27] Inq. a.q.d. file 387, no. 8.

[28] *Feud. Aids*, v, 318; *Lay Subs. R.* 1428 (Worcs. Hist. Soc.), 33, 41.

[29] Chan. Inq. p.m. 22 Edw. IV, no. 40.

[30] Ibid.

[31] De Banco R. Mich. 24 Hen. VII, m. 155 d.

[32] Feet of F. Worcs. Mich. 36 Hen. VIII.

[33] Ibid. East. 10 Eliz.

[34] Recov. R. Mich. 18 & 19 Eliz. rot. 1116.

[35] Feet of F. Div. Co. East. 25 Eliz.; Hil. 26 Eliz.; Recov. R. Mich. 25 Eliz. rot. 15; Add. MS. 36645, fol. 158; Feet of F. Div. Co. Trin. 38 Eliz.

[36] Notes of Fines, Worcs. Hil. 13 Jas. I.

[37] Ibid.; Rudder, *Hist. and Antiq. of Glouc.* 265; Cherry, 'Prosapiae Bercherienses,' ii, 77.

[38] Recov. R. D. Enr. Trin. 15 Chas. II, m. 2; Recov. R. Trin. 15 Chas. II, rot. 32; East. 4 Anne, rot. 263; Feet of F. Div. Co. Mich. 14 Geo. II; Recov. R. Mich. 14 Geo. II, rot. 205; East. 6 Geo. III, rot. 303.

[39] Close, 7 Geo. III, pt. xxi, no. 2.

[40] See above.

[41] *Testa de Nevill* (Rec. Com.), 41, 42.

[42] Eccl. Com. Rec. bdle. 121, no. 43698, fol. 186.

[43] Feet of F. Worcs. East. 12 Hen. III.

[44] Eccl. Com. Rec. bdle. 121, no. 43698, fol. 176.

[45] *Lay Subs. R.* 1332–3 (Worcs. Hist. Soc.), 6; *Feud. Aids*, v, 310.

[46] Feet of F. Worcs. Hil. 38 Hen. III.

[47] Ibid.

[48] *Feud. Aids*, v, 310; *Lay Subs. R.* 1346 (Worcs. Hist. Soc.), 29.

[49] Habington, op. cit. i, 60; Mins. Accts. (Eccl. Com. Rec.), 92007.

[50] Anct. D. (P.R.O.), C 2130.

[51] Mins. Accts. (Eccl. Com. Rec.), 92008.

[52] Close, 21 Hen. VIII, no. 19. This William Childe was the son of Edmund and grandson of the elder William (ibid.).

[53] Ibid.

[54] Chan. Inq. p.m. (Ser. 2), cxxii, 77; *Visit. of Worcs.* (Harl. Soc.), 81.

[55] Feet of F. Worcs. Mich. 6 & 7 Eliz.

[56] Ibid. Trin. 25 Eliz.; Habington, op. cit. i, 62; *Visit. of Worcs.* (Harl. Soc.), 81.

[57] Feet of F. Worcs. East. 35 Chas. II.

[58] Ibid. East. 4 Jas. II; Mich. 1 Anne; Recov. R. D. Enr. Hil. 1 Geo. III, m. 75; Nash, op. cit. i, 99–100; G.E.C. *Complete Peerage.*

BLOCKLEY CHURCH : THE SOUTH DOORWAY

BLOCKLEY CHURCH FROM THE SOUTH-EAST

Lady Northwick in May 1912 the property passed under the will of her late husband, the last Lord Northwick, to her grandson Mr. George Spencer-Churchill.

There were twelve mills attached to Blockley in 1086,[59] but it is not possible to trace the descent of more than half that number.

RUSHOUT, baronet. *Sable two leopards in a border engrailed or.*

There is a mill now called Snugborough at the bottom of the slope on which the village is built which may possibly stand on the site of the 'mill in Blockley,' valued in 1364 at 10s. yearly.[60] This mill seems always to have been attached to the bishop's manor. In 1299 mention is made also of Frenismill, afterwards French Mill,[61] in 1383, of the mill called 'Peomull,'[62] and in 1506 of the fulling-mill.[63] There were two water corn-mills in Blockley in 1707.[64] The Chantry Mill in Blockley, which was probably the ancient Spina Mill (*vide supra* in Aston), belonged in 1375 to John of Blockley, who granted it to Henry Rose the chaplain and his successors.[65] At the dissolution of the chantry Edward VI gave the mill to Thomas Watson and William Adys and their heirs,[66] but it is difficult to trace its later history. There are still two disused silk-mills in Blockley village, the only traces now left of an industry which flourished here during the 18th century. The first of these was built by Henry Whatcot, who died in 1718, and by 1780 there were five mills working with great success,[67] but the trade has now entirely disappeared.

A water corn-mill is mentioned among the appurtenances of the manor of Middle Ditchford in 1376,[68] and this followed the descent of that manor until 1580[69] and again from 1662 to 1821.[70] Possibly this was Bran Mill (Braundes Mill, xvi cent.), which now stands about three-quarters of a mile from the hamlet of Upper Ditchford and was leased to the Crown between 1587 and 1662.[71] Bran Mill was said to be attached to Draycott in 1634,[72] but there is no other mention of any mill in connexion with that hamlet.

Northwick Mill is first mentioned in 1227, when Robert de Northwick granted it in marriage with Maud his daughter to Roger de Draycott.[73] It subsequently followed the descent of the so-called manor of Northwick,[74] and was probably on the site of the present mill.

There is now a water corn-mill in Paxford known as Pye Mill which perhaps marks the site of a mill mentioned about 1182, when it was worth 10s., though its previous value had been 5s. only.[75]

Walter Cantilupe, Bishop of Worcester, in 1239 obtained from Henry III a grant of a yearly fair on the three days before the vigil of St. Michael and on the vigil and feast,[76] which was confirmed to his successor Giffard in 1270.[77] In 1286 mention occurs of another fair on the eve, day and morrow of St. Matthew and the five days following, which had already been granted to the Bishops of Worcester, presumably in extension of the grant of 1239, and was further extended over another eight days at Giffard's request.[78] The two fairs were thus amalgamated. By 1692 another fair seems to have been held,[79] possibly that which is mentioned by Nash as taking place on the second Tuesday after Easter.[80] Both fairs were still held at the beginning of the 19th century, though the duration of the autumn one had apparently shrunk to one day, Michaelmas, and neither was of much importance except for the hiring of servants.[81]

The woodland belonging to the manor of Blockley was described at the time of the Domesday Survey as 'half a league in length and in width,'[82] but the date of its inclosure as a *PARK* is uncertain. Walter Cantilupe, Bishop of Worcester, obtained a grant of free warren in Blockley from Henry III in 1248,[83] and this grant was afterwards confirmed and extended.[84] His successor, Godfrey Giffard, who cared as little as Chaucer's monk for 'the text . . . that seyth that hunters ben nat hooly men,' seems to have been the first to stock the park with deer.[85] In 1277 he obtained for that purpose a gift from Edward I of twenty bucks and does from the neighbouring forest of Wychwood.[86] There is more than one reference to the deer kept in this park during the next three centuries,[87] but after the Reformation the stock seems to have been allowed to decline, though John Bell, Bishop of Worcester, in granting a lease of the park to Humphrey Talbot and Thomas Hungerford, made a condition that 100 deer should be inclosed.[88] After the death of Talbot, Hungerford assigned his interest to John Stevens, who seems to have conveyed the unexpired term of the lease to Oliver Dawbney, retaining the under-tenancy for himself.[89] John Stevens, however, while in possession of the lease, had failed to inclose the deer according to the terms of the agreement, and after the expiration of the year's notice, as provided in the lease, the bishop re-entered and granted a new lease to William

[59] *V.C.H. Worcs.* i, 293.
[60] Rentals and Surv. R. 724.
[61] Eccl. Com. Rec. bdle. 121, no. 43698, fol. 175.
[62] Mins. Accts. (Eccl. Com. Rec.), 92007.
[63] Ibid. 92009.
[64] Feet of F. Worcs. Hil. 6 Anne.
[65] Inq. a.q.d. file 390, no. 13 ; Mins. Accts. (Eccl. Com. Rec.), 92009.
[66] Pat. 3 Edw. VI, pt. i, m. 23.
[67] Nash, op. cit. i, 101.
[68] Chan. Inq. p.m. 50 Edw. III (1st nos.), no. 21.
[69] Ibid. 6 Ric. II, no. 32, &c.
[70] Feet of F. Worcs. Trin. 30 Chas. II, &c.
[71] Chan. Proc. (Ser. 2), bdle. 235, no. 1.

[72] Pat. 10 Chas. I, pt. xvi, no. 20.
[73] Feet of F. Worcs. East. 12 Hen. III.
[74] *Vide supra.*
[75] Eccl. Com. Rec. bdle. 121, no. 43698, fol. 250.
[76] Chart. R. 24 Hen. III, m. 4 ; *Ann. Mon.* (Rolls Ser.), iv, 431.
[77] Chart. R. 54 Hen. III, m. 9.
[78] Ibid. 14 Edw. I, m. 6, no. 38.
[79] Richard Castell was steward of the fairs in that year (*Hist. MSS. Com. Rep.* xiv, App. vi, 364).
[80] Nash, op. cit. i, 98.
[81] Ibid.
[82] *V.C.H. Worcs.* i, 293.
[83] Chart. R. 32 Hen. III, m. 3.
[84] Ibid. 39 Hen. III, m. 6 ; Pat. 37 & 38 Hen. III, pt. ii, m. 2. The bishops'

warren is occasionally mentioned in later documents (Pat. 8 Edw. III, pt. i, m. 2 d. ; pt. ii, m. 38 d.). In 1693 it was leased to Richard Castell (*Hist. MSS. Com. Rep.* xiv, App. vi, 364).
[85] Close, 5 Edw. I, m. 11.
[86] Ibid. Possibly the request was made on the occasion of the king's visit ; he stayed at Blockley for some days in January of that year (Pat. 5 Edw. I, m. 24 ; *Cal. Fine R. 1272–1307*, p. 77).
[87] Pat. 8 Edw. III, pt. i, m. 2 d. ; pt. ii, m. 38 d. ; 13 Edw. III, pt. i, m. 36 d. ; Habington, op. cit. i, 63 ; Chan. Proc. (Ser. 2), bdle. 51, no. 92.
[88] Chan. Proc. (Ser. 2), bdle. 51, no. 92.
[89] Ibid.

Sheldon,[90] which was confirmed by the dean and chapter.[91] John Stevens was thereupon expelled by Richard Hecks, sub-lessee for five years under William Sheldon, and the park became the subject of proceedings in the Court of Chancery.[92]

John Stevens was still in possession of a moiety of Blockley Park in 1572[93]; this was afterwards leased for thirty-five years to John Talbot, who conveyed his interest in the lease together with property in Bromsgrove to William Sebright for £200 in 1574.[94] Talbot subsequently complained that the money was unpaid, and that Sebright had coaxed him into giving a release of the debt to be shown to Mistress Bowyer, on the plea that 'the said Mistress Bowyer was doubtfull of his estate and feared that he was indebted, and that if he might by any meanes satisfy her therein he was like to marry.'[95] This story was of course emphatically denied by Sebright, who declared that it was well known to Mrs. Bowyer, then his wife, that he was, long before his marriage, able to pay far greater sums.[96]

CHURCHES The church of *ST. PETER AND ST. PAUL* consists of a chancel 32 ft. by 18 ft. 6 in., north vestry 11 ft. by 12 ft., nave 58 ft. by 25 ft., north aisle 12 ft. wide by 71 ft. long, north and south porches and a western tower 14 ft. square. These measurements are all internal.

The church dates from about 1180, and work of that period still remains in the four walls of the chancel, and in the east, south and west walls of the nave. There was probably a contemporary western tower, the two eastern buttresses of which appear inside the west wall of the nave. The church apparently stood unaltered until the 14th century, though a note in the Worcestershire Episcopal Registers[3] records the dedication of a high altar in Blockley in 1285. About 1310 several alterations were made and enlargements begun. These included the insertion of the large east window and the widening of those on the south. The piscina and sedilia were inserted, a south priest's door built, and a new vestry added on

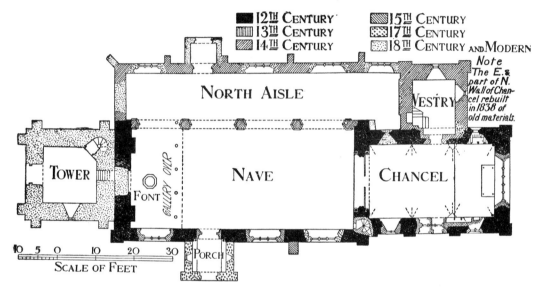

■ 12ᵀᴴ CENTURY ▨ 15ᵀᴴ CENTURY
▥ 13ᵀᴴ CENTURY ▦ 17ᵀᴴ CENTURY
▧ 14ᵀᴴ CENTURY ░ 18ᵀᴴ CENTURY ᴀɴᴅ MODERN

Note
The E. &
part of N.
Wall of Chancel rebuilt
in 1838 of
old materials.

NORTH AISLE

VESTRY

TOWER   NAVE   CHANCEL

FONT

GALLERY OVER

10 5 0 10 20 30   PORCH
SCALE OF FEET

PLAN OF BLOCKLEY CHURCH

In 1587 a lease of Blockley Park, together with the site of the manor of Tredington, was granted to the Crown by Edmund Freke, Bishop of Worcester,[97] and the two estates subsequently followed the same descent (q.v. in Tredington) until the expiration of the lease in 1679.[98] The site of the park was afterwards leased to the Rushouts of Northwick in this parish, and was held by Sir John Rushout at the end of the 18th century.[99] The park has from that time followed the descent of the manor.

A free fishery in Blockley Park is mentioned in a lease of the 15th century,[100] and in later documents concerning the park.[1] There are still the remains of a fish-pond near Blockley Park Farm. Another fishery 'on the bank of the stream by Paxford' is mentioned in 1383.[2]

the north side. This last dates from 1320, the upper part being a chantry for Ralph de Balleton. The north aisle, of the same length as the nave, with an arcade of four bays, was built about the end of the same century. Later on came the usual enlargement of windows, the middle one in the south wall of the chancel being an insertion of the 15th century. Those in the north walls, and perhaps the easternmost on the south side of the nave, were probably put in when the clearstories were added in 1636, although they are of rather good work for that date. The 12th-century south doorway was filled in with a square-headed one in the 15th century, the south porch being added in 1630. The western tower was pulled down in 1724, and the present structure built in the following year against the western wall of the nave. Somewhat

90 Chan. Proc. (Ser. 2), bdle. 51, no. 92.
91 Ibid.
92 Ibid.
93 Ct. of Req. bdle. 26, no. 72.
94 Ibid.
95 Ibid.

96 Ibid.
97 Pat. 30 Eliz. pt. iv, m. 20.
98 Ibid.; Chan. Proc. (Ser. 2), bdle. 235, no. 1; Exch. Dep. Mich. 8 Chas. I, no. 47; Hil. 8 & 9 Chas. I, no. 26; Mich. 14 Chas. J, no. 22; Pat. 10 Chas. I,

pt. xvi, no. 20; *Cal. S. P. Dom.* 1661-2, p. 366.   99 Nash, loc. cit.
100 Habington, op. cit. i, 63.
1 Chan. Proc. (Ser. 2), bdle. 51, no. 92.
2 Mins. Accts. (Eccl. Com. Rec.), 92007.
3 op. cit. Giffard, fol. 234.

later, probably about 1790, the east wall of the north aisle was taken down, the aisle being extended eastward to the vestry, as a chapel for the Northwick family. It was inclosed by an iron fence, recently removed. The last addition was the north porch, built in 1871.

The east window is of five lights with trefoiled tracery under a two-centred arch. There were three 12th-century windows on either side of the chancel; two of those in the north wall have been blocked, the easternmost alone remaining open. It is a round-headed single light, with widely splayed jambs, and an outer order, both within and without, of a quarter-round attached shaft, with moulded bases and carved foliage capitals of the late Norman type. The middle window is blocked to the face of the splay inside, so that the side shafts show, and the one to the west is blocked flush with the wall face, and has lost its eastern jamb. The middle window in the south wall has been displaced by a 15th-century insertion of three lights, with traceried head, under a four-centred arch, and elaborate mouldings. The other two windows, whilst retaining their 12th-century jambs inside, have been cut away on the outer face in the 14th century to form two-light windows with traceried heads and pointed rear arches. In each angle at the east end is a detached round vaulting shaft with carved capitals, of the 12th century, and between the two eastern windows on either side the upper portions of a second pair remain. They consist of three attached shafts, with elaborately carved capitals, separated by small rolls. About 6 ft. above the chancel floor is a horizontal string-course banding these shafts, and below it they have been cut away into conical points, probably in the 14th century.

The piscina and sedilia date from about 1310. The former has a trefoiled ogee head, and the latter three bays with plain ogee heads, all with crocketed labels and finials. In the north wall is a square aumbry about a yard wide and divided into four compartments.

The 14th-century south priest's doorway has a two-centred arch, and the north doorway leading to the vestry is similar. The wall behind this doorway, in the vestry, has been cut back, and is partly arched over. In the south-east corner of the vestry was the stone stair to the room above, but this has been closed up, and is now obscured by a cupboard. In the east and north walls are trefoiled lancet windows, apparently old, and in the west wall (now hidden by the wooden stair) is a small square aumbry with rebated edges. The upper chamber, approached by a modern stair, is lighted by a trefoiled lancet in the east wall and a modern two-light window on the north. The responds of the chancel arch belong

to the 12th century. They consist of two square orders, with two half-round shafts on the inner face and detached shafts in the angles. The latter have been cut away about 6 ft. above the floor, probably to receive the Jacobean panelling below. The capitals are elaborately carved, each jamb differing in design. The two-centred arch is 14th-century work of three orders.

The nave arcade dates from about the year 1390. It is of four bays and has hexagonal piers with moulded bases and capitals. The arches are two-centred and of two chamfered orders, the inner being cut away to form an edge on the soffit like the angle of a hexagon; the unusual section of the arches and capitals may indicate a later date, and they are

BLOCKLEY CHURCH : THE NAVE LOOKING EAST

perhaps contemporary with the clearstory. In the eastern respond is a piscina for the original side altar with the basin and canopy cut away. The head is moulded and at the back is a small shelf.

There are three lower windows in the south wall; the first (from the east) is of three lights, with a square head, and is probably contemporary with the clearstory, the other two date from the middle of the 15th century and have three lights and traceried four-centred heads.

The south doorway dates from the 12th century with a 15th-century insertion. The earlier work has rebated jambs with detached shafts and foliage capitals. The arch is semicircular with a plain chamfered label and later head stops. The 15th-century doorway, which is flush with the inner order of the earlier work, has a two-centred arch in a square head, with traceried spandrels.

In the clearstory there are four windows on either side, each with three lights under a square head. Below the easternmost on the north side is the inscription 'AF AL 1635,' and under the one opposite 'AL TF 1636.' Between these windows on both sides are wide pilasters built on moulded corbels at the level of the window sills, and projecting from the face of each is a corbel about 3 ft. below the ceiling. These doubtless once supported the trusses of the former roof, which was replaced by a flat plastered ceiling, probably in 1702, when the Bishop of Worcester 'beautified the church.' At the west end below the gallery is a blocked doorway with rebated jambs of the 12th century, having detached shafts with scalloped capitals; the arch has been replaced by a pointed one. This was the entrance to the former tower, and on either side of it the shallow Norman buttresses of its east face still project into the church. The gallery at the west end is of Renaissance design and was put up in 1735. The west wall formerly supported the tower, but the later one was built up against it, the two walls being together 9 ft. 3 in. thick.

The easternmost window in the north aisle, of three plain square-headed lights, was inserted in the 18th century, when the aisle was extended eastwards. The second, third and fourth windows are of three lights under square heads, the lights of the second being ogee-headed. These, like the south-east window of the nave, are probably of the 17th century. The window in the west wall has been blocked up.

The 14th-century north doorway is of two continuous orders, with a two-centred head. In the upper part of the north wall is a range of clearstory windows, an unusual feature in an aisle; they appear to be of the same date as those to the nave and were evidently built to light a gallery. The windows are of two lights each, the easternmost differing somewhat from the other three.

Of the two porches the northern was built in 1871, but the southern dates from 1630. It is embattled and pinnacled, with a round-headed outer doorway (on which is inscribed the date), and above it is a sundial.

The tower, built in 1725, is of four stages, with two buttresses on each face. It has a plain parapet with square pierced angle and intermediate pinnacles surmounted by crocketed finials.

Some 12th-century work has apparently been re-used in the west doorway and in a square-headed light in the south wall. The west window has a semicircular head and the belfry windows are of three lights, of which the centre one is blocked.

The roof of the chancel is wagon-headed, of modern date; that to the north aisle is a low-pitched roof with moulded timbers, and the nave has a flat plaster ceiling.

Externally the 12th-century shallow buttresses still remain on the south side of the chancel and inclosing the eastern angles. Between and flush with them, below the parapet, is the original corbel tabling of pairs of small half-round arches between moulded corbels. It is carried along both side walls and round the vestry, where it appears to be partly old work re-used and partly 14th-century imitation. The 12th-century moulded plinth is also copied

in the 14th-century work. The east wall and part of the north wall of the chancel were rebuilt in 1838 with the old materials. The parapet of the chancel is plain and bears an inscription recording its erection in 1738. The walling is of rough-coursed ashlar with dressed quoin stones.

The font is octagonal in plan, the 14th-century bowl having quatrefoil panelled sides, each panel with a square flower. The stem and base are modern.

There is a fine 15th-century oak screen across the chancel arch, consisting of five bays on either side of a central doorway, which has a two-centred cusped arch. The details are somewhat thin in appearance, and it has been varnished in recent times; the carved work at the top was added in 1870. The chancel fittings are modern, but around the walls is some panelling of the 17th century, which is also the date of the carved oak pulpit.

There are two monumental brasses in the chancel, one on the floor to Philip Worthim, M.A., who died in 1488, with a small figure of a priest kneeling in eucharistic vestments, and a scroll above. Engraved on the slab is a chalice, and a small plate of the Virgin and Child is missing. The second brass, to William Neele, vicar here and rector of Bourton-on-the-Water, who died in 1510, is set in the back of the sedilia and consists of a small figure of a priest with the inscription and portions of scrolls. There are said to be the remains of another brass, undated, to William Jombhaste, rector of Stretton on the Fosse. In front of the two blocked north windows are modern mural monuments to Lord Northwick and his daughter.

At the east end of the north aisle is a large monument to William Childe and Elizabeth his wife, 1633 and 1622, with kneeling figures, and next to it, on the east wall, is a triple arcade of modern date inclosing monuments to members of the Rushout family of Northwick dating from 1698 to 1878.[4] On the north wall is another monument to William Childe, said to have died in 1601, with an armed kneeling figure and shields of Childe, Gules a cheveron ermine between three eagles close argent, impaling Folliott and Childe impaling Jeffereys. East of it is a monument with the reclining figure of a lady, to Anne Jenkinson, wife of Thomas Childe of Northwick, who died in 1659. To the north of the chancel arch is another to Edward and Maria Carter, 1667 and 1675, and on the south wall are others of later date.

There are six bells: the treble by Matthew Bagley, 1683; the second, 1679; the third by Abel Rudhall, 1729; the fourth and fifth by Henry Bagley, 1638, and the tenor, 1854, by Mears.

The communion plate comprises two cups and patens, two flagons, a plate and an almsdish, all given in 1732 by Elizabeth Countess Dowager of Northampton; also a plate given by Elizabeth Martyn of Upton Wold in 1706.

The registers are as follows: (i) baptisms and burials 1538 to 1812, marriages 1539 to 1753; (ii) marriages 1754 to 1768; (iii) marriages 1769 to 1800; (iv) marriages 1800 to 1812.

The church of ST. JOHN at Aston Magna, erected in 1846, consists of a chancel, nave, west tower and

[4] The floor above the Rushout vault is 3 ft. above the general level, and when it was made some 2,000 skulls were discovered, indicating the site of a former charnel-house.

BLOCKLEY CHURCH : THE PISCINA AND SEDILIA

south-east porch, which serves as a vestry. The design is Early English in character, the materials being stone and the roofs slated.

The plate consists of a silver cup, paten and alms-dish of 1842 and a silver flagon of 1841.

ADVOWSONS There was a church at Blockley in 1086, served by a priest who held 1 hide of the manor.[5] The living was in the gift of the Bishop of Worcester, and was a valuable one. In 1279,[6] when the rector, Gregory of Caerwent, died at the Papal Court,[7] the pope granted the presentation for that turn to the Archbishop of Canterbury.[8] Giffard thereupon made a heated protest, declaring that he had himself received an indulgence to exercise the patronage,[9] but a few weeks later he gave way and instituted the arch-bishop's nominee.[10] In this case, however, residence was enforced,[11] and when the living fell vacant in 1291 the bishop was able to present his kinsman William Greenfield, afterwards Archbishop of York.[12] Greenfield resigned in 1294, and Giffard then gave the living to Piers de Escote, who, though not a kinsman, had been a member of his household.[13] Escote died at Rome in the following year, 'pro-curando ecclesias episcopi fieri prebendales contra commodum ecclesie Wygorniensis,'[14] according to the monks of Worcester, who evidently considered his death an awful warning. Giffard was then trying to make the churches of his patronage, including Blockley, prebendal to the college of Westbury-on-Trym,[15] but the prior and convent appealed against it, stating that they had always possessed the right of instituting rectors to those churches during a vacancy of the see and the bishop's action deprived them of the privilege.[16] It does not, however, appear from Giffard's register that Escote was sent to Rome on this mission; the only correspondence between them concerns a dispensation for the rector's illegitimacy. He had allowed himself to be ordained without saying that such a dispensation was necessary, and the bishop having discovered this wrote reproaching him 'that so, by withholding the truth,' he had obtained orders.[17] The letter betrays a gentleness of which Giffard is not often suspected, but the writer was obviously very anxious about the consequences of Escote's

action; he hinted that the affair must be kept as secret as possible, lest the living should 'rightfully be reputed vacant' and the papal chaplains clamour for it.[18] Escote in reply acknowledged that he had not been regularly ordained, and declared that he would never lay claim to the living if Giffard chose to give it to another, but the bishop declined to take this advantage,[19] and Escote ultimately obtained from the pope not only his dispensation but a recognition of his position as rector.[20] His death in the summer of 1295 threw the patronage once more into the hands of the pope,[21] and for the next fifty years the living was filled by a succession of non-resident foreigners.[22] In 1333 Adam Orlton, then Bishop of Worcester, petitioned John XXII for leave to appropriate Blockley Church to the episcopal income, and a licence was granted to take effect on the resignation of the Bishop of Porto, then rector.[23] It was not until 1352 that the vicarage of Blockley was ordained,[24] but after this date there was no further interference with the bishop's patronage there.[25] The advowson still belonged to the Bishop of Worcester in 1904, but passed in the following year from the Bishop of the newly created see of Birmingham to the vicar of Bromsgrove, the present patron, in exchange for the advowson of Moseley and some of the other churches in the Birmingham part of the old parish of Broms-grove.[26]

Aston Magna was formed into a separate ecclesiastical parish in 1847.[27] The living is a vicarage in the gift of Lord Redesdale.

A chantry was founded about 1314 in the parish church of Blockley in honour of the Blessed Virgin by William de Ditchford and Ralf de Baketon, who gave lands in Middle Ditchford, Northwick and Blockley for the maintenance of the chaplain.[28] This endowment proved insufficient, and further lands were granted by Baketon in 1324[29] and by John de Blockley in 1356 and 1375.[30] The right of presenting a chantry priest belonged to the incumbent of Blockley, or if the living were vacant to the bishop.[31] The yearly value of the chantry lands at the time of the Dissolution was £9 2s. 6d.[32] The property was granted to Thomas Watson and William Adys in 1549,[33] but after this date its history becomes obscure.

[5] V.C.H. Worcs. i, 293.
[6] It was valued at £36 13s. 4d. in 1291 (Pope Nich. Tax. [Rec. Com.], 219).
[7] In cases when the incumbent died at Rome the presentation for that turn belonged to the pope (Reg. G. Giffard [Worcs. Hist. Soc.], 120, 463).
[8] Cal. Papal Letters, i, 460; Reg. G. Giffard, 120.
[9] Reg. G. Giffard (Worcs. Hist. Soc.), 222.
[10] Ibid. 121.
[11] Cal. Papal Letters, loc. cit.
[12] Dict. Nat. Biog.; Reg. G. Giffard (Worcs. Hist. Soc.), 447.
[13] Reg. G. Giffard, 447.
[14] Ann. Mon. (Rolls Ser.), iv, 523.
[15] Ibid. passim; Worc. Epis. Reg. passim; V.C.H. Gloucs. ii, 107.
[16] Reg. G. Giffard, 492. It is difficult to see how this could be the case, as the prior and convent by the agreement of 1260 had a right to the spiritualities of the bishopric only (Sede Vacante Reg. [Worcs. Hist. Soc.], 3), which did not include patronage (Bracton's Note Bk.

passim; Maitland, 'Canon Law in the Ch. of Engl.' Engl. Hist. Rev. xi, 647; Stubbs, Select Charters, 138). Nor do they seem to have received a special grant of the patronage, as the king certainly presented to Blockley—which Giffard did not succeed in making prebendal—during vacancies of the see (Worc. Epis. Reg. Morgan, ii, fol. 5 d.; Inst. Bks. [P.R.O.]; Nash, op. cit. i, 104).
[17] Reg. G. Giffard (Worcs. Hist. Soc.), 451.
[18] Ibid.
[19] Ibid. He sent the pope letters testimonial in favour of Escote (ibid. 449).
[20] Ibid. 463; Cal. Papal Letters, i, 559.
[21] Reg. G. Giffard (Worcs. Hist. Soc.), 463; Cal. Papal Letters, loc. cit.; Ann. Mon. (Rolls Ser.), iv, 523.
[22] Reg. G. Giffard, loc. cit.; Ann. Mon. loc. cit.; Cal. Papal Letters, i, 559; ii, 222, 319, 337, 370, 382. The only exception was Benet de Pastone, who was probably an Englishman; but he was a pluralist (Cal. Papal Letters, ii, 222), and there is no evidence that he

ever resided. He was certainly a papal chaplain and died at Rome (ibid. 319).
[23] Cal. Papal Letters, ii, 382; Pat. 9 Edw. III, pt. i, m. 10; Close, 11 Edw. III, pt. ii, m. 41.
[24] Worc. Epis. Reg. Thoresby, fol. 26 d., 41; Whittlesey, fol. 15.
[25] Ibid. Brian, fol. 25 d.; Inst. Bks. (P.R.O.). The living was worth £87 14s. 6½d. in 1535 (Valor Eccl. [Rec. Com.], iii, 218).
[26] Inform. from Mr. J. W. Willis-Bund.
[27] Lond. Gaz. 29 June 1847, p. 2375.
[28] Pat. 8 Edw. II, pt. i, m. 31; 13 Edw. II, m. 5; 17 Edw. II, pt. ii, m. 27; Inq. a.q.d. file 97, no. 10; 163, no. 16; Worc. Epis. Reg. Maidstone, fol. 14 d.; Cobham, fol. 65.
[29] Pat. 17 Edw. II, pt. ii, m. 27.
[30] Inq. a.q.d. file 317, no. 13; 387, no. 8; 390, no. 13; Worc. Epis. Reg. Wakefield, fol. 7.
[31] Worc. Epis. Reg. Morgan, fol. 16; Bourchier, fol. 50 d.; Carpenter, fol. 59, 173; Silvester de Gigliis, fol. 25.
[32] Chant. Cert. 60, no. 28.
[33] Pat. 3 Edw. VI, pt. i, m. 23.

Habington says that there was a chapel of St. Michael besides St. Mary's chantry.[34]

Stretton on the Fosse (co. Warwick) was formerly a chapelry annexed to Blockley, but in 1351 the parishioners there obtained from Bishop John Thoresby leave to bury their dead at Stretton on account of the distance from Blockley Church, to which burials had previously belonged.[35] Bourton on the Hill, Moreton-in-Marsh and Batsford formerly buried at Blockley and still paid mortuaries there in the 18th century.[36]

There is a Baptist chapel in Blockley and mission chapels in connexion with it in Draycott and Paxford.

CHARITIES Educational Charities.—It appeared from the church table that Erasmus Saunders, D.D., vicar of the parish, erected a new schoolhouse in 1715, to which Jane Croft, by a codicil to her will, gave £3 yearly for clothing and 10s. yearly for buying Bibles for the children. The sums are paid out of the Northwick estate. The same table also mentioned that Goddard Carter, by his will dated in 1723, gave £10 yearly out of his estate in Upton Wold for the school ; also that Mrs. Mary Carter gave £100 for the school and for buying books for the poor. This gift is represented by £194 7s. 1d. consols with the official trustees, arising from the sale in 1899 of cottages and gardens, formerly the site of the workhouse, towards the building of which the £100 had been applied.

The official trustees also hold a sum of £154 3s. 11d. consols, representing two legacies of £50 each by wills of Mrs. Ann Martyn, 1727, and Mrs. Elizabeth Martyn, 1747. They also hold £200 consols left by will of Ann Boughton and £103 7s. 2d. consols left by will of Mrs. Lucy Russell, proved at Worcester 15 September 1858.

The several sums of stock produce in annual dividends £16 5s. 8d., which is remitted to trustees for application for purposes in connexion with the elementary schools.

Eleemosynary Charities.—Richard Perkins, who died in 1710, by his will directed £400 to be laid out in land, the rents to be applied in clothing aged or impotent poor or children of the poor who were regular attendants of the parish church. The legacy was laid out in the purchase of 9 acres or thereabouts at Mickleton, county of Gloucester, producing £28 a year. The net income is applied in the distribution of coats for men and gowns for women.

In 1723 Goddard Carter, above mentioned, gave a further annuity of £10 out of his estate in Upton Wold for clothing the poorest old people.

Elizabeth Countess of Northampton, who died in 1750, left to the parish £200 to be disposed of as her brother Sir John Rushout, bart., should think proper. The legacy remains as a charge on the Northwick estate, in respect of which twenty two-penny loaves were distributed every Sunday morning.

The five charities next mentioned are administered together, namely—

1. Mrs. Martha Scattergood, will, 1753, trust fund, £171 7s. 11d. consols.

2. Rebecca Baroness Northwick — mentioned on the church table—trust fund, £175 2s. 5d. consols, income for distribution among twenty women.

3. Mrs. Frances Bowhay, deed, 1836, trust fund, £538 2s. 11d. consols, for distribution in coal among the poor of the township.

4. Mrs. Lucy Russell, will proved at Worcester 15 September 1858, trust fund, £193 5s. 9d. consols, for distribution of bread, clothing and fuel among the poor of the township.

5. The Hon. Anne Rushout, will, 1840, trust fund, £180 consols, for blankets for the poor at Christmas.

The several sums of stock are held by the official trustees, producing in annual dividends £30 18s. 8d., which is applied proportionately in accordance with the trusts of the respective charities.

In 1909–10 twenty women received 5s. each, 12 tons of coal were distributed at a cost of £13, and the remainder, after payment of 12s. 4d. to the vicar and churchwardens of Aston Magna in respect of Mrs. Russell's charity, was applied in coals, blankets, quilts and sheets.

The four charities next mentioned are also administered together, namely :—

1. William Boughton, will, in or about 1831, trust fund, £297 18s. 2d. consols, income to be applied primarily in repair of tablet to be erected in the church to the memory of testator's sister and himself, surplus for the poor.

2. Admiral Sir Edward Collier, K.C.B., founded by codicil to will proved at London 29 October 1872, trust fund, £323 17s. 9d. consols, dividends to be applied during the term of 100 years from the day of testator's decease in the distribution of coal or other necessaries at Christmas.

3. Mrs. Elizabeth Sperry, will proved at Gloucester 19 March 1873, trust fund, £108 16s. 11d. consols, dividends to be applied, subject to repair of her husband's tomb and tablet in the church, in the distribution of blankets or warm clothing at Christmas.

4. Mrs. Ellen Phillips, will, 1878, trust fund, £97 13s. 6d. consols, dividends to be distributed to the poor.

The several sums of stock are held by the official trustees, producing together in annual dividends £20 13s. 4d., of which £2 10s. was in 1909 paid to the vicar and churchwardens of Aston Magna for distribution, 5s. in cleaning tomb and the remainder in the distribution of coal and clothing for the poor.

Church Lands.—Under the Inclosure Act, 1772, 10 a. 3 r. 21 p. was awarded to the vicar and churchwardens in lieu of certain lands mentioned on the church table as given for the reparation of the church. The land is let at £24 15s. yearly.

This parish is also entitled to share in the apprenticing charity of George Townshend in Cheltenham, co. Gloucester.

---

[34] Habington, op. cit. i, 68.   [35] Worc. Epis. Reg. Thoresby, fol. 22 d.   [36] Nash, op. cit. i, 102.

BREDICOT

Bradingecotan, Bradigcotan (xi cent.) ; Bradecote (xiii cent.) ; Bradicot, Bradecot, Brodecot (xiv cent.).

Bredicot is a small parish lying almost in the centre of Worcestershire and about 4 miles east of Worcester. It covers an area of 399 acres, of which 212 are laid down in permanent grass, 33 are woods and plantations and 111 are arable land,[1] and the chief crops are wheat, oats, beans and peas. The soil is marl and clay and the subsoil clay. The village, consisting of the church, rectory and court farm and a few cottages, lies in the centre of the parish on a branch road from the Worcester and Alcester high road.

The main settlement, which lies about a quarter of a mile south-east of the church, forms a picturesque group of houses mostly of half-timber and brick dating from the 16th and 17th centuries. Bredicot Court, to the south of the village, is an early 17th-century half-timber and brick house of two stories and an attic with tiled roofs, added to on the south in the 18th century and plastered and modernized on the west front. The original timber work is exposed on the east and north. The stairway, in the 18th-century addition, has a moulded handrail and retains in part its original slender turned balusters. East of the house there is a 17th-century half-timber and brick barn with a tiled roof. On the opposite side of the road is an L-shaped half-timber house dating probably from the 16th century, but restored with brickwork in the 18th century. It has an original projecting chimney on the north terminating in two diagonal shafts and retains its heavy oak timbers and floors. The stairway has square newels with shaped finials ; of its original shaped pierced balusters only one remains. Over a fireplace in an upper room is a piece of an oak moulded beam.

The nearest station is at Worcester, although the Midland railway passes near the village, crossing the parish from north to south. The parish was inclosed under Acts of 1836 and 1840, and the award is dated 1 December 1846.[2]

A Roman urn was dug up in 1839 near Bredicot Court.[3]

Among the place-names occur Goding's Mere[4] (x cent.), Spert Meadow[5] (xv and xvii cent.), Upper Stocking, Nether Stocking, Wyorsland Close, New Tyning, the Hill Ways and Kimbersley Coppice[6] (xvii cent.).

Prattinton, writing in the 19th century and quoting the Parliamentary Survey of 1650, says : 'There is a waste ground or common within the said manor called Ridley containing about 18 acres, in which the tenants of the said manor have common of pasture for their cattle at all times of the year appertinent to their copyholds, but the lessee of the farm hath pasture there only for one mare and colt.'[7]

MANOR There is no recorded grant of the manor of BREDICOT to the church of Worcester, but it had certainly been acquired before 985, when Bishop Oswald granted the vill to a priest named Goding on condition that he did any writing that was necessary. To this, it is said, he willingly assented, and wrote many books for the monastery.[7a] He retained the vill until his death,[8] and his heirs are said to have held Bredicot after him of the church of Worcester until it was taken away by the Normans.[9] The record adds that the church of Worcester thus lost the lordship, but in 1086 it was held of the bishop's manor of Northwick.[10] Brictwold the priest, who held it in the time of King Edward, performing such service for it as the bishop willed, was possibly one of Goding's heirs.

The manor was still held of the manor of Northwick at the end of the 13th century,[11] but after that time the bishop's overlordship seems to have lapsed.

In 1086 Walter Poer (Ponther) held the manor under the Bishop of Worcester,[12] and it formed part of the two and a half fees which Hugh Poer held of the bishop in 1166.[13] Early in the 13th century John Poer held this manor.[14] The chief seat of this branch of the family was at Battenhall in Worcester, and Bredicot became a member of that manor, the Poers' interest in Bredicot passing with Battenhall to the Prior and convent of Worcester in 1330.[15] This intermediary lordship lapsed in 1377, when the prior and convent acquired the manor in fee.

The early history of the tenants under the Poers is obscure. John de Bredicot presented to the church in 1288 and 1289,[16] and was probably lord of the manor at that time, as the advowson was apparently an appurtenance of the manor. He was holding the manor in 1298.[17] He granted the rent and services of one of his tenants at Bredicot to John de Everley in 1304–5,[18] but in 1317 Reginald Baldewyn as 'former lord of Bredicot' gave the manor to John de Dufford and his wife Cecily.[19]

[1] Statistics from Bd. of Agric. (1905).
[2] *Blue Bk. Incl. Awards*, 189.
[3] Noake, *Guide to Worcs.* 57.
[4] Nash, *Hist. of Worcs.* ii, App. xliv ; Heming, *Chartul.* (ed. Hearne), 347.
[5] Nash, op. cit. i, 125 ; Close, 1650, pt. xxii, no. 16.
[6] Close, 1650, pt. xxii, no. 16 ; Prattinton Coll. (Soc. Antiq.), Survey of Bredicot in possession of Rev. A. Wheeler, 1812.
[7] Prattinton Coll. (Soc. Antiq.) ; Nash, op. cit. i, 120.
[7a] This story is complicated by the fact that in the boundaries of a charter of about 840 relating to Crowle reference is made to 'Godings boundary at Bradigcotan' (Birch, *Cart. Sax.* ii, 2). If Heming's tale is to be trusted the boundaries must be a later addition to the extant text of the charter. The whole question deserves critical investigation because of its bearing upon the general authenticity of Heming's texts. As Goding, first as deacon and then as priest, attests documents issued by Bishop Oswald, Heming's tale deserves to be taken seriously (inform. from Mr. F. M. Stenton).
[8] Heming, op. cit. 139, 265 ; Dugdale, *Mon. Angl.* i, 567. Heming gives the boundaries of the land in Anglo-Saxon (op. cit. 357). [9] Heming, op. cit. 265.
[10] *V.C.H. Worcs.* i, 294.
[11] *Testa de Nevill* (Rec. Com.), 41*b* ; Habington, op. cit. i, 110, 150.
[12] *V.C.H. Worcs.* i, 295.
[13] *Red Bk. of Exch.* (Rolls Ser.), 300 ; Red Bk. of Bishopric of Worc. (Eccl. Com. Rec. Var. bdle. 121, no. 43698), fol. 253, 18.
[14] *Testa de Nevill* (Rec. Com.), 41*b*.
[15] *Cal. Pat.* 1327–30, p. 470 ; Dugdale, op. cit. i, 616.
[16] Nash, op. cit. i, 121. John and William de Bredicot paid subsidies at Bredicot in 1280 (*Lay Subs. R. Worcs.* c. 1280 [Worcs. Hist. Soc.], 39).
[17] Habington, op. cit. i, 110.
[18] Add. MS. 28024, fol. 148 ; Prattinton Coll. (Soc. Antiq.), Deeds of D. and C. of Worc. no. 10.
[19] B.M. Harl. Chart. 111, D 16. In 1295 licence was granted to Matthew Besill and Elizabeth his wife to grant the manor of Bradecote, held by them in chief, to John Wogan for life (*Cal. Pat.* 1292–1301, p. 151). As the manor of Bredicot was not held in chief and these names do not occur again in connexion with Bredicot, it is possible that this reference refers to Radcot in Oxfordshire, where the king granted Matthew Besill a weekly market in 1272 (*Cal. Chart. R.* 1257–1300, p. 183).

John de Dufford was escheator in Ireland,[20] and in 1324 became indebted for 40 marks to William de Kirkby.[21] He evidently mortgaged Bredicot Manor as security for the payment of this debt, for in 1327 William de Kirkby and Hugh de Dufford, whom John had nominated in 1327 as his attorney in England during his absence in Ireland,[22] were in possession of the manor.[23] In 1330 William de Kirkby transferred the debt owed to him by John de Dufford to Sir William de Walkington,[24] who accordingly entered into possession of the manor.[25]

As Sir William Walkington presented to the church in 1337,[26] he was probably still in possession of the manor at that date, but it seems to have been redeemed by the Duffords before 1346, when William de Dufford held it.[27] In 1346 William de Kirkby gave to William de Dufford and his wife Katherine messuages and lands in Bredicot formerly belonging to Richard Chasteleyn.[28] In 1352 William de Dufford released his life interest in the manor to his son Thomas, to his brother of the same name and to William de Kirkby.[29] It is possible that Thomas de Dufford the younger became a priest and gave up his rights in the manor to the Prior of Worcester in consideration of a yearly allowance, for in 1370 Thomas Dufford, chaplain, acknowledged 40s. in part payment of £4, a yearly pension which he received from the prior,[30] and the Dufford family afterwards ceased to hold property in Bredicot. In 1377 Richard II gave licence to the priory to acquire the manor and advowson of Bredicot of William de Astley, chaplain, John de Kirkby and John de Wellesbourgh.[31]

The Prior and convent of Worcester remained in possession of the manor until the Dissolution,[32] when it passed to the Crown. It was granted in 1542 to the Dean and Chapter of Worcester[33] and was confirmed to them in 1609.[34]

During the Commonwealth the dean and chapter were deprived of their possessions and Bredicot was sold to Richard Higgons in 1650.[35] It was restored on the accession of Charles II to the dean and chapter and was confirmed to them in 1692.[36] The dean and chapter remained in possession of the manor until 1859, when it was transferred to the Ecclesiastical Commissioners,[36a] who are the present owners.

In 1773 the 'leasehold manor or site of the manor held for eleven years and renewable every seven years' was put up for sale.[37] It appears to have been bought by Samuel Brampton, who became

a bankrupt in 1816, and the Bredicot Court estate was then sold.[38] In the middle of the 19th century Bredicot Court was for many years the residence of Henry Chamberlain, and the estate was purchased of his trustees in 1864 by Robert Berkeley of Spetchley, father of the present owner.

The church of *ST. JAMES THE LESS* is a simple rectangular structure 41 ft. long by 15 ft. wide inside. It has been very much restored in modern times, but its walls probably contain 13th-century material. In its east wall is a pointed window of three lights with plain heads and intersecting tracery over. The other five windows, two in each side and one in the west wall, are of two lights each with a plain piercing over. To the south of the chancel is a piscina with a trefoiled ogee head and a mutilated basin. The south doorway has a pointed head of two orders. The porch is of wood, and on the floor are some old tiles with the monogram R.E. The font is octagonal with shallow trefoiled panels on the side of the bowl and a small square diaper above. The bowl may be as early as the 13th century, but the stem and base are modern. All the other furniture is of recent date.

There is one bell above the west gable.

The communion plate includes an Elizabethan cup and cover paten of 1571, a stand paten of 1842, a plated flagon of 1869, and a brass almsdish of 1867.

The registers[39] before 1812 are as follows: (i) baptisms 1702 to 1812, burials 1702 to 1810 and marriages 1713 to 1753; (ii) marriages from 1754 to 1805.

ADVOWSON The advowson of the church of Bredicot seems from early times to have belonged to the owners of the manor,[40] and was granted in 1542 with the manor to the Dean and Chapter of Worcester, who are patrons at the present day.[41]

In 1585 Edward Dalton of Holbury presented to the church by a grant of the dean and chapter, and another grant of the advowson was made by them to John Archibold, whose widow Eleanor presented in 1624.[42] The living is a rectory, and was united in 1841 to the vicarage of Tibberton.[43]

Until 1543 Bredicot had all parochial rights except that of sepulture, the parishioners being obliged to carry their dead to the churchyard of the church of Worcester.[44] In that year the right of burial was granted to the parish and a piece of land adjoining

---

[20] *Cal. Pat.* 1321–4, p. 140.
[21] *Cal. Close,* 1323–7, p. 167.
[22] *Cal. Pat.* 1327–30, p. 187.
[23] Ibid. 1324–7, p. 352. William and Hugh jointly presented to the church in 1326, and are then stated to have been holding the farm of the manor and advowson for seven years (Nash, op. cit. i, 121).
[24] *Cal. Close,* 1330–3, pp. 141, 145.
[25] Ibid. 416, 527; Dugdale, *Mon. Angl.* i, 616. John Wyard had also had some property here early in the 14th century, but he was among those who joined the Earl of Lancaster's rebellion in 1322, and his goods at Bredicot were seized by the king, who issued orders that he should be arrested if he tried to escape at any port (*Cal. Close,* 1330–3, pp. 165, 416). His possessions at Bredicot were purchased by John Dufford, and in 1331 William de

Walkington was distrained for these goods, John Wyard having been pardoned in 1331 (ibid. p. 416; *Cal. Pat.* 1330–4, p. 53).
[26] Nash, op. cit. i, 122.
[27] *Feud. Aids,* v, 308.
[28] Prattinton Coll. (Soc. Antiq.), Deeds of D. and C. of Worc. no. 139.
[29] Ibid. no. 89. In the deed is mentioned Beatrice mother of William de Dufford, then wife of Thomas de Pentridge. Nash states that these three together presented to the church in 1361 and in 1395 (Nash, op. cit. i, 122).
[30] Prattinton Coll. (Soc. Antiq.), Deeds of D. and C. of Worc. no. 59.
[31] Pat. 1 Ric. II, pt. vi, m. 36; Chan. Inq. p.m. 1 Ric. II, no. 127.
[32] *Valor Eccl.* (Rec. Com.), iii, 223.
[33] *L. and P. Hen. VIII,* xvii, g. 71 (29).

[34] Pat. 6 Jas. I, pt. xii, no. 2.
[35] Close, 1650, pt. xxii, no. 16.
[36] Pat. 4 Will. and Mary, pt. i, no. 6.
[36a] Inform. from the late Mr. J. H. Hooper, Chapter Clerk of Worcester.
[37] Prattinton Coll. (Soc. Antiq.).
[38] Ibid.
[39] There are copies of earlier entries among the Bishops' Transcripts.
[40] Nash, op. cit. i, 121, 122; *Reg. G. Giffard* (Worcs. Hist. Soc.), 355; *Sede Vac. Reg.* (Worcs. Hist. Soc.), 237; Pat. 1 Ric. II, pt. vi, m. 36.
[41] *L. and P. Hen. VIII,* xvii, g. 71 (29); Inst. Bks. (P.R.O.).
[42] Inst. Bks. (P.R.O.); Nash, op. cit. i, 122.
[43] *Parl. Papers* (1872), xlvi, no. 227, p. 2.
[44] Noake, op. cit. 56.

BREDICOT CHURCH C. 1810
(From a Water-colour by Thos. Rickards in Prattinton Collection)

BREDON'S NORTON MANOR HOUSE

the church was consecrated. For this the parishioners paid to the dean and chapter a yearly pension of 6*d.* under pain of excommunication for non-payment.[45]

CHARITIES

Poor's Land.—This parish is in possession of about a quarter of an acre, producing £2 3*s.* yearly, which is distributed in coal to the poor.

BREDON

Breodun (xi cent.) ; Bredune (xii cent.) ; Breedon (xiii cent.) ; Breuton (xiv cent.).

The parish of Bredon lies on the southern margin of the county of Worcester, and is bounded on the west by the River Avon running south and on the south by a small stream called Carrant Brook running into the Avon on its left bank.

Included in this parish are the village of Bredon, which stands on a plain at the south-west base of Bredon Hill on the left bank of the Avon, and the hamlets of Bredon's Norton, Bredon's Hardwick, Kinsham, Mitton and Westmancote. Cutsdean, until recently a detached part of this parish, though geographically in Gloucestershire, was part of Worcestershire[1] until 1912, when by Order in Council it was annexed to the parish of Temple Guiting in Gloucestershire.

The area of the parish is 5,853 acres, of which 30 acres are covered with water; 3,187 acres are in Bredon, 1,106 acres in Bredon's Norton and 1,560 acres in Cutsdean. Bredon includes 851 acres of arable land, 1,678 acres of permanent grass and 40 acres of wood, while Bredon's Norton contains 317 acres of arable, 612 acres of permanent grass and 24 acres of wood, and Cutsdean 717 acres of arable land, 312 acres of permanent grass and 145 acres of woodland.[2] The soil is loam, sand and clay, and the subsoil is Keuper Sandstone. The chief crops are corn, fruit, vegetables and flowers.[3] The slope of the land is from east to west, and at Bredon Hill to the north-east, in Bredon's Norton, the land is 700 ft. above the ordnance datum. The highest point in the detached part of the parish, Cutsdean, is Cutsdean Hill, 1,000 ft.

The high road from Worcester enters the parish from the north and meets the Evesham and Tewkesbury high road in Bredon village close to the station on the Midland railway.

In the northern portion of the parish, near a wood called Aldwick Wood,[3a] on Bredon Hill, are some stones of a curious shape called King and Queen Stones.[4]

The village of Bredon is situated about 8½ miles south-west of Evesham and 3 miles north-east of Tewkesbury, overlooking the valley of the Avon. The church stands in a large churchyard near the western end of the village. To the west of the church, in the yard of the Manor Farm, is a magnificent stone barn of the 14th century, still in a fine state of

preservation, and almost unaltered since the period of its erection. It is placed with its greatest length from north to south, and measures internally about 124 ft. 3 in. by 37 ft. 11 in. The walls are of rubble masonry, with the exception of the buttresses, which are of ashlar work. The end walls, on the north and south, are gabled, and a stone-slated ridge roof, with dripping eaves, covers the building. The western side wall is divided into nine bays by ten buttresses of two offsets, and there are wagon entrances in the third bay from either end. The corresponding bays of the eastern side wall are occupied by two large porches, which also contain wagon entrances, the southernmost having a room with a fireplace above it. Between the porches and on either side of them were

14TH-CENTURY BARN, BREDON

originally six buttresses, opposite to the corresponding buttresses on the west wall, but three of these have been removed and lean-to sheds erected against the wall. On the exterior of the north wall are three buttresses, a central buttress of four offsets rising to about half the height of the gable, and two smaller buttresses, each of two offsets, on either side. The wall is terminated on the east and west by the end buttresses of the side walls, which are flush with it. In the centre of the south wall is a buttress of one offset, extending only to about the base of the gable, the flanking buttresses being placed at the extremities of the wall and at right angles to the end buttresses of the side walls, with which they correspond in height. In each bay of the side walls are plain narrow slits, unglazed, about 5 in. in width and widely splayed on the inside. In the north wall are three similar openings, one on either side of the

[45] Nash, op. cit. i, 126 ; Prattinton Coll. (Soc. Antiq.) ; Noake, op. cit. 57.

[1] Stat. 7 & 8 Vict. cap. 61.

[2] Statistics from Bd. of Agric. (1905).

[3] The allotment system is extensively

carried out here, nearly 300 persons being occupiers of small plots.

[3a] It is also called Aldick, and possibly takes its name from an old ditch running along the hill above it.

[4] One of the leets for Oswaldslow

Hundred was formerly held at this place (Eccl. Com. Ct. R. [P.R.O.], bdle. 195, no. 6), and the court leet for the manor of Bredon was also held here until about 100 years ago, when the stones were whitewashed with some ceremony.

central buttress and one above it in the apex of the gable. The arrangement is varied in the south wall, where there is a pair of openings on either side of the central buttress, one immediately over it, and a second smaller slit in the apex of the gable. The putlog holes in these walls, and here and there in the side walls, are also left unfilled. The walls have a chamfered plinth and a cornice of similar form, beneath the eaves of the roof; gablet finials crown the gables. Internally the barn is divided into three longitudinal divisions, corresponding to nave and aisles, by two rows of posts, about 1 ft. 1½ in. square, carrying purlins which support the principal rafters at the middle of their length. The posts, which stand upon stone plinths about 1 ft. 9 in. square, are stiffened transversely by collars at the purlin level and a little below. These, with the purlins, are strutted from the posts by curved braces, while the rafters are again strutted from the collars. The lower halves of the rafters, which form the roofs of the aisles, are stiffened by horizontal timbers at their feet, abutting upon the posts, from which both they and the rafters are strutted. The side walls of the wagon porches on the eastern side are of stone, their gable ends being filled with half-timber work. The room above the southern porch was probably originally entered by a staircase in the square chamber which occupies the internal angle made by the porch with the main building on the north. This has long been blocked, and an external stair of stone against its south wall now gives the sole access to it. The fireplace on the north side of the porch has also been built up; the chimney stack is corbelled out, and rises square for a few feet above the eaves of the roof. Here it is surmounted by an octagonal shaft crowned by a lantern-like cap of the same form, each face of which is gabled, and has a small opening to let the smoke out. This is in turn surmounted by a pyramidal finial. On the ground floor are small doorways in each side wall. The north porch is of similar character, but being without an upper room is consequently of less height.

The old rectory-house, on the north-east of the church, is an interesting building of various dates. The earliest portion, which is on the north-east and partly surrounds three sides of a court-yard, is of half-timber covered with rough-cast, and probably dates from the late 15th century. It has, however, been so altered and modernized at subsequent periods that the determination of its date must remain a matter of conjecture. A gabled two-storied porch gives entrance to the house from the court-yard. The outer entrance has a moulded segmental head and jambs; above is a window with a pointed head of two trefoiled lights, the spandrel in the head being blocked. This appears to be reset 15th-century work, though the main structure can hardly be earlier than the end of the 16th century. A small bellcote surmounts the gable, in which is hung a bell without date or inscription, commonly reported to be of silver and to have been found in the bed of the Avon. The whole of the western part of the house appears to be an enlargement of the 17th century, and is of stone covered with rough-cast. A complete remodelling of the interior appears to have taken place in the early 19th century, when large sash windows were formed in the wall of the entrance front on the south, to give the appearance of a single lofty story. The entrance-porch is of stone, gabled, with moulded coping, and a ball finial upon the apex of the gable. The outer doorway has a semicircular head, with moulded archivolt and imposts, and is flanked by Ionic pilasters elevated upon pedestals and supporting an entablature. Above is a shield with a lion rampant impaling a cross charged with a leopard's head. Below the shield is the date cIɔ Iɔ c Lxxxiii. The general style of the porch and the characters in which the date is written would lead one to suppose that it was about 100 years earlier, the whole character being Elizabethan. It is possible that the date is actually intended to be cIɔ Iɔ Lxxxiii, a c having been placed after the Iɔ in error. Little original detail remains inside the house. The room on the north side of the stable-yard, known as the 'panelled room,' retains its early 17th-century panelling, upon which is a shield with these arms: a bend cotised between three lions and a crescent on the bend.

The house known as the 'Mansion House' is a good early 17th-century building of brick with stone dressings and stands to the east of the rectory. In the centre of the village are Reed's almshouses, a pleasant block of 17th-century buildings, one story in height with an attic over. The eight houses form three sides of a quadrangle. The front, with its projecting wings, is faced with stone, but the back is of plain brickwork. In the wall of the eastern projecting wing is a shield carved in stone: quarterly (1) and (4) a winged lion, (2) and (3) three cross-bows. The windows are mullioned and the doorways have straight-sided four-centred heads.

There is also at Bredon an old village pound.

At Mitton, 2 miles south of Bredon, in what is now the yard of Mitton Farm, a good late 17th-century house of brick, is the site of an ancient chapel, now covered by farm buildings.

Bredon's Norton Manor House is a 16th-century house of stone and half-timber three stories in height, and consists of a central block, the ground floor of which is occupied by a large entrance-hall, with wings at the north and south, the latter of which appears to have been entirely rebuilt. The north wing appears to be of half-timber, while the centre portion and the later south wing are of stone. With the exception of this wing the walls are covered with rough-cast. The chimney stacks are of stone and are surmounted by brick chimney shafts. The external appearance has been much altered by the insertion of sash windows, though some of the mullioned windows of the centre block have been left undisturbed. At the south-east of the hall is a central newel stair, probably of original date, while there are later stairs on the north. In a room on the first floor is a stone fireplace on which are carved the initials t.c. m.c. and the date 1585, with a shield in the centre charged with a cross paty. The same shield and initials occur on a chimney stack on the north side of the house. With the exception of some panelling belonging to this period the house has retained few other features of interest. The forecourt remains much as it was laid out at the end of the 16th century, with its elaborate gateway and plain inclosing walls, with buildings at the north and south angles. The gateway, which was blown down about twenty-five years ago and carefully re-erected, is an excellent example of Elizabethan work. It has a semicircular head, and is surmounted by an entablature with a fluted frieze, supported by short pilasters, stopped at the level of the moulded imposts of the arch. In the gable over the entablature, which has a moulded coping, is carved the date 1585, with three blank shields in a panel beneath. In the side walls of the forecourt are gateways with segmental heads and crowned by weathered copings. On the north side of the house is a good stone barn.

This manor-house is now occupied as a residential club and belongs to Miss Z. M. Woodhull of Norton Park in this parish.

An Inclosure Act for Bredon was passed in 1808,[5] for Bredon's Norton in 1814,[6] and for Cutsdean in 1775.[7]

Roman remains have been found on Bredon Hill and on the top of the hill there are some extensive

MANORS According to Worcester tradition, between 715 and 717,[12] Ethelbald, King of Mercia, gave land at *BREDON* to his kinsman Eanulf to found a monastery there.[13] Offa grandson of Eanulf endowed the monastery with lands in Worcestershire in 780.[14] In 781, 12 *manses* at Bredon were confirmed by Offa to the see of Worcester in settlement of a dispute which had arisen between him and the bishop.[15]

On Christmas Day 841 Berhtwulf, King of Mercia, freed the monastery of Bredon and its lands from the duty of entertaining persons sent by the king, in return for which the abbot and brethren gave him a large *discus* of silver, finely worked, 120 *mancusae* of pure gold, and promised to sing in twelve turns 100 psalms and 120 masses for the king and the people of Mercia.[16]

BREDON : THE OLD RECTORY

earthworks.[8] Roman remains were also found in 1882 at Bredon village near the station.[9]

Various Anglo-Saxon relics have been found at Bredon's Norton. They were presented to the museum of the Worcestershire Natural History Society in 1838 by one of the engineers employed in making the Birmingham and Gloucester railway.[10]

Dr. Prideaux, who became Bishop of Worcester in 1641, died in 1650 at Bredon, where he had retired to the house of his son-in-law Dr. Henry Sutton after his deprivation in 1646.[11]

A few years later King Berhtwulf granted the monastery further privileges, including freedom from the burdens called *cum feorme et eafor*, in return for which they paid 180 *mancusae* of pure gold and certain lands.[17] The monastery of Bredon continued under an abbot of its own for some time,[18] but before 844 it seems to have become in some way subject to the see of Worcester, for Heming gives a charter of that year by which Aelhun Bishop of Worcester gave to the monks of Worcester 12 *cassata* of land in Bredon, or rather confirmed it, for it appears that the gift was

[5] Priv. Act, 48 Geo. III, cap. 24. The award is dated 4 July 1811 (*Blue Bk. Incl. Awards*, 189).

[6] Priv. Act, 54 Geo. III, cap. 36. The award is dated 18 Feb. 1815 (*Blue Bk. Incl. Awards*, 191).

[7] Priv. Act, 15 Geo. III, cap. 69. The award is dated 27 Feb. 1776 (*Blue Bk. Incl. Awards*, 189).

[8] *V.C.H. Worcs.* i, 218.   [9] Ibid. 189.

[10] Ibid. 230–1.   [11] *Dict. Nat. Biog.*

[12] The gift was made in the pontificate of Egwin (693–717). [13] Dugdale, *Mon.* i, 607.

[14] Ibid. 586, 587; Birch, *Cart. Sax.* i, 329. Offa also granted the reversion of land at Evenlode to Bredon Monastery in 772 (Birch, op. cit. i, 297).

[15] Birch, op. cit. i, 335.

[16] Ibid. ii, 8.   [17] Ibid. 37.

[18] Eanmund was abbot in 841 (Birch, op. cit. ii, 8).

made by Coenwulf, King of Mercia.[19] Three years later the monks restored to Bishop Aelhun twelve *manses* of the land belonging to the monastery of Bredon on condition that after his death and the death of one other to whom he might bequeath the land it should return to the monks of Worcester.[20] In 964 Bredon was included by King Edgar in his famous charter, granting the hundred of Oswaldslow to the church of Worcester.[21]

Some confusion has been caused by a charter of King Edgar granting land at 'Bredone' and implying the existence of a church there in 966. The site has been wrongly identified with the Worcestershire Bredon. It is, however, certain that the place referred to is Breedon on the Hill, co. Leicester, land at Diseworth in that county being conveyed by the same grant.[22] In 1086 the manor of Bredon with its members was in the possession of the Bishop of Worcester.[23]

By 1118 the bishop had increased his demesne lands at Bredon by 3 hides,[24] and in 1254 and 1255 free warren was granted to him there.[25] In 1275 the Bishop of Worcester complained that the Earl of Warwick had impeded him from having free warren at Bredon, and had tried to get possession of his demesne lands there,[26] and in the same year certain persons (unnamed) came to the bishop's manor of Bredon, assaulted his servants, and carried away his goods.[27]

The manor remained in the possession of successive Bishops of Worcester[28] until under the Act of 1558–9 empowering the queen to take into her hands temporal possessions of any bishopric, in exchange for parsonages impropriate, Bredon Manor passed to the Crown.[29] It was leased in 1569–70 for twenty-one years to Richard May,[30] and in 1570–1 the site of the manor and all rents of assize belonging to it were granted to him and his sons Richard and John for their lives at a rent of £20 9s. 10d. yearly.[31] The site and demesne lands of the manor were leased in 1575 to John Morley from 1607 for twenty years, and the capital messuage called Bishopshouse was leased to him for a similar term, beginning in 1613.[32]

The manor was granted in 1577 to Henry Knollys and Edward Williams at a fee-farm rent of £59 12s. 0½d.[33] They sold it a few days later to Thomas Copley and George Hornyold.[34] Copley

and Hornyold seem to have alienated large estates, formerly parcels of the manor of Bredon.[35] The part retained by Hornyold, known as half the manor of Bredon, included the site and capital messuage of the manor, and passed from George Hornyold in 1618 to his son Thomas.[36] Thomas was succeeded in 1632 by his son Thomas,[37] who was dealing with this moiety of the manor in 1655.[38] He sold the greater part of the estate in 1667 to Thomas Turvey and the rest to Richard Harris, John Mason and others.[39]

HORNYOLD. *Azure a bend counter-embattled argent with a wolf passant between two scallops sable thereon.*

Thomas Turvey's daughter Elizabeth married Other son of Thomas Lord Windsor, and in 1673 Thomas Turvey conveyed his share of Bredon Manor to Sir William Coventry and Sir Francis Russell,[40] as trustees for its sale in payment of Other's debts.[41] Other was still in possession in 1680–1.[42] This moiety of the manor afterwards passed to the Darkes, and was dealt with in 1792 by John Darke and Anne his wife and Richard Darke.[43] Before 1850 the manor had passed to Nathan Dyer. Between 1863 and 1868 it seems to have passed to Nathan Nathaniel Dyer,[44] who held it till after 1880. It had passed before 1892 to William Dyer of Bickerton Hall, co. Hereford. Nathan Dyer had succeeded before 1904, and is at present lord of the manor of Bredon.

Part of the manor which was alienated by Copley and Hornyold in the 16th century afterwards became known as a moiety of the manor of Bredon. In 1578 Thomas Copley and George Hornyold sold Bishopswood,[45] Penny Land and Strange Acre to Thomas Cockes and his son Seth.[46] Seth died in 1599 and Thomas in 1601 holding 'the manor of Bredon.'[47] Thomas son of Thomas succeeded, but the estate had passed before 1616–17 to Sir Edward Fisher, Thomas Allen and William Allen his son, who joined in conveying it in that year to William Allen.[48]

William Allen forfeited all his lands to the king for debt in June 1631, and his estates in Bredon, comprising a capital messuage and land called the Downes,

[19] Heming, *Chartul.* (ed. Hearne), 562.
[20] Dugdale, *Mon. Angl.* i, 608.
[21] Birch, op. cit. iii, 380.
[22] Ibid. 592 ; 'Type of Manorial Structure in the Northern Danelaw' (*Oxford Studies in Social and Legal History*, ii, 78). It is also probable that the monastery of Briudun in Mercia, where Tatwine, Archbishop of Canterbury, had been abbot before his elevation, was situated in the Leicestershire Breedon. Bede, to whom we owe this information (*Opera Historica* [ed. Plummer], i, 350), would certainly have described the Worcestershire Bredon as 'in the province of the Hwiccas' (inform. from Mr. F. M. Stenton).
[23] *V.C.H. Worcs.* i, 291a.
[24] Ibid. 324b.
[25] *Cal. Pat.* 1247–58, p. 345 ; *Cal. Chart. R.* 1226–57, p. 443.
[26] *Reg. G. Giffard* (Worcs. Hist. Soc.), 75.
[27] *Cal. Pat.* 1272–81, p. 103.
[28] *Testa de Nevill* (Rec. Com.), 42a ;

Pope Nich. Tax. (Rec. Com.), 225a ; *Feud. Aids*, v, 306, 318. In 1291 the bishop received £28 a year from this manor, but before 1535 it had increased in value to £56 15s. 8½d. (*Valor Eccl.* [Rec. Com.], iii, 218b).
[29] *V.C.H. Worcs.* ii, 48 ; Pat. 4 Eliz. pt. vi.
[30] Pat. 12 Eliz. pt. v, m. 15.
[31] Ibid. 13 Eliz. pt. ix, m. 19. In 1586 Richard May complained that Richard Dawks, to whom he had entrusted the leases of Bredon in order that he might raise money on them, 'lay in waite for Richard in a desert place as he was riding to keep courte at Breedon . . . and so riding over a great flud the said Dauckes cam behinde unawares and strocke him neer to death meaning to have murthered him in the water if rescue had not cum,' and 'he continualye doth procure vagrant persons to murther him' (Ct. of Req. bdle. 123, no. 46).
[32] Pat. 17 Eliz. pt. xi, m. 21.
[33] Ibid. 19 Eliz. pt. xiii, m. 17.

[84] Ibid. pt. iv, m. 38.
[35] Ibid. 20 Eliz. pt. v, m. 4, 40 ; Chan. Inq. p.m. (Ser. 2), cclxx, 103.
[36] Chan. Inq. p.m. (Ser. 2), ccclxxii, 156 ; Fine R. 20 Jas. I, pt. iii, no. 45.
[87] Chan. Inq. p.m. (Ser. 2), cccclxxxvi, 57.
[38] Feet of F. Worcs. Hil. 1655.
[39] Exch. Dep. East. 32 Chas. II, no. 26.
[40] Feet of F. Div. Co. Hil. 25 & 26 Chas. II.
[41] Ibid. Mich. 33 Chas. II ; Priv. Act, 9 Anne, cap. 5.
[42] Exch. Dep. East. 32 Chas. II, no. 26.
[48] Recov. R. East. 32 Geo. III, rot. 269.
[44] Noake, *Guide to Worcs.* 60.
[45] Bishopswood existed under this name in the time of Henry II, when Peter de Saltmarsh held assarts there (Habington, op. cit. i, 526).
[46] Pat. 20 Eliz. pt. v, m. 4.
[47] Chan. Inq. p.m. (Ser. 2), cclxx, 103.
[48] Notes of Fines, Worcs. East. 14 Jas. I.

Bishop's Field, &c., were granted in the following month to Lady Constance Lucy and Francis Lucy as long as they remained in the king's hands.[49] In 1637 this estate was sold by Sir Richard Lucy, bart., executor of Lady Constance, to George and Roger Corbett.[50] Before William Allen's forfeiture the estate was sold by him to Sir Thomas Bowyer and Nathaniel Studley in trust for Pedael Harlow.[51] They seem to have recovered it from Allen's creditors, for in 1638-9 Sir Thomas Bowyer gave up his claim to Pedael Harlow.[52] Edward Andrews and his wife Elizabeth and John Harlow were dealing with this moiety of the manor in 1660-1.[53] The Harlows' estate passed before 1676 to William Dowdeswell[54] of Pull Court, with which estate it descended[55] until 1786, when Thomas Dowdeswell sold it to Mr. Morris, who was possibly an agent for John Darke, who eventually acquired it.[56] It thus became united with the other moiety of the manor.

The part of the manor retained by Thomas Copley, which included an estate called the manor of *HALL COURT alias BRACE'S LAND* in Norton,[56a] and carried with it the advowson of the church, was settled by him in 1587 upon his son John.[57] Thomas died in 1593, and John died without issue in 1606, when Thomas son of Thomas succeeded.[58] He and Thomas Copley, jun., who was probably his son, sold the manor of Hall Court in 1649 to William Hancock, sen., and William Hancock, jun.[59] The two latter had to compound in 1649 for two-thirds of the estate which had been sequestered for the recusancy of the two Copleys.[60] William Hancock, who dealt with the manor of Hall Court in 1678-9,[61] was son of the younger William,[62] and was probably the William Hancock who died in 1719.[63] Peter Hancock and Anna his wife were in possession in 1765.[64] The former died in 1775, leaving two daughters,[65] one of whom, Charlotte, married John Embury. Charlotte and John dealt with a moiety of the manor of Hall Court in 1776-7.[66]

When the manor of Bredon was granted in 1577 to Henry Knollys and Edward Williams, a fee-farm

COPLEY. *Argent a cross sable with a martlet or thereon.*

rent of £59 12s. 0½d. was reserved to the Crown.[67] It was granted by James I to his queen, Anne, for life[68] in 1614, and by Charles I to Queen Henrietta Maria in 1627.[69] Later it was confiscated by Parliament, and sold in 1651 to Arthur Hollingworth of London.[70]

At the Restoration this fee-farm rent returned to the Crown, and was in 1670 vested in trustees,[71] who sold it in 1672 to Peter Lely of St. Paul's, Covent Garden, the well-known painter.[72] This rent afterwards passed to the Vernons of Hanbury, who were in possession in 1745 and 1819.[73]

The manor of Bredon was surveyed in 1563, shortly after it came into the hands of Queen Elizabeth.[74] It was found that the mansion-house, called Bishop's House, was very ruinous and almost fallen down for want of repair. The house was then held under a sixty years' lease by the Hornyolds.[75]

At the date of the Domesday Survey Urse held 4 hides at *WESTMANCOTE* (Westmonecot, xi cent.; Westmancote, Westmecote, xiv cent. ; Westmoncote, xv cent. ; Westencote, xvi cent.) which one Brictuine had held, and for which he had done service to the Bishop of Worcester on such terms as could be obtained.[76]

Urse's interest in the manor passed with his other estates to the Beauchamps, afterwards Earls of Warwick, and Westmancote was held of the barony of Elmley until 1612-13, when the overlordship is mentioned for the last time.[77]

Under the lords of Elmley this manor was held by the Pendocks of Pendock for knight service. Robert de Pendock was holding 4 hides there early in the 13th century,[78] and the manor then followed the same descent as Pendock until 1346, when it was held by John de Pendock.[79]

In 1371-2 the manor was held by Roger Marshal and his wife Margaret in her right.[80] It would seem probable that Margaret Marshal was the widow of John or William de Pendock, and held only a life interest in the manor, for in 1402-3 she, then a widow, and John son of William de Westmancote *alias* Pendock sold the manor to Sir John Cheyne.[81]

Anne daughter of Sir John Cheyne married Thomas Rous of Ragley,[82] and the manor of Westmancote was settled upon them in 1427.[83] They were succeeded by a son Thomas, who died without issue, the manor then passing to his brother William, who brought an action against his father's trustees as

[49] Pat. 14 Chas. I, pt. xxiv, no. 2.
[50] Add. Chart. 14752.
[51] Ibid. 15007 ; Chan. Proc. (Ser. 2), bdle. 396, no. 155.
[52] Feet of F. Worcs. Trin. 14 Chas. I.
[53] Ibid. Trin. 12 Chas. II.
[54] Exch. Dep. East. 32 Chas. II, no. 26 ; inform. from the Rev. E. R. Dowdeswell.
[55] Recov. R. D. Enr. Hil. 10 Anne, m. 6 ; Recov. R. East. 16 Geo. III, rot. 28, 29.
[56] Inform. from the Rev. E. R. Dowdeswell.
[56a] The manor of Hall Court or Brace's Land had been bought by Thomas Copley in 1567 of Francis Brace (Feet of F. Worcs. East. 9 Eliz.).
[57] Pat. 29 Eliz. pt. xiii, m. 32.
[58] Chan. Inq. p.m. (Ser. 2), cccvi, 155 ; Fine R. 8 Jas. I, pt. i, no. 44.
[59] Feet of F. Worcs. Mich. 1649.
[60] Cal. Com. for Comp. 2102.

[61] Feet of F. Worcs. Trin. 30 Chas. II.
[62] Metcalfe, *Visit. of Worcs.* 53.
[63] M.I. quoted by Nash (*Hist. of Worcs.* i, 133).
[64] Recov. R. Mich. 6 Geo. III, rot. 182.
[65] Nash, op. cit. i, 130.
[66] Feet of F. Worcs. Mich. 17 Geo. III.
[67] Pat. 19 Eliz. pt. xiii, m. 17.
[68] Ibid. 11 Jas. I, pt. xiii.
[69] Ibid. 2 Chas. I, pt. iv.
[70] Close, 1651, pt. lv, no. 25.
[71] Pat. 22 Chas. II, pt. ii (1st roll).
[72] Close, 24 Chas. II, pt. ix, m. 23. In 1680 there were proceedings taken to settle in what proportions this rent-charge should be paid by the owners of the manor of Bredon (Exch. Dep. East. 32 Chas. II, no. 26).
[73] Recov. R. Trin. 18 & 19 Geo. II, rot. 48 ; East. 59 Geo. III, rot. 289.
[74] Rentals and Surv. portf. 4, no. 7.
[75] Ibid.

[76] V.C.H. Worcs. i, 292a.
[77] Testa de Nevill (Rec. Com.), 41b ; Cal. Inq. p.m. 1-9 Edw. II, 403 ; Chan. Inq. p.m. (Ser. 2), xix, 74 ; cccxxvi, 48.
[78] Testa de Nevill (Rec. Com.), 41b.
[79] Cal. Inq. p.m. 1-9 Edw. II, 403 ; Cal. Pat. 1317-21, p. 523 ; Feet of F. Worcs. 16 Edw. III, no. 13 ; Feud. Aids, v, 307. The manor of Westmancote does not seem to have been held by John de Pendock, who died seised of Pendock in 1322. It probably remained in the elder branch of the family, to which Pendock ultimately seems to have reverted.
[80] Feet of F. Worcs. 45 Edw. III, no. 10.
[81] Phillipps, Index to Worcs. Fines, p. x, East. 4 Hen. IV ; see also Close, 4 Hen. IV, m. 36.
[82] Visit. of Worcs. 1569 (Harl. Soc. xxvii), 113.
[83] Feet of F. Div. Co. East. 5 Hen. VI.

to this manor towards the end of the 15th century.[84] Later he had difficulty in obtaining the manor from Margaret wife of Richard Barneby, who claimed it under the will of Thomas Rous the son.[85] William Rous died in 1505–6,[86] and the manor passed with Rous Lench[87] until it was sold with the other Worcestershire estates in 1861–70 by Sir Charles Rouse-Boughton.

Rous. *Argent two bars engrailed sable.*

Another estate at Westmancote, known as a manor in the 16th century and later, belonged to the Poers and Washbournes of Wichenford. Its origin is obscure, and nothing is known of it until the end of the 14th century. In 1390–1 William son of John Poer and Philippa his wife conveyed land in Westmancote, Moreton and Bredon to John Poer of Wichenford.[88] In 1410–11 John and his wife Eleanor conveyed the same estate to John Washbourne.[89] It then followed the same descent as

POER of Wichenford. *Gules a fesse or with two molets argent in the chief.*

WASHBOURNE. *Argent a fesse between six martlets gules with three cinqfoils argent upon the fesse.*

Wichenford until 1675, when William Washbourne and his wife Susan sold it to William Hancock.[90] It then passed with the Hancocks' manor of Bredon until 1776–7, when a moiety of it was conveyed with Hall Court by John Embury and his wife Charlotte to John Windus.[91]

Both the estates at Westmancote seem to have passed before 1872 to Miss Martin, who was then lady of the manor of Westmancote. She continued to hold the manor until 1891, and was succeeded by her brother, Mr. Robert Martin of Overbury, who died in 1897, leaving it to his son John Biddulph Martin. He survived his father only by three days

and left his property to his widow, the present owner of the manor.[91a]

A manor called *MORETON*, which is mentioned in deeds of the 16th century and later relating to the Washbournes' manor of Westmancote, was probably in the parish of Bredon, the present Moreton Farm in Lower Westmancote no doubt marking its site.

Among the charters of the see of Worcester is one by Athelstan, King of Britain (926–40), to his servant Ethelnoth of two *manses* in Moreton.[92] This land evidently passed subsequently to the church of Worcester, and is probably to be identified with the 2 hides at Moreton granted by Bishop Oswald in 990 to two brothers, Beorhnaege and Byrhstan.[93] These two charters probably relate to Moreton in Bredon, as the church of Worcester does not seem to have held any other estate of that name.

Two hides at Moreton were held in the time of Henry II of the manor of Bredon by Robert son of Richard.[94] These 2 hides were held in the beginning of the 13th century by Robert de Moreton, David son of Robert also holding half a hide in Moreton.[95] Walter de Westmancote held the 2 hides in 1299[95a] and both estates had passed by 1346 to John de Moreton.[96] It was perhaps the same estate which, as land in Moreton, was settled in 1390–1 on William son of John Poer and his wife Philippa with contingent remainder to John Poer of Wichenford.[97] It followed the same descent as the Poers' manor of Westmancote from that time until 1599,[98] when it is mentioned for the last time as a manor. It afterwards seems to have become annexed to Westmancote, for in an inquisition of 1622 'the manor of Westmancote in Norton and Moreton' is mentioned,[99] and at the present day Moreton Farm is the property of Mrs. J. B. Martin, lady of the manor of Westmancote.

CUTSDEAN (Codestune, x cent.; Codestone, xi cent.; Cuttesden, Cutsdowne, Cuttson, xvii cent.) is said to have been given to the church of Worcester by Offa.[100] In 974[1] Oswald Bishop of Worcester granted 5 *manses* at Cutsdean for three lives to one Wulfheah with reversion to the church of Worcester.[2] In 987 the bishop granted the same land to Ethelmund for two lives.[3] Shortly after Bishop Brihteah (Beortheah) leased this land to one Dodo, but Archbishop Ealdred recovered it from his son in the reign of William I.[4] At the date of the Domesday Survey Aeilric the archdeacon held 2 hides at Cutsdean of the bishop's manor of Bredon.[5] Before 1118 these hides had apparently reverted to the bishop,[6] and they are said to have been given by Bishop John de Pageham, who

84 Early Chan. Proc. bdle. 52, no. 68.
85 Ibid. bdles. 56, no. 9; 53, no. 284; 51, no. 154; 59, no. 15; 84, no. 11. It is not clear from the Chancery proceedings whether Margaret had ever actually married Thomas Rous, but she appears to have been betrothed to him.
86 Chan. Inq. p.m. (Ser. 2), xix, 74.
87 Recov. R. Trin. 2 Geo. IV, rot. 148; D. Enr. m. 55.
88 Phillipps, Index to Worcs. Fines, p. viii, East. 14 Ric. II.
89 Ibid. p. xi, East. 12 Hen. IV. John Washbourne married Margaret daughter and one of the heirs of John Poer (see Wichenford).
90 Exch. Inq. p.m. (Ser. 2), file 1190,

no. 2; Feet of F. Worcs. Mich. 3 Edw. VI; Hil. 11 Eliz.; Hil. 41 Eliz.; Mich. 15 Chas. I; Hil. 1658; Chan. Inq. p.m. (Ser. 2), clix, 75; Feet of F. Worcs. Trin. 27 Chas. II.
91 Feet of F. Worcs. Trin. 30 Chas. II; Recov. R. Mich. 6 Geo. III, rot. 182; Feet of F. Worcs. Mich. 17 Geo. III.
91a Inform. by Sir Richard Martin of Overbury.
92 Heming, Chartul. (ed. Hearne), 567.
93 Ibid. 180, 558.
94 Habington, op. cit. i, 526; Red Bk. of Bishopric of Worc. (Eccl. Com. Rec. Var. bdle. 121, no. 43698), fol. 66.
95 Testa de Nevill (Rec. Com.), 42.
95a Red Bk. of Bishopric of Worc. fol. 56.

96 Feud. Aids, v, 309.
97 Feet of F. Worcs. East. 14 Ric. II.
98 Phillipps, Index to Worcs. Fines, p. xi, East. 12 Hen. IV; Feet of F. Worcs. Hil. 11 Eliz.; Hil. 41 Eliz. Moreton is first called a manor in 1569.
99 Jas. Davenport, Hist. of the Washbourne Family, 138.
100 Heming, op. cit. i, 515.
1 The date is given as 977 by Heming.
2 Birch, Cart. Sax. iii, 618; Heming, op. cit. 167. The boundaries of the land are given.
3 Heming, op. cit. 166.
4 Ibid. 302; V.C.H. Worcs. i, 291b.
5 V.C.H. Worcs. i, 291b.
6 Ibid. 324, n. 12.

died in 1158, to the priory of Worcester.[7] According to the Red Book of the bishopric, however, Cutsdean was given to the monks in the time of Bishop Pageham by Peverell de Beauchamp.[8] In 1212, on the death of William de Wetmora, Cutsdean is said to have returned into the hands of the Chamberlain of Worcester Priory,[9] William having probably held it under a lease for life. In 1240 the monks held 2 hides at Cutsdean[10] and in 1256 they obtained a grant of free warren in this manor.[11] About 1291 Godfrey Bishop of Worcester released to the prior and convent all his rights of scutage, homage, &c., in the vill of Cutsdean.[12] In 1291 the chamberlain of the priory held at Cutsdean a carucate of land worth £1.[13]

The manor remained in the hands of the successive Priors of Worcester until the dissolution of the priory in 1539–40,[14] when it was granted by Henry VIII in 1541 to Richard Andrews.[15] In the following year he sold it to William Freeman,[16] who settled it in 1561 upon himself and his wife Ann and their issue male.[17] He was succeeded by his grandson Thomas Freeman.[18] Thomas Freeman, his grandmother Anne Freeman, and Edward Freeman, who may have been his son, conveyed the manor of Cutsdean in 1582[19] to Robert Ashfield and Francis Kettleby. Edward Freeman married Catherine sister of Humphrey Coningsby and in 1604–5 conveyed the manor to his brother-in-law.[20] Humphrey Coningsby died seised of the manor of Cutsdean in 1611,[21] his heir being his sister Catherine Freeman. She and her husband had livery of the manor in 1617,[22] but only seem to have retained a third of it, the other two thirds passing to the Coningsbys. Edmund Freeman and Catherine were dealing with a third of the manor in 1628,[23] and Coningsby Freeman, who sold this third in 1633 to John Kite, was probably their son.[24] This third was sold in 1665 by Francis Kite and his wife Alice to William Dobbins.[25] William or a descendant of the same name held in 1721 an estate at Cutsdean,[26] which was conveyed in 1775–6[27] by John and Samuel

CONINGSBY. *Gules three sitting conies argent in a border engrailed sable.*

Dobbins and Henry Timme and his wife Elizabeth to John Darke.[28]

Edward Dobbins West still held an estate at Cutsdean in 1872 and 1880, but William Price is said to have been lord of the manor in 1872 and his widow Mrs. Price held the manor in 1876 and 1892. This estate was bought soon after by the Earl of Wemyss,[28a] who owned the other part of the manor, and Lord Elcho, his eldest son, is now the lord of the whole.

The other two thirds of the manor were held by Sir Thomas Coningsby at the time of his death in 1626.[29] His son Fitz William Coningsby held the estate in 1658, when he and his son Humphrey agreed to assign a rent from this manor to Sampson Wise.[30] Humphrey son of Fitz William was in possession in 1660.[31]

The estate had passed before 1691 to Lady Tracy,[32] and appears to have still belonged to her in 1721.[33] In 1735 Robert son of John Tracy of Stanway held the manor,[34] and from him it passed to his brother Anthony. Henrietta Charlotte, one of the daughters and heirs of Anthony, married Edward Devereux Viscount Hereford, who held the manor in her right in 1775 and at the end of the 18th century.[35] The viscount died without issue, and on the death of his widow in 1817 Cutsdean passed to her sister Susan wife of Francis Charteris Lord Elcho.[36] Francis son of Susan was created Lord Wemyss in 1821 and became Earl of Wemyss, Lord Wemyss of Elcho and Lord Elcho and Methel in 1826 by the reversal of the attainder of David Wemyss, his collateral

CHARTERIS-WEMYSS-DOUGLAS, Earl of Wemyss. *Argent a fesse azure within a double tressure counter-flowered gules* for CHARTERIS, *quartered with Or a lion gules* for WEMYSS.

ancestor, who joined in the Stuart rising, and was attainted after the battle of Culloden in 1745.[37] He was dealing with the manor of Cutsdean in 1821,[38] and it now belongs to Lord Elcho, eldest son of the present Earl of Wemyss.

An estate which lay partly in Cutsdean, sometimes known as Cutsdean Manor, which appears to have included *HINCHWICK* Manor or Farm, belonged

[7] *Dict. Nat. Biog.* under John de Pagham.
[8] Red Bk. of Bishopric of Worc. fol. 254; Habington, op. cit. i, 524, 525, and see Hale, op. cit. 103a.
[9] *Ann. Mon.* (Rolls Ser.), iv, 401; see also *Testa de Nevill* (Rec. Com.), 42a.
[10] Hale, loc. cit.
[11] *Cal. Pat.* 1354–8, p. 266.
[12] Ibid. 1281–92, p. 451; *Reg. G. Giffard* (Worc. Hist. Soc.), 393.
[13] *Pope Nich. Tax.* (Rec. Com.), 227b.
[14] *V.C.H. Worcs.* ii, 111. At this date the manor with the farms of Berrow and Mitton was worth £11 13s. a year to the priory (*Valor Eccl.* [Rec. Com.], iii, 223a).
[15] *L. and P. Hen. VIII,* xvi, g. 878 (36).
[16] Ibid. xvii, g. 362 (54).
[17] Feet of F. Worcs. Hil. 4 Eliz.; Pat. 3 Eliz. pt. xiii, m. 6.

[18] William Freeman had settled the manor of Cutsdean on his eldest son John on the occasion of his marriage with Joan daughter of Thomas Bonner. John died before his father, and there were proceedings in the Court of Chancery between Joan and her son Thomas and William Freeman to compel him to grant the manor to his grandson Thomas (Chan. Proc. [Ser. 2], bdle. 67, no. 8).
[19] Feet of F. Worcs. Hil. 24 Eliz.; East. 24 Eliz.
[20] Feet of F. Worcs. Hil. 2 Jas. I.
[21] Chan. Inq. p.m. (Ser. 2), cccxxxvi, 52.
[22] Fine R. 15 Jas. I, pt. ii, no. 27.
[23] Feet of F. Div. Co. East. 4 Chas. I.
[24] Ibid. Worcs. East. 9 Chas. I.
[25] Ibid. Hil. 16 & 17 Chas. II.
[26] Exch. Dep. Mich. 8 Geo. I, no. 11.
[27] In 1775 Edward Dobbins or the heir at law of William Dobbins, deceased, was one of the lords of the manor of

Cutsdean (Priv. Act, 15 Geo. III, cap. 69).
[28] Feet of F. Worcs. Hil. 16 Geo. III.
[28a] Inform. by Mr. B. C. Cobb.
[29] Chan. Inq. p.m. (Ser. 2), ccccxxiv, 93.
[30] Recov. R. East. 1658, rot. 195; Close, 22 Chas. II, pt. xxiii, no. 28.
[31] Feet of F. Worcs. Hil. 12 Chas. II.
[32] Exch. Dep. Mich. 3 Will. and Mary, no. 48. Anne daughter of Thomas Coningsby and sister of Fitz William married Richard son of Paul Tracy of Stanway, co. Glouc. (*Visit. of Worcs.* 1569 [Harl. Soc. xxvii], 44).
[33] Exch. Dep. Mich. 8 Geo. I, no. 11.
[34] Recov. R. Trin. 9 Geo. II, rot. 178; Close, 9 Geo. II, pt. i, no. 15.
[35] Priv. Act, 15 Geo. III, cap. 69; Nash, *Hist. of Worcs.* i, 129b.
[36] G.E.C. *Complete Peerage,* iv, 218; viii, 87. [37] Ibid. viii, 87.
[38] Recov. R. Trin. 2 Geo. IV, rot. 196.

early in the 18th century to John Dutton of Sherborne, co. Glouc. He settled it in 1710 upon himself and his heirs.[39] It appears to have been formerly held by his father Ralph and belonged to John, then Sir John, in 1721.[40] He died in 1742–3 and James Lenox Naper, his nephew and successor, who assumed the name Dutton,[41] was dealing with the manor of Cutsdean in 1762.[42] James son and heir of James Lenox Dutton was created Lord Dutton of Sherborne in 1784,[43] and it was probably his son John who was dealing with the manor (as John Dutton, esquire) in 1800.[44] The estate passed

DUTTON of Sherborne. *Quarterly argent and gules fretty or.*

before the end of the century to the Dugdales, and now belongs to Colonel James Dugdale of Sezincote House, Moreton-in-Marsh, co. Glouc. The present Hinchwick is in the parish of Condicote, co. Glouc., the part of the estate which lay in Cutsdean being marked by Hinchwick Plantation and Hinchwick Hill Barn.

At the date of the Domesday Survey Durand held 2 hides at *BREDON'S NORTON*[45] (Nortune, xi cent.; Northton, xiii cent.) which had apparently passed into the hands of the Bishop of Worcester by 1108–18.[46] This manor was given as 2 hides and a virgate of land by Bishop Samson (1096-1112) to Illi de Turre.[47] It passed from him before the end of the 12th century to Hamo de Turre,[48] and probably not long after to William Poer of Wichenford.[49] Early in the 13th century Richard Poer was in possession.[50]

James Poer held the estate in 1299,[51] and it seems to have followed the same descent as Wichenford[52] (q.v.) until 1663, when William Washbourne sold it to William Hancock.[53] It then passed with Westmancote and Hall Court to John Embury and his wife Charlotte, who were dealing with it in 1776–7.[54] The manor seems afterwards to have followed the descent of the manor of Westmancote. Norton Park, now the residence of Mrs. John Biddulph Martin, was built by the Misses Ann and Penelope Martin and finished in 1839.

In 1362 the manor comprised a capital messuage and a carucate of land, and the pleas and perquisites of court were worth 16*d.*[55]

Half a hide of land in Norton was held of the manor of Bredon in the time of Henry II by Robert son of Richard.[56] It was evidently closely connected with the

2 hides at Moreton held by the same owner. It was perhaps part of this estate which was claimed in 1224 by Robert son of Thomas against his cousin Richard son of David, both claiming descent from a certain Robert who held the land in the time of Henry II.[57]

In 1274–5 Nicholas de Kingsley claimed 3 acres of land in Norton Robert against Geoffrey Fitz Robert, who said that Alice de Kingsley, to whom Nicholas had given the land, had granted it to him.[58] The half-hide at Norton had passed with Moreton before 1299 to Walter de Westmancote,[59] and afterwards came to the Washbournes, who owned the other estate at Norton.[60]

MITTON (Myttun, Multon, ix cent.; Muttune, Mitune, xi cent.) was granted by Berhtwulf, King of Mercia, to the Bishop and monks of Worcester in 841,[61] and was included by King Edgar in his famous charter of 964, granting the hundred of Oswaldslow to the church of Worcester.[62] In 965 Oswald, then Bishop of Worcester, granted 2 *manses* in 'Muctune,' which may perhaps be identified with Mitton, to one Athelstan for three lives.[63] Mitton is mentioned as one of the manors which were restored to Bishop Wulfstan in the time of William the Conqueror.[64] At the date of the Domesday Survey 1 hide at Mitton belonged to the monks of Worcester,[65] having been granted to them by Ealdred,[66] who was Bishop of Worcester from 1044 to 1061.[67] It was confirmed to them by Bishop Simon in 1148.[68] The tenant of this manor owed the special service of keeping the field of battle (*custodire campum*) whenever a trial by wager of battle was fought as to any of the lands of the priory.[69]

The monks subinfeudated this manor from very early times, and their interest was represented by a rent of 40*s.* received by the chamberlain of the monastery from the 13th to the 16th century.[70] At the Dissolution it passed to the dean and chapter and was confirmed to them in 1608–9.[71]

The tenant under the church of Worcester of this hide at Mitton in the time of Henry II was a certain Robert Stilia,[72] and Robert de la Folie held it early in the 13th century.[73] In 1235 Philip de Mitton died and his wife purchased the wardship and marriage of his heir of the Prior of Worcester.[74] It is doubtless this transaction to which the Register of Worcester Priory refers thus : 'Prior William received for the premises [Mitton] 10 marks of silver at the instance and petition of the bishop, who married one of his kinsmen to the heir of Mitton in 1235.'[75] Sir Nicholas de Mitton was in possession of the

[39] Recov. R. Trin. 9 Anne, rot. 47.
[40] Exch. Dep. Mich. 8 Geo. I, no. 11.
[41] G.E.C. *Complete Baronetage*, iv, 104.
[42] Recov. R. Trin. 2 Geo. III, rot. 51.
[43] G.E.C. *Complete Peerage*, vii, 130.
[44] Recov. R. Hil. 40 Geo. III, rot. 342. He succeeded to the barony in 1820.
[45] *V.C.H. Worcs.* i, 292*a.* One Leofwine had held these 2 hides and had served as bishop's radman (ibid.).
[46] Ibid. 324*b* n.
[47] Red Bk. of Bishopric of Worc. fol. 243.
[48] Ibid.
[49] Ibid. 254.
[50] *Testa de Nevill* (Rec. Com.), 41*b.*
[51] Red Bk. of Bishopric of Worc. fol. 55.
[52] *Feud. Aids*, v, 308, 319 ; Chan. Inq. p.m. 36 Edw. III, pt. ii (1st nos.),

no. 18 ; Feet of F. Worcs. Hil. 41 Eliz. ; Exch. Dep. Mich. 22 Chas. II, no. 35 ; Recov. R. Mich. 6 Geo. III, rot. 182.
[53] Davenport, *Hist. of Washbourne Family*, 145.
[54] Feet of F. Worcs. Mich. 17 Geo. III.
[55] Chan. Inq. p.m. 36 Edw. III, pt. ii (1st nos.), no. 18.
[56] Habington, op. cit. i, 526 ; Red Bk. of Bishopric of Worc. fol. 66.
[57] Maitland, *Bracton's Note Bk.* iii, 30.
[58] Assize R. 1026, m. 20.
[59] Habington, op. cit. i, 527 ; Red Bk. of Bishopric of Worc. fol. 56.
[60] Habington, loc. cit.
[61] Birch, *Cart. Sax.* ii, 7 ; Heming, *Chartul.* (ed. Hearne), ii, 400.
[62] Heming, op. cit. ii, 520 ; Birch, op. cit. iii, 379.

[63] Heming, op. cit. i, 233.
[64] Ibid. ii, 407.
[65] *V.C.H. Worcs.* i, 291*a.*
[66] Heming, op. cit. ii, 395.
[67] Stubbs, *Reg. Sacr. Angl.* 35.
[68] Thomas, *Surv. of Cath. Church of Worc.* A 109. Bishop Walter de Grey (1214–16) is said to have restored Grimley and Mitton to the monks (ibid. A 124).
[69] Hale, *Register of Worc. Priory* (Camd. Soc.), 79*b.*
[70] Ibid. ; *Pope Nich. Tax.* (Rec. Com.), 227*b* ; *Valor Eccl.* (Rec. Com.), iii, 223*a.*
[71] Pat. 6 Jas. I, pt. xii ; see also Chan. Proc. (Ser. 2), bdle. 37, no. 26.
[72] Red Bk. of Bishopric of Worc. fol. 66.
[73] *Testa de Nevill* (Rec. Com.), 42*a.*
[74] *Ann. Mon.* (Rolls Ser.), iv, 427.
[75] Hale, loc. cit.

BREDON CHURCH : THE SOUTH DOORWAY

BREDON CHURCH : THE NORTH PORCH

estate in 1275 and 1287,[76] and sold it in 1290–1 to John son of Sir John de Thorndon.[77] In the following year a controversy arose between John and Nicholas le Chamberlain as to the manor. In settlement of this dispute John gave up his claim to this manor and that of Kinsham in exchange for a rent of £10 from the manor of Fladbury.[78] Simon le Chamberlain seems to have been in possession in 1299,[79] but must have sold the manor shortly after to Walter de Beauchamp of Powick, who obtained a grant of free warren there in 1300.[80] He died two years later,[81] and Alice de Beauchamp, who paid a subsidy at Mitton in 1327, was probably his widow.[82] In 1329–30 the manor was settled on her third son Giles, on condition that he paid her £100 yearly during her life.[83] However, in 1337–8 Giles was ejected from the manor by his brother Sir William,[84] who settled it in 1348[85] upon himself for life with reversion to Thomas de Bradeston and his heirs.[86] Sir Thomas de Bradeston died seised of it in 1360–1.[87] His grandson and heir Thomas died in 1374–5, leaving a daughter Elizabeth,[88] who afterwards became the wife of Walter de la Pole.[89] The manor passed from her to her grandson Edmund Inglethorpe,[90] who sold it in 1452 to John Beauchamp Lord Beauchamp of Powick.[91] John died in 1475,[92] and his son and successor Richard settled the manor in 1495 upon Robert Willoughby Lord Brooke, who had married his eldest daughter Elizabeth.[93] Her granddaughter Elizabeth, widow of Sir Fulk Greville, died seised of the manor in 1563 and was succeeded by her son Fulk,[94] who sold the manor in 1571 to Giles Reed.[95] Giles died seised of it in 1611, when it passed to his son John.[96] John Reed seems to have been

REED. *Azure a griffon or.*

succeeded by Edward Reed, probably his son, before 1627.[97] Richard Reed and his wife Eleanor and Edward Reed and others conveyed the manor in 1638–9 to Thomas Lord Coventry and others.[98]

No further deeds have been found relating to this manor of Mitton, but in 1779 the Earl of Coventry was one of the principal landowners in Mitton, and an important estate at Bredon called Mitton Farm has descended with the title of Earl of Coventry to the present day.[99] There is, however, no longer a manor at Mitton.

Another estate at Mitton, sometimes called a manor, belonged during the 18th century to the Dowdeswells of Pull Court. It seems to have originated in land acquired by the Davis[99a] family in 1590. In 1636 Giles Davis sold the capital messuage of Little Mitton with other land to Richard Dowdeswell, as agent for Mrs. Catherine Savage. The property was made over in 1660 to Richard Dowdeswell, and it passed with the Pull Court estate[100] until about 1788, when it was sold by Mr. Dowdeswell as Mitton Farm, containing 101 acres, worth £144 a year.[1] The further descent of this estate has not been traced, the manorial rights, if any ever existed, having long since lapsed.

A hide of land at *KINSHAM* (Kilmesham, Chelmesham, xii cent.; Kelmesham, xiii cent.; Kilmesham, xiv cent.; Kensham, xvi cent.) was held of the manor of Bredon[2] in the time of Henry II by Juliane de Ponville.[3] Early in the 13th century it was in the hands of John de Bonville.[4] In 1254–5 Parnel wife of John de Caldecote gave up to Nicholas de Caldecote all her claim to dower in Caldecote and Kinsham in exchange for an annuity of 10s.[5] This estate afterwards seems to have passed to Nicholas de Mitton, who gave it with Mitton to John de Thorndon.[6] With Mitton, Kinsham passed to Nicholas le Chamberlain in 1296–7,[7] and from it was to be paid half the rent which Nicholas agreed to pay to John in exchange for the two manors.[8] Shortly after

[76] Add. MS. 28024, fol. 129*b*; *Lay Subs. R. Worcs.* 1280 (Worcs. Hist. Soc.), 70; *Ann. Mon.* (Rolls Ser.), iv, 493.

[77] Add. MS. 28024, fol. 172.

[78] Ibid.

[79] Red Bk. of Bishopric of Worc. fol. 56.

[80] *Cal. Chart. R.* 1257–1300, p. 489.

[81] Dugdale, *Baronage*, i, 249.

[82] Ibid.; *Lay Subs. R. Worcs.* 1327 (Worcs. Hist. Soc.), 29*b*.

[83] Feet of F. Worcs. 3 Edw. III, no. 16.

[84] Co. Plac. Chan. Misc. bdle. 85, file 1, no. 8.

[85] De Banco R. 356, m. 3.

[86] Feet of F. Worcs. Mich. 22 Edw. III, no. 15.

[87] Chan. Inq. p.m. 34 Edw. III (1st nos.), no. 61. His widow Agnes held the manor during her lifetime (Feet of F. Worcs. 35 Edw. III, no. 18).

[88] Chan. Inq. p.m. 48 Edw. III (1st nos.), no. 10.

[89] Wrottesley, *Ped. from Plea R.* 204.

[90] Chan. Inq. p.m. 12 Hen. VI, no. 33.

[91] Close, 31 Hen. VI, m. 6; Feet of F. Worcs. 32 Hen. VI, no. 47. This John was the great-grandson of Giles Beauchamp mentioned above.

[92] G.E.C. *Complete Peerage*, i, 278.

[93] Ibid. 279; Close, 10 Hen. VII, m. 24, 25.

[94] Chan. Inq. p.m. (Ser. 2), cxliii, 12. The manor was leased by Fulk Greville and Elizabeth in 1545–6 for seventy years at a rent of £27 19s. 7d. to William Reed (Feet of F. Worcs. East. 37 Hen. VIII). It was probably this William Reed who is called of Mitton and Winniard and died in 1557 (Habington, op. cit. i, 112).

[95] Feet of F. Worcs. East. 13 Eliz. Giles had married Catherine Greville, who died in the same year as her husband (M.I. given in Habington, op. cit. i, 114).

[96] Chan. Inq. p.m. (Ser. 2), cccxxii, 143.

[97] Feet of F. Div. Co. Trin. 10 Jas. I; Recov. R. Mich. 3 Chas. I, rot. 101.

[98] Feet of F. Worcs. Hil. 14 Chas. I; Div. Co. Trin. 14 Chas. I.

[99] Nash, op. cit. i, 129; information from Mr. W. Hill.

[99a] The Davis family were settled at Mitton in 1563, and in 1607 Thomas Copley conveyed 'Hallys Place' to Richard Davis (inform. from the Rev. E. R. Dowdeswell).

[100] Information from the Rev. E. R. Dowdeswell from deeds at Pull Court. Recov. R. D. Enr. Hil. 10 Anne, m. 6.

[1] Recov. R. East. 16 Geo. III, rot. 28, 29.

[2] Kinsham was held of the manor of Bredon until the middle of the 16th century (Chan. Inq. p.m. [Ser. 2], cxliii, 12).

[3] Habington, op. cit. i, 526; Red. Bk. of Bishopric of Worc. fol. 66. In an undated survey, probably of the 12th century, Peter de Upton is returned as holding 1 hide at Kinsham, 1 hide at Mitton and half a hide at Norton (Red Bk. of Bishopric of Worc. fol. 244).

[4] *Testa de Nevill* (Rec. Com.), 42*a*.

[5] Assize R. 1022, m. 4. The 14th and 15th-century manor of Caldecote, which perhaps originated in this land at Caldecote, seems to have been situated in the parish of Bredon, but its site no longer exists. It followed the descent of Kinsham in the 14th and 15th centuries, being first called a manor in 1334–5 and appearing for the last time in 1494–5 (Feet of F. Worcs. 8 Edw. III, no. 13; Close, 31 Hen. VI, m. 6; 10 Hen. VII, m. 24, 25). In 1374–5 it seems to have been included in the manor of Kinsham, as rent from the tenant of 'Coddecote' is included in an extent of the manor of Kinsham (Chan. Inq. p.m. 48 Edw. III [Add. nos.], no. 37). Various members of the family de Caldecote paid subsidy at Westmancote in 1280 (*Lay Subs. R. Worcs.* 1280 [Worcs. Hist. Soc.], 69).

[6] Add. MS. 28024, fol. 172.

[7] Ibid. fol. 172, 172 d.

[8] Ibid.

Nicholas must have sold the manor to Peter Crok, for he was holding it in 1299,[9] and in 1301–2, when John de Thorndon gave the rent of £10, half of which he received from this manor, to Guy de Beauchamp Earl of Warwick.[10] Peter must have sold his estate in the manor soon after this time to Walter de Beauchamp or his wife Alice, for in 1304–5 Guy Earl of Warwick was receiving the rent from Alice de Beauchamp, and in that year gave up all his claim in it to her.[11] Lady Alice de Beauchamp was apparently still in possession in 1327,[12] but the manor had passed before 1334–5 to William de Beauchamp,[13] and from that time it followed the same descent as the manor of Mitton (q.v.) until 1570–1, when Sir Fulk Greville sold it to Anthony Freeman.[14] The further history of this manor has not been traced.

In 1086 the Bishop of Worcester had a mill in Bredon worth 6s. 8d.[15]; it had increased in value to £2 a year by 1291.[16] In 1302 the tolls amounted to 5s. 11d. and the millstone was renewed.[17] The mill was worth 20s. a year in 1511–12.[18]

At the present day there is no mill in Bredon, though Mill End to the north of the village evidently marks the site of a former one.

Two mills and a fishery were leased with the manor of Mitton in 1545–6,[19] and a mill at Mitton appurtenant to the manor is mentioned in 1627.[20]

The *RECTORY MANOR* of Bredon, which belongs to the rector, was valued in 1535 at £72 11s., the glebe land being worth £12.[21] In the 18th century the glebe land included 520 acres, with tithes of 3,200 acres, and the rectory was valued at £1,143 2s.[22] The rectory estate is now to a large extent divided into allotments and let to over 300 people.

CHURCHES — The church of *ST. GILES* consists of a chancel 45½ ft. by 20½ ft., nave 60½ ft. by 23 ft., a central tower 13½ ft. square between them, a north aisle 33 ft. by 10½ ft., south aisle 32½ ft. by 18½ ft. and a north porch. These measurements are all internal.

The original 12th-century church consisted of an aisleless nave, of which a large part still remains, the existing north porch, and a chancel and central tower; but of the two last no traces now remain, with the exception of the western tower arch. The first addition to the church was the south aisle with its arcade of two bays, which was added about 1220. In the 14th century the chancel was enlarged and rebuilt and the central tower reconstructed, the north aisle with its arcade of two bays being added at the same time. A window was inserted above the west doorway in the 15th century and a rood stair constructed, while the west window of the south aisle was blocked for the Reed tomb in 1611.

The east window of the chancel has four lights and geometrical tracery under a two-centred arch. The opening is of the 14th century, but the tracery is modern. The side walls are each pierced by three original two-light windows with trefoiled heads. The piscina and sedilia are also of the 14th century; the former has a trefoiled head and bowl. The sedilia have heads of the same form with cusped spandrels

between them. The eastern tower arch has half-round attached shafts to the jambs with moulded bell capitals and bases and a two-centred arch of three orders.

In the north wall of the tower is a small doorway with a two-centred arch, and above is a trefoil-headed window. The 12th-century western arch is of three pointed orders with a label on which there are traces of red painting; the inner order springs from a scalloped capital with a keeled shaft, and the second order on the western face is enriched with cheveron ornament. On the east side the orders are plain and die into the tower walls.

The north arcade of the nave is of two bays with pointed arches of three chamfered orders and shallow chamfered capitals. The north aisle windows—one of three lights in the east wall and three of two lights on the north—are all 14th-century work with traceried heads. The string of the 12th-century porch and nave remains in the west wall of the aisle.

The north, south and west doorways of the nave all date from the 12th century and have shallow rolls on the internal rear arches and jambs. A roll string on the north and south walls breaks over the door heads; but on the west wall the string is higher and clears the doorway, which has a billet label. Still higher up in the wall is a second string. The north door is externally of two orders, the outer having cheveron ornaments with keeled shafts to the jambs and early carved foliated capitals. The west doorway is recessed in three orders, the middle one enriched with zigzag and springing from scalloped capitals. The south doorway only differs from the western in having a lozenge zigzag mould to the middle order. In the western bay on each side of the nave is an original 12th-century light with plain round head and wide splayed jambs.

The north porch, which is contemporary, has an outer doorway of two orders, with one pair of side shafts and foliated capitals. Above it is a horizontal zigzag string, and the cornice has a nail-head decoration on its upper member. The porch is vaulted, with wall and diagonal ribs, springing from late scalloped and carved foliated capitals and keeled shafts. The stone benches on either side do not extend for the whole length.

The south arcade, of two bays, has a pier and responds of clustered shafts with moulded capitals and bases and pointed arches of two orders. In the wall against the eastern respond is a small shallow piscina. A 15th-century rood-stair turret projects at the north-east corner of the aisle and partly covers a moulded arched recess probably of 14th-century date. In the east wall are three trefoiled lancet windows, and between them on the inner face are independent marble shafts with moulded capitals and bases; the rear arches are trefoiled. In the south wall are four pairs of lancets of similar detail, and to the south-east is a large trefoiled piscina. Below the other windows are three arched recesses. In the east wall is a rough blocked arch, probably a barrow-hole. The west pair of lancet windows is blocked by the Reed monument.

[9] Habington, op. cit. i, 527; Red Bk. of Bishopric of Worc. fol. 56.
[10] Add. MS. 28024, fol. 171.
[11] Ibid. 171 d.
[12] *Lay Subs. R. Worcs.* 1327 (Worcs. Hist. Soc.), 24b.
[13] Feet of F. Worcs. 8 Edw. III, no. 13.
[14] Ibid. East. 13 Eliz.
[15] *V.C.H. Worcs.* i, 291a.
[16] *Pope Nich. Tax.* (Rec. Com.), 225a.
[17] Mins. Accts. bdle. 1143, no. 18.
[18] Prattinton Coll. (Soc. Antiq.).
[19] Feet of F. Worcs. East. 37 Hen. VIII.
[20] Recov. R. Mich. 3 Chas. I, rot. 101.
[21] *Valor Eccl.* (Rec. Com.), iii, 267a.
[22] Nash, *Hist. of Worcs.* Suppl. 15.

BREDON CHURCH : THE CHANCEL LOOKING EAST

BREDON CHURCH : THE CHANCEL ARCH AND SOUTH ARCADE

The roof of the south aisle is plastered, and those of the nave and north aisle are modern. In the nave are corbels carved with dragons and human figures.

The gable end of the porch is rubble-faced, but the rest of the building is of ashlar, and on the north side of it is a small square blocked window, formerly lighting the room over the porch. The room has been recently opened up through the west wall. On the south side, in the north wall of the nave, is a blocked doorway with staples for the hinges of a door. From this it is evident that the room was entered by stairs from the inside of the nave. On either side of this doorway are shelved aumbries. There are also small cupboard recesses in each side wall and on either side of the blocked window in the north wall. There is no made floor, a fact which seems to indicate that, whatever its intended use, it was abandoned soon after its construction.

The exterior of the nave generally is of rough rubble with wide jointing. At the west end the clasping buttresses are carried up as square pinnacles

trefoiled head enriched with crockets and ball-flower ornament. The lower part of the north wall has evidently been rebuilt at a later date than the 14th century, as the masonry is of square ashlar with coarser jointing. The north wall of the north aisle has three ashlar-faced buttresses, and the walling generally is of rough ashlar.

The monuments are numerous and interesting. In the north wall of the chancel is a recess with a segmental-pointed feathered arch, enriched with ball-flower, under a gabled and crocketed head. The finial and the flanking pinnacles have been broken off. In the recess is a plain blue marble coffin slab, evidently not in its original position. On the south side of the chancel is a slab set up against the wall bearing a rood of unusual design under a crocketed canopy. To the west of this is a small canopied and recessed altar tomb of about the year 1500, with a panelled front, on which rest three recumbent effigies —the first a bearded man with a long cloak and close tunic with long sleeves buttoned on the under-

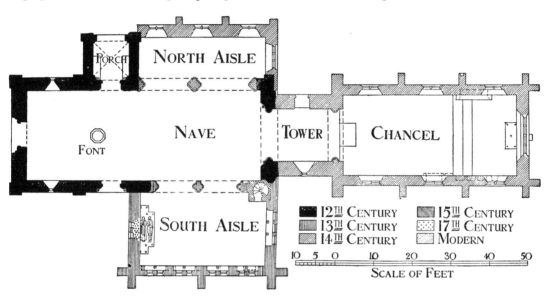

PLAN OF BREDON CHURCH

in two stages, with angle shafts and foliated capitals, and terminate in plain square spires. The gable cross is apparently original 12th-century work. The side buttresses are carried up to the eaves, which have tabling with moulded roll corbels. The south aisle is faced with coursed and squared rubble. In the west wall of this aisle is part of a round-headed opening now blocked up, and apparently not *in situ*. On the south walls are traces of several ancient sundials.

The tower, divided externally into two stages, has an embattled parapet, and is surmounted by an octagonal spire, with roll angles. The walls of the tower have been plastered, and above the window in the north wall is the doorway giving access to the ringing chamber, which is approached by an iron stair outside. The belfry is lit by a two-light window in each wall, the lights of which have been half filled in in recent years. The spire is pierced with three sets of four lights with gabled heads, diminishing in size at each stage. The chancel walls of squared rubble are much covered with ivy. In the second buttress on the north side is a niche of 14th-century date, with a

side, hose, and a sword with a jewelled belt; the second a lady; at their feet is a man, and a child bare to the waist with a long flowing gown below; beneath is a pedestal with a stem, and a leopard's head at its base. In the ceiling of the canopy is a figure of our Lord in glory.

At the west end of the south aisle of the nave is a handsome alabaster and black marble monument of great size to Giles Reed and Catherine (Greville) his wife, both of whom died in 1611. It has life-sized recumbent effigies on a panelled sarcophagus. The arched canopy is carried on Corinthian columns, and bears in the spandrels the arms of Reed quartering Or three crossbows proper, and the shield of Greville, quartered with Arderne, Ufford and Beauchamp of Powick. Above the cornice is a central arched panel with Reed's quartered coat, surmounted by a black eagle displayed, which is Reed's crest, between two obelisks. On either side of the main arch under which the effigies lie are small side canopies with Ionic capitals carrying ball obelisks, and beneath them are the kneeling figures of eight children, with an inscription recording that John Reed set up the tomb to his parents and that he lies in the south wall near by.

In one of the recesses of the south chapel is a slab, probably of 14th-century date, on which are carved two arms holding a heart, and in another is a tall coffin slab with an elaborate cross of similar date.

In the chancel over the sedilia is a mural monument to Thomas Copley, 1593. In the floor of the chancel are several slabs, and a brass to John Prideaux, Bishop of Worcester, 1650, with a mitre and shields of the arms of the see of Worcester, Prideaux, Goodwin and Reynell. In the sedilia is a 12th-century cross-head.

In the churchyard to the south of the nave is a tomb with a coped top and a roll cross, and next to it an old slab with a plain cross.

Several of the windows contain fragments of ancient stained glass. In the second, on the north side of the chancel, are two figures under 14th-century canopies of St. Mary (? of Egypt) and St. Mary Magdalene, a shield of arms, Barry argent and gules. In the next window to the west are the arms of Tatteshall, Checky gules and or a chief ermine. The window opposite to the latter contains the arms of Beauchamp Earl of Warwick. In the second on the south is a shield with uncertain arms, while in the easternmost on this side are the letters IHS in gold on white.

The wall at the east end of the chancel bears ancient diapering in red below the string.

Set in the treads and risers of the sanctuary steps are numerous 14th-century heraldic tiles, with the arms of England, Castile and Leon, France, Beauchamp, Fitz Alan, Warenne, Bohun, Mortimer, de Vere, Cantelow, Newburgh, Clare, Hastings, Berkeley, Graunson, and many others. There are also other patterns, some of the tiles being arranged in groups of five. Frequently an inscription is to be traced, and some bear the names of the months, but their original arrangement has been disturbed.

There are six bells in all : the first cast by Abraham Rudhall, 1733 ; the second, third and fifth by an otherwise unknown William Whitmore, 1624, the inscription on the third being 'W. Witmore made us all' ; the fourth is by Abraham Rudhall, 1706 ; the sixth is a 'ting-tang' without inscription.[23]

The plate includes a silver cup of 1567 and a cover paten probably of the same date, though the date letter is worn away. There is also a silver paten of 1779, presented by S. Smith, rector, in 1799, which appears to have been made originally for secular use.

The registers up to 1812 are as follows : (i) baptisms from 1563, marriages 1562 and burials 1559, all to 1700 ; (ii) baptisms and burials 1701 to 1812 and marriages 1700 to 1754 ; (iii) marriages 1754 to 1812.

The church of *ST. GILES* at Bredon's Norton consists of a chancel, nave, west tower and south porch. The earliest details now surviving are the south doorway and parts of the outer doorway of the south porch, which belong to the end of the 12th century. A chancel appears to have been added early in the 13th century, to which period the chancel arch is to be referred. The nave was rebuilt from the foundations in 1883, the 12th-century work above referred to, together with some

[23] Inform. from Mr. H. B. Walters.

13th-century work, being incorporated into the new structure. The west wall, with the tower, were, however, left untouched.

The chancel is lighted from the east by a modern three-light window ; a portion of the head is of original early 13th-century date. On the north and south are two-light square-headed windows with modern tracery, and there is also a south doorway. The chancel arch is sharply pointed and of three moulded orders, with angle-shafts on both faces of the responds, having curiously stilted bases and foliated capitals of good early 13th-century character.

In the north wall of the nave is a reset lancet of the 13th century, and beneath it is a portion of a scroll string-course contemporary with it. The south doorway is of the late 12th century and is of two round-arched orders, with angle-shafts in the outer order having scalloped capitals. The head is moulded with sunk quarter-rounds. A sundial stone has been set on the inside of the west jamb. The outer doorway of the porch contains stones of the same period. The jamb-shafts are ornamented with zig-zags, and their scalloped capitals have chamfered and pelleted abaci, and the arch has the cheveron and pellet enrichment. In the west wall of the nave is a small original lancet looking into the tower, and below it is a plain chamfered pointed doorway, also of original date.

In the south and west walls of the ground stage of the tower are modern lancets, and at the north-east are the stairs, entered originally from within by a square-headed doorway probably of the 14th century. The entrance is now from the outside. The second stage of the tower is lighted by a small square-headed window and the bell-chamber by two-light windows with heads of similar form. The string-course above and the crowning embattled parapet are of the 15th century. The exterior is faced with squared stone.

On the north wall of the chancel is a marble monument to William Hancock, who died in 1719, and to his wife, who died in 1685. It is inclosed by a good wrought-iron railing. On the monument are his arms : Gules a hand argent and a chief argent with three cocks gules therein, impaling Argent a fesse nebuly with three hares' heads or thereon, for Harewell of Wootton Wawen.

There are six bells. The treble, by Mears & Stainbank, was added in 1885, the gift of Mrs. Martin ; the other five are by Abel Rudhall, all dated 1738 except the fourth, which is of 1739.

The plate consists of a silver cup of 1708 inscribed 'Norton juxta Bredon 1709,' a paten of the same date inscribed on the foot 'IHΣ,' a plated paten inscribed 'Norton juxta Bredon,' and a small modern flagon of 1889.

The registers date from 1754 to 1812.

The church at *CUTSDEAN* consists of a chancel 19 ft. by 13 ft. internally, nave 28 ft. by 14½ ft., and a west tower about 6 ft. square. The tower alone remains of the original building and appears to date from the 15th century. It is built of coursed rubble and the stages are unmarked by external string-courses. In the west wall of the ground stage is a doorway with a two-centred head, and above is a single light with a square external head. The ringing stage is lighted by a small plain light on the west and the bell-chamber by windows of two lights, with traceried two-centred heads, in the north, west and south walls. A similar window in the east wall was blocked on the rebuilding of the nave. The nave and chancel were rebuilt on the old foundations in 1863 and do not appear to reproduce the character of the demolished work.

There are two bells, both apparently cast in the year 1865, by Bond of Burford.

The plate includes a silver cup of 1767, a paten of the same date, a flagon, not of silver, and a pewter almsdish.

The registers previous to 1812 are as follows : (i) mixed entries from 1696 to 1758 ; (ii) mixed entries from 1759 to 1812.

ADVOWSON The advowson of Bredon belonged to the Bishops of Worcester. In 1287 Bishop Giffard obtained licence to appropriate the church of Bredon with its chapels of Sutton (? Mitton), Norton and Westmancote to the collegiate church of Westbury.[24] This was followed by a petition of the Prior and convent of Worcester to Pope Nicholas IV complaining that by making the church of Bredon prebendal to the college of Westbury the bishop had deprived them of their right to institute to the church during a vacancy in the see.[25] The appropriation of Bredon never seems to have taken place, and the advowson remained with successive Bishops of Worcester[26] until it passed with the manor into the hands of Queen Elizabeth. It was granted with the manor in 1577 to Henry Knollys and Edward Williams and sold by them to Thomas Copley and George Hornyold.[27] It then followed the same descent as the Copleys' moiety of the manor until 1626–7, when Thomas Copley sold it to William Sutton, clerk.[28] Between this date and 1749 the presentations were made by various persons,[29] but they were perhaps feoffees of the Suttons and patrons for one turn only, for Mary Sutton presented in 1642 and Mary Sutton widow in 1749,[30] and in 1670 a rent from the glebe lands of the rectory was paid by Dr. Henry Sutton.[31] Benjamin Pearkes was patron in 1781,[32] having purchased the advowson about 1780 from William Davenport.[33] Pearkes sold it in 1783–4 to John Durand,[34] who presented in 1787.[35] Before 1806 the advowson had passed to John Keysall,[36] and he sold it between 1836 and 1842 to Rev. Thomas Arthur Strickland.[37] Eight years later the right of presentation passed to Jacob Jones,[38] and was purchased of him in 1858 by the Duke of Portland,[39] from whom it has passed to the present duke.

The date of the foundation of the chantry of the Blessed Virgin Mary in the church of Bredon is not known. The earliest mention of it occurs in 1287, when Thomas de Hardwick was collated to it by the bishop.[40] Possibly this chantry was augmented by a bequest by William de Loriaco, rector of Bredon, for finding a chaplain to celebrate in the church of Bredon for the repose of his soul,[41] as there is no record of a second foundation. The advowson of the chantry belonged to the Bishops of Worcester[42] until 1458, when the chantry was annexed to the church of Bredon, because the lands belonging to it had become so reduced in value by plague and from other causes that they did not bring in 40s. a year, and were insufficient to maintain a priest. The rector of the church was to possess the chantry on condition that he found a chaplain to celebrate at the altar of the Blessed Virgin when the chaplains of the chantry were accustomed to celebrate there.[43] At the date of the suppression of the chantries in the reign of Edward VI the chantry priest was still supported by a rent-charge of 40s. from the glebe land of the parsonage, to which the chantry land had evidently been added.[44] This rent-charge of 40s. passed to the Crown on the suppression of the chantry, and was vested in trustees for sale in 1670.[45] The rent was sold in 1672 to Sir John Banks of Aylesford, bart.[46]

There was a chapel at Mitton, dedicated in honour of the Holy Cross,[47] the remains of which are still in existence. It was a chapelry of the church of Bredon.[48] The first mention of it occurs in 1287,[49] and in 1290 Sir Nicholas de Mitton left by his will 1 mark to the work of the chapel of Mitton, and made bequests to the chaplain and clerk of Mitton.[50]

In 1427 the inhabitants of Mitton petitioned that they might have a cemetery at their chapel of Mitton, as the town was about 2 miles from the parish church of Bredon. Their petition was granted by the pope.[51] The only other reference to the chapel of Mitton is in 1571, when its advowson was included in the sale of the manor of Mitton by Sir Fulk Greville to Giles Reed.[52]

A chapel in Westmancote was dependent on the church of Bredon in 1287,[53] and in 1290 Sir Nicholas de Mitton made bequests to the chaplain and clerk of Westmancote.[54] No further reference to this chapel has been found.

There is at present a mission room at Westmancote attached to the chapelry of Norton-by-Bredon.

---

[24] *Reg. G. Giffard* (Worcs. Hist. Soc.), 336.
[25] Ibid. 362. See under Blockley advowson.
[26] *Cal. Pat.* 1301–7, p. 28 ; 1313–17, p. 94 ; 1317–21, p. 50 ; 1348–50, p. 51 ; *Reg. Ginsborough* (Worcs. Hist. Soc.), 83.
[27] Pat. 19 Eliz. pt. xiii, m. 17 ; pt. iv, m. 38.
[28] Ibid. 29 Eliz. pt. xiii ; Feet of F. Worcs. Trin. 29 Eliz. ; Chan. Inq. p.m. (Ser. 2), cccvi, 155 ; Feet of F. Worcs. Mich. 22 Jas. I ; Mich. 2 Chas. I.
[29] See Inst. Bks. (P.R.O.). Nash (*Hist. of Worcs.* i, 131) says that Dr. Henry Sutton's grandson sold the advowson to John Webb, after whose death John Webb, junior, was patron, but the advowson afterwards returned to the Suttons. [30] Inst. Bks. (P.R.O.).
[31] Pat. 22 Chas. II, pt. ii (1st roll).

[32] Inst. Bks. (P.R.O.).
[33] Nash, op. cit. i, 131a.
[34] Feet of F. Worcs. Mich. 24 Geo. III.
[35] Inst. Bks. (P.R.O.). [36] Ibid.
[37] *Clerical Guide*, 1836 ; *Clergy Lists.*
[38] *Clergy Lists.* [39] Ibid.
[40] *Reg. G. Giffard* (Worcs. Hist. Soc.), 305. By his will dated 1290 Sir Nicholas de Mitton directed that his body should be buried in the chapel of the Blessed Mary of Bredon, and left 10s. to the work of the chapel (ibid. 388).
[41] Worc. Epis. Reg. Reynolds (1308–13), fol. 31 d.
[42] Ibid. Cobham (1317–27), fol. 119 ; Orlton (1327–33), i, fol. 20 d. ; ii, fol. 35 ; Montagu (1333–7), i, fol. 16 ; Brian (1352–61), fol. 34 ; Winchcomb (1395–1401), fol. 42.
[43] Nash, op. cit. i, 135–6 ; Worc. Epis. Reg. Carpenter (1443–76), i, fol. 160.

[44] Aug. Off. Chant. Cert. 60, no. 41. There were also five cows, valued at 12s. each, which had been given by various persons for finding lights in the church (ibid. 60, no. 72).
[45] Pat. 22 Chas. II, pt. ii (1st roll). It was then said to be applied to the use of funerals at Bredon.
[46] Close, 24 Chas. II, pt. xvii, m. 19.
[47] *Cal. Papal Letters,* vii, 524.
[48] *Reg. G. Giffard* (Worcs. Hist. Soc.), 336.
[49] It is evidently intended by the 'chapel of Sutton' (*Reg. G. Giffard* [Worcs. Hist. Soc.], 336).
[50] Ibid. 388.
[51] *Cal. Papal Letters,* vii, 524.
[52] Feet of F. Worcs. East. 13 Eliz.
[53] *Reg. G. Giffard* (Worcs. Hist. Soc.), 336.
[54] Ibid. 388.

The chapel at Norton was also dependent on the church of Bredon,[55] and to the chaplain and clerk of this chapel Sir Nicholas de Mitton bequeathed money in 1290.[56] Bredon's Norton is still a chapelry of Bredon.

At the date of the Domesday Survey there was a priest at Cutsdean.[57] The chapel was in the 13th century attached to the church of Bredon,[58] and so remained until 1912, when it became a separate parish in the patronage of the Bishop of Worcester.[59]

There is a Baptist chapel in Cutsdean, which was opened in 1839, and also one in Westmancote, opened in 1779. The Wesleyan Methodists have a chapel at Bredon, and there is also a Baptist mission chapel in Kinsham, opened in 1849.

CHARITIES The almshouses founded by Catharine Reed, and endowed in 1696 by her nephew, Richard Reed, are regulated by a scheme of the Charity Commissioners 6 May 1884.

The endowments consist of about 90 a. at Aston and Pamington, 35 a. at Tredington, and 16 a. at Fiddington, bringing in a gross rental of £142 a year, or thereabouts ; also tithes on land at Ashchurch, co. Gloucester, amounting to £11 0s. 3d. a year. The official trustees also hold £579 12s. 4d. consols, producing £14 9s. 8d. yearly, and a sum of £235 17s. 3d. like stock on an investment account for replacing amount expended on the farm at Tredington. The income—subject to the payment of an annuity of £4 to Brasenose College, Oxford—is applied for the benefit of eight poor widows or maids, inmates of the said almshouses.

In 1731 Charles Parsons—as mentioned on the church table—by his will gave 40s. a year for the distribution of bread on the first Sunday in every month ; also a Mr. Gatley, by his will, gave 6s. 8d. a year for the distribution of bread on St. Thomas's Day.

In 1743 Mary Sutton, by her will, left £200 to be laid out in land, out of which the testatrix directed that £1 should be paid to the minister for preaching a sermon on 2nd February each year, the residue of the rents to be distributed to poor residents of Bredon and Norton. The sum of £7 a year is paid by the proprietor of an estate in Bredon and distributed in sums of 1s. among 140 poor people.

Church Lands.—On the inclosure in 1808 an allotment of 6 a. or thereabouts was awarded in exchange for certain lands, known as Church Lands, which had been in the possession of the parish from time immemorial. The land is let at £35 a year, which is carried to the churchwardens' account.

The Free School, or Blue Coat School, founded by a codicil to the will of William Hancock, dated in 1718, was originally for the education and clothing of twelve boys, and for apprenticing, the schoolmaster to be a member of the Church of England, but not in ecclesiastical orders.

The endowment consists of the school buildings and land in Bredon, and 37 a. or thereabouts in Ashchurch, co. Gloucester, the rental value being about £140 a year.

The official trustees also hold £70 11s. 5d. consols, arising from the sale of timber, producing £1 15s. yearly.

The chapel of Norton is in possession of 6 a. in Bredon Meadow, acquired in exchange for certain lands mentioned on the church table as anciently given to the chapel of Norton, and for half an acre derived in 1646 under the will of John Jennings.

The land is let at £16 a year, of which £2 is distributed in bread to the poor and the remainder is applied towards the repairs of the church.

John Haydon, by his will proved at Worcester 9 February 1782, bequeathed his residuary estate to trustees, the income to be paid to a Baptist minister, who should duly and statedly preach to the congregation at Westmancote, and for teaching fifteen poor children gratis reading, writing and arithmetic and the principles of the Christian religion. The charity is regulated by a scheme of the Charity Commissioners 26 October 1904. The trust funds are now represented by £1,159 Bristol Corporation 2½ per cent. stock, held by the official trustees, producing £28 19s. 6d. yearly, of which one moiety is payable absolutely to the Baptist minister and the other moiety to the same minister so long as he shall conduct an efficient Sunday school.

BROADWAS

Bradewesse (viii cent.) ; Bradewasse (x cent.) ; Bradewesham (xi cent.) ; Bradewa, Bradewasse (xii cent.) ; Bradwas, Bradwes (xvii cent.) ; Bredweys (xviii cent.).

Broadwas is a parish in the west of Worcestershire on the left bank of the River Teme, which forms its southern and part of its western boundary. It is watered, also, by a small tributary of the Teme, and covers 1,108 acres, much of the land near the river being liable to floods. The southern part of the parish lies in the valley of the Teme, but the rest is hilly, reaching a height of 200 ft. above the ordnance datum to the north of the village and on the northern boundary. The greater part of the parish consists of rich pasture land, 683 acres being laid down in permanent grass. Only 9½ acres are covered by woodland, distributed for the most part in small copses, but the fields are well planted with timber ; 312 acres are arable land,[1] the chief crops being wheat, beans and hops. The parish was at one time famous for its cider. The soil is loam and marl with gravel and marl subsoil.

The village is picturesque and lies chiefly on the north and south of the main road from Worcester to Bromyard, the land becoming higher and more irregular as the hills on the west are approached. The church lies in a wooded hollow to the south-west of the village close to the River Teme.

On the north side of the village is a half-timber house known as 'The Butts.' It consists of a centre and two larger wings projecting irregularly from the front. The chimney stacks are of ashlar work and

---

[55] *Reg. G. Giffard* (Worcs. Hist. Soc.), 336.
[56] Ibid. 388.
[57] *V.C.H. Worcs.* i, 291b.
[58] Hale, *Reg. of Worc. Priory* (Camd. Soc.), 103b.
[59] Inform. from Mr. J. W. Willis-Bund.
[1] Statistics from Bd. of Agric. (1905).

BROADWAS CHURCH : THE PULPIT

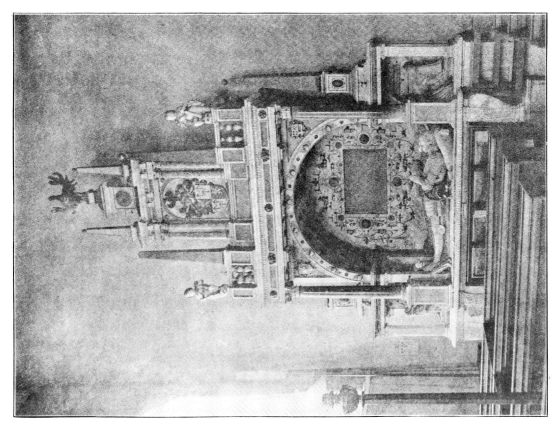

BREDON CHURCH : MONUMENT TO GILES REED AND CATHERINE
(GREVILLE) HIS WIFE

each is surmounted by twin shafts of brick. The curved beams springing from the ground to the gable, as well as the roof beams in the attic, render it very probable that the centre and part of the northern wing were originally an open hall of 15th-century date or even earlier, the chimney stacks being 17th-century additions.

In 1884 the part of Broadwas lying south of the River Teme was, by order of the Local Government Board, amalgamated with Leigh, and the part of Alfrick to the north of the Teme was united to Broadwas. At the same time part of Broadwas was transferred to Cotheridge.[2]

Former place-names in this parish include Foxbaece (viii cent.), which had become Foxbatch in the 18th century[3]; Rugghey Glebe and Rugg Hill[4] (xviii

is not mentioned by name in the charter, it was probably freed, like Hallow, from all secular services in 816 by King Coenwulf.[7] The monks of Worcester held Broadwas at the time of the Domesday Survey,[8] and it was confirmed to them in 1148 by Simon Bishop of Worcester.[9] In 1240 the demesne included a court with an orchard and vineyard,[10] 3 carucates of land with the land of Doddenham, a meadow, grove, fulling-mill and corn-mill.[11]

The prior obtained a grant of free warren in the manor in 1256.[12] From that time until the dissolution of the monastery the manor remained with the priory. Its value at the Dissolution was £35 18s. 10½d. yearly.[13] Henry VIII granted it in 1542, with other possessions of the priory, to the Dean and Chapter of Worcester.[14] This grant was

THE 'BUTTS,' BROADWAS

cent.). Other place-names found in the 18th century are Brach, Hopyards and Noyts, Cilliers, Grumspleck and Taberness.[5]

Offa, King of the Mercians, granted MANOR land at BROADWAS to the monks of Worcester about 786.[6] It was at an early date annexed to the manor of Hallow, and, though it

confirmed by James I,[15] but under the Commonwealth the manor was sold by the Parliamentary Trustees in 1650 to Henry Pitt.[16] In the previous year the farm-house of the manor had been sold to Edmund Pitt.[17] The manor was then charged with a yearly payment of £20 towards the maintenance of a free grammar school in the city of Worcester.[18] It was

---

[2] *Census of Engl. and Wales,* 1891, ii, 657.
[3] Heming, *Chartul.* (ed. Hearne), 329.
[4] Prattinton Coll. (Soc. Antiq.).
[5] Ibid.
[6] Birch, *Cart. Sax.* i, 325; Heming, op. cit. 328.
[7] Birch, op. cit. i, 494. In the annals of Worcester Priory a charter of Coenwulf

relating to the manor is mentioned (*Ann. Mon.* [Rolls Ser.], iv, 367).
[8] *V.C.H. Worcs.* i, 295.
[9] Thomas, *Surv. of Worc. Cathedral,* App. no. 18.
[10] The tenants in villeinage of the prior at Doddenham did two days' reaping at Broadwas and worked two days a year in the vineyard there (Hale, *Reg. Worc. Priory* [Camd. Soc.], 21a).

[11] Hale, *Reg. Worc. Priory* (Camd. Soc.), 32a.
[12] *Cal. Pat.* 1354–8, p. 266.
[13] *Valor Eccl.* (Rec. Com.), iii, 221.
[14] Pat. 33 Hen. VIII, pt. v, m. 19.
[15] Ibid. 6 Jas. I, pt. xii, no. 2.
[16] Close, 1650, pt. xxvii, no. 10.
[17] Ibid. pt. xxii, no. 44.
[18] Ibid. pt. xxvii, no. 10.

restored to the Dean and Chapter of Worcester on the accession of Charles II, William and Mary confirming to them the manor and manorial rights in 1692,[19] and they have continued to hold the manor until the present day.

Court baron and court leet for the manor were still held in the 18th century.[20]

About 1561 the Dean and Chapter leased the site of the manor to John Cratford and his daughters Elizabeth and Joan for £8 14s. 4d., and the third and tenth sheaf of corn growing on the arable land, these sheaves being afterwards commuted for £2 10s. 10d.[21] After John's death his daughter Joan wife of William Doughtie instituted proceedings to recover the property, which had been seized by her kinsman John Cratford, son of Humphrey Cratford of Croome, co. Worcester, and by her sister Elizabeth wife of Richard Whitney. It does not appear whether she was successful, but in 1636 Charles Cratford obtained from the dean and chapter a lease of the farm of the manor.[22] Cratford was indicted about 1618–19 for an alleged tampering with a book containing the assessment of lands in the parish and

in Broadwas about which there were Chancery proceedings in the middle of the 16th century.[27] Nash, writing at the end of the 18th century, deplored the state of the farms at Broadwas in spite of the good quality of the soil, 'but the estates,' he says, 'are held by lives under the church, and the fields belonging to the several farms very much dispersed, they are not so much improved as they might be.'[28]

There were two mills in the manor of Hallow with Broadwas in 1086,[29] and in 1240 the Prior of Worcester had two mills at Broadwas, one being a corn-mill and the other a fulling-mill.[30]

Whenever the tenants of the manors of Grimley, Hallow and Henwick were prevented from grinding corn at their own mills they were obliged to do it at Broadwas. If the corn was carried elsewhere the villein who carried it was liable to the forfeiture of his horse to the prior and of the meal to the steward of the manor. In the use of the mill for grinding corn the prior had the precedence, next to him the parson and the heirs of one Alan; after them the lord of Suckley, the dam of the mill extending to his land. Malt ground at the mill and brewed for private use paid no toll; but if the beer was sold (whether it was by the parson, a freeman, or any other person permitted to use the mill) a toll was then payable of 1d. or 4 gallons of beer, double toll being due from a villein. Whenever a millstone was fetched from Worcester, all the freemen and villeins (the parson excepted) were bound to attend the steward's summons, and help in turn with men and oxen, the cart, attended by one man, with two oxen to draw it, being furnished by the prior.[31] There was a mill existing in the parish in 1776.[32]

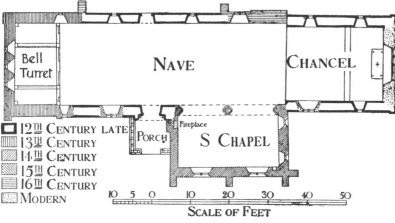

PLAN OF BROADWAS CHURCH

The church of *ST. MARY MAGDALENE* consists of a chancel 25 ft. by ·18½ ft., a nave 70½ ft. by 20½ ft. wide (the western end being occupied by the framing of a square wooden tower), and a south chapel 26 ft. by 13 ft. These measurements are all internal.

The earliest church of which traces now remain dates from c. 1170 and was an aisleless building with a chancel and nave extending as far west as the present tower. Of this church part of the north and south nave walls with the south door remain, and the chancel is of the same date, though much repaired and refaced. The western part of the nave inclosing the tower is probably of the 13th century. The south chapel was added in the first half of the 14th

the rules and customs to guide the parishioners. He was then said to have come into the parish six years previously.[23] The prior and monks of Worcester acquired several pieces of land and rents in the parish during the 13th century. John de la Pulle sold to the prior and monks 'Lutle forlonge with a messuage above Holeweie,' for which he paid yearly 4d.[24] The deed of sale is undated, but it was probably before 1240, as the register of the priory of that date records the fact that Brother Ralph had bought one messuage from John de la Pulle.[25] Hugh the son of Siward, with the consent of Cecily his wife, released to the prior all his lands in Broadwas, in return for which the prior gave him 30 marks of silver.[26] The prior also acquired land of Adam de Ancredham.

Richard Habington, grandfather of Thomas Habington, the Worcestershire historian, owned property

[19] Pat. 4 Will. and Mary, pt. i, no. 6.
[20] Nash, op. cit. i, 137.
[21] Chan. Proc. (Ser. 2), bdle. 57, no. 30.
[22] Close, 1650, pt. xxii, no. 44.
[23] Exch. Dep. East. 19 Jas. I, no. 3. A monument in the church records that Elizabeth wife of Charles Cratford was

buried there in 1623 (Habington, *Surv. of Worcs.* [Worcs. Hist. Soc.], i, 109).
[24] Prattinton Coll. (Soc. Antiq.), Deeds of D. and C. of Worc. no. 112, 336.
[25] Hale, *Reg. Worc. Priory* (Camd. Soc.), 33a.
[26] Prattinton Coll. (Soc. Antiq.); *Ann. Mon.* (Rolls Ser.), iv, 423.

[27] Chan. Proc. (Ser. 2), bdle. 96, no. 11.
[28] Nash, *Hist. of Worcs.* i, 137.
[29] *V.C.H. Worcs.* i, 295b.
[30] Hale, *Reg. of Worc. Priory* (Camd. Soc.), 32a.
[31] Ibid.
[32] Prattinton Coll. (Soc. Antiq.).

century. The deed for the foundation in 1344 is quoted by Prattinton,[33] and refers to the newly-erected chapel of the Blessed Virgin Mary in St. Mary Magdalene's Church at Broadwas. A porch to the south door was built at the same time as the chapel, but a line of corbelling is all that is now left. The chancel arch was probably removed in the 16th century, and the north nave wall, having been thrust out of the perpendicular, was partially rebuilt with the easternmost window at the same time. The walling inclosing the base of the present tower is of doubtful date, but the three lancet lights in the present west wall probably belong to the 13th century. The present woodwork of the tower is modern, but the wood gable and some balusters with part of the west gallery are

have been widened. West of this door is another lancet window, and at the point where the wood framework of the tower begins is a third which has perhaps been rebuilt.

The tower framework occupies the west end of the church, leaving a vestry in the middle and a small gallery above. In the west wall are three small lancets of 13th-century date.

The south chapel opens into the chancel by an arcade of two bays, with a pier of four engaged shafts with moulded capitals and bases. In the east wall are two trefoil-headed windows, the labels being cut away on the wall above the altar. Immediately above is a circular traceried window and below a narrow course where the altar slab tailed into the wall. In

BROADWAS CHURCH FROM THE SOUTH-EAST

of 16th and 17th-century date. The existing south porch is modern.

The modern east window of the chancel is of four lights in 14th-century style. On either side of the altar is some 17th-century panelling. In the north wall are two late 12th-century lights with round rear arches and stepped sills. One similar window occupies the south side with a two-light window with modern tracery to the west of it. The jambs are probably of the 15th century. In the same wall is a trefoiled piscina, probably contemporary with the chancel, and to the west of it a small projection, perhaps a portion of a destroyed sedile.

The easternmost window in the north nave wall is a 16th-century two-light window with a square head, the second is an original lancet with a round rear arch. The north door has chamfered jambs and a round head ; the jambs are splayed and appear to

the south wall are two traceried two-light windows, and on the west is a fireplace of uncertain date, though later than the original chapel wall. The pointed south door is of three moulded orders with early foliated capitals and two shafts on each side. It is set in a gabled projection covered by a modern wood porch. To the west of the south doorway is a two-light 15th-century window, and there is an original lancet immediately to the east of the commencement of the tower frame-work.

The font, of uncertain date, has a plain octagonal bowl and a round stem with scallops at the top.

In the north-east corner of the nave is an octagonal wood pulpit, the two panels to each face having good 17th-century carving. Above the panels is inscribed 'Anno Dom 1632, William Noxon, Roger Prince, Church Warden.' On the tester above the pulpit is ' Blessed are they that heare the word of God and keepe it.'

[33] op. cit. See also below under the advowson.

On the floor of the chancel are sets of 16th-century tiles in patterns of fours and sixes, with *Deo gratias*, the arms of Berkeley, and other devices. One set of four are border tiles. On another set is inscribed 'Adjuva nos deus salutaris noster et propter gloriam nominis tui delibera nos,' with the shields of Berkeley, John Nailheart and Robert Eliot.

At the north-west end of the nave are some 17th-century pews, one bearing the letters c c on a shield and probably referring to the Cratford family, to whom there is an early 17th-century tomb slab. There are remains of other tomb slabs at the west end, including one dated 1610.

The external roofs of nave and chancel are continuous, of a steep pitch and tiled ; the south chapel has also a steep gable roof of remarkable height. The bell tower is weather-boarded. The buttresses of the chapel have gabled weatherings with tracery on the face.

Before 1896 there were four bells, three by John Rudhall and the old bell described below. In that year one of the Rudhall bells was recast and a treble added. Thus at present the bells are five in number : the first and third cast in 1822 and 1820 respectively by John Rudhall, the second and fourth by Charles Carr of Smethwick, 1896, and the ancient tenor, inscribed '✠ IOHANNIS : PRECE : DVLCE : SONET : ET : AMENE,' which was cast at Gloucester about 1350, probably by 'Master John of Gloucester.'[34]

The plate consists of a cover paten of 1571, a plated cup, paten and flagon and a pewter flagon.

The registers[35] before 1812 are as follows : (i) mixed entries 1676 to 1755 ; (ii) baptisms and burials 1755 to 1812 ; (iii) marriages 1754 to 1811.

ADVOWSON The advowson of the church of Broadwas belonged to the Prior and convent of Worcester until the dissolution of the monasteries.[36] Henry VIII granted it, with the manor, in 1542 to the Dean and Chapter of Worcester.[37] This was confirmed by James I,[38] and the dean and chapter hold the patronage at the present day.

The church of Broadwas was free, ' by authority of St. Wulfstan,' from all jurisdiction of the archdeacon and rural dean, the parson being archdeacon of his parish and receiving all the emoluments of the archdeaconry[39] and one-fifth of the Whitsun farthings from the parish. He also received a part of the great tithes, all the small tithes, mortuaries and the Paschal eggs, the latter being collected by the steward of the prior. Broadwas was returned in the archdeaconry of Worcester in the Valor Ecclesiasticus of 1535, but made no payments to the archdeacon.[40]

In 1628 there was a dispute between two ministers, Richard Potter and Thomas Archbold, both desiring to be presented to the rectory of Broadwas. The latter appealed to the king, who wrote to the dean telling him to signify to the bishop the king's pleasure for Archbold's institution.[41] The parish contributed one 'cronnum,' or half quarter of grain, to St. Wulfstan's alms, which were distributed to the poor from the gate of the priory on St. Wulfstan's Day, and 18*d.* to St. Peter's pence.[42]

In 1450 Bishop Carpenter granted an indulgence to any who should give or assign any property to the fabric, lights, bells, &c., in the parish church of Broadwas.[43]

In 1340 licence was granted to John de Broadwas, clerk, to give 120 acres in Cotheridge for the maintenance of a chaplain to celebrate divine service daily in the church of St. Mary Magdalene, Broadwas, for the good estate of the king, Queen Philippa, William de Kyldesby, Master John de Broadwas, Peter de Grete, Margery Drew of Housele and John and William her sons, while living, and for their souls when dead.[44] Three years later John de Broadwas gave further portions of land with a messuage in Broadwas to two chaplains for the same purpose.[45] John reserved to himself the right of presentation, and it was arranged that after his death the Prior of Worcester should present, and if he did not appoint for two months the right should afterwards be in the bishop's hands. The priests were to find wax, &c., and on All Souls' Day 5*s.* (or bread or corn to that amount) to be distributed to the poor inhabitants of the parish. Having given to the first two priests, on their appointment to the chantry, 10 marks with all the growing crops and produce of the lands, John de Broadwas required that each priest, on giving up the chantry, should leave for his successor ' 8 proper oxen, a wain, a cart, a plough and a harrow, and various household requisites, the best of which he should have on leaving the chantry besides a half of all his other goods.' He also required the two chaplains to reside and spend the profits of the lands in their *manse* at Broadwas, recite their benefactions and take an oath to observe all the conditions.[46] John de Broadwas made the first presentation[47] in 1344, but five years later the advowson had passed into the hands of the Prior of Worcester,[48] who continued to appoint until 1457,[49] after which time there is no record of the chantry.

CHARITIES In 1775 the Rev. Henry Roberts, by his will, left £2 yearly to the poor at Christmas. The legacy is represented by £66 13*s.* 4*d.* consols with the official

---

[34] Inform. from Mr. H. B. Walters.

[35] Earlier entries for the 17th century will be found among the Bishops' Transcripts.

[36] Hale, *Reg. of Worc. Priory* (Camd. Soc.), 32*b* ; *Ann. Mon.* (Rolls Ser.), iv, 447, 496 ; *Sede Vac. Reg.* (Worcs. Hist. Soc.), Introd. 101.

[37] Pat. 33 Hen. VIII, pt. v, m. 19 ; *L. and P. Hen. VIII*, xvii, g. 71 (29).

[38] Pat. 6 Jas. I, pt. xii, no. 2. In 1561 the presentation was made by William Cratford of Chelmarsh, co. Salop, by grant of the dean and chapter, the former incumbent, ' an unlearned and stubborn priest confined to the County of Here-

ford,' having been deprived of the living (Nash, op. cit. i, 135).

[39] Hale, *Reg. of Worc. Priory* (Camd. Soc.), 32*b*. The parson as archdeacon may have held an ecclesiastical court with jurisdiction in criminal, matrimonial and testamentary causes from which these emoluments were perhaps derived (Hale's notes on *Reg. of Worc. Priory* [Camd. Soc.], p. lxiv).

[40] *Valor Eccl.* (Rec. Com.), iii, 233.

[41] *Cal. S. P. Dom.* 1628–9, pp. 60, 95, 382.

[42] Hale, *Reg. of Worc. Priory* (Camd. Soc.), 98*a*, 107 ; Introd. p. xciii.

[43] Worc. Epis. Reg. Carpenter (1443–76), i, fol. 83 *d.*

[44] *Cal. Pat.* 1338–40, p. 477.

[45] Ibid. 1343–5, pp. 49, 215. In 1405 the question arose whether these lands were free alms belonging to the chantry (De Banco R. 579, m. 389 ; Prattinton Coll. [Soc. Antiq.]).

[46] Prattinton Coll. (Soc. Antiq.). Nash gives a full transcript of the deed of ordination of the chantry (op. cit. i, 140–3).

[47] Nash, op. cit. i, 139.   [48] Ibid.

[49] Worc. Epis. Reg. Wulstan Bransford (1339–49), i, fol. 82 d. ; Brian (1352–61), fol. 41 ; Wakefield (1375–95), fol. 48 d. ; Winchcomb (1395–1401), fol. 9 d. ; Carpenter, xxii, fol. 144 d.

trustees, producing £1 13s. 4d. yearly, which is distributed in money doles to about twenty-eight recipients.

In 1797 Sarah Roberts, by her will, gave £5 yearly to the poor, to be distributed on New Year's Day. The legacy is represented by £166 13s. 4d. consols with the official trustees, producing £4 3s. 4d. yearly, which is distributed in money doles to about thirty-two recipients.

In 1892 John Francis Greswolde-Williams, by his will proved at Worcester 12 August, bequeathed

£1,000 for the benefit of the poor. The legacy was invested in £1,030 18s. 7d. consols with the official trustees, and the annual dividend, amounting to £25 15s. 4d., was in 1908–9 distributed as to £11 10s. in cash to thirteen recipients, £5 7s. 6d. in orders on tradesmen and £8 17s. 10d. to coal and clothing clubs.

The same testator bequeathed £1,000 for the benefit of the Church of England school. This legacy was invested in £1,030 18s. 7d. consols with the official trustees, producing £25 15s. 4d. yearly.

CHURCHILL

Circehille (xi cent.); Cherchull, Chirchehull, Cershull-juxta-Humelbrok (xiii cent.).

Churchill, usually spoken of as Churchill in

there is a chalybeate spring and in the east of the parish a petrifying spring.

The village is very small, and consists of a few

CHURCHILL : WOOD FARM SHOWING DOVECOT

Oswaldslow to distinguish it from Churchill in Halfshire, is a small parish 5 miles to the east of Worcester. Bow Brook runs south along the eastern side and the Evesham and Worcester road forms the boundary on the south. The parish covers an area of 670 acres, of which 251 acres are laid down in permanent grass and 56 are woods and plantations,[1] Churchill Wood being the largest of these ; 202 acres are arable land, the chief crops being wheat, barley and beans. The parish lies partly on the Keuper Marls and partly on the Lower Lias formation, the soil being clay. The eastern part of the parish lies on the right bank of the Bow Brook, but to the west the land rises, reaching a height of 200 ft. above the ordnance datum at Churchill Wood in the north-west. No railway line touches the parish, the nearest station being at Stoulton on the Great Western line, 3 miles distant. At Churchill Spa in the north-east

[1] Statistics from Bd. of Agric. (1905).

farm-houses and half-timbered cottages. The church stands on the summit of a slight hill on the east side of the road along which the cottages forming the village are grouped. To the north-east of the church is the site of the former manor-house, the surrounding moat of which may still be traced in its entirety. On the west side of the road, nearly opposite the church, is a two-storied L-shaped half-timber house, probably of 16th-century date. On the same side of the road, at the southern extremity of the village, is a small half-timbered farm-house of picturesque appearance. At the foot of the hill to the north of the church, where the road takes a turn to the eastward, is a late 17th-century farm-house or brick. At Churchill Wood, on the north side of the Alcester road, about half a mile to the north of the main village, is Wood Farm, a 17th-century house of brick, and adjoining it is a fine brick dovecot and stable combined. The dovecot forms a tower at the west end of the stable, and is crowned by a tiled roof gabled on each face, the gable ends being filled with half-timber work. A small central lantern surmounts the whole. The lower story forms part of the stables.

Among former place-names were Le Mershe, Wythewell[2] and Small Elms, now contracted to Smellums.[3] In 1811 an Act was passed for inclosing lands in the parish and for making compensation for tithes.[4]

MANOR Three hides at *CHURCHILL* were held of the Bishop of Worcester's manor of Northwick in Claines at the time of the Domesday Survey.[5] Churchill still formed part of Northwick in the 13th century,[6] and in 1488 the bishop was still said to be overlord of the fee.[7] Azor held this manor in the time of Edward the Confessor, but Walter Poer (Ponther) was the bishop's tenant in 1086.[8] As at Bredicot, Walter's interest in the manor as mesne lord became annexed to the Poers' manor at Battenhall, and passed with it to the Prior of Worcester,[9] the manor being said in 1501 and 1574 to be held of the manor of Battenhall.[10] The manor was perhaps held by the Poers in demesne until the 13th century, for no mention has been found of any tenant until about the middle of that century.

Sir John de Churchill, who was evidently lord of the manor,[11] had a long quarrel with the Bishop of Worcester over the patronage of the church, and 'incurred the sentence of excommunication for contumacy' because he insisted on presenting John de Farley, the rector of Stanton near Oxford, to Churchill, although the bishop refused to admit him. In 1269 'the said John, having at length sought and obtained absolution, the bishop, although having the right to collate to the church, out of clemency admitted the said John on the presentation of the same knight.'[12] Sir John joined the rebellious barons during the Barons' War and forfeited all his estates. He was in prison in 1266, when part of his land was assigned to his wife Maud.[13] He died before 1272, when his property was given to his widow.[14] Maud was still holding a third of the manor in 1321,[15] but the rest passed between 1280 and 1289 to the heir of Sir John de Churchill, Joan wife of Giles de Argentein.[16] Joan was holding the manor in 1297-8,[17] and it

seems probable that Maud wife of John de Burwell, who released her right in the manor in 1304 to Joan de Argentein, then a widow, was Maud, formerly the wife of Sir John de Churchill.[18]

Joan in 1321 gave two-thirds of the manor and the reversion of the other third after Maud's death to Richard de Westbury.[19] Six years later John de Westbury, probably a son of Richard, gave the manor to Sir John de Wisham and his wife Hawise,[20] and in 1328 Sir John obtained from the king a grant of free warren in this manor.[21] He died about 1333, leaving a son and heir John,[22] who obtained a pardon for marrying without the king's licence in 1334, when only fifteen years old.[23] Hawise, widow of the elder John, retained a life interest in the whole manor, which was confirmed to her by her son when he came of age.[24] In 1356 she settled the manor on herself and her son John and his heirs, with remainder to Sir Robert Bures.[25] She died three years later, when John succeeded.[26] The manor had passed from him to another John before 1415.[27] This John[28] married Margaret daughter and heir of Sir John Beauchamp of Holt, and after his death the manor was divided, like Holt (q.v.), between the Guise and Croft families.[29]

WISHAM. *Sable a fesse between six martlets argent.*

The part which passed to the Guise family was sold by John Guise in 1543 to George Habington.[30] Of him it was purchased by Jane Stanford,[31] and she with her husband Edward Stanford sold it to Sir John Bourne in 1555.[32] The right of the last-named was unsuccessfully contested by William Guise, the son of John Guise, who claimed that his father had made a settlement of the property in 1554 on his sons Anselm and William in tail-male successively, and that Anselm had died childless.[33] Sir John Bourne was in possession of the estate at his death in 1575,[34] and was succeeded by his son Anthony, who sold 'some of these lands to his tenants creating them freeholders,'[35] and this portion of the manor therefore disappears.

The moiety of the manor which belonged to the Crofts was purchased by William Cooksey.[36] The date of the purchase is not known, but it evidently

[2] Prattinton Coll. (Soc. Antiq.), Deeds of D. and C. of Worc. no. 127.
[3] Inform. supplied by Rev. R. C. Bates.
[4] Priv. Act, 51 Geo. III, cap. 59.
[5] *V.C.H. Worcs.* i, 295.
[6] *Testa de Nevill* (Rec. Com.), 41.
[7] De Banco R. Hil. 3 Hen. VII, m. 344.
[8] *V.C.H. Worcs.* i, 295.
[9] See Bredicot and Battenhall in St. Peter's, Worcester.
[10] Chan. Inq. p.m. (Ser. 2), xv, 100; clxxii, 142; see also ibid. 56 Hen. III, no. 38; *Testa de Nevill* (Rec. Com.), 41; *Cal. Pat.* 1327-30, p. 470; 1343-5, p. 254; Chan. Inq. p.m. 6 Edw. III (1st nos.), no. 53.
[11] It was probably this John who, as Sir John son and heir of John de Churchill, gave two water-mills with some land to the church of Churchill, the gift having perhaps been made in expiation for his controversy with the bishop. The gift was confirmed in 1344 (*Cal. Pat.* 1343-5, p. 254).

[12] *Reg. G. Giffard* (Worcs. Hist. Soc.), 32, 33.   [13] *Cal. Pat.* 1258-66, p. 546.
[14] *Cal. Inq. p.m. Hen. III*, 282. Sir John's widow Maud obtained part of these lands by gift of the king. Half the estate had been held by Hamo Lestrange, who had received it from Thomas Boterel, to whom the king gave it during the minority of Sir John's heir (*Cal. Close,* 1272-9, pp. 42, 43).
[15] Feet of F. Worcs. 15 Edw. II, no. 32.
[16] *Lay Subs. R.* 1280 (Worcs. Hist. Soc.), 40; Feet of F. Worcs. 15 Edw. II, no. 32; *Reg. G. Giffard* (Worcs. Hist. Soc.), 355. Giles de Argentein presented to the church in 1289.
[17] Add. MS. 28024, fol. 148.
[18] Feet of F. Worcs. 33 Edw. I, no. 21.
[19] Ibid. 15 Edw. II, no. 32.
[20] Ibid. 1 Edw. III, no. 3; De Banco R. Trin. 1 Edw. III, m. 78.
[21] Chart. R. 2 Edw. III, m. 17, no. 59.
[22] Chan. Inq. p.m. 6 Edw. III (1st nos.), no. 53. The manor contained at this time a capital messuage with a moat

round it (*Cal. Close,* 1330-3, p. 516; 1333-7, p. 454; *Cal. Inq. p.m.* 1-9 Edw. III, 320).
[23] *Cal. Pat.* 1334-8, p. 10.
[24] *Cal. Close,* 1341-3, p. 133.
[25] Feet of F. Div. Co. Hil. 30 Edw. III; see also *Cal. Close,* 1341-3, p. 525.
[26] Chan. Inq. p.m. 33 Edw. III (1st nos.), no. 22.
[27] Nash, op. cit. i, 196. In 1398 John Luttley and his wife presented to the church (ibid.).
[28] *Lay Subs. R. Worcs.* 1427-8 (Worcs. Hist. Soc.), 35.
[29] For references see Holt.
[30] Com. Pleas D. Enr. Hil. 34 Hen. VIII, m. 7.
[31] Chan. Proc. (Ser. 2), bdle. 77, no. 40.
[32] Feet of F. Worcs. Trin. 2 & 3 Phil. and Mary.
[33] Chan. Proc. (Ser. 2), bdle. 77, no. 40.
[34] Chan. Inq. p.m. (Ser. 2), clxxii, 142.
[35] Habington, *Surv. of Worcs.* i, 151.
[36] Ibid.; Chan. Proc. (Ser. 2), bdle. 17, no. 66.

took place before 1565–6.[37] William Cooksey died without issue and this estate passed to his sister Alice wife of Humphrey Acton[38] or to her son John, for William Acton, apparently the son of John, was dealing with it in 1607,[39] and John Acton and his son William sold it in 1610 to Rowland Berkeley.[40] The manor has since followed the descent of Spetchley,[41] and now belongs to Mr. Robert Valentine Berkeley.

In 1086 there was a mill at Churchill worth 4*s*.[42] About the middle of the 13th century Sir John de Churchill and his wife Maud gave two water-mills under one roof at Churchill for the support of a chantry priest in the church of Churchill.[43] This grant was ratified by the king in 1344.[44] The parson of Churchill apparently remained in possession of these mills until the dissolution of the chantries in the time of Edward VI.[45] In the 16th century this mill was the subject of Chancery proceedings. Sir John Bourne and William Cooksey claimed the ownership, but Thomas Harewell and his wife Margaret, who were in possession, replied that it had come into the hands of Edward VI by virtue of the statute made for the dissolution of chantries, and that Queen Elizabeth had granted it in 1565 to them for twenty-one years.[46] The result of this suit is not known, but in 1590 the queen granted two water-mills to John Williams and John Wells and their heirs for ever.[47] A water-mill still stands in the parish.

CHURCH   The church of *ST. MICHAEL* consists of a chancel 20½ ft. by 15½ ft. and a nave 37 ft. by 20 ft. These measurements are internal. The chancel was rebuilt a few years ago, and the nave, which dates from the 14th century, is now undergoing a complete restoration. It appears to have replaced an earlier structure, probably of the 12th century, as a few worked stones of that date were re-used in the 14th-century walling. Lying in the churchyard is a knee-stone of a gable, once painted and carved with a small couchant lion.

The east window of the chancel is of three lights under a pointed head, without tracery, and the two windows on the south are single lights. The north wall is plastered externally and is without openings. The chancel arch is modern, of two chamfered orders.

The nave has a single 14th-century window in each side wall of two lights with a quatrefoil above. To the east of each is a small hole through the wall about 7 in. square and about 3 ft. above the ground. The purpose of these openings is doubtful. A piscina in the south wall appears to be original and has a trefoiled head. The 14th-century north doorway has been lately reopened; it is of a single chamfered order with a pointed arch. The south doorway is similar and the jambs of both have deep holes for the reception of wooden draw-bars. The south wall has recently been rebuilt, owing to its serious

inclination outwards, but the old materials have been carefully re-used. In the side walls several worked stones, including jambs and shafts, of an earlier building have been found in the 14th-century work. The two-light west window is modern. The church was ceiled throughout, but the plaster of the nave roof has been stripped and the old timbers exposed. A small modern turret capped by a pyramidal roof rises above the west end and contains two bells, one dated 1711 and the other undated but probably somewhat older.

The stone font is octagonal and appears to be of 15th-century date. The altar rails are of the early 18th-century baluster type.

There are several monuments in the chancel, the oldest to Thomas Barker, died 1688.

A small piece of ancient glass in the east window bears a shield of the arms of Wisham.

A gravestone in the churchyard commemorates George Apedaile, a Roman Catholic priest who died in 1799, and some English nuns of the order of Poor Clares, who, when banished from Dunkerque by the fury of the French Revolution about 1792, found, by the kindness of Mr. Berkeley, a refuge at Churchill, and William Southworth, their chaplain, who died in 1814. They lived at Wood Farm in this parish.

The communion plate includes an Elizabethan cup with the date 1571 inscribed on it and the date letter for the same year and an exact copy of the same cup inscribed 1905. There are also a pewter flagon and two small pewter almsdishes.

The registers before 1812 are as follows : (i) baptisms 1565 to 1794, burials 1566 to 1792 and marriages 1564 to 1750 ; after this the baptisms and burials before 1813 are missing ; (ii) marriages 1761 to 1812.

ADVOWSON   In the 11th century Churchill was a chapelry of the church of St. Helen, Worcester.[48] It seems to have become separated from St. Helen's before 1269, for it is then called a church, and its advowson was in dispute between the bishop and Sir John de Churchill.[49] After this time, however, the advowson followed the same descent as the manor,[50] and was divided in the same way at the end of the 15th century between the families of Guise and Croft.[51] The moiety which ultimately passed to the Crofts followed the same descent as their share of the manor to Rowland Berkeley.[52] The moiety held by the Guise family seems to have been sold by John Guise with his share of the manor to George Habington, though it is not mentioned in the conveyance, for Edward and Jane Stanford sold it with the Guise moiety of the manor to Sir John Bourne,[53] who died seised of it in 1575.[54] It must have passed shortly after to Philip Sheldon, for he presented to the church in 1581[55] and sold the advowson in 1606 to

[37] Chan. Proc. (Ser. 2), bdle. 17, no. 66. John Croft had married Margaret, a sister of William Cooksey (*Visit. of Worcs.* 1569 [Harl. Soc. xxvii], 44).
[38] *Visit. of Worcs.* 1569 (Harl. Soc. xxvii), 44.
[39] Ibid. 7 ; Feet of F. Worcs. East. 5 Jas. I.
[40] Feet of F. Worcs. Trin. 8 Jas. I.
[41] Chan. Inq. p.m. (Ser. 2), dccxviii, 155 ; Recov. R. D. Enr. East. 18 Geo. III, m. 27 ; Recov. R. Trin. 48 Geo. III, rot. 37.

[42] *V.C.H. Worcs.* i, 295.
[43] *Cal. Pat.* 1343–5, p. 254 ; Pat. 32 Eliz. pt. xi, m. 8.
[44] *Cal. Pat.* 1343–5, p. 254.
[45] *Cal. Close*, 1272–9, pp. 42, 43 ; Chan. Proc. (Ser. 2), bdle. 17, no. 66.
[46] Chan. Proc. (Ser. 2), bdle. 17, no. 66.
[47] Pat. 32 Eliz. pt. xi, m. 8.
[48] Heming, op. cit. 427.
[49] *Reg. G. Giffard* (Worcs. Hist. Soc.), 32, 33.

[50] Ibid. 355, 451 ; Feet of F. Worcs. 15 Edw. II, no. 32 ; 1 Edw. III, no. 3 ; Div. Co. 30 Edw. III, no. 11.
[51] De Banco R. East. 14 Hen. VII, m. 21 ; Chan. Inq. p.m. (Ser. 2), xv, 100 ; Feet of F. Worcs. Hil. 27 Hen. VIII.
[52] Feet of F. Worcs. East. 5 Jas. I ; Trin. 8 Jas. I.
[53] Ibid. Trin. 2 & 3 Phil. and Mary.
[54] Chan. Inq. p.m. (Ser. 2), clxxii, 142.
[55] Nash, op. cit. i, 196.

Rowland Berkeley.[56] From that time the advowson has remained with the Berkeley family.[57]

CHARITIES The charities of Thomas Barker and others, mentioned on a table in the church, are now represented by £200 consols with the official trustees, arising from the sale of a cottage and garden in the parish of White Ladies Aston, which had been purchased with £55 given by Thomas Barker and others for the poor. The annual dividends of £5 are, under a scheme of 1 July 1864, distributed to the poor on the eve of St. Thomas's Day.

In 1867 Mrs. Maria Dineley, by her will, bequeathed £150 consols, the interest to be applied in the first place in keeping in repair the Dineley tomb in the churchyard, and any residue to be distributed to the poor. The stock is in the name of the official trustees, and the income, £3 15s. yearly, is applied in aid of the sick poor. The tomb is kept in repair.

It was recorded on another table in the church that in 1733 a sum of £6 was given to the parish to remain a stock for ever, the use thereof to be laid out in books of devotion and piety to be distributed by the minister.

The church land consisted of about an acre situate in the glebe, in respect of which £1 was paid to the clerk in part payment of his salary.

CLAINES

Cleinesse (xi cent.) ; Cleines, Cleynes, Claynes (xiii cent.).

The parish of Claines, on the left bank of the Severn and to the north of Worcester, has been considerably reduced at different times. In 1880, under the Divided Parishes Act, Smite Hill was annexed to Hindlip.[1] The tithing of Whistones was taken into the city of Worcester under the Municipal Corporation Act, 1832, and in 1885 Claines was divided into North Claines and South Claines, the latter being added to the city under the Worcester Extension Act.[2]

North Claines covers 3,403 acres, of which 814½ are arable land, 2,174¾ permanent grass, and 10¼ woods and plantations.[3] The chief crops are wheat, barley and beans. Its western boundary is the Severn and its northern the River Salwarpe, which, running south-west, enters the Severn near Hawford Lodge. To the south of the Salwarpe and following approximately the same direction is the Droitwich Canal, which was constructed in accordance with the Act of 1767.[4] Barbourne Brook enters the parish on the east and runs south-west through Perdiswell Park, joining the Severn near the City Waterworks. The Worcester and Birmingham Canal follows the same direction as the Barbourne Brook.

The Droitwich road enters the parish in the north-east at Fernhill Heath, and after passing Perdiswell Park it meets at Barbourne the Kidderminster road, which enters this parish at Hawford. The two roads, when united at Barbourne, cross the brook at Barbourne Bridge where Charles II first halted after the battle of Worcester (the present bridge is a modern structure), and then form the tithing of Whistones, on the left hand side of which is the old Cistercian nunnery of the White Ladies, now the endowed grammar school of Queen Elizabeth, and runs on to a street formerly called Salt Lane (now Castle Street).

There were many complaints in the 17th century of the bad state of the roads in Claines.[5] Prattinton mentions an advertisement for the erection of two toll-houses at Barbourne in 1814, and these houses remain at the junction of the Kidderminster and Droitwich roads. The Turnpike Acts were still in force here until the final abolition of the turnpikes in 1868.[6]

The Oxford, Worcester and Wolverhampton branch of the Great Western railway crosses the parish from north to south, passing through Rainbow Hill Tunnel before it reaches the city. There are stations at Worcester and Fernhill Heath.

The village of Claines is in the centre of the parish on a branch road connecting the Kidderminster and Droitwich high roads. It stands at about 100 ft. above the ordnance datum, and to the north and west the land falls to the valleys of the Salwarpe and the Severn. Perdiswell Hall, formerly the property of the Wakemans, stands in a large park south of the village on the borough boundary.

The house known as Porter's Mill stands on a tributary of the Severn, with the actual mill on the opposite side of the road. The building is of half-timber work plastered, and is entered by a wood porch, with 18th-century moulded balusters fitted in the sides. There is a small hall, with stair and large fireplace on the left, and above the latter are the royal arms encircled by the Garter and flanked by the crowned initials E. R. One of the rooms contains a 17th-century plaster ceiling of interlacing design, enriched with fleurs de lis, crowns, fruit, Prince of Wales' feathers, mermaids, &c. There is also some good moulded oak panelling ornamented with lions and crowns. The short stair has good twisted balusters.

To the west of the village is the hamlet of Bevere. It contains Bevere House, the seat of Mr. F. Curtler, formerly the residence of the historian Treadway Nash. A picture of it is given in the frontispiece of the first volume of his history. Bevere Island in the Severn afforded shelter to the inhabitants of Worcester in 1041, when their city was attacked by Hardicanute,[7] and again in 1637, when the city was visited by plague.[8] To the north of the village is Hawford House, the residence of Mrs. Castle.

---

[56] Feet of F. Worcs. Mich. 4 Jas. I ; see also Recov. R. East. 6 Jas. I, rot. 83.

[57] Inst. Bks. (P.R.O.). Robert Dormer presented in 1711, Richard Nash in 1739, and the University of Oxford in 1745 (ibid.), probably for the Berkeleys.

[1] Pop. Ret. 1891, ii, 657. An account of Smite Manor will be found under Warndon.

[2] Stat. 48 & 49 Vict. cap. 164.

[3] Statistics from Bd. of Agric. (1905).

[4] Loc. and Pers. Act, 8 Geo. III, cap. 37.

[5] Quart. Sess. R. (Worcs. Hist. Soc.), 526, 557, &c.

[6] Prattinton Coll. (Soc. Antiq.) ; Bibl. of Worc. (Worcs. Hist. Soc.), i, 137.

[7] Roger de Hoveden, Chron. (Rolls Ser.), i, 92.

[8] Prattinton Coll. (Soc. Antiq.) ; Quart. Sess. R. (Worcs. Hist. Soc.), 639.

CHURCHILL CHURCH C. 1810
(*From a Water-colour by Thos. Rickards in Prattinton Collection*)

CLAINES CHURCH FROM THE SOUTH-EAST

Fernhill Heath is a hamlet to the north-east on the Droitwich road near the railway station, the greater part of which adjoins Hindlip and is the property of Lord Hindlip. It contains the kennels of the Worcestershire Hunt. In the hamlet of Astwood to the south-east of Claines is Moat House Farm, where remains of a moat still exist. The Blanquettes in Barbourne, standing in large grounds watered by the Barbourne Brook, is being cut up for building.

The common pound still standing in North Claines was put up for sale in 1820 among the effects of Mr. Handy, the auctioneer.[9]

Thomas Morris, vicar of Claines in 1689, was one of those who refused to take the oath of supremacy and was deprived of his living. He is said to be the person buried in Worcester Cathedral under a gravestone inscribed at his own request only with

dine, Tollardine) [12] (xiv cent.) ; Pichecroft,[13] Hawford (Havard, Haforde),[14] Barroe Cope,[15] Kent Grounds,[16] Hallow Claines,[17] le Breche, Tooseland, Cowmedowyate, Portwellisley [18] (xvi cent.) ; Muncke Meadowe, The Neyte, Edicros [19] (xvii cent.), Jacob's Ladder.

MANORS It is not known when the church of Worcester acquired the great manor of NORTHWICK, which seems in early times to have included the present manor of WHISTONES (Wistan, Whytston, xiii cent. ; Wyston, xiv cent.), the principal manor in the parish of Claines.[20] In 1086 it consisted of 25 hides, of which the bishop held 3½ in demesne with houses in Worcester and salt pans at Droitwich.[21] Henry III granted to the bishop free warren in his demesne lands here in 1254 and in 1255.[22]

PORTER'S MILL, CLAINES : HALL AND STAIRCASE

the word 'Miserrimus,' which formed the subject of a sonnet by Wordsworth. Thomas Biddulph, the Evangelical preacher, was born at Claines in 1763.[10]

Among the place-names found at Claines are Losmar (Losemore) [11] (xiii cent.) ; Tolwardyn (Tala-

Before the end of the 13th century the principal manor of the Bishops of Worcester in Claines had acquired the name 'Northwick and Wistan.' [23] The manor was surveyed under this name in 1484–5,[24] but before the middle of the 16th century the name

[9] Prattinton, op. cit. [10] Dict. Nat. Biog.
[11] Cal. Chart. R. 1226–57, p. 173 ; Chan. Proc. (Ser. 2), bdle. 115, no. 14 ; Pat. 7 Jas. I, pt. xvi.
[12] Prattinton Coll. (Soc. Antiq.) ; Chan. Inq. p.m. (Ser. 2), xxi, 19 ; Exch. Spec. Com. 30 Eliz. no. 2491 ; Exch. Dep. East. 30 Eliz. no. 19.
[13] Valor Eccl. (Rec. Com.), iii, 223 ; Pat. 7 Jas. I, pt. xvi.
[14] Cal. S. P. Dom. 1547–65, p. 439 ; Quart. Sess. R. (Worcs. Hist. Soc.), 656 ; Close, 1650, pt. xxii, no. 14.

[15] Memo. R. Recorda Hil. 2 Eliz. rot. 36.
[16] Exch. Dep. Mich. 32 & 33 Eliz. no. 35.
[17] Ibid. Hil. 33 Eliz. no. 4.
[18] Pat. 36 Hen. VIII, pt. xxii (grant to Rich. Taverner).
[19] Close, 1650, pt. xxii, no. 14.
[20] A manor of Northwick is mentioned in Edgar's charter (964) among the manors of the priory of Worcester (Heming, Chartul. [ed. Hearne], 520), but as it was 'in monte Wiccisia' and is followed in

the charter by Evenlode, Daylesford, Dorn and Iccomb it seems more probable that Northwick in Blockley is intended.
[21] V.C.H. Worcs. i, 294a.
[22] Chart. R. 39 Hen. III, m. 6 ; Cal. Chart. R. 1226–57, p. 443 ; Cal. Pat. 1247–58, p. 345.
[23] Red Bk. of Bishopric of Worc. (Eccl. Com. Rec. Var. bdle. 121, no. 43698), fol. 1.
[24] Rental of Northwick in Prattinton Coll. (Soc. Antiq.).

Whiston or Whistones had superseded that of North-wick.[25] The manor-house at Northwick seems to have been disused as a residence of the Bishops of Worcester before the Dissolution. Leland writing soon after says, 'This Northewike was one John of Wodds *in hominum memoria* and bought of a Bysshope for lake of a Howse in Claynes. It is motid and had a Parke.'[26] In the time of Elizabeth the house was in ruins, and in a lease to Gilbert Lyttelton was described as ' all that house . . . within our mote within the scite and precincts of the manor of Northwick in the parish of Claines where of late our old capital mansion did stand.'[27]

The site was conveyed in 1612 by John Weme and his wife Margery, who evidently held it under lease from the bishop, to John Stampe,[28] and four years later John Weme and John Stampe sold it to Hum-phrey Baker.[29] In 1648 the site was still leased by the Bakers,[30] and was sold in that year as a late possession of the see of Worcester to Richard Vernon and Anthony Feare.[31] At the present day nothing is left of the manor-house at Northwick but a portion of the moat.

The manor of Whistones remained in the pos-session of the Bishops of Worcester until under the Commonwealth it was confiscated and sold in 1648, as ' the manor of Whitstons and Claynes,' to George Pike,[32] the site of the manor of Whistones having been sold a month before to Thomas Newsam, Edward Berkeley, Richard Vernon and Edward Harwood.[33] The manor was restored to the bishop on the acces-sion of Charles II.[34] The manor, still known as Claines and Whistones in the 18th century, is now called the manor of Claines, and belonged to the Bishops of Worcester[35] until it was taken over in 1860 by the Ecclesiastical Commissioners,[36] who are the present owners of the manor, and courts are still held.

The site of the manor of Whistones seems to have been held before the Dissolution by the Dean of Westbury College under the Bishops of Worcester.[37] This lease afterwards came to the Blounts, Robert Blount dying seised of the site of the manor or farm of Whistones in 1573.[38] In 1616 the bishop leased the site of the manor for three lives to George Smith, who shortly after assigned the lease to William Warmestry.[39] Warmestry afterwards assigned the lease to Thomas Cheatle,[40] to whom it was re-newed by the bishop in 1623.[41] The Cheatles were still in possession in 1648,[42] and the site was granted

for a long lease in 1668 by the bishop to Sir Rowland Berkeley and members of the Vernon family, the Vernons having inherited the bulk of the Cheatle property.[43]

Though the nuns of Whistones obtained grants of land from time to time during the 13th and 14th centuries[44] they never seem to have had a manor in the parish of Claines, their possessions there in 1535 being represented by a rent of 42s. 6d.[45] After the Dissolution the lands of the nunnery were dispersed,[46] but the site was leased in 1537 to Walter Welshe,[47] and granted in 1543 to Richard Callowhill.[48] On his death in 1548 his brother John inherited the property,[49] and in the following year gave it to his son John,[50] who was succeeded in 1573 by his son, a third John.[51] He was succeeded by Nicholas Callow-hill (probably his cousin and son of his uncle Nicholas), on whose death in 1593 his daughter Elizabeth, the wife of Giles Acton, inherited this land.[52] Before the death of John Callowhill in 1573 the site of the priory appears to have passed to the governors of the free school at Worcester, for they received the profits after the death of John,[53] and it was probably held under them by lease by John's descendants. The governors of Queen Elizabeth's school in Worcester are the present owners of the estate.[54]

It was leased in 1662 by the governors to Richard Blurton and his wife Mary. The lease was renew-able, and in 1700 their daughter Anne, who married John Cooksey, renewed it, and it was afterwards again renewed by her son Richard Cooksey in 1714.[55] His daugh-ter Anne married Edward Ingram in 1745, when the lease was transferred to her.[56] Their son Richard Ingram, who appears to have taken the name Cooksey,[57] held it until his death in 1811, and his widow renewed it in the following year. Her daughter Mary, who married John Thomas, lived at the White Ladies until the lease fell in between 1848 and 1858. It was then taken by Mr. Everill of Worcester, who was the occupier in 1865.[58] On the termination of that lease the governors rebuilt the school and almshouses on the site, the old house becoming the head master's residence.[59]

COOKSEY. *Argent a bend azure with three cinqfoils or thereon.*

[25] *Valor Eccl.* (Rec. Com.), iii, 217.
[26] Leland, *Itin.* (ed. Hearne), viii (2), 100.
[27] Noake, *Monastery and Cathedral of Worcester*, 521.
[28] Feet of F. Worcs. Mich. 10 Jas. I.
[29] Ibid. Mich. 14 Jas. I.
[30] Close, 24 Chas. I, pt. xiv, no. 17.
[31] Ibid.
[32] Ibid. 1649, pt. iv, no. 13.
[33] Ibid. 24 Chas. I, pt. xv, no. 2.
[34] Recov. R. D. Enr. East. 3 Will. and Mary, m. 3.
[35] *Diary of Francis Evans* (Worcs. Hist. Soc.), 26, 37, 38, 109.
[36] Stat. 23 & 24 Vict. cap. 124.
[37] Chan. Proc. (Ser. 2), bdle. 115, no. 14.
[38] Chan. Inq. p.m. (Ser. 2), clxv, 191.
[39] Chan. Proc. (Ser. 2), bdles. 353, no. 6; 309, no. 26.

[40] Ibid. bdle. 353, no. 6.
[41] Close, 24 Chas. I, pt. xv, no. 2.
[42] Ibid.
[43] Recov. R. D. Enr. East. 3 Will. and Mary, m. 3.
[44] *Ann. Mon.* (Rolls Ser.), iv, 443; *Reg. G. Giffard* (Worcs. Hist. Soc.), 301; Inq. a.q.d. files 19, no. 6; 34, no. 2; 228, no. 20; 234, no. 1; *Cal. Pat.* 1405–8, p. 260; see *V.C.H. Worcs.* ii, 155.
[45] *Valor Eccl.* (Rec. Com.), iii, 230.
[46] *L. and P. Hen. VIII*, xiii (1), p. 586; xiv (1), p. 604; xix (2), g. 527 (25); xx (1), g. 282 (52).
[47] Ibid. xiii (1), p. 588.
[48] Ibid. xviii (1), g. 981 (47).
[49] Chan. Inq. p.m. (Ser. 2), lxxxvii, 95.
[50] Pat. 3 Edw. VI, pt. v.
[51] Chan. Inq. p.m. (Ser. 2), dcclxiv, 20.

[52] Ibid. cccxxv, 199.
[53] Ibid. dcclxiv, 20. Unfortunately this inquisition is so much torn that it is impossible to find out from it exactly what were the respective interests of the governors of the school and the Callow-hills in the site.
[54] Mr. Lees erroneously states that the site was given to the governors of the school by Queen Elizabeth (*Assoc. Archit. Soc. Rep.* viii, 359).
[55] Prattinton Coll. (Soc. Antiq.); Met-calfe, *Visit. of Worcs.* 1682–3, p. 39.
[56] Ibid.
[57] Ibid.; he is called Richard Cooksey in Metcalfe's *Visit. of Worcs.* (p. 39), and all his descendants bore the name of Cooksey according to this pedigree.
[58] *Assoc. Archit. Soc. Rep.* viii, 359. Paper by Edwin Lees.
[59] Inform. from Mr. J. W. Willis Bund.

A description of such remains of the nunnery as now exist will be found with the city of Worcester.

The hospitals of St. Wulfstan [60] and St. Oswald [61] in Worcester held land in this parish, which they acquired from various donors during the 13th and 14th centuries; the latter house, originally situated in this parish, was receiving rents amounting to £4 12s. 8d. from Claines in 1535,[62] and Nash says that their estate was once 'esteemed a manor.' [63]

Land at *BARBOURNE* (Beferburna, x cent.; Beverburne, Berborne, xiv cent.) was granted by Werefrith, Bishop of Worcester, in 904 to Ethelred ealdorman of Mercia and his wife Æthelflæd.[64] Barbourne afterwards became part of the manor of Northwick, of which it was held in the 13th century.[65]

From early times land at Barbourne was included in the manor of White Ladies Aston, the two manors being held for the service of a fifth part of a knight's fee.[66] Ralph de Wilington was holding Barbourne early in the 13th century, and it had formerly belonged to his father-in-law, Robert de Evercy,[67] having probably been granted at the same time as Aston to the ancestors of Robert by Theulf, Bishop of Worcester (1115–23).[68] It followed the same descent as White Ladies Aston, passing with it to the nuns of Whistones.[69] It then seems to have been incorporated in the demesnes of Whistones Priory, and is probably to be identified with land lying at le Barbours Brook, granted in 1543 with the site of Whistones Priory to Richard Callowhill.[70] Its further descent has not been traced.

Land in *PORTEFIELDS* was the property of Whistones Priory until the suppression of the nunnery. It was sold by Henry VIII in 1544 to Richard Andrews and John Howe,[71] who in the same year alienated it to the tenant, Thomas Hill.[72] John Callowe bought this land from Thomas Hill shortly before the death of the latter in 1557.[73] Some time before 1642 Portefields had come into the hands of Robert Waldegrave *alias* Fleet, but in that year he was considerably in debt, and he sold a property of 52 acres at Portefields.[74] In 1818 this estate was sold for building sites, the occupier at that time being Miss Strickland.[75]

PERDISWELL (Perdeswell, xii cent.; Persewell, xvi cent.) seems to have been a manor held of Northwick at least as early as the 15th century, as it is so called in a rental of Northwick in 1484–5.[76] John Comin was holding three-quarters of a yardland at Perdiswell of the manor of Northwick in the time of Henry II by grant of Bishop Alfred (1158–60).[77] The

estate was afterwards, according to Prattinton, held by the Perdiswells,[78] then by the Attwoods, and shortly before 1484 by Thomas Acton,[79] but no original deeds have been found throwing light on its early history. In 1526–7 John Wood conveyed it to trustees in trust for his younger sons Anthony, Robert, Ralph and Richard.[80] John died in 1527,[81] and Anthony Attwood, who was dealing with the manor in 1596, was probably his son.[82] The manor remained in the possession of the Attwood family (see Wolverley) until 1684, when Henry Attwood sold it to Edward Hammond.[83] Thomas Hammond was in possession in 1736,[84] and was succeeded by Henry Hammond, clerk, on whose death, about 1769, the estate was sold pursuant to a decree in Chancery.[85] The purchaser may have been Charles Freeman Wakeman, who was in possession of the manor in 1812.[86] Before 1828 it had passed to Henry Wakeman of Perdiswell, who was created a baronet in that year.[87] He was succeeded in 1831 by a son, Sir Offley Penbury Wakeman, on whose death in 1858 the manor passed to his son Sir

WAKEMAN, baronet. *Paly vert and argent a saltire engrailed ermine.*

Offley Wakeman,[88] who shortly after sold it with the bulk of the Wakeman property in Claines. It was purchased by Henry Walker, and has recently been sold.

The manor of *BEVERE* (Beverege, xi cent.) probably originated in gifts made to the Prior and convent of Worcester in the 11th and 12th centuries. One was made by Bishop Wulfstan, who gave the monks the fishery of Beverburn with 12 acres of land belonging to it, the other in 1117 by Bishop Theulf, who gave a fishery in the Severn with the weir of Beverburn, and the island [89] (evidently Bevere Island). At the Dissolution this manor was valued with Lippard as 'Bevrey cum Barborn' at £10 14s.[90] With the rest of the estates of the priory it was granted as the manor of Bevere in 1542 to the Dean and Chapter of Worcester.[91] It was confirmed to them in 1608–9,[92] but was sold in 1650 by the trustees for the confiscated lands of the dean and chapter to William Dineley of Hanley Castle. The estate was then apparently only a farm.[93] It was, however, confirmed to the dean and chapter in 1692 as the manor of Bevere.[94] The manor of Bevere was

[60] *Cal. Chart. R.* 1226–57, p. 173; Inq. a.q.d. file 226, no. 1; *Cal. Pat.* 1330–4, p. 506.
[61] *Cal. Pat.* 1330–4, p. 283.
[62] *Valor Eccl.* (Rec. Com.), iii, 229.
[63] Nash, op. cit. i, 225.
[64] Birch, *Cart. Sax.* ii, 266.
[65] *Testa de Nevill* (Rec. Com.), 41.
[66] Ibid.; Red Bk. of Bishopric of Worc. (Eccl. Com. Rec. Var. bdle. 121, no. 43698), fol. 255.
[67] Ibid. [68] See White Ladies Aston.
[69] *Feud. Aids*, v, 308.
[70] *L. and P. Hen. VIII*, xviii (1), g. 981 (47).
[71] Ibid. xix (1), g. 1035 (107).
[72] Ibid. (2), p. 87.
[73] Pat. 3 & 4 Phil. and Mary, pt. iv, m. 35; Chan. Inq. p.m. (Ser. 2), cx, 162.

[74] Exch. Dep. Trin. 1651, no. 5; Mich. 1652, no. 11.
[75] Prattinton Coll. (Soc. Antiq.).
[76] Ibid.
[77] Habington, *Surv. of Worcs.* (Worcs. Hist. Soc.), ii, 41; Red Bk. of Bishopric of Worc. (Eccl. Com. Rec. Var. bdle. 121, no. 43698), fol. 18.
[78] Cecily de Perdiswell and her daughter Isabel held land in the manor of Northwick in 1299 (Red Bk. of Bishopric, fol. 2), and Walter de Perdiswell paid a subsidy of 2s. there in 1327 (*Lay Subs. R. Worcs.* 1327 [Worcs. Hist. Soc.], 12).
[79] Prattinton Coll. (Soc. Antiq.).
[80] Feet of F. Worcs. Trin. 18 Hen. VIII; Chan. Inq. p.m. (Ser. 2), xlvii, 24.
[81] Chan. Inq. p.m. (Ser. 2), xlvii, 24.
[82] Feet of F. Worcs. Trin. 38 Eliz.

[83] Ibid. Mich. 36 Chas. II; Recov. R. Mich. 36 Chas. II, rot. 302; Chan. Proc. (Ser. 2), bdles. 348, no. 25; 379, no. 13.
[84] Recov. R. Mich. 10 Geo. II, rot. 281.
[85] Prattinton Coll. (Soc. Antiq.).
[86] Recov. R. Trin. 52 Geo. III, rot. 142.
[87] Burke, *Peerage*, 1906. [88] Ibid.
[89] Hale, op. cit. 40; Heming, *Chartul.* (ed. Hearne), 533. The mills at Barbourne were demolished about the middle of the 17th century (Exch. Dep. East. 1659, no. 30).
[90] *Valor Eccl.* (Rec. Com.), iii, 223.
[91] *L. and P. Hen. VIII*, xvii, g. 71 (29).
[92] Pat. 6 Jas. I, pt. xii, no. 2.
[93] Close, 1650, pt. xxii, no. 14.
[94] Pat. 4 Will. and Mary, pt. i, no. 6.

held under leases from the dean and chapter by the Attwoods of Perdiswell in the 16th and 17th centuries.[95]

A rent reserved by the Crown from this manor, under the grant of 1542, was vested in trustees for sale in 1674.[96] This was in 1739 in the hands of Charles Earl of Tankerville and his wife Camilla, who then granted it to Charles Clarke,[97] and thirty years later Samuel Bayes and his wife Theodosia with Thomas Cotton and his wife Rebecca conveyed a rent from Bevere Manor to Anne West, a widow.[98]

Dr. Treadway Russell Nash bought an estate at Bevere shortly after his marriage in 1758 and died there in 1811. His property passed to his daughter Mary, whose husband, John Somers Cocks, had succeeded to the title of Lord Somers in 1806.[99] Prattinton, writing at the beginning of the 19th century, states that Bevere, the late residence of William Cary, was then for sale.[100] It was subsequently purchased by Thomas Gale Curtler and is now in the possession of his grandson.

The manor of *BLANKETTS*, which appears for the first time in 1548, probably originated in half a hide of land held of the manor of Northwick by the Blankett family. Osbert Blankett held an estate near Barbourne at the end of the 12th or early in the 13th century,[1] and Robert Blankett paid a subsidy about 1280 and was the owner in 1299.[2] Beatrice Blankett is returned as tenant in a later survey,[2a] and John Blankett gave land in Northwick to the hospital of St. Oswald in 1310.[3] Agnes Blankett paid a subsidy of 1s. 6d. at Northwick in 1327,[4] and John Blankett still appears to have had an estate at Claines in 1339.[5] In 1484 Humphrey Frere or Friar was holding a messuage which had lately belonged to Agnes Blankett.[6] The manor remained with the Friar family, whose pedigree is given in the Visitation of Worcester of 1569,[7] until 1589, when Richard Friar and his wife Anne sold it to George Langford.[8] It belonged in 1831 to Henry Evans and his wife Mary Anne and Charlotte Elizabeth Stewart.[9] It passed through several hands and became the property of the Stallards. Its site is marked by the Blanquettes, an estate in Barbourne, now being developed for building.

FRIAR. *Sable a cheveron between three dolphins argent.*

Bishop Wulfstan gave a mill at Tapenhall[10] to the priory of Worcester in the 11th century.[11] The tenant of the mill was obliged to supply the master of the kitchen of the monastery with 30 'stiches' of eels or their equivalent in money, and the miller had to feed the horses which brought meal to be ground at the mill.[12] This mill evidently passed with the rest of the prior's estates to the Dean and Chapter of Worcester, for they had a water corn-mill at Tapenhall on Salwarpe Brook in 1613.[13] This mill was leased by the Nashes in the 17th century, George Nash and his nephew Thomas each having built an additional mill during his tenure of the lease.[14] The mill built by Thomas about 1609 was called Mildenham Mill.[15] Before 1659 Thomas Nash owned four water corn-mills at Mildenham, while a Mr. Porter had three mills at Tapenhall.[16] He made a settlement of these three mills and the capital messuage called Tapenhall Mills in 1672.[17] This capital messuage may have been the old half-timbered house called Porter's Mill.[18] Two corn-mills belonged to the manor of Whistones and Claines in 1649.[19] There were three water corn-mills at Hawford in 1659, of which Richard Jones was the owner.[20] In 1815 a mill at Hawford was the property of the Bishop of Worcester. It was put up for sale with 6 acres of land and was equipped with three pairs of French stones and one pair of French and Welsh, being capable of grinding 300 bags of corn per week.[21]

Four mills, which at one time belonged to the nuns of Whistones, were evidently granted with the site of the priory to the Callowhills.[22] Mildenham, Hawford and Porter's Mill exist at the present day on the River Salwarpe.

The church of *ST. JOHN THE BAPTIST* consists of a chancel 23 ft. 8 in. by 17 ft. 2 in., north and south chapels 9 ft. 2 in. and 9 ft. 3 in. wide respectively, of the same length with the chancel, a modern north vestry on the north side of the north chapel, nave 43 ft. 10 in. by 15 ft. 10 in., north and south aisles 8 ft. 10 in. wide, a modern additional north aisle, west tower 10 ft. 7 in. square and a modern south porch. These measurements are all internal.

The present church appears to have been entirely rebuilt in the early 15th century upon the site of an older building, some fragments of which, dating from the late 12th century, and consisting of the moulded base and capital with a few of the drum stones of an arcade pier and some arch stones of a doorway, with an embattled moulding, were discovered beneath the north wall of the north aisle on its demolition for the modern extension. The north and south chapels

[95] Close, 1650, pt. xxii, no. 14 ; Chan. Proc. (Ser. 2), bdle. 232, no. 2.
[96] Pat. 26 Chas. II, pt. iv.
[97] Feet of F. Div. Co. Trin. 13 Geo. I.
[98] Ibid. Worcs. East. 9 Geo. III.
[99] *Dict. Nat. Biog.*
[100] Prattinton Coll. (Soc. Antiq.).
[1] Habington, op. cit. ii, 42 ; Red Bk. of Bishopric of Worc. (Eccl. Com. Rec. Var. bdle. 121, no. 43698), fol. 255.
[2] *Lay Subs. R. Worcs.* c. 1280 (Worcs. Hist. Soc.), 78 ; Red Bk. of Bishopric of Worc. fol. 2.
[2a] Habington, op. cit. ii, 43.
[3] *Cal. Pat.* 1307-13, p. 289.
[4] *Lay Subs. R.* 1327 (Worcs. Hist. Soc.), 12.
[5] Prattinton Coll. (Soc. Antiq.), Deeds of D. and C. of Worc. no. 305.

[6] Prattinton Coll. (Soc. Antiq.), Rental of Northwick and Whistones.
[7] *Visit. of Worcs.* (Harl. Soc. xxvii), 57.
[8] Feet of F. Worcs. Trin. 31 Eliz. ; see also Mich. 2 Edw. VI.
[9] Recov. R. Mich. 2 Will. IV, rot. 315.
[10] Land at Tapenhall was granted by Bishop Kenwald to the priest Behstan for four lives in 957 (Birch, *Cart. Sax.* iii, 187), and Bishop Lyfing leased an estate there to Carcytel in 1038 (Add. Chart. 19798).
[11] Heming, op. cit. 424, 523, 407.
[12] Hale, *Reg. Worc. Priory* (Camd. Soc.), 41a.
[13] Exch. Dep. Trin. 11 Jas. I, no. 9. Tapenhall Mill had belonged to — Childe

before the Nashes became possessed of it (ibid. Mich. 20 Jas. I, no. 27).
[14] Exch. Dep. Trin. 11 Jas. I, no. 9.
[15] Ibid. A mill at 'Moldenham' had been held by the Prior of Worcester about 1182 (Red Bk. of Bishopric of Worc. fol. 18).
[16] Exch. Dep. East. 1659, no. 30.
[17] Close, 24 Chas. II, pt. xi, m. 25.
[18] See above ; *Birm. and Midl. Inst. Trans. of Arch. Sect.* 1892, p. 58.
[19] Close, 1649, pt. iv, no. 13.
[20] Exch. Dep. East. 1659, no. 30.
[21] Prattinton Coll. (Soc. Antiq.). The same authority states that it was part of the bishop's property at Whistones in 1511, and then leased to John Hawford.
[22] Pat. 4 & 5 Phil. and Mary, pt. xv, m. 20.

were added early in the 16th century, and a rood gallery constructed or enlarged at the same period. In 1887–8 a new north aisle was added to the existing aisle, the north wall of which was moved outwards and rebuilt practically stone for stone. The walling throughout the church is of large squared sandstone, laid in more or less regular courses.

The east window of the chancel is of three trefoiled ogee lights with vertical tracery within a two-centred head. At the south-east is a plain piscina recess with a square basin, originally projecting, but now cut back flush with the wall. The north and south walls are occupied by the chapel arcades, each of two bays with two-centred arches. Those of the north arcade are of two orders, the outer hollow-chamfered and the inner wave-moulded, an interesting example of the reversion to type characteristic of early 16th-century work. The column and responds continue the orders, which are interrupted by bell capitals of a clumsy section. The south arcade has arches of one order only, moulded with a plain chamfer, set back a little from the wall face and supported by an octagonal column, with responds of the same form. The two-centred chancel arch is of a single chamfered order, with semi-octagonal responds having moulded capitals and bases, of the same plain section as those of the nave arcades. Externally there were originally diagonal buttresses at both the eastern angles, but that at the south-east appears to have been taken down and set square with the east wall on the addition of the south chapel. This is shown both by the disturbance of the facing here and by a short portion of the original return of the plinth mould, which surrounds the whole of the early 15th-century building.

The east window of the north chapel has a straight-sided four-centred head, and is of three trefoiled lights with vertical tracery over. The mullions are hollow-chamfered, and the tracery is set near the middle of the wall with a wide external casement. The square-headed window of three trefoiled ogee lights at the north-east is one of the original north windows of the chancel reset, and is of the same general type as those used throughout the church in the work of the earlier period. The remainder of the north wall is occupied by an arch opening into the modern vestry. At the north-west is a doorway with an elliptical head opening into the rood stairs, which are contemporary with the chapel. A two-centred arch of two chamfered orders, with responds of the same form as those of the chancel arcade, opens into the north aisle. The wall at the south-west angle is said to have been cut away and two squints cut from the aisle to the chapel, and from the chapel to the chancel, in the first half of the 19th century, when a small font was placed here. A portion of the plinth mould of the north wall of the chancel is visible at the south-east. Both here and in the case of the south chapel the whole of the length of chancel wall occupied by the arcade has been cut away and rebuilt. Externally the east wall has a plainly moulded cornice, now surmounted by a gable, which is evidently of later date, the present high-pitched roof being an addition. A piece of quatrefoil panelling at the north-east shows that there was originally a panelled parapet, similar in type to that which crowns the walls of the south chapel. The pinnacles which surmounted it have been reset at the angles of the tower parapet. At the eastern angle is a diagonal buttress of two offsets, and at the west end of the north wall a buttress of a similar number of offsets is visible inside the modern vestry, one of the east windows of which, removed originally from the north wall of the chancel to the chapel, has again been removed to its present position. The plinth of the chapel is of the same section as that of the chancel, the stones having probably been re-used. Over the north-east window is a large grotesque gargoyle.

The south chapel has one east window similar to that of the north chapel, but the tracery is more symmetrically set out, and generally shows traces of a slightly earlier date. The two square-headed windows in the south wall, of three and two lights respectively, are the reset south windows of the chancel, and are similar in detail to the reset north windows. Between them is a blocked doorway. An acute two-centred arch with semi-octagonal responds opens into the south aisle. Externally the walls are crowned by a heavily-moulded cornice and a pinnacled parapet panelled with quatrefoils. The pinnacles are crocketed, gabled and panelled ; on each is carved a blank shield below a rose. The parapet is unpanelled on the east, and appears to have been disturbed, the coping being set at a less inclination than the cornice, which follows the slope of the low-pitched lean-to roof. There is a diagonal buttress at the south-east, one between the two windows of the south wall and one at the junction of the chapel with the aisle, all of two offsets. A plain chamfered plinth runs round the walls.

The nave arcades are each of four bays with acute two-centred arches of a single chamfered order, supported by octagonal columns and responds having moulded capitals and bases, similar in section to those of the chancel arch. In the apex of the east gable is a single cinquefoiled light. The north wall of the north aisle has been taken down and re-erected as the north wall of the additional aisle, added in 1887. Its three-light square-headed windows, three in number, are reset in this wall, with the original buttresses between them, and a diagonal buttress at the north-west angle, all of two offsets. The west window, which occupies its original position, is of similar design. All correspond in type to those of the chapels described above. An arcade of four-centred arches divides the two aisles. The south aisle has a west and three south windows of the same pattern as those of the north aisle, with buttresses between them and at the south-west angle. Between the two western windows is the south doorway, which has a plain chamfered two-centred head and segmental rear arch.

The tower is of three stages with an embattled parapet, at the angles of which are placed the four pinnacles of the north chapel. At the west are diagonal buttresses of four offsets. The tower arch is of a single acute two-centred order, and the west window of the ground stage is a square-headed three-light window of the type prevailing throughout the building. In the north and south walls are blocked doorways. The ringing chamber is lighted on the north, west and south by single ogee-headed lights, and the belfry by square-headed windows of three trefoiled ogee lights. The plinth mould of the chancel, nave and aisles is continued round the base of the tower.

The roofs of the chancel and chapels are modern ; the ceiling of the north chapel conceals internally its later high-pitched roof. The nave has its original trussed rafter roof, and some of the timbers of the aisle roofs are also of original date. Externally the roofs of chancel, nave and aisles are tiled, those of the chapels being leaded.

In the north porch are preserved some fragments of encaustic tiles of the 15th century, including the four-tile Talbot design so common in the neighbourhood. In the vestry is some early 17th-century panelling.

In the east bay of the south chancel arcade, moved here from the churchyard, where it had been for many years, is the elaborate table tomb of John Porter, who died in 1577. It is now very imperfect, part only of the panelled sides remaining. Upon the top is his recumbent effigy. Of the inscription only the fragment—'IOHN PORTER WHICH WAS A LAWYER 1577'—survives. The panels of the sides have semi-circular heads with shells in their tympana and blank shields inclosed in smaller trefoiled panels below, the whole exhibiting a curious and characteristic mixture of Gothic and Renaissance. Above the three shields on the north side are the initials 'I.,' 'I.P.' and 'P.' Below is decipherable 'Anno Domini 1577.' That this tomb has always been a cenotaph is shown by a tablet now in the north chapel inscribed as follows : ' Subtus requiescit sed in erectissima | spe resurrectionis Iohannes Porter | Iurisconsultus qui Obiit Anno Dom͞ | 1577 | Omnia transibunt, nos ibimus, ibitis, ibunt | Ignari, gnari, conditione pari.' |

In the floor at the west end of the nave is a slab with a Passion cross having a shield in the centre and the arms crossed at the ends incised in outline upon it. The slab is probably of the 13th century. Upon the east wall of the north aisle is an elaborate mural tablet to Mary Porter, widow of John Porter, who died in 1668. Other mural tablets include those to Henry Wynne ' of Clifford's Inn,' who died in 1693 ; to Elizabeth wife of Phineas Jackson, who died in 1714, and several of her children who died young ; and to George Porter, who died in 1709, and his wife Elizabeth, who died in 1720. In the nave floor are many slabs, none earlier than the late 17th century.

There is a ring of five bells inscribed as follows : treble, ' Francis Wythes, William Reynolds, Churchwardens 1686 ' ; second, recast by Warner of London in 1886 from a bell said to have been of the late 14th century ; third, ' Gloria in Excelsis Deo 1622 ' ; fourth, ' Jesus be oure spede 1623 ' ; tenor, ' God bless oure Nobell King 1623.'

The plate consists of an Elizabethan cup, the foot gone and the rim renewed, the hall-mark of which has disappeared ; a cover paten, which doubtless belonged to it, inscribed on the foot 1571, with the mark of 1570 ; two silver cups, a flagon, and a paten of 1846, a chalice and paten of silver-gilt of 1902, a silver paten, a silver chalice and paten formerly used at the mission room at Fernhill Heath, three mounted cruets and a silver bread box, all modern.

The registers before 1812 are as follows : (i) all entries 1538 to 1656 ; (ii) a fragmentary paper book with all entries 1641 to 1647 ; (iii) all entries 1661 to 1684 ; (iv) all entries 1684 to 1740 ; (v) baptisms and burials 1740 to 1784, marriages to 1752 ; (vi) baptisms and burials 1785 to 1812 ; (vii) marriages 1752 to 1787 ; (viii) marriages 1787 to 1812.

Descriptions of the churches of St. George, South Claines, St. Stephen, Barbourne, St. Mary Magdalene, the Tything, and St. Barnabas, Rainbow Hill, now in the city of Worcester, will be found with the account of the city.

ADVOWSON Claines was originally a chapelry annexed to the church of St. Helen, Worcester.[23] When the controversy between the bishop and the prior as to the church of St. Helen was finally settled in 1234 the chapel of Claines was assigned to the bishop, and it was agreed that he should ordain a vicarage there.[24] Instead of doing this the bishop gave the vicarial and some of the great tithes to the nuns of Whistones, on condition that they provided a fit chaplain to serve the chapel of Claines. This arrangement seems to have been made, possibly only temporarily, before 1269, as in that year the Dean of Worcester was ordered to provide a priest on the advice of the nuns, who were to give him a competent portion of the tithes,[25] and in 1271 the bishop's former grant of tithes was confirmed until their debts should be paid. In 1275 the tithes were appropriated to them on condition that they undertook to provide a chaplain.[26] Thus, though Claines was called a vicarage, it was in reality a perpetual curacy, the curates being provided by the owner of the vicarial tithes until 1874, when Sir Offley Wakeman granted the advowson to the Bishop of Worcester.[27] From that time the living has been a vicarage in the gift of the bishop.

The vicarial tithes remained with the nuns of Whistones until the dissolution of their house.[28] In 1545 all the tithes belonging to Claines Vicarage, which still carried with them the obligation to support a chaplain,[29] were granted to George Tresham,[30] who sold them in the same year to Richard Callowhill,[31] then owner of the site of the priory. Most of these tithes, some having already been sold, were purchased of John Callowhill, nephew of Richard,[32] by John Porter in 1558.[33] In 1567 John Porter sold the property to John Habington, the Callowhills confirming the sale.[34] Thomas and Richard Habington, sons of John, gave it to Queen Elizabeth in 1590 for a term in payment of a debt.[35] In 1595 Thomas and

[23] Heming, op. cit. 427.
[24] *Ann. Mon.* (Rolls Ser.), iv, 426, 427 ; Hale, op. cit. 36*b*, 37*a*.
[25] *Reg. G. Giffard* (Worcs. Hist. Soc.), 35.
[26] Nash, op. cit. i, 210 ; *Reg. G. Giffard* (Worcs. Hist. Soc.), 190. In 1291 the portion of the nuns in the chapel was £2, while that of the priest was £2 13s. 4d. (*Pope Nich. Tax.* [Rec. Com.], 239).
[27] *Lond. Gaz.* 15 May 1874, p. 2586. The living was endowed in the same year with £170 per annum out of the

common fund of the Ecclesiastical Commissioners (ibid. 29 May 1874, p. 2827).
[28] *Valor Eccl.* (Rec. Com.), iii, 230. Procurations amounting to 6s. 8d. were then paid to the church of St. Helen.
[29] This is probably what was meant by the statement in 1573-4 that the owner of the vicarial tithes held also 'the advowson of the priory church of Claines' (Memo. R. [L.T.R.], Hil. 16 Eliz. rot. 34).
[30] *L. and P. Hen. VIII*, xx (1), g. 846 (11).

[31] Ibid. p. 672.
[32] See site of priory.
[33] Com. Pleas D. Enr. Hil. 4 & 5 Phil. and Mary ; Memo. R. Recorda, Hil. 3 Eliz. rot. 36. The purchase was confirmed in 1561 (Feet of F. Worcs. Hil. 3 Eliz.).
[34] Memo. R. (L.T.R.), Hil. 16 Eliz rot. 34.
[35] Feet of F. Div. Co. East. 32 Eliz. ; Prattinton Coll. (Soc. Antiq.). Elizabeth gave it to Sir Thomas Flud and others in the same year (Pat. 32 Eliz. pt. xi).

Richard sold it to Robert Wilde.[36] On the death of the latter in 1608 the vicarage passed to his son Thomas,[37] who only survived him two years.[38] His son Robert afterwards held it, and in 1639 some disagreement seems to have arisen between him and the curate as to the parsonage-house, but the exact nature of the dispute is not known.[39] In 1653 the vicarage and tithes belonging were included in the marriage settlement of Robert's son Thomas and Mary Savage.[40] Six years later Thomas was still holding it.[41] His son Robert died, leaving no children,[42] and until 1789 nothing is known of the vicarage, which may, however, have remained, like the rectory (see below), in the possession of the Wilde family. Nash states that the Wildes sold it to Mr. Denne, a banker,[43] and it was probably this estate which, as 'the advowson of the vicarage of Claines,' was sold in 1789 by Cornelius Doune and his wife Elizabeth to Henry Wakeman,[44] who probably bought the rectorial tithes shortly afterwards (see below).

The greater part of the rectorial tithes of Claines were given by the bishop to the hospital of St. Wulfstan, Worcester. This gift had been made before 1291, when the portion of the hospital in the chapel was valued at £3 13s. 4d.[45] These tithes remained in the possession of the hospital until the Dissolution, when they were valued at £12 1s. 4d., from which 26s. 8d. was paid yearly to the churchwardens.[46] The rectory with the so-called advowson of the vicarage was granted in 1540 to Richard Morrison, and confirmed to him in 1541,[47] but the grant was surrendered in 1544,[48] in order that it might be made to him afresh without the reservation of any rents.[49] In the following year he gave the rectory to the king in exchange for other lands.[50] It was granted in 1546–7 to the Dean and Chapter of Christ Church, Oxford,[51] who leased it from time to time. Robert Wilde held the lease in 1590.[52] As stated above, he acquired the vicarage five years later, and the lease of the rectory remained in the Wilde family until 1750 or later.[53] Charles Freeman Wakeman was dealing with the rectory or parsonage of Claines in 1812.[54] Prattinton states that he gave £2,000 to the Dean of Christ Church for their portion of the tithes under the Land Tax Redemption Act.[55] His descendant, Sir Offley Wakeman, bart., is now the impropriator of the tithes of Claines.[55a]

A third portion of the tithes of Claines, valued in 1535 at 50s., belonged at that date to the church of St. Swithun, Worcester,[56] having been given to the parson who acted as their confessor by the nuns of Whistones.[57] The vicar of St. Swithun's still claimed these tithes in 1577 and in 1590.[58]

A fourth portion of the tithes of Claines belonged to the hospital of St. Oswald, and was valued at £4 12s. 8d. in 1535.[59] The hospital was still in possession of these tithes in 1590.[60]

The parishioners of Claines had been obliged to carry their dead to Worcester for burial, until in 1400 they obtained licence from the pope to have a churchyard of their own.[61] For this right they paid to the priory of Worcester an annual sum of 6s. 8d.[62] Henry VIII granted this rent to the Dean and Chapter of Worcester in 1542.[63] The Worcester Cemetery is now in North Claines parish.

A chantry of our Lady was founded in Claines by John Williams, who endowed it with lands valued at £6 3s. 1d. at the time of the dissolution of the chantries. It was then found that £5 6s. 6½d. was employed in payment of a priest and for the repairs of the church 'and other good works at the will of the parishioners.'[64] The lands with which it was endowed included Luttringhall, and these were sold by Edward VI in 1549[65] to Robert Wood. Habington states that Ellen Frogmore and her brother John gave land in Northwick in 1421–2 towards the endowment of this chantry.[66]

CHARITIES In 1677, as recorded on a benefaction table, William Swift gave a tenement and four closes for providing twelve penny loaves every Lord's Day, and twenty-four more such loaves on Christmas Day, Easter Day and Whitsunday, the overplus to be given to the minister. The vicar distributes a sum of £2 18s. yearly in bread in respect of this charity.

The same table further recorded that John Cox in 1634 gave £20 and Walter Thomas in 1656 gave £30 for the poor, and that Edward Thomas by will (1656) left £50 for apprenticing, and that Timothy Wood by will (1677) left £50 for the poor. These legacies, amounting to £150, were in 1678 laid out in the purchase of a rent-charge of £7 10s. issuing out of land adjoining the churchyard, of which £3 10s. is applied in doles and £4 in apprenticing.

The church table further recorded that George Wingfield and Ann his wife gave £100, now represented by £105 consols in the names of the trustees, the annual dividends, amounting to £2 12s. 4d., to be applied on St. Thomas's Day in the distribution of gowns to poor women, no woman to have a gown two years together.

The other charitable gifts mentioned on the church table appear to have been expended or lost.

[36] Feet of F. Worcs. Hil. 37 Eliz. ; Mich. 41 & 42 Eliz. Thomas Habington referring to these tithes says the property brought with it 'a part of troubles, . . . wheareof I thancke God I have acquitted my sealfe, for some of thease seeme to bee haunted with a spirit of dissention' (Habington, op. cit. ii, 47).
[37] Chan. Inq. p.m. (Ser. 2), cccv, 124.
[38] Ibid. cccxv, 166.
[39] Cal. S. P. Dom. 1639, pp. 109, 110.
[40] Recov. R. Mich. 1653, rot. 244 ; Visit. of Worcs. 1569 (Harl. Soc. xxvii), 152.
[41] Exch. Dep. East. 1659, no. 30.
[42] Visit. of Worcs. (Harl. Soc. xxvii), 152.
[43] Nash, op. cit. i, 210.

[44] Feet of F. Worcs. Mich. 30 Geo. III.
[45] Pope Nich. Tax. (Rec. Com.), 239.
[46] Valor Eccl. (Rec. Com.), iii, 228.
[47] L. and P. Hen. VIII, xv, g. 831 (64) ; xvi, g. 678 (25).
[48] Ibid.
[49] Ibid. xix (1), g. 444 (10).
[50] Ibid. xx (2), g. 266 (32).
[51] Pat. 38 Hen. VIII, pt. viii.
[52] Exch. Dep. Mich. 32 & 33 Eliz. no. 35 ; Hil. 33 Eliz. no. 4.
[53] Prattinton Coll. (Soc. Antiq.).
[54] Recov. R. Trin. 52 Geo. III, rot. 142.
[55] Prattinton Coll. (Soc. Antiq.).
[55a] Inform. by the Rev. O. A. Moore, vicar of Claines.
[56] Valor Eccl. (Rec. Com.), iii, 231.
[57] Nash, Hist. of Worcs. ii, App. cxvii.

[58] Chan. Proc. (Ser. 2), bdle. 1, no. 47 ; Exch. Dep. Hil. 33 Eliz. no. 4.
[59] Valor Eccl. (Rec. Com.), iii, 229.
[60] Exch. Dep. Mich. 32 & 33 Eliz. no. 35 ; Hil. 33 Eliz. no. 4.
[61] Cal. Papal Letters, v, 374. The right seems to have been disputed by the prior and convent until 1408, when a final agreement was made (Habington, op. cit. ii, 53).
[62] Valor Eccl. (Rec. Com.), iii, 226. The prior and convent also received half the mortuaries.
[63] L. and P. Hen. VIII, xvii, g. 71 (29) ; Pat. 6 Jas. I, pt. xii.
[64] Aug. Off. Chant. Cert. 25, no. 9 ; 60, no. 9 ; 61, no. 8.
[65] Pat. 3 Edw. VI, pt. ix.
[66] Habington, op. cit. ii, 53.

A HISTORY OF WORCESTERSHIRE

The charity of William Norton, founded by will 1721, consists of an annuity of £7 issuing out of The Grange and land adjoining, which is applicable in the payment of 20s. a year to the minister for a sermon on 13 November every year, being the anniversary of the testator's funeral, and 20s. to the poor in bread on the same day and the residue in clothing five poor men.

Mary Walker, by her will proved at Worcester in May 1736, demised a cottage and garden at Dennis Green, the rents to be applied in providing four gowns for four poor widows and any surplus in bread to the poor. The trust property consists of two cottages, producing £10 yearly, which is duly applied.

In 1767 Moses Hyett by his will left £80 for the poor, which is invested in £90 6s. consols in the names of the trustees, producing £2 5s. yearly.

The charity known as the 'Housedwellers' Charity' is now endowed with £561 7s. 4d. consols, arising from the sale in 1891 of two tenements and land comprised in a deed of trust 7 December 1856. The annual dividends, amounting to £14 0s. 8d., together with the income of Moses Hyett's charity, are applied in the distribution of groceries, &c.

In 1786 Thomas Cooke by his will left £20, the interest to be applied on St. Thomas's Day in purchasing a coat and gown for a poor man and woman having the names of Thomas and Mary. The principal sum is deposited in the Post Office Savings Bank, the interest being accumulated and applied in accordance with the trust from time to time.

The charity known as the Parish Land Charity is now endowed with £756 4s. 7d. consols, arising from the sale in 1891 of 3 a. 2 r. comprised in a deed of trust 17 December 1822. The annual dividends, amounting to £18 18s., are with the other apprenticing charities applied in premiums of £10 each.

In 1831 Sir Henry Wakeman, bart., by his will proved in the P.C.C. 11 May, bequeathed £200, the income to be applied for the benefit of the poor on 27 February in each year. The legacy was invested in £214 18s. 6d. consols, producing £5 7s. 4d. yearly.

In 1869 Thomas Oldham by his will left a legacy, now represented by £539 1s. 8d. consols, producing £13 9s. 4d. yearly, which is applicable as to two-thirds in providing on Whit Tuesday a tea with games for the children of the parochial school and one-third in augmenting the salary of the master.

In 1888 Mrs. Susanna Jolley, by her will proved at Gloucester 16 August, bequeathed to this parish a reversionary and contingent interest in a sum of £1,600 railway stock, which has not yet come into operation.

In 1901 Edward Wrey Whinfield by his will bequeathed £152 17s. 3d. India 3 per cent. stock, the annual dividends, amounting to £4 11s. 8d., to be applied for the benefit of the Church Institute.

The Martin Mence Charity for the Poor is endowed with £204 1s. 7d. India 3 per cent. stock, the annual dividends, amounting to £6 2s. 4d., being, under a deed of trust of 8 March 1905, applicable in the distribution of coal among the poor of the ecclesiastical district of Claines.

The several sums of stock are, unless otherwise stated, held by the official trustees.[67]

CLEEVE PRIOR

Clyve (xi cent.); Clive Prioris (xiii cent.); Priors Cleve (xvi cent.).

'Clive surnamed Prior, seated in the fruytful Vale of Evesham and the large spredinge medows of the ryver Avon, runneth out as a foreland between the countys of Gloucester and Warwicke.'[1] The parish lies mainly on the left bank of the Avon, but a part of the north-west boundary is formed by the Arrow, about 100 acres of land known as Worcester Meadows, on the right bank of the Avon, being thus included.

The village of Cleeve Prior stands about a quarter of a mile from the river, backed by the long low ridge of Cleeve Hill with its crest of trees. A road, locally said to be Roman,[2] runs along the length of the ridge to Marlcliff Hill in the north-eastern corner of the parish; the hamlet of Marlcliff lies just beyond the eastern border in Warwickshire. The boundary here coincides for an unusual distance with the limits of various fields, though in this respect the southern border is even more remarkable, lying as it does entirely along the edges of the fields in an almost straight line. Possibly it marks the end of the old common lands inclosed in 1775.[3] The parish contains about 1,521 acres of land, of which 685 are arable and 711 under permanent grass.[4] The soil is clay and the subsoil lower lias,[5] and the chief crops are wheat, barley and beans.

An old road runs from the Icknield Street through Marlcliff to Cleeve Prior and enters the village close to the 'King's Arms,' where the beehive yew-tree and quaintly cut bird above the hedge emulate the glory of the 'Prior's Garden' at the manor-house.

The older houses and cottages of Cleeve Prior are built of limestone quarried in the neighbourhood, and their rubble walls present a marked contrast to the half-timber construction elsewhere so abundant. On the north-east of the church, which stands in a large churchyard surrounded by stone walls, is the manor-house, a T-shaped two-storied building of Elizabethan and earlier date, with its principal front towards the east. The oldest portion appears to be the entrance hall, with the apartments on the south side, the walls of which, though plastered inside and out, seem to be half-timber. The house probably assumed its present shape towards the end of the 16th century, when the north wing, containing, on the ground floor, the kitchen and offices, appears to have been remodelled and an entrance porch added at the

[67] For charities in Barbourne and Whistones see Worcester City, *V.C.H. Worcs.* iv.
[1] Habington, *Surv. of Worcs.* i, 153.
[2] A large hoard of gold and silver coins, principally of the 4th century, was found at a little distance from this road in 1811 (*V.C.H. Worcs.* i, 216–18).

[3] Priv. Act, 15 Geo. III, cap. 36. The landowners then freed themselves of all payments in lieu of tithe by the allotment of land to the dean and chapter (Nash, *Hist. of Worcs.* i, 236).
[4] Statistics from Bd. of Agric. (1905).

[5] Blue lias and limestone are quarried in the district, and the stone was well thought of in the 18th century (Nash, loc. cit.). Nash mentions the quarries at Cleeve Prior in 1780 and describes a fossil fish which had been found in one of them (ibid.).

CLEEVE PRIOR MANOR : THE ENTRANCE

CLEEVE PRIOR : OLD GRANARY

south-east of the hall ; perhaps, also, the rooms at the south end belong to this period. All this later work is of stone rubble masonry ; the windows, where left in their original form, have stone mullions. In the north wing, approached from a lobby opening into the hall, is a staircase of original Elizabethan date. In the old court room, opening out of the hall on the south, is some panelling of the same date, now painted and grained. A second staircase leads out of this room, entered by a door in the panelling at the side of the chimney stack in its south wall. The hall appears to have been repaired internally in the first half of the 18th century, to which date the bold marble architrave of the fire-place belongs. There is also good panelling of the same period in the room at the east end of the north wing. Under one of the floors there is a hiding hole where Thomas Bushell is said to have been concealed for many months in 1650. The most interesting feature from an architectural point of view is the two-storied Elizabethan entrance porch on the east side. The side walls are of rubble, but the front wall is of ashlar work in a remarkably good state of preservation. The outer doorway has a semicircular head with slightly sunk spandrel panels, each occupied by a bust in high relief. The head of the bust in the left-hand spandrel has been broken off. Over the head of the doorway is an entablature, supported by three carved consoles, the frieze enriched with human heads and lions' heads alternately. The room over the porch has a stone-mullioned and transomed window of four lights with a moulded sill, beneath which is a delicately modelled strapwork panel inscribed ' DWE + ETTE + MW | NE + DROITE ' (Dieu et mon droit). The whole is surmounted by a gable with bracketed kneelers and moulded coping, crowned by the figure of a winged boy. The entrance doorway within the porch has a moulded wood frame and straight-sided four-centred head with foliated spandrels. The door itself is a fine specimen of 16th-century joinery. A magnificent avenue of clipped yews, known as the 'Apostles and Evangelists,' borders the flagged path leading to this entrance. In the yard on this side of the house are some stone stables with external stairs of the same material leading to the loft above. From the detail of the woodwork remaining, these appear to be of early 16th-century date. On the north side of the house is a circular pigeon-house of stone in excellent preservation.

On the east side of the road which leads out of the village past the rectory in the direction of Marlcliff is a stone house, now an inn, with the sign of the 'King's Arms,' and in the gable is inscribed the date 1691 with the initials W.A. At the western extremity of the village, on the north side of the main street, is an interesting stone house, dated 1619, and formerly the residence of the Charlett family, but now derelict and used as a store-house for farm purposes. It is of two stories with an attic story in the roof ; each floor contains two rooms, one on either side of the stair-

case, which is in the centre of the house. The room at the east end of the ground floor has a stone fire-place with a moulded four-centred head and jambs, and on the walls is a good plaster frieze, unfortunately in an advanced state of decay. In the room above is a fireplace of similar form. The handrail of the stairs appears to be of the 18th century. The house is gabled at each end and the single ridge-roof by which it is crowned is covered with stone slates. The windows throughout are mullioned, the attics being lighted by windows in the end gables and the stair-case landing on this floor by stone dormers. The building is remarkable as an almost unaltered example of a small early 17th-century house. To the west of this, on the brow of Cleeve Hill, overlooking the valley of the Avon, is the base of an octagonal cross, probably of the 14th century.[5a] Cleeve Mill, by the River Avon, is chiefly interesting from the beauty of its surroundings. The older portion of the building, which appears to be of the 17th century, is of stone, and in the gable of this part are pigeon-cells. The channels in which the mill-wheels work, or rather used to work, for it is no longer in active use, are covered by arched roofs of stone rubble masonry. A later addition has been made of brick.

The following place-names occur in local records : Burgerd,[6] Styacre, Pewytelowe[7] (xiii cent.) ; Lowes and Waye, Blackberd, Forendell-in-the-Moor, Prutz and Rysam[8] (xvi cent.).

The Barnt Green, Evesham and Ashchurch Branch of the Midland railway touches the north-west corner of the parish. The nearest station is Salford Priors, about a mile and a half from the village on the opposite side of the Avon.

The monastery of Worcester held land *MANOR* at *CLEEVE PRIOR* in early times ; the monastic chartulary credits Ethelred with the gift.[9] In 1086 the church held in Cleeve Prior and Atch Lench 10½ hides, of which 2 hides less 1 virgate were waste,[10] but by the time of the survey of Oswaldslow (1108–18) the assessment of this holding had been reduced to 10 hides.[11]

King John came to Worcester in January 1207, and, after a solemn procession, prayed at the tomb of St. Wulfstan until Prior Ralf of Evesham, thinking the king's mind sufficiently softened for benevolence, came to him asking for liberties in Cleeve and three other manors,[12] which John granted, though not until he had received 100 marks and a palfrey.[13]

In 1220 a violent quarrel arose between the Worcester monastery and their bishop, William of Blois, who deposed Simon the prior and put in his own nominee, William Norman.[14] Eventually, how-ever, it was agreed, by the mediation of the arch-bishop, that William of Blois should appoint another prior from outside the Worcester community, and that the convent should grant the manor of Cleeve Prior as compensation to William Norman for his life.[15] He died in 1233, and the estate then reverted to the prior and convent,[16] in whose possession it

[5a] It is said to mark the spot where Prince Edward advancing from Alcester first saw the barons' position at Evesham.
[6] Hale, *Reg. of Worc. Priory* (Camd. Soc.), 87.
[7] Prattinton Coll. (Soc. Antiq.), no. 320.
[8] Ct. of Req. bdle. 104, no. 25.
[9] Heming, *Chartul.* 574 ; Habington

(op. cit. i, 458) also describes the following inscription in the cloister of Worcester Cathedral, 'Ethelfrithus Rex dedit Clivam.'
[10] *V.C.H. Worcs.* i, 297.
[11] Ibid. 326.
[12] *Ann. Mon.* (Rolls Ser.), iv, 395 ; Hale, *Reg. of Worc. Priory* (Camd. Soc.), 11a ; Thomas, *Surv. of Worc. Cathedral,* 122.

[13] Pipe R. 9 John, m. 19 d. ; *Cal. Rot. Chart.* 1199–1216 (Rec. Com.), 168.
[14] *Ann. Mon.* (Rolls Ser.), iv, 414.
[15] Hale, op. cit. 27 ; *Reg. G. Giffard* (Worcs. Hist. Soc.), 61 ; *Ann. Mon.* (Rolls Ser.), iv, 416.
[16] *Ann. Mon.* iv, 425.

remained until the Dissolution.[17] Henry VIII granted it to the Dean and Chapter of Worcester,[18] who continued to be the lords of the manor until 1650,[19] when it was sold by the Parliamentary Commissioners to Peter Langston.[20] At the Restoration the dean and chapter once more became the owners, and they continued to hold the estate until 1859,[21] when it was taken over by the Ecclesiastical Commissioners, who are the present lords of the manor.[22]

At the time of the Domesday Survey the church of Worcester held a mill in Cleeve which rendered a *sextaries* of honey.[23] It seems to have been granted with the manor to William Norman,[24] but was not included in the lease made after his death to the men of the vill[25]; in 1237 it was let to the son of Thomas the miller for his life.[26] By this time the nature of the rent had been altered twice at least, and the changes illustrate the process of commutation. During the early part of the 13th century the rent was paid partly in money, and the amount, probably up to 1233, was 3 marks and 40 'stiches' of eels yearly[27]; this was finally altered in the lease of 1237 to a payment of 1 mark quarterly.[28]

The history of the mill after this date is difficult to trace, but Cleeve corn-mill near the ford over the Avon in the north-west of the parish probably stands on the same site.

The privileges granted to the monks of Worcester in Cleeve by King John during his visit to the city in 1207 were very extensive. They included ' soc et sac, thol et theam et infangenethef cum judicio aque et ignis et furcarum et ferri, et cum quitancia de visu thethingarum, et de murdris et misericordiis et cum omnibus aliis libertatibus et libris consuetudinibus.'[29] A grant of free warren in their demesne lands was obtained by the monks from Henry III in 1256,[30] and confirmed to them in 1355 by Edward III.[31]

An interesting ' custom of the manor from time out of mind ' is mentioned in 1585: if a tenant seised of any custumary land took a wife and died during her confinement, the wife had the right of holding all such custumary lands and tenements for her life, unless she married again or had surrendered her estate in the premises of her own free will during her husband's life.[32]

In the register of Worcester Priory full details are given of the tenants holding land in Cleeve under the prior and of the services due from them in respect of their holdings in 1240.[33] During the whole of the 13th century the work of consolidating the monastic possessions in Cleeve was actively carried on. In the reign of John the prior and convent had granted to William Ruppe for his good service a hide of land.[34] This was afterwards let to Richard de Saunford and Hugh his brother, against whom an action for the recovery of the land was brought in 1211 by Thomas Ruppe.[35] The court, however, held that the prior's charter did not bind him to warrant to the heirs of William Ruppe, and the land was left at the disposal of the monastery.[36] A little later the prior and convent obtained a small holding from Henry de Cleeve, the son of Sweyn de Littleton,[37] and this gift was afterwards confirmed by Robert the Franklin and Alice his wife.[38] In 1240 Hugh de Cleeve did homage for certain lands in the parish which he held of the prior.[39] He died about 1240, when his lands passed to his widow Olive,[40] who demised them after the death of her son Thomas to Geoffrey Pipard.[41] The prior, however, declared that Thomas had sold the land to him, and brought a successful action for its recovery against Olive and Geoffrey.[42]

More difficult to acquire was a carucate of land belonging to Robert de Bellewe, which the priory was anxious to hold in mortmain, but which Robert, regardless of the health of his soul, seems to have been most unwilling to sell. In 1293 the convent tried to obtain licence for this alienation, but the jury declared that it would be the loss of the king ' because if the said Robert be hanged the King would have the year's waste and chattels,' and of the county, ' because if he live on the land he may be useful in assizes and summonses.'[43]

Fortunately for the monastery Edward I came to Worcester in the following year, and the prior, Philip Aubyn, apparently seized this golden opportunity to coax him into granting the desired licence,[44] though even then it was only *sub condicionibus satis duris* that the obdurate Robert at last agreed to give up his land.[45]

Further grants in mortmain were made to the monastery during the 14th century by Richard de Hawkeslowe,[46] William the Freeman[47] and Henry Austen.[48]

The manor-house and certain lands in Cleeve were rented from the dean and chapter in the 16th century by Edward Bushell, the second son of Edward Bushell of Broad Marston, co. Gloucs.[49] Thomas Bushell,

[17] *Ann. Mon.* iv, 428; Hale, op. cit. *passim*; Habington, op. cit. i, 154; Prattinton Coll. (Soc. Antiq.), Deeds of D. and C. of Worc. no. 320; *Ann. Mon.* iv, 433, 442–3, 514; Inq. a.q.d. files 19, no. 13; 145, no. 18; Pat. 16 Edw. II, pt. i, m. 15; 29 Edw. III, pt. ii, m. 12; 33 Hen. VIII, pt. v, m. 19.

[18] *L. and P. Hen. VIII,* xvii, g. 71 (29).

[19] Ct. of Req. bdle. 104, no. 25; Pat. 5 Jas. I, pt. xii, no. 2.

[20] Close, 1651, pt. l, no. 30.

[21] Pat. 4 Will. and Mary, pt. i, no. 6; Nash, *Hist. of Worcs.* i, 236.

[22] Inform. from Ecclesiastical Commissioners; *Lond. Gaz.* 16 Dec. 1859, p. 4757; Stat. 31 Vict. cap. 19.

[23] *V.C.H. Worcs.* i, 297.

[24] Hale, op. cit. 27.

[25] *Ann. Mon.* (Rolls Ser.), iv, 425.

[26] Ibid. 428.

[27] Hale, op. cit. 87.

[28] Ibid.; *Ann. Mon.* iv, 428.

[29] Hale, op. cit. 11.

[30] Pat. 29 Edw. III, pt. ii, m. 12.

[31] Ibid.

[32] Ct. of Req. bdle. 104, no. 25.

[33] Hale, op. cit. 86–7.

[34] Habington, op. cit. i, 154; Hale, op. cit. 62–3.

[35] Hale, loc. cit.

[36] Ibid.

[37] Habington, op. cit. i, 154; Hale, op. cit. 87.

[38] Habington, loc. cit.

[39] Hale, op. cit. 87.

[40] Ibid.; *Ann. Mon.* (Rolls Ser.), iv, 433.

[41] Hale, op. cit. 157–8. Olive had previously granted them to Thomas after the death of her mother, Emma de Bellewe, who held them in dower (ibid.).

[42] Ibid. 158; *Ann. Mon.* iv, 443; Prattinton MSS. Deeds of D. and C. of Worc. no. 320. Emma de Bellewe seems to have retained a dower of 50s. yearly in the holding (Habington, op. cit. i, 155).

[43] Inq. a.q.d. file 19, no. 13; *Worcs. Inq. p.m.* (Worcs. Hist. Soc.), i, 46. It appears, however, that Robert had never lived on the land and was not likely to do so, because he had other estates in Oxon. and Gloucs. (ibid.).

[44] Pat. 22 Edw. I, m. 10. The licence is dated ' Worcester 2 September.'

[45] *Ann. Mon.* (Rolls Ser.), iv, 514. The conditions were that Robert should receive 40 marks down and 10 marks yearly during his life (ibid.).

[46] Inq. a.q.d. file 145, no. 18; Pat. 14 Edw. II, pt. ii, m. 23.

[47] Pat. 16 Edw. II, pt. i, m. 15.

[48] Habington, op. cit. i, 155.

[49] *Visit. of Warws.* (Harl. Soc.), 139; *Visit. of Gloucs.* (Harl. Soc.), 238; *Visit. of Worcs.* (Harl. Soc.), 27.

CLEEVE PRIOR: 17TH CENTURY HOUSE FORMERLY THE RESIDENCE OF THE CHARLETT FAMILY

CLEEVE PRIOR CHURCH: THE NAVE LOOKING EAST

the servant and admirer of Francis Bacon, is said to have been a younger son of this family.[50] He became the farmer of the royal mines, and did the king much service during the Civil War, having the so-called silver mines in Cardiganshire, and coining money at the mint in Aberystwyth Castle. After the Commonwealth was proclaimed he went into hiding for a time,[51] according to a local tradition, at Cleeve Prior, but eventually gave securities for his good behaviour and obtained a renewal of his lease of the mines from the Protector.[52]

BUSHELL. *Argent a cheveron between three water-bougets sable.*

The manor-house at this time was held by Anthony Bushell,[53] a less ardent Royalist who deserted the king's service before the battle of Naseby, and compounded for his delinquency in 1649.[54] He lived to see the Restoration, and in 1662 'post multa sub regiis vexillis fortiter gesta placide in Domino obdormivit.'[55] His descendants were still in the parish in 1720,[56] as tenants of the dean and chapter, but seem to have disappeared before the end of the century.[57]

Another family that was established for some time in the parish was that of Charlett, of whom Habington says that his 'forefathers were of Cleeve Prior.'[58] Their name occurs in the 16th century,[59] and they were still living in the parish in 1698.[60] They continued in other parts of the county to a much later date.

The church *CHURCH of ST. AN-DREW* consists of a chancel 30 ft. by 16 ft., a nave about 40½ ft. by 15¼ ft., a south transept 16¼ ft. by 11½ ft. and a western tower 12 ft. square. These measurements are all internal.

The earliest work visible is a 12th-century buttress at the north-east angle of the nave. It is probably not *in situ*, and the details of its rounded angles suggest the jamb of a chancel arch rather than an external member. The existing nave, however, is but little later, dating probably from the first years of the 13th century, and, from its proportions and the irregular set-out with regard to the later chancel, may possibly have been the complete church without a structural chancel. Later in the 13th century the present chancel and small north and south transepts were added, the priest's door and chancel windows being inserted in the following century. The tower dates from late in the 15th century. After the Reformation the transepts were destroyed, and the present brick south transept was constructed in the 18th

century. The church has been repaired and restored in recent years.

The three-light east window of the chancel is modern and is in the style of the 14th century. The north-east window has modern tracery, also of 14th-century detail, but the jambs of the reveal are original. On the south side is a round-headed piscina, and in the same wall a two-light window, identical with its counterpart on the north. The south chancel door is of the late 14th century, and has a chamfered round head and jambs. The western windows in the north and south chancel walls are also 14th-century work, re-tooled, and have trefoiled heads. The chancel arch is two-centred and of two chamfered orders, of which the outer is continuous, but the inner dies on to flat responds.

On the north side of the nave the first window is of two lights under a square head and contains some fragments of old glass. Between the first and second windows traces indicating the position of a north transept are visible in the wall. The second and third windows are 13th-century lancets with wide splays, and below the former begins a rough string-course carried west to the tower and repeated on the

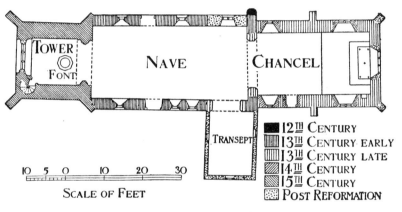

■	12TH CENTURY
▥	13TH CENTURY EARLY
▤	13TH CENTURY LATE
▨	14TH CENTURY
▧	15TH CENTURY
▦	POST REFORMATION

SCALE OF FEET

PLAN OF CLEEVE PRIOR CHURCH

south wall. The north door has a rebuilt round head. The two-centred arch to the south transept springs from 13th-century capitals, but the transept itself is modern. The three windows in the south wall of the nave are lancets similar to those on the north, and the south door repeats the type of the north on a larger scale. The tower arch is two-centred and of two orders, and the west window has three lights with modern tracery in the 15th-century style. The west door has a square external head, but is now blocked up.

Externally the tower is the finest feature of the church and is an excellent example of 15th-century work. The angles are supported by diagonal buttresses, and the parapet is embattled and had originally eight pinnacles, four of which now remain. The four belfry windows are of two transomed lights, with 15th-century tracery. Below the belfry are single-light windows and niches decorated with crocketed canopies. The chancel roof is modern, but that over

[50] *Dict. Nat. Biog.*
[51] Ibid.
[52] Ibid.
[53] *Cal. Com. for Comp.* 2006.
[54] Ibid.
[55] M. I.
[56] Ibid.
[57] Nash (op. cit. i, 237) says, 'The
Bushells were the chief tenants of the manor.' [58] op. cit. ii, 40.
[59] Ct. of Req. bdle. 104, no. 25.
[60] M. I.

the nave is of open timber, with moulded tie-beams, dating from the end of the 14th century.

The tower and nave are built of large ashlar work, but the chancel is of rubble masonry. The transept is mainly of modern red brick. On the north side of the eastern nave buttress, as stated above, are several 12th-century stones re-used. The font has an octagonal bowl with a moulding round the lower edge and a stem of the same form.

The tower contains four bells and a clock : the treble is inscribed, 'Cantate domino canticum novum, 1658'; the second, 'God be our good speed 1658, H. B.'; the third, 'Richard Sanders made me 1722,' with the churchwardens' names ; the fourth, with the churchwardens' names, 1658.

CHURCH TOWER, CLEEVE PRIOR

The plate consists of a cup of 1728 presented by Mrs. Elizabeth Bromwell in 1729, a silver paten of 1858, a modern plated flagon, a pewter flagon and two pewter almsdishes.

The registers before 1812 are as follows : (i) baptisms 1598 to 1717, burials and marriages 1599 to 1717 ; (ii) mixed entries 1717 to 1793, marriages extending only to 1754 ; (iii) baptisms and burials 1794 to 1812 ; (iv) marriages 1754 to 1812. There are no entries between 1641 and 1661. There is a book of churchwardens' accounts from 1695 to 1823.

ADVOWSON At the time of the Domesday Survey there was a priest at Cleeve Prior who held 1 hide of land.[61] From the earliest date of which we have record the advowson of the church belonged to the priory of Worcester,[62] and in 1214 the living was appropriated to the monks by Walter Gray, Bishop of Worcester.[63] The church, which was worth £6 in 1291,[64] was reserved to the priory when the manor was granted to William Norman,[65] and its appropriation was confirmed in 1216 by Honorius III.[66] A vicarage was immediately ordained,[67] but there is no record at this time of a royal licence for the appropriation. This was probably not gained until 1308, when it seems to have been acquired through the agency of Walter Reynolds, afterwards Archbishop of Canterbury.[68] The church was dedicated to St. Andrew, and a graveyard consecrated there by Bishop Walter Maidstone in September 1315.[69] The advowson remained in the possession of the prior and convent until the Dissolution,[70] when it was granted to the dean and chapter,[71] who retained it until the Commonwealth.[72] It was recovered by them at the Restoration, and has ever since that date remained in their possession.[73]

Bishop John of Coutances is said to have granted to the prior and convent out of the revenues of their church at Cleeve 17s. for pittances and 3s. for the maintenance of a light [74] called the light of St. Romain. The latter grant was perhaps represented at the date of the suppression of the chantries, in the reign of Edward VI, by the rent of 1s. arising out of the lands of the Dean and Chapter of Worcester, which was applied to the maintenance of a lamp in the church of Cleeve Prior.[75]

There do not appear to be any endowed charities in this parish.

---

[61] *V.C.H. Worcs.* i, 297.
[62] *Ann. Mon.* (Rolls Ser.), iv, 403 ; Nash, op. cit. i, 238. The rhymed chronicle of benefactors (Heming, op. cit. 574) says, 'Persone Clyve sumus ex Constante Johanne,' which may possibly mean that the advowson was given to the convent by Bishop John of Coutances. Habington (op. cit. i, 469) mentions an inscription in a window in the west cloister : 'Berwulfus Rex dedit ecclesiam de Clive.'

[63] Hale, op. cit. 86 ; *Ann. Mon.* iv, 403.
[64] *Pope Nich. Tax.* (Rec. Com.), 217.
[65] Hale, op. cit. 27.
[66] Heming, op. cit. 536, 545.
[67] Hale, op. cit. 86.
[68] This is probably the explanation of a charter of appropriation from Walter Reynolds, 1308, mentioned by Habington (op. cit. i, 155), and of the confirmation by him in 1318 of 'the gift of the church of Cleve which he made while Bishop of

Worcester to the prior and convent of that place' (Add. Chart. 41381).
[69] Worc. Epis. Reg. Maidstone, fol. 37.
[70] *Sede Vac. Reg.* (Worcs. Hist. Soc.), 380, 426. The clear annual value of the vicarage in 1536 was £8 (*Valor Eccl.* [Rec. Com.], iii, 264).
[71] *L. and P. Hen. VIII*, xvii, g. 71 (29).
[72] Inst. Bks. (P.R.O.).
[73] Ibid.; *Clergy Lists.*
[74] Thomas, op. cit. 121 ; Hale, op. cit. 109a. [75] Chant. Cert. 60, no. 69.

CROOME D'ABITÔT

Cromma (x cent.) ; Crumbe (xi cent.) ; Crumba, Crombe Abetot, Crombe Osbert (xiii cent.) ; Croumbe, Crombe Osbern (xiv cent.) ; Croom Dabitot, Abytotescrombe (xv cent.) ; Abbotts Crome (xvii cent.).

This parish, covering an area of 1,178 acres, lies to the south of the county, 8 miles south-east from Worcester. The land rises towards the north and west ; at the south-east of the parish it is only 51 ft., rising to over 100 ft. above the ordnance datum to the north of Croome Court, on the Pershore road. To the west of this road, on the border of the park, is the new church of St. James, built in 1763, the site of the old church near Croome Court being now only marked by two trees. The high road from Severn Stoke to Defford passes along the north side of the park, and on it is the hamlet of High Green.

The village of Croome D'Abitôt, which lies on the northern borders of the park of Croome Court, the residence of the Earl of Coventry, is altogether devoid of architectural interest. Croome Court itself is a fine stone mansion, erected about 1750. The plan is of the dignified and symmetrical character which was then in favour, consisting of a central block two stories in height, with four three-storied pavilions at the angles, crowned by pyramidal slated roofs. The whole is elevated upon a basement, and the principal entrance, in the centre of the north front, is approached by a balustraded flight of stone steps. In the centre of the south or garden front is a tetrastyle portico of the Ionic order. The banqueting-hall, which occupies the whole of the western front, is a beautiful example of the Adam style. The walls are painted in monochrome, in imitation of sculpture, and the ceiling is richly coffered. The chimney-piece, of white marble, with caryatid figures, is an extremely good and characteristic piece of design. The yellow drawing room and saloon are also very perfect examples of the same style. The library, which occupies the ground floor of the south-east pavilion, still retains its specially designed book-cases. The staircase is at this end, and occupies the centre of the east front. The decoration of these rooms seems to have been undertaken some years subsequently to the first erection of the house. The panelling of the green dining room and billiard room on either side of the entrance hall is of the earlier date. The park was laid out by 'Capability' Brown, and, it must be confessed, with very successful results. The 'properties' include an artificial river, several temples and a ruined castle at Dunstall, half a mile away. The park is thickly wooded and abounds with deer. There is an arboretum which includes many rare trees and shrubs.

The soil in this parish is loam and clay with subsoil of Lower Lias ; 832¾ acres are laid down as permanent grass, 169½ acres are arable land,[1] the chief crops being wheat, barley and beans, and 54¾ acres are covered with woods and plantations.

MANOR The church of Worcester had evidently acquired land in *CROOME D'ABITÔT* before 969, when Bishop Oswald leased land there for three lives to the thegn Cynelm.[2] This land formed part of the bishop's manor of Ripple in 1086,[3] and was still said to be held of that manor in 1640.[4] In 1471 land in Croome D'Abitôt and Kerswell was said to be held of the Bishop of Worcester as of his manor of Kempsey,[5] but it is doubtful whether the manor of Croome D'Abitôt was ever so held.

In the reign of Edward the Confessor Croome D'Abitôt was held by Sirof. On the death of the latter the bishop gave his daughter with this land to a certain knight on condition that he should support her mother and render service to the bishop.[6] Siward was holding the manor in 1086,[7] but early in the 12th century the estate was held by Walter de Beauchamp.[8] His interest in the manor passed with the barony of Elmley Castle until 1530, when it is mentioned for the last time.[9]

Under the lords of Elmley the manor was held by the family of D'Abitot. Robert D'Abitot is mentioned in the Pipe Roll for Worcestershire in 1165–6,[10] and was probably the Robert whose heir was holding 5 hides in Croome D'Abitôt (Moldecrombe) of William Beauchamp about 1182.[11] This heir was, perhaps, Osbert, who was living in 1172.[12] He or a descendant of the same name was holding the manor about the middle of the 13th century,[13] and Sir William D'Abitot was probably the owner in 1254, when an agreement was made with the Abbot of Pershore as to tithes.[14]

D'ABITOT, of Croome. *Ermine a chief bendy or and sable.*

In 1283 Osbert D'Abitot was patron of the church of Croome D'Abitôt,[15] and continued to hold property in Croome during the early 14th century.[16] He had been succeeded before 1319 by his son William D'Abitot,[17] who in 1325 was called the lord of Croome and was patron of the church.[18] William held half a fee in Croome in 1346,[19] and was still living in 1361.[20] Eight years later he had been succeeded by Thomas D'Abitot,[21] who was still living in 1388,[22] and was

---

[1] Statistics from Bd. of Agric. (1905).

[2] Birch, *Cart. Sax.* iii, 526 ; Heming, *Chartul.* (ed. Hearne), 181, 182. The boundaries of the land are given in this charter.

[3] *V.C.H. Worcs.* i, 292.

[4] Habington, op. cit. i, 235 ; ii, 266 ; Chan. Inq. p.m. (Ser. 2), dxciv, 68.

[5] Chan. Inq. p.m. 11 Edw. IV, no. 61.

[6] *V.C.H. Worcs.* i, 292.

[7] Ibid.   [8] Ibid. 324.

[9] *Testa de Nevill* (Rec. Com.), 41 ; *Cal. Inq. p.m.* 1–9 *Edw. II*, 403 ; Add. R. 25964 ; Chan. Inq. p.m. (Ser. 2), lxxx, 106.

[10] *Pipe R. 12 Hen. II* (Pipe R. Soc.), 82.

[11] Habington, op. cit. i, 235 ; Red Bk. of Bishopric of Worc. (Eccl. Com. Rec. Var. bdle. 121, no. 43698), fol. 252. Srreve Crombe, where Maud de Croome held 5 hides at about the same date, is probably Croome D'Abitôt (fol. 96).

[12] *Pipe R. 19 Hen. II* (Pipe R. Soc.), 163.

[13] *Testa de Nevill* (Rec. Com.), 41.

[14] Aug. Off. Misc. Bks. lxi, fol. 110.

[15] *Reg. G. Giffard* (Worcs. Hist. Soc.), 216.

[16] *Cal. Inq. p.m.* 1–9 *Edw. II*, 403.

It was to this Osbert that Nicholas de Mitton in his will left a silver cup, six silver spoons, &c. ; to his wife a silk girdle with a golden buckle, and to each of his children 40s. (*Reg. G. Giffard* [Worcs. Hist. Soc.], 389).

[17] Prattinton Coll. (Soc. Antiq.), Deeds of D. and C. of Worc. no. 301.

[18] Worc. Epis. Reg. Cobham (1317–27), fol. 106a.

[19] *Feud. Aids*, v, 307.

[20] Worc. Epis. Reg. Brian, fol. 32 d.

[21] Ibid. Lynn, fol. 3 ; Wakefield, fol. 10 d.

[22] Ibid. Wakefield, fol. 54 d.

followed by William D'Abitot.[23] Before 1412 Richard D'Abitot had become the lord of Croome.[24] He was still living in 1424,[25] but William D'Abitot held the manor in 1428.[26] In 1434–5 Richard D'Abitot presented to the church.[27] Joan Verney, who presented to the church in 1452, was perhaps the widow of one of the D'Abitots.[28] It is probable that after her death the manor was divided among the heirs of William D'Abitot, who were apparently descendants of another branch of the D'Abitot family, for among the four persons who presented jointly to the church in 1467 was Thomas Rice,[29] who is said to have married Margaret the daughter and heir of John D'Abitot.[30] Simon Rice, the son of Thomas, held a share of the manor at the beginning of the 16th century. This appears to have been the main portion of the estate, and passed under his will at his death in 1530 to Gilbert Clare.[31] His son Simon Clare was lord of the manor in 1554, when he leased it to Edward Young for sixty years.[32] Simon and John Clare conveyed it to John Blunt in 1559.[33] In 1584 Simon's son Francis was holding this manor,[34] then called 'Clares Crome.' This he sold to Thomas Coventry eight years later.[35] The latter, who married Margaret Jeffery of Earl's Croome, was a justice of the Common Pleas and was knighted in 1606, dying in December of that year.[36] His son Thomas, who succeeded to the estate,[37] was Lord Keeper of the Great Seal, and was created Lord Coventry of Allesborough in 1628.[38] He settled the manor of Croome D'Abitôt in 1627 on his son Thomas on his marriage with Mary Craven.[39] George son of Thomas and Mary inherited the property on the death of his father in 1661.[40] His son John dying unmarried in 1687, the property reverted to the latter's uncle, Thomas Coventry, who was in 1697 created Earl of Coventry and Viscount Deerhurst,[41] and was succeeded in 1699 by his son Thomas. Thomas, son of the latter, died unmarried in 1711,

CLARE. *Or three cheverons gules and a border engrailed azure.*

COVENTRY, Earl of Coventry. *Sable a fesse ermine between three crescents or.*

when the next heir was his uncle Gilbert.[42] He died in 1719, leaving only a daughter, and the manor passed to William Coventry, a descendant of Walter, a younger brother of Sir Thomas Coventry, first Lord Coventry.[43] William Earl of Coventry died in 1750–1. His elder son having died unmarried six years previously, he was succeeded by his second son George William. The Earls of Coventry continue to hold the manor of Croome D'Abitôt, George William, the ninth earl (of the 1697 creation), who succeeded his grandfather[44] in 1843, being the present lord.

Very little trace can be found of the other portions of the estates of the D'Abitots in Croome, but some light is thrown upon their descent by the records dealing with the advowson. Associated with Thomas Rice (son-in-law of John D'Abitot) in the patronage of the church in 1467 were John Langston, Joan Childe of Blockley and Margery Tounley.[45] Of these Margery Tounley had been succeeded by Joan Pereson in 1472. Joan Childe was then a widow, William Childe (probably her son) presenting alone four years later.[46] John Langston was represented by Joan Langston in 1472, after which their interest in the advowson ceased, although a family of the same name held a considerable extent of land in the parish in the 17th century.[47] It seems probable that these three portions of the manor and advowson were purchased by John Young of Worcester about 1486, when he presented alone to the church, being styled John Young of Croome D'Abitôt in the Visitation of 1569.[48] This property was sometimes called Young's Croome, and in 1523 John's son Humphrey held the patronage of the church jointly with Simon Rice,[49] who at that date owned the chief portion of the manor (see above), and Edward Young, the son of Humphrey, held it in 1545 with Rice's successor, Simon Clare.[50] In 1549 Edward Young quitclaimed his interest in the manor to Conan Richardson, probably as security for a debt of £300.[51] Four years later William Sheldon, Edward Grevill and Anthony Ashfield leased the manor for sixty years to Edward Young,[52] and he (as stated above) in the following year obtained a lease of the Clares' part of the manor from Simon Clare.[53] After

YOUNG, of Croome D'Abitôt. *Argent a bend sable with three griffons' heads razed or thereon.*

[23] *Sede Vac. Reg.* (Worcs. Hist. Soc.), 235.
[24] Worc. Epis. Reg. Peverell, fol. 48 d.
[25] Ibid. Morgan, fol. 29 d.
[26] *Feud. Aids,* v, 319.
[27] *Sede Vac. Reg.* (Worcs. Hist. Soc.), 425.
[28] Nash, op. cit. i, 263.
[29] Ibid.
[30] *Visit. of Worcs.* (Harl. Soc. xxvii), 37.
[31] Chan. Inq. p.m. (Ser. 2), 80, 106. The relationship between Simon Rice and Gilbert Clare is not known. According to the *Visitations of Shropshire* and *Worcestershire* (Harl. Soc. *Publ.* xxviii, 113; xxvii, 38) Gilbert was Simon's grandson, and according to the *Visitation of Warws.* he was his nephew (ibid. xii, 136),

but as he is not given as Simon's heir in the inquisition taken on the latter's death the relationship was probably not so close. The heirs of Simon as given in the inquisition were his nephew Richard Mucklowe and his aunt Margaret Pye.
[32] Feet of F. Worcs. East. 1 & 2 Phil. and Mary.
[33] Ibid. Div. Co. East. 2 Eliz.
[34] Ibid. Worcs. Mich. 27 & 28 Eliz.; Recov. R. Mich. 27 Eliz. rot. 79.
[35] Feet of F. Worcs. Trin. 35 Eliz. In 1594 Henry Clare brother of Francis released all his claim in the manor to Thomas Coventry (ibid. Hil. 36 Eliz.).
[36] *Dict. Nat. Biog.*
[37] Feet of F. Worcs. Trin. 8 Jas. I.
[38] G.E.C. *Complete Peerage,* ii, 391.
[39] Chan. Inq. p.m. (Ser. 2), dxciv, 68.

[40] G.E.C. loc. cit.
[41] Ibid. 392, 388.
[42] Ibid. 389.
[43] Ibid.
[44] Recov. R. Trin. 1 Will. IV, rot. 285.
[45] Nash, op. cit. i, 263.
[46] Ibid.
[47] Feet of F. Worcs. Hil. 18 & 9 Chas. II; East. 25 Chas. II; East. 3 Jas. II.
[48] *Visit. of Worcs.* (Harl. Soc. xxvii), 153.
[49] Nash, loc. cit.
[50] Ibid.
[51] Feet of F. Worcs. Hil. 3 Edw. VI; Anct. D. (P.R.O.), A 13214.
[52] Feet of F. Worcs. East. 7 Edw. VI.
[53] Ibid. East. 1 & 2 Phil. and Mary.

CROOME D'ABITÔT : CROOME COURT : THE SOUTH FRONT

this time the descent of Young's Croome has not been traced.

Another estate in Croome D'Abitôt can be traced from the 14th century. In 1371 Thomas D'Abitot sold 40s. rent in Croome D'Abitôt to John Marshal, who granted it six years later to John Marsh of Feckenham for life with remainder to John Clopton.[54] His son Sir William Clopton died in 1419 holding of the lord of Croome D'Abitôt a messuage and a carucate of land called Abovedoune of the yearly value of 20s.[55] Thomas son and heir of William must have died without issue, for one of his sisters, Jane, inherited this estate,[56] and on the death of her husband, Sir John Burgh, in 1471[57] his grandson John Newport obtained these lands, which at this time were described as the manor of Croome D'Abitôt.[58] It was found by Prattinton among some papers lent to him by Capt. Lingen of Redbrook that the estates of Sir John Burgh were divided among his heirs 'by Lotts close (? lots chosen) in balls of Worc.'[59] John Newport was succeeded by a son Thomas,[60] who settled the manor on his son Sir Richard Newport and his wife Margaret.[61] On the death of Sir Richard Newport in 1570 his heir was his son Francis, then thirteen years of age,[62] but after this there are no further traces of this estate.

In 1584 there were two mills at Croome D'Abitôt which were at that time held with the manor by Francis Clare.[63] No earlier record has been found of these mills and no trace of them occurs again.

The church of *ST. MARY MAGDA-CHURCH LENE* consists of a chancel 22½ ft. by 18 ft., nave 39½ ft. by 18 ft., north and south aisles 8½ ft. wide, and a western tower, which is square outside but octagonal within and 11 ft. across. These measurements are all internal.

The building was erected in 1763 by Lancelot Brown for the Earl of Coventry. It is an interesting example of an 18th-century building in the Gothic style, and the result, while not altogether incongruous, shows some peculiar features. The former church stood near the present site and was entirely removed.

The chancel is lit by a three-light traceried window in the east wall, and the chancel arch is pointed, with an attached shaft on the west face supporting the crocketed and finialled label.

On either side of the nave are piers of four engaged shafts with moulded bases and capitals, supporting horizontal lintels, with ornamental plaster soffits. The ceiling is curved and enriched with three plaster pendants. The aisle windows are of two lights, with traceried heads. The lowest stage of the tower forms an octagonal west porch, with a vaulted roof springing from round angle-shafts. The tower is three stages high, and is strengthened by a pair of buttresses on each face and finished with an embattled parapet and pinnacles. The belfry is lit by four-light transomed windows and the stage below by quatrefoil openings. In the west end of the north aisle is a round-headed recess with a vaulted canopy. The exterior of the church is ashlar-faced, but the internal walls are plastered. The elegant carved wood font, with

the seats, pulpit, &c., are all contemporary with the building.

The church contains numerous monuments to members of the founder's family, some of them removed from the former church. Of the four large altar tombs in the chancel, the earliest is to Thomas first Lord Coventry, lord keeper, who died in 1639. It is of Renaissance design in black and white marble. The base supports a reclining figure in cap and robe with a mace and cushion in white marble. Above the figure is a large arched canopy, flanked by female figures representing Wisdom and Justice, the latter holding, besides her sword, the great seal of England. Above is a shield of the arms, and on either side of the arch an angel.

Another tomb, to Mary (Craven) wife of Thomas second Lord Coventry, who died in childbed, 1634, bears her reclining effigy holding an infant, with two children kneeling at the feet. The canopy is supported on black marble twisted columns. The third monument, to Thomas second Lord Coventry, who died in 1661, is also in black and white marble, with an effigy in coronet and robes. The fourth commemorating John fourth Lord Coventry, who died in 1687, has a similar effigy under a canopy, all in white marble, flanked by figures of Hope and Mercy. On the walls of the nave and aisles are various other monuments to different members of the same family.

There are six bells and a small broken 'sanctus' bell : the treble is dated 1812; the second is inscribed 'Iesvs be our good speed, Iohn Langston c.w. 1652'; the third '+ singe we meryly toe God on hie Ralph Goodall c.w. 1652'; the fourth '+ in time of need God be our speed John Pensham c.w. 1651,' and below the inscription a heart inclosing the initials IM and a bell; the inscription on the fifth reads 'Soli Deo Gloria Pax Hominibus 1651,' with the same stamp as the fourth; and on the tenor is 'Renata et Restaurata impensis Prae honorabilis Thomae Comitis de Coventre et Vicecomitis Deerhurst et Baronis Coventrye de Allesborough Anno 1699.'

The plate consists of a large communion cup with paten cover and a tankard-shaped flagon, silver gilt, of 1635, bearing the Coventry arms.

The registers before 1812 are as follows : (i) mixed entries 1560 to 1591 ; (ii) baptisms 1592 to 1733, marriages 1593 to 1729, burials 1592 to 1701 ; (iii) baptisms 1741 to 1812, burials 1678 to 1812, marriages 1741 to 1754 ; (iv) marriages 1754 to 1812.

The advowson of the church *ADVOWSON* of Croome D'Abitôt followed the descent of the manor from 1283,[64] the earliest time at which we have any mention of it, being divided in the same way as the manor in the 14th century. Towards the end of the 16th century the Clares appear to have become sole possessors of the advowson, which evidently passed with the manor in 1592 to Thomas Coventry.[65] The Earl of Coventry is patron at the present day.

In 1384 Richard Loke, the chaplain, was cited to appear before the bishop to show cause why he held the chapel of Croome D'Abitôt with the

[54] Prattinton Coll. (Soc. Antiq.).
[55] Chan. Inq. p.m. 7 Hen. V, no. 46.
[56] *Visit. of Worcs.* (Harl. Soc. xxvii), 71.
[57] Chan. Inq. p.m. 11 Edw. IV, no. 61 ; Close, 11 Edw. IV, m. 2.
[58] Prattinton Coll. (Soc. Antiq.).
[59] Ibid.
[60] *Visit. of Shropshire*, 1623 (Harl. Soc.), i, 60.
[61] Chan. Inq. p.m. (Ser. 2), clviii, 38.
[62] Ibid.
[63] Feet of F. Worcs. Mich. 27 & 28 Eliz.
[64] *Reg. G. Giffard* (Worcs. Hist. Soc.), 216.
[65] Nash, op. cit. i, 264.

rectory of Harsfield contrary to canonical institution. He stated that Croome D'Abitôt was within the bounds and limits of the parish church of Ripple, and that there were certain provisions and tithes arising in the manor of Croome for the officiating chaplain, but without cure of souls, and therefore it was tenable with any other benefice. This was allowed by Bishop Wakefield.[66] Although described as a church in 1283 it was usually called a chapel or a free chapel up to the middle of the 15th century,[67] 'the church or chapel' of Croome D'Abitôt occurring in 1467.[68] The rectory was valued in the middle of the 16th century at £8 2s. It was then still, to a certain extent, dependent upon the church of Ripple, paying a yearly pension of 20s. to the rector.[69]

Nash says that in 1771 the parish of Croome was united with that of Pirton, not by Act of Parliament, but by consent of the bishop and patron.[70] The living is still annexed to that of Pirton.

At the suppression of chantries it was found that land worth 1s. 4d. yearly was in the tenure of the churchwardens of Croome D'Abitôt for the maintenance of a lamp in the church there.[71] This was granted in 1588 to Richard Branthwaite and Roger Bromley,[72] and in 1637 to Francis Braddock and Christopher Kingscote.[73]

CHARITIES It appears from the Parliamentary returns of 1786 that a William Tustin charged certain lands, then the property of the Earl of Coventry, with the payment of 3s. 6d. a year to the poor. This payment, however, is not now made as a definite charge.

EARL'S CROOME

Crumbe (xi cent.); Crumba, Croumbe Adam (xiii cent.); Croumbe Simond, Symondescrombe (xiv cent.); Erles Crombe (xv cent.); Ellyscrove, Yrlyscrome, Erles Crowme (xvi cent.); Jeffrey Croombe, Jefferry Crombe, Earley Crome (xvii cent.); Irliscroome (xviii cent.).

This parish, lying near the left bank of the Severn in the south of Worcestershire, covers 1,153 acres. Of these 329 acres are arable land, 697 are permanent grass and 39 are laid out in woods and plantations.[1] The parish lies on the Keuper Marl formation with Alluvium near the river. Wheat, beans and barley are the chief crops. The main road from Pershore to Upton-on-Severn passes through the parish to the south of the village of Earl's Croome, meeting the road from Tewkesbury to Worcester to the southwest of Earl's Croome. The village stands at about 50 ft. above the ordnance datum, but to the north and west the land rises to 100 ft.

The village of Earl's Croome contains nothing of any particular interest, with the exception of Earl's Croome Court, a half-timber house of the early 17th century, which has, however, been considerably altered and modernized. This was formerly the residence of the Jeffery family, and on a plaster panel, in what is now the servants' hall, is their shield, party fessewise embattled gules and or, in chief three leopards' heads, in base three hawks' lures, countercoloured.

Part of Ripple was transferred to Earl's Croome in 1884.[2]

Among 15th and 16th-century place-names in this parish were Silbefeld, Holewell, Haledowne, Herdwell[3] and Paynes Meadow.[4]

MANOR Æthelswith wife of Burgred, King of Mercia, daughter of Æthelwulf, King of Wessex, is said to have granted Croome to the church of Worcester in the middle of the 9th century.[5] This possibly included the three later manors of Earl's Croome, Croome D'Abitôt and Hill Croome, and their connexion with Ripple may have dated from this time, for Bishop Aelhun had recovered Ripple at about the same time from Burgred.[6] In 1086 *EARL'S CROOME* was a member of the manor of Ripple,[7] and so continued until the 13th century,[8] when its connexion with Ripple seems to have ceased. It was, however, said to be held of the Bishop of Worcester in 1406-7.[9]

Godric, the bishop's tenant before the Conquest, was followed in Earl's Croome by Ordric, who held 1 hide there in 1086.[10] This estate had lapsed to the Bishop of Worcester as overlord early in the 12th century, when he was holding it in demesne.[11]

Bishop Samson (1096-1112) gave a hide of land at Croome to Adam de Croome.[12] Simon son of Adam was holding this land about 1182,[13] and this manor was probably among the lands for which he paid sums of 90s. yearly from 1158 to about 1172.[14] Simon and Adam de Croome both occur in 1175 and 1176 as paying fines for trespass in the king's forest.[15] In 1196-7 Adam de Croome was holding a fee and a half of the Bishop of Worcester in Worcestershire,[16] and early in the 13th century Adam de Croome was holding this manor with those of Tidmington and Armscote for the service of one knight's fee.[17] In 1252 he obtained a grant of free warren in this manor,[18] and was probably succeeded soon after by a son Adam, for in 1273 Simon son of the younger Adam was holding the manor,[19] which was said to have been held by his father Adam.[20] In 1273 the bishop confirmed to Simon the liberties which Adam his grandfather had held in this manor,[21] and in the Hundred Roll of about that time Simon is returned as

[66] Worc. Epis. Reg. Wakefield, fol. 24 d.; Prattinton Coll. (Soc. Antiq.).

[67] *Reg. G. Giffard* (Worcs. Hist. Soc.), 216, 546; Worc. Epis. Reg. Gainsborough, fol. 33; Brian, fol. 23; Peverell, fol. 48 d.; *Sede Vac. Reg.* (Worcs. Hist. Soc.), 425.

[68] Worc. Epis. Reg. Carpenter, fol. 214; Inst. Bks. (P.R.O.).

[69] *Valor Eccl.* (Rec. Com.), iii, 266.

[70] op. cit. i, 262; Bacon, *Liber Regis,* 971.

[71] Chant. Cert. (Aug. Off.), 60, no. 44a.

[72] Pat. 30 Eliz. pt. xvi, m. 114.

[73] Ibid. 12 Chas. I, pt. i, m. 1.

[1] Statistics from Bd. of Agric. (1905).

[2] *Census of Engl. and Wales,* 1891, ii, 657.

[3] Mins. Accts. bdle. 644, no. 10457.

[4] Anct. D. (P.R.O.), A 12736; Ct. of Req. bdle. 122, no. 23.

[5] Dugdale, *Mon. Angl.* i, 609; *Angl. Sax. Chron.* (Rolls Ser.), ii, 57, 68.

[6] Dugdale, *Mon. Angl.* i, 609.

[7] *V.C.H. Worcs.* i, 292.

[8] *Testa de Nevill* (Rec. Com.), 41b; Habington, op. cit. i, 137.

[9] Chan. Inq. p.m. 8 Hen. IV, no. 68.

[10] *V.C.H. Worcs.* i, 292.

[11] Ibid. 324.

[12] Red Bk. of Bishopric of Worc. (Eccl. Com. Rec. Var. bdle. 121, no. 43698), fol. 242.

[13] Ibid. fol. 96.

[14] See *Pipe R.* 5 *Hen. II*-19 *Hen. II* (Pipe R. Soc.).

[15] Ibid. 22 *Hen. II*; 23 *Hen. II.*

[16] *Red Bk. of Exch.* (Rolls Ser.), 108.

[17] *Testa de Nevill* (Rec. Com.), 41b.

[18] *Cal. Chart. R.* 1226-57, p. 400.

[19] *Reg. G. Giffard* (Worcs. Hist. Soc.), 54.

[20] Add. MS. 28024, fol. 125b.

[21] *Reg. G. Giffard* (Worcs. Hist. Soc.), 54.

EARL'S CROOME COURT : GARDEN FRONT

EARL'S CROOME CHURCH : CAPITAL OF CHANCEL ARCH

claiming pleas relating to hue and cry and effusion of blood and the assize of bread and ale and free warren in this manor.[22] He had married a niece of Bishop Giffard,[23] and in 1301 one of the articles brought by the prior and convent against the bishop was that he had granted to Simon the assize of bread and ale without the consent of the convent. The bishop justified himself on the ground that Simon's ancestors had had this privilege from ancient times.[24]

In 1291 Simon de Croome granted this manor to Geoffrey de Hambury,[25] who shortly after regranted it to Simon and his wife Maud, daughter of Alexander de Escote,[26] but in 1319 Simon settled the manor on himself and his wife Christine and their issue with remainder to John and Simon, his sons by former marriages.[27] Simon and Christine had a son Godfrey, who in 1333 granted the manor to John Hamond of Elmley.[28] John was a villein of the Earl of Warwick, who on this account seized the manor of Earl's Croome,[29] but Godfrey seems to have recovered the seisin shortly after.[30] The three manors of Croome, Tidmington and Armscote were returned in 1346 as held by John de Croome and Roger de Ledbury,[31] but Croome was probably never held by them, but remained with Godfrey de Croome until his death. It then seems to have passed to Thomas Beauchamp Earl of Warwick, who was dealing with it in 1369 as the manor of Croome Adam,[32] and had presented to the church of Earl's Croome in 1353.[33] Reginald de Hambury, who claimed the estates of the Croomes on Godfrey's death (see Tidmington), released all his right in the manor of Earl's Croome (Crombe Simond) in 1375–6 to Thomas Earl of Warwick, Sir Hugh de Segrave, Sir Henry de Arderne and others,[34] and in 1382 Ellen widow of Sir Henry de Arderne gave up all her claim in the manor to William de Cooksey and others, to whom the manor had been granted by Thomas Earl of Warwick.[35] They were evidently feoffees in trust for the earl, for he held the manor until his forfeiture in 1396,[36] when it passed to the Crown. At this date the manor was still held for life by Christine widow of Simon de Croome and by John Russell, who probably had a life grant of it from the earl.[37] In 1397 the king granted it in fee to John for his good service and a sum of 200 marks.[38] In the following year John settled it upon himself and his wife Elizabeth and their issue.[39] John Russell probably died

about 1400, when his son William confirmed the advowson to Elizabeth.[40] Thomas Earl of Warwick was restored in 1399[41] and died seised of this manor in 1401.[42] It then followed the same descent as Elmley Castle, passing into the possession of Henry VII in 1487.[43] The manor remained in the Crown[44] until December 1546, when it was granted by Henry VIII to Thomas Wymbish and his wife Elizabeth Lady Tailboys.[45] In the following February it was sold by Edward Lord Clinton, stepfather of Lady Tailboys, to Thomas Jeffery,[46] Lord Clinton perhaps acting on behalf of his stepdaughter.

Thomas was succeeded in 1548 by his son William,[47] on whose death in 1570 his heir was his son Leonard.[48] In 1583 Leonard had livery of the manor.[49] He died in 1629, leaving a son Thomas,[50] who owned the manor until his death in 1650.[51] It was probably this Thomas Jeffery, who was a justice of the peace, with whom Samuel Butler, the author of *Hudibras*, spent some years of his early life, acting as his clerk.[52] William the son of Thomas Jeffery was in possession of the manor in 1657,[53] his sister and heir Hester, wife of Sir Robert Barkham, holding it in 1689.[54]

JEFFERY. *Party fessewise and battled gules and or with three leopards' heads or in the chief and three hawks' lures gules in the foot.*

She, who died in 1691,[55] was the last of the Jeffery family, and in 1694 the manor was vested in trustees to be sold.[56] It appears to have been bought by the Rev. William Marten, who was living there in 1700.[57] After his death the property was divided between his two daughters. This occurred before 1738, for in that year half the manor was owned by Marian Marten.[58] She afterwards married Thomas Dunne of Gatley Park and died in 1744. Her eldest son Martin died unmarried in 1814 and was succeeded by his nephew Thomas Dunne.[59] The second son of the latter, the Rev. Charles Dunne, took the name of Amphlett in 1855[60] on inheriting the property of Four Ashes Hall (co. Salop),[61] and the manor has from that time remained in the Amphlett family, the Rev. George le Strange Amphlett being the present lord of the manor.

[22] *Hund. R.* (Rec. Com.), ii, 283.
[23] *Reg. G. Giffard* (Worcs. Hist. Soc.), 57.
[24] Ibid. 548.
[25] Add. MS. 28024, fol. 125b.
[26] Ibid.
[27] Feet of F. Worcs. 13 Edw. II, no. 10.
[28] Add. MS. 28024, fol. 126a.
[29] Ibid.
[30] Ibid.
[31] *Feud. Aids,* v, 309.
[32] Close, 43 Edw. III, m 8 d.
[33] Habington, op. cit. i, 137.
[34] Add. MS. 28024, fol. 126b.
[35] Ib'd. fol. 147a.
[36] Chan. Inq. p.m. 21 Ric. II, no. 137.
[37] Ibid. no. 97.
[38] *Cal. Pat.* 1396–9, p. 275; see also p. 222.
[39] Feet of F. East. 22 Ric. II, no. 57.
[40] Close, 2 Hen. IV, pt. ii, m. 7 d.
[41] G.E.C. *Complete Peerage,* viii, 58.
[42] Chan. Inq. p.m. 2 Hen. IV, no. 58.
[43] Ibid. 18 Edw. IV, no. 47; Cal.

Pat. 1476–85, pp. 124, 379; Close, 3 Hen. VII, m. 11; Anct. D. (P.R.O.), A 11056. From 1431 to 1466 a quarter of this manor was held by Isabel wife of Richard Curson, evidently under a grant for life by the Earl of Warwick (*Feud. Aids,* v, 334; Feet of F. Div. Co. Mich. 6 Edw. IV, no. 41).
[44] *L. and P. Hen. VIII,* i, 3613; ii, 1074, 3483; iii (1), 1081 (27); Priv. Act, 28 Hen. VIII, cap. 22; *L. and P. Hen. VIII,* xii (1), g. 1330 (32); xvi, g. 1391 (56); xviii (2), g. 449 (8). The site of the manor was leased in 1519–20 for twenty-one years to William Honyman and others (Pat. 11 Hen. VIII, pt. ii, m. 20) and in 1536 to Richard Winslow and others for a similar term (*L. and P. Hen. VIII,* xii (1), g. 539 [35]).
[45] Pat. 38 Hen. VIII, pt. vii, m. 25; *L. and P. Hen. VIII,* xxi (2), g. 648 (38).
[46] *L. and P. Hen. VIII,* xxi (2), g. 771 (37).

[47] W. and L. Inq. p.m. v, 24.
[48] Chan. Inq. p.m. (Ser. 2), cliv, 112.
[49] Fine R. 25 Eliz. pt. i, no. 42.
[50] Chan. Inq. p.m. (Ser. 2), ccccliv, 31.
[51] Fine R. 7 Chas. I, pt. i, no. 3; Feet of F. Worcs. Trin. 16 Chas. I; Nash, op. cit. i, 268, quoting M.I.
[52] *Dict. Nat. Biog.*; *Quart. Sess. R.* (Worcs. Hist. Soc.), Introd. p. xlix.
[53] Feet of F. Worcs. Hil. 1657; Nash, loc. cit.
[54] Feet of F. Worcs. East. 1 Will. and Mary; G.E.C. *Complete Baronetage,* iii, 222.
[55] G.E.C. loc. cit.
[56] Priv. Act, 6 & 7 Will. III, cap. 8.
[57] Burton, *Bibl. of Worcs.* (Worcs. Hist. Soc.), i, 32.
[58] Recov. R. Mich. 12 Geo. II, rot. 483.
[59] Burke, *Landed Gentry* (ed. 11).
[60] Phillimore and Fry, *Changes of Name,* 6.
[61] Burke, loc. cit.

The other daughter of William Marten married the Rev. Francis Welles, and half the manor of Earl's Croome passed into this family. Edmund Marten Welles, probably the son of Francis Welles, owned the property in 1770.[62] The next owner was Edmund Francis Welles, possibly son of the former owner, and he is known to have held the property between 1805 and 1817.[63] Shortly after this time this moiety of the manor appears to have lapsed to the Dunnes.[64]

In the 15th century a fair was held at Herdwell in Earl's Croome at the feast of St. Lawrence.[65]

CHURCH The church of *ST. NICHOLAS* consists of a chancel measuring internally 15 ft. by 13½ ft., a nave 34½ ft. by 18½ ft., a modern western gallery, a western tower built within the nave walls and a modern vestry. The nave and chancel are those of a 12th-century church, which remained practically untouched till the first half of the 19th century, when the west wall was rebuilt. The remains of the old west front, preserved in the vicarage grounds, are sufficient to show that it was shafted and arcaded in an elaborate manner. At the same time the western tower was

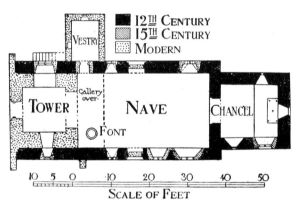

PLAN OF EARL'S CROOME CHURCH

built within the nave walls, a western gallery erected and the vestry added. New tracery was also inserted in several windows, which had already in some cases been enlarged at various dates in the 14th and 15th centuries.

The east window of the chancel is a single light. The rear arch is of 12th-century date and round-headed, but the window itself has a trefoiled head, inserted probably in the 14th century. Above this is a small loophole window, with an elaborately carved 12th-century head, jambs and sill. Below this, externally, is a portion of an enriched cable-moulded string-course of the same period. In the north wall is a small untouched 12th-century window with a round head and an external rebate for a wooden frame. To the south are two windows, the eastern having a two-light wooden frame of the 15th century with trefoiled heads, and the western a single 12th-century light with a modern head of 13th-century character. The chancel arch is semicircular and elaborately ornamented on its western face, with

zigzag ornament and a roll moulding. The responds have angle-shafts on the west, with cushion capitals, richly carved with interlacing floral designs, surmounted by deep square abaci, ornamented with 'arabesque' designs in low relief, and, in the case of the southern one, with a well-formed lion looking backwards. The bases are also moulded and carved and the shafts are ornamented with the cheveron. There are two 12th-century openings in the north wall of the nave, both enlarged to two lights. The eastern has modern tracery in the style of the 14th century and the tracery of the other is made up of later work. The north door between the windows is blocked, and though somewhat restored is similar in style and date to the chancel arch. Of the three windows in the south wall the first is of 15th-century date with modern tracery. It is of two lights with traces of flowing decoration in colour on the jambs and rear arch. West of this is a two-light modern window of 14th-century detail, while the third is similar to the corresponding window in the north wall. The 12th-century south door is also blocked, and has a round head enriched with roll and cheveron, the side shafts having scalloped capitals and moulded bases. The old wooden door retains a portion of its ironwork.

Built in the western portion of the nave is the modern tower, and opening into it are two old nave windows, both somewhat restored. The northern is of two lights with a quatrefoil over, and the southern is a single light of a lancet type, the external jambs and head being modern. The west wall is almost entirely modern with a doorway of 12th-century detail. A rough sketch (preserved at the rectory) of the west front previous to the rebuilding shows a double arcade of 12th-century design. The tower is three stages high and has an embattled parapet.

On the north wall of the chancel is a small tablet with a well-designed inscription, in Roman capitals, to Thomas Jeffery, died 1650, and on the south a painted inscription, and over it, carved in low relief, a shield of his arms.

There are five bells: the treble dated 1746, the second 1739, and the third, fourth and fifth 1707.

The plate consists of a cup with a paten cover (hall-marked for 1571), a small plated paten and a plated flagon.

The registers before 1812 are as follows : (i) baptisms from 1647 to 1785, burials 1658 to 1785, marriages 1659 to 1785 ; (ii) baptisms and burials from 1785 to 1812 ; (iii) marriages from 1754 to 1812. Some earlier 17th-century entries will be found among the Bishops' Transcripts.

ADVOWSON The advowson of the rectory of Earl's Croome has always followed the same descent as the manor,[66] the Welles and Dunne families presenting alternately when the manor was divided between them.

In 1670 Fleetwood Sheppard presented to the church,[67] and Thomas Wheat did so in 1701,[68] but it seems probable that this was by arrangement with the Jeffery family, for Sir Robert Sheppard and Thomas

[62] Recov. R. East. 10 Geo. III, rot. 201.
[63] Ibid. Trin. 45 Geo. III, rot. 216 ; Mich. 51 Geo. III, rot. 314 ; *Clerical Guide*, 1817.
[61] See *Clerical Guide* and Noake, *Guide to Worcs.* 102.
[65] Mins. Accts. bdle. 644, no. 10457.
[66] See manor and *Reg. G. Giffard* (Worcs. Hist. Soc.), 330 ; Inst. Bks. (P.R.O.).
[67] Inst. Bks. (P.R.O.).
[68] Ibid.

Earl's Croome Church : Blocked South Doorway

Earl's Croome Church : The Chancel from the South-east

Wheat were trustees or the marriage settlement of Sir Robert Barkham and Hester Jeffery in 1689.[69]

Nash writing in 1779 states that there was then in the registry of the church of Worcester a deed of composition between the rectors of Ripple and Earl's Croome concerning the burial of their dead.[70]

CHARITIES In 1796 the Rev. F. Welles— as appeared from the church table —by his will left £20, the interest to be distributed in bread on Christmas Eve. The

trust fund now consists of £31 on deposit at a bank, the annual interest of about 15s. being duly applied.

The Church Lands—also mentioned on the church table—consist of 8 a., or thereabouts, producing £1 1 5s. yearly. The official trustees also hold the sums of £44 15s. 6d. consols and £225 2½ per cent. annuities, arising from sales in 1898 and 1902 of cottages and lands, producing in annual dividends £6 15s.

The income is applied towards the repair and upkeep of the church.

HILL CROOME

Hylcromban, Hilcrumbe (xi cent.) ; Hullecrembe, Hollecrumbe (xii cent.) ; Hulecrumb, Hulcrombe (xiii cent.) ; Hull (xiv cent.) ; Hylle Crumbe, Hylcrome (xv cent.) ; Croome Montis, Croomb (xviii cent.).

The parish of Hill Croome, covering an area of 993 acres, lies in the south of the county near the Gloucestershire border. The Horse Brook, crossing the western side of the parish, flows south from Baughton and enters the parish of Ripple near Naunton. A small stream which falls into Bourne Brook forms the eastern boundary of the parish and the main road from Pershore to Upton-on-Severn that on the north.

The land is low-lying for the most part, being about 50 ft. above the ordnance datum, but rising to 100 ft. at Baughton Hill. In 1905 573½ acres were laid down as permanent grass, 275¾ acres were arable land,[1] the chief crops being wheat and beans, and 13¾ were covered by woods and plantations. The parish lies partly on the Lower Lias and partly on the Keuper Marls, the soil being clay and loam.

The village is small and scattered, containing, besides the church, but two farm-houses and one or two cottages. Opposite the church, and separated from it by the by-road about which the few houses are grouped, is the house formerly known as the ' Glebe Farm.' It is of half-timber, two stories in height, and of L-shaped plan. The main limb is the earliest part of the house and appears to date from the 14th century. The insertion of the floors and fireplaces and the addition of the western wing appear to have taken place at the end of the 16th century ; the main timbers of the older portion have been much cut about by the later alterations. A little distance to the north of the church are the remains of the moat of the former manor-house. The Manor Farm, formerly known as the Court House, upon the west side of the road about a quarter of a mile to the north of the church, is a modernized building of little interest. The hamlet of Baughton, about half a mile again to the north of the Manor Farm, contains some interesting half-timber work, and is considerably larger than the parent village. Here is a good half-

timber farm-house of L plan with the date 1540 upon it. The chimney stacks are of stone and are surmounted by brick shafts of the intersecting diagonal plan so common to the county and the period.

An Inclosure Act for the parish was passed in 1770,[2] and the award is dated 1771.[3]

Among former place-names in this parish were Mylles or Myboards and Golds or Goldwynes [4] (xvi cent.) ; Cow Leasow, Nuns Close, Cooks Close, Fryer's Acre, the Eleven Lands, the Fiddle [5] (xviii cent.).

MANORS A grant of 972, by which King Edgar confirmed to the abbey of Pershore land in ' Cromban,' [6] may perhaps refer to HILL CROOME, but there is no further evidence that the abbey ever held land in this parish, and in 1038 Lyfing, Bishop of Worcester, granted 5 mansae at Hill Croome and Baughton to his faithful servant Ethelred for three lives.[7]

In 1086 Hill Croome was a member of the manor of Ripple,[8] and continued to be held of that manor until the 17th century.[9] In 1480 a chief rent of 7s. from the manor of Hill Croome was paid to the Master of Balsall Preceptory.[10]

In 1086 Roger de Lacy was tenant under the bishop of 3 hides at Hill Croome,[11] and his descendant Hugh de Lacy held it early in the 12th century.[12] This manor was evidently one of those which Hugh Poer took from the Lacys and gave to Walter de Meduana (see Himbleton), for Walter de ' Marine ' is mentioned as an owner in the Red Book of the Bishopric of Worcester,[12a] and the overlordship afterwards apparently passed to the Monchenseys with Walter's other estates (see Spetchley), for Denise daughter of William son of Warin de Monchensey, wife of Hugh de Veer, who succeeded William in 1289,[13] was mesne lady of the manor.[14] On her death in 1313 without issue her interest in Hill Croome passed to her cousin [15] Aymer de Valence Earl of Pembroke, who died in 1324. Among the fees held of him was half a fee in Hulle, probably to be identified with Hill Croome.[16] It was assigned to his niece and co-heir Elizabeth Comyn, and became annexed to Goodrich Castle, which also fell to her share.[17]

[69] Feet of F. Worcs. East. 1 Will. and Mary.   [70] Nash, op. cit. i, 268.

[1] Statistics from Bd. of Agric. (1905).

[2] Priv. Act, 11 Geo. III, cap. 17.

[3] Blue Bk. Incl. Awards, 190.

[4] Chan. Proc. (Ser. 2), bdle. 190, no. 11.

[5] Prattinton Coll. (Soc. Antiq.). A small piece of the Fiddle was called the Cheese Cake, and there were 'two meer-

stones on the east side of the Cheese Cake for setting out the same which is to be exactly square.'

[6] Cott. MS. Aug. ii, 6 ; Dugdale, Mon. Angl. ii, 416.

[7] Kemble, Codex Dipl. no. 760 ; Heming, Chartul. (ed. Hearne), 599.

[8] V.C.H. Worcs. i, 292.

[9] Habington, op. cit. i, 235, 236 ; ii, 266 ; Chan. Inq. p.m. (Ser. 2), dxciv, 68.

[10] Mins. Accts. bdle. 1117, no. 15.

[11] V.C.H. Worcs. i, 292.

[12] Ibid. 324.

[12a] Habington, op. cit. i, 235.

[13] G.E.C. Complete Peerage, vi, 204.

[14] Habington, op. cit. i, 236.

[15] G.E.C. loc. cit.

[16] Cal. Inq. p.m. 10-20 Edw. II, 336.

[17] Cal. Close, 1323-7, p. 275.

She afterwards married Sir Richard Talbot, and died about 1372, when her son Sir Gilbert succeeded as lord of this fee.[18] The manor was still held of the Talbots of Goodrich Castle in 1410,[19] but a fourth part of it was said in 1461 to be held of Richard Earl of Warwick for a twentieth part of a fee,[20] and in 1542 it was held of the king as of Elmley Castle.[21]

Under the Lacys the manor was held about 1182 by William son of Hereman.[22] A later owner was Almeric son of William.[23] In 1194 William de la Hulle handed over the manor for six years to Richard Hagernier as surety for a debt for 40 marks.[24] This William or a successor known as William de Hill Croome demised the manor for ten years to Nicholas de Wilington, whose ward he had been and whose daughter he had married.[25] This feoffment evidently took place before 1203, when Nicholas sued William for not keeping the agreement made between them as to this land.[26] Later William gave the manor to Eudes de Beauchamp. William de Hill Croome was succeeded before 1220 by his son Richard, who in that year claimed a third of the manor against Ivo de Beauchamp.[27] In 1232 Richard disputed the right of Eudes de Beauchamp to the manor, but he lost his case.[28] Eudes died about 1241–2,[29] and was succeeded by Robert de Beauchamp, against whom Maud widow of Eudes recovered a third of the manor in 1242.[30] Robert must have been succeeded shortly after by William de Beauchamp, for in 1243 he and Maud gave land and wood in the manor of Hill Croome to Richard de Hill Croome.[31] In 1255 Maud, then the wife of Odo 'de Monte,' released all her dower in Hill Croome to Margery widow of Richard de Hill Croome and her son John,[32] and in the following year William de Beauchamp of Eaton sold the manor to the same John for a rent of 1d. yearly and foreign service.[33]

It was possibly this mesne lordship which was sold in 1276 by Ralph de Beauchamp to William son of Warin de Monchensey, as the wardship of the land and heir of John de Hill Croome and of his heirs for ever.[34]

Amy widow of John de Hill Croome married William de Monchensey in 1279, and thus for a short time the mesne lordship and tenancy of the manor were vested in the same owners. Amy's marriage was the subject of a celebrated decision of Bishop Giffard, who declared it to have been legal, although the service was performed at the church door. The ceremony took place, we are told, in the morning before sunrise at the church of Hill Croome, 'the same William being then dressed in a robe of black camlet, and the lady Amy in a robe of murry colour.'[35]

The heir of John de Hill Croome was apparently Nicholas de Hill Croome (Hulle), who held the manor in 1299.[36] He was succeeded before 1324 by a son John,[37] who obtained in 1347 a charter of free warren at Hill Croome.[38] The next owner appears to have been William Wilcote, who held the manor in 1406[39] in right of his wife Elizabeth, who was a daughter of Sir John Trillow of Chastleton, co. Oxford.[40] William Wilcote died in 1410, leaving two sons Thomas and John.[41] They both died without issue before their mother,[42] who continued to hold the manor until her death in 1445.[43] As a second husband she had married Sir John Blaket, and as Elizabeth Blaket had granted certain annuities from the manor of Hill Croome to Thomas Pope and Thomas Boteler.[44] The heirs of Elizabeth Blaket were her grandchildren William Wykeham, Richard Beaufo, Thomas Conyers, Elizabeth wife of Thomas Palmer, Philippa wife of William Catesby, and her daughter Isabel Burton.[45] In 1480 land in Hill Croome which had belonged to William Catesby, son of Philippa and William Catesby, was apparently in the king's hands.[46] Three years later, however, property described as the manor of Hill Croome was settled on William Catesby and his heirs by Roger Townesend.[47] William forfeited all his estates on the accession of Henry VII,[48] and after this time all trace of this portion of the manor is lost.

In 1453 William Wykeham and his wife Joan quitclaimed 'the manor of Hill Croome' to William Brown,[49] to whom two years later Margaret the daughter of William Wykeham, and her husband Sir William Fiennes, also released their right in the manor,[50] but after this time the descent of this estate is lost.

Richard Beaufo,[51] a third co-heir of Elizabeth Blaket, died in 1460 holding a quarter of the manor,[52] his son Humphrey being then a minor in the custody of Thomas Archbishop of Canterbury and Anne Duchess of Buckingham.[53] Humphrey was succeeded in 1485 by his son John,[54] on whose death in 1516 his son John inherited this portion of the manor of Hill Croome.[55] This John Beaufo

---

[18] Chan. Inq. p.m. 46 Edw. III, no. 66.
[19] Ibid. 12 Hen. IV, no. 41.
[20] Ibid. 1 Edw. IV, no. 3.
[21] Ibid. (Ser. 2), lxvii, 154.
[22] Habington, op. cit. i, 235; Red Bk. of Bishopric of Worc. (Eccl. Com. Rec. Var. bdle. 121, no. 43698), fol. 96.
[23] Red Bk. of Bishopric of Worc. fol. 253; Habington, op. cit. ii, 266. William son of Almeric was grandson of William son of Hereman (cf. Shell in Himbleton). Habington also states that Walter Aumerei was an owner of Hill Croome (ibid. ii, 266), but the date of his tenancy is not known.
[24] Rot. Cur. Reg. (Rec. Com.), i, 46; Abbrev. Plac. (Rec. Com.), 6.
[25] Maitland, Bracton's Note Bk. ii, 524.
[26] Pipe R. 5 John, m. 4 d.
[27] Ibid. 4 Hen. III, m. 14 d.
[28] Maitland, loc. cit.
[29] Excerpta e Rot. Fin. (Rec. Com.), i, 364.
[30] Cur. Reg. R. 123, m. 3.

[31] Feet of F. Worcs. 28 Hen. III, no. 9.
[32] Ibid. 40 Hen. III, no. 42.
[33] Ibid. 41 Hen. III, no. 2.
[34] Ibid. 5 Edw. I, no. 5.
[35] Reg. G. Giffard (Worcs. Hist. Soc.), iii, 359–60.
[36] Habington, op. cit. i, 138; Red Bk. of Bishopric of Worc. fol. 85.
[37] Habington, op. cit. i, 236; Cal. Close, 1323–7, p. 272; Cal. Inq. p.m. 10–20 Edw. II, 336.
[38] Cal. Pat. 1345–8, p. 529; Pat. 21 Edw. III, pt. iv, m. 21.
[39] Cal. Pat. 1405–8, p. 235.
[40] Berks., Bucks. and Oxon. Arch. Journ. iii, 98.
[41] Chan. Inq. p.m. 12 Hen. IV, no. 41.
[42] Thomas died in 1415 (Chan. Inq. p.m. 3 Hen. V, no. 21) and John before 1438 (Cal. Pat. 1436–41, p. 306).
[43] Feud. Aids, v, 334; Chan. Inq. p.m. 24 Hen. VI, no. 33.

[44] Mins. Accts. bdle. 1117, no. 15.
[45] Chan. Inq. p.m. 24 Hen. VI, no. 33; Berks., Bucks. and Oxon. Arch. Journ. iii, 99.
[46] Mins. Accts. 20 Edw. IV, bdle. 1117, no. 15; Berks., Bucks. and Oxon. Arch. Journ. iii, 101.
[47] De Banco R. D. Enr. Hil. 1 Ric. III, m. 1.
[48] Dugdale, Hist. of Warw. 789.
[49] Feet of F. Div. Co. Trin. 32 Hen. VI; Croke, Hist. of Croke Family, no. 42.
[50] Feet of F. Div. Co. Hil. 34 Hen. VI; Croke, loc. cit.
[51] Visit. of Warw. (Harl. Soc. xii), 131.
[52] Chan. Inq. p.m. 1 Edw. IV, no. 3.
[53] Cal. Pat. 1467–77, p. 211; Early Chan. Proc. bdle. 47, no. 4.
[54] Visit. of Warw. (Harl. Soc. xii), 203; Cal. Inq. p.m. Hen. VII, i, 52.
[55] Chan. Inq. p.m. (Ser. 2), xxxi, 20.

died in 1583, leaving a son Thomas,[56] but this portion of the manor also disappears after this date.

In 1521 Edmund Lee and his wife Ellen granted to Edward Saxilby, Henry White, Thomas Bountayn and others the so-called manor of Hill Croome.[57] Saxilby and the others were probably acting for Thomas Walshe and his wife Katherine, Saxilby's sister,[58] for Thomas died seised of the manor in 1542.[59] His widow held the manor during her life, and after her death it passed to her son Thomas. In 1591 Thomas Walshe bargained with his great-nephew Thomas Lambert[60] for the sale of this manor for £1,900.[61] After paying the first instalment of £100, Lambert found that he had made a bad bargain on account of a lease to Joan Tusten, which was still running, and instituted Chancery proceedings against his uncle for release from his bargain and recovery of the £100.[62] He was apparently successful, the manor returning into the possession of Thomas Walshe, as had been agreed in 1591, if Lambert failed to pay the £1,900. Thomas Walshe died in 1593,[63] apparently leaving co-heirs.

Before 1615 the manor had been divided into three parts, one part being in the possession of the above-mentioned Thomas Lambert and his wife Margaret.[64] Another third was held by Sir Thomas Jervoise and his wife Lucy, and Sir William Young and his wife Anne.[65] No connexion can be traced between Thomas Walshe and these holders. Thomas Bromley and his wife Anne, one of the heirs at law of Thomas Walshe, held the remaining third.[66] All three portions were bought between 1615 and 1618 by Thomas Trevor, Richard Shilton and others, trustees for Thomas Coventry,[67] who as Lord Coventry obtained in 1630 a confirmation of a third of the manor from Henry Bromley, son of Thomas and Anne.[68] From that time until the present day the manor has remained in the Coventry family,[69] the present owner being the Earl of Coventry.

The manor of BAUGHTON (Bocctun, xi cent.; Boctun, Broctona, xiii cent.; Brocton, xiv cent.; Boghton, xv cent.) was held of the manor of Ripple.[70] Land there was given by Bishop Lyfing in 1038 with Hill Croome to Ethelred.[71] It was probably included in the 3 hides at Hill Croome in 1086. It seems to have followed the same descent as Hill Croome to the Beauchamps, Ivo de Beauchamp holding 3 hides there in the beginning of the 13th century.[72] It has apparently since followed the same descent as Hill Croome.[73]

Another estate at Baughton was held in 1319–20 by the Croome family of Earl's Croome. Simon de Croome and his wife Christine held 6 marks of rent in Baughton at that date,[74] and the estate seems to have followed the descent of the manor of Earl's Croome, being granted as the manor of Baughton to John Russell in 1397.[75] Sir John Burgh died about 1471 holding three messuages and 2 carucates of land at Earl's Croome and Baughton,[76] but it is not certain whether this was the same estate, for a manor of Baughton passed with Earl's Croome to the Jeffery family,[77] and afterwards Baughton Court became the seat of the Welles family.[78]

Prattinton gives the following account of Baughton : 'It was the property of the Turbervilles, whose ancestors, according to their pedigree, lent to Dr. Nash, came over with the Conqueror. Their heiress married Captain Roger Brooke, whose son James Brooke, rector of Hill Croome, died, leaving the property (but not the manor of Baughton) to two daughters, who married James Skey and Mr. Wells.'[79]

This account probably refers to a capital messuage called Turvills Place in Hill Croome, mentioned in 1640 as belonging to Lord Coventry.[80] This was probably the land for which Thomas Turberville sued Richard Turberville of Baughton in 1468, the latter claiming the estate by descent from his grandfather Richard Turberville.[80a] A messuage and close in Baughton were held in 1591 by John Turberville and his wife Joan and their daughter Margaret under a lease from Thomas Walshe, lord of Hill Croome.[81]

The church of ST. MARY THE VIRGIN consists of a chancel 24¼ ft. by 14½ ft., nave about 35 ft. by 17 ft., a west tower 8 ft. by 6¼ ft. and a modern north porch. These measurements are all internal.

CHURCH

---

[56] Chan. Inq. p.m. (Ser. 2), cc, 27.

[57] Feet of F. Worcs. Mich. 13 Hen. VIII.

[58] Chan. Inq. p.m. (Ser. 2), lxvii, 154; *Visit. of Worcs.* (Harl. Soc.), 140. Katherine Walshe let the site and demesne of the manor to Joan Tusten, a widow, and her daughter Elizabeth. Elizabeth married John Gawton, who, after the death of Katherine, gave her son Thomas £6 13s. 4d. for the right to enjoy the estate. Shortly afterwards Elizabeth, the wife of John Gawton, was 'stolen away and persuaded to disagree with the marriage of the complainant and to promise herself to another,' and her husband was expelled from the premises. He tried to come to some agreement with Thomas Walshe to recover possession, but without success, and thereupon brought a successful action against him in Chancery (Chan. Proc. [Ser. 2], bdle. 72, no. 15; see also bdle. 86, no. 14). Elizabeth afterwards married Michael Ree or Rey, who was holding the remainder of this lease in 1591 (Close, 33 Eliz. pt. xxi, Lambert and Walshe; Chan. Proc. [Ser. 2], bdle. 244, no. 8).

[59] Chan. Inq. p.m. (Ser. 2), lxvii, 154. In this document his heir is said to be a

son Anthony, but he does not appear to have succeeded to the estate.

[60] Lambert called Thomas Walshe his uncle, but from the pedigree of the family given in the Worcestershire visitation of 1569 it appears that he was his great-uncle, being brother of Lambert's grandmother (*Visit. of Worcs.* 1569 [Harl. Soc. xxvii], 140; Chan. Proc. [Ser. 2], bdle. 244, no. 8).

[61] Close, 33 Eliz. pt. xxi, Lambert and Walshe.

[62] Chan. Proc. (Ser. 2), bdle. 244, no. 8.

[63] Nash, op. cit. ii, 377, quoting monumental inscription in Stockton Church.

[64] Feet of F. Worcs. Trin. 15 Jas. I; *Visit. of Worcs.* (Harl. Soc.), 140.

[65] Feet of F. Worcs. Trin. 16 Jas. I.

[66] Chan. Proc. (Ser. 2), bdle. 432, no. 60; Feet of F. Worcs. Mich. 13 Jas. I. Anne was a daughter and co-heir of Sir Richard Walshe of Shelsley Walsh, the Walshes of Hill Croome being a younger branch of that family (Metcalfe, *Visit. of Worcs.* 1682, p. 24).

[67] Feet of F. Worcs. Mich. 13 Jas. I; Trin. 15 Jas. I; Trin. 16 Jas. I; Close, 13 Jas. I, pt. viii, no. 13.

[68] Feet of F. Worcs. Hil. 6 Chas. I.

[69] Chan. Inq. p.m. (Ser. 2), dxciv, 68;

Recov. R. Mich. 1653, rot. 193; Trin. 16 Geo. II, rot. 210; Trin. 1 Will. IV, rot. 285.

[70] *Testa de Nevill* (Rec. Com.), 42; Chan. Inq. p.m. (Ser. 2), dxciv, 68.

[71] Heming, *Chartul.* (ed. Hearne), 599.

[72] *Testa de Nevill* (Rec. Com.), 42. The 3 hides probably included part of Hill Croome, for which there is no other return in the *Testa de Nevill*.

[73] Maitland, *Bracton's Note Bk.* ii, 524; *Lay Subs. R. Worcs.* 1280 (Worcs. Hist. Soc.), 27; *Feud. Aids,* v, 309; Feet of F. Worcs. Mich. 13 Hen. VIII; Chan. Inq. p.m. (Ser. 2), dxciv, 68.

[74] Feet of F. Worcs. 13 Edw. II, no. 10.

[75] *Cal. Pat.* 1396–9, p. 275.

[76] Chan. Inq. p.m. 11 Edw. IV, no. 61; Close, 11 Edw. IV, m. 2.

[77] Priv. Act, 6 & 7 Will. III, cap. 8.

[78] Recov. R. East. 10 Geo. III, rot. 201.

[79] Prattinton Coll. (Soc. Antiq.).

[80] Chan. Inq. p.m. (Ser. 2), dxciv, 68. The land of Richard de Turberville in Croome is mentioned in a deed of about 1319 (Prattinton Coll. [Soc. Antiq.], Deeds of D. and C. of Worc. no. 301).

[80a] Wrottesley, *Pedigrees from Plea R.* 424.

[81] Close, 33 Eliz. pt. xxi, Lambert and Walshe.

The earliest details are of the 14th century, to which date the whole building probably belongs. In the year 1907 a thorough restoration and repair was entered upon, when part of the north wall of the nave was rebuilt and the north porch was added. At the same time the chancel roof was ceiled with oak, in place of the former plaster ceiling, and the nave roof was entirely renewed. The east window of the chancel is of two lights with a lozenge opening above and probably dates from the 14th century. The other chancel windows are square-headed and fitted with wood lintels and mullions. In the south nave wall are two square-headed two-light windows with a lancet opening in the west tower wall. This last, together with the tower, is of 14th-century date. The font is circular with a tapering bowl.

The bells are three in number: the first inscribed 'Ave Maria' with a flowered cross stop; the second without inscription or mark; the third having RI divided by a bell and 'Peace and Good Neighbourhood.'

The plate consists of a very small cup and cover paten made in 1571 and a modern chalice.

The registers before 1812 are as follows: (i) baptisms and burials 1721 to 1812, marriages 1721 to 1753; (ii) marriages 1754 to 1807. Very much earlier books are known to have been recently in existence.[82]

ADVOWSON About 1235 Eudes de Beauchamp granted to Roger, Abbot of Pershore, the advowson of the church of Hill Croome, 'together with his own body.'[83] This grant was evidently acknowledged by his widow Maud, who after his death claimed the manor but not the advowson.[84] In 1246 William de Beauchamp of Eaton confirmed the grant.[85] The abbot and convent appear to have held it until the Dissolution,[86] when it passed into the king's hands, and it has remained in the gift of the Crown ever since.[87]

In 1274 the Abbot of Pershore granted licence to Sir John de Hill Croome to have divine service celebrated in his chapel in the court of Hill Croome.[87a]

A terrier of 1714 found in the small parish chest by Prattinton in 1820 records that 'there is a prescription of 6d. per house for dovehouses and 1s. for a double house. A pigeon loft lately erected upon a small estate of William Cotterill's pays pigeons in kind.' An old pear tree between Fryers Acre and the Eleven Lands was a 'parting tree,' and the fruit (when any) was to be divided.[88]

CHARITIES This parish has long been in possession of certain lands supposed to have been the gift of one Cotterill for relief of the poor. The property consists of three closes of land containing about 5 a., producing £13 5s. yearly. The net rents are distributed in coal.

The charity of Mrs. Harriet Welles, founded by will proved at Gloucester 18 August 1864, is endowed with £192 15s. 4d. consols with the official trustees, producing £4 16s. 4d. yearly. The charity is regulated by a scheme of the Charity Commissioners 1 October 1907, which directs that the income shall be applied primarily in keeping in repair a tablet and windows in the church, put in since the decease of testatrix's husband, and subject thereto in maintaining and keeping in repair the churchyard and fabric of the church.

CROPTHORNE

Cropponthorne, Croppethorne (viii cent.); Croppanhorne (ix cent.); Croppethorne (xii cent.).

The parish of Cropthorne lies in the south-east of the county and is bounded on the north by the Avon and a stream called Merry Brook, the latter also forming the greater portion of the eastern boundary of the parish and flowing into the Avon on its left bank.[1]

The area of the parish of Cropthorne, excluding Charlton and Netherton, is 1,538 acres,[2] of which 777 acres are arable land, 515 acres are permanent grass, and 23 acres are wood.[3] The soil is light and sandy in some parts, in others it is stiff clay; the subsoil is sand, gravel, clay and blue limestone. The north of the parish lies in the valley of the Avon, but to the south the land rises, reaching a height of 200 ft. at Haselor Hill in the south of Charlton. The chief crops are wheat, beans and barley, but much of the land in the parish is used for market gardening.

Cropthorne village, which lies in the valley of the Avon, is extremely picturesque and contains many interesting examples of half-timber work. The church stands at the eastern end of the village and in the churchyard are the remains of a stone cross. Adjoining it on the north-east are the grounds of Cropthorne Court, an 18th-century house, with later additions, which possesses no features of architectural interest. The manor-house, which is on the west side of the churchyard, is a good brick house of the 18th century. Upon the same side of the road a little further to the west is a small two-storied cottage of half-timber with a thatched roof, which is probably 14th-century work, the framing being of quite an early type. On the opposite side of the road, near the modern schools and parish room, is a good half-timber house, now divided into cottages, which is probably of similar date. Here, too, the roof is thatched. Near this spot, which is about the middle of the village, upon a blind lane leading northwards, is an interesting small two-storied house of the early 17th century. It is of half-timber, L-shaped on plan, and stands upon a basement course of stone. A triple chimney stack of the same material rises from the centre of the ridge roof of the main block. A weather-mould of typical section follows

---

[82] A number of entries will also be found among the Bishops' Transcripts at Worcester.

[83] Anct. D. (P.R.O.), B 3995; Aug. Off. Misc. Bks. lxi, fol. 110; his gift was confirmed by John de Hulle (Misc. Bks. loc. cit.).

[84] Cur. Reg. R. Worcs. 123, m. 3.

[85] Feet of F. Worcs. 31 Hen. III, no. 18.

[86] Nash, op. cit. i, 270. In 1342 the presentation was made by Joan formerly wife of John de Wilington (Nash, loc. cit.).

[87] Inst. Bks. (P.R.O.).

[87a] Aug. Off. Misc. Bks. lxi, fol. 111 d.

[*] Prattinton Coll. (Soc. Antiq.).

[1] There is another unnamed stream which runs through the parish from south to north and joins the River Avon near the village of Cropthorne.

[2] 16 acres are covered by water.

[3] Statistics from Bd. of Agric. (1905).

the slope of the roof on either side of the ridge, having at the apex a simple circular finial. The stacks are crowned by a small cornice of the same section as the weather-mould. Above this is one course of stone crowned by later brickwork. The gabled end of the projecting wing has been refaced with brick, probably towards the latter part of the 17th century, when the small stone-mullioned windows of this portion were inserted. A small barn near the house has framing of the same type, and is probably contemporary with it. The main street slopes sharply to the westward, and at the foot of the hill, where it turns to the south to join the Worcester road, is a fine half-timber farm-house. The earlier part of the building appears to have been of an L-shaped plan, and is certainly of a date anterior to the 16th century. Early in the 17th century a second wing was added at the opposite end to the original wing, by which the type of plan has been transformed. The ground story walls of this addition are of stone with mullioned windows. Externally the whole has been

imparts a quaint and unusual air. Some of the cottages are half-timbered. Charlton House is a brick mansion of the latter half of the 17th century, containing no features of extraordinary interest. There is a square stone pigeon house, much restored. At the entrance of the drive are fine stone gate-piers.

Netherton, which includes the southern part of the parish of Cropthorne, was annexed to the parish of Elmley Castle for ecclesiastical purposes in 1864.[6]

Near Chapel Farm in Netherton, now forming part of the out-buildings and in a lamentable state of ruin, are the remains of a mid-12th-century chapel. The building consisted of a chancel measuring internally about 16 ft. by 13 ft. and a nave about 44 ft. by 15 ft. The walls are of rubble masonry about 2½ ft. thick. At some period early in the 17th century the chapel was converted into a dwelling-house and a floor was inserted which has since disappeared, though the pockets for the joists are clearly to be seen on the inside of the nave walls. At the same time a chimney stack containing one fireplace for each floor was built

HALF-TIMBER COTTAGE IN CROPTHORNE VILLAGE

covered with rough-cast, including the half-timbered upper story, which has had wood-mullioned windows inserted to match those of the ground story. In a large upper room, now cut up by modern partitions, is a stone fireplace with a straight-sided four-centred head and jambs of stone. Elsewhere the older open fireplaces have been built up and small modern grates take their place. The original stairs remain in this wing.

Charlton, which comprises the eastern portion of the ancient parish of Cropthorne, was formed into a separate ecclesiastical parish in 1882,[4] and has an area of 1,599 acres, of which 17 acres are covered by water, 917 acres are arable land, 678¾ acres permanent grass and 5 acres woodland.[5]

The village or hamlet of Charlton lies about a mile to the east of Cropthorne proper, and is situated on both banks of Merry Brook. The osier-bordered stream which runs down the centre of the street

into the west wall of the nave and a wing was built out on the north side of the nave. The north wall has been cut away for this purpose immediately to the east of the north doorway, and made good again with fragments of 12th-century moulded stones. The stone paving of this wing is still *in situ*.

Two square-headed windows in the south wall of the chancel, now blocked, appear also to belong to the 17th-century alterations. The east window, which is a single light with a cusped head and ribbed rear arch, is probably a late 13th-century insertion. Between the two square-headed windows in the south wall above referred to is a very early 13th-century lancet, with external rebates for shutters. The accompanying illustration, taken from a photograph of four years ago, shows a similar window in the north wall, but this portion has since fallen. A broken fragment of masonry shows the position of the west wall of the chancel, and there are the remains of a buttress at this

---

[4] *Lond. Gaz.* 22 Aug. 1882, p. 3911.   [5] Statistics from Bd. of Agric. (1905).   [6] *Parl. Papers* (1872), xlvi, no. 345, p. 3.

point on the south wall. The corresponding portion of the wall on the north side is gone.[7] The north doorway of the nave, now blocked, is a beautiful specimen of late Norman work. The arch, which springs from keeled jamb shafts with delicately carved capitals, is of two orders externally, the outer enriched with the cheveron and lozenge, each lozenge inclosing a sculptured leaf or flower. More than half the stones of the western limb of the arch have fallen out, and the jamb shaft on this side has disappeared. The inner order is also enriched. The doorway itself had a square head, and the tympanum, carved with a wyvern, is now lying in a stable hard by. The rear arch is enriched with a double cheveron. In the eastern half of the south wall the jambs of two original windows may be traced. The blocked south doorway seems to have been of the same character as that on the north, but only the external jambs of its inner order remain, and these seem to have been reset. To the west of this, apparently reset in the blocking of a 17th-century window, is a plain narrow round-headed light, the head formed of a single stone, which may be a survival from a smaller and earlier chapel.

The west wall is now partly occupied by the stone fireplaces added in the 17th century, the chimney stack projecting externally. At the south-west is an angle buttress, probably of the 15th century. What remains of the roofing of the chancel appears to be of the same date. The wall-plates are moulded. Of the two remaining trusses, the eastern, or wall, truss is of the simple tie-beam and collar construction. The western truss has the collar stiffened by curved braces forming a two-centred arch. The roofing of the western portion of the nave, which is otherwise roofless, is modern. In the wall of a neighbouring stable is a reset small round-headed light of the 12th century.

The road from Pershore to Evesham runs through the parish from west to east, and from it at a short distance from the village of Cropthorne a road branches off southwards to Smoky Farm. Salt Way[8] runs from north to south through Netherton, a branch from it running west through the village into the Elmley Castle Road, which passes through the southern portion of the parish from west to east.

The following place-names occur in the 14th century :—Rokkeplace and Lynneplace[9] ; and in the 16th century Twenty Lands and Witche Meadow

Furlong in Estfield,[10] Inch Meadow, Colhill Way, Sharforde Meadow.[11]

A bronze celt of early type has been found at Cropthorne,[12] and at Charlton an urn containing charred bones 6 ft. below the surface. Near it was a bronze celt.[13]

MANOR In 780 Offa, King of Mercia, is said to have granted 7 *manentes* at CROP-THORNE to the church of Worcester,[14] but this charter may be a forgery.[15] Cropthorne was still a royal estate in 841, when King Beorhtwulf dated from there a genuine charter giving land in Wychwood to Bishop Heahbeorht of Worcester.[15a] The 50 hides at Cropthorne[16] which then comprised the hundred of Cuthbergehlawe were included in the spurious charter of 964, ascribed to King Edgar, granting the hundred of Oswaldslow to the church of Worcester.[17] In 1086 the church held Cropthorne with Netherton.[18]

The manor was confirmed to the prior and convent by Bishop Simon in 1148.[19] King Stephen is said to have freed 5 hides in Cropthorne from taxes.[20] The manors of Cropthorne and Netherton seem to have been leased early in the 13th century to William de Wetmora, for on his death in 1212 they returned to the prior.[21] A grant of free warren here was made to the prior in 1256,[21a] and in 1291 he held 7 caru-cates of land at Cropthorne and Netherton.[22] The prior increased his holding in Cropthorne by various purchases during the 14th century,[23] and in 1355 the grant of free warren was confirmed.[24]

On the dissolution of the priory in 1539–40[25] the manor passed to the Crown and was granted to the dean and chapter in 1542.[26] This grant was confirmed in 1609.[27] The dean and chapter continued to hold the manor of Cropthorne until it was sold under the Commonwealth in 1649 to Thomas Kempe.[28]

The site and demesne lands of the manor were sold in the following year to William Dineley,[29] and his nephew Edward Dineley of Charlton was in possession in 1658,[30] and was dealing with half the site of the manor in 1676–7.[31] At the latter date he was probably a tenant under the dean and chapter, for their estates had been given back to them at the Restoration, and the manor of Crop-thorne was confirmed to them in 1692.[32] The manor remained with the dean and chapter[33] or their

---

[7] Prattinton (Coll. Soc. Antiq.), who visited Cropthorne in 1817, gives a full description of the chapel. At that period the north wall of the chancel was intact, and there was a ‘stone bell-turret, capable of holding two bells.’ He also states that there was an ‘additional building added on the north.’ As mentioned above, the floor of this building alone survives at the present day.

[8] Not the Roman road so called.

[9] Prattinton Coll. (Soc. Antiq.), Deeds of D. and C. of Worcester, no. 252.

[10] Chan. Proc. (Ser. 2), bdle. 158, no. 36.   [11] Ibid. bdle. 51, no. 37.

[12] V.C.H. Worcs. i, 194.

[13] Ibid.

[14] Heming, Chartul. (ed. Hearne), i, 95 ; ii, 319 ; Birch, Cart. Sax. i, 327.

[15] Mr. Round supposes that this charter was forged by the monks for production in the dispute with the Abbot of Evesham with regard to Hampton and Bengeworth (V.C.H. Worcs. i, 254–5).

[15a] Birch, op. cit. ii, 6, 7.

[16] In Offa’s grant was included land at Netherton, Elmley, Criddesho, Charlton, Hampton and Bengeworth, together making up 50 or rather 49 hides.

[17] Hale, Reg. of Worc. Priory (Camd. Soc.), 22b ; Heming, op. cit. ii, 519 ; Birch, Cart. Sax. iii, 377.

[18] V.C.H. Worcs. i, 296b. Robert le Despenser held Elmley Castle and Charl-ton of this manor (ibid.), and the Abbot of Evesham held Hampton and Bengeworth (ibid. 297a) in the same way.

[19] Thomas, Surv. of Worc. Cath. App. no. 18.

[20] Heming, op. cit. ii, 526 ; Nash, Hist. of Worcs. i, 271.

[21] Ann. Mon. (Rolls Ser.), iv, 401.

[21a] Cal. Pat. 1354–8, p. 266.

[22] Pope Nich. Tax. (Rec. Com.), 227b.

[23] Adam son of Guy de la Folye granted to the Prior of Worcester a messuage, a carucate of land and 20s. rent in Cropthorne in 1305 (Cal. Pat. 1301–7,

p. 361 ; Chan. Inq. p.m. 33 Edw. I, no. 145 ; Inq. a.q.d. file 52, no. 21) ; John de Bransford gave land in 1336 (Cal. Pat. 1334–8, p. 222 ; Inq. a.q.d. file 228, no. 23) ; and in 1345 Alexander, vicar of the church of Hallow, Richard de Hindlip, chaplain, John de Totenham, chaplain, and John Trenchefoil, clerk, gave 34s. 9d. rent in Cropthorne (Cal. Pat. 1343–5, p. 449).

[24] Cal. Pat. 1354–8, p. 266.

[25] V.C.H. Worcs. ii, 111.

[26] L. and P. Hen. VIII, xvii, g. 71 (29); Pat. 33 Hen. VIII, pt. v. Ralph Parsons was their tenant for life in 1560 (Chan. Proc. [Ser. 2], bdle. 52, no. 26).

[27] Pat. 6 Jas. I, pt. xii, no. 2.

[28] Close, 1649, pt. xiv, no. 15.

[29] Ibid. 1650, pt. xxxiv, no. 23.

[30] Feet of F. Worcs. East. 1658.

[31] Ibid. Mich. 28 Chas. II.

[32] Pat. 4 Will. and Mary, pt. i, no. 6.

[33] Nash, op. cit. i, 271 ; Priv. Act, 19 Geo. III, cap. 33.

CROPTHORNE : NETHERTON CHAPEL, RUINS FROM THE NORTH-WEST

CROPTHORNE CHURCH C. 1810
(*From a Water-colour by Thos. Rickards in Prattinton Collection*)

lessees until 1859, when their estates were transferred to the Ecclesiastical Commissioners.[34] In 1861 the Commissioners sold to Francis Holland, lessee of the Cropthorne Court estate, the reversion of Cropthorne Court manor-house and the lord's interest in certain copyhold lands. In 1864 and 1866 Mr. Holland purchased the Commissioners' interest as lords of the manor in other lands, and his grandson Francis Corbett Holland is now lord of Cropthorne.[35] Up till 1859 a court leet was held yearly for the manor of Cropthorne.

In 1086 there was a mill at Cropthorne which paid 10s. and 20 'stiches' of eels yearly.[36] In 1240 the Prior of Worcester owned a mill there, which paid 35s. and 30 'stiches' of eels yearly,[37] and he had two other mills.[38] In 1261 the prior bought of William de Beauchamp a quarter of a virgate of land and half of two mills at Cropthorne,[39] and this gift was confirmed by John son of Nicholas de Pebbesworth, who had sold the mills to William de Beauchamp.[40] The mill of Cropthorne is again mentioned in the time of Queen Elizabeth,[41] and there is still a water corn-mill to the north of the village.

CHARLTON (Ceorletune, viii, xii cent. ; Chereleton, xiii cent. ; Cherlinton, xiv, xv cent.) was included in King Offa's probably spurious charter of 780 granting Cropthorne to the church of Worcester.[42] Heming the monk in his chartulary says that the *villa* called Ceorlatun belonged to the church of Worcester, half of it being held by the monks, and the other half, though possessed by strangers, owing service to the monastery. He goes on to say that the latter part which the Frenchmen possessed— namely, 7 hides—had been leased to a certain rich man for three lives, and after his death was held by his son, who was succeeded by a certain Godric, surnamed Finc. After his death Bishop Wulfstan received it back again, and because certain of the Normans who invaded the estates of the English strove to oppose him he went to the king and gave him a golden goblet of great worth, and after he had got a writ from the king under his seal he returned and possessed this part of Charlton. Later, however, he tells us, Robert le Despenser, brother of Urse the sheriff, seized it with the assistance of the queen, and so the church lost it, but Robert still professed to be ready and willing to do service to the church for it.[43] In 1086 Robert le Despenser held these 7 hides at Charlton[44] under the manor of Cropthorne. Later

this manor became annexed to the manor of Fladbury, and was held of that manor during the 12th and 13th centuries.[45] In 1541 the manor was said to be held of the manor of Cropthorne,[46] but in 1624 the jurors did not know of whom it was held.[47]

On the death of Robert le Despenser his lands were divided, and the early 12th-century survey of the hundred of Oswaldslow shows Robert Marmion as owner of these 7 hides at Charlton.[48] The overlordship remained in the Marmion family[49] until the death of Sir Philip Marmion about 1292.[50] The Marmions' interest in the manor then seems to have lapsed.

Under the Marmions the manor was held from very early times by the Botelers of Oversley. Robert Boteler held the manor of Robert Marmion about 1182.[51] It was probably his son Ralph who in 1140 endowed the abbey of Alcester with half the tithes of his lordship of Charlton.[52] The mesne lordship of Charlton remained in this family[53] until about 1380, when William Boteler died, leaving a daughter Elizabeth, who married Robert de Ferrers.[54] They were succeeded by their daughter Mary, who married Ralph Nevill.[55] The estate passed from Ralph about 1457–8 to his son John Nevill,[56] who died in 1482,[57] leaving as his heir Sir William Gascoigne, son of his daughter Joan[58] and William Gascoigne.[59] In 1484–5 Sir William brought an action against Robert Throckmorton and John Hardwyk on a 'plea why they took away William Dineley a minor,' son and heir of William Dineley, who had been seised of the manor of Charlton and had held it as of the manor of Oversley by the service of a knight's fee.[60] This is the last mention of the Gascoignes' interest in the manor.

The manor of Charlton does not seem to have been held by the Botelers in demesne. As early as the 12th century Robert son of Hubert held the manor of Robert Boteler.[61] Nothing more is known of the tenants of the manor until 1240, when William de Handsacre held it.[62] In 1267–8 he was accused of carrying off the goods of Thomas de Arderne from this manor.[63] William did not appear to answer the plea, and the sheriff was commanded to take all his lands and tenements into the king's hands.[64] William had evidently fallen under the king's displeasure before this time, for in 1266 he was granted a safe conduct coming to the king's court to stand his trial.[65] William paid a subsidy of 30s. at Cropthorne in 1280,[66] and

[34] *Lond. Gaz.* 16 Dec. 1859, p. 4757, confirmed by Stat. 31 & 32 Vict. cap. 19.
[35] Inform. by the late Mr. J. H. Hooper and the Ecclesiastical Commissioners.
[36] *V.C.H. Worcs.* i, 296b. There were twenty-five eels to a 'stiche.'
[37] The parson of Cropthorne received the tithes of the mill and eels.
[38] Hale, *Reg. of Worc. Priory* (Camd. Soc.), 70a. There is a charter in this register by which the prior and convent granted to Hugh de Furches a virgate of land in Cropthorne in exchange for the moiety of the mill in Cropthorne and the land which attached to it, Hugh paying the priory 8s. a year. This charter is undated (ibid. 73b).
[39] *Ann. Mon.* (Rolls Ser.), iv, 447.
[40] Prattinton Coll. (Soc. Antiq.), Deeds of D. and C. of Worc. no. 207 ; Add. MS. 28024, fol. 128a.
[41] Chan. Proc. Eliz. Pp. 2, no. 35.
[42] Birch, *Cart. Sax.* i, 327 ; Heming, op. cit. i, 70 ; and see *ante*.

[43] Heming, op. cit. i, 268–9.
[44] *V.C.H. Worcs.* i, 296b and n. ; J. H. Round, *Feud. Engl.* 176.
[45] Habington, *Surv. of Worcs.* (Worcs. Hist. Soc.), i, 226 ; *Testa de Nevill* (Rec. Com.), 41b ; *Worcs. Inq. p.m.* (Worcs. Hist. Soc.), i, 42.
[46] Chan. Inq. p.m. (Ser. 2), lxiv, 103.
[47] Ibid. ccccxxiii, 74.
[48] *V.C.H. Worcs.* i, 325b n.
[49] For a pedigree of the Marmions see Round, op. cit. 191.
[50] Round, loc. cit. ; *Worcs. Inq. p.m.* (Worcs. Hist. Soc.), i, 42 ; Habington, op. cit. i, 226. Lady Avice de Charlton, who held the manor early in the 13th century (*Testa de Nevill* [Rec. Com.], 41b), was probably the widow of Robert Marmion.
[51] Habington, op. cit. i, 226 ; Red Bk. of Bishopric of Worc. (Eccl. Com. Rec. Var. bdle. 121, no. 43698), fol. 81, 253.
[52] Dugdale, *Hist. of Warw.* 854 ; Dugdale, *Mon.* iv, 172, 175. In 1240 these tithes were still paid to the abbey (Hale,

Reg. of Worc. Priory [Camd. Soc.], 70a), and are last mentioned in 1291, when they were worth £7 6s. 8d. (*Pope Nich. Tax.* [Rec. Com.], 217b).
[53] *Worcs. Inq. p.m.* (Worcs. Hist. Soc.), i, 42.
[54] Dugdale, *Hist. of Warw.* 854.
[55] Ibid.
[56] Chan. Inq. p.m. 36 Hen. VI, no. 21.
[57] Ibid. 22 Edw. IV, no. 26.
[58] Ibid. ; De Banco R. Trin. 2 Ric. III, m. 317.
[59] De Banco R. Trin. 2 Ric. III, m. 317.
[60] Ibid.
[61] Red Bk. of Bishopric of Worc. fol. 253.
[62] Hale, *Reg. of Worc. Priory* (Camd. Soc.), 70a.
[63] *Abbrev. Plac.* (Rec. Com.), 170b, 175b.
[64] Ibid. 175b.
[65] *Cal. Pat.* 1258–66, p. 533.
[66] *Lay Subs. R. Worcs.* 1280 (Worcs. Hist. Soc.), 71.

was holding the manor in 1292 and in 1299.[67] Sir Simon Handsacre, possibly his son, is said to have been lord of Charlton in 1331–2,[68] and William de Handsacre was in possession in 1346.[69] Sir Simon, who succeeded William, died before 1383–4, leaving three daughters, Eleanor wife of Richard Dineley, Elizabeth wife of Roger Colmon, and afterwards of Peter de Melburn, and Isabel wife of Lawrence Frodley.[70] Richard Dineley and Elizabeth were dealing with a third of the manor in 1386–7,[71] and three years later the co-heirs conveyed the manor to

HANDSACRE. *Ermine three chess-rooks sable.*

DINELEY. *Argent a fesse sable with a molet between two roundels sable in the chief.*

trustees,[72] evidently for the purpose of settling it on the Dineleys, to whom the whole afterwards passed.

A pedigree of the family of Dineley is given in the Worcestershire visitation of 1569.[73] According to this pedigree Thomas Dineley, who held Charlton in 1431,[74] was the son of Richard and Eleanor. Thomas married a member of the family of Throckmorton,[75] and seems to have settled Charlton upon himself and his wife.[76] He was succeeded by a son and grandson, both named William.[77] The latter was a minor in 1484–5,[78] and in 1498 was in controversy with the Prior of Worcester as to common of pasture in Penmere.[79] In 1514 he settled the manor on his son John on his marriage with Elizabeth Tate, daughter of Roger St. Nicholas of Thanet.[80] John died in 1541, when his son Sir Henry succeeded to the manor.[81] He was Sheriff of Worcestershire in 1553 and 1568.[82] On 5 July 1575 Henry Dineley settled the manor on his son Francis on his marriage with Elizabeth Bigge, daughter of Thomas Bigge of Lenchwick.[83] Francis Dineley, who was Sheriff of Worcester in 1597,[84] died 28 October 1624 seised of the manor of Charlton, his heir being his grandson Edward, son of his elder son Henry.[85] Edward died

in 1646,[86] and his son and successor Samuel died about 1654, leaving two daughters, Mary, who afterwards married Henry Collins, and Elizabeth wife of Whitlock Bulstrode.[87] In 1674 Mary Dineley conveyed her moiety of the manor to her uncle Edward Dineley,[88] who acquired the other moiety in 1676 from Whitlock Bulstrode and Elizabeth.[89]

Edward Dineley was knighted in 1681,[90] and served as Deputy Lieutenant for Worcestershire in 1682.[91] His daughter and heir Helen or Eleanor married Edward Goodere of Burhope in Herefordshire, who was created a baronet in 1707 and died in 1739, at the age of nearly ninety.[92] He was followed by his eldest surviving son John, who having succeeded to the Charlton estates took the name of Dineley about 1708.[93] He married Mary daughter and heir of — Lawford of Stapleton in Gloucestershire,[94] by whom he had a son, who joined with him in disentailing the estate and died soon afterwards.[95] Samuel Goodere, who was a captain in the Royal Navy and at that time commanded a ship called the *Ruby,* expected to inherit the manor from his brother Sir John Dineley, but the latter threatened to disinherit him and leave his property to his nephew John Foote of Truro in Cornwall, the son of his sister Eleanor.

It so alarmed and disgusted the said Samuel that he came to the bloody resolution of murdering him, which he executed on the 17th Jan. 1741. A friend at Bristol who knew their mortal antipathy had invited them both to dinner, in hopes of reconciling them, and they parted in the evening in seeming friendship, but the captain placed some of his crew in the street near College Green with orders to seize his brother, and assisted in hurrying him by violence to his ship, under pretence that he was disordered in his senses, where when they arrived he caused him to be strangled in the cabin by White and Mahony, two ruffians of his crew, himself standing sentinel at the door while the horrid deed was perpetrated.[96]

But the cooper of the ship and his wife happened to be in the next cabin, and by the help of an open crevice saw the whole transaction.[97]

Samuel Goodere and his accomplices, Mahony and White, were arrested, and, having been tried in Bristol on 26 March and found guilty, were executed on 15 April 1741.[98] John Foote succeeded his uncle and took the name of Dineley. He was dealing with the manor in 1741 and 1745,[99] but Dame Mary Dineley-Goodere, Sir John's widow, held the Charlton estate in dower [100] and married William Rayner, a printer in White Friars, London. He alleged that he became owner of the manor of Charlton by the purchase from John Foote-Dineley of his reversionary

[67] *Worcs. Inq. p.m.* (Worcs. Hist. Soc.), i, 42 ; Habington, op. cit. i, 228.
[68] *Visit. of Worcs.* 1569 (Harl. Soc. xxvii), 50.
[69] *Feud. Aids,* v, 309.
[70] De Banco R. 491, m. 204 d.
[71] Feet of F. Div. Co. Mich. and East. 10 Ric. II.
[72] Ibid. East. 13 Ric. II.
[73] op. cit. (Harl. Soc. xxvii), 50.
[74] *Feud. Aids,* v, 332.
[75] *Visit. of Worcs.* 1569 (Harl. Soc. xxvii), 50.
[76] De Banco R. Trin. 2 Ric. III, m. 317.
[77] Ibid.
[78] Ibid.
[79] Ibid. Hil. 14 Hen. VII, m. 416.
[80] Chan. Inq. p.m. (Ser. 2), lxiv, 103.
[81] Ibid.

[82] P.R.O. *List of Sheriffs,* 158.
[83] Feet of F. Div. Co. Mich. 17 & 18 Eliz. ; Chan. Inq. p.m. (Ser. 2), ccccxxiii, 74.
[84] P.R.O. *List of Sheriffs,* 158.
[85] Chan. Inq. p.m. (Ser. 2), ccccxxiii, 74.
[86] Metcalfe, *Visit. of Worcs.* 1682, p. 42.
[87] Ibid.
[88] Ibid. ; Feet of F. Worcs. Hil. 25 & 26 Chas. II.
[89] Feet of F. Worcs. Mich. 28 Chas. II.
[90] Shaw, *Knights of Engl.* ii, 256.
[91] Nash, op. cit. i, 272.
[92] G.E.C. *Complete Baronetage,* v, 5.
[93] Ibid.
[94] She later set up a fraudulent claim to the Charlton estate (as his widow) on behalf of an alleged surviving son (J.

Latimer, *Annals of Bristol in the Eighteenth Century,* 233–4).
[95] G.E.C. *Complete Baronetage,* v, 5.
[96] Nash, op. cit. i, 272–3.
[97] *The Bristol Fratricide,* printed by J. Hart, 1741, p. 11.
[98] There is in the library of the British Museum a full report of the trial published by H. Goreham. *The History of the Life and Character of Samuel Goodere, the Bristol Fratricide,* and *The Fratricide, or the Murderer's Gibbet,* published at the *Bristol Mirror* office in 1839, also refer to this case.
[99] Recov. R. Hil. 15 Geo. II, rot. 193 ; Mich. 19 Geo. II, rot. 468.
[100] Sir John Dineley, the fifth and last baronet, who was insane, described himself as of Charlton (*Dict. Nat. Biog.*), but had no claim to the estate.

interest, and sold it to Joseph Biddle of Evesham,[100a] from whose executors it was purchased in 1774 by Thomas Beesley, Richard Sockett, William Lilly, and Timothy Bevington of Worcester.[1] They or their descendants were the owners in 1775–6,[2] and in 1787 Thomas Beesley, Timothy Bevington, Richard Sockett, Thomas Griffith, clerk, and Thomas Brewster conveyed the manor to John Sparling, Robert Rolleston and Thomas Barton.[3]

About this time one wing of the manor-house was burnt down. In 1825 Robert Dent was the owner.[4] The manor had been purchased before 1868 by Henry Workman,[5] who sold it in 1873 to William Carey Faulkner. His second son James Faulkner is now lord of the manor.

The other half of the vill of Charlton which was said by Heming to have been kept by the church of Worcester was probably included at the time of the Domesday Survey in the manor of Cropthorne. It may, however, have been the land at Charlton which, having been lost by the college of Westbury, was restored in 1093 by Bishop Wulfstan when he refounded the college and made it subject to the church of Worcester.[6] Charlton was, however, confirmed to the prior and convent by Bishop Simon in 1148,[7] and formed part of the manor of Cropthorne in 1240.[8] On the dissolution of the priory in 1539–40[9] the manor of Charlton was granted to the dean and chapter.[10] · The grant was confirmed in 1608–9,[11] and in 1641 the dean and chapter granted a lease of the manor to Edward Dineley for the lives of his children, John, Edward, and Joyce.[12] In 1649 this manor was sold by the Parliamentary commissioners to William Dineley,[13] the uncle of Edward Dineley of Charlton, but was recovered by the dean and chapter, to whom it was confirmed in 1692.[14] The manor remained with them until the manorial rights lapsed, the last mention of it being in 1779.[15] It was then held under a lease from the dean and chapter by Mr. Dineley, and was not easily distinguishable from the other manor of Charlton, since the lands of the two manors were intermixed.[16]

An estate at Charlton was held by the nuns of Pinley in Warwickshire. There is no record of any grant to them of this land, but in 1291 they held rents of assize at Charlton,[17] and in 1535 their estate there and at Beoley was valued at 30s. 4d. yearly.[18]

These lands, which fell to the Crown at the Dissolution, were granted to Henry Best in 1589–90.[19]

NETHERTON (Neotheretune, viii cent. ; Neotheretune, xi cent.) is included with Cropthorne in King Offa's supposed forged grant of 780 to the church of Worcester,[20] and at the date of the Domesday Survey the church held Netherton.[21] In the Register of the priory of 1240 it is stated that Netherton 'gelded' with Cropthorne, and that there were 2 carucates in demesne.[22] In the Taxation of 1291 Netherton is included in Cropthorne.[23] In 1255–6 the prior obtained a grant of free warren at Netherton, and it was confirmed in 1355.[24] After the dissolution of the priory in 1539–40[25] the manor of Netherton was granted in 1542 to the Dean and Chapter of Worcester,[26] and this grant was confirmed to them in 1609.[27]

In 1549–50 the manor was granted by the dean and chapter to George Willoughby at a fee-farm rent of £20 8s. 2d.[28] This rent was sold by the Parliamentary trustees in 1655 to Richard Salwey,[29] but was restored to the dean and chapter at the Restoration, and was still held by them in 1779.[30] After the death of George Willoughby the manor passed to his widow Anne Willoughby.[31] She married as a third husband Sir Francis Bulstrode, who was concerned in several suits in Chancery as to this estate.[32] Sir Francis Bulstrode and Anne his wife and Paul Raynsford, who had married Frances second daughter of George Willoughby,[33] sold the manor to Henry Willoughby in 1569–70.[34] He sold it to William Savage of Elmley Castle in 1591–2.[35] The manor then followed the same descent as that of Elmley Castle[36] until the manorial rights lapsed, the last mention of it being in 1822, when Robert Clavering Savage was the owner.[37]

CHURCHES

The church of *ST. MICHAEL* consists of a chancel about 34 ft. by 14½ ft., nave 47 ft. by the same width, north and south aisles 9½ ft. and 9 ft. wide respectively, south porch, and a western tower 11 ft. square. These measurements are all internal.

The earliest portion of the present building was begun about the year 1100, and appears to have been a rebuilding of an earlier structure, beginning with the north arcade and aisle, followed soon afterwards by those on the south side. About 1170 the chancel

[100a] It was contended that no rights passed in this sale, as Samuel Goodere when in prison on the charge of murder accepted surrender of all leases and regranted them on payment of very light fines. After long litigation the court annulled the contention, holding that while in treason the attainder dated from the commission of the offence, in felony it begins with the actual sentence.

[1] Nash, op. cit. i, 273. Included in the sale were the mansion-house and over 1,000 acres of land. The soil is said to be 'chiefly of the best of that kind which farmers call Turnep Land' (Prattinton Coll. [Soc. Antiq.]).

[2] Priv. Act, 16 Geo. III, cap. 47.
[3] Feet of F. Worcs. Hil. 27 Geo. III.
[4] Recov. R. Hil. 5 & 6 Geo. IV, rot. 138.   [5] Noake, op. cit. 104.
[6] Heming, op. cit. 422.
[7] Thomas, op. cit. App. no. 18.
[8] Reg. of Worc. Priory (Camd. Soc.), 70a, 71a.
[9] V.C.H. Worcs. ii, 111.

[10] Pat. 33 Hen. VIII, pt. v ; L. and P. Hen. VIII, xvii, g. 71 (29).
[11] Pat. 6 Jas. I, pt. xii, no. 2.
[12] Close, 1650, pt. xxxiv, no. 23.
[13] Ibid.
[14] Pat. 4 Will. and Mary, pt. i, no. 6.
[15] Nash, op. cit. i, 273. The dean and chapter are mentioned as lords of one of the manors of Charlton in the Inclosure Act for Charlton dated 1775–6 (Priv. Act, 16 Geo. III, cap. 47).
[16] Nash, op. cit. i, 273.
[17] Pope Nich. Tax. (Rec. Com.), 230. The entry is cancelled and against it is written 'hoc est error quia pauper et mendicans.'
[18] Valor Eccl. (Rec. Com.), iii, 90.
[19] Pat. 32 Eliz. pt. ix.
[20] Heming, op. cit. i, 95 ; ii, 319 ; and see ante note.
[21] V.C.H. Worcs. i, 296b.
[22] Reg. of Worc. Priory (Camd. Soc.), 72b.
[23] Pope Nich. Tax. (Rec. Com.), 227b. The place is here spelt 'Setherton,' and

each carucate is said to be worth £1 a year (ibid.).
[24] Cal. Pat. 1354–8, p. 266.
[25] V.C.H. Worcs. ii, 111.
[26] Pat. 33 Hen. VIII, pt. v.
[27] Ibid. 6 Jas. I, pt. xii, no. 2.
[28] Ibid. 3 Edw. VI, pt. ix ; Close, 1656, pt. xii, no. 2.
[29] Close, 1656, pt. xii, no. 2.
[30] Nash, op. cit. i, 273.
[31] Chan. Proc. (Ser. 2), bdle. 4, no. 37, 57.
[32] Ibid. bdles. 148, no. 16 ; 4, no. 37, 57 ; 186, no. 94 ; 5, no. 8.
[33] Ibid. bdle. 148, no. 16.
[34] Feet of F. Div. Co. Trin. 12 Eliz.
[35] Ibid. Worcs. Hil. 34 Eliz. The sale was confirmed by Robert Willoughby in the following year (ibid. East. 35 Eliz.).
[36] Chan. Inq. p.m. (Ser. 2), ccclvi, 121 ; cccclxvii, 186 ; Feet of F. Div. Co. Mich. 21 Chas. II. For the pedigree of the Savages see Elmley Castle.
[37] Recov. R. Hil. 2 & 3 Geo. IV, rot. 123.

arch was inserted, and a few years later the tower added, the chancel being rebuilt and widened about 1200. The church stood thus, with chancel, nave with narrow aisles, and west tower, till the middle of the 14th century, when the chancel was again rebuilt and the nave aisles widened.

Late in the 15th century the church seems to have been much altered, and it is not improbable, from the character of the bases, that the north arcade was then rebuilt with the old stones before the clearstory was added. The tower also was raised to its present height, with the intention of adding a spire, but the last work was never carried out. The south porch seems to be the work of a later date, probably with older materials, and in the 18th century the north range of clearstory windows was renewed in the 'churchwarden' style of the time. In 1894 the chancel was rebuilt with the old materials, and the church also underwent restorations in 1900 and 1903, and a further one has lately been completed.

The three-light east window has modern tracery, but the jambs belong to the 14th century. On either side are plain brackets in the east wall, and in the northeast corner is a square plastered recess with a shelf.

In the north wall is a small lancet window dating from about the year 1200, and on the south side are three square-headed windows, each of two lights; the heads of the two eastern are modern, while the third is of later date than the chancel. Under the easternmost window is a 13th-century piscina in the form of a round moulded capital.

The chancel arch has 12th-century jambs, of two orders, the inner with an engaged shaft on the west angle. The outer order has been cut away on the west face. The engaged shafts have scalloped capitals, but the arch, of two chamfered orders, is of much later date and is very unevenly built, and above it the wall is set back on the west face.

The north arcade of the nave consists of four bays with circular piers and semicircular arches of two square orders. The western respond, and the second pier from it, have meagre 12th-century moulded capitals, but the others are apparently later copies. The south arcade is also of four bays and has half-round arches of two orders, and circular piers with moulded capitals and bases differing somewhat from those opposite. The tower arch has jambs and a pointed arch of two chamfered orders with a square and chamfered abacus carved with tooth ornament.

In the clearstory on the north side are three large plain windows with square panes and arched heads, of 18th-century design. On the south side the three windows, of late 15th-century date, are each of two lights with blank spandrels within a square internal head and an external elliptical head. The square-headed east window of the north aisle is of three lights, and the two windows in the north wall are of two lights under square heads, differing slightly in design. The 14th-century north doorway has a two-centred chamfered arch, considerably restored.

The east window of the south aisle differs but slightly from that of the north, and the three side windows are each of two ogee-headed lights. The 14th-century south doorway has a two-centred arch of one chamfered order. The remains of an old piscina basin still exist in the south-east corner of the south aisle, with an arch over, of much later date. In the east wall is a square recess with rebated jambs.

A large groove in the north wall of the aisle, next to the east wall, seems to suggest that the wall has been reconstructed east of its original position.

The south porch seems to have been much altered in the late 15th century. The outer doorway has jambs and an elliptical arch of two continuous chamfered orders. In the side walls are narrow rectangular lights, the western one being blocked. The diagonal buttresses are modern, and the wall over the archway finishes abruptly with a plain horizontal parapet in front of the gabled roof.

The tower is of three stages, the lower two dating from the 12th century and the upper being a late 15th-century addition. The lowest stage has shallow buttresses in the middle of the three outer walls. They reach only to the first offset and are pierced by small round-headed windows, with wide splays inside. The second stage has a small round-headed 12th-century light in its west wall. The belfry is lit by transomed windows of two lights with vertical tracery, the lights beneath the transoms having trefoiled heads and quatrefoil spandrels. The labels are returned round the tower as a horizontal string at the transom level. The parapet is embattled with continuous coping and grotesque gargoyles. At the angles are small square pinnacles. The walling of the church generally is rubble with dressed quoins, &c., parts of it being rough-cast.

The chancel has a modern open timbered roof, while the nave and aisles have plastered ceilings.

The font is also modern. Some of the traceried bench ends and front and back panelling to the nave seats date from the 15th century.

There are several large tombs in the church. The most prominent, to Edward Dineley, 1646, is placed askew in the first bay of the north arcade, and is of Renaissance design, with kneeling figures under a flat canopy, supported on marble columns of the Corinthian order. On the front face of the base are the kneeling figures of four sons and three daughters in high relief. Above the canopy is a cleft pediment with a shield bearing the Dineley arms impaling those of his wife. The pedestals at the angles also support shields. The tomb is evidently not in its original position, and was probably removed from the chancel.

At the east end of the north aisle is another altar tomb to Francis Dineley, died 1624, with recumbent effigies of a man and woman, the former in armour. On the base are the kneeling figures of nine sons and seven daughters, and cradles for three children, who died in infancy.

In the north wall, to the west of the first window, is a 14th-century tomb recess with a flattened ogee arch, enriched with ball flowers. The arch springs from square blocks of stone supported on carved corbels, and at the apex is a human head. In the recess is an ancient slab carved with a long round-headed cross, a hand and a chalice, but it is apparently not in the original position. There are many other slabs of 18th-century date and other modern wall monuments.

There are six bells : the first by Abel Rudhall, 1746 ; the second, 1898, by Bond ; the third, 1703 ; the fourth by Abel Rudhall, 1750 ; the fifth by Bond, 1898, and the sixth by Rudhall, 1746.

The plate consists of a very small cup of 1571 with a cover paten without a hall mark, but inscribed

CROPTHORNE CHURCH FROM THE SOUTH-WEST

CROPTHORNE CHURCH : THE NAVE LOOKING NORTH-EAST

1571, and a plated modern set of a cup, two plates, standing paten and a flagon.

The registers are as follows : (i) mixed entries 1557 to 1717 and burials 1752 to 1754; (ii) baptisms and burials 1718 to 1812, marriages 1718 to 1756 ; (iii) marriages 1754 to 1801 ; (iv) marriages 1801 to 1812.

The modern church of *ST. JOHN THE EVAN-GELIST*, Charlton, is a small rectangular building of stone, designed in the style of the 13th century. It was converted from an old barn by Mr. Workman and was opened by licence in 1872.[38] The ecclesiastical parish of Charlton was formed from Cropthorne in 1882, and the church was consecrated in the following year.[39] The patronage was vested in Henry Workman for life, and then in the Bishop of Worcester.[40]

ADVOWSON   In 1086 there was a priest at Cropthorne, who had half a hide with one plough.[41] The Prior and convent of Worcester were patrons of Cropthorne until the Dissolution.[42]

In 1350 the prior and convent received a licence from the Crown to appropriate the church of Cropthorne, according to a Bull of Pope Clement.[43] The vicarage was ordained in 1365.[44] In 1427–8 the church was valued at £7 6s. 8d.,[45] and it was worth £21 4s. 8d. in 1535.[46] After the dissolution of the priory in 1539–40,[47] the advowson of the church of Cropthorne was granted to the Dean and Chapter of Worcester in 1542.[48] This grant was confirmed in 1609,[49] and the dean and chapter have presented ever since,[50] with the exception of once in 1642, when they granted the presentation to Francis Kite and Stephen Richardson for that turn only.[51]

Chapels at Charlton and Netherton, which belonged to the church of Cropthorne, are mentioned in the 13th century.[52] This seems to be the only reference to them in the records. Netherton chapel was in ruins in the middle of the 17th century,[53] and some remains of it can still be seen in a farm-house at Netherton (see above).

There is a mission Baptist chapel at Charlton in connexion with Cowl Street, Evesham.

CHARITIES   The Widow Lye's Charity.—It appears from the church table in the parish of All Saints in Evesham that the Widow Lye gave a tenement in Cowl Street, the rent to be distributed in bread to the poor of the parish of St. Lawrence and the town of Cropthorne for ever. A sum of about £9 10s. is annually received from Evesham St. Lawrence, which is applied in the distribution of bread and money.

Holland's School.—In 1735 Mrs. Mary Holland, by her will, bequeathed £50 to be laid out in building a schoolhouse. The testatrix likewise bequeathed £200 as an endowment.

The trust property now consists of the old schoolhouse and garden and 1 r. 20 p., producing £10 per annum, and £175 13s. 2d. consols with the official trustees, producing £4 7s. 8d. yearly.

The church land consists of 2 a. of land which has been in the possession of the parish from time immemorial. The rents, amounting to £1 15s. yearly, are carried to the churchwardens' accounts.

CROWLE

Croh Lea, Crohleye (ix cent.) ; Crohlea, Croelai (xi cent.) ; Croulega (xii cent.) ; Crauley, Croley (xiii cent.) ; Croull (xiv cent.) ; Croll (xv cent.) ; Crowley, Crolle, Crowel (xvi cent.).

The parish of Crowle is bounded on the south and west by Crowle Brook, a tributary of Bow Brook, which runs from north to south through the centre of the parish. Its area is 1,735 acres,[1] of which 481 are arable, 895 are permanent grass, and 104 acres are woodland.[2] The land rises from the Bow Brook in the east to a height of over 200 ft. above the ordnance datum near the western boundary. The subsoil is Lower Lias, and the chief crops are wheat and beans.

The inclosure award for Crowle is dated 9 August 1808[3] under an authorizing Act of 1806.[4]

Habington, in his Survey, says of the village of Crowle that it 'lyethe between the vale of Evesham and the woodland, deep in the one and warme by the other.'[5] The church is at the south end of the village, which extends for about a quarter of a mile north-wards along the road from Broughton Hackett. This road then joins that leading westwards to Worcester and eastwards in the direction of Himbleton. Here are the green and the Chequers Inn, a modernized building of little interest. There is some half-timber work in the main street of the village, which possesses no remarkable features.

Crowle Court, the manor-house of the Priors of Worcester, was destroyed about 1864. It was surrounded by a moat, still remaining, and is supposed to have been built in the 13th century and rebuilt on the old foundations shortly before Prior Moore's time. It included a chapel and tithe-barn. A portion of the house remained in 1868 and was then used as a cider-house.[6]

Habington mentions a coffin found in Crowle ' made of a Burford stone beeinge the best of England and covered with the same lyinge Southe and Northe whearein weare the bones or rather dust of a man upon a sheete of leade and sheetes of leade by his sydes with an earthen pychar at hys heade, hys stature

[38] *P.O. Dir. Worcs.* 1872.

[39] *Parl. Papers* (1890–1), lxi, no. 386, p. 38 ; *Lond. Gaz.* 22 Aug. 1882, p. 3911.

[40] *Lond. Gaz.* 22 Aug. 1882, p. 3911.

[41] *V.C.H. Worcs.* i, 296b.

[42] *Ann. Mon.* (Rolls Ser.), iv, 428, 434, 539 ; *Reg. G. Giffard* (Worcs. Hist. Soc.), 507 ; ibid. *W. Ginsborough*, 145 ; *Cal. Pat.* 1348–50, p. 573.

[43] *Cal. Pat.* 1348–50, p. 573 ; *Cal. Papal Pet.* i, 195 ; *Cal. Papal Letters*, iii, 334 ; Heming, op. cit. ii 544 ; *Hist.*

MSS. Com. Rep. xiv, App. viii, 168. Nash gives the licence and the Bull in full (op. cit. i, 276–7).

[44] Worc. Epis. Reg. Carpenter (1443–76), i, fol. 193.

[45] *Lay Subs. R. Worcs.* 1427, 1429 (Worcs. Hist. Soc.), 11.

[46] *Valor Eccl.* (Rec. Com.), iii, 222.

[47] *V.C.H. Worcs.* ii, 111.

[48] *L. and P. Hen. VIII*, xvii, g. 71 (29); Pat. 33 Hen. VIII, pt. v.

[49] Pat. 6 Jas. I, pt. xii, no. 2.

[50] Inst. Bks. (P.R.O.).

[51] Ibid.

[52] Hale, *Reg. of Worc. Priory* (Camd Soc.), 70a.

[53] Habington, op. cit. i, 180.

[1] Of these 3 acres are covered by water.

[2] Statistics from Bd. of Agric. (1905).

[3] *Blue Bk. Incl. Awards*, 189.

[4] Priv. Act, 46 Geo. III, cap. 49.

[5] *Surv. of Worcs.* (Worcs. Hist. Soc.), i, 532.

[6] Noake, *Guide to Worcs.* 107.

not extraordinary for the coffin was little more then syx foote in lengthe, but hee excelled in authority who was not onely interred in leade but allso in a stony coffyn brought from Burford in Oxfordshyre. This greate personage was by all lykelihoode a Dane.'[7]

Place-names which occur in connexion with this parish in the 17th century are Impey, Bredicott Piece,[8] Mill Meadow, Lott Meadow, Crimnell Withies Close.[9]

MANORS Five *mansae* at CROWLE were given to Eadberht, Bishop of Worcester (822–46), by Beortulf, King of Mercia.[10] The boundaries of these five *mansae* extended from Crohwella to Maidenbridge; from there all round Snoddeslea to Hymelbrook; from Hymelbrook to Honeybourn and thence to Godinges boundary at Bredicot; thence to the drain (sice) at Crowle Wood and from that drain to Oddingley Wood; along the old inclosure place (aldan geard stealles) to Huddington boundary and thence east to Crohwell.[11] Bishop Eadberht bestowed this estate upon the priory of Worcester.[12]

As has already been remarked, the reference to the boundary of Goding's land shows that these boundaries cannot be contemporary with Beortulf of Mercia. The language of the charter is very inflated —too inflated to be easily assigned to this early date— and the terms of the grant are not easily reconciled with the reference to Crowle made in a grant of undoubted authenticity issued a few years earlier. In 836 King Wiglaf of Mercia granted certain liberties to the monastery of Hanbury. Gifts of land were made by the Bishop of Worcester to the king and to two ealdormen who obviously would suffer from the grant of immunities to Hanbury. In particular Mucel the ealdorman, otherwise described as Mucel the son of Esne (Mucel Esninz), received 10 hides at Crowle.[12a] This fact is of great interest, for this Mucel may fairly be identified with the father of Ealdorman Æthelred, surnamed Mucel, whose daughter married King Alfred. We thus obtain a hint as to the local position of the Gaini over whom the second Mucel was ealdorman, a standing crux in old English topography. It is only reasonable to assume that the second Mucel succeeded to the same ealdormanry as his father, and that Hanbury lay within the latter's government. Later evidence[12b] connects the family with the Severn valley. It is natural to conclude that the territory of the Gaini included part of the later Worcestershire.[12c]

During the rule of the Danes Crowle was divided into two parts, of which Simund, a Dane by birth, and a thegn of Earl Leofric, held one,[13] the other being apportioned to the support of the monks of Worcester. Simund, coveting the monks' portion, harried it, was impleaded for doing so, and finally at the entreaty of Earl Leofric obtained it for his life from Prior Ethelwine, agreeing to serve the monastery in expeditions by land and sea and to pay annually some pecuniary acknowledgement or a horse to the prior.[14] This service seems to have been transferred to the Bishop of Worcester, for in the Domesday Survey it is stated that Simund had rendered for the manor service and geld to the bishop, and could not transfer his services.[15] It seems not improbable that the priory, by this grant to Simund, lost the manor, for it is said to have been given to them by Bishop Wulfstan.[16]

In 1086 the monks of Worcester held 5 hides at Crowle as a berewick of their manor of Phepson.[17] Attached to this manor was a salt-pan at Droitwich worth 3s., and woodland half a league long and 1 furlong wide, lying in the king's forest.[18] Though the monks of Worcester seem at this time to have been overlords of the manor and still were in the time of Henry I,[19] it afterwards became separated from Phepson, and was annexed in the reign of Henry II to the bishop's manor of Northwick,[20] the monks once more losing their rights of overlordship. Successive bishops continued to be overlords until the middle of the 14th century, the overlordship being mentioned for the last time in 1336.[21]

Under the priory of Worcester the manor was held in 1086 by Roger de Lacy.[22] Roger was banished in 1091–2 and succeeded at Crowle by his brother Hugh.[23] In the Domesday Book of the bishopric (temp. Henry II) Hugh de Lacy, probably grand-nephew of Roger and Hugh above named, was tenant immediately under the bishop,[24] but since that time the Lacys' interest in the manor has not been traced.

Under the Lacys Crowle was held in 1086 by one Odo.[25] His interest had passed before 1182 to Hugh Tirel, who then held the manor under Hugh Lacy.[26] In 1194 Eudes Tirel paid 5 marks for having judgement in the king's court against Roger Tirel for a knight's fee in Crowle.[27] Richard Tirel held the estate early in the 13th century, apparently immediately of the Bishop of Worcester,[28] and in 1213 Richard son of Roger Tirel gave a palfrey for having a 'precipe' against Richard Tirel for a knight's fee in Crowle.[29] At about this time the manor must have passed to Stephen Devreux, whether by descent or by a grant from the Crown is not known, for in 1214 Stephen obtained licence to assart 40 acres in his wood of Crowle.[30] This grant was perhaps made to Stephen in recognition of his services with the king in Poitou.[31] In 1214 he was acquitted of scutage for one fee

[7] op. cit. i, 136. Nash mentions this and says that Dr. Thomas imagined this person to be Simund the Dane (*Hist. of Worcs.* i, 282).
[8] Close, 1650, pt. xvi, no. 1.
[9] Ibid. 1658, pt. xxxvi, no. 5.
[10] Birch, *Cart. Sax.* ii, 1; Heming, *Chartul.* (ed. Hearne), 345–6.
[11] Ibid.
[12] Heming, op. cit. 572; *Ann. Mon.* (Rolls Ser.), iv, 563.
[12a] Birch, op. cit. i, 581–3.
[12b] Ibid. ii, 218.
[12c] The above paragraph is from information supplied by Mr. F. M. Stenton.

[13] For descent of this part see Froxmere Court.
[14] Heming, op. cit. 264; *V.C.H. Worcs.* i, 297, n. 10.
[15] *V.C.H. Worcs.* i, 297.
[16] Thomas, *Surv. of Cath. Church of Worc.* S 14, 32. The gift was registered in the sixth window of the west cloister of Worcester Cathedral.
[17] *V.C.H. Worcs.* i, 297.
[18] Ibid.   [19] Ibid. 326.
[20] Habington, op. cit. ii, 41, 42; i, 134; *Testa de Nevill* (Rec. Com.), 41b; Red Bk. of Bishopric of Worc. (Eccl. Com. Rec. Var. bdle. 121, no. 43698), fol. 18.

[21] Worc. Epis. Reg. Montacute (1333–7), fol. 29.
[22] *V.C.H. Worcs.* i, 297.
[23] Dugdale, *Baronage*, i, 95; *V.C.H. Worcs.* i, 326.
[24] Habington, op. cit. ii, 41; Dugdale, loc. cit.
[25] *V.C.H. Worcs.* i, 297.
[26] Habington, op. cit. ii, 41; Red Bk. of Bishopric of Worc. fol. 253, 18.
[27] Pipe R. 6 Ric. I, m. 9 d.
[28] *Testa de Nevill* (Rec. Com.), 41b.
[29] *Rot. de Oblatis et Fin.* (Rec. Com.), 501.
[30] *Rot. Lit. Claus.* (Rec. Com.), i, 168.
[31] Ibid. 623.

CROWLE CHURCH C. 1810
(*From a Water-colour by Thos. Rickards in Prattinton Collection*)

which he held of the Bishop of Worcester in chief.[32] In 1228 Stephen's lands were taken into the king's hands until it could be found who rightfully held the custody of them.[33]

In 1240-1 William Devreux acknowledged that 2 carucates of land in Crowle were the right of Joan Devreux and her heirs.[34] From this it seems possible that Joan was an heiress of the Tirels and the widow of Stephen Devreux. In 1299 John Siward held the manor in right of Joan Devreux his mother,[35] and in 1304-5 it was settled on John and his wife Joan.[36] Joan widow of John Siward held the manor as dower in 1324-5, and it was in that year settled on John son of Richard Siward and his wife Olive and their heirs with contingent remainder to the heirs of Olive.[37] It was probably this Olive who as the wife of Peter Nevill conveyed the reversion of the manor of Crowle Siward[38] after the death of Joan wife of John Siward to Thomas de Evesham and John de Bransford in 1335.[39] In the same year Thomas and John obtained licence to grant this reversion to the Prior and convent of Worcester,[40] the licence of the bishop, as overlord, being obtained in the following year.[41] For this the prior and convent granted to the bishop a pension of a mark yearly from the manor of Tibberton,[42] and inserted his name in their Martyrology, and promised to keep his anniversary with mass and chant in their quire.[43]

The manor remained in the possession of the prior and convent[44] until 1536, when it was granted to William Moore, Prior of Worcester, on his resignation of the office.[45] In the valuation of the priory lands taken in 1535 the clear value of this manor was given as £16 8s. 5d.[46] After the dissolution of the priory in 1540 this manor was granted in 1542 to the Dean and Chapter of Worcester.[47] This grant was confirmed in 1609,[48] and the manor remained in the possession of the dean and chapter until 1650, when it was sold by the Parliamentary commissioners to Major Richard Salwey.[49] He and his wife Anne conveyed the manor in 1655 to Richard Sturt and John Woolfe,[50] and in 1657 and 1658 Richard Gilman and his wife Hester conveyed it to John Okey.[51] At the Restoration the lands of the dean and chapter were restored to them, and this manor was confirmed to them in 1692.[52] It remained in their possession until 1859, when it was taken over by the Ecclesiastical Commissioners,[53] who are now lords of the manor.

The manor of *FROXMERE COURT* or *CROWLE*

HACKETT.—At the date of the Domesday Survey a second holding in Crowle, which in the time of King Edward had belonged to Chetelbert, was held by Urse under Osbern Fitz Richard.[54] This was doubtless the manor of Crowle, held, as mentioned above, by Simund the Dane, who is probably to be identified with Simon, who had preceded Osbern Fitz Richard at Shelsley.[55] It was assessed at 5 hides, and attached to it were a burgess and two salt-pans, probably at Droitwich.

Osbern Fitz Richard's interest in the manor followed the same descent as the manor of Wychbold in Dodderhill to the families of Say, Mortimer, Talbot and Lucy, by whom it was held as part of the honour of Richard's Castle, and is last mentioned in 1428.[56] It is possible that before this date the sub-tenancy of the manor lapsed, and it was held by the overlords in demesne.[57] In 1593 the manor was said to be held of the Dean and Chapter of Worcester.[58]

In 1086 Urse was tenant of the manor under Osbern Fitz Richard.[59] His interest passed to his descendants the Beauchamps,[60] but their rights of overlordship seem to have lapsed after 1309.

The Poers seem to have been intermediary tenants early in the 13th century between the Beauchamps and the Hackets, who held the manor in demesne, but their overlordship is mentioned only in the *Testa de Nevill.*[61]

William Hacket was a tenant under William de Beauchamp in 1166,[62] but it is not known whether his holding then included Crowle. Early in the 13th century Walter Hacket held the manor of Crowle,[63] and in 1233 he was pardoned for the death of Adam de la Kersonera.[64] Walter sold part of the wood of Crowle in 1237 to the monks of Worcester Priory,[65] and in 1240-1 his widow Margery gave woodland at Crowle to the brethren of the hospital of St. Wulfstan in Worcester.[66] William son of Walter Hacket with the consent of his wife Alice gave to the Prior and convent of Worcester all his wood in Crowle called Northwood, lying between Oddingley Wood and Huddington Wood.[67] In 1300 Walter Hacket obtained a grant of free warren in his demesne lands of Crowle.[68]

This is the last mention of the Hacket family in connexion with the manor, which may perhaps have lapsed to the overlords soon after this time, for John Talbot was said to be holding it in 1346,[69] and no mention is made of any sub-tenant. His daughter Elizabeth wife of Sir Warin Archdekne held a fee at

[32] *Rot. Lit. Claus.* (Rec. Com.), i, 167.
[33] *Excerpta e Rot. Fin.* (Rec. Com.), i, 168.
[34] Feet of F. Worcs. 25 Hen. III, no. 41.
[35] Habington, op. cit. ii, 42 ; Red Bk. of Bishopric of Worc. fol. 2.
[36] Feet of F. Worcs. 33 Edw. I, no. 19.
[37] Ibid. 18 Edw. II, no. 16, 17.
[38] The manor bore this name during the 14th and 15th centuries (Feet of F. Worcs. 18 Edw. II, no. 16 ; Cal. Pat. 1334-8, p. 130 ; Feud. Aids, v, 308, 319).
[39] Feet of F. Worcs. 9 Edw. III, no. 16.
[40] Cal. Pat. 1334-8, p. 130.
[41] Worc. Epis. Reg. Montacute (1333-7), i, fol. 29. It is here stated that the manor had been taken from the convent by malice and fraud.
[42] Ibid. ii, fol 20.
[43] Dugdale, *Mon. Angl.* i, 576.

[44] *Feud. Aids,* v, 308, 319.
[45] Dugdale, op. cit. i, 581 ; Nash, *Hist. of Worcs.* i, 280. William Moore was buried in the church of Crowle (Noake, *Guide to Worcs.* 107).
[46] *Valor Eccl.* (Rec. Com.), iii, 220.
[47] *L. and P. Hen. VIII,* xvii, g. 71 (29).
[48] Pat. 6 Jas. I, pt. xii, no. 2.
[49] Close, 1650, pt. xvi, no. 1 ; Cal. S. P. Dom. 1652-3, p. 336.
[50] Feet of F. Worcs. Mich. 1655.
[51] Ibid. Mich. 1657 ; East. 1658.
[52] Pat. 4 Will. and Mary, pt. i, no. 6.
[53] *Lond. Gaz.* 16 Dec. 1859, p. 4757, confirmed by Stat. 31 Vict. cap. 19.
[54] *V.C.H. Worcs.* i, 314a.
[55] Ibid. 297 and 313 n.
[56] Ibid. 328 ; Red Bk. of Exch. (Rolls Ser.), 567 ; Testa de Nevill (Rec. Com.), 40a ; Worcs. Inq. p.m. (Worcs. Hist. Soc.),

ii, 29 ; *Feud. Aids,* v, 302, 323 ; Chan. Inq. p.m. 9 Hen. IV, no. 39.
[57] See below.
[58] Chan. Inq. p.m. (Ser. 2), ccxxxvi, 90.
[59] *V.C.H. Worcs.* i, 314, 328.
[60] Testa de Nevill (Rec. Com.), 40a ; Worcs. Inq. p.m. (Worcs. Hist. Soc.), i, 27 ; ii, 29.
[61] (Rec. Com.) 40, 42b.
[62] Red Bk. of Exch. (Rolls Ser.), 299.
[63] Testa de Nevill (Rec. Com.), 40a.
[64] Excerpta e Rot. Fin. (Rec. Com.), i, 248.
[65] Hale, Reg. of Worc. Priory (Camd. Soc.), 55b ; Ann. Mon. (Rolls Ser.), iv, 429.
[66] Feet of F. Worcs. 25 Hen. III, no. 21.
[67] Nash, op. cit. i, 280.
[68] Cal. Chart. R. 1257-1300, p. 489.
[69] Feud. Aids, v, 302.

Crowle at the time of her death in 1407–8,[70] and again no sub-tenant is mentioned, and her son-in-law Sir Walter Lucy held it in 1428.[71] In 1431, however, an eighth of a knight's fee at Crowle Hackett was held by John Froxmere of Droitwich,[72] and it was evidently from him or his descendants that the manor took the name Froxmere Court, by which it was subsequently known.

From this time until 1575 documents relating to this manor are wanting, but it probably passed from John Froxmere, who died without issue, to his brother Thomas,[73] who left daughters as his co-heirs. This manor passed to the eldest daughter Anne wife of Edward Cockett of Ampton.[74] Her eldest son Anthony died in her lifetime, and on her death a disagreement arose between her grandson and heir, Arthur son of Anthony, and his uncle, her younger son Thomas, as to the division of her estate, and the dispute was not settled until 1580.[75] Each seems to have claimed half the manor of Crowle, for in 1575 Arthur sold half to William Banaster,[76] and in October 1579 Thomas Cockett sold his moiety to Arthur,[77] of whom it was purchased in November of the same year by William Penrice *alias* Glover of Crowle.[78] Banaster's moiety was purchased in 1584 by Richard Gardener,[79] who sold it in 1587 to William Penrice.[80]

The Penrices had been settled some time at Crowle, William Penrice, grandfather of the purchaser of Froxmere Court, having held a messuage called Tenburyes in the manor of Froxmere by demise of Anne Cockett.[81] William Penrice died in 1593, leaving a son Thomas.[82] Thomas and his son and heir-apparent John conveyed the manor of Froxmere Court to John Green and John Blanchard in 1630,[83] and in 1655, after the death of Thomas Penrice, his son John conveyed it to Thomas Bridges

PENRICE. *Party indented gules and argent.*

and Hugh Phillipps.[84] Both these conveyances were evidently made for settlements, for in 1662 John Penrice and his wife Susan sold the manor to John Holmden.[85] It passed in the Holmden family [86] until the death of John Holmden about the middle of the 18th century. He left two daughters, Elizabeth and Lydia, both unmarried in 1777.[87] This manor fell to the share of Elizabeth,[88] who appears to have

married Rawson Parke, for in 1802 he and his wife Elizabeth conveyed the manor of Froxmere Court to John Exley.[89] In 1813 they made a further conveyance of the manor to William Welles.[90] Froxmere Court afterwards passed to Colonel Clowes, who died there about 1868, when the estate passed under his will to his niece, who married Captain Castle,[91] the father of Captain Norton C. Castle, the present owner of the manor.[92]

The hospital of St. Wulfstan in Worcester obtained land at Crowle from various donors. Walter Hacket of Crowle gave a virgate and a half of land, Stephen son of Hugh de Crowle gave a virgate of land in Crowle, and another virgate there, being one of two which his father pledged to the hospital. Hugh [93] son of Nicholas de Crowle gave 3 virgates in Crowle, and Emma de Hales gave all the land which she purchased of Henry son of Herce in Crowle. Hamo the Hunter gave a rent of 4*s.* and Baldwin Hacket a rent of 2*s.* in Crowle. The date of none of these gifts is known, but they were all confirmed to the hospital by the king in 1232.[94] These possessions, and a further gift of woodland in Crowle made by Margery widow of Walter Hacket in 1240–1,[95] subsequently became a manor held by successive masters of the hospital until the Dissolution.[96] In 1406–7 it was held, for the service of one knight, of Margaret widow of Thomas Earl of Warwick.[97] In 1535 the property of the hospital at Crowle was valued at 119*s.*[98]

The manor was confiscated by the Crown on the dissolution of the hospital in 1540,[99] and granted in June of that year to Richard Morrison, a gentleman of the privy chamber.[100] The grant was renewed in 1541,[1] but was surrendered in 1544, when another was made to him with the rents reserved in the previous grants.[2] Morrison sold the manor in the same year to John Combes,[3] who died in 1550,[4] being succeeded by his son John, to whom livery was made in 1553.[5] On his death in 1588 the manor passed to his son Edward,[6] who died in 1597, leaving as his co-heirs three daughters, Joyce wife of John Garner (afterwards of Francis Cornewall), Anne and Elizabeth.[7] The manor had, however, been entailed in 1590 upon the heirs male of Edward and his brothers,[8] and though in May 1601 two parts of the manor were delivered to Joyce and Anne,[9] their sister Elizabeth having died in 1598,[10] the manor passed under the entail to Thomas brother of Edward Combes. He died seised of it in 1609,

[70] Chan. Inq. p.m. 9 Hen. IV, no. 39.
[71] *Feud. Aids,* v, 323.
[72] Ibid. 330. In 1398 all the goods and chattels of John Froxmere of Droitwich, forfeited for felony, were granted to Thomas Duke of Surrey, the king's nephew (*Cal. Pat.* 1396–9, p. 316).
[73] *Visit. of Worcs.* 1569 (Harl. Soc. xxvii), 39.
[74] Ibid. ; Close, 22 Eliz. pt. xi, Brace and Cockett.
[75] Close, 22 Eliz. pt. xi, Brace and Cockett.
[76] Feet of F. Worcs. Mich. 17 & 18 Eliz.
[77] Close, 21 Eliz. pt. xviii, Cockett and Cockett.
[78] Ibid. pt. xvi, Cockett and Penrice.
[79] Feet of F. Worcs. East. 26 Eliz.
[80] Ibid. Mich. 29 Eliz.

[81] Close, 21 Eliz. pt. xvi, Cockett and Penrice.
[82] Chan. Inq. p.m. (Ser. 2), ccxxxvi, 90. He was then said to be holding half the manor of Froxmere Court.
[83] Close, 6 Chas. I, pt. xix, no. 26.
[84] Feet of F. Worcs. Hil. 1655 ; Close, 1655, pt. xii, no. 7.
[85] Feet of F. Worcs. Mich. 14 Chas. II.
[86] Ibid. Div. Co. Mich. 16 Chas. II ; Worcs. East. 15 Geo. II.
[87] Ibid. Worcs. East. 17 Geo. III ; Nash, *Hist. of Worcs.* i, 281.
[88] Nash, loc. cit.
[89] Feet of F. Worcs. East. 42 Geo. III.
[90] Ibid. East. 53 Geo. III.
[91] Inform. from Mr. J. W. Willis-Bund.
[92] Inform. from Mr. W. A. Gadesden.
[93] Hugh de Crowle held an estate at Crowle in 1220–1 (Assize R. 1021, m. 3).
[94] *Cal. Chart. R.* 1226–57, p. 173.

[95] Feet of F. Worcs. 25 Hen. III, no. 21.
[96] *Pope Nich. Tax.* (Rec. Com.), 231*a* ; Chan. Inq. p.m. 8 Hen. IV, no. 68 ; Habington, op. cit. i, 134 ; *Lay Subs. R. Worcs.* 1280 (Worcs. Hist. Soc.), 22*a.*
[97] Chan. Inq. p.m. 8 Hen. IV, no. 68.
[98] *Valor Eccl.* (Rec. Com.), iii, 228.
[99] *V.C.H. Worcs.* ii, 176.
[100] *L. and P. Hen. VIII,* xv, g. 831 (64). [1] Ibid. xvi, g. 678 (25).
[2] Ibid. xix (i), g. 444 (10).
[3] Feet of F. Worcs. Mich. 36 Hen. VIII.
[4] Chan. Inq. p.m. (Ser. 2), xciv, 98.
[5] Fine R. 7 Edw. VI, no. 18.
[6] Chan. Inq. p.m. (Ser. 2), ccxix, 79.
[7] Ibid. ccli, 54.
[8] Ibid. cclii, 54 ; cclix, 43.
[9] Fine R. 43 Eliz. pt. ii, no. 29.
[10] Chan. Inq. p.m. (Ser. 2), cclxi, 30.

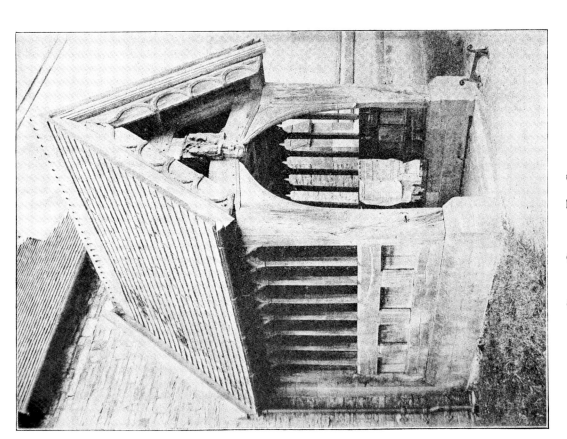

CROWLE CHURCH : 12TH CENTURY MARBLE LECTERN

CROWLE CHURCH : THE PORCH

and was succeeded by his son William.[11] William sold the site of the manor and capital messuage of Crowle with closes called Commanders Furlong, Fryer Jennings, Nineland and the Wincey to Thomas Penrice of Crowle,[12] and this estate subsequently descended with the manor of Froxmere Court.[13] William Combes and Katherine his wife and Thomas Combes conveyed the manor in 1620 to Sir Thomas Bigg, bart., and John Savage,[14] but this conveyance was perhaps made only for a settlement, for William Combes presented to the church, whose advowson was appurtenant to this manor in 1621.[15] He must have sold the manor at about this time to William Keyt, for he presented to the church in 1622.[16] The manor then descended in the Keyt family in the same way as the manor of Church Lench until 1727.[17] It was sold in that year by William Keyt, bart., to Thomas Gem.[18] The further descent of the estate is not known : its site is perhaps marked by the present Commandry Farm at Crowle.

There was a mill worth 2s. in the manor of Crowle held under the monks of Worcester in 1086.[19] In 1220–1 Peter de Wick built a mill at Crowle, and with his pond swamped the land of Hugh de Crowle.[20] There are now no mills in Crowle.

The church of *ST. JOHN BAPTIST CHURCH* (formerly dedicated to St. Peter) consists of a chancel, north and south transepts, nave, west tower, and a north porch. The porch, a magnificent example of late 14th-century timber work, alone survives of the fabric of the original building, which was entirely rebuilt between the years 1881 and 1885. A remarkable marble lectern of the late 12th century, locally said to have come from Pershore Abbey at the time of the Dissolution, and a fine 15th-century font have also been preserved, while parts of the old windows have been reset in the modern walls.

Portions of the mullions and tracery of the three-light east window of the chancel appear to be original and to date from about 1300. The external label and sill-string, with their leaf stops, are also partly original. The north-east window is of two coupled cinquefoiled lights. The head and mullion are original and probably contemporary with the east window. The south-east window, also of two lights, is entirely modern. Modern segmental arches open into the two transepts.

In the east wall of the north transept is reset a 15th-century piscina head with plain spandrels contained within a square. Portions of the three-light north window are original 15th-century work, and the jamb and mullion of the two-light west window are of similar date. The windows of the south transept are the most perfect of the re-used work and preserve their original rear arches. All have two-centred heads, and appear to be of late 14th-century date. The south window is of three lights, with tracery of an early vertical character. The east and west windows are each of two lights, with an elongated quatrefoil in the head.

Of the two windows in the north wall of the nave the eastern is entirely modern, while the western

window has remains of early 14th-century work in the tracery. In the south wall all three windows are modern. The original early 15th-century tower arch has been reset, and is of two chamfered orders. The responds are hollow-chamfered, and their plain bell capitals fit them very ill. The modern tower is of three stages, and is crowned by an embattled parapet, both belfry and ringing stage being lighted by two-light traceried windows. On the east wall, above the apex of the nave roof, is an elaborate niche with a trefoiled head, crocketed and finialled, and small pinnacled flanking buttresses, all apparently reset work of the 15th century. Parts of the three-light west window of the ground stage appear to be of the same date, but the tracery is entirely modern.

The north porch, which measures internally 8 ft. by 7 ft., is a fine specimen of late 14th-century carpentry. At about half their height the corner posts are cut back to receive curved pieces, which form two-centred arches at the entrance and against the north wall of the nave. These pieces brace the cambered collars resting on the corner posts. Out of the lower part of the side plates are formed the trefoiled ogee heads and pierced and foliated spandrels of the eight open lights which occupy the upper half of each side wall. The lower half is filled by four square panels, which with the mullions of the open lights have been renewed. Framed on to the collar above the entrance arch, and forming a sort of key, is a large block of wood carved with an Annunciation. The barge-boards are enriched with semicircular foliations, culminating in an ogee at the apex of the gable. The ceiling is divided into four main compartments by richly moulded ribs with carved bosses at their intersections. Each main compartment is further subdivided into six by subordinate hollow-chamfered ribs. The porch has been very carefully restored and re-erected on a stone basement.

The most remarkable survival from the original church is the marble lectern. The desk is formed of a large block of blue-grey marble, sunk to receive the book. The front and sides are sculptured with a conventional vine, springing on each face from the mouth of an inverted lion's head. In the centre of the front is a bearded figure, with the knees bent forward, holding with both arms to the vine. The desk is supported by a central and four angle-shafts, all of the same diameter, with foliated capitals of Romanesque character. The shafts are modern and the moulded bases have leaf-spurs at the angles and rest on a common plinth. The 15th-century font has an octagonal bowl supported by a stem of the same form. The sides of both have traceried panelling, the cardinal faces of the stem being the most elaborated.

In the west window of the north transept are some fragments of 15th-century glass. The only perfect piece is a shield—Gules a saltire argent within a border sable charged with stars. The other fragments include two crowned female heads.

There is a ring of eight bells. The first three were cast by Barwell of Birmingham, who rehung the whole peal in the year 1887. The remaining bells are inscribed as follows : the fourth 'Iesvs be our good speed 1667'; fifth 'All prayse and glory be to

---

[11] Chan. Inq. p.m. (Ser. 2), cccxi, 91.

[12] Close, 6 Chas. I, pt. xix, no. 26.

[13] Feet of F. Worcs. Mich. 6 Chas. I ;

Hil. 1655; Mich. 14 Chas. II ; East. 17 Geo. III ; East. 42 Geo. III.

[14] Feet of F. Worcs. Mich. 18 Jas. I.

[15] Inst. Bks. (P.R.O.).   [16] Ibid.

[17] Recov. R. Trin. 14 Chas. II, rot. 10.

[18] Feet of F. Worcs. East. 13 Geo. I ; Trin. 1 Geo. II.   [19] *V.C.H. Worcs.* i, 297.

[20] Assize R. 1021, m. 3.

God for ever 1667'; sixth 'Soli deo gloria pax hominibvs 1667'; seventh 'Iohn Manley Henry Prescott churchwardens 1667'; eighth 'Francis Reynolds vicar of Crowle William Wagstaffe assistant 1667 Iames Reynolds.' All these bells are stamped with a heart-shaped shield, with a bell in the middle and the founder's initials I.M.

The plate consists of a silver chalice and cover paten of 1571 and a silver flagon of 1783 presented to the church in 1883 by William Lee, Archdeacon of Worcester.

The registers before 1812 are as follows : (i) mixed entries 1539 to 1640, with fragmentary entries to 1661 [21]; (ii) mixed entries 1663 to 1751; (iii) baptisms and burials 1752 to 1812, marriages 1752 to 1754; (iv) marriages 1754 to 1812.

ADVOWSON The church of Crowle was evidently originally appurtenant to the manor known as Crowle Siward, for the advowson was granted to the hospital of St. Wulfstan in Worcester by Stephen Devreux, a grant confirmed in 1232 by the king,[22] and it subsequently followed the same descent as the manor in Crowle held by the hospital of St. Wulfstan until 1727,[23] when it was sold by Sir William Keyt to Thomas Gem. It apparently passed from him to George Gem, who presented to the church in 1749.[24] Edward Pearce presented in 1770 [25] and Richard Harrison in 1798 and 1803.[26] Edmund Pearce was patron in 1817,[27] and the Rev. Richard Harrison presented in 1822.[28] The advowson passed in 1845–6 from him to Edwin Crane,[29] who sold it in 1854 to A. H. Green,[30] and he in 1861 to W. H. Woolrych.[31] His representatives made the presentation in 1889,[32] but in 1892 they sold the advowson to the Rev. James Stephenson,[33] from whom it passed in 1896 to the Rev. John Bamber,[34] who is now the owner.

The date of the appropriation of the church of Crowle to the hospital of St. Wulfstan is not known, but it had taken place before 1289.[34a] The rectory followed the same descent as the advowson [35] until 1727 or later. In 1802 and 1813 it belonged to Rawson Parke and Elizabeth his wife, owners of the manor of Froxmere Court.[36]

By an undated charter Baldwin de Akeny and Joan his wife gave to the church of St. Mary, Worcester, and to the prior and convent there, a yearly rent of 2s. from their manor of Crowle, for keeping a light before the tomb of St. Wulfstan.[37]

CHARITIES The charities subsisting in this parish (with the exception of Caleb Baylis's charity) are regulated by a scheme of the Charity Commissioners 14 August 1863, comprising the following charities :

1. The parish lands, which are recorded on a stone upon the north wall of the church, now consist of 19 a. called Towthan Land, allotted under the Inclosure Act in exchange for the lands so recorded. They are let at £27 10s. a year, and the official trustees hold a sum of £166 5s. 8d. consols in trust for this charity.

2. Mrs. Elizabeth Attwood, recorded on the church table, will 1720, trust fund, £22 15s. 5d. consols.

3. The Rev. Richard Harrison, will proved in the P.C.C. 5 February 1835, trust fund, £61 5s. 5d. consols.

4. Robert Smith, will proved at Worcester 7 February 1862, trust fund, £110 7s. consols.

The several sums of stock are held by the official trustees, producing £9 0s. 10d. in annual dividends.

The scheme directs that the income of the parish lands shall be applied in equal shares for the maintenance of the fabric of the church, the repair of highways and support of provident clubs. In 1910 the sum of £8 6s. 6d. was applied for each of those purposes, and gifts were made to twenty-one widows and spinsters and to ten men.

The charity of Caleb Baylis, founded by will proved at Worcester 11 March 1889, consists of £101 15s. 7d. consols with the official trustees, the annual dividends, amounting to £2 10s. 8d., being applicable in the distribution of bread on St. Thomas's Day.

DAYLESFORD

Daeglesford, Deilesford, Eilesford (xi cent.); Daeilesford, Dayleford (xii cent.); Dalysford, Dailsford, Dallifford, Dallisford (xvii cent.).

The parish of Daylesford, containing 670 acres, of which 266 acres are arable land, 258 under permanent grass and 47 woodland,[1] lies between Oxfordshire and Gloucestershire on the left bank of the little River Evenlode, which forms its southwestern boundary. The Oxford, Worcester and Wolverhampton branch of the Great Western railway runs alongside the river, which makes a great curve to the east and is twice crossed by the line within half a mile south of Adlestrop station. Close to this curve of the river and rather more than a quarter of a mile from the main road is the neat village of Daylesford, which was entirely built by the late Mr. Grisewood on the road leading to Daylesford Park, the old houses being pulled down one by one as the new were finished. At its western end on slightly rising ground stands the church of St. Peter

[21] At the year 1619 is the following note : 'The Register booke was not kepte : Mr. Thornburgh and Mr. Haries beinge att suite for the vicaridge.'
[22] *Cal. Chart. R.* 1226–57, p. 173.
[23] *Reg. G. Giffard* (Worcs. Hist. Soc.), 335, 445; *L. and P. Hen. VIII,* xv, g. 831 (64); Feet of F. Worcs. Mich. 36 Hen. VIII; Chan. Inq. p.m. (Ser. 2), xciv, 98; ccxix, 79; cclii, 54; cccxi, 91; Inst. Bks. (P.R.O.); Feet of F. Div. Co. Trin. 14 Chas. II; Worcs. Trin. 1 Geo. II.

[21] Inst. Bks. (P.R.O.). [25] Ibid.
[26] Ibid. [27] *Clerical Guide* (ed. 1).
[28] Ibid. (ed. 2).
[29] *Clergy List,* 1846.
[30] Ibid. 1854. For a short period at this time the living was united with Upton Snodsbury, of which the Greens were also patrons (inform. by the Rev. John Bamber).
[31] *Clergy List,* 1861. [32] Ibid. 1889.
[33] Ibid. 1892. [34] Ibid. 1896.
[34a] *Reg. G. Giffard* (Worcs. Hist. Soc.), 335.

[35] *L. and P. Hen. VIII,* xv, g. 831 (64); Feet of F. Worcs. Mich. 36 Hen. VIII; Chan. Inq. p.m. (Ser. 2), xciv, 98; cccxi, 91; Feet of F. Worcs. Mich. 18 Jas. I; East. 13 Geo. I.
[36] Feet of F. Worcs. East. 42 Geo. III; East. 53 Geo. III.
[37] Prattinton Coll. (Soc. Antiq.), Deeds of D. and C. of Worc. no. 46. Baldwin de Akeny and Joan his wife paid 20s. for a writ in Cornwall in 1250 (*Excerpta e Rot. Fin.* [Rec. Com.], ii, 94).
[1] Statistics from Bd. of Agric. (1905).

with its depressed spire looking down on the double row of well-built comfortable cottages which suggests a succession of park lodges rather than a village street.

A road from Kingham (co. Oxon.) separates the church from the village, and runs north-west to join the main road from Stow-on-the-Wold to Banbury, which crosses the Evenlode a little south of Adlestrop station and forms the greater part of the northern boundary of Daylesford. The ground slopes gradually up from the river till it reaches a height of about 700 ft. above the ordnance datum in the north corner of the parish. From this point a footpath leads along the north-eastern boundary to meet the road from Chipping Norton, which runs almost due west along the borders of Daylesford Park to Norton Gap, where it joins the road to Stow-on-the-Wold. Both roads are well shaded, and in the park there are many fine trees, especially beeches.

Daylesford House is a handsome late Georgian building standing in the middle of a well-timbered park. The house was built about 1793 by the East India Company for Warren Hastings, and in it he spent the last years of his life. It is built on the slope of rising ground, the main rooms facing south and west. The entrance front has been added to and altered since Hastings was there. The elevations are of a plain and somewhat heavy classical type, and the interior is decorated with the severe classical plaster detail of the period. The state bedroom is a very good example of the domestic work of this time with a high-domed ceiling and a segmental bay. The old furniture has for the most part disappeared, but many of the pictures remain. Particularly notable is a large collection of exquisite miniatures of Indian workmanship.

The gardens at the back of the house were planned and laid out by the ex-governor. Possibly he regarded such improvements as a part of his inheritance, for there is a local tradition that his great-great-grandfather John Hastings busied himself with agricultural improvements as far as his limited means would allow, and was the first to introduce into England the sainfoin which has now become so thoroughly naturalized in the country round Daylesford.[2] Corn and root crops are also at the present time grown in the parish, but a large proportion of the land is pasture. The subsoil is Oolite and Lias, with beds of Chipping Norton limestone.

The following place-names occur in local records : Combe Grove,[3] the Parsons Seete, Hillis Close, Wills Close, Gallaunce, Bickerstaffe Coppice, Baywell[4] (xvii cent.) ; Great Hill, the Picked Piece, Proctor's Farm, and Halifax's Farm[5] ; the Pike, Hunger Bean, Hangings, Mazey Ground, Tipsey Hill, Sparkwell and Slinket[6] (xviii cent.).

MANOR The history of *DAYLESFORD* during the centuries preceding the Domesday Survey depends almost entirely on the conflicting statements of the two religious houses between whom its possession was for many years disputed. According to the Abbot and convent of Evesham it had been granted to their house for the support of the monks by Earl Ælfgar with the consent of King Edward the Confessor,[7] while the Worcester monks stated that it had belonged to them ever since the end of the 9th century, though they do not seem to have been quite certain whether the original grant had been made to Bishop Eadberht by Beorhtwulf, King of the Mercians, in 841,[8] or to the monastery

DAYLESFORD HOUSE

before 875 by King Ceolwulf II of Mercia.[9] Both statements could be supported by charters in the Worcester chartulary, which also contained leases made by St. Oswald the Bishop to his brothers between 961[10] and 979,[11] as well as a charter of King Ethelbald granting the land to Bœge (Bœgia) in 718 for the foundation of a monastery.[12] In comparison with so ancient a title the claim made by Evesham Abbey seems modest, but the charter of Ælfgar which her monks were able to produce stated that the earl had made the gift because he 'had heard and knew that the land belonged of old time to that church'[13] ; and it

---

[2] Among the Prattinton Collection belonging to the Society of Antiquaries there is a letter written in 1732 to Dr. Thomas by Penyston Hastings, stating that the 'french grass called saintfoin' was first brought to England by John Hastings and planted at Daylesford in 1650.

[3] Probably the plantation now known as Combe Wood, in Adlestrop parish.

[4] Chan. Inq. p.m. (Ser. 2), dlii, 113.

[5] Exch. Dep. Mich. 1 Geo. II, no. 2.

[6] Add. MS. 29232, *passim*.

[7] Heming, *Chartul.* (ed. Hearne), 640.

[8] Birch, *Cart. Sax.* ii, 11 ; Heming, op. cit. 69.

[9] Heming, op. cit. 369. There is a grant of privileges (ibid. 57) dated 875 from Ceolwulf II to the monks of Worcester in return for a four lives' lease of the property : the king is said to have paid in addition 60 *mancuses* of gold.

[10] Heming, op. cit. 562.

[11] Ibid. 211–12.

[12] Ibid. 68 ; Birch, op. cit. i, 204. It is needless to say that Daylesford was also included in the famous 'charter of King Edgar' (Heming, op. cit. 520).

[13] Heming, op. cit. 640. Birch gives a charter of King Offa (777) granting land at Daylesford to the abbey of Evesham (*Cart. Sax.* i, 311), but this is certainly a forgery.

was witnessed by almost every person of the day who had any claim to distinction.[14]

Of these varying statements the claim of Evesham receives the most support from the Domesday Survey, where it is said that Daylesford was assigned to the support of the monks and was held by the abbot of the Bishop of Worcester until Odo of Bayeux took it from the abbey.[15] The Bishop of Worcester appears to have been still recognized as overlord in the 12th century,[16] but after the Hastings family obtained the manor it is usually said to be held of the Earl of Pembroke.[17] Godfrey Giffard revived the episcopal claims, and succeeded in 1290 in obtaining an acknowledgement from Sir Miles de Hastings that he owed suit at the court of Blockley.[18] Daylesford was also included in the bishop's hundred of Winburntree,[19] and appears on the court rolls as late as 1680, though its owners seem usually to have evaded their duty.[20] The last mention of the overlordship of Pembroke occurs in 1541,[21] and in 1637 the wardship of John Hastings belonged to the Crown,[22] though Habington says his inheritance was held 'partly of the Bishop of Worcester.'[23]

Stephen the son of Fulchered held Daylesford in 1086,[24] but it seems probable that the land was afterwards acquired by Urse D'Abitot, or his brother Robert Despenser, for the Worcester chartulary records that Walter de Beauchamp held 3 hides there in the time of Henry I.[25] It subsequently passed to Robert Marmion, who was the tenant in 1182.[26] At the same date Philip de 'Haster' (? Hastings) was said to hold Daylesford of the bishop, possibly as a tenant under Robert Marmion.[27] Eutropius Hastings, who held half a fee of the Bishop of Worcester in 1166, may have been owner of Daylesford.[28] William Hastings was holding lands in the neighbourhood in 1216,[29] and in 1275 Miles de Hastings granted the manor, on condition that he himself should hold it for life, to his younger son Thomas and the heirs of his body with remainder in default to another younger son Nicholas.[30] Miles died in 1305,[31] and was succeeded

in Daylesford by Thomas,[32] who died before 1310, leaving the manor to Roland Hastings, probably his son.[33] Roland was still living in 1333,[34] but died before 1335[35]; his heir was another Thomas Hastings, who died in 1362, leaving a son Bartholomew in his minority.[36] Bartholomew came of age in 1368,[37] but the history of the manor during the next twenty years is difficult to trace. By 1393 the property had passed to John Mirye of Lyneham (co. Oxon.), who settled it in that year on himself and Agnes his wife with reversion to his own heirs[38]; and before 1408 it was held by Richard Milton and Katherine his wife in right of Katherine, who was perhaps the daughter of John Mirye.[39] She and her husband sold Daylesford in 1408 to Thomas Hastings,[40] traditionally said to have been a member of the old family, though it is not clear whether he was a descendant of Bartholomew or Nicholas.

The manor subsequently continued in the possession of the Hastings family for over 300 years. It was held by Edward Hastings in 1466[41] and 1494,[42] and successively by his son[43] and grandson,[44] both John Hastings. Simon the son of John the younger succeeded in 1585,[45] and made a settlement of the estate in 1618 on himself for life and his wife Susanna during her widowhood and to the use of his younger sons and daughters for sixteen years with reversion to his eldest son John and John's son Edward.[46] Simon Hastings died in 1628[47] and John in the following year[48]; Edward had died during his father's lifetime, and John's heir was his infant son and namesake,[49] whose long minority only ended in 1648. He married Elizabeth, the daughter of Sir Thomas Penyston,[50] whose surname was given to his son and continued in the family for three

HASTINGS. *Argent a sleeve sable.*

[14] The list of witnesses includes Edith the queen, Stigand and Aldred archbishops, and Earls Leofric, Harold, Tostig and Leofwine (Heming, loc. cit.).

[15] *V.C.H. Worcs.* i, 293.

[16] Ibid. 325; Eccl. Com. Rec. Var. bdle. 121, no. 43698, fol. 254. It is possible that even in 1166 there was some uncertainty about the episcopal rights, for it is recorded that Robert Marmion owed the bishop two knights but denied one (*Red Bk. of Exch.* [Rolls Ser.], 300; *Reg. G. Giffard* [Worcs. Hist. Soc.], 470). Daylesford was described as one knight's fee in 1305 (Chan. Inq. p.m. 33 Edw. I, no. 64).

[17] In 1305 it was held of John Hastings, ancestor of the Earls of Pembroke, who is said to have held of the king in chief (Chan. Inq. p.m. 33 Edw. I, no. 64); in 1368 of John Earl of Pembroke (ibid. 42 Edw. III, no. 72); and in 1541 of the Countess of Pembroke (ibid. [Ser. 2], lxiv, no. 177). In 1637 it was held of the king in chief, and this is the last mention of the overlordship (ibid. dlii, no. 113).

[18] *Reg. G. Giffard,* op. cit. 336; Miles had obtained a remission of this suit in 1288 (ibid. 318).

[19] Eccl. Com. Ct. R. (P.R.O.), bdles. 189, no. 5; 200, no. 7.

[20] Ibid. bdles. 189–200, *passim.*

[21] Chan. Inq. p.m. (Ser. 2), lxiv, 177.

[22] Ibid. dlii, 113.

[23] Habington, *Surv. of Worcs.* i, 184.

[24] *V.C.H. Worcs.* i, 293; Heming, op. cit. 494.

[25] Heming, op. cit. 314.

[26] *Red Bk. of Exch.* (Rolls Ser.), 300; *Reg. G. Giffard* (Worcs. Hist. Soc.), 470; Habington, op. cit. i, 183; Eccl. Com. Rec. Var. bdle. 121, no. 43698, fol. 254.

[27] Eccl. Com. Rec. loc. cit. fol. 254.

[28] *Red Bk. of Exch.* (Rolls Ser.), 300.

[29] In 1216 William de Hastings received seisin of a knight's fee in Oxfordshire which had been held by Miles de Hastings and Walter Murdac, opponents of King John (*Rot. Lit. Claus.* [Rec. Com.], i, 282), and William de Hastings was afterwards seised of land at Westwell (co. Oxon.) on the Gloucestershire border (*Testa de Nevill* [Rec. Com.], 102).

[30] Feet of F. Worcs. Trin. 3 Edw. I.

[31] Chan. Inq. p.m. 33 Edw. I, no. 64.

[32] Close, 33 Edw. I, m. 8. The heir to Miles's other lands (with the exception of Yelford, co. Oxon., which had also been granted to Thomas) was his grandson Miles (Chan. Inq. p.m. 33 Edw. I, no. 64).

[33] Feet of F. Oxon. Trin. 3 Edw. II.

[34] *Cal. Inq. p.m.* 1–9 *Edw. III,* 368.

[35] Nash, *Hist. of Worcs.* i, 287.

[36] Chan. Inq. p.m. 36 Edw. III, pt. i, no. 96.

[37] Ibid. 42 Edw. III (1st nos.), no. 72; Close, 42 Edw. III, m. 7.

[38] Feet of F. Div. Co. Mich. 17 Ric. II.

[39] Ibid. Worcs. Hil. 9 Hen. IV. Richard Mitton was concerned in the abduction of the young Earl of March and his brother in 1406, and his lands were forfeited on that account, but were afterwards restored to him (Pat. 7 Hen. IV, pt. i, m. 13).

[40] Feet of F. Worcs. Hil. 9 Hen. IV.

[41] Chan. Misc. bdle. 85, no. 41; *Cal. Pat.* 1467–77, p. 2; Nash, op. cit. i, 288.

[42] Nash, loc. cit.

[43] Chan. Inq. p.m. (Ser. 2), lxiv, 177.

[44] Ibid. ccx, 121.

[45] Ibid.

[46] Feet of F. Div. Co. Trin. 16 Jas. I; Chan. Inq. p.m. (Ser. 2), ccccxl, 75. See also Chan. Proc. (Ser. 2), bdle. 446, no. 129.

[47] Chan. Inq. p.m. (Ser. 2), ccccxl, 75.

[48] Ibid. dlii, 113. Of Simon's younger sons, Hercules died in 1634 (ibid.) and the other three were living in 1637 (ibid.); Charles, who was still alive in 1646 (Inst. Bks. [P.R.O.]), seems to have been the last survivor.

[49] Chan. Inq. p.m. (Ser. 2), dlii, 113.

[50] Metcalfe, *Visit. of Worcs.* 1683, p. 54.

generations. Penyston Hastings succeeded his father before 1674,[51] but his fortune was so much reduced by 1709 that he and his sons Samuel, Penyston and Theophilus were obliged to convey the estate to trustees to raise money for the payment of £3,345 6s. to the Misses Eaton of Oxford,[52] and subsequently to sell it to Jacob Knight,[53] from whose trustees it was bought back in 1793 by Warren Hastings, the great Governor - General of India and grandson of the younger Penyston.[54]

IMHOFF. *Argent three buffaloes' heads sable cut off at the neck.*

Warren Hastings died at Daylesford in 1818. In accordance with a settlement of 1798 he left the property to his wife Marian for her life with reversion to Charles Imhoff, her son by her first husband.[55] Mrs. Hastings died in 1837, and Sir Charles Imhoff subsequently remained in possession of the manor until 1853,[56] when he sold it to Mr. Harman Grisewood, who retained it till his death in 1874.[57] It was afterwards bought from his trustees by Mr. R. Nichol Byass,[58] who sold it in 1884 to Mr. Charles Edward Baring Young, the present lord of the manor.[59]

Five messuages and 4 virgates of land in Daylesford were settled in 1275 by 'the younger Miles de Hastings' on Margery de Hastings and her heirs, to be held for the rent of a rose at Midsummer for all service.[60] She granted her holding in 1286 to William de Chyrinton, clerk,[61] and it afterwards passed to John le Boteler and Margaret his wife,[62] who settled it in 1353 on William of Evenlode and his wife Felice.[63] Its subsequent history is obscure.

There was a water-mill attached to the manor of Daylesford in 1275,[64] which seems to have followed throughout the descent of the manor.[65] It is mentioned in the sale of the estate to Jacob Knight in 1715,[66] but had apparently disappeared before 1797.[67] There is now no trace of the building, but it probably stood on the left bank of the Evenlode near the rectory, where there are sluices and a second stream which looks like a mill-race.

CHURCH The church of *ST. PETER* consists of a chancel measuring internally $10\frac{1}{2}$ ft. by 13 ft., a central tower about 11 ft. square, north and south transepts 10 ft. deep and 12 ft. wide, and a nave 30 ft. by 15 ft. There are also a vestry and organ bay on the north side of the chancel and a south porch.

The present building, designed by J. L. Pearson in 13th-century style, was built in 1860 by Harman Grisewood to replace another erected in 1816 on the site of a very much older church. The east window consists of three large lancets, each under an elaborate rear arch, and on each side of the chancel is a wall arcade with an alabaster dado below. Some remains of 12th-century work exist in the north wall of the chancel, consisting of two capitals and one bay of a Norman arcade of two square orders.

The transepts are divided off by screens of open

DAYLESFORD CHURCH FROM THE NORTH

ironwork and the responds of the tower arches are enriched with polished marble shafting.

[51] Recov. R. Mich. 26 Chas. II, rot. 268; Feet of F. Worcs. Hil. 29 & 30 Chas. II.

[52] Close, 3 Geo. I, pt. xii, no. 27.

[53] Feet of F. Worcs. Trin. 2 Geo. I.

[54] Add. MS. 29232, fol. 162–8 ; Priv. Act, 33 Geo. III, cap. 55.

[55] Add. MS. 29232, fol. 221 ; Feet of F. Worcs. Hil. 37 Geo. III.

[56] Inform. from the Rev. A. G. Grisewood, rector of Daylesford.

[57] Ibid.

[58] Ibid.

[59] Ibid.

[60] Feet of F. Worcs. Trin. 3 Edw. I. It is not clear if this Miles was the father or one of the brothers of Thomas.

[61] *Abbrev. Plac.* (Rec. Com.), 212.

[62] Feet of F. Worcs. East. 27 Edw. III.

[63] Ibid.

[64] Ibid. Trin. 3 Edw. I.

[65] Chan. Inq. p.m. 33 Edw. I, no. 64 ; 36 Edw. III, pt. i, no. 96, &c.

[66] Feet of F. Worcs. Trin. 2 Geo. I.

[67] Ibid. Hil. 37 Geo. III.

In the south porch some fragments of 13th-century work are embodied in the present jambs and capitals. Several tablets and monuments have been transferred from the original church, including a well-preserved brass to William Gardiner of Lagham, Surrey, who died aged twenty-six in 1632. It is engraved with a large figure in short cloak and riding boots, a crest and three coats of arms, two being Gardiner (azure) a griffon passant (or) and one Gardiner impaling Hastings (argent) a maunch (sable). The following inscription forms a border to the brass :—

' A full carrouse, vain world,
    Let those drink up that like thy sweets,
    I did but miss ye cup,
    Thy best I tasted and disliked, for when
    Thy enjoyed pleasures do but weary men,
    What will thy labours doe ?
    This made me soone to seek for rest
    Before my age's noone.
    Should any blame my haste let it suffice
    I went to bed betimes, betimes to rise.'

On the west wall of the south transept is a tablet to Abel Makepeace, gent., 1708. On the north wall of the chancel is a tablet to Warren Hastings, acknowledging him as founder of the previous church. His actual grave, in the churchyard close to the east end, is marked by a stone urn inscribed 'Warren Hastings' and mounted on a square pedestal.[68]

Two monuments of the Imhoff family commemorate General Sir Charles Imhoff, kt., died 1853, and Anna Maria Apollonia Baroness Imhoff, died 1837, ' relict of the Right Honourable Warren Hastings.' The church is built of Broadway stone and has a square pyramidal spire with gables over the four belfry lights.

There is a set of tubular bells and two ordinary bells without inscriptions.

The plate consists of a modern cup, paten and flagon (1860).

The registers[69] before 1812 are as follows : (i)
baptisms from 1674 to 1788, burials 1679 to 1785, marriages 1684 to 1748, many pages being missing ; (ii) baptisms from 1787 to 1812 ; (iii) marriages from 1755 to 1812.

ADVOWSON   At the time of the Domesday Survey there was a church in Daylesford, of which the advowson then belonged to Stephen the son of Fulchered,[70] and afterwards followed for the most part the descent of the manor. It was granted by Miles de Hastings to his son Thomas in 1275,[71] but was not included in the life grant which Thomas made to his father in return.[72] Thomas presented in 1281,[73] but Miles seems nevertheless to have considered that he had some right to the patronage, for he sued his son for its recovery in 1302.[74] During this suit the patronage devolved by lapse of time on the Prior of Worcester,[75] the see being vacant, and the Abbot of Westminster wrote asking that the living might be given to William of Evenlode.[76] The prior, however, gave it to Wulfstan of Worcester, together with a licence for seven years' absence for study.[77] But the king sent a writ of prohibition for the duration of the lawsuit,[78] and Wulfstan the incumbent resigned in 1305, when Thomas de Hastings again presented.[79] After this date the advowson followed the descent of the manor until the 18th century,[80] though Sir Francis Russell, bart., presented for one turn in 1679.[81] It was conveyed in 1716 to the younger Penyston Hastings,[82] who presumably sold it, for in 1753 Miss Elizabeth Selfe was the patron,[83] and in 1766 the Rev. Thomas Brooks presented in right of his wife Mary.[84] The advowson was afterwards bought by Warren Hastings, who presented in 1814,[85] and was bequeathed to Sir Charles Imhoff.[86] It was sold with the manor in 1853 to Mr. Harman Grisewood,[87] who left it in his will to his brother Mr. Henry Grisewood.[88] The Rev. Arthur George Grisewood, rector of Daylesford and son of Mr. Henry Grisewood, is now the patron.

There do not appear to be any endowed charities in this parish.

ELMLEY CASTLE

Aelmleage, Elmlaege, Elmlege, Elmleia (viii cent.) ; Emlaeh (ix cent.) ; Almeya (xii cent.) ; Elmele, Elmeley, Aumeleghe, Aumley, Annelegh (xiii cent.) ; Castell Emlegh (xiv cent.).

The parish of Elmley Castle lies in the south-east of the county. It is watered by an unnamed tributary of the Avon and has an area of 2,062 acres, of
which 717 acres are arable, 1,792 permanent grass, and 184 wood.[1] The parish lies to the north of Bredon Hill, the southern part of it being on the hill at about 900 ft. above the ordnance datum. To the north the ground falls to 200 ft. The soil is clay and the subsoil Lower and Middle Lias. The chief crop is beans. There are stone quarries on Bredon Hill.[2]

[68] The *Dict. Nat. Biog.* states that his tomb was included in the new church in 1860, but it is still to be seen outside. The monument is inscribed only with his name and the date of his death, ' but what hathe so worthy a name neede of an heraught to blazon itt ?' (Habington, op. cit. i, 184, a description of the 'playne tomb' of Simon Hastings).

[69] Many earlier entries will be found in the Bishop's Transcripts.

[70] *V.C.H. Worcs.* i, 293.

[71] Feet of F. Worcs. Trin. 3 Edw. I.

[72] Ibid.

[73] *Reg. G. Giffard* (Worcs. Hist. Soc.), 134.

[74] *Sede Vac. Reg.* (Worcs. Hist. Soc.), 14.

[75] Ibid. 36.

[76] Ibid. The abbot speaks of 'the Chapel of Daylesford,' and in an inquisition Nonarum of 1340 (*Lay Subs.* R. 1340 [Worcs. Hist. Soc.], 55) 'the church of Evenlode with the chapel of Daylesford' is mentioned, but in other documents both earlier and later Daylesford is called a church. It was not, however, included in Pope Nicholas's Taxation. In 1428 it was valued at 6 marks (*Feud. Aids*, v, 318).

[77] *Sede Vac. Reg.* (Worcs. Hist. Soc.), 27, 34.

[78] Ibid. 14.

[79] Worc. Epis. Reg. Gainsborough, fol. 102.

[80] Nash, op. cit. i, 287–8 ; Worc. Epis. Reg. *passim* ; Inst. Bks. (P.R.O.). The
church was valued at £6 in 1536 (*Valor Eccl.* [Rec. Com.], iii, 257).

[81] Inst. Bks. (P.R.O.).

[82] Close, 3 Geo. I, pt. xii, no. 27.

[83] Ibid.

[84] Inst. Bks. (P.R.O.) ; Add. MS. 29232, fol. 72.

[85] Inst. Bks. (P.R.O.).

[86] Ex inform. Rev. A. G. Grisewood.

[87] Ibid.   [88] Ibid.

[1] Statistics from Bd. of Agric. (1905).

[2] These quarries were a source of revenue to the lords of Elmley Castle in the 15th and 16th centuries. There was one called Brandon Hill Quarry, another in Wodeyate and one on Bredon Hill (Add. R. 25962, 25965 ; Duchy of Lanc. Mins. Accts. bdle. 645, no. 10468).

The village of Elmley Castle is situated about 5¼ miles south-west of Evesham at the foot of the northern slopes of Bredon Hill, on an outlying spur of which is the site of the ancient castle. The church stands on the east side of the existing Elmley Castle, the churchyard adjoining the park. At the fork of the road a little to the north of the church is the base and stem of a cross, probably of late 14th-century date. A square sundial appears to have been substituted for the cross in the first half of the 17th century. Upon the stem is carved in Roman characters ' A.DOM. MCXLVIII,' an obvious error, by the omission of D after the M, for 1648. In the village is some good half-timber work, including the building now used as the village hall. A cottage, now the police-station, may be of the 14th century.

The signboard of the Queen's Head Hotel contains portraits of Queen Elizabeth and the then lord of the manor William Savage and his wife, who received

CASTLE Elmley Castle, which stood on the summit of a hill in the deer park to the south of the village, is supposed to have been built by Robert le Despenser, brother of Urse the Sheriff.[8] After the castle at Worcester fell into decay Elmley was for a time the chief seat of the Beauchamps, and it followed the same descent as the manor of Elmley Castle (q.v.) until the death of Thomas Byrche Savage in 1776. The house and park went to his widow, who sold them to Richard Bourne Charlett, at whose death in 1822 they were purchased of his executors by Colonel Thomas Henry Hastings Davies, M.P. for Worcester.[9] He died in 1846 without issue, leaving the estate to his widow for life, then in succession to his two brothers, Warburton, who died in 1870, and General Francis John Davies, who died in 1874. Colonel Davies's widow married Sir John Pakington, afterwards Lord Hampton, and died in 1892, when the castle passed to the

VILLAGE HALL, ELMLEY CASTLE

the queen on her visit to the village on 20 August 1575.[3] The painting, which is modern, is much above the usual level of sign-painting.

There is no Inclosure Act for Elmley Castle. Netherton was annexed to Elmley Castle for ecclesiastical purposes in 1864.[4]

Edmund Bonner, Bishop of London (1540–59), was born at Elmley Castle.[4a]

Place-names occurring in deeds relating to Elmley Castle are Pychweye[5] (xiv cent.); Wyndemulle-furlong, Wodeyate,[6] Edmundes Place Beauchamp[7] (xv cent.); Wormstall, Worrall, Puppy's Parlour, Fiddler's Knap (xx cent.).

present owner, Lieut.-General Henry Fanshawe Davies, J.P., D.L., son of General Francis John Davies.[10]

In 1216 the king committed the custody of Elmley Castle to Walter de Lacy, Hugh de Mortimer and Walter de Clifford to keep while Walter de Beauchamp went to the Papal Legate to obtain absolution for his lapse from fidelity to the king.[11] In 1298 the castle was found to be in need of much repair,[12] and after the death of Guy de Beauchamp Earl of Warwick in 1315 it was in such a bad state as to be valued at only 6s. 8d., evidently a nominal valuation, as in another survey taken at the same time it was

---

[8] Queen Elizabeth spent Saturday night and the whole of Sunday in the village of Elmley Castle (Green, *Hist. of Worc.* App. xlii).
[4] *Parl. Papers* (1872), xlvi, no. 345, p. 3. A description of Netherton which

was formerly in Cropthorne will be found under the account of that parish.
[4a] Information by Lt.-General H. F. Davies.   [5] Add. R. 25961.
[6] Ibid. 25962.   [7] Add. Chart. 20431.
[8] Mackenzie, *Castles of Engl.* i, 382.

[9] Information by the Rev. Hugh Bennett, rector of Pirton.   [10] Ibid.
[11] See below; *Rot. Lit. Pat.* (Rec. Com.), i, 192.
[12] *Worcs. Inq. p.m.* (Worcs. Hist. Soc.), i, 63, 64.

said to be worth nothing.[13] The castle was granted by the king to the executors of Guy's will in 1315–16 on condition that they should not grant it to any other without the king's licence.[14] The custody of the castle was, however, taken from them and granted to Hugh le Despenser the elder about 1317.[15] In November of that year Hugh was ordered to fortify it,[16] and to put in twenty fencible footmen to be retained at the king's wages until further orders.[17] Hugh le Despenser having been banished in 1321 the Sheriff of Worcester was ordered to take the castle into the king's[18] hands, and to cause it to be safely guarded and to make an inventory of the arms and victuals and other goods contained in it.[19] Later in the same year Elmley Castle was taken by the rebel barons under Humphrey de Bohun Earl of Hereford, and suffered considerable damage.[20] It is not known whether it underwent a siege, but the gates and some of the houses were burned and many of the defenders slain.[21] Peace having been restored, order was given in 1322 to the keeper of the castle to disband the extra men-at-arms placed there during the war.[22]

Some slight repairs were made in the castle in 1413 and 1425,[23] and again in 1480 and 1492.[24] William Adams was appointed keeper and Thomas Brugge steward in 1478, the castle being then in the hands of the king on account of the minority of Edward Earl of Warwick.[25] Sir John Savage, the younger, received a grant of the constableship in 1488.[25a] In 1528 the castle seems to have been still habitable, for Walter Walshe was then appointed constable and keeper,[26] and ten years later Urian Brereton succeeded to the office.[27] In 1544, however, prior to the grant to Sir William Herbert and Christopher Savage, a survey was made of the manor and castle of Elmley, and it was found that the castle, strongly situated upon a hill surrounded by a ditch and wall, was completely uncovered and in decay.[28] Leland writing at about this time says, 'Ther stondithe now but one Tower, and that partly broken. As I went by I saw Carts carienge Stone thens to amend Persore Bridge about ii miles of. It is set on the Tope of a Hill full of Wood, and a Townelet hard by.'[29]

Of the fabric of the ancient castle, which stood on the summit of the hill about half a mile to the south of the existing building, only a very small amount of masonry, probably forming part of the keep wall, remains. The outer and inner ditch and the site of the barbican can be distinctly traced.

The present mansion of Elmley Castle is a large stone Elizabethan[29a] house of two stories with gabled attics. The plan seems to have been originally E-shaped, but in 1702 the house was entirely remodelled and the character of the plan transformed by filling the arms of the E with brick additions, the south or garden front being refaced with brick to harmonize in appearance with the new building. At the same time large sash-windows were substituted for the original mullioned openings, one or two of which still survive in the attic story and in the cellar. The finest feature of the house is the handsome staircase hall added at this period to the south of the entrance hall. The ceiling is a particularly good example of Queen Anne plaster work. The stairs are of oak with twisted balusters supporting the hand-rail. The east wing contains the principal apartments, and the panelling, where not replaced by later work, dates from the 1702 remodelling. The drawing room at the south end of this wing has been increased to its present size by the removal of a partition. In the southernmost of the two rooms out of which it has been formed Queen Elizabeth is said to have slept when she visited Elmley Castle. Between the drawing room and the dining room is a small room called the cedar parlour from the panelling of this material which lines its walls. At the side of the doorway opening from the hall to the staircase was originally an entrance to a secret chamber or hiding hole which can now be entered from one of the first floor bedrooms. The kitchen and offices are in the west wing, which retains some original 16th-century detail, including a stone fireplace with moulded jambs and a four-centred head, and a small external doorway now partly masked by a brick porch.

The *PARK* at Elmley, which belonged to the lords of Elmley Castle, was possibly made about 1234, for in that year Walter de Beauchamp received from the king a gift of ten does and three bucks for stocking his park at Elmley.[30] In 1298 the wood in the park was worth 4s. yearly.[31] Thomas de Beauchamp Earl of Warwick complained in 1349 that several persons, including Robert de Amyas, parson of the church of Great Comberton, had hunted in his free chase at Elmley Castle and carried away deer.[32] The park was enlarged about 1480 by the addition of part of the demesne land of the manor called Court Close.[33] In 1478 William Adams was appointed keeper of the park and warren at Elmley Castle.[34] In 1480 John Mortimer was appointed master of the game in Elmley Park,[35] and in 1484 John Hudelston succeeded to this office,[36] but it was granted in the following year to Richard Naufan, and in 1488 to Sir John Savage.[36a] Henry VIII appointed Sir John Savage and his son John Savage keepers of the park and warren in 1512.[37] Walter Walshe was appointed keeper in 1528.[38] He died in 1538, and Thomas Evans[39] and Rowland Morton both wrote to Cromwell asking for his aid in obtaining the position, the

[13] *Worcs. Inq. p.m.* (Worcs. Hist. Soc.), ii, 61, 74.
[14] *Abbrev. Rot. Orig.* (Rec. Com.), i, 223.
[15] *Cal. Close*, 1313–18, p. 491.
[16] Ibid. 505.   [17] Ibid. 512.
[18] *Abbrev. Rot. Orig.* (Rec. Com.), i, 260.
[19] *Cal. Close*, 1318–23, p. 311.
[20] Ibid. 511, 512, 513, 516.
[21] Ibid.
[22] Ibid. 1318–23, p. 437.
[23] Add. R. 26898, 26899.
[24] Duchy of Lanc. Mins. Accts. bdle. 645, no. 10461, 10466.
[25] *Cal. Pat.* 1476–85, pp. 76, 124.

[25a] *Materials for Hist. of Hen. VII* (Rolls Ser.), ii, 245.
[26] *L. and P. Hen. VIII*, iv, g. 4687 (19).
[27] Ibid. xiii (2), g. 734 (28).
[28] Add. R. 25965.
[29] Leland, *Itinerary* (ed. Hearne), vii, 13.
[29a] In the inquisition taken on the death of Christopher Savage in 1545 there is no mention of a house. Francis Savage in his will dated 1557 bequeathed to his wife for life the mansion-house of Elmley.
[30] *Cal. Close*, 1231–4, p. 529. There is a charter by King Henry given in the Beauchamp Chartulary, by which the

king forbade anyone to take the pheasants (fesandos) of Walter de Beauchamp, which he had placed in his manor of Elmley (Add. MS. 28024, fol. 127 d.).
[31] *Worcs. Inq. p.m.* (Worcs. Hist. Soc.), i, 63.
[32] *Cal. Pat.* 1348–50, p. 311.
[33] Duchy of Lanc. Mins. Accts. bdle. 645, no. 10461.
[34] *Cal. Pat.* 1476–85, p. 76.
[35] Ibid. 211.   [36] Ibid. 379.
[36a] *Materials for Hist. of Hen. VII* (Rolls Ser.), i, 25 ; ii, 245.
[37] *L. and P. Hen. VIII*, i, 3613, 3483.
[38] Ibid. iv, g. 4687 (19).
[39] Ibid. xiii (1), 424.

ELMLEY CASTLE : FRAGMENT OF CASTLE KEEP

ELMLEY CASTLE HOUSE FROM THE SOUTH-EAST

latter saying, 'if it please the King by your Lordship's mediation to prefer me, I and mine shall stand balanced *in alto et basso*, live and die in your Lordship's retinue.' He also begs credence for his messenger 'and will give your Lordship £20.'[40] Neither of these suppliants received the post, which was granted to Urian Brereton.[41] The park was included in the sale to Christopher Savage,[42] and remained in his family until 1822, when it was sold with the castle to Colonel Thomas Henry Hastings Davies. It now belongs to Lieut.-General Henry Fanshawe Davies, J.P., D.L.

HONOUR Elmley Castle was the *caput* of the Worcestershire honour of the Beauchamps. The chief part of the honour descended to them from Urse the Sheriff, but Elmley Castle came to them from Robert, Urse's brother. The honour seems to have consisted of the land which Urse held of the Bishop of Worcester in 1086,[43] and was held in 1166[44] and in the 13th century[45] by the Beauchamps for fifteen knights' fees. The manor[46] and castle were included in the honour[47] and followed the same descent. A rent roll of the honour in 1698 is preserved at the British Museum.[48] When the castle was purchased by Colonel Davies he revived the claim to chief rents due to the honour, which had been allowed to lapse. The owners of most of the manors compounded and their lands were enfranchised.

The court of the honour of Elmley seems to have been held at Worcester in the 14th century, for in the inquisition taken on the death of Guy de Beauchamp in 1315 it was said that the pleas and perquisites of the court of the castle of Worcester called the court of knights pertained to the manor of Elmley.[49]

MANORS King Offa is said to have granted the land of two *manentes* in *ELMLEY* to the Bishop of Worcester in 780,[50] and the overlordship of the manor remained with the see of Worcester[51] until the middle of the 15th century.[52] In 1478–9 the manor was said to be held of the king in chief.[53]

Brihteah, Bishop of Worcester (1033–8), gave the vill of Elmley to a certain servant of his, but Bishop Lyfing, his successor, restored it to the monastery. Later, however, on the entreaties of his friends, he gave it to Aegelric Kiu, one of his knights, to hold for his life only, with reversion to the monastery.[54] 'After the death of Kiu, it was restored to the monastery and one Witheric was bailiff, but Robert le Despenser, the brother of the sheriff, with the authority of the King took it away from the monastery.'[55] This Robert held 4 hides in the manor of Cropthorne, evidently representing the manor of Elmley,[56] at the

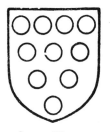

SEE OF WORCESTER. *Argent ten roundels gules.*

date of the Domesday Survey. He died without issue, and the manor of Elmley Castle passed to the Beauchamps, the heirs of his brother Urse D'Abitot, the Sheriff of Worcester. Emmeline daughter and heir of Urse married Walter de Beauchamp,[57] who is mentioned as the owner of these 4 hides in an early 12th-century survey of Oswaldslow.[58] He was succeeded in 1129–39 by his son William.[59] For his zeal in the cause of the Empress Maud William was dispossessed of his lands by King Stephen, but was afterwards restored to them. His son William succeeded him in 1170,[60] and dying before 1211[61] was followed by his son Walter, a minor.[62] In 1211 Roger de Mortimer gave 3,000 marks for having the wardship of Walter de Beauchamp and the custody of his lands, and married Walter to his daughter.[63] Walter de Beauchamp seems to have taken the part of the barons against John for a short time in 1216, but made his peace with the king in August of that year.[64] He died in 1235, and in the following year the king took the homage of his son William for the estates in Worcestershire.[65] In 1254 this William obtained from the king a grant of a weekly market on Wednesdays at Elmley and a fair for three days at the feast of St. Leonard in the summer.[66] He married Isabel daughter of William Mauduit and sister and heir of William Mauduit Earl of Warwick,[67] and

---

[40] *L. and P. Hen. VIII*, xiii (1), 479.

[41] Ibid. xiii (2), g. 734 (28). There were proceedings in the Court of Star Chamber taken by George Willoughby and Anne his wife, the widow of Thomas Lyttelton, against Urian Brereton, on the ground that he had forcibly entered and prohibited them from using a lodge in Elmley Castle, which the defendant alleged had always been used as the residence of the keeper of the park (Star Chamb. Proc. Hen. VIII, bdles. 21, no. 48 ; 32, no. 105 ; 24, no. 209 ; 17, no. 236 ; Edw. VI, bdles. 1, no. 96 ; 7, no. 56). [42] See below.

[43] Four exceptions seem to be Hampton Lovett, Rushock, Doverdale and Coston Hackett, all of which were held by Urse in chief in 1086 and by William de Beauchamp in chief in the 13th century. All of these manors were said to be held of the barony of Elmley in the 15th, 16th and 17th centuries (for refs. see under the manors).

[44] *Red Bk. of Exch.* (Rolls Ser.), 300.

[45] *Worcs. Inq. p.m.* (Worcs. Hist. Soc.), i, 63.

[46] The descent is given under the manor.

[47] The term barony of Elmley was used in the 15th and 16th centuries. Duchy of Lanc. Mins. Accts. bdle. 645, no. 10461, 10468 ; Rentals and Surv. portf. 16, no. 89. The nuns of Cookhill held the tithes of the *fercula* of the barony of Elmley.

[48] Add. R. 27517. This includes rent from many places which do not seem to have been formerly included in the honour.

[49] *Worcs. Inq. p.m.* (Worcs. Hist. Soc.), ii, 62, 75. [50] Heming, op. cit. 95.

[51] Birch, *Cart. Sax.* i, 328.

[52] *V.C.H. Worcs.* i, 296b, 325 ; *Cal. Inq. p.m.* 1–9 *Edw. II*, 410 ; Chan. Inq. p.m. 8 Hen. IV, no. 68 ; 18 Hen. VI, no. 3. In 1269 William de Beauchamp did homage for his lands to the Bishop of Worcester in the church of Bredon (*Reg. G. Giffard* [Worcs. Hist. Soc.], 9).

[53] Chan. Inq. p.m. 18 Edw. IV, no. 47.

[54] Heming quotes the charter of Bishop Lyfing to Aegelric (op. cit. 599).

[55] Ibid. 267–8.

[56] *V.C.H. Worcs.* i, 296b, n. 8. It would seem, however, that Elmley had formerly been held by Keneward.

[57] Round, *Feud. Engl.* 175.

[58] *V.C.H. Worcs.* i, 325b.

[59] Add. MS. 28024, fol. 127 d.

[60] *Ann. Mon.* (Rolls Ser.), iv, 382.

[61] A William de Beauchamp died in 1197 (ibid. 389).

[62] *Red Bk. of Exch.* (Rolls Ser.), 567 ; *Testa de Nevill* (Rec. Com.), 41b.

[63] *Ann. Mon.* (Rolls Ser.), iv, 400.

[64] *Rot. Lit. Claus.* (Rec. Com.), i, 280.

[65] *Excerpta e Rot. Fin.* (Rec. Com.), i, 300.

[66] *Cal. Pat.* 1247–58, p. 272. In 1274–5 the jurors of Oswaldslow presented that William held a market at Elmley and took amends of the assize of bread and ale. William produced the charter of 1254 (Assize R. 1026, m. 37 d.). Nothing further is known of a market or fair at Elmley Castle.

[67] G.E.C. *Complete Peerage*, viii, 56. Leland says that 'the olde Lord Beauchampe of Helmeley sent 3 or 4 of his sunnes to the Batel of Eovesham to help King Henry the 3 and Prince Edwarde againe Simon Monteforte and the Barons ; and these Brether and their Band did a greate feate in vanquischsing the Host of Montefort' (Leland, *Itin.* [ed. Hearne], vi, 63).

dying in 1269 was succeeded by his son William de Beauchamp,[68] who had previously inherited the earldom of Warwick from his uncle.[69]

In 1275 Bishop Godfrey Giffard renewed the suit against the Beauchamps, which had been begun by Walter de Cantilupe, alleging that they held the assize of bread and ale at Elmley Castle without authority, and claiming the redress of sundry other grievances.[70] In 1279 the decision of the arbitrators was given in favour of the bishop.[71]

BEAUCHAMP. *Gules a fesse between six crosslets or.*

This William de Beauchamp died in 1298.[72] His son Guy did homage for his father's lands in October 1298,[73] and died 10 August 1315, leaving as his heir his eldest son Thomas, then aged two years.[74] Thomas Earl of Warwick was knighted in January 1330 and had livery of his lands in the following year.[75] He conveyed this manor among others to trustees for the payment of portions to his daughters after his death.[76] He was marshal of the army in France in 1346 and distinguished himself at Crecy and at Poitiers in 1356. He died at Calais in November 1369 and was succeeded by his second but eldest surviving son Thomas.[77] The latter was arrested for treason and imprisoned in the Tower in 1396, and his estates were forfeited.[78] In August 1397 the manor of Elmley Castle was granted to Thomas Lord le Despenser.[79] In September of that year Thomas was created Earl of Gloucester, and the manor was confirmed to him under that title.[80] Thomas Earl of Warwick was, however, reinstated in all his possessions on the accession of Henry IV, and died in 1401.[81] The manor of Elmley was held by his widow until her death in 1406–7, when her son Richard succeeded.[82] In 1423 the manor was settled on him and his second wife Isabel le Despenser Countess of Worcester.[83] He died in April 1439, and on the death of Isabel in the following December Elmley Castle passed to their son Henry, aged fifteen years.[84] In 1444 he was created Premier Earl of England, and advanced to the dignity of Duke of Warwick in the following year. He is supposed to have been crowned King of the Isle of Wight by Henry VI.[85] He died 11 June 1446, when the dukedom and the male line of this branch of the family expired, but

his other honours devolved on his only daughter Anne Countess of Warwick, then aged three years.[86] She died an infant in 1448–9, and the manor of Elmley Castle passed to her aunt Anne, the wife of Richard Nevill Earl of Salisbury.[87] After his death at the battle of Barnet in 1471, Elmley Castle was settled on his daughter Isabel wife of George Duke of Clarence, the right of his widow Anne being ignored. Isabel died in 1476,[88] and Elmley Castle was held by her husband until his death on 4 March 1478.[89] Edward his son and heir being a minor the castle and manor passed into the king's hands.[90] In 1487, however, Anne Countess of Warwick obtained an Act of Parliament for her restoration to the Warwick estates, but this seems only to have been done to enable her to convey them to the Crown,[91]

CLARENCE. *FRANCE quartered with ENGLAND with the difference of a label argent having a quarter gules upon each pendant.*

for in the same year she surrendered the manor and castle of Elmley with the other Warwick estates to Henry VII.[92] The manor remained in the king's possession until 1544,[93] when it was sold by Henry VIII to Sir William Herbert of the Privy Chamber and Christopher Savage.[94] The grant included the lordship and manor, castle and park, of Elmley Castle, the water of the Avon beside Peryforde, from Cropthorne Field to le Lytle Neytesende and thence to the lower end of Peryforde Meadow, and thence as far as Chalforde, with all 'lez neytes' pertaining to the said water and free fishery in it, a parcel of land called 'le Nocke' beyond the Avon, the site of the manor of Elmley otherwise called the lodge of Elmley Park.[95] On 6 November 1544 Sir William Herbert quitclaimed his share of the manor to Christopher Savage, who died on 23 November 1545, leaving a son and heir Francis Hardwyk Savage.[96] The latter died August 1557 and was followed by his eldest son William Savage.[97] William Savage died 7 August 1616,[98] when the estate passed to his eldest son Sir John Savage. He on 15 June in the following year settled the manor on his brother Giles in tail-male with contingent remainder to another brother George and his son William. Sir John Savage died without issue at Elmley Castle on 2 April 1623

[68] *Excerpta e Rot. Fin.* (Rec. Com.), ii, 487.
[69] G.E.C. *Complete Peerage*, viii, 56. He assumed the title Earl of Warwick in the lifetime of his parents.
[70] *Reg. G. Giffard* (Worcs. Hist. Soc.), 75; Thomas, op. cit. App. no. 47.
[71] Thomas, op. cit. 137.
[72] *Worc. Inq. p.m.* (Worcs. Hist. Soc.), i, 63, 64.
[73] Add. MS. 28024, fol. 127.
[74] *Cal. Inq. p.m.* 1–9 *Edw. II*, 398. Guy de Beauchamp was nicknamed 'the Black Cur of Arden' by Piers Gaveston, the favourite of Edward II. He had Gaveston beheaded, and is supposed to have died of poison administered by the latter's friends (*Dict. Nat. Biog.*). A tenant at Wadborough held his land by service of being hornblower without the gate of Elmley Castle at the feast of the

Trinity (*Worcs. Inq. p.m.* [Worcs. Hist. Soc.], ii, 93).
[75] G.E.C. *Complete Peerage*, viii, 57.
[76] Add. MS. 28024, fol. 15a.
[77] G.E.C. op. cit. viii, 57.
[78] Chan. Inq. p.m. 21 Ric. II, no. 137, m. 6.
[79] *Cal. Pat.* 1396–9, p. 186.
[80] Ibid. 219.
[81] G.E.C. op. cit. viii, 58.
[82] Chan. Inq. p.m. 8 Hen. IV, no. 68.
[83] Feet of F. Div. Co. Mich. 2 Hen. VI.
[84] Chan. Inq. p.m. 17 Hen. VI, no. 54; 18 Hen. VI, no. 3.
[85] G.E.C. op. cit. viii, 59.
[86] Chan. Inq. p.m. 24 Hen. VI, no. 43. In 1447 the manor was granted to the duke's widow Cecily (*Cal. Pat.* 1446–52, p. 38).
[87] G.E.C. op. cit. viii, 60.
[88] Chan. Inq. p.m. 18 Edw. IV, no. 47.

[89] Ibid.
[90] *Cal. Pat.* 1476–85, pp. 76, 124, 379; Mins. Accts. 3 & 4 Hen. VII, no. 989.
[91] G.E.C. op. cit. viii, 63.
[92] Close, 3 Hen. VII, m. 11; De Banco R. Hil. 3 Hen. VII, m. 208.
[93] *L. and P. Hen. VIII*, i, 3613; ii, 3483; iv, g. 1049 (28), 3006 (12), 4687 (19); xiii (2), g. 734 (28). An Act was passed in 1536 assuring the possessions of the Earls of Warwick to the king (Stat. 28 Hen. VIII, cap. 22).
[94] Pat. 36 Hen. VIII, pt. xxi, m. 10; *L. and P. Hen. VIII*, xix (2), g. 527 (41).
[95] Pat. 36 Hen. VIII, pt. xxi, m. 10.
[96] Chan. Inq. p.m. (Ser. 2), lxxii, 101.
[97] Ibid. cxii, 168; ccclvi, 121. In 1548 John Earl of Warwick purchased a messuage and lands in Elmley Castle from the Crown (Pat. 2 Edw. VI, pt. v).
[98] Chan. Inq. p.m. (Ser. 2), ccclvi, 121.

ELMLEY CASTLE CHURCH FROM THE NORTH

ELMLEY CASTLE CHURCH : THE NAVE LOOKING EAST

and was succeeded by his brother Giles, who died 31 January 1631–2.[99] Thomas son of Giles raised a troop of horse for Charles I at the beginning of the Civil War, being then only seventeen years old and a ward of the king. He deserted, however, on the publication of the Declaration of Grace and lived at his mother's house near Tewkesbury. When the county committee came to Worcester he compounded for his estate and gave them £100 for the support of the garrison of Evesham. He came before the Committee for Compounding on 29 November 1645, and it was proved that his corn, barns and other houses had been burnt in September by soldiers from Evesham and that he was £600 in debt. Nevertheless he was fined £1,500 on 4 June 1646. His fine was reduced to £1,487 on 30 October 1649.[100] The estate remained with the Savage family[1] until 1742,[2] when Thomas Savage died without male issue and left the manor to his daughters Elizabeth and Margaret.[3] Some litigation followed, but under an Act of Parliament in 1743[4] the manor of Elmley Castle went to Thomas Byrche son of Elizabeth.[5] He assumed the name of Savage, and dying in 1776 without issue left the manor to his widow Dorothy and afterwards to Robert Clavering, the eldest son of Jane, his youngest sister.[6]

Robert Clavering took the additional surname of Savage,[7] and was succeeded by his son also Robert Clavering Savage, who sold the manor to his tenant and agent Mr. Moore, of whom it was purchased about 1867[8] by Joseph Jones of Oldham. From him it passed to his heir John Joseph Jones in 1880.[9] He was succeeded by his cousin William Jones, and on the death of Frederick William son of the latter in 1910 the manor passed to his brother Arthur, the present owner,[10] who, however, claims no manorial rights.

In 1298 there were two mills at Elmley Castle, one water-mill and one windmill.[11] Fisheries between the banks of Nassebrook and Burne are mentioned as belonging to Guy Earl of Warwick in 1315.[12] The mills are not again mentioned in deeds relating to the manor, but a fishery in the Avon belonged to Elmley Castle in 1646.[13] The site of Castle Mill is still to be seen near the ruins of the castle, and there are two water-mills at Elmley Castle at the present day.

A hide of land at *KERSOE* (Criddesho, viii cent. ;

SAVAGE. *Argent six lions sable.*

Crideshoth, xii cent. ; Creddeshey, xv cent.) was given with Elmley by King Offa in 780 to the church of Worcester.[14] It evidently followed the descent of Elmley Castle,[15] being part of that manor in the 15th century.[16] It was granted with Elmley in 1544 to William Herbert and Christopher Savage,[17] and apparently followed the same descent until 1822, when under the name of 'the manor of Kersoe'[18] it occurs for the last time.

At the Dissolution the Abbot of Westminster was receiving a fee-farm rent of £17 6s. 0¾d. from Elmley and the neighbouring parishes of Bricklehampton and Comberton.[19] It was perhaps paid by the lords of Elmley Castle for his tenants at Bricklehampton and Little Comberton in the abbot's fee.[20] The fee farm was granted in 1542 to the Dean and Chapter of Westminster.[21] This rent has not been traced later.

'A manor of Elmley,' which has not been identified, was granted by Queen Mary to the refounded abbey in 1556–7,[22] and by Queen Elizabeth regranted to the dean and chapter in 1559–60.[23] It was sold in 1650 among many other of the dean and chapter's manors to Cheney Colepeper of Hollingbourne, co. Kent,[24] and then seems to have formed part of the manor of Binholme in Pershore. It was restored to the dean and chapter on the accession of Charles II, and is mentioned among their possessions in 1690, being then leased with Bricklehampton and Comberton at a rent of £16.[24a]

The church of *ST. MARY* consists of a chancel 25 ft. by 16 ft., nave 57 ft. by 19½ ft., north transept 20 ft. deep by 16½ ft. wide, north aisle to the west of it, 9 ft. 10 in. wide, and south aisle 10 ft. wide, a north porch, and a western tower 18½ ft. wide by 14 ft. deep ; all the measurements are internal.

The church dates from a very early period, the walling of the chancel, which was shorter than the present one, belonging to about the end of the 11th century. The plan at that time consisted simply of nave and chancel, and doubtless much of the original stonework remains in the present nave, though many of the carved stones belong to 12th-century alterations. The first addition of which there is any definite evidence took place early in the 13th century, when the unusually wide tower was erected at the west end of the nave, which may have been lengthened at the same time. About 1340 the church was considerably enlarged, the north transept and the south aisle being added. The chancel also was lengthened by some 5 ft., evidently to form a narrow vestry behind the high altar. The north aisle was an addition of the latter part of the 15th century, the

---

[99] Chan. Inq. p.m. (Ser. 2), cccclxvii, 186. Thomas, brother and next heir of Sir John, was a lunatic.
[100] Cal. Com. for Comp. 1030.
[1] Nash gives a pedigree of the family (op. cit. i, 384). A pedigree has also been printed by Sir Thomas Phillipps in his *Genealogia.*
[2] Feet of F. Div. Co. Mich. 21 Chas. II ; *Index to Worcs. Fines* (Worcs. Hist. Soc.), 244.
[3] Nash, op. cit. i, 383.
[4] Priv. Act, 16 Geo. II, cap. 31.
[5] Ibid. ; Recov. R. Trin. 26 & 27 Geo. II, rot. 284.
[6] Nash loc. cit.

[7] Phillimore and Fry, *Changes of Name,* 280.
[8] Noake, *Guide to Worcs.* 146.
[9] Information from Lt.-General H. F. Davies.
[10] Ibid.
[11] *Worcs. Inq. p.m.* (Worcs. Hist. Soc.), i, 63.
[12] *Cal. Inq. p.m.* 1–9 Edw. II, 398.
[13] Recov. R. Trin. 22 Chas. I, rot. 54.
[14] Birch, op. cit. i, 328.
[15] Red Bk. of Bishopric of Worc. (Eccl. Com. Rec. Var. bdle. 121, no. 43698), fol. 253 ; Chan. Inq. p.m. 18 Hen. VI, no. 3 ; 17 Hen. VI, no. 54 ; 24 Hen. VI, no. 43.

[16] Mins. Accts. 3 & 4 Hen. VII, no. 989 ; ibid. bdle. 645, no. 10466, 10468.
[17] Pat. 36 Hen. VIII, pt. xxi.
[18] Recov. R. Hil. 2 & 3 Geo. IV, rot. 123.
[19] Dugdale, *Mon.* i, 325.
[20] Mins. Accts. 3 & 4 Hen. VII, no. 989.
[21] *L. and P. Hen. VIII,* xvii, g. 714 (5).
[22] Pat. 3 & 4 Phil. and Mary, pt. v, m. 1.
[23] Ibid. 2 Eliz. pt. xi, m. 16.
[24] Close, 1651, pt. lvi, no. 19 ; 1654, pt. xi, no. 13.
[24a] Deeds of D. and C. of Westm. no. 21912.

earlier transept arch being retained as the easternmost bay of the arcade and a cross arch constructed in place of the west transept wall. At the same time a new column was substituted for the first pier in the south arcade and the top stage was added to the tower, a new west door and window being inserted. In the early part of the 16th century the transept was heightened and new windows inserted to form a chapel for the Savage family, the alterations amounting practically to a rebuilding. The north porch underwent considerable repair in the first half of the next century, and it is not improbable that the western half of the south aisle was rebuilt in 1629, the date inscribed upon a stone between the two westernmost windows in the south wall. To the same date belongs also the embattled parapet of the north aisle. Prattinton, who wrote in 1817, mentions a semi-circular end to the chancel; it was probably an 18th-century addition and has now been removed. The chancel was restored in 1863, when the east

the late 11th century, and at the west end of the south wall is a short length of plinth course. The chancel arch is modern and springs from corbels. In the east wall of the nave flanking it are niches for figures; the one to the south is complete with its square head, but of the other only the lower parts of the jambs remain.

The nave arcades each consist of four bays. The first bay on the north side has a square jamb on the east with a 14th-century pointed arch of two chamfered orders dying on it. The rest of the arcade is of late 15th-century date and has octagonal columns with simple capitals and bases and pointed arches of two chamfered orders. The arches on the south side are similar to the first bay on the north, but the first column is octagonal and similar in detail to the later work opposite. The second and third piers and the western respond are square, the arches dying on them, and the east respond is dispensed with. The rood stair formerly existing in the angle of the north tran-

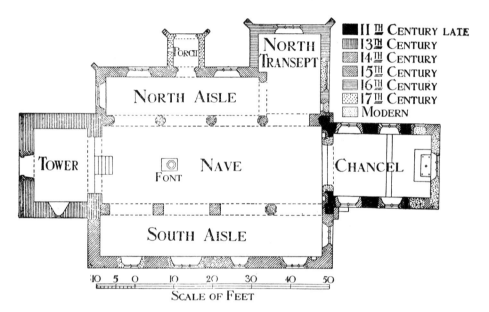

II<u>TH</u> CENTURY LATE
13<u>TH</u> CENTURY
14<u>TH</u> CENTURY
15<u>TH</u> CENTURY
16<u>TH</u> CENTURY
17<u>TH</u> CENTURY
MODERN

SCALE OF FEET

PLAN OF ELMLEY CASTLE CHURCH

wall was rebuilt, a new roof put up, and new tracery inserted in the side windows. The round chancel arch, which is said to have been of wood, was rebuilt at the same time. The chancel also underwent a general restoration in 1878, when the nave and aisles were re-roofed.

The modern east window, put up by Lieut.-General Davies to the memory of his parents and brothers, is of three lights with a traceried head; a 14th-century doorway opening into the former vestry behind the altar is now walled up, and traces remain of a corresponding door in the south wall. The first of the two windows on the north is of two lights under a traceried two-centred head; the second also has two lights with a quatrefoil over; the tracery and mullions of both are modern, but the jambs are old, those of the easternmost dating probably from the early 15th century, while those of the western window appear to be of the 14th century. The two windows on the south side correspond in all respects with those opposite. Between these windows and visible on both sides of the wall is the herring-bone work of

sept and the nave has been removed, but the blocked doorways remain. The east and north windows of the transept are both 16th-century insertions, though not quite contemporary. The former, which was of five lights, is now blocked by the large tomb of the first Earl of Coventry[24b]; the north window has three lights with sunk spandrels under a flat head. The transept has an embattled parapet both to its side walls and to the low north gable. In the aisle wall west of the transept is a raking stone showing the position of the former steep gabled roof. The cross arch towards the aisle, which stands somewhat east of the line of the transept wall, belongs to the 15th-century work and springs from the first column of the arcade. The two north windows and the west window of the north aisle are all original and have three lights with feathered tracery in a square head. The entrance doorway between the two north windows has a two-centred drop arch, and is evidently a 14th-century doorway removed here from the former

[24b] In this window was formerly a Jesse tree. See Nash, *Hist. of Worcs.* i, 386.

nave wall. The porch has in its west wall a diminutive and almost shapeless light. The outer doorway has continuous mouldings and a semicircular head with a moulded label. Set in the side walls are many 11th and 12th-century stones carved with various beasts, foliage, and diapering.

The porch is strengthened by diagonal buttresses, and its parapets, with those of the aisle, are embattled with continuous copings ; above the porch doorway is a small trefoiled niche. Set in the aisle wall below the string are two gargoyles with grotesque human and animal figures.

The east window of the south aisle is a 15th-century insertion of three lights under a pointed traceried head. To the north of it outside is a shallow buttress, above which can be seen the quoined angle of the original nave. In the south wall of the aisle is a small ogee-headed piscina of 14th-century date the bowl of which has been cut away. The first window on the south is a later insertion with three lights under a square traceried head. The second window appears to be contemporary with the aisle and has two narrow lights with a quatrefoil above them, the jambs being of two chamfered orders. The third window is modern, and the fourth, of two lights under a pointed head, appears to be an insertion of the 16th or 17th century. Between the last two windows is a stone inscribed 1629 F.F.

The tower is of three stages with a pointed tower arch of two chamfered orders springing from moulded abaci. The respond of the inner order is corbelled back to the face of the jambs a little below the level of the abacus. It is evidently part of the original early 13th-century tower, as is also the small lancet window in the south wall. The west doorway and window above it are 15th-century insertions. The doorway has a two-centred drop arch with a moulded label, and the jambs are of two orders. In the north and south walls of the second stage are large 13th-century lancet windows now filled in. The third stage or bell-chamber is lighted by transomed windows of two lights in each wall, with a quatrefoil above them in a pointed head. The parapet is embattled and has grotesque gargoyles at the angles. The walling of the lower part of the tower is of small rubble with wide jointing, and the third stage is ashlar faced.

The walling of the church generally is of rubble, varying in the different parts of the building. Besides the herring-bone work in the chancel wall the other parts of the earlier work are of uncoursed rubble. In the east gable of the nave are several ancient carved or worked stones. The parapets generally are of ashlar. The roofs are all gabled and modern.

The font has a 13th-century square base carved with four dragons around a circular stem. The bowl dates from about 1500, and is octagonal, with plain panels inclosing shields carved with the Five Wounds, the rose, feathers, a portcullis, a trefoiled leaf with a bar on the stem, an indented fesse, and a ragged staff. In the pewing of the south aisle are four turned legs, which probably belonged to the 1637 communion table mentioned in the churchwardens' accounts. There are also four standards for misericordes. A large number of 16th-century pews with moulded rails remain in use. An old stone bowl now in the transept was brought from a farm at Kersoe.

In the north window of the transept are two pieces of old glass ; one is a panel inclosing the arms of Westminster, and over it is a crowned rose, party palewise red and white, a royal badge of the Tudors. In the south-east window of the south aisle are a few other old fragments, including a crowned red rose and the quartered lilies and leopards of France and England.

In the transept are two large monuments. The first is an alabaster altar tomb, with a black marble slab on which rest the three recumbent effigies of William Savage, Giles Savage, who died in 1631, and his wife Catherine. The latter holds the figure of a posthumous daughter. At their feet are the kneeling figures of their four other children. On mural slabs above the tomb are placed the inscriptions, arms, &c. The second large monument, against the east wall, is to the first Earl of Coventry, who died in 1699 ; it is of Renaissance design, and has a white marble effigy of the earl reclining on his elbow under a canopy of the same material, supported on Ionic columns flanked by large allegorical female figures. In the cleft pediment are the Coventry arms and crest with allegorical figures at the sides. The monument, which was refused admittance to Croome D'Abitôt Church by the second earl, was erected by the countess dowager, who in 1700 married Thomas Savage of Elmley Castle. On the south wall of the chancel is a mural monument to Anne daughter of Sir Richard Fetyplace, 1609 ; and another, opposite, to E. G. died 1668, has Corinthian capitals and a broken pediment, but has lost its columns. An undated slab in the floor commemorates William Ganderton. In the north aisle below the second window is a tablet to Elizabeth wife of Thomas Harper, vicar of Elmley, who died in 1609.

Part of a 14th-century coffin slab with a cusped cross stands in the north transept.

Mention may be made here of the curious sundial which stands in the churchyard ; it is a square pillar, on the south face of which is the dial above a carving of the Savage arms in a shield of ten quarters as they appear on the tomb in the north transept.

The bells are six in number : the first a treble of 1700 ; the second cast by Henry Farmer, 1619 ; the third with the inscription ' Eternis annis,' &c. (upon this bell are the heads of a king and queen) [24c] ; the fourth by Matthew Bagley, 1686 ; the fifth an old bell, said to have been of 1556, recast in 1886 ; and the sixth a tenor bell of 1620.

The communion plate comprises a silver cup given in 1633 with a salver, a standing paten of 1635, and a flagon of 1770.

The registers before 1812 are as follows : (i) all entries 1665 to 1740 ; (ii) baptisms and burials 1741 to 1812 and marriages to 1754 ; (iii) marriages 1754 to 1812. There are also some old churchwardens' accounts and some 17th-century papers found in the church in 1817, which include inventories of church goods and property. In the inventory of 1633 among the churchwardens' accounts are mentioned 13 dozen and 2 organ pipes, also a silver flagon, and in 1637 a new rail for the communion table is mentioned ; there is also note of repair to the tower in 1666.

[24c] Said by Ellacombe to be those of Edward I and Eleanor. The same heads and cross are on a bell at Dynham (Gloucs.).

345

ADVOWSON The advowson of the church of Elmley Castle evidently belonged to the lords of the manor in early times,[25] for in 1308 Guy de Beauchamp granted it to his newly-founded chantry in the chapel of the castle of Elmley.[26] Licence was given for this gift, although it was found that it would be to the king's damage, because in case of forfeiture or during a minority the presentation would belong to the king.[27] In the following year the church was appropriated to the warden and chaplains of the chantry,[28] and the vicarage was ordained in 1312.[29] The vicar was presented by the warden of the chantry.[30] In 1530 an inquiry was made as to the advowson of Elmley, which was found to belong to the warden of the chantry. John Brereton, then warden, had apparently neglected the interests of the parishioners.[31] The chantry was surrendered to Henry VIII in May 1545,[32] and the advowson of the church with the rectory was granted in that year to Sir Philip Hoby.[33] In 1558, however, the advowson was granted to Richard Pates, Bishop of Worcester.[34] On the accession of Elizabeth Pates was deprived, but the rectory was granted to his successor Edwin Sandys in part compensation for certain manors which the queen retained.[35] This grant seems to have included the advowson of the church, for presentations have since that time been made by the Bishops of Worcester.[36]

There was also a chapel in the castle of Elmley, and in 1308 Guy de Beauchamp Earl of Warwick founded there a chantry of eight chaplains and four clerks. In addition to the advowson of the parish church of Elmley he endowed this foundation with a rent of £20 from the manor of Childs Wickham, co. Gloucester,[37] but this proved insufficient to meet the needs of the chaplains, and in 1311, though the rectory of Elmley had been added to the endowment in 1309, it was found necessary to reduce the chantry by one priest and two clerks.[38] The chantry was under the care of a master or warden appointed by the lords of Elmley,[39] and the warden had the power to admit and remove the chaplains.[40]

In 1463 Richard Nevill Earl of Warwick obtained licence to grant land to the value of 20 marks to the warden of the chantry to find an additional chaplain,[41]

and George Duke of Clarence gave the manor and advowson of Naunton Beauchamp.[42] In 1536 the chantry was valued as 'the Rectory of Elmley' at £55 13s. 3d. clear.[43] It was surrendered by the warden Robert Bone in 1545,[44] and all its possessions were granted in the same year to Sir Philip Hoby.[45] In 1546 Sir Philip was in controversy with William Tattersall, lessee under the late warden, as to the chantry lands.[46] The mansion-house, which had belonged to the warden, was granted to Sir Ralph Sadleir by Henry VIII, but he surrendered it to Edward VI in 1547.[47]

The chantry with the mansion was granted in 1564 to Anthony Daston and Anne his wife, widow of Francis Savage of Elmley, for their lives, with remainder to William Savage and his heirs.[48] Anthony died in 1572, and Anne granted her interest for a term of years to Richard Daston and Thomas Savage of Nobury.[49] William Savage died seised of 'the chantry of Elmley called Le College' in 1616,[50] and it then followed the same descent as the manor, with which it seems soon to have become incorporated.[51]

A parcel of land given for the maintenance of lamps and lights in the church of Elmley Castle was valued in 1549–50 at 3s. 4d.[52] This or another estate given for the same purpose was valued in another survey at 7s. 4d., 2s. 4d. being set aside for the poor.[53]

CHARITIES In 1821 Richard Bourne Charlett —as stated on the church table—by his will left £100, the interest to be paid annually to poor persons not on the parish books. The legacy was lent on the security of certain lands in the parish of Claines, into which the trustees entered into possession and eventually sold. The proceeds, with accumulated rents, were invested in £260 8s. consols with the official trustees, producing £6 10s. yearly.

Church Lands.—The church table further stated as follows : — 'One land in King's-hedge Furlong, in the Fields of Elmley Castle, one land in a Furlong called Crowel ; one land and four leys in a field called Bartlett's Field, in Bricklehampton, the donor out of memory.'

These lands do not now appear to be capable of identification.

[25] Chan. Inq. p.m. (Ser. 2), lxxx, 107.
[26] Campb. Chart. xxix, 2 ; Inq. a.q.d. file 67, no. 2.
[27] *Cal. Pat.* 1307–13, p. 136.
[28] Worc. Epis. Reg. Reynolds (1308–13), fol. 21.
[29] Nash, op. cit. i, 391. A transcript of the ordination is here given.
[30] Worc. Epis. Reg. Bransford (1339–49), fol. 12 ; Nash, op. cit. i, 382 ; Chan. Inq. p.m. (Ser. 2), lxxx, 107.
[31] Chan. Inq. p.m. (Ser. 2), lxxx, 107.
[32] *L. and P. Hen. VIII,* xx (1), 718.
[33] Ibid. g. 846 (79). The advowson of the rectory of Elmley had been included, as a late possession of the Earl of Warwick, in the grant of the manor and castle to Sir William Herbert and Christopher Savage in 1544 (ibid. xix [2], g. 527 [41]), but by this the advowson of the chantry was intended, the master of the chantry being rector of Elmley.

[34] Pat. 5 & 6 Phil. and Mary, pt. ii, m. 30.
[35] Ibid. 4 Eliz. pt. vi. The rectory was leased by the bishop to the Savages of Elmley (Add. Chart. 25966 ; Recov. R. Trin. 22 Chas. I, rot. 54). In 1646 Thomas Savage was offered an abatement of £400 from his fine if he assigned his rectory of Elmley, worth £60 a year, to the vicar there (*Cal. Com. for Comp.* 1030). Mr. Arthur Jones, lord of the manor, is now the owner of the rectorial tithes.
[36] Inst. Bks. (P.R.O.) ; *Clergy Lists.* The advowson of the vicarage of Elmley was, however, included in a conveyance of the manor of Elmley in 1753 (Recov. R. Trin. 26 & 27 Geo. II, rot. 284).
[37] *Cal. Pat.* 1307–13, p. 136 ; Inq. a.q.d. file 67, no. 2.
[38] Worc. Epis. Reg. Reynolds (1308–13), fol. 48 d.

[39] Ibid. fol. 78 d. ; Cobham (1317–27), fol. 30 d. ; Bransford (1339–49), i (3), fol. 102 ; *Sede Vacante Reg.* (Worcs. Hist. Soc.), 361 ; *Cal. Pat.* 1396–9, p. 212 ; 1476–85, p. 159.
[40] Nash, op. cit. i, 382.
[41] *Cal. Pat.* 1461–7, p. 296.
[42] Chan. Inq. p.m. (Ser. 2), lxxx, 107.
[43] *Valor Eccl.* (Rec. Com.), iii, 267.
[44] *L. and P. Hen. VIII,* xx (1), 718.
[45] Ibid. g. 846 (79).
[46] Ct. of Req. bdle. 2, no. 191.
[47] Pat. 1 Edw. VI, pt. ix, m. 42.
[48] Ibid. 6 Eliz. pt. x, m. 9.
[49] Chan. Inq. p.m. (Ser. 2), ccclvi, 121.
[50] Ibid.
[51] Ibid. ccclxvii, 186. It is mentioned for the last time in 1632.
[52] Chant. Cert. 60, no. 46.
[53] Ibid. 61, no. 33.

Elmley Castle Church: Tomb of William Savage, Giles Savage and his Wife, Catherine

Elmley Castle : The Police-station

EVENLODE

Eowlangelade (x cent.) ; Eowinlode, Eowinglade, Evnelade (xi cent.) ; Evenlode (xiii cent.) ; Ewnelode (xiv cent.) ; Emlode (xv cent.).

Evenlode is one of the detached parishes of Worcestershire which touch the western border of Oxfordshire and are separated by Gloucestershire from the main part of their own county.

'Meethincketh,' wrote Habington, 'I see our Shyre as mounted on a Pegasus flyinge over the neighbouring counties, and coming to the confines of Oxfordshire . . . he caryethe the authority of our county about and over Coteswould . . . as at Evenlode [1] . . . which altho' seperated with parishes not attending our county yet is wholy ours. It joynethe on Morten Henmarsh heath on the stone which touches four sheeres,' [2] and marks the northern limit of the parish. The boundary thence runs along field edges and the green path by Stuphill Covert till it reaches the Chastleton road, whence it turns south along the fields by Horn Farm and Evenlode Grounds to the little river which winds gently about the western border of the parish—

'The tender Evenlode, that makes
  Her meadows hush to hear the sound
Of waters mingling in the brakes
  And binds my heart to English ground.' [3]

The village of Evenlode stands on the hillslope looking across to Crowthorn Wood, close to the left bank of the stream from which it is locally said to derive its name.[3a] The road here forms a rough triangle inclosing a wide space now largely given up to orchards ; this is crossed by several footpaths connecting the southern part of the village with the main street, which climbs in a north-easterly direction up the slope from the river. On the right-hand side is a stately row of poplars known locally as the Eleven Apostles, the representative of Judas Iscariot being a twisted tree of later growth which stands back from the straight rank formed by the others. The village for the most part is built like its neighbours of the warm grey Cotswold stone ; but a black and white house in the lower street and an outlying half-timbered farm show a Worcestershire influence. At the bottom of the hill is the church of St. Edward with the rectory, a pleasant stone house of the 18th century, much modernized and added to during the 19th century, to which a verandah, now covered with creepers, has been added. Close to the church is the old manor-house now the property of Mr. R. E. B. Yelf. The house is of L-shaped plan and has two stories and an attic. The west wing containing the kitchen dates from the 17th century and appears to be the earliest part of the building. The main limb of the plan, containing a central hall and stairway with a room on either side, is of the early 18th century. The contemporary stairs, which are of oak, and rise from the hall to the attics, are of the open well type with moulded handrails and turned balusters. At the stairway to the cellar in the earlier part of the house is some re-used 17th-century panelling. The garden at the back of the house stretches almost down to the Worcester branch of the Great Western railway, which runs along the river bank close to the village ; the nearest station is, however, at Adlestrop, 2 miles away.

Evenlode Farm, at the north end of the village, is an L-shaped house of about 1600. The west front with its central entrance has been modernized, but the house still retains its original fittings and stone mullioned windows on the east and north ; the southern part of the house was probably added later in the same century. In one of the windows is some leaded glass with a glazier's name and the date 1727 inscribed upon it. At the south end are two oval blocked lights. The Home Farm on the west side of the road to the north of the church is a house of similar date and type, two stories in height with an attic. The original stone mullioned windows and oak stairs still remain. The latter has a moulded handrail and flat balusters in the form of twisted columns.

Evenlode House is a stone building of about the middle of the 16th century with mullioned windows and stone shingle roofs. In the centre of the main block is the hall, with a room on the north, and the main entrance, modern stairs, and another room on the south ; the kitchen is contained in a wing projecting towards the east. The west front appears to have been altered early in the 17th century, when timber bays were added ; these have been repaired and the front and north walls covered with rough-cast. The original stairs were probably contained in the gabled projection on the north-east. On this side of the house is a stone barn probably of the 16th century with original rough roof timbers. Fletcher's Farm is a good example of a small 16th-century house which has retained its original character practically unaltered, with stone mullioned windows, oak floors, stairs and beams. The entrance, a little to the east of the south front, admits to a passage which has the principal rooms on the west, the kitchen on the east and the staircase at the back on the west. A wing on the north, completing the plan, has an external stone stair. Another farm to the east of this, a rectangular two-story house, is probably of the early 17th century, and has a central hall with the parlour on the west and the kitchen on the east. Some of the rooms have been cut up by modern partitions, but much of its original character is retained. There is a row of seven slate-roofed cottages rebuilt by Evenlode parish in 1834, on the east side of the green, an open space connected with the southern end of the village by a footpath. The pasturage here together with that on the wide strips of turf by the roadsides, amounting to 5 acres, is let every year and the rent applied in providing fuel for the poor.[4] There is much excellent pasture land in the parish ; of 1,619 acres no fewer than 1,108½ are under permanent grass.[5] The arable land amounts to 322 acres, the chief crops being cereals and beans, and there are only 20½ acres

---

[1] *Surv. of Worcs.* (Worcs. Hist. Soc.), i, 211.   [2] Ibid. ii, 68.
[3] Hilaire Belloc, *Lambkin's Remains*, dedication.

[3a] In a charter of 969 the name of the stream is given as Bladene (Birch, *Cart. Sax.* iii, 529).

[4] Inform. from Rev. H. J. Kelsall, rector of Evenlode.
[5] Statistics from Bd. of Agric. (1905).

of woodland,[6] for, though the village of Evenlode is well shaded and the hedgerows are thickly set with trees, there are no woods except Brookend and Evenlode Mane within the boundaries of the parish. The common lands were inclosed under a Private Act of Parliament in 1765,[7] in which provision was made for the above charitable application of the rents for roadside pasturage.[8] The subsoil is chiefly Lower Lias, but the bed of Middle Lias at Chastleton (co. Oxon.) extends slightly into the eastern corner of Evenlode parish near Harcomb Wood.

The following place-names occur in local records: Heortwelle and Mules Hlaewe [9] (viii cent.); Sealt-strete, Gildbeorh, Grenanstige,[10] Lafercan beorh, and Brocenan beorh [11] (x cent.); Typedale Foss [12] and Heth Ynd [13] (xv cent.); Salley meade, Broades Leyes, Mill Holme Close, and Langett or Northfeild Slade [14] (xvii cent.).

The early history of *EVENLODE, MANOR* like that of Daylesford, depends almost entirely on the charters produced in support of their respective claims by the monks of Worcester and Evesham at the close of the 11th century. According to the house of Worcester the land had been granted for three lives by King Offa to his thegn Ridda in 772 with reversion to the monastery at Bredon,[15] but Evesham stated that the gift had been made in 784 to Earl Esne (Esme) with reversion in default of heirs male to their own church.[16] The Worcester account is probably nearer the truth, for in 969 St. Oswald was in possession of land at Evenlode, which he granted to Ealhstan,[17] and a charter of Bishop Lyfing (1038–44) concerning the same property is also mentioned in the chartulary.[18] Possibly it was by a grant from this bishop that Wulfgeat of Donnington came into possession of this land, which he left in his will to his wife.[19] It passed shortly afterwards to Eamer, from whom it was bought between 1044 and 1053 by Mannig, Abbot of Evesham, and his monks.[20] They continued to hold it of the Bishop of Worcester until it was taken from them by Odo of Bayeux,[21] and it was perhaps under them that it was held by Hereward, who is mentioned in 1086 as the former tenant.[22]

At this date Evenlode was one of the members of the great episcopal manor of Blockley,[23] and the overlordship long remained in the hands of the bishop. The holding at Evenlode, assessed at 5 hides, was, however, granted by Bishop John of Pageham (1151–8) to Hugh Poer, who married his niece.[24] After this enfeoffment the overlordship is rarely mentioned, though the tenant of Evenlode was still supposed to pay suit of court at Blockley.[25] This was commuted during the life of Bishop Giffard for the payment of 40s. in 1288,[26] and during the 14th century it is possible that the episcopal rights fell somewhat into disuse. They were revived in 1455 by John Carpenter, at whose request an inquiry was made 'touching the persons of whom the manor of Evenlode was held.' [27] Probably he considered that the wardship of Thomas Petyt ought to have belonged to him, but this was in the possession of the Prior and convent of Worcester, who had succeeded the Poers in the mesne lordship, and the bishop contented himself with confirming their grant to John Gloucester.[28] There seems to be no mention of the overlordship after this date.

The interest of the Poers followed throughout the descent of the mesne lordship of Bredicot [29] (q.v.), the manor of Evenlode being held of the lord of Batten-hall as late as 1641.[30]

The tenancy of Evenlode belonged for over a century to a branch of the Deyvile family, who were also known by the name of the manor. Before 1182 Hugh Poer had enfeoffed Matthew of Evenlode,[31] who was succeeded by Nicholas of Evenlode, possibly his son.[32] The estate passed about 1288 to Richard of Evenlode, also called Richard Deyvile,[33] who was still living in 1309, in which year he settled the manor on himself and his wife Eugenie for life with reversion to their son William.[34] This William took part against the Despensers in the troubles of the reign of Edward II, and in 1327, 'at the request of Roger Mortimer,' he received as his reward a pardon of 'the fine which he was compelled to make by procurement of Hugh le Despenser and others of his confederacy for a certain trespass maliciously charged upon him by the said Hugh.' [35] William Deyvile died about 1348 seised of the manor of Evenlode, which he left to his eldest son Piers.[36] Piers was still living in 1398,[37] but probably

[6] Statistics from Bd. of Agric. (1905).
[7] 5 Geo. III, cap. 63.
[8] Inform. from the Rev. H. J. Kelsall, rector of Evenlode.
[9] Birch, *Cart. Sax.* i, 298. These names occur among the boundaries given in the Worcester chartulary under the date 772. The parish boundary still passes a spring (locally 'well') near Horn Farm and a mound near the Evenlode, now overlooking the railway.
[10] The 'Green Way' may still be traced near the Chastleton road.
[11] Birch, op. cit. iii, 529, 530.
[12] Eccl. Com. Ct. R. (P.R.O.), bdle. 189, no. 5.
[13] Early Chan. Proc. bdle. 372, no. 42.
[14] Chan. Inq. p.m. (Ser. 2), dcvi, 59.
[15] Birch, op. cit. i, 297; Heming, *Chartul.* (ed. Hearne), 35, 552.
[16] Birch, op. cit. i, 338; Heming, op. cit. 638. This charter is an obvious forgery. Birch also gives a charter of Offa, granting Evenlode with Daylesford and other estates to the abbey of Evesham in 777 (op. cit. i, 311). It is also a forgery. The authenticity of these and

other charters has been determined by Mr. F. M. Stenton.
[17] Birch, op. cit. iii, 529. Evenlode was also included in the 'Charter of King Edgar' (Heming, op. cit. 520).
[18] Heming, op. cit. 582.
[19] Harl. Chart. 83 A 2; Birch, op. cit. iii, 652.
[20] Heming, op. cit. 639. The authenticity of this charter has been doubted, but it receives so much support from the Domesday Survey that it seems reasonable to suppose that it may represent the facts. [21] *V.C.H. Worcs.* i, 293.
[22] Ibid. [23] Ibid.
[24] Eccl. Com. Rec. Var. bdle. 121, no. 43698, fol. 253.
[25] Ibid. fol. 175. He had also to pay 10 doddocks of oats yearly in the name of Chirsete, and do suit at the hundred court of Winburntree (ibid.). Evenlode was included in the hundred rolls until 1520 (Eccl. Com. Rec. Ct. R. *passim*), but is not mentioned in those of 1525 or later.
[26] Eccl. Com. Rec. Var. bdle. 121, no. 43698, fol. 185; Habington, op. cit. i, 59.

[27] Pat. 35 Hen. VI, pt. ii, m. 13; Nash, *Hist. of Worcs.* i, 394.
[28] Nash, loc. cit.
[29] *Red Bk. of Exch.* (Rolls Ser.), i, 300; Red Bk. of Bishopric of Worc. (Eccl. Com. Rec. Var. bdle. 121, no. 43698), fol. 253, 261; *Testa de Nevill* (Rec. Com.), 42; Habington, op. cit. i, 213; Pat. 3 Edw. III, pt. ii, m. 4; Dugdale, *Mon.* i, 616.
[30] Chan. Inq. p.m. (Ser. 2), dcvi, 59.
[31] Eccl. Com. Rec. Var. bdle. 121, no. 43698, fol. 253.
[32] Ibid. fol. 186, 244, 253.
[33] Ibid. fol. 175, 185; Habington, op. cit. i, 59.
[34] Feet of F. Worcs. Mich. 3 Edw. II.
[35] Pat. 1 Edw. III, pt. iii, m. 1.
[36] William was still living in 1346 (*Feud. Aids*, v, 309; *Lay Subs. R.* 1346 [Worcs. Hist. Soc.], 27), but was certainly dead before 1361 (*Sede Vacante Reg.* [Worcs. Hist. Soc.], i, 206), and in 1398 Piers stated that his father had been dead about fifty years (Habington, op. cit. i, 212).
[37] Habington, loc. cit.

died shortly afterwards; he seems to have left a widow, Amice, who subsequently married William Lisle.[38] In 1415 John Petyt and Philippa his wife, the heir of Piers Deyvile, settled certain lands in Evenlode on William Lisle and Amice with reversion to Philippa and her heirs,[39] and a little later a life grant of the manor seems to have been made to Amice and her husband, for William Lisle was described as lord of Evenlode in 1416.[40] He seems to have died about 1421,[41] and by 1425 Amice had probably married a third husband, Richard Eton,[42] who held the manor until 1431,[43] in which year it reverted to John Petyt and Philippa.[44] In 1441 they settled it on themselves and the heirs of the body of Philippa, with contingent remainder to her right heirs.[45] John Petyt survived his wife and died about 1455, leaving as his heir his grandson Thomas Petyt, a minor, whose wardship was granted by the Prior and convent of Worcester to John Gloucester.[46] Thomas Petyt died young, and in 1473 the manor was held by William Petyt, probably his brother, who conveyed it for one year to William Rollesley with reversion to himself and his wife Eleanor and their heirs.[47] William Petyt supported the Yorkist cause during the Wars of the Roses, and was in some favour with Edward IV.[48] He was not mentioned in any of the Acts of Attainder passed by Parliament during the reign of Henry VII, but for some reason he lost his property at Evenlode about this time. After an unsuccessful attempt to recover it against Lawrence Albrighton and William Leicester,[49] he, named as William Petyt of Knowle, co. Warw., conveyed his interest to Robert Tate,[50] and between 1501 and 1509 John Tate and Richard Petyt were concerned in more than one cattle-driving expedition to the estate of which they had been dispossessed.[51]

Before 1528, however, Evenlode had passed to Sir William Compton of Compton Wyniates (co. Warw.), who died seised of it in that year, leaving as his heir his son Peter.[52] In 1539 Peter was succeeded by his infant son Henry,[53] afterwards created Lord Compton, who made a settlement of the manor on himself and his wife Frances in 1568.[54] He took part as a peer in the trial of Mary Queen of Scots in 1587, and was subsequently one of the four chief attendants at her

COMPTON of Compton Wyniates. *Sable a leopard or between three helms argent.*

funeral.[55] He died in November 1589, and was succeeded by his son William,[56] who sold the manor of Evenlode in 1601 to John Croker,[57] from whom it was bought in 1605 by Edward Freeman.[58]

In 1618, on the marriage of his son Coningsby with Beatrice the daughter of Thomas Cludd, Edward Freeman made a settlement of the manor to his own use with remainder to the young couple and their heirs in tail-male.[59] Coningsby Freeman succeeded his father in 1631 [60] and died in 1639 [61]; his wife survived him, and was seised of the manor for her life.[62] She obtained a grant of the wardship of her son Edward Freeman, which John Riley afterwards tried to get annulled on the ground that she had concealed some of the lands.[63] Edward Freeman seems to have died before 1675, in which year his sister and co-heir Joyce the wife of Thomas Owen was dealing with part of the manor,[64] probably for the purpose of a settlement. By 1682 the whole estate had come into the hands of Ursula Poer, another of Edward's sisters, and Robert Lawrence, who was perhaps the son of the third sister Eleanor.[65] Robert Lawrence was still living in 1702, when he was co-vouchee in a recovery with Thomas Karver and his wife Beatrice Katherine.[66] The manor subsequently passed to Mrs. Ellen Biggs,[67] and from her to her kinswoman Ellen the wife of Thomas Fothergill.[68] In 1786 it was bought from Thomas Fothergill by Mr. John Jones of Chastleton (co. Oxon.),[69] who bequeathed it in 1827 to his cousin Mr. John Henry Whitmore-Jones, the grandfather of the present owner.[70] In 1900 Miss Mary Elizabeth Whitmore-Jones, who had succeeded to the estates in accordance with a settlement of 1872,[71] surrendered them to her nephew Mr. Thomas Whitmore Harris, who then assumed the name of Whitmore-Jones and is now the lord of the manor.[72]

WHITMORE. *Vert fretty or.*

A holding containing 2½ virgates of land and 14 acres of meadow was granted in 1431 by John Petyt and his wife Philippa to William Haynes and the heirs of his body for a yearly rent of 13s. 4d. with remainder in default to John and Philippa and their heirs.[73] It is possible that this was the same holding as that of which Richard Haynes died seised in 1633 [74]; it was occupied after his death by his

[38] She was called 'Amice Deyvile' in 1421 (Nash, op. cit. i, 395).
[39] Feet of F. Div. Co. Mich. 3 Hen. V.
[40] Nash, loc. cit.
[41] In that year Amice as 'domina de Evenlode' presented to the church (ibid.).
[42] Ibid.
[43] Feud. Aids, v, 320, 333; Lay Subs. R. 6 & 7 Hen. VI (Worcs. Hist. Soc.), 39, 45; Habington, op. cit. i, 68.
[44] Feet of F. Worcs. Mich. 10 Hen.VI.
[45] Ibid. 20 Hen. VI.
[46] Pat. 33 Hen. VI, pt. ii, m. 13; Nash, op. cit. i, 394.
[47] Feet of F. Worcs. Trin. 12 Edw. IV.
[48] Parl. R. v, 531, 583.
[49] Early Chan. Proc. bdle. 153, no. 22.
[50] Ibid. bdle. 170, no. 8.

[51] Ct. of Req. bdle. 1, no. 59. The Petyts remained at Evenlode after they had lost the manor, and their descendants were still living in the parish in 1708 (Parish Reg.).
[52] L. and P. Hen. VIII, iv (2), 4442 (5); vii, 923 (ii); Chan. Inq. p.m. (Ser. 2), xlviii, 129.
[53] G.E.C. Complete Peerage.
[54] Recov. R. Hil. 10 Eliz. rot. 153; Feet of F. Worcs. Hil. 10 Eliz.
[55] G.E.C. op. cit.
[56] Chan. Inq. p.m. (Ser. 2), ccix, 130.
[57] Feet of F. Worcs. Trin. 43 Eliz. He had previously mortgaged the estate to John Bishop (Recov. R. D. Enr. Trin. 36 Eliz. m. 1 d., 2, 3).
[58] Feet of F. Worcs. Hil. 2 Jas. I.

[59] Chan. Inq. p.m. (Ser. 2), dcvi, 59.
[60] Ibid.   [61] Ibid.   [62] Ibid.
[63] Cal. S. P. Dom. 1640–1, p. 240.
[64] Feet of F. Worcs. Trin. 27 Chas. II.
[65] Ibid. Mich. 34 Chas. II; Fosbroke, Hist. of Glouc. ii, 331.
[66] Recov. R. Trin. 1 Anne, rot. 73.
[67] Feet of F. Worcs. East. 27 Geo. II; ex inform. Mr. T. W. Whitmore-Jones.
[68] Recov. R. East. 27 Geo. II, rot. 367; Feet of F. Worcs. East. 27 Geo. II.
[69] Feet of F. Div. Co. East. 26 Geo. III.
[70] Ex inform. Mr. T. W. Whitmore-Jones.
[71] Ibid.
[72] Ibid.
[73] Feet of F. Worcs. Mich. 10 Hen.VI.
[74] Chan. Inq. p.m. (Ser. 2), ccccxcv, 65.

widow Frances[75] and his son Richard, who died in 1650,[76] but its subsequent history is obscure.

There was a water-mill at Evenlode in the 11th century, which had perished by the time of the Domesday Survey,[77] and after this date there is no mention of any mill in the parish until 1568, when another water-mill had been built, possibly on the site of the old one.[78] This building has also perished, and there is now no mill in Evenlode, but its site has been commemorated in the name 'Mill Holme Close' borne by one of the fields on the river bank near the Manor Farm.

The church of *ST. EDWARD* con-
CHURCH sists of a chancel 23½ ft. by 14¼ ft., a nave 39 ft. by 17 ft., a short south aisle 24 ft. by 12¼ ft., a western tower about 11½ ft. square, and a modern porch and north organ chamber. These measurements are all internal. Late in the 12th century the church consisted of a nave with a narrower chancel, but towards the end of the 14th century the church was largely rebuilt, the south aisle added and windows inserted, the western

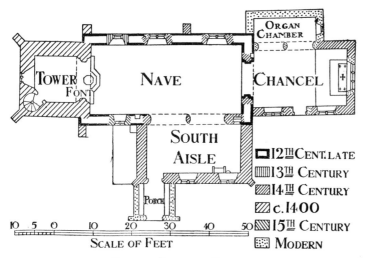

PLAN OF EVENLODE CHURCH

shows that it was originally of greater span. The outer of the two orders is decorated with a boldly executed cheveron ornament. The responds have square pilasters, and at their western angles are engaged shafts with moulded bases mitred around the pilasters, which both have scalloped capitals of slightly varied design on the north and south. In the eastern face of the north respond is a small square rough niche. Externally the chancel has been considerably repaired and restored.

The north wall of the nave has two windows of two lights each, of which the jambs are old, the tracery and rear arch being modern, in 14th-century style. Below the western window are the chamfered jambs of the blocked-up north door, and further west again is a lancet window of 13th-century detail, the jambs of which are old but the head modern. In the eastern respond of the south arcade is a square door to the rood-loft opening into the south aisle. The 14th-century arcade is of two bays with pointed arches of two chamfered orders, dying into a plain chamfered pier of lozenge form. The third bay of the nave beyond the aisle contains a crude two-light window of 15th-century date.

The south aisle is lighted by two 14th-century windows in the south wall, each of two lights with flowing tracery and a quatrefoil over. In the sill of the first is a projecting circular piscina drain and beneath it a sedile constructed of slabs of stone, which is probably as old as the aisle. West of these windows is the contemporary south door with a two-centred head and an external label, above which is a small niche with a cusped head. Externally the aisle has diagonal buttresses.

The late 14th-century western tower has a tower arch of two chamfered orders, and is three stages high with an embattled parapet and diagonal buttresses reaching to the second stage. In the south-west angle is a newel staircase to the belfry. Above the small west door is a two-light window with a quatrefoil in the head and the belfry lights are of similar detail. There is also a two-light window on the south side of the second stage with a small trefoil-headed light above it. The south porch is entirely modern.

The roofs and seating are all modern, but the pulpit is an interesting example of 15th-century work, with tracery cut from the solid in low relief and trefoil panelling with trefoils and quatrefoils over. The 15th-century octagonal font has quatrefoil panels on its faces, and beneath these, on the chamfered undercutting, are floral bosses, alternating with shields, one of which is charged with two ragged staves set upright.

There are five bells, all recast and rehung in 1897. A clock was placed in the tower in commemoration of the coronation of King George V, 1911.

The plate includes a large cup of 17th-century shape, the hall mark illegible, a cover paten, an alms-dish or paten made in 1690 with a monogram T.A., and a small plain dish with marks illegible.

tower being erected a few years later about the year 1400. The various 19th-century restorations account for the organ chamber, south porch and much of the window tracery. It is probable that work was done between the two earlier dates, as the lancet window in the nave and the dog-tooth ornament built into the chancel wall imply alterations in the 13th century.

The modern east window of the chancel is of three lights and of early 14th-century detail. The north wall is of three bays, the two western being filled with a modern arcade, of 14th-century detail, opening to the organ chamber. In the south wall are two two-light windows with original jambs and modern tracery of 14th-century type. Between them is a modern priest's door, and in the external wall is a fragment of 13th-century dog-tooth ornament. The chancel arch is of late 12th-century date, but has evidently been rebuilt at some later period, perhaps in the 14th century when the chancel itself may have been reconstructed.. The arch is now pointed, but the mutilated condition of the two crowning voussoirs

[75] Chan. Inq. p.m. (Ser. 2), ccccxcv, 65.   [76] Parish Reg.   [77] *V.C.H. Worcs.* i, 293.   [78] Feet of F. Worcs. Hil. 10 Eliz.

The registers before 1812 are as follows : (i) baptisms 1604 to 1721, burials 1561 to 1721, marriages 1562 to 1721 with a gap 1631 to 1666 ; (ii) baptisms 1722 to 1789, burials 1722 to 1792, marriages 1722 to 1754 ; (iii) baptisms 1788 to 1812, burials 1792 to 1812 ; (iv) a marriage book 1754 to 1812.

ADVOWSON   The church of Evenlode is first mentioned in 1270, when Bishop Giffard committed the custody of it to William de Saltmarsh [79] ; it was valued in 1291 at £4 yearly.[80]   In 1301 the advowson belonged to Richard Deyvile,[81] and it continued to follow the descent of the manor until 1601.[82]   In 1541 it was in the possession of Sir Philip Hoby,[83] who had married Elizabeth widow of Sir William Compton.[84] William Lord Compton sold it in 1601 to John Croker,[85] from whom it was bought in the following year by Margaret Farre, widow.[86]   She sold it to

to Henry Hurst, who sold it in 1665 to Richard Cocks.   Cocks conveyed it to Charles Nevill for £110 in 1680, and subsequently mortgaged it to Thomas Greenwood of Chastleton, who presented in 1696.[89]   Charles Nevill,[90] the rector of the parish, settled it in 1716 on his second son Ralph Nevill, the trustee for the settlement being Philip Woodman,[91] who presented in 1717.[92]   Ralph Nevill presented in 1727 [93] and subsequently sold his right to George Pye, the patron in 1735.[94]   In 1744 the patronage was conveyed by Pye to Mrs. Mary Hughes, who exercised the right in 1767 [95] ; she granted it to her daughter Miss Mary Hughes, who presented until 1817.[96]   She had, however, conveyed the advowson in 1786 to Richard and Mary Davis in trust for Mary Davis and William Horton : they sold it in 1801 to Mr. George Perrott, who released it in 1809 to Mr. Joseph Pitt.[96a]   Mr. Pitt presented in

EVENLODE CHURCH : SOUTH AISLE

John Smyth in 1637,[87] but after this date the history of its descent becomes obscure.   King Charles presented in 1661,[88] and the advowson afterwards passed

1825 [97] and Mr. Perrott in 1829.[98]   Mr. Pitt released it in 1825 to Mrs. Ann James, patron until 1857,[99] when she sold it to Mr. John Hambrough,

[79] *Reg. G. Giffard* (Worcs. Hist. Soc.), 39, 48.
[80] *Pope Nich. Tax.* (Rec. Com.), 240.
[81] *Reg. G. Giffard* (Worcs. Hist. Soc.), 547.
[82] *Sede Vacante Reg.* (Worcs. Hist. Soc.), 206, 362 ; Nash, op. cit. i, 395 ; Feet of F. Worcs. Mich. 20 Hen. VI ; Habington, op. cit. i, 211 ; Chan. Inq. p.m. (Ser. 2), ccxxix, 130. In 1317 Richard le Porter was the patron (*Sede Vacante Reg.* [Worcs. Hist. Soc.,], 183), but this was probably only for one turn, as another Richard Deyvile was rector in 1350, when he obtained an indult to choose a confessor who should give him, being penitent, plenary remission at death

(*Cal. Papal Letters*, iii, 404). William Petyt presented by a grant from Robert Tate in 1505 and Richard Bray of Taynton presented in 1596 (Nash, loc. cit.).
[83] Nash, loc. cit.
[84] *Visit. of Worcs.* 1569 (Harl. Soc. xxvii), 80, 140.
[85] Feet of F. Worcs. Trin. 43 Eliz.
[86] Ibid. Hil. 44 Eliz.   William Farre, perhaps her husband, was rector in 1560. Ex inform. Rev. H. J. Kelsall.
[87] Ibid. East. 13 Chas. I.
[88] Inst. Bks. (P.R.O.).   The king had also presented by lapse in 1636 (ibid.).
[89] Inst. Bks. (P.R.O.) ; inform. from Rev. H. J. Kelsall.

[90] Feet of F. Worcs. Hil. 1 Geo. I ; Parish Reg.
[91] Feet of F. Worcs. Hil. 1 Geo. I ; inform. from Rev. H. J. Kelsall.
[92] Nash, loc. cit.
[93] Inst. Bks. (P.R.O.) ; Parish Reg.
[94] Habington, op. cit. ii, 69 ; Inst. Bks. (P.R.O.).
[95] Inst. Bks. (P.R.O.) ; inform. from Rev. H. J. Kelsall.
[96] Inst. Bks. (P.R.O.) ; *Clerical Guide* ; Parish Reg.
[96a] Inform. from Rev. H. J. Kelsall.
[97] Parish Reg.   [98] Ibid.
[99] Ibid. ; inform. from Rev. H. J. Kelsall.   She presented in 1858 (Parish Reg.).

who presented in the following year.[100] In 1867 it was the property of Mr. Meaburn Staniland,[1] from whom it was bought in 1869 by the Rev. T. E. Buckworth,[2] after whose death it passed in 1878 to the Rev. Charles Peach.[3] The Rev. Henry James Kelsall, who has been rector of the parish since 1895, is now the patron.[4]

The Congregational chapel at Evenlode was opened in October 1865.[5] It is a mission chapel worked from Moreton-in-Marsh, Gloucestershire.

CHARITIES In 1751 M— Greenwood, as stated in the Parliamentary Returns of 1786, by will left £50 for the poor. An annual sum of £2 is paid in respect of this charity out of Campden Close in this parish.

It appears from the same Returns that Thomas Barker by will, 1700, left 10s. yearly for the poor, issuing out of land known as Caswells in Longborough, county of Gloucester.

Poor's Allotment.—Upon the inclosure of the parish in 1765 an allotment of 5 a. o r. 16 p. was awarded for the use of the poor in lieu of certain rights of cutting fuel on the common. The allotment produces £7 10s. a year ; a sum of about £6 is also received yearly for the right of pasturing on the roadsides and village green.

The charities are administered together. In 1908–9 about 22 tons of coal were distributed among twenty-six recipients.

FLADBURY

Fledanburg, Fledanbyrig (vii cent.) ; Fladbyrig (viii cent.) ; Fledanburh (ix cent.) ; Fledebirie (xi cent.) ; Fladdebir (xiii cent.).

The parish of Fladbury lies in the south-east of the county between Evesham and Pershore and was described in the 17th century as 'a paryshe very large, richly seated in the vale of Evesham.'[1] The area of the parish with its hamlets and chapelries is 6,879 acres,[2] of which 1,573 acres lie in Fladbury, 1,368 in Hill and Moor, 1,522 in Throckmorton, 381 in Wyre Piddle, 1,151 in Stock and Bradley, and 884 acres in Ab Lench.[3] In Fladbury, including Hill and Moor, 1,070 acres are arable land, 1,234 acres are permanent grass and 93 acres are woodland.[4] Throckmorton includes 1,017 acres of arable land and 492 acres of permanent grass ; Wyre Piddle, 270 acres of arable and 161 acres of permanent grass ; Stock and Bradley, 90 acres of arable land and 945 acres of permanent grass.[5] The soil is chiefly light clay with a little sand ; the subsoil is Lower Lias, producing crops of wheat, beans, barley, hops, market garden produce and fruit. Vines were formerly grown at Fladbury, for in the register of Worcester Priory occurs the statement that the sacrist received two parts of the tithes of the land where vines once grew at Fladbury, Ripple and Westbury.[6] At the end of the 18th century about 2 acres of land called the Vineyard belonged to the rector of Fladbury.[7]

The Avon forms the southern boundary of the parish, and from the valley of the river the land rises slightly to the north. The highest point in the parish is Craycombe Hill to the north-east of the village of Fladbury, about 300 ft. above the ordnance datum.

The main road from Worcester to Evesham runs through the parish from west to east. On a branch from this road on the right bank of the River Avon is the village of Fladbury. A bridge over the Avon to the south of the village, erected in commemoration of the 1897 Jubilee, connects it with Cropthorne. In the open space between the Anchor Inn and the

church a market is said to have been held in former times on Wednesdays.[8] The rectory was built by the son of Bishop Lloyd in 1710.[9] There are several half-timber and brick houses dating mostly from the 17th century ; one opposite the church, the front of which has been covered with rough-cast, has a good oak stairway with moulded handrails and turned balusters of about 1700 ; another near the junction of the roads has an early 18th-century brick front with original window frames and leaded lights in small squares. A half-timber barn on the roadside north of the village has been much repaired and modernized, but probably dates from the 15th century.

The hamlet of Wyre Piddle in the west of the parish contains some good half-timber houses. The Avon bounds it on the south, Piddle Brook, a tributary of that river, forming its western boundary. In the centre of this hamlet is the shaft and base of an old stone cross. It was restored in 1844, and is now surmounted by an iron cross.

Of the hamlet of Hill and Moor the most populous portion is Lower Moor, which lies near the railway to the south of the Worcester road. It contains one or two interesting old houses. At Hill, in the north of this hamlet, is Court Farm, which bears the date 1681 on the weather vane.

The chapelry of Throckmorton is to the north of the parish of Fladbury. To the north-east of the church is a moated inclosure, and to the south of Court Farm are the remains of another moat.

The village of Ab or Abbots Lench, formerly a hamlet and chapelry of Fladbury, but since 1865[10] ecclesiastically part of Church Lench, is completely isolated from Fladbury, part of the parish of Bishampton lying between them. It is divided from Bishampton by Whitsun Brook, over which there is a bridge called Stakamford Bridge. The village consists of a few houses on a branch road from that leading from Rous Lench to Fladbury.

The now separate parish of Stock and Bradley is also completely cut off from Fladbury, of which it

---

[100] Parish Reg.
[1] Ibid. He had bought it in that year from the Rev. W. E. Hambrough, to whom it had been conveyed by Mr. John Hambrough in 1863 (inform. from Rev. H. J. Kelsall).
[2] Parish Reg.
[3] Ibid.
[4] Inform. from Rev. H. J. Kelsall.

[5] Information from Mr. Joseph Williams, pastor.
[1] Habington, *Surv. of Worcs.* (Worcs. Hist. Soc.), i, 225.
[2] Of which 49 are covered by water. This includes Ab Lench now in Church Lench.
[3] *Census of Engl. and Wales Worcs.* 1901, pp. 22, 23.

[4] Statistics from Bd. of Agric. (1905).
[5] Ibid.
[6] Hale, *Reg. of Worc. Priory* (Camd. Soc.), 110b.
[7] Nash, *Hist. of Worcs.* i, 446.
[8] Noake, *Guide to Worcs.* 164.
[9] Inscr. on the monument of Bishop Lloyd in the vestry.
[10] *Parl. Papers* (1872), xlvi, 27.

was formerly a part, and lies to the west of the parish of Feckenham. The Salt Way, now the high road from Droitwich to Alcester, runs through it from west to east, and from it a road runs south along the eastern border of the parish to the village of Bradley. A stream forms part of the western boundary of Stock and Bradley, and another brook flows through the parish from east to west, being crossed south of the village of Bradley by Priest Bridge. In 1680 this bridge was first built of stone, and an agreement was made between the inhabitants of Bradley and the lord of Fladbury Manor by which the latter found the materials and the former supplied the labour. The lord of Fladbury was relieved of liability to further contributions in consideration of his payment of a lump sum.[11] Bradley Green is to the north of the parish, and Stock Green lies to the south on the Inkberrow boundary.

The disafforestation of the forest of Horewell, which formerly covered part of the parish of Fladbury, took place in 1229[12]; the parish is still, however, well wooded.

An Inclosure Act was passed for Fladbury in 1788, and the award is dated 23 May 1789[13]; for Stock and Bradley in 1825,[14] for Hill and Moor in 1832,[15] for Throckmorton in 1772,[16] and for Wyre Piddle in 1836 and 1840, the award being dated 5 August 1841.[17]

MANORS

There was a monastery at FLADBURY in early times. It was given, together with 44 *cassati* of land at Fladbury, to Bishop Oftfor in 691–2 by King Ethelred,[18] for the welfare of his soul and that of his wife Osthryth.[19] In the early part of the 8th century Bishop Æcgwine, Oftfor's successor, exchanged the monastery and its lands with a noble named Æthelheard for 20 *cassati* at Stratford-on-Avon.[20] He explained the apparently unprofitable nature of the exchange by pointing out that he and the king had agreed that both places should revert to the church after the death of the noble.[21] In the Annals of Evesham, however, we are told that Bishop Æcgwine, who was the founder of Evesham, gave up Fladbury to Æthelheard in order to secure Stratford, both vills being claimed by Æthelheard as heir of Queen Osthryth.[22] The monks of Evesham further stated that Fladbury had been given by Ethelred to Æcgwine and the abbey of Evesham in 703, and attributed their inability to

recover it to the superior strength of the Bishop of Worcester.[23] About 780 Bishop Tilhere consented and subscribed to a deed by which Aldred, *subregulus* of the Hwiccas and a descendant of Æthelheard, granted the monastery of Fladbury to his kinswoman Æthelburh for her life, with reversion to the church of Worcester.[24] At about this time Bishop Tilhere made a great feast for King Offa and his chieftains at Fladbury, where the king granted to the church the royal vill of Cropthorne with land amounting to 50 *mansae* and a very choice Bible with two clasps of pure gold.[25] After Æthelburh's death the monastery reverted to the church of Worcester and was con-

OLD HOUSE AT LOWER MOOR, FLADBURY

firmed in the early part of the 9th century to Bishop Deneberht by Coenwulf, King of Mercia, in an undated charter,[26] by which he also granted to the bishop

[11] Prattinton Coll. (Soc. Antiq.).
[12] *Cal. Chart. R.* 1226–57, p. 102.
[13] Priv. Act, 28 Geo. III, cap. 16; *Blue Bk. Incl. Awards,* 190.
[14] Priv. Act, 6 Geo. IV, cap. 1. The award is dated 11 July 1829 (*Blue Bk. Incl. Awards,* 191).
[15] Priv. Act, 2 & 3 Will. IV, cap. 13. The award is dated 12 Dec. 1833 (*Blue Bk. Incl. Awards,* 190).
[16] Priv. Act, 12 Geo. III, cap. 37.

The award is dated 31 Oct. 1772 (*Blue Bk. Incl. Awards,* 191).
[17] *Blue Bk. Incl. Awards,* 192. The Inclosure Acts for Wyre Piddle have not been found among the printed Acts of Parliament.
[18] Heming, *Chartul.* (ed. Hearne), 21; Birch, *Cart. Sax.* i, 110.
[19] In a forged Evesham charter the land is said to have belonged to Ethelred in right of his wife (Birch, op. cit. i, 193).
[20] Ibid. 111; Heming, op. cit. 590.

[21] Dugdale, *Mon. Angl.* i, 585; Heming, op. cit. 591; Birch, op. cit. i, 111, 191.
[22] *Chron. of Evesham* (Rolls Ser.), iv, 73.
[23] Ibid. 18, 71, 73, 95.
[24] Birch, op. cit. i, 331; Heming, op. cit. 591, 585. This deed is certainly genuine.
[25] Birch, op. cit. i, 328. This charter is, however, a forgery. See above under Cropthorne.
[26] *Arch. Journ.* xix, 247.

the reversion after his death of the land of thirty tributaries at Fladbury.[27] The see of Worcester continued to hold the manor until the date of the Domesday Survey, when it paid geld for 40 hides.[28] In the 12th century the bishop still held these 40 hides at Fladbury.[29] Richard I freed 13½ acres from *essartum*,[30] and King John confirmed this grant.[31] On 15 March 1214 he gave leave to the bishop to plough up 29½ acres of his wood.[32] In 1254 the bishop received a grant of free warren at Fladbury.[33] The manor was confirmed to the church by Pope Gregory in 1275,[34] and in 1291 was worth £29 6s. a year.[35] It remained in the possession of successive Bishops of Worcester,[36] and was in 1535 worth £53 1s. 2d. yearly.[37] In 1632 the bishop granted a lease of it to William Sandys for his life and that of his brother Thomas, and of William's wife Cicely daughter of Sir John Steed.[38] During the Civil War the manor was seized by Parliament, and a survey was taken in 1648.[39] In the same year the manor was sold to Robert Henley and Edward Smith for £1,082 9s. 6d.[40] After the Restoration the Bishop of Worcester recovered the manor, which he then seems to have leased to the Henleys and afterwards to the Hales.[41] The lease was purchased by Nicholas Lechmere in 1681,[42] and four years later he sold to Thomas Earl of Plymouth, the lease then running for the lives of Robert Henley of the Grange (co. Hants), of George brother of Sir John Hales deceased, and of William Peck.[43] In 1699 the lease was held by Other Windsor Earl of Plymouth, grandson and successor of Thomas.[44] His daughters sold the remainder of the lease to George Perrott, one of the barons of the Exchequer, who died 28 January 1780.[45]

The manor remained with the successive Bishops of Worcester until it was taken over by the Ecclesiastical Commissioners under the Act of 1860,[46] and they are still lords of the manor,[47] but the lease remained in the Perrott family until 1861, when it passed by exchange to the Commissioners.[48]

There was a mill at Fladbury in 1086 which was

worth 10s. and 20 stiches[49] of eels a year.[50] Bishop William of Blois purchased a mill there from Adam de Evesham in the early part of the 13th century.[51] In 1302 there were two mills at Fladbury farmed at £3 19s. 6d., and the fishery in the Avon brought in a rent of 19s. 6d.[52] Two water corn-mills were included in the sale to Robert Henley and Edward Smith.[53] There is now a corn-mill in Fladbury, to the south of the village on the Avon, and Wyre Mill is a corn-mill on the Avon in the south of Wyre Piddle.

AB LENCH or *ABBOT'S LENCH* (Abeleng, xi cent.; Habbelenche, xiii cent.; Hob Lench, xvi and xvii cent.; Abs Lench, xviii cent.; Abbot's Lench,[54] xviii and xix cent.) seems to have belonged to the church of Worcester from an early date, and was probably comprised in the 5 *mansae* at Lench which Oswald gave to Gardulf for three lives in 983.[55] It appears in the Domesday Survey as the property of the bishop, of whom it had been held by Godric. It is said that he did 'service for it to the bishop (on such terms) as he could obtain.'[56] At the actual time of the Survey Urse D'Abitot, the Sheriff of Worcestershire, held it of the bishop as of his manor of Fladbury.[57] It appears to have afterwards passed to Urse's descendants, the Beauchamps, and may possibly have been included in the 22 hides which Walter de Beauchamp held of the bishop in Fladbury early in the 12th century.[58]

The overlordship of Ab Lench descended in the Beauchamp family until the 16th century,[59] but the superior lordship of the Bishops of Worcester seems to have lapsed in the 13th century.[60]

The manor of Ab Lench was held towards the end of the 12th century under William de Beauchamp by Stephen de Beauchamp.[61] It must shortly afterwards have passed to William de Belne, who was said in a survey of Fladbury taken at about that time to be holding these 5 hides, which gelded at only 1 hide and had formerly been pasture for kine.[62]

It was afterwards held by Roger de Lench, who, according to the *Testa de Nevill*, held one knight's

---

[27] Birch, op. cit. i, 507; Heming, op. cit. 25.

[28] *V.C.H. Worcs.* i, 289b. The bishop had all the proceeds of hunting and honey as well as the timber used for the salt-pans at Droitwich (ibid.).

[29] Ibid. 324a.

[30] Cart. Antiq. RR 15.

[31] Ibid. I 31.

[32] Thomas, *Surv. of Cath. Ch. of Worc.* 123; *Hist. MSS. Com. Rep.* xiv, App. viii, 194.

[33] *Cal. Pat.* 1247–58, p. 345. This grant was confirmed in the following year (*Cal. Chart. R.* 1226–57, p. 443). The warren was probably made on Craycombe Hill, where it remained until the commons of Fladbury were inclosed in 1788 (Priv. Act, 28 Geo. III, cap. 16).

[34] Thomas, op. cit. 138.

[35] *Pope Nich. Tax.* (Rec. Com.), 225b.

[36] *Feud. Aids*, v, 306, 318.

[37] *Valor Eccl.* (Rec. Com.), iii, 218a.

[38] Close, 24 Chas. I, pt. xiv, no. 5. In 1639–40 William Sandys and his wife Cicely conveyed the manor to Henry Sandys, who had married William's sister Jane (Feet of F. Worcs. Trin. 15 Chas. I; *Visit. of Worcs.* 1569 [Harl. Soc. xxvii], 124). This William Sandys spent £20,000 in making the Avon navigable for vessels of 50 tons from Tewkesbury to Stratford, a distance of 24 miles (*Cal. S. P. Dom.*

1635–6, p. 280; Noake, *Guide to Worcs.* 164; Nash, *Hist. of Worcs.* i, 446–7).

[39] Nash, op. cit. i, 447. There were then twenty-four copyhold tenants in the manor (ibid.).

[40] Close, 24 Chas. I, pt. xiv, no. 5.

[41] In 1671–2 Sir John Hales and his wife Anne and Richard Hopkins and his wife Mary were dealing with six parts of the manor of Fladbury (Feet of F. Worcs. Mich. 23 Chas. II).

[42] Shirley, *Hanley and the House of Lechmere*, 47.

[43] Recov. R. D. Enr. East. 1 Jas. II, m. 3. The bishop reserved from the lease the advowson of the church and the rights to 'chase, hawke and hunt' upon the premises.

[44] Nash, op. cit. i, 447a. In 1700 the manor was valued at £450 a year (*Diary of Francis Evans* [Worcs. Hist. Soc.], 25). In 1749 the manor of Fladbury was conveyed by Valens Comyn and his wife Mary, widow of Francis Colston, to Hugh Watson (Feet of F. Worcs. Hil. 23 Geo. II; Close, 23 Geo. II, pt. iii, no. 23).

[45] *Dict. Nat. Biog.*

[46] Stat. 23 & 24 Vict. cap. 124.

[47] Inform. supplied by Ecclesiastical Commissioners.

[48] Ibid.; Priv. Act, 28 Geo. III, cap. 16; 6 Geo. IV, cap. 1; 2 & 3 Will. IV, cap. 13.

[49] There were 25 eels to the stich.

[50] *V.C.H. Worcs.* i, 289b.

[51] Thomas, op. cit. A 129. In 1291 the mill of Fladbury was worth £2 (*Pope Nich. Tax.* [Rec. Com.], 225b).

[52] Mins. Accts. bdle. 1143, no. 18.

[53] Close, 24 Chas. I, pt. xiv, no. 5.

[54] The name Abbot's Lench is a corruption unknown until about 1796. Dr. William Kyle Westwood Chafy, who now owns this hamlet, is desirous of restoring the ancient name Ab Lench. The county council tried to get this done, but the Ordnance Survey officials refused.

[55] Heming, op. cit. 187; Kemble, *Cod. Dipl.* no. 637.

[56] *V.C.H. Worcs.* i, 289b.

[57] Ibid.

[58] Ibid. 324a.

[59] *Testa de Nevill* (Rec. Com.), 41; *Cal. Inq. p.m.* 1–9 Edw. II, 403; Exch. K. R. Misc. Bks. xxii, fol. 1; *Cal. Inq. p.m. Hen. VII*, i, 345; Chan. Inq. p.m. (Ser. 2), lxxv, 98.

[60] *Testa de Nevill* (Rec. Com.), 41.

[61] Red Bk. of Bishopric of Worc. (Eccl. Com. Rec. Var. bdle. 121, no. 43698), fol. 252. Church scot at Ab Lench was given by Stephen de Beauchamp to the nuns of Cookhill (Nash, op. cit. ii, 17).

[62] Red Bk. of Bishopric of Worc. fol. 81.

fee and 2 hides of William de Beauchamp, who held of the Bishop of Worcester.[63] The entry probably refers to Ab Lench and Rous Lench, both of which the Lay Subsidy Roll of 1346 conclusively proves to have been held by Roger de Lench.[64]

Possibly it was this Roger who with Stephen de Lench successfully resisted the encroachment of the Abbot of Halesowen on the common pasture of Ab Lench in 1230.[65] Ankaretta de Beauchamp paid a subsidy of 20s. at Ab Lench in 1280.[66]

In 1299–1300 Ab Lench had passed into the hands of Simon le Bruyn,[67] to whom the Belnes' land at Belbroughton also passed. He was still in possession of it in 1315, according to the inquisition taken on the death of Guy de Beauchamp Earl of Warwick, which states that he held half a knight's fee there.[68] John le Bruyn paid a subsidy at Ab Lench in 1327,[69] and in 1346 he or a descendant of the same name paid 20s. for half a knight's fee in Ab Lench which Roger de Lench had formerly held.[70]

Henry Bruyn of Brians Bell held land in Ab Lench in 1405–6,[71] and it passed by the marriage of his 'cousin' and heir Joan to Sir Nicholas Burdett,[72] Great Butler of Normandy, who was slain in 1440.[73] His son Thomas Burdett[74] was a servant or follower of George Duke of Clarence; on 20 April 1474 he was attainted of high treason[75] and executed in the early part of 1477.[76] One of the charges brought against the Duke of Clarence on his attainder in the same year was that he sent his servants 'into diverse parties of this Royaulme to assemble the King's subjects to Feste theym and chere theym and by theise policies and reasonyng enduce them to beleve that the said Burdett was wrongfully executed and so to putte it in noyse and herts of the People.'[77] Burdett's lands were forfeited, but the attainder seems to have been afterwards reversed, as on 17 June 1478 the custody of his son and heir Nicholas, a minor, and of all his possessions was granted to Sir Simon Mountfort.[78] Nicholas died without issue and was succeeded by his brother John Burdett,[79] who in 1483–4 released to his half-brother Richard Burdett and others all his right in the manor of Ab Lench.[80]

On 1 October 1487 the manor was settled upon

BURDETT. *Azure two bars or with three martlets gules upon each bar.*

this Richard Burdett and Joyce his wife and his heirs.[81] Richard died in 1492, leaving his son Thomas, aged fourteen years and more, as his heir. Joyce survived her husband,[82] and held the manor until her death under the terms of the deed referred to.

Thomas Burdett, who was in possession of the manor in 1534,[83] died without issue, and it passed to his sister Anne,[84] who became the wife of Edward Conway.[85] She predeceased her husband, who held the manor by courtesy until his death in 1546. John Conway, their son and heir, was stated to be then thirty-five years of age.[86] He was knighted in 1560,[87] and sold the manor in 1565 to John Rous[88] of Rous Lench, with which manor Ab Lench has since descended,[89] Dr. William Kyle Westwood Chafy, D.D., of Rous Lench Court, being the present lord of the manor.

In 1227 Warin son of William de Upton granted jointly with his wife Hawisia 40 acres of land in *AB LENCH* to the Abbot and convent of Halesowen, with common of pasture,[90] and his grant was confirmed by William Marshal Earl of Pembroke for the souls of himself and Eleanor his wife on condition that a rent of 4s. should be paid yearly at his manor of Inkberrow.[91] He afterwards relinquished his claim to this rent in favour of the abbey.[92]

The Abbot and convent of Halesowen were in possession of property in Ab Lench in 1228–9, when they were fined 20s.[93] The abbot is stated to have afterwards erected houses for the storage of grain on the common pasture of Ab Lench, and an action was brought against him by Roger and Stephen de Lench, perhaps on behalf of the inhabitants; they recovered seisin of the pasture, and the houses were ordered to be removed, but on 18 September 1230, on the petition of the abbot, leave was granted for the houses to remain standing until 2 February in the next year.[94] On 20 September 1233 the abbot paid 2s. for assarts made at Lench,[95] from which it would appear that his land included a part of the woodland mentioned in Domesday. In 1272–3 the abbot conveyed to Ralph de Hengham a messuage and land in Church Lench and Ab Lench.[96] Though land at Ab Lench is not mentioned among the possessions of the abbey in 1291[97] or in 1535, it is possible that they retained some estate there, which passed in the same way as their manor of Church Lench to the Scudamores, for John Scudamore held in 1596 a manor called Hob Lench,[98] which passed with the manor of Church Lench until 1627, when it is mentioned for the last time.[99]

[63] *Testa de Nevill* (Rec. Com.), 41.
[64] *Lay Subs. R.* 1346 (Worcs. Hist. Soc.), 19 ; *Feud. Aids*, v, 307.
[65] *Cal. Close*, 1227–31, p. 373.
[66] *Lay Subs. R. Worcs.* c. 1280 (Worcs. Hist. Soc.), 35.
[67] Habington, *Surv. of Worcs.* (Worcs. Hist. Soc.), i, 326.
[68] Chan. Inq. p.m. 9 Edw. II, no. 71 ; *Cal. Inq. p.m.* 1–9 *Edw. II*, 403.
[69] *Lay Subs. R.* 1327 (Worcs. Hist. Soc.), 6.
[70] Ibid. 1346 (Worcs. Hist. Soc.), 19 ; *Feud. Aids*, v, 307.
[71] Habington, op. cit. i, 326.
[72] *Feud. Aids*, v, 319, 333.
[73] Habington, loc. cit. ; Dugdale, *Hist. of Warw.* 847 ; *Visit. of Warw.* (Harl. Soc. xii), 101.
[74] *Visit. of Warw.* (Harl. Soc. xii), 101.

[75] Pat. 17 Edw. IV, pt. i, m. 8 d.
[76] Chan. Inq. p.m. 17 Edw. IV, no. 66.
[77] *Parl. R.* vi, 193.
[78] Pat. 18 Edw. IV, pt. i, m. 9.
[79] *Visit. of Warw.* (Harl. Soc. xii), 101.
[80] Dugdale, *Hist. of Warw.* 847 ; De Banco R. Chart. Enr. East. 1 Ric. III, m. 2.
[81] *Cal. Inq. p.m. Hen. VII*, i, 345.
[82] Ibid.
[83] Recov. R. Hil. 26 Hen. VIII, rot. 144.
[84] Dugdale, *Hist. of Warw.* 847.
[85] Chan. Inq. p.m. (Ser. 2), lxxv, 98 ; Early Chan. Proc. bdle. 291, no. 69.
[86] Chan. Inq. p.m. (Ser. 2), lxxv, 98.
[87] Metcalfe, *Bk. of Knights*, 117.
[88] Feet of F. Worcs. East. 7 Eliz. A second conveyance took place in 1585 (ibid. Mich. 26 & 27 Eliz.).

[89] Chan. Inq. p.m. (Ser. 2), cccxxvi, 48 ; Recov. R. Trin. 4 Geo. II, rot. 14 ; 2 Geo. IV, rot. 148 ; Feet of F. Worcs. Mich. 11 Chas. I ; Div. Co. Hil. 1650 ; East. 5 Anne.
[90] *Will. Salt Arch. Soc. Coll.* iv, 227.
[91] Jeayes, *Lyttelton Chart.* no. 7.
[92] Ibid. no. 8.
[93] Nash, op. cit. ii, App. xx, quoting Pipe R. 13 Hen. III.
[94] *Cal. Close*, 1227–31, p. 373.
[95] Nash, op. cit. ii, App. xx, quoting Fine R. 17 Hen. III, m. 2.
[96] Feet of F. Worcs. 1 Edw. I, no. 1.
[97] *Pope Nich. Tax.* (Rec. Com.), 230.
[98] Feet of F. Div. Co. Trin. 39 Eliz.
[99] Chan. Inq. p.m. (Ser. 2), cccciv, 114 ; Feet of F. Worcs. Trin. 3 Chas. I.

In a catalogue of the charters of the monastery of Worcester there is mentioned one by Wulfstan called the Archbishop, who was Bishop of Worcester from 1062 to 1095, relating to three *mansae* at THROCK-MORTON [100] (Throcmortune, xi cent. ; Trokemard-tune, xii cent. ; Trockmerton, Trochmerton, xiii cent. ; Throkmarton, xiv cent.), but the nature of this charter is not known. Throckmorton is not mentioned in the Domesday Survey, being then probably included in Fladbury, of which it was part until the 15th century.[1] After 1415 the manor was held of the Bishops of Worcester at a fee-farm rent of £12.[2]

Throckmorton gives its name to the family of Throckmorton, who were tenants of the Bishop of Worcester at an early date, Reoland Throckmorton appearing as a juror for the hundred of Oswaldslow in the middle of the 12th century.[3] Raulyn, who held 2½ hides in Throckmorton about 1182, may have been a member of this family, possibly identical with Reoland.[4] Adam de Throckmorton apparently owned land in Worcestershire in 1174–5,[5] and John and Joscelin de Throckmorton appear in 1175–6 and 1176–7,[6] but it is not known that they held land in Throckmorton. Henry son of John de Throckmorton at the beginning of the 13th century obtained from Mauger Bishop of Worcester (1199–1212) half a hide of land in Fladbury,[7] and he is probably the Henry son of John who is mentioned in the Testa de Nevill as holding a virgate of land in Throckmorton.[8]

Adam son of Robert, who also held at that time a virgate of land in Throckmorton,[9] was possibly the Adam de Throckmorton who was dealing with a third of a fee in Upton and Throckmorton in

THROCKMORTON.
Gules a cheveron argent with three gimel bars sable thereon.

1232–3.[10] According to a pedigree of the family given by Nash, Adam died before 1248, and was succeeded by his son Robert, who was alive in 1252.[11] Robert appears to have been succeeded before 1266 by a son Simon.[12] Robert de Throckmorton, who obtained a dispensation from the Bishop of Worcester in 1275,[13] was son of Simon.[14] He was living in 1315–16,[15] and is perhaps identical with the Robert de Throckmorton who in 1333–4 settled four messuages and land in Throckmorton upon his son John and Maud his wife, with remainder to his other children, Nicholas, Sybil, Alice and Joan.[16] The manor of Throckmorton seems, however, to have passed to Robert's son Giles, for a messuage and 2 carucates of land in Throckmorton were settled in 1341–2 upon Giles and his wife Agnes, and upon their sons Robert, John, Thomas and Richard in tail-male.[17]

Thomas Throckmorton, who, according to the pedigree of the family given in the *Visitation of Warwickshire*,[18] was a son of John Throckmorton, was of the retinue of Thomas Beauchamp Earl of Warwick in 1396, was escheator for the county of Worcester in 1402, and Constable of Elmley Castle in 1404–5.[19] He seems to have made a lease of the manor in 1410–11,[20] and was succeeded by his son Sir John Throckmorton,[21] who was also of the retinue of the Earl of Warwick.[22] In 1415 the Bishop of Worcester obtained licence to grant fourteen messuages and 2 carucates of land in Throckmorton to Sir John de Throckmorton, to be held of the bishop at a fee-farm rent.[23] This was probably the estate which the bishop had held in demesne in the 12th century.[23a] Habington evidently refers to this transaction when he says that John Carpenter, who succeeded as Bishop of Worcester in 1444, so much disliked the alienation of Throckmorton that he threatened to excommunicate the Prior and monks of Worcester on account of it, whereupon they sued to the Archbishop of Canterbury to send for Thomas son of John Throckmorton [23b] and command him to give satisfaction to the Bishop of Worcester. But 'thys lounge contention

---

[100] Heming, op. cit. ii, 580.

[1] *Testa de Nevill* (Rec. Com.), 41*b* ; Mins. Accts. bdle. 1143, no. 18 ; *Cal. Pat.* 1413–16, p. 340 ; Chan. Inq. p.m. (Ser. 2), xiv, 6 ; Exch. Inq. p.m. (Ser. 2), file 1179, no. 1.

[2] See below.

[3] *V.C.H. Worcs.* i, 291. According to Sir William Dugdale a John Throckmorton was lord of the manor of Throckmorton in 1130, but there seems to be no authority for this assertion (Betham, *Baronetage of Engl.* i, 486).

[4] Habington, *Surv. of Worcs.* (Worcs. Hist. Soc.), i, 226 ; Red Bk. of Bishopric of Worc. fol. 81. The bishop, who at this time held a manor at Throckmorton in demesne, had other tenants at Throckmorton ; Norman held half a hide of land and Osmund the Chamberlain half a hide (ibid.). In a later survey the heir of Osmund the Chamberlain was holding at Throckmorton a hide and a half of land which Osmund son of Gervaise held of him. Bishop John (c. 1151) confirmed this tenement to Osmund for the service which Malgetus did for it (ibid. 255). Osmund son of Gervaise still held a virgate at Throckmorton at the beginning of the 13th century (*Testa de Nevill* [Rec. Com.], 41*b*).

[5] *Pipe R.* 21 *Hen. II* (Pipe R. Soc.), 130.

[6] Ibid. 22 *Hen. II*, 36 ; 23 *Hen. II*, 65.

[7] *Hist. MSS. Com. Rep.* xiv, App. viii, 194.

[8] *Testa de Nevill* (Rec. Com.), 41*b*. William son of Joscelin held a virgate in Throckmorton at this time (ibid.).

[9] Ibid.

[10] Feet of F. Worcs. 17 Hen. III, no. 14.

[11] Nash, op. cit. i, 452.

[12] *Excerpta e Rot. Fin.* (Rec. Com.), ii, 447.

[13] *Reg. G. Giffard* (Worcs. Hist. Soc.), 81.

[14] Habington, op. cit. i, 227. In 1299 Robert was holding 3 virgates in Throckmorton which had belonged to William de Westhill, and he also held 2½ hides for which he had to defend the manor of Fladbury from suit at the county court (Red Bk. of Bishopric of Worc. fol. 69). John de Pikersham held in 1299 a hide of land in Throckmorton which afterwards passed to the Throckmortons (Habington, op. cit. i, 227, 228 ; Red Bk. of Bishopric of Worc. fol. 69).

[15] *Cal. Inq. p.m.* 10–20 Edw. II, 409.

[16] Feet of F. Worcs. Hil. 7 Edw. III, no. 9.

[17] Ibid. Trin. 15 Edw. III, no. 5. In

1346 John Huband was said to be holding a fifth of a knight's fee at Throckmorton corresponding to the 4 virgates of the Testa de Nevill (*Feud. Aids*, v, 309). Members of this family paid subsidy at Throckmorton in 1280 and 1327 (*Lay Subs. R. Worcs.* 1280 [Worcs. Hist. Soc.], 36 ; ibid. 1327, p. 5), and in 1332–3 John Huband granted a messuage and a carucate of land in Throckmorton to Thomas de Morton and Denise his wife for life at a rent of a rose, with reversion to John (Feet of F. Worcs. Mich. 6 Edw. III, no. 41).

[18] op. cit. (Harl. Soc. xii), 87.

[19] Betham, *Baronetage of Engl.* i, 487.

[20] Feet of F. Worcs. 12 Hen. IV, no. 26.

[21] *Cal. Pat.* 1446–52, pp. 168, 169.

[22] *Dict. Nat. Biog.*

[23] *Cal. Pat.* 1413–16, p. 340. This fee-farm rent was doubtless the £12 received from the manor by the Bishop of Worcester in 1535 (*Valor Eccl.* [Rec. Com.], iii, 218). It was still paid to the bishop in 1685 (Recov. R. D. Enr. East. 1 Jas. II, m. 3).

[23a] See note 4 above.

[23b] John Throckmorton had died in 1445 (see M. I. in church).

FLADBURY CHURCH : THE NAVE LOOKING WEST

THROCKMORTON CHURCH : THE CHANCEL

beeinge in the end utterly extinguished, thys good Bishopp entred into such a leauge of fryndshyp with Thomas Throckmorton as in Testimony of his charitye he enterteyned him to be Stuarde of all hys Castelles, Mannors etc. with a fee of 10 li. per annum.'[24] In 1440 Sir John was styled chamberlain of the Exchequer and under-treasurer of England. He died in 1445, and was buried in the church of Fladbury, where there is an inscription to his memory.[25] Sir John Throckmorton was succeeded by a son Thomas,[26] who in 1467 obtained a general pardon for all offences committed by him before 23 June.[27] He died in 1472,[28] and his son Sir Robert was in possession of the manor in 1500.[29] Sir Robert died in 1518, and was succeeded by his son George,[30] who settled the manor of Throckmorton on his son Robert on his marriage with Elizabeth Hungerford.[31] Robert succeeded his father in 1552,[32] and died in 1581, leaving a son Thomas.[33] Thomas Throckmorton was involved in difficulties owing to his religious opinions, his estate being frequently sequestrated and his person imprisoned.[34] He died in 1615, and was succeeded by his grandson Sir Robert Throckmorton,[35] who was created a baronet in 1642,[36] and suffered severely at the hands of the Parliamentary forces during the Civil War.[37] He died 16 January 1650, and was followed by his son Sir Francis Throckmorton,[38] who died 7 November 1680.[39] His eldest surviving son Sir Robert,[40] who was one of the 'Catholic non-jurors,' died 8 March 1720–1,[41] and was succeeded by his only surviving son Sir Robert,[42] on whose death on 8 December 1791 the manor probably passed to his grandson and successor to the title Sir John Courtenay Throckmorton.[43] He died without issue in 1819, and his brother and successor Sir George also died issueless in 1826.[44] The manor of Throckmorton then seems to have passed to his nephew Robert George Throckmorton, who was dealing with it in that year.[45] He succeeded to the baronetcy on the death of his uncle Sir Charles in 1840,[46] and in 1862 the manor passed from him to his eldest surviving son Sir Nicholas William George Throckmorton, ninth baronet, who is now lord of the manor of Throckmorton.[47]

At the date of the Domesday Survey HILL (Hulla, xiii cent.; Hulle near Fladbury, xiv cent.) and MOOR was part of the 5 hides formerly belonging to Keneward held by Robert le Despenser of the Bishop of Worcester's manor of Fladbury.[48] Hill and Moor has apparently always been part of the manor of Fladbury.[49]

At the beginning of the 13th century an agreement was made between Henry son of John Throckmorton and Mauger Bishop of Worcester by which half a hide of land at Hill passed into the possession of Henry, who was to hold it of the bishop.[50] Henry afterwards granted a virgate of this land to William Heye for life, and in 1237–8 Richard and Adam Roland were in controversy as to the ownership of this estate, which Richard claimed as grandson of Henry Throckmorton. The suit was terminated in favour of Richard.[51] He died in 1254,[52] and his widow agreed with Richard Cristot in 1254–5 that a third of a tenement in Throckmorton and Hill which Emma held for life should revert to him at her death.[53] In the previous year Richard had agreed with the Bishop of Worcester that he should hold a carucate of land in Hill and elsewhere by suit at the bishop's court of Worcester, the bishop giving a warranty against the claims of Emma wife of Richard Roland for dower if she survived Richard.[54] The whole or part of the Rolands' estate at Hill afterwards passed to Simon Chamberlain, who had it in frank marriage by gift of Henry Roland.[55] The Chamberlains also held land in Hill and Fladbury under the Poers of Wichenford,[56] and it was probably this estate which Richard Poer held in Hill of the bishop's manor of Wick early in the 13th century.[57] Simon le Chamberlain was holding a virgate of land in Fladbury in 1221–2,[58] and Nicholas le Chamberlain held a so-called manor at Fladbury in 1291–2.[59] In 1299 Sir Simon le Chamberlain, brother and successor of Nicholas,[60] held 3 virgates of land in Fladbury and 1 in Hill of Sir John Poer, besides the half-hide which came to his family through the Rolands.[61] Sir Simon le Chamberlain still held an estate at Fladbury in 1301–2,[62] but the Chamberlains afterwards exchanged this land for that of John de Haseley in Wichenford.[63] Possibly this name should be Basely, for that family was already in possession of land at Fladbury. In 1278–9 Henry Basely was successful in proving his right to an estate there which he had inherited from his father Roger against Maud la Turre,[64] and in 1280 he paid a subsidy of half a mark

[24] Habington, op. cit. i, 425.
[25] Dict. Nat. Biog.
[26] Cal. Pat. 1446–52, pp. 168, 169.
[27] Ibid. 1467–77, p. 20.
[28] Chan. Inq. p.m. 12 Edw. IV, no. 33.
[29] Ibid. (Ser. 2), xiv, 6.
[30] Exch. Inq. p.m. (Ser. 2), file 1179, no. 1.
[31] Chan. Inq. p.m. (Ser. 2), xcviii, 75.
[32] Ibid.
[33] Ibid. cxciii, 89.
[34] Burke, Peerage (ed. 1906).
[35] Chan. Inq. p.m. (Ser. 2), ccclxvii, 100.
[36] G.E.C. Complete Baronetage, ii, 197. In 1637–8 Robert Throckmorton obtained a grant of two-thirds of the manor of Throckmorton, in the king's hands on account of the recusancy of Robert, for forty-one years if the manor remained in the king's hands so long (Pat. 13 Chas. I, pt. xxiii, no. 7).
[37] G.E.C. op. cit. ii, 198.

[38] Ibid.; Feet of F. Div. Co. Hil. 1654; Hil. 21 & 22 Chas. II.
[39] G.E.C. loc. cit.
[40] Feet of F. Div. Co. Hil. 36 & 37 Chas. II.
[41] G.E.C. loc. cit.
[42] Feet of F. Worcs. Hil. 6 Geo. I; Recov. R. Mich. 10 Geo. I, rot. 239; East. 16 Geo. II, rot. 254.
[43] G.E.C. loc. cit.
[44] Ibid.
[45] Recov. R. Mich. 7 Geo. IV, rot. 264, 183. The baronetcy passed to Charles brother of Sir George (G.E.C. op. cit. ii, 199).
[46] G.E.C. loc. cit. [47] Ibid.
[48] V.C.H. Worcs. i, 290b.
[49] Testa de Nevill (Rec. Com.), 41b; Habington, op. cit. i, 227; Priv. Act, 2 & 3 Will. IV, cap. 13.
[50] Hist. MSS. Com. Rep. xiv, App. viii, 194.
[51] Maitland, Bracton's Note-Bk. iii, 235–6; Abbrev. Plac. (Rec. Com.), 105.

[52] Feet of F. Worcs. 38 Hen. III, no. 16; 39 Hen. III, no. 28.
[53] Ibid. 39 Hen. III, no. 28.
[54] Ibid. 38 Hen. III, no. 16.
[55] Habington, op. cit. i, 228; Red Bk. of Bishopric of Worc. fol. 69.
[56] Habington, loc. cit.
[57] Testa de Nevill (Rec. Com.), 41b. This land had been given as 2 hides and a virgate in Fladbury by Bishop Samson (1096–1112) to Illi de Turre and passed with Norton in Bredon from Turre to Poer (Red Bk. of Bishopric of Worc. fol. 243). It was held about 1182 by Walter de Turre (ibid. fol. 81).
[58] Feet of F. Worcs. East. 6 Hen. III.
[59] Add. MS. 28024, fol. 172, 172 d.
[60] Ibid. 172 d.
[61] Habington, loc. cit.; Red Bk. of Bishopric of Worc. fol. 69.
[62] Add. MS. 28024, fol. 171.
[63] Red Bk. of Bishopric of Worc. fol. 69.
[64] Assize R. 1029, m. 1 d.

at Fladbury.[65] This seems to have been the same estate which afterwards passed to the Sodingtons.[66] According to Habington, Richard de Sodington was at one time the owner.[67] In 1327 Isabel de Sodington paid a subsidy of 3s. 4d. in Fladbury,[68] and about 1337–8 William de Sodington and his wife Elizabeth bought an estate at Fladbury of the Bishop of Worcester.[69] Elizabeth died in 1371 holding a cottage called Baselond in Fladbury of the king for the service of a seventh part of a knight's fee, her heir being her daughter Isabel wife of Robert Aleyn.[70] Before this time, however, part of the estate held by the service of a tenth of a knight's fee had passed to Alexander de Besford.[71]

A parcel of land in Hill was forfeited in 1396 by Thomas Earl of Warwick.[72] The earl had granted it for life to his bastard brother John de Athereston, and the king granted the reversion in 1397 to Sir John Russell.[73]

An estate at Hill consisting of 2 hides was given by Bishop Samson (1096–1112) to Frederick or Freri de Bishopsdon.[74] William de Bishopsdon held the estate early in the 13th century,[75] and it followed the same descent as the manor of Waresley in Hartlebury (q.v.), passing with it to the Catesbys.[76] The estate at Hill and Moor was sold in 1501 by George Catesby to Robert Throckmorton.[77] The Throckmortons were dealing with land in Moor in 1558,[78] and the estate seems to have remained with them until about the middle of the 19th century, for Sir Charles Throckmorton was said to be lord of the so-called manor of Hill and Moor in 1832.[79] The manor-house is a 17th-century half-timber building with good panelled rooms. Cromwell is said to have slept here in 1651. It was acquired by Benjamin Johnson, town clerk of Worcester, before 1832. He died in 1835 and left it by his will to Thomas Henry Bund, whose grandson Mr. John Willis-Bund now holds it.

WYRE PIDDLE (Pidele, xi and xiii cent. ; Wyre Pydele, xiv cent. ; Wirepedill, Werpedell, xv cent. ; Werepedyll, Wyre Pydle, xvi cent. ; Wire Puddell, Warpdale, xvii cent.). At the date of the Domesday Survey Robert le Despenser held 5 hides at Wyre Piddle and Hill and Moor of the Bishop of Worcester's manor of Fladbury.[80] The overlordship of the bishop

was still recognized at the end of the 13th century, but it afterwards seems to have lapsed.[81]

The manor followed the same descent as Elmley Castle until 1487–8, when it passed into the hands of Henry VII.[82] It remained in the Crown[83] until 1550, when it was granted by Edward VI to Ralph Sadleir and Lawrence Wenington.[84] They seem to have conveyed it to Bartholomew Hales, who sold it to John and Thomas Folliott in 1571.[85] John Folliott died on 7 March 1578 seised of the manor of Wyre Piddle,[86] which then passed with the manor of Stone in Halfshire Hundred (q.v.) in the Folliott family,

FOLLIOTT. *Argent a lion purpure with a forked tail and a golden crown.*

COURTEEN. *Or a talbot passant sable.*

and subsequently to the Courteens and Rushouts.[87] On the death of Sir James Rushout in 1711 this manor, instead of passing with Stone to his sister Elizabeth St. John, passed with the baronetcy to his uncle Sir John Rushout, and from that time followed the same descent[88] as Northwick Park in Blockley (q.v.). Lady Northwick, widow of George third Lord Northwick, held the manor until her death in 1912, when it passed by will to her grandson Mr. George Spencer Churchill.

The rent of £5 reserved from the manor of Wyre Piddle in the grant of 1550 was vested in trustees for sale in 1670–1.[89] It was sold by them in 1672 to John Jones of Whitehall,[90] and in 1807 it belonged to Frances Hearne Bettesworth.[91]

BRADLEY (Bradanleah, Bradanlege, viii cent.; Bradelege, xi cent. ; Bradeleghe, xiii cent.), afterwards *STOCK* and *BRADLEY*. In the pontificate

[65] Lay Subs. R. Worcs. 1280 (Worcs. Hist. Soc.), 36. Other members of the Basely family paid subsidies at Fladbury at this date (ibid. 36, 37).
[66] Habington, loc. cit. [67] Ibid.
[68] Lay Subs. R. Worcs. 1327 (Worcs. Hist. Soc.), 4.
[69] Abbrev. Rot. Orig. (Rec. Com.), ii, 114, 134 ; Cal. Pat. 1338–40, p. 260.
[70] Chan. Inq. p.m. 49 Edw. III, pt. ii (1st nos.), no. 34a.
[71] Feud. Aids, v, 308. Richard Poer had once held this estate. John de Besford paid a subsidy of 1s. 6d. at Hill in 1327 (Lay Subs. R. Worcs. 1327 [Worcs. Hist. Soc.], 4).
[72] Cal. Pat. 1396–9, pp. 314, 359.
[73] Ibid.
[74] Red Bk. of Bishopric of Worc. fol. 243 ; see also fol. 81.
[75] Testa de Nevill (Rec. Com.), 41b.
[76] Anct. D. (P.R.O.), A 7245, 5908, 5883 ; Close, 49 Edw. III, m. 20 d.; Feud. Aids, v, 308, 320, 333 ; Habington, op. cit. i, 227.
[77] Anct. D. (P.R.O.), A 6470.
[78] Com. Pleas D. Enr. East. 4 & 5 Phil. and Mary, m. 15.

[79] Priv. Act, 2 & 3 Will. IV, cap. 13. At this time the lord of Fladbury and the lord of the manor of the rectory of Fladbury both claimed rights in Hill and Moor, as their respective manors extended into that hamlet.
[80] V.C.H. Worcs. i, 290b. One Keneward had held it in the same manner (ibid.). Pidelet Radulfi mentioned in the 12th-century survey of Pershore Hundred has been wrongly identified as Wyre Piddle in a former volume (ibid. 328a).
[81] Testa de Nevill (Rec. Com.), 41b ; Habington, op. cit. i, 228 ; Red Bk. of Bishopric of Worc. fol. 69.
[82] Testa de Nevill (Rec. Com.), 41b ; Feud. Aids, v, 306, 318, 332 ; Cal. Pat. 1396–9, pp. 314, 359 ; Feet of F. Div. Co. Mich. 6 Edw. IV ; Chan. Inq. p.m. 18 Edw. IV, no. 47 ; Close, 3 Hen. VII, m. 11. Early in the 13th century the manor, with Moor, was held of William de Beauchamp for the service of a knight's fee by William Fitz Warin (Testa de Nevill [Rec. Com.], 41b), and in 1230 William son of this William leased certain meadow land above Piddle called 'La

brode dole' for eighteen years to the sacristan of Pershore (Anct. D. [P.R.O.], D 282). In 1240 William leased the 'manor' of Piddle for twenty-three years (Cur. Reg. R. 122, m. 10 d.), but this may have been the manor of Wick Piddle held by the Fitz Warins (see St. Andrew, Pershore, V.C.H. Worcs. iv).
[83] Duchy of Lanc. Mins. Accts. bdles. 10465, 10467, 10468 ; L. and P. Hen. VIII, i, 3613 ; ii (2), 3483.
[84] Pat. 4 Edw. VI, pt. iv, m. 26. A rent of £5 was reserved to the Crown.
[85] Feet of F. Worcs. Mich. 13 & 14 Eliz.; Chan. Inq. p.m. (Ser. 2), clxxxiii, 96.
[86] Chan. Inq. p.m. (Ser. 2), clxxxiii, 96.
[87] Ibid. ccclxxviii, 137 ; ccccxxix, 96 ; Feet of F. Worcs. Mich. 22 Jas. I ; Div. Co. East. 12 Chas. I ; Worcs. Trin. 6 Will. and Mary ; Pat. 22 Chas. II, pt. ii (1st roll).
[88] Recov. R. Trin. 4 Geo. I, rot. 116 ; Hil. 1 Geo. III, rot. 298.
[89] Pat. 22 Chas. II, pt. ii (1st roll).
[90] Close, 24 Chas. II, pt. xxix, no. 10.
[91] Recov. R. Mich. 48 Geo. III, rot. 417.

of Wilfrid (717–43) Ethelbald, King of Mercia, gave 6 cassates of land in Bradley to Cyneburh.[92] As this grant is included among the charters of the monastery of Worcester,[93] and Ethelbald is said to have given Bradley to the church,[94] it may be supposed that after Cyneburh's death these 6 cassates at Bradley passed to the see of Worcester.

At the famous Council of Celchyth in 789 Heathored, Bishop of Worcester, proceeded against Wulfheard, son of Cussa, who had endeavoured to deprive the church of land at Bradley which had been bequeathed to it by Hemele and Duda. The bishop proved his right to the lands, but agreed that Wulfheard should hold them for life, and that at his death they should be restored to the church where the bodies of Hemele and Duda were buried.[95]

In 962 Bishop Oswald granted to his servant Eadmaer the wood from Bradley necessary for the preparation of salt in four vats at Droitwich which belonged to certain land in Bentley which the bishop had granted to Eadmaer.[96] At the date of the Domesday Survey Aelfric the Archdeacon held a hide at Bradley of the bishop's manor of Fladbury.[97] The manor seems to have remained with the see of Worcester [98] until the reign of Edward VI, when by some means it passed to the Crown. Edward VI granted it in 1553 to John Earl of Bedford and Edmund Downing.[99] On 1 February 1554 Edmund sold it to Roger and Robert Taverner of London.[100]

The date at which the manor returned to the possession of the Bishops of Worcester is not known. It was perhaps before 1628, when an agreement was made by which the bishop and Sir William Sandys conveyed to the king 110 acres of the waste of Bradley in Feckenham Forest on condition that they should hold the remainder on certain terms.[1] In 1825 the Bishop of Worcester claimed the hamlet of Stock and Bradley as a member of his manor of Fladbury.[2] The Ecclesiastical Commissioners, who took over the estates of the see of Worcester in 1860,[3] are now the principal landowners in Stock and Bradley.

In the time of Henry II, Randolph son of Roger (of Rous Lench) held a hide of land at Bradley.[4] Roger son of Ralph de Lench gave the tithes of Bradley which belonged to the chapel of Chadwick to the hospital of St. Wulfstan, Worcester, his grant being confirmed in 1232 by the king.[5]

In the time of Bishop Baldwin (1180–90) Alured Levet claimed to hold of his nephew (*nepos*), the son of Ralph de Levet, a hide of land at Fladbury.[6] It was probably this estate which was held at the time

of the Testa de Nevill by William of Bradley as a hide at Bradley.[7] An estate at Bradley belonged about the middle of the 13th century to the Walton or Wauton family. Master Simon de Walton purchased half a carucate of land in Bradley of Richard le Archer in 1244–5,[8] and in 1248–9 he acquired land there from John Copty, Stephen Alewy, Hugh de Seler,[9] Ralph de Eccleshal [10] and Ralph Marsh.[11]

In 1253 Master Simon obtained from Henry III a grant that his garden with the grove therein which he had caused to be inclosed in the circuit of his house at Bradley in the forest of Feckenham should remain inclosed, bounded by a hedge without a deer leap like a park, with the 'beasts of the wood' in the park if he liked.[12] Simon de Wauton appears to have been succeeded by John, who was dealing with land at Bradley in 1274–5,[13] and paid a subsidy of 8s. in 1280 at Bradley.[14] John de Wauton, who in 1294 obtained licence from Simon Bishop of Norwich to do homage to the chief lords for land in Bradley and elsewhere,[15] was perhaps son of John above mentioned. John Knight held a hide of land in Bradley in 1299,[16] and Robert Knight paid a subsidy of 1s. there in 1327.[17] In 1346 William Knight of Bradley was in possession of the land at Bradley which William de Bradley had held,[18] but it is not certain that this was the same estate as that held by the Wautons, and its further descent has not been traced.

In 1086 the priest at Fladbury held half a hide of land.[19] In 1772 the rector of Fladbury received an allotment in consideration of 70 acres which he held in Throckmorton as part of the *RECTORY MANOR*.[20] In 1788, when Fladbury was inclosed, he obtained a further allotment in consideration of his right of common in Fladbury belonging to the rectory manor.[21] Nash in his *History of Worcestershire* mentions that it was a custom of the rectory manor for the rector to grant for three lives and the widow to have her free bench.[22] The manorial rights have now apparently lapsed.

CHURCHES
The church of *ST. JOHN BAPTIST* consists of a chancel 38½ ft. by 19½ ft., a modern north vestry and south organ chamber, nave 57 ft. by 20 ft., north aisle 9 ft. and south aisle 8½ ft. in width, south porch and a western tower 12½ ft. wide and 13½ ft. deep; all the measurements are internal.

A church stood here in the 12th century, but of this building only the tower remains, the three lower stages dating from that period; it was probably attached to an aisleless nave and chancel. About

[92] Birch (*Cart. Sax.* i, 221) dates this charter 723, 729, 735 or 740.
[93] Heming, op. cit. 15.
[94] Dugdale, *Mon. Angl.* i, 607.
[95] Birch, op. cit. i, 356; Heming, op. cit. 16, 17, 18. This charter was confirmed by Bishop Deneberht at the Council of Cloveshoo in 803 (Heming, op. cit. 19; Dugdale, *Mon. Angl.* i, 587). In the Worcester chartulary there is a note of a charter dated 789 by Ceolwulf (afterwards King of Mercia) relating to land at Bradley (Heming, op. cit. 579), but it was probably only a confirmation of this agreement (see Dugdale, loc. cit.).
[96] Heming, op. cit. 144; Birch, op. cit. iii, 318.
[97] *V.C.H. Worcs.* i, 290b. Archbishop

Ealdred had leased it to his reeve in the time of Edward the Confessor (ibid.).
[98] *Testa de Nevill* (Rec. Com.), 41b; *Valor Eccl.* (Rec. Com.), iii, 217.
[99] Pat. 7 Edw. VI, pt. xiii, m. 7.
[100] *Cal. S. P. Dom.* 1547–80, p. 58.
[1] Ibid. 1628–9, p. 248.
[2] Priv. Act, 6 Geo. IV, cap. 1.
[3] Stat. 23 & 24 Vict. cap. 124.
[4] Habington, op. cit. i, 316; Red Bk. of Bishopric of Worc. fol. 81.
[5] *Cal. Chart. R.* 1226–57, p. 172.
[6] Red Bk. of Bishopric of Worc. fol. 257.
[7] *Testa de Nevill* (Rec. Com.), 41b.
[8] Feet of F. Worcs. 29 Hen. III, no. 10.
[9] Ibid. 33 Hen. III, no. 21.

[10] Ibid. no. 44.
[11] Ibid. no. 29.
[12] Cart. Ant. QQ 7; *Cal. Pat.* 1247–58, p. 180.
[13] Feet of F. Worcs. 3 Edw. I, no. 17.
[14] *Lay Subs. R. Worcs.* 1280 (Worcs. Hist. Soc.), 38.
[15] *Reg. G. Giffard* (Worcs. Hist. Soc.), 443; see also p. 445.
[16] Red Bk. of Bishopric of Worc. fol. 69; Habington, op. cit. i, 228.
[17] *Lay Subs. R. Worcs.* 1327 (Worcs. Hist. Soc.), 42.
[18] *Feud. Aids,* v, 309.
[19] *V.C.H. Worcs.* i, 289b.
[20] Priv. Act, 12 Geo. III, cap. 37.
[21] Ibid. 28 Geo. III, cap. 16.
[22] op. cit. i, 449a.

the year 1340 the whole of the pre-existing structure (except the tower) was swept away to make room for the new work. The present nave with both its aisles, and the chancel with a vestry to the north-east of it (which has now disappeared), were then erected, the clearstory being added immediately afterwards. The south porch was built with the south aisle, but it was refaced some time in the 17th century, and since that period has undergone restoration. A board in the ringing-chamber records that the steeple [23] was taken down and the parapet to the tower built in 1752, and that galleries were added in 1783 and 1824. Much restoration work has been carried out in modern times, chiefly in 1865 and

FLADBURY CHURCH TOWER FROM THE NORTH-WEST

1871. The east and south walls of the chancel, the vestry and the organ chamber are all of recent date, as are also several of the windows and doorways and other parts specifically mentioned below. The present four-light east window replaced a seven-light one, probably itself of no great age; the gable wall over is pierced by a small quatrefoil opening. In the south wall is a modern double piscina in 14th-century style and a sedile formed by the window-ledge; the two windows in this wall, both modern, have each two lights with cusped piercings over in a pointed arch. There is also a small priest's doorway with a pointed head. On the north side is a 14th-century window of two lights with a cusped opening over in

[23] Which was of wood.

a pointed head. The doorway into the vestry appears to be of 14th-century workmanship, but has probably been reset, and has two continuous moulded orders. To the east of the vestry, outside, in the north wall of the chancel is an original 14th-century piscina, the basin of which has been removed. The chancel arch and the arch opening into the organ chamber are both modern.

The 14th-century nave arcades consist of four bays, the first three of each being of equal span and the fourth pair narrower. The arches are of two pointed chamfered orders, and the columns are octagonal with moulded bases and bell capitals; there are no respond shafts, the inner order springing from moulded corbels except at the north-west, where it dies on to the wall of the tower stair turret. The two eastern corbels are modern. The original doorway into the tower stair turret opens towards the east into the nave, but a modern one has been inserted in the west aisle wall outside. The tower arch has three continuous chamfered orders, and over it is a wide opening into the ringing chamber with a pointed segmental arch, which is evidently modern, as above it a similar arch is visible, now filled in. The clearstory has four windows on either side, of two lights each, with square heads; the westernmost pair are modern, the others original.

The three-light east and west windows of the north aisle are modern, as is the westernmost of the four two-light north windows, the other three being of late 14th-century date.

In the south wall of the south aisle next the arch opening into the modern organ chamber is a small locker with rebated edges, and west of it are the remains of a piscina with a concave back and pointed head. The two south windows of the aisle are both in part old, each with two lights in a square head. The south doorway has been completely modernized, and to the east of it is a small square blocked doorway, which evidently once opened to a stair leading to a room over the porch. The jambs only of the west window are old, and above it externally is a string-course, all modern except the piece at the south-west corner, carved with the head and shoulders of an angel. Above the string-course are remains of a blocked opening, probably connected with an 18th-century gallery. The south porch, although much repaired, is of the same date as the aisle and has a ribbed vault, springing from corner shafts with moulded bases and capitals. In the east wall is a window of two small lancets and in the west a quatrefoil window, both partly renewed. The outer archway appears to be an 18th-century rebuilding, and this again has been repaired in modern times. Over the doorway is a circular traceried piercing with a square moulded label. The front wall of the porch is finished with a curved pediment, capped by a pedestal sundial.

The tower is of four stages, the lowest being strengthened by shallow clasping and intermediate buttresses, the latter pierced by small round-headed lights, surrounded internally by large shallow recesses with pointed arches. The next two stages are both pierced by narrow rectangular lights, and on the west face of the third stage is a clock. Here the outlines of the former belfry windows can still be traced ; these were evidently filled in when the tower was heightened. The top stage or bell-chamber is lit by a two-light window in each wall with a plain spandrel in a pointed arch. The parapet is embattled with a continuous coping, the lower part being panelled and the merlons pierced with trefoiled openings. At the angles are square panelled pinnacles with smaller ones in the centre of each face. The walling of the church is mainly of rubble, but the tower is ashlar faced and the clearstories, above the windows, are built of red brick.

The buttresses of the north aisle wall are original, but most of the others are modern. The roofs are also modern, the chancel and nave having low-pitched gables ; the roof of the latter is ceiled. The aisle roofs are flat, lead covered, and plastered internally. All the roofs have eaves with stone cornices.

The altar table, marble reredos, stone pulpit and font are all of recent date.

Under the tower is a large altar tomb of grey marble to John Throckmorton, who died in 1445, Eleanor his wife, and Thomas his son. It was moved from its former position in the chancel at the last restoration of the church. The sides of the tomb are panelled and the moulded plinth contains a band of quatrefoils. In the slab are the brass figures of a man in armour and a lady with five shields, one of which is missing ; the other four have the arms of Throckmorton impaling Azure a fesse or with three pheons thereon. In the chancel floor is a slab with the half figure of a coped priest in brass and an inscription below to Thomas Mordon, Bachelor of Law and Treasurer of St. Paul's, London, a former rector of this church, who died in 1458. The arms in the shields over are a cheveron between two molets in the chief and a lion in the foot.

A second brass has a Latin inscription to William Plewine, M.A., rector, who died in 1504, whose figure is represented in mass vestments ; and a brass inscription commemorates Olive wife successively of Edward Harris and John Talbot, who died in 1647.

At the west end of the nave is a brass to Edward Peyton, in armour, the figures of the wife and children with three shields being missing. Another undated Latin inscription is to Godytha (Bosom) wife of Robert Olney (her daughter Margaret married Thomas Throckmorton) surrounded by three reversed shields. The other monuments include one, in the vestry, to

Bishop William Lloyd, 1707, and another in the south aisle to John Darby, 1609.

In the north-west window of the chancel are six shields of 14th-century glass, of the arms of Beauchamp, Mountford, Moigne, Mortimer, Montfort, and Despenser. They were removed from the east window to make way for the present stained-glass window, and are said to have come from the abbey of Evesham at the Dissolution. They are mentioned in Symonds's Diary in 1644.[23a]

There were a number of encaustic tiles about the church ; most of them have been collected and placed in the north doorway, now blocked.

In the churchyard is a fine row of yew trees with a pathway between it and the old brick boundary wall.

There is a ring of six bells, all cast by Mears in 1807, and in addition a small sanctus bell hung in the south window with a black letter inscription, ' Sancta Katerina Ora pro me Edwardo Gregion.'

The old communion plate was in 1801 removed to the chapels of Throckmorton and Wyre Piddle.[24]

THROCKMORTON CHURCH FROM THE SOUTH-WEST

The registers are as follows : (1) baptisms and marriages from 1560 to 1630, burials 1560 to 1629 ; (ii) baptisms and burials from 1630 to 1713, marriages 1630 to 1712, with gaps from 1640 to 1660 in this book ; (iii) baptisms and burials from 1713 to 1803, marriages 1713 to 1753 ; (iv) marriages from 1754 to 1812 ; (v) baptisms and burials from 1804 to 1812.

The church of *THROCKMORTON* consists of a chancel 12½ ft. by 16 ft., a central tower 11½ ft. by 13½ ft., a nave about 45 ft. by 17½ ft., and a small south aisle 4½ ft. in width. These measurements are all internal.

The chancel is of the 13th century, but the tracery of the windows is all modern, the eastern being of three lights, with one of two lights in each side wall. The trefoiled piscina at the east end of the south wall has a square head with pierced spandrels and a half-octagonal bowl. The eastern arch of the contemporary central tower which is included within the

23a op. cit. (Camden Soc.), 25.
24 Prattinton Coll. (Soc. Antiq.), Church Notes.

chancel is of two chamfered orders, the outer order dying upon the walls and the inner springing from plain corbels. The western arch is similar, with the exception that the inner order also dies upon the face of the responds, and a little above its springing it is interrupted on both sides by large plain corbels which must have originally supported the rood-beam. In the south wall of the tower is a window of two trefoiled lights with modern tracery. The projecting chamfered course on the north and south walls evidently supported a floor below the level of the crowns of the arches.

In the north wall of the nave is a window of similar form to the east window of the chancel. The north doorway is of the 14th century and is of two chamfered orders. The south arcade of the nave is of five bays with two-centred arches of two plain chamfered orders and dates from the 13th century. The centre bay is considerably narrower than the rest. Above the columns where the labels, had they existed, would have intersected, are face-corbels. These have been recently placed in this position for their better preservation. They were formerly lying loose in the building, and had probably been detached from the fabric at some repair or restoration. The columns are quatrefoil on plan with moulded capitals and water-holding bases. The three-light west window dates from early in the 14th century.

Both aisle windows are modern. The south doorway is reset 14th-century work and has a chamfered two-centred head and jambs. The embattled tower is three stages high, with good gargoyles at the angles. The belfry is lighted by two-light windows, and the stage below by two small square-headed lights in the south wall.

Externally the chancel is built of coursed rubble with an intermixture of brick and tile. The walls of both chancel and nave have been heightened in brick. The nave and tower are both covered with rough-cast, and the south aisle is modern.

The cylindrical font with its thick tapering stem is perhaps of 14th-century date.

The tower contains four bells : the first is uninscribed, the second has fallen from its frame and is broken at the crown, the third is dated 1622 with the churchwardens' names, the fourth is cracked and inscribed,

'Be it known to all that shall us see
That Henrie Farmer made we 4 of 3.'

The plate consists of an Elizabethan cup with cover paten without hall mark, a small paten of plain beaten silver, also without hall mark, and an almsdish of brass.

The registers before 1812 are as follows : (i) baptisms from 1546 to 1717, marriages 1545 to 1717, and burials 1661 to 1717 ; (ii) baptisms from 1717 to 1812, burials 1721 to 1750, and marriages from 1718 to 1754.

The church at WYRE consists of a chancel 14½ ft. by 15½ ft., nave 41½ ft. by 18 ft., and a north porch.

The walls appear to follow the plan of a 12th-century building, but the whole structure has been rebuilt in modern times. The three-light east window is in 14th-century style with modern tracery and original jambs. In the north wall is a modern two-light window. The first window on the south side is of three lights in the style of the 14th century and the second is modern. In the same wall

is set half of a 13th-century capital, used as a credence table, and a typical 12th-century pillar piscina, with square bowl. The chancel arch is round-headed, of one plain order, with a chamfered label, and springs from square chamfered impost mouldings. On each side of it is a square squint.

All the nave windows are modern restorations, there being three in the north wall and four in the south. The western pair are modern lancets ; the remaining windows are each of two lights, the eastern pair having quatrefoil tracery. The north door is the only entrance to the nave, and is covered by a modern porch. The 15th-century west window is of two lights and contains some fine pieces of contemporary stained glass. The font is circular, with a moulded rim and cheveron ornament below. The stem and base are also circular, and beneath the bowl are fluted scallops. In a recess in the north wall are preserved some fragments of early work, with the boss of a shield and a light spearhead, discovered in the churchyard. There is also one of a pair of 14th-century candlesticks in the churchwarden's house. The chancel floor is largely paved with mediaeval tiles, the better preserved being within the altar rails.

The church has a bellcote above the chancel, with spaces for two bells. The work is contemporary with the chancel, but has been restored. It contains one 18th-century bell by Rudhall.

The plate includes a reconstructed cup, the old stem Elizabethan, the cup itself comparatively modern, a plain plate hall-marked 1673 and a large flagon of 1651.

The registers before 1812 are as follows : in one book, baptisms 1670 to 1709, burials 1680 to 1713, marriages 1684 to 1709.[25]

The church of ST. JOHN BAPTIST, Bradley, consists of a chancel, nave, north porch and north-east tower. The church was erected in 1864–5 on the site of a former building, which is stated by Nash to have been of timber with a wooden tower.[26] The materials are Inkberrow stone, and the design is in the style of the early 14th century. The east window of the chancel is of three lights with tracery over, and the nave is lighted from the west by a large rose-window. The tower is surmounted by a broach spire of stone. The north porch contains portions of two mediaeval tomb slabs. The earliest of these has a double cross with a wheel head, and probably dates from about 1300. The later and more elaborate slab has a cross approximating to the Maltese shape, and upon its stem a shield charged with three crosslets upon a bend. In the church is a monument from the former building to Joseph James, who died in 1776.

There is one bell of 1865, replacing three cast in 1771.

The plate consists of a chalice and cover of Reformation pattern, the cover (usable as a paten) bearing the date 1571, a paten dated 1865, and a modern metal flagon, never used.

The registers before 1812 are as follows : (i) mixed entries 1562 to 1644 ; (ii) 1645 to 1718 ; (iii) 1719 to 1812.

ST. THOMAS'S Church at Lower Moor was opened on 21 December 1869. It was built on a

[25] Some earlier 17th-century entries will be found in the Bishops' Transcripts.
[26] op. cit. i, 453 ; Prattinton Coll. (Soc. Antiq.).

WYRE PIDDLE CHURCH : THE PILLAR PISCINA

WYRE PIDDLE CHURCH : FRAGMENTS OF 15TH-CENTURY GLASS IN
WEST WINDOW

site given by Robert Wagstaff, and service is held there every Sunday afternoon by the rector and curates of Fladbury. Parish rooms at Fladbury, Moor and Wyre Piddle are used for meetings.

ADVOWSONS There was possibly a church at Fladbury in 1086, as there was then a priest there.[27] The advowson has always belonged to the see of Worcester.[28] In 1291 the church was valued at £26 13s. 4d.[29] In 1317 the Crown presented owing to the vacancy of the see of Worcester,[30] and in 1535 the presentation was granted to Thomas Cromwell and others on the petition of Thomas Bagard, LL.D., vicar-general of Worcester.[31] In 1535 the rectory of Fladbury, with the chapels attached to it,[32] was worth £81 0s. 8d. yearly.[33] In 1543 Christopher Hales, the rector, received a licence to travel abroad for seven years, and take with him one servant and two horses.[34]

On 14 May 1448[35] Eleanor wife of John Throckmorton and her son Thomas obtained licence to found in the parish church of Fladbury a chantry of one chaplain to celebrate divine service daily at the altar of St. Mary. The chantry was to be called 'Throkmerton Chaunterie,' and Eleanor and Thomas were to endow it with rents to the value of £10 a year.[36] The advowson belonged to the lords of the manor of Throckmorton.[37] In 1535 the chantry was valued at £9 3s. 4d.[38] William Lane, the chantry priest, obtained licence in 1547 to grant all the lands belonging to the chantry to George Throckmorton.[39] Two years later the chantry was dissolved, and the chantry-house seems to have been granted to Stephen Hales, for he and his wife Joan conveyed a messuage called the Chantry House in 1553 to John Ayland,[40] and in 1588 the chantry of Fladbury was granted by the queen, at the request of Edward Dyer, to Edward Wymarke.[41] In 1601 it was granted to Robert Stanford or Stamford.[42]

There was an obit in the church in connexion with this chantry supported by a sum of 5s. from the endowment of the chantry.[43] There was also a rent of 4d. from an acre of land in Fladbury given for the maintenance of a lamp in the church.[44]

A chapel, to which the rectors of Fladbury presented, was in existence at Ab Lench as early as 1269, when the first presentation of which we have any record took place.[45] Presentations were made to this vicarage until 1419.[46] The remains of the chapel were visible in 1812,[47] and are still remembered by some of the inhabitants. Carlisle, writing in 1808, mentioned a demolished chapel.[48] Ab Lench was annexed to Church Lench for ecclesiastical purposes in 1865.[49]

The chapels of Throckmorton, Bradley and Wyre Piddle were mentioned in the Valor of 1535.[50] The chapels of Throckmorton and Wyre Piddle are still annexed to Fladbury. Bradley was separated from Fladbury in July 1862,[51] and the living was declared a rectory in 1866.[52] It is in the gift of the Bishop of Worcester.

CHARITIES The amalgamated charities are administered by the rector and churchwardens, comprising

1. The charity known as Holt's charity, consisting of £49 13s. 6d. consols, representing donations mentioned on the church table of £5 each by Miss Martin, Nicholas Perks and Mrs. Hester Jones, improved by offertories to £50.

2. The charity of Richard Bourne Charlett, will 1821, also mentioned on the church table, trust fund, £100 consols.

3. The charity of Mrs. Joyce Evans, will proved at Worcester 15 July 1848, trust fund, £44 14s. consols.

4. The charity of Robert Wagstaff, will proved at Worcester 26 July 1880, trust fund, £500 consols.

The several sums of stock are held by the official trustees, the annual dividends of which, amounting to £17 7s., were in 1908–9 applied in gifts of 4s. to 8s. among twenty-eight widows, 10s. each to two poor residents and other money gifts.

In 1825 the Rev. Martin Stafford Smith by deed gave a sum of £1,125 1s. consols with the official trustees, the annual dividends, amounting to £28 2s. 4d., to be distributed in coals, bread and meat, and religious books to the poorest inhabitants of Fladbury, Hill and Moor, Wyre Piddle and Throckmorton on or about 23 December. Contributions to the income are made by residents, the distributions being made chiefly in coal by the rector and churchwardens, and Bibles, Prayer books and hymn books by the rector.

In 1865 the Rev. Frederick Gauntlett by deed gave £100 consols (with the official trustees), the annual dividend of £2 10s. to be applied towards the support of the parochial schools.

The Church Lands—referred to on the church table as the gift in 1403 of Thomas Wilcox and Grysels his wife, and devise by will of John Hopkins, 1710—now consist of 11 acres let in allotments, acquired by exchange on the inclosure in 1787 for other lands called the Cherry Orchard and Rick Ground; also 2 acres in the hamlet of Hill and Moor. The net rental of about £18 yearly is carried to the churchwardens' accounts.

Hamlet of Hill and Moor.—In 1681 William White of London, vintner—as appeared from the church table—gave £5 for the use of the poor, subsequently augmented to £17.

In 1841 William George, by will proved in the P.C.C., left £50 for the poor. These gifts are now represented by £72 8s. 8d. consols.

27 *V.C.H. Worcs.* i, 289b.

28 Worc. Epis. Reg. Bransford (1339–49), ii, fol. 12 ; Inst. Bks. (P.R.O.).

29 *Pope Nich. Tax.* (Rec. Com.), 218.

30 *Cal. Pat.* 1313–17, p. 657.

31 *L. and P. Hen. VIII*, viii, g. 962 (24).

32 See below.

33 *Valor Eccl.* (Rec. Com.), iii, 268.

34 *L. and P. Hen. VIII*, xviii (1), g. 623 (69).

35 The actual foundation does not appear to have taken place until 1460 (Chant. Cert. 25, no. 16).

36 *Cal. Pat.* 1446–52, pp. 168, 169.

37 Worc. Epis. Reg. Morton (1486–97), fol. 41 ; Silvester de Gigliis (1498–1521), fol. 29 d.

38 *Valor Eccl.* (Rec. Com.), iii, 266.

39 Pat. 1 Edw. VI, pt. iii, no. 57.

40 Feet of F. Worcs. Mich. 1 Mary.

41 Pat. 30 Eliz. pt. vii, m. 1.

42 Ibid. 43 Eliz. pt. vi, m. 26.

43 Chant. Cert. 25, no. 16.

44 Ibid. 60, no. 40.

45 *Reg. G. Giffard* (Worcs. Hist. Soc.), 7.

46 Ibid. 446 ; *Sede Vac. Reg.* (Worcs. Hist. Soc.), 184, 232 ; Worc. Epis. Reg. Reginald Brian (1352–61), fol. 27 ; Nash, *Hist. of Worcs.* ii, 83.

47 Prattinton Coll. (Soc. Antiq.).

48 Carlisle, *Topog. Dict.* under Hob Lench. Lewis, writing in 1849, says, 'Here was a chapel which fell into decay about two centuries ago. Divine service is performed in a cottage by the rector of Fladbury' (ibid.).

49 *Parl. P.* 1872, xlvi, 27.

50 *Valor Eccl.* (Rec. Com.), iii, 267.

51 *Parl. P.* 1872, xlvi, 21.

52 *Lond. Gaz.* 3 Apr. 1866, p. 2210.

In 1885 Miss Mary Wagstaff, by will proved at Worcester, left £200, which was invested in £198 10s. 2d. consols.

In 1888 Miss Ann Wagstaff, by a codicil to her will proved at Worcester, left £200, invested in £206 9s. consols.

The several sums of stock are held by the official trustees, the annual dividends of which, amounting to £11 18s., are applied proportionately in pursuance of the trusts of the respective charities. The distribution is made in bread and money in the month of January in each year, a preference being given to widows. In 1909 sixteen needy families benefited under Miss Ann Wagstaff's charity.

This hamlet also participates in the benefit of the charity of the Rev. Martin Stafford Smith. (See under parish of Fladbury.)

Chapelry of Stock and Bradley.—The Poor's Land—referred to on the church table as the gift in 1621 of William Jones and in 1653 of Henry Collier—now consists of 2½ acres, known as the Parish Close, and two plots of garden land, containing together 1 acre, or thereabouts, of the annual rental value of £8 10s., which is applied in the distribution of bread, beef and coal.

The Church Lands.—The chapelry has been in possession from time immemorial of about 5½ acres of land, now let at £19 a year, which is carried to the chapel-wardens' account.

Hamlet of Wyre Piddle.—The Chapel Lands consist of a garden plantation containing 1 a. 2 r. 8 p. let at £8 a year, which is applied towards the repair of the chapel, the sum of 10s. being paid to the rector as tithe.

This hamlet also participates in the benefits of the charity of the Rev. Martin Stafford Smith. (See under the parish of Fladbury.)

GRIMLEY

Grimanlege (ix cent.) ; Grimanleag (x cent.) ; Grimanleh (xi cent.) ; Grimele (xiii cent.).

The parish of Grimley on the right bank of the Severn to the north of Hallow covers an area of 2,471 acres. Of these 865 acres are arable land, the chief crops being wheat, barley, beans and roots. The soil is loam and gravel, the subsoil red marl and clay. There are 1,187 acres of permanent grass and the woods and plantations cover 180 acres.[1] Grimley Brook, a tributary of the Severn, rises to the north of Monk Wood and forms the northern boundary of Grimley, the Severn forming the eastern boundary. The land near the river is very low-lying and liable to floods, being only 48 ft. above ordnance datum. The village itself stands about 70 ft. above the ordnance datum. To the west the ground rises, reaching a height of 200 ft. at Oakhall Green near Monk Wood. A road from Worcester to Stourport runs north past the vicarage and crosses Grimley Brook near Ball Mill. At Camp House a ferry leads to Bevere.

The village of Grimley is situated on the right bank of the Severn to the east of the road from Stourport to Worcester. The church stands at the north end of the short street which constitutes the village. Sinton[2] is a hamlet to the west of the village. Sinton Court, a 19th-century house of moderate size, is the residence of Mr. Thomas MacBean. Thorngrove, the property of Mrs. Lee Williams, now occupied by Mr. Herbert Whiteley, was for several years the residence of Lucien Bonaparte, Prince of Canino, younger brother of Napoleon I, when a prisoner of war in this country.

It is a plain stone mansion of the late 18th century standing in extensive grounds.

The Priors of Worcester visited Grimley frequently in the 14th century, and transacted business here. Many letters and orders in 1302, 1307 and 1375 are dated from Grimley.[3] The manor-house built in the reign of Henry VIII was destroyed towards the close of the 17th century and replaced by a cross-timbered building called 'The Palace.'[4]

George Hooper, Bishop of Bath and Wells, was born here in 1640,[5] and Sir Samuel White Baker, F.R.S., F.R.A.S., the African explorer, is buried in the churchyard, his father Samuel Baker being then the owner of Thorngrove in this parish.

Former place-names in the parish include Ocholt or Okholtesgrove, Sechenhal, Bertrithestoking, Erthelond, Smocacra, Storteland, Werle, Hashulle, Heldedeshashull, Boygrava, Rugmore, Smethemor, Ailwinch, Holithurn, Marshell, Butholt, Leintewirthin[6] (xiii cent.) ; Pritch[7] (xvi cent.) ; the Vineyard,[8] Monk-redding and Holy Well[9] (xix cent.).

MANOR   Bertwulf, King of the Mercians, in 851 gave 3 cassata at GRIMLEY to the church of Worcester for the salvation of his soul. It was to be free of all service except military service and the building of bridges.[10] Possibly King Offa also granted land at Grimley to the monastery, as a charter of that king relating to Grimley is noted among the charters of the church of Worcester.[11]

Bishop Oswald (961–72) leased four manses at Grimley and one at Moseley[12] to his brother Oswulf for three lives,[13] but Bishop Wulfstan redeemed it in

---

[1] Statistics from Bd. of Agric. (1905).

[2] Sinton is probably to be identified with the 13th-century Suthintun or Sudintun (*Reg. of Worc. Priory* [Camden Soc.], 44a). In the 13th century Matthew de Hallow gave land there to his daughter Joan, by whom it was afterwards given to the priory of Worcester (Prattinton Coll. [Soc. Antiq.], Deeds of D. and C. of Worc. no. 81, 250, 133).

[3] *Sede Vacante Reg.* (Worcs. Hist. Soc.), 78, &c.

[4] Noake, *Guide to Worcs.* 171.

[5] *Dict. Nat. Biog.*

[6] Hale, *Reg. of Worc. Priory* (Camden Soc.), 42a, 42b, 43a, 46b, 47a.

[7] Chan. Inq. p.m. (Ser. 2), ccxl, 63. Pritch may have derived its name from J. Prich, a rod-knight of the prior, in 1240 (Hale, *Reg. of Worc. Priory* [Camden Soc.], 44b).

[8] The vineyard at Grimley is mentioned in 1240 (*Reg. of Worc. Priory* [Camden Soc.], 43b).

[9] Prattinton Coll. (Soc. Antiq.).

[10] Heming, *Chartul.* (ed. Hearne), 416; Birch, *Cart. Sax.* ii, 55. The bounds of the land are given in this charter.

[11] Heming, op. cit. 584.

[12] Moseley, though not mentioned by name, seems to have been included in King Coenwulf's grant of 816, freeing Hallow and its members from secular services (Thomas, *Surv. of Worc. Cath.* A 25).

[13] Birch, op. cit. iii, 385 ; Heming, op. cit. 596, 147. The boundaries of the land are given in this charter.

the time of William the Conqueror and gave it to Thomas, Prior of Worcester.[14]

Grimley was among the possessions of the monastery of Worcester in 1086,[15] and was confirmed to the monks by Bishop Simon in 1148.[16] It is difficult to account for the statement found in one of the cloister windows of Worcester Cathedral that Bishop Walter (1214–16) gave Grimley to the priory of Worcester.[17] In 1240 the priory held at Grimley a court and 2 carucates of land, one of which was held by the tenants at will and the other let to them at farm.[18] In 1256 the monks obtained a grant of free warren at Grimley.[19] From that time until the Dissolution Grimley remained in the possession of the priory of Worcester.[20]

The manor was granted by Henry VIII to the Dean and Chapter of Worcester in 1542,[21] but in 1547 they gave it back to the king in exchange for the rectory of Kempsey and other lands,[22] and Edward VI gave the manor of Grimley in the same year to the Bishop of Worcester.[23] Bishop Heath was deprived of his see when he refused to subscribe to the Edwardian Prayer Book, but on the appointment of Bishop Hooper Edward VI gave him the lands of the bishopric.[24] Grimley remained in episcopal hands until 1648, when it was sold to John Corbett.[25] The bishop recovered it at the Restoration, and it was taken over in 1860 by the Ecclesiastical Commissioners,[26] who are the present lords of the manor.

Bishop Pates gave a long lease of the rent-corn from Grimley to 'Master Abingdon,' Cofferer to Elizabeth, but John Whitgift, on being appointed to the see, found the bishopric so much impoverished by this and other leases, the rent-corn of Hallow and Grimley being 'the chief upholding of the bishop's hospitality,' that he appealed to the queen to restore it to the see. Notwithstanding that Habington 'was a great man then to contend withal, his wife being sometimes the Queen's Bedfellow,' the queen supported the bishop, and Habington was obliged to surrender his lease in return for £300.[27]

The monks of Worcester held Monk Wood in demesne in the 13th century.[28] They bought James de Wichenford's rights of pasturage in 1300[29] and obtained licence to impark Monk Wood in 1309.[30] When the manor of Grimley was granted to William Moore, the retiring prior, in 1536,[30a] he petitioned the king to allow him 'the mansion place' of Grimley with sufficient fuel from the wood called Monk Wood.[31] Monk Wood was evidently granted with the manor to the Dean and Chapter of Worcester, for in 1546 they surrendered it to the king.[31a] Nash states that when he was writing at the end of the 18th century Monk Wood contained 145 acres, of which about 50 acres were coppice wood.[32]

In 1086 the church of Worcester owned a mill at Grimley, which yielded no profit,[33] and half a fishery. In the 13th century the mill was leased at 24s. yearly.[34] The inhabitants of Grimley were obliged to take their corn to be ground at Broadwas when their own mill was out of repair.[35] When the manor of Grimley was sold in 1648 by the Parliamentary Commissioners the mill of Grimley, then known as Ball Mill, was included in the sale.[36] The present Ball Mill is a corn-mill on Grimley Brook, to the west of the village.

The church of *ST. BARTHOLOMEW* CHURCH consists of a chancel 27 ft. by 15½ ft., north vestry, nave 45½ ft. by 19½ ft., north aisle 9¼ ft. wide, south porch, and a western tower 13 ft. by 10 ft. These dimensions are all internal. The only remains of the 12th-century church are the south doorway and the lower part of the south wall of the nave. The chancel appears to have been rebuilt in the 13th century, assuming that the restored lancet windows in its walls are copies of their predecessors. The south wall of the nave was partly rebuilt in the 14th century, when the three existing windows were inserted, and a larger window was inserted in the east wall of the chancel in the 15th century. The tower was probably erected at the same time. The north aisle and vestry were added in 1886, and at the same time the rest of the building underwent a drastic restoration.

The 15th-century east window of the chancel is of three lights under a traceried four-centred head. In each side wall are two lancet windows renovated almost wholly with modern stonework. One now opens into the modern vestry on the north side. The pointed chancel arch is modern.

In the south wall of the nave are three windows of two lights under traceried pointed heads ; they appear to be of 14th-century date, but are of unusually rough workmanship. Below the first window outside is the lower part of a 12th-century shallow buttress, and to the east of it and also below the second window are some indications of blocked openings. The 12th-century south doorway is of two orders, and has detached shafts to the jambs with modern capitals. The modern south porch is designed to harmonize with it in style, as is the stairway which gives access to the west gallery. The modern arcade north of the nave is of three bays, and the aisle is lighted by three two-light windows on the north and a single light at the west end. The tower has been entirely modernized ; it is in four stages, supported by diagonal buttresses. The west doorway has a four-centred head, with a two-light traceried window over it. The bell-chamber is lighted by pairs of two-light transomed windows, with a quatrefoil in the head of each. Their ogee labels terminate in

[14] Heming, op. cit. 407.
[15] V.C.H. Worcs. i, 295b.
[16] Thomas, op. cit. App. no. 18.
[17] Ibid. S. 32 ; Habington, Surv. of Worcs. ii, 366.
[18] Reg. of Worc. Priory (Camden Soc.), 41a.   [19] Cal. Pat. 1354–8, p. 266.
[20] Valor Eccl. (Rec. Com.), iii, 221. At this time the manor was valued at £55 15s. 9½d. It had been assigned to William Moore in 1536 when he resigned the priorship, and he continued to hold it far into the reign of Elizabeth (L. and P.

Hen. VIII, x, 1272 ; Dugdale, Mon. i, 581).
[21] Pat. 33 Hen. VIII, pt. v, m. 19.
[22] Close, 38 Hen. VIII, pt. ii, no. 51 ; Pat. 1 Edw. VI, pt. ix, m. 5 ; L. and P. Hen. VIII, xxi (2), g. 770 (50), 326.
[23] Pat. 1 Edw. VI, pt. iv ; L. and P. Hen. VIII, xxi (2), g. 770 (67).
[24] Ibid. 6 Edw. VI, pt. vii.
[25] Close, 24 Chas. I, pt. xiv, no. 26.
[26] Stat. 23 & 24 Vict. cap. 124.
[27] Sir Geo. Paule, Life of Archbishop Whitgift, 27, 28.

[28] Hale, Reg. of Worc. Priory (Camden Soc.), 47a.
[29] Ann. Mon. (Rolls Ser.), iv, 549.
[30] Inq. a.q.d. file 71, no. 18; Cal. Pat. 1307–13, p. 200.
[30a] See note 20 above.
[31] L. and P. Hen. VIII, x, 1272.
[31a] Ibid. xxi (2), 326.
[32] op. cit. i, 471.
[33] V.C.H. Worcs. i, 295b.
[34] Hale, Reg. of Worc. Priory (Camden Soc.), 41b.   [35] Ibid. 32a.
[36] Close, 24 Chas. I, pt. xiv, no. 26.

carved finials. The parapet is embattled and a gargoyle projects from each face.

The roofs are gabled and modern.

The font is apparently an old one recut. It is octagonal in plan, with a moulding of 15th-century character on the lower ridge of the bowl ; the base is new. The pulpit and the other furniture are modern, and under the tower is a gallery. The monuments are all of the late 18th century or modern.

Two of the 14th-century windows contain 15th-century stained glass. One has the kneeling figure of a saint in the western light holding a cup and paten. In its east light is a figure of God the Father in the act of blessing ; the two lights appear to be part of a single subject. Another window has a representation of the Annunciation.

There are six bells : the first three cast by John Rudhall in 1820 ; the fourth dated 1599 and inscribed ' God be our good spede, William Wogan, I.G. ' ; the fifth bears the inscription ' + Jesus ba (sic) our sped 1626 ' ; the tenor is a well-known dated pre-Reformation bell, it is inscribed in Lombardic capitals ' O Beate O Sancte Gregori laus tibi in gloria,' with winged dragons and a cross ; below it in script letters is another small inscription reading ' T. Clyvegrove, Tempore dñi Roberti Multon Prioris Wygornae Anno Dñi millimo CCCCmo LXXXIJ.'

The communion plate comprises a large silver cup of 1635 with the initials $_{RA}^{F}$, a plated paten, and a silver flagon of 1812.

The registers are as follows : (i) mixed entries 1573 to 1731 ; (ii) baptisms and burials only 1731 to 1812; (iii) marriages for the same period.

ADVOWSON In 1238 there was a free chapel at Grimley.[37] The advowson belonged to the Priors of Worcester[38] until the monastery was dissolved. It was appropriated to the priory in 1268 under the title of ' church,' and to it was attached the chapelry of Hallow.[39] In 1269 the bishop assigned to the vicar 10 marks from the priory until a certain portion of the tithes had been provided,[40] and the vicarage was ordained in the following year.[41] In the 16th century 20s. was paid to the vicar out of the rectory.[42] After the Dissolution the advowson and rectory passed with the manor to the Bishop of Worcester. In 1549 the advowson was sold to William Sheldon by Bishop Heath,[43] but in the following year the bishop recovered the patronage by exchanging for it certain land in Ditchford.[44] From that time until the present day the Bishops of Worcester have been patrons of the church.[45] In the 18th century the rectory of Grimley seems to have been leased to members of the Davis family, Francis Davis[46] dealing with it in 1741 and Thomas and Edwin Davis and others in 1776.[47]

During the Commonwealth a grant of £50 was

made for the maintenance of the minister of Grimley.[48] Hallow was a chapelry of Grimley until 1876.[49]

Question arose in 1733 about the tithes of hops, which, it was claimed, should not pay tithe because they had been introduced into the parish recently and after the time at which a composition in money had been made for the small tithes. Dr. Thomas took counsel's opinion, but he does not state how the matter was settled.[50]

CHARITIES The Poor Land.—In 1732 Mrs. Rebecca Clarke, as stated on the church table, gave land in Grimley Field and Broadley, the rents whereof to be laid out in bread to poor housekeepers. The land was sold in 1880, and the proceeds invested in £151 6s. 5d. consols with the official trustees, producing £3 15s. 8d. yearly.

In 1812 Thomas Berrow, as stated on the same table, gave £40 for the poor. This sum was invested in £40 5s. 7d. consols in the name of the official trustees, producing £1 yearly.

Thomas Bourne, by his will (date not stated), gave £100, the interest to be distributed in flannel and linen to the poor. The legacy was invested in £100 15s. 1d. consols, with the official trustees, producing £2 10s. 4d. yearly.

In 1875 Susannah Garmston, by her will proved at Worcester 21 August, bequeathed £1,000, the interest to be applied in the purchase of coal for the poor. This sum was invested in £1,036 5s. 4d. consols, with the official trustees, producing £25 18s. yearly.

The church allotments consist of 2 a. 2 r. 28 p., producing £4 4s. yearly.

In 1910 the net income of the preceding charities, amounting to £35 13s. 10d., was applied as to £4 10s. 6d. in money gifts, £5 3s. 4d. in bread and flannel, and £26 in coal.

The church table further stated that Anna Bull, by her will, gave £100 to purchase lands, the yearly rents whereof were to be laid out for teaching poor children of Hallow and Grimley to read English and to learn the Church Catechism. The money was laid out in 1722 in land at Newland in Leigh, which, with an allotment under the Inclosure Act, consisted of about 3 acres. The land has been sold, and the endowment now consists of £2,886 16s. 1d. consols, with the official trustees, producing £72 3s. 4d. yearly, of which two-fifths is applied for educational purposes in Grimley, two-fifths in Hallow, and one-fifth in the parish of Madresfield.

In 1864 Susan Bourne, by her will proved at Worcester 22 June, left £300, the interest to be applied in clothing or relief in money, or both, to sick and other poor persons. The legacy, less duty, was invested in £303 15s. 11d. consols, with the official trustees. The income, amounting to £7 11s. 8d. yearly, is applied at Christmas in clothing to about twenty widows or other needy persons.

[37] Ann. Mon. (Rolls Ser.), iv, 430.
[38] Hale, Reg. of Worc. Priory (Camden Soc.), 44a.
[39] Ann. Mon. (Rolls Ser.), iv, 458 ; Reg. G. Giffard (Worcs. Hist. Soc.), 1.
[40] Reg. G. Giffard (Worcs. Hist. Soc.), 26.
[41] Worc. Epis. Reg. Carpenter (1443–76), i, 193 d.
[42] Valor Eccl. (Rec. Com.), iii, 224.
[43] Pat. 3 Edw. VI, pt. v.
[44] Ibid. 4 Edw. VI, pt. ii, m. 21.
[45] Inst. Bks. (P.R.O.).
[46] Feet of F. Worcs. Mich. 15 Geo. II.
[47] Ibid. Trin. 16 Geo. III.
[48] Cal. S. P. Dom. 1658–9, p. 112.
[49] Parl. Papers (1890–1), lxi, no. 386, p. 50.
[50] Prattinton Coll. (Soc. Antiq.).

HALLOW

Halhegan, Heallingan, Halnegan (ix cent.); Halhegan, Hallhagan (xi cent.); Hallawe, Hallaye, Hallag (xiii cent.).

The parish of Hallow, now known as North Hallow, lies to the north-west of Worcester, part of it, including Henwick, having been comprised in the city of Worcester by the Extension Act of 1885.[1] The parish of North Hallow contains 3,358 acres, 950 being arable land, of which the chief crops are wheat and beans, and 2,257 acres permanent grass.[2] The subsoil is Keuper Marl. There are no extensive woods, but the copses and plantations cover 32 acres. The inclosure award for Hallow is dated 16 August 1816.[3]

The land on the banks of the Severn is low-lying and subject to floods, being not more than 44 ft. above sea level at Henwick. It rises considerably to the west, and at Peachley a height of 205 ft. is reached. The Severn forms the eastern boundary of the parish. Laughern Brook waters the northern part, flowing in an easterly direction until it reaches Hallow Mill, where it turns to the south. No railway lines pass through Hallow, but the main road from Stourport to Worcester enters the parish on the north, and, after passing through Hallow Heath, reaches the village which lies on either side of it. The church of St. Philip and St. James is to the south, and near it is the village pound. Behind the church is Hallow Park, an old house remodelled in the 18th century. The road from Worcester to Tenbury runs north-west from the city through Lower Broadheath and Peachley.

Hallow, while in their possession, was one of the retreats of the monks of Worcester. Habington in the 17th century described the house as being raised on a small hill at a short distance from the river, 'so that it was nowaye annoyed with the contagion vaporinge from the water.'[4] It was placed in a little park 'whose higher ground aboundinge in mynte yeeldethe a sweete savor, and whose sandy pathes are eaver drye, in so muche as Queene Elizabethe huntinge theare (whylest the abundance of hortes beatinge the mynt dyd bruse but a naturall perfume) gave it an extraordinary commendation, a deynty situation scarce secound to any in England.'[5]

Parkfield, near the city boundary, was built by the late Mr. Charles Wheeley Lea, a member of the firm of Lea & Perrins, makers of the celebrated Worcestershire sauce. His widow now resides there, and has purchased a great deal of the parish, including Hallow Park. A working men's club hall for local meetings and a house for a district nurse were established by Mrs. Lea in 1904.

Sir Charles Bell, the discoverer of the distinct functions of the nerves, died at Hallow Park in 1842. He was staying there, and was buried in the churchyard of the parish. There is in Hallow Church a tablet to his memory with an English inscription by Lord Jeffrey.[6]

Among former place-names in the parish were Lamput,[7] Bradeburn, Chiseburn, Dorlingeshall, Denesmedwe, Gateslegercroft[8] (xiii cent.); Flanebrok, Cumbwelle, Sparkebroc, La Roedinge, Hetherwelleforlong, Le Schawe, Orleye, Hunwaldeleye, Aunsacre[9] (? xiii cent.); Wickenshorne[10] (xvii cent.).

MANORS   *HALLOW* was evidently acquired by the church of Worcester before 816, when Coenwulf, King of the Mercians, freed it and all its vills on the west of Severn from all secular services except building of bridges and strongholds and military service.[11] This manor had apparently become the property of the monks by the 10th century, being included in their lands as set forth in King Edgar's charter.[12] In 1086 the priory held 7 hides at Hallow and Broadwas, to which belonged ten houses and a salt-pan at Droitwich.[13] Hallow with all its members was confirmed to the prior by Bishop Simon in 1148.[14] In 1240 the demesne of the manor, consisting of a court and 2 carucates of land, was leased to the villeins at farm for a rent of grain of different kinds.[15] In 1256 the prior obtained a grant of free warren here.[16] The history of the manor is the same as that of Grimley[17] (q.v.), and it is now in the hands of the Ecclesiastical Commissioners.

Among the rights of the Prior of Worcester in Hallow was that of the service of riding men. In other manors these rod-knights usually compounded with him for a sum of money in the 13th century, but at Hallow Simon de Peachley still performed the service, and Nicholas David and Osbert de Barbourne rode in turns for the tenement which they held.[18] It is interesting to find that the prior still claimed a sum of money in the place of service of the villeins in the vineyard in the 13th century,[19] although the vineyard had ceased to exist.

The Prior of Worcester obtained licence to inclose and impark 60 acres of land and 40 acres of wood in Hallow in 1312.[20] Leland in his Itinerary enumerates among the places belonging to the priory 'Halow, a park without a howse, a two myles from Worcester.'[21] Hallow Park does not seem to have been granted with the other possessions of the priory to the Dean and Chapter of Worcester, but was given with the manor in 1547 to Nicholas Heath, Bishop of Worcester.[22] It remained in the possession of the Bishops

---

[1] Stat. 48 & 49 Vict. cap. 164.
[2] Statistics from Bd. of Agric. (1905).
[3] Blue Bk. Incl. Awards, 190.
[4] Habington, Surv. of Worcs. (Worcs. Hist. Soc.), i, 544.
[5] Ibid.
[6] Dict. Nat. Biog.
[7] Hale, Reg. Worc. Priory (Camd. Soc.), 47a.
[8] Ibid. 49a, 49b, 51a, 51b.
[9] Prattinton Coll. (Soc. Antiq.), Deeds of D. and C. of Worc. 25, 108, 123, 142, 154, 158, 251, 277, 287, 309.

[10] Quarter Sess. R. (Worcs. Hist. Soc.), 75.
[11] Birch, Cart. Sax. i, 494; Heming, Chartul. (ed. Hearne), 337. The bounds of Hallow are given in this charter.
[12] Birch, op. cit. iii, 379.
[13] V.C.H. Worcs. i, 295, 296.
[14] Thomas, Surv. of Worc. Cath. App. no. 18.
[15] Hale, op. cit. 47a; see also Ann. Mon. (Rolls Ser.), iv, 409, 445.
[16] Cal. Pat. 1354-8, p. 266.
[17] For references see Grimley. The

manor-house and site of the manor were sold in 1648 to William Combe (Close, 24 Chas. I, pt. iv, no. 37), the manor having been sold with that of Grimley to John Corbett.
[18] Hale, op. cit. 50a.
[19] Ibid. 51b.
[20] Cal. Pat. 1307-13, p. 517; Inq. a.q.d. file 94, no. 23; Abbrev. Rot. Orig. (Rec. Com.), i, 199.
[21] Leland, Itin. (ed. Hearne), viii (2), 100.
[22] Pat. 1 Edw. VI, pt. iv.

of Worcester, being leased with the site of the manor from time to time until 1648, when it was sold by the Parliamentary Commissioners to William Combe.[23]

A lease of the site of the manor and park of Hallow, granted by the bishop in 1550 to William Hett, afterwards came into the possession of John Habington, who held it at the time of his death in 1582.[24] Queen Elizabeth visited him there and hunted in the park.[25] This lease expired in 1620, and in 1648 Anne Fleet was holding the site and park under a lease for fifty-one years granted by Queen Elizabeth in 1583.[26] In 1678 the park was held by the co-heirs of Thomas Fleet, Magdalene wife of Richard Williams and Anne wife of Ambrose Scudamore.[27] Before the end of the century it had passed to Edward Bull, who died there in 1700.[28] In the 19th century Hallow Park was the property of the Lygons, Earls Beauchamp, and remained in their possession until it was sold by the present earl in 1912 to Mrs. C. W. Lea.[29]

There were two mills in the manor of Hallow in 1086,[30] and mills seem to have existed at Hallow and at Henwick in the 13th century, for the men there were forced to take their corn to be ground at Broadwas when they were unable to grind it at their own mills.[31] There was a mill at Eastbury at that time, and one in Woodhall in 1648 which had belonged to the Bishop of Worcester, and was then sold by the Parliamentary trustees to William Combe.[32] Water corn-mills still exist in Hallow, Henwick and Woodhall.

Bishop Ealdred in the middle of the 11th century gave to the priory of Worcester fisheries at Hallow, known in the 13th century as Chiterling and Scadewell.[33] These two fisheries were confirmed to the priory by Bishop Simon in 1148.[34] In the 13th century Walerand, a sokeman of Henwick, owed service at the fish-pools. The prior made complaint in 1346 against men of the town of Worcester that they not only attacked him and his monks with bows and arrows and tried to burn down their priory, but they also fished in his fishery at Hallow and hunted and carried away hares and rabbits from his warren there.[35]

Though not mentioned by name in the charter, *HENWICK* (Hynewike, xiii cent.) is said to have been included in Coenwulf's grant freeing Hallow and its vills from all secular services.[36] It was probably included in Hallow in the Domesday Survey, but is mentioned as a separate manor in Bishop Simon's confirmation grant of 1148.[37] In 1206 Henwick

was leased to the men of the vill for fifteen years at a rent of grain,[38] and this term was prolonged by twelve years in 1217.[39] In 1240 the manor consisted of a court and carucate of land in demesne,[40] and eight years later the prior added to his estate the land of John Chiterling at Henwick.[41] Henwick was among the manors in which the Prior of Worcester obtained a grant of free warren in 1256.[42] In 1261 the grange of Henwick was destroyed by a great storm.[43]

The manor of Henwick, though it must still have belonged to the Prior of Worcester, was not separately valued in 1535, and is not mentioned in the grant of the priory lands to the Dean and Chapter of Worcester in 1542. It must, however, have been included in that grant, as the dean and chapter ceded it to the king in 1546,[44] and it was given by Edward VI in 1547 to the Bishop of Worcester.[45] In 1648 the manor was sold as a late possession of the bishopric of Worcester to William Combe.[46] It was restored to the bishop at the Restoration, and still belonged to the see at the end of the 18th century.[47]

The manor or farm-house of Henwick was held during the 16th and 17th centuries under leases from the bishop by members of the Hall family. John Hall seems to have acquired the remainder of a lease about 1575 from Edward Darnell, but both Thomas and John Hall, father and grandfather of this John, appear to have been seated at Henwick. The lease was renewed to Edward Hall son of John in 1610 for the lives of his sons Edward, Arthur and John, and about 1638 the lease was again renewed for the lives of John, Edward and Richard Hall.[48]

HALL of Henwick. *Argent crusilly azure three talbots' heads razed sable.*

The Halls' lease was surrendered to the bishop in 1665 by Nicholas Bayly and his wife Dorothy, who held it by grant of Martha Hall.[49] A third of the site of the manor of Henwick was conveyed in 1785 by John Barneby, Bartholomew Lutley Sclater, and Penelope Lutley Sclater to Abraham Winterbottom.[50]

The Prior and convent of Worcester had a conduit from Henwick over Worcester Bridge, and in 1407 they obtained the king's protection when repairing the conduit on the lands of other people.[51]

A cassate of land at *GRIMHILL* (Grimanhylle, x cent.; Gremanhil, xi cent.; Grimhull, xiii cent.; Grymmyll, xvi cent.) evidently belonged to the church

[23] Close, 24 Chas. I, pt. iv, no. 37.
[24] Exch. Spec. Com. 24 Eliz. no. 2479.
[25] Habington, op. cit. i, 3.
[26] Close, 24 Chas. I, pt. iv, no. 37. It is not clear how the queen obtained the right to grant such a lease.
[27] Feet of F. Worcs. Trin. 30 Chas. II ; see Redmarley D'Abitôt.
[28] Nash, op. cit. i, 475, quoting M.I.
[29] Information from Mr. J. W. Willis-Bund.
[30] *V.C.H. Worcs.* i, 296.
[31] Hale, *Reg. Worc. Priory* (Camd. Soc.), 32*a*, 50*a*, 153*a*. The Prior of Worcester had a mill at Hallow, Grimley or Henwick in 1291, but as the manors were valued together it is impossible to say in which manor the mill was situated (*Pope Nich. Tax.* [Rec. Com.], 227).

[32] Close, 24 Chas. I, pt. ix, no. 4.
[33] Heming, *Chartul.* (ed. Hearne), 517 ; Hale, op. cit. 40*a*. Chiterling pool appears to have been in Henwick. There was a John Chiterling in Henwick in 1248 (Feet of F. Worcs. 33 Hen. III, no. 39).
[34] Thomas, *Surv. of Worc. Cath.* App. no. 18.
[35] *Cal. Pat.* 1348–50, pp. 246, 250.
[36] *Ann. Mon.* (Rolls Ser.), iv, 367.
[37] Thomas, loc. cit.
[38] *Ann. Mon.* (Rolls Ser.), iv, 394.
[39] Ibid. 409.
[40] Hale, *Reg. Worc. Priory* (Camd. Soc.), 52*a*.
[41] *Ann. Mon.* (Rolls Ser.), iv, 439 ; Feet of F. Worcs. 33 Hen. III, no. 39.
[42] *Cal. Pat.* 1354–8, p. 266.

[43] *Ann. Mon.* (Rolls Ser.), iv, 447.
[44] *L. and P. Hen. VIII,* xxi (2), 326, 770 (50) ; Pat. 1 Edw. VI, pt. ix ; see also Close, 38 Hen. VIII, pt. ii, no. 51.
[45] Pat. 1 Edw. VI, pt. iv.
[46] Close, 24 Chas. I, pt. iv, no. 37.
[47] Nash, op. cit. i, 473.
[48] Ct. of Req. bdle. 127, no. 54 ; Close, 24 Chas. I, pt. iv, no. 37 ; *Kyre Park Chart.* (Worcs. Hist. Soc.), 86 ; Chan. Proc. (Ser. 2), bdle. 361, no. 11 ; bdle. 372, no. 7. A pedigree of the Halls of Henwick is given in *Visit. of Worcs.* 1596 (Harl. Soc. xxvii), 64, 65.
[49] Feet of F. Worcs. Mich. 17 Chas. II.
[50] Ibid. Trin. 25 Geo. III.
[51] *Cal. Pat.* 1405–8, p. 324 ; Heming, op. cit. 548.

To the Memory of
Edward Bull Gentleman late of
Hallow Hake in this Parish Who dyed
the 24ᵗʰ day of July 1700.

Anne the youngest daughter of
William Lygon late of Maddresfield
in this County Efqr his sorrowfull
Widow dedicates this
Who died ẏ 17ᵗʰ of April 1707.
in ẏ 59ᵗʰ Year of her Age

Hallow Church : Mural Tablet to Edward Bull

of Worcester before 957, when Cynewold, Bishop of Worcester, granted it to the priest Behstan for four lives.[52] This vill was invaded by Urse when he became Sheriff of Worcester, and, fearing his power, the monks gave it up to him on condition that he would discharge all service due for it to the king.[53] In 1086, however, a hide at Grimhill was held by Urse of the Bishop of Worcester's manor of Wick Episcopi, and it was said that Eddid (Edith) had held it before the Conquest, rendering customary dues to the church.[54] Urse's interest in the manor passed with his other estates to the Beauchamps, lords of Elmley, and Grimhill continued to be held of the barony of Elmley until 1601, when the overlordship is mentioned for the last time.[55]

In 1086 Godfrey held this land under Urse.[56] About the middle of the 13th century Richard de Grimhill held it under the Beauchamps.[57] He must have been succeeded shortly after by Robert de Grimhill, under whom land in Grimhill was held by Robert de Hallow. Robert de Hallow, who was a mason, on leaving the country in pursuit of his business, left this estate in charge of his brother Peter. Peter, however, became a leper, and Robert on his return committed the care of it to another brother Reginald. The latter failed to carry out his charge, and the land being left waste was taken by Robert de Grimhill, the overlord, who cultivated part of it himself and gave part to Master Matthew de Grimhill. On the death of Robert de Hallow his daughters Ingreth and Mabel wanted to enter upon this land, but were not permitted to do so by Robert de Grimhill. A jury in 1220–1, however, found in their favour, and Robert was ordered to compensate Matthew de Grimhill with other land.[58] In 1276 Simon son of Master William de Grimley tried to recover his land at Grimhill which had been taken by the king on account of his default against Matthew de Grimley.[59] A Richard de Grimhill died about 1307–8, leaving three daughters his co-heirs,[60] but it is doubtful whether he was an owner of this manor, for it remained in the family of Grimhill, being held in 1315 by Richard de Grimhill.[61] In 1335 John le Young was lord of Grimhill.[62] The next mention of this manor occurs in 1346, when William Brown was in possession. In 1526–7 a relief of 25s. was paid to the lord of Elmley on the death of John Valaunce, who had held Grimhill.[63] The manor, however, returned to the Grimhills,[64] and in 1537–8 Robert de Grimhill

sold it to John Gower,[65] who settled it in 1544 upon himself and his wife Anne.[66] On John's death in 1548 the estate passed to his son John, then six months old.[67] This boy died in 1561, and his step-sister Elizabeth, the wife of Richard Ingram, inherited his property.[68] Elizabeth died in 1601,[69] and ten years later her son William sold the manor to Thomas Cheatle,[70] whose grandson Thomas sold it in 1653 to Anthony Ball, of whom it was purchased in 1655 by Edward Hall.[71]

In the following year Edward sold to John Corbett for a sum of £1,245 the manor of Grimhill with the messuage called the Hall House, Henry Ingram and Henry Gower being parties to the conveyance.[72]

The name Grimhill has now disappeared, but the manor is known to have extended into Grimley, and the site may perhaps be marked by the present Greenhill Farm, which lies near the Grimley boundary.

Two estates at *EASTBURY* (Earesbyri, Esebyr, ix cent. ; Eresbyrie, xi cent. ; Esseburi, xiii cent. ; Estbury, Aylesbury, xvi cent.) were claimed by the monks of Worcester as having been included in Coenwulf's grant freeing Hallow and its vills from all secular services.[73] Later they stated that an estate at ' Earesbyri ' had been taken from them by Æthelwig, Abbot of Evesham,[74] who had in turn been deprived of it by Odo of Bayeux.[75] Another account, which may refer to the other estate, recounts that Eastbury was subject to the church of Worcester in the time of Edward the Confessor until Urse took it, and it was lost by the church.[76] Neither of these accounts is borne out by the Domesday entry for Eastbury, which represents it as half a hide of land held of the manor of Hallow by Walter de Burh, as successor of Aelfric.[77] From the subsequent history of the manor it seems probable, however, that Urse did hold some estate at Eastbury, for, though the mill of Eastbury belonged to the Prior of Worcester in the middle of the 13th century,[78] the monks held no manor there, and the manor of Eastbury became part of the barony of Elmley,[79] the honour of Urse's descendants, the Beauchamps.

The tenants of the manor under the lords of Elmley are not known until 1315, when John de Kekingwik held this manor and Kenswick for two knights' fees.[80]

The descent of Eastbury is identical with that of Kenswick[81] (q.v.) until about the middle of the 16th century,[82] when it was sold by Humphrey Stafford to

---

[52] Birch, op. cit. iii, 187 ; Kemble, *Cod. Dipl.* no. 466 ; Heming, op. cit. 164.

[53] Heming, op. cit. 257.

[54] *V.C.H. Worcs.* i, 289. The manor had been separated from the manor of Wick Episcopi before the beginning of the 13th century.

[55] *Testa de Nevill* (Rec. Com.), 41b ; Chan. Inq. p.m. 9 Edw. II, no. 71, m. 53 ; Rentals and Surv. portf. 16, no. 89 ; Chan. Inq. p.m. (Ser. 2), lxxxix, 156 (1) ; cxxxii, 42 ; cclxx, 102.

[56] *V.C.H. Worcs.* i, 289.

[57] *Testa de Nevill* (Rec. Com.), 41b.

[58] Assize R. 1021, m. 3 d.

[59] *Cal. Close, 1272–9*, p. 409.

[60] *Cal. Inq. p.m.* 1–9 Edw. II, 2.

[61] Ibid. 403.

[62] Prattinton Coll. (Soc. Antiq.), Deeds of D. and C. of Worc. no. 288.

[63] *Feud. Aids*, v, 307 ; Rentals and Surv. (Gen. Ser.), portf. 16, no. 89.

[64] Early Chan. Proc. bdle. 513, no. 33.

[65] Com. Pleas D. Enr. Hil. 29 Hen. VIII, m. 8.

[66] Feet of F. Worcs. East. 36 Hen. VIII.

[67] Chan. Inq. p.m. (Ser. 2), lxxxix, 156 (1).

[68] Ibid. cxxxii, 42. The Gowers or Ingrams seem to have leased the site of the manor to the Monoux family, for about the middle of the 16th century Thomas Monoux stated that his father William had held a capital messuage called Grimhill with a messuage adjoining called the Hall House, the latter of which he granted to Henry Rowles and his wife for life (Chan. Proc. [Ser. 2], bdle. 124, no. 79).

[69] Fine R. 3 Jas. I, pt. ii, no. 36 ; Chan. Inq. p.m. (Ser. 2), cclxx, 102.

[70] Feet of F. Worcs. Mich. 9 Jas. I.

[71] Ibid. Mich. 1655 ; Close, 1657,

pt. xxxvii, no. 9 ; Chan. Proc. (Ser. 2), bdle. 446, no. 23.

[72] Close, 1657, pt. xxxvii, no. 9.

[73] Heming, op. cit. 516.

[74] Ibid. 272.

[75] Thomas, *Surv. of Worc. Cath.* A 85.

[76] Heming, op. cit. 257.

[77] *V.C.H. Worcs.* i, 296.

[78] Hale, op. cit. 50b.

[79] *Cal. Inq. p.m.* 1–9 Edw. II, 403 ; Chan. Inq. p.m. (Ser. 2), xxiv, 83.

[80] *Cal. Inq. p.m.* 1–9 Edw. II, 403. Eastbury was probably included in the 2½ hides at Kenswick held by Walter de Kekingwik in the beginning of the 13th century, for Kenswick in 1086 contained only 1 hide (*Testa de Nevill* [Rec. Com.], 41b).

[81] In Knightwick parish.

[82] *Feud. Aids*, v, 307, 319, 332 ; Pat. 2 Hen. VII, pt. i.

Thomas Hall.[83] Thomas was succeeded between 1616 and 1631 by Edward Hall, probably his son,[84] on whose death in 1636 the messuage or farm of Eastbury passed to his son John.[85] John was probably succeeded by a brother Thomas Hall, for, in answer to a request from Thomas Habington for information about his title to the manor, Thomas Hall, the owner in 1641, stated that it had been purchased by his grand-father Thomas Hall.[86] The further descent of the estate has not been traced until 1826, when it belonged to Thomas Henry Cookes.[87] Thomas Cookes of Bentley held the manor at the end of the 18th century,[88] but the manorial rights of Eastbury have now lapsed.

PEACHLEY (Pecesleia, Petcheslee, xii cent. ;

HALLOW CHURCH FROM THE SOUTH

Petchesleg, xiii cent.) is said to have been bought by Alfstan, Prior of Worcester, brother of Bishop Wulfstan, for the priory of Worcester.[89] It does not appear that there was ever a manor at Peachley, but an estate there was in the 13th century owned by the priory of Worcester,[90] to which portions of it were given at different times by Nicholas the son of David de Peachley, John Murieweder, Henry de Dumbleton, Richard de Peachley and others.[91] Margaret the wife of David de Peachley and Alice the wife of William Hibernius or Ibernius appear to have been daughters of a certain Ingram, from whom they had inherited property here in 1194.[92] The heirs of William Hibernius were holding land at Peachley in 1240. During the 13th and 14th centuries the prior obtained licence to acquire land in Peachley on many occasions.[93] The Peachley estate formed part of the manor of Hallow, and Peachley Farm was sold with Hallow Manor in 1648 to John Corbett.[94] An estate there consisting of 30 acres of land and an orchard was sold in 1625 by Thomas Saunders and his wife Mary to John Elfe.[95] In 1632 Thomas sold half of Peachley Farm to Henry Best.[96] A messuage in Peachley was settled on Samuel Pytts by his mother Katherine Pytts in 1699,[97] and in 1732 Peachley Farm was owned by Edmund Pytts.[98]

Habington states that in the mansion-house of Peachley, belonging to the Peachley family, there was a chapel.[99]

There existed at one time a manor of *WOODHALL* (Wodehalle, xiii cent.) which in the 13th century was a pos-session of the priory of Worcester. In 1240 it consisted of a court and 2 carucates of land,[100] and in 1291 was included in the valuation of Broadwas.[1] In 1256 the prior obtained a grant of free warren in this manor.[2] It was evidently given in 1542 to the Dean and Chapter of Worcester, though not mentioned by name in the grant, for in 1547 they surrendered it to Edward VI.[3] A few months later the king gave it to the Bishop of Worcester.[4] The Bishops of Worcester remained in possession of this estate, which formed part of their manor of Hallow, until it was confiscated under the Common-wealth and sold to William Combe in 1648, the manor being then held under lease by the Evett family.[5] Thomas Chambers and his wife Joan and Thomas Allen were probably lessees under the bishop in 1720, when they conveyed the manor to William Worth.[6] The manorial rights have long since lapsed.

[83] Habington, op. cit. i, 546 ; ii, 106 ; Chan. Inq. p.m. (Ser. 2), xi, 87 ; xxiv, 83 ; lxxv, 96.

[84] *Quarter Sess. R.* (Worcs. Hist. Soc.), 216 ; Chan. Inq. p.m. (Ser. 2), dli, 110.

[85] Chan. Inq. p.m. (Ser. 2), dli, 110.

[86] Habington, op. cit. ii, 106.

[87] Recov. R. Trin. 7 Geo. IV, rot. 134.

[88] Nash, op. cit. i, 474.

[89] Heming, op. cit. 407.

[90] Hale, op. cit. 47a.

[91] Add. Chart. 41396 ; Feet of F. Worcs. 25 Hen. III, no. 19 ; Prattinton

Coll. (Soc. Antiq.), Deeds of D. and C. of Worc. no. 20, 142, 155, 312, &c.

[92] *Abbrev. Plac.* (Rec. Com.), 6 ; *Rot. Cur. Reg.* (Rec. Com.), i, 28 ; Hale, op. cit. 151b.

[93] *Abbrev. Rot. Orig.* (Rec. Com.), i, 207 ; *Cal. Pat.* 1313–17, p. 80 ; 1330–4, p. 116 ; Inq. a.q.d. file 228, no. 23.

[94] Close, 24 Chas. I, pt. xiv, no. 26.

[95] *Kyre Park Chart.* (Worcs. Hist. Soc.), 87.

[96] Ibid.

[97] Ibid. 88.

[98] Ibid.

[99] Habington, op. cit. i, 544.

[100] Hale, op. cit. 34b.

[1] *Pope Nich. Tax.* (Rec. Com.), 226.

[2] *Cal. Pat.* 1354–8, p. 266.

[3] Pat. 1 Edw. VI, pt. ix ; see also Close, 38 Hen. VIII, pt. ii, no. 51 ; *L. and P. Hen. VIII*, xxi (2), 326.

[4] Pat. 1 Edw. VI, pt. iv.

[5] Close, 24 Chas. I, pt. ix, no. 4. The manor had been held by the Evetts as lessees under the Bishops of Worcester since the time of Edward IV (Habington, op. cit. i, 545).

[6] Feet of F. Worcs. Hil. 6 Geo. I.

The church of *ST. PHILIP AND*
CHURCH *ST. JAMES* consists of a chancel 36 ft.
by 17½ ft., a nave 60 ft. by 18 ft., north
and south aisles 10½ ft. wide, a south porch and a
western tower 14½ ft. square, all measurements being
internal. The church was built in 1869, the material
being of the local red sandstone. The original
building, which was destroyed in 1830, stood on a
site some 300 yards to the north-east and was replaced
by an aisleless building pulled down when the present
structure was erected. Judging from the sketches
preserved in the vestry neither of these older
churches was of any architectural importance.

The present chancel is designed in the style of the
14th century, the east window being of three lights.
The nave of four bays is in the style of the 13th
century and has a series of five stone pointed arches
supporting the roof. The thrust is taken by flying
buttresses arching over the aisles. The nave has a
clearstory with four windows on each side. The
principal entrance is on the south with an open
arcaded porch, and in the west wall is an elaborate
window of three lights, with geometric tracery.
The tower is surmounted by a stone broach spire
and angle pinnacles.

The church contains some interesting monuments
removed from the old building. In the south aisle
is a small slab to John Pardoe, who died in 1680,
his daughter Elizabeth, wife of Thomas Bund, and
their daughter Anne, with a well-designed border of
flowers and fruit. Near it is a slightly earlier slab
with a characteristic border of the scrolled-leather
type to John Evett (died 1657). In the tower is an
elaborate monument to Edward Hall (died 1616)
with columns, pediment and a kneeling figure. The
inscription, which had become completely defaced,
has been restored, from the account of the monument
given by Nash. A mural tablet to Edward Bull, died
1700, is an excellent and typical example of the period.

There is a ring of eight modern bells. The
original 16th-century bell from Hallow Chapel was
taken to Broadheath Chapel in 1901.

The plate comprises a cup and cover paten, of
mid-17th-century shape, with a large handle paten
of perhaps the same date, the marks being defaced,
a flagon made in 1807 and a modern cup with cover
paten.

The registers before 1812 are as follows: (i) baptisms from 1583 to 1644, burials 1596 to 1651,
marriages 1584 to 1647; (ii) baptisms from 1644 to
1702, burials and marriages 1652 to 1702; (iii)
baptisms from 1703 to 1797, burials 1703 to 1799,
marriages 1703 to 1751; (iv) baptisms from 1798
to 1812, burials 1800 to 1812; (v) marriages
from 1754 to 1790; (vi) marriages 1791 to 1812.

A chapel of ease was erected at Broadheath in
1837. It consisted only of a nave and was reseated
and improved in 1861. It is now used as a schoolroom. A new church, *CHRIST CHURCH*, was
built in 1904. Broadheath was formed into a separate ecclesiastical parish in 1910, and the living is a
vicarage in the gift of the Bishop of Worcester.
There is also in Broadheath a chapel belonging to

Lady Huntingdon's Connexion, which was built in
1825.

Hallow was a chapelry annexed
ADVOWSON to the church of Grimley[7] until
1876, when it was constituted a
separate vicarage,[8] in the gift of the Bishop of
Worcester.

A supposed claim by the Prior and convent of
Worcester to archidiaconal rights in Hallow[9] was
probably due to confusion between this manor and
Broadwas, the two being closely connected. In the
latter the prior had archidiaconal rights.

There was a chapel dedicated to St. Giles in
Peachley in the 13th century.[10] In 1448 an indulgence was granted to all assisting in the construction,
repair and maintenance of the chapel.[11] It was still
in existence in 1535, when the oblations from it
amounting to 6s. were paid to the chapel of Hallow.[12]
In 1574 a cottage and a parcel of land called
St. Giles Chapel Yard were granted to John and
William Marsh.[13]

John Fleet, as stated on the church
CHARITIES table, gave a tenement with a close,
orchard and gardens in Henwick, a
moiety of the rents to be paid to the minister for
preaching every other Sabbath, and the other moiety
for the poor at Easter and Christmas. The property
is now represented by a house in Henwick Road
known as 'The Cedars,' which is subject to a ground-
rent of £27 10s. 2d. yearly.

The church table further recorded that Thomas
Fleet, Henry Evett, by will 1768, John Ingram, and
four other donors gave for the poor donations
amounting together to £42, which with considerable
additions from the parish stock were in 1689 laid
out in the purchase of a tenement and about 6 a. at
Broadheath. The trust property now consists of
3 a. 1 r. 3 p. at Broadheath let in allotments, a
cottage and garden, and a warehouse, bringing in
a rental of about £20 a year. Also £76 13s. 2d.
consols and £264 Furness Railway 4 per cent.
preference stock, arising from sales of land in 1894
and 1903 held by the official trustees, producing in
dividends £12 9s. 6d. yearly.

It was further recorded on the church table that
Thomas Tillam, by will 1689, gave £3 to the poor,
Magdalen Evett, relict of Henry Evett in 1692, gave
£10, Susannah Ingram, relict of John Ingram, by
will 1701, gave £10, Mrs. Harrison gave £55, £1
to be paid to the minister for a sermon on 10 May
yearly, and that Richard Bourne in 1811 gave £20,
the interest to be given in bread to the poor on
St. Thomas's Day.

A sum of £98, comprising the gifts of Thomas
Tillam and others, above referred to, was in 1857
invested in £105 4s. 8d. consols with the official
trustees, producing £2 12s. 4d. yearly.

The above-mentioned charities are administered
together, a moiety of the income of John Fleet's
charity being paid to the minister, who also receives
£1 for a sermon on 10 May. The distribution of
the remaining income is made chiefly in money, also
in bread and coals, and in clothing for poor widows.

---

[7] *Ann. Mon.* (Rolls Ser.), iv, 434, 458;
Hale, op. cit. 50a; *Pope Nich. Tax.* (Rec.
Com.), 216b; *Valor Eccl.* (Rec. Com.),
iii, 224.

[8] *Parl. P.* 1890–1, lxi, no. 386, p. 50.

[9] Prattinton Coll. (Soc. Antiq.), Deeds
of D. and C. of Worc. no. 41; *Hist. MSS.
Com. Rep.* xiv, App. viii, 191.

[10] Hale, *Reg. Worc. Priory* (Camd.
Soc.), 50a; Prattinton Coll. (Soc.

Antiq.), Deeds of D. and C. of Worc.
no. 251.

[11] Worc. Epis. Reg. Carpenter, i, fol. 65.

[12] *Valor Eccl.* (Rec. Com.), iii, 235.

[13] Pat. 16 Eliz. pt. xii.

This parish is entitled to two-fifths of the income of the charity of Anna Bull for educational purposes amounting to £28 17s. 4d. (See under parish of Grimley.)

The official trustees also hold a sum of £650 consols arising from the sale of land belonging to the Free School, producing £16 5s. yearly.

HANBURY

Heanburg (vii cent.) ; Heanberi (viii cent.) ; Heanbyrg (ix cent.) ; Hambyrie, Heanbyri, Hambury-juxta-Witham (xii cent.) ; Hambir (xiii cent.).

Hanbury is a large hilly parish east of the town of Droitwich. The following account of it in the 17th century is given by Habington :—

And althoughe our country (sic) is graced with so many pleasaunt prospectes as scarce any shyre the lyke, in so muche as allmost eaverey littell hyll largely affourdethe the same, yet aspyringe Hambury obtaynginge the Principality overlookethe them all, A stately seate meete for a Kinges pallace ; and had it but the commodity of our Severne, might compare with that of Wyndesore. Neyther wanted theare for recreation of our Kynges a fayre Parcke, which though in thys paryshe is styled Feckenham Parcke,[1] sootinge in name with the Kynges vast forest, reachinge in former ages far and wyde. A large walk for savage beastes, but nowe more commodyously chaunged to the civill habitations of many gentell-men, the freehoulds of wealthy yeomen, and dwellinges of industryous husbandmen.[2]

The area of the parish is 7,790 acres,[3] of which 1,661 acres are arable, 5,526 permanent grass and 251 woods.[4] Huntingdrop Common, a detached part of the parish of Dodderhill, was annexed to Hanbury in 1880, under the Divided Parishes Act.[5] The soil is clay with a subsoil of Keuper Marl, and the land slopes downward from the north towards the south, the highest point, about 385 ft. above the ordnance datum, being on the Stoke Prior Road north of the village. The chief crops are wheat, beans and barley.

The main road from Droitwich to Alcester runs through the parish from west to east and meets that from Bromsgrove to Alcester near Carter's Hill. From it a branch road leads past Hanbury Park to the village. This is scattered about three roads, forming a rough triangle, the base of which is the Droitwich to Alcester Road on the south. Hanbury Park occupies the whole of the western side of the triangle, and the church of St. Mary the Virgin stands at its apex near the north-east corner of the park. Habington,[6] writing in the 17th century, says that the church 'invironed with highe and mighty trees and able to terrifye a far of ignorant enimy with a deceytful showe of an invincible Castell may rightly be called the Lanthorne of our county.' Near the main entrance to the park upon the opposite side of the road is 'The Moorlands,' a good half-timber house, two stories in height, with a triple-gabled attic and tiled roof. In the central attic gable is the date 1619. The house has been converted into an almshouse for old women. The date of the alteration (1879) and the initials H. F. V. are placed on one of the gables. At the Pump-house Farm, on the south side of the

lane to which it gives its name, is a brick-nogged, half-timber dovecot. At the foot of the hill on the road leading to the church are the base and shaft of an ancient cross.

Hanbury Hall,[7] built about 1700, is a fine Queen Anne house of brick with stone dressings, two stories in height, with an attic floor in the roof. William Rudhall, of Henley-in-Arden, was the architect, and the original drawings are still preserved in the house. The entrance front faces south-east, and the plan consists of a central block with two wings projecting at the front and back. The central portion of the entrance front is crowned by a pediment, rising from the wooden cornice, which is continued round the whole building. The lower members of the entablature are of stone. A stone string-course divides the elevations externally into two stages, and the large sash windows have architraves and moulded sills of the same material. At the angles are plain stone quoins. The dormer windows have small pediments, and the slopes of the roof are tiled, the flat at the top being lead-covered, and surmounted by a clock-turret. The chief feature of the interior is the hall, which occupies the whole of the ground floor of the centre of the entrance front. At the west end are the stairs, which have carved console spandrel brackets and finely-turned balusters. The walls of the staircase are painted with scenes from the life of Achilles, set in architectural borders, the work of Sir James Thornhill. The ceilings of the hall and dining room are also decorated in the same manner. Over the fireplace of a small study on the west side of the house is an early Jacobean chimney-piece, elaborately carved and divided into three compartments, separated by caryatid figures and crowned by a carved frieze, enriched with fruit, flowers and strapwork, carved consoles supporting the cornice. In the centre panel are the Prince of Wales's feathers, and below each caryatid figure are the thistle, rose, fleur de lis and pear of Worcestershire with Stuart crowns. This is said to have been brought here from Ticknell House, Bewdley,[8] which was appointed by King James I as a residence for his eldest son Prince Henry. The fact that he was the first Prince of Wales who would be entitled to use the thistle as a badge gives strong support to the tradition. It may also be stated that Ticknell was being dismantled at the time that Hanbury Hall was in building and that a near kinsman of the Vernon who built it was living near Ticknell at the time. A view made in 1732 shows an oblong forecourt, about the width of the frontage of the house, with a bowling-

[1] From the Domesday Survey it appears that there was woodland 1 league in length and half a league in width, which had been included in the king's forest of Feckenham (V.C.H. Worcs. i, 298a). Feckenham was disafforested in 1629, and Edward Leighton, as lord of Hanbury, received a grant of 360 acres, which included Queen's coppice, Ranger's

coppice, Timber coppice, Fearful coppice and Red Slough coppice (Prattinton Coll.).
[2] Habington, Surv. of Worcs. (Worcs. Hist. Soc.), i, 253, 254.
[3] Of which 24 acres are covered by water.
[4] Statistics from Bd. of Agric. (1905).
[5] Census of Engl. and Wales, 1891, ii, 658 ; Stat. 44 & 45 Vict. cap. 62.

[6] op. cit. i, 254.
[7] Nash, op. cit. i, 548. In a letter dated 29 September 1733 Bishop Hough speaks of it as 'a sweet place and a noble estate' (J. Wilmot, Life of the Rev. John Hough [1812], 213).
[8] Information kindly furnished by Sir Harry Foley Vernon, bart.

HANBURY : MERE HALL FROM THE NORTH-EAST

green and formal garden on the west and a stable court on the east. This arrangement was abolished about 1850. In the smaller of two rooms in a detached building to the north-west is some plain Jacobean panelling, probably from the original house which formerly stood upon the site, a portion of the moat of which still remains. In the grounds is a handsome orangery, 72 ft. by 21 ft., with a central pediment carved with fruit and flowers in the style of Grinling Gibbons.

To the south of the parish is the hamlet of Broughton Green, on a branch road from the Droitwich and Alcester road. On this branch road, approached by an avenue of fine old elms, is Mere Hall,[9] the seat of Col. Edward Hugh Bearcroft, C.B., J.P., a fine half-timber house, facing north, two stories in height, with an attic floor in the roof. The plan is of the central hall type with projecting wings on the east and west and a central newel stair on the south-west. The central part of the house may date in part from the 14th century, but the original arrangement seems to have been largely altered in the early 17th century, to which date belong the row of gabled attic windows on the entrance front and the structure of the wings. On the sill of the attic floor, which projects beyond the wall below and is supported by carved console brackets, is carved in Arabic numerals the date 1337. It is unfortunate that a piece of timber so manifestly renaissance in character should have been selected for this attribution. About 1700 a general repair appears to have been undertaken, when the present entrance porch and the small timber lantern surmounting the roof of the central block were added and the forecourt formed with its inclosing walls, gates and summer-houses. It is probable that the majority of the present sash windows were then substituted for the original openings, though the quasi-Gothic arrangement of their bars belongs to the early 19th century. About this latter period additions were made to the west wing and to the rear of the central block, by which passages were formed on the ground and first floors to secure communication between the two wings without the necessity of passing through the hall, and to give readier access to the bedrooms above it. The interior of the hall retains no features of interest. On either side of the present entrance doorway in the north wall, which dates from the Queen Anne repair, is a range of leaded lights with ovolo-moulded mullions, dating from the early 17th century. In the west wing is the present dining room, which has a fine carved chimney-piece and good wainscoting of the same date. Both appear to have been refixed and to have been brought here from the east wing, as it seems probable that the kitchen was originally on this side of the house and that the lobby which divides the dining room from the hall was made with the intention of 'trapping' the offices from the living rooms at some period in the first half of the 17th century. A sideboard recess in the east wall of the dining room has been taken out of this lobby, which terminates on the north in a small closet contained in the porch-like bay which fills the internal angle

made by the wing with the central block and extends to the first floor, being crowned by a gable. That this is of slightly later date than the rebuilding of the front is evident from the fact that the closet on the first floor incloses portions of the moulded attic sill with its supporting console bracket. In the bedroom over the east end of the hall is some good panelling of the late 16th or early 17th century. The east wing has been completely modernized on the ground floor. The front elevation, crowned by its central row of gabled attics and flanked by the large end gables of the wings, presents an appearance of great picturesqueness, from which the Queen Anne entrance porch, with its twisted Corinthian columns and pediment filled by the Bearcroft shield, in nowise detracts. A recess is formed in the east side of the closet projection adjoining the west wing to allow room for an additional light to the range of windows lighting the hall. The remaining elevations present no features of particular interest.

BEARCROFT. *Sable a cheveron between three bears' heads razed argent with three swans sable upon the cheveron.*

The forecourt is inclosed on the east, north and west by brick walls with garden-houses of the same material at the northern angles, and fine wrought-iron gates and railings in the centre of the northern or entrance side. The garden-houses correspond with each other in design. A cupola of fanciful outline, covered with ornamental tiles, rises from a wood cantilever cornice. The sides which face on the forecourt are open to the cornice, the upper part being filled by a wooden arch with a central turned pendant. Inside are refixed Jacobean benches which have been cut to fit their present position. The whole lay-out is an interesting example of the Queen Anne period. The fine avenue of trees which leads up to the entrance gate is no longer used for the drive.

A little to the south-east of Mere Hall is Broughton Court, a half-timber house of the normal central entrance-hall type, probably of the early 16th century, which has been much altered and pulled about at various subsequent periods. The original stairs have disappeared; the present stairs are of the early 18th century.

The Worcester and Birmingham Canal and the Bristol and Birmingham branch of the Midland railway run through the western portion of the parish.[10]

An Inclosure Act for Hanbury was passed in 1781,[11] and the award is dated 27 July 1783. There is a parish club at Carter's Hill, which was opened in 1891, and a recreation ground of about 6 acres opened in 1895. The cricket and football clubs occupy part of it and the remainder is for the general use of the parishioners.

Roman coins have been found in the parish near the church, and also modern coins, one a half-crown of Charles I with the Worcester mint mark.[12]

---

[9] Mere Hall or Meer Green Hall has been in the possession of the Bearcroft family since the 14th century. A pedigree of the family from the time of Edward III is given in Metcalfe's *Visit. of Worcs.*

1682, pp. 12–15, and in Sir Thomas Phillipps' *Genealogia.*

[10] In 1852 an Act was passed for making a canal from Droitwich to join this canal at or near Hanbury Wharf

(Local and Pers. Act, 15 & 16 Vict. cap. 22).

[11] Priv. Act, 21 Geo. III, cap. 41.

[12] *V.C.H. Worcs.* i, 219; Nash, op. cit. i, 547.

The following place-names occur : Eston Ricardi,[13] in the 12th century ; Stocking,[14] Goshull,[15] in the 13th century ; Nether Wallynge,[16] Britmore, Russhe, Syley, Clarydole, Barthhurste,[17] Morewisend, Reven Innyng, Swancombe, Menske,[18] Elvyns,[19] Beart,[20] and Wawemore,[21] in the 16th century.

MANORS There was perhaps a monastery at Hanbury in the 7th century, when Wulfhere, King of Mercia, who died in 675,[22] granted 50 'manses' at Hanbury to Abbot Colmannus, who was possibly Abbot of Hanbury.[23] The only record specifically mentioning this monastery seems to be a grant, preserved in a contemporary text, in the time of Wiglaf, King of Mercia, dated 836, by which the monastery of Hanbury was freed

MERE HALL, HANBURY : GARDEN HOUSE

from 'pastu regis, et principium, et ab omni constructione regalis villae, et a difficultate illa, quam nos saxonicè, fæstingmen dicimus.'[24] The monastery was soon after merged in the church of Worcester.[25] A grant made in the pontificate of Milred and in the reign of Offa of Mercia, i.e. between 757 and 775, by which Abbot Ceolfrith[26] gave to the church of Worcester 20 *manentes* at HANBURY which had descended to him from his father Cyneberht[27] is an earlier reference to this Hanbury. Cyneberht, Ceolfrith's father, had received an estate at Ismere from King Ethelbald of Mercia.[27a] At the date of the Domesday Survey the church of Worcester held Hanbury, where there were 14 hides that paid geld, 2 of which were waste.[28] Attached to the manor were salt-pits in Droitwich, which rendered 105 'mits' of salt yearly.[29] In the 12th-century survey of the hundred of Oswaldslow the church still held these 14 hides.[30] In 1189–90 Richard I freed 34½ acres there from forest exactions.[31] In 1237–8 the bishop increased his holding by a purchase from Henry son of Geoffrey de Hanbury,[32] and in 1291 the manor was worth £24 a year.[33] In 1287 Geoffrey the son of Guy de Hanbury leased to Bishop Giffard a meadow called 'Dole' for five years, and in 1292 the lease was renewed for a further term of five years.[34] The manor remained with the successive Bishops of Worcester[35] until the deprivation of Bishop Pates on the accession of Queen Elizabeth. Under an Act of Parliament passed in 1558–9 Queen Elizabeth retained this manor, compensating the see with certain impropriate rectories.[36]

On 25 April 1590, at the request of Sir Francis Knollys and Sir Thomas Leighton and Elizabeth his wife, daughter of Sir Francis Knollys, the queen granted the manor in fee farm to Robert Cecil, Sir Francis Knollys, jun., and Henry Killigrewe to the use of Sir Francis Knollys, the Treasurer of the Household, with the condition that if Sir Thomas Leighton and Elizabeth paid Sir Francis Knollys £941 within seven years the manor should be theirs.[37] Sir Thomas had become possessed of the manor before 1594, when he received a grant of timber in the woods of Hanbury for building and repairing the houses there.[38] He settled the manor on his son Thomas on the

---

[13] *V.C.H. Worcs.* i, 327.
[14] Prattinton Coll. (Soc. Antiq.). William of Blois, Bishop of Worcester, 1218–36, purchased these lands from Reginald de Merstham for 3 marks.
[15] Ibid. Henry de Goshull gave all his lands at Goshull to Walter Cantilupe, Bishop of Worcester, 1237–66. The site is still indicated by Goosehill and Little Goosehill Wood in the south-west of the parish.
[16] Star Chamb. Proc. Hen. VIII, bdle. 20, no. 5.
[17] All these lands were alienated by Thomas Badger, Thomas Fowler and Robert Dyson, the grantees of the manor of Holloway, in 1545 (*L. and P. Hen. VIII,* xx [1], p. 672). [18] Pat. 21 Eliz. pt. iii.
[19] Ibid. 30 Eliz. pt. x.
[20] Star Chamb. Proc. Hen. VIII, bdle. 29, no. 25.
[21] Com. Pleas D. Enr. East. 1 Mary, m. 9.
[22] *Angl.-Sax. Chron.* (Rolls Ser.), ii, 318.
[23] Heming, op. cit. 567.
[24] Kemble, *Codex Dipl.* i, no. 237; Birch,

op. cit. i, 581 ; Cott. MS. Aug. ii, 9 ; Heming (op. cit. 47) gives the date as 833.
[25] It was probably a 'family' monastery like those of Bredon and Fladbury (*V.C.H. Worcs.* ii, 3).
[26] It is possible that he was abbot of the monastery of Hanbury.
[27] Birch, op. cit. i, 308 ; Heming, op. cit. ii, 474. [27a] Birch, op. cit. i, 222.
[28] *V.C.H. Worcs.* i, 298a. Urse held of the bishop 2 hides, which Ralf held of him (ibid.).
[29] Ibid. In 1295 Bishop Giffard leased one of these salt-pits to Agnes daughter of Stephen Croune. It was 'situated between the bishop's salt-pit and the way which is before the gate of a close called Vinstalstude' (*Reg. G. Giffard* [Worcs. Hist. Soc.], 467).
[30] *V.C.H. Worcs.* i, 326b.
[31] Thomas, *Surv. of Worc. Cath.* App. no. 27 ; Cart. Antiq. RR, 15.
[32] Feet of F. Worcs. 22 Hen. III, no. 10. Habington, speaking of this

family, says, 'I have read this name so often witnessed in the evydences of the Churche of Worcester as none so much, but theyre estate I feare it is nowe extenuated, which I wyshe maye bee agayne augmented, for other wyse Pitty is a poore releyfe' (op. cit. i, 257). There is a pedigree of the family given in *Visit. of Worcs.* 1569 (Harl. Soc. xxvii), 65.
[33] *Pope Nich. Tax.* (Rec. Com.), 225b.
[34] *Reg. G. Giffard* (Worcs. Hist. Soc.), 327, 423.
[35] *Cal. Pat.* 1317–21, pp. 374, 493 ; *Feud. Aids,* v, 306, 318 ; *Cal. Pat.* 1377–81, p. 404 ; *Cal. Close,* 1346–9, p. 231. In 1536 the manor was worth £34 17s. 7d., of which William Savage received £2 3s. 4d. as collector (*Valor Eccl.* [Rec. Com.], iii, 217a).
[36] *V.C.H. Worcs.* ii, 48; Pat. 4 Eliz. pt. vi.
[37] *Cal. S. P. Dom.* 1581–90, p. 660 ; Pat. 32 Eliz. pt. xxii, m. 4.
[38] *Cal. S. P. Dom.* 1591–4, p. 539 ; Pat. 36 Eliz. pt. xv.

HANBURY : MERE HALL, ENTRANCE FRONT

HANBURY : MERE HALL, ENTRANCE GATES

occasion of his marriage in 1608–9,[39] and died on 1 February 1610.[40] His son Thomas Leighton held the manor[41] until his death in 1617–18, when he was succeeded by his son Edward.[42] The latter had livery of the manor of Hanbury in 1631,[43] and sold it in the same year to Edward Vernon, the eldest son of Richard Vernon, rector of Hanbury.[44] Edward Vernon suffered at the hands of both parties during the Civil War,[45] and died in 1666,[46] being followed by his son Richard Vernon.[47] On the death of the latter in 1678[48] the manor of Hanbury passed to his son Thomas Vernon,[49] who was a celebrated lawyer,[50] and ' by his profession added much to the estates of the family.' [51]

VERNON of Hanbury, baronet. *Or a fesse azure with three sheaves or thereon and a crosslet fitchy gules in the chief.*

He died without issue in February 1721, and left the manor of Hanbury to Bowater Vernon,[52] eldest son of his first cousin William Vernon of Caldwell, near Kidderminster, who died in 1735,[53] being succeeded by his son Thomas Vernon.[54] The latter dying in 1771 [55] left an only daughter Emma, who married Henry Cecil, first Marquess of Exeter, and died in 1818, when her estates passed to her cousin Thomas Shrawley Vernon, who died in 1825.[56] Thomas Tayler Vernon, his eldest son, succeeded him, and on his death in 1835 Hanbury passed to his elder son Thomas Bowater Vernon, who died unmarried in 1859.[57] He was succeeded by his brother Harry Foley Vernon, who represented the county in Parliament for some years, and was created a baronet in 1885. He is now lord of the manor of Hanbury.[58]

The fee-farm rent of £35 17s. 6d. reserved from the grant of the manor in 1590 was held in 1655 by John Johns and Mary his wife and John Houghton and Sarah his wife, to whom it had perhaps been sold by the Parliamentary trustees. They sold it in that year to Edward Hall,[59] of whom it was purchased in 1658 by Nicholas Heaton.[60] It returned to the Crown at the Restoration, and was sold in 1672 by the trustees for the sale of fee-farm rents to Peter Lely,[61] probably the famous portrait painter.

The Bishops of Worcester had a *PARK* at Hanbury. The bishop obtained a grant of free warren there in 1255,[62] and in 1315 Bishop Maidstone ordered that ' certain presumptuous sons, who had impeded and molested the bishop's peaceful possession of his wood in Hanbury, should be denounced as excommunicate within the diocese of Worcester.' [63] During the early part of the 14th century several commissions were appointed to inquire regarding trespassers in the park or forest of Hanbury,[64] the park being mentioned for the first time in 1339.[65]

In 1377 the bishop granted John Webb the custody of the bishop's wood of Hanbury for life at a weekly rent of a bushel of wheat and 1d.[66] In 1379 and again in 1406 the bishop received a licence to sell his wood to the value of 200 marks.[67] The park passed to the Crown with the manor in the reign of Elizabeth, and has since belonged to the owners of the manor of Hanbury.[68]

In 1086 the manor of *HOLLOWAY* (Haloede, xi cent. ; Holewya, xii cent. ; Holeweye, xiii and xiv cent. ; Hollway, xvi cent.) belonged to the king, who had succeeded the Saxon lord Siward, ' a thegn and kinsman of king Edward ' (teinus et cognatus regis E.).[69] Domesday Book gives a full account of the manor among the king's other property in Herefordshire. With the manor of Feckenham, of which it was originally a member, it rendered at the town of Hereford ' 18 pounds of pennies at 20 to the ounce.' There were 3 hides, four villeins, one bordar, a reeve, a beadle, with three ploughs, six serfs and bondwomen, a park for wild animals, four salt-pans and one ' hoch ' in Droitwich, and one house in Worcester rendering two plough-shares.[70] Holloway was granted to the abbey of Bordesley by the Empress Maud at its foundation [71] (1136). Although there is no mention in the charter of a rent reserved on the manor, the abbot rendered £6 3s. for it every year between 1159 and 1221.[72] In 1233 the abbot and convent obtained a charter from Henry III exempting them from ' giving or carrying litter to Fecham on the coming of the king there,' a service which had been exacted from them ' contrary to their charter ' by the king's bailiffs of Feckenham.[73] By a further charter of Henry III the abbot obtained the custody of the wood of Holloway in the forest of Feckenham.[74] In 1291 the abbot and convent held at Holloway

[39] Feet of F. Worcs. Hil. 6 Jas. I.

[40] Chan. Inq. p.m. (Ser. 2), cccxxiv, 126.

[41] Feet of F. Worcs. Mich. 9 Jas. I.

[42] Chan. Inq. p.m. (Ser. 2), ccclxvi, 173.

[43] Fine R. 6 Chas. I, pt. iii, no. 2.

[44] Feet of F. Worcs. Trin. 7 Chas. I ; Metcalfe, op. cit. 97.

[45] Though he denied having assisted Charles I with arms, men or money, in February 1645 he appeared before the Committee of Worcester and compounded with them for £200. In May 1645 Prince Rupert ordered his confinement in Ludlow Castle until he paid £500 for the king's service, and in July 1646 he was fined £400 by the Committee for Compounding. On 20 Sept. 1646 Prince Maurice signed an order for his seizure for disaffection (Cal. Com. for Comp. 1373).

[46] M. I. in Hanbury Church, quoted by Nash, op. cit. i, 550.

[47] Close, 24 Chas. II, pt. ix, no. 23.

[48] M. I. in Hanbury Church quoted by Nash, loc. cit.

[49] Metcalfe, op. cit. 97.

[50] He was called to the Bar 30 Oct. 1679 and became a bencher of the Middle Temple Inn in 1703. His *Reports of Cases decided in Chancery*, 1681–1718, was published in 1726–8 and a new edition appeared in 1806–7 (*Dict. Nat. Biog.*).

[51] Nash, op. cit. i, 549 ; Pat. 9 Anne, pt. vi, no. 15. In 1710 this Thomas Vernon received a licence to inclose a road running through his estate on condition that he replaced it with another road equally convenient (Harl. MS. 2264, fol. 272).

[52] M. I. in Hanbury Church quoted by Nash, op. cit. i, 551.

[53] Ibid.

[54] Ibid.

[55] Ibid. 552.

[56] Burke, *Peerage*, 1906.

[57] Ibid.

[58] Ibid.

[59] Feet of F. Worcs. Trin. 1655.

[60] Ibid. East. 1658.

[61] Close, 24 Chas. II, pt. ix, no. 23.

[62] Cal. Chart. R. 1226–57, p. 443.

[63] Worc. Epis. Reg. Maidstone (1313–17), fol. 35.

[64] Cal. Pat. 1317–21, pp. 374, 483, 543 ; 1321–4, pp. 251, 380 ; 1338–40, p. 273.

[65] Abbrev. Rot. Orig. (Rec. Com.), ii, 133 ; Cal. Pat. 1338–40, p. 273.

[66] Cal. Pat. 1377–81, p. 64.

[67] Ibid. 404 ; 1405–8, p. 204.

[68] Feet of F. Worcs. Hil. 6 Jas. I ; Recov. R. Trin. 18 & 19 Geo. II, rot. 48.

[69] V.C.H. Worcs. i, 321a and b. This phrase is most unusual.

[70] Ibid.

[71] Ibid. ii, 152 ; Cal. Chart. R. 1257–1300, p. 63.

[72] Pipe R. 5 Hen. II–24 Hen. II (Pipe R. Soc.) ; Pipe R. Worcs. 25 Hen. II–5 Hen. III.

[73] Cal. Pat. 1232–47, p. 18.

[74] Cart. Antiq. FF 17 ; Cal. Chart. R. 1226–57, p. 116.

3 carucates of land each worth a mark.[75] In 1323 the abbey leased the manor for eighty years to Henry de Hanbury,[76] and in 1467–8 granted a rent of 100s. from the manor to Thomas Webb, the grant to be void if the monks celebrated masses for Thomas's soul according to a form prescribed.[77]

The manor remained with the abbey of Bordesley until the Dissolution, when it was valued at the large sum of £50 1s. 8d.[78] Being surrendered to the king in 1538,[79] the manor and grange were in 1545 granted to Thomas Badger, Thomas Fowler and Robert Dyson.[80] These grantees sold away the manor to various purchasers,[81] and it became so subdivided that Habington says of it ' I have scarce seene an entyre thynge severed in so many partes.'[82] The site of the manor seems, however, to have remained with the Dysons.[83] Robert son of Henry Dyson, by his will dated 25 June 1558, left Great and Little Holloway to his wife Fortune.[84] He was succeeded by a son Henry, who died in 1561 seised of the reversion, after the death of his mother Fortune, of land in Holloway, and was succeeded by his five sisters.[85] Another Henry Dyson died in 1597 holding land at Holloway which passed to his son Henry.[86] The Henry Dyson who was dealing with land in Holloway in 1651[87] was probably he who is said by Habington to have been the owner of the site of the manor in his time.[88] Edward Dyson held land in Holloway in 1654,[89] and in 1660–1 Henry Dyson made a conveyance of land there.[90] Other members of this family held land at Holloway until 1692–3.[91]

DYSON. *Azure the sun party sable and or.*

The descendants of Thomas Fowler also seem to have retained some interest in Holloway until 1670, when Thomas Fowler was paying a fee-farm rent from the manor.[92] The Badgers may also have retained some land in the manor, for in 1789 Richard Badger sold the manor of Holloway to Edward Bearcroft.[93] Nash, writing at the end of the 18th century, states that Holloway then belonged to Henry Cecil in right of his wife Emma Vernon,[94] but early in the 19th century it was claimed by the Bettesworth family.[95]

Holloway Grange, formerly part of the manor of Holloway, was sold by Thomas Badger and his co-grantees in 1545 to John Hunt and his wife Agnes.[96] John was succeeded by his son Henry Hunt, who died in 1581, leaving a son Raphael Hunt, then aged fifteen.[97] He had livery of the manor in 1588,[98] and settled it in 1628 on his son Henry, on the occasion of his marriage with Joan daughter of Thomas Cooke the elder of Redmarley Oliver. Raphael died 30 March 1638,[99] and was succeeded by a son Henry, who died in 1646.[100] His son and successor Jonathan was also seated at Holloway and died in 1676.[1] John Hunt was dealing with land in Holloway in 1683–4,[2] and in 1690 William Hunt of London sold to Thomas Shuckforth all his lands in Hanbury and Bradley, including a house called the Stone House.[3] This estate was purchased in 1705 of Thomas Shuckforth by Thomas Vernon of Spernall Hall,[4] and probably became merged in the manor of Hanbury.

The name Holloway has disappeared, and the site of this once important manor is now marked by Upper, Lower and Middle Hollowfields Farms in the south-east of the parish.

The estate afterwards known as the manor of *PARKHALL* was perhaps ' the land of the parker' excepted from the foundation grant by the Empress Maud to the abbey of Bordesley.[5] Parkhall belonged to the hereditary keepers of the park of Feckenham until the park was granted by Edward I to his consort Eleanor. Henry atte Park, the hereditary parker, was then removed, and the office was from that time granted at the queen's will.[6] It is not known when Parkhall became severed from the office of parker of Feckenham, but the separation probably took place about 1376–7, when John Wawe of Bradden (Northants) granted to trustees all his lands and tenements called Parkhall,[7] and in the same year these trustees gave the estate, which was then said to have been granted to them by King Edward III for that purpose, to the Abbot and convent of Bordesley.[8] The convent retained this manor until 1538, when it was surrendered by the last abbot to Henry VIII.[9]

The messuage or tenement called Parkhall was included in the grant of the manor of Holloway to Thomas Badger and his co-feoffees.[10] They immediately sold it to Henry Gardener.[11] He was succeeded in 1559 by his son Richard Gardener,[12] who died in 1595, having settled the manor on his wife Joyce with remainder to his son John.[13] John Gardener died in 1599, leaving three daughters, Ann, Alice, and Ursula.[14] Ursula died in 1599–1600,[15] and John Gardener's lands were divided between his

[75] *Pope Nich. Tax.* (Rec. Com.), 230a. The tithes of Holloway were given by William Fitz Osbern to the abbey of Cormeilles (Dugdale, *Mon.* vi, 1076, 1077). They were purchased afterwards by the monks of Bordesley, who promised in exchange to pay a rent of 6s. 8d. a year (Madox, *Formulare Angl.* 300). It was probably this rent which was released in 1296 by the Prior of Newent (a cell of Cormeilles) to the Abbot of Bordesley (Anct. D. [P.R.O.], B 1570).
[76] *Cal. Pat.* 1321–4, pp. 239, 437.
[77] Madox, *Formulare Angl.* no. 486.
[78] *Valor Eccl.* (Rec. Com.), iii, 272.
[79] Feet of F. Div. Co. Trin. 30 Hen. VIII.
[80] Pat. 37 Hen. VIII, pt. iv, m. 39; *L. and P. Hen. VIII,* xx (1), g. 1081 (49).
[81] *L. and P. Hen. VIII,* xx (1), p. 672.
[82] op. cit. i, 260.
[83] Ibid.

[84] Chan. Inq. p.m. (Ser. 2), cxxxii, 41.
[85] Ibid.
[86] Ibid. cclxiv, 168.
[87] Feet of F. Worcs. Mich. 1651.
[88] op. cit. i, 260.
[89] Feet of F. Worcs. Hil. 1654; Mich. 1654.
[90] Ibid. East. 12 Chas. II.
[91] Ibid. Div. Co. Mich. 17 Chas. II; Worcs. Mich. 19 Chas. II; Div. Co. East. 4 Will. and Mary.
[92] Palmer's Indices (P.R.O.), lxxiii, fol. 79.
[93] Feet of F. Worcs. Mich. 30 Geo. III.
[94] op. cit. i, 549.
[95] Prattinton Coll. (Soc. Antiq.).
[96] *L. and P. Hen. VIII,* xx (i), p. 672.
[97] Chan. Inq. p.m. (Ser. 2), cxciii, 44.
[98] Fine R. 30 Eliz. pt. ii, no. 8.
[99] Chan. Inq. p.m. (Ser. 2), dcclix, 7.
[100] Metcalfe, op. cit. 64.

[1] Ibid.
[2] Feet of F. Worcs. Mich. 35 Chas. II.
[3] Close, 2 Will. and Mary, pt. xiv, no. 13.
[4] Ibid. 4 Anne, pt. xv, no. 11.
[5] *Cal. Chart. R.* 1257–1300, p. 63.
[6] Chan. Inq. p.m. 11 Edw. III (2nd nos.), no. 103b. Habington mentions a lease for 100 years granted by Sir William de Sareshull to James del Park of a sixth part of the manor of Parkhall in 1343–4 (op. cit. i, 260).
[7] Anct. D. (P.R.O.), B 4161.
[8] Ibid. 1574.
[9] Feet of F. Div. Co. Trin. 30 Hen. VIII.
[10] Pat. 37 Hen. VIII, pt. iv, m. 39.
[11] *L. and P. Hen. VIII,* xx (1), p. 672.
[12] Chan. Inq. p.m. (Ser. 2), cxxiv, 215.
[13] Ibid. cxlii, 89.
[14] Ibid. cclvii, 78.
[15] Ibid. cclix, 108.

HANBURY HALL : STAIRCASE WITH PAINTINGS BY SIR JAMES THORNHILL

HANBURY HALL : OVERMANTEL IN STUDY

surviving daughters,[16] Ann wife of James Harley, and Alice, who afterwards married Peter Warburton.[17]

Before the middle of the 17th century Parkhall had passed to the Hunts of Holloway Grange, having probably been acquired with the manor of Hill Court in Grafton Flyford of the co-heirs of John Gardener in 1616–17. In Habington's time it belonged to Raphael Hunt,[17a] and it seems to have passed to John, a younger son of Raphael, as he is called in the Visitation of 1682 John Hunt of Parkhall,[18] and was dealing with land in Holloway and Parkhall in 1654 and 1657,[19] and his son John was also seated at Parkhall.[20] The latter was perhaps the John Hunt of Parkhall who died in 1721.[21] Parkhall still belonged to the Hunts at the end of the 18th century,[22] but all manorial rights, if such ever existed, have long since fallen into abeyance.

The manor of *TEMPLE BROUGHTON* (Broghton, Temple Brocton, xiv cent.) was probably part of the manor of Hanbury in 1086. It is said to have been granted by Bishop Theulf (1115–23) to Peverell de Beauchamp,[23] and it was held in the time of Henry II by Peter de Beauchamp.[24] It seems to have been forfeited about 1170–1 by Walter de Beauchamp,[25] and remained in the king's hands until 1189 or later.[26] It was apparently given by Richard I to Peter de Beauchamp, Walter's uncle,[27] but it was taken from him by King John and given to Hugh Pantulf and Hamo Cocus.[28] They were apparently in possession in 1220–1,[29] and according to the Red Book of the Bishopric of Worcester the estate, then consisting of 5 hides, was held in 1299 by the Knights Templars by the gift of Sir Hugh Pantulf.[30] Sir Hugh's gift had perhaps been made before 1237, when Henry III granted to the Templars 2½ acres of

THE TEMPLARS. *Argent a cross gules and a chief sable.*

THE HOSPITALLERS. *Gules a cross argent.*

clearing in his forest of Feckenham which William Fitz Robert had held at a rent of 6d. per annum.[31]

This manor was probably granted with the rest of the Templars' possessions in 1312 to the Knights Hospitallers,[32] for it belonged to them at the time of the Dissolution. It was not valued separately in 1536, but was then included in the Preceptory of Balsall in Warwickshire, of which it was parcel.[33] The manor was granted in 1554 to John Butler,[34] and he and his son William sold it in 1571 to Sir John Throckmorton and his wife Margery.[35] Sir John died in 1580, and was succeeded by his son Francis Throckmorton,[36] who conspired against Queen Elizabeth, and was executed at Tyburn 10 July 1584.[37] The manor of Temple Broughton thus forfeited to the Crown was granted in 1586–7 to Edward Heron and John Nicholas.[38] No further mention of the manor has been found until 1616, when Edmund Bell sold it to George Lench.[39] The latter was succeeded by William Lench, who sold the manor of Temple Broughton to Mary Stanhope in 1654.[40] A Thomas Gwynne is mentioned as the owner in 1705,[41] and also in 1737, when he and William Gwynne conveyed the manor to Lucy Rodd, widow, and Thomas Williams.[42] By 1754 the manor had passed to Edward Bearcroft,[43] who died without issue in 1793, and the estates came into the family of his cousin Elizabeth wife of Robert Longcroft.[44] Her grandson Edward Henry assumed the name Bearcroft in 1822, and died in 1832, when his son Edward succeeded.[45] On the death of the latter in 1886 the estate passed to his son Colonel Edward Hugh Bearcroft, who is the present owner.[46]

In 1317 the custody of 'the manor of Broghton' which Thomas de Clinton held for life by grant of Guy de Beauchamp Earl of Warwick was granted by the king, in whose hands the manor was on account of the minority of the earl's heir, to Giles de Beauchamp, to enable him to remain in the king's service.[47] In the following year commissioners were ordered to make inquiry touching the persons who expelled the escheator's servants from an estate in Temple Broughton and Hanbury (evidently the manor mentioned above, as Thomas de Clinton held it for life).[48] In 1319–20 the custody of the manor of Temple Broughton was committed to John Spark during the minority of the heir of Guy Earl of Warwick.[49] It was probably this estate which under the designation of a messuage and a carucate of land in Hanbury was the subject of a suit in 1352 between Sir Baldwin de Frevile and Sir Giles de Beauchamp.[50] Baldwin asserted that William de Ablinton gave the estate to Maud Devreux and Alexander de Frevile and the heirs of Alexander's body, and claimed it as

[16] Fine R. 10 Jas. I, pt. iii, no. 16 ; 14 Jas. I, pt. i, no. 27.
[17] See Hill Court in Grafton Flyford, *V.C.H. Worcs.* iv.
[17a] op. cit. i, 260.
[18] Metcalfe, op. cit. 64.
[19] Feet of F. Worcs. Mich. 1654 ; Hil. 1657.
[20] Ibid. [21] Nash, op. cit. i, 554.
[22] Ibid. 549.
[23] Habington, op. cit. i, 256 ; Red Bk. of Bishopric of Worc. (Eccl. Com. Rec. Var. bdle. 121, no. 43698), fol. 254.
[24] Red Bk. of Bishopric of Worc. fol. 109.
[25] *Pipe R.* 17 *Hen. II* (Pipe R. Soc.), 98.
[26] See Pipe R. for Worcs. 18 Hen. II–35 Hen. II.

[27] Pipe R. 6 Ric. I, m. 1 ; 9 Ric. I, m. 13 d. ; Assize R. 1021, m. 8 d.
[28] Assize R. 1021, m. 8 d.
[29] Ibid.
[30] Red. Bk. of Bishopric of Worc. fol. 100.
[31] Cart. Antiq. QQ 8.
[32] *Cal. Close,* 1313–18, p. 89.
[33] Pat. 1 & 2 Phil. and Mary, pt. ii, m. 8 ; see Ct. R. (Gen. Ser.), portf. 207, no. 9.
[34] Pat. 1 & 2 Phil. and Mary, pt. ii, m. 8.
[35] Feet of F. Worcs. Mich. 13 & 14 Eliz.
[36] Chan. Inq. p.m. (Ser. 2), cxci, 114.
[37] *Dict. Nat. Biog.*
[38] Pat. 29 Eli pt. viii, m. 31.

[39] Feet of F. Worcs. Mich. 13 Jas. I.
[40] Ibid. Trin. 1654.
[41] *Index to Worcs. Fines* (Worcs. Hist. Soc.), 371.
[42] Feet of F. Worcs. Mich. 11 Geo. II.
[43] Ibid. Hil. 28 Geo. II ; Recov. R. Mich. 28 Geo. II, rot. 341.
[44] Metcalfe, op. cit. 12, 14, 15 ; inform. from Rev. F. S. Colman, rector of Hanbury ; Recov. R. East. 52 Geo. III, rot. 287.
[45] Metcalfe, loc. cit. ; Sir T. Philipps, *Genealogia.*
[46] Burke, *Landed Gentry* (1906).
[47] *Cal. Pat.* 1317–21, p. 65.
[48] Ibid. 173.
[49] *Abbrev. Rot. Orig.* (Rec. Com.), i, 249.
[50] *Cal. Close,* 1349–54, p. 407.

grandson and heir of Alexander. Giles pleaded that he held the estate of the king's gift for a yearly payment at the Exchequer, and produced his Letters Patent.[51] The further descent of this estate at Temple Broughton has not been traced.

A tenement called *HILL HOUSE*, held of the manor of Temple Broughton, belonged from the 16th to the 18th century to a family named Watkins. Thomas Watkins died seised of it in 1587, leaving a son John,[52] on whose death in 1601 it passed to his son, another John.[53] Francis Watkins compounded for his estate in Hanbury in 1649.[54] There are monumental inscriptions to various members of the family in the church of Hanbury; among them one to John Watkins of Hill House, who died in 1708, and another to John Watkins of Hill House, who died in 1721.[55]

In 1431 Humphrey Stafford held certain land in Hanbury for the service of a quarter of a knight's fee.[56] This estate, afterwards known as the manor of Hanbury, was forfeited by Humphrey Stafford and granted with the rest of his Worcestershire estates in 1486–7 to John Darrell and John Pimpe.[57] It then followed the same descent as the manor of Hawkesley in King's Norton[58] (q.v) until the death of Sir Humphrey Stafford in 1545.[59] He was then succeeded by a son Humphrey, who with his wife Elizabeth and John Cooper and Margaret his wife conveyed the manor of Hanbury to Sir William Stafford and others.[60] At the same date Humphrey Stafford conveyed land in Wawemore in Hanbury to Thomas Carwe.[61]

The Staffords also seem to have held an estate in Hanbury known as the manor of *WEBHOWE* or *WEBBHOUSE*. Early in the 16th century Maud Stafford, widow, brought a suit against Thomas Stafford for detaining deeds relating to this manor.[62] Habington gives the following descent of this estate. It passed from the Webbs or Wybbes[63] by the marriage of Alice daughter and heir of Thomas Webb with Thomas Jennettes. Thomas and Alice had an only daughter Maud, who married John Stafford, and is evidently Maud the plaintiff in the above-mentioned suit. Her daughter Agnes married Richard Andrews.[64] The manor of 'Wybbes' was conveyed by Gilbert Andrews in 1580 to William Andrews and John Kemett.[65] According to Nash it was sold by a member of the Andrews family to Richard Vernon,[66] and there is an inscription in Hanbury Church to Richard Vernon of Webbhouse, who died in 1660.[67]

The site of the manor is probably marked by the

ANDREWS. *Argent a bend between cotises sable with three molets argent on the bend.*

present Webbhouse Farm in the north of the parish on the Dodderhill boundary.

The church of *ST. MARY THE VIRGIN* consists of a chancel 36½ ft. by 17 ft., nave of equal width and 45½ ft. long, north vestry and organ chamber 24½ ft. by 16½ ft., south chapel 21 ft. by 20½ ft., north and south nave aisles, the former 17¾ ft. wide, the latter 20 ft. wide, and a western tower 16 ft. square; all the dimensions being internal.

The earliest part of the fabric is the south arcade, which dates from about 1210, and was probably an insertion in the south wall of an earlier structure. The aisle itself has evidently been rebuilt and widened at a much later period (probably in the 18th century), but portions of the windows date from the 13th and 14th centuries. The north aisle was evidently added in the 14th century, but later rebuilding has probably much increased the original width.

The tower was rebuilt in 1793[68] against the west wall of the nave on old foundations, and other work was done at the same time, Thomas Johnson of Worcester being the architect. Since then several restorations have been carried out, and the chancel was rebuilt by Street in 1860, with the addition of the organ chamber and south chapel.

The modern chancel is in the style of the 13th century with the most elaborate details. The east wall is pierced by three lancets with marble shafting and carved foliage capitals. In the south wall are a credence, piscina and three sedilia and an arcade of two bays dividing the chancel from the south or Vernon chapel, which is itself divided by an arcade running north and south.

The chancel arch is modern. The nave is clearstoried and has an arcade of four bays on either side dividing it from the aisles; that on the north has octagonal columns on which are 14th-century capitals designed to fit much larger piers and cut back before the necking; the arches are pointed and of two chamfered orders. The south arcade has round columns with modern bases. The capitals are moulded 13th-century work except the middle one, which has large fluted scallops; the arches are pointed and chamfered.

The north aisle has four side windows, the easternmost of which has been filled in. Both it and the third window have pointed heads without tracery and some remains of 14th-century stonework. The two remaining windows are square-headed, and at the west end is a blocked pointed doorway. The wall leans outwards and has been strengthened by four large raking buttresses.

In the south wall is a blocked doorway with 14th-century mouldings to the external jambs, and two windows, the eastern of which is probably of the same date and has a pointed head, devoid of tracery, The west window of the aisle has been reconstructed

[51] *Cal. Close*, 1349–54, p. 407.
[52] Chan. Inq. p.m. (Ser. 2), ccxlii, 36.
[53] Ibid. cclxxxii, 56.
[54] *Cal. Com. for Comp.* 2079.
[55] Nash, op. cit. i, 553, 554.
[56] *Feud. Aids*, v, 332.
[57] Pat. 2 Hen. VII, pt. i.
[58] Chan. Inq. p.m. (Ser. 2), xi, 87; xxxiii, 4.
[59] Exch. Inq. p.m. file 1198, no. 8.

[60] Feet of F. Worcs. East. 1 Mary.
[61] Com. Pleas D. Enr. East. 1 Mary, m. 9.
[62] Early Chan. Proc. bdle. 357, no. 32.
[63] William Webb paid a subsidy of 2s. 6d. at Hanbury in 1280 (*Lay Subs. R. Worcs.* 1280 [Worcs. Hist. Soc.], 33). In 1432 Thomas Webb of Hanbury was summoned to answer Humphrey Duke of Gloucester for a debt (*Cal. Pat.* 1429–

36, p. 167). He was afterwards outlawed, but was pardoned in 1455 (*Cal. Pat.* 1452–61, p. 233).
[64] Habington, op. cit. i, 257.
[65] Feet of F. Worcs. Mich. 22 & 23 Eliz. [66] Habington, loc. cit.
[67] Ibid. 552.
[68] An Act for the purpose was obtained in that year (Loc. and Pers. Act 33 Geo. III, cap. 45).

VIEW OF HANBURY HALL FROM A SURVEY MADE IN 1732
(*In the possession of Sir Harry Foley Vernon, Bart.*)

HANBURY HALL FROM THE SOUTH-WEST

of 13th-century materials, and the internal jambs have shafts with moulded capitals. In the west wall is a doorway below the gallery, and on either side of it a recess. Above is the blocked arch of the former tower with a pointed head of three chamfered orders.

The present tower of three stages is built of red sandstone. The ground floor serves as a porch to the church. The second stage is pierced by a west window of two lights under a pointed head, and the bell-chamber has also pointed windows of two lights. The stair rises in the north-west angle, and the parapet is embattled with corner pinnacles.

The font is modern in 13th-century style. In the first floor of the tower are some remains of 17th-century pew panelling.

The Vernon chapel contains numerous monuments to members of that family. They include memorials of Edward Vernon, 1666, and his wife Eleanor, 1673, Richard Vernon, 1678, John Vernon, 1681, and a large monument to Thomas Vernon, 1721, with a recumbent effigy between two females, all in white marble, and a lofty pediment supported on columns above. It bears a shield of Vernon impaling Keck, Sable a bend ermine between two cotises counterflowered or. On the west wall is a monument to Bowater Vernon, 1735, with a life-size figure in classic dress by Roubilliac, and a medallion of his second wife Jane Cornwallis. There is also a monument by Chantry to Thomas Tayler Vernon, died 1835. In the chancel on the north wall a tablet commemorates Richard Vernon, for forty-six years parson of Hanbury, died 1627, and his wife Frances (Wylde). At the east of the south aisle is a tablet to Thomas Vernon, 1771.

There are eight bells: the treble and second by Mears, 1819; the third and fourth by Richard Sanders of Bromsgrove, 1720; the fifth by Matthew Bagley, 1678; the sixth, seventh and tenor by J. Rudhall, 1792.

The plate is most massive, of Georgian pattern and gilt. It comprises two very large cups and paten covers, two large almsplates, and four very large flagons, all hall-marked 1721 and inscribed 'E dono Bowater Vernon Arm.'

The registers are as follows: (i) mixed entries from 1577 to 1715; (ii) 1716 to 1812.

There is a chapel of ease to the parish church at Woolmere Green, and in 1872 the school at Broughton Green was made suitable for public worship by the addition of a partitioned chancel and wooden bell-turret.

ADVOWSON   There was a priest at Hanbury at the date of the Domesday Survey.[69]
The advowson has always followed the descent of the manor.[70]

The parish of Hanbury was a peculiar exempt from the jurisdiction of the archdeacon but not of the bishop.[70a] In 1301 the rector received a licence to be absent for study,[71] and in 1326 Bishop Cobham

wrote to the Dean of Wych (Droitwich) 'concerning the public scandal occasioned by W. de Bever, rector of the church of Hanbury, that he makes no residence at his church, but wanders about in London and elsewhere leading a most dissolute life.'[72] In 1375 another rector of Hanbury was in trouble owing to his way of living.[73]

One Richard Yate gave two cows, valued in 1549-50 at 12s. each, for the maintenance of certain lamps and lights in the parish church of Hanbury.[74]

In 1287 Bishop Giffard confirmed the appropriation of certain land in the demesne of Hanbury which Nicholas de Aylesbury, parson of Hanbury, had assigned to build a house for a priest to celebrate the office of the Glorious Virgin.[75]

CHARITIES   The Hanbury parochial charities are regulated by a scheme of the Charity Commissioners 7 February 1896, whereby the church lands are continued as a separate charity under the administration of the rector and churchwardens. The remaining charities are divided into the educational branch and the poor branch under the administration of a body of ten trustees, constituted as therein mentioned.

In the educational branch are comprised the following charities, namely:—

The Charity school founded in or about 1627 by the Rev. Richard Vernon, a former rector, and further endowed by will of Thomas Vernon, and by will of Madam Mary Bearcroft, dated respectively in 1711 and 1714, is endowed with 10 a. or thereabouts in Hanbury let at £12 a year, an annuity of £2 4s. issuing out of a tenement in the chapelry of Stock and Bradley in Fladbury, and an annuity of £1 out of Astwood Farm. The income is applicable under the scheme towards the maintenance of the National schools.

Charity of the said Thomas Vernon for apprenticing, by will 1711, consisting of 19 a. in Dodderhill let at £25 a year and £439 10s. 10d. consols, producing £10 9s. 8d. yearly. The income if not required for apprenticing is applicable towards the outfit of any poor child, technical instruction, or exhibitions for higher education.

Charity of Henry Collier—mentioned on the church table—consisting of a cottage and 2 a. 2 r. in Stock and Bradley, producing £10 yearly and £90 consols, producing £2 5s. yearly.

Charity of Mrs. Ann Dyson—also mentioned on the church table—consisting of 3 a. known as The Fling, let at £5 5s. a year and £40 consols, producing £1 a year, and the charity known as the Forest Money, or the charity of Sir Miles Fleetwood, founded in or about the year 1672, being an annuity of £6 13s. 4d. issuing out of the Forest Farm, and £60 consols, producing £1 10s. yearly.

The income of the three last-mentioned charities is by the scheme made applicable in the advancement of children attending public elementary schools by means of prizes, payments to encourage continuance at

[69] *V.C.H. Worcs.* i, 298a.

[70] *Testa de Nevill* (Rec. Com.), 44a; *Reg. G. Giffard* (Worcs. Hist. Soc.), 427, 439; *Cal. Pat.* 1385-9, p. 458; Inst. Bks. (P.R.O.). The church of Hanbury appears to have been one of those which Bishop Giffard attempted to make prebendal to the college of Westbury-on-Trym (*Reg. G. Giffard* [Worcs. Hist. Soc.], 427).

[70a] Inform. from Rev. F. S. Colman, rector. The seal of the peculiar is in the British Museum, and is described in *Proc. Soc. Antiq.* (Ser. 2), v, 247. Wills proved in the rector's court are now at the Probate Registry, Worcester.

[71] *Sede Vacante Reg.* (Worcs. Hist. Soc.), 73.

[72] Worc. Epis. Reg. Cobham (1317-27), fol. 115.

[73] *Sede Vacante Reg.* (Worcs. Hist. Soc.), 340.

[74] Chant. Cert. 60, no. 74.

[75] *Reg. G. Giffard* (Worcs. Hist. Soc.), 311; Habington, op. cit. i, 255; Red Bk. of Bishopric of Worc. fol. 99.

school, and by conditional payments to public elementary schools.

In the poor branch are comprised the following charities, namely :—

Charity of the said Thomas Vernon, founded by codicil dated in 1720, for clothing and for fuel for the poor, consisting of 84 a. known as Astwood Bank Farm in Feckenham, and a farm at Foster's Green, containing 13 a., of the gross rental of £110 a year.

Charity of Sir John Hanbury—mentioned on the church table—founded by will in or about the year 1639, consisting of an annual payment of £6 10s. by the Merchant Taylors' Company, and a sum of £25 consols, producing 12s. 6d. yearly.

Charity of John Staverton, founded by will dated in 1672, being an annual payment of £4 10s., part of the rent-charge of £20 mentioned below under the church lands, and £25 consols, producing 12s. 6d. yearly.

Charity called Berrifield's clothing, being an annual payment of 16s., further part of the said rent-charge of £20.

The several sums of consols, amounting together to £679 10s. 10d., are held by the official trustees.

The income of the poor branch is by the scheme directed to be applied for the benefit of the poor in such way as the trustees should consider most conducive to the formation of provident habits, by donations to hospitals, &c., to coal and clothing clubs, or by contributions towards the provision of nurses and medical aid in sickness.

The church lands.—In consideration of certain parcels of land being given up to the proprietors of Hanbury Manor, an annuity of £20 was by deed 7 July 1812 secured upon an estate called Beck's Farm, of which £4 10s. and 16s. is applied for the benefit of the poor in respect of the charities of John Staverton and Berrifield mentioned above, the balance of £14 14s. being carried to the churchwardens' accounts.

HARTLEBURY

Heortlanbyrig (x cent.) ; Heortlabiri, Huerteberie (xi cent.) ; Herclebery (xii cent.) ; Hertlebur, Hertlebyr (xiii cent.) ; Herthulbury (xiv cent.) ; Hertylburie (xv cent.) ; Hartilbury, Hurtbery (xvi cent.).

The parish of Hartlebury has an area of 5,355 acres. Upper Mitton, with an area of 359 acres, formerly a hamlet of Hartlebury, was constituted a civil parish under the Local Government Act of 1894.[1] From the low-lying banks of the Severn and the Stour on the western side of Hartlebury the land rises towards the east, reaching a height of 200 ft. above the ordnance datum on the eastern border and of 300 ft. at Bishop's Wood on the southern boundary. The eastern part of the parish is on the Keuper Sandstones, the western on the Bunter Pebble Beds. There are 1,618 acres of permanent grass and 2,810 acres of arable land, the chief crops being wheat, barley, peas and potatoes. The woods and plantations, of which the largest is Bishop's Wood, cover 172 acres.[2] The Oxford, Worcester and Wolverhampton branch of the Great Western railway passes through the parish, and is joined at Hartlebury station by the Severn Valley branch. The main road from Worcester to Kidderminster enters the parish on the south near the Mitre Oak, where the road from Stourport meets it, and running north is joined in the village of Hartlebury by another road from Stourport, on the left of which near the smithy is the old pound.

The village of Hartlebury is on the Worcester and Kidderminster high road. The church stands in the centre of the village in a churchyard of moderate size. The village itself contains few features of particular interest ; the best house is, perhaps, the rectory, a good building of the late 17th century built by Bishop Stillingfleet (1689–99). Hartlebury Castle is situated a little to the north-west of the main village, surrounded by an extensive park. On the east side of the road ascending to the southward out of the village, which is built at the foot and upon the sides of small hills of sandstone, is the old grammar school, a small and much modernized building of brick. On the same side of the road, a little distance to the southward again, new and elaborate buildings for the accommodation of the school have been erected, and were opened in 1912.

There used to be in the village an old cross bearing the date 1666, but it was pulled down by a farmer's team in 1839 because it was thought to be in the way, and with it went also the stocks and whipping-post which stood below it.[3] A sundial covered with quaint inscriptions used to stand in a cottage garden surrounded by a yew hedge. It was called the Wizard's Pillar, being put up in 1687 by a man named Fidkin, who was considered to be a wizard. This now stands in the churchyard of Areley Kings.[4] On the glebe farm there is a hermit's cave called Hardwick's Cell. The roof is supported by sandstone pillars, and a door and window have been cut in the rock. Two giant oak trees stand in this parish, one in the bishop's park, called the Prior's Oak, and the other called the Mitre Oak, on the high road to Worcester. Probably they marked the boundaries of the bishop's rights in the forest. The Mitre Oak is said, but certainly erroneously, to have been the oak under which Augustine met the Welsh bishops.

In Wilden (Wildon, Wildons, xvi cent.),[5] a hamlet on the north-west of Hartlebury, near the Stour and the Worcestershire and Staffordshire Canal, are the ironworks of Messrs. Baldwin, Limited.

Torton, on the north-east of the parish, was the 'Torchinton' named in a 13th-century charter as one of the boundaries within which the forest of Ombersley was to be disafforested.[6]

Titton, another hamlet, and part of the episcopal manor of Hartlebury in the 16th century, was then called 'Titton, Tiddington or Teddington.'[7]

[1] Stat. 56 & 57 Vict. cap. 73.
[2] Statistics from Bd. of Agric. (1905).
[3] Rev. D. Robertson, 'Hist. of Parish of Hartlebury,' Assoc. Archit. Soc. Rep. xxvi, 223.
[4] Ibid.
[5] Wilden was part of the bishop's manor of Hartlebury in the 16th century and was leased to John Walker (Chan. Proc. [Ser. 2], bdle. 193, no. 10).
[6] Cal. Chart. R. 1226–57, p. 102.
[7] Chan. Proc. (Ser. 2), bdle. 70, no. 15.

Waresley is a hamlet and ancient manor to the south of the village. Waresley House was for many years in the latter half of the 19th century the residence of Dr. John Peel, D.D., Dean of Worcester. From about 1876 until his death in 1912 the Rev. Benjamin Gibbons lived there. Waresley Court is now occupied by Lord Hampton.

Whitlench House,[8] to the east of the village, is the residence of the Rev. J. P. E. Bulteel, M.A., a secretary of the Bishop of Worcester. Charlton House in the hamlet of Charlton is the residence of Mr. R. M. Danks, J.P.

On Hartlebury Common, on the west of the parish, were the rifle ranges of the County Rifle Association, but they are now closed. The common is held by the county council under a lease from the Ecclesiastical Commissioners. The parish was inclosed under an Act of 1815,[9] the award being dated 27 July 1821.[10]

Upper Mitton is separated from Hartlebury by the River Stour. The whole of the northern part of the parish is occupied by a sewage farm. The town, which lies on the outskirts of Stourport, is in the south of the parish, with a station on the Severn Valley branch of the Great Western railway.

Among former place-names in this parish were Werkmangreve, the Cross of Waresle, Cheyshoute, Euchencroft, la Chesehouse [11] (xiii cent.); Murkhous, le Bruche, Killyngham, Carenforlong, le Brodemore in Carentesmede, Briddesgrene, Welhegge,[12] Escherugg or Asscherugge [13] (xiv cent.); Lynnall or Lynholt Wood,[14] Nordalls and Payton or Paynter's Grove,[15] Perches [16] (xvi cent.).

Hartlebury Castle was originally the CASTLE manor-house of Hartlebury, and has always followed the same descent as the manor. Walter Cantilupe began to build in the time of Henry III,[17] the castle being finished by Bishop Giffard, who in 1268 obtained a royal licence to complete its fortification.[18] The first royal visitor to the castle was Edward I, who came here on his way to suppress the Welsh rebellion of 1282. He then called upon Bishop Giffard to have ready his forces to join the expedition.[19] Twelve years later Edward again spent a day here when he was journeying to Wales.[20]

In the middle of the 16th century the castle is described as a 'fayre Maner Place . . . having ii lyttel Towers covered with Leade, and the Chamber cauled the Bishop's Chamber also covered with Leade, and there is a Chappell annexed to the said Chamber lykewyse covered with Leade, where ys a lyttell Bell weying by estimacion dimid. hundred Weight. Also there is a Mote and a Ponde adjoyning to the said Castell well stored with Fyshe.'[21]

Elizabeth stayed at Hartlebury for a week on one occasion, being entertained by Bishop Bullingham.[22] The castle was the principal residence of the Bishops of Worcester during the 16th and first half of the 17th century,[23] until it fell into the hands of the Parliamentarians in 1646. In 1644 the Commissioners of Array, being pursued, fled here from Ombersley, considering it a safer place than Worcester,[24] but William Sandys, the governor of the castle, surrendered it in May 1646 to Colonel Thomas Morgan without a shot having been fired.[25]

The castle is said to have been destroyed by the Parliamentary army, but it was afterwards used as a prison for Royalist plotters, and from a survey taken in 1648 it is evident that the building was still standing. It was then described as a strong castle situated upon a rock with a moat round about it filled with water. The Commissioners intended to have it pulled down, and the value of the materials was estimated at £820 15s. 10d.[26] In 1647 the castle was sold with the manor to Thomas Westrowe.[27]

Bishop Lloyd was in residence in the reconstructed castle in 1699, and a list of the household goods found there by him is given in Francis Evans's diary.[28] Bishop Hurd was visited at the castle on 2 August 1788 by George III and the queen accompanied by the Duke of York, the Princess Royal and the Princesses Augusta and Elizabeth.[29] It is said that in 1803, during the panic caused by the projected invasion of the Emperor Napoleon, his Majesty contemplated removing to Hartlebury with the royal family for greater security.[30] Bishop Hurd actually made the offer, and the king, though considering that he himself ought to be nearer the centre of action, said that in so unhappy an event he would feel much confidence in placing the queen and princesses under the care of the bishop. In 1846 Hartlebury was made the sole palace of the see of Worcester,[31] and some lands in the parish were vested in the bishop in 1870.[32]

There has been a chapel in the castle from very early times. In 1285 Bishop Giffard held an ordination in his chapel of Hartlebury.[33] Bishop

---

[8] A *manse* at 'Hwitan hlinc' was leased in 969 by Bishop Oswald to the thegn Brihtmar for three lives (Birch, *Cart. Sax.* iii, 532). Walter de Wytelynge held a hide of land in the manor of Hartlebury in 1299 (Red Bk. of Bishopric of Worc. [Eccl. Com. Rec. Var. bdle. 121, no. 43698], fol. 112), and land at Whitlench was given in 1323 as part of the endowment of the chantry in Hartlebury Church (*Cal. Pat.* 1321–4, p. 296).

[9] Priv. Act, 55 Geo. III, cap. 43.

[10] *Blue Bk. Incl. Awards*, 190.

[11] Red Bk. of Bishopric of Worc. fol. 111.

[12] Chan. Inq. p.m. 48 Edw. III (Add. nos.), no. 37.

[13] *Reg. G. Giffard* (Worcs. Hist. Soc.), 336; *Cal. Pat.* 1377–81, p. 346.

[14] In this wood (now in Ombersley) there was common of pasture of the whole parish (Red Bk. of Bishopric of Worc. fol. 111).

[15] Anct. D. (P.R.O.), A 13523.

[16] Ct. of Req. bdle. 24, no. 48.

[17] Dugdale, *Mon. Angl.* i, 574. Sir J. Mackenzie states that the building was begun in 1255 (*Castles of Engl.* i, 383), but Dugdale gives the date as 1263 (loc. cit.).

[18] Thomas, *Surv. of Worc. Cath.* App. 44; Prattinton Coll. (Soc. Antiq.). Bishop Giffard was accused of appropriating some of the goods of the sacrist to meet the expense of building Hartlebury Castle (Thomas, op. cit. App. no. 67).

[19] *Reg. G. Giffard* (Worcs. Hist. Soc.), Introd. 147.

[20] *Cal. Pat.* 1292–1301, p. 126. Mr. Robertson states that Edward III also visited the castle ('Hist. of Parish of Hartlebury,' *Assoc. Archit. Soc. Rep.* xxvi, 216).

[21] Rev. D. Robertson, op. cit. 215.

[22] Ibid. 217.

[23] *Cal. S. P. Dom.* 1566–79, p. 568; 1581–90, p. 509; 1603–10, p. 558; 1619–23, p. 72, &c.

[24] *Hist. MSS. Com. Rep.* iv, App. i, 270.

[25] *Cal. Com. for Comp.* 1512; *Hist. MSS. Com. Rep.* xiii, App. i, 359; K. Watson, *Statist. and General Hist. of Worc.* (Topog. Tracts, vol. iv [Soc. Antiq.], 13). According to the account of a grandson of 'a martial' of Col. Sandys the castle was only surrendered after many hot onsets by storm and battering by cannons (Rev. D. Robertson, op. cit. 218).

[26] Nash, op. cit. i, 568.

[27] Close, 23 Chas. I, pt. xvi, no. 16.

[28] op. cit. (Worcs. Hist. Soc.), 12, 24.

[29] *Dict. Nat. Biog.*

[30] Sir J. Mackenzie, op. cit. i, 383; Rev. D. Robertson, op. cit. 221.

[31] *Lond. Gaz.* 3 Feb. 1846, p. 365.

[32] Ibid. 12 Aug. 1870, p. 3755.

[33] *Reg. G. Giffard* (Worcs. Hist. Soc.), 252.

Hemenhale received in this chapel the vow of the widowed Lady Isabella de Stepilton in 1337, and blessed her in *forma benedicendarum viduarum*. As she was not 'of the lord's jurisdiction' Lord William de Birmingham swore that such vow should be kept under penalty of 100*d*. 'in subsidy of the Holy Land to be applied.'[34] Orders were frequently celebrated by the bishops in this chapel.[35]

Hartlebury Castle stands on a plateau of red sandstone, surrounded on three sides by a moat partly filled with water. On the east side the moat has been filled up. The remaining part is about 100 ft. wide, and incloses a space of about 4 acres, on the west side of which the house is placed, the ground at the back falling away sharply to the level of the moat, while on the east or entrance side, towards the village of Hartlebury, there is a large forecourt. The whole of this space seems originally to have been inclosed by a wall, of which the north-west bastion alone remains. The character of its masonry suggests that it belongs to the period of Giffard. Of the house itself, which does not seem to have been more than a fortified manor-house, the earliest portions which can be definitely dated are the hall, the chapel, with the apartments to the west of it, and a small piece of the west wall of the present kitchen. They appear, from the few original details which have survived, to be of the 15th century, though much altered and incorporated into later work. Bishop Carpenter built a gate-house and draw-bridge on the east side of the house, near the present entrance gates, and he may perhaps have been the builder of the hall. The drastic rebuildings and alterations to which the castle was subjected in the last half of the 17th century have rendered the evidence of the structure itself difficult to read. Bishop Carpenter's gate-house has long disappeared, and Bishop Hurd is said to have removed in 1781 the last vestiges of the original keep, which is described as having stood to the east of the present house.[35a] As the buildings stand at present they consist of the hall, with the principal entrance at the south-east, the chapel wing on the south, projecting towards the east, and connected with the hall by a range of buildings of nearly equal length, and a north wing, answering to the chapel wing.

The only original detail remaining in the hall is the timber roof, now partly concealed by a plaster ceiling at the level of the collars. There are six principals, two being against the wall at either end. They have wall posts, resting upon corbels, from which the collars are strutted by modern curved braces forming four-centred arches. The moulded ribs of the original ceiling following the slope of the sides of the roof are still visible, though the panels are plastered. The entrance is now at the south-east; the original entrance and the screens were probably at the north end, on which side was, and still is, the kitchen, though completely rebuilt. Two recesses with moulded four-centred heads and jambs, plastered and painted, opposite to each other at the south end of the hall, and containing the entrance and garden doorways, may perhaps point to the former existence of oriels at the daïs end. The north wall is now occupied by an early 19th-century stone geometrical staircase, leading to a doorway giving entrance to the first floor of the north wing.

There are three plain pointed windows in the east wall. In the centre of the north wall is a fine stone chimney-piece of the late 17th century, placed there by Bishop Hough, with his shield over the opening, Worcester impaling argent a bend sable. South of the hall is the saloon, lighted by three pointed windows in its east wall, balancing those of the hall. The walls and ceiling are fine examples of early 18th-century plaster work. At the rear of the hall and saloon is a long corridor, divided by a lobby, through which the hall is entered from the moat or garden side. Previously to the end of the 18th century this would seem to have been of one story only. At this period Bishop Hurd added the library on the first floor above it. This is a fine apartment, long and narrow, divided into a central and two shorter end bays by Ionic columns, and having a semicircular bay window in the centre of the west wall. The ceiling is coved and flat, and the design is in the Adam manner. The original drawings which have been preserved are dated 1782, and are signed by one James Smith of Shifnall; the plaster work was executed by Joseph Bromfield of Shrewsbury. The elevation presented to the forecourt by this range of buildings is long, low, and uninteresting. The sandstone facing, which renders the earlier and later work externally indistinguishable, is probably the work of Bishop Fleetwood (consecrated 1675), whose shield is placed over the entrance porch. On either side of the porch are the plain pointed windows of the hall and saloon. A print of 1731 shows these as square-headed; by the end of the 18th century the testimony of another print shows that they had assumed their present form. The whole is crowned by an embattled parapet. The elevation towards the moat is of two stories, with the semicircular bay window of Bishop Hurd's library in the centre. The windows are plain square openings, and the parapet is likewise embattled. The slope of the roof towards the forecourt is slated, while the slope on the moat side is tiled. A flèche of Strawberry Hill Gothic, surmounted by a vane, and exhibiting a dial and pointer to show the direction of the wind, is perched on the centre of the ridge.

Adjoining the saloon on the south is a projecting two-storied portion containing the drawing room, a small library, and the principal stairs, while south of this again is the chapel, two stories in height, which projects nearly its whole length into the forecourt. At the west end of the chapel is a two-storied range of apartments of equal height, the west wall of which is flush with the west wall of the central range of buildings described above. Neither the drawing room nor the adjoining apartment possesses any feature of interest. The stairs appear to be of the last half of the 17th century, at which date this block appears to have been rebuilt. The chapel is a good example of the 'Gothic taste' of the 18th century. The date of the walls is uncertain. The print of 1731 referred to above shows an east window of four lights with intersecting tracery in the head and a gable over it. If any reliance can be placed on this view, it would put the date well back into the 14th century. Here again the refacing of the walls inside and out renders it impossible to dogmatize. The buttresses, of which there are five, two angle buttresses

34 Worc. Epis. Reg. Hemenhale, fol. 12 d.
35 Worc. Epis. Reg. *passim*.

35a The record of this is probably based on a confusion between a supposed keep and the ruins of Carpenter's gate-house.

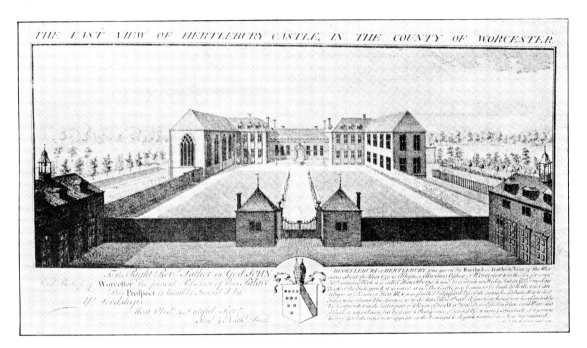

HARTLEBURY CASTLE IN 1731
(*Drawn and Engraved by S. & N. Buck*)

at the east end and three on the south wall, one belonging to the apartments at the west end, are suspiciously wiry in their proportions, but their mouldings seem too good for the 18th century. Some of the windows of the west part of the chapel range are evidently openings of the 15th century, having four-centred heads ; on the whole, it seems most likely that the whole of the range, chapel included, may be assigned to that date. The chapel in its present form has an east window of three pointed lights, with three pointed two-light windows in each side wall, all of the 18th century. The chapel and the adjoining apartments on the west are covered by one hipped roof covered with slate. Internally the chapel is wainscoted with 'Gothic' panelling of the Batty Langley school. The ceiling is a plaster fan-vault. In the upper lights of the side windows are the shields of some of the most noteworthy of the former bishops. These, which are by Price, are good specimens of 18th-century glass painting. In the west wall is a window opening into the first floor of the adjoining apartment.

The northern wing balances the chapel wing and seems to be almost entirely of the 17th century, with the exception of part of the west wall of the kitchen, against which is a large buttress of one offset, which may belong to the 15th century.

The forecourt is inclosed by low brick walls on the north and south ; on the east side are the entrance gates with small lodges on either side. These are the work of Fleetwood, though, like the rest of his work, Gothicized in the 18th century. An outer court is formed by stables running east and west on either side of the lodges. Those on the north side have been altered into a clergy-house. All trace of the moat on this side has disappeared.

There has for long been a *PARK* at Hartlebury. In the 16th century there was a 'lyttell Parke conteanying one Myle abowte . . . wherein be lxxvi Deare.' The keeper, Francis Blount, had pasture there for one horse and two kine by a grant of the dean and chapter, and by a grant for life from the bishop pasture for 5 kine.[36] In a deposition of the reign of Charles II it was said that the park of about 100 acres was impaled and well stocked with deer in early times, the bishop paying to the rector in lieu of tithes one shoulder of every deer killed there. It was disparked before it was sold with the manor to Thomas Westrowe in 1647, and was then divided up, one half of it being fenced.[37] In 1701

the park pale was in a state of dilapidation and Bishop Lloyd allowed timber for its repairs to be taken from Monks Wood and his demesne at Grimley and Hartlebury.[38] A detailed account of the deer in Hartlebury Park from 1699 to 1709 was kept by the bishop's secretary and is still preserved.

HARTLEBURY is said to have been
MANORS   given to the Bishop of Worcester by Burhed, King of Mercia (c. 850).[38a] It certainly belonged to the bishopric in 985, when Bishop Oswald granted half a 'mansa' there to his 'familiar friend' Leofwine for three lives.[39] The manor is enumerated among the lands of the see in the Domesday Survey,[40] and in 1199 John granted to the bishop in this manor such liberties as he enjoyed in his other manors.[41]

The bishop obtained a grant of free warren at Hartlebury in 1254 and 1255.[42] In 1291 the manor, containing 2 carucates of land, was worth £25 13s. 4d.[43] It remained in the possession of successive bishops[44] until Bishop Hooper, during his short occupation of the see, gave it to Edward VI,[45] who in 1553 granted it to the Duke of Northumberland.[46] In the same year the duke sold it to Sir Francis Jobson.[47] On the restitution of Bishop Heath he re-entered into possession of the manor,[48] but Sir Francis Jobson, through the influence of the Earl of Leicester, obtained an Act confirming his title in March 1558,[49] in spite of the protests of the bishop. Sir Francis died in 1573,[50] and before 1578 the manor again became a possession of the see of Worcester.[51] In 1647 the Parliamentary Commissioners sold it to Thomas Westrowe.[52] At the Restoration it was given back to the see,[53] and passed in 1860 into the hands of the Ecclesiastical Commissioners,[54] who are the present lords of the manor.

Five 'manses' at *WARESLEY* (Waresley, x cent. ; Wearesleah, xi cent. ; Waereslege, xii cent. ; Warbelsley, Warvysley, Wardesley, xvi cent.) were given by Bishop Oswald in 980 to his clerk Wulfgar. The land[55] remained subject to the church until shortly before the Conquest, when, Bishop Wulfstan having granted it to Alfwine son of Beorhtmœr, it was seized on the death of Alfwine by Urse the sheriff.[56] Thus, according to the monastic chronicler, the church lost this land. The bishop's right of over-lordship seems, however, still to have been recognized, for in the 12th century the land was held of the manor of Hartlebury,[57] and was still said to be held of the bishop in 1505.[58]

[36] Rev. D. Robertson, op. cit. xxvi, 215.

[37] Exch. Dep. East. 28 Chas. II, no. 8; Trin. 31 Chas. II, no. 2.

[38] *Diary of Francis Evans* (Worcs. Hist. Soc.), 48, 146, &c.

[38a] Heming, *Chartul.* (ed. Hearne), 480. An early reference to this place occurs among the boundaries of Waresley, 'the street that goes to Heortlabyrig.' The exact date of these boundaries is uncertain (Birch, op. cit, 502).

[39] Heming, op. cit. 172. The Anglo-Saxon boundaries of Hartlebury are given by Heming (op. cit. 354). Habington supposed that Hartlebury was annexed to the bishopric from its foundation in 679, but that the fact was 'somewhat obscured by reason of the king's prerogatives in the forest of Ombersley,' which adjoined Hartlebury (Habington, op. cit. i, 281).

Prattinton adds a note of Dr. Thomas in the Habington MSS. stating that Hartlebury was given to Bishop Aelhun by Burhed, King of the Mercians, about 850 (Prattinton Coll.), but no grant of Hartlebury has been found in the Worcester chartulary.

[40] *V.C.H. Worcs.* i, 298.

[41] *Cal. Rot. Chart.* 1199–1216 (Rec. Com.), 10.

[42] *Cal. Pat.* 1247–58, p. 345 ; *Cal. Chart. R.* 1226–57, p. 443. In 1647 this warren was called Charlton and Tainton Warren (Close, 23 Chas. I, pt. xvi, no. 16).

[43] *Pope Nich. Tax.* (Rec. Com.), 225.

[44] *Feud. Aids*, v, 306, 312, 318.

[45] *Cal. S. P. Dom.* 1547–65, p. 575.

[46] Prattinton Coll. (Soc. Antiq.) ; *Cal. S. P. Dom.* 1547–65, p. 575; Pat. 7 Edw. VI, pt. viii, m. 28.

[47] Pat. 7 Edw. VI, pt. vi.

[48] *Cal. S. P. Dom.* 1547–65, p. 575.

[49] Ibid. ; Prattinton Coll. (Soc. Antiq.).

[50] Prattinton Coll. (Soc. Antiq.).

[51] *V.C.H. Worcs.* ii, 52.

[52] Close, 23 Chas. I, pt. xvi, no. 16.

[53] In 1699 Bishop Lloyd appointed a gamekeeper in his manor of Hartlebury (*Diary of Francis Evans* [Worcs. Hist. Soc.], 6).

[54] Stat. 23 & 24 Vict. cap. 124. Mr. Watson stated in 1839 that the manor then belonged to George Talbot (K. Watson, op. cit. 4).

[55] Dugdale, *Mon. Angl.* i, 569; Heming, op. cit. 143. The bounds of the land are given in Anglo-Saxon (see also p. 354).   [56] Heming, op. cit. 261.

[57] *V.C.H. Worcs.* i, 325b, 327a ; Red Bk. of Bishopric of Worc. fol. 253.

[58] Chan. Inq. p.m. (Ser. 2), xix, 63.

Urse's interest passed to the lords of Elmley, and the manor was held of the honour of Elmley until the end of the 14th century.[59]

Towards the end of the 12th century Walter de Bromsgrove held Waresley of William de Beauchamp.[60]

The family of Bishopsdon held land under the Beauchamps at the beginning of the 13th century, if not earlier, for in 1208 a writ of mort d'ancestor was brought by William Black and his wife Eleanor in the name of Neste, the mother of Eleanor, against William de Bishopsdon for 2½ hides in Pepwell and Waresley. William called to warranty the son of William de Beauchamp to prove that the latter had given the land to Frarinus[61] de Bishopsdon. The plea concludes :· 'William Black being asked by what warranty he married Eleanor said that he found her penniless and married her for herself.'[62] William de Bishopsdon, in the rebellion of the barons against John, followed his lord Walter de Beauchamp, and on that account forfeited his lands, but they were restored to him in 1216.[63] William was dealing with land in Waresley in 1220,[64] and it was perhaps his son William who granted land at Waresley in 1225 to Hawisia daughter of Eleanor,[65] who may have been his sister. William de Bishopsdon joined the barons against Henry III, and forfeited his lands, which were, however, restored to him in 1268, under the 'Dictum of Kenilworth.'[66] Thomas de Bishopsdon afterwards held the manor, his widow Joan holding dower of his lands in 1339.[67] John de Bishopsdon, who obtained a grant of free warren in his demesne lands here in 1319, was probably grandson of Thomas.[68] In 1339 this John, then Sir John, settled land in Waresley upon himself and his wife Beatrice for life, with remainder in tail-male to his sons Roger and John.[69] Beatrice survived her husband and her son Roger, and was still holding land at Waresley in 1374, when Thomas son of Roger de Bishopsdon conveyed the reversion after her death to trustees.[70] Thomas died in 1386 in possession of the manor of Waresley.[71] His son William succeeded and granted all his land in Waresley to his daughter Iseult in frank marriage.[72] Iseult apparently left no children, for the manor passed into the Catesby family through the marriage of Philippa daughter of William de Bishopsdon with Sir William Catesby.[73]

Their son William Catesby was attainted and forfeited all his estates in 1486, but they were restored to his son George in 1495.[74] He died in 1505, leaving a son William,[75] on whose death in 1517 the estate passed to his brother Richard.[76] Richard died in 1553, leaving as his heir his kinsman William Catesby, then a minor. This William was his grandson, son of his son William.[77] The manor of Waresley was assigned as dower to Katherine widow of William son of Sir Richard Catesby, who afterwards became the wife of Anthony Throckmorton.[78] William (then Sir William) Catesby leased the manor in 1577 to

CATESBY. *Argent two leopards sable with golden crowns.*

Edmund Catesby and others for twenty-one years after the death of Katherine Throckmorton, who still held the manor as jointure.[79] This lease was assigned in 1591 to Thomas Best.[80] Habington states that Sir William Catesby sold the manor to Mr. Henry Cookes, 'in whose heirs Waresley for the greatest part continued,'[81] but it seems probable that the property was sold to Thomas Best by Sir William Catesby, for in 1619 William Best and his wife Margery were holding the manor,[82] and in 1646 Gervase Wheeler and his wife Joyce had come into possession of it,[83] and continued to hold it as late as 1694.[84] In 1764 William Wheeler was owner of the manor.[85] In 1817 it was conveyed by Thomas Harward and his wife Anne to William Prattinton.[86] Mr. Watson writing in 1839 said the manor then belonged to the Rev. Thomas Harward of Winterfold.[87] Part of the manor passed under his will to the Rev. Thomas Littleton Wheeler, whose son Canon Thomas Littleton Wheeler acquired the rest under the will of Miss Mary Jane Harward in 1908. On the death of Canon Wheeler in 1910 the property was vested in trustees for sale, his widow Mrs. Katherine Ewart Wheeler being tenant for life.[87a]

There is no mention of *PEPWELL* (Pipewell, xiii cent. ; Peopwell, Pepewell, xiv cent. ; Peppwall, Popewelle, xv cent.) in the Domesday Survey, but it was probably one of the berewicks belonging to the manor of Hartlebury at that time, as it was held of that manor in 1281, when William de Portes did suit at the bishop's court of Hartlebury by reason of

[59] *V.C.H. Worcs.* i, 325b, 327a ; *Testa de Nevill* (Rec. Com.), 41b ; Chan. Inq. p.m. 17 Ric. II, no. 6.
[60] Red Bk. of Bishopric of Worc. fol. 253.
[61] Probably to be identified with Fraericus de Bishopsdon, who flourished in the reign of Henry II (see Hill in Fladbury).
[62] *Abbrev. Plac.* (Rec. Com.), 62b.
[63] *Rot. Lit. Claus.* (Rec. Com.), i, 280. Early in the 13th century William de Bishopsdon held half a knight's fee in Waresley of William de Beauchamp, and Stephen de Waresley was holding a knight's fee there at the same date, as well as a virgate of land of the Bishop of Worcester (*Testa de Nevill* [Rec. Com.], 41b, 42). No further trace of Stephen's possessions has been found, and it may be assumed that his lands were acquired by the Bishopsdons.
[64] Feet of F. Worcs. 5 Hen. III, no. 17.

[65] Ibid. 10 Hen. III, no. 12.
[66] Anct. D. (P.R.O.), A 9858.
[67] Ibid. 7245.
[68] Chart. R. 13 Edw. II, m. 7, no. 27 ; De Banco R. Mich. 2 Edw. III, m. 148; Wrottesley, *Ped. from Plea R.* 42.
[69] Anct. D. (P.R.O.), A 7245.
[70] Add. Chart. 14006 ; Anct. D. (P.R.O.), A 5883, 5908 ; Close, 49 Edw. III, m. 20 d. Beatrice had perhaps married John de Peyto as a second husband, as he was said to be holding the manor in 1346 (*Feud. Aids*, v, 307).
[71] Chan. Inq. p.m. 17 Ric. II, no. 6.
[72] Anct. D. (P.R.O.), A 9750.
[73] *Visit. of Warw.* (Harl. Soc. xii), 126, 131.
[74] Chan. Inq. p.m. (Ser. 2), xxxii, 21.
[75] Ibid. xix, 63.
[76] Ibid. xxxii, 21.
[77] Ibid. c, 47 ; ci, 85 ; *Visit. of Warw.* (Harl. Soc. xii), 126.

[78] Anct. D. (P.R.O.), A 12373.
[79] Ibid. 13108.
[80] Ibid. ; see also Feet of F. Worcs. Trin. 32 Eliz. ; Anct. D. (P.R.O.), A 13523 ; Recov. R. Mich. 33 Eliz. rot. 81. The Best family had been seated at Waresley since 1511 (Ct. R. [Gen. Ser.], portf. 210, no. 99 ; Ct. of Req. bdle. 122, no. 16 ; Chan. Proc. [Ser. 2], bdle. 16, no. 19 ; Ct. of Req. bdle. 55, no. 66).
[81] Habington, op. cit. i, 283.
[82] Feet of F. Worcs. Mich. 17 Jas. I.
[83] Ibid. Hil. 22 Chas. I.
[84] Ibid. Trin. 17 Chas. II ; East. 5 Will. and Mary.
[85] Recov. R. Hil. 4 Geo. III, rot. 187.
[86] Feet of F. Worcs. Mich. 58 Geo. III.
[87] op. cit. 14.
[87a] Inform. from Mr. Gainsborough Harward, and Messrs. Holloway, Blount and Duke, solicitors.

HARTLEBURY CASTLE FROM THE SOUTH-WEST

HARTLEBURY CASTLE : THE HALL

his tenure of Pepwell.[88] No other mention of the overlordship occurs.

As early as 1208 the Bishopsdon family held land here as well as in Waresley,[89] and it continued in their hands until about the end of the 14th century, when William de Bishopsdon gave it to his daughter Iseult in free marriage. After this little connexion can be made out between the successive owners. John Lench, who was attainted in 1461 and put to death 'for having followed his holy king and master Henry VI,'[90] owned a messuage and land in Pepwell.[91] In 1537 John son and heir of William 'Stapull' granted the manor to Richard Hunt for £30, part of it being then held by Elizabeth Grewell, John's grandmother.[92] John Stapleton sold it in 1538 to Henry Morgan,[93] who with his wife Agnes is known to have owned the property until 1549.[94] William Cookes had acquired it before 1595, and after his death in 1619 he was succeeded by his son Edward.[95] Prattinton, writing at the beginning of the 19th century, states that Pepwell then belonged to Mr. Glasebrook.[96]

The manor of UPPER MITTON (Mutton, xiv cent.) is in the hundred of Lower Halfshire, and is separated from the rest of the parish of Hartlebury by the River Stour. It is not mentioned by name in the Domesday Survey, but it was probably one of the six berewicks of Hartlebury, of which manor it was held until the 17th century.[97]

In 1359–60 John Sapy and his wife Isabel sold a messuage, a mill, and a carucate of land in Over Mitton to Edmund de Brugge.[98] John Lench held land at Mitton at the time of his attainder in 1461,[99] and this was granted in the following year to Sir Walter Scull.[100]

Agnes widow of John Dombleton died seised of the manor of Over Mitton in 1495.[1] Her heir and successor Margery daughter of William Dombleton was involved in the following year in a lawsuit with Richard Habington and Richard Brown as to a watermill belonging to this manor.[2] According to the Visitation of Worcester of 1569 the two plaintiffs were sons of Elizabeth or Parnell and Perino, daughters of John de Dombleton and his wife Agnes.[3] The manor of Over Mitton seems eventually to have passed to Richard Brown, for he and his wife Anna sold it in 1522 to Henry White, William Jefson, and Edward Saxilby,[4] who conveyed it three

years later to Simon Rice.[5] It then passed with Croome D'Abitot (q.v.) to Sir Francis Clare, who inherited it in 1580.[6] From that date it followed the same descent as Caldwall Hall in Kidderminster (q.v.) until 1777, when it passed with that manor from Anthony Deane to Matthew and Thomas Jeffreys.[7] Its descent after that time has not been found.

POOLLANDS FARM was leased by John Pooler from the Bishop of Worcester in 1655, when he was accused of being an adherent of the King of Scotland and his estates sequestered.[8] Evidence having been brought before the Treasury Commissions to prove the accusation groundless, his estates were restored, but four years later they were again sequestered for his complicity in Sir George Booth's rising.[9] Hugh Pooler was holding a lease of Poollands in 1664,[10] and in 1710 an Act was passed for the sale of the estate of Humphrey Pooler.[11]

There were belonging to the Bishop of Worcester[12] in this parish in 1086 two mills worth 4s. and 10 horseloads of grain yearly. They were worth £3 in 1291.[13] Eight years later one water-mill 'next the vivary' was leased by the bishop to Adam de Hartlebury and his wife Agnes.[14] This mill was known as 'Polemulne,' and there was also a fulling-mill in the manor.[15] In 1302 the water-mill was leased for 58s. and the fulling-mill for 23s.[16] In 1644 an order was issued to all commanders in the service of the king and Parliament to forbid the plunder of cloth in the fulling-mills in Hartlebury belonging to Robert Wilmot.[17] At the present day there is a corn-mill at Titton on a tributary of the Severn and another on the Stour.

The bishops had fishing rights in Hartlebury, a weir in the Severn being leased at 16s. in 1299,[18] and at 11s. 3d. in 1302.[19] There were four fishponds in the manor in 1299.[20] In 1359 Bishop Brian wrote denouncing 'certain sons of iniquity who have incurred excommunication' for entering his manor and taking away fish.[21]

The tenants of the bishop in the 16th century were allowed common pasture for their cattle on the bishop's meadow of 16 acres from Michaelmas to Candlemas, in return for which they cut and made the hay on 10 acres of the meadow without payment, the bishop supplying them with meat and drink during this work.[22]

[88] Reg. G. Giffard (Worcs. Hist. Soc.), 129.
[89] cf. Waresley. Pepwell was not among the lands of Thomas de Bishopsdon in 1386, but William de Bishopsdon had held lands here a little earlier (Anct. D. [P.R.O.], A 9750).
[90] Habington, op. cit. i, 190.
[91] Chan. Inq. p.m. 3 Edw. IV, no. 15. It is here called 'Peppwall alias Hertilbury.'
[92] Close, 29 Hen. VIII, pt. iii, no. 50.
[93] Recov. R. Hil. 30 Hen. VIII, rot. 151.
[94] Feet of F. Worcs. Hil. 3 Edw. VI.
[95] Chan. Inq. p.m. (Ser. 2), ccclxxxi, 161.
[96] Prattinton Coll. (Soc. Antiq.).
[97] Chan. Inq. p.m. (Ser. 2), cccxli, 54.
[98] Feet of F. Worcs. Mich. 33 Edw. III, no. 14.
[99] Chan. Inq. p.m. 3 Edw. IV, no. 15.
[100] Cal. Pat. 1461–7, pp. 91, 388.

[1] Cal. Inq. p.m. Hen. VII, i, 472.
[2] De Banco R. Mich. 11 Hen. VII, m. 261.
[3] Visit. of Worcs. 1569 (Harl. Soc. xxvii), 63, 13.
[4] Feet of F. Worcs. Mich. 14 Hen. VIII.
[5] Ibid. Hil. 17 Hen. VIII.
[6] Chan. Inq. p.m. (Ser. 2), lxxx, 106; cxci, 117; Feet of F. Div. Co. East. 2 Eliz.
[7] Chan. Inq. p.m. (Ser. 2), cccxli, 54; Fine R. 15 Jas. I, pt. ii, no. 37; Close, 20 Jas. I, pt. xvi, no. 4; Feet of F. Worcs. Trin. 1654; Recov. R. Trin. 1654, rot. 149; Feet of F. Worcs. Trin. 1655; Recov. R. Trin. 3 Jas. II, rot. 36; Notes of Fines Worcs. Trin. 18 Geo. III.
[8] Cal. S. P. Dom. 1655, pp. 70, 112, 160.
[9] Cal. Com. for Comp. 3250.
[10] Add. Chart. 38980. This document was evidently used as a draft for a lease to Samuel Wall in 1697.

[11] Priv. Act, 9 Anne, cap. 16.
[12] V.C.H. Worcs. i, 298.
[13] Pope Nich. Tax. (Rec. Com.), 225.
[14] Reg. G. Giffard (Worcs. Hist. Soc.), 519.
[15] Red Bk. of Bishopric of Worc. fol. 112.
[16] Mins. Accts. bdle. 1143, no. 18.
[17] Hist. MSS. Com. Rep. iv, App. i, 267.
[18] Red Bk. of Bishopric of Worc. fol. 112.
[19] Mins. Accts. bdle. 1143, no. 18.
[20] Red Bk. of Bishopric of Worc. fol. 112.
[21] Worc. Epis. Reg. Brian, xi (1), 94 d. In 1562 Thomas Burghill owned half the passage over the Severn with appurtenances in Hartlebury (Feet of F. Worcs. East. 4 Eliz.), and in 1655 Ralph Clare had free fishing in Hartlebury (Feet of F. Worcs. Trin. 1655).
[22] Rev. D. Robertson, op. cit. 216.

CHURCHES

The church of *ST. JAMES* [23] consists of a chancel, with south chapel and north organ chamber and vestry, nave with north and south aisles, continued west to form staircases to the side galleries, a western tower and a west porch. The building is almost completely modern, having been designed by Rickman in 1836, and as such is not without interest. The detail is scholarly but the general design is poor. The chancel is three bays long with open arcades to the two eastern bays. On the north side this is original early 14th-century work with pointed arches of two chamfered orders resting on piers of four half-round columns with moulded circular capitals and bases, and is the only part of the chancel not entirely modern. The arcading on the south is a modern copy. The east window is of four lights with geometrical tracery, and the moulded chancel arch has shafted jambs. The nave, of similar design, is four bays long with attenuated sandstone piers supporting two-centred moulded arches, above which is a groined and vaulted plaster ceiling. The north and south aisles are lit by five three-light windows divided horizontally by the north and south galleries. The tower is of 16th-century date and bears on a pedimented tablet the arms of Bishop Sandys and the date 1587. It is of three stages with diagonal buttresses and an embattled parapet with modern angle pinnacles. The belfry openings are of two lights under a three-centred main arch. Against the west side of the tower is a modern two-storied porch, and above the west door is a window of three lights. Only the lower part of the bowl of the font is original 12th-century work. It is circular with nail-head ornament.

The tower contains a ring of eight bells with a sanctus. The treble and second are modern, and were cast in 1900 by Mears & Stainbank of Whitechapel when the belfry was restored. The third was cast by J. Briant of Hertford in 1812, and the fourth was recast in 1900. The fifth and seventh are dated 1640, and are the work of Thomas Hancox, the latter bearing the inscription in Roman capitals 'Master Eyre the coroner gave to this bell thirty pounds.' The sixth is an interesting mediaeval bell by a 16th-century Worcester founder, and bears the inscription in Lombardic capitals 'SANCTA MARIA VIRGO INTERCEDE PRO TOTO MUNDO QVEYA (*sic*) GENVISTI REGEM ORBIS.' The eighth was cast by Abraham Rudhall in 1704, and the sanctus bears the churchwardens' names and the date 1678.

The plate consists of a set presented by William Lloyd, Bishop of Worcester, and Ann his wife, 1714, having been made in the previous year. The set comprises two cups, one handle paten and one flat paten, two flagons and an almsdish, all silver gilt.

The registers are as follows : (i) mixed entries from 1540 to 1754 with gaps 1553 to 1560 and 1672 to 1673 ; (ii) baptisms and burials 1755 to 1787 ; (iii) baptisms and burials 1788 to 1812 ; (iv) marriages 1754 to 1803 ; (v) marriages 1803 to 1812.

The church of *ALL SAINTS* at Wilden was built in 1879 by the late Mr. Alfred Baldwin as a chapel of ease to St. Michael, Stourport. It consists of chancel, nave, organ chamber, south porch and western bell-turret. Wilden was constituted a separate ecclesiastical parish in 1904, the living being a vicarage in the gift of Mr. Stanley Baldwin.

The Mission Church of *ST. MARY*, Bishop's Wood, was presented to the parish by Bishop Philpott, who opened it in 1882. It is built in the half-timbered style of the surrounding houses, on a beautiful site overlooking the Severn. Bishop Philpott was buried in the churchyard, which was added in 1892. Archdeacon Lea presented a little silver cup said to be of 1571 for use in this church. [24]

There is a church mission room at Summerfield.

ADVOWSON

A priest at Hartlebury is mentioned in 1086, [25] and the church was granted by Bishop Samson in 1097 to the monks of Worcester with a hide of land and the tithes. [26] In 1148 Bishop Simon confirmed to them the church with a chapel and lands belonging. [27] Bishop Giffard consecrated a church at Hartlebury in honour of St. James the Apostle in 1269. [28] Wishing to enrich the college of Westbury-on-Trym Giffard tried to appropriate the rectory of Hartlebury to it, [29] and for a short time Hartlebury became a vicarage, the rector presenting a vicar in 1280. [30] On account of the expostulations of the monks of Worcester the bishop revoked the appropriation, and in 1290 he presented John de Rodeberewe [31] to the church, having previously given it to him as a prebend of Westbury. [32] The advowson of the church of Hartlebury has belonged from that time to the Bishops of Worcester. [33]

The living of Hartlebury was a peculiar, the rector holding concurrent jurisdiction with the chancellor in proving wills and granting administrations. It was visited by the bishop triennially, the other two years by the rector of Hartlebury. [34]

In 1291 the church of Hartlebury was valued at £20, [35] and at 30 marks in the 14th century. [36] In 1535 the rectory was valued at £30. [37] At this time the rector of Hartlebury received from the rectory of Elmley Lovett 20s. 6d. and from the rectory of Doverdale 2s. [38] The rector of Hartlebury sued the

[23] It is also apparently referred to as the church of St. Mary the Virgin (see 'Advowson').

[24] Rev. D. Robertson, op. cit. 223. Archdeacon Lea obtained this cup from a house in Droitwich, but it seems to have come originally from Gloucestershire.

[25] *V.C.H. Worcs.* i, 298.

[26] Heming, op. cit. 391, 426 ; Dugdale, *Mon. Angl.* i, 572. This was probably the hide of land called Herdewicha which Roger Bishop of Worcester (1164–79) recognized as the demesne of the church of Hartlebury. Absalon, who had held it, gave it to Ralph, Prior of Worcester, who restored it to him for life at a rent of

6d. (Prattinton Coll.). In 1274 Adam son of Absalon released his claim in this hide of land to the parson of Hartlebury (Feet of .F. Worcs. 3 Edw. I, no. 55), but in 1299 Elias Absalon still held a hide of land at Hartlebury (Red Bk. of Bishopric of Worc. fol. 112).

[27] Thomas, op. cit. App. no. 18.

[28] *Reg. G. Giffard* (Worcs. Hist. Soc.), 28.

[29] Ibid. 492.

[30] Ibid. 123.

[31] This John de Rodeberewe was a person of considerable importance, being appointed as the bishop's official to act as his representative and hear causes in the

Consistory Court. He was also appointed one of Bishop Giffard's executors (*Reg. W. Ginsborough* [Worcs. Hist. Soc.], 25, 29, 60).

[32] *Reg. G. Giffard* (Worcs. Hist. Soc.), 370.

[33] *Cal. Pat.* 1313–17, p. 648 ; 1385–9, p. 219 ; Inst. Bks. (P.R.O.).

[34] *Valor Eccl.* (Rec. Com.), iii, 512.

[35] *Pope Nich. Tax.* (Rec. Com.), 217.

[36] *Inq. Nonarum* (Rec. Com.), 295.

[37] *Valor Eccl.* (Rec. Com.), iii, 274.

[38] Ibid. 274, 275.

HARTLEBURY CHURCH : THE NAVE LOOKING EAST

HARVINGTON CHURCH : THE NAVE LOOKING WEST

rector of Doverdale in 1450 for this latter sum, which he claimed had been paid from time immemorial.[39] Bishop Simon in the 12th century granted all tithes of hay in his vill of Hartlebury to the use of the monks and for hospitality.[40] These tithes were said in 1303 to be worth 16*s*.[41] A rent of £1 6*s*. 8*d*. was paid to the monks of Worcester out of the rectory of Hartlebury in 1291,[42] and in 1542 Henry VIII granted this rent to the Dean and Chapter of Worcester.[43] This gift was confirmed by James I.[44]

A chantry dedicated to St. Mary the Virgin was founded in the church of St. Mary the Virgin of Hartlebury in 1323 by Richard Mayel for the souls of John de Rodeberewe[45] and his father and mother and all the faithful departed, certain lands in Waresley 'Wetelyng' (?Whitlench), Stone, Shenston, Walton and Lychmor being granted to a chaplain to celebrate daily service there.[46] In 1337 Richard Mayel and Maud, formerly wife of Alexander D'Abitot, presented the chantry priest,[47] but before 1457 the patronage had devolved upon the bishop.[48] The chantry is mentioned again in 1472,[49] but appears to have been dissolved before 1549, its revenues having, perhaps, been granted before that time to Hartlebury School, for among the property of the governors of the school are Chantry Meadow and the meadow of St. Mary.[50] Kenrick Watson, writing in 1839, states that in the churchyard under an arch in the wall of that part of the church which was formerly called St. Mary's chantry was a monument of John de Rodeberewe, but that the monument was destroyed when the old church was taken down.[50a] It is uncertain whether this chantry was the same as the chantry of Waresley to which the bishop presented in 1362.[51]

In 1548 there was an obit in the parish maintained by the rent of a piece of meadow then worth 1*s*. 6*d*.,[52]

and in 1638 Charles I granted to Sir Edward Sawyer a meadow called Netherton in the parish of Kidderminster, which had been given for obits in Hartlebury Church.[53]

Upper Mitton, part of the benefice of Hartlebury, was transferred to Lower Mitton in 1877.[54]

The Congregationalists have a mission chapel at Crossway Green in connexion with Baxter Chapel, Kidderminster, erected in 1860, and there is a Baptist chapel at Upper Mitton.

CHARITIES The Free Grammar School and charity of Mrs. Hannah Eyre for education.[55]

In 1634 Samuel Manninge, by will proved at Worcester, gave a close of land to the poor. The trust property consists of about 5 a. in St. Peter, Droitwich, producing £10 yearly, which is distributed in sums of 4*s*. each to poor widows.

The Almshouse Charity—as recorded on the table of benefactions—about 2 a. of land with two cottages thereon in the manor of Waresley were appropriated to the use of the poor. The property is let at £11 6*s*. a year, which is also distributed in sums of 4*s*. each to poor widows.

In 1821 William Hyde by will left a legacy of £400, now represented by £430 13*s*. 8*d*. consols with the official trustees, the annual dividends of which, amounting to £10 15*s*. 4*d*., are applied as to £2 5*s*. to the bell-ringers for ringing peals on the anniversary of testator's birth, 10*s*. to the parish clerk and 2*s*. to the sexton for attending to the grave of testator's mother, the residue being distributed in bread.

In 1874 Mary Hurst by deed gave a sum of £50 for coals for the poor. It was invested in £53 16*s*. 6*d*. consols with the official trustees, producing £1 6*s*. 8*d*. yearly.

HARVINGTON

Herefortune, Hereforda (ix cent.) ; Herefordtun-juxta-Avene (x cent.) ; Herferthun (xi cent.) ; Herfortune (xii cent.) ; Hervertun (xiii cent.) ; Hervyngton (xv cent.).

The parish of Harvington lies on the eastern boundary of the county. It is divided from Warwickshire by a tributary of the River Avon,[1] forming the greater part of the eastern and northern boundaries of the parish. The Avon itself bounds it on the south and east, while one of its tributaries, flowing south-east, forms the western boundary. There is a ferry across the Avon in the extreme south of the parish.

The area of Harvington is 1,310 acres,[2] of which 780 are arable, 383 permanent grass and 2 acres are

woodland.[3] The village of Harvington stands at a height of some 100 ft. to 150 ft. above the ordnance datum. To the north-west the land rises slightly, attaining near the northern border a height of 200 ft. The soil is sand, with a subsoil of gravel and Keuper Marl, and the chief crops are wheat, barley and beans.

Harvington village spreads over a series of steep and irregular slopes, the houses being scattered along several by-roads. The roads run between banks and hedges, and the country is wooded close to the village.[4] The church stands prominently on a ridge at the meeting of three roads, the rectory in wooded ground on the west at the foot of the hill. In the village are several houses of 15th and 16th-century date, the half-timber work being well preserved.

[39] Worcs. Epis. Reg. Carpenter, i, fol. 84.

[40] Heming, op. cit. 533.

[41] *Reg. W. Ginsborough* (Worcs. Hist. Soc.), 35.

[42] *Pope Nich. Tax.* (Rec. Com.), 217.

[43] Pat. 33 Hen. VIII, pt. v ; *Valor Eccl.* (Rec. Com.), iii, 225, 275.

[44] Pat. 6 Jas. I, pt. xii, no. 2.

[45] Rector of Hartlebury (see above).

[46] Inq. a.q.d. file 157, no. 7 ; *Cal. Pat.* 1321-4, p. 296. Mr. Watson states that John de Rodeberewe died in 1290, but he

is known to have been alive in 1306 (*Reg. W. Ginsborough* [Worcs. Hist. Soc.], 29, 60).

[47] Worc. Epis. Reg. Montagu (1333-7), fol. 27 d.

[48] Ibid. Carpenter, i, fol. 142.

[49] Ibid. ii, fol. 29 d.

[50] Rev. D. Robertson, op. cit. 224.

[50a] K. Watson, op. cit. 25.

[51] Worc. Epis. Reg. Barnet (1362-3), fol. 22 d.

[52] Chant. Cert. 60, no. 53.

[53] Pat. 14 Chas. I, pt. vii.

[54] *Lond. Gaz.* 22 June 1877, p. 3785.

[55] See 'Schools,' *V.C.H. Worcs.* iv.

[1] Perhaps the Noryebroc of the 13th century (Prattinton Coll. [Soc. Antiq.], Deeds of D. and C. of Worc. no. 254).

[2] Of which 12 are covered by water.

[3] Statistics from Bd. of Agric. (1905).

[4] The wood called Longlands to the south-east of the village existed under that name in the 13th century (Prattinton Coll. [Soc. Antiq.], Deeds of D. and C. of Worc. no. 254). In 1224 Harvington among other of the new forests of England was disafforested (*Ann. Mon.* [Rolls Ser.], iv, 417).

Adjoining the churchyard on the south-east is Harvington Manor, a fine two-storied house of stone and half-timber, dating in part from the 14th century, but much altered by the insertion, probably in the 17th century, of new floors and partitions. The floors throughout appear to be hung up by iron straps to the tie-beams of the roof principals. The original arrangement of the plan seems to have consisted of a large open hall on the north with a two-storied block of buildings on the south. The position of the original screens is marked by a passage across the house, and the present door on the east is a later opening. The walls of the ground story are of stone-rubble masonry, the first floor being of half-timber construction. The roof is covered with stone slates. Two of the original window openings with their moulded oak mullions still remain. The entrance doorway at the north-east of the original hall still retains its moulded frame and door of oak. To the north of the entrance is a central newel stair, probably of later date, leading to the loft over this portion of the house. A little to the north of the house, imme-

observed at Harvington ; the children used to go round to all the houses on St. Thomas's Day and St. Valentine's Day repeating a doggerel rhyme as follows [5]: —

'Wissal, wassail, through the town,
  If you've got any apples throw them down,
  Up with the stocking and down with the shoe,
  If you've got no apples money will do.'

An Inclosure Act for Harvington was passed in 1786,[6] and the award is dated 19 March 1787.[7]

Thomas James, head master of Rugby School, was presented in 1797 to the rectory of Harvington, where he died in 1804.[8]

A bronze celt was found in the ditch which divides Harvington from Warwickshire.[9]

The following place-names occur in the 17th century : Harfordes, Mowes, the Meere, Hingle, Bitton, Portway Peece, Haynes Close, and Sherrowes.[10] Wistanes Brycge, Heopanhylle, Hunighommesstreote, Caersawealla are places mentioned on the boundaries of Harvington in an Anglo-Saxon charter.[11]

THE MANOR HOUSE, HARVINGTON

diately adjoining the churchyard on the east, is a fine pigeon-house of rubble masonry lined internally with stone cells and having a ridge roof covered externally with stone slates. This is probably contemporary with the house, and is an extremely fine example. In the garden of the rectory, an old house with modern additions, are portions of early 14th-century tracery, removed from the east window of the church at the time of its restoration.

The village contains a reading room, opened in 1887.

There is a wharf on the Avon and to the north of the village a disused gravel-pit. There is a sand-pit in the north-west of the parish.

In 1868 there was a curious old custom still

MANOR

In 799 Balthun Abbot of Kempsey gave to King Coenwulf of Mercia, in return for privileges for his house, 12 'manentes' at 'Hereford.' [11a] At the beginning of the 9th century Deneberht, Bishop of Worcester (798–822), gave 2 cassates of land at *HARVINGTON* to Eanswyth for her life on condition that if she survived him it should pass to the church of Worcester after her death.[12] Harvington is included in King Edgar's spurious charter of 964, granting the hundred of 'Oswaldslow to the church[13] of Worcester. At the date of the Domesday Survey Harvington, which then included Wiburgestoke, was held by the monks of Worcester.[14] In 1207 they let it at a farm of 24 marks and 12 quarters of oats to the men of the

[5] *Worcs. Nat. Club Trans.* (1847–96), 268–9.
[6] Priv. Act, 26 Geo. III, cap. 23.
[7] *Blue Bk. Incl. Awards,* 190.
[8] *Dict. Nat. Biog.*
[9] *V.C.H. Worcs.* i, 193.
[10] Close, 1652, pt. xv, no. 19.
[11] Heming, *Chartul.* (ed. Hearne), 347.
[11a] Birch, *Cart. Sax.* i, 411–12. Mr.

F. M. Stenton identifies 'Hereford' with Harvington.
[12] Kemble, *Cod. Dipl.* i, no. 182 ; Birch, *Cart. Sax.* i, 426 ; Heming, op. cit. 330, 572.
[13] Heming, op. cit. 520 ; Birch, op. cit. iii, 379 ; Kemble, op. cit. ii, no. 514. The Saxon boundaries of the manor are given in the chartulary of Heming, p. 347.

[14] *V.C.H. Worcs.* i, 295*b*. Heming mentions a charter of 852, by which King Berthulf granted 3 *cassates* of land in Werburge or Werburghstoce to his faithful thegn Edgar (op. cit. pp. 567, 584). This land evidently passed to the church of Worcester, as this grant is found among the charters of the monastery.

vill for twelve years.[15] This lease was renewed in 1230 for ten years.[16] In 1240 the annual money rents from the manor amounted to £2 14s. 10d.[17] In 1254 the prior leased the manor to Simon de Wauton, afterwards Bishop of Norwich.[18]

At about this time John D'Abitot made an exchange with the monks of Worcester of 4 acres of land for a part of a messuage in Harvington, and a case[19] in which this John appears was taken at the Worcester Eyre of 1254. Roger de Pershore and Marchia his wife complained to the judges that on the Thursday before St. Peter ad Vincula last certain strangers had stolen away Maud their daughter and abandoned her at Harvington, where John D'Abitot kept her at his house against her will. John D'Abitot, however, denied any fault of his. On the Thursday he was leaving his courtyard at Harvington, when he heard a great noise, and on looking for the cause beheld a monk and some Welshmen dragging along an unwilling girl who made a great outcry. Seeing D'Abitot her captors fled and she, left alone, begged him for shelter. This he willingly gave her till she could return to her own friends. The girl confirmed the story ; so the parents, who had sued the rescuer for 100s., went disappointed away.

In the Taxation of 1291 Harvington was included with Cleeve Prior.[20] After the dissolution of the priory in 1540[21] the manor of Harvington was granted to the Dean and Chapter of Worcester in 1542,[22] and was confirmed to them in 1609.[23] On 23 June 1641 they granted it to Kempe Harward for three lives, but in 1652 the commissioners for the sale of the dean and chapter lands sold it to Thomas Bound.[24] He still held in 1658,[25] but at the Restoration the manor was recovered by the dean and chapter,[26] and remained with them until 1859,[27] when it was taken over by the Ecclesiastical Commissioners. In 1862 the commissioners sold to the trustees of the Duc D'Aumale the reversion of certain leasehold land and the lord's interest in some copyhold land and a fishery in the Avon.[28] This estate has since passed with Bishampton Manor (q.v.) to Sir Charles Swinfen Eady.

At the date of the Domesday Survey there was a mill at Harvington which was worth 10s. a year.[29] This mill was granted by David, Prior of Worcester (1143–5), to William Rupe at a yearly rent of 17s. and 30 'stiches' of eels,[30] and in 1212 was the subject of a lawsuit between Thomas Rupe and his wife Joan and Richard and Hugh Sandford and their wives Maud and Olivia. It was finally settled by Thomas Rupe acknowledging the right of the Sandfords to the mill, while they yielded to him certain lands which were part of his mother's dowry.[31] In

1294–5 an agreement was made between William Lench and Alice his wife, on the one hand, and Henry de Chester, John his son and Henry Austyn on the other,[32] concerning mills in Harvington, which may have been those acquired by the prior and convent from Henry Austyn of Sandford in 1311.[33] After the dissolution of the priory both these mills passed to the dean and chapter, who sold them to George Willoughby in 1549–50.[34] In 1818 corn-mills at Harvington were advertised for sale, a paper-mill there being at that time held under a lease for thirty years by a Mr. Phillips.[35] There is still a mill in the parish to the south of the village, and near it is a weir which is said to have been repaired with fragments and even some of the statues from Evesham Abbey.[36]

The church of *ST. JAMES* consists
CHURCH of a chancel measuring internally 32 ft. by 20½ ft., south vestry, nave 25 ft. by 40 ft., north porch, and west tower 9 ft. by 9½ ft. The earliest existing remains belong to the 12th century or earlier, and the church at that date was considerably smaller than the present building, the nave being about 16 ft. wide. The extreme height of the early nave, the west wall of which is still clearly visible, would even suggest a pre-Conquest date, but the earliest detail, that of the tower (which has been rebuilt in recent years), is of the first quarter of the 12th century. Early in the 14th century the whole church was rebuilt, with the exception of the tower, and enlarged to its present dimensions. The east window was replaced by a modern one at a recent restoration, and the tower was largely restored and crowned with a modern timber spire.

The three-light east window is modern, replacing a 14th-century window, the remains of which are in the vicarage garden. On either side of the chancel are three single-light windows, of 14th-century date, with trefoiled heads. At the east end of the south wall is a curious 14th-century piscina with a trefoiled head and an abnormal development of the cusps into a thin stone shelf. There is no sedile, but the sill of the south-east window was originally carried down to form a seat. The north door to the chancel and the pointed chancel arch of two chamfered orders both date from the 14th century.

In the east wall of the nave is a small image bracket and at the east end of both north and south walls appear the sockets for the rood beam. The nave is lit by four 14th-century windows, each of two lights with traceried heads, and though all are of similar detail the eastern one in the south wall is of notably

[15] *Ann. Mon.* (Rolls Ser.), iv, 396.
[16] Ibid. 422.
[17] Hale, *Reg. Worc. Priory* (Camd. Soc.), p. vii.
[18] *Ann. Mon.* (Rolls Ser.), iv, 442.
[19] Assize R. 1022, m. 17 (39 Hen. III).
[20] *Pope Nich. Tax.* (Rec. Com.), 227b. In 1311 the prior purchased 6 acres from William le Chaplain (*Cal. Pat.* 1307–13, p. 338). John de Bransford made several grants of land in Harvington to the priory in the early years of the reign of Edward III (Inq. a.q.d. files 195, no. 10 ; 205, no. 26 ; 228, no. 23 ; 215, no. 9).
[21] *V.C.H. Worcs.* ii, 111. Harvington Manor at this time was valued at

£28 11s. 2d. yearly (*Valor Eccl.* [Rec. Com.], iii, 222).
[22] *L. and P. Hen. VIII*, xvii, g. 71 (29) ; Pat. 33 Hen. VIII, pt. v.
[23] Pat. 6 Jas. I, pt. xii, no. 2.
[24] Close, 1652, pt. xv, no. 19. The sale included the site of the manor and free warren (ibid.). The manor was charged with a yearly rent of £3 6s. 8d. payable towards the maintenance of the Free Grammar School at Worcester, for which Thomas Bound was allowed £77 10s. on condition that he continued to pay it. [25] Feet of F. Worcs. Hil. 1658.
[26] Pat. 4 Will. and Mary, pt. i, no. 6.
[27] *Lond. Gaz.* 16 Dec. 1859, p. 4757 ; confirmed by Stat. 31 Vict. cap. 19.

[28] Inform. supplied by the Ecclesiastical Commissioners.
[29] *V.C.H. Worcs.* i, 295b.
[30] *Abbrev. Plac.* (Rec. Com.), 84b ; Hale, op. cit. 63a.
[31] *Abbrev. Plac.* (Rec. Com.), 87b.
[32] Anct. D. (P.R.O.), B 4025.
[33] Inq. a.q.d. file 83, no. 4 ; *Cal. Pat.* 1307–13, p. 338 ; see also Prattinton Coll. (Soc. Antiq.), Deeds of D. and C. of Worc. no. 51.
[34] Pat. 3 Edw. VI, pt. ix. The Willoughbys also owned a free fishery at Harvington (Feet of F. Worcs. Mich. 28 & 29 Eliz.).
[35] Prattinton Coll. (Soc. Antiq.).
[36] Ibid.

finer design. There are 14th-century north and south doors to the nave, the latter blocked, with chamfered jambs and heads and labels with curiously mitred drips. The north porch is modern. The circular tub-font at the west end of the nave is of doubtful date. The west wall of the nave bears clear traces of the earlier church, the line of the nave walls and the pitch of the roof being quite distinct. There is also a blocked-up square door which must originally have opened on to a western gallery and above this is a small round-headed window, originally external.

The door between tower and nave is of late 12th-century date with a plain slightly pointed arch of two square orders and chamfered capitals. The early 12th-century west window is a single deeply splayed light with a round head. The original belfry windows

HARVINGTON CHURCH : WEST TOWER

in the second stage of the tower are of two round-headed lights, the mullion taking the form of a column. The broach spire, added in 1855, is covered with oak shingles. On the west wall of the nave are two monuments, to Thomas Ferriman, who died in 1619, and to Thomas his son, both rectors of the church.

The belfry contains a peal of tubular bells.

The plate consists of a chalice without marks, of late 17th-century design, a plated salver and a pewter flagon.

The registers before 1812 are as follows : (i) baptisms from 1573 to 1733, burials 1570 to 1731, marriages 1570 to 1729 (1633 to 1660 missing) ; (ii) baptisms from 1653 to 1690, burials 1653 to 1687, marriages 1678 to 1687 in a dilapidated minute book ; (iii) baptisms and burials from 1734 to 1812, marriages 1734 to 1752 ; (iv) marriages from 1755 to 1812.

There is a Baptist chapel in the parish with 160 sittings, erected in 1886.

ADVOWSON According to the register of Worcester Priory, Deneberht, Bishop of Worcester, gave the church of Harvington to the priory at the same time as he gave the manor.[37]

The prior and convent were the patrons until the Dissolution.[38] After the dissolution of the priory the advowson was granted to the Dean and Chapter of Worcester in 1542[39] and confirmed to them in 1609.[40] The dean and chapter have made the presentations[41] ever since, and are still the patrons of the church of Harvington.

A cottage at Harvington given for the maintenance of lights in the church was valued at 3s. 4d. at the time of the dissolution of the chantries.[42]

CHARITIES The eleemosynary charities are regulated by a scheme of the Charity Commissioners 6 May 1884. They comprise the charities of (1) William Chaunce[43] and others, trust fund, £120 consols, representing the gifts of various donors mentioned on the church table ; (2) Mrs. Lydia Ward, gift in 1841, trust fund, £22 7s. 4d. consols, and (3) Mrs. John Marshall, gift in 1857, trust fund, £26 18s. 7d. consols. The several sums of stock are held by the official trustees, producing £4 4s. 8d. yearly, of which in 1909 £2 4s. 8d. was distributed in coal and £2 was paid as bonuses to clothing and boot clubs.

In 1887 the Rev. Arthur Henry Winnington-Ingram, by his will proved at London 16 April, bequeathed £100, now £100 consols, with the official trustees, the annual dividend of £2 10s. to be applied in memory of Mrs. Winnington-Ingram in adornment of the churchyard with trees, shrubs and flowers and in maintaining the churchyard in beautiful order.

A reading room with site was by deed dated 3 September 1887 conveyed to trustees by Mrs. Winnington-Ingram in memory of her husband, the Rev. Arthur Henry Winnington-Ingram, for the use of the parishioners.

[37] Hale, *Reg. Worc. Priory* (Camd. Soc.), 60a.
[38] *Reg. G. Giffard* (Worcs. Hist. Soc.), 120, 128 ; *Sede Vac. Reg.* (Worcs. Hist. Soc.), 141, 361.
[39] *L. and P. Hen. VIII*, xvii, g. 71 (29); Pat. 33 Hen. VIII, pt. v.

[40] Pat. 6 Jas. I, pt. xii, no. 2.
[41] Inst. Bks. (P.R.O.). In 1619, to corroborate a presentation, and in 1677, by a lapse, the Crown presented. After the Restoration of 1660 Stephen Baxter, the rector of Harvington, was ejected. 'He was one of a solid understanding,

and a calm peaceable spirit. After he was silenced, he practis'd Physick' (Edmund Calamy, *Account of Ministers Ejected* [ed. 1713], ii, 770).
[42] Chant. Cert. 60, no. 45.
[43] This name is incorrectly given as Clarke on the table.

HIMBLETON

Hymeltun (ix cent.) ; Hymeton (x cent.) ; Humeton (xiii cent.) ; Hemelton (xiv cent.) ; Humilton (xvi cent.).

Himbleton parish is watered in the north by Dean Brook, a tributary of Bow Brook, which it joins in the hamlet of Shell. Another tributary of Bow Brook called Little Brook forms part of the southern boundary. Bow Brook itself passes through the village of Himbleton, and Habington says of this parish, 'She is well watered yf not to muche in winter.'[1] The parish is low in the valleys of these brooks, Neight Hill to the south-east of the village being the highest point, about 190 ft. above the ordnance datum.

The area of the parish is 2,373 acres,[2] of which 631 are arable, 1,302 permanent grass and 133 woods.[3] The soil is principally clay on the Lower Lias formation, and the chief crops are wheat, beans and barley.

An Inclosure Act for Himbleton was passed in 1779,[4] and the award is dated December 1780.[5]

The village of Himbleton lies about 5 miles south-east of Droitwich and 7½ miles north-east of Worcester. The village, though a small one, is particularly rich in examples of half-timber work of the 16th and 17th centuries. Of these the finest is Shell Manor Farm, which stands about a mile to the north of the church, by the side of Bow Brook, and is approached by a ford, with a stone footbridge. Roughly the plan resembles an H, and consists of a central entrance hall facing south with rooms on either side of it, the eastern limb of the plan projecting considerably further northward than that on the west. The house is half-timbered and two stories high with wattle and daub filling, the sills resting on a plinth of local limestone. It appears to date from the 16th century, but there is a brick addition of the 19th century at the north end of the east wing. The ground floor of the west wing is divided into a larger and a smaller room by an original stud partition with a four-centred doorway, now blocked, in the centre. The walls of the former room are lined with early 17th-century panelling, having a well-carved frieze ; panelling of similar date and character exists in the room above. The original entrance doorway at the south-east of the hall has been blocked,

but the early 17th-century porch remains untouched. The posts and head of the outer doorway are ogee-moulded, and the room above is brought slightly forward, the sill being supported by plain console brackets. The interior has been entirely modernized, and the present entrance and stairs are in the east wing. The lower portions of the chimney stacks on the north and east are of rubble masonry, and are surmounted by fine brick shafts, those on the east being formed by the intersection of two squares, while those on the north are plain diagonal shafts. The chimney stack on the west side of the house is more elaborate. The base is of ashlar work surmounted by a capping of brick, with gablets at the angles, above which rise two diagonal shafts of the same material. The roof timbers of this wing have arched braces, and generally there is more elaboration on this side, which probably included

SHELL MANOR FARM, HIMBLETON

the private apartments, while the kitchen and offices were on the opposite side of the hall, beneath which portion there is a cellar. The half-timbered front of the house with its tiled roof, flanked by the two gabled wings, is extremely picturesque. Of the farm buildings the weather-boarded barn on the east of the forecourt appears to be contemporary in date with the house.

Court Farm, standing to the west of the church in Himbleton itself, is an L-shaped two-storied half-timber house of very similar arrangement, and appears to date entirely from the late 16th century. The entrance porch is of three stories, the attic gabled and windowless. A new entrance and stairs have been constructed on the east of the original hall. A cellar exists beneath this portion of the house, with walls of rubble masonry. Brook Farm, also of half timber and of similar date, has a fine projecting gable, supported by richly carved console brackets.

[1] *Surv. of Worc.* (Worcs. Hist. Soc.), i, 285.

[2] 10 acres are covered by water.
[3] Statistics from Bd. of Agric. (1905).

[4] Priv. Act, 19 Geo. III, cap. 31.
[5] *Blue Bk. Incl. Awards*, 190.

The Manor Farm, now divided into two cottages and known as the Church Cottages, is another half-timbered house, with a large pigeon-house of the same material. Until lately there was a pair of handsome chimneys of triangular section, but these, though not dilapidated, have been pulled down. To the east of the village stands Himbleton Manor, formerly the residence of the late Sir Douglas Galton, K.C.B., and now occupied by his daughter Mrs. Gascoigne.

The hamlet of Dunhampstead is partly in Oddingley. A moat still existed on the site of the ancient manor-house in 1865, when Himbleton was visited by the Worcester Naturalists' Club,[6] but it now seems to have disappeared. Shernal Green is a hamlet to the extreme north-west, and Phepson and Shell[7] are in the north of the parish. Earl's Common is a hamlet to the east of the village, and near it

COURT FARM, HIMBLETON

are several woods, the largest of which are Harnil Wood, Saldon Wood, Rabbit Wood, Bossil Wood, and King's Wood.

Lime-burning is carried on to some extent in the

parish,[8] but there are no traces of the coal mines said to have been worked here in the 17th century. In 1868 and at the present day glove-sewing employs some of the female population.[9] In 1744 the house of Thomas Baker was licensed for Baptists,[10] but there is no Dissenting chapel there now.

A considerable quantity of Roman pottery was found in a limestone quarry in 1865,[11] and at the same place some prehistoric implements made from the horns of red deer were discovered.

Places mentioned as being on the boundary of Himbleton in the 9th century are Egcbrihtingethyrne, Scipenelea, Maigdenbrycge, Bercrofte, Cestergeate, Ceasterwege, Langenleage, Deorleage, Midlestanwicwege,[12] Baddon Aesc, Wadlege, Ennanpol, Wynnastigele, Lytlanbrook, Hymelbroc, Henruc,[13] Blacanpyt, Aescbed, Biscespeswuda, Ealdandic, Maerford, Ipwaelhylle.[14]

Seventeenth-century names are Puckhill, Finch Grove, Quarter Grove, Ansells, Dunnam Grove, Harnell, Great and Little Moone Shaft, Nether Held, Fower Men's Coppice, Nynteene Lands, Alcott Wood, Oaken Vallett Coppice, Fursale Coppice, Light Grove Coppice,[15] Court Orchard, Oldberry, Wallsett, Stocking.[16]

MANORS According to the Register of Worcester Priory, Coenwulf, King of Mercia, gave HIMBLETON to the church of Worcester at the beginning of the 9th century.[17] This statement probably refers, however, to a charter of Coenwulf dated 816, by which he freed this among other estates from all royal exactions except the building of strongholds and bridges and military service,[18] and from this it would seem that the manor had been given to the church prior to 816. By a charter dated 884 Ethelred Ealdorman (dux) of Mercia granted the land of five 'manentes' at Himbleton to Ethelwulf, making it free of tribute.[19] This land probably passed afterwards to the church of Worcester, for in 975–6 Archbishop Oswald[20] demised a hide of land at Himbleton to his servant Wulfgeat for two lives.[21] According to the historian of Worcester Priory, Himbleton was among the lands alienated by Bishop Brihteah (1033–8). He gave it to his brother Aethelric or Alric, who was, however, deprived of it by Earl William of Hereford, 'so that,' continues the historian, 'the possession is up till now alienated from the church.'[22] This story is to some extent substantiated by the fact that Aethelric had held Himbleton in the time of King Edward, but in 1086 Roger de Lacy, who then held the manor, did service for it to the monks at their manor of

[6] *Worc. Naturalists' Club Trans.* i, 96.

[7] In the *Census Returns* of 1831 Shell was returned as a hamlet of Himbleton, but it then claimed to be extra-parochial (op. cit. ii, 719). In 1884 it was annexed to the parish of Himbleton (ibid. 1891, ii, 657). Its claim to be extra-parochial may have originated in the action of William de Valence, who was said in 1275–6 to have appropriated Morton and Shell to his liberty of Newbury (*Hund. R.* [Rec. Com.], ii, 284). The chapel of Shell was annexed to the church of Hanbury. In 1325 there seems to have been some doubt as to this, and an inquisition

was taken to find out the truth (Worc. Epis. Reg. Cobham [1317–27], fol. 104).

[8] In 1865 some fossilized remains of the Ichthyosaurus were found in a limestone quarry at Himbleton (*Worcs. Naturalists' Club Trans.* i, 97).

[9] Noake, *Guide to Worcs.* 200–1.

[10] Ibid. 201.

[11] *V.C.H. Worcs.* i, 219; *Worcs. Naturalists' Club Trans.* i, 97.

[12] Nash, *Hist. of Worcs.* ii, App. 52; Heming, *Chartul.* (ed. Hearne), 355.

[13] Nash, loc. cit.; Heming, op. cit. 356. [14] Birch, *Cart. Sax.* ii, 175.

[15] Close, 1651, pt. liii, no. 18.

[16] Ibid. 1650, pt. xxxviii, no. 14.

[17] op. cit. (Camden Soc.), 55b; *Ann. Mon.* (Rolls Ser.), iv, 367.

[18] Heming, op. cit. 337.

[19] Ibid. 593–4; Birch, op. cit. ii, 174. This charter, in which the bounds of Himbleton are given, was issued at Risborough, co. Bucks. Dugdale quotes a statement that 'Earedus' and his wife Tunthrytha gave Himbleton and Dunhampstead to the church of Worcester in 896 (*Mon. Angl.* i, 609).

[20] Oswald Bishop of Worcester became Archbishop of York in 972.

[21] Heming, op. cit. i, 151; Thomas, *Surv. of Worc. Cath.* A. 44.

[22] Heming, op. cit. 266.

Hallow.[23] Himbleton was then waste, and, together with Spetchley, was assigned to the support of the monks.[24]

Roger de Lacy still held the manor at the beginning of the 12th century,[25] but his descendant Hugh de Lacy lost it before the time of Henry II, for it was then stated that Hugh ought to hold of the Bishop of Worcester 3½ hides of land in Himbleton and Spetchley, which Roger de Lacy anciently held, but that Hugh Poer then held them of Walter de 'Marine.'[26] This Walter de 'Marine' was evidently Walter de Meduana, who was said in a survey of about the same date to be holding Himbleton and Spetchley in right of his wife Cecily late Countess of Hereford, evidently by grant of Hugh Poer, who stated that he acquitted Walter against the Bishop of Worcester for the service of one knight's fee.[27]

Isnard Parler is said to have held half the vill of Himbleton in the time of Henry I,[28] and with his wife Emma to have bestowed it upon the monastery of Worcester,[29] but this hardly agrees with a charter of Brian de Brompton and his wife Margery, by which they gave to the church of Worcester their part of Himbleton which Isnard and Emma had bequeathed to them, reserving to themselves a rent of 3s. yearly during their lives. William son of Guy de Offern grandson of Isnard confirmed this grant, which was also ratified by Hugh Poer, who claimed some interest in the land, evidently as overlord, by descent from his grandfather Walter Poer.[30]

The monks of Worcester were holding 2 carucates of land at Himbleton in 1240 and 1291,[31] and in 1248 the king granted that 3½ acres of assarted land there in the metes of Feckenham Forest should be held rent free by the prior and convent.[32] In 1378–9 the prior leased the manor to William Hull for a term of thirty years at a yearly rent of £14 2s. 8d.[33] It remained in the possession of the prior and convent until the dissolution of the priory in 1539–40.[34] It was granted in 1542 to the Dean and Chapter of Worcester,[35] with whom it continued until sold in 1654 by order of the Parliament, described by Prattinton as 'that ever infamous and destructive Parliament and great enemy to all Hierarchy order and decency in church and state.'[36] It was purchased by Nicholas Lockyer,[37] a Puritan divine of some note, chaplain of Oliver Cromwell.[38] As mistakes had been made in its valuation, the lands being charged with payments to charitable uses, he was allowed in 1655 to reconvey the manor to the State.[39] At the Restoration it was recovered by the dean and chapter. It was confirmed to them in 1692–3,[40] and remained in their possession until it was taken over in 1859 by the Ecclesiastical Commissioners,[41] who are now lords of the manor of Himbleton.[42]

A *cassata* of land at DUNHAMPSTEAD (Dunhamstyde, Dunhamstede, ix cent.; Dunestead, xvi cent.) was granted to the church of Worcester by Coenwulf, King of Mercia, in 814.[43] Land at Dunhampstead is also said to have been given to the monastery by Earedus and his wife Tunthrytha in 896.[44] Alfstan brother of Bishop Wulfstan, who succeeded as Prior of Worcester in 1062, purchased land in Dunhampstead for the priory.[45] It is not mentioned by name in the Domesday Survey, but seems with Ravenshill to be included in 2 hides held by two *radmanni* in the manor of Hallow.[46] The overlordship remained in the possession of the prior and convent.[47] It seems to have become annexed to the manor of Phepson, for in 1148 Bishop Simon confirmed Phepson with Dunhampstead[48] to the prior and convent.

By an undated charter John Rous of Ragley gave up to Ralph de Dynbergh and Joan his wife all his right in the manors of Dunhampstead and la Sale.[49] It was probably towards the end of the 13th century that Hugh de Caveruche gave to Peter de Saltmarsh of Dunhampstead and Alice his wife certain land in Dunhampstead.[50] Peter de Saltmarsh paid a subsidy of 3s. at Dunhampstead in 1280, and at the same date Lady Parnel de Dunhampstead paid 5s. 6d.[51] Alice, who is called in a deed of 1310–11 lady of Dunhampstead, was evidently the widow of Peter de Saltmarsh.[52]

Edward de Dunhampstead by a charter without date gave to Walter de Lench and his wife Joan certain lands in Dunhampstead,[53] and in 1329–30 John Lench son and heir of Walter gave all his land in Dunhampstead and la Sale to William de Eccleshall, chaplain.[54] Ten years later Walter Lench

---

[23] *V.C.H. Worcs.* i, 296a. The connexion of this manor with Hallow dated from the 9th century (Heming, op. cit. 337). In the 12th century, however, it was held of the Bishop of Worcester's manor of Northwick (Red Bk. of Bishopric of Worcester [Eccl. Com. Rec. Var. bdle. 121, no. 43698], fol. 253).

[24] *V.C.H. Worcs.* i, 296a.

[25] Ibid. 325b. It is difficult to account for the fact that Himbleton was held towards the end of the 12th century of the Bishop of Worcester's manor of Kempsey (Red Bk. of Bishopric of Worcester, fol. 253).

[26] Red Bk. of Bishopric of Worc. fol. 253.   [27] Ibid.

[28] Habington, op. cit. i, 285.

[29] Hale, *Reg. of Worc. Priory* (Camd. Soc.), 55b.

[30] Habington, op. cit. i, 285.

[31] Hale, *Reg. of Worc. Priory* (Camden Soc.), 55b; *Pope Nich. Tax.* (Rec. Com.), 227.

[32] *Cal. Pat.* 1247–58, p. 5.

[33] Prattinton Coll. (Soc. Antiq.). The lease gives details of the stock then on the manor.

[34] *Valor Eccl.* (Rec. Com.), iii, 221; *V.C.H. Worcs.* i, 111.

[35] Pat. 33 Hen. VIII, pt. v; *L. and P. Hen. VIII*, xvii, g. 71 (29). The manor was worth £32 19s. 3¼d. a year (*Valor Eccl.* [Rec. Com.], iii, 221), and the grant was confirmed in 1609 (Pat. 6 Jas. I, pt. xii, no. 2).

[36] op. cit. (Soc. Antiq.). In 1581–2 the dean and chapter granted the manor of Himbleton to Henry Gardiner for three lives (ibid.).

[37] Close, 1654, p. xxvi, no. 8. In 1650 certain parcels of the manor were sold to Henry Evett (ibid. 1650, pt. xxxviii, no. 14), in 1651 a further portion was sold to Edward Greene of London (ibid. 1651, pt. liii, no. 18).

[38] *Dict. Nat. Biog.*

[39] *Cal. S. P. Dom.* 1655–6, pp. 24, 377.

[40] Pat. 4 Will. and Mary, pt. i, no. 6.

[41] *Lond. Gaz.* 16 Dec. 1859, p. 4757: confirmed by Stat. 31 & 32 Vict. cap. 19.

[42] Information supplied by the Ecclesiastical Commissioners.

[43] Heming, op. cit. 415, 416, 574; Birch, op. cit. i, 487. The boundaries of the land are given.

[44] Dugdale, *Mon. Angl.* i, 609.

[45] Heming, op. cit. 407.

[46] *V.C.H. Worcs.* i, 296; Heming, op. cit. 307.

[47] Hale, *Reg. of Worc. Priory* (Camden Soc.), 55b. In 1408 the manor of Dunhampstead was held of the Prior and convent of Worcester as of their manor of Himbleton by service of rendering 7s. and suit of court twice a year (Inq. a.q.d. file 439, no. 24).

[48] Thomas, op. cit. App. no. 18.

[49] Prattinton Coll. (Soc. Antiq.), Deeds of D. and C. of Worc. no. 255. La Sale was probably the modern Saleway, or perhaps Sale Green now in Huddington.

[50] Ibid. no. 140.

[51] *Lay Subs. R. Worcs.* 1280 (Worcs. Hist. Soc.), 38. By an undated charter of the 13th century Peter de Saltmarsh gave his brother William all his land in Dunhampstead (*Hist. MSS. Com. Rep.* v, App. i, 302).

[52] Prattinton Coll. (Soc. Antiq.), Deeds of D. and C. of Worc. no. 35.

[53] Ibid. 25.

[54] Ibid. 39.

acquired land in la Sale of William son of Richard Saundyes,[55] and in 1342–3 land near the churchyard of Dunhampstead from John de Mone.[56] In 1347–8 Nicholas de la Sale, rector of Spernore (Spernall, co. Warw.), gave to Walter all his property in la Sale,[57] and at the same date Thomas de Beauchamp gave him 30 acres in Dunhampstead.[58] It was probably his widow who as Joan wife of Ralph Dynbych granted in 1368–9 to Walter de Lench a third of a messuage which she held as dower.[59] Ralph and Joan were dealing with land in Dunhampstead in 1404–5,[60] but Ralph died soon after and his widow conveyed the manors of Dunhampstead and Sale to trustees in 1406.[61] This was probably a preliminary to the gift of the manor in 1408 by Joan, then called Joan de Dunhampstead, to the Prior and convent of Worcester.[62] This manor is not mentioned in the Valor of the priory lands in 1535, but probably remained in the possession of successive priors until the Dissolution, and was granted with the other priory lands to the Dean and Chapter of Worcester, for in 1575 the dean petitioned Burghley that his college might not be deprived of the farm of Dunhampstead on Mr. Ralph Holliwell's pretence of concealed lands.[63] This petition was probably made on account of a grant by the Crown in 1574 to John and William Marsh of land in Dunhampstead held by Richard Halliwell.[64] No further reference to Dunhampstead has been found, but the so-called manor was sold by Judge Amphlett, K.C., of Wychbold Hall, in 1911 to Mr. Gibbs of Tibberton, the present owner.[65]

PHEPSON (Fepsetnatune, x cent.; Fepsintun, xii cent.; Fepsynton, xiii cent.; Phepston, xvii cent.) was granted by King Eadwig to the monastery of Worcester in 956,[66] and at the date of the Domesday Survey the monks owned 6 hides there, 5 of which paid geld, Walter Poer being their under-tenant.[67] Henry I freed 4 hides at Phepson from 'geld,'[68] and by a charter without date William son of Almaric confirmed the gift of his grandfather William son of Herman to the monks of Worcester of all the land in Phepson which was of the hide of Trunchet,[69] free from all services.[70]

Bishop Simon confirmed Phepson to the prior and convent in 1148.[71] In 1231 the manor of Phepson was let to farm to the men of the vill for eight years.[72] They were still holding it in 1240,[73] and the lease fell in in 1253.[74] From that time all trace of the manor disappears, and it probably became merged in the manor of Himbleton. In the 13th century Phepson seems to have been a member of the manor

of Stoke Prior,[75] and is said to have been in the liberty of the hundred of Stoke.[76]

A tithe barn and close at Phepson were sold in 1656 as late possessions of the Dean and Chapter of Worcester to George Hooper of Westminster.[77]

In 1086 Roger de Lacy owned *SHELL* (Scelves, xi cent.; Shelne, Schelne, xiii cent.; Shelbe, xvi cent.), and Herman held it of him. In the time of King Edward it had been held as two manors by Aelfwig.[78] The Lacys' interest in the manor evidently passed like their lordship at Spetchley to the lords of Inkberrow, Shell being held of that manor in 1375–6[79] and in the 15th century.[80] It probably continued to be held of the manor of Inkberrow until 1536, when a rent of 1d. was paid from the manor to Lord Bergavenny.[81] In 1275–6 the jurors of the hundred court presented that William de Valence, who then owned Inkberrow, had appropriated Shell and Morton Underhill to his liberty of Nobury in Inkberrow.[82]

Herman's tenancy of the manor evidently passed to William son of Herman, who by an undated charter, which was confirmed by his grandson William son of Almaric, gave land in Phepson to the monks of Worcester, promising to acquit Phepson from all royal services, which should from henceforth be supplied from his land of Shell.[83]

Shell, which seems to have followed the same descent as Hill Croome in early times, is probably to be identified with the 'Solive' which was held by William de la Hull in 1194–5.[84] Whether William's interest in the manor was that of overlord or tenant is not clear, but he sold the vill of Shell in 1206–7 to William Marshal Earl of Pembroke.

The tenancy of the manor afterwards passed to a family who took their name from the estate. Alexander de Shell settled a messuage, a mill and half a virgate of land in Shell in 1268–9 upon himself and his wife Alice and Alexander his son.[85] Simon de Shell paid a subsidy of 2s. at Shell and Crowle in 1280, and at the same date Geoffrey de Shell paid 2s. 6d. at Phepson,[86] while in 1282 William de Shell came before the king and sought to recover his land in Shell which he had forfeited for his default against John de Haulton.[87] In 1292 Richard de Berton presented to the chapel of Shell,[88] whose advowson appears to have belonged to the lords of the manor, and in 1295 Richard 'called Barcham' presented.[89] The usual form of the name seems to have been Bartram. Richard de Bartram held the manor in 1297–8.[90] Maud Bartram is called lady of Shell

[55] Prattinton Coll. (Soc. Antiq.), Deeds of D. and C. of Worc. no. 181.
[56] Ibid. 185.
[57] Ibid. 222.
[58] Ibid. 268.
[59] Ibid. 12.
[60] Ibid. 221.
[61] Ibid. 135.
[62] *Cal. Pat.* 1408–13, p. 31.
[63] *Cal. S. P. Dom.* 1547–80, p. 497.
[64] Pat. 16 Eliz. pt. xii.
[65] Information supplied by the Rev. Gordon H. Poole, late vicar of Himbleton.
[66] Heming, op. cit. ii, 333, 516; Birch, op. cit. iii, 114. The grant included 5 'cassates' of land and five salt-pans in Droitwich (ibid.). The bounds are given in the charter.
[67] *V.C.H. Worcs.* i, 297b. The five salt-pans at Droitwich still belonged to

the manor and are returned as worth 10s. a year (ibid.).
[68] Hale, *Reg. of Worc. Priory* (Camden Soc.), 58b; Heming, op. cit. ii, 524. This explains the entry in the 12th-century survey of the hundred of Oswaldslow, when the monks were holding 1 hide only at Phepson (*V.C.H. Worcs.* i, 326a).
[69] Trench Lane and Trench Wood still exist in Oddingley.
[70] Hale, *Reg. of Worc. Priory* (Camden Soc.), 58b; Heming, op. cit. 525.
[71] Thomas, op. cit. App. no. 18.
[72] *Ann. Mon.* (Rolls Ser.), iv, 422.
[73] Hale, *Reg. of Worc. Priory* (Camden Soc.), 57a.
[74] *Ann. Mon.* (Rolls Ser.), iv, 442.
[75] Hale, *Reg. of Worc. Priory* (Camden Soc.), 5, 157b. [76] Ibid. 57a.
[77] Close, 1657, pt. xxxvii, no. 31.

[78] *V.C.H. Worcs.* i, 312a.
[79] Chan. Inq. p.m. 49 Edw. III (pt. i), no. 70.
[80] Ct. R. (Gen. Ser.), portf. 210, no. 46; Chan. Inq. p.m. 12 Ric. II, no. 135; 19 Ric. II, no. 43; 14 Hen. VI, no. 35.
[81] *Valor Eccl.* (Rec. Com.), ii, 432.
[82] *Hund. R.* (Rec. Com.), ii, 284.
[83] Hale, *Reg. of Worc. Priory* (Camden Soc.), 59a.
[84] *Abbrev. Plac.* (Rec. Com.), 6; *Rot. Cur. Reg.* (Rec. Com.), i, 46.
[85] Feet of F. Worcs. Trin. 53 Hen. III
[86] *Lay Subs. R. Worcs.* 1280 (Worcs. Hist. Soc.), 22, 38.
[87] *Cal. Close,* 1279–88, p. 185.
[88] *Reg. G. Giffard* (Worcs. Hist. Soc.), 430.
[89] Ibid. 450.
[90] Add. MS. 28024, fol. 148.

in 1325,[91] and two years later Agnes Bartram paid a subsidy of 40*d.* at Shell.[92] Roger de Butterley, who was lord of Shell in 1344,[93] was holding in 1346, jointly with the Prior of Worcester, a thirteenth of a fee in Shell which Richard 'Herthram' once held.[94] Lucy Bartram held the manor in 1361,[95] and John Bartram seems to have been in possession in 1375–6.[96] John son of John de Shell and grandson of Richard Shell or Bartram, who presented to the chapel in 1382,[97] died in 1384–5, leaving a son John, aged ten.[98] The latter died a minor in 1395–6, his heir being his cousin Thomas Best, grandson of Maud sister of Richard Bartram, John's great-grandfather.[99] The advowson of the chapel, and possibly also the manor, soon afterwards passed to the Webbs, Henry Webb presenting in 1399 and 1400.[100] In 1410 and 1413 William Webb, whose relationship to Henry is not known, and Thomas Hawkeslow, who had married Sibil sister of Henry Webb, were patrons of the chapel of Shell.[1] The manor subsequently passed to the college of Westbury, but neither the donor nor the date of the gift is known. In 1535 it brought in a rent of £6 9*s.* 11*d.* to the college.[2]

The college was surrendered to Henry VIII on 10 February 1544,[3] and its possessions, including the manor of Shell, were granted on 22 March to Sir Ralph Sadleir,[4] who sold the manor of Shell to Thomas and Richard Finch or Fincher in 1549–50.[5] The shares of these two brothers follow a different descent.[6] Thomas Fincher died in 1590, having previously, in 1567, settled the manor on his wife Joan, with remainder to his third son Robert.[7] The latter, dying in 1593, was followed by his sons Thomas and John in succession.[8] John was followed about 1663 by his grandson John Fincher,[9] who died before 1717,[9a] when his son Philip and his five daughters were dealing with the manor.[10] Philip died in 1755, and the manor passed to co-heirs, Mary wife of Thomas Hornblower, Mary Fincher and Anne Fincher.[11] Thomas Hornblower conveyed a third of the manor in 1801–2 to William Humphreys,[12] and Anne wife of Nicholas Pearsall, who conveyed the manor of Shell in 1795–6 to Matthew Jefferys,[13] was perhaps Anne Fincher mentioned above. Later the whole manor passed to Henry Payton, who died in 1819,[14] when it was sold to Edward Bearcroft,[15] whose grandson, Colonel Edward Hugh Bearcroft, C.B., is now lord of the manor of Shell.[16]

The moiety of the manor of Shell bought by Richard Fincher from Sir Ralph Sadleir was given by the former in 1563 to his prospective son-in-law Ralph Lench.[17] Richard, however, seems to have retained a life interest, for Ralph Lench and Elizabeth his wife did not enter into possession of the manor until after Richard's death in 1581.[18] George Lench, who was the owner of the manor in Habington's time,[19] was possibly Ralph's son. John Lench was the owner in 1651[20] and in 1655.[21] In 1671 John Kerver and his wife Elizabeth, Elizabeth Lench, only daughter and heir of George Lench, deceased, and John Lench of Doverdale conveyed the manor to Paul Foley.[22] Paul died in 1699, leaving a son Thomas, who died in 1737.[23] His son Thomas was created Lord Foley of Kidderminster in 1776, and his grandson Thomas Lord Foley was dealing with the manor of Shell in 1802.[24] This portion of the manor seems also to have passed to the Bearcrofts.

There was a mill in the Prior of Worcester's manor of Himbleton in the middle of the 13th century,[25] but it seems to have disappeared before the middle of the 16th.

There is a water corn-mill on Bow Brook at Shell. The first mention of it seems to be in 1268–9, when it was in the possession of Alexander de Shell and his son Alexander.[26] It afterwards belonged to the college of Westbury, and was evidently granted to Sir Ralph Sadleir with the manor.[27]

The church of *ST. MARY MAGDA-CHURCH LENE* consists of a chancel and nave without division 70¾ ft. long (of which about 27 ft. belong to the chancel) by 18 ft. in width, north aisle 40 ft. by 10½ ft., with a modern vestry, communicating with it by a passage, south transept 12 ft. deep by 11 ft. wide, and a south porch. A small bell-turret of wood rises above the roof at the west end of the nave. All the measurements are internal.

The 12th-century church consisted of a nave, with a narrower chancel to the east of it, but of this building only the south doorway and part of the south nave wall remain. About 1240 the chancel appears to have been entirely rebuilt of the same width as the nave. The next addition was about 1370, when the south transept was built as a chapel, and at the same period the arch of the early south door was reconstructed and the porch added. The west and south-west walls of the nave were rebuilt, probably

[91] Worc. Epis. Reg. Cobham (1317–27), fol. 104.
[92] *Lay Subs. R. Worcs.* 1327 (Worcs. Hist. Soc.), 42.
[93] Worc. Epis. Reg. Wulstan de Bransford (1339–49), fol. 73d.
[94] *Feud. Aids,* v, 304.
[95] *Sede Vacante Reg.* (Worcs. Hist. Soc.), 207.
[96] Chan. Inq. p.m. 49 Edw. III (pt. i), no. 70.
[97] Nash, op. cit. i, 555.
[98] Chan. Inq. p.m. 12 Ric. II, no. 135. In a later inquisition the date of his death is given as 1386–7 (ibid. 13 Ric. II, no. 143).
[99] Ibid. 19 Ric. II, no. 43.
[100] Nash, loc. cit.
[1] Ibid.; *Visit. of Worcs.* 1569 (Harl. Soc. xxvii), 9.
[2] *Valor Eccl.* (Rec. Com.), ii, 432.
[3] *V.C.H. Gloucs.* ii, 108.
[4] *L. and P. Hen. VIII,* xix (1), g. 278 (68).

[5] Pat. 3 Edw. VI, pt. viii, m. 13.
[6] For Richard Fincher's portion see below.
[7] Chan. Inq. p.m. (Ser. 2), ccxxxi, 99. His wife Joan predeceased him. According to a Fine Roll of 1591 Hugh Fincher, the eldest son, had livery of the manor of Shell in 1591 (Fine R. 33 Eliz. no. 76), but the manor finally went to the third son.
[8] Chan. Inq. p.m. (Ser. 2), ccxxxiv, 58; Fine R. 42 Eliz. pt. ii, no. 54 ; Chan. Inq. p.m. (Ser. 2), cclxxxii, 48 ; Fine R. 4 Jas. I, pt. iii, no. 35.
[9] Metcalfe, op. cit. 44 ; *Index to Worcs. Fines* (Worcs. Hist. Soc.), 41.
[9a] It was probably this John who died in 1703 (M. I. in Himbleton Church).
[10] Metcalfe, loc. cit. ; Feet of F. Worcs. Mich. 4 Geo. I.
[11] M. I. in Himbleton Church ; Feet of F. Worcs. Trin. 30 & 31 Geo. II.
[12] Ibid. Hil. 42 Geo. III.

[13] Ibid. East. 36 Geo. III.
[14] *Himbleton Parish Mag.* May 1905.
[15] Prattinton Coll. (Soc. Antiq.).
[16] Information from Colonel Bearcroft.
[17] Pat. 5 Eliz. pt. v, m. 7.
[18] Fine R. 25 Eliz. pt. i, no. 17.
[19] *Surv. of Worcs.* (Worcs. Hist. Soc.), i, 259.
[20] Feet of F. Worcs. Mich. 1651.
[21] Ibid. Trin. 1655.
[22] Recov. R. D. Enr. Mich. 23 Chas. II, m. 1 d.
[23] Burke, *Peerage* (1906).
[24] Recov. R. Hil. 42 Geo. III, rot. 21.
[25] Hale, *Reg. of Worc. Priory* (Camden Soc.), 55*b*; see also *Pope Nich. Tax.* (Rec. Com.), 227*b*.
[26] Feet of F. Worcs. 53 Hen. III, no. 23.
[27] Pat. 3 Edw. VI, pt. viii. It is not mentioned in the grant to Sadleir, but was sold by him with the manor to the Finchers.

when the wood turret was first erected in the 15th century. The aisle was an addition of the 16th century, and many of the windows were altered at the same or a later period. The chief restoration during the past century was undertaken in 1893 ; the vestry is quite a modern addition.

The east window, of three pointed lancets, is mainly of 13th-century date, but the buttresses at the eastern angles of the chancel are modern. Of the four windows in the side walls the first pair are original, each being of two lights with a square head. The second on the north is also a square-headed, two-light opening, but the window opposite is entirely modern. The archway to the transept appears to be 14th-century work and has two continuous chamfered orders. The south transept or chapel has a window

CHURCH PORCH, HIMBLETON

in each wall ; that to the east has three square-headed lights and is original. To the south is a 14th-century window of two lights with a quatrefoil over. The two-light west window, of similar date, has a plain spandrel in the head, and in the sill is a piscina basin. Cut on the south-west diagonal buttress of the transept is a sundial. The south window of the nave is a plain square-headed opening of two lights, the stonework of which is old. The south doorway has 12th-century jambs of two square orders, with shafts in the angles, having carved capitals and moulded bases. The western shaft is modern and the pointed arch is of late 14th-century date. The contemporary wood door is divided into nine main panels by rails, each subdivided into four by muntins, the thirty-six panels thus formed being quatrefoiled. The north arcade

consists of three bays, with arches of two chamfered orders, resting on slight octagonal columns, with chamfered bases and moulded capitals. The responds have been partly cut away, and beyond the eastern respond is the blocked square-headed doorway to the former rood stair. The west window of the nave has three square-headed lights and has been much repaired.

The east window of the aisle is of three lights with plain four-centred heads under a flat lintel. The first window in the north wall is similar, and the other two resemble it in type, but are of two lights each. The west window of the aisle is entirely modern. The north doorway is old and has a four-centred arch of a single chamfered order. It now opens into the passage to the new vestry.

The south porch is of timber on low stone walls, each side having an arcade of trefoiled openings ; the outer doorway is arched, and above it is an open timbered gable. The bargeboard is panelled with quatrefoils and the roof is tiled. The sloping sides of the lower part of the bell-turret are covered with oak shingles, and above this rises the belfry, which is of half-timber work filled in with rough-cast and crowned by a pyramidal tiled roof. The belfry windows are of two lights under flat lintels. The walls generally are of rubble, but the west wall of the nave and the south wall west of the porch, which were rebuilt in the 15th or 16th century, are of ashlar, chiefly red sandstone.

The gabled roofs retain some of their old 15th or 16th-century timbers. Both chancel and nave have ancient pointed barrel trusses, once plastered, and the chancel wall-plates are moulded and embattled. The corresponding feature in the nave has carved flowers at intervals, but is largely modern. The transept has a gabled roof with plain embattled wall-plates, and the aisle is roofed with barrel trusses, the timbers of both being old but plain. Across the chancel is a modern rood beam.

The font is square in plan, the sides of the bowl being chamfered below and having a Paschal Lamb carved on the east face. The stem is moulded at the top and the base is modern. The original portion may be as early as the 12th century. An 18th-century marble font on a carved baluster stem now stands in the vestry. This was made for Hanbury Church, and afterwards went to the new church at Finstall, in each case making way for a modern Gothic font.

In the church is a quantity of old stained glass [27a] and other modern glass, very closely resembling it. The only old piece in the east window is a small figure of St. Mary Magdalene with the name inscribed below. In the north-west window of the chancel are some fragments including the greater part of the figures of St. Anne and the Virgin. The east window of the transept has ancient glass in the side lights. On the north is St. Mary with two kneeling figures in blue below and the words in black letters ' Sancta Maria ora pro nobis,' and on the south St. John with two similar figures and the inscription ' Sancte Johannes ora pro nobis.' Below all three lights is the inscription ' Orate pro animabus Henrici Godd

[27a] A description of the stained glass in Himbleton Church is given in the Prattinton Collection.

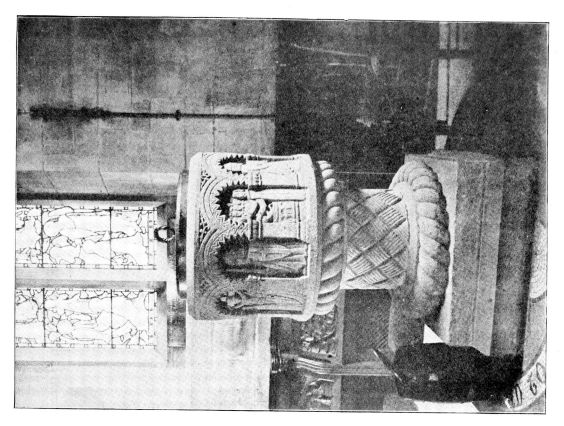

HINDLIP CHURCH : THE FONT

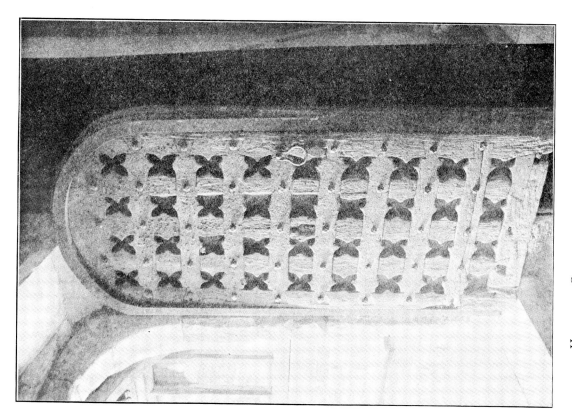

HIMBLETON CHURCH : 14TH-CENTURY SOUTH DOOR

et Agnetis uxoris ejus.' In the south window of the transept are a few old fragments, while the north-east window of the aisle contains in its western light an eagle on a tower said to be a badge of the Winters of Huddington ; below this is a head on a geometrical figure, and under this the head, hand, spear and shield of St. George, with the dragon and skull of a human victim below, all mixed up with fragments of a robe, of which part of a nimbus and veil belong to the St. Anne and the Blessed Virgin in the chancel windows. In the middle light is a large R. E. with a W,[27b] and below it the crowned figure of St. Catherine. Under these is a mantled helmet with the crest of an eagle and a shield : Quarterly : 1 and 4 quarterly: (1) Argent a bend azure with three cinq-foils or thereon, for Cooksey ; (2) and (3) Gules a saltire argent in a border sable charged with molets or, for Hoddington ; (4) Argent a bend gules with three buckles or thereon, for Cassey ; 2 and 3. Sable two bars argent with three roundels argent in the chief, and the difference of a molet argent, for Hungerford. In the east light is the headless figure of St. John the Evangelist in blue vestments holding a chalice with a serpent issuing from it, and in the head of the light is a rebus of Cooksey ; a kitchen table in a cock-boat ; between them the word ' Mā ' in a geometrical figure. Over the east window is a remarkable painting of the royal arms of Queen Elizabeth, executed on the plaster. Unfortunately this is fast fading away.

In the south transept are a number of gravestones to members of the Fincher family ; one to Philip Fincher, died 1660, and others to John Fincher of Shell, died 1703, John died 1705, and Elizabeth his wife 1709. On the wall is a monument to Philip, the last male of the family of Fincher of Shell, died 1755, and other wall monuments of later date.

There are four bells, all cast by John Martin of Worcester in 1675. The inscriptions read : on the treble, 'Jesus be our good speed' ; the second, 'Prayse and glory be to God for ever' ; the third, ' Bee it known to all that doth we see, John Martin of Worcester hee made wee,' and the tenor, 'All men that heare my rorin sound, Repent beefore you ly in ground.'

The communion plate includes a cup and cover paten, inscribed 'Mr. John Fincher's gift to ye Church and Parish of Himbleton 1656 augmented 1688 ' (it bears no hall-mark, but the stamp S R four times), and a paten, also with no hall-mark, but inscribed 1688.

The registers before 1812 are as follows : (i) baptisms 1713 to 1791, marriages 1713 to 1753, and burials 1713 to 1790 ; (ii) marriages 1754 to 1812 ; (iii) baptisms and burials 1792 to 1812.

ADVOWSON The advowson of Himbleton belonged to the priory of Worcester until the dissolution of their house,[28] when it passed to the Crown. It was granted with the manor in 1542 to the Dean and Chapter of Worcester,[29] who are still the patrons.

In November 1389 the Prior and convent of Worcester obtained a licence to appropriate the church of Himbleton [30] to the guest-house of the monastery, which was then insufficiently endowed. The appropriation was confirmed by the pope in 1395.[31] In 1403 the vicarage was ordained, a pension of 10 marks and 16 acres of arable land being assigned to the vicar.[32] Shortly after the pension of 10 marks was doubled and the prior and convent undertook to pay 3s. 4d. to the poor parishioners of the parish.[33] In 1535 the rectory was annexed to that of Tibberton.[34]

In 1536 Cromwell wrote asking the Prior of Worcester to lease the tithe and parsonage of Himbleton to Robert Sturges. The prior replied that the rectory was always kept in his own hands and could not be spared, as the monks did not obtain sufficient corn from their tenants to meet their needs.[35]

There was a chapel at Shell annexed to the church of Hanbury.[36] The first presentation which has been found was made in 1292 by Richard Bartram, lord of the manor of Shell, and successive lords of the manor seem to have been patrons of this chapel [37] until 1413, when the last recorded presentation took place.[38] The chapel is not mentioned in the valuation of Hanbury rectory taken in 1535. The tithes of Shell continued, however, to belong to the lords of the manor until 1717 or later.[39] It was probably after the destruction of the chapel at Shell that a chapel in the church of Himbleton was assigned to the use of the inhabitants of Shell.

From entries in the register of Worcester Priory it seems possible that there were chapels at Phepson and Dunhampstead in the 13th century, for the Prior and convent of Worcester are said to have been patrons of the former by collation of King Edwy and of the latter by collation of King Coenwulf.[40] It is to be observed, however, that no mention is made of any chapel in the survey of either of these manors given in this register. No further reference to a chapel at Phepson has been found, but in a deed of 1342–3 land near the churchyard of Dunhampstead is mentioned.[41]

CHARITIES It appeared from the church table that the Rev. William Maschall, the vicar in 1633, the Rev. Samuel Wilkins (a former vicar) and Francis Mince gave certain donations for the use of the poor which cannot now be traced. A cottage with two dwellings situate near Road Bridge was subsequently purchased with a sum of £30, presumably representing these gifts with interest thereon. They were occupied by two poor persons rent free.

An annuity of 20s., stated on the same table to have been devised by will of Andrew Baker of Hill Court, Grafton Flyford, for bread for the poor, has ceased to be paid.

The church lands, formerly consisting of 3 r. 15 p., held by the vicar and churchwardens since 1657, were sold in 1907 and the proceeds invested in £59 11s. 1d.

27b Probably for Roger and Elizabeth Winter, as the donors of the window.
28 *Ann. Mon.* (Rolls Ser.), iv, 430, 446, 447, 506, 548 ; *Reg. G. Giffard* (Worcs. Hist. Soc.), 201, 539.
29 Pat. 33 Hen. VIII, pt. v ; *L. and P. Hen. VIII*, xvii, g. 71 (29).
30 *Cal. Pat.* 1388–92, p. 164 ; Inq.a.q.d. 13 Ric. II, file 408, no. 10 ; Heming, op. cit. 546.

31 *Cal. Papal Letters*, iv, 519.
32 Nash, op. cit. i, 582.
33 Worc. Epis. Reg. Clifford (1401–7), fol. 73.
34 *Valor Eccl.* (Rec. Com.), iii, 224.
35 *L. and P. Hen. VIII*, xi, 262.
36 Worc. Epis. Reg. Cobham (1317–27), fol. 104.
37 Ibid. ; Nash, op. cit. i, 555 ; *Reg.*

G. Giffard (Worcs. Hist. Soc.), 430, 450.
38 Nash, loc. cit.
39 Pat. 3 Edw. VI, pt. viii ; Feet of F. Worcs. Hil. 27 Eliz. ; Mich. 4 Geo. I.
40 Hale, *Reg. of Worc. Priory* (Camden Soc.), 55b, 57a.
41 Prattinton Coll. (Soc. Antiq.), Deeds of D. and C. of Worc. no. 185.

Birmingham Corporation 3 per cent. stock with the official trustees, producing £2 1s. 8d. yearly, which is used for church repairs in accordance with the description of the church lands in the 18th-century map of the parish, where the piece of land is labelled 'for church repairs.'

HINDLIP

Hindehlep (x cent.); Hundeslep (xii cent.); Hindelupe (xiii cent.); Henlipp (xvi cent.).

The parish of Hindlip, containing about 1,380 acres, of which 481 are arable, 856 under permanent grass and 42 woodland,[1] lies to the east of North Claines ; the Worcester and Birmingham Ship Canal runs through the southern part of the parish, and the nearest station is at Fernhill Heath, on the Great Western railway, about a mile away. Hindlip Hall, the seat of Lord Hindlip, stands about three-quarters of a mile to the north of the canal on the site of the old house ; it is beautifully situated on rising ground in a well-wooded park and has a fine view of the Malvern and Abberley Hills and the surrounding country. The house, which was entirely rebuilt in the first half of the 19th century, is a square building of brick with stone dressings ; two wings, connected with the main building by crescent-shaped walls, were added in 1867. The church of St. James is in the park and stands close to the house, but the rectory is about three-quarters of a mile distant, near the western border of the parish. A bronze Roman coin was found in the grounds here in 1840.[2]

The village has been almost entirely rebuilt and possesses no features of architectural interest with the exception of Cummins Farm, a half-timber building of the 16th century with a later brick casing. In the room at the north end of the ground floor is a fine plaster ceiling of the mid-17th century. It is divided by beams and cross-beams into seven compartments. The beams are cased with plaster and enriched with the egg and tongue. The central compartment is occupied by a boldly modelled wreath. Over the fireplace is a scroll pediment with swags of fruit and flowers flanked by caryatid figures bearing baskets of acanthus on their heads, which give apparent support to the main beams. On the enriched plaster frieze which partly surrounds the walls of the room are small oval shields which may originally have borne genuine coats of arms, but have since been painted with random charges and tinctures. The newel staircase, with its turned oak balusters, is of original 17th-century date. There is a hiding-place at the side of the chimney stack on the east side of the house. In one of the first floor bedrooms, on the wall of this hiding-place, which is of lath and plaster, is a plaster panel with a lion rampant holding a sword and the date 1615. The chimney stack on the north side of the house is surmounted by three diagonal shafts of brick.

At the north-east is a brick addition of the 18th century.

Offerton Farm lies about 1½ miles south-east of Hindlip, and about half a mile north of it on the road which runs east through the parish to Oddingley are the two farms of Smite. They were included in Hindlip parish in 1880,[3] and previously formed a portion of Warndon. Smite Hill was transferred to Hindlip from Claines at the same date.[4]

The soil is strong clay and marl, the subsoil Keuper Marl. The chief crops are wheat, barley and oats, but much of the parish is woodland.

Among place-names which occur in local records are : Wyboldeshale,[5] Scynardeshul,[6] Oldebury,[7] Bekleshill, Benhull and Swyllecroft,[8] found in the 13th century ; and Poche, Caylbours, and Jack's Close[9] in the 16th century.

MANORS — The manor of *HINDLIP* belonged before the Conquest to the see of Worcester, and Bishop Oswald granted a lease of the land there for three lives to a woman named Ælfhild in 966.[10] In the time of Edward the Confessor it was held by Edric, the steersman of the bishop's ship.[11] He was present at the trial between the houses of Worcester and Evesham, and as Edric de Hindlip subsequently took part in the final settlement before the Domesday Commissioners.[12] At the time of the Survey Urse D'Abitot held 5 hides at Hindlip and Offerton in the bishop's manor of Northwick, and Godfrey held them of him.[13] Urse's interest passed to his descendants, the Earls of Warwick, the manor of Hindlip being held of their manor of Elmley Castle, the descent of which was followed by the overlordship until 1557, when it is last mentioned.[14]

William de Beauchamp was apparently holding Hindlip in demesne in 1164–79,[15] but in 1197 Margaret 'of Hindlip' paid 5 marks to have the right of half a knight's fee there against John D'Abitot and Maud his wife.[16] John D'Abitot, who subsequently held Hindlip for a knight's fee,[17] probably died about 1230, when his son and heir Geoffrey is described as lord of Hindlip.[18] Geoffrey was afterwards knighted.[19] Both he and his son Alexander, who seems to have succeeded him about 1250,[20] gave lands in Hindlip to the hospital of St. Wulfstan, Worcester.[21]

Geoffrey D'Abitot, probably the son of Alexander, was holding the manor in 1277[22] ; he died before 1305, in which year the lord of Hindlip was another Alexander D'Abitot, who then settled the estate on himself and his wife Maud with reversion to his heirs.[23]

---

[1] Statistics from Bd. of Agric. (1905).
[2] *V.C.H. Worcs.* i, 219.
[3] *Census of Engl. and Wales*, 1891, ii, 657.
[4] Ibid. A history of Smite will be found under Warndon.
[5] *Cal. Bodl. Chart.* 590.
[6] Ibid.   [7] Ibid. 591, 592.
[8] Ibid.
[9] Chan. Proc. (Ser. 2), bdle. 37, no. 18.
[10] Birch, *Cart. Sax.* iii, 443 ; Heming, *Chartul.* (ed. Hearne), 170.

[11] *V.C.H. Worcs.* i, 294.
[12] Ibid. ; Heming, op. cit. 80.
[13] *V.C.H. Worcs.* i, 294 ; Heming, op. cit. 305. Hindlip was still held of the manor of Northwick in the 12th century (Red Bk. of Bishopric of Worc. [Eccl. Com. Rec. Var. bdle. 121, no. 43698], fol. 252), but does not seem to have been so held in the 13th century.
[14] *Testa de Nevill* (Rec. Com.), 41b ; Chan. Inq. p.m. 9 Edw. II, no. 71, m. 53; (Ser. 2), cxiv, 70.

[15] Red Bk. of Bishopric of Worc. fol. 252.
[16] Pipe R. 8 Ric. I, m. 4 d.
[17] *Testa de Nevill* (Rec. Com.), 41.
[18] *Cal. Bodl. Chart.* 591.
[19] Ibid. 592.
[20] Ibid.
[21] Ibid. 590, 591, 592.
[22] *Abbrev. Plac.* (Rec. Com.), 193.
[23] Feet of F. Worcs. Trin. 33 Edw. I ; Add. MS. 28024, fol. 20b.

SOUTH-EAST VIEW OF HINDLIP HOUSE (NOW DESTROYED) IN 1776
(From an engraving by J. Ross in Prattinton Collection)

Maud survived her husband and was in possession of the manor in 1346,[24] but by 1351 she had been succeeded by her son Robert, who in that year released his right in Hindlip to Thomas Beauchamp Earl of Warwick, apparently, however, retaining a life interest in the estate.[25] The earl obtained a grant of free warren in the manor in 1352,[26] and in 1370 his son and successor Thomas granted the reversion after Robert's death to trustees.[27] In a settlement of the earl's lands in the following year Hindlip Manor is not mentioned, and it may have passed before that time to William Walsh of Hindlip, who in 1412 granted all his lands except one meadow in the manor of Hindlip to William son of Thomas Solley.[28] The heir of Maud D'Abitot was said to be holding Hindlip in 1428,[29] but —— Solley was in possession in 1431.[30] Possibly this was Thomas Solley, son of the above-mentioned William, who is said by Habington to have died in 1479, leaving as his heir a son of the same name.[31] This Thomas married a daughter of Thomas Coningsby.[32] He seems to have been succeeded about 1538[33] by a third Thomas Solley, who died in 1557, leaving Hindlip to his cousin Humphrey, the son of John Coningsby of North Mimms[34] (Herts.), upon whom he had settled it ten years earlier.[35] This settlement was disputed by Edward Hanbury, the son of Thomas Solley's sister Joan, who 'entered into the manor' after his uncle's death, whereupon Humphrey 'came armed with a company and drove him away.'[36] The dispute was, however, settled by fine in 1562,[37] and in the following year Humphrey sold the estate to John Habington, treasurer of Queen Elizabeth's household.[38] John Habington died in 1582, leaving as his heir his son Edward,[39] who was hanged for his share in Babington's Plot in 1586.[40] Edward was succeeded by his brother Thomas Habington or Abington, another of the conspirators, who on account of his youth and because he was Queen Elizabeth's godson was pardoned.[41] Thomas Habington married Mary daughter of Edward Lord Morley and granddaughter of Lord Monteagle, and she is said to have written the famous letter betraying the Gunpowder Plot.[42] In his time Hindlip House was

HABINGTON. *Argent a bend gules with three eagles or thereon.*

fitted up by Nicholas Owen as a refuge for Roman Catholic priests,[43] and after the discovery of the Gunpowder Plot it was carefully searched by Sir Henry Bromley of Holt for Garnet and Oldcorne, who were at last found in it.[44] Thomas Habington, who was away from home at the time, was subsequently arrested for concealing traitors, but he was released at Monteagle's intercession.[45] His pardon was conditional on his not leaving the county, and this enforced residence led him to write his *Survey of Worcestershire.*

Thomas Habington died in 1647; his wife Mary survived him, and suffered great losses under the Commonwealth.[46] Hindlip House was plundered after the battle of Worcester in 1651,[47] and she lost her money, plate and jewels; while in 1652 she complained that the rent for which she had received back her estate after its sequestration had been raised so high that she could not pay it and maintain her family.[48] She continued to petition the commissioners at intervals until 1655, complaining that a new lease had been made of the manor, from which she had been ejected without being allowed to reap the harvest she had sown. In July 1655 she obtained an order reinstating her in the manor-house and garden Her son, William Habington the poet, is said to have taken the republican side[49]; he died in 1654, and was succeeded by his son Thomas.[50] Thomas Habington died childless, leaving his estate to his cousin Sir William Compton of Hartbury (Gloucs.), who was the son of Mary sister of William Habington.[51] Sir William Compton, created a baronet in 1686, was succeeded by his son of the same name, who died in 1731, leaving as his heir his son, a third William.[52] This Sir William, the fourth baronet, died in 1758,[53] and his son and heir of the same name in 1760[54]; the manor then passed

COMPTON, baronet. *Argent a fesse wavy and a chief gules with a helm between two lions' heads razed or in the chief.*

to Sir Walter Abington Compton, a younger son of the fourth baronet. He died childless in 1773,[55] and his sisters, Catherine the wife of Edward Bearcroft, and Jane the wife of John Berkeley, were his heirs.[56] Catherine died childless before 1779,[57] but Jane left

[24] *Lay Subs. R.* 1346 (Worcs. Hist. Soc.), 21.

[25] Add. MS. 28024, fol. 6*b*, 7; Close, 43 Edw. III, m. 8 d.

[26] Chart. R. 26 Edw. III, m. 10, no. 23.

[27] Close, 43 Edw. III, m. 8 d.

[28] Habington, *Surv. of Worcs.* i, 293.

[29] *Feud. Aids,* v, 319.

[30] Ibid. 333.

[31] Ibid.

[32] *Visit. of Worcs.* (Harl. Soc.), 43.

[33] Recov. R. Trin. 20 Hen. VIII, rot. 100.

[34] Chan. Inq. p.m. (Ser. 2), cxiv, 70.

[35] Feet of F. Worcs. Mich. 1 Edw. VI.

[36] Habington, op. cit. i, 294; Chan. Proc. (Ser. 2), bdles. 37, no. 18; 86, no. 15.

[37] Feet of F. Worcs. Trin. 4 Eliz.

[38] Ibid. Hil. 5 Eliz.; Recov. R. Hil. 5 Eliz. rot. 131.

[39] Chan. Inq. p.m. (Ser. 2), cc, 53.

[40] *Dict. Nat. Biog.*

[41] Habington, op. cit. i, Introd. A lease of the manor was made by the Crown in 1607 to Sir John Dromond (Pat. 4 Jas. I, pt. ix), and in the same year it was granted to William Kynnesman (Memo. R. [Exch. L. T. R.] East. 11 Jas. I, rot. 41; Pat. 5 Jas. I, pt. xxx), as a late possession of Thomas Habington, attainted.

[42] Habington, loc. cit.; *Dict. Nat. Biog.* His sister Dorothy married Thomas Winter, afterwards one of the conspirators in the Gunpowder Plot.

[43] *Dict. Nat. Biog.*

[44] Ibid.

[45] Ibid. Hindlip seems to have been at this time the home of unpopular opinions, for the noted astrologer John Lambe was living there in 1608, when he was arraigned for having 'invoked and entertained certain evil and impious spirits.' He was convicted and imprisoned in Worcester Castle, but the local authorities petitioned for his removal on the ground that after his conviction 'the high sheriff, the foreman of the jury and divers others of the justices gentlemen died within a fortnight.' Lambe was accordingly removed to London, where he was eventually killed by the mob, owing to his connexion with the Duke of Buckingham (*Dict. Nat. Biog.*).

[46] *Cal. Com. for Comp.* 2941.

[47] Ibid.

[48] Ibid.

[49] *Dict. Nat. Biog.*

[50] Ibid.

[51] Nash, *Hist. of Worcs.* i, 585.

[52] G.E.C. *Complete Baronetage,* iv, 141.

[53] Ibid.

[54] Ibid.

[55] Ibid.; Recov. R. Trin. 10 Geo. III, rot. 149.

[56] Com. Pleas D. Enr. Mich. 11 Geo. III, m. 151; Mich. 20 Geo. III, m. 48.

[57] Ibid. Mich. 20 Geo. III, m. 48.

two daughters, Catherine and Jane, who were in joint possession of the manor in 1809.[58] Catherine married Robert Canning ; she predeceased her sister, who died seised of the manor in 1853,[59] leaving it to her husband Thomas Anthony, third Viscount Southwell, on whose death in 1860 it was bought by Mr. Henry Allsopp, afterwards Lord Hindlip. His grandson, the present Lord Hindlip, is now the owner of the manor.

ALLSOPP, Lord Hindlip. *Sable three pheons set cheveronwise or between three doves rising argent each holding an ear of wheat or.*

A windmill was among the appurtenances of the manor in 1601,[60] and there was a water corn-mill in 1809[61]; both these have perished,

Dissolution,[67] when it was granted to Richard Morrison,[68] who sold it in 1544 to Thomas Solley.[69] It has since that date followed the descent of the manor of Hindlip,[70] though John Habington's right to it was at first disputed by John Brooke, who declared that it had been granted to his grandfather, Edmund Brooke, by the brethren of St. Wulfstan's Hospital in 1530.[71]

THE CHURCH The church of *ST. JAMES THE GREAT* consists of a chancel with a south chapel, north vestry and organ chamber, a nave, south aisle and a western tower. The original church appears to have consisted of chancel, nave and tower, but was almost entirely rebuilt in 1864, when a south transept was added. In 1887 the church was further enlarged, the chancel lengthened eastward, the transept pulled down and the present aisle, chapel and vestry added. The church was also re-roofed and the tower considerably restored, so that little of the original fabric remains.

The modern east window is of three lights, with tracery of 14th-century detail, and there are two modern single-light windows in the north and south walls. West of these are modern arcades, each of two bays, opening to the organ chamber on the north and the chapel on the south. There is no chancel arch, but the chancel is divided from the nave by an elaborate brass grille. The nave is three bays long and is lit on the north by two windows, a single light of 15th-century date and a modern two-light window. On the south is the modern south arcade, which is designed in the style of the 14th century. The south chapel has two modern windows of 15th-century type, one in the east wall and one in the south, and is separated from the south aisle by a small moulded archway. The south aisle is lit by two-light modern windows, two on the south and one at the west end, with an original 15th-century single light between the two former.

The tower is in part old, but is not, apparently, earlier than the 15th century and has been much restored. It is of three stages, with diagonal buttresses

HINDLIP CHURCH FROM THE WEST

and there is now no mill in the parish. A free fishery is first mentioned in 1775.[62]

In the Saxon period *OFFERTON* (Alhfretune, Alcrinton, xi cent. ; Alcreton, xiii cent. ; Alfreton, xvi cent. ; Auferton, xvii cent.), now a farm in Hindlip, seems to have formed part of the Hindlip estate.[63] It was held of Urse D'Abitot by Godfrey at the time of the Domesday Survey,[64] and was afterwards in the tenure of Henry, the younger son of John D'Abitot,[65] and others, who granted it between 1232 and 1250 to the hospital of St. Wulfstan in Worcester.[66] It remained in the possession of the hospital till the

[58] G.E.C. loc. cit.
[59] M. I.
[60] Recov. R. Hil. 42 Eliz. rot. 27 ; Feet of F. Worcs. Mich. 42 & 43 Eliz.
[61] Recov. R. Trin. 49 Geo. III, rot. 285.
[62] Feet of F. Worcs. Trin. 15 Geo. III.
[63] Heming, op. cit. 355.

[64] *V.C.H. Worcs.* i, 294.
[65] Prattinton Coll. (Soc. Antiq.) ; Hale, *Reg. of Worc. Priory* (Camden Soc.), 36b.
[66] *Cal. Chart. R.* 1226–57, p. 173 ; *Cal. Bodl. Chart.* 590, 591, 592.
[67] *Lay Subs. R. c.* 1280 (Worcs. Hist. Soc.), 41 ; *L. and P. Hen. VIII*, xv, g. 831 (64) ; xvi, g. 678 (25).

[68] *L. and P. Hen. VIII*, xix (1), g. 444 (10).
[69] Ibid. (2), g. 690 (67) ; Chan. Proc. (Ser. 2), bdle. 37, no. 18.
[70] Recov. R. Hil. 5 Eliz. rot. 131 ; Chan. Proc. (Ser. 2), bdle. 3, no. 69 ; Exch. Spec. Com. 4 Jas. I, no. 4759 ; Pat. 4 Jas. I, pt. ix.
[71] Chan. Proc. (Ser. 2), bdle. 3, no. 69.

HINDLIP: PANEL AT CUMMINS FARM

HINDLIP: CEILING AT CUMMINS FARM

and an embattled parapet, with angle pinnacles. The belfry lights are square-headed, and the west window is of four lights, with late 15th-century tracery over. The west door, which is the main entrance to the church, is modern. The three-centred tower arch is of three chamfered orders, the inner having an octagonal moulded capital. The font at the west end of the south aisle is modern. Fixed to the walls of the tower, in the lowest stage, are a number of 15th-century glazed tiles of the usual Worcestershire type.

There are eight modern bells.

The plate consists of two modern cups and patens.

The registers before 1812 are as follows : (i) a copy of the Bishops' Transcripts at the Diocesan Registry, the original being missing, it contains mixed entries from 1612 to 1737 ; (ii) mixed entries from 1736 to 1812.

ADVOWSON Hindlip was a chapelry belonging to the church of St. Helen, Worcester, at the end of the 11th

century,[72] but it had become a rectory before 1269.[73] The advowson seems to have followed the same descent as the manor until 1294,[74] when the Countess of Warwick was the patron.[75] It remained in the possession of the Earls of Warwick until about 1344,[76] but Thomas Robins *alias* Thomas of Salwarpe (see Salwarpe Chantry) presented in 1349 and 1356,[77] and in 1357 he and his brother William obtained licence to grant the advowson to three chaplains to celebrate daily in the church of Hindlip.[78] The grant was probably never made, for Richard Hussingtree, lord of Martin Hussingtree, presented in 1375,[79] and the advowson followed the descent of Martin Hussingtree until the beginning of the 16th century.[80] Gilbert Talbot of Salwarpe presented to the church in 1539,[81] but the right of presentation was bought before 1547 by Thomas Solley.[82] It has since that date followed the descent of the manor of Hindlip.[83]

There are apparently no endowed charities subsisting for the benefit of this parish.

HOLT

Holte (xi cent.) ; Hoult (xvii cent.).

The parish of Holt, containing nearly 1,999 acres, of which 661 are arable, 1,041 under permanent grass and 202 woodland,[1] covers a strip of land lying between Grimley Brook and Shrawley Brook ; the River Severn forms its eastern boundary. The road to Ombersley and Droitwich runs along the northern edge of the parish and crosses the Severn by a fine iron bridge of a single span, built about 1826 at Holt Fleet.[2] Not far from the bridge a lane branches off from the road to Holt village,[3] whence it turns at right angles to join the road from Shrawley to Worcester, which runs through the parish in a south-easterly direction. The hamlet of Holt Heath has grown up at the junction of this road with that to Ombersley. Holt Fleet, which stands close to the river, is a place of call for steamers between Worcester and Stourport during the summer months, but the nearest station is at Droitwich on the Great Western railway, 6½ miles away.

The church of Holt stands in what was originally part of the grounds of Holt Castle, the ' praty pile ' of Leland, immediately opposite the west front of the house and a little distance to the east of the main Worcester road, about which the majority of the houses are grouped.

The soil is loam and gravel, the subsoil sandstone and gravel. The chief crops are wheat, barley and oats, but hops and fruit are also grown. The common lands were inclosed by an Act of 1810.[4] Little Witley lies 2 miles west of Holt ; it was a chapelry attached to the church here in 1831, but

was transferred in 1904 to the parish of Great Witley. The hamlet of Little Witley is extremely picturesque, containing some good half-timber work. From the chapel here a good half-timber building known as ' Chapel Farm ' takes its name.

The following place-names occur in local records : Hearoc hricge[5] (x cent.) ; le Rode[6] (xiv cent.) ; Hawkerydge Wood,[7] now Ockeridge, Chappellyardes,[8] Newnton,[9] Wyrkins Mill[10] (xvi cent.).

CASTLE Holt Castle was never apparently brought into prominence and little is known of its history. It followed the descent of the manor (q.v.), and is now the property of Lord Dudley. The castle consists of a rectangular block of buildings, partly of the 15th century and partly of the early 18th century, with a massive square 14th-century tower in the centre of the west front (probably built by John Beauchamp, first Lord Beauchamp of Kidderminster, who was executed in 1388), and a modern addition on the north. The tower is evidently a survival from an earlier fortified building, which was replaced in the 15th century by a house with a central hall of moderate size, having the principal apartments on the north and in all probability a wing containing the kitchen and servants' apartments on the south. Of this building the solar portion and the lower walls at least of the hall survive, forming an L-shaped fragment of the plan incorporated into the later additions. Sufficient detail remains in the solar portion at the north end of the hall to show with certainty that it is of the 15th century, while the disposition of the hall itself and the thickness of its side walls practically

[72] Heming, op. cit. 427.
[73] *Reg. G. Giffard* (Worcs. Hist. Soc.), 27. [74] Ibid. 27, 144.
[75] Nash, op. cit. i, 589 ; Add. MS. 28024, fol. 162 d.
[76] Nash, loc. cit. Thomas of Salwarpe presented in 1349.
[77] Ibid.
[78] Inq. a.q.d. file 325, no. 6.
[79] Nash, loc. cit.
[80] Ibid. Richard Lechmere, the rector presented by Edmund Ruding in 1501, was a witness in the trial of William

Peynton of Ombersley for heresy (Worc. Epis. Reg. Silvester de Gigliis, fol. 70).
[81] Nash, loc. cit.
[82] Habington, op. cit. i, 294 ; Feet of F. Worcs. Mich. 1 Edw. VI.
[83] Nash, loc. cit. ; Inst. Bks. (P.R.O.). Queen Elizabeth presented in 1586, and her grantees in 1590 by reason of the attainder of Edward Habington (Nash, loc. cit.).
[1] Statistics from Bd. of Agric. (1905).
[2] Local and Personal Act, 7 Geo. IV, cap. 59 ; Burton, *Bibl. of Worcs.* 102.

[3] A looped bronze celt was found here in 1844 (*V.C.H. Worcs.* i, 195).
[4] Burton, op. cit. 87 ; Priv. Act, 50 Geo. III, cap. 24.
[5] Heming, *Chartul.* (ed. Hearne), 144.
[6] Chart. R. 47–51 Edw. III, no. 28, m. 12 ; Feet of F. Worcs. Trin. 22 Eliz.
[7] Star Chamb. Proc. Hen. VIII, bdle. 23, no. 108.
[8] Pat. 5 Eliz. pt. v.
[9] Feet of F. Worcs. Mich. 2 & 3 Eliz.
[10] Chan. Proc. (Ser. 2), bdle. 13, no. 75.

amount to proof that it is of similar date. The south wall, which is thinner than the side walls of the hall, was probably erected about 1700, when the interior of the house was almost entirely remodelled to suit the fashion of the time, and it is not unreasonable to suppose that the kitchen wing was then removed. Towards the end of the 16th century floors appear to have been inserted n the solar portion, new chimney stacks constructed, and in all probability the original hall roof was taken down, the walls being raised to accommodate an upper floor. At the period of the Queen Anne restoration, referred to above, the remaining portion of the plan seems to have been squared up by the addition of a staircase and withdrawing room on the east side of the hall, and the whole exterior refaced, sash windows being inserted throughout. The facing is of a reddish sandstone. Within the last fifty years the present kitchen and offices were rebuilt in a style corresponding with the

corner originally led from the basement to the first-floor level ; its upper flight is now broken away, and the entrances to it on both ground and first floors have been blocked. At the first-floor level a second vice leads to the upper floors and out on to the leads. The upper stages are lighted on the west by good pointed windows of two trefoiled ogee lights with flowing tracery in their heads, and on the north and south by single trefoiled lights, also with ogee heads. There are blocked windows in the east wall. The whole is crowned by a moulded cornice with grotesque heads at the four angles surmounted by an embattled parapet. The facing is of large squared sandstone rubble. The entrance doorway and the tracery of the windows have been considerably restored.

The room at the north-east of the tower, beneath the west end of the original solar, is the only room on the ground floor which retains any visible detail of the 15th century. In addition to the cupboard recess in the west wall above described there is a blocked doorway immediately to the north which probably opened originally upon stairs leading to the cellar which occupies the internal angle made by the tower with the house on this side. A blocked doorway immediately beneath lends support to this supposition. The present cellar stairs are entered from the modern part of the house by a doorway at the north-east, the west jamb of which is of original 15th-century date, and the stairs themselves, inclosed by a brick partition, are taken

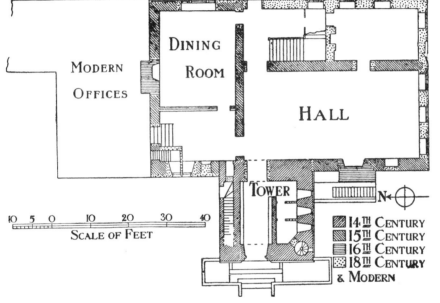

PLAN OF HOLT CASTLE

14TH CENTURY
15TH CENTURY
16TH CENTURY
18TH CENTURY & MODERN

SCALE OF FEET

rest of the building, with the exception that the windows have stone mullions.

The tower measures internally 16 ft. by 14 ft. 10 in. The thickness of the walls at the ground stage averages about 4 ft. It is of four stories, with a basement, and the floors are unmarked by external string-courses. The entrance doorway and vaulted corridor dividing the ground stage into two compartments are most likely alterations of the 15th century, when the nucleus of the present house was erected, and were constructed with the view of transforming the tower into the principal entrance of the new building. The narrow chamber thus formed on the south side of the corridor is lighted by three narrow loopholes, and is now cut up by modern brick partitions. In the thickness of the north wall is a straight flight of stone stairs leading to the first floor, now entered by a modern external doorway. That a staircase has existed here from the 15th century is shown by a blocked doorway, now used as a cupboard, by which it was entered from the solar end of the house. A vice at the south-west

out of the room. A partition, probably of the 16th century, divides this room from the dining room, to which it now serves in the place of a serving lobby. The dining room has good panelling of the early 18th century. The hall, staircase and withdrawing room all have panelling and finishings of the same date. They present a particularly pleasing example of the Queen Anne style.

The timbers of the roof of the solar portion of the house are of original 15th-century date and must have originally been open to the solar below, the present attic floor having been inserted in the 16th century. It is now divided by a partition of that date into two rooms. The eastern, which is also the larger room, is known as the ' chapel,' and is lighted by a 16th-century four-light mullioned window in the east gable. The roof was originally gabled on both east and west, but the western gable has been removed and the roof hipped to conform with the surrounding roofing. The cutting of the timbers is immediately obvious from the inside. In both rooms are remains of 16th-century plastering. Few other details of interest exist elsewhere in the house. Some 15th-century glazed tiles, probably taken up from hearths, are preserved.

Externally the elevations are flat and uninteresting. An embattled parapet crowns the walls, behind which rises a tiled, hipped roof with small dormer windows. A moulded string-course marks the level of the first floor. The large sash windows impart an 18th-century air to the whole of the exterior, which is curiously at variance with the embattled parapet. The front elevation is rendered interesting by the juxtaposition of the 14th-century tower and the 16th-century stone stack of the hall, surmounted by its diagonal brick chimney shafts. All that portion of the older house to the north of the tower has been refaced at the period of the modern additions on this side. The east, or garden, front has its embattled parapet interrupted by the 'chapel' gable and by the long, narrow windows of the staircase hall. A flight of steps, with good wrought-iron railings, leads from the staircase hall to the garden. On the west side of the house a stone wall running westwards at right angles from the house, against which it abuts, divides the forecourt from the garden, and communication is secured by a stone doorway with a straight-sided two-centred head. The portion of walling in which this is contained measures about 2 ft. 10½ in. in thickness. Its distance from the house, with which it is connected by about 84 ft. of thinner walling, precludes the possibility of its having originally formed a portion of the kitchen wing which has presumably disappeared ; probably it originally formed part of the north wall of an outhouse or barn. The terraced garden on the east side of the house slopes down to the Severn ; that on the south seems still to preserve much of its original 16th-century arrangement.

MANORS At the time of the Domesday Survey Urse D'Abitot held of the manor of Wick 5 hides at *HOLT* which Ailric had previously held, 'rendering the customary rent except the peasants' labour, as it could be obtained from the reeve.'[11] The estate passed with the rest of Urse's possessions to the Beauchamps, who held it in demesne[12] until William Beauchamp gave it to his younger son John between 1235 and 1269.[13] John de Beauchamp was succeeded by his son Richard, who died in 1327, leaving as his heir his son John, then eight years old.[14] This John was in the sea fight at Sluys in 1340, and served in the French wars 'from the time of the passage to Normandy all the while the king was abroad'[15]; he fought in the king's company at Crecy, and was subsequently at the siege of Calais.[16] He had returned to England by Michaelmas 1348, at which time he bought a small estate at Hanley Child, and settled it on himself and his wife Isabel for life, with successive

HOLT CASTLE : WEST FRONT

remainders to his sons William and Thomas.[17] He was one of the knights of the shire in the Parliament of 1352.[18] Afterwards, however, he went back to the wars in France, and seems to have served in the Poictiers campaign[19] ; in 1357 he obtained a grant of £12 yearly for his good service.[20] He was still living in 1361, but seems to have died before 1367.[21]

[11] *V.C.H. Worcs.* i, 288.
[12] Eccl. Com. Rec. Var. bdle. 121, no. 43698, fol. 252 ; *Testa de Nevill* (Rec. Com.), 41b.
[13] Add. MS. 28024, fol. 155b; see Elmley Castle and Dugdale, *Baronage,* i, 250.
[14] Chan. Inq. p.m. 1 Edw. III (1st nos.), no. 20. His wardship was given to Sir Robert Attwood, whose daughter Isabel he married (Nash, op. cit. i, 600). Dower in the manor was assigned to Eustacia, widow of Richard (*Cal. Close,* 1327-30, pp. 192, 558).
[15] Close, 15 Edw. III, pt. i, m. 8 ; Dugdale, *Baronage,* i, 250 ; Memo. R.

(Q.R.), 27 Edw. III, m. 11 ; *Will. Salt Arch. Soc. Coll.* xviii, 175.
[16] *Vide* Wrottesley, *Crecy and Calais,* in which the French and Norman Rolls, 1346-7, are printed. John Beauchamp of Holt is included in the list of knights who served in the king's division at Crecy, but there does not seem to be any subsequent mention of his knighthood, and in the grant of 1357 (Pat. 31 Edw. III, pt. ii, m. 7) he is addressed as an esquire.
[17] Feet of F. Worcs. Mich. 22 Edw. III. There is no mention in this deed of John, the son who ultimately succeeded.

[18] *Ret. of Memb. of Parl.* i, 151.
[19] Exch. Accts. (Army), bdle. 27, no. 8.
[20] Pat. 31 Edw. III, pt. ii, m. 7.
[21] *Vide* Exch. Accts. (Wardrobe and Household), bdle. 393, no. 11, fol. 74 d., where mention is made of both him and his son, and bdle. 395, no. 10, where only one John Beauchamp of Holt is named. It is possible that the elder died in Gascony, where, according to Dugdale (who, however, constantly confuses him with his son), he went on the king's service in 1363 (*Baronage,* loc. cit.).

He was succeeded by his son of the same name, who married, about 1370, Joan daughter and heir of Robert Fitz With, then a minor in the king's wardship.[22] This John Beauchamp served under John of Gaunt in the Spanish campaign of 1372,[23] and in 1373 obtained a grant of a yearly fair at a place called ' le Rode ' in the parish of Holt, on the day of St. Mary Magdalene.[24] It was, however, after the accession of Richard II that he made his most rapid rise in the royal favour. He was knighted in the summer of 1385,[25] at which time he obtained a grant of land in Carnarvonshire to the annual value of £100 in aid of the honourable maintenance of his rank [26]; this was supplemented, after he had been made Justice of North Wales,[27] by a grant of all the temporalities of the alien Priories at Deerhurst (Gloucs.) and Astley.[28] In October 1387, ' in consideration of the noble and trusty family from which he sprang, and of his own great sense and circumspection,' he was created a peer and baron of the realm under the style of Lord Beauchamp and Baron of Kidderminster,[29] an estate which he had lately acquired.[30] In December of the same year he was summoned to Parliament, but he never took his seat,[31] and in the following March, upon the seizure of authority by the Lords Appellants, he was attainted of high treason,[32] and after imprisonment in Dover Castle [33] was brought to London and beheaded on Tower Hill.[34]

BEAUCHAMP of Kidderminster. *Gules a fesse between six martlets or.*

The manor and advowson of Holt were subsequently restored to his son and heir John,[35] during whose minority they were delivered to the Earl of Warwick as overlord [36]; a moiety of the goods was, however, granted in 1390 to Elizabeth the sister of John Lord Beauchamp towards the maintenance of herself and her nephew.[37] John Beauchamp was declared of full age in January 1397,[38] but it was found that he had married Isabel Ferrers, a niece of the Countess of Warwick, without leave, and decided that the earl should keep the manor of Holt until he had received 250 marks.[39] John denied that he had married without leave, but he did not have livery of his lands until Michaelmas 1398.[40] By the reversal of the proceedings of the Merciless Parliament in the same year he became lord of Kidderminster,[41] but in 1399 his father's attainder being reaffirmed after the accession of Henry IV, his honours were again forfeited.[42] He died in August 1420, leaving as his heir his daughter Margaret,[43] whose second husband John Wysham was holding the manor in her right in 1428.[44]

Alice daughter and co-heir of Margaret married John Guise of Aspley Guise (Beds.), and succeeded to a third part of the manor of Holt [45] in 1472 after the death of her mother's third husband Sir Walter Skull.[46] Alice Guise died in 1487, leaving as her heir her son John,[47] who died in 1501 seised of a moiety of the manor of Holt, which he left to his son of the same name.[48] Anselm, the son and heir of this John Guise,[49] sold his property in Holt to Sir John Bourne in 1557.[50] Of this moiety Sir John died seised in 1575, leaving as his heir his son Anthony,[51] from whom it was bought in 1578 by Thomas Fortescue and Edmund Hardy,[52] probably for the purpose of a settlement on Elizabeth, Fortescue's daughter, on her marriage with Sir Thomas Bromley, the lord chancellor. Sir Thomas Bromley died seised of the estate in 1587, leaving as his heir his son Henry.[53]

Joan, a second daughter and co-heir of Margaret Beauchamp, married before 1487 John Croft,[54] and was seised of a third of the manor of Holt in that year. Her sister Elizabeth married Thomas Croft,[55] ranger of Woodstock, and after his death in 1488 probably Nicholas Crowemer [56]; she seems to have died childless about 1500, for after this date the manor was divided in moieties between John and Joan Croft and John Guise.[57]

John Croft survived Joan, and died in 1531,[58] having settled a moiety of the estate on Elizabeth his second wife for her life.[59] She, with his son and heir John, granted to Thomas Evans a lease of the premises in 1535,[60] and in 1537 apparently the

[22] Anct. D. (P.R.O.), A 9265 ; Close, 15 Ric. III, m. 42 ; 49 Edw. III, m. 21 ; Feet of F. Div. Co. Mich. 49 Edw. III ; Misc. Inq. p.m. file 241, no. 91.

[23] Dugdale, loc. cit.

[24] Chart. R. 47–51 Edw. III, no. 162, m. 12.

[25] Pat. 9 Ric. II, pt. i, m. 36.

[26] Ibid. 31.

[27] Ibid. 5 ; pt. ii, m. 8.

[28] Ibid. 11 Ric. II, pt. i, m. 23. Astley had previously been leased to him for a term of years (ibid. 8 Ric. II, pt. i, m. 18).

[29] Ibid. 11 Ric. II, pt. i, m. 12. This was the first barony created by patent.

[30] Feet of F. Worcs. Mich. 8 Ric. II, no. 22.

[31] G.E.C. Complete Peerage.

[32] Rolls of Parl. iii, 241–3.

[33] Close, 11 Ric. II, m. 10.

[34] G.E.C. Complete Peerage.

[35] Rolls of Parl. iii, 358 ; Chan. Inq. p.m. 12 Ric. II, no. 91 ; Close, 12 Ric. II, m. 33.

[36] Close, 12 Ric. II, m. 33 ; Misc. Inq. p.m. file 241, no. 151 ; Chan. Inq. p.m. 21 Ric. II, file 266, no. 6.

[37] Cal. Pat. 1388–92, p. 287. Apparently the Earl of Warwick subsequently

claimed the wardship of John Beauchamp the younger, for he seems to have been a member of the earl's household in 1396 (Exch. Memo. R. [L.T.R.], Mich. 22 Ric. II, rot. 10).

[38] Exch. Memo. R. (L.T.R.), Mich. 22 Ric. II, rot. 10. The inquisition taken in August 1388 after his father's death stated that he was then ten years old (Chan. Inq. p.m. 12 Ric. II, no. 91).

[39] Exch. Memo. R. (L.T.R.), Mich. 22 Ric. II, rot. 10 ; Chan. Inq. p.m. 21 Ric. II, file 266, no. 6.

[40] Exch. Memo. R. (L.T.R.), Mich. 22 Ric. II, rot. 10.

[41] G.E.C. Complete Peerage.

[42] Ibid. ; Pat. 1 Hen. IV, pt. i, m. 12 ; pt. v, m. 25. He, however, continued to sit in Parliament as knight of the shire (Ret. of Memb. of Parl. i, 261).

[43] Chan. Inq. p.m. 8 Hen. V, no. 70.

[44] Lay Subs. R. 1427–8 (Worcs. Hist. Soc.), 35.

[45] Chan. Inq. p.m. (Ser. 2), xxiii, 70.

[46] He presented to the church of Holt in 1472 (Nash, op. cit. i, 601), but died before October of that year (Feet of F. Div. Co. Mich. 12 Edw. IV).

[47] Chan. Inq. p.m. (Ser. 2), xxiii, 70.

[48] Ibid. xv, 100.

[49] Chan. Proc. (Ser. 2), bdles. 77, no. 40 ; 72, no. 20.

[50] Feet of F. Worcs. Trin. 3 & 4 Phil. and Mary.

[51] Chan. Inq. p.m. (Ser. 2), clxxii, 142.

[52] Feet of F. Worcs. Hil. 19 Eliz. Fortescue and Hardy together with Sir Thomas Bromley also obtained a quit-claim from John, nephew and heir of Anselm Guise, in 1583 (ibid. Trin. 25 Eliz.).

[53] Chan. Inq. p.m. (Ser. 2), ccxiii, 114.

[54] De Banco R. Hil. 3 Hen. VII, m. 344. She had previously been married to — Westcote (Chan. Inq. p.m. [Ser. 2], xxiii, 70).

[55] Feet of F. Div. Co. Mich. 12 Edw. IV.

[56] P.C.C. Wills, 17 Milles ; De Banco R. Trin. 10 Hen. VII, m. 162.

[57] De Banco R. Trin. 16 Hen. VII, m. 346 ; Feet of F. Div. Co. Trin. 16 Hen. VII ; Chan. Inq. p.m. (Ser. 2), xv, 100.

[58] Chan. Inq. p.m. (Ser. 2), li, 67.

[59] Feet of F. Worcs. East. 29 Hen. VIII.

[60] Habington, op. cit. ii, 127.

Holt Church : The Chancel Arch

reversion after the death of Elizabeth.[61] In 1549 John Croft seems to have bought back the lease,[62] which his son and heir Martin granted ten years later to Sir John Bourne,[63] the owner of the other moiety of the manor. Sir John Bourne at his death in 1576 left the lease to his son and heir Anthony, who subsequently sold it to Sir Thomas Bromley.[64]

Henry, the son and heir of Sir Thomas Bromley, who succeeded his father in 1587,[65] was the magistrate appointed to search Hindlip House, after the discovery of the Gunpowder Plot, for Garnet and Oldcorne,[66] whom he brought to his house after their arrest to restore their strength before their journey to London.[67] Sir Henry Bromley bought the reversion of the Croft moiety of Holt from Ezechiel Evans in 1613,[68] and died seised of the whole manor in 1615.[69] He left as his heir Thomas his son by his second wife Elizabeth, who

BROMLEY of Holt.
Quarterly fessewise indented gules and or.

succeeded to the castle and manor of Holt[70] after the death of his father's widow Anne, upon whom the estate had been settled for life.[71] Sir Thomas Bromley died about 1629,[72] leaving as his heir his son Henry, then under age ; the custody of the land was granted to Richard Downes.[73]

Henry Bromley afterwards became Sheriff of Worcestershire.[74] He took the Royalist side in the Civil War, and was accordingly sentenced to a fine amounting to £4,000 (one-sixth of his property) in 1646.[75] An order for his arrest on account of non-payment was issued in 1648,[76] but he subsequently paid his fine and was allowed to receive his rents ' on security of two years' value for the real estate and double the value of the personal estate.'[77]

Henry Bromley died before 1657, leaving as his heir his son of the same name,[78] who in that year settled the manor on himself and his wife Mercy and their heirs male.[79] He was succeeded in 1683 by his son William,[80] whose daughter and heir Mercy married John Bromley of Horseheath.[81] Their son Henry, who was created Lord Montfort in 1741, had inherited the estate by 1726[82] ; he was still in possession of it in 1740,[83] but seems to have sold it before 1764 to Thomas Lord Foley.[84] It has since

followed the descent of Witley Court[85] (q.v. in Great Witley), and is now the property of the Earl of Dudley.

At the time of the Domesday Survey there was a water-mill in Holt, which was then worth 40*d.*,[86] and by 1499 another mill had been built.[87] Both these followed the descent of the manor,[88] but one of them, called Wyrkins Mill, was leased for three lives by Sir John Bourne to Martin Croft in May 1557[89] ; they are perhaps represented by the two water-mills known respectively as Holt Mill and Hollingshead Mill at the present day.

The fish-pond belonging to the manor is first mentioned in 1329,[90] when it formed part of the dower of Eustacia widow of Richard de Beauchamp, together with one-third of the pleas and profits of court and the liberties belonging to the manor, which included the fines for bloodshed and breach of the assize of bread and ale.[91] A dovecot worth 3*s.* 4*d.* yearly is mentioned among the appurtenances of the manor in 1420.[92]

The last Sir John Beauchamp of Holt had a park attached to his manor in the early part of the 15th century. It was worth 6*s.* 8*d.*, besides the keep of the deer there at his death in 1420,[93] but no mention of it occurs after this date.

LITTLE WITLEY was probably included in the grant said to have been made in 964 by Edgar to the church of Worcester[94] of Witley and Grimley, which were subsequently leased by Bishop Oswald to Eadmer for three lives.[95] One hide of land at Witley was held of the bishop of the manor of Wick Episcopi in 1086 by Urse D'Abitot,[96] and had formerly been held by Arnwin the priest, who is said to have been a priest of Edric the Wild and to have received Witley from Bishop Aldred at Edric's request.[97] Little Witley followed the descent of Holt until the beginning of the 13th century, when William de Beauchamp enfeoffed Hugh de Cooksey.[98] Hugh's son and heir of the same name married Julian daughter of Hugh le Poer,[99] who brought him as her marriage portion the manor of Great Witley[100] (q.v.), the descent of which has since been followed by Little Witley.[1] The Earl of Dudley is the present lord of the manor.

BENTLEY (Beonet Laege, ix cent.), now represented by a farm in the parish of Holt, was given in perpetual alms by Burghred to Aelhun, Bishop of Worcester, in 855.[2] It was leased for three lives by

[61] Feet of F. Worcs. East. 29 Hen. VIII. In spite of this deed John Croft does not seem to have given up all his interest, for Martin Croft was dealing with the reversion in 1559 (ibid. Mich. 2 & 3 Eliz.) and 1564 (ibid. Mich. 7 & 8 Eliz.).
[62] Ibid. Mich. 3 Edw. VI.
[63] Ibid. Mich. 2 & 3 Eliz. ; Chan. Proc. (Ser. 2), bdles. 27, no. 25 ; 13, no. 75 ; Habington, op. cit. ii, 127.
[64] Habington, loc. cit. Bromley obtained a quitclaim from Edward, brother and heir of Martin Croft, in 1580 (Feet of F. Worcs. Trin. 22 Eliz.).
[65] Chan. Inq. p.m. (Ser. 2), ccxiii, 114.
[66] Cal. S. P. Dom. 1603–10, p. 284.
[67] Ibid.
[68] Feet of F. Worcs. East. 10 Jas. I.
[69] W. and L. Inq. p.m. lv, 245.
[70] Ibid.   [71] Ibid.
[72] Pat. 6 Chas. I, pt. xiv, no. 4.
[73] Ibid.

[74] *Cal. of Com. for Comp.* ii, 1220.
[75] Ibid.
[76] Ibid.
[77] Ibid.
[78] Feet of F. Worcs. Mich. 1657 ; Add. MS. 277.
[79] Feet of F. Worcs. Mich. 1657.
[80] M. I. in Holt Church ; *Kyre Park Chart.* (Worcs. Hist. Soc.), 135.
[81] M. I. in Holt Church.
[82] Recov. R. Hil. 13 Geo. I, rot. 228 ; G.E.C. *Complete Peerage*, v, 349.
[83] Inst. Bks. (P.R.O.).
[84] Ibid.
[85] Recov. R. Hil. 42 Geo. III, rot. 21 ; Hil. 10 & 11 Geo. IV, rot. 255.
[86] *V.C.H. Worcs.* i, 288.
[87] Feet of F. Div. Co. East. 14 Hen. VII.
[88] *Cal. Close*, 1327–30, p. 559 ; De Banco R. Trin. 16 Hen. VI, m. 21, 346 ; Feet of F. Worcs. Trin. 3 & 4 Phil. and Mary ; Mich. 2 & 3 Eliz. ;

Hil. 19 Eliz. ; Trin. 22 Eliz. ; Trin. 25 Eliz. ; East. 10 Jas. I.
[89] Chan. Proc. (Ser. 2), bdle. 13, no. 75.
[90] *Cal. Close*, 1327–30, p. 558.
[91] Ibid.
[92] Chan. Inq. p.m. 8 Hen. V, no. 70.
[93] Ibid.
[94] Heming, op. cit. 520.
[95] Ibid. 159 ; Birch, *Cart. Sax.* iii, 533.
[96] *V.C.H. Worcs.* i, 288.
[97] Heming, op. cit. 256.
[98] De Banco R. Hil. 6 & 7 Edw. III, m. 283.
[99] Ibid.   [100] Ibid.
[1] Chan. Inq. p.m. 9 Edw. II, no. 71, m. 53 ; Chart. R. 9 Edw. III, no. 3, m. 1 ; Chan. Inq. p.m. 50 Edw. III (1st nos.), no. 20 ; 24 Hen. VI, no. 41 ; L. and P. Hen. VIII, xiv (1), p. 304 ; Feet of F. Div. Co. Trin. 21 Eliz. ; Recov. R. Mich. 22 Jas. I, rot. 99, &c.
[2] Heming, op. cit. 436.

Bishop Oswald to Eadmer in 962,[3] and in 1017 Archbishop Wulfstan gave to his brother Elfwig 6 'manentes' at Bentley.[3a] Bentley seems to have become incorporated with the manor of Holt by the time of the Domesday Survey.[4]

The church of *ST. MARTIN* CHURCHES consists of a chancel 25¼ ft. by 16 ft., a nave 49½ ft. by 18½ ft., a south chapel 42 ft. by 11 ft. and a western tower 12 ft. square. These measurements are all internal.

The mid-12th-century church consisted of the still existing nave and a chancel somewhat shorter than the present one. In the 13th century the chancel was lengthened eastward and the sills of the old chancel window were lowered. The south chapel was added in the middle of the 14th century and the tower in the 15th, when the old west wall of the nave was rebuilt.

The 15th-century east window of the chancel is of two lights with a four-centred head, and on either side are two much defaced niches. In the north wall of the chancel are three single-light windows. The eastern one is of 13th-century date, and the two

capitals of the smaller shafts on the south are also scalloped, but the middle one is of a foliated type.

There are three single-light windows in the north wall of the nave, the first of which is modern, while the other two are original 12th-century windows with round heads and wide splayed reveals, and below the sills externally is an enriched cable moulding. The north door between these windows is of the same date and has a round head of two orders richly ornamented with cheverons and shafted jambs with elaborate cushion capitals, on the eastern of which is carved the fable of the fox and the stork. At the east end of the south wall are two bays of 14th-century arcading to the south chapel, with arches of two chamfered orders and an octagonal pier. The responds are octagonal to within about 4 ft. of the ground and square below. In the western face of the upper part of the east respond is a shallow niche with a plain pointed head. Further west is the 12th-century south door, which has a round head of two orders enriched with both the horizontal and vertical cheveron and double shafted jambs with cushion capitals carved with grotesque heads. West of the south door is a modern single-light window of 12th-century detail.

The south chapel has a well-designed 14th-century east window of three lights with flowing tracery over, and in the south wall are three two-light windows of the same date with a blocked south doorway. Between the middle and easternmost window is a small blocked light which may have opened at one time

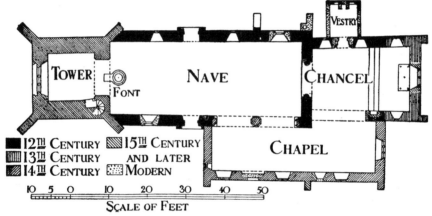

PLAN OF HOLT CHURCH

western are 12th-century windows with round heads, but they have been lengthened to bring their sills level with that of the later window. The lengthening of the easternmost has cut into a 12th-century round-headed niche, and both have cut through an external embattled moulding of the same date. In the south wall is a lancet light similar to that on the north, and west of this a 15th-century trefoil-headed piscina. A segmental arch of two chamfered orders opens into the south chapel. The semicircular chancel arch is of 12th-century date. The eastern face is comparatively plain, only the inner order being enriched, but both orders on the west, with the soffit, are elaborately ornamented with the cheveron, and above is a sunk label enriched with medallions. The jambs have two half-round columns to the inner order and two angle shafts to each jamb, all having elaborate capitals and circular bases. On the north the capital of the eastern angle-shaft is scalloped, those of the western angle-shaft and the inner half-round column being carved with an interlacing ornament. The

into an anchorite's cell. Externally the 14th-century string-course stops square a few feet on either side of this, and the adjoining buttress is evidently not contemporary with the original building of the aisle; these facts tend to prove the existence at some time later than the 14th century of some small building against this part of the south wall. There is also a small blocked loophole at the south-west corner of the chapel, but in this case the string-course is broken over it, and it is evidently a part of the original building.

The tower is of three stages with an embattled and pinnacled parapet and angle buttresses up to the second stage with small flat buttresses on corbels from the base of the third stage to the parapet. The belfry openings are of two lights with a quatrefoil over and are filled with pierced freestone slabs. There are also single-light openings in the second stage under square heads and filled in the same manner as the belfry lights. The handsome west window is of three lights and dates from the 15th century. The tower arch is of two chamfered orders.

[3] Heming, op. cit. 144; Birch, op. cit. iii, 317.
[3a] Kemble, *Cod. Dipl.* no. 1313.
[4] There is no mention of this Bentley in Domesday Book (*V.C.H. Worcs.* i, 288); it is, however, possible that it was the same as the Holt estate. The boundaries given in the charter of 962 show that Bentley lay on the western bank of the Severn and extended from the Severn to 'Hearochricge' (? Ockeridge).

Holt Church : The Font

Holt Church : The South Doorway

The 12th-century font is circular in form, carved with well-drawn grotesques and having a twisted fluted stem and cable mouldings. There are some interesting fragments of 15th-century glass in the windows of the south chapel, including a portion of an Annunciation and a well-drawn achievement of the arms of Brayley. In the south-west corner of the chapel is a wall monument to Henry Bromley, died 1683, and his wife Mercy (Pitts), and in the chancel another to Sir Henry Bromley, kt., died 1615, erected by his wife Anne Beswicke, and in the floor of the chancel a slab to John Washbourne, 1619, rector of this church with the arms : A fesse with three molets thereon between six martlets impaling a cheveron between three scallops. There is also preserved in the south chapel a tabard emblazoned with the Brayley arms and quarterings, and in the same place is a life-size effigy of 15th-century date of

in the previous year, a small modern paten and a brass almsdish, presented in 1721.

The registers before 1812 are as follows : (i) baptisms and burials 1538 to 1812 and marriages 1538 to 1753 ; (ii) a marriage book 1754 to 1812.

The chapel of the *HOLY TRINITY*, Little Witley,[5] consists of an apsidal chancel, north vestry, nave and western bellcote. The present building was entirely rebuilt in 1867, partly upon the old foundations, some of the old stones being re-used. The only original detail remaining is the blocked north doorway of the nave, which has a two-centred head, roll-moulded continuously with the jambs, and is of early 13th-century date. Portions of the lower courses of the nave and chancel walls appear to belong to the former building. These are of red sandstone, the material employed for the rebuilding, which is designed in the mid-Victorian 13th-century convention.

HOLT CHURCH FROM THE NORTH-EAST

a lady in a long robe and wearing a wimple, coif and veil. This has lately been painted in various colours by the wife of a deceased rector.

The bells are five in number, including a sanctus, undated and without inscription : the first, a treble, bears the inscription 'Robart Dugard, Whitney Kinnersley, C.W. 1713,' and the mark of the maker R.S. ; the second has neither date nor inscription ; the third is inscribed 'Jesus Be Our Speed 1632, IH. IW.' ; the fourth is of 1603 and bears the inscription 'God Save Our King James, 1603,' and the maker's mark A.W.

The plate consists of a large cup, paten and flagon, presented in 1699 by Margaret Bromley and made

There is one bell by Richard Sanders of Bromsgrove, 1733.

The plate includes an Elizabethan cup of 1571 with cover paten. The inscription on the cup is 'Poculum sacrum capellanae (*sic*) de Witley Parva Humph. Hill Warden 1708.'

The registers before 1812 are as follows : (i) mixed entries 1680 to 1753, burials to 1764, baptisms to 1812 ; (ii) marriages 1756 to 1811. Burials were recorded at Holt after 1764.

ADVOWSONS Holt was originally a chapelry belonging to the church of St. Helen, Worcester.[6] It had become a rectory before 1269,[7] the presentation belonging to

---

[5] Formerly under the invocation of All Saints (*Cal. Papal Letters*, v, 317).

[6] Heming, op. cit. 427.

[7] *Reg. G. Giffard* (Worcs. Hist. Soc.), 28.

the lords of the manor.[8] The advowson has since followed the same descent as the manor,[9] the Earl of Dudley being the present patron.

During the 13th, 14th and 15th centuries it was the practice for the rector of Holt to present a vicar or curate to perform the services.[10] The church was valued at £9 6s. 8d. in 1291[11] and at £11 13s. 11d. in 1536.[12]

A chapel of St. Mary Magdalen in the church of Holt was mentioned in 1366, when a relaxation of penance was granted to those who gave alms and visited it on certain days,[13] but there is no reference to it after this date.

The chapelry of Little Witley was formerly attached to Holt. It is mentioned in the 11th century as being a chapelry of St. Helen, Worcester.[14] In 1375 the inhabitants of the village obtained licence to erect a baptismal font in the chapel and to have a cemetery near, as their parish church was 2 miles distant and the road, especially in winter, watery and muddy.[15] The chapelry was transferred to the parish of Great Witley in 1904, but the advowson has followed the same descent as that of Holt[16]; it is now the property of the Earl of Dudley.

CHARITIES In 1620, as recorded on the church table, Mr. Moscrop gave £10 for the poor, and in 1683 the Hon. Beatrice Bromley gave £20 for the poor.

These gifts were laid out in the purchase of 5 a. known as Hare Close. The land was sold in 1884, and the proceeds with accumulations of income were invested in £543 14s. 1d. consols with the official trustees. The annual dividends, amounting to £13 11s. 8d., are distributed in coal at Christmas to about forty recipients.

The gifts for the poor of £20 by Mrs. Mercy Walsh and £10 by John Bromley, also mentioned on the church table, and of £5 by one Pillett, have been lost owing to the insolvency of the holder.

In or about 1825 Mrs. Susannah Gabb, by her will, gave £20 for the poor. The principal sum is in the post office savings bank, the interest being distributed in bread on Good Friday.

In 1863 Mrs. Elizabeth Cowell, by her will, left £50 for the poor, which sum is also in the savings bank; the interest is from time to time distributed in money to the poor.

HUDDINGTON

Hudintuna, Huntintune, Hudintune, Hudigtun (xi cent.); Hodintone (xiii cent.); Hodyngton (xiv cent.).

The parish of Huddington lies near the centre of the county to the south-east of the town of Droitwich. The area of the parish is 981 acres,[1] of which 166 are arable, 637 permanent grass and 111 woods.[2] Bow Brook and Little Brook,[3] one of its tributaries, form the north-eastern boundary of the parish.

The chief road in the parish is Trench Lane, which runs from Huddington village north-west to Droitwich, being intersected at Shaftland Cross, to the north-west of the village, by a road running south-west to Worcester.

The village of Huddington lies in the valley of Bow Brook and the whole parish is low-lying, the highest part being in the north-west, where the land rises to 200 ft. above the ordnance datum. The parish is on the Lower Lias, the soil being stiff clay and limestone. The land is chiefly pasture.

The village is situated on either side of the road to Droitwich. It contains Huddington Court, the church of St. James, Hall Farm, a corn-mill[4] and a few cottages. The church stands a little back from the south side of the road in a small inclosed churchyard. The village itself forms a small street of a few cottages running northwards from the church, and includes some good specimens of half-timber work, but the chief architectural feature is Huddington

Court, now a farm-house, which, surrounded by a moat, stands immediately to the west of the church.

It is a small late 15th-century house of half-timber, two stories in height, with an attic floor in the roof. The plan is T-shaped, the tail of the T appearing to be a later addition, probably of the early 17th century. The original part consists of a large hall, with an entrance in the centre, and two rooms on either side, the kitchen on the west, and a parlour on the east, both now cut up by modern partitions. This appears to be itself a rebuilding of an earlier house, to judge by the series of shields reset over the fireplace of the room above the parlour. The hall is now mainly occupied by a late 16th-century staircase, to which date the present entrance doorway and porch belong. The latter is gabled and of half-timber on a brick base, with small attached Ionic columns of wood and well-carved capitals. An original oaken gate with turned balusters is still in position. The stairs, also of oak, are wide, and have an easy ascent. The first floor is supported by richly moulded 15th-century beams, one of which has been moved out of its original position to make room for the later stairs and chamfered away on one side to give the utmost amount of head-room. The room on the east side of the first-floor landing has been divided into two by a modern partition which cuts into a large open fireplace with moulded jambs and head. Above this is reset the older work before-

---

[8] *Reg. G. Giffard* (Worcs. Hist. Soc.), 342.

[9] Nash, op. cit. i, 600; *Sede Vacante Reg.* (Worcs. Hist. Soc.), 223, 224, 231, 288, 423; Chan. Inq. p.m. (Ser. 2), xv, 100; Feet of F. Worcs. Trin. 3 & 4 Phil. and Mary; Inst. Bks. (P.R.O.).

[10] *Reg. G. Giffard* (Worcs. Hist. Soc.), 28, 51, 347; *Sede Vacante Reg.* (Worcs. Hist. Soc.), 149, 183, 378.

[11] *Pope Nich. Tax.* (Rec. Com.), 216.

[12] *Valor Eccl.* (Rec. Com.), iii, 234.

[13] *Cal. Papal Letters*, iv, 55.

[14] Heming, op. cit. 427.

[15] *Cal. Papal Letters*, v, 317.

[16] Heming, loc. cit.; *Inq. Nonarum* (Rec. Com.), 296, &c. The chapel was valued at £4 11s. 8d. in 1535 (*Valor Eccl.* [Rec. Com.], iii, 236).

[1] Four of these are covered by water.

[2] Statistics from Bd. of Agric. (1905).

[3] The fishing in these brooks is mentioned in the 15th century, when it seems to have been of considerable value. In 1487–8 Robert Winter proceeded against one William Somer for fishing and carrying away fish, to the value of £5, from Huddington (De Banco R. Hil. 3 Hen. VII, m. 55).

[4] This mill is mentioned in the Domesday Survey, when it rendered three horse-loads of grain as rent (*V.C.H. Worcs.* i, 294b). It apparently followed the same descent as the manor (Recov. R. Mich. 5 Anne, rot. 219). In 1650 two water grist mills under one roof called Huddington Mills were worth £10 a year (Parl. Surv. Worcs. 1650–1, no. 6).

HUDDINGTON COURT FROM THE NORTH-EAST

HUDDINGTON COURT : HERALDIC FRIEZE OVER FIREPLACE

mentioned. This consists of a 14th-century frieze with four quatrefoiled panels, each containing a shield hanging from a head : (1) Hodington ; (2) a cheveron between three roses ; (3) England ; (4) Cromelyn. The quatrefoils themselves are enriched with the ball-flower, and in their foliations on either side of the shields, as well as in the spandrels, are large ball-flowers. On the west side of the landing was a room of smaller dimensions ; both these rooms were originally lighted by bay windows on the north side, only that to the eastern room now remaining ; it is of five transomed lights, with a narrower light in each return. The projecting sill rests on richly carved brackets with a plastered soffit following their curve. The main uprights of the house divide the ceilings of these rooms into three and two bays respectively. The ceiling beams are slightly cambered to a central ridge rib, and each bay on either slope is subdivided into four panels by subsidiary ribs. All the timbers are moulded, and have masons' mitres at their intersections. The chimney stack at the south-east is a beautiful example of late 15th-century brickwork. The lower portion is of stone ashlar, with a bold base-mould. At about the level of the first floor is a weathered offset, and above the gutter level rise the brick octagonal bases of the twin shafts, each face of the octagon panelled with a trefoiled panel. The shafts themselves are circular and elaborately moulded, but their cappings again become octagonal with concave sides. The main portion of the house is roofed by a tiled ridge-roof, gabled at either end. The windows, with the exception of the bay window above described, are mostly 17th-century insertions, the positions of the former windows having been altered in many cases. A moat filled with water surrounds the house.

A survey [5] of the manor made in 1650 shows that the court-house then possessed ten rooms below stairs and twelve above. There were two barns, two stables and a pigeon-house. The house was surrounded by an orchard, a green court and a small hopyard, a close called Parke Close on the south, and a croft called the Oat Crofte on the west and Piggs Close on the east. The house was at that time much out of repair. The avenue of trees by which the house is approached is known as Lady Winter's Walk. According to the local legend one of the Winters at the time of the Gunpowder Plot, not daring to appear by day, used to meet his wife here at night, and Robert Winter, who was executed in 1606, still walks with his head in his hand.

The hamlet of Sale Green, consisting of a farm and a few cottages, is 1 mile to the north-west of the village of Huddington and lies partly in Crowle and Oddingley.

A skeleton, buried about 3 ft. beneath the surface, was found in January 1903 in the churchyard, with the remains of a purse on the thigh bone, which was broken. Thirty-two coins were found, thirty Scotch bodles of Charles I, a Scotch turner of James I and a double turnois of Louis XIII dated 1637.

Place-names which occur at Huddington in the 17th century are Parke Close, Great Charsleyes, Shatherlong Field, Dry Slowes, Mawbridge or Maybridge Close, Windmill Field.[6]

A reference to *HUDDINGTON* [7] *MANOR* occurs amongst the boundaries given in a charter relating to Crowle,[8] which seems to date from the 11th century.[9] In 1086 Alric the archdeacon held a hide of land at Huddington, which had formerly been held by Wulfric, as a villein, of the Bishop of Worcester's manor of Northwick.[10] The overlordship of the Bishop of Worcester was recognized until the 17th century.[11]

In the reign of Henry II this hide at Huddington was held by Alan de Warnestre.[12] It must have passed before the end of that reign to Simon son of Adam de Croome, for Simon was holding a hide at Huddington without doing service for it, and this land he said he held of Roger de St. John, who held it of the bishop.[13] Richard de Hodington was in possession of the estate in 1299,[14] and is probably to be identified with Richard de Cromelyn, who was holding the vill of Huddington in the previous year,[15] and paid a subsidy there in 1327.[16] He must have been succeeded shortly afterwards by John de Hodington, who paid subsidy in Huddington in 1332-3.[17] Walter de Hodington, who was a witness to a deed of 1339-40, was probably son of this John.[18] In 1390-1 the manor was settled on Walter's son Thomas and his wife Joan daughter of Richard Thurgrim and their issue, with contingent remainders to Thomas son of Alexander de Besford and Thomas son of John Moraunt, sons of Margaret sister of Thomas Hodington.[19] Thomas Hodington left two daughters, Agnes wife of William Russell and Joan wife of Roger Winter.[20] Nicholas Stokes and Robert Russell, probably the son of William and Agnes, were said to be holding the manor of Huddington in 1431.[21] The Russells received as their share a rent of 22s.[22] from the manor, while the manor itself passed to the Winters. Robert Winter was apparently in possession in 1487-8, as he then claimed certain fishing rights at Huddington.[23] Roger Winter, son of this Robert,[24] died in 1535 holding the manor of Huddington, which then passed to his son Robert.[25]

[5] Parl. Surv. Worcs. 1650-1, no. 6.
[6] Ibid.
[7] Thomas (*Surv. of Worc. Cath.* A 16) identifies Huddington with the 'Huntenatune' which Aldred gave to Beornheard about the middle of the 8th century (Birch, *Cart. Sax.* i, 306 ; Heming, Chartul. [ed. Hearne], 106) and which Ecgferd King of Mercia gave in 796 to Ethelmund (Heming, op. cit. 106 ; Birch, op. cit. i, 384, 385). In a survey of the manor of Northwick, which appears to be of the same date as the Domesday Survey or a copy of it, Huddington is spelt Huntintune (Heming, op. cit. 305).
[8] Birch, *Cart. Sax.* ii, 2.
[9] Inform. from Mr. F. M. Stenton.
[10] *V.C.H. Worcs.* i, 294.

[11] Chan. Inq. p.m. (Ser. 2), lvii, 11 ; cccxcii, 98 ; cccxxxix, 60.
[12] Red Bk. of Bishopric of Worc. (Eccl. Com. Rec. Var. bdle. 121, no. 43698), fol. 18 ; Habington, *Surv. of Worcs.* (Worcs. Hist. Soc.), ii, 41. Alan and his wife Cecily gave church scot of Huddington to the nuns of Cookhill (Nash, op. cit. ii, 17).
[13] Red Bk. of Bishopric of Worc. fol. 254.
[14] Habington, op. cit. i, 288 ; Red Bk. of Bishopric of Worc. fol. 3.
[15] Add. MS. 28024, fol. 148. In the visitation of Worcester 1569 Sir Richard Cromelyn is said to have had a daughter Lucy who married Sir Richard Hodington (*Visit. of Worcs.* [Harl. Soc.], 118).

[16] *Lay Subs. R. Worcs.* 1327 (Worcs. Hist. Soc.), 12.
[17] Ibid. 1332-3 (Worcs. Hist. Soc.), 6.
[18] Prattinton Coll. (Soc. Antiq.), Deeds of D. and C. of Worc. no. 181 ; *Visit. of Worcs.* 1569 (Harl. Soc. xxvii), 118.
[19] Feet of F. Div. Co. Mich. 14 Ric. II ; *Visit. of Worcs.* 1569 (Harl. Soc. xxvii), 118.
[20] *Visit. of Worcs.* 1569 (Harl. Soc. xxvii), 118.
[21] *Feud. Aids*, v, 332.
[22] *Cal. Inq. p.m. Hen. VII*, i, 381 ; Chan. Inq. p.m. (Ser. 2), xvi, 11, 106. This rent was paid until 1502.
[23] De Banco R. Hil. 3 Hen. VII, m. 55.
[24] See Chan. Inq. p.m. (Ser. 2), ccxlii, 75. [25] Ibid. lvii, 11.

Robert was succeeded in 1549 by his son George Winter.[26] Robert had settled the manor in 1542 upon

HODINGTON. *Gules a saltire argent and a border azure bezanty.*

RUSSELL. *Argent a cheveron between three crosslets fitchy sable.*

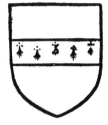

WINTER. *Sable a fesse ermine.*

his wife Catherine,[27] who afterwards married Thomas Smith and held some estate in the manor in 1567.[28]

George died in 1594, being followed by Robert Winter, his eldest son by his first wife, Jane daughter of Sir William Ingleby.[29] This Robert Winter and his brother Thomas were deeply implicated in the Gunpowder Plot. When they were fully satisfied that the plot was discovered the conspirators fled to Huddington, where they stayed on 6 November 1605. Thomas Winter was captured on the following day at Holbeach, and taken to the Tower on 8 November, but Robert, less resolute than his younger brother, escaped from Holbeach before the encounter with the sheriff's men,[30] and in company with Stephen Lyttelton hid for two months in barns and poor men's houses in Worcestershire.[31] He was finally captured at Hagley, at the house of Mrs. Lyttelton, through the treachery of John Finwood, one of her servants.[32] He was attainted of high treason, and executed on 30 January 1606, the day before

his brother.[33] His estates were restored in the same year[34] to his widow, Gertrude Winter, who seems to have forfeited the manor in 1607 for recusancy.[35] Her son John Winter, however, died seised of the manor in 1622,[36] being followed by his sons John, Robert and George successively.[37] George Winter was created a baronet 29 April 1642,[38] took the side of the king in the Civil War,[39] and died without issue on 4 June 1658, when the baronetcy became extinct.[40]

Sir George Winter, by his will dated 13 March 1657, left the manor of Huddington to his wife Mary and his aunt Helen for their lives, with remainder to Francis Earl of Shrewsbury, his first wife's brother, and to Gilbert Talbot, brother of Francis, in tail-male, with contingent remainder to the English Fathers of the Society of Jesus.[41] Helen Winter and Francis Earl of Shrewsbury and his brother Gilbert were dealing with the manor in 1660.[42] The issue male of Francis Earl of Shrewsbury failed on the death of his son

TALBOT, Earl of Shrewsbury. *Gules a lion and a border engrailed or.*

Charles in 1717–18,[43] and Gilbert Talbot, son of Gilbert above mentioned, succeeded to the title and estates.[44] The manor has since descended with the title, and now belongs to Charles Henry John Chetwynd-Talbot, twentieth Earl of Shrewsbury.

In 1232 the king confirmed to the hospital of St. Wulfstan, Worcester, a grant of land made to them by Roger the clerk of Huddington. The land lay in Ryecroft, Heringshame, Derhamme, Pichethorn, Frewinspit and Hemmingesik,[45] and, though the parish in which it was situated is not stated, it was probably in Huddington, for in 1291 the hospital of St. Wulfstan owned 2 carucates of land in Crowle and Huddington worth 20s. a year.[46] The lands at Huddington and a building thereon were worth 26s. 8d. in 1535,[47] and after the suppression of the hospital in 1540[48] passed to the Crown. The estate was granted to Richard Morrison in the same year,[49] and the further descent of it has not been traced.

CHURCH The church of *ST. JAMES*[50] consists of a chancel 20½ ft. by 15 ft., a nave 40 ft. by 17 ft., a south chapel 21 ft. by 14 ft. and a north porch. These measurements are all internal.

[26] Chan. Inq. p.m. (Ser. 2), lxxxix, 157.
[27] Ibid.
[28] Feet of F. Worcs. Hil. 9 Eliz.
[29] Chan. Inq. p.m. (Ser. 2), ccxlii, 75.
[30] *Dict. Nat. Biog.* under Thomas Winter.
[31] *Cal. S. P. Dom.* 1603–10, p. 281.
[32] Ibid. 1580–1625, p. 474.
[33] *Dict. Nat. Biog.*; Stat. 3 Jas. I, cap. 2; *Cal. S. P. Dom.* 1603–10, pp. 242–5, 247, 254, 264, 266, 274, 280, 281, 282, 297.
[34] Parl. Surv. Worcs. 1650–1, no. 6.
[35] Pat. 6 Jas. I, pt. vii. The manor was granted to Sir Walter Leveson for forty-one years.
[36] Chan. Inq. p.m. (Ser. 2), cccxcii, 98. In an inventory taken on the death of his widow in 1629 a small striking watch clock and a watch, a 'whipping wheele' and a spinning wheel are mentioned (*Var. Coll.* [Hist. MSS. Com.], ii, 299).

[37] Chan. Inq. p.m. (Ser. 2), ccccxxxix, 60; ccclix, 24b. John died in 1628 and Robert in 1630.
[38] G.E.C. *Complete Baronetage*, ii, 169.
[39] *Cal. Com. for Comp.* 2124. In 1650–1 a survey of the manor was taken by the Parliamentary Commissioners, who evidently based their claim on the forfeiture of 1606. The manor was worth £490 a year, and attached to it were twenty-four 'bullaries' of salt in Droitwich worth £144 a year (Parl. Surv. Worcs. 1650–1, no. 6).
[40] G.E.C. *Complete Baronetage*, ii, 169.
[41] *Hist. MSS. Com. Rep.* x, App. iv, 198; *Cal. S. P. Dom.* 1666–7, p. 422. At the Restoration Gervase Holles, the Master of Requests, petitioned the king for the reversion of 'the manor of Huddington entailed on the Crown after one life' (*Cal. S. P. Dom.* 1660–1, p. 112). This

was evidently an attempt to revive the claim of 1650–1 (see *ante*).
[42] Recov. R. Trin. 12 Chas. II, rot. 108.
[43] G.E.C. *Complete Peerage*, vii, 144.
[44] Ibid. [45] *Cal. Chart. R.* 1226–57, p. 173.
[46] *Pope Nich. Tax.* (Rec. Com.), 231.
[47] *Valor Eccl.* (Rec. Com.), iii, 228.
[48] *V.C.H. Worcs.* ii, 176.
[49] *L. and P. Hen. VIII*, xv, g. 831 (64); xvi, g. 678 (25); Pat. 32 Hen. VIII, pt. v, m. 1.
[50] That St. James is the correct invocation appears from a will of a former vicar proved in 1545 and other evidence. See *Himbleton and Huddington Parish Mag.* Feb. 1901. The Rev. G. H. Poole there points out that the mistaken notion that the church is under the patronage of St. Michael and All Angels is probably owing to the fact that King Henry VIII ordered all wakes and feasts to be kept at Michaelmas.

HUDDINGTON COURT : THE ENTRANCE PORCH

HUDDINGTON CHURCH : THE PORCH

The earliest church of which traces remain was of late 12th-century date, parts of the north and south nave walls, with the two doorways, being of that period. The chancel was probably of the same size as the present one, which was rebuilt late in the 15th century. The south chapel was a 14th-century addition, and within the last few years the whole building has been repaired and restored.

The east window of the chancel is of three lights with a 15th-century traceried head, and on each side are defaced image niches with shields above. The north and south chancel walls have each two windows of two lights, with tracery above under a square head, of the same date as the east window. In the south-east corner is a plain piscina supported on a square pillar with chamfered angles. The 15th-century chancel arch is of two moulded orders.

In the north wall of the nave the western window and the north door are original 12th-century work, the latter having a round head and jambs chamfered in the 14th century. The other two windows, with that in the west wall, are of the 14th century, but the tracery of the easternmost is modern, and all are of two lights. The arcade of two bays to the south chapel has pointed arches of two moulded orders with moulded capitals. The work is probably of the 14th century, but has apparently been recut in the 17th century.

The east window of the chapel is of two lights, and perhaps dates from the 14th century, but the two-light windows to the south and west both date from the late 16th century. In the west window is some 15th and 16th-century heraldic glass comprising three shields : (1) Cassey impaling Cooksey ; (2) Winter and Hungerford, being the arms of Roger and Elizabeth Winter ; (3) the arms of George Winter, the father of the conspirators. These shields are part of the large quantity of glass removed from the church about seventy years ago, and recovered in 1906 by the late vicar, the Rev. G. H. Poole. Some of this glass is now in one of the windows of the Raven Hotel, Droitwich.

In the south wall are some remains of a blocked piscina, and in the east wall is an image bracket. The round-headed south door dates from the 12th century and is partly restored. The roofs are 16th-century woodwork, and have at one time been plastered.

The other fittings include a 17th-century chancel screen with balusters, the remains of a 16th-century screen, some linen pattern panels re-used for the front of the quire stalls, and some 17th-century panelling on either side of the altar.

In the south chapel is a monument to Sir George Winter, bart., who died in 1658.

There is also a brass tablet to the same man, and another to the 'honorabilissima heroina' Mary

daughter of Charles Viscount Carrington and second wife of Sir George Winter of Huddington, who died in 1642. Two other brass tablets record respectively Frances first wife of Sir George Winter, who died in 1641, with her infant son and Adrian Fortescue, who died in 1653. The timber porch, which stands on modern dwarf walls of stone, dates from the 16th century. The embattled cross beam on the front is carved with an ogee arch on the under side. The barge-boards of the gable form a cinquefoiled arch with an ogee head, and the open sides of the porch are divided by three moulded wood shafts.

The exterior of the building has been repaired, though the chancel retains its original ashlar facing

HUDDINGTON CHURCH : CHANCEL FROM THE SOUTH-EAST

with diagonal buttresses and a plinth ; the western portions of the nave and aisle are rebuilt or refaced with small coursed rubble. The roofs are tiled.

There is one bell by Richard Sanders of Bromsgrove, cast in 1723.

The plate consists of a cup without hall-mark, but with a shaped punch stamped s r above a star and two dots, repeated four times. There are also a modern paten and a small plated dish.

The registers [51] before 1812 are as follows : (i) mixed entries 1695 to 1799, which appear to overlap book ii, which has entries 1785 to 1812 ; (iii) a marriage book 1756 to 1810.

[51] Earlier 17th-century entries will be found among the Bishops' Transcripts.

ADVOWSON

Huddington was originally a chapelry of the church of St. Helen Worcester.[52] It is said afterwards to have become annexed to the church of Crowle,[53] but is called a church in 1291, 1340, and 1428.[54] Before 1291 the church appears to have been appropriated to the hospital of St. Wulfstan, Worcester.[55] In 1428 it was not taxed because there were not ten inhabitants at Huddington.[56] The facts that the church of Huddington is not mentioned in the valuation of the possessions of St. Wulfstan's Hospital made in 1535, and that no presentations to it have been found, confirm the opinion that it was a chapelry of Crowle. It seems to have passed with the church of Crowle (q.v.) to the Combes, for John Combes and his wife Rose and Edward Combes sold the advowson and tithes in 1570 to George Winter.[57] The living then seems to have been severed from that of Crowle, and the advowson remained in the possession of successive owners of the manor,[58] belonging at the present day to the Earl of Shrewsbury, while the rectory belongs to Lord Edmund Talbot.

CHARITIES

In 1744 the Rev. — Wilkins, by his will, left £5 to remain as a stock for ever, the interest to be yearly distributed in money on Good Friday to the poor by the minister and churchwardens. The principal sum came into private hands without security, and no interest has been received for many years.

ICCOMB

Iccecumbe, Iccacumb (viii cent.) ; Iacumbe (xi cent.) ; Ikcoumbe (xiii cent.).

The parish of Iccomb or Icomb lies in a valley of the Cotswolds about 2 miles south-east of Stow-on-the-Wold ; the boundary is formed on the western side by the road from Stow to Burford, and on the south by Westcote Brook, but it runs for the most part along the borders of various fields. The parish, which is now entirely in Gloucestershire, contains about 1,184 acres, of which 513 were in Worcestershire until 1844.[1] This part, Church Iccomb, is divided from the rest of the parish by a small stream which is crossed by a footbridge near the village and flows southwards into Westcote Brook. Both Church Iccomb and the adjoining hamlet stand on the lower slopes of Iccomb Hill, near the top of which are the remains of an ancient camp. There is a round tower in the sham Gothic taste of the early 19th century on the hill at the point where the boundary between Iccomb and Church Iccomb touches the road to the village. Further down the hill this road winds about to form a rough quadrangle, at the south-east corner of which stands the church, while two of its sides form the main streets of Church Iccomb, a grey stone village set comfortably in a valley of orchards and backed by the bare wold.

The soil is clay and stone brash, the subsoil lias. The chief crops are wheat, barley and turnips, but the greater part of the land is pasture. The common lands in Church Iccomb were inclosed in 1810 under the Act of 1809.[2]

Iccomb Place, which has been conservatively restored by its present owner, Mr. George Simpson-Hayward, stands to the south of the brook which formed the old county boundary and was always in Gloucestershire; it is a fine two-storied stone house of the early 15th century, and was probably built by Sir John Blaket, who resided here from 1400 to the year of his death, 1430.[3] The original plan included two courtyards, divided from each other by the hall, the principal or entrance court being on the north and the office court on the south. The entrance court with the buildings surrounding it survives in its entirety. At the west end are the withdrawing room and solar, on the east were the buttery, larder and cellar, while the northern range, which is pierced by the entrance gateway, contained the private apartments of the family, with a porter's lodge at the eastern end opening out of the gateway. Of the office court the eastern range, which contained the kitchen, and a portion of the western range alone remain, the southern range having been pulled down within living memory. The surviving portion of the house, including as it does the most important apartments, is externally in a fine state of preservation, and the details are characteristic of the best work of the period. Unfortunately the interior has suffered severely, and much fine panelling has been removed.

The entrance gateway is a little to the east of the centre of the north front, of which it forms the most important feature. The wall is here broken forward to about the projection of the eaves of the roof, and is crowned by a well-moulded cornice and embattled parapet. The gateway itself has an elaborately moulded four-centred head, and is flanked by buttresses of one offset, rising to a little above the string-course, which here marks the level of the upper floor. In the upper stage thus formed is a square-headed window of four lights with good vertical tracery in the head, both lights and tracery being uncusped. The label is formed by the lower members of the crowning cornice which are returned downwards on either side to the usual level. This gatehouse-like projection separates the façade into two unequal lengths. Immediately to the east of it is the corbelled-out chimney stack of a first-floor fireplace, surmounted by a square stone shaft. Nearly in the centre of the western part of the façade is a similar chimney stack. Both floors are lighted by square-headed windows of two and three lights. The more important have

[52] Heming, op. cit. 427.
[53] Habington, op. cit. i, 290.
[54] *Pope Nich. Tax.* (Rec. Com.), 218 ; *Inq. Nonarum* (Rec. Com.), 295; *Feud. Aids,* v, 316.
[55] The church was then taxed at £1, but the entry is cancelled 'quia infirmorum' (*Pope Nich. Tax.* [Rec. Com.], 218 ; see also Bacon, *Liber Regis,* 975).

[56] *Feud. Aids,* v, 316.
[57] Feet of F. Worcs. Hil. 12 Eliz.
[58] Chan. Inq. p.m. (Ser. 2), ccxlii, 75 ; cccxcii, 98 ; ccccxxxix, 60 ; cccclix, 24*b* ; *Cal. S. P. Dom.* 1666-7, p. 422 ; Recov. R. Mich. 5 Anne, rot. 219.
[1] *Pop. Ret.* 1851, i (vi), 27 ; Stat. 7 & 8 Vict. cap. 61.

[2] Priv. Act, 49 Geo. III, cap. 43 ; *Blue Bk. Incl. Awards,* 190.
[3] The 'manor house at Iccumbe with the hall, chambers, bakehouse and kitchen' are mentioned in Edmund Blaket's will in 1444 (*Bristol and Gloucs. Arch. Soc. Trans.* vii, 179).

ICCOMB PLACE : NORTH FRONT, BEFORE RESTORATION IN 1884

ICCOMB PLACE : NORTH FRONT IN 1912

labels; the mullions have been in some cases restored. The walls of this and the other portions of the house are of rubble masonry, with ashlar quoins, and have in some instances been covered with rough-cast. The roof of the range is terminated at either end by gables with moulded copings and foliated gablet finials. The interior of the gateway is ungroined and plain; doorways in the east and west sides lead to the porter's lodge and to the private apartments on the west. A four-centred arch, plainly chamfered and the whole width of the gateway, opens into the courtyard, which within its narrow compass presents all the characteristic features of the domestic architecture of the 15th century. On the south side is the hall with its richly moulded entrance doorway and tall traceried windows; on the west the withdrawing room and solar upon whose oriel have been lavished the utmost pains of mediaeval mason-

two-centred heads and vertical tracery over. In the south wall is one similar window. The twin doorways in the east wall leading to the kitchen and buttery have been blocked and are no longer visible from the hall. In the south wall is a fireplace with a 17th-century stone chimney-piece, removed here recently from the withdrawing room, which is reached by a doorway at the west end of the north wall. A corridor has been erected against the ground-stage of the south wall to connect the remaining portions of the east and west ranges of the former office-court. A flat plaster ceiling conceals the trusses of the roof, which have collars stiffened by curved braces, moulded purlins, and arched wind-braces.

The withdrawing room occupies the whole of the ground floor of the range at the west end of the entrance-court. It is now divided by brick partitions into a larder and pantry. At the south-east it

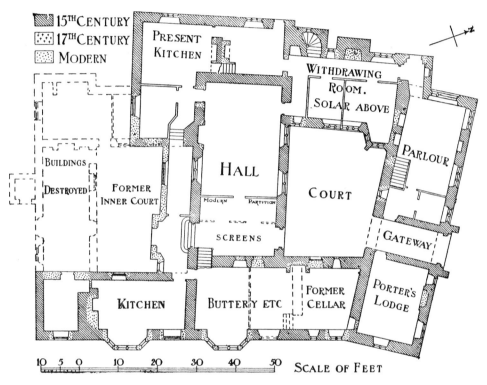

PLAN OF ICCOMB PLACE

craft. The plainer elevations of the east and north sides mark their more utilitarian purpose. The walls here are covered with rough-cast.

The hall is entered at the south-east of the courtyard by a doorway with a two-centred head within a square containing casement mould and label. The spandrels are traceried and each has a blank shield. In the opposite wall is a similar doorway. The screens and gallery have disappeared, and their place has been taken by a modern gallery, communicating with the rooms on the first floor of the eastern range, and continued externally in half-timber across the east end of the courtyard. An entrance hall has been formed by the insertion of a modern partition; the remaining and larger portion of the hall is now used as a dining room. In the north wall are two lofty square-headed windows with casement-moulded jambs, each of two transomed lights, with uncusped

is lighted by the lower part of the oriel window which forms the principal feature of the courtyard. To the south is a window of four lights with depressed three-centred heads. At the south-west is a doorway opening on to the stone stairs which lead to the solar. The fireplace in the west wall is now blocked up, the stone chimney-piece having been re-erected in the hall as mentioned above. The stack projects externally, and is surmounted by diagonal chimney shafts of brick, probably of the 16th century. The oriel window which lights both withdrawing room and solar is designed in a style of the greatest elaboration. It abuts on the north upon the south wall of the northern range, and thus has but one return. A base-mould of bold section is continued round the whole oriel, which is divided into two stages by a moulded string-course, and there are small buttresses of two offsets at the eastern angles. In the principal face of the ground stage is a square-headed window of two uncusped ogee lights with pierced quatrefoil spandrels, and in the return is a single light of similar character. Lighting the solar are square-headed windows of a corresponding number of cinquefoiled lights with vertical tracery in their heads. These have bold labels with spirited head-stops, and the whole is surmounted by a plain parapet with a moulded coping.

The stone central newel stairs leading to the solar are contained in a square projection on the west side of this range. The solar itself is lighted by the upper part of the oriel, and to the southward of it by a labelled window, originally of three cinquefoiled ogee lights with vertical tracery within a square head. The tracery has been much restored, and the window has been enlarged by the addition of two southern lights. At the north-west is a small closet, probably a garderobe. In the west wall is a stone fireplace with a wave-moulded square head and jambs, and to the north of it a modern three-light window. At the south-west of the solar, adjoining the upper part of the hall on the west, is a smaller room, which has a stone fireplace with a four-centred head, and is lighted by a plain two-light window in the west wall.

The northern range has been much altered internally, and retains few features of interest. The large room on the west side of the gateway has been curtailed at its eastern end by modern partitions and by the insertion of a staircase. This room seems originally to have communicated with the withdrawing room by a doorway in the south wall immediately to the west of the oriel. The western range is now entered through the small closet at the north-east, which has been transformed into a back entrance. The first floor, formerly occupied by a long room extending the whole length of the range, and covered by an elaborate open-timber roof, communicates with the solar by a doorway at the south-west. The roof, if it still exists, is now concealed by a plaster ceiling.

The room on the east side of the gateway, occupying the remainder of the ground floor of this range, probably served as a porter's lodge. A fireplace in the north wall has been blocked and the original stonework removed to the adjoining room in the east range. A doorway at the south-east leads into this range, the ground floor of which has been completely remodelled and turned into one large room. Here were originally the buttery, larder, and cellars, but all partitions have been removed, a doorway leading from the cellars to the courtyard blocked, and a new fireplace constructed. The doorways leading to the hall, as mentioned above, have also been blocked. A modern bay window has been inserted at the south end of the east wall and a second modern window at the opposite end of the same wall. On the first floor

is the room known as 'the panelled room,' which contains painted panelling of a crude type, dating from the latter half of the 17th century. An external doorway in the east wall with moulded architraves, now blocked, appears to have originally opened on to a flight of steps leading to the garden. A parallel to this curious arrangement exists at Norgrove Court, near Feckenham, where there are similar blocked doorways in the external wall of the first floor.[3a] There is an attic floor over this range, and on the walls of one of the rooms known as 'Dyke's chamber' is a 17th-century painting in a red pigment of a ship in full sail.

The buildings at the west end of the hall, the ground floor of which is now occupied by the kitchen and offices, contain little original detail, with the exception of the room over the first floor adjoining the solar mentioned above. The eastern range of the disappeared office-court containing the original kitchen has been completely modernized internally, and several modern windows have been inserted. The roofs of the whole building are of Stonesfield slate.

MANORS Offa, King of the Mercians, in 781 gave land at *ICCOMB* in exchange for Sapey [Pitchard] to Bishop Heathored,[4] who gave it to the cathedral monastery of Worcester[5]; Wiles Well is mentioned as a boundary on the north.[6] Algar son of Leofric, Earl of Mercia, about 1060 and King Harold in 1066 were later credited with making additions to this grant.[7]

At the time of the Domesday Survey Church Iccomb belonged to the episcopal manor of Blockley with which it was valued, but it was apportioned to the support of the monks.[8] In 1256 the Prior and convent of Worcester obtained a grant of fee warren in their demesne lands in Iccomb from Henry III.[9]

The manor continued in the possession of the cathedral monastery until the Dissolution, when it was granted by Henry VIII to the Dean and Chapter of Worcester.[10] They returned it to him in 1545 in consideration of his acquittance of their obligation to maintain students at Oxford,[11] but received it back again in 1547 in exchange for a grant to the king of the manors and parsonages of Grimley and Hallow.[12]

Iccomb was sold in 1650 by the trustees for the sale of church lands to Thomas Marsh,[13] from whom it passed to Thomas and Stephen Robins, who were still in possession of it in 1659.[14] It was, however, recovered after the Restoration[15] by the Dean and Chapter of Worcester, who held it until 1859, when it was transferred to the Ecclesiastical Commissioners,[16] the present lords of the manor.

At the time of the Domesday Survey there were three manors of *ICCOMB* in Gloucestershire,[17] two of which were formed into the parish of Westcote before 1444.[18] The third belonged in the reign of

3a See above.

4 Birch, *Cart. Sax.* i, 334; Heming, *Chartul.* (ed. Hearne), 412, 445.

5 Heming, op. cit. 572.

6 Ibid. The northern boundary of the parish still passes across a 'well' or spring at the edge of Maugersbury Grove.

7 Heming, op. cit. 370, 390, 404.

8 *V.C.H. Worcs.* i, 293; Dugdale, *Mon.* i, 604.

9 Habington, op. cit. i, 337; ii, 359; *Cal. Pat.* 1354–8, p. 266.

10 *L. and P. Hen. VIII*, xvii, g. 71 (29); Dugdale, *Mon.* i, 620; Pat. 6 Jas. I, pt. xii, no. 2. A rent of £1 from the rectory of Iccomb was included in this grant.

11 *Hist. MSS. Com. Rep.* xiv, App. viii, 185.

12 *L. and P. Hen. VIII*, xxi (2), g. 770 (50); Dugdale, op. cit. i, 620. The bishop afterwards recovered the advowsons of Grimley and Hallow, and a rent from the manor of Iccomb, which had been granted

to him by the dean and chapter, from William Sheldon in exchange for land in Blockley (Pat. 4 Edw. VI, pt. ii, m. 21).

13 Close, 1650, pt. xxxvi, no. 25.

14 Exch. Dep. East. 1659, no. 12.

15 Feet of F. Div. Co. Trin. 13 Geo. I.

16 *Lond. Gaz.* 16 Dec. 1859, p. 4757.

17 *Domesday Bk.* (Rec. Com.), i, 167b, 168, 168b; Atkyns, *Gloucestershire*, 255.

18 Edmund Blaket left 'ii boves optimos fabrice ecclesie' there by his will (*Bristol and Gloucs. Arch. Soc. Trans.* vii, 179).

Iccomb Place : North-west Angle of Court

Edward the Confessor to Turstan and in 1086 to Durand de Gloucester; it was held of him by Walter,[19] probably his nephew, whose granddaughter Margaret de Bohun was overlord in 1166.[20] In 1331 the manor was held in moieties of the lords of Williamscot in the parish of Cropredy (co. Oxon.) and Southam in the parish of Bishop's Cleeve,[21] but before 1353 the overlordship had passed to the Earls of Kent,[22] and it was perhaps on the extinction of this earldom in 1408 that it came to the Crown. It is last mentioned in 1608, when the manor was held in socage of James I as of the manor of Slaughter.[23]

In 1166 Ellis Cokerel held in Gloucestershire half a knight's fee of the fee of Miles of Gloucester, of which a feoffment had been made in the time of Henry I.[24] He seems to have been succeeded by another Ellis, who in 1213 gave 20 marks to the king and 12 lampreys to the Bishop of Winchester and Geoffrey Fitz Peter that he might be delivered from prison, where he had been confined owing to 'a certain false judgement made before the King's Justices in Gloucestershire.'[25] The heir of this Ellis was perhaps William de Iccomb, whose daughter Maud dealt with a virgate of land in the parish in 1221,[26] but by 1246 the widow of Ellis Cokerel was holding the half fee in Cotes which belonged to the same family,[27] and she was succeeded very shortly afterwards by Fulk Cokerel.[28] At the time of Kirkby's Quest Iccomb was held by another Ellis,[29] who was succeeded before 1303 by Thomas de Iccomb.[30] Thomas was still living in 1316,[31] but died before 1330.[32] His heir, another Ellis, seems to have died very shortly afterwards,[33] leaving a widow Margaret and perhaps a son Ellis, who died in 1331 and was succeeded by his son and namesake, then eighteen years old.[34] This Ellis was still living in 1336,[35] but died before 1346, in which year Roger Blaket and Margaret his wife, probably the sister and heir of Ellis, were seised of the estate.[36]

Sir John Blaket, who was perhaps the grandson of Roger and Margaret, had succeeded to the estate by 1410.[37] He married Elizabeth widow of William Wilcote of Wilcote in the parish of North Leigh (co. Oxon.), and was killed in the French wars in the summer of 1430.[38] He left a son Edmund, who

died at Wilcote in 1444.[39] His heir was his sister Anne, the wife of Ralph Baskerville, a younger son of the lord of the adjoining manor of Combe Baskerville in Westcote.[40] Anne's daughter and heir Jane married Simon Mylborne[41]; they had eleven daughters and co-heirs, one of whom, Blanche, the wife of James Whitney, succeeded to Iccomb.[42] Her son Robert Whitney died in 1541 seised of the manor, which he left by his will to his wife Margaret for life.[43] His son and heir Sir Robert Whitney died about 1565, having settled the manor two years before his death on his second wife Mary, the widow of Sir Thomas Jones, for her life.[44] Sir James Whitney, the son of Sir Robert by his first wife Sibylla Baskerville, succeeded to the estate after Mary's death and died seised of it in 1587, leaving as his heir his brother Eustace,[45] who was succeeded in 1607 by his son, another Sir Robert Whitney.[46] Sir Robert Whitney died before 1653[47]; his son and heir Richard early in the following year conveyed the manor to William Cope, the father-in-law of Thomas Whitney, Sir Robert's younger son, possibly in order to raise money for the Royalist cause.[48] Sir Henry Cope made a conveyance of the manor in 1692,[49] probably for the purpose of settling it upon Elizabeth daughter of William Cope, then the widow of Thomas Whitney and wife of Thomas Geeres. She and her daughter Elizabeth, who married firstly William Gregory and secondly Richard Hopton,[50] were dealing with the manor in 1707,[51] and the younger Elizabeth had succeeded before 1725.[52] The manor was divided after the death of this Elizabeth between her sons William Gregory and Edward Cope Hopton.[53] The moiety belonging to Gregory descended to John Stackhouse, who held it in 1807,[54] and subsequently sold it to Henry Stokes, of whom it was purchased by William Cambray,[55] while Hopton's moiety was inherited by his son Richard Cope Hopton, who held it in 1807,[56] and left it at his death to his cousin the Rev. John Parsons, grandson of Deborah the sister of Edward Cope Hopton,[57] who, as John Hopton, was seised of it in 1819.[58] Both moieties were apparently bought before 1883 by Mr. Hambidge,[59] who sold them before 1890 to Dr. Hayward of Stow-on-the-Wold. Mr. George Simpson Hayward is now lord of the manor.

---

[19] *Domesday Bk.* (Rec. Com.), i, 168 *b*; Atkyns, loc. cit.

[20] *Red Bk. of Exch.* (Rolls Ser.), 294.

[21] Chan. Inq. p.m. 5 Edw. III, file 26, no. 6.

[22] Close, 27 Edw. III, m. 14.

[23] Chan Inq. p.m. (Ser. 2), cccv, 109.

[24] *Red Bk. of Exch.* (Rolls Ser.), 294.

[25] *Rot. de Oblatis et Fin.* (Rec. Com.), 470.

[26] Feet of F. Gloucs. Trin. 5 Hen. III.

[27] *Testa de Nevill* (Rec. Com.), 74.

[28] Ibid. 82.

[29] *Bristol and Gloucs. Arch. Soc. Trans.* xiii, 321.

[30] *Feud. Aids*, ii, 252.

[31] Ibid. 274.

[32] *Cal. Inq. p.m.* 1–9 *Edw. III*, 228.

[33] An Ellis Cokerel of Iccomb was holding Colesburn in 1330 (ibid.), but a few years later Walter Clement and Margaret his wife, formerly wife of Ellis de Iccomb, were summoned to answer Ellis Eliesaunt (? Ellison) de Iccomb, kinsman and heir of the said Ellis, for waste in the lands held of his inheritance in

Iccomb by Margaret for her life (*Bristol and Gloucs. Arch. Soc. Trans.* vii, 174); this seems to show that the Ellis who succeeded in 1331 was the grandson or cousin of Thomas's heir.

[34] Chan. Inq. p.m. 5 Edw. III, file 26, no. 6; Close, 5 Edw. III, pt. ii, m. 4.

[35] Pat. 10 Edw. III, pt. ii, m. 36 d.

[36] *Feud. Aids*, ii, 287.

[37] Chan. Inq. p.m. 12 Hen. IV, no. 35.

[38] Pat. 17 Hen. VI, pt. ii, m. 7. His will is dated Wednesday in Easter week, 1430, and was proved by his widow 8 July following. He bequeathed his body to Iccomb Church and desired that the funeral service should be celebrated by the Abbot of Bruern (P.C.C. Wills, 13 Luffenham).

[39] *Bristol and Gloucs. Arch. Soc. Trans.* vii, 179.

[40] Ibid.; Habington, op. cit. ii, 323.

[41] Habington, loc. cit.

[42] *Bristol and Gloucs. Arch. Soc. Trans.* vii, 176.

[43] Chan. Inq. p.m. (Ser. 2), lxiii, 40.

[44] Ibid. cxlvi, 126.

[45] Ibid. ccxix, 76; *Bristol and Gloucs. Arch. Soc. Trans.* vii, 176.

[46] Chan. Inq. p.m. (Ser. 2), cccv, 109.

[47] Feet of F. Gloucs. Hil. 1653.

[48] Recov. R. East. 1654, rot. 108.

[49] Feet of F. Div. Co. East. 4 Will. and Mary.

[50] *Bristol and Gloucs. Arch. Soc. Trans.* vii, 181.

[51] Feet of F. Div. Co. Hil. 5 Anne.

[52] Ibid. Trin. 12 Geo. I. The younger Elizabeth was a party to the fine of 1707.

[53] *Bristol and Gloucs. Arch. Soc. Trans.* vii, 181; Recov. R. Trin. 12 Geo. I, rot. 104; Hil. 6 Geo. II, rot. 215, 217; Mich. 11 Geo. III, rot. 452.

[54] Fosbrooke, *Gloucestershire*, ii, 403.

[55] *Bristol and Gloucs. Arch. Soc. Trans.* vii, 181; inform. from Mr. G. Simpson-Hayward.

[56] Fosbrooke, loc. cit.

[57] *Bristol and Gloucs. Arch. Soc. Trans.* vii, 181.

[58] Recov. R. Mich. 60 Geo. III, rot. 12.

[59] *Bristol and Gloucs. Arch. Soc. Trans.* vii, 181.

The church of *ST. MARY THE CHURCH VIRGIN* consists of a chancel measuring internally 28½ ft. by 15½ ft., a nave 38½ ft. by 19½ ft., a western tower 7½ ft. by 8¼ ft., a

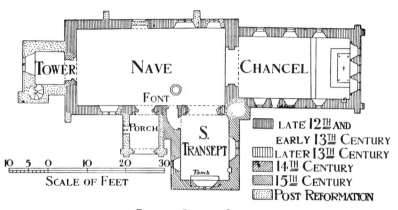

TOWER   NAVE   CHANCEL

FONT

PORCH   S. TRANSEPT

Tomb

10   5   0   10   20   30

SCALE OF FEET

▦ LATE 12TH AND EARLY 13TH CENTURY
▥ LATER 13TH CENTURY
▨ 14TH CENTURY
▧ 15TH CENTURY
▤ POST REFORMATION

PLAN OF ICCOMB CHURCH

south transept 16½ ft. by 12½ ft., and a south porch. The nave and chancel are part of one design and were set out at the end of the 12th century, the nave being finished first and the chancel following early in the 13th century. The south transept was added immediately on the completion of the chancel, but forms no part of the original design. In the 14th century a west tower was built, but of this no trace remains except the door from the nave. The transept was completely rebuilt as a chapel for the Blaket family in the middle of the following century, and the tower was rebuilt in the 17th century.

In the east wall is a triplet of 13th-century lancets, with shafted internal jambs and elaborately moulded rear arches. The shafts are detached and have moulded circular capitals and bases and an annulet at half their height. Externally the windows have a common label and the verge of the gable is decorated with dog-tooth ornament. There are also three single lancet windows on either side of the chancel with rear arch ribs supported upon carved corbels of varying designs. The pointed chancel arch of late 12th-century date is of two chamfered orders with square pilasters to the responds and square capitals. In the south wall is a 13th-century priest's door, and further east a double trefoil-headed niche with a piscina drain in the eastern compartment. Previous to the restoration of 1870 there appears to have been a passage from the chancel to the south transept through the rood staircase, but this is now blocked up.

In the north wall of the nave are two 17th-century square-headed two-light windows and affixed to the jamb of the eastern one is a plain iron hour-glass stand

with a modern glass. West of these is a blocked north door of 12th-century date with a round head and plain chamfered capitals to its external jambs. South of the chancel arch are the remains of a doorway which must have opened on to the rood-loft, and there are traces of the stair, entered originally from the south transept. The arch opening from the nave into the south transept is of mid-13th-century date and of two moulded orders. The jambs continue the mouldings, the rolls becoming shafts with circular bell capitals and moulded bases. West of the transept arch is a small opening to a low curved passage leading to the south transept, and following on this is the early 13th-century south door, which has shafted jambs and a moulded two-centred head of two orders. The only window in this wall of the nave is a 17th-century insertion of two square-headed lights. The door to the western tower is an excellent example of early 14th-century work and has a two-centred head of two moulded orders.

Of the original south transept, built in the middle of the 13th century, only the arch and the west window now remain, but the numerous fragments of this date discovered imbedded in the walls [60] at a recent restoration showed the original design to have been similar to that of the chancel. The character was, however, wholly altered at the 15th-century

ICCOMB CHURCH : ARCH AND PASSAGE TO TRANSEPT

rebuilding. Across the north-east corner is the blocked entrance to the rood stairs. The east window of the transept, of mid-15th-century date, is of two lights under a square head. To the north of it are

[60] Paper read before the Worc. Dioc. Arch. Soc. 11 Aug. 1860.

the remains of a blocked-up image niche and to the south a plain piscina.[61] The two-light south window is of the same date, and has a four-centred head ; beneath it is a niche with a moulded and cusped four-centred head lighted at the back by a small opening. Inserted in this is a life-size, full-length effigy of a man in 15th-century armour, his head resting on a helm and his feet on a hound. The slab rests upon a plinth ornamented in front with seven cinquefoil-headed panels. In the centre panel is a representation of the Trinity, with the figures of a man and his wife in the two panels on either side ; these again are flanked by angels bearing shields, while the two outer panels contain figures of St. Agnes and St. Michael. Two panels on the return have figures of angels with shields, for the plinth and slab project from the niche, for which they were evidently not originally intended, though approximately of the same date. A modern brass marks this as the tomb of Sir John Blaket, lord of the Gloucestershire manor of Iccomb, died 1431.[61a] There is one window in the west wall, a single lancet light of 13th-century date, and at the north-west angle is the opening of the passage to the nave. The south porch is largely modern ; there is, however, a small opening in the west wall, the two lights being separated by a pair of plain shafts in which there are a number of ancient stones reset.

The 17th-century west tower is three stages high ; the west window is of two square-headed lights under a square label and at the south-west angle is a staircase to the belfry. The octagonal font, which is of late 15th-century date, has quatrefoil panelling on the faces of the bowl and trefoil-headed panels on the stem.

The tower contains a peal of tubular bells.

The plate includes a cup of 1616 inscribed 'Icomb D.D. T.I. Rect'. 1758,' a paten of 1713 with the same inscription, a modern plated flagon, two glass flagons and two almsdishes, one pewter and one brass.

The registers before 1812 are as follows : (i)[62] baptisms 1545 to 1789, burials 1602 to 1788, marriages 1563 to 1753, with occasional gaps ; (ii) a marriage book 1754 to 1812 ; (iii) baptisms and burials 1788 to 1812.

ADVOWSON There was a church at Iccomb before 1240, at which time it was free from the jurisdiction of the archdeacon and dean.[63] The patronage belonged in

the 13th century to the Prior and convent of Worcester,[64] but they were not always able to exercise it ; in 1285, for instance, their nominee was not instituted because of a collation in the Roman Court on the death of Nicholas Chilbolton there.[65] Whether Nicholas himself had been presented by the prior and convent does not appear, but he seems to have been living for some time in Rome.[66] The episcopal register of 1283 contains a note to the effect that he had 'three churches in this diocese and a fourth in Bath and Wells, two of which he received after the Council,[67] and is not yet promoted to priest's orders, but went without the leave of his diocesan to the court of Rome : where he still remains.'[68]

The advowson continued in the possession of the prior and convent until the Dissolution, when it was granted by Henry VIII to the Dean and Chapter of Worcester.[69] When the manor was sold to Thomas Marsh by the trustees for the sale of church lands the advowson and tithes were reserved.[70] Possibly they were subsequently sold to the Whitneys, owners at that

ICCOMB CHURCH : THE BLAKET TOMB

time of the Gloucestershire manor of Iccomb (q.v.), who seem to have dealt with the advowson in 1653.[71]

The right of presentation to the living continued to be mentioned in deeds relating to the Gloucestershire manor at least as late as 1805,[72] but it had in reality been restored in 1660 to the Dean and Chapter of Worcester,[73] who are the present patrons.[74]

A messuage and half a virgate of land in Iccomb were assigned in 1260 by Gilbert of Woodford and

[61] This piscina was possibly for the altar to which the chantry of Gilbert Woodford was attached in 1260 (see under advowson).

[61a] This date seems to be an error. See above under manor.

[62] There is a note prefixed to the first book : 'This Regester booke of the Parishe of Icombe was made in the 19 yeare of his Maiesties raigne Anno Dñi 1621. In which allsoe is written all the old Regester booke which beganne 1545 and continued untill this praesent' yeare 1621.'

[63] Hale, *Reg. of Worc. Priory* (Camden Soc.), 104*b*.

[64] *Reg. G. Giffard* (Worcs. Hist. Soc.), 276.

[65] Ibid. 278. In cases where the incumbent died at Rome the next presentation belonged to the pope (ibid.).

[66] He was, however, in England in 1282, when he was the bearer of a prohibition concerning Mickleton (ibid. 145).

[67] The Council at Lyons in 1270.

[68] *Reg. G. Giffard* (Worcs. Hist. Soc.), 283. Possibly he wished to be at a safe distance from his creditors ; the living of

Iccomb was afterwards sequestered for the payment of his debts (ibid. 273).

[69] *L. and P. Hen. VIII*, xvii, g. 71 (29).

[70] Close, 1650, pt. xxxvi, no. 25.

[71] Feet of F. Gloucs. Hil. 1653. In 1657 the Trustees for the Maintenance of Ministers granted an increase of £10 to the incumbent of Iccomb (*Cal. S. P. Dom.* 1657–8, p. 242).

[72] Feet of F. Div. Co. Trin. 12 Geo. I ; Recov. R. Mich. 11 Geo. III, rot. 455 ; Feet of F. Gloucs. East. 45 Geo. III.

[73] Inst. Bks. (P.R.O.).

[74] *Clergy Lists*.

Emma his wife for the maintenance of a chaplain to celebrate to the honour of the Virgin Mary in the church for their souls and the souls of the ancestors and heirs of Emma.[75] In 1343 the chantry chaplain was Elias Walters, a somewhat disorderly person who thought fit to take up arms in the interest of his kinsman Robert Walters, a Papal nominee to the living of Little Compton.[76] To this rectory Philip de Alcester had already been presented by the king,[77] but the two Walters, with other clerks from the neighbourhood, broke into the house and maintained themselves there for ten days.[78] They are further said to have plotted, after Philip had been put in possession, 'to kill him or do him such other irrevocable injury as they could'; an order was therefore given for their arrest.[79] Elias was taken in June 1347[80] and Robert in August of the following year.[81] They seem to have agreed to pay compensation to Philip[82]; but it may be doubted whether they left him undisturbed in his rectory. His successor, John Paty, resigned the living in December 1350, whereupon the king at last presented Robert to the coveted post which had been his by Papal provision eight years earlier.[83]

The chantry, which was of the clear yearly value of £6,[84] was dissolved in the time of Edward VI,[85] after which the rents and profits were taken by Robert Whitney, lord of the Gloucestershire manor of Iccomb (q.v.), and his successors Robert and William,[86] until 1568, when an inquiry was made into their rights.[87] Queen Elizabeth subsequently granted leases of the chantry lands to Richard Barnerd,[88] Richard Brian[89] and John Lee successively,[90] but William Whitney was in possession of the estate in 1598.[91] It is possible that he afterwards came to an agreement with John Sotherton, who obtained a grant in fee from the Crown in 1600,[92] but the history of the chantry lands after this date is obscure.

In the 13th century the Prior and convent of Worcester claimed that there was a charge of 3 marks a year from Iccomb Church payable to the almoner of Worcester Priory for the use of poor pilgrims.[93] Richard de Sycham, rector of Iccomb, neglected to make this payment, and in 1292 the almoner of the

cathedral monastery appealed to the bishop,[94] who decided the matter in favour of the priory in accordance with a charter given by his predecessor Bishop Walter Cantilupe.[95]

The charity of William Cope, *CHARITIES* founded by deed poll 15 January 1690. A yearly sum of £10 is, under a scheme of the Charity Commissioners dated 21 June 1889, for the administration of the parochial charities of Stow-on-the-Wold, co. Gloucester, paid to the minister of Iccomb.

A yearly sum of £5 is also received from the trustees of the same charities for apprenticing poor boys or girls of this parish, or, failing such, the same to be applied in prizes or rewards to children attending a public elementary school.

Shepham's Educational Charity is endowed with a sum of £141 16s. 2d. consols, representing the proceeds of the sale of schoolhouse and buildings, and £334 South Eastern Railway 4 per cent. stock, arising from the redemption of an annuity of £13 6s. 8d.

The sums of stock are held by the official trustees, producing £16 17s. 10d. yearly, which, under the scheme above referred to, is applicable in exhibitions for children of Stow-on-the-Wold and Iccomb attending a public elementary school.

In or about 1829 the Dean and Chapter of Worcester gave £50 towards the repair of the parish church. The gift was invested in 1867 in £56 9s. 10d. consols with the official trustees, producing £1 8s. yearly.

In 1858 Richard Phillips, by his will proved at Oxford 13 October, bequeathed £108 16s. 10d. consols, the annual dividends, amounting to £2 14s. 4d., to be distributed at Christmas in coals to the poor.

The stock is held by the official trustees, who also hold a sum of £113 11s. 3d. consols, known as the Iccomb Homes of Rest Fund, producing £2 16s. 8d. yearly, which by a scheme of 31 May 1904 is also applied in supplying coal to the poor, so long as the funds available are insufficient to provide a home of rest.

The two charities are administered together, the coal being distributed to about forty recipients.

INKBERROW

Intanbeorgan (viii, ix cent.); Inteberg (xi cent.); Inkbarewe (xiii cent.); Inkeberwe, Inkebergh, Incebarrow (xiv cent.); Ynkebarrow (xvi cent.).

The parish of Inkberrow is situated on the eastern boundary of the county, due east from the town of Worcester. It covers an area of 6,879 acres,[1] of which 2,168 are arable land, 4,085 permanent grass and 203 woods.[2] The soil is sand, clay and marl, with a subsoil of Keuper Marl with occasional bands

of sandstone.[3] The chief crops are wheat, barley, oats, roots and beans. The land rises from about 200 ft. above the ordnance datum in the west of the parish to 450 ft. at New End on the Ridge Way. Stone quarries are worked, for local purposes only, at the Stone Pits about half a mile from the village. Papermaking was carried on at Inkberrow during the first half of the 19th century, but the industry became extinct about 1850. The mills were at

[75] Feet of F. Gloucs. Mich. 45 Hen. III.
[76] Pat. 16 Edw. III, pt. iii, m. 12 d.; 19 Edw. III, pt. ii, m. 12 d.; pt. iii, m. 11 d.
[77] Ibid. 19 Edw. III, pt. ii, m. 12 d. The king claimed the advowson on the ground that the temporalities of Deerhurst Priory, to which it belonged, were in his hands on account of the French war (ibid. 24 Edw. III, pt. iii, m. 5).
[78] Ibid. 19 Edw. III, pt. iii, m. 11 d.; 21 Edw. III, pt. i, m. 34 d.

[79] Ibid. 21 Edw. III, pt. i, m. 34 d.
[80] Ibid. pt. ii, m. 20.
[81] Ibid. 22 Edw. III, pt. iii, m. 16.
[82] Cal. Close, 1346–9, p. 296.
[83] Pat. 24 Edw. III, pt. iii, m. 5.
[84] Chant. Cert. 60, no. 29; 61, no. 25.
[85] Exch. Spec. Com. 26 Eliz. no. 890.
[86] Ibid.
[87] Ibid.
[88] Pat. 10 Eliz. pt. iv, m. 16.
[89] Ibid. 20 Eliz. pt. ix, m. 8.

[90] Cal. S. P. Dom. 1581–90, p. 666; Pat. 32 Eliz. pt. vii, m. 25.
[91] Exch. Spec. Com. 40 Eliz. no. 2898.
[92] Pat. 42 Eliz. pt. xxx, m. 1.
[93] Reg. G. Giffard (Worcs. Hist. Soc.), 412.   [94] Ibid.
[95] Ibid.; Hale, Reg. of Worc. Priory, 104b.
[1] Of which 4 acres are covered by water.
[2] Statistics from Bd. of Agric. (1905).
[3] V.C.H. Worcs. i, 16.

Midsummer Meadow, Pool Mill and Little Nobury, the last surviving a long time after the others were demolished. Glove-sewing employs some of the female population of Inkberrow, and a large proportion of the residents at the northern part of the parish, both male and female, work in the needle factories at Astwood Bank.

Brandon Brook forms part of the northern boundary, and another brook, unnamed, runs through the parish from north to west, finally joining Piddle Brook in the south. From the Ridge Way, now the high road from Redditch to Evesham, which forms the eastern boundary of this parish, the Salt Way[4] runs west through Edgiock and Shurnock to Droitwich. Another road leads westward from the Ridge Way through the village of Inkberrow to Worcester.

The village of Inkberrow is pleasantly situated on undulating ground and contains some good examples of half-timber work. The church stands on the east side of the village in a large churchyard surrounded by stone walls. To the north of the church on the opposite side of the by-road leading to it is the vicarage,[5] a house of some size, enlarged and altered externally in 1837. A previous rebuilding took place in 1762. Some of the internal walls, however, are of oak-framed timber work, which must have formed part of a much earlier building. Upon the south side of the same road, between the church and the main street of the village, is the Old Bull Inn, a half-timbered house probably of 16th-century date. At the junction of this by-road with the main street is a small triangular green, on the south side of which is a good house of c. 1600. At the south end of the village a second by-road leads off to the eastward, and here are some picturesque cottages of half-timber with thatched roofs, most of them on bases of local white sandstone. At Little Inkberrow, about half a mile to the north-west of the main village, is a good stone farm-house of the first half of the 17th century known as the 'Stone House' Farm. The plan is of the normal central entrance-hall type, and the interior has been much modernized. The windows, where they remain in their original condition, have stone mullions.

From Inkberrow, which lies in the centre of the parish, roads branch off to the hamlets of Edgiock and Holberrow Green in the north, to Stockwood in the west, and to Cookhill in the east.

There are moats at Holberrow Green Farm and Dragon Farm, and at Morton Underhill and Thorne. There is also a moat in good preservation on the glebe at the foot of the hill, below the vicarage.

Cookhill Priory, about 3 miles to the east of Inkberrow, stands on the site of the nunnery founded by Isabel Countess of Warwick in the 13th century. Of the original buildings all that remains above ground are portions of the east and north walls of the chapel and probably the nucleus of the adjoining range, which is of half-timber cased with brick. The greater part of the buildings of Cookhill nunnery

excepting the chapel appear to have been demolished when the site of the monastery was granted to Nicholas Fortescue in 1542. A new house was erected, which incorporated portions of the original establishment, and seems to have inclosed a courtyard, open on the north. The eastern range is flush with the east wall of the chapel, which it adjoins, and dates, in part at least, from the 15th century. The buildings upon the south and west sides appear to have been demolished by Captain John Fortescue in 1763 when a new hall and drawing room were built on the west side of the eastern range. In 1783 the chapel was rebuilt by the same owner, and within the last few years a new addition has been made by which the west front of the remaining part of Nicholas Fortescue's original house has been almost entirely hidden.

The chapel, as it stands at present, is of red brick, with the exception of the original portion of the east and north walls. It is lighted on the north by two windows, each of two lights, with pointed heads, and there is a pointed doorway in the stone-faced west wall, with a quatrefoil window above it. The whole

INTERIOR OF CHAPEL, COOKHILL PRIORY, INKBERROW

is crowned by an embattled parapet, behind which rises a hipped roof covered with slates. All these details date from the 18th-century rebuilding referred to above. The lower part of the splayed jambs of a large east window, now blocked, with image brackets on either side, and the east respond of a north arcade, are visible internally. From this the arches appear to have been of two orders, separated by a casement, the outer continuous and moulded with a swelled chamfer and the inner supported by an attached semicircular shaft with a plain bell capital and moulded semi-octagonal abacus. The aisle, into which this arcade must have opened, has disappeared, but on the external face of the space of wall included between the respond and the east end of the chancel is a piscina with a trefoiled ogee head and plain circular basin, probably earlier than the arcade, the remaining respond of which can hardly date from an earlier time than the last decade of the 14th century, to which period the jamb of the blocked east window

[4] V.C.H. Worcs. i, 213.
[5] Charles I is said to have slept in the

vicarage at Inkberrow on 10 May 1645 (Symonds's Diary [Camden Soc.], 166).

An old book of maps left behind on that occasion is still preserved.

419

may belong. At the north-east internal angle is a curious recess, about 5 ft. in height, with plain square head and jambs, the purpose of which it is difficult to determine. In the blocked east window is placed a painted alabaster bas-relief of the Virgin, in the style of the early 15th century, which may have formed part of a reredos. Some fragments of tiles of the same date are also preserved, including portions of the four-tile Talbot pattern so often met with in the county. In a vault beneath are buried many members of the Fortescue family. In the floor are slabs commemorating John Fortescue, who died in 1692, his wife, who died in 1664, William Fortescue, who died in 1706, and a slab now almost illegible commemorating a John Fortescue, the date of whose death cannot now be deciphered. On the south wall is a mural tablet to the Captain John Fortescue who rebuilt the chapel ; the inscription states that he was 'one of the last Survivors of the memorable Crew of the Centurion, which sailed round the World under the Command of Commodore Anson.' He died in 1808 in his 87th year. His youngest daughter is commemorated on the same tablet. On this wall are also tablets to his wife, who died in 1780, his eldest daughter, and to the wife of a preceding John Fortescue, who died in 1764. On a wooden panel, still hung upon the wall, is recorded the history of the house, drawn up and painted under the direction of Captain John Fortescue.

In the east wall of the garden which runs in a southerly direction from the south-west angle of the house, and is put together of fragments of masonry of the original buildings, is a portion of a late 14th-century bas-relief of the Annunciation. Only the upper part now remains, and the whole is much decayed. The heads of the angel Gabriel and the Virgin, with the top of a lily, can, however, be plainly distinguished. The roof of the older portion of the house appears to be of the 15th century, a fact which would seem to show that this is a portion of the original conventual buildings, remodelled by the Fortescues when they took possession of the estate. Some 16th and 17th-century panelling still remains. In the year 1765 a portrait of Charles I was discovered in the double panelling of the room on the first floor at the north end of the house adjoining the chapel. In a room at the south end of the house he is said to have slept.

Captain John Fortescue's addition, two stories in height, is of red brick with stone dressings, and is designed in a simple and dignified style. The walls are crowned by a stone cornice surmounted by a parapet of brick. The new portion to the south of this is designed in a corresponding style.

A bell, which local tradition asserts to have belonged to the Centurion, is still preserved. It is, however, inscribed 'William Ffortescue August 9 Anno 1619,' which shows it to have been the personal property of the family more than a hundred years before the Centurion expedition, nor is it likely that Captain Fortescue, who sailed in a subordinate capacity, took the bell with him.[6]

Under the northern half of the garden on the south side of the house is the basement of the southern range of buildings demolished in the 18th century. At the south-west angle of the garden is a brick garden-house of the 17th century. The ground falls away in terraced slopes on the west side of the house, which is situated near the summit of the hill from which it takes its name. The line of the moats may be very plainly distinguished. The area which they include is subdivided by a cross moat on the west, while a small branch at the north-west corner of the system originally fed the stew-ponds, two of which can still be traced by depressions in the ground. A portion of the moat is still filled with water. On the summit of the hill, to the east of the house, is an ancient camp, in a very perfect state of preservation, the circle of the moat being entire. The main road, called the Ridge Way, which runs from north to south, and forms the eastern boundary of the grounds, divides Worcestershire from Warwickshire ; from the front of the house a very extensive prospect is commanded over the whole county, the horizon being terminated by the Malvern Hills.

Cladswell and New End lie to the north of Cookhill.[7] Knighton and Little Nobury[8] are two small hamlets in the south-east of the parish. Morton Hall, now the property of Mr. Gilbert Player, and Morton Farm lie in the north to the east of the hamlet of Morton Underhill. Thorne lies in the extreme south of the parish. Another hamlet named Stockwood is in the north-west.

A Roman coin of the time of Hadrian was found at Inkberrow about 1810, and is now in the possession of Mr. G. L. Eades of Evesham.[9]

An Inclosure Act for Inkberrow was passed in 1814,[10] and the award is dated 6 August 1818.[11]

The following place-names occur : Tokene Ok,[12] Russhemore Causey,[13] in the 14th century.

MANORS The manor of *INKBERROW* formed part of the inheritance of Hemele and Duda, who bequeathed it to the church of Worcester. It was, however, later claimed by Wulfheard son of Cussa, and the contention between him and the bishop was settled in 789 at the Synod of Calchyth (Chelsea).[14] There it was agreed that Wulfheard should hold the land for his life, and after his death it should pass to the church of Worcester.[15] This agreement was confirmed in 803 at the Council of Clovesho by Bishop Deneberht,[16] and again by King Ceolwulf I of Mercia (821-3).[17]

[6] Walter's account of the voyage of the *Centurion* does not mention Fortescue's name.

[7] In the 13th century William de Twyford gave to William Molyns 18*d*. rent from land called 'Ehgisht' in Cladswell (Prattinton Coll. [Soc. Antiq.], Deeds of D. and C. of Worc. no. 282).

[8] Nobury seems at one time to have been a place of some importance, and is perhaps to be identified with the 'Neubir' where William de Valence had a liberty, to which he attached the men of Morton, Shell and Witton, about the middle of the

13th century (*Hund. R.* [Rec. Com.], ii, 284). The Zouches held land at Nobury, which probably passed to them about 1276, when Millicent wife of Eudo le Zouche obtained certain land in Inkberrow as co-heir of Eva de Braose, one of the co-heirs of Anselm Earl of Pembroke (*Abbrev. Plac.* [Rec. Com.], 266 ; see also Chan. Inq. p.m. 5 Ric. II, no. 62; 19 Ric. II, no. 52 ; 3 Hen. V, no. 46). In Habington's time (17th century) Lord Bergavenny was lord of the manor of Nobury, but the house was inhabited by the Savages (op. cit. ii, 144).

[9] *V.C.H. Worcs.* i, 219.

[10] Priv. Act, 54 Geo. III, cap. 5.

[11] *Blue Bk. Incl. Awards*, 190.

[12] Felons were hung at Tokene Ok in the 14th century (Ct. R. [Gen. Ser.], portf. 210, no. 46).

[13] Rentals and Surv. (Duchy of Lanc.), bdle. 14, no. 3.

[14] Birch, *Cart. Sax.* i, 356.

[15] Birch, op. cit. i, 356 ; Heming, *Chartul.* (ed. Hearne), 16, 17.

[16] Heming, op. cit. 17, 19 ; Birch, op. cit. i, 427.

[17] Heming, op. cit. 19.

INKBERROW : ALABASTER IN THE CHAPEL OF COOKHILL PRIORY

In 977 Bishop Oswald granted one *mansa* of land in Inkberrow to his servant Athelstan.[18] Seven years later the same bishop granted the land of four *manentes* to a certain matron named Wulfflaed.[19]

At the time of the Domesday Survey there were two manors at Inkberrow, both being held by the Bishop of Hereford. One, comprising 5 hides, he held of the Bishop of Worcester's manor of Fladbury[20]; the other, which gelded for 15½ hides, of the king in chief.[21] The latter holding had been wrongfully held by Earl Harold, but King William restored it to the bishopric of Hereford.[22] The Bishops of Worcester seem afterwards to have claimed the overlordship of both manors. The manor of 5 hides was held of the manor of Fladbury until the beginning of the 14th century or later.[23] About 1186 a dispute arose between the Bishops of Worcester and Hereford as to the overlordship of Inkberrow, and it was decided that the latter owed the service of a knight's fee to the former.[24] This agreement apparently included both the Domesday manors, and in 1323–4 the overlordship of the Bishop of Worcester was still recognized.[25]

The Bishops of Hereford apparently continued to hold the manor in demesne[26] until towards the end of the 12th century, when Bishop Robert Folliot gave it in exchange for 'Eston' to John son of John Marshal, who was to hold it of the bishop for the service of half a knight's fee.[27] This agreement was confirmed in 1253[28] and again in 1355,[29] and the overlordship of the Bishop of Hereford was recognized until about the end of the 14th century,[30] the manor in 1397–8 being said to be held of the Prior of Hereford.[31] In 1307–8 it was said, evidently

SEE OF HEREFORD.
Gules three fleurs de lis coming out of leopards' heads reversed or.

in error, to be held of the king in chief as of the marshalsy of England.[32] In 1435–6 the overlord of Inkberrow was not known,[33] and in 1476 the manor was said to be held of George Duke of Clarence for the service of one knight's fee.[34]

John Marshal, who by the agreement mentioned above became tenant of the manor of Inkberrow, died without issue in 1193–4, when he was succeeded by his brother William, who in right of his wife Isabel became Earl of Pembroke.[35] He or one of his predecessors had erected a castle at Inkberrow, and

in 1216 William Cauntelow was ordered to provide him with wood for repairing it.[36] William Marshal died three years later, and his son William obtained in 1230 a grant from the king by which his manor of Inkberrow was freed from the regard and view of the foresters.[37] The earl died in 1231, and his widow Eleanor daughter of King John[38] received permission from her brother Henry III to reside at Inkberrow Castle until the king should assign her dower of her husband's lands.[39]

MARSHAL. *Party or and vert a lion gules.*

Richard Marshal, brother and successor of William, being a firm opponent of the king's foreign advisers, was proclaimed a traitor in 1233,[40] and the custody of Inkberrow Castle (then called *domus*) was given to Baldwin de Lisle.[41] In October of that year, however, the Sheriff of Worcester was ordered to convoke his whole county at Inkberrow, and to destroy the castle and cause the wood in the park to be sold for the king's use.[42] A grant of this manor or that of Begeworth, whichever he should select, was made in January 1234 to Morgan de Carleon.[43] Richard Earl of Pembroke died in Ireland in April of that year,[44] and the manor of Inkberrow was restored to his brother and successor Gilbert,[45] who seems to have remade the park there, as in 1234 he obtained a grant of ten does and five bucks from Feckenham Forest to stock it.[46] In the following year he was evidently building a residence, for the bailiffs of Feckenham were ordered to give him ten oaks from Werkwood to roof his houses at Inkberrow.[47] On his death in 1241 his brother Walter succeeded, but he died without issue four years later.[48] His widow Margaret (formerly wife of John de Lacy Earl of Lincoln) appears to have held the manor until her death in 1267.[49] Anselm, brother and heir of Walter Earl of Pembroke, died shortly after his brother, his heirs being his five sisters or their descendants.[50]

The manor of Inkberrow probably fell to the share of the youngest sister Joan wife of Warin Monchesney, and was forfeited by her son Sir William de Monchesney, for in 1274–5 it was in the possession of William de Valence, who had married Monchesney's sister Joan, and received in 1265 a grant of his brother-in-law's forfeited estates.[51] In 1274–5 William was accused of appropriating about 5 acres of common land in the manor,[52] and about the same time others of the co-heirs of the Earl of

[18] Heming, op. cit. 185.
[19] Ibid. 186.
[20] *V.C.H. Worcs.* i, 289b.
[21] Ibid. 299a.
[22] Ibid.
[23] Habington, op. cit. i, 226, 228.
[24] Ibid. 229; *Reg. G. Giffard* (Worcs. Hist. Soc.), 351; Red Bk. of Bishopric of Worc. (Eccl. Com. Rec. Var. bdle. 121, no. 43698), fol. 69.
[25] Chan. Inq. p.m. 17 Edw. II, no. 75, m. 56.
[26] Habington, op. cit. i, 226.
[27] *Cal. Pat.* 1247–58, p. 259.
[28] Ibid.
[29] Ibid. 1354–8, p. 197.
[30] Chan. Inq. p.m. 17 Edw. II, no. 75,

m. 56; *Cal. Inq. p.m.* 10–20 *Edw. II,* 387.
[31] Chan. Inq. p.m. 21 Ric. II, no. 2.
[32] Ibid. 1 Edw. II, no. 58.
[33] Ibid. 14 Hen. VI, no. 35.
[34] Ibid. 16 Edw. IV, no. 66.
[35] G.E.C. *Complete Peerage,* vi, 200.
[36] *Rot. Lit. Claus.* (Rec. Com.), i, 280b.
[37] Cart. Antiq. QQ. 6; *Cal. Chart. R.* 1226–57, p. 113.
[38] She afterwards married Simon de Montfort Earl of Leicester.
[39] *Cal. Close,* 1227–31, p. 492. Gilbert Marshal Earl of Pembroke, then lord of Inkberrow, assigned her the issues of the manor in 1235 (*Cal. Pat.* 1232–47, p. 125).
[40] G.E.C. *Complete Peerage,* vi, 201.

[41] *Cal. Close,* 1231–4, p. 253.
[42] Ibid. 543. The castle was probably only an earthwork with wooden defences, and was so completely destroyed that its site is not now known.
[43] *Cal. Pat.* 1232–47, p. 36.
[44] G.E.C. op. cit. vi, 201.
[45] Ibid. 202.
[46] *Cal. Close,* 1231–4, p. 518.
[47] Ibid. 1234–7, p. 144.
[48] G.E.C. op. cit. vi, 203.
[49] Ibid.; *Cal. Inq. p.m. Hen. III,* 149.
[50] G.E.C. loc. cit.
[51] Ibid. 205. William restored Monchesney's estates some two years later, but must have retained Inkberrow.
[52] Assize R. 1026, m. 47.

Pembroke claimed, and apparently obtained, certain rents and services in the manor.[53] In 1290 the steward of Feckenham was ordered to restore to William de Valence his wood pertaining to the manor of Inkberrow,[54] and two years later William obtained licence to inclose his fish stew and 80 acres around it to enlarge his park of Inkberrow.[55] He died in 1296, and a third of the manor was assigned to his widow Joan,[56] who held it until her death in 1307–8.[57]

Aymer de Valence Earl of Pembroke, her son and successor, died in 1324,[58] having previously in 1310 granted the manor to John de Hastings,[59] lord of Bergavenny, and the heirs of his body, with remainder to the earl, who retained a life interest in the estate.

VALENCE.   *Burelly argent and azure an orle of martlets gules.*

HASTINGS.   *Argent a sleeve sable.*

John de Hastings died in January 1324–5 holding the manor of Inkberrow, which then passed to his son Lawrence, a child of six.[60] The custody of the manor during his minority was granted in 1331 to the Bishop of Worcester,[61] and later to the Bishop of Winchester.[62] Lawrence proved his age in May 1341,[63] and held the manor until his death in 1348.[64] John, his son and successor, died in 1375, leaving a son John.[65] He died childless in 1389, being killed in a tournament at Woodstock. Disputes arose between his co-heirs as to the partition of his estate,[66] but the manor of Inkberrow appears to have been among the estates which with the lordship of Bergavenny had been settled by John Earl of Pembroke, father of the last earl, in default of his issue upon his cousin William de Beauchamp, his mother's sister's son.[67] Reginald Grey de Ruthyn was found to be cousin and heir of the whole blood to John Earl of Pembroke, and he and other claimants to the

estate of the earl were dealing with the manor of Inkberrow in 1400–1,[68] but in 1428 it was in the possession of Joan Lady Bergavenny, widow of William de Beauchamp above mentioned,[69] and she held it until her death in 1435.[70] She was succeeded by her granddaughter Elizabeth, wife of Sir Edward Nevill, and the manor has since descended in the same family,[71] being now in the possession of William Nevill Marquess of Abergavenny.

A survey of the manor was made in 1392, and the house appeared then to be in a ruinous state. There was a chapel outside the wall, built of stone and roofed with shingles and slate.[72]

The lord and tenants of Inkberrow enjoyed common pasture in the waste land of Stock in Fladbury, but about 1382 the Bishop of Worcester appropriated the waste of that manor and made no reservation of common for the tenants of Inkberrow, though he had common in Valence Wood or Kereford Wood in the manor of Inkberrow.[73]

The manor of *LITTLE INKBERROW* was held of the manor of Fladbury in the 12th century,[74] and was so held until the beginning of the 14th century.[75] Before the end of that century the overlordship was vested in the lords of Great Inkberrow.[76]

The manor seems to have been held at an early date by the Beauchamps, for in the Domesday Book of the bishopric of Worcester compiled about 1182 William de Beauchamp held 5 hides in Little Inkberrow of the land of Hebrand of the manor of Fladbury, and under him they were held by Nicholas Oute.[77] In 1259 William Beauchamp of Elmley granted to John de Bereford for life a messuage and 2 carucates of land in Inkberrow at a rent of a sparrow-hawk.[78] John in 1274–5 restored the estate to William's son, William de Beauchamp Earl of Warwick.[79] John, lord of Little Inkberrow, is mentioned in 1290,[80] and in 1298–9 William Davey[81] and John de Inkberrow were holding these 5 hides in 'Lesser Inkberrow and Davids Inkberrow,' probably as under-tenants of the Beauchamps.[82] William Davey is doubtless to be identified with the William David or William de Inkberrow whose son Peter in 1304–5 recovered land in Inkberrow against John de Inkberrow and his son Philip.[83] In 1311–12 John de Inkberrow gave to Guy de Beauchamp Earl of Warwick a messuage and 2 carucates of land in Little Inkberrow, and all the tenement which Margery wife of Henry de Stoke held of him for her life.[84] Guy, who died

[53] *Abbrev. Plac.* (Rec. Com.), 189, 192, 196, 266. In 1297–8 the manor of Great Inkberrow was held by Joan de Valence, Agatha de Mortimer and Milicent de Monhaut (Add. MS. 28024, fol. 148). The last two were descended from Sibyl de Ferrers and Eva de Braose respectively, two of the sisters of Anselm Marshal.
[54] *Cal. Close,* 1288–96, p. 74.
[55] *Cal. Pat.* 1281–92, p. 465.
[56] *Cal. Close,* 1296–1302, p. 3.
[57] Chan. Inq. p.m. 1 Edw. II, no. 58.
[58] Ibid. 17 Edw. II, no. 75, m. 56.
[59] John was a nephew of Aymer de Valence, being the son of his sister Isabel (G.E.C. op. cit. vi, 209).
[60] Chan. Inq. p.m. 18 Edw. II, no. 83, m. 21.   [61] *Cal. Pat.* 1330–4, p. 106.
[62] *Cal. Close,* 1339–41, p. 66.
[63] Ibid. 1341–3, p. 77.
[64] *Feud. Aids,* v, 308 ; *Cal. Pat.* 1348–50, p. 239.

[65] Chan. Inq. p.m. 49 Edw. III, pt. i, no. 70.
[66] Ibid. 14 Ric. II, no. 134 ; 15 Ric. II, pt. ii, no. 179.
[67] G.E.C. op. cit. vi, 211 n. ; see also Chan. Inq. p.m. 49 Edw. III, pt. i, no. 70 ; Close, 11 Ric. II, m. 16, 29 d.
[68] Feet of F. Div. Co. Mich. 2 Hen. IV. In 1397 Richard Earl of Arundel died holding a third of the manor of Inkberrow in right of his wife Philippa, widow of John de Hastings, the last earl (Chan. Inq. p.m. 21 Ric. II, no. 2).
[69] *Feud. Aids,* v, 320.
[70] Chan. Inq. p.m. 14 Hen. VI, no. 35.
[71] Ibid. 16 Edw. IV, no. 66 ; (Ser. 2), cccxcix, 157.
[72] Rentals and Surv. (Duchy of Lanc.), bdle. 14, no. 3.
[73] Ct. R. (Gen. Ser.), portf. 210, no. 46.
[74] Habington, op. cit. i, 226 ; Red Bk. of Bishopric of Worc. fol. 69 et seq.

[75] Habington, op. cit. i, 228.
[76] Chan. Inq. p.m. 49 Edw. III, pt. i, no. 70 ; 8 Hen. V, no. 85 ; Exch. Inq. p.m. (Ser. 2), file 1183, no. 7. In the Red Book of the Bishopric of Worcester there is a memorandum (c. 1288) that John de Inkberrow held Little Inkberrow of Henry de Mortimer, son of Agatha de Mortimer, one of the co-heirs of Walter Marshal Earl of Pembroke (fol. 80).
[77] Habington, op. cit. i, 226 ; Red Bk. of Bishopric of Worc. fol. 81, 252.
[78] Feet of F. Worcs. 44 Hen. III, no.11 ; Add. MS. 28024, fol. 121.
[79] Add. MS. 28024, fol. 121.
[80] *Cal. Fine R.* 1272–1307, p. 281.
[81] William David paid a subsidy of 3s. at Inkberrow in 1280 (*Lay Subs. R. Worcs.* 1280 [Worcs. Hist. Soc.], 34).
[82] Habington, op. cit. i, 228.
[83] *Abbrev. Rot. Orig.* (Rec. Com.), i, 145b.
[84] Add. MS. 28024, fol. 121 d.

seised of the manor of Little Inkberrow in 1315, seems to have obtained a confirmation of John's grant from his widow Agnes la Holylond of Worcester.[85] The manor then followed the same descent as Elmley Castle[86] (q.v.) and was granted by Thomas de Beauchamp, twelfth Earl of Warwick, about 1370 to Ralph de Tangelegh for life.[87] On the earl's forfeiture in 1396 the reversion of the manor passed to the Crown,[88] and was granted in 1398 to the king's nephew Thomas Duke of Surrey.[89]

In 1420–1 Sir Ralph Arderne died seised of the manor,[90] but it is not known how he acquired it. His son Robert succeeded, and from that time the manor followed the same descent as Pedmore (q.v.) until the death of Robert Arderne in 1643.[91] It was divided like Pedmore among his four co-heirs.[92] The quarter which fell to the share of Dorothy Bagot was sold in 1680 by Arderne Bagot to Nathaniel Tomkins, B.D.,[93] and he probably acquired another quarter from one of the other co-heirs, for his

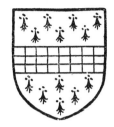

ARDERNE. *Ermine a fesse checky or and azure.*

widow Margaret Tomkins settled half the manor in 1711 on her son Pakington Tomkins.[94] George son of Pakington seems to have acquired the rest of the manor, as he was dealing with the whole in 1758.[95] He died unmarried ten years later, when his brother Thomas succeeded.[96] Pakington George Tomkins, LL.D., son of Thomas, sold it in 1791–2 to William Smith.[97] Thomas Smith conveyed the manor in 1819 to Daniel Winter Burbury and William Whateley,[98] but William Smith was still in possession later in the same year.[99] The further descent of the manor has not been traced.

In 1382–3 it was presented at the manorial court that the lord of Inkberrow had waif and stray, outfangthef and infangthef throughout the demesne of Little Inkberrow.[100]

MORTON UNDERHILL (Morton-next-Inteberg, xiii cent.; Comynes Morton, xiv cent.; Mourton

Underhill, xv cent.) was held of the manor of Great Inkberrow.[1]

In 1274–5 Henry de Bradlegh and Margery his wife[2] conveyed to Geoffrey del Park land in 'Holberwe Morton,' which Geoffrey was to hold of them at a rent of a clove gillyflower.[3] At the end of the 13th century the manor of Morton Underhill was held by Richard, lord of Morton, his surname not being given.[4] Early in the following century the manor passed to Thomas West,[5] who granted it for life to Roger Podde,[6] and sold it in 1334–5 to John Comyn and Joan his wife.[7] John Comyn presented to the chapel of Morton in 1338,[8] but died before 1346, when Philip Irreys held the manor.[9] Philip was perhaps the second husband of Joan Comyn, for she as Joan Comyn presented to the chapel in 1349,[10] and was succeeded before 1355 by John Comyn.[11] After his death towards the end of the 14th century the manor was divided between his four daughters, Millicent wife of William Aghton, and afterwards of Richard Massey, Ellen wife of James Dineley, Joan wife of John Farrington, and another whose name is not known.[12]

James Dineley and Ellen in 1408 conveyed their quarter of the manor to Roland Dineley.[13] Both this quarter and another seem to have passed to Robert Dineley, for in 1420 he and his wife Joan sold a moiety of the manor to Thomas Gower of Woodhall.[14] This moiety followed the same descent as Woodhall[15] (q.v.) in the Gower family[16] until 1628 when Woodhall was sold. Morton Underhill was retained by William Gower, who then took up his residence at Holdfast in Ripple,[17] and it passed under his will to his widow Anne. Conveyances of the manor made by his son William in 1647 and 1648 were probably connected with the fulfilment of this will.[18] The further descent of this moiety of the manor has not been traced.

John and Joan Farrington settled their quarter in 1402 upon themselves for life with remainder to their sons Christopher and Richard in tail-male.[19] Christopher and his wife Alice sold it in 1436 to Thomas Hugford.[20] John Hugford, who was probably son of Thomas,[21] died about 1485–6, leaving as his heirs his

[85] *Cal. Inq. p.m.* 1–9 *Edw. II*, 410, 411.

[86] In 1369–70 Thomas Colman was paying a rent of 10 marks a year for the manor of Little Inkberrow (Close, 43 Edw. III, m. 8).

[87] Ibid. 46 Edw. III, m. 15d.

[88] Mins. Accts. bdle. 1123, no. 5.

[89] *Cal. Pat.* 1396–9, p. 336.

[90] Chan. Inq. p.m. 8 Hen. V, no. 85.

[91] For references see Pedmore. Little Inkberrow Manor never belonged to Thomas Arderne, having been settled by his father John, who died in 1525, upon William son of Thomas (Exch. Inq. p.m. file 1183, no. 7; Chan. Inq. p.m. [Ser. 2], lxxxv, 75).

[92] Feet of F. Worcs. Trin. 1645; Mich. 1658; East. 31 Chas. II; East. 32 Chas. II; Div. Co. East. 1651; Trin. 12 Chas. II.

[93] Feet of F. Worcs. East. 32 Chas. II; Recov. R. Mich. 32 Chas. II, rot. 46.

[94] Recov. R. D. Enr. Hil. 10 Anne, m. 10; Duncumb, *Hist. of Heref.* ii, 73.

[95] Recov. R. Trin. 31 Geo. II, rot. 162.

[96] Duncumb, loc. cit.

[97] Ibid.; Feet of F. Worcs. East. 32 Geo. III.

[98] Feet of F. Worcs. Mich. 59 & 60 Geo. III.

[99] Recov. R. Mich. 60 Geo. III, rot.164.

[100] Ct. R. (Gen. Ser.), portf. 210, no.46.

[1] Chan. Inq. p.m. 21 Ric. II, no. 2; 14 Hen. VI, no. 35; Exch. Inq. p.m. (Ser. 2), file 1183, no. 5.

[2] The nuns of Cookhill received land at Morton Underhill by gift of Robert son of Odo before 1288 (*V.C.H. Worcs.* ii, 157). They retained this land until the Dissolution (*Valor Eccl.* [Rec. Com.], iii, 262), and it was granted with the site of the priory to Nicholas Fortescue (see Cookhill).

[3] Feet of F. Worcs. 3 Edw. I, no. 28.

[4] *Reg. G. Giffard* (Worcs. Hist. Soc.), 507, 525, 526; Prattinton Coll. (Soc. Antiq.), Deeds of D. and C. of Worc. no. 44. Gilbert de Morton and Robert de Morton were returned as former owners of the manor in inquisitions as to knights' fees belonging to the manor of Inkberrow in 1397 and 1435 (Chan. Inq. p.m. 21 Ric. II, no. 2; 14 Hen. VI, no. 35).

[5] Worc. Epis. Reg. Cobham (1317–27), fol. 34.

[6] Ibid. fol. 114 d.

[7] Feet of F. Worcs. 8 Edw. III, no. 12.

[8] Worc. Epis. Reg. Hemenhale (1337–8), fol. 20 d.

[9] *Feud. Aids,* v, 303.

[10] *Sede Vacante Reg.* (Worcs. Hist. Soc.), 237.

[11] Worc. Epis. Reg. Brian (1352–61), xi, fol. 15 d., 21; Barnet, xii, fol. 5 d.

[12] Dugdale, *Hist. of Warw.* 368.

[13] Feet of F. Div. Co. East. 9 Hen. IV.

[14] Ibid. Trin. 8 Hen. V.

[15] In the parish of Norton by Kempsey.

[16] Exch. Inq. p.m. (Ser. 2), file 1183, no. 5; Feet of F. Worcs. East. 16 Eliz.; Div. Co. East. 19 Eliz.; East. 4 Jas. I; Mich. 14 Jas. I; East. 19 Jas. I.

[17] Inform. from Mr. R. Vaughan Gower. This moiety of the manor was then in the tenure of Thomas Dyson.

[18] Feet of F. Worcs. Trin. 23 Chas. I; Notes of F. Worcs. Trin. 24 Chas. I.

[19] Feet of F. Div. Co. Mich. 4 Hen. IV.

[20] Ibid. Trin. 14 Hen. VI.

[21] *Visit. of Warw.* (Harl. Soc. xii), 337.

two daughters Alice and Anne, and his grandson John Beaufo, son of Joan, his eldest daughter.[22] The quarter of the manor eventually passed to John Beaufo, who died in 1516, and was succeeded by a son and grandson of the same name.[23] Thomas Beaufo, son of the last John, sold the manor in 1592 to Richard Gower.[24]

The descent of the remaining quarter of the manor has not been traced from the end of the 14th century until 1537, when it belonged to John Hyde and his wife Ellen.[25] It is possible, however, that this estate is referred to in a grant by the Crown in 1546 to Oliver Lawrence of land at Morton Underhill, 'parcel of the lands of Robert Bonhull, lord of the town of Morton Underhill,' seized by Henry VI because granted by the said Robert without licence to a certain chantry in that town.[25a] John and Ellen Hyde sold it in 1543–4 to Richard Wagstaff and George Hunt,[26] who conveyed it in 1544 to William Gower.[27] This William was probably William Gower of Woodhall, to whom a moiety of the manor already belonged, but on his death this quarter, instead of passing with Woodhall to his eldest son John, probably passed to a younger son Richard,[28] who, as stated above, bought the other quarter of Thomas Beaufo. This moiety of the manor passed from Richard Gower to his son Edmund,[29] who sold it in 1612 to Thomas Ailworth.[30] In 1624–5 Thomas Ailworth and Edward and Thomas Ailworth, who were perhaps his sons, sold half the manor of Morton Underhill to Thomas Dyson.[31] Thomas Dyson,[31a] or a descendant of the same name, was dealing with half the manor in 1685,[32] and it was perhaps this moiety which was conveyed in 1768 by Alexander Jesson and Jane Jesson, spinster, to Thomas Farrer.[33] The manor subsequently passed to the Cowley family, who held it for some 150 years. It is now the property of Mr. Charles Loxley, who bought it a few years ago from the Perks family.[34]

Oswald, Bishop of Worcester, granted a lease for three lives to the thegn Athelstan of land at *THORNE* (Thorndune, ix cent.; Torendune, xii cent.; Thorneden, Thorne, xvi cent.; Thorn, xix cent.) in 963.[35] This manor, which is not mentioned in the Domesday Survey, was held of the Bishop of Worcester as of the manor of Fladbury.[36]

It was held under the Bishops of Worcester from early times by members of the family of Marshal, John Marshal holding 3 hides of land there in the time of Henry II.[37] William Marshal held half a fee there early in the 13th century.[38] The Marshals' interest passed with Great Inkberrow Manor to the Earls of Pembroke,[39] and Thorne was held of that manor until the 16th century.[40]

The tenant under the lords of Great Inkberrow in the middle of the 13th century was perhaps Adam le Boteler, as he granted to the hospital of St. Wulfstan a load of corn annually at Thorne.[41] In a return of knights' fees belonging to the manor of Inkberrow taken in 1375–6 it is stated that James de Boys had held Thorne, and, as a James de Boys paid a subsidy of 4s. 6d. at Inkberrow in 1280,[42] he was probably holding Thorne at that time. Part of the manor passed before 1346 to Christine de Boys, for at that date she held it jointly with John Gerard, Nicholas Somery, Philip le Freeman and Geoffrey Colman.[43] The last-named had been dealing with land in Thorne in 1330–1,[44] and was evidently a descendant of Roger Colman, who paid a subsidy of 2s. 6d. at Inkberrow in 1280.[45] In 1357–8 Geoffrey Colman seems to have transferred his interest in the manor to Thomas son of John de Throckmorton.[46] In 1428 William Gerard and Edmund Crowley held half a fee in Thorne which John Gerard and his coparceners had held,[47] and John Gerard still held land at Thorne in 1431,[48] but at the same date John D'Abitot of Croome was said to be holding the manor of Thorne.[49]

Robert Russell died in 1493–4 seised of this manor, which then passed to his son Robert,[50] who died in 1502–3, leaving a son John.[51] He (then Sir John Russell) died in 1556,[52] and was succeeded by a son Sir Thomas. The manor then followed the same descent as Strensham[53] (q.v.) until the death of Sir Thomas Russell in 1633.[54] The further history of this manor has not been traced, but Prattinton records a sale of 'the manor or reputed manor of Thorn' in 1812.[55]

The Throckmortons seem

RUSSELL of Strensham. *Argent a cheveron between three crosslets fitchy sable.*

to have retained the interest in the manor acquired from Geoffrey Colman in 1357–8, for, though no deeds have been found relating to this part of the manor from that time until 1581, Sir Robert Throckmorton then died seised of the manor,[56] which followed the same descent as Throckmorton[57] until 1604–5, when it was sold by Thomas Throckmorton to Edward Turvey and John Surman.[58]

COOKHILL (Cochul, xiv cent.; Cokehill, xv cent.; Cockhilla, Cookehill, xvi cent.). About the middle of the 13th century Osbert D'Abitot held a knight's fee in Inkberrow and Croome under William

[22] *Cal. Inq. p.m. Hen. VII,* i, 54.
[23] *Visit. of Warw.* (Harl. Soc. xii), 203.
[24] Feet of F. Worcs. East. 34 Eliz.
[25] Ibid. Mich. 29 Hen. VIII.
[25a] *L. and P. Hen. VIII,* xxi (1), g. 302 (64).
[26] Feet of F. Worcs. Hil. 35 Hen. VIII.
[27] Ibid. Mich. 36 Hen. VIII.
[28] *Visit. of Worcs.* (Harl. Soc. xxvii), 60. [29] Ibid.
[30] Feet of F. Worcs. Trin. 10 Jas. I. Eleanor sister of Richard Gower had married Richard Ailworth (*Visit. of Worcs.* [Harl. Soc. xxvii], 60).
[31] Feet of F. Worcs. Hil. 22 Jas. I.
[31a] A Thomas Dyson died 1651 (see M.I. in porch of Inkberrow Church).
[32] Recov. R. East. 1 Jas. II, rot. 43.
[33] Feet of F. Worcs. Hil. 8 Geo. III.

[34] Information supplied by Rev. Canon John J. Burton.
[35] Birch, op. cit. iii, 343.
[36] Habington, op. cit. i, 226; *Testa de Nevill* (Rec. Com.), 41b.
[37] Habington, op. cit. i, 226; Red Bk. of Bishopric of Worc. fol. 81.
[38] *Testa de Nevill* (Rec. Com.), 41b.
[39] Habington, op. cit. i, 228.
[40] *Cal. Inq. p.m. Hen. VII,* i, 381; Chan. Inq. p.m. (Ser. 2), xvi, 11.
[41] *Cal. Bodleian Chart.* 593.
[42] *Lay Subs. R. Worcs.* 1280 (Worcs. Hist. Soc.), 34.
[43] *Feud. Aids,* v, 309.
[44] Sir T. Phillipps, *Index to Worcs. Fines,* 1.
[45] *Lay Subs. R. Worcs.* 1280 (Worcs. Hist. Soc.), 34. Various members of this

family paid subsidy in 1327 (ibid. 1327 [Worcs. Hist. Soc.], 34).
[46] Sir T. Phillipps, op. cit. 6. The further descent of this part of the manor will be found below.
[47] *Feud. Aids,* v, 320.
[48] Ibid. 334. [49] Ibid. 333.
[50] *Cal. Inq. p.m. Hen. VII,* i, 381.
[51] Chan. Inq. p.m. (Ser. 2), xvi, 11.
[52] Exch. Inq. p.m. (Ser. 2), file 1203, no. 1.
[53] W. and L. Inq. p.m. xv, 109; Chan. Inq. p.m. (Ser. 2), ccxli, 126; ccxxxix, 124.
[54] Chan. Inq. p.m. (Ser. 2), ccccclxxxviii, 97. [55] Prattinton Coll. (Soc. Antiq.).
[56] Chan. Inq. p.m. (Ser. 2), cxciii, 89.
[57] Ibid. ccclxvii, 100.
[58] Feet of F. Worcs. Hil. 2 Jas. I.

de Beauchamp, who owed service for it to the Bishop of Worcester.[59] Osbert was still holding the estate, which then included land in Cookhill, in 1315–16.[60] Maud of Croome D'Abitôt, who was perhaps Osbert's widow, gave 2½ hides at Cookhill to the nuns of Cookhill,[61] who in 1346 held 'the half fee in Inkberrow which Osbert D'Abitot formerly held.'[62] The manor remained in the possession of Cookhill Priory until its dissolution about 1538,[63] when it passed to the Crown. It was granted in 1542 to Nicholas Fortescue, a member of the king's household, in tail-male.[64] He died in 1549 and was succeeded by his son William,[65] who died in 1605.[66] The latter's eldest son and successor, Nicholas Fortescue, had considerable difficulty in proving he was not concerned in the Gun-powder Plot, he being a zealous Roman Catholic and a near neighbour of the Winters and Catesbys,[67] and having a considerable quantity of armour in his house at Cookhill.[68] He was knighted in 1618–19[69] and died in 1633, leaving a son and heir William.[70] John Fortescue son of William, who succeeded his

FORTESCUE of Cookhill. *Azure a bend engrailed argent between cotises or in a border gobony argent and azure.*

father in 1649,[71] took an active part in the Civil War as a Royalist leader,[72] and was forced to compound for his estates in 1650 for £234 15s. 5d.[73] He took the 'oath of abjuration' on 20 March 1650.[74] In 1663 he petitioned for and obtained a grant of the remainder, in default of issue male of Nicholas Fortescue, vested in the Crown, of Cookhill Priory, 'long pertaining to his ancestors,' because 'he had suffered for his loyalty and had been active in promoting the Restoration.'[75] He died soon afterwards, and was succeeded by John, who disinherited his eldest son Nicholas, and dying in 1692 left the manor of Cookhill to his second son William.[76] On his death in 1706 he was succeeded by his only son John,[77] who died in 1758, leaving as his successor his son Captain John Fortescue.[78] He was followed in 1808 by his only son John Fortescue,[79] who was dealing with the manor of Cookhill in 1821 and 1823,[80] and sold it about that time. The purchaser

was evidently Sir Thomas Cotton Sheppard, who sold it in 1829 to John Phillips.[81] He died in 1836, and his daughter Miss Phillips held it for life under the terms of his will. On her death in 1907 it passed under the above-mentioned will to Mr. Frederick Griffiths, who sold it in that year to Mr. Philip Antrobus, the present owner.[82]

Another estate at Cookhill held of the manor of Great Inkberrow,[83] sometimes known as the manor of Cookhill, belonged to the Russells of Thorne. It is mentioned for the first time in 1493–4 when Robert Russell died seised of the manor of or land in Cookhill.[84] It followed the same descent as Thorne until 1592–3,[85] when it is mentioned for the last time.

EDGIOCK (Eggoke, Egeoke, Edgeock, xvi cent.; Egioke, xvii cent.; Eiock, xviii cent.) is first mentioned in 1543–4, when Sir George Throckmorton mortgaged the so-called manor of Edgiock to John Legh of London.[86] In 1580 Sir John Throckmorton, sixth son of Sir George,[87] died seised of a capital messuage in Edgiock.[88] His son and heir Francis was attainted and executed for high treason in 1584,[89] and his possessions in Edgiock were granted to Thomas Combes in 1587.[90] William and John Combes sold them to John Edgiock,[91] whose family had long been settled at Edgiock.[92] John died in 1596,[93] and his son Sir Francis Edgiock[94] sold the manor in 1609[95]

EDGIOCK. *Azure two cinqfoils in the chief and a fleur de lis in the foot all or.*

SAVAGE. *Argent six lions sable.*

to John Savage, who settled it in 1613 on his second son John.[96] John Savage the elder died in 1631,[97] and in 1634 John Savage the son settled the manor on his wife Mary daughter of Sir John Rous.[98] John died before 1656, and in November of that year

[59] *Testa de Nevill* (Rec. Com.), 41b.
[60] Chan. Inq. p.m. file 71, no. 53 (9 Edw. II).
[61] *V.C.H. Worcs.* ii, 157.
[62] *Feud. Aids*, v, 307.
[63] *Valor Eccl.* (Rec. Com.), iii, 262.
[64] *L. and P. Hen. VIII*, xvii, g. 556 (1); xvi, p. 728; Pat. 34 Hen. VIII, pt. i, m. 22.
[65] Chan. Inq. p.m. (Ser. 2), xcii, 112.
[66] Ibid. ccc, 183.
[67] See Huddington.
[68] *Dict. Nat. Biog.*; *Cal. S. P. Dom.* 1603-10, p. 253.
[69] Shaw, *Knights of Engl.* ii, 71.
[70] Chan. Inq. p.m. (Ser. 2), dlv, 86.
[71] Thomas, Lord Clermont, *Works of Sir John Fortescue*, ii, 19.
[72] Ibid. 21.
[73] *Cal. Com. for Comp.* 2217.
[74] Ibid.
[75] *Cal. S. P. Dom.* 1663-4, pp. 49, 75; Pat. 15 Chas. II, pt. ix, no. 3.

[76] Thomas, Lord Clermont, op. cit. ii, 22.
[77] Ibid.; Recov. R. Hil. 6 Geo. I, rot. 120; East. 23 Geo. II, rot. 256; Feet of F. Worcs. East. 23 Geo. II.
[78] Clermont, loc. cit.; Recov. R. Hil. 20 Geo. III, rot. 150; Trin. 27 Geo. III, rot. 157; see above under Cookhill Chapel. [79] Clermont, loc. cit.
[80] Recov. R. Trin. 2 Geo. IV, rot. 29; Feet of F. Worcs. Hil. 3 & 4 Geo. IV.
[81] Feet of F. Worcs. Mich. 9 Geo. IV.
[82] Information from T. C. Hyde & Sons, solicitors, Worcester.
[83] *Cal. Inq. p.m. Hen. VII*, i, 381.
[84] Ibid.
[85] W. and L. Inq. p.m. xv, 109; Chan. Inq. p.m. (Ser. 2), ccxli, 126; ccxxxix, 124.
[86] Close, 35 Hen. VIII, pt. vi, no. 10.
[87] Dugdale, *Hist. of Warw.* 749; and see Chan. Inq. p.m. (Ser. 2), ccclxvii, 100.
[88] Chan. Inq. p.m. (Ser. 2), cxci, 114.
[89] *Dict. Nat. Biog.*

[90] See Pat. 30 Eliz. pt. xv, m. 31.
[91] Prattinton Coll. (Soc. Antiq.).
[92] John de Edgiock paid a subsidy of 20d. at Inkberrow in 1327 (*Lay Subs. R. Worcs.* 1327 [Worcs. Hist. Soc.], 34), and Habington mentions a Thomas Edgiock of Inkberrow who flourished in 1468 (op. cit. ii, 139). Edward Edgiock was succeeded in lands at Edgiock by his son Thomas early in the 16th century (Early Chan. Proc. bdle. 305, no. 27). A pedigree of the family is given in *Visit. of Worcs.* 1569 (Harl. Soc. xxvii), 52.
[93] M. I. in Inkberrow Church, quoted by Habington, op. cit. i, 314.
[94] *Visit. of Worcs.* 1569 (Harl. Soc. xxvii), 52. It is probably this Francis whose death in 1622 is recorded on a mural tablet in the north aisle of the church of St. Margaret, Westminster.
[95] Pat. 7 Jas. I, pt. xxiii, no. 5.
[96] Prattinton Coll. (Soc. Antiq.).
[97] Monument in Inkberrow Church.
[98] Prattinton Coll. (Soc. Antiq.).

his widow conveyed the manor to Sir Thomas Rous for a settlement on her daughter Hester and her husband Thomas Appletree.[99] On 1 March 1685 the latter's son John settled the manor on his wife Ann, with remainder to his sons Thomas, John and William. John gave the estate to his son Thomas on 10 March 1711.[100] The latter raised a mortgage for £1,450 on the manor in 1713 and died about 1728, when it was sold.[1] Francis Baber was probably the purchaser, as he made a conveyance of the manor in 1740.[2] On his death about twenty years later the manor was sold by Hugh Baber to Thomas Petty,[3] but the manorial rights have now fallen into abeyance.

George Louis Fawdrey of New End, Astwood Bank, Redditch, now owns the site of the old manor-house, and the manor farm forms part of an estate belonging to University College, Oxford.[4]

The manor-house at Lower Edgiock was taken by the parish in 1787 and used as a workhouse. It was a half-timber building, and the last remains of it were demolished about 1890.[5]

Gilbert Marshal Earl of Pembroke held land in *KNIGHTON* (Cnitteton) at the time of his death in 1241,[6] and Robert de Wyneby held a knight's fee at Knighton of the lord of Great Inkberrow in 1375–6.[7] Later this estate must have reverted to the lords of Great Inkberrow, for in 1476 Sir Edward Nevill Lord Bergavenny died seised of the park of Knighton, parcel of the manor of Inkberrow.[8] The park still existed in the middle of the 17th century,[9] and was said in 1392 to contain 78 acres and to be stocked with deer.[10] An estate at Knighton is still held by the Marquess of Abergavenny, but Little Knighton Farm belongs to Mr. Philip Antrobus.

There was an old manor-house near Knighton, which was burnt down many years ago. The site can still be recognized by some stones, a well and some trees which must have been in the garden. Local tradition has called it the manor of *CANK*, and the site is so marked in the ordnance map, but in deeds belonging to Mr. Philip Antrobus, whose family has owned the property for many years, the estate is called Barrel's Manor. The present Barrel's Wood, adjoining Cank, is part of Lord Abergavenny's property.[10a]

Land at Inkberrow, with the manor of Dormston, was conveyed in 1271–2 by Reginald de Imworth and his wife Maud to John de Bottelegh, who was to hold it at a rent of 10 marks.[11] In 1283–4 Maud widow of Reginald de Imworth sold this rent to Philip de Nevill.[12] It was possibly this estate or part of it which was given in 1328–9 by

Robert de Okley to Richard de Hawkeslow and his wife Nichola.[13] From Richard and Nichola the estate passed to their three sons, Richard, William and John, in succession.[14] John was succeeded by a son Geoffrey, whose son Thomas was in 1405–6 in controversy with William Russell as to this estate.[15] Possibly it passed, like the manor of Hawkesley in King's Norton, to the Staffords, for an estate at Inkberrow was forfeited by Humphrey Stafford at the beginning of the reign of Henry VII, and granted with his other Worcestershire estates to John Pimpe and John Darell.[16] It then seems to have followed the same descent as Hawkesley in King's Norton (q.v.), and may have passed with it to the Middlemores, as land in Little Inkberrow was included in the marriage settlement of John Middlemore of Hawkesley when he married Amphillis daughter of John Goodwin in 1553.[17]

An estate at Inkberrow was held by the Mortimers. It probably originated in land and rent in the manor of Inkberrow assigned to Agatha wife of Hugh de Mortimer, as one of the co-heirs of Anselm Earl of Pembroke.[18] It was said in 1300–1 and 1398 to be held of the king in chief,[19] and in 1360–1 to be held of the Bishop of Worcester.[20] The estate is called a manor in 1300 and in 1405. In 1284–5 John de Mortimer and Geoffrey de Parco made an agreement by which the estate was to belong to Geoffrey for life, with reversion to John.[21] Maud de Mortimer died seised of this estate in 1300–1, when her son Edmund succeeded.[22] He died about four years later,[23] and this land was assigned to his widow Margaret,[24] who granted it for life to Thomas de Stokeslee. On the death of Thomas about 1359 the land was delivered to Roger de Mortimer Earl of March, as heir of Edmund Mortimer,[25] and it passed with the title of Earl of March until about 1414, when it is mentioned for the last time.[26]

A water-mill is mentioned in Inkberrow in 1307–8,[27] and by 1323 there were two water-mills and one windmill there[28] belonging to the lords of the manor. A windmill belonged to the manor of Little Inkberrow in the 14th century.[29] There is a ruined windmill at Holberrow Green, and another, which stood on a hill near the Mearse Farm in the lane leading to Cladswell, was pulled down quite recently.

The vicar of Inkberrow as early as 1375–6 held a manor at Inkberrow, for which he did the service of a quarter of a knight's fee to the lord of Great Inkberrow.[30] The glebe land belonging to the vicarage was valued at 24s. in 1535–6,[31] and a manor was still held by the vicar at the end of the 18th century.[32]

[99] Recov. R. D. Enr. Mich. 1656, m. 10 d. ; see also original deed in Prattinton Coll.

[100] Thomas Appletree was dealing with the manor in 1703 (Recov. R. Hil. 2 Anne, rot. 29).

[1] Prattinton Coll. (Soc. Antiq.).

[2] Feet of F. Div. Co. Trin. 13 & 14 Geo. II.

[3] 'Hist. of Inkberrow,' *Assoc. Archit. Soc. Trans.* xxvi, 473.

[4] Information supplied by Rev. Canon John J. Burton.

[5] 'Hist. of Inkberrow,' &c., 474.

[6] *Cal. Close,* 1237–42, p. 351.

[7] Chan. Inq. p.m. 49 Edw. III, pt. i, no. 70.

[8] Ibid. 16 Edw. IV, no. 66.

[9] Habington, op. cit. ii, 144.

[10] Rentals and Surv. (Duchy of Lanc.), bdle. 14, no. 3.

[10a] Inform. from Rev. Canon J. J. Burton.

[11] Feet of F. Worcs. 56 Hen. III, no. 39.

[12] Ibid. 12 Edw. I, no. 6.

[13] Sir T. Phillipps, *Index to Worcs. Fines,* 1.

[14] Wrottesley, *Ped. from Plea R.* 241.

[15] Ibid.

[16] Pat. 2 Hen. VII, pt. i.

[17] Phillimore, *Account of Middlemore Family,* 179.

[18] *Abbrev. Plac.* (Rec. Com.), 192.

[19] Chan. Inq. p.m. 29 Edw. I, no. 53 ; 22 Ric. II, no. 34.

[20] Ibid. 34 Edw. III (1st nos.), no. 86.

[21] Feet of F. Worcs. East. 13 Edw. I.

[22] Chan. Inq. p.m. 29 Edw. I, no. 53.

[23] Ibid. 32 Edw. I, no. 63a.

[24] *Cal. Close,* 1302–7, p. 176.

[25] Ibid. 1354–60, p. 553.

[26] Chan. Inq. p.m. 34 Edw. III (1st nos.), no. 86 ; 5 Ric. II, no. 43 ; 22 Ric. II, no. 34 ; *Cal. Pat.* 1405–8, p. 101; Mins. Accts. bdles. 1069, no. 6 ; 1236, no. 5.

[27] Chan. Inq. p.m. 1 Edw. II, no. 58.

[28] Ibid. 17 Edw. II, no. 75, m. 56 ; 18 Edw. II, no. 83, m. 21.

[29] Ibid. 9 Edw. II, no. 71.

[30] Ibid. 49 Edw. III, pt. i, no. 70.

[31] *Valor Eccl.* (Rec. Com.), iii, 267.

[32] Nash, op. cit. ii, 9. The Diocesan records at Worcester contain a complete list of vicars of Inkberrow from 1268 to the present time.

CHURCHES

The church of *ST. PETER* consists of a chancel 26½ ft. by 19½ ft., north chapel 15 ft. wide by about 19 ft. in length, nave 61½ ft. by 23½ ft., south transept opening out of the nave 19 ft. by 15 ft., north aisle 14 ft. wide, north porch, and western tower 14 ft. square ; these measurements are all internal.

Evidence of a 12th-century building upon the site is seen in the south wall of the nave, which has a plinth of the extraordinary projection of 18 in. There is little doubt that the courses below the plinth-mould, where the wall is over 4 ft. thick, belong to the 12th century, the wall above having been thinned down when it was rebuilt in the 15th century. The earliest architectural feature of the church, with the exception of the north doorway, is the chancel, which replaced the former one about 1390. Its axis inclines to the north from that of the nave, and it

of the aisle were re-used in the new east wall, and the place of the latter occupied by a buttress of different detail. A wide archway was opened into the chancel, and the wall north of the chancel arch was cut back on the slope. Beyond the rebuilding of the south transept, known locally as the Dormston chapel, in 1784, nothing else appears to have been done structurally until 1887, when the east and south walls of the chancel were rebuilt, the latter being moved a few inches outward ; at the same time the chancel arch was reconstructed, using many of the old stones, while the north porch was rebuilt, a west gallery removed, and the tower archway opened out. The south and west doorways were also re-opened and other restoration work done to the walls and roofs, the roof of the chancel being entirely renewed.

The three-light east window with the whole of the east wall is modern, but the north-east window has two lights in a square head of late 14th-century date.

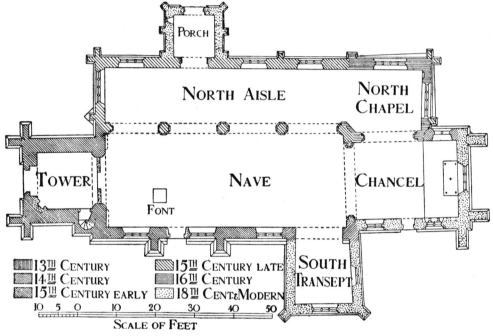

PLAN OF INKBERROW CHURCH

had a vestry against the north wall. It is probable that the addition of a south transept was made about the same time, but of this only the arch opening into it remains, the rest having been rebuilt in 1780. The east jamb of this archway shows the thinning of the wall from 4 ft. at the floor level to about 2 ft. 10 in. at its upper part, and a straight joint outside at the thicker face shows the return of the nave wall, and points to the transept being a later addition. About 1420 the south wall of the nave was rebuilt and the tower added shortly after. Later in the century, about 1480, the north aisle and the north porch were built, the earlier (probably 13th-century) doorway being moved outwards with the wall. Early in the next century the aisle was extended eastwards over the site of the earlier vestry. The old foundations were retained, but as they were square with the chancel and not with the nave and aisle it became necessary to set the new walls askew on the older work. The east and the two angle buttresses

The 16th-century archway to the westward of it has a four-centred arch of two chamfered orders, the inner carried by shafts with moulded capitals.

The south-east window is of two lights under a traceried head of 15th-century character. The piscina and sedilia below the window, with the south priest's doorway, are practically modern. The sedilia contain one old stone, which suggested the design of the new work, while the jambs of the doorway at the ground level are original. The south-west window is like that at the north-east, but only the outer orders of the jambs and lintel are old. As stated above, the east and south walls are modern ; the north wall is of uncoursed square ashlar with a moulded plinth. The open-timbered roof is modern.

The pointed arch spanning the south transept is of two chamfered orders, the inner of which springs from modern corbels on square jambs. The east window of the transept is a modern one of two trefoiled lights under a square head ; the south window is poor, of three trefoiled lights under a three-centred head. There are three windows in the south wall of the nave, all of 15th-century date ; each has three lights under a pointed traceried head. The doorway between the second and third window has modern jambs and an original four-centred head. The wall is divided externally into three bays by buttresses, of which the upper portions are new. The north arcade of the nave consists of four bays with large octagonal columns having moulded bases and capitals. The arches are two-centred and of two chamfered orders. The roof of the nave is comparatively modern and has a pointed barrel vault plastered between the timbers.

INKBERROW CHURCH FROM THE NORTH-EAST

The chapel north of the chancel is lighted in its east and north walls by windows of four lights with traceried two-centred heads. In the east wall north of the window and partly obscured by an 18th-century monument is a shallow recess for a figure. The three north windows of the aisle are each of three lights and have two-centred heads with vertical tracery.

The north doorway is an earlier one re-used, with square jambs, continuous mouldings, and a four-centred rear arch. The west window of the aisle, which is of four lights, has been considerably restored. The buttresses of the aisle are all of two stages and are surmounted by pinnacles broken by grotesque beasts at the parapet string-course level and topped by crocketed finials. The second buttress from the east is, however, finished with a trefoiled gablet. The

parapet is embattled with returned copings, and a moulded plinth is carried round the walls. The southern of the pair of buttresses against the west wall stands on a diagonal plinth, which can only be the base of a former nave angle buttress, removed when the aisle was added.

The roof is a modern flat one, but the corbels of the former 15th-century roof remain in position on both sides.

The north porch, which was rebuilt at the restoration, was of similar date and design to the aisle, with pinnacled buttresses and an embattled parapet. The outer archway is of modern stonework, with the exception of the label, which has carved human head stops. Over the doorway a diagonal pinnacle rises from a carved corbel in the string-course.

The tower is three stages high with two buttresses on each outer face, carried up to the third stage ; the stair turret projects at the south-east corner. The archway to the nave has a pointed head of two chamfered orders and is closed by a modern screen. The west doorway, which is of original date, is of two moulded orders with a four-centred arch, and above it is a four-light traceried window. The second stage has small rectangular lights on its outer faces, and the third or bell-chamber is lit by two-light windows with four-centred heads in the north, west and south walls ; the east window differs slightly from these. The parapet is embattled, with pinnacles at the angles, and is enriched with grotesque gargoyles at the level of the string-course, placed at the angles and near the centre of each side. The tower is ashlar-faced.

The font is apparently of early 13th-century date. It is square in plan, the bowl having vertical sides partly moulded, and hollowed on the lower edge. On each face are three circular carvings, all with varying flower patterns, except on the east side, where the second one bears the Agnus Dei. The hollow chamfer below is enriched with dog-tooth flowers. At the top of the font is the beginning of an inscription, ✠ EST HIC FON. . . . The stem is square and plain and the base has a roll and splay on its upper edge. The pulpit may be of 18th-century date, and there is some 17th-century oak panelling around the north chapel, which now serves as a vestry.

There are several fragments of 15th-century glass in the church, the largest being in the west window of the north aisle with figures of St. Catherine and another female saint (? St. Margaret) crowned and holding a staff. Other fragments remain in the east and south-west windows of this aisle.

There is a large altar tomb of painted white marble in the south-east corner of the transept to John Savage 'of Edgioke, who had by his three wives six sonnes and four daughters.' He died in 1631. On the base is his effigy in full armour ; the hands and feet are missing. On the sides of the base were formerly the kneeling figures of the children, but these have been removed, and some of them are lying loose on the top of the canopy. The arched canopy rests on Corinthian columns and has Gothic cusping to the coffered soffit, and surmounting it are small figures representing 'Time,' 'Hope,' and 'Faith.' The tomb is evidently not in its original position and was formerly either standing entirely free or touching the wall at one end only. On the tomb are the arms of Savage. In the transept also is a small brass inscription to George third son of Sir Francis Edgiock of Shurnock Court, died 1638, and another 17th-century brass to William Willis, an old servant of Sir Francis. Another wall monument is to Frances wife of John Sheldon of Nobury, 1690.

In the floor are several 17th-century and later slabs and in the porch is a stone to Thomas Dyson, 1651.

The six bells in the tower were cast in 1868.

The communion plate consists of a silver cup of 1592 with a baluster stem and a cover (originally gilt), a silver cup of 1629, a stand paten of the same date, a salver paten with an indistinct hall-mark, but engraved with the date of 1665, and a flagon of 1851.

The registers [33] before 1812 are as follows : (i) baptisms and burials 1675 to 1778, marriages 1675 to 1754 ; (ii) baptisms and burials 1779 to 1812 ; (iii) marriages 1754 to 1792 ; (iv) marriages 1792 to 1812.

The district church of *ST. PAUL* at Cookhill is a well-built stone fabric of a simple Gothic design, consisting of a chancel with an organ chamber and vestry on the north side, a nave with a bell-turret on the west gable and a south porch. It was erected and consecrated in 1876, on a site given by the late Marquess of Hertford, as a chapel of ease to the church of St. Peter.

ADVOWSON In 1086 there was a priest in the Bishop of Hereford's manor of Inkberrow.[34] Part of the tithes [35] were appropriated to a prebend in Hereford Cathedral. The advowson of both prebend and vicarage was apparently vested in the Bishops of Hereford until the manor passed in the 12th century to John Marshal ; the advowson of the vicarage then passed to him, that of the prebend remaining with the Bishops of Hereford.[36] The prebend remained in the gift of the Bishop of Hereford at least as late as 1562.[37] The advowson of the vicarage has since followed the descent of the manor.[38] In 1305 the vicar received a licence from the Bishop of Worcester to let his church to farm and make a journey to Rome.[39]

By his will, dated August 1558, Richard Moore, vicar of Inkberrow, bequeathed 'the rood loft as I bought' to the church of Inkberrow to be set up within the half-year or else sold and the money given to the poor.[40]

There was a chantry chapel dedicated to St. Blaise at Morton Underhill, the advowson of which belonged to the lords of the manor.[41] The first recorded presentation was made in 1298 [42] and the last in 1362.[43] It was probably to this chantry that Robert Bonhull granted land in Morton Underhill, without licence, the land being on that account seized by Henry VI.[43a]

There is said to have been a chapel at Little Nobury in the 13th century,[44] but it was in ruins in the 17th century, when Habington wrote, 'it hath byn graced with a chapell, whose deade carckas is withered to Haye.' [45]

In 1357 Thomas Colman obtained licence to alienate a messuage and a carucate of land in Holberrow and elsewhere to a chaplain to celebrate divine service daily in the chapel of St. Catherine in the church of Inkberrow for the souls of various members of the Colman family.[46]

In 1720 the house of R. Windle in Inkberrow was licensed for Dissenting worship.[47] A Baptist chapel was built there in 1861, and another at Cookhill was built in 1841. A Methodist chapel existed at Stock Wood in 1868.[48] It is now converted into a dwelling-house.

CHARITIES The parochial charities are regulated by a scheme of the Charity Commissioners 19 February 1886. They comprise the charities of :—

1. The Poor's Land, including the charities of the Conway family ; Walter Smith, will, 1729 ; Mrs. Sarah Roper, will, 1782, and others. The trust estate consists of 51 a. 2 r. 12 p., situate in Knowlefield in this parish, awarded on the inclosure in 1818, let at £30 a year.

2. The Rev. — Vaughan.—Mentioned in the Parliamentary Returns of 1786, consisting of a rent-charge of 20s. issuing out of a farm called Morton Underhill.

3. Moses and Alice Mansell.—Founded in 1672, mentioned in the same returns and on the benefaction table, consisting of an annuity of 20s. issuing out of an estate at Cookhill.

4. John Phillips.—Mentioned in the same Returns, being an annuity of 20s. issuing out of the Pinhill Estate.

5. John Hobbins, by will 1735, gave 20s. a year charged on a close called Brook Meadow End at Great Alne, county of Warwick.

[33] Many 17th-century entries of much earlier date will be found among the Bishops' Transcripts.

[34] *V.C.H. Worcs.* i, 289b.

[35] The tithes were divided about equally between the prebend and the vicar (Nash, op. cit. ii, 9). The property of the prebend was sold about 1856 (*Lond. Gaz.* 11 Nov. 1856, p. 3655), and the Dean and Chapter of Hereford were impropriators of the tithes in 1868 (Noake, *Guide to Worcs.*), 208.

[36] *Cal. Pat.* 1247–58, p. 259 ; Worc. Epis. Reg. Cobham (1317–27), fol. 13 ; Nash, op. cit. ii, 9 ; *Reg. G. Giffard* (Worcs. Hist. Soc.), 55, 447.

[37] *Anct. D. (P.R.O.), A* 12477.

[38] *Reg. G. Giffard* (Worcs. Hist. Soc.), 4, 152, 277 ; *Cal. Pat.* 1338–40, p. 2 ; Inst. Bks. (P.R.O.) ; *Cal. S. P. Dom.* 1635–6, p. 408. In 1625 Henry Lord Bergavenny demised to Edward Bawtre the advowson of Inkberrow for forty years. In 1636 Bawtre assigned the remainder of the lease to Sir John Lambe.

[39] *Reg. W. Ginsborough* (Worcs. Hist. Soc.), 116.

[40] 'Hist. of Inkberrow,' *Assoc. Archit. Soc. Trans.* xxvi, 496.

[41] *Reg. G. Giffard* (Worcs. Hist. Soc.), 507, 525, 526 ; Worc. Epis. Reg. Cobham (1317–27), fol. 34, 114 d. ; Montacute (1333–7), fol. 14, 16 d. ; Hemenhale (1337–8), fol. 20 d. ; Brian (1352–61), xi, fol. 15 d., 21 ; *Sede Vacante Reg.* (Worcs. Hist. Soc.), 237.

[42] *Reg. G. Giffard* (Worcs. Hist. Soc.), 507.

[43] Worc. Epis. Reg. Barnet, xii, 5 d.

[43a] *L. and P. Hen. VIII,* xxi (1), g. 302 (64).

[44] Noake, op. cit. 207.

[45] Prattinton Coll. (Soc. Antiq.).

[46] *Cal. Pat.* 1354–8, p. 574 ; Inq. a.q.d. file 326, no. 12.

[47] Noake, op. cit. 208.

[48] Ibid.

6. Daniel George, will proved at Worcester 8 November 1851, trust fund, £107 10s. 6d. consols.

7. Richard Adcock, jun.—Gift in 1861 ; trust fund, £53 15s. 4d. consols.

The sums of stock are held by the official trustees, producing together £4 0s. 4d. yearly. The net income was in 1909–10 distributed as to £8 15s. in bread, £12 15s. in coal, £1 4s. in widows' gowns and the remainder added to the coal and clothing clubs.

In 1851 Robert Hunt by deed gave £100 upon trust that the income should be distributed on St. Thomas's Day among the poor residing within Inkberrow and Morton Limit in bread, meat, fuel and clothing. The principal sum was invested in £107 13s. 5d. consols, held by the official trustees, producing £2 13s. 8d. yearly, which is distributed in half-crowns.

The church lands now consist of 40 a. 0 r. 30 p., allotted on the inclosure in 1818 in respect of other lands. There are no deeds showing the origin and trusts of the original lands, but in a terrier dated 1749 they are stated to have been given 'for the repairs and beautifying of the parish church.' The land is let at £30 a year.

In 1899 Lilla Haynes by her will devised certain real estate for the support of the Baptist chapel. The property was sold in 1901 and the proceeds invested in £268 9s. 8d. Birmingham Corporation 3 per cent. stock with the official trustees, producing £8 1s. yearly.

KEMPSEY

Kemesei, Kemeseg (viii cent.) ; Kemesege (ix cent.) ; Chemesege (xi cent.).

Kempsey is a parish on the left bank of the Severn, containing 3,238 acres of land, of which 32 are covered with water. The parish is watered by the Severn and a tributary, the Hatfield Brook. The village of Kempsey lies on the high road from Worcester to Tewkesbury. This road is mentioned in 1427 and 1448, when an indulgence was granted to all who should assist in repairing the old highway leading from Worcester to Kempsey.[1] In 1634 and 1635 it was presented at the county court of Worcester that this road was in great decay,[2] and in 1640 it was still out of repair.[3] The site of the bishop's palace is near the church of St. Mary in the middle of the village. Close to the church are traces of a Roman camp where urns and coins were found in 1835–6. Kempsey House, the residence of Mrs. Boucher, stands west of the high road, in grounds through which flows Hatfield Brook, supplying a small piece of artificial water.

Kerswell Green with its mission church and Methodist chapel is on the southern border of the parish. Most of the houses there lie on the north side of a small green. Between Kerswell and Baynhall is The Nash, the seat of Lieut.-Col. Sir Richard Carnac Temple, bart. The house is now an irregularly shaped building running east and west with the porch and entrance on the south. It is of red brick partly on a stone base. The existing building is of various dates, and consists of three independent half-timbered blocks, standing partly on a stone base and recased in red brick, which have been joined together by covering in the spaces between them under connected pent roofs, now showing twenty stepped gables with brick copings. The present hall was thus formed. To the left of it is the dining room, and over it the 'oak bedroom,' forming one of the old houses, apparently a 'hall.' In the dining room was an ingle, now covered in, and traces of a stair leading from it to the room above still exist. Both rooms are panelled with early oak, covering earlier walls of half-timber. They are ceiled with fine Italian plaster-work with plaster friezes of about 1600, and are of the same pattern as a ceiling at Madresfield Court : vine, rose, oak and thistle. The dining room frieze is of Tudor roses and Prince of Wales' feathers. The over-doors are of plaster with figures. In the oak bedroom is a large Italian painted plaster mantel of figures and strap-work dated 1598. Above this room and under the present roof are the timbers of the original roof, showing curved tie-beams and wind-braces. The hall is half-panelled in linen pattern oak, and contains a good 'Queen Anne' staircase, a leaded stained glass window of unusual construction, and a fireplace in an ingle with a window (restored) dated 1648 carved with figures and foliage. Here is also an early font originally in Pershore Abbey. The bowl is circular with a line of interlacing arches enriched with nail-head ornament and having thirteen seated figures within them. The stem, resting on a modern base, has a band of scallops and cable moulding. There is much panelling elsewhere and furniture of the 17th and 18th centuries. The bay windows and other openings chiefly date from the extensive changes made in 1831. The chimneys are very tall and are set diagonally.

An extensive museum of Burmese carvings and savage implements from the islands in the Bay of Bengal has been recently added to the house.

Draycott lies to the south. Draycott House is the residence of Lieut.-Col. Charles Edmund Southouse Scott, R.A. Napleton, with the seat of Mr. Philip Seymour Williams, and Stonehall are in the east, Brook End in the north-east and Upper Ham in the north. Lower Ham is a large common meadow, subject to floods, to the south-west of the village. There is a ferry there to Pixham and Malvern. At Clerkenleap, Treadway Russell Nash, the historian of Worcestershire, was born on 24 June 1725.[3a]

Kempsey Common is a large piece of rough grass-land south-east of the town. There is another smaller common at Stonehall, and Normoor Common is north of Kerswell Green.

The village and a large part of the parish lie very low in the Severn Valley 50 ft. or less above the ordnance datum. Kempsey Common is about 100 ft. above the ordnance datum, and the land rises north-eastward to a height of 200 ft. at Stonehall Common. In 1905 the parish of Kempsey contained 877 acres of arable land, 1,677 of permanent grass and 20 of woods and plantations.[4] The soil is various and the

[1] Worc. Epis. Reg. Thos. Pulton (1425–33), fol. 34 f ; John Carpenter (1443–76), fol. 61 d.   [2] Worcs. Quarter Sess. R. (Worcs. Hist. Soc.), 572, 598.   [3] Ibid. 684.
[3a] Dict. Nat. Biog.
[4] Statistics from Bd. of Agric. (1905).

Kempsey : The Nash from the South

subsoil Keuper Marl, producing crops of wheat, barley and beans.

At Upper Broomhall Farm in the north of the parish there are remains of a moat.

Beanhall in Kempsey was purchased with a sum of £100 bequeathed to the poor of the parish of St. Michael, Worcester, in 1712 by Mrs. Henrietta Wrottesley. The rent from this land was to be distributed upon All Saints' Day and at the Feast of the Purification of the Blessed Virgin by the minister and churchwardens and two of the feoffees of the charity.[5]

During the siege of Worcester in June 1646 the house of a Mrs. Andrews at Barneshall was fortified by the besieging army, who stationed troops of horse and dragoons at Kempsey in order to cut off communications towards the south.[6]

Richard de Marisco, who may have been related to the family of that name holding land at Norton-juxta-Kempsey, was presented in 1212 to the rectory of Kempsey. He was one of King John's worst advisers, becoming Chancellor in 1214 and Bishop of Durham in 1217.[7]

Various antiquities, of which an account has been given in a former volume, have been found at Kempsey.[8]

Place-names which occur in deeds relating to Kempsey are the Lode Ground[9] (xvi cent.); Carlsome,[10] Garston Bridge, Ripple Gate Close,[11] and Byrdley Hall[12] (xvii cent.).

MANORS — Thirty manses belonging to the 'monasterium' called *KEMPSEY* were given in 799 by Coenwulf, King of Mercia, to Abbot Balthun, and at the same time this land was freed from all secular services, except military service and the building and repairing of bridges and strongholds.[13] The same king gave all the monasteries which belonged to Worcester to the monks of Worcester in 814.[14] This grant evidently included the monastery of Kempsey, which was given by the monks to their Bishop Deneberht (798–822) and his assigns for two lives, with reversion to the monastery.[15] The gift of Beormodeslea and Colesburna to Balthun by the bishop and monks may have been made to compensate him for the loss of Kempsey.[16] The manor evidently passed from Deneberht to his successors in the see, Eadberht and Aelhun, and the latter gave the manor back to the monks in 844.[17] In 847, however, they gave it again to Bishop Aelhun for two lives, on condition that his heirs should pay yearly to the monks on his anniversary certain specified provisions.[18] The manor seems to have passed into the possession of the Bishops of Worcester, possibly on account of these grants by the monks, and at the time of the Domesday Survey the large manor of Kempsey, including 24 hides, was held by the Bishop of Worcester.[19] In 1189 Richard I gave licence to assart 161½ acres in the manor of Kempsey,[20] and this grant was confirmed by King John in 1199.[21] Henry III in 1255 granted to the bishop free warren in his manor of Kempsey, provided it did not lie within the king's forest.[22] The bishop held 4 carucates of land, a mill, and a dovecot at Kempsey in 1291.[23] Kempsey remained in the possession of successive bishops[24] until 1648, when it was confiscated and sold by the Parliamentary trustees to Christopher Meredith of London.[25] It was conveyed in 1656 by Richard Harlakenden to Herbert Pelham and John Joscelyn,[26] but was restored to the bishop on the accession of Charles II. Since that time the successive bishops remained in possession of the manor until it was transferred in 1860 to the Ecclesiastical Commissioners,[27] in whose possession it still remains.

The Bishops of Worcester had a park at their manor of Kempsey.[28] A manor-house evidently existed here in early times, for Bishop Leofric died at Kempsey in September 1033.[29] A house in the village still called the Palace probably marks its site. It seems to have been a favourite seat of the Bishops of Worcester,[30] and it was here that Simon de Montfort, accompanied by Bishop Cantilupe, brought Henry III as a prisoner in 1265 before the battle of Evesham.[31] Henry II issued from Kempsey a charter relating to Inkberrow,[32] and Edward I appears to have been a frequent visitor here as the guest of Bishop Godfrey Giffard.[33]

The estate called *HOWDENS* probably originated in two messuages and a virgate of land at Broomhall in the manor of Kempsey granted by William, Bishop of Worcester (1302–7), to his chamberlain Adam de Howden, and confirmed to Adam by the prior and convent in 1313[34] and by the king in 1320.[35] A tenement called Howdens in Kempsey and Broomhall seems to have been in the possession of Adam Moleyns, Dean of Salisbury, in 1444.[36] The capital messuage of Howdens afterwards passed to the Mucklow family of Martley. Richard Mucklow died seised of it in 1556, when it passed to his son Simon.[37] He settled it in 1570 upon his son John and upon Appollina wife of the latter. John died in 1579, leaving a son Simon, a minor.[38] The further descent of this estate has not been found.

A messuage called *BROOMHALL* at Clerkenleap in Kempsey belonged to the monastery of Tewkesbury, but it is not known how the monks became

[5] Nash, *Hist. of Worcs.* ii, 322.
[6] Ibid. App. 99, 100.
[7] *Dict. Nat. Biog.*
[8] *V.C.H. Worcs.* i, 196, 210.
[9] Chan. Proc. (Ser. 2), bdle. 21, no. 27.
[10] Close, 1650, pt. xxxviii, no. 4.
[11] Ibid. 24 Chas. I, pt. xiv, no. 9.
[12] Chan. Inq. p.m. (Ser. 2), ccc, 81.
[13] Birch, *Cart. Sax.* i, 411; Heming, *Chartul.* (ed. Hearne), 452.
[14] Dugdale, *Mon. Angl.* i, 608.
[15] Ibid.
[16] Ibid.
[17] Heming, op. cit. 562.
[18] Dugdale, *Mon. Angl.* i, 608.
[19] *V.C.H. Worcs.* i, 288.
[20] Cart. Antiq. RR, 15.
[21] Ibid. I, 31.

[22] *Cal. Chart. R.* 1226–57, p. 443.
[23] *Pope Nich. Tax.* (Rec. Com.), 225.
[24] *Abbrev. Rot. Orig.* (Rec. Com.), ii, 133; *Feud. Aids,* v, 306, 318; *Cal. Close,* 1346–9, p. 231; Pat. 6 Edw. VI, pt. vii, m. 21; *Valor Eccl.* (Rec. Com.), iii, 218; Chan. Proc. Eliz. Dd. 8, no. 52.
[25] Close, 24 Chas. I, pt. xiv, no. 9.
[26] Feet of F. Div. Co. Hil. 1656.
[27] Stat. 23 & 24 Vict. cap. 124.
[28] *Abbrev. Rot. Orig.* (Rec. Com.), ii, 133; Pat. 6 Edw. VI, pt. vii, m. 21.
[29] Dugdale, *Mon. Angl.* i, 570.
[30] Worc. Epis. Reg. *passim.*
[31] Rishanger, *Chron. et Ann.* (Rolls Ser.), 35; *Reg. G. Giffard* (Worcs. Hist. Soc.), Introd. p. xx.

[32] Habington, *Surv. of Worcs.* (Worcs. Hist. Soc.), ii, 145.
[33] *Cal. Chart. R.* 1300–26, p. 9; *Cal. Pat.* 1396–9, p. 85.
[34] *Hist. MSS. Com. Rep.* x, App. iv, 445.
[35] *Cal. Pat.* 1317–21, p. 522. A hide of land in Kempsey had been held towards the end of the 12th century by Roger Chamberlain, to whom it had been given by Bishop Simon (1125–50) (Red Bk. of Bishopric of Worc. [Eccl. Com. Rec. Var. bdle. 121, no. 43698], fol. 49).
[36] *Hist. MSS. Com. Rep.* x, App. iv, 445. Adam Moleyns was rector of Kempsey in 1434 (*Cal. Papal Letters,* viii, 506).
[37] Chan. Inq. p.m. (Ser. 2), cvi, 91.
[38] Ibid. clxxxvii, 109.

possessed of it. In 1535 it was leased out at a rent of 24s. a year,[39] and it was granted in 1544 to John Thatcher.[40]

William de Kerswell and Taillefer [41] held 2½ hides at *KERSWELL* of the manor of Kempsey in the time of King Henry III.[42] In 1299 Nicholas de Hulle or Hill held land at Kerswell,[43] and was probably succeeded by a son of the same name, for in 1311 Nicholas de Hulle of Kerswell did homage to the bishop [44] for lands held of him in the manor of Kempsey.[45] He seems to have been succeeded by a son John,[46] and the estate had passed before 1346 to John son of John de Hulle,[47] who obtained a grant of free warren in the manor in 1347.[48] From this time it would appear from the few deeds which have been found relating to the estate that it passed in the same way as the manor of Hill Croome [49] to Thomas Lord Coventry, who died seised of it in 1640.[50] It has since descended with the title, and now belongs to the Right Hon. George William Earl of Coventry.[51]

Habington states that according to an undated survey of Kempsey Manor the heirs of John Clopton held there.[52] Sir William son of John Clopton died in 1420 holding a messuage and a carucate of land in Kerswell of the Bishop of Worcester as of his manor of Kempsey for knight service.[53] He left a son Thomas, aged thirteen, but he apparently died without issue, for the estate passed to his sister Joan, who married Sir John Burgh.[54] Sir John outlived Joan, and died in 1471, leaving four co-heirs.[55] This estate apparently passed to John Newport, son and heir of Elizabeth, one of the daughters of Sir John, for Habington states that he had heard that this land passed to Sir Richard Newport, grandson of John Newport,[56] and was sold by him to Kenelm Winslow, of whom it was purchased by Sir John Buck.[57]

The estate at Kempsey called the *NASH* (Atenasche, Asshe) was held of the manor of Kempsey.[58] References to inhabitants of the hamlet of Nash occur in early times. Robert de Fraxino was a tenant of Kempsey Manor in the time of Henry II.[59] In 1299 John son of Ralph de Ash was holding 3 virgates in Kerswell,[60] and in 1302–3 he was dealing with land in the field of 'Asshe.' Part of his estate afterwards passed to his brother Walter, who gave it in 1311 to his mother Alice and his sister Margery.[60a] Land held by the Ash family at Kempsey seems to have passed to John

de Kempsey, the founder in 1316 of the chantry at Kempsey, for he endowed this chantry with a messuage which he had bought of Adam de Fraxino.[61] The estate now known as the Nash seems to have been identical with that land at Kerswell held in the time of Henry III by Taillefer,[62] who may have been a member of the Ash family, Taillefer de Fraxino occurring in a deed in the parish chest of Kempsey, quoted by Prattinton. A messuage and 6 acres of land at Kempsey were held in the 13th century under John Taillefer by Peter de Frechnie, whose son John gave it up to John Taillefer, the chief lord. He afterwards gave this tenement to Osbert Buck, from whom it descended to Richard Buck, the owner in 1274. John Taillefer's interest in the land was then vested in his son Ralph.[63] Richard Buck paid a subsidy for this land in 1280.[64] John Buck and Isabel his wife levied a fine concerning land in Kempsey in 1356–7,[65] and in 1358–9 the king committed to them a messuage and a virgate of land in Kempsey, to be held during pleasure.[66] According to the pedigree of this family given in the Visitation of Worcestershire (1569),[67] which starts from this John Buck and Isabel, the estate descended from father to son in the family for many generations, but there are no documents which throw any light on the history of the estate from 1359 until 1535 when Kenelm Buck did homage to the king for a messuage in Kempsey.[67a] Kenelm died in 1550 holding an estate described as a capital messuage and land called Nash, held of the Bishop of Worcester as of his manor of Kempsey.[68] Kenelm was succeeded by his son Francis, on whose death in 1580 it passed to his son John, then a minor.[69] He was afterwards knighted,[70] and sold the estate to Humphrey Baker of Worcester.[71] Charles Bentley held it about the middle of the 17th century.[72] About 1738 it was bought by Sir William Temple.[73] He succeeded to the baronetcy in 1749 on the death of his cousin Viscount Cobham, and died in 1760. His only daughter by his second wife, Anna Sophia,

BUCK of the Nash. *Party fessewise and wavy argent and sable with three pairs of bucks' horns with the scalps countercoloured.*

[39] *Valor Eccl.* (Rec. Com.), ii, 473.
[40] *L. and P. Hen. VIII*, xix (1), g. 812 (57).
[41] For Taillefer's part see below under the Nash.
[42] *Testa de Nevill* (Rec. Com.), 42.
[43] Red Bk. of Bishopric of Worc. fol. 35.
[44] This land was held of the bishop as of his manor of Kempsey in 1411, but the overlordship is not mentioned after that date (Chan. Inq. p.m. 12 Hen. IV, no. 41).
[45] Worc. Epis. Reg. Walter Reynolds (1308–13), fol. 43 d.
[46] Habington, op. cit. ii, 148.
[47] *Feud. Aids*, v, 309.
[48] *Cal. Pat.* 1345–8, p. 529.
[49] Chan. Inq. p.m. 12 Hen. IV, no. 41 ; Feet of F. Worcs. Mich. 13 Hen. VIII ; Chan. Inq. p.m. (Ser. 2), ccccxcii, 68.
[50] Chan. Inq. p.m. (Ser. 2), ccccxcii, 68.

[51] Exch. Dep. Hil. 7 & 8 Will. III, no. 18 ; inform. from Mr. W. Hill.
[52] Habington, op. cit. ii, 148.
[53] Chan. Inq. p.m. 7 Hen. V, no. 46 ; *Visit. of Worcs.* 1569 (Harl. Soc. xxvii), 71. The estate was so held in 1471, but no further mention of the overlordship has been found (Chan. Inq. p.m. 11 Edw. IV, no. 61).
[54] *Arch. Journ.* xxxiv, 373.
[55] Chan. Inq. p.m. 11 Edw. IV, no. 61.
[56] Bridgeman, *Hist. of Princes of South Wales*, Table viii.
[57] Habington, loc. cit.
[58] *Testa de Nevill* (Rec. Com.), 42 ; Chan. Inq. p.m. (Ser. 2), xciv, 102.
[59] Habington, op. cit. ii, 148.
[60] Red Bk. of Bishopric of Worc. fol. 35.
[60a] Deeds in parish chest of Kempsey quoted in Prattinton Coll. (Soc. Antiq.).
[61] Habington, op. cit. ii, 153. Adam was holding a messuage and land at

Kempsey in 1274–5 (Assize R. 1026, m. 22).
[62] *Testa de Nevill* (Rec. Com.), 42 ; Prattinton Coll. (Soc. Antiq.).
[63] Assize R. 1026, m. 14.
[64] *Lay Subs. Worcs. c.* 1280 (Worcs. Hist. Soc.), 79.
[65] Sir T. Phillipps, *Index to Worcs. Fines*, 6.
[66] *Abbrev. Rot. Orig.* (Rec. Com.), ii, 248. [67] op. cit. (Harl. Soc. xxvii), 26–7.
[67a] Prattinton Coll. (Soc. Antiq.).
[68] Chan. Inq. p.m. (Ser. 2), xciv, 102.
[69] Ibid. cxci, 121.
[70] *Worcs. Quarter Sess. R.* (Worcs. Hist. Soc.), Introd. p. xxx.
[71] Habington, op. cit. ii, 148.
[72] Nash, op. cit. ii, 20. Charles Bentley was dealing with land at Kerswell in 1657 (Feet of F. Worcs. Mich. 1657), and Edward and Charles Bentley in 1695–6 (ibid. East. 7 Will. III).
[73] G.E.C. *Complete Baronetage*, i, 84.

KEMPSEY CHURCH : THE NAVE LOOKING EAST

KEMPSEY CHURCH : THE 13TH CENTURY PISCINA AND SEDILIA

married her cousin Sir Richard Temple, who succeeded to the baronetcy on the death of Sir Peter Temple, brother and heir of Sir William above named.[74] The estate of the Nash passed to her. She died in 1805 without surviving issue,[75] and the estate passed to John Dicken, son of her half-sister Henrietta, wife of William Dicken of Sheinton, co. Salop.[76] John Dicken took the name and arms of Temple by royal licence 23 September 1796,[77] and his grandson Richard Temple was created a baronet in 1876.[78] He died in 1902, and his son Lieut.-Col. Sir Richard Carnac Temple succeeded to the estate,[79] where he now resides.

TEMPLE of the Nash, baronet. *Or an eagle sable quartered with Argent two bars sable with three martlets or upon each bar.*

CLERKENLEAP (Clarconleppo, xvi cent.) at one time belonged to the Winslows.[80] Edward Winslow, grandson of Kenelm Winslow of Kempsey, sailed in the *Mayflower* and became Governor of Plymouth Colony.[81] The estate was purchased about 1650 by John Nash of Worcester, and left by him to his nephew Richard Nash, from whom it passed to his grandson Dr. Treadway Russell Nash, the historian of Worcestershire. It descended with his other estates to Lady Henry Somerset, the present owner.[82]

There was a windmill worth 13s. 4d. at Kempsey in 1299.[83] In 1324 pardon was granted to John de Mareys 'mouner' for acquiring in fee from Godfrey Bishop of Worcester two mills in Kempsey held in chief of the king.[84] In 1690 a water grist-mill at Kempsey belonged to William Yarranton.[85] A weir-pool at Clerkenleap called Wheler's Weare was granted in 1545 to John Bourne,[86] and passed at his death in 1575 to his son Anthony.[87] There were two wind-mills at Kempsey in 1821,[87a] but the last was pulled down about 1875.

The manor of the *RECTORY* of Kempsey seems to have existed from quite early times. Godfrey the archdeacon, who may have been rector of Kempsey, held a hide and a half in the manor about 1182, and he also held 8 acres which had been given by Bishop John (1151–8) at the dedication of the church.[88] In 1223 Boidin, parson of Kempsey, was summoned to answer the Abbot of Pershore as to a claim set up by the parson to common in the abbot's manor of Wadborough. Boidin claimed it in exchange for common of pasture which he said the abbot enjoyed in his land at Kempsey.[89] In 1305 free warren was granted to Peter de Collingburn, parson of the church of Kempsey, in the demesne lands of the church of Kempsey.[90] In 1334 the privilege was granted to the parson of Kempsey that the rectory-house should be quit of livery of stewards, chamberlains, &c., so

that none of them should lodge there against his will.[91] When the church of Kempsey was appropriated to the college of Westbury by the founder John Carpenter, Bishop of Worcester, in 1473,[92] the manor of the rectory passed to this college. The farm of the manor brought in £46 13s. 4d. at the time of the Dissolution, and from it various payments were made in alms. A sum of 4s. 4d. was given to six poor men and six widows by the ordination of Bishop John Carpenter, and alms to the value of 20s. were distributed on the anniversaries of Edward IV and the Duke of York his father. A sum of 9s. was paid for the diets of six senior priests, six poor men and six widows twice a year.[93]

The manor was confiscated by the Crown on the suppression of the college, and was granted in 1544 to Sir Ralph Sadleir and his wife Ellen.[94] Sir Ralph exchanged it with the king for other property in 1547,[95] and in the same year it was granted to the Dean and Chapter of Worcester.[96] It was confiscated by the Parliamentary trustees and sold in 1650 to George Wylde of Gressenhall, co. Norfolk.[97] The manor then included a mansion-house, fields called Butchers Meadows on the banks of the Severn, Windmill Fields, Carlsome, a tithe-barn and a wood near Jagg Mills.

At the Restoration the manor was given back to the dean and chapter, in whose possession it remained until it was transferred in 1859 to the Ecclesiastical Commissioners,[98] who are the present owners.

The church of *ST. MARY THE CHURCH VIRGIN* consists of a chancel 47½ ft. by 21 ft., a south organ bay, a nave 60¾ ft. by 28½ ft., a north transept 35 ft. long and 19 ft. wide, a south transept 26½ ft. long and 18¼ ft. wide, north and south aisles 10¾ ft. and 9½ ft. wide respectively, a west tower 15 ft. square, and a north porch. These measurements are all internal.

That the present building has been developed from an aisleless cruciform church of the 12th century is shown by the remaining jamb of a window in the west respond of the south arcade. Additional evidence may be seen in the plinth and buttresses at the western angle of the nave, the plinth of the south transept, and the south-east buttress of the north transept.

The chancel appears to have been rebuilt about 1250, and towards the end of the same century a south aisle was added to the church and the existing south arcade built. Soon after this a similar addition was made to the north side of the church, the north aisle and existing arcade being added early in the 14th century. During the 15th century extensive repairs became necessary, and the whole of the north and south transepts and aisles were rebuilt. A little later in the same century the west tower was rebuilt and heightened, much of the older masonry being re-used. In modern times an organ chamber has been added to the south of the chancel, the chancel arch

[74] G.E.C. *Complete Baronetage*, i, 84.
[75] Ibid. 85.
[76] Ibid. 84 n. (a).
[77] Ibid.
[78] Burke, *Peerage*, 1909.
[79] Ibid.
[80] Nash, op. cit. ii, 21.
[81] *Dict. Nat. Biog.*
[82] Nash, loc. cit. ; inform. from Mr. J. W. Willis-Bund.
[83] Red Bk. of Bishopric of Worc. fol. 35.

[84] *Cal. Pat.* 1324–7, p. 51 ; Inq. a.q.d. file 173, no. 14.
[85] Recov. R. East. 2 Will. and Mary, rot. 83.
[86] *L. and P. Hen. VIII*, xx (1), g. 465 (80).
[87] Chan. Inq. p.m. (Ser. 2), clxxii, 142.
[87a] Prattinton Coll. (Soc. Antiq.).
[88] Red Bk. of Bishopric of Worc. fol. 49.
[89] Maitland, *Bracton's Note-Bk.* iii, 462–3.

[90] *Cal. Chart. R.* 1300–26, p. 49.
[91] *Cal. Pat.* 1330–4, p. 534.
[92] Worc. Epis. Reg. John Carpenter (1443–76), fol. ii, 25 f.
[93] *Valor Eccl.* (Rec. Com.), ii, 432.
[94] *L. and P. Hen. VIII*, xix (1), g. 278 (68).
[95] Pat. 1 Edw. VI, pt. ix, m. 42.
[96] Ibid. m. 5.
[97] Close, 1650, pt. xxxviii, no. 4.
[98] *Lond. Gaz.* 16 Dec. 1859, p. 4757.

and parts of the transepts rebuilt, new windows inserted and a porch added on the north side.

The chancel walling is of fine coursed rubble, the arcade walling of large random rubble, and the greater part of the later work faced with red sandstone ashlar. Parts of the internal details are in oolite, and greenstone is used in the arcades and elsewhere.

The east window of the chancel is of five grouped lancets under a moulded arch with shafted jambs ; the external labels have leaf stops and a moulded inclosing arch. In the north wall are three double lancet windows with internal and external inclosing labels. The south wall contains two similar windows and a south door, the latter with a segmental rear arch and continuously moulded jambs.

KEMPSEY CHURCH : 13TH-CENTURY PISCINA

The trefoil-headed piscina has three moulded brackets, one foliated, and a slot for a shelf. The sedilia are of similar design but with moulded labels and head stops, the spandrels being filled in with foliage. A moulded string-course runs round the chancel, breaking over the piscina, sedilia and doorway, and on the exterior is a corresponding course, apparently modern. The details of the chancel have been much repaired throughout, but the sedilia and piscina are excellent examples of 13th-century work. The chancel arch is modern.

The early 14th-century north nave arcade is of three bays, with arches of two chamfered orders, springing from square piers, with a half shaft against each face, and moulded capitals. The south arcade,

also of three bays, has similar piers with mouldings of rather earlier date. The arches, of two moulded orders, are built of green and white stone alternately.

The 15th-century east and west windows of the north transept are of three lights, and in the modern north wall is a large window of the same type. The two north aisle windows, one on each side of the porch, are similar to the old windows in the transept. The north door, which may be of 15th-century date, but suggests a later copy, opens into a modern porch. The 15th-century west window is of three lights.

The south transept has a window on the south only, a large modern five-light opening, set in modern walling. In the east and west walls are traces of 13th-century windows with filleted shafts to the jambs, and on the east is a trefoiled piscina of similar date. The south aisle has been rebuilt with two windows similar to those opposite and a modern south door. The west wall, which is original, has a lancet light. The transverse arches at the eastern end of the aisles are contemporary with the adjoining arcades.

The tower is of three stages, with angle buttresses and an embattled parapet, having crocketed pinnacles at the four corners. The two-centred tower arch has flat panelled jambs and soffit, and the west window of the ground stage is of four large cinquefoiled lights with vertical tracery in the head. At the north-east is a blocked entrance to the vice, which is now entered by a modern external doorway. The bell-chamber is lighted on all four sides by windows of two trefoiled lights with traceried two-centred heads, and the ringing chamber beneath by windows of similar design on the north, west and south.

The roofs are all modern.

The second window from the east in the north wall of the chancel, and the corresponding window on the south, contain some exceedingly fine remains of 14th-century glass. In the north window are the figures of St. Margaret and an archbishop, probably St. Thomas of Canterbury, both with well-designed cusped and crocketed canopies. Below in small trefoiled panels are the figures of a bishop and St. Catherine. These are earlier in style, and probably belong to the latter part of the previous century. The southern window contains figures of St. Catherine and St. Cuthbert of the same size as the figures in the opposite window, and with canopies of a similar design. Below are small trefoiled panels, with the figures of a bishop and a king, perhaps St. Edward. All have red backgrounds, with the exception of the St. Catherine in the southern window. The heads, grounds and borders of the windows are made up of various fragments of canopy and border work.

The seating and fittings are all modern. On the north chancel wall is a monument to Sir Edmund Wylde, 1620, consisting of an armed effigy on an altar tomb with arch and cornice above, and two kneeling figures of his sons Edmund and Walter, and in the pediment the quartered arms and crest of Wylde. The wife of Sir Edmund was Dorothy Clarke of Houghton Conquest, Bedfordshire. Out of this tomb for some years there formerly grew a horse chestnut tree, which was considered one of the great ornaments of the church. Under the tower is a large modern bronze bust of Sir Richard Temple, bart., who died in 1902.

The bells are six in number : the first inscribed 'Cantate Domino Canticum Novum 1686'; the second, ' Fear God, Honour the King 1686'; the third, 'Matthew Bagley made me 1686 '; the fourth, ' Henricus Bagley me fecit 1686'; the fifth, the churchwardens' names. These bells have the same lettering and are probably of the same date. The sixth is by Mears, 1821, and the sanctus is inscribed T, R, K, W, I, L, with rose and fleur de lis stops, and a bell between the initials I. B.

bishopric of Worcester.[100] John Devreux, nephew of the Bishop of Worcester, was made rector of Kempsey in 1284.[1] He was apparently non-resident, for he appointed a vicar whose portion consisted of part of the tithes, mortuaries, Peter's pence and two loads of hay, a manse and garden.[2] In 1288 the bishop made the church of Kempsey prebendal to the college of Westbury and bestowed the prebend upon John Devreux.[3] In the following year an inquiry was instituted by the Pope, Nicholas IV, regarding a petition of the Prior and convent of Worcester stating that they had had the right of instituting rectors and vicars during a vacancy in the see of Worcester, but the bishop had constituted the church of Kempsey, which was subject to the church of Worcester, prebendal to the church of Westbury-on-Trym and assigned it to his clerk, John Devreux, whom he had made rector of the church of Kempsey and a new canon in the church of Westbury, so that the

KEMPSEY CHURCH FROM THE NORTH-EAST

The plate consists of a 1571 cup repaired and recently gilt, a paten, apparently of 1639, a large flagon, 1732, a modern silver gilt copy of the 1571 cup, a small flat paten, and two large almsdishes. All the plate except the flagon is silver gilt.

The registers before 1812 are as follows : (i) baptisms 1688 to 1782, burials 1688 to 1783, marriages 1690 to 1753 ; (ii) baptisms and burials 1783 to 1812, marriages 1783 to 1807 ; (iii) marriages 1754 to 1812. Many earlier 17th-century entries will be found among the Bishops' Transcripts.

ADVOWSON

There was a priest at Kempsey at the time of the Domesday Survey.[99] The advowson belonged to the

church of Kempsey was no longer immediately subject to the church of Worcester as it ought to be.[4] Kempsey, however, remained a prebend of Westbury in the gift of the Bishops of Worcester,[5] the vicars being appointed by the rectors,[6] and in 1434 it was declared by a papal letter at the petition of Adam Moleyns, rector of the church, that the church of Kempsey as a prebend of Worcester might be held with other benefice or dignity without papal dispensation.[7] In 1473 the church of Kempsey was appropriated to the college of the Holy Trinity, Westbury, by Bishop John Carpenter, who had refounded the college, the revenues being found insufficient,[8] and from that time the presentations to

[99] V.C.H. Worcs. i, 288.
[100] Reg. G. Giffard (Worcs. Hist. Soc.), 249, 250 ; Thomas, Surv. of Worc. Cath. App. no. 49.
[1] Reg. G. Giffard (Worcs. Hist. Soc.), 249, 294.

[2] Ibid. 250 ; Nash, op. cit. ii, 26 n b.
[3] Reg. G. Giffard (Worcs. Hist. Soc.), 343. [4] Ibid. 362. See above, p. 275.
[5] Cal. Pat. 1301-7, pp. 29, 63 ; 1313-17, p. 47 ; 1429-36, p. 322 ; Reg. G. Giffard (Worcs. Hist. Soc.), 461 ;

Worc. Epis. Reg. Wulstan de Bransford (1339-49), fol. 10 f.
[6] Nash, op. cit. ii, 26-7.
[7] Cal. Papal Letters, viii, 506.
[8] Worc. Epis. Reg. John Carpenter (1443-76), ii, fol. 25 f.

the vicarage were made by the Dean and Chapter of Westbury.[9]

In February 1544 the college with all its possessions was surrendered to the king,[10] and the rectory and advowson of Kempsey were granted in that year to Sir Ralph Sadleir and his wife Ellen.[11] They exchanged them with the king in 1547 for other property,[12] and in the same year they were granted to the Dean and Chapter of Worcester.[13] The presentations have been made by the dean and chapter from that time until the present day.[14]

An oratory at Kempsey was built and dedicated to St. Andrew by Aelhun, Bishop of Worcester, in 868.[15]

In 1316 a chantry of one chaplain was founded in the parish church of Kempsey by John de Kempsey, treasurer of the cathedral of Hereford. He endowed it with two messuages, 40 acres of land, 2 acres of meadow and 9s. 8d. rent in Kempsey.[16] The first presentation to this chantry was made by John de Kempsey,[17] but subsequent collations seem to have been made by the Bishops of Worcester.[18] In 1362–3 Roger de Otery, clerk, granted a messuage and land at Norton by Worcester to the chaplain of the chantry at the altar of St. Mary in the church of Kempsey.[19] At the time of the dissolution of the chantries in the reign of Edward VI the endowment of this chantry amounted to £6 10s. 11d., of which 26s. was paid to the bishop and 11s. 4¾d. to the king for tenths. In one return of the value of the chantry it is stated that the parish of Kempsey contained 400 'houseling people' and that the one parish priest was not sufficient,[20] but in another the number of householders is returned as 120.[21] The chantry was granted in 1548 to Sir John Thynne and Laurence Hide as a late possession of Kenelm Buck of The Nash.[22] They must shortly afterwards have transferred it to Kenelm Buck, for he died in 1550 in possession of the chantry lands of Kempsey which he held of the Bishop of Worcester as of his manor of Kempsey.[23] Francis his son succeeded him, and appears to have been in possession of the chantry in 1566.[24]

A messuage called the Church House was granted with the chantry to Sir John Thynne in 1548.[25] It passed with the chantry to the Bucks and was conveyed in 1558 by Francis Buck to trustees, for the use of the inhabitants of Kempsey. It was then described as containing four bays, and every bay 15 ft. in length. The trustees leased the church-house from time to time, retaining the right to enter into possession on a quarter's notice, for the purpose of holding a church ale.[26]

There is a Baptist chapel at Kempsey erected in 1860.

CHARITIES The Church Lands.—The parish has been possessed from time immemorial of certain lands and hereditaments under this title. The trust estates now consist of six cottages situate in different parts of the parish, also of twelve tenements in Church Street and at The Greens; 3 a. 3 r. 20 p., known as Lammas Land, or Ann's Acre; 1 a. 0 r. 20 p., known as Southam Lammas Lands, and allotments, Church Street, containing 3 a.

The official trustees also hold a sum of £427 10s. 3d. consols, producing £10 13s. 8d. yearly, arising from sales of land and accumulations.

The net income, amounting to about £110 a year, is applied towards repairs of the church and general church expenses.

The trust is regulated by a scheme of the Charity Commissioners 17 June 1902.

Christopher Meredith's Charity.—In pursuance of the will of this donor, dated 24 January 1652, Bibles and Prayer books to the value of £3 a year were received from the Stationers' Company for distribution amongst the tenants of the manor of Kempsey, and the like books of the same value among the scholars of the school. By an order of the Charity Commissioners 5 December 1905 this branch of the charity was constituted the Meredith Educational Foundation.

A free school was carried on in this parish as far back as memory goes, the master of which received £1 a year from a gift of John Winslow in 1717. The official trustees also hold a sum of £105 9s. 6d. consols, producing £2 12s. 8d. yearly, bequeathed in 1839 by will of Rebecca Sargent as a subscription to the Charity school.

Eleemosynary Charities.—Sir Edmund Wylde, kt., as stated on the church table, in 1620 gave £20 for the poor, and other donors (twenty in number) gave smaller sums, amounting in the aggregate to £94 10s. In 1679 a tenement and 1 a. 2 r. in the hamlet of Kerswell were purchased therewith. In 1902 the sum of £4 4s. was received as rent, and the official trustees hold a sum of £42 15s. 3d. consols in respect of these charities; also a sum of £4 16s. 5d. consols in respect of William Giles's gift of £5 for bread on New Year's Day.

The church table further mentioned that Charles Geary by his will 1788 left £20, the interest to be laid out in bread and coals at Christmas among ten poor women. The legacy is represented by £19 10s. 2d. consols.

In 1789 Elizabeth Eaton, by her will and a codicil thereto, bequeathed £150 and £50 respectively for the poor, which are represented by £195 11s. 11d. consols.

In 1822 William Hay by his will left £19 19s., the interest to be applied in the distribution of shoes to poor men. The legacy is now represented by £35 19s.

The several sums of stock are held by the official trustees, producing together in annual dividends £7 9s. These five charities are administered together and applied mainly in the distribution of coals.

An annual sum of 20s. is distributable in bread to the poor in respect of the charity of John Winslow,

[9] Nash, op. cit. ii, 27.
[10] V.C.H. Gloucs. ii, 108.
[11] L. and P. Hen. VIII, xix (1), g. 278 (68). [12] Pat. 1 Edw. VI, pt. ix, m. 42.
[13] L. and P. Hen. VIII, xxi (2), g. 770 (50).
[14] Nash, op. cit. ii, 27; Inst. Bks. (P.R.O.).
[15] Matt. Paris, Chron. Maj. (Rolls Ser.), i, 391.
[16] Cal. Pat. 1313–17, p. 387; Worc.

Epis. Reg. Walter Maidstone (1313–17), fol. 54 f.
[17] Worc. Epis. Reg. Walter Maidstone (1313–17), fol. 45 d.
[18] Ibid. Simon de Montacute (1333–7), fol. 20; Thos. Pulton (1425–33), fol. 148 d.; John Carpenter (1443–76), i, fol. 8 d., 124 d.; John Alcock (1476–86), fol. 50 d.
[19] Inq. a.q.d. file 346, no. 1; Cal. Pat. 1361–4, p. 237.

[20] Chant. Cert. 25, no. 10.
[21] Ibid. 60, no. 8.
[22] Pat. 2 Edw. VI, pt. v, m. 60.
[23] Chan. Inq. p.m. (Ser. 2), xciv, 102.
[24] Chan. Proc. (Ser. 2), bdle. 30, no. 98.
[25] Pat. 2 Edw. VI, pt. v, m. 60.
[26] Deeds in the parish chest of Kempsey quoted in Prattinton Coll. (Soc. Antiq.).

KEMPSEY CHURCH : REMAINS OF 14TH CENTURY GLASS

which is payable out of the rents of 4 a. 2 r. in the tithing of Draycott in this parish belonging to the charities of George Lloyd and Richard Spencer, comprised in deed of 21 August 1762. The annual rent, amounting to about £12, is applicable in moieties for the benefit of the poor of Kempsey and Severn Stoke.

Edward Hurdman by his will (date not stated) left £100, the interest to be applied in clothing on St. Thomas's Day for three or four poor men. The legacy has been invested in £102 13s. 11d. consols.

In 1839 Rebecca Sargent by her will left £100, the interest to be applied on St. Thomas's Day in clothing six poor old women ; invested in £105 9s. 6d. consols.

In 1853 Frances White left a legacy, now represented by £30 3s. 11d. consols, the income to be applied in bread.

In 1880 Mrs. Mary Handy Mercer, by her will proved at Gloucester 27 August, bequeathed £100, the interest to be distributed to the poor. The legacy has been invested in £97 18s. 4d. consols.

In 1883 Miss Caroline Wigley Bell, by her will proved at Gloucester 15 November, left £100 for the poor. The legacy, less duty, is represented by £88 6s. 10d. consols.

The several sums of stock are held by the official trustees, who also hold a sum of £10 13s. 2d. consols in respect of a legacy under the will of Sarah Mills, proved at London 23 August 1876.

The annual dividends of the six preceding charities, amounting together to £10 17s., are applied mainly in the distribution of doles, with a preference to widows.

In 1859 Joseph Munn, by his will proved at Worcester 18 February, bequeathed £100, the interest to be applied in bread for the poor. It was invested in £94 19s. 9d. consols, producing £2 7s. 4d. yearly.

In 1898 Thomas Crisp, by his will proved 11 November, bequeathed £20 consols, the annual dividend of 10s. to be applied in the purchase of shoes to be given on Good Friday to a poor man of not less than fifty years of age, any residue to be distributed in bread.

These sums of stock are also held by the official trustees.

KNIGHTWICK

Cnihtawiche (x cent.) ; Cnihtewica (xi cent.) ; Chenitwica (xii cent.) ; Knythwyk, Knhittewyk (xiii cent.).

Knightwick is a parish containing 857 acres, of which 8 acres are covered with water, on the Herefordshire border of the county, on the right bank of the River Teme. Sapey Brook forms part of its western boundary. The Worcester and Bromyard branch of the Great Western railway passes through the parish and has a station called Knightwick station just outside the parish boundary on the east. Suckley station, on the southern boundary, is in this parish at Knightwick Row. Two roads branch off from the Bromyard road near Woodford House in the north of the parish. One branch passes over the Teme at Knightsford Bridge and leads north to Martley, and the other branch leads southwards past Knightwick station to Malvern. From the latter road a branch passes south-west to Knightwick Row, and is connected by a cross road with the village of Knightwick. At the south-east of the parish near Suckley station is an early 17th-century half-timber cottage of one story with an attic, known locally as 'the old house.' Adjoining it to the west is a cart-shed, also of half-timber. The village contains a few cottages and houses, of no architectural interest, the rectory, a mortuary chapel erected in 1879 on the site of the old church of St. Mary the Virgin and a graveyard. The present church of St. Mary the Virgin for this parish and Doddenham is at Knightsford Bridge in Doddenham and was built in 1856. The manor-house, the residence of Mr. Thomas Lawson Walker, J.P., stands to the west of the village. It is a red brick two-story house of ⊔ plan with tiled roofs, built in the Queen Anne period partly on the foundations of an earlier 17th-century building. The entrance front is on the south-east, with the main doorway covered by a light wooden porch in the centre. The four angles of the main block are pilastered, while the windows are long and narrow and glazed with small square panes ; at the ends and

back of the house are blank window recesses designed to complete the symmetry of the elevation. Above the hipped roofs two chimneys rise from the centre of the main block and two from the ends of the projecting wings at the back. There is a cellar under the south part of the house, the two-light mullioned openings to which on the south side retain the sandstone dressings of the earlier building. The hall, which is entered directly from the main doorway, has the parlour and dining room on the south, some domestic apartments on the north, and the staircase on the west, with a modern addition at the back filling the space between the two wings. Above the hall fireplace there is a carved oak panelled chimney-piece of the latter half of the 17th century, the panels being divided by pairs of slender turned balusters supporting a cornice. The walls of the parlour are covered entirely with Jacobean panelling in small squares with a fluted frieze. A recess on the south flanked by fluted Ionic columns supporting a cornice surmounted by a broken curved pediment is contemporary with the rebuilding of the house in the Queen Anne period. At the back of this recess is a painting of four nude children, probably of contemporary date. The plaster ceiling is divided into four deep panels with moulded edges. Above the modern fireplace is a piece of carved oak overmantel of the Charles II period. The stairs to the first floor are modern, but above there is an early 18th-century dog-legged stair with a moulded handrail and turned balusters.

The scenery of the valley where the River Teme has broken its way through the hills is very beautiful. The hills are usually rounded and wooded, but in places precipitous cliffs fall straight to the river as at Rosebury Rock. To the north are some old brickworks.

The north of the parish lies in the valley of the Teme, but the land rises rapidly to the south, reaching a height of 400 ft. above the ordnance datum at the south-eastern boundary. In 1905 Knightwick contained 290 acres of arable land and 487 of permanent grass.[1] The subsoil is Keuper Sandstone, the soil loam, clay and marl, producing crops of wheat, beans, fruit and hops.

Kenswick, formerly a chapelry of Knightwick and an extra-parochial district, became a separate parish in 1857.[2] It lies to the south-east of Wichenford, and is separated from Knightwick by the parishes of Lulsley and Broadwas. It contains 425 acres, of which 96 are arable land, 276 permanent grass and 21 woodland.[3]

The Tenbury and Worcester high road passes through it, and Kenswick House, the seat of the Hon. Mrs. Britten, on the south side of this road, and the Kedges on the north are the only two houses of any importance in the parish. Kenswick House is a stuccoed three-story building dating probably from the early 17th century, but so modernized inside and out that it is difficult to say of what the original house consisted. The lower parts of two brick chimney stacks surmounted by square shafts, which belong to the rooms on either side of the entrance-hall, are of the original date. The dining room, which is contained in a projecting wing on the north-east, is lined with Jacobean panelling brought here from Wichenford Court. The elaborate oak over-mantel has a carved shield upon it, which suggests that it may have been erected by Anthony Washbourne (d. 1573) or his son John (d. 1633), but the heraldry is not quite clear. Various modern additions have been made at the rear, the present kitchen and offices being contained in a projecting wing on the east, and a billiard room in a corresponding wing on the west. A stable to the south-west of the house occupies the site of a Roman Catholic chapel ; some parts of the original brick walls appear to be incorporated in the present building. Portions of the original moat remain, out of which the two ponds to the south-east of the house are formed. The road is carried over the Laughern Brook, which forms the southern boundary of Kenswick, at Pig Bridge.

The soil is clay with a subsoil of Keuper Marl, and the chief crops are wheat, beans, peas, barley and roots.

Seventeenth-century place-names which have been found in connexion with Knightwick are Dales, Hollowe Orchard, Stitching Furlong, Coppearn Grove, the Lakes, the Holmes, Howley, Wallcroft.[4]

MANORS Amongst the manors said to have been freed for the monks of Worcester by King Edgar in 964 from all royal exactions Knightwick was included.[5] At this time and in 1086 it formed part of the manor of Grimley,[6] and so was probably included in the grant of Grimley to the church of Worcester by Beorhtwulf, King of Mercia, in 851.[7] The manor was assigned to the support of the monks, and had been leased by them to

a certain Eadgyth, a nun, who held it, performing the services due for it, as long as the brethren could dispense with it. In the time of King William, however, their number increased and Eadgyth restored the manor to them. She was living at the time of the Domesday Survey and was willing to testify to this. At the time of the Survey, however, the hide of Knightwick was in the hands of Robert le Despenser, brother of Urse the Sheriff. This hide rendered in the manor of Grimley sac and soc and all services due to the king.[8]

Like most of the rest of Robert's possessions in Worcestershire, Knightwick passed to Walter de Beauchamp, son-in-law of Urse the Sheriff.[9] The overlordship remained with Walter's descendants the Earls of Warwick, the manor being held of their honour of Elmley,[10] but the overlordship is not mentioned after 1325.

Walter de Beauchamp apparently held the manor in demesne in the time of Henry I.[11] From this time until about 1280 the history of the sub-tenants of this manor is very obscure. In 1220–1 John Clerk and his sister Julia released to Henry Fitz Ralph all their claim in a virgate of land at Knightwick,[12] and in 1255 Auda widow of Godfrey de Gamages granted the manor of Knightwick to William de la Were.[13] William died in 1269, and his brother Peter succeeded to the estate,[14] which he apparently held in 1274–5.[15] These deeds do not appear to refer to the capital manor of Knightwick, which was probably already in 1274–5 in the possession of the Prior of Great Malvern.[16] The prior probably derived his title from the family of Mans, who held the chapel of Knightwick in the 12th century and endowed the priory of Little Malvern with land at Knightwick towards the end of that century.[17] Simon de Mans, the benefactor of Little Malvern Priory, had two sons Walter and William. Walter, the elder son, had a son William, who died childless, a daughter, Avice wife of Bartholomew Marshall, and a second daughter, who married Walter Mapnor and had a son Walter.[18] The estate at Knightwick evidently passed to the Mapnors, and was given by Walter de Mapnor or his daughter Lucy to the Prior of Great Malvern before 1274–5.[19] Lucy apparently still lived at Knightwick or held some estate there in 1280, for she paid 12d. in that year towards the lay subsidy, while the Prior of Great Malvern paid 20s.[20] In 1283 the manor was given by the Prior of Great Malvern to Bishop Godfrey Giffard in compensation when the title of Westminster to Great Malvern was finally settled.[21]

The bishop leased the manor in 1318 to Master Peter Fillol, rector of the church of Martley,[22] and in 1324–5 to John Collan for life.[23] It was again leased in 1336 for the lives of William de Massington

[1] Statistics from Bd. of Agric. (1905).
[2] Stat. 20 Vict. cap. 19.
[3] Statistics from Bd. of Agric. (1905).
[4] Pat. 6 Chas. I, pt. xiv, no. 3.
[5] Birch, Cart. Sax. iii, 379.
[6] Ibid. ; V.C.H. Worcs. i, 295b.
[7] Kemble, Codex Dipl. ii, no. 266.
[8] V.C.H. Worcs. i, 295b. A charter of 1023 whereby Wulfric, on his marriage with the sister of 'the Archbishop,' undertook to obtain for her the land at Knightwick 'for three men's day' from the convent of Winchcomb, seems to

relate to this Knightwick (Thorpe, Dipl. Angl. Aevi Sax. 320).
[9] V.C.H. Worcs. i, 325, 265–6.
[10] Cal. Close, 1279–88, p. 238 ; Cal. Inq. p.m. 1–9 Edw. II, 403 ; Inq. a.q.d. file 181, no. 1 (19 Edw. II).
[11] V.C.H. Worcs. i, 325.
[12] Feet of F. Worcs. 5 Hen. III, no. 21.
[13] Ibid. Trin. 39 Hen. III, no. 25.
[14] Excerpta e Rot. Fin. (Rec. Com.), ii, 484.
[15] Assize R. 1026, m. 9.
[16] Ibid. m. 18. [17] See below.
[18] Prattinton Coll. (Soc. Antiq.), Deeds

of D. and C. of Worc. no. 311, 53 ; Habington, Surv. of Worcs. (Worcs. Hist. Soc.), i, 194.
[19] Assize R. 1026, m. 18.
[20] Lay Subs. R. Worcs. 1280 (Worcs. Hist. Soc.), 45.
[21] Cal. Pat. 1281–92, p. 85 ; Cal. Close, 1279–88, p. 238 ; Ann. Mon. (Rolls Ser.), iv, 488 ; Thomas, Surv. of Worc. Cath. A. 140–1 ; Reg. G. Giffard (Worcs. Hist. Soc.), 218.
[22] Worc. Epis. Reg. Cobham (1317–27), fol. 54 f.
[23] Inq. a.q.d. files 172, no. 2 ; 181, no. 1.

and Agnes his wife.[24] In 1460–1 the bishop leased the site of the manor to Thomas Romney of Lulsley, Isabel his wife and John their son for a term of seventy years.[25] The manor was valued at £8 in 1535.[26] It was confiscated by Edward VI[27] on Bishop Heath's deprivation in 1552 and was granted in the following year to Lord Robert Dudley and his heirs and William Glasyer.[28] Lord Robert Dudley was attainted and sentenced to death in the same year for taking the part of Lady Jane Grey, and though he was pardoned in October 1554[29] this manor seems to have remained in the Crown until 1560.[30] It was among the manors taken from the bishopric by Queen Elizabeth under the Act of 1558–9, which enabled her to take into her hands certain of the temporalities of any bishopric which fell vacant, recompensing the value with parsonages impropriate.[31]

Lord Robert Dudley was restored in blood in March 1557–8 and created Earl of Leicester in 1564.[32] The manor of Knightwick must have been restored to him,[33] and his and William Glasyer's interest passed to Sir Richard Sackville, whose son Thomas Sackville Lord Buckhurst sold the manor in 1568 to Lancelot Romney.[34] Lancelot died seised of it in 1595, when it passed to his son John,[35] to whom livery was made in 1605.[36] It was probably this John who was outlawed for felony and murder in January 1628. By an inquisition taken in 1630 it was found that John on the day of his outlawry was seised for life of a capital messuage and land in Knightwick. This estate was granted in September 1630 to Thomas Cooke during the lifetime of John Romney.[37] John was evidently restored, for he died seised of the manor about 1640, when it passed to his son Lancelot.[38] Lancelot died in 1643, leaving a son John, aged eleven, and three years after the estate was sequestered for Lancelot's delinquency in arms. In 1648 John Evett, grandfather and guardian of John Romney, begged to compound for the estate, but before the sum could be raised Evett was imprisoned for debt in Worcester Castle. The guardianship of the child passed to Henry son of John Evett, and he in March 1651 offered to pay the debt. When Charles came to Worcester in 1651 John Romney joined his standard, under compulsion, as he stated, by the Scotch soldiers quartered at his uncle's house. Though he did not take part in the battle his estate was forfeited, and when in 1659 his property was ordered to be sequestered for his complicity in Sir George Booth's rising it was found that it was already sequestered for his engagement with the Scots.[39]

In 1666 John Romney and Elizabeth his wife, William Robbins and Joan his wife, Henry Evett and

Francis Powle sold the manor of Knightwick to Thomas Foley.[40] His grandson Thomas Foley was created Lord Foley of Kidderminster in 1712,[41] and the manor descended with the title[42] until 1830[43] or later. It must soon after have been purchased by John Williams of Pitmaston, from whom it passed under a settlement made in 1838 to his son Francis

FOLEY, Lord Foley. *Argent a fesse engrailed between three cinqfoils and a border all sable.*   WILLIAMS. *Gyronny ermine and erminees a lion or sprinkled with drops of blood.*

Edward Williams. He was lord of the manor until his death in 1885,[44] when the estate passed to his son John Francis, who assumed the additional surname Greswolde. He died without issue in 1892, having devised the manor to his nephew Francis Wigley Greswolde Greswolde-Williams of Bredenbury Court, Herefordshire.[45]

At the time of the Domesday Survey a hide of land at KENSWICK (Checinwiche, xi cent. ; Kekingwyk, xiii and xiv cent. ; Kekonwyche, Kekynwych, xv cent. ; Kengewyk, xvi cent.), which formed part of the manor of Wick Episcopi, was held by Urse.[46] His heirs the Beauchamps, afterwards Earls of Warwick, held the overlordship as part of their honour of Elmley, and it followed the same descent as that honour.[47] William Savage at the end of the 16th century claimed the wardship of Giles Blount, forcing the latter's friends to compound with him for this right,[48] but this appears to have been the last occasion on which the rights of overlordship were exercised.

Wulfwine is the earliest known tenant of Kenswick, but before 1086 he had been succeeded by a certain Walter.[49] Walter de Kekingwik occurs in 1205,[50] and held 2½ hides at Kenswick in the time of Henry III,[51] and it may be assumed that Sir Walter de Kekingwik, who was patron of the church in 1270,[52] was also lord of the manor. Walter was succeeded apparently by John de Kekingwik, and it may have been this John and his son William who were keepers of the king's goshawks in 1306.[53] John died about 1316, and his son William inherited the property,

[24] *Cal. Pat.* 1334–8, p. 276.
[25] Habington, op. cit. ii, 169.
[26] *Valor Eccl.* (Rec. Com.), iii, 218.
[27] Habington states that the Bishop of Worcester had a manor in Knightwick in the middle of the 17th century (op. cit. ii, 168).
[28] Pat. 7 Edw. VI, pt. x, m. 3.
[29] G.E.C. *Complete Peerage*, v, 47.
[30] Mins. Accts. 2 & 3 Eliz. no. 38, m. 12.
[31] Ibid. ; Pat. 4 Eliz. pt. vi, m. 24.
[32] G.E.C. *Complete Peerage*, v, 47–8.
[33] Close, 10 Eliz. pt. xxvii, no. 1.
[34] Ibid. ; Feet of F. Worcs. Hil. 11 Eliz.
[35] Chan. Inq. p.m. (Ser. 2), ccxlvii, 51.
[36] Fine R. 3 Jas. I, pt. ii, no. 22.

[37] Pat. 6 Chas. I, pt. xiv, no. 3.
[38] Chan. Inq. p.m. (Ser. 2), dxcv, 90.
[39] *Cal. Com. for Comp.* 1823–4.
[40] Feet of F. Worcs. East. 18 Chas. II.
[41] G.E.C. *Complete Peerage*, iii, 387.
[42] The title became extinct on the death of Thomas Lord Foley in 1766, but was revived in 1776 for his cousin and heir Thomas Foley.
[43] Recov. R. Hil. 42 Geo. III, rot. 21 ; Hil. 10 & 11 Geo. IV, rot. 255.
[44] Inform. from Mr. Arthur Lord ; Burke, *Landed Gentry* (1906).
[45] Burke, *Landed Gentry* (1906).
[46] *V.C.H. Worcs.* i, 288b. The connexion of this manor with Wick Episcopi

and the bishop's overlordship in right of this connexion seem to have lapsed in the 13th century (*Testa de Nevill* [Rec. Com.], 41b).
[47] *Testa de Nevill* (Rec. Com.), 41b ; Add. MS. 28024, fol. 190a ; *Cal. Inq. p.m.* 1–9 *Edw. II*, 403 ; Chan. Inq. p.m. 21 Ric. II, no. 36, 137 ; (Ser. 2), xxiv, 83 ; lxxv, 96.
[48] Habington, op. cit. ii, 106.
[49] *V.C.H. Worcs.* i, 288.
[50] *Rot. de Oblatis et Fin.* (Rec. Com.), 285.
[51] *Testa de Nevill* (Rec. Com.), 41b.
[52] *Reg. G. Giffard* (Worcs. Hist. Soc.), i, 41.   [53] *Cal. Close*, 1302–7, p. 385.

which then consisted of a messuage and a carucate of land at Kenswick.[54] It was probably this William de Kekingwik who was rewarded in 1339 for good service at Carisbrooke Castle and was custodian of the port of Yarmouth in the Isle of Wight in 1340.[55] John de Kekingwik held a fourth and a twentieth part of a knight's fee in Kenswick and Eastbury in 1346, and Walter de Hoklington held a tenth of a fee at Kenswick.[56] John presented to the chapel of Kenswick in 1361,[57] but Alice Spelly, lady of Kenswick, presented in the following year. William Vallet presented in 1366[58] and styled himself lord of Kenswick in 1366-7.[59] It would seem that Alice and William must have held the manor during the lifetime of John de Kekingwik, for his daughters and co-heirs were minors in the custody of Thomas Earl of Warwick when the latter forfeited his possessions in 1396,[60] and the inquisition on John's possessions, which included Kenswick Manor, was taken in 1397, though the date of his death is not given.[61] In 1411–12 John Aston, clerk, conveyed the manor, which was then held for life by William Yoxhale, to Fulk Stafford, clerk.[62] William Yoxhale was still holding the manor in 1428,[63] but it had passed before 1431 to Sir Humphrey Stafford of Grafton,[64] nephew of Fulk Stafford, mentioned above.[65] Sir Humphrey was slain in Jack Cade's rebellion in 1449-50,[66] and by his will dated 1442 he had bequeathed Kenswick to his son Sir Humphrey.[67] The latter was attainted and executed in 1485, and his lands became forfeited to the king.[68] The manor of Kenswick was granted by Henry VII in 1486 to John Darell and John Pympe in tail-male.[69] Pympe died in 1496, leaving a son Henry, two years of age.[70] He died in 1518, and the property reverted to Sir Humphrey Stafford, son of the attainted Sir Humphrey, who had been restored to favour by Henry VIII in 1514–15.[71] Sir John Darell died in 1509, leaving a son and heir John,[72] but this part of the manor was also restored to Sir Humphrey Stafford.[73] It is doubtful whether John Darell was ever recompensed, for in 1515 he found it necessary to obtain a pardon for all entries on the manor of Kenswick.[74] Sir Humphrey Stafford died in 1546,[75] and his son Humphrey sold the manor in 1565 to George Blount.[76] Francis son of George died during the lifetime of his father, his son Giles inheriting the manor from his grandfather George while still a minor.[77] It was the wardship of this boy which was claimed by William Savage.[78] Giles Blount was indicted in 1633 at quarter sessions for neglecting to repair the highway from Martley which passed through his estate, and three years later

he was presented on account of the ruinous state of Blackmore Bridge.[79] Giles died about 1650,[80] when he was succeeded by his son Robert Blount,[81] who sold the manor in 1669 to Robert Foley.[82] The latter died about 1676 and was succeeded by his son Robert,[83] who conveyed the manor in 1679 to Roger North, probably for a settlement on his marriage with Anne daughter of Dudley Lord North.[84] Robert was succeeded by his eldest son North Foley in 1702.[85] He died in 1727, when the manor passed to his son Thomas Talbot Foley,[86] who died without issue, the manor passing to his sister Anne before 1789.[87] In that year she and Francis Plowden conveyed the manor to James Seton and others.[88] The manor was purchased about 1872 by Daniel Britten, who was succeeded in 1892 by his son Rear-Admiral Richard Frederick Britten, J.P. On his death in 1910 the manor passed to his widow, the Hon. Mrs. Britten, the present owner.

An estate at Knightwick afterwards called *PIT-HOUSE* was apparently held of the Despensers, for Thurstan Despenser and Alda Bluet his mother confirmed a grant of the estate to the Prior and convent of Little Malvern, and apparently thereby renounced their overlordship, as nothing further is heard of it.[89]

Under the Despensers the land was held by Simon Mans, who granted it towards the end of the 12th century, as a virgate of land in Knightwick which had belonged to Robert de la Putte, to the Prior and convent of Little Malvern.[90]

The estate remained in the possession of the Priors of Little Malvern until the Dissolution, when it passed to the Crown.[91] It was granted in 1544 to William and Francis Sheldon, and then consisted of a messuage called 'Pyte-house' and a virgate of land and a grove called 'Pytegrove.'[92] William and Francis sold it in the same year to John Alderfull or Alderford,[93] who died seised of it in 1556, leaving a son John his heir.[94] John Alderford sold the Pithouse in 1578 to John Washbourne,[95] who obtained licence to alienate it in 1587 to Roland Berkeley,[96] but it had passed before 1617 to Simon Clent, who died seised of it in that year, leaving as his heir his nephew John son of his brother William.[97] It is probable that at about this time Pithouse became annexed to the manor of Mapnors (q.v.), for further references to it have not been found.

An estate called the manor or capital messuage of *MAPNORS* in Knightwick was held by John Alderford at the time of his death in 1556. It was held as of Elmley Castle,[98] and, from its name, had evidently been held at one time by the Mapnors,

[54] Chan. Inq. p.m. 10 Edw. II, no. 12.
[55] Cal. Close, 1339-41, pp. 32, 574.
[56] Feud. Aids, v, 307.
[57] Nash, op. cit. i, 477 ; Sede Vacante Reg. (Worcs. Hist. Soc.), 203.
[58] Nash, loc. cit.
[59] Habington, op. cit. ii, 154.
[60] Chan. Inq. p.m. 21 Ric. II, no. 137.
[61] Ibid. 36.
[62] Feet of F. Worcs. 13 Hen. IV, no. 32.
[63] Feud. Aids, v, 319.
[64] Ibid. 332.
[65] Nash, op. cit. i, 157.
[66] Ibid.
[67] Chan. Inq. p.m. (Ser. 2), lxxv, 96.
[68] Ibid.
[69] Pat. 2 Hen. VII, pt. i ; Materials for Hist. of Hen. VII (Rolls Ser.), ii, 33.
[70] Chan. Inq. p.m. (Ser. 2), xi, 87.

[71] Ibid. xxxiii, 4 ; Memo. R. Hil. Recorda, 6 Hen. VIII, rot. 53.
[72] Chan. Inq. p.m. (Ser. 2), xxiv, 83.
[73] Memo. R. Mich. Recorda, 36 Hen. VIII, rot. 70 ; Chan. Inq. p.m. (Ser. 2), lxxv, 96.
[74] L. and P. Hen. VIII, ii, 1182.
[75] Chan. Inq. p.m. (Ser. 2), lxxv, 96.
[76] Feet of F. Worcs. Mich. 7 & 8 Eliz.
[77] Habington, op. cit. ii, 106-7.
[78] See above.
[79] Quart. Sess. R. (Worcs. Hist. Soc.), 509, 614.
[80] Metcalfe, Visit. of Worcs. 1682-3, p. 19.
[81] Ibid.
[82] Feet of F. Worcs. East. 21 Chas. II.
[83] Metcalfe, op. cit. 47.

[84] Ibid. ; Feet of F. Worcs. Mich. 31 Chas. II.
[85] Nash, op. cit. ii, 465.
[86] Ibid. ; Recov. R. Hil. 12 Geo. III, rot. 391.
[87] Nash, loc. cit. ; Recov. R. East. 29 Geo. III, rot. 319.
[88] Recov. R. D. Enr. East. 29 Geo. III, m. 107.
[89] Coll. Topog. et Gen. iv, 239, 240.
[90] Ibid. 238.
[91] Valor Eccl. (Rec. Com.), iii, 243.
[92] L. and P. Hen. VIII, xix(1), g. 80(50).
[93] Pat. 35 Hen. VIII, pt. xviii, m. 12.
[94] Chan. Inq. p.m. (Ser. 2), cviii, 127.
[95] Pat. 20 Eliz. pt. iii, m. 19.
[96] Ibid. 29 Eliz. pt. vi, m. 45.
[97] Chan. Inq. p.m. (Ser. 2), ccclx, 25.
[98] Ibid. cviii, 127.

KNIGHTWICK CHURCH C. 1810
(From a Water-colour by Thos. Rickards in Prattinton Collection)

KENSWICK CHURCH C. 1810
(From a Water-colour by Thos. Rickards in Prattinton Collection)

once lords of Knightwick. Habington states that the Alderfords came into possession of this manor by the marriage of Walter Alderford, father of John (the purchaser of Pithouse), with Joan daughter and heir of Thomas Brooke of Knightwick.[99] The manor passed with Pithouse to John Clent,[100] and belonged in 1802 to Lord Foley,[1] but does not now exist.

The first mention of a mill at Knightwick occurs in 1630, when a water grain-mill on the Teme was granted with the capital messuage of Knightwick to Thomas Cooke.[2] Ten years later this mill is described as a water-mill on the brook of Thunder near Knightwick.[3] There is now a corn-mill, called Knightwick Mill, on the Teme in the north of the parish.

The church of *ST. MARY THE VIRGIN*, built in 1856 at Knightsford Bridge in Doddenham, serves for both Knightwick and Doddenham, and will be described with the latter parish, which is in the hundred of Doddingtree.

The site of the previous church is on a small hill about a mile to the east of Knightsford Bridge. It was an old black and white timbered structure with a fine wooden porch, and was pulled down by John Francis Greswolde-Williams in 1879, and a mortuary chapel built on its site in the churchyard. On the floor of the chapel is a portion of the circular bowl of a 12th-century font with wide lines of zigzag ornament. On the west walls are slabs from the previous church to Grace and Dorothy Lane of Bentley, Staffordshire, who died in 1721, and are said to be sisters of Jane Lane, who did so much to secure the escape of Charles II after the battle of Worcester.

There is one bell in a western bellcote.

The plate consists of a silver cup of 1676, inscribed 'Knightwick Chalice 1676,' a cover paten of the same date, a paten of 1874, a flagon of 1882, a bread-knife with an agate handle, a plated almsdish, a pewter almsdish, and one of tin. There is no separate plate for Doddenham.

The registers before 1812 are as follows : (i) baptisms 1539 to 1687, burials 1617 to 1687, marriages 1542 to 1684; (ii) baptisms 1695 to 1812, burials 1702 to 1812, marriages 1695 to 1753 ; and (iii) marriages 1756 to 1811.

ADVOWSONS The advowsons of the chapels of Knightwick and Doddenham were given by Simon de Mans about 1177 to the Prior and convent at Worcester for the souls of his father and mother and himself.[4] This grant was confirmed by Roger 1164–79,[5] Robert 1191–3,[6] and Henry 1193–5, Bishops of Worcester, and by William de Mans, grandson of the donor, in

1231.[7] The advowson remained in the possession of the Prior and convent until the Dissolution,[8] when it passed to the Crown. It was granted in 1542 to the Dean and Chapter of Worcester,[9] and confirmed to them in 1609 by James I,[10] and has since remained in their possession.[11]

The living is united with that of Doddenham, the union having perhaps taken place about 1655, when it was found by inquisition that the cure of Knightwick was always supplied by the minister of Doddenham, and that the two churches were ' neere about equal bigness, and fit to be united together.'[11a]

Land given for lights and obits in the church of Knightwick was leased in 1560–1 to William Dalby.[12] This land afterwards formed part of the endowment of Martley grammar school.[13]

The chapel of Kenswick was subject to the church of St. Helen, Worcester,[14] in the 11th century. The advowson has always belonged to the lords of the manor,[15] but it is not mentioned in deeds of conveyance of the manor after 1411–12, though the site of the chapel is mentioned in such deeds until 1669.[16] The last presentation to the chapel was made in 1415 by William Yoxhale,[17] but Nash notes that Anthony Moggridge was incumbent of Kenswick in 1675.[18] In 1782 the chapel was in ruins, but fifty years before service was performed in the chapel once a month, the owner of Kenswick paying £10 a year.[19] The chapel was taken down about 1860.[20]

A pension from the chapel was paid yearly to the Prior and convent of Worcester until the Dissolution.[21] This pension was granted in 1542 to the Dean and Chapter of Worcester.[22] By an Order in Council 25 October 1898, to take effect on the next voidance of the benefice, Kenswick became part of Wichenford for ecclesiastical purposes.[23] The order took effect in 1908, but since 1910 Kenswick has been part of the new ecclesiastical parish of Broadheath, formed in that year from Hallow, Wichenford, and St. John's, Worcester.

CHARITIES This parish is entitled to receive, as stated in the church table, 20s. a year from land in Much Marcle, co. Hereford, under the gift of the Rev. Isaac Ailway. This sum was applicable in the purchase of coats for three poor men.

In 1726 Mrs. Dorothy Lane, as stated in the same table, left £20, the interest to be given to the poor. The legacy is on deposit at the Worcester Old Bank, producing 10s. a year.

In 1761 John Freeman by deed charged certain property, known as the Gaines Estate, in the neighbouring parish of Whitbourne in Herefordshire, with an annuity of £2 10s. for the benefit of the poor.

[99] Habington, op. cit. ii, 169 ; *Visit. of Worcs.* 1569 (Harl. Soc. xxvii), 8.

[100] Chan. Inq. p.m. (Ser. 2), ccclx, 25 ; Fine R. 15 Jas. I, pt. i, no. 40.

[1] Recov. R. Hil. 42 Geo. III, rot. 21.

[2] Pat. 6 Chas. I, pt. xiv, no. 3.

[3] Chan. Inq. p.m. (Ser. 2), dxcv, 90.

[4] Thomas, *Surv. of Worc. Cath.* A 115.

[5] Ibid.

[6] Habington, op. cit. ii, 365 ; Thomas, op. cit. A 120 and App. no. 29.

[7] Prattinton Coll. (Soc. Antiq.), Deeds of D. and C. of Worc. no. 311 ; *Ann. Mon.* (Rolls Ser.), iv, 423.

[8] *Ann. Mon.* (Rolls Ser.), iv, 438, 439,

441, 523 ; *Valor Eccl.* (Rec. Com.), iii, 226.

[9] Pat. 33 Hen. VIII, pt. v, m. 19 ; *L. and P. Hen. VIII,* xvii, g. 71 (29).

[10] Pat. 6 Jas. I, pt. xii, no. 2.

[11] Inst. Bks. (P.R.O.).

[11a] Prattinton Coll. (Soc. Antiq.) quoting inquisition in the possession of Sir T. Winnington.

[12] Pat. 3 Eliz. pt. v.

[13] Nash, op. cit. ii, 167.

[14] Heming, op. cit. 427.

[15] *Reg. G. Giffard* (Worcs. Hist. Soc.), i, 41 ; Nash, op. cit. i, 477 ; Chan. Inq. p.m. 10 Edw. II, no. 12 ; 21 Ric. II, no. 36 ; *Sede Vacante Reg.* (Worcs. Hist.

Soc.), 203 ; Feet of F. Worcs. 13 Hen. IV, no. 32. Though Francis Blount apparently never held the manor of Kenswick, he made a conveyance of the chapel in 1611 (Feet of F. Worcs. Mich. 9 Jas. I).

[16] Feet of F. Worcs. Mich. 7 & 8 Eliz. ; East. 21 Chas. II.

[17] Nash, op. cit. i, 477.

[18] Ibid.   [19] Ibid. ii, 458.

[20] Noake, *Guide to Worcs.* 354.

[21] Hale, *Reg. of Worc. Priory* (Camden Soc.), 35a ; *Valor Eccl.* (Rec. Com.), iii, 225.

[22] *L. and P. Hen. VIII,* xvii, g. 71 (29).

[23] *Census of Engl. and Wales,* 1901, Worcs. 8.

The income of these two charities is distributed in money gifts.

The charities of John Francis Greswolde-Williams. —In 1890 John Francis Greswolde-Williams by deed founded six almshouses situated in the parish of Doddenham, and endowed the same with £6,000 2½ per cent. annuities, four of the almshouses to be allotted to residents of Knightwick and Doddenham, or either of them, and two to residents in the chapelry of Lulsley.

The same donor erected a residence for a nurse for poor sick persons resident in the same three parishes, but died without completing a conveyance to trustees. In 1893 the premises were duly conveyed by Thomas Suckling, who, in conjunction with Agnes Elizabeth Baynton, provided a sum of £2,040 15s. 10d.

2½ per cent. annuities as an endowment fund, producing £51 a year.

The same donor, by his will proved at Worcester 12 August 1892, bequeathed £1,000, the interest to be distributed to the poor of Knightwick and Doddenham on 23 October yearly, in the form of orders upon tradesmen, or in the form of money for paying rent. The legacy was invested in £1,030 18s. 7d. consols with the official trustees, producing £25 15s. 4d. yearly, which is applied chiefly in providing flannel petticoats and serge gowns.

The official trustees also hold a sum of £1,030 18s. 7d. consols, representing a legacy by the will of the same testator, for the benefit of the Church of England school at Doddenham, in the hundred of Doddingtree.

LINDRIDGE

Lindericgeas (xi cent.) ; Lynderug, Linderugge (xii cent.) ; Lindruge, Lindrigg (xiii cent.) ; Lyndrugge, Lindriche (xiv cent.) ; Lynderige (xvi cent.).

The two new ecclesiastical parishes of Knighton-on-Teme and Pensax were formed from the ancient parish of Lindridge in 1843.[1] In 1879 Menith Wood was ecclesiastically annexed to Pensax.[2] Knighton, which includes 2,593 acres of land, 28 acres of which are covered by water, comprises the western portion of the original parish, and Pensax, containing 1,197 acres, occupies the eastern part of the ancient Lindridge. The present parish of Lindridge comprises 2,496 acres of land, of which 21 are inland water.

The River Teme forms the southern boundary of the parish, which is also watered by the River Rea and its tributaries the Trapnell and Marl Brooks, each forming part of the northern boundary, and by Corn Brook, Dumbleton Brook and other tributaries of the Teme. An old canal passes through Knighton, and the Tenbury and Bewdley branch of the Great Western railway has a station at Newnham Bridge in Knighton.

The land rises northwards from the valley of the Teme to heights varying from 300 ft. to 500 ft. above the ordnance datum on the Mamble border. At Knighton, which is almost surrounded by brooks and rivers, the land does not rise much above 300 ft. In 1905 the parish contained 1,225 acres of arable land, 3,382 of permanent grass and 308 of woodland.[3] The soil is marl, clay and sandstone, the subsoil Old Red Sandstone, and large crops of hops are produced, especially on the banks of the Teme, where there are some of the finest hop gardens in the county. Fruit and beans are also cultivated, and some wheat and barley at Knighton and Pensax. There is much meadow land both at Knighton and Lindridge.

There is no village at Lindridge, but at Eardiston, a hamlet about a mile and a half east of the church on the road to Droitwich, is a small settlement of red brick cottages. These, however, are of no antiquity. The church stands on a small but sharp hill on the north side of the road ; the vicarage, the garden of which adjoins the churchyard on the east, is a late Georgian red brick building three stories

high with a tiled roof. The oldest building in the parish appears to be Lower Lambswick, a two-story red brick farm-house, standing on the east side of a small by-road leading north about a quarter of a mile east of the church. It was built in the latter part of the 17th century, and, although in bad repair, it has been little altered since its first erection. The plan roughly resembles a **T** in shape, the head being represented by a wing running east and west at the north end of the main block, from the centre of which projects a brick porch, the upper part forming a bay to the room over. Both the porch and the western end of the north wing have shaped gables. The entrance to the porch has a round head with stone springing blocks and keystone, and the windows have flat brick arches with a central wood mullion and transom to each. At the south-east of the north wing is a good oak staircase—now painted—with moulded handrail and string and turned balusters.

Moor Farm House, Eardiston, is a good 18th-century red brick building. It is of two stories and is roofed with tiles. Though modernized inside it still retains its original oak staircase, a fine piece of 18th-century woodwork. The house was originally surrounded by a moat, but most of this is filled in, only a part in the north-east corner remaining ; this piece still holds water.

At Pensax the church stands at a height of over 500 ft. on the high land north of the Teme valley. To the north and east the land rises gently, but on the south the road descends for a mile, very steeply in places, to the level of the Teme valley at the village of Stockton. The western end of the churchyard is on the edge of a precipitous descent where the land drops to a deep-wooded valley trending to the west, with fine views across the broken country beyond. There have been coal-pits at Pensax for more than 300 years. They were worked in 1744, being then esteemed some of the best in Worcestershire.[4] Three pits were at work in 1868, but were disused twenty years later.[5] At present one pit is worked by Mr. Samson Yarnold.

At Knighton-on-Teme, about half a mile north-west of the church, is the Jewkes, a good half-timber house with three gables.

---

[1] *Census of Engl. and Wales,* 1901, *Worcs.* 6, 7.
[2] *Lond. Gaz.* 26 Aug. 1879, p. 5202.
[3] Statistics from Bd. of Agric. (1905).
[4] *Exch. Dep. Mich.* 18 Geo. II, no. 10.
[5] Noake, *Guide to Worcs.* 252.

Cornwood and Frith Commons were inclosed under an Act of 1797, the award being dated 1803.[6] The Act for the inclosure of Menith Wood is dated 1816 and the award 21 July 1823.[7]

Edward Milward, physician and Fellow of the Royal Society, who died in 1757, was buried in Knighton chapel.[8] Nash connects John Lowe, who was Bishop successively of St. Asaph (1433–44) and Rochester (1444–67), with the Lowe family of the Lowe in Lindridge.[9]

Place-names which occur in deeds relating to Lindridge are Pleistude, Seieginchwuck, Stierckewrchelond, Sleddelick,[10] Menhey, Le Seken,[11] Havecleg, Buterden, Linleg, Twichene,[12] Depecroft, Prothehale, Oxenhale, Cawneie, Espedele, Bikelege, Worthin, Bordele, Orhope[13] (xiii cent.); Fortelett[14] (xvi cent.); Upper and Lower Warmshall, Ebold, Mallandfield, Tynning, Longstaffe, Menney Wood,[15] Milne Leasowes[16] (xvii cent.).

MANORS The manor of *LINDRIDGE* was claimed by the monks of Worcester as the gift of Wiferd and Alta his wife.[17] By Wiferd's grant (781–98) 15 cassata of land at Newnham, Knighton and Eardiston, in Lindridge, passed to the church of Worcester, but no mention is made of Lindridge itself.[18] From the boundaries given in this grant it is, however, clear that it included the whole of Lindridge. This manor became lost to the monks, and was not recovered until William the Conqueror restored it to Bishop Wulfstan, who gave it to Thomas the prior.[19] This restoration probably took place before 1086, for at that time the monks held 15 hides at Knighton and Eardiston, and these probably included the whole manor of Lindridge.[20]

Bishop Simon in 1148 confirmed Lindridge to the priory,[21] and the issues of the manor were assigned to the cellarer.[22]

King Stephen acquitted 5 hides of land in Lindridge from all temporal exactions.[23]

King John visited Worcester in August 1207,[24] and at the request of the prior he granted to the convent, among other liberties, sac and soc, tol and team, infangenthef, quittance from view of tithing, and from suits at shire and hundred court.[25] This seems to have had the effect of constituting Lindridge a liberty[26] independent of the hundred court.

Henry III granted to the monks a market on Wednesdays at Lindridge in 1236[27] and free warren in the manor in 1256.[28]

In 1291 the prior and convent held at Lindridge 6 carucates of land and two mills, but this included the whole liberty of Lindridge.[29] The manor was not valued separately at the Dissolution, but appears to have been then included in the manors of Moor and Newnham,[30] as it also was in 1542, when the possessions of the late Priory of Worcester in this parish were granted to the Dean and Chapter of Worcester.[31] The manor after that time remained in the possession of the dean and chapter[32] until it was transferred in 1859 to the Ecclesiastical Commissioners, the present owners.[33] The manor of Lindridge *cum membris* now includes the manors of Moor with Pensax and Newnham with Knighton.

Habington, in his account of the cloister windows which in his time still remained at Worcester, gives the following inscription from the seventh window: ' Huthridus Dux More Nuenham cum . . .' betokening the gift of the manor of *MOOR* to the church of Worcester by Duke Uhtred.[34] The date of this gift is not known, but Uhtred joined with his kinsmen Eanberht, King of the Hwiccas, and Aldred about 757 in giving Tredington to the Bishop of Worcester,[35] so possibly Uhtred's grant was made at about the same time. The manor was evidently leased by the prior and convent, for in 1215 they prolonged the lease for sixteen years.[36] In 1240 'Mora' is entered among the possessions of the convent as a member of the liberty of Lindridge. There was at Moor a court with a chapel and 3 carucates of land.[37] It would seem that Moor was the principal manor of the prior at Lindridge, for in 1280 his subsidy of 5 marks for this parish was paid for his tenement at ' la More.'[38] The manor remained in the possession of the prior and convent until the Dissolution,[39] and was granted in 1542 to the Dean and Chapter of Worcester,[40] on condition that they should maintain ten poor men bruised in war, maimed by old age or the like, which men together with the petty clerks and other ministers of the church and together with the choristers and grammar scholars should each receive for their garments[41] three yards of cloth, at 3s. 4d. a yard. The manor remained in the possession of the dean and chapter[42] until it was confiscated under the Commonwealth and sold in 1650 to Philip Starkey.[43] Philip and his wife Edith and Timothy Robinson

---

[6] Priv. Act, 37 Geo. III, cap. 107; *Blue Bk. Incl. Awards,* 190.

[7] Priv. Act, 56 Geo. III, cap. 59; *Blue Bk. Incl. Awards,* 190.

[8] *Dict. Nat. Biog.*   [9] Ibid.

[10] Nash, op. cit. ii, 103.

[11] Ibid. 94 (iv).

[12] Hale, *Reg. of Worc. Priory* (Camden Soc.), 16b, 19a.

[13] Nash, op. cit. ii, 91.

[14] Chan. Proc. (Ser. 2), bdle. 22, no. 20.

[15] Close, 1650, pt. xxxviii, no. 12.

[16] Ibid. 1649, pt. xi, no. 26.

[17] Hale, *Reg. of Worc. Priory* (Camden Soc.), 10b. See below under Newnham.

[18] Birch, *Cart. Sax.* iii, 207; Kemble, *Codex Dipl.* no. 952.

[19] Dugdale, *Mon. Angl.* i, 600; Heming, *Chartul.* (ed. Hearne), 407.

[20] *V.C.H. Worcs.* i, 298. In a copy of the Domesday Survey made probably in the time of Henry I the entry relating to Knighton and Eardiston is headed

'de Linderyge,' though this does not appear in the original survey (Heming, op. cit. 309).

[21] Thomas, *Surv. of Worc. Cath.* App. no. 18.

[22] Dugdale, *Mon. Angl.* i, 607.

[23] Heming, op. cit. 526; Habington, *Surv. of Worcs.* (Worcs. Hist. Soc.), i, 338.

[24] *Rot. Lit. Pat.* (Rec. Com.), i, Itinerary of King John.

[25] *Cal. Rot. Chart.* 1199–1216 (Rec. Com.), 168; Pipe R. 9 John, m. 19d.; Habington, op. cit. i, 333–4.

[26] Hale, *Reg. of Worc. Priory* (Camden Soc.), 12a, 15b, 16b.

[27] Close, 20 Hen. III, m. 7; *Cal. Chart. R.* 1226–57, p. 220.

[28] *Cal. Pat.* 1354–8, p. 265. This grant was confirmed by Edward III in 1355 (ibid.), and by Richard II in 1391–4 (Chart. R. 15–17 Ric. II, no. 2).

[29] *Pope Nich. Tax.* (Rec. Com.), 163.

[30] The courts of the Prior of Worcester

for Lindridge were held at Moor and Newnham (Nash, op. cit. ii, 90).

[31] *Valor Eccl.* (Rec. Com.), iii, 221; L. and P. Hen. VIII, xvii, g. 71 (29).

[32] Chan. Proc. (Ser. 2), bdle. 22, no. 20; Eliz. Rr. bdle. 8, no. 35.

[33] *Lond. Gaz.* 16 Dec. 1859, p. 4757; confirmed by Stat. 31 & 32 Vict. cap. 19.

[34] op. cit. i, 334, 356; Thomas, op. cit. S. 32.

[35] Birch, op. cit. i, 260.

[36] *Ann. Mon.* (Rolls Ser.), iv, 405.

[37] Hale, *Reg. of Worc. Priory* (Camden Soc.), 16b.

[38] *Lay Subs. R. Worcs.* c. 1280 (Worcs. Hist. Soc.), 48.

[39] *Valor Eccl.* (Rec. Com.), iii, 221.

[40] L. and P. Hen. VIII, xvii, g. 71 (29).

[41] Nash, op. cit. ii, 90.

[42] Chan. Proc. (Ser. 2), bdle. 79, no. 13; Chan. Proc. Eliz. Mm. 15, no. 58; Pat. 6 Jas. I, pt. xii, no. 2.

[43] Close, 1650, pt. xxxviii, no. 12.

sold the manor in 1659 to Sir Edward Sebright, bart.,[44] who had obtained a lease for twenty-one years from the dean and chapter about 1644.[45] The manor was restored to the dean and chapter at the Restoration, and now belongs to the Ecclesiastical Commissioners, but it was still held under a lease by the Sebright family in 1782.[46] Under these lessees the manor was long inhabited during the 18th century by the Wheelers.[47] It now includes the manor of Pensax and is itself included in the manor of Lindridge *cum membris*.

Fifteen 'cassata' of land at Knighton, *NEWNHAM* (Neowanham, x cent. ; Neweham, xiii cent.) and Eardiston were granted to the church of St. Peter of Worcester by Wiferd,[48] ealdorman of the Hwiccas, and Alta his wife.[49] This grant was claimed by the monks of Worcester to have been made in the time of King Offa during the bishopric of Heathored (781–98),[49a] but the date and position of Wiferd (O.E. Wigfrith) are both uncertain. No person of rank bearing this name is recorded in the Mercia of the 8th century, and 'Wiferd' cannot possibly have been ealdorman of the Hwiccas in this period. Most probably Wiferd lived in the 10th century.[49b] The boundaries of the land mentioned in this grant were from Temede to Cornabroc[50] ; along the brook to Cornwood, from there to Cornlith ; along that lith to the other Cornabroc, and along the middle of the stream to Nen[51] ; from Nen to Maerabroc,[52] and thence along Momele[53] boundary to Suthintun[54] boundary ; from that boundary between Stilla dune[55] to Holanbrok,[56] and to the boundary at Holignan ; from Holigena boundary to the brook and to Worfesleahges[57] boundary and so to Stoctune,[58] and from Stoctune east to Temede.[59] Newnham was also included in Duke Uhtred's grant of Moor to the church of Worcester.[60]

The manor is not mentioned in the Domesday Survey, but was probably then included in the 15 hides of land at Knighton and Eardiston held by the Prior and convent of Worcester. It was confirmed in 1148 to the prior and convent by Bishop Simon,[61] and assigned to the cellarer.[62] In 1215 the prior prolonged the lease of Newnham for sixteen years.[63] In 1241 the prior made peace with the parson and freemen of Newnham concerning the assart of Cornwood.[64] In 1240 there were at Newnham a court and chapel with 3 carucates of land in the demesne.[65]

At the Dissolution the manor was valued at £47 17s. 8d. clear.[66] It was granted in 1542 to the Dean and Chapter of Worcester,[67] and was confirmed

to them in 1608–9 by James I.[68] The manor was confiscated under the Commonwealth, and sold in 1649 to George Cony of London.[69] It was restored to the dean and chapter on the accession of Charles II, and remained with them until 1859, when it was transferred to the Ecclesiastical Commissioners.[70] It now includes the manor of Knighton, and is itself included in the manor of Lindridge *cum membris*.

Newnham Court has long been the residence of the Wheeler family. Vincent Wood Wheeler of Kyrewood House was sometimes resident at Newnham Court. He was succeeded in 1853 by his son Edward Vincent Wheeler,[71]

WHEELER of Newnham. *Or a cheveron between three leopards' heads sable.*

father of Edward Vincent Vashon Wheeler, D.L., J.P., now of Newnham Court.[72]

The manor of *KNIGHTON-ON-TEME* (Cnithtatun, x cent. ; Cnistetone, xi cent. ; Cnichteton, xii cent. ; Knichteton, Knihteton, xiii cent.) was granted by Wiferd and Alta his wife to the monks of Worcester,[73] and was held by the prior and convent at the Domesday Survey and in the time of Henry I, when it was assigned to the support of the monks.[74] They seem to have subinfeudated or sold the estate to the Knightons. Alexander de Knighton was holding in Worcestershire in 1180–1,[75] and Ketelburn de Knighton held the manor in the reign of Henry II. Half a hide of land at Knighton passed from him to his son Thomas, and from Thomas to his son Hugh, who gave it to the Prior of Worcester in 1208.[76] This gift was confirmed by his mother Miracula.[77] Half a virgate at Knighton descended to Osbert de Knighton son of Ketelburn, and passed from him to his son Ralph. This half virgate was held of the Prior and convent of Worcester, and Ralph granted it to them about 1195–1205, retaining for himself a life interest which expired on his death in 1220.[78] A rent of 60s. from the manor was adjudged in 1211 by the prior to the infirmarer of the priory.[79] Richard, another son of Ketelburn de Knighton, unsuccessfully claimed part of the manor in 1220–1.[80] In 1229 the prior made an agreement with Christine de Knighton, who was possibly the widow of Hugh de Knighton, that she should give up all claim in the manor in exchange for a yearly portion of three 'crannocks' of wheat during

[44] Feet of F. Worcs. Hil. 1659.
[45] Nash, op. cit. ii, 90.
[46] Ibid.
[47] Ibid. 96, 97.
[48] Near the stone cross placed over the tomb of Wiferd, Bishop Oswald was wont to preach during the building of the new cathedral at Worcester (Birch, op. cit. iii, 208).
[49] Ibid. 207 ; Kemble, op. cit. no. 952. This charter, though somewhat suspicious in structure, probably represents Wiferd's grant to Worcester.
[49a] Hale, *Register of Worc. Priory* (Camden Soc.), 10b.
[49b] Inform. from Mr. F. M. Stenton.
[50] Cornbrook on the western boundary of Knighton-on-Teme.
[51] Neen Sollars.
[52] Now Marl Brook.

[53] Mamble.
[54] Sodington in Mamble.
[55] Now Stildon.
[56] There still exist Upper and Lower Hollin Farms in Rock, near which flows a brook unnamed in the ordnance map.
[57] Now Worsley Farm in Rock.
[58] Stockton-on-Teme.
[59] Kemble, op. cit. no. 952. These boundaries include the whole of the ancient parish of Lindridge, and can easily be traced at the present day.
[60] Habington, op. cit. i, 334, 356.
[61] Thomas, op. cit. App. no. 18.
[62] Dugdale, *Mon. Angl.* i, 607.
[63] *Ann. Mon.* (Rolls Ser.), iv, 405.
[64] Ibid. 432–3.
[65] Hale, *Reg. of Worc. Priory* (Camden Soc.), 12a.

[66] *Valor Eccl.* (Rec. Com.), iii, 221.
[67] *L. and P. Hen. VIII*, xvii, g. 71 (29).
[68] Pat. 6 Jas. I, pt. xii, no. 2.
[69] Close, 1649, pt. viii, no. 22.
[70] *Lond. Gaz.* 16 Dec. 1859, p. 4757 ; Stat. 31 & 32 Vict. cap. 19.
[71] Burke, *Landed Gentry* (1906).
[72] Ibid.
[73] Birch, op. cit. iii, 207.
[74] *V.C.H. Worcs.* i, 298, 326.
[75] *Pipe R. 27 Hen. II* (Pipe R. Soc.), 22.
[76] Assize R. 1021, m. 5 ; *Ann. Mon.* (Rolls Ser.), iv, 397.
[77] Nash, op. cit. ii, 91.
[78] Ibid. 103 ; *Ann. Mon.* (Rolls Ser.), iv, 412.
[79] *Ann. Mon.* (Rolls Ser.), iv, 400.
[80] Assize R. 1021, m. 5.

Knighton on Teme Church : The Chancel Arch

her lifetime.[81] By an undated charter William, Prior of Worcester, confirmed to Adam Parmentarius of Knighton all the land in Knighton which he had bought of Hugh de Knighton, paying yearly to the prior and convent 7s. at the four terms.[82] The manor appears subsequently to have become annexed to Newnham,[83] whose descent it follows.[84]

EARDISTON (Eardulfestun, x cent. ; Ardolvestone, xi cent. ; Eardulfestun, xii cent.) was granted with Knighton and Newnham by Wiferd to the monks of Worcester,[85] and was held by them at the time of the Domesday Survey.[86] It is not subsequently mentioned as a manor, and it seems probable that it became incorporated in the manor of Moor. Sir William Smith, bart., resided at Eardiston House from the 18th to the middle of the 19th century. His estate was purchased shortly before 1868 by Mr. George Wallace,[87] who resided at Eardiston House until his death. The house is now occupied by the Misses Wallace.

The manor of *PENSAX* (Pensex, xiii cent. ; Pensokes, xvi cent.) was given to the Prior and convent of Worcester by Ralph son of Osbert de Knighton by a charter of 1195–1205.[88] Ralph retained a life estate in the manor, but he died in 1220,[89] and in 1230 the monks leased the manor for life to Edwin, a wheelwright, for the third sheaf.[90] In 1240 Pensax was a member of the liberty of Lindridge, and in demesne there were a grange and 1 carucate of land.[91] It followed the same descent as the manor of Moor, to which it is now annexed.[92]

An estate at Pensax was held in the 18th and 19th centuries by the Clutton family, who resided at Pensax Court.[93] The Clutton heiress married a Mr. Brock, whose son, Colonel Brock, sold it about the middle of the 19th century to John Higginbottom. In 1868 there were coal-pits at work on his estate which produced between 3,000 tons and 4,000 tons annually.[94] Mr. Higginbottom resided at Pensax Court. He apparently purchased part of the manorial rights of Pensax, as he is called lord of the manor in 1872 and 1876. He sold all his interest in the property to John Joseph Jones, who had purchased the Abberley estate. It has since passed to Elmley Castle and now belongs to Mr. James Arthur Jones of Abberley Hall. Pensax Court is occupied by Captain Baldwin John St. George.

Land at *PENHULL*[95] in Lindridge was apparently given with Knighton and Newnham by Wiferd to the church of Worcester.[96] Like Lindridge this land was lost by the convent before the Conquest, but was restored by King William to Bishop Wulfstan.[97] This estate was held in the reign of Henry III by Alured de Penhull, but in consequence of debt the property became mortgaged to the Jews, and Alured

being freed from his obligations to them by the Prior of Worcester granted his estate about 1231 to the convent in exchange for an undertaking by the prior to provide him with a ' crannock' of grain, half wheat and half *siligo*, every six weeks during his life, and a rent of half a mark at Michaelmas during the lifetime of his mother, and 10s. at the same feast every year after her death. Alured was also to retain a house and croft belonging to the dower of his mother, to inhabit during his life.[98]

Habington assigns a very ancient lineage to the family of Lowe, who held *THE LOWE* in Lindridge until 1724. He states that their ancestor was one of the captains who fought under Duke William of Normandy in the conquest of England, ' as appeareth in a Rowle most carefully and exactly kept in Flanders.'[99] In the time of Henry III, Stephen son of Alan Lowe (de Lawa) ' being detained in heavy chains [by the Jews] and compelled to make payment by exquisite torments,' was released owing to the exertions of the Prior of Worcester on his behalf. In gratitude for this benefit Stephen gave the prior part of his land at ' Lawa.'[100] At about the same time Stephen granted to the prior and convent all the land which he held of them in Moor in Lawefield.[1] In a survey of the liberty of Lindridge taken in 1240 there were many sokemen ' of the land of Stephen' paying rent for land at ' Lawa.'[2]

LOWE of The Lowe. *Or a bend cotised sable with three wolves' heads razed or on the bend.*

In 1220–1 John Lowe (de la Lawe) conveyed land in the Lowe to Alditha widow of David Lowe.[3] At the beginning of the 16th century a suit took place between Thomas Pakington and John Walker as to the ownership of a messuage and land called the Lowe in Lindridge.[4]

Nash in his history[5] gives a pedigree of the family of Lowe from very remote times. The estate at Lowe, now consisting of a single farm, Lowe Farm, was held by this family until the death of Arthur Lowe in 1724.[6] It passed to his daughter Elizabeth, who had married Joshua Lowe. Her two sons died without issue, and on her death in 1727 the estate passed to her daughters, Elizabeth wife of the Rev. William Cleiveland, and Mary Pakington Lowe. Mary died unmarried in 1768 and Elizabeth died in the following year, when the estate devolved upon her son, the Rev. William Cleiveland, who was the owner in 1782.[7] This property now belongs to the Eardiston Farming Co., Ltd.

[81] Feet of F. Worcs. Trin. 14 Hen. III, no. 6 ; *Ann. Mon.* (Rolls Ser.), iv, 421.
[82] Prattinton Coll. (Soc. Antiq.), Deeds of D. and C. of Worc. no. 306.
[83] Information from Ecclesiastical Commissioners.
[84] Chan. Proc. Eliz. Mm. 15, no. 58.
[85] Birch, op. cit. iii, 207.
[86] *V.C.H. Worcs.* i, 298.
[87] Noake, op. cit. 247.
[88] Nash, op. cit. ii, 103.
[89] *Ann. Mon.* (Rolls Ser.), iv, 412.
[90] Ibid. 422–3.
[91] Hale, *Reg. of Worc. Prior* (Camden Soc.), 19a.

[92] Chan. Proc. Eliz. Mm. 15, no. 58 ; information from Eccl. Commissioners.
[93] M.I. in Pensax chapel, printed by Nash in his *History of Worcestershire* (ii, 98). A pedigree of the family is given in Burke, *Landed Gentry* (ed. 5, 1871).
[94] Noake, op. cit. 252.
[95] Now Penn Hall on the east of Menith Wood.
[96] Heming, op. cit. 574.
[97] Dugdale, *Mon. Angl.* i, 600 ; Heming, op. cit. 407.
[98] Nash, op. cit. ii, 103.
[99] op. cit. i, 335.
[100] Nash, op. cit. ii, 94 (v). Nash

quotes the charter in full, and gives the exact extent of the land.
[1] Ibid. 94 (iv).
[2] Hale, *Reg. of Worc. Priory* (Camden Soc.), 16b.
[3] Feet of F. Worcs. 5 Hen. III, no. 22.
[4] Early Chan. Proc. bdle. 347, no. 5.
[5] *Hist. of Worcs.* ii, 94 (i and ii).
[6] Ibid. 92–3, 95 ; Dorothea Lowe, widow, paid a subsidy of £3 in 1603 (*Lay Subs. R. Worcs.* 1603 [Worcs. Hist. Soc.], 32). Arthur Lowe of Lowe took the oath of allegiance in 1633 (*Cal. S. P. Dom.* 1633–4, p. 190).
[7] Nash, op. cit. ii, 94 (ii).

The estate now represented by *UPPER* and *LOWER WOODSON FARMS* belonged during the 16th and 17th centuries to the Penell family. Habington mentions a William de Wodeston, who died in 1302, and a John Pascall of Wodeston, who 'in his pious charity to the priory of Worcester granted them by consent of his wife Christine for the benefit of their souls' land at Lindridge, Wodeston, Wodenhull [8] and elsewhere—i.e. his lands in Lindridge, a noke in Wodenhull held of Godfrey de Wodenhull [9] with Pulecrosse and a noke between Munckmedowe and Godmer and other lands held of Godfrey de Wodenhull and half a yardland in Wodeston.[10] There are several monuments to the Penells of Woodson in Lindridge Church,[11] and Nash in his history gives a pedigree of the family.[12] Elizabeth daughter of

LINDRIDGE CHURCH FROM THE SOUTH

Edward Penell, who died in 1666, married Acton Cremer, and joined with her son Henry in 1704 in selling this estate to Thomas Baker, in whose family it still remained in 1782.[13]

Mr. James Adams held the Woodson House estate in 1872, and twenty years later it had passed to James Adams Partridge. Mr. Charles George Partridge is a landowner at Lindridge at the present day, but Woodson House is the residence of Mr. Edward Francis Ingleby.

There were a mill and a fishery on the prior's estate at Knighton and Eardiston in 1086.[14] In the reign of King John, Ralph son of Osbert de Knighton

granted to the Prior and convent of Worcester all his right in the mill of Newnham,[15] and in October 1212 this mill was granted to O. Bolt for ten years for 60s.[16] Besides this mill at Newnham there were also two mills at Moor in 1240, one outside the court and the other called the mill of Medeweye, and another at Pensax.[17] The three former mills were exempt from vicar's tithes by an agreement made between the Prior of Worcester and the vicar of Lindridge in the time of Giles Bishop of Hereford (1200–15).[18] In 1291 only two mills are mentioned at Lindridge in the survey of the prior's lands there at that date.[19] There is still a corn-mill at Newnham on the River Rea, and another, Meadows Mill, on the Teme in the south of Eardiston. This is doubtless on the site of the ancient Medeweye Mill. There is a disused corn-mill in Pensax on a tributary of the Teme. Cutmill House, on Dumbleton Brook, may perhaps mark the site of the second mill at Moor.

The church of *ST. LAWRENCE* consists of a chancel, north vestry and organ chamber, nave with south aisle of two bays and a south-west tower, in the south wall of which is the main doorway. The present building was erected in 1861 on the site of an earlier church, from which four brass tablets survive : the first to Elizabeth wife of John Giles (died 1651) ; the second to William Penell of Woodson (died 1623) ; the third to Margaret wife of Edward Penell (died 1625) ; and the fourth to Edward Penell (died 1666). They bear the following coats of arms : the first, on a fesse three sheaves with a molet for difference impaling Rowndon, a griffon ; the second, Penell quartering a wolf passant for Lowe, impaling quarterly 1. and 4. Rowndon, 2. six martlets, 3. on a bend cotised three stags' heads caboshed. Margaret Penell's brass has two shields : Penell impaling Greville and Penell quartering Lowe with an escutcheon of pretence of Greville. The fourth brass bears : Penell and Lowe quarterly with Greville in pretence impaling a fesse ermine within a border engrailed ermine for Acton, with a greyhound's head for crest.

There are four bells in all : the first cast by Robert Oldfeild, 1626 ; the second by Abraham Rudhall, 1702 ; the third by John Martin, 1663 ; and fourth an ancient sanctus bell, the only relic of the mediaeval church. It is inscribed in very small Lombardic capitals : + AVE MARIA GRACIA PLENA DOMINVS TECVM, with stamps representing royal heads, perhaps Henry VI and Queen Margaret. The letters are the same as on the second bell at Wichenford, and the bell was cast at Worcester about 1480.

The plate consists of a silver cup and cover paten, both of 1698—the cup is inscribed 'Lindridge' ; a silver flagon of 1771, inscribed 'The Gift of Mrs. Mary Winwood Widd. of Eardiston to the Parish Church of Lindridge,' while in the middle of the inscription is a shield charged with a cross fleury

[8] In all probability Dodenhull should be read for Wodenhull. The name Doddenhill still exists at Lindridge.

[9] Godfrey de Dodenhull (temp.Hen.III) gave land for a light in the church (see advowson).

[10] Habington, op. cit. i, 336.
[11] Nash, op. cit. ii, 95.
[12] Ibid. 94.
[13] Ibid.
[14] V.C.H. Worcs. i, 299.
[15] Nash, op. cit. ii, 103.

[16] Ann. Mon. (Rolls Ser.), iv, 400–1.
[17] Hale, Reg. of Worc. Priory (Camden Soc.), 16b, 18b.
[18] Ibid. 11b.
[19] Pope Nich. Tax. (Rec. Com.), 163.

impaling ermine a lion rampant; and two silver credence patens, one a little larger than the other, but both of the same date and engraved with the same inscription and arms as the flagon.

The registers before 1812 are as follows: (i) all entries 1574 to 1612; (ii)[20] baptisms 1638 to 1711, marriages 1648 to 1711; (iii) burials 1654 to 1728, baptisms 1712 to 1728, marriages 1712 to 1727; (iv) a paper volume in which are also entered many parish collections and rates, births and burials 1695 to 1706, marriages 1696 to 1706; (v) baptisms 1728 to 1786, burials 1728 to 1787, marriages 1728 to 1753; (vi) marriages 1754 to 1812; (vii) baptisms 1786 to 1812, burials 1787 to 1812. There are also two loose parchment leaves; the one, though almost illegible, appears to contain all entries from 1636 to 1641, and the other all entries from 1628 to 1633.

The church of *ST. MICHAEL* at Knighton-on-Teme consists of a chancel 22 ft. by 18¼ ft., a nave 54 ft. by 21¾ ft. and a wooden west tower, the lower part of which has been inclosed by walls forming an extension of the nave 25¾ ft. long and approximately of the same width as the rest of the nave. These measurements are all internal.

early work. The later inclosing walls, which probably date from the 15th century, indicate the existence at that period of a similar feature. The wooden doorway in the screen which now separates the nave from the tower is perhaps of the same date. The two lancet lights in the west tower wall are probably late copies of the original windows of the church.

The eastern wall of the chancel has two modern wide round-headed single-light windows. In the north wall are two single-light windows, the heads of which appear to have been changed from round to pointed. In the south wall is a modern trefoiled piscina, with a shelf and a two-light window with quatrefoil tracery, of about 1360. The modern sedile formed in the sill represents an ancient feature, as the west jamb is also cut away. The south door has a plain segmental inner arch, and to the west of it is a small square window, probably of the 14th century; it is rebated for a shutter, the hooks of which remain. The sill is splayed downwards, and there are two cinquefoils painted in dark red on the soffit of the window head. The chancel arch, which has a flattened semicircular head, is of two orders, each enriched with a line of sunk star work, and has jamb

12TH CENTURY EARLY   14TH CENTURY
12TH CENTURY LATE   15TH CENTURY
13TH CENTURY   MODERN

10 5 0 10 20 30
SCALE OF FEET

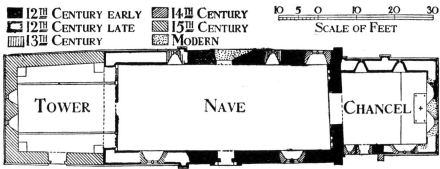

PLAN OF KNIGHTON ON TEME CHURCH

The earliest church of which portions now remain dated from the early 12th century,[21] and consisted of a chancel and nave probably of the same size as those now existing, with perhaps an external wood tower at the west end.

The present nave as far west as the external pilaster buttresses, together with the chancel arch and an adjoining portion of the south chancel wall, represent the remains of the original building. The rest of the chancel dates from the end of the 12th century, when it was rebuilt, the north wall being made thicker than the south, which conforms to the earlier portion remaining. Probably at the same period the west end of the nave was rebuilt, the pilaster buttresses covering the junction.

This rebuilding would include the west wall, which occupied the position of the present wood partition. The walling of this date has a plinth, which is not used in the earlier work. The exact date of the present wood tower is uncertain, but the rough construction, with the four massive oak struts, indicates

shafts with cushion capitals and chamfered abaci to the inner order on the nave side. The abaci, which have been cut back flush with the capitals on the west, are elsewhere enriched with star work. The shafts have conical bases with spurs. On either side of the arch, and possibly of slightly earlier date, are small wall arcades, each of two bays, with small round arches formed out of single stones supported by columns with cushion capitals without abaci and conical bases, the complete arcade being inclosed in a round arch with the tympanum thus formed left quite plain and unornamented.

The first window in the north nave wall is of two lights and is similar to that in the south chancel wall. It contains some fragments of original glass consisting of canopy and border work. The second and third windows are pointed lancets, both probably insertions of the 13th century, and between them is the north door, now blocked, showing an external segmental arch, which has been altered. At the south-east is a window of two lights similar to the corresponding

[20] This volume is anything but complete, and the leaves have been bound together in no chronological order. Most of the baptisms appear to have been entered from 1649 to 1651, 1653 to 1665, and 1669 to 1711, but the intervening years are missing. The entries between 1638 and 1651 are only fragmentary, and there is also one baptism in the year 1630. In the case of the marriages the entries between 1654 and 1669 are very fragmentary, and there are no records of any marriages between 1707 and 1710.

[21] There was a priest and possibly a church at Knighton in 1086 (*V.C.H. Worcs.* i, 298).

window in the north wall. The south door is narrow and high, measuring 9 ft. to the spring of the external arch and 11½ ft. to the spring of the rear arch. It is of two round-arched orders, the outer set in a projection from the wall which rises above the doorway and includes a wall arcade. This order is enriched with sunk star work, and springs from cushion capitals and plain shafts. The inner has a double line of cable moulding. The eastern jamb and shaft are cut away for a stoup. Above the doorway are the remains of a billeted string-course, upon which is a row of five circular shafts carrying a small wall arcade. The arches are cut from single stones and worked with a tooth moulding. The capitals, without abaci, are of differing designs, and the shafts, which have cushion bases, are enriched with cheveron, spiral and sunk star designs.

West of the doorway is a two-light 15th-century window. The west end of the nave is cut off from the tower by a 15th-century wood partition, in which is an ogee-headed doorway, which leads into the central part of the ground floor of the tower, now used as a vestry. It is lighted from the west by two pointed lancets with sills cut down and contains some 18th-century pews taken from the nave and an old chest of plain oak planks.

Flanking the vestry are two narrow spaces, from the southern of which, entered by a doorway in the south wall, access is obtained to the upper stages of the tower. In these spaces are the struts or legs of the tower framework, which rise slantwise across each other.

The nave roof is of the 15th century, with moulded tie-beams ; the wall-plates and purlins are moulded, and the principals have moulded cambered tie-beams, with braced collars and plain struts above.

The eastern bay has canted boarding in panels, with moulded battens painted alternately red and green and embattled wall-plates. Originally, to allow an uninterrupted view of the rood-loft, there was no tie-beam across the eastern bay, but a modern beam has now been inserted. On the battens is a spiral pattern, and the panels have been diapered. Nailed to the jacklegs below the ties are reversed shields bearing crowned tuns and roses. The west end is wattled in above the wood partition. Above the chancel arch are two beams which once carried part of the rood-loft.

The font has a shallow bowl and a baluster stem, with a round moulded base. The communion table has late 17th-century baluster legs, and the rails are of 18th-century date.

On the north chancel wall is a monument to John Cecil, High Sheriff of Bristol, who died in 1697.

Externally the older walls are built of red sandstone, the later of red sandstone and tufa. The south-eastern nave window has a label with large worn stops, and above it an angel holding a defaced shield, the lower part of which seems to bear a cheveron with a molet in base. The roof is tiled and the sides of the tower boarded.

In the churchyard to the south of the church are the steps and lower part of the stem of a cross. On the west face of the steps is a niche with a crocketed gable and side pinnacles.

There were formerly three bells : the first cast by John Martin, 1661, the second mediaeval, dedicated in honour of St. Michael, and the third dated 1625. At present only two exist, a bell originally of 1625 recast by James Barwell of Birmingham in 1885, and a small 'ting-tang' without inscription.[22]

The plate consists of a silver cup and cover paten of the Elizabethan period, which have no plate-marks, but the paten bears the date 1577, and a chalice, paten and flagon of 1865.

The registers before 1812 are as follows : (i) all entries 1559 to 1642 (an unbound parchment volume, much decayed and in places illegible) ; (ii) all entries 1653 to 1700 on parchment and 1703 to 1716 on paper (this too is an unbound volume) ; (iii) all entries 1717 to 1748 ; (iv) baptisms and burials 1748 to 1789 ; (v) baptisms and burials 1790 to 1812 ; (vi) marriages 1757 to 1811.

The church of *ST. JAMES* at Pensax was built in 1832 and is of little architectural interest. The building consists of a chancel with north vestry and organ chamber, nave and west tower with a porch on the south. The east window is of five lights in 15th-century style. The chancel roof is panelled in oak. The chancel arch has shafted jambs. On each side of the nave are three windows of 15th-century type, and there is a similar window in the west wall of the tower.

There are three bells : the treble, by John Martin of Worcester, is inscribed with the three church-wardens' names and the date 1669 ; the second is inscribed '1627 I.P. God is my hope' ; the third, by John Martin, is inscribed 'All praise and glory be to God for ever' with a churchwarden's name, 1681.

The plate comprises a large chalice and paten given by Priscilla Childe, 1720, and made in the preceding year, and a modern plated flagon.

The registers are as follows : (i) mixed entries 1563 to 1707, which is bound up with a fragment of a 13th-century manuscript ; (ii) 1707 to 1746 ; (iii) 1747 to 1771, the marriage entries extending only to 1754 ; (iv) marriages 1754 to 1811 ; (v) and (vi) baptisms and burials 1772 to 1791 and 1791 to 1812.

ADVOWSON The Prior and convent of Worcester claimed the church of Lindridge as the gift of Wiferd.[23] There was a priest on the prior's estate at Knighton and Eardiston in 1086,[24] but it does not appear whether he ministered at the church at Lindridge or at the chapel of Knighton. Possibly when the monks lost the manor of Lindridge the church was also taken from them, for in 1132 Robert de Bethune, Bishop of Hereford, 'to make a perfect union of charity between the Prior of Worcester and the church of Hereford,' gave to David, Prior of Worcester, and the monks the parsonage of Lindridge for ever.[25] This grant was confirmed by Pope Lucius (1144-5) and by Pope Innocent.[26] In 1205 Giles Bishop of Hereford confirmed to the monks a pension of 40s. from the church of Lindridge,[27] and in the following year an agreement was made between the parson of Lindridge and the prior, by which the prior was to receive yearly 10s. from the church and the parson was to have all the tithes of Moor

---

[22] Inform. from Mr. H. B. Walters.
[23] *Reg. of Worc. Priory* (Camden Soc.), 10b. See above under Newnham.
[24] *V.C.H. Worcs.* i, 298.
[25] Habington, op. cit. i, 338.
[26] Heming, op. cit. 536.
[27] *Ann. Mon.* (Rolls Ser.), iv, 393.

K<small>NIGHTON</small> <small>ON</small> T<small>EME</small> C<small>HURCH</small> : T<small>HE</small> S<small>OUTH</small> D<small>OORWAY</small>

and Newnham except tithes of hay.[28] The presentations were made by the prior and convent,[29] and in 1307 they obtained licence to appropriate the church in order to augment the convent by three monks and to find two wax lights continually burning before the shrine of St. Wulfstan.[30] The vicarage was ordained in 1310. The vicar was to have a court with a garden and dovecot which the rector of the church formerly had as a rectory; he was also to have 24s. from the chapel of Knighton and 8s. from the chapel of Pensax, besides the support of two chaplains, 20s. from the mother church of Lindridge, and tithes from certain fields and a fulling-mill. The houses in which the chaplains of Knighton and Pensax had been accustomed to live were to be at the disposition of the vicar, so that his chaplains might live there without paying rent. The vicar was to appoint suitable chaplains to serve the two chapels.[31]

The advowson was granted in 1542 to the Dean and Chapter of Worcester,[32] and has remained in their possession ever since.[33]

In the time of Henry III Godfrey de Dodenhull gave an acre of land in Benhales field to maintain the light on the altar of St. Mary.[34] Land to the yearly value of 8d. was held for the support of lights in the church at the time of the dissolution of the chantries.[35]

The chapel of Knighton was attached to the church of Lindridge in the time of Edward I,[36] and was served by a chaplain appointed by the vicar of Lindridge.[37] In the time of Edward VI it was returned that there were 160 'houselyng people' at Knighton and there was a chantry of our Lady in the church there.[38]

In the return made to Parliament during the Commonwealth the inhabitants of Knighton stated that their chapel of Knighton was appendant to Lindridge; that the township of Knighton and the village thereunto belonging were distant from Lindridge Church about 2 miles and some parts 3 miles, 'and the ways thereof very fowle and deepe in time of winter'; that the church of Lindridge was not large enough to contain half the parishioners of Knighton and Lindridge; that as their chapel was larger than the church of Lindridge and had a fair gallery and had all parochial rights belonging to it, and stood near about the middle of the township, they conceived it fit to be made a parish church.[39] The parish was not, however, ecclesiastically separated from Lindridge until 1843.[40] Since that time the living has been a vicarage in the gift of the vicar of Lindridge.

A parcel of land given for the maintenance of certain lights in the church at Knighton was granted in 1550 to William Winlove and Richard Feld.[41]

The date when Pensax chapel was first built is not known. It was a chapel of Lindridge in the time of Edward I,[42] and was served by a chaplain appointed by the vicar of Lindridge.[43] Nash says, 'Pensax chapel stands very high with a small spire. It has the privilege of burials.'[44] This old chapel under the invocation of St. James was of the Norman period, and was pulled down in 1829.[45] Pensax was formed into an ecclesiastical parish in 1843.[46] The living is a vicarage in the gift of the vicar of Lindridge.

There is a Wesleyan chapel at Frith Common. There is also a mission church at Menith Wood where services are held on Sunday evenings.

CHARITIES In 1718 Arthur Lowe, by his will, directed six penny loaves to be distributed among six poor people, also that £1 a year should be paid to the vicar for preaching a sermon on St. Thomas's Day and Good Friday.

The testator also directed that the same six people should every third year receive a garment, a coat for men and a waistcoat with long skirts for women.

These payments were charged on a tenement and lands belonging to the Lowe Estate in the Upper Clay Wood, lying above the Lowe, and are duly made.

LITTLE MALVERN

Malvern Minor, Parva Malvern, Lesser Malvern (xvi cent.); Milberne Parva (xvii cent.).

Little Malvern is a small parish on the Herefordshire border of the county containing 721 acres. The village lies under the Malvern Hills about 500 ft. above the ordnance datum. It consists of Little Malvern Court, the seat of Captain William Berington, J.P., the Priory church of St. Giles, a farm and one or two cottages.

Little Malvern Court, which was probably the prior's house of the demolished priory, stands to the south-west of the surviving fragment of the church, on the west side of the former cloister-garth. The plan has a small central court, somewhat in the nature of a light-well, with a hall and undercroft on the east, which would have adjoined the western range of the cloister, having a four-storied building on the south, with a spur projecting eastwards, which probably marks the position of the southern range of the cloister. The buildings on the north side of the court are of two stories with an attic at the northwest. The ground story of all this portion is of stone, the upper stories being of half-timber. The roof of the hall, now concealed, is of the 14th century, to which date the greater part of the original house probably belongs. Adjoining the building at the south of the hall and forming the centre of the south front is a three-storied portion, now covered with rough-cast, but apparently entirely of stone, with a circular garderobe turret at the south-west. To the west of this is a modern wing, which, with the one-storied entrance hall on the west side of the house, was

[28] *Ann. Mon.* (Rolls Ser.), iv, 394.
[29] Ibid. 398, 447, 493.
[30] *Cal. Pat.* 1301–7, p. 523.
[31] Nash, op. cit. ii, 101.
[32] *L. and P. Hen. VIII*, xvii, g. 71 (29).
[33] Pat. 6 Jas. I, pt. xii, no. 2; Inst. Bks. (P.R.O.). [34] Nash, op. cit. ii, 90.
[35] Chant. Cert. 60, no. 55.

[36] Nash, op. cit. Introd. p. xxxvi.
[37] Ibid. ii, 101.
[38] Chant. Cert. 60, no. 23.
[39] Noake, op. cit. 250.
[40] *Pop. Ret. Worcs.* 1901, p. 6; *Parl. Papers* (1872), xlvi, 18 d.
[41] Chant. Cert. 60, no. 57; Pat. 4 Edw. VI, pt. iv.

[42] Nash, op. cit. Introd. p. xxxvi. The 'churchwei' of Pensax is mentioned in a deed c. 1231 (ibid. ii, 103).
[43] Ibid. ii, 101.
[44] Ibid. 98.
[45] Noake, op. cit. 251.
[46] *Parl. Papers* (1872), xlvi, 18 d.; *Pop. Ret. Worcs.* 1901, p. 7.

added about fifty years since. A staircase was formed on the south side of the court in the 18th century, and a second staircase contained in a brick addition has, within comparatively recent years, been constructed on the east side. The interior of the house has been much modernized, very little original detail surviving.

The hall has been divided by modern partitions into a chapel, in which mass is said weekly, and an oratory, with an entrance passage on the north and a corridor on the west side adjoining the court. Plaster ceilings conceal the fine timber roof, which has tie-beams and collars with foiled struts and wind braces. Over the partition at the north end of the chapel, which is lighted by modern sash windows, is an exposed tie-beam with an embattled moulding. The reredos of the altar is put together of fragments of 15th and 16th-century woodwork. At the south-east of the hall, projecting into the court, is the original central newel stair. The half-timber work of the hall is not now exposed. The roof of the four-storied building to the south of the hall is terminated on the south by a gable hipped at the apex. Adjoining the hall is a gabled spur, three stories in height, projecting to the eastward, on the first floor of which was probably a small private chapel. The half-timber work is exposed on the north side, the other three sides, as well as the whole of the remaining part of this block, being covered with rough-cast. The upper story overhangs on the same side. In the ground story of the south or garden front are original stone-mullioned windows. The stone buildings to the westward on the same front project slightly and there is a circular garderobe turret at the western angle, crowned by a modern pyramidal tiled roof. A modern bay window has been added to the two lower floors and the walls are of rough-cast. The chimney stack at the south-east angle has built into it a piece of stone canopy work, a head corbel and a lion, all probably fragments of the former nave of the church. The rooms at the north end of the hall are faced with brick and have modern sash windows. Externally the most imposing features of the house are the apartments at the north-west angle, which are gabled on both faces and have a massive chimney stack of brick and stone, dating probably from the 16th century, on the north. The barge-boards appear to be modern, but the wood-mullioned window in the gable lighting the second or attic floor is of original date. Generally the exterior of the house has been much restored and many new windows inserted, while most of the original openings have been renewed at different periods. The character of the west front has been almost entirely destroyed by the modern entrance hall and south-west wing, which are faced with rubble and have quoins of wrought stone and large mullioned windows. Many fragments of the destroyed portion of the church are preserved in the house or worked into the walls. In the entrance hall is a leather-covered trunk ornamented with brass-headed nails, on the lid of which is the Tudor Crown and Rose with the initials K.R. This is said to have belonged to Katherine Parr.

The Roman Catholic Priory with St. Wulstan's Church and the school are to the north of the village on the road to Malvern Wells, and the Grange and pound are to the east on the Upton-upon-Severn road.

The Shire Ditch, which passes along the top of the Malvern Hills, forms the western boundary of the parish. Broad Down and Hangman's Hill are two pieces of common land on the Malvern Hills. Behind the church the ground rises very steeply through dense wood and the road leads upward with a steep gradient and a very sharp bend to the south. This road crosses the hills by a gap known as Wind's Point. There is a large earthwork on the summit of the ridge to the south, known as the British Camp.

In 1905 the proportion of arable, grass and woodland in the parish was returned as 94 acres of arable land, 335 acres of permanent grass and 60 acres of woodland and plantations.[1] The soil is loamy with a subsoil of gravel, producing crops of wheat and barley.

The Rev. Prior Williams, the last prior of the English Carthusians of Nieuport, Flanders, died 2 January 1797 at Little Malvern.[2]

Place-names occurring in deeds relating to Little Malvern are Colierfield, Oxmore, Cowmore, Fermery Furlonge[3] (xvi cent.).

The present manor of LITTLE MALVERN MANOR was included in Malvern Chase until the time of its disafforestation in 1631–2.[4] It was given to the monks of Little Malvern in 1171, on the foundation of their house, by the Bishop of Worcester, being taken out from the bishop's fee.[5] Mauger, Bishop of Worcester (1200–12), granted to the monks of Little Malvern firewood and an oak tree yearly from his wood of Malvern-super-Montem.[6] In 1291 the prior's estate at Little Malvern included a carucate of land worth 6s.[7] The manor remained in the hands of successive priors[8]

LITTLE MALVERN PRIORY. *Argent a fesse between three cocks' heads razed sable having their beaks and combs and wattles or with a mitre or upon the fesse.*

RUSSELL of Little Malvern. *Argent a cheveron between three crosslets sable and a border gules engrailed and bezanty.*

until the suppression of their house in 1537,[9] when it was valued at £18 12s. 10d.[10]

In September 1537 John Russell addressed a letter to Cromwell asking for his assistance in obtaining the priory and manor of Little Malvern.[11] The manor, however, seems to have remained in the Crown until 1554, when it was granted to Henry Russell and Charles Brockton or Broughton.[12] Henry Russell

[1] Statistics from Bd. of Agric. (1905).
[2] *Hist. MSS. Com. Rep.* ii, App. 73.
[3] Aug. Off. Misc. Bks. ccx, fol. 82.
[4] Nash, *Hist. of Worcs.* Introd. p. lxix, note g., 75, 81 ; *V.C.H. Worcs.* ii, 319; Leland, *Itin.* vii, 12.

[5] Thomas, *Surv. of Worc. Cath.* A 108 ; Habington, *Surv. of Worc.* (Worcs. Hist. Soc.), ii, 193.
[6] Worc. Epis. Reg. Orlton, 1327–33, fol. 9 d., 10.
[7] *Pope Nich. Tax.* (Rec. Com.), 228.

[8] *Lay Subs. R. Worcs.* c. 1280 (Worcs. Hist. Soc.), 45.
[9] *L. and P. Hen. VIII,* xvi, 617.
[10] *Valor Eccl.* (Rec. Com.), iii, 242.
[11] *L. and P. Hen. VIII,* xii (2), 769.
[12] Pat. 1 & 2 Phil. and Mary, pt. x, m. 31.

LITTLE MALVERN COURT FROM THE SOUTH

LITTLE MALVERN PRIORY CHURCH FROM THE SOUTH-EAST

died in 1558,[13] and Charles Broughton conveyed the manor in 1566 to John Russell, son and heir of Henry.[14] John died in 1588 holding the manor of Little Malvern and his brother Henry succeeded.[15] The manor passed to John son of Henry in 1608,[16] and from him to his son Thomas in 1641.[17] John Russell, son of this Thomas,[18] conveyed the manor in 1683 to Charles Trinder and others.[19] John Russell's sons John and Thomas both died without issue,[20] and the manor passed to his daughter Elizabeth, who married Thomas Berington.[21] She was succeeded by her daughter Elizabeth wife of Thomas Williams of Trellynia, co. Flint,[22] who conveyed the manor of Little Malvern in 1766–7 to Edmund Lechmere,[23] evidently for the purposes of some settlement. She as a widow held the manor with her daughter Mary in 1771.[24] Mary married Walter Wakeman, but died without issue, leaving Little Malvern Court to her kinsman William Berington of Hereford, son of her second cousin Charles.[25] William died in 1847, when the manor passed to his son Charles Michael, who enjoyed it until his death in 1897, when he was succeeded by his son Captain William Berington, J.P., the present owner.[26]

In 1537 John Russell applied to Cromwell for the site of the *PRIORY* of Little Malvern,[27] and in 1538 a lease of the house and site of the priory for twenty-one years was granted to him.[28] The site was granted in 1543 to Richard Andrews and Nicholas Temple,[29] who sold it before 1552 to Henry Russell.[30] He settled it in that year upon himself and his wife Milbore.[31] He died in 1558; and Milbore held the site of the priory until her death in 1575,[32] when it passed to her son John. From that point it descended with the manor, with which it finally became incorporated.[33]

There was a mill at Little Malvern annexed to the site of the priory, with which it was granted in 1543 to Richard Andrews and Nicholas Temple.[34] It afterwards passed with the site of the priory to the

Russells,[35] and a water-mill and a windmill are mentioned in a deed of 1683.[36]

CHURCH The priory church of *ST. GILES,* when complete, had a quire with chapels to the north and south and a presbytery projecting one bay beyond them, nave with north aisle only, north and south transepts and a central tower. The eastern arm with the central tower is the only part still in use, the quire aisles, transepts and nave being in more or less complete ruin. The quire measures internally about 40 ft. by 18 ft. 3 in., the north chapel 26 ft. 9 in. by 13 ft. 6 in., the south chapel 28 ft. by 13 ft. 6 in., the tower 18 ft. by 18 ft. 6 in., and the north and south transepts each 24 ft. 6 in. by 19 ft.

The earliest portions of the building now standing appear to be the two late 12th-century cloister doors, one opening into the south transept and the other into the nave, and the contemporary eastern respond of

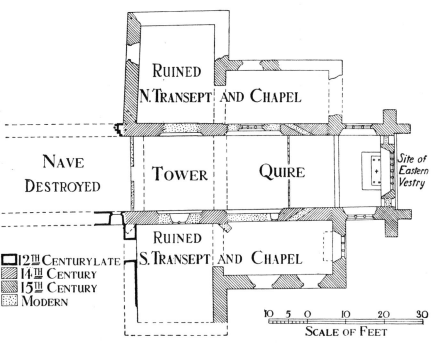

PLAN OF LITTLE MALVERN PRIORY CHURCH

the nave arcade on the north. The remaining portions of the structure appear to have been reconstructed on older lines by Bishop Alcock late in the 15th century.

The east window is of six transomed lights with a traceried head ; on either side of it are doorways once opening into an eastern vestry, which is now destroyed. The north-east and south-east windows are of three lights with net-tracery heads (of c. 1330) re-used, the rest of the windows, which are very high, being of

[13] W. and L. Inq. p.m. xviii, 1.
[14] Pat. 8 Eliz. pt. ix, m. 8.
[15] Chan. Inq. p.m. (Ser. 2), ccxxii, 36.
[16] Ibid. ccciii, 130.
[17] Ibid. dcclx, 32. Thomas Russell of Little Malvern, a recusant, petitioned to compound for his estate in 1654 (*Cal. Com. for Comp.* 3197).
[18] Nash, op. cit. ii, 141.
[19] Recov. R. East. 35 Chas. II, rot. 215.
[20] Nash, loc. cit.

[21] Burke, *Landed Gentry* (1906).
[22] Ibid.
[23] Recov. R. D. Enr. Mich. 7 Geo. III, m. 214.
[24] Recov. R. Trin. 11 Geo. III, rot. 36.
[25] Burke, *Landed Gentry* (1906).
[26] Ibid.
[27] *L. and P. Hen. VIII*, xii (2), 769.
[28] Aug. Off. Misc. Bks. ccx, fol. 82.
[29] *L. and P. Hen. VIII*, xviii (1), g. 981 (57).

[30] Mins. Accts. Worcs. Phil. and Mary, no. 313.
[31] Pat. 1 Mary, pt. xiv, m. 21.
[32] W. and L. Inq. p.m. xviii, 1.
[33] Chan. Inq. p.m. (Ser. 2), ccxxii, 36; ccciii, 130 ; dcclx, 32.
[34] *L. and P. Hen. VIII*, xviii (1), g. 981 (57).
[35] Pat. 33 Eliz. pt. ii, m. 17.
[36] Recov. R. East. 35 Chas. II, rot. 215.

the same date as the east window. The sill of the south window is cut down to form a seat, and to the east of it is a small shallow recess, used as a credence.

From this point westwards the chancel is overlapped by the side chapels and is lighted by two late 14th-century clearstory windows of three lights on each side. Arches of the same date, now blocked, opened from the west bay of the chancel into the chapels. The capitals of these arches are carved with scrolls, doubtless once bearing painted inscriptions. In the blocking of the north arch is a three-light window of Alcock's date, taken from the ruined chapels. It contains a figure of God the Father in contemporary stained glass, from a coronation of our Lady, whose figure is lost; on the south side a single lancet is set in the blocking. The tower is carried on four arches of like detail, the east and west dying into the side walls, while the north and south are

stained glass. The arms are those of Arthur Prince of Wales, Henry VII, and Bishop Alcock, and below them is a figure of Prince Arthur, a part of one of Margaret Tudor, and the whole of those representing Katherine of Aragon and her ladies.

Externally the chancel buttresses display gaps as if for the heads of flying buttresses over the chapel roofs. The chancel windows all have plain labels.

The tower is in three stages with angle buttresses and a pyramidal slated roof. The upper stage is divided on each face into nine panels with trefoiled heads, each angle having in addition a panelled continuation of the buttress; the belfry lights occupy the middle of the panelling on each face and are of two lights with a quatrefoil above. On each side of the windows and forming the external edge of the splay are small square pilasters, terminating in crocketed gables a short distance below the roof.

LITTLE MALVERN PRIORY CHURCH : THE CHANCEL

segmental and now blocked, a two-light window of early 14th-century style being inserted in the southern.

Immediately to the east of the chapel arches is a 15th-century screen, the head being richly carved with fruit and foliage and each bay having a pierced trefoiled head. On either side of the chancel are five stalls with carved elbows, one of which represents two pigs feeding from a bowl, but all the misericorde bosses have been cut away. The west end of the present church is occupied by an organ and vestry. The roof is hidden by a flat plaster ceiling on which are fastened some mediaeval carved bosses of wood arranged in a cross, and at the east end is a cornice of pierced quatrefoils. The floor is paved with mediaeval tiles, now much worn, the best preserved being within the altar rails. One is inscribed 'Spontaneam honorem et mentem sanctam Deo et patriae liberacionem.' In the east window is some good ancient

The two chapels flanking the chancel were each two bays long and were apparently both rebuilt by Bishop Alcock. They opened from the transept by low-pitched half arches against the base of the central tower, and in the eastern bay of each was a squint opening into the chancel and now blocked. The southern chapel is the best preserved and retains its three-light traceried east window and the base of the altar. The two windows in the south wall were of two lights each.

The north transept is of the same date as the chapels and retains an altar platform and part of the altar block.

In the west wall of the south transept is a 12th-century doorway formerly opening into the cloister, and in the south nave wall adjoining it is a second archway of similar date.

Of the nave itself only this door and the respond of the north arcade remain standing, but the blocking of the western tower arch may cover the base of the pulpitum.

There is one bell of pre-Reformation date inscribed + AVE : MARIA : GRACIA : PLENA : DOMINVS : TECVM, cast at Gloucester about 1350 by Master John of Gloucester.[37]

The plate consists of a cup and cover paten of 1571, a modern paten, two mounted glass flagons and a spoon.

The only volume of registers before 1812 is very imperfect, and contains entries from 1735 to 1811. Some entries of the 17th century will be found among the Bishops' Transcripts.

ADVOWSON The parish of Little Malvern had apparently no church apart from the conventual church. After the Dissolution the parish was served by a curate, to whom a payment of £5 per annum was due from the manor of Little Malvern.[38]

Earl Somers was patron of Little Malvern from 1841 until about 1872.[39] The living became a vicarage in 1868,[40] and the advowson passed into the hands of Charles Michael Berington, the lord of the manor, in whose son Captain William Berington, J.P., it is now vested.[41]

Though no appropriation of the church of Little Malvern has been found, it was evidently appropriated to the priory, probably under the foundation charter,[42] the tithes, as a late possession of the priory, being leased for twenty-one years in 1550–1 to William Doddington.[43] The reversion after the expiration of the lease was granted with the manor in 1554 to Henry Russell and Charles Broughton,[44] and the tithes have since followed the descent of the manor, being now in the possession of Capt. Berington.

The church of Little Malvern was apparently rebuilt in the episcopacy of Bishop Giffard, for he visited the priory and dedicated the church there in 1282.[45]

Mr. Fowke, vicar of Little Malvern, applied in 1911 for a faculty to enlarge and restore the church. The scheme was resisted by Capt. Berington as lay rector and owner of the ruins, on the site of which a proposed vestry was to stand, and by the parishioners, and the faculty was refused by the Chancellor of the Consistory Court of Worcester on the ground that there was no demand for any enlargement and no need for any restoration.

After the suppression of Little Malvern Priory the parishioners made suit to the king for the five bells which had always served the parish as well as the monastery, and were worth, after 20s. the hundred, £45 0s. 6¾d.[46]

In 1274 John the prior and the convent of Little Malvern granted that Henry Fitz Geoffrey Bernard should present a suitable secular chaplain in the conventual church, who should celebrate divine service at the altar of St. Cross for the souls of Henry, Geoffrey, Maud and Nicholas de Mitton, Edith and Robert de Clipston, Alice and Richard de Boudon and Elena. After the death of Henry, Sir Nicholas de Mitton and his heirs and assigns were to present successive chaplains. The chaplain was to receive 20s. and to have a decent chamber within the close of the court, and an assistant, either lay or clerical, to serve him.[47] This charter was confirmed by the bishop.[48]

In 1791 Mary Williams of Little Malvern certified that she had set apart rooms in her house for Roman Catholic worship.[49]

The Roman Catholic Priory Church of St. Wulstan at Little Malvern was built in 1862.[50]

CHARITIES This parish is entitled to send seven poor children to the Free school at Colwall, co. Hereford, founded in 1612 by will of Humphrey Walwyn.

NORTON-JUXTA-KEMPSEY

Norton-juxta-Kempsey is a small parish containing 1,844 acres of land lying to the north-east of Kempsey. The Oxford, Worcester and Wolverhampton branch of the Great Western railway meets the Abbots Wood branch of the Midland railway at Norton Junction, where there is a station. The Bristol and Birmingham branch of the Midland railway also passes through the parish, but has no station at Norton. The only high road which passes through Norton is that from Worcester to Pershore.

The village of Norton lies near the railway. Hatfield and Littleworth are districts to the south. To the north-west are Norton Barracks, the dépôt of Regimental District no. 29 (the Worcester Regiment), built in 1876. The village of Norton, which includes a few half-timber houses, stands at a height of 130 ft. to 150 ft. above the ordnance datum, and the land rises slightly north and south. Woodhall, the seat of Mr. Walter Holland, D.L., J.P., stands in wooded grounds commanding views of Malvern and the surrounding hills. The mansion is a modern erection of brick in the Tudor style. An avenue of trees leads from the house northward to the Worcester and Pershore high road. There is a small park with a fish-pond at Norton Hall, the residence of Mr. Francis Joynson, and the districts of Hatfield and Littleworth are well wooded. At Newlands Farm near the barracks are the remains of a moat.

In 1905 Norton-juxta-Kempsey contained 532 acres of arable land and 1,294 acres of permanent grass.[1] The soil is various, the subsoil Keuper Marl, and the chief crops are barley, beans and wheat. Hatfield in Norton was inclosed in 1840, and 70 acres in Eastfield were inclosed in 1854.[2]

[37] Inform. from Mr. H. B. Walters.
[38] Pat. 1 & 2 Phil. and Mary, pt. x, m. 31, 32; Chan. Inq. p.m. (Ser. 2), cccxiii, 130; dcclx, 32.
[39] Clergy Lists.
[40] Stat. 31 & 32 Vict. cap. 117, sect. 2.
[41] The presentations seem to have been made by Earl Somers and others, probably as trustees.

[42] Valor Eccl. (Rec. Com.), iii, 244.
[43] Aug. Off. Misc. Bks. ccxxiii, fol. 360.
[44] Pat. 1 & 2 Phil. and Mary, pt. x, m. 31, 32.
[45] Reg. G. Giffard (Worcs. Hist. Soc.), 165.
[46] L. and P. Hen. VIII, xii (2), 769.

[47] Reg. G. Giffard (Worcs. Hist. Soc.), 114.
[48] Ibid. 65.
[49] Worcs. N. and Q. 126.
[50] The Catholic Dir. 1912.
[1] Statistics from Bd. of Agric. (1905).
[2] Blue Bk. Incl. Awards, 190; Slater, Engl. Peasantry and Encl. of Common Fields, 307.

Cookes Holme was transferred in 1885 from Stoulton to Norton-juxta-Kempsey, and at the same date part of Old Home Farm was transferred from Norton to Whittington.[3]

NORTON-JUXTA-KEMPSEY has *MANORS* apparently never been looked upon as a separate manor, but has always formed part of the manor of Kempsey.[4]

The manor of *WOODHALL* was held of the manor of Kempsey.[5] Beatrix de Pirton held a hide of land in Norton, in the manor of Kempsey, early in the 13th century.[6] It was stated in 1220–1 that the ancestors of Reginald de Pirton, son of this Beatrix, had held the manor since the conquest of England. Reginald deduced his claim from his grandmother Beatrix, mother of Beatrix de Pirton, but Boidin, parson of the church of Norton, said that Beatrix, grandmother of Reginald, who held the estate as dower, knowing that it rightfully belonged to the church, restored it to the church as free alms, and Beatrix her daughter confirmed this grant. The jurors had, however, no knowledge of these gifts, and Reginald was adjudged to be the rightful owner.[7] William de Pirton paid a subsidy at Norton in 1280,[8] and was still holding the manor in 1299.[9] Giles son of this William[10] seems to have assumed the name 'de la Wodehall,' for in 1317–18 'the manor of Norton' was settled upon Giles de la Wodehall and Sybil his wife for their lives, with reversion to Robert de Aston and Katherine his wife and their heirs *de se*, with contingent remainders to Robert de Pirton and his heirs.[11] It seems probable that Katherine de Aston was daughter of Giles, and that Robert de Pirton was his brother. In 1346 the manor was held by Henry Wyvill.[12] Thomas Gower, escheator of Worcestershire in 1419–20,[12a] settled it in 1410 upon himself and his wife Katherine, in whose right he appears to have held it.[13] She was, according to a pedigree of the Gower family given in the Visitation of Worcestershire, 1569, a daughter of Lord Dudley.[14] Habington mentions that he has seen in a book of the bishopric of Worcester the Lady Dudley called lady of Woodhall.[15] Thomas Gower died before 1431, and his widow married John Finch, who is called

GOWER of Woodhall. *Azure a cheveron between three wolves' heads razed or.*

'of Woodhall' in 1431.[16] Thomas left a son Thomas, who married Alice daughter of John Attwood of Northwick and died in 1440, leaving a son Thomas, a minor at the time of his father's death.[17] John son of Thomas died in 1526–7 seised of the manor of Woodhall.[18] His son and successor William was Sheriff of Worcestershire in 1549.[19] He was succeeded by his son John,[20] who died in 1569.[20a] His son John, who then succeeded to the manor, conveyed it in 1577 to Richard Lygon and others for a settlement on his marriage with Margaret Harewell, a relative of Richard Lygon.[21] He died in 1620, and was buried at Norton-by-Kempsey.[21a] His son William Gower and his wife Anne, who was the daughter of Sir William Whorwood,[21b] sold the manor of Woodhall to William Stevens in 1628–9.[22] William seems to have followed by a son Randall, who died in 1653,[23] and had been succeeded before 1676 by Thomas Stevens, who conveyed the manor in that year to William Bagnall for a settlement upon Thomas and his heirs.[24] Thomas died in 1711.[25]

The Woodhall estate had passed before 1868 to Thomas Adams,[26] and the house was occupied by his widow in 1888 and 1896. It was purchased in 1903 by Mr. Walter Holland, D.L., J.P., the present owner.

The manor of *NEWLAND* probably originated in land in the manor of Kempsey held by the family 'de Newland.' There was litigation in 1220 between Simon de Newland and Boidin, parson of Kempsey, as to a curtilage and garden in Norton.[27] William de Newland gave a messuage and a carucate of land in Norton to Walter Cantilupe, Bishop of Worcester (1237–66),[28] and this property the bishop assigned to the sacristy of Worcester. It was claimed in 1274 by William's brother Robert de Newland, who stated that when his brother made the gift he had been in durance at Colchester. Robert's plea was rejected, and it was found that William was 'in bono statu et extra vincula et extra prisonam ad voluntatem suam propriam.'[29] Bishop William's grant was confirmed to the sacrist in 1336 by the bishop and by the prior and convent.[30] The estate seems to have been held of the prior and convent,[31] and the bishop's confirmation was made in order that the grantee might be quit of suit of court and any other service beyond rent and scutage.[32] In 1536 the convent was receiving a rent of 69*s.* 4*d.* from the demesne lands at Newland.[33] The manor, with a rent of 16*d.* for the carriage of four wagon loads of

[3] *Pop. Ret.* 1891, ii, 657.
[4] Information given by Ecclesiastical Commissioners; *Testa de Nevill* (Rec. Com.), 42.
[5] *Testa de Nevill* (Rec. Com.), 42; Habington, *Surv. of Worcs.* (Worcs. Hist. Soc.), ii, 147.
[6] *Testa de Nevill* (Rec. Com.), 42.
[7] Assize R. 1021, m. 3.
[8] Lay Subs. R. *Worcs.* c. 1280 (Worcs. Hist. Soc.), 80.
[9] Red Bk. of Bishopric of Worc. (Eccl. Com. Rec. Var. bdle. 121, no. 43698), fol. 35.
[10] Habington, op. cit. ii, 147.
[11] Feet of F. Worcs. 11 Edw. II, no. 22.
[12] *Feud. Aids*, v, 309.
[12a] Nash, op. cit. Introd. p. xiii.
[13] Feet of F. Worcs. 12 Hen. IV, no. 29.

[14] *Visit. of Worcs.* 1569 (Harl. Soc. xxvii), 60; a pedigree of the Gowers of Woodhall and Boughton is in the possession of Mr. Robert Vaughan Gower.
[15] op. cit. ii, 147.
[16] *Cal. Pat.* 1429–36, p. 159.
[17] *Visit. of Worcs.* 1569 (Harl. Soc. xxvii), 60; Chan. Inq. p.m. 33 Hen. VI, no. 9.
[18] Exch. Inq. p.m. (Ser. 2), file 1183, no. 5.
[19] P.R.O. *List of Sheriffs*, 158.
[20] *Visit. of Worcs.* 1569 (Harl. Soc. xxvii), 60.
[20a] A commission was granted to his son John to administer his estates in 1570 (inform. from Mr. R. Vaughan Gower).
[21] Feet of F. Div. Co. East. 19 Eliz.; Hardwicke MS. (Add. MS. 37940).

[21a] Par. reg. and pedigree in the possession of Mr. R. Vaughan Gower.
[21b] M.I. in church of Upton on Severn; pedigree in possession of Mr. R. Vaughan Gower.
[22] Feet of F. Worcs. East. 5 Chas. I. Baptiste Viscount Campden and his wife Elizabeth were parties to this fine.
[23] Nash, op. cit. ii, 25–6.
[24] Recov. R. D. Enr. Hil. 27 & 28 Chas. II, m. 5.
[25] Nash, loc. cit.
[26] Noake, *Guide to Worcs.* 286.
[27] Assize R. 1021, m. 6.
[28] Ibid. 1026, m. 20.
[29] Ibid.
[30] *Cal. Pat.* 1338–40, p. 46.
[31] *Valor Eccl.* (Rec. Com.), iii, 224.
[32] *Cal. Pat.* 1338–40, p. 46.
[33] *Valor Eccl.* (Rec. Com.), iii, 224.

NORTON-JUXTA-KEMPSEY ·CHURCH C. 1810
(*From a Water-colour by Thos. Rickards in Prattinton Collection*)

fuel from Newland to the sacristy of the priory, was granted in 1545 to John Bourne, the lessee under the priory.[34] He died in 1575, and the estate passed to his son Anthony, who sold it in 1577 to Sir Thomas Bromley, kt., Lord Chancellor of England.[35] He with his son Henry conveyed it in 1587 to trustees for a settlement upon Elizabeth wife of Sir Thomas for life. It may have passed in the same way as Hill Croome from the Bromleys to Lord Coventry, for the Earl of Coventry now holds Newland Farm, but all manorial rights have lapsed.[36]

William de Marisco about 1182 held half a hide of land in Norton, which he had received from Bishop Simon (1125–50).[37] The estate was held of the manor of Kempsey, and Joseph de Marisco was the owner early in the 13th century.[38] In 1232 the bishop attorned Richard de Cumpton and Richard de Alvechurch against Thomas de Marisco and Alice his wife of half a virgate and 12 acres of land in Kempsey.[39] John de Marisco held it in 1299,[40] and Habington states that his land was given to the chantry of Kempsey,[41] but in 1346 William de Marisco held a fifth of a fee in Norton which Joseph de Marisco had formerly held.[42]

CHURCH The church of *ST. JAMES* consists of a chancel 21 ft. by 12 ft., north vestry, nave 50½ ft. by 16½ ft., south aisle 11½ ft. wide, south porch and western tower 7 ft. wide by 9¾ ft. deep. These measurements are all internal.

The church has been a great deal repaired during the past century, and the south aisle, porch and vestry were added in 1875. The oldest portion of the existing church is the 12th-century nave, which appears to have been lengthened in the 13th century. The chancel appears to have been rebuilt in the 14th century, and the tower may have been added late in the same century.

The east window has two lights with modern tracery and mullions. The east wall sets back 6 in. about 5 ft. above the ground outside. In the north wall is a square-headed late 14th-century window of two lights, now opening into the vestry. In the south wall is a similar window of two lights ; the jambs, which are of white stone, and the sill and lintel, which are of red sandstone, appear to be old work recut. The chancel arch is pointed and of modern date. The nave is lighted in its north wall by three windows ; the first, the stonework of which is modern, is of two lights with a quatrefoil over. The second is apparently of the 12th century, and is the only window of that date left ; it is very small and has a round head. The third window is a lancet with a pointed head, and is evidently of 13th-century date. Between the two last is a round-headed doorway covered by two wood doors bolted together. A modern arcade of four bays divides the nave from the aisle, which is lit by three windows in the south wall and one at each end. The round-headed south doorway is of 12th-century design, and the capitals and a few stones of the outer order are old, and evidently belonged to a doorway formerly in the south wall of the nave. The south porch is of timber on stone foundation walls.

A modern doorway in the west wall of the nave admits to the tower, which is unbroken horizontally from ground to parapet. The latter is pierced by quatrefoils and has square pinnacles at the angles, gabled and crocketed. The west window in the ground floor is of two lights with rough heads, apparently recut, and a modern mullion. The chamber above has two unglazed rectangular lights in the west wall and one in the north, all with original red sandstone jambs. The bell-chamber is lighted by windows of two lights under pointed heads.

The roofs are all modern and gabled ; that over the chancel is panelled, and the nave and aisle have low pointed barrel ceilings. All the furniture is modern except the 13th-century font, which is octagonal and of irregular form.

In the chancel is a slab to Randall Stevens of Woodhall, who died in 1653, and others to later members of the same family. There are also many wall monuments of the 18th century and later. On the east wall outside is a memorial to William March, who was buried in 1661, and his son William, 1673.

There are three bells : the first by Abel Rudhall, 1716 ; the second inscribed 'Sancta Anna ora pro nobis' and bearing a stamp of four fleurs de lis set saltirewise in a square ; the third is dated 1682 and has a stamp with the maker's initials I. M. for John Martin.

The communion plate consists of a silver cup with a baluster stem, and a cover paten, dated 1677, and stamped with the hall mark of 1675, a paten of 1677, the gift of Bishop Fleetwood, a set of a cup, paten, almsdish and flagon given in 1876, and a pewter flagon of older date.

The registers before 1812 are as follows: (i) baptisms 1540 to 1710, burials 1538 to 1710 (with a gap between 1638 and 1652) and marriages 1572 to 1709 with gaps between 1640 and 1653 and 1658 to 1661 ; (ii) baptisms 1711 to 1812, burials 1711 to 1812 and marriages 1711 to 1754 ; (iii) a marriage book 1754 to 1812. There are also preserved several old deeds, and the will of Mrs. Stephens, 1668, bequeathing various gifts to the parish.

ADVOWSON The church or chapel at Norton-by-Kempsey was dependent upon the church of Kempsey.[43] In 1269 the inhabitants of Norton complained that Maurice de Tapenhale, vicar of Kempsey, had taken from them baptisms, weddings and churchings which by ancient custom were celebrated at Norton, and it was decided by the bishop's commissioners that the parishioners had such customs, and that mass ought to be celebrated on every Sunday and feast day in the said chapel.[44] In 1368 further trouble arose between the men of Norton and the rector and vicar of Kempsey as to the rights of their chapel. The inhabitants claimed that their chapel from time immemorial had all rights belonging to a parish church except that of sepulture, and they affirmed that they ought to have a priest there continually to celebrate the services. The rector of Kempsey, however, maintained that services ought to be celebrated there only three days in the week. The bishop again decided in favour of

[34] *L. and P. Hen. VIII*, xx (1), g. 465 (80).
[35] Chan. Inq. p.m. (Ser. 2), clxxii, 142 ; Close, 19 Eliz. pt. iii.
[36] Pat. 32 Eliz. pt. xxi, m. 4 ; inform. from Mr. W. Hill.

[37] Red Bk. of Bishopric of Worc. fol. 35.
[38] *Testa de Nevill* (Rec. Com.), 42.
[39] *Cal. Close*, 1231–4, p. 150.
[40] Red Bk. of Bishopric of Worc. fol. 35.

[41] Habington, op. cit. i, 147.
[42] *Feud. Aids*, v, 309.
[43] *Reg. G. Giffard* (Worcs. Hist. Soc.), 11.
[44] Ibid.

the men of Norton.[45] In 1556 Bishop Pates granted the parishioners of Norton the right of sepulture.[46]

The living of Norton-juxta-Kempsey was a perpetual curacy until 1867–8, when it became a vicarage.[47] The Dean and Chapter of Worcester have always been patrons of this parish.

There is a Wesleyan chapel at Littleworth.

CHARITIES The charities subsisting in this parish are regulated by a scheme of the Charity Commissioners 28 July 1882, as varied by scheme of 23 December 1908, namely, the charities of : —

1. Thomas Knight, will, 1652, endowment consisting of £336 11s. 7d. consols, arising from the sale in 1881 of land purchased with the original bequest.

2. Elizabeth Stephens, by will, 1668, trust fund, consisting of £49 3s. 9d. consols.

3. The parish lands appear by a feoffment made 7 January 1568 to have been originally granted towards the relief of the poor, the setting forth and furnishing of soldiers, the amending of highways, and other such like works of charity, within the town and parish. The trust estate consists of 5 a. 18 p. at Whittington and 6 a. at Norton-juxta-Kempsey and £370 2s. 7d. consols.

The sums of stock, amounting together to £755 17s. 11d. consols, are held by the official trustees. Of this £600 stock was, by an order of the Charity Commissioners 17 January 1905, directed to be set aside for providing £15 a year for educational purposes, leaving a sum of £155 17s. 11d. stock, producing £3 17s. 8d., for the other charitable purposes.

The parish lands are let at £21 a year, out of which, by an order of the Charity Commissioners 22 February 1898, £6 a year was made applicable towards church expenses and the remainder of the income of the charities for eleemosynary purposes was in 1910 applied in the distribution of bread and coals.

ODDINGLEY

Oddungahlea, Oddungalea, Oddungalea (x cent.) ; Oddunclei (xi cent.) ; Oddinglegh, Oddingesle, Oddingle (xiii cent.) ; Oddingleye (xiv cent.).

Oddingley is pleasantly situated about 3½ miles to the south-east of Droitwich on the slopes of a valley through which run the Worcester and Birmingham Canal and the Bristol and Birmingham branch of the Midland railway, which has a goods station at Dunhampstead, but no passenger station at Oddingley. A road from Droitwich to Huddington passes through the north of the parish, and another road connects the village of Oddingley with Droitwich.

The village is in the centre of the parish, and besides the church of St. James and Church Farm contains brick and tile works on the canal. The old rectory is about half a mile from the church to the north-west. The present rectory and the school are at some distance from the village to the north on the Droitwich road.

The village itself stands at a height of about 185 ft. above the ordnance datum, and the land rises slightly in the north, the rectory at the extreme north being 203 ft. above the ordnance datum.

The church lies a little to the south of the by-road along which the main part of the village is built, and is surrounded by a small churchyard. Immediately to the south-east of the church is a farm-house of brick and half-timber, which appears to date from about 1600. It is of two stories with attics, and latterly has been divided up into three cottages. In the meadow adjoining is a fine dovecote of half-timber work, rectangular in plan, with a pyramidal tiled roof, surmounted by a flèche affording entrance to the birds. The timbering is of simple uprights and cross-beams, with occasional straight struts, and the filling appears to have been originally wattle and daub, though this has been replaced in many places by brick. The structure is probably contemporary with the adjacent farm-house. The few cottages which make up the main portion of the village are situated a little to the north of the church. Here are some good examples of half-timber work. A small cottage standing a little way back on the west side of the road has two remarkably fine late 15th-century moulded brick chimney stacks with circular shafts, spirally fluted, and octagonal cappings with concave sides. The plan is a simple oblong containing two rooms on the ground floor with fireplaces at either end of the building, a central staircase, and a small out-house on the north. There is an attic story in the roof. The ceilings are open-joisted. About three-quarters of a mile south-east of the church, on the opposite side of the railway and canal, is Netherwood Farm, a modernized 17th-century building of red brick ; in an adjoining barn was committed a murder consequent on the 'Oddingley murder' in 1806. A man was tried for this in 1830 at the Worcester assizes, but was acquitted. This barn has been since demolished and a new one erected on its foundations.

The vill of Oddingley is said to have been thrown into the forest of Feckenham by Henry II,[1] but was disafforested at the beginning of the reign of Henry III.[2] A part of Trench Wood, which lies chiefly in Huddington, is in Oddingley. Oddingley Heath was inclosed before 1817, and until its inclosure the inhabitants of Oddingley, Tibberton, Hindlip, Hadzor and Salwarpe enjoyed rights of common there.[2a] The parish contains 894 acres, of which 357 are arable land, 423 permanent grass and 75 woodland.[3] The soil is loamy and the subsoil Keuper Marl, producing crops of cereals and roots.

Place-names at Oddingley are : Stigeley, Greenway, Deorleage, Longandic, Caltham Hill, Crohheama[4] (ix cent.) ; Nufeld[5] (xv cent.) ; Horsham Valez, Mortymers Coppice[6] (xvi cent.).

MANOR The manor of *ODDINGLEY* was apparently given to the see of Worcester before 816, for at that date Coenwulf, King of Mercia, granted to Bishop Deneberht and the

---

45 Worc. Epis. Reg. William Whittlesey (1364–8), fol. 32 d., 33 f. ; Nash, op. cit. ii, 28.
46 Prattinton Coll. (Soc. Antiq.).

47 Stat. 31 & 32 Vict. cap. 117.
1 Nash, *Hist. of Worcs.* Introd. pp. lxv–vi.   2 *V.C.H. Worcs.* ii, 315.
2a Prattinton Coll. (Soc. Antiq.).

3 Statistics from Bd. of Agric. (1905).
4 Birch, *Cart. Sax.* iii, 341.
5 Ct. R. (Gen. Ser.), portf. 210, no. 69.
6 Pat. 3 Edw. VI, pt. vii.

church of Worcester that Oddingley should be free of all secular services except building of strongholds and bridges and military service.[7] Cynewold, the fifteenth Bishop of Worcester (929–57), is said to have given this manor about 940 to the monks of Worcester,[8] and in 963 Bishop Oswald, with the permission of the convent, of Edgar, King of England, and of Alfhere, ealdorman of Mercia, gave this estate for three lives to Cynethegn with reversion to the church of Worcester.[9] A more detailed account of this alienation is given in the registers of the monastery. A certain clerk of noble birth called Cynethegn came to Godwin, the venerable dean of the monastery, and asked for a *cassata* of land called Oddingley. Godwin being unwilling to deny him, as he knew him for a powerful man of great prudence, granted it to him without delay, on condition that he should pay 5s. a year for the land. This agreement Cyne-

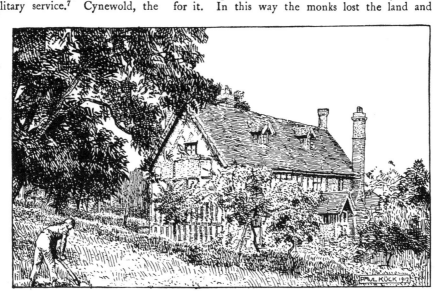

ODDINGLEY : OLD FARM-HOUSE NEAR THE CHURCH

thegn kept as long as he lived, but on his death his heirs usurped the land and would not do any service for it. In this way the monks lost the land and the service due for it.[10] The manor was, however, included in the land of the church of Worcester at the time of the Domesday Survey. It was held by Ordric, and his predecessor Turchil had done service for it to the bishop.[11]

The tenure by which this manor was held seems to have been doubtful. Towards the end of the 12th century it was returned as belonging to the Bishop of Worcester's great manor of Northwick in Claines, but the tenant did no service for it.[12] In 1330–1 it was said to be held of the Abbot of Wigmore,[13] but in 1346 it was granted to John de Beauchamp for the service of serving the king with his cup whenever he should come to the manor.[14] In 1360 and 1424–5 it was not known of whom the manor was held,[15] while in 1398–9 it was said to be held of the king in chief by knight service.[16] In 1432–3 it was held of Richard Earl of Warwick and others, as of their manor of Bromsgrove, for a service unknown.[17]

Adam de Croome is the first undertenant of the manor whose name is known. He claimed a hide at Oddingley of the bishop's fee as the land of his cousin. This apparently happened in the time of Bishop Samson (1096–1112),[18] and Adam later gave the estate to William Hacket, who was in possession towards the end of the 12th

HALF-TIMBER DOVECOTE, ODDINGLEY

[7] Heming, *Chartul.* (ed. Hearne), 337.

[8] *Ann. Mon.* (Rolls Ser.), iv, 564 ; Habington, *Surv. of Worcs.* (Worcs. Hist. Soc.), i, 440.

[9] Birch, op. cit. iii, 341 ; Heming, op. cit. 160.

[10] Dugdale, *Mon. Angl.* i, 595 ; Heming, op. cit. 264.

[11] *V.C.H. Worcs.* i, 294b.

[12] Red Bk. of Bishopric of Worc. (Eccl. Com. Rec. Var. bdle. 121, no. 43698), fol. 18.

[13] Chan. Inq. p.m. 28 Edw. III (1st nos.), no. 53.

[14] *Cal. Pat.* 1345–8, p. 123.

[15] Chan. Inq. p.m. 34 Edw. III (1st nos.), no. 86 ; 35 Edw. III, pt. ii (2nd nos.), no. 1 ; 3 Hen. VI, no. 32.

[16] Ibid. 22 Ric. II, no. 34.

[17] Ibid. 11 Hen. VI, no. 39.

[18] Red Bk. of Bishopric of Worc. fol. 242.

century.[19]   In 1226–7 Alda widow of Thomas Hacket claimed a third of a hide of land at Oddingley as dower from Ralph Hacket.   It was agreed between them that Alda should have half a knight's fee in Coston and a rent of 1 mark yearly in Eckington in satisfaction of her dower.[20]   In 1254–5 William Cassy sued Philip Hacket for land in Oddingley,[21] and in 1274–5 Philip Hacket brought a writ of novel disseisin against Roger Mortimer for land in Oddingley.[22]   The manor of Oddingley had, however, been sold before this time, probably in the reign of Henry III,[23] by Robert Hacket to Roger Mortimer, but the charter recording this grant is undated.[24] This Roger Mortimer was evidently Roger Mortimer of Wigmore, and he gave the manor to his younger son Roger Mortimer of Chirk, who in 1284 applied to his brother Edmund for a confirmation of their father's grant.[25]   Margery widow of Gregory de Caldwell sued Roger son of Roger Mortimer in 1274–5 for a third of the manor of Oddingley which she claimed as dower.   Roger said that she had no right to this dower, as Gregory had been outlawed, but Margery said that the manor had been taken away from Gregory before his outlawry by Roger de Mortimer, sen.[26]   Gregory possibly held a lease of the manor under the Hackets. His son Edmund claimed two-thirds of the manor in 1279, stating, as his mother had done, that Gregory had been unjustly disseised of the manor by Roger Mortimer the elder.[27]   It would seem that Margery Caldwell secured a third of the manor, for in 1284 she was sued for this third by John Costentyn and Margery his wife, as Margery's right, and Margery Caldwell called Roger Mortimer to uphold her right.[28]   Roger Mortimer had probably recovered possession of the manor in 1300, for he presented to the church in that year,[29] and granted the manor for life to Adam de Harvington in 1304–5.[30]   Roger Mortimer of Chirk forfeited all his possessions in 1322 for taking up arms against the Despensers.[31]   He died in prison in August 1326,[32] and, though he left a son Roger, his nephew Roger Mortimer of Wigmore was declared his heir, and presented to the church of Oddingley in December 1326,[33] the king having

MORTIMER.   *Barry or and azure a chief or with two pales between two gyrons azure therein and a scutcheon argent over all.*

presented in October of that year by reason of the lands of Roger Mortimer of Wigmore[34] being in his hands.[35]   Roger Mortimer of Wigmore was restored on the accession of Edward III and was created Earl of March in 1328,[36] but he was convicted of treason and hanged in 1330.[37]   The manor of Oddingley was enumerated among his possessions at that time,[38] but was probably still held by Adam de Harvington. On the death of Adam the manor reverted to the Crown on account of Roger's forfeiture, and was granted for life by Edward III in 1344–5 to Thomas de Hawkeston for his good services, at a rent of £6 6s.[39]   This rent was remitted in 1345.[40]   In 1346 the reversion after the death of Thomas was granted to John de Beauchamp.[41]   John died in December 1360,[42] and the reversion of the manor had evidently been granted to Roger Mortimer, grandson of Roger the first Earl of March, when he was created Earl of March, and his grandfather's attainder reversed in 1354,[43] for he had confirmed the king's grant to John de Beauchamp, and died seised of the manor in February 1360.[44]   His son and successor Edmund died in 1381, leaving a son Roger, aged seven,[45] and the manor passed into the king's custody.[46]   Roger, then Earl of March, died seised of the manor in 1398,[47] and it was assigned as dower to his widow Eleanor, who married as her second husband Edward Charleton Lord Powys.[48] Edward and Eleanor granted an annuity of 100s. from the manor to Alice Bremle for her good service to Eleanor, and this grant was confirmed to her by the king in 1405,[49] probably on account of the manor coming into his hands by the death of Eleanor Lady Powys in that year, her son Edmond being still a minor.[50]   Edmond died without issue in 1425, his heirs being his sisters Joan wife of Sir John Grey and Joyce wife of Sir John Tiptoft and his nephew Richard Duke of York.[51]   This manor was assigned to Richard Duke of York, but Anne widow of Edmond Earl of March held a third of it as dower until her death in 1432–3.[52]   Richard Duke of York died in 1460,[53] and his son Edward was proclaimed King of England in March 1460–1.   In June 1461 he, as Edward IV, granted the manor of Oddingley to his mother Cicely Duchess of York,[54] and this grant was confirmed by Richard III in 1484.[55]   The manor was probably held by Elizabeth, queen consort of Henry VII, as she presented to the church in 1499.[56] Henry VIII granted the manor in 1509 to Katherine of Aragon,[57] and it evidently also formed part of the jointure of Jane Seymour.[58]   In January 1540 it was

[19] Red Bk. of Bishopric of Worc. fol. 18.
[20] Feet of F. Worcs. 11 Hen. III, no. 15.
[21] Assize R. 1022, m. 4.
[22] Ibid. 1026, m. 22 d.
[23] *Hund. R.* (Rec. Com.), ii, 284.
[24] Add. MS. 6041, fol. 28*b*.
[25] De Banco R. 55, m. 107 d.
[26] Assize R. 1026, m. 2 d.
[27] De Banco R. 17, m. 54.
[28] Ibid. 55, m. 83.
[29] Nash, op. cit. ii, 201.
[30] Add. MS. 6041, fol. 28*b*.
[31] G.E.C. *Complete Peerage*, v, 380; *Cal. Close*, 1318–23, p. 594; *Cal. Pat.* 1321–4, p. 271.
[32] Trokelowe, *Chron. et Ann.* (Rolls Ser.), 147; *Chron. of Edw. I and Edw. II* (Rolls Ser.), i, 312. G.E.C. following

Dugdale and chronicles of priory of Wigmore gives the date of Roger's death as 1336 (op. cit. v, 380).
[33] Nash, op. cit. ii, 201; Worc. Epis. Reg. Cobham (1317–27), fol. 117.
[34] Probably Chirk was meant, as Roger Mortimer of Wigmore would hardly have obtained his uncle's possessions until after the arrest of the king in Nov. 1326.
[35] *Cal. Pat.* 1324–7, p. 333.
[36] G.E.C. *Complete Peerage*, v, 243.
[37] Ibid.
[38] Chan. Inq. p.m. 28 Edw. III (1st nos.), no. 53.
[39] *Abbrev. Rot. Orig.* (Rec. Com.), ii, 165.
[40] *Cal. Pat.* 1343–5, p. 532.
[41] Ibid. 1345–8, p. 123.
[42] Chan. Inq. p.m. 35 Edw. III, pt. ii (2nd nos.), no. 1.

[43] G.E.C. *Complete Peerage*, v, 243.
[44] Chan. Inq. p.m. 34 Edw. III (1st nos.), no. 86.
[45] G.E.C. *Complete Peerage*, v, 244.
[46] Nash, op. cit. ii, 201.
[47] Chan. Inq. p.m. 22 Ric. II, no. 34.
[48] De Banco R. 582, m. 463 d.
[49] *Cal. Pat.* 1405–8, p. 101.
[50] G.E.C. *Complete Peerage*, v, 244.
[51] Chan. Inq. p.m. 3 Hen. VI, no. 32.
[52] Ibid. 11 Hen. VI, no. 39.
[53] G.E.C. *Complete Peerage*, v, 244.
[54] *Cal. Pat.* 1461–7, p. 131.
[55] Ibid. 1476–85, p. 459.
[56] Nash, op. cit. ii, 201.
[57] *L. and P. Hen. VIII*, i, 155; Duchy of Lanc. Misc. Bks. xxii, fol. 1.
[58] *L. and P. Hen. VIII*, xiv, g. 1192 (20).

granted for life to Anne of Cleves on her marriage with the king,[59] and in 1541 to Katherine Howard.[60] In 1544 it was granted to Katherine Parr.[61]

Edward VI granted the manor in 1549 to John Earl of Warwick,[62] and confirmed it to him in 1552 and 1553,[63] having created him Duke of Northumberland in 1551. He was attainted and beheaded in 1553 for taking the part of Lady Jane Grey,[64] but this manor seems to have remained in the possession of his widow Joan, for in 1553–4 Queen Mary granted to her other manors in exchange for the manors of Yardley and Oddingley,[65] the latter of which the queen granted in 1554 to her secretary Sir John Bourne.[66] He died in 1575,[67] and his widow Dorothy and her son Anthony sold the manor in 1575–6 to George Winter.[68] It then followed the same descent as the manor of Huddington[69] until the death of Sir George Winter in 1658.

By his will dated 1657 Sir George had charged the manor of Oddingley with his debts and legacies,[70] and it evidently passed with Huddington to his aunt Helen Winter, for it was sold by her to Thomas Foley,[70a] who was in possession in 1661.[71] The manor followed the same descent as that of Great Witley (q.v.) from this time until 1806 or later.[72] It was purchased about 1837 by John Howard Galton of Hadzor.[73] He died in 1867, and the manor was held until her death in 1877 by his widow.[74] It then passed to her son Theodore Howard, who was succeeded in 1881 by his son Major Hubert George Howard Galton, R.A., of Hadzor House, the present owner of the manor.[75]

Some 16th-century Court Rolls of the manor are preserved at the Public Record Office.[76]

CHURCH The church of *ST. JAMES* consists of a chancel 17½ ft. by 12½ ft., nave 37½ ft by 14½ ft., north transept 9½ ft. deep by 11½ ft. wide, south transept 11 ft. wide by 12 ft. deep, and a western tower 8½ ft. by 9 ft. These measurements are all internal.

No part of the fabric is earlier than the 15th century, when the existing building, with the exception of the tower, was erected. The nave, judging from the position of the doorways, was originally longer, and was shortened when the tower was added, probably in the 17th century. Although the church retains its original windows, they have been much

restored and their stones recut, doubtless when the chancel was rebuilt in 1861.

The east window of the chancel is wholly modern and is of three lights under a four-centred traceried head. The two 15th-century windows in the south wall have been reset; each is of two lights under a square head. Between them is a reset 15th-century doorway with a four-centred arch. The window in the north wall is similar to the south-west window opposite. There is no chancel arch, but the wall returns on both sides to the walls of the wider nave.

The north transept is entered by a plastered archway and has an east window of two lights similar to those of the chancel and apparently old. The north window is of three lights with cusped cross-tracery and a two-centred arch; much of its stonework appears to be original. The west window is probably a later insertion, and is of two lights with unpierced spandrels. Across the opening to the south transept is a 15th-century moulded timber archway or screen, the western post being placed against the west jamb

ODDINGLEY CHURCH FROM THE NORTH-EAST

of the opening, while the eastern stands free and gives access to the pulpit. This arrangement appears to be original, the narrow opening being evidently left for the passage of a rood-loft stair. The east and west windows of the south transept, both original, are of two lights and resemble those in the chancel. The south window has three lights with pierced spandrels within a two-centred head. The lower part of the lights is filled in with modern stonework.

The two-light north window of the nave, which is apparently old, conforms to the general type. The south window is square-headed with three lights.

[59] *L. and P. Hen. VIII*, xv, g. 144 (2), p. 52. [60] Ibid. xvi, g. 503 (25).
[61] Ibid. xix (1), g. 141 (65).
[62] Pat. 3 Edw. VI, pt. vii.
[63] Ibid. 5 Edw. VI, pt. iv; 7 Edw. VI, pt. viii.
[64] G.E.C. *Complete Peerage*, vi, 87.
[65] Pat. 1 Mary, pt. v, m. 1.
[66] Ibid. 2 Mary, pt. i, m. 29; Nash, op. cit. ii, 199.

[67] Chan. Inq. p.m. (Ser. 2), clxxii, 142.
[68] Close, 18 Eliz. pt. iii, Winter and Bourne.
[69] Chan. Inq. p.m. (Ser. 2), ccxlii, 75; Pat. 6 Jas. I, pt. xxiii, no. 13; Chan. Inq. p.m. (Ser. 2), cccxcii, 98; ccccxxxix, 60; ccccclxiv, 24b.
[70] *Hist. MSS. Com. Rep.* x, App. iv, 198.
[70a] Prattinton Coll. (Soc. Antiq.).

[71] Thomas presented to the church at that date (Nash, op. cit. ii, 201).
[72] Feet of F. Worcs. East. 16 Chas. II; Recov. R. Hil. 42 Geo. III, rot. 21; *Worcs. Guide*, 1797, p. 46.
[73] *Clergy List*, 1841.
[74] Burke, *Landed Gentry* (1906).
[75] Ibid.
[76] Ct. R. (Gen. Ser.), portf. 210, no. 40, 69.

The north and south doorways (of which the former is filled in) have each a single chamfered order and a four-centred arch and appear to be original. The timber porch to the south doorway is modern. To the east of the doorway is a round-headed niche partly repaired, but the stoup which occupied it is now gone. To the west of these doorways are low buttresses flush with and not bonded to the nave walls.

The tower, of rough rubble without quoins, is three stages high with square string-courses to mark the divisions. The plastered archway towards the nave has a pointed head and the partly restored west window is of three lights with tracery above. It was probably the original west window of the nave removed and reset when the tower was added. The second stage is lighted by plain rectangular lights to the north and south and the bell-chamber or third stage by a pair of round-headed windows in each wall. The roof is of pyramidal form, tiled, and with plain eaves. The rest of the church is rubble faced with quoins. The chancel walling is all modern, and the upper part of the transept has also been rebuilt. The gabled roofs are plastered internally with ornamental trusses at intervals. The font is octagonal and is apparently original work recut. The moulded lower edge to the bowl is carved with roses and fetterlocks alternately. Some of the oak seats are made up with 17th-century re-used woodwork. There are two old plain chests in the church made from solid tree trunks, and in the nave is a wrought-iron hour-glass stand. The other furniture is modern.

In the east window of the chancel are some fragments of 15th-century glass, including complete figures of St. Martin and St. Catherine. Above the latter in the north light is a shield of the king's arms impaling Nevill, and below are the half-length figures of a man and wife praying and the inscription ' Orate pro animabus Johannis Yarnold et Johanne uxoris eius '; below these again is another figure in a blue habit and scapular kneeling before a prayer desk. Below St. Martin in the middle light is part of the figure of an archbishop. In the south light is the fragmentary figure of a female saint holding a cross staff over her with the arms of Mortimer. Below are inscribed the words ' Dñs Johñes Haryes ' and under this are the kneeling figures of a man and his wife without inscription. Below these is a priest in sub-deacon's vestments. Among the other fragments are a small head of Christ with the crown of thorns and part of an inscription

referring to a rector. In the north window of the chancel is an Assumption of our Lady, with a Majesty to the east. There are also bits of old glass in the spandrels of all the chancel window heads.

There are three bells : the treble is inscribed ' Prayse and glory be to God for ever I.P. 1661,' and on the waist is the mark of the founder, John Martin of Worcester. On the second bell is a cross with the letters H K, a lion passant, G O, H O, and another lion passant. The tenor is dated 1713 and was cast by Richard Saunders of Bromsgrove.

The plate[77] includes a plain cup of peculiar pattern, gilt inside, with the hall mark of 1802 ; also a salver paten standing on three feet with an embossed ring 6 in. in diameter, inscribed on the reverse ' Hadzor 1816,' and having the hall mark of 1754. There is in addition a curious pewter flagon with a pear-shaped body, made of two pieces joined together, also a pewter plate.

The registers[78] before 1812 are as follows : (i) all entries 1661 to 1745 ; (ii) baptisms 1745 to 1812, burials 1748 to 1812, marriages 1748 to 1754 ; (iii) marriages 1756 to 1812.

ADVOWSON The descent of the advowson of the church of Oddingley is substantially the same as that of the manor.[79] It was apparently excepted from the grants of the manor to Adam de Harvington, Thomas de Hawkeston and John de Beauchamp. Elizabeth consort of Henry VII presented to the church in 1499[80] and Queen Katherine in 1523,[81] but it was not included in the grants of the manor to the other consorts of Henry VIII. The advowson of the church was granted with the manor to Sir John Bourne in 1554[82] and has since descended with the manor. The living is a rectory, united in 1864 to Hadzor.[83]

CHARITIES In 1631 Henry Button, as stated on the church table, by his will gave 2s. 6d. per annum out of certain land in the parish for the poor on Good Friday for ever, to be distributed by the churchwardens and overseers.

The same table also stated that Margaret Parker in 1657, by her will, gave to the poor 10s. per annum issuing out of land known as Aves Hills, to be distributed to the poor on Christmas Day and Whit Sunday. Upon non-payment thereof a power of distress was given to the churchwardens and overseers. It is understood that the annuity is paid by the proprietor of the farm charged.

OMBERSLEY

Ambresl', Ombresleya, Ambreslege (viii cent.) ; Ambreslege (xi cent.) ; Aumbresleg, Humbresl' (xiii cent.) ; Ombresleye (xiv cent.).

Ombersley is a large parish containing 7,129 acres, of which 86 acres are covered by water. It is bordered on the west by the River Severn, on the south by the Salwarpe and on the east by Hadley Brook. The high road from Stourport to Worcester passes through the parish from north to south and in the village of

Ombersley it crosses at right angles the high road from Droitwich to Tenbury, which is carried over the Severn by Holt Fleet Bridge. This bridge consists of one iron arch with stone piers. The country round is very beautiful and is much frequented by visitors. The bridge was built under an Act of 5 May 1826.[1]

The village of Ombersley stands in the middle of the parish at the junction of the two above-men-

---

[77] Part of the old communion plate was stolen in July 1830.

[78] Earlier entries for the 17th century will be found among the bishop's transcripts.

[79] See Institutions, Nash, op. cit. ii, 201.

[80] Ibid.

[81] Ibid.

[82] Pat. 2 Mary, pt. i, m. 29.

[83] *Parl. Papers* (1872), xlvi, 14 d.

[1] Burton, *Bibl. of Worcs.* i, 102 ; Loc. and Personal Act, 7 Geo. IV, cap. 59.

tioned high roads. The remains of the old church of St. Andrew, which was superseded in 1825 [1a] by a new structure built near the site of the old one, are still to be seen on the west side of the Worcester and Stourport road. Near it is a cross. Two stone coffins were found on the site of the old church in 1834.[1b] The vicarage is on the opposite side of the road. Nearly opposite the church is the King's Head Inn, a fine half-timber building of two stories, the earliest part of which appears to date from the 15th century. King Charles is said to have stopped here after the battle of Worcester,[1c] and upon the plaster ceiling of the ground-floor room at the northern end of the building the royal arms, which still exist, were placed in memory of the event. Elsewhere, upon the same ceiling, is a small figure of

the stack. In the ground-floor room to the west of the hall is a fine stone fireplace, and the enriched ceiling is divided into compartments by the plastered beams supporting the joists of the floor above. The room over this has also a fine fireplace of stone. Much of the original woodwork still remains. The original staircase has been replaced by modern stairs, which occupy the greater part of the entrance hall. At the corner of the main street and the Holt Fleet road is a late 15th-century half-timber house of two stories with a fine spirally-fluted chimney shaft of brick. A little distance to the north of the cross-roads, upon the east side of the main street, is a half-timber house with a thatched roof, probably of a somewhat later date. The village abounds in half-timber work of the Elizabethan and Jacobean periods,

OMBERSLEY : THE DOWER HOUSE

a mermaid with comb and mirror and a design of roses and thistles. To the north of the church in a beautifully wooded park stands Ombersley Court, a building of the time of William and Mary, re-fronted with stone in the early 19th century. Upon the north side of the Holt Fleet road, a little to the west of the main street, is the house known as the Dower House, a good two-storied half-timber building of the early 17th century. It is of the normal central entrance-hall type with a fine fireplace at its western end ; the jambs are of stone, but the four-centred arch is of brick. The entrance is to the south of the fireplace, a small lobby being formed by

most of which has been kept in excellent repair. At Hadley, about a mile to the eastwards, there are also many good specimens of similar work. There is here an old-fashioned inn called 'The Bowling Green,' with a fine bowling green attached.

Suddington, Chatley Green and Hawford are districts to the south, Hadley is in the east, Uphampton, Oldfield, Northampton, Sytchampton, Dunhampton, Cornhampton, Brookhampton, Acton, Owlhill and Lineholt are to the north, and Boreley and Holtfleet are to the west. At Hawford there is a square timber-framed dovecot on a stone base, with a roof of four gables and a square open lantern. The lower

[1a] Prattinton Coll. (Soc. Antiq.). In 1814 an Act was passed for taking down the old church tower and steeple of Ombersley, erecting a new church, enlarging the churchyard, and for building a workhouse (Loc. and Personal Act, 54 Geo. III, cap. 218).

[1b] Prattinton Coll. (Soc. Antiq.).

[1c] Charles certainly passed through Ombersley, and it was here that Massey left him and rode away to Droitwich.

part is used as a coach-house, the pigeon-holes being on two sides in the upper part. There are also timber-framed dovecotes at Chapel Farm and at Pipstile Farm, Uphampton, and at Northampton, but the two latter are ruined. At Sytchhampton are several half-timber cottages and farm-houses. Acton Hall is an irregular half-timber and brick house. There is a square timber-framed dovecote. The nesting-holes, now brick and slate, were formerly wooden rails with small baskets. An inn on the main road near Acton is partly of half-timber and partly of brick, with false timbers painted on the brickwork.

The land rises from the valley of the Severn in the west to a height of 300 ft. above the ordnance datum at Lineholt Common on the north. The southern part of the parish is at about 100 ft. above ordnance datum.

permanent grass and 223 acres of woodland.[7] The subsoil is Keuper Sandstone, the soil various, chiefly a rich loam, producing crops of wheat, peas, beans and barley, fruit and potatoes. Agriculture is now the principal industry, but some women and girls were in the middle of the 19th century engaged in glove-making and slopwork for Worcester tradesmen.[8]

The Queen Dowager and the Duchess of Kent visited Ombersley in September 1843.[9]

Doctor Johnson visited Lord Sandys at Ombersley in 1774. He observes that the house was large and the hall a very noble room, and ' we were treated with great civility.' Piozzi relates that he heard Dr. Johnson protest that he never had quite so much as he wished of wall fruit except once in his life ' when we were all together at Ombersley.' [10]

OMBERSLEY : THE VILLAGE STREET

This parish gave its name to an ancient forest which had originally formed part of the great forest of Wyre.[2] Nash gives the boundaries of the forest of Ombersley.[3] This forest not being ancient demesne of the Crown was disafforested by the charter of Henry III of 1217,[4] but the actual disafforestation did not take place until 1229.[5] Though the parish is well wooded at the present day, there are no large tracts of woodland. An Inclosure Act for Ombersley was passed in 1814, and the award is dated 11 October 1827.[6] In 1905 Ombersley contained 3,291 acres of arable land, 3,082 acres of

Edward III in 1354 granted to the Abbot of Evesham a market on Mondays and a fair for four days at the feast of St. Barnabas (11 June) at Ombersley.[11] This grant was confirmed in 1467 by Edward IV.[12] The market has long been discontinued. It apparently was not held at the time of the Dissolution, as no mention of it is made in the valuation of the manor taken at that time. A pleasure fair was held until recently on 29 May, but has now been discontinued.

There was a prison at Ombersley in 1203.[13] It was one of the duties of the oxmen (*bovarii*) on the

[2] *V.C.H. Worcs.* ii, 316.
[3] *Hist. of Worcs.* Introd. p. lxviii.
[4] *V.C.H. Worcs.* ii, 315 ; *Rot. Lit. Claus.* (Rec. Com.), i, 359.
[5] *Cal. Close,* 1227–31, p. 220 ; *Cal. Chart. R.* 1226–57, p. 102.

[6] Loc. and Pers. Act, 54 Geo. III, cap. 227 ; *Blue Bk. Incl. Awards,* 191.
[7] Statistics from Bd. of Agric. (1905).
[8] Noake, *Guide to Worcs.* 292.
[9] Ibid.

[10] Boswell, *Life of Johnson* (ed. Bell), v, 455.
[11] Chart. R. 28 Edw. III, m. 4.
[12] *Cal. Pat.* 1467–77, p. 67.
[13] *Chron. de Evesham* (Rolls Ser.), 127.

manor of Ombersley to guard any thieves who might be taken on the manor.[14]

It was presented in 1612–13 that the tenants of the manor were bound to repair all the bridges standing in any highway in the manor. Two of these, called Hawford's Bridge and Wade Bridge, 'are now ruyned and not passable without great danger.'[15]

At Hadley Heath Common there is the site of a camp with entrenchments.[16] Near this camp were several mounds, which were levelled in 1815, when 'red earth' ware was discovered.[17] A prehistoric ringed palstave, now in the Worcester Museum, was dug up on Lineholt Common.[18]

The following place-names occur in the boundaries of Ombersley in 706: Lincumbe, Geofandene, Blacamore, Merbroc, Uffanheale.[19] Other place-names are Owood[20] (xvi cent.) ; Fowles,[21] Jerves, Redenhurst, Cutnull,[22] Vicars Park,[23] Suddington Orchard, Swirdland, Lilhalle, Linchford, Tapenhill, Knights Grove, Birchen Vallett in Linholt,[24] Wynnald[25] (xvii cent.).

Twelve *cassata* of land at OMBERSLEY, MANORS were granted to Abbot Ecgwine and the abbey of Evesham in 706 by Ethelward, *subregulus* of the Hwiccas, with the consent of King Coenred.[26] This grant was confirmed by Ceolred and Ethelbald, Kings of Mercia, and by King Offa.[27] The fate of Ombersley is not known during the troubled times in the middle of the 10th century, when Evesham Abbey so often changed hands, but in 976, when the monks were expelled for the second time by Alfhere, ealdorman of Mercia, Ombersley was given to Alfward, Alfhere's brother.[28] Subsequently the lands of Evesham Abbey were given to Earl Godwin in exchange for Towcester,[29] and evidently Ombersley thus passed into the hands of the earl, and the various grantees of the abbey after this time were unable to recover it.[30] It remained in Godwin's hands until redeemed by Abbot Brihtmar after long suit.[31]

The estate which the abbey of Evesham had at Ombersley in 1086 had been reckoned at 15 hides in the time of Edward the Confessor. Three of these hides were free of geld, but in ancient times, so it was said, the whole manor was assessed at only 3 hides.[32]

Free warren at Ombersley was granted in 1251 to the Abbot of Evesham,[33] and in 1275–6 it was presented at the assizes that he had made a new warren without licence.[34] Various improvements were made in the manor of Ombersley during the 13th and 14th centuries. Abbot Ralph (1214–29) made a fish stew at Lineholt and two other stews under the

court.[35] His successor, Abbot Thomas of Marlborough, asserted 2 carucates of land at Chattesley, having obtained the permission of Walter de Beauchamp, who had common at Chattesley.[36] John de Brokhampton (1282–1316) erected a room with a vault at Ombersley Manor,[37] and Abbot John Ombersley (1367–79) added a hall and two rooms, one in the west and one in the north, a stable outside the lower door and a small grange in the outer court. He also obtained licence from the king in 1376 to inclose 300 acres of land and water in the manor called the wood of Lineholt and to make a park there.[38] Abbot Roger Zatton (1379–1418) restored the fish-pond called Trylpole and mills at Ombersley, and rebuilt the dovecot, kitchen and chapel.[39] Abbot William de Bois died at Ombersley in 1367.[40] At the time of the surrender of Evesham Abbey the manor of Ombersley was bringing in the considerable revenue of £121 7s. 9¾d. to its owners.[41]

In 1546–7 the manor-house was leased for twenty-one years to Philip Brace of Doverdale, on the surrender of a lease for ninety-two years granted by the abbot in 1538. In the same year the manor was leased for the same period to Robert Constable.[41a] A thirty-one years' lease of the manor, after the expiration of Robert Constable's lease, was granted, probably by Queen Mary in 1554, to Sir John Bourne.[42] Queen Elizabeth leased it for twenty-one years in 1560 to William Garrard and others, but in 1562 they surrendered it to the Crown,[43] and in 1574–5 it was granted to John Hamond and John Hill for thirty-one years after the expiration of Sir John Bourne's lease.[44] In 1594 a lease for thirty-one years from Michaelmas 1619 was granted to Sir Samuel Sandys.[45] Sir Samuel had evidently obtained Hamond's lease, for in 1608 he was in possession of the manor, and his lease had still above forty years to run, and he expressed himself willing to renew it if the king wished.[46]

In 1610 Ombersley Manor formed part of the large estate granted by James I to his son Henry, Prince of Wales.[47] Prince Henry died in 1612, and in 1614 the manor was granted to Sir Samuel Sandys at a fee-farm rent of £26 19s. 3d.[48] Sir Samuel was the eldest son of Edwin Sandys, Bishop of Worcester, and afterwards Archbishop of York.[49] The manor was confirmed to

SANDYS of Ombersley, Lord Sandys. *Or a fesse dancetty between three crosslets fitchy gules.*

[14] *V.C.H. Worcs.* i, 274.
[15] Exch. Dep. East. 11 Jas. I, no. 3.
[16] Noake, op. cit. 293.
[17] *V.C.H. Worcs.* i, 220.
[18] Ibid. 195.
[19] Birch, *Cart. Sax.* i, 172.
[20] Chan. Proc. (Ser. 2), bdle. 188, no. 20.
[21] Exch. Dep. Hil. 4 Jas. I, no. 13.
[22] Ibid. East. 5 Jas. I, no. 9.
[23] Ibid. East. 9 Jas. I, no. 11.
[24] Pat. 11 Jas. I, pt. ix, no. 1.
[25] Nash, op. cit. i, 569.
[26] Birch, op. cit. i, 171 ; *Chron. de Evesham* (Rolls Ser.), 72 ; Haddan and Stubbs, *Councils*, 278.
[27] Birch, op. cit. i, 172–3. This

charter is a forgery (inform. from Mr. F. M. Stenton).
[28] *Chron. de Evesham* (Rolls Ser.), 79.
[29] *V.C.H. Worcs.* ii, 114. [30] Ibid.
[31] *Chron. de Evesham* (Rolls Ser.), 80–1.
[32] *V.C.H. Worcs.* i, 307.
[33] *Cal. Chart. R. 1226–57*, p. 364.
[34] *Hund. R.* (Rec. Com.), ii, 283 ; Assize R. 1026, m. 44 d.
[35] *Chron. de Evesham* (Rolls Ser.), 261.
[36] Ibid. 275. [37] Ibid. 288.
[38] Ibid. 300–1 ; Pat. 50 Edw. III, pt. i, m. 8. A licence for this inclosure had been obtained by the Abbot of Evesham in 1358 (*Cal. Pat. 1358–61*, p. 15).
[39] *Chron. de Evesham* (Rolls Ser.), 304.

[40] Ibid. 299.
[41] *Valor Eccl.* (Rec. Com.), iii, 249.
[41a] *L. and P. Hen. VIII*, xxi (2), pp. 439, 441.
[42] Exch. Spec. Com. 26 Eliz. no. 129 ; Pat. 17 Eliz. pt. i, m. 19.
[43] Pat. 2 Eliz. pt. xiii, m. 13.
[44] Ibid. 17 Eliz. pt. i, m. 19. John Talbot seems to have succeeded Sir John Bourne as lessee (Exch. Dep. Mich. 20 Jas. I, no. 28 ; East. 9 Jas. I, no. 11).
[45] Pat. 36 Eliz. pt. ii, m. 14 ; *Cal. S. P. Dom. 1591–4*, p. 513.
[46] *Cal. S. P. Dom. 1603–10*, p. 489
[47] Pat. 8 Jas. I, pt. xli.
[48] Ibid. 11 Jas. I, pt. ix, no. 1.
[49] Nash, op. cit. ii, 221.

Edwin son and heir of Sir Samuel by Letters Patent in April 1614,[50] in the lifetime of his father, who did not die until August 1623.[51] Edwin died in September 1623, and was succeeded by his son Samuel,[52] who died in 1685, when the manor passed to his eldest son Samuel.[53] Edwin, son of the latter, married Alice daughter of Sir James Rushout in 1694, when a settlement of the manor was made.[54] He died in 1699, before his father, and on the death of the latter in 1701 the manor of Ombersley passed to Samuel son of Edwin.[55] He was chancellor of the exchequer and one of the Lords of the Treasury in 1742–3, and was created Lord Sandys in December 1743.[56] He died in 1770, and was succeeded by his son Edwin.[57] He was M.P. for Droitwich 1747–54 and for Westminster 1762–70[57a] and Lord of the Admiralty in 1757. He died without issue at Ombersley Court in 1797, when the title became extinct. His estates passed to his niece, Mary daughter of Martin Sandys, fourth son of the first Lord Sandys.[58] Mary married Arthur Hill, second Marquess of Downshire, and shortly after the death of her husband, in June 1802, she was created Baroness Sandys of Ombersley, with remainder to her second, third, fourth and fifth sons respectively, with a final remainder to her eldest son, the Marquess of Downshire.[59] She died in 1836, and the manor of Ombersley descended with the title of Lord Sandys to her second son, Arthur Moyses William Hill. He was succeeded in 1860 by his next younger brother, Arthur Marcus Cecil Hill, who took the surname Sandys in 1861.[60] He died two years later, and the manor passed to his son Augustus Frederick Arthur Sandys, on whose death without issue in 1904 the estate passed to his brother Michael Edwin Marcus Lord Sandys, the present owner.[61]

The fee-farm rent payable by the owners of the manor from the site and demesne lands was granted in 1637–8 to James Duke of Lennox,[62] and in 1664 to Catherine queen consort of Charles II.[63] In 1670 the fee-farm rents belonging to the Crown were vested in trustees,[64] who sold the reversion after the death of Queen Catherine of the rent due from Ombersley Manor to Charles Lord St. John, Ralph Bucknall and others in July 1672.[65] Benjamin Bathurst and Elizabeth his wife made a conveyance of this rent in 1747[66]; in 1753 it belonged to James Brydges Marquess of Carnarvon.[67] It passed from him on his death in 1789 to his only daughter Anna Eliza, who married Richard Marquess of Buckingham.[68] Their son Richard Earl Temple was in possession of the fee-farm rent in 1818.[69]

A fishery and two weirs, one where the spring called Ombreswelle falls into the Severn and the other at the ford called Leverford, were included in Ethel-ward's grant of the manor in 706.[70] In 1086 there were a fishery and a half at Ombersley yielding 2,000 eels and two mills worth 8s.[71] Abbot Thomas of Marlborough in 1230–1 recovered into his own hands the mill of 'Haddeley' in Ombersley.[72] In 1291 two mills belonged to the abbot's manor of Ombersley.[73] Abbot Zatton (1379–1418) rebuilt the mills at Trylpole.[74] A mill called Pig Mill is mentioned in grants of the manor in 1574–5 and 1593–4.[75] In 1613 the mills called Squint Mill, Tirle Mill, and Pig Mill were granted to William Whitmore and others at a fee-farm rent of 7s. 4d.,[76] but they must have sold them afterwards to Edwin Sandys, for the three mills were included among his possessions at the time of his death.[77]

Watered as it is on all sides by rivers or brooks, Ombersley still has many mills. Winnall Mill, a corn-mill, is on the tributary of the Severn in the north-western corner of the parish, near Hampstall Ferry. Hadley Mill is at Hadley on Hadley Brook on the eastern border. New Mill on the Salwarpe is also on the eastern border. Turn Mill, probably the same as Trylpole Mill and Tirle Mill, is a corn-mill on a tributary of the Severn.

A part of a weir at Ombersley which Thomas Gugun had given him was granted by Absalon de Bevere to Marjory his daughter by an undated charter of the 13th century.[78] In 1348 William the fisherman of Ombersley gave to William ate Tolle of Salwarpe, clerk, all his land and tenements with a rent and fishery at Ombersley.[79] Richard de Hansforde, son and heir of Richard de Hansforde, in 1357–8 granted to Sir William Rome of Ombersley, chaplain, a portion of his weir in Ombersley, for which he paid a yearly rent to the Abbot of Evesham.[80]

An interesting survey of the mansion-house of Ombersley was taken in 1584.[81] There was a hall built of timber and covered with tile, a house at the south end of the hall, a room on the east of the hall adjoining the outer court, an old chapel built of stone with a timber roof covered with tiles, and a vaulted room beneath, rooms on the south and east of the chapel, and a room on the north of the hall. All this part of the manor was considered fit to remain standing, though the repairs would be costly, but a house on the east of the court with a passage built upon posts leading from it to the hall was in a state of ruin past repair.[82] The present mansion, Ombersley Court, was built by the first Lord Sandys.[83]

The lord of the manor had free warren in the manor, in Oldfield, in the Haye by Trehampton, in the Winyards, in Birchin Lane, in Lineholt, and in the Heath by Woodham field.[84] In 1752 an Act was passed to extinguish the right of the lord of the manor of Ombersley of keeping a warren on Linall

[50] Pat. 12 Jas. I, pt. i, no. 6.
[51] Nash, op. cit. ii, 222 ; Chan. Inq. p.m. (Ser. 2), ccccv, 154.
[52] Chan. Inq. p.m. (Ser. 2), ccccv, 154.
[53] Nash, op. cit. ii, 221.
[54] Feet of F. Div. Co. Mich. 6 Will. and Mary.
[55] G.E.C. Complete Peerage, vii, 54 ; Recov. R. East. 11 Geo. I, rot. 150.
[56] G.E.C. loc. cit.
[57] Ibid. ; Recov. R. Mich. 9 Geo. III, rot. 141.
[57a] Ret. of Members of Parl. ii, under date.
[58] G.E.C. loc. cit.
[59] G.E.C. op. cit. vii, 55.
[60] Ibid.
[61] Burke, Peerage.
[62] Pat. 13 Chas. I, pt. xiii.
[63] Ibid. 15 Chas. I, pt. xiv, no. 1.
[64] Palmer's Indices (P.R.O.), lxxiii, fol. 83 ; see also Pat. 22 Chas. II, pt. ii (1st roll).
[65] Close, 24 Chas. II, pt. xii, m. 10.
[66] Recov. R. East. 20 Geo. II, rot. 145.
[67] Ibid. Hil. 26 Geo. II, rot. 472.
[68] G.E.C. Complete Peerage, ii, 206.
[69] Recov. R. East. 58 Geo. III, rot. 189.
[70] Birch, op. cit. i, 171.
[71] V.C.H. Worcs. i, 307.
[72] Chron. de Evesham (Rolls Ser.), 275.
[73] Pope Nich. Tax. (Rec. Com.), 229.
[74] Ibid. 304.
[75] Pat. 17 Eliz. pt. i, m. 19 ; 36 Eliz. pt. ii, m. 14.
[76] Ibid. 10 Jas. I, pt. xxv, no. 2.
[77] W. and L. Inq. p.m. xl, 49 ; Exch. Dep. East. 11 Jas. I, no. 3.
[78] Anct. D. (P.R.O.), B. 2671.
[79] Ibid. 2692.   [80] Ibid. 2673.
[81] Exch. Spec. Com. 26 Eliz. no. 2480
[82] Ibid.
[83] Noake, op. cit. 292.
[84] Exch. Dep. East. 11 Jas. I, no. 3.

Ombersley : Cross near the Old Church

Common, the Birchin Valley and the Lyth, and for securing to him the rent then paid for the warren, and for annexing Birchin Valley to several ancient copyholds in the manor.[85]

Rents called Honysilver and Hundred silver were due by his tenants to the lord of the manor of Ombersley.[86] The latter rent was a composition paid by the tenants at Ombersley for exemption from suit at the Abbot of Evesham's distant hundred of Blackenhurst, to which Ombersley belonged until the middle of the 18th century.[87]

Habington gives a mythical origin of the family and manor of *ACTON*,[88] but the earliest authentic reference is to Philip de Acton, who appears to have been a landowner in Worcestershire in 1175–6.[89] Ellis de Acton is given as a juror in 1219, and an Ellis de Acton assigned rent which he held in Ombersley to the support of a chaplain in a certain chapel there. In 1274–5 Iseult widow of Ellis de Acton son of Ellis mentioned above sued John de Acton, son of the younger Ellis,[90] for a third of this rent, which she claimed

ACTON of Acton. *Or three bars wavy gules.*

as dower. It appeared that Ellis the son had never held the rent, but had merely acted as collector for his father, so that Iseult's claim was void.[91] In 1342 John de Acton and Isabel his wife settled the manor of Acton upon themselves with reversion to their son Walter and his heirs male, with contingent remainders in tail-male to their sons Edmund, William and Simon.[92] Richard de Acton and Isabel his wife, to whom there was a monument in the old church of Ombersley,[93] may have owned the manor of Acton. In 1513 an award was made by the Abbot of Evesham in termination of a dispute which had arisen between Francis Acton and the two daughters of Walter Acton as to the manor of Acton. The abbot awarded the manor, which had descended to Walter from William Acton, probably his father,[94] to the co-heirs, Isabel wife of Thomas Broughton of Belbroughton, and Joyce Acton.[95] Joyce afterwards married Thomas Barneby, and they were dealing with the manor in 1547–8,[96] and in 1554–5 they and Richard Barneby their son conveyed half the manor to Ellis Evans and others [97] for some settlement. Thomas Barneby was dead before 1578, and his widow Joyce conveyed the moiety of the manor to Thomas Pury.[98] Pury may have been a

trustee for her son Charles, to whom she gave part of the manor.[99] Charles gave this estate to his eldest brother Richard,[100] evidently before 1581, for Richard was then dealing with the manor.[1] It passed from him to his son William,[2] who conveyed it in 1602 to Abel Gower and John Sheldon.[3] They were probably trustees for some settlement, for Sir William Barneby was dealing with the manor in 1624,[4] and his son John sold it in 1649 to Richard Bourne the elder.[5]

Part of the other moiety of the manor appears to have been alienated by Thomas Broughton, Isabel Acton's first husband, to Richard Bourne the elder.[6] Walter Blount, the second husband of Isabel, died in 1561, and she died in the following year.[7] On their tomb in Astley Church are two sons and five daughters,[8] who apparently all died young except the youngest daughter Margery, who is the only child of Walter Blount mentioned in the Worcester Visitation of 1569. She is there given as wife of Roger Stamford,[9] but she also must have died without issue, for the estate retained in this family passed to Robert Blount, who was presumably Walter's brother.[10] Robert sold part of the manor to Thomas Clent about 1572, and part of it to James Nash.[11]

Richard Bourne seems to have acquired the whole manor before 1663, when he conveyed it to Robert Wylde and others.[12] Richard's son Richard, who married Anne daughter of Robert Wylde, died at about this time,[13] and on the death of his father in 1669 [14] the estate passed to John son of the younger Richard.[15] John conveyed the manor of Acton in 1678 to Robert Wylde and Arthur Charlett,[16] possibly on the occasion of his marriage with Elizabeth daughter of Arthur Charlett.[17] Elizabeth Bourne, widow, and Richard Bourne, who conveyed the manor in 1721 to Allen Cliffe and other trustees,[18] were probably the widow and son of John Bourne. Richard Bourne of Acton was Sheriff of Worcestershire in 1730.[19] It was probably this Richard who died in 1754 and was buried in Ombersley Church.[20] Francis Bourne of Acton, whose relationship to Richard is not known, changed his name to Page about 1741 in accordance with the will of his grand-uncle Sir Francis Page.[21] He held the manor in 1782 [22] and died unmarried in 1803.[23] In 1868 Acton Hall belonged to T. Amphlett,[24] and it is now the property of Mr. Thomas Edward Amphlett.

Richard son of Maurice de Ombersley held half a knight's fee of the Abbot of Evesham in 1166.[25] In 1281–2 Simon de Ombersley gave John de Grafton two-thirds of a messuage and 2 carucates of land which Simon held, and the reversion of a third of the

[85] Burton, *Bibl. of Worcs.* i, 52 ; Priv. Act, 25 Geo. II, cap. 22.

[86] Dugdale, *Mon. Angl.* ii, 45 ; Pat. 17 Eliz. pt. i, m. 19 ; 12 Jas. I, pt. i, no. 6.

[87] Burton, op. cit. i, 55.

[88] op. cit. ii, 226.

[89] *Pipe R. 22 Hen. II* (Pipe R. Soc.), 39.

[90] Assize R. 1025, m. 1.

[91] Ibid. 1026, m. 11.

[92] Feet of F. Worcs. East. 16 Edw. III.

[93] Habington, op. cit. ii, 227.

[94] *Visit. of Worcs.* 1569 (Harl. Soc. xxvii), 3. This William may have been the son of Richard and Isabel (ibid.).

[95] Deed quoted in Prattinton Coll. (Soc. Antiq.).

[96] Feet of F. Div. Co. Mich. 1 Edw. VI.

[97] Ibid. Worcs. 1 & 2 Phil. and Mary.

[98] Com. Pleas D. Enr. East. 20 Eliz. m. 37.

[99] Exch. Dep. Hil. 38 Eliz. no. 3.

[100] Ibid.

[1] Feet of F. Div. Co. East. 23 Eliz.

[2] Metcalfe, *Visit. of Worcs.* 1682–3, p. 8.

[3] Feet of F. Worcs. Mich. 44 & 45 Eliz.

[4] Recov. R. Mich. 22 Jas. I, rot. 92.

[5] Feet of F. Worcs. Mich. 1649 ; Metcalfe, loc. cit.

[6] Exch. Dep. Hil. 38 Eliz. no. 3.

[7] Nash, op. cit. i, 43. [8] Ibid.

[9] op. cit. (Harl. Soc. xxvii), 19.

[10] Ibid. ; Exch. Dep. Hil. 38 Eliz. no. 3.

[11] Exch. Dep. Hil. 38 Eliz. no. 3.

[12] Feet of F. Worcs. Trin. 15 Chas. II.

[13] Metcalfe, op. cit. 19.

[14] Nash, op. cit. ii, 219.

[15] Ibid.

[16] Feet of F. Worcs. Mich. 30 Chas. II.

[17] Metcalfe, loc. cit.

[18] Feet of F. Worcs. Mich. 8 Geo. I.

[19] P.R.O. *List of Sheriffs*, 159.

[20] Nash, op. cit. ii, 219.

[21] *Dict. Nat. Biog.* under Sir Francis Page.

[22] Nash, op. cit. ii, 218.

[23] *Dict. Nat. Biog.* under Sir Francis Page.

[24] Noake, op. cit. 293.

[25] *Red Bk. of Exch.* (Rolls Ser.), 302.

tenement which Peter de Lench and Margaret his wife held of Simon's inheritance. John agreed to let Simon and his wife Margaret hold the two parts of the tenement for their lives with reversion to John.[26] In 1349–50 Sir John, lord of Grafton, granted to John Searle, rector of Grafton, and others certain of his manors and lands including the manor of Ombersley,[27] and in 1350 Thomas de Beauchamp Earl of Warwick granted land and rent in Evesham and Ombersley held for life by Roger de Grafton to the Abbot and convent of Evesham to find chantries and alms and other pious works in their abbey as he should ordain.[28] This estate, which is called the 'manor of Oversudington' within the manor of Ombersley, had come into the earl's hands by surrender.[29]

CHURCH

The church of *ST. ANDREW* consists of a chancel 30 ft. by 20 ft. with vestries north and south of it, nave 69 ft. by 21 ft.. north and south aisles 15 ft. wide and a

rises an octagonal spire strengthened by flying buttresses at the angles.

The stone and marble font is a recent gift replacing the mean font dating from 1828 which now stands in the mortuary chapel. The pulpit and quire seats are also modern, but the box pews date from 1828.

The remaining portion of the former church includes about two-thirds of the chancel and measures 29 ft. by 21½ ft. inside. It is of late 13th-century date with the exception of the east wall, which was probably rebuilt in the 18th century. The east window, which was square, is now filled in. In each side wall are two trefoiled lancets with detached shafts having moulded capitals and bases to the internal jambs, supporting rear arches, moulded in each case with a filleted bowtel. Their labels are returned as a string-course on each wall, while at the level of their sills is a second string-course, which leaps the heads of the sedilia and piscina in the south wall and

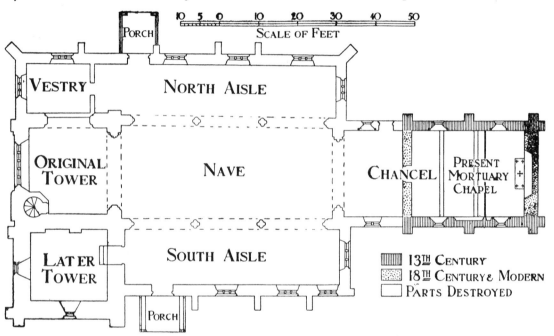

PLAN OF OMBERSLEY OLD CHURCH (based on Prattinton's plan)

western tower 12 ft. square. These measurements are all internal. The building was erected by Rickman in 1825 for the Marchioness of Downshire, near the site of the former church, which was pulled down with the exception of the eastern portion of the chancel, which now serves as a mortuary chapel to the family of Lord Sandys.

The new building is of the most florid 14th-century style and is ashlar faced. The nave has a clearstory of four two-light windows on each side, and the arcades of four bays are divided by a gallery which runs round the north, west and south sides of the church. The east window of the chancel is of four lights, and in each side wall are four three-light windows, the buttresses between them having crocketed pinnacles. The roofs of the nave and chancel are stone vaulted, but those of the aisles are flat. The tower is three stages high with an embattled parapet and angle pinnacles. Above this

forms their labels. On the north side the sill-string rises as though over a square-headed tomb recess, but the wall is filled in flush. The piscina has a trefoiled head and the basin is in the form of a moulded bell capital. The three sedilia are also trefoiled. The east and west jambs have detached shafts with moulded bases and capitals. The capitals between the seats rest on diminishing corbels, which are in turn supported on carved human heads. The head appears to have been dropped in a later alteration or rebuilding. The inclosing west wall with its doorway is modern, and the ceiling is plastered. Outside the walls are almost entirely hidden by ivy. They are finished with a modern embattled parapet and are supported on either side by three buttresses, with two on the east wall.

A 17th-century oak altar table still stands against the east wall. It has carved baluster legs and around the top rail is the text 'Whosoever shall eat this

[26] Feet of F. Worcs. 10 Edw. I, no. 24.   [27] Add. MS. 28024, fol. 135a.   [28] Cal. Pat. 1348–50, p. 565.   [29] Ibid. 1350–4, p. 60.

bread and drink this cup of the Lord unworthily shall be guilty of the Body and Blood of the Lord.' There are several monuments and gravestones to members of the Sandys family, all of 17th or 18th-century date.

According to Dr. Prattinton the nave of the old church was three bays long with north and south aisles and arcades resting on piers of quatrefoil plan. The main roof was arched and panelled in oak. The tower apparently stood at the west end of the nave, opening to it by a lofty arch with a respond of clustered shafts on the north. It appears, however, to have been subsequently rebuilt at the west end of the south aisle. The nave also possessed north and south porches.

In the churchyard is a tall cross raised on a platform of four steps; the 15th-century square base is moulded and its faces are panelled with quatrefoils.

1630, a stand paten dated 1704 with the hall mark of 1697 and two flagons dated 1685, and having the hall mark of 1682.

The registers before 1812 are as follows : (i) baptisms 1574 to 1674, burials 1574 to 1675 and marriages 1574 to 1676 (the entries from 1649 to 1660 being entered from 'hearsay' by Edward Pilkington, 'the routed vicar') ; (ii) baptisms and burials 1676 to 1752 and marriages 1677 to 1752 ; (iii) baptisms and burials 1753 to 1812 ; (iv) marriages 1754 to 1789 ; (v) marriages 1789 to 1812.

ADVOWSON It would seem that originally the advowson of the church of Ombersley belonged to the Bishops of Worcester, for in 1207, in the settlement of the dispute between the bishop and the Abbot of Evesham as to the churches of the Vale of Evesham, the bishop agreed to give the church of Ombersley to the

THE SANDYS MAUSOLEUM, OMBERSLEY OLD CHURCH

The shaft is octagonal, chamfered out to the square above and below, and supports a red sandstone head, surmounted by a hollow-sided pyram'd. The cornice and the pyramid are 18th-century work and the lower part of the head probably 17th-century. A dial is set on the south face.

The six bells were brought from the old church, but the second, fourth and the tenor were recast by John Rudhall before the rehanging in 1828. The treble is by Henry Bagley and has fifteen bronze Charles I coins in the shoulder and mouth of the bell ; the third and fifth are dated 1628, the former with Matthew Bagley's name as the founder.

The communion plate consists of a silver Elizabethan cup and cover paten of 1571, a silver-gilt cup of

abbot.[30] Ranulph, Abbot of Evesham (1214–29), converted to the use of the poor and the convent an ancient pension of 60s. from the church which his predecessors had been accustomed to bestow upon their kinsmen and clerks.[31] In 1248 Pope Innocent IV granted an indulgence to Theodisius, canon of Beauvais, the pope's grand-nephew, to serve by fit vicars his church of Ombersley and any other benefices which he might hold or in future obtain, and to receive all the benefits and profits of such benefices ; it also exempted him from being compelled to take orders or make residence on these benefices.[32] In December 1269 the church of Ombersley was consecrated by the bishop in honour of St. Andrew.[33] It was committed by the bishop in 1283 to William de Cherinton, as

[30] *V.C.H. Worcs.* ii, 119; *Chron. de Evesham* (Rolls Ser.), 223.

[31] *Chron. de Evesham* (Rolls Ser.), 260.

[32] *Reg. G. Giffard* (Worcs. Hist. Soc.), 107. [33] Ibid. 30.

the bishop's sequestrator, until he should be certain of the death of the rector,[34] but Theodisius was still rector, and trouble arose between him and William in 1285.[35] The bishop declared in the following year that neither by authority of the pope, nor of the Archbishop of Canterbury, nor of the bishop himself, was William instituted to the church of Ombersley, nor by authority of the bishop had he any title to it,[36] and Theodisius was restored to his possession.[37] Cherinton became Abbot of Evesham in 1317 and immediately endeavoured to get the church of Ombersley appropriated to the abbey.[38] The abbot pleaded the poverty of his house owing to excessive taxation and calls on its hospitality due to its situation near the public way,[39] but it was not until 1326 that licence was finally given for him to appropriate the church.[40] For this privilege he had to pay 30s. a year to the Bishops of Worcester.[41] The vicarage was ordained in 1327 and a portion of the tithes assigned to the vicar.[42] William de Cherinton bequeathed the churches of Ombersley and Badby (Northants) in 1344 to his prior and convent to dispose of as might seem best to them. In accordance with the will of the abbot it was ordained in full chapter at Christmas 1344, that at Ascensiontide and at the feast of St. Peter ad Vincula, £24 from these churches should be distributed between the prior and monks.[43] The advowson remained with the Abbot and convent of Evesham until the Dissolution,[44] when it passed to the Crown. It was granted in 1558 to Richard Bishop of Worcester, who presented in that year.[45] The rectory and church were included in Robert Constable's and Sir John Bourne's leases of the manor,[46] and the advowson was probably also included, for Sir John's successor as lessee, John Talbot, evidently held it, as the presentation was made in 1587 by the grantees of his executors.[47] The rectory and advowson were granted in 1609 at a fee-farm rent of £32 18s. 4d. to Francis Philipps and Richard Moore,[48] but they sold it a month later to Thomas Coventry, Thomas Sandys and others.[49] They were probably trustees for Sir Samuel Sandys, to whom the

advowson and rectory passed at about this time.[50] The subsequent descent of the advowson and rectory is the same as that of the manor.[51]

The fee-farm rent of £32 18s. 4d. from the rectory of Ombersley was granted in 1613–14 to Queen Anne, consort of James I, for life,[52] and in 1627 to Queen Henrietta Maria.[53] In 1675–6 it was sold by the Crown to Sir Walter Wrottesley, Richard Congrave and John Gifford.[54]

There is a Congregational church in the town, opened in 1823.

CHARITIES In 1768 John Amphlett by his will gave £30 in trust for the poor. This was augmented in 1773 by a legacy of £100 under the will of Thomas Amphlett. These legacies were secured on Southall Farm, part of the Westwood Estate, in respect of which an annuity of £5 17s. is paid, and applied in the distribution of tickets on tradesmen of the value of 10s. 6d. each.

A further sum of 10s. is applied with these charities as interest on a further sum of £20 on deposit in the Post Office Savings Bank. This is understood to be a legacy under the will of another John Amphlett.

The Church Estate, the origin of which is not precisely known, consists of a house and shop, twelve cottages, 1 a. 2 r. let in allotments, and a building known as the Parish Institute, bringing in a total gross income of £88 a year, which is applied to church expenses.

Lloyd's Charity School, founded by Richard Lloyd by deed, 1723, is regulated by a scheme made under the Endowed School Acts of 7 July 1874, whereby the charities of Thomas Clent and others, recorded on the church table as having been given for the benefit of the poor, were directed to be applied for the advancement of education.

In addition to the schools and land, a sum of £3,499 6s. 5d. consols, producing £87 9s. 8d. yearly, is held by the official trustees as part of the endowment.[55]

OVERBURY

Uferabyrig, Uferebreodun, Uferebiri (ix cent.) ; Uverabreodun (x cent.) ; Ovreberie (xi cent.) ; Werebyri (xii cent.) ; Uverbyri (xiii cent.).

The parish of Overbury lies in the south of the county. Habington in his survey describes it as ' seated at the foote of Breadon Hill in a beautiful vale, and the extreme southe of our shyre, in so muche as three of her chappelles, being Tedington, Aulston, and Washbourn, are severed from the continent of our shyre by the county of Gloucester.'[1] The Carrant Brook, mentioned by this name in a

9th-century charter,[2] forms the southern boundary of Overbury, separating it from Teddington. This stream formerly supplied the power for paper, silk and corn-mills.

The area of the parish, exclusive of Little Washbourne and Alstone, is 2,817 acres.[3] The village lies at about 200 ft. above the ordnance datum. To the north and west the land rises rapidly to Bredon and Conderton Hills, the northern border of the parish being at a height of 900 ft. above the ordnance datum. The soil varies. The southern part of the

[34] *Reg. G. Giffard* (Worcs. Hist. Soc.), 204.
[35] Ibid. 264.
[36] Ibid. 284.
[37] Ibid. 299.
[38] *Cal. Papal Letters*, ii, 148.
[39] Worc. Epis. Reg. Cobham (1317–27), fol. 112 d.
[40] *Cal. Pat.* 1324–7, p. 256 ; *Cal. Papal Letters*, ii, 397.
[41] Worc. Epis. Reg. Wulstan de Bransford (1339–49), fol. 20 f.

[42] Ibid. Cobham (1317–27), fol. 124 d.; Nash, op. cit. ii, 226.
[43] Dugdale, *Mon. Angl.* ii, 31.
[44] *Valor Eccl.* (Rec. Com.), iii, 253 ; Nash, op. cit. ii, 220.
[45] Nash, loc. cit. ; Pat. 5 & 6 Phil. and Mary, pt. ii, m. 30.
[46] *L. and P. Hen. VIII*, xxi (2), p. 441 ; Pat. 17 Eliz. pt. i, m. 19.
[47] Nash, op. cit. ii, 220.
[48] Pat. 7 Jas. I, pt. ix, no. 12.
[49] Recov. R. D. Enr. Trin. 7 Jas. I, m. 9.

[50] Exch. Dep. East. 11 Jas. I, no. 23.
[51] Inst. Bks. (P.R.O.).
[52] Pat. 11 Jas. I, pt. xiii.
[53] Ibid. 2 Chas. I, pt. iv.
[54] Ibid. 27 Chas. II, pt. v.
[55] See 'Schools,' *V.C.H. Worcs.* iv.
[1] op. cit. ii, 229.
[2] Heming, *Chartul.* (ed. Hearne), 456.
[3] Overbury itself contains 1,271 acres, Conderton 799 acres, and Teddington 747 acres.

OMBERSLEY OLD CHURCH : THE SOUTH WALL OF THE CHANCEL

OVERBURY CHURCH : THE NAVE LOOKING EAST

parish is on the Lower Lias and the northern on Inferior Oolite, the chief crops being wheat, oats, barley and roots. The inhabitants are chiefly employed in agriculture. In the middle of the 19th century some of the women were employed in glove-sewing.[4]

The village of Overbury lies on the Tewkesbury and Evesham high road at the foot of Bredon Hill. The church stands near the centre of the village, and on its north side standing in its park is Overbury Court, the seat of Sir Richard Biddulph Martin, bart., J.P. The house is of the early 18th century with modern additions. The cottages which compose the village have been for the most part rebuilt with great taste and judgement by the present lord of the manor. The post office, on the south side of the Bredon road, is an old cottage added to and enlarged in half-timber from the designs of the late Mr. Norman Shaw. On the north side of the same road, to the east of the church, is a pair of stone cottages, with a four-centred entrance gateway upon which is carved 'E.R. I.R. 1639.' Upon the road which leads northward up the side of Bredon Hill, parallel with the eastern boundary of the grounds of Overbury Court, are many houses and cottages, none, however, architecturally of any importance.

At the hamlet of Conderton, to the eastward of the village of Overbury, is Conderton Manor, an H-shaped Carolean house of stone, two stories in height, with an attic in the roof. Some early 18th-century panelling and a staircase of oak with twisted balusters remain, but the house has been much restored and modernized. It is now the residence of Mrs. Franklin.

The hamlet of Teddington lies to the south of Overbury on the southern side of the high road from Tewkesbury to Stow-on-the-Wold. At the point where this road crosses that from Evesham to Cheltenham and meets Crashmore Lane leading north to Overbury village stands an ancient guide-post of stone called Teddington Hands,[5] bearing the inscription :

' Edmund Attwood,[6] of the Vine Tree,
    At the first time erected me,
    And freely he did this bestow
    Strange travellers the way to show ;
    Ten generations passed and gone,
    Repaired by Alice Attwood of Teddington,
                            August 10th 1876.'

The village is situated on a branch road from the Evesham and Cheltenham road at about 100 ft. above the ordnance datum, and the church stands on rising ground to the south of the road along which the cottages are grouped. To the south the land rises abruptly to Oxenton Hill, which is just over the southern boundary. The Tirle Brook flows through the west of the hamlet.

Little Washbourne is a small village to the north of the road from Tewkesbury to Stow-on-the-Wold, to the east of Teddington. It is still a chapelry of Overbury, but was transferred to Gloucestershire for Parliamentary purposes in 1832,[7] and for all purposes in 1844.[8] The chapel of Little Washbourne now stands in the orchard of a farm which with one or two cottages comprises the entire hamlet.

The village of Alstone, which became part of Gloucestershire at the same date, is south-west of Little Washbourne. On the north side of Alstone Church is a fine L-shaped half-timber farm-house of the 15th century, and there are several stone-built cottages of 17th-century date in the village.

On Conderton Hill to the north of the village of Conderton is a small oval camp, near which Roman remains have been found. Fragments of Roman pottery and coins have been picked up in the arable fields near Overbury and Conderton, and it is probable that there was a villa here.[9]

An Inclosure Act for Overbury was passed in 1811,[10] and the award is dated 29 March 1815.[11]

Among the place-names are Butthay, Stanthall, Berry Furlong,[12] Lower Meron[13] (xvii cent.).

Ceolwulf II, King of Mercia, gave MANORS OVERBURY in 875 to the monks of Worcester,[14] who in 1086 held Overbury with Pendock,[15] where there were 6 hides that paid geld.[16] The manor was confirmed to the prior and convent in 1148 by Simon Bishop of Worcester.[17] In 1240 there was a curia with 3 carucates of land.[18] The manor remained with the priory until the Dissolution in 1540.[19] It was granted to the Dean and Chapter of Worcester in 1542[20] and confirmed to them in 1609.[21] The manor was sold in 1652 by the commissioners for the sale of church lands to William Horton, Henry Smith and Anthony Dickins,[22] the site and warren of the manor having been sold in the previous year to Giles Parsons.[23] At the Restoration it was recovered by the dean and chapter, and confirmed to them in 1692–3.[24] In 1859 the lands of the dean and chapter were taken over by the Ecclesiastical Commissioners,[25] now lords of the manor.[26]

The Parsons family held the manor under lease from the dean and chapter from 1641.[27] William Parsons, the last survivor of the family, died in 1714, leaving an only daughter Mary, an infant, who married in 1735 William Bund. William Parsons was the last life in the lease

PARSONS. *Azure a cheveron ermine between three trefoils argent.*

[4] Noake, *Guide to Worcs.* 294.
[5] In 1789 an Act was passed for amending and widening the road leading from Cross Hands in Teddington Field to the London turnpike road between Evesham and Pershore (Local and Personal Act, 29 Geo. III, cap. 102).
[6] The Attwoods held the manor of Teddington by lease from the Dean and Chapter of Worcester in the 17th century.
[7] Stat. 2 & 3 Will. IV, cap. 64.
[8] Stat. 7 & 8 Vict. cap. 61.
[9] *V.C.H. Worcs.* i, 218.

[10] Priv. Act, 51 Geo. III, cap. 5 (not printed).
[11] *Blue Bk. Incl. Awards*, 191.
[12] Close, 1650, pt. xxxiii, no. 18.
[13] Ibid. 1651, pt. liii, no. 35.
[14] Heming, op. cit. 331 ; Birch, *Cart. Sax.* ii, 160. The bounds of the land are given in this charter. [15] Now a separate parish.
[16] *V.C.H. Worcs.* i, 295a.
[17] Thomas, *Surv. of Worc. Cath.* App. no. 18.
[18] Hale, *Reg. of Worc. Priory* (Camd. Soc.), 74a.

[19] *V.C.H. Worcs.* ii, 111 ; *Valor Eccl.* (Rec. Com.), iii, 222.
[20] *L. and P. Hen. VIII*, xvii, g. 71 (29) ; Pat. 33 Hen. VIII, pt. v, m. 19.
[21] Pat. 6 Jas. I, pt. xii, no. 2.
[22] Close, 1652, pt. i, no. 1.
[23] Ibid. 1651, pt. liii, no. 35.
[24] Pat. 4 Will. and Mary, pt. i, no. 6.
[25] *Lond. Gaz.* 16 Dec. 1859, p. 4757 ; Stat. 31 & 32 Vict. cap. 19.
[26] Information supplied by the Ecclesiastical Commissioners.
[27] Close, 1651, pt. liii, no. 35.

from the dean and chapter, and at his death it was not renewed. A new lease was then granted to John Martin, a banker, who built at Overbury a house which was burnt down in 1735. A few years afterwards a second house, called Overbury Court,[28] was built, and is now occupied by his descendant, Sir Richard Biddulph Martin, who was created a baronet in 1905.[29]

MARTIN of Overbury, baronet. *Paly erminois and azure a chief engrailed gules with three martlets argent therein.*

Free warren in the manor of Overbury was granted to the Prior of Worcester in 1256,[30] and confirmed by Edward III in 1355[31] and by Richard II.[32] The warren was sold by the Parliamentary Commissioners to Giles Parsons in 1651.[33]

CONDERTON[33a] (Cantuaretun, ix cent.; Cantertun, xii cent.; Kanterton, Canterton, xiii cent.) was granted in 875 with the manor of Overbury to the church of Worcester by King Ceolwulf.[34] It was confirmed to the monks in 1148 by Bishop Simon.[35] In 1212 Ralph Prior of Worcester gave to Godfrey son of Stephen de Canterton half a hide of land which Stephen his father had held, for the rent of a mark yearly at the four terms.[36] In 1220–1 Peter son of Peter and Emma de Bellewe (Bella Aqua) recovered half a hide of land here against Richard le Scot and his wife Alice.[37] Peter son of Peter was in possession in 1240, when he paid 16*d.* four times a year to the prior for the estate.[38]

By an undated charter Walter de Bradewell gave to William de Fescamp all his land in Conderton, saving to the Prior of Worcester a rent of a mark at the four terms and to Walter and his heirs a rent of 20*s.* 8*d.*[39] William de Fescamp was holding the estate, half a hide, of the prior in 1240.[40] It was possibly the rent reserved by Walter in the above-mentioned grant which was given by him to William de Aqua, whose widow Margery gave it to the almoner of the priory of Worcester.[41] By an undated charter William Herun gave to the prior and convent 1¼ acres of land in Conderton in exchange for a place called the Chapel Heye in Conderton.[42] The prior obtained further grants of land in Conderton in 1322.[43]

Conderton was probably always part of the manor of Overbury, and in 1652, when the latter was sold

by the Parliamentary Commissioners, it was called the manor of Overbury and Conderton.[44]

In 780 Offa, King of Mercia, gave 5 'manses' at *TEDDINGTON* (Teottingtun, viii cent.; Tidinctune, Tidantun, x cent.; Teodintun, Theotinctun, Teotintune, xi cent.; Tedinton, xiii cent.) to the monastery of Bredon.[45] The possessions of the monastery afterwards passed to the see of Worcester,[46] but this manor was taken from the church by Beorhtwulf, King of Mercia, about 831. Bishop Eadberht (Heaberht) went to Tamworth and at Easter 840 proved his right to the manor before the king and the assembled nobles, and the land was restored to him.[47] It was confirmed to the monks in King Edgar's famous charter of 964 granting the hundred of Oswaldslow to the church of Worcester.[48] In 969 Oswald, Bishop of Worcester, granted land there to one Osulf and to his two children, and after them to his wife Eadleofu and her two brethren.[49] In 977 he leased three 'manses' at Teddington to one Eadric for three lives,[50] and eight years later the same Eadric received a further grant of 5 'manses' for three lives.[51] In the time of Edward the Confessor one Toki, a rich and powerful minister of the king, left by his will 3 hides in Teddington and Alstone to Ealdred, Bishop of Worcester, but his son Aki,[51a] also a powerful servant of the king, claimed them as his hereditary possession, and endeavoured to set the will aside. Finally, with the consent of the 'great men,' Aki gave up the property, and in return for 8 marks of gold confirmed the possession of it to the bishop, who made it over to the monks.[52] At the same time the bishop freed it from all services to the episcopal vill of Bredon, to which it was said to have belonged in ancient times, though no man then living could remember it.[53] In 1086, however, these 3 hides were still held by the monks of the bishop's manor of Bredon.[54]

In 1240 William de Godeshalve held a virgate in this manor freely for the service of going bail in the county of Gloucester for the prior's men of Teddington and Alstone wherever they should be attached. The lord of Oxenton (a manor in Gloucestershire near Teddington) from ancient times received a cart-load of hay yearly from the meadow of Teddington in exchange for an undertaking to protect the manor in time of war.[55]

In 1256 the prior obtained a grant of free warren here, and this was confirmed in 1355.[56]

The subsequent history of this manor is the same as that of others belonging to the priory. On the

---

[28] Nash, op. cit. ii, 235.
[29] Burke, *Peerage.*
[30] *Cal. Pat.* 1354–8, p. 266.
[31] Ibid.
[32] *Cal. Rot. Chart. et Inq. a.q.d.* (Rec. Com.), 192.
[33] Close, 1651, pt. liii, no. 35.
[33a] Mr. F. M. Stenton points out that a most interesting fact in connexion with this place is its name, which means, the town of the Kent-people (cf. Canterbury). It thus proves that before 875 a settlement of Kentishmen had already been established in this distant part of England.
[34] Heming, op. cit. 331; Birch, op. cit. ii, 160.
[35] Thomas, op. cit. App. 18.
[36] Prattinton Coll. (Soc. Antiq.), Deeds of D. and C. of Worc. no. 220*.

[87] Assize R. 1021, m. 1 d.; see also Maitland, *Bracton's Note-Bk.* iii, 358.
[38] Hale, *Reg. of Worc. Priory* (Camd. Soc.), 74*b.*
[39] Prattinton Coll. (Soc. Antiq.), Deeds of D. and C. of Worc. no. 115.
[40] Hale, *Reg. of Worc. Priory* (Camd. Soc.), 74*b.*
[41] Prattinton Coll. *ut supra,* no. 73.
[42] Ibid. 241.
[43] *Cal. Pat.* 1321–4, p. 218; *Hist. MSS. Com. Rep.* v, App. i, 302; see also *Reg. of Worc. Priory* (Camden Soc.), 158*a*–160*b,* for a long suit as to 2 virgates in Conderton.
[44] Close, 1652, pt. i, no. 1.
[45] Heming, op. cit. 456; Birch, op. cit. i, 329. The Anglo-Saxon boundaries of Teddington are given in Heming, op. cit. 362.
[46] See Bredon.

[47] Heming, op. cit. 26, 27; Birch, op. cit. ii, 4.
[48] Heming, op. cit. 520.
[49] Ibid. 177–8; Birch, op. cit. iii, 523; Add. Chart. 19792.
[50] Heming, op. cit. 204.
[51] Ibid. 203.
[51a] Toki and Aki are Scandinavian names, and Mr. Stenton points out that they form part of the evidence which proves a strong Danish element among Worcestershire landowners in the 11th century.
[52] Heming, op. cit. 395, 396, 517. The grant included a house in Worcester.
[53] Ibid. 396.
[54] *V.C.H. Worcs.* i, 291*a.*
[55] Hale, *Reg. of Worc. Priory* (Camden Soc.), 78*b.*
[56] *Cal. Pat.* 1354–8, p. 266.

dissolution of the house in 1540[57] Teddington passed to the Crown, and it was granted to the dean and chapter in 1542.[58] This grant was confirmed in 1609,[59] and the manor was sold by the Parliamentary Commissioners in 1650 to William Clarke and James Stanford.[60] The farm-house of the manor was sold in the same year to William Attwood[61] and Conan Daubeney.[62] The manor was recovered by the dean and chapter at the Restoration, confirmed to them in 1692–3,[63] and was taken over by the Ecclesiastical Commissioners in 1859.[64] The commissioners do not now own a manor at Teddington, the ancient manor having perhaps become merged in that of Overbury.[65]

ALSTONE (Aelfsigestun, x cent.; Alsestun, Elfsiston, xiii cent.; Alston, xvii cent.) was granted with Teddington in 969 by Bishop Oswald to Oswulf,[66] and was given with it by Bishop Ealdred to the priory of Worcester.[67] It evidently formed part of the manor of Teddington, being assessed with it in 1240 at 3 hides,[68] and sold in 1650 as the manor of Teddington and Alstone.[69]

LITTLE WASHBOURNE (Wassanburna, viii and ix cent.; Wasseburne, x cent.; Waseburne, xi cent.; Wasseburne Militis, xiv cent.; Knyghtes Wasshebourne, xv cent.; Knyghtyswasshebourne, xvi cent.). Offa, King of Mercia, gave 10 *cassates* of land at Little Washbourne (which had on the east a ford called Geolwaford and on the west a spring called Gytingbroc) to the monks of Worcester in 780.[70] This land, like Teddington, was afterwards taken from the monks by King Beorhtwulf, but was recovered by them in 840.[71] In 977 Bishop Oswald granted 3 'manses' there to a monk named Winsig for three lives.[72]

In the reign of Edward the Confessor one Elmer held 3 hides in Washbourne. He afterwards became a monk, and the Bishop of Worcester took his lands,[73] but in 1086 Urse the Sheriff held the estate, of the manor of Bredon.[74] His interest passed with his other possessions to the Beauchamps of Elmley,[75] and followed the descent of Elmley Castle until the 15th century, the manor of Washbourne being held of the honour of Elmley in 1492.[76]

Under the lords of Elmley the manor was held in the time of Henry II by William son of Sampson,[77]

and it afterwards passed to the Washbournes, whose ancestor Sampson may have been.[78] The first member of the family who is known to have held Little Washbourne is Roger Washbourne, who is mentioned as a juror in an inquisition of 1259,[79] and paid a subsidy of 15*s.* at Washbourne about 1280.[80] He was succeeded before 1299 by his son John Washbourne.[81] Roger Washbourne, son of John, to whom his father granted the manor in 1315–16,[82] seems to have taken part in the rebellion against the Despensers, and forfeited his estate to the king, for in 1322 his forfeited lands were restored to him.[83] Roger paid a subsidy of 3*s.* at Washbourne in 1327, and Isabel Washbourne, who paid a similar sum, was no doubt his mother.[84]

Roger Washbourne afterwards became a coroner for Worcestershire, and in 1347 the king commanded that another coroner should be elected in place of Roger, who was 'so sick and broken by age' that he could not fulfil the duties of his office.[85] His son John, who probably succeeded soon after, died without issue, and the manor of Little Washbourne passed to his uncle Peter, who in his turn was succeeded by his son John.[86] In 1368 John Washbourne was engaged in a suit against Katherine, widow of his cousin John, with regard to this manor.[87] By his first

WASHBOURNE. *Argent a fesse between six martlets gules with three cinqfoils argent on the fesse.*

wife Joan John had a daughter Iseult, who married firstly John Salwey, and secondly Thomas Harewell, the last-named being returned as owner of this manor in 1428.[88] In 1426–7, however, John Washbourne had conveyed the manor of Knights Washbourne to Norman Washbourne,[89] his son by his second wife Margaret Poer, and Norman was returned as the owner in 1431.[90] Humphrey Salwey son of Iseult claimed this manor in right of his mother, and finally in 1479, after much controversy between the two families, it was agreed between John son of Norman Washbourne and Humphrey Salwey that John should have the manor of Little Washbourne, while Humphrey

[57] *V.C.H. Worcs.* ii, 111. In 1535 the annual value of the manor of Teddington was £37 15*s.* 5*d.* (*Valor Eccl.* [Rec. Com.], iii, 222).

[58] *L. and P. Hen. VIII,* xvii, g. 71 (29); Pat. 33 Hen. VIII, pt. v, m. 19.

[59] Pat. 6 Jas. I, pt. xii, no. 2.

[60] Close, 1650, pt. xxv, no. 11.

[61] The site of the manor had been held by the Attwoods under the dean and chapter since the time of Queen Elizabeth (Chan. Proc. [Ser. 2], bdle. 3, no. 63; Feet of F. Worcs. East. 43 Eliz.; Close, 1650, pt. xxxiii, no. 18).

[62] Close, 1650, pt. xxxiii, no. 18.

[63] Pat. 4 Will. and Mary, pt. i, no. 6.

[64] *Lond. Gaz.* 16 Dec. 1859, p. 4757; Stat. 31 & 32 Vict. cap. 19.

[65] Inform. supplied by Ecclesiastical Commissioners.

[66] Birch, op. cit. iii, 523.

[67] Heming, op. cit. 396.

[68] Hale, *Reg. of Worc. Priory* (Camden Soc.), 78*a.*

[69] Close, 1650, pt. xxxiii, no. 18; xxv, no. 11.

[70] Heming, op. cit. 456; Birch, op. cit. i, 330.

[71] Heming, op. cit. 26, 27; Birch, op. cit. ii, 4.

[72] Heming, op. cit. 175.

[73] *V.C.H. Worcs.* i, 292*a.*

[74] Ibid. The connexion of this manor with Bredon seems still to have been recognized in Habington's time (op. cit. i, 525). In 1571 the manor was held of the Bishop of Worcester for the service of the tenth of a knight's fee and suit at the hundred court of Oswaldslow (Chan. Inq. p.m. [Ser. 2], clix, 75).

[75] *V.C.H. Worcs.* i, 324 n.; Habington, op. cit. i, 525.

[76] *Cal. Inq. p.m. Hen. VII,* i, 361.

[77] Habington, op. cit. i, 525; Red Bk. of Bishopric of Worc. (Eccl. Com. Rec. Var. bdle. 121, no. 43698), fol. 66.

[78] Habington, op. cit. i, 525; Red Bk. of Bishopric of Worc. fol. 66. There is a tradition that the founder of this

family was knighted on the field of battle by William the Conqueror and endowed by him with the manors of Great and Little Washbourne (J. Davenport, *The Washbourne Family,* 2).

[79] *Worcs. Inq. p.m.* (Worcs. Hist. Soc.), i, 4.

[80] *Lay Subs. R. Worcs.* 1280 (Worcs. Hist. Soc.), 71.

[81] *Visit. of Worcs.* 1569 (Harl. Soc. xxvii), 142; see also *Cal. Close,* 1302–7, p. 347; 1307–13, p. 216; *Feud. Aids,* v, 305.

[82] Davenport, op. cit. 5.

[83] *Cal. Close,* 1318–23, p. 419.

[84] *Lay Subs. R. Worcs.* 1327 (Worcs. Hist. Soc.), 25; *Visit. of Worcs.* 1569 (Harl. Soc. xxvii), 142.

[85] *Cal. Close,* 1346–9, p. 232.

[86] Co. Plac. (Chan.), Worcs. 27 Hen. VI, no. 9.

[87] Ibid.

[88] *Feud. Aids,* v, 321.

[89] Davenport, op. cit. 25; and see Feet of F. Worcs. 7 Hen. VI, no. 21.

[90] *Feud. Aids,* v, 332.

should have Stanford.[91] The manor then followed the same descent as Wichenford in the Washbourne family[92] until 1712, when Wichenford was sold by William Washbourne. The manor of Little Washbourne was retained by the Washbourne family. William Washbourne died about 1726,[93] but seems to have given the manor before this time to his son Ernle, who was dealing with it in 1717.[94] Ernle died without issue in 1743,[95] and left this property to his three sisters, Susannah, Hester Soame and Ann Sheppard, in equal shares for their lives, with remainder to their children. In the event of the three sisters leaving no issue, Richard Washbourne, son of Goodwin Washbourne of St. Ann's Lane, Westminster, was to inherit, with remainder to his heirs male. Failing such heirs the property was to go to John Robinson the younger, son of John Robinson the elder of Cransley and his heirs.[96] Six months after Ernle's death the three sisters leased the manor of Little Washbourne to Timothy Shury for eighteen years at a rent of £225.[97] The three sisters left no children, Hester, the last of the three, dying in 1782, and the estate presumably passed under Ernle's will to the Robinsons.[98] It belonged in 1791–2 to Richard Hill,[99] and it was sold by him or his son at the beginning of the 19th century to Samuel Gist Gist,[100] who was holding it in 1823.[1] He died in 1845, and was succeeded by a son Samuel,[2] who was owner of the manor in 1897. The manor of Washbourne has since this date been sold to Mrs. Eyres Monsell of Dumbleton.

In 1240 there were four mills at Overbury belonging to the manor and one which belonged to the church.[3] In 1291 three mills at Overbury were valued at £1 4s.[4] A water corn-mill was included in the sale of the site of the manor in 1651.[5] At the end of the 18th century there was a paper-mill on the Carrant Brook, and also a corn-mill and malthouse.[6] The paper-mill had disappeared before 1868, as had a silk-mill which once flourished at Overbury. There were then two grist-mills on the Carrant Brook.[7] The only mill in the parish at the present day is Overbury Mill, a corn-mill on the eastern boundary of Overbury Park.

CHURCHES The church of *ST. FAITH* consists of a chancel 24 ft. by 16½ ft., nave 56½ ft. long and tapering from 16¾ ft. at the west to 15¾ ft. at the east, with a central tower 12 ft. wide by 13½ ft. from east to west, north aisle to the nave 10 ft. wide, south aisle 9¾ ft. wide and a modern south porch. All the dimensions given are internal.

The earliest part of the building is the nave, with its two arcades and clearstory, which dates from the latter part of the 12th century, but the variation in the width probably indicates the pre-existence of an aisleless building. A tower also appears to have been built on the site of the present one at the same time, and doubtless there was a sacrarium to the east of it. The latter was rebuilt in the 13th century, when it was widened and lengthened, but from an entry in the Worcester Episcopal Registers[8] it does not appear to have been consecrated before the year 1315. The west wall of the nave was also rebuilt, probably at the same time.

About 1330–40 the narrow 12th-century aisles were widened to their present size, the original south doorway being brought out with the wall and rebuilt. The clearstory had to be abandoned as a source of light, and was inclosed below the new aisle roofs. Nothing important was subsequently done to the structure until the latter half of the 15th century, when the central tower was entirely rebuilt. The capitals of the former 12th-century half-round responds were reversed and reset in the bases of the present arches, and the angle shafts in the chancel were turned slightly to fit the skew walls joining the chancel to the tower. The large east window was inserted at much the same time.

A gallery stood at the east end of the nave in the early part of the last century, and was removed to the west end in 1835, but in 1850 it had entirely disappeared. The church has been restored during the past century, chiefly in 1879–80. The porch is presumably of this date.

The east window is of four main and eight sublights with 'Perpendicular' tracery above under a four-centred main arch. The mullions are continued down below the sill to form a series of blind panels with quatrefoils over. The plinth outside has a moulded top member with two splays below. At the corners are 13th-century shallow clasping buttresses, and a shallow buttress divides each side wall into two bays. Two large and apparently modern buttresses have been added to each side wall. The jambs and arches of the two 13th-century lancets in either wall are richly moulded. Each jamb has detached round shafts both within and without and another engaged shaft flush with the inner face of the wall. All three have carved foliated capitals and moulded bases. The external labels mitre with a moulded string-course of the same section which runs along the wall at the springing level. A similar string-course is carried along the wall a few feet higher. The groined stone vault of the chancel is in two bays and springs from vaulting shafts attached to the wall. The

[91] Davenport, op. cit. 11. George Duke of Clarence, brother of Edward IV, was the arbitrator. His full award is given on pp. 11–17. A rent of 8 marks from the manor of Little Washbourne was assigned to Humphrey Salwey and passed to his son John in 1493 (*Cal. Inq. p.m. Hen. VII*, i, 361). John was succeeded by three daughters: Cecily wife of Thomas Coningsby, Joyce wife of William Ashby, and Margaret (Chan. Inq. p.m. [Ser. 2], xxix, 72). It was perhaps Joyce who, as the wife of Ralph Worsley, sold a third part of this rent in 1557 to Humphrey Coningsby, son of Cecily and Thomas Coningsby (Feet of F. Worcs. Mich. 4 & 5 Phil. and Mary; *Visit. o*

Worcs. [Harl. Soc. xxvii], 43). In 1658 Fitz William Coningsby, grandson of Humphrey, assigned a rent of £4 6s. 8d. from the manor of Knights Washbourne to Sampson Wise (Close, 22 Chas. II, pt. xxiii, no. 28).

[92] Feet of F. Worcs. East. 10 Eliz.; Chan. Inq. p.m. (Ser. 2), clix, 75; Feet of F. Worcs. Hil. 41 Eliz.; Close, 2 Will. and Mary, pt. xii, no. 17.

[93] Davenport, op. cit. 169.

[94] Recov. R. Mich. 4 Geo. I, rot. 139.

[95] Davenport, op. cit. 170.

[96] The will is given in full by Davenport, op. cit. 172–6.

[97] Ibid. 219–20. The owners undertook to pay all taxes and charges other

than window tax, to allow timber for the repair of 'the bridge over the Brooke out of the Lord's Mead' and to allow the tenant 'ffive tunns of Coal at the Key yearly.' [98] Ibid. 171.

[99] Feet of F. Worcs. East. 32 Geo. III.

[100] Prattinton Coll. (Soc. Antiq.).

[1] Recov. R. Hil. 3 & 4 Geo. IV, rot. 38.

[2] Burke, *Landed Gentry* (ed. 7).

[3] Hale, *Reg. of Worc. Priory* (Camd. Soc.), 74a, b.

[4] *Pope Nich. Tax.* (Rec. Com.), 227b.

[5] Close, 1651, pt. liii, no. 35.

[6] Nash, op. cit. ii, 232.

[7] Noake, op. cit. 294.

[8] op. cit. Maidstone, fol. 37.

angle shafts are single and filleted, but the intermediate shafts form clusters of three. All have moulded bases and carved foliated capitals. The faces of the window ledges are moulded and continued along as a string-course, which is carried up vertically by the side of the vaulting shaft and around the arch of the vault to form the wall rib. The vaulting ribs are moulded, and at the junction of the diagonals are carved bosses, both with female heads. The chancel walls are rubble-faced inside, outside they are cemented. The two-centred archways east and west of the tower are of two chamfered orders with plain bases and moulded capitals of late 15th-century form.

In the south wall of the tower is a small doorway with moulded jambs and pointed arch. Above it, and also on the opposite side, are windows of three lights under traceried two-centred heads. These light the space below the modern groined stone vault which spans the lowest story of the tower. The room above the vault is lighted by single square-headed lights in the north and south walls below the moulded string-course which marks the first of the three stages of the tower. In this string are carved square flowers at intervals. In the second stage is a similar small light to the west. The third stage or bell-chamber has a square window in each wall of four lights entirely filled with small and elaborate tracery in stone. At the angles are diagonal buttresses. Grotesque winged gargoyles project at the four corners of the moulded parapet string, and lower down on the south-western buttress is a curious carved reptile. The parapet is embattled with a moulded returned coping, and at the angles are slender square pinnacles with crocketed finials. The tower is of rubble, ashlar-faced outside.

The nave arcades each consist of four bays; both are of the 12th century, but differ slightly in detail, and one (probably the south) was evidently finished before the other was begun. Both have circular columns and half-round responds. The moulded bases on the north side have a very decided 'water-table,' and the scalloped capitals are square with a grooved and chamfered abacus. The capitals on the south side are also scalloped, but in this case the vertical face of the capital is very deep and the flutes are almost horizontal. The arches on both sides are semicircular and of two square orders.

Above each column and over the eastern respond are the small semicircular-headed lights to the former clearstory; their jambs and head are splayed all round inside and rebated and chamfered towards the aisle; the easternmost, on the north side, is partly obscured by the angle wall of the later rood stair turret, in which is a square-headed doorway. In the

west wall of the nave are three lancet windows with plain pointed heads. The outside stonework is all new. Inside the shafts between the lights are detached, and are square in plan, with chamfered edges and a filleted roll on the face, the latter having a moulded base and capital. These rolls or shafts are repeated on the jambs.

The 14th-century east window of the north aisle is of three lights with a traceried head. To the south of it is the doorway to the rood-loft stair set on the skew. Another doorway is inserted in the angle buttress of the tower outside. The two north windows of the aisle are of similar detail and date to the east window, and between them is the north doorway with a two-centred drop arch. The modern west window is of two lights in 14th-century style.

The three-light east window of the south aisle has all been renewed except the jambs. The two southern windows are similar, and in each case the inner stones of the tracery and the mullions are modern. The round-headed south doorway is the original late 12th-century entrance reset in the 14th

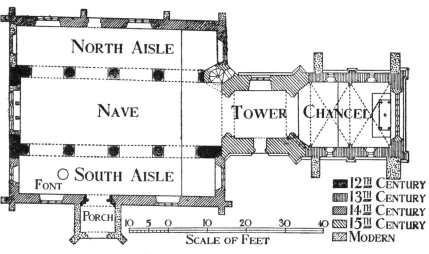

PLAN OF OVERBURY CHURCH

NORTH AISLE

NAVE

TOWER CHANCEL

FONT ○ SOUTH AISLE

PORCH

10 5 0 10 20 30 40

SCALE OF FEET

■ 12TH CENTURY
▨ 13TH CENTURY
▨ 14TH CENTURY
▧ 15TH CENTURY
▨ MODERN

century; the jambs are of three orders, the two outer each having a keeled shaft in the angle. The shafts and edge rolls have carved capitals, most of which have been partly or wholly renewed. The west window resembles that in the other aisle, and with the south porch is entirely modern. The buttresses of the aisles have been renewed with the exception of the eastern buttress of the north aisle. The north wall of this aisle is of rubble or rough ashlar in small square stones and the east end of the south aisle is also in small ashlar. The roof of the nave is gabled, and has a plastered ceiling below, cut up into panels by wood ribs. The aisle roofs are flat and of modern date.

The font is large, and has a bowl which appears to date from the 11th century on a 14th-century stem and base. On the curved sides of the bowl are carved two figures, one holding two croziers and the other a small model of a building; there are also a flower scroll ornament, partly repaired, and a cross and dove wholly modern. The stem is octagonal with ball flowers on the faces and the base has a moulded octagonal sub-base.

The tub-shaped pulpit is octagonal and rests on a stone base. Parts of the woodwork date from the 15th century, and the panels have traceried heads with carved spandrels and small roses at the cusp points. The cornice is carved with a running vine pattern, with inverted cresting below. The nave seats are also made up with much fine late 15th-century woodwork.

There are six bells : the treble, by Robert Hendlet of Gloucester (c. 1450), is inscribed 'Sancte Egidi ora pro nobis'; the second, which is probably of late 16th-century date, has an alphabet; the third and fourth are by Roger Purdue and dated 1641, the former is inscribed 'Come when I call to serve God all,' the latter 'Halleliah'; the fifth is by Abraham Rudhall, 1719; the tenor was added in 1903 and

OVERBURY CHURCH FROM THE SOUTH-WEST

bears the following chronogram : 'CaMpana sanCtae f I De I Ceter I s Consonare parata.'

The communion plate includes a silver cup and a cover paten, the latter bearing the date 1571. There are also two patens and a flagon of 1876.

The registers before 1812 are as follows : (i) includes entries 1563 to 1681, with a single baptism entered in 1557; (ii) marriages 1686 to 1755, baptisms and burials 1683 to 1794; (iii) baptisms and burials 1795 to 1812, and (iv) marriages 1755 to 1812.

The church of ST. NICHOLAS, Teddington, consists of a chancel measuring internally 19¾ ft. by 14 ft., nave 36¾ ft. by 19½ ft., west tower 10 ft. by 8 ft. and a south porch 9 ft. 7 in. by 8 ft.

The earliest detail of the building is the plain

semicircular chancel arch, which seems to indicate an 11th-century origin. The presence of moulded arch-stones of the early 12th century in the facing of the wall on either side of it shows that a drastic repair has taken place at some subsequent period, perhaps at the time the present west tower was built, the ground stage of which is constructed of re-used 13th-century stones. The four-centred doorway leading to the vice gives the 15th century as the date of this reconstruction. The source from which these stones were brought is uncertain. The elaborate nature of the tower arch and the west window shows that it must have been a building of considerable importance. The north-east window of the nave and the north porch are of the middle of the 13th century. The east window of the chancel dates from the latter half of the 14th century. New windows were inserted in the south wall of the nave and in both side walls of the chancel in the 16th or early 17th century.

The east window of the chancel is of three trefoiled ogee lights with tracery of a transitional type within a two-centred head. The two north windows are each of two plain square-headed lights, and between them is a small doorway with an elliptical head and moulded external jambs. In the south wall are two similar windows, the sill of the easternmost having been lowered to serve as a credence table. These features are all of the 16th century. The chancel arch, which probably dates from the late 11th century, is semicircular and perfectly plain with unmoulded imposts and plain responds. Built into the wall on either side of it are several fragments of early 12th-century moulded arch-stones and a piece of a moulded impost. Externally there are two small buttresses of one offset on either side of the east window and below the level of its sill, while at the angles of the wall are buttresses of two offsets. The walls are faced with irregularly coursed rubble.

The mid-13th-century north-east window of the nave is a single lancet light with a trefoiled head and plain wide internal splays. The rear arch is formed by wood lintels. Below the sill is a plain oblong recess in the face of the wall. The north doorway appears to be of the late 12th century. The external head is two-centred and is roll-moulded continuously with the jambs. There is a label with a head-stop on the east and a mask-stop on the west, both partaking more of the Norman than the Early English character. The rear arch is semicircular. In the south wall are two 16th-century windows with square heads and external labels. The eastern of these is of three elliptical-headed lights and the western of two similar lights. Internally the wall sets off with a chamfer about 3 ft. above the floor level. Between these is a blocked doorway of the same date as that in the wall opposite with a two-centred external head and label and a segmental two-centred rear arch. Externally a string-course runs

OVERBURY CHURCH : CHANCEL WINDOWS

TEDDINGTON CHURCH : THE NAVE LOOKING EAST

along the western half of the north wall and is twice lifted as if to meet the sills of two windows. There are, however, no traces in the wall above of any openings. The plinth is here swept back to the face above by a deep double chamfer. On the south wall are three buttresses of two offsets, probably of the 13th century.

The tower appears to have been built in the late 15th century. Many 13th-century details are used up in the ground stage, including the west window and the tower arch and the lower stages of the buttresses. The responds of the tower arch are formed of cylindrical piers with attached circular shafts at the cardinal points, and are built clumsily into the angles made by the west wall of the nave with the side walls of the tower, exposing two only of the attached shafts on either side. Their capitals, which are finely moulded, show them to be of the middle of the 13th century. The bases are gone and they stand on rude square blocks of stone. The arch itself fits the improvised responds very ill. It is of the same date and of two elaborately moulded orders. The west window, which is also of the same period, is a particularly fine example of early bar tracery. It is of two cinquefoiled lights surmounted by a multifoiled circle within a two-centred head. Both jambs and mullions are shafted internally and externally and the tracery is richly moulded. At the south-east of the ground stage is a vice leading to the ringing stage, entered by a doorway with a four-centred head. This is contained within a stone-roofed westward extension of the nave, with a diagonal buttress of two offsets at the western angle. There is a similar feature on the north, by which the nave is made to clasp the tower on both sides. The tower is divided externally into three receding stages by moulded string-courses, and there are diagonal buttresses of three offsets at the western angles. The whole is crowned by a cornice with gargoyles at the four corners surmounted by an embattled parapet. The bell-chamber is lighted by two-light windows with two-centred heads containing tracery of a very poor and debased type. The walls are faced with ashlar work.

The north porch, as stated above, is of mid-13th-century date. The outer entrance has a two-centred head and is chamfered continuously with the jambs.

The roofs of both chancel and nave are of the trussed-rafter type and probably date from the 14th century. The nave roof has been considerably repaired by the insertion of ties at various later dates.

The base and stem of the font belong to the 14th

century, but the bowl is modern. The pews, though much restored, are all of the late 15th century. The top-rails are elaborately moulded, but they are otherwise quite plain, with the exception of two ends, which have linen-pattern panels. The altar rails and the priest's stall in the chancel are Jacobean. On the front of the desk is carved 'Quench not ye spirit, Despise not prophecyĩg'; on the seat, 'pray continually.' The pulpit, which has been cut down and set on a stone base, was made in 1655. The date, with the names of the churchwardens, Michael Tyller and William Awoode (sic), is carved on the panels which form the back. The desk-cloth with its gold-tasselled fringe has worked upon it $^{C.W.}_{E.A.}$ 1717.

On the plaster of the south wall, occupying the whole of the space between the two windows and above the head of the blocked doorway, are painted the royal arms of William and Mary within a crude architectural frame. On the north wall are the Lord's Prayer and the General Confession inscribed in black letter, the work of the early 17th century.

TEDDINGTON CHURCH FROM THE SOUTH

There are two bells, inscribed as follows : (1) 'Christus est Via, Veritas, Vita 1605,' (2) 'God Save King James 1609.'

The plate consists of a silver cup and cover paten of 1571, a modern paten and flagon and a pewter almsdish.

The registers previously to 1812 are in one volume containing mixed entries from 1560 to 1793.

The church of ST. MARGARET, Alstone, consists of a chancel measuring internally 15¼ ft. by 15 ft., nave 29¼ ft. by 17 ft., a north aisle 30¼ ft. by 8½ ft., a south porch 8¼ ft. by 7¼ ft. and a modern timber belfry over the east end of the nave.

The responds of the chancel arch and the south doorway of the nave date from the middle of the 12th century. No other details of this period remain in position. A rebuilding appears to have taken place in the 13th century, when the chancel and nave were rebuilt, a new two-centred arch being fitted to the existing responds of the chancel arch, the south doorway of the nave being retained in its original position. The south wall of the nave appears to have been again rebuilt at some later period, and the north aisle with the arcade of the nave probably dates from the latter half of the 16th century. The south porch was added in 1621.

The east window of the chancel is of two trefoiled lights and dates from the middle of the 13th century. The north-east window has modern tracery of the same character, but the jambs appear to be original. In the south wall is a window of three square-headed lights, probably of the early 17th century. At the south-east is a 12th-century projecting piscina basin, reset in the wall. A supporting shaft has evidently

TEDDINGTON CHURCH, WEST WINDOW

ing, runs round the walls and is interrupted by the buttresses, which have independent plinths of slighter projection. The walling is of ashlar work in deep courses. The east gable has a chamfered coping and is crowned at the apex by a stone cross, probably of original 13th-century date.

The 16th-century north arcade of the nave is of three bays, with two-centred arches of two orders and octagonal columns and responds. The mouldings are of a simple and nondescript type. The easternmost window of the south wall has three four-centred lights within a square head and appears to be contemporary in date with the north arcade and aisle. The south doorway has a semicircular head, and is of two orders externally, the outer order having shafted jambs. The details are very similar to those of the chancel arch, with which it is evidently contemporary. The opening itself is square-headed, the arch being filled with a plain tympanum. This has been cracked at the head, and the stones generally bear evident marks of having been reset. The westernmost window is of two plain lights with modern mullions. It is probable that the whole of this wall was rebuilt at the time the north aisle was added, various fragments of window mullions and other moulded stones being worked into the internal facing. In the west wall is a single trefoiled light of the 13th century with an external chamfered label. The thrust of the nave arcade is taken on the east by a buttress of two offsets set with its south side against the north wall of the chancel. The west wall is crowned by a modern half-timber gable and is flanked by buttresses of two offsets. There is a buttress of a single offset at the south-west.

The north aisle is lighted by square-headed windows of two four-centred lights in the east, north, and west walls. There are angle buttresses of two offsets at the east and west and one in the centre of the north wall. The whole aisle has the appearance of having been put together of fragments.

The south porch has stone seats on either side, and the outer doorway has a four-centred head. Above the arch is carved the date 1621. The open timber roofs are tiled. The stone font is octagonal, simply moulded, and of original 13th-century date. In the south-west window of the nave are some fragments of 15th-century stained glass. The 16th-century pulpit has linen-pattern panels. Some of the bench-ends appear to be of the same date.

disappeared. The chancel arch is of two orders towards the west. The responds alone date from the 12th century. The jambs of the outer order are shafted and the shafts have enriched scalloped capitals, cabled neckings and moulded bases. Their abaci, which are enriched with the star ornament, are continued round the responds. The southern shaft, with its capital and abacus, is a modern restoration. The arch itself is of the 13th century; it is two-centred, and the orders are moulded with deep chamfers. The wall on either side is pierced by large square-headed squints. Externally there are buttresses of two offsets at the eastern angles. A deep chamfered plinth, surmounted by a small roll mould-

LITTLE WASHBOURNE CHAPEL : THE NAVE LOOKING EAST

ALSTONE CHURCH : THE CHANCEL ARCH

On the north wall of the north aisle is a monument with a long inscription in verse to the wife of 'T. D.' (Darke ?), who died in 1662. Among the other monuments is one to Elizabeth daughter of 'Mr. Smith, Minister of this Parish,' who died in 1682, and to Humphry Smith, evidently the 'Mr. Smith' of the preceding inscription, who died in 1729. There is also a fragment of an inscription in verse, from which the name has gone, to a child of nine, who died in 1696.

There is one bell, inscribed : 'Jnº New Churchwarden, 1790.'

The plate includes a cup with a floral band but without date and probably Elizabethan. There is also a plated paten as well as a silver flagon of 1880, the gift of Miss Levett of Cheltenham.

The registers previous to 1812 are as follows : (i) baptisms, burials and marriages 1546 to 1734 ; (ii) baptisms, burials and marriages 1782 to 1804.

The chapel of *ST. MARY THE VIRGIN* at Little Washbourne consists of a chancel 13 ft. by 18 ft., a nave 28½ ft. by 18½ ft., and a timber bell-turret over the west end of the chancel.

The building dates from the middle of the 12th century, but seems to have been largely rebuilt at later periods. The earlier work is of rubble masonry, but the north wall of the nave and the greater part of the south wall are faced with ashlar. The present windows are modern enlargements of the older openings and probably date from the late 18th century. The building is now in a very bad state of repair. The walls have been pushed very much out of the perpendicular by the thrust of the roof-trusses, to counteract which massive buttresses have recently been erected. The outward movement seems, however, to have ceased, as the buttresses themselves have commenced to fall away from the walls.

The east window of the chancel is a large pointed light without tracery, and there are no windows in the side walls. The timber bell-turret is supported by uprights rising from the floor. The chancel arch is semicircular and of a single plain order with jamb shafts on the nave side, having scalloped capitals and chamfered abaci. The walls are of rubble masonry, and a small blocked semicircular-headed light, with a rebate for a shutter, is visible externally in the north wall. The east gable is crowned by a 14th-century cross.

There are no windows in the north wall of the nave. In the south wall is a modern doorway, and to the east of it a window of the same character as the chancel window. There is a similar window in the west wall. The north wall and the greater part of the south wall appear to be later rebuildings, perhaps of the 15th century. They are faced with ashlar work, in deep courses. The west wall, which is of rubble, still remains much in its original condition ; there are pilaster buttresses at the north and south and one in the centre, the upper part of which has been cut away for the sill of the window. A plain cross with arms of round section crowns the gable.

The roof of the chancel has trusses with tie-beams and collars strutted by arched braces. The roof of the nave seems to have undergone many repairs at various periods. The collars of the trusses are stiffened by straight struts, and there are cambered tie-beams. Externally the roofs are stone-slated. The pulpit and pews are extremely good examples of late 18th-century joinery. The altar table, which has a marble top with a narrow

LITTLE WASHBOURNE CHAPEL FROM THE SOUTH-WEST

edge of wood, is a fine piece of furniture of the same date.

The original bell, which is seriously cracked, is still preserved in the building. It is inscribed in black letters : 'made 1584.' The present bell was cast in 1892.

The plate includes an Elizabethan cup without hall mark or date and a pewter plate or paten.

The registers are kept with Alstone.

ADVOWSON In 1086 the Prior and convent of Worcester had on their manor of Overbury a priest who had half a hide of land.[9]

In 1194 the Bishop of Worcester granted the prior an annual rent of 2 marks in his church of Overbury and half a mark in his chapel of Berrow (Berga) for a special feast on the Feast of the Transfiguration, and for doles to the poor.[10] In 1291 the church of Overbury with its chapels [11] was valued

9 *V.C.H. Worcs.* i, 295a.   10 Prattinton Coll. (Soc. Antiq.), Deeds of D. and C. of Worc. no. 314.   11 See below.

at £16, and the prior received £3 6s. 8d. a year for the great tithes.[12] In 1315 Bishop Maidstone consecrated the high altar in the church of Overbury.[13]

The advowson of Overbury belonged to the Prior and convent of Worcester, and remained in their possession until the Dissolution, when it passed to the Crown.[14] In 1330 the prior and convent obtained licence to appropriate the church of Overbury with its chapels,[15] but the appropriation does not seem to have taken place immediately, for in 1344 the Letters Patent granting the licence were exemplified,[16] and in 1346 Queen Philippa petitioned the pope that the appropriation might be made for the payment of the debts of the priory, and for the support of two monks at the University of Oxford.[17] The appropriation was made in the same year,[18] and the vicarage was ordained in 1368.[19] The advowson was granted to the Dean and Chapter of Worcester in 1542[20] and has since remained in their possession.[21]

In 1240 there were chapels at Alstone, Teddington and Little Washbourne[22] attached to the church of Overbury.[23] The chapel of Alstone is not mentioned in 1330 in the licence to appropriate the church of Overbury, though the other two are then said to be chapels of Overbury,[24] but in 1535 the chapels of Alstone and Teddington were said to be chantry chapels.[25] The three chapels are still annexed to the church of Overbury.

In 1868 Noake records a chapel in Overbury used by Baptists and Independents.[26] At the present day there is a Baptist chapel, which was opened in 1861.

CHARITIES Elizabeth Wood, who died in 1824, by her will bequeathed £200 bank stock, the dividends to be applied, subject to keeping in repair certain vaults, in the distribution of clothes for labouring poor who support their families without parish relief.

The stock was sold out and the proceeds thereof, with accumulations of income, were invested in £444 6s. 3d. consols, which is now held by the official trustees, producing £11 2s. yearly. In 1908 the income was distributed in clothing to twenty-six recipients.

Church Lands.—The parish is in possession of about 5 acres, acquired on the inclosure in 1811, in exchange for land intermixed with other lands in the common fields. The land is let at £12 10s. a year, which is carried to the churchwardens' accounts and applied in cleaning, lighting and heating the church.

Mrs. Agg, as stated on the church table, gave £10, the annual interest to be laid out in bread to be distributed to poor widows. The principal sum, with other sums, appears to have been applied towards defraying the expenses of building the poor-house.

PENDOCK

Penedoc, Peonedoc (ix, x and xi cent.) ; Penedok, Penedoch (xiii cent.).

Pendock is a parish containing 1,145 acres, with a detached part to the south-west. It is bounded on the south and east by an unnamed stream, a tributary of the Severn. This stream is crossed at Horse Bridge by the high road from Ledbury to Tewkesbury, which passes north-west through the parish past Prior's Court to Sledge Green, a district on the north-west border of the parish.[1] The church and rectory lie back from this road. A branch road from the Ledbury high road runs past the rectory westward to the detached part of Pendock where the village of Pendock is situated. The church is approached by a footpath and stands in an isolated position, the only building near being a farm a short distance to the north-east. The rectory is about a quarter of a mile to the north-west. On the south side of the church is a steep descent, and on the west connecting with the declivity thus formed is an artificial fosse of some size.

In the village of Pendock at Cromer Green are the schools and a Wesleyan Methodist chapel. A road leads north-west from the village to Portway. To the east is Cleeve House, where there is a moat. Frogmore is a district in the south of the detached part of Pendock.

The parish is undulating but low-lying. The church stands a little over 100 ft. above the ordnance datum, and the land falls in the south towards the brook.

Pendock Moor is a small piece of rough grassland in the north of the main part of Pendock ; to the west of it is a moat, but no building remains. In 1905 the parish contained 223 acres of arable land, 526 of permanent grass, and 18 of woodland.[2] The soil is mixed and the subsoil Keuper Marl, producing crops of wheat, barley and beans. The inclosure award for the parish is dated 1843.[3] In 1882 part of Pendock was transferred to Berrow.[4]

Roman coins and some indications of buildings have been found near the church.[5]

Ninth-century place-names are Elfstansbridge, Osric's Pool, Duca's Pit, Rushole, Wenbrook, Hinmere, Ashapalderley, Dinggarston, Wanding Hole.[6]

[12] Pope Nich. Tax. (Rec. Com.), 217b. In 1271 Thomas Bushley, a sub-deacon, was convicted of stealing ornaments from the church of Overbury and degraded (Reg. G. Giffard [Worcs. Hist. Soc.], 46). Geoffrey de Northwick, rector of Overbury, obtained licence in 1302 to absent himself from his church to visit the Roman Court (Sede Vacante Reg. [Worcs. Hist. Soc.], 27).
[13] Worc. Epis. Reg. Maidstone (1313–17), fol. 37.
[14] Reg. G. Giffard (Worcs. Hist. Soc.), 433 ; Cal. Pat. 1327–30, p. 536 ; Hale, Reg. of Worc. Priory (Camd. Soc.), 74a ;

Ann. Mon. (Rolls Ser.), iv, 513 ; L. and P. Hen. VIII, xvii, g. 71 (29).
[15] Cal. Pat. 1327–30, p. 536.
[16] Ibid. 1343–5, p. 210.
[17] Cal. Papal Pet. i, 121.
[18] Cal. Papal Letters, iii, 225 ; Hist. MSS. Com. Rep. xiv, App. viii, 168 ; Heming, op. cit. 536, 545, 551.
[19] Nash, op. cit. ii, 238.
[20] L. and P. Hen. VIII, xvii, g. 71 (29).
[21] Inst. Bks. (P.R.O.).
[22] The prior received half the tithes of the demesne of Washbourne, and the church of Nafford had the other half (Reg. of Worc. Priory [Camd. Soc.], 74b).

[23] Ibid. ; Pope Nich. Tax. (Rec. Com.), 217b. Berrow was also a chapelry of Overbury. [24] Cal. Pat. 1327–30, p. 536.
[25] Valor Eccl. (Rec. Com.), iii, 227.
[26] op. cit. 294.
[1] It was presented at the county court in 1633 that this road was in decay at Pendock between Crommen Pytt and Birtsmorton (Worcs. Quart. Sess. R. [Worcs. Hist. Soc.], 512).
[2] Statistics from Bd. of Agric. (1905).
[3] Blue Bk. Incl. Awards, 191.
[4] Pop. Ret. 1891, ii, 657.
[5] Noake, Guide to Worcs. 296.
[6] Nash, Hist. of Worcs. App. 57.

Ceolwulf II, King of the Mercians, gave
MANOR to the monks of Worcester land at Overbury with Conderton and Pendock in
875.[7] Among the Anglo-Saxon charters in the
archives of Worcester Cathedral is one dated 888
whereby King Alfred granted to the priory of
Worcester land at Pendock,[8] and King Edgar in 964
granted the monks freedom from all royal exactions in
their manor of *PENDOCK*.[9] In 967 Bishop Oswald
leased two *mansae* at Pendock to his servant Hœhstan
for three lives.[10] At the time of the Domesday Survey
2 hides in the manor of Pendock were held by Urse
D'Abitot the sheriff, and had formerly been held by
Godwine,[11] apparently of the Bishop of Worcester's
manor of Bredon. Another manor of Pendock seems
to have been included in the manor of Overbury and
was held by the monks of Worcester.[12] This estate
was still annexed to Overbury in 1148.[13]

The following account given by the monks of the
loss of Pendock probably refers to the part held by
Urse in 1086. Pendock had been taken by violence
from the church of Worcester by the ancestors of a
certain Northman, but he restored it to the monastery
when his son became a monk there, at the time when
Wulfstan (afterwards bishop) was dean. The manor
was, however, again taken from them by Rawulf the
Sheriff, with the help of William Earl of Hereford.[14]

Urse's manor of Pendock passed with his other
estates to Walter de Beauchamp,[15] and from him to
the Earls of Warwick,[16] who held this manor as overlords. The overlordship of the Earls of Warwick is
last mentioned in 1436.[17] The connexion of this
manor with that of Bredon seems to have been lost at
an early date. It was still held of the manor of
Bredon in the time of Henry I,[18] and early in the
13th century William de Beauchamp held it under
the Bishop of Worcester,[18a] but after that time the
interest of the Bishops of Worcester in the manor
seems to have ceased.

Under the Beauchamps the manor of Pendock was
held by a family[19] taking their name from the manor.
The brothers Robert and Walter de Pendock appear
in 1175–6,[20] and a certain Robert held the estate
about 1182.[21] Robert de Pendock was holding the
manor early in the 13th century,[22] and the Abbot of
Pershore sued him in 1248–9 for arrears of rent.[23]
William de Pendock appeared as a juror in 1264.[24]

In 1290 Robert de Pendock son of John de Hanley
presented to the church of Pendock,[25] but he had
previously (before 1275) sold half the manor to the
Prior of Little Malvern, who was to hold it of Robert
at a rent,[26] and this grant was confirmed by William
de Beauchamp.[26a] The monks of Little Malvern
continued to hold this moiety of the manor under the
Pendocks until the Dissolution,[27] and their interest,
then represented by a rent of 6s. 3d., was granted in
1554–5 to Henry Russell and Charles Broughton.[28]

Robert de Pendock retained the other moiety of
the manor. He presented to the church in 1290,[29]
and was perhaps succeeded about that time by Sir
Henry de Pendock, who was witness to a charter in
1291.[30] William son of Henry de Pendock was
holding Pendock in 1316,[31] but the manor afterwards
passed to the heirs of Robert de Pendock by his son
John. John son of John son of Robert de Pendock
died in 1322, leaving a son John, a minor.[32] John
son of William de Pendock held the manor in 1342
and 1346,[33] and had been succeeded before 1357 by
William de Pendock, who presented to the church at
that date and in 1369.[34]

A long gap then occurs in the history of the manor.
The heir of John de Pendock was said to be
holding it in 1428.[35] Guy Spencer held the manor
in 1431[36] and presented to the church in 1452.[37]
John Clapam presented to the church of Pendock
in 1461 and Guy Spencer again in 1465,[38] and in
1493 John Spencer and Elizabeth his wife conveyed
land and rent in Pendock and the advowson of the
church to Christopher Throckmorton.[39] This part
of the manor then became united to the part held by
the D'Abitot family, the descent of which is given
below.

The estate at Pendock held in 1086 by the monks
of Worcester was confirmed to them by Bishop Simon
in 1148.[40] Subsequently this manor seems to have
been held by the Beauchamps as mesne lords between
the Bishops of Worcester and the D'Abitots, but this
mesne lordship of the Beauchamps is mentioned only
twice in the 13th century,[41] and may have been due
to confusion between this part of the manor and that
held by the Pendocks, which was certainly held under
the Beauchamps. The whole manor of Pendock
comprising the two estates was held of the bishopric
of Worcester in 1513 and in 1637.[42]

[7] Birch, *Cart. Sax.* ii, 160; Heming, *Chartul.* (ed. Hearne), 331.

[8] Heming, op. cit. 580; Harl. MS. 4660, Chart. 10.

[9] Birch, op. cit. iii, 379; Heming, op. cit. 520.

[10] Birch, op. cit. iii, 485; Heming, op. cit. 183.   [11] *V.C.H. Worcs.* i, 291b.

[12] Ibid. 295.

[13] Thomas, *Surv. of Worc. Cath.* App. no. 18.

[14] Dugdale, *Mon. Angl.* i, 593.

[15] *V.C.H. Worcs.* i, 324.

[16] *Testa de Nevill* (Rec. Com.), 41b; *Cal. Close,* 1313–18, p. 277; *Cal. Inq. p.m.* 1–9 Edw. II, 403; Add. MS. 28024, fol. 190a, 133b; Chan. Inq. p.m. 15 Hen. VI, no. 36.

[17] Chan. Inq. p.m. 15 Hen. VI, no. 36.

[18] *V.C.H. Worcs.* i, 324; Cott. MS. Vesp. B xxiv, fol. 7. At about this time the manor consisted of two parts : 'pars Warneri,' worth 20s., and 'pars Gualteri,' worth 6s.

[18a] *Testa de Nevill* (Rec. Com.), 41b.

[19] In the time of Henry I the manor was probably held by two tenants called Warner and Walter. (See note 18 above.)

[20] *Pipe R.* 22 *Hen. II* (Pipe R. Soc.), 39.

[21] Red Bk. of Bishopric of Worc. (Eccl. Com. Rec. Var. bdle. 121, no. 43698), fol. 252.

[22] *Testa de Nevill* (Rec. Com.), 41b.

[23] Feet of F. Worcs. 33 Hen. III, no. 42.

[24] *Worcs. Inq. p.m.* (Worcs. Hist. Soc.), i, 8.

[25] Nash, op. cit. ii, 242; *Reg. G. Giffard* (Worcs. Hist. Soc.), 379.

[26] *Hund. R.* (Rec. Com.), ii, 284; Assize R. 1026, m. 14 d.

[26a] Add. MS. 28024, fol. 133b.

[27] Ibid. fol. 190a; *Cal. Pat.* 1321–4, p. 64; Feet of F. Worcs. Mich. 14 Edw. III; Mich. 16 Edw. III; *Valor Eccl.* (Rec. Com.), iii, 243.

[28] Pat. 1 & 2 Phil. and Mary, pt. x, m. 31.

[29] Nash, op. cit. ii, 242.

[30] *Cal. Pat.* 1281–92, p. 451.

[31] *Cal. Close,* 1313–18, p. 277.

[32] Chan. Inq. p.m. 16 Edw. II, no. 16; Nash, op. cit. ii, 242. A third part of the manor, including a 'waighhous' and a chapel in the cemetery, was assigned to Cecily wife of John.

[33] Feet of F. Worcs. case 260, file 21, no. 13; *Feud. Aids,* v, 307.

[34] Nash, op. cit. ii, 242.

[35] *Feud. Aids,* v, 319.

[36] Ibid. 332.

[37] Nash, op. cit. ii, 242.

[38] Ibid.

[39] Feet of F. Worcs. Trin. 9 Hen. VII.

[40] Habington, *Surv. of Worcs.* (Worcs. Hist. Soc.), ii, 363; Thomas, op. cit. App. no. 18.

[41] *Testa de Nevill* (Rec. Com.), 41b; Red Bk. of Bishopric of Worc. fol. 55.

[42] Exch. Inq. p.m. (Ser. 2), file 1176, no. 1; Chan. Inq. p.m. (Ser. 2), dxlviii, 11.

Geoffrey D'Abitot held half a knight's fee in Pendock early in the 13th century,[43] and the estate passed with Redmarley D'Abitôt (q.v.) to the Sapy family.[44] It would seem that the manor passed from the last John Sapy to Sir Richard Dudley, for Habington states that Geoffrey D'Abitot's land at Pendock afterwards passed to R. Dudley,[45] and in 1373-4 Sir John Sapy settled certain of his possessions on himself for life with remainder to Sir Richard Dudley.[46] It seems to have been this manor which was sold in 1405 by Walter Toky and Joan his wife as five parts of a messuage and land in Pendock to Thomas Brydges.[47] The estate was held by Walter and Joan in right of Joan, who may have been the heiress of Sir Richard Dudley. Thomas Brydges evidently settled Pendock upon his issue by his second wife Alice, for in 1431 Giles Brydges, son and heir of Thomas and Alice, was holding the manor.[48] Giles must have conveyed it before his death, which did not occur until 1466-7,[49] to his step-brother Edward, for the latter died in 1436-7 holding half the manor of Pendock, a messuage called Morecourt,[50] and two-fifths of a messuage called Wavepolles in Pendock.[51] Edward left a daughter Isabel,[52] who afterwards married John Throckmorton.[53] He died in 1472 holding an estate in Pendock which passed to his son Christopher,[54] on whose death in 1513 his son William succeeded.[55] Thomas son and successor of William[56] sold the manor in 1571 to Thomas Bartlett.[57] Thomas died in 1582-3,[58] leaving the manor and advowson of Pendock to Thomas Bartlett, younger son of his brother Richard,[59] who sold it in 1590 to Giles Nanfan.[60] Giles purchased the site of the manor in 1598 from John Beale and Margery his wife and Edward Halliday,[61] and sold it in 1601 to Giles Parker.[62] Giles Nanfan died seised of the manor in 1614,[63] and from that time until 1769 it followed the same descent as Birtsmorton[64] (q.v.). Pendock was sold in 1769 by Judith daughter and heir of Richard third Earl of Bellamont to Robert Bromley.[65] Judith Bromley, daughter of William Bromley of Ham Court, married John Martin of Overbury Park, and brought Pendock Manor into the family.[66] It seems to have passed from John Martin to his nephew Thomas,[67] and James Thomas Martin who sold it in 1827 to Samuel Beale,[68] may have been the son of Thomas.[69] Samuel Beale had presented to the church in 1810.[70] He was apparently succeeded by Mary Anne Beale, who married William Symonds of Elsdon. On her death about the middle of the 19th century the estate passed to her son the Rev. William Samuel Symonds, the eminent geologist and author.[71] He

died in 1887, and his daughter Hyacinth wife of Sir Joseph Dalton Hooker is now lady of the manor of Pendock.

Richard de Berking, Abbot of Westminster (1222-46), bought a quit-rent of 24s. at Pendock, with two tenants who held their land of the sacrist. This rent remained with the abbey until the Dissolution, when it amounted to 13s. 3½d. It was granted in 1542 to the Dean and Chapter of Westminster, and is entered among their possessions in 1690 as 'certain concealed lands in Pendock which cannot be discovered, for which the farmer pays out of purse yearly to the church 10s.'[71a]

CHURCH The church (dedication unknown) consists of a chancel 18 ft. by 12 ft., modern north vestry, nave 37 ft. by 18 ft., a west tower and a north porch. These measurements are internal.

The chancel and nave appear to date from the middle of the 12th century. New windows were inserted in the 14th and 15th centuries, and at one or other of these periods the chancel arch seems to have been rebuilt, the original jambs being left, and some of the earlier arch stones built into the new work. The west tower is of the 15th century.

The east window of the chancel is of two trefoiled lights, with a quatrefoil in the head. The jambs and arch are of original 14th-century date, but the tracery is modern. In the north wall is a single light, probably of the same period, with a wood lintel for rear arch. The modern vestry is entered by a doorway with a four-centred head. In the south wall is a square-headed window of two lights, also with a wood lintel, the tracery of which is modern. At the south-east is a piscina recess with a head apparently made up of old stones at a comparatively recent period. The bowl, which has a square drain, appears to be part of a late 12th-century pillar piscina. Part of the carved face with interlacing arches is exposed. The jambs of the chancel arch date from the middle of the 12th century and have angle-shafts on the nave side. The arch itself, which is two-centred, appears to have assumed its present form at some period subsequent to the date of the jambs, perhaps in the 14th century, when the majority of the later windows were inserted. At the south-east of the nave is a square projecting turret containing the rood-stair. In the north wall to the west of the north doorway is a window of two trefoiled lights with a quatrefoil in the head, rough work, probably of the 15th century. The north doorway is of the original 12th-century date. The opening is square, with a plain tympanum contained

43 *Testa de Nevill* (Rec. Com.), 41b.
44 Habington, op. cit. ii, 254; Red Bk. of Bishopric of Worc. fol. 55; *Cal. Close*, 1330-3, p. 21; *Feud. Aids*, v, 308.
45 Habington, op. cit. ii, 254.
46 Inq. a.q.d. file 380, no. 3.
47 Feet of F. Worcs. Hil. 6 Hen. IV.
48 *Feud. Aids*, v, 332; Chan. Inq. p.m. 6 Hen. V, no. 57; 2 Hen. V, no. 7; *Visit. of Gloucs.* (Harl. Soc. xxi), 233.
49 Chan. Inq. p.m. 7 Edw. IV, no. 15.
50 Held of the Prior of Great Malvern.
51 Held of Guy Spencer. John Wavepol paid a subsidy of 18s. at Pendock in 1280 (*Lay Subs. R. Worcs.* 1280 [Worcs. Hist. Soc.], 44), and Peter Wavepol witnessed a deed of 1318-19 (Prattinton Coll. Deeds of D. and C. of Worc. no. 65).

52 Chan. Inq. p.m. 15 Hen. VI, no. 36.
53 Ibid. 16 Hen. VI, no. 70.
54 Ibid. 13 Edw. IV, no. 16.
55 Exch. Inq. p.m. (Ser. 2), file 1176, no. 1.
56 Nash, op. cit. i, 452.
57 Feet of F. Worcs. Mich. 13 & 14 Eliz.
58 His will is dated 1582 and proved 1583.
59 P.C.C. Wills, 20 Rowe.
60 Feet of F. Worcs. Mich. 32 & 33 Eliz.   61 Ibid. Mich. 41 Eliz.
62 Ibid. Mich. 43 & 44 Eliz.
63 Chan. Inq. p.m. (Ser. 2), ccccliii, 72.
64 Feet of F. Worcs. Mich. 1659; Div. Co. Hil. 33 & 34 Chas. II; Recov. R. East. 12 Anne, rot. 188.

65 Feet of F. Worcs. Hil. 9 Geo. III.
66 Nash, op. cit. ii, 445; Burke, *Landed Gentry* (1906).
67 Burke, loc. cit.; Recov. R. Hil. 11 Geo. III, rot. 354.
68 Recov. R. Mich. 8 Geo. IV, rot. 36.
69 Burke, loc. cit.
70 Inst. Bks. (P.R.O.). Thomas Beale was holding a messuage and farm in Pendock in 1738 (Recov. R. D. Enr. East. 11 Geo. II, m. 1).
71 *Dict. Nat. Biog.*
71a Cott. MS. Claud. A viii, fol. 48 d.; *Valor Eccl.* (Rec. Com.), i, 414; *L. and P. Hen. VIII*, xvii, g. 714 (5), p. 394; Pat. 3 & 4 Phil. and Mary, pt. v; 2 Eliz. pt. xi, m. 15; Deeds of D. and C. of Westminster, no. 21912.

within a cheveron-moulded external round-arched order having a pelleted label. The jambs of this order have angle shafts with scalloped capitals and moulded bases. Their abaci are cut back flush. The nail-studded door with its plain band straps is old. The under edge of the tympanum and the jamb of the doorway are cut back for fitting a square wood frame. There are two windows in the south wall, one on either side of the south doorway. The easternmost is of two trefoiled lights and dates from the 14th century. The south-west window is a modern copy of a similar number of lights. The south doorway is quite plain and has a semicircular head. Generally the exterior has quoins and dressings of sandstone. On the south side of the nave are two buttresses probably of the 16th century ; the wall here leans over a little.

The tower is of three stages with diagonal buttresses at the western angles. The tower arch is two-centred and of two chamfered orders, with a moulded string at the springing. The west window of the ground stage has a traceried two-centred head, and is of two cinquefoiled lights. The bell-chamber is lighted by windows of two trefoiled lights, and internally the squinches for a spire may be seen. The intermediate stage is lighted by single square-headed lights. The facing is of large sandstone, and the weathering of an earlier and more steeply pitched nave roof is visible on the east wall. The porch is of timber, probably of the 15th century, with a modern roof.

The nave and chancel roofs are plastered. Both have moulded plates, probably of the 15th century, and at the south-east of the nave roof, which has three moulded tie-beams, the plate is moulded with extra elaboration, as if on account of its contiguity to the demolished rood. Externally the roofs are tiled.

The font is circular, and stands on a base of the same form. The workmanship is rude, and no more can be said of its date than that it belongs to the middle ages. The communion rails, with their balusters and deep-carved top rail, may perhaps be Laudian. There are some pieces of old woodwork in the reading-desk, with linen pattern panels and tracery, and the lower panels of the 15th-century chancel screen are still preserved.

There are four bells : the first and third by Abel Rudhall, 1753 and 1745 ; the second, a roughly-cast bell by an unknown founder dated 1686, some of the letters being black letter smalls ; the fourth, originally of 1745, was recast by H. Bond of Burford, 1908.[72]

The plate includes a cup of porringer shape with the hall mark of 1766. There are also a plate for paten and a large tankard flagon hall-marked 1748, both given by Lord Bellamont, as well as a silver-handled bread knife of 1750.

The registers previous to 1812 are in four volumes : (i) all entries 1558 to 1684 ; (ii) all 1668 to 1735 ; (iii) baptisms and burials 1735 to 1813, marriages 1735 to 1754 ; (iv) marriages 1755 to 1813.

A wooden church was erected at Pendock in 1889 on a site given by Miss Higgins.

ADVOWSON There was possibly a church at Pendock at the time of the Domesday Survey, for a priest held half a hide of land in the manor of Pendock belonging to the monks of Worcester Priory.[73] The advowson was annexed to the part of the manor held by the Pendock family.[74] In 1211 there was an assize to discover whether Geoffrey D'Abitot presented the last parson to the church of Pendock in his own right or on account of the custody of Maud wife of Hugh Bonvalet. Judgement was given in favour of Hugh and Maud and they recovered the presentation.[75] From this it would seem that Maud must have been a member of the Pendock family.

William de Pendock, who presented to the church in 1357 and 1369, had recovered by law the advowson of the church against the Prior of Little Malvern.[76] The advowson was sold by John Spencer and Elizabeth his wife to Christopher Throckmorton in 1493,[77] and from that time has followed the descent of the united manor of Pendock,[78] the present patron being Lady Hooker.

In 1576–7 a cottage and land at Pendock given for obits in the church were granted to Edward Grimston.[79]

CHARITIES The church table stated that a pious benefactor gave lands to repair the church and towards the support and maintenance of the poor, comprised in an ancient feoffment, temp. James I. The property now consists of 4 a. in Longdon, 2 r. in Little Wilkin, three cottages and 1 a. in Pendock, and an old schoolroom, producing in the aggregate £14 17s., of which about £2 yearly is distributed among the sick and needy, and the net residue is carried to the churchwardens' account.

The Wesleyan Methodist chapel comprised in an indenture of 28 July 1823 has, under an order of the Charity Commissioners, been settled upon the trusts of the Wesleyan chapel model deed.

REDMARLEY D'ABITÔT

Reode moere leage, Ryde mereleage (x cent.) ; Rydmer lege, Hrydmearlea, Ridmerleye (xi cent.) ; Rudmerleg (xiii cent.); Redmerley Dapetot (xiv cent.).

Redmarley D'Abitôt lies in the extreme south-west of the county on the Gloucestershire border. It covers an area of 3,800 acres, which includes 12 acres of inland water, 1,165 acres of arable land, 2,432 acres of permanent grass, and 89 acres of woods and plantations.[1] The soil is sand and clay on a subsoil of clay and shale and raises crops of wheat, beans, peas and barley. The parish is watered by the River Leadon, which divides Redmarley from Pauntley,

[72] Inform. from Mr. H. B. Walters, F.S.A.
[73] V.C.H. Worcs. i, 295.
[74] Institutions given in Nash, op. cit. ii, 242.
[75] Cur. Reg. R. 54, m. 8 d. ; 55, m. 7 ; Abbrev. Plac. (Rec. Com.), 80a.
[76] Nash, loc. cit.
[77] Feet of F. Worcs. Trin. 9 Hen. VII.
[78] Exch. Inq. p.m. (Ser. 2), file 1176,
no. 1 ; Feet of F. Worcs. Mich. 13 & 14 Eliz. ; Inst. Bks. (P.R.O.).
[79] Pat. 19 Eliz. pt. v ; Chant. Cert. 60, no. 61 ; 61, no. 33.
[1] Statistics from Bd. of Agric. (1905).

(Gloucs.), on the south and by the Glynch Brook,[2] a tributary of the Leadon, and the Wynd Brook.

CHURCH HOUSE, REDMARLEY D'ABITÔT

30 ft. by 17 ft. 8½ in. It is vaulted in three bays, with chamfered transverse and diagonal ribs springing from moulded corbels. In one side wall is a plain round-headed doorway, and close to it a small round-headed light. There are two similar lights in the opposite wall, now blocked by later additions. One end wall is also covered by modern buildings, but the other retains an original window. The hall door was reached by an outside stair; of the hall itself no original features remain.

There is a moated inclosure near Heart's Farm in the south of the parish.

In 1636 a certain John Jackman, yeoman, was indicted for obstructing the highway by erecting a pound in the road from Redmarley D'Abitôt to Tewkesbury.[3]

There are various notes in the registers of historic interest with regard to the parish. In the year 1644 'the battle of Redmarley,' in which between 2,000 and 3,000 troops were engaged, was fought among the fields outside the village. In the fight the Royalist leader Major-General Mynn was killed.[4] The name of Feargus O'Connor, Chartist agitator, is connected with the locality, and in 1847 the Lowbands estate was purchased by the National Land Company. Wakes were originally held on the village green (inclosed 1838) on the Sunday before St. Bartholomew's Day.[5]

Among the ancient place-names are Assendene[6] (xiv cent.); Le Mere,[7] Moreheldende or Morellynde[8] (surviving as Murrellsend) (xv cent.); Overhouse, The Held, Tondens, Slade, Neth Gramell, le

The western part of the parish is hilly, rising from the valley of the Leadon to over 200 ft. above the ordnance datum. In the east the land is lower, standing at about 100 ft. above the ordnance datum. The main road from Ledbury to Gloucester passes through Redmarley. A branch from it to the west leads to the village, and another branch leads north-east across Glynch Brook to Pendock. The parish contains houses of various types and sizes scattered along several winding roads. In the south-west corner of the churchyard there is a 17th-century brick and timber house, and there are several other houses of this type in the parish, with large picturesque chimney stacks of red brick. The rectory lies about a quarter of a mile to the east of the church, the present building occupying an old site which was originally moated.

At Bury Court Farm are the remains of a late 12th-century hall over a vaulted cellar, measuring

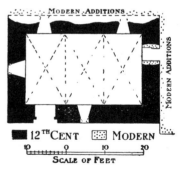

BURY COURT: PLAN OF VAULTED CELLAR

ynde[8] (surviving as Murrellsend) (xv cent.); Overhouse, The Held, Tondens, Slade, Neth Gramell, le Mort Medowe, Darcombe[9] (xvi cent.); Glasham, Howhill, Longeland, Thatchcroft[10] (xvii cent.).

---

[2] The Glynch Brook is mentioned in a charter dated 963 (Birch, *Cart. Sax.* iii, 342). There were two bridges over this brook in 1609 (*Quart. Sess. R.* [Worcs. Hist. Soc.], i, 130).

[3] *Quart. Sess. R.* (Worcs. Hist. Soc.), ii, 613.
[4] See *Cal. S. P. Dom.* 1644, pp. 397, 413.
[5] The wake was still held in 1868 (see Noake, *Guide to Worcs.* 308).

[6] Add. Chart. 24758.
[7] Ibid. 24770.
[8] Sloane Chart. xxxiii, 70; Add. Chart. 24789–91, 24775, 24785–6.
[9] Ibid. 24791.   [10] Ibid. 24799.

REDMARLEY D'ABITÒT : VAULTED CELLAR AT BURY COURT

REDMARLEY D'ABITÒT : VAULTED CELLAR AT BURY COURT

MANORS Land at *REDMARLEY* belonged in the 10th century to the see of Worcester, a 'mansa' there 'near the Glynch Brook' being leased by Bishop Oswald in 963 for three lives to a certain thegn named Eadmœr.[11] A similar lease was made by the same bishop to his thegn Æthelmund in 978.[12] Among the Worcester charters is one of Bishop Lyfing in 1038 dealing with land in Redmarley,[13] but the nature of the charter is not known.

Before the Conquest Azor and Godwine held Redmarley of the bishop's manor of Bredon, but by 1086, when it consisted of 7 hides, it had come into the possession of Urse the Sheriff.[14] The manor was still held of Bredon in 1299,[15] but the overlordship of the Bishops of Worcester is not mentioned after that time. Urse's interest passed to his descendants the Beauchamps, who continued as mesne lords until they acquired the manor at the beginning of the 15th century.[16]

In 1086 2 of the 7 hides of which the manor consisted were held under Urse by a certain William,[17] and subsequently the whole 7 passed to the D'Abitots, from whom the manor derived its name. Osbert D'Abitot held the manor about 1164–79.[18] The Geoffrey D'Abitot who held the manor early in the 13th century[19] was perhaps he who in 1204 gave 40 marks and a palfrey for having seisin of lands of which he had been deprived by the king's command.[20] His name also occurs in 1199 and 1200.[21] In 1241 Osbert D'Abitot released to Geoffrey D'Abitot all his claim in the manor of Redmarley.[22] This Geoffrey was perhaps succeeded by Ralph, for in 1274 it was said that the Earl of Gloucester had appropriated all the land belonging to Ralph D'Abitot and put it into his chase, and the land evidently lay in the neighbourhood of Redmarley, as the Glynch Brook is mentioned.[23] Probably, however, Ralph never held the manor, for it seems to have belonged in 1274[24] to Geoffrey grandson of Geoffrey D'Abitot above mentioned.[25] He went in 1277 with William de Beauchamp Earl of Warwick against the Welsh,[26] receiving in the same year a respite for a few months from becoming a knight,[27]

and three years later exemption for life from being put on assizes, juries and recognizances.[28] It was probably this same Geoffrey who in 1320 sued his uncle Geoffrey D'Abitot for a messuage and 2 carucates of land in Redmarley (evidently the manor) which the latter claimed by gift of his father Geoffrey. His nephew, however, stated that Geoffrey had been out of his mind when he made the gift,[29] and was apparently successful in proving his claim, for in 1321–2 he as Geoffrey son of John D'Abitot settled the manor on himself for life with remainder to John de Sapy and

D'ABITOT. *Ermine a chief bendy or and sable.*

STREET IN REDMARLEY D'ABITÔT

[11] Birch, op. cit. iii, 342 ; Heming, *Chartul.* (ed. Hearne), 179.
[12] Heming, op. cit. 176.
[13] Dugdale, *Mon. Angl.* i, 582 n.
[14] *V.C.H. Worcs.* i, 291 b.
[15] Red Bk. of Bishopric of Worc. (Eccl. Com. Rec. Var. bdle. 121, no. 43698), fol. 55.
[16] *V.C.H. Worcs.* i, 324 b n.; *Testa de Nevill* (Rec. Com.), 41 b ; *Cal. Inq. p.m.* 1–9 *Edw.* II, 403 ; *Cal. Close,* 1313–18, p. 277 ; *Feud. Aids,* v, 307, 319.

[17] *V.C.H. Worcs.* i, 291 b.
[18] Red Bk. of Bishopric of Worc. fol. 252.
[19] *Testa de Nevill* (Rec. Com.), 41 b.
[20] *Rot. de Oblatis et Fin.* (Rec. Com.), 225.
[21] Ibid. 67 ; *Rot. Cur. Reg.* (Rec. Com.), i, 276.
[22] Feet of F. Worcs. East. 25 Hen. III, no. 33.
[23] *Hund. R.* (Rec. Com.), ii, 283.
[24] Assize R. 1025, m. 1. See *Lay Subs.*

R. *Worcs.* c. 1280 (Worcs. Hist. Soc.), 41.
[25] De Banco R. 236 (Mich. 14 Edw. II), m. 141 d. See also *Cal. Close,* 1296–1302, pp. 443, 444. Lucy widow of Geoffrey the grandfather was still living in 1321–2 (*Cal. Pat.* 1340–3, p. 474).
[26] *Cal. Pat.* 1272–81, p. 190.
[27] *Cal. Close,* 1272–9, p. 368.
[28] *Cal. Pat.* 1272–81, p. 367.
[29] De Banco R. 236 (Mich. 14 Edw. II), m. 141 d.

his wife Sibyl, daughter of Alice D'Abitot, Geoffrey's aunt.[30] Geoffrey evidently took an active part in the rebellion against the Despensers, and in 1321 a warrant was issued for his arrest as a ' rebel and enemy of the king.'[31] He was imprisoned at Gloucester, and only released after he had been obliged by ' force and duress' to give up the manor of Redmarley to Hugh le Despenser the younger,[32] who to make his title more secure obtained grants from the king[33] and from John de Sapy and Sibyl his wife.[34]

Immediately after the accession of Edward III John de Sapy and Sibyl received a grant of Redmarley in 'consideration of his losses in the service of the late king.'[35] This naturally led to quarrels with Geoffrey D'Abitot, who was probably among the 'malefactors' accused by John de Sapy of breaking his houses at Redmarley and taking away his goods.[36] Geoffrey petitioned in 1327 for a restoration of the manor,[37] but, although his lands were restored,[38] this manor does not appear to have been among them, and he was still trying to recover it in 1329.[39] He evidently did not succeed in establishing his claim, and in 1330 John de Sapy and Sibyl received a new grant of the manor for their lives only,[40] with a grant of free warren in 1332,[41] while in 1340 and 1342 the king confirmed the fine under which the manor had first been settled on them.[42] John de Sapy was knighted and received other marks of royal favour.[43] He was holding in 1346[44] and died some time before 1350, when the fealty of his grandson John Sapy son of Thomas was taken for certain lands in Caldecot.[45] From the last-named John,[46] who was a justice of the peace for the county of Worcester,[47] and was still holding the manor in 1381,[48] it passed, probably by purchase, to Elizabeth widow of Edward Lord le Despenser, on whom it was settled in 1393.[49] She was succeeded in turn by her grandson Richard le Despenser, who died childless and while still a minor in 1414,[50] and by her granddaughter Isabel, through whose marriage with Richard Earl of Warwick[51] the manor came into the possession of the Earls of Warwick, who were already the overlords. It then followed the same descent as Elmley Castle[52] (q.v.), passing with it to Henry VII in 1487.

It was granted in exchange for other manors to Edmund Bonner, Bishop of London, in 1545.[53]

Bishop Ridley, who succeeded Bonner, leased the park and a mill at Redmarley to his sister Alice and her husband George Shipside,[54] and they were living there when Bonner again became bishop on the accession of Queen Mary. Bonner wrote to Richard and Robert Lechmere requesting them to look after Redmarley and not to allow 'sheep's head or shipes side (alluding to Ridley's brother-in-law) to be any medler there or to sell or carry away anything from thence.'[55] Shortly afterwards he made a fresh lease of the park and mill to Thomas Sherle and others, but on the accession of Queen Elizabeth both park and mill were restored to the Shipsides.[56] In 1591 John, Bishop of London, surrendered the manor to the queen,[57] who immediately granted it in exchange for other lands to Thomas Crompton, Robert Wright and Gelley Meyrick.[58]

For a few years after this date the descent of the manor is not quite clear, but by 1612 it was in the possession of William Horton of the neighbouring parish of Staunton.[59] His son Thomas Horton sold it in 1615 to George Shipside's son George,[60] who had succeeded his father as lessee of the park and mill in 1609[61] and was living at Redmarley in 1615.[62] After holding it for a year only, George Shipside, with Margaret his wife, sold the manor to a certain John Fleet, known also as Waldegrave,[63] but continued to live at the manor-house, then known as Redmarley Park.[64] John Fleet died at Hallow in 1619 and was succeeded by his son Thomas,[65] who died in the following year, leaving an infant son John.[66] The manor had been settled on Thomas and Jane his wife on their marriage in 1617.[67] She married secondly a certain William Bodenham,[68] whose name occurs on the Quarter Session Rolls as a recusant,[69] and also as refusing to contribute towards the repair of the roads in Redmarley.[70] Before 1676 the manor had been divided between Magdalen wife of Richard Williams and Anne wife of Ambrose Scudamore,[71] sisters and co-heirs of Thomas Fleet. They sold it to George Wellington of London, of whom it was purchased in 1698 by Sir Nicholas Lechmere of Hanley Castle.[71a] It was in the possession of his great-grandson Edmund Lechmere in 1732[72] and passed from him to his son Nicholas.[73] The latter, who took the name of Charlton in 1784, was succeeded by his son Edmund Lechmere Charlton, who

---

[30] *Cal. Pat.* 1340–3, p. 474 ; *Visit. of Warw.* (Harl. Soc. xii), 136.

[31] *Cal. Pat.* 1321–4, p. 102.

[32] *Parl. R.* ii, 411 ; *Cal. Pat.* 1327–30, p. 477.

[33] *Cal. Chart. R.* 1300–26, p. 464.

[34] Feet of F. Worcs. Trin. 17 Edw. II.

[35] *Cal. Pat.* 1327–30, p. 40. John de Sapy was one of the king's yeomen who had held various official posts (see *Cal. Pat.* 1307–13, pp. 201, 362, 620).

[36] Ibid. 1327–30, p. 73.

[37] *Parl. R.* ii, 411.

[38] Ibid. 421*a*, 422*b*, 423*a*.

[39] *Cal. Pat.* 1327–30, p. 477.

[40] Ibid. p. 543.

[41] Chart. R. 6 Edw. III, m. 26, no. 51.

[42] *Cal. Pat.* 1340–3, pp. 510, 474.

[43] Ibid. 1330–4, p. 437 ; 1338–40, p. 55.

[44] *Feud. Aids*, v, 307.

[45] *Cal. Close*, 1349–54, p. 134.

[46] Worc. Epis. Reg. Alcock, fol. 104 d. ; Anct. D. (P.R.O.), A 11389.

[47] *Cal. Pat.* 1381–5, pp. 138, 246.

[48] Chan. Inq. p.m. 5 Ric. II, no. 29.

[49] Feet of F. Worcs. East. 16 Ric. II. She obtained protection for one year for herself and her tenants in this and other manors in 1400 (*Cal. Pat.* 1399–1401, p. 178).

[50] G.E.C. *Complete Peerage*, iii, 93. One-third of Redmarley was assigned to his widow Eleanor in dower (Chan. Inq. p.m. 4 Hen. V, no. 52).

[51] G.E.C. loc. cit.

[52] For refs. see Elmley Castle.

[53] Pat. 37 Hen. VIII, pt. vii, m. 13 ; *L. and P. Hen. VIII*, xx (2), g. 496 (13).

[54] Chan. Enr. Decrees Eliz. pt. xiii, no. 27.

[55] Ridley, *Life of Bishop Ridley*, 429.

[56] Chan. Enr. Decrees Eliz. pt. xiii, no. 27.

[57] Feet of F. Div. Co. East. 33 Eliz.

[58] Pat. 33 Eliz. pt. vi, m. 17 ; see also ibid. 32 Eliz. pt. ix, m. 11.

[59] *Quart. Sess. R.* (Worcs. Hist. Soc.), i, 172.

[60] Close, 13 Jas. I, pt. iv, no. 36. Thomas granted that George and his heirs should hold the manor without any hindrance from the heirs of Sir Thomas Gresley, kt., deceased, or Richard Bartlett, who, it is probable, held the manor before William Horton.

[61] Habington, op. cit. ii, 264.

[62] Close, 13 Jas. I, pt. iv, no. 36.

[63] Feet of F. Worcs. Trin. 14 Jas. I.

[64] Chan. Inq. p.m. (Ser. 2), ccclxxviii, 115.

[65] Ibid.

[66] Ibid. ccclxxx, 135.

[67] Ibid.

[68] W. and L. Inq. p.m. xcv, 181.

[69] op. cit. (Worcs. Hist. Soc.), ii, 612.

[70] Ibid. 560.

[71] Feet of F. Worcs. Trin. 28 Chas. II ; Trin. 30 Chas. II ; Mich. 32 Chas. II.

[71a] Close, 10 Will. III, pt. xv, no. 5.

[72] Recov. R. East. 5 Geo. II, rot. 236.

[73] Ibid. Mich. 4 Geo. III, rot. 391.

was holding Redmarley in 1811.[74] He sold it in the following year to William Lord Beauchamp,[75] and it is now in the possession of William, the present earl.

A family named D'Abitot owned property in the parish in the 16th century, and lived at Down House.[76] According to Nash, the last member of the family died in the 18th century.[77]

LYGON, Earl Beauchamp. *Argent two lions passant gules with forked tails.*

INNERSTONE (Inarde-stone, xiii cent.), now a farm in the parish, is first mentioned in 1229–30, when William de Kardiff conveyed a knight's fee there to Geoffrey D'Abitot.[78] Since that date it has always belonged to the lord of Redmarley.[79] It is called a manor until 1416,[80] and then apparently became merged in the more important manor of Redmarley.

The park at Redmarley is first mentioned in 1457.[81] It has always belonged to the lords of the manor,[82] various appointments of park-keepers being made by Edward IV [83] and Henry VIII.[84]

A mill in Redmarley worth 5s. 8d. is mentioned in the Domesday Survey.[85] In 1359 there was a mill known as Pauntleys belonging to the lord of Redmarley,[86] while in the 15th and 16th centuries there were two mills, one called Bury Mill, the other Flaxeorde Mill.[87] Bury Mill, Blackford Mill [88] and Farm Mill, on the Glynch Brook, are still in use. Besides the manorial mills the D'Abitots owned another mill called Thurbache, which John D'Abitot purchased from Thomas Bradford in 1549.[89] In 1654 Francis Dineley sued Thomas D'Abitot for detaining deeds relating to Thurbache Mill, claiming that the defendant had sold the reversion after his death to him, and afterwards leased the mill to him on condition that he would repair it.[90] It belonged to Charles Dineley and Frances his wife in 1685.[91] It was probably this mill which was owned by Edmund Cowcher in 1715.[92] There is at present a disused corn-mill called Durbridge Mill on the Leadon. In the 17th century the D'Abitots had the right of free fishing in the River Leadon,[93] which with Thurbache Mill passed from them to Charles and Frances Dineley.[94]

The church of *ST. BARTHOLO-*
CHURCH *MEW* consists of a chancel measuring internally 28 ft. by 17½ ft., nave 49½ ft. by 23½ ft., a west tower 14 ft. square, a north aisle

16 ft. wide, a north vestry and a south porch. The whole church, with the exception of the tower, was rebuilt in 1855.

The east window of the chancel is of three lancet lights, and in the north and south walls are single lancets. The furniture includes a 17th-century credence table, two chairs (one dated 1632) and some 17th-century baluster altar-rails re-used in the quire desks.

The nave has a north arcade of three bays, and is lit by two-light windows, all in the style of the 14th century.

The timber south porch and the octagonal stone font are both modern, as are also the arches to the chancel and tower. The two-light west window, with a four-centred head, is probably of 18th-century date.

The only monument of importance is that to George Shipside, who died in 1609, aged eighty-four, on the north wall of the chancel. It is a framed slab headed *Memento Mori*, with a rhyming epitaph.

The exterior of the tower is in three stages, with an embattled parapet and angle pinnacles ; there is a stair at the north-west angle entered from the outside by a segmental-headed door. The belfry windows are of two lights and similar to the window in the west wall. The tower was rebuilt early in the 18th century, but the lower part is perhaps of earlier date. The roof of the church is tiled.

The bells are six in number, the first, second, fourth and fifth by Abel Rudhall, 1743, the third 1739 and the tenor 1793.

The plate consists of a cup and cover paten engraved with the date 1571 ; there are also a modern paten, flagon and almsdish.

The registers before 1812 are as follows : (i) baptisms 1542 to 1695, burials 1539 to 1691, marriages 1539 to 1693, and from these dates the entries are continued promiscuously to 1702 ; (ii) mixed entries 1703 to 1800, marriages extending to 1753 ; (iii) baptisms and burials 1800 to 1812 ; (iv) marriages 1755 to 1797 ; (v) marriages 1798 to 1812.

ADVOWSON   The first mention of the church of Redmarley occurs in 1290, when the Bishop of Worcester dedicated three altars there.[95] The advowson followed the same descent as the manor [96] (q.v.) until 1590, when the manor was granted to Thomas Crompton and the advowson retained by the queen. It belonged to the Crown [97] until James I granted it to William Teynton or Taunton in 1610.[98] The descent for some time after this date is not clear. William Teynton had been succeeded before 1662 by Henry

[74] Recov. R. Hil. 51 Geo. III, rot. 254.

[75] Inform. from the Rev. A. M. Niblett.

[76] Feet of F. Div. Co. East. 3 Edw. VI. This property is called a manor in 1549, but not again (Add. Chart. 24789, 24790, 24791, 24794, 24799 ; *Quart. Sess. R.* [Worcs. Hist. Soc.], ii, 507, 612).

[77] op. cit. ii, 305.

[78] Feet of F. Worcs. case 258, file 4, no. 12.

[79] *Abbrev. Rot. Orig.* (Rec. Com.), i, 113 ; Chart. R. 17 Edw. II, no. 9 ; Feet of F. Worcs. East. 16 Ric. II, no. 43 ; Chan. Inq. p.m. 4 Hen. V, no. 52.

[80] Chan. Inq. p.m. 4 Hen. V, no. 52.

[81] *Cal. Pat.* 1476–85, p. 97.

[82] For reference see manor.

[83] *Cal. Pat.* 1476–85, pp. 161, 319.

[84] *L. and P. Hen. VIII,* iii, g. 1081 (27) ; ix, g. 729 (2) ; xv, g. 436 (4) ; xx

(2), g. 496 (13) ; Chan. Enr. Decrees Eliz. pt. xiii, no. 27.

[85] *V.C.H. Worcs.* i, 291b.

[86] Anct. D. (P.R.O.), A 11389. This mill may have been in Pauntley on the site of the present (disused) corn-mill near Pauntley Court on the Redmarley border.

[87] Mins. Accts. (Gen. Ser.), bdles. 644, no. 10457 ; 1068, no. 9 ; ibid. Hen. VII, no. 989.

[88] This mill is mentioned in Chan. Enr. Decrees Eliz. pt. xiii, no. 27, and Close, 10 Will. III, pt. xv, no. 5. For other references to Bury Mill see *L. and P. Hen. VIII,* iii, 1215 (4) ; x, g. 226 (37) ; xx (2), g. 496 (13). In *Quart. Sess. R.* (Worcs. Hist. Soc.), i, 130, one of these mills is called 'the Bean Mill.'

[89] Add. Chart. 24789, 24790, 24791, 24794.

[90] Chan. Proc. (Ser. 2), bdle. 441, no. 9.

[91] Feet of F. Div. Co. East. 1 Jas II.

[92] Recov. R. Mich. 2 Geo. I, rot. 115.

[93] Feet of F. Worcs. Mich. 1649.

[94] Ibid. Div. Co. Mich. 33 Chas. II ; East. 1 Jas. II.

[95] *Reg. G. Giffard* (Worcs. Hist. Soc.), 372. The church was valued at £11 13s. 4d. in 1291 (*Pope Nich. Tax.* [Rec. Com.], 216), and at £16 1s. 3½d. at the Dissolution (*Valor Eccl.* [Rec. Com.], iii, 245).

[96] Feet of F. Worcs. 17 Edw. II, no. 11 ; *Cal. Pat.* 1340–3, pp. 474, 510 ; Feet of F. Worcs. East. 16 Ric. II ; Chan. Inq. p.m. 4 Hen. V, no. 52 ; *Cal. Pat.* 1408–13, p. 285 ; Pat. 37 Hen. VIII, pt. vii, m. 13.   [97] Inst. Bks. (P.R.O.).

[98] Pat. 8 Jas. I, pt. lv, no. 20 ; *Cal. S. P. Dom.* 1603–10, p. 631.

Jackson, clerk,[99] in whose family the advowson remained until 1739, when Thomas Jackson and his wife sold it to Francis Morton.[100] The latter was the patron from 1745 to 1750,[1] but Michael Biddulph presented to the living in 1789 and George Monro in 1801.[2] Between 1829, when George Monro still owned the advowson,[3] and 1836 it was purchased by the Nibletts,[4] and is now in the possession of the rector, the Rev. Henry Morton Niblett.

The rector of Redmarley claimed among other liberties the right of pasturing eight oxen and two cows in all the demesne pastures of Redmarley and Innerstone and 'lawegrist' in all the mills of the lords, and these were confirmed to him by John Sapy, kt., in 1358.[5]

In the 15th century there was a chapel at Innerstone which was the cause of a dispute between the inhabitants of that place and the rector of Redmarley. It was decided in 1466 that the rector should find a chaplain to serve the chapel.[6] It seems to have been disused before the Dissolution, and its site may be marked by the present Chapel Farm.

At the time of the Dissolution there was a chantry dedicated in honour of our Lady in the church of Redmarley D'Abitôt.[7] It seems to have been founded by Walter D'Abitot and Thomas Mon' and others, but the foundation charter has not been found.[8] The parish then contained 230 'houseling people,' and the salary of the chantry priest, who was 'competently learnyd and of honest conversacon,' was derived from lands valued at £6 10s. 4d. yearly,[9] which were granted in 1549 to Thomas Watson and William Adys.[10]

A Bible Christian chapel was built about the middle of the 19th century for the Chartist colonists on the Lowbands estate,[11] and was afterwards used by Primitive Methodists. It was bought by the late Colonel Scobell in 1908, and is now used for church services and other purposes. There is a Wesleyan Methodist chapel near the village, erected in 1859 and rebuilt in 1889.

CHARITIES The church and poor's land charities are regulated by scheme of the Charity Commissioners 24 April 1896. They comprise the five charities following, which were recorded on the church table, namely:—

1. John Bower, founded by deed 29 April 1462, consisting of a parcel of land known as Nottin Dole, toward the repair of the church and for the use of the poor.

2. Walter Ryley, by deed 11 December 1469, gave lands known as Carter's Close, Bean Pits, Bell Acre and two other pieces of land.[12]

3. An unknown donor gave several pieces of land containing about 2 acres, and there were other parcels of land given for charitable purposes.

The lands above referred to were sold in 1873 and the proceeds invested in £857 18s. 2d. consols with the official trustees.

4. William Church, will dated in 1727, being a rent-charge of 20s. issuing out of a tenement known as Church's, for putting out poor children to school, constituting the educational foundation of William Church.

5. Margaret Birchett, will dated in 1732, being a rent-charge of 10s. issuing out of a messuage known as The Folly. This money is given to four poor widows who are not in receipt of parish pay.

Also the charity of John Reginald Pindar Earl Beauchamp, founded by will proved in the P.C.C. 22 February 1853, trust fund £124 17s. consols with the official trustees. This includes a small investment from sale of timber.

By the scheme a moiety of the dividends of £857 18s. 2d. consols, amounting to £10 14s. 4d., is made applicable towards the repair and maintenance of the church, and the other moiety, together with the dividends on £124 17s. consols, amounting together to £13 16s. 8d., is distributed in coal. The rent of the post office, representing the old poorhouse, amounting to about £9 a year, is likewise distributed in coal.

RIPPLE

Rippell (vii cent.); Repell (xiii cent.); Ryppull (xiv–xv cent.).

The parish of Ripple, lying in the south of the county on the borders of Gloucestershire, formerly included the now separate ecclesiastical parish of Queenhill with Holdfast formed in 1880[1] on the opposite side of the Severn. Part of Ripple was transferred to Earl's Croome in 1884 and at the same date Twyning Meadow was transferred from Ripple to Twyning (Gloucs.).[2] The present parish of Ripple is on the left bank of the Severn, which divides it from Upton upon Severn and Queenhill.

The parish is also watered by the Horse Brook and its continuation the Ripple Brook.

Ripple is a long, narrow parish, and with Queenhill and Holdfast covers an area of 3,847 acres, which includes 1,214 acres of arable land, 2,064 of permanent grass and 10 of woods and plantations.[3] On the banks of the Severn the land lies very low and is liable to floods, being in some places not more than 31 ft. above the ordnance datum. The highest point is 100 ft. in the north, near Earl's Croome. The soil and subsoil are gravel and grey sandstone.

---

[99] Inst. Bks. (P.R.O.).
[100] Feet of F. Worcs. Mich. 13 Geo. II.
[1] Inst. Bks. (P.R.O.). [2] Ibid.
[3] Gorton, Topog. Dict. of Great Britain, 1829.
[4] Lewis, Topog. Dict.; inform. from the Rev. A. M. Niblett.
[5] Nash, op. cit. ii, 307; Worc. Epis. Reg. Alcock, fol. 104 d.
[6] Worc. Epis. Reg. Alcock, fol. 105.
[7] Chant. Cert. Worcs. 60, no. 30; 61, no. 26.

[8] Valor Eccl. (Rec. Com.), iii, 247.
[9] Ibid.
[10] Pat. 3 Edw. VI, pt. i, m. 23.
[11] Noake, op. cit. 308.
[12] In 1654 Thomas D'Abitot, the churchwarden, stated that one Ruly and — Bowier 100 years ago had enfeoffed certain persons with land in Rylies field, Darcombe, Westfield, Church Grove, Notlinge Dale, Prince Hill and Bellacre in Redmarley, the profits to be laid out on the repair of the church and for the

poor. He complained that certain persons had obtained possession of the deeds, and prevented him from receiving the rents, so that the church was 'like to be ruinated, and the poor starved.' Thomas had himself spent £20 to save the church from utter decay (Chan. Proc. [Ser. 2], bdle. 440, no. 1).
[1] See under advowson.
[2] Census of Engl. and Wales, 1891, ii, 657.
[3] Statistics from Bd. of Agric. (1905).

Ripple : The Village Cross

Ripple Church from the North-West

The village, which is on the Ripple Brook, extends into Twyning (Gloucs.), and has a station on the Midland railway. In the centre of the village of Ripple is a cross standing to nearly its full height, with the stocks and whipping-post beside it within a railing. Remains of three other crosses exist in the village, two in the churchyard and one near the rectory.[4]

The rectory, to the north-east of the churchyard, is a fine square building of early 18th-century date (1726) and contains at its north-east angle considerable remains of 15th-century walling, while in the cellars are several fragments of 12th-century stonework and a chimney-breast apparently of 15th-century date. In the village, near the cross, is Ripple Hall, the residence of Miss Behrens, a good half-timbered house of the type commonly built in South Worcestershire at the end of the 15th and during the 16th century. It has recently been stripped of the ivy which obscured it and judiciously repaired. The hamlet of Uckinghall is extremely picturesque, and contains many cottages of half-timber with thatched roofs. At the cross-roads at the south end of the settlement is the base and lower part of the octagonal stem of a cross, probably of the 15th century, but now much decayed. Naunton is almost entirely composed of small thatched half-timber cottages. There is a Baptist chapel here, built in 1863, and a Wesleyan chapel at Ryall Grove.

Queenhill with Holdfast is on the right bank of the Severn. The church at Queenhill is situated within the park of Pull Court, the southern portion of which, with the mansion, is in the parish of Bushley. To the north of the church is a brick farm-house of no architectural interest, while further still to the northward, just outside the gate of the park, is a half-timbered cottage now transformed into a school. Here is also a gabled brick house of the 17th century, with plastered walls and modern bargeboards. At Holdfast, which is about a mile to the north of Queenhill, is some half-timber work of the normal type. On the east side of the road which runs northwards through the hamlet is a fair-sized H-shaped brick house of the later 17th century. Here the ground varies in height from 38 ft. on the banks of the river to 170 ft., the highest part of Heath Hill. The subsoil is Keuper Marl, the soil near the river alluvial, and in the west red marl. Agriculture and market gardening are the only industries.

Perry was probably made at Ripple at the beginning of the 17th century, when a certain John Raynolds was indicted for stealing perry-tree stocks there,[5] and one William Franklin was said to have sold perry to his neighbours without a licence.[6]

Salmon fishing in the Severn was one of the industries of the parish in the 16th and 17th centuries, and several fishermen were among the recusants there in 1593.[7] In 1582 the Bishop of Worcester wrote to Walsingham complaining of two brothers called Moore, who were 'watermen dwelling hard upon Severn syde' and had masses said in their house which many Papists attended. He describes them as 'pore men but very dangerous,' and adds, 'I think there are not two woorse assorted anywhere of their calling that doo more harm.'[8] In 1613 many of the fishermen in the counties of Worcester and Shropshire complained that the men of Ripple, Holdfast and other places on the Severn were destroying the fish in the river by netting them 'with forestalling nets which reach from one side of the river to the other and from the top to the bottom,' taking about sixty salmon at a time.[9] Ripple Lock Stake was a well-known point on the River Severn, above which only nets of a certain mesh might be used.[9a]

The commons of Ripple were inclosed under an Act of 1801,[10] the award being dated 4 September 1807,[11] those of Queenhill in 1807[12] and those of Holdfast in 1812.[13] The main road from Worcester to Tewkesbury passes through Ripple from north to south, and the road from Gloucester to Upton upon Severn through Holdfast.

Roman remains have been discovered near Bow Bridge.[14]

MANORS The manor of *RIPPLE* is said to have been granted in 680 by Oshere, King of the Hwiccas, to Frithowald, a monk of Wynfrid, ex-Bishop of Lichfield,[15] but the charter is spurious. Frithowald evidently gave the estate to the Bishop of Worcester, and it belonged to the see in 1086. With Upton upon Severn it contained at that time 25 hides which paid geld. The woodland was included in the king's forest of Malvern, and the bishop only had pannage and wood for firing and repairs, instead of 'the honey and the hunting and all the profits, and 10s. over and above,' which had belonged to him before the Conquest.[16]

The manor was valued at £36 3s. 4d. in 1291,[17] at £57 11s. 10d. in 1535, the last sum including 100s. for the fee farm at Upton.[18] Ripple belonged to the Bishops of Worcester[19] until 1860, when it was transferred to the Ecclesiastical Commissioners,[20] who are the present lords of the manor.

There was a mill at Ripple in 1086[21] and a watermill and windmill in 1299.[22] Only one mill is mentioned in 1291,[23] and in 1302-3 a mill there was repaired.[24] There does not seem to have been any mill at Ripple in 1535 or in 1648.

[4] See below under architectural account of church.

[5] *Quart. Sess. R.* (Worcs. Hist. Soc.), i, 128.

[6] Ibid. ii, 615.

[7] Recusant R. (Pipe Office Ser.), no. 2.

[8] S. P. Dom. Eliz. clvi, 29.

[9] *Quart. Sess. R.* (Worcs. Hist. Soc.), i, 187.

[9a] It is mentioned in the Act of 1778 for the preservation of fish in the Severn (Stat. 18 Geo. III, cap. 33).

[10] Priv. Act, 41 Geo. III, cap. 109.

[11] *Blue Bk. Incl. Awards,* 191.

[12] Priv. Act, 47 Geo. III, cap. 28 ; *Blue Bk. Incl. Awards,* 191.

[13] Priv. Act, 52 Geo. III, cap. 4.

[14] *V.C.H. Worcs.* ii, 220.

[15] Birch, *Cart. Sax.* i, 84 ; Heming, *Chartul.* (ed. Hearne), 46. Worcestershire was then in the diocese of Lichfield. Wynfrid had been deposed by Archbishop Theodore in 675 (Thomas, *Surv. of Worc. Cath.* A 6).

[16] *V.C.H. Worcs.* i, 292a.

[17] *Pope Nich. Tax.* (Rec. Com.), 225. In 1302-3 the value was about the same when £15 18s. 9d. had been deducted for expenses (Mins. Accts. [Gen. Ser.], bdle. 1143, no. 18).

[18] *Valor Eccl.* (Rec. Com.), iii, 218.

[19] Heming, op. cit. 533 ; *V.C.H. Worcs.* i, 324 ; Cart. Antiq. RR. 15 ; *Cal. Close,* 1346-9, p. 231 ; *Feud. Aids,* v, 306, 312,

318 ; Chan. Proc. Jas. I, S. 6, no. 34 ; Feet of F. Worcs. Mich. 13 Geo. I ; Hil. 6 Geo. II ; East. 7 Geo. II ; *Acts of Parl. rel. to co. Worc.* (Worcs. Hist. Soc.), 104. In 1648 it was sold by Parliament to William Dormer (Close, 24 Chas. I, pt. xv, no. 11), but was restored to the bishop in 1660.

[20] Stat. 23 & 24 Vict. cap. 124.

[21] *V.C.H. Worcs.* i, 292.

[22] Red Bk. of Bishopric of Worc. (Eccl. Com. Rec. Var. bdle. 121, no. 43698), fol. 85.

[23] *Pope Nich. Tax.* (Rec. Com.), 225.

[24] Mins. Accts. (Gen. Ser.), bdle. 1143, no. 18.

There appears to have been a park at Ripple Manor in 1339.[25] The bishop had obtained a grant of free warren there in 1254.[26]

HOLDFAST (Holenfesten, x cent. ; Holefest, xi cent. ; Halleffest, Holefeld, xiii cent. ; Holfaste, xvi cent.) apparently belonged in the 10th century to the monks (*clerici*) of Worcester, for they gave it in exchange for Spetchley to Bishop Oswald, who leased it in 967 for three lives to his kinsman Osulf, with reversion to the bishop.[27] A similar lease was made in 988 by the same bishop to his nephew Alfwin.[28] Before the Conquest Holdfast was held by two priests of the bishop, but in 1086 the priests had been succeeded by Urse the Sheriff.[29] The bishop was still overlord at the end of the 13th century,[30] but after that date his rights appear to have lapsed. Urse's interest passed to the Beauchamps of Elmley, the manor being held of Elmley Castle until 1568, when the overlordship is mentioned for the last time.[31]

Holdfast was held of the Beauchamps by the Bracys. William Bracy held a hide of land at Holdfast about 1166,[32] and was still living in 1175-6,[33] but the land had passed by about 1182 to Richard Bracy.[34] Early in the 13th century the manor was held by Robert Bracy,[35] and from that time until 1315–16 it followed the same descent as Warndon [36] (q.v.). In that year Robert Bracy settled the reversion after his death on his son Fulk and Margery his wife.[37] Robert Bracy was still living in 1328, when he obtained a grant of free warren in Holdfast,[38] but died before 1346, when the manor was in the possession of William son of Robert Bracy.[39] From 1346 until the beginning of the 16th century there is no mention of Holdfast, but it is probable that it passed with Warndon (q.v.) to the Lygons, for Richard Lygon died seised of it in 1512.[40] It then descended with Warndon [41] until 1580, when Richard Lygon sold it to Henry Field,[42] whose niece and heir Anne married Sir William Whorwood.[43] Sir William sold it before 1610 to William Gower of the Woodhall family, who married Ann, Sir William Whorwood's daughter.[44] William Gower is described as 'the head of that spreadinge and lounge continuinge family' who 'made it [Holdfast] his habitation.'[45] William Gower died in 1647, and was succeeded by his son William, who died about 1679.[45a] In 1683 it was purchased from George Gower son of William by Sir

Nicholas Lechmere, the judge,[46] whose great-grandson Edmund [47] was holding it in 1732.[48] In 1763, although Edmund was still living, Holdfast appears to have been in the possession of his eldest son Nicholas,[49] but finally passed with the rest of Edmund's unentailed property to Anthony, his eldest son by his second wife, who was lord of the manor in 1812.[50] After that time the manor disappears, and probably became merged in that of Queenhill, which was also held by the Lechmeres.

QUEENHILL (Cunhille, Chonhelme, xi cent. ; Queinhull, Cuhull, Kuhull, xiii cent. ; Quenhull, xiv cent. ; Quinhill, Quhill, Cuhull, xvii cent.) was a berewick of the manor of Ripple and held before the Conquest by Ailric or Æthelric, brother of Brihteah, Bishop of Worcester.[51] Soon after the Conquest it was evidently seized by William Earl of Hereford, since he gave the tithes to the abbey of Lire.[52] He must have granted the manor to Ralph de Bernai, one of his followers, who is said to have been tenant of Queenhill after the Conquest. The whole of Earl William's estate was forfeited by his son Roger in 1074,[53] and at the time of the Domesday Survey Queenhill was in the hands of the king, who held it of the bishop,[54] this being one of the few manors which the king so held.[55] The bishop's rights as overlord continued until the end of the 13th century,[56] but seem to have lapsed soon after. The king's interest in the manor passed with the manor of Hanley Castle (q.v.) to the Earls of Gloucester, the manor being said to be held of the honour of Gloucester in 1210–12.[57] Subsequently it was said to be held of the king in chief by the serjeanty of rendering one dog yearly.[58] In the 14th century this service was found to have been unpaid for several years, and both William de Kardiff and Edward his brother received pardons of the arrears due from them.[59] It was still paid in 1629,[60] but after that date there is no trace of it, and it was evidently allowed to lapse.

Robert Fitz Roy Earl of Gloucester gave this manor to William de Kardiff,[61] who was paying 2 marks for scutage in the county of Worcester [62] in 1158–9. He or a namesake held the manor in 1182 and at the beginning of the 13th century.[63] In 1275 Paul de Kardiff granted to the Master of St. Wulfstan's, Worcester, a rent in kind from the manor of Queenhill.[64] In 1279 he was one of the

[25] *Cal. Pat.* 1338–40, p. 273.
[26] Ibid. 1247–58, p. 345 ; *Cal. Chart. R.* 1226–57, p. 443.
[27] Heming, op. cit. 596 ; Birch, op. cit. iii, 482.
[28] Heming, op. cit. 173.
[29] *V.C.H. Worcs.* i, 292b.
[30] *Testa de Nevill* (Rec. Com.), 41b ; Red Bk. of Bishopric of Worc. fol. 85.
[31] Red Bk. of Bishopric of Worc. fol. 85 ; Chan. Inq. p.m. (Ser. 2), xxvii, 22 ; cxlviii, 1.
[32] Red Bk. of Bishopric of Worc. fol. 252.
[33] *Pipe R.* 22 *Hen. II* (Pipe R. Soc.), 37.
[34] Red Bk. of Bishopric of Worc. fol. 96.
[35] *Testa de Nevill* (Rec. Com.), 41b.
[36] *Lay Subs. R. Worcs.* c. 1280 (Worcs. Hist. Soc.), 43.
[37] Feet of F. Worcs. 9 Edw. II, no. 35.
[38] Chart. R. 2 Edw. III, m. 1, no. 4.
[39] *Feud. Aids*, v, 307.
[40] Chan. Inq. p.m. (Ser. 2), xxvii, 22.
[41] Exch. Inq. p.m. (Ser. 2), file 1203,

no. 2 ; Chan. Inq. p.m. (Ser. 2), cxlviii, 1 ; Feet of F. Worcs. Hil. 16 Eliz.
[42] Recov. R. Hil. 22 Eliz. rot. 519.
[43] P.C.C. 41 Watson ; Feet of F. Div. Co. Hil. 29 Eliz. ; Worcs. Mich. 2 Jas. I.
[44] Feet of F. Worcs. Mich. 8 Jas. I. ; M. I. in church of Upton upon Severn (Nash, op. cit. ii, 447).
[45] Habington, *Surv. of Worcs.* (Worcs. Hist. Soc.), ii, 275.
[45a] M. I. in church of Upton upon Severn (Nash, loc. cit.) ; pedigree in the possession of Mr. Robert Vaughan Gower. The will of William Gower was proved in P.C.C. 17 March 1647.
[46] Close, 36 Chas. II, pt. xvi, no. 32 ; Shirley, *Hanley and the House of Lechmere*, *passim*.
[47] Son of Anthony (ob. 1720), son of Edmund (ob. 1703), son of Nicholas, the purchaser of Holdfast (Shirley, loc. cit.).
[48] Recov. R. East. 5 Geo. II, rot. 236.
[49] Ibid. Mich. 4 Geo. III, rot. 391.
[50] Priv. Act, 52 Geo. III, cap. 4.
[51] *V.C.H. Worcs.* i, 293a, 322a.

[52] Ibid. ; *Testa de Nevill* (Rec. Com.), 43.
[53] *V.C.H. Herefs.* i, 270.
[54] *V.C.H. Worcs.* i, 293a, 322a.
[55] Ibid. 257.
[56] *Testa de Nevill* (Rec. Com.), 41 ; Red Bk. of Bishopric of Worc. fol. 85.
[57] *Testa de Nevill* (Rec. Com.), 43.
[58] *Red Bk. of Exch.* (Rolls Ser.), ii, 568 ; *Testa de Nevill* (Rec. Com.), 43. See also references to inquisitions below.
[59] *Cal. Pat.* 1327–30, p. 439 ; 1350–4, p. 491.
[60] Chan. Inq. p.m. (Ser. 2), cccliii, 71.
[61] Exch. Q.R. Misc. Bks. i, fol. 195.
[62] *Red Bk. of Exch.* (Rolls Ser.), i, 18. See also Pipe R. 7 Hen. II (Pipe R. Soc.), 54 ; 13 Hen. II, 68.
[63] Red Bk. of Bishopric of Worc. fol. 96 ; *Red Bk. of Exch.* (Rolls Ser.), ii, 568 ; Exch. K.R. Misc. Bks. i, fol. 195.
[64] Feet of F. Div. Co. Trin. 3 Edw. I, no. 29. It is uncertain how long this payment was continued ; there is no trace of it at the time of the Dissolution.

RIPPLE CHURCH : THE CHANCEL

RIPPLE CHURCH : THE NAVE LOOKING EAST

commissioners appointed to inquire into the conduct of the Sheriff of Worcester in distraining people to become knights.[65] He died about 1291, when his son William had seisin of his lands.[66] The latter died about 1309,[67] and his son Paul, who succeeded him, about 1315.[68] William son and heir of Paul was a supporter of Thomas Earl of Lancaster, and was imprisoned in Pickering Castle in 1322.[69] His estates were forfeited to the Crown, but restored on the accession of Edward III.[70] He died about 1331, leaving an only daughter Joan,[71] who was already married to John de Wincote,[72] and three years later she settled the manor on the heirs of her body.[73] After the death of John, about 1343,[74] Joan married Sir John de Hampton, who had purchased the custody of the lands and heirs of John de Wincote from Laurence Earl of Pembroke, and he also predeceased her.[75] John de Wincote is said to have had four daughters,[76] but only three, Margaret, Elizabeth and Eleanor, were living at the time of Joan's death in 1349,[77] and they all died of the Black Death within a year after her.[78] Soon after Joan's death a commission had been issued to two of the king's serjeants-at-law to find and bring to Gloucester Castle the heirs of John de Wincote, who had been taken away by some persons unknown and 'moved from place to place to prevent their being apprehended and brought to the king.'[79] Elizabeth, the last surviving daughter, is said to have died in the king's custody. In one inquisition her heirs are said to have been her sisters Margaret, afterwards called Elizabeth, and Ivetta, who were evidently her half-sisters and the daughters of John de Hampton, and in another her mother's uncle Edward Kardiff.[80] According to the settlement of 1334 Queenhill should have belonged to the sisters, but in 1350 Edward de Kardiff had seisin of it,[81] and in 1363 Elizabeth, then wife of John Bawdrip, and Ivetta wife of Robert Underhill surrendered their claim to him and his wife Joan.[82] He died seised in 1369, leaving a son Paul,[83] but the latter evidently died childless before his father's widow Joan,[84] who afterwards became the

wife of Henry Grendour.[85] On her death in 1395 Queenhill was divided between the representatives of Elizabeth and Ivetta, viz. John Basset son of Agnes daughter of Elizabeth Bawdrip and Richard Ruyhale and Elizabeth his wife,[86] who had purchased the reversion of one moiety from Robert de Underhill and Ivetta.[87] John Basset died unmarried in 1396 and was succeeded by his brother Thomas,[88] who settled his property here on his wife Elizabeth in 1410.[89] His half of Queenhill appears to have been acquired before 1484 by Thomas Lygon [90] and sold by him or one of his successors to William Gower of Woodhall before 1544.[91]

Richard Ruyhale died seised of the other half in 1408, leaving a son Richard,[92] who died childless in 1424-5.[93] On the death of the latter his mother and her third husband, Richard Oldcastle, obtained a grant of this half of Queenhill from his uncle and heir Edmund Ruyhale.[94] Richard Oldcastle died childless in 1422,[95] and on the death of his widow Elizabeth, six years later,[96] the property reverted to John Merbury, Edward Brugge and William Poleyn, the trustees of Edmund.[97] In 1443 Katherine widow of William Stoughton held it for life, of these trustees, who granted the reversion after her death to the Abbot and convent of Tewkesbury.[98]

This moiety passing to the Crown at the Dissolution was granted in 1543 to William and Thomas Sheldon,[99] being then valued at £6 1s. 10d.[100] They sold it in 1548 to Robert Gower son of the William Gower who held the other moiety,[1] and thus the two parts were reunited. The real value of the manor is said to have been £8 18s. 6d.,[2] and shortly after purchasing it Robert Gower brought an action in the Court of Chancery against William Sheldon to gain possession of a meadow called Quenehome *alias* Underhome, which, owing to the wrong valuation, had been omitted in the sale of the manor to him.[3] At the time of his death in 1599 he was seised of the whole manor,[4] which followed the same descent as Colmers [4a] in King's Norton (q.v.) until 1720, when the property of his descendants

[65] *Parl. Writs* (Rec. Com.), i, 219.

[66] Robertson, *Cal. Gen.* ii, 755; *Abbrev. Rot. Orig.* (Rec. Com.), i, 67; *Cal. Fine R.* 1272–1307, p. 297.

[67] Chan. Inq. p.m. 2 Edw. II, no. 27; *Abbrev. Rot. Orig.* (Rec. Com.), i, 164; *Cal. Fine R.* 1307–19, p. 38.

[68] Chan. Inq. p.m. 9 Edw. II, no. 42; *Abbrev. Rot. Orig.* (Rec. Com.), i, 222, 225; *Cal. Fine R.* 1307–19, pp. 259, 276. His widow Eleanor survived him and evidently held one-third of Queenhill in dower; Chan. Inq. p.m. 5 Edw. III (1st nos.), no. 26; *Lay Subs. R.* 1332–3 (Worcs. Hist. Soc.), 25.

[69] *Parl. Writs* (Rec. Com.), ii (2), 214.

[70] *Parl. R.* ii, 420.

[71] Chan. Inq. p.m. 5 Edw. III (1st nos.), no. 26; *Abbrev. Rot. Orig.* (Rec. Com.), ii, 50.

[72] *Abbrev. Rot. Orig.* (Rec. Com.), ii, 54.

[73] Sir T. Phillipps, *Index of Worcs. Fines*, 3; Chan. Inq. p.m. 24 Edw. III (1st nos.), no. 65.

[74] Chan. Inq. p.m. 24 Edw. III (1st nos.), no. 65.

[75] Ibid. 23 Edw. III, pt. ii (1st nos.), no. 4; Fine R. 23 Edw. III, m. 20. The Warw. Inq. and Fine Roll say that John de Hampton's widow was called Eleanor (Chan. Inq. p.m. 24 Edw. III [1st nos.], no. 65).

[76] *Cal. Close*, 1349–54, p. 52.

[77] Chan. Inq. p.m. 23 Edw. III, pt. ii (1st nos.), no. 4. The Worcs. Inquisition only gives Margaret, aet. 11, and Elizabeth, aet. 9, but the Gloucester Inquisition mentions a younger daughter Eleanor. The custody of the eldest and her lands was granted to Thomas Moigne (*Cal. Pat.* 1348–50, p. 275).

[78] Chan. Inq. p.m. 24 Edw. III (1st nos.), no. 65. The manor was valued at 60s. only, because of the Plague.

[79] *Cal. Pat.* 1348–50, p. 317.

[80] Chan. Inq. p.m. 24 Edw. III (1st nos.), no. 65.

[81] *Abbrev. Rot. Orig.* (Rec. Com.), ii, 210.

[82] Feet of F. Div. Co. Mich. 37 Edw. III. Joan was the daughter of John de Saltmarsh (Wrottesley, *Ped. from Plea R.* 83).

[83] Chan. Inq. p.m. 43 Edw. III, pt. i, no. 61*b*.

[84] *Abbrev. Rot. Orig.* (Rec. Com.), ii, 307.

[85] Feet of F. Worcs. 7 Ric. II, no. 18.

[86] Chan. Inq. p.m. 18 Ric. II, no. 19; Close, 18 Ric. II, m. 14.

[87] Chan. Inq. p.m. 18 Ric. II, no. 19; Feet of F. Worcs. 7 Ric. II, no. 18; *Cal. Pat.* 1391–6, p. 554.

[88] Chan. Inq. p.m. 20 Ric. II, no. 5.

[89] *Cal. Pat.* 1408–13, p. 196.

[90] Ibid. 1476–85, p. 480.

[91] Chan. Inq. p.m. (Ser. 2), cclvii, 74; Memo. R. (Exch. Q.R.) Hil. 10 Eliz. m. 230.

[92] Chan. Inq. p.m. 9 Hen. IV, no. 26.

[93] *Cal. Pat.* 1429–36, p. 281.

[94] Ibid.; *Cal. Pat.* 1416–22, p. 440.

[95] Chan. Inq. p.m. 10 Hen. V, no. 16.

[96] Ibid. 7 Hen. VI, no. 41.

[97] *Cal. Pat.* 1429–36, p. 281.

[98] Chan. Inq. p.m. 21 Hen. VI, no. 5; *Cal. Pat.* 1441–6, p. 152. Its value at that time is said to have been 40s.

[99] Pat. 35 Hen. VIII, pt. x, m. 30; *L. and P. Hen. VIII*, xix (1), g. 80 (50).

[100] See Aug. Off. Misc. Bks. ccccxliv, fol. 113.

[1] Chan. Proc. (Ser. 2), bdle. 77, no. 4; Memo. R. (Exch. Q.R.) Hil. 10 Eliz. m. 230.

[2] *Valor Eccl.* (Rec. Com.), ii, 482.

[3] Chan. Proc. (Ser. 2), bdle. 77, no. 4.

[4] Chan. Inq. p.m. (Ser. 2), cclvii, 74.

[4a] John Gower made a conveyance of Queenhill in 1656 (Feet of F. Worcs. Mich. 1656), but Robert Gower seems to have been owner of Colmers at that time. Again in 1681 Queenhill was held by William Gower, possibly son of Richard, who held Colmers (Recov. R. Trin. 33 Chas. II, rot. 126).

William and John Gower was sold for the payment of their debts.[5] Queenhill, which had been heavily mortgaged, was at first excepted from the sale and settled on William brother of John, with the request that if he died unmarried he should leave it to their kinsman Edward Thomas Hawkins, second son of Thomas Hawkins of Nash, co. Kent, on condition that he took the name of Gower.[6] However, in 1722 an Act was passed for the sale of Queenhill,[7] and it was purchased in 1724 by Nicholas Lord Lechmere.[7a] In 1787 it was in the possession of Lord Lechmere's nephew and heir, Edmund Lechmere, who settled it on Anthony, his eldest son by his second wife.[8] The latter, who was created a baronet in 1818,[9] was holding the manor at that date,[10] but his son Sir Edmund Hungerford Lechmere sold it in 1852 to William Dowdeswell of Pull Court in Bushley, to whose son the Rev. Edmund Richard Dowdeswell it now belongs.[10a]

LECHMERE. *Gules a fesse or with two pelicans or in the chief.*

A windmill at Queenhill was held with the manor in the 14th century, but is not mentioned again.[11]

A small estate at Queenhill, with a house called Barnes' House, was held for more than 200 years by the family of Barnes. In 1583 it was sold by Richard Barnes of Hindlip to John Barnes of Upton upon Severn, son of Nicholas Barnes, the late owner of the estate. From John it passed to his daughter Joan Etheridge, who was succeeded by her uncle Thomas Barnes. The estate remained with the family of Barnes until 1792, when it was sold by Thomas Barnes to Anthony Lechmere, who added it to his other estate at Queenhill. Twelve years before this sale Thomas Barnes had acquired, by his marriage with Dorothea daughter of John Knottesford, an estate at Holdfast,[11a] held since the beginning of the 17th century by the Knottesfords. On the death of John Knottesford Barnes, son of Thomas and Dorothea, there was a lawsuit as to the next of kin, and eventually in 1857 the estate was bought by William Dowdeswell. It now belongs to his son the Rev. Edmund Richard Dowdeswell.[11b]

RYALL (Ruyhale, xii cent.; Ryhal, xiii cent.; Ruhale, Ruyhale, xiv cent.; Rehale, xv cent.; Royall, Royalles Court, Ryolles Court, xvi cent.) is not mentioned in the Domesday Survey and was probably included in the manor of Ripple. It was held of the Bishop of Worcester,[12] the last mention of the overlordship being in 1641.[13]

Jordan held half a hide in Ryall about 1182, and for it had to go to the county and hundred courts for the bishop's men, and was one of the bishop's 'radmen.'[14] This half hide belonged to Roger Golafre in 1299.[15] No further deeds have been found connecting this family with Ripple until the 15th century, but it probably descended from father to son[16] until William Golafre sold or gave it to Robert Arderne[17] and John Spetchley, who were in possession in 1431.[18] They sold it in 1448–9 to John Vampage of Wick near Pershore and his son of the same name.[19] The latter brought a suit in Chancery against a certain Reynold, one of his father's trustees, for refusing to deliver up his estates.[20] He died before 1505, when his son Robert obtained from the king an inspeximus of the charters to his father and grandfather.[21] Robert died seised of the manor in 1516, leaving a son John,[22] who died childless in 1548 and was succeeded by his two sisters Mary and Dorothy widow of John Hugford or Higford, then wife of Thomas Winchcombe,[23] and by his nephew Edmund Harewell son of another sister Margaret.[24] Mary died childless,[25] and Ryall was divided between her sisters' children, Margaret daughter of Dorothy and wife of Thomas Hanford and Edmund Harewell.[26] Thomas and Margaret sold their share to Margery Lechmere in 1570,[27] and Edmund Harewell, son of the above Edmund, sold his to Thomas Coventry and his son Thomas in 1601.[28] The latter,[29] who became Lord Coventry in 1628,[30] died seised of this moiety in 1639–40 and was succeeded by his eldest son Thomas,[31] who in 1656 sold his share of Ryall to Nicholas Lechmere,[32] who had inherited the other half from his great-grandmother Margery Lechmere.[33] The so-called manor formed part of the settlement on Edmund Lechmere son of Nicholas on his marriage with Lucy Hungerford in 1674, and from that date until 1811 it passed with Holdfast[34] (q.v.). In 1816, however, it was conveyed by John Glasse and Susan his wife to Sir James Graham and Sir Edmund Antrobus.[35]

[5] Fine R. 44 Eliz. pt. i, no. 9; Chan. Proc. Jas. I, G. 16, no. 73; Feet of F. Worcs. Hil. 14 Jas. I; Mich. 1 Chas. I; Pat. 1 Chas. I, pt. xxi, no. 86; Chan. Inq. p.m. (Ser. 2), ccccliii, 71; Fine R. 6 Chas. I, pt. iii, no. 1a; *Cal. Com. for Comp.* 1857; Feet of F. Div. Co. Trin. 7 Will. III; Recov. R. D. Enr. Hil. 5 Geo. I, m. 9; Mich. 6 Geo. I, m. 11; Recov. R. East. 5 Geo. I, rot. 52.
[6] Recov. R. D. Enr. Trin. 6 Geo. I, m. 15 d.
[7] *Acts of Parl. rel. to co. Worc.* (Worcs. Hist. Soc.), 46; Priv. Act, 9 Geo. I, cap. 22.
[7a] Inform. from the Rev. E. R. Dowdeswell from deeds at Pull Court.
[8] Feet of F. Worcs. Mich. 28 Geo. III.
[9] Burke, *Peerage and Baronetage.*
[10] Recov. R. Trin. 58 Geo. III, rot. 439.
[10a] Inform. from the Rev. E. R. Dowdeswell.
[11] Chan. Inq. p.m. 9 Edw. II, no. 42; 23 Edw. III, pt. ii (1st nos.), no. 4.

[11a] The estate included 84 acres and a very good house.
[11b] Information about the Barnes' and Knottesfords' estates has been kindly supplied by the Rev. E. R. Dowdeswell from deeds at Pull Court.
[12] Chan. Inq. p.m. 9 Hen. IV, no. 26; 10 Hen. V, no. 16; 7 Hen. VI, no. 41; (Ser. 2), xxxi, 118.
[13] W. and L. Inq. p.m. xcv, 181.
[14] Red Bk. of Bishopric of Worc. fol. 96.
[15] Ibid. 85.
[16] For pedigree of Golafre family see Baker, *Hist. and Antiq. of Northants,* ii, 22.
[17] For connexion between Ardernes and Golafres see *Visit. of Warw.* (Harl. Soc. xii), 74.
[18] Pat. 20 Hen. VII, pt. iii, m. 12; *Feud. Aids,* v, 334.
[19] Pat. 20 Hen. VII, pt. iii, m. 12.
[20] *Cal. Pat.* 1452–61, p. 288.
[21] Pat. 20 Hen. VII, pt. iii, m. 12; *Visit. of Worcs.* 1569 (Harl. Soc. xxvii), 138.

[22] Chan. Inq. p.m. (Ser. 2), xxxi, 118.
[23] *Visit. of Worcs.* 1569 (Harl. Soc. xxvii), 70.
[24] W. and L. Inq. p.m. iii, 108; Recov. R. Mich. 6 & 7 Eliz. rot. 123.
[25] *Visit. of Worcs.* 1569, p. 138.
[26] Feet of F. Div. Co. Hil. 13 Eliz.
[27] Ibid. Worcs. East. 12 Eliz.
[28] *Visit. of Worcs.* 1569 (Harl. Soc. xxvii), 72; Feet of F. Div. Co. Mich. 42 & 43 Eliz.; Close, 44 Eliz. pt. v, Harewell and Coventry. This moiety included the hall with the cellars and rooms over and the 'Crosse House' at the east end of the same.
[29] Feet of F. Worcs. Trin. 8 Jas. I.
[30] G.E.C. *Complete Peerage,* ii, 391.
[31] W. and L. Inq. p.m. lxiv, 181.
[32] Feet of F. Worcs. Hil. 1656.
[33] Shirley, op. cit. 13, 14.
[34] Feet of F. Worcs. Hil. 25 & 26 Chas. II; Recov. R. East. 5 Geo. II, rot. 236; Mich. 4 Geo. III, rot. 391; Hil. 51 Geo. III, rot. 254.
[35] Ibid. Trin. 56 Geo. III.

RIPPLE CHURCH : DETAIL OF NORTH DOORWAY

RIPPLE CHURCH : SOUTH RESPOND OF WESTERN TOWER ARCH

Before 1831 it had been acquired by George William Earl of Coventry,[36] to whose grandson, the present earl, a farm called Ryalls Court now belongs.

In 1249 the Bishop of Worcester gave a carucate of land in Ryall to John de Ruyhale in exchange for a hide of land in Alvechurch.[37] This John died before 1254, when we have a reference to his widow.[38] The estate seems to have been in the possession of Isabel de Ruyhale c. 1280,[39] and of Joan Ruyhale in 1332–3.[40] In 1399, when it is first described as a manor, it was settled with a moiety of Queenhill (q.v.) on Richard Ruyhale and Elizabeth his wife,[41] and afterwards on the latter's second and third husbands, John Philipot[42] and Richard Oldcastle.[43] It is uncertain what became of it on the death of Elizabeth, but it probably passed to the Harewells and Hanfords, owners of the other manor of Ryall, who are stated by Nash to have been heirs of the Ruyhales.[44]

The right of free fishing in the Severn was held with the estate at Ryalls Court in 1603,[45] and was conveyed by Edmund and Thomas Lechmere to Sir Nicholas Overbury and Giles Overbury in 1635.[46]

Half a hide of land at *NAUNTON* (Newentone, xii cent.; Nounton, xiii cent.) was given by Bishop Theulf (1115–25) to Auda 'Vitrarius,' from whom it was bought in the time of Bishop Simon (1125–50) by Adam de Croome.[47] It followed the same descent as Earl's Croome until 1299,[48] but its descent after that time has not been traced. It may have formed part of the endowment of the chantry of Ripple, which is called in 1374 and 1375 the chantry of Newton or Newynton and Ripple.[49]

At the time of the Domesday Survey the king held of the bishop 1 hide of land at a place called *BURSLEY* (Burgelege) which had belonged to Brictric son of Algar.[50] It is mentioned in 1182 and again in the Testa de Nevill and in 1299 as being held by the king,[51] and probably after that date was annexed to the manor of Queenhill. The name has now disappeared, but Mr. Round identifies it with Borsley Lodge, which occurs in an inscription quoted by Nash, and with Borley House, which is marked on the earlier ordnance survey maps and was between Holdfast and Queenhill.[52]

The hamlet of *SAXONS LODE* (Cestrelade, xii cent.; Sextaneslade, xiii cent.) was held at the end of the 12th century as half a hide of land by Jordan of Ryall and had previously been held by Martin Coti for the service of being 'radman.'[53] It was held in the 13th and 14th centuries by a family called De la Lode, atte Lode or Sestanslade.[54] In 1590 it was in the possession of John Woodward *alias* Smyth,[55] who settled it on his son Thomas. The latter died in 1636 seised of the capital messuage or farm called 'Sextons Loade,'[56] which passed to his daughter Katherine,[57] who married John Dormer and was the mother of Sir Robert Dormer the judge.[58]

The parish church of *ST. MARY CHURCHES THE VIRGIN* consists of a chancel 41 ft. by 16 ft. 6 in., central tower 15 ft. 6 in. by 16 ft., north and south transepts, each 16 ft. by 20 ft. 6 in., nave 68 ft. 10 in. by 20 ft., aisles 70 ft. 6 in. by 7 ft. 10 in., and a north porch 12 ft. by 11 ft. These measurements are all internal.

The whole of the structure, which is built of limestone with stone-slabbed roofs, is of the original date, c. 1195–1200, and is a good example of a complete transition church. A local tradition that the church was part of a Benedictine establishment is without foundation, though colour is lent to it by the length of the chancel.

The original building has been very little altered. In the latter part of the 13th century the chancel appears to have been remodelled by the insertion of ranges of large windows on the north and south, and of a priest's door on the north, forming part of the scheme. These alterations are in Kenilworth stone, which is also used for heavy buttresses, added, doubtless at the same time, to the chancel, north transept, and west and south walls of the nave, which are considerably out of the perpendicular. The east window of the chancel and the west window of the nave are of the 15th century, when buttresses were added at the north-east and south-east angles of the chancel, and the pitch of the roofs was altered throughout the church. In the 16th century the easternmost windows of the aisles were enlarged and two-light windows were inserted at the east end of the clearstory. In 1713 the top of the tower, whose spire had been struck by lightning on 18 December 1583, was taken down and was rebuilt to a greater height, and in 1797 the tower was again repaired and raised, the uppermost stage being now of the latter date. The upper stage of the porch was built at the same time, blocking one of the clearstory windows. It was probably at this time that the south transept was walled off from the tower crossing up to the crown of the arch, and a vestry, since removed, built on the south side. The modern repairs, recently undertaken, include the unblocking and repair of the south transept window and the clearing out of the external plaster blocking of the south aisle door and the clearing of the south arch of the crossing from the crown to the spring.

The east wall of the chancel has a large 15th-century window of five lights, set within the shafted jambs of the original 13th-century set of arcaded lancets. There is a moulded string at the sill level. The north and south walls each contain at the east a single-light window of the latter half of the 13th century, with tracery in the head, and three windows each of three lights in a drop-centred head, with clumsy chamfered mullions and spandrels roughly pierced with quatrefoils and trefoils. The western-

---

[36] Recov. R. Trin. 1 Will. IV, rot. 285.

[37] Feet of F. Worcs. East. 23 Hen. III, no. 15.

[38] *Excerpta e Rot. Fin.* (Rec. Com.), ii, 189.

[39] *Lay Subs. R.* c. 1280 (Worcs. Hist. Soc.), 27.

[40] Ibid. 1332–3, p. 12.

[41] Chan. Inq. p.m. 9 Hen. IV, no. 26.

[42] Mins. Accts. (Gen. Ser.), bdle. 1074, no. 20.

[43] Chan. Inq. p.m. 10 Hen. V, no. 16; 7 Hen. VI, no. 41.

[44] op. cit. ii, 250.

[45] Feet of F. Worcs. Mich. 1 Jas. I.

[46] Ibid. Trin. 11 Chas. I.

[47] Red Bk. of Bishopric of Worc. fol. 242.

[48] Ibid. 85, 96.

[49] *Sede Vacante Reg.* (Worcs. Hist. Soc.), 289, 304, 351.

[50] *V.C.H. Worcs.* i, 293.

[51] *Testa de Nevill* (Rec. Com.), 41a;

see also *V.C.H. Worcs.* i, 324b n.; Red Bk. of Bishopric of Worc. fol. 85, 96.

[52] *V.C.H. Worcs.* i, 293a n.

[53] Red Bk. of Bishopric of Worc. fol. 96.

[54] Ibid. 85; *Lay Subs. R.* c. 1280 (Worcs. Hist. Soc.), 27; 1332–3, p. 12; *Cal. Pat.* 1345–8, p. 350.

[55] Exch. Dep. East. 32 Eliz. no. 18.

[56] Chan. Inq. p.m. (Ser. 2), ccclxxix, 94.

[57] Ibid.

[58] *Dict. Nat. Biog.*

most window on each side is much distorted by a settlement of the tower, and is blocked, that on the north showing the tracery on both sides, but that on the south on the exterior only. Under the second three-light window, in the north wall, and having a hood rising into its sill, is a priest's door. A moulded string runs at the sill level on each side, that on the north rising over the segmental outline of the hood of the priest's door. The stones of the original walling are visible in the splays of the windows and are of bluish-white hard limestone.

The central tower rests on massive piers having keel-moulded responds with scalloped capitals of a late type, and angle shafts with stiff-leaf foliage on the inner angles and on the nave faces of the western piers. The capitals of the shafts in all four internal angles of the tower remain, but the eastern pair of shafts are gone. The western pair which remain are keel-moulded. Above the capitals are signs of the spring of a crossing-vault, but the crossing

The upper stages of the tower, accessible by a ladder from the north transept, have been altered in level, probably when the vaulting was removed, and the heavy floor corbels and the stepped splays of the original windows of the first stage, now blocked, are visible internally. The bell-chamber, which is in the 18th-century part, is well lighted by two-light pseudo-Gothic windows on all four sides, filled with wooden lattice, and the tower is surmounted by a balustrade and pinnacles of bad but not ineffective design. The weathering of all the original roof is visible on the faces of the tower.

The north and south transepts are to all intents and purposes identical. Each has a broad shallow altar recess (5 ft. 1 in. by 1 ft.) low down in the east wall, with a plain round head. On the north side of the arch of the recess in the north transept is a face with some other traces of early 13th-century painting. In the north wall of the north and the south wall of the south transept are large and well-

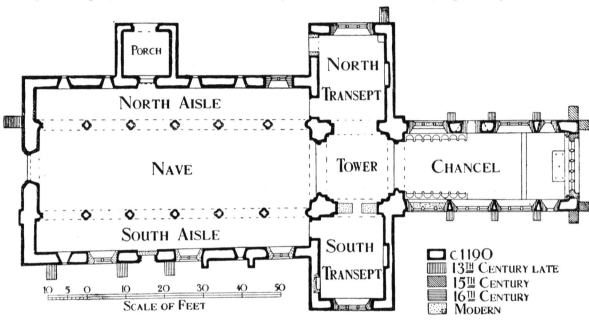

PLAN OF RIPPLE CHURCH

is now ceiled, with a heavy beam running from crown to crown of the north and south arches. The east and west arches are pointed and of two orders, plain on the east. The western arch on the nave side is contained within a continuous sunk quarter-round, under a hood mould returned at the ends to the nave walls. The arch itself is of two orders, the inner resting on the large keeled responds with square scalloped capitals, and the outer on a small angle shaft like those in the internal angles of the crossings. The inner order is plain and the outer a three-quarter round. Outside them both is a continuous sunk quarter-round, and the whole is inclosed in a label returned to the north and south walls of the nave. The north and south arches of the crossing are of plain orders on plain hollow-chamfered imposts. Behind the northern arch is the organ, which stands in the north transept. The southern arch has a filling of brick to the springing level, pierced by a narrow doorway to the south transept, now the vestry.

designed windows, slightly later in date than the north and south windows of the chancel; both are of three acutely-pointed lights in a two-centred head, with pierced spandrels between the heads of the lights. In the north end of the west wall of the north transept is a modern round-headed external doorway, and high up in the southern end of the wall is a wide round-headed window of original date. In the south transept is a similar window, now blocked. In each transept is a wide doorway with a semicircular head, plain on the transept side, but continuously moulded with a sunk quarter-round on the side towards the aisles, into which the doorways open. The voussoirs of these arches are of green, grey and white limestone set at random. Externally there is a large Kenilworth stone buttress of late 13th-century date at the east end of the north wall of the north transept, which leans outwards.

The nave arcades are of six bays with labelled two-centred arches of two orders, the outer moulded in

RIPPLE CHURCH : MISERERES

RIPPLE CHURCH : MISERERES

each case with a small chamfer and a roll at the angle, and the inner with a deep plain chamfer resting on piers quatrefoil on plan, with capitals of various late scalloped types, some looking almost like the roughing out of stiff-leaf foliage. The east responds are semi-circular, but those at the west had originally sunk and detached shafts, one on the face and one in each angle, with corresponding capitals and bases. The shafts are now all gone, but the foliated capitals remain. The clearstory has six windows on each side, the easternmost in each case being 16th-century two-light insertions and the remainder original single pointed lights with internal splays. The latter are set over the piers, not over the arch-crowns. The west window is of five lights with vertical tracery in a pointed head. The west doorway is original and has a deeply-moulded external pointed head on moulded jambs having two detached shafts with good foliated capitals on either side. There is a hood mould with grotesque head stops of an early character, and of a different stone from the rest, apparently re-used.

The aisles are both alike. In the east wall of each is the round-headed doorway described with the transepts to which they open. In the north wall the easternmost window is of two lights, and is a 16th-century insertion. To east and west of the north doorway, which is raised two steps above the floor level, and has a round head, with well-developed external mouldings on shafted jambs with foliated capitals, are two original single pointed lights considerably repaired with wide internal splays. The north porch, which is nearly square, has an entrance doorway with chamfered jambs and a pointed head with billet moulding over it. In the four angles are the original corbels for a vault now gone. The upper story, which has a pseudo-Gothic window in the north face over the door, is an 18th-century addition, and is only accessible by a doorway high up in the north end of the east wall, to which there is no permanent stairway. The walls of the upper story are carried across the aisle roof without other support than its timbers, and are only lath and plaster in their southernmost portion. The roof of the porch blocks part of one of the clearstory windows.

The south aisle windows are also five in number, the easternmost, third and fourth being modern and of two lights, copied from the 16th-century window in the north aisle, and the second and fifth original single lights like those of the north aisle. Between the third and fourth windows is the south doorway, now blocked, and showing a pointed recess internally, while externally it has a pointed head of two moulded orders resting on shafted jambs with foliated capitals. Externally there are original buttresses between the first and second and second and third windows, and on either side of the south door, and to the west of the last window are heavy Kenilworth stone buttresses of four offsets, added in the second half of the 13th century for the support of the wall, which leans considerably outwards. On the west front of the church a similar buttress of five offsets and of 4 ft. 6 in. projection counteracts a similar tendency at the junction of the nave and north aisle, and is matched at the junction of the nave and south aisle by a flat pilaster buttress of original date.

All the roofs are eaved and appear to date from the 15th century. The kneelers of the east gable of the chancel, carved with grotesques, are original, together with the coping and gable cross. The corbel tables of nave and chancel are also original throughout, and consist of a plain double roll.

In the chancel are fourteen fine stalls with moulded elbow rests and carved misereres of 15th-century date. The misereres, which appear to represent the twelve months, together with the sun and moon, are in very fine condition. There are two duplicate misereres, apparently also original, hanging in the south transept. There was a screen within living memory, but this has been destroyed, and fragments of it worked into the door to the south transept from the crossing, and into a partition in the transept itself, show it to have been of early 15th-century work. The altar rail, of a slender baluster pattern, is said to be Laudian, but is probably of the late 17th century, together with the panelling along the walls from the sanctuary to the stalls.

In the south windows of the chancel are some fragments of white and gold 15th-century glass, including some very beautiful heads. In the blocking of the north-west window of the chancel are two brass inscriptions, one commemorating John Woodward, yeoman of the guard to King Philip and Queen Elizabeth, who died in 1596, and another commemorating his grandson, who died in 1668. There are no other monuments of interest. In the churchyard are the bases of two crosses, one to the north of the north porch, retaining the lower part of the shaft, the other at the north-east corner of the churchyard, having an 18th-century sundial set in it. The base of a third cross is hollowed out and used as a pump-trough in the yard on the north side of the rectory.

The six bells are all of 1808, and bear inscriptions reading from one bell to another. They were cast at Gloucester by John Rudhall.

The communion plate includes an Elizabethan silver cup of the usual pattern, bearing the London date letter for 1571, and a cup, paten, flagon and almsdish inscribed 'Sacrum Ecclesiae de Ripple in com. Vigorn. Rectore Roberto Lucas S.T.P. 1793.' Besides these pieces there are two copper almsdishes, one of the 15th century, the other a modern copy. They were at one time lined with red velvet, but this has been removed. In a large plain 17th-century chest in the south transept, which also contains the registers and churchwardens' accounts, are kept a spherical bronze censer [59] of early 13th-century workmanship, which was found when an 18th-century vestry was demolished, and a 17th-century pewter flagon.

The registers include several volumes of the registers of Queenhill. They are as follows :—Ripple : (i) mixed entries 1558 to 1701, with a note of the first burial in Hill Croome churchyard, 1591, and register of briefs 1660 to 1662 ; (ii) baptisms and burials 1702 to 1802, marriages 1702 to 1762 ; (iii) marriages 1755 to 1789 ; (iv) marriages 1789 to 1812 ; (v) baptisms 1803 to 1812. There are

---

[59] Illustrated in *Proc. Soc. Antiq.* vol. xi (Ser. 2), p. 25, where it is ascribed to the 15th century. It has a four-gabled top and pinnacle and three arches in the upper part filled with pierced designs. There is a hole burnt or rusted in the bottom.

also two books of banns from 1754 to 1774 and 1775 to 1794. Queenhill: (i) mixed entries 1585 to 1701 ; (ii) burials 1789 to 1812, baptisms 1791 to 1811 ; (iii) marriages 1754 to 1782.

The church of *ST. LAURENCE*, Queenhill, formerly dedicated in honour of St. Nicholas, consists of a chancel 22 ft. 11 in. by 14 ft. 8 in. ; nave 35 ft. by 18 ft. 4 in. ; west tower 8 ft. 9 in. by 7 ft. 10 in. ; and a modern south porch of timber. These measurements are all internal.

It is probable that a church has stood on this site since the end of the 11th century. A fragment of the sculptured head of a small round-arched light, now built into the north wall of the nave, cannot well be later. The earliest details now *in situ* are the late 12th-century south doorway and the jambs of a blocked north doorway of the same date. The former has evidently been reset, probably in the 14th century, to which date belong the original windows of the nave, the walls of which were probably rebuilt

under a square head, and dates from the late 14th century. At the north-west is a modern window of the same design. Between them are the internal jambs and semicircular rear arch of a blocked doorway. The head has been much restored. In the south wall are two windows, each of two lights, of the same general type as those of the north wall. The jambs of the easternmost appear to be original, but the tracery is modern. The westernmost window appears to have been entirely renewed. The south doorway between these two windows is of the late 12th century, and was probably reset in the 14th century. It seems originally to have been of two elaborately moulded round-arched orders, the outer having shafted jambs with a pelleted label. As reset, the stones of the orders have been mixed up, with the result that the present outer order has had to be made out with two stones from the inner, suggesting that their positions have been reversed. The jamb shafts have scalloped capitals ; the chamfered abaci

QUEENHILL CHURCH, RIPPLE, FROM THE SOUTH

at this period. The chancel is a rebuilding of the 13th century, and the west tower is contemporary with the renovation of the nave. The church was thoroughly restored and repaired in 1854.

The east window of the chancel, inserted late in the 15th century, is of three cinquefoiled lights under a straight-sided pointed head. There are two original early 13th-century lancets with square external rebates in each side wall. Between the two south windows is a small doorway with a plain chamfered two-centred external head and a rear arch of the same form. At the south-east is a plain square piscina niche, from which the basin has disappeared. There is no chancel arch. The walling is of rubble masonry with wrought sandstone dressings, and there is a plain chamfered plinth-mould. The east gable, which is of ashlar work, was probably rebuilt when the east window was inserted.

The north-east window of the nave is of three trefoil-headed ogee lights with pierced spandrels

have been misplaced, and their bases have disappeared. A two-centred segmental head has been inserted under the semicircular head of the inner order. Externally there are restored buttresses of two offsets at the east end of the north and south walls. The walling is of rubble, and the lower courses are perhaps those of the original building. The western angles have been very drastically repaired.

The tower is of three stages, with diagonal buttresses of three offsets at the western angles, and a plain chamfered plinth. The tower arch has a single continuously moulded chamfered order on the nave side, with an outer order on the west dying on to the wall face. The ringing-stage is lighted by a single trefoiled light on the west and the bell-chamber by windows of two trefoiled lights. A modern saddleback roof crowns the whole.

The roof of the chancel is modern. That of the nave has a plaster ceiling, but the tie-beams, which are exposed, are probably of the 14th century.

RIPPLE CHURCH : MISERERES

RIPPLE CHURCH : MISERERES

In the churchyard to the south of the church are the base and lower part of the stem of a 14th-century cross. The upper part, with the cross itself, has recently been renewed.

The bowl of the font is modern, but the cable-moulded circular base is probably of the 12th century. The altar-table, rails and pulpit are Jacobean, the latter crowned by fragments of a carved and pierced vine cornice, probably belonging to the chancel screen, which is an excellent specimen of late 15th-century woodwork in very fair preservation. The central opening has a four-centred head with plain spandrels, while the bays of the screen on either side have traceried open lights with plain panelling below. In the north-west window of the nave are fragments of late 14th-century glass, including the head of a female figure in a green robe, wimple, and white hood with a yellow border, and the hands of another figure pointing to an alphabet, evidently portion of a St. Anne teaching the Virgin. There are also several bits of canopy work of the same period and a fragment of an inscription in Gothic capitals.

Set against the south wall of the nave is a curious incised alabaster slab, which was formerly in the floor of the church, commemorating Henry Field of King's Norton, who died in 1584, his first wife Anna, who died in 1572, and his second wife Sybil, who apparently survived him, as the date of her death is left blank. Upon the slab are their three figures incised in outline ; the inscription is much decayed. At the south-west of the chancel, upon the wall, is a small brass plate with the following inscription :—

' If any aske who lyes wthin this tombe
Tell them Nick Barnes hath taken up ye roome,
Who godly dide & lived an honest life
& soe did prove to kindred frend & wife,
his body rests, his soule still daily singes
glory and praise unto ye king of kinges
Obiit xv die decembris a. d̄n̄ MDCXXIII.'

On the north wall of the nave is an elaborate mural tablet to Margaret Knottesford, who died in 1725, aged eighteen, and below, on a brass plate, are commemorated her parents, Richard Knottesford, who died in 1768, and Martha his wife, who died in 1761. The remaining monuments, ranging in date from the end of the 17th century to modern times, are of no great interest.

There are four bells, inscribed as follows : treble : ' Peace and good Neighbourhood A. R. 1718 ' ; (2) ' Edwd. Serman Michaell Powell Ch:Wardens 1718 ' (these two were evidently cast by Abraham Rudhall of Gloucester) ; (3) ' William Such William Cox C:W: 1680 I.M.' (for John Martin of Worcester) ; tenor :

' John Barnes and Nicholas Toune churchwardens 1602.'

The plate consists of a small silver cup, with the date-letter much worn, but probably of about 1650 ; a silver paten, the marks of which are also indecipherable, probably of the same period ; a modern silver chalice ; a pewter flagon, inscribed ' Queenhill 1679 ' ; and a pewter almsdish, inscribed ' Ex dono Jo : Harding 1677.'

Besides the registers at present kept at Ripple there is at Queenhill a volume containing baptisms and burials from 1733 to 1789 and marriages from 1733 to 1754.

ADVOWSONS The church of St. Mary, Ripple, may have existed at the time of the Norman Conquest, having possibly been served by the two priests here, mentioned in the Domesday Survey.[60] The advowson has always belonged to the Bishops of Worcester.[61] In 1291 the value of the church with a chapel was £26 13s. 4d.,[62] and by the time of the Dissolution it had increased in value to £42 6s. 8d.[63]

In the 12th and 13th centuries the parson of Ripple held 2 acres, for which he was bound to provide a lamp burning before the altar of St. James in the church of Ripple.[64] There was formerly a custom in the parish that on the death of the head of any family who owned live stock his second best animal, or the best if the lord did not claim it, should be given to the rector.[65] In 1437 John Baldwin was excommunicated for trying to evade this by giving his animals, during his illness, to a cousin. On his recovery he was made to walk round the churchyard with bare head and feet for three Sundays, holding a torch in his hand.[66]

Among the well-known men who have been rectors of Ripple were Thomas Rotherham, afterwards Archbishop of York, Robert Lucas the poet, and John Webb the antiquary. Edmund Bonner, Bishop of London (1540–59), is also said to have held the living.[67]

In 1319 John Salemon, clerk, obtained licence to found a chantry in the church of St. Mary, Ripple, dedicated in honour of our Lady.[68] The chantry was ordained in 1320, and the endowment, consisting of a messuage and land in Stratford in the parish of Ripple, supported two chaplains to celebrate divine service daily. The advowson belonged to the said John Salemon during his life,[69] then to Philip David, one of the first chantry priests, and after his death to the Bishop of Worcester.[70] In 1438–9 the chantry is called that of St. Peter,[71] and in 1448 the chantry, which had been ' desolated by poverty of emoluments,' was newly ordained by the bishop, who provided that there should be one chantry priest only, appointed by

---

[60] *V.C.H. Worcs.* i, 292a.

[61] *Cal. Pat.* 1313–17, p. 652 ; 1327–30, pp. 415, 440 ; 1334–8, p. 300 ; 1354–8, p. 409 ; 1388–92, p. 107 ; 1391–6, p. 260 ; *L. and P. Hen. VIII*, xii (1), 38 ; Inst. Bks. (P.R.O.).

[62] *Pope Nich. Tax.* (Rec. Com.), 218.

[63] *Valor Eccl.* (Rec. Com.), iii, 265.

[64] Red Bk. of Bishopric of Worc. fol. 87, 98.

[65] A survey was made in 1648 of the manor of the rectory of Ripple (Nash, op. cit. ii, 296), but no other reference to

this manor has been found. It probably originated in half a hide of land given by Bishop Simon (1125–50) to the church (Red Bk. of Bishopric of Worc. fol. 98). This land appears to have been in Uckinghall (Ogginhale) (ibid. 87).

[66] Worc. Epis. Reg. Bourchier, fol. 34 d. ; Nash, op. cit. ii, 300.

[67] *Dict. Nat. Biog.*

[68] Inq. a.q.d. file 138, no. 19 ; *Cal. Pat.* 1317–21, pp. 388, 389 ; *Abbrev. Rot. Orig.* (Rec. Com.), i, 251 ; *Hist. MSS. Com. Rep.* v, App. i, 303. The charter gives a list of goods which were

to be left by the chantry priest to his successor.

[69] Worc. Epis. Reg. Cobham, fol. 22 ; Montagu, fol. 22 ; Hemenhale, fol. 16 ; Wulstan de Bransford, i (2), fol. 27 ; i (3), fol. 82, 142.

[70] Ibid. Wakefield, fol. 50; Peverell, fol. 25 d. The Prior of Worcester presented in 1375 during a vacancy in the see (*Sede Vacante Reg.* [Worcs. Hist. Soc.], 351).

[71] Worc. Epis. Reg. Bourchier, fol. 55. At the time of its dissolution it was called our Lady's chantry.

himself and his successors, to celebrate masses twice a week, on feast days and on the Thursday in Pentecost for the anniversary of the founder.[72] The possessions of the chantry were granted in 1549 to John Harford of Bosbury, Hereford, and Richard Willison of Ledbury.[73]

There was formerly a chapel, dedicated in honour of St. Laurence, at Holdfast, dependent upon the mother church of Ripple.[74] In Habington's time the inhabitants of Holdfast attended the church of Queenhill, and their chapel was 'so dangerously deformed with ruins' that he 'scarce durst looke into itt.' He mentions a painting on the south wall of a 'younge Kinge ryding on a red lyon.'[75] The chapel has now entirely disappeared, but the site is still called Chapel Ground.

The church at Queenhill is probably the chapel which was valued with the church of Ripple in 1291.[76] It became the church of the newly-formed parish of Queenhill in 1880,[77] and is in the gift of the Bishop of Worcester.

The tithes of Queenhill were granted with half a virgate of land there to the abbey of St. Mary, Lire, by William Earl of Hereford,[78] and were included with the other possessions of Lire in the endowment of Sheen Priory by Henry V. After the Dissolution they were granted to John Williams and Anthony Stringer,[79] but must have been alienated by them shortly afterwards, as in 1554 Philip King sold them to Henry Field.[80] Before 1605 they were in the possession of Henry Shawe and Elizabeth his wife, who then sold them to Francis and William Symcox,[81] and they, after holding for about six years, conveyed them to Henry Hobday and Humphrey his third son.[82] In 1650 they were purchased by Thomas Barnes,[83] and they were subsequently acquired by the rector of Ripple and the lord of the manor of Queenhill.[84]

CHARITIES The charity lands derived under the will of Thomas Morris *alias* Woodward, dated in 1675, and from other sources, now consist of cottages and 37 a. 3 r. 26 p. situated in the parishes of Ripple, Twyning, Upton upon Severn and Earl's Croome, acquired for the most part under the Inclosure Act, of the gross yearly rental value of £118. The charity is regulated by a scheme of the Charity Commissioners 26 January 1892, as varied by orders of 1896 and 1902, whereby one moiety of the net income is directed to be paid to the vicar and churchwardens for the maintenance and repair of the fabric of the church, and the other moiety to be applied for the general benefit of the poor. In 1910 the sum of £39 was paid to the churchwardens, £19 15s. was distributed in coal, £4 4s. was paid to the Worcester Infirmary, £7 to a boot club, £2 2s. to a pig club and the residue in money gifts.

The Rev. Dr. Holt, at a date unknown, gave £20 for the use of poor persons not in receipt of parochial relief. This gift is represented by £19 18s. consols with the official trustees, the annual dividends of which, amounting to 9s. 8d., are paid to the National school account.

In 1882 Mrs. Henry Frances Clifton, by her will proved at London 21 March, left a legacy, now represented by £979 3s. 10d. consols with the official trustees, the annual dividends, amounting to £24 9s. 4d., to be applied in the distribution of coals on 12 February in memory of donor's husband, who died on that day.

In 1884 Mrs. Mary Woodward, by deed dated 17 May in that year, declared the trusts of a sum of £250 London and North Western Railway 4 per cent. debenture stock, the annual dividends thereof, amounting to £10 a year, to be applied for the benefit of the poor not in receipt of parochial relief in such manner as would encourage thrift, education and temperance.

There are also in this parish four almshouses for four aged persons.

Hamlet of Holdfast.—Mrs. Ann Bowyer *alias* Gower, at a date unknown, gave to the poor 1 a. lying in Upton Lower Ham and also two beasts' pastures. A sum of £4 4s. yearly is received as rent, which is distributed in doles of money varying from 2s. 6d. to 10s. to each recipient.

Naunton.—In 1870 Philip Roberts, by will proved at Gloucester 17 December, left a legacy, now represented by £287 12s. 4d. consols with the official trustees, the annual dividends, amounting to £7 3s. 8d., to be applied as to £1 in payment to the minister of the Baptist chapel, Barton Street, Tewkesbury, for preaching a sermon yearly on the anniversary of the donor's death, and on the following Lord's day a sermon at the Baptist chapel, Naunton, 5s. for keeping in order his burial-place, and the residue in promoting the preaching of the Gospel at Naunton Baptist Chapel.

Queenhill.—The charity of — Grice, date of foundation unknown, consists of £31 11s. 9d. consols with the official trustees, producing 15s. 8d. a year, which is applied by the vicar and churchwardens for the benefit of the poor of this hamlet.

---

[72] Worc. Epis. Reg. Carpenter, i, fol. 46.
[73] Pat. 3 Edw. VI, pt. vii, m. 25. The value of the chantry at the Dissolution is variously given as £3 15s. 4d. (Chant. Cert. 25, no. 17), £4 6s. (ibid. 60, no. 26), and £5 11s. 5d. (*Valor Eccl.* [Rec. Com.], iii, 266). [74] Inst. Bks. (P.R.O.).
[75] op. cit. ii, 275.
[76] *Pope Nich. Tax.* (Rec. Com.), 218. The possessions of the chapel in 1552

included a silver chalice and four small bells in the steeple (Exch. Q.R. Church Goods, 9, no. 21, m. 22).
[77] *Census of Engl. and Wales, Worcs.* 1901, p. 7. An order for this separation was issued in 1863, but does not seem to have taken effect (*Parl. Papers* [1872], xlvi, no. 227, p. 11).
[78] *V.C.H. Worcs.* i, 322b; *Testa de Nevill* (Rec. Com.), 43b.

[79] *L. and P. Hen. VIII*, xviii (1), g. 226 (79, p. 131); Pat. 34 Hen. VIII, pt. xi, m. 23.
[80] Pat. 1 Mary, pt. xiv, m. 16.
[81] Feet of F. Div. Co. Mich. 3 Jas. I.
[82] Memo. R. Hil. 9 Jas. I, rot. 14.
[83] Inform. by the Rev. E. R. Dowdeswell.
[84] Priv. Act, 47 Geo. III, cap. 28.

RIPPLE CHURCH : WEST DOORWAY

ROUS LENCH CHURCH : CHANCEL ARCH AND NAVE ARCADE

ROUS LENCH

Lenc, Biscopesleng (xi cent.) ; Lench Randulf, Lelenz (xii cent.) ; Randulves Lench (xiii cent.) ; Lench Rondolf (xiv cent.) ; Rouslench, Randolphs Lench (xvi cent.).

The parish of Rous Lench lies in the east of the county. Piddle Brook forms its northern and an unnamed stream, a tributary of Whitsun Brook, its western boundary. The road from Worcester to Alcester passes through the north of the parish, and from it a road runs north to Radford and Inkberrow, crossing Piddle Brook by a ford. A second branch road runs southwards to the village of Rous Lench

magnificent group of elms, of which only one now remains. To the north of the green lies the church, in a churchyard an acre in extent, bounded on one side by an ancient stone wall and on the remaining sides by the moat and park. A little way off on the Fladbury road is the now ruinous pound. At the south-west angle is a picturesque red brick building built by Sir Charles Rouse-Boughton as a public-house on the site of an earlier one. It was closed as an inn by Dr. Chafy, and enlarged and opened by him in 1882 as a parish-room and workmen's club, now known as Chafecote.

ROUS LENCH COURT FROM THE NORTH-WEST

The area of the parish is 1,494 acres,[1] and the land is chiefly arable, the principal crops being cereals. Fruit and flower farming are carried on to some extent, and the women were employed in glove-stitching in the middle of the 19th century, but the industry has now died out. The soil is sand and marl and the subsoil Keuper Marl and Lower Lias.

The village of Rous Lench is situated on a plateau about 200 ft. above the ordnance datum. To the east the land rises to 300 ft. ; to the west and north it is undulating and lies between 170 ft. and 200 ft. above ordnance datum.

The village lies on a branch road from the Worcester and Alcester high road. The houses, many of which are half-timbered and some still thatched, are built round a triangular green, formerly crowned by a

Rous Lench Court. the property and residence of the Rev. William Kyle Westwood Chafy, D.D., situated on the northern slope of a hill to the south of the village, is a much-modernized two-storied half-timber house of the early 16th century. The original house appears to have been a large building, inclosing two quadrangles, divided from each other by a great hall. The greater part of the house was pulled down about a hundred years ago, and the buildings on the south and west sides of the western or entrance quadrangle, forming an L-shaped block, alone survive. Remains of the lesser quadrangle were standing within living memory, and traces of the demolished servants' wing and of the flagging of the great hall were found by Dr. W. K. W. Chafy in the course of laying out the grounds on the east side of the house. The existing remains seem to have contained the private

---

[1] Two acres are covered by water.

apartments; the kitchen and offices seem to have adjoined the quadrangle on the east side of the hall. In the west wing is the original entrance gateway, with the porter's lodge on the north side giving access to the former servants' wing. On the first floor is a large room known as the 'matted gallery,' with two fireplaces contemporary with the earliest building, one having its original moulded jambs and a four-centred head. The walls are lined with Elizabethan panelling. Practically no other original detail of interest remains internally, and modern additions have been made at the eastern and western ends of the southern range. Externally the timbering has been much restored and the chimney shafts are mostly new. The terraced gardens with their clipped yew hedges, laid out under the direction of Dr. W. K. W. Chafy, form an almost unique example of topiary art. The splendid yew ring surrounding a summer-house on the south-east side of the house, together with a few single trees here and there and a fine avenue, remain as survivals of the original gardens, which could never have been large. The whole now covers about 7 acres. In the park is still to be seen the moat which surrounded the old manor-house. It incloses an area of about half an acre in extent. About 1647 Richard Baxter, the Nonconformist, wrote part of his 'Saint's Everlasting Rest' while staying here.[2] In 1646 he says in *Reliquiae Baxterianae*, ' my quarters fell out to be at Sir Thomas Rous' at Rous Lench, where I had never been before. The Lady Rous was a godly, grave, understanding woman, and entertained me not as a soldier but a friend.'[3] A tree in the garden, which has now disappeared, was known as Baxter's Tree.

Radford is a hamlet to the north on the Worcester and Alcester road, and in the east of it is a brick and drain pipe works.

An Inclosure Act for Rous Lench was passed in 1778,[4] and the award is dated 27 February 1779.[5]

Among the place-names are Pittmeade and Le Widowes End, found in the 16th century.[6]

MANORS   The manor of *ROUS LENCH* is probably to be identified with the 'Lenc' which was acquired by Alfstan the prior, brother of Bishop Wulfstan, for the church of Worcester about 1062.[7] This estate became annexed to the manor of Fladbury, and in the time of Edward the Confessor the bishop held 2 hides in demesne, while the rest of the manor, 5 hides, was held by Frane, who did all the services due for it. By 1086 the whole manor had passed into the hands of Urse the Sheriff, under whom it was held by Alvred.[8] It was, however, still held under the manor of Fladbury,

and continued to be so held until the end of the 13th century.[9]

Urse's interest in the manor passed with his other possessions to the Beauchamps (see Elmley Castle), and was held by them and their descendants until the end of the 15th century, when the overlordship of Rous Lench passed with most of their other possessions into the hands of Henry VII.[10]

The tenants of the manor under the lords of Elmley adopted the name Lench. Randolf son of Roger de Lench held the manor in the time of Henry II,[11] and is probably to be identified with Randolf de Lench, who paid 40 marks in 1175–6 for pardon for trespass in the forest.[12] Roger de Lench was the representative of this family early in the 13th century.[13] It was probably he who with Stephen de Lench resisted the claim of the Abbot of Halesowen to common pasture at 'Hale Lench' in 1230.[14] Two years later he obtained from the king a grant of protection against Jews who held his lands as security for debt.[15] Peter de Lench paid a subsidy of 4s. at Lench Randolf in 1280,[16] and a Peter de Lench held land in Worcestershire in 1290.[17] Thomas de Lench was holding the manor in 1315,[18] and still seems to have been in possession in 1329, as he presented to the church at that date.[19] In 1346 it was returned that William son of John de Lench, Sir John de Hampton, Richard de Lench, John de Chester[20] of Lench and Henry Norreys held the manor,[21] but Richard de Lench presented to the church three years later.[22] In 1366–7 Robert de Derlaston settled the manor of Rous Lench on Thomas Snodhull of Rous Lench and Lucy his wife and their issue, with remainder in default to Henry Bruyn and his heirs.[23] In

Rous of Ragley. *Sable two bars engrailed argent.*

1381–2 Thomas and Lucy sold the manor and advowson of the church to John Rous.[24] John seems to have granted this manor for life to his father John Rous of Ragley, for on the death of the younger John in 1396–7 John Rous and Christina his wife were holding the manor by their son's gift. Robert Rous was brother and heir of the younger John,[25] but the manor of Rous Lench seems to have passed to Henry, a younger brother.[26] Henry was succeeded by his son Thomas,[27] who obtained licence in 1445 to have divine service celebrated in the chapel or oratory in his manor of Rous Lench.[28] William son of Thomas

[2] *Dict. Nat. Biog.*

[3] op. cit. (ed. 1696), 58.

[4] Priv. Act, 18 Geo. III, cap. 101.

[5] *Blue Bk. Incl. Awards*, 191.

[6] Pat. 31 Eliz. pt. iii.

[7] Heming, *Chartul.* (ed. Hearne), 407.

[8] *V.C.H. Worcs.* i, 290.

[9] *Testa de Nevill* (Rec. Com.), 41; Red Bk. of Bishopric of Worc. (Eccl. Com. Rec. Var. bdle. 121, no. 43698), fol. 81.

[10] *Testa de Nevill* (Rec. Com.), 41*b*; *Cal. Inq. p.m.* 1–9 Edw. II, 403; Chan. Inq. p.m. 20 Ric. II, no. 45; Exch. Q.R. Misc. Bks. xxii, fol. 1; Chan. Inq. p.m. (Ser. 2), xix, 74.

[11] Habington, *Surv. of Worcs.* (Worcs. Hist. Soc.), ii, 171; i, 316; Red Bk. of

Bishopric of Worc. fol. 81. The manor had apparently previously belonged to William Herce (Red Bk. of Bishopric of Worc. fol. 81).

[12] *Pipe R. 22 Hen. II* (Pipe R. Soc.), 37. It was probably from this owner that the manor acquired the alternative name of Lench Randolf.

[13] *Testa de Nevill* (Rec. Com.), 41.

[14] *Cal. Close*, 1227–31, p. 373.

[15] Ibid. 1231–4, p. 123.

[16] Lay Subs. R. *Worcs.* 1280 (Worcs. Hist. Soc.), 35.

[17] *Cal. Close*, 1288–96, p. 128.

[18] *Cal. Inq. p.m.* 1–9 Edw. II, 403; *Cal. Close*, 1313–18, p. 277.

[19] Nash, op. cit. ii, 87. Thomas paid a subsidy at Rous Lench in 1327 (Lay Subs.

R. *Worcs.* 1327 [Worcs. Hist. Soc.], 34).

[20] William de Chester paid a subsidy at Rous Lench in 1327 (Lay Subs. R. Worcs. 1327 [Worcs. Hist. Soc.], 34).

[21] *Feud. Aids*, v, 307.

[22] Nash, op. cit. ii, 87.

[23] Feet of F. Worcs. 40 Edw. III, no. 34.

[24] Ibid. 5 Ric. II, no. 13.

[25] Chan. Inq. p.m. 20 Ric. II, no. 45.

[26] Dugdale, *Hist. of Warw.* 853; *Parl. R.* iv, 410*b*, 412*a*.

[27] *Visit. of Worcs.* 1569 (Harl. Soc. xxvii), 113. Thomas Serchesden was said to be holding this manor in 1428 (jointly with Agnes Throckmorton), and in 1431 (*Feud. Aids*, v, 318, 333).

[28] Chafy, *Hist. of Rous Lench*, 38.

ROUS LENCH CHURCH : THE SOUTH DOOR

died seised of the manor in 1505–6, leaving Thomas his son and heir.[29] Thomas was succeeded by his son John.[29a] Edward son and successor of John died in 1611, leaving a son Sir John Rous.[30] He served as Sheriff of Worcestershire in 1610 and 1636,[31] and died in 1645.[32] His son Sir Thomas Rous, who had been created a baronet in 1641, was the friend and host of Richard Baxter and an ardent opponent of the Royalists during the Civil War.[33] He died in 1676.[34] Sir Edward Rous, his son by his first wife, followed him and died without issue 5 November 1677, when the baronetcy and estates devolved on his half-brother Sir Francis Rous. He was succeeded in 1687 by his brother Sir Thomas Rous,[35] who died without issue on 29 December 1721, when the baronetcy became extinct and the estates passed to his sister Elizabeth,[36] who, dying unmarried in 1729, was succeeded by Thomas Philipps,[37] a descendant of the last baronet's half-sister. He took the surname of Rouse and died unmarried 30 December 1768, leaving his estates to his distant cousin Charles William Boughton, who took the additional surname of Rouse.[38] He was created a baronet (Boughton-Rouse of Rous Lench) in

BOUGHTON. *Sable three crescents or.*

1791,[39] but three years later he succeeded, on the death of his brother, to the baronetcy of Boughton and transposed the order of the name to Rouse-Boughton.[40] He died on 26 February 1821,[41] but the manor seems to have passed before his death to his son William Edward Rouse-Boughton, who was dealing with it in 1810.[42] He died 22 May 1856, and was followed by his eldest son Sir Charles Henry Rouse-Boughton.[43] The latter sold the manor of Rous Lench to the present owner, Dr. William Kyle Westwood Chafy of Sherborne, in 1876.[44]

CHAFY. *Party gules and azure a griffon argent and a chief engrailed ermine with three lozenges azure therein.*

In 1410–11 Thomas Throckmorton and his wife Agnes were dealing with two messuages and 4 carucates of land in Rous Lench.[45] Agnes Throckmorton held half a fee in Rous Lench jointly with Thomas Serchesden in 1428,[46] and John Throckmorton presented to the church in 1433.[47] It was perhaps this

estate which, as the manor of Rous Lench, was held by Francis Folliott of Pirton at the time of his death in 1545.[48] His son John succeeded him and died in 1578, leaving a son Thomas.[49] Thomas and his wife Katherine were dealing with the manor in 1593,[50] when it is mentioned for the last time. It possibly passed to the Rous family and became incorporated with the capital manor.

In 1243–4 the Bishop of Worcester gave to William de Norwich and his wife Prudence half a hide of land in *RADFORD*.[51] Geoffrey de Lyttelton and his wife Eugenie sold messuages and land there and at Rous Lench to Richard Austin and his wife Constance in 1274–5.[52] An estate at Radford called a manor was held in 1545 by Francis Folliott,[53] but seems to have been sold by his son John, as it is not mentioned among his possessions at the time of his death. Sir John Rous was dealing with it in 1635,[54] and it followed the same descent as the manor of Rous Lench until 1821 or later.[55]

There was a mill worth 4s. at Rous Lench in 1086.[56] No further mention of it has been found until 1730, when it occurs in a conveyance of the manor.[57] There is now a corn-mill at Radford on the Piddle Brook.

CHURCH The church of *ST. PETER* consists of a chancel about 25 ft. by 16 ft., a nave 38½ ft. by 18½ ft., a north aisle 12 ft. wide, a north chapel and a vestry. These dimensions are all internal.

Nearly the whole church has been rebuilt in recent years, but enough remains to prove the existence of a church in the middle of the 12th century consisting of a chancel and nave with a north aisle of about the dimensions of the present structure. Practically no additions were made, except the insertion of one or two windows in the 14th century, until the modern rebuilding. At a late date the structure was allowed to get much out of repair and the north aisle was destroyed, the arcade being filled up. In 1885 the arcade was reopened, a new north aisle was built, the nave and chancel walls and arcade repaired and restored, a north chapel (for the Rous monuments) and a vestry and sacristy added, and the nave re-roofed. A bellcote was also constructed above the west wall of the chancel.

The east window of the chancel has been removed to the west end of the north aisle and the opening filled up. The eastern end of the north wall is built of brick and at the west end is a modern squint from the north aisle. In the south wall are two single-light windows, the eastern showing traces of 12th-century work in the head. The south-west window is of the 13th century and is rebated for a shutter ;

[29] *Visit. of Worcs.* 1569 (Harl. Soc. xxvii), 113 ; Chan. Inq. p.m. (Ser. 2), xix, 74.
[29a] Exch. Inq. p.m. file 1198, no. 6 ; *Visit. of Worcs.* 1569 (Harl. Soc. xxvii), 114.
[30] Chan. Inq. p.m. (Ser. 2), cccxxvi, 48
[31] P.R.O. *List of Sheriffs*, 159.
[32] G.E.C. *Complete Baronetage*, ii, 108.
[33] Ibid. ; Feet of F. Div. Co. Hil. 1650.
[34] G.E.C. loc. cit.
[35] Ibid. ; Feet of F. Div. Co. East. 5 Anne.
[36] Sir Thomas and Elizabeth had been dealing with the manor in 1706 (Feet of F. Div. Co. East. 5 Anne).

[37] G.E.C. loc. cit. ; Recov. R. Trin. 4 Geo. II, rot. 14.
[38] G.E.C. op. cit. ii, 108 n.
[39] Ibid. 123.
[40] Ibid.
[41] Ibid.
[42] Recov. R. East. 50 Geo. III, rot. 130.
[43] G.E.C. op. cit. ii, 123.
[44] This family is descended from John Chafy of Sherborne, who was buried 26 September 1558 (Burke, *Landed Gentry* [1906]). Dr. Chafy still retains portions of the old family property in Dorset and Somerset.
[45] Feet of F. Worcs. Hil. 12 Hen. IV.
[46] *Feud. Aids*, v, 318.

[47] Nash, op. cit. ii, 87.
[48] Exch. Inq. p.m. file 1198, no. 6. The manor was held of John Rous as of his manor of Rous Lench.
[49] Chan. Inq. p.m. (Ser. 2), clxxxiii, 96.
[50] Feet of F. Worcs. Hil. 35 Eliz.
[51] Ibid. 28 Hen. III, no. 7.
[52] Ibid. 3 Edw. I, no. 49.
[53] Exch. Inq. p.m. file 1198, no. 6.
[54] Feet of F. Worcs. Mich. 11 Chas. I.
[55] Ibid. Div. Co. Hil. 1650 ; East. 5 Anne ; Recov. R. Trin. 4 Geo. II, rot. 14 ; East. 50 Geo. III, rot. 130 ; Trin. 2 Geo. IV, rot. 148.
[56] *V.C.H. Worcs.* i, 290.
[57] Recov. R. Trin. 4 Geo. II, rot. 14.

east of it is a small rough niche with a shelf and triangular-shaped head, which may have belonged to an earlier building on the site. The round-headed chancel arch is of 12th-century date and of two square orders, the responds being semicircular with scalloped capitals. At the present time there is a second chancel arch east of the original one, of similar detail but constructed of plaster, as a temporary expedient to support the roof of the chancel.

The nave is three bays long with a 12th-century arcade to the north aisle having semicircular arches of two plain square orders and round piers with scalloped capitals and moulded bases. The whole arcade is of one date with the exception of the western respond, which is largely modern, a portion of the old capital being preserved in the Rous chapel. It is possible that this bay was altered, and perhaps narrowed, at a rebuilding of the west wall of the nave, beneath which the capital was found. At the eastern end of the south nave wall is the rood stair; this, with the turret containing it, which leaned as much as 2 ft. out of the perpendicular, was taken down stone by stone and re-erected when the adjoining nave wall was rebuilt. There are two windows in the south wall, both of two lights. The westernmost is entirely modern. Beneath the other window is a piscina-like niche with a plain two-centred head, but there were no traces of a drain in the old wall, which was taken down. The south door is a remarkably fine example of 12th-century work of about 1130, and has a round head decorated with zigzag ornament and twisted shafts with carved capitals and billet-moulded abaci. Above this is a well-executed 'Majesty' within an elaborate oval frame formed of wings, the whole design being inclosed in a round-headed enriched arch resting on ornate columns with cushion capitals. The west window of the nave is of early 14th-century date and has three lights under a two-centred head.

The north aisle is modern and is terminated towards the east by a semicircular apse with an elaborate arch opening into the aisle. Over the altar here is a semi-octagonal stone canopy, erected under the direction of Dr. Chafy in imitation of the well-known example in the nave of St. Mark's, Venice. The old north door has been restored and reset, the shafted jambs being largely modern, while the head, of two orders, is old. The west end of this aisle is railed off to form a baptistery and contains the original octagonal 15th-century font. The reset west window, which is of two plain pointed lights with a quatrefoil over, is probably of the late 13th century.

The Rous chapel is also modern, and was built to receive the monuments of the Rous family removed from the chancel at the recent restoration. They include a monument to Edward Rous of Rous Lench, who died in 1611, his wife Mary (Haselrigg), who died in 1580, three daughters and one son, with coloured effigies and an inscription within an elaborately carved cartouche, above which appear the arms: sable two bars engrailed argent; crest, a Moor's head. There is also a monument, with a crude Doric entab-

lature, to Sir John Rous, who died in 1645, and his wife Esther (Temple), and a wall slab to Sir Thomas Rous, son of the above (the first baronet), who died in 1676, and his three wives, Jane (Ferrers), Frances (Murray) and Anne, of whom nothing is known. There are other wall slabs to Sir Edward Rous, his eldest son, the second baronet, who died in 1677, and his wife Elizabeth (Lisle), who died in 1691. Preserved in the Rous chapel are a number of early 12th-century carved window heads and some capitals and bases of the same date, also an elaborately carved stone, already noted in a previous article,[58] and a carved window head of an early date.

The bellcote over the west wall of the chancel takes the place of a former rude wooden belfry built inside the west end of the nave and contains two bells, both by John Martin of Worcester, the treble dated 1661 and the second bearing the inscription 'God be our Speed.'

The church plate includes a cup and paten with the hall mark of 1570, and inscribed with the date 1571; a paten inscribed as the gift of Thomas Wall in 1704, but with the hall mark of 1693, a flagon given by a second Thomas Wall in 1756, with the hall mark of the previous year, and a three-legged paten of 1727, given by an unknown donor in 1748.

The registers before 1812 are as follows: (i) containing entries of births in the Rous family from 1513 and all entries from 1539 to 1778 except the marriages, which end in 1754; (ii) baptisms and burials 1779 to 1812; (iii) a marriage book 1754 to 1812.

ADVOWSON At the date of the Domesday Survey Urse had a priest on his manor of Rous Lench.[59] The first recorded presentation took place in 1286, when Sir Walter de Cooksey presented.[60] His name has not been connected with the manor, but it is probable that he had some interest in it, as the advowson afterwards belonged to the lords of the manor, Thomas de Lench presenting in 1329.[61] From that time the advowson has followed the same descent as the manor.[62] John Throckmorton, who was at that time holding a manor at Rous Lench, presented to the church in 1433.[63]

In 1291 the church was valued at £4 6s. 8d.[64] In 1309 the church for some reason was consecrated by Bishop Reynolds,[65] possibly after some desecration by bloodshed or otherwise.

CHARITIES The official trustees hold a sum of £30 15s. 10d. consols, which represents a legacy of £300 by will of John Pitts proved 19 May 1884. Nearly all of this was lost in the collapse of a firm to which it had been entrusted, and only £8 16s. 9d. was recovered. This was handed to the rector and churchwardens in 1901. Dr. Chafy has from time to time augmented this sum to its present figure. The annual dividends amounting to 15s. 4d. are applicable in the distribution of coals, bread or other articles in kind among the poor on 12 December in each year.

[58] *V.C.H. Worcs.* ii, 184 et seq.
[59] Ibid. i, 290a.
[60] *Reg. G. Giffard* (Worcs. Hist. Soc.), 277.
[61] Nash, op. cit. ii, 87.
[62] Ibid.; Feet of F. Worcs. 5 Ric. II, no. 13; Chan. Inq. p.m. (Ser. 2), xix,

74; cccxxvi, 48; Feet of F. Worcs. Mich. 11 Chas. I; Div. Co. Hil. 1650; East. 5 Anne; Recov. R. Trin. 4 Geo. II, rot. 14; East. 50 Geo. III, rot. 130; Trin. 2 Geo. IV, rot. 148; Inst. Bks. (P.R.O.). In 1640 George Wall presented under a grant from Sir John Rous,

and in 1772 Charles Fortescue presented for one turn only (Inst. Bks.).
[63] Nash, op. cit. ii, 87.
[64] *Pope Nich. Tax.* (Rec. Com.), 217b.
[65] Worc. Epis. Reg. Reynolds (1308–13), fol. 12.

ST. JOHN IN BEDWARDINE

The parish of St. John in Bedwardine, containing about 3,775 acres, of which 901 are arable, 1,745 under permanent grass and 99½ woods and plantations,[1] lies on the right bank of the Severn and stretches up the Teme, which forms its southern boundary from its junction with the Severn, as far as Cotheridge. On the north it is bounded by Broadheath, the Tenbury road and a tributary of Laughern Brook.[2] The chief roads, those from Worcester to Great Malvern, Hereford, Bromyard and Tenbury respectively, are old roads, and so apparently is the by-road to Oldbury; these are all mentioned in the court rolls of the 14th century, when the bridges by which some of them were carried over Laughern Brook and the Teme seem to have been in a state of chronic insecurity.[3] The Worcester, Malvern and Hereford branch of the Great Western railway passes through the parish, but there is no station nearer than Henwick.

The western part of the parish is made up of the hamlets of Upper and Lower Wick; the latter and part of the former were once parcel of the manor of Wick Episcopi.[4] 'A house with its garden and curtilage . . . and two fish ponds' is mentioned as early as 1299.[5] At Wick the Bishops of Worcester had a manor at which Godfrey Giffard often stayed, and where he entertained Archbishop Winchelsey in 1300.[6] He seems to have spent a good deal on building; the money, according to the Worcester monks, had been stolen from the sacrist of the priory, but apparently their judgement was warped by the joy of condemning a fault-finder.[7] The house now standing on the site known as Wick Episcopi is a ⌐⌐-shaped building, but nothing except the foundations is older than the 16th century. The present house at Lower Wick is modern, but has an extensive moat on the south. Standing in the farmyard is an ancient building long used as stables, which, it is claimed, is the remains of the church of St. Cuthbert. It is a rectangular building, probably of the early 13th century, built of red sandstone ashlar. The walls have been taken down to within about 5 ft. of the window sills and a half-timber and brick story erected upon them in the 17th century. The western portion of the south wall seems to have been rebuilt. The east and west windows are blocked, but the north external jamb of the latter, probably a lancet, has a filleted edge roll, and the internal jambs of the east window seem to have been

similarly enriched; internal chamfered jambs of north and south windows remain, and on the old portion of the south wall there are two original buttresses. It is possible, however, that the building may be that of a small house having a hall and two-storied block at its east end.

There are at Upper Wick several 17th-century half-timber cottages with thatched roofs and some 18th-century brick ones with tiled roofs. Upper Wick manor-house to the west is an L-shaped brick building of about 1700, with a slightly later addition on the south. It is of two stories with an attic. The house has been somewhat modernized internally, but retains some old beams and the upper part of a fine oak stairway of the original date which has square newels with ball finials, heavy moulded handrail and twisted balusters. A long, narrow pond extending round the south for some distance was probably a moat.

On the western side of the parish, where the Malvern road crosses the Teme, is Powick Old Bridge. The two arches of the bridge on the St. John's side were broken down during the Civil War and subsequently rebuilt.[7a]

Rushwick, which is first mentioned about 1299,[8] lies on the Hereford road between Laughern Brook and the Teme. A branch lane connects this hamlet with the Bromyard road, which it joins a little to the north-east of Crown East Court. The road here passes between the Grove Covert and Crown East Wood, at the western edge of which the ground after sloping steadily upwards from the Teme bank reaches the highest point in the parish; hence perhaps the name of the place, properly Crow Nest.[9] This ridge is well set with trees, for the greater part of the woodland in the parish lies about Crown East and Oldbury, though there is a strip of wood at Broadheath, and Birchen Grove, once the property of the Preceptor of Balsall (co. Warw.),[10] is still to be seen near the northern boundary of Temple Laughern. The soil is alluvium, the subsoil Keuper Marls. The common fields at Upper Wick were inclosed in 1789.[11]

The following place-names occur in local records: Portstraet[12] (x cent.); Nonham, Buttemefield, Bromlingfield, Colewyke, Chirnemore, Pitemauston, Pyrefield[13] (xiii cent.); Croppecroft,[14] Prichescroft,[15] Kynaresfelde or Kynewardesfelde, Sleyhull, Eorthenbrugge, Hurdelemebrugge and Noggensbrugge[16]; Boddecroftesend, Pullestrete or Poelstret, Cloptones-

---

[1] Statistics from Bd. of Agric. (1905).

[2] It is tempting to regard this as the boundary mentioned in an early charter of Laughern—'from the heath by the field haye to the wood and thence to the highway, along the road . . . across Onip burn and along the burn to Lawerne' (Birch, *Cart. Sax.* iii, 341; Heming, *Chartul.* [ed. Hearne], 160, 349), but, after all, there are many brooks and more than one highway in the parish.

[3] Eccl. Com. Ct. R. (P.R.O.), bdle. 193, no. 8–10, *passim*.   [4] Ibid.

[5] Red Bk. of Bishopric of Worc. (Eccl. Com. Var. bdle. 121, no. 43698), fol. 21. The kitchen and bake-house are also mentioned at this date (ibid.), and a much

later survey (Pat. 28 Eliz. pt. x, m. 32) mentions that the former was 'of two bays,' and that there was also a hall of three bays.

[6] *Ann. Mon.* (Rolls Ser.), iv, 548.

[7] Thomas, *Surv. of Worc. Cath.* App. 64.

[7a] Inform. from Mr. J. W. Willis-Bund.

[8] Red Bk. of Bishopric of Worc. fol. 31.

[9] The form Crowneast is not found till the 17th century (Habington, *Surv. of Worc.* ii, 134), when it is evidently only a variant of spelling, as Habington says that the name is 'poor.' The proper name was used up to the middle of the 19th century, when the estate was bought

by A. H. Royds, who changed the name to Crown East. Nash (*Hist. of Worcs.* ii, 311) says the place is 'vulgarly called Crow's Nest.'

[10] Pat. 36 Hen. VIII, pt. xx, m. 2.

[11] Original deed *penes* Mr. J. W. Willis-Bund.

[12] Heming, op. cit. 160; 'le port way' is mentioned in the 15th century (Eccl. Com. Ct. R. [P.R.O.], bdle. 193, no. 10).

[13] Red Bk. of Bishopric of Worc. fol. 21.

[14] Prattinton Coll. (Soc. Antiq.), Deeds of D. and C. of Worc. no. 218.

[15] Chan. Inq. p.m. 7 Ric. II, no. 22.

[16] Eccl. Com. Ct. R. (P.R.O.), bdle. 193, no. 8.

lone,[16a] Blakefield, Doddecroft and Clokhull[17] (xiv cent.) ; le ffortey, Russhwycrosse or Rushwyke Crosse and Waterelone,[18] Leystonesfelde, Ladycroft, Dynes Grene, Standefast Brigge, Barewardyn and Parok Diche[19] (xv cent.) ; Kychyns, Moncke Orchard, Le Mytre, Leighton Corte[20] (xvi cent.) ; Pool Close and Sling Meadow[21] (xvii cent.).

The manor of *WICK EPISCOPI MANORS* (Wiche, xi cent. ; Wyke, xii cent. ; Wyke by Worcester, xiii cent. ; Wyke Episcopi, xiv cent.) belonged to the church of Worcester before the Conquest,[22] and its site is said to have been granted by Offa, King of the Mercians, to Bishop Milred before 775.[23] It continued to be held by the Bishops of Worcester until 1558,[24] when Queen Elizabeth assumed possession of it during a vacancy of the see under the Act of 1558,[25] after which it was held on lease from the Crown by Richard Maye till 1586.[26] In that year the queen granted it to Sir Thomas Bromley,[27] whose

BISHOPRIC OF WORCESTER. *Argent ten roundels gules.*

descendants (q.v. in Holt) remained in possession of Wick until 1743,[28] when Henry Lord Montfort sold the larger part of the estate to Richard Vernon,[29] who was probably a trustee for Thomas Vernon of Hanbury, for the latter was in possession in 1745.[30] Other parts were sold by Lord Montfort to William Bund.[30a] The Vernon part followed the descent of Hanbury[31] until recently, when the greater part was sold to the tenant, Mr. John Edward Powell.[31a]

It was the custom of the manor of Wick Episcopi as well as the other manors belonging to the see that the demesne lands should be let by indenture and convent seal and all other tenantries of copyhold by court roll.[32] In the 15th century some of the parishioners obtained the convent seal for the purpose of making fraudulent indentures 'by which the bishop

looses his heriots and fines and the King's pore subjects hath no habytacons'[33] ; a commission of inquiry was appointed, with the result that the culprits were commanded to appear before the council in 1522.[34]

The 15th-century court rolls give an interesting record of the growth of inclosures ; towards the end of the period several tenants were accused of encroaching on the common land almost as regularly as the court was held,[35] and in spite of fines the practice seems to have increased steadily. In 1387 the jurors presented

BROMLEY of Holt. *Quarterly fessewise indented gules and or.*

that Geoffrey Binn had 'built a dovecot by his cottage to the damage of the whole community, wherefore he was commanded to pull it down.'[36]

There were two fisheries attached to the manor of Wick Episcopi in 1086,[37] and one followed the descent of the manor throughout.[38] The other passed by the grant of Bishop Giffard to the priory of Malvern, and has since the suppression of that house descended with the mills. It now belongs to Mr. Willis-Bund.[39] In 1348 the prior had also a fishery at Bedwardine.[40] A park at Wick belonging to the Bishop of Worcester is mentioned in 1339,[41] and free warren in the demesne lands there was

BUND. *Ermine a pile gules from the foot between two like piles from the chief with an eagle's leg razed or upon each.*

granted to Walter Cantilupe by Henry III in 1254.[42]

The manor of *UPPER WICK* (Goldhine Wic, xii cent. ; Goldginewike, Goldinewyke, xiii cent. ; Wyke Dabitot, Sapynswyk, Wick Sapey, Overwyke, xiv cent. ; Weeke Sapi, Gowld Weeke, Upper Week, xvii cent.) is said to have been granted to Osbert

---

[16a] In 1086 Urse held a hide at Cloptune in the manor of Wick in succession to Brictmar (*V.C.H. Worcs.* i, 289). This is mentioned about the middle of the 12th century as being held by William Beauchamp (Red Bk. of Bishopric of Worc. fol. 252). See also Heming, op. cit. 253–4.

[17] Ct. R. as above, no. 9.   [18] Ibid.

[19] Ibid. bdle. 194, no. 3.

[20] *Valor Eccl.* (Rec. Com.), iii, 220.

[21] *Charters of D. and C. of Worc.* (Worcs. Hist. Soc.), 166.

[22] *V.C.H. Worcs.* i, 288.

[23] Birch, *Cart. Sax.* i, 307. The boundaries are given in this charter.

[24] *V.C.H. Worcs.* loc. cit. ; Heming, *Chartul.* (ed. Hearne), 313 ; Red Bk. of Bishopric of Worc. fol. 31, 254, 21 ; *Reg. G. Giffard* (Worcs. Hist. Soc.), *passim* ; *Reg. W. Ginsborough* (Worcs. Hist. Soc.), *passim* ; Close, 21 Edw. III, pt. i, m. 2 ; White Bk. of the Bishopric of Worc. (Eccl. Com. Rec. Var. bdle. 121, no. 43696), fol. 101 ; Eccl. Com. Ct. R. (P.R.O.), bdle. 193, no. 8–10; bdle. 194, no. 1–6. The manor was assessed in 1086 at 15 hides, and was then worth £8 (*V.C.H. Worcs.* loc. cit.). In 1299

it was worth £52 5s. 2½d. yearly (Red Bk. of Bishopric of Worc. fol. 21).

[25] Pat. 4 Eliz. pt. vi, m. 24. She afterwards granted to Bishop Sandys the rectories of Hanley Castle and other places in compensation (ibid.).

[26] Pat. 12 Eliz. pt. v, m. 15 ; Exch. Dep. Worcs. East. 33 Eliz. no. 21.

[27] Pat. 28 Eliz. pt. x, m. 32.

[28] Chan. Inq. p.m. (Ser. 2), ccxiii, 114 ; Exch. Dep. Worcs. Hil. 15 Jas. I, no. 4 ; East. 16 Jas. I, no. 8 ; Mich. 4 Chas. I, no. 5 ; Recov. R. Mich. 4 Jas. II, rot. 226 ; Nash, *Hist of Worcs.* ii, 311 ; Close, 16 Geo. II, pt. xviii, no. 1. Sir Thomas Bromley seems to have let or mortgaged the manor in 1616 to John Grove (Feet of F. Worcs. Mich. 14 Jas. I), who was said to have died seised of the reversion thereof in 1617 (Chan. Inq. p.m. [Ser. 2], ccclxv, 147), but Henry Bromley entered into the manor after the death of his father's widow (Chan. Proc. [Ser. 2], bdle. 402, no. 85).

[29] Close, 16 Geo. II, pt. xviii, no. 1.

[30] Recov. R. Trin. 18 & 19 Geo. II, rot. 48.

[30a] Inform. from Mr. J. W. Willis-Bund.

[31] Recov. R. Mich. 20 Geo. II, rot. 44 ; East. 59 Geo. III, rot. 289 ; Feet of F. Worcs. Hil. 25 Geo. III ; Nash, loc. cit.

[31a] Inform. from Mr. J. W. Willis-Bund.

[32] Ct. of Req. bdle. 7, no. 51.

[33] Ibid.

[34] Ibid. The lease which was the subject of this lawsuit had been made about 1498 ; the plaintiff stated that the lands in question, Salmons and Brittisland, were not of the demesne, and had been let to his grandfather by copy of court roll 12 Oct. 1481 (ibid.).

[35] Eccl. Com. Ct. R. (P.R.O.), bdle. 194, no. 1–4.

[36] Ibid. bdle. 193, no. 8.

[37] *V.C.H. Worcs.* i, 288.

[38] Eccl. Com. Ct. R. (P.R.O.), bdle. 193, no. 8–10 ; Red Bk. of Bishopric of Worc. fol. 21 ; Pat. 28 Eliz. pt. x, m. 32 ; Recov. R. Mich. 20 Geo. II, rot. 44.

[39] Inform. from Mr. J. W. Willis-Bund.

[40] Pat. 22 Edw. III, pt. iii, m. 13 d.

[41] Ibid. 13 Edw. III, pt. i, m. 36 d. ; *Abbrev. Rot. Orig.* (Rec. Com.), i, 133.

[42] Pat. 37 & 38 Hen. III, pt. ii, m. 2.

ST. JOHN IN BEDWARDINE CHURCH C. 1810
(*From a Water-colour by Thos. Rickards in Prattinton Collection*)

ST. JOHN IN BEDWARDINE CHURCH FROM THE SOUTH

D'Abitot by Bishop Alfred, probably about 1158[43]; it afterwards followed the descent of Redmarley D'Abitôt (q.v.) until 1389,[44] when it passed on the death of John de Sapy to Ellen de Arderne, who was perhaps his daughter and heir.[45] Her descendants, the owners of Pedmore (q.v. in Halfshire Hundred), remained in possession of the manor until 1563,[46] when it seems to have been sold by Edward Arderne to John Nanfan,[47] who sold it in 1571[48] to Jasper Gower. Nine years later it was purchased of Jasper by John Hall[49] of Henwick. His son Edward demised part of the manor about 1614 to Paul Tracy of Stanway (co. Glouc.), bart.,[50] and died seised of the remainder in 1617, leaving as his heir his son and namesake.[51] This Edward Hall together with Sir Paul Tracy conveyed the manor in 1633 to Henry Best,[52] whose only child Kathe-rine was married before 1650 to Scudamore Pytts, the younger son of James Pytts of Kyre Wyard.[53] Henry Best was still living in 1669, when he was a party to the fine by which certain lands in Wick were settled on Katherine Cliffe,[54] afterwards the wife of his grandson James Pytts.[55] She seems to have lived here during her widowhood,[56] and died here, being buried in St. John's Church. Her heir was her son Samuel Pytts, then owner of Kyre Wyard,[57] and he sold the site of the manor and other land at Wick to Thomas Bund, whose great-grandson Mr. John W. Willis-Bund is now the owner.[58]

According to the register of Worcester Priory the manor of *HARDWICK* (Hordewik, Herdewyk, Hardewik, xiii cent.; Hardeswyke, xvi cent.) was granted to the monks of that house by King Edgar between 961 and 975.[59] It is not, however, mentioned in the Domesday Survey, nor does there seem to be any reference to it earlier than 1236, at which date it

PYTTS of Kyre.
*Azure three bars argent
with three stars or in the
chief.*

certainly belonged to the priory.[60] In 1256 the monks obtained from Henry III a grant of free warren in their demesne lands there,[61] which was con-firmed by Edward III in 1355.[62] The manor remained in the possession of the priory till the Dissolution,[63] when Henry VIII granted it to the dean and chapter.[64] During the Commonwealth it seems to have been occupied by John Oldbury,[65] who had obtained a long lease of it from Dean Potter in 1638,[66] but after the Restoration it was re-covered by the dean and chapter.

A court baron was held there as late as 1857,[67] and there are still (1912) at least two copyhold tenants.[67a]

In 1291 the proceeds from the manor of Hardwick, except the profits from stock, were assigned to the pittancer of the priory,[68] from which it may perhaps be concluded that *PITTENSARYS FARM*, for which there is no separate entry in the Taxation, was at that time regarded as a member of this manor. Its early history was, however, quite distinct from that of Hardwick, for there can be little doubt that this small estate, which contained rather more than 31 acres in 1860,[69] was the odd virgate of the bishop's demesne held by Urse D'Abitot at the time of the Domesday Survey.[70] This land, which had been held of Urse by his chaplain Alfred,[71] was granted by his son-in-law Walter de Beauchamp to the Priory of Worcester[72]; it is described as being on the west side of the chapel of St. John,[73] and the 14th-century court rolls show that it stretched as far as the bridge called Hereford Bridge over Laughern Brook.[74] It followed the descent of Hard-wick until 1860,[75] and though called a manor in the 16th century never seems to have had a separate court; it was, however, always leased to tenants as a separate estate by the dean and chapter.[76] In 1857 a lease for twenty-one years was granted by them

WORCESTER PRIORY.
*Argent ten roundels gules
and a quarter azure with
our Lady and the Child
or therein.*

[43] Red Bk. of the Bishopric of Worc. fol. 31. On fol. 257 Osbert is said to have held it 'de novo a tempore Johannis Episcopi' (1151–8), which looks as if it had either been granted at the beginning of Alfred's episcopate (1158–64) or held by Osbert previously for some rent of which Alfred had discharged him.

[44] *Testa de Nevill* (Rec. Com.), 41*b*; White Bk. of the Bishopric of Worc. fol. 8; Feet of F. Worcs. Hil. 7 Edw. I; *Reg. G. Giffard* (Worcs. Hist. Soc.), 243, 356; *Feud. Aids*, v, 308; Eccl. Com. Ct. R. (P.R.O.), bdle. 193, no. 1–9; Deeds of D. and C. of Westm. no. 22545.

[45] John de Sapy was still seised of Wick in 1388 (Eccl. Com. Ct. R. [P.R.O.], bdle. 193, no. 8, m. 34), and as Ellen Arderne was in possession a year after-wards (ibid. no. 9, m. 10), she probably entered immediately after his death, which occurred during the year (Deeds of D. and C. of Westm. loc. cit.). Her title to Wick is not given in the court roll.

[46] White Bk. of Bishopric of Worc. fol. 102; Early Chan. Proc. bdle. 26, no. 139; Ct. of Req. bdle. 10, no. 13; Feet of F. Worcs. Mich. and Hil. 1 & 2 Phil. and Mary; Trin. 5 Eliz.

[47] Feet of F. Worcs. Trin. 5 Eliz.

[48] Ibid. Mich. 13 & 14 Eliz.

[49] Ibid. Mich. 22 & 23 Eliz.; Habing-ton, *Surv. of Worcs.* (Worcs. Hist. Soc.), i, 500, states that 'thro' dyvers hands it came to Mr. Thomas Hall of Henwyke,' the father of John Hall.

[50] Chan. Inq. p.m. (Ser. 2), ccclxvi, 162.

[51] Ibid.

[52] *Kyre Park Charters* (Worcs. Hist. Soc.), 86, no. 316.

[53] Ibid. p. viii.

[54] Ibid. 87, no. 320.

[55] Ibid. p. viii.

[56] Ibid. 88.

[57] He had succeeded to Kyre in 1685 on the death of James Pytts, his father's first cousin (ibid. p. viii).

[58] Original deeds *penes* Mr. J. W. Willis-Bund.

[59] 'Apud Hordewik curia (est) cum pertinentiis *ex* collatione Adgari Regis tempore Sancti Oswaldi' (Hale, *Reg. of Worc. Priory*, 37*b*). The manor is not included in 'King Edgar's charter' (Birch, *Cart. Sax.* iii, 377).

[60] Hale, op. cit. 110*b*, 120*b*, 123*a*.

[61] *Cal. Pat.* 1354–8, p. 266.

[62] Ibid.

[63] *Pope Nich. Tax.* (Rec. Com.), 227;

Habington, op. cit. ii, 133; *Valor Eccl.* (Rec. Com.), iii, 220.

[64] Pat. 33 Hen. VIII, pt. v; *Charters of D. and C. of Worc.* (Worcs. Hist. Soc.), 163.

[65] *Charters of D. and C. of Worc.* (Worcs. Hist. Soc.), 166.

[66] Ibid.

[67] A. W. Isaac, *Boulton in St. John's*, 21.

[67a] Inform. from Mr. J. W. Willis-Bund.

[68] *Pope Nich. Tax.* (Rec. Com.), 227.

[69] A. W. Isaac, op. cit., plan of Pitten-sarys in 1860.

[70] *V.C.H. Worcs.* i, 289.

[71] Hale, op. cit. 92*a*.

[72] Ibid. William de Beauchamp was, however, returned as the owner about 1164 (Red Bk. of the Bishopric of Worc. fol. 252).

[73] Hale, op. cit. 39.

[74] Eccl. Com. Ct. R. (P.R.O.), bdle. 193, no. 8–10, *passim*.

[75] Ibid. bdle. 194, no. 1–7; *Charters of D. and C. of Worc.* (Worcs. Hist. Soc.), 165, 129; A. W. Isaac, op. cit. 21.

[76] Ibid.

to Mr. Francis Williams of Laughern Hill,[77] who enfranchised the estate in 1860.[78]

The manor of *CROWN EAST* (Crawenest, Crowe Nest, xiii cent. ; Crowneast, xvii cent.) or *RIDGE HALL* (Rugge, xii cent.; Rughall, Ruggehall, xiv cent.; Rygehalhide,[79] Riggehallhide, xvi cent.) seems to have been a collection of holdings bought during the 13th century by Baldwin de Frevile and his son Alexander. One carucate of this land belonged in 1236 to Walter Bufle[80] ; his son and heir Robert sold it in 1255 to Baldwin de Frevile,[81] who settled it at the same time on himself and his wife Maud with remainder to their younger son Alexander.[82] Baldwin died shortly afterwards,[83] and before 1265 his widow had married Sir William Devereux, who was killed fighting for the king at

FREVILE. *Or a cross gules with five lozenges vair thereon.*

Evesham.[84] Maud released her right in Crown East to her son Alexander before 1286, in which year he obtained from Edward I a grant of free warren in his demesne lands there.[85] These lands were said in 1349 to be held of the Prioress of White Nuns at Whistones.[86] Alexander seems also to have acquired before 1286 another virgate of land, which he held of the Bishop of Worcester in 'Rugge' in 1299[87] ; it had been held of Bishop Baldwin about 1182 by William of St. John's.[88] A second virgate of land in 'Rugge' was added to the estate before 1349, either by Alexander or his son Baldwin[89] ; this was probably the virgate held of the bishop in 1299 by Thomas son of Walter le Fleming.[90] Alexander Frevile spent a great part of his long life in the king's service both in France and Scotland,[91] and it was

perhaps as a reward that he received in 1305 a pardon of the debts due from him to the Exchequer.[92] He served in the Bannockburn campaign,[93] and was again summoned to march against the Scots in 1327, when he must have been at least seventy-three.[94] He died in the following year and was succeeded by his son Baldwin,[95] who died seised of 'Croweneste and Rughall' in 1346, leaving as his heir his son and namesake.[96] This Baldwin Frevile, who was afterwards knighted, granted the manor to his cousin John Hillary *alias* Grey of Sandiacre (co. Derby).[97] John Grey died in 1403, leaving as his heirs his daughters Isabel, who married first John Walsh and afterwards Humphrey Halloughton, and Alice the wife of John Leeke.[98] Isabel died in March 1435, when the jurors presented that her son was of full age and might hold when he had satisfied his lord of his homage.[99] She had not, however, been living in the neighbourhood for some time,[100] and her son had presumably died before her, for by the inquisition taken in the following May her sister Alice was found to be her heir.[1]

Alice settled the manor on her younger son Thomas Leeke, who was seised of it in 1453,[2] and was apparently succeeded about 1459 by another Thomas Leeke, perhaps his son.[3] This Thomas may have been still living in 1472, as there is no mention

LEEKE of Sandiacre. *Argent a saltire engrailed sable with five rings or thereon.*

of Crown East among the possessions of the Leekes of Sandiacre at that date[4] ; by 1513, however, the Worcestershire manor seems to have reverted to the elder branch.[5] John Leeke of Sutton-en-le-Dale, the

---

[77] A. W. Isaac, loc. cit.

[78] Ibid. 22. Mr. J. S. Isaac bought part of the land from Mr. J. F. Williams in 1875, and the rest was sold to Mr. Hopton (inform. from Mr. J. W. Willis-Bund).

[79] Possibly the 'hide' refers to Crown East ; in the court roll of March 1436 (Eccl. Com. Ct. R. [P.R.O.], bdle. 193, no. 10) Isabel Halloughton is said to have 'died seised of two messuages, one called Rugehale and the other la Huyde,' but Crown East was extended at 2 carucates and Ridgehall at 3½ virgates in the same year (Chan. Inq. p.m. 14 Hen. VI, no. 17).

[80] Hale, op. cit. 105, 106.

[81] Feet of F. Worcs. Mich. 39 Hen. III; MSS. of Lord Middleton (Hist. MSS. Com.), 65.

[82] Feet of F. Worcs. Mich. 39 Hen. III. The settlement was probably made shortly after Alexander's birth, as Baldwin's marriage to Maud took place in 1253 (Pat. 37 Hen. III, m. 5), and Alexander was their second son (De Banco R. Mich. 6 Edw. III, m. 448).

[83] MSS. of Lord Middleton, loc. cit.

[84] Yr. Bks. 20 Edw. I (Rolls Ser.), 193 ; Flores Hist. (Rolls Ser. 95), iii, 6.

[85] Pat. no. 105a ; Yr. Bks. 20 Edw. I (Rolls Ser.), 158. Maud died in 1297 and was buried in Worcester Cathedral (Ann. Mon. [Rolls Ser.], iv, 534). She was the sister of Godfrey Giffard, whose determination to be buried beside her (ibid.) caused some scandal at the time of his

death, as there was no place for his tomb there until the bones of John of Coutances had been moved.

[86] Chan. Inq. p.m. 17 Edw. III, file 69, no. 37.

[87] Pat. no. 105a ; Red Bk. of Bishopric of Worc. fol. 21.

[88] Ibid. fol. 260. It is entered in the Testa de Nevill as a virgate in 'Brugge' held of the manor of Wick Episcopi by William of St. John's (p. 41).

[89] Chan. Inq. p.m. 17 Edw. III, no. 37.

[90] Red Bk. of Bishopric of Worc. fol. 257.

[91] Cal. Pat. 1281–92, p. 240 ; 1292–1301, p. 309 ; Pat. no. 105a ; Dugdale, Baronage, ii, 103. G.E.C. Complete Peerage shows that there is no evidence for Dugdale's statement that Alexander was ever summoned to Parliament as a baron.

[92] Cal. Pat. 1301–7, p. 308.

[93] Dugdale, loc. cit. ; Scutage R. 12–19 Edw. II, m. 2.

[94] G.E.C. loc. cit.

[95] Chan. Inq. p.m. Edw. III, file 11, no. 4 ; Pat. 2 Edw. III, pt. ii, m. 33. Baldwin had evidently taken part in the rebellion of 1322 (Cal. Close, 1318–23, p. 608).

[96] Chan. Inq. p.m. 17 Edw. III, no. 37. There is no mention of a manor court at this date, but courts were certainly held at Crown East between 1353 and 1370 (MSS. of Lord Middleton [Hist. MSS. Com.], 287). In the Feud. Aids of 1346 (v, 308) 'William' Frevile is said to hold the land at Rughall formerly

held by William of St. John's, but this was probably a mistake.

[97] Misc. Inq. file 242, no. 101. John was the grandson of Joan wife of Henry Hillary, a daughter of Philip Marmion, another of whose daughters was Mazera de Cromwell, the mother of Joan wife of Alexander de Frevile (Wrottesley, Ped. from Plea R. 510 ; Close, 11 Edw. III, pt. ii, m. 1 ; Pat. 17 Edw. III, pt. ii, m. 17). John Grey granted the manor of Ridge Hall to William Gunthorpe and others, who transferred their interest to Sir John Beauchamp of Holt, to hold during their pleasure. He died seised of the manor in 1387 (Chan. Inq. p.m. 12 Ric. II, no. 91).

[98] Chan. Inq. p.m. 4 Hen. IV, no. 1 ; 14 Hen. VI, no. 17.

[99] Eccl. Com. Ct. R. (P.R.O.), bdle. 193, no. 10.

[100] Ibid.

[1] Chan. Inq. p.m. 14 Hen. VI, no. 17.

[2] Eccl. Com. Ct. R. loc. cit. ; Thoroton, Notts. i, 49.

[3] Eccl. Com. Ct. R. loc. cit. William Leeke, Alice's eldest son, had a younger son called Thomas (Thoroton, loc. cit.), who may have been the one summoned to do homage in 1459, but he could not have been of age to hold the land, as his elder brother John was only eight in 1460 (Chan. Inq. p.m. 38 & 39 Hen. VI, no. 18).

[4] Jeayes, Derbyshire Charters, 181.

[5] Thoroton, Notts. i, 145.

grandson of Alice's eldest son William, dealt with it in that year,[6] but it subsequently passed to his younger brother Thomas Leeke, who sold it in 1518 to John Mucklowe.[7]

William Mucklowe, John's heir, died in 1529 seised of the manor of Crown East, which he left by his will to Peter Mucklowe.[8] Peter was succeeded by William Mucklowe's eldest son Richard, who was seised of Crown East and Ridge Hall (described at this time as separate manors) at his death in 1556.[9] The estate afterwards followed the descent of Martley in Doddingtree Hundred (q.v.) until 1619,[10] when it was sold by Simon Mucklowe to Edmund White.[11]

Edmund White died in 1633, leaving the manor by will to his son Edmund, with successive remainders to Edmund's son and namesake and his heirs male and James White, the testator's son.[12] In 1676 the third Edmund White sold Crown East, with the consent of his cousin and heir-apparent John the son of James White, to Edward Barton,[13] who dealt with it by fine in 1704.[14] The descent of the manor after this date is not easy to trace, but as Nash states that the family of John Wowen, owner of the estate in 1801, had held it for nearly 150 years,[15] Wowen was perhaps descended from Barton. His father, another John Wowen, was in possession in 1765,[16] but the history of the manor during the first half of the 18th century is obscure. The Wowens had considerable property in the parish. It was, however, sold to various persons about 1820. The largest lot, Crown East, with about 300 acres of land, was bought by Josiah Patrick. It passed from him to a solicitor in Worcester named Hughes, who sold it about 1860 to A. H. Royds. At his death it was sold to the present owner, Mr. Henry Bramwell, J.P.[16a]

According to the chartulary of Worcester Monastery half a hide of land at *LAUGHERN* (Lawerne, x cent. ; Laure, xi cent.; Lauwern, Lauerne, xii cent. ; Lawerne Almoners, Lawerne Elemosinary, xv cent.) was granted by Offa, King of the Mercians, to Bishop Heathored between 781 and 796,[17] and bestowed on the prior and convent by Bishop Cynewold before 957.[18] In the time of King Edward the Confessor Kineward held it, 'doing such service as the bishop willed.'[19] The monastic chartulary states that it had been held by him of the convent, and reverted to the monks at his death,[20] but they were deprived of it shortly afterwards by Robert le Despenser,[21] who held it at the time of the Domesday Survey.[22] Between

1108 and 1118[23] it was held by Nicholas,[24] probably of Walter de Beauchamp, whose son William de Beauchamp was in possession of it before 1180.[25]

In 1299 the Prior of Worcester held half a hide in Laughern by service of a quarter of a knight's fee[26]; this seems to have been the same estate and was probably the land granted by John D'Abitot (living 1197)[27] to the priory.[28] Among the property of the prior taxed in 1291 were certain lands in 'Lawerne debetok' (? D'Abitot) held by the almoner,[29] and the monks paid a rent of 2 marks yearly to the heirs of Lord Beauchamp as late as 1536.[30] 'The Almoner's manor in Lawerne' is mentioned in the 14th-century court rolls,[31] but at a later date it probably lapsed; it is not mentioned by name in the priory accounts of the 16th century,[32] or in the Valor,[33] though it was evidently included at this time among the priory lands in Hardwick and St. John's.[34]

TEMPLE LAUGHERN (Lauwerne, xii cent. ; Lauuarne, Lawerne Willelmi, xiii cent. ; Temple Lauherne, Holberie Lawerne, xv cent. ; Temple Lawghern, xvi cent. ; Holberie, Templars Lawerne, xvii cent.).

According to the chartulary of Worcester Priory a manor in Laughern was 'returned' to the cathedral monks by Bishop Simon between 1125 and 1151,[35] but, as both the manors mentioned in Domesday Book were still held at that date by William de Beauchamp,[36] this was probably a fresh grant from the bishop's demesne. It seems to have been this property which the prior and convent afterwards claimed to have granted to William the son of Miles de Laughern before 1236 at a yearly rent of half a mark.[37] William was succeeded by another Miles, who sold the manor in 1249 to the Master and brethren of the Temple for £100.[38]

In 1253 the Templars received from Henry III a grant of free warren in their demesne lands in Laughern,[39] but after the death of Miles their right to their property was disputed by his sister and heir Sabine and her husband John de Donyngton, who occupied the manor,[40] and it was not until 1275 that the master obtained a quitclaim from them, promising in return to pay a rent of

THE KNIGHTS TEM-
PLARS. *Argent a cross gules and a chief sable.*

[6] Thoroton, *Notts.* i, 145.
[7] Feet of F. Worcs. Trin. 10 Hen.VIII ; Chan. Inq. p.m. (Ser. 2), l, 158.
[8] Chan. Inq. p.m. (Ser. 2), l, 158.
[9] Ibid. cvi, 91.
[10] Ibid. clxxxvii, 109 ; Habington, op. cit. ii, 134. In 1568 Simon Mucklowe obtained a quitclaim from Sir Francis Leeke, the son of John Leeke of Sutton-en-le-Dale (Feet of F. Worcs. Hil. 10 Eliz.).
[11] Feet of F. Worcs. East. 16 Jas. I ; Close, 16 Jas. I, pt. v, no. 48.
[12] Chan. Inq. p.m. (Ser. 2), dccxxiv, 11.
[13] Feet of F. Worcs. Trin. 28 Chas. II ; Com. Pleas D. Enr. East. 28 Chas. II, m. 10. John White had dealt with the manor by fine in 1671 (Feet of F. Div. Co. Hil. 23 & 24 Chas. II).
[14] Feet of F. Worcs. East. 3 Anne.
[15] Nash, *Hist. of Worcs.* ii, 311.

[16] Recov. R. Hil. 5 Geo. III, rot. 143.
[16a] Inform. from Mr. J. W. Willis-Bund.
[17] Heming, op. cit. 515, 575.
[18] Ibid. 390, 573 ; *Ann. Mon.* (Rolls Ser.), iv, 564. The chartulary also contains a lease from St. Oswald to Cynethegn (Heming, op. cit. 160, 349 ; Birch, *Cart. Sax.* iii, 341).
[19] *V.C.H. Worcs.* i, 267, 289.
[20] Heming, op cit. 252–3.
[21] Ibid.
[22] *V.C.H. Worcs.* i, 289.
[23] It is said to have been held of the church of St. Helen, Worcester, in the 12th century by Fritheric, who left it to the priory at his death (Heming, op. cit. 427).
[24] *V.C.H. Worcs.* i, 324.
[25] Red Bk. of the Bishopric of Worc. fol. 252.

[26] Ibid. fol. 31.
[27] Pipe R. 8 Ric. I, m. 4 d.
[28] Hale, *Reg. of Worc. Priory*, 36b ; Prattinton Coll. (Soc. of Antiq.), Deeds of D. and C. of Worc. no. 219.
[29] *Pope Nich. Tax.* (Rec. Com.), 227.
[30] *Valor Eccl.* (Rec. Com.), iii, 220.
[31] Eccl. Com. Ct. R. (P.R.O.), bdle. 193, no. 8, m. 21.
[32] Printed by the Worcs. Hist. Soc. in *Accounts of Worc. Priory.*
[33] *Valor Eccl.* (Rec. Com.), loc. cit.
[34] Ibid.
[35] Thomas, *Surv. of Worc. Cath.* App. 6 ; Heming, op. cit. 535.
[36] Red Bk. of the Bishopric of Worc. fol. 252.
[37] Heming, loc. cit.
[38] Feet of F. Worcs. Mich. 34 Hen. III.
[39] Chart. R. 37 Hen. III, m. 16.
[40] Feet of F. Worcs. Trin. 3 Edw. I.

8 marks yearly during the lives of John and Sabine.[41] To this settlement the Prior of Worcester opposed his claim,[42] but though he was unsuccessful the Templars were not yet able to enjoy their manor in peace, as the Donyngtons re-entered during 1276,[43] and the new master was obliged to come to terms with them in the autumn of that year.[44]

The Templars remained in possession of the manor till 1311,[45] when it was granted on the fall of the order with the Preceptory of Balsall, to which it had become attached, to the Knights Hospitallers,[46] who retained it till the Dissolution.[47] In 1544 it was sold by Henry VIII to Richard Goodyere and William Gower.[48] In 1558 Richard Goodyere obtained licence to alienate his moiety of the manor to Roger Goodyere *alias* Onyon,[49] who in 1583 settled certain lands there on his son Richard Onyon *alias* Unwyn, retaining the rest of the property to his own use for life.[50] Roger was succeeded in 1611 by his son Richard,[51] who together with Roger his son sold much of the land to John Gower, the owner of the other moiety of the manor.[52] The descent of Unwyn's own share after this date is difficult to trace ; it was held in 1629 by Robert Stanford, who left it at his death to his daughter Frances the wife of George Middlemore.[53] By 1655 some of the land seems to have come into the possession of Francis Earl of Shrewsbury,[54] and this had passed before 1679 to Jane Cotes, who with her son Henry Cotes conveyed it in that year to Sir Edward Sebright, bart.[55] The so-called manor was settled on Richard Sebright, Sir Edward's younger son, in 1707,[56] but its history after this date is obscure.

William Gower, who bought the second moiety of Temple Laughern in 1544, was also the owner of Boughton or Boulton (q.v. *infra*), and his property in Laughern afterwards became known as the manor of

THE KNIGHTS HOS-PITALLERS. *Gules a cross argent.*

Boulton Colemarsh.[57] It followed the descent of Queenhill in Ripple [58] (q.v.), and was still held by the Gower family in 1766.[59] They sold it early in the 19th century to the Harrisons, who held it till about 1840, when it was sold to the Munns. On the death of the last brother about 1900 it was bought by James Best, whose widow now lives there.[59a]

In 1086 Urse D'Abitot held 3 virgates at *LAUGHERN* (Laure, xi cent. ; Lawerne, xii cent. ; Lauerne, Lawarne Dabtot, Bechameslawerne, xiv cent. ; Lawarne Beuchamp, xv cent. ; Lawgherne, xvi cent.) which had previously been held by Sawine as of the bishop's demesne.[60] This was afterwards held by William de Beauchamp by John D'Abitot[61] and followed the descent of Hindlip (q.v.) until 1286,[62] when it was resumed by the Earl of Warwick, who settled it on his third son Walter.[63] In 1300 Walter de Beauchamp obtained a grant of free warren in his demesne lands in Laughern.[64] By 1346 the estate had passed to William de Beauchamp, Walter's second son, who settled it in that year on himself and the heirs of his body with successive remainders to William de Bradewell and his own right heirs.[65] Before 1379 the rents issuing thence were in the possession of Sir Roger Beauchamp, who is said to have been a younger

BEAUCHAMP of Powick. *Gules a fesse and six martlets or.*

son of Giles Beauchamp of Powick.[66] Sir Roger died in 1379, leaving as his heir his grandson Roger, then sixteen.[67] John Beauchamp, the grandson of the younger Roger, died during his minority, leaving as his heir his sister Margaret.[68] She married Oliver St. John, who was seised of the manor of Laughern Beauchamp in 1431.[69] They had several sons, but the manor passed by settlement or purchase to their cousin Richard Lord Beauchamp of Powick, who settled it on his daughter Margaret and William Rede on their marriage.[70] Margaret predeceased her

---

[41] Feet of F. Worcs. Trin. 3 Edw. I.

[42] Ibid.

[43] Ibid. Mich. 4 Edw. I.

[44] Ibid.

[45] *Abbrev. Rot. Orig.* (Rec. Com), i, 189.

[46] The manor of Temple Laughern was enumerated among the possessions of Guy de Beauchamp Earl of Warwick at his death in 1315 (*Cal. Inq. p.m.* 1–9 Edw. II, 411).

[47] Eccl. Com. Ct. R. (P.R.O.), bdle. 193, no. 8–10 ; bdle. 194, no. 1–5.

[48] L. and P. Hen. VIII, xix (1), g. 80 (44) ; Pat. 35 Hen. VIII, pt. x, m. 8 (29).

[49] Pat. 5 & 6 Phil. and Mary, pt. iv, m. 16.

[50] Feet of F. Worcs. East. 25 Eliz. ; Chan. Inq. p.m. (Ser. 2), cccxxiv, 124.

[51] Chan. Inq. p.m. (Ser. 2), cccxxiv, 124.

[52] Feet of F. Worcs. Trin. 10 Jas. I ; Notes of F. Worcs. Trin. 13 Jas. I ; Chan. Proc. (Ser. 2), bdle. 352, no. 6.

[53] Chan. Inq. p.m. (Ser. 2), ccccliii, 54.

[54] Feet of F. Worcs. East. 1655.

[55] Ibid. Trin. 31 Chas. II. It is possible that these lands had never been part of Unwyn's estate, but had been

inherited by Shrewsbury from his great-grandmother Eleanor Baskerville, daughter and heir of Richard Habington (*Visit. of Worcs.* [Harl. Soc.], 63–4 ; G.E.C. *Complete Peerage*), grandson of William Habington, who had held land in the neighbourhood in the 15th century (Habington, op. cit. i, 129, 135). In this case Sebright's connexion with the Shrewsbury property probably ceased before 1707, as the place-names in the settlement on Richard Sebright (Com. Pleas D. Enr. Hil. 6 Anne, m. 9) are the same as those in Stanford's inquisition (Chan. Inq. p.m. [Ser. 2], ccccli, 54).

[56] Com. Pleas D. Enr. Hil. 6 Anne, m. 9.

[57] Ibid. Hil. 5 Geo. I, m. 9 d., 10 ; Mich. 6 Geo. I, m. 11, 8 ; East. 23 Geo. II, m. 85.

[58] Ex inform. Mr. R. Vaughan Gower ; P.C.C. Wills, 19 Alen ; Chan. Proc. (Ser. 2), bdles. 69, no. 28 ; 98, no. 10 ; Chan. Inq. p.m. (Ser. 2), cclvii, 74 ; ccccliii, 71 ; Feet of F. Worcs. Hil. 14 Jas. I ; Mich. 1 Chas. I ; Mich. 1656 ; Fine R. 6 Chas. I, pt. iii, no. 1a ; Recov. R. Mich. 1656, rot. 1 ; Trin. 33 Chas. II, rot. 126 ; Com. Pleas D. Enr. Hil. 5 Geo. I, m. 9 d., 10 ; Mich. 6 Geo. I,

m. 8, 11 ; Trin. 6 Geo. I, m. 15 d. ; East. 23 Geo. II, m. 85.

[59] Com. Pleas D. Enr. Mich. 7 Geo. III, m. 192.

[59a] Inform. from Mr. J. W. Willis-Bund. [60] *V.C.H. Worcs.* i, 289.

[61] *Testa de Nevill* (Rec. Com.), 41 ; White Bk. of Bishopric of Worc. fol. 105.

[62] Prattinton Coll. (Soc. of Antiq.), Deeds of D. and C. of Worc. no. 289 ; Add. MS. 28024, fol. 157a (162).

[63] Add. MS. 28024, fol. 157a (162). The exact descent of the manor at this point is not quite clear, as the only recorded grant to Beauchamp is from William the son of Hugh, to whom it had been given 'for the life of himself and his wife Christine' by Geoffrey D'Abitot (ibid.).

[64] Chart. R. 28 Edw. I, m. 2, no. 93.

[65] *Feud. Aids,* v, 307 ; Feet of F. Worcs. East. 22 Edw. III, no. 13.

[66] Chan. Inq. p.m. 7 Ric. II, no. 22 ; G.E.C. *Complete Peerage,* under Beauchamp of Bletsoe ; Dugdale, *Baronage.*

[67] Chan. Inq. p.m. 7 Ric. II, no. 22.

[68] G.E.C. loc. cit.

[69] *Feud. Aids,* v, 332.

[70] Chan. Inq. p.m. (Ser. 2), xxiv, 81 ; Exch. Inq. p.m. (Ser. 2), file 1171, no. 1.

husband, who died in 1508 seised of the manor.[71] His heir was his son Richard Rede,[72] whose wardship and marriage were granted to his uncle Richard Lygon.[73] Richard Rede died before 1544, leaving a widow Joan, who held the estate for her life.[74] William Rede, Richard's heir, conveyed the reversion to Thomas Solley and other trustees in 1544,[75] but the descent of the manor after this date is obscure. Some of the land seems to have been bought by the owners of Earl's Court (q.v. *infra*), and may have formed the so-called manor of Laughern Grove[76]; the rest perhaps passed to the Dean and Chapter of Worcester.

The reputed manor of *LAUGHERN GROVE* or *THE GROVE* is first mentioned in 1564, and seems to have derived its name from the 20 acres of woodland which had previously formed part of the manor of Laughern Dabitot[77]; the part of the property to the south side of the Bransford road had probably been bought by John Bund, whose family had held it of the Bishops of Worcester as parcel of the manor of Wick at least as early as 1457,[78] and in whose descendant Mr. J. W. Willis-Bund it still remains.[78a] In 1546 John Bund *alias* Walcrofte and William Gower were parties to a fine concerning this part,[79] and by 1616 the estate had acquired the alternative name of Bunde Grove.[80] The other part on the north side of the Bransford road was held in that year by William Ingram of Earl's Court[81] (q.v. *infra*), and subsequently followed the descent of that property.[82]

The reputed manor of *EARL'S COURT* seems to have been a collection of holdings bought by Arnold Gower before 1542 and settled by him in that year on his illegitimate son John Gower,[83] who afterwards conveyed the estate to Arnold and his wife Eleanor for their lives.[84] John Gower died before 1559[85] and was succeeded by his son John, who died childless, leaving as his heir his sister Elizabeth the wife of Richard Ingram.[86] Elizabeth's right to the property was disputed about 1561 by William Gower, the grandson of Arnold's brother and heir William,[87] but in 1599 she and her son William Ingram succeeded in obtaining a quitclaim.[88]

Henry Ingram, the son of William, succeeded before 1637[89]; he mortgaged his property in that year to Richard Briggenshawe, who entered in default of payment in 1639, though he is said not to have paid the extra money agreed upon for the absolute purchase,[90] and conveyed it in trust to his son William Briggenshawe.[91] But Timothy Colles, who had married Margaret the daughter of Henry Ingram, expressed himself willing to redeem the estate and complained that Ingram and Briggenshawe prevented him.[92] The descent of the reputed manor after 1649 is not clear. Sara the daughter and heir of Timothy Colles married Thomas Geers,[93] and Eleanor the daughter of William Briggenshawe became the wife of Francis Geers,[94]

INGRAM. *Ermine a fesse gules with three scallops or thereon.*

who dealt by fine with Earl's Court in 1691[95]; the estate does not, however, seem to have been in the possession of the heirs of either. Thomas Geers married as his second wife Elizabeth the widow of Robert Whitney,[96] and her grandson Edward Cope Hopton was the owner of the property in 1745[97]; it afterwards descended with Iccomb (q.v.) to the Rev. John Parsons, afterwards Hopton.[98] On the death of his son and successor John in 1891 the estate passed to the latter's daughter Bertha Maria wife of Walter Thomas Mynors Baskerville of Clyro Court, Radnorshire. She died in 1892, and her daughter Sybil Maud is now the owner of Earl's Court. Sybil Maud Baskerville assumed the name Hopton in 1898, and Colonel John Dutton Hunt, whom she married in the following year, also took the name Hopton.[98a]

BOUGHTON or *BOULTON* originally belonged to the manor of Wick Episcopi.[99] William de Pechesleye had tenements there in 1345 of the gift of Alexander vicar of Hallow and Richard de Hindlip, chaplain,[100] and William de Habington held lands in the neighbourhood about 1431.[1] At about the end of the 15th century John Gower of Suckley, second son of Thomas Gower of Woodhall by Catherine daughter of John Lord Dudley,[2] bought lands here, and, in the words of Habington, built 'a faire house at Boulton.'[3] Several adjoining holdings were bought during the 16th century by Arnold and William Gower, sons of John Gower,[4] and William Gower eventually succeeded to the

[71] Chan. Inq. p.m. (Ser. 2), xxiv, 81 ; Exch. Inq. p.m. (Ser. 2), file 1171, no. 1.
[72] Ibid.
[73] *L. and P. Hen. VIII*, i, 1174; Lygon had married Anne the sister of Margaret Rede (Chan. Inq. p m. [Ser. 2], xxiv, 81).
[74] Feet of F. Worcs. Mich. 36 Hen. VIII.
[75] Ibid.
[76] Notes of F. Worcs. Mich. 7 & 8 Eliz.; Feet of F. Worcs. Mich. 13 Jas. I. The Grove estate included, apparently, the 20 acres of wood which had belonged to Laughern Dabitot (Feet of F. loc. cit.).
[77] Notes of F. Worcs. Mich. 7 & 8 Eliz. Nash (op. cit. ii, 309) states that the Grove belonged to John D'Abitot, but does not give his authority.
[78] Eccl. Com. Ct. R. (P.R.O.), bdle. 193, no. 10.
[78a] Inform. from Mr. J.W.Willis-Bund.
[79] Notes of F. loc. cit.
[80] Feet of F. Worcs. Mich. 13 Jas. I.
[81] Ibid.

[82] Ibid. Hil. 13 Chas. I ; Mich. 21 Chas. I ; Chan. Proc. (Ser. 2), bdle. 438, no. 63, 78 ; Recov. R. East. 8 Geo. II, rot. 31 ; Mich. 6 Geo. IV, rot. 47, &c.
[83] Com. Pleas D. Enr. East. 33 Hen. VIII, m. 4 d.
[84] Ibid. Trin. 33 Hen. VIII, m. 8.
[85] Richard Ingram was then the owner of and resided at Earl's Court (Chan. Proc. [Ser. 2], bdle. 98, no. 42).
[86] Chan. Proc. (Ser. 2), bdle. 69, no. 28.
[87] Ibid.
[88] Feet of F. Worcs. Mich. 41 & 42 Eliz.
[89] Chan. Proc. (Ser. 2), bdle. 438, no. 78.
[90] Ibid.
[91] Ibid.
[92] Ibid. bdle. 438, no. 63.
[93] Duncumb, *Hereford* (Hundred of Grimsworth), iv, 30.
[94] Ibid.
[95] Feet of F. Worcs. Mich. 3 Will and Mary. The Briggenshawes dealt both

with this manor and the Grove between 1645 and 1691 (Feet of F. Worcs. Mich. 21 Chas. I ; East. 1657 ; East. 14 Chas. II ; Mich. 3 Will. and Mary), while Timothy Colles was a party to fines concerning it between 1648 and 1658 (ibid. Trin. 23 Chas. I ; Trin. 1649 ; Trin. 1658).
[96] Duncumb, loc. cit. ; *Bristol and Gloucs. Arch. Soc. Trans.* vii, 181.
[97] Feet of F. Worcs. Hil. 19 Geo. II.
[98] Ibid. 37 Geo. III ; Recov. R. Mich. 6 Geo. IV, rot. 47 ; Feet of F. Worcs. Trin. 10 Geo. IV.
[98a] Burke, *Landed Gentry* (1906) ; inform. from Mr. J. W. Willis-Bund.
[99] White Bk. of the Bishopric of Worc. fol. 166.
[100] Ibid.
[1] Habington, op. cit. ii, 129.
[2] *Visit. of Worcs.* 1569 (Harl. Soc. 27), 60.
[3] Habington, *Surv. of Worcs.* ii, 129 ; Nash, *Hist. of Worcs.* ii, 308.
[4] Habington, op. cit. ii, 129.

whole estate,[5] which was afterwards termed a manor. William Gower died in 1546,[6] and it then passed to his son Henry Gower,[7] who sold it in 1617 to his cousin Abel Gower, son of George Gower of Colemarsh.[8] Abel Gower was succeeded in 1632 by his eldest son Abel,[9] who died in 1669.[9a] He was succeeded by his eldest son Robert Gower, who married Catherine daughter of Sir William Childe of Kinlet, co. Salop,[10] and, dying in 1689,[10a] was succeeded by his eldest son Abel Gower,[11] who died in 1710, having two sons Abel Eustace and William Gower, both minors.[11a] Abel Eustace Gower dying some few months after his father, the estate passed to his brother William Gower.[12] John Gower of Queenhill was dealing with the manor of Boughton in 1719.[12a] The manor was sold in 1729 by William Gower, then of Chiddingstone, co. Kent, to Joseph Weston, a merchant of Worcester.[12b]

GOWER of Suckley. *Argent a cheveron between three wolves' heads razed gules with the difference of a crescent.*

In 1778 Mary Weston, Joseph's widow, and her son Joseph sold a portion of the estate to William Lilley [13] and the remainder to Thomas Bund. The Rev. John Lilley, son of William, sold part of the land in 1810 to Mr. Elias Isaac [14]; the remainder with the reputed manor he had already sold in 1808 to Mr. Joseph Helm,[15] from whom Mr. Elias Isaac bought it in 1814.[16] The present owner is his great-grandson Mr. Arthur W. Isaac.

Two mills in Wick were attached to the bishop's manor in 1086 [17]; these seem to have been Wick Mill on the Teme and Cut Mill (Cottemulne, Cuttemill, xiii cent.; Cuttenmill, xiv cent.) on Laughern Brook, both of which followed the descent of Wick Episcopi till the end of the 13th century.[18]

About that time another mill was built on the Teme,[19] and in 1300 Giffard granted all three to the Prior of Great Malvern.[20]

In 1475 the tenants in Wick Episcopi complained that the prior had dug a canal from the Teme to Wick Mills, greatly to the damage of their land,[21] and that he had not paid the yearly sum agreed on before he had obtained leave to do this, or repaired the bridge over the water as he had promised.[22] In 1536 the prior paid 4s. rent for his water-course and held the mills (Powick Mill and Cut Mill), valued at £5 4s. 8d. yearly, at a fee-farm rent of £4 0s. 8d. to the bishop.[22a] In 1543 the two water-mills called Powick Mills in the tenure of William Moore were granted to Richard Andrews and Nicholas Temple,[22b] who had licence to alienate them to William Moore in the same year.[22c] He died in 1565 seised of three water-mills called Powick Mills,[22d] and his son Richard sold two of them in 1578 to William and Anthony Gower.[22e] The reversion of two mills at Wick was granted by Queen Elizabeth to Sir Thomas Bromley in 1586,[23] and they afterwards passed with part of the manor of Wick Episcopi to William Bund.[24] Three mills at Wick were sold by Mr. J. W. Willis-Bund in 1904 to the City of Worcester, and are now their electricity works.[24a] Cut Mill seems to have been one of those sold by Richard Moore to William Gower in 1578,[25] and afterwards followed the descent of Boughton,[26] until it was sold about 1760 by Mary Weston to William Bund. The mill was then pulled down and the mill-pond filled up. About 1780 Thomas Bund redeemed the quit-rent payable from it to the Crown.[27] With Cut Mill William Gower also acquired another water-mill,[28] which like Cut Mill followed the descent of Boughton till 1693,[29] but no mention of it occurs after this date.

The New Mill in Laughern D'Abitot was probably the mill that formed part of that manor in 1086.[30] It was granted before 1294 to the cathedral monastery [30a] and probably descended to the dean and

[5] Chan. Proc. (Ser. 2), bdles. 69, no. 28; 98, no. 10; Feet of F. Worcs. Mich. 40 & 41 Eliz.

[6] Will dated 16 Aug. 1546, proved 1546, P.C.C. 19 Alen.

[7] *Visit. of Worcs.* 1569 (Harl. Soc. 27), 61.

[8] Feet of F. Worcs. 15 Jas I; Nichols, *County Families of Wales,* ii, 90.

[9] Chan. Inq. p.m. (Ser. 2), lix, 31.

[9a] M. I. in church of St. John Baptist, Worcester. Will dated 29 Sept. 1669, and proved P.C.C. 2 Mar. 1670-1, P.C.C. 36 Duke.

[10] Entry in Kinlet reg.

[10a] Entry in parish reg. and will dated 23 Mar. 1684 and proved P.C.C. 1690.

[11] Feet of F. Worcs. Hil. 4 Will. and Mary.

[11a] Entries in parish reg. [12] Ibid.

[12a] Recov. R. East. 5 Geo. I, rot. 52. He was probably acting as guardian of William Gower, who did not attain his majority until 1722.

[12b] A. W. Isaac, loc. cit.; deeds *penes* Mr. R. Vaughan Gower.

[13] Ibid.; Recov. R. Trin. 18 Geo. III, rot. 347. [14] A. W. Isaac, loc. cit.

[15] Ibid. [16] Ibid. 18.

[17] *V.C.H. Worcs.* i, 288.

[18] Hale, op. cit. 35b; Red Bk. of Bishopric of Worc. fol. 21, 31; White Bk. of Bishopric of Worc. fol. 83.

[19] There were only two mills in 1291

(*Pope Nich. Tax.* [Rec. Com.], 225) and in 1299 (Red Bk. of Bishopric of Worc. fol. 21), one being Cut Mill (ibid.), but there were two besides Cut Mill in 1300. In 1338 the Prior of Great Malvern stated that he had built this mill himself (Close, 12 Edw. III, pt. i, m. 34), but it is certainly mentioned in Giffard's charter (White Bk. of Bishopric of Worc. loc. cit.). Probably, as it was in the old house called Wykemill (Close, loc. cit.), the prior had not troubled to get a separate licence to acquire it.

[20] White Bk. of Bishopric of Worc. loc. cit. This charter is undated, but the mills had not been granted to the prior in 1299 (Red Bk. of the Bishopric of Worc. loc. cit.), and the grantee died before mid-March 1301 (*Ann. Mon.* [Rolls Ser.], iv, 548). The mills were worth £5 in 1299 (Red Bk. of the Bishopric of Worc. fol. 31), beyond the rent of £4 (ibid. fol. 21) which Giffard reserved to himself and his successors (White Bk. of Bishopric of Worc. loc. cit.).

[21] Eccl. Com. Ct. R. (P.R.O.), bdle. 194, no. 1, m. 22.

[22] Ibid. The bridge in some way became repairable by the parish of Powick. There are various entries in the Powick parish accounts of moneys spent for the repair of 'Wykefield Bridge.' It is now repaired by Mr. J. W. Willis-Bund (inform. from Mr. J. W. Willis-Bund).

[22a] *Valor Eccl.* (Rec. Com.), iii, 237.

[22b] *L. and P. Hen. VIII,* xviii (1), g. 981 (20).

[22c] Ibid. xviii (2), g. 449 (40).

[22d] Chan Inq. p.m. (Ser. 2), cxlii, 67.

[22e] Pat. 21 Eliz. pt. i, m. 7.

[23] Ibid. 28 Eliz. pt. x, m. 32.

[24] Ibid. 22 Chas. II, pt. ii; Recov. R. Mich. 4 Jas. II, rot. 226; inform. from Mr. J. W. Willis-Bund.

[24a] Inform. from Mr. J. W. Willis-Bund.

[25] Pat. 21 Eliz. pt. i, m. 7.

[26] Feet of F. Worcs. Mich. 15 Jas. I; Trin. 16 Chas. I; East. 33 Chas. II; Hil. 4 Will. and Mary; Chan. Inq. p.m. (Ser. 2), dix, 31; Recov. R. Hil. 4 & 5 Will. and Mary, rot. 59; A. W. Isaac, op. cit. 15.

[27] Original deeds *penes* Mr. J. W. Willis-Bund.

[28] Pat. 21 Eliz. pt. i, m. 7.

[29] Feet of F. Worcs. Mich. 15 Jas. I; Trin. 16 Chas. I; East. 33 Chas. II; Hil. 4 Will. and Mary; Chan. Inq. p.m. (Ser. 2), dix, 31.

[30] *V.C.H. Worcs.* i, 289.

[30a] Prattinton Coll. (Soc. Antiq.), Deeds of D. and C. of Worc. no. 290. The deed is undated, but Sir Giles Berkeley, who died in 1294 (*Reg. G. Giffard* [Worcs. Hist. Soc.], 449), was one of the witnesses.

St. John in Bedwardine : Wick Episcopi

St. John in Bedwardine : Remains of St. Cuthbert's Chapel, Lower Wick

chapter.[31] It seems to have been on the site of St. John's Mill ; the court rolls show that it stood on a high road near a bridge close to the borders of Laughern D'Abitot and the Pittensarys.[31a] St. John's Mill, on the Bromyard road, is now the Worcester Cold Storage Works.

Ambrose Mill (Aumbreyesmille, Awmbreys, xiv cent.) was perhaps part of the tenement in Laughern granted to the Prior and convent of Worcester by John son and heir of Geoffrey Ambrose.[32] After the Dissolution it came into the possession of the dean and chapter.[32a] It still exists on the road from Worcester to Dines Green.

Wandesford Mill is first mentioned in 1236[33] ; it was situated in the same tithing as the New Mill and Ambrose Mill,[34] and like them paid tithes to Worcester Priory.[35] It is last mentioned by name in 1392,[36] but may have been one of the three unnamed mills belonging to the dean and chapter after 1630.[37]

A water-mill called Ivall's Mill is mentioned in 1630, when it was occupied by George Worfield[38] ; it had previously been held by William Worfield and Michael Worfield,[39] and was afterwards apparently in the possession of the dean and chapter.[40] Another water-mill was attached to the manor of Earl's Court in 1647.[41]

A windmill outside Hardwick is mentioned in 1236, when it belonged to the priory of Worcester.[42] It was perhaps this mill which was 'removed from its place by means of Mr. Richard Cupper' about 1626,[43] and set up on some copyhold lands in the manor of Wick Episcopi.[44] No further mention of it occurs.

The church of *ST. JOHN BAPTIST* in Bedwardine consists of chancel with *CHURCH* south chapel, nave with south aisle and a western tower, with a wide north aisle of modern work. The north arcade of three bays is of the 12th century, but the arches were destroyed some years ago, so as to give more view from the pulpit. The south arcade is of the 14th century, and the south wall has two large windows under gables of which the eastern represents the transept. On a pillar of the south arcade is a shield with the Gower arms. The south chapel of the chancel is of the 14th century with the original roof.[44a] The font is modern. There is a good monument in the north aisle, and there are several monuments to the Bund family, which with others have been moved from their original positions when the church was restored and

the chancel built about twenty years ago. At the same time some old glass in the east window was taken out and worked up in the chancel windows. The parish chest of 1693 is plain with iron straps.

The 15th-century tower at the west end is wide and low and contains a ring of six bells by Thomas Mears of London, dated 1816 (the second 1815), also a small bell by John Greene, a Worcester founder, dated 1626. The former bells were by Richard Sanders of Bromsgrove, 1707.

The plate consists of an Elizabethan flagon, a cup and cover for paten of 1571, a paten of rude work and inscribed 'The gift of G. Wryfall, 1736.' There are also a cup, cover and flagon of recent date.[45]

The registers before 1812 are as follows : (i) baptisms and burials 1558 to 1774, marriages 1559 to 1754 ; (ii) baptisms and burials 1775 to 1812 ; (iii) marriages 1754 to 1812. All are in good condition.[46]

ADVOWSON The church of St. John the Baptist in Bedwardine was originally a chapel of ease to the church of St. Cuthbert, Wick Episcopi. St. Cuthbert had in its turn been a chapelry attached to the church of St. Helen, Worcester, and as such had been granted by Fritheric to the monks of Worcester Priory, according to their chartulary, in the 12th century.[47] William of Blois, however, seems to have disputed the right of the convent to the chapelries belonging to St. Helen, for in 1234 he made an agreement with them by which they should hold only those of Wick and Wichenford.[48]

Wick was still a chapelry in 1236,[49] and seems to have been appropriated about this time to the Prior and convent of Worcester together with the chapels of St. John, Golden Wick and Laughern.[50] The chapel of St. Cuthbert at Wick became the parish church before 1283,[51] though the vicarage-house was always at St. John's.[52]

It is not clear when the chapel in St. John's began to be more important than the mother church ; possibly an increase in the population of the suburb and the duties of its vicar led to Bishop Giffard's suggestion in 1283 that his work was underpaid.[53] This was also the opinion of William Lynn, bishop in 1370, who stated that the prior and chapter took so large a proportion of the tithes that there was not enough left to support a separate vicar at all.[54] He therefore determined, at the request of the parishioners, to abandon the church of Wick, which was already 'half deserted and attended by very few,' and make

[31] *Valor Eccl.* (Rec. Com.), iii, 220 ; *Charters of D. and C. of Worc.* (Worcs. Hist. Soc.), 127. Habington (op. cit. ii, 133) states that it belonged to the priory manor in Laughern.

[31a] Eccl. Com. Ct. R. (P.R.O.), bdle. 193, no. 1-6, *passim.*

[32] Prattinton Coll. (Soc. of Antiq.), Deeds of D. and C. of Worc. no. 141.

[32a] *Charters of D. and C. of Worc.* (Worcs. Hist. Soc.), 129.

[33] Hale, op. cit. 35*b*.

[34] Eccl. Com. Ct. R. (P.R.O.), bdle. 193, no. 8, m. 21.

[35] Hale, op. cit. 151*b*.

[36] Eccl. Com. Ct. R. (P.R.O.), bdle. 194, no. 9, m. 16.

[37] *Charters of D. and C. of Worc.* (Worcs. Hist. Soc.), 127.

[38] Chan. Inq. p.m. (Ser. 2), cccclvi, 81.

[39] Ibid.

[40] *Charters of D. and C. of Worc.* (Worcs. Hist. Soc.), 127.

[41] Feet of F. Worcs. Trin. 23 Chas. I.

[42] Hale, op. cit. 38.

[43] Exch. Dep. Spec. Com. 2 Chas. I, no. 5717.

[44] Ibid.

[44a] It is said to have been built by Sir Reginald Bray, who was a native of St. John in Bedwardine, but his date is much later.

[45] Lea, *Church Plate of Worcs.* 76.

[46] *Digest of Parish Reg. in Diocese of Worcester,* 61.

[47] Heming, op. cit. 427 ; Nash, op. cit. ii, App. 145.

[48] *Ann. Mon.* (Rolls Ser.), iv, 426.

[49] Hale, *Reg. of Worc. Priory* (Camden Soc.), 35*a*.

[50] There is apparently no licence for appropriation extant, but the chapel was appropriated between 1234 (*Ann. Mon.* [Rolls Ser.], loc. cit.) and 1236 (Hale, *Reg. of Worc. Priory,* 35*a*).

[51] *Reg. G. Giffard* (Worcs. Hist. Soc.), 176.

[52] Hale, loc. cit.

[53] *Reg. G. Giffard,* loc. cit. As early as 1256, in the foundation charter of Crown East Chantry, the 'parish church of St. John's' is mentioned, which looks as if it had already begun to overshadow the mother church (*MSS. of Lord Middleton* [Hist. MSS. Com.], 65).

[54] Worc. Epis. Reg. Lynn, fol. 30. The church with the chapel was valued at £8 13s. 4d. in 1291 (*Pope Nich. Tax.* [Rec. Com.], 225), and at 18 marks in 1340 (*Inq. Nonarum* [Rec. Com.], 301).

St. John's Chapel the parish church.[55] The new church was consecrated in 1371.[56]

The advowson belonged to the priory till the Dissolution,[57] and was granted in 1542 to the Dean and Chapter of Worcester,[58] who are still the patrons.[59]

The chapels of Golden Wick and Laughern are mentioned in 1236.[60] These were both private chapels belonging to the lords of those manors, who paid a certain sum yearly to the priory for leave to hear divine service.[61] The latter chapel was at Laughern Willelmi,[62] and probably fell into disuse after the estate was granted to the Templars. The chapel at Golden Wick is not separately mentioned after this date. Another chapel was attached to the manor of Crown East; in 1256 Maud de Frevile founded a chantry there for the health of her husband's soul.[63] The licence for this chantry was to last only during her life,[64] and probably after her death the chapel too was disused, as her son cannot have spent much time there, and the manor-house itself was a ruin in 1349.[65] There was also a private chapel belonging to the bishop's house at Wick.[66]

CHARITIES The United Charity School was founded by deeds of Milberrow Doelittle, 1719, and Mercy Herbert, 1722.[67]

In 1852 Mary Harrison, by her will proved 19 May, left £50 for the benefit of the Sunday school. The legacy is on deposit in the Post Office Savings Bank; the income of £1 5s. yearly is applied to the Sunday schools.

The charities of John Carwardine and others are now represented by £508 9s. 6d. consols with the official trustees, arising from the sale in 1904 of certain lands and hereditaments comprised in deeds of lease and release 4 and 5 November 1719. These had been purchased with sums given by several charitable persons for the use of the poor. The annual dividends, amounting to £12 14s., are applied

as to £1 in the distribution of Bibles in respect of a gift of £20 by Margery Carwardine for that purpose, as to £5 in the distribution of bread on St. Thomas's Day, and the residue towards repairs of the church.

This parish participates in the general charity of Henry Smith. In 1909 £12 12s. was received and applied in the distribution of twenty-four gowns and in bread to the value of £2 10s.

In 1698 Timothy Nourse by his will devised an annuity of £25 for binding poor children as apprentices and for clothing poor old men and women. The annuity was redeemed in 1866 by the transfer to the official trustees of £833 10s. consols, now producing £20 18s. 6d. yearly, which is applied chiefly in the distribution of coats and in subscriptions to the clothing club.

In 1701 Henry Johnson by his will devised 3 r. of land, the rents to be distributed equally among twelve poor widows. The land was sold in 1874 and the proceeds invested in £162 12s. consols with the official trustees. In 1877 a sum of £78 14s. 10d. consols was sold out and the proceeds remitted to the trustees, leaving a sum of £83 17s. 2d. with the official trustees, producing £2 1s. 8d. yearly.

In 1880 Mrs. Janet Amelia Meredith, by her will proved at London 13 May, bequeathed £300 in augmentation of one or more of the parochial charities. The legacy was invested in £303 0s. 7d. consols, producing £7 11s. 4d. yearly.

The Church Lands.—The parish has from time immemorial been in possession of certain lands and hereditaments for the repairs of the church and such other godly uses as the major part of the parishioners approve, the earliest deed extant being dated in 1640. In 1910 the gross income, including the dividends on a sum of £113 12s. 9d. consols with the official trustees arising from the sale of a cottage and garden at Dines Green, exceeded £200.

ST. MARTIN

The parish of St. Martin lies in the east part of the city of Worcester and stretches into the country as far as the borders of Spetchley and Bredicot. It contains about 1,093 acres, of which about two-thirds are under permanent grass, rather less than one-third arable and the rest woodland.[1] The parish, or the greater part of it, was at one time within the limits of the forest of Feckenham. Some of the plantations lie about Woodgreen and Elbury Hill, but the greater part of the woodland is on the lower ground in the south of the parish. The southern boundary skirts the edge of Perry Wood close to the battle-field of 1651 and passes along the Alcester road almost as far as the hamlet of Swinesherd, which stands a little to the south of Nunnery Wood, and is said to have formed one of the boundaries of the Cudley estate as early as 974.[2] A footpath branching off from this road about a quarter of

a mile beyond Swineshesd leads to Cudley Court, which is connected by another path with the road from Crowle. This road passes through the hamlets of Newtown and Ronkswood, and runs almost due west across the parish, entering the city close by Shrub Hill station on the Great Western line. The ground rises gradually from the east and south-west, the highest point in the parish being reached at Leopard Hill about a quarter of a mile south of the Tolladine road, which there forms the northern boundary.

Leopard Grange, about 2 miles east of the city by this road, is a rectangular brick house of two stories and an attic built in 1705, with a later 18th-century addition on the north and a modern single-story wing on the east. On a keystone of an upper floor window are the date 1705 and the initials W... M., the second letter being obliterated. The

[55] Worc. Epis. Reg. loc. cit.
[56] Ibid. Lynn states that neither church nor chapel had been previously dedicated (ibid.).
[57] *L. and P. Hen. VIII*, xvii, g. 71 (29); Pat. 33 Hen. VIII, pt. v, m. 19. The church was valued at £13 7s. in 1536 (*Valor Eccl.* [Rec. Com.], iii, 234).

[58] Pat. 33 Hen. VIII, pt. v, m. 19.
[59] *Clergy List*, 1912.
[60] Hale, loc. cit.
[61] Ibid. [62] Ibid.
[63] *MSS. of Lord Middleton*, loc. cit.
[64] Ibid.
[65] Chan. Inq. p.m. 17 Edw. III, no. 37.

[66] *Reg. G. Giffard* (Worcs. Hist. Soc.), 451.
[67] See article on Schools, *V.C.H. Worcs.* iv.
[1] Statistics from Bd. of Agric. (1905).
[2] Birch, *Cart. Sax.* iii, 617; Heming, *Chartul.* (ed. Hearne), 155.

house contains a fine oak staircase with moulded hand-rail and twisted balusters. Ponds on the east and west of the house and a depression filled with soft earth on the north are probably the remains of an encircling moat.

Nunnery Farm north of the junction of the Alcester and Pershore roads is a two-story early 18th-century brick house with a 19th-century three-story addition.

The soil is partly alluvium, the subsoil Keuper Marls.

The following place-names occur in local records : Goldbourn,[3] Æglardes Marsh [4] (? xi cent.) ; Red Hill,[5] Losemere,[6] Scomeleswey, Stocking,[7] Endel' [8] (xiii cent.); Incentis Lane, Pirie Brook,[9] Le Oeure [10] (xiv cent.) ; Twenty Lands, Plackmedowe, the Pike, Woodgreen, Stockt Coppice, Wallreadinge [11] and Windmill Hills [12] (xvii cent.).

The church of Worcester was in *MANORS* possession of *CUDLEY* (Cudinclea, x cent. ; Cudelei, xi cent. ; Codeley, Cudeleg, Codele, xiii cent. ; Cudley Bethnall, xvi cent.) before the Conquest, and it is said that as early as 974 the bishop had certain lands there, which St. Oswald leased to Brihtlaf for three lives.[13] At the time of the Domesday Survey Urse D'Abitot held 1 hide there of the bishop's manor of Northwick [14] ; it had previously been held by Ælfgifu the nun.[15] The bishop's overlordship is mentioned about 1212,[16] but seems to have been allowed to lapse during the 13th century ; there is no reference to it after this date. The lordship of the Earl of Warwick, the descendant of Urse, is mentioned in 1315.[17] In 1212 Cudley was held of William de Beauchamp by John de Cudley,[18] who with his wife Maud unsuccessfully claimed common of pasture in Leopard against the Prior of Worcester.[19] John was perhaps succeeded by Jordan de Cudley, whose name appears in various deeds about 1259,[20] but before 1282 Thomas de Cudley seems to have been the chief landholder there.[21] Before 1297 John de Cudley, called also John de Everley, was in possession of the manor.[22] He married Philippa de Spetchley,[23] by whose name his descendants were sometimes known.

Thomas de Cudley, who seems to have been the second son of John de Everley,[24] held the manor in 1315.[25] He died before 1330, at which date another John de Cudley was lord of the manor, which he and his wife Alice settled on Marjory the wife of Philip de Peopleton, probably their daughter, and her heirs.[26] This Philip was no doubt the Philip de Spetchley who held the manor in 1346,[27] at which date Spetchley itself was still held by William de Everley, the son of John and Alice.[28] William de Everley died in 1349,[29] and his property afterwards came to William de Spetchley, who was perhaps the son of Philip and Marjory. This William in 1363 settled all his lands in Cudley and Spetchley on himself and his wife Parnel and their children with remainder to William, rector of Peopleton, and his heirs.[30]

The descent of the manor during the 15th century is very difficult to trace. Habington says that it descended to the Hubauds,[31] but does not give the date at which they became possessed of it. It was, however, held in his own day by Sir John Hubaud,[32] who sold it between 1553 and 1585 to Ralph Wyatt, at one time high bailiff of the city of Worcester.[33] He was succeeded at Cudley by his son William Wyatt,[34] whose daughter and heir Frances married Richard Wyatt.[35] They sold the manor to Sir Robert Berkeley in 1635,[36] and it has ever since followed the descent of Spetchley [37] (q.v.). The present owner is Mr. R. V. Berkeley, who holds it as part of the Spetchley estate.[38]

The earliest reference to *LEOPARD* (Lipperd, x cent. ; Lippard, xiii cent. ; Luppard, Lyppard, xiv cent. ; Lypards, Lypperdes Farm, Lippiards, xvi cent. ; Leppards, Leopards, xvii cent.) occurs in a charter dated 969, where it is mentioned among the boundaries of Battenhall.[39] It is also given among the boundaries of Perry in a charter of Wulfstan Bishop of Worcester between 1003 and 1016,[40] but is not entered as a separate manor in Domesday Book.[41] Probably it was at that time included in Whittington and Warndon, for in 1236 part of it was said to have been given to the priory of Worcester by John Poer [42] and part by Sir H. Poer [43] ; while another half-virgate near Whittington,

---

[3] Heming, op. cit. 357.

[4] Ibid. 358 ; Add. Chart. 19795.

[5] Red Bk. of Bishopric of Worc. (Eccl. Com. Rec. Var. bdle. 121, no. 43698), fol. 4.

[6] Ibid. fol. 17.

[7] Hale, *Reg. of Worc. Priory*, 53a.

[8] Ibid. 54b.

[9] Add. MS. 28024, fol. 145.

[10] Cal. Bodl. Chart. 592 ; Marsh, *Ann. of St. Wulstan's Hospital*, 55.

[11] *Chart. of D. and C. of Worc.* (Worcs. Hist. Soc.), 129.

[12] Chan. Inq. p.m. (Ser. 2), dccxviii, 155.

[13] Birch, op. cit. iii, 617 ; Heming, op. cit. 155.

[14] *V.C.H. Worcs.* i, 294.

[15] Ibid.

[16] Red Bk. of Bishopric of Worc. fol. 253, 259 ; White Bk. of Bishopric of Worc. (Eccl. Com. Rec. Var. bdle. 121, no. 43696), fol. 7 ; *Testa de Nevill* (Rec. Com.), 41.

[17] *Cal. Inq. p.m.* 1–9 Edw. II, 403.

[18] Red Bk. of Bishopric of Worc. loc. cit. ; White Bk. loc. cit. ; *Testa de Nevill*, loc. cit.

[19] Hale, op. cit. 54b.

[20] Habington, *Surv. of Worcs.* (Worcs. Hist. Soc.), ii, 20 ; *Charters of D. and C. of Worc.* (Worcs. Hist. Soc.), 116.

[21] *Lay Subs. R. Worcs.* c. 1280 (Worcs. Hist. Soc.), 40.

[22] Add. MS. 28024, fol. 148.

[23] *Vide* Spetchley.

[24] Feet of F. Worcs. Trin. 9 Edw. I.

[25] Add. MS. 28024, fol. 190 d. ; *Cal. Inq. p.m.* 1–9 Edw. II, 403.

[26] Feet of F. Worcs. Trin. 4 Edw. III.

[27] *Feud. Aids*, v, 307. He is here called Philip de Pechesley, but this is probably a mistake, as Philip de Spechesley of St. Martin's parish is mentioned in 1340 (*Inq. Nonarum* [Rec. Com.], 301).

[28] *Vide* Spetchley.

[29] Close, 23 Edw. III, pt. i, m. 16.

[30] Feet of F. Worcs. East. 37 Edw. III.

[31] Habington, op. cit. ii, 294.

[32] Ibid.

[33] Ibid. Habington does not give the date, but Sir John Hubaud succeeded his father in 1553 (Dugdale, *Warwickshire*, 737–9) and died in 1585 (Chan. Inq. p.m. [Ser. 2], ccviii, 202).

[34] Habington, loc. cit.

[35] Ibid.

[36] Ibid. ; Nash, *Hist. of Worcs.* ii, 317 ; ex inform. Mr. R. V. Berkeley.

[37] Chan. Inq. p.m. (Ser. 2), dccxviii, 155 ; Recov. R. Mich. 10 Geo. II, rot. 147 ; Mich. 17 Geo. II, rot. 160 ; Trin. 48 Geo. III, rot. 37 ; Com. Pleas D. Enr. East. 18 Geo. III, m. 27 ; ex inform. Mr. R. V. Berkeley.

[38] Ex inform. Mr. R. V. Berkeley.

[39] Birch, op. cit. iii, 531.

[40] Add. Chart. 19795.

[41] 'Lappewrte,' entered among the possessions of the church of Worcester, has been identified as Leopard (*V.C.H. Worcs.* i, 296), but the singular likeness of this entry to that concerning Lapworth (*V.C.H. Warw.* i, 326) suggests that this is the Warwickshire manor, mentioned here only because it was of the bishop's soke and paid 8d. chirset to the church of Worcester. There is no record of this payment from Leopard, but Lapworth still paid 8d. chirset in 1236 (Hale, op. cit. 79b) and 1299 (Red Bk. of Bishopric of Worc. fol. 145, 151–2, 271) ; and the bishop held lands and a wood there as part of his manor of Old Stratford (ibid.).

[42] Hale, op. cit. 53a.   [43] Ibid.

for which the priory paid 1*d.* yearly to the heirs of Adam de Throckmorton,[44] had been the gift of Richard Marmion.[45]

In 1204 Randulf Prior of Worcester obtained from Robert de Bracy a quitclaim of his rights of common of pasture in Leopard, and in return quitclaimed to Robert his own common rights in Warndon.[46] The prior's manor was disafforested in 1224, according to the annals of the monastery,[47] and in 1256 he and his monks obtained a grant of free warren in their demesne lands 'without the bounds of the king's forest.'[48] These bounds, however, seem to have been still somewhat doubtful, for it is recorded in the perambulation of 1297 that Leopard ought to be disafforested according to the charter of Henry III.[49] The prior and convent remained in possession of Leopard until the Dissolution,[50] and the manor was afterwards granted to the dean and chapter,[51] who remained in possession until the 17th century.[52]

The manor of *PERRY* (Pirian, Pirie, xi cent. ; Purie, Perye, xiv cent.) belonged before the Conquest to the Bishops of Worcester, though according to the monastic chartulary it had been granted to the monks by ' Sexwulf the first bishop of Worcester' before 680.[53] It was leased for three lives to Wulfgifu by Wulfstan Bishop of Worcester between 1003 and 1016,[54] and was afterwards held by Godric[55] ; at the time of the Domesday Survey Herlebald was the tenant.[56] The manor passed before 1212 to William de Beauchamp, of whom it was perhaps held by Stephen de Beauchamp.[57] The overlordship of the bishop is mentioned for the last time at this date[58] ; the Beauchamps were afterwards regarded as the overlords until 1350, when the Earl of Warwick resumed a moiety of the manor.[59] Perry was held in the 14th and perhaps the 13th century by a family who took their surname from the place ; William de Perry is mentioned in 1241[60] and Ralf de Perry in 1292.[61] Before 1307 Nicholas de Perry had succeeded to the manor,

PERRY. *Argent a bend sable with three pears or thereon.*

which he settled in that year on himself and his wife Agnes, with successive remainders to his sons John and Richard.[62] Before 1334 John de Grafton was in possession of Perry.[63] He afterwards granted half the manor to the hospital of St. Wulfstan[64] ; the remaining moiety was perhaps already in the hands of his son Roger, who settled it in 1350 on himself and Thomas Robins for life, with reversion to the Earl of Warwick.[65] In 1352 the earl received from Edward III a grant of free warren in his demesne lands there.[66]

The Beauchamp moiety of the manor followed the descent of Elmley Castle (q.v.) until 1487,[67] when Anne Countess of Warwick released her right in it to Henry VII.[68] It was afterwards held on lease from Henry VIII by Richard Came,[69] but was granted by the king in 1545 to William Forthe and Richard Morrison.[70] Probably Forthe shortly afterwards released his right to his coparcener, for two weeks later Morrison, who had obtained a grant of the other moiety of Perry on the dissolution of St. Wulfstan's Hospital,[71] exchanged the whole manor with the Crown for other lands.[72] In the following year Henry VIII granted it to the Dean and Chapter of Christ Church, Oxford,[73] who were still the owners at the end of the 18th century.[74] All manorial rights in connexion with this estate have now apparently lapsed.

Frog Mill is mentioned as an appurtenance of the manor of Perry in 1423[75] ; it followed throughout the descent of the Beauchamp moiety.[76]

CHURCHES

The church of *ST. MARTIN* is in the Cornmarket, and was rebuilt in red brick with stone dressings in 1771 from the designs of Anthony Keck.[77] It consists of nave with vaulted aisles in five bays and carried by Ionic columns with entablatures. There is a tower at the west end, finished through the grant of £300 by the Rev. Benjamin Lane. The fittings are old, but the seats, font and east window are recent. The entire cost of building the church was £2,215, including the old materials.[78] The old church had three aisles, with three gables to the south, an open timbered south porch with a parvise, and a western tower capped with open balustrades and corner urns.[79] Sir Robert Berkeley, the judge, gave twenty trees towards the rebuilding of the north aisle in 1616, and spent over

44 Hale, op. cit. 53*a.*
45 Ibid.   46 Ibid. 53*b.*
47 *Ann. Mon.* (Rolls Ser.), iv, 417.
48 Cart. Antiq. NN 75.
49 Add. MS. 28024, fol. 148.
50 *Lay Subs. R. Worcs.* 1280 (Worcs. Hist. Soc.), 39 ; *Early Compotus R. of Worc. Priory* (Worcs. Hist. Soc.), 20, 28 ; *Compotus R. of Worc. Priory, 14th and 15th centuries* (Worcs. Hist. Soc.), 14, 17, 22, 54–5, 70, 73 ; Habington, op. cit. i, 327 ; Pat. 33 Hen. VIII, pt. v, m. 19.
51 Pat. 6 Jas. I, pt. xii, no. 2. Only the tithes of the demesne lands of Leopard were included in the grant of the priory lands to the dean and chapter in 1542.
52 Chan. Proc. (Ser. 2), bdle. 159, no. 71 ; Notes of F. Worcs. Hil. 12 Jas. I ; *Charters of the D. and C. of Worc.* (Worcs. Hist. Soc.), 105, 129.
58 Heming, op. cit. 390. Worcester was at that time included in the diocese of Lichfield, of which Sexwulf was consecrated bishop in 675 (Stubbs, *Reg. Sacrum Anglicanum*).

54 Add. Chart. 19795.
55 *V.C.H. Worcs.* i, 295.
56 Ibid.
57 Red Bk. of Bishopric of Worc. fol. 253. In the White Bk. fol. 7, however, the land held by Stephen of William de Beauchamp is said to have been at ' Piryton' (Pirton), and this statement is repeated in the *Testa de Nevill* (Rec. Com.), 41.
58 Red Bk. of Bishopric of Worc. loc. cit.
59 Feet of F. Worcs. Trin. 24 Edw. III.
60 Ibid. East. 25 Hen. III.
61 *Ann. Mon.* (Rolls Ser.), iv, 510.
62 Feet of F. Worcs. 1 Edw. II, no. 1.
63 Marsh, *Ann. of St. Wulstan's Hospital,* 55 ; Add. MS. 28024, fol. 130 ; Inq. a.q.d. file 366, no. 13 ; file 372. no. 12.
64 Marsh, loc. cit. ; Add. MS. loc. cit.
65 Feet of F. Worcs. Trin. 24 Edw. III, no. 25 ; Close, 43 Edw. III, m. 8 d.
66 Chart. R. 26 Edw. III, m. 10, no. 23.
67 Close, 43 Edw. III, m. 8 d. ; 46

Edw. III, m. 16 d. ; Pat. 21 Ric. II, pt. iii, m. 21 ; Feet of F. Div. Co. Mich. 2 Hen. VI ; Chan. Inq. p.m. 2 Hen. IV, no. 58 ; 17 Hen. VI, no. 54 ; 18 Hen. VI, no. 3 ; Pat. 25 Ric. VI, pt. i, m. 1 ; Feet of F. Div. Co. Mich. 6 Edw. IV ; Pat. 1 Ric. III, pt. iii, m. 15 ; 2 Ric. III, pt. iii, m. 22, 23.
68 De Banco R. Hil. 3 Hen. VII, m. 208.
69 Rentals and Surv. portf. 16, no. 89.
70 Pat. 37 Hen. VIII, pt. vii, m. 11.
71 Ibid. 32 Hen. VIII, pt. viii, m. 11 ; *L. and P. Hen. VIII,* xvi, g. 678 (25).
72 Pat. 37 Hen. VIII, pt. vii, m. 11.
73 Ibid. 38 Hen. VIII, pt. viii, m. 19 ; *L. and P. Hen. VIII,* xxi (2), g. 648 (25).
74 Nash, *Hist. of Worcs.* ii, 319.
75 Feet of F. Div. Co. Mich. 2 Hen. VI.
76 Chan. Inq. p.m. 2 Hen. IV, no. 58, &c.
77 V. Green, *Hist. and Antiq. of Worc.* ii, 62.
78 Ibid. 63.
79 V. Green, *Surv. of Worc.* 223.

£100 in rehanging the ring of bells and adding the tenor and treble bells in 1640.[80]

The bells are six in number : the first by Thomas Rudhall, 1780 ; the second by Thomas Mears of London, 1833 ; the third is of the 14th century, probably cast at Lichfield, and is inscribed ' Sancte Martine Hora Pro Nobis ' ; the fourth and fifth are by Hugh Watts of Leicester, inscribed respectively ' Durantia Dona in Honorem, 1638,' and 'The Gifte of Robert Durant for the honour of God, 1638 ' ; the tenor is by the same founder, inscribed ' Deo Gloriam et Gratias Sono Berkeley, 1640.' There is also a ' ting-tang ' inscribed 'The gift of Richard Durant, 1621.'

The plate consists of a modern cup, paten and large flagon, which are reported to have been made out of the old plate.[81]

The registers before 1812 are as follows : (i) baptisms 1538 to 1634, burials 1545 to 1626, marriages 1538 to 1628 ; (ii) all entries 1637 to 1680 ; (iii) all entries 1681 to 1744 ; (iv) baptisms 1745 to 1788, burials 1745 to 1775 ; (v) baptisms 1788 to 1812, burials 1789 to 1812 ; (vi) marriages 1776 to 1807 ; (vii) marriages 1807 to 1812. Two volumes of marriages, 1754 to 1762 and 1762 to 1776, are missing.[82]

The new church of *ST. MARTIN* in the London Road now supersedes the old one in the Cornmarket as the parish church. It was consecrated on 18 April 1911 and was erected from designs by Mr. G. H. Fellowes Prynne. The old church has been united to the parish of St. Swithun.

ADVOWSON It is possible that St. Martin was the church mentioned among the boundaries of Perry in the charter of Bishop Wulfstan.[83] The advowson belonged to the priory of Worcester until the Dissolution,[84] and was granted in 1542 to the dean and chapter,[85] who are still the patrons.[86] A chantry was founded in this church before 1349[87] ; the advowson belonged to the rector.[88] It is mentioned in 1355,[89] but seems to have been disused before the Dissolution ; there is no reference to it in the chantry certificates, though the profits from the leases of certain tenements were employed for the celebration of an obit.[90]

CHARITIES The united charities are regulated by a scheme of the Charity Commissioners 4 January 1910. They comprise the charities of :—

1. Alice Houghton, gift before 1673. The endowment consists of an inn, known as the ' Swan with Two Necks,' situate in New Street, Worcester, let at £30 a year.

2. Unknown donor, gift before 1672. Endowment originally a house in New Street, which was sold in 1893 and proceeds invested in £508 Great Western Railway 4½ per cent. debenture stock.

3. Edward Thomas Moore. Founded by deed-poll 1613. The property consists of a shop and yard, a warehouse adjoining, and two cottages in Silver Street, a workshop in Watercourse Alley, and a warehouse, the whole producing £47 4s. 6d. yearly.

4. Charities of Robert Bell and others, comprised in deed 19 October 1685, in which it was recited that certain charitable donations, amounting in the aggregate to £189 13s. 4d., were given for the poor, including £100 by Joshua Gun, £10 by Robert Berkeley, £5 by Robert Bell, and £25 by Mary Salway for the instruction of poor children. The principal was laid out in the purchase of land. The trust estate now consists of 13 a. 2 r. 13 p., called ' The Greens,' at Upton-on-Severn, an allotment of 2 a. 1 r. at Upton Ham, and 1 a. 2 r. 33 p. adjoining, of the gross yearly rental of £44.

5. Richard Durant. Will 20 October 1617.

6. John Greenway, date unknown, but before 1830. The property of these two charities consists of a house and land called ' The Vineyards ' at Powick, producing £35 yearly.

7. Mrs. Johnson. Will before 1772. The endowment consists of Lake House Farm, Welland, containing 11 a. 2 r. 26 p., an allotment in Tildridge containing 3 a. 0 r. 4 p., and 1 acre of land known as Upper Tildridge, Upton-on-Severn, the whole producing £43 yearly.

8. Sir Robert Berkeley. Gift before 1685, consisting of a rent-charge of £5 10s. out of Red Witchend Estate at Much Cowarne.

9. Mrs. Ann Moore. Will in or about 1638, being a rent-charge of £2 10s. out of Red Witchend Estate at Much Cowarne, co. Hereford.

10. William Bagnall. Will 1654, being a rent-charge of £4 for the parishes of St. Martin and St. Nicholas, issuing out of the Old Pheasant Inn, Worcester, applicable in apprenticing in these parishes alternately. There is also a sum of £99 1s. 4d. consols, representing accumulations belonging to the parish of St. Martin.

11. John Pomfrey. Will before 1718, being a rent-charge of £1 15s. out of Gaunt's Land, at Martin Hussingtree.

12. Elizabeth Mary Grismond. Deed 1726, being a rent-charge of £1 5s. out of the Mile End Estate at Kempsey.

13. John Woodward. Gift before 1830, being a rent-charge of £2 12s. out of the Railway Bell Inn, Worcester.

14. Ann Russell. Will 1792, a legacy of £100, which, together with an addition from the parish, was invested in £200 consols.

15. Robert Vellers. Will 1815, trust fund £91 5s. 7d. consols.

16. George Wingfield and Anne Sumner. Will before 1813, trust fund, £149 18s. consols.

17. Christopher Henry Hebb. Codicil to will, 1849, trust fund, £200 consols.

18. Susan Hartshorne. Will proved at Worcester 14 November 1879, trust fund, £198 0s. 4d. consols.

[80] V. Green, *Hist. and Antiq. of Worc.* ii, 61 n.
[81] Lea, *Church Plate of Worcs.* 70.
[82] *Digest of Par. Reg. in Dioc. of Worc.* 55. [83] Add. Chart. 19795.
[84] *Reg. G. Giffard* (Worcs. Hist. Soc.), 106, 428 ; *Ann. Mon.* (Rolls Ser.), iv, 511 ; Habington, op. cit. ii, 421.

[85] Pat. 33 Hen. VIII, pt. v, m. 19.
[86] *Clergy List*, 1912.
[87] *Sede Vacante Reg.* (Worcs. Hist. Soc.), 234. Nash (*Hist. of Worcs.* ii, 139) states that William Roculf was the founder of this chantry. In 1269 a chaplain was admitted to a chantry which William Roculf had founded by his will

(*Reg. G. Giffard* [Worcs. Hist. Soc.], 34), but the place of the foundation is not mentioned, and the name Roculf suggests Church Lench (see under Church Lench).
[88] Ibid.
[89] Worc. Epis. Reg. Brian, fol. 12.
[90] Chant. Cert. 60, no. 7.

The several sums of stock are held by the official trustees, producing in dividends £46 6s. a year. The scheme directs that after providing for a 'Repair Fund' one-eighth of the net yearly income of the charities of Robert Bell and others shall be applied to education and called the Educational Foundation of Mary Salway ; and that one-half of the net income of the charities of Richard Durant and John Greenway and Alice Houghton, and the unknown donor's charity, together with the yearly sum of £2 13s. out of the income of the charity of

Sir Robert Berkeley, shall be applied towards the maintenance, &c., of the parish church, the remaining income being applicable for the general benefit of the poor.

In 1910 £4 10s. was paid to poor widows (Hartshorne's charity), £13 4s. 2d. in relief tickets, £4 15s. 6d. in travelling expenses of patients to hospitals, &c., in clothes, &c., and in relief in money, £3 4s. in maintenance of patients at convalescent home, and the balance in subscriptions to certain institutions.

ST. PETER with WHITTINGTON

The parish of St. Peter, Worcester, lies to the south and south-east of Worcester city. Together with the civil parish of Whittington it covers an area of 2,313 acres. The north-western corner of the parish, including the church of St. Peter, lies within the city and forms the southern quarter of Worcester adjoining the main thoroughfare of Sidbury or Sudbury Street (Suthebury, xiii cent.). At Sidbury lived the earliest family of bell-founders known to have exercised their trade in the city.[1] A chapel or oratory dedicated in honour of St. Katherine stood there in the 17th century.[2] At right angles to Sidbury ran La Knole or Studemery's Knoll (now Edgar Street), the approach to the Great Gate of the priory.[3] Sidbury Gate stood at the south end of Sidbury[4] and was the chief entrance to the city from the south. It was commanded on the east by the earthwork called Fort Royal. On the other side of the gate Sidbury becomes the London Road and leads on towards Battenhall. The hospital of St. Wulfstan lay just without the gate.

The meadow called Digleys or Dudleys, now Diglis, south-west of Sidbury by the river, was partly demesne of the Bishop of Worcester. Bishop Godfrey granted pasture rights over his lands there to the hospital of St. Wulfstan and the priory of Worcester.[5] Part of it was apparently appurtenant to the castle of Worcester,[6] and the Prior of Worcester had a rent of £6 accruing from it in 1535.[7] In 1542 the 'first crop of the field called Digley' was granted to the Dean and Chapter of Worcester.[8] The close called Diglis, described as parcel of Warwick's and Spencer's lands, was leased to John Bourne in 1546.[9] In 1669 the dean and chapter had three closes called Diglis lying between Green Lane on the east and the river on the west.[10] There was a hermitage of St. Ursula at Diglis, but no record has been found of it until the 16th century, when it was in decay.[11]

The southern part of St. Peter's parish is entirely

rural and consists chiefly of pasture land. There is now no woodland within it,[12] although it was formerly in the ambit of the forest of Feckenham, which came up to Sidbury Gate. On the west the parish is bounded by the River Severn, and the land adjoining the river does not average more than 50 ft. above the ordnance datum. In the north-east it rises to about 200 ft. The road to Tewkesbury runs south from Worcester through the parish on its western side, and the London road cuts through it in a south-easterly direction, leading towards Pershore. Indulgences to those who should assist in the repair of the latter road between Worcester and Kempsey, where the bishop had a palace, were granted in 1427 and 1448.[13] This road passes the farms of Barneshall and Timberdine.[14]

The manor-house of Battenhall, a 17th-century half-timber house of two stories and attic, with modern additions on the south and west, stands between the roads from Pershore and Kempsey. To the north and south of the manor-house are Middle Battenhall and Upper Battenhall Farms.

The civil parish of Whittington has an area of 1,108 acres. Ecclesiastically Whittington is now a chapelry of St. Martin's, but before its transference in 1910 it had been attached from an early date to St. Peter's.[15] Other parts of St. Peter's were at the same time transferred to the newly-formed parish of St. Martin (q.v.). The church of St. Philip and St. James stands on the east of the road to Pershore, occupying the site of the ancient chapel of the same name. To the south-west, on the other side of the road, is Crookbarrow Hill, a very large elliptical mound with artificial top ; its character and origin are unknown. Crookbarrow manor-house, now a farm, stands under Crookbarrow Hill to the east of the main road. It is a late 17th-century brick building of two stories and attic with modern additions ; it is partly surrounded by a moat which begins on the north and goes round the west to the south side. In

[1] Orig. Chart. relating to Worc. (Worcs. Hist. Soc.), pp. xvi, 10, 143. Simon Campanarius lived between 1225 and 1266.
[2] Chan. Inq. p.m. (Ser. 2), cxiv, 73 ; clxxii, 142 ; ccclvi, 99.
[3] See J. Harvey Bloom, Orig. Chart. ut supra, Introd. p. ix. In the 16th and 17th centuries a house belonging to the dean and chapter called 'The Sign of the Cock' stood in La Knole at Knole End (ibid. 107, 109).
[4] Habington describes it as 'an ancient gate where a king's statue appeareth.'

'Within it,' he says, 'is a stately gatehouse, sometimes the king's court, raised on a knoll and opening into the college green' (Surv. of Worcs. [Worcs. Hist. Soc.], ii, 418).
[5] Habington, op. cit. ii, 41.
[6] Cal. Pat. 1476–85, p. 461.
[7] Valor Eccl. (Rec. Com.), iii, 224.
[8] Pat. 33 Hen. VIII, pt. v, m. 19.
[9] L. and P. Hen. VIII, xxi (1), g. 1383 (62).
[10] Orig. Chart. ut supra, 109 ; see Hist. MSS. Com. Rep. xiv, App. viii, 200 ;

Exch. Dep. Spec. Com. Mich. 5 Jas. I, no. 40.
[11] Pat. 16 Eliz. pt. xii, m. 18 ; 17 Eliz. pt. iii, m. 9. The hermitage was sold with the manor of Battenhall in 1577 by Anthony Bourne to Thomas Bromley (Close, 19 Eliz. pt. iii).
[12] cf. the meagre area of woodland in the Domesday extent (V.C.H. Worcs. i, 288a, 294b).
[13] Worc. Epis. Reg. Polton, fol. 34 ; Carpenter, i, fol. 61 d.
[14] See under manors.
[15] See under advowson.

the village on the main road are some 18th-century brick houses.

At Swinesherd on the north-eastern boundary of Whittington one of the leets for Oswaldslow Hundred was held.[16] Swinesherd (Swinesheasdan) is mentioned among the boundaries of Whittington in 989,[17] and a 'cultura called Swynesheved' in the manor of Whittington occurs in the 13th century.[18]

Where the London and Alcester roads join at Red Hill in the north-eastern corner of the parish was the spot at which all the county criminals were executed until the early half of the 18th century. The gibbet on which such of them as were hung in chains were suspended also stood here.

MANORS   The manor of *BATTENHALL* (Battenhale, x cent.) was in the possession of the church of Worcester in 969, when a lease for three lives of one 'mansa' there was made by Bishop Oswald to a clerk named Wulfgar.[19] The Domesday Survey makes no mention of Battenhall ; possibly it is one of the two estates given under the name of Whittington (q.v.), both of which were held under the Bishop of Worcester by Walter Poer, with whose descendants the manor is next found. In 1249 Hugh Poer quitclaimed 2 carucates of land in Battenhall to William Poer.[20] Sir William Poer, son of Roger Poer, was holding the manor at the end of the 13th century[21] and settled it on his brother Roger for life with reversion to William Walens and Walter Hacket successively.[22] Afterwards, however, by a sequence of grants of portions of the manor from Sir William Poer, the whole estate seems to have passed to Richard le Mercer, a citizen of Worcester.[23] In 1306 John de Merton and Elizabeth his wife, possibly a daughter[24] and co-heir[25] of Sir William Poer, quitclaimed the manor to Richard le

POER.   *Or a fesse gules with two molets gules in the chief.*

Mercer, his wife Margaret and his son John le Mercer.[26]   Richard was apparently dead by 1327 when John le Mercer conveyed the manor through his feoffees Bikerton and Braunsford to the priory of Worcester,[27] a grant followed in 1330 by a quitclaim of all the knights' fees appurtenant to the manor.[28] The manor was appropriated to the cellarer[29] and remained with the priory until the Dissolution.[30]

Battenhall was excepted from the grant of the priory lands to the Dean and Chapter of Worcester,[31] and in 1545 was granted in fee to John Bourne,[32] who had been lessee under the prior[33] and afterwards under the king.[34] In 1555 it was confirmed by Queen Mary,[35] under whom Sir John Bourne served as a Secretary of State. At his death in 1575 the manor descended to his son Anthony Bourne,[36] who in January 1576-7 sold it to Thomas Bromley,[37] then Solicitor-General and afterwards Lord Chancellor. Henry Bromley his son, who succeeded him in 1587, alienated the manor in 1614 to William Sebright of Besford.[38] It then followed the descent of Besford[39] (q.v.)

SEBRIGHT of Besford, baronet. *Argent three cinqfoils sable.*

until the last quarter of the 19th century, when it was sold in lots to a number of small proprietors, a large part becoming building land.[40]

A park pertained to the manor of Battenhall in the time of the Prior and convent of Worcester[41] and was granted with the manor to John Bourne.[42] The 16th-century manor-house stood within the park,[43] but it had been destroyed before the end of the 18th century.[44]

William Poer was presented before the justices for his warren in 1275, but is said to have shown his warrant.[45] Free warren was exercised by the Priors of Worcester and was the subject of a suit for trespass brought by their successor Sir John Bourne[46]

---

[16] Eccl. Com. Ct. R. (P.R.O.), bdle. 195, no. 6.

[17] Heming, *Chartul.* (ed. Hearne), 359.

[18] Nash, *Hist. of Worcs.* ii, 325.

[19] Birch, *Cart. Sax.* iii, 531 ; Heming, op. cit. 136. The boundaries are given, beginning from the south wall of St. Peter's Church.

[20] Feet of F. Worcs. 33 Hen. III, no. 60 (case 258, file 6).

[21] Assize R. 1026, m. 35 ; *Orig. Chart. ut supra,* 115 ; Feet of F. Worcs. 3 Edw. I, no. 37 (case 258, file 9).

[22] Prattinton Coll. (Soc. Antiq.), Deeds of D. and C. of Worc. no. 304.

[23] Dugdale, *Mon.* i, 617. The lands within the manor granted by William Poer included 'Old Battenhall.' Richard le Mercer also obtained small portions of land from other grantees (ibid.).

[24] In 1299 Elizabeth Poer is returned as tenant of Battenhall under the Bishop of Worcester (Eccl. Com. Rec. Var. bdle. 121, no. 43698, fol. 2). The transfer to Richard le Mercer had apparently not been officially noticed. It is possible, however, that Elizabeth was widow of William Poer and held a life interest in the manor which she afterwards exchanged for a rent of 10 marks.

[25] William Poer had a daughter Aline (*Cal. Close,* 1296–1302, p. 130).

[26] Feet of F. Worcs. 34 Edw. I, no. 15 (case 259, file 13). A rent-charge of 10 marks on the manor was reserved by Elizabeth for her life (ibid. ; *Orig. Chart. ut supra,* 118).

[27] See collection of documents relating to the transfer printed by Dugdale, *Mon.* i, 614. Words are used at the end of Richard le Mercer's abstract of title printed on p. 617 which seem to indicate that a grant was made to the convent by Richard le Mercer, but his name does not appear in any existing documents recording the transaction.

[28] Ibid. In 1369 Thomas le Carter granted six messuages and 2 carucates of land in Battenhall, Whittington and Northwick to the prior and convent (*Orig. Chart. ut supra,* 118).

[29] *Compotus R. of Priory of Worc. of xiv and xv cent.* (Worcs. Hist. Soc.), 11. See ibid. 18.

[30] *Valor Eccl.* (Rec. Com.), iii, 224. The manor was valued with demesne and herbage of park at £18 6s. 8d. and the forinsec rents pertaining to it at £20 12s. 10d.

[31] *L. and P. Hen. VIII,* xvii, g. 71 (29), p. 32.

[32] Ibid. xx (1), g. 465 (80).

[33] Ibid. xvi, p. 719.

[34] Ibid. xvii, 1258, p. 692.

[35] Pat. 1 & 2 Phil. and Mary, pt. ii, m. 15.

[36] Chan. Inq. p.m. (Ser. 2), clxxii, 142.

[37] Feet of F. Worcs. Hil. 19 Eliz. ; Close, 19 Eliz. pt. iii. For settlement on his wife Elizabeth Fortescue see Pat. 32 Eliz. pt. xxi, m. 4.

[38] Feet of F. Worcs. East. 12 Jas. I ; Com. Pleas D. Enr. East. 12 Jas. I, m. 1.

[39] In Pershore Hundred, *V.C.H. Worcs.* iv.

[40] Feet of F. Hil. 18 & 19 Chas. II ; Feet of F. Div. Co. Trin. 6 Will. and Mary ; Recov. R. Trin. 3 Geo. III, rot. 274 ; Trin. 33 Geo. III, rot. 40 ; inform. from Mr. J. W. Willis-Bund.

[41] *Accts. of Priory of Worc.* 1521-2 (Worcs. Hist. Soc.), 34 ; *Valor Eccl.* (Rec. Com.), iii, 224. An earlier deed (*Orig. Chart. ut supra,* 80) mentions Robert the Parker.

[42] *L. and P. Hen. VIII,* xx (1), g. 465 (80).

[43] Harl. Chart. 77 H. 10.

[44] Nash, op. cit. ii, 327. The park is mentioned in the sale of 1614 (Com. Pleas D. Enr. East. 12 Jas. I, m. 1).

[45] Assize R. 1026, m. 35.

[46] For free warren confirmed to him see *L. and P. Hen. VIII,* xx (1), g. 465 (80).

against the lessee of certain demesne lands called Warwick Furlong, Gylden Acrefield and Gyldenfield, where contrary to the terms of the lease the lessee had hunted conies.[47]

The manor of *WHITTINGTON* (Huitington, ix cent. ; Widinton, xi cent.) was granted to Deneberht Bishop of Worcester by Coenwulf King of the Mercians in 816 in exchange for other lands.[48] In 989 Oswald Bishop of Worcester leased Whittington for three lives to Gardulf,[49] and later Bishop Britheah gave it to his brother Ailric, but the latter was dispossessed by King William.[50] In 1086 it consisted of two estates attached as members to the bishop's manors of Kempsey and Northwick,[51] both held under the bishop by Walter Poer.[52] Hugh Poer is returned as tenant of the Kempsey member in an early 12th-century survey of Oswaldslow,[53] and another Hugh, possibly his son, was holding both members at the end of the same century.[54] About the middle of the 13th century Sir Roger Poer appears as witness to a grant of land called Stocking in Whittington made to the Prior and convent of Worcester,[55] and is probably the Roger Poer who was called upon by Walter Poer to warrant to him 2 virgates of land in Whittington in 1226.[56] About the same time John Poer appears as tenant of the Northwick member,[57] possibly by subfeoffment.

Whittington was one of the knights' fees granted to the priory of Worcester by John le Mercer in 1330,[58] when a toft and a carucate of land there were held by Roger Poer, clerk, as a quarter of a knight's fee. Later this estate does not seem to have preserved its identity as a manor. Part of it seems to have been attached to the manor of Spetchley[59] and part to Woodhall in Norton.[60] Nash says that the 'principal farm' in his time was held by Richard Ingram, who had bought it of Randall Stevens.[61] Mr. R. V. Berkeley of Spetchley Park is now the principal landowner.

The manor of *TIMBERDON* or *TIMBERDINE* consisted of lands granted at various times to the Prior and convent of Worcester, chiefly to the use of the almoner.[62] A weir there (possibly the fishery mentioned under Whittington in the Survey of 1086) is said to have been given to them by Walter Poer.[63] In 1535 the convent's demesne lands at Timberdine were valued at £5.[64]

LECHMERE. *Gules a fesse or with two pelicans or in the chief.*

The site of the manor with the fishery in the Severn and a wood called Pylgrove was granted to John Bourne in 1545.[65] It descended with Battenhall[66] (q.v.) to Henry Bromley, who as Sir Henry Bromley, kt., sold it in 1611 to Edward Mytton.[67] Mytton died seised in 1620[68] and his son Edward[69] in 1627,[70] the latter leaving a son and heir of the same name. In 1799 the manor was in the possession of Anthony Lechmere, who with his wife Mary conveyed it in that year to Isaac Pickering.[71] The Lechmeres, however, retained the manor-house and a considerable part of the land until 1912, when Mr. Anthony Lechmere sold the property in lots.[71a]

In this manor on the Kempsey road is a public-house called the Ketch, in a low window of which looking down the river Samuel Butler is said to have written part of 'Hudibras.'[71b]

The manor of *BARNES* or *BARNES HALL* was another priory estate originating in a carucate of land at 'La Neweberne' and Timberdine granted with the manor of Battenhall to the convent of Worcester in 1327.[72] In the 14th century this estate was, as the name suggests, the priory stock farm.[73] In 1535 the lands called 'Le Barnys' were farmed out by the priory for £5.[74]

The site of the manor was granted with Battenhall (q.v.) to John Bourne in 1545.[75] It descended with that manor to Sir Henry Bromley,[76] who sold it in 1611 to Thomas Andrewes.[77] Andrewes died seised in January 1636–7, leaving a son and heir Jonathan.[78]

---

[47] Star Chamb. Proc. Edw. VI, bdle. 1, no. 94.

[48] Birch, *Cart. Sax.* i, 497 ; Heming, op. cit. 2.

[49] Heming, op. cit. 156. The boundaries of this land are given (ibid. 156, 359) and translated by Nash (*Hist. of Worcs.* ii, App. lv).

[50] Heming, op. cit. 266 ; *V.C.H. Worcs.* i, 288, 294.

[51] Half a hide of the estate of Whittington held of Northwick Manor was at Rodeleah (*V.C.H. Worcs.* i, 294), and Hugh Poer still held an estate at Radleya at the end of the 12th century (Red Bk. of Bishopric of Worc. [Eccl. Com. Rec. Var. bdle. 121, no. 43698], fol. 253). Radley is mentioned in 989 among the boundaries of Whittington (Heming, op. cit. 359), and evidently lay on the northern border of that parish not far from Swinesherd in the neighbourhood of the present Red Hill.

[52] *V.C.H. Worcs.* i, 288, 294.

[53] Ibid. 324.

[54] Red Bk. of Bishopric of Worc. fol. 253.

[55] Deed quoted by Habington, op. cit. i, 426.

[56] Feet of F. Worcs. 11 Hen. III, no. 35 (case 258, file 3).

[57] *Testa de Nevill* (Rec. Com.), 41. It is possible that the Poers kept in their own hands one member which formed the manor of Battenhall, and that they granted the other member to another branch of their family, and that this was the one held under them by John Poer and his descendants.

[58] Dugdale, *Mon.* i, 614.

[59] Sir T. Phillipps, *Index to Worcs. Fines*, p. vi ; Feet of F. Worcs. 37 Hen. VI, no. 50 (case 260, file 27). Spetchley was also held by the Poers under the lords of Northwick. Part of Spetchley Park is in Whittington.

[60] Feet of F. Worcs. 12 Hen. VI, no. 29 (case 260, file 26) ; Mich. 14 Jas. I. Crookbarrow also lay within Whittington and may have been part of the original manor.

[61] Nash, op. cit. ii, 325, ; cf. Woodhall and Crookbarrow.

[62] *Hist. MSS. Com. Rep.* v, App. i, 302, 302b ; Orig. Chart. ut supra, 149 ; Lay Subs. R. Worcs. c. 1280 (Worcs. Hist. Soc.), 40 ; Dugdale, *Mon.* i, 614 ; Chan. Inq. a.q.d. file 228, no. 23 (8 Edw. III) ; Cal. Pat. 1334–8, p. 222 ; cf. Harl. Chart. 112 B. 20.

[63] *Reg. of Worc. Priory* (Camden Soc.), 37b. A 'cribarium' of fish due on the feast of St. Anne was among the rents payable to the infirmarer of the convent (ibid. 98b). [64] *Valor Eccl.* iii, 223.

[65] *L. and P. Hen. VIII*, xx (1), 465 (80) ; Pat. 1 & 2 Phil. and Mary, pt. ii, m. 15.

[66] Chan. Inq. p.m. (Ser. 2), clxxii, 142 ; Close, 19 Eliz. pt. iii ; Pat. 32 Eliz. pt. xxi, m. 4.

[67] Feet of F. Worcs. Hil. 8 Jas. I.

[68] Chan. Inq. p.m. (Ser. 2), ccclxxx, 111.

[69] See Fine R. 19 Jas. I, pt. i, no. 39.

[70] Chan. Inq. p.m. (Ser. 2), ccccxxxviii, 110.

[71] Feet of F. Worcs. Trin. 39 Geo. III.
[71a] Inform. from Mr. J. W. Willis-Bund. [71b] Ibid.

[72] Dugdale, *Mon.* i, 614 ; see above under Battenhall.

[73] Comp. R. of Priory of Worc. xiv and xv cent. (Worcs. Hist. Soc.), 10, 23 ; Nash, op. cit. ii, 327.

[74] *Valor Eccl.* (Rec. Com.), iii, 223.

[75] *L. and P. Hen. VIII*, xx (1), g. 465 (80) ; Pat. 1 & 2 Phil. and Mary, pt. ii, m. 15.

[76] Close, 19 Eliz. pt. iii ; Pat. 32 Eliz. pt. xxi, m. 4.

[77] Nash, op. cit. ii, 327. The deed was not enrolled in Chancery.

[78] Chan. Inq. p.m. (Ser. 2), dxlviii, 25.

The manor descended in this family [79] until it came to two heiresses—Abigail, who married John York, and Anne, who married William Hopton. It was sold by Hopton and by York's eldest son to Treadway Nash, D.D., in 1767.[80] Nash settled it on his daughter Margaret, who married John Lord Somers.[81] Their eldest son Edward Charles Cocks, on whom a settlement was made in 1811,[82] was killed the following year at the siege of Burgos. It descended with the other Somers estates and is now the property of Lady Henry Somerset.

ANDREWES of Barnes Hall. *Gules a saltire or voided vert.*

The manor of *CROOKBARROW* (Crokbarwe, Crockebergh, xiv cent.) was one of the knights' fees granted with the manor of Battenhall to Worcester Priory in 1330.[83] In 1314 it was held in demesne by Alexander de Montfort and his wife Elizabeth. They in that year granted it to Edmund Hakelut,[84] who in 1330 received a grant of free warren in his demesnes of Crookbarrow and Whittington.[85] The manor remained in the hands of tenants under the priory. Thomas Gower died seised of it in February 1439–40, when it descended to Thomas his son and heir.[86] It then followed the descent of Woodhall Manor in Norton by Kempsey[87] until 1676, when both manors were settled upon Thomas Stevens.[88] It is said by Nash to have been bought by Edward Ingram of Upper Home, Clifton.[89] His son Richard Ingram suffered a recovery of it in 1799,[90] and in 1814 it was in the possession of John Richard Ingram.[91] It afterwards passed to the Berkeleys of Spetchley, who now own it.

A park was appurtenant to the manor of Crookbarrow in 1504.[92]

CHURCHES The church of *ST. PETER* stands at the extreme south-east corner of the city upon the walls, and is a large barn-like structure of brick and stucco, erected about 1820. The old church consisted of chancel and nave with north and south aisles, and had a 15th-century tower at the north-west angle panelled in the Somerset manner.[93]

There are three bells : the first by Godwin Baker, inscribed 'LORDE IN THEE IS OVR HOOP 1615,' with the churchwardens' names ; the second by John Martin, 1661, and the third by the same, 1693 (his latest bell) ; also a 'ting-tang' by Warner, 1885.

The plate consists of a cup without cover and illegible hall mark, a large paten, and an almsdish inscribed 'The gift of Mrs. Anna Dennis of the Commandry in Worcester, 1721.' There are also a cup, paten and flagon in plated ware.[94]

The registers before 1812 are as follows : (i) all entries 1686 to 1745 ; (ii) baptisms 1745 to 1797, burials 1745 to 1782, marriages 1745 to 1754 ; (iii) marriages 1754 to 1783 ; (iv) marriages 1783 to 1812 ; (v) burials 1783 to 1812 ; (vi) baptisms 1798 to 1812.[95]

The church of *ST. PHILIP AND ST. JAMES*, Whittington, erected in 1842, stands 100 yards east of the main road upon the site of the ancient chapel. It is built of coursed rubble with sandstone dressings in 13th-century style, and consists of chancel, nave, south porch and small west tower. The walls are plastered internally and have open-timber tiled roofs. There are some early 19th-century mural monuments in the nave ; one on the north wall is to Francis Best, 1795, Ann his wife, 1819, and their two daughters ; and one on the south wall is to Henry West, 1798, and Ann his wife, 1817. On the nave floor are two 18th-century slabs to the Hampton family.

There is one bell by G. Mears of London.

The plate consists of silver chalice, paten and almsdish, all Victorian.

The registers previous to 1812 are as follows : (i) all entries 1653 to 1708 ; (ii) baptisms 1709 to 1796, marriages 1710 to 1755, and burials 1710 to 1795, rather confusedly intermingled ; (iii) marriages 1755 to 1811 ; (iv) baptisms 1796 to 1812 and burials 1796 to 1811.

ADVOWSON The advowson of St. Peter's Church was granted to the convent of Pershore by John Poer in the first half of the 13th century.[96] In 1384 the abbot obtained licence to appropriate the church.[97]

The rectory and advowson were granted in 1542 to the Dean and Chapter of Worcester,[98] with whom they have since remained.[99] Leases were made of the advowson, the rectorial tithe and parts of the glebe lands during the 16th and 17th centuries.[100]

The chapel of Whittington was originally appurtenant to the church of St. Helen in the city of Worcester.[1] A pension of 2s. from it is said to have been granted to Worcester Priory by Hugh Poer.[2] Later it seems to have been held as a chapel to St. Peter's by the Abbot of Pershore,[3] but at the end of the 15th century the inhabitants claimed parochial status for it. The matter was compromised

---

[79] See Nash, loc. cit. Jonathan Andrewes died in 1667 (M.I. quoted by Nash, op. cit. ii, App. cliii). Another Jonathan, probably his son, died in 1701 (ibid.).

[80] Nash, op. cit. ii, 327.

[81] Feet of F. East. 25 Geo. III ; see Impney in Dodderhill, Halfshire Hundred.

[82] Com. Pleas D. Enr. East. 51 Geo. III, m. 8 ; Recov. R. East. 51 Geo. III, rot. 24.

[83] Dugdale, *Mon.* i, 614.

[84] Feet of F. East. 8 Edw. II, no. 22 (case 259, file 15). Hakelut was a contrariant (Assize R. 1037, m. 4 d.).

[85] Chart. R. 4 Edw. III, m. 34, no. 92 ; see *Feud. Aids*, v, 308, where Edmund Hakelut is given as holder of one of a list of knights' fees formerly of John

Poer. This may refer to Crookbarrow (see under Whittington).

[86] Chan. Inq. p.m. 33 Hen. VI, no. 9.

[87] De Banco R. 970, m. 434 ; Chan. Inq. p.m. (Ser. 2), xlviii, 139 ; Feet of F. Div. Co. East. 19 Eliz. ; Worcs. East. 4 Jas. I ; Mich. 14 Jas. I ; East. 19 Jas. I ; East. 5 Chas. I.

[88] Com. Pleas D. Enr. Hil. 27 & 28 Chas. II, m. 5 ; Recov. R. Hil. 27 & 28 Chas. II, rot. 140.

[89] Nash, loc. cit. i, 243.

[90] Recov. R. Trin. 39 Geo. III, rot. 121.

[91] Ibid. Mich. 55 Geo. III, rot. 198.

[92] De Banco R. 970, m. 434.

[93] The church of St. Peter, Worcester, was dedicated in 1420 (Worc. Epis. Reg. Morgan, fol. 3).

[94] Lea, *Church Plate of Worcs.* 76.

[95] *A Digest of Parish Reg. within Diocese of Worcester*, 56.

[96] During the abbacy of Gervase, 1204–34 ; Misc. Bks. (Aug. Off.), lxi, fol. 51 d. Confirmation by Roger Poer (ibid. fol. 51 d., 106 d.).

[97] *Cal. Pat.* 1381–5, p. 374 ; *Cal. of Papal Letters*, iv, 524. In 1535 the vicarage was valued at £12 3s. 0½d., the rectory at £5 4s. 8d. only (*Valor Eccl.* [Rec. Com.], iii, 234, 261).

[98] *L. and P. Hen. VIII*, xvii, g. 71 (29).

[99] See Inst. Bks. (P.R.O.).

[100] *Orig. Chart. ut supra*, 109 ; Feet of F. Worcs. East. 28 Eliz. ; Inst. Bks. (P.R.O.). [1] Heming, op. cit. 427.

[2] *Reg. of Worc. Priory* (Camden Soc.), 92a ; Heming, op. cit. 544.

[3] See Habington, op. cit. i, 27.

by an agreement with Pershore that the latter should pay 20s. yearly towards the support of a chaplain.[4] The living was held with St. Peter's until 1910, when it was annexed to St. Martin's.

CHARITIES The following charities are distributed on St. Thomas's Day, namely, John Hughes', mentioned on the church table as founded by will, 1636, consisting of a rent-charge of 40s., issuing out of the Crown Inn, Friar Street.

Sarah Hodgkins' (date of foundation unknown, but mentioned in Parliamentary returns of 1786), consisting of a rent-charge of 20s., payable out of the Red Lion Inn, Sidbury.

Richard Adams' (mentioned on the same table), will 1702, being 20s. yearly issuing out of a farm at Alfrick in Suckley.

Charities of Henry Staunton and others, which consist of a freehold house, 5 Edgar Street, Worcester, producing £28 10s. a year, one moiety of the net income being applicable for the poor and the other moiety for expenses in connexion with the church.

Mrs. Sarah Hall's (mentioned on the church table), will 1776, trust fund, £350 consols, the dividends to be applied in warm gowns for six poor maids or widows.

Charles Geary's, will date unknown, mentioned on church table as a legacy of £20, now represented by £30 11s. 9d. consols, the interest to be given to ten poor women.

Thomas Taylor's, date of foundation not stated, trust fund, £103 9s. 10d. consols, arising from sale of two cottages in Meadow Row, Worcester, dividends applicable in the distribution of articles in kind.

William Otley's, will proved at Worcester 19 September 1864, trust fund, £49 11s. 1d. consols, dividends applicable in the distribution of bread.

Anna Farrell's, will proved at London 10 March 1894, trust fund, £176 5s. 1d. consols, dividends applicable in the distribution of bread and coal.

The several sums of stock are held by the official trustees, producing in annual dividends £17 4s. 4d. In 1910 the sum of £23 was expended on St. Thomas's Day in the distribution of dresses, sheets and petticoats, £4 13s. on bread and groceries and £10 towards church expenses.

Other donations mentioned on the church table appear to have been lost.

In 1855 William Dent, by his will proved 22 January, bequeathed £1,000, the interest to be applied in the purchase of coats, gowns and blankets for poor men, women and housekeepers. The legacy

was invested in £1,063 16s. 7d. consols with the official trustees, producing £26 11s. 8d. yearly.

In 1861 Robert Allies, by his will proved 18 March, bequeathed £500, the interest to be distributed in October in blankets to poor housekeepers. The legacy was invested in £514 2s. 9d. consols, producing £12 17s. yearly. The stock is with the official trustees, who also hold a sum of £514 2s. 9d. like stock, arising from a legacy by the same testator, for the benefit of the Church of England day schools.

The official trustees likewise hold a sum of £594 15s. 10d. consols, representing a legacy of £600 by will of Thomas Nicholls Stratford, proved at Worcester 8 March 1883, producing £14 17s. 4d. yearly, of which two-thirds are applied in the distribution of groceries to the poor of St. Peter's and one-third for the poor of the chapelry of Whittington.

In 1908 John Darke, by his will proved at London 24 March, left as an endowment fund for St. Mark's Mission Church a legacy which is represented by £348 17s. 2d. India 3½ per cent. stock and a sum of £67 5s. 7d. cash with the Worcester Diocesan Trustees. The charity is regulated by a scheme of the Charity Commissioners 23 March 1910.

Chapelry of Whittington.—In 1668 Elizabeth Stephens by her will left £50, now represented by £51 5s. 5d. consols, for the poor. The annual dividends, amounting to £1 5s. 8d., are distributed in small money doles.

In 1881 Miss Alice Bateman, by her will proved at Worcester 31 May, left a legacy, represented by £95 9s. 8d. consols, the annual dividends, amounting to £2 7s. 8d., to be applied towards the salary of the organist.

In 1883 Thomas Nicholls Stratford, by his will proved at Worcester 8 March, bequeathed £600, which was invested in £594 15s. 10d. consols, the annual dividends, amounting to £14 17s. 4d., being applicable as to two-thirds for the poor of St. Peter the Great, city of Worcester, and one-third for the poor of Whittington.

In 1888 Miss Fanny Clifton, by a codicil to her will proved at Wells 13 March, bequeathed £900, the interest to be applied in the purchase of coal and fuel for distribution on St. Thomas's Day, with power for the trustees to provide a fund for any special time of want. The legacy is, with accumulations, represented by £955 7s. 6d. consols, producing £23 17s. 8d. yearly. In 1910 5 cwt. of coal was distributed to each of seventy-one recipients.

The several sums of stock are held by the official trustees.

SEDGEBERROW

Segcgesbearuue, Secgesbearuue (viii cent.); Secgesbearawe (x cent.); Seggesbarwe (xi cent.); Seggesbereg, Shegeberwe (xiii cent.); Seggeberugh (xiv cent.); Segebarowe (xv and xvi cent.); Sedgborowe (xvii cent.).

The parish of Sedgeberrow lies in the south of the county, and is almost surrounded by Gloucestershire, being connected with Worcestershire by a narrow

strip of land. It is bounded on the east by the River Isbourne,[1] which flows north and joins the Avon near Bengeworth. The Carrant Brook forms part of the southern boundary. The village of Sedgeberrow lies on the left bank of the River Isbourne on the road from Winchcomb to Evesham, which joins the Cheltenham and Evesham high road to the north of the village. The Court House, which stands on the site

---

[4] Epis. Reg. quoted by Nash, op. cit. ii, 325; *Valor Eccl.* (Rec. Com.), iii, 261.

[1] This river is mentioned under the name Esegburna in King Offa's grant of 777 (see below).

of the old manor-house of the Priors of Worcester adjoining the churchyard on the west, is a rectangular half-timber building of the later 16th century. The house is now divided into two cottages and the interior has been much altered to suit its present use. A secret chamber or 'hiding hole' is constructed by the side of one of the stone chimney stacks. On a stack on the west side of the house is carved the date 1572. At the north end of the village are some good half-timber cottages with thatched roofs, one of which contains elaborate Jacobean panelling on the ground floor. The house at present occupied by Miss Ashwin at the south end of the village is a rectangular half-timber building of the early 17th century, with a brick wing added early in the succeeding century. The older portion contains little of its original detail internally, but there is a fine staircase in the later wing.

In a cottage at the same end of the village are some interesting 13th-century remains, probably part of a former chapel. These consist of a rectangular building of rubble with wrought stone quoins, surmounted by later half-timber work. In the east wall is a window of two trefoil-headed lights with a plain quatrefoil between the heads. Internally the jambs and mullion have a square rebate with two holes formed in the back of the mullion as if for shutter bolts. The lights measure 8½ in. in width and 3 ft. in height; the width of the whole opening is about 2 ft. 4 in. externally, splaying internally to 4 ft. 3 in. The head is cut out of a single semicircular stone, the jambs are each of three stones, and the mullion and sill are each single stones. Externally on either side were originally corbels, one of which still exists, but that on the south has disappeared, and the pocket has been filled. At the southern angle of the wall, and at about the same level, is a similar corbel, cut out of one of the quoin stones. At the north-east is a small trefoiled light, probably of the same date. The walling contemporary with these details appears only to extend westwards about 13 ft. on the north and 11 ft. 3 in. on the south, the width of this portion being 13 ft. 10 in. and the thickness of the walls varying from 2 ft. 1 in. to 2 ft. 4 in. All the western part of the ground floor, the walls of which are about 1 ft. 8 in. thick, is probably contemporary with the half-timber upper story and dates from c. 1600. The present division of the ground floor probably belongs to the same period. There is a large room on the east into which the entrance opens, a living room on the west, with the staircase and a smaller room in the centre. A brick kitchen has been added on the north side, probably in the 18th century. A fine Jacobean settle with baluster legs, apparently an original fixture, occupies a large recess formed on the east side of the western room, which has a large fireplace in the west end wall, where is the only chimney stack of the house with the exception of that in the later kitchen on the north. The building

has recently been restored and put in thorough repair by the present rector of Sedgeberrow.

The village and the greater part of the parish lie low in the valleys of the River Isbourne and the Carrant Brook, about 100 ft. to 120 ft. above the ordnance datum, but the land rises slightly to the west and south.

The area of the parish is 1,020 acres,[2] of which 611 acres are arable land and 347 permanent grass-land.[3] The subsoil is Keuper Marl and the soil is clay, producing crops of wheat, oats, beans and barley.[4]

Some implements of the Stone and Bronze Ages have been found in the parish.[5]

The following place-names have been found : Horsham[6] (xiii cent.) ; Bightwell Furlong, Bridge Pleck Furlong, Hinton Mill Leasow, Barrew Leyes[7] (xvii cent.).

SEDGEBERROW : 13TH-CENTURY WINDOW OF COTTAGE

An Inclosure Act for Sedgeberrow was passed in 1810.[8]

In 777 Offa, King of Mercia, gave *MANOR SEDGEBERROW* to the under-king Aldred, ealdorman of the Hwiccas, who bestowed it on the Bishop of Worcester.[9] It was confirmed to the church in King Edgar's famous charter of 964,[10] and was assigned to the support of the monks. One Dodd held it, and his son Brictric tried to dispossess the monks, but Ealdred, Bishop of Worcester (1044–69), restored it to them.[11] At the date of the Domesday Survey the monks of Worcester held Sedgeberrow, where there were 4 hides that paid

[2] 2 acres of which are covered by water.

[3] Statistics from Bd. of Agric. (1905).

[4] Habington, writing about 1640, says Sedgeberrow is 'deeply taynted with the fowle wayes of Eweshame's vale, whence springethe a most fayre and fertile commodity of corne' (*Surv. of Worcs.* [Worcs. Hist. Soc.], i, 355).

[5] *V.C.H. Worcs.* i, 193.

[6] *Reg. of Worc. Priory* (Camden Soc.), 106b.

[7] Close, 1654, pt. xv, no. 19.

[8] Priv. Act, 50 Geo. III, cap. 28.

[9] Kemble, *Cod. Dipl.* no. 131 ; Birch, *Cart. Sax.* i, 311 ; Heming, *Chartul.* (ed. Hearne), 401, 403. This charter is genuine and important.

[10] Heming, op. cit. 520.

[11] *V.C.H. Worcs.* i, 295a ; Heming, op. cit. 395.

geld.[12] The manor remained in the possession of the prior and convent until the dissolution of their house.[13] The register of 1240 gives full particulars of the tenants and their holdings. At that date there were 2 carucates and half a virgate of demesne land.[14] In 1256 the monks obtained a grant of free warren at Sedgeberrow, and this right was confirmed to them in 1355.[15] In 1535 the manor was worth £27 4s. 8d. a year,[16] and after the dissolution of the priory in 1539–40 [17] was granted to the Dean and Chapter of Worcester in 1542.[18] It was confirmed to them by James I in 1609.[19] On 23 June 1641 they granted a lease of it to Judith Langston for three lives.[20] In 1654 the commissioners for the sale of the dean and chapter lands sold the manor of Sedgeberrow for £1,164 14s. to Henry Sealey,[21] who sold it to Edwin Baldwyn and Edward Feild in 1657.[22] The site of the manor had been sold by the commissioners in 1651 to Giles Parsons of Overbury.[23] At the Restoration the dean and chapter recovered it, and it was confirmed to them in 1692,[24] and in 1859 was taken over by the Ecclesiastical Commissioners,[25] who are lords of the manor at the present day.[26]

At the date of the Domesday Survey the monks of Worcester had in their manor of Sedgeberrow two mills which were worth 10s.[27] In 1240 there appears to have been only one mill,[28] and both had disappeared before 1535.

The church of ST. MARY THE VIRGIN is of a simple rectangular plan 71 ft. long (of which 26½ ft. is to the east of the chancel step) and 22½ ft. wide inside, a north porch, modern south vestry and a small western tower 10½ ft. wide outside covered by a stone spire.

An entry in the Worcester Episcopal Register records the dedication of the church with its three altars in 1331,[29] and the building has remained almost intact from that time. Licence was granted to Thomas de Evesham for celebration ' in his Chapel of Seggeberewe ' in 1335.[30] The tracery of the east window is somewhat later in appearance than the usual work of this date, and may be a reconstruction of the next century. The vestry was built in 1900, and the church had been previously restored in 1868.

The east window has a two-centred head and is of five trefoiled lights, the heads rising toward the middle light ; the tracery over is of vertical character, each piercing except the spandrels being trefoiled. The jambs and arch are of two chamfered orders with a label. The stone reredos in front of the window is an exceptional example of 14th-century work, and, though somewhat over-restored and painted, its lines and carving are substantially original. It consists of three recessed semi-hexagonal bays (the centre bay raised to correspond with the arrangement of the lights of the window above), divided from each other by small square buttresses, finished with gabled and crocketed finials and flanked by taller outer buttresses of the same form at the angles of the window jambs.

Each bay has a vaulted canopy completing the hexagon with three hanging arches, ogee-shaped and cinque-foiled on the face and enriched with crockets and foliated finials, separated by small pinnacles with leaf bosses below. The canopies have vaulted soffits with small ribs springing from miniature vaulting shafts, having moulded bases but no capitals, and there are bosses at the intersections of the ribs. In the wall on either side of the reredos is a moulded corbel for an image. The piscina in the south wall, which is also painted, has a projecting ogee-vaulted canopy, with carved crockets and finial, and a fan-shaped basin. The two sedilia in the window recess appear to be modern. There are four windows in each side wall and each window is the counterpart of the one opposite. They are all of two lights under pointed arches of two chamfered orders, and the second pair has vertical tracery similar to that in the east window. The others have leaf tracery of trefoils and quatre-foils in the heads, and the two western pairs have somewhat larger lights.

Just east of the third window in the south wall of the nave are the remains of a piscina, evidently once resembling that in the chancel. The projecting part of the canopy and basin have been cut away. The pointed north doorway in the bay between the third and fourth windows is of one chamfered order, and the label is continued around the porch as a moulded wall-plate. In the side walls are rectangular lights and a holy-water stoup is set in the west wall. The outer doorway appears to be old, and has a pointed head of two chamfered orders. The side walls of the church are divided into five bays externally by buttresses in four stages besides the plinth, all apparently original. The moulded drip-stones of the windows are continued as strings along the walls between the buttresses. The roofs are gabled, with pointed curved trusses below the rafters. They are modern, but some of the plain timbers are, perhaps, original.

The modern vestry is lighted on its east wall by three lancets and at its south end by a three-light pointed window.

The tower is of four stages and is octagonal above the roof, five of the sides continuing up from the plinth. The first and second stages both have door-ways towards the nave. The lower one has a single chamfered order and a pointed arch, while the upper is square-headed, and to the south of it a large corbel remains, which may have supported a gallery. The first and third stages are lighted only by slits, but the second has a rectangular light in addition. The fourth has a rectangular light in each of the four cardinal faces. The spire rises directly from the hollowed cornice and has a roll at each angle.

The whole of the church is faced with ashlar.

A large modern screen reaching to the wall-plates divides the nave from the chancel and stands on a low stone wall.

[12] V.C.H. Worcs. i, 295a.
[13] Ibid. 325 ; Cal. Pat. 1354–8, p. 266; Valor Eccl. (Rec. Com.), iii, 222a. It was confirmed to them by Simon, Bishop of Worcester, in 1148 (Thomas, Surv. of Cath. Church of Worc. App. no. 18).
[14] Reg. of Worc. Priory (Camden Soc.), 59a.
[15] Cal. Pat. 1354–8, p. 266.
[16] Valor Eccl. (Rec. Com.), iii, 222a.

[17] V.C.H. Worcs. ii, 111.
[18] L. and P. Hen. VIII, xvii, g. 71 (29) ; Pat. 33 Hen. VIII, pt. v.
[19] Pat. 6 Jas. I, pt. xii, no. 2.
[20] Close, 1654, pt. xv, no. 19.   [21] Ibid.
[22] Feet of F. Worcs. Mich. 1657.
[23] Close, 1651, pt. liii, no. 35.
[24] Pat. 4 Will. and Mary, pt. i, no. 6.
[25] Lond. Gaz. 16 Dec. 1859, p. 4757 ; Stat. 31 Vict. cap. 19.

[26] Information supplied by the Ecclesiastical Commissioners.
[27] V.C.H. Worcs. i, 295a.
[28] Reg. of Worc. Priory (Camden Soc.), 59a.
[29] Worc. Epis. Reg. Orlton, fol. 37 d.
[30] Ibid. Montagu, ii, fol. 9a. This may refer to the chapel of which the remains have been described above.

SEDGEBERROW CHURCH : THE CHANCEL

The font appears to be original with the church, though the simplicity of its detail suggests an earlier period. It is round in plan, with a cup-shaped bowl, a cylindrical stem and a base with a large rounded upper mould.

There are a few modern wall monuments, the oldest of which commemorates John Parsons, who died in 1713.

There are three bells : the first by Henry Bagley of Chalcombe, cast in 1665 ; the second by Abraham Rudhall, 1718 ; and the third inscribed 'IESVS BEE OVR SPEED 1623,' cast by Godwin Baker of Worcester and bearing his stamp, the crossed keys of St. Peter.[31]

The plate includes a cup and cover paten inscribed with the vicar's and churchwardens' names and the date 1664 and stamped with the hall mark of that year ; also a modern cup, paten and flagon, the gift of Mary Barber, 1869.

The registers before 1812 are as follows : (i) baptisms from 1566 to 1783, marriages 1566 to 1751 and burials 1567 to 1783, with many gaps ; (ii) marriages 1756 to 1782 ; (iii) baptisms and burials 1783 to 1812 and marriages 1785 to 1812.

ADVOWSON   At the date of the Domesday Survey there was a priest at Sedgeberrow who held half a hide of land.[32] The advowson belonged to the Prior and convent of Worcester until the Dissolution.[33] It was granted with the manor in 1542 to the Dean and Chapter of Worcester, who have since been patrons of the church.[34]

CHARITIES   The official trustees hold a sum of £11 5s. 7d. India 3 per cent. stock derived under the will of John Pitts, proved 19 May 1884. This is in course of being accumulated at compound interest.

SHIPSTON-ON-STOUR

Scepwaeisctune (viii cent.) ; Scepwestun (xi cent.) ; Sipestone, Sepwestun, Schipton (xiii cent.) ; Sepeston-on-Sture (xiv cent.).

The parish of Shipston-on-Stour, which was formed out of the large parish of Tredington in 1719,[1] is one of the detached parishes of Worcestershire and lies to the south-east of the county proper. The River Stour, flowing north, forms the eastern boundary, and it is joined by a small tributary called Pig Brook, flowing east, which forms the southern boundary. The parish consists of 1,220 acres,[2] of which 110 are arable and 900 permanent grass.[3] The soil is clay, lying on a substratum of Lower Lias. The chief crops are wheat, barley and oats, but during the last twenty years much of the land has been put down to grass. At one time shag or plush weaving was largely carried on at Shipston-on-Stour, but the industry was declining in the middle of the 19th century,[4] and has now died out.

The township of Shipston-on-Stour is on the left bank of the River Stour, on the high road from Woodstock to Stratford-upon-Avon. The church of St. Edmund, near the river bank, is about 200 ft. above the ordnance datum. To the west and south the land rises steadily to Waddon Hill and Hanson Hill, 300 ft. above the ordnance datum. The main square is situated on the west side of Church Street ; the George Inn and the 'White Bear' stand on the east side of the square and the 'Black Bear' on the west. Adjoining the Bell Inn is a good 18th-century house, and not far distant, in the Bell Inn road, is a house with a tablet over the porch bearing the date 1678. The rectory stands at the corner of the Chipping

Camden and Chipping Norton roads. On the Stratford road, which is known in the town variously as Stratford Road, Church Street, New Street and London Road, is the Ellen Badger Memorial Cottage Hospital, erected in 1896, and to the south of the town a cemetery, consecrated 5 April 1865, with two mortuary chapels for members of the Church of England and Nonconformists. The Shipston-on-Stour union workhouse lies to the north-west of the town.[5] There is no town hall, but the 'Hostel' in Sheep Street, the property of the trustees of the late Mrs. Townsend of Honington Hall, is used for meetings and musical entertainments. Petty sessions are held in the police station on alternate Saturdays.

There is a Baptist chapel in Shipston-on-Stour, which was first formed in 1781. The present chapel was built in 1867. There is also a Wesleyan Methodist chapel, built in 1880, and a meeting-house for the Society of Friends.[6]

An Inclosure Act for Shipston was passed in 1812, and the award is dated 1815.[7]

Place-names occurring in the 17th century are Boggies, Oddenhall, Fell Mill Grounds.[8]

Francis Hickes, the translator, was born at Shipston-on-Stour in 1566. William Parry, the calligrapher and numismatist, was presented to the rectory in 1739.[9]

MANOR   Huthrid (Uhtred), *subregulus* of the Hwiccas, granted to the church of Worcester two 'manses' near the ford of the River Stour, called Scepeswasce (i.e. Sheepwash),[10] and this grant was confirmed by King Edgar in his famous charter of 964.[11] At the date of the

[81] Inform. from Mr. H. B. Walters.
[32] *V.C.H. Worcs.* i, 295a.
[33] *Reg. of Worc. Priory* (Camden Soc.), 132a ; *Reg. G. Giffard* (Worcs. Hist. Soc.), 103, 226, 242. In 1288 the bishop presented, owing to the priory being vacant (*Reg. G. Giffard* [Worcs. Hist. Soc.], 325).
[34] *L. and P. Hen. VIII*, xvii, g. 71 (29) ; Inst. Bks. (P.R.O.).
[1] Priv. Act, 6 Geo. I, cap. 9.
[2] Of which 6 acres are covered by water. In 1901 there were 338 inhabited houses in the parish, with a population of 1,564

(*Census of Engl. and Wales*, 1901, *Worcs.* 25).
[3] Statistics from Bd. of Agric. (1905).
[4] Noake, *Guide to Worcs.* 320.
[5] In 1618 it was stated that the town was charged with a multitude of poor people to the number of seven score households that were weekly relieved there, and that the inhabitants were not able to continue without help, as there were only thirty householders able to contribute to the rates. It was ordered that Blockley was to pay a third part (*Var. Coll.* [Hist. MSS. Com.], i, 298).

[6] In 1689 three houses in Shipston-on-Stour, one being in Shap Street, were registered as places of worship for Quakers (*Var. Coll.* [Hist. MSS. Com.], i, 325).
[7] Priv. Act, 52 Geo. III, cap. 12 ; *Blue Bk. Incl. Awards*, 191.
[8] Close, 1650, pt. xxxiii, no. 17.
[9] *Dict. Nat. Biog.*
[10] Birch, op. cit. i, 290 ; Heming, op. cit. 324, 325. The date of this charter is between 764 and 775. The Anglo-Saxon boundaries of Shipston are given by Heming, op. cit. 347.
[11] Heming, op. cit. II, 520.

Domesday Survey the monks of Worcester held 2 hides in *SHIPSTON-ON-STOUR*,[12] and these they also held at the beginning of the 12th century.[13] In 1201 the manor was leased to Sir Thomas de Erdington for sixteen years.[14] In the register of the priory full details are given as to the services and rents due from the tenants of this manor.[15] The annual money receipts in 1240 were £2 11s. 7d.[16] In 1291 the Prior of Worcester owned 3 carucates here and at Blackwell worth £3 per annum,[17] and in 1345 he increased his holding in Shipston-on-Stour by the purchase of a messuage and 3 virgates of land from John de Tottenham and William de Hull.[18] At the beginning of the 15th century a dispute arose between the prior and his tenants as to customs and services.[19] The manor of Shipston-on-Stour remained with successive priors until the dissolution of the priory in 1540.[20] It then passed to the Crown, and was granted in 1542 to the Dean and Chapter of Worcester,[21] with whom it remained until 1650, when it was sold by the Parliamentary commis-

1692.[23] It was taken over in 1859 by the Ecclesiastical Commissioners,[24] to whom it now belongs.[25]

In 1268 Henry III granted to the Prior of Worcester a market in Shipston-on-Stour to be held weekly on Saturdays and a fair to be held there yearly on the vigil, feast and morrow of Saint Barnabas (10–12 June).[26] This grant was confirmed in 1400[27] and again in 1461.[28] On the dissolution of the priory in 1540[29] the stallage of the market was worth £4 10s.[30] About the middle of the 16th century the tolls of the market were in the hands of members of the Morris family under a long lease.[31] In 1573 Edward and Richard Morris, two brothers, were the lessees, taking the profits in alternate years.[32] The tolls are now leased by the Ecclesiastical Commissioners, the present owners,[33] to the parish council.[34] At the present day there is a market every Saturday and a monthly cattle fair, but the three statute fairs are a horse fair on the first Tuesday after 10 April, a horse and pleasure fair on 22 June, a pleasure fair and the old annual Michaelmas fair on the first Tuesday after 10 October.[35] The October fair is called 'bull roast,' as an ox is then roasted in the market. At this fair servants are hired.[36]

The mill at Shipston-on-Stour was worth 10s. in 1086, and in 1240 its value was the same.[37] There is no mill mentioned in the valor of the manor taken in 1535. At the present day there is a corn-mill in the town on the River Stour.

The church of *CHURCH ST. EDMUND*, which stands on the east side of the Stratford road, between it and the River Stour, consists of a chancel 27½ ft. by 19 ft., a north chapel 15½ ft. square, a vestry to the north of this 12 ft. by 9½ ft., south chapel 15½ ft. by 12½ ft., nave 71 ft. long and of similar width to the chancel, north aisle 15½ ft. wide, south aisle 17 ft. wide, south porch and a western tower 9½ ft. by 8¾ ft., all these measurements being taken within the walls.

SEVENTEENTH-CENTURY HOUSE, SHIPSTON-ON-STOUR

sioners for the sale of dean and chapter lands to Maurice Gething.[22] After the Restoration the manor of Shipston-on-Stour was restored to the Dean and Chapter of Worcester and confirmed to them in

[12] *V.C.H. Worcs.* i, 295a.

[13] Ibid. 325a.

[14] *Ann. Mon.* (Rolls Ser.), iv, 391.

[15] *Reg. of Worc. Priory* (Camden Soc.), 68a–69b. The 'bovarii' of this manor held on the same terms as those at the prior's manor of Blackwell (see below).

[16] *Reg. of Worc. Priory* (Camd. Soc.), Introd. p. vii.

[17] *Pope Nich. Tax.* (Rec. Com.), 227b.

[18] *Cal. Pat.* 1343–5, p. 449.

[19] Ibid. 1401–5, p. 197; see also ibid. 1413–16, p. 111. Habington, writing about 1640, says that the discontented tenants broke out again, 'but all theese beeinge longe synce buryed shall not bee revived by my pen, which shall neaver preiudice or blot any with infamy' (op. cit. i, 363).

[20] *V.C.H. Worcs.* ii, 111.

[21] *L. and P. Hen. VIII*, xvii, g. 71 (29).

In the same year the king granted a lease of certain rents of grain in this manor to John Burne (ibid. p. 692).

[22] Close, 1650, pt. xxvii, no. 1. The demesne lands of the manor had been sold a month before to William Hicks (ibid. pt. xxxiii, no. 17).

[23] Pat. 4 Will. and Mary, pt. i, no. 6.

[24] *Lond. Gaz.* 16 Dec. 1859, p. 4757; confirmed by Stat. 31 Vict. cap. 19.

[25] Information supplied by Ecclesiastical Commissioners.

[26] *Hist. MSS. Com. Rep.* xiv, App. viii, 169; Habington, op. cit. i, 363.

[27] *Cal. Pat.* 1399–1401, p. 384. About this time the fair was discontinued owing to the riotous behaviour of the tenants (see above); Habington, loc. cit.

[28] *Cal. Pat.* 1461–7, p. 160.

[29] *V.C.H. Worcs.* ii, 111.

[30] *Valor Eccl.* (Rec. Com.), iii, 222.

[31] Ct. of Req. bdle. 120, no. 31.

[32] Chan. Proc. (Ser. 2), bdle. 129, no. 95. In this year Edward Morris brought proceedings against one William Tydsall, who erected eight stalls every Saturday and on fair days, and charged each holder of them 1d. (ibid.). In 1581 Edward Morris gave Richard all his lands, &c., in Shipston-on-Stour provided that he might quietly hold two shops and the profits of the criership of Shipston-on-Stour which Richard had demised to him (Anct. D. [P.R.O.], A 5955).

[33] Information supplied by Mr. William Ellis Coe.

[34] Ibid.

[35] Ibid.

[36] Information supplied by Mr. F. S. Parsons.

[37] *V.C.H. Worcs.* i, 295; *Reg. of Worc. Priory* (Camd. Soc.), Introd. p. xv.

The whole of the church, except the 15th-century tower, was rebuilt in 1855 in the style of the 14th century. Beyond the tower there are now no old remains. From notes made by Prattinton in 1812 the former church appears to have been of early date, consisting of a chancel and chapel and a nave separated from a north aisle by a round-arched arcade. The font, however, was of 1707. Habington mentions two raised tombs in the churchyard to John White, who died in 1632, and Thomas White his son, who died in 1631. The present chancel has an east window of five lights with a traceried head and a single light on the south. The sedile in the same wall has a segmental head, while on the north side is a flat pointed arch. On either side of the chancel are arches opening to the chapels, and that opening to the nave is of one order. The nave has arcades on both sides of five bays, and each of the chapels has a western cross arch and is lighted by a four-light traceried east window.

Both aisles have four two-light traceried windows in their side walls, with north and south entrances at the west ends. The west window of the north aisle is of two lights and the corresponding window of the south aisle of four lights, both with traceried heads.

The tower arch is old and of two orders, the outer of which is continuous and the inner interrupted by a moulded capital of late form. The tower is two stages high, and is supported on its west face by diagonal buttresses which rise to about half its height. It has a western window of three lights with modern tracery and arch, but with an old two-centred rear arch. Over the west window, and also on the north side, are small rectangular lights of a single chamfered order. The belfry is lighted on each side by a two-light window with a plain spandrel in the pointed head. The parapet of the tower is embattled, and at each corner is a small square pinnacle rising from the coping only, and surmounted by a crocketed finial. There are also intermediate pinnacles set diagonally and rising from grotesque heads in the parapet string. Grotesques project likewise from the western angles at the same level.

The pulpit and the font are modern and both of stone.

There are six bells in the tower, all by Matthew Bagley, and of 1754, except the third, which is of 1774.

The plate consists of a communion cup inscribed 1824 with the hall mark for 1822, a salver of 1823 and a flagon of the same date.

The registers before 1812 are as follows : (i) baptisms and burials 1572 to 1797, marriages 1572 to 1754 ; (ii) baptisms and burials 1798 to 1812 ; (iii) marriages 1754 to 1805 ; (iv) marriages 1806 to 1812.

ADVOWSON Shipston-on-Stour was a chapelry of Tredington, and from very early times difficulties seem to have arisen as to the provision of a chaplain for Shipston. In 1299 it was agreed that the chaplain was to be chosen by the Prior and convent of Worcester,[38] and to be presented every year to the rector of Tredington and admitted by him, and to owe him canonical obedience. The chaplain was to receive all tithes and oblations from Shipston except tithes of sheaves, hay, fleeces and lambs and all mortuaries and the oblations of the parishioners on St. Gregory's Day. The chaplain was also to pay the rector a yearly pension of 12d. The rest of his stipend was to be paid by the parishioners.[39] This agreement was confirmed in 1363.[40] In 1516, at the request of the inhabitants, permission was given them to bury their dead at Shipston.[41] Though it seems to have been looked upon as a separate vicarage in 1535,[42] and its advowson was granted to the dean and chapter in 1542 as a late possession of the prior and convent,[43] Shipston was in reality a chapelry of Tredington until 1719, when Shipston and Tidmington were formed into a separate rectory and endowed with a third of the rectory of Tredington.[44] At the same time an agreement was made between the fellows of Jesus College, patrons of Tredington, and the Dean and Chapter of Worcester, by which the dean presented every third time to the rectory of Shipston-on-Stour,[45] and this arrangement still holds.

CHARITIES Educational Charities.—In 1706 John Pittway by his will devised four houses and 2 a. of land for the instruction, books and clothing of six scholars and for other charitable purposes.

The trust property, applicable for education, now consists of land in Horn Lane let in allotments, a building used as an engine-house producing in rents about £30 a year, and £1,501 13s. 9d. consols, producing in annual dividends £37 10s. 8d., arising from the sale also of three houses in the High Street.

In 1789, as stated on the benefaction table, the Rev. Thomas Jones left £60 in augmentation of the salary of the schoolmaster. The legacy with voluntary contributions is represented by £100 consols.

These charities are regulated by a scheme of the Board of Education 19 May 1910, whereby £5 a year is directed to be applied towards religious instruction by means of a Sunday school, and the residue of the income is made applicable in apprenticing, in school fees, exhibitions, &c.

In 1747 George Marshall, by will proved in the P.C.C., left certain securities for establishing and supporting a free school. The trust fund now consists of £1,412 2s. 5d. consols, producing yearly £35 6s., which is applied for educational purposes under the provisions of a scheme of the Charity Commissioners of 5 January 1886.

Eleemosynary Charities.—The above-mentioned John Pittway, by his will, dated in 1706, also directed that a portion of the rents of the devised property should be applied in clothing and bread for the poor, and for a sermon, the trust funds of which, derived from the sale of the three houses in the High Street, were by an order of the Charity Commissioners 9 March 1906 apportioned as follows :—

Pittway's clothing dole, £140 consols, the annual dividends of £3 10s. being applied in clothing three poor men and three poor women ; Pittway's bread dole, £215 6s. 8d. consols, producing £5 7s. 8d. yearly ; and Pittway's ecclesiastical charity, £20

[38] The prior and convent agreed to pay 8s. to the rector.
[39] Nash, op. cit. ii, 435, quoting White Book of bishopric. [40] Nash, loc. cit.
[41] Nash, op. cit. ii, 434 ; Worc. Epis. Reg. Silvester de Gigliis (1498–1521), fol. 123 d.
[42] Valor Eccl. (Rec. Com.), iii, 257.
[43] Pat. 33 Hen. VIII, pt. v ; L. and P. Hen. VIII, xvii, g. 71 (29).
[44] Priv. Act, 6 Geo. I, cap. 9.
[45] Bacon, Liber Regis, 984.

consols, the annual dividends of 10s. being paid to the rector for a sermon on Good Friday.

The several sums of stock above mentioned are held by the official trustees.

In 1555 William Willington, by his will, devised an annuity of £1 13s. 4d. for the poor, issuing out of land at Brailes, co. Warwick.

In 1747 George Marshall, by his will, left £100 South Sea new annuities, now represented by £105 19s. 2d. consols with the official trustees, producing £2 13s. yearly. The two charities are administered together and applied every three years in the distribution of meat.

In 1719 Sarah Halford, by her will, devised an annuity of £10 4s. issuing out of a farm in Willersey, co. Gloucester, 50s. to be given in clothing to each of four poor widows and a sum of 1s. in money to each.

In 1729 William Hobbins, by his will, devised an annuity of £4 out of his copyhold estate in the parish to be applied in clothing four poor men. The property charged is now in the possession of five different owners, who each pay a certain proportion.

The three charities next mentioned are administered together, namely : Thomas Hodgkins', will proved in 1811, trust fund, £113 16s. 7d. consols ; Thomas Sabin's, will proved in 1820, trust fund, £105 consols ; William Horniblow's, will dated in 1826, trust fund, £88 15s. 7d. consols.

The several sums of stock are held by the official trustees, the annual dividends of which, amounting together to £7 13s. 4d., are applicable in gifts of clothing, usually of the value of 5s. each.

In 1891 Edward Vere Nicoll bequeathed £600, the interest to be applied for the benefit of the poor. The legacy was invested in £633 4s. 11d. consols

with the official trustees ; the annual dividends amounting to £15 16s. 4d. are applied in the distribution of grocery, drapery, coal and clothing.

The charities founded by will of Richard Badger, proved at London 7 December 1907.

This testator bequeathed for the benefit of the poor of certain parishes in this county, and in the counties of Warwick and Gloucester, a considerable sum which has been invested in the following railway securities, now held by the official trustees : £5,000 Buenos Ayres Great Southern Railway 4 per cent. stock, £6,000 Canadian Pacific Railway 4 per cent. stock, £5,000 Grand Trunk Railway of Canada 4 per cent. stock, and £4,711 London and North-Western 3 per cent. stock, producing £781 a year. This parish is entitled to one-fourteenth part of such income, amounting to £55 16s. 2d. yearly, for the benefit of the poor ; this is distributed in meat and coal ; also to one-twenty-first part, amounting yearly to £31 4s., which is applicable to the Church Restoration Fund.

The church is also entitled to a moiety of the income of allotments made under the Inclosure Act, known as the Church Piece and Pound, producing £5 a year, the poor being entitled to the other moiety.

The Curfew Bell Charity consists of £81 14s. 9d. consols with the official trustees, derived under the will of the above-mentioned William Horniblow for a bell-ringer for ringing one of the bells in the morning and in the evening at certain specified hours.

Nonconformist Charities.—The Baptist chapel is endowed with land in Church Street and a messuage thereon let at £30 a year, also with £161 10s. 2d. consols with the official trustees, producing £4 0s. 8d. yearly, arising under the will of Miss Martha Sabin.

SPETCHLEY

Speacleatun (ix cent.) ; Spæclea (x cent.) ; Speclea (xi cent.) ; Spechele, Spechelegh (xiii cent.) ; Spechesleye (xiv cent.) ; Speachley (xvii cent.).

Spetchley is a small parish about 3 miles east of Worcester. It covers an area of 780 acres, of which 13 are covered by water, 189 are arable land, 539 permanent grass and 37 woods and plantations.[1] Almost the whole of the south-west of the parish is included in Spetchley Park, which contains 196 acres, 117 of which are in the deer park, where there are herds of red and fallow deer. The mansion at Spetchley Park, a house in the Grecian manner of the early 19th century, is the seat of Mr. Robert Valentine Berkeley. The village itself, though prettily situated, possesses no buildings of architectural interest. The main road from Worcester to Alcester forms the northern boundary of the park and the chief street of the village. There is a Roman Catholic chapel of St. John the Baptist attached to the house at Spetchley Park. It was registered for marriages in 1841.[2] Agriculture is the only industry, the chief crops being wheat, barley and beans. The soil is various, the subsoil marl and clay.

The land varies in height from 138 ft. in parts of the park to 207 ft. in the north of the village. The nearest passenger station is at Worcester, 3 miles west. There is a goods station on the Midland railway in this parish.

SPETCHLEY was among the manors
MANOR   belonging to the church of Worcester freed in 816 by Coenwulf, King of the Mercians, from secular services.[3] Bishop Oswald granted three 'manses' at Spetchley in 988 to the monks of Worcester in exchange for other land which he wished to give to his nephew Alfwin.[4] Bishop Brihteah gave it to his brother Agelric, Ethelric or Alric, who was deprived of it by William Earl of Hereford.[5] It must, however, have been restored to the church, and by the time of the Domesday Survey was a member of the prior's manor of Hallow, being assigned for the support of the monks of Worcester, and in the possession of Roger de Lacy.[6]

The Prior of Worcester soon seems to have lost all rights in the overlordship of Spetchley, which was said towards the end of the 12th century to be held of the bishop's manor of Kempsey,[7] and

---

[1] Statistics from Bd. of Agric. (1905).
[2] *Lond. Gaz.* 9 Apr. 1841, p. 947.
[3] Heming, *Chartul.* (ed. Hearne), 2, 337, 382, 588.

[4] Ibid. 174.
[5] Ibid. 266.
[6] *V.C.H. Worcs.* i, 296a. There were two Frenchmen on the manor in 1086.

[7] Red Bk. of Bishopric of Worc. (Eccl. Com. Rec. Var. bdle. 121, no. 43698), fol. 253.

SPETCHLEY PARK FROM THE SOUTH-WEST

SPETCHLEY CHURCH : THE CHANCEL AND SOUTH CHAPEL

in the 13th century was held of the manor of Northwick.[8]

Roger de Lacy still owned Spetchley at the beginning of the 12th century,[9] but his descendant Hugh Lacy, as at Himbleton, lost this fee, which passed with Himbleton to Hugh Poer, who held it of Walter de Meduana.[10] Walter de Meduana's interest passed with the rest of his possessions to William de Monchensey.[11] Warin de Monchensey held the fee in 1245–6,[12] and it afterwards passed to his son-in-law William de Valence. It then followed the descent of Inkberrow (q.v.) until the death of Aymer de Valence Earl of Pembroke in 1324, and was assigned in 1325 to his kinswoman Elizabeth Comyn.[13] After this time this mesne lordship seems to have lapsed.

Hugh Poer's interest descended in the Poer family,[14] and the fee became annexed to their manor of Battenhall, passing with that manor to the Prior of Worcester.[15] The overlordship of the lords of Battenhall was recognized until 1579 or later.[16]

Under these lords the manor was held by the Spetchleys. It is probable that Robert Spetchley, who was one of the justices of assize in 1230,[17] was lord of the manor. He had been succeeded before 1245–6 by Richard Spetchley.[18] Richard Spetchley belonged to the household of Maud de Cauntelow and went with her to Scotland in attendance on the king's daughter Margaret in 1252,[19] and abroad in 1255.[20] In the summer of 1252 he obtained exemption for life from being put on juries and assizes.[21] He seems to have left an only daughter Philippa, wife of John de Everley,[22] king's yeoman, who received a grant of free warren in Spetchley in 1271,[23] and twelve years later licence to hunt foxes, hares, badgers and cats in the king's forests in the counties of Worcester and Hampshire.[24] In 1280–1 John and Philippa settled Spetchley on their son John with contingent remainders to Thomas and Agnes, their other children.[25] It was probably this son John who was made coroner for the county of Worcester, but removed from that office in 1320 for 'insufficient qualifications,'[26] and who with many other men of the county was compelled by the Despensers to pay a large sum of money to the king for a 'certain trespass maliciously charged against them.'[27]

He was succeeded before 1346 by William de Everley,[28] probably his son, who took part in the riots of 1345 against William Beauchamp.[29] In 1346 a warrant was issued for his arrest, and he was found to have fled the county.[30] In 1348 he was still in possession of Spetchley, and was then concerned in the riots between the men of Worcester and the priory,[31] but he died in the following year,[31a] and his property passed to William Spetchley, a descendant of the former owners, who was dealing with tenements in the parish in 1363.[32] Another William Spetchley presented to the living in 1419[33] and was succeeded before 1433 by John Spetchley,[34] who may have been his son. The latter in 1454 sold the reversion of the manor after his death to Sir Thomas Lyttelton of Frankley and Joan his wife,[35] and with his wife Maud confirmed the sale in 1459.[36] Sir Thomas Lyttelton settled Spetchley on his younger son Thomas and Anne his wife.[37] The younger Thomas died in 1524,[38] leaving three sons, Thomas, who died without issue in 1535,[39] John and Anthony. John succeeded his brother in the manor and with Anthony sold it to Richard Sheldon in 1544–5.[40] By his will, proved in February 1562, Richard left it to his wife Margaret for her life or as long as she remained unmarried, with reversion to Philip, his eldest son.[41] The latter with his wife Elizabeth and son William sold Spetchley in 1606 to Rowland Berkeley, a clothier of Worcester,[42] who left it to his second son Robert in 1611.[43] Sir Robert Berkeley was made serjeant-at-law in 1627 and justice of the King's Bench in 1632.[44] He was among the judges committed to the Tower for their support of the ship-money tax and was fined £20,000, the fine being afterwards reduced to £10,000.[45] He was a Royalist, but in 1651 Spetchley was the head quarters of Cromwell before and at the battle of Worcester, and at that time Sir Robert Berkeley's house was burnt down by some Presbyterian soldiers in the king's army. He made his stables habitable and lived there until his death in 1656.[46] A 'capital messuage and buildings, with a moat about half-way encompassing the same,' mentioned in an inquisition taken soon after his death,[47] must evidently have been this dwelling. A picture of the stables in which Sir Robert lived, and which the family occupied

---

[8] Red Bk. of Bishopric of Worc. (Eccl. Com. Rec. Var. bdle. 121, no. 43698), fol. 2 ; Testa de Nevill (Rec. Com.), 41b.
[9] V.C.H. Worcs. i, 325a.
[10] Red Bk. of Bishopric of Worc. fol. 253 ; see Himbleton.
[11] Red Bk. of Exch. (Rolls Ser.), 96.
[12] Feet of F. Worcs. Hil. 30 Hen. III. For pedigree of the Monchenseys see V.C.H. Bucks. ii, 273.
[13] Chan. Inq. p.m. 17 Edw. II, no. 75, m. 109 ; Cal. Close, 1323–7, p. 273.
[14] Testa de Nevill (Rec. Com.), 41b ; Feet of F. Worcs. Hil. 30 Hen. III ; Red Bk. of Bishopric of Worc. fol. 2 ; Feud. Aids, v, 308.
[15] Cal. Pat. 1327–30, p. 470 ; Chan. Inq. p.m. 21 Edw. IV, no. 55 ; (Ser. 2), lvii, 27.
[16] Chan. Inq. p.m. (Ser. 2), clxxxvii, 111.
[17] Cal. Pat. 1225–32, p. 366.
[18] Feet of F. Worcs. Hil. 30 Hen. III, no. 14.
[19] Cal. Pat. 1247–58, p. 123.
[20] Ibid. 417.
[21] Ibid. 141.

[22] Assize R. 1026, m. 20. Emma widow of Richard married John Young, and in 1274–5 gave up her share of Spetchley to John Everley and Philippa.
[23] Cal. Chart. R. 1257–1300, p. 178. In 1274 his right to have a warren in Spetchley was questioned, but he proved his claim by producing the charter of Henry III (Assize R. 1026, m. 35).
[24] Cal. Pat. 1281–92, p. 71.
[25] Feet of F. Worcs. 9 Edw. I, no. 20.
[26] Cal. Close, 1318–23, p. 195. In 1319 he was one of the assessors in co. Worcester of the eighteenth granted to the king for the war in Scotland (Cal. Pat. 1317–21, p. 349).
[27] Cal. Pat. 1327–30, p. 203.
[28] Feud. Aids, v, 308.
[29] Cal. Pat. 1345–8, pp. 36, 97.
[30] Ibid. 1345–8, p. 118.
[31] Ibid. 1348–50, p. 249.
[31a] Cal. Close, 1349–54, p. 23.
[32] Sir T. Phillipps, Index to Worcs. Fines, p. vi.
[33] Sede Vacante Reg. (Worcs. Hist. Soc.), 403. William Golafre and William Wyrehall had presented as lords of the

manor in 1401 (ibid. 379), but were probably trustees of the Spetchleys.
[34] Ibid. 408.
[35] Feet of F. Worcs. Mich. 33 Hen. VI, no. 48.
[36] Ibid. East. 37 Hen. VI, no. 50.
[37] Hist. MSS. Com. Rep. v, App. i, 295 ; Chan. Inq. p.m. 21 Edw. IV, no. 55.
[38] Chan. Inq. p.m. (Ser. 2), xli, 10.
[39] Exch. Inq. p.m. (Ser. 2), file 1190, no. 7.
[40] Recov. R. East. 30 Hen. VIII, rot. 138 ; Feet of F. Worcs. East. 36 Hen. VIII.
[41] P.C.C. 9 Chayre ; Chan. Inq. p.m. (Ser. 2), cxxxii, 40. Margaret afterwards married Thomas Harewell (Feet of F. Worcs. East. 27 Eliz.).
[42] Feet of F. Worcs. Mich. 4 Jas. I ; Recov. R. East. 6 Jas. I, rot. 83.
[43] Chan. Inq. p.m. (Ser. 2), cccxxv, 181.
[44] Dict. Nat. Biog.
[45] Clarendon, Hist. of the Rebellion, iii, 209.
[46] Dict. Nat. Biog. ; Nash, op. cit. ii, 359.
[47] Chan. Inq. p.m. (Ser. 2), dccxviii, 148.

until the present house was built in 1821, is now in the possession of Mr. R. V. Berkeley.[48] Robert Berkeley, grandson of Sir Robert,[49] married Elizabeth daughter of Sir Richard Blake, the authoress of *A Method of Devotion* and other works.[50] He died childless in 1694[51] and was succeeded by his brother Thomas, who left two sons John and Thomas.[52] Thomas Berkeley, the only son of John, died without issue in 1742 and Spetchley passed to his uncle Thomas.[53] Robert Berkeley, son of Thomas, died childless in 1804 and was succeeded by his nephew Robert.[54] The manor now belongs to Mr. Robert Valentine Berkeley, great-grandson of the last-named Robert.[55]

BERKELEY. *Gules a cheveron between ten crosses formy argent.*

A mill at Spetchley was sold with the manor to Rowland Berkeley in 1608,[56] but is not mentioned in any other documents relating to the manor.

The *PARK* at Spetchley was made or enlarged by Robert Berkeley, the judge, who in 1625 received licence to impark any part of the parish for deer, rabbits and pheasants.[57] It extends into the parishes of Whittington and St. Martin, Worcester, and covers an area of 196 acres.

CHURCH The church of *ALL SAINTS* consists of a chancel 24½ ft. by 15¾ ft., a south chapel of equal length with the chancel and 13 ft. in width, nave 29 ft. by 21¾ ft., inclosing at its west end a tower 9 ft. wide by 9½ ft. deep. Over the west doorway is a wooden porch. The measurements here given are all internal.

The nave and chancel date from about 1330, and there is no evidence of older work on the site. The south chapel, dedicated in honour of the Holy Trinity, was added by Sir Robert Berkeley in 1614, as recorded on the tomb set up by him to his father and mother. His own tomb stands against its south wall, and his arms are carved above the doorway at the west end of the chapel. The tower is also attributed to him, but is very inferior in design to the chapel, and a later date, 1714, for which there seems to be some evidence, is on the whole more likely to be correct.

The church had no rights of burial till 1561, and the churchyard is very small, which is no doubt the reason why it was found more convenient to block up the west part of the nave with a tower than to encroach on the very restricted area of the graveyard.

The east window of the chancel, which has three lights with tracery of 15th-century style, is modern. There were originally two north windows, the western of which, a tall trefoiled single light, yet remains, but only a few stones of the east jamb of the other are now to be seen, it having been destroyed in the latter part of the 16th century, about 1580, when the existing rectangular bay window was inserted. It is a curious and unusual feature, and was built by one

of the Sheldons to contain his tomb, though Habington records that he was not actually buried there. It has a moulded cornice and a flat roof. On the jambs inside are four shields; the upper on the east face has three axes impaling a cheveron between three stars and the lower three lions' heads razed and a chief impaling three axes. The upper on the west side bears a fesse between three eagles impaling a cheveron between three stars in the chief, and crusilly formy three lozenges fessewise in the foot; the lower shield has a cheveron between three stars impaling a fesse between three eagles. In the bay is an altar tomb with no inscription; its base is divided into three panels, the middle one of which incloses an almost obliterated shield of six quarters of which the first four seem to be three lions' heads, three axes, a cheveron between three stars and a fesse between three eagles. To the east of the bay are the quoin stones of an earlier blocked window. The other window at the western end of this wall is of a single trefoiled light, the jambs and head being of two chamfered orders. The large opening on the south side into the chapel is spanned by a flat wood lintel, moulded like the stone jambs, with a sunken half-round in the centre and chamfered outer edges. On the top of the latter, below the lintel, are chamfered cornices. The pointed chancel arch probably dates from the 14th century, and is in red sandstone of two continuous chamfered orders.

The chapel is lighted through its east wall by a window of three trefoiled lights under a pointed head. It is contemporary with the chapel and is chiefly of white sandstone. The two windows in the south wall are each of two trefoiled lights with a feathered spandrel over in the pointed head. The west doorway has a four-centred flat arch, and over it is carved a Berkeley shield of fourteen quarterings.

The first window on either side of the nave is of two lights with a pointed head. Both date from the 14th century, and below the southern is an old piscina with a trefoiled pointed head and a sill cut away flush with the wall. The second north window is a single light with a plain pointed head, and is probably an insertion of the 16th century or later. The north doorway, which has a two-centred head, has been blocked, but has a wood threshold in position. The third window is a single light, blocked on the building of the tower. The second window on the south is also a single light with a plain triangular head, presumably a late reconstruction. The south doorway, of a single chamfered order, has a pointed head like that opposite, and is also filled in, with its wood door retained in position. The third window is similar to the blocked opening opposite, the space between the tower and the nave wall on this side being used for the stairway up to the first floor. The doorway in the east wall of the tower is a square plastered opening with a 'church-warden' Gothic window of three lights over it. The west doorway, now the only entrance to the nave, has a round head of a single chamfered order and has been partly renewed. The window over it is perhaps

[48] Inform. from Mr. R. V. Berkeley.
[49] Chan. Inq. p.m. (Ser. 2), dccxviii, 155; Feet of F. Worcs. East. 31 Chas. II.
[50] *Dict. Nat. Biog.* She afterwards married Gilbert Burnet, Bishop of Salisbury.
[51] M. I. in Spetchley Church.
[52] Recov. R. Mich. 10 Geo. II, rot. 147; Burke, *Landed Gentry.*
[53] Burke, *Landed Gentry*; Recov. R. Mich. 17 Geo. II, rot. 160.
[54] Recov. R. D. Enr. East. 18 Geo. III, m. 27; Hil. 19 Geo. III, m. 94, 95; Recov. R. Trin. 48 Geo. III, rot. 37.
[55] Burke, *Landed Gentry.*
[56] Recov. R. East. 6 Jas. I, rot. 83.
[57] Pat. 1 Chas. I, pt. ix, no. 24.

Spetchley Church : Monument to Rowland Berkeley and Katherine Haywood his Wife

of late 14th-century date ; it has two lights with a quatrefoil over in a two-centred head. The tower passes through the nave roof, and has an embattled parapet with a moulded string and square corner pinnacles, enriched with crocketed finials. The bell-chamber is lighted by plain square-headed lights.

The walling generally is of rubble ; that in the east chancel wall is of very small slaty material with large quoin stones. The embattled parapet of the chapel has large square stones with tiles between. The roofs are gabled, with plaster cradle-vaulted ceilings below to the chancel and nave, and a flat ceiling also of plaster to the chapel ; the latter is divided into panels by moulded wood beams. A few fragments of 14th and 15th-century glass remain in the nave windows.

In the chancel floor are nine old painted tiles of red and white patterns bearing the Berkeley arms, the same with a partly obliterated inscription 'adjuva nos Deus,' an oak leaf, a rose, a lily and a sword with cross keys. The altar table dates from the 18th century, and the east wall is panelled in oak of the same date. The font is modern except the bowl, which may be as early as the 12th century ; it is cup-shaped with a small roll around its lower edge and a modern moulded rim.

The church contains numerous ancient monuments, including several to members of the Berkeley family ; the most prominent is that of Rowland Berkeley, who purchased the Spetchley estate, and Katherine Haywood his wife, which stands between the chancel and chapel. It is an altar tomb with diagonal pedestals, on which are obelisks surmounted by balls. It bears the effigies of the pair in the dress of the period, with dogs at their feet, and above is a half-round canopy supported on each side by square fluted columns with Ionic capitals. The soffit is coffered, and at the springing on each side is a shield with Berkeley impaling Haywood. Rowland was buried in 1611 and his wife in 1629, and a slab in the floor of the chancel with their arms marks their grave. On the upper edge above the canopy are Gothic crockets, and in the middle of the arch on both sides are draped cartouches bearing the arms and crest.

Against the south wall of the chapel is the altar tomb of the founder, Serjeant Robert Berkeley, who died in 1656. The tomb is of black and white marble, and on it is his recumbent effigy in white marble robed in a judge's gown and holding a scroll. The epitaph is on the wall above, and over it is the shield of Berkeley with thirteen quarterings and thirteen shields around it, one for each quarter. In the north-west corner of the chapel is another large monument in white marble to Thomas Berkeley, who died in 1693, and his wife Anne, who died in 1692. Over the tomb is the shield of fourteen quarters and two lozenges, one with the arms Azure a sleeve or with a crescent for difference, for Elizabeth Conyers, his mother, and the other Azure a lion

or, for Anne Dayrell, his wife. In the opposite corner is the monument of his son Robert, who died in 1694, and Elizabeth his wife, who died in 1708. The arms over are Berkeley impaling Argent a cheveron between three wheat sheaves sable, for Blake. The other Berkeley monuments in the chapel are modern. In the chancel is a mural monument on the south wall to Anne daughter of Rowland and Katherine Berkeley, and wife of William Smyth, who died in 1638. In the floor are slabs of various dates, one with a brass inscription to Dr. William Smyth, rector of Tredington, Warden of Wadham and Vice-chancellor of Oxford, who died in 1658. Other slabs commemorate Thomas Berkeley, who died in 1719, the wife of Roland Crosby, who died in 1689, and Anna Smyth (undated).

In the Berkeley chapel is a 15th-century chest with a good lock plate.

There are four bells : the first, second and fourth with no inscription, the third with the inscription partly gone ; it is in crowned Lombardic capitals and reads 'Sancte Petre ora pro nobis.' [58]

The communion plate consists of a silver cup with no date mark, but apparently of about 1640, the maker's initials being R. T., a cover paten, a tankard flagon of the same make, and two stand patens of 1688, with the maker's initials D.B.

The registers before 1812 are as follows : (i) all entries, containing baptisms, burials and marriages 1539 to 1745 (with one baptism of 1784); (ii) baptisms and burials 1746 to 1812, marriages 1748 to 1753 ; (iii) marriages 1764 to 1810. There is also an account book with entries of gifts to the poor from 1801.

ADVOWSON The advowson of the church of Spetchley has always belonged to the lords of the manor,[59] and the present patron is Mr. Robert Valentine Berkeley.

The rectory of Spetchley was united with Warndon in 1874.[60]

Spetchley was originally a chapelry,[61] dependent upon the cathedral church of Worcester. The date at which it became parochial is not known, but it is called a church in 1291.[61a]

From the 13th century the priory of Worcester had a pension of 2s. from the church or chapel of Spetchley,[62] probably as a recognition of the rights of the mother church. This rent was granted after the Dissolution to the Dean and Chapter of Worcester.[63] Right of sepulture was granted to the inhabitants of Spetchley in 1561.[64]

In 1397 the rector of Spetchley obtained licence from the pope to let the rectory while he was studying at any university or in the service of any prelate in England or living at the Roman court.[65]

In 1574 an acre of land at Spetchley held by the churchwardens, formerly given for the maintenance of lights in the church, was granted to John and William Marsh.[66]

---

[58] Mr. H. B. Walters suggests the uninscribed bells are of the same date as the third, which was cast by John Barker of Worcester late in the 15th century (*Assoc. Arch. Soc. Papers*, xxv, 562).

[59] Feet of F. Worcs. Mich. 33 Hen. VI, no. 48 ; East. 37 Hen. VI, no. 50 ; and other references to the manor ; *Reg. G. Giffard* (Worcs. Hist. Soc.), 496 ; *Sede Vacante Reg.* (Worcs. Hist. Soc.), 379,

403, 408 ; Inst. Bks. (P.R.O.). In 1286 Maud de Churchill presented to the church of Spetchley (*Reg. G. Giffard*, 285). She had in 1266 obtained a grant of a yearly rent of 4s. from Spetchley, which had been forfeited by John her husband (*Cal. Pat.* 1258-66, p. 546).

[60] *Lond. Gaz.* 15 May 1874, p. 2574.

[61] *Reg. of Worc. Priory* (Camd. Soc.), 92a, 156a.

[61a] *Pope Nich. Tax.* (Rec. Com.), 216.

[62] *Reg. of Worc. Priory* (Camd. Soc.), 92a, 156a ; *Valor Eccl.* (Rec. Com.), iii, 225.

[63] Pat. 33 Hen. VIII, pt. v, m. 19 ; *L. and P. Hen. VIII*, xvii, g. 71 (29) ; Pat. 6 Jas. I, pt. xii, no. 2.

[64] Nash, op. cit. ii, 364.

[65] *Cal. Papal Letters*, v, 25.

[66] Pat. 16 Eliz. pt. xii, m. 18.

CHARITIES In 1767 Moses Hyett, by his will, gave £80, the interest thereon to be distributed to the poor. An unknown donor, as mentioned in the Parliamentary Returns of 1786, gave £30 to the poor. A sum of £110,

representing these two gifts, was in 1872 invested in £119 4s. 10d. consols with the official trustees. The annual dividends, amounting to £2 19s. 4d., are distributed in coal on St. Thomas's Day to about ten recipients.

STOKE PRIOR

Stochan (ix cent.) ; Stoche (xi cent.) ; Stoka (xiii cent.) ; Stoke Prior (xvi cent.).

Stoke Prior is a large parish lying in mid-Worcestershire to the north-east of the town of Droitwich. It has an area of 3,835 acres,[1] of which 994 are arable land, 2,232 permanent grass and 1½ woods.[2] The village of Stoke Prior, in the west of the parish, lies in the valley of the Salwarpe, at about 200 ft. above the ordnance datum, but the land rises in the north, reaching a height of over 400 ft. at Finstall. The subsoil is Keuper Marl and the upper soil is clay, growing crops of wheat, barley and turnips.

The village lies on the Bromsgrove and Alcester high road, which passes through the parish from north to south, connecting the village with the hamlet of Sharpway Gate on the southern boundary of the parish. A branch from this road at Stoke Heath leads north-east to Aston Fields and Finstall.

The River Salwarpe, which rises in the Lickey Hills, flows south-west through the parish. On its course through Stoke Prior it is fed by several tributaries, of which the most important is Sugar Brook. On the banks of the Salwarpe lies the village of Stoke Prior, the inhabitants of which are almost exclusively engaged in the manufacture of salt. A new village has sprung up in the course of the last century to the south of the original settlement, clustering round the Stoke Prior Salt Works. These were built by Mr. Corbett, and now belong to the Salt Union. Salt was found here in 1828,[3] and the works are now the most complete and compact in the world.[4]

The Stoke Farm Reformatory for Boys, to the south of the village, was founded by Joseph Sturge about the middle of the 19th century,[5] and is managed by a committee under Government inspection. It contains on an average eighty inmates, who are employed in gardening, tailoring, carpentry, shoemaking, and general work on the farm. Near the Reformatory is the Colonial Training College, which has for its object the practical training in domestic work of ladies desiring to proceed to the colonies. To the north of the village at Stoke Heath[6] is the Grange, the residence of Mr. Arthur James Norton. To the west are needle-scouring mills,[7] and to the

south-east is an old pound. To the south of the village are workshops and a wharf on the Worcester and Birmingham Canal, which passes through a great many locks in its passage through the parish of Stoke Prior.

Finstall, now a separate ecclesiastical parish, lies in the north, and practically constitutes a suburb of Bromsgrove. It includes Finstall Park, of 120 acres, the property of Mr. Ernest Montague Everitt, J.P., and now occupied by Mr. John Boultbee Brooks, J.P. The village hall was presented to the parish in 1904 by Miss Albright, and is used for religious services on Sundays and as a men's social club during the week.

The newer portion grouped round Bromsgrove station is locally known as Aston Fields and lies to the south of Finstall. It is a populous district, inhabited by the employees of the Midland Railway's wagon works, which are in this parish. The Aston Fields Workmen's Club was opened in 1891.

The Bristol and Birmingham branch of the Midland railway runs through the parish from south-west to north-east, with a station called Stoke Works near the salt works. This is also the terminus of the Stoke branch of the Great Western railway. Bromsgrove station lies in this parish, to the west of Aston Fields, and to the north of Finstall is the beginning of the Lickey incline on the Midland railway, with a gradient of 1 in 37.

An Inclosure Act for Stoke Prior was passed in 1772,[8] and the award is dated 9 December 1772.[9]

Two armlets have been found, with the remains of a skeleton, near Stoke Prior.[10]

The following place-names have been found : La Syche[11] (xiii cent.) ; Casbridge and Kinchfords[12] (xviii cent.) ; and Lower and Upper Gambolds (xix cent.).

The land of ten tributaries at STOKE MANOR PRIOR was given to the monks of Worcester by Huthrid (Uhtred), subregulus of the Hwiccas, in 770.[13] Bishop Oswald leased 6 cassates at Stoke[14] to the thegn Eadmaer for three lives in 967,[15] and at the date of the Domesday Survey the monks of Worcester held Stoke Prior, which, with its berewicks of Eston[16] and Bedindone,[17] contained 10 hides.[18]

[1] 29 acres are covered by water. The part of Stoke Prior in Bromsgrove Urban District, containing 2 acres, became a separate civil parish under the Local Government Act, 1894, and is now called Stoke in Bromsgrove (Census of Engl. and Wales, 1901, Worcs. 23 note).
[2] Statistics from Bd. of Agric. (1905).
[3] V.C.H. Worcs. ii, 263.
[4] In 1561-2 there were forty-nine families in this parish, and in 1776 110 (Nash, op. cit. ii, 381). The population in 1901 was 2,744 (Census of Engl. and Wales, 1901, Worcs. 23).
[5] Noake, Guide to Worcs. 328.
[6] There are disused brickfields in this part of the parish.
[7] These mills belonged to Richard

Wagstaff and were burnt down at a loss of £500 in 1772 (Prattinton Coll. [Soc. Antiq.]).
[8] Priv. Act, 12 Geo. III, cap. 97.
[9] Blue Bk. Incl. Awards, 191.
[10] V.C.H. Worcs. i, 197.
[11] Nash, op. cit. ii, 379. [12] Ibid. 380.
[13] Heming, Chartul. (ed. Hearne), 322 ; Birch, Cart. Sax. i, 289. The boundaries of the land are given in this charter.
[14] This entry may refer to Stoke Prior.
[15] Heming, op. cit. 234 ; Birch, op. cit. iii, 481. Eadmaer was succeeded by Brihtmær (Birch, loc. cit.).
[16] Land at Aston on the River Salwarpe was granted in 767 by Uhtred, subregulus of the Hwiccas, to Ethelmund son of Ingeld, an ealdorman and praefectus of King Ethel-

bald (Birch, op. cit. i, 286). The grant was renewed for three lives in 770, and in this charter, which is incomplete, there seems to be a clause granting the reversion to the church of Worcester (ibid. 287), to which it certainly afterwards passed. The name still remains at Aston Fields, but the manor must have become incorporated with that of Stoke Prior at an early date.
[17] The berewick of Bedindone evidently became merged in Stoke Prior Manor, but the mill of Bodinton or Baddington followed the descent of the manor until the middle of the 17th century or later (Habington, op. cit. i, 385 ; Close, 1650, pt. xx, no. 36).
[18] V.C.H. Worcs. i, 298a.

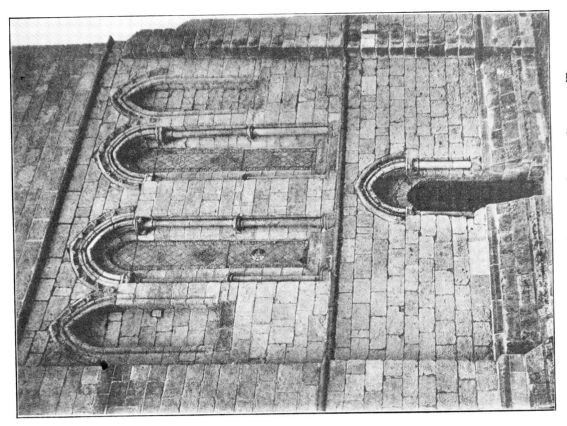

STOKE PRIOR CHURCH : DETAIL OF GROUND STAGE OF TOWER

STOKE PRIOR CHURCH FROM THE SOUTH-EAST

In 1207 King John acquitted the manor from suits at shire and hundred and from aids of sheriff, reeve and bailiff, and granted the monks sac and soc, thol and theam, infangentheof and other liberties.[19] In the time of Henry III the prior appropriated about 5 acres in the common of forest (communa foreste) at Stoke,[20] and about the same time he assarted about half a virgate in Woderewe at Stoke in Feckenham Forest.[21] It was probably the latter land (called half an acre) which was released by Henry III in 1248 from all rents usually levied on assarted land in the forest, on condition that the prior should appropriate no more land without licence.[22]

The chamberlain of the monastery, to whom this manor belonged,[23] leased it from time to time.[24] In 1225 it returned to his hands on the death of Reginald de Shortgrave, the farmer.[25] There were over fifty villeins on the manor,[26] and two free tenants, who paid 10s. a year rent.[27]

The manor remained in the possession of the priory[28] until the dissolution of the house in 1540,[29] and was granted to the Dean and Chapter of Worcester in 1542.[30] This grant was confirmed by James I in 1609,[31] and the manor remained with the dean and chapter until 21 March 1650, when it was sold by the Parliamentary Commissioners to John Fownes for £685.[32] At the Restoration it was recovered by the dean and chapter, and was confirmed to them in 1692.[33] They continued to hold it until 1859,[34] when it was taken over by the Ecclesiastical Commissioners, who still own it.[35]

In 1780 both courts leet and courts baron were still held for this manor,[36] but they have lately fallen into disuse. Some court rolls and rentals of this manor are preserved in the muniment room of the Dean and Chapter of Worcester.[37]

At the date of the Domesday Survey the Prior of Worcester had two mills on his manor of Stoke Prior, rendering 2 ounces of silver yearly.[38] In 1240 Robert the chaplain held these mills for the term of his life, and paid an annual rent of 32s.[39] There was also a fulling-mill, which brought in 40s. a year.[40] A corn-mill called Baddington Mill on 'Salop' Brook was included in the sale of the manor to John Fownes in 1650.[41] The present Stoke Prior Mills are on the River Salwarpe, to the south-west of the village. Bant Mill on Spadesbourne Brook is on the eastern boundary, Sugarbrook Mill is at the junction of Sugar Brook with the Salwarpe, and Fish House Mill is a corn-mill on the Salwarpe to the north-east of the village. The needle-scouring mill in the village has been mentioned above.

The church of ST. MICHAEL
CHURCHES   consists of a chancel 40 ft. by 13½ ft., north vestry 8½ ft. by 9½ ft., north chapel (St. Catherine's) 18 ft. by 10 ft., tower (south of the chancel) 16¼ ft. by 15½ ft., with a small Lady chapel east of it 7 ft. wide by 8½ ft., nave 56 ft. by 18½ ft., north aisle of the whole length of the nave and 8½ ft. wide, with a modern vestry to the north of it, south aisle to the eastern half of the nave 29 ft. long and 9 ft. wide, and a south porch. These measurements are all internal.

The earliest church of which there are any remains dates from the first half of the 12th century, at which time it consisted of a chancel and nave with a north aisle.

About 1180 a small chapel was added at the east end of the north aisle with an archway opening into the chancel. At the same time the building of the tower was begun, the north and west arches being the first work ; whether the latter really opened into an existing aisle is doubtful. More probably it was inserted preparatory to the addition of an aisle at a later date. The building of the tower seems to have lingered for some time, and the greater part of the superstructure is work of about 1200. The small chapel to our Lady east of it is a peculiar feature, but seems to have been part of the original plan. About thirty years later the chancel was lengthened eastwards and the north vestry built, and this was followed by the addition of the south aisle with its arcade of two bays about 1250, which is one of the most beautiful portions of the church. In the 14th century the east window was enlarged, a new window inserted in the south wall of the chancel, and the space between the 13th-century vestry and the north chapel was closed in and roofed over, the east wall of the latter being removed and the archway from the chancel considerably widened. The outer walls of the south aisle were rebuilt in the 15th century, and the former wood porch in the angle of the nave and aisle was, perhaps, of the same period.

At various times in the 19th century the church underwent much rebuilding and repair, the north and west walls being rebuilt, the nave reroofed, a new vestry added, and a new south porch being erected in place of the ancient porch, the woodwork of which now serves as a lych-gate.

The 14th-century east window is of five lights under a pointed head filled with net tracery, and has been considerably restored. The north-east window is a 13th-century lancet with widely splayed internal jambs. The pointed segmental rear arch has apparently been lowered.

The pointed doorway into the vestry of a single chamfered order has been recut, and a straight joint in the walling between it and the lancet window possibly marks the length of the former chancel. The south window is of two lights under a traceried head

[19] Cal. Rot. Chart. 1199–1216 (Rec. Com.), 168 ; Pipe R. 9 John, m. 19 d.
[20] Hund. R. (Rec. Com.), ii, 284a.
[21] Ibid. 286.
[22] Cal. Pat. 1247–58, p. 5.
[23] Reg. of Worc. Priory (Camd. Soc.), 99b.
[24] Ann. Mon. (Rolls Ser.), iv, 397, 404.
[25] Ibid. 418.
[26] Reg. of Worc. Priory (Camd. Soc.), 100, 101, 102. This was the largest number of villeins on any of the manors belonging to the priory.
[27] Ibid. Introd. p. xvii.
[28] The customs of the manor are set

out in a survey made in 1240 (Reg. of Worc. Priory [Camd. Soc.], Introd. p. xv ; 102a and b).
[29] V.C.H. Worcs. ii, 111.
[30] L. and P. Hen. VIII, xvii, g. 71 (29); Pat. 33 Hen. VIII, pt. v.
[31] Pat. 6 Jas. I, pt. xii, no. 2.
[32] Close, 1650, pt. xx, no. 36. The manor was then chargeable with an annuity of £13 6s. 8d. towards the maintenance of the Free Grammar School, Worcester.
[33] Pat. 4 Will. and Mary, pt. i, no. 6.
[34] Lond. Gaz. 16 Dec. 1859, p. 4757 ; confirmed by Stat. 31 Vict. cap. 19. In

1836 an Act was passed empowering the dean and chapter to enfranchise and sell to the British Alkali Company 8 acres of land called Lower Leasow (Priv. Act, 6 & 7 Will. IV, cap. 33).
[35] Information supplied by the Ecclesiastical Commissioners.
[36] Nash, op. cit. ii, 380.
[37] Hist. MSS. Com. Rep. xiv, App. viii, 184.   [38] V.C.H. Worcs. i, 298a.
[39] Reg. of Worc. Priory (Camd. Soc.), 99b.   [40] Ibid.
[41] Close, 1650, pt. xx, no. 36. It had been leased to Henry Hodback for three lives on 23 June 1631.

of the 14th century. Below it are the 13th-century piscina and sedilia ; the former has a rough trefoiled head, a circular basin and a modern shelf. The three sedilia are divided by detached octagonal shafts supporting pointed and moulded heads ; above the shafts, in the spandrels, are small grotesque crouching figures. A moulded string-course runs along the wall face on either side of the sanctuary, and to the east of the 14th-century window in the south wall are signs of a blocked 13th-century lancet window. Square clasping buttresses support the angles of the east wall ; their upper halves with the gable end have been renewed. The archway into the north chapel has jambs with bowtels and a half-round shaft on the inner face ; the west jamb appears to be the original transitional one, the capital of the half-shaft being carved with a pointed leaf decoration and the other capitals with bold projecting flowers. In the east jamb the bases differ slightly and may be later, and the capital of the half-shaft here is plain. The two-centred drop arch has been widened and is obviously later. The jambs of

The north chapel or chapel of St. Catherine has a two-light 14th-century window resembling the south-east window of the chancel, but differently moulded ; the window is set above the eaves course in a gabled head. To the west of it is a small round-headed light with a square external order ; the jambs are old, and probably belonged to the original transitional light of the chapel. The arch from the aisle has been much modernized and a rood stair which stood here early in the 19th century [42] has been cleared away, but the upper door can still be seen above the north jamb of the chancel arch.

The western arch of the tower has jambs similar to those of the north arch, but with an extra chamfered outer order. The northern capital to the half-round shaft is scalloped, but that to the south jamb is moulded. The arch is pointed and of three orders. The building east of the tower probably served only as an altar recess to the chapel formed by the base of the tower. It has a pointed barrel vault and a moulded pointed arch opening into it. In the east wall are two lancets, all modern outside, and a third, original, in the south wall. To the west of the last is a trefoiled piscina. Over the chantry or altar recess is a large lancet window which has a later and lower rear arch below the wood ceiling, the upper part of the window, which is visible in the chamber above, being filled in. The external jambs have detached shafts with moulded bases and carved capitals ; the arches are moulded and have labels carved with square flowers. Externally on either side of this window are blind recesses with a continuous edge roll to the jambs and arches and moulded labels. In the south wall of the tower is a small doorway, the jambs of which contain detached shafts on the outer face with bases and carved capitals. The head has a moulded outer arch forming a sort of tympanum. The deeply splayed plinth around the tower is cut through square by this doorway, which appears to be an insertion of slightly later date. Above it are a moulded string and two lancet windows with banded jamb shafts like that in the east wall ; they are, however, at a lower level and of greater length. These windows are also flanked by two recesses (resembling those in the east wall) carried down to the level of the bands of the window shafts. Higher up another string-course marks the second stage outside, and the shallow clasping buttresses at the angles stop below it. The stair turret rises in the south-west corner, projecting slightly both ways, and is lighted by narrow slits. The third stage of the tower was till recently a blind story, but two modern lancets

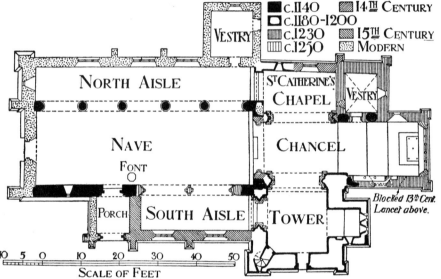

Legend:
■ c.1140   ▨ 14TH CENTURY
☐ c.1180-1200
▥ c.1230   ▧ 15TH CENTURY
▥ c.1250   ▨ MODERN

VESTRY · NORTH AISLE · NAVE · FONT · PORCH · SOUTH AISLE · St CATHERINE'S CHAPEL · VESTRY · CHANCEL · TOWER · *Blocked 13th Cent. Lancet above.*

SCALE OF FEET

PLAN OF STOKE PRIOR CHURCH

the tower arch, though of greater thickness, are similar to those opposite. The capitals are, however, quite different, some being scalloped and others foliated. The arch is pointed and of three orders with a moulded label. The chancel arch is probably a 14th-century alteration of an earlier one and has been much repaired with modern stonework.

The 13th-century vestry is lighted in its east wall by an old lancet with a triangular pointed head ; another lancet on its west side has been filled in, probably when the north chapel was enlarged in the 14th century. The chamber is vaulted in stone with chamfered diagonal ribs springing from angle corbels moulded with some elaboration. There is a chamber above, which is lighted on its east side by a lancet with old jambs and a new head. It was probably entered by an outer doorway on the north side, but its traces have been concealed by the modern stonework in the upper part of the wall. The north-eastern corner is strengthened by a clasping buttress, but that to the other angle has been displaced by a 14th-century buttress greatly repaired.

[42] Prattinton Coll. (Soc. Antiq.), v, 31 (1811).

STOKE PRIOR CHURCH : THE SOUTH ARCADE

STOKE PRIOR CHURCH : THE NAVE LOOKING EAST

now admit the light from the north side. The fourth stage or bell-chamber is lighted by a triplet of lancets on each side with jambs of two orders, the outer having engaged shafts with moulded bases and bell capitals. Edge rolls are cut on the external angles in this stage. The upper part of the parapet is modern and plain, but the ancient corbel tabling still remains; each space is trefoiled and the corbels are carved as billet moulds with human heads and rams' heads arranged in irregular sequence. On the face of the stair turret is a sundial, apparently of cement, dated 1663. A tall timber spire covered with oak shingles crowns the tower; it is square at the base and splayed back to octagonal form from the parapet.

The nave has an early 12th-century north arcade of five bays with circular columns and half-round arches of two square orders. There are indications in the last pier to the west that the end bay is slightly later in date and the mouldings of the western respond base differ from the others. There is, however, nothing else left to verify this extension of the nave. The capitals are all of plain section with grooved and chamfered abaci and follow the forms of the piers. The 13th-century south arcade consists of two bays of graceful proportions and rich detail. The middle column is circular with four engaged shafts, and the responds are similar to half the column. The bases are of the water-table type, and the capitals have moulded bells with overhanging abaci. Part of the eastern respond, which had been cut away to let light into the pulpit, was restored in 1848. The arches are pointed and of two elaborately moulded orders, with a moulded label on the nave face, stopping on a bunch of foliage above the central column. The 12th-century south doorway of the nave has jambs of two orders, the outer with detached shafts in the angles, partly restored, and with capitals carved with stiff-leaf foliage. The arch is of two semicircular orders, and on the face of the wall to the west is cut or scratched an interlacing pattern. The south-west window to the west of the south doorway is a small 12th-century round-headed lancet, chamfered outside, and with splayed jambs and semicircular rear arch inside. The modern west doorway is said to have replaced a late 15th-century one. The window over, also modern, has three lights under a traceried head.

The south aisle is lighted by two 15th-century windows, each of three lights beneath a four-centred arch. A buttress of one stage between these windows has a niche upon its face with a trefoiled head. The parapet of the aisle is embattled, with pinnacles above the two buttresses, both set diagonally, that over the middle buttress being alone original. The three side windows of the north aisle are modern, and have each three lights in a square head. Below the middle window are the jambs of a 12th-century doorway, which were discovered and left in position at the rebuilding of the wall. The west window is a modern round-headed single light. The deep raking plinth to the west walls of the aisle and nave appears to be old, but the upper walling is nearly all new. The walling throughout is of ashlar stonework, and the south-west portion of the nave has been picked to receive plaster. All the roofs appear to be modern except the flat roof of the south aisle, which retains its original moulded

principal timbers. The chancel is gabled and open timbered below and the nave is barrel-vaulted.

The octagonal font is of the 15th century. The sides of the bowl are panelled, and carved with two censing angels and four bearing shields. On the north the subject represented appears to be a baptism, in which a figure stands before a small font with angels in the top corners holding up his robe. The south face is quite blank, suggesting that the font originally stood against the wall. The under edge of the bowl is carved with Tudor roses, with a row of ornamental cresting above, and in the middle of the stem is a projecting band with carved flowers on its face. The other fittings are modern. In the vestry off the chancel is an old chest cut from a solid tree trunk.

In the south aisle lies an ancient stone coffin lid or slab, on which is the recumbent effigy of a priest; he appears to be holding a chalice, but the whole is much mutilated. On the east wall of St. Catherine's chapel, and hidden by the organ, is a brass with figures of Robert Smith, citizen and draper of London and 'free of the famous company of Marchant Adventurers,' who died in 1609, and his two wives[43] and children. The brass is set in a panelled stone slab. In the south aisle is another brass commemorating Henry Smith, also citizen and draper of London, who died in 1606; this brass must also have been set in a stone slab, which has now gone.

In the east lancet of the tower is some ancient glass, brought from the Priory Church, Great Malvern, including the inscription 'letabor in misericordia.'

Of the eight bells the first two are of 1897, the third and fourth 1886, the fifth was cast by Henry Bagley, 1676, the sixth is dated 1663, the seventh has the motto 'Honi soit qui mal y pensi (sic) 1620' and the tenor was a 1663 bell recast in 1886.

The communion plate consists of a silver-gilt cup and paten of 1848 and a pewter flagon and almsdish.

The registers before 1812 are as follows : (i) baptisms from 1564, burials from 1557, marriages from 1574, all to 1710; (ii) baptisms and burials 1710 to 1812, marriages 1712 to 1754; (iii) marriages 1755 to 1812.

The new church of *ST. GODWALD* at Finstall, built in 1883, consists of a chancel, south transept (containing the organ and vestry), nave and south porch. The style is of the early 14th century, and the materials are red sandstone with tiled roofs, the interior being faced with white bricks. A south vestry and north transept are included in the design, but not yet completed. The disused church of St. Godwald, which stands a short distance to the eastward, close to the railway, is a small rectangular building of red brick with stone dressings, lighted by plain pointed windows, and having a gallery at the west end. The roof is slated, and over the west door is a stone tablet recording the rebuilding of the church in 1773. The 18th-century fittings still remain, and the whole building is in the last stage of disrepair. It is now used as a mortuary chapel.

ADVOWSONS At the date of the Domesday Survey the Prior of Worcester had a priest on his manor of Stoke Prior.[44] A church there is mentioned in 1240, and to it

[43] The first wife was Thomasin daughter of Arthur Dedicoate of Hackney and the second Susan daughter of Richard Pipe, kt., and Lord Mayor of London.

[44] *V.C.H. Worcs.* i, 298a.

belonged a *curia* and half a hide of land and the tithes of Crufting, as a composition for the tithes of the demesne.[45] The advowson belonged to the prior and convent,[46] and remained in their possession until the Dissolution.[47] In 1389 the prior and convent received a licence from the Crown to appropriate the church for the use of the chamberlain.[48]

The advowson and rectory[49] were granted to the dean and chapter in 1542,[50] and the advowson has remained with them ever since.[51]

John Toy, who was vicar in 1641, was the author of a poem describing the Plague in Worcester.[52] In July 1656 the council ordered that the sum of £40 a year should be settled on Richard Dowly, the minister, to augment the very small value of the vicarage.[53]

The chapel dedicated to St. Godwald at Finstall in this parish is mentioned in 1390, when all oblations received there were assigned to the vicar as part of his stipend.[54] These oblations amounted to 23s. 4d. in 1535.[55] The chapel and chapel yard formerly called St. Godwald's Chapel in Stoke Prior were granted in 1575–6 to John Mershe and others.[56] Under the Stoke Prior Inclosure Act of 1772 5 acres of the common were allotted to the chapel of St. Godwald, and the allotment was to be held by the vicar of Stoke Prior or his nominee.[57] A district was assigned to the chapel in 1868,[58] and it was endowed with £50 out of the common fund of the Ecclesiastical Commissioners in 1869,[59] and with a further sum of £150 in 1879.[60] The living is a vicarage in the gift of the vicar of Stoke Prior.

In Stoke Prior Works there is a Wesleyan Methodist chapel. At Aston Fields there is a Primitive Methodist Sunday school, built in 1891, and a council school.

CHARITIES Henry Smith, citizen and draper of London, who died in 1606, as recorded on a brass plate in the parish church, gave by will to Stoke Prior, where he was born, £100 to be laid out in land, the rent whereof should be employed in the payment of 40s. a year for four or six sermons a year to be preached by strangers, 'the rest of the rent to be employed for the freeing the poorer sort of boys' schooling, to be elected as therein mentioned.'

The legacy was laid out in the purchase of a close called Mott's Furlong, containing 7 a. or thereabouts.

The land is let at £15 a year, which, subject to the payment of 40s. for sermons, is applicable for educational purposes.

Charity of John Saunders for apprenticing.—In the table of benefactions it is stated that Mr. John Saunders, grocer, of London, gave by his will £10 a year for the placing of a boy of Upton Warren, Stoke Prior, or Chaddesley Corbett at May Day. An annual payment of £10 is made by the Grocers' Company, and is applied in the first-named parish. (See under Upton Warren, Halfshire Hundred.)

It is further stated in the same table that Joseph Fownes by his will left for the poor £20, and that the Rev. James Johnson, a former vicar, left £5. A cottage and land at Stoke Heath were purchased therewith, and are now represented by two plots containing together 1 a. 3 r. 36 p., producing yearly £6, which is distributed in bread to about fifty recipients.

In 1874 Joseph Page, by his will proved at Worcester 22 August, bequeathed £300, the interest to be applied for the benefit of agricultural labourers, their wives and children on St. Thomas's Day. The legacy was invested in £316 12s. 6d. consols with the official trustees, the annual dividends, amounting to £7 18s. 4d., being duly applied.

The official trustees also hold a sum of £194 14s. consols, arising from the sale of the old National school buildings at Finstall comprised in a deed of 9 September 1848. The annual dividends, amounting to £4 17s. 4d., are, under a scheme of 15 November 1898, applied in prizes and rewards to school children.

STOULTON

Stoltun (ix and xi cent.); Stulton (xv cent.); Stowton (xvii cent.).

Stoulton is a small parish lying between Worcester and Pershore and covering an area of 1,959 acres, of which the greater part is arable land, 961 acres being permanent grass and 16 woodland.[1] The soil is chiefly clay, gravel and sand, and the subsoil Lower Lias, producing crops of wheat, beans, barley, turnips and fruit. The ground varies in height from 79 ft. above the ordnance datum in the south-east near Stonebow Bridge to about 200 ft. on the borders of White Ladies Aston in the north.

The parish is watered by the Bow Brook, which divides it from Peopleton, and by two of its tributaries, one of which, known as the Saw Brook, forms the boundary between Stoulton and White Ladies Aston. The village is situated on rising ground on the main road from Worcester to Pershore.[2] A wooden bridge and 'causey' over the stream near Hawbridge, where the road enters Holy Cross, were built in 1625 by George Allen, curate of Stoulton, with £5 given by the Dean and Chapter of Worcester and 5s. 4d. of his own money.[3] The main road from Worcester to Evesham forms the north-eastern

---

[45] *Reg. of Worc. Priory* (Camd. Soc.), 100a.   [46] Ibid.

[47] *Reg. G. Giffard* (Worcs. Hist. Soc.), 58, 429; *Cal. Pat.* 1388–92, p. 164; *L. and P. Hen. VIII*, xvii, g. 71 (29).

[48] *Cal. Pat.* 1388–92, p. 164; Inq. a.q.d. file 408, no. 112; *Cal. Papal Letters*, iv, 519. The vicarage was ordained in 1390 (Nash, op. cit. ii, 384).

[49] The rectory of Stoke Prior was valued with that of Berrow in 1535 (*Valor Eccl.* [Rec. Com.], iii, 225).

[50] *L. and P. Hen. VIII*, xvii, g. 71 (29); Pat. 33 Hen. VIII, pt. v.

[51] Pat. 6 Jas. I, pt. xii, no. 2; Inst. Bks. (P.R.O.). In 1641 Christopher Potter made the presentation for one turn only (Inst. Bks.).

[52] *Dict. Nat. Biog.*

[53] *Cal. S. P. Dom.* 1656–7, p. 15.

[54] Nash, op. cit. ii, 384.

[55] *Valor Eccl.* (Rec. Com.), iii, 269.

[56] Pat. 18 Eliz. pt. ii.

[57] Priv. Act, 12 Geo. III, cap. 97.

[58] *Lond. Gaz.* 11 Dec. 1868, p. 6586.

[59] Ibid. 21 May 1869, p. 2952.

[60] Ibid. 15 Aug. 1879, p. 4984.

[1] Statistics from Bd. of Agric. (1905).

[2] In 1637 the highway in Little Wolverton between Worcester and Stonebow was in great decay through the default of Thomas Acton and Thomas Riborn (*Quart. Sess. R.* [Worcs. Hist. Soc.], 643).

[3] Note on the fly-leaf of the first book of registers at Stoulton; Nash, *Hist. of Worcs.* ii, 24.

STOULTON CHURCH : THE SOUTH DOORWAY

STOKE PRIOR CHURCH : INTERIOR OF GROUND STAGE OF TOWER
SHOWING CHAPEL TO EAST

boundary of Stoulton for some distance. The Great Western railway passes through the parish and has a station on the south-eastern boundary.

The village is composed of scattered houses and cottages, many of half-timber and brick dating from the 17th century. On the north side of the church, which stands a little distance to the east of the main road, is the vicarage ; the nucleus of the house appears to be of the 17th century, but there is an early 19th-century addition on the west. At the corner where the by-road to the church joins the main road is a square 18th-century plastered brick house of three stories with a tiled roof and a large central chimney stack, and off the main road, about a quarter of a mile to the west, is a two-storied half-timber house, dating probably from the 16th century, with 18th-century brick nogging. The plan is L-shaped, and there are projecting chimney stacks in the end walls. The roof is partly thatched and partly tiled. Inside are the original heavy ceiling beams and rafters and three wide fireplaces. A projecting beam on the east has the letter W cut on its face and a date, which may be intended for 1710, probably the date of the brickwork. About half a mile south of Stoulton station is a good three-story brick house of the 18th century, now tied with iron bolts and glands, and at Wolverton Magna is a 16th-century half-timber house with later brick nogging and modern chimney stacks. Wolverton Hall, the property of Mr. William Walter Acton, a descendant of the Thomas Acton who in 1637 neglected to repair the road at Stonebow, and now occupied by Mr. Anthony H. Lechmere, D.L., stands about a mile north-east of the station ; it is a plain square three-story house of the first half of the 18th century built of brick with stone rusticated quoins, brick string-courses and a plain parapet. On the garden front the string-courses are of stone and the windows have keystones of the same material.

Cookes Holme, formerly part of Stoulton, was transferred to Norton by Kempsey in 1885.[4]

Among the many complaints brought against the last Abbot of Pershore in 1533 is one by the tenants of Stoulton of 'great injuries, wrongs and oppressions' done to them in driving their cattle from the heaths of Thornton, Wolverton, Wadborough, Mucknell and Over Wolverton. The abbot's answer shows that the matter had already been submitted to arbitration.[5]

The first mention of STOULTON MANORS occurs in 840, when Bertwulf, King of the Mercians, is said to have restored it to the Bishop of Worcester, who had been unjustly deprived of it.[6] Before the Conquest Stoulton was a berewick belonging to the Bishop of Worcester's manor of Kempsey and was assigned with Mucknell and Wolverton, two other berewicks of the same manor, to the support of the monks of Worcester, the three berewicks together containing 7 hides. At the time of the Domesday Survey these 7 hides were in the possession of Urse the Sheriff.[7] The overlordship belonged to the Bishops of Worcester until it lapsed, probably in the 15th century.[8] In 1280 William Earl of Warwick, then lord of the manor, acknowledged that he owed 6 marks yearly to Godfrey, Bishop of Worcester, and agreed to pay it to the nuns of Wroxall,[9] giving a bond to the bishop for the payment of the same in 1298.[10] No later mention of this rent has been found, and there is no trace of it among the possessions of Wroxall at the Dissolution.

Urse's interest passed with the rest of his possessions to the Beauchamps of Elmley, and followed the descent of Elmley Castle[11] until the death of Henry Duke of Warwick in 1446.[12] It was assigned in 1447 to his widow Cecily,[13] and after her death in 1450 it seems to have passed to Elizabeth wife of George Lord Latimer, a half-sister of Henry Duke of Warwick,[14] for she died seised of the manor of Wadborough, of which Stoulton formed part,[15] in 1480,[16] and the manor remained with her descendants in spite of the fact that it is included among the manors which Anne Countess of Warwick granted to Henry VII, and which were confirmed to Henry VIII by Act of Parliament in 1536.[17]

Elizabeth Lady Latimer was succeeded by her grandson Sir Richard,[18] who was dealing with the manor in 1523,[19] and on whose death in 1530 it passed to his son Sir John Nevill, Lord Latimer.[20]

He, by his will dated September 1542, left it to his eldest son John.[21] The latter died in 1577, leaving four daughters, Katherine, Dorothy, Lucy and Elizabeth, between whom his property was divided.[22] Stoulton was assigned to Katherine and settled on her first husband, Henry Percy Earl of Northumberland, in 1579,[23] and on her second husband, Francis Fitton of Binfield, co. Berks., in 1586.[24] By the second settlement it was arranged that the reversion should belong to the heirs of Katherine, but in 1595 she sold it to Francis Fitton to increase the portions of her younger sons William and Jocelyn Percy and her daughter Eleanor.[25] Accordingly the manor passed to Sir Edward Fitton, bart., nephew of Francis, who held it in 1625,[26] and he sold it to Samuel Sandys of Ombersley for £7,300 in 1636.[27] The latter was a prominent Royalist, a colonel in the king's army, and for a time governor

[4] *Census of Engl. and Wales,* 1891, ii, 657.
[5] *L. and P. Hen. VIII,* vi, 298 (vi).
[6] Birch, *Cart. Sax.* ii, 4 ; Heming, *Chartul.* (ed. Hearne), 26.
[7] *V.C.H. Worcs.* i, 288a.
[8] Ibid. 324a ; *Worcs. Inq. p.m.* (Worcs. Hist. Soc.), i, 63 ; ii, 66 ; Chan. Inq. p.m. 8 Hen. IV, no. 68 ; 18 Hen. VI, no. 3.
[9] *Cal. Close,* 1279–88, p. 43.
[10] *Reg. G. Giffard* (Worcs. Hist. Soc.), 489.
[11] For references see Elmley Castle. In 1396 the manor of Stoulton was granted to Thomas Earl of Kent (*Cal. Pat.* 1396–9, pp. 200, 215).

[12] Chan. Inq. p.m. 24 Hen. VI, no. 43.
[13] *Cal. Pat.* 1446–52, p. 38.
[14] G.E.C. *Complete Peerage,* v, 25.
[15] In the 15th century Stoulton is said to have been included in Wadborough (Anct. D. [*V.P.R.O.*], C. 714, 3323), and from the 16th to the 18th century is described as Stoulton with Wadborough.
[16] Chan. Inq. p.m. 20 Edw. IV, no. 73.
[17] De Banco R. Hil. 3 Hen. VII, m. 208 ; Stat. 28 Hen. VIII, cap. 22.
[18] Chan. Inq. p.m. 20 Edw. IV, no. 73.
[19] Recov. R. Trin. 15 Hen. VIII, rot. 353. [20] G.E.C. *Complete Peerage,* v, 25.
[21] Chan. Inq. p.m. (Ser. 2), lxv, 81 ; P.C.C. 17 Spert ; Chan. Proc. (Ser. 2), bdle. 133, no. 80.

[22] G.E.C. *Complete Peerage,* v, 26.
[23] Pat. 22 Eliz. pt. xii, m. 11 ; Feet of F. Div. Co. Trin. 21 Eliz. Richard Nevill cousin and heir male of John gave up any right he might have in the manor to Henry and Katherine in 1580 (Feet of F. Div. Co. Hil. 22 Eliz.).
[24] Pat. 28 Eliz. pt. iv, m. 21 ; Feet of F. Div. Co. Trin. 28 Eliz. ; see also Trin. 34 Eliz.
[25] Feet of F. Worcs. Trin. 37 Eliz. ; Chan. Inq. p.m. (Ser. 2), ccxlviii, 22.
[26] Feet of F. Worcs. East. 1 Chas. I ; Trin. 10 Chas. I ; Recov. R. Trin. 10 Chas. I, rot. 111.
[27] Close, 12 Chas. I, pt. xi, no. 7.

of Worcester.[28] He had to compound for delinquency, and mortgaged Stoulton, which passed to the family of Somers, who were solicitors in Worcester and engaged in mortgage transactions.[29] It was probably acquired from the Sandys family by John Somers, who died in 1716, leaving his property to his two sisters, Elizabeth wife of Sir Joseph Jekyll, who died childless, and Mary wife of Charles Cocks,[30] who finally inherited the whole. Her grandson Charles Cocks was created Lord Somers of Evesham in 1784, and his son John Somers Cocks was created Earl Somers in 1821.[31] Stoulton has since remained in his family,[32] and now belongs to his great-granddaughter Lady Henry Somerset, one of the two surviving daughters of Charles the last Earl Somers.

Cocks, Earl Somers. *Argent a cheveron between three pairs of harts' horns sable.*

A water-mill and windmill, together worth 8*s.* yearly, belonged to the manor in 1298,[33] but were both in ruins in 1315,[34] and are not mentioned again.

From the 16th century the lords of Stoulton had the right of free fishing in the 'Hymbell Brook' from 'Fecknam' Pool to the Avon.[35] 'Hymbell' is evidently another name for the Bow Brook which flows through Himbleton. Possibly it is this fishery which is mentioned in an extent of the manor in 1315.[36]

WOLVERTON (Wulfrintun, x cent. ; Uulfrinton, Ulfrinton, Wlfrinton, xi cent. ; Wolferton, xiv cent. ; Wollerton, xvi cent.) may have been included in the grant of Stoulton to the Bishop of Worcester. It was certainly in the possession of Bishop Oswald in 984, when he granted 3 manses there to his kinsman Eadwig and Wulfgifu his wife for their lives and the lives of two heirs after them.[37] Before the Conquest and at the time of the Domesday Survey there were two separate estates in Wolverton afterwards known as Over and Little Wolverton, both held of the bishop's manor of Kempsey. One of these, probably Over Wolverton, was with Stoulton and Mucknell assigned to the use of the monks of Worcester in the time of Edward the Confessor, and belonged to Urse the Sheriff in 1086.[38] The other is said to have been granted by Bishop Brihteah to his brother Alric,[39] who continued to hold it after the Conquest,[40] but he was deprived of it by William Earl of Hereford,[41]

and at the time of the Domesday Survey it was in the possession of Aiulf, who held it of Roger de Lacy.

The overlordship of Over Wolverton passed from Urse to his descendants the Beauchamps, and was probably included in 7½ hides at Mucknell and Stoulton held by William de Beauchamp in demesne early in the 13th century. Later it was held under them by a family called Bruly or Brayly. About 1280 and in 1315–16 it belonged to Walter de Bruly, who held it by service of keeping the Earl of Warwick's warren at Stoulton.[42] He was succeeded by John de Bruly, who with Joan his wife settled it on his son John and Alice his wife in 1336.[43] There appears to be no later mention of it as a separate holding, but it evidently came into the possession of the Beauchamps, and was annexed to their manor of Stoulton.[44]

The 2 hides at Little Wolverton were lost by the Lacys before 1108–18, when Walter de Beauchamp held them.[45] About 1182 it was said that William de Beauchamp held this land, though Hugh de Lacy ought to have held it of the bishop.[46] The rights of the bishop in this manor were recognized until the 13th century,[47] and William de Beauchamp's interest followed the descent of Elmley Castle, Little Wolverton being held of that manor until 1616.[48]

Aiulf, the Domesday tenant, was followed by a family who took their name from the manor. Philip de Wolverton probably held it in 1174–5, when his name occurs on the Pipe Rolls for the county of Worcester,[49] and early in the 13th century William de Wolverton was holding 2½ hides at Little Wolverton.[50] The extra half hide was perhaps the half hide of the demesne of Kempsey given by Bishop Simon (1125–50) to a certain son of Walter de Beauchamp called Simon, whom he had baptized. This land lay near Oswaldslow, and was locally called 'Beane' because all *hernasii* (*tota hernesse*) ploughed it at the summons of the steward and reeve.[51] Simon de Beauchamp probably died childless, for about 1182 this estate belonged to William de Beauchamp,[52] and was perhaps given with Little Wolverton to the Wolvertons. This family was succeeded before 1220 by the Folyes, who were lords of the manor for about 100 years.

In 1220 Nicholas de la Folye surrendered all his right in half a knight's fee in Little Wolverton to Richard de la Folye,[53] and about 1280 the manor belonged to Robert de la Folye.[54] Robert appears to have been succeeded by Peter de la Folye, whose widow Alice was holding part of the manor in dower in 1329.[55] At that date the reversion of the manor was divided between Sibyl wife of Peter le Harpour

[28] *Cal. Com. for Comp.* 1296.
[29] Inform. from Mr. J. Willis-Bund.
[30] G.E.C. *Complete Peerage*, vii, 167 ; Feet of F. Worcs. Mich. 4 Geo. I.
[31] G.E.C. *Complete Peerage*, vii, 166 ; Recov. R. Trin. 32 & 33 Geo. II, rot. 179 ; Trin. 22 Geo. III, rot. 164.
[32] Recov. R. D. Enr. Trin. 47 Geo. III, m. 38.
[33] *Worcs. Inq. p.m.* (Worcs. Hist. Soc.), i, 63.
[34] Ibid. ii, 66.
[35] Feet of F. Div. Co. Trin. 21 Eliz. The fishery is mentioned in most of the 17th-century documents relating to the manor (q.v.).
[36] *Worcs. Inq. p.m.* (Worcs. Hist. Soc.), ii, 66.

[37] Heming, op. cit. i, 153. The boundaries of the land are given.
[38] *V.C.H. Worcs.* i, 288*a*.
[39] Heming, op. cit. i, 266.
[40] *V.C.H. Worcs.* i, 288*a*. Alric is said to have rendered the same customary rents as his predecessors, except the peasants' labour, as it could be obtained from the reeve.
[41] Heming, op. cit. i, 266 ; *V.C.H. Worcs.* i, 288*b* n.
[42] *Lay Subs. R.* c. 1280 (Worcs. Hist. Soc.), 25 ; *Cal. Inq. p.m.* 1–9 *Edw. II*, 403 ; Add. MS. 28024, fol. 190*b*. In 1302 Walter was in prison at Worcester on the charge of murdering a certain Walter Botte (*Cal. Close*, 1296–1302, p. 564).

[43] Feet of F. Worcs. Mich. 10 Edw. III.
[44] Close, 9 Will. III, pt. ix, no. 15.
[45] *V.C.H. Worcs.* i, 324 n.
[46] Red Bk. of Bishopric of Worc. (Eccl. Com. Rec. Var. bdle. 121, no. 43698), fol. 253.
[47] *Testa de Nevill* (Rec. Com.), 41*b*.
[48] Chan. Inq. p.m. (Ser. 2), ccclv, 50.
[49] *Pipe R.* 21 Hen. II (Pipe R. Soc.), 128.
[50] *Testa de Nevill* (Rec. Com.), 41*b*.
[51] Red Bk. of Bishopric of Worc. fol. 49.
[52] Ibid.
[53] Feet of F. Worcs. 5 Hen. III, no. 18; Assize R. 1021, m. 1.
[54] *Lay Subs. R.* c. 1280 (Worcs. Hist. Soc.), 26.
[55] Feet of F. Worcs. East. 5 Edw. III, no. 36.

and Joan wife of Henry Bole, the heirs of Peter de la Folye,[56] who sold it in 1327-9 to John de Wysham and Hawisia his wife.[57] From this time the manor followed the descent of Churchill in Oswaldslow,[55] being divided between the Croft and Guise families. The moiety held by the Crofts passed with a moiety of Churchill to William Cooksey, who purchased the other moiety of John Guise in 1531.[59]

By his will dated September 1581 he left the manor and house at Little Wolverton to his wife Alice for life with reversion to Anne Croft, widow of his nephew Martin Croft, for her life, and afterwards to the heirs male of his sister Alice wife of Humphrey Acton. The will gives some idea of the size of the house at Little Wolverton. It mentions the parlour, the chapel, the old chamber over the porch, the chambers over the 'compasse windowe' and over the chapel, the buttery, tavern, kitchen, 'larder howse, deyhowse, mylnehowse and bakehowse.'[60] In 1583 a certain Edmund Croft who had acquired Alice Cooksey's interest in the manor asserted that the reversion had been settled on the heirs male of Martin Croft and his wife Anne with contingent remainder to himself,[61] but in 1585 he appears to have given up his claim to John son of Humphrey and Alice Acton.[62] William Acton [63] son of John died seised of the manor in 1615, leaving a son Thomas,[64] who in 1632 settled it on Elizabeth daughter of John Weedon, whom he afterwards married.[65] He fought on the side of the Royalists in the Civil War and in 1650 his estates were sequestered.[66] He died some time before 1657, when his son William was holding Little Wolverton.[67]

ACTON of Little Wolverton. *Gules a fesse in an engrailed border ermine.*

The latter was succeeded in 1679 by a son William,[68] whose grandson of the same name, son of another William, was lord of the manor in 1811.[69] He died in 1814,[70] and his son William Joseph was succeeded in 1871 by his eldest son William Robert Acton, whose son Mr. William Walter Acton is the present owner of Little Wolverton.[71]

MUCKNELL (Mucenhil, xi cent.; Mokenhull, xvi cent.), now a farm in the parish of Stoulton, was a berewick of the manor of Kempsey at the time of the Domesday Survey.[72] It afterwards became merged in the manor of Stoulton and has always followed the same descent.[73]

CHURCH The church of *ST. EDMUND* consists of a chancel 31 ft. by 19¾ ft., nave 51 ft. by 27½ ft., west tower 12½ ft. deep by 9 ft. wide, and a small timber north porch. These measurements are all internal.

The history of the church is simple, as it has never been enlarged since it was built about the year 1120. Larger windows were inserted in the south wall of the chancel and also on either side of the nave in the 14th century, c. 1320. The tower is about 120 years old; marks of fire on the north-west buttress of the nave suggest that the former tower was destroyed by fire. The church was restored in 1848, when new windows were inserted in the east wall of the chancel, the north and south walls of the nave, and in the west wall of the tower; at the same time the flat ceiling which then existed was removed.

The east window is of four lights under a pointed head, and below its sill externally is a shallow buttress of 12th-century date. There are shallow clasping buttresses at the angles, the upper parts being of brick. The side walls of the chancel are divided into three bays by similar buttresses; in the first and second bays on the north side and in the second on the south are the round heads of the original 12th-century windows, but the jambs have been cut away to widen the lights at a later period. The first intermediate buttress on the south side has been cut away and an early window filled in to make room for the 14th-century window, which is of three lights under a pointed head. The walling of the chancel is of lias stone with wide joints plastered over outside. The former east wall was of brick. The chancel arch is semicircular, and of two square orders, the rebate being carried down on the east side only, while the jambs are plain and square on the nave side, and the simple abacus is continued to the side walls.

The north-east and south-east windows of the nave are 14th-century insertions of three lights under two-centred arches. The north doorway is round-headed and of two square orders with a chamfered string at the springing; the outer order is set in an ashlar projection, which is continued up to the old eaves level. It has an arcade of two round-headed bays in the upper part, the shafts having scalloped or cushion capitals. A cross cut in the eastern jamb of the doorway may possibly be a consecration cross. The south doorway has been filled in with brick; it is of two round-headed orders; the inner is square and the roll-moulded head of the outer order was carried by jamb shafts, of which the cushion capitals remain, but the shafts have gone. Over the doorway is a similar arcade to that on the north side, but with lozenge and zigzag enrichments cut on the abaci. The two western windows are modern insertions. The side walls are divided into three bays by shallow buttresses and have clasping buttresses at the angles, splayed off below the old roof line. Near the tops of the buttresses are string-courses variously enriched. The present eaves of the nave are about 18 in. higher than the former ones, and on the east faces of the north-east and south-east buttress is another string,

[56] Add. MS. 28024, fol. 190b.
[57] Feet of F. Worcs. East. 2 Edw. III; East. 15 Edw. III; De Banco R. 268, m. 25; 272, m. 13. John de Wysham obtained a grant of free warren in Little Wolverton in 1328 (Chart. R. 2 Edw. III, m. 17, no. 59).
[58] Feud. Aids, v, 307, 319, 332; for other refs. see Churchill.
[59] Feet of F. Worcs. Hil. 23 Hen. VIII; Recov. R. Hil. 23 Hen. VIII, rot. 141.

[60] P.C.C. 5 Rowe.
[61] Chan. Proc. Eliz. Aa. 7–13.
[62] Feet of F. Worcs. Mich. 27 & 28 Eliz.
[63] Ibid. East. 5 Jas. I; Recov. R. East. 5 Jas. I, rot. 120.
[64] Chan. Inq. p.m. (Ser. 2), ccclv, 50.
[65] Burke, Landed Gentry (1906); Recov. R. D. Enr. East. 8 Chas. I, m. 15; Recov. R. East. 8 Chas. I, rot. 15.
[66] Cal. Com. for Comp. 2399.

[67] Feet of F. Div. Co. Mich. 1657; Recov. R. Mich. 1657, rot. 50.
[68] Exch. Spec. Com. Chas. II, no. 6542; M. I. in Stoulton Church.
[69] Recov. R. Trin. 51 Geo. III, rot. 302.
[70] Burke, Landed Gentry. [71] Ibid.
[72] V.C.H. Worcs. i, 288a.
[73] Ibid. 324a n.; Testa de Nevill (Rec. Com.), 41b; Feud. Aids, v, 308; Red Bk. of Bishopric of Worc. fol. 253.

below the last mentioned, the use of which is doubtful. The tower is of three stages, the lowest of lias stone, perhaps old material re-used, and the upper two of brick. The archway opening into the nave is of the full width of the tower with a semicircular arch of two square orders springing from a chamfered abacus. The stair turret rises in the south-east corner. The west window is a three-light insertion of 1848 and the bell-chamber is lighted by single lights on the north, south and west. The parapet is plain and has a stone coping and small angle pinnacles. The gabled roofs are modern, that of the chancel being of a lower pitch than formerly. The walls inside are plastered.

All the furniture is modern except the font, which dates from the erection of the church ; it is cut

chancel hang a sword and a funeral helmet with the crest of an arm holding a sword piercing a boar's head ; a hatchment below bears the arms of William Acton. The same arms are carved on the 1679 gravestone.

There are five bells, the tenor recast in 1897, the other four dating from 1799.

The plate includes an Elizabethan cup with cover paten, hall marked, probably of 1571, a salver paten, hall marked 1732, and a plated flagon.

The registers before 1812 are as follows : (i) baptisms 1542 to 1663, burials 1542 to 1651 and marriages 1542 to 1652 ; (ii) all entries 1677 to 1707 ; (iii) baptisms and burials 1707 to 1765 and marriages 1707 to 1755 ; (iv) marriages 1755 to 1811 ; (v) baptisms and burials 1765 to 1812.

STOULTON CHURCH FROM THE SOUTH-EAST

from one block 2¾ ft. wide by 2½ ft. high, and is round on plan, with sides tapering to the base. It is moulded at the base and near the top. There are several gravestones and monuments in the chancel ; one dated 1679 to William Acton has the words ' Pray for his soule,' an unusual form for the date ; they also occur on the slab to another person of the same name, dated 1725. Other slabs are to Barbara Vincent, who died in 1702, and William Acton, 1721. In the nave passage-way below the chancel arch is a stone to Alianor Desmasters, who died in 1667, and outside by the south doorway is a defaced mural slab. In the tracery of the south chancel window are some pieces of ancient painted glass. To the south of the

ADVOWSON Stoulton was formerly a chapelry of the church of Kempsey and is first mentioned on the appropriation of that church to the college of Westbury in 1473.[74] It was not separately valued for Pope Nicholas's taxation in 1291, but at the time of the Dissolution was worth £4 1s. 6d.[75] The advowson, with that of Kempsey (q.v.), probably passed on the dissolution of Westbury to Sir Ralph Sadleir and later to the Dean and Chapter of Worcester, to whom it certainly belonged in 1683. At that date the chapel is said to have been endowed with tithes of hay and other tithes except corn, all of which had been commuted for money, and the profits of some meadow ground in Great Wolverton.[76]

74 Nash, op. cit. ii, 28.
75 *Valor Eccl.* (Rec. Com.), iii, 236.

76 Exch. Spec. Com. Chas. II, no. 6542. The tithes of Stoulton and Little

Wolverton evidently belonged to the Dean and Chapter of Worcester.

According to Nash [77] the chapel was in his time 'in many respects independent of the Mother Church' and elected its own curate and other officers.

In 1814 an Act was passed vesting the advowson in John Lord Somers, from whom it has passed with the manor to Lady Henry Somerset.[78]

CHARITIES The charity of Thomas Blyzard, founded in 1859 by declaration of trust, is endowed with £164 11s. 8d.

consols, producing £4 2s. yearly, which in pursuance of a scheme 10 May 1907 is applied for the general benefit of the poor.

In 1886 Miss Ann Hemus by her will left £50, the interest to be distributed to the poor at Christmas in coals, blankets and other necessaries. The legacy is represented by £51 19s. consols, producing £1 6s. yearly, which is usually applied in clothing.

The sums of stock are held by the official trustees.

TIBBERTON

Tidbrihtingctune (x cent.) ; Tidbertun (xi cent.) ; Titbrictune, Tibrithtun (xii cent.) ; Tiburtone, Tibritton, Tybryton (xiii cent.) ; Tyberton (xvi cent.).

The parish of Tibberton lies in the middle of the county to the north-east of the town of Worcester. Its area is 1,271 acres,[1] of which 473 are arable land and 747 permanent grassland.[2] The soil is clay with a subsoil of Keuper Marl, and the chief crops are wheat, beans and oats.

The village lies to the west of the Droitwich road, which turns westward to Worcester at Ravenshill Farm, south of the village. The church and vicarage stand on an eminence, about 200 ft. above the ordnance datum, but the land falls to the east and south to the valleys of the brooks which form the eastern and part of the southern boundaries of the parish. The vicarage, which lies near the church, was built in 1884, mainly at the cost of the Ecclesiastical Commissioners. To the south of the church is a good half-timber farm-house of the early 17th century ; a house of similar type and date stands a little distance to the north of the church. Ravenshill Farm is a red brick house, built on a sandstone base, of two stories and an attic, with twin tiled roofs. The eastern half, dating from the 17th century, has a brick string-course between the ground and first floors and two gables on the east front, while the west part, added early in the 18th century, has no string-course or gables. Some windows on the east and south are blocked. Internally the house retains its original oak floors, stairs and doors. In the first floor rooms of the earlier part of the house are two panelled oak fireplaces with cornices. In the centre panel of the overmantel of the fireplace in the southern room is a painting on canvas of Europa and the bull. To the north-east of the house is a 17th-century half-timber and brick barn with a thatched roof, and to the south is a sheet of water extending in three directions in the form of a Y, which may be the remains of a moat. There is a parish room, opened in 1905.

Foredraught Lane is a district in the north of the parish near the Worcester and Birmingham Canal, which here passes through Tibberton, and Moor End is a district to the south.

An Inclosure Act for Tibberton was passed in 1810.[3] Chaunters Close is a place-name found in the 17th century.[4]

MANORS Though there is no record of a grant of *TIBBERTON* to the church of Worcester, it must have owned it before the end of the 10th century, when Oswald, Bishop of Worcester and Archbishop of York,[5] leased 7 acres of meadow there to a priest named Godinge for three lives,[6] on condition that he should be amanuensis to the see. At the date of the Domesday Survey Tibberton was a member of the bishop's great manor of Northwick,[7] and probably had been granted to the church with that manor. It doubtless remained part of Northwick until Bishop Samson (1096–1112) gave it to the Prior and convent of Worcester.[8] It was confirmed to them by Bishop Simon in 1148.[9]

Waleran Count of Mellent in the reign of Stephen directed William de Beauchamp to give to the Prior and monks of Worcester the 'forestage' of Tibberton, and he pardoned the prior the king's geld in the forest which belonged to him.[10]

Richard I made the church's lands in Tibberton free from all forest dues, pleas and exactions.[11] In 1244 the prior bought some heathland near Tibberton of Alexander D'Abitot.[12] Four years later William de Bracy gave the prior a pasture in Tibberton, and gave him licence to inclose a field called Purnewude and to make a path 8 ft. wide through the wood of Warndon from the manor of Tibberton to the king's highway which goes to Worcester. The prior was to make a bec to protect the corn, and to give William a messuage and croft in Trotteswell and 10 marks of silver.[13] In the same year the king granted that the prior might hold free of rent 7 acres of land in Tibberton which he had assarted in the forest of Feckenham.[14] It was the custom in the 13th century for the prior to lease the manor to the villeins for 102s. a year.[15]

The manor remained in the possession of the Prior and convent of Worcester until the Dissolution,[16] when it passed to the Crown. It was granted in 1542 to the Dean and Chapter of Worcester,[17] and confirmed to them in 1609.[18] In 1650 the Parliamentary commissioners sold the manor of

[77] op. cit. ii, 24.

[78] *Acts of Parl. rel. to co. Worc.* (Worcs. Hist. Soc.), 90; Priv. Act, 54 Geo. III, cap. 51.

[1] Three acres are covered by water.

[2] Statistics from Bd. of Agric. (1905).

[3] Priv. Act, 50 Geo. III, cap. 72.

[4] Close, 1657, pt. xliv, no. 31.

[5] *V.C.H. Worcs.* ii, 5.

[6] Heming, *Chartul.* (ed. Hearne), 140.

[7] *V.C.H. Worcs.* i, 294a.

[8] Heming, op. cit. 575.

[9] Thomas, *Surv. of Cath. Church of Worc.* App. no. 18.

[10] *Hist. MSS. Com. Rep.* v, App. i, 301a.

[11] Cart. Antiq. D. 43.

[12] *Ann. Mon.* (Rolls Ser.), iv, 435.

[13] *Hist. MSS. Com. Rep.* v, App. i, 301 ; *Ann. Mon.* (Rolls Ser.), iv, 439.

[14] *Cal. Pat.* 1247–58, p. 5.

[15] *Reg. of Worc. Priory* (Camd. Soc.), 54b.

[16] *Pope Nich. Tax.* (Rec. Com.), 226a; *Valor Eccl.* (Rec. Com.), iii, 221a.

[17] *L. and P. Hen. VIII*, xvii, g. 71 (29).

[18] Pat. 6 Jas. I, pt. xii, no. 2.

Tibberton to William Garland and John Houghton for £1,033 5s. 3d.[19] At the Restoration the dean and chapter recovered the manor. It was confirmed to them in 1692,[20] and remained with them until 1859, when it was taken over by the Ecclesiastical Commissioners,[21] who are in possession of the manor at the present day.[22]

The lords of the manor of Tibberton held a court baron which was included in the sale of 1650.[23] In 1812 this court was held at Himbleton, and the tenants of Tibberton presented the Dean of Worcester with 6s. 8d. saddle money.[24] No court is held at the present day.

In 1291 the prior owned a windmill in Tibberton.[25] This mill is again mentioned in 1315,[26] but seems to have disappeared before 1535.

RAVENSHILL (Raefneshyl, ix cent.; Raeveneshyll, xi cent.) was evidently given to the church of Worcester before 816, when Coenwulf, King of Mercia, freed it from all secular services except building of bridges and strongholds and from military service.[27] It was then a vill of Hallow. It was given by Bishop Brihteah (1033–8) to his kinsman Brihtwine,[28] but afterwards Urse the Sheriff seized this land and the church lost it.[29] Shortly afterwards, however, they must have recovered it, for it is evidently to be identified with part of the 2 nameless hides in the manor of Hallow which two *radmanni* held in 1086.[30] The mesne lordship, however, passed with Urse's other estates to the Beauchamps of Elmley, for in the 12th century it was held under William de Beauchamp by Osbert D'Abitot, of whom it was held by John Haltham.[31] A certain John rendered 40s. for Ravenshill in 1166–7,[32] and may perhaps have been John Haltham.

Habington mentions a Richard de Ravenshill who flourished in 1305,[33] and Robert de Ravenshill (Reveshutt) paid a subsidy of 8d. at Tibberton in 1327.[34] Richard Baugh held the estate in Habington's time (17th century), and it had been in his family for some time before that.[35] It was purchased of the Baughs by the Berkeleys of Spetchley,[36] and is perhaps included in the land at Tibberton of which Rowland Berkeley died seised in 1611. Ravenshill was the residence in 1655 of Thomas son of Sir Robert Berkeley of Spetchley, and in 1681 it is recorded that there was a Roman Catholic chapel at the house of Mr. Thomas Berkeley at Ravenshill.[36a] In 1689 a warrant was issued for the protection of Mrs. Anne Berkeley of Ravenshill and her son Thomas.[37] The estate has since remained in the possession of the Berkeley family, and now belongs to Mr. Robert V. Berkeley of Spetchley Park.

An estate belonging in the 16th century to the Winters, and known as the manor of *TIBBERTON*, is said by Habington to have been the half hide of land in 'Ivelinge' granted by Ralph Prior of Worcester to Thomas Fitz Aldred for 8s. yearly.[38] In 1240 Alexander de Iveling was paying this rent to the prior for half a hide of land at Tibberton,[39] and in 1280 Richard de Iveling paid a subsidy at Tibberton.[40] He had been succeeded before 1327 by John de Iveling.[41] Habington states that this property afterwards passed to the Hodingtons, and descended with the manor of Huddington (q.v.) to the Winters.[42] Certainly Roger Winter held it at the time of his death in 1535,[43] and it then passed with Huddington in the Winter family until the middle of the 17th century.[44] After the Revolution of 1688 the Jesuit fathers of the Catholic Mission at Worcester retired to Evelench.[44a] Nash writing at the end of the 18th century does not give the owner of the Evelench estate, which was purchased in 1851 by the Rev. H. W. Walmesley and others. It is now in the possession of the Jesuits of St. George's, Worcester.[44b]

The small church of *ST. PETER AD CHURCH VINCULA*, built in 1868, consists of a chancel, nave, porch and west bell-turret. The walls are of brick faced with stone, and it is in 13th-century style. In the east wall of the chancel is a pointed window of three lights, and in the side walls are two lancets on the north side and one on the south, with a square-headed two-light window further west.

The nave is lighted by three pairs of lancets on the north and two pairs on the south, while to the west are single lancets on either side. In the west wall are four lancets with a traceried circular window above. The entrance is by a pointed doorway in the south wall covered by a wood porch. A timber turret stands above the roof at the west end and above it is an octagonal spire. Some oak work from the old church is said to have been used in the present flooring and altar rails.

The former building is described by Dr. Prattinton in 1818 as consisting of a nave, chancel and south porch, with a timber bell-turret at the west end. The chancel was lit by a three-light east window and three single-light openings in the side walls. He also mentions two uninscribed bells in the turret.

The font is now octagonal, but from the remains of a horizontal roll at the corners it would appear to have formerly been round in plan and was probably of the 13th century.

There are two modern bells, both by J. Taylor.

[19] Close, 1650, pt. xxviii, no. 19.
[20] Pat. 4 Will. and Mary, pt. i, no. 6.
[21] *Lond. Gaz.* 16 Dec. 1859, p. 4757; confirmed by Stat. 31 Vict. cap. 19.
[22] Information supplied from the Ecclesiastical Commission.
[23] Close, 1650, pt. xxviii, no. 19.
[24] Prattinton Coll. (Soc. Antiq.).
[25] *Pope Nich. Tax.* (Rec. Com.), 226a.
[26] Nash, op. cit. ii, 426. Tithes of the prior's windmill were assigned to the vicar when the vicarage was ordained.
[27] Heming, op. cit. 337.
[28] Ibid. 267.
[29] Ibid.
[30] *V.C.H. Worcs.* i, 296; Heming, in an abbreviated transcript of Domesday Survey, gives these 2 hides at Ravenshill and Dunhampstead (op. cit. 307).
[31] Red Bk. of Bishopric of Worc. (Eccl. Com. Rec. Var. bdle. 121, no. 43698), fol. 252.
[32] *Pipe R. 13 Hen. II* (Pipe R. Soc.), 67.
[33] op. cit. i, 441.
[34] *Lay Subs. R. Worcs.* 1327 (Worcs. Hist. Soc.), 27.
[35] Habington, loc. cit.
[36] Nash, op. cit. ii, 422.
[36a] Inform. from Mr. R. V. Berkeley; Chan. Inq. p.m. (Ser. 2), cccxxv, 181; Foley, *Rec. of the Engl. Province,* iv, 282.
[37] *Cal. S. P. Dom.* 1689–90, p. 167.
[38] op. cit. i, 441. Ralph, Prior of Worcester, died in 1143; another Ralph succeeded in 1146 and died 1189; Ralph de Evesham was prior from 1203 to 1214 (*V.C.H. Worcs.* ii, 111).
[39] *Reg. of Worc. Priory* (Camd. Soc.), 55a and b.
[40] *Lay Subs. R. Worcs.* 1280 (Worcs. Hist. Soc.), 39.
[41] Ibid. 1327, p. 27.
[42] op. cit. i, 441.
[43] Chan. Inq. p.m. (Ser. 2), lvii, 5. The manor was then held of the Prior of Worcester.
[44] Ibid. lxxxviii, 69; Pat. 7 Jas. I, pt. vii.
[44a] Foley, loc. cit.
[44b] Inform. from Mr. R. V. Berkeley.

STOULTON CHURCH : THE NAVE LOOKING EAST

TIBBERTON : 17TH CENTURY HOUSE NEAR THE CHURCH

The communion plate consists of an Elizabethan cup and cover paten dated 1571, the maker's initials being H.W., a stand paten of 1839, and a flagon of 1869.

The registers before 1812 are as follows : (i) baptisms 1680 to 1760, burials 1684 to 1760, and marriages 1683 to 1754 ; (ii) baptisms and burials 1761 to 1812 ; (iii) marriages 1756 to 1811.

ADVOWSON The advowson of the church of Tibberton belonged to the Prior and convent of Worcester until the Dissolution.[45] In 1314 the church was appropriated to the office of precentor of the convent[46] for the provision of new books and rolls, the repair of the old ones, and the keeping of horses for the business of the convent.[47] A vicarage to the value of 5 marks was ordained in the following year.[48] In 1535 the rectory of Tibberton was returned as annexed to that of Himbleton.[49] The advowson and rectory[50] were granted to the Dean and Chapter of Worcester in 1542,[51] and the advowson has remained with them ever since.[52] The vicarage was annexed on 6 October 1841 to the rectory of Bredicot.[53]

The precentors of Worcester seem to have had a residence at Tibberton, for in 1657 the Parliamentary trustees sold to Robert Urwyn the site of the rectory of Tibberton and the mansion-house belonging to the same, with land called Chaunters Close, which had been leased by the dean and chapter in 1641 for three lives to Mary Gibson.[54] The rectory seems to have been leased from time to time by the dean and chapter, and was in 1666 and at the beginning of the 19th century in the possession of the Bearcroft family.[55]

The church house of Tibberton was granted in 1573–4 to John and William Mersh.[56]

There is a Wesleyan Methodist chapel in the parish.

CHARITIES In or about 1813 Mrs. Anne Sumner, late wife of the Rev. Dr. Sumner of King's College, Cambridge, and widow of Mr. George Wingfield, by her will, in pursuance of her first husband's will, bequeathed £500, the interest to be applied in buying gowns to clothe poor women, the said £500 to be equally divided between the several parishes of St. Martin and St. Nicholas, Worcester, and the parishes of Claines, Warndon and Tibberton in the county of Worcester.

The sum of £100 coming to this parish, reduced by the legacy duty, is represented by £105 consols with the official trustees, the annual dividends of £2 12s. 6d. being duly applied.

TIDMINGTON

Tidelminc Tune (x cent.) ; Tidelintun, Tidelmintun (xi cent.) ; Tydamintun (xiii cent.) ; Tydilmynton, Tydlemynton (xiv cent.).

The parish of Tidmington, which was formed out of the parish of Tredington in 1719,[1] is one of the outlying parishes of Worcestershire, being surrounded by Warwickshire on the east and west and by Gloucestershire on the south, with the parish of Shipston-on-Stour, another of the detached parishes of Worcestershire, on the north. The River Stour forms the southern and the greater part of the eastern boundary, while Pig Brook, a small tributary, forms the northern boundary of the parish.

The area of Tidmington is 774 acres, of which 4 are covered with water, 2 are woodland, 64 arable and 630 pasture land.[2] The soil is stiff loam on a subsoil of Lower Lias.

The village, which consists of a few scattered houses, mostly modern, is situated on the high road from Woodstock to Shipston-on-Stour, on the left bank of the Stour. Near the church to the east of the high road is Tidmington House, the residence of Miss Staunton, a large three-story stone building of c. 1600, much altered and added to in the Queen Anne period, and refronted on the west later in the 18th century. The three gables on the east with their stone-mullioned windows are of the early date, while there is a Queen Anne brick addition on the north and a wing at the south-east with a semicircular termination. The wooden balustraded verandah on the south side of the house is of the same date as these additions. The later west front has projecting wings at either end, the recessed central space being occupied by a Tuscan portico, over which is a Venetian window. The village is about 250 ft. above the ordnance datum. To the west the land rises to 300 ft. or more.

MANORS *TIDMINGTON*, which was a member of the manor of Tredington, was probably granted with that manor to the church of Worcester by Eanberht.[3] In 977 Archbishop Oswald[4] gave five manses at Tidmington to Alfward for three lives.[5] In 1086 the Bishop of Worcester held Tidmington as a member of his

[45] *Ann. Mon.* (Rolls Ser.), iv, 418, 439 ; *Sede Vacante Reg.* (Worcs. Hist. Soc.), 199 ; *Reg. of Worc. Priory* (Camden Soc.), 54*b* ; *Cal. Pat.* 1313–17, p. 217 ; *L. and P. Hen. VIII*, xvii, g. 71 (29). In the register of Worcester Priory it is stated that the church of Tibberton was free and had a *curia* and land, and received all tithes, paying 2s. yearly to the prior (op. cit. 55*a*). In 1291 the church was valued at £6 13s. 4d. (*Pope Nich. Tax.* [Rec. Com.], 239*a*). In the 16th century the church was still a peculiar, the dean and chapter having concurrent jurisdiction with the Chancellor in proving wills and granting administrations, and the church being exempt from archidia-

conal jurisdiction (*Valor Eccl.* [Rec. Com.], iii, 512).
[46] *Cal. Pat.* 1313–17, p. 217 ; *Abbrev. Rot. Orig.* (Rec. Com.), i, 212 ; Inq. a.q.d. file 102, no. 1.
[47] Worc. Epis. Reg. Maidstone (1313–17), fol. 23.
[48] Ibid. 23, 27, 35 d.
[49] *Valor Eccl.* (Rec. Com.), iii, 224.
[50] The rectory and tithes, which had been leased by the dean in 1609 to Richard Harris for lives, were in 1638 the subject of a dispute between his widow and granddaughter (Chan. Proc. [Ser. 2], bdle. 403, no. 65).
[51] *L. and P. Hen. VIII*, xvii, g. 71 (29) ; Pat. 33 Hen. VIII, pt. v.

[52] Pat. 6 Jas. I, pt. xii, no. 2 ; Inst. Bks. (P.R.O.). The presentation was made by the Crown in 1699 by reason of a lapse (Inst. Bks.).
[53] *Parl. Papers* (1872), xlvi, no. 227, p. 2. [54] Close, 1657, pt. xliv, no. 31.
[55] Feet of F. Worcs. Mich. 18 Chas. II; Prattinton Coll. (Soc. Antiq.).
[56] Pat. 16 Eliz. pt. xii.
[1] Priv. Act, 6 Geo. I, cap. 9.
[2] Statistics from Bd. of Agric. (1905).
[3] See under Tredington.
[4] Also Bishop of Worcester.
[5] Kemble, *Cod. Dipl.* no. 614; Heming, *Chartul.* (ed. Hearne), 192. The bounds of the land are given (see also Heming, op. cit. 348).

manor of Tredington,[6] and the bishop's overlordship was recognized in 1636, when he still received a rent of wheat from the manor.[7]

The family of Croome were under-tenants of the bishop in this manor from very early times. Bishop Samson (1096–1112) gave 3 hides at Tidmington to Adam de Croome with Earl's Croome.[8] Ellis de Croome held it about 1182,[9] but it must soon after have passed to Simon son of Adam de Croome, who was probably an elder brother of Ellis, for Simon is returned as holding the manor in a survey of about the same date.[10] Early in the 13th century it was held by Adam de Croome of Earl's Croome.[11] Adam obtained a grant of free warren there in 1252.[12] The manor then passed with that of Earl's Croome to Adam's grandson Simon, who in 1291 granted it to Geoffrey de Hambury. Geoffrey in the same year regranted it in free marriage to Simon and his wife Maud daughter of Alexander de Escote.[13] Simon settled it in 1314–15 upon himself and his wife Joan,[14] and, as Sir Simon, granted it in 1328–9 to his son John and his wife Joan daughter of Richard Hawkeslow, and to their eldest child, with reversion to the donor.[15] John de Croome and Roger de Ledbury were joint owners in 1346.[16] It is not known whether John's son Richard[17] ever held the manor, which passed under the above grant to John's brother Godfrey son of Simon de Croome and Maud de Escote.[18] On his death without issue the manor was claimed by Thomas Corbett in right of his wife Joan, but in 1364 Reginald de Hambury instituted a successful claim against them, on the ground that the manor had been granted by his grandfather Geoffrey de Hambury in frank marriage to Simon and Maud de Croome, and by the form of the gift ought to revert, on the failure of Godfrey de Croome's issue, to the heir of the donor.[19] In 1366 the manor was given by Richard Patty, who was evidently acting for Roger[20] de Hambury,[21] to the Abbot of Evesham.[22]

It remained in the possession of successive abbots until the dissolution of the abbey in 1540.[23] It was granted by the king in 1545 to Richard Ingram and Anthony Foster.[24] Richard died seised of the manor in 1562, and was succeeded by his son Anthony,[25] who settled it in 1565 on himself and his wife

Dorothy and their heirs.[26] In 1596 Anthony settled the manor on his son John on his marriage with Cecily daughter of Robert Williamson, but John predeceased his father,[27] on whose death in 1600 the reversion of the manor on the death of Cicely, then wife of Simon Clifford, passed to Hastings son of John Ingram.[28] Hastings and his wife Katherine conveyed the manor in 1626 to William Baldwin.[29] In 1636 George Savage and his wife Eleanor conveyed it to Edward, Richard and John Walker.[30] Richard Walker was still in possession in 1650,[30a] but after this date the history of the manor is very obscure. In 1716 Thomas Wentworth[31] of Wentworth Woodhouse, co. York, settled it on himself and his wife Alice Proby for their lives.[32] The manor afterwards passed to the Snow family,[33] and in 1794 was held by Thomas Lambert Snow.[34] He was succeeded by the Rev. Thomas Lambert Snow, probably his son, whose eldest daughter Mary Ann married John Staunton of Longbridge. On the latter's death in 1888[35] the Tidmington property was divided between his two

STAUNTON of Longbridge. *Argent two cheverons in an engrailed border sable.*

daughters Anne Elizabeth, now Mrs. Thomas Tufnell Staunton, and Caroline Standert Staunton, who are at present joint owners of the manor.[36]

The church, the invocation of which *CHURCH* is unknown, is a small one, and consists of a chancel, nave, west tower and south porch.

The building dates from about the year 1200, and was then probably of the same size and plan as at present except that the chancel may have been shorter. This was rebuilt at the beginning of the 16th century. The nave windows have all been restored with modern stonework and the early 13th-century tower has been repaired. The south porch is modern. The east window of the chancel has three lights under a traceried square head. On either side is a plain stone bracket and below the southern a small recess.

[6] *V.C.H. Worcs.* i, 293*b*.

[7] Habington, *Surv. of Worcs.* (Worcs. Hist. Soc.), i, 430, 431 ; Chan. Inq. p.m. 39 Edw. III (2nd nos.), no. 42 ; Exch. Dep. Hil. 11 & 12 Chas. I, no. 24 ; 12 Chas. I, no. 23. In the *Testa de Nevill* (Rec. Com.), 41*b*, the manor was said to be held of the manor of Ripple, but it was certainly held of the manor of Tredington in the latter part of the century (Habington, loc. cit.). The tenants of this manor owed suit at the court of Winburntree (ibid. 431).

[8] Red Bk. of Bishopric of Worc. (Eccl. Com. Rec. Var. bdle. 121, no. 43698), fol. 242.

[9] Ibid. 173. Ellis was not holding Earl's Croome at this time, and was probably a younger son of Adam de Croome.

[10] Ibid. 254.

[11] *Testa de Nevill* (Rec. Com.), 41*b*.

[12] *Cal. Chart. R.* 1226–57, p. 400.

[13] Add. MS. 28024, fol. 125 d.

[14] Feet of F. Worcs. 8 Edw. II, no. 19 ; *Cal. Bodleian Chart.* 687.

[15] Add. MS. 28024, fol. 125.

[16] *Feud. Aids*, v, 309.

[17] Add. MS. 28024, fol. 125.

[18] De Banco R. 418, m. 176 d.

[19] Ibid. ; Anct. D. (P.R.O.), D 645.

[20] Possibly this should be Reginald.

[21] *Chron. de Evesham* (Rolls Ser.), 295.

[22] Pat. 40 Edw. III, pt. i, m. 37 ; Chan. Inq. p.m. 39 Edw. III (2nd nos.), no. 42.

[23] *Feud. Aids*, v, 320 ; *Valor Eccl.* (Rec. Com.), iii, 248*b* ; *V.C.H. Worcs.* ii, 126. It was valued at £10 16s. 8d. in 1535.

[24] Pat. 36 Hen. VIII, pt. xiv, m. 12 ; *L. and P. Hen. VIII*, xx (1), g. 621 (7). The manor had been held on lease by the Ingrams before this time, for in 1540 John Ingram of Little Wolford assigned to his son Richard a lease of the manor, acquired from Walter Taylor, on condition of obtaining within seven years an estate in the manor in fee simple from the king (Add. Chart. 24312).

[25] Chan. Inq. p.m. (Ser. 2), cxliii, 11.

[26] Pat. 8 Eliz. pt. i, m. 15 ; Feet of F. Worcs. Hil. 8 Eliz.

[27] Chan. Inq. p.m. (Ser. 2), cclii, 7. The Ingrams seem to have lived at Little

Wolford, co. Warwick, and evidently leased the manor of Tidmington, as Jane Blabie, farmer of the manor, held the courts in 1608–9 (Ct. R. [Gen. Ser.], portf. 210, no. 98), and died soon after, having held the manor for about twelve years (Exch. Dep. Hil. 11 & 12 Chas. I, no. 24).

[28] Chan. Inq. p.m. (Ser. 2), cccxlv, 123.

[29] Feet of F. Div. Co. East. 2 Chas. I.

[30] Feet of F. Worcs. Hil. 12 Chas. I.

[30a] Chan. Proc. (Ser. 2), bdle. 466, no. 23.

[31] He was third son of Sir Edward Watson and took the name Wentworth on succeeding to the estates of his uncle William Wentworth (Foster, *Yorks. Pedigrees*, ii, under Wentworth of Wentworth Woodhouse).

[32] Recov. R. Trin. 2 Geo. I, rot. 179.

[33] Nash, op. cit. ii, 4.

[34] Recov. R. Trin. 34 Geo. III, rot. 12.

[35] Burke, *Landed Gentry* (1906).

[36] Information supplied by Miss Caroline Staunton.

TIDMINGTON CHURCH FROM THE SOUTH-WEST

The side walls are pierced by three windows of two lights under square heads, one on the north and two on the south. To the east of the south-east window is the bowl of an early 13th-century pillar piscina, with a part of the shaft re-used. The chancel arch is pointed and of two chamfered orders, dying on to the jambs, the lower parts of which may be of the early 13th century. The north-east window of the nave and the two south windows are modern and of two lights each ; the north-west window appears to be a restored and widened single light. The north entrance is modern, but the south doorway is early 13th-century work ; the head is round within and square outside, with a tympanum above it, on which is an incised cross. An acute arch of three chamfered orders, the inner springing from octagonal corbels, opens into the tower from the nave.

The tower is of three stages, the lowest having a small square-headed west window and being strengthened by clasping buttresses at the angles. A later buttress has been added in the middle of the south wall. The second stage is lighted by plain square-headed loops on the north, south and west. The belfry windows are apparently original, each being of two lancets with a common semicircular label and divided by a semi-octagonal shaft with moulded base and capital. The pyramidal roof rests on the original corbel tabling, the corbels being moulded or carved with heads. The lowest stage of the tower is of ashlar, the upper stages of rubble with quoin stones. To the north of the tower is a small modern vestry. The font is round and tub-shaped and quite plain.

There are a few old seats with traceried ends, and a good chest, with the initials and date ' R B 1692,' is preserved in the church.

There are four bells,[37] one of which is a sanctus bell. The first was cast by Robert Atton of Buckingham, 1619 ; the second is inscribed ' + Bartelmew Aton' (crown), with the lettering and marks used by the Newcombes of Leicester, and was cast there about 1580 (Atton, who afterwards set up a foundry at Buckingham, was then acting as foreman to the Newcombes) ; the third is inscribed in black letter ' Sancte Petre ora pro nobis,' with a shield bearing a cheveron between three laver-pots, originally used by W. Dawe of London (1385–1420). As some of his stamps went to Reading and occur on other bells cast there in the 16th century, probably this bell is the work of William Welles of that town about 1550. The sanctus bell has an unintelligible inscription in early Roman capitals, and probably dates from the reign of Elizabeth.

The plate consists of a silver cup of 1753 and a paten of 1845.

The registers[38] before 1812 are as follows : (i) baptisms 1691 to 1803, burials 1691 to 1801 and marriages 1693 to 1777 ; (ii) baptisms 1804 to 1811 and burials 1806 to 1812 ; (iii) a smaller book, of which the first page is missing, containing marriages 1762 to 1773, banns 1762 to 1771 and a baptism of 1790. There are also some church-wardens' accounts from 1704.

ADVOWSON Tidmington was a chapelry annexed to the church of Tredington until 1719, when Tidmington and Shipston-on-Stour were formed into a separate parish and endowed with a third of the rectory of Tredington.[39] Tidmington is still a chapelry annexed to the rectory of Shipston-on-Stour.

Towards the end of the 13th century the Croomes seem to have had a manorial chapel at Tidmington, for the advowson of the chapel of Tidmington was included in conveyances of the manor in 1291[40] and 1328–9.[41]

CHARITIES This parish is entitled to an eighty-fourth part of the dividends arising from several sums of stock forming the endowment of Richard Badger's charity, founded by will proved at London 7 December 1907. This is applicable for church purposes. In 1910 a sum of £9 6s. was received.

The parishes of Tidmington and Burmington, in the county of Warwick, are also entitled to receive a forty-second part of the dividends arising from the endowment of the same charity for distribution to the poor in coal. In 1910 a sum of £18 12s. was received. (See under Shipston-on-Stour.)

TREDINGTON

Tredingctun (viii cent.) ; Tredinctune (x cent.) ; Tredinton (xiii cent.) ; Tredynton, Tradynton (xiv cent.).

The parish of Tredington is one of the detached parishes of Worcestershire and lies to the south-east of the county proper. Included in this parish are the township of Tredington and the hamlets of Blackwell, Darlingscott, Newbold-on-Stour and Armscote.

Fosse Way, the old Roman road between Moreton-in-Marsh and Leicester, runs through the parish from south to north and crosses the present high road from Stratford to Shipston-on-Stour to the north of the village of Tredington, which is situated on the latter road. Newbold-on-Stour is also on the Stratford road, from which a branch leads south through Armscote, Blackwell and Darlingscott. The River Stour, flowing north, forms the greater part of the eastern and northern boundaries of the parish.

The Stratford-upon-Avon and Moreton-in-Marsh tramway runs through the parish, the Shipston-on-Stour branch joining the main line at Darlingscott. There are brick-fields and lime-kilns near the tramway.

The area of the parish of Tredington is 5,347 acres,[1] of which 1,639 are arable, 3,430 permanent grass and 17 woods.[2] The chief crops raised are wheat, beans, barley and oats. The soil is stiff clay and the subsoil is Lower Lias ; in Armscote Field white lias limestone is obtainable.

The village of Tredington is situated about 2 miles north of Shipston-on-Stour upon the main road to

---

[37] Inform. from Mr. H. B. Walters.
[38] There are some earlier 17th-century entries among the Bishops' Transcripts.
[39] Priv. Act, 6 Geo. I, cap. 9.
[40] Add. MS. 28024, fol. 125 d.

[41] Ibid. 125. It is here called a chantry chapel.
[1] Of which 19 are covered by water.
[2] Statistics from Bd. of Agric. (1905). In the 13th century there was no wood-

land in Tredington, the tenants of the manor having house and heybote at Blockley and Lapworth (Red Bk. of Bishopric of Worc. [Eccl. Com. Rec. Var. bdle. 121, no. 43698], fol. 173).

Stratford. The church stands on high ground a little to the east of the main road in a churchyard surrounded by an old stone wall with a weathered and stepped coping. Between the churchyard and the main road is the rectory; the original building, which must have been a particularly fine example of a large 15th-century house, was unfortunately demolished in the 'forties of the last century, when the present building was erected, a few of the windows of the old house being re-used. In the window of the hall, which is an original 15th-century window of two lights with a square traceried head, is some 17th-century heraldic glass, comprising the following shields : (1) Gules a bend or between two scallops argent impaling gules a cheveron argent between three cinquefoils argent ; (2) Sable a fesse argent

north-west of the church. The manor-house is a fine L-shaped early 17th-century house of stone, two stories in height with an attic. The windows throughout have moulded labels and ovolo-moulded mullions. The southern or principal front has two gabled bays, extending above the eaves of the roof and lighting the attics. The ground stage of the eastern bay contains the entrance porch. Between the windows of the first and attic floors is a sundial. The interior has been much cut about and modernized. On a fireback still preserved is inscribed '1631 $\frac{\text{N.}}{\text{AM.}}$' Armscote House, known locally as the 'Pool House' from the ponds to the south-east, is an early 17th-century building of two stories with an attic, H-shaped on plan, with an original entrance passage on the east side of the central room or hall. The stairs are at

ARMSCOTE HOUSE, TREDINGTON, SOUTH FRONT

between three sheldrakes in their proper colours impaling the first charge of the foregoing shield; (3) Gules two swords argent in saltire impaling sable three crosslets fitchy on a cheveron or between three stars or with the crest of a mitre, for William Laud, Bishop of London ; (4) the Stuart royal arms. The coach-house, to the south-east of the rectory, appears to be a fragment of the original out-buildings. The cottages which compose the village are mostly of stone, with low mullioned windows and stone-slated roofs after the regular Cotswold type. To the east of the church is a good stone farm-house two stories in height, with an attic in the roof, dating from the early 17th century. To the south-west of the village are the Tredington Hills, where the land rises to 300 ft. above the ordnance datum. Armscote is a picturesque hamlet about three-quarters of a mile

the north-west of the hall in the west wing. The fireplaces are mostly of stone, with straight-sided, four-centred heads. On a beam in one of the rooms in the east wing is carved the date 1606. The front, with its stone-mullioned windows, each with a label, and its gabled wings at either end, is characteristic of the period. The roofs are stone-slated on the front, but tiled at the back, where the windows have oak frames, mullions and ledges. The chimney stacks are of stone with moulded cappings. The inclosing wall of the garden on the entrance side appears to be of the original date, though the gate-piers, crowned by ball finials, are probably later. The original farm buildings still remain.

The hamlet of Newbold, situated about 1½ miles north of Tredington upon the Stratford road, contains many modern brick cottages and some older work.

Opposite the church is a good stone farm-house of the early 17th century, and to the north of this, a little to the east of the main road, is a small stone house of c. 1700, with mullioned and transomed windows of the old type on the principal front, and a large sash-window, apparently contemporary, in the gabled end wall on the south.

At Talton near Newbold is Talton House, a modernized gabled building with sash-windows inserted in the 18th century A short distance to the west of the house is a water-mill, partly old.

Blackwell, about 1 mile west of Tredington, is a hamlet of moderate size, containing some good examples of the Cotswold type of stone cottages. There is a green at the west end of the settlement, where the cottages have been largely rebuilt.

Darlingscott, about 1 mile south-west of Blackwell, contains many picturesque stone farm-houses and cottages of the early 17th century.

Roman remains have been found at Newbold-on-Stour and at Talton.[3]

An Inclosure Act for Tredington was passed in 1836, the award being dated 26 April 1878.[4] The award for Armscote Field is dated 31 July 1865,[5] that for Blackwell 24 October 1868,[6] for Darlingscott 27 August 1846,[7] and for Newbold-on-Stour 20 June 1850 (amended 9 December 1850).[8]

Humphrey Owen was rector of Tredington from 1744 until 1763, when he became librarian of the Bodleian Library. Peter Vannes, Dean of Salisbury, the well-known Latin secretary to Henry VIII and Edward VI, was rector of Tredington in 1542. Vice-Admiral Sir Hyde Parker was younger son of Hyde Parker, rector of Tredington, and was born there in 1713–14.[9]

The following place-names occur in the 14th century : Bithelongesithers, Underchirchehull, Wydycombe, Baldricheswelle, the Chirchehulleweye,[10] Menecroft,[11] and Heyfordusland.[12]

MANORS A spurious charter purporting to date from the 8th century relates that Eanbeorht, under-king of the Hwiccas, and his brothers Uhtred and Aldred granted land in *TREDINGTON* to Milred, Bishop of Worcester.[13] Tredington was in the hundred of Winburntree, and by the charter of King Edgar of 964 was freed from royal exactions.[14] In 1086 the Bishop of Worcester held 23 hides in Tredington.[15] In 1254 the bishop obtained in this manor a grant of free warren, which was confirmed to him in the following year.[16] In 1351 the bishop complained that though he had infangentheof and outfangentheof in this manor, as in all his other Worcestershire manors, some goods found

in the possession of thieves arrested in the manor of Tredington had been taken away by force by other malefactors, so that justice had never been done.[17] In 1409 he again had reason for complaint, as Richard Wych, parson of the church of Tredington, late farmer of the manor of Tredington, with others broke into the manor-house, dovecot and mill at Tredington, carried off the windows with their iron fastenings, sealed the door of the mill, stole the doves, and assaulted the bishop's servants and Simon Colyns, then farmer of the manor.[18]

In 1423 the manor of Tredington, with the water-mill and fishery, was leased to Richard Cassey, rector of Tredington.[19]

The manor remained part of the possessions of the see of Worcester [19a] until it was sold by the Parliamentary Commissioners in 1649 to John Baker and William Dyer,[20] but the bishop recovered it at the Restoration. It remained in the possession of successive bishops until 1860, when it was transferred to the Ecclesiastical Commissioners,[21] who are at present lords of the manor.[22]

In 1588 Edmund, Bishop of Worcester, leased the site of the manor of Tredington and other lands to Queen Elizabeth for ninety years, after the expiration of certain leases then running.[23] A month later she assigned the lease to her physician Roger Lopes,[24] who was attainted and forfeited it in 1590. In 1635 Charles I granted the remainder to William Warmestry and William Barnes.[25] In 1633, however, William Sheldon claimed to hold a lease of the site of the manor, supposed to have been granted to Katherine Hornyold, as trustee for the Sheldons, before the lease to the queen in 1588.[26] This claim resulted in long litigation. Bishop Stillingfleet claimed that the queen's lease began in 1607 and expired in 1697, but Sir Henry Parker, who held the remainder of this lease, said that it began in 1642 on the death of Edward Sheldon, the last life mentioned in Katherine Hornyold's lease, and therefore the bishop had no power to lease the manor as he had done to his son James Stillingfleet.[27] Bishop Stillingfleet died while the suit was still pending, and between 1699 and 1703 there were various suits between James Stillingfleet and Sir Henry Parker, the matter being apparently decided in 1703–4 in favour of Sir Henry.[28] In 1710 the bishop granted a lease of the site for three lives to Sir Henry Parker, in whose family it still remained at the end of the 18th century.[29]

BLACKWELL (Blace Wellan, x cent. ; Blacanvella, Blachewelle, xi cent. ; Blakewelle, Blacwell, xiii cent.) was included by King Edgar in his charter of 964 granting the hundred of Oswaldslow to the church of

[3] *V.C.H. Worcs.* i, 220.
[4] *Blue Bk. Incl. Awards,* 191.
[5] Ibid. 188 ; Authorizing Act (Local and Personal), 24 & 25 Vict. cap. 38.
[6] *Blue Bk. Incl. Awards,* 189; Authorizing Act (Local and Personal), 27 & 28 Vict. cap. 1.
[7] *Blue Bk. Incl. Awards,* 189.
[8] Ibid. 190, 191 ; Authorizing Acts (Local and Personal), 8 & 9 Vict. cap. 118 ; 10 & 11 Vict. cap. 25.
[9] *Dict. Nat. Biog.*
[10] *Cal. Pat.* 1317–21, p. 499.
[11] Jeayes, *Lyttelton Charters,* no. 31.
[12] *Chron. de Evesham* (Rolls Ser.), 295. This land was given in 1364 by Joan daughter of William Heyford to Thomas

de la Morehall, rector of Quinton (*Cal. Close,* 1364–8, p. 68), and Henry de la Morehall soon after gave it to the Abbot of Evesham. It included a carucate of land on the Stour (*Chron. de Evesham,* 295).
[13] Heming, *Chartul.* (ed. Hearne), 36–9; Birch, *Cart. Sax.* i, 260. The boundaries of the land are given in this charter (Birch, op. cit. 262). Tyrdda the Earl formerly held it.
[14] Birch, op. cit. iii, 380.
[15] *V.C.H. Worcs.* i, 293*b*.
[16] *Cal. Pat.* 1247–58, p. 345 ; *Cal. Chart. R.* 1226–57, p. 443.
[17] *Cal. Pat.* 1350–4, p. 95.
[18] Ibid. 1408–13, p. 177.
[19] Nash, *Hist. of Worcs.* ii, 433.

[19a] *Mins. Accts.* bdle. 1143, no. 18 ; *Feud. Aids,* v, 306, 312, 318 ; *Valor Eccl.* (Rec. Com.), iii, 218.
[20] *Close,* 1650, pt. xxiv, no. 13.
[21] Stat. 23 & 24 Vict. cap. 124.
[22] Inform. supplied by Ecclesiastical Commissioners.
[23] Pat. 30 Eliz. pt. iv, m. 20.
[24] Ibid.
[25] Pat. 10 Chas. I, pt. xvi, no. 20.
[26] Exch. Spec. Com. 9 Chas. I, no. 5909 ; Exch. Dep. Hil. 8 & 9 Chas. I, no. 26.
[27] Exch. Dep. East. 2 Anne, no. 21.
[28] Ibid. ; Nash, op. cit. ii, Suppl. 81.
[29] Nash, loc. cit.

Worcester,[30] and was granted by Oswald, Bishop of Worcester, to his thegn Aelfnoth for three lives in 978.[31] Within the next few years the monks were deprived of their holding by Earl Leofwine, whose son Earl Leofric also kept Blackwell from the monks for some time, but later he and his wife the Countess Godiva restored the manor in the time of Wulfstan, who succeeded as prior on the eve of the Conquest.[32] At the date of the Domesday Survey 2 hides were assigned to the support of the monks of Worcester.[33]

The manor of Blackwell remained with the prior and convent until the dissolution of the priory in 1540,[34] when it passed to the Crown. In 1542 it was granted to the Dean and Chapter of Worcester,[35] who continued to hold it until 1654, when it was sold by the Parliamentary Commissioners to Nicholas Lockyer of London.[36] He seems to have made a bad bargain, for in the following year the Protector's Council ordered that as these lands were charged with payments to charitable uses, whereby he could not have the benefit of his purchase, he should receive the sum of £2,500 out of any discoveries he might make for the Committee for Discoveries, and should then reconvey the manor of Blackwell to the Commonwealth.[37] A further order was made in 1656 to the same effect, but it was not carried out.[38] At the Restoration the dean and chapter recovered their estates, and this manor was confirmed to them in 1692.[39] It is now annexed to the manor of Shipston-on-Stour, and belongs to the Ecclesiastical Commissioners.[39a] In the 13th century a full survey of this manor was taken.[40]

TALTON (Taetlintune, x cent.; Tatlinton, Tatlington, xiii cent.; Tadlington, Talton, xvi cent.) was probably included in Tredington at the time of its grant to the church of Worcester and at the time of the Domesday Survey. In 991 Archbishop Oswald[41] gave to his thegn Eadric 3 hides at Talton and Newbold for two lives.[42]

The manor was held of the Bishop of Worcester of the manor of Tredington[43] until the 14th century.

It was possibly held by the Bishops of Worcester in demesne until early in the 12th century, when Bishop Theulf (1115–23) gave it to William de Armscote.[44] William was holding the estate in 1166,[45] and his son Auger was in possession towards the end of the 12th century.[46] He was probably an ancestor of William son of Auger, who held the manor at the beginning of the 13th century.[47] In 1226–7 Thomas son of William gave the manor of Talton to Clemencia de Broc, widow of William de Talton, in dower.[48] Clemencia had two sons, Auger and Simon,[49] and in 1255 William son of Thomas de Talton, who evidently represented the elder branch of the family, gave the manor to Auger.[50] The latter subinfeudated it to Robert Waleraund, who died seised of it about 1272–3, leaving as his heir his nephew Robert son of William Waleraund.[51] The manor of Talton was, however, assigned to his widow Maud.[52] Robert apparently died without issue and was succeeded by his brother John, on account of whose idiocy the manor was taken into the king's hands.[53] The custody was delivered in 1303 to Adam de Harvington,[54] but John Waleraund died about 1308–9.[55] His heir of the whole blood was found to be his cousin Alan Plogenet.[56]

The interest of the Taltons in the manor passed to Walter de Gloucester, who died seised of it in 1311, being succeeded by his son Walter.[57] The manor was assigned to Walter's widow Hawisia,[58] and she in 1323 obtained licence from the king to grant it to the Abbot and convent of Evesham to find two chaplains to pray in the abbey church for the souls of Walter and Hawisia and their family.[59] In 1329–30 the abbot's right to the manor was disputed by Sybil widow of Alan Plogenet, then wife of Henry de Penbridge, who claimed a third of the manor as dower. The abbot appealed to Hawisia de Gloucester to uphold his claim, but the suit was decided in Sybil's favour.[60] The abbot seems to have recovered the manor shortly after, being in possession in 1332,[61] and his successors held until the dissolution of the abbey in 1540,[62] when the manor passed to the Crown. In 1535 the manor, with its members in Darlingscott, Armscote and Newbold, was valued at £30 7s. 7d. The site and demesne land of the manor and a water-mill were leased at a rent of £7 13s. 4d.[63] In 1544 the manor was granted to William and Francis Sheldon,[64] and they in the same year sold the site to William Barnes.[65]

[30] Heming, op. cit. 520.
[31] Ibid. 193; Kemble, Cod. Dipl. no. 620. The boundaries of the estate, which belonged to Tredington, are given.
[32] Heming, op. cit. 261, 406, 409.
[33] V.C.H. Worcs. i, 293b. This manor owed suit at the hundred of Winburntree (Reg. of Worc. Priory [Camd. Soc.], 64b).
[34] V.C.H. Worcs. i, 325a; Reg. of Worc. Priory (Camden Soc.), 64b; Sede Vacante Reg. (Worcs. Hist. Soc.), 398. In 1291 the prior had 3 carucates here and in Shipston worth £3 (Pope Nich. Tax. [Rec. Com.], 227b). In 1535 the manor was worth £24 8s. 7½d. (Valor Eccl. [Rec. Com.], iii, 222a).
[35] L. and P. Hen. VIII, xvii, g. 71 (29); Pat. 33 Hen. VIII, pt. v. This was confirmed in 1609 (Pat. 6 Jas. I, pt. xii, no. 2).
[36] Close, 1654, pt. xxvi, no. 8.
[37] Cal. S. P. Dom. 1655–6, pp. 24, 377.
[38] Dict. Nat. Biog.
[39] Pat. 4 Will. and Mary, pt. i, no. 6.

[39a] Inform. from Ecclesiastical Commissioners.
[40] Reg. of Worc. Priory (Camden Soc.), pp. 64b–68a.
[41] Also Bishop of Worcester.
[42] Heming, op. cit. 195; Kemble, op. cit. no. 676.
[43] Testa de Nevill (Rec. Com.), 42; Cal. Inq. p.m. 1–19 Edw. I, 6; 1–9 Edw. II, 72, 198; Inq. a.q.d. file 158, no. 13. The tenants of the manor owed suit at the hundred of Winburntree (Habington, op. cit. i, 431).
[44] Red Bk. of Exch. (Rolls Ser.), 301; Red Bk. of Bishopric of Worc. fol. 243. William also received 5 virgates at Armscote from Bishop Simon (1125–50) (Red Bk. of Bishopric of Worc. fol. 173).
[45] Red Bk. of Exch. (Rolls Ser.), 301.
[46] Red Bk. of Bishopric of Worc. fol. 255.
[47] Testa de Nevill (Rec. Com.), 42.
[48] Feet of F. Worcs. 11 Hen. III, no. 45. Thomas was probably son of William by a former wife.
[49] Ibid.; Cal. Inq. p.m. Hen. III, 99, 100.
[50] Feet of F. Worcs. 40 Hen. III, no. 47.

[51] Cal. Inq. p.m. 1–19 Edw. I, 6.
[52] Cal. Close, 1272–9, pp. 8, 67.
[53] Abbrev. Rot. Orig. (Rec. Com.), i, 128; Cal. Pat. 1301–7, p. 155. Agnes de Talton was holding the manor in 1299 as mesne lady between the bishop and the Waleraunds (Red Bk. of Bishopric of Worc. fol. 165).
[54] Cal. Pat. 1301–7, p. 155.
[55] Chan. Inq. p.m. 2 Edw. II, no. 80.
[56] Ibid. Alan was grandson of Alice, sister of William Waleraund, John's father.
[57] Chan. Inq. p.m. 5 Edw. II, no. 66.
[58] Cal. Close, 1307–13, p. 380.
[59] Cal. Pat. 1321–4, p. 285; Inq. a.q.d. file 158, no. 13.
[60] De Banco R. 276, m. 141.
[61] Abbrev. Rot. Orig. (Rec. Com.), ii, 64, 75; Cal. Pat. 1343–6, p. 435.
[62] Feud. Aids, v, 310, 320; Valor Eccl. (Rec. Com.), iii, 249.
[63] Valor Eccl. (Rec. Com.), iii, 249.
[64] Pat. 35 Hen. VIII, pt. x, m. 30; L. and P. Hen. VIII, xix (1), g. 80 (50).
[65] L. and P. Hen. VIII, xix (1), g. 610 (116), p. 384.

TREDINGTON : ARMSCOTE HOUSE FROM THE SOUTH-EAST

TREDINGTON CHURCH : THE NAVE AND CHANCEL

William died in 1562,[66] leaving the manor to his widow Alice for life with reversion to his son William.[67] William seems to have entered into possession before 1584,[68] and died in 1621, having settled the manor on William Barnes, son of his brother Richard.[69] William Barnes, apparently the grandson of this William, sold the manor in 1663 to Henry Parker.[70] Henry died in 1670 and was followed by his son Henry of Honington, co. Warw.,[71] who succeeded in 1696-7 to the baronetcy granted to his uncle Hugh, a merchant of London,[72] in 1681. He died in 1713 and was succeeded by his grandson Sir Henry John Parker,[73] who held the manor in 1729[74] and in 1741.[75] He died in 1771 without male issue, and the baronetcy passed to his cousin Sir Henry Parker. It is not known when Talton passed from this family, but it ultimately came into the hands of Georgica Hawkes, on whose death in 1878 it passed to one of his daughters, Mrs. George Lainson Field, the present owner.[75a]

PARKER of Honington, baronet. *Sable a hart's head cabossed between two flaunches argent.*

Two hides of land at *ARMSCOTE* (Edmundescote, xiii cent.; Admundescote, xiv cent.; Advescott, Admyscote, Armyscote, xvi cent.; Armescott, Armscoate, xvii cent.) were granted in 1042 by Lyfing, Bishop of Worcester, with the consent of King Harthacnut, to his thegn Ægelric for three lives.[76] Mr. Stenton points out that the original text of this grant has been preserved and is of high importance. The gift is attested by the king and his mother, the 'hired' of Worcester, Evesham and Winchcomb, Bishop Lyfing of Worcester, Ælfweard Abbot of Evesham and Bishop of London, Earl Leofric, 'and all the thegns in Worcestershire both English and Danish.' The latter phrase is of extreme interest, for it shows that under the house of Cnut Danish settlers formed a recognized element among the magnates of Worcestershire, a county placed under a Danish earl. It is also remarkable as an anticipation of the phrase 'all faithful people French and

English,' which is common in post-Conquest grants. It thus shows that already in 1042 men were accustomed to the presence of alien settlers in the country, a fact which must have gone far to make for the acceptance of Norman lords after 1066.

The hamlet of Armscote was at an early date divided into two moieties. Both were held under the manor of Tredington, one by the owners of Talton,[77] the other by the Croome family.[78] The first manor, which included 2 hides of land, followed the same descent as Talton (with which it seems to have become incorporated in the 14th century) from the 12th century, when it first makes its appearance,[79] until 1544.[80] It was granted as part of Talton in that year to William and Francis Sheldon,[81] and they sold various parcels of land there in the same year to Thomas Smith,[82] William and Richard Morres[83] and Robert Dave.[84] In 1587 Stephen Halford died seised of tenements in Armscote which had belonged to his father Robert, and had formerly been parcel of the manor of Talton. He was succeeded by his son John.[85]

The second manor of Armscote, which also consisted of 2 hides of land, was given to Adam de Croome with Tidmington by Bishop Samson[86] (1096–1112). It followed the same descent as Tidmington,[87] being granted with that manor in 1365 to the Abbot and convent of Evesham.[88] The manor seems to have retained its separate identity until about 1428,[89] but probably became merged soon after in the abbot's other estate at Armscote.

A hide of land at *DARLINGSCOTT* (Derlingiscote, Berlingescote, Derlyngescot, xiii cent.; Darlingascote, Derlescote, Derlyngscott, xiv cent.) was held with Talton by William de Armscote, in the time of Henry II, of the manor of Tredington.[90] It followed the same descent as the manor of Talton,[91] passing with it to the Abbot of Evesham,[92] and was in 1535 a parcel of that manor[93] (q.v.).

Another estate at Darlingscott belonged to the Bishop of Worcester. In 1284 he granted to William de Westhill a messuage and land in Darlingscott,[94] which had formerly belonged to Simon de Throckmorton, at a rent of 1*d*.[95] William sold the estate in 1292 to Matthew Checker.[96] At the same date Matthew transferred his interest in the estate to Godfrey, Bishop of Worcester.[97] This land was

[66] According to Habington the date is given as 1561 on his tomb.
[67] Exch. Inq. p.m. file 1160, no. 5.
[68] Recov. R. Mich. 26 Eliz. rot. 116. In 1613 Sir Edward Marowe of Barkeswell sold the manor, capital messuage and mill of Talton to William Barnes, but there is no record of a previous sale by the Barnes to Sir Edward (Close, 10 Jas. I, pt. xiv, no. 44).
[69] Chan. Inq. p.m. (Ser. 2), ccclxxxviii, 85; Fine R. 20 Jas. I, pt. i, no. 44.
[70] Feet of F. Worcs. Hil. 15 & 16 Chas. II; Close, 16 Chas. II, pt. x, no. 22. William Barnes, grandfather of the vendor of the manor, was still alive, and had a life interest in certain parcels of the manor, under a settlement of 1640 between him and his son William, father of the vendor.
[71] G.E.C. Complete Baronetage, iv, 120.
[72] In 1671 Hugh Parker had bought the rent of £3 2s. 3d. reserved to the Crown from the grant to the Sheldons (Pat. 22 Chas. II, pt. ii [1st roll]; Close, 3 Chas. II, pt. xiv, m. 12).

[73] G.E.C. Complete Baronetage, iv, 120.
[74] Feet of F. Div. Co. Trin. 2 & 3 Geo. II.
[75] Ibid. Trin. 14 & 15 Geo. II; Recov. R. East. 14 Geo. II, rot. 330.
[75a] Inform. from the Rev. W. A. Edwards, rector of Tredington.
[76] Add. Chart. 19799.
[77] Testa de Nevill (Rec. Com.), 42; Habington, Surv. of Worcs. (Worcs. Hist. Soc.), i, 430, 431.
[78] Habington, loc. cit. In the Testa de Nevill the second manor was returned as held under the manor of Ripple (p. 41b), but in 1299 both estates were held of the manor of Tredington (Red Bk. of Bishopric of Worc. fol. 173).
[79] Red Bk. of Bishopric of Worc. fol. 173. [80] For references see Talton.
[81] L. and P. Hen. VIII, xix (1), g. 80 (50). [82] Ibid. g. 141 (77).
[83] Ibid. g. 610 (116). [84] Ibid. g. 278 (76).
[85] Chan. Inq. p.m. (Ser. 2), ccxviii, 27.
[86] Red Bk. of Bishopric of Worc. fol. 242.
[87] For references see Tidmington.
[88] Chan. Inq. p.m. 39 Edw. III (2nd

nos.), no. 42; Chron. de Evesham (Rolls Ser.), 295.
[89] Feud. Aids, v, 320.
[90] Habington, op. cit. i, 430; Red Bk. of Bishopric of Worc. fol. 173.
[91] Habington, op. cit. i, 431; Cal. Inq. p.m. 1-19 Edw. I, 6.
[92] Inq. a.q.d. file 158, no. 13; Cal. Pat. 1321-4, p. 285.
[93] Valor Eccl. (Rec. Com.), iii, 249.
[94] This may have been the same estate as half a hide at Darlingscott, which was held in the time of Henry II by Richard de Darlingscott, a 'radman' (Habington, op. cit. i, 430). There was a 'radman' in the manor of Tredington in 1086 (V.C.H. Worcs. i, 293).
[95] Reg. G. Giffard (Worcs. Hist. Soc.), 222.
[96] Ibid. 419; Feet of F. Worcs. 11 Edw. I, no. 35. The estate which passed by this fine was two messuages and 3 carucates of land in Darlingscott, Tredington and Alvechurch.
[97] Reg. G. Giffard (Worcs. Hist. Soc.), 419.

afterwards acquired by William Chiriton, Abbot of Evesham (1317–44),[98] who doubtless added it to his other estate at Darlingscott. In 1331 the abbot acquired land in Darlingscott of Henry de Ombersley.[99]

LONGDON (Longedun, xi cent. ; Langeton, xiii cent. ; Longdon Travers, xiv cent. ; Longdon Travers, Longdon Parva, xvii cent.) was held of the manor of Tredington, this overlordship being mentioned for the last time in 1629.[100]

In 969 Oswald, Bishop of Worcester, granted 4½ manses there to one Byrnicus for three lives.[1] Before the Conquest Leofric the reeve held 4 hides at Longdon at the will of the bishop. In 1086 this estate was held by Gilbert son of Turold.[2] Ralph Travers held it in 1166,[3] having received it from Bishop Theulf (1115–23),[4] and he or a descendant of the same name was in possession in 1174–5.[5] Towards the middle of the 13th century it belonged to William Travers.[6]

It was probably this William who was succeeded by a son William and a grandson Alexander. The last going to Ireland and marrying there a daughter of Reginald de Hanwood, gave to Reginald his land at Longdon for life in exchange for land in Ireland.[7] Reginald paid a subsidy at Longdon in 1280[8] and died about 1297,[9] and Maurice Travers son of Alexander gave the Bishop of Worcester 6 marks for an acknowledgement that he was Reginald's heir to this land.[10] The manor, however, passed to Geoffrey Spenser,[11] who paid a subsidy of 6s. 8d. at Longdon in 1327,[12] and had been succeeded before 1346 by Sir William Spenser.[13] In 1367–8 John son of Sir William conveyed the manor to Alina widow of Thomas de Newynton.[14] The next mention of the manor occurs in 1398, when Robert Walden of Warwick granted it to the chaplain of a chantry which he had founded in the previous year in the church of Tredington.[15]

In 1487 John Brown, John Smith, Humphrey Coningsby and Richard Palmer recovered a manor of Longdon Travers against Richard Burdet.[16] In 1533 an estate called the manor of Longdon Travers was assured to Elizabeth widow of Sir William Compton, then the wife of Walter Walshe,[17] and two

years later Edward Conway and Anne his wife conveyed the manor to Thomas Burdet and others,[18] but this does not seem to have been the same estate as that held by the chantry priest of Tredington, as that still belonged to the chantry in 1535,[19] and was granted in 1547 to Sir Philip Hoby, who had married Elizabeth widow of Walter Walshe.[20] In 1551–2 Sir Philip sold the manor to Thomas Andrews of Charwelton, co. Northants,[21] who was knighted before 1555[22] and died about 1564.[23] He was followed by a son Thomas, who settled the manor in 1603 upon his son John on his marriage with Anne daughter of John Reade. John succeeded on his father's death in 1609,[24] and, as Sir John, he obtained livery of a third of the manor in 1610, probably on the death of his mother.[25] Sir

ANDREWS of Charwelton. *Gules a saltire or voided vert.*

John continued to hold the manor until 1634, when he and his wife Mary conveyed it to William Loggin and others.[26] In 1705 and 1715 the manor belonged to William and Thomas Baldwin,[27] and in 1743 Thomas Baldwin and William Baldwin and his wife sold it to Joseph Townsend.[28] In 1809 Gore Townsend and Thomas Townsend conveyed it to William Waltham Atkinson.[29] The later descent of this estate is not known, and it is believed that the manorial rights have now lapsed.

A hide of land at *NEWBOLD-ON-STOUR* (Neoweboldan, x cent. ; Neubolde, Neubolt, xiii cent.; Nuwebolde, xiv cent.) was granted with Talton by Oswald, with the consent of the monks of Worcester, to Eadric for two lives in 991,[30] and like Talton was probably included in 1086 in the 23 hides in Tredington held by the Bishop of Worcester.[31]

Two hides at Newbold were granted with Talton to William de Armscote.[32] The estate followed the same descent as the manor of Talton, to which it seems at an early date to have become annexed, until 1544.[33] It was granted as part of the manor of

[98] *Chron. de Evesham* (Rolls Ser.), 289.

[99] *Cal. Pat.* 1330–4, p. 50. This land was held by Henry of the Abbot of Evesham, who held it of the Bishop of Worcester (Inq. a.q.d. file 210, no. 8).

[100] *V.C.H. Worcs.* i, 294a ; *Testa de Nevill* (Rec. Com.), 42 ; Chan. Inq. p.m. (Ser. 2), ccccxlvii, 76.

[1] Heming, op. cit. 209, 561 ; Kemble, op. cit. no. 553.

[2] *V.C.H. Worcs.* i, 294a.

[3] Habington, op. cit. i, 430 ; *Red Bk. of Exch.* (Rolls Ser.), 300.

[4] *Red Bk. of Bishopric of Worc.* fol. 243.

[5] *Pipe R.* 21 *Hen. II* (Pipe R. Soc.), 129.

[6] *Testa de Nevill* (Rec. Com.), 42a.

[7] *Reg. G. Giffard* (Worcs. Hist. Soc.), 488.

[8] *Lay Subs. R. Worcs.* 1280 (Worcs. Hist. Soc.), 73.

[9] In 1299, however, Reginald was still returned as holding the manor (Red Bk. of Bishopric of Worc. fol. 165).

[10] *Reg. G. Giffard* (Worcs. Hist. Soc.), 488.

[11] Habington, op. cit. i, 431.

[12] *Lay Subs. R. Worcs.* 1327 (Worcs. Hist. Soc.), 22.

[13] *Feud. Aids,* v, 310.

[14] *Feet of F. Worcs.* 41 Edw. III, no. 37.

[15] *Cal. Pat.* 1396–9, p. 317.

[16] *De Banco R.* Hil. 2 Hen. VII, rot. 346.

[17] Stat. 24 Hen. VIII, cap. 14. William Lord Compton was in possession of land in Longdon Travers in 1600 (Add. Chart. 19423).

[18] *Feet of F. Worcs.* Hil. 26 Hen. VIII.

[19] *Valor Eccl.* (Rec. Com.), iii, 257.

[20] *Pat.* 1 Edw. VI, pt. ix, m. 10 ; *Visit. of Worcs.* 1569 (Harl. Soc. 27), 80.

[21] *Pat.* 5 Edw. VI, pt. ii, m. 41 ; *Feet of F. Worcs.* Mich. 5 Edw. VI.

[22] *Recov. R.* Hil. 2 & 3 Phil. and Mary, rot. 543 ; *Feet of F. Div. Co.* East. 3 & 4 Phil. and Mary.

[23] *Chan. Inq. p.m.* (Ser. 2), cxxxix, 141.

[24] *Visit. of Worcs.* 1569 (Harl. Soc. 27), 10 ; *Feet of F. Worcs.* Mich. 1 Jas. I ; Chan. Inq. p.m. (Ser. 2), cccxv, 163.

[25] *Fine R.* 8 Jas. I, pt. iii, no. 4.

[26] *Feet of F. Worcs.* Hil. 22 Jas. I ; East. 9 Chas. I.

[27] *Recov. R.* Hil. 4 Anne, rot. 121 ; Feet of F. Worcs. East. 1 Geo. I.

[28] *Feet of F. Worcs.* Trin. 16 & 17 Geo. II.

[29] *Recov. R.* Hil. 49 Geo. III, rot. 222.

[30] Heming, op. cit. 195 ; Kemble, op. cit. no. 676.

[31] The estate was held of the manor of Tredington in the 13th century (*Testa de Nevill* [Rec. Com.], 42 ; Habington, op cit. i, 430, 431).

[32] *Red Bk. of Bishopric of Worc.* fol. 173.

[33] Habington, op. cit. i, 430, 431 ; *Testa de Nevill* (Rec. Com.), 42 ; *Cal. Inq. p.m.* 1–19 *Edw. I,* 6 ; Inq. a.q.d. file 158, no. 13 (16 Edw. II) ; *Abbrev. Rot. Orig.* (Rec. Com.), ii, 64, 75 ; *Feud. Aids,* v, 310, 320 ; *Valor Eccl.* (Rec. Com.), iii, 249 ; *L. and P. Hen. VIII,* xix (1), g. 80 (50). Auger de Talton gave land in Newbold to Simon Levelaunce in 1268–9 (Feet of F. Worcs. 53 Hen. III, no. 28). The Abbots of Evesham having acquired Newbold-on-Stour from Hawisia de Gloucester bought

TREDINGTON CHURCH : THE SOUTH DOOR

TREDINGTON CHURCH FROM THE SOUTH-EAST

Talton to William and Francis Sheldon,[34] but they in the same year sold some land there to Henry Sych or Such.[35] The Such family continued to hold land in Newbold-on-Stour for many years,[36] the last mention of their estate being in 1714, when Robert Such was the owner.[37]

In 1086 there were three mills in the bishop's manor of Tredington[38]; one of these was probably at Talton (see below). There seems to have been only one mill in Tredington Manor in 1291, and it was worth £1.[39] The mill was broken into by thieves in 1409.[40] It is not mentioned in the valor of the manor in 1535, but a water corn-mill was sold by the Parliamentary trustees in 1649 as a parcel of the manor of Tredington to Sir Edward Estopp.[41] Later in the same year another mill at Tredington was sold with the manor to John Baker and William Dyer.[42] At the present day there are two corn-mills on the Stour, one to the north, the other to the south of the town.

The water-mill at Talton is first mentioned in 1308–9, when it formed part of the possessions of John Waleraund.[43] It passed with the manor to the abbey of Evesham,[44] and was repaired several times by Abbot Roger Zatton (1379–1418).[45] In 1535 the mill was leased with the site of the manor and demesne lands.[46] It passed with the manor into the possession of the Barnes family.[47] The present Talton Mill is on the Stour in the north of the parish.

A mill at Armscote is mentioned in 1328–9, when Simon de Croome excepted it from a grant of the manor to his son John.[48]

In 1240 the Prior and convent of Worcester had a mill at Tredington belonging to the manor of Blackwell which was leased to W. the miller at a rent of 16s.[49] In 1291, however, the mill brought in only 8s.[50] Another mill at Tredington was purchased by the prior in 1259 of William de Tredington.[51] Possibly this last was the water corn-mill at Tredington sold in 1654 by the Parliamentary trustees with the manor of Blackwell.[52] There is no mill at Blackwell at the present day.

The mill at Newbold-on-Stour, which was leased for 26s. 8d. in 1299,[53] is a corn-mill on the Stour on the northern boundary of the parish.

CHURCHES The church of ST. GREGORY consists of a chancel 45 ft. by 21½ ft., with a north vestry 16½ ft. by 12½ ft., nave 58 ft. by 21 ft., north aisle 16 ft. wide, south aisle 17 ft. wide, north porch, and western tower 16½ ft. square ; these dimensions are internal.

The remains of the Saxon church consist of the ranges of windows above the nave arcades, which were discovered at the last restoration of the church. Of this building a unique feature was the high gallery

at the west end, the doorways to which still exist in part, and could only have been approached by external staircases or ladders. A window in either wall at a higher level than the others lighted this gallery.

Late in the 12th century (c. 1170–80) aisles were added on both sides, the arcades being inserted in the earlier walls and the Saxon windows and doorways closed up. In the beginning of the 14th century the chancel was lengthened and entirely rebuilt, beginning with the east wall. The dedication of the high altar (and a chapel), which cannot now be located, at Tredington (Trediton) is recorded in 1315.[54] The west tower was erected about the same time. About 1360 both aisles were rebuilt and widened, the 12th-century doorway being reset in the later south wall. A block of masonry west of the porch marks the west wall of the north aisle, which was doubtless re-erected partly on the old 12th-century foundations, but both aisles were extended westwards to the tower about thirty years later, an additional half-bay being added to either arcade to match the rest. The clearstory, north porch and vestry are all additions of the 15th century, but the two latter appear to have been altered in the 17th or 18th century. The west wall of the south aisle also appears to have undergone a later rebuilding. Several restorations have taken place during the past century, the last and most extensive being in 1899.

The east window of the chancel is of five lights under a two-centred head filled with modern tracery; the jambs have shafts on the inner face with foliated capitals and with the arch are of 14th-century date. Internally on either side of the window are contemporary niches with moulded ogee heads. Both the window and the niches show traces of red colour. In the north wall are three tall 14th-century windows, each of two lights with a quatrefoil above in a pointed head having a moulded drop rear arch. The easternmost window now looks into the vestry. The 15th-century doorway into the vestry has a two-centred arch of a single chamfered order. The vestry is lighted by an east window of three lights under a square head, the moulded label of which has been reset with the vertical parts reversed, the return ends being turned inwards. In the north wall near the west angle is a small blocked window of two lights under a square head, set low down in the wall, its iron bars remaining inside. Above it is a modern window of two lights, and in the west wall a modern door. The three south windows of the chancel are contemporary with those opposite and of similar detail. Below the middle one is a 14th-century priest's doorway with a pointed head, and west of the

various other properties there during the 14th century (see *Chron. de Evesham* [Rolls Ser.], 295, 297; *Cal. Close*, 1364–8, p. 68; Inq. a.q.d. file 287, no. 19; 418, no. 35 ; Chan. Inq. p.m. 16 Ric. II, pt. i, no. 155). Richard de Blackwell was in possession of a hide of land at Newbold in the time of Henry II (Habington, op. cit. i, 430).

[34] *L. and P. Hen. VIII*, xix (1), g. 80 (50).
[35] Ibid. g. 141 (77). The first mention of this family is in 1384, when John atte Syche *alias* Chelmescote was in possession of land in Newbold and Armscote (Anct. D. [P.R.O.], D 616).

[36] Chan. Inq. p.m. (Ser. 2), cxv, 79 ; Pat. 12 Eliz. pt. ix ; Chan. Inq. p.m. (Ser. 2), clxxii, 150 ; cxci, 110 ; Pat. 26 Eliz. pt. xvii ; Chan. Inq. p.m. (Ser. 2), cccxli, 15 ; d, 26 ; Feet of F. Worcs. Hil. 5 Will. and Mary ; Mich. 7 Anne ; Hil. 12 Anne ; Trin. 13 Anne.
[37] Feet of F. Worcs. Trin. 13 Anne.
[38] *V.C.H. Worcs.* i, 293.
[39] *Pope Nich. Tax.* (Rec. Com.), 226.
[40] *Cal. Pat.* 1408–13, p. 177.
[41] Close, 1649, pt. xxvii, no. 6.
[42] Ibid. 1650, pt. xxiv, no. 13.
[43] Chan. Inq. p.m. 2 Edw. II, no. 80.

[44] Ibid. 5 Edw. II, no. 66 ; Pat. 16 Edw. II, pt. ii, m. 13.
[45] *Chron. de Evesham* (Rolls Ser.), 304.
[46] *Valor Eccl.* (Rec. Com.), iii, 249.
[47] Pat. 3 Eliz. pt. v, m. 39.
[48] Add. MS. 28024, fol. 125.
[49] *Reg. of Worc. Priory* (Camd. Soc.), 65a.
[50] *Pope Nich. Tax.* (Rec. Com.), 227b.
[51] Feet of F. Worcs. 44 Hen. III, no. 10 ; *Ann. Mon.* (Rolls Ser.), iv, 446.
[52] Close, 1654, pt. xxvi, no. 8.
[53] Red Bk. of Bishopric of Worc. fol. 165.
[54] Worc. Epis. Reg. Maidstone, fol. 37.

third window is a small low-side window of lancet form. There was also one opposite, but this is now blocked and is not visible outside. Stone benches stopping at the low-side windows are built against the side walls in the western part of the chancel. The walling of the chancel is of ashlar; the two east and the south-east buttresses are of two stages, the lower with a gableted offset, but the other side buttresses are without the gablet. The chancel arch is sharply pointed and of two chamfered orders, the inner continuous from the floor, the outer dying on the jambs; the stonework is perhaps of the 13th century, but the arch has been subsequently widened, probably when the chancel was rebuilt.

The arcades to the nave are of three and a half bays on each side; the columns are round with moulded bases, square scalloped capitals, and chamfered

west of the third windows over the second piers from the east. They are of oolite stone with hollow-chamfered jambs and semicircular arches, the continuity of the chamfer being broken by projecting square blocks or imposts at the springing level of the arch. This springing level is 18 ft. above the ground floor and the heads of the windows $20\frac{1}{2}$ ft., the outer arrises being about $2\frac{1}{2}$ ft. apart. The windows to the west of the doorway on either side are higher than the others and apparently of slightly less width. The 15th-century clearstory has five windows a side, each of three lights under a square head. In the eastern respond of the south arcade is a corbel which supported the former rood-loft. The square-headed entrance to the loft is through the wall above the north-east respond, being approached by a stairway from the north aisle; the lower doorway in the

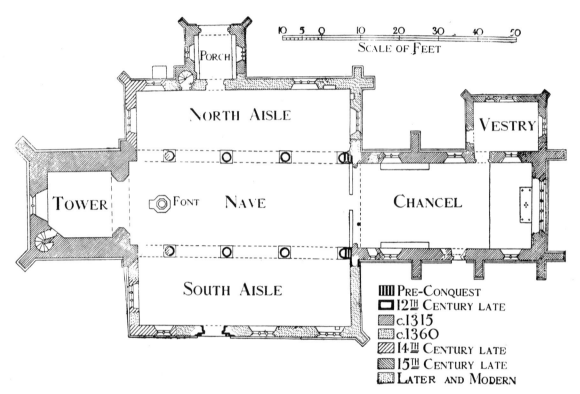

PLAN OF TREDINGTON CHURCH

abaci. The arches are pointed and of two square orders with chamfered labels on both sides. The half-round west responds of the original arcades were completed to form circular piers when the western half-arches were inserted in the late 14th century. Over the arcades and partly cut away for the arches are the remains of the Saxon clearstory windows. There are three main windows on each side, visible both in the nave and the aisles; the easternmost on the south has been opened out and shows the jambs to be splayed on both sides of the wall. The arches are of lias rubble and are chamfered like the jambs, and although they are roughly semicircular the voussoirs do not radiate from the centre, necessitating the insertion of wedge-shaped keystones in the crowns of the arches. The eastern jambs and part of the arches of both Saxon doorways to the western gallery remain in position immediately

east wall of the aisle retains its wood door, but the stair has been removed.

The late 14th-century east window of the north aisle has three lights with tracery above in a pointed arch and the north-east window is similar. To the north of the window in the east wall is a small square recess, probably once a locker, and near it in the north wall, to the east of the north-east window, is a large plain niche for a figure with a trefoiled segmental arch.[55] The north doorway is contemporary with the aisle; it has a two-centred arch and a richly moulded segmental rear arch. The wood door is old and has vertical ribs studded with square nail-heads. To the west of it is the 15th-century doorway to the stair leading up to the chamber over the porch.

[55] In this recess possibly stood the image of our Lady of Pity, and at the east end of this aisle may have been the altar of the chantry of St. Mary and St. Michael (see under advowson).

It has a four-centred arch and a wood door with a traceried head. The north-west window has two lights with a quatrefoiled spandrel within a two-centred arch, and is probably mainly a restoration. The west window has three lights and three quatrefoils above of a late 14th-century form under a two-centred head.

There is no east window to the south aisle. The first south window is very close to the east wall; it is original and has three lights under a pointed head filled with flowing tracery. Below it is a trefoiled piscina with an ogee head, a shelf and a mutilated basin.[56] The second window is old and of similar design to the east window of the north aisle. The south doorway is of late 12th-century date reset; it has two orders, the outer with modern shafts in the angles, the capitals of which are original and crudely carved with foliage. The arch is semicircular with a roll between the cheveron enrichment on the face and soffit, the cheverons being carved with foliage. The south-west window is of two lights with a quatrefoil above in a two-centred head, and the west window of this aisle is similar to the corresponding window of the north aisle. This wall has apparently been rebuilt and has not been reset on the former plinth, the northern part of the wall being moved more to the east.

The tower is of three stages with square buttresses to the north and south flush with the east face, and diagonal buttresses to the western angles. The two-centred tower arch has plain splayed jambs, on to which die the three chamfered orders. The stair turret recess is in the south-west angle and the west window has two lights with cusped tracery above in a pointed head. Below the first string-course on the north and south sides are small trefoiled loops, and on the west face a disused diamond-shaped clock dial.

The marks of the old steep gabled roof of the nave show on the east external face of the tower. The belfry is lighted in each wall by a window of two sharply pointed lights with a quatrefoiled spandrel in a two-centred arch. The parapet is pierced with quatrefoils and at the angles are square pinnacles with embattled cornices and plain pointed finials. Above the tower rises a tall stone spire divided by string-courses into three stages; at the foot are four gabled spire lights of two openings with a quatrefoil over. There are also diminutive lights near the top of the spire, which terminates in a carved finial.

The north porch is lighted on either side by windows; the western has two lights under a square head, the eastern was originally similar, but has been altered into three lights. Both have shouldered rear arches, the eastern having shields carved on the jambs in addition. The archway of the outer entrance has moulded jambs and head, with a wide hollow containing carved flowers with angels at the apex. Over the archway is a canopied niche with the remains of the figure of the patron saint. The bracket has three pointed corbels below. Above the niche is a blocked square-headed window formerly lighting the parvise. The porch has a plain moulded parapet and the roof is flat below and panelled with moulded ribs and carved bosses. The chancel roof is gabled and modern. The nave roof is of very low

pitch and retains most of its 15th-century timbers; the tie-beams are moulded and are strengthened with curved braces and moulded jacks resting on stone corbels carved with grotesques. The roof of the south aisle is of the same low pitch and has a moulded stone wall-plate, the tie-beams being supported by braces and jacks on moulded wood corbels. The north aisle has old moulded tie-beams, wall-plates and purlins.

The 15th-century font is octagonal with traceried sides to the bowl. Across the chancel arch is a low stone wall faced with modern wood panelling towards the west, and above it is the remaining portion of the traceried 15th-century rood screen. The pulpit with its canopy is a good example of 17th-century work. The oak lectern is also old; the chains were formerly attached to the copy of Jewell's *Apology*, which now rests upon it. The church contains many 15th-century bench ends and pew fronts with traceried panels and moulded top rails.

In the chancel is a brass effigy of a priest with a marginal inscription incorrectly fitted together, the date and name being lost. This is given by Nash as Richard Cassey, rector, who died c. 1427. There is also a brass, with a kneeling effigy and inscription in Latin to Henry Sampson, rector, died 1482, and a figure of a lady in ruff, full skirt and puffed sleeves, with a fragment of an inscription, the only remains of a brass to William Barnes, died 1561, and Alice his wife.

On the west wall of the south aisle is a 17th-century painted scroll with the inscription, 'One thing is needfull. They have chosen that good part.'

There are six bells: the treble by Matthew Bagley, 1683; the second by Mears, 1858; the third and fourth by George Purdye (Purdue), 1622; the fifth dated 1624, and tenor (undated) by George Purdye with the inscription 'Drawe neare to God.'

The communion plate includes a silver cup with a cover paten, large paten and two flagons, all except the cover bearing the inscribed date of 1638. The hall mark on the large paten is for the same year, but the others have the hall mark for 1591; there is also a second modern cup.

The registers before 1812 are as follows: (i) baptisms and burials 1541 to 1781 and marriages 1541 to 1784; (ii) baptisms 1781 to 1812 and burials 1782 to 1812; (iii) marriages 1754 to 1788; (iv) the same 1789 to 1812.

The chapel or church of *ST. GEORGE* at Darlingscott consists of a chancel, nave, north porch and a western bell-turret containing one bell. There is also a south transept, used as a schoolroom, which opens into the church by folding doors. The style is of the 13th century, and the material stone, with the exception of the transept, which is of brick The earlier pre-Reformation chapel may have been demolished as early as the 16th century.

The church of *ST. DAVID* at Newbold-on-Stour consists of a chancel, north vestry, nave, north aisle and north-west tower. The design is in the style of the 13th century, and the tower is surmounted by an octagonal lead-covered spire.

ADVOWSON The advowson of Tredington belonged to the Bishops of Worcester,[57] and remained in their hands until

[56] This piscina probably belonged to the altar of St. Nicholas, to which was attached the well-endowed chantry founded by Robert Walden in 1397 (see under advowson).
[57] *Rot. Lit. Pat.* (Rec. Com.), 165a. In 1216 the presentation was in the king's hands on account of a vacancy of the see of Worcester.

1328.[58] In January of that year a collation to the rectory made by Wulstan, Bishop-elect of Worcester, was confirmed by the king,[59] but in March of the same year this presentation was revoked, and the king presented Master Adam de Harvington,[60] giving as his reason that Tredington was in his gift because of the late voidance of the see.[61] The king, having again presented in 1339 [62] during a vacancy of the see, seems to have claimed the advowson as his right, but this was disputed by Wulstan, Bishop of Worcester. He was, however, unable to prove the right of the see of Worcester to the advowson, which the king recovered by a judgement in the courts.[63]

In 1345 a writ was issued against certain persons who had assaulted Thomas de Baddeby, whom the king had presented to the living.[64] In the following year the appointment of Thomas de Baddeby was ratified,[65] and in 1347 a commission was appointed to arrest all those who prosecuted appeals contrary to the judgement of the Bench.[66] In May of the same year the king, being informed that certain persons meant to induct one Thomas Dunclent,[67] who had been appointed by the pope,[68] issued a commission to arrest them.[69] In June a band of men entered the house of the king's nominee, Thomas Baddeby, collected the tithes,[70] and prevented the holding of the sessions.[71] There were probably further proceedings in the courts, and finally the king had to give way, for in January 1348 Thomas Dunclent,[72] the nominee of Rome, was appointed parson, the presentation by the king to Thomas de Baddeby was revoked,[73] and in August 1348 all those concerned in the riots were pardoned.[74]

From this time the advowson of the church of Tredington remained in the hands of the successive Bishops of Worcester [75] until 1549, when it passed by exchange to John Earl of Warwick.[76] He was created Duke of Northumberland in 1551, but was attainted and executed in 1553,[77] when all his estates were forfeited. In 1558–9 the advowson was granted to Bridget Morrison,[78] but the queen presented in 1581 by a lapse.[79]

The advowson afterwards passed to the Sheldons, the grantee of Ralph Sheldon presenting in 1606 and 1607.[80] Though the king presented in 1620 and again in 1660,[81] the advowson seems to have remained in the Sheldon family until 1702, when Ralph and Edward Sheldon sold it to Sir Henry Parker.[82] The presentation was made in 1703 by John Verney and Richard Freeman,[83] and in 1706 by John Verney.[84]

The advowson was purchased in 1713 from Sir Thomas Cooke Winford of Astley, Robert Hyde of Hatch (co. Wilts.), Harry Parker of the Inner Temple and Nathaniel Pigot for £1,540 by the Principal of Jesus College, Oxford, with whose successors it still remains.[85]

During the 18th century it appears to have been the practice to present two clerks to the church of Tredington, one being called the senior and the other the junior portionist.[86] The latter was probably a perpetual curate.

The pope in 1399 [87] granted an indulgence to those who should visit the chapel of St. Mary the Virgin in the church of Tredington, where there was great devotion to an image (*ymaginem*) of our Lady of Pity (*Pietatis*) holding a figure of Christ crucified.[88]

In 1415 Richard Cassey, rector of Tredington, obtained licence to have a portable altar.[89]

In 1397 Robert Walden of Warwick founded a chantry of one chaplain in the parish church of Tredington to pray for the king and his progenitors and Thomas Dunclent, late rector of Tredington.[90] The chantry, later called Walden Chantry or St. Nicholas Chantry, was dedicated to St. Nicholas,[91] and the chantry priest was bound every year on the day of the anniversary of Thomas Dunclent to celebrate Requiem Mass and say the full office of the dead, i.e. *Placebo* and *Dirige* (Sarum Use), and on all other high days and feasts to say service according to the Sarum Ordinal.[92] The advowson of the chantry was vested in Robert and his heirs,[93] and probably passed from him to John Walden of Warwick, for in 1465 John Upton of Warwick, who had married Agnes, one of the daughters and heirs of John Walden, presented to the chantry.[94]

Isabel daughter and heir of John Upton married as a second husband Hugh Dalby, and in 1507–8 sold the advowson of Walden chantry to John Spenser.[95] The advowson remained with the Spensers until the chantry was dissolved in 1547.[96] At that time the clear yearly revenue of the chantry was £14 4s. 7½d.[97] The chantry with the capital messuage and endowment was granted in 1547 to Sir Philip Hoby,[98] who sold it in 1551–2 to Thomas Andrews.[99] Land in King's Norton belonging to the chantry was granted in 1571–2 to William James and John Grey,[100]

[58] *Reg. G. Giffard* (Worcs. Hist. Soc.), 69, 265, 450, 461, 467, 488.
[59] *Cal. Pat.* 1327–30, p. 205.
[60] In 1332 Adam de Harvington was constituted the bishop's vice in the diocese during his absence from England (Worc. Epis. Reg. Orlton [1327–33], fol. 27).
[61] *Cal. Pat.* 1327–30, p. 347.
[62] *Sede Vacante Reg.* (Worcs. Hist. Soc.), 265; *Cal. Pat.* 1338–40, p. 175.
[63] De Banco R. 344, m. 440.
[64] Ibid. 344, m. 440; 346, m. 328 d.; 345, m. 81.
[65] *Cal. Pat.* 1345–8, p. 475.
[66] Ibid. 313.   [67] Ibid. 322.
[68] Ibid. 313.
[69] Ibid. 322.
[70] Ibid. 383.
[71] Ibid. 386.
[72] In 1348 Thomas obtained an indult to study at a university for three years without being ordained deacon or priest

or residing on his benefice (*Cal. Papal Letters*, iii, 301).
[73] *Cal. Pat.* 1345–8, p. 447.
[74] Ibid. 1348–50, p. 220.
[75] Nash, op. cit. ii, 431.
[76] Pat. 3 Edw. VI, pt. iii, m. 3.
[77] G.E.C. *Complete Peerage*, viii, 64.
[78] Pat. 1 Eliz. pt. vi.
[79] Nash, op. cit. ii, 432.
[80] Habington, op. cit. i, 434; Nash, op. cit. ii, 432.
[81] Nash, loc. cit.; Pat. 17 Jas. I, pt. vi; Inst. Bks. (P.R.O.).
[82] The sale took place in 1702 (Feet of F. Worcs. East. 1 Anne), but Sir Henry had presented in 1701 (Inst. Bks. [P.R.O.]).
[83] Inst. Bks. (P.R.O.). This presentation was confirmed by the Crown.
[84] Ibid.
[85] Information supplied by Mr. W. Hawker Hughes, bursar, Jesus Coll., Oxford.
[86] Inst. Bks. (P.R.O.).

[87] *Cal. Papal Letters*, v, 207.
[88] Ibid.
[89] Ibid. vi, 363.
[90] *Cal. Pat.* 1396–9, p. 68.
[91] Worc. Epis. Reg. Silvester de Gigliis (1498–1521), fol. 90 f.
[92] Ibid. Winchcombe (1395–1401), fol. 17 f.
[93] *Cal. Pat.* 1396–9, p. 68.
[94] *Visit. of Warw.* (Harl. Soc. 12), 229; Worc. Epis. Reg. Carpenter (1443–76), fol. 188 d.
[95] Feet of F. Worcs. Mich. 23 Hen. VII; De Banco R. Mich. 23 Hen. VII, m. 21.
[96] Worc. Epis. Reg. Silvester de Gigliis (1498–1521), fol. 90 f.; *L. and P. Hen. VIII*, xvi, g. 107 (2); xxi (2), g. 771 (11).
[97] Chant. Cert. 25, no. 14.
[98] Pat. 1 Edw. VI, pt. ix, m. 10.
[99] Ibid. 5 Edw. VI, pt. ii, m. 41.
[100] Ibid. 14 Eliz. pt. vii.

Tredington Church : The North Arcade

Tredington Church : The South Arcade

and in 1582–3 the chantry and lands belonging were granted to Theophilus and Robert Adams.[1] It may afterwards have passed to the Sheldons, for the Chantry Farm House in Tredington was among the estates forfeited by William Sheldon and discharged from sequestration and bought of the treason trustees in 1653.[2] The name of the purchaser of the estate is not given.

There may have been a second chantry in the church of Tredington, for in 1487 John Upton presented to the chantry of our Lady and St. Michael, a pension of 4 marks from the revenues of the chantry being assigned to the retiring chaplain.[3]

The chapel of Blackwell was in existence before 1240. It was a demesne chapel (*dominica capella*) of the Prior of Worcester, but belonged to the church of Tredington. Service was celebrated there by a chaplain of Tredington on the day of dedication (26 January), on the day of the deposition of St. Wulfstan (19 January) and on the feast of St. Anne (26 July).[4]

There were other chapels belonging to the church of Tredington at Newbold, Armscote and Darlingscott,[5] but the date of their foundation is not known. The four chapels were granted in 1549 to Richard Field and others,[6] and were probably demolished.

In 1833 Newbold and Armscote were constituted a separate ecclesiastical parish, and a church, parsonage-house and churchyard were built at Newbold.[7] The living is a rectory in the gift of Jesus College, Oxford.

Shipston-on-Stour and Tidmington were chapelries of Tredington until 1719, when they were formed into a separate parish and endowed with a third of the rectory of Tredington.[8]

The Society of Friends hold a meeting at Armscote on the first Sunday in August. The Quakers seem to have been established there at an early date, for George Fox and his friend Thomas Lower were arrested there in 1673 and imprisoned at Worcester Gaol for more than a year.[9] In 1689 the house of John Bennett at Tredington was licensed for Quaker worship.[10]

CHARITIES In 1831 John Jordan by a codicil to his will, proved in the P.C.C. 25 November, bequeathed (among other things) such a sum of money as would purchase sufficient Government stock to produce £50 a year to be applied towards the support of a day school. A sum of £1,666 13s. 4d. 3 per cent. consols was purchased, and the endowment is now represented by a like amount of 2½ per cent. consols, producing £41 13s. 4d. yearly, with the official trustees. Three-fifths of the income is applied in aid of the National school of Tredington and two-fifths for the National school in the hamlet of Newbold.

In 1859 the Rev. William Hopkins by his will proved at London 8 September, gave a sum of money, now represented by £314 18s. 10d. consols

with the official trustees, the dividends to be applied for the benefit of the poor. The annual dividends, amounting to £7 17s. 4d., are distributed in coal and money doles. In 1909 coal was distributed among fifty-three families.

This parish is entitled to a twenty-first part of the dividends arising from several sums of stock forming the endowment of Richard Badger's charity founded by will, proved at London, 7 December 1907. A moiety of the proportion due to this parish is applicable for church purposes and the other moiety for the poor. In 1910 a sum of £37 4s. 2d. was received. (See under Shipston-on-Stour.)

Hamlet of Newbold.—In 1773 Thomas Eden by deed provided for the instruction of poor children in three several parishes in the county of Gloucester, in one parish of the county of Warwick, and in the hamlet of Newbold. An annual payment of about £8 a year is made by the trustees of the charity at Pebworth, Gloucestershire, and applied in aid of the National school.

A sum of £16 13s. 4d., being two-fifths of the dividends of John Jordan's charity, is applied for the same purpose. (See under Tredington.)

Henry Eden, a son of Thomas Eden above mentioned, by his will dated in 1788, and by a codicil dated in 1791, proved in the P.C.C., made certain bequests for schools and the support of the Methodist cause which do not appear to have come into operation.

In 1859 the Rev. William Hopkins, by his will proved at London 8 September, bequeathed £200, now represented by £209 14s. consols with the official trustees, the annual dividends, amounting to £5 4s. 8d., to be distributed in coal.

This hamlet with Armscote is entitled to receive one twenty-first part of the dividends from the endowment of Richard Badger's charity, founded by will proved 7 December 1907. In 1910 a sum of £37 4s. 2d. was so received and applied as to one moiety for church purposes and the other moiety in the distribution of coal. (See under Shipston-on-Stour.)

Hamlet of Darlingscott.—In 1872 T. Edwin Gibbs, by his will proved at London 22 April, bequeathed £294 6s. 10d. consols with the official trustees, the annual dividends, amounting to £7 7s., to be applied towards the salary of a mistress and maintaining a preparatory school at Darlingscott for younger children unable to attend the school at Tredington.

This hamlet with Blackwell is entitled to receive one twenty-first part of the dividends from the endowment of Richard Badger's charity, founded by will proved 7 December 1907. In 1910 a sum of £37 4s. 2d. was so received, of which £10 was applied for church purposes and £27 4s. 2d. distributed in coals to the poor on St. Thomas's Day.

---

[1] Pat. 25 Eliz. pt. iv, m. 4.
[2] Cal. Com. for Comp. 1955.
[3] Worc. Epis. Reg. Moreton (1486–97), fol. 17 d.
[4] Reg. of Worc. Priory (Camd. Soc.), 64 b.

[5] Pat. 3 Edw. VI, pt. v.
[6] Ibid.
[7] Loc. and Personal Act, 3 & 4 Will. IV, cap. 30.
[8] Priv. Act, 6 Geo. I, cap. 9.

[9] Dict. Nat. Biog. The original indictment is still among the Worcester Session records.
[10] Var. Coll. (Hist. MSS. Com.), i, 325.

WARNDON

Warmedon, Wermindun (xiii cent.) ; Warnington (xvi cent.) ; Warnton (xvii cent.).

Warndon is a small parish in mid-Worcestershire, about 2 miles east of the town of Worcester. It has an area of 827 acres, of which in 1905 302 were arable land, 385 permanent grass and 30 woods.[1] The soil is clay with a subsoil of Keuper Marl, growing crops of wheat and beans. A road from Droitwich to Worcester forms part of the southern boundary of the parish, and from it another road runs north to the village of Warndon, which lies in the centre of the parish. In the village there is a cross. The hamlet of Trotshill lies in the south. Most of the land in the parish is flat, but there is a slight rise towards the south, the highest point being 185 ft. above the ordnance datum on the Worcester road in the extreme south.

There is no Inclosure Act for Warndon.

The Worcestershire Naturalists' Club visited Warndon on 18 June 1885, and its *Transactions* contain a description of the present manor-house erected in the 17th century on the site of that once inhabited by the Lygons. Remains of the moat that once surrounded the house and church were then visible, as well as a cellar and a heavy large-hinged iron-studded door, relics of the original house.[2]

MANOR At the date of the Domesday Survey Urse held *WARNDON* of the Bishop of Worcester's manor of Northwick.[3] The bishop's overlordship continued until the 13th century,[4] but it is not mentioned afterwards, and it apparently lapsed, Urse's descendants the Beauchamps, formerly intermediary lords,[5] holding directly of the king. The manor was held of the Beauchamps' manor of Elmley Castle,[6] until the overlordship lapsed,[7] probably soon after 1611, when the last mention of it occurs.[8]

The manor of Warndon was held in 1086 under Urse the Sheriff by Robert.[9] There is some indication that the Poers held the manor in the time of Henry II. Habington quotes a grant by Hugh Poer to the priory of Worcester of 2s. yearly from his chapel of Warndon, and assigns the date of this charter to the time of Henry II.[10] Further, in 1284–5 John Poer held land of the manor of Northwick in Warndon and elsewhere,[11] but the manor of Warndon was probably held by the Bracys (between whom and the Poers Habington deduces some connexion from a similarity in their coats of arms)[12] as early as the time of Henry I, for William de Bracy in 1166 held half a knight's fee in Worcestershire of William de Beauchamp, of ancient feoffment from the time of Henry I[13]; indeed, Robert, who held at Warndon and Aston in 1086 under Urse the Sheriff, was probably an ancestor of the Bracy family, who held both at Warndon and Aston early in the 13th century.[14]

In 1205 Robert Bracy gave up to the Prior of Worcester all his claim to common of pasture at Lippard in exchange for a similar quitclaim by the prior as to common in Warndon.[15] From this time the manor followed the same descent[16] as that of Madresfield[17] (q.v.) until 1594, when Sir William Lygon sold it to Rowland Berkeley.[18] Rowland acquired the manor of Spetchley in 1606, and the descent of Warndon has been identical with that of Spetchley (q.v.) from that time,[19] the present owner being Mr. Robert Valentine Berkeley, J.P., D.L.

In 978 Bishop Oswald gave to Aethelnoth 1 *mansa* at *SMITE*.[20] This formed part of the manor of Northwick, and was held of the Bishops of Worcester as of that manor.[21] In the time of Henry II, Godfrey the Archdeacon held half a hide of land at Smite,[22] which had passed by 1299 to John Washbourne, also known as John de Dufford, son of Roger de Washbourne, who claimed to have held it of John de Dossigh and his wife Salima, who was a daughter of William de la Verne, though in 1299 he held it of the bishop in chief.[23] In 1327 Hugh de Dufford complained that certain persons broke his house at Smite and assaulted him.[24]

John Washbourne, by his will dated 1532, bequeathed the manor of Smite to his wife Margaret for her life. She afterwards married John Kettleby, and they were in possession of the manor at the time of the death of John Washbourne's son Anthony, upon whom they had settled the reversion in 1547.[25] John son of Anthony Washbourne was dealing with the manor in 1573,[26] and conveyed it in 1598 to his brother Robert.[27] Robert and his wife Mary sold it in 1601 to Rowland Berkeley,[28] who died seised of it ten

---

[1] Statistics from Bd. of Agric. (1905).
[2] op. cit. 1847–96, p. 322.
[3] *V.C.H. Worcs.* i, 294*b*.
[4] *Testa de Nevill* (Rec. Com.), 41*b*.
[5] Ibid.
[6] Chan. Inq. p.m. (Ser. 2), xxi, 19 ; cccxxv, 181.
[7] *Cal. Inq. p.m.* 1–9 *Edw. II*, 403 ; Add. MS. 28024, fol. 190*a* ; Chan. Inq. p.m. (Ser. 2), xxi, 19.
[8] Chan. Inq. p.m. (Ser. 2), cccxxv, 181.
[9] *V.C.H. Worcs.* i, 294*b*.
[10] *Surv. of Worcs.* (Worcs. Hist. Soc.), i, 450–1.
[11] Ibid. ii, 41.
[12] Ibid. i, 448.
[13] *Red Bk. of Exch.* (Rolls Ser.), 299.
[14] *Testa de Nevill* (Rec. Com.), 41*b*.
[15] Nash, *Hist. of Worcs.* ii, 318 ; *Reg. of Worc. Priory* (Camd. Soc.), 53*b*.
[16] Thomas Lygon seems to have acquired this manor earlier than that of Madresfield, possibly on his marriage

with Joan Bracy, as he was holding it in 1428 (*Feud. Aids*, v, 319).
[17] *Testa de Nevill* (Rec. Com.), 41*b* ; *Hist. MSS. Com. Rep.* v, App. i, 301 ; Feet of F. Worcs. Trin. 10 Edw. II ; Chart. R. 2 Edw. III, m. 1, no. 4 ; *Feud. Aids*, v, 307 ; *Sede Vacante Reg.* (Worcs. Hist. Soc.), 350 ; Chan. Inq. p.m. (Ser. 2), xxi, 19 ; xxvii, 22 ; cx, 172 ; cxlviii, 1 ; ccvi, 8 ; Chan. Proc. Eliz. Ww. 15, no. 54.
[18] Feet of F. Worcs. Mich. 36 & 37 Eliz. This was confirmed by another fine five years later (ibid. East. 41 Eliz.).
[19] For references see Spetchley.
[20] Dugdale, *Mon. Angl.* i, 569; Heming, *Chartul.* (ed. Hearne), 150. The boundaries of Smite were as follows : from Althreton in the middle to the Oldbury, from thence to Impanleg, from there to Thornley. From there to Babel's Hill and from that hill to the broad slough in Kilmer's mere. From the slough to Smite and thence

to the hill. From the hill to Brooks Croft and from that croft to Hefancroft and so to the Gleden (Heming, op. cit. 150–1, 355 ; Nash, op. cit. App. 51).
[21] Habington, op. cit. ii, 41, 42, 43.
[22] Red Bk. of Bishopric of Worc. (Eccl. Com. Rec. Var. bdle. 121, no. 43698), fol. 18.
[23] Habington, op. cit. ii, 42, 43 ; Red Bk. of Bishopric of Worc. fol. 2.
[24] *Cal. Pat.* 1324–7, p. 352. Hugh was attorney in England for John de Dufford at this time (see Bredicot).
[25] Chan. Inq. p.m. (Ser. 2), clix, 75 ; *Valor Eccl.* (Rec. Com.), iii, 229 ; a manor at Smite seems to have belonged to the hospital of St. Oswald, Worcester, in 1535 (*Valor Eccl.* [Rec. Com.], iii, 229).
[26] Feet of F. Worcs. Trin. 15 Eliz.
[27] Ibid. Hil. 40 Eliz. ; *Visit. of Worcs.* (Harl. Soc. 27), 143.
[28] Feet of F. Worcs. Mich. 43 & 44 Eliz.

WARNDON CHURCH C. 1810
(*From a Water-colour by Thos. Rickards in Prattinton Collection*)

WARNDON CHURCH FROM THE SOUTH-WEST

years later.[29] An estate at Smite afterwards passed to the Solley family. Humphrey son of John Solley of Smite died unmarried about 1647, and was succeeded by his brother Thomas, from whom the estate passed to his son Thomas.[30]

Habington gives the following account of Smite : 'there lyethe in the north east of Warndon half a township called Smite, straungly divided, the one part in Warndon, the other in Claynes, and wheare the landes in theyre medowes weare yearely altered from one to another : the tythes interchangeably altered so theyre courses, thys yeere in Warndon the next in Claynes.'[31]

Smite is now in the parish of Hindlip, Upper and Lower Smite having been transferred from Warndon in 1880 and Smite Farm from Claines in the same year.[32]

The Grey Friars and Black Friars of Worcester owned land in Warndon in the 16th century, but it is not known at what date they acquired it or by whom it was given. After the Dissolution it was included in the grant of their possessions by Henry VIII in 1539 to the bailiffs and citizens of Worcester.[33]

CHURCH The church of *ST. NICHOLAS* consists of a chancel and nave in one range, with a north porch of brick, and a west bell-tower constructed of timber. The earliest part of the church is the nave, which dates from the 12th century. Early in the 15th century the chancel was rebuilt, and probably about a century later the bell-tower was added. The porch is probably of the 17th century.

The east window of the chancel is of three lights, and has been considerably restored. In it are inserted some interesting fragments of 15th-century glass, including a beautifully coloured figure of the Virgin and Child and figures of St. Peter, St. Paul and St. Andrew. The north and south walls of the church contain five windows, three on the north and two on the south, all of two lights, with four small lights and flowing tracery above them under a square head. The 12th-century north and south doors (the latter blocked) have each a roll-moulded round head and jambs. There is a brick porch, apparently of the 17th-century, with wooden sprockets forming an arched entrance to the south door. The font at the west end of the nave is of 15th-century date, heptagonal in form and has a stem of the same thickness as the bowl, both being moulded and treated as a single member. The tower is of half-timber construction with hewn oak studding from 7 in. to 10 in. square and lath and plaster filling and is probably of 16th-century date. On the west is a two-light window with a plain square head.

A curious feature of the church is a chamber formed between the flat ceiling over the western part of the nave and the roof, and entered from the tower. The rest of the nave and chancel has a barrel-shaped plaster ceiling. The seating of the church is of 18th-century date, but the lower part of the posts of the rood screen remain in the back of one of the pews, and above this is a single tie-beam with struts rising to the ceiling, the spaces between the struts being filled in with lath and plaster. The oak altar-rails, of 17th-century date, are supported on turned balusters, and there is an oak communion table of the same date. There are also some carved cherubs, of the Grinling Gibbons type and a pelican in piety preserved in the tower, which are said to have come from the Cathedral at Worcester.

The belfry contains two bells and space for a third. The treble bears the name 'John Brook c w 1710' and the mark of Richard Saunders, the second is a pre-Reformation bell inscribed 'Sancte [Nicholas ?] Ora Pro nobis.' The original treble was sold in the middle of the 19th century, and, according to Prattinton, who visited the church in 1818,[34] bore the inscription 'Ave Maria Ora Pro nobis.'

The church plate consists of a chalice, hall marked for 1669, inscribed as the gift of Thomas Wilde, and a modern paten of 1893.

The registers before 1812 are as follows : (i) baptisms 1561 to 1812, burials 1563 to 1812, marriages 1567 to 1757 ; (ii) a marriage-book 1759 to 1812.

ADVOWSON The chapel of Warndon was originally annexed to the church of St. Helen Worcester. After the death of Bishop Wulfstan the monks committed the care of St. Helen's vicarage and all its members, in which the chapel of Warndon in Northwick was included, to Frithericus, priest of St. Helen's, for their use.[35] The chapel seems later on to have passed to Hugh Poer.[36] The first recorded institution is dated 1300, and the chapel had by that time become a church.[37] The presentation was made by Robert Bracy, lord of Warndon, and from that time the advowson has followed the same descent as the manor.[38]

The rectory was united with that of Spetchley in 1874.[39]

In 1374 the Prior of Worcester warned Thomas Feld, the rector, to return to his duties, which he had neglected. He, however, exchanged his living for St. Clement's, Worcester, in the following year.[40]

In 1542 Henry Holbeche, last Prior and first Dean of Worcester,[41] consecrated the church and churchyard, which were dedicated in honour of St. Nicholas.[42] This may have been when the tower was added to the church.

CHARITIES The legacies of £5 and £10 mentioned on the church table as having been left for the poor by the will of Richard Berwick, proved 1663, and by the will of

[29] Chan. Inq. p.m. (Ser. 2), cccxxv, 181.

[30] Metcalfe, *Visit. of Worcs.* 1682-3, p. 87.

[31] op. cit. i, 450.

[32] *Pop. Ret.* (1891), ii, 657.

[33] Pat. 31 Hen. VIII, pt. i ; *L. and P. Hen. VIII*, xiv (2), g. 780 (9).

[34] Prattinton Coll. (Soc. Antiq.), xxxiv.

[35] Nash, op. cit. App. 145 ; Heming, op. cit. 427.

[36] Habington, op. cit. i, 450-1. The

deed quoted is accompanied by others of the reign of Henry II.

[37] *Reg. G. Giffard* (Worcs. Hist. Soc.), 525.

[38] Nash, op. cit. ii, 452-3 ; *Reg. W. Ginsborough* (Worcs. Hist. Soc.), 124 ; Feet of F. Worcs. Mich. 36 & 37 Eliz. ; East. 41 Eliz. ; East. 20 Chas. I ; East. 31 Chas. II ; Recov. R. Mich. 10 Geo. II, rot. 147 ; Mich. 17 Geo. II, rot. 160 ; Trin. 48 Geo. III, rot. 37 ; Hil. 2 & 3 Geo. IV, rot. 39. Presentations were

made between 1726 and 1791 by members of the Nash family, and in 1888-9 by William Odell, possibly as trustees for the Berkeleys (Inst. Bks. [P.R.O.] ; *Clergy Lists*).

[39] *Parl. Papers* (1890-1), lxi, no. 386, p. 47.

[40] *Sede Vacante Reg.* (Worcs. Hist. Soc.), 320, 349.

[41] *V.C.H. Worcs.* ii, 111.

[42] *Worcs. Naturalists' Club Trans.* 1847-96, p. 321.

Robert Berkeley, proved 1693, respectively, to be used as a permanent stock, appear to have been expended for some parochial object.

Charities of George Wingfield and Mrs. Anne Sumner.—In or about 1813 Mrs. Anne Sumner, in pursuance of the will of George Wingfield, her first husband, bequeathed £100, the interest to be applied in gowns to clothe poor women, no woman to have a gown for two years together. The legacy is represented by £141 10s. 9d. consols, producing £3 10s. 8d. yearly. In 1909 fourteen gowns at 5s. 6d. each were distributed.

In 1822 Colonel Henry Barry, in fulfilment of the wishes of his sister Elizabeth Barry, by deed, gave £50 for the poor. This gift is represented by £54 0s. 4d. consols, the annual dividends of which, amounting to £1 7s., are distributed in bread.

The church table stated that a piece of meadow ground in the parish of Claines of about one-third of an acre, known as Church Meadow, was given to the poor. The land was sold in 1878, and the proceeds invested in £64 13s. 4d. consols, since augmented by accumulations to £76 10s. 9d. consols. The interest, amounting to £1 18s. yearly, is applied towards the maintenance of the church. The several sums of stock are held by the official trustees.

WELLAND

Wenlond (ix cent.) ; Weneland (xii cent.) ; Went-lande, Wenlond (xiii cent.).

The parish of Welland lies in the south-west of the county. It has an area of 1,888 acres, of which in 1905 498 were arable land, 1,068 permanent grass and 17½ wood.[1] The parish was formerly part of Malvern Chase,[2] which was disafforested in 1631–2,[3] and is studded with small woods. The soil is loam, and the subsoil Keuper Marl, producing crops of wheat, beans and barley. The numerous old clay-pits in the parish indicate that clay was worked for manure. The land rises from about 100 ft. above the ordnance datum on the eastern border of the parish to a height of 276 ft. on the western boundary near Marl Bank. The high road from Upton-on-Severn to Malvern Wells, which passes through the village, is here called Drake Street, and is continued through Marl Bank, a district to the north-west of the village.

Mere Brook, running east into the River Severn, near Upton-on-Severn, forms the northern boundary of the parish. A stream runs through the village of Welland, which is situated in the centre of the parish, at the foot of the eastern slopes of the Malvern Hills, upon the main road, about 2 miles west of Upton-on-Severn. Upon the south side of the road is the modern church of St. James. The original church stood upon a by-road, about half a mile to the eastward, a little to the south of the main road. Only the gravestones in the surrounding churchyard mark the site of the original building, no vestige of which is now left. On the north is the old vicarage, a half-timber building covered with rough-cast, and on the south Welland Court, a good brick house of the early 18th century. At the junction of this by-road with the main road is a fine half-timber farm-house with later brick additions. The houses here are mainly modern, though one or two are of half-timber, modernized and cased with brick.

An Inclosure Act for Welland was passed in 1847,[4] and the award is dated 1852.[5]

The Ashchurch, Tewkesbury and Malvern branch of the Midland railway runs through the north of the parish, and the nearest stations are at Upton-on-Severn and at Malvern Wells.

Among the place-names that have been found are Fauxhalle, le Prioris Fulmer, le Hooke wood [6] (xvi cent.), The Mere and the Vicar's Hill [7] (xvii cent.).

MANORS The manor of WELLAND formed part of the inheritance of King Coenwulf, and is said to have been given in 889 with Upton-on-Severn to the see of Worcester by Ealdorman Athulf, kinsman of King Coenwulf.[8] Welland is not mentioned in the Domesday Survey, and was probably then included in the manor of Bredon, for in a survey of the lands of the bishopric taken in 1299 it is stated that all the tenants of Welland owed suit at the court of Bredon,[9] and in valuations of Bredon Manor taken in 1299, 1408 and 1529 Welland is included.[10] The manor had probably been separated from Bredon before 1535, for in the valuation of the bishop's lands taken at that time it is entered apart from Bredon, and it had then and in 1560 a separate bailiff.[11]

Richard I in 1189 freed 34 acres at Welland from all forest exactions,[12] and King John confirmed this charter.[13] The manor of Welland was confirmed to the bishop by Pope Gregory (1272–6).[14] The successive Bishops of Worcester [15] remained in peaceful possession of the manor [16] until Bishop Heath was deprived by Edward VI in 1552 for refusing to subscribe to the Edwardian Prayer Book.[17] Edward VI, instead of restoring it to Bishop Hooper, Heath's successor, granted it to John Duke of Northumberland in exchange for other lands in 1553.[18] The duke sold the manor to Sir John Throckmorton for over 200 marks.[19] Bishop Heath was restored in July 1553 on Queen Mary's accession, and, in the words

---

[1] Statistics from Bd. of Agric. (1905).
[2] Nash, *Hist. of Worcs.* ii, 454, and Introd. p. lxxv.
[3] *V.C.H. Worcs.* ii, 320.
[4] Burton, *Bibl. of Worcs.* i, 114 ; Priv. Act, 10 & 11 Vict. cap. 25.
[5] *Blue Bk. Incl. Awards,* 192.
[6] *L. and P. Hen. VIII,* xx (2), g. 496 (49) ; Pat. 37 Hen. VIII, pt. x.
[7] Prattinton Coll. (Soc. Antiq.).
[8] Dugdale, *Mon. Angl.* i, 609.
[9] Nash, op. cit. ii, 454 ; Habington,

Surv. of Worcs. (Worcs. Hist. Soc.) i, 551.
[10] Habington, op. cit. i, 529 ; Red Bk. of Bishopric of Worc. (Eccl. Com. Rec. Var. bdle. 121, no. 43698), fol. 65, &c.
[11] *Valor Eccl.* (Rec. Com.), III, 218 ; Mins. Accts. 2 & 3 Eliz. no. 38.
[12] Cart. Antiq. RR. 15.
[13] Ibid. I, 31.
[14] Thomas, *Surv. of Cath. Church of Worc.* App. 49.

[15] In 1460 John, Bishop of Worcester, gave to his servant John Gower the office of keeper of his woods at Welland and elsewhere in the chase of Malvern (Nash, op. cit. ii, 137).
[16] *Reg. G. Giffard* (Worcs. Hist. Soc.), 519 ; Thomas, op. cit. A 120 ; Habington, op. cit. i, 551 ; ii, 295, 135 ; *Valor Eccl.* (Rec. Com.), iii, 218.
[17] *V.C.H. Worcs.* ii, 45.
[18] Pat. 7 Edw. VI, pt. viii, m. 25.
[19] *Cal. S. P. Dom.* 1601–3, p. 575.

of Sir John Throckmorton, 'entered without law or order into all again,' and so Sir John lost his land and money also and had no recompense.[20]

Queen Elizabeth took the manor from Bishop Pates under the Act of Parliament of 1559, which empowered the queen to take into her hands certain of the temporal possessions of any bishopric which fell vacant, recompensing the value with parsonages impropriate.[21] This manor was not, however, retained by the Crown,[22] but passed again to the see of Worcester. It was sold in 1648[23] as a possession of the bishopric by the Parliamentary commissioners for the sale of the bishops' lands to Nicholas Lechmere of Hanley Castle, Thomas Lechmere and Matthew Smith for £110 13s. 6d.[24] At the Restoration the manor of Welland returned to the bishopric, and still forms part of the possessions of the see.[25]

The Bishops of Worcester had a mill in their

of John son of John Walpole of Welland, who claimed a third of a messuage and land at Welland against Maud wife of John Walpole, and a third of a messuage and land there against William son of John Walpole. This she claimed as dower, and, as the legality of her marriage was proved, it may be supposed that she obtained her third part in the estate.[31] This is probably the estate which subsequently became known as the manor of *DAUNCIES*, and was released in 1463 by John son and heir of Thomas Sugwas to Robert Hanley for life, and after his death to William Walpole and his heirs.[32] Some twenty to thirty years later the manor of Dauncies was claimed by Christiana Smith daughter of Alice daughter of Hugh son of William Walpole, who complained that Thomas Pauncefoot, a trustee in the conveyance of 1463, and others refused to allow her to have possession of the manor. Thomas, however, stated that the manor

WELLAND COURT

manor of Welland, which is mentioned in 1197.[26] In 1299 Bishop Godfrey Giffard leased it to William le Donnare of Bredon.[27] There is no mill at the present day.

Robert Walpole or Wavepol (Bagepol) held land at Welland towards the end of the 12th century.[28] John Walpole paid a subsidy of 12s. 6d. there in 1280,[29] and in 1299 he held a messuage and land in Welland 'of the ancient feoffment.'[30] In 1306 a writ was issued to the Bishop of Worcester to hold an inquisition as to the lawful marriage of Margery wife

had been sold to him by William Walpole.[33] In 1515–16 the manor was sold by William Wicombe and his wife Christine, cousin and heir of Henry Walpole *alias* Wenland, to William Mucklow.[33a]

The priory of Little Malvern also owned land in Welland. It is not known by whom it was given, but in 1322 the Crown granted the prior 'protection in his manor of Welland.'[34] In 1535 this land was valued at 18s. 8d. a year,[35] and, having come into the king's hands on the dissolution of the house in 1537,[36] was granted in 1545 to William Pinnock and Elizabeth

[20] *Cal. S. P. Dom.* 1601–3, p. 575.
[21] Mins. Accts. 2 & 3 Eliz. no. 38.
[22] Pat. 4 Eliz. pt. vi, m. 24 ; Rentals and Surv. portf. 16, no. 87.
[23] Close, 24 Chas. I, pt. xiv, m. 32.
[24] Ibid.
[25] Welland does not seem to have been among the manors taken over by the Ecclesiastical Commissioners in 1860.

[26] Thomas, op. cit. A 120 ; Habington, op. cit. i, 553.
[27] *Reg. G. Giffard* (Worcs. Hist. Soc.), 519.
[28] Red Bk. of Bishopric of Worc. fol. 66.
[29] *Lay Subs. R. Worcs.* 1280 (Worcs. Hist. Soc.), 44.
[30] Red Bk. of Bishopric of Worc. fol. 62.

[31] *Reg. W. Ginsborough* (Worcs. Hist. Soc.), 232–3.
[32] Close, 2 Edw. IV, m. 19.
[33] Early Chan. Proc. bdle. 109, no. 72.
[33a] Feet of F. Worcs. Hil. 7 Hen. VIII.
[34] *Cal. Pat.* 1321–4, p. 64.
[35] *Valor Eccl.* (Rec. Com.), iii, 243.
[36] *L. and P. Hen. VIII*, xvi, 617.

his wife.[37] The estate included land called Fauxhall and Prioris Fulmer near le Hooke wood. Its further descent is not known.

CHURCH The church of *ST. JAMES* consists of a chancel 31 ft. by 20 ft., a nave 61 ft. by 25 ft., north and south aisles 10 ft. wide, a tower with a wooden spire built over the westernmost bay of the south aisle, an organ chamber north of the chancel and a vestry below the chancel. The church was erected in 1875 from the designs of J. W. Hugall, half a mile from the old church, which was then destroyed. The material of the building is stone, and the detail is in 13th-century style.

The chancel has a large three-light window with two smaller windows to north and south. On the south side is an arched opening to a quadrant passage to the south aisle, which is now closed by the quire

chalice with a high spire-like cover, both of elaborate repoussé work, with the hall marks for 1613; a blown glass flagon with a silver-gilt lid, neck-band and foot, with the hall marks of 1582, both bearing the Taylor arms. There are also a silver cup of the usual type dated 1571 and a modern silver-gilt cup, flagon and paten—the last three the gift of Mrs. Forsyth—and a modern paten partly made from an old one melted down.

The registers [38] before 1812 are as follows: (i) all entries from 1670, the baptisms and burials to 1770 and the marriages to 1754; (ii) baptisms and burials 1771 to 1813; (iii) a printed marriage book 1754 to 1812.

ADVOWSON The chapel of Welland is thought by Habington to have been bestowed upon the priory of Little Malvern by Simon, Bishop of Worcester (1125–50).[39] In 1288 a

WELLAND CHURCH FROM THE SOUTH-WEST

seats. The nave is of four bays and has round piers built in alternating bands of grey and white stone, with elaborately carved capitals. The north aisle is conterminous with the nave, but the western bay of the south aisle is occupied by the tower, the lower stage of which is utilized as a porch. In it is a simple wall monument to Walter Evans, who died in 1614, Joan his wife, and Sampson his son, removed from the old church on its destruction.

The tower contains a clock and a modern ring of six bells.

The church plate consists of a handsome silver-gilt

dispute arose between Walter de Berton, rector of the church of Bredon, and the Prior and convent of Little Malvern as to the right to present to the chapel of Welland.[40] It was settled by an agreement, under which the rector of Bredon nominated a clerk who was presented by the Prior and convent of Little Malvern.[41] This practice continued at least as late as 1473,[42] and probably until the Dissolution. It would appear from this that Welland was originally a chapelry of Bredon.[42a] It is called a chapel until 1304–5,[43] but in 1340 the church of Welland is mentioned.[44] Prattinton says that the chapel was

[37] *L. and P. Hen. VIII*, xx (2), g. 496 (49).
[38] Earlier 17th-century entries will be found in the Bishops' Transcripts.
[39] op. cit. i, 552.
[40] *Reg. G. Giffard* (Worcs. Hist. Soc.), 318. [41] Ibid. 531.

[42] Nash, op. cit. ii, 457; *Sede Vacante Reg.* (Worcs. Hist. Soc.), 379.
[42a] A pension of 6s. 8d. from the rectory of Welland was paid to the rector of Bredon in 1535 (*Valor Eccl.* [Rec. Com.], iii, 244).

[43] *Reg. W. Ginsborough* (Worcs. Hist. Soc.), 183, 190, 222; *Pope Nich. Tax.* (Rec. Com.), 218.
[44] *Inq. Nonarum* (Rec. Com.), 294.

appropriated to the priory in 1463-4,[45] but the living was already a vicarage in 1300.[46]

The priory of Little Malvern was suppressed in 1537,[47] and the advowson of the church of Welland was confiscated by the Crown, with which it has remained ever since,[48] with the exception of one presentation made in 1548 by William Pinnock of Hanley, to whom had been granted in 1545 the estate of the priory of Little Malvern at Welland,[49] though the advowson was not included in this grant. Habington states that in his time the advowson of Welland belonged to the Dean and Chapter of Westminster,[50] but nothing has been found to confirm this statement.

A church mission-room was built at Assarts Common in 1886, and has seating accommodation for ninety persons.

In 1787 the house of William Purser at Welland was licensed for Protestant Dissenters.[51]

A Wesleyan chapel was built in Welland in 1886.

CHARITIES The poor's land, founded by deed poll 7 January 1624, whereby John Castle *alias* Salter granted to trustees 4 a. 2 r., called Ayleworth-houne, 1 a. 2 r. 27 p. in Tippers Croft, 2 r. 14 p. now known as Fourteen Shilly Piece, all in Welland, and 2 r. 32 p. known as Welland Meadow in Castle Morton.

Under the Welland Inclosure Act, 9 a. 1 r. 32 p. were awarded for the benefit of the poor in respect of these lands. The gross rental in 1910 amounted to £20 10s., and a sum of £77 9s. 1d. consols is held by the official trustees, producing £1 18s. 8d. yearly, arising from sale of timber and accumulations.

The charity is regulated by a scheme of the Charity Commissioners 5 October 1906. The net income was in 1910 applied in donations to coal and clothing clubs, also in gifts of coal and money and in paying the expenses of patients sent to hospitals or convalescent homes.

WHITE LADIES ASTON

Eastun, Estun (xi cent.) ; Eston (xii and xiii cent.) ; Bishop's Aston, Aston Episcopi (xiv cent.) ; Bysshopus-aston, Byshoppes Aston (xv cent.) ; Aston Episcopi, Whiteladiaston (xvi cent.).

The parish of White Ladies Aston lies to the south-east of the town of Worcester. Bow Brook, running southwards into the River Avon near Defford, forms the eastern, and Saw Brook, a tributary of Bow Brook, forms the southern boundary. The area of the parish is 1,236 acres. In 1905 the parish contained 446 acres of arable land and 772 of permanent grass.[1]

The soil is clay with a little sand and the subsoil is Lower Lias. The chief crops are wheat, beans and barley. The slope of the land is from west to east, the highest point, 205 ft. above the ordnance datum, being on Low Hill, on the western boundary of the parish.

The village of White Ladies Aston lies near the centre of the parish, a little distance to the south of the Alcester and Stratford road. The houses are grouped along a winding by-road, running roughly north and south, with the church at the east side of the road at the north end of the village, to which the many half-timber cottages with their thatched roofs give a characteristic and unspoiled appearance. Aston Hall, a farm-house at the lower end of the village, is a half-timber L-shaped house two stories in height, with tiled roofs. The north wing, containing the kitchen and dairy, though encased in 18th-century brickwork, dates probably from the 16th century, and originally formed a rectangular cottage of the normal central chimney type. The south wing, comprising a large hall and connecting staircase with apartments above, was added early in the 17th century, the house being

then transformed into one of greater importance. The timbers of this latter part of the house are exposed, and the square panels which they form are filled with lath and plaster work. Against the gabled west wall is an original square brick chimney stack with a long vertical panel on the outer face in which the brickwork is arranged in a lattice pattern. The hall has a cellar under the east part, and is now divided into two apartments with a modern chimney stack on the east. The dog-legged stairs between the hall and kitchen are of early 17th-century date, and have square newels with moulded finials, chamfered rails, and plain flat balusters. Between this and the kitchen is a doorway made through the south wall of the original building, one of the horizontal timbers being partly cut away. The kitchen has a fine ceiling with a heavy beam along the centre about 12 in. square supporting the cross members, and a wide open fireplace. The brick chimney above is mainly original. Some of the old half-timber work of this part of the house is exposed at the north gable. At the north-west of the house there is a timber barn with a thatched roof, which dates probably from the 17th century, and at the north-east there is another of similar character and date. An old stone cider press in another barn near the house is still in use.

A little to the north of Aston Hall, facing a bend of the road, is the house known as the 'Moat Farm,' which appears to have been rebuilt early in the 19th century to the west of the moated site from which it takes its name. The moat, which is still filled with water, is nearly perfect. Aston Court[2] is a modern red brick house of no architectural interest. Sneachill is a hamlet in the north-west of

[45] Prattinton Coll. (Soc. Antiq.). In 1535 the rectory of Welland brought in a revenue of 10s. to the priory (*Valor Eccl.* [Rec. Com.], iii, 244).

[46] *Reg. G. Giffard* (Worcs. Hit. Soc.), 531. [47] *L. and P. Hen. VIII*, xvi, 617.

[48] Inst. Bks. (P.R.O.).

[49] See above ; Nash, op. cit. ii, 457.

[50] op. cit. i, 552.

[51] *Worcs. N. and Q.* 126.

[1] Statistics from Bd. of Agric. (1905).

[2] Aston Court was formerly the residence of the Goods. During the Civil War the Goods took the Royalist side, and Aston Court was plundered. 'The Puritan commander, noticing a pretty Miss Good, became very rude in his attentions, and to save herself from out-

rage she fled into a neighbouring wood, where she climbed into a tree and shrouded herself among the thick foliage and thus escaped further notice. The tree was long honoured in the family, but yielding to time and age like all sublunary things, only its stump was at last left in the wood' (*Worcs. Nat. Club Trans.* 1847-96, p. 243).

the parish on the Worcester and Evesham road. The nearest railway station is Stoulton, 1½ miles from the village, on the Great Western railway.

The Worcester and Evesham road forms the western boundary, and from it in the north of the parish another road branches off and runs east to Naunton Beauchamp, crossing Bow Brook by Edward's Bridge and ford. In the south another branch from the Worcester and Evesham road runs to Pershore. Other roads lead from the village of White Ladies Aston north to Churchill and south-east to Peopleton, the latter crossing Bow Brook near Hays Brake by Barrel Bridge and Barrel Ford.

An Inclosure Act for White Ladies Aston was passed in 1825.[3]

CHIMNEY STACK AT ASTON HALL, WHITE LADIES ASTON

The following place-names have been found : Farmelandes [4] (xvi cent.); Hunt Place and Cock [5] (xvii cent.).

MANORS The manor of *ASTON* formed at the time of the Domesday Survey a part of the manor of Northwick,[6] and was probably given with Northwick to the Bishop of Worcester, as no separate grant of it has been found. Before 1086 Urse D'Abitot the Sheriff had obtained possession of part of the manor of Aston, and though this land was included under the possessions of the see of Worcester it does not appear that Urse did any service for it. Three hides and a virgate in the manor were held under the Bishop by Ordric, and this land had been and then was part of the demesne of the capital manor of Northwick.[7] King William I restored land at 'Eastun' to Bishop Wulfstan,[8] and this was probably Ordric's holding at Aston, for the land held in the manor of Northwick by the bishop in demesne had increased between 1086 and the time of Henry I by 3 hides, approximately the amount of Ordric's holding at White Ladies Aston.[9] Part of the manor of White Ladies Aston was given by Bishop Theulf (1113–23) to Robert de Evercy,[10] but a manor called 'the manor of Aston Episcopi' was retained by the bishop and remained in the possession of the see of Worcester[11] until 1648. It was then sold by the Parliamentary trustees for the sale of the lands of the bishops to Thomas Rawlins, Edmund Giles and Christopher Giles.[12] It was restored to the see at the Restoration and remained in the hands of successive bishops until the death of Henry Pepys, Bishop of Worcester, in 1860, when it became vested in the Ecclesiastical Commissioners, who are the present owners.[12a]

Walter, Bishop of Worcester, obtained a grant of free warren at 'Eston' in 1255.[13]

The part of the manor given by Bishop Theulf to Robert de Evercy[14] probably comprised half the vill of Aston,[15] and afterwards became known as the manor of *WHITE LADIES ASTON.* It was held of the Bishop of Worcester's manor of Northwick by knight's service.[16] Robert de Evercy held the manor in 1166,[17] and he or a descendant of the same name obtained a recognition of his right to present to the church of Aston in 1204.[18] Olimpia daughter and heir of Robert de Evercy married Ralph de Wilington,[19] and in 1205 Robert granted half the vill of Aston to Ralph and Olimpia, retaining for himself a life interest in the estate,[20]

[3] Burton, *Bibl. of Worcs.* i, 101 ; Priv. Act, 6 Geo. IV, cap. 79.

[4] *L. and P. Hen. VIII*, xix (1), g. 1035 (107).

[5] Close, 24 Chas. I, pt. xii, no. 31.

[6] *V.C.H. Worcs.* i, 294. [7] Ibid.

[8] Heming, *Chartul.* (ed. Hearne), 407.

[9] *V.C.H. Worcs.* i, 325, n. 8.

[10] For subsequent descent of this part see below.

[11] *Pope Nich. Tax.* (Rec. Com.), 225 ; Exch. Dep. East. 8 Jas. I, no. 30 ; Nash, *Hist. of Worcs.* Introd. p. xxxvi ; *Valor*

Eccl. (Rec. Com.), iii, 218. The Bishop of Worcester in 1324 leased the manor of Aston Bishop to Thomas de Hever and John Berking for their lives (Inq. a.q.d. file 172, no. 18).

[12] Close, 24 Chas. I, pt. xii, no. 31.

[12a] Inform. from Ecclesiastical Commissioners. In 1804 the Bishop of Worcester claimed to be lord of the manor of Upper Aston. Inform. from Mr. R. V. Berkeley.

[13] *Cal. Chart. R.* 1226–57, p. 443.

[14] *Red Bk. of Exch.* (Rolls Ser.), 301 ;

Red Bk. of Bishopric of Worc. (Eccl. Com. Rec. Var. bdle. 121, no. 43698), fol. 243.

[15] *Rot. de Oblatis et Fin.* (Rec. Com.), 316–17.

[16] *Red Bk. of Exch.* (Rolls Ser.), 301 ; *Feud. Aids*, v, 308 ; *Testa de Nevill* (Rec. Com.), 41b.

[17] *Red Bk. of Exch.* (Rolls Ser.), 301.

[18] Pipe R. 6 John, m. 7 d.

[19] *Ann. Mon.* (Rolls Ser.), iv, 404.

[20] *Rot. de Oblatis et Fin.* (Rec. Com.), 316–17 ; Pipe R. 8 John, m. 20 d.

and this was confirmed by a fine in 1207.[21] Ralph de Wilington received seisin of the manor in 1208,[22] Robert de Evercy having died at about that time.[23] In 1215 Walter Gray, Bishop of Worcester, recovered from Ralph de Wilington the manor and advowson of Aston,[24] and in March 1215 the Sheriff of Worcester was commanded to give the bishop seisin of the manor, which, it was said, his predecessor Bishop Mauger had held before he fled the country in 1208.[25] In 1216 the sheriff was ordered to restore the land to Ralph,[26] but between 1216 and 1218 Ralph with the consent of his wife Olimpia granted the manor and the advowson of the church to Silvester of Evesham, Bishop of Worcester,[27] and Cecily de Evercy, widow of Robert de Evercy, released all her claim to a third of the manor to William of Blois, who succeeded Silvester as bishop in 1218.[28] This estate evidently formed part of the manor at Aston granted about the middle of the 13th century by Bishop Walter Cantilupe (1237–66) to the newly-founded nunnery at Whistones,[29] for in 1346 it was stated that the Prioress of Whistones held a fifth of a knight's fee in Aston Bishop and Barbourne which ' Ralph de Wilymet ' once held.[30] The estate of the nunnery also included half a hide at Aston held in the time of Henry II by Robert de Burford,[31] and early in the 13th century by Walter de Burford, of the Bishop of Worcester's manor of Northwick, for the service of a tenth of a knight's fee,[32] this land having been acquired by the nuns before 1299.[33] Whistones Nunnery was suppressed in October 1536,[34] and at that time the nuns' manor of White Ladies Aston consisted of demesne lands worth £6 7s. 10d., a rent of 64s. 4d. and king's alms amounting to £10.[35] The manor was granted on 14 July 1544 to Richard Andrews and John Howe,[36] and they on 30 July sold it to Thomas Hill.[37] Thomas died in 1557,[38] but this manor does not seem to have passed to his son and heir William, but to a younger son Francis, who had joined with his parents in buying the manor.[39] Francis Hill died in 1611, leaving a daughter Alice wife of Richard Andrews of Piddington, co. Northants.[40] Richard and Alice sold the manor in 1612 to Robert Berkeley of Spetchley,[41] and the manor has since descended in the same way as Spetchley to Robert Valentine Berkeley.[42]

Land at White Ladies Aston, afterwards known as the manor of *ASTON BRULEY* (Nether Aston, xvii cent.), was held under the Bishop of Worcester as of his manor of Northwick[43] by the Bruleys from very early times. In the Bishop of Worcester's Domesday (c. 1182), Richard de Bruley is entered as holding a hide at Aston,[44] and Richard ' Brusle ' is mentioned in the Pipe Roll of 1175–6.[45] In the early 13th century a descendant of Richard's bearing the same name held a hide at Aston for the service of a fifth part of a knight's fee.[46] Milicent widow of Richard de Bruley sued Henry de Bruley in 1274–5 for not keeping a covenant made between them as to 3 virgates of land at Aston under Oswaldslow.[47] No further mention has been found of this manor until 1346, but it probably passed from Henry Bruley to his son Henry,[48] and from him to his eldest son William.[49] Henry Bruley son of William left a daughter Agnes, who married a cousin William Bruley,[50] and William in 1346 held the land in Aston which Richard Bruley had formerly held.[51] In 1413–14 he and Agnes conveyed a toft and 2 virgates of land in Aston Bishop to John Lynton and John Bertelmewe.[52] William and Agnes Bruley had a son John, whose daughter and heir Joan married John Danvers of Ipswell and Calthorpe, co. Oxon.[53] John Danvers died about 1448,[54] and Thomas, the eldest son of John and Joan Danvers, died in 1502 without issue, being succeeded by his brother Sir William Danvers.[55] The manor passed in 1504[56] from Sir William to his son John, who died in 1508, leaving an infant son John.[57] On his death while still a minor in 1517[58] this manor passed to his youngest sister Dorothy, who married Nicholas Hubaud or Hubold.[59] It was settled in 1532 upon them and the heirs of their bodies with remainder in default to Dorothy's heirs.[60] Nicholas died in 1553 and Dorothy in 1558,[61] and the manor was sold by their son Sir John Hubaud to William Solley,[62] whose son Leonard Solley held it at the time of Habington's Survey of Worcestershire.[63] In 1610–11 Sir — Fitton, kt., was lord of the manor

DANVERS. *Argent a bend gules with three martlets or thereon.*

[21] Feet of F. Div. Co. Mich. 9 John, no. 48.
[22] Rot. de Oblatis et Fin. (Rec. Com.), 430, 440.
[23] Ibid. 438.
[24] Ann. Mon. (Rolls Ser.), iv, 404 ; Rot. Lit. Claus. (Rec. Com.), i, 189.
[25] Rot. Lit. Claus. (Rec. Com.), i, 189.
[26] Ibid. 275.
[27] Habington, *Surv. of Worcs.* (Worcs. Hist. Soc.), ii, 19.
[28] Ibid.
[29] V.C.H. Worcs. ii, 154 ; Ann. Mon. (Rolls Ser.), iv, 443. Habington states that Godfrey Giffard, the successor of Walter Cantilupe, gave the manor of Aston to the nuns (op. cit. ii, 20).
[30] Feud. Aids, v, 308.
[31] Red Bk. of Bishopric of Worc. fol. 18.
[32] Ibid. ; Habington, op. cit. ii, 41 ; Testa de Nevill (Rec. Com.), 41b. Walter de Burford's estate was called ' Whitefe' (Habington, op. cit. ii, 43).
[33] Red Bk. of Bishopric of Worc. fol. 2.

[34] L. and P. Hen. VIII, xvi, 617 (ii).
[35] Valor Eccl. (Rec. Com.), iii, 230.
[36] L. and P. Hen. VIII, xix (1), g. 1035 (107).
[37] Ibid. xix (2), g. 166 (82).
[38] Chan. Inq. p.m. (Ser. 2), cx, 162.
[39] Exch. Dep. East. 8 Jas. I, no. 30. The manor was claimed by William Hill, but Francis and his mother Anne recovered it (Chan. Proc. [Ser. 2], bdle. 210, no. 19).
[40] Chan. Inq. p.m. (Ser. 2), cccxxxi, 120.
[41] Feet of F. Worcs. Mich. 10 Jas. I.
[42] Ibid. East. 1656 ; Recov. R. Mich. 10 Geo. II, rot. 207 ; Mich. 17 Geo. II, rot. 160 ; Recov. R. D. Enr. East. 18 Geo. II, m. 27.
[43] Habington, op. cit. ii, 41 ; Testa de Nevill (Rec. Com.), 41b.
[44] Red Bk. of Bishopric of Worc. fol.18. Richard Bruley held this estate of William Bracy, and afterwards of Robert de Lucy, to whom Bracy's estates passed (ibid. 256, 257).

[45] Pipe R. 22 Hen. II (Pipe R. Soc.), 36.
[46] Testa de Nevill (Rec. Com.), 41b.
[47] Assize R. 1026, m. 20 d.
[48] Visit. of Oxfordshire (Harl. Soc. 5), 186.
[49] Wrottesley, Ped. from Plea R. 465.
[50] Ibid. ; Macnamara, Memorials of Danvers Family, 224.
[51] Feud. Aids, v, 308.
[52] Feet of F. Div. Co. Mich. 1 Hen.V.
[53] Wrottesley, loc. cit. ; Macnamara, loc. cit.
[54] Macnamara, op. cit. 101.
[55] Ibid. 165, 177.
[56] Ibid. 180 ; Chan. Inq. p.m. (Ser. 2), xxiv, 62 (2).
[57] Chan. Inq. p.m. (Ser. 2), xxiv, 82.
[58] Ibid. xxxii, 43.
[59] Burke, Landed Gentry (1846).
[60] Feet of F. Div. Co. Trin. 24 Hen. VIII.
[61] Dugdale, Hist. of Warw. 741.
[62] Habington, op. cit. ii, 21.
[63] Ibid.

of Aston Bruley.[64] Its further descent has not been traced, and the manor no longer exists.

The manor at White Ladies Aston held in 1086 by Urse, in the manor of Northwick, remained part of that manor probably till about the middle of the 13th century.[65] The bishop's overlordship seems to have lapsed after that time. Urse's interest in the manor passed with his other possessions to the Beauchamps, who were overlords of this manor until about 1316, when the overlordship is mentioned for the last time.[66]

This manor was held under Urse D'Abitot by a certain Robert, and, like the manor which he held at Warndon, this manor passed subsequently to the Bracy family.[67] It descended apparently in the same way as Warndon until, according to Habington, it was sold by Robert Bracy to Walter Cantilupe, Bishop of Worcester (1237–66), who endowed Whistones Nunnery with it.[68] Robert de Bracy was said to be holding Aston about 1316,[69] and in 1346 the manor was again returned as held by Robert Bracy,[70] but all records of the estate cease after this time.

Habington refers to another property in White Ladies Aston, which he states was held by Sir Hugh de Eston in 1269, and descended to Richard de Eston, whose heir Isabel married Adam de Clifton. He adds that ' Clyfton injoyed thease landes in Eston tyll thys family once worthy but nowe synckinge with theyre ruinatinge house, Mr. Francis Clyfton sould thease in Eston called Clyfton's place to Richard Wagstaffe, and Wagstaffe to Mr. Thomas Simonds who now inhabiteth theare.'[71]

There seems to be little evidence to confirm this account beyond a claim by Elena daughter of Richard de Aston in 1313–14 from John son of Richard le Clerk of Aston Bishop of a third of two messuages and land in Aston Bruley which Isabel wife of Richard le Clerk claimed as dower.[72] In 1594 Eleanor and Anne Clifton had livery of three messuages in White Ladies Aston or Nether Aston (Aston Bruley), which had belonged to their grandfather Nicholas Clifton at the time of his death in 1588.[73] The Thomas Symonds who purchased from Wagstaffe was probably Thomas Symonds of Aston Bishop, who died in 1640.[74] In 1656 George Symonds and Jane his wife and Thomas Symonds conveyed a moiety of the manor of White Ladies Aston to Jasper Brittaine and Thomas Harris,[75] evidently for the purpose of some settlement. George Symonds died in 1664,[76] and was apparently succeeded by Thomas Symonds, Sheriff of Worcester, in 1669.[77] Mr. Symonds of White Ladies Aston was executed in 1708 for the murder of Mrs. Palmer of Upton Snodsbury,[78] and his estate escheated to Bishop Lloyd as lord of the manor. He founded therewith in 1713 two schools called the Bishop's Charity Schools in Worcester.[79] The estate still belongs to the trustees of the Charity, and is leased to Mr. Robert V. Berkeley.

A very fine old black and white timbered house was the residence of the Symonds family. Here it was that Cromwell slept on his way from Evesham to Worcester before the battle, Symonds being a great Roundhead. The house and some land came to Thomas Henry Bund, who pulled down the house, and ultimately sold all his land in the parish about 1836 to Mr. Berkeley of Spetchley.[79a]

There is some indication that there was a manor of the RECTORY in this parish. When the manor of White Ladies Aston was granted to Richard Andrews in 1544 the mansion and chief messuage of the rectory of Aston Bishop was included in the grant,[80] and this mansion is mentioned in the inquisition taken on the death of Francis Hill in 1611.[81] In a deposition taken in 1610–11 there is mention of a court held for Francis Hill in his house called the Parsonage House in White Ladies Aston.[82]

The church of *ST. JOHN BAPTIST CHURCH* consists of a chancel measuring internally 23 ft. by 13 ft., nave 40 ft. by 17 ft., north aisle 10 ft. wide, and a vestry north of the chancel. The aisle and vestry were added in 1861, up to which date the church had stood unaltered in plan since the 12th century. Larger windows had, however, been inserted, one in the south wall of the chancel at the end of the 14th century and another to the nave in the 15th. The timber tower and spire, which rise above the roof at the west end of the nave, have no distinctive features, but probably the oldest timbers date from the 15th century.

During the incumbency of the Rev. Henry Martin Sherwood, who was vicar from 1839 to 1911, the church was restored and enlarged. Besides the addition of the aisle and vestry the west wall was rebuilt in 1861 and the south porch added in 1864. The walling of the chancel is small, wide-jointed rubble work. The east window is a single round-headed light, probably original. A small round-headed light of modern stonework in the north wall is either a repair or an insertion, and in the south wall of the chancel is a two-light window under a square head. Further west is another round-headed window with modern stonework. The chancel arch has square jambs with square abaci and a three-centred arch. The modern arcade to the north aisle is of three bays with round and octagonal piers and responds. The aisle is lighted by pairs of lancet windows and the north doorway is of modern stonework in the style of the 12th century. The south window of the nave is square-headed and of two lights partly restored. The round-headed south doorway is evidently of the 12th century, but only the abaci and a few other stones are old. In the modern west wall are two lancet windows with a quatrefoil in the gable above.

The tower is supported on strong wood posts which stand in the church. Its sides are boarded and covered

---

[64] Exch. Dep. East. 8 Jas. I, no. 30.
[65] Habington, op. cit. ii, 41 ; *Testa de Nevill* (Rec. Com.), 41b.
[66] *Testa de Nevill* (Rec. Com.), 41b; Add. MS. 28024, fol. 190a.
[67] Ibid. ; *Feud. Aids*, v, 307.
[68] Habington, op. cit. ii, 20.
[69] Add. MS. 28024, fol. 190a. His under-tenant may have been the Prioress of Whistones.

[70] *Feud. Aids*, v, 307.
[71] Habington, op. cit. ii, 22.
[72] De Banco R. Mich. 7 Edw. II, m. 72; Hil. 7 Edw. II, m. 1 d.
[73] Fine R. 36 Eliz. no. 23, 24 ; Exch. Dep. East. 8 Jas. I, no. 30.
[74] Nash, op. cit. App. 150.
[75] Feet of F. Worcs. Trin. 1656.
[76] Nash, op. cit. i, 51.

[77] P.R.O. *List of Sheriffs*, 157.
[78] Nash, op. cit. ii, 438.
[79] Ibid. i, 50.
[79a] Inform. from Mr. J. W. Willis-Bund.
[80] *L. and P. Hen. VIII*, xix (1), g. 1035 (107).
[81] Chan. Inq. p.m. (Ser. 2), cccxxxi, 120.
[82] Exch. Dep. East. 8 Jas. I, no. 30.

White Ladies Aston Church c. 1810
(From a Water-colour by Thos. Rickards in Prattinton Collection)

with lead on the west and south faces; the windows to the bell-chamber are square and luffered. The upper corners are chamfered off to the octagonal spire, which is covered with wood shingles. The roofs are gabled and have plastered ceilings.

The font, probably of the 13th century, is of a dark red sandstone with a twelve-sided bowl. The other fittings are modern.

There are three bells: the first dated 1707; the second 1636, inscribed 'Give prays to God'; the third 'Sancte Jacobpe, ora pro nobis,' with a crowned female head and a cross.

The communion plate includes an Elizabethan cup and cover paten with the hall mark of 1571.

The registers before 1812 are as follows: (i) mixed entries 1558 to 1660 and baptisms 1661 to 1717, marriages 1661 to 1705 and burials 1661 to 1709; (ii) baptisms and burials 1718 to 1812 and marriages 1719 to 1753; (iii) marriages 1755 to 1812.

ADVOWSON The advowson of the church of Aston was evidently granted with the manor of White Ladies Aston to Robert de Evercy, for in 1204 Robert paid two palfreys for having a confirmation of his right to present to the church, which seems to have been questioned by the Bishop of Worcester.[83] From that time the advowson followed the same descent as the manor of White Ladies Aston,[84] Mr. Robert Valentine Berkeley being the present patron.

There do not appear to be any endowed charities for the benefit of this parish. The children attend the National school at Bredicot.

WICHENFORD

Wychynford (xiv cent.); Wychenford (xvi cent.); Winchenford, Whichingford, Witchenford (xvii cent.); Wickingford, Wickenford (xviii cent.).

The parish of Wichenford lies 6 miles to the north-west of the town of Worcester. Its area is 2,866 acres,[1] of which in 1905 656 acres were arable land, 1,761 permanent grass and 119 woods.[2] The soil is clay, with a subsoil of Keuper Marl, growing crops of wheat, beans and fruit and a few hops. The slope of the land is from north-west to south-east, the highest point, 363 ft. above the ordnance datum, being in the extreme north-west.

The road from Martley to Worcester runs through the middle of the parish, and from it another road branches off to the hamlet of Wants Green in the south, and forms part of the western boundary of the parish. From Wants Green it runs south-east, and forms part of the southern boundary, being joined at Tinkers' Cross by a branch road. From Castle Hill on the Worcester road another road runs north-east to the village of Wichenford.

Laughern Brook, flowing east to join the River Teme near Powick, divides the parish into two parts, and is crossed at Pig Bridge by the Worcester road. To the south of the bridge there are fish ponds[3] and a weir. Woodhall Farm[4] and Woodend Farm lie still further south, and at both there are the remains of moats. The village of Wichenford is situated on the eastern boundary of the parish on the banks of Laughern Brook.

A quarter of a mile south-east of the church is Wichenford Court, formerly the residence of the Washbournes, when it was one of the largest mansions in the county and had a moat and drawbridge.[5] It was evidently to a great extent rebuilt about 1712, and at one time covered more space than it does now.[6] By 1866 it was only a farm-house,[7] but the remains of the moat are still in existence. The present house is in the main a red brick building of about 1700, with wood mullioned and transomed windows and leaded lights with good wrought-iron fasteners. The east room on the first floor contains early 17th-century panelling and a plain but good carved mantel. The middle room on this floor is also panelled, and has a carved frieze, used as a skirting board, all now painted. The stair has good 18th-century balusters. Among the farm buildings is a fine timber and wattle barn put up in 1695. There is also near the house a half-timber dovecote on a red sandstone base, surmounted by a glazed lantern.

When Wichenford Court was visited by the Worcestershire Naturalists' Club on 7 June 1866, around two sides of a panelled room under the ceiling were a number of carved grinning heads with teeth, said to be human.[8] The tradition is that during the wars with the Welsh under Owen Glendower in the reign of Henry IV one of the Bourbon princes was confined here for some time, and was afterwards put to death by the then Lady Washbourne. After her death her ghost, with a dagger in its hand, is said to have been seen in the murdered prince's chamber.[9] This tale was later connected with an old portrait of one of the Washbournes. The ghost of Lady Washbourne, wife of John the Royalist, is said to frequent the moat with a golden harp, in a

[83] Pipe R. 6 John, m. 7 d.

[84] *Ann. Mon.* (Rolls Ser.), iv, 404; *Valor Eccl.* (Rec. Com.), iii, 230; *L. nd P. Hen. VIII,* xix (1), g. 1035 (107); xix (2), g. 166 (82); Chan. Inq. p.m. (Ser. 2), cx, 162; cccxxxi, 120; Feet of F. Worcs. Mich. 10 Jas. I; Worc. Epis. Reg. Montagu, fol. 13 d.; Inst. Bks. (P.R.O.). In 1772 Robert Berkeley leased the advowson for ninety-nine years to Sir Chandos Hoskins (Recov. R. D. Enr. Trin. 12 Geo. III, m. 129), but this lease must soon have been given up, for in 1775 Robert Berkeley granted the advowson for the same term to Rev. S. Stephens (Recov. R. D.

Enr. Hil. 16 Geo. III, m. 129). Robert Dormer presented to the church in 1723, William Bund in 1759, and Thomas Elrington in 1808, probably for those turns only, by grants from members of the Berkeley family (Inst. Bks. [P.R.O.]).

[1] 6 acres are covered by water.

[2] Statistics from Bd. of Agric. (1905).

[3] These ponds, together with another in Churchfield, formed part of the manor of Wichenford and were reserved by George Dowdeswell for his own use when he leased the manor to William Rider in 1695 (Jas. Davenport, *The Washbourne Family,* 187).

[4] Woodhall Farm is now in the parish of North Hallow, but may mark the site of the ancient manor of Wyard's Woodhall, Wyat's Wood being in the vicinity. There was, however, another manor of Woodhall in Hallow, to which Woodhall Farm may have belonged.

[5] Noake, *Guide to Worcs.* 353.

[6] Davenport, op. cit. 185.

[7] *Worcs. Nat. Club Trans.* 1847–96, p. 101.

[8] Ibid. This wainscoting was removed by Rear-Admiral Britten to his house at Kenswick in 1895 (Davenport, op. cit. 193).

[9] Davenport, op. cit. 191.

silver boat drawn by four white swans.[10] To the south of Wichenford Court is Abbinton's Farm, the old manor-house of the Habington family. Most of the house was taken down in the 18th century, and the remaining portion was converted into a couple of cottages about 1865.[11]

Two Roman coins of the time of Victorinus and Constans have been found in Wichenford.[12]

There is no Inclosure Act for Wichenford. In 1884 Ossage Farm was transferred from the parish of Cotheridge to that of Wichenford.[13]

Among the place-names that have been found are the Lady Meadow, the Tineing, the Upper and Lower Hassells Meadow and the Malenders[14] (xvii cent.), and Coldbrook, Ockeridge Waste, Rugg's Place and Bournescroft (xix cent.).

This probably refers to the confiscation of the manor by Edward VI,[16] but Habington assigns the date of the severance of the two manors to the beginning of the reign of Queen Elizabeth, when Wick Episcopi passed by exchange to the queen.[17] Walter Cantilupe, Bishop of Worcester, claimed to be lord paramount at Wichenford,[18] and in 1288 Bishop Giffard granted land there to one Matthew Choke.[19] In 1535 the manor of Wichenford belonging to the bishop was valued apart from that of Wick Episcopi.[19a]

In 1552 Bishop Nicholas Heath was deprived of his see by Edward VI,[20] who seems to have confiscated the manor of Wichenford, which he granted in 1553 to John Dudley Duke of Northumberland.[21] Habington says that the latter in 1551–2, when Earl of Warwick, obtained licence to alienate the manor to

WICHENFORD COURT

MANORS The manor of *WICHENFORD* was no doubt included at the time of the Domesday Survey in that of Wick Episcopi belonging to the see of Worcester. It continued to form part of the latter manor until the 16th century, for in a commission taken in 1594–5 it is stated that 'the manors of Wike Episcopi and Wichingforde were the same manor of Wike Episcopi and had the same court baron until the manor of Wike Episcopi came to the hands of the king.'[15]

Walter Blount. The duke was executed in 1553,[22] and this manor was restored to the see of Worcester probably in 1554–5, when the temporalities of the bishopric were restored to Bishop Heath.[23]

It was sold in 1651 by the Parliamentary trustees[24] to Richard Turner and Thomas Davies for £574 12s. 7½d.[25] The manor was recovered by the see of Worcester at the Restoration, and passed in 1860 to the Ecclesiastical Commissioners,[26] who are still lords of this manor.[27]

[10] Davenport, op. cit. 191–2.
[11] Noake, op. cit. 353.
[12] V.C.H. Worcs. i, 220.
[13] Pop. Ret. (1891), ii, 657.
[14] Davenport, op. cit. 187.
[15] Exch. Spec. Com. 37 Eliz. no. 2501.
[16] See below.

[17] Habington, Surv. of Worcs. (Worcs. Hist. Soc.), ii, 135 ; Pat. 4 Eliz. pt. vi, m. 24. [18] Habington, op. cit. i, 500.
[19] Reg. G. Giffard (Worcs. Hist. Soc.), 319.
[19a] Valor Eccl. (Rec. Com.), iii, 217.
[20] V.C.H. Worcs. ii, 45.

[21] Pat. 7 Edw. VI, pt. viii, m. 25.
[22] Dict. Nat. Biog.
[23] Pat. 1 & 2 Phil. and Mary, pt. i.
[24] Close, 1651, pt. lvi, no. 21.   [25] Ibid.
[26] Stat. 23 & 24 Vict. cap. 124.
[27] Inform. supplied from the Ecclesiastical Commission.

A manor at *WICHENFORD* held by the Poer family of the bishop's manor of Wick Episcopi[28] seems to have originated in a virgate of land there given by Samson, Bishop of Worcester (1096–1112), to Illi de Turre.[29] This land probably passed with Norton in Bredon to Hamo de Turre, and towards the end of the 12th century was like Norton in the possession of William Poer.[30] Richard Poer, who may perhaps be identified with the Richard who was holding half a knight's fee of the bishop in 1196–7,[31] was holding 4 hides at Wichenford, Norton and Hill in Fladbury early in the 13th century.[32] The date of Richard's death is not known, but he was still alive in 1220,[33] and a Richard Poer was holding land at Lemington, co. Gloucester, in 1241.[34] Richard was succeeded, according to the pedigree of the family given in the visitation of 1569, by his son John,[35] who in 1244 agreed with the Bishop of Worcester as to an exchange of land at Fladbury and Wichenford.[36] James Poer was in possession of the manor in 1299.[37] Roger son of John Poer[38] died about 1342, leaving John his son and heir a minor.[39] Maud wife of Roger held the manor until her death in 1362,[40] when livery was made to her son John.[41] John Poer of Wichenford is mentioned in 1404–5,[42] but the exact date of his death is not known.[43] He left two daughters Margaret and Agnes his co-heirs.[44] Wichenford evidently fell to the share of the former, who became the second wife of

POER. *Gules a fesse or with two molets or in the chief.*   WASHBOURNE. *Argent a fesse between six martlets gules with three cinqfoils argent on the fesse.*

John Washbourne, for in 1428 her son Norman Washbourne held the manor.[45] He died before 1480,[46] and his son and successor John[47] died in 1517, leaving as his heir his grandson John son of Robert Washbourne.[48] John died in 1532,[49] leaving this manor to his widow Margaret, who afterwards married John Kettleby of Cotheridge. Anthony son and heir of John Washbourne and Margaret died at Wichenford in 1570 in the lifetime of his mother.[50] The exact date of Margaret's death is not known, but before 1598–9 the manor had passed to John eldest son of Anthony.[51] He died in 1633–4, leaving as his heir his great-grandson John,[52] who married Elizabeth Childe in 1639, while still a minor.[53] He was an ardent Royalist, and compounded for his estates in 1649–50.[54] He probably took part in the battle of Worcester in September 1650, as he was among those present before the battle at the review at Pitchcroft. He disappeared from that time, and his fate is not known, but he was dead before 1653.[55] His son William succeeded to the manor and died in 1702.[56]

It would seem that the manor passed to his son and heir William during his lifetime, for in September 1695 William Washbourne the younger made it over to George Dowdeswell for five years at a peppercorn rent in return for the latter's services in helping him meet debts amounting to £800.[57] Three months later George Dowdeswell leased the manor and its appurtenances to William Rider for three years at a yearly rent of £108.[58] William Washbourne sold the manor in 1712 to Edmund Skinner.[59] The latter was Sheriff of Worcestershire in 1726.[60] He was succeeded by a daughter, Anna wife of Plukenett Woodroffe, on whose death in 1787 the manor passed to her third but eldest surviving son Skynner Woodroffe.[61] He died in 1822, and was succeeded by his brother George, who, dying in the same year, was followed by his son Skynner George.[62] The latter was succeeded on his death in 1848 by his son George William Plukenett,[63] who sold Wichenford Court about 1856 to Daniel Britten.[64] Rear-Admiral Richard Frederick Britten, J.P., son and successor of Daniel Britten, died in 1910, and the manor now belongs to his widow, the Hon. Mrs. Britten.

An estate called *WYARDS*[65] or *WYARDS WOODHALL* in Wichenford seems to have consisted of a yardland held of the Bishop of Worcester in the manor of Wichenford by the widow of John Wyard in 1299.[66] By an undated deed Robert son of

[28] Red Bk. of Bishopric of Worc. (Eccl. Com. Rec. Var. bdle. 121, no. 43698), fol. 243, 254; *Testa de Nevill* (Rec. Com.), 41*b*; Chan. Inq. p.m. 36 Edw. III, pt. ii (1st nos.), no. 18; Exch. Inq. p.m. file 1178, no. 7. This overlordship is mentioned for the last time in 1518.

[29] Red Bk. of Bishopric of Worc. fol. 243.

[30] Ibid. 254.

[31] *Red Bk. of Exch.* (Rolls Ser.), 108.

[32] *Testa de Nevill* (Rec. Com.), 41*b*.

[33] *Excerpta e Rot. Fin.* (Rec. Com.), i, 50.

[34] *Ann. Mon.* (Rolls Ser.), i, 119.

[35] *Visit. of Worcs.* 1569 (Harl. Soc. xxvii), 62.

[36] Wharton, *Angl. Sacra,* i, 492; *Ann. Mon.* (Rolls Ser.), iv, 435.

[37] Red Bk. of Bishopric of Worc. fol. 22.

[38] *Visit. of Worcs.* (Harl. Soc. xxvii), 62.

[39] Chan. Inq. p.m. 16 Edw. III (1st nos.), no. 4.

[40] Ibid. 36 Edw. III, pt. ii (1st nos.), no. 18.

[41] *Abbrev. Rot. Orig.* (Rec. Com.), ii, 269.

[42] Habington, op. cit. i, 42.

[43] He was still alive in 1410–11 (Phillipps, *Index to Worcs. Fines,* p. xi, East. 12 Hen. IV).

[44] *Visit. of Worcs.* 1569 (Harl. Soc. xxvii), 63; Davenport, op. cit. 20.

[45] *Feud. Aids,* v, 319; *Visit. of Worcs.* 1569 (Harl. Soc. xxvii), 143.

[46] Davenport, op. cit. 17.

[47] Ibid. 30.

[48] Exch. Inq. p.m. file 1178, no. 7.

[49] Ibid. 1190, no. 2.

[50] Chan. Inq. p.m. (Ser. 2), clix, 75.

[51] Feet of F. Worcs. Hil. 41 Eliz.; Davenport, op. cit. 84.

[52] Davenport, loc. cit.

[53] Ibid. 137; Recov. R. Mich. 15 Chas. I, rot. 80.

[54] *Cal. Com. for Comp.* 1930.

[55] Davenport, op. cit. 145.

[56] Ibid. 148, 164; Recov. R. Hil.

13 & 14 Chas. II, rot. 52; East. 2 Will. and Mary, rot. 218.

[57] Davenport, op. cit. 166. This debt included a sum of £400 owing to his father for five years' board for himself, his wife and his children, and a further debt of £200 for hay and provender supplied for his horses (ibid. 186).

[58] Ibid. 187. All trees are excluded from the lease 'saveinge allwaies out of this exception reasonable estrovers of hedgboot, plowboot, cart boote and fire boote,' and sufficient timber for the repair of gates, stiles and bridges.

[59] Close, 12 Anne, pt. xii, no. 12.

[60] P.R.O. *List of Sheriffs,* 159.

[61] Burke, *Family Records,* 637.

[62] Ibid.

[63] Ibid. 638.

[64] Inform. kindly supplied by the late Rear-Admiral Britten.

[65] The name is still retained at Wichenford at Wyat's Coppice near Woodhall Farm.

[66] Red Bk. of Bishopric of Worc. fol. 22.

Robert Wyard gave to Robert de Cowsden 3 acres of land held by Walter son of Walter the Miller in la Buriende in the vill of Wichenford, to be held of Robert Wyard for the rent of a rose.[67] Stephen Wyard acquired land in Wichenford from William Habington, but the date of this transaction is not known.[68] In 1320–1 Thomas Habington owed for a messuage called the Hawe Place suit of court and heriot to the manor of Wyards Woodhall.[69] John Wyard forfeited all his possessions in 1322 for his adherence to Roger de Mortimer Earl of March,[70] and in 1323 Woodhall was granted to Simon de Reding, king's serjeant-at-arms, for life.[71] Free warren at Woodhall was granted to Simon in the following year.[72] John Wyard was

pardoned, and his lands were restored to him in 1331,[73] and in the same year he conveyed to John de Stone and Joan his wife his manor of Woodhall.[74] This conveyance must have been made for the purpose of some settlement, for the estate passed from John Wyard to his daughter Elizabeth, who married William de la Lowe.[75] Richard de la Lowe, her son,[76] sold to William Habington in 1417–18 all his lands called Wyards Woodhall.[77] This is probably the William Habington of the pedigree in the Worcester Visitation of 1569 called 'of Wichenford.'[78] His descendant of the same name was in possession of a house lately belonging to John Wyard at Wichenford in 1519–20,[79] and Richard son of William Habington held a house

DOVECOTE AT WICHENFORD COURT

or mill called Wyards in Wichenford.[80] The further descent of this estate is identical with that of the manor of Woodend[81] (q.v.) until 1628. It was then called the manor of Wyors.[82]

An estate subsequently known as the manor of WOODEND or HABINGTONS PLACE in Wichenford, held of the see of Worcester,[83] apparently consisted of a quarter of a yardland in Wichenford held by Nicholas Attwood or de Boys in 1299.[84] There was a monument without date to John de Boys, lord of Wichenford, in the church of Hindlip,[85] and John Gannon and Margery his wife by an undated conveyance sold certain lands in the manor of Wichenford, of the fee of Nicholas de Boys, to William Habington and Margery his wife.[86] This William Habington was of Bedwardine, co. Worcester, and, according to Habington, had obtained an estate at Wichenford before 1286 by his marriage with Margery daughter of William Beaufitz of Eastleach, co. Gloucester, by Margery daughter and co-heir of Richard Wood of Wichenford.[87] William Habington held a yardland at Wichenford in 1299.[88] The estate descended in the Habington family,[89] of whom a doubtful pedigree is given in the Visitation of Worcester of 1569,[90] until the death of Richard son

[67] Prattinton Coll. (Soc. Antiq.), Deeds of D. and C. of Worc. no. 201.
[68] Habington, op. cit. ii, 130.
[69] Ibid. i, 503.
[70] Cal. Pat. 1330–4, p. 53.
[71] Ibid. 1321–4, p. 275.
[72] Cal. Chart. R. 1300–26, p. 462.
[73] Cal. Pat. 1330–4, p. 53. John had recovered some of his land before this date (ibid. 1327–30, p. 419) and see Kyre Wyard.
[74] Habington, op. cit. i, 503.
[75] Wrottesley, Ped. from Plea R. 426.
[76] Habington states that Richard was the son of Henry de la Lowe of Stone (op. cit. i, 503).

[77] Wrottesley, loc. cit.; Habington, op. cit. i, 503.
[78] Visit. of Worcs. (Harl. Soc. xxvii), 62.
[79] Ct. R. See of Worcester (Eccl. Com.), bdle. 195, no. 7.
[80] Chan. Proc. (Ser. 2), bdle. 96, no. 11.
[81] Ibid.; Exch. Inq. p.m. file 1198, no. 5.
[82] Chan. Inq. p.m. (Ser. 2), ccccxliii, 47a.
[83] Exch. Inq. p.m. file 1198, no. 5.
[84] Red Bk. of Bishopric of Worc. fol. 22; Habington, op. cit. i, 504. In 1274–5 Alice de Boys claimed against Agnes wife of Jordan de Boys and others land and a messuage at Wichenford, and she had previously tried to recover it against Thomas de Boys. Judgement in each

case was against her (Assize R. 1026, m. 20 d.).   [85] Habington, op. cit. i, 296.
[86] Ibid. 504. William Habington was holding a yardland in the manor of Wick Episcopi in 1299 (Red Bk. of Bishopric of Worc. fol. 22).
[87] Habington, op. cit. i, 296.
[88] Ibid. 503.
[89] Ibid.; Chan. Proc. (Ser. 2), bdle. 96, no. 11.
[90] op. cit. (Harl. Soc. xxvii), 62–3. James de Habington married Agnes daughter and co-heir of John Poer at the beginning of the 15th century, but it does not appear that any land at Wichenford passed to the Habingtons through this marriage.

of Richard Habington in 1545. Richard left his co-heirs three daughters,[91] Mary wife of Richard Barneby of Acton in the parish of Ombersley, co. Worcester, Jane wife of Edward Stamford of Rowley, co. Staff., and Eleanor married first to John Dancey, secondly to Sir Thomas Baskerville of Brinsop, co. Hereford,[92] and thirdly to John Gage. It appears that the manor had been settled by Richard Habington, grandfather of these co-heirs, upon his son Richard in tail-male with contingent remainders to his other sons George, Edward and John. On the death of Richard Habington the son, John his only surviving brother laid claim to the manor, but it does not seem that he was ever able to establish his right,[93] though he subsequently acquired the third of the manor held by Edward Stamford in right of his wife Jane in 1565.[94] John Habington died in 1581,[95] and his sons Thomas and Richard conveyed this portion of the manor in 1596 to John Talbot.[96] Robert Barneby, son of Richard Barneby and Mary Habington,[97] sold his third of the manor to John Steyner of Worcester,[98] and the history of this third has not been further traced. Eleanor the third daughter of Richard Habington had issue by Sir Thomas Baskerville, a daughter Eleanor, who married the above-mentioned John Talbot,[99] and in 1599 John and Eleanor Talbot conveyed two thirds of the manor, one which John had acquired by purchase from the Habingtons and the other, of which it would seem they held only the reversion, to Eleanor Talbot's mother Eleanor, who was then the widow of John Gage.[100] These two thirds of the manor passed from Eleanor to Edward Gage her son by her third husband.[1] He died in 1628 holding two thirds of the manor of Wyors and two thirds of land in Wichenford, leaving a son and heir William,[2] who conveyed a third of the manor of Wichenford in 1653 to Augustine Belston and William Nevill.[3] Nash states that the Gages long enjoyed this estate and sold some of it to Mr. Gyles, a clothier in Worcester, whose estate is called 'the Wooden Farm.'[4]

Another estate in Wichenford is mentioned in 1530, when William Mucklowe died, owning the so-called manor of Wichenford, which he had previously settled on his wife Margery.[5] Richard was his son and heir, and was then aged thirty.[6] Richard died in 1556,[7] and the estate evidently passed to his son and heir Simon, for a little later Lettice wife of John Page, daughter of Richard Mucklowe, claimed against Simon a share of the manor, which, she said,

HABINGTON of Woodend. *Argent a bend gules with three eagles or thereon.*

under the will of her father, ought to have been divided amongst his seven children.[8] Habington in his survey gives the following account of it : 'Leyke's armory maye showe howe Leyke deryvethe hys tytell to thease landes which after they inioyed tyll Leyke sould the same to Mr. Richard Mucklowe, whose heyre in our age dispersed by sale thease possessyons amounge others.'[9] Nash continues the history of this estate : 'One parcel was purchased by Mr. Andrews, who sold it to Mr. Nash, whose only daughter Elizabeth married John Moulding, a very ingenious antiquary.'[10]

The Prior and convent of Worcester held certain lands at Wichenford, probably included at the Dissolution in the manor of 'St. Jonys cum Wichenford.'[11] These lands were granted to the Dean and Chapter of Worcester in 1542.[12]

In an undated deed, probably of the 13th century, Walter son of Walter the Miller of la Buriende in Wichenford is mentioned.[13] In 1545 a water-mill belonged to Richard Habington's manor of Wichenford,[14] and in 1787 two mills were annexed to the Woodroffes' manor there.[15] In 1636 it was presented at the county court that George Sherwood of Wichenford ought to repair part of Blackmore Bridge over the River 'Lawrne,' lying in Wichenford parish, by reason of the tenure of his mill there.[16] The present Woodhall Mill on Laughern Brook, now in the parish of North Hallow, is probably the successor of Habington's mill. There are no mills in the parish of Wichenford at the present day.

The church of *ST. LAWRENCE* CHURCH consists of a chancel measuring internally 27¾ ft. by 16½ ft., a north vestry, a nave 49 ft. by 21½ ft., a west tower 10 ft. wide and a south porch.

The nave is the oldest part of the present church and dates from about 1320. The east part of the contemporary chancel has been rebuilt in modern times. The present tower was added at the end of the 14th century, the original west wall of the nave being removed. In 1791 the steeple was removed as being unsafe, and in 1863 the upper part of the tower was rebuilt and a new spire added. There is some evidence of the existence of a 12th-century church in the capitals of that date preserved at the rectory.

The modern east window is of three lights. The side walls are each pierced by two lancets, all of 13th-century date, except that on the north-east, which is modern. In the south wall are a 13th-century door and a piscina. The chancel arch is modern. In the north wall of the early 14th-century nave are three modern two-light windows, one replacing the north door. The tower arch has two massive orders springing from chamfered abaci. In the north and south walls of the ground stage are single ogee lights. The west window is also a single light ; the door

91 Exch. Inq. p.m. file 1198, no. 5.
92 Chan. Proc. (Ser. 2), bdle. 96, no. 11 ; *Visit. of Worcs.* (Harl. Soc. xxvii), 13 ; Feet of F. Div. Co. East. 8 Eliz. ; Worcs. Trin. 15 Eliz.
93 Chan. Proc. (Ser. 2), bdle. 96, no. 11.
94 Recov. R. Trin. 7 Eliz. rot. 727.
95 Habington, op. cit. i, 3 ; Exch. Spec. Com. 24 Eliz. no. 2479.
96 Feet of F. Worcs. Hil. 38 Eliz.
97 *Visit. of Worcs.* 1569 (Harl. Soc. xxvii), 14.

98 Habington, op. cit. i, 504.
99 Ibid. ; *Visit. of Worcs.* 1569 (Harl. Soc. xxvii), 64.
100 Feet of F. Worcs. East. 41 Eliz.
1 *Visit. of Worcs.* 1569 (Harl. Soc. xxvii), 64.
2 Chan. Inq. p.m. (Ser. 2), ccccxliii, 47a.
3 Feet of F. Div. Co. East. 1653.
4 Nash, op. cit. ii, 458.
5 Chan. Inq. p.m. (Ser. 2), l, 158.
6 Ibid.
7 Ibid. cvi, 91.

8 Chan. Proc. (Ser. 2), bdle. 145, no. 72.
9 op. cit. i, 502.
10 op. cit. ii, 458.
11 *Valor Eccl.* (Rec. Com.), iii, 220.
12 *L. and P. Hen. VIII,* xvii, g. 71 (29).
13 Prattinton Coll. (Soc. Antiq.), Deeds of D. and C. of Worc. no. 201.
14 Chan. Inq. p.m. (Ser. 2), lxxv, 94.
15 Recov. R. Trin. 27 Geo. III, rot. 324.
16 *Worcs. Quart. Sess. R.* (Worcs. Hist. Soc.), 614.

beneath it is modern. The south door of the nave and the porch are modern. To the east of the south door is a two-light window with a quatrefoil over of the 14th century. The south-west window of the nave is a single light of the same date with a restored head. At the south-east is a contemporary trefoiled piscina.

The roofs and fittings are modern. In the south-west corner of the nave is a tomb with two recumbent effigies, to John Washbourne, who died in 1615, and Alice his wife and their three children. The inscribed slab above has been replaced by a brass plate. Mounted on a board close to the tower arch are the old clappers of the bells, which have recently been fitted with new ones.

On the north side of the chancel is an altar tomb with two effigies in 17th-century armour, one on the slab and one beneath it. Behind are two female figures kneeling in recesses, with a classic cornice and ornament above crudely coloured and gilt. An inscription records that John Washbourne at the age of eighty-four built the monument for himself (the upper figure), his two wives Mary Savage and Eleanor Lygon, and his father Anthony (the lower figure).

There are four shields, the centre and highest one of the Washbourne arms. Below this is a shield quarterly of Washbourne quartered with Poer and Dabitot. To the west is a shield of these arms impaling the six lions of Savage. To the east is the same impaling the two lions passant of Lygon.

On the north side of the chancel is an alabaster slab used as a credence and fitted to the sill of a window. It is stated to have been found in the rectory garden and probably formed the top of an altar tomb.

There are three bells,[17] the first and third by John Martin of Worcester, dated respectively 1673 and 1664, but only the third has his foundry mark. The second is a mediaeval bell inscribed ' + Sancte Michael Ora Pro Nobis,' with fleur de lis and head of Prince Edward (son of Henry VI) as stops ; on the shoulder is an inscription in smaller letters of a similar character to those at Lindridge, ' Tempore Dñi Thome Feld,' with similar stops. Thomas Feld was vicar until 1489, and the bell was cast at Worcester about 1480.

The plate consists of an early Elizabethan cup with a leaf band under the rim and a thistle below and a cover paten with a pricked band ornamentation, both being without hall marks. There are also a large flat paten, made in 1747, and presented by Plukenett Woodroffe in 1748, and a modern plated flagon.

The registers [18] previous to 1812 are as follows : (i) mixed entries 1690 to 1788, marriages stopping at 1754 (an earlier book beginning 1539 is recorded by Nash, but is known to have been missing since 1847) : (ii) baptisms and burials 1788 to 1812 ; (iii) a marriage book 1754 to 1812.

ADVOWSON
A church or chapel [19] has existed at Wichenford from early times. The chapel of Wichenford, which was attached to the church of St. Helen, Worcester, was granted by the monks after the death of Bishop Wulfstan to Fritheric, the priest of St. Helen's, who was to make provision for them during his lifetime. After his death all the possessions which he held in trust for the monks were to return to the prior and convent.[20] In 1234 a division was made of the chapelries annexed to St. Helen's, between the Bishop and the Prior and convent of Worcester. Wichenford, as lying on the west bank of the Severn, fell to the share of the prior and convent,[21] who presented to the vicarage until the dissolution of their house.[22]

The advowson of Wichenford was evidently granted to the Dean and Chapter of Worcester, though no record of this grant has been found,[23] for the presentations from 1573 until the present day have been made by the dean and chapter.[24]

The surveys taken at the time of the dissolution of the chantries in the reign of Edward VI mention a piece of land in this parish worth 3s. 4d. a year which had been given to maintain an obit light in the parish church of Wichenford.[25] This land was leased to William Dalby in 1560,[26] but after that date all trace of it is lost.

An image of St. Michael the Archangel in the chancel of Wichenford Church is mentioned in the will of John Washbourne dated 1532,[27] and John Washbourne, by will dated 1517, bequeathed his body to be buried in the chancel of St. Michael in Wichenford and 40d. to the high altar of St. Michael at Wichenford.[28]

CHARITIES
The gifts of William Evett and other donors, including a legacy of £20 by will of Mrs. Ann Groves, proved at Worcester 12 February 1814, amounting together to £86, as recorded on the church table, were with other benefactions invested in the purchase of £178 1s. 10d. consols. The annual dividends, amounting to £4 9s., are distributed in money doles.

The Rev. John Pritchett and Mrs. Pritchett, the relict, by their respective wills (date not stated), bequeathed legacies of £100 and £100, the interest to be applied annually in clothing two poor old men and two poor old women.

The two legacies, less duty, were in 1857 invested in £196 14s. 5d. consols, producing yearly £4 18s. 4d., which is duly applied.

---

[17] Inform. from Mr. H. B. Walters.

[18] Many 17th-century entries will be found in the Bishops' Transcripts.

[19] It is called indiscriminately church or chapel, but the living was a vicarage (*Ann. Mon.* [Rolls Ser.], iv, 435, 441, 541, 426 ; *Pope Nich. Tax.* [Rec. Com.], 219b, 239 ; *Reg. G. Giffard* [Worcs. Hist. Soc.], 495, 512, &c.).

[20] Heming, *Chartul.* (ed. Hearne), 427 ; Nash, op. cit. App. 145.

[21] *Ann. Mon.* (Rolls Ser.), iv, 426.

[22] Worc. Epis. Reg. *passim* ; *Ann. Mon.* (Rolls Ser.), iv, 435, 441, 541, 427 ; *Valor Eccl.* (Rec. Com.), iii, 235.

[23] In a grant to the dean and chapter in 1542 land at Wichenford lately belong-ing to the priory of St. Mary, Worcester, was included, but there is no mention of the advowson of the church.

[24] Inst. Bks. (P.R.O.).

[25] Chant. Cert. 61, no. 33.

[26] Pat. 3 Eliz. pt. v.

[27] Davenport, op. cit. 67.

[28] Ibid. 32.

WICHENFORD COURT : 17TH CENTURY PANELLING

WICHENFORD CHURCH : TOMB OF JOHN WASHBOURNE

WOLVERLEY

Uluardele (viii cent.) ; Ulwardileia, Wulfferdinleh (ix cent.) ; Wlfereslawe, Welwardel (x cent.) ; Uulfordilea (xi cent.) ; Wlfwardill, Wulfardeley (xii cent.) ; Wluarle, Ulwardell, Wolvardelegh, Wluuard, Wulewarde, Wulwardesleg, Wluardele (xiii cent.) ; Woluardel, Woluardeley (xv cent.) ; Woluley (xvi cent.).

This parish, covering an area of 5,543 acres,[1] of which 52 acres are covered with water, lies on the northern boundary of Worcestershire, with Staffordshire to the north and the borough of Kidderminster to the south. The Stour enters the parish on the north-east and flows through it in a southerly direction, passing through the hamlets of Caunsall and Cookley and through the village of Wolverley, where it is joined by the Horsebrook. Below Wolverley Court the Honey Brook meets it, and after traversing the parish it enters Kidderminster near the Broadwaters. On the eastern side of the parish is a series of large pools of water, Benson's Bath, the Stew and Sleepy Mill Island, and there are four or five large pools at the Broadwaters on the Wannerton Brook. On either side of the river the land is rich pasture, liable to floods at certain seasons of the year, and it is along its course that the lowest ground of the parish lies, at a height of only 118 ft. above the ordnance datum near Wolverley Lock. The land rises from the river banks, especially to the west, where it reaches heights of over 500 ft. The Staffordshire and Worcestershire Canal, projected in 1766, follows the course of the river through the parish and is spanned at Cookley by an aqueduct in connexion with the Birmingham waterworks scheme. The welded steel pipes form a bridge with a span of 112 ft. Great difficulty was experienced in building the bridge owing to the gravelly nature of the ground, through which the water from the surrounding marshes percolated.[1a]

The parish is well wooded, 372 acres being laid out in woods and plantations.[2] Some of these woods are ancient, namely Birch Wood,[3] Bodenham Wood and Cookley Wood, which comprises Spring Coppice and Solcum Coppice. Axborough Wood on the east is a plantation made since the Inclosure Act in 1775. The soil is light and the subsoil sandstone and gravel ; 2,830 acres are arable land and 1,715 permanent grass.[4] Barley and wheat with market garden produce are the chief crops grown.

The roads from Kidderminster to Wolverhampton and Stourbridge pass through the eastern side of the parish and the Kidderminster and Bridgnorth road touches its western edge.

The River Stour flows through the centre of the village, which lies in a pleasant hollow surrounded by numerous trees. On the south there is an outcrop of sandstone forming a small cliff, and the church and churchyard are prominently situated upon it, over-looking the village to the north and the valley of the Stour to the east. The main approach to the village is from the east, off the road running between Broadwaters and Wribbenhall. This approach, after entering the village, rises sharply to the north, the road being cut through the sandstone hill. At the top of this hill on the east side of the road stands the old tithe barn, a mediaeval timber structure with a tiled roof. The cottages are of no great antiquity, and are generally built of red brick with tiled roofs, though the local red sandstone is also used. The church is approached from the north by an old path[5] hewn out of the sandstone hill. Hollowed out of the hill on the south side is the pound. The stocks used within the memory of some of the older inhabitants were placed opposite the Queen's Head Inn, but have now disappeared.

Wolverley Court, the property of the trustees of Mr. A. Cameron Hancocks, stands on the south side of the road leading from the Kidderminster and Wolverhampton road about a quarter of a mile east of the church. Though the south-east corner is late 16th-century work with stone mullioned windows, the house was almost entirely rebuilt early in the 19th century, the interior of the old building being all remodelled and most of the windows blocked up. In the conservatory are the remains of an alabaster effigy of a member of the Attwood family, popularly considered to be the Sir John Attwood mentioned below. It is of the latter part of the 14th century, and was taken from the church at the rebuilding. Unfortunately, most of the lower part of the figure is missing. The head of the effigy rests on a crowned helm, of which the mutilated crest was evidently that of his house, a swan's head and neck between two wings. The steel bascinet has an aventail attached, and over the mail shirt is a jupon, but this is too worn for the charge to be made out. The feet rest on the back of a small lion. There is at Wolverley Court a curious piece of old coloured glass representing the Attwood arms, apparently also removed from the old church.

A short distance above the court is Heathfield, the well-situated modern residence and property of Mr. Edward James Morton, M.A., D.L., J.P., and on the summit of the incline is Sion Hill House, the property and residence of Mr. T. A. Carless Attwood, M.A., F.S.A. It is an 18th-century two-story building, but has been much altered in the 19th century. The stables are a good piece of 18th-century brickwork, and the farm is also of that date. The farm was formerly known as Upton House.

Standing back on the east side of the road, at the top of the hill on the north side of the village, adjoining the mansion-house of the rectory,

---

[1] On the tithe map the area is 5,530 acres.
[1a] *Guide to Cookley and Wolverley.*
[2] Statistics from Bd. of Agric. (1905).
[3] Birchwood Coppice was the subject of litigation in 1674, when 'Master Foley' was said to have contracted for wood there and agreed not to 'cole' the parson's tithes should they be claimed for the wood felled (Exch. Dep. Mich. 26 Chas. II, no. 14). The underwood at Birchwood was leased to Thomas Hooke in 1579 for 20s. by the dean and chapter. In 1668 Birchwood was leased to William Thornborough and afterwards to William Talbot, who surrendered it, when a fresh lease was made to James Nash for twenty-one years at a rent of 20s. The bailiff of the manor of Wolverley stated in 1683 that for a long time no taxes had been assessed upon Birchwood, but that any taxes levied had been assessed upon him (ibid. Mich. 35 Chas. II, no. 47 ; East. 35 Chas. II, no. 37).
[4] Statistics from Bd. of Agric. (1905).
[5] This path must date from pre-Reformation days, the following being an extract from the will of Humfrey Sebright made in 1545 : 'I bequethe to the meynteynying of the holowe way in the church hill iijs iiijd.'

is Wolverley House, the property and residence of Major Eric A. Knight, M.P., J.P. It is a large three-story Georgian house built of red brick with red sandstone quoins, a modillion cornice and a porch of the Doric order.

Lea Castle, the property and residence of Mr. George Montagu Brown-Westhead, B.A., LL.M., is a large brick castellated mansion, standing in extensive and well-wooded grounds near Sion Hill House. It was erected early in the 19th century.

A curious feature of Wolverley are the rock dwellings scattered over the parish, of which the most picturesque are at Blakeshall and Drakelow.[6] Cut in the side of the sandstone hill, some of these primitive dwellings are dry and warm, others, owing to the porous nature of the rock, become very damp, especially in winter.

Wolverley includes the hamlets of Woodfield (Wodehamcake),[7] Blakeshall, Cookley, Lowe, Caunsall, Kingsford, Horseley, The Sladd, Little Hoboro, Austcliff (Alsclyne) and a portion of Broadwaters,[8] formerly known as Upton, but not Broadwaters House, which is in the foreign of Kidderminster, and has long been in the possession of the Homfray family.

On the north-west of the parish, about a mile from Kingsford, is Castle Hill, the residence of Mr. James Albert Lycett, J.P., with the remains of an old castle.

Common lands in the parish are mentioned early, Fantesruding[9] and Whitfield[10] being the names of some of these in the 13th century. In a survey of 1649 the commons in the manor included about 160 acres in Cookley Wood, another common adjoining of 50 acres, a great waste of heath or gorse of 400 acres and Horseley Heath containing 20 acres.[11]

An Inclosure Act was passed in 1775, but inclosing was not completed until 1779 owing to dissensions.[12] There is now on Blakeshall Common a pillar erected to the memory of Richard Baxter, who became a minister of Kidderminster in 1641. John Baskerville was born at Upton House, known latterly as Sion Hill Farm, in Wolverley in 1706, but he removed to Birmingham, where he established a japanning business, and later set up his celebrated printing press. He died in 1775, and ' agreeable to the singularity of his opinions he was buried under a windmill in his garden, on whose top after it fell into disuse he had erected an urn.'[13]

Among former place-names in this parish have been found Horsebrook, Smythescrok, Vroggemore[14] (xiv cent.) ; Lords Meadow, High Holborough[15] (xvi cent.). Socombe, Aylesbury, Buryton, Berrington, The Flosses or Flaws, Draclow and Buryhalle have been found on the manorial rolls.[16]

The early history of *WOLVERLEY MANORS* presents difficulties. There was a confused tradition current at Worcester in the 11th century that the place had been the subject of a grant by Æthelbald of Mercia to one of his ealdormen named Hwita.[17] Otherwise the earliest references to Wolverley are dated 866. Two charters issued by Burhred of Mercia are preserved in a corrupt form : (1) granting to one ' Wulfferd' two *manentes* at ' Soegeslea ' belonging to Wolverley[18] ; (2) granting the same estate under the name of ' Secceslea ' to the monks of Worcester.[19] Secceslea, the correct form of this name, has been identified with Seckley Wood near Wolverley. Although the charters have been modernized in spelling they contain features which seem to come from the 9th century.[20] In each grant the boundaries of the land are given,[21] and the two evidently refer to the same estate. Possibly the exchange between the king and Wulfferd never took place, thus leaving the king free to bestow Wolverley upon the monks.

During the time when the Danes were ravaging England the monks of Worcester lost many of their manors, Wolverley being among them, but 5 hides there were restored to them by Leofric Earl of Mercia and his countess Godiva in the time when Wulfstan was prior.[22] The charter of Leofric is undated, but he died in 1057.[23] These 5 hides were assigned to the refectory of the monastery,[24] and, though it is stated that shortly after Leofric's grant they were seized by the Danes,[25] they were held by the monks in demesne at the time of the Domesday Survey.[26]

The manor with its members Horseley, Cookley and Burton was confirmed to the prior and convent by Simon, Bishop of Worcester, in 1148,[27] and in 1207 King John granted them in this manor sac and soc, thol and theam, infangentheof, with judgement by fire and water, gallows[27a] and iron, freedom from view of tithing and of murders and fines and all other liberties and customs which they enjoyed in their other manors. This manor was also freed for ever

---

[6] Brassington, *Historic Worcestershire*, 201.

[7] The alternative names have been supplied by Mr. Thomas Cave, from the court rolls of the manor in the Worcester Cathedral Library.

[8] Little Wolverley was a hamlet in the parish in the 18th century (Nash, *Hist. of Worcs.* ii, 470). A property called the manor of Little Wolverley passed in 1598 from John Ingram to his son Hastings (Chan. Inq. p.m. [Ser. 2], cclii, 7).

[9] Heming, *Chartul.* (ed. Hearne), 525.

[10] *Ann. Mon.* (Rolls Ser.), iv, 421, 435. A freeman of Kidderminster recovered his right of pasture in Whitfield in 1230.

[11] Nash, op. cit. ii, 471.

[12] Ibid. ; Burton, *Bibl. of Worcs.* (Worcs. Hist. Soc.), i, 65 ; *Blue Bk. Incl. Awards*, 192.

[13] *British Topog.* ii, 300.

[14] Prattinton Coll. (Soc. Antiq.) ; Nash, op. cit. ii, 476.

[15] Chan. Proc. (Ser. 2), bdle. 85, no. 56. The rent of Lords Meadow was entertainment for a night and a day for the retinue attending the lord's court (inform. from Mr. Thomas Cave). See also Exch. Dep. Mich. 35 Chas. II, no. 47.

[16] Inform. from Mr. Thomas Cave.

[17] Dugdale, *Mon. Angl.* i, 607 ; Heming, op. cit. 583.

[18] Kemble, *Cod. Dipl.* no. 292 ; Heming, op. cit. 593 ; Birch, *Cart. Sax,* ii, 125.

[19] Kemble, op. cit. no. 291 ; Heming, op. cit. 410 ; Birch, op. cit. ii, 127.

[20] Inform. from Mr. F. M. Stenton.

[21] 'From the Stour to Hunig Brook, then up the brook to the old hedge, along the hedges quite up to the Oldway or Road, along the Oldway to the great street, along the street to the four ways (or boundaries), from thence to Calebrook, along the same to Horsebrook, from thence to the Dyke, along the Dyke

to the Stour, again from the Stour to the Dyke, along the same to Cuthred's Tree, and still along the same to Hesecan Hill, from Hesecan Hill to the Dyke, along the Dyke to Wenforth, and so to the Stour.' Prattinton identifies Hesecan Hill with Sion Hill (Prattinton Coll. [Soc. Antiq.]).

[22] Dugdale, *Mon. Angl.* i, 595, 609 ; Heming, op. cit. 261, 406, 409 ; Kemble, op. cit. no. 766.

[23] *Angl.-Sax. Chron.* (Rolls Ser.), ii, 287.

[24] Heming, op. cit. 409.

[25] Dugdale, *Mon. Angl.* i, 600.

[26] *V.C.H. Worcs.* i, 298b.

[27] Thomas, *Surv. of Cath. Church of Worc.* App. no. 18.

[27a] The gallows stood on the high road through the village near Buckers Arbour (inform. supplied by Thomas Cave from evidence in manorial rolls at Worcester Cathedral Library).

from suits at shire and hundred courts and from all aids and exactions of sheriff and bailiff.[28]

From that time until the Dissolution the manor of Wolverley was the property of the Priors of Worcester.[29] In 1542 Henry VIII granted it to the dean and chapter,[30] and this was confirmed by James I in 1609.[31]

The trustees for the sale of church lands sold the manor in 1650 to William Moore of Alvechurch,[32] but the dean and chapter appear to have recovered it at the accession of Charles II, as it was again in their hands in 1683.[33] The manor was confirmed to the dean and chapter in 1692,[34] and remained with them until 1859, when it was transferred to the Ecclesiastical Commissioners,[35] in whose possession it still remains.

Nash states that in the 18th century the court baron and court leet were held at Bury Hall Farm at the will of the lord.[36] Until 1768 copyhold estates in this manor were held by Borough English, but in that year an Act was passed to make the succession follow that of the common law.[37]

From the 13th century occasional notices appear of the descent of a property in Wolverley (afterwards described as a manor) held under the prior.[38] It seems to have originated in a messuage at Wolverley which Thomas de Northgrave sold to Malcolm de Harley for 100 marks in 1274, retaining the rent of a rose.[39] Prattinton, on the authority of MSS. belonging to the dean and chapter, states that in 1298–9 Sir Richard de Harley released his right in these lands to Malcolm de Wasteneys, to whom Margaret, lady of Pitchford, also released all claim in the manor in the same year.[40] He further says that in 1331 Malcolm de Wasteneys, lord of Tixhall, granted all his land in Wolverley to Robert Attwood (de Boys), Joan his wife and Robert their son.[41] John Attwood, king's yeoman, and possibly of the same family, obtained a grant of free warren in his manor of Wolverley in 1362, with licence to inclose and make a park of 600 acres.[42] John Attwood died in 1369 and Sir John Attwood in 1391.[43] The knight whose alabaster effigy, now at Wolverley Court, has been described above was a member of this family. There is a tradition in the village that one of the Attwoods went on a crusade and remained away so long that his wife, supposing him to be dead, was about to marry again. A milkmaid, however, going into the meadows early one morning, found a man, emaciated and fettered, asleep in the grass. The sleeping figure was recognized as the knight by his dog, but being so changed, his wife was only convinced of his identity when he produced the half

of a ring which they had broken at parting. The Crusader related that he had been imprisoned by the infidels and kept in a dungeon until released by the Virgin, who transported him in a trance to his own fields.[44] Another version of the quaint old legend is that when it was reported that Sir John Attwood had been brought back by an angel he piously denied it, and said it was by a swan. Hence the origin of the swan crest used by several families of the name Attwood, in slightly differing forms. Although unable to identify the alabaster figure as that of a Crusader, Habington thus concludes the story : ' But that theare was one Sir John Atwode who beeinge imprisoned by the Infydelles was miraculously caryed from that far remote dungeon of his captivity to Trimpley, losed of his gyves, and restored to lyberty, the same is so publycke, the chappell buylded in remembrance theareof so notable, the gyves themselves reserved as a trophy of thys glorious redemption so cleere a testimony as none but willfull obstinate can denye itt.' [45] Iron fetters said to have been worn by the knight are still shown, and there was at one time a rent-charge on ' The Knight's Meadow,' where the knight was said to have been found. This rent was ' paid to someone who should keep the irons polished and show them to all who would like to see them.' [46] The original fetters have long been lost.

The family of Attwood occupied a prominent position in the county during the 15th century, but there is little to connect them with this estate, although they probably continued to hold it. John and Thomas Attwood obtained land in the parish in 1452 from Sir Walter Scull and his wife Margaret,[47] but in 1504 John Wood conveyed the manor of Wolverley to Sir Thomas Englefield,[48] and Francis, the son of the latter, with his wife Catherine released their right in it to Anthony Attwood forty-three years later.[49] Anthony Attwood had been succeeded by his son Anthony in 1595,[50] and Samuel Attwood, the son of the latter, was living there when Habington wrote in the 17th century.[51] The Attwoods continued to hold land in the parish until 1714, when Abel Attwood and his wife were in possession.[52] This Abel was the son of Henry Attwood, and was the last heir male of the elder branch [53] of the house of Attwood.[54] He died

ATTWOOD of Wolverley. *Gules a lion argent with a forked tail.*

---

[28] Heming, op. cit. 541 ; *Cal. Rot. Chart.* 1199–1216 (Rec. Com.), 168. For this grant the prior paid to the king 100 marks and a palfrey. The 100 marks the king restored for the repairs of the church and conventual buildings of Worcester (*Rot. de Oblatis et Fin.* [Rec. Com.], 397).

[29] *Ann. Mon.* (Rolls Ser.), iv, 399, 404 ; *Pope Nich. Tax.* (Rec. Com.), 227*b* ; *Valor Eccl.* (Rec. Com.), iii, 221.

[30] *L. and P. Hen. VIII*, xvii, g. 71 (29).

[31] Pat. 6 Jas. I, pt. xii, no. 2.

[32] Close, 1650, pt. xx, no. 26.

[33] Exch. Dep. Mich. 35 Chas. II, no. 47.

[34] Pat. 4 Will. and Mary, pt. i, no. 6.

[35] *Lond. Gaz.* 16 Dec. 1859, p. 4757; confirmed by Stat. 31 Vict. cap. 19.

[36] Nash, op. cit. ii, 471.

[37] *Acts of Parl. rel. to co. Worc.* (Worcs. Hist. Soc.), 59.

[38] Chan. Inq. p.m. (Ser. 2), lx, 26.

[39] Feet of F. Worcs. 3 Edw. I, no. 61.

[40] Prattinton Coll. (Soc. Antiq.) ; Habington, op. cit. i, 498.

[41] Prattinton Coll. (Soc. Antiq.). In 1393 Roger Wasteneys sued John de Okedene, clerk, and others for lands and rents in Wolverley which Ralph de Pitchford had given to Geoffrey Wasteneys and Eleanor his wife and their heirs (Wrottesley, *Ped. from Plea R.* 192).

[42] Chart. R. 36 Edw. III, no. 154.

[43] Prattinton Coll. (Soc. Antiq.).

[44] Brassington, op. cit. 201.

[45] Habington, op. cit. ii, 321.

[46] Brassington, op. cit. 204.

[47] Feet of F. Worcs. 31 Hen. VI, no. 46.

[48] De Banco R. East. 20 Hen. VII, m. 148. Sir Thomas at the time of his death in 1537 held the reversion of the manor after the death of Joan widow of Henry Leynham (Chan. Inq. p.m. [Ser. 2], lx, 26).

[49] Feet of F. Worcs. Trin. 1 Edw. VI.

[50] Ibid. Trin. 38 Eliz.

[51] op. cit. ii, 50.

[52] Feet of F. Worcs. East. 13 Chas. II ; East. 13 Anne. M. I. in the old church of Wolverley printed in Nash, op. cit. ii, 472.

[53] Another branch of the family was settled at Claines.

[54] Inform. by Mr. T. A. C. Attwood of Sion Hill House.

in 1726, at the age of sixty-six, having outlived his son (or sons) and only grandson Holborough Attwood.[55]

Wolverley Court, the seat of the Attwoods, has for some time belonged to the Hancocks family, though they have not of late years occupied the house,[56] which is at present vacant.

Early in the 18th century the Knight family acquired land at Wolverley in succession to the Jewkes, who were then the chief family at Wolverley. Edward Knight of Wolverley died in 1780,[57] and Nash, writing in 1782, states that Edward Knight, son and successor of Edward, whose ancestors had acquired a large fortune by the iron trade and had built a good house, was then the principal landowner in the parish.[58] In 1809 John Knight obtained from the Dean and Chapter of Worcester a lease of their messuage called The Lee at Wolverley for twenty-one years, and seven years later he acquired the lease of an estate in Caunsall and Broadwaters from John Smith.[59] Lea Castle, which was for some time occupied by the Knights, was built by John Knight, probably at about this time.[60] It was sold about 1818[61] to Mr. John Brown, from whose sister Ann Brown, afterwards Mrs. Westhead, the present family of Brown-Westhead of Lea Castle is descended.[62] The castle is now the seat of Mr. George Montagu Brown-Westhead.

KNIGHT of Wolverley. *Argent three pales gules in a border engrailed azure with a quarter gules having a spur or therein.*

The Sebrights[63] claimed to have held land in BLAKESHALL from the end of the 13th or early 14th century, when Mabell (here a man's name) Sebright of Blakeshall married Catherine daughter of Ralph Cowper of Blakeshall.[64] It is known that the Sebrights were living in the parish of Wolverley in 1302, when John Sebright, the son of John Sebright of Wolverley, became a monk in the priory of Dodford.[65] The same family continued to hold in Blakeshall, Cookley and elsewhere at least as late as the middle of the 17th century.[66]

Edward Sebright held Byrds Farm and Newmans Farm in the lordship of Kingsford in 1569.[67] John

Sebright of Blakeshall was succeeded by a son Edward,[68] who was created a baronet in 1626.[69] He had succeeded his uncle William at Besford in 1620,[70] and was one of the executors of the will of the latter, who left certain lands for the maintenance of a free grammar school at Wolverley.[71] In 1634 Sir Edward received a lease from Charles I of free warren, fishing, fowling and hunting in Wolverley for a rent of two brace of partridges and one brace of cocks to the value of 3*s*.[72] In 1651 he had to compound as a Royalist for an estate at Wolverley.[73] The Sebrights subsequently from time to time parted with their Worcestershire estates, and took up their residence on their Hertfordshire property. Blakeshall was the property of John Smith in 1809,[74] and it now belongs to Mr. William Hancocks, in whose family it has been for some time.

The present COOKLEY WOOD near Kingsford has been identified with a place called in the 10th century Culnan Clif.[75] Land here was granted by King Edgar to Earl Beorhtnoth in 964, and was then described as being on the River Stour near Wolverley.[76] In 1067 2 hides of land at 'Culla Clif' were granted by King William to Bishop Wulfstan, who gave them to the monks of Worcester on condition that they should pray for the soul of the donor.[77] The estate (Culclive) was in the hands of the Prior of Worcester in the 13th century, his tenants there being Fulk, Edith the widow and others.[78] It probably remained part of the manor of Wolverley and followed its descent, passing into the hands of the Dean and Chapter of Worcester at the dissolution of the priory, for in 1650 Cookley Wood, valued at £20, was a part of the lands of the Dean and Chapter of Worcester.[79] This wood was sold at this time to William More.[80]

The Cookley Ironworks were founded towards the end of the 17th century, and from that time Cookley became a centre of the iron and tinplate industry. Joseph Piper, a native of this village, invented and perfected the patent tinning process. The mill at Cookley was originally a corn-mill, erected in the time of Elizabeth. It was still a corn-mill in 1649, when it and a slitting-mill were held by Sir Edward Sebright. It had been converted into an iron-mill before 1706. These mills were subsequently leased and held by the Knights.[80a] Edward Knight owned these mills about 1750–80, in which latter year he

[55] Inform. by Mr. T. A. C. Attwood of Sion Hill House; Nash, op. cit. ii, 473.

[56] Inform. by Mr. T. A. C. Attwood of Sion Hill House.

[57] Burke, *Landed Gentry.* Richard Knight of 'Brindgwood,' co. Hereford, was admitted at a court held for the manor in 1731 to the holdings of William Rea, but the family seems to have come to Wolverley ten years earlier. In a comparatively short time the Knights were working all the forges in the parish, with the exception of one or two worked by the Homfray family (inform. from Mr. T. A. C. Attwood and Mr. Thomas Cave).

[58] Nash, op. cit. ii, 471.

[59] Priv. Act, 56 Geo. III, cap. 32.

[60] Inform. from Mr. T. A. C. Attwood.

[61] A descendant of the Knights, Major Eric Ayshford Knight, still owns and resides at Wolverley House.

[62] Inform. from Mr. T. A. C. Attwood.

[63] John Sebrist was a surety for the

Prior of Worcester in 1277 (Habington, op. cit. i, 492).

[64] *Visit. of Worcs.* 1569 (Harl. Soc. xxvii), 126 ; Habington, op. cit. i, 493. The marriage took place before 1293–4.

[65] *Sede Vacante Reg.* (Worcs. Hist. Soc.), 7. The name frequently occurs in the court rolls (inform. from Mr. Thomas Cave).

[66] *Visit. of Worcs.* (Harl. Soc. xxvii), 126 ; Habington, op. cit. i, 494. A pedigree of the family from the time of Henry VII is given by Nash, op. cit. i, 79.

[67] Star Chamb. Proc. Eliz. bdle. 73, no. 10.

[68] G.E.C. *Complete Baronetage,* ii, 4.

[69] Ibid.

[70] Chan. Inq. p.m. (Ser. 2), ccclxxxvi, 85.

[71] Chan. Proc. Mitford, lxiii, no. 33.

[72] Close, 1650, pt. xx, no. 26.

[73] Royalist Comp. Papers (Ser. 2), xlvii, no. 275 ; Cal. Com. for Comp. 2374.

[74] Priv. Act, 56 Geo. III, cap. 32.

[75] Nash (op. cit. ii, 35) identifies it as Cookley hamlet. Mr. Thomas Cave, however, by reference to the court rolls, has proved its identity with Cookley Wood. The district is frequently referred to in the court rolls, sometimes as Culclewood.

[76] Birch, op. cit. iii, 376 ; Heming, op. cit. 561. The boundaries of the land are given. Places mentioned on the boundaries are Usmere (now Ismere), Heasecanbeorh, Cuthredestreow, the Stour, Horssabroc, Cenungaford, Kynefordes Stane or Cynefares Stane, Maerdene, Windofre and Lytlandune.

[77] Heming, op. cit. 407, 413. The bounds are again given here as in the grant of 964.

[78] *Reg. of Worc. Priory* (Camd. Soc.), 94*b*. [79] Close, 1650, pt. xx, m. 26.

[80] In 1670 Lord Windsor had a passage over the Stour with appurtenances in Cookley (Feet of F. Div. Co. Mich. 22 Chas. II).

[80a] Inform. from Mr. Thomas Cave.

died,[81] and the last of this family connected with these works was Sir Frederic Winn Knight. On his death in 1897 the Wolverley estates passed to his nephew Eric Ayshford Knight of Wolverley.[82] The industry gradually declined in the 19th century, owing to lack of railway communication, and in 1886 the entire works were removed to the neighbourhood of Brierley Hill in the midst of the Staffordshire coalfields, but of late years part of Cookley Mill has been used by Messrs. Brampton. Cookley has again become busy, as new works have been erected there.

HORSELEY (Horselega, Horselee, xii cent. ; Horsleg, xiii cent.) was said to be a member of the liberty of the hundred of Wolverley in 1240 and was assessed at one-third part of it.[83] Ralph the Prior of Worcester[84] granted to Fulk de Horseley that land which his father and afterwards he had assarted from the wood of the prior, to be held for a sextar of honey besides those two which he owed for Horseley. In order that there should be no future disagreement as to the boundaries of Fulk's land they were set forth in the grant.[85] Horseley was confirmed to the priory as a member of Wolverley by Bishop Simon in 1148.[86] In 1189 the sheriff rendered 36s. for land which had belonged to Fulk de Horseley,[87] and in 1196 Osbert de Adleya rendered account of 2½ marks for the custody of the heir of Fulk de Horseley, so that Robert, who was heir of that land, might have his land in Horseley.[88] Afterwards Horseley seems to have passed to the Ribbesford family.[89] An assize of novel disseisin was brought against Henry de Ribbesford in 1223 by Simon de Cove.[90] In 1239 the monks of Worcester took Horseley at farm for twenty years.[91] The heirs of Ribbesford were tenants under the prior at Horseley in 1240,[92] and in 1300 Ralph de Streche was holding land at Horseley of Henry de Ribbesford.[93] Ralph Streche died seised of land at Horseley about 1300,[94] leaving a son and heir Robert, and in 1315–16 Robert sold the manor to the Prior of Worcester.[95] In 1321 the prior obtained licence to purchase land at Horseley, held of him and his convent, from Richard de Hawkeslow.[96] From this time Horseley seems to have become incorporated with the manor of Wolverley.

KINGSFORD (Cenungaford, Cynefares, x cent. ; Kynefordes, xi cent. ; Kyngvard, xvi cent. ; Kyngefort, xvii cent.). William de Tracy was a freeman in Wolverley in the 13th century, when he paid an annual rent and did homage to the prior for 'Walter de Keingford.'[97] The Tracys appear to have held land at Wolverley through the next two centuries. In 1530 William Tracy the younger

died seised of the manor of Kingsford held of the priory of Worcester, his father William having settled it on him on his marriage in 1517.[98] Henry the son of William Tracy the younger afterwards held Kingsford, but after his death his son John was obliged to institute Chancery proceedings to obtain possession of it. He stated that the deeds of enfeoffment had come into the hands of Katherine Jones, who claimed to hold a lease of it, and that she and others had made secret sales of the manor.[99] He appears to have obtained possession of it again, for in 1569 he sold it to Thomas Whorwood,[100] on whose death in 1616 it was said to be held of the lord of Hampton Lovett by fealty and socage and a yearly rent of 4s.[1] Gerard the son of Thomas Whorwood sold the manor in 1622 to Roger Fowke,[2] to whom he appears to have mortgaged it six years before.[3] Roger Fowke sold it in 1633 to Richard Foley of Stourbridge,[4] who had amassed a fortune as an ironmaster. Richard Foley sold the manor in 1648[5] to his third son Thomas[6] for £500. Thomas died in 1677.[7] His grandson Thomas was made Lord Foley of Kidderminster in 1712,[8] and the manor passed with the title until 1830.[9] Prattinton states that Lord Foley sold the manor to Miss Perry of Wolverhampton, who afterwards sold the whole manor, including the Court Farm, to Mr. Knight.[10]

DEBDALE (Depedal, xiii cent.), now a farm, was the property of the monks of Worcester in the 13th century. Half a virgate there was rented by John the son of Edith for 9½d. quarterly, and a certain Leonin also had a rent of the same amount there.[11] In an undated deed Richard son of Richard de Debdale gave to Leonin the son of Philip all his land there, for which the latter paid 47d. to the convent quarterly and a pair of gauntlets to Richard at Easter.[12]

There was a mill at Wolverley in the possession of the church of Worcester at the time of the Domesday Survey, when it was worth 6s.[13] In the 13th century the mills were rented out,[14] one being leased for 13s. 4d. quarterly, a fulling-mill for 11d., and other mills for 10s. quarterly.[15] In 1291 the rent of assize of two mills went to the almoner's fund.[16] In 1482–3 a new corn-mill was erected on the Horsebrook near Cookley Wood by John Fleming of Tatenhill, co. Staff. The mill known as Lords Mill, probably that which existed in 1086, was demised as two water corn-mills under one roof to John Attwood for his life and the lives of his mother and his brother Samuel in 1641.[17] It was converted into iron-mills in 1656 by Joshua Newbrugh, and these

[81] Inform. from Mr. T. A. C. Attwood.
[82] Burke, *Landed Gentry* (1906).
[83] *Reg. of Worc. Priory* (Camd. Soc.), 95a.   [84] He died in 1143.
[85] Heming, op. cit. 429–30. Places mentioned on the boundary are Mulpol, Waringesruding, Imbe Oak, Surftro, Caverudinge, Hennelega, Holesiche, Stodfolda, Edwineshuse, Wibbecumbeshavede.
[86] Thomas, op. cit. App. no. 18.
[87] *Gt. R. of the Pipe*, 1 Ric. I (Rec. Com.), 249.
[88] Pipe R. 8 Ric. I, m. 4 d.
[89] See under Ribbesford in hundred of Doddingtree.
[90] *Cal. Pat.* 1216–25, p. 410.
[91] *Ann. Mon.* (Rolls Ser.), iv, 431.
[92] *Reg. of Worc. Priory* (Camd. Soc.), 95a.

[93] Chan. Inq. p.m. 28 Edw. I, no. 18.
[94] Ibid.
[95] Habington, op. cit. i, 495.
[96] *Cal. Pat.* 1314–21, p. 560; Inq. a.q.d. file 145, no. 18.
[97] *Reg. of Worc. Priory* (Camd. Soc.), 93a.
[98] Chan. Inq. p.m. (Ser. 2), lxxx, 104.
[99] Chan. Proc. (Ser. 2), bdles. 181, no. 87 ; 184, no. 51.
[100] Feet of F. Worcs. East. 11 Eliz.
[1] Chan. Inq. p.m. (Ser. 2), ccclⅳ, 104.
[2] Feet of F. Div. Co. Trin. 20 Jas. I.
[3] Ibid. Mich. 13 Jas. I.
[4] Ibid. East. 9 Chas. I ; Hil. 11 Chas. I.
[5] Close, 24 Chas. I, pt. xiv, no. 16.
[6] Burke, *Peerage* ; Feet of F. Worcs. East. 16 Chas. II.

[7] Burke, *Peerage*.
[8] Ibid.
[9] Recov. R. Hil. 42 Geo. III, rot. 21 ; Hil. 10 & 11 Geo. IV, rot. 255.
[10] Prattinton Coll. (Soc. Antiq.).
[11] *Reg. of Worc. Priory* (Camd. Soc.), 94.
[12] Prattinton Coll. (Soc. Antiq.), Deeds of D. and C. of Worc. no. 160. This appears to have been about the same date as the register, the name of Walter de Kingsford occurring in both.
[13] *V.C.H. Worcs.* i, 298b.
[14] *Ann. Mon.* (Rolls Ser.), iv, 442.
[15] *Reg. of Worc. Priory* (Camd. Soc.), 92b, 153a.
[16] *Pope Nich. Tax.* (Rec. Com.), 227b.
[17] Close, 1650, pt. xx, m. 26.

passed before 1713 to Talbot Jewkes. A lease of this forge was granted in 1727 to Edward Knight. The corn-mill known as Sleepy Mill on Wolverley Heath was built about 1660 by Samuel Jewkes. In 1669 another iron-mill was erected by Joshua New-brugh and Philip Foley at the Lowe. The mill is now disused. There was another corn-mill at Drake-low on the Horsebrook, and Upton Mill at Broad-waters was used as a fulling-mill until converted in 1746 by Thomas Smart into a corn-mill. In 1753 it was made into an iron forge by John Homfray, and used until about twenty-five years ago, when it was dismantled. Part of it has been used of late years by Mr. William Birkett, a saddle flock manu-facturer.[17a]

WOLVERLEY CHURCH FROM THE SOUTH-EAST

CHURCHES

The church of ST. JOHN BAP-TIST is a red brick building con-sisting of a chancel, south vestry, nave with arcades, north and south aisles containing galleries continued round the west end, and a west tower.

The present church, which replaces an older one

pulled down in 1769, is built in the Italian style and was completed in 1772 [18] ; it forms an excellent example of local work and design, the tower being particularly good.

The tester of an older pulpit is preserved ; on it is inscribed ' Be of one mind. Live in Peace and the God of Peace and Love shall be with you. 1638.' In the church is a chained copy of Jewell's *Apology*.

The bells are six in number : the first by R. S. (Saunders), 1737 ; the second and fifth by John Rud-hall, 1788 ; the third by the same maker, 1789 ; the fourth recast 1896 ; and the sixth by Richard Sanders, 1737.

The plate consists of a cup made in 1661 inscribed ' William Sebright Armig. Wolverley,' and bearing a shield with three roses, a standing paten of similar date, and a modern cup, paten, flagon and almsdish. There is a pewter almsdish, and the bowl of the font is lined with the same material.

The registers previous to 1812 are as follows : (i) mixed entries 1539 to 1655 ; (ii) 1653 to 1696 ; (iii) bap-tisms and burials 1697 to 1769 and marriages 1697 to 1754 ; (iv) marri-ages 1754 to 1812 ; (v) baptisms and burials 1770 to 1812 ; (vi) a private register containing mixed entries 1678 to 1712.

The church of ST. PETER, Cookley, is a building of brick in early 14th-century style, consisting of chancel, nave, aisles, north porch and north-west tower. An organ chamber was added in 1872.

ADVOWSON

There was a priest at Wolverley in 1086.[19] The church with its tithes and lands was given by Bishop Roger (1164–79) to the priory.[20] The priory held the patronage until the Dissolution,[21] and it was given with the manor to the Dean and Chapter of Worcester in 1542.[22] This gift was confirmed by James I,[23] and the patron-age has remained in the same hands up to the present day.[24]

Geoffrey Bacoun, called de North-wick, the vicar of Wolverley, exchanged his benefice for that of Overbury in 1293 because the latter church was on wet land while the former was on dry soil.[25] Although he was non-resident he had held Wolverley by special dis-pensation of the Bishop of Norwich on condition that he would be ordained, but he was not ordained until after he was transferred to Overbury. He had in 1303 to obtain a dispensation from the pope to hold the benefice as an absentee.[26]

In 1351 the church was appropriated to the priory on payment of 20 marks yearly to the bishop, the

17a Information about the mills of Wolverley has been kindly supplied by Mr. Thomas Cave.
18 Nash, op. cit. ii, 472.
19 *V.C.H. Worcs.* i, 298*b*.
20 Heming, op. cit. 526 ; Dugdale, *Mon.* i, 572.
21 *Ann. Mon.* (Rolls Ser.), iv, 443, 510,

&c. ; *Reg. G. Giffard* (Worcs. Hist. Soc.), 50, 423, &c.
22 *L. and P. Hen. VIII*, xvii, g. 71 (29).
23 Pat. 6 Jas. I, pt. xii, no. 2. In the 16th century Roger Juckes claimed that the dean and chapter had granted the presentation to Richard Ewer, clerk, who gave it with the deed of gift to John

Juckes, who gave it to Roger. Roger entrusted the deed to Thos. Waterson for safe keeping and he afterwards refused to give it up (Chan. Proc. [Ser. 2], bdle. 100, no. 32).
24 Inst. Bks. (P.R.O.).
25 *Ann. Mon.* (Rolls Ser.), iv, 513.
26 *Cal. of Papal Letters*, i, 608.

prior being in great need of money for the repair of the monastery.[27] The vicarage was ordained in 1354,[28] when the bishop assigned to the vicar for his residence the houses and manse which had belonged to Thomas de Hale. They were to be rebuilt and altered at the expense of the priory. The prior and convent were bound to repair the chancel and to discharge the vicar from all payments of tithes.[29] In 1535 it was said to be a peculiar, subject to the jurisdiction of the dean and chapter.[30] An increase of £10 to the minister of Wolverley was recommended by the Council in 1656.[31]

There was a chantry in the parish in 1485, when James Nash was appointed chaplain to pray for the good estate of the king. His salary was an annuity of 9 marks from a quit-rent of £9 5s., payable by the manor of Kings Nordeley in the parish of Alveley, co. Salop, to be paid at the hands of the heirs of John Lee of Coton in that parish or of the Sheriff of Worcester.[32]

The ecclesiastical parish of Cookley was formed from Wolverley in 1849.[33] The living is a vicarage in the gift of Mr. William Hancocks of Blakeshall House.

On Blakeshall Common there is a mission chapel built by the late Mr. William Hancocks. It is now used by the vicar for church purposes. Another mission room at Broadwaters was built in 1908 in connexion with the church of St. John the Baptist, Wolverley. The Wesleyan Methodist chapel at Cookley was built in 1814 and rebuilt in 1874, and there is a Primitive Methodist chapel at Broadwaters built in 1858. A Primitive Methodist chapel erected at Cookley in 1860 has been converted into a private house.

CHARITIES Sebright's Endowed Schools, founded by will 1620, were regulated by a scheme of 11 July 1877, under the Endowed Schools Acts.[34] In consequence of the leases of a considerable London estate now falling in the endowments are now large and are rapidly increasing, and the school will be very rich. This has made a new scheme necessary, the terms of which are being settled between the governors, the County Council and the Board of Education. Out of the income an annual sum of £3 0s. 8d. is applicable

in the distribution of bread and 6s. 8d. is paid to the parish clerk for his trouble. An annual sum of £10 is likewise applicable towards the repairs of the parish church. (See also under Old Swinford.)

In 1704 Richard Bibb by deed gave a house and land in Shenstone, the rents and profits to be distributed to the poor. The trust property was sold in 1898 and proceeds invested in £303 7s. 8d. India 3 per cent. stock. The annual dividends, amounting to £9 2s., are distributed on St. Thomas's Day in groceries, meat, &c.

In 1823 John Smith by his will bequeathed £600, out of the income thereof £12 to be paid to the minister for a sermon every Sunday afternoon and the remaining income to be applied in clothing or relieving superannuated husbandmen or widows. The legacy, less duty, is represented by £577 10s. 10d. consols, producing £14 8s. 8d. yearly.

In 1835 John Longmore by his will left a legacy, now represented by £539 1s. 8d. consols, the annual dividends, amounting to £13 9s. 4d., to be applied in the distribution of bread to poor regular attendants at the parish church.

In 1883 William Hancocks, by his will proved at Worcester 15 September, bequeathed £1,000, the income to be distributed among the needy poor, being Protestants, of Wolverley and Cookley St. Peter. The legacy was invested in £998 2s. 8d. consols, producing £24 19s. yearly, which is applied in moieties in the distribution of coal, clothing and other articles in kind among the poor of the respective parishes.

The same testator bequeathed a further sum of £1,000, one moiety of the income to be applied towards the support of the National schools at Wolverley and the other moiety towards the National schools at Cookley. This legacy was invested in £838 14s. 8d. consols, producing £20 19s. 4d. yearly.

The charity is regulated by a scheme of the High Court (Chancery Division) 18 December 1900, whereby the Charity Commissioners are empowered to vary the proportions in which the income may be divided between the two parishes.

The several sums of stock above mentioned are held by the official trustees.

[27] Prattinton Coll. (Soc. Antiq.) ; *Cal. Pat.* 1350–4, p. 173 ; *Cal. Papal Letters,* iii, 430.
[28] Worc. Epis. Reg. Carpenter, i, fol. 194 f.
[29] Prattinton Coll. (Soc. Antiq.) ; Nash, op. cit. ii, 476–7.
[30] *Valor Eccl.* (Rec. Com.), iii, 275, 512.
[81] *Cal. S. P. Dom.* 1656–7, p. 15.
[32] *Cal. Pat.* 1476–85, p. 496.
[33] *Pop. Ret.* 1901, *Worcs.* 5.
[34] See 'Schools,' *V.C.H. Worcs.* iv.